A detail from the twelfth-century illuminated bible of St. Andre au Bois.
(© Michael St. Maur Sheil/CORBIS)

NEW
CATHOLIC
ENCYCLOPEDIA

NEW
CATHOLIC
ENCYCLOPEDIA

SECOND EDITION

4
Com–Dyn

GALE®

Detroit • New York • San Diego • San Francisco • Cleveland • New Haven, Conn. • Waterville, Maine • London • Munich

in association with
THE CATHOLIC UNIVERSITY OF AMERICA • WASHINGTON, D.C.

The New Catholic Encyclopedia, Second Edition

Project Editors
Thomas Carson, Joann Cerrito

Editorial
Erin Bealmear, Jim Craddock, Stephen Cusack, Miranda Ferrara, Kristin Hart, Melissa Hill, Margaret Mazurkiewicz, Carol Schwartz, Christine Tomassini, Michael J. Tyrkus

Permissions
Edna Hedblad, Shalice Shah-Caldwell

Imaging and Multimedia
Randy Bassett, Dean Dauphinais, Robert Duncan, Leitha Etheridge-Sims, Mary K. Grimes, Lezlie Light, Dan Newell, David G. Oblender, Christine O'Bryan, Luke Rademacher, Pamela Reed

Product Design
Michelle DiMercurio

Data Capture
Civie Green

Manufacturing
Rhonda Williams

Indexing
Victoria Agee, Victoria Baker, Lynne Maday, Do Mi Stauber, Amy Suchowski

While every effort has been made to ensure the reliability of the information presented in this publication, The Gale Group, Inc. does not guarantee the accuracy of the data contained herein. The Gale Group, Inc. accepts no payment for listing; and inclusion in the publication of any organization, agency, institution, publication, service, or individual does not imply endorsement of the editors or publisher. Errors brought to the attention of the publisher and verified to the satisfaction of the publisher will be corrected in future editions.

LIBRARY OF CONGRESS CATALOGING-IN-PUBLICATION DATA

New Catholic encyclopedia.—2nd ed.
    p. cm.
        Includes bibliographical references and indexes.
        ISBN 0-7876-4004-2
        1. Catholic Church—Encyclopedias. I. Catholic University of America.
BX841 .N44 2002
282' .03—dc21
2002000924

ISBN: 0-7876-4004-2 (set)
0-7876-4005-0 (v. 1)
0-7876-4006-9 (v. 2)
0-7876-4007-7 (v. 3)
0-7876-4008-5 (v. 4)

0-7876-4009-3 (v. 5)
0-7876-4010-7 (v. 6)
0-7876-4011-5 (v. 7)
0-7876-4012-3 (v. 8)
0-7876-4013-1 (v. 9)

0-7876-4014-x (v. 10)
0-7876-4015-8 (v. 11)
0-7876-4016-6 (v. 12)
0-7876-4017-4 (v. 13)
0-7876-4018-2 (v. 14)
0-7876-4019-0 (v. 15)

Printed in the United States of America
10 9 8 7 6 5 4 3 2 1

For The Catholic University of America Press

EDITORIAL STAFF

CONTRIBUTING EDITORS

Foreword

This revised edition of the *New Catholic Encyclopedia* represents a third generation in the evolution of the text that traces its lineage back to the *Catholic Encyclopedia* published from 1907 to 1912. In 1967, sixty years after the first volume of the original set appeared, The Catholic University of America and the McGraw-Hill Book Company joined together in organizing a small army of editors and scholars to produce the *New Catholic Encyclopedia*. Although planning for the *NCE* had begun before the Second Vatican Council and most of the 17,000 entries were written before Council ended, Vatican II enhanced the encyclopedia's value and importance. The research and the scholarship that went into the articles witnessed to the continuity and richness of the Catholic Tradition given fresh expression by Council. In order to keep the *NCE* current, supplementary volumes were published in 1972, 1978, 1988, and 1995. Now, at the beginning of the third millennium, The Catholic University of America is proud to join with The Gale Group in presenting a new edition of the *New Catholic Encyclopedia*. It updates and incorporates the many articles from the 1967 edition and its supplements that have stood the test of time and adds hundreds of new entries.

As the president of The Catholic University of America, I cannot but be pleased at the reception the *NCE* has received. It has come to be recognized as an authoritative reference work in the field of religious studies and is praised for its comprehensive coverage of the Church's history and institutions. Although Canon Law no longer requires encyclopedias and reference works of this kind to receive an *imprimatur* before publication, I am confident that this new edition, like the original, reports accurate information about Catholic beliefs and practices. The editorial staff and their consultants were careful to present official Church teachings in a straightforward manner, and in areas where there are legitimate disputes over fact and differences in interpretation of events, they made every effort to insure a fair and balanced presentation of the issues.

The way for this revised edition was prepared by the publication, in 2000, of a Jubilee volume of the *NCE,* heralding the beginning of the new millennium. In my foreword to that volume I quoted Pope John Paul II's encyclical on Faith and Human Reason in which he wrote that history is "the arena where we see what God does for humanity." The *New Catholic Encyclopedia* describes that arena. It reports events, people, and ideas—"the things we know best and can verify most easily, the things of our everyday life, apart from which we cannot understand ourselves" (*Fides et ratio,* 12).

Finally, I want to express appreciation on my own behalf and on the behalf of the readers of these volumes to everyone who helped make this revision a reality. We are all indebted to The Gale Group and the staff of The Catholic University of America Press for their dedication and the alacrity with which they produced it.

Very Reverend David M. O'Connell, C.M., J.C.D.
President
The Catholic University of America

Preface to the Revised Edition

When first published in 1967 the *New Catholic Encyclopedia* was greeted with enthusiasm by librarians, researchers, and general readers interested in Catholicism. In the United States the *NCE* has been recognized as the standard reference work on matters of special interest to Catholics. In an effort to keep the encyclopedia current, supplementary volumes were published in 1972, 1978, 1988, and 1995. However, it became increasingly apparent that further supplements would not be adequate to this task. The publishers subsequently decided to undertake a thorough revision of the *NCE*, beginning with the publication of a Jubilee volume at the start of the new millennium.

Like the biblical scribe who brings from his storeroom of knowledge both the new and the old, this revised edition of the *New Catholic Encyclopedia* incorporates material from the 15-volume original edition and the supplement volumes. Entries that have withstood the test of time have been edited, and some have been amended to include the latest information and research. Hundreds of new entries have been added. For all practical purposes, it is an entirely new edition intended to serve as a comprehensive and authoritative work of reference reporting on the movements and interests that have shaped Christianity in general and Catholicism in particular over two millennia.

SCOPE

The title reflects its outlook and breadth. It is the *New Catholic Encyclopedia,* not merely a new encyclopedia of Catholicism. In addition to providing information on the doctrine, organization, and history of Christianity over the centuries, it includes information about persons, institutions, cultural phenomena, religions, philosophies, and social movements that have affected the Catholic Church from within and without. Accordingly, the *NCE* attends to the history and particular traditions of the Eastern Churches and the Churches of the Protestant Reformation, and other ecclesial communities. Christianity cannot be understood without exploring its roots in ancient Israel and Judaism, nor can the history of the medieval and modern Church be understood apart from its relationship with Islam. Interfaith dialogue requires an appreciation of Buddhism and other world religions, as well as some knowledge of the history of religion in general.

On the assumption that most readers and researchers who use the *NCE* are individuals interested in Catholicism in general and the Church in North America in particular, its editorial content gives priority to the Western Church, while not neglecting the churches in the East; to Roman Catholicism, acknowledging much common history with Protestantism; and to Catholicism in the United States, recognizing that it represents only a small part of the universal Church.

Scripture, Theology, Patrology, Liturgy. The many and varied articles dealing with Sacred Scripture and specific books of the Bible reflect contemporary biblical scholarship and its concerns. The *NCE* highlights official church teachings as expressed by the Church's magisterium. It reports developments in theology, explains issues and introduces ecclesiastical writers from the early Church Fathers to present-day theologians whose works exercise major influence on the development of Christian thought. The *NCE* traces the evolution of the Church's worship with special emphasis on rites and rituals consequent to the liturgical reforms and renewal initiated by the Second Vatican Council.

Church History. From its inception Christianity has been shaped by historical circumstances and itself has become a historical force. The *NCE* presents the Church's history from a number of points of view against the background of general political and cultural history. The revised edition reports in some detail the Church's missionary activity as it grew from a small community in Jerusalem to the worldwide phenomenon it is today. Some entries, such as those dealing with the Middle Ages, the Reformation, and the Enlightenment, focus on major time-periods and movements that cut across geographical boundaries. Other articles describe the history and structure of the Church in specific areas, countries, and regions. There are separate entries for many dioceses and monasteries which by reason of antiquity, size, or influence are of special importance in ecclesiastical history, as there are for religious orders and congregations. The *NCE* rounds out its comprehensive history of the Church with articles on religious movements and biographies of individuals.

Canon and Civil Law. The Church inherited and has safeguarded the precious legacy of ancient Rome, described by Virgil, "to rule people under law, [and] to establish the way of peace." The *NCE* deals with issues of ecclesiastical jurisprudence and outlines the development of legislation governing communal practices and individual obligations, taking care to incorporate and reference the 1983 *Code of Canon Law* throughout and, where appropriate, the *Code of Canons for the Eastern Churches*. It deals with issues of Church-State relations and with civil law as it impacts on the Church and Church's teaching regarding human rights and freedoms.

Philosophy. The Catholic tradition from its earliest years has investigated the relationship between faith and reason. The *NCE* considers at some length the many and varied schools of ancient, medieval, and modern philosophy with emphasis, when appropriate, on their relationship to theological positions. It pays particular attention to the scholastic tradition, particularly Thomism, which is prominent in Catholic intellectual history. Articles on many major and lesser philosophers contribute to a comprehensive survey of philosophy from pre-Christian times to the present.

Biography and Hagiography. The *NCE,* making an exception for the reigning pope, leaves to other reference works biographical information about living persons. This revised edition presents biographical sketches of hundreds of men and women, Christian and non-Christian, saints and sinners, because of their significance for the Church. They include: Old and New Testament figures; the Fathers of the Church and ecclesiastical writers; pagan and Christian emperors; medieval and modern kings; heads of state and other political figures; heretics and champions of orthodoxy; major and minor figures in the Reformation and Counter Reformation; popes, bishops, and priests; founders and members of religious orders and congregations; lay men and lay women; scholars, authors, composers, and artists. The *NCE* includes biographies of most saints whose feasts were once celebrated or are currently celebrated by the universal church. The revised edition relies on Butler's *Lives of the Saints* and similar reference works to give accounts of many saints, but the *NCE* also

provides biographical information about recently canonized and beatified individuals who are, for one reason or another, of special interest to the English-speaking world.

Social Sciences. Social sciences came into their own in the twentieth century. Many articles in the *NCE* rely on data drawn from anthropology, economics, psychology and sociology for a better understanding of religious structures and behaviors. Papal encyclicals and pastoral letters of episcopal conferences are the source of principles and norms for Christian attitudes and practice in the field of social action and legislation. The *NCE* draws attention to the Church's organized activities in pursuit of peace and justice, social welfare and human rights. The growth of the role of the laity in the work of the Church also receives thorough coverage.

ARRANGEMENT OF ENTRIES

The articles in the *NCE* are arranged alphabetically by the first substantive word using the word-by-word method of alphabetization; thus "New Zealand" precedes "Newman, John Henry," and "Old Testament Literature" precedes "Oldcastle, Sir John." Monarchs, patriarchs, popes, and others who share a Christian name and are differentiated by a title and numerical designation are alphabetized by their title and then arranged numerically. Thus, entries for Byzantine emperors Leo I through IV precede those for popes of the same name, while "Henry VIII, King of England" precedes "Henry IV, King of France."

Maps, Charts, and Illustrations. The *New Catholic Encyclopedia* contains nearly 3,000 illustrations, including photographs, maps, and tables. Entries focusing on the Church in specific countries contain a map of the country as well as easy-to-read tables giving statistical data and, where helpful, lists of archdioceses and dioceses. Entries on the Church in U.S. states also contain tables listing archdioceses and dioceses where appropriate. The numerous photographs appearing in the *New Catholic Encyclopedia* help to illustrate the history of the Church, its role in modern societies, and the many magnificent works of art it has inspired.

SPECIAL FEATURES

Subject Overview Articles. For the convenience and guidance of the reader, the *New Catholic Encyclopedia* contains several brief articles outlining the scope of major fields: "Theology, Articles on," "Liturgy, Articles on," "Jesus Christ, Articles on," etc.

Cross-References. The cross-reference system in the *NCE* serves to direct the reader to related material in other articles. The appearance of a name or term in small capital letters in text indicates that there is an article of that title elsewhere in the encyclopedia. In some cases, the name of the related article has been inserted at the appropriate point as a *see* reference: (*see* THOMAS AQUINAS, ST.). When a further aspect of the subject is treated under another title, a *see also* reference is placed at the end of the article. In addition to this extensive cross-reference system, the comprehensive index in volume 15 will greatly increase the reader's ability to access the wealth of information contained in the encyclopedia.

Abbreviations List. Following common practice, books and versions of the Bible as well as other standard works by selected authors have been abbreviated throughout the text. A guide to these abbreviations follows this preface.

The Editors

Abbreviations

The system of abbreviations used for the works of Plato, Aristotle, St. Augustine, and St. Thomas Aquinas is as follows: Plato is cited by book and Stephanus number only, e.g., Phaedo 79B; Rep. 480A. Aristotle is cited by book and Bekker number only, e.g., Anal. post. 72b 8–12; Anim. 430a 18. St. Augustine is cited as in the Thesaurus Linguae Latinae, e.g., C. acad. 3.20.45; Conf. 13.38.53, with capitalization of the first word of the title. St. Thomas is cited as in scholarly journals, but using Arabic numerals. In addition, the following abbreviations have been used throughout the encyclopedia for biblical books and versions of the Bible.

Books

Acts	Acts of the Apostles
Am	Amos
Bar	Baruch
1–2 Chr	1 and 2 Chronicles (1 and 2 Paralipomenon in Septuagint and Vulgate)
Col	Colossians
1–2 Cor	1 and 2 Corinthians
Dn	Daniel
Dt	Deuteronomy
Eccl	Ecclesiastes
Eph	Ephesians
Est	Esther
Ex	Exodus
Ez	Ezekiel
Ezr	Ezra (Esdras B in Septuagint; 1 Esdras in Vulgate)
Gal	Galatians
Gn	Genesis
Hb	Habakkuk
Heb	Hebrews
Hg	Haggai
Hos	Hosea
Is	Isaiah
Jas	James
Jb	Job
Jdt	Judith
Jer	Jeremiah
Jgs	Judges
Jl	Joel
Jn	John
1–3 Jn	1, 2, and 3 John
Jon	Jonah
Jos	Joshua
Jude	Jude
1–2 Kgs	1 and 2 Kings (3 and 4 Kings in Septuagint and Vulgate)
Lam	Lamentations
Lk	Luke
Lv	Leviticus
Mal	Malachi (Malachias in Vulgate)
1–2 Mc	1 and 2 Maccabees
Mi	Micah
Mk	Mark
Mt	Matthew
Na	Nahum
Neh	Nehemiah (2 Esdras in Septuagint and Vulgate)
Nm	Numbers
Ob	Obadiah
Phil	Philippians
Phlm	Philemon
Prv	Proverbs
Ps	Psalms
1–2 Pt	1 and 2 Peter
Rom	Romans
Ru	Ruth
Rv	Revelation (Apocalypse in Vulgate)
Sg	Song of Songs
Sir	Sirach (Wisdom of Ben Sira; Ecclesiasticus in Septuagint and Vulgate)
1–2 Sm	1 and 2 Samuel (1 and 2 Kings in Septuagint and Vulgate)
Tb	Tobit
1–2 Thes	1 and 2 Thessalonians
Ti	Titus
1–2 Tm	1 and 2 Timothy
Wis	Wisdom
Zec	Zechariah
Zep	Zephaniah

Versions

Apoc	Apocrypha
ARV	American Standard Revised Version
ARVm	American Standard Revised Version, margin
AT	American Translation
AV	Authorized Version (King James)
CCD	Confraternity of Christian Doctrine
DV	Douay-Challoner Version

ERV	English Revised Version	NJB	New Jerusalem Bible
ERVm	English Revised Version, margin	NRSV	New Revised Standard Version
EV	English Version(s) of the Bible	NT	New Testament
JB	Jerusalem Bible	OT	Old Testament
LXX	Septuagint	RSV	Revised Standard Version
MT	Masoretic Text	RV	Revised Version
NAB	New American Bible	RVm	Revised Version, margin
NEB	New English Bible	Syr	Syriac
NIV	New International Version	Vulg	Vulgate

C

COMBONI, DANIELE, BL.

Missionary bishop in Africa; founder of Comboni Missionaries of the Sacred Heart and the Missionary Sisters Pie Madri della Nigrizia; b. Limone del Garda (near Lake Garda), northern Italy, March 15, 1831; d. Khartoum, Sudan, Oct. 10, 1881. Daniele was the only one of the eight children of his farmer parents to live. With a view to dedicating his life to evangelizing Africa, he studied languages and medicine, as well as theology, at the diocesan seminary and Verona Institute for missionary preparation before his ordination to priesthood (1854).

In 1857 he went to Khartoum with four other priests via the Holy Land. The five labored along the White Nile, suffering deplorable shortages of food and water in an unfamiliar climate and a hostile environment that left three dead within a short time. The failed mission was aborted by the Propaganda Fide, and Comboni and his companion returned to Italy (1859) to train more missionaries.

On Sept. 15, 1864 Comboni conceived of a plan for the evangelization of Africa that involved ''saving Africa with Africans.'' Europeans would establish missions along the coast and make expeditions inland to educate Africans to evangelize others. The plan included the use of female missionaries. In 1867, with papal approval, he founded the Verona Fathers because the new bishop of Verona no longer allowed the Institute for missionary preparation to have its own seminarians or priests. The first group left before the end of the year to establish a mission post at Cairo.

Returning to Europe to seek funding, Comboni established the Missionary Sisters of Verona or Pie Madri della Nigrizia (1872). He prepared a document for Vatican Council I that included his plan, and it received approval on July 18, 1870 from Pope Pius IX. Comboni was appointed provicar apostolic (1872), then vicar apostolic (1877) of the Vicariate Apostolic of Central Africa embracing Sudan, Nubia, and territories south of the great lakes. The following year he was involved in famine re-lief in Khartoum. Besides traveling widely in his vicariate and establishing missions at Khartoum, El-Obeid, Berber, Delen, and Malbes, Comboni sought to end the widespread slave trade and its abuses. This led to his abduction by a Freemason in Paris during one of his fundraising trips.

Comboni was also a linguist, geographer, and ethnologist, and contributed extensively to scientific journals. He compiled a dictionary of the Nubian language, and published studies on the Dinka and Bari tongues. His reports, such as *Un passo al giorno sulla via della missione* (Bologna, 1997) and *Gli scritti* (Bologna, 1991), and correspondence provide much information on the history of African civilization.

Comboni succumbed to malaria during his journey from El-Obeid to Khartoum in July of 1881. Nevertheless, he continued to work for several months before he died. Pope John Paul II beatified Comboni on March 17, 1996.

Feast: Oct. 10.

Bibliography: D. AGASSO, *Un profeta per l'Africa* (Milan 1993). A. BARITUSSIO, *Cuore e missione: la spiritualità del cuore di Cristo nella vita e negli scritti di Daniele Comboni* (Bologna 2000). O. BRANCHESI, *Safari for Souls* (Cincinnati 1951). A. CAPOVILLA, *Daniele Comboni,* 6th ed. (Verona 1923). C. FUSERO, *Daniele Comboni,* 3rd ed. (Bologna 1961). L. FRANCESCHINI, ''Il Comboni e lo schiavismo,'' in *Archivo Comboniano* (Verona 1961): 27–65. MONS. M. GRANCELLI, *Daniele Comboni e la missione dell'Africa Centrale* (Verona 1923). S. LUCIANI and I. TADDIA, eds., *Fonti comboniane per la storia dell'Africa nord-orientale,* 2 v. (Bologna 1986 and Cagliari 1988). V. MILANI, ed., *Mozambico: un imperativo di coscienza* (Bologna 1976). A. MONTONATI, *Il Nilo scorre ancora* (Bologna 1995).

[J. M. CARILLO/K. I. RABENSTEIN]

COMBONI MISSIONARIES OF THE HEART OF JESUS

(MCCJ, Official Catholic Directory #0380); popularly known as the Verona Fathers. The Comboni Missionaries of the Heart of Jesus (Missionarii Comboniani Cordis Jesu), a pontifical congregation of priests and brothers devoted exclusively to missionary work, was founded by Bp. Daniele COMBONI in Verona, Italy, in 1867. Originally founded as a secular institute for African missions, the institute was changed in 1885 into a religious congregation under the guidance of the Jesuits. Final approval of the Holy See was given in 1910.

From its inception, the congregation gave priority to missionary work in Africa, establishing its mission in Sudan, but a revolution there in 1881 disrupted the work. In 1899, the congregation returned to Sudan to rebuild the missions and establish schools. In 1910 they expanded their work to Uganda, and later to Ethiopia and Mozambique. In Latin America the society has missions in Mexico, Brazil, and Ecuador. Members of the society have written works on the ethnology and languages of the African tribes whom they have evangelized.

When they came to the United States in 1940, the congregation established themselves in Cincinnati, Ohio, where the provincial house is located. The generalate is in Rome.

Bibliography: O. BRANCHESI, *Safari for Souls* (Cincinnati 1951).

[J. M. CARILLO/EDS.]

COMENIUS, JOHN AMOS (KOMENSKÝ)

Exponent of sense realism, writer, educator, and last bishop of Moravian Brethren; b. Niwnitz, Moravia (or at Coma, Moravia), March 28, 1592; d. Amsterdam, Netherlands, Nov. 15, 1670. Because he was orphaned very young, his formal education at the hands of relatives was irregular. Only at 17 did Comenius begin to study Latin at the Stráňice Latin School because of a desire to prepare for the ministry of the Moravian Brethren. His higher education took place at Herborn, Nassau, and Heidelberg, Germany, where he earned his degree. On returning to Moravia, Comenius taught in the Brethren's schools in Prerau, where he was ordained in 1614. As a pastor he opened his own school at Fulneck. To aid his students Comenius published *Grammaticae facilioris praecepta,* the first of his educational treatises.

In 1618 the Thirty Years' War broke the peaceful ways of Moravia; Spanish invasion and Protestant harrassment drove the Moravian Brethren into exile. Comenius settled with the Brethren at Lissa, in Poland, where their schools reopened according to their own curricula. In 1630 he published *Pansophiae prodromus,* a work on

education. In 1631 *Janua Linguarum reserata,* a textbook to teach Latin by means of the vernacular, received international acclaim and was translated during his lifetime into 12 European and four Oriental languages. The *Eruditionis scholasticae vestibulum,* an edition of the *Janua* meant for younger children, and the *Atrium* for those who had advanced beyond the *Janua,* increased his reputation as a new leader in educational thought and practice.

Comenius used the same method in these three works: sentences conveying practical information arranged in parallel columns in both the vernacular and the language to be learned, e.g., Latin or Greek or another modern language. Most scholars credit Comenius with the discovery of this technique for teaching languages. To advance this method of language study, based on induction and learning real objects before learning the nouns that describe them, in 1658 Comenius produced the *Orbis sensualium pictus,* the first children's picture book, in which the objects in each picture bore a number that referred to a word. This system was then introduced into later editions of the *Janua, Vestibulum,* and *Atrium.* The *Orbis sensualium pictus* was printed in Europe for more than 200 years as a basic school textbook.

In his philosophy Comenius adopted a form of pansophism, a doctrine based on universal knowledge and teaching. Convinced that peace could exist on earth only when mankind united under the service of one God, in one religion, the Moravian exile advocated compulsory education for both sexes and all social classes, on a ladder plan in which each school led to a higher level and terminated with the College of Light, a haven for the learned of all nations. He reasoned that education would provide an equal level of knowledge for all men and thus lead to the acceptance of the unity of mankind and one universal religion. The *Didactica magna* (1638) is the best summary and presentation of Comenius's pansophism.

His educational theories and practices and his philosophical works led the nations of Europe to invite the Moravian leader to offer advice on their schools. In 1638 Swedish authorities, hoping to establish a national system of education, invited Comenius to reform their schools. England extended a similar invitation in 1641, but the political situation forced him to withdraw. His brief stay in England nevertheless resulted in the publication of *The School of Infancy,* the purpose of which was to instruct mothers how to teach young children correct speaking, observation, and religion. The pansophic group that welcomed Comenius to England was later influential in establishing the Royal Academy in 1662.

In 1648 John Winthrop, Jr., touring Europe in search of an outstanding theologian-educator to be president of Harvard (Cambridge, Mass.), is believed to have invited

Comenius to accept the incumbency. In 1644 the Poles banished him from Lissa because he had welcomed Swedish troops when they captured the city during the Thirty Years' War. The Swedes again welcomed him, but after his attacks on Lutheranism, revoked their hospitality. In 1648 he was elected bishop of the Moravian Brethren, the last in the Bohemian-Moravian episcopal line.

Comenius had more influence on the educational theorists of the 19th century, which adopted his ideal of free, compulsory, universal education, than on his contemporaries. His pansophic and religious ideas, however, never attracted a wide following.

Bibliography: J. A. COMENIUS, *Analytical Didactic*, ed. and tr. V. JELINEK (Chicago 1953); *The School of Infancy*, ed. E. M. ELLER (Chapel Hill, N.C. 1956); *The Great Didactic*, tr. M. W. KEATINGE (London 1896). M. SPINKA, *John Amos Comenius: That Incomparable Moravian* (Chicago 1943).

[E. G. RYAN]

COMENSOLI, GERTRUDE CATERINA, BL.

Known in religion as Gertrude of the Blessed Sacrament, foundress of the Sacramentine Sisters of Bergamo; b. Biennio, Brescia, Lombardy, Italy, Jan. 18, 1857; d. Bergamo, Lombardy, Feb. 18, 1903. Gertrude, the fifth of ten children in a poor family, learned to love and revere the Blessed Sacrament from her parents' example. She was a Maria Bambino Sister of Charity until ill health forced her from the convent. Upon her recovery, she taught in association with the Company of Angela Merici while serving as a lady's companion to a countess. After meeting Francesco SPINELLI (1879), founder of the Sisters of Perpetual Adoration of the Blessed Sacrament, she founded the Sacramentine Sisters of Bergamo (1882), dedicated to Christian education and adoration. The first sisters received the religious habit in 1884. From Bergamo, where they had started, the sisters moved to Lodi where they received episcopal approval in 1891. They returned to Bergamo the following year, expanded the congregation's ministries, and received papal approval in 1908. When financial difficulties beset the Sacramentine Sisters, Spinelli was removed from their direction by the bishop. The beatification process for Gertrude Comensoli was opened in 1928. She was declared venerable by John XXIII and beatified by John Paul II on Oct. 1, 1989.

Bibliography: C. COMENSOLI, *Un'anima eucaristica, madre Gertrude Comensoli* (Monza 1936). *La Suora Sacramentina alla scuola della Serva di Dio Madre Gertrude Comensoli* (Bergamo 1960). *Acta Apostolicae Sedis* (1989): 1030.

[K. I. RABENSTEIN]

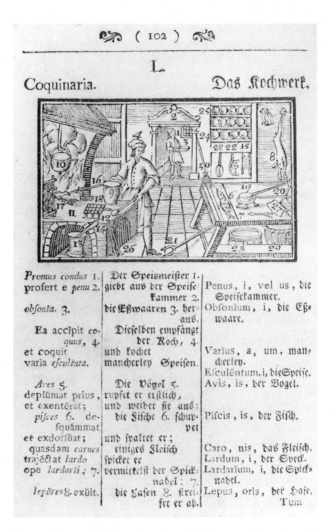

Page with text and illustration from "Orbis sensualium pictus," by John Amos Comenius, 1780.

COMGALL, ST.

Sixth century Irish monastic founder; b. Ulster, *c.* 520; d. Bangor, Ireland, *c.* 602. St. Comgall founded the monastery of Bangor about 555 on the southern shore of Belfast Lough. Its rule, derived from Clonenagh in Leix, was very severe. He helped St. COLUMBA OF IONA to convert the pagan Picts of Scotland and about 590 dispatched a group of 12 under a leader, St. COLUMBAN, to renew religious life in Merovingian Gaul. The excellence of the education given in Bangor is apparent in Columba's writings. It appears, too, in the Antiphonary of Bangor, compiled in the monastery within the years 680 to 691. Comgall is mentioned in the *Life of Columbanus* by Jonas and commemorated in the Stowe Missal and the Martyrology of Tallaght.

Feast: May 10.

Bibliography: C. PLUMMER, comp., *Vitae sanctorum Hiberniae*, 2 v. (Oxford 1910) 2:3–21. *Acta Sanctorum* May

2:577–587. J. P. BUTE, *Acta sanctorum Hiberniae ex Codice Salmanticensi,* ed. C. DE SMEDT and J. DE BACKER (Edinburgh 1888).

[J. RYAN]

COMITOLI, PAOLO

Jesuit moral theologian and exegete; b. Perugia, 1544; d. there, Feb. 18, 1626. He entered the Society of Jesus in 1559 and took part in the papal commission charged with producing a new edition of the Septuagint in 1587. He was a staunch defender of papal authority in the controversy occasioned by Paul V's interdict of 1606 against the Venetian doge and senate. But so captious were some of his arguments in the *Trattato apologetico,* which he wrote on the subject (Venice 1606), that Bellarmine had to intervene to clarify his position. Comitoli was an opponent of PROBABILISM. Among his other works were *Catena in Job* (Venice 1587), *Responsa moralia* (Lyons 1609), and *Doctrina contractuum* (Lyons 1615).

Bibliography: P. BERNARD, *Dictionnaire de théologie catholique,* ed. A. VACANT et al. (Paris 1903–50) 3.1:388. C. SOMMERVOGEL et al., *Bibliothèque de la Compagnie de Jésus* (Brussels-Paris 1890–1932) 2:1342–43.

[L. B. O'NEIL]

COMMA PIANUM

Comma pianum are words that evoke the controversies that arose in the 16th and 17th centuries over the interpretation of the bull *EX OMNIBUS AFFLICTIONIBUS,* of Oct. 1, 1567, by which Pope Pius V condemned 76 propositions taken from the works of BAIUS and his followers. After the enumeration of the condemned propositions, the bull contained the following clause, which according to the custom of the chancellery was not punctuated: "quas quidem sententias . . . quamquam nonnullae aliquo pacto sustineri possent in rigore et proprio verborum sensu ab assertoribus intento haereticas . . . respective . . . damnamus. . . ." If a comma is placed after "possent," the sense is that the propositions, some of which in some way are tenable, are condemned in the full rigor of the terms and the proper meaning of the words such as the authors had in mind. If a comma is placed after "intento," the sense is that the propositions are condemned, although some are tenable in a certain manner in the rigor of the terms and in the proper meaning desired by the authors. The displacement of the comma, then, leads to two opposite interpretations; the second, since it was favorable to Baius, was defended by him and by his defenders, especially by Jacques Janson in 1618

and by C. JANSEN (JANSENIUS) in *AUGUSTINUS.* Since the bull of Pius V was renewed in 1643 (date of promulgation) in the bull of Urban VIII, *In eminenti,* this document was printed under the direction of the nuncio Fabio Chigi with the comma after "possent," which provoked violent reactions from the Jansenists. The investigation ordered by Urban VIII agreed to the presence of the comma in this place. However, the controversies continued, and it was not until 1701, under the influence of M. Steyaert, that the Faculty of Louvain definitely accepted this punctuation. It must be noted, however, that the recent works of Edouard van Eijl, OFM, have completely reopened the question and have shown that in fact it was the interpretation favorable to Baius that should have been retained as in accord with the intentions of Pius V without, however, thereby diminishing the force of the condemnation.

Bibliography: E. VAN EIJL, "L'Interprétation de la bulle de Pie V portant la condamnation de Baius," *Revue d'histoire ecclésiastique* 50 (1955) 499–542. J. ORCIBAL, "De Baius à Jansénius: Le *Comma pianum,*" *Revue des sciences religieuses* 36 (1962) 115–139.

[L. J. COGNET]

COMMANDMENTS, TEN

A group of moral precepts in the Pentateuch, known also as the Decalogue, always regarded as of basic importance in both Judaism and Christianity. This article treats the Biblical data, the moral theology, and the catechistic role of the Ten Commandments.

IN THE BIBLE

The group of precepts traditionally known as the Ten Commandments are found in the Bible in two separate pericopes: Ex 20.1–17 and Dt 5.6–21. Both these pericopes are contained in narrations of the Sinaitic revelation and making of the COVENANT. The importance of these laws is shown by the fact that they are presented as written by Yahweh Himself on two tablets of stone (Ex 24.12; 31.18; Dt 4.13; 5.22). In fact, these laws represent a substantial part of the covenant, so that the covenant itself could be referred to as the Ten Commandments in Dt 4.13; 10.4; Ex 34.28. They correspond to the stipulations of obligation in the Hittite suzerainty treaty form.

A comparison of the two lists of commandments shows that, while they are very similar, there are some variations between them. The principal variations are the different motives assigned for the Sabbath observance and the different ways of considering possessions. In Exodus a man's wife is ranked with his servants and his animals as forming part of his "house," i.e., his possessions, whereas in Deuteronomy she is placed first as distinct

Moses receiving the Ten Commandments (upper) and reading the Ten Commandments (lower) to the Israelites inside a basilica, full-page miniature from the "Bible of Charles the Bald," second half of the 9th century, in the Bibliotheque Nationale, Paris. (MS Latin 1, fol. 27v)

from the rest of his possessions. This indicates that, behind the present form of the laws, there was a process of formation from more primitive forms.

Apodictic Law. The basic characteristic of the Ten Commandments is that they are apodictic laws, that is, they are in the form of brief imperatives or prohibitions, complete in themselves without any explanation. Studies have shown that this form of law is closely, though not exclusively, bound up with the history of Israel, in contrast to the form of casuistic law usually found in the ancient Near East. The apodictic form of the Ten Commandments thus gives important insight into their background and time of composition.

Their form, coupled with the realization that these precepts reflect ideas known in the ancient Near East as witnessed by the 125th chapter of the Egyptian Book of the Dead [J. B. Pritchard, *Ancient Near Eastern Texts Relating to the Old Testament* (2d, rev. ed. Princeton 1955) 34–36], the Babylonian hymn to Shamash (*ibid.*, 387–389), and the Assyrian exorcisms [H. Gressmann, *Altorientalische Texte zum Alten Testament* (2d ed. Berlin 1926) 9–12], has today led critical scholars generally to abandon the position that the Ten Commandments resulted from the preaching of the later classical Prophets. Rather, it is affirmed that they had their origin in Mosaic times and that there is no reason to doubt the tradition that connects them with Moses' activity as law-giver.

Since several of the commandments still retain their characteristically brief, negative form, the amplifications and assignment of motives to several others can be considered as secondary. Note, however, that the complete text as found in the Bible is certainly inspired and the consideration of certain phrases as secondary is done only to see more clearly the work of the inspired redactor(s).

The Number Ten. With this understanding, it is possible to proceed to an examination of the principal difference between the two lists with regard to the last commandment. This commandment is given in Ex 20.17 as a general prohibition against the desire of another's property, including his wife. In Dt 5.21 this commandment has a more elevated moral sense: the wife is considered first and separately, followed by a prohibition against the desire of another's property. The use of two different verbs to achieve this separation naturally leads to an apparent increase in the number of commandments. What then of the number ten, which seems to be the traditional number as appears from the use of the phrase "ten words" in Dt 4.13; 10.4; Ex 34.28? Some scholars hold that ten is only a round number in this context, especially when considered alongside of other lists of apodictic laws that appear in the Pentateuch.

The reality of this problem is felt even today, since the acceptance of the enumeration of commandments as found in Deuteronomy by St. Augustine and many Fathers of the West has led the Latin Church, as well as the Lutherans, to use this enumeration. Confusion arises from the fact that the enumeration as presented by the text of Exodus, which appears also in Jewish Rabbinic tradition, was adopted by St. Jerome and the Greek Fathers and so has resulted in a usage by the Greek Church differing from that of the Latin Church. Protestants other than Lutherans and the Jews also use the enumeration of Exodus.

Jewish tradition maintains the number ten by considering the first commandment to be Ex 20.2, which is viewed by others as a prologue to the Commandments. The Christians who follow the tradition of Exodus seek to maintain the tradition of ten by splitting into two commandments—Ex 20.3 and Ex 20.4–6—what is considered as one commandment by the tradition of the West, namely, Dt 5.7–10. Such a split is considered to represent the more original form of the Decalogue. The fusion into one commandment would have taken place after the dividing of the last one as an attempt to maintain the number ten.

This opinion, that Ex 20.4a was originally a separate commandment, seems to be a satisfactory solution, especially if it is maintained that it represents a prohibition against making idols of Yahweh, since it would then conform to the nature of apodictic law by regulating a matter different from that of the first commandment.

Nothing definite can be said regarding the division of the original ten commandments on the two stone tablets, even though the tablets are mentioned several times in the Pentateuch, e.g., Ex 34.29 and Dt 4.13.

Bibliography: J. J. STAMM, *Le Decalogue*, tr. P. REYMOND (Cahiers Théologiques 43; Neuchâtel 1959). G. E. MENDENHALL, *Law and Covenant in Israel and the Ancient Near East* (Pittsburgh 1955) repr. from *Biblical Archeology* 17 (1954) 26–46, 49–76. G. VON RAD, *Old Testament Theology,* tr. D. M. G. STALKER, 2 v. (New York 1962–) v.1.

[S. M. POLAN]

IN MORAL THEOLOGY

Among all the directives of God, the Ten Commandments—the Decalogue, from the Greek δέκα and λόγοι, literally "the ten words"—are given preeminence in the Scriptures of the Old Testament and especially in the theological reflection of the people of the covenant. Indeed, the literary genre of the account makes this clear: in the midst of the mighty revelation of the holiness and goodness of God, the Commandments as the conclusion of the covenant of Sinai were directly announced to

Moses alone, who in turn communicated them to the people, imposing them as a perpetual remembrance (Exodus ch. 19, 25). In Ex 20.1–17 they are found in their oldest redaction. In contrast with the other ancient legal maxims that were handed down along with "the ten words" only the Decalogue was said to have been written by the finger of God upon the two tablets (Ex 24.12; 31.18). In the account of the renewal of the tablets, Exodus says explicitly that God "wrote on the tablets the words of the covenant, the Ten Commandments" (34.28).

The Law of the Covenant and Moral Norms. The Decalogue must be viewed basically in terms of the covenant of God with the people. The covenant is a pure gift. And thus also the observance of the Ten Commandments of God is not primarily an accomplishment through which man first merits membership in the covenant. The negative character of the formulation has a deep theological meaning. The Israelite must be careful lest he fall out of the unique reality of the covenant. And yet the fulfillment of the Decalogue is eminently positive: gratefully remaining within the covenant and acting according to the gift of the covenant. Primarily the Decalogue concerns the people as a whole; each individual is personally addressed as a member of the people. Belonging to the salvific community is the most manifest basis of his personal obligation. Solidarity and personal obligation are united in perfect synthesis. The salvific-social basis determines the individuals place, duties, and rights in the community. The community of the Israelites with one another has its ultimate and strongest basis in the covenant of God with His people.

Structure and Meaning. From antiquity there has been a diversity of opinion with respect to the enumeration and ordering of the individual Commandments. Catholics consider the Commandment "You shall not have other gods besides me" along with the First Commandment as a positive specification or explanation, following St. Augustine. Others—above all, the Reformers—consider this as the Second Commandment. (Accordingly, what Catholics consider as the Second Commandment, others consider as the Third, etc.) Likewise, they then take the Commandment forbidding the coveting of a neighbor's wife together with that regarding the coveting of a neighbor's goods. In so doing they follow the oldest tradition, going back to Philo and Origen.

The first three Commandments (according to the other reckoning, the first four) govern the relation to the covenant of God. In them the primacy of the religious sphere is clearly expressed. The observance of the whole of the Decalogue, but especially and in a unique way the absolutely exclusive worship of Yahweh, is an act of thanksgiving for liberation from Egypt and for the gift of the covenant. The following Commandment forbidding idolatry serves as a protection for the exclusive worship required of the people with whom God has entered into covenant. The destiny of the people of the covenant is shaped by the purity of the worship of God. Honoring the name of God and keeping holy the Sabbath are expressions of worship and loving reverence for the God of the covenant—expressions of fidelity to Him. As indicated in the first tablet, the purity of divine worship decides the destiny of the people. The focal point of the second tablet is the relation of the members of the people of the covenant to each other, family sense, piety toward one's parents. It bears the promise for prosperity in the social order and participation in the land of the covenant. The next Commandments protect life, marital fidelity, property, and the trustworthiness of testimony. At the conclusion, morality of the heart is enjoined: an evil act and an evil desire are both opposed to the fidelity owed to the God of the covenant and the people of the covenant. The close juxtaposition of the Commandments concerning the desire for one's neighbors wife and for his property and home is to be understood in terms of the sociological background, which imposes certain limitations upon his freedom of action. Basically, it is a question of the social aspect of marital chastity in conjunction with the morality of the heart.

The Decalogue and the Law of Christ. Already among the teachers of the Old Testament there was great freedom in formulating the Decalogue. Distinguished exegetes believe that the primitive form of the Decalogue was as short as that in the catechism today. In any case, both of the main texts (Ex 20.1–17; Dt 5.6–21) present noticeable variations—for example, the different bases for the Sabbath Commandment: in one place the basis is considered to be the transcendence of God the Creator; in the other, it is considered to be the salvific acts of God, which lay the foundation for a salvific-social thought. Deuteronomy (5.21) displays a finer sense of the dignity of womanhood, while Exodus (20.17) first forbids desiring the neighbor's house and then his wife. It would be an understatement to say that in presentation of the Decalogue Christ offered a still greater freedom, and in a manner still clearer than that of the teachers of the Old Testament, He gathered all together under the law of love. Jesus pedagogically began with the knowledge of the Decalogue proper to the Jews. But He is infinitely more than a promulgator of law: He is Himself "the new law and the new Covenant" (Justin, *Dial.*, 11, 43; *Patrologia Graeca* 6:497–499, 568). For the Christian, the greater reality on which his duty is founded is life in Christ. Christ has expressed this blessed reality in the form of the new law through His words and example, and above all through the Sermon on the Mount (cf. Matthew ch. 5–7) and the farewell discourse (John ch. 14–17) The Decalogue falls far short of this directive toward perfection. To attempt to represent it as a *summa* of Christian morality implies an inadmissible impoverishment. Whoever wishes to consider it, following Augustine, as the basis for a moral schema must present it in the light of the New Testament and New Testament law (Sermon on the Mount and the farewell discourse) and this in the light of Christ and of life in Christ. Each individual Commandment must be seen as demanding that love that God has given us in Christ.

When it is said that the Decalogue is not the characteristic expression of the New Testament and the Law of the New Testament, it should not be understood, however, that the Ten Commandments do not apply to the Christian [H. Denzinger, *Enchiridion symbolorum* (32 ed. Freiburg 1963) 1569]. Apart from the two commandments of purely positive law forbidding the veneration of images and commanding observance of the Sabbath, which were abolished and indirectly fulfilled in a higher mode of divine worship, the Commandments of the Decalogue remain as an enduring expression of the natural law and thus are contained, though surpassed as a part—modest indeed—of the New Testament law.

Bibliography: P. ALTHAUS, *Gebot and Gesetz* (Gütersloh 1952). M. P. BUTLER, "Must We Teach Morality according to the Decalogue," *Worship 37* (1964) 293–300. W. DRESS, "Die Zehn Gebote und der Dekalog," *Theologische Literaturzeitung* 79 (1954) 415–422. L. HARTMAN, "The Enumeration of the Ten Commandments," *The Catholic Biblical Quarterly* 7 (1945) 105–108. H. H. ROWLEY, "Moses and the Decalogue," *The Bulletin of the John Rylands Library* 34 (1951–52) 81–118, also separately pub. (Manchester 1951).

[B. HÄRING]

IN CATECHESIS

The *Catechism of the Catholic Church* states, "Ever since St. Augustine, the Ten Commandments have occupied a predominant place in the catechesis of baptismal candidates and the faithful"(2064). The statement needs to be qualified because it was only when the Church's penitential rites became linked to confessional practice, sometime about the beginning of the 8th century, that the Decalogue became a standard formula in catechesis.

The Twofold Commandment of Love. Although a number of passages in both the Gospels and the Epistles cite individual commandments, the Ten Commandments are not listed in their entirety anywhere in the New Testament nor are they referred to collectively. In the gospels of Mark and Matthew Jesus identifies love of God and love of neighbor as the two commandments that are the basis of the law and prophets. In response to the scribe in Mark's gospel who asks, "Which is the first of all the commandments?," Jesus replies quoting the *Shema* and Deuteronomic text (6.4–5): "The first is this: 'Hear, O Israel! The Lord our God is Lord alone! You shall love the Lord your God with all your heart, with all your soul, with all your mind, and with all your strength' The second is this: 'You shall love your neighbor as yourself.' There is no other commandment great than these" (Mk 12.28–31). In Matthew's gospel a Pharisee asks much the same question and Jesus responds in much same way again quoting Deuteronomy, calling it "the greatest and the first commandment," and then adds, "The second is like it: You shall love your neighbor as yourself. The whole law and the prophets depend on these two commandments"(Mt 22.33–40).

Augustine's *Enchiridion* (c. 419/422) outlines the contents of catechesis on the basis of the Creed (faith), the Lord's Prayer (hope), and the twofold commandment of love. The last section is by far the shortest. He writes, "every commandment concerns charity" (par. 120). The only explicit reference to the Decalogue, and it is by way of example, is the text, "You shall not commit adultery" (Ex 20.14; Dt. 5.18). Augustine repeatedly cites the twofold commandment of charity in his sermons and in a text quoted in the Catechism (2067), he clearly links it to the Ten Commandments.

> As charity comprises the two commandments to which the Lord related the whole Law and the prophets . . . so the Ten Commandments were themselves given on two tablets. Three were written on one tablet and seven on the other (*Sermo* 33, 2, 2).

> For him the first three commandments (through to Sabbath-observance) center on love of God, the remaining seven on love of neighbor.

St. Thomas Aquinas expounded the Decalogue in the context of the twofold commandment of love in a series of catechetical instructions delivered in the vernacular during Lent of 1273. At the beginning of the sermons on the Commandments he quoted Augustine's *Enchiridion*, "Three things are necessary for salvation, knowledge of what must be believed; knowledge of what must be hoped for; and knowledge of what must be done." The first written catechism, *The Lay Folks' Catechism* commissioned by the Archbishop of York, John Thoresby (1357), continued the tradition of listing the Commandments in groups of three and seven. But as the sacrament of penance and confession became an occasion for catechesis, the division was lost sight of and the list of the Ten Commandments became a free-standing formula to be memorized. *The Lay Folks' Catechism* directed confessors to ask whether the penitents knew the Ten Commandments. They were one of six items that parish priests were to inquire about when people made their annual Lenten confession. If not always observed in practice, the tradition of examining the laity about the Ten Commandments became well established in the late Middle Ages. In 1518 Martin Luther had a poster printed with the heading, ''A Short Explanation of the Ten Commandments'' as an aid to assist people preparing for confession.

Reformation and Post-Reformation Catechisms. Luther's catechisms—both large and small—gave new prominence to the Ten Commandments. His theology of Law and Gospel caused him to position the Ten Commandments first, before his explanation of the Creed and the Lord's Prayer. Catholic catechisms generally continued to follow the traditional order of treating the Creed before the Commandments. The *Summa* of St. Peter Canisius which exercised a major influence on the contents of post-Reformation catechisms adopted the Augustinian pattern of Faith, Hope, and Charity but added a fourth element, Sacraments. The Catechism of the Council of Trent, the so-called Roman Catechism, has four parts but in a different sequence: Creed, Sacraments, Commandments and the Lord's Prayer. The first edition of the Baltimore Catechism (1885) that provided the syllabus for Catholic religion textbooks in the United States for half a century followed the basic plan of Trent. The revised edition (1941), however, changed the order to Creed, Commandments, Sacraments and Prayer, again to give greater emphasis to the Decalogue.

To the extent that the Ten Commandments became the only and almost exclusive framework for teaching Catholic moral doctrine, the emphasis on the Decalogue in catechesis was criticized. The principal criticisms were two. First, in making the Ten Commandments a stand-alone list of moral norms to be committed to memory, they became dissociated from the *Shema* and Covenant theme in Exodus and Deuteronomy of which they were an integral part. Second, they overshadowed, even displaced, the twofold commandment of love, that in the New Testament is clearly the basis on which the law and prophets depend. The *Catechism of the Catholic Church* corrects the one-dimensional presentation of the Ten Commandments and rejoins them to the twofold commandment of love (2052–2074). The *CCC* acknowledges that the Decalogue is one of the ''four pillars of catechesis.'' It follows the order of the Catechism of the Council of Trent—Creed, Liturgy, Commandments, and Lord's Prayer—and it reaffirms St. Augustine's dictum, ''every commandment concerns charity.''

Bibliography: J. A. SLATTERY, *The Catechetical Use of the Decalogue from the End of the Catechumenate through the Late Medieval Period* (PhD. dissertation, The Catholic University of America, 1980). B. L. MARTHALER, *The Catechism Yesterday and Today* (Collegeville, MN 1995). W. LANGER in J. GEVAERT, ed., *Dizionario di catechetica* (Turin 1986).

[B. L. MARTHALER]

COMMENDATION

The act of giving benefices *in commendam* (in trust) or the condition of such during the absence of a titular authority. The practice existed in the early Church and became common especially during the barbarian invasions (see Gregory I, *Reg.* 2.37 [Ewald 1:132]). Essentially it was a temporary arrangement. The holder drew the revenue during the vacancy and exercised some jurisdiction. Subsequently, from the Carolingian period onward, the practice fell into disrepute when it was used to reward those who clearly could not fulfill the duties (e.g., granting an abbey to a layman) and when it lost its temporary character. These developments were part of the feudalization of ecclesiastical institutions during the Middle Ages. Attempts were made to remedy the situation (cf. LYONS COUNCIL II, c.14 [*Conciliorum oecumenicorum decreta* 298] and LATERAN COUNCIL V, *Supernae dispositionis arbitrio* [*Conciliorum oecumenicorum decreta* 59]), but the papacy found the system useful, and it was flagrantly abused, especially during the financial crises of the later Middle Ages. The practice of giving commendatory abbeys continued after the Reformation and lasted into the 18th and 19th centuries.

Bibliography: R. LAPRAT, *Dictionnaire de droit canonique*, ed. R. NAZ, 7 v. (Paris 1935–65) 3:1029–85. G. MARIÉ, *Catholicisme. Hier, aujourd'hui et demain*, ed. G. JACQUEMET (Paris 1947–) 2:1340–42. P. HOFMEISTER, *Lexikon für Theologie und Kirche*, ed. J. HOFER and K. RAHNER, 10 v. (2d, new ed. Freiburg 1957–65) 6:407. H. E. FEINE, *Kirchliche Rechtsgeschichte*, v. 1 *Die katholische Kirche* (4th ed. Cologne 1964).

[J. GILCHRIST]

COMMENDATION OF THE DYING

The Rite for the Commendation of the Dying has been revised within the post-conciliar liturgical reform of the rites of the sick, the dying, and burial. The emergence of this reformed rite as it appears in the 1983 *Pastoral Care of the Sick: Rites of Anointing and Viacticum* is the result of the adaptations made to the 1972 *Ordo commendationis morientium*, found in the Latin *editio typica* of *Ordo Unctionis infirmorum eorumque pastoralis curae*, which itself was a revision of the *Ordo commendationis animae*, found in the Title V, chapter vi of the 1614 *Rituale Romanum*. Early ritual evidence of commending the dying person to God appears in *Ordo Romanus XLIX* (*c.* 800), in which the dying person is communicated, and then has "the passions of the Lord" read "until the soul departs from the body," followed by, at the moment of expiration, the responsory *Subvenite*, Ps 114 *In exitu*, and the antiphon *Chorus angelorum*. As Frankish practices came to dominate Roman ones, the reading of the passions of the Lord were replaced by other liturgical texts, such as the litany prose prayer *Proficiscere/Libera*, whose source can be traced to the fourth-century *Orationes pseudocyprianae*, which, in their original context, were exorcisms that asked protection against the powers of hell for catechumens. While the continued practice of reading the passions of the Lord to the dying person is evidenced largely through monastic rituals and the twelfth-century *Roman Pontifical*, the pervasiveness of the Frankish pattern of rites for the dying can be seen in the absence of the reading of the passions in the thirteenth-century *Pontifical of the Roman Curia*, as well as in the *Franciscan Ritual of the Last Sacraments* (1260), which drew from and was very influential in disseminating this thirteenth-century curial rite. Despite this influence, however, two important predecessors to the 1614 *RR*, the *Liber Sacerdotalis* of Alberto Castellani (1523) and Giulio Santori's *Rituale Sacramentorum Romanum* (1602), both include the readings of the passions of the Lord in their rites for the dying. While the 1614 *RR* incorporates the litany of the saints and the six commendation prayers from the Franciscan ritual, it also includes a subunit composed of Jn 17:1–26 (Jesus' farewell discourse), the passion of John, the passion prayer, and Pss 118 and 119, as well as three devotional prayers, whose origins can be traced to the fourteenth-century *Ars moriendi*.

Consisting of multiple short texts and biblical readings, the litany of saints, four commendation prayers, a devotional prayer, and prayers at expiration, the postconciliar reform of the commendation of the dying involves a changed ritual context, for it is once again associated, not with the *Sacramentum extremae unctionis*, but with viaticum, seeking to sustain this union with Christ until it is brought to fulfillment after death. Further, the reformed commendation rite involves a changed ritual and changed texts that reflect changing attitudes to death and the afterlife. No longer as concerned about the need for forgiveness of sins and deliverance from the pains and punishments of hell, the reformed rite invites the dying person to share in the paschal mystery, completing what was begun in baptism, and to share in the hope of eternal communion with God and of the resurrection of the body. In order to accomplish this goal, the prayers and readings attempt to assist the dying person to overcome the anxiety and fear of death in the power of Christ, who in dying destroyed death, encouraging the dying person to imitate Christ in his suffering and death and to accept his or her own fear and anxiety about death in the hope of heavenly life and of resurrection. Offered by the Church to strengthen and comfort a dying Christian in passage from this life, this rite helps the dying person to "embrace death in mysterious union with the crucified and risen Lord, who awaits them in the fullness of life" (*PCS*, no. 163). Even in the absence of a priest or deacon, other members of the community should be prepared to carry out this ministry, for their presence shows more clearly that this Christian dies in the communion of the Church (*OUI*, no 142; *PCS* no. 213).

Bibliography: M. ANDRIEU, *Ordo Romanus XLIX*, in *Les Ordines romani du haut moyen-âge: Les textes (Ordines XXXV–XLIX)*, (Spicilegium Sacrum Lovaniense 28; Louvain 1956), 4:529–530. *Sacramentarium Rhenaugiense*, ed. A. HÄNGGI and A. SCHÖNHERR (Spicilegium Friburgense, no. 15; Freiburg 1970). M. ANDRIEU, *Le pontifical de la curie romaine au XIIe siècle*, vol. 1, *Studi e Testi* 86 (Vatican City 1938). M. ANDRIEU, *Le pontifical de la curie romaine au XIIIe siècle*, v. 2, *Studi e Testi* 87 (Vatican City 1940). *Sources of the Modern Roman Liturgy: The Ordinals by Haymo of Faversham and Related Documents (1243–1307)*, ed. S. J. P. VAN DIJK, *Studia et documenta Franciscana*, 2 v. (Leiden 1963). A. CASTELLANO, *Liber Sacerdotalis* (Venice 1523; Paris 1973). J. A. CARDINAL SANTORI, *Rituale Sacramentorum Romanum Gregorii Papae XIII Pont. Max. iussu editum* (Rome 1584–1602; Paris 1973). *Rituale Romanum Pauli V. Pont. Max. iussu editem* (Romae 1614; Paris 1973). *Ordo Unctionis infirmorum eorumque pastoralis curae*, Rituale Romanum ex decreto sacrosancti oecumenici Concilii Vaticani II instauratum auctoritate Pauli PP. VI promulgatum, editio typica (Rome 1972). *Pastoral Care of the Sick: Rites of Anointing and Viaticum*, the Roman Ritual Revised by Decree of the Second Vatican Ecumenical Council and Published by Authority of Pope Paul VI, Approved for Use in the Dioceses of the United States of America by the National Conference of Catholic Bishops and Confirmed by the Apostolic See, Prepared by the International Commission on English in the Liturgy: A Joint Commission of Catholic Bishops' Conferences (New York 1983). Literature. B. BOTTE, "The Earliest Formulas of Prayer for the Dead," in *Temple of the Holy Spirit: Sickness and Death of the Christian in the Liturgy,* trans. M. J. O'CONNELL (New York 1983): 17–31. J. M. DONOHUE, "The Rite for the Commendation of the Dying in the 1983 *Pastoral Care of the Sick: Rites of Anointing and Viaticum*," (Ph.D. diss., The Catholic University of America, 1999). F. S. PAXTON, *Christianizing Death: The Creation of a Ritual Process in Early Medieval Europe* (Ithaca 1990). D. N. POWER, "Commendation of the Dying and the Reading of the Passion," in *Rule of Prayer, Rule of Faith: Essays in Honor of Aidan Kavanagh, O.S.B.*, ed. N. MITCHELL and J. F. BALDOVIN (Collegeville, Minn. 1996): 281–302. D. SICARD, *La Liturgie de la mort dans l'église latine des origines à la réforme carolingienne* (Liturgiewissenschaftliche Quellen und Forschungen 63; Münster 1978).

[J. M. DONOHUE]

COMMENDONE, GIOVANNI FRANCESCO

Cardinal, papal diplomat; b. Venice, March 17, 1524; d. Padua, Dec. 25, 1584. His father, Antonio, came from a family in Bergamo; his mother, Laura Barbarigo, belonged to the old Venetian aristocracy. After a well-rounded education at the University of Padua, Commendone went to Rome in 1550 and entered the "famiglia" of Pope Julius III in 1551. His first and rather sensational test as a diplomat took place in 1553 when, traveling to Brussels in the suite of the Cardinal Legate Girolamo Dandino, he went to London on a secret mission. His assignment was to see Queen Mary Tudor and subsequently to report to the Curia about religious and political conditions in England and the prospects of a Catholic restoration. After a mission to Portugal in 1554, Paul IV gave him a position in the Secretariat of State. In 1556 he accompanied the Cardinal Legate Scipione Rebiba to Brussels. Because of the conflict between the pope and the House of Hapsburg, the journey was interrupted in Maastricht and ended with the sudden flight of the legate through the Ardennes to France, where thanks to Commendone's skill he arrived safely. Appointed bishop of Zante in 1555, he came to Venice on a mission to win over the city for the anti-Hapsburg coalition led by Paul IV and Henry II. Here Commendone came into conflict with the unscrupulous Cardinal Carlo CARAFA, who owed his appointment to the nepotism of the age. There followed a time of withdrawal and studies that ended with his reentry into the Secretariat of State under Pius IV.

Pius commissioned Commendone to invite participation of North and West Germany in the conciliar sessions at Trent. Traveling by way of Vienna, the nuncio came to Naumburg, where the Protestant princes, gathered in convention, met the papal invitation with a firm refusal (January–February 1561). Further travels to the courts of spiritual and temporal princes (Berlin, Lübeck, Cologne, Brussels, Reims, Nancy, Mayence, Bamberg, Munich) yielded a variety of views from Protestants and Catholics alike regarding the question of a council, which views Commendone gathered in a final report to Pius IV (spring 1562). From Trent he visited Emperor Ferdinand I, whom he tried to win over to the same solution of the conciliar crisis that Cardinal Giovanni MORONE later successfully proposed.

From 1563 to 1565 Commendone was nuncio in Poland, where in cooperation with Cardinal Stanislaus HOSIUS he laid the permanent foundation of Catholic reform. Pius IV elevated him to the cardinalate and sent him as papal legate to the Imperial Diet at Augsburg, where the German estates of the empire were deliberating about the confirmation of the Peace of Augsburg (1555). The newly elected Pius V inclined to the opinion that the decrees of the Council of Trent were incompatible with the resolutions of the Augsburg Peace and recommended his legate to raise a protest. Commendone and the majority of his theological advisers saw the possibility of having the decrees of Trent adopted by the Catholic estates without op-posing the Religious Peace. With the help of the general of the Jesuits, Francis Borgia, and Spanish diplomacy, Commendone succeeded in convincing Pius V of this viewpoint. The protest was not raised, the estates accepted the decrees, and the road of Catholic reform in Germany was open. In the years 1568 and 1569 Commendone was sent as legate to Emperor Maximilian II in the matter of the Austrian religious concessions, and again from 1571 to 1573 to Vienna and to Poland in the matter of the Polish succession and a League against the Turks. After 1574 he was an active member of the Roman Congregation of Cardinals for Germany. Through his untiring and selfless zeal, his realistic evaluation of political and ecclesiastical situations, his diplomatic skill, and his deeply religious sense of responsibility, Commendone made a substantial contribution to the beginnings of regeneration of the Catholic Church in central Europe.

Bibliography: *Nuntiaturberichte aus Deutschland*, Abt.1, v.13, ed. H. LUTZ (Tübingen 1959); Abt.2, v.2, ed. A. WANDRUSZKA (Vienna 1953); v.5–6, ed. I. P. DENGEL (1928–39). A. M. GRAZIANI, *De vita J. F. Commendoni* (Paris 1669), French tr. (1694). L. PASTOR, *The History of the Popes from the Close of the Middle Ages* (London-St. Louis 1938–61) bibliog. K. REPGEN, *Die Römische Kurie und der Westfäische Friede* (Tübingen 1962–) 1:87–153. L. VAN MEERBEECK, *Dictionnaire d'histoire et de géographie ecclésiastiques*, ed. A. BAUDRILLART et al. (Paris 1912–) 13:367–378, bibliog. J. WODKA, *Lexikon für Theologie und Kirche*, ed. J. HOFER and K. RAHNER (2d, new ed. Freiburg 1957–65) 3:19 20.

[H. LUTZ]

COMMER, ERNST

German philosopher and theologian; b. Berlin, Feb. 18, 1847; d. Graz, April 24, 1928. He became doctor of civil and Canon Law (1869) and of theology (1880), was ordained (1872), and studied at Berlin, Bonn, Göttingen, Tübingen, Würzburg, Breslau, and Rome. He taught philosophy at Regensburg (1875) and Liverpool (1877), apologetics and general ethics at Münster (1884), and dogmatic theology at Breslau (1888) and Vienna (1900–11). Commer was cofounder, editor, and frequent contributor to the *Jahrbuch für Philosophie und spekulative Theologie* (Münster 1886), later called *Divus Thomas* (Fribourg 1914) and then the *Freiburger Zeitschrift für Philosophie und Theologie* (1954). He is remembered for his critical examination of the works of the Catholic reformer Hermann SCHELL, for which he won the respect of Pope Pius X (1907), and for his answer to Professors F. Kiefl and K. Hennemann, defenders of Schell (1909). In his philosophical and theological writings Commer gives evidence of his strong adherence to Aristotle, St. Albert the Great, and St. Thomas Aquinas; he is regarded as a faithful expositor of THOMISM.

See Also: SCHOLASTICISM, 3.

Bibliography: Works. *Die Katholizität nach dem heiligen Augustin* (Breslau 1873); *Die philosophische Wissenschaft* (Berlin 1882); *System der Philosophie,* 4 v. (Münster 1883–86); *Die Logik* (Paderborn 1897); *Hermann Schell und der fortschrittliche Katholizismu* (Vienna 1907); *Die jünste Phase des Schellstreites* (Vienna 1909). Literature. S. SZABÓ, *Divus Thomas,* 3d series 6 (1928) 257–291. J. HASENFUSS, *Lexikon für Theologie und Kirche,* ed. J. HOFER and K. RAHNER (2d, new ed. Freiburg 1957–65) 3:20. *Der Grosse Herder*² 2:925. *Enciclopedia filosofica* (Venice-Rome 1957) 1:1111.

[F. J. ROENSCH]

COMMINGLING

In the Roman Mass a ceremony which forms part of the Fraction Rite, in which the celebrant breaks the consecrated bread and drops a broken particle into the chalice, saying: "Haec commixtio Corporis et Sanguinis Domini nostri Iesu Christi fiat accipientibus nobis in vitam aeternam" ("May this commingling of the body and blood of our Lord Jesus Christ bring eternal life to us who receive it").

It is remarkable that the same ceremony is found in some form among all the liturgies of East and West. This fact indicates that it was a generally accepted practice in Christian antiquity before the Church became divided. Actually, it started in Syria and quickly became the property of the universal Church.

Unfortunately the theological significance of this rite was lost sight of in the course of time. According to Syrian documents, the Commingling is the connecting link between Sacrifice and Communion. Commingling, with the Consignation as its initial act, symbolizes that the sacrificial chalice has been accepted by the Father and returned to the participants at Mass as "spiritualized," i.e., filled with the Spirit of God ("May. . . avail us unto eternal life").

Our earthly gifts are returned to us as heavenly food. Whereas the double consecration of bread and wine is the twofold sign of Christ's Body and Blood, the Commingling symbolizes the union of the two Species and therefore the glorified humanity of the risen Christ, laden with gifts that lead humanity to a participation in Christ's divinity and immortality. In this symbolic sequence of ceremonial, the Commingling was intended to express the sacramental effect of Communion. Commingling, then, symbolizes the transfiguring Resurrection of Christ, his humanity's being taken up by the Spirit of God, thereby able to fill the human race with the same Spirit. Hence, this rite of Commingling was meant to be a visual representation of what was verbally expressed in the EPICLESIS, namely, that God's Spirit descends upon the elements and transforms them into the life-giving Christ. Both epiclesis and Commingling are situated on the symbolic level, pointing to and unfolding the same reality of the Eucharist as Sacrament of humanity's spiritual transfiguration through eating and drinking Christ's glorified Body and Blood.

Bibliography: J. P. DE JONG "Le Rite de la commixtion de la messe romaine dans ses rapports avec les liturgies syriennes," *Archiv für Musikwissenschaft* 4.2 (1956) 245–278; 5.1 (1957) 33–79. J. A. JUNGMANN, *The Mass of the Roman Rite,* tr. F. A. BRUNNER (rev. ed. New York 1959) 475–479.

[J. P. DE JONG/EDS.]

COMMISSARIAT OF THE HOLY LAND

A Franciscan monastery that is the headquarters of a duly appointed Franciscan official—called a commissary—whose special function, together with his staff, is to interest the public in the holy places in Jerusalem, to collect funds for their support, and to recruit missionaries for work in the Holy Land. Such commissariats have been established for centuries in Europe. At the beginning of the 21st century, there were 82 commissariats in some 44 countries; the one in Washington, D.C. (Franciscan Monastery of the Holy Sepulchre), is considered one of the most important and is the principal commissariat in the United States. It was founded in New York City in 1881, and later was moved to Washington in 1899 by the builder of the Monastery of the Holy Sepulchre, Godfrey Schilling, OFM.

Besides transferring the Good Friday collections and other donations from the United States to the Holy Land, the commissariat in Washington, D.C., recruits missionaries for work in Jerusalem. The principal publication of the commissariat in Washington, D.C., is the *Crusader's Almanac,* a quarterly magazine about the Holy Land.

Bibliography: *The Rule and Constitutions of the Order of Friars Minor* (Rome 1953). *Famiglie religiose della custodia di Terra Santa* (Jerusalem 1963). G. CLEARY, *The Catholic Encyclopedia,* ed. C. G. HERBERMANN et al., 16 v. (New York 1907–14) 4:164.

[P. KINSEL/EDS.]

COMMISSARY APOSTOLIC

Title given to a delegate of the holy father, i.e., an ecclesiastic who receives a papal commission to handle a special affair (generally judicial) in the pope's name. Originally the commissaries apostolic were charged with judging all appeals from tribunals of the first instance; because of this important duty, Pope Boniface VIII (1294–1303) decreed that they be endowed with some ecclesiastical dignity. This was confirmed by the Council of Trent. Nowadays a commissary apostolic is normally a cardinal, residing in Rome, judging the appeal of a special case (e.g., one involving heads of state) that has already passed through the Supreme Tribunal of the Apostolic Signature and that by sovereign order is to be revised.

[P. C. VAN LIERDE]

COMMISSION OF REGULARS

A French royal commission created in 1766 to regulate religious orders with solemn vows. Five archbishops and five lay councilors of state were members of the Commission, which lasted until 1780, when it was replaced by the Commission of Unions. This in turn was replaced in 1784 by the Bureau of Regulars, attached to the chancery until its abolition in 1790. To discover the condition of the orders, the Commission gathered an enormous amount of information from religious and their superiors, and from the hierarchy. Replies to its detailed questionnaires convinced the Commission of the decadent state of religious orders. Religious complained that superiors abused their authority and misappropriated community goods; superiors decried the disobedience of their subjects; and the bishops objected to the exemptions and wealth of the religious houses. In 1768 a regal act fixed the minimum age for religious profession at 21 years for men and 18 for women. Also it decreed that a religious house outside of a congregation must have at least 15 in its community, and in a house under a general chapter, at least nine. No order was permitted to have more than one house in a town. Exemption was practically ended in 1773. The Commission insisted that general chapters meet and revise constitutions in a more democratic sense. Mendicant orders, however, whose headquarters were in Rome, attempted to thwart this design. The Commission obliged orders to reestablish conventual life by suppressing some houses and uniting members in other houses. Several orders were suppressed because they were considered incapable or reconstituting conventual life.

Parlement, especially the Parlement of Paris, exercised control over the Commission's activity. After the fall of the Duke of Choiseul in 1770, the Parlements became hostile. Rome felt obliged to tolerate the Commission and recognized the legality of its changing of constitutions and suppressions of orders. The papal nuncio to Paris was unable to obtain any substantial concessions from the Commission, however, despite his constant efforts.

Archbishop Étienne LOMÉNIE DE BRIENNE, *rapporteur* of the Commission and an instrument of Choiseul, was the prime mover in its activities. The 111 volumes extant in the Collection de Brienne in the National Archives are adequate proof of his industry. Accusations that he aimed at the total ruin of the orders are unjust. In good faith Loménie believed that constitutional reform and renewed social utility would suffice to revivify monastic life. As an organ of the *ancien régime* the Commission of Regulars was animated by a spirit of enlightened despotism and accomplished unwittingly a task whose tendency was revolutionary. The French Revolution, in a different spirit, completed the suppression of religious life.

Bibliography: S. LEMAIRE, *La Commission des réguliers, 1766–80* (Paris 1926). P. CHEVALLIER, *Loménie de Brienne et l'ordre monastique, 1766–89* (Paris 1959–).

[P. CHEVALLIER]

COMMISSION OF THE BISHOPS' CONFERENCES OF THE EUROPEAN COMMUNITY (COMECE)

The Commission of the Bishops' Conferences of the European Community, in French, *Commission des épiscopats de la Communauté européenne,* thus COMECE, was established on March 3, 1980 with the agreement of the Holy See. COMECE consists of a delegate bishop from each of the episcopal conferences in the member states of the European Community, or the *European Union (EU), as it is now known. Acting for the episcopal conferences of the member states, COMECE's fundamental aim is to interact with the European political institutions concerning important issues surrounding the construction of Europe, especially in the socio-economic, political, legal, and cultural spheres.

Purpose and Aims. An instrument in the process of ongoing evangelization of Europe, COMECE seeks to ensure that the process of European construction is value based and endowed with a soul. While not having an official status vis-à-vis the institutions of the EU, the COMECE Secretariat is a listening post for the local churches of the member states concerning all matters of interest to the Chruch treated by the institutions of the EU (especially the European Commission, the European Parliament, the Council of Ministers, and the European Court). The Secretariat also monitors the work of the institutions of the Council of Europe in Strasbourg. Article One of the COMECE statutes states:

> The Bishop's Conferences of the countries belonging to the European Community excercise

their pastoral task in the framework of that Community, as a complement to their pastoral duties in their own countries, so as to attain a reciprocal openness and fraternal cooperation among themselves in the service of the evangelization of the new Europe.

COMECE is an instrument of that process and as such has five aims. First, it seeks to inform the bishops and, through them, the local churches about issues of common pastoral concern being dealt with in the various EU institutions and the Council of Europe. Second, it helps the bishops reflect on the pastoral issues and challenges arising from the process of European integration. Third, it facilitates collegiality among the bishops' conferences with regard to pastoral decisions and action to be taken in the context of a community of nations characterized by an ever-deepening political union. Fourth, it establishes contacts with European civil servants and politicians in order to present to them the concerns of the bishops' conferences and the local churches on issues of importance in contemporary Europe and, at the same time, to discover the EU perceptions of the same issues and ascertain the questions that the civil servants or politicians might wish to address to the Church. Fifth, it makes statements or produces responses to particular issues in the EU political sphere in the name of the bishops' conferences, as deemed necessary and fitting by COMECE in consultation with the national bishops' conferences.

Structure. The membership of COMECE consists of the bishops delegated for three-year terms by each conference of the EU member states. Observers are invited from other European countries that have applied, but have not yet been approved, for membership in the EU. A Swiss observer has always attended the plenary meetings, which are held twice a year to set out the main areas of work. Elections are held once every three years to elect the Executive Committee.

The Executive Committee, consisting of the president, two vice presidents, and the secretary general, carries out the decisions taken by COMECE. It meets twice yearly between the two plenary sessions. The staff of the Secretariat carries out work under the direction of the secretary general. The president is responsible for the Secretariat and its service to the Commission and its Executive Committee. Based in Brussels, the Secretariat also has a small office in Strasbourg.

Franz Cardinal Hengsbach (Essen, Germany) was elected as the first president of COMECE in March 1980. He was assisted by Archibishop Jean Hengen (Luxembourg) and Cahal B. Cardinal Daly (then bishop of Ardagh and Clonmacnoise, Ireland). At the plenary meeting in April 1983, Hengen was elected president and Bishop Dante Bernini (Albano, Italy) and Hengsbach as vice presidents. Hengen was re-elected for a second term as president in 1986 with Archbishop Charles A. Brand (Strasbourg, France) and Bishop José da Crus Policarpo (Lisbon, Portugal) as vice presidents. In November 1990 Brand became president with Bishop Joseph Duffy (Clogher, Ireland) and Bishop Luc de Hovre (Mechelen-Brussels, Belgium) as vice presidents. At the plenary meeting in November 1993 Bishop Josef Homeyer (Hildesheim, Germany) was elected president, and Archbishops Fernand Franck (Luxembourg) and Elias Yanes Alvarez (Zaragoza, Spain) were elected as vice presidents.

Origin and Activities. As with many Church-related organizations surrounding the European institutions, the role of lay Christians in COMECE's inception is significant. Its direct origins, however, are to be found within the already existing postconciliar *Council of the Bishops' Conferences of Europe (CCEE). Some of the members of the latter from the then member states of the European Economic Community (EEC) recognized the need for an instrument to ensure information, presence, and interaction with the evolving EEC. Thus, discussions in the mid-1970s led initially to the establishment in 1976 of an information service, *Service d'Information Pastorale Catholique* (SIPECA) under the aegis of the Apostolic Nunciature in Brussels. Four years later, when COMECE was set up, the work of the SIPECA was entrusted to COMECE. By continuing to publish the twice-quarterly SIPECA review, *Europe, Current and Coming Events,* in French, English, and German, COMECE was able to fulfill its task as an information service for the European bishops of the main issues dealt with in the work of the EU and of the Council of Europe. COMECE distributes the review to all the bishops of the EU member states and the presidents and secretaries of the Bishops' conferences of the countries of Central and Eastern Europe.

A part of COMECE's regular work as an information service, the Secretariat organizes general information visits to the Brussels, Luxembourg, and Strasbourg institutions for bishops, groups involved in specific pastoral activities, and for individuals and groups involved with specific issues where the EU is competent.

COMECE's central task is that of articulating contributions of the bishops' conference to the evolving political agenda of EU policy making. In this regard, the agenda of COMECE's work is set to a large extent by the agenda of the EU itself. Social and economic policy issues, political union, deepening and enlargement of the EU, subsidiarity, security, peace and disarmament, equality of opportunity for men and women, audiovisual and media policy, education and training, refugee and asylum policy, EU relations with Central and Eastern Europe and with the developing countries, biotechnology and bio-ethical issues, ecological and environmental policy, and the preservation of Sunday observance are among the many issues to which COMECE seeks to contribute to the shaping of EU political policy-making. Such contributions are made chiefly through meetings and exchanges with officials of the EU institutions and on occasion by means of statements or position papers.

COMECE has a particular function with respect to the nine European schools located in six of the members states of the EU. The governing body of these schools recognizes COMECE as an official interlocutor in matters pertaining to the teaching of Catholic religion on behalf of the bishops in whose dioceses the European schools are located. As necessary COMECE organizes meetings and seminars for these bishops or their delegates to ensure adequate coordination and organization. In June 1990 COMECE drew up a framework program for the teaching of religion in these schools to assist religion teachers with their tasks.

Cooperation and Links. Since its foundation COMECE has had close links with the representatives of the Holy See to the institutions of the European Union in Brussels and of the Council of Europe in Strasbourg. Good working relations with the episcopal conferences of the member states of the EU, their presidents, Secretariats, and commissions are also fostered. In the case of those bishops' conferences where there exists a Committee for European Affairs, the COMECE Secretariat contributes to their work and when possible participates in the realization of their objectives. COMECE has always enjoyed close links with the CCEE. The continuation of such cooperation was foreseen in the statutes of the CCEE as redrafted in 1993. COMECE is the authorized interlocutor on behalf of the bishops' conferences of the EU member states with the European Ecumenical Commission for Church and Society (EECCS), the consultative commission of the non-Catholic churches in the EU member states.

Bibliography: R. ASTORRI, ed. *Gli statuti delle conferenze episcopali l* (Padova 1987); G. BAUER, "Consitution de la commission des épiscopats de la Communauté européenne," *SIPECA, Bulletin d' Information mensuel* 31 (1980); H. E. CARDINALE, "Une nouvelle initiative pastorale de l'Eglise en Europe," *SIPECA, Bulletin d' Information mensuel* 31 (1980). COMECE, *Statutes of the Commission of the Bishops' Conferences of the European Community; Standing Orders of the COMECE*. P. HUOTPLEUROUX, "Le Cardinal Hengsbach et la COMECE," in *Zeugnis des Glaubens Dienst an der Welt: Festschrift für Franz Kardinal Hengsbach*, ed. B. HERMANS (Essen 1990). C. THIEDE, "Bischöfe–kollegial für Europa. Der Rat der Europäischen Bischofskonferenzen im Dienst einer sozialethisch konkretisierten Evangelisierung," *ICS Schriften* 22 (Münster 1991).

[N. TREANOR]

COMMITMENT

Commitment is an act of the will by which a person orients the total personality in response to a reality deemed absolute. Christian faith asserts God's self-communication in Jesus Christ as an absolute invitation to humanity addressed to the totality of human existence. This self-communication brings an actual sharing of divine life. Commitment, then, as the free and full acceptance of and witness to God's Revelation, forms an essential and characteristic element of Christian faith. It is both affirmation and activity appropriate to the recognition of the call to participate in the creative and redemptive plan of God.

The Christian engages in communal participation in this divine plan through the mission of the Church. Sacramental life concretizes the call that all receive to associate themselves with Christ in his saving mission and also elicits the response inspired by grace. The documents of VATICAN COUNCIL II, stressing the Church as the Sacrament of salvation, essentially state that the commitment that the Church signifies is one of perfect charity. The individual willingly accepts the fact that love of God and love of neighbor cannot be separated. The Christian, in faith, recognizes the call to holiness that is only achieved through self-giving love. This recognition is the beginning of the actualization of the Church's mission to be a sign of the unity of humankind and of the Kingdom of God.

Individuals are to enact this faith commitment as social beings. With hope and confident freedom, the Christian is a realist regarding life in the world and seeks to bring the meaning of God's revealed promises to the variety of social situations and responsibilities in which he or she is involved. Human existence, in its varied forms and contexts, is neither denied nor tolerated, but is the basis of an obedient faith. In both single and married life choices, each person thus recognizes the historical character of his or her vocation in light of the Gospel. All vocation is essentially the historical responsibility undertaken in openness to God's presence in human existence.

The public profession of religious states of life specifically signifies commitment as an essential element of Christian faith. Here the person accepts a particular ecclesial structure as the chosen form of commitment to God. This structure is not the object of religious commitment, but is vital to the historical efficacy of that commitment. Public by nature, the commitment is asserted as an intensification of the baptismal commitment of Christian life. Ordinarily, the evangelical counsels of poverty, chastity, and obedience are vowed perpetually to God through the Church. The perpetual nature of the vows stresses the totality more than the temporality of this commitment of men and women religious. In contemporary expression, this commitment is directed to the liberation of persons from all forms of oppression. This accounts for the plurality of forms of religious life within the Church today.

Bibliography: M. FARLEY and D. GOTTEMOELLER, ''Commitment in a Changing World.'' *Reviews in Religion and Theology* 34 (1975) 846–867. K. RAHNER, *Foundations of Christian Faith,* tr. W. V. DYCH (New York 1978).

[C. WREN]

COMMON GOOD

In the twentieth century, reflection on the concept of the common good was advanced in a particularly important way during the pontificate of Pope JOHN XXIII, who implicitly defined the common good as the sum total of those conditions of social living whereby men are enabled more fully and more readily to achieve their own perfection (*Mater et Magistra* 65). The concern with the perfection of men is limited in this article to particular aspects of human beings insofar as they ''are by nature social beings . . . raised . . . to an order of reality which is above nature'' (*ibid.* 219). The exposition assumes the principle that ''individual human beings are the foundation, the cause and the end of every social institution'' (*ibid.* 219). It also presupposes that the perfection of man and society consists in a ''right ordering of man's conscience with God . . .'' (*ibid.* 215).

Notion. The concept of the common good is not static. Pope John noted that the common good itself progresses and that the general norms by which it is defined are in accord with the nature of things and the changed conditions of man's social life (*ibid.* 220, cf. 65). Among the particular conditions to which Pope John had reference are ''scientific and technical progress, greater productive efficiency and a higher standard of living'' (*ibid.* 59). These factors have produced the principal characteristic of the mid-20th century: the ''increase in social relationships, in those mutual ties, that is, which daily grow more numerous and which have led to the introduction of many and varied forms of associations in the lives and activities of citizens, and to their acceptance within our legal framework'' (*ibid.* 59).

The same factors that have produced a growing interdependence among the citizenry at a national level have also caused a growing international interdependence. Consequently, the common good of a single political community can no longer be achieved in isolation from the world family of political communities. ''Hence there will always exist the objective need to promote in sufficient measure the universal common good, that is, the common good of the entire human family'' (*Pacem in terris* 132).

The encyclicals of Pope John clearly state that a correct understanding of the common good rests on seeing the true nature of a human being as a member of a society, the need for expanding social organizations and institutions, the growth of concern in a national political community, and the requirement of an international authority to unite the family of nations. This list of required elements must be immediately distinguished from the forces of cohesion that unify a society. A political community may be stabilized on such grounds as ethnic kinship, common language and history, or shared religious persuasion. But the common good is the set of concrete ends or goals at which political communities aim rather than the grounds on which societies were founded. This distinction obviates the possibility of misunderstanding the basic nature of the common good. For the common good is achieved through principles and directives regarding social affairs that should be adapted to the changing times, whereas the foundations of political unity are historically fixed and do not require similar modifications.

Plato and Aristotle. A historical survey of the notion of the common good reveals both that it is an ancient notion and that it is variously understood and formulated. PLATO identifies the common good with the total virtue of the citizenry. He bases his analysis on the primacy of the polis (Gr. πόλις, STATE or city) over the citizen, since it is the polis that has been divinely sanctioned by Hermes's gifts of justice and reverence. The individual man has worth and dignity if he lives within a political community that is intrinsically just. The Republic allegorically argues for this sense of community based primarily on an analysis of JUSTICE. The GOOD and the end of man is the virtuous life achieved through ''the care of the soul.'' But the just law of the polis is the ultimate sanction for virtuous living. Hence the *Crito* has the laws say to Socrates: ''You are our child and slave.''

For Plato society is natural, and Athenian society is based on just laws. The common good is the virtuous life of the entire community. Since Plato is convinced that only a very few gifted men can achieve the life of VIRTUE, the limited communal good must be directed by LAW. Because laws are formulated by men, and hopefully by virtuous men, virtue is more a force of cohesion in the community than a set of conditions for individual self-fulfillment, i.e., a common good.

ARISTOTLE, like Plato, sees society as natural and the virtuous life as the end of man. But, unlike Plato, he looks to the autonomy of human reason rather than to the just society as the sanction for the good life. It is the capacity of individual reason in a man within the society that distinguishes the citizen from the natural slave. And it is only the citizens, or those who have a share in the constitution, among whom the commonwealth, such as honor and money, is divided (*Eth. Nic.* 1130b 30–1031a). Aristotle does say that ". . . if the end is the same for a single man and for a state, that of the state seems at all events something greater and more complete whether to attain or to preserve; though it is worthwhile to attain the end merely for one man, it is finer and more godlike to attain it for a nation or for city states" (*ibid.* 1094b 6–9). In the *Politics,* Aristotle asserts that the happiness of the individual and the state are identical, but he also insists that there is a qualitative difference between the capacities of a statesman and the master of the household. Although happiness, i.e., the virtuous life, is the identical goal for both individual men and society, it cannot properly be said to be the common good in the sense of those conditions whereby men are enabled to realize their own perfection. By definition, the good of the state is the cumulative good of the individual citizens, and the restrictive qualification of citizenship makes impossible the notion of a good common to all men. The sense in which the good of the state is "finer and more godlike," and hence to be preferred to the good of the individual, is neither a relation of substantive priority nor one of entitative subsidiarity. It is rather a preferential judgment based on an analogy to science, in which meaning and significance are found in the universal and not the particular. In the achievement of moral goals, as in scientific accomplishments, the measure of worth is the universality of its conclusions.

Understandably, neither Plato nor Aristotle saw in every man an intrinsic worth and dignity consequent on creation. They did see a need to maximize civic worth extensively. To this end Plato turned to the most just law capable of enforcement; Aristotle, to the functionally best form of government. By turning to law or government as the norms of self-fulfillment, Plato and Aristotle unwittingly began a tradition that progressively inverted the proper relation between human beings and society. The principles of political order and unity are not identical with the purposes of human society. The effect of confusing political principles with societal goals is to invest the political community with an intrinsic worth that properly belongs only to a human being. Such a fallacious concretization puts an indefensible premium on national sovereignty that has the immediate effect of restricting the range of responsibility the nation owes to every member of the political community. The common good under such assumptions has historically been identified only with those aspects of human existence that contribute to the stability of the nation, and not with the total conditions of self-fulfillment.

Cicero and Augustine. CICERO, for example, speaks of the commonwealth as the "people's affair," and "the people is not every group of men, associated in any manner, but is the coming together of a considerable number of men who are united by a common greement about law and rights and by the desire to participate in mutual advantages" (*On the Commonwealth,* 1.25). Cicero explicitly says that the purpose of rule is the endurance of the state, which is in no way equatable with maximizing the conditions for each man's self-perfection. In fact, for Cicero, only law may be equally shared by all citizens. In all other matters inequality is natural and ought to be preserved by the state.

St. AUGUSTINE, in viewing Cicero's conception of the commonwealth, finds a serious fault. Augustine insists that "there never was in Rome any true 'weal of the people,'" and hence never any Roman Republic. For Augustine the "common good whose common pursuit knits men together into a 'people'" is absolutely restricted to those who are subject to God and who live religiously, and Augustine insists that the Romans did not serve God but demons (*Civ.* 19.2).

Augustine, unlike Cicero, does insist that "the bond of a common nature makes all human beings one" (*Civ.* 17.2). He is, therefore, concerned with world community. This concern is basically limited to the attainment of peace, but because of the passions endemic to human beings, universal peace is beyond permanent achievement, and "the city of man remains in a chronic condition of civil war." It is the duty of the political community to seek peace, which is "an ordered harmony of authority and obedience between citizens." And earthly peace, however tenuously obtained, is enhanced by the enjoyment of temporal goods that include "health, security and human fellowship." Yet such temporal goods are specifically spoken of as gifts of God, and Augustine does not seem to think that it is the business of the political community to enhance programmatically the opportunity for all men to acquire such gifts. Evidence for this view can be found in Augustine's admission without censure that: "Our holy Fathers in the faith had slaves, but in the regulation of domestic peace it was only in matters of temporal importance that they distinguished the position of their children from the status of their servants" (*Civ.* 19.16). In matters of worship of God, the Fathers had the same loving care for all the household. For Augustine, the common good of the city of man was peace, but a peace that had to be judged by the divine law and serve as a vehicle to the "eternal life" that is the end of the city of God. Because of Augustine's preoccupation with the permanence of the end of the city of God, he found little reason to concern himself with changing social conditions that would call for a redefinition of the norms by which the end of the city of man could be more fully realized.

Aquinas. St. THOMAS AQUINAS, in his comments on Aristotle's *Ethic,* observes that "nothing is good unless it is a likeness to and a participation in the highest good." The same formula is used in the *Summa theologiae:* "Everything is therefore called good from the divine goodness, as from the first exemplary, effective and final principle of all goodness" (1a, 6.4). Aquinas is unquestionably indebted to Augustine for his notion of the common good. It consists essentially in the ordination of all men to God. Such an ordination is achieved and preserved by love of God and love for men. Consequently, Thomas interprets Aristotle's remark that the good of the city-state is "finer and more godlike" in terms of what is extensively the most lovable: God. He concludes, then, that when Aristotle spoke of "that good which is common to a single man or to many states, he intended a method, i.e., an art, which is called politics. Hence it belongs to politics in a most special way to consider the ultimate end of human life" (*In 1 eth.* 2.30). In considering the characteristics of a good ruler, Aquinas says that the primary concern is "to establish a virtuous life in the multitude subject to him." The reason for this charge is that "men form a group for the purpose of living well together" and "the good life is the virtuous life." Aquinas is not oblivious to the fact that a single man must live in a group because he is in no way self-sufficient and that physical accouterments are required for living the good life. But he identifies sufficiency of material goods with the necessities of life, i.e., with the minimal requirements for social existence. He states "that a society will be the more perfect the more it is sufficient unto itself to procure the necessities of life." Aquinas seems not to be concerned with the need for a world community of political organizations, for he calls any political entity, a city or a province, a perfect community if the ruler can defend the community against its enemies in addition to providing the necessities of life for the citizenry.

Aquinas's identification of the common good with the virtuous life of the citizenry is the key to the interpretation of his remarks that "it is impossible that a man be good, unless he be well ordered to the common good, nor can the whole be well ordered unless its parts be proportioned to it. Consequently, the common good of the State cannot flourish, unless the citizens be virtuous, at least those whose business it is to govern. But it is enough for the good of the community that the other citizens be so far virtuous that they obey the commands of their rulers" (1a2ae, 92.1 ad 3). The latter part of the quotation could leave the mistaken impression that Aquinas was defending absolute monarchy. Such is not the case, but it must be said that Aquinas had little practical concern with the exigencies of social change and political organization. For example, he does hold that the private good can be prior to the common good if the private good is not in the same genus as the common good. His telling example is the priority of VIRGINITY over carnal fecundity. However, in every case in which the good of the individual and the common good are in the same genus, the common good is prior, and the search for the common good is indispensable for achieving man's own good, the virtuous life.

Aquinas, like Augustine, was primarily concerned with the common good in the specific sense of setting down the invariable principles governing man's relation to society. The perspective of those principles was mainly limited to man's relation to God as his ultimate end and his relation to society as a natural and necessary means of achieving his end. In this light, the principles of Augustine and Aquinas can be taken only as necessary presuppositions for the task of the redefinition of norms for which Pope John called. But in themselves they do not suffice as constituting the explication of the common good in the changed social conditions of the 20th century.

Modern Thinkers. To call the principles of Augustine and Aquinas presuppositions serves to reinforce their indispensability in contemporary discussion. For to deny the true nature of man is to make impossible the proper considerations of the true relation of man to society, and a fortiori to redefine the norms of the common good. Evidence for this assertion can be found in the treatment of the common good in the Enlightenment, when society was regarded as contractual rather than natural and its ends were declared to be determined by self-interest rather than by divine ordination (*see* ENLIGHTENMENT, PHILOSOPHY OF).

According to T. HOBBES, government was established to remedy a defective human nature. The function of formed government is simply to reduce the natural brutishness of man against man. Organized society is thus united by a common power that is supposed "to defend [the citizens] from the invasion of foreigners, the injuries of one another, and thereby to secure them in such sort, that by their own industry and by the fruits of the earth they may nourish themselves and live contentedly" (*Leviathan,* 1.17). A common power is certainly not a common good that is essentially different from the aggregate of private goods. Hobbes says: "The nature of man being as it is, the setting forth of Publique land, or of any certain Revenue for the Commonwealth is in vaine: and tendeth to the dissolution of Government'' (*ibid.* 2.24).

J. LOCKE, as Hobbes, sees the common good as definable in terms of the private good. He insists that in society the source of value is private: ''Labor puts the difference of value on everything.'' Locke does make one concession to the common good. He sets a limiting condition on what a man has a right to keep, even if he has produced it. Using agriculture as his model, he says that a man can keep only what he can use, and if there is a danger of spoilage, the surplus that cannot be privately consumed reverts to common possession.

J. BENTHAM is most explicit in deriving the meaning of the common good from that of private interest. ''The interest of the community then is—what? The sum of the interests of the several members who compose it. . . . It is vain to talk of the interest of the community, without understanding what is the interest of the individual. A thing is said to promote the interest or to be *for* the interest of an individual, when it tends to add to the sum total of his pleasures; or what comes to the same thing, to diminish the sum total of his pains'' (*Principles of Morals and Legislation,* 1.4–5).

By the middle of the 18th century the notion of the common good was completely modeled on that of the private good, especially the material goods that men accumulated. Adam SMITH in *The Wealth of Nations* dealt with the problem of the public interest in strictly economic terms, for these had become the pervasive language in which the goals of society were defined. He noted that there were three classes of people differentiated by their source of income: landowners, who received rent; laborers, who worked for wages; and dealers, who lived by profit. Smith declared that the interest of the first two groups is inseparably connected with the general interest of the society, but that the interest of the profit makers is ''always in some respects different from, and even opposite to that of the public.'' He went on to warn that the public should be suspicious of any legislative proposal originating with the profit makers because they ''have generally an interest to deceive and even to oppress the public . . .'' (bk. 1, concl.). Although Smith was clear that the common good was not the simple aggregate of private interests, he saw moral suasion as the only remedy for the inevitable injustice resulting from the doctrine of the priority of private interests.

The 19th century inherited and advanced the doctrine that the main business of government was to do for the multitude what no one citizen could do for the corporate person, viz, defend the nation from attack and maintain domestic order. The notion that government should do for the individual what he could not do for himself or that government should provide the social conditions for universal self-fulfillment was unthinkable. The notion of the common good and its priority over private interests had completely disappeared, and its loss involved the denial of the belief that every man has intrinsic worth and dignity.

Modern Catholic Teaching. In 1891 Pope LEO XIII wrote *RERUM NOVARUM* in an effort to correct the abuses that had arisen from economic liberalism (laissez-faire capitalism) and as an alternative solution to that proposed by the socialists. The encyclical noted that the spirit of the times was revolutionary, both politically and economically. The focus of the encyclical was on the condition of labor and, in that context, Pope Leo redefined the norms of the common good—guidelines that his successors have followed. He reasserted the intrinsic dignity of every man; he called for an expanded but flexible range of concerns on the part of the government; and he asserted the right and the need of workmen's associations and other social institutions that would aid each man in his right to self-fulfillment.

Pius XI. Forty years later, Pope PIUS XI wrote the encyclical *QUADRAGESIMO ANNO* to commemorate the anniversary of *Rerum novarum.* Again social changes demanded a redefinition of the norms of the common good. Industrial capitalism had affected the social sphere to the extent that even those living outside its ambit were affected by ''its advantages, inconveniences and vices.'' The basic issue was ''a right distribution of property and a just scale of wages.'' Pius recalled Leo's formulation and then added his own development. He was particularly insistent that ''the public institutions of the nations must be such as to make the whole of human society conform to the common good, i.e., to the standard of social justice'' (*Quadragesimo anno* 110). Economic and social individualism was singled out as the dominant evil that had weakened or destroyed social institutions concerned with the welfare of particular segments of society. Pius called for a reform of institutions but ''principally the State.'' He was not opposed to state intervention in social and economic affairs, but was convinced that not ''all salvation is to be hoped for from its intervention'' (*ibid.* 78). His proposed solution was the principle of SUBSIDIARITY. ''The State should leave to these smaller groups the settlement of business of minor importance. It will thus carry out with greater freedom, power and success the tasks belonging to it, because it alone can accomplish these, directing, watching, stimulating and restraining, as circumstances suggest or necessity demands'' (*ibid.* 80).

Pius insisted on a revitalization of institutions within the political community and on an extended range of concerns for the state. He suggested further that the various nations promote economic cooperation, for he saw that the economic aspect of the universal common good could no longer be achieved at a national level.

Maritain. The rise of totalitarian regimes—Facist, Nazi, and Communist—and the consequent World War II demanded a contemporary restatement of the intrinsic dignity of man without which the common good of nations simply could not be achieved and, even less, the universal common good. Jacques MARITAIN was probably the most influential writer of this period (*see* THOMISM). He carefully distinguished the temporal common good from the supernatural common good; and, within the temporal concern, he separated the political structure of the state from the economic organization of society. The key term in Maritain's definition of a society of free men was "personalist," by which he intended to reaffirm man's ordination to God as an end—an end that transcends every common good. But it is only in virtue of that ordination, says Maritain, that any ordination to other common goods is possible. Maritain saw that the political erosion of man's dignity led to totalitarianism and also that changes in the systems of property and production would inevitably occasion political reorganization. He noted that such changes "will in any case give way to a new system of life, better or worse according to whether it is animated by the personalist or totalitarian spirit" (*Rights of Man and Natural Law,* 95). Whether or not the democracies would be able to give man his due as a person was problematic. Maritain hoped they would, but saw as an indispensable condition a reorientation away from the individualism of the 19th century.

Maritain's "personalism" came under considerable attack from scholastic philosophers, notably Charles DE KONINCK. The burden of the differences, however, were mainly metaphysical and not immediately concerned with the interpretation of the social changes to which Pope John XXIII subsequently addressed himself.

John XXIII. The notion of the common good is almost entirely absent in contemporary philosophical discussion. When it does appear, it is usually in a context concerning justice or law, as was the case for the Greeks and Romans. Moreover, the depth of contemporary discussion concerning the common good is severely limited by the acceptance of at least the technical language that was the legacy of economic liberalism, social Darwinism, and legal positivism. Examples can be found in four principal aspects of the common good selected by Pope John for his presentation, viz, (1) neglect of the person in favor of the individual, (2) the multiplication of social institutions, (3) increased governmental intervention, and (4) the growth of nationalism.

First, "it is agreed that in our time the common good is chiefly guaranteed when personal rights and duties are maintained. . . . For *to safeguard the inviolable right of the human person, and to facilitate the fulfillment of his duties, should be the essential office of every public authority*" (*Pacem in terris* 60). The pope's use of the word person must be sharply differentiated from the more commonplace term individual (*see* INDIVIDUALITY). The social connotations of the term individual are those of an instrument of production or a possessor of property. Manuals of jurisprudence consistently define person as "the substances of which rights and duties are the attributes." The legal attribution of rights and duties, however, is radically distinct from the assertion of God-given inviolability. In the latter case it must be asserted that a human being has an intrinsic dignity or worth that transcends and takes priority over every form of political association, whereas in the case of attribution a man has a social or political value that is contingent on a particular political or economic system. The functional definition of man in the systematic terms of any science emphasizes his needs and acquisitive desires, which are satisfied by material goods. Such definitions omit the inherent richness of the person that is the basis of fruitful interpersonal association. Persons have the duty of giving and sharing, but individuals can rest on their right to acquire. Since the person is the end of all social institutions, person must be understood as transcending every particular form of social and economic institution, whatever it may be.

Second, the failure to distinguish between individual and person results in divergent interpretations concerning the natural multiplication of social organizations that are directed to the satisfaction of many personal rights, including health services, education, leisure, and recreation. Technological developments and economic affluence are two of the reasons why persons can reasonably aspire to a greater share of the common wealth, but which they cannot obtain without banding together in common action. Pope John made it clear that the proliferation of such organizations is not a threat to personal responsibility and absolutely rejected the notion that increased communal action will cause a man to lose his initiative and consequently become an automaton. Since the emerging complex social organization is the creation of persons, it has as its purpose making the accouterments of the good life more accessible to the greatest number of persons. It is not intended as providing a more facile way for individuals to acquire a disproportionate share of the common wealth. If institutions are seen as the fitting way for a person to carry out his rights and duties "and to fully develop and perfect his personality," then it follows that every institution is obliged to enter into dialogue with all other institutions. For only through the institutional expansion of concerns can the person fully receive his due. The tradition of economic individualism, however, views such expansion with suspicion because it conceives the function of institutions to be concerned primarily with the means of retaining what was individually acquired. Consequently, individualism stresses institutional independence rather than interdependence, and thus prefers silence to dialogue in the face of social change.

Third, Pope John observed that "this development in the social life of man is at once a symptom and a cause of the growing intervention of the State, even in matters which are of intimate concern to the individual, hence of great importance and not devoid of risk" (*Mater et Magistra,* 60). He saw that opportunity for free action by individuals is restricted by governmental intervention. But that danger is not serious enough to offset the advantages that governmental intervention brings. The problem, at least in the economic sphere, is that "the economic prosperity of a nation is not so much its total assets in terms of wealth and property, as the equitable division and distribution of this wealth. This it is which guarantees the personal development of the members of society, which is the true goal of a nation's economy" (*ibid.* 74). The propriety of governmental intervention was defended by the pope on the factual ground that the common good evolves in correspondence with the growth of economic prosperity. Such an evolution makes possible a national focus on distributive justice, according to which all members of the community are given a proportionate share of the communal goods. The theory of individualism, however, rejects the evolutionary concept and insists that the business of government ought to be restricted to the tradition of noninterference in the modes of acquisition and retention of private goods. On this view governmental concern with justice should be mainly directed to correcting the inequities arising from illegal modes of acquisition. This emphasis on corrective justice disallows an organic view of a national polity and consequently insists on an isolated national autonomy rather than on any international organization that would benefit equally the family of nations.

Fourth, Pope John observed: "At the present time no political community is able to pursue its own interests and develop itself in isolation, because its prosperity and development are both a reflection and a component part of the prosperity and development of all the other political communities" (*Pacem in terris* 131). He pointed out that a national common good is no longer achievable without concern for the universal common good and that the universal common good in concrete form is a "public authority, having world-wide power and endowed with the proper means for the efficacious pursuit of its objec-

tive . . ." (*ibid.* 138). It is clear that Pope John held that the intrinsic worth and dignity of each person can be realized if and only if national political organizations transcend their own domestic concerns. Just as all men form the human family, so the common good must be universal if it is to be maximally achieved at any national level. The corollary is that the more powerful states have a moral obligation to assist the less privileged communities, but according to the principle of subsidiarity. The proponents of individualism, having rejected an organic notion of a political community and an evolutionary concept of the common good, see no justification for any nationally transcendent obligations. Instead, they would pursue a policy of economic accommodation and military reaction that is intended to defend the integrity of national rights, particularly the right of property.

Recent Developments. Church leaders, pastoral letters, and synodal documents since Vatican II have largely echoed and extended the analysis of the concept of common good offered by Pope John XXIII. The Second Vatican Council's Pastoral Constitution on the Church in the Modern World (*Gaudium et spes*) repeats verbatim John XXIII's definition of the common good and dedicates several paragraphs (see nos. 26 and 74) to a careful explanation of the proper role of public authorities and government agencies in protecting and enhancing the conditions that foster human flourishing and fulfillment. In his encyclical *Populorum progressio* (1967), Pope Paul VI reminds us that "the right to property must never be exercised to the detriment of the common good" (no. 23). He also amplifies his predecessor's insight about the ever-widening extent of internationalized obligations to promote the common good by authoring the stirring phrase "the social question has become worldwide" (*Populorum progressio*, no. 3). Pope John Paul II has likewise frequently couched his own exhortations to social justice and assistance to the needy in terms of advancing the common good, often offering substantial reflections on aspects of contemporary economic, political, and cultural life which so tragically detract from greater attainment of the common good.

A number of documents emanating from various gatherings and groupings of bishops have likewise made substantial reference to the common good. *Justice in the World*, the document of the 1971 Synod of Bishops, emphasizes the temporal obligations we all have, as both citizens and believers, to promote the common good (no. 39). In recent decades, episcopal conferences in several parts of the world have issued pastoral letters that use the category of the common good to analyze economic and social realities in their own distinctive contexts. The U.S. bishops, in their 1986 pastoral letter on the American economy, *Economic Justice for All*, called attention to the special obligations of leaders of industry to use their wealth and influence to promote the common good, declaring: "Business people, managers, investors, and financiers follow a vital Christian vocation when they act responsibly and seek the common good. We encourage and support a renewed sense of vocation in the business community" (no. 117). Finally, the 1994 *Catechism of the Catholic Church* uses the concept of common good extensively in its section on social life in the human community (nos. 1878-1912). Here the master concept of common good emerges as a privileged lens through which we may view and make judgments about political and economic realities and events.

Conclusion. It is simply impossible to define the common good in a final way irrespective of the changing social conditions. However, the social encyclicals on which this exposition rests completely reject the philosophy of individualism and insist that the norms for the common good of individual political communities as well as the universal common good "cannot be determined except by having regard to the human person" (*Pacem in terris* 139).

See Also: AUTHORITY; COMMUNITY; MAN, NATURAL END OF; PERSON (IN PHILOSOPHY); SOCIETY.

Bibliography: *Seven Great Encyclicals* (Glen Rock, N.J. 1963). J. MARITAIN, *The Rights of Man and Natural Law,* tr. D. C. ANSON (New York 1943); *The Person and the Common Good,* tr. J. J. FITZGERALD (New York 1947). C. DE KONINCK, *De la primauté du bien commun* (Quebec 1943). E. WELTY, *Gemeinschaft und Einzelmensch nach Thomas v. Aquin* (Salzburg 1935). T. ESCHMANN, "In Defense of Jacques Maritain," *The Modern Schoolman* 22 (1944–45) 183–208. W. FARRELL, "Person and the Common Good in a Democracy," *American Catholic Philosophical Association, Proceedings of the Annual Meeting* 20 (1945) 38–47. S. HOOK, ed., *Law and Philosophy* (New York 1964).

[A. NEMETZ/T. MASSARO]

COMMON SENSE

For Aristotle, one of the internal SENSES that discerns the differences among proper SENSIBLES, as, for example, between sweetness and whiteness, which are perceived respectively by the external senses of smell and sight (*Anim.* 425b 8, 427a 12). Aristotle does not use the expression κοινὴ αἴσθησις, which was employed by the scholastics in the Latin form, *sensus communis;* used in Aristotle's sense, especially by St. THOMAS AQUINAS (*In 2 anim.* 13.390), it designates the unity of sense knowledge: "for by common sense we perceive that we live" (*see* CENTRAL SENSE). For Thomas REID and the Scottish school (*see* SCOTTISH SCHOOL OF COMMON SENSE), common sense is the assembly of beliefs (such as realities of objects, spirits, etc.) that man irresistibly holds to be true

by reason of instinct or immediate suggestion. According to Reid, the perception of an object includes belief in its real existence, and this is not the result of any reasoning, but the immediate effect of man's natural bent (*Inquiry,* 6.20). This belief comes from nature; it is bound up with perception as the body is bound up with earth. In Reid, common sense is identified with universal consensus, but he dogmatizes the notion by assuming that it is the absolute criterion of truth, having its justification in itself.

[M. F. SCIACCA]

COMMONWEAL

Commonweal (originally *The Commonweal*; name shortened in 1965) is the oldest independent lay Catholic journal of opinion in the United States. Founded in 1924 by Michael Williams (1877–1950) and the Calvert Associates, it reflected a growing sense of self-confidence among American Catholics as they emerged from a largely immigrant status to become highly successful members of the American mainstream. Modeled on the *New Republic* and the *Nation,* the magazine's goal was to be a weekly review "expressive of the Catholic note" in covering literature, the arts, religion, society, and politics. Never bound by a strict ideology, it became a forum for thoughtful, urbane discussion, and had a distinguished roster of editors and writers.

Liberal in temperament, the magazine's editorial strategy was to reject sectarianism and to rely on reasoned discussion. It never shrank, however, from taking strong and controversial positions. When it declared its neutrality during the Spanish Civil War (1938), circulation plummeted by 20 percent. During World War II, it condemned the firebombing of Dresden and the use of atomic weapons at Hiroshima and Nagasaki. It criticized American racism, the anti-Semitism of Father Charles Coughlin, and the smear tactics of Senator Joseph McCarthy; supported resistance to U.S. involvement in Vietnam; and took issue with the 1968 papal encyclical *Humanae vitae.*

The magazine benefited from long editorships: Michael Williams (1924–38); Edward S. Skillin (1938–67); James O'Gara (1967–84); Peter Steinfels (1984–88); and Margaret O'Brien Steinfels (1988–); it was also energized by a variety of remarkable supporting editors, including George N. Shuster, John Cogley, Daniel Callahan, and Paul Baumann. Edward Skillin's association with the journal was unique. He joined the staff in 1933, became editor and a principal owner in 1938, served as publisher from 1967–99, and transferred ownership to the nonprofit Commonweal Foundation in 1982.

Part of the price for the magazine's independence was its periodic ostracism from various church and political circles, and its chronic sense of financial precariousness (it was forced to become a biweekly in 1974). The Commonweal Associates, established in the 1960s, met the magazine's annual revenue shortfall through donors' gifts, and an endowment fund was inaugurated in 1994 to assure greater long-term financial viability. Its circulation in the 1990s was 20,000.

Commonweal was credited with helping prepare American Catholics for Vatican II and its aftermath, and for introducing readers to a new level of literate Catholic discussion. It published such authors as Nicholas Berdyaev, Emmanuel Mournier, Francois Mauriac, Georges Bernanos, Hannah Arendt, Luigi Sturzo, G. K Chesterton, Hilaire Belloc, and Graham Greene. It printed the short fiction of Evelyn Waugh and J. F. Powers, the poetry of W. H. Auden, Josephine Jacobsen, and John Updike. Its cultural columnists included Walter Kerr, Wilfrid Sheed, and Richard Alleva; there were illustrations by Jean Charlot and Emil Antonucci.

On the occasion of *Commonweal*'s fiftieth anniversary (1974), historian John Tracy Ellis wrote that, with the exception of the nineteenth-century lay trustee movement and lay congresses, *Commonweal* "was the American Catholic laity's most ambitious undertaking, and to date remains the most successful one."

Bibliography: P. JORDAN and P. BAUMANN, eds., *Commonweal Confronts the Century* (New York 1999). R. VAN ALLEN, *The Commonweal and American Catholicism* (Philadelphia 1974); *Being Catholic: Commonweal from the Seventies to the Nineties* (Chicago 1993).

[P. JORDAN]

COMMUNICATION, PHILOSOPHY OF

In its ordinary usage, "communication" refers to all the means that serve to bind human beings together, especially through the spread of information by mass media such as the internet, radio, television, press, and motion pictures; in a philosophical sense, it refers to the process of intellectual intercourse between individuals or groups, resulting in the transmission and interchange of information, experiences, affections, goods, and services. Communication as such has become the object of special philosophical interest since World Wars I and II. Yet it has always been regarded as one of the basic phenomena of human existence, as reflected, for example, in analyses of speech as expressive of man's social nature, of the individual good as a participation in the common good, and of the origin of the common good in cooperative human endeavor.

Philosophical Analysis. Man is distinguished from animals in that his nature requires that he attain full stature as a person through CULTURE. Culture itself is entirely social in origin, even in its material aspects; its basis is communication, that is, intellectual cooperation and exchange. Culture is possible only for beings composed of body and soul, for such a composition requires cooperation with others to develop its potentialities and achieve its full perfection. Culture, then, is peculiar to the human being, who is incomplete in himself; a purely intellectual being, such as an angel, being complete in itself, cannot have a culture.

Social individualistic theories see man as a reasonable being, complete in himself and as such entering into social relations. In fact, however, man becomes a fully human and a cultural being through communication, first at the level of the family and then at the level of society as a whole. By communication from generation to generation, a growing set of truth and value insights, ideas, morals, and customs is built up. This development depends equally on participation and on a common sharing by the members of society. Only on the basis of such a developed social mentality are works such as those of Michelangelo, Shakespeare, and Beethoven possible. These are not merely eruptions of individual genius; rather they grow out of a culture, and then go on to repay that culture by contributing to it new forms as well as new contents of communication.

Basis of Communication. In philosophical anthropology and social philosophy the question arises as to the human characteristics that make communication possible. Here the self-evident truth that all men have in common an intellectual nature as human persons is not at question; rather what is sought is the concrete potentiality whose actualization is necessary for communication. The primary characteristic is that man is capable of judging his own experience reflectively and, in consequence, of generalizing his sense experiences by means of concepts and words; thus, as distinct from animals, he is able to accumulate knowledge and experience from one generation to another. Hence social tradition becomes a fundamental category for the explanation of communication. Only by participating in such tradition is the full development of the individual made possible.

Closely related to the characteristic just mentioned is the second: to strive for happiness is a natural impulse in man, and the progressive satisfaction and actualization of such striving are entirely dependent on communication. This is seen in the fact that man's natural impulse is basically one to love and to be loved. Besides, man's aspirations toward happiness, arising as they do from his powers of knowing and desiring in the realm of values, can be realized only by way of communication. Such communication is effective in satisfying the human desire for creative fulfillment by the works of art, literature, science, and technology. To assume, therefore, that the interchange of knowledge is the only function of communication is a one-sided view; love in all its forms, of persons and of things, is no less significant.

Philosophically speaking, there is also a third basis for communication, namely, man's need for FREEDOM. Communication depends on freedom because a nature that must complete itself through cooperative activity must also be free in its endeavors for self-fulfillment through social means. Hence communism, in restricting natural free communication in intellectual, economic, and associated matters, cannot continue indefinitely as a social system. The system is bound slowly to dissolve from within because normal patterns of communication will gradually develop and so will the freedom that these entail.

To the foregoing should be added a fourth, even more basic requirement, viz, the knowledge of the NATURAL LAW, which imposes upon men a basic mode of conduct toward one another. This, together with the imperatives associated with the dignity of the human person, is basic to all communication.

Thomistic Thought. The notion that communication is essential for all social relations is fundamental to the social philosophy of St. THOMAS AQUINAS. Aquinas often uses the word *communicatio* for *communio* and *communitas.* For him, communication implies an imparting as well as an interacting, thus including different forms of natural love and even supernatural love, or CHARITY. Although the basic relations of communication are strongest in kinship, they are found also in civil intercourse in a political society and in the spiritual union of all men in the Church, either actually or potentially (*Summa theologiae* 2a2ae, 31.3). On the civil level, a double bond of communication is emphasized by Aquinas: that based on law and authority on the one hand, and that existing through free intercourse on the other (*Summa theolgiae* 1a2ae, 105.2 and ad 3), with particular stress on commercial exchange. Again, besides the communication that arises through kinship, which he calls *naturalis,* that of individual love *per modum amoris* takes on a special importance (*In 1 sent.* 13.1.2 ad 2). All forms of communication are connected with the love of FRIENDSHIP (*In 3 sent.* 29.6). Communication should unite men in the universal love of God, since they are destined to strive for one common end (*C. gent.* 3.117); more, the love of God is the very basis of all communication (*In 4 sent.* 46.1.1.2).

At the center of St. Thomas's doctrine on communication is the notion of the image of God (*Summa theologiae* 1a, 93). Man is the image of God by virtue of his reason, which, by an innate God-given law, is directed to communicate with God (*Summa theologiae* 1a2ae, 100.2); he is also the image of God in the sense that, like God, he is the principle of life to others (*principium alterius*) through procreation, as well as by instruction and guidance (1a, 94.3). In virtue of man's supernatural sonship, communication among men is established by charity and the common possession of truth (2a2ae, 184.1 and ad 1); communication with God, on the other hand, is established by PARTICIPATION in the divine nature, in divine knowledge through faith, and in divine love through charity (1a2ae, 110.4).

Modern Theories. Arnold Gehlen (1904–1976) accounts for the origin of communication through the biological theory that man developed sounds as forms of movement, thus evolving above the animal stage. In the beginning man's lingual utterances were mere motions; then thought evolved out of man's communicating with himself. This theory postulates what has to be explained: how man, in communication with himself, came to be reflectively conscious of his own experiences and to form the concepts that are expressed verbally in human communication.

According to Max SCHELER, communication is constitutive of the person, i.e., of the individual as well as of the social person. The person is existent only in performing intentional acts, hence only as a member of a society of persons and by way of communication. Although this theory of person and communication does not deny the existence of the concrete individual, the resemblance of Scheler's great work to the philosophy of actualism is undeniable.

The French "philosophy of the spirit," initiated by R. LE SENNE and developed by L. LAVELLE, holds that man, by virtue of his personal experience of being, knows in the very act of knowing that he participates in being as such. Such a philosophy thus approaches a metaphysics of communication, according to which man not only knows himself to be in union with God as the source of all being but also knows himself to be in union with all being as created by God. He is therefore aware of his responsibility, as cocreator, for the state of the world and society. The weakness in this philosophy is that it gives too little attention to the ANALOGY of being, though it does open up metaphysics, particularly within CHRISTIAN PHILOSOPHY, to new interests.

Martin BUBER sees communication as an "I-Thou" relationship, ontologically making possible man's being as man, theologically making possible the fullness of man's being through his relationship to God. Thus man's situation is a kind of twofold dialogue. The much spoken of "I-Thou" relationship and man's dialogue form of being tend to obscure the fact that in Buber's system the ontological nature of SOCIETY itself is not really established.

According to the Christian existentialism of Gabriel MARCEL, man learns in his daily communication with other men how indispensable are devotion and truth toward one another and consequently toward the absolute Thou. This experience of communication becomes the basis for an optimism motivated by hope.

The atheistic existentialism of J. P. SARTRE approaches human existence pessimistically, rendering a negative judgment on communication. The basic fact of the being of man is loneliness. Man finds himself in anguish because he is condemned to freedom as his peculiar form of existence. Being without cognizance of his essence, man knows nothing about the order of his existence; rather he sees himself faced with NONBEING and ABSURDITY. In interhuman relations and in society Sartre does not see fruitful communication but rather an encroachment upon free existence that makes man an "it." This blatantly false philosophy may be taken as an expression of man's depersonalization in the contemporary industrial world.

According to the ontology of Martin HEIDEGGER, the interhuman relation belongs to the existence of man, but communication is limited to the level of care for one another. It is not understood in terms of the social nature of man.

Karl JASPERS distinguishes between objective communication, in which man has a part in the being and the values of society as a whole, and existential communication, in which man freely opens himself to another self and thereby also attains his own existence, freeing himself from loneliness, but also creating new loneliness. From existential communication there originates personal (transcendental) truth; thus, it is the origin of philosophy. However, truth can be perceived by man only in the freedom of self-persuasion. This holds good also in relation to truth about God; hence, philosophical belief alone is possible (*see* EXISTENTIALISM).

What J. de Tonquédec has said of the philosophy of Jaspers applies to all kinds of existential philosophy in which communication is regarded only as a means of achieving individual existence in freedom. It reveals itself basically as a "despairing individualism," in which man experiences only his own truth, his own morality, his own God, all as incommunicable. This reservation, however, does not mean that the existential philosopher has nothing significant to say about communication in either its socio-phenomenological or its socio-philosophical aspect.

Bibliography: R. C. KWANT, *Encounter,* tr. R. C. ADOLFS (Pittsburgh 1960). W. A. M. LUIJPEN, *Existential Phenomenology* (Pittsburgh 1960). M. DE CORTE, "Les Bases préjudicatives de la communication," *Giornale di metafisica* 5 (1950) 1–17. A. GUZZO, "Il problema della communicazione delle coscienze," *ibid.* 18–28. R. JOLIVET, "La Communication avec autrui," *ibid.* 29–44. M. NÉDONCELLE, "Les Données de la conscience et le don des personnes," *ibid.* 70–80. A. GEHLEN, *Der Mensch: Seine Natur und seine Stellung in der Welt* (Bonn 1950). M. SCHELER, *Der Formalismus in der Ethik und die materiale Wertethik,* ed. M. SCHELER (Bern 1954). R. LE SENNE, *La Destinée personelle* (Paris 1951). L. LAVELLE, *La Dialectique de l'éternel présent,* 4 v. (Paris 1945–57), especially volume 1, *De l'être.* M. BUBER, *I and Thou,* tr. R. G. SMITH (2d ed. New York 1958). G. MARCEL, *Homo viator* (Paris 1945). J. P. SARTRE, *Being and Nothingness,* tr. H. E. BARNES (New York 1956). M. HEIDEGGER, *Being and Time,* tr. J. MACQUARRIE and E. ROBINSON (New York 1962). K. JASPERS, *Von der Wahrheit,* v. 1 of his *Philosophische Logik* (Munich 1958); *Der philosophische Glaube* (Munich 1958). J. DE TONQUÉDEC, *Une Philosophie existentielle: L'Existence d'après K. Jaspers* (Paris 1945).

[J. MESSNER]

COMMUNICATION OF IDIOMS

An idiom, in theological usage, is equivalent to a natural property or attribute. Because of the mysterious union of natures in the one person of JESUS CHRIST, the question inevitably arises whether and under what conditions one may assign divine properties to Christ the man, and human properties to God. The special difficulty connected with this communication of idioms lies precisely in the fact of two natures in one person. The natures must not be confused by attributing to one nature what is proper to the other. Yet the one person must not be multiplied by denying to it the possession of anything included in the two natures, thereby implying the existence of another subject or person. It follows that the present question is not entirely a matter of correctness in terminology. Propriety or impropriety in the communication of idioms is also the clearest indication of the presence or absence of orthodox faith in the INCARNATION. It is the expression of the mystery of the HYPOSTATIC UNION itself.

Development. The New Testament makes use of the communication of idioms in attributing to God such natural human characteristics as birth in time according to the flesh, possession of a physical body, human life, sufferings, and death; and to the Son of Man such divine properties and operations as eternity, divine power and authority, elevation above all creatures, creation, and the sanctification of souls. The same usage was followed quite naturally by the earliest Fathers and in the primitive creeds and symbols of faith. More speculative development came only in time. Among the earliest to elaborate the theory of the communication of idioms were Origen, Ephraem, Athanasius, Cyril of Jerusalem, and most explicitly, Gregory of Nyssa in the East, along with Tertullian, Hilary, and especially Augustine in the West. Among those who accepted the true divinity and integral humanity of Christ, no critical difficulty arose concerning the communication of idioms until the Nestorian heresy.

Heresies. The Nestorians, by envisioning in Jesus two physical persons, inevitably destroyed His true unity and, quite as inevitably, the communication of idioms became purely a matter of words. When they said of the so-called moral person-of-union named Christ, Lord, or Son that man is God or God is man, they intended these expressions in a highly improper sense: God, who is not man, is closely joined with this man, or this man, who is not God, is morally joined with God. They especially denied that things belonging to Christ according to His humanity could be attributed to God. According to them, it ought not be said that the Word of God was born or suffered. Finally, a crucial point for both Nestorians and their opponents, Mary was not to be called Mother of God, θεοτόκος (*see* THEOTOKOS), but, at most, Mother of Christ, χριστοτόκος. At the opposite extreme, in attempting to restore the unity of Christ destroyed by the Nestorians, Monophysites and Eutychians confused and mixed the divine and human natures of Christ so that there was no longer a question of a communication of idioms, but of a simple attribution of both divine and human properties to the one resulting nature.

Magisterium. The reaction of the teaching Church to these two erroneous extremes is found mainly in the Councils of Ephesus (431) and Chalcedon (451). Ephesus, rejecting the moral union of two physical persons suggested by the Nestorians, declared that "the Word, according to hypostasis, united to Himself a body animated by a rational soul and so became man in an unexplainable and incomprehensible way. . . . And although the natures are different, they have been brought together into true unity, making for us one Christ and Son; not because the difference of natures is removed in virtue of the union, but rather because the divinity and humanity by a mysterious and ineffable conjoining have achieved, in one person, our one Lord and Son Jesus Christ" (H. Denzinger, *Enchiridion symbolorum*, ed. A. Schönmetzer [Freiburg 1963] 250). Thus, the union in the Incarnation is in and according to person, and there are not found two real persons, divine and human, merely cloaked or covered by the Nestorian person-of-union. Consequently, by a true communication of idioms, the Council asserted that Mary is and is to be called Mother of God. The Council of Chalcedon declared against the Monophysites that the "one and same only-begotten Son, Christ the Lord, must be recognized in two natures without confusion, without change, without division or separation. The difference of the natures is in no way removed by the union, but the

proper characteristics of each are the more preserved thereby; they are united in one person" (*Enchiridion symbolorum* 302). The union of the Word with human nature is not then a union in nature, but after the union, there remain in Christ whole, unmixed, and without change both human nature and divine nature, each preserving what is proper to itself. This vindication of the basis of the communication of idioms was later repeated in a number of places, including the Second Council of Constantinople (553) and the Council of Florence (1442).

It is a clear conclusion from the teachings of the Church that the real communication of idioms in Catholic dogma is not between the natures of Christ, that is, the properties of one nature never become the properties of the other. The true communication of idioms is in the one person of Jesus. He who is truly God, the only-begotten Son, Second Person of the Trinity, became truly man and the Son of Mary. God the Word is man and this man Jesus Christ is God, but divinity is not humanity nor is humanity divinity. Therefore, once the Incarnation has taken place, whatever is affirmed of this one person when He is named or indicated according to one nature can be affirmed of the same person when He is named or indicated according to the other nature. The person is always one and the same even though at one time called God because of His divine nature and at another time called man because of His human nature. What is affirmed of one nature cannot rightly be affirmed of the other nature since the natures always remain different and distinct.

Rules. Since the hypostatic union is itself the deepest mystery, it is unlikely that any set of rules governing the manner of speech about Christ can be completely adequate. However, certain generally accepted norms should be observed so that faith in the Incarnation does not suffer from faulty expression. (1) The communication of idioms is generally legitimate for concrete affirmations, illegitimate for abstract affirmations. One says that the Son of Man is omnipotent and eternal, but not that humanity is omnipotent and eternal; that God was born and died, but not that divinity was born and died. (2) There is an important difference between affirmative and negative propositions. The negatives are more sweeping. Therefore, whatever belongs to Christ according to one nature may be simply affirmed of Him; but what does not belong to Him according to one nature should not be simply denied. One says that Christ died, but not that He did not die, even though in His divine nature He did not die. (3) When the person is named with an additional expression emphasizing one nature, the communication of idioms ceases. One may properly say that Christ is eternal, but not that Christ as man is eternal. (4) While safeguarding the distinction of natures, one may attribute opposed and contrary properties to the one person. Christ is uncreated, eternal, and omniscient; Christ was created, mortal, and grew in knowledge. (5) The communication of idioms supposes that the hypostatic union has already taken place and should not be extended to the time before the Incarnation. In addition to these norms, good theological judgment would suggest that curiosities and novelties not be indulged, that accepted and traditional usages be followed, and that ambiguous expressions be clarified or avoided.

Moment. The communication of idioms is of deeper significance than correctness in the formalities of speech. It concerns the heart of the dogma of the Incarnation. The true foundation for communication is the hypostatic union. By virtue of this, divine and human natures are found in Jesus Christ in one person. All the properties of both natures consequently belong to this one person, and the communication of idioms is fundamentally nothing other than the hypostatic union itself. To be deficient or erroneous in it is necessarily to be deficient or erroneous in faith in the Incarnation. Scripture, the Fathers, and the teaching Church have employed the communication of idioms to stress the reality and the important consequences of the hypostatic union. Historically it has provided the clearest test of orthodoxy about the Incarnation. It is significant that Mary's title as MOTHER OF GOD is nothing other than a proper communication of idioms. Even the greatest vigilance in observing the norms for correctness of expression about the person and natures of Jesus Christ is therefore more than justified. One's desire must be not only to avoid erroneous expressions, but to express the mystery of two natures in one person as fully as one is able to grasp it.

See Also: NESTORIANISM; MONOPHYSITISM; EUTYCHIANISM.

Bibliography: A. MICHEL, *Dictionnaire de théologie catholique*, ed. A. VACANT et al., (Paris 1903–50) 7.1:595–602; Tables générales 2:2574–75. K. FORSTER, *Lexikon für Theologie und Kirche*, ed. J. HOFER and K. RAHNER (Freiberg 1957–65) 5:607–609. I. SOLANO, *Sacrae theologiae summa*, ed. Fathers of the Society of Jesus, Professors of the Theological Faculties of Spain (Madrid 1962) 3:1, 370–407. B. M. XIBERTA Y ROQUETA, *Enchiridion de Verbo Incarnato* (Madrid 1957) Index doctr. 16.

[J. F. RIGNEY]

COMMUNIO

Every adequate theology of the Church must begin with the proper beginning: not with Mt 16.16 (the promise of the Petrine primacy) but with 1 Tm 2.4 (the promise of universal salvation: "God our savior: he wants everyone to be saved . . ."). Traditionally the Church has been considered the Sacrament of this divine saving will,

an insight revived by VATICAN COUNCIL II in the *Dogmatic Constitution on the Church*: "By her relationship with Christ, the Church is a kind of sacrament or sign of intimate union with God, and of the unity of all mankind" (*Lumen gentium* 1); "through this Spirit [Christ] has established His body, the Church, as the universal sacrament of salvation" (ibid. 48). Accordingly the being of the Church is symbol and source of a twofold union—of God with man and of man with man. Hence, the Church is essentially a communion.

Ontology of *Communio*. Both Christ and the Church are called Sacrament, and each, analogously, is also called primal and original Sacrament (*Ursakrament*). The designation is not merely one among many others, equally valid; rather it is the key term in that ontology implicitly contained in the salvation history revealed in the Judaeo-Christian religious tradition. The meaning of Sacrament implies that the divine and the human are so compatible that they can be united in human experience as one event in which the human shares in and manifests the divine being to the world and invites it to participate in this sharing. Clearly, then, the Church can be understood only within the horizon of this Judaeo-Christian ontology.

Ontology of Salvation. Nowhere is the importance of philosophy more striking than in that ecclesiology which explains the Church as *communio* (*koinonia*). All theology, and ECCLESIOLOGY most of all, is liable to trivialize itself as soon as it forgets that it is essentially an answer to the fundamental human question (Man as the *Seinsfrage*), "What is it all about?" Generally, and unfortunately, salvation is understood too narrowly, restricted to what is called either supernatural salvation or redemption. In reality, for the Judaeo-Christian ontology, salvation includes all that is customarily parceled out as creation, grace, and glory. These three designate the three stages or degrees of created participation in uncreated being, which theologians have discerned to be implicitly revealed in the biblical account of history. Hence, the history of the world is correctly called "salvation-history."

If the importance of philosophy for theology is nowhere more obvious than here, likewise is the inadequacy of a "pagan" philosophy. Decisive for every philosophy is the perceived relation between the being of God and the being of the world. The Judaeo-Christian tradition offers the classic formulation of this mutuality in Gn 1.26–27, where the human creation is explicitly stated to be in the image and likeness of the divine creator. Although this formal insight is common to every philosophy and religion, the material content varies enormously. One need only compare typical Mesopotamian, Greco-Roman, Aryan, and Judaeo-Christian theories about the originating pattern, the deity, and the originated imitation, the world.

The Divine Being, Relationship. Since the being of God is decisive for the being of whatever is not God, the being or nature of the Judaeo-Christian God must be elucidated. The first and decisive assertion is that this God is triune, three Persons in one God. Thus are avoided the inadequacies inherent in both polytheism and even certain traditional monotheisms. In Greek philosophy substance denotes a being that stands on its own, that does not inhere in nor form part of another being. It tends to connote independence and even separation, apartness, isolation. Baneful results for certain religious approaches to God are obvious, for the deity becomes not only the One, but the Alone, even the Alien. The Judaeo-Christian God, on the other hand, and precisely as triune, emphatically reveals that by virtue of his divine unicity God is not reduced to the isolated and phthisic status of a monad. In Greek philosophy substance and relation tend to be mutually hostile, so that the more one really is (substance), the less one is related (relation). The ontology implicit in the triune God simply undoes this. For this God, substantial being is being related; relation is substance. Thus, God's very being is the relationships of the Father, Son, and Holy Spirit, for God is not first Father, and then only derivatively and subsequently Son and Holy Spirit (cf. Ratzinger). Rather, the very substance of God is originally communicated Being. Hence, all being, wherever it is in being, is inescapably "being with."

Perichoresis and *Communio*. In order to describe this triune God, theologians have had recourse to many images and terms. One of the happiest has been the Greek word "perichoresis," for it surpasses all others in indicating that one of the classical problems of theoretical philosophy is reconciled in the triune God. Yet, it is not only a problem of theoretical philosophy, but also of practical living, namely the relation of the one and the many, of unity and diversity. Elsewhere considered contraries and even contradictories are revealed to be congenial and harmonious in the triune God. This is aptly expressed by perichoresis, which comes from Greek words meaning "to dance around with." If the anthropomorphism be permitted, PERICHORESIS means that God is so full of being that his oneness is manyness, a manyness that in no way divides or separates, negates or isolates his oneness. Thus a term from "to dance" expresses God's being happy with himself, with his shared being—the being together of the Father, Son, and Holy Spirit. It is this kind of joyful unity in diversity that Genesis (esp. ch. 1 and 2) describes as the creation and which the Hebrew calls *shalom*.

Within this view it is perfectly "natural" that God, whose very being is communicated plenitude, should also communicate being to that which of itself is not God and, hence, which otherwise is simply not at all. To describe this communication in its various stages and degrees theologians have developed the terms "creation," "Christ," and "Church." If Christ, by his HYPOSTATIC UNION, is the most intense and unsurpassable instance of this theandric communication and communion of the divine with the human, then creation and Church are but the necessary antecedent and subsequent conditions: creation as the supposition and inception (protology) and Church as the consequence and completion (eschatology). Only in this context can the traditional distinction between nature and grace, the natural and the supernatural, be properly understood. It is legitimate to refer to the creation as nature and to redemption and glory as grace, but only with the understanding that all being other than the simply divine is gratuitous and, hence, grace. Thus, humanity lives in a gracious world, and always has. The distinction between natural and supernatural remains legitimate only as long as it is clearly understood that the "super" refers not to God the Creator giving the gift, but to man the creature receiving the gift. The gift is being, the full "being with" that God intends to communicate. Hence, the creature's capacity for the "supernatural" does not demand supernatural life from a presumably reluctant God; rather, the generous God's desire to give creatures this superabundant life (Jn 1.16; 10.10) provides that there be a "nature" created to receive it.

Thus the dispute over whether the Creed's *communio sanctorum* refers to holy things or holy persons, though historically pertinent, is theologically and really otiose. All being is communion in the holy being of God, and the Church is precisely where this holy communion is celebrated. As effect and symbol of God's inward communion outwardly communicated, the Church is the Sacrament of salvation. The eternal, immanent trinity is the savingly historical, economic Trinity.

For this reason earliest theology speaks of the Church as "a people united by the unity of the Father, Son and Holy Spirit" (Cyprian, *De Orat. Domin.* 23). Tertullian says, "For the Church is itself, properly and principally, the Spirit Himself, in whom there is a trinity of one divinity, Father, Son and Holy Spirit" (*De pud.* 21). These texts can be taken as but the logical development of John's assertion that God is love (1 Jn 4.8, 16). Both really and gnoseologically the salvation-historical Trinity is the immanent Trinity.

Such lengthy Trinitarian and Christological considerations may seem excessive in a discussion of the entry on the Church as *communio*. However, as soon as such insights are even obscured, ecclesiology deteriorates into debates about lordship in the body politic of the Church, whereas it should be a *lectio divina* about the brotherhood of humanity in Christ celebrating the communion of man with God in the union of the Holy Spirit.

Being of the Church as *Communio*. If the Judaeo-Christian revelation understands that being as such is gift and communion, then it automatically follows that the being of the Church must also be gift and communion. If the divine and theandric sources of the Church are not grudging givers (Phil 2.6), then the Church must also strive for the "more" *perisseuma* that must distinguish the followers of Christ who want to enter the Kingdom of God definitively (Mt 5.20).

***Communio*, Giving and Forgiving.** In neither the institutions of its officials nor in the holiness of its members, however, does the Church expect paradisal innocence or utopian perfectionism. The true Church is not gnostic, but has always (Mt 12.36 43) known that it is, in the words of Augustine, a *corpus mixtum* of saints and sinners. The Church is aware that it is an *ecclesia reformata semper reformanda*. In the customary course of events the holiness of the Church, even as the communion of the saints, is not sinlessness, but forgiveness. For it is the Church of God, who wills not the death, but the life of the sinner (Ez 18.23); the Church of Jesus, who is the friend of sinners (Mt 11.19); and the Church of the Holy Spirit, who is the forgiveness of sins (the Postcommunion of the Roman Liturgy for Whit Tuesday, based on Jn 20.19 with Lk 20.19; 24.47 and Acts 1.8). Disastrously throughout the Church's history this precise nature of its holiness has been misunderstood, by both liberals and conservatives, reformers and integralists. The result has been presumption in those who identify the pilgrim Church with the eschatological Kingdom; despair, in those who identify the sinful Church with the Synagogue of Satan (H. Denzinger, *Enchiridion symbolorum* [32d ed. Freiburg 1963] 1187). Both types are responsible for rending the seamless garment which Christ's Church is to be. Asserting their own holiness, both desert the holiness of that patient (2 Pt 3.9 with Wis 11.15–12.27), divine Wisdom which "sweetly and powerfully disposes all things" (Wis 8.1) and of whose goods and mysteries the Church is the sacramental communion. Rightly, then, the Church is most intensely Church through the Communion in the life-giving Body received at the banquet table spread by the (incarnate) divine Wisdom himself (Prv 9.1–6; Sir 24.19–22 with Lk 22:14–20 and 1 Cor 1.19–31). The gift of the Christian Church, although simultaneously sinful and holy, still the communion of saints, illuminates the fundamental insight of the Judaeo-Christian ontology, namely, that being is both divinely given and forgiven.

A Lived *Communio*. The mission of this Church is to practice this ontology. In both its structure and its life the Church is to be a communion of giving and forgiving. The officer in the Church is to be a shepherd, mindful that Jesus alone is the absolute Sacrament (Jn 10.1 10) of the Divine Shepherd (Ez 34.1). Hence, popes, bishops, pastors, and leaders of whatever kind "are not dictators over your faith, but fellow workers with you for your happiness" (2 Cor 1.24), "administrators of this new covenant" (2 Cor 3.6), who coordinate the many gifts of the one Spirit for the building up of the one Body of Christ. The members are to remember that as members they are also the fellow workers, equally responsible for the completion of the Body of Christ (Col 1.24), for it is not a monarchy, but a communion. Having been loved first by God and brought into communion with him, they are all henceforth able to love others and bring them into the same communion so that the joy of all may be complete (1 Jn 4.7, 10, 19; 1.4).

Vatican II Documents. As used in the council documents, *communio* has, amid a broad range of meaning, two major divisions: communion with God and communion among human persons. In general understanding, humanity is called to communion with God (*Gaudium et spes* 19). Specifically, humanity is called to communion with God who is Father, Son and Spirit (*Unitatis redintegratio* 7, 15). Through the Eucharist, individuals are taken up into communion with Christ, and with one another (*Lumen gentium* 7). This is the communion of believers (UR 2) which has its source and center in Christ (UR 20) and was established by him as a communion of life, love, and truth (LG 9), having the Holy Spirit as the principle of unity (UR 2). *Communio* is used to designate the entire mystical body of Jesus Christ (LG 50): those in glory, those being purified, and those still on pilgrimage. Thus the meaning of *communio* includes that invisible union with God and among believers, as well as the visible manifestation of that union which is membership in the Church (*Sacrosanctum concilium* 69; LG 14).

Communio is also used to designate the relationships between groups within the PEOPLE OF GOD. Religious are bound together in a fraternal communion (LG 43). There is a communion among the Catholic Eastern Churches (*Orientalium ecclesiarum* 2) and between those churches and the pope (OE 24). There was a communion between the West and all the churches of the East before the Schism and even now there exists a communion among the separated churches themselves (UR 14). *Communio* refers to the relation of particular churches among themselves (*Ad gentes* 19) as well as their relationship with the universal Church (AG 38).

The council expresses the structure of the People of God with the term "hierarchical communion" (*Presbyterorum ordinis* 15) applied in several contexts. An individual becomes a member of the episcopal college through sacramental consecration and hierarchical communion with the head of the college and its members (LG 22). He likewise exercises his ministry of teaching, sanctifying, and ruling only in hierarchical communion with the head and members of the episcopal college (LG 21). *Communio* in this context is not to be understood as a vague goodwill, but as something organic which calls for a juridical structure (*Nota praevia* 2). There exists also a bond of hierarchical communion between the priests of a diocese and the bishop (PO 7). Among bishops themselves (LG 25) and among priests themselves (LG 41), the bond of *communio* should abound in every spiritual good and bear living witness of God to all.

In the area of ecumenism, the concept of *communio* plays an important role. The most frequent designation for non-Catholic Christians is "brothers not yet in full communion" (GS 92). This use of *communio non plena* conveys a positive element, that there is communion of prayers and spiritual benefits (LG 15) between the churches, and they are joined in some real way in the Holy Spirit. The council also recognizes that this communion is imperfect and that obstacles hinder full communion (UR 3). But terms like "excommunication," "heretic," and "schism" are never used. *Communio* is used in the Decree on Ecumenism to designate all Christian communities (including the Roman Church: UR 1; 4); to designate all separated churches and ecclesial communities (UR13); and to designate the Anglican communion (UR 13).

The Code and Other Church Documents. Present in the debates and in the texts of Vatican II was a tension between a "juridical ecclesiology" which describes the Church as a "perfect society" structured like a monarchy with its starting point as the primacy of the pope, and an "ecclesiology of communion" which describes the Church as *communio,* emphasizes collegiality and has the local church as its starting point. In a commentary on the 1983 code, James Provost makes the judgment that the ecclesiology of *communio* is "clearly more influential and provides a more consistent perspective for interpreting the council's teaching." Because the teaching of the Second Vatican Council became the foundation for the revisions in canon law, the same tensions present in the conciliar documents are evident in the code, especially in Book II, on the People of God. The code focuses on the external, juridically enforceable dimensions of full communion in canon 205: "Those baptized are fully in communion with the Catholic Church on this earth who are joined with Christ in its visible structure by the bonds of profession of faith, of the Sacraments, and of ecclesiastical governance (cf. LG 14)." There is also a spiritual dimension to communion which is possessing the Spirit of

Christ (LG 14). This forms the living context for the juridical aspects found in the code and is to be seen as complementary to it.

In the apostolic constitution *Sacrae discipline leges* accompanying the promulgation of the code, Pope John Paul II listed among those elements which characterize the true and genuine image of the Church the "doctrine in which the Church is seen as a communion." This was also a major theme in *The Final Report of the Extraordinary Synod of Bishops of 1985* which celebrated the 20-year anniversary of the conclusion of the Second Vatican Council. In assessing the implementation of the teaching of the council, the Bishops reaffirmed the ecclesiology of communion as "the central and fundamental idea of the council's documents" which is the foundation for order and a correct relationship between unity and pluriformity in the Church. In this context the bishops discussed collegiality and coresponsibility and called for continued study of the theological status and doctrinal authority of episcopal conferences; they encouraged continued ecumenical dialogue; and they acknowledged the vocation and mission of women and the emergence of "basic communities." Because the Church, as *communio* is a sacrament for the salvation of the world, the bishops emphasized the Church's mission, particularly its preferential option for the poor and its solidarity for those who suffer. As Bishop James Malone, President of the U.S. Bishops' Conference, stated: "We are a *communio* in which the Spirit of the churches is present to each and all and in which the successor of Peter represents Christ's care for the entire Church. No Catholic can deny any of that; it is the substance of our ecclesiology" [*Origins* 16 (Nov. 20 1986) 394–398].

Since the council, theologians have deepened the Church's self-understanding as *communio* and sought to express more fully and clearly the connections and consequences of this many-sided concept. The community of believers throughout the world forms a communion of local churches, the bishops in communion with the bishop of Rome whose primacy serves the unity of the whole Church. *Communio* not only expresses what the Church is, visibly and invisibly, it also expresses the Church's goal, not only among all Christian communions, but for men and women of every time and place. It is for this reason that, precisely as communion, the Church is a sacrament for the salvation of all. The clearest expression of the Trinitarian character of the Church is the Eucharist, where invisible communion with God and visible communion with one another form a sacramental unity. It is a sign and instrument, possessing within itself the reality of communion with Father, Son, and Spirit, but always as sign and never perfectly. Thus *communio* implies laws, rituals, apostolates and our work in building up the People of God. But at the same time, *communio* is grace and gift, for God has established his people as the Body of Christ through the power of the Holy Spirit. The *communio* that Christians receive is their present task and future goal. It alone fulfills the human heart, for it extends beyond death.

Bibliography: H. DE LUBAC, *Catholicism: Christ and the Common Destiny of Man* (New York 1950). D. L. SCHINDLER, *Heart of the World, Center of the Church: Communio Ecclesiology, Liberalism, and Liberation* (Grand Rapids, Mich. 1996). R. KRESS, *The Church: Communion, Sacrament, Communication* (New York 1985). J. M. R. TILLARD, *Church of Churches: The Ecclesiology of Communion* (Collegeville, Minn. 1992). Y. CONGAR, *Diversity and Communion* (Mystic, Conn. 1985). J. M. MCDERMOTT, "The Biblical Doctrine of 'koinonia,'" *Biblische Zeitschrift* 19 (1975): 64–77; 219–233. J. PROVOST, ed., *The Church as Communion* (Washington, D.C. 1984). E. CORECCO, *Canon Law and Communio: Writings on the Constitutional Law of the Church* (Vatican City 1999). J. RATZINGER, "The Ecclesiology of Vatican II," *Origins* 15 (1985): 370–376. G. ALBERIGO and J. PROVOST, "Synod 1985—An Evaluation," *Concilium* 188 (1986). O. SAIER, *"Communio" in der Lehre des zweiten vatikanischen Konzil* (Munich 1973).

[R. KRESS/G. MALANOWSKI]

COMMUNIO: INTERNATIONAL CATHOLIC REVIEW

Communio, an international federation of journals that now includes editions in Germany, Italy, North America, France, Croatia, Belgium, Spain, Poland, Brazil, Portugal, Slovenia, Hungary, Chile, Argentina, and the Czech Republic, began publication in 1972. In the late 1960s, Hans Urs von BALTHASAR had planned a small book of essays by prominent Catholics that would address the essentials of the faith in light of the controversies following the Second Vatican Council. When it became clear that an anthology would not suffice, but that a continuing conversation with different currents was necessary, he turned to the idea of a journal. The journal began to take concrete form in a conversation arranged during a session of the International Theological Commission in Rome in 1970, followed by a second meeting in Paris in 1971. Theologians called together for the first conversation were Balthasar, H. de LUBAC, L. Bouyer, J. Medina, M. J. Le Guillou, and J. RATZINGER. Balthasar was made father of the joint project with special responsibility for the German branch. Le Guillou was charged with responsibility for the French. Because of Le Guillou's subsequent illness, the French edition was delayed. An Italian partner then emerged, made up partly of members of the movement Comunione e Liberazione. *Communio* thus was finally launched in 1972, with two editions, German and Italian, followed in 1974 by the North American and the French. With the help and en-

couragement of then-archbishop of Krakow, Karol Wojtyła, a group of Polish theologians eventually secured government permission and founded an edition some ten years later in 1983 and 1984.

In the words of Balthasar, the purpose of *Communio* is "negatively: to resist at all costs the deadly polarization brought on by the fervor of traditionalists and modernists alike; positively: to perceive the Church as a central *communio,* a community originating from communion with Christ ('given from above'); as a *communio* enabling us to share our hearts, thoughts and blessings." The journal is theological in nature, intended for specialists as well as for all those concerned with fundamental questions of the faith in its engagement with contemporary culture. In keeping with the spirit embodied in the review's title, the editors sought from the beginning to form a community among themselves and their authors that would proceed on the basis of *communio.* In North America, this has led to the formation of study circles. For the same reason, the editors chose a federated rather than centralized administration for the review, allowing for the coincidence of unity and difference among the many language areas. The different editions frequently publish translations of each other's articles.

Bibliography: H. URS VON BALTHASAR, "Communio: International Catholic Review," *Communio* 19 (1992): 507–8 NC; "The Mission of Communio," *Communio* 19 (1992): 509 NC. JOHN PAUL II, "Address to the Group Representing the Journal *Communio,*" *Communio* 19 (1992): 433–435. A. SICARI, "A Reflection on the Ideals of Communio," *Communio* 16 (1989): 495–498. J. RATZINGER, "*Communio*: A Program," *Communio* 19 (1992): 436–449.

[D. L. SCHINDLER]

COMMUNION AND LIBERATION

An English translation of *Communione e Liberazione*, the name of a spiritual and apostolic movement that had its origins in Italy, where it is also known by its acronym CL. *Communione e Liberazione*, an outgrowth of an experiment in Catholic Action (3:262a), was founded by Luigi Giussani (b. 1922) in the 1950s, and approved as a Confraternity by the Pontifical Council for the Laity, Feb. 11, 1982.

Concerned about the declining influence of the Catholic majority on the social and cultural life of Italy, Giussani, a priest of the archdiocese of Milan, began to work with young people. He resigned his post as a lecturer at the theological school in Venegono, near Milan, to take a teaching assignment in a Milan high school. There he started a catechetical program within the young girls section of the Catholic Action (*Azione Cattolica*) movement, and for over a decade Giussani's experiment was known simply by the acronym GS (*Gioventu' Studentesca*), as the young women's section of Catholic Action was called. His program became prominent in most schools in Milan and spread to Romagna and other parts of the country.

Giussani's basic principle is the totality of Christian life commitment: faith cannot be confined to some interior recesses of one's being, but must engage all aspects of a Christian's life and action. Giussani identified the enemy as a kind spiritual schizophrenia, a situation which he blamed on some Italian apostolic movements that separated personal commitment from public policy: Giussani's movement split from the Catholic Action movement in 1964–65 over his disregard of its rigid structure, which organized its members according to sex, age, and education. Shortly afterwards *Communione e Liberazione* faced another major crisis, in 1968, when its failure to come to grips with the widespread student protests and demonstrations caused some of its most promising leaders to leave the movement for secular and leftist groups. Nonetheless CL became more and more prominent in the Church and Italian society because of its dynamism and readiness to confront moral issues like divorce and abortion. Members gained influential positions in some sectors of the press, labor, education, and political parties. With the accession of Pope John Paul II (1978), CL found favor in Vatican circles, and began to spread outside Italy. In the 1980s CL had adherents in 20 or more countries, including the United States (Boston, New York, aand Washington, D.C.).

Structure. The *Communione e Liberazione* is loosely organized, with an International Council in Milan, where the different branches are represented. At the local level, the strength of the movement is the study groups, "Schools of Communion," where members meet to study and reflect on important Church documents and materials provided by Giussani's central headquarters. The weekly community meeting of the members is regarded as the culminating point of communion and personal commitment. The "Schools of Communion" are linked with one another in a loose organization that gives CL influence and strength far beyond the strict canonical scope of a confraternity. Some members form special interest groups, addressing issues of labor relations, family problems, and Italian and European politics. The official organ of the movement is the bulletin *Litterae Communionis CL,* but its ideology is also strongly promoted in some highly successful Italian periodicals such as *Il Sabato, 30 Giorni, L'Avvenire*, and a series of books published by Jaca Book, a publishing house in Milan.

Bibliography: F. PERRENCHIO, "Communione e Liberazione," A. FAVALE, ed., *Movimenti ecclesiali contemporanei. Dimensioni storiche teologico-spirituali ed apostoliche* (2d ed. Rome 1982) 375–401. R. RONZA, *Communione e Liberazione. Interviste a Luigi Giussani.* (Milan 1976). G. RIVA, *Don Giussani* (Milan 1986).

[G. ELDAROV]

COMMUNION ANTIPHON

The chant (a psalm, hymn, or antiphon) that was historically sung by a soloist, the choir, or the congregation during the Communion of the priest and the faithful in the Roman Mass. In the Roman liturgy this chant is called the Communion antiphon (*antiphona ad communionem*) or simply the Communion.

Origin and Psalmodic Practice. The ancient practice of chanting a psalm during the distribution of Communion is common to both Eastern and Western liturgies. It is mentioned in the *Apost. Const.* (8:13, 16), by St. Cyril of Jerusalem (*Catech. Myst.* 5:20) and by St. Augustine [*Serm.* 225; *Patrologica Latina*, ed. J. P. Migne, 217 v., (Paris 1878–90) 38:1098, cf. 46:828]. In the East as in the West, Psalm 33 was often sung because of the relevant verse, *Gustate et videte quoniam suavis est Dominus,* which still serves for the eighth Sunday after Pentecost. Severus of Antioch composed hymns for the Communion [*Patrologia orientalis*, ed. R. Graffin and F. Nau (Paris 1903–) 7:678]. It is known that a hymn was sung in the ancient Gallican liturgy (*Antiphonary of Bangor,* ed. H. Warren, Bradshaw Society, 4, fol. 10v). At Milan an antiphon without psalmody, the *Transitorium,* is sung during Communion. The double Ambrosian series of *Transitoria* and *Confractoria* (the latter an antiphon sung during the breaking of the Host) presents numerous analogies with the Roman series of Communion antiphons.

According to the *Ordines Romani* of the 8th and 9th centuries, the Communion song was carried out in the following manner: Communion antiphon sung by the schola; psalmody, with repetition of the antiphon after each verse; *Gloria Patri. . .Sicut erat. . .*; a *versus ad repetendum;* and a last repetition of the antiphon. The psalm selected was the same as that from which the antiphon had been drawn. When the antiphon was not from the Psalter but from the Gospels or St. Paul's Epistles, or even from the Old Testament, the INTROIT psalm provided the verses. The alternation of psalms with the Communion antiphon did not persist for long. In France the psalm was preserved only until the 10th century—except in certain churches on Christmas and Easter, days of general Communion. At St. Gall (*see* SANKT GALLEN, ABBEY OF) the psalm was still being sung in the 11th century, and in southern France and southern Italy the use of the psalm was known until the 12th century.

Musical Relation to Office Chants. In the Old Roman chant there are 38 Communion antiphons that are repeated as responses—with the addition of a versicle—in the antiphonary. In GREGORIAN chant, where the distinction of genres is better observed, one finds far fewer selections common to the gradual and to the antiphonary. Such an example is the Communion *Ego sum pastor* (second Sunday after Easter), which is found again as a responsory in the Office, and the Communion *Vos qui secuti* (Common of Apostles), found also as an Office antiphon. The Communion of Holy Thursday, *Dominus Jesus,* is also an antiphon during the Mandatum. It is this distinction of musical genres in Gregorian chant that explains why eight Communions with Gospel texts and in syllabic style exactly like the Office antiphons were later clothed in ornate melodies that differ from one another according to the region where they are found. Five of them replaced Communion antiphons (now lost) from the Psalter on weekdays of Lent. For these Communions there are in medieval MSS ten different melodies for *Oportet te,* six for *Qui biberit,* five for *Nemo te,* seven for *Lutum,* and four for *Videns.* For the three remaining antiphons there are three different melodies for *Mirabantur* (third Sunday after Epiphany), four for *Spiritus qui a Patre* (Tuesday of Pentecost week), and six for *Vos qui secuti* (Common of Apostles).

To account for this multiplicity of melodies, it has been claimed that at the time the psalm-Communions of Lent were replaced by the Gospel-Communions, the new texts did not have melodies; hence the musical composition must have been effected subsequently and independently in each region. Such an explanation must be rejected, since in the Middle Ages the text of a chant was never set down without its being clothed at the same time with its melody. The true explanation is simpler: the primitive melodies of the five Lenten Communions—preserved in the oldest French, German, and Italian MSS—and the melodies of the other three Communions cited above, were syllabic in nature, resembling the antiphons of the Office rather than the other Communions of the Gradual book. In various churches it was thought desirable to replace this simple melody by a more elaborate one that would conform to the style of the other Communions.

Musical Analysis. The musical style of the Gregorian Communion antiphon is very much like the style of the Introit and is related to the style of the responsories of the Office; in fact, certain formulas of intonation and of cadence are identical with those of the Introit, and certain Communion cadences are found also in the responsories. Yet, Gregorian composition cannot be reduced to a mere linking together of ready-made formulas: creative inventiveness also had a large role to play. The pentatonic

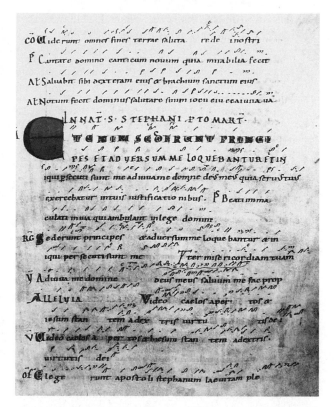

Manuscript, Communion antiphon, 11th-century versiculary, used for the feast of St. Stephen.

melodies (e.g., *In splendoribus, Tu es Petrus*) are perhaps from the oldest strata of the Gregorian repertory. The Communions of the Lenten weekdays (except those of Holy Week and the Gospel-Communions cited above) are by one and the same composer.

The modal division of the 144 Communion antiphons of the primitive Gregorian repertory is as follows: modes on D, 41; modes on E, 26; modes on F, 31; pieces sometimes classed on F, sometimes on G, 11, modes on G, 27. To this total of 136 antiphons must be added the 8 Communions mentioned above. A number of Communion melodies are merely adaptations of new texts to already existing melodies; thus, the Communion *Per signum crucis* (Exaltation of the Holy Cross) was adapted to the melody of the Communion *Ab occultis* (Lent). Likewise, the Communion *Ego sum vitis vera* (St. Vitalis) has borrowed its melody from *Ego sum pastor bonus* (second Sunday after Easter); here, the same initial text has understandably introduced the same melody. This manner of adaptation, which obviates original composition, was repeated at all epochs. The Communion for the Feast of the Holy Trinity, introduced in the 9th century, took its melody from the Communions *Feci judicium* and *Invocabit.* In the 13th century, the text *Quotiescum-*

que (feast of Corpus Christi) was adapted, a bit awkwardly, to the Communion *Factus est repente* (Pentecost).

Bibliography: P. M. FERRETTI, *Esthétique grégorienne* (Tournai 1938) 266–90. J. FROGER, "Les Chants de la messe aux VIIIe–IXe siècles," *Revue Grégorienne* 27 (1948) 104–06. R. J. HESBERT, ed., *Antiphonale missarum sextuplex* (Brussels 1935) 46. M. HUGLO, "Antifone antiche per la *Fractio panis*," *Ambrosius* 31 (1955) 85–95. J. A. JUNGMANN, *The Mass of the Roman Rite,* tr. F. A. BRUNNER, 2 v. (New York 1951–55) 2:391–400. P. WAGNER, *Einführung in die gregorianischen Melodien,* 3 v. (Leipzig) v.1 (3d ed. 1911), v.2 (2d ed. 1912), v.3 (1921); repr. (Hildesheim 1962) 116–20.

[M. HUGLO]

COMMUNION OF SAINTS

The article of the Apostles' Creed that in Latin reads "Credo in . . . sanctorum communionem," is translated as "I believe in . . . the communion of saints." The Christian reality underlying this article is so central and so pervasive in the life of the Church that it was lived and borne along in the movement of the Church's life long before it became the object of theological reflection. Once such reflection did begin, the very amplitude of the doctrine favored a variety of emphases, kindred enough, in evolving its many aspects; and the same cause often resulted in a treatment more piecemeal than synthetic.

The present treatment sets forth only the general outlines of the doctrine, with special aspects left to other headings. The order is the following: (1) communio as mutual interchange, (2) New Testament foundation, (3) patristic and creedal origins, and (4) later historical developments.

Communio as Mutual Interchange. Beginning in the 19th century, the main emphasis has been on the mutual interchange and interplay of supernatural energies and goods among all the members of the tripartite Church, triumphant in heaven, expectant in purgatory, and militant on Earth. The stress is on what some theologians came to refer to as "horizontal" sharing by all the members in the varied common life of the Church. It is succinctly explained in Pope LEO XIII's encyclical on the Eucharist, *Mirae caritatis* (May 28, 1902, *Acta Sanctae Sedis* 34:649):

> As everyone knows, the communion of saints is nothing else but a mutual sharing in help, satisfaction, prayer and other good works, a mutual communication among all the faithful, whether those who have reached heaven, or who are in the cleansing fire, or who are still pilgrims on the way in this world. For all these are come together to form one living city whose Head is Christ, and whose law is love.

Explanations in the writings of Leo's successors in the 20th century develop along similar lines. Vatican II's Dogmatic Constitution on the Church (*Lumen gentium*) while looking to the Lord's coming in glory states "at the present time some of his disciples are pilgrims on earth," some "have died and are being purified," while still others "are in glory" contemplating God as He is. All, "in varying degrees and different ways" share in the same charity toward God and neighbor. "The union of the wayfarers with the brethren who sleep in the peace of Christ is in no way interrupted, but on the contrary, according to the constant faith of the Church, this union is reinforced by an exchange of spiritual goods." Those who have been "received into their heavenly home" and are "present to the Lord" (cf. 2 Cor. 5:8) do not cease to intercede for us with the Father, sharing the merits they acquired on Earth through Christ Jesus (LG, 49).

In explaining the Creed the *Catechism of the Catholic Church* links the *communio sanctorum* to the Church to the point of stating explicitly, "The communion of saints is the Church" (n. 946). It presents the twofold meaning of *communio sanctorum*—sharing in holy things (*sancta*) and among holy persons (*sancti*) as complementary.

> *Sancta sanctis!* ("God's holy gifts for God's holy people") is proclaimed by the celebrant in most Eastern liturgies during the elevation of the holy Gifts before the distribution of communion. The faithful (*sancti*) are fed by Christ's holy body and blood (*sancta*) to grow in the communion of the Holy Spirit (*koinonia*) and to the world (n. 948).

The Catechism describes in some detail the "goods" that are shared under the headings: communion in the faith, communion of the sacraments (especially the Eucharist), communion of charisms, communion in charity, and, alluding to the primitive Christian community in Jerusalem, holding all things in common (nn. 949–953).

New Testament Context. Though the emphasis is on the members' solidarity and vital interdependence, it is clearly taught that this horizontal sharing of goods and life is real only as suspended from a "vertical" communion, i.e., from a sharing in Jesus Christ and in His Spirit, realized in and through FAITH and the Sacraments (*see* SACRAMENTAL THEOLOGY), especially the Eucharist. If in Christ's social Body, under the quickening Spirit of love, there is a radial diffusion of love and of its goods, it is fundamentally because there is in Christ a descent of divine love poured forth into men's hearts by the Spirit of Christ, a rebirth from above communicated in water and the Spirit, a force from on high that makes Christ's glory in His various members turn to the service and benefit of all (Rom 5.5; Jn 3.5; Ti 3.5–6).

The ground is found in the divine life that the Father has communicated to the fallen world, drawing people afresh into a real, though distant, sharing in the one life that the Father and His Son in their one Spirit live together as their own (Jn 17.20–26). It is only in His Son made Man that the Father has brought men into the sphere of divine life (Jn 14.6–24; 1 Jn 2.23; 5.11–13), made them "partakers of the divine nature" (2 Pt 1.4), and given them communion with Himself and with His Son (1 Jn 1.1–3; 1 Cor 1.9). The Christian shares, through faith and the Sacraments, in all the stages of Christ's life from His lowliness in suffering and death (Phil 3.10; 1 Pt 4.13) to His risen glory (1 Pt 5.1; Rom 8.17). The Christian shares initially in all the blessings of the New Covenant, brought by Jesus and already realized in Him, the dead and risen Lord (1 Cor 9.23). It is a communion with Christ most intensely realized by partaking sacramentally of the Lord's body and blood (1 Cor 10.16–17); it is a communion sealed in the gift that is the Spirit of Christ (2 Cor 13.13; Phil 2.1; Gal 4.6; Rom 8.14–17).

The common life that Christians share with Christ and with His Father in their one Spirit (Eph 2.18) leads of itself to a sharing of life among all those quickened by the same Spirit of Christ (1 Jn 1.3, 7). Among Christ's members there exists a most varied inward-outward interplay of new life; an interchange of supernatural energies and gifts, of helps and services of all forms (Phlm 17; Rom 12.13; 15.26–27; 2 Cor 8.4; 9.13; Phil 4.14–20; Gal 6.6; Heb 13.16; Acts 2.42). Sharing in the "trials" of Jesus brings into play a communion in suffering with the social Body of Christ that turns to the good of the whole (Col 1.24; 2 Cor 4.12, 15; 1.5, 7). The interchange of new life to the "building up the body of Christ" (Eph 4.12) is shown and realized in mutual prayer and almsgiving (Eph 6.18–19; Rom 15.30; 2 Cor 8.13–15). "The Church is in its truest being both a shared destiny and a shared existence with Christ, and with one another in Christ".

Patristic Period. The Apostles' Creed in its present form, conventionally labeled T (H. Denzinger, *Enchiridion symbolorum,* ed. A. Schönmetzer [32d ed. Freiburg 1963] 30), is an expanded version of the old Roman baptismal creed, labeled R (see H. Denzinger, *Enchiridion symbolorum* 12 for a 4th-century Latin text of R). R's development into T took place, seemingly, in southwestern Gaul during the 5th to the 8th centuries. Among the additions that T makes to R is the article "sanctorum communionem."

This addition presents a difficult problem of the history and interpretation of T. First, the provenance of the clause is debated, some holding for an eastern and Greek origin, others for a western and Latin.

Second, the original meaning of the clause is disputed. There are two main opinions held. The first view puts a personal construction on the clause and translates it "fellowship or common life with the saints." In this personal interpretation the "saints" are either the martyrs and confessors proper, both living and departed, or all the baptized faithful without exception. The second view, sometimes called the "real" interpretation, and commonly proposed by those holding a Greek origin of the clause, translates it "a sharing in, or partaking of, holy things." The holy things or realities (hence the "real") are either the faith and Sacraments in general, or, in particular, the consecrated elements of the Eucharist.

This real interpretation is not apersonal. In the thought and sensibility of the early Church, sharing in holy things, and above all in the Eucharist, meant a deeply personal meeting with the glorious Christ sanctifying His members through His mysteries present in His Church. "You have shown yourself to me face to face, O Christ," wrote St. Ambrose, "I find you in your Sacraments" (*Apologia prophetae David* 12.58; *Patrologia Latina,* ed. J. P. Migne, 271 v., indexes 4 v. [Paris 1878–90] 14: 875). Sharing in the Eucharist was also a profession and a realization of a profound personal union with all Christ's members and with the whole present company of the saints in the Church. Finally, sharing in the Eucharist had a deeply personal eschatological direction, grounding the faithful's hope in the full communion of the coming kingdom with the Father and the Lord in their one Spirit, and with all the blessed.

An exclusively linguistic approach to the problem of original meaning is inconclusive. If the original meaning is sought in the extant creedal commentaries and homilies, chiefly of a south Gallic provenance, dating from the 5th to the 8th centuries, the personal interpretation predominates, but even in the West the words were often taken as referring to the sacrament (see J. N. D. Kelly, *Early Christian Creeds* [3d ed. London 1972] 393).

But one must also consider the living background of early Christian belief and practice, which came to a focus in this creedal article. Before the clause was introduced into the creed, what it stood for was long since part of the living faith of the Church.

In the thought and devotion of the early Church, the mystery of holy Church is the sacrament of the glorious Savior, giving His light and life to the world ("What was visible in the work of our Redeemer, passed over into the Sacraments," wrote St. Leo the Great [*Serm.* 74.2; *Patrologia Latina* 54:398]). It is only through the faith and Sacraments of holy Church that one is made a sharer in Him who is "the holy one of God" (Jn 6.69); it is only under His headship that His members, once consecrated through His Spirit in the Sacraments, are enabled to adore and to serve the movement of His life in and through His whole Body, with an outreach of love compassing their fellow members who have gone ahead, and looking forward in hope to the full communion of the coming great kingdom. Above all it is in the Eucharist that the glorious Lord is supremely present and active in communicating His holiness to men; it is here that the Christian shares in Christ's lordship over the newness of life, and is qualified to serve the range of that new life over the whole Body, both in those that live here below and in those that live beyond.

This awareness of sacramental communion with Christ carried with it a vivid sense of the diffusive sanctity of the whole Body of Christ sharing in the mystery of Christ. In a study of the Church's saving mediation, as the early Fathers portrayed it under the image of the Church as Mother, Karl Delahaye writes:

> The early Church considers all the saints as both subject and object of her own saving action. . . . The Church as mother, comprising all united to Christ in faith and Baptism, is the communion of saints. If her motherhood is grounded on her inward mysterious union with Christ, then all who have entered into this communion with Christ share in the Church's motherhood. . . . The communion of the saints is always at the same time a communion which saves and sanctifies. (*Erneuerung der Seelsorgsformen aus der Sicht der frühen Patristik* [Freiburg 1958] 142–143. See 134, 148–149.)

If the whole Church is, to adapt a word of Ignatius of Antioch, a fruitful "bearer of holy things" (ἁγιοφόρα: *To the Smyrnaeans,* introd.), the reason is that the whole Church shares in the Spirit of Christ. As Pope Martin I (649–655) wrote to the Church of Carthage: "Whatever is ours, is yours, according to our undivided sharing in the Spirit" (*Ep.* 4; *Patrologia Latina* 87.147).

Subsequent Developments. In the Middle Ages the two orientations lived on. In Alexander of Hales's *Summa theologica* the two are merely juxtaposed (lib. 3, p. 3, inq. 2, tr. 2, q. 2, t. 1–2; tom. 4 [Quaracchi 1948] 1131, 1136). Both St. Albert and St. Thomas give a more synthetic view, indicating that the real-sacramental communion is the ground of the varied horizontal sharing. For St. Albert, see *In Ioannem* 6.64; *In 4 sent.* 45.1; *De sacramento Eucharistiae* 1.5; 4.1–7. St. Thomas writes: "The good of Christ is communicated to all Christians . . .; and this communication is realized through the Sacraments of the Church, in which the power of Christ's Passion is at work . . ." (*Exp. symb. apost.* 10). But the good that Christ communicates is chiefly "the Holy Spirit, who through the unity of love communicates the blessings of Christ's members one with another" (*Summa theologiae* 3, 82.6 ad 3).

From the Reformation onward, the emphasis is strongly on the validity and the modes of the interplay of life among the members of the tripartite Church. Theologians were aware that the article "is variously explained by the doctors" (J. de Lugo, *De virtute fidei divinae* 13.4.112), but generally their preference is for the personal interpretation (see F. Suárez, *De virtutibus infusis* 13.4.10; R. de Arriaga, *De fide divina* 13.3.16). The catechisms, from Bellarmine on, reflect this trend (see M. Ramsauer, "Die Kirche in den Katechismen," *Zeitschrift für katholische Theologie* 73 [1951] 129–169, 313–346). In the early 19th century the two orientations begin to come together. In J. A. Möhler's phrase, "a communion in the holy and of the saints" (*Die Einheit in der Kirche,* ed. J. R. Geiselmann [Cologne 1957] 315) they are seen as complementary one to the another.

Bibliography: A. PIOLANTI, *Il mistero della comunione dei santi* (Rome 1957). L. HERTLING, *Communio. Chiesa e papato nell' antichità cristiana* (Rome 1961). A. MICHEL, "La Communion des Saints," *Doctor Communis* 9 (1956) 1–125. J. P. KIRSCH, *The Doctrine of the Communion of Saints in the Ancient Church* (St. Louis 1910). H. SEESEMANN, *Der Begriff* κοινωνία *im Neuen Testament* (Giessen 1933). L. S. THORNTON, *The Common Life in the Body of Christ* (3d ed. London 1950). A. R. GEORGE, *Communion with God in the New Testament* (London 1953). S. MUÑOZ IGLESIAS, "Concepto biblico de κοινωνία," *XIII Semana Biblica Española, 1952* (Madrid 1953) 195–224. M. THURIAN, *The Eucharistic Memorial,* tr. J. G. DAVIES (2 v., Richmond, Va. 1961). *Communio* (English) 15 (Summer 1998), issue devoted to the Communion of Saints. R. GOIZUETA, *Caminemos con Jesús: Toward a Hispanic/Latino Theology of Accompaniment* (Maryknoll 1995). E. ILOGU, *Christianity and Ibo Culture* (Leiden 1974). M. BROWNE, ed., *African Synod: Documents, Reflections, Perspectives* (Maryknoll 1996). E. A. JOHNSON, *Friends of God and Prophets: A Feminist Theological Reading of the Communion of Saints* (New York 1998).

[F. X. LAWLOR/EDS.]

COMMUNION SERVICE

A liturgical service within which eucharistic bread reserved from a previous celebration is shared by a congregation when the Eucharist cannot be celebrated. A lay person normally presides. The Anglican communion speaks of "communion by extension." Many churches of the Reformation tradition use "Communion Service" for the celebration of the EUCHARIST at Sunday worship and most do not allow communion outside the Eucharist.

The practice of sharing communion outside Mass can be traced to the second and third centuries. The remote origins lie in an "emergency" situation, sending eucharistic bread from the Sunday celebration to those who were absent (Justin, 1 Apol. 1, 67), and in a domestic setting, laity bringing it home for family communion during the week (Tertullian, *Ad uxorem* 2, 5; *De oratione* 19).

Communion outside the liturgy for the sick, imprisoned, and dying has remained common throughout history. However, from the ninth-century Carolingian reformation on only priests were allowed to perform this ministry. Domestic weekday communion declined with less frequent communion and the introduction of weekday Mass (beginning in the late fourth century), although desert monks (Basil, Letter 93) and other recluses continued the practice. We do not know what type of service took place, if any.

In the Christian East, both clergy and laity have shared presanctified bread at Evening Prayer in the Liturgy of the Presanctified on noneucharistic weekdays, especially during Lent. The Latin Church adopted this practice for Good Friday in the seventh and eighth centuries. From the thirteenth century on it was customary for only the priest to receive communion and this became law in the Missal of Pius V, not changing until the Holy Week reform of PIUS XII in 1955. The practice in both East and West has involved bringing the reserved Eucharist to the altar in procession at the end of the service, praying the Lord's Prayer, and then sharing communion.

In the Christian West, beginning in the ninth century, those not receiving communion on Sundays were sometimes dismissed with the priest's blessing, and communion then followed. This became common on Sunday communion days in the twelfth and thirteenth centuries. Monasteries and convents without a resident priest sometimes used similar prayer services for weekday communion from the reserved sacrament or associated it with the Liturgy of the Hours. A similar short service, usually penitential, was generally inserted into the Mass itself when laity were to receive and is found in the Missal of Pius V. As communion became more frequent after the Council of Trent, such a service was often held on weekdays apart from Mass or even immediately before or after Mass for the convenience of those who were unable to be at Mass or preferred not to be. It was also often customary in some parishes to distribute communion throughout the weekday Mass without any link to the Mass itself.

All these practices presume that some of the bread sanctified at Mass is kept back (reserved) for subsequent use. For the first millennium the Eucharist was normally reserved only for the communion of the sick and dying. Beginning in the eleventh century, partly for convenience and partly because of the growing distinction between the Eucharist as sacrifice and the Eucharist as sacrament, communion from the reserved sacrament became common at Mass as well. With the increased frequency of communion after the Council of Trent this became the rule rather than the exception, despite the preference expressed in the Missal of Pius V and in documents of Benedict XIV (1742) and Pius XII (*Mediator Dei*). This preference was repeated in stronger language at Vatican II (SC 55), in GIRM 56h, and in *Holy Communion and Worship of the Eucharist outside Mass* 13, but the practice continues.

The current Communion Service differs from the tradition in allowing such a service on Sundays for a community, not just certain individuals. As liturgical ministries were increasingly reserved to the priest, especially from the ninth century on, communities without a priest generally used a devotional service on Sundays in place of the Eucharist; e.g., the rosary. Sometimes these services were more clearly liturgical; e.g., part of the Liturgy of the Hours or, in Europe and Latin America in modern times under Protestant influence, a scripture service. In 1965 lay eucharistic ministers were authorized in East Germany and a Communion Service began to be added to the scripture service when Eucharist could not be celebrated because of the shortage of priests. Permission for this was extended worldwide in 1967 and became increasingly common as a substitute for Sunday Eucharist. However, in much of the world the Communion Service is not possible because the Eucharist cannot be reserved, either because of infrequent visits by a priest or the climate.

The Congregation for Divine Worship's *Directory for Sunday Celebrations in the Absence of a Priest* (1988), the U.S. bishops' *Gathered in Steadfast Faith: Statement on Sunday Worship in the Absence of a Priest* (1991), the Canadian bishops' *Sunday Celebrations of the Word: Gathering in the Expectation of the Eucharist* (1992), and similar documents gave reluctant approval to the practice of the Sunday Communion Service, warning against the danger of separating communion from Mass. The documents recommended Morning or Evening Prayer or a Liturgy of the Word when Sunday Eucharist cannot be celebrated and permitted a Communion Service to be added. They emphasized a particular concern that the Communion Service could be confused with the Mass or lead to a decreased appreciation of the Eucharist.

Although weekday Communion Services have a base in the tradition, the Sunday Communion Service apart from the celebration of Eucharist is a late twentieth-century development that is the consequence of the ordination discipline and a clergy shortage. Although the service provides a means of eucharistic participation and access, it is derivative and passive. Theological criticism, based on the importance of the assembly's celebration of Eucharist on the Lord's Day, calls attention to the practice obscuring the assembly's role, diminishing the link between ecclesial and eucharistic communion, deemphasizing the significance of the laity in the celebration of the eucharistic sacrifice and reducing their role to receiving communion, minimizing the roles and significance of both ordained and lay ministers (e.g., the priest as one who consecrates), and promoting an individualistic devotional spirituality. Bishops have warned against coming to accept this practice as common or adequate. Many critics suggest a residual clericalism: the Sunday Communion Service gives a higher priority to an exclusively male ordained priesthood than to communities celebrating Eucharist on Sunday. These critics point out that the Roman and U.S. documents highlight this priority by naming the service according to its leader, departing from the older tradition of naming a service according to its nature.

Bibliography: J. DALLEN, *The Dilemma of Priestless Sundays* (Chicago 1994). M. HENCHAL, *Sunday Celebrations in the Absence of a Priest* (Washington DC 1992); W. MARREVÉE, ''Priestless Masses'—At What Cost?'' *Église et Théologie* 19 (1988) 207–222; N. MITCHELL, *Cult and Controversy: The Worship of the Eucharist outside Mass* (New York 1982).

[J. DALLEN]

COMMUNITY

Community in its most generic significance pertains to the personal relationship experienced among individuals that is essential to the constitution of human society. Thus all of man's activities insofar as they affect two or more individuals exhibit various dimensions of community; the more such activities affect the personhood of the individuals, the more intense and demanding is the sense of community. All religious traditions are, therefore, characterized by a concern with community, at least as the natural situation of society. There is also a tendency in the social organization of religion to develop specifically religious forms of community. This is true even of traditions that are doctrinally centered upon the isolation of the individual seeker, as is the case in Buddhism with the *Sangha*—''The Holy Order'' or ''Brotherhood'' which in a variety of community forms, most notably the cenobitic monastic, is regarded as one of Buddhism's three irreducible principles (along with the Buddha himself and the Dharma or law).

Christian. The Christian concern for community is two-fold: involvement in the historic socio-cultural condition of man which is always communal, and the affirmation of the essential extension of INCARNATION through community as an incorporation of individuals into Christ. The Christian doctrinal understanding of man's relationship to the sacred embraces senses of community proper to both man and God. The doctrine of the

Trinity affirms community of God: the absolute oneness of the Godhead is not a static isolate, but a self-communication—God who is Father communicates himself in his own internal Self Image, the Son or LOGOS, and self and image are in internal dynamic unity, the power or spirit. The doctrine of the Incarnation affirms community of God and creation together: the Logos is the creative center of all things that, as manifestations of God, have been created through the Logos or God's perfect Image. The Logos is also the unifying center of creation by the union of Logos and the man Jesus of Nazareth, so that there is but one hypostasis, Jesus-Logos, in the fullness of both human and divine natures. The doctrine of incorporation affirms the open extension of Incarnation to all men: each human being is called to participate fully in Christ-life by becoming member-for-member the Body of Christ. From this flows the understanding of the Church as the community-in-Christ and the inter-individual relationship of community as *koinonia* or the sharing of life in unity.

Contemporary. The contemporary concern for community includes a rejection of the rationalist concept of society that has dominated Western thought since the formulation of Rousseau's doctrine of the social contract. The rationalist concentration on man as a self-contained individual, each essentially interchangeable with all others and each possessed of the same faculty of reason and will to natural goodness, called for a negative evaluation of society. Society was regarded as a pragmatic necessity to overcome the practical limitations of individuals who entered a social contract, so that through a combination of their efforts they might achieve a common benefit. Such a society results in an inevitable curtailment of the individual's independence and thus is a limited evil, tolerated insofar as the common goal is agreed upon as valuable to each participant. The failure of continental enlightenment republicanism to achieve a ''contractual society'' prompted further development of a negative vision of society, most notably the Nazi reduction of individuality to the natural superiority of the Leader, the *Fuehrerprinzip,* and the Marxist reduction of individuality to mass society as the ''new socialist man,'' the collectivity.

Moving beyond this merely negative reaction, the new direction in religious community is responsive both to the development of the personalist vision of man and to the discovery of the inter-personalist constitution of society. Through the existentialist reorientation whereby man was not thought of as an example of an abstract nature, but as a personal existent, a new concern for individuality in terms of personal authenticity and individual values has become one of the fundamental elements in the theology of community and attempts for renewal. The

"I and Thou" motif of BUBER's EXISTENTIALISM typifies this sensitivity. Complementing the existentialist emphasis on the personal is the reevaluation of the nature of society as a community of persons and the gathering of personal communities as the basis for a new type of mutation in the evolution of human species. TEILHARD DE CHARDIN's concept of the process toward collectivity as an inter-personal creative union has provided theology with a new perspective on community renewal in the context of predictable socio-cultural change. Emerging in the growing understanding of personal community is the realization that man is constitutionally inter-personal and his inter-relation in community extends the process of the individual's interior self-reflectivity. Thus communities can now be recognized as a force that, through a conscious sharing of values, can bring these values to a greater level of individual reflection. Religious communities are called to a new creativity in both the personal visibility of their members and shared consciousness in the collectivity.

Bibliography: M. BEHA, *Dynamics of Community* (New York 1970). G. MORAN, *Experiences in Community* (New York 1969). R. NIEBUHR, *Man's Nature and His Communities* (New York 1965). L. ORSY, *Open to the Spirit: Religious Life after Vatican II* (New York 1968). C. PEIFER, *Monastic Spirituality* (New York 1966). A. VAN KAAM, *Personality Fulfillment in Religious Life* (Pittsburgh 1967).

[R. E. WHITSON]

COMMUNITY CHURCHES

Common name for independent local congregations with no formal denominational affiliation. Their growing number and influence are a typical phenomenon of American democracy in the field of religion. While the term community church goes back to the 19th century, systematic grouping of such bodies is a recent development. The guiding principles of the Council of Community Churches (1950) faithfully reflect the spirit of its member churches and may be taken as representative of the individual congregations.

History and Program. The Council of Community Churches was organized at Lake Forest, Ill., on Aug. 17, 1950, in a merger of the National and Biennial Councils of Community Churches. Through the merger, the scope of membership was extended to likeminded religious bodies throughout the world. Its voting membership of several hundred congregations is only the nucleus of many times the number of churches that share its ideals and with which the council is in associated fellowship. At its national headquarters, the council maintains business offices from which a full-time minister-at-large directs a national program of services along lines determined by the churches through their council. Among other services, the council publishes a monthly periodical, the *Christian Community,* the *Pastor's Journal* for clergy, and other publications from the Community Church Press.

Objectives and Principles. As outlined in its constitution, the Council of Community Churches is a fellowship that seeks to realize Christian unity in local, national, and world relations. Believing that communities require united churches, the council is committed to Christian unity, and works toward a united church "as comprehensive as the spirit and teachings of Christ and as inclusive as the love of God." It welcomes all congregations that seek to make the church an instrument for discovering and putting into practice the will of God in community life.

On invitation, the council helps communities without any church to form one all-inclusive church that is free to provide all Christian forms of religious expression. In the same way the council assists overchurched communities to federate and combine into one community-centered congregation. Accordingly, community churches arise in different ways, and the council is ready to promote their establishment. When a disaffected minister in one of the traditional churches severs relations with the parent body, or a congregation is unsympathetic with the teaching of its pastor, or the residents of some locality find themselves too varied in religious outlook to organize a denominational parish, the council takes action and supports the community venture along strictly nonsectarian lines.

The cardinal principle of community-church policy is that an individual speaks only for himself. To move beyond that point is to make him liable to the charge of encroachment on religious liberty. Community churches are regularly described as "of the people, for the people, and by the people." Pastors in these congregations believe themselves commissioned to fulfill a particular task, that of reinterpreting the Gospels for Christians who no longer find denominational Protestantism satisfying to their needs. Liberty of thought and expression are encouraged, yet generally within a framework that is remarkably close to the Inner Light theories of George FOX and the Quakers (*see* FRIENDS, RELIGIOUS SOCIETY OF). Unlike the Unitarians, community churches place considerable emphasis on faith in Christ and acceptance of His teaching; but, like the Unitarians, they favor a personal approach to Christianity with no semblance of authoritarian creeds or prescribed forms of worship.

Bibliography: F. S. MEAD, S. S. HILL, and C. D. ATWOOD, *Handbook of Denominations in the United States, 11th ed* (Nashville 2001).

[J. A. HARDON/EDS.]

COMOROS, THE CATHOLIC CHURCH IN THE

> **Capital:** Moroni, Grande Comore.
> **Size:** 690 sq. miles.
> **Population:** 578,400 in 2000.
> **Languages:** French, Arabic, Comoran.
> **Religions:** 250 Catholics (.04%), 577,960 Sunni Muslims (99%), 190 Protestants (.03%).
> **Apostolic administration:** Mayotte.

The Comoros, which encompasses the islands of Grande Comore, Anjouan, Mayotte and Mohéli, is a group of volcanic islands located in the Indian Ocean 190 miles off the east coast of Africa between Mozambique and Madagascar. The islands, which range in terrain from steep mountains to rolling hills, are visited by cyclones during the rainy season which lasts from November to April. Grande Comoro, which houses the seat of government, is heavily forested, and produces much of the vanilla, cloves, coconuts, bananas and cassava which are the region's main agricultural products. A live volcano, Le Kartala, is also located on the island. An overseas territory of France until 1975, Comoros became divided politically when the island of Mayotte voted to retain ties to France. The remaining three islands gained independence as the Federal Islamic Republic of Comoros. More than half of all Comorians resided on the island of Grande Comore; by 2000 less that half the population was literate. One of the world's poorest countries, Comoros was heavily dependent on foreign aid.

History. The Arabs, who arrived in the Comoros in the 14th century, established long-lasting dominance over the region, despite the appearance of Africans, Indonesians and Portuguese explorers in the 16th century. In 1843 the French began their control when they established a protectorate over Mayotte; they extended it to the other three islands in 1886. From 1912 until 1947 when they became a French overseas territory, the colonies were administered from Madagascar. Grande Comore, Anjouan and Mohéli gained political autonomy in 1960, and declared independence on July 6, 1975. At that point the islands became politically divided; Mayotte, with a Christian majority, voted to remain an overseas territory of France. Under the constitution dated October 6, 1976, religious freedom was granted to all Comorians.

Following independence, the region was rocked by a series of 19 military governments and the economy weakened due to a decline in exports. By the late 1990s the political situation had deteriorated still further and in August of 1997 Anjouan and Mohéli both declared independence and requested a return to French rule, which France declined. The government in Grande Comoro was overthrown by the Comoro Army, and in April of 1999 General Azaly Assoumani took control of the government. In October a new constitution was promulgated under which the right of Christians to practice their faith was curtailed. By 2000 Anjouan had not yet agreed to return to the Comoros, and the Organization of African Unity began efforts to bring about a resolution to the political strife in the region.

The Comoros islands were made part of the prefecture apostolic of the Little Malagasy Islands (created in 1848), and were entrusted first to the Jesuits, then to the Holy Ghost Fathers in 1879. In 1901 the islands became part of the vicariate apostolic of Northern Madagascar, which was advanced to a prefecture in 1938, and was created the diocese of Ambanja, Madagascar, a suffragan of Diego Suarez, in 1955. During the mid-20th century two mission stations existed on the Comoros to tend to the region's 800 Catholics, and an apostolic administration was established at the time of Mayotte's independence. By 2000 there were two religious priests tending to the region's small Catholic population, the center of the faith a church in the capital city of Moroni. These priests were aided in their efforts by approximately ten members of religious orders. In February of 1998 a second church, located on Anjouan, was burned by arsonists. Because of the restrictions on the Church, which included a ban on possessing Christian printed materials, charges of "anti-Islamic activity" were leveled against several Catholics engaged in practicing their faith. Christians of all faiths were discriminated against in employment and elsewhere, and in some cases were publicly blacklisted and harassed. Despite such repression, Comoros celebrated 16 baptisms in 1999.

Bibliography: *Bilan du Monde.*

[J. BOUCHAUD/EDS.]

COMPAGNIE DU SAINT-SACREMENT

A society, clerical and (mainly) lay, active in 17th-century French Catholic renewal. In part the company's aims and methods of promoting personal holiness and Christian social ideals anticipated those of today's lay apostolate groups. Proposed in 1627 by Henry de Lévis, Duke of Ventadour, supported by Fathers Philippe

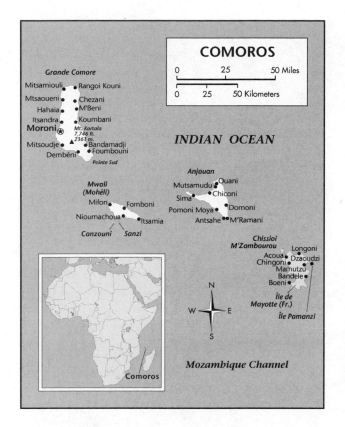

table projects of every kind. The company's aims led it to oppose freethinkers, Jansenists, Protestants, nobles given to dueling, and unscrupulous merchants. Sometimes concern for good gave way to zealotry. Thus many enemies were made. In 1660 two publications attacked the company by name as a conspiracy and inflamed public sentiment; Jules MAZARIN, already hostile to the society, had the Parlement forbid all secret meetings (December 1660). This was the death blow. Although some meetings could be held until 1665, the company disappeared after 1666. A number of the institutions it started, however, continued to function, among them the PARIS FOREIGN MISSION SOCIETY.

Bibliography: R. DE VOYER D'ARGENSON, *Annales de la compagnie du Saint-Sacrement,* ed. H. BEAUCHET-FILLEAU (Paris 1900). R. ALLIER, *La Cabale des dévots, 1627–1666* (Paris 1902), important but biased. A. FLICHE and V. MARTIN, eds., *Histoire de l'église depuis les origines jusqu'à nos jours* (Paris 1935–) 19.2: 545–556, *passim.* A. LATREILLE et al., *Histoire du Catholicisme en France,* 3 v. (Paris 1957–62) 2:316–318. G. WAGNER, *Catholicisme. Hier, aujourd'hui et demain,* ed. G. JACQUEMET (Paris 1947–) 2:1413–15. E. LÉVESQUE and R. HEURTEVENT, *Dictionnaire de spiritualité ascétique et mystique. Doctrine et histoire,* ed. M. VILLER et al. (Paris 1932–) 2.1:1301–11. C. LEFEBVRE, *Dictionnaire d'histoire et de géographie ecclésiastiques,* ed. A. BAUDRILLART et al. (Paris 1912–) 13:405–412.

[W. H. PRINCIPE]

d'Angoumois, Charles de CONDREN, and Jean Suffren, the company was definitively established in 1630. Its statutes called for a superior, usually a layman; a director, always a cleric, to foster the spirit of the rules; meetings every Thursday, the day dedicated to the Blessed Sacrament, devotion to which inspired the company and gave it its name. Meetings included prayer, reports on activities and new needs, spiritual reading, and alms. Works were to embrace every kind of Christian social action—practical charity for the afflicted, concern for magistrates' administration, settling of disputes, and repression of vice. Absolute secrecy was enjoined for both spiritual motives and practical efficacy in sensitive areas of public life. The local ordinary's permission was required. Louis XIII and RICHELIEU lent support and Pope URBAN VIII gave his blessing but no official approval to the society. From Paris the company spread to more than 50 provincial centers linked by correspondence. Meetings attracted bishops, priests, nobles, parliamentarians, judges, bourgeois, and craftsmen; SS. VINCENT DE PAUL and John EUDES were members, as were Jean Jacques OLIER, Charles de Condren, and Jacques Bénigne BOSSUET.

Judgment of the true extent of the company's influence is restricted by reason of its rule of secrecy. Not all Christian social action of the period derived from it (St. Vincent's works, e.g., though aided by the company were independent of it); yet its members shared in many chari-

COMPANY OF MARY

Official Catholic Directory #0700; Abbreviation: ODN; Founded in 1608 by St. Jeanne de LESTONNAC (1556–1640), the order was dedicated to the education of youth and was intended to complement the work of the Society of Jesus. From its initial foundation in Bordeaux, France, the order spread rapidly through western Europe. After a long existence in this area, tentative foundations were made in Cuba and Mexico; and finally, in 1926, the first U.S. foundation was established in Douglas, Ariz. The rule of the community was originally adapted from that of the Jesuits; and when papal approval was granted for its foundation, it was affiliated with the Order of St. Benedict. The sisters are under papal jurisdiction. The generalate is located in Rome.

Bibliography: P. HOESL, *In the Service of Youth,* tr. J. CARR (London 1951). I. DE AZCARATE RISTORI, *El origen de las órdenes femeninas de enseñanza y La Compañía de María* (San Sebastián, Spain 1963). R. A. RUBLE, *A Woman in Love* (Albuquerque 1961)

[R. A. RUBLE/EDS.]

COMPENSATION, OCCULT

Occult compensation is the act of appropriating secretly what is owed to one in strict justice by another who

Grand Comore, Comoros Islands, photograph by Wolfgang Kaehler. Reproduced by Permission.

will not satisfy his obligation. It amounts, in fact, to the secret collection of a debt. Moral theologians are agreed that it is licit under certain conditions; otherwise an individual would be without means to defend himself against flagrant violations of his property rights and the unjust oppressor would be protected in his iniquity by the moral law.

The conditions under which it is licit to compensate oneself occultly are: (1) What is to be recovered must be owed in strict justice, i.e., not in fidelity, equity, or charity; (2) Recourse to other and legal means for the collection of the debt must be morally impossible, or it must be foreseen that such recourse would be unavailing; (3) What is taken must be substantially of the same order as what is owed. Thus it is not considered licit to take money or its equivalent to compensate oneself for the loss of reputation caused by another; (4) The debt must be certain, i.e., a merely probable claim to indemnification does not suffice; (5) Care must be taken to see that the debtor suffers no loss other than that of the property taken, and that no harm is done to a third party or to the common good.

Although moral theologians agree in admitting the licitness of occult compensation under the foregoing conditions, they hold that it should rarely be practiced and even more rarely counseled. The reasons for their caution are: (1) The bypassing of ordinary legal steps to recover a debt, even when these would be ineffectual, seems to involve an element of social disorder; (2) People are prone to take a prejudiced view when their own interests are concerned and to think that their strict rights have been violated when such is not the case; (3) Occult compensation is generally imprudent because the person practicing it exposes himself to the risk of discovery and prosecution for theft.

Pope Innocent XI condemned a proposition to the effect that domestic servants can secretly steal from their employers to compensate themselves for work that they judge to be worth more than the salary paid them. Nevertheless Innocent XI's condemnation has not been understood by moralists as a denial of the right of employees to compensate themselves under some circumstances. It is generally agreed that if workers not engaged simply out of pity are forced by the employer to work for a wage less than just, and other workers could not be found to do the same work for the same pay, or if they are forced to do work not envisioned in their employment contract, they may legitimately compensate themselves if the employer will not do so. However, if the employee freely enters into a low-wage contract, or if he freely undertakes extra work, he has no claim in strict justice to additional compensation.

Bibliography: D. M. PRÜMMER, *Manuale theologiae moralis,* ed. E. M. MÜNCH, 3 v. (12th ed. Freiburg–Barcelona 1955) 2:88–90. H. DAVIS, *Moral and Pastoral Theology,* rev. and enl. ed. by L. W. GEDDES (New York 1958) 2:281–284. E. DUBLANCHY, *Dictionnaire de théologie catholique,* ed. A. VACANT et al., 15 v. (Paris 1903–50; Tables générales 1951–) 3.1:601–604.

[F. C. O'HARE]

COMPENSATIONISM

Compensationism is the moral system according to which in a doubt of conscience concerning the morality of a certain course of conduct, one may follow the opinion for liberty when there are sufficient reasons to compensate for the danger of a material transgression of the law. The proponents of this system teach that a doubtful law, being imperfectly known, binds imperfectly. Hence, per se it must be obeyed. But, *per accidens,* there can be sufficient reasons for running the risk of a material sin by following the opinion for liberty. The sufficiency of the reasons must be judged for each particular case in accordance with the circumstances, especially the gravity of the law and the grade of probability of the opinion for liberty. Thus, this system is based on the principle of the double effect. Accordingly, in some instances the opinion for liberty could not be followed even if it were equally probable; in other instances it could be followed even if it were the less probable. Because of the difficulty of computing the compensating benefits for each case, this system has few adherents. Its most prominent exponent in the twentieth century was D. PRÜMMER, O.P.

See Also: CONSCIENCE; MORALITY, SYSTEMS OF; DOUBT, MORAL; REFLEX PRINCIPLES.

Bibliography: D. M. PRÜMMER, *Manuale theologiae moralis,* ed. E. M. MÜNCH, 3 v. (10th ed. Barcelona 1945–46) 1:344. J. AERTNYS and C. A. DAMEN, *Theologia moralis,* 2 v. (16th ed. Turin 1950) 1:101, 124. M. ZALBA, *Theologiae moralis compendium,* 2 v. (Madrid 1958) 1:677. A. TANQUEREY, *Synopsis theologiae moralis et pastoralis,* 3 v. (Paris 1925) 2:441–442.

[F. J. CONNELL]

COMPÈRE, LOYSET

Renaissance composer of the Flemish school; b. Flanders(?), *c.* 1450 (christened Louis); d. Saint-Quentin, Aug. 16, 1518. He was a singer at the Milanese court in 1474–75, and became *chantre ordinaire* to Charles VIII of France (1486). As a priest he received prebends in Cambrai (1498) and Douai (1500), and a canonry at the collegiate church of Saint-Quentin, where he is buried. He was celebrated in the writings of Gafurius, Aaron, Cretin, Molinet, Rabelais, and others. His works include two Masses, individual Mass movements, three *motetti missales* cycles, twenty-three motets, five motet-chansons, forty-nine chansons, and two frottole (which are quoted in a quodlibet of L. Fogliano). The religious works exhibit Italian as well as Franco-Flemish traits: sonorous chords, canonic writing, and advanced parody technique. His chansons range from Burgundian types to the newer syllabic genre, with repeated notes and rapid declamation. Though not considered Josquin Desprez's equal, he represents an important link between the generations of Okeghem and Attaingnant.

Bibliography: *Opera omnia,* ed. L. FINSCHER, *Corpus Mensurablis musicae,* ed. American Institute of Musicology (Rome 1958–) 15. L. FINSCHER, "Loyset Compère and His Works," *Musica Disciplina* 12 (Rome 1958) 105–143; 13 (1959) 121–154; 14 (1960) 135–157; 16 (1962) 93–113. *Die Musik in Geschichte und Gegenwart,* ed. F. BLUME (Kassel-Basel 1949–) 2:1594–98. *Histoire de la musique,* ed. ROLAND-MANUEL v.1 (Paris 1960–63). G. REESE, *Music in the Renaissance* (rev. ed. New York 1959). D. M. RANDEL, ed., *The Harvard Biographical Dictionary of Music* (Cambridge, Massachusetts 1996) 171. J. RIFKIN and B. HUDSON, "Loyset Compère," in *The New Grove Dictionary of Music and Musicians, vol. 4,* ed. S. SADIE 595–598, (New York 1980). M. STEIB, "Loyset Compère and His Recently Rediscovered *Missa De tous biens plaine,*" *The Journal of Musicology* 11 (1993), 437–454. N. SLONIMSKY, ed., *Baker's Biographical Dictionary of Musicians, Eighth Edition* 350 (New York 1992). A. ZUCKERMAN WESNER, *The Chansons of Loyset Compère: Authenticity and Stylistic Development* (Ph.D. diss. Harvard University, 1992).

[I. CAZEAUX]

COMPIÈGNE, MARTYRS OF

A group of 16 beatified discalced Carmelite nuns who were martyred (July 17, 1794) during the FRENCH REVOLUTION (feast, July 17). The Carmelite community at Compiègne in northern France, established in 1641, had 21 members in 1789. On Aug. 4, 1790, government officials took an inventory of the community's goods. After all the nuns subscribed to the oath of *Liberté-Egalité* (August 9), they departed the convent and dispersed through the town in four groups. During the next four years they dressed in secular attire, but each group continued the former regular manner of religious life. The local Jacobins then accused them of violating the law by living as a religious community and imprisoned all but five of them in the Visitation Convent (June 22, 1794). In prison the nuns retracted their oaths and practiced in common their usual religious exercises until July 12, when they were placed on two hay carts and sent under guard to Paris to be detained in the Conciergerie. While awaiting trial, they recited together nightly the Divine Office and composed religious couplets and sang them to the air of the Marseillaise. At the brief trial (July 17), held without witnesses, they were sentenced to death as counterrevolutionists and religious fanatics for living as religious under obedience to a superior. Immediately after the trial they went to the guillotine chanting the *Miserere, Salve Regina,* and *Te Deum.* Each nun in turn obtained her superior's blessing before mounting the scaffold chanting the Psalm *Laudate Dominum, omnes gentes.*

The 16 martyrs were: Mother Thérèse of St. Augustin, the prioress (Marie Lidoine, b. 1752), and Sisters St. Louis (Marie Madeleine Brideau, b. 1752), Jesus Crucified (Marie Piedcourt, b. 1715), Charlotte of the Resurrection (Anne Thouret, b. 1715), Euphrasia of the Immaculate Conception (Marie Brard, b. 1736), Henrietta of Jesus (Marie de Croissy, b. 1745), Thérèse of the Heart of Mary (Marie Hanisset, b. 1742), Thérèse of St. Ignatius (Marie Trézelle, b. 1743), Julie of Jesus (Rose de Neufville, b. 1741), Marie Henrietta of Providence (Annette Pebras, b. 1760), Marie of the Holy Spirit (Angélique Roussel, b. 1742), St. Martha (Marie Dufour, b. 1741), St. Francis (Elisabeth Vérolot, b. 1764), Constance, a novice (Marie Meunier, b. 1765), and the two extern sisters, Catherine Soiron (b. 1742) and Thérèse Soiron (b. 1748). All were beatified May 27, 1906.

Bibliography: *Acta Sanctae Sedis* 40 (1907) 457–465. V. PIERRE, *Les Seize carmélites de Compiègne* (Paris 1905). G. DE GRANDMAISON, *Les Bienheureuses carmélites de Compiègne* (Paris 1906). H. LECLERCQ, *Les Martyrs,* 15 v. (Paris 1902–27) v.12 *La Révolution 1794–1797* (1913). J. L. BAUDOT and L. CHAUSSIN, *Vies des saints et des bienheureaux selon l'ordre du calendrier avec l'historique des fêtes,* ed. by the Benedictines of Paris, 12 v. (Paris 1935–56) 7:399–405. M. ANDRÉ, *La Véridique histoire des carmélites de Compiègne* (Paris 1962).

[M. LAWLOR]

COMPLINE

The last prayer of the day; it closes the day's liturgical office. Its content shows it is meant to be prayed just before retiring for the night. Compline originated in monastic circles. John CASSIAN (d. 435) is the first to refer to it. In describing monastic practices of his day he mentions that Eastern monks were accustomed on Sunday nights to join in singing a few Psalms in their dormitory (*De instit. cenob.* 4.19; *Patrologia Latina,* 49:179). The rule of Aurelian of Arles (d. 585) called for monks to recite Psalm 90 and *Preces* before retiring (*Patrologia Latina,* 68:395, 405).

Historically, Compline had two distinct parts, first a preliminary period of spiritual reading and confession of

faults, and lastly the prayers for retiring. As to the first part, St. BENEDICT (d. 543) is the first witness to this practice and he prescribed four or five pages of Cassian's Conferences or the lives of the Fathers (Rule, ch. 42). A custom developed also of having the monks publicly accuse themselves of the day's faults and receive an absolution before the chanting of the Psalms (*S. Fructuosi Regula monachorum,* 2; *Patrologia Latina,* 87:1099). The second part of Compline arose from the basic structure of the Benedictine hours—three Psalms, a hymn, a lesson and responsory, the canticle of Simeon (Lk 2.29), an oration, and final blessing. In his rule, St. Benedict (Rule, ch. 18) prescribed the same Psalms daily (4, 90, 133: Sunday's Psalms in the Roman Office), a hymn, lesson, responsory, and blessing.

The *Constitution on the Sacred Liturgy* decreed that Compline was to be revised so that it would be a suitable prayer at end of the day. In its revised form in the LITURGY OF THE HOURS (1970), it is a beautiful night prayer of profound trust in the protecting presence of Christ.

[G. E. SCHIDEL/EDS.]

COMPLUTENSES

A name referring to the professors of philosophy in the Discalced Carmelite College of St. Cyril at Alcalá de Henares (Complutum), who published a complete course of philosophy in the 17th century. Principal among them were Michael of the Most Holy Trinity (1588–1661), regent of the College of Alcalá; Anthony of the Mother of God (1587–1641), a theologian at the University of Salamanca; Blaise of the Conception (1603–94), the French visitator general of the Carmelites; and John of the Annunciation (1633–1701), one time general of the Spanish congregation. Their *Cursus artium,* as it came to be known, first appeared in four volumes between 1624 and 1628 and was entitled *Collegium Complutense philosophicum, hoc est artium cursus, sive disputationes in Aristotelis dialecticam et philosophicam naturalem, juxta Angelici Doctoris D. Thomae doctrinam et ejus scholam.* It was frequently edited and reprinted. A two-volume commentary by Blaise of the Conception on Aristotle's *Metaphysics* was added as a fifth volume to the Lyons editions of 1651 and 1668. But because it was less well adapted to beginners, John of the Annunciation excluded it in publishing a five-volume edition augmented with special questions in metaphysics and natural philosophy (Lyons 1669–71). Henceforth the complete *Cursus* consisted of seven volumes (John's five and Blaise's two) and became a classic introduction to the *Cursus theologicus Salmanticensis,* for which it had served as a model (*see* SALMANTICENSES). The Complutenses wrote in the traditional scholastic form of a commentary on the works of Aristotle and St. Thomas Aquinas and maintained a close adherence to the doctrine of Aquinas. The *Cursus* was entirely lacking in personal opinions peculiar to the authors; it constitutes a veritable encyclopedia of Thomistic philosophy.

Bibliography: E. DE JÉSUS-MARIE, *Catholicisme. Hier, aujourd'hui et demain,* ed. G. JACQUEMET (Paris 1947–) 2:1426–28. H. HURTER, *Nomenclator literius theologiae catholicae,* 5 v. in 6 (3d ed. Innsbruck 1903–13) 3:918–920. A. MARCHETTI, *Enciclopedia filosofica,* 4 v. (Venice-Rome 1957) 1:1118. O. MERL, *Lexikon für Theologie und Kirche,* ed. J. HOFER and K. RAHNER, 10 v. (2d, new ed. Freiburg 1957–65) 3:29. P. MARIE-JOSEPH, *Dictionnaire d'histoire et de géographie ecclésiastiques,* ed. A. BAUDRILLART et al. (Paris 1912–) 2:4–5. *Enciclopedia de la Religión Católica,* ed. R. D. FERRERES et al., 7 v. (Barcelona 1950–56) 2:903–904. *Wetzer und Welte's Kirchenlexikon,* 12 v. (2d ed. Freiburg 1882–1901) 3:769–771.

[F. J. ROENSCH]

COMPULSION

An imperative urge to perform against one's will an unreasonable act repetitiously in spite of knowledge that the act is senseless. Common compulsions are frequent handwashing, touching or counting certain objects, MASTURBATION, etc. Compulsions are characteristic of obsessive-compulsive neuroses. They can develop when resistance against obsessions in the preceding stage of the illness has diminished to such an extent that the motor act suggested in the obsession no longer can be prevented. Like obsessions, compulsions result from repeated repression over a long period of feelings that are mistakenly considered unacceptable, harmful, or morally wrong.

Since it is not the will, but the act of repression that is at the root of the compulsive acts, attempts to prevent them by willpower are of no avail and merely increase the tension associated with the compulsion. Although performance of the compulsive act relieves this tension temporarily, complete cure of the obsessive-compulsive neurosis, leading to true freedom of choice, is usually achieved by the individual through psychotherapy.

Bibliography: A. A. A. TERRUWE, *The Neurosis in the Light of Rational Psychology,* tr. C. W. BAARS, ed. J. AUMANN (New York 1960). A. P. NOYES and L. C. KOLB, *Modern Clinical Psychiatry* (6th ed. Philadelphia 1963). J. C. FORD and G. A. KELLY, *Contemporary Moral Theology* (Westminster, Md. 1958–). F. J. BRACELAND and M. STOCK, *Modern Psychiatry* (New York 1963).

[C. W. BAARS]

COMPUNCTION

In ecclesiastical usage "compunction" has a wider connotation and is found more frequently in the works of the Fathers of the Church than the later theological term "contrition," though both are employed, often as synonyms, primarily to express sorrow felt for sin. The basic meaning of the Greek and Latin verb equivalents is to "prick" or "pierce." On the day of Pentecost, those who heard St. Peter's explanation of the events leading up to the coming of the Holy Spirit "were pierced to the heart (*compuncti sunt corde*) and said to Peter and the rest of the Apostles, 'Brethren, what shall we do?'" (Acts 2.37). St. Benedict (d. *c.* 547), in his *Rule for Monks,* used the word in the same sense to encourage his followers to stir up within themselves sorrow and repentance for their past sins (*compunctione lacrimarum,* ch. 20: *compunctioni cordis,* ch. 49). But it is Cassian (d. *c.* 435) and St. Gregory the Great (d. 604) who give the classic formulation of the full import of compunction. For these two writers in particular, compunction is one of the elements of affective prayer. They never lose sight of the primary idea of pain felt at the remembrance of the sins one has committed. This, however, is always accompanied by a fervent aspiration toward God as the soul realizes its need for Him. When one reads Cassian on prayer (*Confederate* 9.11, 26–33), it is difficult to determine whether the word compunction means pain caused by remorse or longing for union with God. Often both notions are intertwined. St. Gregory the Great distinguishes four stages of compunction: (1) the soul is overcome with shame when it recalls former sins (*ubi fuit*); then (2) it realizes the just punishment it has deserved for these sins (*ubi erit*); (3) it sees that amid the miseries of the present life there is a possibility of its falling again (*ubi est*); finally, (4) it is affected with intense longing for its heavenly home (*ubi non est*) (*Mor. in Job, Patrologia Latina,* ed. J. P. Migne, 76:275B–277A). St. Gregory underscores the point that a person can never understand fully the effects of sin unless he has experienced in contemplative prayer a foretaste of the joys of heaven. Again, he contrasts compunction caused by fear, *compunctio per timorem,* and compunction brought about by desire, *compunctio per amorem* (*Mor. in Job, Patrologia Latina,* 76:291D–292C; *Hom. in Ezech., Patrologia Latina,* 76:1060B–C, 1070A–1071B). Later spiritual writers concentrated, for the most part, on the elements of remorse and fear in the concept of compunction without including the nostalgia of the soul for God and heaven that should naturally follow. Many have emphasized the importance of the "gift of tears"; there is a set of prayers in the Roman Missal whose petition is to obtain this favor. St. Teresa of Avila, alone among the postscholastic mystics, has written of the wounding of the heart by the love of God and the unbearable but joyful pain this love can cause (see, for example, *Autobiography* 29:17; *Relations* 8:16).

See Also: CONTRITION.

Bibliography: GREGORY I THE GREAT, *Morales sur Job,* ed. R. GILLET, tr. A. DE GAUDEMARIS (*Sources Chrétiennes,* ed. H. DE LUBAC et al. 32; Paris 1952) 72–79. J. LECLERCQ, *The Love of Learning and the Desire for God,* tr. C. MISRAHI (New York 1961). G. MORIN, *The Ideal of the Monastic Life Found in the Apostolic Age* (Westminster, Md. 1950). *Thesaurus linguae Latinae* (Leipzig 1900–) 3:2171–72; 4:779–780. I. HAUSHERR, *Penthos: La Doctrine de la componction dans l'Orient chrétien* (Rome 1944).

[D. HURST]

COMPURGATION

Compurgation is a judicial proof of innocence commonly permitted in medieval ecclesiastical courts. Owing something to Germanic law, but deriving from the apostolic statement that "an oath for confirmation is the end of all controversy" (Heb 6.16), it allowed a defendant to clear himself (*purgare*) of an accusation by calling on specified "oath-helpers" (*coniuratores, compurgatores, Eidhelfer*) to substantiate his oath to his own innocence (see *Corpus iuris canonici,* ed. E. Friedberg (Leipzig 1879–81; repr. Graz 1955) C.2 q.5 for the chief patristic and papal texts). These "helpers" as a rule were not to exceed the "canonical number" of seven and had to be from the social stratum of the accused; their oath was not to testify to the truth as such, in the manner of witnesses or jurors, but simply to the truth of the oath sworn by the accused. In essence compurgation (*purgatio canonica*) was the ecclesiastical counterpart of ORDEALS (*purgatio vulgaris*), for in either case the judgment was referred to God; on occasion an accused was presented with a choice of one or the other. Likewise, compurgation was just as hazardous a method of discovering the truth, and by the 14th century it was almost wholly discredited. A form survives in modern civil law in the institution of character witnesses.

Bibliography: R. RUTH, *Zeugen und Eideshelfer in den deutschen Rechtsquellen des Mittelalters* (Breslau 1922). F. POLLOCK and F. W. MAITLAND, *A History of English Law Before the Time of Edward I* (2d ed. Cambridge, Eng. 1898; repr. 1952) 1:443–444; 2:633–637. N. DEL RE, A. MERCATI and A. PELZER, *Dizionario ecclesiastico,* 3 v. (Turin 1954–58) 3:389. J. LEDERER, *Lexikon für Theologie und Kirche,* ed. J. HOFER and K. RAHNER 10 v. (2d, new ed. Freiburg 1957–65) 3:731.

[L. E. BOYLE]

COMPUTUS

The science of determining (Lat. *computare*) time. In ecclesiastical usage it covers the ensemble of rules by which the date of Easter is reckoned. The earliest-known ecclesiastical computus is the Easter table of HIPPOLYTUS for 222–233, which was engraved by his admirers on his statue (now in the vestibule of the Vatican Library). The next known is the *De pascha computus,* written in 243 by an African writer (pseudoCyprian) to correct a three-day error arising from Hippolytus's choice of a 16-year lunar cycle (*Patrologia latina* 4:939–74). More important, however, is the computus (*Patrologia latina* 10:209–32) of ANATOLIUS, bishop of Laodicea. This introduced, about 258, the Alexandrian 19-year cycle (Golden Number), which later, through the *Liber de paschate* of DIONYSIUS EXIGUUS in 526, became standard. Since the Gregorian Calendar of 1582, however, a more practical system has obtained, based on the epact, i.e., the age of the moon on January 1. Other influential computists were BEDE (*De ratione computi, Patrologia latina* 90:579–600); William DURANTI THE ELDER (1230–96), bishop of Mende [bk. 8 of his *Rationale divinorum officiorum* (ed. Lyons 1672) 468–485]; Helperic of Auxerre (9th century); JOHN DE SACROBOSCO; ROGER BACON; and ROBERT GROSSETESTE.

A knowledge of the computus was until recently part of every cleric's training. Charlemagne imposed the computus in his schools; a passage attributed in Gratian's *Decretum* (*Corpus iuris canonici* D.38 c.5) to Augustine but which is mostly from Bede's *Penitentiale,* specifies a computus as one of the books without which a priest "scarcely is worthy of the name." Ready-made computus tables, listing epact and Golden Number, DOMINICAL LETTERS, and Indications, preface present-day Missals, Breviaries, and Martyrologies.

See Also: LITURGICAL CALENDAR I, CATHOLIC.

Bibliography: A. BUCHERIUS, *De doctrina temporum commentarius* (Antwerp 1634). N. NILLES, *De computo ecclesiastico* (2d ed. Arras 1864); *Kalendarium manuale utriusque ecclesiae orientalis et occidentalis,* 2 v. (Innsbruck 1896–97). C. H. TURNER, "The Paschal Canon of Anatolius of Laodicea," *English Historical Review* 10 (1895) 699–710. J. MAYR, "De computo ecclesiastico," *Zeitschrift für katholische Theologie* 77 (1955) 301–330. A. CORDELIANI, "Les Traités de comput du haut moyen âge (526–1003)," *Archivum latinitatis medii aevi* 17 (1943) 51–72. E. HUFMAYR, *Die pseudocyprianische Schrift "De pascha computus,"* (Augsburg 1896). M. NOIROT, *Catholicisme* 2:1430–31.

[L. E. BOYLE]

COMTE, AUGUSTE

French social philosopher, often called the father of modern systematic sociology; b. Montpellier, Jan. 19, 1798; d. Paris, Sept. 5, 1857.

Life. The son of devoutly Catholic and Royalist parents, from earliest school age Comte was known for his intellectual brilliance and also for habitual defiance of authority. The first quality won him many academic prizes as well as precocious admission to the famous École Polytechnique in Paris; the second, however, brought about his early dismissal for leadership of a student insurrection. Added to these was a third quality, possibly of psychotic nature, that led to a temporary mental breakdown in early manhood and, in later life, to messianic delusions that alienated all but the most zealous of his followers.

Shortly after his academic dismissal in 1816, Comte took up residence in Paris, when he became acquainted with the utopian socialist C. H. SAINT-SIMON. Although the exact influence of this extraordinary mind on Comte is subject to scholarly dispute, it was during his association with Saint-Simon that Comte acquired the interest in social reconstruction that subsequently governed his life. The two men broke in extreme bitterness, however, about 1823, and Comte, thereafter, never acknowledged Saint-Simon in any way as an influence on his work. The major intellectual influences on him (which he himself fully acknowledged) were the ENLIGHTENMENT, from which came his interest in social development, and the early 19th-century French Catholic conservative reaction to the Enlightenment, from which he derived his interest in order and stability (*see* TRADITIONALISM).

Thought. Comte's earliest writings were essays, of which the most notable was the ''Prospectus of the Scientific Works Required for the Reorganization of Society,'' published in 1822 with an introduction by Saint-Simon. In this learned and original piece, Comte set forth germinally most of the ideas that he later incorporated in his more systematic works. He disclosed his underlying vision of a Europe disorganized and alienated by the forces of modernism—nationalism, centralization, religious dissent, secularism, revolution—that had broken up the consensus of the Middle Ages without producing anything to replace it. The prime requirement of the modern age, he declared, was a new philosophy, one rooted in science, that would do for the present and future of Europe what Christianity had done in the medieval period, that is, serve as the basis of intellectual certainty, moral consensus, and social stability. Comte had no use for the democratic ideas of the Enlightenment and the FRENCH REVOLUTION. He saw in them metaphysical fallacies that could only subvert the social order. It was his attack on the Revolution and its equalitarian ethos that made him, for all his anti-Catholic, antimonarchist ideas, a favored name of the extreme right in French politics at the end of the 19th century.

The New Science. The outlines of Comte's new science—which he referred to variously as social physics or sociology, having expressly coined the latter word—are to be found in the *Cours de philosophie positive,* pub-

A portion of the Easter tables engraved on the sides of a 3d-century statue of Hippolytus in the Vatican Library.

lished between 1830 and 1842. This work rests on Comte's ''law of the three stages,'' undoubtedly the best-known of all his contributions. The ''law'' states that society and, within it, all disciplines of thought must pass with iron necessity through three stages of development: the religious, the metaphysical, and finally the ''positive,'' or scientific. According to Comte, each of the natural sciences—astronomy, physics, chemistry, and biology, in precisely that order—had already passed through these stages. Each had attained its third, that is, its scientific stage, and the intellectual scene was therefore ripe, for the first time in history, for the emergence of a science of SOCIETY—the one area of knowledge still confined to the realms of religion and metaphysics. This new science of sociology Comte proposed to organize, like each of the preceding natural sciences, into a statics and a dynamics, the first sphere being the study of order and stability; the second, the study of societal movement or, as Comte called it, progress. Comte, like many other intellectuals in the 19th century, was preeminently a philosopher of progress, but, unlike the others, he posited his law of progress upon intellectual rather than social or economic factors. Because of the boldness and the extraordinary sweep of knowledge displayed in his work, Comte's philosophy (which became known far and wide as POSITIVISM) was honored by some of the leading

The remainder of the Easter tables on the sides of the 3d-century statue of Hippolytus.

minds of Europe, among them Alexander von Humboldt and John Stuart MILL. Mill indeed, in his *Logic,* made Comte's work the very basis of his own prescription of the method of the social sciences.

Maturity. The final period of Comte's intellectual life was marked by the publication of the *Système de politique positive* (1851–54). Although remarkable in its conception and its learning, it is the most bizarre and controversial of Comte's works, infused with messianic visions that were absent from his earlier writings. This vast work may be seen from any one of three perspectives: utopian, religious, or scientific.

Under the utopian perspective there is a detailed preview of life in the positivist society that Comte never doubted would develop, first in Europe, then throughout the world. Comte foresaw the positivist society as one governed by scientists and intellectuals working in close harmony with industrialists. It would be hierarchical, not equalitarian; republican, not democratic. Its underlying theme would be consensus and articulation, rather than individual rights or freedom, which Comte regarded as "metaphysical fallacies." Every possible detail of life in the positivist utopia is spelled out, down to the names of the months and days of the reformed positivist calendar

and the colors of the vestments to be worn by luminaries at public assemblies.

The *Positive Polity* is also a religious work, for by middle age Comte's view of positivism had become suffused with a profoundly religious flavor. Much of its emphasis is on the hieratic and liturgical, and it reveals an appreciation of the Middle Ages and of Catholicism that was lacking in Comte's earlier writings. Positivism, he declared, would, in scientific fashion, carry on the work of Catholicism. Society became for him the true deity; he prescribed modes of worship and scientist-rulers called priests. It was this emphasis that produced, following the book's publication, scores of "positivist societies," especially in England and the United States, all of them founded on Comte's "religion of humanity." Not without reason, his work was called by some critics "Catholicism minus Christianity."

Nevertheless, the *Positive Polity* is a work of social science—protoscience, perhaps—for along with its messianic cast and its religious and utopian leanings, it contains frequent penetrating analyses of the social order. The division between "statics" and "dynamics," drawn from the earlier work, is carefully maintained. Under the first, Comte analyzes kinship, social class, religion, morality, language, and other elements of the social bond. Stripped of their bizarre locutions and worshipful value contexts, these analyses are incisive and sometimes profound. Comte's treatment of the political, social, and psychological character of the family was unequaled in the century, save possibly by Frédéric LE PLAY. Comte's "dynamic sociology," although it took up the familiar 19th-century theme of inevitable progress, included insights into European history, particularly into the social nature of the Middle Ages and its breakup, that were the equal of any in his age. There is, in short, ample justification for Comte's subtitling his work "a treatise on sociology," the first such use of the term to be found in European thought.

Comte cannot be placed with Alexis de Tocqueville, Karl MARX, or Le Play as a foremost influence in laying the foundations on which such men as Ferdinand Tönnies, Max WEBER, Georg Simmel, and Émile DURKHEIM subsequently built the structure of contemporary sociology. His unstable commitment to causes and values that subverted his own ideal of science—such as his messianic utopianism and religion of humanity—prevented that. But no one in the century more successfully conveyed the desideratum of a science of society and of the necessity of science—rather than revolution—as an element in the building of the good society.

Bibliography: F. S. MARVIN, *Comte* (London 1936). F. E. MANUEL, *The Prophets of Paris* (Cambridge, Mass. 1962). M. DE-

GRANGE, *The Curve of Societal Movement* (Hanover, N.H. 1930). L. LÉVY-BRUHL, *The Philosophy of Auguste Comte* (New York 1903).

[R. A. NISBET]

CON, GEORGE

Papal agent at the English court; b. Aberdeen, Scotland, date unknown; d. Rome, Jan. 10, 1640. Con (Conn, Connaeus) was educated at Douai, the Scots College in Paris and Rome and at Bologna University. After tutoring the son of the Duke of Mirandola, Con went to Rome in 1623, entering the service of Cardinal Francesco Peretti Montalto and later that of Cardinal Francesco Barberini (secretary of state to Urban VIII). Barberini sent him in July 1636 as papal agent to Henrietta Maria, Queen of England, in succession to Gregorio PANZANI. Though not sharing the latter's optimism about reunion with Rome, Con succeeded in making individual converts, chiefly among the courtiers, and enlisted the queen's influence in easing the lot of English papists. At the same time the king, Charles I, found in Con a fellow Scot of charm and diplomatic skill, with whom he could talk freely. Their conversations on questions such as a proposed new oath of English Catholics, the suggestion of a cardinal's hat for Con, and a papal loan to aid the king against the Puritan Parliamentarians were reported at length by Con in fortnightly dispatches to Rome. Late in 1639 Con retired to Rome a sick man; there he died. His tomb, with marble bust and a long epitaph, is in San Lorenzo in Damaso, of which church he was a canon. Con published in Latin between 1621 and 1629, tracts on Scottish affairs and a life of Mary, Queen of Scots.

Bibliography: S. R. GARDINER, *The Dictionary of National Biography from the Earliest Times to 1900* (London 1885–1900; repr. with corrections, 1908–09, 1921–22, 1938) 4:945–946. G. ALBION, *Charles I and the Court of Rome* (London 1935) *passim.* M. J. HAVRAN, *The Catholics in Caroline England* (Stanford 1962).

[G. ALBION]

CONATY, THOMAS JAMES

Educator and bishop; b. Kilmallough, Cavan, Ireland, Aug. 1, 1847; d. Coronado, Calif., Sept. 18, 1915. He was the eldest of eight children of Patrick and Alice (Lynch) Conaty, who settled (1850) with their family in Taunton, Massachusetts. In 1867, after studies in the local public school and the minor seminary of Montreal, Canada, he entered Holy Cross College, Worcester, Massachusetts, graduating in 1869. He completed his studies in Montreal and was ordained for the Springfield diocese on Dec. 21, 1872. In Worcester, after assisting at St.

John's, he became (1880) the first pastor of the Church of the Sacred Heart. He was a member of the board of the Worcester Free Public Library for 12 years and of the school board for 14 years. Besides actively participating in the Irish National Movement, he was president both of the diocesan temperance society (1877) and of the Catholic Total Abstinence Union of America (1887–89). His work as a founder and president of the Catholic Summer School of America attracted the attention of the hierarchy. In 1896, as an acceptable compromise candidate to replace the dismissed Bp. John J. KEANE, Conaty was appointed second rector of the CATHOLIC UNIVERSITY OF AMERICA, Washington, D.C. He was made a domestic prelate June 2, 1897, and consecrated titular bishop of Samos Nov. 24, 1901.

As rector, amid many controversies, Conaty coordinated the departments of the newly established schools. Into the university complex, he welcomed four major religious institutions and ably assisted the founding of the neighboring Trinity College. The NATIONAL CATHOLIC EDUCATIONAL ASSOCIATION owes its origin (1904) to the unification of three groups formed by Conaty: the Educational Conference of Seminary Faculties (1898), the Association of Catholic Colleges (1899), and the Parish School Conference (1902). Under his leadership, Catholic University became a charter member of the Association of American Universities (1900).

At the end of his first term as rector Conaty was appointed sixth bishop of Monterey-Los Angeles on March 27, 1903 (*see* LOS ANGELES, ARCHDIOCESE OF). Conaty kept the Church abreast of the Los Angeles population growth between 1903 and 1915. Catholics increased from 65,000 to 178,000, priests from 118 to 271, churches and missions from 130 to 266, and educational institutions from 34 caring for 4,500 to 73 serving 10,545. He was active also in preserving the old missions and other historic Catholic landmarks of California.

Bibliography: P. E. HOGAN, *The Catholic University of America, 1896–1903: The Rectorship of Thomas J. Conaty* (Washington 1949).

[P. E. HOGAN]

CONCEIÇÃO, APOLINÁRIO DA

Franciscan lay brother and author; b. Lisbon, Portugal, July 23, 1692; d. probably in Brazil, not before 1759. Conceição went with his parents to Brazil where he became a lay brother in the Franciscan Province of the Immaculate Conception of Rio de Janeiro. Despite the insistence of friends that he study for the priesthood, he was content to remain a lay brother, and endeavored to exalt that state through the most important of his published works, *Pequenos na terra, grandes no céu.*

At St. Anthony's Convent in Rio de Janeiro he began to collect biographies of Franciscan lay brothers noted for their saintly lives. He was encouraged by confreres to publish his collection, and was sent to Europe in 1724 to care for the interests of his province and to continue the collection. The first volume of 500 biographies was published in 1732. He spent a large part of his life in Lisbon devoted to research and publication. He journeyed to France, Spain, and Italy in search of material. During the years 1735, 1738, 1744, and 1754 he published a total of 2,350 brief biographies of lay brothers in the four-volume *Pequenos na terra, grandes no céu*. It is more a compilation than a personal and critical research study; its historical value is entirely dependent upon the accuracy of the authors consulted.

Apolinário published another work, *Primazia seráfica* (Lisbon 1733), concerning the Franciscans of Brazil. This is of more historical value despite the fact that its title is apologetical. He wrote also *Claustro franciscano ereto no domínio da Coroa portuguesa* (1740), *Doze instruções para os que deixam o mundo* (1740) *Flor peregrina* (1744), and a few other books. He left some unedited works, the most important of which is *Epitome do que em breve summa contêm a Santa Província da Imaculada Conceção do Brasil* (1730). Some of these writings are known only because the author mentioned them in the volumes of *Pequenos na terra*. His literary style reflects the exuberance of the epoch.

Bibliography: D. DE FREITAS, *Elenco biográfico* (Petrópolis 1931).

[I. SILVEIRA]

CONCELEBRATION

Concelebration refers to verbally expressed joint sacramental action of several priests in celebrating the Eucharist. Both the *Constitution on the Sacred Liturgy* (*Sacrosanctum Concilium* 57) and the declaration of the Sacred Congregation for Divine Worship on concelebration of Aug. 7, 1972, recommend concelebration as a fuller manifestation of the unity of the priesthood, the church, and the one Sacrifice of Christ. The basic principle of the declaration, however, is that a concelebrated Mass follows the same norms as Mass by one priest; it determines only which parts have to be said aloud, although in a subdued voice, or sung, or accompanied by gestures on the part of the concelebrants.

In the West, the earliest recorded account of concelebration (Eusebius, *Histoire ecclesiastique* 5.24.17) seems to be that of Anicetus who "conceded the Eucharist" to Polycarp, bishop of Smyrna (c. 155), an expression that

can be explained best as concelebration. Church legislation from the 3rd century onward prescribed that visiting bishops be allowed to concelebrate the Eucharist with the local bishop (e.g., the Council of Arles [314], 19; the 5th-century *Statuta ecclesiae antiqua*, 56). In the East, the 3rd-century Syrian *Didascalia Apostolorum* (2.58.3) describes a Eucharist at which one bishop consecrates the bread, another the wine. The Council of Neocaesarea (315) prescribed that visiting bishops be invited to concelebrate (c. 18). Documents of the 4th to the 6th centuries indicate that concelebration of the priests with their bishop was customary in Asia Minor, Syria, and Egypt. In the 9th century John VIII (d. 882) permitted his delegates to concelebrate with the Patriarch of Constantinople (*Epist. 248 ad Photium*).

In Rome concelebration of the priests with the pope was the rule until the 6th century, and on great feasts until the 12th century. The simultaneous audible recitation of the Canon of the Mass, however, is mentioned for the first time in the 8th-century *Ordo Romanus III*: "On feast days . . . the cardinal priests . . . recite the canon with him . . . and together they consecrate the body and blood of the the Lord." The practice spread quickly to the rest of Europe. The ancient rite of Lyon (in France) prescribed the sacramental concelebration of six priests with the archbishop on great feasts, a practice that gradually fell into disuse after the 12th century. Until the liturgical reforms of the Second Vatican Council, concelebration in the Roman Rite was restricted to the Masses for the ordination of priests and consecration of bishops. The Constitution on the Sacred Liturgy broadened eucharistic concelebration in the Latin Church (n. 57), and directed that a rite be drawn up and inserted in the Roman Pontifical and Missal (58), thereby effectively suppressing the previous form of concelebration as it had existed for the ordination of presbyters and bishops.

In the 1969 revision of the ROMAN RITE of Mass, concelebration is specified in three instances: (i) when it is required by the liturgical context, as in ordinations of presbyters and bishops; (ii) on Holy Thursday at the chrism Mass and the evening celebration, at councils, meetings of bishops, and synods, and the blessing of abbots; (iii) with the permission of the ordinary, at conventual Masses, the principal Masses in churches and oratories, and at gatherings of presbyters. Current church legislation prohibits Catholic priests from concelebrating at Eucharist with clergy of churches which are not in full communion with the See of Rome.

Bibliography: A. A. KING, *Concelebration in the Christian Church* (London 1966). K. GAMBER, "Concelebration in the Continuity of the Ancient Church" *Christian Orient* 2 (1981) 57–62. G. OSTDIEK, "Concelebration Revisited" In *Shaping English Liturgy*, eds. P. C. FINN and J. SCHELLMAN (Washington, DC 1990),

139–171. R. F. TAFT, "Ex Oriente Lux? Some Reflections on Eucharistic Concelebration" *Worship* 54 (1980) 308–25.

[A. CORNIDES/EDS.]

CONCEPT

A concept is a representation that the mind forms within itself, in which it simply apprehends the nature of something without affirming or denying anything of it. Aristotle called this mental entity by several names, each highlighting a different aspect of it. He most frequently called it a "thought" (νόημα, *Interp.* 16a 10) because it was produced by thinking; a "word" (λόγος, *Eth. Nic.* 1096b 21) because it was a mental expression of meaning; occasionally an "idea" (εἶδος, *Anim.* 429a 28) because the intellect "sees" by means of it; "receptions of the soul" (παθήματα τῆς ψυχῆς, *Interp.* 16a 3) to emphasize the intellect's initial passivity; at times a "conception" (ὑπόληψις, *Topica* 114a 18) because of the many similarities between mental and physical conception.

St. THOMAS AQUINAS latinized most of the above and added "intention" (*intentio, C. gent.* 1.53) because through it the intellect "tends" to the thing; "species" (*ibid.*) from the little-used verb *specere,* "to see"; "notion" (*notio, In Heb.* 1.1) for the mind knows by this means; "reason" (*ratio, Summa Theologiae* 1a, 44.3), because concepts are the material for reasoning. But most frequently the Angelic Doctor employs "concept" or "conception" (*conceptus, conceptio, In 1 perih.* 2.3). The same similarity between intellectual and physical conception that the Greek verb λαμβάνω expressed, St. Thomas found in the Latin *concipere.* He explained the comparison as follows: "That which is thus comprehended by the intellect, existing as it does within the intellect, is conformed both to the moving intelligible object, of which it is a certain likeness, and to the quasi-passive intellect, which confers on it intelligible existence. Hence what is comprehended by the intellect is not unfittingly called the conception of the intellect. . . . Therefore, when the intellect understands something other than itself, the thing understood is, so to speak, the father of the word conceived in the intellect, and the intellect itself resembles rather a mother, whose function is such that conception takes place in her" (*Comp. theol.* 1.38–39).

Nature and Kinds of Concept. These various expressions emphasize the basic Aristotelian-Thomistic position that concepts (and UNIVERSALS) exist formally in the mind but fundamentally in things themselves. The concept has been formed under the influence of the thing (so it resembles and represents the thing), but it exists as such only in the mind. In this way THOMISM steers a middle path between ultrarealism, which ascribes too much reality to the concept (i.e., it exists as such outside the mind), and nominalism, which ascribes too little reality to it (i.e., there are no universal concepts, only general names). The moderate REALISM of St. Thomas recognizes that things can be and are known by the human intellect as these things exist really and in themselves. But it also recognizes that for such real things to be known, they must be brought before the mind as objects, "for knowledge occurs according as the known is in the knower" (*Summa Theologiae* 1a, 12.4).

The concept is both knowledge and the means by which knowledge is attained (*see* KNOWLEDGE, PROCESS OF); "it is not only 'that which' is understood, but also that 'by which' the thing is understood" (*De ver.* 4.2 ad 3). The Thomistic commentators signified these two values of the concept as "formal" and "objective." Tommaso de Vio CAJETAN explained: "In order to understand the terms involved, note that the term 'concept' has a two-fold meaning: formal and objective. The formal concept is a certain image which the possible INTELLECT forms in itself as objectively representative of the thing known: it is called an intention or concept by philosophers and a word by theologians. But the objective concept is the thing represented by the formal concept as terminating the act of understanding. For example, the formal concept of a lion is that image of a lion which the possible intellect forms of the QUIDDITY of a lion when it wishes to understand it; the objective concept is the very leonine nature represented and understood. Nor should it be thought that when it is said that a name signifies a concept that it signifies one or the other only; for it is a sign of the formal concept as a means or a *quo,* and it is a sign of the objective concept as an ultimate, or *quod*" (*In de ente* 1.14).

It is only the formal concept that is properly a concept, an intellectual offspring that bears a resemblance to both father and mother. It alone is a real entity, an entitative modification of the intellect. Yet clarity requires distinctions. For just as one can view a statue materially as a piece of marble, and formally as an image that signifies some personage, so one must distinguish between the concept as an entity and its formal or intentional function. This could be set forth as follows:

1. Materially or entitatively considered, the concept pertains to the category of quality, and thus differs from the external thing, which can pertain to any category (*see* CATEGORIES OF BEING).
2. Formally or intentionally considered, the concept is similar to the external thing:
   a. As an essence, representative of the external thing, it is identical with the essence of that thing; yet

b. As existent intentionally in the mind, it differs in not having the natural mode of existence of the thing.

The history of modern philosophy shows the need for such careful distinction. In DESCARTES the intentional function disappears, and the concept is treated as a portrait for whose validity divine veracity is needed. Consequently BERKELEY saw no need for keeping the external thing as a double of the idea. Kant admitted, with Descartes, a thing hidden behind the object. But because he regarded the object as constructed by the mind according to its a priori laws, he made the thing-in-itself unknowable. Neorealists, such as Perry and Montague, by disregarding the distinction between thing and object, somehow made the extramental thing itself immanent to thought. Phenomenologists and the critical realists stop knowledge at an object, which is no longer a product of the mind, but some irreducible datum, still separate from the extramental thing.

Concepts and Intentionality. The Thomistic theory of knowledge constantly bears on the real; INTENTIONALITY is of its essence. A thing first exists in itself, then it impresses itself upon the knower. Consequently those characteristics that belong to a thing in its first state, i.e., as it exists in itself—that man is an animal—are called first intentions. Those formalities that belong to a thing in its second state, i.e., as it exists in knowledge—being universal, being a species, being a subject—are called second intentions (John of St. Thomas, *Cursus phil.* 1:290–293). In both first and second intentions there is need to distinguish again between the formal and the objective, between the SIGN and the signified. While formal first intentions or concepts are modifications of the intellect, their objective intentions are realized extramentally. On the other hand, the formal second intention is likewise a real modification of the intellect, while the objective second intention is a relation of the object known precisely as it is known. This relation is produced by thought, exists only in thought and only as long as thought of.

Extension and Comprehension. In objective first intentions—essences of real things—two different features can be considered: their comprehension or intension and their extension. A concept's comprehension consists in the intelligible aspects or elements necessarily included in its structure; it is what must be "comprehended" to have an accurate notion of the thing. The extension of a concept is its breadth in relation to the individuals in which it is realized, and which it groups into a unity. Thus the one concept "animal" extends to all sentient beings. Since each additional note added to the comprehension restricts its applicability, the general rule has been formulated: as the extension of concepts increases, their comprehension decreases, and vice versa.

Care must be taken to avoid the error of NOMINALISM in understanding comprehension. Following nominalist theory, the concept contains only what man puts into it; accordingly it does not grasp essences or natures as these are in themselves, independent of the manner of apprehending them. Consequently nominalists understand the comprehension of a concept only in a subjective sense; they consider it as merely a group of notes that have been collected and that, given man's present state of knowledge, constitute the concept for him. But, on the contrary, if it be true that essences or natures are real, and that concepts grasp them to some degree, then comprehension must be understood in an objective sense. In other words, the comprehension of a concept is in effect the sum of all the notes that constitute the objective concept itself.

Much of modern logic, especially symbolic or mathematical logic, in its quest for "pure form" has concentrated exclusively on extension and ignored comprehension (*see* LOGIC, SYMBOLIC). Boolean algebra treats of the relations between classes wholly in extension (membership of the classes), and not in intension (meaning of the classes). Nominalistic tendencies are also evident in many semanticists, such as Tarski and Carnap, who are concerned with the relations between the sign and the *designatum* (i.e., the external thing). They lose sight of the capital distinction between thing and object, and the mediatorial function of concept between language and the extramental thing (*see* SEMANTICS). St. Thomas made no such leap: "Words immediately signify conceptions of the intellect, and by means of them things" (*In 1 perih.* 2.5).

Categories and Predication. Since first intentions are perfections characteristic of things as they exist outside the mind, Aristotle enumerated ten basic modes of real (finite) being, and called them the categories. For the Aristotelian tradition these categories are completely different from Kantian a priori mental forms; they are real modes of finite being. Since they form ten supreme genera, they serve as the starting point for an orderly classification of all essential predicates attributed to an individual. Such a procedure is exemplified for the category of substance by the famous PORPHYRIAN TREE.

When the mind ponders how two concepts are related to each other, it discovers that there are five and only five ways in which a predicate can be attributed to a subject. These are the five PREDICABLES: genus, specific difference, species, property, and accident. Since it is only in the mind that concepts are so related, the predicables are clearly second intentions.

Simple apprehension seeks a clear and distinct knowledge of objective concepts by an explicit grasp of their comprehensive notes and extensive parts (*see* APPRE-

HENSION, SIMPLE). The act whereby the intellect explicitly expresses the comprehension of a concept is the act of defining that concept. The act of DEFINITION produces a complex concept that shows what the thing defined has in common with other things and in what it differs from them. The act whereby the intellect explicitly expresses the distribution of a concept into its subjective parts or components is the act of logically dividing that concept. The act of DIVISION likewise produces a complex concept or imperfect discourse that shows the distribution of a concept into its subjective parts.

In every phase of its analysis of the concept, Thomism shows a consistent moderate realism that makes due allowance for both the IMMANENCE and the TRANSCENDENCE of thought.

See Also: KNOWLEDGE, THEORIES OF; TERM (LOGIC); WORD.

Bibliography: J. MARITAIN, *Distinguish to Unite, or the Degrees of Knowledge,* tr. G. B. PHELAN from 4th French ed. (New York 1959); *Formal Logic,* tr. I. CHOQUETTE (New York 1946). J. F. PEIFER, *The Concept in Thomism* (New York 1952). B. J. F. LONERGAN, ''The Concept of *Verbum* in the Writings of St. Thomas Aquinas,'' *Theological Studies* 7 (1946) 349–392; 8 (1947) 35–79, 404–444; 10 (1949) 3–40, 359–393. G. RABEAU, *Species, Verbum: L'activité intellectuelle élémentaire selon s. Thomas d'Aquin* (Paris 1938). E. GILSON, *Réalisme thomiste et critique de la connaissance* (Paris 1938).

[J. F. PEIFER]

CONCEPTUALISM

A philosophical position on the nature of UNIVERSALS maintaining, against NOMINALISM, that universal terms signify universal concepts and, against REALISM, that concepts, as such, signify nothing actually, potentially, or virtually universal outside the mind.

For WILLIAM OF OCKHAM, who is generally called a conceptualist, universal concepts correspond to no ontological root of universality in things; they are intentionalities of the soul, predicable of individuals by reason of resemblances caused by God, but devoid of objective universality (*In 1 sentences* 2.9). In the conceptualism of John LOCKE, agnosticism about the reality of essences is combined with the conviction that men do fashion universal, general ideas, abstracted from particular ones and idealized in a fixity of meaning; such mental constructs correspond to no objective universality, but they are the object of universal and certain knowledge (*Essay Concerning Human Understanding,* 3.3.11). In the idealistic conceptualism of Immanuel KANT, universality and necessity, required for all scientific propositions of mathematics and physics, are a priori categories of the mind

that are imposed on contingent phenomena; this conceptual universality and necessity corresponds to nothing outside the mind. For Henri BERGSON, the constantly evolving reality of temporal duration cannot be represented in any universal concept, but such abstract concepts are useful to indicate practical attitudes of a knower toward objects known. Unlike traditional introspective conceptualism, the dispositional version of H. H. Price (1899–) does not consider concepts to be entities, or occurrent ideas, but memory dispositions operating *in* minds without ever being present to minds (330–358).

The moderate realist tradition of St. THOMAS AQUINAS agrees with conceptualism that no universal nature exists as such outside some mind, divine or created. It disagrees, however, with the subjectivist position of conceptualism that universal concepts have no foundation in individual realities outside the mind. For the moderate realist, only individuals exist as such outside the mind. But each existent individual possesses a nature that is manifested through characteristic properties and activities. For the moderate realist, individuals manifesting the same characteristics, generic or specific, are the real foundation for forming universal concepts. This objective foundation justifies predicating a single intelligible term of many individuals. In moderate realism, analogical concepts as well presuppose an objective foundation in things outside the mind both for UNDERSTANDING and for PREDICATION.

See Also: KNOWLEDGE, THEORIES OF.

Bibliography: R. I. AARON, *The Theory of Universals* (Oxford 1952). H. H. PRICE, *Thinking and Experience* (Cambridge, Mass. 1953). A. A. MAURER, *Medieval Philosophy,* v.2 of *A History of Philosophy,* ed. É. H. GILSON, 4 v. (New York 1962–). É. H. GILSON and T. LANGAN, *Modern Philosophy: Descartes to Kant, ibid.,* v.3.

[R. G. MILLER]

CONCILIARISM (HISTORY OF)

Conciliarism is a doctrine asserting that a general council constitutes the supreme authority in the Church. The word is used especially to designate a complex of medieval ideas that grew up in the 13th and 14th centuries and found wide acceptance at the time of the Western Schism (1378–1417).

Sources. These theories had many different sources. Most fundamental of all was a conviction that the Church, the whole Christian people, formed one body sustained by the Holy Spirit, and that it was proper for this corporate nature to find some appropriate expression in the institutional structure of Church government. With the exception of Marsilius of Padua, however, all the greater medieval conciliarists believed wholeheartedly

Manuscript illustration from "Concilium Buch," by Ulric of Reichenthal, depicting procession of conclave that elected Martin V at Constance, printed by Anton Sorg, Augsburg, 1483.

also in the doctrine that the pope, as successor to St. Peter, was the divinely willed head of the Church. The "conciliar theory" was an attempt to reconcile these fundamental insights. Some of its characteristic propositions began to be formulated in the works of the canonists of the age of INNOCENT III (1198–1216), a pope who exercised with unusual vigor all the judicial and legislative powers of his office. The canonists in general warmly approved of his activity and themselves contributed much to a growing theory of papal "plenitude of power." But these same lawyers who, in some contexts, exalted the authority of the papal office in the most extreme language showed themselves deeply concerned also over the grievous harm that might befall the Church if all the power that the popes were coming to exercise fell into evil hands. Their great collection of canon law, Gratian's *Decretum,* told of popes who had sinned and erred in the past (*see* GRATIAN, DECRETUM OF). The circumstances in which a pope's pronouncements could be regarded as infallible had been neither defined nor much discussed. It was generally accepted that a pope could err in faith and it seemed intolerable that the whole Church should be thrown into confusion as a result. There was a need then to find norms that might set proper limits to the powers even of a pope. In seeking such norms the canonists

turned to the general councils of the past and it became commonplace around 1200 to assert that the pope was bound by the canons of councils "in matters touching the faith and the general state of the Church."

This raised the problem of how to deal with a pope who offended against such canons. The most eminent canonist of the age, HUGUCCIO, discussed the problem at length. He concluded that a pope who publicly professed his adherence to a known heresy could be deposed by the Church and, further, that a pope who contumaciously persisted in notorious crime could likewise be deposed since "to scandalize the Church is like committing heresy." Huguccio also considered the question of how the possibility of a pope erring in faith, which he admitted, could be reconciled with the ancient doctrine that the true faith would always live on in the Roman Church. His answer was based on a distinction between the local Roman Church and the universal Roman Church. "The Roman Church is said to have never erred in faith . . . but I say that the whole Catholic Church which has never erred *in toto* is called the Roman Church." And again, "Wherever there are good faithful men there is the Roman Church." This distinction between the proneness to error of a pope and the indefectibility of the whole Church became a most important element in later conciliar theories.

Huguccio's views were repeated with various modifications by the canonists of the early 13th century. Some taught that a pope could be condemned only for heresy, not for notorious crimes in general. Others held that he could be deposed for professing a new heresy and not for only adhering to an old one. All agreed that a doctrinal definition of a general council, that is of pope and bishops acting together, possessed a higher authority than the bare word of a pope alone. A few accepted the more radical view that a decision of the fathers of a council acting in concert against the pope should be preferred to the pope's decision. Sometimes the language employed was ambiguous, and perhaps deliberately so. The *Glossa Ordinaria* to the *Decretum* of JOANNES TEUTONICUS, a work used as a standard text in canon law schools throughout the Middle Ages, declared simply, "Where a matter of faith is involved a council is greater than a pope."

The 13th and 14th Centuries. All this argumentation in the years around 1200 was essentially academic, a preoccupation of intellectuals in the schools. Two developments during the course of the next century gave it a more practical significance. In the first place, the increasing centralization of authority in the Roman Curia—the growing burden of papal taxation and the growing number of papal PROVISIONS to benefices—stimulated protests among diocesan bishops and some of them began to look to general councils as a means of permanently limiting papal power. William DURANTI THE YOUNGER developed a whole conciliar theory on this basis in 1310. He suggested that general councils should meet every ten years and that all legislation for the universal Church and all general taxation should be approved by the councils.

The second major factor influencing the growth of conciliar thought was a persistent friction between Church and State during the 13th and 14th centuries. Already in 1239 the emperor FREDERICK II appealed in vague terms to a general council against Pope GREGORY IX. In the conflict between PHILIP IV of France and BONIFACE VIII (1294–1303) the supporters of the French king quite explicitly demanded that the pope be put on trial before a general council and they drew up a whole list of charges against him including one of heresy. From this time onward conciliar ideas were expressed not only in isolated legal glosses and in polemical royal letters but also in substantial treatises on political theory. The most important such work produced *c.* 1300 was that of the Dominican JOHN (QUIDORT) OF PARIS. He described the pope as a *dispensator* or steward appointed to administer the property of the Church and to guard its faith. The papal office was established by God, he held, but the designation of the person who was to fill the office was left to human choice. The cardinals acted on behalf of the whole Christian people in electing a pope and, just as consent of the Church was effective in establishing a pope, so too the withdrawal of consent could have the effect of deposing him if he had proved an unjust steward. According to John, bishops, like the pope, held their authority ''from God immediately and from the people who elect or consent'' and, diffused among them, there was an authority ''equal to or greater than'' that concentrated in the papacy.

Marsilius of Padua and William of Ockham. The most radical conciliar theories of the Middle Ages were developed a little later by MARSILIUS OF PADUA and WILLIAM OF OCKHAM, writing as partisans of the emperor Louis IV the Bavarian during his struggle with Pope JOHN XXII. Marsilius asserted that all power, ecclesiastical and civil, was vested primarily in the whole community and secondarily in governors appointed by the community. He maintained that clerics were fully subject to the jurisdiction of the State and themselves disqualified from exercising coercive jurisdiction. He denied that the papacy was of divine origin and regarded such little authority as he conceded to it as being dependent solely on the continuing consent of the people. He held that the highest authority in matters of faith was that of a council in which laity as well as clergy were represented.

Marsilius's theory, if implemented, might have led to a secularist absolutism. William of Ockham's ideas tended more to mere anarchy. In his voluminous *Dialogus* he presented every conceivable argument against papal power and, although Ockham did not explicitly endorse all the ideas that he publicized, his subtle and skeptical mind exploited with corrosive effect the widely accepted opinion that the pope could err in faith and that only the whole Church was indefectible. According to Ockham, Christ's promise that his Church would never fail meant only that somewhere within the Church the true faith would live on—perhaps in an idiot or a child. He refused to admit that a general council could represent the Church so perfectly as to be endowed with the Church's indefectibility.

Conciliar Movement. The early 15th century saw a serious attempt to put earlier conciliar theories into practice, that is to assert for the general council a dominant role in the government of the Church. The immediate cause of this conciliar movement was the WESTERN SCHISM. After 1378 there were two contending lines of popes and, from 1409 onward, three. As the schism became inveterate it seemed that it could never be ended if the doctrine of absolute papal sovereignty were adhered to with its corollary that the pope (whoever he was) was immune from all human judgment. In these circumstances many moderate thinkers turned to the alternative theory that ultimate authority rested with a general council. As early as 1380 the theologian CONRAD OF GELNHAUSEN argued that, if a council could be assembled by any means, it would be empowered to judge between the rival popes. To refute the objection that a legitimate council had to be convoked by the pope in the first place, he appealed to equity and the principle that ''necessity knows no law.'' Subsequently, eminent leaders of the Church in many lands put forward similar proposals, among them the Frenchmen PETER OF AILLY (Alliaco) and Jean GERSON, the German Dietrich of NIEHEIM (Niem) and the Italian Francesco ZABARELLA. The conciliarists differed in the details of their systems of thought but they all agreed that the universal Church possessed a more ample authority than the local Roman Church and that, in the circumstances then existing, a general council could wield all the Church's power. The most impressive statement of conciliar ideas was the *De concordantia catholica* of NICHOLAS OF CUSA, a subtle and harmonious work in which the principles of representation and consent were interwoven with the basic doctrine of the indefectibility of the whole Christian people in such a fashion as to produce a detailed theory of constitutional government for the Church. There has been much discussion concerning the influence of Marsilius and Ockham on the 15th-century theories. The conciliarists did indeed borrow many arguments from these two formidable predecessors but did not typically adopt their more extreme positions, e.g., Marsilius's denial of the divine origin of papal power or Ockham's skepticism about the ability of a general council truly to represent the Church.

In 1415 a council met at CONSTANCE and it succeeded in ending the schism by deposing two of the rival popes and accepting the abdication of the third. It also enacted a decree (*Sacrosancta*) declaring that a general council held its authority directly from Christ and that every one, even the pope, was bound to obey its decrees. The fathers further laid down the norm that in future general councils were to meet frequently to ensure the good government of the Church. The enactment of these decrees was the high-water mark of the conciliar movement. In 1418 Pope MARTIN V refused to countenance an appeal from the pope to a future general council and such appeals were formally prohibited by Pope PIUS II in 1460. Considered as a practical program aiming to control the central machinery of Church government, conciliarism petered out with the disintegration of the faction-ridden Council of BASEL. As a theory it lived on and continued to attract the support of some leading canonists and theologians in the late 15th and 16th centuries. Its theses influenced the subsequent development of GALLICANISM and FEBRONIANISM.

Judgment. Different aspects of the conciliar theory call forth different judgments from modern scholars. Later developments in theology and canon law seem to have provided no adequate alternative answer to the central problem that the conciliarists faced—how the intrinsic authority of the Church can be exercised during a prolonged vacancy or quasi vacancy in the Apostolic See. The demand that councils should play a regular part in the government of the Church may have been a reasonable reaction against excessive centralization in a bureaucratic Roman Curia. Insofar as the conciliar theory asserted the supremacy of an assembly of bishops over a certainly legitimate pope it seems out of accord with Catholic tradition. But the more moderate view that pope and bishops together constitute the highest authority in the Church would be accepted by many modern theologians.

See Also: BISHOP (IN THE CHURCH); CONCILIARISM (THEOLOGICAL ASPECT); COUNCILS, GENERAL (ECUMENICAL), THEOLOGY OF.

Bibliography: F. BLIEMETZRIEDER, *Das Generalkonzil im grossen abendländischen Schisma* (Paderborn 1904). J. N. FIGGIS, *Studies of Political Thought from Gerson to Grotius* (2d ed. Cambridge, Eng. 1916). H. HEIMPEL, *Dietrich von Niem* (Münster 1932). G. HOFMANN, *Papato, conciliarismo, patriarcato, 1438–1439* (Rome 1940). J. LECLERCQ, *Jean de Paris* (Paris 1942). *Marsilius of Padua,* ed. and tr. A. GEWIRTH, 2 v. (New York 1951–56). H. JEDIN, *History of the Council of Trent,* tr. E. GRAF, v. 1–3 (St. Louis 1957–80); *Geschichte des Konzils von Trient,* 2 v. (Freiburg 1949–57; v. 1, 2d ed. 1951). B. TIERNEY, *Foundations of the Conciliar Theory* (Cambridge, Eng. 1955). P. DE VOOGHT, "Le Conciliarisme aux Conciles de Constance et de Bâle," *Le Concile et les conciles* (Paris 1960) 143–181. J. B. MORRALL, *Gerson and the Great Schism* (Manchester, Eng. 1960). E. F. JACOB, *Essays in the Conciliar Epoch* (rev. ed. Notre Dame, Ind. 1963). P. E. SIGMUND, *Nicholas of Cusa and Medieval Political Thought* (Cambridge, Mass. 1963).

[B. TIERNEY]

CONCILIARISM (THEOLOGICAL ASPECT)

Conciliarism is essentially a false theory about the possessor of supreme authority in the Church. Also called the conciliar theory, it attributes the highest power of jurisdiction to a general assembly of the bishops acting independently of the POPE and denies it to the pope and to a genuine ecumenical council.

Sometimes conciliarism is defined as a theory that asserts the superiority of an ecumenical council over the pope. Although this definition has been used for centuries and is still currently found in theological and canonical texts, it is better avoided, since the term ecumenical council is used in it in a loose sense. There cannot be an ecumenical council without the active participation of the pope, at least by way of approving the council's decisions. An assembly of the bishops without the pope is not an ecumenical council.

Another definition, found mainly in legal texts, says that conciliarism is the theory that admits an appeal from the judgment of the pope to that of an ecumenical council. The same objection against the incorrect use of this term is also valid here, and it is to be noted that the definition states a practical consequence of the conciliar theory rather than describing its substance.

Theological Analysis. In subjecting conciliarism to a critical analysis this article sets its essential elements against the background of present-day knowledge of the structure of the Church in order to better understand the defects of this theory. The conclusions are valid for every form of conciliarism, since there is a sufficient unity of thought in all its historical manifestations to justify a common approach to its various schools.

A classical formulation of the conciliar theory can be found in the decree *Sacrosancta* of the fifth session of the Council of CONSTANCE in 1415:

> This Holy Synod of Constance . . . declares that, being gathered together according to the law and in the Holy Spirit, and being a general council representing the Catholic and militant Church, it has

its power directly from Christ; [therefore] every person of whatever status or dignity, be it even papal, has to obey [this synod] in all that concerns the faith, the rooting out of the present schism, and the general reform of this Church of God in its head and members. [J. D. MANSI, *Sacrorum Conciliorum nova et amplissima collectio* (Graz 1960–) 27:590.]

The next paragraph in the Council's declaration says that all persons of whatever condition, status, or dignity, the pope included, are subject to penance and punishment if they are found disobedient (*see* H. Denzinger, *Enchiridion symbolorum*, ed. A. Schönmetzer [Freiburg 1963] 1151, introd. note).

This and similar texts that could be quoted (e.g., from the 39th session of the same Council) show that the fundamental error of conciliarism is that it attributes the supreme power of jurisdiction to a general assembly of bishops who are acting independently of the pope. Theologically, the error springs from a mistaken concept of the episcopal college: it assumes that this college can be fully in existence and be the subject of rights and duties when it is deprived of its head. This is not so: the collective power given to the Catholic episcopate is present in their midst only when the hierarchical communion between the head and the members, the pope and the bishops, is intact. When this communion is absent, the corporate power of the episcopate cannot be present. Therefore, a general assembly of bishops acting independently of the pope cannot be a genuine ecumenical council.

The other fundamental error of conciliarism is the misrepresentation of the office of the pope. By the will of Christ, he is the keeper of the keys to the use of all power of jurisdiction in the Church, even to that of an ecumenical council. It follows that he cannot be subject to any assembly of the bishops, and that, rather, they are subject to him in the use of the power given to them by their consecration and the hierarchical Church. This is why the pope has the power to convoke a universal council, to direct its work, and to confirm its decisions.

The right to appeal from a sentence of the pope to a general assembly of bishops is the practical consequence of conciliarism. Since this theory clothes the general assembly of bishops with the supreme power of jurisdiction and denies it to the successor of Peter, it is logical that it should advocate the possibility of appeal from the pope to his fellow bishops, who would be sitting as the supreme court of the Church.

In some of its more radical forms the conciliar theory is based on the idea of representation. The owner of power would be God's people, the congregation of the faithful, who would entrust this power to the bishops, and the bishops in their turn to the pope—with the right of revocation all along the line should there be abuses on the part of the trustees. Thus the bishops are considered the representatives of the faithful, and the pope the representative of both the faithful and the bishops. Naturally enough the bishops would be entitled to sit in judgment over the pope and deprive him of his office should they think it necessary for the good of the Church.

The error of the theory of representation is to conceive of the structure of the Church as if it were a political community. Although it is true to say that in a state the citizens are the source of political power and they entrust it to their government, it is wrong to conceive of the Church as a democratic institution. Christ has given all power of jurisdiction to the bishops, and made one of them, the successor of Peter, the universal bishop of the whole Church with power over all the others.

Pronouncements of the Church. The error of conciliarism has been condemned several times, but its doctrinal deficiency in explaining the structure of the Church can be best seen not through the condemnations of it but through consideration of the positive pronouncements on the power of the Church made by the ecclesiastical teaching authority.

VATICAN COUNCIL I defined, in its *Dogmatic Constitution on the Church, Pastor aeternus* (*Enchiridion symbolorum* 3050–75), the full and supreme power of jurisdiction of the pope over the universal Church, both in defining the faith and in practical legislation. This power was declared by the Council to be ordinary and immediate, reaching all Churches, their shepherds and faithful. Since this definition is incompatible with any conciliar theory that would admit the superiority of an episcopal assembly over the pope and the possibility of an appeal from the pope's sentence to the bishops, conciliarism has to be excluded as incompatible with the Catholic faith.

VATICAN COUNCIL II, in its *Dogmatic Constitution on the Church, Lumen gentium,* describes the internal structure of the Church and asserts that there is a permanent unity between the members and the head of the episcopal body. It states clearly and emphasizes that the members participate in the corporate power of the episcopate, but only if and when they are in hierarchical communion with its head. It follows that an assembly of bishops without the pope would be powerless.

Finally, both Vatican Councils exclude any theory of representation in the government of the Church. The power of jurisdiction, the right and duty to feed and to govern the flock, is not possessed by the faithful, but was given to the bishops personally, to the episcopal college as a corporate unity, and to the vicar of Christ, the pope. They have their power from God without any mediation on the part of the faithful. In having their power, they are the trustees of God, not of the congregation. However, their power should be used for the benefit of God's people. If sometimes they are called representatives of the Church, the term should be applied to them in a loose sense only; it should not imply that they receive their power from their subjects.

Among the explicit condemnations of conciliarism perhaps the most important document is the bull *Exsecrabilis,* promulgated by Pius II in 1460. In his earlier life, before he was ordained a priest, Enea Silvio de' Piccolomini (Pius II) was an ardent advocate of conciliarism. As pope he condemned it, calling erroneous and detestable the doctrine that admits the legitimacy of an appeal from the pope's sentence to a universal council (*Enchiridion symbolorum* 1375).

The attitude of the Church toward conciliarism has not changed since the time of Pius II. Today it is reflected in several canons of the Code of Canon Law. "There is no appeal from the Roman pontiff's sentence to an ecumenical council" (c.228.2). Those who attempt such an appeal are excommunicated and under suspicion of heresy (c.2332), and the chapter on ecclesiastical courts begins with c.1556: "The First See is not subject to any judge." Those practical provisions are the manifestations of a deep doctrinal conviction.

It would be false to conclude, however, that the theologians who embraced the conciliar theory in one of its historical forms were all formal heretics. Some of them were persons of great spiritual stature and intellectual integrity, seeking anxiously a solution to the problems of their time. They failed to find the right solution, and they embraced a theory alien to the Catholic faith, but one should remember that they did not have the same theological armory that exists today, and that to some extent they were pioneers in the study of the mysterious nature of the Church.

See Also: CONCILIARISM (HISTORY OF); COUNCILS, GENERAL (ECUMENICAL), HISTORY OF; COUNCILS, GENERAL (ECUMENICAL), THEOLOGY OF; PRIMACY OF THE POPE.

Bibliography: Vatican Council II, *Lumen gentium, Acta Apostolicae Sedis* 57 (1965) 5–71. H. JEDIN, *Lexikon für Theologie und Kirche,* ed. J. HOFER and K. RAHNER (Freiberg 1957–65) 6:532–534. G. ALBERIGO, *Lo sviluppo della dottrina sui poteri nella chiesa universale* (Rome 1964). B. TIERNEY, *Foundations of the Conciliar Theory* (Cambridge, Eng. 1955). V. MARTIN, "Comment s'est formée la doctrine de la supériorité du concile sur le pape," *Revue des sciences religieuses* 17 (1937) 121–143, 261–289, 405–427.

[L. M. ÖRSY]

CONCILIUM MONASTICUM IURIS CANONICI

Even before the Second Vatican Council concluded its work, the Canon Law Society of America sponsored a Concilium Monasticum Iuris Canonici to give monks around the world an opportunity to have some say in the formulation of the new law proper to them. Monastic canonists of all nations were invited to share in its work and questionnaires were sent to large cross sections of monastic communities.

In 1966 the Pontifical Commission for the Revision of the Code of Canon Law received the *Propositum monasticum de Codice iuris canonici recognoscendo* prepared by the Concilium. Presuming that the new Code would take the same form as the 1917 *Codex iuris canonici,* the *Propositum* formulated 42 canons divided into sections, chapters, and articles. The fundamental question put by the *Propositum* was the delineation of those who were to be included within the category of monks. Some wanted the monastic state to be identified with the contemplative state. However, the *Propositum* followed the lead of Vatican Council II which spoke of monks who devote themselves entirely to divine worship in a life that is hidden or those who lawfully take up some apostolate or works of Christian charity; (*Perfectae caritatis* 9). There was a strong desire to provide adequately for the contemplative life, and for the eremitical vocation. Thus, the second section of the *Propositum: De vita monastica in specie,* has three chapters: *De vita coenobitica, De vita eremetica, De vita unice contemplativa.* The first section of the *Propositum* concerns itself with law for monasteries and federations, and such matters as admission, formation, and transfer. Although nuns had little opportunity to take part in the work of the Concilium its members held strongly that dispositions concerning monks apply equally to nuns. As a result there was no distinct provision in the *Propositum* for nuns.

The *Propositum* was one of the first concrete proposals received by the Pontifical Commission. It was taken up at the first meetings of the subcommission concerned with the section on religious life. By its presence it affirmed the right to be heard of those who were being legislated for. By its demands for a provision that fully respected the specific nature of a God-given vocation it called for a complete rethinking of this section of the *Codex iuris canonici* and an abandoning of the prevalent terminology and categories. The result was that the *Schema canonum de institutis vitae consecratae per professionem consiliorum evangelicorum* (Canon Law for Religious) was universally applauded. It fulfilled the general norms proposed for the new Code, and reassured monks that monastic life is quite distinct from other forms of religious life. It recognized that monastic life must have a distinct structure and a framework sufficiently flexible to allow its free development under the guidance of the Spirit. The due autonomy of the local community under its Spiritual Father is capital in this regard.

Bibliography: "Propositum Monasticum de Codice Iuris Canonici Recognoscendo," *Jurist* 26 (1966) 331–357; "Monastic Proposal for Canon Law," *Review for Religious* 26 (1966) 19–45. J. BEYER, "De institutorum vitae consecratae novo jure," *Periodica de re morali canonica liturgica* 62 (1974) 145–168, 179–222; K. D. O'ROURKE, "The New Law for Religious: Principles, Content, Evaluation," *Reviews in Religion and Philosophy* 34 (1974) 23–49. M. B. PENNINGTON, "The Canonical Contemplative Life in the Apostolate of the Church Today," *Jurist* 24 (1964) 409–422; "The Integration of Monastic Law in the Revised Code," *Jurist* 25 (1965) 345–350; "Monastic and Contemplative Life and the Code of Canon Law," *Revue de l'Université d'Ottawa* 36 (1967) 529–550, 757–770; "The Structure of the Section Concerning Religious Life in the Revised Code," *Jurist* 25 (1965) 271–290. M. SAID, *Progetto della riforma della legislazione codiciale "De religiosis," un giro d'orizzonte* (mss. of a talk given in 1974 to an international conference of major superiors). J. P. BEAL, J. A. CORIDEN, and T. J. GREEN, *New Commentary on the Code of Canon Law* (New York 2000).

[M. B. PENNINGTON]

CONCINA, DANIEL

Dominican preacher, theologian, controversialist, leader of antiprobabilists in 18th century; b. Clauzetto, Italy, Oct. 2, 1687; d. Venice, Feb. 21, 1756. On the completion of his preparatory studies at the Jesuit college in Goritz, Austria, he entered the Dominican congregation of strict observance in Venetian territory, drawn to its austerities by love of evangelical poverty. While teaching philosophy to Dominican students at Forli, he prepared for the preaching career in which he achieved much popularity in Rome and northern Italy. His sermons were aimed at renewing the ancient Christian spirit of heroic self-denial, penance, and uncompromising separation from worldly contamination.

He was a prolific writer, mainly on the moral questions in controversy in his day: the vow of poverty, the Lenten fast, usury, the theater, and especially PROBABILISM. He first published the *Commentarius historico-apologeticus* (Venice 1736–45), which contains two dissertations. The first disproves the fiction, then accepted by the BOLLANDISTS, that St. Dominic borrowed his ideas of poverty from St. Francis of Assisi. The other refuted the claim of De Pornasio, OP, that Dominican observance of poverty was the same in the 18th as it had been in the 13th century. In this work and in his *Disciplina apostolico-monastica* (Venice 1739–40) the reprobation of the

peculium (money permitted to a religious to use as he pleases) allowed in some religious institutes, gave rise to a lengthy polemic with those who favored its legitimacy. Benedict XIV terminated the Lenten-fast dispute with his encyclical letter *Non ambigimus,* May 30, 1741, which favored Concina. The *Storia del probabalismo e rigorismo* (2 v. Venice, 1743) contains the history and principles of probabilism, its doctrinal indefensibility and the papal condemnation, a dissertation on the Church's true moral doctrine, and a commentary on some propositions censured by the Church as lax or rigorous. The Jesuits, recognized champions of probabilism, vigorously resisted this attack on the system.

Concina's greatest work, the 12-volume *Theologia Christiana dogmatico-moralis* [Rome (Venice) 1749–51, 1755], brought the 18th-century phase of the probabilist controversy to a climax. The author conceived it as a definitive exposition of sound Christian moral theology. It was accepted and used as such by many seminaries and schools of theology, either in the principal edition or in a two-volume compendium (Venice 1760). The Jesuits petitioned the pope to condemn it for its errors and anti-Jesuit bias. The pope, after examining Concina's reply to these charges, personally dictated a declaration in Italian that closely follows the language of Concina's reply. The pope requested that this declaration be translated into Latin, and it appeared in a subsequent edition. Few changes were made in the text of this new edition, but the author added a chapter to its preface expressing high esteem for the Society of Jesus, declaring his intention was not to attack persons but opinions that he judged perniciously lax, and professing willingness to retract any error in his doctrine and to right any wrong unwittingly done to anyone. Concina, in all his controversies, had the encouraging support of Benedict XIV and other illustrious personages. He was tainted neither with Jansenism nor the rigorism condemned in 1690 by Alexander VIII. The opening sentence of the *Storia* states his position: "Nothing is more alien to my mind than excessive rigor in deciding moral controversies and directing consciences. . . . The law of Jesus Christ is our one and only rule of morals. To make that law too strict is as sinful as to make it too easy. . . . Between the two extremes [rigorism and laxity], benignity is a lesser evil than excessive rigor" (*Storia,* introd.).

See Also: MORALITY, SYSTEMS OF.

Bibliography: R. COULON, *Dictionnaire de théologie catholique,* ed. A. VACANT et al. (Paris 1903–50) 3.1:676–707. D. SANDELLI, *De Danielis Concinae vita et scriptis commentarius,* 4 v. (Brescia 1767). A. VECCHI, *Correnti religiose nel Sei-Settecento Veneto* (Venice 1962).

[P. O'BRIEN]

CONCLAVE

A term referring either to the locked place within which a papal election occurs or to the assembly of cardinals who carry out the election. Conclaves originated in 1274 in Gregory X's attempt to ensure that cardinals avoided delay in choosing a pope. They are regulated by the constitution *Universi dominici gregis* of John Paul II. The CAMERLENGO, assisted by one cardinal bishop, one cardinal priest, and one cardinal deacon, controls the conclave, which takes place in a sealed-off portion of the Vatican palace. It meets 15 days (if necessary a five-day extension may be allowed) after the pope's death. The election is by secret ballot. Each cardinal writes only the name of the candidate of his choice on the ballot paper, which he places in a chalice on the altar of the Sistine Chapel, where the voting takes place. A vote takes two to three hours. If the first vote is inconclusive, another vote immediately follows; there are two each morning and each evening, the ballot papers being burned after every second vote. An election occurs when a candidate receives two-thirds of the total votes or two-thirds plus one when the total votes are not divisible by three. All cardinals must vote at each ballot. No contact with the outside world is allowed during the conclave; all audiovisual equipment is banned, and any notes concerning the election must be placed in the papal archives. The elected candidate closes the conclave by receiving the homage of the individual cardinals.

See Also: POPES, ELECTION OF.

Bibliography: JOHN PAUL II, "Universi dominici gregis" (apostolic constitution, Feb. 22, 1996), *Acta Apostolicae Sedis* 88 (1996) 305–343.

[B. FORSHAW/EDS.]

CONCORD, FORMULA AND BOOK OF

The fragmentation of the Lutheran movement after the death of Martin Luther, the disastrous defeat of the Lutheran estates of the Holy Roman Empire in the Schmalkaldic War (1546–47), and the imposition of the Augsburg Interim (1548) on many of the Lutheran territories threatened the Lutheran movement with extinction (*see* INTERIMS). Although the Convention of Passau (1552) and the Peace of AUGSBURG (1555) saved the Lutheran movement politically, theological reunification proceeded more slowly. Initial efforts at reunion through the authority of the princes foundered on the bitter opposition of the Gnesiolutherans, led by Matthias FLACIUS (Vlačić) Illyricus, and the extremist disciples of Philipp MELANCHTHON, the Philippists (*see* GNESIOLUTHERANISM; PHILIPPISM; CRYPTO-CALVINISM).

Gradually a group of moderates—among them James Andreae (1528–90), Martin CHEMNITZ, Nicholas Selneccer (1530–92), and David Chytraeus—took over the theological leadership of the Lutheran movement. Their efforts at reunion received generous financial support from the Lutheran princes. Andreae rewrote six sermons on Lutheran reunion into the "Swabian Concordia" (1573), which Chemnitz reworked into the "Swabian-[Lower-]Saxon Concordia" (1575). A combination of the latter document with the "Maulbronn Formula" (1576) produced the "Torgau Book" (1576), which was submitted to the Lutheran churches throughout the Empire for criticism. The critiques were incorporated in a final draft—the Formula of Concord, *Formula Concordíae* (1577)—produced at Bergen Abbey (hence the name "Bergic Book") by the four theologians named above, and Andrew Musculus (1514–81) and Christopher Cornerus (1518–94).

The Formula of Concord consists of a condensation, called the Epitome, prepared by Andreae, and of the Solid Declaration; each is divided into a preface, an introductory article, ten numbered articles on the controverted issues (original sin, free will, the righteousness of faith, good works, the distinction between the law and the gospel, the "third use" of the divine law, the Holy Communion, the person of Christ, His descent into hell, ecclesiastical ceremonies), an 11th article on predestination, and a 12th, which disavows the ANABAPTISTS, SCHWENCKFELDERS, and "New Arians and Antitrinitarians." The Formula was conceived of not as a new symbol, but as an authoritative interpretation of the Augsburg Confession of 1530. The final document received general, although not universal, endorsement in Lutheran circles. A carefully formulated preface (1580), signed by three electors, two prince-bishops, four margraves, a palsgrave, 13 dukes, 24 counts, four barons, and 35 imperial cities, was added.

The Book of Concord (*Concordia*), in which the Formula with its preface is the largest individual document, was formally published on June 25, 1580, the 50th anniversary of the presentation of the AUGSBURG CONFESSION. It contains, in addition to the Formula, the three Catholic Creeds (Apostles', Niceno-Constantinopolitan, and Athanasian), the Augsburg Confession (1530), the Apology of the Augsburg Confession (1531), Luther's Schmalkald Articles (1536–38), Melanchthon's Treatise on the Authority and Primacy of the Pope (1537), and Luther's Large and Small Catechisms (1529). An appended "Catalog of Testimonies" provides documentation, chiefly in the form of citations from Eastern and Western theologians from the second through the 14th centuries, in support of the Formula's Christology and its doctrine on the Sacrament of the Altar. The official Latin translation of the German 1580 edition came out in 1584. Before the end of the 16th century the Book of Concord had been translated into French, Wendish, Czech, Greek, Spanish, and Magyar. It is the most complete collection of Lutheran symbolical books and the most authoritative expression of the mind of the Lutheran Church. In the history of Lutheran theology, its publication ushers in the era of classic Lutheran orthodoxy (1580–1713). In 1584 an elaborate four-part Apology of the Book of Concord against its Reformed and Gnesiolutheran critics came out over the signatures of Chemnitz, Selneccer, and Timothy Kirchner (1533–87).

Bibliography: H. LIETZMANN, ed., *Die Bekenntnisschriften der evangelisch-lutherischen Kirche,* 5th ed. E. WOLF (Göttingen 1963), critical Lat. and Ger. text; Eng. T. G. TAPPERT, ed. and tr., *The Book of Concord* (Philadelphia 1959). W. D. ALLBECK, *Studies in the Lutheran Confessions* (Philadelphia 1952). J. L. NEVE, *Introduction to the Symbolical Books of the Lutheran Church* (2d ed. Columbus, Ohio 1926; repr. 1956). V. VAJTA and H. WEISSGERBER, eds., *The Church and the Confessions* (Philadelphia 1963). E. SCHLINK, *Theology of the Lutheran Confessions,* tr. P. F. KOEHNEKE and H. J. A. BOUMAN (Philadelphia 1961). F. E. MAYER, *The Religious Bodies of America,* ed. A. C. PIEPKORN (4th ed. St. Louis 1961) 139–182.

[A. C. PIEPKORN]

CONCORDAT OF 1801 (FRANCE)

Concordat between PIUS VII and Napoleon Bonaparte (*see* NAPOLEON I), which regulated Church-State relations in France for more than a century.

Negotiations. In arranging this agreement Napoleon was inspired solely by political considerations; Pius VII, entirely by religious aims. While terminating the FRENCH REVOLUTION, the First Consul intended at the same time to consecrate the principles of 1789, which had characterized its start; but the pope sought to safeguard the Church's principles. Progress to final accord, despite the disparity of the two men's views and the lively opposition that Napoleon met in Paris and the pope in Rome, required strong determination on both sides. Ever since the pacification of the Vendée by Bernier, Bonaparte had secretly formed a plan of coming to an understanding with the Holy See, but he waited until his authority was firmly established before initiating negotiations. The victory at Marengo (1800) supplied his regime with the desired strength. Before returning to France Napoleon stopped at Vercelli in Italy, where he exposed his plan to Cardinal Carlo della Martiniana, whom he delegated to transmit his overtures to the pope. Pius VII immediately welcomed the First Consul's advances, although he had no illusions about the obstacles ahead. When he ordered Martiniana to notify Napoleon of his acceptance and to

seek further details, he also sent Giuseppe SPINA to Vercelli, since he had slight confidence in the capabilities of the bishop of Vercelli. The First Consul insisted that negotiations be conducted in Paris, where the papal representative would be isolated and more accommodating; he then furnished the envoy with passports for Paris without informing the Holy See. This was the first of many improper acts.

Spina arrived in Paris (Oct. 20, 1800) accompanied by the Servite Father (later Cardinal) Carlo Caselli (who replaced Martiniana) and supplied with instructions limiting his powers. Thus he was authorized to discuss the French government's proposals, but not to pass final decision on them. In discussions with the industrious BERNIER, who represented the French government, Spina was circumspect and patient. Four successive schemes were studied, modified and then rejected. Thanks to Spina, definitive agreements were attained on some points, although not on the crucial ones where conflict existed between the principles of the civil and religious powers. In his impatience Bonaparte then drew up a fifth project and sent it to Rome to obtain approval without any amendment. When the Holy See delayed its response, Napoleon dispatched an ultimatum that ordered Cacault, his representative, to quit Rome and commanded the army of MURAT to march on the Eternal City. Cacault saved the situation by advising Cardinal CONSALVI, the papal secretary of state, to go to Paris and reopen the negotiations. Consalvi rejected Bernier's sixth plan but accepted the seventh one after two revisions. But when Consalvi presented himself (July 13, 1801) to sign it, he perceived that many alterations had been introduced into the text agreed upon and refused his assent. Bonaparte flung an eighth scheme into the fire and then produced a ninth one, which was also judged inadmissible. The tenth one proved acceptable to both sides and it was signed at midnight on July 15. Pius VII ratified it on Aug. 15; Napoleon, on Sept. 8. The French legislature approved the concordat, along with the Organic Articles, on April 8, 1802. Solemn promulgation on Easter Sunday (April 10) was marked by a *Te Deum* in Notre Dame cathedral.

Contents. In the brief preamble opening the concordat the French government admitted that Roman Catholicism was the religion of the majority of Frenchmen, and the pope expressed his expectation that the greatest good would follow the establishment of the Catholic cult in France and the particular profession that the consuls make. The 17 articles in the concordat treated the following subjects. The agreement permitted freedom of action for the Catholic religion and for public worship, but public worship must be conducted in conformity with such police regulations as the government might judge necessary for public tranquility (art. 1). New boundaries for dioceses (art. 2) and parishes (art. 9) were to be drawn in collaboration with the government. All titulars of French dioceses must resign. If they refused to do so, the pope was to replace them (art. 3). Bishops were to be nominated by the First Consul (art. 4) and then receive canonical institution from the pope (art. 5). Pastors were to be named by their bishops acting in accord with the government (art. 10). Each diocese was authorized to have a chapter and a seminary, but the government did not obligate itself to endow them (art. 11). A new regime of ecclesiastical properties was introduced whereby all churches that were not already alienated were placed at the disposal of the bishops (art. 12). The pope promised not to disturb those who had acquired alienated ecclesiastical goods (art. 13). The government, on its part, assured a suitable income to bishops and pastors (art. 14) and promised to take steps so that Catholics could endow ecclesiastical foundations but only in the form of government bonds (art. 16). The First Consul and the Republic were given the same rights and privileges as former governments but provision was made for a new agreement in case Napoleon should have a non-Catholic successor (art. 17). Bishops and priests were required to take an oath of obedience and loyalty to the government (art. 6). The prayer *Domine salvam fac Rempublicam, salvos fac consules* (O Lord, save the Republic and our consuls) was to be recited in all churches at the end of the Divine Office (art. 8).

Application. Agreements are worth as much as the application they receive. To facilitate and accelerate the concordat's application, Bonaparte asked that a papal LEGATE *a latere* be sent to Paris and endowed with wide powers. The person he designated was Cardinal CAPRARA, whom he knew to be conciliating to the point of weakness. Napoleon created a minister of cults and confided the post to Jean Portalis, a legist imbued with GALLICANISM but very well disposed toward the Church. Bernier was appointed to act as the unofficial but shrewd liaison man between Caprara and Portalis.

The first problem to be resolved was that of the boundaries of dioceses, whose total number was reduced to 60. The solution was inspired mainly by political considerations in order to give more dioceses to the Vendée region and to the territories along the eastern and northern borders. All the constitutional bishops agreed to resign, but 45 of the 97 nonjuring bishops of the *ancien régime* refused to do so (*see* CIVIL CONSTITUTION OF THE CLERGY). Opposition to this section of the concordat gave rise to the schismatic PETITE ÉGLISE. Bonaparte selected the new hierarchy in accordance with his principle of amalgamation to avoid the appearance of favoring any party. As a result he nominated as bishops 16 who had been bishops during the *ancien régime,* 12 who had been con-

stitutional bishops and 32 priests. The government sought men who were morally irreproachable, moderate and good administrators.

It was with considerable difficulty that Rome resigned itself to accepting former constitutional bishops. It demanded that before these prelates receive canonical institution they must subscribe to an act of submission to Roman decisions concerning French religious affairs, which was equivalent to a condemnation of the Civil Constitution of the Clergy and to a retraction. As matters turned out the majority of the constitutional bishops refused to make the retractions that Bernier claimed to have obtained; it was not until 1805 that they received from the Holy See their confirmation; Pius VII was unable to obtain from the most tenacious among them formal disavowals previous to their consecration. Napoleon was so anxious for appeasement that he did not permit any further demands besides the acceptance of the concordat, arguing that this in itself implied the renunciation of the Civil Constitution. Motivated by the same principles of appeasement and amalgamation the government insisted that bishops reserve to constitutional priests some of the positions as canons, vicars-general, pastors and curates; it also forbade that jurors be obliged to make retractions. To the Holy See's great discontent Caprara gave way on this last point.

At Napoleon's urging Rome regularized the situation of the hundreds of secular priests who had contracted marriage during the Reign of Terror in order to escape persecution. By his brief to Spina, *Etsi apostolici principatus* (Aug. 15, 1801), Pius VII conferred the necessary powers to remove the censures incurred by these clerics and permitted the delegation of these powers to bishops and pastors. All priests who had married before Aug. 15, 1801, were laicized, but they could have their marital unions validated. The papal brief *Inter plura illa mala* (Oct. 27, 1802) regulated the status of religious of both sexes who had married before Aug. 15, 1801. In the case of TALLEYRAND, the pope granted his wish to be laicized, but he refused to relieve the famous statesman, who was also bishop of Autun, of his vow of chastity or to authorize him to marry.

So slowly were seminaries organized that clerical recruitment was retarded. Bishops lacked priests and priests lacked resources. For a while curates (*desservants*) had no assured income. Their status improved when the emperor provided an annual remuneration of 500 francs to 23,000 of them in 1804 and to 30,000 of them in 1807. The laws that prohibited religious congregations remained in force, except for those engaged in teaching and hospital work and some dedicated to the foreign missions.

Results. For the Church the concordat represented a mixed blessing. It involved huge financial sacrifices in its renunciation of all claims for the restitution of alienated ecclesiastical goods. Pius VII made another temporal sacrifice when he did not seek to obtain the restoration of the legations, the sections of the STATES OF THE CHURCH ceded by the Treaty of Tolentino. AVIGNON and Venaissin remained in French possession. Great personal sacrifices were imposed by the clause requiring the resignation of the entire hierarchy. It was a sacrifice for the Church to concede to Napoleon the right of making episcopal nominations. The concordat did not recognize Catholicism as *de jure* the state religion but only as *de facto* the religion of most Frenchmen. The Organic Articles, soon joined to the concordat by Napoleon's unilateral action, still further diminished the value of the agreement.

On the other hand the disavowal of the Civil Constitution ended a dangerous schism. The papal right to institute and to depose bishops was officially admitted. The government issuing from the Revolution recognized the authority of the head of the Church. It was also a great advantage for the Church in France to regain legal existence, which enabled it to undertake a badly needed religious regeneration of the country. Religious unity was gradually attained.

The Concordat of 1801 served as a model for concordats concluded with about 30 other countries during the 19th century. It remained in force in France until 1905, because Rome repudiated the so-called CONCORDAT OF FONTAINEBLEAU (1813) and that which Louis XVIII tried to obtain in 1817 in order to abrogate the concordat of the usurper Napoleon. Successive French governments put into effect with more or less benevolence the provisions of the Concordat of 1801, as well as those of the Organic Articles. During the Restoration period (1815–30) Catholicism regained recognition as the state religion, but the July Monarchy (1830–48) reverted to the text of the Concordat of 1801, which spoke of Catholicism merely as the religion of the majority of Frenchmen. The Bourbons reestablished 30 former sees in 1823. Laval was created as a new diocese in 1854; sees were erected also in Algeria, Martinique and Carthage. The concordat was applied to Algeria in 1848 and to Nice and Savoy in 1860. The Third Republic proposed in 1878, 1902 and 1904 to abolish the concordat and finally did so by vote of the Chamber of Deputies (Dec. 6, 1905). In his encyclical *Vehementer nos* Pius X protested against this unilateral action and renewed the condemnations of Gregory XVI and Pius IX against separation of Church and State. The Concordat of 1801 is still in force in Alsace-Lorraine, which was annexed by Germany in 1871 and restored to France in 1918.

Bibliography: A. MERCATI, *Raccolta di Concordati...* (Rome 1954) 1:561–565 has the text of the concordat. Eng. tr. in F. MOURRET, *A History of the Catholic Church,* tr., N. THOMPSON, v.7 (St. Louis 1955) 562–564. A. BOULAY DE LA MEURTHE, *Documents sur la négociation du Concordat et les autres rapports de la France avec le Saint Siège en 1800 et 1801,* 6 v. (Paris 1891–1905); *Histoire de la négociation du Concordat de 1801* (Tours 1920). A. THEINER, *Histoire des deux Concordats de la République française et de la République cisalpine,* 2 v. (Paris 1869). I. RINIERI, *La diplomazia pontifica nel secolo XIX,* 2 v. (Rome 1902), v.1; *Concordato tra Pio VII e il primo console anno 1800–1802.* F. D. MATHIEU, *Le Concordat de 1801* (Paris 1903). C. CONSTANTIN, *Dictionnaire de théologie catholique,* ed. A. VACANT et al., 15 v. (Paris 1903–50) 3.1:744–779. H. H. WALSH, *The Concordat of 1801* (New York 1933). R. NAZ, *Dictionnaire de droit cannonique,* 7 v. (Paris 1935–65) 3:1404–30. J. LEFLON, *Étienne-Alexandre Bernier, évêque d'Orléans,* 2 v. (Paris 1938); *Monsieur Émery,* 2 v. (Paris 1945–46), v.2; *La Crise révolutionnaire, 1789–1846* [*Histoire de l'église depuis les origines jusqu'à nos jours,* eds., A. FLICHE and V. MARTIN, 20; 1949]. A. LATREILLE, *L'Église catholique et la révolution française,* 2 v. (Paris 1946–50), v.2; et al., *Histoire du catholicisme en France,* v.3 (Paris 1962). S. DELACROIX, *La Réorganisation de l'Église de France après la Rèvolution, 1801–1809* (Paris 1962–), v.1. A. DANSETTE, *Religious History of Modern France,* tr., J. DINGLE, 2 v. (New York 1961) v.1.

[J. LEFLON]

CONCORDAT OF FONTAINEBLEAU

Misleading title given to a tentative agreement in 1813 between Pope PIUS VII and NAPOLEON I. These two men had concluded the French CONCORDAT OF 1801 to which Napoleon had attached the Organic Articles. When Napoleon returned from Russia (December 1812), he wanted to arrange with the imprisoned Pius VII a new compact that would incorporate adherence to GALLICANISM, the designating of two-thirds of the cardinals by Catholic sovereigns, the disavowal of the "black" cardinals, the establishment of the papal residence in Paris, and the institution of bishops by metropolitans. When the negotiations conducted by Duvoisin proved inconclusive, the emperor went to Fontainebleau, 35 miles from Paris, to overcome the pope's resistance (Jan. 19, 1813). Contrary to some accounts, Napoleon did not stage any violent scenes. After five days of discussions, he succeeded in having the exhausted pope subscribe on January 25 to ten articles, which were to be kept secret and were to serve as the basis of a definitive arrangement.

According to this preliminary agreement, the pope would exercise his office in France and in the kingdom of Italy in the same manner as his predecessors; he would also maintain diplomatic representation. His agents would administer those papal domains that had not been alienated. To compensate for alienated possessions, the pope would receive two million francs. He would accord to newly named bishops canonical institution within six months, or else the metropolitan would supply it. The pope was to have the exclusive right to nominate to the six suburbicarian sees and to titular sees. He would act in concert with the emperor to reduce the number of dioceses in Tuscany, Genoa, Holland, and in the Hanseatic departments. The emperor promised to restore to his good graces those cardinals and prelates who had discontented him. Finally, the Congregation for the Propagation of the Faith, the Sacred Penitentiary, and the papal archives would be reestablished "in the place where the Holy Father sojourned."

These ten articles indicated that Napoleon had withdrawn some of his first claims but had obtained the canonical institution of bishops by metropolitans, the concession he wanted most. Although this was supposed to be merely a preliminary, secret agreement, Napoleon published it as a new concordat concluded with Pius VII. Contrary to the affirmations by Bartolomeo PACCA in his memoirs, the "black" cardinals who returned to France were not the ones responsible for the pope's disavowal of his concessions. A declaration in the pope's handwriting has been found recently among Pacca's papers proving that on January 28 Pius VII insisted that the articles of January 25 were to be set aside, abrogated, and annulled. At this time the pope decided to await the return of his cardinals in order to consult them, not about the revocation of this act, but about the best procedure to follow in order to render less grave the consequences of his disavowal. After deliberating with the cardinals, Pius VII sent to Napoleon on March 24 a letter retracting what he had admitted, but adding that he was prepared to make accommodations on other bases in conformity with his duty. Napoleon ordered this letter kept secret and proclaimed the Concordat of Fontainebleau as a law of the empire. Napoleon's downfall prevented the so-called concordat from ever being put into effect.

Bibliography: A. MERCATI, *Raccolta di Concordati . . .* (Rome 1954) 1:579–585, has text of concordat. L. PASZTOR, "Per la storia del *Concordato* di Fontainebleau," *Chiesa e stato nell'ottocento: Miscellanea in onore di P. Pirri,* ed. R. AUBERT et al., 2 v. (Padua 1962) 2:597–606. J. LEFLON, *La Crise révolutionnaire, 1789–1846* (*Histoire de l'église depuis les origines jusqu'à nos jours* 20; 1949). A. LATREILLE, *L'Église catholique et la Révolution française,* 2 v. (Paris 1946–50) v.2. P. FÉRET, *La France et le Saint-Siége sous le premier Empire, la Restauration et la monarchie de Juillet,* 2 v. (Paris 1911) v.1.

[J. LEFLON]

CONCUBINAGE

The enduring state or practice of sexual intercourse between a man and a woman not bound to each other by legitimate marriage. This article is not concerned with the historical or sociological dimensions of the practice of concubinage, but confines its attention to the subject as it is viewed in Canon Law.

Concubinage occurs in different forms, the common and essential element of which is an agreement, at least virtual, between a man and a woman to engage regularly or habitually in sexual intercourse outside of the bond of marriage. The illicit relationship may or may not involve cohabitation; it may or may not be covered by some sort of legality, as in the case of a purely civil marriage between persons bound by the canonical form. It is referred to as "qualified" concubinage if the relationship exists between persons who could not be legitimately married to each other because of an existing marriage bond, or a relationship of consanguinity or affinity, or an impediment arising from Holy Orders or religious profession. When the relationship is unknown to others, or is known only to a few and is unlikely to become more generally known, it is said to be private or occult; if it is actually known to many, or if there is a good probability that it will become so, it is said to be public.

Canon Law. The Church has always held that sexual relations are lawful only within the state of marriage. Nevertheless, at all times in the history of the Church, there have been some who, in spite of their profession of Christianity, have engaged in the practice of it. So far as the clergy was concerned, this was particularly so during the Middle Ages in consequence of local resistance to the introduction of the law of clerical celibacy.

When investigating the history of concubinage in the early canonical texts of bishops and councils, one should keep in mind that it was possible for a Christian to be considered by Roman law to be in concubinage, while according to canon law he was not. This was because Roman law did not recognize as full marriage (*iustae nuptiae*) certain unions (e.g., between a man and a woman of lower social state). Thus the Council of Toledo (400) allowed a man living in concubinage to be admitted to the Eucharist as long as the union did not fail to meet some condition essentially required for Christian marriage (*Codex iuris canonici,* D.34 c.4).

Laity. For a long time the only type of concubinage among the laity that received specific condemnation was adulterous and incestuous. Not until the Council of Trent was there a general condemnation of concubinage in all its forms (sess. 24, c.8). This decree states that anyone who would not dismiss his concubine, after having received three warnings from the ordinary, was to be excommunicated, and the concubine was to be expelled from the city with the aid of the secular authorities. This rule and procedure was not adopted into the Code of Canon Law. Instead the *Codex iuris canonici* (c.2357.2)

64

NEW CATHOLIC ENCYCLOPEDIA

simply states that those who are living in public concubinage are to be prohibited from legitimate ecclesiastical acts (e.g., sponsors at baptism). However, by reason of the fact that those living publicly in concubinage are also considered public SINNERS, they are also to be prevented from the reception of the Eucharist (c.851.1), from receiving ecclesiastical burial (c.1240. 1n6), and from joining associations officially approved by the Church (c.693.1). Moreover, public or notorious concubinage gives rise to the matrimonial impediment of PUBLIC PROPRIETY.

Clergy. There is considerably more material to be found in canonical sources concerning concubinage on the part of the clergy. Condemnations of this practice began in the 4th century and culminated in the decrees of the Council of Trent. The council formulated a series of measures designed to combat clerical concubinage: admonitions, suspensions, and privation of office and benefice (sess. 25, c.14. *De reform*). According to the present legislation, clerics in minor orders who are guilty of concubinage are to be reduced to the lay state and are subject to the same penalties as the laity (1917, *Codex iuris canonici* c.2358). Clerics in major orders are also to be reduced to the lay state (c.2359) with the consequent loss of the benefices the offender may theretofore have enjoyed. The procedure to be followed by the ordinary against clerics living in concubinage is stated in canons 2176–81. Finally, whenever a cleric, despite the admonitions of his ordinary, continues to frequent the residence of a woman whose reputation is suspect, he is to be presumed guilty of concubinage (c.133.4); as such, he is subject to the same penalties as those actually convicted of concubinage.

Morality. Concubinage has been a grave moral and social problem at different times and in different areas and cultures. The subjective guilt of some who have practiced it may be modified to a degree by the complexities of the human and cultural situations in which they lived. But the objective morality of the practice is clear. It is gravely sinful, for it involves all the moral disorder involved in habitual indulgence in the sin of FORNICATION, and in some cases this malice is aggravated by that of ADULTERY, INCEST, or SACRILEGE. Theologians have debated as to whether simple concubinage (uncomplicated by the malice of adultery, etc.) is objectively a greater or a lesser sin than promiscuous fornication. Some have argued that it is a greater sin, because it includes per se a greater pertinacity and obstinacy in the intention of the sinner. Others have argued that it is less sinful because by reason of the enduring relationship of one person with another it retains a greater likeness to marriage than does promiscuous fornication and is thus a lesser violation of the natural law.

Bibliography: G. JACQUEMET, *Catholicisme* 2:1473–77. R. BROUILLARD, *ibid.* 1477–78. É. JOMBART, *Dictionnaire de droit conanique*, ed. R. NAZ (Paris 1935–65) 3:1513–24, with bibliog. J. A. MACCULLOCH et al., *Encyclopedia of Religion and Ethics*, ed. J. HASTINGS (Edinburgh 1908–27) 3:809–820. *Enciclopedia del diritto* 8:695–697. A. VERMEERSCH, *Theologiae moralis principia, responsa, consilia* (Rome 1944–48). H. LECLERCQ, *Dictionnaire d'archéologie chrétienne et de liturgie* (Paris 1907–53) 3.2:2494–2500.

[J. M. BUCKLEY]

CONCUBINE (IN THE BIBLE)

In Biblical usage, a concubine (Heb. *pīlegeš*) is a true wife, although of secondary rank. Accepted without question as part of Israel's culture, the concubine regularly lived in the household and was recognized and provided for by Israelite custom. This article treats, in order, of the concubine living in her husband's house, the concubine in her father's house, and the inheritance of the concubine's sons.

Living in Her Husband's House. The Biblical references to concubines are confined to the Old Testament and connote an institution that was an offshoot of polygamy. The English word concubine may give a false connotation, suggesting a kept mistress. In reality, a concubine was a genuine wife. She was not a woman who cohabited with a man while unmarried to him. In the family the concubine held an intermediate place between the wife of first rank and an ordinary slave. In most cases she was a slave raised to a higher dignity by marriage to the master (Gn 16.3). The concubine held position as a wife of inferior or secondary rank. As such, she did not have the full legal status held by the wife of first rank. It is not certain what constituted the difference in rank. Most probably it was based upon the question of whether the wife was considered a purchase, having been sold (in the strict sense) to her husband. (The *mōhar* or dowry given for the wife was not actually a payment in purchase, although it appears similar.) The possession of numerous concubines in a harem was a sign of wealth. They were purchases exhibited as status symbols (2 Sm 3.7; 16.21). Such would have been the case with Solomon's 300 concubines (1 Kgs 11.3).

Living in Her Father's House. A concubine may have originally been a wife who continued to live in her father's house while her husband lived elsewhere and periodically visited her for conjugal relations. This was a genuine marriage, but without permanent cohabitation. The practice is sometimes found today among the Arabs where the husband is called a "visiting husband." Samson's marriage to the Philistine woman (Jgs 15.1) seems to have been of this type. The Middle Assyrian laws refer to such a custom (J. B. Pritchard, *Ancient Near Eastern Texts Relating to the Old Testament* [Princeton 1955] 182:25–36).

Her Son's Inheritance. The sons of concubines who were slaves had no right to inheritance as such, but the father could, if he chose, raise them to equal status with the sons of the wife of first rank. Such was the case with the sons of Jacob. No distinction was made between the sons of the concubines Bala and Zelpha and those of Rachel and Leah. All had an equal share in the land of Canaan (Gn 49.1–28). Sarah did not wish Ishmael, the son of the concubine Hagar, to share in the inheritance with her son Isaac. Although Ishmael had a right to the inheritance, in this instance Abraham sent him away, believing it was Yahweh's will (Gn 21.10–12). The Old Testament mentions the following as having concubines: Nahor (Gn 22.24), Abraham (Gn 25.6), Jacob (Gn 35.22), Eliphaz (Gn 36.12), an unnamed Levite (Jgs 19–20), Saul (2 Sm 3.7; 21.11), David (2 Sm 5.13; 15.16; 16.21; 19.5; 20.3), Solomon (1 Kgs 11.3), Manasseh (1 Chr 7.14), Caleb (1 Chr 2.46, 48), and Rehoboam (2 Chr 11.21). Concubines in the royal harem are mentioned also in Est 2.14; Dn 5.3, 23; Ct 6.8.

See Also: INHERITANCE (IN THE BIBLE); SEX (IN THE BIBLE).

Bibliography: R. PATAI, *Sex and Family in the Bible and the Middle East* (New York 1959). L. M. EPSTEIN, *Sex Laws and Customs in Judaism* (New York 1948). R. DE VAUX, *Ancient Israel, Its Life and Institutions*, tr. J. MCHUGH (New York 1961) 24–40, 53–54.

[R. H. MCGRATH]

CONCUPISCENCE

From the classical Latin *concupiscere,* meaning to long much for a thing, to be desirous of, to covet, to aspire to, to strive after. This article indicates the doctrinal sources on the subject of concupiscence, discusses the various senses of the word, explains in some detail its technical sense, and finally, treats in brief fashion the views of St. Augustine.

Sources. There are three declarations of the Church that must be mainly attended to: (1) the *Decree on Original Sin* of the Council of Trent, session 5, June 17, 1546 (see H. Denzinger, *Enchiridion symbolorum,* ed. A. Schönmetzer [32d ed. Freiburg 1963] 1515–16); (2) the condemnation of the errors of Baius in St. Pius V's *Ex omnibus afflictionibus,* Oct. 1, 1567 (propositions 26, 74–75; Denzinger, 1974–75); (3) the condemnation of the errors of the Synod of Pistoia in Pius VI's *Auctorem fidei,* Aug. 28, 1794 (see Denzinger, 2614). Another major source is the scriptural material furnished by Genesis ch. 2 and 3, and Romans ch. 6, 7, 8, especially 7.14–25 (cf. Gal 5.16–25). Finally, there are certain very pertinent portions of the writings of St. Augustine. Concerning these last, see below and bibliography.

Senses of the Word. In current English usage, the word "concupiscence" sometimes has an unfortunate ring. According to Webster's *Third New International Dictionary,* it means "strong or ardent desire: **a:** a longing of the soul for what will give it delight or for what is agreeable especially to the senses—used chiefly by Scholastic philosophers **b:** sexual desire: LUST." *The Oxford English Dictionary* says that concupiscence means "especially libidinous desire, sexual appetite, lust." This usage might shelter under the patronage of Augustine, who often speaks of concupiscence as an evil and sometimes as "bestial desire" (*C. Julian* 4. 16.82).

There are three gradings of the theological concept of concupiscence. In its broadest sense, it comprises the whole sweep and range of appetite, or desire (stressing its activity as against the relative passivity of knowledge), both sensory and spiritual, both faculty as well as its acts—and these latter whether deliberate or spontaneous. It includes not only the seeking of a good but also the rejecting of what is judged to be harmful.

In the next and narrower sense, concupiscence, while it can still be either sensory or spiritual, is nevertheless tied by a twofold restriction: first insofar as it is limited to the *act* of desire; second, insofar as this is *in*deliberate. This unfree act belongs to the mechanism or raw material of man's deliberate choosing. The personal decision, in order to come to birth, must be heralded not only by an act of knowing, but also by some automatic, vital reaction of the appetitive faculty, some spontaneous stretching out toward, or turning away from, an object held in the gaze of the mind. The indeliberate act of desire, springing from the very dynamism of man's nature, gives to the will the object about which it deliberates and decides. Every human being (therefore Christ in His human nature, Our Lady, Adam prior to his fall) must have concupiscence in this sense; absence of it would spell paralysis of the will.

Finally, in its third and technical sense (which alone is the concern of the rest of this article), concupiscence again is involved in the indeliberate act of desire but only and precisely insofar as this is pitted against the free decision, hindering and hampering it, wrestling with and diverting it. In this technical sense, then, concupiscence acts three ways. (1) It forestalls the free decision; already before any choice is finally made, concupiscence is present threatening liberty of action. (2) In the very process of one's choosing, concupiscence is at work as a counter-tension. (3) Even when vanquished, it still asserts itself and is not totally submissive.

The salient feature of concupiscence in this technical sense lies in the tenacity, persistence, and obduracy with which it withstands the free decision. This latter, be it noted, seeks to shape and stamp one's whole being, to affect one through and through, to seize on one and commit one in one's entirety, to possess and master one as wholly as it can. When man chooses, he aims at throwing into that choice everything that is in him, even his blind, spontaneous elements. He strives to articulate himself in his choice, to make it express and advertise him and all that he wants to be and stand for. He endeavors to impregnate with his freely selected convictions even the darkest recesses of his being. And he encounters the defiance of concupiscence.

Technical Sense. Through a series of affirmations and elaborations of them, it may be possible to elucidate the purport of concupiscence in its technical sense.

Partial and Adequate Presentations. One must distinguish between a partial and an adequate presentation of concupiscence. Preachers, ascetical writers, and spiritual directors are rightly concerned only with a pastoral approach to concupiscence. Their purpose is to put people on their guard against falling into its snares by self-indulgence, especially fleshly. Hence they underscore its dangers, vilifying it as unbridled passion and rebel desire. Given their scope, their one-sided picture of concupiscence is, in itself, legitimate. Furthermore it is authorized by Scripture and tradition. It must be stressed, however, that this is only a limited account of concupiscence; it neither is, nor should it claim to be, complete and well-rounded.

Human Phenomenon. Concupiscence is a characteristically human phenomenon. It is found neither in the angels, above man, nor in the animals, below man. The angel is a pure spirit, owning a nature of unruffled harmony, jangled by no inner tension or clash. Its personal decision, therefore, achieves what every personal decision innately gropes after: that the whole nature should, so to speak, be poured into and shaped by, this decision, nothing at all withstanding or escaping its molding. There is, consequently, a lofty irrevocability about the election of an angel; if he sins, his sin is a sin of strength, not of weakness; his self-commitment is so lucidly entire and entirely lucid as to preclude the bare possibility of any retraction.

The complex organism of the brute beast likewise exhibits a wonderful harmony. Instinct gives coherence to its behavior. Nothing it does is excessive, nothing unreasonable, because it has no dictate of reason to violate. Nothing it does is blameworthy, for such an epithet is emptied of meaning when applied to the blind functioning of a nature coerced by its instinct.

Man is a creature apart; in his nature there is no nicely balanced harmony, but a raw and radical dualism of flesh and spirit. Never is he perfectly at ease within himself, never serenely integrated, never wielding "solely sovereign sway and masterdom."

Concupiscence is not, therefore, as some are inclined to suppose, man's egoism and pride at war with his yearning towards God. Lucifer and his followers fell victims to such self-assertiveness, which cannot, then, figure as an exclusively human weakness.

Natural to Man. That concupiscence is natural to man is deducible, first of all, with certitude from the teaching of the Church that Adam's immunity from concupiscence was a gratuitous, unowed endowment and, second, with probability from the fact that man is at once flesh and spirit. The angel lacks concupiscence because he is sheer spirit; the beast, because it is in nowise spirit. One has no more right to label concupiscence bestial than angelic. It is simply human. And since it is native to man, he would have it were he to be created in some other, purely natural, order.

Operative in the Whole. Concupiscence should not be classed as an exclusively sensory event. Man is a composite being whose coefficients of flesh and spirit both condition him continuously and all-pervasively (as psychosomatic medicine keeps one aware). No human action can be exclusively sensory or exclusively spiritual. Man's knowledge of the most crassly material object is partly spiritual, piercing down to its essence; his knowledge of the purely spiritual is partly sensory (when he studies the nature of God or of an isosceles triangle, his imagination inveterately provides him with a picture of perhaps an old gentleman or a diagram traced in red chalk). Likewise his spiritual desires are shaded with sensory; his sensory, with spiritual. The most physical of human acts (e.g., sexual intercourse, a woman suckling her baby, a laborer devouring a meal) are, because they are shot through with the spiritual, essentially different from parallel actions in other mammals. Just as the water of a lake, no matter how vast and meandering, no matter how cut by headlands or studded with islands, seeks its own level—so man: in all he does, there is the inflow and interplay of both flesh and spirit. Hence concupiscence cannot be exclusively sensory. It is as much at work in the temptation to disbelieve an article of faith (where the object is purely spiritual) as in a solicitation to lust.

It is misleading to make concupiscence exactly coincidental with sexual desire. The unruly movements of sex do, of course, thrust before man concupiscence in its most humiliating and seductive dress. It is thus that Genesis adumbrates that immunity from concupiscence with which the first parents were endowed and which they forfeited by sin. Gn 2.25: Adam and Eve are naked and unashamed; Gn 3.7: they are naked but now ashamed—solely as the outcome of sin. The shame or modesty here referred to is not the acquired or infused virtue of that name, which resides in the spiritual region of man. Rather it is something instinctive, an element in his sensory mechanism, a check on the sex instinct causing distress or fear; it is universal among adults, growing alongside the sex instinct, with whose exercise it is linked. Clothing, though not identical with modesty, is its individuation. Everything in Genesis ch. 2 and 3 shows man's first parents as responsible adults. If, then, they were naked but unabashed, this was not due to the immaturity of childhood, but to the privilege of integrity, of which they were deprived through their own grievous fault.

Not Exclusively a Proneness to Evil. Because natural to man, concupiscence cannot be adequately represented as exclusively a proneness to evil or a thwarting of right reason. The all-wise and holy God could not create man with an inborn drive diametrically counter to his last end. Moreover, a characteristic of concupiscence is its spontaneity, which is ambivalent. Concupiscence defies and challenges a wicked, as much as a good, purpose. It is as much in evidence at one's blush because one has lied, as in the promptings of lust.

Metonymy. In both Scripture (especially Romans ch. 6, 7, 8) and tradition (especially Augustine), concupiscence is called sin. This must not give one the wrong impression that it is sin strictly and formally so-called. A sort of metonymy is at work for which three reasons can be alleged; concupiscence is (1) the fruit, (2) the punishment, and (3) the seed of sin. This last reason relates to personal sin; the first two, to ORIGINAL SIN, and they apply equally to DEATH. For whatever might be held about human death in a state of PURE NATURE, in the present, supernatural order, it is both the result and punishment of original sin. Unlike concupiscence, however, death does not incline to frequent sins of weakness. Though it may be the result, it is scarcely the cause of sin. Neither death nor concupiscence can be accurately described as moral evil—for such a qualification belongs only to deliberate choices. Nevertheless it would be rash to infer that death and concupiscence are equally amoral. For, in a way that death does not, concupiscence trenches on the field of morality, seeing that it can incline to evil and persist against the dictate of right reason.

Relation to Willfulness. Concupiscence is certainly not the root of all sin, nor is it the cause of the worst sins.

The proof of this twin statement lies in the devil's sin and in that of the first parents: despite their immunity from concupiscence, they sinned. Indeed it was precisely this immunity that enabled them to climb to the very acme of calculated malice. Where there is concupiscence, there is no total self-commitment, and consequently, no "perfect" sin.

Other Elements. Likewise, concupiscence is certainly not the sole source of TEMPTATION and tendency to sin. The option of the angels against God involved some sort of temptation, at least in the sense of an encounter with the dilemma: either to let God be God, accepting one's very being from His hands; or to aspire to God-head, repudiating one's radical dependence on Him. Genesis makes it plain that Adam and Eve, while endowed with integrity, were liable to temptation.

Compensating Aspects. Concupiscence is not without its compensations. (1) It cannot hurt man unless he decides to be in league with it. It cannot force his will, and available are God's multiple helps. (2) It provides an incentive to progress in the spiritual life. The merits of holy Christians arise, under God, from the steadfastness with which they overcome the obstacles arising from concupiscence. Always there, it constitutes a constant challenge to asceticism, prayer, and the frequentation of the Sacraments. (3) Even when a man has a mind to sin mortally, concupiscence implies a twin advantage. On the one hand, its stubborn resistance diminishes the malice of a wicked resolve. (It may be mentioned, incidentally, that, obsessed with the risks of concupiscence, one overlooks those of integrity. This latter gift was granted to Adam so that he might dedicate himself utterly to God; but it was bivalent, and there lay its risk. For when Adam used it to sin, he was able to commit a sin of surpassing heinousness.) On the other hand, by hindering the evil decision's seizing on and stamping the whole man with malice, it furnishes the psychological basis for a retraction of the will. There is no basis for repentance in the sinful angel, whose apostasy is voiced in his whole being. A change of heart was, however, feasible in Adam's case, because integrity in him was a sheerly gratuitous gift, lost, therefore, in the very flush of sin. (4) It is because of concupiscence that, quite often, transgressions of gravely binding commandments are in reality only venially sinful. Concupiscence saves man from a full-blooded consent. Such venial sins of weakness are unthinkable in an angel or Adam before his fall. Without concupiscence, one consents fully or not at all. (5) Concupiscence, finally, belongs to the complex state of restoration in Christ and the Church. This is so much more wonderful (cf. *mirabilius reformasti* of the Offertory at the Mass) than the state of ORIGINAL JUSTICE that the liturgy can acclaim Adam's sin as fortunate: *felix culpa.* To counterpoise his dualism, Adam received integrity as a lump gift, i.e., intended to be permanent and conferring complete self-dominion. Christians do not have one gift once and for all; it comes in installments. It is found especially in the daily Eucharist. Whereas Adam was given something, they are given somebody, Christ Himself.

Duality. Once again one notices how concupiscence is pervasively dual in aspect: it is both sensory and spiritual; for both good and ill; if it explains many sins of weakness, it also explains why many sins either stop short of being mortal, or, if mortal, are not irremediably so. It further explains why the most abandoned sinners surprise one occasionally with some instinctive good deed. On the other hand, even in those indwelt by the Holy Ghost, even in the heroically holy and in the mystics, concupiscence stays on. Consequently, they never succeed in concentrating everything within them under their personal orientation to Christ. Something escapes, some small, peripheral element. Hence they must lament those daily, semideliberate venial sins that the Council of Trent, session 6, Jan. 13, 1547, assigns even to the holiest (*Decree on Justification* 11; Denzinger, 1537). Even the Apostles, even after their unforgettable personal experiences during the Passion, Resurrection, and Ascension of Our Lord, even after Pentecost, when they were transformed by the Holy Ghost and confirmed in grace, still had to, and in fact did, describe themselves as sinners (1 Jn 1.8–10; Jas 3.2).

St. Augustine (354–430). Perhaps no Christian writer at all, certainly none of comparable intellectual caliber, authority, and influence, has dealt with concupiscence at such length and so frequently as St. Augustine. Hence, he deserves special attention. Repeatedly and acutely he commented upon the relevant passages in Genesis and Romans; his attitude has commanded that of most Western thinkers, whether medieval or modern. Among these must be included especially St. Thomas Aquinas. By more than 1,000 years Augustine anticipated the Catholic rebuttals of Luther's error that concupiscence is formally original sin. His very phrases on concupiscence are echoed by, and enshrined in, the *Decree on Original Sin* issued by the Council of Trent.

Augustine's doctrine of concupiscence, however, is not free from difficulty—as is evident in that both M. BAIUS and C. JANSEN have (wrongly) attributed to him their own blunders (see C. Boyer). Hence the Church, while honoring him as it has honored few of its Doctors, places express reservations on his handling of deeper and more thorny questions (Denzinger, 249; Portalié, *A Guide to . . . St. Augustine,* 323–326).

The main objections against Augustine's position are four. (1) He seems to identify concupiscence with fleshly desire in general and with lust in particular. (2) He seems to regard it as evil and nothing but evil, persisting as evil even after baptism and in wedlock. (3) He seems to undermine the dignity of Christian wedlock, because, while on the one hand marriage (in his theory) cloaks concupiscence with respectability, it is itself degraded by its traffic with what he continues to castigate as evil. (4) He exaggerates the role of concupiscence in the transmission of original sin, giving the impression that the two are one and the same reality.

In Augustine's vast prolixity on concupiscence, there undoubtedly occur some unfortunate emphases. Nevertheless many difficulties yield before growing familiarity with his whole thought. Thus he expressly recognizes that Paul's idea of "flesh" and "walking" or "living according to the flesh" takes in more than body and bodily sin (cf. Gal 5.19–20). It is the great error of Platonists and Manichees to debit all man's wickedness against the body (*Civ.* 14.1–6). And although monotonously vociferating against concupiscence as an evil, Augustine refused to call it a formal sin. Here is the formula of his predilection: "the justified man is without all sin, though not without all evil [*omni peccato caret, non omni malo*]" *C. Julian* 6.16.49. For a just assessment of Augustine's theory, one must set it in its historical context of the Pelagian heresy. This proclaimed that all is well with man, that concupiscence is in every sense innocent, that it has no connection with original sin, which, moreover, is not a transmitted race-sin but the purely private misdemeanor of a forebear who disedified his posterity by shabby behavior. Against such falsehoods Augustine eloquently protests that concupiscence is the fruit and seed of sin, that it is morally imputable to men through their solidarity with the head of the human race, Adam, in whom they lost integrity. So much for the actual state of mankind, at any rate. He admits that, absolutely speaking, God could create man with concupiscence (*Retract.* 1.9.6) and that integrity is a grace (*C. Julian.* 4.16.82). As a sample both of Augustine's basic soundness and at the same time of his tendency to mislead the unwary through his one-sidedness, the reader should ponder the last dozen lines or so, n. 71 in Book 1, of his *Incomplete Work against Julian.*

See Also: AUGUSTINE, ST.; AUGUSTINIANISM, THEOLOGICAL SCHOOL OF; GRACE AND NATURE; INTEGRITY, GIFT OF.

Bibliography: E. PORTALIÉ, *Dictionnaire de théologie catholique,* ed. A. VACANT et al., 15 v. (Paris 1903–50; Tables générales 1951–) 1.2:2268–2472; Eng. tr., R. BASTIAN, *A Guide to the Life and Thought of St. Augustine* (Chicago 1960). J. B. METZ, *Lexikon für Theologie und Kirche,* ed. J. HOFER and K. RAHNER, 10 v. (2d, new ed. Freiburg 1957–65) suppl., *Das Zweite Vatikanische Konzil: Dokumente und Kommentare,* ed. H. S. BRECHTER et al., pt.

1 (1966) 2:108–112. AUGUSTINE, *Civ.* 14; *Nupt. et concup.*; *C. Iulian,* esp. 4 and 5; *C. Iulian op. imperf.* esp. 4 and 5. C. BOYER, *Tractatus de Deo creante et elevante* (5th ed. Rome 1957). I. F. SAGÜÉS, *Sacrae theologiae summa,* ed. Fathers of the Society of Jesus, Professors of the Theological Faculties in Spain, 4 v. (3d ed. Madrid 1958) 2.2:727–752. M. SCHMAUS, ''Konkupiszenz,'' *Katholische Dogmatik,* 5 v. in 8 (Munich 1953–59) 2.1:355–360. J. DE LA VAISSIÈRE, *Modesty: A Psychological Study of Its Instinctive Character,* tr. S. A. RAEMERS (St. Louis 1937). J. P. KENNY, ''The Problem of Concupiscence: A Recent Theory of Professor Karl Rahner,'' *Australasian Catholic Record* 29 (1952) 290–304; 30 (1953) 23–32; abridged in *Theology Digest* 8 (1960) 163–166. P. DE LETTER, '''Concupiscence,' Clergy Monthly,'' *Ranchi* 31 (1957) 211–220. J. P. MACKEY, ''Original Sin: Nature and Grace,'' *Irish Theological Quarterly* 30 (1963) 191–204. L. BOROS, *Mysterium mortis* (Freiburg 1964).

[J. P. KENNY]

CONCURRENCE, DIVINE

The influence God exercises upon the activities of creatures; God not only creates and conserves creatures, but He also cooperates with their actions. The doctrine of divine concurrence is opposed to two extremes: DEISM, which admits creation by God as the origin of the universe at its first moment, but denies all subsequent influence of God on creatures, and OCCASIONALISM, which denies that creatures have any true CAUSALITY of their own and holds that on the occasion of creatures' presence to one another, God as sole and total cause effects whatever comes into being.

Common Teaching. Just as creatures are never self-sufficient for existing, but owe the fact that they are actually existent to the creative and conserving causality of God, so likewise, creatures are never self-sufficient for acting, but owe the fact that they are actually agents to the concurrent causality of God. Still, just as creatures are not themselves parts or intrinsic elements of God's own being, but are substances that exist in themselves, likewise creatures are truly agents and exercise a causality of their own with respect to their own proper effects.

God's concurrence is a transcendent kind of causality; it is not additive to that of the creature, as though the creature produced half of the effect, and God produced the other half (*see* CAUSALITY, DIVINE). The real duality of causes justifies one's speaking of the cooperation of God with creatures; this is not a mechanistic juxtaposition of causes or equal distribution of labor, but rather a radical subordination of the created cause to the uncreated cause. There is a complete compenetration of created causes and their activities by the causality of the Creator. God's causality and creatural causality are an organic activity, constituting one principle of action. The activity is single, but it has a two-fold relation of dependence. The whole activity is attributable to God, and the whole activity is attributable to the creature. That the activity and what it produces are in the order of reality, or exist at all, is attributable to the activity of God; that this reality is of this or that nature or kind is attributable, under God, to the activity of the created cause. This latter is attributable ''under God,'' for what God does is absolutely prerequisite for what the creature does; BEING is what is most interior to, most deeply within, most constitutive of, a thing, and being is what God first and foremost and indispensably produces as His own proper effect. Since being is radically presupposed by all the operations of the creature, the actions and effects of created agents depend even more on God than they do on these created agents. Concurrence is demanded not because of the lack of any natural power or disposition, but because of the radical dependence of secondary causes (created and finite) on the primary or first CAUSE (uncreated and omnipotent). It is the relationship of creature to Creator extended to the realm of activity.

Common Distinctions. The divine concurrence that Christian theologians and philosophers commonly defend is something physical, not merely moral; that is, it is not a mere command on the part of God, or a threat, or some advice, or some other moral suasion; rather it is a physical influence affecting all created agents, whether these be rational beings or subhuman, and it is a cause of the objective physical entity of the effect and of the action, to the extent that this is an entity.

The divine concurrence may be universal, general, and natural; and it may be particular, special, and supernatural. General concurrence is given by God to every created agent in every one of its activities. Special concurrence is given only with regard to certain kinds of activities. Actual GRACE is a case of special and supernatural concurrence.

Divine concurrence is almost universally considered to be immediate. Here the common doctrine is opposed to that of DURANDUS OF SAINT-POURÇAIN, who defends only a mediate concurrence, since he holds that the divine creation and conservation of a thing's being and natural powers suffice for the creature to go ahead and act on its own. [For a different interpretation of Durandus, see J. Stufler, ''Bemerkungen zur Konkurslehre les Durandus von St. Pourçain,'' *Beiträge zur Geschichte der Philosophie und Theologie des Mittelalters* (Münster 1891–) Suppl. 3.2 (1935) 1080–90.]

The distinction is sometimes made between concurrence in first act and concurrence in second act. The former refers to God's own internal will act: the eternal, free, actual decision on the part of God to concur with created causes in the manner conforming with their nature. Concurrence in second act is a contingent reality, the actual terminus produced by the eternal decree, a quality received in the created cause itself (according to Thomists) or the action itself of producing an effect insofar as this action is due to God's simultaneously operating with the created cause (according to Molinists). Similarly, reference is often made to hypothetical concurrence, or the concurrence that God offers, i.e., that He is prepared to confer (*concursus oblatus*), and to the actually conferred concurrence (*concursus collatus, exhibitus*). These distinctions assume importance when one investigates the disagreements on the nature of divine concurrence and allied matters such as PREDESTINATION and the efficaciousness of grace.

Disputed Area. St. THOMAS AQUINAS treats of divine concurrence especially in *In 2 sent.*, 37.2.2; *C. gent.* 3.66, 67, 70; *Summa Theologiae* 1a, 105.5; and *De pot.* 3.7. In this last place Aquinas summarizes his teaching: "God causes the action of everything inasmuch as He gives to everything its power to act and conserves it in being and applies it to its action, and inasmuch as it is through His power that every other power acts. If we add to this the fact that God is His own power, and that He is present in all things not as an essential part of them but as maintaining them in their being, we should conclude that He acts in every agent immediately, but without eliminating the action of the will and of nature."

In the development of this doctrine, theologians and philosophers have divided into two main camps, although there are several subdivisions and even deviations. The divisions are traceable fundamentally to the differing ways thinkers view created causality, but they are especially accentuated in discussions about God's concurrence with man's free acts. The differences center on the meaning of God's "application of created agents to their actions," and on created agents' "operation in virtue of the power of God."

Molinists. The 16th-century Jesuit theologians Luis de Molina (*Concordia*, 14.13.25–35), Francisco SUÁREZ (*Disp. meta.* 22; *Opusc. de concursu et efficaci auxilio gratiae Dei; De auxiliis gratiae*, 3), and Leonard LESSIUS (*De perf. moribusque divinis*, 11.3–7) teach that God's concurrence with creatures is a "simultaneous concursus" that, considered in first act and with regard to human free acts, is "indifferent," i.e., is not effective of some particular determinate act rather than some other equally possible one, but is requisite for the production of any action and effect. These authors and their followers (including many modern Jesuits, especially Spaniards and Germans) argue that secondary causes are complete in the order of causing, once they have been endowed with their natural active powers and have been properly disposed and applied to their subject matter, that these dispositions and applications are usually effected by other created causes, and that the transition from this naturally complete and aptly disposed capacity for acting to the status of actually acting is a transition requiring no further modification in the secondary agent itself. What is required is the simultaneous influence of God directly on the created activity itself and, through this, on the effect. The action and the effect thus proceed from two simultaneously operating causes. The created cause is not intrinsically "elevated" by God in order to "operate in virtue of the power of God"; rather God cooperates with the action that proceeds from the creature. The primacy in the order of causality is still God's, since the action as proceeding immediately from Him accounts for the fact that both the action and the effect are real beings rather than nothing at all, whereas the action, as proceeding from the creature, accounts only for why the action and effect are of such and such a kind. (*See* MOLINISM.)

Thomists. In contrast with the Molinists, or defenders of "simultaneous concursus," there are the Thomists, who defend a concurrence that is a "physical premotion" of the created cause. This school includes especially the Dominicans, but also many others including numerous French and Italian Jesuits. The Thomists maintain that the divine concurrence is a strict MOTION, an intrinsic, transitory modification of the created cause itself, an accidental quality received immediately from God by the created cause prior to its actual operation, and needed for two major reasons: (1) in order that the finite cause may be "applied" to the act of operation, on the score that of itself the finite cause, even when all other natural conditions are fulfilled, is only in potency for operating, whereas to be actually operating implies that the cause is made more perfect; and (2) in order to elevate the created cause intrinsically so that, as an instrument permeated by the divine power, it may produce an effect not proportionate to its own native powers but surpassing them, namely, the being of the thing generated (*see* INSTRUMENTAL CAUSALITY).

The Thomists are subdivided into two very different groups. There are those who, in general, follow the interpretation given to St. Thomas by Domingo BÁÑEZ (*Comm. in S.T.* 1.14.13; 1.19.8; 1.23.3) and who are sometimes termed "Bañezians" by their opponents. See, e.g., A. Goudin, *Philosophia juxta inconcussa tutissimaque divi Thomae dogmata*, 4.4; J. B. Gonet, *Clypeus Thomisticus*, 4.5, 9; and John of St. Thomas, *Curs. phil.*, *Phys.* 1.25.2, 1.26. These teach that the physical premotion, or divine concurrence in second act, of its very nature physically predetermines the secondary cause to its individual actions, doing so even in the case of the free acts of men. Others, sometimes vaguely called Neothomists (or even Neo-Molinists) maintain physical PREDE-TERMINATION for all nonfree actions, but claim that the divine concurrence in the case of the free-will acts of finite agents is an "indifferent" premotion of the secondary cause, moving it to actual operation, but not determining the specification of the act. Among these latter are L. Billot [*De gratia Christi* (4th ed., Rome 1928) 3–25, 124–139] and A. D' Alès [*Providence et Libre Arbitre* (2d ed. Paris 1927)].

In the Thomist doctrines the concurrence, though immediately affecting the created cause itself, also carries over into the action and effect, and in that sense partakes of the nature of a "simultaneous concursus" as well. (*See* PREMOTION, PHYSICAL.)

To the above divisions, one should add that there is a tendency among certain recent writers to reduce all premotion and simultaneous concursus to the transcendent "creative" activity of God. [See A. Van Hove, "De motione divina in ordine cum naturali tum supernaturali animadversiones," *Divus Thomas*, (Piacenza 1880–) ser. 3, 10 (1933) 248–264; also, J. H. Nicolas, "La Permission du péché," *Revue thomiste* 60 (1960) 9–13.]

Relation to Other Doctrines. The teaching on divine concurrence is especially relevant to other doctrines, particularly to those concerned with grace, sin, and human freedom.

Grace. Since the divine concurrence, according to the strict Thomists, contains the predetermining of an activity even to its individual details, it is easy to see why in this view concurrence in the supernatural order is an intrinsically efficacious grace, and how God has thereby a ready and infallible means of bringing about His ends, including the predestination of the elect. The Jesuits, holding that divine concurrence is intrinsically indifferent, so that, although it is a positive inclination, it is not an irresistible determination, have to explain the efficaciousness of supernatural concurrence or grace by appealing not only to the intrinsic nature of the grace, but also to God's knowledge of the hypothetical future (SCIENTIA MEDIA). With this knowledge, God knows the graces whose congruousness so tallies with the dispositions of the man's will in the particular circumstances in which the grace is bestowed, that the man infallibly and freely consents to it (*see* CONGRUISM).

Sin. As activities, sins have being and are positively caused in this being; hence they require God's physical and immediate concurrence for this, their material aspect. The malice, which is the formal element of sin, is attributable entirely to the bad will of the creature; it is a negative activity, a deficiency of causality, requiring no concurrence from God. For this element, the creature's moral malice is alone responsible. God's relation to the EVIL of the sinful act is not causative, but permissive: out of respect for human freedom God does not, although absolutely speaking and by an extraordinary intervention He could, prevent the sin.

Human Freedom. All Catholics agree that human FREEDOM is not absolute self-sufficiency; like man's being it is something loaned, something dependent in its inmost nature and operations on the independent Being and, therefore, in need of divine concurrence if it is to act. The nature of the concurrence with free acts is debated consistently with the special doctrines of the various schools. The question at issue is one in which the paradox of the coexistence of the finite and the infinite is seen in its most acute form. All Catholics will admit the following teaching of St. Thomas: "Since the divine will is perfectly efficacious, it follows not only that those things are done, which God wills to be done, but also that they are done in the way that He wills. Now God wills some things to be done necessarily, some contingently, to the right ordering of things, for the building up of the universe. Therefore, to some effects He has attached necessary causes, that cannot fail; but to others defectible and contingent causes, from which arise contingent effects" (*Summa theologiae*, 1a, 19.8; cf. 1a2ae, 10.4).

See Also: CONSERVATION, DIVINE; CREATION, 2; EXISTENCE; FREE WILL.

Bibliography: V. FRINS, *Dictionnaire de théologie catholique*. ed. A. VACANT et al., (Paris 1903–50) 3.1:781–796. R. GARRIGOU-LAGRANGE, *Predestination*, tr. B. ROSE (St. Louis 1939). L. LERCHER, *Institutiones theologiae dogmaticae*, v.2 (4th ed. Barcelona 1945) 258–270. A. M. DUMMERMUTH, *S. Thomas et Doctrina Praemotionis Physicae* (Paris 1886). L. RASOLO, *Le Dilemme du concours divin* (Analecta Gregoriana 80; Rome 1956). B. LONERGAN, "St. Thomas' Theory of Operation," *Theological Studies* 3 (1942) 375–402. R. P. PHILLIPS, *Modern Thomistic Philosophy*, 2 v. (Westminster, Md. 1934–35; repr. 1946) 2:342–351. W. J. BROSNAN, *God Infinite: The World and Reason* (New York 1943).

[A. J. BENEDETTO]

CONDILLAC, ÉTIENNE BONNOT DE

Philosopher, member of the French Academy (1768), third son of Gabriel Bonnot, Viscount of Mably; b. Grenoble, Sept. 30, 1715; d. Flux, near Beaugency, Aug. 3, 1780. After studies at Saint-Sulpice and the Sorbonne, he was ordained in 1740. His intellectual interests and writings gave him entry into the salons, friendship with J. J. ROUSSEAU, acquaintance with D. Diderot, and the tutorship of Ferdinand of Parma; but he was ill disposed toward Paris's secular atmosphere and returned to his estate in the provinces. Influenced by R. DESCARTES, J. LOCKE, and I. Newton, Condillac became the leading

French advocate of SENSISM, a theory of knowledge claiming that man's mental activity is explained by an analysis of sense experience. In his *Essai sur l'origine des connaissances humaines* (Amsterdam 1746) he taught that SENSATION is the unique source of knowledge, thus departing from Locke, who included also REFLECTION. In his *Traité des systèmes* (Amsterdam 1749), a criticism of rationalist philosophies, he doubted that substance could be properly defined; moreover, he expressed his preference for systems based on observation. His most important work, *Traité des sensations* (Paris 1754), presented his theory that the mind is a product of sense experience, contains no innate ideas, and may even lack incorporeity. Condillac, a man of faith, repudiated the determinist and atheistic consequences of this theory, but his ideas were developed along such lines by the atheist Marquis de Sade (1740–1814) in France and by J. S. MILL and H. SPENCER in England.

Bibliography: *Oeuvres philosophiques*, ed. G. LE ROY, 3 v. (Paris 1947–51). É. H. GILSON and T. D. LANGAN, *Modern Philosophy: Descartes to Kant* (New York 1963). G. DE BAGUENAULT DE PUCHESSE, *Condillac: Sa vie, sa philosophie, son influence* (Paris 1910).

[R. J. MARAS]

CONDITION

Broadly understood, a condition is that which makes possible, makes ready, or prepares the way for an efficient cause to act, or for its action to be efficacious. A condition may be referred to the AGENT or to the patient, and so is intimately related to efficient and material CAUSALITY. However, the primary referent of a condition is the patient or subject that is acted upon (*see* ACTION AND PASSION). A condition may indicate a state or DISPOSITION of a patient or subject that permits the subject to receive the action of an agent. It may also connote the absence or the removal of an obstacle that would otherwise block the agent's activity or render it ineffective. This latter description is commonly referred to as a *removens prohibens*. Often, in order for a cause to function and produce an effect, some impediment must be removed; e.g., for a parachute to open, it is a necessary requirement that its risers not be tangled. Similarly, for a pen to write, it is a condition that it be not clogged. The removal of the impediment, i.e., the entanglement of the parachute shrouds or the clogging of the pen, demands a cause. But the removal of the impediment is not a cause as such of the effect that follows, namely, of the parachute opening or of the pen writing. Scholastics designate the removal of an impediment as a cause *per accidens* of the effect that is the result of the agent; the air opening the parachute would be the cause *per se* of the parachute opening.

Although a condition is not strictly a proximate cause, it may provide an absolute requirement that must be met if the cause is to function effectively. When such is the case, the condition is termed a *conditio sine qua non*. A condition does not influence the effect so much as it influences the action of the agent, either in itself or in the subject. Some examples that will clarify this are presented.

It is a condition for a man to see that his eyelids be open, or that the lens of the eye be not clouded with scar tissue. Neither condition strictly causes man to see; rather they render the act of seeing possible. Again, it is a condition of certain types of food that they be prepared in a special manner to be edible. This condition is not a cause of the food being eaten and digested, but it does make possible such a process. In still another sense, the academic preparation of a student listening to a lecture may influence the extent of his grasp of the lecture. Thus the academic training is a condition for the lecture's being understood in detail.

From what has been said it is evident that when one looks for concrete examples of conditions, it becomes increasingly difficult to distinguish remote and comparatively insignificant causality from certain types of conditions. For example, the physical and mental condition of an athlete will influence and be a cause of the stamina he shows in sports activity. Ovulation is a necessary condition for conception, yet it also contributes toward that end in the fashion of a cause. Hence, condition, OCCASION, PRINCIPLE, and cause must be understood in relation to each other.

See Also: EFFICIENT CAUSALITY.

Bibliography: J. M. BALDWIN, ed., *Dictionary of Philosophy and Psychology,* 3 v. in 4 (New York 1901–05; repr. Gloucester 1949–57). L. DE RAEYMAEKER, *The Philosophy of Being,* tr. E. H. ZIEGELMEYER (St. Louis 1954). B. GERRITY, *Nature, Knowledge and God* (Milwaukee 1947). T. N. HARPER, *The Metaphysics of the School,* 3 v. (New York 1879–84; reprint 1940).

[G. F. KREYCHE]

CONDORCET, MARIE JEAN ANTOINE CARITAT

Marquis Condorcet, a mathematician, philosopher, and statesman whose classical statement of the theory of progress influenced 19th-century thinkers; b. Ribemont, Picardy, Sept. 17, 1741; d. Bourg-la-Reine, March 29, 1794. Condorcet was educated by the Jesuits at Reims and their Collège de Navarre in Paris. He attracted the attention of great mathematicians, such as J. L. Lagrange and J. d'Alembert, with his *Essai sur le calcul integral,* and soon became acquainted with prominent thinkers of the French ENLIGHTENMENT. In 1769 Condorcet was elected to the Academy of Sciences, and in 1782 to the French Academy. His *Essai sur l'application de l'analyse à la probabilité des decisions rendues à la pluralité des voix* (1785) was a notable contribution to the theory of probability. His biographies, *Vie de M. Turgot* (1786) and *Vie de Voltaire* (1787), were widely read.

In 1791 Condorcet was elected to the legislative assembly. He prepared a scheme for state education and was one of the first to advocate a republic. He was the leading member of the convention's committee on drafting a constitution. Condorcet sided with the Girondins against the Jacobins, and when the former were arrested in June 1793, he went into hiding. Here he wrote his famous *Esquisse d'un tableau historique des progrès de l'esprit humain,* which sketches history as man's ascent from barbarism to an age of enlightened reason through a progress that is irreversible and inescapable. He himself was then arrested and the following day found dead, either from suicide or from exhaustion.

Bibliography: *Oeuvres,* ed. A. C. O'CONNOR and M. F. ARAGO, 12 v. (Paris 1847–49); *Sketch for a Historical Picture of the Progress of the Human Mind,* tr. J. BARRACLAUGH (New York 1955). P. FAGGIOTTO, *Enciclopedia filosofica* (Venice-Rome 1957) 1:1180–81.

[T. P. NEILL]

CONDREN, CHARLES DE

Oratorian preacher and spiritual director; b. near Soissons, France, Dec. 15, 1588; d. Paris, Jan. 7, 1641. Condren's father, a convert, was governor of Monceaux, canton of Meaux. Too frail as a child to attend school, Charles entered college only for philosophy, after which he wished to study for the priesthood. His father refused permission, urging him to enter the service of the king, whereupon Condren fell gravely ill. After his recovery he was permitted to continue his studies, and in 1614 he was ordained. He earned his doctor's degree in a year at the Sorbonne, and in 1617 he entered the Oratory, which had been founded in France by Cardinal Pierre de BÉRULLE in 1611. Assigned to preaching, teaching, and spiritual direction, Condren was soon in great demand and became confessor to many leaders of the court and Church. On the death of Bérulle in 1629, Condren was elected second superior general of the Oratory.

Condren established the Oratory on a firm basis, put the constitutions in order, and defined clearly the aims of the congregation. Convinced that its chief work was the conducting of seminaries and the building up of a spiritually strong clergy devoted to the Church, he sought whenever possible to prevent its engagement in other types of work. In 1631 Condren wished to resign as superior general, but the Oratory not only confirmed him in office but also made the position a life appointment. Condren tried twice to escape from the burden of his position, even attempting to hide, but Richelieu's threat to make him a cardinal and the command of his confessor forced him to continue in office until his death. Condren was the most effective interpreter of the teaching of his master Bérulle, yet his basic principle and emphasis were slightly different. At the heart of Condren's spirituality was a strong consciousness of the fact of creation and the nothingness of man the creature, who is wholly dependent on God. This led to a great devotion to the Word Incarnate, the supreme priest and perfect victim, who in a state of interior annihilation and total immolation offered to God the only sacrifice worthy of the Creator. Man's duty is to imitate this sacrifice by reflecting continually on his own nothingness and by giving himself wholly as a victim to the service of God. Priests above all must endeavor by continual prayer and self-surrender to unite themselves to the perfect victim, and they can best do this by complete obedience to their bishops. In this teaching lies the essential aim and spirit of the Oratory.

Condren was not a Jansenist, nor did he despise human nature, though his teaching is, in part at least, a reaction against the exaggerated humanism of his time. He was moderate in action and speech, and by his sweetness of manner and simplicity of life, in which nothing extraordinary was apparent, he concealed the austerity of his doctrine. St. Vincent de Paul esteemed him highly, and St. Jane Francis de Chantal said that God had given him to the Church to teach not men but angels.

Condren published nothing, but after his death his followers saw to the publication of 169 of his letters and some of his conferences: *Discours et lettres* (Paris 1643); *L'Idée du sacerdoce et du sacrifice de Jésus-Christ par P. Condren* (Paris 1677, ed. Quesnel); *Considérations sur les mystères de Jésus-Christ* (Paris 1899, ed. P. Bonnardet). The works of his most prominent disciples, including Jean Jacques Olier and St. John Eudes, were inspired by Condren and reflect his teachings.

Bibliography: A. MOLIEU, *Dictionnaire de spiritualité ascétique et mystique. Doctrine et histoire,* ed. M. VILLER et al. (Paris 1932–) 2:1373–88, with extensive bibliog. P. POURRAT, *Christian Spirituality,* tr. W. H. MITCHELL, v.3 (New York 1927; repr. 1953) 350–352, 371–377. H. BREMOND, *Histoire littéraire du sentiment réligieux en France depuis la fin des guerres de religion jusqu'à nos jours* (Paris 1911–36) 3:284–418. D. AMELOTE, *La vie du Père Charles de Condren* (Paris 1643).

[M. J. BARRY]

CONFERENCE FOR PASTORAL PLANNING AND COUNCIL DEVELOPMENT (CPPCD)

This organization is the result of a merger in 1989 to 1990 between members of the National Pastoral Planning Conference (NPPC) and the Parish and Diocesan Council Network (PADICON). At least since the 1960s, when some dioceses in the United States began opening pastoral planning offices, coordination and development of accurate research data on parish life in the local church was needed on a national scale. Under the sponsorship of the Diocese of Pittsburgh and the Center for Applied Research in the Apostolate (CARA), representatives of 17 dioceses met at Duquesne University on May 16 to 17, 1971, to address this concern. Those gathered issued a document, "Planning for Planning: Perspectives on Diocesan Research and Planning," which helped launch the idea for the collection of empirical data on trends in ecclesial life.

Meanwhile, in a seminar on Pastoral and Parish Councils at Catholic University, another group recognized the need for outreach to diocesan personnel who minister to parish councils. Participants took the name Diocesan Parish Council Personnel in 1974, then PADICON in 1983. Its first annual meeting took place the following year in conjunction with the NPPC. Beginning in 1984, the two groups met simultaneously. Formal discussions for joining the two groups began in 1986, though a vote among members to unite did not occur until 1989. The present CPPCD met for the first time from March 4 to 7, 1990 in Orlando, Florida. Arthur Deegan chaired and eventually became the first Executive Director of the CPPCD (1992–1997).

A coordinating committee functions as the governing board. There are several standing committees, including one for awards. The CPCCD administers the Yves Congar award for distinguished service to the Church by a member of the CPPCD and the *Lumen Gentium* award for an outstanding contribution by a group or person outside the ranks of the CPPCD. Past recipients have included Sharon Euart, RSM, The Leadership Conference of Women Religious, Bishop Kenneth Untener, and Monsignor Philip Murnion.

Since 1992, the CPCCD has published a quarterly newsletter, *Conference Call*. In 2001, the CPCCD was engaged in research on parish reorganization. It also participated in ecumenical research projects, including surveys on various types of faith communities together with an examination of international church life, particularly congregational vitality, in order to obtain a portrait of the American religious landscape. CPPCD is presently based in St. Louis, Mo.

Bibliography: National Pastoral Planning Conference. *Proceedings* (1974–); *Resource Bulletin* (1977–); *Conference Call* (1992–). *Building a Vibrant Parish Pastoral Council* (Mahwah, New Jersey 1995). Conference for Pastoral Planning and Council Development, *Laity, Parish & Ministry* (New York n.d.). There is archival material for the NPPC at Marquette University.

[P. J. HAYES]

CONFERENCE OF ROMAN CATHOLIC CATHEDRAL MUSICIANS

An association of professional musicians serving Roman Catholic cathedral churches in the U.S. and Canada. The inspiration and impetus for the Conference of Roman Catholic Cathedral Musicians (CRCCM) came from the initial collaboration of Peter LaManna, Gerald Muller, and Richard Proulx in the search process for a new director of music for the Basilica of the National Shrine of the Immaculate Conception in spring 1983. This led to the establishment of the CRCCM by 17 cathedral musicians who met at the Cathedral-Basilica of St. Peter and St. Paul in Philadelphia, Penn. in November 1984. In collaboration with other liturgical and musical organizations, the CRCCM provides professional support and resources for cathedral musicians in their quest for beauty and excellence in liturgical worship in Roman Catholic cathedrals.

[EDS.]

CONFESSION, AURICULAR

Like its Greek and Latin equivalent, EXOMOLOGESIS, confession has a variety of meanings, but ordinarily it signifies an avowal of sin, made either to God or to man. Etymologically exomologesis denotes open declaration and implies public confession. In the primitive Church it was employed for confession of offenses and for the sacramental procedure involving austere discipline. From the 8th century onward the term confession designated a disclosure of sins to the priest, but more especially the entire Sacrament of Penance. Confession is a manifestation of personal sins to the Church in the person of a duly authorized priest for the purpose of obtaining sacramental absolution by virtue of the power of the keys. There are two types: public, made before an assembly; and private or secret confession, made to the priest alone and called auricular since it is spoken.

Great difficulty is caused by varying terminology and practice during the lengthy time expanse under consideration. The word "penance" was used to designate both the entire sacramental procedure and the satisfaction

An elderly woman confesses after Orthodox religious procession on Easter Sunday night, Kiev, Ukraine. (AP/Wide World Photos)

performed by the penitent. Three steps in sacramental PENANCE have to be kept clearly distinct: confession, satisfaction, and reconciliation. Though confession was a necessary presupposition to reception of the Church's sacramental Penance, it is not always certain what sort of confession was required. At one time and place it could have been that acknowledgement by a person of his sin expressed by the mere fact that he took his place among the ranks of public penitents; it might also have been a verbal but generic admission of sinfulness similar to our Confiteor (a possible interpretation of the Didache 14.1; J. Quasten, ed., *Monumenta eucharista et liturgica vetusissima*, 13). Some documents suppose or clearly call for a detailed confession of grievous sins. But to repeat, documents of the patristic period are difficult to interpret on this score, and unanimous agreement has not been reached among scholars.

Public Confession. The view that the administration of sacramental Penance in the first six centuries was nor-

mally public in the West enjoys wide acceptance. Some kind of confession is today almost unanimously admitted to have been coextensive with and part of this discipline. Whether confession was secret or public still divides historians. Some hold that up to the end of the 4th century public confession of even secret sins was generally required, and in evidence thereof they cite the *Didascalia*, the *Apostolic Constitutions*, Irenaeus, Tertullian, Cyprian, Origen, Ambrose, and others. But this testimony is inconclusive, since it can be interpreted as imposing public satisfaction or as merely counseling public confession. Perhaps Irenaeus (*Adv. Haer.* 1.6.3; *Patrologia Graeca,* ed. J. P. Migne, 7:507) and Origen (*In ps. 37 homil.* 2.6; *Patrologia Graeca* 12:1386) envisioned an obligatory public confession.

Secret Confession. That secret confession was the more general practice in the early Church is the more common view of scholars. B. Poschmann regards favorably E. Vacandard's opinion that the only publicity required was in the acts of satisfaction, not in the confession. In this connection two episodes are relevant. According to the historian Sozomen (*Hist. Eccl.* 7.16; *Patrologia Graeca* 67:1459) the office of priest-penitentiary was instituted in the East to restrict public confession of sins, since it was burdensome to announce one's sins "as in a theatre with the congregation of the Church as witness." The duration of the practice of public confession is uncertain because of the wide difference of opinion as to the time when the priest-penitentiary was introduced. O. Watkins is convinced that this does not tell in favor of public confession, since Sozomen cited Chrysostom's words and confused the meaning of exomologesis. In a letter written in 459 to some Italian bishops, Leo the Great, while sternly condemning the abuse of compelling penitents to read publicly a detailed catalogue of personal sins, admits that a voluntary public confession might be laudable in some cases, but that it must not be demanded, since secret confession to priests alone is sufficient (*Epist.* 168.2; *Patrologia Latina* ed. J. P. Migne, 54:1210). This decree, although variously interpreted, is evidence of public confession practiced in some churches.

In the new mode of penance introduced in the 6th century by the Celtic monks, the characteristic elements are private: a secret confession to the priest, the acceptance of satisfaction, and reconciliation without defamatory or juridical consequences. In contrast to the ancient system, the Celtic mode gave greater prominence to confession which, owing to the influence of Alcuin and his successors, eventually became its most significant feature.

Bibliography: B. POSCHMANN, *Penance and the Anointing of the Sick*, tr. and rev. F. COURTNEY (New York 1964). O. D. WATKINS, *A History of Penance*, 2 v. (New York 1920). E. F. LATKO, "Trent and Auricular Confession," *Franciscan Studies* (St. Bonaventure, N.Y. 1940–) 14 (1954) 3–33. P. F. PALMER, *Sacraments of Healing and of Vocation* (Englewood Cliffs, N.J. 1963); ed., *Sacraments and Forgiveness,* v.2 of *Sources of Christian Theology,* 2 v. (Westminster, Md. 1955–60). J. T. MCNEILL and H. M. GAMER, trs., *Medieval Handbooks of Penance* (New York 1938). E. VACANDARD, *Dictionnaire de théologie catholique,* ed. A. VACANT et al., 15 v. (Paris 1903–50) 3.1:838–894. P. GALTIER, *Dictionnaire apologétique de la foi catholique,* ed. A. PALÈS 4 v. (Paris 1911–22) 3:1784–1865; *Aux origines du sacrement de pénitence* (Rome 1951). K. RAHNER, *Lexikon für Theologie und Kirche,* ed. J. HOFER and K. RAHNER, 10 v. (2d, new ed. Freiburg 1957–65) 2:805–815. J. A. JUNGMANN, *ibid.* 2:823–826.

[E. F. LATKO/EDS.]

CONFESSIONS OF FAITH

PART I: NEW TESTAMENT TO MIDDLE AGES

In the language of the New Testament the word confession signifies the open acknowledgement of FAITH in Christ and of SALVATION through Him (cf. 1 Tm 6.13; 2 Cor 9.13). Thus it soon came to mean public WITNESS to the faith even at the risk of martyrdom.

Occasionally the word is used for the ancient ecumenical CREEDS and for the formal PROFESSIONS of faith drawn up by the Church, for example, that prescribed for Berengarius of Tours in 1079. But it is more generally used for the Protestant professions of faith of the 16th and 17th centuries. In trying to reestablish religious unity, Emperor Charles V asked the various groups to draw up official statements of doctrine. These were known as "confessions of faith." That of the Lutherans at Augsburg in 1530 was the first. This is the famous AUGSBURG CONFESSION. These confessions enjoy official status, and members are often asked to subscribe to them in order to hold official position. However, they are viewed less rigidly today than formerly, and frequently are not the ultimate norms for acceptance or rejection of members.

From this meaning of confession is derived the use of the term for the religious body or church holding to it. This designation was originally political, for the civil authorities simply referred to each religious body as a confession—whether Lutheran, Calvinist, or Zwinglian.

[W. F. DEWAN/EDS.]

PART II: PROTESTANT CONFESSIONS OF FAITH

The doctrinal declarations and symbols of the several Protestant communions. Beginning in the era of the Reformation, such confessions have been set forth both in response to doctrinal controversy within and between various churches and in justification of separations or reunions. Many confessions adopted for specific needs have been forgotten; others have become dead letters; still others continue to be decisive factors in the theological and organizational life of their communions. In German the term *Konfession* has become the usual designation for a denomination or communion; the comparative study of the various denominations, with special attention to their doctrinal declarations, is called *Konfessionskunde,* in English usually Symbolics or Comparative Symbolics. This article surveys the Lutheran confessions of the Reformation period, the confessions of the Reformed churches, the Anglican confessions, the confessions of the radical Reformation, the confessions of Continental Protestantism since the Reformation, and the confessions that have arisen within American Protestantism. It concludes with a discussion of the role of confessions in the churches and of their relation to ecumenical (or interconfessional) theological movements. The bibliography includes the standard editions and translations of the confessions, as well as the historical and theological introductions to them.

Lutheran Confessions (Reformation Period). Martin Luther and his followers explained and defended the cause of their Reformation in thousands of personal treatises and books, but they also presented the case for their movement in several official statements of doctrine. Significantly, most of these were occasioned by challenges to the Reformation that were political as well as religious in character; both the addressees and the signatories of several of the Lutheran confessions were secular rulers.

Luther's Catechisms. The beginnings of the Lutheran confessions are to be found in the work of Luther himself. Three of the documents included in the Book of CONCORD are directly by him. Of these, the most influential and important was certainly his Small Catechism of 1529. During the autumn of 1528 Luther had carried out a visitation in Saxony of parishes that adhered to the Reformation, and had been shocked at the religious illiteracy of the lay people, who "do not know the Our Father, the Creed, or the Ten Commandments." To correct this condition, he composed two catechisms, the Small Catechism for the instruction of the laity and the Large Catechism principally for the clergy. Each consisted of an explanation of the Decalogue, an exposition of the Apostles' Creed, a petition-by-petition commentary on the Lord's Prayer, and a presentation of the meaning of Baptism, Penance, and the Eucharist. Both were written in German and were later translated into Latin, eventually into many other languages as well. They have the status of confessions of faith because they, more fully and precisely than any of the other Lutheran confessions, set forth what is the *publica doctrina* that has been preached in Lutheran pulpits and taught to Lutheran catechumens.

Schmalkaldic Articles. The third of the confessions from Luther's own hand is the set of articles prepared by him in anticipation of the general council convoked by Pope Paul III to meet in Mantua in May 1537. Although the council did not meet until 1545, and in Trent, Luther's articles were taken by his prince, the Elector of Saxony, to a meeting of the SCHMALKALDIC League early in 1537. The League did not adopt them, but they have acquired the title Schmalkaldic Articles because many of those in attendance did sign them. The Schmalkaldic Articles are perhaps the most vigorously polemical of the Lutheran confessions, summarizing with sharpness and force the attack upon the teachings and the practices of Roman Catholicism.

Augsburg Confession. Although Luther was not the author of the AUGSBURG CONFESSION in the same sense as he was of the three confessions just enumerated, the basis of that confession lies in several documents in preparation of which he had a part. In 1528 he had written a lengthy treatise defending the real presence of the Body and Blood of Christ in the Eucharist against Huldrych ZWINGLI and others, to which he appended a confession of faith. This served as a model for the so-called Schwabach Articles of 1529, which dealt with the doctrinal disputes; a second set of articles, dealing with disputes over church practice and adopted at Torgau in March 1530, are called the Torgau Articles. From these several sources Luther's colleague Philipp MELANCHTHON composed the confession that was presented by seven German princes and the representatives of two free cities at the Diet of Augsburg on June 25, 1530, before the Holy Roman Emperor, CHARLES V. The Augsburg Confession strove to put the dispute between Rome and the Reformation into the context of the dogmatic consensus of the ancient Church. Its language and tone are moderate and traditionally Catholic. But its clear intent was to demonstrate that the Reformers stand in continuity with that consensus and that their opponents did not. Demonstration of this thesis was likewise the theme of the Apology of the Augsburg Confession, which Melanchthon composed as an answer to the Confutation of the Augsburg Confession. The Apology, published in the spring of 1531, gives special attention to the doctrine of justification, with lengthy articles also on original sin, the Church, the Mass, and other controverted issues. The Augsburg Confession is the basic confession of Lutheranism; in several countries Lutherans are even specifically designated as "Evangelicals of the Augsburg Confession."

Formula and Book of Concord. During the decades that followed, and especially during the 30 years after Luther's death (1546), the theologians of the Augsburg Confession were involved in a series of controversies among themselves; in addition, the rise of new varieties of Protestantism, especially of CALVINISM, as well as the work of the Council of TRENT, necessitated a further clarification of the Lutheran position. This was accomplished in the Formula of Concord of 1577. During the preceding five years a number of statements of doctrine had been drawn up in an effort to resolve the controversies. James Andreae (1528–90) compiled the Epitome of the Formula of Concord from these statements, including his own proposals. Although Andreae was thus technically the author of the Formula, its principal architect was Martin CHEMNITZ. The Formula of Concord, especially in its second part, the Solid Declaration, is of all the Lutheran confessions the most learned theologically and the most precise. On each of the disputed doctrines it seeks first to clarify the *status controversiae,* goes on to define the central terms, and adjudicates the dispute. The Epitome and the Solid Declaration made the rounds of the Lutheran states of Germany, gaining the signatures of more than 8,000 clergy, theologians, and teachers. On the 50th anniversary of the presentation of the Augsburg Confession, June 25, 1580, the Book of Concord, containing all the confessions enumerated above plus the three "ecumenical creeds" (the Apostles', Nicene, and Athanasian), was published. Although Lutherans have continued to write doctrinal declarations (see below), the Book of Concord is still their only confessional norm.

Confessions of the Reformed Churches. By the very nature of the movement, the confessions of faith drawn up by the churches calling themselves "Reformed in accordance with the Word of God" have had a more international and less homogeneous history, and no individual Reformed confession has been accorded the universal acceptance granted by Lutherans to the Augsburg Confession and to Luther's Catechisms. Thus the collection of Reformed confessions by Böckel contains 32 statements of faith; the collection by Niemeyer contains fewer, but includes some that are not in Böckel. Perhaps the most helpful procedure is, with Böckel, to arrange the Reformed confessions according to the nations where they arose.

Switzerland. The earliest Reformed confessions were written in Switzerland. Zwingli himself prepared several confessional statements, notably his *Expositio Christianae fidei,* written shortly before his death. But the most widely accepted of the confessions of Swiss Protestantism were the First Helvetic Confession of 1536 and the Second Helvetic Confession of 1566. The First spoke as the united voice of all the Reformed cantons of Switzerland and was drafted and published in Basel. The Second, which Philip Schaff called "the most elaborate and most catholic among the Swiss confessions," is a careful and detailed summary, written by Heinrich BULLINGER, of Reformed theology as it had been reshaped through the work of John CALVIN. More than a century later, in 1675, the Helvetic Consensus Formula articulated in confessional form the characteristic teachings of orthodox Calvinism as these had been promulgated by the Synod of Dort (see below). Of the Swiss confessions, the Second Helvetic has probably enjoyed the most nearly universal acceptance both in Europe and in Great Britain.

Germany. Far more universal than any of the Swiss confessions, however, was the German contribution to the Reformed standards, the HEIDELBERG CATECHISM of 1563. It has been translated into most of the languages of Europe, as well as into Hebrew, Arabic, and Persian. It was the result of a literary collaboration between Zacharias URSINUS and Caspar Olevianus (1536–85). The Heidelberg Catechism omits such Calvinistic doctrines as double predestination and limited atonement, concentrating instead on the central tenets of evangelical faith, or, as the very first question puts it, the "only comfort in life

and in death." Its exposition of the Apostles' Creed forms its central and chief part; this is preceded by questions and answers dealing with sin, and is followed by an explanation of the Decalogue and of the Our Father. Although it was intended for the instruction of the young and has been used for this purpose throughout the Reformed tradition, its careful use of language and its comprehensive, largely irenic tone have made it useful as a public confession of faith.

France and the Low Countries. Whether or not it was, as some traditions claim, actually written by Calvin, the Gallican Confession of 1559 does present, more accurately perhaps than any other confession, the distinctive doctrines of the Genevan Reformer. Scholars have pointed to its Christocentricity and its orderly balance as its most striking characteristics. Because it was used there as a statement of the faith of French Reformed Protestantism, it is called also the Confession of La Rochelle of 1571. Also written in French was the Belgic Confession of 1561, whose chief author was Guido de Brès. In 1562 it was presented to Philip II as a defense of the Reformed churches in the Low Countries. These churches still subscribe to it, together with the Heidelberg Catechism, as their confessional standard. It shows traces of earlier Reformed confessions and was in fact partly based on the Gallican Confession. The Low Countries were also the locale for the international conclave of Reformed theologians and churchmen that codified predestinarian Calvinism, the Synod of Dort, which lasted from Nov. 13, 1618, to May 9, 1619. The synod was provoked by ARMINIANISM, which had attacked the doctrines of predestination and reprobation in the form in which they were being taught by orthodox Calvinists. Against the Arminians the decrees of the Synod of Dort, with great care and learning, affirmed the doctrines of predestination, limited atonement, total depravity, irresistible grace, and the perseverance of the saints.

British Isles. For Reformed Christians in the English-speaking world, the most important confession is the WESTMINSTER CONFESSION of Faith of 1646. Instead of the revision of the Anglican THIRTY-NINE ARTICLES, for which it had been appointed, the Westminster Assembly, which met from 1643 to 1653, was ordered by Parliament to draw up "a Confession of Faith for the three Kingdoms, according to the Solemn League and Covenant." Its 33 articles combine the Calvinist emphases of Dort with the covenantal theology of the PURITANS. The Presbyterians of Scotland adopted it in 1647, and the English Parliament approved it a year later. Thus it established itself as the chief confessional statement of Scotch PRESBYTERIANISM, replacing the Scots Confession of 1560; in America ch. 23, "Of the Civil Magistrate," and ch. 31, "Of Synods and Councils," have been revised.

Eastern Europe. Other Reformed confessions that should be mentioned are those of the Reformed churches in Eastern Europe. These include the Czech Confession of 1535, to which Luther wrote a preface, and the Czech Confession of 1575. The Reformed Church of Hungary, which had to clarify its position not only in relation to Roman Catholicism and to other forms of Protestantism but also in contrast with Anti-Trinitarianism, published the Confession of Czenger in 1557. And in Poland the effort to achieve reunion of the churches brought about the Consensus of Sandomierz of 1570, which represented a temporary agreement between the Reformed Church, the Lutheran Church, and the Unity of BOHEMIAN BRETHREN.

Anglican Confessions. As already noted, it was in England that the Westminster Confession, now the hallmark of Scotch Presbyterianism, was prepared. But the Church of England had, by 1646, developed its own standards of correct teaching and worship.

Early Articles. These began with various sets of articles prepared under Henry VIII, of which the Ten Articles of 1536 were the first. The most important for the future were the Thirteen Articles of 1538, which were drafted as a statement of agreement between a group of Anglican and a group of Lutheran theologians; they are adapted from the Augsburg Confession. Under Edward VI a new and longer statement of faith, the Forty-Two Articles, was drawn up, principally by Thomas CRANMER; these, too, manifest a dependence on the Augsburg Confession. They were completed in 1552 and published in 1553, but they do not seem to have been officially adopted by Convocation. In 1553, with the accession of Queen Mary, England became officially Roman Catholic again, until 1558. Thus the Forty-Two Articles could not be sanctioned or applied, and by the time ANGLICANISM was restored some of the antitheses of the Forty-Two Articles were no longer relevant and a revised confession of faith became necessary.

Thirty-Nine Articles. That revised confession of faith came in the Thirty-Nine Articles. The first version of these was presented to Convocation by Matthew PARKER, the Archbishop of Canterbury, who was largely responsible for their composition, at the behest of ELIZABETH I. They were written in Latin. Essentially, they were an adaptation and abbreviation of the Forty-Two Articles. The bishops and Convocation adopted them in 1563, but with the insertion of a statement affirming the right of the Church to legislate on her own rites and with the omission of an article denying that the unworthy communicant receives the true Body and Blood of Christ (the so-called *manducatio indignorum*). Later the Thirty-Nine Articles were translated into English, the controversial article restored, and the final form of the Articles was adopted in

1571. In their theological content the Thirty-Nine Articles display what an Anglican writer has called "masterful ambiguity," with the result that various positions across the spectrum of Anglican thought have been able to claim support from them. But it would be a mistake—and a mistake sometimes committed by Continental theologians—to use the Thirty-Nine Articles as the key to the understanding of the Anglican communion. Two other creations of the English Reformation, the Authorized Version of the Bible and, above all, the Book of COMMON PRAYER, perform that function as precisely for Anglicanism as the Augsburg Confession and Luther's catechisms do for Lutheranism. An indication of the problematic role actually played by the Thirty-Nine Articles is the designation of Anglicanism as "Reformed" in the textbooks of German writers in comparative symbolics.

Confessions of the Radical Reformation. Perhaps even less concerned than Anglicanism about confessions of faith, though for quite opposite reasons, was the left wing of the Reformation. For while most of the "magisterial Reformers," whether Lutheran, Reformed, or Anglican, sought to establish their legitimacy by appealing to the Catholic tradition, it was characteristic of the radical Reformers that they quite self-consciously broke with that tradition, denounced it as apostate, and saw themselves as the restorers of a Christianity that had been lost for a long time, perhaps since apostolic days.

Racovian Catechism. The most radical of the confessions of faith to come from the left wing was probably the Racovian Catechism of 1574, which asserts what one writer has called "the communitarian, immersionist, anti-Nicene Anabaptism in the most radical center" of the Reformation sectarians. Its full title is: "Catechism and confession of faith of the congregation gathered throughout Poland, in the name of Jesus Christ, our crucified and risen Lord." Rigidly Biblical in its conception of authority, it asserts an adoptionistic view of the person of Christ and rejects the doctrine of the Trinity as inconsistent with Sacred Scripture. The threefold office of Christ as prophet, priest, and king determines the basic outline of the Racovian Catechism. Its author was George Schomann, who drew upon suggestions of Faustus Socinus (*see* SOCINIANISM). The most distinctive feature of the Racovian Catechism is its break with the fundamental dogmatic presupposition of virtually all previous Christian confessions of faith, viz, the orthodox doctrine of the Trinity.

Other Confessions. Although they were not so radical in their break with the Trinitarian dogma, the other confessional documents of the left wing of the Reformation were no less vigorous in asserting that the development of the doctrine and practice of the Church was a betrayal of apostolic faith. In 1527 the Swiss ANABAPTISTS, meeting at Schleitheim, adopted a confession, whose author was Michael Sattler. The chief concern of this brief statement of faith was the doctrine of the Church as a gathered community of true and committed believers. In its defense of this doctrine, the confession sets forth its views on seven issues: Baptism, excommunication, the breaking of the bread, separation from the abominations, pastors in the Church, the use of the sword, and oaths. A more comprehensive confession of the faith held by Anabaptists was adopted more than a century later at Dort in 1632. Reviewing in sequence the central affirmations of Christian belief about God, man, Christ, the Church, and the Sacraments, it asserts in largely Biblical language the characteristic Mennonite emphases upon faith as commitment, upon the imitation of Christ in His life and death as the mark of the true Christian, and upon the community of love and faith. It is still regarded by MENNONITES as the most nearly adequate summary of the doctrine taught in their churches.

Confessions of Continental Protestantism since the Reformation. Most of the Protestant communions whose doctrinal declarations have been reviewed thus far went on producing confessions of faith even after the Reformation. Among the Lutherans, for example, the Wittenberg theologian Abraham CALOV composed a new confession in 1655, the "Reiteration of the Consensus of the Lutheran Faith," which attempted to formulate the position of Lutheranism in antithesis to new teachings of the 17th century. The Declaration adopted at the Colloquy of Thorn in 1645 has been accepted in some Reformed churches as a new Reformed confession. In most Protestant communions the new doctrinal and moral challenges of a new day have seemed to demand a new confessional statement; but when the challenge had been met or had passed, the confession had outlived its usefulness and could be forgotten. For present purposes in this survey, therefore, the most significant of the post-Reformation confessions are the recent ones, for they embody the witness of the Protestant churches in response to modern issues and are still a living force in the teaching and practice of these churches.

Confessional Basis of the Prussian Union. When, for example, the King of Prussia, Frederick William III, sought to unite the Reformed and the Lutheran churches and to provide them with a common confession and a common agenda, the confessional basis of the Prussian Union was taken to be, not a new confessional document, but the consensus of the historic Reformation confessions. The theological mentor of the Union, Friedrich SCHLEIERMACHER, felt able to declare in the preface to his dogmatics of 1821, *The Christian Faith,* that there was "no wall of separation between the two ecclesiastical communions" and that therefore he could compose a systematic theology "in accordance with the fundamental principles of the evangelical church," using the word "church" in the singular to denote the common ground between the Reformed and the Lutheran confessions. Such declarations of an interconfessional concord themselves assume confessional status, especially when they are opposed by the strict constructionists in the confessional tradition, in this case almost exclusively the Lutherans.

Barmen Declaration of May 1934. But the most historic of modern confessions in European Protestantism came in the 20th century, in the Barmen Declaration of May 1934. Under pressure from National Socialism and with an awareness of the temptation, represented by the "German Christians," to accommodate the Christian witness to the neopaganism of the Third Reich, spokesmen of Reformed and Lutheran churches met at Barmen to affirm the independence of the Christian message from the ideologies of the state and to declare its distinctive content, "Jesus Christ, as He is testified to us in Holy Scripture . . . the one Word of God, whom we are to hear." The theology of Barmen was that of Karl Barth, and in the years during and after World War II the Barmen Declaration came to have a confessional status in several German churches.

American Confessions. Among the Protestant denominations of America, confessions of faith have frequently been revisions or adaptations of earlier British or Continental standards; other confessions have been produced in the course of discussions about the merger of denominations, or in justification for withdrawal or separation from merger. Characteristically, many American confessions have concentrated on questions of polity rather than of dogma. Thus the Cambridge Platform, adopted by representatives of the four Puritan colonies in New England in 1648, confined itself to the issues of polity, the nature of the gathered congregation, the authority of the clergy, and related matters. As a statement of its teaching on other matters, the synod declared its acceptance of the recently formulated Westminster Confession. The Westminster Confession likewise satisfied the dogmatic requirements of the synod held at Saybrook, Connecticut, in 1708; the "Saybrook Articles" could thus deal with questions of church government and, when combined with the Confession, became the Saybrook Platform, published in 1710. Among Methodists, the question of a confessional standard has been less clear (*see* METHODISM). As early as 1763 John WESLEY's *Notes on the New Testament* and his four volumes of sermons had played a quasi-confessional role, but behind these standards lay Anglican statements of faith, especially the Homilies and the Thirty-Nine Articles, which Wesley revised into the Twenty-Five Articles of Religion, adopted by American Methodists in 1784. Baptists, too, adapted earlier formulations to their purposes; the Philadelphia Confession of 1688, first published in London in 1677, was a revised version of the Westminster Confession. Perhaps the most widely accepted doctrinal declaration among American Baptists was the New Hampshire Confession of 1833, which was written by John Newton Brown; the Confession is a brief summary of the chief articles of faith.

Ecumenical (Interconfessional) Movements. Efforts at reunion among Protestant denominations during the 19th and 20th centuries were responsible for several confessions of faith. In 1903 the Westminster Confession was revised by the [Northern] Presbyterian body by a modification of its teachings on predestination and related issues. This made it possible for Presbyterian reunion to proceed, in several stages, toward the creation of a single body and the adoption of a single confession. In 1925 the United Church of Canada brought together Presbyterians, Congregationalists, and Methodists; its Basis of Union served as the confessional consensus of the new body. In addition to the analogous statements drawn up by the other mergers of the 20th century, some mention should be made of the ''messages to the churches'' and other statements of a confessional nature that have come from meetings of the WORLD COUNCIL OF CHURCHES and its predecessors, especially of the confession on ''the Church's unity'' adopted at New Delhi in 1961 and of the doctrinal clauses in the constitution of the World Council, a ''fellowship of churches which accept our Lord Jesus Christ as God and Savior.''

Significance of the Confessions. Even from this brief survey, it should be evident that confessions of faith have played and continue to play a prominent part in the life and teaching of the Protestant communions, but that this role has varied greatly from one body to another as well as from one century to another. Most Protestants share the hostility of the Reformers to the formal authority of tradition, even when they accept much of its content. As they oppose the claims of the Greek and Latin Churches, so they are obliged to qualify any claims of normativeness for their own confessions. Thus even confessional Lutherans, who are probably the most confessionally oriented among Protestants, describe their confessions *as norma normata,* in distinction from Sacred Scripture, which is *norma normans.* As the history of Protestant theology makes clear, moreover, individual theologians have frequently defied or ignored the authority of their confessions, sometimes with impunity and sometimes at the price of expulsion from their denomination. Despite the cases that can be cited from ecclesiastical history of lay support for the confessional principle,

it is by no means obvious just what the confessions of faith have meant to the general body of Protestant laity. But it is clear that confessions have served as a decisive mark of differentiation between Protestant churches or from Roman Catholicism, and therefore as a barrier to the reunion of Christendom.

Yet such an interpretation of the function of confessions is an oversimplification, for during the 19th and 20th centuries the confessions of various Protestant communions have sometimes served to remind them of Christians from whom they are separated. In one way or another, virtually every confession affirms that the Church is one as Christ is one, even though it may go on to justify schism. That affirmation of unity carries with it the admission that there are Christians outside the boundaries of one's own ecclesiastical organization. By their declarations of loyalty to the early centuries of the Church and to the ancient creeds, the confessions also connect the faith of the Church to its past—and thus, inevitably, to others who declare the same loyalty. The very polemics of the Reformation confessions may also serve the cause of Christian reunion. Every confessional antithesis, whether of Augsburg or Westminster or, for that matter, Trent, was called forth by a teaching that, however heretical it may have been, was a critique of something amiss in the life of the Church. A historical recognition of this situation and of the meaning of the confessions in the light of it enables one simultaneously to ''confess'' (in the sense of making a confession of individual and corporate sins) and to ''confess'' (in the sense of pledging one's allegiance to Christ).

Bibliography: The standard coll. of confessions, outdated but indispensable, is P. SCHAFF, *Bibliotheca symbolica ecclesiae universalis: The Creeds of Christendom,* 3 v. (6th ed. New York 1919), the creeds of the Protestant communions are in v.3; their history is included in v.1. The Lutheran confessions in the original Latin and German appear in the many eds. of the Book of Concord, the most recent and textually most authoritative being *Die Bekenntnisschriften der evangelisch-lutherischen Kirche* (4th ed. Göttingen 1959–). The standard English translation is that of T. G. TAPPERT, ed. and tr., *The Book of Concord: The Confessions of the Evangelical Lutheran Church* (Philadelphia 1959). Reformed collections. H. A. NIEMEYER, *Collectio confessionum in ecclesiis reformatis publicatarum* (Leipzig 1840). E. G. A. BÖCKEL, ed., *Die Bekenntnisschriften der evangelisch-reformirten Kirche* (Leipzig 1847). E. F. K. MÜLLER, ed., *Die Bekenntnisse der reformierten Kirche* (Leipzig 1903). Brief but convenient collections. B. A. GERRISH, ed., *The Faith of Christendom* (pa. New York 1963). J. H. LEITH, ed., *Creeds of the Churches* (pa. Garden City, NY 1963). C. FABRICIUS, ed., *Corpus Confessionum: Die Bekenntnisse der Christenheit* (Berlin 1928–).

[J. PELIKAN/EDS.]

CONFESSOR

A term stemming from the Latin verb *confiteri* (to declare openly); it came to be applied to all male saints who were not martyrs, but who, by their Christian lives, had publicly proclaimed their faith. This precise signification of the word confessor only gradually developed in the Church.

In the New Testament the Church taught the necessity of confessing one's faith by living it (1 Jn 2.14), and particularly of confessing it in the face of opposition (1 Jn 2.22–25). Peter and Stephen set the example by facing suffering and death to proclaim their belief (Acts 4.20; 7.56). Denying Christ risked denial by Christ before the Father (Mt 10.32).

First and Second Centuries. In the First century of the Church there seems to have been no fine distinction between the terms confessor and martyr. A Christian who suffered imprisonment, torture, exile, or hard labor in the mines, yet had not given his life for Christ, was called a martyr just as if he had shed his blood for his faith. Eusebius of Caesarea, in several places, attests that the term martyr was applied to the living. According to Eusebius, Hegesippus stated that the descendants of St. Jude, dragged before Domitian and dismissed as harmless after the emperor's interrogation, were venerated as martyrs (*Ecclesiastical History.* 3.20). Themison and Alexander, two acolytes strongly suspected of MONTANISM, called themselves martyrs (*Ecclesiastical History* 5.18). Eusebius pointed out that some heretics coveted the title of martyr to obtain gifts and money (*Ecclesiastical History* 5.18).

In the second half of the second century, Christians began to make a distinction between those who died for the faith and those who simply suffered. According to the letter from the churches of Vienne and Lyons, the martyrs of Lyons, while still alive, begged their co-religionists not to give them the title of martyr. This, they said, should be reserved only for those who had proclaimed Christ by their deaths. They themselves were only lowly and humble confessors (*Ecclesiastical History* 5.2).

Tertullian stated that no one still subjected to the temptations of this world had the right to call himself a martyr (*De pudicitia* 22.3). Origen taught that only those who had proved their faith by pouring forth their blood could properly be called martyrs (*Comment. in Joh.* 2.34). Nevertheless, this distinction in terminology was not religiously observed. Martyr and confessor continued to be used indiscriminately. Tertullian addressed his book *Ad martyres* (197) to confessors whom he called candidates for martyrdom (*benedicti martyres designati*). He frequently used the term martyr in the sense of confessor. Origen himself admitted that the word martyr could be applied to all who in any way witnessed to the truth (*Comment. in Joh.* 2.34).

In the *Passio SS. Perpetuae et Felicitatis* (ch. 2), Quintus, who died in prison, was called a martyr. St. Cyprian wished those who died in prison, even if not tortured, to enjoy the same honors as martyrs. Nevertheless, he calls those who languish in prison confessors. According to Cyprian, there are two grades of confessors: those who publicly proclaim Christ before a pagan judge, and those who privately confess him by fleeing to the desert to escape offering pagan sacrifices (*De lapsis 3*).

Third Century and Later. From the middle of the third century, the distinction between martyr and confessor became more common. Eusebius tells of a certain Seleucus, who first was a confessor, then a martyr (*De mart. Palest.* 2.20). Optatus of Milevis records a persecution that made martyrs of some people, confessors of others (*De schism.* Donat. 1.13). By the third century, then, although there was still some confusion of terminology, the word confessor gradually became associated with one who, although suffering for the faith, had not given his life for it.

After the termination of the Roman persecutions, Christian writers used the term confessor in a metaphorical sense, applying it to Christians who proclaimed their faith by their spiritual lives. Still living in the era of the martyrs, CLEMENT OF ALEXANDRIA (*c.* 150–215) in *Stromata* (4.15.3) spoke of the Christian who testifies to Christ with a kind of spiritual martyrdom consisting of a pure life spent in observing the Commandments. Therefore, hermits and monks, who spent their lives in penance and prayer, took on the proportions of confessors of Christ.

In the Eastern Church, the first Christians to receive public veneration as confessors outside the times of persecution were Anthony (d. 356), Hilarion (d. 371), and Athanasius (d. 373). In the West the first publicly venerated confessors were bishops of the fourth century: Sylvester at Rome (d. 335), Martin in Gaul (d. 397); then, Severus at Naples (d. *c.* 409), Augustine in Africa (d. 430), and Apollinaris at Ravenna (fifth century). These confessors had often suffered persecution in the defense of orthodoxy. The anniversaries of their deaths were kept, and their bodies were buried beneath altars. In his *De gloria confessorum* Gregory of Tours (538–594) described bishops, abbots, monks, virgins, and holy women as confessors.

Though it was once thought that the term confessor was also to be identified with a medieval *cantor* chanting God's praise in the Divine Office, Bernard Botte has disproved it.

Bibliography: H. LECLERCQ, *Dictionnaire d'archéologie chrétienne et de liturgie,* ed. F. CABROL, H. LECLERCQ and H. I. MARROU (Paris 1907–53) 3.2:2508–15. F. M. CAPPELLO, *Enciclopedia*

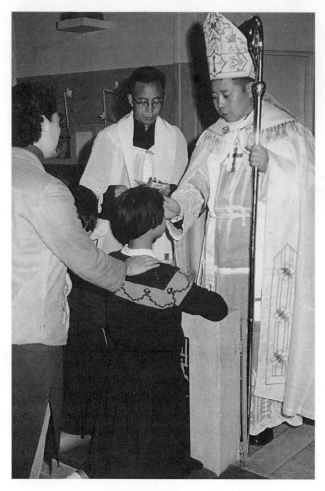

Bishop anointing a confirmand, Taipei, Taiwan.

Italiana de scienzi, littere ed arti (Rome 1929–39) 11:119. B. BOTTE, *Archivum latinitatis medii aevi* 16 (1941) 137–148. W. DÜRIG, *Lexikon für Theologie und Kirche*, ed. J. HOFER and K. RAHNER (Freiberg 1957–65) 2:142. F. L. CROSS, *The Oxford Dictionary of the Christian Church* (London 1957) 327.

[E. DAY]

CONFIRMATION

One of the three sacraments of Christian initiation. In the Christian East, the sacrament is called "chrismation." Through this sacrament, Christians "are more perfectly bound to the Church and are enriched with a special strength of the Holy Spirit" (LG 11). The *Rite of Christian Initiation of Adults* explains the significance of confirmation in its relationship to baptism. "The conjunction of the two celebrations signifies the unity of the paschal mystery, the close link between the mission of the Son and the outpouring of the Holy Spirit, and the connection between the two sacraments through which the Son and the Holy Spirit come with the Father to those who are baptized" (215).

Confirmation is conferred at different occasions, depending on the circumstances. In all the Eastern churches, the presbyter who baptizes, also chrismates (confirms) in the same ceremony, whether the one being baptized is an infant or an adult. In the Latin church, confirmation follows baptism immediately only for adults and children of catechetical age, and in the extraordinary circumstance of an unbaptized infant in danger of death. Ordinarily, the confirmation of those baptized as infants is deferred to increase the preparedness of the child and accessibility of the bishop. If a baptized but unconfirmed Catholic is in danger of dying, a presbyter may confirm. When those baptized in another Christian community are received into the full communion of the Catholic Church, they receive Confirmation as well (unless they have already received a valid Confirmation; for example, in one of the Orthodox Churches).

Origins of the terms "confirm" and "Confirmation." The term "confirm" first came into usage in the fifth-century Gallic councils of Riez (CChr.SL 148:67–68), Orange (CChr.SL 148:78), and Arles III (CChr.SL 148:133). It pertained to a ritual performed by a bishop when another minister had baptized on a separate occasion. In practice, the bishop had been the primary minister of an elaborate rite of initiation. But when another minister baptized due to danger of the candidate's death or distance from the cathedral, the bishop would "confirm" the Baptism. If candidates formerly adhered to a heresy with inauthentic initiation, the bishop would "confirm" them, reconciling them with orthodox Christianity. The term originated as a juridical concern in documents written by bishops concerning the ministry of bishops.

An early homily expressed the difference between Baptism and Confirmation. Inserted into a seventh-century collection attributed to a pseudonymous "Eusebius Gallicanus" and thought by some to come from Faustus of Riez (*c.* 490), the work presumes a developed complex of prayer for the Holy Spirit, hand-laying, and anointing (CChr.SL 101:337–338). The combination of these elements makes a sixth-century date more plausible. This homily is the earliest elaborate explanation uniting "Confirmation" with "the descent of the Holy Spirit." By this time, the term "Confirmation" had backed into the baptismal ceremony to identify the anointing within that ritual that bishops were now frequently performing outside of Baptism.

A confirmation is celebrated outside a Roman Catholic church in Lucca, Italy. (©Richard Bickel/CORBIS)

Historical Developments

New Testament. Theological and liturgical sources propose Acts of the Apostles 8:14–17 and 19:5–6 as evidence for the apostolic practice of Confirmation. In the first, Peter and John imposed hands on a group of previously baptized Christians in Samaria, and they received the Holy Spirit. In the second, Paul imposed hands on 12 new Christians in Ephesus, immediately after their Baptism, and the Holy Spirit came upon them. In this case, Luke explains that the group spoke in tongues and prophesied. In both stories, some kind of apostolic intervention was needed for a group whose formation was thought to be incomplete, resulting in an outpouring of the Holy Spirit as had happened on Pentecost. Hebrews 6:1–2 links instruction about baptisms (a peculiar use of the plural) with hand-laying, but the relationship among the terms in the list is not clear.

At the same time, other passages appear not to show hand-laying after Baptism. In Acts 10:47–48, hand-laying and the gift of the Holy Spirit actually precede Baptism. Many other reports of Baptism (Acts 2:38–42, 4:4, 8:12–13, 8:36–39; 9:18–19; and 22:16) make no reference to hand-laying for the gift of the Holy Spirit at all. Consequently, it is difficult to argue that the apostles reg-

ularly imposed hands on the baptized, much less anointed them.

The scriptures do refer to a symbolic anointing of Jesus Christ with the Holy Spirit (Acts 4:27 and 10:38). Hebrews 1:9 applies a psalm about a royal anointing to Jesus, and Jesus applies a text about a prophetic anointing to himself (Lk 4:18 citing Is 61:1). Paul tells of the anointing he and Timothy received, giving them the Spirit (2 Cor 1:21–22). John speaks of the anointing the Christian community received, enabling them to gain understanding (1 Jn 2:20 and 27). Although there is no record of the physical anointing of Jesus or his followers, some scholars think that the custom of anointing Christians probably grew from the poetic language of these texts.

Early Church. Whatever the case may be, the ritual elaboration of Baptism came to include a prebaptismal anointing, sometimes with hand-laying. This was especially the case in the Syrian baptismal rites of the third and fourth centuries. The Syriac *Didascalia apostolorum* 16 (*Corpus Scriptorum Christianorum Orientalium* 401:156f), the *Recognitions* of Pseudo-Clement 3:67 (*Patrologia Graeca* 1:1311–12), the *Acts of Judas Thomas* (*The Apocryphal Acts of the Apostles* ed. William

Wright. Amsterdam: Philo Press, 1968, pp. 166–167; 188–189; 258–259; 267–268; 289–290), the *History of John Son of Zebedee* (Wright, pp. 52–55), and Homily 12 of Aphrahat (*Patrologia Syriaca* 1:538) all indicate that the anointing preceded baptism. After the Council of Laodicea called for a postbaptismal anointing in canon 48 (Hefele, *Histoire des Conciles* 1:2,1021), the Syrian rites of initiation came more to resemble those in the West, as evidenced by the *Apostolic Constitutions* 3:16 (Funk 1:210–211), Theodore of Mopsuestia 2:17 (*Studi e Testi* 145:396–397), and the *Testament of the Lord* 2:8 (ed. Johannes Quasten. *Florilegium Patristicum tam veteris quam medii aevi auctores complectens*, 5:270).

A similar shift may have occurred in Egypt, although the evidence from Origen (*Commentariorum in epistolam B. Pauli ad Romanos*, 5:8; 5:9, *Patrologia Graeca* 14:1038; 1047 and *Homélies sur le Lévitique*, 6:5, *Patrologia Graeca* 12:472), Didymus of Alexandria (*De Trinitate*, 2:15, *Patrologia Graeca* 39:719–720), and the *Canons of Hippolytus* (cf. Thomas M. Finn, *Early Christian Baptism and the Catechumenate: Italy, North Africa, and Egypt* [Collegeville, Minn. 1992] 6:221–223) is less conclusive.

Contemporaneous to these traditions, the Western churches developed a sequence of Baptism followed by anointing, which eventually became the norm. Tertullian (*De baptismo* 7:1 and 8:1 [SC 35:76]) and Cyprian (*Epistola* 37:9 [*Corpus scriptorum ecclesiasticorum latinorum* 3/2:784–785]) give the earliest testimony for this custom. It appears most elaborately in the *Apostolic Tradition* (21 [SC 11bis:78; 80; 86–91]) and the works of Ambrose, Cyril, Egeria, and Augustine, to name a few.

In his *Ecclesiastical History*, Eusebius tells of the ailing Novatus, who was baptized by a minister, but when he recovered he did not receive remaining rites, including the sealing of the bishop (6:43 [ed. Eduard Schwartz and Theodor Mommsen, *Die griechischen christlichen Schriftsteller der ersten drei Jahrhunderte* [Berlin, Leipzig 1903] 9:619–621]). Thus, as early as the third century, for a grave reason, bishops may have finished an incomplete initiation on a later occasion. Whether this can be interpreted as giving rise eventually to a ceremony called Confirmation referred to by the fifth-century Gallic councils cannot be resolved in the absence of further conclusive evidence.

Development. The celebration of Confirmation developed throughout the early Middle Ages. A letter from Pope Innocent I (401–417) to Decentius of Gubbio treated the custom of ''consigning'' those who were baptized to bestow the Holy Spirit (ed. Robert Cabié, Bibliothèque de la revue d'histoire ecclésiastique, [Louvain 1973] 58:22, 24). Innocent permitted presbyters to anoint those whom they baptized, but not on the forehead. The consigning of the forehead with chrism was reserved to bishops, in faithfulness—so he believed—to a tradition dating to the Acts of the Apostles. This letter influenced the decision in the West to restrict Confirmations to bishops, whereas the Eastern churches permitted presbyteral confirmation.

By the late sixth or seventh century, ''confirming'' appeared in a baptismal context in *Ordo XI* (*Les Ordines Romani du Haut Moyen Âge*, 2:445–447). After Baptism, the bishop confirmed with the invocation of the Holy Spirit and then anointed the candidates. This document, a description of the Roman initiations rites over which the bishop presided, thus borrowed the term that had formerly been applied to an anointing apart from Baptism, and used it to name the anointing that immediately followed Baptism by a bishop.

By the ninth century, orders and sacramentaries commonly described the initiation rites over which a bishop presided as moving from Baptism through Confirmation to Eucharist, all in the same ceremony, usually on Easter or Pentecost. See, for example, *Ordo XXXB* from southwest France c. 780 (*Les Ordines Romani du Haut Moyen Âge*, 3:473–474), the Frankish Gelasian Sacramentary of Gellone c. 790 to 800 (CChr.SL 159:100–101), the sacramentary of Autun c. 800 (CChr.SL 159B:70), and the Frankish *Ordines XXVIII* (*Les Ordines Romani du Haut Moyen Âge*, 3:407–409) and *XXVIIIA* c. 800 (*Les Ordines Romani du Haut Moyen Âge*, 3:423–424). The candidate's age was not a factor: All the baptized, infants and seniors, were confirmed and shared communion if the bishop presided. When he did not, the presbyter offered Communion, no matter the candidate's age, and Confirmation was deferred to a time when the bishop was available. As a result, even though the written documentation of the Middle Ages suggests that Confirmation followed Baptism and preceded sharing the Eucharist, in actual practice Confirmation probably commonly followed the baptismal Eucharist by some years.

During the same period, however, the Communion of infants began to disappear. And by the thirteenth century, the practice all but vanished in the West. The churches of the Christian East continued offering Confirmation and Communion to infants on the occasion of baptism.

Also during the same period there arose a growing concern about the numbers of those who were never confirmed. Councils like that of Aix-la-Chapelle (836, canon 2) (J. D. Mansi, *Sacrorum Conciliorum nova et amplissima collectio* [Florence-Venice 1757–98] 14:681) and documents like the *False Decretals* (*Decretales pseudo-*

Isidorianae et capitula angilramni, ed. Paulus Hinschius [Leipzig 1863] 63–64; 146) stressed the importance of being confirmed, suggesting that many people were not participating in the ritual. In his collection of canons, Archbishop Ruotger of Trier (915–956) urged people to present their infants for Confirmation, before the children learned how to sin (canon 33, *Pastor Bonus* 52 [1941]:61–72). This is perhaps the earliest reference to a preferred age for Confirmation.

The earliest preserved independent rites of Confirmation come just before the eleventh century (e.g. *The Pontifical of Egbert* [Surtees Society, Durham] 1853, 27:67). Others must have preceded because Confirmation was administered apart from Baptism for some time.

In 1274 the Second Council of Lyon listed Confirmation among the seven sacraments of the Church (DS 860). The ritual was appearing in written collections among the blessings that bishops gave, and its relationship to Baptism remained obscure. Although the early Church imposed hands, prayed for the gift of the Holy Spirit, and anointed in the baptismal rite, the later Church did so only if the bishop were present. The sole factor determining the occasion for the administration of Confirmation was not the age or readiness of the candidate, but the availability of the bishop to perform a ritual that had become associated with his ministry: conferring the Holy Spirit on the baptized.

Some minor developments continued, but the ceremony remained essentially the same throughout the remainder of its history. The subtle shifts that emerged related to three issues surrounding the sacrament: the minister, the age of the candidate, and its sequence with the first sharing of Communion.

Issues. Both in the origins and the development of Confirmation, its ministry in the West has always been associated with that of the bishop. In its origins, all the uses of the term referred to something a bishop did: anointing those previously baptized by another minister, anointing those moving from heterodox adherence to orthodox Christianity, and invoking the Spirit and anointing those whom they themselves baptized.

However, there are examples of occasions when presbyters confirmed, or when some communities judged anything beyond the presbyters' baptisms inessential. For example, the first Council of Toledo (400) forbade anyone but the bishop to make chrism, but permitted presbyters to use it (canon 20) (J. D. Mansi, *Sacrorum Conciliorum nova et amplissima collectio* 3:1002). The same canon's prohibition against deacons' using chrism suggests that some of them had been doing so. Innocent's letter (see above) restricted the ministry of consigning to

bishops, again suggesting that other ministers had assumed this responsibility. Letter 9 of Pope Gelasius I (492–496) repeated the prohibition (*Patrologia Latina* [Paris 1878–90] 59:50). All these examples indicate that fifth-century presbyters in some communities imitated the bishop's Confirmation ministry.

In Gaul, the Council of Orange (441) permitted presbyters to sign heretics in danger of death. It also permitted any minister who baptized to also use chrism. The bishop would not do so again at Confirmation (canons 1–2) (CChr.SL 148:78). The Council of Epaone (517) repeated the permission for presbyters to confirm heretics (canon 16) (CChr.SL 148A:28), but the Second Council of Paris (573) reserved confirming to bishops (CChr.SL 148A:213).

In Italy, a sixth-century Life of St. Sylvester says presbyters anointed those they baptized in danger of death (*Liber Pontificalis* 1:171). Gregory the Great said presbyters should not anoint the forehead of the baptized with chrism (Letter 4:9) (CChr.SL 140:226). However, in 594 he permitted the presbyters of Sardinia to continue the same practice (Letter 4:26) (SL 140:245). But writing to the bishops of Sicily, he forbade deacons to consign (Letter 13:20) (SL 140:1021).

In Spain, the Second Council of Braga (572) forbade presbyters to anoint only if the bishop were present (canon 52) ("Concilium Bracarense secundum duodecim episcoporum," Claude W. Barlow, Papers and Monographs of the American Academy in Rome [New Haven, Conn. 1950] 12:137). The Second Council of Barcelona (599) assumed that presbyters anointed with chrism (canon 2) (*Concilios Visigóticos,* ed. José Vives, España Cristiana [Barcelona-Madrid 1963] 1:159). In 619, under Roman influence, the Second Council of Seville ruled that presbyters were neither permitted to sign foreheads with chrism, nor to impose hands and pray for the Holy Spirit (canon 7) (J. D. Mansi, *Sacrorum Conciliorum nova et amplissima collectio* 10:559). Ildephonse held that only bishops could anoint the newly baptized (*Book on the Understanding of Baptism* 128–9, 131, 136; *Patrologia Latina* 96:164–166, 168). Braulio of Saragossa (after 651), though, believed that presbyters could anoint (Epistula 2:3; *Patrologia Latina* 87:406–407).

In Great Britain, Bede says that Augustine asked the local converts to have their Baptism "completed" (*Ecclesiastical History* 2:2)—possibly an allusion to the bishop's Confirmation (*Bede's Ecclesiastical History of the English People,* ed. Bertram Colgrave and R. A. B. Mynors [Oxford 1969] 138). One plausible explanation is that the local community did not see the necessity of Confirmation after Baptism.

Several missals from the end of the seventh to the ninth centuries described the presbyter's role in the baptismal rites. Because they do not allude to the bishop's Confirmation at all, they suggest that the presbyter's role sufficed. These include the *Ordo scrutiniorum* (*North Italian Services of the Eleventh Century; Recueil d'ordines du XIᵉ siècle provenant de la haute-Italie*, ed. C. Lambot [London 1931] 67:31, 34f); the *Missale Gallicanum Vetus* (ed. Leo Mohlberg, *Rerum Ecclesiasticarum Documenta*, Series maior: Fontes III [Rome 1958] 42 and 50); the *Bobbio Missal* (ed. E. A. Lowe [Suffolk 1991] 58 and 61:75); the *Missale Gothicum* (ed. Leo Cuthbert Mohlberg, *Rerum Ecclesiasticarum Documenta*, Series maior, Fontes V [Rome 1961] 54–67 passim); and the *Stowe Missal* (ed. George F. Warner [London 1906] 32/2:31–32).

The Spanish *Liber ordinvm episcopal* from 1072 has the presbyter anointing the baptized on the forehead with chrism, a practice accepted earlier in Spain's history (ed. Jose Janini [Stvdia Silensia XV 1991] 84 and 192).

Intensifying the ministerial question was the increasing difficulty bishops faced in fulfilling their responsibilities to confirm. Boniface (*c.* 680–*c.* 754) required bishops to visit their dioceses at least once a year to confirm ("Letter to Cuthbert" in *Monumenta Germaniae Historica: Epistolae Merowingici et Karolini aevi* [Berlin—] 3/1:351). Charlemagne repeated the directive in 769 ("First Directive of Charlemagne" 7; *Monumenta Germaniae Historica: Capitularia* 1:45). So did the Council of Chelsea in 787 (canon 3) (*Councils and Ecclesiastical Documents Relating to Great Britain and Ireland*, 3:448–449). All these reminders, repeated in successive centuries, indicate that bishops found it difficult to confirm as they were expected.

Throughout the twentieth century, the occasions on which presbyters confirmed gradually increased. In 1929 Pope Pius XI gave Latin American bishops authority to appoint some priests to assist in the ministry of Confirmation (AAS 21 [1929] 555). In 1947 the Sacred Congregation on the Propaganda of the Faith permitted bishops of mission territories to empower all their priests to confirm those they baptized (AAS 40:41). This began a practice still found in some places where Confirmation is made available to infants. In 1946, the Sacred Congregation on the Discipline of Sacraments gave presbyters permission to confirm infants and adults in danger of death (AAS 38 [1946] 350–357 passim). After the Second Vatican Council, the *Rite of Christian Initiation Adults* (International Commission on English in the Liturgy and Bishops' Committee on the Liturgy, Chicago 1988) and the canon law of the church (Washington 1983) actually obliged presbyters to confirm when they baptized adults

and children of catechetical age (*Codex Iuris Canonicis* c. 883 §2 and c. 885 §2). The revised *Rite of Confirmation* permitted certain priests to confirm when the number of those for the bishop to confirm was large (Vatican City 1973). Although the bishop is canonically the ordinary minister of the sacrament (*Codex Iuris Canonicis* c. 882), the occasions on which presbyters confirm have increased dramatically.

The history of the age of Confirmation demonstrates even broader variation. As already noted, early Church history demonstrates no association between the age of candidates for Confirmation and the occasion of its celebration. The occasion for Confirmation simply had to do with the availability of the bishop.

Later in the Middle Ages, theologians began to make a connection between childhood and Confirmation. The sacrament became interpreted as strengthening ("confirming") against the struggles of life. "We are reborn in baptism for life, and we are confirmed after baptism for the strife. In baptism we are washed; after baptism we are strengthened" (Gratian *De cons.* 5:2) (ed. Emil Friedberg [Graz 1955] 1:1413). Although the word entered ritual vocabulary to refer to the bishop's confirming (or affirming) of another's Baptism, the meaning shifted to strengthening those who now had some even limited experience in the spiritual life. Otto of Bamberg (after 1168) may have been the first to suggest confirming adolescents (Sermon to the Pomeranians) (*Patrologia Latina* 173:13580), but a younger age probably prevailed. With this interpretation of the meaning of the sacrament, its celebration began to be deferred more commonly from infancy.

Opinions about the age for Confirmation diversified by the thirteenth century. Those who preferred an age younger than seven included the Council of Worcester (1240) (J. D. Mansi, *Sacrorum Conciliorum nova et amplissima collectio* 23:527), Richard of Chichester (1246) (*Concilia Magnae Britanniae et Hiberniae a synodo Verolamiensi* A.D. *CCCCXLVI ad Londinensem* A.D. *MDCCXVII*, ed. David Wilkins, 1:688), the Council of Durham (1249) (*Concilia Magnae Britanniae et Hiberniae a synodo Verolamiensi* A.D. *CCCCXLVI ad Londinensem* A.D. *MDCCXVII*, ed. David Wilkins, 1737, 1:575–576), the Council of Arles (1260) (J. D., *Sacrorum Conciliorum nova et amplissima collectio* 23:1004–1005), the Synod of Exeter (1287) (*Concilia Magnae Britanniae et Hiberniae a synodo Verolamiensi* A.D. *CCCCXLVI ad Londinensem* A.D. *MDCCXVII*, ed. David Wilkins, 2:131–1320), the statutes of John of Liège (3:1) (J. D. Mansi, *Sacrorum Conciliorum nova et amplissima collectio* 24:889), and the Synod of Winchester (1308) (*Concilia Magnae Britanniae et Hiberniae a*

synodo Verolamiensi A.D. *CCCCXLVI ad Londinensem*
A.D. *MDCCXVII*, ed. David Wilkins, 2:293). The Synod
of Cologne (1280) was the first to fix the age at seven
years or older (J. D., *Sacrorum Conciliorum nova et amplissima collectio* 24:349). Others tolerated a later age.
The Roman Catechism (1566) after the Council of Trent
eventually said, ''It is less profitable when [Confirma-
tion] is done before children have the use of reason. If it
seems that one should not wait for the age of twelve, it
is certainly most fitting that this sacrament be deferred to
age seven'' (2:3) (ed. Petrus Rodriguez [Vatican City
1989] 230).

At the same time, the age for the first sharing of
Communion was accelerating. Infant Communion, once
required at Baptism, had become forbidden. Opinions
about the proper age for sharing Communion for the first
time also varied widely, but most commonly ages ten to
twelve were recommended during this period. Gradually,
that age increased even more in some places, and it was
not until the early twentieth century when first Communion reverted to about age seven with the publication of
Quam singulari by the Sacred Congregation of the Discipline of the Sacraments in 1910 (AAS 2 [1910]
577–583). Although the decree did not address the question of Confirmation directly, it created a situation which
pastoral ministers instinctively questioned. It placed a
profusion of sacraments at around age seven: Confession,
Confirmation, and first Communion. And it left a void
around the age of puberty, when the church had a transitional rite in the form of first Communion ceremonies,
first organized in grassroots efforts in the seventeenth
century.

Into that void moved Confirmation. The 1917 Code
of Canon Law proposed seven years as the age of Confirmation and urged bishops to travel throughout their dioceses every five years, tacitly setting the normal age
between seven and twelve (Rome 1917). In 1934 the Sacred Congregation of the Sacraments clarified that the occasions for younger Confirmation were danger of death
and the inaccessibility of a bishop (AAS 27 [1935] 16).
In 1952 the Pontifical Commission for Authentically Interpreting the Canons of the Code ruled that no bishop
could forbid Confirmation to those younger than ten
(AAS 44 [1952]:496). By the second half of the twentieth
century, however, many dioceses around the world began
to defer the age of Confirmation until even later, although
the universal age remains seven years or another age determined by the conference of bishops.

The advance in the age of Confirmation appears to
come with a concern about catechetical formation. With
the lowering of the age of First Communion the Church
lost a sacramental celebration to accompany the maturing

of Christians and the completion of school age catechesis.
Confirmation, reinterpreted through the Middle Ages as
a sacrament for strengthening, became popularly reinterpreted again as a sacrament of commitment to the church.
Those who were baptized as infants were invited to profess the self-appropriation of their faith.

Rome has never endorsed this opinion and has even
cautioned against it: ''Although confirmation is sometimes called the 'sacrament of Christian maturity,' we
must not confuse adult faith with the adult age of natural
growth, nor forget that the baptismal grace is a grace of
free unmerited election and does not need 'ratification'
to become effective'' (*Catechism of the Catholic Church*
1308.) In 1999 the Sacred Congregation for Divine Worship approved the appeal of the family of an eleven-year-
old who requested Confirmation at an age younger than
that established by the diocese (*Notitiae* 400–401
Nov.–Dec. 1999/11–12, 536–538). Still, the large number of those celebrating Confirmation in adolescent years
has affected the popular mind to believe that this sacrament is now the rite of commitment to the Catholic
Church.

A third issue that has shaped the history of the sacrament of Confirmation is its sequence with the first sharing
of Communion. This concern began to surface only late
in the twentieth century, but in retrospect it sheds light
on how the sacrament was understood throughout its history.

Examples of concern about sequence before the
nineteenth century are few. John Peckam in 1279 (''Constitutions of the Council of Lambeth: The Sacrament of
Confirmation'' *Concilia Magnae Britanniae et Hiberniae
a synodo Verolamiensi* A.D. *CCCCXLVI ad Londinensem*
A.D. *MDCCXVII*, ed. David Wilkins, 2:53), the four-
teenth- or fifteenth-century York Manual ([Durham
1875] 63:20–22), and the Salisbury Manual of 1543 (ed.
A. Jeffries Collins [Chichester 1960] 43) expected Confirmation to precede Communion, probably to encourage
the celebration of the former. The 1751 synodal constitutions of Saint-Paul-Trois-Châteaux, edited in Avignon
(R. Levet, ''L'âge de la confirmation dans la législation
des diocèses de France depuis le Concile de Trente,'' *La
Maison-Dieu* 54 [1958] 124), preferred to have Confirmation follow first Communion, whereas the synodal
statutes of Valence in France (1727) accepted no one for
first Communion who had not been confirmed (*ibid.*,
121).

By the nineteenth century opinions diverged, however. The councils of Tours (1849) (J. D. Mansi, *Sacrorum
Conciliorum nova et amplissima collectio* 44:392), Avignon (1849) (J. D. Mansi, *Sacrorum Conciliorum nova
et amplissima collectio* 43:745), Sens (1850) (J. D.

Mansi, *Sacrorum Conciliorum nova et amplissima collectio* 44:230), Rouen (1850) (J. D. Mansi, *Sacrorum Conciliorum nova et amplissima collectio* 44:45), Auch (1851) (J. D. Mansi, *Sacrorum Conciliorum nova et amplissima collectio* 44:617–618), Prague V (1860) (J. D. Mansi, *Sacrorum Conciliorum nova et amplissima collectio* 48:269–270), Mende (1863) (R. Levet, ''L'âge de la confirmation dans la législation des diocèses de France depuis le Concile de Trente,'' *La Maison-Dieu* 54 [1958] 130), and Utrecht (1865) (J. D. Mansi, *Sacrorum Conciliorum nova et amplissima collectio* 48:706–707, 710) preferred Communion to take place before Confirmation for spiritual, traditional, and catechetical reasons. Rome, however, preferred the other sequence. In 1854 the Sacred Congregation of the Council reversed the sequence in *La Réunion 9 Collectanea S. Congregationis de Propaganda Fide* [Rome 1907] 588) and in 1873 the same decision was made for the province of Algiers in North Africa (R. Levet, ''L'âge de la confirmation dans la législation des diocèses de France depuis le Concile de Trente,'' *La Maison-Dieu* 54 [1958] 132). An 1897 letter of Pope Leo XIII commended the bishop of Marseilles who moved confirmation to a position before first communion (*Codicis iuris canonici fontes*, ed. Peter Gasparri, Rome 1925, 3:515–516). The 1899 statutes of Lyon and the 1902 statutes of Paris also acceded and placed Confirmation before Communion (R. Levet, ''L'âge de la confirmation dans la législation des diocèses de France depuis le Concile de Trente,'' *La Maison-Dieu* 54 [1958] 134). The 1913 Synod of Laval in France reversed its earlier custom and placed Confirmation before Communion (*ibid.* 136). The Statutes of Limoges changed to the same pattern in 1948 (*ibid.* 138). The Sacred Congregation on the Sacraments exchanged letters with the bishops of Spain in 1932 (AAS 24 [1932]:271–272), in which it became clear that seven years old was not just the minimum age for Confirmation, but the ideal age as well.

None of these decisions was influenced by an argument about Baptism. They all simply sought fidelity to a previous custom. The Church has a long history of Communion before Confirmation, but whenever Rome intervened, it preferred the other sequence.

Instrumental to the twentieth-century discussion of sequence is the *Rite of Christian Initiation of Adults*, which yokes the celebration and meaning of Confirmation to Baptism (215). In the East, Confirmation consecrates the baptized for sharing the Eucharist. The same is true for those baptized in other churches and ecclesial communities who celebrate the Rite of Reception into the Full Communion of the Catholic Church. Their Confirmation leads the way to eucharistic Communion.

Some, then, began to place the celebration of Confirmation before or with first Communion even for children.

Although this was not unheard of in the past, the practice shows another development in the history of the sacrament. What developed was not the sequence Confirmation-before-First Communion, which has clear precedents, but that this sequence would be observed completely apart from the celebration of Baptism and on distinct occasions. The trend to honor the sequence of Confirmation-before-First Communion has merit, but it will only raise the question about why Confirmation should be deferred from Baptism at all.

Theology. Confirmation is a gift of the Holy Spirit that orients the baptized toward mission. An examination of the texts in the liturgy of Confirmation establishes this conclusion. The sacrament is administered with the words, ''N., receive the gift of the Holy Spirit'' (Rite of Confirmation, 27). Many of the liturgical texts remind the one being confirmed that this gift comes with an expectation, that it will be used for service to the church and the world (e.g. 22, 30 and 33).

The activity of the Holy Spirit is ritualized especially in the aforementioned text and its accompanying gestures. Pope Paul VI explicitly stated, ''The sacrament of confirmation is conferred through the anointing with chrism on the forehead, which is done by the laying on of the hand, and through the words: 'Accipe Signaculum Doni Spiritus Sancti''' (Apostolic Constitution). The work of the Holy Spirit is signified both in hand-laying and in anointing. The imposition of hands signifies the prayer for the descent of the Holy Spirit upon the candidates. The anointing signifies the sealing and staying power of the Spirit. It consecrates the candidate for exercising the challenge of the gospel.

Chrism, which may be consecrated only by a bishop, is traditionally a blend of olive oil and balsam, but today any plant oil and perfumed oil may be used. It is the oil used in the Baptism of children, Confirmation, presbyteral and episcopal ordination, and in the anointing of the altar and walls of a church. It carries with it the unifying ministry of the bishop.

In addition to its pneumatic purpose, Confirmation also unites the candidates more firmly to Christ (*Catechism of the Catholic Church* 1303). The very word ''Christ'' means ''anointed one,'' and Confirmation gives the candidate a share in this anointing, and hence in the mission of Jesus to bring good news to the poor (Lk 4:18).

Confirmation also renders one's bond with the Church more perfect (*Catechism of the Catholic Church* 1303). That bond, established by Baptism, becomes stronger through this gift of the Holy Spirit. This sacrament more strongly obliges the candidates to spread their faith by word and deed (*Lumen gentium* 11).

Confirmation imparts a character like Baptism and Holy Orders. So effective is its power that it is celebrated only once (*Catechism of the Catholic Church* 1304–1305). Canonically, this sacrament carries certain privileges. Those who are unconfirmed may not serve as godparents (874/3), enter religious life (645/1), enter a seminary (241/2) or be ordained (1033). The sacrament of Confirmation is required for full Christian initiation (842/2).

The meaning of Confirmation has settled into three different categories: initiation, maturity, and reception to communion. The initiatory function of Confirmation is most clearly seen when it is celebrated in conjunction with Baptism during the *Rite of Christian Initiation of Adults*, Eastern baptismal rite, and the Baptism of infants in danger of death. It appears to be a maturity rite whenever it is separated from Baptism, no matter the candidate's age. Some preparation is required for its celebration, and the sacrament is deferred until the candidate is able to renew baptismal promises and is properly disposed for it (*Codex Iuris Canonicis* c. 889 §2). Confirmation is a reception into communion when it is celebrated by those baptized in other churches or ecclesial communities who are making their profession of faith and being received into the full communion of the Catholic Church.

Rite of Confirmation. The Rite of Confirmation was revised and promulgated in 1975. The publication includes a decree, the apostolic constitution, an introduction, and several chapters. The first chapter treats the rite of Confirmation within the Mass. The second treats the rite of Confirmation outside of the Mass. The third chapter considers Confirmation by a minister who is not a bishop. The fourth provides the service for confirming a person in danger of death. The final chapter contains texts for the celebration of the sacrament.

The sources for the ritual come from every period of Church history. The third- or fourth-century *Apostolic Tradition* provides for two post-baptismal anointings with chrism. The second, administered by the bishop before the Eucharist, is a major source for the development of the Confirmation rite. The fifth-century letter of Innocent to Decentius explicitly mentions signing the forehead with a cross. The sixth-century *Ordo XI* and the eighth-century *Gelasian Sacramentary* (ed. Leo Cunibert Mohlberg, *Rerum Ecclesiasticarum Documenta*, Series maior, Fontes IV [Rome 1981]) compiled significant texts for the sacrament, including the ancient prayer for the sevenfold gift of the Spirit (451), with antecedents already in Ambrose (*De mysteriis* 7:42 [SC 25:121]; *De sacramentis* 3:2,8 [SC 25:82]). A prayer from the mid-tenth-century Reichenau Sacramentary, "Deus, qui apos-

tolis tuis," (*Patrologia Latina* 138:957–958) endured through the Roman-Germanic Pontifical (*Studi e Testi* 227:388, ed. Cyrille Vogel and Reinhard Elze) and other versions of the rite. An adaptation of the prayer concludes the general intercessions of the 1975 rite (30).

In later years, further development of the rite occurred. Durand replaced hand-laying with an extension of hands over the group and introduced a gesture borrowed from the ceremony of making a knight: The bishop gave a light slap to the cheek of the candidate, signifying their readiness to bear trouble for the sake of the Gospel (*Le Pontifical Romain au Moyen-Âge: Le Pontifical de Guillaume Durande*, ed. Michel Andrieu, *Studi e Testi* 88, 3:333–335). Benedict XIV suggested placing the hand on the head of the candidate while anointing, thus blending hand-laying with sealing (*Ex quo primum tempore, Bullarium*, t. III [Prato 1847] 320). Paul VI changed the words that accompany the administration of the sacrament. Prior to the Second Vatican Council, the words were, "I consign and confirm you in the name of the Father and of the Son and of the Holy Spirit." The new text more closely resembles that of the chrismation rite of the Christian Eastern and underscores the role of the Holy Spirit more than that of the bishop (*Apostolic Constitution*).

The ritual unfolds very simply. After the Liturgy of the Word, the candidates are presented (Rite of Confirmation 21). In the homily, the bishop leads everyone to a deeper understanding of Confirmation (22). The renewal of baptismal promises follows, and the beginning of the third question is expanded into an independent question concerning belief in the Holy Spirit, "the Lord, the giver of life, who came upon the apostles at Pentecost and today is given . . . sacramentally in confirmation" (23). After silent prayer, the bishop and any priests present extend their hands over those to be confirmed (24) while the bishop sings the Confirmation prayer for the sevenfold gift of the Holy Spirit (25). Then the candidates are anointed on the forehead with chrism (26–29). General intercessions come next (30). If the Confirmation takes place at Mass, the Liturgy of the Eucharist follows (31–32). Blessings conclude the ceremony (33). The first two chapters of the Rite of Confirmation explain this ceremony inside and outside of the Mass.

The third chapter of the Rite of Confirmation considers the presidency of a minister who is not a bishop. However, it simply refers the reader to the earlier chapters. There is no difference in the ritual. Ordinarily, the minister of this rite (apart from Baptism) is a bishop, but he may appoint presbyters to lead it in his absence, or to join him in its celebration.

In danger of death, the scenario that the fourth chapter faces, the priest or bishop may follow the full rite, or a much abbreviated format involving only an imposition of hands, the prayer for the sevenfold gift of the Spirit, and the anointing with chrism. In extreme necessity, one may simply anoint and use the formula, ''N., be sealed with the Gift of the Holy Spirit.'' The texts that fill the fifth chapter of the rite offer options for the antiphons, prayers, blessings, and readings.

To be confirmed one must not have been confirmed before, be prepared, be able to renew baptismal promises, and to desire the sacrament. The ideal sponsor is the baptismal godparent (*Codex iuris canonicis* c. 893 §2). Although no mention of the traditional practice ''taking of a confirmation name'' is found in the rite, this practice continues to thrive in many places.

Other churches. A rite of confirmation exists in several other Christian denominations. Most do not regard it as a sacrament as the Catholic Church does. The Anglican communion reserves the administration of confirmation to a bishop. Other communities do not. Some offer variations on the theme of confirmation, calling the ceremony an ''affirmation of baptism,'' and providing multiple opportunities for its celebration. The Eastern Churches generally keep Confirmation with Baptism in all instances. The Latin Rite recognizes the validity of all the Confirmations of the Eastern Churches, both Catholic and Orthodox.

Bibliography: M. HAUKE, *Die Firmung: Geschichtliche Entfaltung und theologischer Sinn* (Paderborn 1999). P. TURNER, *Confirmation: The Baby in Solomon's Court* (Mahwah, N.J. 1993); *Ages of Initiation: The First Two Christian Millennia* (Collegeville, Minn. 2000). C. FABRIS, *Il Presbitero ministro della Cresima? Studio giuridico teologico pastorale* (Padua 1997). GERALD AUSTIN, *The Rite of Confirmation: Anointing with the Spirit* (New York 1985). A. KAVANAGH, *Confirmation: Origins and Reform* (New York 1988). P. CASPANI, *La pertinenza teologica della nozione di iniziazione cristiana* (Milan 1999).

[P. TURNER]

CONFORMITY TO THE WILL OF GOD

The idea that human goodness involves a harmonious relationship between the human will and the will of God is a commonplace of Christian thought. In its most obvious application it is realized in obedience to the divine will as this is made known through prohibition and command; but there is a sense in which conformity goes beyond obedience, which it supposes, and signifies not only exterior compliance to an order, but also interior attitudes of harmony in willing and thinking.

The notions of conformity, abandonment, and resignation are closely related. Abandonment is generally understood to differ from simple conformity in implying the renunciation of one's own judgment and will, and allowing God to lead one blindly, without one's having any desire to know the reasons or ends God has in view. Abandonment, therefore, describes a passive or mystical state, while conformity is usually associated with the idea of an active state. The terms are, however, used differently by different authors, and it is necessary to discover just what a given writer means when he is using them. Resignation differs from conformity and abandonment in referring only to the willing acceptance of unpleasant things.

Scripture and the Fathers. There are numerous passages in Scripture in which there is reference to conformity to the will of God. Among the principal ones can be noted Heb 10.5–9, with its reference to Ps 39.7; Jn 5.30 and 6.38; Acts 9.6, but these passages all seem to refer simply to obedience and hence do not involve conformity in the more technical sense.

Most of the Fathers also touched upon the idea of conformity only under the more general notion of obedience to the Commandments. A few expressions are, however, worthy of particular note. Origen (*In Rom.* 12.1, *Patrologia Graeca*, ed J. P. Migne [Paris 1857–66] 14:1207) remarked that to discover without error what the will of God is requires the illumination of wisdom and the possession of the gnosis. He implied that this is quite rare and not found in the ordinary Christian. Among the Fathers writing in the tradition of Oriental monastic spirituality, SS. Pachomius, Basil, and John Chrysostom, a relationship is established between conformity to the will of God and Christian perfection. St. Augustine spoke of the importance of willing what God directs (*Conf.* 10.26 and *In Psalm.* 44.17, *Patrologia Latina*, ed. J. P. MIGNE [Paris 1878–90] 36:503–504), and in his *Enchiridion* he discussed the possibility of a good man willing what God does not will. This last passage was incorporated by Peter Lombard into his *Sentences* (1.48) and thus served as a starting point for much of the later medieval speculation on the problem of man's conformity to the divine will.

Medieval Theologians. St. Bernard seems to be the first to have used the term *conformitas*, in his 83d sermon on the Canticle, but he used the expression simply to describe the love whereby the soul is joined to God in spiritual marriage. St. Albert the Great spoke of conformity as the highest rule of moral action and distinguished three grades of the spiritual life according to three degrees of conformity: the conformity of imperfection, of sufficiency, and of perfection (*Summa theologiae* 1.20.80.3). It is with Peter Lombard, however, and his commentators that one finds the first real development of the idea of conformity. The Master of the Sentences spoke of the distinction of the divine will of good pleasure (*voluntas* *beneplaciti*) and of the signified will (*voluntas signi*) with its various subdivisions (1.45), while elsewhere (1.48) he raised the question, suggested by the remark of St. Augustine in the *Enchiridion*, of how there can be some disagreement between the will of God and that of a good man, and indicated the distinction, to be developed by the later scholastics, between conformity relative to the thing willed and conformity in the motive or end of willing.

This distinction received its clearest treatment in St. Thomas Aquinas, who discussed it in his *Commentary on the Sentences* as well as in the *De veritate* (23.7–8) and more compendiously in the *Summa theologiae* (1a2ae, 19.9–10). St. Thomas noted that the goodness of the divine will is the measure and norm of every good will. A created will is good when it wills what God wants it to will. The problem of conformity, then, consists in discovering the obligation to will objects and events that God wills and wants men to will. Here St. Thomas proposed some distinctions. Since the goodness of an object or event depends upon the end, that which is formally good about any object or event is its order to a right end and ultimately its order to the end for which God wills all things, namely His own divine goodness. Concerning this end, a man is obliged to conform his will to the divine will simply speaking and absolutely; i.e., he cannot, without sin, refuse to will this order or will anything contrary to it. Regarding particular objects or events, it is of obligation to will them only as they come under this order and, indeed, only as man sees them as coming under this order. Regarded from this viewpoint, any object or event willed by God must be agreeable to man; but regarded from a different viewpoint, such an object or event may, and perhaps even should, displease man.

This diversity of viewpoints can come from either of two sources. First, since men in this life, even the just, do not see the divine goodness perfectly, they do not clearly perceive the order of all things as related to the divine goodness. Consequently, the possibility of conforming one's will to that of God is limited by one's lack of ability to recognize in all cases the relationship of a particular object or event to the end that is the divine goodness. Until this relationship is clear, man can without fault, albeit conditionally, will otherwise than God has willed. Secondly, things that are good when viewed simply according to their particular nature may be bad when viewed as part of a more universal picture, and vice versa. God's viewpoint is, of course, the universal one; man's is more frequently a limited and particular one, concerned with a particular good suited to him according to his nature. This may make for some differences between the divine and the human will, and for a certain lack of complete conformity, even though it may become clear to man, at least after something unpleasant to him

has taken place, that it has indeed been willed by God as part of a more general plan. St. Thomas remarks that this contrary affection of will in the just man may even be termed praiseworthy because of the other viewpoint from which the object can be regarded. Yet he notes that this affection is not pursued with obstinacy, but supposes an acceptance of the divine will, since it is pleasing to the just man that the divine will be fulfilled in all things. In a more basic sense, moreover, these movements of appetite, so long as they are not immoderate, are themselves in conformity with the divine will, since God has given His creatures these appetites and wills them to be attracted to their proper objects. It is in this sense that St. Thomas explained the reluctance in the will of Christ relative to the sufferings of His Passion, even though He knew that it was His Father's will that He should suffer, and also the "dissent" relative to the Passion in the will of the Blessed Virgin Mary.

St. Thomas also treated explicitly one of the more obvious difficulties about conformity: the problem of conforming to God's will when He has willed a man's eternal punishment. He answers by saying, first of all, that no one in this life can know that God has so willed; but even if this should be revealed to him, he should regard the revelation rather as a warning than as an indication of accomplished fact. Even granting that the fact were revealed as a certainty, one would not be obliged to will his own damnation absolutely, but only according to the order of justice whereby God wills to punish those who persist in sin.

This idea of conforming to the divine will relative to damnation, and more particularly relative to sin, gave rise to certain errors in the late medieval and early modern period. Among these are the 14th and 15th condemned propositions attributed to Meister Eckhart (*Enchiridion symbolorum* 964, 965), and the proposition attributed to Peter of Bonagenta and condemned by the Spanish Inquisition [De Guibert, *Documenta ecclesiastica christianae perfectionis spectantia* (Rome 1931) 313]. Quietist notions about the total suppression of human willing in order to achieve perfect conformity can be found in the work of Benet of Canfield and in the 61st of the condemned propositions of Miguel de Molinos (*Enchiridion symbolorum* 2261). Similar exaggerations were attributed to the French semiquietists, as is evidenced in the 26th of the Articles of Issy (De Guibert, *op.* cit. 496) and in the condemned propositions taken from the works of Fénelon (*Enchiridion symbolorum* 2354–55).

On the positive side, an active and wholly orthodox notion of conformity was proposed by St. IGNATIUS LOYOLA, whose *SPIRITUAL EXERCISES* reach their climax in leading the soul to make "a choice in conformity to His most holy will and good pleasure" (Second Week). This teaching was further elaborated by Alfonso RODRIGUEZ, who developed the idea in *Ejercicio de perfección y virtudes cristianas* and by Jeremias DREXEL, who, in his *Heliotropium*, saw the soul, under the symbolism of that flower, constantly keeping itself turned to God in conformity to the divine will.

Bibliography: F. M. CATHERINET, *Dictionnaire de spiritualité ascétique et mystique. Doctrine et histoire*, ed. M. VILLER et al. (Paris 1932–) 2:1441–69. THOMAS AQUINAS, *Summa theologiae* 1a2ae, 19.9–10; *De ver.* 23.7–8; *In 1 sent.* 48.

[P. M. STARRS]

CONFORTI, GUIDO MARIA, BL.

Founder of the XAVERIAN MISSIONARY FATHERS; archbishop. b. Casalora di Ravadese (near Parma), Italy, March 30, 1865; d. Parma, Italy, Nov. 5, 1931. Son of Rinaldo and Antonia Conforti, Guido attended the Christian Brothers' school at Parma. Fascinated by a biography of St. Francis XAVIER, he desired to become a missionary to foreign lands. In 1876 he entered the diocesan seminary and was ordained on Sept. 22, 1888. He aided Paul Manna, PIME, in founding the Pontifical Missionary Union of the Clergy, of which he later became the first national president (1918).

Missionary activity *ad gentes* was still his great ideal, although his precarious health prevented him from undertaking such a strenuous activity. On the feast of St. Francis Xavier, Dec. 3, 1895, he established a seminary for training missionaries, and in 1898 he founded the Pious Congregation of St. Xavier for Foreign Missions. He was consecrated archbishop of Ravenna in 1902, but ill-health forced his resignation two years later. In 1907, after Conforti's health improved, Pope PIUS X personally asked him to accept an appointment as archbishop of Parma. For the next twenty-four years he worked with admirable zeal and prudence for the flock entrusted to his care. In addition, he continued to oversee the Xavieran Fathers, visiting their missions three years before his death. In 1941, ten years after his demise, the diocesan process for his beatification began. The apostolic process opened in Rome in 1960, leading to his beatification, March 17, 1996, by Pope John Paul II.

Feast: Nov. 5.

Bibliography: L. BALLARIN, *L'anima missionaria di G. M. Conforti* ((Parma 1962). G. BARSOTTI, *Il servo di Dio G. M. Conforti* (Rome 1953); *L'anima di Guido Maria Conforti* (Rome 1975); *Più vivo dei vivi* (Rome 1970). G. BONARDI, *Guido Maria Conforti* (Parma 1936). P. BONARDI, U. DELSANTE, and E. FERRO, eds., *A Parma e nel mondo* (Parma 1996). F. TEODORI, ed. *Il beato Guido Maria Conforti arcivescovo vescovo di Parma: nomina e possesso* (Vatican City 1996); *Beato Guido Maria Conforti: missioni in Cina e legislazione saveriana* (Vatican City 1995). V. C. VANZIN, *Un pastore, due greggi* (Parma 1950).

[F. G. SOTTOCORNOLA/K. I. RABENSTEIN]

CONFRATERNITY OF CHRISTIAN DOCTRINE (CCD)

The Confraternity of Christian Doctrine, an association of the faithful devoted to the work of Catholic religious education, traces its origins to sixteenth-century Italy. Prompted by the need to counteract widespread ignorance of Church teachings and indifference toward religious practice, zealous individuals began to organize groups of catechists, priests and laity, for the instruction of youth. The movement spread in many Italian cities including Rome, where about 1560 a Society of Christian Doctrine (*Compagnia della Dottrina Cristiana*) was established that gained the approval of Pope Pius V in 1571. Meanwhile the reform-minded Archbishop Charles BORROMEO was promoting a similar group, the Sodality of Christian Doctrine, in Milan, where he directed that it be established in every parish church. It was St. Charles more than anyone who gave the association it early structure, pastoral guidelines, and juridical status.

In 1607 Pope Paul V with the apostolic brief *Ex credito nobis* established the Society of Christian Doctrine as an archconfraternity with headquarters in St. Peter's Basilica. The pope thereby implicitly recognized that even its members participated in the teaching mission of the Church. He further encouraged its members by extending to them a number of indulgences. At the beginning of the twentieth century Pope Pius X breathed new life into the confraternity. His encyclical letter *Acerbo nimis* (1905), regarded as the magna carta of the modern CCD, lamented the neglect of catechesis and ordered that the confraternity be established in every parish as a way of providing the pastor with lay helpers in teaching the catechism. The 1917 Code of Canon Law (c. 711.2) incorporated the command, directing that parish units be established by formal decree of the local ordinary and affiliated with the archconfraternity in Rome. During the pontificate of Pope Pius XI, the congregation of the council further decreed that diocesan and national offices be established to promote, support, and coordinate the work of the confraternity at local levels (*Provido sane*, 1935).

CCD in the USA Shortly after the publication of *Acerbo nimis* the individual parishes in the U.S. began to organize the confraternity and in time it became a national movement. In the initial stages, the CCD was promoted in dioceses like New York and Pittsburgh where there were a great number of recent immigrants. In 1922 the confraternity was organized in the diocese of Los Angeles under the auspices of the Office of Catholic Charities to reach out to the immigrant families from Mexico who were moving into the area. The diocesan and parochial structure of the Los Angeles CCD became the model for other dioceses.

By the early 1930s the CCD had become a national movement, and Bishop Edwin V. O'HARA of Great Falls, Montana, gained permission from the Holy See to establish a national office to coordinate its activities. An episcopal committee with O'Hara as president was named in 1934, and it in turn established the national center for CCD under the auspices of National Catholic Welfare Conference in 1935. Throughout the first quarter century of its existence the national center reflected the zeal of Bishop O'Hara, the guiding spirit in its foundation, and that of Miss Miriam MARKS, early aide to Bishop O'Hara and executive secretary from 1935 to 1960.

The national center developed a highly structured model for the confraternity at the parish level. At its head was the priest-director, the pastor or his delegate, whose function was to direct the members' activity and form them spiritually. Collaborating with him was a lay executive board consisting of the officers and the chairs of each of six departments: teachers, fishers, helpers, parent-educators, discussion clubs, and the Apostolate of Good Will for those who were not members of the Church. After the Second Vatican Council diocesan directors of the confraternity formed the National Conference of Diocesan Directors–CCD to coordinate their efforts. Its executive secretary acted as liaison with the national center. It was the forerunner of the NATIONAL CONFERENCE OF CATECHETICAL LEADERSHIP.

The national center offered many support services to the field in the way of congresses, handbooks, catechetical resources, and graded catechisms. Every year from 1935 to World War II it organized national congresses, the first held at Rochester, N.Y.; after the war, the national congresses were held every five years, the last in 1971 in Miami. To make the Scriptures more accessible to both CCD teacher and student, Bishop O'Hara took the initiative in organizing the Catholic Biblical Association and commissioning it to produce the confraternity edition of the New Testament, which was later subsumed into the NEW AMERICAN BIBLE. In 1964 the national center began publication of *The Living Light*, a quarterly under the editorship of Mary Perkins RYAN designed to provide resources and pastoral counsel to catechists.

Although the early focus of the confraternity in the U.S. was on immigrant families, its principal concern came to be the religious instruction of children who were not attending Catholic schools. It designed programs to meet a variety of situations, urban and rural: Sunday school, released time, and summer vacation school. In addition, the CCD had three other special areas of concern: preschool children and their parents, the further Catholic education of adults in general, and, greatest of all, the hardly touched harvest of those outside the Church.

In no other country was the confraternity as highly organized as in the U.S. Yet with the publication of the *General Catechetical Directory* in 1971, which made no mention of the CCD, the structures of the confraternity went into decline. In 1975 the National Center of Religious Education–CCD was suppressed and its ministry assigned to the department of education of the United States Catholic Conference. For a while CCD served as a generic term for non-school programs, but it no longer signified the highly organized and, in many places, very successful program of the early years.

Bibliography: *The Confraternity Comes of Age: A Historical Symposium* (Paterson, NJ 1956). J. B. COLLINS, *Religious Education and CCD in the United States: Early Years (1902–1935)*, American Ecclesiastical Review 169 (1975) 48–67; *Bishop O'Hara and a National CCD, ibid.*, 237–255.

[J. E. KRAUS/EDS.]

CONFUCIANISM AND NEO-CONFUCIANISM

The term "Confucianism" was originally coined by 16th century Jesuits missionaries to China as a neologism for the venerable, all-encompassing tradition rooted in Chinese culture and philosophical-religious thought that is variously referred to in the Chinese language as *rujia* (School of the *Literati*), *rujiao* (Traditions of the *Literati*), *ruxue* (Teachings of the *Literati*) or simply as *ru (literati)*. While the vision and ideas of CONFUCIUS and his followers such as MENCIUS (Mengzi) and Xunzi (Hsüntzu) played a key role in animating and enriching the *ru* tradition, the *ru* tradition itself *predated* Confucius. The efforts of Matteo RICCI and his Jesuit companions to canonize Confucius as the "founder" of Confucianism had more to do with missiological exigencies than being an accurate description of the *ru* movement in its socio-historical setting. In the absence of an appropriate term, the term "Confucianism" is used as a convenient label for the Chinese cultural-philosophical tradition shaped by Confucius and his followers beginning from the period of the Warring States (481–221 B.C.) and leading up to the Song dynasty (A.D. 960–1279).

The term "Neo-Confucianism" is often used to refer to the developments in Confucian thought from the Song

A traditional Confucian spring rite. (©Nathan Benn/CORBIS)

dynasty to the collapse of the Qing dynasty (1644–1911). It has been similarly criticized for its misleading portrayal of a unified and normative movement, overgeneralizing the reality of a diverse plurality of vibrant, competing schools of thought in China during the period from that included *Daoxue* (School of the Way), *Lixue* (School of Principle), and *Xinxue* (School of the Mind), to name a few. These schools regarded Confucius as their inspiration and his teachings as a common cultural-philosophical heritage, but developed his ideas in innovative ways that he would never have recognized. The problem is compounded by the fact that the Chinese themselves never saw fit to coin a single term to describe the diversity of competing schools.

Canonical Texts. One major characteristic of Confucianism and Neo-Confucianism is the absence of any creeds or official dogmas. The traditional Confucian corpus is identified with the Five Classics (*Wu jing*) that Confucius supposedly edited: Book of Poetry (*Shijing*),

Book of History (*Shujing*), Book of Rites (*Liji*), Book of Changes (*Yijing*) and the Spring and Autumn Annals (*Chunqiu*). A sixth Classic, the Book of Music (*Yuejing*) is no longer extant. Although *Zhu Xi (Chu-hsi)*, the great Neo-Confucian philosopher formulated a canonical list of the Four Books (*Si shu*)—*Lunyu* (Confucian Analects), *Mengzi* (Mencius), *Daxue* (''Great Learning'') and *Zhongyong* (''Doctrine of the Mean'') for use in the Chinese civil service examinations from 1313 to 1905, there was no official orthodoxy or revealed dogmas on how these Four Books or the Five Classics were to be interpreted and appropriated. This paved the way for the emergence of diverse creative and novel interpretations, all claiming to be faithful to the teachings of the First Teacher himself.

Existential Quest. The point of convergence of various schools within Confucianism and Neo-Confucianism is the existential-religious questions of the ultimate values that shape human living: ''What does it mean to be human as opposed to barbarians or animals?'' ''What makes life worth living as humans?'' ''What are the ideals and virtues that are needed to inspire everyone from emperor to peasant to participate in the creation and maintenance of a harmonious and civilized society as opposed to chaos and destruction?'' ''Where are these ideals and virtues to be found?''

The responses to these questions that Confucius and his successors formulated reveal a dynamic, relational understanding of ''knowing'' in Chinese thinking that is not concerned with discovering the truth via abstract, essentialist conceptualizations of the natural world. Instead, ''knowing'' for Confucius and his followers is about knowing how to be adept in one's relations with others, how to make use of the possibilities arising from these relations, and how to trust in the validity of these relations as the cornerstone for familial and social harmony. Hence, knowing how to be a ruler or a parent is not knowing the proper behavioral qualities that define an ideal-type ruler or parent, but knowing how to relate genuinely to one's subjects or one's children, fulfill one's responsibilities toward them, and in turn to earn their respect, deference and their trust.

All schools of Confucianism and Neo-Confucianism never begin their quest for authentic human living *ex nihilo*, but rely on innovative, contextualized appropriations of ancient folk traditions and the traditions of the Former Kings (*Xianwang*)—the legendary sage-kings Yao, Shun and Yu, and the first three rulers of the Zhou dynasty, Wen, Wu and Zhou Gong (the Duke of Zhou)—to provide answers as to what is appropriate in each age. Confucians and Neo-Confucians have been adept at adding interpretive layers of meaning to the classic terminology rather than creating entirely new systems of thought in their existential quest for meaningfulness in human living.

Achieving the Fullness of Being Human. It is important to recognize the interrelationality and intersubjectivity of the Confucian and Neo-Confucian quest that seeks to realize the fullness of *renxing* (*jen-hsing*, ''human nature''). The ideal Confucian is always and everywhere one among many, to be fully human in relation to others within the wider world of humanity, and seeking the ultimate, existential values within human living. Confucius called this existential quest the highest virtue of *ren* (*jen*, ''human-ness''). Not to seek *ren* (''humanness'') is tantamount to a denial of the fullness of one's humanity in relation to others. Various schools of Neo-Confucianism would propose different methodological approaches and call it by different names (e.g., ''principle'' or *li*), but the quest remains the same.

Human Nature. While Confucius himself never spoke much about human nature (*renxing, jen-hsing*), it became a major contentious point between Mencius (Mengzi) and Xunzi (Hsün-tzu), the two major Confucian philosophers representing the idealist and rationalist wings of Confucianism during the period of the Warring States (481–221 B.C.). Mencius argued that ''original human nature'' (*benxing*) at one's birth is good but incipient and underdeveloped. At birth, the *benxing* comprises the four virtuous tendencies of commiseration, shame, deference and preference that are incipient, underdeveloped and fragile. With proper education and self cultivation, these tendencies could mature and blossom into the four cardinal virtues of ''human-ness'' (*ren*), appropriateness (*yi*), propriety (*li*) and wisdom (*zhi*) in a fully developed human nature (*renxing*). Xunzi rejected Mencius' position, insisting that the inherent human tendency is toward evil, and goodness can only be imposed externally through education and disciplined self-cultivation. Although Mencius and Xunzi had diametrically opposite understandings of human nature, they converged in agreement on the need for proper education and personal self-cultivation. While Xunzi's position found a receptive response during the Han Dynasty, his interpretation was marginalized and eventually supplanted by Mencius' idealist understanding, which became the authoritative interpretation accepted by the various Neo-Confucian schools.

Five Constants (*Wu chang*). The Confucian existential quest for meaningfulness is not limited to the human-self, but is contextualized in a unity of the cosmological, social, familial and individual dimensions of human living. Confucius and his followers called this the Way of Heaven and its Mandate (*Tianming*) for virtuous living. The classical Confucian paradigm for virtuous living is the proper self-cultivation of the ''Five Constants'' (*Wu chang*)—*ren* (*jen*, ''human-ness''), *yi* (*i*, ''appropriateness''), *li* (propriety), *zhi* (*chih*, ''wisdom in thought and action''), and *xin* (*hsin*, ''keeping to one's word''). Merely knowing these virtues in an intellectual, theoretical sense is not enough. Each school within Confucianism and Neo-Confucianism insists on the need for *actual* personal self-cultivation of the ''Five Constants,'' each proposing different approaches to this quest.

Five Relations (*Wu lun*). Another classical Confucian paradigm is the Five Relations (*Wu lun*), which defines the five foundational relations of a Confucian society: parent-child, ruler-subject, husband-wife, elder-younger sibling, and friend-friend. The first four relations are hierarchical relations, while the fifth is a relation of equals. Within the Confucian conception of society, there are no strangers in society, the basic relation is at least friend-to-friend. The Five Relations reveals that the hierarchical ordering of familial relations is the principal foundation upon which complex, interlocking human relations in the Chinese society are constructed. Before a person is able to do great things in society, that person must first be a proper spouse, parent, child, sibling or friend to another.

Filiality and Ancestor Veneration. For Confucians and Neo-Confucians, the proper relational ordering of society as a human macrocosm takes the family as its inspiration and starting point. Society is ordered and harmony is promoted based at all levels based on *filiality*, the source of order and harmony within a family. Ritually, filiality is expressed through ancestor veneration offered by son to father, by scholar-gentry to Confucius as ancestor *par excellence*, and by emperor to his ancestors and to *Tian* (Heaven) for the well-being of the nation. Because filiality together with its public ritual expression of ancestor veneration became the glue that held religion, culture and society together in imperial China, the attempts by some missionaries in the 17th and 18th centuries to prohibit Chinese Catholic converts from participating in ancestor veneration were viewed as attacks on filiality and on the very cohesion of Chinese culture and society. This triggered the CHINESE RITES CONTROVERSY that lasted more than three centuries.

Emergence of Neo-Confucian Schools. After centuries of competing intellectually and spiritually with Daoism and BUDDHISM, Confucian scholars in the Song Dynasty initiated a process of reinterpreting traditional Confucian classical texts to formulate new answers that responded to the challenges brought by Daoism and Buddhism. This process gave rise to new innovative schools of thought. This revival and revitalization of Confucianism started with the writings of the Northern Song scholars Zhou Dunyi (Chou Tun-i, 1017–73), Shao Yong (Shao Yung, 1011–77), Zhang Zai (Chang Tsai, 1020–77), and the brothers Cheng Hao (Ch'eng Hao, 1032–85) and Cheng Yi (Ch'eng I, 1033–77).

Early Neo-Confucian Developments. While overtly condemning Buddhism and Daoism, these scholars were busy combining metaphysical elements borrowed from those two religions with traditional themes from Confucian classics such as the Analects, the Mencius, the Book of Changes, the Book of Rituals. In doing so, the Neo-Confucians did not view their actions as distorting and betraying their predecessors' vision. On the contrary, the innovations were adopted to justify and strengthen the Confucian vision of life that was under threat from its two main rivals. Nevertheless, what emerged from the ruminations of these scholars was a novel and innovative metaphysical framework for Confucianism that was designed to counter the attractiveness of rival Daoist and Buddhist metaphysical systems. Zhou Dunyi (Chou Tun-i) and Shao Yong (Shao Yung) had reinterpreted

Daoist metaphysical diagrams to offer an nascent metaphysical cosmology for Confucianism. Zhang Zai (Chang Tsai) proposed a materialist understanding of *qi* (*chi*, "energy") as the building block of everything (i.e., spirit, matter and energy) in the universe. The two brothers Cheng Hao and Cheng Yi formulated the theory of "principle" (*li*) as the universal and primordial potentiality from which all living things are ordered.

Zhu Xi and the School of Principle. It was the great Neo-Confucian scholar Zhu Xi (Chu-hsi, 1130–1200) who synthesized the efforts of these five Neo-Confucian scholars into a coherent metaphysical framework that later became the foundational tenets of his rationalist School of Principle (*Lixue*). The starting point for Zhu Xi is "principle" (*li*) as predictable and observable patterns of potentialities in the world upon which *qi* (energy) crystallizes and forms all living things. There was one universal and primordial *li* (principle) that is *objectively descriptive* (i.e., it describes *why* things are) and *morally prescriptive* (it prescribes *what* can be done to these things). Adapting the Mencian assertion that "original human nature" (*benxing*) is wholly good, Zhu Xi claimed that *li* (principle) is wholly good, and evil arises not from *li* (principle) but turgid *qi* (bad energy), which can be clarified through disciplined self-cultivation. The purpose of education is to acquire knowledge of the descriptive and prescriptive aspects of *li* (principle) through the "investigation of all things" (*ge wu*). He insisted on the necessity of investigating all things, arguing that if one merely investigate one thing, there is no basis for differentiating particularity from universality within the *li* (principle) that constitutes that one thing.

Wang Yangming and the School of the Mind. Wang Yangming (1472–1529), the idealist Neo-Confucian scholar of the Ming dynasty who synthesized the principal teachings of the School of the Mind (*Xinxue*), rejected the rationalist approach of Zhu Xi. He propounded a doctrine of the "unity of knowledge and action" (*zhi xing he yi*) based on the notion that principle (*li*) is found wholly within the mind (*xin*), because the mind is the repository of the innate knowledge of all goodness (*liangzhi*). To investigate these moral principles is to "rectify the mind" (*chengyi*). Thus, for Wang Yangming, the "investigation of things for attaining knowledge" (*ge wu zhi zhi*) is unnecessary, all that is needed is a contemplative and introspective "rectification of the mind" (*chengyi*).

See Also: BUDDHISM.

Bibliography: W. T. CHAN, *A Sourcebook in Chinese Philosophy* (Princeton 1963). W. T. DE BARY et al, *The Unfolding of Neo-Confucianism* (New York 1975). J. CHING, *To Acquire Wisdom: The Way of Wang Yang-ming* (New York 1976). W.-M. TU, *Neo-

Confucian Thought in Action: Wang Yang-ming's Youth (1472–1509) (Berkeley, Calif. 1976). W.-M. TU, *Confucian Thought: Selfhood as Creative Transformation* (Albany, N.Y. 1985). B. I. SCHWARTZ, *The World of Thought in Ancient China* (Cambridge, Mass. 1985). I. EBER, *Confucianism, the Dynamics of Tradition* (New York 1986). D. K. GARDNER, *Chu-Hsi and the Ta-hsueh: Neo-Confucian Reflection on the Confucian Canon* (Cambridge, Mass. 1986). W. T. CHAN, ed. *Chu-Hsi and Neo-Confucianism* (Honolulu 1986). W. T. CHAN, *Chu Hsi, Life and Thought* (Hong Kong 1987). W. T. CHAN, *Chu Hsi: New Studies* (Honolulu 1989). A. C. GRAHAM, *Disputers of the Tao: Philosophical Argument in Ancient China* (La Salle, Ill. 1989). W. T. DE BARY, *The Trouble with Confucianism* (Cambridge, Mass. 1991). D. L. HALL and R. T. AMES, *Thinking Through Confucius* (Albany N.Y. 1987). D. L. HALL and R. T. AMES, *Anticipating China: Thinking Through the Narratives of Chinese and Western Culture* (Albany, N.Y. 1995). D. L. HALL and R. T. AMES, *Thinking from the Han: Self, Truth and Transcendence in Chinese and Western Culture* (Albany, N.Y. 1997). L. M. JENSEN, *Manufacturing Confucianism: Chinese Traditions & Universal Civilization* (Durham 1997). J. H. BERTHRONG, *Transformations of the Confucian Way* (Boulder, Colo. 1998). X. YAO, *An Introduction to Confucianism* (Cambridge, Eng. 2000). J. CHING, *The Religious Thought of Chu Hsi* (New York 2000).

[J. Y. TAN]

CONFUCIUS (KONGFUZI)

Honorific title for China's preeminent philosopher, teacher, social thinker and political theorist; real name *Kongqiu* (K'ung Ch'iu); literary name *Zhongni* (Chungni); b. 551 B.C., Qufu (Ch'ü-fu) in the state of Lu (modern-day Shandong province in northeastern China); d. 479 B.C. Confucius is the Latinization form of the Chinese *Kongfuzi* (K'ung Fu-Tzu) or *Kongzi* (K'ung-Tzu), in English, "Master Kong."

Biographical Information

Confucius lived during China's Spring and Autumn Period (722–481 B.C.), the twilight years of the Zhou (Chou) Dynasty that witnessed the gradual disintegration of the Zhou feudal structure into the turbulent Warring States period. Born into a family of petty aristocracy that had fallen upon hard times, he was a prolific scholar who had distinguished himself in learning as a member of the class of *ru (ju)*, i.e., itinerant scholars who were usually sons of petty aristocratic families that had fallen upon hard times and were now wandering from court to court, offering their services as teachers, masters of ritual, astronomers and specialists in calendrical computations.

A firm believer in education as the *sine qua non* for one's self-cultivation, Confucius achieved fame by establishing China's first school of learning more than a century before Plato had established his academy in Athens. Before this, education was available only to the wealthy

Confucius. (Archive Photos/Popperfoto)

Chinese aristocratic families who could afford to hire a *ru* as a private tutor for their children. An enthusiastic and charismatic teacher, Confucius was able to gather some thirty men as his first batch of students. As a teacher, he made no distinction between the sons of nobility or peasantry, accepting whatever payment they could afford for his services (see *Analects* 7:7, 15:38). In return, he expected a high degree of commitment toward learning and self-cultivation from his students, and was intolerant of those who were lazy or unenthusiastic (*Analects* 7:8). His curriculum of the traditional "six arts," (1) ritual and ceremony (*li*), (2) music, (3) archery, (4) charioteering, (5) calligraphy and (6) mathematics, was geared as much toward personal cultivation and character refinement as toward training for employment as government functionaries. Viewing himself as a transmitter rather than an innovator ("following the proper way, I do not forge new paths," *Analects* 7:1), he made his students study the ancient Chinese classics—the Book of Poetry (*Shijing*), the Book of History (*Shujing*) and the Book of Changes (*Yijing*).

Confucius firmly believed that everyone could benefit from self-cultivation and insisted that everyone could aspire to be leaders by proper training and education. For him education was more than mere acquisition of knowledge or a means of acquiring power. Rather, education is primarily about character building and self-cultivation, and only secondarily about acquiring skills for career advancement. His twofold legacy of proper education as a cornerstone of socio-political transformation, and teaching as the highest and most noble calling continues to animate the East Asian societies that venerate him as teacher and philosopher *par excellence*.

Confucius did not achieve fame and recognition in his lifetime, failing to secure any influential administrative position where he could implement his vision of life and socio-political theories. His idealistic socio-political vision did not endear him to these rulers. For him, a ruler had to rule in the manner of the Former Kings (*Xianwang*), i.e., the ancient sage-kings Yao, Shun and Yu, and the first three rulers of the Zhou (Chou) Dynasty, viz., King Wen, his son King Wu, and Zhou Gong (the Duke of Zhou), the younger brother of King Wu. He regarded these rulers as having governed by observing propriety (*li*) rather than by imposing laws and using force. He associated governing by propriety with the maintenance of cosmological harmony and natural order between "Heaven" (*Tian*) and earth, while using force was associated with the corruption and chaotic disorder that led to the downfall of wicked kings. Very little is known about the twilight years of life, except that later biographers recorded him as dying a broken and dejected man, having no inkling of the tremendous impact his teachings would subsequently have throughout East Asia to the present.

While Confucius claimed to be a transmitter rather than an innovator (Analects 7:1), the originality and vitality of his overarching vision of life, characterized by a threefold principle—the love of tradition, the love of learning, and the love of self-cultivation—was to transform China and the other East Asian societies of Korea, Japan and Vietnam indelibly. Although he personally did not found any mass movement, his teachings was disseminated by his admirers among the *ru* (literati) and co-opted by them, gradually evolving to become the foundational tenets of the *rujiao* ("Teachings of the *Literati*," commonly but inaccurately translated as CONFUCIANISM). His vision also caught the imagination of the masses and was appropriated by them in their popular folk traditions and customs centered around rites of passage, filiality and ancestor veneration.

Confucius himself did not appear to have written anything that can be clearly attributed to him. The only extant collection of his sayings is the *Lun Yu* (Analects), a later compilation by his disciples of sayings attributed to him.

Philosophy and Vision of Life

The core of Confucius' teachings centers on the self-cultivation of *li, xiao (hsiao), yi (i)* and *ren (jen)*, commonly translated as propriety, filiality, appropriateness and human-ness. The objective of such self-cultivation is to become a *junzi (chün-tzu)* or "superior person."

Propriety (li). This refers to the ritualized norms of proper conduct regulating all aspects of human interactions according to relations of position and rank in family and society. For Confucius, *li* is the proper expression of sincere emotion, distinguishing the civilized person from barbarians who gave free and undisciplined vent to their emotions. He condemned empty and formalistic displays of rituals (see Analects 3:12), insisting that *li* must combine the *external* aspect of performing the proper ritual form with the *internal* disposition of heartfelt inner attitude. Indeed, Analects 2:7 criticizes empty and insincere ritualized displays of filiality toward one's parents. There is no separation or contradiction between external propriety and inner disposition. The goal of propriety is social harmony:

> Achieving harmony (*he*) is the most valuable function of observing ritual propriety (*li*). In the way of the Former Kings, this achievement of harmony made them elegant, and was a guiding standard in all things large and small. But when things are not going well, to realize harmony just for its own sake without regulating the situation through observing ritual propriety will not work (Analects 1:12).

Filiality (xiao). Filiality is defined as the primacy of the parent-child relations in the indivisible personal, social and religious realms of one's life. For Confucius, filiality undergirds one's obligations of reverence, obedience, and love toward one's parents when they are still alive, venerating them with the proper rituals when they are dead, and perpetuating this veneration by producing descendants (see Analects 2:5). At the same time, filiality is more than merely giving material support to one's parents. It also involves the self-cultivation of proper respectful and reverential inner dispositions toward them:

> Ziyou asked about filial conduct (*xiao*). The Master replied: "Those today who are filial are considered so because they are able to provide for their parents. But even dogs and horses are given that much care. If you do not respect your parents, what is the difference? (Analects 2:7).

It does not mean an uncritical obsequiousness:

The Master said, "In serving your father and mother, remonstrate with them gently. On seeing that they do not heed your suggestions, remain respectful and do not act contrary. Although concerned, voice no resentment (Analects 4:18).

The practice of ancestor veneration as a ritualization of filiality became a defining characteristic of Chinese culture and the cornerstone of the Chinese family. Attempts by some missionaries in the 17th century to prohibit Chinese Catholic converts from participating in ancestor veneration were viewed as attacks on Chinese culture and family structure, triggering the CHINESE RITES' CONTROVERSY that lasted more than three centuries.

Appropriateness (yi). The term *yi (i)* is commonly translated by Western scholars as "benevolence," "morality," or "moral." However, traditional Chinese dictionaries, e.g., the *Ci Hai* ("Sea of Words") translate this term "right," "fitting," or "proper." Etymologically, the word comprises the ideograph of a sheep (*yang*) above the ideograph for the first person pronoun (*wo*) that can be translated both in the first-person ("I," "me") or the third-person ("we," "us"). Sinologists think that the ideograph for *yi* represents a community doing something proper or fitting by sacrificing a sheep (see e.g., Analects 3:17). On this basis, the term *yi*—"appropriateness," or doing something "proper" or "fitting"—undergirds such other virtues as propriety and filiality, enabling one to do what is proper and fitting in relation to others:

> The Master said, "Exemplary persons (*junzi*) understand what is appropriate (*yi*), petty persons understand only what is of personal advantage" (Analects 4:16).

Human-ness (ren). The concept of *ren (jen)*, often translated as "humanity" or "human-ness," refers to the attribute of "being fully human," in contrast with barbarians or animals acting on instincts. The *Shuowen jiezi* suggests that etymologically, the Chinese character for *ren* comprises the character for "person" and the number "two," indicating perhaps a relational quality that marks the "human" character of persons in community. Herbert Fingarette expresses this succinctly as follows: "For Confucius, unless there are at least two human beings, there can be no human beings." Confucius himself defined *ren* as "loving people" (*ai ren*) (Analects 12:22), emphasizing the *inter-relationality* and *intersubjectivity* of human living, where one is always *one among many* and seeking to achieve full humanity in one's relations with others. For him, *ren* is the highest moral virtue and the totality of all moral virtues embodying an ideal moral life. In practical terms, *ren* embodies *yi* (appropriateness), *li* (propriety) and *xiao* (filiality).

Superior Person (junzi). Confucius consistently extolled and upheld the *junzi (chün-tzu)* or "superior person" as the goal of self-cultivation. For him, a *junzi* is someone who embodies the virtues of propriety, filiality, appropriateness and human-ness (*see* Analects 1:2, 1:8, 1:14, 2:11, 2:13, 4:5, 4:24, 6:16, 9:13, 13:3, 14:30, 15:17, 15:20, 15:31, 16:8, 16:10). Originally, the term referred to the son of a ruler who was heir to the throne. Confucius appropriated and relativized this political term to communicate his belief in meritocracy, viz., real leaders are formed, not born. For him, a true leader is one who has perfected himself through a life-long engagement of moral self-cultivation. Anyone, even the son of a peasant could aspire to be a *junzi*, the epitome of perfection. Here, the quest to become a *junzi* should not be understood as a selfish, individualistic quest for its own sake, but rather within a wider context of human relations in society. Confucius often contrasted the *junzi* with the *xiaoren* (*hsiao-jen*, or "petty person"), a self-centered and individualistic person whom he portrayed as selfish, calculative, unrefined and vindictive (*see* Analects 2:14, 4:11, 4:16, 8:6, 12:16, 13:23, 13:26, 14:24, 15:20, 17:23).

Bibliography: Sources. D. C. LAU, *Confucius: The Analects* (Hong Kong 1992). C. HUANG, *The Analects of Confucius* (Oxford 1997). R.T. AMES and H. ROSEMONT, JR., *The Analects of Confucius: A Philosophical Translation* (New York 1998). W. T. CHAN, *A Sourcebook in Chinese Philosophy* (Princeton 1963). Studies. H. A. FINGARETTE, *Confucius: The Secular as Sacred* (New York 1972). B. I. SCHWARTZ, *The World of Thought in Ancient China* (Cambridge, Mass. 1985). A. C. GRAHAM, *Disputers of the Tao: Philosophical Argument in Ancient China* (Chicago 1989). D. L. HALL and R. T. AMES, *Thinking Through Confucius* (New York 1987). D.L. HALL and R. T. AMES, *Anticipating China: Thinking Through The Narratives of Chinese and Western Culture* (New York 1995). D. L. HALL and R. T. AMES, *Thinking from the Han: Self, Truth and Transcendence in Chinese and Western Culture* (New York 1997). X. YAO, *An Introduction to Confucianism* (Cambridge, Eng. 2000).

[J. Y. TAN]

CONGAR, YVES MARIE-JOSEPH

Theologian, ecumenist, author; b. in Sedan (Ardennes), France, April 13, 1904; d. in Paris, June 22, 1995; son of Georges and Lucie (Desoye) Congar. He studied at the minor seminary in Rheims and the Institut Catholique in Paris, and in 1925 joined the Dominican Order, completing his studies and earning a doctorate in theology at the Dominican Studium of Saulchoir. He was ordained a priest in 1930, and from 1931 to 1939 he taught fundamental theology and ecclesiology at Le Saulchoir. Drafted into the army in 1939, he spent five years as a prisoner of war.

At the end of World War II, Congar returned to Le Saulchoir, where he taught until 1954, when a series of ecclesiastical decisions forced him into exile in Jerusalem, Rome, and Cambridge before being given a regular

Yves Marie-Joseph Congar. (Agence France Presse/Archive Photos)

assignment in Strasbourg (1956–58). He was invited, at the express wish of Pope John XXIII, to help in the preparations for the Second VATICAN COUNCIL. At Vatican II he served on the Doctrinal Commission and made major contributions to the council's documents on the Church, ecumenism, revelation, missions, the priesthood and the Church in the modern world.

Congar contributed a running commentary on the theological discussions and events of the Council to the bi-weekly *Informations catholiques internationales* (collected in *Le concile au jour le jour* 1963–66). Vatican II represented a thorough rehabilitation of his reputation in Catholic circles; after the council he was able to devote himself peacefully to historical and theological scholarship until a chronic bone disease made it difficult for him to write.

Writings and Thought. The list of Congar's published titles numbers more than 1,700 books and articles, among which may be found works of first-rate historical scholarship, theological exploration, contemporary ecclesial interpretation, and essays in spiritual theology. For almost fifty years he reported regularly on ecclesiology in the *Revue des sciences philosophiques et théologiques.*

On the eve of his priestly ordination, Congar received what he considered to be a divine vocation to work for the reunion of Christians. He understood that ecumenical rapprochement would require a thorough renewal in ecclesiology, and it is his research into the history of the theology of the Church and his efforts to recover a fuller ecclesial vision than had prevailed in the baroque theology of the modern era that provided the chief focus of his writings.

Congar's first major contribution, *Chrétiens desunis: Principes d'un "oecuménisme" catholique* (1937; English translation 1939), was a watershed in the Catholic Church's attitude towards ecumenism. In this work Congar offered an historical interpretation of the great schisms which have split the Church, a sympathetic presentation of the distinctive characters of Protestantism, Anglicanism, and Orthodoxy, and a statement of principles for Catholic participation in the ecumenical movement. This work also caught the attention of Roman authorities, and it seems it was only his wartime imprisonment that enabled him to escape the condemnations which in 1942 fell upon Le Saulchoir and his colleague, Marie Dominique CHENU.

Upon his return to France after the war, Congar threw himself into the very heady atmosphere of Church life. In the late 1940s, French Catholicism was alive with the promise of Biblical, liturgical, and patristic revivals, the so-called new theology, the worker-priest experiment, and efforts to construct a new pastoral theology and practice. Congar attempted to propose principles and criteria for an authentic reform and renewal in the Church in his next great work, *Vraie et fausse reforme dans l'Église* (1950). Much of what he proposed would later be sanctioned by Vatican II, but in 1950 this was hardy stuff; and he was one of those considered to indulge in the "false irenicism" condemned that year in *Humani generis.* In 1952 all translations and re-editions of the work were forbidden by Rome.

Nonetheless in 1953 he was able to publish his very influential work, *Jalons pour une théologie du laïcat* (1953; rev. ed. 1964; English translation 1957 and 1965), which was later to find many echoes at Vatican II. The work provides a critique of the reduction of ecclesiology to "hierarchology" (a term which he seems to have coined), and a validation of the laity's participation in the threefold office of Christ.

A year later, however, the series of denunciations, warnings, and restrictive measures which he had received from Rome was crowned by an order that he desist from teaching and leave Le Saulchoir. He was ordered successively to Jerusalem, Rome, and to England. All his writings were made subject to stringent censorship. In 1956, Archbishop Weber took him under his protection in Strasbourg.

During these difficult years, Congar published, after long delays caused by the censors, a profound study of the Church under the title, *Le mystère du Temple* (1958; English translation 1962). Unable to participate directly in ecumenical activities, he devoted himself to historical scholarship. A first fruit of this was his two-volume work, *La tradition et les traditions* (1960 and 1963; English translation 1966). This work and several lengthy essays on episcopal collegiality, on authority as service, on poverty in the Church, on the local church, and on catholicity as universal inculturation were to contribute greatly to the elaboration of the documents of the Second Vatican Council. His participation in the preparation and unfolding of the Council was to make up for the years of neglect and suspicion, and he could rightly claim the Council as the triumph of many causes for which he had been working.

Post Vatican II. After the Council, Congar continued his scholarly work and participated actively in the great debates occasioned by the remarkable changes that took place in the Church. He published two major works on the history of ecclesiology, *L'ecclésiologie du haut moyen-âge* (1968) and *L'Église de Saint-Augustin à l'époque moderne* (1970). Several collections of his published works include essays on ministry, salvation, diversity and communion, the theology of Luther, and the ecclesiology of Vatican II. A three-volume work on the Holy Spirit, *Je crois en l'Esprit-Saint* (1979–80; English translation 1983), attempts to redress the neglect of pneumatology in Western theology. Many other scholarly essays remain scattered in various journals and volumes.

Congar never regarded Vatican II as an unsurpassable moment and with a remarkable openness he continued to speak and write on post-conciliar developments and problems, as for example, the challenge of Archbishop Lefebvre, political and liberation theology, and the charismatic movement.

His contribution to 20th-century theology is difficult to summarize or to synthesize. Congar's most widely acknowledged contribution is the vast work of historical recovery of the great and broad Catholic tradition before it began to be straitened by the schisms of the 11th and 16th centuries. He regarded this *ressourcement* as crucial to the life of the Church today, and all his life he has brought to the discussion of contemporary events a mind informed by a broad and deep knowledge that has enabled him to be what J.-P. Jossua calls "a prophet of tradition," that is, a theologian exercising a critical and constructive role precisely as a mediator of the achievements of the past. In all these respects, as the event of the Second Vatican Council itself illustrates, Yves Congar proved a model of a perennially necessary theological effort. Pope John Paul II named Congar to the College of Cardinals on Nov. 24, 1994.

Bibliography: Y. CONGAR, *Le Concile se Vatican II: Son Église, Peuple de Dieu et Corps du Christ* (Paris 1984); *Dialogue Between Christians: Catholic Contributions to Ecumenism* (Westminster, Md. 1966): 1–51; *Diversity and Communion* (Mystic, Conn. 1985); *Une passion: L'unité: Réflexions souvenirs 1929–1973* (Paris 1974). E. FOUILLOUX, "Friar Yves, Cardinal Congar, Dominican: Itinerary of a Theologian," *U.S. Catholic Historian* 17 (1999): 63–90. J.-P. JOSSUA, *Le Père Congar: La théologie au service du Peuple de Dieu* (Paris 1967). T. I. MACDONALD, *The Ecclesiology of Yves Congar: Foundational Themes* (Lanham, Md. 1984). A. A. NICHOLS, *A. Yves Congar* (Wilton, Conn. 1989); "An Yves Congar Bibliography 1967–1987," *Angelicum* 66 (1989): 422– 66.

[J. A. KOMONCHAK]

CONGO, DEMOCRATIC REPUBLIC OF, THE CATHOLIC CHURCH IN

Located in central Africa along the equator, the Democratic Republic of the Congo borders the Central African Republic and Sudan on the north, Uganda, Rwanda, Burundi and Tanzania on the east, Zambia and Angola on the south and the Republic of the Congo on the west. Possessing only a few miles of South Atlantic Ocean coastline in its southwest at the mouth of the River Congo, the Democratic Republic of Congo also benefits from access to Lake Tanganyika, which separates it from Tanzania in the southeast. In the rich Congo River drainage basin running its northern width, hot, humid temperatures prevail, while it is cooler and drier in the higher elevations to the south. The region's wealth of natural resources include cobalt, copper, cadmium, oil reserves, diamonds, gold, silver, zinc, tin, uranium, bauxite, coal, iron ore and timber, while agricultural produce consists of coffee, sugarcane, palm oil, rubber, tea, quinine, bananas, fruits and vegetables. Live volcanoes exist in the south.

Traversed first by the British missionary and explorer David Livingstone and then by Henry Morton Stanley in 1871, the Congo Basin was partitioned among Portugal, France and King Leopold II of Belgium in 1884. As the Congo Free State, the region was exploited under the personal rule of Leopold, leading to an international scandal after which the Belgian government assumed control in 1908. While the Belgians improved the lot of the region's native population in the areas of education, health care and economic development, they failed to train an intellectual or professional elite able to lead the government. The African nationalism movement of the 1950s and the hasty granting of independence in 1960 caused a breakdown of public order: due to corruption and a se-

---

Capital: Kinshasa.
Size: 905,000 sq. miles.
Population: 51,965,000 in 2000.
Languages: French; Ciluba, Kikongo, Lingala, Swahili, and Bantu languages are spoken in various regions.
Religions: 25,982,500 Catholics (50%), 5,200,000 Muslims (10%), 10,393,000 Protestants (20%), 5,180,000 Kimbanguist (10%), 5,209,500 adhere to indigenous beliefs.

Archdioceses	Suffragans
Bukavu	Butembo-Beni, Goma, Kasongo, Kindu, Uvira
Mbandaka-Bikoro (formerly Coquilhatville)	Basankusu, Bukungu-Ikela, Budjala, Lisala, Lolo, Molegbe
Lubumbashi (formerly Elisabethville)	Kalemie-Kirungu, Kamina, Kilwa-Kasenga, Kolwezi, Kongolo, Manono, Sakania-Kipushi
Kinshasa (formerly Léopoldville)	Boma, Idiofa, Inongo, Kenge, Kikwit, Kisantu, Matadi, Popokabaka
Kananga (formerly Luluabourg)	Kabinda, Kole, Luebo, Luiza, Mbujimayi, Mweka, Tshumbe
Kisangani (formerly Stanleyville)	Bondo, Bunia, Buta, Doruma-Dungu, Isangi, Isiro-Niangara, Mahagi-Nioka, Wamba

ries of political upheavals, the Belgian Congo became, successively, the Republic of the Congo (1960–64), the Democratic Republic of the Congo (1964–71) and the Republic of Zaire (1971–97). International interest in the region due to its mineral wealth was also involved: The mutiny of the Congolese army in July of 1960 necessitated the intervention of a UN peacekeeping force; a secessionist movement in Katanga (now Shaba) from 1960–63 was supported by mining interests; and the separatist movement led from 1961–62 by Patrice Lumumba was aided by the Soviet bloc and by aggressively anti-colonial African nations. The departure of the UN forces in 1964 started another leftist and tribal uprising in the Kivu and eastern provinces that required the intervention of foreign mercenaries. The economy of the Congo, among the strongest in Africa before 1960, suffered seriously, and did not begin to recover until 1967 when a military dictatorship under General Mobutu Sese Seko nationalized the region's copper mining industry. Upheaval continued through 2000: in 1977 French troops were called in to quell rebellion; multiparty elections in 1991 resulted in riots and larson; and the rivalry between ethnic Tutsi and Hutu resulted in the overthrow of the government in 1997 and the renaming of the country. Economic problems continued to be exacerbated by an influx of refugees from wars in Rwanda and Burundi through the 1990s, and a civil war waged by eastern separatists was only temporarily brought to a halt by a cease fire in July of 1999.

History to Vatican II

Although Portuguese explorer Diogo Cão discovered and claimed the region around the mouth of the Congo River in 1484, attempts to explore and to develop the interior would be only partially successful until the explorations of David Livingstone and Henry Morton Stanley in the 1860s and 1870s. Cão sent some of the native leaders to Lisbon, where they were treated royally at the court and were instructed in the Catholic faith. When these men returned the following year, they converted the local king. Portuguese Franciscans, Canons Regular and secular priests began a systematic and very successful evangelization around the mouth of the Congo in 1490. King Nzinga was baptized in 1491, and had the church

of São Salvador (now in northern Angola) erected in his capital, which became the seat of a bishopric in 1597. He developed along the left bank of the Congo a Christian kingdom modeled on Portugal. Christianity spread widely in this area under King Alfonso (1506–43). His son Don Henrique was ordained, and in 1518 he was consecrated titular bishop of Utica, becoming the first native bishop of black Africa. Until his death c. 1535, he remained in the Congo.

Development of the Missions. In the Congo, as in Angola to the south, the missions experienced alternating gains and reverses, in part due to the difficulty in communicating the faith to native peoples, the demoralizing effects of the slave trade and the ceaseless tribal wars. Despite frequent petitions by Congolese kings for more missioners, Portugal insisted on its rights of *padroado,* and admitted only Portuguese as missioners, even though it became less and less capable of supplying them. In 1640 the Congregation for the Propagation of the Faith created the Prefecture Apostolic of the Congo, which was confided to Italian Capuchins. A seminary, opened in 1682, supplied a number of native priests. However, in the 1760s the anticlerical policies of the Marquis de POMBAL seriously injured the Church throughout all Portuguese territories, and the rapid decline of the mission continued in the 19th century (*see* PATRONATO REAL).

Rebuilding the Missions. By 1865 The Congo had in good part reverted to paganism when the Holy Ghost Fathers assumed responsibility for the lower Congo River region and established a mission at Boma ten years later. By 1878 Belgian White Fathers had penetrated the east-

DEMOCRATIC REPUBLIC OF THE CONGO

ern sections from Lake Tanganyika; their province was entrusted with the Vicariate Apostolic of the Upper Congo, created in 1888. After King Leopold II of Belgium was given control of the Congo Free State, most of the region was confided to the Congregation of the Immaculate Heart of Mary (Scheut Fathers). Missionary efforts, which continued after Belgium assumed control of the region in 1908, continued to be hampered by the ruthless slave trade continued by the Arabs and Portuguese, and additional hardships, such as climate, disease and travel, took a heavy toll on the missionaries.

During World War I the missions languished, but the improved roads and communications infrastructure constructed following the war facilitated evangelization, resulting in rapid growth. The Catholic population, 350,000 in 1921, had increased to 1,700,000 by 1941 and reached 4,000,000 during the mid-1950s. The first native priest was ordained in 1917, and a Congolese bishop was consecrated in 1956. The hierarchy was established in 1959. By the mid-20th century the Congo had the largest Catholic community in the world. Catholic education, especially in the elementary schools, progressed greatly after 1924, when it began to receive government subsidies.

Two-thirds of the elementary teaching came to be Catholic, compared to one-fourth Protestant. Unfortunately, the stability of the region ended with the movement toward independence from Belgian rule, which culminated in a new government on June 30, 1960.

Bibliography: J. VAN WING, *Dictionnaire d'histoire et de géographie ecclésiastiques,* ed. A. BAUDRILLART et al. (Paris 1912–) 13:444–450. E. WEBER, *Die portugiesische Reichsmission im Königreich Kongo* (Aachen 1924). G. GOYAU, "Les Débuts de l'apostolat au Congo et dans l'Angola," *Revue d'historie des missions,* 7 (1930) 481–514. J. CUVELIER and L. JADIN, *L'Ancien Congo, d'après les archives romaines (1518–1640)* (Brussels 1954). B. M. BIERMANN, "Zur Geschichte der alten Kongo-Mission," *Neue Zeitschrift für Missionswissenschaft,* 4 (1948) 98–104; 8 (1952) 67–68. K. S. LATOURETTE, *A History of the Expansion of Christianity,* 7 v. (New York 1937–45) v.5, 7. G. NOIRHOMME et al., *L'Église au Congo en 1963* (Léopoldville 1963).

[L. JADIN]

The Modern Church

Civil disorders throughout the region after independence resulted in the abandonment of many missions and a return to the practice of indigenous tribal religions, which tolerated polygamy. Many priests and religious men and women were slaughtered amid a rising swell of African nationalist fervor. In November of 1965 a military coup brought to power President Mobutu Sese Seko, who quelled the rebellion and the civil war in Katanga, Stanleyville and the Kwilu and allowed the country to begin to rebuild itself. By the early 1970s the region had one of Africa's strongest economies.

The Suppression of the Church. Several years into his administration, Mobutu initiated the politics of "authenticity," which combined the writings of African nationalist Patrice E. Lumumba, the negritude movement, and the influence of Chinese communist leader Mao Tse Tung into a political philosophy designed to foster political revolution and cultural identity. In the end, Mobutu's policy of nationalization, an integral component of the politics of authenticity disintegrated into economic mismanagement, corruption and a cult of personality.

In 1972, because of his protest against the distorted vision of the politics of authenticity, Cardinal Malula was forced into exile in Rome. Two years later the central committee of Mobutu's Mouvement Populaire de la Révolution (MPR) adopted a new, anti-Christian constitution embodying the so-called "great decisions of radicalization." Mobutu was declared a Messiah; "mobutuism" was granted the status of a religion, and the MPR was made a church. The MPR was also declared the only legal political party. Freedom of information ceased to exist and Church property was confiscated. Christian names, including those of many towns and cities in the country, were suppressed, religion was removed from school curricula and all Christian solemnities were transferred to Sunday so that even Christmas ceased to be a holiday. Holy pictures and images were replaced by a picture of Mobutu. Confiscated minor seminaries were converted by the state into public schools, while the MPR's youth units were introduced in the major seminaries. Meetings of the Zairean Episcopal Conference were forbidden.

The Influence of Vatican II. For the church, Mobutu's anti-Christian policies were a tragedy. The Second Vatican Council of the mid-1960s had sparked positive transformations, such as the Commission on Evangelization's 1969 undertaking of a monumental project of INCULTURATION of the eucharistic liturgy in Zaire that would culminate in Vatican approval of the MISSAL FOR THE DIOCESES OF ZAIRE in 1988. Torn from the inspiring themes of Vatican II, the Zairean Episcopal Conference was forced to focus on defending religious freedom, the freedom of the Church and the rights of individuals in a time of political upheaval and economic recession by 1972. Despite the restrictions placed on them, bishops, as well as the outspoken Cardilan Malula (c. 1989) repeatedly addressed social and economic issues, reaffirmed foundational principles and attacked the secular character of Mobutuism. The pastoral letters *Tous solidaires et responsables* (1977) and *Appel au redressement de la Nation* (1978) courageously named the "Zairean Evil" and its causes while renewing the Church's commitment to fight evil and promote a sustainable development. In 1985 they published a pastoral letter on the meaning of political independence and an evaluation of 25 years of independence in Zaire. Most documents from the 1990s had the predominant theme of democracy and the rebuilding of the nation. Other pastoral letters dealt more directly with religious matters. Another indication of the Catholic Bishops' Conference's relevance was the joint statement on reconciliation made during the National Conference with the leaders of other religious denominations including the Orthodox, the Protestants, Kimbanguists and Muslims.

Resurgence of the Church. By the late 1970s the regional economy declined due to falling copper prices. Faced with rebellions in 1977 and 1978 that required the government to call in French mercenary troops, Mobutu began to moderate his stance. A new constitution promulgated in April of 1978 further moderated government views in the face of Church opposition that rallied almost half of the country's population. In 1980, the anniversary of 100 years of missionary activity in Central Africa, prompted Pope John Paul II's first pastoral visit to Africa. The pope was welcomed by the government, of then Zaire, for a second visit five years later.

Before independence, the Church operated almost all schools in the region, with its goals the elimination of illiteracy, the creation of the first national university in the country, the promotion of cross-cultural understanding and the increasing use of native languages in society. While control of education shifted to the state in 1974, and Church schools and seminaries were placed under strict government control, by 1986 the state reversed itself, restoring private education and resuming the pre-1961 policy permitting children to be educated in conformity with their religious beliefs. Catholic bishops played an important part in the reversal, issuing a declaration that reaffirmed what they considered indefeasible rights and principles of education for the child, the parents, the state and the Church. They encouraged the stimulation of private initiative in education as a replacement for the state's exclusive control. Subsequently, the number of private schools increased significantly.

Major state universities in the region were located in Kinshasa (founded as Lovanium University under Catholic auspices), Lubumbashi and Kisangani (Protestant). While the government had attempted, in 1971, to merge these schools into the National University of Zaire under the jurisdiction of the government, the experiment failed and the three universities eventually regained their autonomy. During the merger, the government suppressed confessional schools within the National University and in 1974 the Catholic bishops determined to organize a school of theology as a separate and autonomous unit. Thus, the first school of theology in black Africa was born and developed into the Catholic Faculties of Kinshasa (1988) under the direct control of the Episcopal Conference of Zaire. One of the most respected universities in the country, it comprised schools of philosophy, theology, development sciences and technology, and social communications. It also maintained a well-respected center for the study of African religions, the aim of which was to provide scientific study and understanding of African traditional religions and culture as a matrix of authentic African theology.

Upheaval Continues into 21st Century. By the mid-1980s the country was once again in chaos. The end of the Cold War, which had given Zaire its strategic importance as heart of the African continent, resulted in a declining concern as to its internal stability by Western superpowers. Extreme poverty, malnutrition and disease became rampant. By 1990 these things combined with the collapse of the country's economy and what the bishops called the ''death'' of the state, evoked renewed opposition to Mobutu and his government. Forced to agree to multi-party elections, Mobutu convened the Sovereign National Conference (Conférence Nationale Souveraine), a 15-month-long meeting of over 2,800 delegates from throughout Zaire to review the nation's plight. By public request, Kisangani Archbishop Laurent Pasinya Monsengwo, then chairman of the Episcopal Conference, presided over this gathering, and by 1992 had aided in drawing up a new constitution under a government led by a high council, a calendar for elections, and a system to deal with the economic crisis. Unfortunately, these plans were not implemented; instead anarchy prevailed, with Mobutu and the council appointing rival governments. The nation was effectively without a working government until 1994, when a transitional government was elected. In 1997 the Hutu government of Mobutu stepped down, forced from the office by Tutsi insurgents led by Laurent Kabila, who assumed the role of dictator and renamed the country the Democratic Republic of the Congo. Backed by Rwandan troops while attempting to oust Mobutu, Kabila soon became a new target of Rwanda. Civil war with neighboring regions to the east continued to leave the nation without a constitution, although the government respected the freedom of Catholics to worship provided they did not become a disruptive influence. Mobutu died in 1997, a year after Archbishop Christophe Munzihirwa Mwene Ngabo died in suspicious circumstances.

By 2000 there were 1,259 parishes tended by 2,350 diocesan and 1,365 religious priests. Other religious included approximately 1,475 brothers and 6,400 sisters, many of whom were engaged in operating the Church's 6,700 primary and 2,046 secondary schools. While bishops continued their efforts to urge all Christians within the nation to work for social justice, a greater sense and respect for life, communion with the ancestors and solid confidence in God, they were also forced to confront the escalation of violence directed toward civilian populations. In January of 1999 rebels attempting to overthrow the Kabila government massacred hundreds of villagers in the southeast. Churches in the eastern regions occupied by troops from Uganda and Rwanda were also targeted by these troops due to their perceived involvement in attacks upon the Tutsi in 1994. Bishop Emmanuel Kataliko of Bukavu was exiled under suspicion of inciting resistance, while reports continued to circulate of other priests and nuns violently attacked and church buildings destroyed. The plight of the thousands of Rwandan and Burundian refugees living camps in the northeast also remained a cause for concern, as humanitarian aid became increasingly rare due to the violence in the region. Reprisals by the Kabila government against Hutu refugees were also suspected. Congolese bishops joined with the country's Protestant and Muslim leaders in March of 2000 to begin a campaign of reconciliation conducive to the formation of a lasting peace. While U.N. forces entered the region in July of 1999, bishops feared that they would be of little deterrence to continued violence within such a vast region.

Bibliography: A. BOLAKOF, *Bakanja martiru wa biso* (Kinshasa 1984). F. BONTINCK, *L'évangélisation du Zaïre* (Kinshasa 1980). CONFERENCE EPISCOPALE DU ZAIRE, *Annuaire de l'Eglise Catholique au Zaïre 1999–2000* (Kinshasa 2000). K. C. DJUNGU-NSIMBA, *Bakanja Isidore. Vrai Zaïrois, vrai chrétien* (Kinshasa 1994). G. IWELE, *Mgr Monsengwo. Acteur et témoin de l'histoire* (Louvain-la-Neuve 1995). S. S. MOBUTU, *Loi-cadre numero 86/005 du 22/9/86 de l'enseignement national* (Kinshasa 1986). K. NGOYI, *L'enseignement de l'Église sur l'éducation, pro manuscripto* (Nganda 1988). *Bakanja Isidoro. Martire per lo Scapolare*, ed. R. PALAZZI (Rome 1994). Also see *Documentation et Information Africaines*.

[G. IWELE]

CONGO, REPUBLIC OF, THE CATHOLIC CHURCH IN

The Republic of the Congo is located in equatorial Africa, and borders the Democratic Republic of the Congo on the east and south, Angola (Cabinda) and the Atlantic Ocean on the southwest, Gabon on the west, and the Central African Republic and Cameroon on the north. The terrain is varied, falling from a coastal plain at the Atlantic northward to a southern basin, then rising again to plateau before falling to lowlands in the far north. Humid and hot, the region's tropical climate is marked by a rainy season in the spring and a dry season that stretches from June to October. Small-scale agricultural concerns produce tapioca, sugar, rice, corn and ground nuts; most of the economy's wealth results from exploiting the region's natural resources, which include petroleum, timber, lead, zinc and uranium.

Once known as Middle Congo, the region became part of French Equatorial Africa from 1910–58 before joining the French Community as a constituent republic. In 1960 the Congo became an independent republic. A sequence of unstable governments culminated in the one-party rule of Marxist leader Col. Denis Sassou-Nguesso in 1979. Sassou-Nguesso dominated the political realm for over a decade before the country's first democratic elections were held in the early 1990s. A civil war in 1997 was quelled following the return of the former leader. While a return to Marxist rule signified a shift away from democratic ideals, efforts were underway by 2000 to privatize parts of the Congo's industrial base.

History. Kongo tribes from the east and Pygmies from the north were the first to inhabit the region, arriving in the 15th century. Portuguese slave traders set up operations along the coast, their efforts hampered by Christian missionaries whose initial efforts proved ineffective in

Capital: Brazzaville.
Size: 122,000 sq. miles.
Population: 2,830,960 in 2000.
Languages: French, Lingala, Monokutuba; local dialects are spoken in various regions.
Religions: 1,613,600 Catholics (57%), 52,700 Muslims (2%), 84,900 Protestants (3%), 1,079,760 follow indigenous faiths.
Archdiocese: Brazzaville, with suffragans Kinkala, Nkayi, Ouesso, Owando, and Pointe-Noire. An apostolic prefecture is located at Likouala.

comparison to the stable missions established to the south in Léopoldville and Angola. In 1663 Capuchin Bernardine of Hungary came at the invitation of the king of Loango (near Pointe-Noire) and converted him and more than 2,000 of his subjects. This brilliant beginning seems to have faded quickly, however; after 1666 no record remained of this community. A century later French missionaries revived the work of evangelization from 1766–76, albeit with slight success.

Another century passed before permanent missionary activity was established. In 1875 French explorer de Brazza initiated treaties with native leaders to bring the region under French control, and in 1883 the Holy Ghost Fathers set up a mission at Loango. Prosper Augouard (1852–1921), the "apostle of the Congo" and first missionary to penetrate the interior, reached Stanley Pool in 1883 and present-day Brazzaville in 1887. The Vicariate Apostolic of the French Congo was created in 1886. In 1890 it was divided into the Vicariate of the French Lower Congo, with its center at Loango, and the Vicariate of the French Upper Congo, with its seat at Brazzaville, where Augouard became the first vicar apostolic. When the hierarchy was established in 1955, Brazzaville became the archdiocese and metropolitan see for the country.

Political instability, communist influences, tribal rivalries and hatred of foreigners were among the main problems facing the mission following the declaration of independence on Aug. 15, 1960. In 1965 all Catholic schools not for the purpose of exclusive training in the faith were made the property of the state. In the 1980s, under a strong Marxist government, political life stabilized, and ties with France remained established. However, in 1990 an agreement was reached to establish a multiparty government. Indicative of the esteem in which Church leaders were held within both society at large and the political realm, Owando Bishop Ernest Kombo was asked to oversee the nation's parliamentary elections in 1992. The outcome was an unstable coalition government, and the results of the new elections held in 1993 were disputed. Violence between competing political fac-

tions escalated during the mid-1990s, resulting in an Angola-backed military coup by Sassou-Nguesso, who returned to his former office. During outbreaks of fighting both before and after the coup, Congolese bishops issued repeated appeals for peace and denied accusations that they had aided efforts to unseat the new president. The Marxist government continued to extend freedom of religion to Congolese through 2000, and a military peace between Sassou-Nguesso and rebel factions was signed in November of 1999. Over 500,000 Congolese were estimated to be in hiding prior to the treaty. In a meeting with Pope John Paul II in 2001, the pope praised the bish-

ops for making ''your voices heard, calling for peace and reconciliation.''

By 2000 there were 126 parishes tended by 185 diocesan and 89 religious priests. Other religious included approximately 50 brothers and 270 sisters, many of whom assisted in running the country's 13 primary and two secondary schools, as the government began to return schools confiscated in 1965 to the Church. Also demanding the attention of the Church was the continuing toll taken by HIV/AIDS; by 2000 the life expectancy for a Congolese was 47 years. Among the country's non-Christian population, many were followers of Kimbangu-

Pope John Paul II is welcomed by the crowd in Brazzaville, Congo, May 1980. (©Vittoriano Rastelli/CORBIS)

ism, a syncretist religion based in the Democratic Republic of the Congo.

Bibliography: J. BOUCHAUD, *Dictionnaire d'histoire et de géographie ecclésiastiques,* ed. A. BAUDRILLART et al., (Paris 1912—) 13:450–455. *Bilan du Monde,* 2:261–264. *Annuario Pontificio,* (1965) 74, 156, 341. For additional bibliography, *see* AFRICA.

[J. BOUCHAUD/EDS.]

CONGREGATIO DE AUXILIIS

The controversies of the Reformation period concerning the operation of God's GRACE and man's FREE WILL, predestination and the many issues that the Council of Trent's Decree on Justification left unsettled forced the subject of the relation between grace and free will on the attention of Catholic theologians of the 16th century. In the years following the council there gradually emerged two opposed explanations of this relationship, one championed by the Dominicans and the other by the Jesuits. The *Congregatio* was a Roman commission established by the pope then reigning, Clement VIII, to examine the orthodoxy of each opinion and to reconcile both parties involved in the dispute. The theological presupposition common to both schools of thought was the absolute, infallible efficacy of the grace or divine help, necessary to effect the meritorious act or the good act. The center of the dispute, God's grace (*auxilium*), gave the name to the controversy; hence the term, the *de auxiliis* controversy. The point of the controversy crystallized around the question as to whether this infallible efficacy of grace is due to the very nature of the grace itself or to God's eternal knowledge of the use each man would make of all possible graces. The course of the debate and the work of the Roman commission can be described in an account of the events that took place in Spain, Portugal and finally Rome itself.

Spain (1582). The controversy is considered to have begun officially during a dispute in Salamanca, on Jan. 20, 1582, when Prudencio de Montmayor, SJ, denied the Dominican teaching of a divine grace, received in the soul, that predetermines the will to the performance of a particular virtuous action (physical PREDETERMINATION), on the grounds that it is irreconcilable with human liberty. He was joined in his position by Luis de León, OESA, Juan de Castaneda, OSB, and Miguel Marcos, SJ, but was vigorously attacked by the Dominican Domingo Báñez. On the basis of a report from the Dominicans, the Spanish Grand Inquisitor, Gaspar de Quiroga, prohibited the further teaching of the reported 16 theses in which De Montmayor's position was contained.

The phase of the controversy occurring at the University of Louvain, Belgium, during 1587–88 is here omitted since Portugal and Spain were the centers of attention in the dispute and the two discussions merged into one.

Portugal (1589). On Dec. 22, 1588, the printing of the Jesuit Luis de Molina's *Concordia liberi arbitrii cum gratiae donis* was halted; this had been ordered by the censor of the Inquisition, Bartholomaeus Ferreira, OP, who suspected that the 16 theses condemned at Salamanca were contained in the *Concordia.* The Portuguese Grand Inquisitor, Cardinal Alberto, had the list of the 16 propositions sent from Spain and commissioned Maestro Francisco Cano to examine the *Concordia* in the light of these theses. The examination proved unfavorable to the work, and in March 1589 Molina received two censures, one from Cano stating that the *Concordia* contained eight of the propositions already condemned in Castile, the other probably from the Dominicans objecting to 17 more points. In answer to these censures Molina protested in a memorandum to Cardinal Alberto that his work did not contain these propositions. Consequently, Alberto declared the *Concordia* free of error in July of 1589. In the following September, Molina had a slightly revised draft of his memorandum published as an *Appendix ad Concordiam.*

Spain (1593–97). In May of 1590 the Inquisition of Castile commissioned the Universities of Alcalá and Salamanca to prepare a new index of forbidden books and in doing so to examine all works that had appeared since 1583. In 1593 Molina learned that all his writings, including the *Concordia* and his commentary on the *Prima pars* of St. Thomas's *Summa theologiae,* published in 1592, were being investigated in Salamanca. As a precaution against his chief opponents, Domingo Báñez and Francisco Zumel, Dominican professors at the university, Molina sent the Grand Inquisitor Quiroga a report, in December of 1593, in which he charged both Báñez and Zumel with Lutheranism. This was followed in May of 1594 with a list of their heresies and in June of that year with charges against Zumel's recently published commentary on the *Summa.* The Inquisitor halted the University of Salamanca's proceedings against Molina and ordered it to submit to the Inquisition the material discussed, as well as the writings of Báñez and Zumel. To aggravate this confusion, Henriquez, the only Jesuit at Salamanca, presented the Inquisition with his own censure of Molina's *Concordia.* Further publicity was given the controversy through the *Proceedings in Valladolid* (1594). Here, Diego Nuno Calbezudo, OP, had attacked Molina's *Concordia* in the spring of 1594. The Jesuit Antonio de Padilla replied to this attack by a defense of six theses from the *Concordia* in a public disputation. On March 28 he followed up this defense with a memorandum to the Inquisition, while Calbezudo on June 7, 1594, gave it a censure of 22 of Molina's propositions. The papal nuncio advised the cardinal secretary of state that the pope reserve the controversy's settlement to himself. On June 28, 1594, the papal secretary of state answered that Rome would reserve the dispute to itself. The Inquisition was directed to forward all documents to Rome; both orders were to send their opinions in writing to the Holy See. On July 21, 1594, Quiroga requested the Universities of Salamanca, Alcalá and Siguenza, as well as 13 bishops and eight doctors of theology, for their opinions of Molina's *Concordia.* One year later, on June 22, 1595, the University of Salamanca completed a censure of nine propositions of Molina. Paradoxically, in that same year the second revised edition of the *Concordia* appeared in Antwerp. In their own behalf, the Dominicans formulated between July of 1594 and September of 1595 the *Apologia fratrum praedicatorum.* To the Inquisition the Jesuits on their part remitted seven written defenses. By the fall of 1597 these documents had been collected and forwarded to Rome.

The Roman Commission (1597–1601). In November of 1597 Clement VIII appointed a commission consisting of two cardinals, three bishops and five theologians to examine the *Concordia* and Molina's commentary on the *Summa.* The commission, after 11 sessions, was convinced that Molina's mode of reconciling divine grace and human liberty was novel, expressly contrary to the teachings of Saints Augustine and Thomas Aquinas, and a censure was drawn up with a view to prohibiting the teaching of the *Concordia* and expurgating several points from the commentary. In the very month that the commission brought its censure to Clement, March of 1598, the last of the documents requested from Spain arrived. In these circumstances, the *Concordia* could not be condemned without taking into account the previous examinations of which it had been the object;

the pope ordered the commission to reevaluate its decision in the light of the new sources. However, far from revising their decision, the members of the papal commission, after a rapid reading of the massive documentation, maintained their decision to condemn the *Concordia.* Report of the commission's decision caused consternation in Spain; the Jesuits appealed to the pope not to condemn Molina without first having heard him. Many influential friends of the society, including King Philip III, are said to have intervened on his behalf. At such insistence, the pope agreed to alter the procedure by substituting friendly colloquia with the express purpose of reconciling the Dominicans and the Jesuits in their differences over actual grace. Four such conferences only proved the irreducibility of the positions taken by the two orders.

With the breakdown of the colloquia, the pope on April 13, 1600, ordered the commission, which was still working, to prepare a shorter list of the condemned propositions; the same day Molina died at Madrid amid reports that he had been condemned as a heretic and his books burned at Rome. But the appeal of the Jesuits against what seemed imminent condemnation of the 20 propositions as well as the defense of the *Concordia* by the Carmelite Antonio Bovius prompted the pope to order an oral defense of the theses still condemned before the full commission. In 15 sessions from Jan. 25 to May 7, 1601, the 20 propositions were fully debated. After 21 more sessions the commission decided eight to two to recommend the condemnation of the propositions. On Oct. 24, 1601, the pope instructed the commission to undertake the final editing of the condemnation without the assistance of Bovius and Piombino (regent of the Carmelite College, a defender of the Jesuits, as was Bovius). This was accomplished in ten more sessions without essential change and approved by the commission on Nov. 19, 1601; the pope received it on Dec. 12, 1601.

But once again the pope hesitated to make the final decision. He was besieged by the intercessions of nobles. Several universities condemned the Dominican teaching on physical premotion and defended Molina; they asked that before condemning him, the theologians of northern Europe be heard.

The Papal Disputations (1602–06). To resolve the impasse, the pope decided to convene the commission in his presence and have the theologians of both orders debate the issues. The commissions eventually consisted of 15 cardinals, five bishops and the seven theologians who had been working with the commission through the earlier stages of the debate. The disputing parties were represented by their superiors general and theologians from each order: for the Dominicans, Diego Alvarez and

Thomas de León spoke; while the Jesuits countered with Gregory of Valencia, Pedro de Arrubal and Ferdinand de la Bastida. The debates began on March 20, 1602. Clement had indicated his desire to hear the comparison of Molina's teaching to that of St. Augustine. He had two questions. (1) Does St. Augustine or Molina give more power to free will? (2) Does one read in Augustine's works or is it in his thought that God has established with Christ the infallible law that every time man does what he is able, God will give him His grace? On the first question, seven propositions of Molina concerning human freedom were to be compared with the teaching of Augustine and were disputed in debates two to eight; the decision of the consultors was that Molina's propositions were irreconcilable with Augustine's teaching. The second question discussed in the ninth debate resulted in the consultors voting that the law of grace mentioned there could not be found in Augustine. Fourteen more propositions of Molina were then examined to test their agreement with the teachings of the Semi-Pelagian John Cassian. These were disputed in debates 9 to 18 with the consultors finding agreement between the teachings of Molina and Cassian. Next, the discussion centered on Molina's teaching on repentance and its agreement with the Council of Trent. This was debated in the 19th session, and the decision of the consultors again was against Molina. The ensuing debates from June 23, 1603, to Jan. 21, 1605, were concerned with the essence and first principle of the supernaturality of the virtuous act (debates 20 to 33); the problem of God's mediate knowledge, SCIENTIA MEDIA (34 to 36); predestination (37); and the origin of the right use of actual grace (38). On all points the votes of the consultors were against Molina. Then Molina's *Concordia* was thoroughly debated. However, on March 4, 1605, Clement died without having promulgated a decision.

After the brief pontificate of Leo XI (April 1–24, 1605), Paul V was elected pope (May 16, 1605). As a cardinal he had attended all the previous debates and on Sept. 14, 1605, he had them resumed. In debates 39 to 47 (Sept. 20, 1605 to Feb. 22, 1606) the Dominican teaching on grace of itself efficacious (*gratia ex se efficax*) was debated. The consultors decided that efficacious grace could be described as *physice determinans,* that the teaching of both Augustine and Thomas supported *gratia ex se efficax,* and that this teaching had nothing to do with Calvinism. The last session took place on March 1, 1606, ending the wearying 85 sessions and 47 debates. The remainder of 1606 was taken up with the pope's obtaining the decision of the consultors, first each consultor's separate vote and then the commission's common vote. The result was that the majority of the consultors recommended the condemnation of the 42 propositions of Molina.

The Decision (1607). On the feast of St. Augustine, Aug. 28, 1607, the pope convened the cardinal consultors at the Quirinal. Of the eight cardinals present only the Dominican Bernerius declared that it was necessary to condemn the 42 propositions of Molina; two others, Givry and Blanchette, favored the Dominican position but thought that a condemnation would be premature; while Bellarmine and Du Perron thought that the physical predetermination was Calvinistic. Paul then declared that the Dominican position was far from Calvinistic and that the Jesuits in their views were not Pelagians. Both orders were allowed to defend their own teachings, but were enjoined not to censure or condemn the opposite opinion and were commanded to await the final decision of the Holy See. No decision on the matter has yet been made. With a view to restoring harmony between Dominicans and Jesuits, Paul, by a decree of the Inquisition in 1611, forbade the publication of books on the subject of efficacious grace without the authority of the Holy See. Pope Urban VIII, by decrees of 1625 and 1641, sustained this prohibition and added penalties to it; Innocent X did the same in 1654.

See Also: BÁÑEZ AND BAÑEZIANISM; MOLINA, LUIS DE; MOLINISM; CONGRUISM; FREE WILL AND GRACE; GRACE, CONTROVERSIES ON; GRACE, EFFICACIOUS; OMNISCIENCE; GRACE, ARTICLES ON; PREDESTINATION, ARTICLES ON.

Bibliography: H. QUILLET, *Dictionnaire de théologie catholique,* ed. A. VACANT et al., 15 v. (Paris 1903–50) 3.1:1120–38. E. VANSTEENBERGHE, *ibid.* 10.1:2094–2187, esp. 2154–66. C. BOYER, *Dictionnaire de théologie catholique,* ed. A. VACANT et al., 15 v. (Paris 1903–50) Tables générales (1862–67). F. STEGMÜLLER, *Lexikon für Theologie und Kirche,* ed. J. HOFER and K. RAHNER, 10 v. (2d, new ed. Freiburg 1957–65) 4:1002–07. L. PASTOR, *The History of the Popes from the Close of the Middle Ages,* 40 v. (London–St. Louis 1938–61) 11:115–385; 12:163–179. D. BÁÑEZ, *Scholastica commentaria in primam partem Summae Theologicae S. Thomae Aquinatis,* 1 (Madrid 1934). L. DE MOLINA, *Liberi arbitrii cum gratiae donis, divina praescientia, providentia, praedestinatione et reprobatione concordia,* ed., J. RABENECK (Madrid 1953). V. MUÑOZ, *Salmanticence,* 1 (Salamanca 1954) 440–449. J. BRODRICK, *The Life and Work of Blessed Robert Bellarmine,* 2 v. (London 1928). J. H. SERRY, *Historia Congregationum de auxiliis,* (Louvain 1700). F. CERECEDA, *Estudios eclesiásticos,* 14 (1935) 257–269. J. RABENECK, *Miscellanea comillas,* 18 (1952) 11–26.

[T. RYAN]

CONGRÉGATION, LA

A pious association of laymen that played a conspicuous part in the French-Catholic revival (1801–30). Initiated February 1801 by six Paris students under the guidance of Jean Baptiste Bourdier-Delpuits, a former Jesuit (1776–1811), it was, at first, merely a new version of those pious sodalities under the invocation of the Blessed Virgin Mary that had flourished since the end of the 16th century in Jesuit colleges. By 1805 membership totaled 180. After the police discovered some young members disseminating Pius VII's document excommunicating NAPOLEON I (1809), the society was suppressed. Revived after Napoleon's downfall under the leadership of Pierre Ronsin, SJ (1771–1846), its ranks enlisted not only students but also clerics and high-ranking lay aristocrats. Although the Congregation confined itself to purely religious activities, it gave birth through its members to a network of charitable, social, and educational organizations, thus anticipating modern CATHOLIC ACTION. In some 60 other French towns similar bodies were founded, often by former Paris members. Among these grew practically independently the Congregation of Lyons, responsible for the creation of the Society for the PROPAGATION OF THE FAITH, and that of Bordeaux, founded by Guillaume CHAMINADE. Around 1824 the Liberal press took to denouncing the Congregation as the tool of the Jesuits for infiltrating governmental administration. This onslaught was made more bitter and dangerous by the confusion arising from the existence of the secret society of the KNIGHTS OF THE FAITH, which did aim at capturing political power. After the Jesuits were forbidden to teach in France (June 1828), the Congregation declined in activity, although one of its leaders, Prince Jules de Polignac, headed the government in August 1829. The revolution of 1830 ended the society, but some of its creations survived.

Bibliography: C. A. GEOFFROY DE GRANDMAISON, *La Congrégation, 1801–1830* (Paris 1889). G. DE BERTIER DE SAUVIGNY, *Un Type d'ultra-royaliste: Le Comte Ferdinand de Bertier (1782–1864) et l'énigme de la Congrégation* (Paris 1948). J. B. DUROSELLE, ''Les 'Filiales' de la Congrégation,'' *Revue d'histoire ecclésiastique* 50 (1955) 867–891.

[G. DE BERTIER DE SAUVIGNY]

CONGREGATION OF MARY, QUEEN

Also known as Trinh Vương, abbreviated CMR. The popular name for the *Congregation of the Missionary Sisters of the Blessed Virgin Mary, Queen of the World* (Dòng Nữ Tu Thừa Sai Đức Mẹ Trinh Vương). Trinh Vương encompasses a number of diocesan institutes of indigenous Vietnamese women religious in Vietnam, Australia and the U.S.

Trinh Vương traces its origins to the LOVERS OF THE HOLY CROSS (Dòng Mến Thánh Giá) of Bùi Chu (in northern Vietnam), a Vietnamese community of women religious founded by Pierre LAMBERT DE LA MOTTE in

1670. Over three centuries, this fledging community survived the vicissitudes of persecution and harassment as it endeavored to serve the pastoral needs of Vietnamese Catholics. In the wake of the French defeat at Điện Biên Phủ, followed by the signing of the 1954 Geneva Accord which divided Vietnam at the 17th parallel, the entire community fled Bùi Chu, joining the mass exodus to South Vietnam. Under the patronage of Bishop Peter Maria Phạm Ngọc Chi of the diocese of Quy Nhơn, the congregation was reorganized as a diocesan institute under its present name.

In the early 1970s, a number of sisters were sent to Sydney, Australia for religious formation. This fortuitous decision paved the way for the survival of Trinh Vương outside of Vietnam. Under the auspices of the then Bishop Bernard F. Law, Bishop of Springfield-Cape Girardeau, Missouri, the Australian community was invited to establish a presence in Missouri. In 1979, three sisters arrived from Australia, establishing the first house in Springfield, Missouri. On Dec. 1, 1986, the Holy See erected the American Region of the Congregation of Mary, Queen, under the supervision of the Bishop of Springfield-Cape Girardeau. Headquartered in Springfield, Missouri, the American Region of Trinh Vương serves the local Vietnamese communities in Missouri in the areas of education, healthcare, parochial, pastoral, and charitable works.

[V. T. PHAM]

CONGREGATION OF THE MOTHER CO-REDEMPTRIX

Also known as Dòng Đồng Công, abbreviated CMC. Dòng Đồng Công is an indigenous Vietnamese congregation of religious priests and brothers with communities in Vietnam and the U.S. Founded by a Vietnamese priest, Đaminh (Dominic) M. Trần Đình Thủ in 1953 in Bùi Chu (in northern Vietnam), the fledging community fled southward almost immediately, joining the mass exodus to South Vietnam in the wake of the French defeat at Điện Biên Phủ, followed by the signing of the 1954 Geneva Accord which divided Vietnam at the 17th parallel. In the south, the congregation operated schools and seminaries, and carried out pastoral work in parishes. A second exodus occurred in the aftermath of the fall of Saigon on April 30, 1975. About 170 priests and brothers of the Dòng Đồng Công fled South Vietnam by boat. Picked up by American naval vessels, they were resettled in the U.S. Under the auspices of the then Bishop Bernard F. Law, Bishop of Springfield-Cape Girardeau, Missouri, the Dòng Đồng Công was given a new lease on life. Headquartered in Carthage, Missouri, the American

branch of the Dòng Đồng Công serves Vietnamese parishes and communities throughout the U.S. Their annual Marian Days pilgrimage celebration every August, mirrored after the traditional Marian Days pilgrimage to the Shrine of Our Lady of LA VANG in central Vietnam, draws an estimated 50,000 Vietnamese Catholics to Carthage. The congregation numbers around 200 priests and brothers in the U.S., and about 400 in Vietnam.

[V. T. PHAM]

CONGREGATIONAL CHURCHES

Those Christians who hold that Christ is the only head of the church; that the Bible is a sufficient rule of faith and practice; that Christian character is the measurement for membership in the church; and that sovereignty in matters of church polity and government rests ultimately in the congregation, or God's chosen people who have covenanted together to walk in the ways of the Lord made known or to be made known to them.

Origin. The origins of Congregationalism are not clear; some trace them back to the primitive Church, or to the secretaries of the 13th century, or to John WYCLIF and the LOLLARDS. Modern Congregationalism, however, began with the Protestant REFORMATION. When the Anglican settlement under Elizabeth I proved unacceptable both to Roman Catholics and to Puritans, the latter divided into those who wished to separate completely from the Anglican Church (Separatists or Independents) and those who wished to purify it from within. The Separatist point of view, early set forth in Robert Browne's famous book, *A Treatise of Reformation without Tarrying for anie . . .* (1582), embodied the principles of what later was called the "Congregational Way." Churches reflecting these views were established early in the 17th century, but government opposition drove them into exile in Holland. Under Cromwell's Protectorate (1653–59), the Congregationalists made some progress; in 1658 more than 100 churches were represented at the Savoy Synod in London. The 19th century was characterized by a movement toward union for mutual support, with the forming of County Associations of Churches and the combination of these associations (1832) in the Congregational Union of England and Wales, and later similar unions in Scotland and Ireland.

Colonial America. Congregationalism was brought to America by the Pilgrim Fathers, who were Separatists, in 1620, when they arrived on the Mayflower. Subsequently the non-Separatists of the Puritan party also began to arrive in large numbers and to settle around Massachusetts Bay, and the differences between the two groups soon disappeared. The English leader John Robinson counseled his followers "rather to study union than division"; and when Dr. Samuel Fuller, deacon of the church at Plymouth, ministered to the sick of the church at Salem, the "right hand of fellowship" was soon extended to all parties. At Plymouth, the MAYFLOWER COMPACT established a form of government by the will of the majority and played an important part in shaping both the religion and the politics of the colony. There William BRADFORD was repeatedly elected governor from 1621 on and William Brewster (1567–1644) acted as lay preacher. The church polity established by the Puritan leaders of the Massachusetts Bay settlements became normative for the entire area and was soon known as the "New England way." Two early leaders, Thomas HOOKER and John COTTON, wrote in defense of the freedom of the New England churches. The CAMBRIDGE PLATFORM of 1648, a declaration of principles of church government and discipline, regularized the practices of the New England churches, forming in fact a constitution for Congregationalists.

Because they themselves were educated, the early Puritans demanded an educated ministry, and to this end Harvard College (later University) was founded in 1636. The Connecticut Congregationalists followed suit in 1701 with Yale (New Haven); and Dartmouth (1769, Hanover, NH), Williams (1785, Williamstown, MA), Bowdoin (1794, Brunswick, Maine), Middlebury (VT, 1800), and Amherst (MA, 1821) all had founders who were Congregationalists. The earliest missionaries included John Eliot (1604–90), known as the "apostle to the Indians" because of his translations of the New and Old Testaments, and his Catechism (1653), the first book to be printed in a Native American tongue; and Thomas Mayhew (1621–57), who, about 1643, converted the natives of Martha's Vineyard. By 1674 there were 4,000 "praying Indians," with 24 native preachers. Another leader of early Congregationalism was John Wise (1652–1725), pastor of the Second Parish Church at Ipswich, MA, who led his fellow townsmen in resisting an attempt to raise money by levying a province tax. He made the word "democracy" respectable by calling it "Christ's government in church and state." His idea of sovereignty as resident in the people was revived in 1772 and had a distinct influence on the American Revolution. He also resisted the Presbyterianizing of the New England Churches, or the attempt to unite them by means of ecclesiastical councils such as those recommended by Increase and Cotton MATHER. Although his essay *The Churches Quarrel Espoused* (1710) dealt a death blow to this whole movement, the Congregational churches (especially in Connecticut) always remained on good terms with the Presbyterian churches to the south of them.

Following the unfortunate witchcraft incidents of the 1690s, religious fervor cooled somewhat in the early part of the 18th century. Doctrinal difficulties arose over who should participate in the Lord's Supper, and a kind of secondary church membership was accorded to those who could give no demonstration of an actual inward rebirth, but who were in sympathy with Christian ideals. The result of this HALF-WAY COVENANT seemed to weaken the ties of church membership, and a revival of genuine religious experience was sought by the eloquent and brilliant Jonathan EDWARDS. The GREAT AWAKENING of the 1740s saw the revival of enthusiasm and religious fervor throughout all the colonies, but eventually this gave way to the preoccupations of the Revolutionary War period.

In the U.S. In 1787 the Northwest Territory attracted many New Englanders, and Marietta, Ohio, became the first permanent settlement in the Northwest Territory (1788). The first Congregational church of Ohio was established there eight years later, and in the following year Muskingum Academy, which eventually became Marietta College (1835). As Congregationalists from New England expanded and moved West, they met Presbyterians moving in from the South. Seeing the futility of competition, both denominations resolved to cooperate by forming a "Plan of Union." At the time it seemed that frontier life lent itself more to a Presbyterian than to a Congregational type of Church government, but neither group found the plan altogether satisfactory. Despite the fact that the Presbyterians profited most by it, they were the first to abrogate it in 1837, although there was partial cooperation until 1852.

Separation of Church and State was not a belief of the early Puritans; on the contrary, the ideal had been a union of Church and State to constitute a Christian commonwealth. This Church-State bond was not broken in New England until the 19th century (1818 in Connecticut, 1834 in Massachusetts), but in spite of the "disestablishment," the denomination continued to expand across the continent. State conferences were formed to build and strengthen new churches, as well as to aid those that were already established. State conferences (or conventions), composed of the churches within a state working together on common matters, first came into being in Connecticut in 1798; the last was in Colorado in 1905.

Education continued to rank high among Congregationalists, and many colleges followed the movement of Congregational Christians across the continent. Among those originally having Congregational connections were Beloit (WI, 1846), Carleton (Northfield, MN, 1866), Defiance (Ohio, 1850), Dillard (New Orleans, LA 1869), Doane (Crete, NE, 1872), Drury (Springfield, MO, 1873), Elon (NC, 1889), Fisk (Nashville, TN 1866), Grinnell

(Iowa, 1846), Huston-Tillotson (Austin, TX, 1877), Illinois (Jacksonville, 1829), Le Moyne (Memphis, TN, 1870), Marietta (Ohio, 1797), Northland (Ashland, WI, 1892), Olivet (MI, 1844), Pacific (Stockton, CA, 1851), Piedmont (Demorest, GA, 1897), Ripon (WI, 1850), Rocky Mountain (Billings, MT, 1883), Southern Union (Wadley, AL, 1934), Talladega (AL, 1867), Tougaloo Southern Christian (MS, 1869), Westminster (Fulton, MO, 1851), and Yankton (SD, 1881). Illinois College was formed by a group of student missionaries known as the Yale band, made up of seven missionaries from Yale Divinity School who, in 1829, started west and furthered educational activities on the Illinois frontier.

During the first half of the 19th century, the Romantic movement and the rise and spread of liberal ideas led many Congregationalists to question the old Calvinist ideas of original sin and total depravity. Traditional values were challenged by many church leaders and teachers, especially in the greater Boston, MA, area. In 1819 William Ellery CHANNING preached a famous sermon at Baltimore, MD, on Unitarian Christianity, and six years later the American Unitarian Association was organized and captured more than a third of the churches that had formerly been Congregational. This resulted in the Dedham Case, a tangled legal situation involving considerable church property. Many Congregational congregations, despite an actual numerical majority, found themselves without funds and church buildings. When the historic church of Plymouth split into two groups, the Unitarian First Church in Plymouth retained the traditional date 1620, while the Pilgrim Church in Plymouth retained the traditional Congregational label, but took the date 1801 (*see* UNITARIANS).

Missions. In the summer of 1806 the possibility of American missions overseas became a reality when a group of five students, headed by Samuel J. MILLS, were driven by a thunderstorm to seek shelter under a haystack, where they talked and prayed together about "the moral darkness of Asia" and the possibility of going there. The result was the organization of the American Board of Commissioners for Foreign Missions in 1810. Two years later the five men who had participated in the famous haystack meeting at Williams College in 1806 were ordained in Salem Tabernacle Church on Feb. 6, 1812, and were the first American missionaries to go overseas. For awhile, the American Board extended its membership into the Presbyterian Church and the Associate Reformed and Dutch Reformed churches, and also acted for the German Reformed Church and the Congregational Churches of Canada (*see* REFORMED CHURCHES II: NORTH AMERICA). In 1961 it joined with the Board of International Missions of the Evangelical and Reformed Church to form the United Church Board for World Min-

istries; its work is worldwide and includes building churches; supporting schools, colleges, and hospitals; and engaging in programs of social welfare.

In 1839 the Spanish slave ship *Amistad,* on which 42 Africans had mutinied, killed the captain, and attempted to sail back to Africa, was brought into New Haven harbor. After two years' litigation, the Supreme Court pronounced them free, and three missionaries returned them to Africa. Several groups of Congregationalists, concerned about the welfare of both Native Americans and African Americans, now combined to form the American Missionary Association (1846), an organization that has continued to foster interracial relations. It became quite active in the South, and after the Civil War began the "Contraband School" for slaves freed by the Union armies, which later became Hampton Institute, at Hampton, VA. Berea College, KY, founded 1855, was one of the first integrated schools.

By 1882 there "was not a western state or territory in which Congregationalism was not represented." This was due largely to the work of the American Home Missionary Society, founded in 1862 in New York. According to the first issue of the *Home Missionary* (May 1828), the society was designated "to promote the religious benefit of a great and growing nation." Although its name has been changed more than once (it is now the Board of Home Missions), it still founds churches; publishes the denominational journal, *United Church Herald;* aids city, town, and country churches; organizes evangelism; conducts schools for pastors in service; works among Native Americans and other underprivileged people; supplies curriculum material for Christian education in the local church and advises in youth education; assists as it can in higher Christian education and campus ministries; agitates and educates for better race relations; administers work camps and voluntary Christian services; coordinates the work of many benevolent institutions; and publishes books under the name of the United Church Press.

One of the divisions of the Board of Home Missions is the Pilgrim Press, which is a publishing and distributing agency of constructively religious materials for children, teachers, parents, pastors, and churches. Publications of the Pilgrim Press include a wide range of curriculum materials, monthly magazines, biweekly story papers, books for the home and for ministers and leaders, and materials needed for Christian education and evangelism.

Other Activities. Preaching has always occupied a very important place in Congregationalism. Mention has already been made of Jonathan Edwards and his connection with the revivalism of the Great Awakening. Of an entirely different temperament was Horace BUSHNELL who staunchly opposed the emotionalism of the revivals and their insistence upon a conscious, dated, emotional experience of conversion. The true principle of Christian education, he maintained is that "the child is to grow up a Christian, and never know himself as being otherwise." This would happen, he believed, if the life of the family in the home was truly Christian. Religious education took much of its inspiration from Bushnell.

Still another important preacher was Washington Gladden, for 36 years pastor of the First Congregational Church in Columbus, Ohio. As early as 1875 he began to use the principle of "applied Christianity," or the SOCIAL GOSPEL, to the relations between employers and workingmen, and to the settlement of strikes. The Council for Social Action, organized in June 1934, owes much of its inspiration to him. This important body conducts institutes, seminars, and conferences on social issues confronting the Christian world, publishes materials for the study of those issues, assists churches and other local groups with studies in this field, and from time to time, when the sentiment of the church comes to a focus on some social question, makes a public statement on the matter.

Attempts at Union. In the 19th century on the American Frontier, Protestant churches tended to divide and multiply into different denominations. Hence it was not until after 1850 that Congregationalists first began to think nationally. The Plan of Union with the Presbyterians, which had placed them at a disadvantage on the frontier, was finally ended by the 1852 Council in Albany, NY. The Boston National Council of 1865 helped to pave the way for national councils that met periodically in order to advise and guide the churches. Although without power to legislate for the churches, the councils fostered education, implemented the social consciousness of the churches, and toward the end of the period related Congregationalism not only to the great religious communions of America, but to English Congregationalism and that of other parts of the world as well.

The 20th century has been characterized by a growing concern for unity in Protestantism. In 1931 the Congregational National Council united with the Christian General Convention to form the Congregational Christian General Council. The Christian Church had been a smaller but important group of churches, holding similar principles of churchmanship, located mainly in the Virginia-North Carolina area and the Illinois-Indiana-Ohio area. It was itself the result of a merger of three groups that sprang up in the early part of the 19th century. North Carolina Methodists under Thomas O'Kelly had separated from the mainstream of Methodists in 1793 in order to preserve a more democratic church polity. Some Baptists in New England also desired greater freedom regarding church membership as well as in theological thinking, especially with regard to the sacraments. And Presbyterians in Kentucky under the partial influence of Barton W. Stone had inaugurated (1804) a small denomination that de-emphasized Calvinistic theology and played up the importance of direct conversions associated with revival meetings. At first, this group was associated with the Disciples of Christ, who were ably led by the Campbells, father and son, and who eventually became one of the nation's largest denominations. These three small groups, Methodist, Baptist, and Presbyterian, joined together to form the CHRISTIAN CHURCH, the idea being that if each denomination would simply call itself "Christian," church unity would be brought one step closer.

The success of this merger helped to pave the way for a union of the Congregational Christian Churches with the EVANGELICAL and REFORMED CHURCH, which was itself a merger. The Reformed Church had originated with the followers of John CALVIN in the 16th century and had spread from Geneva into southwestern Germany and the Netherlands. On arriving in the U.S., members of these churches established new local churches that used the Reformed hymnals, prayer books, and the HEIDELBERG CATECHISM. An early leader, John Philip BOEHM, held the first communion service at Falkner Swamp, a farming community 40 miles north of Philadelphia, PA. In 1793 the denomination had become completely independent of European aid. Mercersburg Academy, Franklin and Marshall College, and Lancaster Theological Seminary owe their origin to this group, which early in the 20th century abandoned German in favor of English for the language of worship.

The Evangelical Synod of North America drew its inspiration from both Calvinists and Lutherans of the Continental Reformation. Its local churches were the product of the foreign-missionary societies of Germany and Switzerland and the American Home Missionary Society cooperating on the frontier in the early part of the 19th century. These local churches took root in the upper Mississippi Valley and in 1877 were united to become the Evangelical Synod. Their doctrine was based on the Augsburg Confession, Luther's Catechism, and the Heidelberg Catechism. Elmhurst College in Illinois and Eden Theological Seminary in Webster Groves, MO, were founded by them.

Similarities in belief, worship, and polity led to the exploration of the possibility of a merger in the 1940s. A document called "The Basis of Union" circulated through each denomination and was amended until generally acceptable by all. When the two denominations independently had given their official acceptance to this, the way was prepared for the uniting meeting of 1957, to form the UNITED CHURCH OF CHRIST.

Bibliography: W. WALKER, *A History of the Congregational Churches in the United States of America* (New York 1894). G. G. ATKINS and F. L. FAGLEY, *History of American Congregationalism* (Boston 1942). G. G. ATKINS et al., *An Adventure in Liberty* (pa. Boston 1961).

[J. R. WILLIS/EDS.]

CONGREGATIONAL SINGING

Numerous directives and exhortations concerning the place of congregational singing in liturgical worship have issued from the Holy See in modern times. They begin with the motu proprio on sacred music by St. Pius X, *Tra le sollecitudini* (1903), and culminate in the *Constitution on the Sacred Liturgy* of VATICAN COUNCIL II, promulgated by Pope Paul VI on Dec. 4, 1963. The most detailed document is the *Instruction of the Sacred Congregation of Rites on Sacred Music and Sacred Liturgy* (Sept. 3, 1958), which offers a blueprint for modern congregational worship by providing specific plans and methods for various types of liturgical services. Although written with the Latin liturgy in view, much of the *Instruction* remains applicable to a vernacular liturgy as well. The *Constitution on the Sacred Liturgy* repeatedly stresses the importance and necessity of congregational participation; no other document in the Church's history is as insistent and clear on this point. Chapter 6, which deals specifically with sacred music, refers several times to congregational singing. Paragraph 118 may be taken as representative: "Religious singing by the people is to be fostered, so that in devotions and sacred exercises, as also during liturgical services, the voices of the faithful may ring out according to the norms and requirements of the rubrics."

Early History. The influence of the Jewish synagogue on early Christian worship, the casual suggestions of St. Paul in Eph 5.19 and Col 3.16, and deductions from the general development of the liturgy in the early centuries entitle us to assume that some kind of singing by the assembled faithful was an accepted part of the earliest Christian liturgy. Modern liturgical scholars, relying on the DIDACHE, Justin Martyr's outline of the early Mass in his *First Apology,* and the *Apostolic Tradition*, and similar scattered texts, conclude that the community-sung Mass early became the normal manner of celebrating the sacred mysteries. In individual cases, however, as pointed out by Bruno Stäblein, one cannot always decide whether the sources, which are literary rather than musical, indicate that the acclamations and responses were spoken, shouted, sung, or proclaimed by some disordered combination of these.

By the fourth century, references to various types of psalm singing, hymns, acclamations, and other sung liturgical activities are to be found with increasing frequency in Patristic writings (along with cautions against contaminations from profane, theatrical music). Much of the testimony is by way of commentary and exhortation, as for instance St. John Chrysostom's advice in his *Exposition of Psalm XLI:* "Even though the meaning of the words be unknown to you, teach your mouth to utter them meanwhile. For the tongue is made holy by the words." Although these references to plural activity suggest some degree of response on the part of the faithful, we have no clearly stated documents (nor musically notated liturgical books) that provide accurate information as to how universally the use of music was employed and encouraged, or how many of the faithful in a given area were capable of joining in the parts assigned to them. The success achieved in this matter by St. Ambrose (and to a certain degree by St. Augustine) was probably not attained in churches where neither clergy nor faithful had sufficient education and background to enable them to perform the music.

From the fifth century on, a gradual diminution of community singing appears in both East and West, although the causes were not always the same. A number of explanations are brought forward: the barbarian invasions, the problem of liturgical language, the lack of books and the multiplicity of texts, the gradual separation of the people from the altar, and especially the incorporation of more difficult music into the liturgy, a practice that gave rise to the formation of SCHOLAE CANTORUM. The *Ordo Romanus I* (c. 700) hardly adverts to the parts traditionally assigned to the faithful. Although in Charlemagne's empire a revival of communal singing was attempted and encouraged, it had no widespread or lasting effect. From the Protestant Reformation to the 20th-century liturgical renewal, congregational singing was hardly a memory.

The Problem in the U. S. Despite the impressive array of papal documents encouraging the restoration of congregational singing, several major obstacles have combined to retard the realization of this goal in the U.S. The most general causes of this failure would appear to be a widespread lack of understanding of the purposes of communal worship, and the consequent lack of conviction concerning its value and necessity—theological shortcomings not restricted to the U. S. To these must be added special American problems arising from customs inherited from earlier generations and from the attitude many American Catholics manifest regarding the place of music in life.

Thus, the Church in America during the 19th century, consisting in the main of many diverse settlements of immigrants from Europe, was incapable of developing a unified tradition of congregational singing, even if the hierarchy had perceived this as a desirable goal. Since the silent low Mass was the usual form of Sunday worship, the congregation was expected to pray both privately and silently; no need for development of a repertory of congregational music for the Mass was felt. Unlike the major white Protestant churches with their hymns and chorales, and also unlike Black Catholics, who took singing in worship for granted, neither the native-born Catholics nor the immigrants possessed a body of service music, written in a contemporary idiom and shared by a majority of the dioceses. The singing of hymns in schools, as well as in churches, during Benediction and other pious devotions, has been fairly widespread; but in parishes where a Sunday *Missa cantata* was celebrated, the performance of the music has customarily been left to a specially trained choir. In those German parishes where the influence of the CAECILIAN movement prevailed, the singing of hymns by the congregation was strongly encouraged; with the change of clergy and the appearance of new generations of the faithful; however, the potency of this movement gradually subsided.

Following upon the legislation of St. Pius X, valiant efforts were put forth in some churches to restore GREGORIAN CHANT as the universal prayer music. Notable success in these efforts was achieved in seminaries, convents, and in those schools and churches in which a program of intensive training could be carried out. In most parishes, however, the singing of chant Masses by the people never took hold; not only was a tradition of singing lacking, but since the chant, written in a medieval style and a dead language, was not an indigenous expression of 20th-century Christians, the modern adult parishioner was incapable of employing it as a personal and meaningful instrument of prayer. By mid-century some leading liturgists began to express openly their doubts about the effectiveness of chant in parochial liturgy; many were also of the opinion that the Latin language was a major deterrent to the spread of communal worship. Their urgent appeals for the use of the vernacular language in the liturgy were coupled with requests that composers of liturgical music should provide simple and rhythmic melodies that the ordinary congregation could master and perform after a short rehearsal. Even before World War II a number of choir-and-congregation Mass settings had been published whose purpose was to enlist the services of the choir while providing an active part in the ceremonies for the congregation. Numerous Masses of this kind, as well as unison Masses for the faithful, were published after the war.

After the *Instruction* of 1958, when a more widespread attempt to achieve congregational participation

was made throughout the U. S., numbers of "people's Masses" made their appearance. The *Constitution on the Sacred Liturgy* of Vatican II finally paved the way for the introduction of the vernacular, and in December 1964 most dioceses began to employ the English language for many parts of the Mass, with congregational participation in the Ordinary. As a significant result of this change, the revival of chant has for the present been sidetracked, whereas the publication of congregational Masses, now being set to English texts, continues apace.

Although, as this brief sketch indicates, much energy has been expended since the publication of the *Constitution,* particularly since the introduction of English, and much attention devoted to the revival of congregational singing, the program was, as a rule, successful only in those parishes where an informed pastor and a competent music director worked together to prepare the people and set an organized plan into motion. In other parishes the response of many adults was less than spontaneous at first. This negative reaction resulted from a variety of causes: omission of positive directives from the bishops, musically indifferent pastors, inadequate musical directors, large and acoustically unsuitable church buildings, lack of time in which to train a majority of the congregation (particularly in large urban parishes), absence of appropriate and practical musical materials, and an inveterate shyness or lack of self-confidence in the people themselves. American Catholic men in particular appear to espouse the notion that singing is the special domain of women, children, and those few who are especially trained for it. For many Americans, the use of song—except in certain types of entertainment and on rare and solemn occasions—is not a customary or spontaneous mode of communication or public expression. This inhibition carries over and affects their conduct in public worship.

In the ensuing years following the Second Vatican Council, the accepted norm for congregational participation was, in most parishes, the so-called four-hymn Mass (entrance-offertory-communion-recessional). Although it originated to fill the need for congregational singing within the context of a pre-Vatican II Latin liturgy, the four-hymn "tradition" is, unfortunately, still all too common today. The revision of the Eucharistic Liturgy itself in 1970 makes it possible to place the emphasis where it belongs—on the congregational singing of those elements that are an integral part of the liturgy. The 1972 statement from the Bishops' Committee on the Liturgy, *Music in Catholic Worship,* followed by a subsequent document, *Liturgical Music Today* both indicate that there are five acclamations that ought to be sung "even at Masses in which little else is sung": the Alleluia; the Holy, Holy, Holy Lord; the Memorial Acclamation; the

Great Amen; and the Doxology to the Lord's Prayer. Congregational participation in the processional chants at the Entrance and the Communion is also encouraged, as is the singing of the Responsorial Psalm after the first reading. Singing by choir or congregation is encouraged, although not demanded, at the Lord, Have Mercy; the Glory to God; the General Intercessions; the song during the Preparation of the Gifts; the Lord's Prayer; the Lamb of God; the song *after* Communion; and the recessional song. Of these, the General Intercessions and the Lord's Prayer should, when sung, always belong to the congregation. How much music a given congregation sings is to be determined by ability and need, rather than by distinctions between high or low Mass. The choir is seen in a role supportive of congregational singing, as well as in its traditional role of singing alone.

The larger part of congregational music used in churches today is taken either from the rich tradition of Reformation hymnody or from the folk-style music that has grown up as a part of the liturgical renewal. Congregational singing of a limited repertory of Latin GREGORIAN chant was recommended for the whole Church.

The question of hymnals and other aids to congregational participation remains a large one, although the recent publication of several fine hymnals has been encouraging (*see* HYMNS AND HYMNALS II: VATICAN II AND BEYOND). The use of missalettes is still prevalent; it is difficult for them to include the variety of options available while maintaining a body of familiar material. The question of a national hymnal has been discussed at length, and the Canadian bishops have actually adopted one. Although a national hymnal can provide music from different publishers in one book, it runs the risk of arresting further development. The proliferation of mimeographed song sheets at the local level, while solving many problems, has brought on the legal problem of copyright infringement.

Many problems remain to be solved, and a body of good congregational music is still being developed, but the 1980s and 1990s have seen American Catholic congregations move from a relatively passive role to one in which their singing is a normal part of worship.

Bibliography: J. A. JUNGMANN, *The Mass of the Roman Rite,* tr. F. A. BRUNNER, 2 v. (New York 1951–55). L. DUCHESNE, *Christian Worship,* tr. M. L. MCCLURE (5th ed. repr. New York 1949). E. ROUTLEY, *The Church and Music* (New York 1950). F. VAN DER MEER, *Augustine the Bishop,* tr. B. BATTERSHAW and G. R. LAMB (New York 1962), pt. 2, ch. 11. J. GELINEAU, *Voices and Instruments in Christian Worship,* tr. C. HOWELL (Collegeville, Minn. 1964). "Music and the Vernacular Liturgy: The Role of the Choir and Congregation," *Musart* 17 (1964), J. H. MILLER, "The Liturgist's View," 8, 48–50 and R. F. HAYBURN, "The Liturgical Musician's View," 9, 51–52. Liturgical Conference, *A Manual for Church Musicians* (Washington 1964). L. DEISS, *Spirit and Song of the New Liturgy* (Cincinnati 1970). Bishop's Committee for Liturgy. *Music in Catholic Worship* (Washington, D.C. 1972); *Liturgical Music Today* (Washington, D.C. 1982). L. DEISS, *Visions of Liturgy and Music for a New Century* (Collegeville 1996).

[F. J. GUENTNER/R. B. HALLER/EDS.]

CONGRUISM

A theological theory chiefly attributed to F. SUÁREZ. It places the difference between sufficient and efficacious grace not only in the free consent of the human will but also in the suitability of the grace for the needs of the individual soul in specific circumstances. The precise point in question is the reconciliation of the movement of the soul by God with the inherent freedom of the soul. Confronted with the authentically Christian character of the Protestant emphasis on personalism in religion and the need for liberation from a legalistic ethos, leading thinkers of the Counter Reformation intensified their efforts on investigating the relationship between nature and supernature; such efforts have continued down to the present day.

Lutherans and Calvinists pinpointed the problem for Catholics by their assumption of an either/or attitude toward the structuring of a good act: either God performs the good act and then it is not human, or man performs it to the exclusion of divine participation. While all theologians in the Catholic tradition hold that God moves the will by grace, various schools have arisen in disputes over the origin of the movement of efficacious grace. Among those who regard it as extrinsic to the will are Molinists, congruists, congruists of the Sorbonne, and modern congruists. Bañezians and Augustinians opt for its intrinsicality.

Suárez, a proponent of mitigated realism, plotted his course by proposing an equilibrium of liberty between Scotist voluntarism and Thomist intellectualism. With almost pedestrian practicality, he argued that God has commanded man to do certain things; He has not simply commanded him to be able to do them. Thus, man must possess a faculty that has within itself the power to act. Here is the core of the Suarezian doctrine on the extrinsicality of grace. The advance from sufficiency to efficiency in the order of grace can come about only when exterior circumstances are such that they lead to fulfillment. The circumstances of God's offering, not the isolated quality of the gift He offers, cause the movement.

In the matter of the divine influence on the human will, Bellarmine with Suárez rejected the idea of physical PREMOTION, postulating a SCIENTIA MEDIA, that is, foreknowledge in God that includes not merely the possible and actual free determinations of man's faculty of choice. This middle knowledge deals with FUTURIBLES, free acts that man would perform in certain circumstances. Given appropriate conditions, they would exist. Bellarmine simply concretized Molina's original contribution on this point by recognizing the validity of a knowledge in God somewhere between that of simple intelligence and that of vision.

Not so Suárez. He opposed Molina by independently asserting that God foresees free futuribles in their formal truth. Where Molina showed God bestowing grace *that* He knows will attain its proper end, Suárez shifted the stress to God giving the grace *because* He knows it will be efficacious. This attitude of Suárez indicated the healthy, if heated, polemical atmosphere generated in the *Congregationes de Auxiliis,* where, in the course of debates, both Jesuits and Dominicans attacked Molinism. In 1613, C. Acquaviva as general of the Jesuits gave his support to Suarezianism as "more conformable to the teaching of Augustine and Thomas."

In the ensuing years, congruists of the Sorbonne tried to harmonize all previous theories by distinguishing between two kinds of efficacious grace. Syncretists, they designated *gratia ab extrinseco efficax* as apt for the realization of good works that are not too difficult. For the completing of a genuinely difficult good work, however, they posited a moral predetermination of the free will through *gratia ab intrinseco efficax.* Cooperation with the first will inevitably lead to the second. Despite its intricacies, this school of thought initiated by N. Ysambert, I. Habert, and H. de Tournely found an eloquent sponsor in St. Alphonsus Liguori.

Theoretically the congruists of the Sorbonne discarded the Suarezian version of *scientia media;* they continued to use it practically, however. Such modern congruists as F. Satolli and B. Lorenzelli reject it utterly, basing their type of congruism on the fact that God unites the state of sanctifying grace with the free exercise of the human will in order to elicit a SALUTARY ACT. Unless man's power of choice concurs with the will of God, grace will remain inefficacious.

See Also: GRACE, EFFICACIOUS; GRACE, SUFFICIENT; GRACE; GRACE, ARTICLES ON; MOLINISM; BÁÑEZ AND BAÑEZIANISM; FREE WILL AND GRACE.

Bibliography: H. QUILLIET, *Dictionnaire de théologie catholique,* ed. A. VACANT et al. (Paris 1903–50) 3.1:1120–38. J. VAN DER MEERSH, *ibid.* 6.2:1671–77. R. GARRIGOU-LAGRANGE, *ibid.* 12.2: 2962–3022. X. LE BACHELET, *ibid.* 2.1:595–599. P. DUMONT, *ibid.* 14.2:2672–91. J. BRODRICK, *Life and Work of Bl. Robert Francis Cardinal Bellarmine,* 2 v. (New York 1928) v. 2. R. GARRIGOU-LAGRANGE, *Predestination,* tr. B. ROSE (St. Louis 1939). T. MUL-LANEY, *Suárez on Human Freedom* (Baltimore, Md. 1950) 170–191. H. RONDET, *Gratia Christi* (Paris 1948) 257–345.

[K. HARGROVE]

CONINCK, GILES DE

Jesuit theologian; b. Bailleul, French Flanders, Dec. 20, 1571; d. Louvain, May 31, 1633. He entered the Society of Jesus in 1592 and studied under Leonard LESSIUS at Louvain. Eventually he succeeded Lessius in the chair of scholastic theology, which he held for 18 years. St. Alphonsus held Coninck's work in high esteem, and it is generally recognized that he made a valuable contribution to moral theology. His principal works are: *Comment. ac disp. in universam doctrinam divi Thomae, de sacramentis et censuris,* a treatise requested by Lessius (Antwerp 1616, enlarged and revised in later editions); *De moralitate, natura et effectibus actuum supernaturalium in genere et fide, spe, ac caritate speciatim* (Antwerp 1623), for which Coninck is supposed to have left extensive additions to be incorporated in later editions; *Responsio ad dissertationem impugnantium absolutionem moribundi sensibus destituti . . .* (Antwerp 1625); and *Disputationes theologicae de sanctissima Trinitate et divini Verbi incarnatione* (Antwerp 1645). The St. Patrick Library in Dublin has a manuscript, dated Aug. 11, 1618, that is said to be Coninck's treatise on grace.

Bibliography: C. RUCH, *Dictionnaire de théologie catholique,* ed. A. VACANT et al. (Paris 1903–50) 3.1:1152–53. C. SOMMERVO-GEL et al., *Bibliothèque de la Compagnie de Jésus* (Brussels-Paris 1890–1932) 2:1369–71. H. HURTER, *Nomenclator literarius theologiae catholicae* (3d ed., Innsbruck 1903–13) 3:881–882.

[F. C. LEHNER]

CONNECTICUT, CATHOLIC CHURCH IN

Connecticut has earned a reputation as the wealthiest of the United States, as the home of Mark Twain, and as the nation's insurance capital. Located in the northeast United States, Connecticut was one of the original 13 states. Connecticut's Catholic Church has also demonstrated steady growth through immigration and institutional management to earn recognition as one of the most Catholic of states. Clerical and lay cooperation allowed Connecticut Catholics to establish firm roots and to confront the challenges resulting from rapid expansion.

Calvinist New England initially appeared as infertile ground for Catholicism, but early 19th-century conditions allowed for Catholic immigration and growth. Although the state's founder, Thomas Hooker, asserted

Archdiocese/Diocese	Year Created
Archdiocese of Hartford	1953
Diocese of Bridgeport	1953
Diocese of Norwich	1953

religious independence from Puritan Massachusetts, Connecticut extended few spiritual freedoms to non-Protestants. Connecticut was clearly seen as mission territory for Catholics, even after the creation of the Diocese of Baltimore, which encompassed the state, in 1789. In 1808, Baltimore was made an archdiocese, and the newly erected Diocese of Boston sent missionaries to Connecticut. Until 1818, the state's constitution granted the Congregational Church status as the established religion. In that year, the end of legal restrictions on Catholic organizations presented opportunities for diverse religious practices. As Irish immigrants increasingly arrived to build the Enfield Canal in the 1820s, Catholicism began to take root in this Yankee Protestant state.

Clerical and lay partnership overcame many anti-Catholic obstacles, and prompted Catholic evangelism in Connecticut. With the support of Boston Bishop Benedict J. Fenwick, S.J., Hartford businessman Deodat Taylor raised funds to create both a newspaper, *The Connecticut Catholic*, and to purchase Hartford's first Catholic church, Holy Trinity, in 1829. The Episcopalian Bishop who sold this church reportedly expressed satisfaction with the business exchange: "Well, Bishop Fenwick, as we have a fine new church building we will let you have the old one." Fenwick replied, with similar contentment, "Yes, and you have a fine new religion and we will keep the old one." During the 1830s, Holy Trinity's second pastor, Rev. James Fitton, S.J., fostered Catholic practice and faith in Connecticut's eastern Tolland, Windham, and New London counties. When establishing New London's first church, Fitton purchased land between two Protestant homes. Though recognizing Protestant resistance to Catholic growth, Fitton believed that this location promised "fire insurance" by discouraging arsonist Protestant gangs. In the following decades, Hartford's Congregational minister Horace Bushnell mobilized anti-Catholicism with aggressive rhetoric: "[O]ur first danger is barbarism—Romanism next." Despite such resistance, the Holy See established the Diocese of Hartford, which encompassed both the states of Connecticut and Rhode Island, in 1843.

Missionary activity received more coordinated direction under the diocese's first bishop, William Tyler (1843–49). Having converted at age 15, Tyler's spiritual development benefited from contact with schoolmate Fitton and the mentoring of Bishop Fenwick. Since Rhode Island contained more than half of this diocese's nearly 10,000 members, Tyler chose this state's capital, Providence—rather than the see city Hartford—as his permanent residence. The bishop's humble example of charity, through regular visits to the poor and the sick, provided the diocese's early direction. In the 1840s, Connecticut's dozens of new mills, factories, and quarries attracted Irish and German immigrants seeking employment. Connecticut soon became the United States' third largest manufacturing state, and experienced greater population growth. Several jobs became available during construction of railroads connecting Connecticut's southeastern cities New London and Norwich to Providence and Worcester, Massachusetts. Jesuit priests from Worcester's Holy Cross College traveled a circuit through eastern Connecticut's Catholic communities. Bishop Tyler's successful financial appeals to Parisian and Viennese benefactors allowed the diocese to recruit priests from Ireland's College of All Hallows. By the end of Tyler's tenure in 1850, the diocese boasted 12 churches and 14 priests.

In the following two decades, Connecticut's rapidly rising Catholic immigration contributed to the diocese's development beyond missionary status. While Tyler's model of humility attracted admiration from some non-Catholics, successors acted more as vocal advocates for an increasing Catholic population in the Diocese of Hartford. More than a million Irish immigrants settled in the United States from 1840 to 1860, and Connecticut's Catholic population doubled during the 1850s alone. When native-born Protestants limited Catholic political and economic freedom, Hartford bishops offered protection to these immigrant Catholics. Bishop Bernard O'REILLY (1850–56) defended Catholics from violations of religious liberty. Under the pseudonym "Roger Williams"—Rhode Island's founder and proponent of religious freedom—O'Reilly wrote to local newspapers in defense of Catholics who suffered religious persecution. For example, O'Reilly sought clemency for a Catholic private whom the U.S Army reprimanded for refusing to attend Sunday Protestant services. In 1855, members of the anti-immigrant KNOW-NOTHING party assembled to "inspect" a Sisters of Mercy convent in Providence. O'Reilly summoned the mayor and city marshall to prevent an imitation of the burning of Boston's Ursuline convent in 1830. NATIVISM, which elevated American-born Anglo-Saxon Protestants above European-born Catholics, reached a peak in pre–Civil War Connecticut. The nativist Know-Nothing party leader, William T. Minor, gained election as Connecticut governor from 1855 to 1858. Despite Catholic protests, Minor supported laws that outlawed Irish-Catholic militia associations and

Aerial view of central skyscrapers and Long Island Sound, New Haven. (Greater New Haven Convention & Visitors Bureau)

proscribed the registration of Catholic property in the name of the bishop. O'Reilly's courageous protection of Hartford Catholics proved critical for resisting these serious challenges to normal Catholic religious practice.

Catholics who sought advanced status in Connecticut political culture benefited from the efforts of O'Reilly's successor, Bishop Francis P. MCFARLAND (1858–74). McFarland's experience as a philosophy professor at St. John's College in Fordham, New York, allowed the new bishop to bring intellectual cachet to the diocese. During the U.S. Civil War, McFarland utilized this scholarly reputation to mobilize Catholics behind the Union cause. McFarland's denunciation of slavery discouraged Catholics in the diocese from violent anti-African attacks, such as those occurring in neighboring New York City in 1863. During the war, Connecticut Catholics sacrificed freedom and life for national unity. This example temporarily quieted anti-immigrant nativism, and the state accepted Catholic militia organizations in the Connecticut National Guard. McFarland also welcomed opportunities to speak at Protestant churches. By engaging non-Catholic Americans in dialogue, both O'Reilly and McFarland frustrated attempts to portray Catholicism as un-American.

The diocese expanded substantially in the following decades, and this growth raised questions about how an increasingly Catholic population would interact with the predominately Protestant U.S. citizenry. In the 1870s, the diocese changed dramatically in response to these dual challenges of immigration and integration. The fruits of growth appeared as the diocese boasted 16 parishes in 1872. Strong state industries—Connecticut produced half of the nation's firearms by 1860—attracted further immigration. In 1874, therefore, the Holy See established the Diocese of Providence, thus leaving the Diocese of Hartford entirely within Connecticut borders. At the same time, immigrants from eastern and southern Europe requested national parishes to preserve immigrant language and culture. Even as second-generation Irish- and German-American Catholics received incremental acceptance into mainstream U.S. political culture, these newest immigrants—from Poland, Italy, Hungary, Lithuania, and Slovakia—revived nativist stereotypes of Catholicism as an alien, immigrant, and un-American faith. Throughout the late 19th and early 20th centuries, Hartford bishops accommodated diverse ethnic and linguistic expressions of Catholic traditions, and established national parishes even in regions where territorial parishes previously existed.

Despite Hartford's advances in size and status, the 1882 initiation of the Knights of Columbus in New Haven revealed how the new challenges of ethnically disparate immigrants threatened Catholic unity in Connecticut. New Haven's Father Michael J. McGivney founded this Catholic lay organization so that increasingly stable Irish Americans could organize in the struggle for acceptance into U.S. society and economy and, at the same time, maintain their faith. While Bishop Lawrence S. McMahon (1879–93) recognized the Knights as a potentially positive force against nativist anti-Catholicism, he discouraged lay Catholic societies from overemphasizing Irish ethnic pride to the detriment of Catholicism's universal appeal. Irish Americans dominated most of the Knights' official positions, but the organization's constitution listed no ethnic or racial requirements for membership. Such assurances satisfied the diocesan leaders that this new organization would welcome participation of an increasingly international Catholic community in Connecticut.

In the final decade of the 19th century, Connecticut's bishops demonstrated strong suspicion that Americanism's emphasis on integration or assimilation into U.S. culture might undermine Catholic identity. From 1891 to 1894, the lay-owned Connecticut Catholic increasingly advocated "Americanization" of Catholicism and characterized U.S. institutions as "the greatest." Bishop Michael Tierney's (1894–1908) installation in 1894 witnessed a sharp change in this publication's editorial tone, and the diocese purchased and renamed its paper The Catholic Transcript in 1896. Subsequent issues emphasized the multinational character of Connecticut's Catholic population. When Tierney inaugurated a petit seminaire in 1897, this six-year seminary emphasized training in language skills and awareness of national differences. Connecticut's seminarians studied in France, Belgium, Germany, Switzerland, Poland, Italy, and French-speaking Canada. Tierney's international emphasis elevated different expressions of Catholicism over integration to American culture.

Steady immigration and church accommodation of these "new immigrants" in national parishes allowed the Catholic Church in Connecticut to grow with great speed at the turn of the century. During Tierney's 14-year tenure, the diocese nearly doubled in the number of parishes and clergy, the number of women religious almost tripled, and he oversaw the construction of five hospitals. From 1908 to 1932, Bishop John J. Nilan (1910–34) continued Tierney's legacy and increased the number of parishes from 221 to 290, including 29 national and four Eastern Rite parishes.

As Connecticut's Catholics became increasingly professional, Nilan also oversaw expanded opportunities in higher education. Nilan approved the establishment of two new Catholic colleges, Albertus Magnus in New Haven and Mount Saint Joseph's in West Hartford. Nilan's permission allowed Connecticut clergy to participate in national education projects. Monsignor Thomas J. Shahan, ordained for Hartford, served as rector of The Catholic University of America in Washington, D.C. from 1909 to 1928. Shahan also was principal editor of The Catholic Encyclopedia, and is considered a founder of the National Shrine of the Immaculate Conception, also in Washington. Another Hartford priest, Father Patrick McCormick, created both The Catholic University's School of Education and the Sister's College summer program (est. 1911), which offered women religious undergraduate training for teaching.

In the 1930s and 1940s, Bishop Maurice F. McAuliffe (1934–44) directed the diocese in serving the predominately second- and third-generation Americans who now represented the majority of Connecticut's Catholic population. Catholics who sought higher education for their children could utilize the newly established Catholic colleges, Annhurst Junior College for women in Woodstock and the Jesuit Fairfield University. Hartford's priests also confronted challenges particular to World War II. McAuliffe maintained correspondence with the 55 wartime chaplains who entered military service from the diocese. On the home front, priests were appointed as counselors to advocate for youth in juvenile courts, and more than 2,000 women religious served in the diocese's educational and health care facilities. While fewer national parishes were founded in this period, the influx of Catholics who worked in defense factories prompted the diocese to establish new territorial parishes in the state's largest cities.

After World War II, Connecticut emerged as an important center for a large influx of postwar Ukrainian immigrants. When the Russian Orthodox Patriarchate of Moscow officially declared legal authority over the Ukrainian Catholic Church based in Galicia (western Ukraine), Ukrainian-Americans maintained this Church's continued allegiance with Rome. In the 1950s, several papal decisions confirmed the enhanced significance of the United States and Canada, and particularly of Connecticut, for Ukrainian Catholics. Connecticut's northwestern city of Stamford became the seat of a second exarchy (the first being in Philadelphia) for Ukrainian-American Catholics in 1956. This exarchy—an organization similar to vicariates apostolic of the Latin Rite—served adherents of Byzantine rites in New York and New England, under the leadership of Bishop Ambrose Senyshyn, O.S.B.M., Stamford's first ordinary (exarch). Divided into seven deaneries, including one in Hartford, the new exarchy included 86,324 Catholics,

101 priests, and 53 parishes. In 1958, the Holy See created an independent Byzantine Rite ecclesiastical province for Ukrainian Catholics in America, establishing the Metropolitan See of Philadelphia (Archeparchy-Archdiocese) and the Eparchy of Stamford.

This period also witnessed the elevation of Hartford to archdiocesan status. During this period, the diocese of Hartford oversaw a Catholic population which grew in size and developed in status. In 1952, 927 priests served in 279 parishes, and 2400 women religious worked in 120 parochial schools. Connecticut's Catholic population reached nearly 750,000—33 percent of the state's 2.25 million residents—in 1953. In that year, the Holy See established the Archdiocese of Hartford and created the Dioceses of Bridgeport, Norwich, and Providence as suffragan sees in the new province. The Diocese of Hartford served Hartford, New Haven, and Litchfield counties. Bridgeport's territory included the wealthy and populous Fairfield County. Eastern Connecticut's four counties—Middlesex, New London, Tolland, and Windham—constituted the Diocese of Norwich.

The Diocese of Norwich expanded pursuit of Catholic education and ecumenism in eastern Connecticut. Bishop Bernard J. Flanagan (1953–59) became the first episcopal leader of Norwich's 53 parishes, 124,000 Catholics, and 24 missions. In six years as ordinary, Flanagan oversaw the creation of six new parishes. Bishop Vincent J. Hines (1960–75) established 11 new parishes, some of which had originally been formed as mission congregations. During these decades, three Catholic high schools—two in Middletown and one in Uncasville—earned solid reputations and substantial numbers of student applicants. Hines's successor, Bishop Daniel Patrick Reilly (1975–94) promoted ecumenical dialogue, most prominently with the Episcopalian Diocese of Connecticut. Reilly's services extended to several national and international Catholic organizations, such as Catholic Relief Services—the world's largest non-governmental relief organization. Reilly also joined a five-member Executive Committee of the National Conference of Catholic Bishops, whose 1983 pastoral on nuclear armaments provoked national discussion among Catholic and non-Catholic scholars and government officials. Despite these extensive responsibilities, Reilly also oversaw the establishment of eight new parishes. In the year 2000, Bishop Daniel A. Hart (1995–) led a diocese which counted 226,000 Catholics, 78 parishes, 139 diocesan and 64 religious priests, and five Catholic high schools.

Erected in 1953, the Diocese of Bridgeport witnessed rapid growth and increased Catholic educational opportunities for Fairfield County. Bishop (later Cardinal) Lawrence Shehan (1953–61) established Notre Dame as the diocese's first Catholic high school, in 1957. Norwalk and Stamford received Catholic high schools soon afterward. Sheehan also opened 15 new parochial elementary schools, and created 15 new parishes. Bishop Walter W. Curtis (1961–88) furthered Shehan's work by creating schools in each diocesan parish, and establishing two more Catholic high schools. After continued efforts by Bishop (later Cardinal) Edward Egan (1988–2000) and Bishop William E. Lori (2001–), the diocese boasted three universities, including Bridgeport's Sacred Heart, and an official newspaper, *Fairfield County Catholic*, with a circulation of 90,000. By the year 2001, this diocese contained 87 parishes, 265 priests, and 365,000 Catholics (43 percent of the county's total population). Parishes offered services in several languages, including Creole, Portuguese, Vietnamese, and Laotian.

The post–World War II Archdiocese of Hartford experienced substantial development in size and status, and also responded to the challenge of immigration of Catholics from Spanish-speaking regions. Bishop—Archbishop after 1953—Henry J. O'Brien (1945–68) founded 45 parishes, expanded hospitals, and promoted racial equality through pastoral letters, clergy retreats and conferences. The diocese created no national parishes for Spanish-speaking immigrants, but sponsored Spanish-language education of priests. Having traveled to Puerto Rico for such language training, these priests could minister more easily to Spanish-speaking communities in Connecticut.

Hartford's leadership has also encouraged laypersons to accept greater responsibilities for church administration. Archbishop John F. Whealon (1969–91), a recognized Scripture scholar, sought to ease pressures on diocesan priests by increasing responsibilities for non-clerics. The archdiocese initiated a permanent diaconate—the fifth in the United States—in 1969, and incorporated laity as eucharistic ministers and lectors. Whealon's appointments to archdiocesan offices established new precedents by including women religious and laypersons. Whealon appointed Sister Dolores Liptak, R.S.M., as archdiocesan historian in 1979 and Vivian Stephenson as the first lay editor of *The Catholic Transcript* in 1981. In 1985, Sister Helen Margaret Feeney, C.S.J., became chancellor of the archdiocese, one of the first women in the United States to receive an appointment to such an important decision-making office.

In the late 20th century, discouraging signs confronted the Archdiocese of Hartford. A study by two Yale University professors reported the existence of substantial work-related anxiety among the clergy. Whealon publicly expressed concern about confusion and apathy among U.S. Catholics. From 1969 to 1994, the archdiocese's

Catholic population decreased from about 830,000 to 810,000. Although the number of parishes grew from 208 to 224 from 1970 to 1990, the number of women religious dropped from nearly two thousand to 950, and Hartford's priests declined in number from 583 to 502.

Archbishop Daniel A. Cronin (1991–) has promoted vocations, evangelization, and social justice as the archdiocese's goals for the 21st century. Despite reversals in the archdiocese's steady growth, making it 14th in population nationally, it ranked fifth in donations to Catholic charities. Emphasis on "human dignity" united Cronin's support for minorities, immigrants, and the disabled with action against abortion, capital punishment, and poverty.

Connecticut's wealth and educational institutions offer opportunities, and responsibilities, for this state's Catholic population. Strong leadership from the Hartford metropolitan, the bishops of Bridgeport and Norwich, and increasingly active laypersons will enable the Catholic Church in Connecticut to harness these resources for further growth and spreading the Catholic faith.

Bibliography: S. M. DIGIOVANNI, *The Catholic Church in Fairfield County, 1666–1961* (New Canaan 1987). C. KAUFFMAN, *Faith and Fraternalism: The History of the Knights of Columbus, 1882–1982* (New York 1982). J. R. KELLEY, *Catholics in Eastern Connecticut: The Diocese of Norwich* (Norwich 1985). D. A. LIPTAK, *Hartford's Catholic Legacy: Leadership* (Hartford 1999). B. P. PROCKO, *Ukrainian Catholics in America* (Lanham 1982).

[T. CARTY]

CONNELL, FRANCIS J.

Theologian; b. Boston, Jan. 29, 1888; d. Washington, D.C., May 12, 1967. He graduated from Boston Latin School with high honors and attended Boston College for two years. In 1907 he entered the Redemptorists and was ordained to the priesthood in 1913 at Mt. St. Alphonsus, Esopus, New York. Following a parish assignment in Brooklyn, he was appointed professor of dogmatic theology at Mt. St. Alphonsus Seminary in 1915. From 1921 to 1923 he studied at the Pontifical Institute of the Angelicum in Rome, where he received the degree of doctor of sacred theology *summa cum laude*. He taught at Esopus (1923–40), The Catholic University of America (1940–58), and St. John's University in Brooklyn (1958–62). He also served in a variety of administrative capacities, including rector of Holy Redeemer College in Washington (1945–50), dean of the School of Sacred Theology at Catholic University (1949–57), and dean for religious communities at Catholic University (1958–67).

Connell was a scholar, writer, administrator, teacher, and preacher. In addition to numerous pamphlets and magazine articles on theological questions, he authored *De Sacramentis Ecclesiae, Morals in Politics and Professions, Outlines of Moral Theology, Spiritual and Pastoral Conferences for Priests,* and *Father Connell's Confraternity Edition of the New Baltimore Catechism.* A selection of his answers to moral problems was published under the title "Father Connell Answers Moral Questions." At the time of his death he was engaged in writing a two-volume text on moral theology. Over the years Connell's opinions on moral questions appeared regularly in the *American Ecclesiastical Review,* of which he was associate editor.

Connell was a pioneer on the national "Catholic Hour" radio program and appeared frequently on radio and television. He was a charter member and first president of the Catholic Theological Society of America. He received from Pope Pius XII the award "Pro Ecclesia et Pontifice" and an appointment as consultor to the Congregation of Seminaries and Universities in Rome. He was designated a peritus for the Second Vatican Council II by Pope John XXIII and served as a member of the briefing panel for English-speaking reporters.

[L. J. RILEY]

CONNELLY, CORNELIA, MOTHER

Foundress of the Society of the Holy Child Jesus; b. Philadelphia, Pa., Jan. 15, 1809; d. St. Leonard's, England, April 18, 1879. Cornelia Augusta Peacock of Philadelphia married Pierce Connelly, Episcopalian rector of Trinity Church, Natchez, Miss., in 1831. They had five children: Mercer (1832); Adeline (1835); John Henry (1837) and Mary Magdalen (1839), who died in infancy; and Pierce Francis (1841). Pierce, after studying the claims of the Catholic Church with Cornelia, renounced his Anglican orders in 1835. That year Cornelia was received into the Catholic Church in New Orleans, La., and Pierce in Rome, Italy, in 1836.

In 1840, Cornelia's husband confided to her his conviction that he had a vocation to the priesthood, a conviction that was approved by his spiritual directors and ultimately by the highest authority in Rome. A papal decree of permanent separation was granted in March of 1844. Cornelia was directed to enter the Sacred Heart convent in Rome as a quasi-postulant, her younger children remaining with her. In 1845, she pronounced her solemn vow of chastity and Pierce was ordained. Her ultimate vocation—to establish a new teaching congregation—was fostered by John Grassi, SJ. At the invitation of Cardinal Nicholas Wiseman she went to England and founded the Society of the HOLY CHILD JESUS in Derby,

Oct. 13, 1846. During her lifetime she established schools in England, the U.S., and France, and subsequently her sisters carried her educational work still farther to Ireland, Wales, Switzerland, Italy, Nigeria, and Ghana.

Her apostolate was accomplished at great personal cost. Her husband apostatized, attempted to regain his conjugal rights, and alienated their children from her and from the Church. In addition, there were temporal anxieties and a delay of the approbation of her rules until after her death. In 1959 the process of her beatification was opened in England. Her congregation then numbered about 900 sisters teaching at all educational and social levels. An African sisterhood, the Handmaids of the Holy Child Jesus, which became independent in 1960, is an outgrowth of her congregation.

Bibliography: M. T. BISGOOD, *Cornelia Connelly* (Westminster, Md. 1963). J. WADHAM, *The Case of Cornelia Connelly* (New York 1957). M. C. GOMPERTZ, *Cornelia Connelly* (4th ed. rev. London 1950). C. MCCARTHY, *The Spirituality of Cornelia Connelly: In God, for God, with God* (Lewiston, N.Y. 1986). R. FLAXMAN, *A Woman Styled Bold: The Life of Cornelia Connelly, 1809–1879* (London 1991).

[M. C. MCCARTHY]

CONNOLLY, JOHN

Second bishop of NEW YORK; b. Slane, County Meath, Ireland, *c.* 1750; d. New York, Feb. 6, 1825. He attended the Dominican School at Drogheda, entered the Order of Preachers, studied at Liège and Louvain, and was ordained probably in 1774. From about 1775 to 1814 he was stationed at San Clemente, the Irish Dominican house in Rome, where he served as prior (1782–96), librarian of the Casanate Library for several years, and Roman agent for some Irish bishops. After being suggested earlier for the episcopacy as bishop of Raphoe, he was appointed to New York on Oct. 4, 1814, and consecrated in Rome by Cardinal C. Brancadoro on November 6. Because he was a British subject, he had to await the end of the War of 1812 before leaving for America. After visits to Liège and Ireland he arrived in New York on Nov. 25, 1815; there he was installed, after 40 years in Rome, as the first resident bishop of a poverty-stricken diocese covering 55,000 square miles, and having 13,000 people, four priests, and three churches. His efforts were harassed by heavy debts on the two churches in New York City, a lack of success in coping with TRUSTEEISM, an acute and chronic shortage of priests and money, and a rapidly increasing population clamoring for churches. Nevertheless, he built 13 churches in eight years, introduced the Sisters of Charity, founded an orphan asylum, and made a visitation of the entire diocese (1823). His remains were interred in old St. Patrick's Cathedral, New York City.

Bibliography: J. T. SMITH, *The Catholic Church in New York* (New York 1906) v. 1. R. H. CLARKE, *Lives of the Deceased Bishops of the Catholic Church in the U.S.* (New York 1887–89) v.1. J. B. CODE, *Dictionary of American Hierarchy* (New York 1940). J. D. G. SHEA, *A History of the Catholic Church within the Limits of the U.S.* (New York 1886–92) v.3.

[F. D. COHALAN]

CONNOLLY, MYLES

Novelist, motion picture script writer; b. Boston, Mass., Oct. 7, 1897; d. Santa Monica, Calif., July 15, 1964. He was the son of Bartholomew and Anne (McManus) Connolly and married Agnes Bevington in 1929. They had three sons and two daughters. He was educated at Boston Latin School (1910–14) and Boston College (1914–18). In World War I he served in the U.S. Navy, and thereafter turned to journalism and wrote for the *Boston Post.* For many years he was a frequent contributor of verse and short stories to national magazines; in 1928 he served on the first board of directors of the Catholic Book Club. From 1928 to 1960, he was responsible for the production and writing of 40 motion pictures. He is best known, however, for *Mr. Blue* (1928), a novel that brought fame to Connolly and became required reading in many schools.

In the world of Hollywood, Connolly stood properly apart as a man of taste and distinction, a brilliant conversationalist who had his own values and could be loyal to them in a forceful, yet charming, manner. His first love was the printed word and he found a wide public for it. In addition to *Mr. Blue,* which was published also in Portuguese, French, and Italian, his works include *The Bump on Brannigan's Head* (1950, also published in Dutch and German); *Dan England and the Noonday Devil* (1951); *The Reason for Ann* (1953); and *Three Who Ventured* (1958). In *Mr. Blue* can be found echoes of St. Francis of Assisi and St. Thomas More. It is filled with a sense of Christian joy, a hope and a certainty of things to come. Or, as Mr. Blue himself says, "there is a glorious Somewhere, and it is far nearer to us than the stars."

[E. LAVERY]

CONNOLLY, THOMAS LOUIS

Archbishop; b. County Cork, Ireland, 1815; d. Halifax, Nova Scotia, Canada, July 27, 1876. He was educated for the priesthood at Rome, where he entered the Capuchin Order, and was ordained at Lyons, France. After serving for several years in Ireland he immigrated to Nova Scotia (1842) as secretary to Bp. (later Abp.)

William Walsh. In 1845 he was appointed vicar-general of the diocese of Halifax. He was consecrated 12th bishop of St. John's, New Brunswick, Aug. 15, 1852. There he founded (1854) a community of Sisters of Charity to whose care he entrusted an orphanage. He began to build a cathedral there but was transferred to the see of Halifax (1859), becoming its second archbishop. His chief work was along charitable and educational lines, but his influence was also great against the secret revolutionary Fenian movement that sought to achieve Irish separation from England. He showed remarkable tact in dealing with the Protestant elements, especially at Halifax. He figured prominently in VATICAN COUNCIL I, where he aligned himself with Abp. Peter R. Kenrick of St. Louis, Missouri, and the minority group on the question of papal INFALLIBILITY. Upon the definition of infallibility, he immediately submitted to the Holy See. He was also influential in Nova Scotia's entry into the Canadian Confederation.

Bibliography: N. F. DAVIN, *The Irishman in Canada* (Toronto 1877).

[J. T. FLYNN]

CONON, POPE

Pontificate: Oct. 23, 686 to Sept. 21, 687. Conon descended from a family whose origins lay in the eastern part of the Roman Empire; his father was an officer who served in a corps of the imperial army based in the East. However, Conon was raised in Sicily and entered the service of the Roman church at an early age, eventually becoming a priest. On the death of Pope JOHN V (685–686) a division occurred in Rome over the election of a successor. Traditionally, papal elections had been the prerogative of the clergy and people of Rome, their decision being subject to confirmation by the exarch of RAVENNA, the emperor's representative in Italy. Generally, the clerical leaders in the city dominated the election process with the laity playing a somewhat indeterminate role. On this occasion the clergy put forward the Archpriest Peter as its candidate, but Peter's candidacy was challenged by a priest named Theodore, who was the choice of what a contemporary source called the "army." This term referred to a new element emerging in Italian affairs, a landed aristocracy whose wealth and power derived from service in the imperial military establishment. During the course of the seventh century the imperial army was increasingly recruited from the local population and led by local officers who used their position to accumulate land, political power, and social status. Such a localized militia had developed in the duchy of Rome and had become increasingly interested in papal affairs. This resulted as a consequence of the important place the papal establishment played in the direction of affairs in Rome and of the increasing irrelevance of imperial policies to the interests of those involved in the militia. For example, the Roman militia played an important role in preventing the exarch from carrying out Emperor CONSTANS II's orders to arrest Pope MARTIN I in 649. Now the leaders of this same segment of Roman society were seeking a decisive voice in the election of the pope. After considerable negotiations the clerical party suggested a compromise candidate who was acceptable to the leaders of the army. He was the priest Conon, already aged, and according to his biography, "of uncomplicated mind." His election was duly confirmed by the exarch in Ravenna.

Conon's brief pontificate was marked by good relationships with the imperial government. Emperor JUSTINIAN II sent Conon a letter informing him that he had discovered the authentic acts of the Sixth Ecumenical Council of 680–681 (Council of CONSTANTINOPLE III) and had required the Byzantine clergy and laity to sign the document so that the council's acts would never be falsified; perhaps the emperor was seeking to assure the papacy of his intentions to abide by the decisions of that council which sought to end the heresy of MONOTHELITISM. Justinian II also made important concessions by lowering taxes on the papal patrimonies in southern Italy and releasing dependents from the papal patrimony in Sicily who were being held by imperial officials as security for payment of taxes.

However, on other fronts things did not proceed so well. Although praised by his biographer for his concern for charitable activities, Conon's illness limited his ability to execute his normal responsibilities, including such things as ordinations. He made an ill-advised appointment when he designated a Sicilian deacon as rector of the papal patrimony of Sicily. This appointment angered the Roman clergy serving in the papal administration, a member of which traditionally filled that office. That resentment was an indication of the importance of the income of the Sicilian patrimony in papal affairs and of the claims of members of the papal administration to rights pertaining to their offices. Conon's choice of a Sicilian rector also angered the Sicilian tillers of the patrimonial lands who were victimized by the rector's greed and deception, an indication of the far-reaching impact of papal administration on Italian affairs. While Conon was still living, a key member of the papal administration, the Archdeacon Pascal, sought to assure his own election to the papal office by bribing the exarch of Ravenna. Pascal's effort resulted in another disputed election which finally settled on Pope SERGIUS I as Conon's successor.

Bibliography: Sources. *Le Liber Pontificalis*, ed. L. DUCHESNE (Paris 1955–1957) 1:368–370, Eng. tr. in *The Book of Pontiffs*

(Liber Pontificalis). Translated Texts for Historians: The Ancient Biographies of the First Ninety Roman Pontiffs to A.D. 715, tr. with intro. R. DAVIS, 5 (Liverpool 1989) 81–82. *Regesta Pontificum Romanorum ab condita ecclesia ad annum post Christum MCXCVIII,* ed. P. JAFFÉ (Leipzig 1885–1888) 1:243. Literature. E. CASPAR, *Geschichte des Papsttums von den Anfängen bis zur Höhe der Weltherrschaft* v.2; *Das Papsttum unter byzantinisches Herrschaft* (Tübingen 1933) 620–623. O. BERTOLINI, *Roma di fronte a Bisanzio e ai Langobardi,* Storia di Roma 9 (Bologna 1941) 396–401. L. BRÉHIER and R. AIGRAIN, *Grégoire le Grand, les États barbares et la conquête arabe (590–757). Histoire de l'église depuis les origines jusqu'à nos jours,* ed. A. FLICHE and V. MARTIN 5 (Paris 1947) 192–193, 406–407. J. RICHARDS, *The Popes and the Papacy in the Early Middle Ages, 476–752* (London, Boston, and Henley 1979) 201–215. T. F. X. NOBLE, *The Republic of St. Peter. The Birth of the Papal State, 680–825* (Philadelphia 1989) 15–16, 185, 190–192.

[R. E. SULLIVAN]

CONQUES, ABBEY OF

Former BENEDICTINE abbey, 24 miles north-northwest of Rodez, Aveyron, France; Diocese of Rodez. Founded in the early 9th century, the abbey came under the authority of BENEDICT OF ANIANE *c.* 820. It became a famous stopping place along one of the "roads to SANTIAGO DE COMPOSTELA" after it was given the head of the Agenais virgin martyr Fides or FOY (hence its name Sainte-Foy), toward the end of the 10th century. Most of the abbey buildings were erected during the next two centuries, notably the famous Romanesque abbey church whose portal of the Last Judgment dates from the end of the 12th century. The abbey suffered much from COMMENDATION, instituted there in 1474. Because of their location in the Rouergue, the monastic buildings barely escaped burning by the Protestants (1568) during the Wars of Religion. By this date the abbey had been secularized (1537), but the collegiate church established there retained large property holdings and numerous dependencies until suppressed during the French Revolution (1790). The abbey church, restored in the 19th century by architects of the Viollet-le-Duc school, serves today as a parish church and since 1873 has been staffed by a small community of PREMONSTRATENSIANS from Frigolet.

Bibliography: *Gallia Christiana,* v. 1–13 (Paris 1715–85), v. 14–16 (Paris 1856–65) 4:288–289. G. DESJARDINS, *Cartulaire de l'abbaye de Conques, en Rouergue* (Paris 1879). É. MÂLE, *L'Art religieux du XIIᵉ siècle en France* (5th ed. Paris 1947). M. AUBERT, "Conques en Rouergue," *Congrès archéologique de France,* 2 v. (Paris 1937) 459–523. F. BOUSQUET, *Dictionnaire d'histoire et de géographie ecclésiastiques,* ed. A. BAUDRILLART et al. (Paris 1912—) 13:472–478.

[L. GAILLARD]

Hernán Cortés (1485–1547), Spanish conqueror of Mexico.

CONQUISTADORES

When Spain undertook the expansion of European civilization into the New World, the conquistadores were her agents. They were not just military conquerors, although military conquest was part of their work. They were explorers, governors, exploiters, Christianizers; men with a mission to spread their faith; men with a desire to gain wealth and position; men with a curiosity that led them into a gigantic project for which their means were quite inadequate. Some were illiterate; some were trained lawyers. They flourished during the first half of the 16th century and for perhaps another half-century or so on the frontier. When a settled society was achieved, the work of the conquistador was done. He had not only lost his place in the New World, but often the respect of the society he had helped to make possible. Few were the conquistadores who lived a long life, enjoying wealth, position, and honor. Columbus was only the first of the founders of the Spanish American empire to see his titles, positions, and prestige dwindle. Death by assassination or murder was a commonplace end for a conquistador.

Mexico and Peru, the centers of population and wealth, attracted the conquistadores. There men such as Hernán Cortés and Francisco Pizarro gained their fame. These adventurers, however, were not limited by geogra-

"The Execution of the Inca," engraving by A.D. Greene.

phy. They spread throughout the islands of the Caribbean, into the southern part of North America, and across the mountains, deserts, and jungles of South America.

Mexico. The conquest of Mexico was achieved by the prototype of the conquistadores, Cortés. Contemporary documents such as Cortés's own letters to Emperor Charles V, the authorized history by Gómara, and the story told by the veteran soldier (in his own words one of the first conquistadores of New Spain) Bernal Díaz del Castillo, give a vivid account of the project.

Cortés was born in Medellín, a small town in Extremadura, the province in Spain from which so many conquistadores came. He spent some time at the University of Salamanca but was in Española by 1504. He went to Cuba with the Velázquez expedition of 1511. Cortés had already gained a reputation for audacity when, at about the age of 33, he was put in charge of the third expedition to Yucatán, being prepared by the governor of Cuba, Diego Velázquez. The governor, prompted by his distrust of the dynamic Cortés and by pressures from relatives, shortly withdrew the appointment. Cortés had anticipated this and sailed before the order could be made effective. Agents of the governor sent after him usually were inveigled by Cortés into joining him instead of arresting him.

Ultimately, with fewer than 700 Spaniards, 16 horses, a few cannons and muskets, but supported by thousands of Native American allies he had cultivated or conquered or both, Cortés led an expedition toward Tenochtitlán, the capital of the Aztec Empire. Before marching inland Cortés founded the city of Villa Rica de la Vera Cruz and the new municipality elected him governor of the area, subject only to the king of Spain.

The Spaniards entered Tenochtitlán peacefully on Nov. 8, 1519. But the conquest was not so easily achieved. While Pedro de Alvarado was in charge of the Spanish forces in the city, their wanton massacres of Aztec nobles during a festival endangered the entire undertaking. Even with reinforcements Cortés could not hold the city. On *la noche triste,* June 20, 1520, the Spaniards tried to fight their way across the causeways and out of the city. Across the water that was gorged with bodies of dead Spaniards, dead Native Americans, dead horses, and baggage of all sorts, the bedraggled remains of Cortés's forces made their way. Muskets and crossbows were lost in the melee. Through it all, "Cortés showed himself very much a man, as he always was," reported Bernal Díaz.

Six months later Cortés had his troops, sheltered during that time by their allies, the Tlaxcalans, ready to return. He had only 550 Spaniards but many Tlaxcalans were trained to fight with them. When siege did not bring the surrender of the Aztecs, Cortés decided that the only way to achieve victory was to level the city. House by house, temple by temple, the Spaniards moved in. Díaz says the siege lasted 93 days; in August 1520 it ended. Tenochtitlán was gone and with it the treasures of the Aztec king.

Cortés immediately set to work establishing the Spanish dominion. He built Mexico City on the site of the old Aztec capital. He sent his captains out in all directions to command the allegiance of the surrounding tribes. He apparently tried to preserve native institutions and to maintain the caciques in their political roles, but these aims, even though supported by royal order, were unsuccessful in the face of demands by his men for vassals. In October 1522 Cortés was appointed governor and captain general of New Spain. While he was away on an expedition to Honduras, however, the Spaniards in Mexico City began to challenge his rule. In 1529 Cortés went to Spain and got his titles and authority confirmed by the emperor. On his return to Mexico he found established there an *audiencia,* even though a venal one, also with royal authority. When the *audiencia* failed to establish order, Charles V appointed a viceroy. Cortés was reduced to conducting exploratory expeditions on the Pacific and to developing his own estates. When he again took his claims to the Spanish court, he was coldly received. He died in Spain in 1547.

In the conquest of Mexico Cortés met the best organized resistance the Europeans ever encountered in America. He multiplied his meager resources by cunning, diplomacy, and force. His men followed him even on vain expeditions such as the one into Central America. W. H. Prescott says of him:

> If he was indebted for his success to the cooperation of the Indian tribes, it was the force of his genius that obtained command of such materials. He arrested the arm that was lifted to smite him, and made it do battle in his behalf . . . . He brought together the most miscellaneous collection of mercenaries who ever fought under one standard; . . . this motley congregation was assembled in one camp, compelled to bend to the will of one man. . . . It is in this wonderful power over the discordant masses thus gathered under his banner, that we recognize the genius of the great commander no less than in the skill of his military operations.

But Cortés did not stop there. Under his direction a political entity was established that preserved organized society and prepared an empire for Spain.

Peru and Chile. The Spanish American empire gained another valuable area in the empire of the Incas. No letters from the conqueror of Peru to the emperor tell us the details of the conquest. Pizarro never even learned to sign his name. His birth date is unknown, but he was born in Extremadura and was an illegitimate son of a military man. He had no inheritance and no education. The New World could offer nothing but an improvement in his station. He was there in Española by 1509 or 1510 and was a member of the unsuccessful expedition led by Alonso de Ojeda. Subsequently he associated himself with Vasco Núñez de Balboa and was with the group that first sighted the South Sea. As an *encomendero* in Panama, Pizarro started a business partnership with Diego de Almagro, another soldier of fortune, and Fernando de Luque, a canon of the cathedral. After having undertaken a number of successful business ventures, the three partners obtained permission from Governor Pedrárias to search for the rich lands reputed to be to the south. Pizarro and Almagro were probably men in their 50s when the first attempt was made in December 1524. In 1528–29 Pizarro went to Spain and got full authorization from the king to continue the planned conquest. He brought back with him his four brothers and a cousin.

It was 1530 before an expedition actually invaded the Inca empire. By then a civil war was in progress there over the succession to the throne. The Spaniards entered the fray when Pizarro and his men seized the Inca Atahualpa, at a meeting in Cajamarca. The Inca's attendants had come unarmed to the ceremonial encounter and thousands, unable to defend themselves, were killed. While Atahualpa's ransom was being collected all over the land (and much of the artistic work of the Incas was being melted into gold ingots by the Spaniards), Almagro arrived with reinforcements. The other claimant to the Inca throne, Huascar, was killed in the south by Atahualpa's orders. Shortly after the Spaniards accused Atahualpa of treason and executed him. Thus the Spaniards lost the key to political control of the highly organized Inca empire. They pushed on with military force. In November they took Cuzco and the men immediately set to work plundering the city. Pizarro left his brothers Juan and Gonzalo in charge there and headed for the sea. Near the harbor he founded Lima, the City of the Kings (1535). Attempts to set up Spanish authority on a regular basis, however, foundered on the revolt of Inca Manco (1536) and on dissension among the Spaniards. As a result of wounds received in the suppression of the Inca revolt, the first of the Pizarro brothers, Juan, died.

Almagro and Francisco Pizarro grew more and more apart. Almagro felt ill-treated in the division of titles and wealth, particularly after his profitless expedition to Chile. On his return he captured Cuzco and imprisoned

Hernando and Gonzalo Pizarro. The civil wars among the Spaniards were underway. Almagro was persuaded by Francisco Pizarro to release Hernando, supposedly to go to Spain. Instead the Pizarros joined forces; Hernando captured Almagro and had him strangled in 1538. The next year Hernando went to Spain bearing the great treasures of Cuzco. Almagro's supporters, however, were already there to accuse him of murder. Hernando spent the next 22 years in prison. The prisons evidently were of varying degrees of rigor for he was married during that time. Imprisonment may have saved his life; supposedly he lived to the age of 100. None of his brothers did. Francisco Pizarro was assassinated June 26, 1541, by the Almagristas; Almagro's son Diego was captured and beheaded in September 1542. When Gonzalo Pizarro assumed control of Peru, he protested against the enforcement of the New Laws of 1542 and led a rebellion against royal authority represented by Viceroy Blasco Núñez de la Vela. In a battle in January 1546, the viceroy was unhorsed and beheaded.

In another attempt to restore order in Peru, Charles V dispatched the priest Pedro de la Gasca. He was given unlimited authority to do whatever should be necessary. The emissary worked slowly and finally persuaded most of the rebellious group to join the royal forces. Gonzalo Pizarro's army deserted him and he had to surrender without a battle. He was beheaded in 1548. Only then could Spain establish a regular administration in Peru and take advantage of the riches that were hers as a result of the work of the indomitable, if bloody, conquistador Francisco Pizarro.

Just before Gonzalo Pizarro's capture, one of his supporters, Francisco de Carvajal, viewing the military force ranged against them, was reported to have said that it must be led by Pedro de Valdivia or the devil. Valdivia was another native of Extremadura. He was probably of a poor noble family and was somewhat unusual among the conquistadores because he had regular military training. He entered the army in 1520 or 1521 and served Charles V both in Italy and Flanders. He was also an educated man. After the battle of Pavia (1525) he returned to Extremadura, married, and lived as a country squire for 10 years. He went to America in 1535, first to Venezuela, and then to Peru the next year with reinforcements for Pizarro. For three years Valdivia supported Pizarro and received position, property, and wealth as a reward. He did not remain on his land long. In April 1539 Valdivia asked permission from Pizarro to explore and conquer Chile. There the enemy were the intractable Araucan people. Valdivia's attempts to colonize Chile ended with his capture by the Araucan at the end of 1553. The rumors about the manner of his death cannot be verified, but they all included torture and the eating of the body by his captors.

Colombia. The conquest of the home of the Chibcha involved no such bloody siege as that of Tenochtitlán or civil war such as that in Peru. The lives lost in the expedition of Gonzalo Jiménez de Quesada were not lost in battle.

Jiménez de Quesada was born in Córdoba about the beginning of the 16th century. He was a lawyer and went to America in 1535 as a magistrate in the company of Pedro de Lugo, the newly appointed governor of Santa Marta. He was in his mid-30s when the governor put him in charge of an expedition of about 900 men to explore and conquer a rich country rumored to be south of Santa Marta, high in the mountains. The expedition started up the Magdalena River in 1536. Nature and indigenous tribes, concealed by the jungle and armed with poisoned arrows, made it a harrowing trip. Almost a year elapsed before the expedition reached the upland plains inhabited by the Chibchas. Only about 166 of the Spaniards were still alive. Jiménez de Quesada gave strict orders that peaceful methods must be used for the conquest and that anyone who violated this policy would be punished by death. By the end of 1538 he had established his authority over the numerous population in the Chibcha country. It was challenged early in 1539 by other groups of Spaniards coming in first from Venezuela and later from Peru. Quesada by judicious use of gifts of gold averted civil war and maintained control.

Out of the 166 who had arrived on the plateau, three or four died on exploring expeditions. One man was hanged on a charge of looting the natives. Jiménez de Quesada had received no reinforcements, but with these few men, almost all preserved through his care, he had conquered the area. Leaving the new city of Santafé de Bogotá in 1539, he went to Spain but did not receive the appointment as governor of the territory. With an honorary title, Jiménez de Quesada returned to the New Kingdom of Granada, where he served in minor offices until his death at about 80.

Other Areas. One of the distinctive conquistadores in the Caribbean and in Panama was Balboa, who moved from being a stowaway into the leadership of the expedition supposedly commanded by lawyer Martin Fernández de Enciso. Balboa gained enough authority and power to arrest Enciso and send him back to Spain and then ensured his position by fairness and consideration in dealing with his men. After he discovered the South Sea and was preparing ships to embark on it in search of the rich lands to the south, Governor Pedrárias sent Francisco Pizarro to arrest him. Balboa was accused of treason and beheaded; it was Pizarro who then went on to the rich lands of the Inca.

The search for the fountain of youth was made by a knight. Juan Ponce de León was a member of the Spanish nobility. He was born about 1460 and went through the training of a page and a squire before going to America. On a return trip to Spain he was knighted by King Ferdinand. Before that he had founded a settlement on the island of Puerto Rico and subjugated the native peoples. Rivalry with Diego Columbus cost Ponce de León the governorship, but the Crown authorized him to undertake other explorations if he wished. On March 3, 1513, he set out from Puerto Rico on the expedition associated with the search for the fountain of youth. Most of the early Spanish American chroniclers mention this as a possible reason for the expedition but only in addition to the desire for economic gain. Bartolomé de LAS CASAS simply states that Ponce de León went for slaves and pearls. The expedition was unsuccessful: 16th-century Florida had no fountains of youth, good slaves, or pearls. In 1521 Ponce de León tried again. He outfitted a colonizing expedition and sailed up the west coast of Florida. The Native Americans attacked, Ponce de León was wounded, and he died in Havana.

The names of many more conquistadores could be added: Pedro de Alvarado in Guatemala, the licentiate Lucas Vázquez de Ayllón in the Carolinas, Pánfilo Narváez in the Floridas, Francisco Vásquez de Coronado in the southwest of the present United States, Hernando de Soto in Florida and the lower Mississippi basin, Álvar Núñez Cabeza de Vaca and Domingo Martínez de Irala in La Plata, and probably hundreds of lesser men who assumed the role of the conquistador in a small area. With them came the priests who served as missionaries but often also as explorers, secretaries, and chroniclers. When the age of the conquistadores was past, the missionaries themselves expanded the empire, particularly from northwest Mexico up into California. But the shadows of the conquistadores seem to reach all the way to the caudillos of independent Spanish America.

Bibliography: F. A. KIRKPATRICK, *The Spanish Conquistadores* (2d ed. London 1946). W. L. SCHURZ, *This New World* (New York 1954). *Hernando Cortés: Five Letters, 1519–1526,* tr. J. BAYARD MORRIS (New York 1962). B. DÍAZ DEL CASTILLO, *The Discovery and Conquest of Mexico, 1517–1521,* tr. A. P. MAUDSLAY (New York 1956). F. LÓPEZ DE GÓMARA, *Cortés: The Life of the Conqueror by His Secretary,* ed. L. B. SIMPSON (Berkeley 1964). W. H. PRESCOTT, *History of the Conquest of Mexico* (New York 1843); *History of the Conquest of Peru* (New York 1847), and later eds. K. ROMOLI, *Balboa of Darién* (Garden City, N.Y. 1953). R. B. C. GRAHAM, *The Conquest of New Granada: Being the Life of Gonzalo Jiménez de Quesada* (London 1922). I. S. W. VERNON, *Pedro de Valdivia: Conquistador of Chile* (Austin, Tex. 1946).

[J. HERRICK]

CONRAD, JOSEPH

Novelist; b. Berdichev, Russian Poland (now the Ukraine), Dec. 3, 1857; d. Bishopsbourne, Kent, En-

Joseph Conrad.

gland, Aug. 3, 1924. Conrad's unhappy Polish childhood shaped his melancholy temperament; his maritime career provided material for nearly all his novels. He was descended on both sides from Roman Catholic landed gentry. Conrad, baptized Józef Teodor Konrad Nałęcz, was the only child of Apollo Korzeniowski (1820–69), editor, translator, romantic poet, and revolutionary nationalist. Conrad was four years old when the family was exiled to Russia for illegal political activity. As a result, both parents died of tuberculosis, his mother, Ewa Bobrowska (1833–65), when he was seven, and his father four years later. Conrad, frequently ill himself, had little formal schooling and few companions. Before he was 17, the restless, undisciplined orphan persuaded his guardian-uncle Thaddeus Bobrowski to let him go to Marseilles and become a sailor. For three years he served as gentleman-midshipman on several voyages to the West Indies; he ran guns to revolutionaries in Spain, and was shot over a woman, either in a duel or, more probably, in attempted suicide.

In 1878 Conrad joined an English ship as able seaman, learned English quickly, and made steady progress in the British Merchant Service, passing examinations as second mate (1880), first mate (1884), and master (1886). He sailed to Eastern ports—Bombay, Bangkok, Singapore, Sydney—and celebrated this life in *The Nigger of* the "*Narcissus*" (1897), "Youth" (1898), *Typhoon* (1902), and *The Shadow-Line* (1917). Voyaging among the East Indies (1887) and on the Congo River (1890), he became fascinated by the psychological and moral deterioration of isolated white traders. He wrote of them in his first novel, *Almayer's Folly* (1895), and in such masterpieces as "Heart of Darkness" (1898), *Lord Jim* (1900), and *Nostromo* (1904), as well as in *An Outcast of the Islands* (1896), *Victory* (1915), and *The Rescue* (1920). He abandoned the sea after the publication of *Almayer's Folly*. On March 24, 1896, he married Jessie George, daughter of a Roman Catholic warehouseman; they had two sons and lived for the most part in Kent. Although his fiction won immediate critical success, he lived in virtual poverty until the large sales of *Chance* (1913).

Conrad presents a complex world, although on the surface his ethic seems simple enough. His novels often portray heroic seamen, "men held together by a community of inglorious toil and by fidelity to a certain standard of conduct." In a godless universe, man's only reward comes from a perfect love of the work. Yet in his best novels Conrad is interested in moral failures, even in criminal betrayers. He condemns them; but he also feels for them a sympathy rooted in skepticism about man's ability to meet life's tests. He sees men defeated chiefly by themselves, by too-active imaginations, by lack of self-knowledge, by twin longings for power and peace, by personal loneliness and moral isolation, and by a fundamental egoism. He doubts equally man's ability to improve his lot through political activity: "In this world of men nothing can be changed." His three political novels, *Nostromo, The Secret Agent* (1907), and *Under Western Eyes* (1911), are antirevolutionary despite their sympathy for certain revolutionists.

His fiction owes something to Henry James and to his collaboration with Ford Madox Ford, but Conrad devised special techniques to convey his dark view. He dramatized misunderstanding and isolation through the use of personal narrators who frequently have to rely on other people's testimony for the facts. He consistently violated normal chronology to convey a sense of complexity and to involve the reader in the moral complications. He developed a distinctive style that, through richly symbolic imagery and overly long sentences, constantly suggests complexity and emotional commitment. Conrad's technique and insights have greatly influenced modern novelists, especially William Faulkner and Graham GREENE (1904–1991).

Conrad was not a practicing Catholic and he sometimes explicitly attacked institutional Christianity, but he never renounced his heritage. While he rarely wrote of religion, one of his finest characters is the saintly Father Romàn in *Nostromo*. Furthermore, Conrad's pervasive insistence on expiation through awareness of guilt seems profoundly Christian.

Bibliography: Works. *The Portable Conrad,* ed. M. D. ZABEL (New York 1946), contains the best introduction. J. M. Dent and Sons has published two collected editions of his works, each in 22 v. (London 1923–38 and 1946–55). Literature. J. BAINES, *Joseph Conrad: A Critical Biography* (New York 1960). A. J. GUERARD, *Conrad the Novelist* (Cambridge, Mass. 1959). E. K. HAY, *The Political Novels of Joseph Conrad* (Chicago 1963). T. MOSER, *Joseph Conrad: Achievement and Decline* (Cambridge, Mass. 1957). J. ALLEN, *The Sea Years of Joseph Conrad* (New York 1965).

[T. MOSER]

CONRAD II, HOLY ROMAN EMPEROR

Reigned Sept. 4, 1024, to June 4, 1039; b. *c.* 990; d. Utrecht, Netherlands. He was the son of Count Henry of Carinthia and the Alsatian Countess Adelheid, founders of the "Salian" dynasty, and was educated by Bp. BURCHARD OF WORMS. Conrad entered a canonically objectionable marriage with Gisela of Swabia in 1015 to 1016. At the instigation of Abp. ARIBO OF MAINZ, he was elected king and successor of HENRY II at Kamba (near Oppenheim) on the Rhine. Crowned on September 8, he was recognized in Germany in spite of the opposition of his son-in-law, Duke Ernst of Swabia. He received homage in Milan in 1025. In 1026 he designated his son Henry III as his successor. Conrad was crowned emperor in Rome by JOHN XIX on Easter Sunday, 1027. Since then the emperor's bull read: *Roma caput mundi regit orbis frena rotundi.* In the East, Conrad was able to win back Lusatia from Poland in 1031 to 1032. He established a personal union of Burgundy with Germany after the death of the Burgundian king, Rudolf III, although he did not exercise his supremacy there. His regime is distinguished by acquisitions of imperial property, uniform laws and statutes, an increase in the flow of money, and in public security, and it laid a foundation for his position in later Germanic legends. The only failure Conrad experienced was in Milan, where he defended the nobles (vavasors) and unsuccessfully fought the wretched excommunicated Archbishop Aribert (1037). Earlier research characterized Conrad as indifferent to the Church, but recently the contrast between him and his predecessors and successors has been denied (Schieffer) or sharply reduced (Vogt). Actually Conrad retained the ecclesiastical control of Henry II without, however, showing any of Henry's personal concern. At synods he was interested only in political issues, neglecting statutes on Church discipline. He delegated monastic reform to

POPPO OF STAVELOT, whom he had sponsored and to whom he had given six imperial abbeys. It is therefore an error to accuse Conrad of irresponsible ecclesiastical administration or (according to Wipo) even of SIMONY, which was more sharply defined only under Henry III. Nevertheless he lacked the necessary knowledge and the correct attitude toward reform in the Church that distinguished both his predecessors and successors.

Bibliography: Sources. *Die Urkunden Konrads II,* ed. H. BRESSLAU, *Monumenta Germaniae Historica: Diplomata* (Berlin 1826–) 4:1–417. WIPO, *Gesta Chuonradi II* in *Die Werke Wipos,* ed. H. BRESSLAU, *Monumenta Germaniae Historica: Scriptores rerum Germanicarum* (Berlin 1826–) 61:1–62. J. F. BÖHMER, *Die Regesten des Kaiserreiches unter Konrad II, 1024–1039,* ed. H. APPELT (Regesta imperii 3.1.1; Graz 1951). Literature. H. BRESSLAU, *Jahrbücher des Deutschen Reichs unter Konrad II,* 2 v. (Leipzig 1879–84). K. HAMPE, *Deutsche Kaisergeschichte in der Zeit der Salier und Staufer,* ed. F. BAETHGEN (10th ed. Heidelberg 1949). T. SCHIEFFER, "Heinrich II. und Konrad II," *Deutsches Archiv für Erforschung des Mittelalters* 8 (1951) 384–437; *Lexikon für Theologie und Kirche,* ed. J. HOFER and K. RAHNER (2d, new ed. Freiburg 1957–1965) 6:466–467. H. SCHREIBMÜLLER, "Die Ahnen Kaiser Konrads II . . . ," in *Herbipolis jubilans: 1200 Jahre Bistum Würzburg* (Würzburg 1952) 173–233. M. LINTZEL, "Zur Wahl Konrads II," in *Festschrift Edmund E. Stengel* (Münster 1952) 289–300. M. L. BULST-THIELE in B. GEBHARDT, *Handbuch der deutschen Geschichte,* ed. H. GRUNDMANN (8th ed. Stuttgart 1954–60) 1:222–230. H. J. VOGT, *Konrad II im Vergleich zu Heinrich II und Heinrich III* (Frankfurt a. M. 1957). H. SCHWARZMAIER, "Reichenauer Gedenkbucheinträge aus der Anfangszeit der Regierung König Konrads II," *Zeitschrift für Württembergische Landesgeschichte* 22 (1963) 19–29.

[G. RILL]

CONRAD BOSINLOTHER, BL.

Abbot and reformer; b. Trier, Germany; d. Oberwang, near Mondsee, Austria, Jan. 15, 1145. A BENEDICTINE monk of the Abbey of Siegburg, he so impressed Abbot Conrad (d. 1132) that the abbot, when he became bishop of Regensburg in 1126, chose him to reform the small episcopal Abbey of Mondsee. Conrad was successful in this undertaking, and to preserve his work he placed the abbey, with the bishop's permission, directly under the Holy See. He was determined to maintain the abbey's rights and thus aroused the hatred of some of its TITHE payers, who set on him as he returned from a service at Oberwang and clubbed him to death. The murderers tried to burn his body, but, according to reports, it was miraculously preserved. His gravestone depicted him with AUREOLE and martyr's palm, and his grave became a place of pilgrimage. Although his body was solemnly raised in 1682 and placed behind the high altar at Mondsee and a plenary indulgence was attached to his veneration by Pope BENEDICT XIV in 1745, his cult is almost extinct today.

Feast: Jan. 15 or 16.

Bibliography: *Chronicon Lunaelacense* (Munich 1748) 117–125, 401–418. A. M. ZIMMERMANN, *Kalendarium Benedictinum: Die Heiligen und Seligen des Benediktinerordens und seiner Zweige,* 4 v. (Metten 1933–38) 1:87, 89–90. V. REDLICH, *Lexikon für Theologie und Kirche,* ed. J. HOFER and K. RAHNER, 10 v. (2d, new ed. Freiburg 1957–65) 6:462. M. PATSCH, "Der selige Konrad Bosinlother, Abt von Mondsee," *Historisch-politische Blätter für das katholische Deutschland* 159 (1917) 534–548.

[J. L. GRASS]

CONRAD OF BAVARIA, BL.

Cistercian monk; b. *c.* 1105; d. Modugno, Italy, March 17, 1154. He was the son of Henry the Black (d. 1126), duke of Bavaria. Conrad studied in COLOGNE and entered the Abbey of MORIMOND in 1125. St. BERNARD took him to CLAIRVAUX when Abbot Arnold of Morimond left the monastery without his superiors' permission, to make a new foundation in the Holy Land. In Clairvaux Conrad led a virtuous life under Bernard's tutelage. Years later Conrad was permitted by the abbot to go to the Holy Land and live there as a hermit, but he remained in contact with Clairvaux. Toward the end of his life, he left Palestine for the West, hoping to die with Bernard at his bedside. On landing in BARI he learned of the death of the saint, whereupon he took up residence at a Marian shrine in Modugno, where he lived as an anchorite and awaited death. His relics rest in a silver shrine under his altar in the cathedral of Molfetta. A mass in Conrad's honor was celebrated already in the 13th century, but his cult was approved only on April 7, 1832. Apart from veneration among the Cistercians, his cult is observed in Molfetta, Bari, and Venosa.

Feast: Feb. 14.

Bibliography: *Historia Welforum,* ed. E. KÖNIG (Stuttgart 1938). A. M. ZIMMERMANN, *Kalendarium Benedictinum: Die Heiligen und Seligen des Benediktinerorderns und seiner Zweige,* 4 v. (Metten 1933–38) 1:211, 213. S. LENSSEN, *Hagiologium cisterciense,* 2 v. (Tilburg 1948–49; sup. 1951) 1:88. J. M. CANIVEZ, *Dictionnaire d'histoire et de géographie ecclésiastiques,* ed. A. BAUDRILLART (Paris 1912–) 13:480. L. GRILL, "Der hl. Bernhard v. Clairvaux. . . ," in *Festschrift zum 800 Jahrgedächtnis des Todes Bernhards von Clairvaux* (Vienna 1953) 31–118. A. BUTLER, *The Lives of the Saints,* ed. H. THURSTON and D. ATTWATER, 4 v. (New York 1956) 1:337–338.

[C. SPAHR]

CONRAD OF CONSTANCE, ST.

Bishop; d. Constance, Switzerland, Nov. 26, 975. He was of the aristocratic Guelf family, son of the founder of WEINGARTEN ABBEY. In 934 Conrad became bishop of Constance through the backing of ULRIC OF AUGSBURG.

Though not a political figure, Conrad spent considerable time with Emperor OTTO I: at Ingelheim in 948, at the royal assembly of Augsburg in 952, and on the Italian expedition in 961 to 962. In 973 he served on a commission appointed by OTTO II to investigate the Abbey of SANKT GALLEN, an incident that exemplified his interest in the contemporary CLUNIAC reform. Tradition associates his name with churches in EINSIEDELN, Rheingau, and St. Trudpert and with the chapel of St. Maurice in Constance. His biography, composed 150 years after his death, speaks also of his pilgrimages to Jerusalem, his relic collection, and his miracles. He was canonized in 1123. All relics, except his head, were thrown into Lake Constance in 1526, during the Reformation.

Feast: Nov. 26.

Bibliography: *Gestalt und Verehrung des heiligen Konrad,* ed. J. SAUER (Karlsruhe, Germany 1975). *Der Heilige Konrad, Bischof von Konstanz,* ed. H. MAURER, W. MÜLLER and H. OTT (Freiburg 1975). E. KELLER, *Der heilige Konrad von Konstanz* (Karlsruhe 1975). *Monumenta Germaniae Historica: Scriptores* 4:430–460; 21:454–477. A. BUTLER, *The Lives of the Saints,* ed. H. THURSTON and D. ATTWATER (New York 1956) 4:425–426. O. FEGER, *Geschichte des Bodenseeraumes* (Lindau 1956–) v. 1.

[R. H. SCHMANDT]

CONRAD OF GELNHAUSEN

Conciliarist and theologian; b. *c.* 1320; d. Heidelberg, April 13, 1390. He studied and taught at the University of Paris and became a canon in Mainz (1359) and procurator of the German nation at the University of Bologna (1369). In a meeting with King Charles V seeking for an effective means of bringing the WESTERN SCHISM to an end, he pronounced himself in favor of CONCILIARISM; in his *Epistola brevis* he summarized his proposals [ed., H. Kaiser, *Historisches Vierteljahrschrift* 3 (1900) 381–394]. In May 1380, he dedicated to the king his treatise *Epistola concordiae* (*Thesaurus novus anecdotorum* 2:1200–26). First, Conrad established the necessity of calling a general council, after the fashion of the Apostles, who assembled four times to seek a solution to difficult questions. Next, he examined the validity of the objections raised against his proposal, the principal one being that the pope alone was qualified to convoke an ecumenical council. The answer was simple: since during the Schism both popes were doubtful, neither had this power; it reverted to the universal Church. It would be desirable that the two pontiffs, acting in concert, convoke the council; but if an agreement was not achieved, the cardinals became responsible for its convocation. The assembly was not to legislate. It should content itself with ending the schism, after which the pope whom it recognized should act in common with it. Conrad's thesis was certainly the inspiration for the ideas expressed by WILLIAM OF OCKHAM in his *Dialogues* concerning the superiority of the council over the pope. It was made public by HENRY HEINBUCHE OF LANGENSTEIN in his *Epistola concilii pacis,* but was never accorded favor until the Council of Constance when one of the papal pretenders was willing to relinquish his claim. The adherence of King Charles VI to the jurisdiction of CLEMENT VII, ANTIPOPE influenced Conrad to leave France in 1386 to lecture at the University of Heidelberg, where be became the first chancellor.

Bibliography: CONRAD OF GELNHAUSEN, *Commentary on the Canticles* (MS Vat. Pal. lat. 77, fol. 1). L. SCHMITZ published one of his letters to PHILIP OF MEZEERES, dated July 18, 1379, *Römische Quartalschrift für christliche Altertumskunde und für Kirchengeschichte* 9 (1895) 185–189. A. KNEER, ''Die Entstehung der konziliaren Theorie,'' *Römische Quartalschrift für christilche Altertumskunde und für Kirchengeschichte,* Supplment 1 (1893). K. WENCK, ''Konrad von Gelnhausen und die Quellen der konziliaren Theorie,'' *Historische Zeitschrift* 76 (1896) 6–61. P. BLIEMETZRIEDER, ''Konrad von Gelnhausen und Heinrich von Langenstein auf dem Konzile zu Pisa, 1409,'' *Historisches Jahrbuch der Görres-Gesellschaft* 25 (1904) 536–541; *Literarische Polemik zu Beginn des grossen abendländischen Schismas* (Vienna 1910). V. MARTIN, *Les Origines du gallicanisme,* 2 v. (Paris 1939). B. TIERNEY, *Foundations of the Conciliar Theory* (Cambridge, Eng. 1955).

[G. MOLLAT]

CONRAD OF OFFIDA, BL.

Franciscan; b. Offida, Italy, *c.* 1237; d. Bastia, near ASSISI, Italy, Dec. 12, 1306. After becoming a friar in 1251, he spent ten years in hermitages in the Marches of ANCONA and Fermo. As a priest he ministered in Ancona, where he directed a saintly tertiary housewife, Bl. Benvenuta (d. 1291; feast: October 30). While assigned to Alvernia (La Verna), he was acquainted with St. MARGARET OF CORTONA, Brother LEO OF ASSISI, and the Franciscan Spiritual leaders UBERTINO OF CASALE and PETER JOHN OLIVI. In 1294 he favored the foundation of a separate eremitical order under Pope St. CELESTINE V, but was persuaded to remain a Franciscan by a decisive letter from Olivi [text in *Archivum franciscanum historicum* 11 (1918) 366–373]. When accused of separatism, Conrad won the confidence of the Minister General John of Murro. With his close friend Bl. Peter of Treia (d. 1304; feast: February 20), he was one of the heroes of the FIORETTI (ch. 42–44). He wrote a one-page letter of ascetical advice, but is not the author of the spiritual polemical *Liber de Flore;* his *Verba* contain prophecies of St. FRANCIS about the future of the order, as reported by Brother Leo. Conrad's cult was approved in 1817.

Feast: Dec. 14.

Bibliography: *Analecta Franciscana* 3 (1897) 422–430. P. SABATIER, "Verba fratris Conradi," *Opuscules de critique historique* 1 (1903) 370–392. A. MACDONNELL, *Sons of Francis* (London 1903) 303–315, 422. B. BARTOLOMASI, "Memorie storiche del B. C. da O.," *Miscellanea Francescana* 15 (1914) 14–21, 54–57, 73–79, 114–121, 152–157; 16 (1915) 22–25, 175–179; 17 (1916) 159–164. H. GRUNDMANN, "Liber de Flore," *Historisches Jahrbuch der Görres-Gesellschaft* 49 (1929) 33–91, esp. 77–79.

[R. BROWN]

CONRAD OF OTTOBEUREN, BL.

Benedictine abbot; d. July 27, 1227. He was elected abbot of OTTOBEUREN in 1191 and held the office for the next 34 years. During his tenure he was twice forced to rebuild his monastery. After completing its first reconstruction, Conrad saw his work destroyed by fire (1217); he again replaced the abbey buildings. In 1204 he was awarded the right to officiate with *pontificalia*. Evidences of his cult date from 1555, when his remains were translated. Since 1772 his body, with that of Bl. Rupert, rest in the same mausoleum at Ottobeuren.

Feast: July 27.

Bibliography: *Chronicon Ottenburanum, Monumenta Germaniae Historica: Scriptores* 23:609–630. A. M. ZIMMERMANN, *Kalendarium Benedictinum: Die Heiligen und Seligen des Benediktinerordens und seiner Zweige* 2:503, 504. A. M. ZIMMERMANN, *Lexikon für Theologie und Kirche*² 6:470.

[O. J. BLUM]

CONRAD OF PARZHAM, ST.

Lay brother; b. Parzham, Germany, Dec. 22, 1818; d. Altötting, Germany, April 21, 1894. John, as he was baptized, was the ninth of ten children born to Bartholomew and Gertrude Birndorfer, both of whom died while John was an adolescent. He worked on the family farm until the age of 30 and then sacrificed his inheritance to enter the CAPUCHINS. He pronounced his solemn vows on Oct. 4, 1852, and for the next 41 years he served the friary of Altötting as doorkeeper. Altötting, a shrine center, brought to the friary door an almost continuous flow of pilgrims and beggars, whom Conrad served with wonderful charity, meekness, and patience. The poor, whom he fed every day, especially experienced his virtues. He was extraordinarily devoted to the Mother of God, and he prayed far into the night before the Blessed Sacrament. He resigned his arduous duties only when physically worn out, three days before his death at the age of 76. Brother Conrad was beatified (June 15, 1930) and canonized (May 20, 1934). His relics are enshrined in the Church of St. Ann, Altötting. He is usually depicted feeding the poor or gazing upon the cross held in his hands.

Feast: April 21.

Bibliography: J. A. VON HARSBERG, *Blessed Conrad of Parzham,* tr. A. NEUFELD (Detroit 1932). G. BERGMANN, *Bruder Konrad von Parzham. Einer der klein genung war* . . . (Altötting 1965); *Bruder zwischen gestern und morgen: Konrad von Porzham* (Passau 1974). C. CARGNONL, *The Capuchin Way: Lives of Capuchins* (North American Capuchin Conference 1996) 180–206.

[T. MACVICAR]

CONRAD OF QUERFURT

Bishop of Hildesheim and Würzburg, chancellor of Emperor Henry VI and Philip of Swabia; d. Würzburg, Dec. 3?, 1202. Son of the burgrave of Magdeburg, he was educated probably at Paris, becoming canon at Magdeburg (1182); royal chaplain (1188); provost at Goslar (1188), at Magdeburg (1190), and at Aachen (1193); and, finally, bishop of Hildesheim (1194). At this same time (1194) he was made imperial chancellor. As imperial legate for all Italy, Conrad led the so-called German Crusade of 1197 and on March 5, 1198, raised the Teutonic Order of St. Mary's Hospital at Jerusalem to the rank of knights (*see* TEUTONIC KNIGHTS). When appointed bishop of Würzburg, he tried to retain the See of Hildesheim also, but was excommunicated and deprived of both sees by Innocent III. He regained Würzburg, however, in 1201 after seeking papal pardon in Rome. When Philip of Swabia incurred papal disapprobation, Conrad shifted his allegiance to the Guelf Emperor Otto IV (November 1202). He was killed by one of his own household.

Bibliography: L. VON BORCH, *Geschichte des kaiserlichen Kanzlers Konrad* . . . (2d ed. Innsbruck 1882). T. MÜNSTER, *Konrad von Querfurt* (Leipzig 1890). A. FRANZEN, *Dictionnaire d'histoire et de géographie ecclésiastiques,* ed. A. BAUDRILLART et al. (Paris 1912–) 13: 498–499.

[M. F. MCCARTHY]

CONSALVI, ERCOLE

Cardinal, secretary of state of Pius VII; b. Rome, June 8, 1757; d. Rome, Jan. 24, 1824. As the son of a Roman noble family, he started early (1783) his career in the Roman Curia under the protection of Henry STUART, cardinal of York. In 1797, having filled with distinction a number of minor positions, he found himself, under most trying circumstances, responsible for the small armed forces of PIUS VI. The murder of the French General Duphot by a Roman mob (Dec. 28, 1797) led to a French invasion of the States of the Church. Pius VI was taken to France in captivity; Consalvi was first imprisoned, later exiled. When he was chosen secretary of the conclave in Venice after Pius VI's death, Consalvi

Ercole Cardinal Consalvi.

worked behind the scenes with consummate patience and skill, paving the way for the election of Cardinal Chiaramonti. PIUS VII immediately made him prosecretary of state, then secretary of state and cardinal (Aug. 11, 1800). He never advanced in Sacred Orders beyond the diaconate.

First Ministry. During his first ministry (March 11, 1800 to June 17, 1806), Consalvi was only moderately successful in his tireless efforts to restore the STATES OF THE CHURCH, ruined by years of chaos and military occupation. His main achievement was the CONCORDAT OF 1801 with France, which made possible the reconstruction of the Catholic Church after the French Revolution. In the last stage of the negotiations, Consalvi went to Paris to confront Napoleon. In their meetings he displayed remarkable subtlety and courage. Another concordat of the same kind was signed (Sept. 16, 1803) with the new Italian Republic created by Bonaparte. But in the following years, Napoleon and his ambassador in Rome, Cardinal FESCH, became increasingly impatient with Consalvi's firmness in resisting abusive demands. Finally Consalvi judged it better to resign the secretariat.

His sacrifice was of no avail. Napoleon's further encroachments terminated with the seizure of Rome and the imprisonment of the Holy Father (July 1809). Consalvi, as well as the other Curia cardinals, was eventually compelled to go to Paris. There he refused a large sum offered by the emperor, and led a completely retired life. In April 1810, he incurred the Emperor's wrath when, with a dozen of his colleagues, he refused to attend the ceremony of Napoleon's marriage to the Archduchess Marie Louise of Austria. Consalvi, considered to be the ringleader of the "black cardinals," was relegated under surveillance to Reims, where he remained until February 1813. Napoleon, returned from Russia, wrested from the weakened Pius VII a preliminary agreement that was deceptively published as the CONCORDAT OF FONTAINEBLEAU. The cardinals were then allowed to regroup around the pope. Pius VII, encouraged by them, recanted his concessions. Once more, Consalvi was exiled, this time to Béziers (February 1814). Upon the downfall of Napoleon, he returned to Italy.

Second Term. Pius VII promptly reinstated him as secretary of state for his second term, May 7, 1814, to Aug. 20, 1823. His first task was to obtain from the victorious allies the restoration of the States of the Church. He had preliminary conversations in London with Metternich and Castlereagh, discussing also the situation of Catholics in the British Isles. Afterward he attended the Congress of Vienna for its duration. European statesmen held him in high respect; they asked him to sit on committees, but he refused to be involved in purely political matters. Instead he concentrated his efforts on the restitution of Church territories. Austria, mainly, was reluctant to hand back the prosperous northern papal provinces, the Legations, which she had taken from the French, after the pope had formally ceded them to France in the Treaty of Tolentino (1797). Finally Consalvi achieved his aims, except for some small tracts of territory on the left bank of the Po River and the former enclaves of Avignon and Comtat Venaissin in France.

Upon returning to Rome, Consalvi confronted two main problems: (1) adaptation of Church status to the new political order in various European states; (2) reorganization and government of the States of the Church. In solving the former, the secretary of state was, on the whole, successful. Concordats or less formal agreements were concluded with Catholic and Protestant powers. Boundaries of ecclesiastical jurisdictions were adjusted to the new political ones. Compromises were devised to share between pope and civil rulers the appointment of bishops and pastors. Former seizures of Church property were either compensated for, or condoned.

Consalvi was less fortunate in dealing with the internal problems of the Papal States. The reactionary party, the *zelanti,* stubbornly resisted all efforts to modernize antiquated administration and laws. Misery and banditry were rampant in the countryside. Liberal secret societies raised frequent disturbances in the towns. Since most of the Curia personnel were hostile, Consalvi had to take upon himself an excessive load of work, which undermined his health. The cardinals resented his "tyranny" and his poor opinion of their capacities.

When Pius VII died, the main preoccupation of the majority in the conclave was to end Consalvi's influence. This was achieved by the election of Cardinal Annibale della Genga, who had been at odds with Consalvi since 1814. Consalvi resigned immediately all his offices. The new pope hastened to undo all his works. Experience, however, soon changed the mind of LEO XII, who recognized Consalvi's merits. Despite the cardinal's grave illness, the pontiff appointed him prefect of the Congregation of the Propagation of the Faith. A few days later, Consalvi was dead. He was a man of exquisite taste and broad culture; a statesman of great courage and industry; a consummate diplomat who ranks as one of the greatest in the papal service in modern times, or in all times; and a devoted servant of the Church.

Bibliography: E. CONSALVI, *Memorie . . .* , ed. M. N. ROCCA DI CORNELIANO (Rome 1950). G. MOLLAT, *Dictionnaire d'histoire et de géographie ecclésiasitques*, ed. A. BAUDRILLART et al. (Paris 1912–) 13:509–523, excellent, with rich bibliog. J. T. ELLIS, *Cardinal Consalvi and Anglo-Papal Relations, 1814–1824* (Washington 1942). M. PETROCCHI, *La restaurazione romana, 1815–1823* (Florence 1943).

[G. DE BERTIER DE SAUVIGNY]

CONSCIENCE

This article deals with conscience (1) in its general concept; (2) in its treatment in the Bible; and (3) in its theological analysis.

1. GENERAL CONCEPT

The treatment of conscience is difficult insofar as it presupposes a certain form of self-experience, without which access, in the strict sense, to the phenomenon itself, as it expresses itself in various ways, is not possible. Yet, in general, the experience mentioned can be analyzed with some precision, since the bonds and relations that give concreteness and possibility to human existence and life are of such a nature that men consider themselves responsible, i.e., they must give an accounting for what they think and do. Therefore, the knowledge of a prescribed order is presupposed, and toward this man adopts a positive or negative attitude. Since this knowledge, on the basis of mythical, personal, and universal experience, does not need to be regarded as reflective in origin, the phenomenon of conscience can be present without a for-

mally defined sphere, i.e., without a name being assigned to it. In such cases, formal analysis of human conduct is required, and especially an analysis of guilt conscience, in order to establish the nature of conscience in the given instance.

University of the Phenomenon. Actually, no culture has yet been found in which conscience is not recognized as a fact, or—in the present age—as at least a problem. Generally among early peoples, expressions such as "heart" and "loins" appear instead of the word conscience, but they are used to indicate the innermost nature of man. An ancient Egyptian text reads: "The heart is an excellent witness," and one must not transgress against its words; "he must stand in fear of departing from its guidance." The divine world order is often employed for conscience; among the Hindus, e.g., it is regarded as "the invisible God who dwells within us." The world order can be represented, as in classical antiquity, also in individual figures, who, reflecting moral awareness of the order that has been impaired or destroyed, are interpreted as the avenging powers employed by the highest divinity (for example, the Erinyes or Eumenides, Furies, and Nemesis).

Formal Recognition of Conscience. In the light of the establishment of the phenomenon of conscience as a presupposed knowledge in respect to the meaning and truth of God, the world, and man, but not yet based on reflection, conscience as "reflective knowledge" must make its appearance by name as soon as the universal validity of knowledge without reflection is questioned. This happened in ancient Greece in the age of the Sophists, when an opposition of φύσις and νόμος (nature and law) was stressed, and when Socrates spoke of his indwelling δαίμονιον (divine monitor). Conscience then received a name, συνείδησις (the scholastic synderesis), a term signifying self-consciousness in its role of making moral judgments. It became the substance and sphere of knowledge in respect to human action, the spiritual-ethical world order, and the existentially experienced correlation of both, either as agreement or difference. Conscience is shared knowledge, referring clearly to the whole, to which man as a morally acting individual (choice of the good) knows that he is responsible, and in a concrete way.

Since feeling and will play a significant role in the application of conscience to human action, conscience is more affirmative than consciousness and abstract knowledge. There can and must be a good and bad conscience, one that is active not only after the deed but also before and during it, because in this kind of knowledge man as a whole, i.e., as an ethical being, is continuously present. Seneca expresses this thought when he speaks of a holy spirit dwelling in man, "an observer and watcher of good and evil in us" (*Epist.* 41.1).

Christianity, naturally, not only took up the question of conscience, but also developed the concept further and defined it more precisely in both theory and practice by its teaching on the virtues. As the numerous manuals of moral theology indicate, it has continued its task along the same lines.

Conscience in Modern Thought. In the process of secularization that characterizes modern times, conscience has received a special position, since the nature and image of man has been affected in a special way. Kant still thought of conscience, although understood as autonomous, as the "consciousness of an interior court of justice in man" FICHTE, as the immediate consciousness of definite human duties, the "oracle of the eternal World." But EMPIRICISM gave it a psychological interpretation, and Darwin and his school evaluated it from the viewpoint of evolution. H. SPENCER, the sociological school of DURKHEIM, and the English Functionalist School all derived it from sociological conditions and needs. F. NIETZSCHE saw in conscience a mark of the degeneration of civilization and created the idea of a superman without a conscience. S. FREUD regarded conscience as the suppression of the libido. Finally, MATERIALISM considered that its deeper meaning was to be sought in its role as a factor in the general process of evolution.

This devaluation of conscience was opposed in the 19th century in part by the romantics, but especially by J. H. NEWMAN and S. Kierkegaard. It is owing to the latter in particular that conscience came to be understood as a phenomenon *sui generis*. As a consequence, philosophy in the 20th century has been concerned with giving justice to the phenomenon of conscience. For M. SCHELER, conscience means not only the capability of moral evaluation but also at the same time serves as a functional guide for action. For N. HARTMANN, it is the "basic form of primary value consciousness." M. Heidegger sees in it the "call of care" that keeps existence from the impersonal "Man," in that it waits for the "voice of being." K. Jaspers understands by conscience that voice speaking to man "which is man himself." The role of conscience in depth psychology was discovered especially by C. G. JUNG and J. A. Caruso.

Significance of Conscience. As the locus of freedom and the intersecting point of mental experiences, conscience has significance not only for philosophy and theology but also for the practical conduct of life, and therefore for the formation of man in the personal and public sphere. Its importance is all the greater, since in conscience the unity of man with himself and with mankind is procured, his personal nature guaranteed, and responsibility for himself, his fellow men, and civilization in general is established. Conscience, which always points to ultimate unity of theory and practice in the ethicoreligious fulfillment of life, can, it is true, be viewed from the concrete situation of action as purely autonomous; but, when viewed from the total nature of existence, it must be understood as heteronomous. If the image-concept of man is assumed, there are found united in conscience both the constitution of its image from the beginning and its independence from its content to its innermost connection. Conscience, therefore, really does not emerge at a given stage, but is already always present in plastic form. Objective heteronomous world order and value order, as regards conscience, are therefore completely compatible with its ultimate—and in this sense autonomous—competence respecting a concrete situation. Conscience, so understood, is the place where man becomes himself, since here the invisible God becomes present for him. Therefore it is proper to the true nature of conscience, with constant effort and submissively, to align itself on what confronts it as claim from the nature of man and his history—for example, the requirement of faith.

Bibliography: J. STELZENBERGER, "Gewissen," H. FRIES, ed., *Handbuch theologischer Grundbegriffe*, 2 v. (Munich 1962–63) 1:519–528. E. WOLF, *Lexikon für Theologie und Kirche*, ed. J. HOFER and K. RAHNER, 10 v. (2d, new ed. Freiburg 1957–65) 2:1550–57, with copious bibliography. H. HÄFNER, *ibid.* 4:864–867, with bibliography. J. H. HYSLOP et al., J. HASTINGS, ed., *Encyclopedia of Religion and Ethics*, 13 v. (Edinburgh 1908–27) 4:30–47, older bibliography. R. EISLER, *Wörterbuch der philosophischen Begriffe*, 3 v. (4th ed. Berlin 1927–30) 1:555–559, with bibliography. G. ERMECKE and J. P. MICHAEL, *Staatslexikon*, ed. GÖRRES-GESELLSCHAFT, 8 v. (6th, new and enlarged ed. Freiburg 1957–63) 3:496–951, with bibliography. J. H. BREASTED, *The Dawn of Conscience* (New York 1934). L. BRUNSCHVICG, *Le progrès de la conscience dans la philosophie occidentale*, 2 v. (2d ed. Paris 1953). M. HOLLENBACH, *Sein und Gewissen* (Baden 1954). H. KUHN, *Begegnung mit dem Sein* (Tübingen 1954). H. HÄFNER, *Schulderleben und Gewissen* (Stuttgart 1956). H. J. SCHOLLER, *Die Freiheit des Gewissens* (Berlin 1958).

[W. DUPRÉ]

2. IN THE BIBLE

The concept of conscience as a kind of other self, a critical voice within one assessing the morality of a concrete situation, finds its clearest Biblical expression in St. Paul. Neither the Old Testament nor the other books of the New Testament treat the subject in any detail.

In the Old Testament and Judaism. Indeed, there is only one certain mention of the word conscience (συνείδησις) in the entire Old Testament (Wis 17.11), and that in a book much influenced by Hellenistic ideas. The word and all the nuances it suggests are more typical of a Greek than of a Hebrew mode of thought. But however theocentric, unreflective, and lacking in introspection the Israelites might have been, they were not unaware of that universal human phenomenon, the experiencing of peace when one has done good or of remorse when one has done evil. Perhaps nowhere else in world literature is remorse of conscience so superbly described as in the recounting of the reaction of Adam and Eve to their disobeying God (Gn 3.7–11).

In the intertestamental period and in the rabbinical literature there are some indications of a developing theory of conscience. But the general tenor of Jewish thought was that of an excessive emphasis on the external act. The paramount importance of one's internal motivation was increasingly neglected. As a result, cultic and ethical activity tended to become increasingly formalistic and to be judged solely on the basis of their external conformity with the Law and its traditional interpretation.

In the New Testament. The Gospels nowhere employ any specific term for conscience, but their spirit is essentially different from that of the rabbinical writings. This spirit lays emphasis, not on the external action, but on the heart, the interior disposition from which it proceeds (Mt 15.7–20; Lk 11.39–42). It insists on the need for purity of intention and bolsters that insistence with a repeated reminder of the omniscience of the transcendent God (Mt 6.1, 4, 6, 18, 33). It is that spirit that animates the Pauline commentary on the Christian conscience.

The Apostle does not offer a systematic treatment of his teaching on the Christian conscience, nor is the word συνείδησις one of his favorite expressions. But he is the first New Testament writer to employ it. And whenever the word is found in the New Testament with the meaning of "conscience" each such use occurs either in a Pauline letter or in a New Testament writing influenced by St. Paul. From his usage of the term the following observations may be made. What the Law is for the Jews, conscience is for the pagans (Rom 2.14–16, a passage that, together with Rom 14.12, may be said to contain the classic Christian understanding of the functioning of conscience with regard to past actions, for pagans and Christians alike). Paul can assert that his own conscience testifies to his having the purity of intention insisted upon in the Gospels (2 Cor 1.12).

In his advice to the Corinthians and the Romans Paul enunciates some of the cardinal principles pertinent to the Christian conscience in its role as regulator of one's moral activity. Whoever acts against his conscience commits sin (Rom 14.23). The conscience is the proximate, subjective norm of moral action; even when it is erroneous, it must be followed (Rom 14.14, 23). Love of God and neighbor must be the supreme regulating principle of Christian conduct and may at times require one to forego

the otherwise legitimate exercise of his Christian freedom (1 Cor 8.1, 3, 9, 11–13; 10.24, 28–29; Rom 14.15, 20–21).

The Biblical doctrine on conscience is obviously not the fully developed Christian understanding of the nature and function of conscience, but the Pauline exposition of what that conscience is and of how it ought to function in the various problems he was called upon to solve is a faithful development of an outline furnished by Jesus Himself.

Bibliography: E. SCHICK, *Lexikon für Theologie und Kirche*, ed. J. HOFER and K RAHNER, 10 v. (2d, new ed. Freiburg 1957–65) 4:859–861. E. WOLF, *Die Religion in Geschichte und Gegenwart*, 7 v. (3d ed. Tübingen 1957–65) 2:1550–52. *Encyclopedic Dictionary of the Bible*, tr. and adap. by L. HARTMAN (New York 1963), from A. VAN DEN BORN, *Bijbels Woordenboek* 412–415. C. A. PIERCE, *Conscience in the New Testament* (London 1955).

[E. R. CALLAHAN]

3. IN THEOLOGY

Perhaps nowhere more than in the theological and philosophical problem of the nature and structure of moral conscience is greater diversity of opinion or greater confusion of thought to be found. In modern times philosophers and theologians as well as religious writers all proclaim in one form or another the absolute supremacy of conscience in the moral life. This they do under the immediate influence of I. KANT, who identified conscience with good will or good intention (see *Groundwork of the Metaphysics of Morals* 1) and in any event completely subjectivized the notion and the reality, separating it in fact from the influence and guiding power of reason and reducing it to a kind of irrational imperative instinct (see *The Metaphysics of Morals* 2.12B), and under the more remote but nonetheless profound influence of NOMINALISM. As a term and concept and as a reality conscience has pertained not only to the field of theoretical and philosophical analysis but also, and perhaps even primarily, to the sphere of folklore or popular wisdom. When an attempt is made to define conscience strictly, its dignity, absolute binding force, and freedom are taken for granted and conscience itself is reduced to a sort of blind instinct that easily becomes the subjective cover for moral cowardice and for innumerable crimes committed in the name of that noble thing called moral conscience or even in the name of Christian conscience.

It is commonly maintained that conscience is the subjective individual consciousness of that which is objectively good or evil, right or wrong; it is the reaction of the human ego vis-à-vis its moral behavior, and as such it is the emotionally conditioned knowledge of the worth or worthlessness of that behavior. Conscience, then, has been reduced to (or, in the minds of some moralists, elevated to) being that faculty by which one is able to judge the goodness or sinfulness of one's actions, by which one is able to determine whether such or such an action is gravely or lightly sinful, and, as a consequence, by which one is able to determine whether any given action in any given circumstances is or is not permitted by the law. An extreme form of this absolutizing of conscience made its appearance in the middle of the 17th century in the atheistic movement begun by a student of Protestant theology, Matthias Knutsen, founder of the so-called *conscientarii.*

In this unwarranted restriction of the function of conscience to determining between the sinfulness or righteousness of one's actions, between their lawfulness or unlawfulness, conscience itself has been emptied of its true nobility and greatness. From being truly the voice of God for an individual and the real guarantee that his life is anchored in God and in the law of Christ, or, as the Germans so pithily put it, of the *Gott- und Christusbezogenheit,* of one's life, it becomes the jealous guardian of one's own petty subjective whims and fancies. Such was not St. Paul's conception of conscience or the notion of conscience found either in Scripture or in the teaching of the early Church Fathers; such was not the idea of conscience held in honor universally among theologians right up to the 17th century and still defended and propounded by a small minority.

C. A. Pierce in his splendid study of conscience in the New Testament, having pointed out the complex structure of conscience and the various subjective elements (both noetical and emotional) that go to make it up or are presupposed to it, remarks judiciously that to erect any one of these elements into an infallible criterion of right or wrong is "woefully to mislead and in any case utterly to distort the conception of the New Testament" (125–126). Most unfortunately, this is what has happened both in Catholic and in non-Catholic theology since the 17th century. It would be true to say that Catholic moral theology has been more profoundly affected by this distortion of the true notion of conscience than corresponding non-Catholic teaching. There were ever non-Catholic theologians to react against this state of affairs, as witness the great Caroline theologians in England (Robert Sanderson and others). Catholic theologians introduced the new conception into moral theology and then forestalled all criticism of it by distinguishing moral theology from ascetical and mystical teaching, thereby unwittingly severing moral theology from its roots and reducing it, too, to a mere shadow of its former noble self.

However, neither this transformation in the notion of conscience nor the true traditional meaning of the term conscience in Christian theology can be properly grasped except by examining the origin of the term and concept and by tracing its development in the history of both profane and Christian thought. The distorted notion of conscience has become so ingrained in common thought that there is danger of reading into the term as used in ancient times (in both sacred and profane literature) the meaning that it has come to have today. Hence the importance of considering the history of the notion of conscience if one wishes to arrive at a proper understanding of it and of its many forms. Any attempt to define or explain and analyze conscience a priori, is, from the nature of the case, doomed to failure.

History of the Term. St. Paul may be rightly considered the author or originator of a systematic teaching, either philosophical or theological, on conscience. He introduced the term and the idea into Christian moral teaching, taking it over from the popular (probably Stoic) philosophy of his time and giving it a new and fuller meaning that it retained up to the 17th century, in spite of many contrary tendencies.

Greek. The term conscience or, better, its Greek correspondent συνείδησις, of which it is the direct translation, is first found in a fragment of Democritus of Abdera toward the middle of the 5th century B.C. It is there used in the specifically moral sense of consciousness of evil life or behavior (συνείδησις τῆς κακοπραγμοσύνης) as distinct from the mere psychological sense of consciousness of the fact of doing or having done something, mere consciousness of self, and as distinct from the nonmoral consciousness of the hardships of life (see H. Diels, *Die Fragmente der Vorsokratiker: Griechisch und Deutsch,* ed. W. Kranz 2:206–207). This is the first-known meaning of the Greek term, and though not the only one, it remained the predominant one up to the period of the New Testament. It was a popular term used in the language of the people to express a very simple idea and a very simple fact of daily experience, namely, the sure knowledge that all men have within and with themselves (hence συνείδησις, *con-scientia*) of the moral quality of their actions and in a special way (precisely because more easily discerned) of the moral quality of their evil actions. However, one does not find, nor should one expect to find, a fully developed notion, worked out in a philosophical or religious context. Such elaborations came much later and very gradually. It should be noted, however, that conscience in the fragment of Democritus was what later became known as a consequent evil conscience, that is, a consciousness of evil action already performed. The explicit notion of either good or antecedent conscience is of much later origin.

Latin. In Latin literature *conscientia* occurs quite frequently in pre-Christian times, and the notion is much more developed than in corresponding Greek literature. The concept of both antecedent conscience and good conscience as the cause of interior peace and joy is found quite commonly in the writings of the Stoics, especially in the works of Cicero and Seneca. Cicero declared that the consciousness of a life well spent and the remembrance of numerous deeds well done (note that the *conscientia bene actae vitae* and the *multorum benefactorum recordatio* are here obviously identified) is the cause of the greatest joy (*iucundissima est—De Senectute* 3.9). Elsewhere he clearly brings out both the antecedent and the religious character of conscience. "On the deeds of evil-doers there usually follow first of all suspicion, next gossip and rumour, then the accuser and the judge. Many wrong-doers have even turned evidence against themselves. . . . And even should any think themselves well fenced and fortified against detection by their fellow-men (*contra hominum conscientiam*), they still dread the eye of the gods (*deorum [conscientiam] horrent*) and are convinced that the pangs of anxiety night and day gnawing at their hearts are sent by the gods to punish them" (*De finibus bonorum et malorum* 1.16). An impressive exhortation addressed by Seneca to his young friend Lucilius brings out in a most striking manner the notion of antecedent and consequent conscience, the notion of good and evil conscience, and finally the notion of conscience as the voice of God within man: "You are doing an excellent and salutary thing if, as you write to me, you strive perseveringly to attain to that health of mind and outlook (*ad bonam mentem*) which it is foolish to desire or wish for, seeing that you can acquire it by your own efforts. It is not a matter of raising hands to heaven nor of beseeching some temple-keeper to give us access to the sanctuary as if in that way we would be more easily heard: God is near you, he is with you, he is within. Thus do I say, Lucilius: a sacred and august spirit resides within us and takes stock of our good and evil actions and is the guardian or avenger of our deeds (*sacer intra nos spiritus sedet, malorum bonorumque nostrorum observator et custos*). Just as he is treated by us so does he treat us" (*Letter* 41.1).

Old Testament. There is no Hebrew word corresponding exactly to *conscientia* or συνείδησις. In the Septuagint the term συνείδησις is found two or perhaps three times (Eccl 10.20; Wis 17.10; Sir 42.18), all of very late date. However, even if the word is missing in the Old Testament, the reality of what is meant by conscience as a fact of universal human experience and as a special experience of the people chosen to enter into special contact with Yahweh is present. It is found in the terms "loins" and "heart" (*kelâyot̲ walḗb*), which are frequently coupled together and signify the inward man made by and known only to God and thus constitute the veritable seat of conscience (cf. Ps 7.10; 25.2; Jer 11.20; 17.10; 20.12 and *passim*) under the watchful eye of God (cf. 1 Sm 16.7; Ps 138). Here three things must be noted: first, for the chosen people, ever conscious of Yahweh and of His law, the voice of conscience, that is, the reaction or feelings of the heart and loins, of the whole inner man, was the voice of Yahweh, their God, and was the answer, in praise or in reproach, on the part of rational man, to His law. Thus conscience for them was intimately linked with the alliance and was essentially conditioned by it. Second, while there was insistence on the concept of consequent conscience that upbraids each one for his evil actions and for his transgressions of Yahweh's law, there was, however, mention also at least implicitly of antecedent and of good conscience, which puts man at peace with himself and with Yahweh, because his life is judged to be in accordance with the demands of the alliance between the people and their God. Third, in the Old Testament conscience, that is, the feelings and the sure knowledge of the heart and the loins, was in no wise set up as an inviolable criterion of one's life and actions. On the contrary, its whole activity was radically conditioned by the objective exigencies of the alliance and by true subjective loyalty to it. It should be remarked here that the priests and the scribes were not slow in exteriorizing, legalizing, and depersonalizing the law of Yahweh by smothering it, as it were, in their own interpretations and traditions. Against this corruptive process the Prophets reacted violently and, in the name of Yahweh and against the priests, recalled the people to a true and inward communion with their God and to a true understanding of His law, which vivifies.

New Testament. It is against this background that one must understand the teaching of the New Testament on conscience. The term is not found in the Gospels, with the exception of one mention in an interpolated text of Jn 8.9. But it is met some 30 times in the rest of the New Testament: 20 times in the Epistles of St. Paul, 5 times in the Epistle to the Hebrews, three times in the first Epistle of St. Peter and twice in the Acts of the Apostles. Whereas the Gospels retain the terminology of the Old Testament and of the Jews in general (heart, cf. Mt 15.18–20; Mk 6.52), St. Paul and the other New Testament authors took over the term συνείδησις, which they found in the Hellenistic culture of the day both as a popular concept and even as a technical term in the writings of the Stoics. There is no reason why they and, in a special way, St. Paul should not have met it in the oral traditions of the Greek Stoics and in the variety of meanings indicated above. However that may be, the fact is that St. Paul took over the term in order to express most appropriately and most fully a central and very complex reality of the Christian moral message. Without a detailed analysis of texts, the three following points should be carefully noted in order to attain to a proper understanding of the real nobility of the Christian conscience and of its full meaning in the Christian context and tradition, as well as of its dependencies and essential limitations.

The first all-important point to be noted is that for the New Testament authors conscience—*syneidesis*—meant a consciousness of the true moral content of human life founded on faith (πίστις) insofar as this faith is conceived as a personal engagement with God coloring man's whole outlook on all of reality—on God, on man, and on the cosmos itself and all that happens in it (cf. Rom 14.1, 23; 13.5; 1 Pt 2.19). In this sense conscience—*syneidesis*—meant very much more than a simple subjective judgment about one's actions. It implied the whole inner religious attitude of man, his whole concept of the world and of human life as seen through the eyes of faith, that is, ultimately through the eyes of God and through the infallible knowledge of God. It might truly be said that, for the authors of the New Testament, Christian conscience was nothing more than the specifically Christian *Weltanschauung,* which in the individual always governs and conditions his reactions to reality and events.

The second point is that in the work of applying this new Christian attitude to the business of daily living, conscience, being a spontaneous reaction of the "new creature" (that is, man re-created and regenerated by grace and living faith) to daily events, frequently needs the corrective of mature consideration of and deliberation on all the varied and changing elements and circumstances of every human action. In other words, it needs the practical guidance of Christian wisdom in the matter of the Christian life. Over and above a good conscience, a wise and prudent evaluation of every human situation, which takes into account not only the demands of the acting individual but also all the exigencies of Christian intersubjectivity and of true Christian charity, is absolutely necessary; and even then it is only in fear and trembling that the Christian works out his salvation (cf. Phil 2.12) and thus attains gradually to the fullness of growth in Christ (cf. Eph 4.13). A very clear example of the existential relation between the applied conscience of him who is born anew in Christ and the corrective power of prudent and wise deliberation is found in St. Paul (1 Cor 8.7–13; 10.27–30).

The final point is that in the New Testament and especially in the teaching of St. Paul conscience is identified with faith, not on the level of application to action, but on that of the general outlook on things mentioned above (see Rom 14.1, 23). All that we do and all that happens to us and all that we are called upon by the circumstances of life to bear must be judged in the light of faith, that is, with reference to God, to His all-wise providence, and to His law, because God spoke to men and became man in Christ in order to teach men how to live and how to order their lives in God and in Christ (cf. Rom 13.5; 1 Cor 14.4), which is only another way of saying in order to redeem and save men. This explains the statement of St. Peter that "this is indeed a grace, if for consciousness of God (διὰ συνείδησιν θεοῦ) anyone endures sorrows, suffering unjustly" (1 Pt 2.19; see also 1 Jn 3.19–22), that is, if one endures in the conviction that he is in the all-seeing and solicitous care of God.

This point (the identification of conscience with faith) is all the more striking when it is recalled that in later centuries almost all the great theologians identified faith with SYNDERESIS on the level of supernatural life (cf. St. Thomas Aquinas, *In 2 Sent.,* 41.1.1; *Summa theologiae* 2a2ae, 10.4 ad 2; *In 1 Sent. prol.* 5) and saw consequently in Christian conscience the application of practical faith to the business of everyday living in Christ (cf. *Summa theologiae* 1a, 79.12, 13, especially ad 3). And in this very precise and theologically exact sense, conscience became known as the voice of God within man, not an autonomous and purely subjective judgment, but an attitude rooted ultimately in the word of God or in faith and in the sure guidance of divine wisdom and infused prudence.

Patristic and Scholastic. Such is the legacy that the early Fathers received and handed on to posterity. It continued in the common teaching of the Fathers and Doctors of the Church in both the East and the West. It should be noted, however, that there was always present the temptation and the tendency (as in the Old Testament) to externalize, to legalize, and to depersonalize the reality of conscience. This danger was more readily present and more acutely felt in the Western Church, where the legal-minded Romans set the tone and determined in great measure the teaching and the organization of Christian ecclesial life. It would, however, be quite incorrect to say that the moral teaching of the Western Church quickly developed into a type of casuistry, while the Oriental Church remained true to the spirit of Christian freedom found in the New Testament. That would be a gross oversimplification of things and a quite unwarranted generalization.

In spite of difficulties and dangers, the Western Church and Western moral teaching ever remained true to the authentic spirit of the New Law. A typical example is that of St. Thomas, who achieved a scientific synthesis of revealed moral teaching, changing it from a simple, direct, and indeed most efficacious moral catechesis to a moral science and rigid analysis. His most brilliant insight was to see in faith the synderesis or intellect (*nous*) of his predecessors and in conscience the spontaneous or quasi-instinctive reaction or application of this attitude (under the all-pervading impulse of charity) to the business of daily living, allowing at the same time for the possibility, if properly understood, of identifying conscience with faith, from which it primarily flows (see *Summa theologiae* 1a, 79.13 ad 3; *In epist. ad Rom* 14.3. 1140–41; for the notion of conscience as a spontaneous or quasi-instinctive reaction, see *Summa theologiae* 2a2ae, 64.5; 64.7; 142.3 ad 2). There are obvious differences in this matter between the East and West, but there is no question of opposition. It is rather a matter of emphasis: the one more social and *communautaire,* the other more individualistic and personal; the one insisting on the part to be played by each member in and for the Christian community, the other insisting more on the personal competence and perfection of each member of the community. The elements found in the New Testament are fully preserved in both East and West. It is true, certainly, that a tendency toward a kind of legalistic casuistry may be traced in the West, but the great theologians of the Western tradition were ever on their guard against it.

After the Reformation. With the religious upheaval of the 16th century, when the structure of the Western Church was shaken to its foundations and when, under the still powerful influence of nominalism, the principles of personal freedom and private judgment were being introduced as the guiding principles of moral living, the Church was faced with a completely new situation. Then appeared, toward the end of the 16th and the beginning of the 17th century, a number of epoch-making and classical juridicomoral treatises on law, right, and justice (Francisco de TOLEDO, GREGORY OF VALENICA, L. LESSIUS, Gabriel VÁZQUEZ, F. SUÁREZ, and others), which laid the foundations of the modern treatise on justice and exercised a most profound influence on the whole future structure of moral teaching in the Western Church. The traditional notion of PRUDENCE and practical personal wisdom, which plays such an important role in Pauline moral teaching, was set aside almost completely and its place taken by a legalistically and casuistically conditioned conscience, put forward now as the ultimate and inviolable norm of moral living. With an overinsistence on the juridical order of things all sense and feeling were lost for the radical subordination of man's life and being to an objective and divine order of things; and at the same time, as a necessary consequence, the true meaning of real personal creative activity realized in the mystery of subjectivity and inter-subjectivity in the dynamism of knowledge and love was forgotten. This reversal of values gave rise to a strange paradox seldom pointed out, but one that should, on no account, be missed or overlooked. On the one side, the ultimate rule of morality became something completely subjective. The all-important condition for good moral action was no longer correspondence with objective reality and the law of God, author of that reality, but rather the subjective good faith or good intention of the individual, whether his moral judgment was objectively right or wrong, true or false. Provided the intention is good, whether the judgment is right or wrong, it is equally the voice of God for the person acting. This is the direct antithesis of traditional moral teaching in the Western Church (cf., for instance, St. Thomas, *Summa theologiae* 1a2ae, 19.5, 6). On the other hand, concrete human activity became completely mechanized and impersonalized through the mechanization of the judgment of conscience, which came to mean nothing more and nothing better than weighing opinions that the individual does not share personally and does not ever live existentially. Thus all sense of the real meaning of creative activity (cf. St. Thomas, *Summa theologiae* 1a2ae, 5.7; 6 prol.; *In 2 Sent.* 34.1.3), which alone can contribute efficaciously to the fulfillment of human life and being, is almost completely lost.

On the level of the so-called spiritual life, a remedy for this state of affairs was sought in the development of a new theological discipline, ascetical and mystical theology, a higher type of moral teaching reserved for the chosen few. There was, then, in the course of the 17th century, a strange shifting of perspective, so that conscience came to mean something it had never meant in the whole of pagan or Christian tradition. Severed from its roots in living practical faith and dependent now on the precepts of positive law and the varying opinions of theologians, conscience inevitably lost its true meaning and was robbed of its true nobility. One could perhaps put the difference this way: whereas the moral teaching of the whole Christian tradition up to the 17th century insisted on the inalienable right of objective truth and of the exigencies of the objective and divine order of things, the new moral teaching, based on a new and legalized notion of conscience, insisted either on security (TUTIORISM) or on the freedom of the individual in the face of the law (LAXISM). And in this way Christian moral teaching came to lose its true existential character.

A strong reaction to this situation appeared among both Catholics and non-Catholics. On the Catholic side the reaction has continued (or better, has been taken up seriously and intensified) until modern times and has been so pressed that the danger exists of falling into quite another extreme by insisting on the primacy of love or charity in moral theology and by leaving out of account altogether that practical wisdom of prudence, through which alone charity can be existentially mediated into the daily life of each Christian. On the non-Catholic side there was an immediate reaction on the part of the great

Caroline theologians in England, who maintained, not without foundation, that they and not their Catholic counterparts on the Continent were the true successors of St. Thomas and the whole authentic tradition of Christian moral teaching.

Systematic Exposition. In the light of what has been said above, a balanced systematic exposition of the nature and structure and division of conscience and, in a special way in the context of moral theology, of Christian conscience (cf. *Patrologia Latina*, ed. J. P. Migne, 13:94 for perhaps the first use of this term) can be worked out without much difficulty.

Conscience began as a popular idea; that is, it belonged to the store of human knowledge, common to all people and to all classes. Fundamentally it has remained such. The term was used to express a variety of mutually cognate concepts and realities from consciousness, self-consciousness, conscientiousness, etc., to the knowledge one has within himself of the specific human (and moral) quality of one's life and actions, whether they are in keeping with the true human dignity of man or not, whether they are worthy of being displayed openly before the critical eyes of one's fellowmen or not. In this last sense it signifies moral conscience as distinct from all its psychological forms. In the Old Testament this moral conscience, expressed in the reaction of the inner man to life and all its vicissitudes, is intimately bound up with the alliance, with God's choice of the Israelites and with His law, given to them as a guide to life and action. In other words, conscience in the Old Testament took on a specifically religious character, which it retained under the New Alliance, with, however, certain important differences. For the New Law, or Alliance, was primarily and fundamentally the grace of the Holy Spirit penetrating every fiber of man's being and transforming it into something divine, a new creation. This new creation, divinized and redeemed man, has a new and transformed consciousness of reality—of God, first of all, and then of himself and of the cosmos in relation to God (cf. Vatican II, *Dogmatic Constitution on the Church* ch. 1, 2, 4). This new consciousness is rooted ultimately in the transformation of human nature by grace, but it comes to act in the reality of faith, which, in its fullness, is the full, personal, and conscious commitment of the human person to God and to Christ the Redeemer. It should be immediately obvious that faith is much more than a mere assent to revealed mysteries; it is also the full acceptance of a way of life worthy of redeemed and divinized man. It must be manifest, too, that faith is fundamentally the Christian's *Weltanschauung,* or outlook on reality, and consequently the fundamental source of his every reaction to reality. This reaction itself is most frequently called "conscience," but St. Paul and the whole Christian tradition down to St.

Thomas saw no difficulty in understanding conscience as faith itself. But in order that man's reaction to concrete reality and events be worthy of one who is called to be a son and a friend of God, his heart and will must be informed with love for the God who calls man to Himself and reveals to him His law as a guide to life and with love for God-made-Man, who died to redeem him. This love of God and of the Redeemer, Christ, implies necessarily a loyal observance of God's law and of Christ's will (cf. Jn 14.15, 21; 1 Jn 5.2; 2 Jn 1.6) as manifested and communicated in Scripture and tradition and in the teaching of the Church, which was instituted by Christ as the guardian of Christian morals and life.

In the business of Christian daily living, with its infinite variety of changing situations and circumstances, it is clearly not sufficient to rely on a spontaneous reaction alone as a guide. For from the very nature of things, this may be faulty and in error on many heads (cf. St. Thomas, *De ver.* 17.2). The corrective of counsel and deliberation, ordained toward fitting Christian living to all the demands of human life, is necessary. In other words, over and above conscience, practical wisdom, also called prudence or discretion in the Christian tradition, is of vital importance. Without this wisdom, which on the one side looks to the objective and divine order of things and on the other is always in the service of charity, mediating it realistically and truly into the flux of life, conscience alone would frequently lead man astray.

In brief résumé: the sources of Christian conscience are grace, faith, and charity; and its most efficacious guardian and corrective, preserving it from pitfalls and forming it to full human maturity, is Christian practical wisdom, or prudence. It follows, then, that the most apt means toward forming a true Christian conscience, enlightened and sure and true, is growth in the spirit of faith and charity and the daily practice of true Christian discretion. This safeguards the true existential character of the Christian life and hinders conscience from exercising, when wrongly understood, a purely subjective tyranny in the lives of Christians.

Bibliography: Of the prolific literature on conscience, the following studies are especially relevant to this article or have full, up-to-date bibliography. E. SCHICK et al., *Lexikon für Theologie und Kirche,* ed. J. HOFER and K. RAHNER, 10 v. (2d, new ed. Freiburg 1957–65) 4:859–867. A. CHOLLET, *Dictionnaire de théologie catholique,* ed. A. VACANT et al. 15 v. (Paris 1903–50) 3.1:1156–74. C. MAURER, G. KITTEL, *Theologisches Wörterbuch zum Neuen Testament* (Stuttgart 1935–) 7:897–918. E. WOLF, *Die Religion in Geschichte und Gegenwart,* 7 v. (3d ed. Tübingen 1957–65) 2:1550–57. P. DELHAYE, *La Conscience morale du chrétien* (Paris 1963). J. STELZENBERGER, *Syneidesis, conscientia, Gewissen* (Paderborn 1963). G. DE LAGARDE, *La Naissance de l'esprit laïque au déclin du moyen âge* 6, *L'Individualisme ockhamiste: Le Morale et le droit* (Paris 1946). C. A. PIERCE, *Conscience in the New Testament* (London 1955). H. R. MCADOO, *The Structure of Caroline*

Moral Theology (London 1949). T. WOOD, *English Casuistical Divinity during the 17th Century* (London 1952). G. LECLERCQ, *La Conscience du chrétien* (Paris 1947).

[C. WILLIAMS]

CONSCIENCE, EXAMINATION OF

Refers to the regular reflection on one's life and action (thoughts, words, deeds, and omissions) in order to recognize areas in need of remediation and to move toward Christian perfection. It also refers to the list of actions or attitudes that serve as the focus of such reflection.

The tradition of an obligation for regular, even daily, examination of conscience evolved from the early Christian communities' concern that the members follow the Christian way of life by avoiding certain attitudes and actions and fostering those in keeping with the teachings of Jesus. Over time this practice became increasingly formalized in different yet fundamentally related expressions: (1) daily examination of conscience with a goal of moving toward Christian perfection; (2) the particular examination of conscience dependent on the SPIRITUAL EXERCISES of St. IGNATIUS OF LOYOLA; and (3) the examination of conscience in the context of proximate preparation for confessing one's sins.

In monastic writings of the 4th to 6th centuries, one finds the roots of the daily self-examination seen as essential to the Christian life. Themes in the authors of the period that recur later in the monastic writings include: the role of daily examination of conscience in helping the neophyte Christian maintain the original vigor and purity of heart (e.g., John CHRYSOSTOM's Baptismal Instructions); the image of the daily self-examination as an experience of judgment in which the person stands as both accuser and accused (e.g., AUGUSTINE, "On the Usefulness of Penance"); and the place of God's presence and grace as aids in the examination process (e.g., GREGORY THE GREAT). While the daily examen is not emphasized in the early monastic writings, it is nevertheless frequently mentioned in the context of confession and spiritual direction. By the time of BENEDICT OF ANIANE (9th century), the monastic Rule calls for daily examination of conscience as part of the process of spiritual growth.

From the 12th century through the REFORMATION in the 16th century, the place of daily examination of conscience continued to take shape and to extend beyond the monastic walls. During this period, three central themes developed that continue to evolve into the modern era. First, there is an emphasis on self-knowledge which leads to knowledge of God; secondly, the examination of conscience is seen in the context of the whole Christian life and as part of the process of growth in faith; and, finally, there is an increasing focus on the method of examination. The Brothers of the Common Life popularized formal schemes for its practice among the faithful in the 14th century, and in the 16th century it is a prominent feature of the Spiritual Exercises of St. Ignatius.

The Ignatian method begins by placing one's self in the presence of God and expressing gratitude for God's grace and goodness. One asks for God's help in recognizing areas of sin in one's life and then proceeds to review one's life and action (thoughts, words, deeds, and omissions) in an attempt to recognize areas in need of forgiveness. The individual asks God for pardon and resolves to attend more faithfully to the grace of God. At the heart of this method is an openness to and reliance upon God's grace active in the person's life. There is the recognition that it is by grace that persons come to awareness of their sinfulness, resolve to make amends, and persevere in being more faithful to God. This is what differentiates an examination of conscience within the Christian tradition from the self-improvement perspective within the secular context.

The particular examination of conscience dates back to the time of the Fathers of the Desert, but as used in the Church today, it depends largely on the Spiritual Exercises. On rising, the focal point of the particular examination is recalled. At noon, and before retiring, one prays according to the scheme of the general examination outlined above, modifying the third point according to the subject matter chosen for a particular examination. St. Ignatius also suggests that a record be kept of progress from day to day and week to week.

Evolving at the same time as daily examinations of conscience was the practice of a focused reflection on one's past in preparation for the practice of sacramental confession. In this context, penitentials with their lists of sins and corresponding penances were developed. Later, in response to the Fourth Lateran Council's (1215) requirement for annual confession and communion, manuals or handbooks of confession were written that contained an examination of conscience or a list of principal sins and virtues. These served as an aid to the confessor in guiding the penitents in the process of confession and in determining the nature of their sins and were in use up to the time of the Reformation.

Drawing from these manuals, small books written for the penitent were designed to act as an aid to the process of self-examination. Some of these books were condensed from larger manuals or were written by those who had authored the manuals. For the people who bought and used these books, a context was established within which the individual could understand what sin was, what repentance involved, and how sins were forgiven. In addition these books contributed to a milieu within which sin was of focal concern. Later brief examinations of conscience to be used as part of night prayer and longer ones to be used in conjunction with confession were added and are present in prayer books up to the present.

Shifts in the way in which the SACRAMENT OF PENANCE is viewed and celebrated, along with a burgeoning interest in spirituality, has lead to changes in the content and the practice of examination of conscience within the present context. Widely circulated printed examinations of conscience tend to reflect a more communal and social nature of sin and are intended to be used both for individual reflection and as part of a community celebration of the sacrament.

Bibliography: H. JAEGER, *Dictionnaire de Spiritualité*, s.v. "Examen de Conscience." J. REGAN, *A Study of the Examination of Conscience as an Element of the Catechesis on Sin in the Prayer Books Published in the United States.* (Ph.D. diss., Washington, D.C. 1989).

[J. REGAN/J. B. WALL]

CONSCIENCE, FREEDOM OF

In a common, although restricted, sense the right to worship God as one prefers. In a more proper and broad usage, however, it denotes the general capacity to follow one's conscience in any matter.

In antiquity, although a large diversity of private beliefs and practices was often tolerated, a right to follow one's conscience on all points was usually not recognized. Even in Greece, the cradle of freedom, citizens had to worship the civic deities. Nevertheless the right to follow conscience was sometimes claimed. In Sophocles' *Antigone* the obeying of the divine over the human law was implicitly condoned. Plato likewise approved of such a choice (*Apol.* 28–30). The Stoics provided a systematic basis to justify such views with their doctrine of a natural law that is above all others and teaches the equality and brotherhood of men. The major fruits of this theory, however, appeared only later in the use made of it by Byzantine jurists and medieval thinkers.

The Hebrews, on the other hand, had always been aware of the priority of doing God's will over obedience to man. The Prophets in particular saw this clearly and did not shrink from acting accordingly. The theocratic organization of Israel restricted freedom of choice in religious matters. Yahweh was a jealous God, and His detailed prescriptions provided severe punishments for those who violated them. The characteristic attitude was to require complete obedience to all the minutiae of the Law, and this eventually degenerated into legalism. Nevertheless, the existence of such sects as the Pharisees, Sadducees, and Essenes shows that some diversity of interpretation was allowed.

Christ rejected unduly literal obedience to the law and instead insisted on peaceful and intelligent love of God and men. Hence there arose a keener appreciation of the role of conscience. Previously, conscience had been thought of mainly in its retrospective aspect. In St. Paul its directive function becomes prominent. His treatment of a case of erroneous conscience (1 Cor 8.9–13) implied two principles: even though conscience is fallible, one should always act according to it, and one should not do violence to the conscience of others. Thus, at first Christians commonly held that all are by natural law free to follow their conscience and that punishments for religious offenses should be left to God. Nevertheless, the early Church did not practice an unlimited tolerance, but it applied only the spiritual sanction of excommunication. Then the Church changed its attitude in the fourth and fifth centuries after it gained its legal freedom and became the established church. It regarded heresy and schism as serious social evils to be punished by the state. This was the view of Augustine, Chrysostom, and Jerome.

In the Middle Ages the Church adhered more firmly to some of its views. It is true that it continued to acknowledge that because faith cannot be forced, non-Christians (i.e., Jews and pagans) were free to follow their beliefs, as long as they did not attempt to pervert true religion. On the other hand, it came to look on heresy and schism as dangerous sins and crimes, since they destroy the unity of both the faith and the social order. The medieval Church, therefore, advocated the death penalty for those who remained obstinate in error, and established the Inquisition to hunt them out.

At the same time, however, progress was made in solving the theoretical issues. Questions about freedom of conscience could be answered only if the nature and functions of conscience were understood. The first treatises on it were written only in the middle of the 13th century; they were full of inconsistencies and often contradicted each other. St. Thomas Aquinas worked out widely accepted solutions. He pointed out (*Summa theologiae* 1a2ae, 19) that the will is good (or evil) only insofar as it tends to what is thought good (or evil). He held, therefore, that one should always follow his conscience, and that an act resulting from an invincibly erroneous conscience is free from guilt; but he did not admit this act to be good. Moreover, he accepted the common opinion that invincible errors arise only in certain unusual cases. He argued elsewhere that Jews and pagans should be tolerated and not forced into the Church. He considered heretics and apostates, however, to be necessarily cognizant of their fault, and so subject to the severest penalties.

The bloody persecutions and religious wars following the Reformation led to a rethinking of these problems. The Protestants worked out the widest variety of arguments, of unequal merits, both pro and con. Many Catholics came to see that the possibilities of error in good faith were much wider than they had been thought previously. They also concluded, from Aquinas's principles, that all conscientious acts are at least subjectively good. Accepting the legitimacy of toleration, they did not, however, advocate full freedom of conscience; they were suspicious of it because of its defense by Protestants, Deists, and "Liberals," on latitudinarian, indifferentist, and relativist grounds. But with the maturing of democratic life after 1800, Catholics and others became increasingly aware of the validity of holding to it on practical grounds: as required by charity, civic peace, democratic government, and especially the integrity of human dignity and of the divine plan. It was maintained that God gave man an intellect and will that he might freely and responsibly work out his own individual salvation.

Among the most dramatic events of Vatican Council II was the conflict that ended with a large majority favoring the *Declaration on Religious Freedom* (*Dignitatis humanae*), thus rejecting the "thesis-hypothesis" theory on religious freedom that had been widely accepted for a century. The Declaration produced several noteworthy results: it achieved doctrinal unity on the point that religious freedom is a universal and natural right; it eliminated a major source of tension with non-Catholics; it fostered a less triumphalist and more humble spirit among Catholics.

The Council's action also cast new light on various theological issues. The establishment of a state religion is seen to be inconsistent with full religious liberty, since it places pressures, open or subtle, on dissidents. There is at least a verbal contradiction between Pius IX's *Syllabus of Errors* and the *Declaration on Religious Freedom*: this requires explanation in terms of the meaning of the theory of development of doctrine. Since the right to freedom of conscience results from man's dignity as a free, rational agent, which precludes that he be ever forced to act contrary to his conscience, difficult questions arise about the nature and limits of discipline within the Church; the cases of Abp. Lefebvre and Hans Küng well illustrate the range and type of issues involved. Other problems arise in regard to mixed marriages, e.g., some requirements imposed in the past are now seen to be inconsistent with the Church's due respect for individual freedom, but there remains the question of how such freedom is to be combined with safeguarding the faith.

Bibliography: J. E. E. DALBERG-ACTON, *The History of Freedom and Other Essays,* ed. J. N. FIGGIS and R. V. LAURENCE (London 1909) 1–60. J. LECLER, *Toleration and the Reformation,* tr. T. L. WESTOW, 2 v. (New York 1960). E. D'ARCY, *Conscience and Its Right to Freedom* (New York 1962). John XXIII Pac Terr. E. J. M. DE SMEDT, "Religious Liberty," *Catholic Mind* 62 (Feb. 1964) 54–63. Vatican Council II, session 4. J. LECLER et al., *Religious Freedom, Concilium* 18 (New York, 1966) with helpful bibliographical survey. E. MCDONAGH, *Freedom or Tolerance?* (Albany 1967). H. MADELIN, "La Liberté religieuse et la sphère du politique," *Nouvelle revue théologique* 97 (1975) 110–126, 914–939. O. MURDICK, "Religious Freedom: Some New Perceptions in Light of Vatican II," *Religious Education* (1976) 416–426. J. C.MURRAY, ed., *Religious Liberty: An End and a Beginning* (New York 1966).

[G. J. DALCOURT]

CONSCIENTIOUS OBJECTION

The term "conscientious objection" was coined in the 1890s in reference to objections to mandatory vaccinations, but during the 20th century the term became generally known as the objection, for reasons of conscience, to participating in war and military service, in the actual or potential intentional killing of other human beings. The term has also been used concerning the refusal to pay taxes for war and military expenditures, for the same reasons. Categories of conscientious objection include *absolute conscientious objection* (opposition to military service and war in any form), *selective conscientious objection* (objection to a particular war or to particular methods of fighting the war, e.g., the use of nuclear, biological or chemical "weapons of mass destruction."), and *in-service conscientious objection* (those who undergo a "crystallization of conscience" while serving in the armed forces and obtain a discharge, as opposed to conscripts who claim conscientious objector status prior to entrance into the military and who then perform alternative civilian service).

In support of their position, Catholic conscientious objectors often point to the statements of Jesus found in the Gospels that summon his followers to do "the things that make for peace" (Lk 19:42). "Blessed are the peacemakers, for they shall be called children of God," he proclaimed in the Sermon on the Mount (Mt 5:9). "You have heard it said, 'You shall love your neighbor and hate your enemy.' But I say to you, love your enemies" (Mt 5:43–44). Commenting on the Gospel call to be peacemakers, the U.S. bishops declared, in their 1983 pastoral letter on war and peace: "We believe work to develop non-violent means of fending off aggression and resolving conflict best reflects the call of Jesus both to love and to justice." Historically, the emphasis of the Christian teaching during the first three centuries was toward peace, though it is not clear that the Church condemned

A crowd of conscientious objectors to military service during World War I at a special prison camp, c. 1915. (©Hulton-Deutsch Collection/CORBIS)

participation in war. MAXIMILLIAN and MARTIN OF TOURS were declared saints in part due to their renunciation of military service; "I am a soldier of Jesus Christ; it is not lawful for me to fight," declared Martin. However, with the recognition given the Church by the Emperor Constantine and with the barbarian invasions, the emphasis was toward legitimate defense by war. From the time of St. Augustine until recently the main teaching in the Catholic Church has been the just-war theory. Still, even in the most militant of times there were pockets of pacifism honored by the Church, as exemplified by the papal privilege given to Franciscan lay tertiaries in the Middle Ages not to fight in feudal wars, or the recognition that clerics, because of the unique dignity and responsibility of their state in life, justly claim an exemption from full military service. In the 20th century, however, the development of increasingly destructive weapons and their intentional and indiscriminate use on civilian populations

led many Catholics to regard conscientious objection in general more favorably.

The Catholic Church has never taught that war is intrinsically evil or that the use of force is always a contravention of the evangelical law of love. The Christian is obliged to love his enemy and to suffer violence patiently when this is conducive to his own salvation and the salvation of others. But if nonviolence is "understood as patiently tolerating injuries done to others, it would be an imperfection, even a vice, if one could efficaciously resist the aggressor" (St. Thomas Aquinas, *Summa Theologiae,* 2a2ae 188.3 ad 1). In the present order of human life, marked by sin, violence does exist. The natural right of self-defense cannot be denied to the individual or to society (cf. Rom 13:1–7). As a general rule, therefore, a Christian living in the world does not have the objective right to adopt an attitude of total nonviolence as the basis for a refusal to fulfill his lawful duties as a citizen. In his Christmas message of 1956, Pope Pius XII affirmed that if a decision to undertake military operations within the limits imposed by the exigencies of legitimate defense against injustice is reached by the freely elected leaders of government, "a Catholic citizen may not appeal to his conscience as grounds for refusing to serve and to fulfill duties fixed by law." However, this explicit statement cannot be taken as a definitive and universal condemnation of the principle of conscientious objection. The pope spoke of a possible situation. The individual, in forming his conscience on the question of his obligation to serve in the defense of his country, must consider the concrete realities of the existing situation.

Basic to the solution of the problem of conscientious objection is the principle of legitimate authority. The authority of civil governments has its source in nature and, consequently, has God for its author. "Those, therefore, who have authority in the state may oblige men in conscience only if their authority is intrinsically related with the authority of God and shares in it. . . . It follows that if civil authority legislates for anything that is contrary to the moral order and therefore contrary to the will of God, these laws cannot be binding on the consciences of the citizens" (Pope John XXIII, *Pacem in terris* 49, 51). It is evident that no rational man could in good conscience take part in any act of war aimed indiscriminately at the destruction of entire cities or of extensive areas along with their populations. The just-war tradition not only provides justification for those who are willing to fight; it also serves as a basis for selective conscientious objection by recognizing that some wars, and some methods of conducting warfare, are unjust.

Vatican Council II, after reaffirming the "right to legitimate defense once every means of peaceful settlement has been exhausted," nevertheless warned of excesses in waging war. They called on governments to recognize the legitimacy of conscientious objection: "it seems right that laws make humane provisions for the case of those who for reasons of conscience refuse to bear arms, provided, however, that they accept some other form of service to the human community" (ibid. 79). In 1980, after issuing several statements during the Vietnam War in support of conscientious objection, the bishops of the United States declared: "We regard this question [conscientious objection] in all its dimensions as a central element in Catholic teaching on the morality of war" ("Statement on Registration and Conscription for Military Service," 1980). The bishops specifically stated their support for the right of selective conscientious objection. Such selective objection has never been legally recognized by the U.S. government. More generally, conscientious objection to military service has been declared by a series of United Nations resolutions, beginning in 1987, as a "universal human right."

Bibliography: R. B. POTTER, *War and Moral Discourse* (Richmond 1973), see the "Bibliographial Essay" pp. 87–123 for extensive references to works on war and peace. J. R. JENNINGS, ed., *Just War and Pacifism: A Catholic Dialogue* (Washington 1973). R. H. BAINTON, *Christian Attitudes Toward War and Peace* (Nashville 1960). J. W. DOUGLASS, *The Non-Violent Cross* (New York 1968). J. J. FAHEY, *Christian Conscience* (New York 1969). L. S. CAHILL, *Love Your Enemies: Discipleship, Pacifism, and Just War Theory* (Minneapolis 1994). D. HOLLENBACH, *Nuclear Ethics* (New York 1983). C. C. MOSKOS and J. W. CHAMBERS III, *The New Conscientious Objection* (New York 1993). R. G. MUSTO, *The Catholic Peace Tradition* (Maryknoll, N.Y. 1986). NATIONAL CONFERENCE OF CATHOLIC BISHOPS, *The Challenge of Peace: God's Promise and Our Response* (Washington, D.C. 1983). T. A. SHANNON, *Render To God: A Theology of Selective Obedience* (New York 1974). L J. SWIFT, *The Early Fathers on War and Military Service* (Wilmington 1983). J. H. YODER, *When War Is Unjust: Being Honest in Just-War Thinking* (Maryknoll, N.Y. 1996).

[R. T. POWERS/T. HEATH/M. W. HOVEY]

CONSCIOUSNESS

From the Latin *conscientia*, a contraction of *cum alio scientia* (i.e., knowledge along with something else), the reflexive knowledge a knower has of himself and of his act in the process of knowing something other than himself. Consciousness has also come to mean (1) mere awareness of something, (2) awareness of the SELF here and now undergoing states of consciousness or emotion, (3) awareness of the self here and now existing that has also undergone other states of thought and emotion, and (4) states of thought or emotion previously experienced and retained in memory even though they are not in the field of awareness. This article considers these various meanings under three main headings dealing with epistemological consciousness, psychological consciousness, and consciousness in modern philosophical thought.

EPISTEMOLOGICAL CONSCIOUSNESS

Among scholastics the most frequent epistemological usage of the term is that designating the simultaneous knowledge a knower has of an object and of himself as knower of the object. This usage is here explained in its historical origins, and then as commonly applied by scholastics to sense knowledge, to intellectual knowledge, and to other internal acts.

Historical Origins. There is no clear notion of consciousness among the early Greek philosophers, who were concerned more with the objective world and its processes of being and becoming than with their own activities of knowing that world. HERACLITUS does make occasional references to consciousness (see H. Diels, *Die*

Fragmente der Vorsokratiker: Griechisch und Deutsch, ed. W. Kranz, 3 v. [8th ed. Berlin 1956]; v. 1 [10th ed. Berlin 1960–61], frgs 1, 110, 117). SOCRATES mentions an experience of himself, recorded by Plato in the *Phaedo* (98B). PLATO himself speaks of self-awareness in the *Charmides* (164D–165B, 167A, 169D), in the *Philebus* (31A–33E, 43AB), and in the *Theaetetus* (185DE, 197BC). Aristotle is more concerned with the subject, notably with sense consciousness as an act of the *sensus communis* (*Anim.* 425B 12). PLOTINUS refers to consciousness in the *Enneads* (1.4.10–11).

Among Christian writers of the Middle Ages there is fuller discussion. St. AUGUSTINE treats of consciousness in *De Trinitate* (10.10.14), *Soliloquies* (2.1.1), and notably in the *Confessions* (10.8–27), where he speaks of plunging into the depths of his own being. Mention of it can be found also in the writings of MATTHEW OF AQUASPARTA, RICHARD OF SAINT-VICTOR, ROGER MARSTON, PETER JOHN OLIVI, and especially St. THOMAS AQUINAS.

Sense Consciousness. Human KNOWLEDGE may be divided into two kinds: SENSE KNOWLEDGE, which man possesses in common with other animals; and intellectual knowledge, which is found in the human species alone. On the sense level man is said to have sense consciousness, or as it is sometimes called, animal consciousness. This, however, is not consciousness in the scholastic definition of the term, since consciousness is reflective knowledge, i.e., knowledge in which the knower, through his knowing power, knows himself in his own act. Such is not the case with sense knowledge, in general. For example, the external SENSES are aware only of other objects, not of themselves or of their own operation. Thus the operation of the external senses, while an act of cognition, is not one of consciousness. On the other hand, a type of sense consciousness, although called such only improperly, is found in the operation of the CENTRAL SENSE (*sensus communis*); this internal sense, when activated by the external senses, becomes aware of their operations. The central sense collects various contents received through the external senses into one common content, which it then refers to one and the same sensing subject.

Intellectual Consciousness. This is consciousness in the more proper meaning of the term. St. Thomas observes that the mind apprehends itself and is aware of its existence in its acts (*De ver.* 10.8). This intellectual awareness, in the terminology of later commentators, may be either direct (sometimes called concomitant), or reflex. Direct consciousness is that by which man primarily knows some object, and secondarily, in the act of knowing that object, knows his act of knowledge and himself as the knower. Reflex consciousness is the know-

ing act in which the mental act itself becomes an object of knowledge.

Different degrees of intensity characterize various states of direct consciousness. In some cases the knower may be so completely absorbed in the object known that, for all practical purposes, he loses awareness of himself as knower. On the other hand, when it is difficult to fix attention on an object, the intense effort involved ordinarily makes the knower more aware of himself. Since direct consciousness always implies at least marginal awareness of a mental state in reference to the self, every state of intellectual consciousness involves some degree of direct consciousness. But it is in reflex consciousness, where the knower deliberately considers his own mental states and himself as objects, that he becomes more completely aware of himself as a person. Consciousness of this kind is found only in man. Some brute animals are aware both of an external object and of an internal state, such as pleasure or pain, but give no acceptable evidence that they distinguish between such feeling and themselves as subjects undergoing it.

Other Internal Acts. Intellectual consciousness is related to freedom of choice. The latter requires that the one choosing be aware of a goal and that he recognize this as an END related to himself. Furthermore, the greater the number of objects of which he may be conscious, the wider the range of objects among which he may choose.

Acts of REFLECTION, in which the knower turns inward upon himself, are often distinguished from acts of ATTENTION, in which the mind turns outward toward objects. Strictly speaking, an opposition should not be set up between these operations, since reflection may well be described as an act of attention to one's own mental processes. Nor should attention, as such, be confused with consciousness, because an individual experiencing a series of mental states may attend to the one that, at that time, is faintest in the field of consciousness. Nor should attention be confused with a voluntary act. While an act of attention may be voluntary, attention itself is a concentration of thought on some object, whereas a voluntary act is a choice to attend to an object. Furthermore, an act of attention need not always be preceded by a voluntary act. In the case of obsessions, for example, a person may attend to some object he wishes he could forget.

Consciousness has been so often identified with the self that some writers (e.g., William JAMES) have described the self as a stream of consciousness. Self-consciousness is not the self, but it is a sign of the self. The PERSON becomes aware of himself as a self by means of his conscious acts.

PSYCHOLOGICAL CONSCIOUSNESS

Whereas the term "consciousness" primarily means reflective awareness for the epistemologist, ordinarily it means simple awareness for the psychologist. Thus it is a generic term applicable to any cognitive or appetitive mental state.

Consciousness. Consciousness is not something distinct from the mental state called conscious. Awareness is the point of distinction between the vegetal and animal kingdoms. In many cases it is extremely difficult to determine whether a living organism is a plant or animal; but the problem in such cases is to discover enough evidence indicating whether or not the organism has at least some rudimentary awareness. Even human beings, capable as they are of a high degree of consciousness, experience different intensities of consciousness at different times. At one time there may be intense concentration of attention on the self whereas at others the diminished consciousness of sleep or twilight zones may intervene.

Subconscious and Unconscious. If consciousness is defined broadly as a state of awareness, it may be contrasted with subconsciousness and unconsciousness, which are states where awareness is lacking. The term "subconscious" usually refers to contents of the mind that are not at the same time in the field of consciousness but are on the threshold. That is to say, if someone is entertaining a train of thought, the next thought that will arise in consciousness, but has not yet appeared, is said to be subconscious. Subconsciousness is sometimes used also as a term referring to marginal states of consciousness. Unconsciousness usually refers to a lack of awareness of those contents of the mind that, at the time, are outside the field of consciousness and beyond the realm of the subconscious.

Freud's Usage. Freudian terminology makes use of two terms, "preconscious" and "unconscious," which are partly equatable with subconscious and unconscious as explained above. The preconscious (Pcs.), in psychoanalysis, refers to what have been called the contents of the subconscious and those unconscious contents of an individual's mind that he himself can raise out of his own mind without resort to psychoanalysis. This does not mean that the contents of the preconscious are always raised without effort; the important factor is that they can be raised by the individual himself. The unconscious (Ucs.), in Freudian terminology, refers to unconscious contents of an individual's mind that are not only out of the field of his awareness but that he cannot bring into awareness without the special techniques of psychoanalysis. These are repressed contents from the individual's own past and the residue of the racial unconscious.

Bibliography: M. STOCK, "Sense Consciousness According to St. Thomas," *Thomist* 21 (1958) 415–486. G. PEDRAZZINI, *Anima in conscientia sui secundum S. Thomam* (Rome 1958). L. LAVELLE, *La Conscience de soi* (Paris 1963). J. M. HOLLENBACH, *Sein und Gewissen* (Baden-Baden 1954). L. KLAGES, *Vom Wesen des Bewusstseins* (4th ed. Munich 1955).

[P. NOLAN]

MODERN PHILOSOPHICAL THOUGHT

There is no question but that the modern transformation of the notion of consciousness began with René DESCARTES. A second stage of development can be distinguished with Immanuel Kant and a third with the phenomenological movement in the 20th century.

Descartes. In his search for an Archimedean point of certitude, Descartes retreated into the "interior world" until he discovered, in the famous *cogito ergo sum,* that while the object of consciousness might be wholly illusory, the consciousness itself is indubitable. Even if I am deceived by what I seem to be conscious of—even if there is no world and I have no body—that I must be in order to be thus deceived is certain. But it was not this bedrock truth (which St. Augustine had already noted) that made Descartes's discovery so important for the course of modern philosophy. It was rather the way in which he conceptualized and articulated it.

First, he understood the presence of the ego to itself in reflection to be the fundamental dimension of all experience. It is into the theater constituted by self-consciousness that all other objects of awareness are introduced as data: perceptions, images, ideas. This image of observing (clearly and distinctly) was rendered by Descartes in terms of *cogitare* and the scholastic-derived terminology of "objective existence." All modes of consciousness are assimilated to the cognitive: "willing, imagining, feeling, etc. . . . agree in falling under the description of thought, perception or consciousness."

Second, Descartes understood the thinking ego, the *res cogitans,* to be identical with the thought-of ego, the *res cogitata.* This identity of the subject and object of self-consciousness, this accessibility of the subject through objective knowledge, makes possible a science of the soul that assimilates reflection to INTROSPECTION and, in contrast to the classical tradition, takes the nature of the soul to be more certainly known than perceptual objects.

In developing the theory that perceptions are contents of consciousness, the British empiricists were led to conclude, with David HUME, that, if the self is the "theater" in which perceptions present themselves, it cannot itself be perceived or presented. Thus there is, in Hume's words, "no such idea," i.e., no perception of the self. It remained for Immanuel Kant to escape from this aporia, and to place the analysis of consciousness on a new path.

Kant. Kant agreed with Hume that the subject, who is the ground of OBJECTIVITY qua that to which all objects are given, cannot himself be an object, i.e., be cognized directly. But man can know that there must be a subject, because how else would the course of his life and experience be unified? How else could the chaos of sensory impressions be organized into the wholes of everyday life? "The synthetic proposition that all of the variety of empirical consciousness must be combined in one single self-consciousness is the absolutely first and synthetic principle of our thought in general." This unifying function of consciousness Kant called the "transcendental unity of apperception" (*see* TRANSCENDENTAL [KANTIAN]).

Kant argued that what is given in self-consciousness is not the subject as he is in himself, but the subject as object, i.e., as organized and subsumed under the categories of objectivity. Thus known, the subject can be material for a science of psychology. Such a science will be an inductive, introspective study of the "empirical ego," but not of the "transcendental ego." Hence, Kant concluded, there is self-certainty in consciousness (the "I think") but no self-knowledge. It is only the self as determined and not the self as determining that is accessible to reflection.

What was left as the unknowable nature of the self by Kant was deciphered by the idealists who followed him as the trans-personal character of the transcendental ego. For G. W. F. HEGEL, man's finite self-consciousness becomes merely a finite mode of God's consciousness of Himself. It was primarily on religious grounds that S. A. Kierkegaard reasserted the irreducibility of the person: "The concept of guilt and sin posits precisely the single individual as the single individual." But he provided no ontological foundation for his notion of the individual consciousness, and it was not until the 20th century that his rebellion against the system acquired an ontology.

Phenomenology. The phenomenological movement denies the primacy of consciousness as *cogito* (Descartes) or *Ich denke* (Kant). Instead it stresses the "prereflective cogito." Whereas, for Descartes, feeling is the consciousness of organic changes and imagination is the consciousness of an image, J. P. Sartre insists that the feeling of hatred is not the consciousness of hatred; rather it is the consciousness of Paul as hateful. Similarly, one's imagining of Peter is not a consciousness of the image of Peter but a specific kind of awareness of Peter himself. Nor can the awareness of the subject of his own existence be defined by the thought he has of existing. The world and one's body are present, according to the existential phenomenologists, not as objects of consciousness or thought, but as constituent elements of one's living awareness. We must not say, writes Gabriel Marcel, that the world is *given* to me as existing, for given normally signifies presented *to* a subject, whereas this assurance of the world *and* myself is constitutive of what we call the subject. The conscious subject is not a gaze for which the world and things exist but a unified life that overflows its explicit knowledge of itself.

The radical schism between this view of consciousness and that of classical modern philosophy is apparent. The epistemological problem loses its primacy since there is no consciousness transparent to itself (as Descartes claimed), confronting its ideas and sensations in the inner world. The self is understood primarily in terms of its "ex-sistence" or ontological union with the world, rather than by the act of reflective self-consciousness in which it "stands back" (in thought) from that junction and views the world as object (*see* EXISTENTIALISM; PHENOMENOLOGY).

Bibliography: S. STRASSER, *The Soul in Metaphysical and Empirical Psychology* (Pittsburgh 1957). J. D. COLLINS, *A History of Modern European Philosophy* (Milwaukee 1954). A. CHOLLET, *Dictionnaire de théologie catholique,* ed. A. VACANT et al., 15 v. (Paris 1903–50; Tables générales 1951–) 3.1:1156–74. J. IVERACH, J. HASTINGS, ed., *Encyclopedia of Religion and Ethics,* 13 v. (Edinburgh 1908–27) 4:49a–58b. A. GUZZO and E. VALENTINI, *Enciclopedia filosofica,* 4 v. (Venice-Rome 1957) 1:1255–70. G. SIEWERTH, *Lexikon für Theologie und Kirche,* ed. J. HOFER and K. RAHNER, 10 v. (2d, new ed. Freiburg 1957–65) 2:329–330. W. ANZ, *Die Religion in Geschichte und Gegenwart,* 7 v. (3d ed. Tübingen 1957–65) 1:1112–15. R. EISLER, *Wörterbuch der philosophischen Begriffe,* 3 v. (4th ed. Berlin 1927–30) 1:207–220.

[F. J. CROSSON]

CONSECRATED LIFE (CANON LAW)

Inspired by the Holy Spirit, some of the Christian faithful are called to a more intimate following of Christ through the profession of the evangelical counsels by vows or other sacred bonds in a stable form of life approved by the Church (*Codex iuris canonici*, c. 573). They possess a special gift in the Church and contribute to its life and mission in accord with the nature, spirit, and end of their respective institutes. Numerous varieties of institutes of consecrated life in the Church manifest Christ praying on the mountain, announcing the kingdom of God, doing good to people, living among men and women in the world, always doing the will of the Father (c. 577). Institutes of consecrated life may be of pontifical right, that is, erected or approved by the Apostolic See; or they may be of diocesan right, that is, erected by the diocesan bishop in his territory (c. 589). Likewise, the institutes may be clerical or lay in accord with the design of the founder and recognition by Church authority (c.

588 §2, §3). Institutes of consecrated life enjoy a just autonomy of life, especially of governance in order to preserve their own patrimony (c. 586). These institutes are subject to the supreme authority of the Church, and their members are bound to obey the pope as their highest superior by reason of their bond of obedience (c. 590). Religious institutes (c. 607), secular institutes (c. 710), and the eremitical lifestyle (c. 603) are forms of consecrated life. While the order of virgins (c. 604) and societies of apostolic life (c. 731) "resemble" or "approach" (*accedunt*) consecrated life, the assumption of the evangelical counsels through vows or other sacred bonds is not a constituent part of their nature. However, some societies of apostolic life do provide for the observance of the evangelical counsels by a bond defined in the constitutions (c. 731 §2).

Religious institutes are societies in which the members in accord with their proper law profess public vows and lead a life of brothers or sisters in common (c. 607 §2). They may be given wholly given over to contemplation (c. 674) or engaged in apostolic action (c. 675).

Secular institutes are institutes of consecrated life in which the Christian faithful living in the world assume the observance of the evangelical counsels through sacred bonds in accord with their constitutions (cc. 710–12). Members of these institutes exercise apostolic activity and act like leaven in the world in their efforts to imbue all things with the spirit of the gospel (c. 713 §1).

The Church also recognizes the eremitical life in which a man or woman is dedicated to God by publicly professing the three evangelical counsels in the hands of the diocesan bishop which profession is confirmed by vow or other sacred bond. In a way of life under the direction of the same bishop, the hermit devotes himself or herself to the praise of God and the salvation of the world through a stricter withdrawal from the world, the silence of solitude, and assiduous prayer and penance (c. 603).

Similar to these forms of consecrated life is the order of virgins by which women resolved to follow Christ through lives of virginity are consecrated to God by the diocesan bishop in the approved liturgical rite. Their lives are given over to service in the Church, and they can associate together for support and assistance in their sacred resolution and service (c. 604).

Societies of apostolic life resemble institutes of consecrated life inasmuch as their members pursue the apostolic purpose of the society and live a life in common as brothers or sisters, striving for charity through the observance of their constitutions. Among these societies, there are some in which the members assume the evangelical counsels by some bond defined in the constitutions (c. 731).

The Church recognizes consecrated life as a gift of the Holy Spirit. While this life does not belong to the Church's hierarchical structure, it is bound inextricably to its life and holiness (c. 574). While the observance of the evangelical counsels may take various forms in the history of the Church, it remains a radical gift of self for love and imitation of Christ, chaste, poor, and obedient. Throughout the centuries, holy men and women have lived the evangelical counsels as ascetics or hermits, monastics, mendicants, contemplatives, and persons engaged in apostolic works in religious or secular institutes. The Church remains open to new forms of consecrated life, the approval of which is reserved to the Apostolic See. Diocesan bishops are encouraged to discern these new gifts and assist their promoters, enabling them to express their inspirations in appropriate statutes (c. 605).

Code of Canons of the Eastern Churches (CCEO). Title XII of the CCEO, "Monks and Other Religious as Well As Members of Other Institutes of Consecrated Life," divides institutes of consecrated life in the following fashion: monasteries, religious houses in which the members strive toward evangelical perfection by the observance of the rules and traditions of monastic life (c. 433 §1); orders, societies in which the members make a profession equivalent to monastic profession (c. 504 §1); congregations, societies in which the members make three public vows which are not equivalent to monastic profession (c. 504 §2); societies of common life according to the manner of religious, societies in which the members profess the evangelical counsels by some sacred bond but not religious vows, imitating the manner of life of the religious state (c. 554 §1); secular institutes, institutes in which the members dedicate themselves to God by profession of the evangelical counsels by a sacred bond and exercise apostolic activity as leaven in the world (c. 563 §1, 1°, 2°); other forms of consecrated life such as ascetics who imitate the eremitical lifestyle without belonging to an institute of consecrated life (c. 570); consecrated virgins and widows who live in the world on their own and publicly profess chastity (c. 570). Finally, the CCEO describes societies of apostolic life whose members without religious vows pursue the particular apostolic purpose of the society and live as brothers or sisters in common according to their constitutions (c. 572). As in the CIC, new forms of consecrated life are reserved to the Apostolic See (c. 571). The typicon is the law proper to monasteries (c. 414 §1, 1°); statutes are proper laws for orders, congregations, societies of common life imitating religious, secular institutes, and other forms of consecrated life (cc. 414 §1, 1°; 511 §1; 554 §1; 563 §1, 1°,

Archdeacon Cox (center) at his consecration as Bishop of Shrewsbury at Westminster Abbey, London, England. (Hulton/ Archive Photos)

3°; 571); constitutions is a term used only for societies of apostolic life without religious vows (c. 572).

[R. MCDERMOTT]

CONSECRATION, PERSONAL

In the strict sense, consecration signifies the total dedication of a person or thing to God and His service, and its consequent separation from ordinary human use. By the act of consecration a state or stable condition is inaugurated: what is consecrated thereafter belongs exclusively to God. In common Christian usage the term is applied to the conversion of bread and wine into the Body and Blood of Christ, to elevation to the episcopate, and to the solemn blessing of churches, altars, sacred vessels, and cemeteries. But the idea of consecration is realized also in Baptism, which may indeed be called the fundamental consecration of the Christian life. Through it the baptized person, by a title distinct from that of creation, belongs and is consecrated to God. CONFIRMATION also, and the Sacrament of Orders, involving the Christian more fully in the service of God, can be considered consecrations, or at least enlargements of the consecration of Baptism.

In addition to this type of consecration, there is another that exists when an individual not only belongs to God, but also sees the relationship and is freely determined by his own choice to accept it, to live in accord with the responsibilities it imposes, and perhaps also to undertake good works or practices that are not obligatory by reason of his baptismal commitment. Thus, from the fourth century, the vow of virginity, accompanied by the liturgical blessing, was called a consecration. Later, the vows of religion were recognized as having a similar character. Similarly, any engagement undertaken by an individual to accept his already existing baptismal obligations, or to enlarge the scope of his service of God, can be considered a kind of consecration, although the idea is less perfectly realized in a determination not stabilized by vow and unratified by the authority of the Church.

Strictly speaking, one can consecrate himself only to God, for only God has the right to man's total dedication and service. Consecration to Christ, to the Sacred Heart, is legitimate because of the Hypostatic Union; but "consecration" to the Blessed Virgin, or even to St. Joseph or to other saints, is not unknown to Christian piety. In the case of St. Joseph or the other saints, this is to be understood as consecration in a broad sense of the term, and it signifies no more than an act of special homage to one's heavenly protector. The case of the Blessed Virgin, however, is not the same. The importance of her role in Christian spirituality is such that formulas of dedication to her appear to have a more profound meaning. Her position in the economy of salvation is inseparable from that of her Son. Her desires and wants are His, and she is in a unique position to unite Christians fully, quickly, and effectively to Christ, so that dedication to her is in fact dedication to Christ.

French spirituality has made much of consecration to Mary. Cardinal BÉRULLE encouraged the vow of servitude to Jesus and Mary. St. John EUDES propagated the devotion of consecration not only to the Sacred Heart, but to the heart of Mary as well. However, the practice achieved its strongest expression in the *Traité de la vraie devotion à Sainte Vierge* of St. Louis Marie GRIGNION DE MONTFORT. The act of personal consecration according to De Montfort, is an act of complete and total consecration. It consists in giving oneself entirely to Mary in order to belong wholly to Jesus through her.

Bibliography: L. M. GRIGNION DE MONTFORT, *Treatise on the True Devotion to the Blessed Virgin Mary,* tr. F. W. FABER (London 1863; rev. ed. Bay Shore, N.Y. 1941). A. TANQUEREY, *The Spiritual Life,* tr. H. BRANDERIS (2d ed. Tournai 1930; repr. Westminster, Md. 1945). A. ROYO, *The Theology of Christian Perfection,* ed. and tr. J. AUMANN (Dubuque 1962). J. DE FINANCE, *Dictionnaire de spiritualité ascétique et mystique. Doctrine et histoire*, ed. M. VILLER et al. (Paris 1932–) 2:1576–83.

[N. LOHKAMP]

CONSEJO EPISCOPAL LATINOAMERICANO (CELAM)

The Latin American Episcopal Council, the Consejo Episcopal Latinoamericano (CELAM), was founded in 1955, following the General Conference of Latin American Bishops that met in Rio de Janeiro. It was formally approved by Pope Pius XII on Nov. 2, 1955. Its main objectives were defined as (1) the study of the problems facing the Church in Latin America, (2) coordinating Catholic activities on the continent, (3) the promotion and support of Catholic charitable activity, and (4) the organization of conferences of Latin American bishops whenever these are summoned by the Holy See.

While CELAM is best known for its role in organizing the General Conferences of Latin American Bishops, Medellín (1968), PUEBLA (1979), and SANTO DOMINGO (1994), milestones in the history of the Latin American Church, it has also had a continuing role in servicing the particular churches of the continent. The council, composed of delegates from each episcopal conference, holds a four-yearly assembly at which it elects a president, two vice-presidents, and a secretary general. The secretary general directs the day-to-day work of CELAM, much of which as of 1994 was carried out by 11 departments: Catechesis, Education, Family, Children and Youth, Liturgy, Missions, Social Action, Consecrated Life, Vocations and Ministries, Ecumenism and Religious Dialogue, and Culture and Media. There are also secretariats for nonbelievers, the military chaplains, migrants, shrines, a radio and television service, and an Institute of Pastoral Theology. Through its departments, CELAM offers courses for bishops and other Church personnel and promotes conferences and publications. It also produces a regular bulletin.

Origins of CELAM. The origins of CELAM and even of episcopal conferences themselves go back to the activities of bishops such as Helder Câmara (Brazil) and Manuel Larraín (Chile), who was president of CELAM from 1963 to 1966. These bishops were determined to end the remoteness of the Church from the bulk of Latin America's population that had resulted from its close relationship with traditional elites. They also sought to bring the Church into the crusade for development that, it was believed, would pull Latin America out of its backwardness through initiatives like the U.S.-sponsored Alliance for Progress. Typical of this approach were proposals at the CELAM meeting in Buenos Aires in 1960 at which Larraín called for studies into the basis of pastoral theology and for sociological research to inform the Church's ministry. At the same meeting, Bishop Alfredo Rubio of Giradot (Colombia) reported the findings of a study that found that most Roman Catholics in rural areas had not been evangelized and called for the Church to support agrarian reform and to organize a Christian rural movement in each country. In 1964 Bishop Leonidas Proaño, of Riobamba, Ecuador, known as the "bishop of the Indians," founded the Latin American Pastoral Institute in Quito, which was to train thousands of Church personnel from all over the continent. In the late 1960s a series of continental meetings were held to discuss reform over the whole area of the Church's life. Particularly significant was the 1966 assembly at Mar del Plata, Argentina, where for the first time the bishops attempted a global vision of the Latin American Church.

The creation of CELAM as an organ of coordination and collegiality for the Church in Latin America had an effect on the Roman Catholic Church worldwide in two ways. First, CELAM and the other Latin American episcopal conferences were prototypes for the structures created after Vatican II to embody the greater degree of autonomy now vested in particular churches. Second, CELAM brought issues of world development on to the agenda of the universal Church. The CELAM bishops caucused at Vatican II and directly influenced the constitution *Gaudium et spes,* especially the commitment to "those who are poor or in any way afflicted." The social concerns behind CELAM were those expressed in Pope Paul VI's encyclical *Populorum progressio* and explored further in the apostolic letter, *Octogesima adveniens* and the apostolic exhortation, *Evangelii nuntiandi.*

The results of the efforts of the CELAM pioneers and a new generation of theologians, economists, and sociologists in Latin America to reassess the role of the Church on the continent were first made visible on a world scale at the Second General Conference of Latin American Bishops, held in Medellín, Colombia, in 1968. The Medellín Fathers committed the Church to participating in the transformation of Latin America into a more humane society by eliminating structures of injustice, a transformation they compared with the liberation of Israel at the Exodus [Medellín, Introduction, 6].

Change and Downsizing. CELAM has undergone drastic changes since its foundation, reflecting both developments within the Latin American Church and the changing relationships between Latin America and Rome. The optimism of the 1960s was to prove short-lived. The democratic and populist movements in Latin American countries were abruptly checked by a series of military coups, starting in Brazil in 1964, followed by Bolivia in 1971, Uruguay in 1973, and—the bloodiest of all—Augusto Pinochet's coup of September 1973 in Chile. In 1975 it was the turn of Peru, followed in 1976 by Ecuador and Argentina. The times were not auspicious for the Sandinista revolution of July 1979 in Nicaragua, especially after the election of Ronald Reagan as U.S. president in 1981.

The early leaders of CELAM were more progressive than the average of Latin American bishops, and their challenge to inherited power structures and attitudes provoked opposition in the Church. An alliance between conservative Latin American prelates and conservative officials of the Roman Curia sought to check what they claimed to be Marxist infiltration into the Church. Their reaction received support in the election in 1978 of the Polish Cardinal Karol Wojtyla as Pope John Paul II. The new pope's experiences in communist Poland had left him fiercely opposed to Marxism and communism and sensitive to the danger that the involvement of Church personnel in community organization would compromise their distinctive religious mission.

Attempts were made to check CELAM. In 1958 a Pontifical Commission for Latin America had been established, a body with no equivalent for any other continent, reflecting the extent to which the future of Catholicism was felt to be closely bound up with Latin America and enabling the Vatican to monitor and influence developments in CELAM. In 1970 the statutes of CELAM were modified to give presidents of episcopal conferences the right to attend the assemblies. This was generally regarded as a move to reinforce conservative tendencies.

In 1972 the Colombian auxiliary Bishop Alfonso López Trujillo was elected secretary general of CELAM, a post he held for an unprecedented seven years. In 1979 he was elected president. As secretary general, López Trujillo embarked, alleging reasons of economy, on a rationalization of CELAM's activities that included the closure of the Pastoral Institute in Quito, the Liturgical Institute in Medellín, and the Catechetics Institute in Manizales. They were combined in 1974 to form the CELAM Theological Institute, operating from the premises of the Liturgical Institute in Medellín. A number of leading intellectuals associated with the theology of liberation claim that they were banned from the new institute. In 1989 the institute was transferred to Bogotá with the exclusion of leading intellectuals associated with the THEOLOGY of liberation.

Bibliography: AA.VV., *CELAM: Elementos para su historia 1955–1980* (Bogota 1982). E. DUSSEL, *The Church in Latin America 1492–1992* (New York and London 1992). J. EAGELSON and P. SCHARPER, eds., *Puebla and Beyond* (New York 1979). G. GUTIÉRREZ, et al., *Santo Domingo and After* (London 1993). F. HOUTART, "CELAM: The forgetting of Origins," in *Church and Politics in Latin America,* ed. D. KEOGH (London 1990). CATHOLIC INSTITUTE FOR INTERNATIONAL RELATIONS, *Reflections on Puebla* (London 1980). P. LERNOUX, *The Cry of the People* (New York 1980). G. MACEOIN, ed., "Puebla: Moment of Decision for the Latin American Church," *Cross Currents* 28/1 (1978). L. MENDES DE ALMEIDA, "A Igreja do Brasil e Puebla," in INSTITUTO NACIONAL DE PASTO-RAL, ed., *Pastoral da Igreja Brasileira nos Anos 70* (Petrópolis 1994). J. B. RESTREPO, *El CELAM: Apuntes para una crónica de sus 25 años* (Medellín 1982). W. URANGA, *Para Interpretar Santo Domingo* (Buenos Aires 1992).

[F. MCDONAGH]

CONSENT, MORAL

From the Latin *consentire,* literally, to feel together. Consent is sometimes understood to include feeling, a sort of sympathy, a complacency with regard to something. Strictly speaking, it is an act of the will acquiescing in a judgment of the mind. Before consenting, one must make up one's mind that what is proposed is good. Consent is the will's determination to implement the verdict of the mind that something is worthwhile.

Consent is an immanent, free movement of the will, and it establishes a certain responsibility for whatever is consented to. It means more than mere willingness and is distinguished from other voluntary acts such as velleity and intention. Volition is sheer willingness, without any thought of ways and means. What a person does of his own volition he is taken as willing to do. Consent enters into the actual doing of it, but the initial willingness to do it comes first. If one analyzes the whole process of willed activity, one sees that velleity itself must presuppose a suggestion by the mind that something might be desirable or good. Whatever is willed must first be known. Velleity is vague, tentative, provisional, leaving undecided whether what is suggested is feasible. It is only when the mind has formed a judgment about the latter that the will goes on to form a firm intention to pursue the proposed objective.

What remains is to explore the ways and means, in case several are available, by which what is suggested can be achieved. The outcome of this investigation is counsel that proposes to the will how its desired objective may be reached. It is at this point only that consent, properly speaking, is given. Aquinas defines it as "the application of the appetitive movement to the decision of counsel" (*Summa theologiae* 1a2ae, 15.3). By his consent, man is determined to secure the desired good. To quote Aquinas again: "Consent denotes the application of the appetitive movement to something that is already in the power of the person applying it. In this process of willed activity, there is first the apprehension of the end; then the desire of the end; then counsel about the means to the end, and then the desire to take the means" (*Summa theologiae* 1a2ae, 15.1).

This desire and decision to take the appropiate steps to achieve one's objective is what St. Thomas understands by consent in the strict sense. It is followed by a further investigation to decide which is the best of all the means available. This discriminating judgment is followed by a further act of the will, election or choice. If there is no choice of means presented, there is no difference between consent and choice. Strictly speaking, in such a case one has no choice, but the consent may still be free. Freedom depends on the possibility of forming another judgment about the desirability of the end proposed. One can always withhold consent from anything proposed to one's will as a good thing if one can judge that something quite different might be a good thing too. (*See* FREE WILL.)

From what has been said about the meaning of consent, it appears that consent always implies freedom of judgment, deliberation, and a freely given acquiescence in what is thought desirable. The first condition of free consent is, therefore, freedom of judgment. If there were no freedom of judgment there could be no free consent. The blessed in heaven, therefore, do not consent to enjoy the vision of God; they are captivated by it; they could not possibly judge anything that would exclude it to be good; their act of enjoyment, therefore, is not free. Here again the distinction must be made between voluntary and free, between volition and consent. The enjoyment of the blessed is perfectly voluntary, being in the will, and proceeding from perfect knowledge; but it is not free. There is free consent only if there is possible dissent, as would not be the case if a person were to be so blinded by passion or intoxication that he could not possibly form any other judgment than that what he proposes to do is good. It might be free in its cause, if free consent were already given to the infatuation, fury, or intoxication that now prevents deliberation. That ignorance can vitiate consent is a corollary to what has been said. Consent implies that one knows what is proposed for one's acceptance and acquiescence. This appears clearly if one considers the mutual consent given by persons who get married. This consent constitutes the essence of the contract. Obviously, it implies that the persons know the meaning and purpose of marriage and also that they know one another. Error either about the purpose or about the person could vitiate the consent necessary to the marriage contract.

Consent being essentially an immanent act cannot be coerced. Violence is incompatible with consent. Violence means force applied from without, without the victim's cooperation. Coercion may either vitiate consent or reduce its willingness and may make it legally rescindable. A general might say that he was coerced into surrendering his army by fear of the consequences of refusal, but consent given reluctantly or grudgingly may still be free consent.

Bibliography: THOMAS AQUINAS, *Summa theologiae* 1a2ae, 15. D. M. PRÜMMER, *Manuale theologiae moralis*, ed. E. M. MÜNCH (Freiburg-Barcelona 1955) 1:48–98; 2:255–258. 1917 *Codex iuris canonici* (Graz 1955) 1081–87, 1089–93.

[A. DOOLAN]

CONSEQUENTIALISM

Consequentialism is a category of moral theories wherein the rightness of acts is judged solely on the basis of the foreseeable consequences of choosing them. The question of how to assess morally the consequences of a human action commands considerable discussion in philosophical ethics, which may be said to move between the extremes of utilitarianism or formalism, between looking at the net profit an action may produce or at one's duty to perform the action. Because she remains committed to an intrinsic teleological morality, the Church may adopt fully neither model in order to determine whether the choice of a concrete kind of behavior is morally good or bad. Though we may be responsible for the consequences that can and should be foreseen, the morality of an act, for good or for bad, is complete before these have begun to appear. St. THOMAS AQUINAS exemplifies the point clearly: "That a beggar misuses and sins with the alms given him detracts nothing from the generosity of the giver; so also if somebody patiently endures a wrong this offers no excuse for him who inflicts it" (*Summa theologiae* I–II, q. 20, a. 5, sc).

The authors of the casuist period (*c.* mid-1500s–1965), represented, for example, by B. H. Merkelbach, had argued that good consequences lay outside of the agent's direct volition, but still warned against committing actions that cause evil consequences. They also stipulated the conditions that must be fulfilled before such evil consequences may be reasonably attributed to the agent. In sum, according to the classical casuists, consequences provided more risks than rewards for the moral agent. The principle of double effect was developed by these same authors to take account of those evil consequences that—so it was affirmed by those who read the tradition loosely—flowed from an exercise of the indirect voluntary. Thomas Aquinas, on the other hand, considered what flows from an indirect voluntary as an enacted nonaction (see *Summa theologiae* I–II, q. 6, a. 3, ad 1), as when a priest grows weak in pastoral charity because he fails to pray, not as grounds for the celebrated *voluntarium in causa*. Casuistry, in any case, accustomed people to think of themselves as somehow involved with bad consequences without imputation of subjective guilt. Scholars have argued that there is a connection between the conception of the indirect voluntary as a kind of negative voluntary (e.g., when a therapeutic operation causes an abortion), and the intrusion of consequentialism and proportionalism into Catholic moral theology in the late twentieth century.

The 1993 papal encyclical letter VERITATIS SPLENDOR, which presents authoritatively the principal methodological issues and substantive questions that shape an adequate Catholic moral theology, excludes these theories, which it characterizes as ''teleological,'' from authentic expressions of Catholic teaching. ''The former [consequentialism] claims to draw the criteria of the rightness of a given way of acting solely from a calculation of foreseeable consequences deriving from a given choice. The latter [proportionalism], by weighing the various values and goods being sought, focuses rather on the proportion acknowledged between good and bad effects of that choice, with a view to the 'greater good' or 'lesser evil' actually possible in a particular situation'' (Veritatis splendor 75). Consequentialist theories comprise a class of teleologisms, each variety of which affords a wrong way of looking at ''ends.'' Although in the encyclical's official English version, the adjectival form of teleologism is rendered ''teleological,'' it would have been better to translate it as ''teleologistic.'' ''Teleology'' describes the setting for sound moral theology; ''teleologism'' is a category that includes repudiated theories.

Christian teleology establishes the framework for a person to establish an act's inner perfection, not a calculus for weighing its consequences. Frequently, though, an appeal to the outcomes of a given action, whether clearly foreseen or unforeseeable, has figured in a ''teleologistic'' approach to morals. Veritatis splendor was written in part to clarify this crucial issue in moral theology. The encyclical provides an admirable summary of Thomas Aquinas's teaching: the object of a given moral act ''is the proximate end of deliberate decision which determines the act of willing on the part of the acting person'' (Veritatis splendor 78). As Thomas Aquinas puts it in Summa theologiae I–II, q.20., a. 1, ad 1: ''The exterior action is the object of the will, inasmuch as it is proposed to the will by the reason, as good apprehended and ordained by the reason.'' The object of the act is not only that aspect of the act under which it is appetible to the agent, but also includes the integral nature of the act itself under this ratio—a consideration that limits the possible remotion of the agent from the act performed and so severely constrains the possibilities for consequentialism.

Bibliography: R. CESSARIO, ''On Bad Actions, Good Intentions, and Loving God: Three Much-Misunderstood Issues about the Happy Life That St. Thomas Clarifies for Us,'' *Logos* 1 (1997) 100–124; *Introduction to Moral Theology* (Washington, D.C. 2001).

[R. CESSARIO]

CONSERVATION, DIVINE

Divine conservation is the activity whereby God keeps creatures in EXISTENCE. It is the continuation, so to speak, or the extension of the creative act whereby God originally gave existence to creatures. Conservation is described also as the first effect of God's providential governance of the universe. The divine CONCURRENCE is the second effect. Divine conservation is almost universally admitted to be something positive; it is not, therefore, God's mere refusal to destroy creatures, even though He is able to do so. Also, God's conservation is usually admitted to be direct and immediate. This means that God does not merely see to it that harmful forces are kept away from the things He wants conserved and that necessary conditions and helpful adjuncts are present when needed, but that He Himself by His own divine causality directly causes the continuation in existence of creatures (*see* CAUSALITY, DIVINE).

Historical Development. That creatures depend upon God not only for their initial creation at the beginning of the world, but also for their present existence and for their every moment, is indicated with greater or lesser clarity in Sacred Scripture when, for example, God's power and freedom are discussed. See: Wisdom 1.7, 13; 11.26; 12.1; Ecclesiastes 1.4; 3.14; John 5.17; Acts of the Apostles 17.27, 28; Romans 11.36; Hebrews 1.3.

Church Fathers. In their comments on such scriptural texts, as well as in their other writings, the Fathers of the Church teach that the permanence in existence of all things depends upon God's free will and power. The Neoplatonic philosophy of Alexandria helped the Fathers to appreciate the finitude of creatures and the purely determinable status of elementary matter. The doctrine of the radical contingency in the existence of all nondivine things thus found support in reason as well as in revelation. (*See* PATRISTIC PHILOSOPHY.)

St. JUSTIN MARTYR points out, in his *Dial. Cum Tryphone,* ch. 6, that the soul participates in life because God wishes it to live and that it will no longer participate in life when God does not wish it to live. St. IRENAEUS states (*Adv. haereses* 2.34.2) that ''all things that have been made had a beginning when they were produced, and they last so long as God wills them to have existence and duration.'' St. JOHN CHRYSOSTOM says [*Cont. Anomoeos,* hom. 12, n. 4; *Patrologia Graeca,* ed. J. P. Migne, 161 v. (Paris 1857–66) 48:810–811] that ''Not only did God produce creatures, He also preserves them and helps them develop; . . . should they be deprived of His efficacious action, they would simply flow away, collapse, perish.''

St. AUGUSTINE (*Conf.* 1.2) speaks thus to God (with a reference to Romans 11.36): ''Without Thee there would exist nothing. . . . I could not exist unless I were in Thee, from whom and through whom and unto whom are all things." Augustine develops the doctrine of conservation in greater detail in his *Gen. ad litt.* 4.12.22 (also see 5.20.40; 8.12.26). He reconciles the passage "And [God] rested on the seventh day from all the work He had done" (Genesis 2.2), with the passage, "My Father works even until now, and I work" (John 5.17), by telling us that God's rest can be understood as meaning that He has ceased to make new species of creatures, but not that He has ceased to operate by governing the universe. God did not cease even on the "seventh day" to exercise His governing power over the heavens and the earth and over all the creatures that He had made. Should He cease to do this, all things would instantaneously fall into nothingness. The cause that keeps every creature in existence is the creative influence of God, the power of God omnipotent and "omnitenant" (the *Pantocrator* of the Greek Fathers). St. Augustine also makes a contrast that is frequently utilized by subsequent writers. God is not like a carpenter who, after constructing a house, goes away without any further care, leaving the house to exist by itself. With regard to the universe, if God were to withdraw His governance it could not last for so much as the blinking of an eye.

Similar testimony could be presented from St. GREGORY THE GREAT (*Moralia* 16.16.18), from St. JOHN DAMASCENE (*De fide orth.* 1.3; 2.29) and from St. BERNARD OF CLAIRVAUX (*Sermo 6 in dedicat. ecclesiae* and *De consideratione* 5.6).

Medieval Scholasticism. With St. ANSELM OF CANTERBURY in the 12th century the doctrine of divine conservation receives a classic statement (*Monologion,* ch. 13), linking together God's creative presence and His conserving presence.

St. THOMAS AQUINAS discusses conservation in several places: *C. gent.* 3.65 (see the commentary of Sylvester FERRARIENSIS ed., Leonina 14:184–188), *De pot.* 5.1–4 and *Summa Theologiae,* 1a, 104.1–4. In this last work Aquinas argues that any effect depends on its cause so far as this is its cause. Now, since all creatures are beings through PARTICIPATION and only God exists by right of essence, all creatures depend on God not merely as on the cause of their coming into being, but also as on the cause of their being, so long as they have this being. Where the cause of a thing is of the same species as the thing (the usual case in the generation of new beings), this cause is not the cause of the effect's form, insofar as this is such and such a form; rather it is the cause merely of the acquisition by matter of this individuated form. The generative cause is the cause of the effect's coming to be, but not of the effect's being. Hence, in addition to

causes that bring things into existence through generation out of previously existing things, there is need of a cause transcending generative causality. In other words, there is need of a cause that directly and immediately accounts for the reality of everything that does not exist by right of its own very essence. Hence, as long as created beings exist, so long are they under the conserving influence of God. This does not preclude the existence of subordinated or secondary conserving causes, but God always remains the primary cause directly conserving the being of things. St. Thomas argues also that since creation is an exercise of God's free will, God can, absolutely speaking, annihilate any creature; but he goes on to argue that God will not annihilate anything, even miraculously, for there is no reason for ANNIHILATION: annihilation would not pertain to the manifestation of God's glory or grace.

St. BONAVENTURE discusses conservation especially in his *In 2 sent.* 37.1.2, but he also brings out that God's conservation presupposes that the creature has some substantiality in itself.

Later Scholasticism. Commenting on *Summa Theologiae* 1a, 104.2, CAJETAN admits that God utilizes the mediation of material substances in the indirect preservation of other material substances. Salt helps preserve meat. But with regard to direct conservation, Cajetan points out that one must distinguish between the case of spiritual and other incorruptible substances on the one hand, and the case of material or corruptible substances on the other. In the former case, these substances (which can originate only by direct and immediate creation) are directly conserved solely by God, with no intermediating causes of conservation; the action of creating these is identical with the action of preserving them. But in the case of corruptible substances (which can originate by way of generation out of other, previously existing, substances and not merely by direct creation) God is not the sole direct conserver: He uses the intermediation of secondary causes as well. In this case the action of creating is not the same as the action of conserving.

Francisco SUÁREZ, in concluding the argument for divine conservation (*Disp. meta.* 21.1.14), stresses the idea that God's OMNIPOTENCE and supreme dominion over creation require that He be able at any moment to annihilate any and every creature. Since annihilation terminates in nothing, it is not a positive action. Therefore, unless God were conserving all creatures for all their duration by a positive and direct action, He could not annihilate them and thus would not have supreme dominion; creatures would in a very real sense be independent of God. Suárez also holds (*ibid.* 21.3.4) that no created substance, even though it is material, can be conserved in its substantial existence by a created cause.

Nature of Conservation. Conservation is described by St. Thomas as "the continuation of that action whereby God gives existence, an action which is without either motion or time" (*Summa Theologiae* 1a, 104.1 ad 4). It cannot be discussed, therefore, in the same terms nor studied according to the same methods that are used by scientists in discussing the conservation of matter or the conservation of energy and by cosmologists in discussing "steady state" theories of the universe.

Conservation is sometimes contrasted with CREATION. Creation is popularly looked upon as the act that brought this universe into its existence at some definite moment of time; and conservation then refers to the act that prolongs the universe through all moments subsequent to the first. Creation and conservation are therefore said to be conceptually distinct. But in themselves, and speaking strictly, the act of creating and the act of conserving are really one and the same act; they both are the a-temporal, direct giving of existence by God to nondivine beings, whenever and for so long as these have existence. It requires the efficacy of the most universal cause, God, to make creatures exist and endure at all, whether they have endured from all eternity or not. God's own activity is outside of TIME; it has no change or succession. Whatever succession there is, is in the terminus willed by God's eternal free act. This terminus is the sum of the contingent, changeable, dynamic, interrelated beings constituting the universe in its totality, past, present and future. Divine conservation contrasts not with creation and not with concurrence but with annihilation.

The maintenance of creatures in their existence is, like their creation, due simply to God alone; the maintenance of the specific nature of a corporeal being is due, under God, to the secondary causes that embody the physical laws of the universe. The stones in an arch mutually support one another, but it is God who gives existence to them all.

In the late Middle Ages, HENRY OF GHENT, Peter Aureoli and GREGORY OF RIMINI asserted that there is a specific difference between creation and conservation. They thought that less effort is required for sustaining a thing in existence than for initiating its existence. Even among the later scholastics there is some obscurity in the way in which they describe God's use of creatures as intermediaries in the direct preservation of other creatures. Their doctrine is further complicated by reason of the false physical and astronomical ideas that these authors entertained. The planets, stars and other heavenly bodies were considered to be agents essentially superior to all terrestrial causes and had, therefore, special roles to play in God's governance. Contemporary scholastics reduce these roles to the ordinary level of the physical and chemical activities of bodies. They also increasingly purify the language of creation and conservation and insist strongly on the transcendence and uniqueness of God's causality. God is not the first link in a succession of causes; neither is He simply the supreme member of a hierarchy of causes (Donceel, 37–38, 80); He belongs to a different dimension from all finite and created causes. For Him to "act through an intermediary in conservation" means that "He simultaneously creates, a-temporally, beings and their causal interdependences" (Sertillanges, 72, n. 1).

Nonscholastic Accounts. René Descartes speaks of conservation as a continuous creation, but his meaning is different from that of the scholastics. Descartes holds that duration and motion are of themselves discontinuous; God's "continual creation" gives them continuity [see F. C. Copleston, *History of Philosophy* (Westminster, Md 1946–) 4:134]. Further, Descartes rejects the notion that things have natures and forms; for him, there is no internal stability in creatures and no true interaction. Such doctrine naturally leads to OCCASIONALISM.

Pierre BAYLE, in his *Dictionnaire* (article "Pyrrhon," end of note B) takes for granted that conservation means that God renews the existence of each creature at every moment, so that conservation is a reiterated creation of things out of the nothingness into which they continually lapse. All creatures thus have a staccato existence. One cannot even be sure of his own identity with the person he used to be a moment before.

Some maintain that DEISM denies the conservation of things by God; but perhaps what deism denies is all special intervention on the part of God.

Special Difficulties. It is argued that since created causes can produce effects that remain in existence without the continued causality of their cause, then certainly God can do so. To this it should be pointed out that a created cause is cause only of the coming into being of its effects; and this process ceases as soon as the created cause ceases its activity. God's proper effect, the existence of creatures, would similarly cease should His activity cease.

But would it not be a more wonderful manifestation of God's power if He were to make a creature that could last without God's direct conservation? No; for instead of being a more wonderful manifestation of power this would be a contradiction. It would require that God produce an unproduced product; it would be calling for a caused being that is not a being caused.

Still, natural objects tend of their very nature toward being. There is no natural tendency toward nothingness. Creatures are truly substances, existing in themselves and they have an innate drive to continue their existence. All this is true enough, but not a serious difficulty; for the very substantiality of creatures and their drive or innate tendency are caused by God. Created existence is not something that can be conferred "once and for all" in the sense that a created thing, once it has been created, could forthwith dispense with its relation to the Creator. Created existence is rather like the sunlight or like an electric current, which cease when contact with the source is severed.

See Also: CAUSALITY; PROVIDENCE OF GOD; SCHOLASTICISM; SUBSTANCE.

Bibliography: A. J. BENEDETTO, *Fundamentals in the Philosophy of God* (New York 1963). A. G. SERTILLANGES, *L'Idée de création et ses retentissements en philosophie* (Paris 1945). J. F. ANDERSON, *The Cause of Being: The Philosophy of Creation in St. Thomas* (St. Louis 1952). R. GARRIGOU-LAGRANGE, *The Trinity and God the Creator: A Commentary on St. Thomas' Theological Summa Ia, q. 27–119,* tr., F. C. ECKHOFF (St. Louis 1952). J. F. DONCEEL, *Natural Theology* (New York 1962). W. J. BROSNAN, *God Infinite, The World and Reason* (New York 1943). H. PINARD, *Dictionnaire de théologie catholique,* ed. A. VACANT et al., 15 v. (Paris 1903–50) 3.1:1187–97. *Cont. Anomoeos,* hom. 12, n. 4; *Patrologia Graeca,* ed. J. P. MIGNE, 161 v. (Paris 1857–66) 48:810–811. F. C. COPLESTON, *History of Philosophy* (Westminster, Md 1946–) 4:134.

[A. J. BENEDETTO]

CONSERVATISM AND LIBERALISM, THEOLOGICAL

Application of these largely political terms to theological statements may be justly resented; yet they will be used, and the attempt must be made to see why and to see how they might be used responsibly. Expressions like "liberal" or "conservative" are especially susceptible of polemical use, and quickly degenerate into labels that are not accurate and should rather be avoided than pursued.

In the measure that theological teaching, however, reflects and affects the spirit of an age, it seems to prompt classification as conservatism or liberalism. "Conservative" and "liberal," then, do not describe theological statements or positions themselves, but rather refer to the way those statements may relate to the spirit of an age. Given that initial clarification, it is fair to say that a liberal theological stance will tend more to accommodate current intellectual movements, while a conservative posture will tend to find them alienating or threatening to theological sanity. Each position, if it is to make genuine theological assertions, must represent itself as carrying forward an authentic tradition; yet they will differ in the strategies employed to elaborate that tradition.

The differences may so polarize them that representatives of either group will come to caricature the other's position polemically. A liberal will be tempted to accuse a conservative of unwillingness to risk a nostalgic attachment to the past by confronting contemporary issues, and a conservative may look upon a liberal as one so anxious to adopt current outlooks that he cares little about the richness of the common heritage. Once these polemical uses have been invoked, the expressions "liberal" and "conservative" quickly become labels and lose descriptive force.

To classify liberal or conservative tendencies in theology with some accuracy, however, calls for attention to the earlier observation: these terms describe the ways in which theological assertions relate themselves to the surrounding intellectual currents. Thus a theological liberal will be prone to distinguish expression from substance and to regard a particular doctrinal expression as culture-bound and thus subject to revision. By contrast, a theological conservative will note how expression in words and in practices so often carry the substance of the matter that they cannot easily be revised without altering the sense of what is being passed on. Because theology is logically tied to a tradition and because traditions develop by a judicious mixture of change and of continuity, theologians will always be divided into conservatives and liberals. Furthermore, the surrounding intellectual currents may shift so that an individual may find himself in one camp or another at different times in his life.

The relatively fixed use for "theological liberalism" refers to a 19th-century movement that sought to accommodate the Scriptures to historical method in such a way as to meet current criteria for scholarly rectitude; Schleiermacher offers the most notable example. Until rather recently the tendency would have been to label Catholic counterparts "Modernists."

Bibliography: J. HITCHOCK, *Decline and Fall of Radical Catholicism* (New York 1971). M. NOVAK, *The Open Church* (London 1964). F. SCHLEIERMACHER, *Brief Outline of the Study of Theology* (Richmond, VA 1966).

[D. BURRELL]

CONSIDINE, JOHN J.

Writer, missiologist, priest; b. New Bedford, Mass., Oct. 9, 1897; d. Maryknoll, N.Y., 1982. In 1917 he entered the newly established society of Maryknoll Missionaries. He studied for the priesthood in Washington, D.C., at the Catholic University of America, where he received the J.C.B. and S.T.L. degrees. He was ordained in 1923. From 1924 to 1934 Considine served as the procurator-general for the society in Rome. He was a member of the society's general council in Maryknoll, New York, from 1934 to 1946.

Although Father Considine was never given a mission assignment, he spent his life establishing and coordinating a network of projects designed to foster understanding and support for the missions. In 1925 he was placed in charge of a permanent mission exhibit on Vatican grounds and later he wrote a book on this project, *The Vatican Missionary Exposition, a Window on the World* (New York 1925). In 1927 he took the lead in establishing the *Fides News Service*, a worldwide organization for the dissemination of mission news, for which he served as director for seven years.

Considine's skill in numerous foreign languages and his firsthand knowledge of far-flung missionary posts brought him a number of diplomatic opportunities. He served as secretary on behalf of the Vatican on a diplomatic mission to Ethiopia in 1929. In the mid-1930s, he spent nearly two years on an expedition that took him across Asia, throughout the East Indies, and over the African continent to learn first-hand of the conditions of missionary life and work. He published a series of articles chronicling his travels, which later appeared as the book *Across a World* (Toronto 1942). In 1934, Considine was called back to Maryknoll headquarters in New York to serve as a member of the general council and was later elected vicar-general, a post he held until 1946.

In the United States, Considine played a key role, along with Bishop Fulton SHEEN and Vincentian Fred McGuire, in organizing the highly successful Mission Secretariat meetings in Washington, D.C. When, at the insistence of Cardinal Cushing, the American Bishop's Conference set up a Latin American Department, Considine was placed at its head and published his *Call for Forty Thousand* (New York 1946). At the end of this term, advanced in years, he returned to Maryknoll where he taught, wrote extensively, and founded *Channel*, a quarterly journal on missionary activity.

Bibliography: A. DRIES, *The Missionary Movement in American Catholic History* (Maryknoll 1998). A. DRIES, "The Legacy of John J. Considine, MM," *International Bulletin of Missionary Research* 21 (1997) 80–84.

[R. E. SHERIDAN]

CONSILIUM

VATICAN COUNCIL II left the implementation of its broad principles and decrees concerning reform of the Roman liturgy to the pope, as the Council of TRENT had done in 1563. Its plan was that the revision of liturgical service books should be undertaken by a postconciliar commission rather than by the Congregation of Rites which had had this function since 1588. The Council's 1963 constitution on the liturgy specified: "Experts are to be employed on the task, and bishops are to be consulted, from various parts of the world" (No. 25).

Organization and Scope. The commission was set up promptly by Pope PAUL VI through the apostolic letter *Sacram Liturgiam* of Jan. 25, 1964, and called the Council (*Consilium*) for the Implementation of the Constitution on the Sacred Liturgy. Its membership included bishops from various parts of the world together with a few curial cardinals; its consultors were largely from Europe. Continuity in members and consultors was preserved with the preparatory (1960–62) and conciliar (1962–63) commissions on the liturgy. The first president was Cardinal Giacomo Lercaro, Archbishop of Bologna (later succeeded by Cardinal Benno Gut); its secretary was Annibale Bugnini, CM, who had served as secretary of the preparatory commission that had drawn up the schema of the liturgical constitution.

The Consilium's relation with the existing Congregation of Rites was defined in a compromise: the Consilium was primarily a study body, with its body of experts distributed by subject matter in subcommittees called *coetus studiorum;* its texts were submitted to the Congregation of Rites and then issued by that dicastery over the signatures of the prefect of the Congregation and the president of the Consilium. Thus, with few exceptions the Consilium did not promulgate the results of its work, but it did have authority to conduct or permit experiments looking to the revision of rites, and it was responsible for the Roman confirmation of decisions taken by episcopal conferences in liturgical matters, especially approval of translations by the conferences. In 1965 the Consilium initiated a monthly journal of information and brief studies, *Notitiae*.

The principal activity of the Consilium was the reform of the corpus of Roman liturgical books, since such revision was conceived as the primary means to achieve the reform purposes of the constitution on the liturgy, as distinguished from its doctrinal and educational purposes. Nevertheless, a certain priority had to be given to the preparation of several instructions, partly to provide an interim simplification of liturgical forms, partly to supplement formal changes with doctrinal guidance.

Instructions. The first of these instructions was dated Sept. 26, 1964 (*Inter Oecumenici,* instruction on the proper implementation of the constitution on the liturgy); it determined procedures for the introduction of the vernacular in the liturgy, enumerated responsibilities of national and diocesan liturgical commissions, and made initial, interim simplifications. This document was followed by a second instruction of implementation (May 4, 1967) and a third instruction, which recapitulated a number of cautions against liturgical excesses (Sept. 5, 1970). A major decree, issued May 7, 1965, determined the rite and norms for concelebration of the Eucharist and Communion under both kinds.

Two lengthy instructions were prepared by the Consilium and issued by the Congregation of Rites in 1967. The first dealt with music in the liturgy (March 5, 1967) and attempted to foster excellence in liturgical music without detriment to artistic freedom; to encourage as much singing, especially congregational singing, as is appropriate to each celebration of worship; and to resolve some of the tensions between Latin and vernacular texts as the basis for musical settings. At the same time the Consilium readied for publication the *Graduale Simplex* (Sept. 3, 1967), which served as a model for similar simplifications of the Mass chants in other languages.

The second major instruction of 1967 was on Eucharistic worship (issued on May 25). It treated the Eucharistic celebration in principle and in detail and also gave revised norms for the Eucharistic cult outside Mass; these norms for Eucharistic reservation, exposition, and processions were simplified. Other instances of instructions dealing with concrete ritual questions for the interim period include: instruction on simplification of pontifical rites and insignia (May 21, 1968); instruction on Masses for special groups (May 15, 1969); instruction on the manner of administering Communion (May 29, 1969).

Revision of Service Books. Although these and similar documents include permanent material and norms, they are secondary in significance to the major work of the Consilium throughout this period, the revision of the service books. This project resembled in scope the work done after the Council of Trent when the modern Roman liturgical books were edited. The passage of four centuries, however, made available critical texts of ancient and medieval liturgies, the insights of the modern liturgical movement, a pastoral and popular dimension enhanced by ecclesiological studies, and a vastly greater measure of consultation and even experimentation. The process regularly included successive stages of drafts prepared by a *coetus studiorum,* examination by consultors and others, practical experimentation in many cases, review by a central body of consultors, and submission to the plenary session of members of the Consilium, in which both consultors and a small number of observers from other Christian communions participated.

The work of the Consilium was guided by the doctrinal, disciplinary, and liturgical principles of the Vatican II constitution on the liturgy. Because contemporary pastoral accommodation had to be taken into account, proposals for revision were sought and received from all parts of the Latin Church, in addition to the investigation of historical precedents. Because modern service books in Latin must serve the whole of the Latin Church—and serve principally as the basis of service books in the modern languages—they cannot envision all the potential needs of various cultures and countries; the Consilium therefore developed both a pattern of adaptations left to the discretion of episcopal conferences, bishops, and priests, and also an extensive provision of options and alternatives. Particular attention was paid to the introductions to the simplified rites; these *praenotanda* are doctrinal and pastoral as well as ritual and juridical. The most notable example is the general instruction of the Roman Missal issued in 1969.

The first result of this program was a section of the Roman Pontifical "revised by decree of the Second Vatican Ecumenical Council and promulgated by authority of Pope Paul VI." It included the rites for the ordination of presbyters, and deacons, and was promulgated Aug. 15, 1968. By 1973 the entire Roman Missal, almost all the Roman Ritual, the Liturgy of the Hours and some parts of the Roman Pontifical had appeared.

The Consilium ceased to be an autonomous body within the Roman Curia with the creation of the Congregation for Divine Worship (May 8, 1969), into which it was integrated.

[F. R. MCMANUS/EDS.]

CONSISTORY

A solemn assembly of all cardinals present in Rome, presided over by the pope, that considers certain of the gravest matters concerning the government of the universal Church. The same name (*consistorium*) was used for a meeting between the emperor and his major counselors in ancient Roman times.

Three kinds of consistories may be distinguished.

(1) The secret, or ordinary, consistory, at which no one may be present except the sovereign pontiff and the cardinals. It is generally held in the Consistorial Hall of the apostolic palace, and after the *extra omnes* the pope generally makes a speech, which is subsequently published. Secret consistories are summoned by the pope when he wishes to create new cardinals, to accept their resignations, to announce a Holy Year, to nominate bishops, and to determine whether a servant of God, already *beatus,* or blessed, should be canonized. Each cardinal individually gives his consent.

(2) The public consistory, generally held in St. Peter's Basilica or in the Sistine Chapel. All the bishops

of Rome and the area around Rome are automatically invited and any others are admitted, as are the papal household and the diplomats accredited to the Holy See. During these public consistories there takes place the *perorationes* for canonizations, the postulations for the pallia, which metropolitans (and some archbishops, non-metropolitans, and bishops who enjoy the privilege) must request after nomination to their see. Here the famous cardinal's hat is imposed on the new cardinals who have been created during a preceding secret consistory.

(3) Semi-public consistories. Besides the cardinals, the above-mentioned bishops are also summoned to these, while all other patriarchs and bishops are also admitted. All have the right to vote. The purpose of these consistories is to ask those present whether the affairs dealt with in the secret consistory, generally held some time beforehand, may proceed.

See Also: CARDINAL.

[P. C. VAN LIERDE]

CONSOBRINO, JOÃO (SOBRINHO)

Theologian; b. Lisbon, beginning of the 15th century; d. Lisbon, Jan. 11, 1486. He entered the Carmelite Order and obtained the master's degree at Oxford in 1449. He became professor of theology and Canon Law in Portugal, and as such was honored with the surname Magister Maximus. He was also court preacher and confessor to King Alfonso V. He became provincial of the Portuguese Carmelite province. Historians praise his devotion to Our Lady and his ability as a preacher and writer. Of the many works attributed to him only one was certainly his, *De iustitia commutativa, arte campsoria ac alearum ludo* (Paris 1483). In it he makes an important contribution to the doctrinal formulation of economic problems.

Bibliography: *Bibliotheca carmelitico-Lusitana* (Rome 1754) 134–136. M. B. AMZALAK, *Frei João Sobrinho e as doutrinas económicas da idade-média* (Lisbon 1945). P. SERVAIS, *Dictionnaire de théologie catholique*, ed. A. VACANT et al. (Paris 1903–50) 3.1:1197.

[H. SPIKKER]

CONSOLATA MISSIONARIES

A congregation whose official title is the Institute of the Consolata for Foreign Missions (IMC), founded at Turin, Italy in 1901 by Blessed Giuseppe Allamano, the nephew of St. Joseph CAFASSO. The plans for the foundation, however, can be traced back to 1891. The institute is a religious congregation, with simple vows, consisting of priests and brothers. Its principal objective is mission and evangelization, especially among non-Christians. The congregation was given final approval by the Holy See on Sept. 7, 1923. Missions were initially established in Africa, followed by the Americas and South Korea. The congregation arrived in the United States in 1946 and in Canada in 1947. Since 1994, the U.S. and Canadian communities have constituted the North American Region, with centers in Montreal, Quebec, Toronto, Riverside, Calif., Buffalo, N.Y., Somerset, N.J., and a house of studies in Washington, D.C. The congregation has communities in 26 countries in Europe (Spain, Great Britain, Italy, Portugal and Switzerland), Africa (South Africa, Ivory Coast, Ethiopia, Guinea, Kenya, Liberia, Libya, Mozambique, Uganda, Somalia, Tanzania and Congo), Asia (South Korea), and the Americas (U.S., Canada, Argentina, Bolivia, Brazil, Colombia, Ecuador and Venezuela). The generalate is in Rome.

The Consolata Missionaries have a special bond of unity and collaboration with the Consolata Missionary Sisters founded by Allamano in 1910. Following the example of their founder, and the teachings of Saints FRANCIS DE SALES, John BOSCO, and Joseph Cafasso, the Consolata Missionaries cultivate a deep devotion to the Virgin Mary.

Bibliography: D. AGASSO, *Joseph Allamano Founder of the Consolata Missionaries* (Turin 1991). L. SALES, *The Spiritual Life: from the Spiritual Conferences of Joseph Allamano* (Turin 1982). G. TEBALDI, *La missione racconta: i missionari della Consolata in cammino con i populi* (Bologna 1999). I. TUBALDO, *Giuseppe Allamano: il suo tempo, la sua vita, la sua opera*, 4 v. (Turin 1986).

[U. VIGLINO/EDS.]

CONSOLATIONS, SPIRITUAL

In general, consolation is the delight or satisfaction experienced when distress or suffering is alleviated or positive support and encouragement are given. The spiritual life alternates between periods of delight and suffering, not only at a given stage but throughout the progress of a soul from the beginning of that life to its culmination in perfection. Consequently, it is lawful to speak of spiritual consolations in the sense of relief from suffering, comfort in the time of trial, or strength for endurance. In this sense spiritual consolations are the counterpart of spiritual desolations.

However, spiritual consolations may also be considered in themselves, either as the concomitant delight that accompanies certain exercises and practices of the spiritual life, or as gifts and favors from God not related to relief from suffering. Psychologically, consolations are experienced in the appetitive faculties of emotions or will, though they may also be of sufficient intensity to overflow to the body itself, as in the case of the gift of tears or ecstatic joy. Knowledge or awareness is required as a necessary disposition, and sometimes the knowledge itself produces a certain delight, as in contemplation, although this is not classified as a spiritual consolation.

Spiritual consolations are always in reference to God or something related to God, though they do not follow by necessity any of man's activities or services in reference to God; rather, the love and service of God may be accompanied by difficulty, suffering, and trials. Therefore, it is important to emphasize the distinction between spiritual consolations and DEVOTION, which is the promptness of the will in reference to those things that pertain to God (i.e., worship, obedience to His laws, performance of duties of state, etc.) and does not necessarily imply delight or sensible consolation. Moreover, spiritual consolations are not a matter of choice, in the sense that one may infallibly experience them through his own efforts, but they tend to proceed naturally from the acts of the spiritual life unless some obstacle prevents them. Some of the more common obstacles are dispositions of temperament (i.e., melancholic or phlegmatic), negative mental attitudes (i.e., sadness, pessimism, scrupulosity, anxiety), internal distractions, habitual sins of intemperance, physical illness or exhaustion, and excessive attachments to worldly things.

As considered in spiritual theology, spiritual consolations are listed as concomitant with activities of the ascetical state (effects of the operations of grace and the infused virtues) or the mystical state (effects of the working of the gifts of the Holy Spirit), or they may be charismatic (extraordinary gifts from God) or preternatural (due to the influence of the devil). Examples of spiritual consolations proper to the ascetical state are (1) the consolation produced by the love of God, known as the fervor or joy of charity; (2) the consolation that accompanies the work of virtue, requiring a relative perfection or facility; (3) the consolation of submission to God's will, experienced usually as a peace and quiet of soul; (4) the consolation that accompanies certain types of prayer, and especially affective prayer and the prayer of simplicity as well as vocal prayer, private or public. Certain physical and psychical factors will foster spiritual consolations: dispositions of temperament (sanguine and choleric), positive mental attitudes (optimism, cheerfulness, empathy, generosity), bodily health, and detachment both from self and from worldly things.

In the mystical state the spiritual consolations are usually experienced as concomitant phenomena of certain grades of mystical contemplation, though immersed sometimes in darkness and alternating with desolations, and in the operations of the virtues perfected by the gifts of the Holy Spirit. In this state also one receives any charismatic consolations that God wishes to give, although His giving is not necessarily restricted to those in a mystical state. Normally the devil does not produce consolations, but sadness and aridity, but if he does produce them, it is to deceive.

Since spiritual consolations are gifts of God and related to the spiritual life, they can be desired legitimately. However, there is such a danger of becoming attached to the consolations themselves, or of taking selfish satisfaction in them, that spiritual writers warn souls to use discretion and humble resignation.

Bibliography: L. POULLIER, *Dictionnaire de spiritualité ascétique et mystique,* ed. M. VILLER et al. (Paris 1932–) 2:1617–34. J. G. ARINTERO, *The Mystical Evolution in the Development and Vitality of the Church,* tr. J. AUMANN, 2 v. (St. Louis 1949–51). J. DE GUIBERT, *The Theology of the Spiritual Life,* tr. P. BARRETT (New York 1953). JOHN OF THE CROSS, *Dark Night of the Soul,* in *Complete Works,* tr. E. A. PEERS, 3 v. in 1 (repr. Westminster, Md. 1963). A. POULAIN, *The Graces of Interior Prayer,* tr. L. L. YORKE SMITH, ed. J. V. BAINVEL (St. Louis 1950). A. TANQUEREY, *The Spiritual Life,* tr. H. BRANDERIS (2d ed. Tournai 1930; repr. Westminster, Md. 1945).

[J. AUMANN]

CONSORS PATERNI LUMINIS

A hymn that was historically sung on Tuesdays at Matins in the medieval Divine Office. It has been attributed to Ambrose, but it is missing from the Ambrosian MSS and, therefore, cannot be claimed as his. It is included in a group of 16 hymns ascribed to Gregory the Great, but Gregory's authorship cannot be proved. The verse is iambic dimeter and has three strophes plus doxology, the latter probably added to bring the number of strophes to four as in other hymns with which it is grouped in the MSS. The text of the hymn escaped the reforms of Pope CLEMENT VIII (1535). The text of the hymn calls upon Christ, the Light and Source of man's light, to dispel the darkness of souls, drive off evil spirits, and remove man's proneness to sloth. The sinner prays also for pardon so that his prayer may win acceptance.

Bibliography: A. S. WALPOLE, ed., *Early Latin Hymns* (Cambridge, Eng. 1922) 268–269.

[M. M. BEYENKA/EDS.]

CONSTABILIS, ST.

Benedictine abbot; b. Tresino, Lucania, Italy, *c.* 1060; d. La Cava, Feb. 17, 1124. He was a member of the Gentilcore family; at the age of seven he entered the Abbey of LA CAVA near Salerno under LEO OF CAVA. In 1118 he was made coadjutor to Abbot Peter, and on March 4, 1122, he was chosen the fourth abbot of the house, but he died after a rule of only two years. Apparently, he built the town of Castel Abbate and is now venerated as its patron. Many miracles have been attributed to Constabilis; his cult was recognized in 1893.

Feast: Feb. 17.

Bibliography: *Acta Sanctae Sedis* Feb. 3:42–46. VENUSINUS, *Vita ss. abbatum Cavensium . . .* (Cava 1912) 71–87. L. P. GUIL-LAUME, *Le navi Cavensi* (Cava 1876). A. M. ZIMMERMANN, *Kalendarium Benedictinum* (Metten 1933–38) 1:225.

[E. J. KEALEY]

CONSTABLE, CUTHBERT

English Catholic landowner and amateur of the arts; b. Wycliffe, North Riding, Yorkshire, *c.* 1666; d. Constable Hall, March 27, 1746. The son of Francis Tunstall, he was educated as a lay pensioner at Douai College and qualified in medicine at the University of Montpellier. In 1714, by an arrangement then common, he succeeded to the very large East Riding estates of his uncle Robert Constable, Viscount Dunbar and changed his surname to Constable. Until his death he devoted himself to improving his houses and estates and to the cultivation of his scientific, antiquarian, and literary tastes. Such activities had been common among the better-educated Catholic gentry for a century or more; he is notable for the quantity of money he was able to spend on his interests. Cuthbert was a constant correspondent of Hearne, the antiquary, and helped Charles Dodd (alias Hugh Tootell) and John Knaresbrough with money and materials for their projects in Church history. He was devoted to the memory of Abraham Woodhead, the Oxford Yorkshire convert and apologist, assidously collected his papers and manuscripts, and built him a new tomb at Oxford. Cuthbert's own literary achievement was apparently limited to an edition of the third part of Woodhead's *Brief Account of Church Government,* including a new biography of Woodhead and a list of his known works (London 1736). Cuthbert also collected books and antiquarian and genealogical manuscripts. His son and successor at Burton Constable, William Constable, to whom he especially bequeathed his library, was an even more earnest patron and collector. It is therefore hard to distinguish the acquisitions of the father from those of the son.

Bibliography: J. KIRK, *Biographies of English Catholics in the 18th Century,* ed. J. H. POLLEN and E. BURTON (New York 1909). J. GILLOW, *A Literary and Biographical History or Bibliographical Dictionary of the English Catholics from 1534 to the Present Time* (London-New York 1885–1902; repr. New York 1961) 1:548–551.

[H. AVELING]

CONSTANCE, COUNCIL OF

An assembly, usually reckoned as the 16th general council of the Church, meeting from Nov. 5, 1414, to April 22, 1418.

Constance was once the see city of the largest diocese in Germany. The see was founded (*c.* 600) as a suffragan to Besançon and was transferred (*c.* 780) to the jurisdiction of Mainz. It was the scene of conflict between Franks and Alamanni, popes and Hohenstaufen, French and Hapsburgs; the jurisdiction of its bishops was contested by the abbots of SANKT GALLEN and REICHENAU and by its cathedral chapter. In the Middle Ages it had its own Breviary and Missal and its excellent library was used by the fathers of the Council of Constance. Chronic financial insecurity and laxity of clerical discipline antedated ZWINGLI's triumph in 1522 and in 1527 bishop and chapter moved permanently to Meersburg, where a seminary was built in 1735. Some reforms followed the Council of TRENT, but after the Napoleonic wars the see was suppressed in 1821, its jurisdiction passing to Freiburg im Breisgau in 1827.

[E. P. COLBERT]

In the course of the council's session more than 300 bishops attended together with 29 cardinals, three patriarchs, 33 archbishops, several hundred doctors of theology and canon law, more than 100 abbots and a dozen ruling princes. It was the greatest representative assembly of medieval Christendom. Three great tasks faced the fathers of the council: to end the WESTERN SCHISM, to combat the new heresies of John Wyclif and John Hus and to reform the institutional structure of the Church. The activities of the council are considered below under these three headings. A final section deals with the authenticity of certain controversial decrees enacted at Constance.

The Council And The Western Schism

In 1414 there were three claimants to the papacy, for the schism arising out of the disputed election of 1378 (*see* URBAN VI, POPE) had been complicated by the creation of a third line of popes at the Council of PISA (summoned in 1409 by dissident cardinals of both Roman and Avignonese obediences). It was the second pope of this Pisan line, styled antipope JOHN XXIII, who summoned the Council of Constance. He did so reluctantly and under extreme pressure from King SIGISMUND, the emperor-elect, who played a leading role at the council as its official protector. Several of the leading theorists of the Conciliarism [*see* CONCILIARISM (HISTORY OF)] were also active in managing the affairs of the assembly, and from the outset many fathers showed themselves determined to end the schism at all costs, even if this involved an attack on the traditional doctrine of papal sovereignty and the substitution of a theory of conciliar supremacy. John XXIII hoped that the council would be content to condemn his two rivals, GREGORY XII and (antipope) BENEDICT XIII; and he relied on the support of the numerous Italian prelates at Constance—nearly half the bishops present at the opening session were Italians—to prevent any attack on his own position. This hope was frustrated when the English and German representatives insisted on a system of voting by nations, each national group casting one vote in the formal sessions of the council. At first the assembly was divided into four nations—English, French, German and Italian—and a fifth was added after Spanish delegates joined the council in October of 1416. All debate was carried on in separate assemblies of the nations and in a steering committee composed of deputies elected from each nation. When unanimity was reached among the nations, a general session of the whole council formally promulgated the decisions arrived at without further discussion. The cardinals complained that this system excluded them from any effective voice in the deliberations of the council and in May of 1415 they were allowed to appoint six representatives to the committee of deputies of the nations. In July, the sacred college began to cast one vote in the general sessions along with the votes of the four nations.

At the beginning of 1415 the council began to attack the grievous problems of the schism. John XXIII was in an especially vulnerable position since he had led a notoriously evil life, and in February it was suggested that the council should appoint a commission to investigate his alleged crimes. Faced with the threat of a public scandal, John solemnly promised to abdicate at the second general session of the council held on March 2, but then he changed his mind and fled from the council on March 20, taking refuge with Duke Frederick of Austria. In these circumstances the prelates assembled at Constance could continue to function as a general council only if they were prepared to assert that the members of a council, separated from the pope, enjoyed direct divine guidance and possessed full authority over the Church. John XXIII intended to disrupt the council by his flight. In fact, his action had the effect of pushing the fathers into extreme statements of conciliar supremacy that many of the moderates would have preferred to avoid.

King Sigismund took the lead in organizing a third general session (March 26), which decreed that the coun-

Woodcut from "Concilium Book," of Ulrich of Reichenthal (Augsburg 1483), depicting scene from Council of Constance, as Antipope John XXIII, prepares to meet with Emperor Sigismund.

cil retained its full authority in spite of the pope's departure and declared that it would not disband until the work of ending the schism and reforming the Church was completed. The French, English and German nations then agreed on a statement asserting in general terms the superiority of general councils over the papacy [*See* COUNCILS, GENERAL (ECUMENICAL), THEOLOGY OF]. The cardinals protested to Sigismund against the enactment of such a decree, and at the fourth general session (March 30) a more moderate one was read by Cardinal Francesco ZABARELLA and approved. This decree asserted only that the particular council then assembled at Constance possessed authority over the pope "in matters pertaining to the faith and the ending of the present schism." That is to say, it claimed supreme authority for a council only in the quite abnormal circumstances then existing, when there was no certainty as to who was true pope. This did not satisfy the more radical conciliarists, and antipapal feeling at Constance reached a new height during the following week as it became evident that John had no intention of rejoining the council and that he might well revoke his promise to abdicate.

At the fifth general session (April 6) the council enacted the decree *Sacrosancta,* containing the full statement on conciliar supremacy originally approved by the nations. Seven cardinals attended the session and acquiesced in the promulgation of the decree, though Zabarella refused to read it. The controversial enactment declared:

> This holy synod of Constance, constituting a General Council and lawfully assembled to root out the present schism and bring about the reform of the church in head and members . . . declares that, being lawfully assembled in the Holy Spirit, constituting a General Council and representing the Catholic Church militant, it holds power immediately from Christ and that anyone of whatsoever state or dignity, even the papal, is bound to obey it in matters which pertain to the faith, the rooting out of the said schism and the general reform of the church in head and members. Further it declares that any person of whatsoever rank, state or dignity, even the papal, who contumaciously refuses to obey the mandates, statutes, ordinances or instructions made or to be made by this holy synod or by any other General Council lawfully assembled concerning the aforesaid matters or matters pertaining to them shall, unless he repents, be subjected to fitting penance and duly punished, recourse being had if necessary to other sanctions of the law. [H. von der Hardt, *Magnum oecumenicum Constantiense concilium,* 7 v. (Frankfurt-Leipzig 1697–1742) 4:98]

The authenticity of the decree is discussed below.

John XXIII's defiance was short-lived. Sigismund made war on Frederick of Austria, who quickly submitted and the pope was arrested in Germany on May 17 and brought back to the council as a prisoner. On May 29 he was declared guilty of perjury, simony and scandalous misconduct and was formally deposed from the papacy. John accepted the sentence meekly and relinquished all claim to the papal throne. Once he was removed from the scene, Gregory XII, the pope of the Roman line, conveyed to the council his willingness to abdicate provided that he was permitted to convoke the assembled prelates for a second time as a general council and so assert once more the legitimacy of his own line of popes. The prelates at Constance were in no mood to make difficulties and they consented to this procedure. Gregory's abdication was formally accepted by the council on July 4, 1415.

There remained only Benedict XIII. Sigismund undertook a journey to Perpignan to try persuading him to abdicate too, but the aged pontiff remained obdurate to the end. At this point (December of 1415) his own cardinals and the Spanish kings and bishops at last abandoned his cause and agreed to join the Council at Constance. On July 26, 1417, Benedict was declared guilty of perjury, heresy and schism and deprived of all rights to the papacy. After complicated disputes about the manner of electing a new pope it was agreed that six deputies from each nation, as well as the cardinals of all three obediences, should participate in the conclave. For a valid election the support of two-thirds of the cardinals and two-thirds of the deputies of each nation was required. The conclave lasted only three days and on Nov. 11, 1417, the electors chose Odo Colonna, a cardinal originally of the Roman obedience who had joined the Council of Pisa and subsequently helped to elect John XXIII. He took the name MARTIN V. With his election the Western Schism came to an end.

The Council And Hersey

The most important doctrinal issues considered at Constance were those raised by WYCLIF and HUS concerning the nature of the Church and the Sacrament of the Eucharist. Wyclif's teachings had already been condemned in England by Archbishop William COURTENAY (1382); they were again condemned at Constance. Meanwhile from the first years of the 15th century, Hus had begun to spread Wyclifite doctrines in Bohemia. His teaching there had an explosive effect because it became identified with a resurgence of Czech national feeling directed against the German and Catholic imperial authority; underlying all the major problems that faced the council was a growing tension between new nationalist loyalties and the old ideal of a united Christendom. Hus traveled voluntarily to Constance in order to defend his position. He received a safe-conduct from Sigismund, but this protected him only from illegal violence not from judicial proceedings before the council and Hus was in fact treated with scant courtesy. He was arrested for presuming to say Mass while under sentence of suspension and then questioned over a period of five weeks by interrogators who showed no interest in exploring the possibilities of a reconciliation but aimed only at Hus's total submission or immediate condemnation. He was finally found guilty of heresy in a general session of the council, and on the same day (July 6, 1415) he was burned at the stake by the secular power. Although Hus's teachings were certainly unorthodox, the extreme harshness of the treatment meted out to him must be explained in part by personal and national antagonisms. Above all, his refusal to accept the authority of the council in a matter of faith struck at the very heart of the conciliar claim to represent the universal Church and to hold its authority directly from

Christ. The council could not acquiesce in such an attitude without abandoning its own pretensions.

The same session that condemned Hus's teachings considered also another doctrinal problem, the licitness of TYRANNICIDE. This was a burning issue in contemporary French politics; in 1407 a partisan of the Duke of Burgundy had murdered the Duke of Orléans and a theologian of Paris, JOANNES PARVUS, had defended the act as justifiable tyrannicide. The council condemned in general terms the proposition that "any subject or vassal can and should licitly and meritoriously kill any tyrant . . . without awaiting the sentence or mandate of any judge" (*Magnum oecumenicum Constantiense concilium,* 4:439). But, in spite of repeated pleas by Jean GERSON, the fathers refused to condemn the writings of Joannes Parvus specifically. A somewhat similar case arose in 1417 in connection with a work of the Dominican John of FALKENBERG. He maintained that it was licit to assassinate the Polish king or exterminate the Polish people because they had allied themselves with pagans against the TEUTONIC KNIGHTS. His tract was denounced as heretical by a commission appointed to examine it and by the nations, but it was not formally condemned in a general session of the council.

The Council And Reform

From the beginning, the leaders of the council had regarded the reform of the Church as one of their principal objectives; and from the point of view of the bishops at Constance, the reforms most obviously needed were a reduction of papal taxation and a diminution of the papal power to make ecclesiastical appointments within their dioceses. The issue of reform became a major topic of discussion in the weeks after Benedict XIII's deposition (July of 1417). A dispute arose then as to whether the council, functioning as sovereign head of the Church, should carry through the work of reform before electing a new pope or whether the task should be undertaken after an election, by pope and council together. The dispute was complicated by a growing antagonism between the French and English nations arising out of the circumstances of the Hundred Years' War, but by early October of 1417 a compromise was reached. It was agreed that the reforms that had already been approved unanimously should be promulgated at once and a decree enacted, stating that further reforms would be undertaken immediately after the election. Accordingly, on Oct. 5, 1417, the council promulgated its first five reform measures. The most important by far was the decree *Frequens,* concerning the frequent summoning of general councils. It laid down that five years after the dispersal of the Council of Constance a second council was to meet, then a third one seven years after the end of the second, and that subsequently a council was to meet every ten years. The obvious intent was to limit the independent power of the PAPACY for the future.

On March 20, 1418, seven additional reform decrees were promulgated by Pope Martin V with the approval of the council. They dealt almost exclusively with papal taxation and abuses of papal PROVISIONS; for example, the pope relinquished his claim to the revenues of vacant sees and undertook to levy general taxation in future only in grave emergencies. Papal dispensations allowing men to hold ecclesiastical benefices for which they were not qualified by the appropriate ordination or consecration were forbidden. And it was decreed that anyone, even a pope or cardinal who participated in a simoniacal transaction, should be *ipso facto* excommunicated.

The reform work of the Council of Constance must be accounted a disappointing failure. The conciliarists always talked of a reform of the Church in head and members, but the only practical measures they proposed aimed solely at weakening the constitutional and financial position of the head and as it turned out, this did not produce any automatic upsurge of vitality in the members. There were indeed abuses of over-centralization to be corrected; but they were only symptoms of a more general malaise, a widespread perversion of the structure of pastoral offices in the Church that was generally tolerated because it provided sinecures for bureaucrats and others at all levels of ecclesiastical and secular government. The reformers of Constance were animated by sincerity and good will, but they did not display an adequate understanding of the kind of institutional change, especially in the members, that was needed to revitalize the whole life of the Church.

Authenticity Of The Council's Decrees

The problem of authenticity has been raised mainly in connection with the decrees *Sacrosancta* and *Frequens* described above. *Frequens,* however, is of relatively minor importance. Although inspired by an extreme conciliarist ideology, it was in essence an administrative reform that, like many other such measures adopted in general councils, was implemented for as long as it seemed to promote the welfare of the Church and abandoned when it apparently did not do so. *Sacrosancta* has more the appearance of a dogmatic definition of a fundamental doctrine of ecclesiology. Two problems are involved in the discussion of *Sacrosancta*'s authenticity. When did the assembly at Constance become a legitimately convoked general council? And which decrees of the assembly did Pope Martin V confirm? Very few Catholic scholars maintain that John XXIII was a legitimately elected pope or that the assembly convoked by him (November of 1414) was, from the beginning, a legitimate general council. Many hold that it became so when Gregory XII convoked it (July of 1415). Others argue that the council acquired an ecumenical character only after the Spaniards joined it (October of 1416). It seems quite certain that the last four sessions, held after the election of Martin V (November of 1417), were sessions of a lawful general council. *Sacrosancta* was enacted before Gregory's intervention. Hence if the majority opinion is accepted, the whole question of its authenticity depends on whether it was subsequently confirmed by Martin V.

Martin was certainly not an ardent or extreme conciliarist..Speaking in consistory on March 10, 1418, he forbade appeals from the pope to a future general council (*Magnum oecumenicum Constantiense concilium,* 4: 1532). On the other hand, there could be no question of his repudiating the work of the council; to have done so would have been to repudiate the validity of his own election. Equally, there could be no question of the council's presenting all its earlier decrees to the pope for his solemn confirmation since the whole achievement of the fathers in ending the schism rested on the assumption that their decrees were valid of themselves, even without papal approval. The most important declaration of Martin himself on the whole question came at the closing session of the council on April 22, 1418. The Polish representatives disturbed the meeting by demanding an explicit condemnation of Falkenberg from the pope. Martin silenced the clamor that arose and then declared "that he would uphold and inviolably observe everything decided, concluded, and decreed in matters of faith by the present Council acting as a Council (*conciliariter*) . . . and not otherwise" (*Magnum oecumenicum Constantiense concilium,* 4:1557). The following arguments have been advanced by those who hold that these words did not constitute an endorsement of *Sacrosancta.* (1) The decree was not a "matter of faith"; that is, it was not intended as a dogmatic definition binding for all time. Here it seems necessary to distinguish. The assertion in *Sacrosancta* that a pope was bound to obey any general council in matters of faith seems clearly to have been proposed as a matter of faith itself, that is, as a permanent definition of doctrine. On the other hand, in the references to "the said Schism" and "the reform of the church," the fathers may well have had in mind only the immediate future of their own work. (2) The cardinals did not support the decree. But the cardinals present acquiesced and other decrees of general councils have been enacted with fewer cardinals present. (3) The pope intended his words to apply only to the case of Falkenberg. But the pope was clearly distinguishing between Falkenberg's condemnation, from which he withheld approval, and the other enactments of council, which he did approve. (4) The

crucial fifth session of the council was not held *conciliariter* because it was disorderly. But there is no reason to suppose that the pope was distinguishing between a session held *conciliariter* and one held *tumultualiter,* as has been suggested. His statement, taken in context, seems clearly to refer to a distinction between decrees enacted *conciliariter,* that is, in a general session of the whole council, and those (such as Falkenberg's condemnation) enacted *nationaliter,* that is, in the preliminary sessions of the nations.

It seems most probable then that Martin V did express his approval of *Sacrosancta.* It seems equally probable that he did not understand it in the sense of the more radical conciliarists. The decree referred to "any other General Council lawfully assembled." Except in the peculiar circumstances prevailing in 1415, such a council would necessarily be summoned by a pope. Its lawful decrees would be those promulgated by the pope and the fathers acting in concert. And it is, of course, entirely proper to assert that a pope, like any other Christian, is bound by such conciliar canons in matters of faith. However this may be, it seems clear that a decree enacted by an assembly of ecclesiastical notables (who probably did not constitute a validly convoked council at the time of the enactment) and subsequently approved by a pope in an unpremeditated speech uttered in the heat of an angry debate cannot be regarded as a solemn dogmatic definition of a legitimate general council. It may be that the decree is susceptible of an orthodox interpretation. It may be that the pope and the prelates assembled at Constance were simply mistaken. One major result of modern scholarship on this whole question has been to emphasize how very rare are the circumstances in which doctrinal pronouncements by popes can be regarded as infallible definitions. For another discussion of the question reaching different conclusions see A. Baudrillart, *Dictionnaire de théologie catholique,* ed. A. Vacant et al., 15 v. (Paris 1903–50) 3:1220–24.

Bibliography: Sources. *Acta concilii Constanciensis,* ed. H. FINKE, 4 v. (Münster 1896–1928). H. VON DER HARDT, *Magnum oecumenicum Constantiense concilium,* 7 v. (Frankfurt-Leipzig 1697–1742). J. D. MANSI, *Sacrorum Conciliorum nova et amplissima collectio,* 31 v. (Florence-Venice 1757–98) v. 27. H. FINKE, *Forschungen und Quellen zur Geschichte des Konstanzer Konzils* (Paderborn 1889). *The Council of Constance,* ed. J. H. MUNDY and K. M. WOODY, tr. L. R. LOOMIS (New York 1961), includes three major narrative sources, Richental's *Chronicle,* Fillastre's *Diary* and Cerretano's *Journal.* Literature. B. HÜBLER, *Die Constanzer Reformation* (Leipzig 1867). M. CREIGHTON, *A History of the Papacy during the Period of the Reformation,* 5 v. (London 1882–94) v. 1. N. VALOIS, *La France et le grand schisme d'occident,* 4 v. (Paris 1896–1902). E. J. KITTS, *In the Days of the Councils* (London 1908). C. J. VON HEFELE, *Histoire des conciles d'après les documents originaux,* tr. and continued by H. LECLERCQ. 10 v. in 19 (Paris 1907–38) v. 7.1. J. HOLLNSTEINER, "König Sigismund auf dem Konstanzer Konzil," *Mitteilungen des Instituts für öster-*

reichische Geschichtsforschung 41 (1926) 185–200. A. C. FLICK, *The Decline of the Medieval Church*, 2 v. (London 1930) v. 2. P. ARENDT, *Die Predigten des Konstanzer Konzils* (Freiburg 1933). K. ZÄHRINGER, *Das Kardinalskollegium auf dem Konstanzer Konzil bis zur Absetzung Papst Johanns XXIII* (Münster 1935). H. FINKE, "Die Nation in den spätmittelalterlichen allgemeinen Konzilien," *Historisches Jahrbuch der Görres-Gesellschaft* 57 (1937) 323–338. L. R. LOOMIS, "Nationality at the Council of Constance," *American Historical Review* 44 (1938–39) 508–527. E. F. JACOB, *Essays in the Conciliar Epoch* (rev. ed. Notre Dame, Ind. 1963). P. H. STUMP, "The Reform of Papal Taxation at the Council of Constance (1414–1418)," *Speculum* 64 (1989): 69–105. E. C. TATNALL, "The Condemnation of John Wyclif at the Council of Constance," in *Councils and Assemblies*, ed. G. J. CUMING and D. BAKER (Cambridge 1971) 209–218.

[B. TIERNEY]

CONSTANS II POGONATUS, BYZANTINE EMPEROR

Reigned 641 to Sept. 15, 668; b. 630; d. Syracuse. Constans, the son of Constantine III, became emperor late in the year 641 at a time when the Empire was gravely troubled from within by the Monothelitic controversy (*see* MONOTHELITISM) and pressed from without by formidable enemies. The Arabs, who had just taken Alexandria, repeatedly invaded northern Africa, Armenia, and Asia Minor. Increasing the pressure, they organized a navy, plundered Cyprus, Rhodes, and Crete and shattered Byzantine naval supremacy in 655 off the coast of Lycia by their decisive victory over the Byzantine fleet, commanded by Constans himself. But the civil war that broke out among the Arabs after 656 gave the Empire some respite and enabled Constans to chastise the Slavs in Macedonia. Meanwhile Constans sought to end the Monothelitic controversy by his TYPOS decree (648), prohibiting discussion on the question of the divine will or energy. This led to a rift with Rome, to Pope MARTIN I's arrest, imprisonment, and exile to far-off Cherson (Crimea), where he died. In 662, for reasons not entirely clear, Constans left for Italy, and visited Rome, but finally settled in Syracuse, where he was murdered in his bath.

Bibliography: F. DÖLGER, *Corpus der griechischen Urkunden des Mittelalters und der neueren Zeit*, series A, *Regesten* (Munich 1924–32) 1:26–27. G. OSTROGORSKY, *History of the Byzantine State*, tr. J. HUSSEY from 2d German ed. (Oxford 1956); American ed. by P. CHARANIS (New Brunswick, N.J. 1957) 98–110.

[P. CHARANIS]

CONSTANS I, ROMAN EMPEROR

Reigned 337 to 350; b. 320; d. *c.* 350. Son of Constantine, coemperor with his brothers Constantine II and Constantius II, he added Gaul, Britain, and Spain to his own jurisdiction over the prefecture of Italy. This he accomplished by defeating and killing Constantine II in 340. In the defense of his frontiers he expelled the Franks from Gaul in 341 and 342 and cleared Britain of barbarian invaders. Constans was an orthodox Catholic who favored churchmen at his court and strove to moderate Constantius II's ARIANISM. Learning from Oriental bishops of the Arians' tampering with the Nicene Creed in 342, he summoned the Council of SARDICA in 343, hoping to vindicate the decisions of Nicaea. He forced Constantius to reinstate St. ATHANASIUS in Alexandria in 345. As long as Constans lived, the West escaped Arianism. At the request of DONATUS he intervened in the Donatist and Circumcellion revolt in North Africa aiding the Catholic recovery. He prohibited public pagan sacrifices, but his domineering character and tyrannical rule cost him his subjects' good will, and in 350 the usurper Magnentius overthrew him.

Bibliography: O. SEECK, *Paulys Realenzyklopädie der klassischen Altertumswissenschaft*, ed. G. WISSOWA et al. 4.1:948–952. J. PALANQUE, *The Church in the Christian Roman Empire*, tr. E. C. MESSENGER (London 1949). E. STEIN and J. PALANQUE, *Histoire du bas-empire* (Paris 1949–59) v.1. J. PALANQUE, *Dictionnaire d'histoire et de géographie ecclésiastiques*, ed. A. BAUDRILLART et al. (Paris 1912–) 13:583–584.

[R. H. SCHMANDT]

CONSTANTINE IV, BYZANTINE EMPEROR

Reigned September 668 to September 685; b. *c.* 652. He succeeded his father, CONSTANS II. His reign is noted for three important developments: the checking of the Arabs before CONSTANTINOPLE, the foundation of the Bulgarian kingdom, and the settlement of the Monothelitic controversy. The Arabs seized Cyzicus in 670 and made it their base of operations against Constantinople. Their repeated attacks against the Byzantine capital, begun in earnest in 674, were finally broken up in 678 with the aid of Greek fire. Their first attempt to break into Europe thus failed. The Bulgars had made their appearance at the mouth of the Danube in the 670s. Constantine's attempt to check them ended in disaster in 680; they crossed the Danube, occupied the territory between it and the Balkan Mountains, already settled by Slavs, and organized the first Bulgarian kingdom. The Monothelitic controversy was settled by the Council of CONSTANTINOPLE III, which Constantine in consultation with Rome convened in 680. The council declared against MONOTHELITISM, which ceased thereafter to be an issue.

Bibliography: F. DÖLGER, *Corpus der griechischen Urkunden des Mittelalters und der neueren Zeit*, series A, *Regesten* (Munich

1924–32) 1:28–31. G. OSTROGORSKY, *History of the Byzantine State*, tr. J. HUSSEY from 2d German ed. (Oxford 1956); American ed. by P. CHARANIS (New Brunswick, N.J. 1957), 110–116.

[P. CHARANIS]

(1954) 151–160. H. G. BECK, *Kirche und theologische Literatur im byzantinischen Reich* (Munich 1959) 301–303.

[P. CHARANIS]

CONSTANTINE V, BYZANTINE EMPEROR

Reigned June 19, 741, to Sept. 14, 775; b. Constantinople, 718; d. Bulgaria. Constantine was the son of Emperor LEO III. He was crowned coemperor on March 20, 720, by his father; when the latter died in 741, Constantine ascended the throne as sole emperor. He was soon challenged, however, by his brother-in-law, Artabasdus, but was able to dispose of him after some fighting. Constantine's first wife was a Khazar princess. He died while on a campaign.

Constantine's reign is noted for the vigor with which the iconoclastic policy was pursued and for the success of the BYZANTINE EMPIRE against its enemies. He made several expeditions against the Arabs in the East, took the frontier towns of Germaniceia, Militene, and Theodosiopolis, and transplanted many of their inhabitants to Thrace. Though these towns were recovered by the Arabs, their capture by the Byzantines showed that Byzantium was no longer on the defensive. It was against the Bulgars in the Balkan Peninsula, however, that Constantine exerted his greatest military activity. He led nine campaigns on Bulgar soil; and though in the end he failed to destroy the Bulgar kingdom, he dealt it crippling blows. In Italy, however, the Empire lost RAVENNA to the LOMBARDS (751), and the *rapprochement* between the papacy and the FRANKS, initiated in 754, further weakened its position in the West.

In promoting ICONOCLASM, Constantine resorted to two expedients: the calling of the Council of Hieria (754), which declared in favor of iconoclasm, and the use of rigorous measures against those who opposed it. Particularly severe were his acts against monastic establishments: monks were persecuted, monasteries were closed, and their properties were confiscated. Constantine himself participated in the theological discussions over iconoclasm and developed ideas somewhat related to MONOPHYSITISM.

Bibliography: A. LOMBARD, *Constantin V, empereur des Romains* (Paris 1902). F. DÖLGER, *Corpus der griechischen Urkunden des Mittelalters und der neueren Zeit*, series A, *Regesten* (Munich 1924–32) 308–337. G. OSTROGORSKY, *History of the Byzantine State*, tr. J. HUSSEY from 2d German ed. (Oxford 1956); American ed. by P. CHARANIS (New Brunswick, N.J. 1957), 147–155. M. V. ANASIOS, "The Ethical Theory of Images Formulated by the Iconoclasts in 754–815," *Dumbarton Oaks Papers*, Harvard Univ., 8

CONSTANTINE VII PORPHYROGENITUS, BYZANTINE EMPEROR

Reigned 908 to Nov. 9, 959; b. Constantinople, probably May 17 or 18, 905. Constantine was the illegitimate son of the emperor Leo VI and his mistress Zoe Karbonopsina ("with the coal-black eyes"); their subsequent marriage (Leo's fourth), caused a doctrinal schism, the *Tetragamy* conflict. Constantine was crowned Byzantine emperor May 15, 908, but was excluded from power variously by his uncle Alexander, the patriarch I Mystikos, his mother Zoe, and Romanus I Lecapenus, whose daughter he married in 919. It was not until Romanus and his sons had been deposed in January 945 that he assumed sole command.

Constantine promised a break with Romanus' administration, calling his officials, "venal, negligent and unwarlike." He passed legislation to safeguard peasant landowners from powerful magnates, and tried to alleviate the burden of taxation, although Romanus had also been concerned with the protection of the rights of small holders.

Constantine achieved little success in foreign affairs. An expedition to Crete in 949 was a failure, and although Byzantine troops captured Germanikeia in 949 and crossed the Euphrates in 952, they were subsequently defeated by Sayf al-Dawla. However, his brilliant diplomacy maintained peace along the northern border from Hungary to the Caucasus, and it was during this time (955 or 957) that Olga, princess of Kiev, visited Constantinople and was baptized.

Constantine's great contribution was in the realm of learning and preservation of antiquity. Once he became the sole ruler with the treasury at his disposal, he ransacked his dominions for manuscripts, gathered a group of scholars, and published his encyclopedias, collections of excerpts from older works of history; agriculture; medicine; horse doctoring, including an epitome (indirect) of Aristotle's "Animals" with additions; and the lives of saints. Constantine himself wrote hymns and sermons, speeches and letters, as well as a description of the provinces (themes) of medieval Byzantium (*de thematibus*). He made substantial contributions to the treatise on statecraft intended for the education of his son, Romanus II, a manual of rubrics for court ceremonies (*de ceremoniis*) and a practical handbook of foreign affairs (*de adminis-*

trando imperio). Constantine's collaborators carried out a new edition of the *Basilica,* the law code of his father, Leo VI. The emperor also commissioned a history in praise of his grandfather Basil I, the founder of the "Macedonian dynasty" which has been ascribed to Genesios, and the encomium of Basil in the work of Theophanes *continuatus* was said to have been written by Constantine himself or under his supervision.

Bibliography: CONSTANTINE, *De Administrando Imperio,* ed. G. MORAVCISK, tr. R. J. H. JENKINS; commentary F. DVORNIK et al. (Washington 1985); *De Ceremoniis,* ed. J. J. REISKE (Leipzig 1829–1830); *De Thematibus,* tr. and comm. A. PERTUSI (Vatican City 1953). O. KRESTEN, *"Staatsempfänge" im Kaiserpalast von Konstantinopel um die Mitte des 10. Jahrhunderts: Beobachtungen zu Kapitel II 15 des sogenannten "Zeremonienbuches"* (Vienna 2000). J. SKYLITZES, *Synopsis historiarum,* ed. H. THURN (Berlin 1973). J. BECKER, ed., *Liuprand of Cremona, Antapodosis* (Hanover 1915), Eng. tr. F. A. WRIGHT (London 1930). I. BEKKER, ed., *Symeon the Logothete (Leo Grammaticus)* (Bonn 1842); *Theophanes Continuatus,* (Bonn 1838). A. KAZHDAN, *Dictionary of the Middle Ages* (New York 1983) 3:546–548. J. FEATHERSTONE, "Ol'ga's Visit to Constantinople," *Harvard Ukranian Studies* 14 (1990) 293–312. P. GRIERSON and R. J. H. JENKINS, "The Date of Constantine VII's coronation," *Byzantion* 32 (1962) 133–138. J. HALDON, *Three Treatises on Imperial Military Expeditions* (Vienna 1990). H. HUNGER, *Die hochsprachliche profane Literatur der Byzantiner* (Munich 1978) 1:360–7. P. LEMERLE, *Byzantine Humanism: The First Phase* (Canberra 1986). G. OSTROGORSKY, *History of the Byzantine State* (Oxford 1968), passim, esp. 169–183. *Oxford Dictionary of Byzantium,* ed. A. KAZHDAN et al. (Oxford 1991) 1:502–503. J. RIPOCHE, "Constantin VII Porphyrogénète et sa politique hongroise au milieu du Xe siècle," *Südost- Forschungen* 36 (1977) 1–12. A. TOYNBEE, *Constantine Porphyrogenitus and His world* (London 1973). M. WHITTOW, *The Making of Orthodox Byzantium, 600–1025* (Basingstoke 1996).

[F. NICKS/M. J. HIGGINS]

CONSTANTINE IX MONOMACHUS, BYZANTINE EMPEROR

June 12, 1042, to Jan. 11, 1055. He was crowned coemperor at his marriage to the Empress-regnant Zoë (1028–50) on June 12, 1042; from that time until his death he was effective ruler of the BYZANTINE EMPIRE. Constantine was a member of the civil aristocracy of Constantinople, which controlled the central administration of the Empire, and as Emperor he was opposed by the military aristocracy of Asia Minor, which sought to gain control of the state. He successfully crushed rebellions but was unable to curb the growing power of the military party, who absorbed the free peasant holdings on which the fiscal and military organization of the Empire was based. The consequent decline of revenue forced Constantine to debase the gold *nomisma* and to neglect the naval defenses of the Empire. Nevertheless, Byzantium appeared strong: independent Armenia was annexed

in 1046, and Patzinak and SELJUK invasions were successfully repulsed during his reign. At the instance of Pope LEO IX Constantine sought an alliance with Rome against the NORMANS who were attacking Byzantine possessions in southern Italy. These negotiations foundered because the Patriarch of Constantinople, MICHAEL CERULARIUS, refused to cooperate (*see* EASTERN SCHISM); however, the Pope's three legates in 1054 (HUMBERT OF SILVA CANDIDA; Frederick of Lorraine, who was later Pope STEPHEN IX; and Peter of Amalfi) praised the Emperor for his orthodoxy and goodwill. Constantine made liberal benefactions to the Church and patronized learning. In 1045 the University of Constantinople was reopened under his aegis.

Bibliography: M. PSELLUS, *Chronographia,* ed. E. RENAULD, 2 v. (Paris 1926–28) Fr. tr.; Eng. tr. without Gk. text by E. R. A. SEWTER (London 1953), chief source for the reign. J. B. BURY, "Roman Emperors from Basil II to Isaac Komnênos," *English Historical Review* 4 (1889) 41–64, 251–285. G. L. SCHLUMBERGER, *L'Épopée byzantine* (Paris 1896–1905) v.3. A. MICHEL, *Humbert und Kerullarios,* 2 v. (Paderborn 1924–30). J. M. HUSSEY, "The Byzantine Empire in the 11th Century," *Transactions of the Royal Historical Society,* series 4, 32 (1950) 71–85. G. OSTROGORSKY, *History of the Byzantine State,* tr. J. HUSSEY from 2d German ed. (Oxford 1956); American ed. by P. CHARANIS (New Brunswick, N.J. 1957), 289–298. S. RUNCIMAN, *The Eastern Schism* (Oxford 1955).

[B. HAMILTON]

CONSTANTINE XI PALAEOLOGUS, BYZANTINE EMPEROR

Born in Constantinople, 1404; d. May 29, 1453. He was the fourth son of Manuel II Palaeologus and Helen Dragases. At his death (1425) Manuel II had divided the empire among his sons, and Constantine received the Greek Peloponnesus, which had been enlarged by his brother John's conquests. Constantine took Patras (1430) and the rest of Achaia (1432), thus obtaining all the Peloponnesus except for four city ports controlled by the Venetians. During John's absence in Italy (1437–40) Constantine was viceregent in Constantinople. He then ruled cities on the Black Sea, which in 1443 he exchanged for the Peloponnesus because of dynastic quarrels. He rebuilt the Hexamilion wall across the Isthmus of Corinth and established himself in northern Greece in 1444 and 1445; but after the Christian defeat at Varna, the Turks destroyed the Hexamilion and invaded the Peloponnesus, making Constantine their tributary. After John's death (October 1448) Constantine was crowned emperor in Mistra on Jan. 6, 1449. In Constantinople he tried unsuccessfully to settle the unionistic controversy in the Church, and the antiunionists refused to pray for him in the Liturgy. He repaired fortifications and doubled

"Christ Pantocrator between Emperor Constantine IX Monomachus and Empress Zoe," Byzantine mosaic, the Church of Hagia Sophia, mid-11th/early 12th century, Istanbul, Turkey. (©Archivo Iconografico, S.A./CORBIS)

his embassies to the West when Muḥammad II began his preparations for the siege of Constantinople. He accepted the promulgation of the union of Florence (Dec. 12, 1452); and fought valiantly and died during the siege (April 7 to May 23).

Bibliography: G. PHRANTZES, *Chronicon, I,* ed. J. B. PAPA-DOPOULOS (Bibliotheca scriptorum Graecorum et Romanorum Teubneriana 1935); *Annales,* ed. I. BEKKER (Bonn 1838), with a Lat. tr. by E. BROCKHOFF. D. A. ZAKYTHINOS, *Le Despotat grec de Morée* (Paris 1932). J. GILL, *The Council of Florence* (Cambridge, Eng. 1959).

[J. GILL]

CONSTANTINE III LEICHUDES, PATRIARCH OF CONSTANTINOPLE

Reigned Feb. 2, 1059, to Aug. 9 or 10, 1063; Byzantine scholar and statesman. Constantine belonged to the group led by Michael Psellus, who promoted learning and reorganized the university in the mid-11th century. Leichudes was prominent in politics during the reign of Michael V (1041–42); he became first minister (*protovestarius*) under Constantine IX until deprived of office by the Emperor's jealousy. Leichudes then turned to scholarship and teaching, apparently again falling from favor toward the end of Constantine IX's reign (*c.* 1055). Like Psellus, he was evidently back at court after Constantine's death and was sent by Michael VI on an embassy to Isaac Comnenus, shortly to displace Michael on the throne. Isaac I selected Leichudes as patriarch of Constantinople on the death of Michael Cerularius (1059); and the patriarch subsequently gave Isaac ecclesiastical tonsure during his illness and abdication. During the reign of Constantine X (1059–67), Leichudes was associated with a policy of persecution adopted toward the Monophysite Syrians and Armenians, and two synodal decrees (1063) ordered the expulsion from Melitene of

Constantine XI Palaeologus, Byzantine Emperor, in battle. (Archive Photos)

all non-Chalcedonians and the burning of their holy books.

Leichudes was a close friend of Michael Psellus, who provided most of the information about him in his *Chronographia* and *Funeral Oration*. It was very probably Leichudes who asked Psellus to write the *Chronographia*. Leichudes was a distinguished scholar and orator, who had studied and taught rhetoric and civil law. He was also a wise administrator and churchman, a man of marked integrity who won the respect of his contemporaries.

Bibliography: M. PSELLUS, *Chronographia,* ed. E. RENAULD, 2 v. (Paris 1926–28), Eng. tr. without Gr. text by E. R. A. SEWTER (London 1953); *Funeral Oration on Likudes,* ed. K. N. SATHAS (Bibliotheca graeca medii aevi 4; Venice 1874). V. GRUMEL, *Les Regestes des actes du patriacat de Constantinople* v.1.1 (1932), v.1.2 (1936), v.1.3 (1947).

[J. M. HUSSEY]

CONSTANTINE, POPE

Pontificate: Mar. 25, 708 to Apr. 9, 715, the fourth Syrian elected pope since 685. The only extant document from his pontificate dates from 713 and authorizes the monastery of Bermondsey and Working in England to choose its own abbot. The LIBER PONTIFICALIS describes the troubles that the Ravenna Exarch, John Rizocopus (d. 710 or 711), caused RAVENNA and its Archbishop, Felix (709–717?, 724?), seeing the misfortunes as retribution for Felix's insubordination at the time of his consecration by Constantine. The Liber indicates that Milan's metropolitan, Archbishop Benedict (685–732), withdrew his protest against papal consecration of the bishop of Pavia. But most of the Liber's account deals with Constantine's visit (October 710 to October 711) to the East on the invitation of Emperor JUSTINIAN II, who warmly received the pope at Nicomedia. Their conversations are unrecorded, but they may well have treated of the relationship between Ravenna and the papacy and of the papal attitude toward the QUINISEXT SYNOD (692). When Justinian was assassinated (Dec. 711) and was succeeded by PHILIPPICUS, who supported MONOTHELITISM, Constantine refused to recognize the new incumbent. Reprisals were avoided, however, when Philippicus was deposed (June 713) and the new emperor, Anastasius II, forwarded to the pope his orthodox profession of faith. According to Bede (*Ecclesiastical History* 5.19), the Mercian King Coinred and the East Saxon Prince Offa made their monastic profession at Rome in 709 during Constantine's pontificate.

Bibliography: *Liber pontificalis,* ed. L. DUCHESNE (Paris 1886–92) 1:389–395, cf. 396; 3:99. P. JAFFÉ, *Regesta pontificum romanorum ab condita ecclesia ad annum post Christum natum 1198* (Graz 1956) 1:247–249. H. K. MANN, *The Lives of the Popes in the Early Middle Ages from 590 to 1304* (London 1902–32) 1.2:127–140. E. CASPAR, *Geschichte de Papsttums von den Anfängen bis zur Höhe der Weltherrschaft* (Tubingen 1930–33) 2:638–643. O. BERTOLINI, *Roma di fronte a Bisanzio e ai Longobardi* (Bologna 1941) 413–423, 767–768. J. HALLER, *Das Papsttum* (Stuttgart 1950–53) 1:349–351, G. BARDY, *Dictionnaire d'histoire et de géographie ecclésiastiques,* ed. A. BAUDRILLART et al. (Paris 1912) 13:589–591. G. OSTROGORSKY, *History of the Byzantine State* (Oxford 1956) 122–127, 135–137. R. AUBERT, *Dictionnaire d'histoire et de géographie ecclésiastiques* (Paris 1995). A. BREUKELAAR, *Biographisch-Bibliographisches Kirchenlexikon* 4 (1992). P. NOVARA, *Dizionario biografico delgi italiani 46* (Rome 1996). S. SCHOLZ, *Lexikon für Theologie und Kirche,* 3d. ed. (1997). J. N. D. KELLY, *Oxford Dictionary of Popes* (New York 1986) 85–86.

[H. G. J. BECK]

CONSTANTINE II, ANTIPOPE

Pontificate: June 28, 767–Aug. 6, 768. We do not have the precise dates of his birth or death. Constantine was the brother of Toto, the Duke of Nepi (northwest of Rome). In the mid-700s central Italy was a highly contested area. The Byzantine Empire and the Lombards had recently (680 or 681) concluded a treaty that recognized the Lombard kingdom in the north. While the Byzantines could not effect a meaningful presence around Rome, the Lombards remained important power brokers who hoped to expand their territory. Meanwhile, the papacy was attempting to solidify its hold on the nascent Papal States, the Franks were becoming an increasingly important presence under Pepin the Short (751–68), and local military magnates, some of whom claimed the title Duke, often used the confusion to expand their power. Within Rome itself, there appears to have been a power struggle between the military elite, whose power base was in the countryside, and various clergy of the Lateran, who hoped to control both the city and the Papal States.

In the midst of this turmoil Duke Toto approached Rome with a large band of troops, hoping to influence the impending papal election, since Pope Paul I (757–67) lay on his death bed. Although he met with the papal chancellor, Christophorus, and agreed not to enter the city or influence the election, Toto broke his oath and entered Rome by force when the pope died on June 28. He and three of his brothers had the fourth, Constantine, elected pope by the mob of soldiers and tenants. Toto himself became Duke of Rome. A few days later, the bishops of Praeneste, Alba, and Porto were forced to consecrate Constantine. Immediately after his election, Constantine wrote King Pepin to confirm alliances made between the two previous popes and the Franks. He did this because military control of Rome, and thus his hold on the papacy, was tenuous: the Lombards still had their eyes on the city, and Lateran officials were hostile to Constantine because he was an outsider.

Soon Christophorus and his son Sergius sought to leave the city, claiming that they would retire to the monastery of St. Savior in Rieti. Once out of Toto's reach, however, the two went to the Lombard duke Theodicius of Spoleto, hoping to find an ally against Toto and his pope. As a result, the Lombard king Desiderius (757–74) instructed Theodicius to supply troops to Sergius, who fought his way into Rome on July 30, 768. Toto was killed in the battle, and Constantine was taken captive in the Lateran. After a failed attempt to install a Lombard pope (Philip, 768), a new pope, Stephen III (IV) (768–72), was canonically elected under the leadership of Christophorus. Stephen was consecrated on Aug. 7, 768. Constantine was formally deposed the day before and imprisoned in a monastery, which was later attacked by a mob that blinded the former antipope.

On April 12 and 13, 769 a synod of 49 bishops was convoked in Rome to consider the issues raised by Constantine's irregular election. The synod, guided by Christophorus, decreed that laymen could not participate in papal elections, and narrowed the criteria required of candidates for the papacy. When Constantine appeared before the synod to defend himself, some of the participants attacked him. The synod then decided to burn all documents of his administration and ruled that his ordinations were invalid. Constantine was sentenced to penance in a monastery, where he disappears from the historical record.

Bibliography: L. DUCHESNE, ed. *Liber Pontificalis* (Paris 1886–92; repr. 1955–57) 1.468–85. P. JAFFÉ, *Regesta pontificum Romanorum* (Leipzig 1885–88; repr. Graz 1956) 1.283–85. J. D. MANSI, *Sacrorum conciliorum nova et amplissima collectio* (Florence and Venice 1759–98; repr. Graz 1960–61) 12.713–20. *Concilium Romanum,* in *Monumenta Germaniae historica, Concilia* 2(1).74–92; also *Monumenta Germaniae historica, Epistolae* 3.649–53. H. K. MANN, *The Lives of the Popes in the Early Middle Ages* (London 1902–32) 1(2) 361–78. O. BERTOLINI, *Roma di fronte a Bisanzio e ai longobardi* (Bologna 1943) 622–38. F. X. SEPPELT,

Geschichte der Päpste von den Anfängen bis zur Mitte des zwanzigsten Jahrhunderts (Munich 1954–59) 2.146–52. G. BARDY, *Dictionnaire d'histoire et de géographie ecclésiastiques* (Paris 1956) 13.591–93. K. BAUS, *Lexikon für Theologie und Kirche* (Freiburg 1957–65) 3.48. H. ZIMMERMAN, *Papstabsetzungen des Mittelalters* (Graz, Vienna, Cologne 1968) 13–25. O. BERTOLINI, *Roma e i longobardi* (Rome 1972). W. ULLMANN, *A Short History of the Papacy in the Middle Ages* (London 1972). T. F. X. NOBLE, *The Republic of St. Peter* (Philadelphia 1984). J. N. D. KELLY, *The Oxford Dictionary of Popes* (New York 1986) 93–4.

[P. M. SAVAGE]

CONSTANTINE I, THE GREAT, ROMAN EMPEROR

Reigned July 15, 306, to May 22, 337; b. Naissus (Nish) in modern Yugoslavia, *c.* 280; d. Nicomedia. Flavius Valerius Constantine was the son of an Illyrian soldier who became emperor as Constantius I (293–306) and a tavern maid (St.) HELENA. Under political pressure Constantius repudiated this clandestine alliance (289), and Constantine was raised at the court of DIOCLETIAN in Nicomedia as a hostage, while his father ruled Gaul, Britain, and Spain. Constantine may have met LACTANTIUS in Nicomedia and probably took part in military operations in the East.

On the abdication of Diocletian (May 1, 305), Constantine joined his father at York in Britain; and on the death of Constantius, he was proclaimed emperor by the army. He led a successful campaign against the Franks on the Rhine and was acknowledged as Caesar in Gaul and Britain by Galerius. At Treves (March 31, 307) he married Fausta, the daughter of the former Emperor Maximian, and was proclaimed Augustus (*see* ROMAN EMPIRE). The panegyric pronounced on this occasion indicated Constantine's withdrawal from the political theology of the tetrarchy; and in keeping with his father's policy, Constantine claimed dynastic descent from the Emperor Claudius the Goth (268–270). In 310 his panegyrist proclaimed Mars in association with the Sol Invictus as Constantine's divine protector, and the Hercules of the tetrarchy disappeared from his coinage.

Constantine refused to accept the rank of caesar given him by Galerius and Licinius (Nov. 11, 308). He practiced forbearance in regard to the Christians; and in 310 at Marseilles he suppressed a rebellion of his father-in-law, whom he executed but declared a suicide. Evidence on a gold coin struck at Tarragona (July 25, 310) indicates a campaign in Spain, which occasioned his brother-in-law, Maxentius, to return from a successful campaign in Africa and to declare Constantine a public enemy. Shortly before death, the Emperor Galerius published (April 30, 311) an edict of religious tolerance for

Constantine I, the Great, Roman Emperor.

Christians signed by Constantine. However, the caesar, Maximin Daia, proclaimed himself emperor in the East, began a propagandist war against the Christians, and attempted to organize the pagan priesthood on ecclesiastical lines (Lact., *De mort.* 36.4–5). Constantine came to an agreement with the co-Emperor Licinius and suddenly marched into Italy with 30,000 soldiers. He defeated Maxentius on the right bank of the Tiber near the Milvian bridge (Oct. 28, 312) and had himself proclaimed senior augustus by the Roman Senate. In 313 he met Licinius at Milan, gave him his sister Constantia in marriage, and agreed to grant equality of rights to all religions; but they issued no edict, probably in order not to interfere prematurely with Maximin Daia. Each emperor issued mandates restoring rights and property to Christians (Lact., *De mort.* 48; Euseb., *Ecclesiastical History* 10.5.1–14), and after two indecisive battles for supremacy (314) reestablished peace and adopted a policy of mutual respect.

Conversion. The religious convictions of Constantine have been the object of numerous controversies. His conversion to Christianity in 312 is now almost universally acknowledged, although the quality of his adherence to the Christian faith is still disputed. That he postponed Baptism until his deathbed is no criterion, for the practice was common, and he late insisted that he had hoped to be baptized in the Jordan.

In reporting Constantine's preparation for the battle of the Milvian bridge, Lactantius claimed (*De morte* 44) that the emperor saw Christ in a dream and was told to paint on his army's shields an inverted "X" with one stem curved over (*transversa X littera summo capite circumflexo*). This formed the Christian monogram (*see* CHI-RHO). In the *Vita Constantini*, Eusebius maintains that at noon, before the battle, Constantine and his army, while he was praying to the god of his father, saw a cross over the sun with the inscription "In this sign, conquer" (τούτῳ νίκα). That night Christ appeared to him and told him to paint the cross on the shields of his soldiers (*Vita* 1.27–32). Eusebius described this sign as the Labarum (used after 325), or staff surmounted with globe, and capped with the Chi-Rho monogram. Eusebius said Constantine told him of the incident. H. Grégoire and W. Seston deny the historicity of the event. However the version of Lactantius (written, probably in Gaul *c.* 318) seems to be authentic: Constantine did have a vision, whether actual, or dictated by anxiety. In later years his convictions gave the story the proportions narrated by Eusebius. The authenticity of the *Vita* (written *c.* 335 or 338) is generally admitted, though its historicity is still open to challenge.

Religious Policy. On entering Rome in 312, Constantine accepted the honors of the Senate but refused a religious ceremony in the temple. He wrote to Maximin Daia opposing the persecution of Christians and gave the palace of Fausta at the Lateran to Pope MILTIADES for a synod, and then, as the papal residence. He completed the building of a civil basilica, constructed new public baths, and erected a Christian church at the Lateran, which he later completed with a baptistery. He published the decree of Galerius giving religious freedom in his realm, and ordered Anullinus, the prefect in Africa, to restore Christian property and aid the bishops. He dedicated a statue of himself in the Forum with the inscription "Through this salutary sign . . . I have freed your city from the yoke of the tyrant" (Euseb., *Ecclesiastical History* 10.4.16; *Vita* 1.40). The vexillum, the first known on the statue of an emperor, apparently was decorated with the Chi-Rho monogram. Silver coins struck at Treves in 312 or 313 depict the emperor's crown with a star-studded helmet on which the Christian monogram appears: the latter caps the decoration of his helmet on a gold medallion from Tivoli (312 or 315). Although the *Sol Invictus* and other pagan signs did not disappear until after 321, the vexillum and monogram appeared regularly after 320; and the Labarum, after 326.

Arch of Constantine. Erected by the Senate and dedicated in 315, the Constantinian arch depicting his victory over Maxentius contains pagan symbols: the attributes of the gods, the crown with sun rays, and the emperor with his right hand held open and upright. But no gods are named; and victory is attributed to an *instinctu divinitatis* (an impulse of divinity), an expression acceptable to both Christians and pagans. But the emperor's involvement in Christian affairs immediately became acute.

In 313 he attempted to settle the Donatist schism in Africa. On an appeal against his recognition of the Catholic Bishop Caecilian, he had Pope Miltiades hold a Roman synod that condemned the Donatist Majorian (Euseb., *Ecclesiastical History* 10.5.18–20). On a second appeal, he ordered a synod in Arles (314) and wrote to the bishops, asking them to achieve unity lest they give occasion to critics to dishonor the Christian religion. Despite several letters in which he demonstrated his increasing adherence to the Christian faith and his desire to follow the decision of the bishops, he decided to use force against the Donatists (316), but in 321 he granted them amnesty.

Not only did he recognize the bishops as counselors of state, but gradually he extended to them juridical rights. He gave legal force to their solution of civil suits in 318 (*Codex Theodosianus* 1.27.1), permitted the emancipation of slaves in church (321), and recognized bequests to the Church (*ibid.* 16.2.4). He seems to have considered himself a colleague of the bishops; Eusebius used the term bishop of those outside (ἐπίσκοπος τῶν ἐκτός), meaning either non-Christians or the things outside the Church. Constantine seems to have felt himself divinely prompted to handle situations beyond the power of the bishops, and he gradually became involved in all the Church's affairs. He wrote to the Persian King Sapor in favor of the Christians in his realm, and supported the Christian kingdom of Armenia.

He did not enroll among the catechumens, evidently believing he had a divinely guided vocation; but he did read the Scriptures and organized religious ceremonies for the Christian community in his palace. He made Sunday a civil holiday and freed Christian soldiers for religious services (*Codex Theodosianus* 2.8.1). While he retained the office of *pontifex maximus* and continued the *Sol Invictus* and *lux perpetua* legends on his coinage and monuments, these were expressions of the eternal quality of the Roman state, which was inconceivable to contemporaries without a religious basis; and the majority of his citizens were pagans. Besides, the *Sol Invictus* had been adopted by the Christians in a Christian sense, as demonstrated in the Christ as Apollo-Helios in a mausoleum (*c.* 250) discovered beneath St. Peter's in the VATICAN.

Byzantium and Jerusalem. After the overthrow of Maximin Daia (313), Licinius had favored the Christians in the Orient. But from 317 the Constantinian coinage indicates conflict between the two emperors, and Licinius gradually resorted to repressive measures against the Christians. War broke out in 324, and Constantine defeated Licinius at Adrianople, then in a naval battle at Chrysopolis (Nov. 18, 324), near Byzantium. To commemorate this victory, Constantine rebuilt Byzantium and changed its name to CONSTANTINOPLE. He then decided to make it the new Rome, discarding a plan to locate his city at the ancient Ilion or Troy in accord with the Homeric and Vergilian legends. In a letter to the Orient, whose authenticity has been supported by the recent discovery of papyri fragments, Constantine spoke of his experience of God's providence (*Vita* 2.24–42) and claimed a divine vocation to protect Christians in the Orient and in the West. In a second letter to the provinces he exhorted pagans to convert to "God's holy law," but proclaimed religious liberty for all (*ibid.* 2.48–60). In an appendix to book 4 of the *Vita,* Eusebius edited an *Oration to the Assembly of Saints* that he attributed to Constantine; its authenticity is disputed, but it is a model of contemporary apologetics.

Despite the enmity of the Roman Senate, whom he offended by refusing religious honors on his anniversaries (*Decennalia* and *Vicennalia*) in 316 and 326, Constantine leveled a cemetery on the Vatican hill and built a vast martyr basilica on the spot where tradition located the grave of St. Peter. He had induced his mother, Helena, to become a Christian, and she built a church on her property near the Lateran known as the Sessorianum, later called Santa Croce in Gerusalemme. On a model of the old hero temples, he also constructed the churches of St. Agnes, St. Paul-Outside-the-Walls, and SS. Peter and Marcellinus in conjunction with Helena's mausoleum. A double church was built in Treves; and in Antioch (328), an octagonal edifice close to the imperial palace. Following the lead of Helena, he aided in the construction of the Nativity basilica in Bethlehem (*Vita* 3.41–43), the Eleona church of the Ascension on the Mount of Olives (*ibid.* 3.41–43), the basilica on the site of Abraham's sacrifice (3.51–53), and the basilica of the Resurrection in Jerusalem (3.25–40), to whose dedication he called the bishops from a synod at Tyre in 335 (*Vita* 4.43–46).

Council of Nicaea. Cognizant of the MELETIAN SCHISM and the outbreak of ARIANISM in ALEXANDRIA, Constantine sent Bishop Hosius of Córdoba with a letter to Bishop Alexander and Arius (323), urging them to make peace for the unity of the realm. After a synod of Oriental bishops at Antioch (324) published a confession of faith (*see* CREED) and suspended Eusebius of Caesarea, Constantine called a general council to meet in Nicaea (June 325); he allowed the bishops to use public transport and housed them in Nicaea (*Vita* 3.6). He opened the Council of NICAEA I with a discourse and presided over its deliberations as if it were a session of the Senate. Ac-

cepting the term homoousios (con-substantial) as key to the problem of the divinity of Christ, he sanctioned the formulation of the Nicene Creed; the settlement of the paschal controversy with the computation of Alexandria and Rome as normative; and the administration of the Church according to civil provinces. He closed the Council with an exhortation to peace and unity in Church and Empire, and in letters of promulgation proclaimed himself as "one of you [Christians] who took part in the deliberations" (*Vita* 3.17–20). He considered the decisions of the bishops as the "judgment of God" (Socrates, *Ecclesiastical History* 1.9.17–25).

The Emperor banished Eusebius of Nicomedia and Theognis of Nicaea, who had been condemned by the Council, and published (probably in 326) an edict against heretics. But he sent a benevolent letter to Arius offering a personal interview (Athanasius, *Decr. Nic. syn.* 40) and in 327 pardoned Eusebius of Nicomedia and Arius. In 328, following a synod, he banished MARCELLUS OF ANCYRA and EUSTATHIUS OF ANTIOCH. When difficulties developed over the election of a new bishop in Antioch, Constantine wrote a letter urging unity on the bishops, and praised Eusebius of Caesarea, who had refused the see because he was already attached to Caesarea (Palestine).

When the Meletians attacked ATHANASIUS OF ALEXANDRIA, Constantine had the matter investigated (Athan., *Apol.* 2.68) and called a synod at Caesarea that Athanasius refused to attend. Summoned to Tyre (335) by the Emperor, Athanasius found the synod there hostile and fled to the imperial court, but was banished to Treves in 336, apparently for his intransigence. Constantine then called the bishops to Jerusalem for the dedication of the basilica of the Savior and informed them that, in view of an acceptable profession of faith, he had restored Arius and his followers.

Constantinople. The decision to found a new city in the East had been dictated by political and military necessity. In the foundation ceremonies (*consecratio Deo*) on November 26, 328, Constantine allowed the imperial astronomers and pagan priests to perform their ancient rites. In the *forum Constantini,* the center of the city, a statue of the Emperor depicted as the *Sol Invictus* was erected on columns; beneath it Constantine had Christian relics and precious objects placed along with the tokens of the ancient city. The new city was dedicated on May 11, 330, in honor of the Christian martyrs (*Vita* 3.48); and although the Emperor allowed the construction of temples to the goddess Rhea and to Fortune (Tyche) brought from Rome, he proscribed bloody sacrifices and did not allow the introduction of the Vestal cult or the colleges of pagan priests.

The new city of seven hills and 14 regions was given a senate; enjoyed the *annona,* or distribution of food; and was designated as the ''Second Rome.'' On taking residence, Constantine made an effort to give the city a Christian character, built the church of St. Irene on the acropolis, and laid plans for the basilica of the Holy Wisdom (Hagia Sophia). While the emperor cult was continued, it was given a Christian interpretation and surrounded with Christian ceremonial. Of Constantinople itself (*Codex Theodosianus*13.5.7), Constantine proclaimed, ''we have endowed [it] with an eternal name at God's bidding'' (*quam aeterno nomine Deo iubente donavimus*).

Constantine continued the toleration of paganism. His laws, however, were gradually influenced by the Christian ethic, although frequently a concurrence with Stoic moral thinking is also evident. The Emperor mitigated the laws dealing with slaves (*Codex Theodosianus* 9.2.) and allowed a mild Christian influence in legislation affecting marriage, celibacy, and the protection of widows and orphans. He prohibited crucifixion, restricted the gladiatorial games, and in part humanized the code of penal law. Yet, generally speaking, he introduced no radical changes.

In keeping with the custom of his predecessors, Constantine built his own mausoleum at Constantinople, and in conjunction with it, a martyr basilica in honor of the Twelve Apostles near a populated area on the highest of the city's hills. He confessed his desire to be remembered by the faithful who came to pray at the shrine of the Apostles (*Vita* 4.60) and so arranged his tomb that on two sides it was flanked by six memorial pillars dedicated to the Apostles. There is question as to whether this tomb was located at first within the church and only removed elsewhere at a later time (R. Krautheimer).

In preparation for death, Constantine had himself baptized by Bishop Eusebius of Nicomedia, and his body was brought to Constantinople, where it received imperial honors. After religious services in the new church, just nearing completion, he was buried in his mausoleum (*Vita* 4.65–73). His burial beside the memorial earned him the title of *Isapostolos* (like an apostle) in the early tradition; and since he had been baptized on his deathbed, he was honored in the Orient as a saint. The Roman calendar never acknowledged him, partly because Eusebius was considered an Arian; but during the Middle Ages, particularly in England and France, churches were dedicated in his honor.

The Eusebian Image. EUSEBIUS OF CAESAREA had gained the emperor's friendship before the Council of Nicaea and seems to have been one of his close advisers thereafter. He preached at the emperor's *Tricennalia,* or 30th anniversary, and in the *Vita* set out to create a new theology of politics with Constantine as the new Moses, a notion current as early as 313. Eusebius portrayed Constantine as consciously inspired by the conviction that he had a divine mission to unify the empire as a manifestation of the kingdom of God on earth. Constantine had expressed this idea in his letter to the bishops at Arles (314; reported by Eusebius) when he pointed to his own life as an example of God's providence leading men *ad regulam justitiae* (to the rule of justice) and punishing evildoers, particularly those who persecuted the Church (Euseb., *Ecclesiastical History* 10.17.1–2; this is also the theme of Lactantius's *De morte persecutorum*).

As a colleague, then as guide of the bishops, the emperor felt he had a vocation to lead all men to unity in honoring the divinity within the Christian Church (*Vita* 2.65.1). In the Scriptures Constantine found justification for his idea of the Church as the peace-bringing house of truth, the unifying element of the state as the kingdom of God (*Vita* 2.56, 67). He respected the decisions of the bishops in synod, particularly the decrees of the Council of Nicaea, and considered all further theological dispute as nugatory. Hence his policy hardened toward pagans and Jews as time wore on. Although he employed pagan terms in speaking of the ''divinity,'' ''the highest god,'' and ''divine providence,'' he had in mind the unique God of the Christians, the creator and judge of all, who saved fallen man through His Son.

Eusebius said nothing about the execution of Fausta and Constantine's eldest, illegitimate son, Crispus, who were accused of mutual adultery (327), or about the violence and barbarity of which JULIAN THE APOSTATE later accused the emperor. But the evidence in regard to Fausta is so confused that it is impossible to sort out the facts. As a soldier and ruler, Constantine was ruthless in practical affairs and resorted to harsh legislation in punishing, for example, adultery on the part of the woman, though, in respect for Helena, he tried to ease the situation of servant girls. In dealing with heretics and in his policy toward the pagans, he exercised astute forbearance. There can be no doubt that he was a convinced Christian, whatever may have been the limitations in his understanding of the full significance of that faith.

Legends. Although there is little indication in the evidence of a relationship between Constantine and Pope SYLVESTER I (314–335), a legend evidently originating in Rome before 500 (W. Levison) credited the Pope with baptizing Constantine in the baths of the Lateran and curing him of leprosy. The story was further elaborated to include the legendary conversion of Helena, who had allegedly been influenced by Jews in Bithynia and went to Rome in 315 to save her son from Christianity; but on a confrontation between Sylvester and Jewish champions, she was converted. Together with the Symmachan forgeries, this story in Latin form, as the *Actus Silvestri,* was incorporated into the *Vita Silvestri* in the *Liber pontificalis.* It was probably partly motivated by a mistranslation of the inscription on the triumphal apse in St. Peter's: "Quod duce te mundus surrexit in astra triumphans, /Hanc Constantinus Victor tibi condidit aulam" (Since under Your guidance a triumphal world has risen toward the stars, /The Conqueror Constantine founded this hall in Your honor). The word *mundus* (world) also means "pure" in Latin.

The Sylvester legend seems also to be at the base of the DONATION OF CONSTANTINE. It gave rise to many wondrous tales during the Middle Ages in which Constantine was considered a great, wise man and the model of the Christian knight.

Bibliography: *Eusebius Kirchengeschichte,* ed. E. SCHWARTZ, 3 v. (*Die griechischen christlichen Schriftsteller der ersten drei Jahrhunderte* [Leipzig 1903–09]) 5th student ed. Berlin 1952; *Über das Leben Constantins,* ed. I. A. HEIKEL (*Die griechischen christlichen Schriftsteller der ersten drei Jahrhunderte* [Leipzig 1902]). J. MOREAU, ed. and tr., *Lactance: De la mort des persécuteurs,* 2 v. (*Sources Chrétiennes,* ed. H. DE LUBAC et al. Paris 1954). E. GALLETIER, ed. and tr., *Panégyriques latins,* 3 v. (Paris 1949–55). O. SEECK, *Regesten der Kaiser und Päpste* (Stuttgart 1919). A. ALFÖLDI, *Pisciculi: F. J. Dölger zum 60. Geburtstag,* ed. T. KLAUSER and A. RUECKER (Bonn 1939) 1–18, *hoc signo; The Conversion of Constantine,* tr. H. MATTINGLY (Oxford 1948). M. R. ALFÖLDI in *Mullus: Festschrift Theodor Klauser* (*Jahrbuch für Antike und Christentum* suppl. 1) 10–16, coinage. P. BATIFFOL, *La Paix constantinienne* (2d ed. Paris 1914). N. H. BAYNES, *Constantine the Great* (London 1930), repr. from *The Proceedings of the British Academy* 15: 341–441. J. BURCKHARDT, *Die Zeit Constantins des Grossen,* ed. F. STÄHELIN (Stuttgart 1929). C. B. COLEMAN, *Constantine the Great and Christianity* (New York 1914). H. DÖRRIES, *Constantine and Religious Liberty,* tr. R. H. BAINTON (New Haven 1961). G. DOWNEY, *Dumbarton Oaks Papers* 6: 53–80, Church of Apostles. P. P. FRANCHI DE CAVALIERI, *Constantiniana* (*Studi e Testi* 171). J. GAUDEMET, *Revue d'histoire de l'Église de France* 33: 25–61. H. GRÉGOIRE, *Revue de l'Université de Bruxelles* 36.2: 231–272, conversion; *L'Antique classique* 1 (1932) 135–143, sign of the cross; *Byzantion* 13 (1938): 561–583, Vita; 14: 341–351, vision "Liquidated." A. H. M. JONES, *The Journal of Ecclesiastical History* 5 (1954): 196–200; *Constantine and the Conversion of Europe* (new rev. ed. New York 1962). F. HALKIN, *Analecta Bollandiana* 77 (1959): 63–107, 307–372; 78: 5–17. H. KRAFT, *Kaiser Konstantins religiöse Entwicklung* (Tübingen 1955). R. KRAUTHEIMER, *Mullus, op. cit.* 224–229. W. LEVISON in *Miscellanea Francesco Ehrle,* v.2 (*Studi e Testi* 38) 159–247. J. MOREAU, *Revue des études anciennes* 55 (1953): 307–333, vision. R. ORGELS, *Bulletin de la Classe des Lettres de l'Académie Royale de Belgique* (1948) 34: 176–208, vision. J. PALANQUE, A. FLICHE and V. MARTIN, eds., *Histoire de l'église depuis les origines jusqu'à nos jours* (Paris 1935–) 3:17–68. E. PETERSON, *Der Monotheismus als politisches Problem* (Leipzig 1935). A. PIGANIOL, *Historia* 1 (1950) 82–95, state of the question. H. U. VON SCHOENEBECK, *Beiträge zur Religionspolitik des Maxentius und Konstantin* (*Klio,* Beiheft 43; Leipzig 1939). E. SCHWARTZ, *Kaiser Constantin und dei christliche Kirche* (2d ed. Leipzig 1936). W. SESTON in *Mélanges Franz Cu-*

mont (Brussels 1936) 373–396, vision; *Relazioni del X congresso internazionale di scienze storiche* 6 (1955) 792–796. E. STEIN, *Histoire du Bas-Empire,* tr. J. R. PALANQUE, 2 v. in 3 (Paris 1949–59) 1:1–130. F. VITTINGHOF, *Rheinisches Museum* 96: 330–373. J. VOGT, *Lexikon für Theologie und Kirche,* ed. J. HOFER and K. RAHNER, 10 v. (2d, new ed. Freiburg 1957–65) 6:478–480; *Constantin der Grosse und sein Jahrhundert* (Munich 1949); in *Mullus, op. cit.* 374–379, *Reallexikon für Antike und Christentum,* ed. T. KLAUSER [Stuttgart 1941– (1950)–] 3:306–379.

[F. X. MURPHY]

CONSTANTINE OF BARBANSON

Capuchin ascetical-mystical theologian; b. Barbanson, near Beaumont in the Hainaut, 1581 or 1582; d. Bonn, Nov. 25 or 26, 1631. He entered the Capuchin Order at the friary in Brussels, Sept. 20, 1600, and several years after ordination to the priesthood (1611) he was sent to the recently established Capuchin province in the Rhineland. There he occupied an eminent position until his death, distinguishing himself as a master of the spiritual life and as a mystical theologian of keen perception, especially in regard to the prequietistic mysticism of the times. His most important writings are *Les Secrets sentiers de l'amour divin* (Cologne 1623); new ed. by the Benedictines of Solesmes (Paris-Tournai-Rome 1932) and *Anatomie de l'âme et des opérations divines en icelle* (Liège 1635).

Bibliography: HILDEBRAND (DE HOOGLEDE), "Le Père Constantin de Barbanson," *Études Franciscaines* 42 (1930) 586–594; 45 (1933) 236–237. WILLIBRORD DE PARIS, "Note sur un MS de Secrets sentiers du P. C. de B.," *ibid.* 1 (1950) 97–102. THÉOTIME DE S'HERTOGENBOSCH, "Le P. C. de B. et le Préquiétisme," *Collectanea Franciscana* 10 (1940) 338–382; "P. C. de B., een oude mysticus," *Franciscaansch leven* 29 (1946) 71–87. *Lexicon Capuccinum: Promptuarium historico-bibliographicum ordinis Fratrum minorum capuccinorum, 1525–1950* (Rome 1951) 451. C. DE NANT, *Dictionnaire de spiritualité ascétique et mystique. Doctrine et histoire,* ed. M. VILLER et al. (Paris 1932–) 2.2:1634–41.

[M. F. LAUGHLIN]

CONSTANTINE THE AFRICAN

Benedictine translator of Arabic medical texts; b. North Africa, between 1010 and 1015; d. MONTE CASSINO, *c.* 1087. From evidence in the *Chronica monasterii Casinensis* (*Monumenta Germaniae Historica: Scriptores* 7:728; *Patrologia Latina,* ed. J. P. Migne, 173:767) and the *De viris illustribus Casinensibus* (*Patrologia Latina,* 173:1034–35) it appears that Constantine spent most of his adult life (perhaps 40 years) traveling in the Middle East, either as a merchant or as a physician. Expelled from Tunis upon his return, he went to Salerno, Italy, where he found service at the court of Robert Guiscard.

Constantine the African conducting urinalysis.

Whether he was a native Christian or a converted Muslim is uncertain; equally doubtful is his relation to the medical school of Salerno. While Desiderius (later VICTOR III) was abbot, Constantine entered Monte Cassino (*c.* 1078); he acknowledged ALPHANUS OF SALERNO as his Latin teacher, and to him he probably owed his monastic vocation. At home in the intellectual milieu created by Desiderius, Constantine enriched the scientific literature of the West by his paraphrase translations of the medical works of Hippocrates, pseudo-Galen (Johannitius and Hubaysh ibn al-Hasan), 'Ali ibn al-'Abbās (d. 994), Ahmed ibn al-Jazzār (d. 1009), Ishāq ben Imran, and ISAAC ISRAELI. Charges of plagiarism, inaccuracy of translation, and "barbarous" Latin aside, Constantine's adaptations of the texts of Greco-Arabic medicine anticipated by several generations the scientific translation literature of the 12th-century renaissance. His reputation and service to medical science in the West are attested by the wide distribution of his works in MS from the 12th century down to the age of printing [cf. L. Thorndike and P. Kibre, *Catalogue of Incipits of Mediaeval Scientific Writings in Latin* (Cambridge, Mass. 1963)]. His works include the following: *De oculis, Megatechne,* and *Michrotechne;* the *Aphorisms, Prognostics,* and *De regimine acutorum* of Hippocrates; the *Pantechni, De gradibus, Viaticum, De oblivione,* and *De melancholia;* and the

Elements, Dietetics, Urines, and *Fevers* of Isaac Israeli. It is probable that the work *De coitu* was not one of Constantine's translations (Steinschneider). An exact estimate of Constantine's role in the history of medicine awaits the critical edition of his texts and of those on which he depended.

Bibliography: Editions. *Omnia opera Isaac* (Lyons 1515). *Constantini Africani . . . opera* (Basel 1536). *Summi in omni philosophia viri Constantini Africani medici operum reliqua* (Basel 1539). Literature. M. STEINSCHNEIDER, *Die europäischen Übersetzungen aus dem Arabischen. . . ,* 2 v. (Vienna 1905–06; repr. Graz 1956). L. THORNDIKE, *A History of Magic and Experimental Science* (New York 1923–58) 1:742–759. R. CREUTZ, "Der Arzt Constantinus Africanus. . . ," *Studien und Mitteilungen zur Geschichte des Benediktiner-Ordens und seiner Zweige* 47 (1929) 1–44; 48 (1930) 301–324; 49 (1931) 25–44; 50 (1932) 420–422. A. MIELI, *La Science arabe et son rôle dans l'évolution scientifique mondiale* (Leiden 1938). P. O. KRISTELLER, "The School of Salerno," *Bulletin of the History of Medicine* 17 (1945) 138–194. H. SCHIPPERGES, "Die frühen Übersetzer der arabischen Medizin in chronologischer Sicht," *Sudhoffs Archiv für Geschichte der Medizin* 39 (1955) 53–93. M. BASSAN, "Chaucer's 'Cursed Monk' Constantinus Africanus," *Mediaeval Studies* (Toronto-London 1938–), 24 (1962) 127–140.

[O. J. BLUM]

CONSTANTINOPLE (BYZANTIUM, ISTANBUL)

Constantinople (modern Istanbul), "Constantine's City" (Lat. *Constantinopolis*), sometimes Byzantium or simply "the City." This article deals with Constantinople (1) as a center of Church history, (2) in its relations with Rome, (3) its break with Rome, (4) as a center of monasticism and (5) as a center of art and archeology.

Early History

The importance of the site of Constantinople as a center of communications and the advantages of its excellent harbor, the Golden Horn, were recognized as early as the seventh century B.C., when Greek merchants founded the colony of Byzantion. As a small commercial city it survived into Roman times.

THE FOUNDING OF CONSTANTINOPLE

On becoming the sole emperor CONSTANTINE I, THE GREAT (306–337), transferred the imperial capital from Italy to the eastern part of the empire for greater administrative and military efficiency. As a result of his conversion to Christianity, he preferred to build a new capital that would be Christian from the beginning, rather than occupy a city with old pagan associations. After considering several sites, he chose Byzantium, since it was not a major city and so could be "refounded" and given a new name, "the city of Constantine." The account of the founding written by Bishop EUSEBIUS OF CAESAREA, Constantine's adviser and biographer, describes the construction of a number of churches, which were supplied with costly copies of the Scriptures specially prepared in Eusebius's *SCRIPTORIUM* in Caesarea. Other sources indicate that Constantine had to take into account that many of his subjects were still pagans and the dedication ceremonies (330) included traditional pagan rites as well as Christian services.

The history of the Church at Constantinople was inevitably colored by the city's being the imperial residence and by the consequent propinquity of the bishop and the emperor. The see inescapably became involved in disputes with other major churches over questions of precedence and authority. A late legend, dating apparently from the early seventh century, attributed the founding of the Church at Byzantium to the Apostle ANDREW. This claim cannot be verified, and its late origin suggests that it arose at the time of the controversy between Rome and Constantinople over the title of "ecumenical patriarch" as used by the patriarch of Constantinople. It is thought that someone at Constantinople, wishing to place the see of the capital among the apostolic foundations and thus raise it to the same level as Rome in this respect, fabricated the legend. The actual situation at the time of the founding of the city is shown by canon six of the Council of NICAEA I (325), which confirmed the traditional authority of the metropolitan of Heraclea over the see of Byzantium.

THE STRENGTHENING OF THE CHURCH IN CONSTANTINOPLE

The controversy over ARIANISM involved Constantinople in tension with the other major churches and had special significance at the capital because of the Emperor CONSTANTIUS II's Arian leanings. Toward the end of the Arian troubles, GREGORY OF NAZIANZUS was installed (381) as bishop in order to direct the restoration of orthodoxy, and the Council of Constantinople I in 381 (later acknowledged as the second ecumenical council) was convoked by THEODOSIUS THE GREAT in order to complete the restoration of religious unity. The Nicene doctrine of the nature of Christ was confirmed and APOLLINARIANISM was condemned. The CREED called Niceno-Constantinopolitan, once thought to have been promulgated at this council, probably originated earlier. The status of Constantinople was elevated by canon three, which decreed that the bishop of Constantinople should have "precedence of honor" after the bishop of Rome "because Constantinople is new Rome."

As patriarch of Constantinople, JOHN CHRYSOSTOM (398–407) encountered political and ecclesiastical diffi-

Engraving of Justinian I. (Bettman/CORBIS)

culties, which led to his condemnation at the Synod of the OAK, followed by his exile and death. Canon 28 of the Council of CHALCEDON (451) indicates that between 381 and 451 Constantinople had extended its jurisdiction over the Dioceses of Thrace, Asia, and Pontus, and that the see of the imperial capital was engaged in a series of hostilities with ANTIOCH and ALEXANDRIA, its natural ecclesiastical rivals in the East. Antioch, by the support it gave to NESTORIANISM and MONOPHYSITISM, provided opportunities for attacks on its own power, while Alexandria brought more strength to its resistance to the capital. The frequent and extended visits of ecclesiastical prelates to the capital led to the formation of a permanent "resident synod" (*synodos endemousa*), which became characteristic of this patriarchate and served both the patriarch and the emperor in the preparation of policy and the issuing of decrees concerning ecclesiastical problems.

Relations With Rome

Relations between Constantinople and Rome were conditioned at an early date by the extension of power of the Constantinopolitan see and by the influence of its patriarch with the emperor. The activities of the patriarch of Constantinople must be viewed in the light of the theory of the nature of the office of the Christian Roman emperor, formulated in the time of Constantine the Great.

According to this theory, which was designed to replace the political theory of the pagan Roman Empire, the Christian emperor was conceived to be the vicegerent of God on earth, divinely chosen for office and ruling by divine inspiration and by virtue of his position responsible for the spiritual as well as the material welfare of his subjects. The competence and right of the sovereign to control or intervene in ecclesiastical affairs was in due course challenged by the Church, but the patriarch of the imperial residence, whether he was considered a partner of the emperor or only an adviser, could on occasion claim authority and jurisdiction, political or spiritual, which the other ancient sees, especially Rome, were unable to accept. Thus the ACACIAN SCHISM, separating East and West from 484 to 519, arose when Pope FELIX III felt it necessary to excommunicate the Patriarch Acacius for the *HENOTICON* or formula of union issued by the Emperor Zeno.

REIGN OF JUSTINIAN (527–565)

This was one of the most brilliant periods in the history of Constantinople and established a new era in Byzantine civilization. JUSTINIAN I sought to complete the process inaugurated by Constantine and Theodosius and to perfect the life of a Christian Roman Empire in which religion, intellectual culture, art, social life, and government were integrated into one harmonious whole under a benevolent emperor who was the all-powerful father of his people and the responsible head of both Church and State. Constantinople was the center in which this achievement was to be realized. In the religious sphere, Justinian's constant preoccupation was the restoration of orthodoxy and the suppression of heresy and paganism. The emperor pursued his goal with autocratic vigor, and in an effort to solve the Monophysite problem, which constituted a breach in both the spiritual and the political unity of the empire, applied himself to theology and ended by issuing unilateral legislation on points of doctrine without consulting the Church, an action that exceeded the most liberal interpretation of his powers. Justinian endeavored to impose his will on Popes AGAPETUS, SILVERIUS and VIGILIUS. Silverius was deposed, while Vigilius was brought to Constantinople and treated with physical violence. The Council of CONSTANTINOPLE II (fifth ecumenical council, 553) was convoked by Justinian to settle the question arising out of the Monophysite problem, as to whether the THREE CHAPTERS, condemned by Justinian in a personal edict in 543, should be condemned, along with their authors, Theodore of Mopsuestia, Theodoret of Cyr and Ibas of Edessa, for their Nestorian sympathies. At the emperor's behest the council condemned the chapters and anathematized their writers.

A new source of difficulty between Constantinople and Rome arose over the use of the title "ecumenical patriarch" by the patriarchs of Constantinople. In existing Greek usage, the term "ecumenical" had a restricted sense, but Pope GREGORY I protested against the patriarchs' use of the title because in the West it would be taken as a claim to universal jurisdiction. This controversy continued for some years, but the patriarchs did not discontinue the use of the title. MONOTHELITISM, growing out of Monophysitism, caused further estrangement between the East and the West, in the course of which Pope MARTIN I and MAXIMUS THE CONFESSOR were arrested by order of the Emperor CONSTANS II, taken to Constantinople and tried for treason. The pope was banished and died from cold and hunger (655).

In 680 the Council of CONSTANTINOPLE III (sixth ecumenical council) was convoked by the Emperor CONSTANTINE IV to settle the Monothelite heresy. The Dogmatic Decree issued by the council reaffirmed the definition of Chalcedon with an additional statement certifying the reality of the two wills and the two operations in Christ. This was followed by the Trullan Synod (692), so called from its meeting in the *trullus* or domed chamber of the imperial palace. It is also referred to as the Quinisext, for its task was to draw up disciplinary decrees on clerical marriage, clerical dress, age of ordination and the like, to supply the canonical measures not handled at the fifth and sixth ecumenical councils (553 and 680). The legislation of this council served to emphasize the difference between Eastern and Western practice.

ICONOCLAST CONTROVERSY (725–843)

This controversy produced tension between the popes, who supported further the traditional use of images as orthodox, and the iconoclast emperors and patriarchs, who sought to abolish sacred images as promoting idolatry (*see* ICONOCLASM). Further cause for discord was the rivalry between Rome and Constantinople for the ecclesiastical control of Illyricum, southern Italy and Sicily, over which from the fifth to the ninth century the See of Constantinople gradually extended its jurisdiction.

PHOTIUS AND THE GREEK SCHISM

The Photian schism was once thought to be the beginning of the definitive schism between the East and the West, but recent research has tended to show that the breach between the East and the West under the Patriarch PHOTIUS (858–869, 877–886) was not permanent, that a recognized schism came about only gradually and that the date when the schism became complete is not easy to establish. Relations between the East and the West at this time reflect the effect of the accumulation of the successive points of difference between Rome and Constantinople, combined with the increasing difficulty of effective communication, as fewer people in the East had a competent knowledge of Latin, while at the same time fewer people in Rome possessed an accurate knowledge of Greek. Thus official correspondence was sometimes not interpreted correctly.

The personal history of the future patriarch Photius was typical of the Constantinople of his day and his appointment illustrates the way in which the affairs of the patriarchate were conducted at that time. A member of a wealthy and distinguished family (his uncle TARASIUS had been patriarch, 784–806), Photius was one of the most learned and cultivated men of his time, a leader in the intellectual and literary revival then taking place in Constantinople. His contributions to scholarship were important. Photius had also shown unusual talents as a diplomat and civil servant. Others of similar background had been called to the patriarchal throne because of their personal prestige and their experience of practical affairs. In the East this was not considered an undesirable practice; but the appointment of such men to the highest ecclesiastical posts seemed strange to the West. Thus, when the emperor MICHAEL III deposed the patriarch IGNATIUS in the course of a quarrel between conservative and moderate elements in the Church, the emperor chose Photius to succeed him, as a man capable of reconciling the discordant groups. Photius was a layman and had to proceed through the necessary series of ordinations in six successive days. When the deposition of Ignatius seemed irregular, Pope NICHOLAS I had additional reason not to recognize Photius as patriarch. Ignatius's friends carried their complaints to Rome. The question of the FILIOQUE was raised; and the case became further complicated by an important administrative question, namely whether the newly established Church of BULGARIA should come under the jurisdiction of Rome or Constantinople. The controversy, protracted and complex, illustrates the way in which the pope was obliged to deal with two powers, the patriarch and the emperor, whereas the patriarch and the emperor had to deal with only a single agent, the pope. Several councils were held in Rome (863, 864, 869, 879) and in Constantinople (859, 861, 869–870, 879–880). The Council of Constantinople IV (869–870) the eighth ecumenical council, confirmed the sentence of the Council at Rome in 869 that anathematized Photius. Ignatius was reestablished as patriarch; but he died in 877 and Photius once again was appointed patriarch and was recognized by Pope JOHN VIII. At a Photian Council at Constantinople in 879–880 the papal legates apparently accepted Photius and annulled the action of the council of 869–870. If the Photian schism did not create a lasting breach between the East and the West the part played by Photius certainly hastened the final schism—he was the first Eastern theologian to bring an accusation that the filioque was an innovation—and it is appropriate that his name is attached to the episode.

PATRIARCHAL STATUS

The careers of Ignatius and Photius illustrate the relations between patriarch and emperor. The patriarch had great power; in the middle of the seventh century he controlled 419 bishoprics, in the early ninth century, more than 500. At the same time, the patriarch often had to defer to the emperor. While a patriarch who had public opinion behind him could when necessary oppose an emperor very effectively, the imperial office could employ constraints that the Church could not always withstand. Under the best conditions, the collaboration of emperor and patriarch could be a harmonious partnership; but emperors might be tyrannical and patriarchs might be servile or contentious. It was possible for heretics such as NESTORIUS, men with heretical tendencies such as ACACIUS and iconoclasts to be patriarchs.

Break With Rome

After the time of Photius, relations between the East and the West further deteriorated. The patriarchate of MICHAEL CERULARIUS (1043–59) has traditionally been taken as the time of the final breach (1054), but recent research has shown that this year did not witness a permanent break and that the final schism developed gradually. Cerularius, a civil servant ordained late in life, brought to the duties of patriarch the strict mentality of the bureaucrat and a strong will that did not defer to the emperor's views. Violently anti-Latin, the new patriarch inaugurated a systematic attack on Latin usages, such as use of unleavened bread in the Eucharist, fasting on Saturdays and the like. When the Latin churches in Constantinople refused to adopt Greek usages, Cerularius closed them, caused a violent letter to be sent to Rome, and instituted further anti-Western propaganda which included some exaggerated and abusive charges.

CONTINUED HOSTILITIES

Pope LEO IX sent three legates to complain to the emperor and reprove the patriarch, their leader being Cardinal Humbert, who disliked the Greeks as strongly as Cerularius disliked the Latins. The Emperor CONSTANTINE IX attempted to act as conciliator but failed. The legates took the unusual step of entering Hagia Sophia just before the singing of the liturgy and laying on the altar a bull excommunicating the patriarch and his followers (but not the emperor). When the contents of the bull became known in the city, there were riots, which the imperial troops put down only with difficulty. After the legates left for Rome, a synod met at Constantinople and anathematized them. Though the synod was careful not to involve the pope, it was later believed in the East that Cerularius had answered the attack on himself by excommunicating the pope. The crisis was taken more seriously in the West than in the East. But political negotiations between the emperor and the Roman See continued, and the evidence indicates that neither the East nor the West looked upon the episode as the beginning of a permanent schism.

CRUSADES

The CRUSADES aggravated the hostility of the patriarch and the Greek people toward Rome. The motives of the crusaders were suspected and their behavior seemed offensive. The emperors made efforts toward conciliation, but the patriarchs did not support these. Feeling became so strong that there was a massacre of Latins in Constantinople in 1182. This was answered by corresponding but much more extensive violence when the members of the Fourth Crusade captured Constantinople in 1204 and pillaged the city for three days. It was the memory of this, more than anything else, that confirmed the breach between Constantinople and Rome. The Byzantine government in exile, with the Greek patriarchs, resided at Nicaea and the Latins, under a Latin patriarch, occupied the principal churches and monasteries of Constantinople. From the beginning of the Latin occupation Pope INNOCENT III attempted to conciliate the Greeks and procure their obedience with as little disturbance of the hierarchy as possible, but the Greeks had no desire for compromise. The patriarchate returned to Constantinople when the city was recaptured by the Byzantines in 1261.

During the remaining years of Byzantine rule in Constantinople the patriarchs joined with the emperors, who in order to secure political and military support against the Turkish threat were seeking union with Rome. At the councils of LYONS (1276) and FLORENCE (1439) the Church of Constantinople recognized the supremacy of the Roman See, but these actions were only accepted by a very small portion of the Byzantine clergy and people. A council, which met in Hagia Sophia in 1450, condemned the union with Rome and deposed the prounion patriarch. Emperor Constantine XII caused the union to be proclaimed again in Hagia Sophia in December of 1452, but again only a few accepted it, and the city was captured by the Turks on May 29, 1453.

Monastic Establishments

A major influence in the political and religious life of Constantinople was the large number of monastic establishments, each with its particular rule. The extant documents preserve the names of 325 monasteries of men and women in the capital between the years 330 and 1453, though some of these may represent the refounding of an existing establishment under a new name. In 1453, when the capital had shrunk to a shadow of its former size, 18 monastic establishments were still active.

INFLUENCE

The monks had a powerful influence on the religious life of the people, for example, in the iconoclast controversy, in which they strongly defended the use of icons. As a rule the monks had a lively sense of independence and could become fanatical when they considered that they must resist unjust actions of ecclesiastical authority. Some of the monasteries, such as the STUDION, were important centers of scholarship and the preservation of manuscripts.

PATRIARCHAL SCHOOL

Along with the university founded by Constantine the Great, there was a patriarchal school, first attested in the seventh century, which offered instruction not only in theology but in secular learning as well. When reorganized by Photius, this school was divided into various branches, which met at different churches in the city.

Art And Archeology

Recent archeological activity in Istanbul has stimulated popular interest in the art of imperial Constantinople and the corpus of known monuments has largely increased. Exploration of the area of the imperial palace has brought to light important mosaics, as well as valuable topographical information. The work of the Byzantine Institute of America in uncovering and restoring mosaics and frescoes in HAGIA SOPHIA (Holy Wisdom) and elsewhere has added new chapters to the history of Byzantine art. A definitive study of the structure and architectural history of Hagia Sophia, carried out by R. L. Van Nice, is nearing publication. Research on many aspects of the history and antiquities of Constantinople is in progress at the Center for Byzantine Studies of Harvard University at Dumbarton Oaks, in Washington, D.C., and at the Institut Français d'Études Byzantines in Paris.

CHURCHES

Numerous churches, as well as other buildings, including a palace, were constructed after the refoundation of the city by Constantine. Extant sources for 11 centuries of the history of Constantinople record the names of 485 churches. The oldest surviving is the Basilica of St. John Baptist Studium, built c. 463. The most important, still standing, is Justinian's great Church of Hagia Sophia. Constructed on a new plan and at a scale never before attempted, it was the greatest church then existing in the world. Contemporary literary accounts of the original construction and decoration by Procopius of Caesarea and Paulus Silentiarius have been preserved. Procopius, who watched the building being constructed and may have been present when it was dedicated, described its effect on the worshipper: "Whenever anyone enters this church to pray, he understands at once that it is not by human power or skill, but by the power of God, that this work has been so beautifully executed. And his mind is lifted up toward God, feeling that He cannot be far away, but must especially love to dwell in this place which he has chosen." Procopius's description is part of his panegyrical account of Justinian's buildings both at Constantinople and throughout the empire, in which we can perceive that the construction of churches and public buildings was one of the main functions of the emperor, illustrating the sovereign's benevolent role as father of his people. Other churches of Justinian still standing are the church of Saints Sergius and Bacchus and the church of St. Irene. Another great undertaking of Justinian's, the church of the Holy Apostles, was destroyed after 1453, but its plan and decoration are known from literary descriptions by Constantine of Rhodes and Nikolaos Mesarites. Some idea of the richness of this church can be gained from St. Mark's at Venice, which was modeled on it in plan and decoration.

SECULAR ARCHITECTURE

The imperial palace facing the Augustaeum, the public square on which Hagia Sophia stood, was begun by Constantine the Great following the quadrangular plan of the Roman fortified camp, exemplified by the palaces at Spalato and Antioch. As at Antioch and Thessalonica, the juxtaposition at Constantinople of the palace, the hippodrome and the "great church" brought together the three places in which the emperor performed his ceremonial functions, both political and religious. In time the palace was enlarged by the addition of public halls, banquet rooms, private chambers, chapels, churches, gardens and a polo field, until it became one of the largest and most magnificent structures in the world of that time. The fortification walls of Constantinople, in large part preserved, give an excellent idea of Byzantine skill in masonry construction and military engineering.

THE ARTS

Constantinople was famous not only for its buildings and their decorations, but for the luxury articles of all kinds which were manufactured in the city and exported throughout the world, the city being one of the most important trading centers of its time. As the largest and most luxurious city in the world in Byzantine times, the Paris of its day, Constantinople possessed both a taste for the work of skilled artists and craftsmen and the wealth to at-

tract them to the city. The spirit of the capital was expressed in a fondness for magnificence and display, and a love of color. Gold mosaic and gold cloth were much in use. Constantinople and Antioch were the two centers for the manufacture of gold and silver Eucharistic vessels and altar furnishings. The workshops of the city—often established in the palace under direct imperial patronage and supervision—produced the finest jewelry and other objects such as book covers inlaid in gold and silver or enamel and ivory, as well as richly illustrated books and figured silks. Icons of all sizes, metal, painted or mosaic were produced. The coins struck at the imperial mint in Constantinople are important both as examples of contemporary art and iconography and as portraits of imperial personages; notable collections are in the British Museum and at Dumbarton Oaks. The illustrations and ornamentation of the manuscripts, both secular and religious, produced at Constantinople, are one of our richest sources for the purpose and methods of Byzantine art.

Byzantine art as it developed in Constantinople illustrates the way in which the capital brought together the artistic traditions of the other great cities of the empire, notably Antioch and Alexandria, and transformed them into a new and distinctive manner, which often went back to the works of classical Greece and Rome for its inspiration. Byzantine Christian art is full of classical motifs and genre scenes in the antique fashion. It was a unified art that was at the same time secular and religious, decorative and didactic. As an official art, centered on the glorification of God and the emperor, Byzantine art found its finest expression in Constantinople.

The iconoclast controversy had two effects on the artistic activity of the capital: a revival of the classical style and the development of a popular style, centered in the monasteries, which flourished alongside the official, imperial art. Thus the end of the iconoclast ban on religious art was followed by a new golden age in the art of Constantinople, from the ninth through the 12th century.

The artistic influence of the capital radiated throughout the world; it is now especially familiar in the early art and architecture of the Slavic lands, whose whole culture was so dependent upon Byzantium, and in the work of the Italian painters, such as CIMABUE, Duccio, Cavallini, GIOTTO, and MANTEGNA, who were familiar with Byzantine work and developed a close affinity with its spirit and style.

See Also: BYZANTINE EMPIRE; BYZANTINE THEOLOGY; BYZANTINE CIVILIZATION; BYZANTINE ART; BYZANTINE LITERATURE.

Bibliography: G. BECATTI et al., *Enciclopedia dell'arte antica, classica e orientale* (Rome 1958—) 2:880–919, with useful bibliog. R. JANIN, *Dictionnaire d'histoire et de géographie ecclésiastiques, ed. A. BAUDRILLART et al. (Paris 1912—) 13:626–768; *Constantinople byzantine: Développement urbain et répertoire topographique* (Paris 1950); *Les Églises et les monastères,* v.3 of *La Géographie ecclésiastique de l'empire byzantin,* pt. 1 (Paris 1953). G. EVERY, *The Byzantine Patriarchate, 451–1204* (2d ed. London 1962). G. DOWNEY, *Constantinople in the Age of Justinian* (Norman, Okla. 1960). F. DVORNIK, *The Idea of Apostolicity in Byzantium and the Legend of the Apostle Andrew* (Cambridge, Mass. 1958); *The Photian Schism* (Cambridge, Eng. 1948). S. RUNCIMAN, *The Eastern Schism* (Oxford 1955). J. EBERSOLT, *Constantinople: Recueil d'études* (Paris 1951); *Constantinople byzantine et les voyageurs du Levant* (Paris 1918). J. BECKWITH, *The Art of Constantinople* (London 1961). A. GRABAR, *Byzantine Painting,* tr. S. GILBERT (New York 1953); *L'Empereur dans l'art byzantin* (Paris 1936). J. A. HAMILTON, *Byzantine Architecture and Decoration* (2d ed. London 1956). C. A. MANGO, *Materials for the Study of the Mosaics of St. Sophia at Istanbul* (Washington 1962); ''The Byzantine Inscriptions of Constantinople: A Bibliographical Survey,'' *American Journal of Archaeology* 55 (1951) 52–66.

[G. DOWNEY]

CONSTANTINOPLE I, COUNCIL OF

From May to July 381, at the invitation of Emperors Theodosius I and Gratian, some 150 bishops of Thrace, Asia Minor, and Egypt met in Constantinople to deal with the Arian heresy, which had prevailed in the East since the reign of CONSTANTIUS II. Under the presidency of Meletius of Antioch, the assembly deposed the Arian bishop of Constantinople, Maximus the Cynic, and replaced him with GREGORY OF NAZIANZUS, who presided over the Council after the sudden death of Meletius. The Council accepted the Nicene Creed, proclaimed Constantinople as the second see in the Empire after Rome, and, upon the resignation of Gregory, whose authority was challenged by Timothy of Alexandria, selected Nectarius, a retired imperial official, as the new bishop. The acceptance by the Council of the teaching on the Holy Spirit occasioned the refusal of the Macedonian bishops to participate.

As the acts of this Council have been lost, its activities are known only through citations in the letter of the synod at Constantinople to Pope DAMASUS the following year (382), which attests that the Council confirmed the faith of Nicaea, accepted the consubstantiality and coeternity of the three divine Persons in the Trinity against the Sabellians, Anomoeans, Arians, and Pneumatics, and clarified the perfect humanity of the Word against those who deny the soul or the manhood of Christ (*see* PNEUMATOMACHIANS).

The so-called Constantinopolitan Creed, which was actually composed after the Alexandrian synod of 362 and which embodied the Creed of Jerusalem, was recited by Nectarius in the baptismal ceremony preceding his consecration during the Council, and then became proper to the Church of Constantinople.

The Council promulgated four canons: (1) against the Arian heresy and its sects; (2) limiting the jurisdictional activities to the civil dioceses for all bishops; (3) favoring Constantinople as the second see after Rome in honor and dignity; (4) condemning Maximus the Cynic and his followers. Three other canons recorded in the Greek MSS belong to the local synod of 382. Canons two through four were intended to prevent the interference of the See of Alexandria in the ecclesiastical dioceses of the East. The Council closed on July 9, 381, and at the bishops' request the emperor promulgated its decrees on July 30.

The Council fathers themselves spoke of it as ''ecumenical,'' this term having been used in reference to a council at CARTHAGE in a letter to Pope CELESTINE by the African bishops, and it was intended to have the meaning of a full or general council, in contrast to the *synodos endemousa,* or particular, local council permanently in session at Constantinople. Gregory of Nazianzus showed annoyance over the use of the term ecumenical, and there is no evidence that the Council's acts were accepted by Pope Damasus in the Roman synod of 382. However, the Council is mentioned in the acts of both the 2d and 5th sessions of Chalcedon, and in those of the 16th session it is joined to Nicaea I. Its regulation concerning the precedence of Constantinople (the so-called 28th canon) became law for the Oriental Churches. However, Pope Leo I strenuously objected to the validity of this regulation and claimed that canon three of Constantinople, upon which it was based, had never been brought to the attention of Rome (*Epist.* 106; *Patrologia Latina,* ed. J. P. Migne, 54:1007). It was Dionysius Exiguus who translated these canons into Latin during the reign of Pope HORMISDAS, and eventually Gregory I acknowledged Constantinople I as one of the four councils that in their spiritual authority paralleled the four Gospels.

Bibliography: C. J. VON HEFELE, *Histoire des conciles d'après les documents originaux,* tr. and continued by H. LECLERCQ, 10 v. in 19 (Paris 1907–38) 2.1:1–48. J. BOIS, *Dictionnaire de théologie catholique,* ed. A. VACANT et al., 15 v. (Paris 1903–50) 3.1:1227–31. G. BARDY, *Dictionnaire de droit canonique,* ed. R. NAZ, 7 v. (Paris 1935–65) 4:424–428. R. JANIN, *Dictionnaire d'histoire et de géographie ecclésiastiques,* ed. A. BAUDRILLART et al. (Paris 1912–) 13:629–740. N. Q. KING, ''The 150 Holy Fathers of the Council of Constantinople,'' *Studia Patristica* 1 (*Texte und Untersuchungen zur Geschitchte der altchristlichen Literatur* 67; 1957) 635–641; *The Emperor Theodosius and the Establishment of Christianity* (Philadelphia 1960). H. D. KREILKAMP, *The Origin of the Patriarchate of Constantinople* (Doctoral diss. microfilm; Catholic University of America 1964) 28–63. N. M. VAPORIS, ed., ''Second Ecumenical Council, Constantinople, AD 381,'' *Greek Orthodox Theological Review* 27 (1982) 341–453. K. LEHMANN and W. PANNENBERG, eds., *Glaubensbekenntnis und Kirchengemeinschaft: Das Modell des Konzils von Konstantinopel* (Freiburg im Breisgau 1982).

[H. D. KREILKAMP]

CONSTANTINOPLE II, COUNCIL OF

The Council, accepted as the fifth general council, was convoked by the Emperor Justinian in 553 and held from May 5 to June 2 with 168 bishops assembled in the great hall of the HAGIA SOPHIA in Constantinople to render judgment, in accordance with the emperor's instructions on the THREE CHAPTERS. All but 11 bishops (including nine recruited by the government from Africa) were from the Orient, since Pope VIGILIUS and his retinue of Western bishops present in the capital refused repeated invitations to attend. Presiding were the Patriarchs EUTYCHIUS OF CONSTANTINOPLE, Apollinaris of Alexandria, Domninus of Antioch, and three bishops representing the newly appointed Eustachius of Jerusalem, in accord with Justinian's decision to give the assembly the appearance of complete freedom by not appointing the customary imperial commissioners to govern the debate.

The Council. The conciliar assembly opened with the emperor's allocution read by the notary Stephen, in which Justinian justified his regulation of religious affairs of the Empire, pointing for precedent to the activities of his predecessors in convoking general councils. Describing NESTORIANISM as the primary danger, reminding the bishops of the written opinion on the Three Chapters he had received from them a year earlier, and deploring the absence of Pope Vigilius, Justinian directed the assembly's attention to the impious writings of THEODORE OF MOPSUESTIA, THEODORET OF CYR, and the letter "falsely attributed" to Ibas of Edessa.

In the first two sessions (May 5 and 8) the bishops concerned themselves with attempts to persuade Vigilius and his entourage to join them in Council; and in the third (May 9), they made a profession of faith based on Justinian's inaugural message, to which they added an anathema against anyone separating himself from the Church, evidently having Vigilius in mind. The fourth session (Monday, May 12) considered 70 passages from the writings of Theodore of Mopsuestia and condemned them as Nestorian teaching, while the fifth session (May 17), after considering the relations between St. CYRIL OF ALEXANDRIA and Theodore, decided that though he was deceased, the person and the works of Theodore should be anathematized. They then decided that the writings of Theodoret of Cyr against Cyril also were heretical and expressed their amazement at the subtlety of the Council of CHALCEDON, which had exonerated Theodoret, but only after his explicit repudiation of Nestorius. The sixth session (May 19) dealt at length with the *Letter to Maris* and the reputation of Ibas of Edessa, deciding that he was not the author of the letter; hence his exoneration at Chalcedon was justified.

Reaction of the Pope. Vigilius, meanwhile, had examined the same matters in his *Constitutum I* (signed May 14, 553) composed with the aid of the deacon and future pope, PELAGIUS I. On May 24 he attempted to send an official copy to the emperor, but was rebuffed with the remark, "If the *Constitutum* agrees with the condemnation of the Three Chapters, it is useless; if it disagrees, Vigilius contradicts himself and is self-condemned." To justify this statement, Justinian in a formal message to the seventh session (May 26) described his relations with the pope since his arrival in Constantinople in 546 and produced secret letters, two signed by the pope in 546 and a third in 550, in which Vigilius had given Justinian and Theodora a guarantee that he would condemn the Three Chapters. This message was followed by a notice that the emperor had ordered Vigilius's name struck from the DIPTYCHS since he adhered to the errors of the Three Chapters, while making it clear that he did not sever communion with Rome: he repudiated the occupant, not the see—*non sedem sed sedentem*—employing a distinction original with Pope LEO I (P. Jaffé, *Regesta pontificum romanorum ab condita ecclesia ad annum post Christum natum 1198*, 483). The bishops supported the emperor's action and condemned the pope until he should repent.

The Conciliar Decrees. In the eighth session (June 2) a doctrinal statement and 14 anathemas prepared under THEODORE ASCIDAS were accepted as the Council's conclusion. The statement gives a long résumé of the Council's actions and a profession of faith in the Incarnation. It explains the attempt to induce Vigilius to attend, but says nothing of his condemnation in the seventh session; finally it insists on the authority of the Council of Chalcedon and Pope Leo I, while making repeated efforts to justify its condemnation of the Three Chapters.

Drawn almost verbatim from the Edict of 551, the anathemas (1 to 10) resume in negative form the Alexandrian Christology aimed at destroying the Nestorian doctrine that divided Christ in two persons and accept the Theopaschite formula "One of the Trinity suffered in the flesh (10)." The last four anathemas condemn a series of heretics from Origen and Arius to Eutyches and Nestorius (11); and along with their heretical teachings, Theodore of Mopsuestia (12) and Theodoret of Cyr (13) are condemned, as is also the *Letter to Maris* of Ibas of Edessa (14). Finally the Council decrees deposition of clerics and anathematization of laymen who defy its decrees.

Acceptance of the Decrees. Justinian delayed publication of the Conciliar Edict until July 14, then demanded the signature of all Metropolitans, bishops, and monastic leaders. Pressure was brought to bear on Vigilius, who, separated from Pelagius, his chief adviser, finally wavered, and on Dec. 8, 553, addressed a letter to the Patriarch Eutyches of Constantinople, in which he accepted the Council and its decisions, blaming his previous obstinacy on the devil's deception; he appealed to St. AUGUSTINE's *Retractions* as precedent for his change of mind.

On Feb. 23, 554, Vigilius published his *Constitutum II,* reaffirming his adherence to the Council's condemnation of the Three Chapters. He accepted its contention that Ibas was not the author of the *Letter to Maris,* that Theodore had been condemned virtually by Pope DAMASUS I (382–386), and that Theodoret was rehabilitated at Chalcedon only after repudiating his former Nestorian teaching. But he said nothing of the doctrine expressed in the first ten anathemas, while explicitly nullifying ''whatever is brought forward in my name in defense of the Three Chapters.''

Reaction in the Orient. The Council was accepted without difficulty everywhere except in the Grand Laura of Egypt, where a group of monks, called *Isochristes* (the same as Christ), because they maintained that in the resurrection all men would be the same as Christ, refused to accept its condemnation of Origen. In the West, and particularly in Africa, Northern Italy, Dalmatia, and Gaul, open rebellion broke out among the bishops. The deacon Pelagius wrote a *Refutatorium* against Vigilius and an *In defensione trium capitulorum,* which, together with the work of the same name by FACUNDUS OF HERMIANE, repudiated the condemnation of the Three Chapters.

Governmental repression exiled Pelagius, VICTOR OF TUNNUNA, Rusticus and Liberatus of Carthage, Facundus of Hermiane, and Abbot Felix of Gillitanum.

On the death of Vigilius (June 7, 555), however, Justinian chose Pelagius as the new bishop of Rome, and with the aid of the Byzantine general Narses had him installed, despite local opposition. On Easter Sunday (April 16, 556) Pelagius cleared himself by oath, was consecrated, and dispatched a *Letter to the Whole Christian People,* in which he declared his adherence to the doctrine of the four ecumenical councils and the faith of Chalcedon, but said nothing of Vigilius and his Constitutions, nor of the Council of 553 (Liber pontificalis 5, Pelagius I). With the aid of the civil power he forced the bishops of Tuscany and Sicily into communion with him; but he was unsuccessful in the provinces of Milan and Aquileia, whose metropolitans cut themselves off completely from communion with Rome.

Despite Pelagius's protest that ''it has never been permitted that a particular synod should judge a General Council'' (Jaffé 1018) and his appeal both to the general Narses and to Justinian, the Milanese remained in schism until 572; while in AQUILEIA, where the metropolitan took the title of patriarch (570), despite the efforts of Popes PELAGIUS II and GREGORY I (590–604) the schism continued until the pontificate of SERGIUS I (687–701), when after a Synod at Pavia legates from Aquileia accepted the Council of Constantinople II as universal and the metropolitan made his submission to Rome.

Evaluation. From a historical standpoint the Council presents several difficulties. The *Acts* are preserved in Latin (J. D. Mansi, *Sacrorum Conciliorum nova et amplissima collectio,* 9:163–658) in two revisions, the shorter of which was probably prepared for Vigilius by Justinian and used by Pelagius, for it makes no mention of Justinian's and the Council's condemnation of Vigilius in the seventh session. It was this version that was employed by theologians in their estimate of the Council's value until the longer version was discovered and published by É. BALUZE in 1683. At the Council of CONSTANTINOPLE III the secret letters of Vigilius to Justinian and Theodora were challenged and pronounced forgeries, but evidence supplied by Facundus of Hermiane (*Adv. Mocianum*) and Justinian (Mansi 9:366) testify to their authenticity. Contemporary evidence (Pelagius, *In def. trium cap.*) likewise witnesses to the authenticity of the letter of Vigilius to Eutyches of Dec. 8, 553, and the *Constitutum II.*

From a theological viewpoint the Council's decisions destroyed whatever Nestorian tendencies may have lingered in Chalcedonian thought. But as Justinian seems to have recognized at the end of his reign, the greater danger lay in Monophysitism. Some modern authors feel the Council represents the triumph of Neo-Chalcedonianism, by which is meant an overstressing of Cyrillan Christology, and as such, a reversion from the accomplishment of Chalcedon.

While Constantinople II settled the fact that the two natures are inviolably united in the person of Christ, it did not come to terms with the qualities of the human nature. Thus it opened the way for the quarrels over the two wills and two energies in Christ that were to be the subject of the next two ecumenical councils and that have returned as problems today in regard to the ''ego'' of Christ.

Bibliography: J. BOIS, *Dictionnaire de théologie catholique,* ed. A. VACANT et al, 15 v. (Paris 1903–50) 3.1:1231–59. É. AMANN, *Dictionnaire de théologie catholique,* ed. A. VACANT et al, 15 v. (Paris 1903–50) 15.2:1268–1924. G. BARDY, *Catholicisme* 3:114–116. L. PETIT and J. B. MARTIN, *Sacrorum Conciliorum nova et amplissima collectio,* 53 v. in 60 (Paris 1889–1927); repr. Graz 1960–) 9:171–657. C. J. VON HEFELE, *Histoire des conciles d'après les documents orginaux,* tr. and continued by H. LECLERQ, 10 v. in 19 (Paris 1907–38). F. DIEKAMP, *Die origenistischen Streitigkeiten im sechsten Jahrhundert* (Münster 1899). L. DUCHESNE, *L'Église au VIe siècle* (Paris 1925). E. STEIN and J. R. PALANQUE, *Histoire du bas-empire,* 2 v. (Paris 1949–59) 2:623–690. *Conciliorum oecumenicorum decreta* 81–98. C. MOELLER, ''Le Cinquième concile oecuménique et le magistère ordinaire au VIe siècle,'' *Revue des* *sciences religieuses* 35 (1951) 413–423; "Le Chalcédonisme et le néochalcédonisme en Orient," A. GRILLMEIER and H. BACHT, *Das Konzil von Chalkedon: Geschichte und Gegenwart*, 3 v. (Würzburg 1951–54) 1:637–700. H. M. DIEPEN, *Douze dialogues de christologie ancienne* (Rome 1960). G. L. C. FRANK, "The Council of Constantinople II as a Model Reconciliation Council," *Theological Studies* 52 (1991) 636–50.

[F. X. MURPHY]

CONSTANTINOPLE III, COUNCIL OF

The sixth ecumenical council, held in Constantinople from Nov. 7, 680, to Sept. 16, 681; it is referred to also as the First Trullan Council. With the support of Emperor HERACLIUS, the Patriarch of Constantinople SERGIUS I (610–638) had introduced MONOTHELITISM into the BYZANTINE CHURCH in an attempt to reunify the MONOPHYSITE and orthodox Christians in the East. The result, however, was the opposite of that hoped for—not only did the East fail to achieve religious unity, but the new doctrine provoked grave complications in the West. And so, with the double-edged purpose of restoring orthodoxy and thus preventing the secession of Italy from the Byzantine Empire, the Emperor Constantine IV (668–685) decided—with the consent of Pope AGATHO—to summon the entire episcopate to a general assembly.

The patriarch of Constantinople duly transmitted the edict convoking this assembly (dated Sept. 10, 680) to his three fellow patriarchs in the East. The Council was held at Constantinople in the Imperial Palace, in the hall of the cupola, and is thus often described as the council *In Trullo* (I). Despite the pressure of the secular authorities, the number of conciliar fathers who attended the Council before the tenth session was extremely small: only 50 (44 bishops and six monks) came to the first session (Nov. 7, 680). The West had been invited to send at least 12 bishops, but only one priest (for the Church of Ravenna), and four Greek monks for the Byzantine monasteries of southern Italy actually came. The Patriarchate of Jerusalem sent only two *apocrisiarii;* Alexandria was represented by only a few clerics. Thus, by contrast, the pope's own delegation appeared imposing, for it consisted of three bishops, two priests, one deacon, and one subdeacon.

The first 11 sessions, as well as the final one, were presided over by the emperor, whose original intention had been to convoke a simple conference; but the assembly insisted on being ecumenical from its first session. In all it held 18 sessions between Nov. 7, 680, and Sept. 16, 681.

Patriarch Macarius of Antioch and his supporters, representing the Monothelite heresy that was to be adjudicated, made their statements at the fifth and sixth sessions (Dec. 7, 680, and Feb. 12, 681). At the following session (March 7, 681), they defended their position. The ensuing debates, hard-fought and meticulous, were protracted. The process against Macarius, who was accused of having misapplied and of having truncated the texts of Scripture and the Fathers of the Church, was begun only during the 11th and 12th sessions (March 20 and 22), but his deposition occurred at the 13th session (March 28). The 17th session (September 11) was occupied with formulating the decree of faith (*horos*) that proclaimed the doctrine of the two wills and the two natural energies in Christ, undivided, inseparable, and without confusion. The document was signed first by the emperor and then by the 178 council fathers then present. Like the fifth ecumenical council, Constantinople II (553), this Council did not promulgate disciplinary canons, an omission that the QUINISEXT SYNOD (691–692), *In Trullo* (II), felt it had to remedy.

One of the most important acts of Constantinople III was the condemnation of Pope HONORIUS I, listed among the real champions of Monothelitism. This condemnation, renewed by the Quinisext Synod and by the eighth ecumenical council, CONSTANTINOPLE IV (869–870), was extensively used at VATICAN COUNCIL I as an argument against papal INFALLIBILITY. There was no protest during the sessions against the condemnation on the part of the papal legates, and Honorius's successor, Pope LEO II, seems to have approved, though he saw Honorius's case only as one of personal failure.

The Council was immediately approved and pronounced ecumenical by Leo II (letter of May 7, 683), subsequently by Pope BENEDICT II and the third Council of TOLEDO (684), and finally by both the Church of the West and the Church of the East, the latter having always recognized it without question as the sixth in the series of general councils of the Church. The *Acta,* of which there is no critical edition, can be consulted most conveniently in J. D. Mansi, *Sacorum Conciliorum nova et amplissima collectio* 11:190–922.

Bibliography: J. BOIS, *Dictionnaire de théologie catholique*, ed. A. VACANT et al., 15 v. (Paris 1903–50) 3.1:1259–74. É. AMANN, *Dictionnaire de théologie catholique* 7.1:93–132. M. JUGIE, *Dictionnaire de théologie catholique* 10.2:2307–23; Tables générales 664–665. C. J. VON HEFELE, *Histoire des conciles d'après les documents originaux*, tr. and continued by H. LECLERCQ, 10 v. in 19, (Paris 1907–38) 3.1:472–538. E. CASPAR, *Geschichte de Papsttums von den Anfängen bis zur Höhe der Weltherrschaft*, 2 v. (Tübingen 1930–33) 2:587–614. A. FLICHE and V. MARTIN, eds., *Histoire de l'église depuis les origines jusqu'à nos jours* (Paris 1935–) 5:183–191. K. BAUS, *Lexikon für Theologie und Kirche*, ed. J. HOFER and K. RAHNER, 10 v. (2d, new ed. Freiburg 1957–65) 6:496, 497, recent bibliog. J. M. A. SALLES-DABADIE, *Les Conciles oecuméniques dans l'histoire* (Geneva 1962) 189–209. On Pope Honorius. K. HIRSCH, "Papst Honorius I. und das VI. allgemeine Konzil,"

Festschrift der 57. Versammlung deutscher Philologen u. Schulmänner in Salzburg (Salzburg 1929) 158–179. A. FLICHE and V. MARTIN, eds., *Histoire de l'église depuis les origines jusqu'à nos jours* 5:120–124, 397–400. P. VIARD, *Catholicisme. Hier, aujourd'hui et demain*, ed. G. JACQUEMET (Paris 1947–) 5:923–925. R. BÄUMER, *Lexikon für Theologie und Kirche*, ed. J. HOFER and K. RAHNER 5:474–475; "Die Wiederentdeckung der Honoriusfrage im Abendland," *Römische Quartalschrift für christliche Altertumskunde und für Kirchengeschichte* 56 (1961) 200–214. On Honorius's letters to Constantinople. V. GRUMEL, "Recherches sur l'histoire du monothélisme. III. Action et rôle d'Honorius," *Échos d'Orient* 28 (1929) 272–282. P. GALTIER, "La Première lettre du pape Honorius," *Gregorianum* 29 (1948) 42–61.

[V. LAURENT]

CONSTANTINOPLE IV, COUNCIL OF

This controversial council, considered by Western canonists as the eighth ecumenical council, convened in Constantinople, Oct. 5, 869, to Feb. 28, 870. As soon as he was master of the empire, Basil I (867–86), whose grand design was endangered by current religious dissensions, demonstrated from the start his resolution to regulate the quarrel that was dividing the BYZANTINE CHURCH and to normalize the relations of this Church with the Holy See. Circumstances seemed favorable to this plan. Pope NICHOLAS I, whom PHOTIUS had anathematized in a synod held in the summer of 867, had died on November 13 of that year, unaware of this condemnation. Photius for his part was soon deposed for having dared to censure Basil, the current ruler and the murderer of Emperor MICHAEL III. It seemed likely that the new ecclesiastical dignitaries, Pope ADRIAN II at Rome and Patriarch IGNATIUS OF CONSTANTINOPLE, should now be able to reach an accord.

Unfortunately, the conduct of Photius, which finally became known in Rome, appeared so offensive to the apostolic see that it seemed to warrant denunciation and eventual condemnation. This was done in the Roman Synod, held in St. Peter's Basilica on June 10, 869. The Photian Synod (867) was condemned, its acts burned, and Photius excommunicated. Thereafter Adrian deferred to the wish of the Byzantine Emperor and agreed to send a mission to Constantinople, but on condition that the council to be held limit itself to confirming the decisions of the Roman Synod.

Sessions. Armed with strict instructions, Donatus, Bishop of Ostia, Stephen, Bishop of Nepi, and especially the deacon Marinus, the most competent member of the mission, were soon on the Bosphorus, where the Council opened at HAGIA SOPHIA. The early sessions were poorly attended (at the 5th session there were still only 21 bishops, and at the 10th and last, 103). But it has not been suf-

ficiently noted that, although the suffragan bishops were conspicuously absent, almost all the metropolitans (37 out of 40) were present when the acts were signed. Photius was required to appear twice, on October 20 and 29. On the second appearance (the 7th session) he was anathematized together with his supporters, and a week later, at the 8th session, all his writings relating to the council of 867 were solemnly burned. Thereafter other meetings were held at intervals until on Feb. 28, 870, the crucial act of the Council took place: this was the publication of the definition (ὅρος), the homage to Pope Nicholas, whose Acts were again accorded the force of law, and the publication of 27 disciplinary canons, which in succeeding centuries had great importance in the West. The Acts were solemnly signed by the Emperor, the papal legates, the Patriarch Ignatius, the representatives (*apocrisiarii*) of the three Eastern patriarchs, the 37 metropolitans, and 65 bishops. An imperial edict promulgated (870) the decisions of the Council as laws of the state. Never had the supremacy of the Roman See over the two great parts of Christendom been so solemnly proclaimed. Convoked essentially to regulate the affair of Photius, the assembly profited by the occasion to take action on several other questions of emergent importance: the liceity of the veneration of IMAGES, still under attack by latent ICONOCLASM; interference by lay persons in episcopal nominations (c.22); and the hierarchy of the five patriarchates, sanctioning the theory of the pentarchy in the government of the universal Church (c.21).

The Acts. The Papal legates were captured and robbed by Slavic pirates on the return journey to Rome, and consequently the copy of the acts destined for Adrian II never reached him. ANASTASIUS THE LIBRARIAN, who had been present at the Council as a representative of the German Emperor Louis II, had better fortune and managed to carry back to Rome a complete copy of the authentic acts; but this copy also has been lost, so that the acts have been preserved only in the translation that the Pope commissioned Anastasius to prepare for him (J. D. Mansi, *Sacrorum Conciliorum nova et amplissima collectio*, 16:16–207), preceded by a preface and a short account of the history of the sessions, composed by Anastasius (*ibid.* 1–16). All that remains of the original Greek is a long fragment abridged by an anonymous author (*ibid.* 308–420).

Ecumenical Status. By calling itself the *universalis octava synodus,* the Council claimed for itself an ecumenical status; it had at least the necessary geographical characteristics because of the authority of all the heads of the Church who were either present or represented. Was it recognized as ecumenical by the Holy See? Three facts are certain and cannot be contested: (1) Adrian II had already approved it in his letter of Nov. 10, 871; in

875 in his letter (P. Jaffé, *Regesta Pontificum romanorum ab condita ecclesia ad annum post Christum natum 1198*, 3012) to the faithful of Salerno and Amalfi, JOHN VIII called it *sancta octava synodus* and thereby formally ascribing to it ecumenicity; (2) since the beginning of the 12th century this council has been listed among the ecumenical councils recognized by the Latin Church; (3) the Byzantine Church itself held this council to be ecumenical until the Photian Synod of 879 to 880, which is thought to have abrogated its Acts; moreover, those portions of the Byzantine Church that have been reunited with Rome in the course of centuries have accepted it and consider it as ecumenical. The problem is reducible to the question whether Pope John VIII, by making use of his supreme power of binding and loosing, actually annulled the acts of the council of 869, thus depriving it of its ecumenical status. The answer is affirmative if the Greek text of the last two sessions of the Photian Synod are considered authentic (Dvornik, Amann); it is negative if reference is had to other documents, especially to the letter (885–886) of Pope STEPHEN V to Emperor Basil I (Grumel). This letter states, in fact, that 20 years after the eighth ecumenical council, Photius was still trying to have it annulled, a step that would be inexplicable if prior to this time John VIII had already taken the initiative in this matter. The least that can be said is that the whole problem centering around the authenticity or nonauthenticity of the last two sessions of the Photian Synod is unresolved.

Bibliography: General. C. J. VON HEFELE, *Histoire des conciles d'après les documents originaux*, tr. and continued by H. LECLERCQ, 10 v. in 19 (Paris 1907–38) 4:481–546. M. JUGIE, *Dictionnaire de théologie catholique*, ed. A. VACANT et al. 15 v. (Paris 1903–50) 3:1273–1307. É. AMANN, *ibid.* 12:1549–82; 16:666–67. A. FLICHE and V. MARTIN, eds., *Histoire de l'église depuis les origines jusqu'à nos jours* (Paris 1935–) 6:493–97. F. DVORNIK, *The Photian Schism: History and Legend* (Cambridge, Eng. 1948); *The Patriarch Photius in the Light of Recent Research* (Munich 1958). K. BAUS, *Lexikon für Theologie und Kirche*, ed. J. HOFER and K. RAHNER, 10 v. (2d, new ed. Freiburg 1957–65) 6:496–97, with recent literature. J. M. A. SALLES-DABADIE, *Les Conciles oecuméniques dans l'histoire* (Paris 1962). Ecumenicity. (1) Favoring the thesis of abrogation by John VIII: F. DVORNIK, "L'Oecuménicité du VIIIᵉ concile (869–870) dans la tradition occidentale du moyen-âge," *Bulletin de l'Académie Royale de Belgique, Section des Lettres* 24 (1938) 445–87, a study included also in *The Photian Schism* (see above). (2) Favoring nonabrogation, and hence ecumenicity: V. GRUMEL, "La Lettre du pape Étienne V à l'empereur Basile Ier," *Revue des études byzantines* 11 (1953) 129–55; "New Light on the Photian Schism," *Unitas* 5 (1953) 140–48. M. JUGIE, *Dictionnaire de théologie catholique*, ed. A. VACANT et al., 15 v. (Paris 1903–50) 3:1304–07. The canons. Extant in a double recension: the one, in 27 canons, in Latin, in the translation of Anastasius the Librarian; the other in a Greek compendium, numbering 14 canons. It has been correctly observed that the abbreviated Greek version, in retaining only the essentials of each article, indeed made a judicious choice. The texts are in J. D. MANSI, *Sacorum Conciliorum nova et amplissima collectio*, 31 v. (Florence-Venice 1757–98); reprinted and continued by L. PETIT and J. B. MARTIN 53 v. in 60 (Paris 1889–1927; repr. Graz 1960–) 16:160–78 and in P. JOANNOU, ed., *Les Canons des conciles oecuméniques* (Sacra Congregazione Orientale, *Codificazione orientale, Fonti* (Rome 1930–); in 3d series, *Pontificia Commissio ad redigendum Codicem iuris canonici orientalis, Fontes* fasc. 9: *Discipline générale antique (IIᵉ–IXᵉ s.,* v.1.1; 1962) 289–342; the editor placed the acts of this council in appendix.

[V. LAURENT]

CONSTANTINOPLE, ECUMENICAL PATRIARCHATE OF

The history of the Ecumenical Patriarchate of Constantinople begins in 324, when the Emperor Constantine I decided to move the seat of governmental administration from Italy to the eastern region of his empire and chose the small town of Byzantium along the Bosporus. Ecclesiastically, Byzantium then was a suffragan of the Exarchate of Heraclea, the capital of Thrace. There is little historical evidence to substantiate the claim that Constantinople had been founded by Saint Andrew, brother of Saint Peter. Most historians today trace this claim back to the apocryphal work of Pseudo-Dorotheus of Tyre, written about 525 in an attempt to place Constantinople on an equal footing with Rome. The bishops of Byzantium gradually withdrew from the jurisdiction of the Arian bishops who controlled the See of Heraclea until finally, with encouragement from the emperors, they succeeded in canon 3 of the Council of CONSTANTINOPLE I (381) to have the bishop of Constantinople granted "precedence of honor after the bishop of Rome because Constantinople is the New Rome."

Jurisdictional Development. With its independence juridically proclaimed, the Church of Constantinople began to assert its jurisdiction in the affairs of the Churches of Ephesus and of CAESAREA IN CAPPADOCIA, on grounds of their position in relation to the imperial court. At the court the bishop of the capital was prevailed upon by the emperor to act as his intermediary in dealing with nearby ecclesiastical provinces. This intervention was gradually extended to territories controlled by the ancient patriarchates of ANTIOCH and ALEXANDRIA and caused jurisdictional troubles among these three patriarchates.

5th Century. In the 5th century ecclesiastical politics rather than zeal for dogmatic truth often caused these churches to take opposite sides. In the Council of EPHESUS (431), Nestorius Patriarch of Constantinople, was condemned through pressure exerted by Saint CYRIL OF ALEXANDRIA; and 20 years later, in the Council of CHALCEDON (451), Constantinople was able to deal a lethal blow to the Patriarchate of Alexandria by securing the condemnation of the Monophysite doctrine held by Dioscorus, Patriarch of Alexandria. In the same council Anatolius of Constantinople succeeded in having the juridical encroachments from 381 to 451 of his patriarchate officially recognized in canon 28, which gave Constantinople jurisdiction over the Dioceses of Thrace, Asia, and Pontus and the right to consecrate bishops for the provinces occupied by the "barbarians."

Antioch, weakened by the two condemned heresies of NESTORIANISM and MONOPHYSITISM, was dismembered even further when, in 451, Jerusalem was made a patriarchate with 57 dioceses that once belonged to the Antiochene Church. The Church of Alexandria subsequently began to disintegrate slowly through the persecutions inflicted upon its adherents to the Monophysite doctrine by the Byzantine emperor and later by the Muslim Arabs. Thus more and more the patriarch of Constantinople extended his ecclesiastical jurisdiction to coincide with the civil power of the emperor. The emperor turned many of his problems over to the patriarch, who developed in the imperial court a permanent synod (*synodos endemousa*). Centralization led the patriarchs of Constantinople to call themselves the Ecumenical Patriarchs.

Ecumenical Patriarch. When Patriarch John IV the Faster in 588 used this title both Pope PELAGIUS II and Pope GREGORY I protested. Historians point out that "ecumenical" in this title did not mean an infringement on the claims of the Pope of Rome to universal jurisdiction; rather it was only an appellation that recognized the reality that the patriarch of Constantinople had jurisdiction throughout the whole of the Byzantine Empire. The Patriarchs of Constantinople have continued to use this title to this day.

Patriarchate under the Turks. The city of Constantinople was sacked by the Turks on May 29, 1453. Under the Muslim sultans the patriarchs of Constantinople were moved from their elegant palace and occupied the small quarters, the Phanar along the Golden Horn. HAGIA SOPHIA became a mosque, later a museum.

Ethnarch under Muslims. Ironically, however, the patriarch began to enjoy more power than he had under the Byzantine emperors, for the sultans drew no distinction between religion and civil state. Christianity was recognized as a separate religious faith, of a rank inferior to Islam, and was organized as an independent political unit with its own administrator. The ecumenical patriarch was chosen as the civil head for all Greeks, becoming the ethnarch, or *millet-bashi*. This arrangement continued until 1923 in Turkey.

The *millet* system had two significant effects on the patriarchate. Faced by a majority of Muslims who im-

posed heavy taxes and discrimination in all areas of life, the Greek Orthodox organized their political life around their Church, with the result that Church and nation, Orthodoxy and Hellenism became synonymous. A new patriarch received the *berat* from the sultan, but for this honor he had to pay a heavy tax that was collected by the sale of bishoprics and the imposition of heavy levies on the people. Out of 160 patriarchs who held the See of Constantinople between the 15th century and the collapse of Ottoman rule, 105 were driven from their thrones; 27 abdicated; and six died violently by hanging, poisoning, or drowning, whereas only 21 died natural deaths still in office.

Jurisdictional Losses. Amid these internal disturbances the patriarch of Constantinople suffered a great loss in his jurisdiction over other Orthodox churches. The principle of philetism, which sanctioned the organization of a separate church for each nationality, was enforced to establish separate patriarchates among Orthodox churches that originally depended on the Patriarchate of Constantinople. Thus Russia erected its own patriarchate (Moscow) in 1589, Serbia in 1830, Romania in 1856, and Bulgaria in 1870; and the Greeks outside the Ottoman Empire set up their own autocephalous synodal Church in 1833. The patriarch of Constantinople was helpless to protest the severing of the bonds of dependence as new nations sought to apply the principle that originally had created the glories of Constantinople. Nevertheless, the Ecumenical Patriarch retains the primacy of honor among the ancient patriarchs of the Christian East. He is formally styled the Archbishop of Constantinople/New Rome and Ecumenical Patriarch.

Present-day Organization. During Ottoman rule, the Ecumenical Patriarchate was governed according to the Constitution approved (1860–62) by Sultan Abd-ul-Aziz, through a synod under the presidency of the patriarch and a mixed council of clergy and laity for temporal affairs. The patriarch was elected by an assembly of the synod, made up of 12 metropolitans and 70 lay delegates. A list is presented to the Turkish state, and those candidates are eliminated who are unacceptable to the government. From the approved candidates three are chosen. The final choice is granted to the metropolitans, who gather in the patriarchal chapel to elect the new patriarch.

The Holy Synod. The Holy Synod, properly speaking, ceased to exist in 1923, when it became impossible for the metropolitans from outside Turkey to meet annually. A permanent synod, composed of the resident prelates of Istanbul and other metropolitans possessing Turkish citizenship, has been substituted. This synod is the official organ of authority for the patriarchate, managing spiritual affairs such as the nomination of the metropolitan members of the synod, electing new bishops, overseeing the monasteries, including Mount ATHOS, and looking after the spiritual life of churches within the patriarchate's jurisdiction.

Bibliography: G. EVERY, *The Byzantine Patriarchate* (2d ed. London 1962). G. HOFMANN, *Griechische Patriarchen und römische Päpste* (*Orientalia christiana*, v.13.2, 20.1, 25.2, 33.1, 36.2; Rome 1928–34). J. PARGOIRE, *L'Église byzantine de 527 à 847* (Paris 1905). R. ROBERSON, *The Eastern Christian Churches: A Brief Survey* (6th ed. Rome 1999).

[G. A. MALONEY/EDS.]

CONSTANTIUS II, ROMAN EMPEROR

Reigned 337 to 361; son of Constantine I, and coemperor with his brothers Constantine II and Constans. Weak and suspicious, he was probably responsible for the murder of rival members of the Flavian dynasty in 337. He governed the East until 350, and thereafter all the Empire, with his nephews Gallus and Julian as Caesars. Although unbaptized until his deathbed, he pursued a vigorous religious policy as an Arian. He attacked paganism, decreeing in 356 that "temples shall be closed at once everywhere" and prescribing capital punishment for the offering of sacrifices. He gave free reign to Arian bishops of the East, and after 350 strove to force the heresy on the West. In 345 he reinstated ATHANASIUS at Constans' insistence, but in 355 exiled him, along with Pope LIBERIUS, HILARY OF POITIERS, and Hosius of Córdoba. He convoked many of the synods of the period. Faced with Julian's rebellion, he died leaving Arianism triumphant everywhere.

Bibliography: J. R. PALANQUE, et al., *The Church in the Christian Roman Empire*, tr. E. C. MESSENGER, 2 v. in 1 (New York 1953). H. LIETZMANN, *History of the Early Church*, tr. B. L. WOOLF, 4 v. (New York 1949–52). A. PIGANIOL, *L'Empire chrétien, 325–395* (Paris 1947).

[R. H. SCHMANDT]

CONSTANTIUS OF FABRIANO, BL.

Dominican; b. Fabriano, Italy, 1410; d. Ascoli, Feb. 24, 1481. A prior of the Dominican congregation of the strict observance, he was an influential peacemaker and counselor because of his personal holiness and extraordinary gifts. He entered the order at the priory of St. Luke, Ascoli, and was taught by St. ANTONINUS of Florence and by Bl. Conradine of Brescia (d. 1429; feast: Nov. 1), whose life he is said to have written. A professor of theology at Bologna and Florence, he was prior at Fabriano (1440 and 1467), Perugia (1459), and Ascoli (1470). Lives of other Dominican *beati* and a collection of sermons are also attributed to him. He was buried in Ascoli, but partial relics were deposited in the cathedral of Fabriano, where they are still venerated. His cult was approved by Pius VIII in 1811.

Feast: Feb. 25.

Bibliography: I. TAURISANO, *Catalogus hagiographicus ordinis praedicatorum* (Rome 1918) 44. *Année Dominicaine*, 23 v. (Lyons 1883–1909) Feb. 2:773–780. J. QUÉTIF and J. ÉCHARD, *Scriptores Ordinis Praedicatorum* (New York 1959) 1.2:858–859.

[B. CAVANAUGH]

CONSUBSTANTIALITY

This term corresponds to the celebrated HOMOOUSIOS (ὁμοούσιος, Latin *consubstantialis*), with which the Council of NICAEA I in 325 (H. Denzinger, *Enchiridion symbolorum*, ed. A. Schönmetzer (32d ed. Freiburg 1963) 125) designated the Son's full divinity and equality with the Father, and which the Council of CHALCEDON in 451 (*Enchiridion symbolorum* 301) used to designate the Son's possession of a true and perfect humanity essentially like ours. The Holy Spirit (e.g., *Enchiridion symbolorum* 853) and the entire Trinity (e.g., *Enchiridion symbolorum* 421, 554, 800, 805, 851) also receive this designation.

Historical Aspects: Trinitarian. Homoousios does not appear in Scripture, though both its Trinitarian and Christological senses are founded on what the New Testament says of the relationships of the Son with the Father (e.g., Jn 10.30; 14.9–10) and with other men (e.g., Gal 4.4). The word, already used by Gnostics and Neoplatonists, was first employed in orthodox Christian circles by Clement and Origen; Origen is the first to apply it to the relationship of Son and Father (*Frag. in ep. ad Hebr.; Patrologia Graeca*, ed. J. P. Migne, 14:1308). It appears thereafter to have won considerable favor at Alexandria, for the anti-Sabellian bishop Dionysius is blamed for his refusal to use it; but his defense, in reply to a letter from his Roman namesake, makes it clear that he admits the conception but avoids the word because it is not found in Scripture (Athanasius, *De sent. Dionysii* 18; *Patrologia Graeca* 25:505). The synod of Antioch in 268 condemned its use in Paul of Samosata, possibly because he gave it a Monarchian sense; the matter is obscure.

At Nicaea I the Fathers, reluctant to have recourse to nonscriptural terms in condemning ARIANISM, felt compelled to do so by the fact that the Arians could accept, in their own meaning, the more traditional formulations. Homoousios was the principal term inserted, along with "from the substance [*ousia*] of the Father," to exclude their denial of the full divinity of the Son. The consubstantiality defined by Nicaea I, then, has an anti-Arian import and affirms essentially that the Son is equal to the Father, as divine as the Father, being from His substance and of the same substance with Him; it follows necessarily that the Son cannot belong to the created, as Arius maintained. At Nicaea I and later, opposition to homoousios arose on four counts (cf. Kelly, *Creeds* 238–42): (1) that it conceived the divine substance as divisible, hence material; (2) that it was Sabellian; (3) that it had been condemned at the synod of Antioch in 268; and (4) that it was nonscriptural. Each of these charges was met successfully either at the Council or later, especially by Athanasius.

Nicaea I said nothing explicitly about the character of the divine unity implied in consubstantiality; this was not its problem. The issue of unity was raised in the post-Nicene polemics, with the final clarification, thanks to ATHANASIUS and the Cappadocians, that there is absolute (and not merely specific) identity in essence (*ousia*), but distinction in HYPOSTASIS (note that Nicaea I had used *ousia* and *hypostasis* synonymously). The view once held by Harnack and others, therefore, contrasting a numerical identity in Nicaea I with a merely specific identity in the "Neo-Nicenes" (Cappadocians), has today generally lost favor; the faith of the Cappadocians in the perfect unity and simplicity of the Godhead (which transcends and excludes that numerical unity which is proper to material being) precludes such an interpretation. Another idea once in vogue is that Athanasius' heroic struggle after Nicaea I was primarily a defense of homoousios; in fact he uses it rarely in his anti-Arian works. It is notable that the first Council of Constantinople in 381 (*Enchiridion symbolorum* 150), in defining against the Macedonians the full divinity of the Holy Spirit, avoided the term homoousios, even though the doctrine of consubstantiality is implicit.

It must not be thought that consubstantiality was a conception peculiar to the Eastern Church. While it seems doubtful that Hosius of Cordoba introduced homoousios at Nicaea I as a direct result of the Western *consubstantialis,* the latter term, and still more *consubstantivus,* was used by Tertullian [*Adv. Hermog.* 44.3 (*Corpus Christianorum. Series latina* (Turnhout, Belg. 1953–) 1:433); *Adv. Valent.* 12.5; 18.1; 37.2 (*Corpus Christianorum. Series latina* 2:764, 767, 778)], whose *unius substantiae* (*Adv. Prax.* 2.4; *Corpus Christianorum. Series latina* 2:1161) represented the leading Western formulation of consubstantiality. The Westerners at Nicaea I most likely welcomed homoousios as apt to express not only the perfect divinity of the Son but the unity of the Godhead, for which they had always been especially concerned. Eastern and Western affirmations of consubstantiality and of Trinitarian unity, while identical in the faith being professed, were different in derivation and formulation. In the Greek conception, the Father is the principle of unity, and Son and Spirit are consubstantial with Him because of generation and procession from Him. In the Latin conception, the divine substance itself is the principle of unity; all three Persons are consubstantial because all three possess equally the divine substance.

Historical Aspects: Christological. It was natural that homoousios, after its long Trinitarian career, should be employed also in Christology to indicate that Christ has the same nature as other men. It is found as early as Eustathius of Antioch (d. 337?; Theodoret, *Eran.* 1.56; *Patrologia Graeca*, 83:88). It was understandably favored by the Antiochene school. Theodoret of Cyr witnesses to the double consubstantiality of Christ, with the Father and with us (*Interp. ep. 1 ad Cor.* 11; *Patrologia Graeca* 82:312), and it was probably due to his influence that this language is found in the Formula of Union (H. Denzinger, *Enchiridion symbolorum* 272) on which John of Antioch and Cyril of Alexandria agreed in 433, and thence in the definition of Chalcedon. The formula is anti-Apollinarian and anti-Eutychean in intent. It counteracts the position of some Apollinarists that the flesh of the Incarnate Son is consubstantial with divinity. Along with "two natures after the Incarnation," it was a touchstone of orthodoxy in the trial of Eutyches under Flavian in 448 (*Acta conciliorum oecumenicorum* (Berlin 1914–) 2.1.1:142–45). Eutyches reluctantly accepted the formula, but evasively, and when pressed on the question of two natures was eventually condemned. The definition of Chalcedon enshrined the double consubstantiality of Christ in the Church's official teaching.

Doctrinal Content. Consubstantiality says identity of substance (nature, essence) between really distinct equals. The three Divine Persons, really distinct from one another, possess equally the one divine substance, or essence, i.e., divinity. Because of the absolute unicity, unity, and simplicity of God, the identity of the substance is not merely specific but absolute, or numerical (provided the latter term be taken analogously). The consubstantiality of Christ according to His humanity with other men, on the contrary, affirms a specific, not numerical, identity of substance, or nature, between Christ and other men. The Chalcedonian assertion of the double consubstantiality of Christ, with the Father according to His divinity, with us according to His humanity, is a more precise way of saying that Christ is true and perfect God, and true and perfect man. In other words, it is, in the context of the Arian and Apollinarist-Eutychean deviations, a dogmatic reaffirmation of the mystery of the Incarnation.

Significance. Implicit in this formulation in terms of consubstantiality of the two basic mysteries of Christianity is a threefold assertion of primary theological and religious significance. (1) It is legitimate and necessary, for the understanding and defense of the Christian faith, to move from the (generally) functional and dynamic conceptions of Scripture to the ontological conceptions typical of Christian dogma. (2) The employment of categories taken from Greek philosophy in the Church's dogmatic pronouncements has represented not a Hellenization of Christianity but a Christianization of Hellenism. (3) A real and not merely verbal doctrinal development is an exigency of the Christian revelation, which has been made to men, who as finite spirits may and must pursue progressive understanding even of divine mysteries, and as incarnate spirits must pursue it under the conditions of human history. Nicaea I and Chalcedon, and the subsequent endorsements of Christian tradition have asserted this legitimacy and exigency as regards the fact; the further penetration and theoretical justification of the fact are a continuing task for historical and theological understanding.

See Also: GENERATION OF THE WORD; INCARNATION; JESUS CHRIST; LOGOS; NATURE; PERSON (IN THEOLOGY); PERSON, DIVINE; PROCESSIONS, TRINITARIAN; THEOLOGY, INFLUENCE OF GREEK PHILOSOPHY ON; TRINITY, HOLY; WORD, THE.

Bibliography: J. N. D. KELLY, *Early Christian Creeds* (2d ed. New York 1960) 242–62; *Early Christian Doctrines* (2d ed. New York 1960) 223–79. H. QUILLIET, *Dictionnaire de théologie catholique*, ed. A. VACANT et al., 15 v. (Paris 1903–50) 3.2:1604–15. J. C. MURRAY, *The Problem of God Yesterday and Today* (St. Thomas More Lectures 1; New Haven 1964) 31–60. G. L. PRESTIGE, *God in Patristic Thought* (Society for Promoting Christian Knowledge 1935; repr. 1959) 197–281. V. C. DE CLERCQ, *Ossius of Cordova: A Contribution to the History of the Constantinian Period* (Washington 1954) 218–89. I. ORTIZ DE URBINA, *El símbolo niceno* (Madrid 1947) 178–216. B. LONERGAN, *De Deo trino*, 2 v. (v.1 2d ed., v.2 3d ed. Rome 1964) 1:75–87, 113–54. R. V. SELLERS, *The Council of Chalcedon* (London 1953) 64–69, 212–13. L. BOUYER, "Omoousios: Sa signification historique dans le symbole de foi," *Les Sciences philosophiques et théologiques* 1 (1941–42) 52–62.

[T. E. CLARKE]

CONSULTATION ON CHURCH UNION

The Consultation on Church Union (COCU) is "a venture in reconciliation" by U.S. churches exploring the formation of a united church. At the beginning of the 21st century, there are nine active members within COCU:

African Methodist Episcopal Church
African Methodist Episcopal Zion Church
Christian Church (Disciples of Christ)
Christian Methodist Episcopal Church
Episcopal Church
International Council of Community Churches
Presbyterian Church (USA)
United Church of Christ
United Methodist Church

Origins. The originating impetus for COCU came from a sermon, "A Proposal Toward the Reunion of Christ's Church," delivered by Dr. Eugene Carson Blake, then stated clerk of the (Northern) United Presbyterian Church in the U.S.A., in Grace (Episcopal) Cathedral, San Francisco, on Dec. 4, 1960, the eve of the fifth triennial assembly of the National Council of Churches. Blake proposed that his own church enter discussions with the Methodist Church, the Episcopal Church, and the United Church of Christ, in view of uniting in a church "truly catholic, truly evangelical, and truly reformed." Blake's proposal envisaged a union of churches of widely different theological and historical traditions; in contrast, previous church unions in the United States involved churches of the same confessional families.

After these four churches officially approved discussion of the proposal, representatives were sent to a plenary meeting in Washington, D.C. (April 9–10, 1962). The meeting established the Consultation on Church Union and explored the theological and other issues that needed to be resolved in view of union. The Washington plenary invited the Christian Church (Disciples of Christ) and the Evangelical United Brethren (which were already, respectively, in union conversations with the United Church of Christ and the Methodist Church) and the Polish National Catholic Church (which is in communion with the Episcopal Church) to become COCU participants; the Disciples and Brethren accepted in 1962. A second invitation urged other North American churches to send observer-consultants to future meetings; about 20 church bodies subsequently sent official representatives. The Roman Catholic Church was first represented in 1964 by two observers: Msgr. William Baum (later Archbishop of Washington) and George Tavard.

Principles of Church Union. At the second plenary at Oberlin, Ohio (March 19–21, 1963), the possibility of union was enhanced when unexpected consensus was achieved on the authority of scripture and tradition in the church. Further consensus was reached at the third plenary in Princeton, N.J. (April 13–16, 1964), on Baptism and the Lord's Supper, and at the fourth plenary in Lexington, Ky. (April 4–8, 1965), on the form on the ministry. The Lexington meeting created a special committee charged with drafting a set of principles of church union that would incorporate the theological agreements and serve as a basis for future union. The fifth plenary at Dallas, Tex. (May 2–5, 1966) approved these *Principles* and commended them to the churches for study and comment.

Meanwhile, the number of participating churches temporarily increased to ten with the membership of the African Methodist Episcopal Church (1965), the (Southern) Presbyterian Church in the U.S., African Methodist Episcopal Zion Church (1966), and the Christian Methodist Episcopal Church (1967). The union of the Methodist and Evangelical United Brethren Churches (as the United Methodist Church) in May 1967 reduced the number of member churches to nine. Except for the temporary withdrawal of the (Northern) United Presbyterians in 1972 and 1973, the nine participants have remained the same.

Organization for the United Church. During its first five years, COCU was primarily concerned with theological issues, which were resolved, after considerable discussion, with widely accepted consensus. Subsequent plenaries focused on practical problems in structuring the proposed united church. The sixth meeting at Cambridge, Mass. (May 1–4, 1967), adopted preliminary "Guidelines for the Structure of the Church." The seventh plenary at Dayton, Ohio (March 25–28, 1968) authorized a commission to draft a plan of union within two years. A preliminary outline of the plan was submitted to the eighth plenary at Atlanta, Ga. (March 17–20, 1969), which adopted "Guidelines for Local Interchurch Action." One of the principal speakers at the Atlanta meeting was Bishop (later cardinal) Jan Willebrands of the Vatican Secretariat for Promoting Christian Unity.

A Plan of Union for the Church of Christ Uniting was approved at the ninth plenary in St. Louis, Mo. (March 9–13, 1970), for transmission to "member churches and to all Christians for study and response. The *Plan* presents doctrinal provisions (on scripture, the church, worship, ministry, etc.), procedures for organizing the "Church of Christ Uniting" (a name proposed to emphasize that union is a continuing process), a "service of inauguration," and an ordinal (for the ordination of presbyters, bishops, and deacons). Subsequent response to the *Plan* indicates broad acceptance of its doctrinal basis but considerable disagreement regarding its organizational procedures.

The plenaries at Denver, Colo. (Sept. 27–30, 1971), and Memphis, Tenn. (April 2–6, 1973), were concerned with engaging all church members in the study and implementation of the *Plan*. The Denver meeting recommended "interim eucharistic fellowship on a regular basis" and "programs leading to the achievement of racial justice and compensatory treatment for minorities in the church and nation." The Memphis plenary, besides mandating further revision of the *Plan*, encouraged active cooperation and contact at every level of church life as a mounting process toward union.

In 1988 the Seventeenth Plenary of COCU approved the document *Churches in Covenant Communion: The Church of Christ Uniting*, as a blueprint for the eventual establishment of a covenant communion of churches. This proposal received a mixed response from the nine members of the consultation. Seven of the member communions [African Methodist Episcopal Church, African Methodist Episcopal Zion Church, Christian Church (Disciples of Christ), Christian Methodist Episcopal Church, International Council of Community Churches, United Church of Christ, and United Methodist Church] approved the proposal with added provisos concerning several issues that needed further reflection and clarification. Although the General Assembly of the Presbyterian Church (USA) approved the covenanting proposal, its presbyteries had rejected the constitutional changes concerning the ministry of ecclesial oversight and episcopate that would have necessitated a significant change in the historic roles of elders in the Presbyterian Church. The 1994 General Convention of the Episcopal Church made it clear that the Episcopal Church had major reservations about the COCU Consensus and Churches in Covenant Communion and declared that although the Episcopal Church would remain a full member of COCU, it was not prepared to enter into covenant communion with the other member churches.

Based on the responses from its nine members, the Eighteenth Plenary of COCU recommended to the participating churches that they agree to enter into a new relationship to be called *Churches Uniting in Christ* (CUIC), to be inaugurated during the Week of Prayer for Christian Unity in 2002. The Presbyterian Church (USA) has already voted to become part of this new relationship. Other members were considering the implications of CUIC, especially the thorny issue of mutual recognition of ordained ministry.

Bibliography: *Digest of the Proceedings of the Consultation on Church Union*, 10 v. (Princeton 1962–71). *A Plan of Union for the Church of Christ Uniting* (Princeton 1970). *COCU: A Catholic Perspective* (Washington, D.C. 1970). *Church Union at Midpoint*, ed. P. A. CROW, JR., and W. J. BONEY (New York 1972). E. TESELLE, "Ecumenical Reflections on the COCU Plan of Union," *Jurist* 31 (1971) 629–637.

[J. T. FORD/EDS.]

CONSULTATION ON COMMON TEXTS

The origins of the Consultation on Common Texts (CCT) lie in the somewhat hesitant decision of Vatican II to permit some use of the vernacular in liturgy, with approved translations (*Sacrosanctum Concilium* 36). This decision led perceptive Protestants to initiate unofficial correspondence with such figures in North American Catholicism as Gerald J. Sigler and Frederick R. McManus, looking toward production of agreed common liturgical texts. The Presbyterian, Scott F. Brenner, writing in 1964, and the Lutheran, Hans Boeringer in 1966, laid the groundwork for a gathering sponsored by the Institute for Liturgical Studies at Valparaiso University in August 1966, attended by representatives from the Inter-Lutheran Commission on Worship, the Episcopal Church, the United Presbyterian Church, the Worship Commission of the Consultation on Church Union (COCU), and the International Commission on English in the Liturgy (ICEL) of the Roman Catholic Church.

In 1967, this group sponsored a widely attended meeting in conjunction with the National Liturgical Week of the Liturgical Conference, also at Valparaiso, Ind.; this became the first of several such meetings. A small working group on ''Agreed Texts'' began meeting semi-annually to prepare English translations of the Lord's Prayer and the Apostles' Creed (released in May 1968), the Nicene Creed and portions of the Ordinary of the Mass (August 1968) and to embark upon the preparation of a common Psalter for liturgical use (November 1968). Its work was first published by the Consultation on Church Union as part of *An Order for the Proclamation of the Word of God and the Celebration of the Lord's Supper* (Forward Movement Publications, Cincinnati 1968).

In 1969 the working group began using the name ''Consultation on Common Texts'' (CCT) and concentrated on its Psalter project, leaving the earlier work of translating common liturgical texts to the newly formed International Consultation on English Texts (ICET). Individual CCT members continued to take part in ICET's various translation projects. The Psalter project came to fruition with the publication of *A Liturgical Psalter for the Eucharist* in 1976. The translator was Dr. Massey Shepherd, Jr., who had been among the founders of CCT and who prepared his translation in close partnership with it.

From 1978 onwards, CCT was asked to prepare an ecumenical lectionary based on the three-year Roman Lectionary (1969), harmonizing the many pericope variations and calendar differences in the various *ad hoc* adaptations that its member churches had made for their own use. This resulted in the publication of the *Common Lectionary* in 1983. A revised edition, incorporating the feedback from its member churches was released in 1992 as the *Revised Common Lectionary*. In 1983, CCT and ICEL jointly organized an international consultation on ecumenical liturgical matters at the Vienna Congress of *Societas Liturgica*. A fruit of this consultation was the formation of the English Language Liturgical Consultation (ELLC) as the successor to ICET, which had ceased to function in 1975. In the mid-1980s, CCT embarked on a project to prepare original ecumenical liturgical texts for adoption by its member churches. This resulted in the publication of *A Christian Celebration of Marriage* (1987), and *A Celebration of Baptism* (1988).

Membership in CTT are drawn from the following churches and agencies: Anglican Church of Canada; Canadian Conference of Catholic Bishops; Christian Church (Disciples of Christ); Christian Reformed Church in North America; Church of the Brethren; Episcopal Church of the United States of America (ECUSA); Evangelical Lutheran Church in America (ELCA); Evangelical Lutheran Church in Canada; Free Methodist Church in Canada; International Commission on English in the Liturgy (ICEL); Liturgy and Life: American Baptist Fellowship for Liturgical Renewal; Lutheran Church—Missouri Synod; Mennonite Church; National Conference of Catholic Bishops of the United States (NCCB); Polish National Catholic Church; Presbyterian Church (U.S.A.); Presbyterian Church in Canada; Reformed Church in America; Unitarian Universalist Christian Fellowship; United Church of Canada; United Church of Christ; United Methodist Church.

[H. A. ALLEN/EDS.]

CONTARINI, GASPARO

Venetian statesman, lay theologian, and reform cardinal; b. Venice, Oct. 16, 1483; d. Bologna, Aug. 24, 1542. At the University of Padua (1501–09), he studied philosophy and philology, natural sciences, and theology. In recognition of his scholarship, he was later appointed to the highest post of the university as *reformatore dello studio*. In spite of his proclivity for scholarship, he entered business life and public service. This descendant of a wealthy and politically prominent family, which had supplied Venice with numerous church dignitaries, magistrates, ambassadors, and six doges, began his public career in 1518 as a surveyor and subsequently held all major offices, except those of procurator and doge.

Diplomatic Skill. He served as an ambassador at the imperial court of Charles V (1520–25), becoming ac-

Gasparo Contarini, by Alessandro Vittoria, church of S. Maria dell'Orto, Venice. (Alinari-Art Reference/Art Resource, NY)

quainted at first hand with German religious problems, and at the papal court of CLEMENT VII (1528–30). In both instances he was charged with the delicate and thankless task of justifying Venice's oppositional policies to the court to which he was accredited. Contarini's common sense and optimism, which enabled him to gloss over contradictions, and his ability to compromise gracefully, inspired confidence in him even on his opponents' side. A grateful Venice bestowed upon him one high position after the other, and Charles V requested his mediating participation, as a papal legate, in the religious talks of Regensburg (1541). Contarini submitted to the Venetian senate the customary comprehensive ambassadorial reports, distinguished by his astute observations and crisp style [see E. Alberi, ed., *Le Relazioni degli Ambasciatori veneti al Senato* Florence, 1.2 (1840) and 2.3 (1846)]. In 1524 he wrote a noteworthy political science text on his native city, *De magistratibus et republica Venetorum* (Paris 1543), skillfully combining description with analysis and theory with practice.

Advocate of Church Reform. The Venetian statesman was as articulately loyal to the Church as he was to his city-state. Although he was appalled by the ecclesiastical abuses and the low level to which the Church had fallen, he was convinced, in his optimistic and pragmatic

way of thinking, that a reform could effect its complete rehabilitation. A year before Luther posted his 95 theses, Contarini dealt with a major aspect of reform in his *De officio episcopi* (1516). Written for his friend Pietro Lippomano on becoming bishop of Verona, he listed the shortcomings of the clergy and outlined the ideal behavior of a bishop as a principal factor to remedy such evil conditions. Frankly acknowledging unsavory conditions, and broadmindedly recognizing virtue in certain views of Luther, Contarini defended the divinely ordained office of the pope, whether under attack by Venetian senators (*De potestate pontificis,* 1530–35) or by the Protestants (*Confutatio articulorum seu quaestionum Lutheranarum,* 1530–35).

This outstanding lay theologian, who spoke more forcefully on behalf of the Church than its own ecclesiastics, was appointed to the College of Cardinals by Paul III on May 21, 1535. He became the center and driving force of reform, and advised the pope on the appointment of other reform-minded men to the cardinalate. He pressed for specific reform measures in the administrative departments of the Curia and ceaselessly urged the calling together of a Church council. As chairman of the newly created Reform Committee (1536), he was responsible for the memorandum *Consilium de emendanda Ecclesia,* which he read before the pope and cardinals (March 9, 1537). A joltingly frank criticism of prevailing ecclesiastical malpractices, the document made specific disciplinary recommendations to erase them. As bishop of Cividale di Belluno (appointed Nov. 23, 1536), Contarini carried out the recommended reforms in his diocese. He also strongly supported papal recognition of the Jesuit Order (1540) as a means of furthering reform. For reform-minded laymen who, like himself, might be named to administer episcopal sees, he wrote *De sacramentis Christianae legis . . .* (1540), to impart an understanding of the Sacraments.

Formula of Double Justification. Contarini's patient attempts to mediate the differences between Catholics and Lutherans at the religious talks of Regensburg in 1541—the last serious "professional" attempt to settle the German religious cleavage peacefully—ended in failure. Despite his diplomatic skill, which led initially to compromises acceptable to both sides, the larger issues concerning dogma (justification), the Sacraments (transubstantiation), and the hierarchical order of the Church could not be resolved. Contarini's compromise formulation of the process of double justification (*Epistola de justificatione,* 1541), stressing *iusticia imputata,* as had Luther, over, but without abandoning, *iusticia inhaerens,* was rejected by both sides. The talks were abandoned on May 22, 1541. Although his stand on justification was severely criticized, Paul III continued to value his counsel and appointed him cardinal legate at Bologna. He remained there until his death, continuing to advocate and work toward a general Church council.

Bibliography: *Opera* (Paris 1571); *Regesten und Briefe des Cardinals Gasparo Contarini,* ed. F. DITTRICH (Braunsberg 1881). H. JEDIN, ed., *Contarini und Camaldoli* (Rome 1953); *Lexikon für Theologie und Kirche,* ed. J. HOFER and K. RAHNER (2d, new ed. Freiburg 1957–65) 3:49–50; *Dictionnaire d'histoire et de géographie ecclésiastiques,* ed. A. BAUDRILLART et al. (Paris 1912–) 13:771–784. F. HÜNERMANN, ed., *Gasparo Contarini, Gegenreformatorische Schriften* (Corpus Catholicorum 7; Munich 1923). F. DITTRICH, *Gasparo Contarini* (Braunsberg 1885). H. HACKERT, *Die Staatsschrift Contarinis und die politischen Verhältnisse Venedigs im 16. Jahrhundert* (Heidelberg 1940). H. RÜCKERT, *Die theologische Entwicklung Gasparo Contarinis* (Bonn 1926). R. STUPPERICH, *Die Religion in Geschichte und Gegenwart* (3d ed. Tübingen 1957–65) 1:1865. A. DUVAL, *Catholicisme. Hier, aujourd'hui et demain,* ed. G. JACQUEMET (Paris 1947–) 3:132.

[F. F. STRAUSS]

CONTARINI, GIOVANNI

Patriarch of Constantinople; b. Venice; d. San Giorgio Maggiore Abbey, Venice, early 1451. Born into the illustrious Contarini family, he went to England in 1392 (by way of SANTIAGO DE COMPOSTELA) to study at Oxford until 1398 or 1399. Having become a master of arts there, he went to Paris (*c.* 1400), becoming a doctor in theology (1409). He returned to Venice, where, although he was still a subdeacon, Pope GREGORY XII named him patriarch of Constantinople (Aug. 26, 1409) and conferred on him the title of *magister theologiae.* Contarini executed various important commissions for the pope: e.g., in October 1414 he was papal nuncio in Germany, and in 1415 he was a member of the delegation at the Council of CONSTANCE commissioned to negotiate Gregory's abdication. Because there were two patriarchs of Constantinople, both appointed during the WESTERN SCHISM, the new pope, MARTIN V, transferred Contarini to the patriarchal see of Alexandria (July 1422); but in 1424 he was restored to his original see. From 1418 to 1427 Contarini was administrator of the diocese of Cittanova nell'Estuario, or Eraclea, near Asolo, Italy. He is buried at the Benedictine Abbey of San Giorgio Maggiore, Venice. Information on his life and activity derives from letters addressed to him; one collection, written to him by his brothers, covers the period 1398 to 1408; another collection belongs to the period 1428 to 1451.

See Also: CONSTANTINOPLE, PATRIARCHATE OF.

Bibliography: C. EUBEL et al., *Hierarchia Catholica medii (et recentioris) aevi* (2d ed. Münster 1913) 1:206–207. G. DELLA SANTA, "Uomini e fatti dell'ultimo trecento e del primo quattrocento . . .," *Nuovo archivio veneto* 32 (1916) 5–99, for the letter collections. P. PASCHINI, "I vescovi di Cittanova d'Istria e di Cittanova nell'Estuario," in *Atti e memorie della società istriana di archelogia e storia patria* 44 (1932) 242–243. J. RUYSSCHAERT, *Dictionnaire d'histoire et de géographie ecclésiastiques,* ed. A. BAUDRILLART et al. (Paris 1912–) 13:784–785. A. B. EMDEN, *A Biographical Register of the University of Oxford to A.D. 1500* (Oxford 1957–59) 1:478.

[M. MONACO]

CONTEMPLATION

Etymologically the word "contemplation" derives from *templum,* which signified the space marked out by a seer with his divining rod as a location for his observation, but which later came to mean the actual observation made by a seer. The Greek origin of the word is θεωρεῖν meaning to regard or look at a spectacle or religious ceremony, though some trace it back to θεός (God) and others to θέα (vision). Both in Latin and in Greek the word has the general meaning of speculative study, admiration of beauty, or consideration of wisdom.

Contemplation in General. Contemplation is a type of knowledge that is accompanied by delight and a certain degree of admiration for the object contemplated. As an operation of the cognitive powers, it may involve bodily vision, imagination, or intellect; by reason of its delight, it may overflow into the appetitive faculties of emotions and will and, if intense enough, affect the body itself. As a type of KNOWLEDGE, it is experimental and connatural, intuitive rather than discursive. In the purely natural order it finds its highest expression in the operation of the habit of wisdom or in the aesthetic response to the beautiful.

Nature of Contemplation. Whether the truth contemplated be of the sensible order, the intellectual order, or the supernatural order, contemplation is not the study of truth by discursive reasoning, but a consideration and delight in truth already grasped; not directed to the practical life of action, but a speculative, disinterested, and delighted gaze upon truth itself. Contemplation involves the following elements: (1) on the part of the object contemplated: truth or some aspect thereof sought for its own sake; (2) on the part of the faculty used: the speculative intellect, not in its function as a reasoning power but of intuitive vision, though utilizing other cognitive powers as auxiliaries; (3) on the part of the experience: a loving gaze that arouses delight and admiration, extending to the appetitive powers by which the delight is intensified.

Types of Contemplation. Both by reason of the truth contemplated and the faculties used, contemplation may be divided into the following types: aesthetic contemplation, which is the delightful vision of truth under the aspect of its beauty; philosophical or scientific contemplation, which is delightful vision of truth as such; theological contemplation, which is the intuitive gaze on God as known through reason enlightened by faith; acquired supernatural contemplation, which is the simple gaze upon God as known through faith and experienced through love; mystical infused contemplation, which is the intuitive experience of union with God through the activity of faith, charity, and the gifts of wisdom and understanding. The contemplation normally signified in the vocabulary of Catholic theology is restricted to that which has God as its object, and God precisely as experienced through the supernatural virtues or gifts, or, in other words, acquired supernatural contemplation and mystical infused contemplation.

Possibility of a Purely Natural Contemplation of God. Both PLATO and PLOTINUS had admitted the possibility of a purely natural contemplation of the divine, but there are reasons for doubting such a possibility. Man's normal method of knowledge is through the external senses and the phantasms of the imagination, and hence he can know immediately and intuitively only those things that can be represented by a phantasm or sense image. But God cannot be attained immediately and intuitively through any sensible image or phantasm of the imagination, and therefore a purely natural contemplation of God is impossible. Moreover, to have an intuitive and immediate experience of God, it would be necessary that God Himself be the intellectual concept, but this would require the elevation of man to the supernatural order or the infusion in man of some supernatural power or species, for such a knowledge is connatural only to God (St. Thomas Aquinas, *Summa theologiae* 1a, 12.4). If the human intellect cannot by its own power attain to a vision of God as He is in Himself (H. Denzinger, *Enchiridion symbolorum,* ed. A. Schönmetzer [32d ed. Freiburg 1963] 895), this would therefore seem to rule out all natural mysticism (see Karl Rahner, *Hörer des Wortes* [Munich 1941] 88).

Can the human intellect attain any natural contemplation of God whatever that is intuitive and delightful? If an object of knowledge is in conformity with the proper object of the human intellect—truth as such—and is at the same time proportionate to man's intellectual capacity, then some kind of natural contemplation seems possible (cf. *Summa theologiae* 1a2ae, 109.3 ad 2). Some authors assert this possibility and base it on the nature of the human intellect and God's providence (see Cuthbert Butler, *Western Mysticism* [2d ed. London 1927]). Others defend this position by positing an immediate apprehension of God or innate ideas (G. Picard, *La Saisie immédiate de Dieu dans les états mystiques* [Paris 1923]; J. Chapmann, "What Is Mysticism," *Downside Review* [1928] 1–28; J. Maritain, *Distinguir pour unir ou les de-*

grés du savoir [3d ed. Paris 1932] 489–573; "Action et contemplation," *Revue thomiste* 43 [1937] 18–50; *Quatre essais sur l'esprit dans sa condition charnelle* [Paris 1939]). According to MARITAIN, this is truly contemplation, though negative and vague and a kind of bridge between philosophical contemplation and infused supernatural contemplation.

The human intellect has a radical capacity or obediential potency for the vision of God through contemplation but the actualization of the potency calls for something above man's natural powers (Thomas Aquinas, *De malo* 5.1c). Therefore, it would seem that the most man can achieve through a natural contemplation of God is the vague knowledge of God acquired by self-reflection. It is possible, however, for natural contemplation to produce a kind of natural ecstasy or alienation from the senses and a relatively intense delight, for which reason some authors have spoken of a "natural mysticism."

Possibility of an Intuitive and Experimental Knowledge of God through the Infused Supernatural Virtues. This would be a contemplation proper to the ascetical rather than the mystical state of the spiritual life, actuated through the operation *modo humano* of the infused supernatural virtues of faith and charity. It would occur either in the practice of some form of prayer or, perhaps, in the meditations of a theologian under the impetus of charity. Most modern authors who defend the possibility of an acquired supernatural contemplation (e.g., Thomas of Jesus, OCD, Philip of the Holy Trinity, OCD, G. B. Scaramelli, SJ, St. Alphonsus Liguori) usually quote St. TERESA OF AVILA to defend their position. She describes the prayer of acquired recollection as distinct from the prayer of infused recollection, but in the 17th century, Scaramelli, who stressed the difference between an ascetical and a mystical perfection, likewise taught the possibility of an acquired contemplation as the perfection in prayer for the ascetical state. As described by St. Teresa, acquired recollection is truly the perfection of ascetical prayer, but neither she nor St. JOHN OF THE CROSS ever used the word "contemplation" in this context. Many authors, chiefly in the Dominican school, prefer to restrict the word "contemplation" to infused mystical prayer and hence judge the expression "acquired contemplation" a contradiction in terms.

An acquired contemplation that operates through faith and charity would involve the following elements: a loving gaze upon God; the absence of *discursus* and the lack of any intervention by other lower faculties; the operation of the supernatural virtues of faith and charity (see St. Teresa, *The Way of Perfection* ch. 28–29; *Interior Castle,* Fourth Mansions, ch. 3). This type of contemplation, however, would be ascetical rather than mystical because it is an actuation of the supernatural virtues of faith and charity only; it would be infused contemplation because it is the operation of virtues that are infused and not acquired; it would be acquired contemplation in the sense that the infused supernatural virtues work in a human manner, that is, at the command of a human agent and through the natural powers or faculties that have been elevated through grace but not replaced by grace.

Mystical Contemplation. In spite of a variety of definitions of mystical contemplation, all agree on the essential note that contemplation is an experimental knowledge of God, which, in turn, admits of varying degrees or grades. Since the time of St. Teresa of Avila, most authors have followed her division of mystical contemplation, though not always using the same terminology. The first degree of supernatural prayer listed by St. Teresa is infused recollection, though Gabriel of St. Mary Magdalen, OCD, maintains that the first degree is the prayer of quiet, and the infused recollection is simply a prayer of transition. According to R. GARRIGOU-LAGRANGE, OP, however, the prayer of acquired recollection or simplified affective prayer is the prayer of transition. Infused recollection is followed by the prayer of quiet, in which the will is captivated, though there may still be some distractions because the intellect remains somewhat free (cf. *The Way of Perfection* ch. 31.5; *Spiritual Relations* ch. 5; *Interior Castle,* Fourth Mansions, ch. 2). The soul then advances to the prayer of union, which admits of the following grades: simple union, ecstatic union terminating in mystical espousal, and transforming union terminating in mystical marriage. Prior to the prayer of union the soul usually experiences a sleep of the faculties, which some authors place as a distinct degree of prayer (e.g., Gabriel of St. Mary Magdalen) while others list it as an effect of the prayer of quiet (e.g., Royo-Aumann), in which the intellect is captivated. In the first degree of the prayer of union the imagination and memory are captivated; in the prayer of ecstatic union the external faculties are alienated to such an extent that ecstasy is a concomitant phenomenon (*see* ECSTASY). In the prayer of transforming union the soul is completely surrendered to God and enjoys a quasi-permanent union in love and confirmation in grace (cf. *Interior Castle,* Seventh Mansions, ch. 1–4; *The Way of Perfection* ch. 10; *Spiritual Canticle* st. 22).

Biblical Sources. Perhaps more than any other mystical theologian St. John of the Cross has interwoven scriptural proofs and examples throughout all his writings. Among the Fathers of the Church, Origen and St. Augustine are noteworthy in defending the existence of contemplation in the Prophets of the Old Testament (see *Patrologia Graeca,* ed. J. P. Migne, 161 v. [Paris 1857–66] 14:201; 11:1425, 1430–31; *Patrologia Latina,* ed. J. P. Migne, 271 v., indexes 4 v. [Paris 1878–90] 33:610–611; 41:221; 42:404, 219, 283, 290–291). Moreover, it would not be difficult to find examples of contemplative or mystical experience in such Old Testament figures as Abraham, Moses, David, Isaiah, Jeremiah, and others (see J. Lebreton et al., *Dictionnaire de spiritualité ascétique et mystique. Doctrine et histoire,* ed. M. Viller et al. [Paris 1932–] 2:1645–73).

In the New Testament Christ is the model of the contemplative life as He is of the active life. In His sacred humanity He enjoyed the beatific vision throughout his earthly sojourn, though the effects were withheld (see *Summa theologiae* 3a, 9.2). His personal prayer was evidently contemplative and in His teaching He encouraged souls to the perfection of prayer, as when He praised Mary for choosing the better part. In His last discourse at the Last Supper He spoke of the union between Himself and the Father and He promised a similar union between the Father and His faithful followers, promising to send them the Sanctifier.

After Christ, perhaps the greatest witness to contemplation in the New Testament is St. Paul, whose conversion was initiated with a vision in ecstasy on the road to Damascus. Most apostolic of men, he was at once a profound contemplative and progressed throughout his life to the highest degrees of prayer, as he bears witness in his Epistles. He is also the great preacher of charity, with St. John, and charity is the imperating power and the culminating joy in contemplation (see *Dictionnaire de spiritualité ascétique et mystique* 2:1698–1716).

Theology of Contemplation. Among the Fathers and theologians the names of GREGORY OF NYSSA, PSEUDO-DIONYSIUS, AUGUSTINE, CASSIAN, GREGORY THE GREAT, Bonaventure, and Thomas Aquinas are outstanding in the theology of contemplation. For St. Thomas contemplation is an operation of either the intellectual habit of wisdom or the gift of the Holy Spirit by the same name. Natural contemplation admits of two types: philosophical and theological (*In 1 Sent.,* prol. 1.1). Some maintain that he admits a further distinction of theological contemplation into the purely speculative and the affective (see *Summa theologiae* 2a2ae, 180). Mystical or infused contemplation is distinguished from natural contemplation by the fact that the former is an operation of infused wisdom and the experience is quasi connatural (cf. *In Dion de div. nom.* 2.4; *In 3 Sent.* 35.2.1.1a; 68.1 ad 4). Like Albert the Great and Gregory the Great, he is careful to insist that there can be no immediate experience of God as He is; but infused contemplation terminates in God Himself, for it is a knowledge of the object present as present (cf. *Summa theologiae* 2a2ae, 45.3 ad

1; *In 3 Sent.* 24.2.3 ad 4). Like others before him, he favors the example of the sense of taste to describe the delight of contemplation, though the notion of connaturality seems to be borrowed from Aristotle.

Since mystical contemplation is an operation of wisdom, it is permeated with charity, of which wisdom is the perfection (*Summa theologiae* 2a2ae, 45). The gift of understanding serves to purify the intellect, but God ever remains transcendent (*In 3 Sent.* 35.2.2.2; *Summa theologiae* 1a2ae, 27.2 ad 2). St. Thomas nowhere describes the grades of contemplation as does St. Teresa of Avila, but he treats of the height of contemplation and follows the doctrine of Gregory the Great in so doing. Like John of the Cross and Pseudo-Dionysius, he refers also to negative contemplation, *per viam remotionis.* Until the 16th century it seems that St. Bonaventure had the greatest influence on the theology of contemplation, but since that time the doctrine of St. Thomas has been more influential.

Carmelite School. Teresa of Avila and John of the Cross are recognized in the universal Church as great masters in the theology of the spiritual life, and Teresa is undoubtedly the greater of the two on the doctrine of prayer. Her approach is more experimental than speculative, more descriptive than deductive. Neither she nor St. John were concerned with the distinction between acquired and infused contemplation, and the earliest Carmelites understood their teaching in terms of infused contemplation. They defined contemplation as a loving knowledge of God that could ultimately reach the transforming union or mystical marriage (*Dark Night* 2.18.5). The distinction of acquired and infused contemplation was introduced into the Carmelite school by Thomas of Jesus, who defined acquired contemplation as a loving knowledge, free of *discursus* and obtained by one's own efforts (*De contemplatione divina* 2:3), and infused contemplation as a loving knowledge produced by the gifts of understanding and wisdom (*ibid.* 2:4). Later, Joseph of the Holy Spirit stressed the superhuman mode of activity in infused contemplation (*Catena mistica* prop. 12). St. John of the Cross had spoken of an affirmative, distinct contemplation and a negative, obscure contemplation, and he divided contemplation into the purgative, illuminative, and unitive stages, thus accommodating it to his doctrine on the passive nights of the senses and of the spirit. He also referred to an imperfect and a perfect contemplation, depending on the degree of passivity in the soul.

For John of the Cross, contemplation is an operation of the supernatural infused virtues of faith and charity and the gifts of the Holy Spirit, and in perfect contemplation there are substantial touches and a high degree of illumination. The contemplation itself is a "passive actuation" of the faculties of the soul through faith, charity, and the gifts of the Holy Spirit; it is also connatural, but not to the extent that contemplation is necessary or even normal in the proper sense of the word. According to Gabriel of St. Mary Magdalen, the Carmelite school maintains that contemplation is not strictly necessary for sanctity but it is usually associated with a high degree of sanctity. This leads to the conclusion that there are two ways to sanctity—ordinary and extraordinary—though all souls receive the grace and virtues that could lead to contemplation (*Dictionnaire de spiritualité ascétique et mystique* 2:2065).

Dominican School. The teaching of Thomas Aquinas on the infused supernatural virtues, the gifts of the Holy Spirit, and the active and contemplative life is the doctrinal foundation for the Dominican school. In general the Dominicans (with the exception of Vallgornera) have always rejected the term "acquired contemplation" because they restrict the word "contemplation" to an infused type of prayer that operates through the virtues of faith and charity and the gifts of understanding and wisdom. Some, however, admit an intermediate stage between meditation and strictly infused contemplation, still predominantly acquired or active but with a latent influence of the gifts of the Holy Spirit (Garrigou-Lagrange, *Christian Perfection and Contemplation* 226–261; Royo-Aumann, *The Theology of Christian Perfection* 528–529). Infused contemplation is defined as a loving knowledge of God that proceeds from the inspiration of the Holy Spirit; its immediate eliciting principle is faith, informed by charity and perfected by the gifts of wisdom, understanding, and knowledge (Royo-Aumann, *op. cit.* 531). Mystical contemplation can be produced only by the operation of the Holy Spirit and this explains the note of passivity as well as its distinction from acquired forms of prayer. For the Dominican school, donal activity is of the essence of contemplation and the mystical state, though all donal activity need not be contemplative in nature (J. Maritain, "Une question sur la vie mystique et la contemplation," *La Vie spirituelle* 7 [1923] 636–650). Infused contemplation does not require infused ideas, but infused light; charisms or *gratiae gratis datae* are not required, for the donal activity suffices; there is no immediate perception of the divine essence but a quasi-experimental knowledge of God as present through His operations. All souls are called to contemplation by at least a general and remote call, for each soul in grace possesses the virtues and gifts that are the immediate principles of contemplation; the passive purifications of the soul necessarily involve contemplation; the beatific vision is the goal of man's life and hence on Earth contemplation is the perfection of faith informed by charity.

Franciscan School. St. BONAVENTURE is the source of Franciscan teaching on contemplation. His spiritual doctrine is overshadowed by and directed to Christ, and souls are brought to the perfection of the Christian life by observance of the commandments and love of Christ. The discourse of Christ at the Last Supper is the compendium of Christian teaching on contemplation and the mystical life (cf. *Dictionnaire de spiritualité ascétique et mystique* 1:1777–91). With John DUNS SCOTUS, Bonaventure states that Christ is the primary object of all the divine decrees and is the final cause of the divine economy and creation, so that man has a connatural desire for Christ, through whom he obtains an existential contact with God (L. M. Berardini, *La nozione del soprannaturale nell'antica schola francescana* [Rome 1943] 186). Through this same desire man has a psychological orientation to God and to contemplation, and the eye of contemplation, which is distinct from the eye of the body or that of the reason, can see God as He is. On the affective side, he also lists three powers, of which one provides the loving ecstasy, though Bonaventure speaks of contemplation as "excessive knowledge," meaning that the intellect is raised above itself through grace and the gifts (*Quaestiones disp., De scientia Christi* 7, concl. and ad 19). Prior to contemplation, God can be experienced as a universal presence, but through grace the soul receives the indwelling of the Trinity and the infused virtues and gifts. The theological virtues are directed to the Trinity; the gifts are directed to evangelical perfection and contemplation. Perfection consists in the operation of the gifts of understanding and wisdom and this is to become transformed into Christ (*Breviloquium* 5.7–10). Grace is not a static, but a dynamic, element (*In 2 sent.* 8.2.1.3 ad 4); the gifts are not receptive or passive powers, but energies that affect, not the infused virtues, but the human faculties themselves. Contemplation is the progressive manifestation of Christ, as promised at the Last Supper, and eventually the soul has an experience of the Trinity in and through Christ. Formally, contemplation is love, affective intuition, and contact, and because it is love, it is immediate, experimental, and existential. It does not give new knowledge of God, but a taste of God, and thus contemplation becomes "excessive love"; since it is an experience of the Trinity in and through Christ, it should rightly be called "Christian experience" rather than mystical experience. For Bonaventure, contemplation is infused because it is Christ working in the soul, though the immediate principles are the gifts of the Holy Spirit. After the 17th century a number of Franciscans adopted the distinction between acquired and infused contemplation (J. Heerynckx, *Dictionnaire de spiritualité ascétique et mystique* 1.836).

Ignatian School. There is no rigid Ignatian teaching on contemplation but there is a common characteristic among Jesuits in this regard, e.g., Scaramelli, Poulain, De Maumigny, Maréchal, Grandmaison, Bainvel, de Guibert, and Truhlar. The early Jesuits followed the doctrine of various theologians and masters who had preceded them and for that reason it is difficult to speak of an Ignatian "school." Contemplation is specifically distinct from other forms of prayer; it is primarily a contact or experience through intimate union with God; it is an immediate awareness of God, not as He is in Himself, but as present through His gifts of grace, the divine indwelling, and the infused virtues. The principle of operation in contemplation is faith, though it is a loving gaze and therefore involves the will and charity, which accounts for the passivity of contemplation. The gifts operate but they have no special function in contemplation and they do not give a superior mode to the activity of the infused virtues. Contemplation is unconditionally and absolutely gratuitous, a special grace, so that it is not essential for salvation, nor can it be the result of one's own preparation. Therefore, it is relatively rare and when given it is an activity of the intellect (Maurice de la Taille) or of both intellect and will (J. Bainvel and J. de Guibert). Yet there is an acquired contemplation for which one can prepare through faith, charity, and purification. This point of doctrine stems from the 17th century, under the influence of the Carmelites, who introduced that distinction. Acquired contemplation is an intermediate state between the ascetical and the mystical or at most the summit of the ascetical state. Contemplation here on Earth, says de la Taille, can never surpass a knowledge of the divine essence through faith, but Maréchal stated that SS. Augustine and Thomas did not definitively rule out the possibility of a direct and immediate vision of the divine essence in contemplation. Since infused contemplation is extraordinary, there are two ways to perfection—the ascetical and the mystical—and hence contemplation is not required for perfection, all souls are not called to infused contemplation, and a soul can be a mystic without being a contemplative.

Benedictine School. Though the monastic life is centered chiefly on the interior perfection of the monk, relatively few Benedictines have treated explicitly of contemplation and the mystical state. Recognizing that such gifts are the work of God, the monks were more concerned with ascetical practices and religious observances by which they could be purified and disposed for the action of God within them. Moreover, the emphasis in spiritual literature by and for monks is usually on the community aspect of life rather than personal holiness, though the latter was recognized as essential. Lastly, the monks were occupied primarily with liturgical prayer, which is collective prayer. There is, therefore, no Benedictine school with a unanimous doctrine or vocabulary concerning contemplation, although certain Benedictines have come to be recognized as authorities in this field. Columba MARMION teaches a Christocentric, Trinitarian, and sacramental spirituality, lived through faith, humility, and abandonment to God, but he does not admit of the double way to perfection. He avoids the word "contemplation" and speaks only of prayer, though he refers to the perfection of prayer in which the soul has a vivid awareness of its adoption as a child of God, through the movement of the Holy Spirit. Prayer begins in the affection, and as one progresses in prayer, discursive reasoning decreases. For advanced souls in the illuminative way the best prayer is the Divine Office, and if the soul is faithful in this prayer, it can reach the prayer of faith or prayer of quiet, which is available to all who are faithful to grace. Then a higher type of activity begins and the soul attains the state of contemplative mystical prayer, wherein it is touched and illumined from above (*Christ the Ideal of the Monk* [St. Louis 1926] 358–371).

For example, Marmion believes that all may lawfully desire the gift of contemplation and all the baptized are called to it in a general way, but when it comes, it is through a gratuitous gift of God and it comes suddenly. John Chapman teaches that contemplation begins with the illuminative way and is perfected in the practice of affective prayer. It is mystical and infused and requires the passive purification of the senses. The original point of his doctrine is that he denies that contemplation is essentially a supernatural gift, but it is the actuation of the preternatural capacity that Adam had and was not completely destroyed in us by original sin. This is effected by grace, the infused virtues, and an inspiration of the Holy Spirit. Cuthbert Butler achieved renown through his classical work, *Western Mysticism,* a treatise on the history of spirituality. His basic conclusions regarding contemplation can be summarized as follows: (1) infused contemplation is passive and extraordinary and is an experimental perception of the presence of God; (2) acquired contemplation is active and ordinary, but mystical so far as it is the immediate disposition for infused contemplation, and it is the normal end of the spiritual life; (3) mystical experience is not a vision of the divine essence, but a direct and immediate perception of the being and presence of God; (4) theoretically no soul is excluded from infused mystical contemplation, and having reached the prayer of recollection, the soul can humbly aspire to it; (5) it is excessive to say that every baptized Christian is normally destined to the transforming union; (6) the best definition of mystical contemplation would be: a prayer without *discursus,* without phantasms and images, without words, and surpassing the laws of natural human psychology.

Anselm Stolz, who relates the mystical state to the condition of Adam before original sin and to Christ, sees it as something essentially sacramental, with its origin in baptism and its culmination in the Eucharist. Mystical contemplation is not a vision of the essence of God but an immediate perception of His presence. Stolz refuses to admit that the ascetical life is merely a prelude to the mystical life, but states that it belongs to the essence of the mystical life. Every true ascetic is also a mystic. It is not permissible to desire extraordinary mystical graces but it is lawful to desire those that constitute the essence of mysticism (cf. *Theologie der Mystik* [Ratisbon 1936]). Alois Mager approaches the study of contemplation and mysticism from a psychological and empirical point of view. He defines the mystical state as the awareness of the soul and its own passivity under the action of God; it is a function of the highest part of the soul, resembling angelic knowledge; the soul attains a spiritualization or "pneumatization" that is effected through the passive purifications of the senses. Mager distinguishes between the mystical order and that of ordinary grace; he denies active contemplation; mystical grace is normal in the development of the spiritual life; the primary essence of the mystical activity is charity, and the awareness of God's action on the soul is its primary effect; mysticism does not pertain to asceticism but it is the work of the Holy Spirit; there is no true mysticism outside of Christianity; authentic mysticism is essentially related to the sacramental and liturgical life (cf. *Mystik als Lehre und Leben* [Innsbruck 1934]; *Mystik als seelische Wirklichkeit* [Graz 1946]).

Vital Lehodey, a Cistercian, defines contemplation as a prayer of simple regard that proceeds from love and reposes in love. He admits two forms of contemplation: acquired contemplation, which he identifies as the prayer of simplicity (the prayer of acquired recollection for St. Teresa), and mystical contemplation, which consists in an awareness of the action of God on the soul and is preceded by the passive purification of the senses. All souls may lawfully desire mystical contemplation, but he insists strongly on total abandonment to the will of God. Are all called to the mystical life? Lehodey calls upon the distinction made by Maritain between the mystical life and mystical prayer, and answers that mystical prayer is the operation of the gifts of knowledge and wisdom and all souls are called to either the mystical life of contemplation or the blending of the two (*Les Voies de l'oraison mentale,* 1917).

Thomas MERTON, also a Cistercian, held that contemplation is the union of mind and will with God in an act of pure love, accompanied by a knowledge of Him as He is in Himself. Infused contemplation begins when God raises this operation above the level of human nature, and its normal terminus is mystical marriage. All souls are called to infused contemplation, which is the reason for their creation by God (see *Seeds of Contemplation*).

A. Saudreau, who has contributed generously to the literature of the theology of the mystical life, defines infused contemplation as a superior knowledge of God, infused in the soul by God through the gifts of the Holy Spirit, together with a love that unites the soul with God. The soul is passive in receiving it, but active in using it. Contemplative knowledge is general and indistinct; contemplative love is a filial love of affection and intimacy. This enables the soul to taste God in His operations, even during periods of passive purification. The resulting union tends to be permanent and this justifies the term "unitive way." Infused contemplation is rightly divided into various forms or degrees. As to acquired contemplation, the words are used to signify different things by various authors, and increasingly it is used to signify a state of prayer in which there are incipient operations of the gifts of the Holy Spirit. The justification of the term depends on the definition given in each case. All souls are called to infused contemplation and to perfection, though not all are culpable for not reaching the goal.

Concomitant Phenomena of Contemplative Prayer. The various grades of contemplative prayer produce definite reactions that are sometimes manifested even in the body. Apart from the extraordinary effects that are not essentially related to contemplative prayer (*see* MYSTICAL PHENOMENA), abstracting from contemplation other than infused and mystical, these are: (1) Infused recollection: awareness of the presence of God; delightful admiration for God; suspension of the operation of the faculties, or spiritual silence of the soul; infused illumination or knowledge of God. (2) Prayer of quiet: sleep of the faculties and inebriation of love (St. Teresa, *Interior Castle,* Fourth Mansions). (3) Prayer of simple union: mystical touches, flights of the spirit; fiery arrows of love; wounds of love (St. Teresa, *The Life* ch. 29; *Spiritual Relations* 5). (4) Prayer of ecstatic union (mystical espousal): suspension of the external faculties by means of ecstatic trance, often accompanied by insensibility and levitation. (5) Prayer of transforming union (mystical marriage): total transformation in God; total surrender to God; permanent union through quasi confirmation in grace.

See Also: MYSTICISM; PRAYER.

Bibliography: J. LEBRETON et al., *Dictionnaire de spiritualité ascétique et mystique. Doctrine et histoire,* ed. M. VILLER et al. (Paris 1932–) 2:1643–2193. J. G. ARINTERO, *The Mystical Evolution in the Development and Vitality of the Church,* tr. J. AUMANN, 2 v. (St. Louis 1949–51); *Stages in Prayer,* tr. K. POND (St. Louis 1957). R. GARRIGOU-LAGRANGE, *Christian Perfection and Contemplation,* tr. M. T. DOYLE (St. Louis 1937); *The Three Ages of the Interior Life,* tr. M. T. DOYLE, 2 v. (St. Louis 1947–48). J. DE GUIBERT,

Trappist monk in solitude.

The Theology of the Spiritual Life, tr. P. BARRETT (New York 1953). G. LERCARO, *Methods of Mental Prayer,* tr. T. F. LINDSAY (Westminster, Md. 1957). A. POULAIN, *The Graces of Interior Prayer,* tr. L. L. YORKE SMITH, ed. J. F. BAINVEL (St. Louis 1950). F. M. MOSCHNER, *Christian Prayer,* tr. E. PLETTENBERG (St. Louis 1962). P. POURRAT, *Christian Spirituality,* tr. W. H. MITCHELL et al., 4 v. (v.1–3, repr. Westminster, Md. 1953; v. 4 pub. 1955). A. ROYO, *The Theology of Christian Perfection,* ed. and tr. J. AUMANN (Dubuque 1962). A. L. SAUDREAU, *The Degrees of the Spiritual Life,* tr. B. CAMM, 2 v. (New York 1907). A. TANQUEREY, *The Spiritual Life,* tr. H. BRANDERIS (2d ed. Tournai 1930; repr. Westminster, Md. 1945). TERESA OF AVILA, *Complete Works,* ed. S. DE SANTA TERESA and E. A. PEERS, 3 v. (New York 1946). JOHN OF THE CROSS, *Complete Works,* ed. and tr. E. A. PEERS from critical ed. S. DE SANTA TERESA, 3 v. (rev. ed. London 1953; repr. 3 v. in 1, Westminster, Md. 1963).

[J. AUMANN]

CONTEMPLATIVE LIFE

A term used to indicate a life characterized by solitude and prayers. Careful distinction should be made between a life of actual solitude and prayer and that state of life in which everything is officially so organized as to create an atmosphere of prayer and quiet. In its canonical form the contemplative life is a state involving the external profession of the religious life. It implies a cloistered existence in which through the exercise of prayer, mortification, and work in some way connected with the cloister, everything is so directed toward interior contemplation that God easily and effectively penetrates the whole of life. Noncanonical forms of the contemplative life are ways of devoting oneself entirely to God by prayer and seclusion. As practiced by those who live in the world, it has been given no juridical status by the Church even though it is approved by her. Pius XII, in the address ''Cedant volontiers,'' cited as an example the holy prophetess Anna in the Gospel of St. Luke, who lived in the temple after the death of her husband and spent her days and nights in prayer and fasting. He also stated explicitly that they lead a truly contemplative life, who, by means of the three vows taken privately, seek perfection in prayer and solitude independently of any canonical status. Both in this manner and in other varying circumstances such men and women have built their own cloister in the midst of the worldly activity around them.

The practice of the contemplative life has roots in the earliest days of Christianity, when both men and women sought to manifest the total consecration of the Christian to Christ by the deliberate choice of perfect continence. Gradually, even in the first centuries, a more formal profession of VIRGINITY brought with it public recognition. Frequent prayer and mortification were joined to the practice of virginity, soon followed by dedication to poverty and obedience. As the need of common life began to be felt, it became rare for consecrated virgins to remain in the world. From the forming of communities of ''ascetics,'' as they were called stem both the active and contemplative forms of the religious life. The contemplative life, however, has roots also in the early movement to the desert where time was devoted totally to prayer and manual labor. St. Anthony of Egypt in the 3d century originated the form of religious life called eremitical, in which an individual practicing it lived alone. Revived in the Middle Ages in the semi-eremitical life of the Camaldolese (1012) and of the Carthusians (1084), it has made a lasting impression on the Church. St. Pachomius in the 4th century, with monasteries of both men and women, founded the cenobitical type of monasticism characterized by the communal life. His work has survived under the various modifications introduced by St. Basil, St. Augustine, and especially St. Benedict. Local regulations for religious men and women eventually led to the imposition of enclosure on all nuns by Boniface VIII in 1298, an action that manifested both the Church's approval of

and her concern for the contemplative life. In the Middle Ages, therefore, the only form of religious life for women was the contemplative. This continued to be the norm even for the second congregations of the mendicant orders, founded in the 13th century. In the 16th and 17th centuries some congregations of women came into being that, although they professed the contemplative life and kept papal cloister, departed from the medieval forms by substituting for the Divine Office certain apostolic and charitable works. Later centuries saw some of the older congregations of women adapt themselves to new needs and take up apostolic work compatible with enclosure, while still others retained the contemplative life in its strictest form. Modern apostolic needs, not always compatible with papal enclosure, have resulted in a distinction between major and minor enclosure, minor enclosure being a modification of the ancient discipline, thus allowing for greater freedom in leaving enclosure for the sake of apostolic works. (*See* CENOBITISM.)

Although external religious profession is essential to the canonical form of the contemplative life, it is not essential to the contemplative life as such. External profession is only a framework for interior contemplation, which is the essence of the contemplative life. The other elements of its canonical form, namely, the cloistered life, the exercises of piety, prayer, mortification, and manual work, are all directed toward interior contemplation. The religious vows, whether solemn or simple, both effect and symbolize in an exterior manner the total consecration of the religious to Christ, which contemplation seeks to bring to an interior reality. Papal enclosure is designed to guard both chastity and silence so that the world cannot disturb or contaminate the monastery. Mental or manual labor satisfies the obligation to work imposed on mankind by the natural law, and also the duty of penance. Work preserves the soul from danger. Undertaken with a holy purpose, it allows the worker to think frequently of God as present with him. It is at once an act of obedience and of mortification. Work done in this fashion is a continual exercise of every virtue. Through it occurs the efficacious union of action with contemplation that is effected by charity. As the perfection of the Christian life, charity is the moving spirit of a contemplative. With a heart open to all mankind, he exercises a universal apostolate: first, by example of a Christian life, second, by public and private prayer, and third, by abnegation and mortification so as to fill up ''what is lacking of the sufferings of Christ . . . for his body which is the Church'' (Col 1.24). In prayerful solitude the contemplative no longer lives, but Christ lives in him.

See Also: ACTIVE LIFE, SPIRITUAL; CONTEMPLATION; RELIGIOUS (MEN AND WOMEN).

Bibliography: Pius XII, ''Sponsa Christi'' (Apostolic Constitution, Nov. 21, 1950), *Acta Apostolicae Sedis* 43 (1951) 5–24; ''Cédant volontiers'' (Address, July 18, 1958), *Pope Speaks* 5 (1958) 61–81. ''Apostolic Constitution, *Sponsa Christi*'', *Review for Religious* 10 (1951) 141–147. ''Instruction on *Sponsa Christi*,'' *Review for Religious* 10 (1951) 205–212. F. B. DONNELLY, ''Changes in the Status of Contemplative Nuns,'' *Homiletic and Pastoral Review* (1951) 734–738. P. POURRAT, *Christian Spirituality*, tr. W. MITCHELL and S. JACQUES, 4 v. (Westminster, Md. 1953–55).

[J. F. CONWELL]

CONTENSON, GUILLAUME VINCENT DE

Dominican theologian and preacher; b. Auvillar, France, 1641; d. Creil-sur-Oise, Dec. 26, 1674. After six years of study under the Jesuits at Montauban, Contenson became a Dominican at Toulouse in 1655. He began teaching philosophy in 1664 at Albi at the invitation of the archbishop but was called back to Toulouse in 1666 to teach theology. He taught in various episcopal seminaries throughout France. His sermons testified to his extensive learning and earned him great popularity. But Contenson's reputation is based primarily on his *Theologia mentis et cordis,* which is still used and highly valued by many. It was completed by Massoulie and published in nine volumes, the last of which appeared posthumously (1681). Basically, the work is a speculative commentary on the *Summa theologiae* of St. Thomas Aquinas. Contenson, believing strongly that theology does not attain its perfection until it unites knowledge and love, attempted to appeal to the heart as well as the mind and to enliven the dry reasoning of scholasticism. He added to his speculative comments, which are accurate and solidly established, asceticomystical reflections drawn from his own opinions and personal experience, illustrating them with imagery borrowed from the Fathers of the Church.

Bibliography: J. QUÉTIF and J. ÉCHARD, *Scriptores Ordinis Praedicatorum*, 5 v. (Paris 1719–23); continued by R. COULON (Paris 1909–); repr. 2 v. in 4 (New York 1959) 2.2:656–657. Á. TOURON, *Histoire des hommes illustrée de l'Ordre de Saint Dominique*, 6 v. (Paris 1743–49).

[C. LOZIER]

CONTINENCE

According to Aristotle, continence is ''a virtue of the appetite, by which men, through thought, control the appetite that induces to evil pleasures'' (*Virt. et vit.* 1250a). Evil pleasures are indulged particularly in immoderate eating and drinking and in seeking unreasonable sexual satisfactions; they are evil because such pleasures pass the bounds laid down by reason. In Christian literature the object of continence is sometimes as comprehensive as it is in Greek philosophy; but in the common parlance of the early Christians, the virtue of continence was associated primarily with sexuality and was synonymous with chastity (Acts 24.25; 1 Cor 7.9; Gal 5.23; Tit 1.8). Today it is variously used in moral theology and popular speech to mean (1) self-restraint in general, or (2) self-restraint with respect to illicit sexual pleasures, or (3) abstention from all sexual pleasure, licit or illicit, or (4) a disposition of the will to resist vehement impulses of the sexual appetite.

In the first of the above senses, continence is identifiable with all virtue, for every virtue implies self-restraint and a holding back from what is repugnant to it. In the second sense it is identifiable with the virtue of CHASTITY, whose function it is to moderate the sexual appetite. In the third sense it can indicate a perfection of chastity, although, as the term is understood in popular usage, the abstention from legitimate sexual activity may have a motive other than that of chastity, in which case it is materially, but not formally, identifiable with that virtue.

Continence in the fourth, and for some moral theologians the most proper, sense of the word, although a most commendable quality, is something less than a virtue inasmuch as it supposes its possessor subject to conditions that would not exist if he were perfectly virtuous. Continence is exercised in holding firm against a riot of disorderly impulses in the sense appetite. In a perfectly chaste man vehement disturbance of this kind would not occur, for it is the function of the virtue of chastity to hold the sense appetite itself under such control that strong irrational movements do not occur in it. Hence continence, which is a quality rooted in the will, is necessary only when chastity has not been equal in its function of controlling the appetite. Continence is therefore a second line of defense, but a necessary one inasmuch as ideally perfect chastity, such as would equip a man to face all manner of circumstances without disorderly reactions of some violence, is a rare quality.

The distinction between continence understood in this sense and temperance was noted by Aristotle (*Eth. Nic.* 7.1), but it was employed also in Christian literature, equivalently at least, from an early date, as can be seen in Cassian's account of the degrees in the practice of chastity (*Collationes* 12, *Patrologia Latina*, ed. J. P. Migne [Paris 1878–90] 49:869–898). St. Thomas Aquinas acknowledged the propriety of speaking of continence both as a virtue in the perfect sense and as something less than perfect virtue, but ordered to the genus of virtue (*Summa theologiae* 2a2ae, 155.1).

The comparative excellence of continence and temperance depends on the sense in which the term is taken. If it is understood to denote abstinence from all venereal pleasures, it is greater than temperance, absolutely speaking; but if it is used in the sense of a strong will to resist lustful impulses, temperance is much greater than continence, for it is more thoroughly in accord with reason. The good of reason is more dominant in the temperate person whose appetite is obedient to reason than in the continent person whose sense appetite strongly resists reason by its evil inclinations. From this point of view, therefore, continence is compared to temperance as something imperfect to something perfect.

See Also: LUST; VIRGINITY; CELIBACY.

Bibliography: THOMAS AQUINAS, *Summa theologiae* 2a2ae, 155–156. B. H. MERKELBACH, *Summa theologiae moralis* (Paris 1949) 2:960–963. *Cursus Theologicus Salmanticensis* (Paris-Brussels 1878) 6:125–126, 266–268. H. LECLERCQ, *Dictionnaire d'archéologie chrétienne et de liturgie.* ed. F. CABROL, H. LECLERCQ and H. I. MARROU (Paris 1907–53) 3:1145–74.

[T. J. HAYES/J. VAN PAASSEN]

CONTINGENCY

In general usage, contingency represents the possible occurrence of future events or conditions that have the character of accidents or emergencies. Viewed as possible or even as probable, although never as certain to occur, contingency involves variability and dependence, and antecedent or concurrent causes or conditions. Because sometimes unforeseen or outside the intention of an agent, it may be identified with CHANCE; in a derived meaning it may be associated with FREEDOM and CHOICE.

Modes of Being. In its metaphysical meaning, contingency represents one of the four modes of being: NECESSITY, contingency, POSSIBILITY, and impossibility. It can therefore best be explained by relating it to the other modes.

Contingency and Necessity. In its opposition to necessity, that condition of fixed, unchangeable being, which is not subordinate to antecedent conditions or prior CAUSALITY, contingency may be viewed either as actual or possible. In terms of possible EXISTENCE, contingency represents the state of an ESSENCE or nature that admits of, but does not demand, actualization; and in this meaning, contingency is coextensive and synonymous with possibility. In terms of actual existence, contingency represents the condition of an essence which, although actualized, is equally disposed toward nonexistence. In short, necessity represents that which cannot not-be; contingency represents that which can be or not-be. In this sense

contingency is predicable of all FINITE BEING that has a beginning, is subject to change, and can perish; that is to say, of all things the mind can conceive as either existing or not existing without thereby falling into contradiction.

Contingency and necessity, however, are not mutually exclusive. The most contingent of things involves at least existential necessity, in the sense that having being it cannot at the same time and under the same aspect not have being. By the same token, contingency involves certain essential necessities: for a triangle to exist, for example, it must have three sides. It may also involve necessity in the sense that certain effects or conditions are relatively necessitated by determined causes or antecedents. This co-presence of necessity and contingency in concrete beings is significant, for it enables the mind to achieve knowledge of the necessary, ranging from universal laws of nature to the existence of God, from the analysis of contingent reality.

Contingency and Possibility. Contingency is sometimes confused with possibility, which also involves the capacity for being. The two may be distinguished in this way: possibility is that which does not imply any contradiction, or that which is not impossible; contingency, on the other hand, is that whose opposite does not imply any contradiction, or that which is not necessary.

Logical Contingency. The logical meaning of contingency closely parallels the metaphysical meaning. In classical logic, it represents one of the modal propositions, i.e., propositions that express a mode of agreement or disagreement between two terms. Necessity and impossibility represent universal modes since the necessary always is and the impossible never is; possibility and contingency represent particular modes, with contingency as the contradictory of necessity, the subcontrary of possibility, and the subaltern of impossibility. In this way the contingent mode of the necessary proposition "It is necessary that S be P" would read: "It is not necessary that S be P and it is possible that S be not P." Modern symbolic logic tends to avoid the metaphysical implications of modal propositions and identifies the contingent proposition with tautology. (*See* LOGIC, SYMBOLIC; OPPOSITION.)

Greek Views of Contingency. Considered historically, contingency in the universe is generally recognized by all philosophers, even those basing their speculation on determinism or necessity. For ARISTOTLE, contingency meant that which is neither necessary nor impossible, or that of which affirmative or negative predication can be made (*Anal. pr.* 46b 40–47b 14). Certain phenomena indicate that the determinate series of causes (formal, final, efficient, and material) does not dominate reality completely, but points to a fifth cause, chance (*Physics* 195b 31–198a 13). Events that thus form exceptions to the usual laws of nature are characterized as happening "neither always nor for the most part" but *per accidens.* Other events seem superficially to conform to purposive causality, but defy analysis to determined principles, as when a farmer plowing his field uncovers buried treasure. Because they are outside of purposive action, such events are attributed to chance (*ibid.; Metaphysics* 1025a 13–34).

Although one need not hold that contingency is treated by Aristotle in his *Physics,* since many of the phenomena referred to are attributable to human ignorance of the determined causes involved or to defects in the material cause, his *Metaphysics* presents a somewhat different view. Here we read that a train of necessary causation may be traced back to a certain point, but cannot be traced further, i.e., to a point that has no cause. There are, for example, conditions already existing which require that all men die, although the time or cause of death cannot be preestablished (*Metaphysics* 1027a 29–1027b 17). All such events are attributed by Aristotle to indeterminate spontaneous forces that derive their existence neither from "nature" nor from "art," but rather "from themselves" and from "chance" (*Metaphysics* 1032a 12–1034b 19). Perhaps, however, the most explicit affirmation of contingency, from both the logical and metaphysical standpoint, is found in the *De interpretatione,* where Aristotle suspends the principle of the EXCLUDED MIDDLE for statements regarding individual future events (17a 25–19b 4). Here he affirms that no proposition with a singular subject concerning the future is necessarily wholly true and its contrary wholly false; otherwise nothing would happen by chance, contingency would be denied, and all events would occur by necessity.

For DEMOCRITUS and the atomists in general, a modification in the size and shape of atoms, reflecting itself in a modulation of their movements, made possible a complex of contingent realities. For EPICURUS, however, the necessary derived from and was contained within the contingent. For he assumed that atoms, unpredictably and for no assignable cause other than self-movement, had the power to deviate from their path of perpendicular descent, and so to form a world of perceptible compounds. This power of declination in the atom, the clinamen, he saw as analogous to will power in man through which movements in the body are initiated.

Contingency in the physical order fortified for Epicurus, as it did for Aristotle, psychological and moral indeterminism by which the human agent retains his freedom and preserves his moral responsibility.

The Aristotelian view of contingency as defect in material causality was continued and developed in the Greco-Arabian tradition, wherein contingency in the universe is due solely to matter, which by lack of proper disposition may prevent effects from taking place.

Medieval Development. The medieval notion of contingency may be summed up in the thesis of St. THOMAS AQUINAS, for whom contingency meant "that which can be and not be" (*Summa theologiae* 1a, 86.3). This definition, however, raised for the scholastics many problems, particularly over the relation between creatures and Creator. Those who defended the real distinction between essence and existence in all created being emphasized the contingent character of such being to show more clearly its dependence on the Creator (*see* ESSENCE AND EXISTENCE). Some, like St. Thomas, used contingency as the basis for a demonstration of the existence of God. Since the essence of the contingent does not itself contain the note of existence, the reason for its existence must be sought in an extrinsic efficient cause. This cause, if in turn contingent, must show reason for its existence in some other antecedent cause. Ultimately a being is reached whose essence includes existence, a first cause whose existence is underived, a being that is necessary and absolute. Such a being is called God. (*See* GOD, PROOFS FOR THE EXISTENCE OF.)

The Epicurean analogy between contingency and will reappeared in the Middle Ages in the VOLUNTARISM of John DUNS SCOTUS and the NOMINALISM of WILLIAM OF OCKHAM. The strain of voluntarism in the outlook of Scotus, however, must be seen in its proper perspective. In the Scotist conception of GOD there is no voluntarism, for the divine will is not elevated above the divine intellect, determining the eternal truths it contains. The essences of creatures are independent of the divine will, for they are necessary and unchangeable, as are the eternal truths deducible from them. Thus, there is a body of necessary speculative truths outside the scope of the divine will. Particular contingent events, however, cannot be explained by such necessary causes as God's intellect and ideas. To account for the actual existence of contingent beings, recourse must be had to His will. God freely chooses certain possible creatures and wills them to exist. In this way God's infinite will accounts for the contingency of creatures. Similarly, in the moral order, certain natural laws are rooted in the very nature of things, the first three Commandments of the Decalogue, for example, but other moral laws are more arbitrary; God simply wills that they should be observed; of such a character are the remaining seven Commandments.

It was William of Ockham who took the final step and reduced the whole moral code to the arbitrary will of God. To do so he found it necessary to eliminate those elements of Scotism that introduce some necessity into God and the universe, namely the divine ideas and the notion of common natures. His efforts in this direction led to charges of nominalism and SKEPTICISM (*see* OCKHAMISM).

Modern Thought. Among modern philosophers as well, these problems are given considerable attention. For LEIBNIZ there subsists in God an infinite number of possibles. All pure essences taken by themselves are subject to an absolute necessity; they are immutably determined and cannot become other than what they necessarily are. Yet ours is a universe of change and contingency. Hence a question arises about the passage from eternal necessity to existential contingency. Leibniz was now placed in a delicate position between DESCARTES and SPINOZA. He sided with Spinoza in removing essences and eternal verities from the free decree of the divine will, yet he did not care to follow Spinoza in affirming that the world emanates from God by absolute necessity. It is a fact that not all possibles are actualized, for certain essences, possible in themselves, are yet incompatible with each other. Such considerations led Leibniz to a position not much different from that of Scotus, wherein the transition from essential to existential existence is through the mediation of the divine will. God created the universe according to a plan, and chose this world as the best of all possible worlds. His choice assures the entrance into existence of the richest system of compatible natures.

With KANT, the orientation of the problem of contingency deviates from its realistic and metaphysical basis. By denying the possibility of metaphysical knowledge and limiting knowledge to the order of PHENOMENA, Kant sees in the modes of contingency, necessity, possibility, and impossibility pure concepts or categories of the understanding that are not derived from experience, but which are a priori and transcendentally deduced from the table of judgments.

In the last half of the 19th century E. BOUTROUX, in an effort to preserve human freedom, proposed a complete "philosophy of contingency" according to which bodies and spirits are governed by no laws of absolute necessity. The supreme principles are rather moral and aesthetical laws; these are expressions of the perfect spontaneity of God in which all creatures participate to varying degrees

See Also: INDETERMINISM; CHANCE; FORTUNE.

Bibliography: C. CARBONARA, *Enciclopedia filosofica* (Venice-Rome 1957) 1:1208–17. R. EISLER, *Wörterbuch der philosophischen Begriffe* (Berlin 1927–30) 1:849–850. E. BOUTROUX, *De la contingence des lois de la nature* (8th ed. Paris 1915). C. DE KONINCK, "Thomism and Scientific Determinism," *American Catholic Philosophical Association. Proceedings of the Annual Meeting* 12 (1936) 58–76. C. FABRO, "Intorno alla nozione 'tomista' di contingenza," *Rivista di filosofia neoscolastica* 30 (1938) 132–149. J. MARITAIN, "Réflexions sur la nécessité et la contingence," *Angelicum* 14 (1937) 281–295. P. H. PARTRIDGE, "Contingency," *Australasian Journal of Psychology and Philosophy* 16 (1938) 1–22. P. H. VAN LAER, *Philosophico-Scientific Problems,* tr. H. J. KOREN (Pittsburgh 1953).

[W. H. TURNER]

CONTINUUM

Broadly speaking, a continuum is a manifold WHOLE whose parts, having continuity, are intrinsically differentiated by their relation to the whole. The various analogical uses of the term continuity, which cover both physical and mathematical domains and encompass extensive and nonextensive manifolds, give breadth to this description. Relative to the primary analogate, which is the extensive continuum, the parts may be understood under two formalities: as analytic or as compositive parts. Thus there are two common definitions of the continuum: (1) a manifold whole that is divisible without end into (analytic) parts, of which there is no smallest; (2) a manifold whole, the extremities of whose (compositive) parts are one. Continuity is logically related to contiguity and consecutiveness, all three referring to extension, but constituting a different ordering of parts. A manifold is consecutive if some element of a different nature intervenes between any part and any other part ordered to the former. The parts are contiguous when nothing of a different nature intervenes, though the parts are bounded; they are continuous when they have a common boundary. A continuum is essentially one, though it has distinguishable parts, whereas both contiguous entities and consecutive manifolds are pluralities, the former with parts distinguished and bounded, the latter with parts separated.

The origin of the notion of continuum is most readily traced to the sensible experience of physical extension, which is the first formal effect of dimensive quantification, manifesting factual material unity but remaining subject to division (*see* EXTENSION). Water provides a good instance, since any sample has parts that are exterior to one another, easily divisible, yet factually not divided: an uninterrupted but divisible extensive whole. Psychological studies show that such continua are grasped by means of a scanning motion, either of the eye or through taction. Though probably secondary, the experience of temporal duration also may be at the basis of man's understanding of the continuum, but this conception differs somewhat from the geometric notion.

Parts Of Extensive Continua

According to the definition given, all continua are divisible into parts that are themselves divisible continua; and since such division does not add anything, the positions of the divisions must be marked by precontained indivisibles. There have been disagreements about the mode of inclusion of the parts in the whole. It would seem that for both ARISTOTLE and St. Thomas Aquinas, the parts as well as the intermediate indivisibles are present only in potency (Aristotle, *Phys.* 233b 33–234b 9; St. Thomas, *In 3 meta.* 13.502–514). Actual existence of parts as parts is understood to be tantamount to actual division, hence loss of continuity. Nevertheless, JOHN OF ST. THOMAS, attempting to represent this position but verbally manifesting a more Platonic tradition, held that both indivisibles and a finite number of extensive parts are actually present, although the boundaries of such parts are shared. This is an interpretation of St. Thomas's remark that an interior point may be the beginning of one and the end of another part of a line (*Cursus phil., Phil. nat.* 1.20). Yet the further divisibility of these parts indicates further potency, and neither the commentator nor more recent expositors of this view seem able to show how or why there should be some actual and some potential parts. Although there is some difficulty concerning terminology, F. SUÁREZ seems to hold that parts are distinct but not in act: . . . *illae partes sunt illo modo in potentia, sed non in actu, quamquam melius ac verius dicentur entia in potentia, quam partes in potentia* (*Disp. meta.* 40.4.9). According to the definition, there can be no minimal parts, but in physical continua there will be minimal integral parts, that is, those whose nature would be changed by any further division. An abstract continuum has only aliquot parts, for example, the ten, one-inch segments of a ten-inch line, or proportional parts distinguished by a measure proportional to some constant or varying numerical ratio, for example, ½, ¼, 1/8, 1/16.

DISTINCTION OF PARTS

No one admits actual division in the sense of separation. Actual division of an abstract continuum is accomplished by the mental removal of a portion of the continuum or the establishment of an indivisible boundary, and this is no more than a simple designation. Division produces two continua that are either contiguous or consecutive. But distinction within a continuum does not require actual determinate boundaries of composite parts; material opposition, called *situs* or position (the differentia of dimensive quantity), suffices [*See* SITUATION (SITUS)]. This will be a distinction with a real, that is, nonmental, basis even though the making of the distinction is a mental act. Because mental being is equivalent to being known, it is easy to confuse the real distinction of parts of a geometrical continuum with their actual division, or make the latter a requirement for the former. While it cannot be said that the parts of a continuum have only potential existence—for then the whole composed of such parts would not be actual—the parts qua parts

cannot be actually present with their own individuality and unity, for this would mean actual division with actual indivisible boundaries.

INDIVISIBLES

Concerning one point, most scholastics agree: a continuum cannot be composed of indivisibles. An infinity of indivisibles can be no more extended than a finite number. G. W. LEIBNIZ (1646–1716) and following him, I. Kant (1724–1804), found a contradiction between a real continuum, which was supposed to be posterior to its simple compositive parts and a mathematical continuum, understood as prior to its analytic parts. Denying composition of the latter, they had to admit it of the former, the composing parts being either real dynamistic points or ideal elements. The continuum, for them, thus became a mere phenomenal unity (G. W. Leibniz, "Letter to Remond," *Die philosophichen Schriften . . .*, ed. Gerhardt, 3:622; I. Kant, *Metaphysische Anfangsgründe der Naturwissenschaft,* 2.4.2). The necessity of composition of a physical continuum is, however, an assumption traceable to the general philosophical position of its proposers, rather than anything proper to the idea of continuum. Arguing on a similar basis, G. BERKELEY (1685–1753) and D. HUME (1711–76) concluded that the continuum is composed of very small extended indivisibles (*See* INDIVISIBLE).

Types Of Continua

In addition to extensive magnitudes, MOTION and TIME are continua. Except for local motion, whose continuity is reducible in part to that of the magnitude being traversed, it is the temporal flux that usually manifests nonstatic continuity. In the static continuum, all parts coexist and are known immediately, while in flowing continua the parts, successive in existence, are known only through the re-presentations of memory. Both types are understood as wholes divisible into parts, distinguished but not interrupted, which have the same nature as the whole; but a flowing continuum is a BECOMING, hence its parts are never a BEING, even when considered abstractly.

Though attained in sensation, the abstracted concept of continuum is primarily mathematical; when used in a physical sense, the term is a secondary analogate. Paradoxically, one must grant notional priority to the mathematical continuum, but experiential priority to the physical continuum. The usual examples are abstractions such as mathematical lines, surfaces or perfectly homogeneous solids. Disagreements about physical continua are often traced to the problem of realization of continuity in matter. It is thought that there can be no continuity where heterogeneity is present. In mathematics this is true because differences would be either qualities proper to quantity (for example, shapes or boundaries), or purely quantitative and hence disruptive. But in the physical order qualitative heterogeneity is consonant with quantitative continuity. The mathematical representation of flowing continua requires greater abstraction than that of static continua, since mathematics abstracts from motion. The mathematical notion is subject to further analogical extensions within that order and has been made to include even discrete quantity.

Mathematical Interpretations

The two mathematical sciences of antiquity, arithmetic (the science of the discrete) and geometry (the science of the continuous), were made to meet in the development of analysis introduced with the conceptions of analytic geometry. The correspondence between points located in a geometric continuum and numbers or sets of numbers suggested an analogous type of continuity in the discrete realm. By a pure convention the integers may be placed in 1 to 1 correspondence with points in a linear continuum marking unit segments; hence, by extension, there should be correspondence between the points within each segment and some numerical value less than one. The genetic development of fractional, irrational and other analogates to natural numbers chronologically followed the requirements for solutions of various algebraic equations of increasing complexity and ultimately involved variables that should assume numerical values continuously according to some functional rule. Thus a function is considered continuous at point t if $F(x)$ has a value at t and approaches $F(t)$ as x approaches t. If the function is continuous at all points in a domain, then it is continuous in the domain. This notion has in turn brought about a new postulational definition of geometric continuity in terms of points rather than parts: a line, for example, is continuous when: (1) between any two points on the line there is a third point and (2) a division of the line always distinguishes an extreme point on one of the parts of the division. The assumption of continuous variability was founded first on the intuitive notions of the calculus and theory of limits, later upon the more rigorous developments in analysis and the theory of functions and series, where transcendental numbers also were explored.

MODERN MATHEMATICS

Until the work of K. Weierstrass (1815–97), R. Dedekind (1831–1916) and G. Cantor (1845–1918), in the latter half of the 19th century, there was no overt attempt to provide a theoretical foundation for a continuum of real numbers. Indeed their theoretical considerations, especially Cantor's, led not only to a definition of a real number continuum, but to a new theory of natural number based upon the concept of "set," which has come to permeate a large part of modern mathematics.

The Dedekind definition of the irrational numbers, which allows a numerical continuum, depends upon the concept of a "cut" in the number field such that two classes are formed: [A] and [C] in which every element a of [A] is numerically less than every element c of [C]. There exists then but one number b that divides the sets, for: (1) either there is a largest rational number a' or a smallest rational c' that divides the sets, or (2) b must be an irrational number defined by the cut since it can be shown that the difference between a' and c' can be made less than any arbitrarily chosen number, that is, that [A] and [C] are arbitrarily close yet divided by a number that is not rational. It is impossible to present the definition rigorously here, but it should be emphasized that there is no proof given but only a rigorous axiomatic definition, which is essentially that of Eudoxus, generalized and freed of its geometric moorings.

Cantor provided an alternate definition of irrational number, which, so to speak, fills the gaps between the elements of the dense set of rational numbers. His theory operates with "nested intervals" that contract toward one element and provides a number system that can be put in one to one correspondence with that of Dedekind. Though the latter accepted an actual infinity of numbers, Cantor first developed an arithmetic of the infinite that operates with infinite sets considered as wholes. If the notion of the continuum is derived in an arithmetic field, as Cantor demands, the geometric continuum will be composed of an infinity of points, a conclusion not universally accepted and philosophically inadmissible.

INSTITUTIONISM AND FORMALISM

H. Weyl (1885–1955) and L. E. J. Brouwer (1881–1966) reject the notion of an actual infinity because it cannot be constructed in intuition, and in their view, the continuum cannot be defined as a system of individual points. The continuum is not a composition for Brouwer, but a matrix in which points can be constructed. The arithmetic continuum does not exist, it "becomes" as it is effectively constructed in intuition, the real numbers being defined in terms of a selective sequence of natural numbers rather than sets. Though more in agreement with the traditional Aristotelian notions, the intuitionist philosophy is largely indebted to Kant, who shared with Aristotle the view that an infinity cannot have the character of a completed whole. The goal of intuitionist mathematics has been to avoid the difficulties inherent in Cantor's set theory.

Early in the 1900s a series of antinomies were discovered that flow from the unguarded use of actual infinities and that are resolved only by postulating certain *ad hoc* axioms (for example, of choice) concerned largely with infinite sets, the legitimacy of which has raised questions that divide the major philosophical positions. The formalist attempt to escape the implications of the thought of R. Dedekind, G. Frege and B. RUSSELL developed parallel difficulties demanding still other assumptions (*see* ANTINOMY; AXIOMATIC SYSTEM).

Physical Continua

The history of attempts to understand the physical universe manifests a constant tension between the continuous and the discrete. The earliest attempt to reduce one to the other is found in the paradoxes of ZENO OF ELEA, the first two of which, *Dichotomy* and *Achilles,* are generated by an unwarranted assimilation of the flowing continua to abstract extension, with the resulting assumption that they are infinitely divided. Mathematical solutions to these paradoxes, based upon convergence theorems of infinite series, make the same baseless assumption. Two others, *Arrow* and *Stadium,* assume that continua are composed of an infinity of indivisible parts, another indefensible reduction.

Again, the concepts of plenum and VOID, found early in natural philosophy, give rise to atomistic versus continuance theories of physical reality. Atoms entail a void—like spatial continuum or arena for local motion, whereas a plenum, or at least a contiguum, may be a continuum heterogeneously and dynamically differentiated. Aristotle countered the atomists, DEMOCRITUS and Leucippus, only by showing that motion could take place in a plenum by "replacement"; in his solution, the obvious discontinuity in the universe would have to be mediated by some sort of interstitial matter or ether. Classical physics, which was thoroughly atomistic, postulated the absolute continua of time and SPACE, and later an ether to serve as a medium for radiation. The failure of the Michelson-Morley experiments to detect such an ether provided the immediate impetus that launched the theories of relativity. A. Einstein's special theory was formulated by H. Minkowski (1864–1909) in terms of a mathematical fusion of space and time, which the general theory interprets as the locale of an energy or force field. Subsequent unsuccessful efforts to construct a unified field theory, had as their goal, the reduction of both gravitational and electromagnetic phenomena to local anomalies and perturbations in an overall curved space-time continuum.

In the 1960s, at least four different fields have to be unified; quantum physics has, moreover, reemphasized the discrete. Classical molecules and atoms have been resolved into subatomic particles that, as models at least,

represent the inner construction of matter. The mass-energy equivalence relation predicted the conversion of matter into radiant energy and the reverse, thereby providing another avenue of reduction. But efforts to explain the details of various radiation phenomena, especially radiant heat, indicated that what must under one form be considered discrete particles, must under another be regarded as a wave governed by a field. Under the first aspect, an unattended space-time continuum is assumed, not different from that of classical physics; while under the second, a continuous field or set of fields is interpreted as a modulation of either a physico-mathematical space-time continuum or of an ether. The development of the quantum theory has not, therefore, settled the issue. In fact, quantum limitations led some physicists to suggest an atomization of space and time themselves, postulating a smallest interval of space, the hodon, of the order of 10^{-13} centimeters (more recently the smallest spatial interval has been set at 10^{-33}—Planck's length), and the smallest temporal interval, the chronon, of the order of 10^{-24} seconds. But such discontinuities only presuppose an underlying continuity, at least as a heuristic device.

The notion of matter as made up of impenetrable bits, though a constantly recurring theme in science, has become unacceptable. In fact, the very notion is considered a gross extrapolation into realms wherein common language is inapplicable. The present classes of subatomic particles, leptons, mesons, baryons and so-called resonance particles, are interrelated in ways that suggest that they are epiphenomenal manifestations of a subject proto-matter or a field. Quantum considerations coupled with general relativity theory have more recently suggested either a compromise "pulsational" universe marked by heterogeneous space-time in which continuity is modified if not completely destroyed, or a rippling universe that manifests foam—like discontinuities in regions of high curvature, identifiable as "particles." It should be borne in mind, however, that all such theories are formally mathematical and explain only dialectically by means of symbolic constructs and models. Thus, for example, the space-time continuum is an abstraction, as Whitehead indicated, and yet it is common to find it considered as an ontological principle similar to primary matter. Though reality cannot be composed of abstractions, it can be explained with the help of constructs that represent abstractions. At present such constructs disclose a modified continuum and hence a plenum as a matrix for the physical universe.

See Also: QUANTITY; MATHEMATICS, PHILOSOPHY OF.

Bibliography: P. HOENEN, *Cosmologia* (5th ed. Rome 1956). F. WAISMANN, *Introduction to Mathematical Thinking,* tr. T. J. BENAC (New York 1959). R. DEDEKIND, *Essays on the Theory of*

Marie Charlotte Carmichael Stopes (1880–1958), pioneer of birth control and family planning, photograph by Underwood & Underwood.

Numbers: I. Continuity of Irrational Numbers, II. The Nature and Meaning of Numbers, tr. W. W. BEMAN (Chicago 1901). G. CANTOR, *Contributions to the Founding of the Theory of Transfinite Numbers,* tr. P. E. B. JOURDAIN (New York 1952). M. ČAPEK, *The Philosophical Impact of Contemporary Physics* (Princeton 1961). A. GRÜNBAUM, *Philosophical Problems of Space and Time* (New York 1963). A. FARGES, *L'Idée de continu dans l'espace et le temps* (5th ed. Paris 1908). E. BODEWIG, "Zahl und Kontinuum in der Philosophie des hl. Thomas," *Divus Thomas,* 13 (1935) 187–207. V. MIANO, *Enciclopedia filosofica,* 4 v. (Venice-Rome 1957) 1:1217–21. R. EISLER, *Wörterbuch der philosophischen Begriffe,* 3 v. (4th ed. Berlin 1927–30) 3:154–158.

[C. F. WEIHER]

CONTRACEPTION

As generally used in Catholic theology, the employment of any of various mechanical, chemical, pharmaceutical, X-ray, or surgical means of preventing sexual intercourse from issuing in the generation of offspring. These means have been understood to include certain distortions of the coital act itself (as in coitus interruptus, or the use of a condom or pseudovagina) as well as other acts before or after intercourse, designed to prevent conception, such as the use of douches and the induction of

sterility. Contraception is to be distinguished from the avoidance of generation by abstention from intercourse, as in the complete or periodic practice of continence. (*See* NATURAL FAMILY PLANNING .)

The reasons for this distinction may chiefly be discovered in history. Major techniques of contraception—coitus interruptus, potions, and pessaries—were known and disseminated, with the inaccuracy of early medicine, in the Greco-Roman world and in medieval Europe. The rule of the Church against contraception developed, in different historical environments, to protect the fundamental values of procreation, life, dignity, and love. Procreation itself was under almost constant attack in the first 1,300 years of Christian experience. In the first 3 centuries its value and dignity were denied by some Gnostic sects outside the Church and by some Gnostic groups within the Church whose sexual morals were attacked by the NT writers in 1 Cor 5.1–8, Gal 5.1–26, Jude 12 and 13, 2 Pt 2.17, and Rv 2.6–15. Alienated from the world and despising its Creator, the Gnostics rejected the OT, claimed an absolute freedom from moral law, and saw procreation as a senseless perpetuation of creation. Against a Gnostic group was written the sole passage explicitly approving procreation in the NT, which declared that "women will be saved by childbearing" (1 Tm 2.15).

Gnostic Teaching. Gnostic currents, repudiated in apostolic times, continued to present a major challenge to the 2nd-century Church. Gnostics of the right, such as Tatian and Marcion, preached an extreme asceticism, prohibiting procreation for all Christians. Gnostics of the left, such as Carprocrates and Valentinus, preached an extreme libertarianism, encouraging sexual intercourse, but totally separating intercourse from procreation. Against both extremes, the first Christian school of theology, that of Clement of Alexandria, insisted that sexual intercourse found its measure in marriage, and that in marriage procreation was a good work of cooperation in the work of a good Creator. In this context, in reaction to the Gnostic denials, Clement adopted the Stoic rule set out by Musonius Rufus: the sole lawful purpose for initiating marital intercourse was procreation (Clement, *Pedagogus* 2.10.95.3). This rule became the dominant opinion of the Fathers and of the medieval theologians on the lawful use of marriage; it effectively excluded contraception.

St. Augustine's Teaching. The Gnostic trauma of the Church, which accounts for so much of the patristic commitment to the procreative purposes of marriage, was repeated and deepened by the Manichaean trauma. Armed with scriptures of its own, organized as a church with a hierarchy, equipped with a theology and a rule of conduct, MANICHAEISM was for more than a century a formidable rival to the Catholic Church. A mind as theologically sophisticated as St. Augustine's could be attracted to it; and that Augustine was a Manichaean from the age of 18 to 29 is of great importance to the history of contraception.

The significant result of Augustine's immersion in Manichaeism was not, as some have asserted, that he carried Manichaean principles into Catholicism, but that his reaction to Manichaeism was so strong, so intense, and so overwhelming that he emphasized, to an extreme degree, the great point on which Catholic morality seemed to him opposed to Manichaean morality. Dualist like Gnosticism, Manichaeaism had for its central moral tenet: you shall not procreate. The difference between this position and that of the Catholics was proclaimed by Augustine in two books written immediately after his conversion, *The Morals of the Manichaeans* (*De moribus Manichaeorum*) and *The Morals of the Catholic Church* (*De moribus ecclesiae catholicae*). Unlike the Manichaeans, the Catholic Church, Augustine said, taught that marriage was good and that procreation was the purpose of marital intercourse. The several explicit passages of Augustine against contraception must be understood in the context of his reaction to the Manichaeans.

In ch. 18 of *The Morals of the Manichaeans,* St. Augustine denounced the Manichaeans for advising use of what physicians in antiquity thought to be the sterile period. He declared that this systematic avoidance of procreation made a wife no more than a harlot. In writing against his old friend, the Manichaean Bishop Faustus, Augustine accused the Manichaeans of practicing coitus interruptus in a "perverse" attempt to avoid imprisonment of their god (*C. Faust.* 22.30). In writing against the Manichaean Secundinus, Augustine asserted that the Manichaeans preferred prostitutes to wives because prostitutes "take steps not to conceive." In two later works, not written against Manichaeans, Augustine employed the same analysis of contraception he had adopted against his former coreligionists. In *Marriage and Concupiscence* (*Nupt. et concup.* 1.15.17), he condemned those who "although they are called husband and wife," avoid children and even abandon the children born to them against their will. "Sometimes," he said, "their lustful cruelty or cruel lust comes to this, that they even procure poisons of sterility." If these do not work they resort to abortion. In this specific denunciation of contraception in marriage, it is not clear whether Augustine condemns individual acts or only a practice of avoiding children. Finally, in a short treatise written in 419 on divorce and remarriage, Augustine made the first reference to the story of Onan by a Christian writer in connection with marriage. It is lawlessness and shameful, he said, to have intercourse with one's wife "where the conception of offspring is avoided: This is what Onan, the son of Judah did, and God killed him for it" (*Adult. coniug.* 2.12.12).

The Manichaean threat merged in the 5th century into the Priscillianist heresy, whose opposition to procreation troubled the western end of the Mediterranean world as late as the first council of Braga in 565, when St. Martin of Braga acted to oppose contraception [*Opera,* ed. C. W. Barlow (New Haven 1950) 142]. Manichaeism itself was still a problem in Africa, Sicily, and the Italian mainland for Gregory the Great, who insisted that procreation alone justified intercourse (*Regula pastoralis* 3.27).

Later Dualist Sects. Varieties of Manichaean and dualistic sects continued to exist in the East. In the 10th century, one of these dualist movements gathered momentum in Bulgaria under the leadership of a priest, Bogomil, and Bogomilism spread east to Constantinople and west to Albania. In the 11th century there appeared in northern Italy and southern France pockets of BOGOMILS, known in the West as CATHARI, that is, "The Pure." By the 12th century the Cathari were a major religious and social problem in western Europe, and from 1140 to 1240—that is, during the most creative era of medieval theology and common law—the Cathari presented a major challenge to the good of procreation.

Reaction to Catharism. Three ecumenical councils dealt with these heretics "denying marriage." From the Second Lateran Council in 1139 (J. D. Mansi, *Sacrorum Conciliorum nova et amplissima collectio* 21:532) to the Third Lateran Council (Mansi 22:476) to the anti-Cathar profession of faith of the Fourth Lateran Council in 1215 (J. D. Mansi, *Sacrorum Conciliorum nova et amplissima collectio* 22:982), the highest authority in the Church was concerned with the repudiation of procreation by the Cathari. While the order of St. Dominic was formed to convert them, secular rulers were urged to suppress them and finally to crusade against them with all the privileges of crusaders for the Holy Land. It was chiefly in this context of the defense of the good of procreation that Gratian inserted in his *Decretum* (2.32.2.7) the canon *Aliquando,* taken from Augustine's *Marriage and Concupiscence,* denouncing absolutely the use of poisons of sterility. It was chiefly in this context that Peter Lombard followed Gratian and made *Aliquando* a central text in the section of the *Sententiae* (4.31.3) dealing with marriage. It was chiefly in this context that Gregory IX enacted the first universal legislation by a pope against contraception. The first of these papal acts, *Si conditiones* (*Decretals* 4.5.7), declared null a marriage entered into with a condition to avoid offspring. The second, *Si aliquis* (*ibid.* 5.12.5), an ancient canon of uncertain origin, declared it to be homicide to prevent generation or cause sterility.

The Values Defended by the Church. It is possible to discern a number of distinct values the Church was concerned to safeguard in its legislation against contraception.

The Transmission of Life. Just as the popularization of the *Ave Maria* in this period was part of the ideological reaction to Catharism—no Cathar could say "Blessed is the fruit of thy womb"—so too were these canons against contraception largely adopted as part of a general program to save and to assert the goodness of the procreative act. If, since the 13th century, there has been no serious large-scale threat to this basic value, it is because the Church so thoroughly established that procreation was a value that must be honored. The absolute prohibition of contraception was part of the process of this defense of the transmission of life.

Life. Life itself, after conception, was a second value that the prohibition of all contraception protected. The defense of innocent life was first undertaken in a Greco-Roman world notoriously insensitive to infant and embryonic life, where the abandonment of young children to beasts or birds of prey or to slave dealers was not uncommon, where infanticide was not viewed as murder, where abortion with paternal consent was lawful. In this milieu the Christians insisted on the sacredness of human life at every stage of its development. In the NT, *pharmakeia,* the use of magical drugs, was severely condemned, and this condemnation may well have included the use of drugs to produce abortions or prevent conception (Gal 5.20; Rv 9.21; 21.8; 22.15). The same opposition to *pharmakeia* appeared in Didache (5.2) and the *Epistle of Barnabas* (20). Abortifacients and probably contraceptives were condemned by Minucius Felix in *Octavius* (30.2). It is clear that contraceptives were referred to in a condemnation in the early 3rd-century *Elenchos* (9.12.5), attributed to St. Hippolytus of Rome.

The desire to preserve life revealed itself strikingly in the Christian extensions of the Roman terms for murder, *parricidium* and *homicidium.* Neither term legally applied to destruction of an infant. But the Christians applied them to infanticide, abortion, and contraception. In the words of Tertullian, "He destroys a man who destroys a man-to-be" (*Apologia* 9.8). Extension of the protection of life to include the interdiction of contraception was all the more necessary because it was impossible to be sure whether the drugs usually employed worked as contraceptives or as abortifacients (Soranos, *Gynecology* 1.19.60). Moreover, according to patristic and medieval belief, a fetus did not receive a human soul until at least 40 days after conception; it was, therefore, difficult to draw a sharp line between the embryo and the seed. To protect the embryo in its earliest stage, language had to be employed that was equally applicable to the seed. In this context the use of contraceptive potions was stigmatized as homicide by St. Ambrose (*Hexaemeron* 5.18.58) and St. Jerome (letter 22, *To Eustochium* 13). Their language, not intended literally, was directed against means that, when employed to prevent conception, often actually attacked existing life.

The same linking of contraception to an attack on life and the same association of contraceptives with evilly magical potions was maintained in the post-patristic period by St. Caesarius of Arles (*Sermons* 1.12) and by numerous penitentials, such as the *Irish Collection of Canons* ("Womanly Questions" 3.3) and the *St. Hubert Penitential* (ch. 56). This approach took definitive form in the decretal *Si aliquis,* already referred to, which from 1232 to 1917 was part of the legislation of the Church. In strong language the canon embodied a defense of life in a prohibition of contraception in any form.

Human Dignity. The prohibition of contraception was undertaken historically also as a defense of human dignity. In the Roman Empire, where slavery, slave concubinage, and easy divorce flourished, women could readily be regarded as objects for male exploitation. The teaching of St. Paul in 1 Cor 7.3–6 on the rendering of the debt of marital intercourse affirmed the fundamental equality of the spouses in sexual matters and in so doing affirmed the personal dignity of the wife. Although many of the Fathers were pessimistic in their judgments concerning woman, they also refused to let woman be considered as a thing. It might be supposed that woman would have been given greater dignity if freed from servitude to procreation, but this supposition does not take account of a milieu where the procreative function constituted a woman's chief claim to be treated other than as an object for pleasure. Anal intercourse was taken as a common occurrence by such Roman moralists as Martial. The Christians showed an abhorrence of such use of a woman. Justin Martyr testified with approbation to a Christian woman leaving her husband for this reason (*Apologia* 2.1). The *Epistle of Barnabas* (10.8) contained a vigorous repudiation of oral intercourse. The teaching of St. Augustine was that anal or oral intercourse was worse than fornication (*Bon. coniug.* 11.12). The monastic penitentials prescribed for such behavior penances more severe than for homicide (e.g., *Penitential of Theodore* 1.2.15). The teaching of Gratian and Peter Lombard was that such intercourse was worse than incest (*Decretum* 2.32.7.11; *Sententiae* 4.38.2).

These kinds of acts were rejected as "unnatural." It was not merely that the acts were not procreative. Intercourse with insemination where procreation was impossible, as in pregnancy, was considered sinful by a majority of theologians, but never rebuked with such vehemence. The characteristic of the acts stamped as unnatural was that insemination itself was avoided. It is possible to find the Christian teaching here focused on the religious significance that should characterize the sexual act: in this view, to have sexual relations where insemination was prevented was a most perverse profanation of what should be in some sense a sacred act. It is possible also to interpret the impulse at the core of this teaching as the impulse to protect and assert human dignity.

Marital Love. The fourth value historically defended by the prohibition of contraception was marital love. The practice of contraception in all ages has been commonly associated with fornication or adultery. It was contraception practiced by unchaste Christian teenagers that was denounced by St. Jerome in his letter to Eustochium. It was contraception practiced by prostitutes that was denounced by St. John Chrysostom ("Homily 24 on the Epistle to the Romans," *Patrologia Graeca* 60:626). The medieval writers often associated interrogation in confession about fornication with interrogation about contraception (e.g., Burchard, *Decretum* 19, "Interrogatory," *Patrologia Latina* 140:972). The strongest papal attack on contraception, the bull *Effraenatam* of Sixtus V, issued Oct. 29, 1588, is probably best understood as part of a papal campaign to repress prostitution in Rome.

As contraception has been so often linked with extramarital sexual behavior, its general prohibition as unnatural may in itself be seen as, in part, a defense of marital fidelity. Beyond that, a common scholastic argument against fornication was that it did injury to the potential child by bringing him into the world without definite parents committed to his education (e.g., Thomas Aquinas, *De malo* 15.2 and 4). If contraception were permissible in extramarital intercourse, the scholastic objection based on injury to the potential child would have less force. This belief, that a main point in the rational case against fornication depends on a prohibition of contraception, has influenced theological thought until recent times. Since 1925, beginning with Dietrich Von Hildebrand's *In Defense of Purity* and Herbert Doms' *The Meaning of Marriage,* a new theory of marital intercourse has made this argument seem less necessary to some theologians. The new theory stressed that the requirements of love of another person can only be met if sexual intercourse occurs within the stable union of marriage. This insight into the demands of love constitutes an objection to extramarital sexual acts that has made it possible to see that the prohibition of contraception is not a necessary part of the argument against fornication. Nevertheless, for centuries the prohibition of contraception had, paradoxically,

served the cause of marital love by providing a basis for the condemnation of sexual acts outside of marriage.

Large Families. In addition to protecting procreation, life, personal dignity, and love, the rule of the Church on contraception, it might be argued, protected the value of the large family. There is one strain of Catholic thought that supports this argument. Duns Scotus declared that procreation was intended to restore the population of heaven, depleted by the fall of the angels (*On the Sentences,* Paris Report, 4.28). The bull *Exultate Deo* of 1439 referred to the Church being "corporally increased through matrimony" (Mansi 31:1054). The encyclical *Casti connubii* taught that Christian parents are not only to propagate the human race, but "to bear offspring for the Church of Christ, to procreate saints and servants of God, that the people adhering to the worship of God and our Savior should daily increase" (*Acta Apostolicae Sedis* 22:544). This was not intended precisely as a plea for large families, but it was a short step in the thinking of many to conclude more or less without qualification that the more numerous the offspring the better.

This valuation of numerous offspring was, indeed, implicit in many Catholic criticisms of contraception in the 19th and 20th centuries. At the same time the normal Catholic judgment set higher store on the perfection of existing offspring than on the procreation of many offspring. Virginity outside of marriage and continence even for life within marriage were traditionally considered more valuable than procreation. Procreation itself was never separated from the duty of education. It has already been noted that the failure to provide education was long the common argument against procreating outside of marriage. A host of authorities taught that the procreation of children *to be educated* in the Lord is the only meritorious act of Christian progenitors as such (Clement, *Stromata* 3.11; St. Augustine, *Gen. ad litt.* 9.7; Peter Lombard, *Sententiae* 4.31; St. Thomas Aquinas, *In epist. 1 ad Cor.* 7.1). Accordingly, in the Christian view, procreation and education were inseparable. If there was a tension between the achievement of one at the expense of the other, this tension was built into the Christian position. The rule on contraception, although sometimes taken to endorse procreation at the cost of the perfection of existing children, cannot, in fact, be isolated from the traditional teaching on education.

The Modern Problem. The practice of contraception on a large scale was a phenomenon that began in France in the last quarter of the 18th century. It was first publicly advocated as a social good in England in 1822 by Francis Place. For most of the 19th century there was still general social, medical, and political hostility to the idea. The Church itself, however, took the position in France that confessors need not interrogate or correct Catholics practicing it in the mistaken good faith conviction that it was innocent, if reform of their behavior seemed unlikely. Contraception became general in France. Then, in the last quarter of the 19th century, Malthusian Leagues began an active advocacy of birth control. Often birth control was presented as a panacea for major social ills, and sometimes, as the name itself indicated, the control of birth rather than conception was the object of the propaganda. However, European governments at the same time were becoming increasingly conscious of the role of population in the European balance of power and tended, therefore, to look with disfavor upon the movement.

Reacting to the careless and crude oversimplifications of the birth control movement and encouraged by nationalist interest in population increase, Church authorities began a vigorous campaign against contraception. In a response dated March 10, 1886, the Penitentiary indicated that the confessor was under obligation to make prudent and discreet inquiries when there was a well-founded suspicion that a penitent was addicted to the crime of onanism, and that he should warn the penitent of the gravity of this sin. The Belgian hierarchy under Cardinal Mercier took a strong and militant stand in a pastoral letter on the duties of married life and in instructions given to curés and confessors on the subject of onanism. This was followed by condemnations of contraception by the German hierarchy in 1913, by the French hierarchy in 1919, and by the hierarchy of the U.S. in 1920. The campaign reached its climax in Pius XI's *CASTI CONNUBII* (1930), drafted largely by Arthur Vermeerch, SJ: "any use whatever of marriage, in the exercise of which the act by human effort is deprived of its natural power of procreating life, violates the law of God and nature, and those who do such a thing are stained by a grave and mortal flaw" (*Acta Apostolicae Sedis* 22:560).

The encyclical was a highpoint of opposition. In the next 35 years the theology of marriage underwent discussion and development. With fear of the population explosion and with the realization that, for some people, children were no longer an economic asset but an economic liability, questions arose as to whether the Church's teaching might change in light of changing socio-economic conditions. Some theologians argued that a newer understanding of man and of his control over his own biological nature required a revision or modification in our understanding of natural law and its requirements. There was also development and argument as to the means of contraception. In 1951 Pope Pius XII approved the systematic use of the sterile period for couples with "serious economic, medical or social reasons" as

a means of birth control (*Acta Apostolicae Sedis* 43:859). He took a different stance regarding the anovulant and therefore contraceptive effects of progestational steroids, denouncing Catholic writers who suggested that possibly "the pill" did not come under the traditional ban on other forms of contraception. Pius XII in an address to hematologists in 1958 labeled such opinions erroneous and affirmed that these preparations are forbidden by the law of God when deliberately used as contraceptives or as temporarily sterilizing agents. With these and other questions in mind, John XXIII established a commission to study the matter and present information and opinions on anything pertinent to the question. In the meantime both he and his successor, Pope Paul VI affirmed that the teaching of preceding popes still held. Paul VI enlarged the commission established by John XXIII to include persons from even more competencies, with a promise to study whatever data they could supply. Addressing this commission on March 27, 1965, the Pope put to them a larger question: "In what form and according to what norms ought spouses to accomplish in the exercise of their mutual love that service of life to which their vocation calls them?" (*L'Osservatore Romano,* March 29, 1965).

Cardinal Julius Döpfner, the co-President of the Commission, presented the Commission's final report to Pope Paul VI on June 28, 1966. It concluded that the Catholic position on artificial contraception "could not be sustained by reasoned argument." Finally in July of 1968, 2 years after the commissions' recommendations had been submitted, Pope Paul issued his formal answer and judgment in his encyclical *HUMANAE VITAE*, again reaffirming the centuries-old teaching that the deliberate positive action of preventing a life-giving effect from a potentially life-giving act between husband and wife is against the law of God. In doing this he agreed with the minority report and rejected the recommendations of the majority statement of the commission as contrary to the teaching of the Church and unacceptable.

Bibliography: H. BATZILL, ed., *Decisiones Sanctae Sedis de usu et abusu matrimonii* (Rome 1944), a collection of Roman documents from 1816 to 1944. L. DUPRÉ, *Contraception and Catholics* (Baltimore 1964), critique of the unchangeability of the prohibition. J. C. FORD and G. A. KELLY, *Contemporary Moral Theology,* 2 v. (Westminster, MD 1958–63), v.2, *Marriage Questions,* a defense of the rule's unchangeability. S. DE LESTAPIS, *Family Planning and Modern Problems,* tr. R. F. TREVETT (New York 1961), sociological arguments against contraception. R. E. MURRAY, SJ, *An Historical and Critical Study of the Lambeth Conferences' Teaching on Contraception* (Rome 1964). D. LINDNER, *Der Usus matrimonii: Eine Untersuchung über seine sittliche Bewertung in der katholischen Moraltheologie alter und neuer Zeit* (Munich 1929), a study of the development of teaching on procreative purpose in marriage. J. T. NOONAN, JR., *Contraception: A History of its Treatment by the Catholic Theologians and Canonists* (Cambridge, MA 1965). C.

CURRAN, ed., *Contraception: Authority and Dissent* (New York 1969). J. E. SMITH, *Humanae vitae: A Generation Later* (Washington, DC 1991). P. HEBBLETHWAITE, *Paul VI. The First Modern Pope* (New York/Mahwah, NJ 1993).

[J. T. NOONAN, JR./EDS.]

CONTRADICTION, PRINCIPLE OF

The principle of contradiction expresses the metaphysical and logical opposition between being and its negation. It is concisely expressed by Aristotle: "A thing cannot at the same time be and not be. . ." (*Meta.* 996b 30); "the same attribute cannot at the same time belong and not belong to the same subject in the same respect. . ." (*Meta.* 1005b 19–20). Formulated in the logical order, it asserts that it is impossible to affirm and at the same time deny the same predicate of the same subject.

Validity of the Principle. The principle of contradiction derives immediately from the abstract, intuitive apprehension of BEING. Since being conceptually involves a positive JUDGMENT or affirmation, it necessarily excludes its own negation. The principle of contradiction is consequently a priori, in a qualified sense, since its apprehension is implicit in the apprehension of being. Its necessity is notional and relational, expressing a basic incompatibility between the positive and the negative, between being and NONBEING. But being, as a transcendental value, extends to every aspect of reality, and intuition of it is implicit in every cognitive act involving thought. Therefore, the principle of contradiction, even though it be regarded as a formal law, has at the same time a concrete universal reference. It is valid for every order of being as well as of knowledge; for every process in the realm of the concrete, the particular, and the practical; in the metaphysical, physical, and moral spheres; in the fields of mathematics, science, and history. Its universal, formal validity is confirmed by concrete experimental evidence, such as that showing the mutual exclusiveness of sweet and sour, healthy and unhealthy, democracy and dictatorship.

The principle of contradiction displays its rigor and its richness above all in METAPHYSICS. This principle alone can initiate the analytic-synthetic process involved in elaborating the concept of being. Under its influence being is grasped in its intrinsic intelligibility, in its absolute condition, and in its possibilities for extension and participation; in the profound interior connection of its constituent principles, essence and existence; in the relationships that are established between being as a substance and its qualitative and operative determinations, whether these be necessary or contingent; and, finally, in its ultimate explanation and absolute foundation—the unparticipated, absolute Being.

Primacy of the Principle. Because of its immediate derivation from the concept of being and its great importance in metaphysics, EPISTEMOLOGY, and LOGIC, St. THOMAS AQUINAS gives the principle of contradiction priority over all other axioms and principles: "For that which first falls under apprehension is being, the understanding of which is included in all things whatsoever a man apprehends. Therefore, the first undemonstrable principle is that the same thing cannot be affirmed and denied at the same time, which is based on the notions of being and not-being; and on this principle all others depend" (*Summa Theologiae* 1a2ae, 94.2; cf. Aristotle, *Meta.* 1005b 32–34). It is the norm and basis of every affirmation, truth, and certainty. It cannot be demonstrated because it is based on a primary concept, i.e., one incapable of logical derivation. It cannot even be denied, because whoever tries to deny it assumes that to affirm is not the same as to deny, and thus implicitly presupposes the principle. Consequently, it is possible to clarify its character only as absolutely intrinsic to understanding itself, and to give an indirect defense of the principle by demonstrating its inevitable acknowledgment by one who attempts to refute it. If the principle of contradiction is rejected, nothing can be affirmed or denied; no expression will any longer have a determined meaning. And, to quote Aristotle, "If words have no meaning our reasoning with one another, and indeed with ourselves, has been annihilated; for it is impossible to think of anything if we do not think of one thing" (*Meta.* 1006b 8–10). The rejection of this principle thus involves the negation of being in the metaphysical order and the denial of thought content in the logical order.

The principle of contradiction is commonly assumed to have priority and precedence over the principle of IDENTITY. From a logical point of view the principle of identity, even when expressed in a nontautological formula such as "being is determined in itself," is dialectically inert. It is not even psychologically first, for in the order of knowledge the original concept of being is followed immediately by the concept of its negation or opposition; hence the principle of contradiction is first known, and this is a relational synthesis of the positive with the negative.

The principle of contradiction comes first as a universal rule of thought, as well as of the dialectical process with which thought penetrates being and conforms itself to it (*see* DIALECTICS). This primacy is not to be confused with that of the first ontological principle, the ABSOLUTE, which is the all-comprehensive principle of truth; nor does it imply a rigorous and strictly psychological INNA-

TISM. The principle of contradiction, in itself, is not the positive source of advances in theoretical knowledge, nor is it productive of thought content or of solutions to particular problems. Instead, it is the condition of the existence and intelligibility of all knowledge, truth, doubt, or certitude in the human intellect. Again, the principle is not something concrete in reality; it exists rather in the logical-objective order and in intellectual CONSCIOUSNESS of the nature of being.

Erroneous Interpretations. The limitations found in the principle of contradiction by some thinkers seem traceable either to inexact expressions of the principle or to exclusively metaphysical interpretations of it. In the philosophy of Aristotle and in traditional, substantialistic, and pluralistic philosophies, the principle of contradiction does receive a plainly ontological interpretation. Thus it is sometimes formulated as the "principle of the determination of substance," according to which every being is definitely constituted in itself as an ontological-operative principle, specifically and numerically distinct from every other being. For this reason Aristotle remarks that those who deny the principle of contradiction "do away with substance and essence" (*Meta.* 1007a 20–21). Yet monistic conceptions of reality, like that of SPINOZA, while not rejecting this principle, necessarily give it a different value and interpretation. In PANTHEISM and IDEALISM as well, it retains its validity relative to the phenomenal manifestations of being; but when nature and the foundation of reality are concerned, diversities and contradictions become dissolved in an original and absolute unity. Accordingly, the meaning of the principle of contradiction changes in the Hegelian dialectical interpretation of reality. For HEGEL, a concrete being is the moment of unity that being and nothingness assume in becoming. In its concrete becoming, reality is a necessary and perpetual synthesis of opposites and contradictories. Hegel thus introduces contradiction into the intimate structure of the real as its most profound and essential determination. Opposites are present not in an objective identity, but rather as overcome in the evolving and creative unity of being. What is real neither is, nor subsists, in contradiction, but necessarily passes through it.

The basic meaning of the principle of contradiction, as already explained, is not refuted by any philosophical system. It is not inconsistent with Hegelianism, nor with LOGICAL POSITIVISM, which holds that laws and metaphysical statements express only verbal relations and not the structure of the real. Hegel's critique, however, betrays at least the possibility of an incorrect interpretation of the principle of contradiction. This must not be understood as a principle of the unchangeability and stability of being, or as a negation of the process of BECOMING. Motion and multiplicity, diversity and composition, are essential to FINITE BEING and are quite evident in the universe. Hence, in the ontological unity of every finite being, a coexistence and succession in time of indefinite, qualitative determinations, both operative and relational, are possible and real, though sometimes in themselves opposed. It is in this sense that even man is called "a living contradiction." One must keep sight of the reality of cosmic and human experience to understand the real meaning of contradiction in being, whether spiritual or material. Such experience does not question, and consequently does not weaken, the universal validity of the principle of contradiction.

See Also: FIRST PRINCIPLES.

Bibliography: U. VIGLINO, *Enciclopedia filosofica,* 4 v. (Venice-Rome 1957) 1:1223–26. J. LAMINNE, "Le Principe de contradiction et le principe de causalité," *Revue Néo-scolastique de philosophie* 19 (1912) 435–88. L. FUETSCHER, "Die ersten Seinsund Denkprinzipien," *Philosophie und Grenzwissenschaft* 3 (1930) 93–376. J. MARÉCHAL, *Le Thomisme devant la philosophie critique* (2d ed.) 491–504, 561–68, v.5 of *Le Point de départ de la métaphysique,* 5 v. (3d ed. Paris 1944–49). M. VERSFELD, *The Mirror of Philosophers* (New York 1960). F. H. BRADLEY, *The Principles of Logic,* 2 v. (2d ed. London 1922).

[U. VIGLINO]

CONTRITION

Contrition (etymologically, rubbing together, grinding so as to pulverize) is the technical term in theology for repentance of sin. In its generic sense, it is "an interior sorrow and detestation of sin with the resolve not to sin any more" [H. Denzinger *Enchiridion symbolorum,* ed. A. Schönmetzer, Freiburg 1963) 1676]. In its specific sense, as distinct from attrition, it is the repentance perfected by charity or love of God, while attrition is imperfect repentance not so perfected by charity (*ibid.*). The present article briefly recalls the meaning of repentance in general—its place in the Scriptures and the Fathers, and its necessary role in every forgiveness of personal sin. It then surveys the history and the theology of the distinction between contrition and attrition. The historical part presents: (1) the origin of the distinction, and the rise of a twofold concept, of contrition-attrition; (2) the position of the Council of Trent; and (3) the controversy of attritionism and contritionism after Trent. The theological part: (1) expounds the two theologies of attrition-contrition accepted today and examines their points of agreement and of difference; and (2) shows the connection of this twofold concept with a corresponding theology of charity, of justification, and of the Sacrament of Reconciliation. In conclusion, a word is said about the pastoral teaching of contrition-attrition.

Contrition in General. Repentance is psychologically complex. It involves two cognitional elements, remembrance of past sinful acts and awareness of the present state of sin; and two volitional elements, sorrow or grief at the presence of the evil of sin, and detestation of sin aiming at its removal now and for the future (purpose of amendment). These volitional elements may be either spontaneous or deliberate, or both. The nature and purpose of repentance, or its metaphysics, is to undo the evil of sin—not to suppress past acts, since this is impossible, but to remove the state of sin. It presupposes the sense of sin, which is different from the sense of guilt.

Repentance, just as sin itself, holds a central place in the scriptural narration of the history of our salvation. Redemption from sin is presented in both the Old and the New Testament as requiring from sinners penance and repentance. In the Old Testament, the Hebrew root *šûb* expresses repentant return to God, as in the collective repentance of Israel returning to Yahweh after repeated infidelities (e.g., 1 Kgs 12.10; 2 Par 15.2–4, 30.9). The example of David (2 Kgs 12) is typical of repentance. So also are the prayers of repentance in the Psalms, e.g., in the seven Psalms known as "penitential" (6, 31, 37, 50, 101, 129, and 142), and the exhortations and objurgations of the Prophets calling for penance (e.g., Ez 18.31; Jer 3.14, 4.1–2, 15.19). In the Gospels, the message of the kingdom of God is in the first place a call to repentance, *metanoia:* (Mt 3.8, 11.20–24; Mk 1.4). The parables of the Prodigal Son (Lk 15.11–32) and of the Pharisee and the Publican (Lk 18.10–14) illustrate its nature and effects. The same call to penance appears in the preaching of the Apostles (e.g., Acts 2.38, 3.19). St. Paul's message is one of mercy and repentance (cf. Rom 2.4, 3.21–26; 2 Cor 7.9–11; 2 Tm 2.25).

No less explicit is the teaching of the Fathers on penance. It suffices to recall the treatises of Tertullian (*De paenitentia*), Cyprian (*De lapsis*), Ambrose, and Chrysostom. Although the term "contrition" occurs rarely in early Christian literature, equivalent terms, such as conversion or compunction, convey the same idea.

The reason repentance is necessary for every forgiveness of personal sin throws some light on its nature. Because sin is a willful turning away from God, through love of self or of some creaturely good, its forgiveness necessarily entails not only God's merciful initiative in remitting sin but also the sinner's voluntary giving up of the disorderly love that severed his union with God. God does not, and in a way cannot, forgive sin for those who do not want to be forgiven; i.e., He cannot reunite to Himself in love those who refuse to be so reunited. The sinner's wish to be forgiven is shown precisely in the voluntary reversal of the disorderly love, a renouncement that includes sorrow and effective detestation. Thus, forgiveness of sin, taking effect in the sinner's reconciliation

with God by the reinfusion of grace, necessarily presupposes the forsaking of sin, that is, repentance.

Contrition and Attrition: History of the Distinction. There is a natural and obvious distinction between a repentance that is so perfect as to achieve its purpose of undoing the state of sin and an imperfect repentance constituting only a step toward the same undoing. Repentance, like any other human endeavor, proceeds to its perfection step by step. As a matter of historical fact, however, the explicit distinction, or at any rate its formulation in the technical terms of contrition and attrition, is not found in theology until well into the 12th century. Yet the distinction was not without antecedents in Scripture and in the Fathers. Scripture knows of an imperfect and insufficient repentance, such as a half-hearted return to God in Hos 6.1–4. In the New Testament, the preaching of St. John the Baptist leads from fear to true repentance (Mt 3.7–12) and the prodigal son rises from self-pity to effective repentance (Lk 15.17–19). Among the Fathers, St. Augustine has immortalized in his *Confessions* the division of the will so characteristic of imperfect repentance and that only grace and love of God can finally heal. In a masterly analysis, he describes the two wills, the old and the new, the carnal and the spiritual; while the spiritual will pleased and overcame his mind (*placebat et vincebat*), the carnal will still attracted and held the spirit bound (*libebat et vinciebat, Confessions* 8), until he could rejoice in gratitude to God for the victory of divine love (*Confessions* 9.1). St. Gregory the Great speaks of two kinds of compunction—one inspired by fear, another inspired by love [*In Ezech. hom.* 2.10.30f; *Patrologia Latina,* ed. J. P. Migne, 271 v., indexes 4 v. (Paris 1878–90) 76:1070).

Origin of the Distinction. Pre-Scholastic and early Scholastic authors, from the 8th to the early 12th century, spoke of one kind of sorrow for sin called contrition (*contritio cordis*) in connection with sacramental or ecclesiastical Penance. They considered this contrition as apt to wipe out sin even before confession and absolution. The preparatory stages leading to such a sorrow were not considered. These preparatory stages received explicit consideration toward the close of the 11th century, however, when, under the influence of Peter Abelard and Peter Lombard, there was a reaction against the view that confession and absolution were more important than contrition. Contrition was then held to be the properly forgiving act, normally preceding absolution. Generally, it was thought that a gradual preparation leads to such a contrition. Fear, for example, may start a penitent on the road to repentance (Anselm, Bernard of Clairvaux, Hugh of St. Victor, Peter Lombard). Alan of Lille (d. 1202) made the first explicit mention of attrition and of its contrast with contrition. He said that sin is either diminished (*remitti-*

tur) by attrition when a sinner is not perfectly repentant, or forgiven (*dimittitur*) by contrition when he is completely converted from sin. The reasons repentance or the break with sin might be incomplete may be various: lack of resolve to confess or do penance, lack of universality of the sorrow, self-centeredness of the sorrow instead of God-centeredness. By the middle of the 13th century, the distinction had become common teaching. William of Auvergne (d. 1248), for example, accepted and explained the difference between the two by the "formation" or "nonformation" by charity. This implies that there is no forgiveness of sin unless a sinner, from being attrite, becomes contrite (*ex attrito fit contritus*). Such was also the position of St. Thomas Aquinas and of the Thomistic school in general: attrition is imperfect sorrow, unformed by charity, for sin; contrition is perfect sorrow formed by charity. If it happens, St. Thomas explained, that a penitent comes to confession attrite only, as is sometimes the case, then the Sacrament itself will bring about the change from attrition to contrition.

Thus, the common teaching in the 13th century distinguished contrition from attrition, not by the motives of fear and love (it considered these also, but rather as principles than as motives of repentance), but by the completeness or incompleteness of the break with sin, and by its formation or nonformation by charity. It considered contrition as the only proper disposition for justification, whether in or outside the Sacrament of Reconciliation. When this disposition is absent from a penitent, as it may be in more or less exceptional cases, then the Sacrament will bring it about before giving grace. This is the medieval "contritionism."

From this common teaching two successive deviations led to another concept and theology of contrition-attrition. Duns Scotus (d. 1308) first put forward the idea that attrition is a sufficient disposition for justification in the Sacrament. Though he still said that an attrite penitent becomes contrite in the Sacrament, he understood this not in the sense that imperfect sorrow makes room for an act of perfect sorrow, but that the same act remaining, the penitent may be called contrite because of the infusion of grace. Another more decisive step lies in the nominalist idea of motive as the distinguishing factor between contrition and attrition (Durandus of Saint-Pourçain, Ockham, Gabriel Biel): contrition is motivated by love of God, attrition by fear of punishment. According to this radically new conception, contrition and attrition were no longer distinguished by the complete or incomplete renouncing of sin, marked by the objective formation or nonformation by charity, but by the psychological motives of love or fear. Nor was attrition essentially a step toward contrition, since the varying motives of the two types of sorrow are not in organic continuity to each

other. Even after justification, attrition retains its proper identity. This new theology, the "attritionism" of the Middle Ages, met with increasing success in the centuries of decadent Scholasticism before the Council of Trent without, however, replacing the ancient common teaching altogether.

Position of the Council of Trent. It is in this setting of two theologies of contrition and attrition that the Council of Trent formulated its teaching. The council deliberately avoided taking sides in any questions disputed among Catholics and aimed only at countering the Protestant views. In this particular case, it meant to rehabilitate the Catholic doctrine on imperfect contrition, or attrition, which the Reformers impugned. Attrition, according to the Protestant opinion, made a man a hypocrite and was only, in Luther's words, a "gallows-repentance." Two main points must be noted in the Tridentine doctrine. First, the council officially sanctioned the distinction between contrition and attrition as part of the Catholic doctrine. Second, in describing either of them, it so formulated its teaching as to make it acceptable to Catholics of both schools [H. Denzinger, *Enchiridion symbolorum,* ed. A. Schönmetzer (Freiburg 1963) 1677].

Accordingly, while Trent teaches that attrition, including the will not to sin, is good because it is an effect of grace and a help toward justification, the council leaves undecided whether it is a proximate or only a remote disposition for the infusion of grace. The description of attrition as coming from "the consideration of the ugliness of sin or from the fear of hell and of punishment" can designate these either as "principles" or as "motives" of repentance. Of contrition, the council said that it is perfected by charity, as both Catholic schools hold, and that it justifies but not without including the desire of the Sacrament. The whole of this teaching is accepted by both schools, but each of them will conceive it in its own way. Concerning the frequency of perfect contrition, the council said that "contrition sometimes happens to be perfected by charity" before the reception of the Sacrament; i.e., occasionally, not regularly, do penitents come to the Sacrament with contrition, which is the exact reverse of what St. Thomas and his contemporaries held. Furthermore, the conciliar text purposely neither affirms nor excludes the change from attrite to contrite at the advent of sanctifying grace, since there was no need to decide the point in order to answer the Protestant views. The council, however, qualified the attrition that disposes for justification. Attrition must exclude the will to sin and include the hope of pardon or else it would not be "sufficient attrition," even in the Sacrament. Since Trent left open many questions concerning contrition, it is small wonder that the doctrine was subjected to further theological reflection. There followed a restatement in novel form of the ancient contritionist-attritionist controversy.

Contritionism and Attritionism after Trent. In the 17th-century controversy known as "attritionists vs. contritionists," the positions were no longer those held before Trent. Partly because of the widespread influence of the Scotist-Suarezian teaching, both the attritionist and contritionist schools followed the psychological motivation approach. Both schools understood the teaching of Trent to mean that attrition is sufficient for justification in the Sacrament. The difference lies in the quality they demand for sufficient attrition. As indicated in the decree of the Holy Office of May 5, 1667 (*ibid.*), which put an end to the heat of the controversy, contritionists are those who require a motive of love, besides the motive of fear, for sufficient attrition. Attritionists are those who do not require this motive of love. Both schools, however, consider attrition as repentance sufficient for justification in the Sacrament. Neither of the two are contritionists in the sense of the medieval Scholastics. The ancient adage about the change from attrite to contrite is bypassed even in so-called Thomistic schools. Since the time of the decree of the Holy Office (1667), both systems have lived in peaceful coexistence, awaiting a further decision of Rome, which has never come.

There have been attempts at reconciling the contritionist position since 1667 with the teaching of St. Thomas. Billuart (d. 1757), and more recently Périnelle, interpreted the motive of love required for sufficient attrition in the Sacrament as being love of benevolence that is not yet charity because it is not reciprocated on the part of God. Reciprocation is brought about by absolution. Contemporary studies (P. de Vooght, H. Dondaine) have shown, however, that this midway position is not faithful to the theology of St. Thomas. The outcome of these more objective and less apologetic studies is the practical relegation of the contritionist-attritionist controversy of the 17th century to the past. Today two theories hold the field: the ancient Thomistic theology of contrition-attrition, and the more common modern theology of the psychological motivation of repentance. This is the revival of the two schools of pre-Tridentine thought.

Contrition and Attrition: Theology of the Distinction. Thomistic theology of repentance considers attrition as a sorrow for sin in its imperfect stage, gradually leading up to contrition in which the break with sin is complete through its formation by charity. The element distinguishing contrition from attrition is the completeness or incompleteness of the break with sin and the formation or the nonformation of the repentance by charity. The distinction does not consist in the psychological mo-

tives of fear and love, which of themselves may be the expression of either attrition or contrition. For every justification, whether sacramental or extrasacramental, the necessary last disposition for grace is contrition. Eventually, absolution and grace make an attrite penitent contrite in the very reception of the Sacrament. In the state of grace, all supernatural repentance for sin is contrition because it is formed by charity. There is no attrition in one in the state of grace.

The other school considers attrition and contrition as two kinds of repentance, the one not related to the other as an imperfect stage leading to the perfect one. They are distinguished, rather, by their motives: fear or self-love in the case of attrition, and love of God in the case of contrition. Attrition is a sufficient disposition for justification in the Sacrament of Reconciliation if, as Trent requires, it excludes the will to sin and includes hope of pardon. Contrition is the disposition required for extrasacramental justification. The Sacrament does not make an attrite penitent contrite; absolution and justification do not change the motives of his repentance. A justified penitent can have attrition when he is sorry for his sins out of interested or self-centered motives.

The two theologies differ first in the very ideas of attrition and contrition. The ancient idea of attrition as sorrow for sin not formed by charity is both narrower and wider than the modern idea of sorrow motivated by fear or other self-regarding motives. It may happen that a sorrow motivated also by fear, but a fear that is not altogether servile, is in fact formed by charity and so is contrition in the Thomistic sense. It may also happen that a sorrow motivated by love of God is not in fact formed by charity. Psychological motive and objective reality do not necessarily coincide. Similarly, the ancient concept of contrition as repentance formed by charity is both wider and narrower than the modern idea of contrition as sorrow motivated by the disinterested love of God. This motive may well be absent psychologically from a repentance objectively formed by charity, and it may be present in a repentance that is not so formed. As a consequence, the contrition that the ancient theology requires as the indispensable last disposition for justification may in fact be the same repentance that the modern theology calls sufficient attrition. When this sufficient attrition is described, for example by Galtier, as demanding "faith, hope, love of desire for God, love of justice, and even the desire of charity," then it will more often than not be contrition in the Thomistic sense [P. Galtier, *De Poenitentia* (Paris 1924)]. If, in some cases, the modern conception of sufficient attrition were not the same as contrition, then it would at least be equivalent to what St. Thomas required for the fruitful reception of the Sacrament, namely, attrition with the signs of contrition. This, he holds, allows the change from attrition to contrition by the Sacrament. It seems that there is only a verbal difference between this modern understanding of sufficient attrition, and the Thomistic doctrine of contrition. Furthermore, when the ancient theology affirms, and the modern theology denies, that by virtue of the power of the keys, operative in the absolution, an attrite penitent becomes contrite, they do not contradict each other in fact but only in words. The change from nonformation to formation by charity required by the Thomistic doctrine does not require the change in the motivation of the repentance.

There is a real difference, however, in the perfection necessary for justifying contrition, and in its frequency, and in the manner of conceiving the efficacy of that contrition. Contrition in the ancient theology is less difficult and more frequent than contrition in the modern sense, because its specific perfection, namely, complete break with sin and formation by charity, does not demand an explicit act of disinterested love of God. Love of God above all things as our Last End suffices. This difference is commanded by a difference in the very concept of charity (see below). The extrasacramental justification by contrition, which the ancient theology conceived as frequent and even as the usual disposition in a penitent, is not in that view purely nonsacramental, as it is for modern theology. Contrition produces its effect by virtue of the power of the keys active in the desire of the Sacrament that it includes. Contrition is part of the Sacrament, and is so transcendentally related to the absolution that it does not detract from the power of the keys.

Two Concepts of Charity, Justification, and the Sacrament. The difference between opposing conceptions of contrition and attrition cannot be properly understood unless one bears in mind the different ways in which charity, justification, and the Sacrament of Reconciliation were conceived.

Charity. In early and medieval theology, the notion of charity inseparably included the disinterested love of benevolence for God, and the love that consists in friendly desire for union, which includes some self-interest. St. Thomas defends this position by showing that charity is the desire for God as our Last End, and that this involves both surrender and union. It is love of friendship that, for all its disinterestedness, seeks union. In this concept, no sooner is there a desire of union with God than the disinterested love of God is also implicitly present. Therefore, a repentance formed by a theologically interested love of God above all things is justifying contrition. Many modern theologians deny this view. Charity is conceived as solely love of benevolence or disinterested love of God, and the interested love of God or desire of union is said to belong to hope. Consequently, the two loves can exist

separately, since hope can exist without charity. A repentance motivated by love of desire for God, therefore, is not perfect or justifying contrition. Here lies the most serious and far-reaching difference between the two concepts of contrition. For modern theology, perfect or justifying contrition is more difficult than it is for ancient and present-day Thomistic theology.

Justification. The infusion of sanctifying grace into a sinner, according to the ancient theology, always supposes the same ultimate disposition for grace, namely, contrition. The difference between sacramental and extrasacramental justification does not lie in the disposition required for the infusion of grace, but in the manner in which this disposition comes about. Justification may be caused either by the actual reception of the absolution when a penitent approaches the Sacrament with attrition only, or by virtue of the desire of the absolution included in contrition elicited before the Sacrament is received. Attrition, however, cannot be the ultimate disposition for justification even in the Sacrament. It must eventually give way to contrition produced by the Sacrament.

According to the modern theology of justification, there are two different manners of justification characterized by different ultimate dispositions for grace: in the Sacrament, the disposition of attrition (with the necessary qualities); and, outside the Sacrament, perfect contrition. Less, therefore, is required of a penitent in the Sacrament than outside it. There is no need for a change from attrition to contrition in sacramental justification. The formal ideas of justification and of the ultimate disposition for it, whether in or outside the Sacrament, are quite different in the two theologies. It may well be, however, that the repentance they both require for sacramental justification is in fact the same, despite the difference in name and in the nature of justification. For extrasacramental justification, the two theologies require the same disposition, but they conceive the efficacy of contrition in a different manner (see below).

Sacrament. The concept of Sacrament in general (*see* SACRAMENTS, THEOLOGY OF) and of the Sacrament of Reconciliation in particular is also different according to these two systems of theology (*see* PENANCE, SACRAMENT OF). In the ancient theology, a Sacrament is conceived not as supplying for the dispositions of the person who receives it, but as an instrument for the infusion of grace to a person already disposed. The reason is that no form, such as grace, can be infused except in a subject properly disposed. The Sacrament may eventually help to produce the needed disposition, but it cannot give grace in the absence of that disposition. Not so for modern theology, which conceives the Sacrament as partly making up for the imperfect dispositions of the recipient, and therefore as making lesser demands for the infusion of grace than extrasacramental justification. The origin of the idea lies in a questionably founded opposition between the efficacy of the Sacrament (*opus operatum*) and the part of the recipient (*opus operantis*). If, for example, in Reconciliation, contrition is always required and justifies by itself, nothing is left for the Sacrament, and there can be no sacramental justification. The answer to this pseudo-difficulty lies in the proper concept of the Sacrament of Reconciliation.

The ancient theology conceives the Sacrament of Reconciliation (made up of the acts of the penitent as matter, and the absolution of the priest as form) by way of one unit, one practical sign of grace. The Sacrament gives grace as one instrumental cause, and its various parts have no separate causality of their own with regard to grace. Accordingly, when contrition justifies prior to the absolution, it does so by the power of the Sacrament. Absolution acts in anticipation through the desire implicit in contrition. This way of causality is possible because the Sacrament is only an instrumental cause of grace, and Christ as the chief Cause can give grace through an incomplete instrument no less than through a complete one. In modern theology this organic unity of the Sacrament is loosened. Justifying contrition remits sin not in virtue of the power of the keys but by itself, namely, by virtue of the love of charity that perfects it. The desire of the Sacrament (*votum sacramenti*) is required, but only as an extrinsic condition for perfect contrition [cf. P. Galtier, *De Poenitentia* (Paris 1924) 3:63).

The differences between the two theologies stem mainly from a difference in approach. The Thomistic approach is in the first place ontological, and secondarily psychological. The modern approach is primarily psychological and only secondarily, if at all, ontological. The difference of approach also affects the respective teachings concerning charity, justification, and Sacrament. But in spite of these differences and of different conceptual and verbal expression, the two teachings are to a large extent identical.

Pastoral Teaching on Contrition-Attrition. The two theologies agree, for all practical purposes, on the repentance required for the Sacrament of Reconciliation. Both say that not just any attrition, even supernatural, is sufficient: attrition must exclude the will to sin and include hope of pardon (Trent). Modern theology interprets this as including faith, hope, and love of desire of God, and calls it attrition. Thomistic theology says: whenever these elements are present, there is contrition or at any rate there are the signs of contrition required and sufficient for the fruitful reception of the Sacrament. In practice, this means that the penitent should not deliberately exclude from his repentance any perfection that with the help of grace he is able to have. He must do what he can. That is exactly what our "acts of contrition" try to express by including motives of repentance both lower and higher. More important than the motives is the sincerity and resoluteness in the break with sin, and this appears more in the purpose of amendment than in the sorrow for the past. Hence the importance of insisting on the resolve not to sin again. Both theologies, therefore, each in its own way, justify an identical pastoral practice with regard to repentance required for the Sacrament.

As regards contrition justifying outside the Sacrament, a difference remains. Here the modern theology of perfect contrition is compelled to make higher demands and insist on the motive of disinterested love of God. Catechetical and moral manuals, written in its spirit, actually do so. Yet such a contrition is presented as not too difficult to achieve: gratitude and similar self-regarding motives may spontaneously lead to disinterested love. Not all theologians will share this optimistic view of an easy transition from imperfect to perfect contrition, unless the traditional Thomistic theology of contrition is silently endorsed. The latter holds that repentance is perfect and justifying contrition when formed by charity, and it is so when it is inspired by the desire of union with God. Such a perfect contrition seems to be more accessible to man. Perhaps even here the two theologies teach the same doctrine in different phraseologies. Perfect contrition, motivated by the pure love of God and yet, allegedly, not difficult to elicit, is perhaps not different from repentance perfected by love of God above all things as our Last End.

Bibliography: P. DELETTER, "Two Concepts of Attrition and Contrition," *Theological Studies* 11 (1950) 3–33. C. R. MEYER, *The Thomistic Concept of Justifying Contrition* (Mundelein, Ill. 1950). C. O'BRIEN, *Perfect Contrition in Theory and Practice* (Dublin 1952). P. F. PALMER, *Sacraments and Forgiveness* in *Sources of Christian Theology* 2 (Westminster, Md. 1960). G. K. SPYKMAN, *Attrition and Contrition at the Council of Trent* (Kampen 1955). P. ANCIAUX, *Le Sacrement de la pénitence* in *Études de théologie sacramentaire* 3 (Louvain 1963). M. TREMEAU, "Attrition et contrition selon saint Thomas," *Ami du clergé* 70.19 (May 1960) 289–294.

[P. DE LETTER]

CONTRITIONISM

Contritionism is a theological doctrine demanding more than attrition as a last disposition to receive fruitfully the Sacrament of PENANCE. Historically, it has had two different meanings.

In high scholasticism: St. Thomas Aquinas (contritionist) wants the penitent to be either contrite or to believe in good faith that he is contrite. CONTRITION, either existing before or brought about by the sacramental AB-SOLUTION (which then "makes the attrite penitent contrite"), is the one disposition for JUSTIFICATION. For Duns Scotus (attritionist), attrition suffices as last disposition for the forgiveness of sin through absolution.

After Trent (17th and 18th centuries): the problem is whether sufficient attrition should or should not contain some love of God (cf. Trent's "they begin to love God"—H. Denzinger, *Enchiridion symbolorum*, ed. A. Schönmetzer [32d ed. Freiburg 1963] 1526). For the contritionists, either incipient CHARITY or love of benevolence is needed; for the attritionists, no act of love or at most love of desire (explicit or implicit). Neither position deserves theological censure (Denzinger 2070).

In practice, penitents should endeavor to have contrition and not rest content with the minimum.

See Also: ATTRITION AND ATTRITIONISM.

Bibliography: V. HEYNCK, *Lexikon für Theologie und Kirche,* ed. J. HOFER and K. RAHNER, 10 v. (2d, new ed. Freiburg 1957–65) 1:1019–21; *ibid.* 6:510–511. B. POSCHMANN, *Penance and the Anointing of the Sick,* tr. and rev. F. COURTNEY (New York 1964). P. F. PALMER, ed., *Sacraments and Forgiveness,* v.2 of *Sources of Christian Theology* (Westminster, Md. 1959).

[G. A. GILLEMAN]

CONTUMELY

Contumely, or reviling, is an offense against the honor or dignity of another by allegation of moral defect, primarily by speech uttered in his presence but also by writings, gestures, or other acts. In certain circumstances even the omission of an act can involve contumely, as when someone speaks to all but one in a group and the circumstances are such that this omission detracts from that person's honor or dignity. Contumely, as opposed to the honor of another, should be distinguished from DETRACTION or backbiting, which is against another's good name or reputation, and from talebearing (*susurratio*), which aims at the destruction of a friendship. These sins consist in speech to someone other than the one offended; but one can be guilty of contumely when speaking only to the one being dishonored, although it is more serious if done in the presence of others.

Contumely is opposed to commutative justice and charity and of its nature is gravely sinful. If only some slight dishonor is intended, the act is venially sinful. In certain circumstances insulting words may be used without intention of dishonoring another. For example, one may use this language in correction, as punishment, or in joking; but due caution must be observed. The intention of dishonoring need not be explicit for a sin of contume-

ly. It suffices that one recognizes that the words or gestures have this effect, even though they may flow from hatred, anger, or envy.

See Also: INSULT.

Bibliography: THOMAS AQUINAS, *Summa Theologiae,* 2a2ae, 72. L. BENDER, in F. ROBERTI et al., *Dictionary of Moral Theology,* ed. P. PALAZZINI et al., tr. H. J. YANNONE et al. from 2d Ital. ed. (Westminster, Md. 1962) 324–325. P. PALAZZINI, ed., *Dictionarium morale et canonicum,* v.1 (Vatican City 1962) 956–961.

[J. HENNESSEY]

CONVENIENTIA, ARGUMENTUM EX

Generally defined as an argument intended to confirm an already established principle or fact by showing the congruity of its results (cf. *Summa theologiae* 1a, 32.1 ad 2). The argument *ex convenientia* is an important and necessary theological tool in two cases: (1) in the case of acts of God that are seemingly gratuitous and might have been different or left undone with the same result, and (2) in the case of mysterious aspects of God's nature that reason cannot understand. Excellent illustrations of the argument *ex convenientia* are, for the first case, St. Anselm's arguments about the Incarnation, and for the second case, St. Augustine's arguments about the Trinity.

The main problem with arguments *ex convenientia* is the difficulty of distinguishing them from similes, analogies, and metaphors. The basis of this difficulty is that arguments *ex convenientia* can often be turned into analogies, and analogies likewise can be turned into arguments *ex convenientia.* Notwithstanding such an interchangeability, there is an essential distinction between analogies and arguments *ex convenientia:* the former pertain to the first operation of the mind, i.e., apprehension; the latter pertain to the third operation of the mind, i.e., reasoning. Analogies (similes and metaphors) are not intended to argue or prove something, but to clarify it; whereas arguments *ex convenientia* are intended to prove something by deducing it from something else, and their inability to show categorical proof does not prevent them from being real proof. Analogies take a fact for granted and try to clarify it; arguments from convenience try to establish the fact itself.

An example that clarifies this difference is that of the mystery of the Holy Trinity and the trinitarian structure of the mind. The argument from convenience tries to understand *why* God is a triune being and finds it reasonable, *since* even the human mind has a triune structure. On the other hand, the analogy accepts the fact that God is a triune being, but tries to understand what that means by *comparing* that triune being to the trinitarian structure of the mind.

The main danger in the use of arguments *ex convenientia* is that one may mistake them for arguments from necessity. When this does happen, reason, instead of the search to understand faith, turns the argument into theological rationalism. However, the fact that many Fathers and scholastics make use in their arguments *ex convenientia* of terms such as *necessarium, necesse est,* and *patet* should not give the impression that they necessarily are guilty of theological rationalism. They may use these terms only to bring out the convenience more forcefully.

The value of arguments *ex convenientia* is different from case to case. There are cases in which their value is very weak, because their congruity may be considered from different standpoints. For instance, the question of the natural perfection of Adam cannot be appreciated in the same way, on the basis of congruity, by one who holds that "the works of God are perfect from the beginning" against another who holds the contrary theory of evolution. In other cases, however, the arguments *ex convenientia* are almost self-explanatory, one example being Aquinas' argument proving the fitness of the Incarnation (*Summa theologiae* 3a, 1). In general, however, if arguments *ex convenientia* are not revealed, they are only probable and of limited force.

See Also: ARGUMENTATION; METHODOLOGY (THEOLOGY); REASONING, THEOLOGICAL; THEOLOGY.

Bibliography: A. CHOLLET, *Dictionnaire de théologie catholique*, ed. A. VACANT et al., (Paris 1903–50) 1.1:1149–54. Y. M. J. CONGAR, *ibid.* 15.1:382–385, 452–456; *La Foi et la théologie* (Tournai 1962). A. GARDEIL, *Le Donné révélé et la théologie* (Paris 1910). M. T. L. PENIDO, *Le Rôle de l'analogie en théologie dogmatique* (*Bibliothèque Thomiste* 15; Paris 1931).

[B. MONDIN]

CONVENT

From the Latin, *conventus,* an assembly or meeting, in current popular usage, designates a residence of religious women. Originally it signified any religious house with members sufficient to maintain monastic observance, and was used principally by the Mendicant Friars in place of the term "abbey" or "monastery," used in the older, monastic orders. Gradually, it was incorporated into the legal vocabulary of the Church and from the 14th century the presence of at least 12 professed religious was required before a house could be designated a *conventus.* Following the Council of Trent and arising from the practice of the Roman CURIA, a distinction was made between a major convent, one having 12 or more religious; and a minor one that lacked this number. This status determined the relation of subjection to the visitation, correc-

tion, and jurisdiction of the local ordinary. The term "convent" does not appear in either the 1917 or the 1983 *Code of Canon Law;* nor does there seem to be an equivalent word in the *Code of the Canons of the Eastern Churches.* Both Latin codes have prescriptions reflecting current usage. In the earlier code a territorial focus gave rise to a distinction among canonical established houses based upon the number and quality of personnel living in that location. A formal house, for example, required at least six professed religious, four of whom had to be priests in a clerical institute; while a nonformal house lacked these qualities (1917 *Codex iuris canonici* [Rome 1918; repr. Graz 1955] c. 488, §5). The 1983 *Codex iuris canonici* approaches the issue more generically by focusing on the life of its members according to particular law of an institute. A religious community must live in a lawfully established house under the authority of a superior designated according to the norm of law, that is, established according to the institute's constitutions and with the written consent of the diocesan bishop (1983 *Codex iuris canonici* cc. 608–609). Two points seem unique in the revised law. The newer legislation permits a flexibility to cover living situations previously described as formal and informal. Pope Paul VI in *Evangelica testificatio* (June 29, 1971), nn. 40–41 permitted two or three religious to live in common and serve in one or more apostolates. Second, an established house of an institute erected by competent authority according to the constitutions of an institute should have greater stability than a residence or faculty house constituted for an apostolic need.

See Also: MONASTERY.

Bibliography: L. SIMEONE, *De condicione iuridica parvarum domorum religiosorum* (Padua 1942). S. HOLLAND, "'Religious' House According to Canon 608," *Jurist* 50 (1990) 524–552. R. M. MCDERMOTT, S.S.J. "Religious Houses and Their Erection and Suppression," *New Commentary on the Code of Canon Law,* ed. J. P. BEAL et al. (New York/Mahwah 2000) 772–779.

[W. B. RYAN/A. ESPELAGE]

CONVERSION, I (IN THE BIBLE)

In the OT and the NT God calls human beings into relationship among themselves and with God. Both testaments show an awareness of the sinful condition of humanity, so much in contrast to the holiness of the God of Israel. The result of a sinful rejection of God's design from the beginning of history (Gn 2:4b–3:24), human beings are born sinners (Ps 51:7). Sin has entered and dominated men and women (Rom 5:12). From that time on, sin has dwelt within the intimate recesses of all human beings (Rom 7:20). Thus, the response to the divine call to enter into communion among themselves and with God demands a "turning away," or a "turning back" from the situation of sin.

Interior view of vaulted scriptorium of the Franciscan convent of Cordeliers, Forcalquier, France. (©Gail Mooney/CORBIS)

The Hebrew verb *sûb* with its noun *tešûbâ,* the Greek verbs στρέφω and ἐπιστρέφω with their associated noun ἐπιστροφή, have an original sense of a physical turning back, or returning. They are found across both the OT and the NT. A similar, but more internal, idea is found in the verb μετανοέω and the noun μετάνοια. These expressions contain the notion of a transformation of the inner self. The verbs and nouns contain a recognition that one is following the wrong path, and is called to turn back, or turn away from that path, in order to return to the original divine plan for communion between human beings (Gn 1:1–2:4a; 2:4b–25) and with God (Gn 1:26–31).

In the Old Testament. Across the development of the OT traditions there is a growth and a deepening of the recognition of sinfulness and the need to turn toward God. Even in ancient times, once there was a sense of a nation in a covenantal relationship with God, individual and collective sinfulness is seen as demanding a recognition of a breakdown in the relationship with God (Jos 7; 1 Sm 5–6). The community establishes punishments for those who offend, including the penalty of death (Ex 32:25–28; Nm 25:7–15; Jos 7:24–26). Divine pardon was also sought by less dramatic signs of conversion: fasting (Jgs 20:26; 1 Kgs 21:8–9), tearing of one's robes and

dressing in sackcloth (1 Kgs 20:31–34; 2 Kgs 6:30; 19:1–7; Is 22:12). There is evidence in the Psalter of crying out formulas of lamentation over collective or personal guilt (Ps 60; 74; 79; 83; Lam 5). There are also collective confessions of guilt (Jgs 10:10; 1 Sm 7:6), and recourse to the intercession of a prophet (Ex 32:30–34). Such practices, which had their beginnings in the earlier epoch of Israelite history, are found throughout the OT (see, for example, Jer 14:1–15:4).

The dramatic experience of the exile, read as punishment for sin, is a turning point in Israel's recognition of the need to "turn back" to God's design. But it had its precedents in the period of David, where prophetic elements in the nation called the sinful king back to the Lord (2 Sm 12:13–23). This is not reserved only to David, as other kings are called to a similar process of conversion (e.g., Is 7:1–25). The pre-Exilic prophets berate Israel's sinfulness: "Ah, sinful nation, a people laden with iniquity, offspring of evildoers, sons who deal corruptly! They have forsaken the Lord, they have despised the Holy One of Israel, they are utterly estranged" (Is 1:4). The preaching of Amos (Amos 5:4, 6, 14, 15), Hosea (Hos 14:2–9), and 1 Isaiah (Is 1:11–15, 16–18; 6:10; 30:15) call for a recognition of sin and a return to the original covenant with God. Isaiah looks forward to the day when a remnant will return to the mighty God (Is 10:21).

Within the context of the final destruction of Judah and Jerusalem, and the subsequent exile, Jeremiah develops more fully the concept of conversion. His unflinching criticism of the sinfulness of the nation and its leaders is that: "It may be that the house of Judah will hear all the evil which I intend to do to them, so that everyone may turn from his evil way, and that I may forgive their iniquity and their sin" (Jer 36:3). It can be claimed that the theme of "turning back" is the leitmotiv of the book of Jeremiah. Rebellious Israel must recognize its sin if it wishes to avert God's anger and punishment (2:23; 3:11–12), but it is not enough for the people and its leaders to shed tears or parade their sins in false penitence and external rituals (3:21–25). They are to reverse every aspect of their behavior, they are to circumcise their hearts (4:1–4). Jeremiah is pessimistic about the possibility of such conversion. Israel prefers to follow the direction of its wicked heart (2:23–25; 18:11–12) as it sinks deeper into wickedness (8:4–7). The call to conversion, however, must be preached (Jer 20:7–10), and the prophet dreams of the day when a vanquished people will pray for its conversion: "You have chastened me, and I was chastened, like an untrained calf; bring me back that I may be restored, for you are the Lord my God" (31:18. See v. 19). The Lord will not be deaf to this prayer. Israel's "turning back" will lead to the establishment of a new covenant, the Lord's law, written on their hearts (31:33). "I will bring them back to this land. . . . I will give them a heart to know that I am the Lord; and they shall be my people and I shall be their God, for they shall return to me with their whole heart" (24:6–7).

The postexilic period deepens the sense of sin and the call to conversion among the Prophets. Ezekiel points to the rebellious nature of the people, and to the reward or punishment they will receive according to their turning to the Lord (Ez 2:4–8; 3:16–21; 18:31–32; 22:1–31; 33:10–20). He also looks forward to the gift of God, a new heart and a new spirit so that they might adhere to the law of God and turn away from their evil ways (11:19–20; 36:26–31). Parallel themes emerge in Second and Third Isaiah's message of consolation and hope (Is 40:1–2; 51:1–3, 7–8). The days of suffering are over and the Lord has blown away the sins of Israel as if they were clouds (40:2; 44:22). A similar message is found in the postexilic work that produced our present Book of Deuteronomy and the so-called Deuteronomistic History. Israel is summoned to an unconditional adherence to the Law. "You shall keep his statutes and his commandments, which I command you this day, that it may go well with you, and with your children after you, and that you may prolong your days in the land which the Lord your

God gives for ever" (Dt 4:40). The major books telling the history of Israel, collected and edited by the same school at about the same time (Deuteronomy, Joshua, Judges, 1 Samuel, 2 Samuel, 1 Kings, 2 Kings), render this theology into narrative. Israel's "history" shows that God has dealt with Israel according to its performance: an original blessing and a call to covenant, the increasing sinfulness of the nation, punishment, followed by suffering and a cry for mercy. This leads to gradual conversion, until the cycle starts again with a further blessing and the restoration of the covenant.

In the same postexilic period a tendency toward the universalization of God's promise emerges. All the nations are called to conversion. If they leave their idols and turn toward the one true God, they will be blessed (Is 45:14–15, 23–24). The pagans will turn to Israel (Is 56:3, 6), and an eschatological vision emerges of the assembly of all the nations turning toward the God of Israel (Ps 22, 28; Jonah). From its original sense of the need to perform ritual acts Israel journeyed long to express its need for conversion and thus purify itself from sin. Behind this journey lies a unique sense of the holiness of God and the sinfulness of human beings. The OT is, in many ways, a continual summons to conversion.

In the New Testament. Much that is central to the OT understanding of conversion flows naturally into the teaching of the NT. The faith of the early Church, however, that Jesus was the Christ, the Son of God (Mk 1:1, 11; Mt 27:54; Lk 1:35; 3:23–38; Rom 1:3–4 Jn 20:31, etc.) radically changes the situation of the sinner before the holiness of God. Fundamental to the teaching of Jesus of Nazareth was his conviction that in his presence, in his word and deed, the Kingdom of God was breaking into the human story (Mk 1:15; Mt 4:17). Yet, only Jesus lives the Kingdom. Everyone else is made aware, by what Jesus says and does, that the Kingdom is "at hand." In order to gain entry to the Kingdom, the believer must repent, turn away from all sinful ways, and enter (Mk 1:15). Luke's Gospel summarizes one of the crucial elements of Jesus' mission: "to call sinners to repentance" (Lk 5:32).

Jesus' teaching attempted to lay bare the subtle but deep reign of human self-sufficiency (Mk 10:21–25: riches; Lk 18:9: pride). He attacks a wicked generation (Lk 11:29–32), rendered public (from the perspective of the Evangelists) by the inability of the Israel of Jesus' and their time to see and accept God's gift of the Kingdom in Jesus (Mt 13:15). Conversion is crucial (Lk 13:1–5) or they will perish like the sterile fig-tree (Lk 13:6–9; Mt 21:18–22). Examples of conversion abound in the Gospels. Simon becomes Peter, a disciple of Jesus, when he falls to his knees and confesses his sinfulness (Lk

5:1–11), the Syrophoenician woman is contrasted with the arrogance of Israel (Mk 7:1–23), as she considers she is of no more worth than the dogs under the table, accepting the crumbs that might fall (Mk 7:24–30). A father cries out, "I believe; help my unbelief" (Mk 9:24), and a centurion confesses, "Lord, I am not worthy to have you come under my roof; but only say the word and my servant will be healed." As in the OT, the coming of the Kingdom in Jesus calls for the recognition of the holiness of God. God's reigning presence is to be found in Jesus' word and person. Thus, the Christian believer is called to a change of heart, a turning back from sinful ways so as to enter the Kingdom of God found in Jesus' word and person.

The Lukan writings are particularly concerned with the theme of conversion. Jesus is the Good Shepherd, in search of the one lost sheep (Lk 15:3–7), a theme eloquently developed in the immediately following parable of the father with two lost sons, only one of whom has come home (15:11–32). Jesus rejoices in the return of the sinful woman (7:36–50) and Zaccheus (19:5–9). On the cross, Jesus hears the cry of the repentant thief, and welcomes him into the Kingdom (23:39–43). As the Gospel of Luke closes, the risen Jesus instructs the disciples that they are witnesses of these things, and "that repentance and forgiveness of sins should be preached in his name to all the nations, beginning from Jerusalem" (24:47). Obedient to this command, the story of the disciples, and then of Paul throughout that Acts of the Apostles, calls for conversion (μετάνοια) so that sin might be forgiven (Acts 2:38; 3:19; 5:31; 28:30–31). The new Christians must turn toward (ηπιστρέφειν) God through faith in Jesus Christ (see Acts 3:19; 9:35).

For Paul, the glory of God's original design has been lost by sin, sin having entered our story in the ongoing story of Adam (Rom 5:12). All, Pagans and Jews, find themselves in a situation of a hopeless "lostness" in sin (Rom 1:18–32 [Pagans]; 2:1–3:20 [Jews]). But that situation has been transformed. Jesus' unconditional obedience to God (Phil 2:5–11) has drawn back God's eschatological restoration of the original glory, due to take place at the end of time, into our history. Now it is possible to be inserted into the Jesus story, where the free gift of God surpasses the judgment following Adam's sin. Where sin abounds, there is also a superabundance of grace (Rom 5:12–21). The Christian is called to "put on" Christ (Col 3:10–11), to enter into a new life "in Christ" (e.g., Gal 3:27–28; Rom 10:12–13; 1 Cor 12:12–13). By entering into the new eschatological people, made possible because of the free act of God and Jesus' response (Rom 3:21–26), the believer becomes part of a "new creation" (Gal 6:15; 2 Cor 5:17). The believer, however, must turn away from idols, "to serve a living and true

God, and wait for his Son from heaven, whom he raised from the dead, Jesus who delivers us from the wrath to come" (1 Thes 1:9–10). Later, in a more theologically developed restatement of the same call to conversion, Paul instructs the Romans, "How can we who died to sin still live in it? Do you not know that all of us who have been baptized into Christ Jesus were baptized into his death? We were buried therefore with him by baptism into death, so that as Christ was raised from the dead by the glory of the Father, we too might walk in newness of life" (Rom 6:2–4). God's eschatological people exists through a process of conversion.

As with the OT, the NT can be read as a long summons to conversion, so that all might believe that Jesus is the Christ, the Son of God, and believing have life in his name (Jn 20:31).

Bibliography: B. R. GAVENTA, "Conversion," in *The Anchor Bible Dictionary,* v. 1 (6 v.; New York 1992) 1131–33; *From Darkness to Light: Aspects of Conversion in the New Testament* (Philadelphia 1986). W. L. HOLLADAY, *The Root šûbh in the Old Testament* (Leiden 1958). S. KIM, *The Origin of Paul's Gospel* (Grand Rapids 1982); "Repentance/Conversion," in *Dictionary of Biblical Theology,* ed. X. LÉON-DUFOUR et al., tr. P. J. CAHILL (2d ed.; London 1988) 486–491. S. L. MCKENZIE, "Deuteronomistic History," in *The Anchor Bible Dictionary,* v. 2 (6 v.; New York 1992) 160–168. H. MERKLEIN, "μετάνοια, μετανοέω," in *Exegetical Dictionary of the New Testament,* v. 2, ed. H. BALZ and G. SCHNEIDER (3 v.; Grand Rapids 1991) 415–419. K. STENDHAL, "Call Rather Than Conversion," in *Paul among Jews and Gentiles* (Philadelphia 1976) 7–13.

[F. J. MOLONEY]

CONVERSION, II (THEOLOGY OF)

Conversion is a word with a variety of meanings. For most Catholics, the word "conversion" means first and foremost "change of religious affiliation," and "convert" is primarily a noun, designating someone who joined the Catholic church as an adult, either from some other Christian denomination, or from some other religion, or from no religion at all. For many Protestants, especially evangelicals, conversion means first and foremost "experience of redemption from sin," and convert is primarily a verb, usually in the past tense and passive voice, describing a personal experience of "having been converted" at a particular point in their lives when they "first accepted Jesus Christ as my personal Lord and Savior." For social scientists of religion, conversion is a psychological experience of dramatic religious change, usually involving both a change of religious attitude and of religious affiliation, to be studied and accounted for.

To understand the variety of ways the word "conversion" is used, and to begin to account for conversion in a coherent and comprehensive theology of conversion, some distinctions need to be made. One may profitably distinguish both a series of kinds of conversion, and a series of levels of conversion.

The most important Catholic theologian for the theology of conversion in the last half of the 20th century was Bernard LONERGAN, S.J. (1904–84). For Lonergan, all conversion is an experience of self-transcendence resulting in a shift of one's point of view, or horizon, which defines the sweep of one's knowledge and interests. In his *Method in Theology,* he distinguishes three kinds of conversion: intellectual, moral, and religious.

Intellectual conversion is the radical change in my intellectual horizon when I move from the world of immediacy, or perceptions, to the world as mediated by meaning, as revealed to me in the processes of experiencing, understanding, judging, and believing.

Moral conversion is the radical change of my criteria for decision making from satisfactions to values. This conversion enables me to rise above asking "Is this good for me here and now?" i.e., immediate satisfaction, and even above asking "Is this good for me in the long run?" i.e., delayed gratification, to ask "Is this good?" and to choose for value even against satisfaction when value and satisfaction conflict.

Religious conversion Lonergan defines as "being grasped by ultimate concern. It is other-worldly falling in love. It is total and permanent self-surrender without conditions, qualifications, reservations." This definition of religious conversion is very similar to the definition of conversion given by Karl RAHNER, S.J.: "the voluntary acceptance of a fundamental religious experience of the inescapable orientation of man toward the mystery which we call God." Lonergan notes that religious conversion is the same reality called in Catholic theological tradition since Augustine "operative" or "sanctifying" grace, the replacement by God in us of a heart of stone with a heart of flesh.

Lonergan suggests that both theory and experience testify that these three kinds of conversion are independent, in that they can occur separately. One can be a brilliant scholar or scientist and a despicable human being at the same time, and a person of great integrity of values can be intellectually naïve. Similarly, an atheist can nonetheless be a person thoroughly devoted to both truth and value. The paradigmatic case, however, is for moral conversion to sublate (i.e., to include, preserve, and carry forward into a new and richer context) intellectual conversion, and for religious conversion to sublate both.

In fact, Lonergan suggests, while the order of explanation is intellectual, moral, and religious, from a causal

Harold II Bluetooth, King of Denmark, converted to Christianity c. 960. (©Archivo Iconografico, S.A./CORBIS)

viewpoint the order is properly the reverse: the gift to us of God's love reveals values to us in their splendor, and enables us to embrace them, and this in turn includes the value of truth.

Such a definition of religious conversion is surely much more fundamental than the decision to change religious affiliation or the description of an emotionally intense religious experience. Still, even this definition is in itself not adequate to make sense of all the uses of the word "conversion" in the Catholic tradition. If religious conversion can be equated to the gift of sanctifying grace, what are we to make of the tradition of calling monastic profession "second conversion," or of the call made by recent popes in various contexts for "continuing conversion"? To situate such uses of the word "conversion," we need to distinguish various levels of conversion.

All conversions, intellectual, moral, or religious, can be fruitfully distinguished on three levels, fundamental, revolutionary, and evolutionary.

Fundamental, or initial, conversion is the foundational act of self-transcendence that opens one up to the reality beyond the self as an object of knowledge, value, or love. Such a conversion creates a horizon. Revolutionary, or subsequent, conversion is a vertical act of self-transcendence that opens one up to a fuller reality beyond the self. Such a conversion creates a new horizon. Evolutionary, or continuing, conversion is an ongoing act of self-transcendence that explores this new or fuller reality. Such a conversion maintains and broadens a horizon, and works out the consequences of living in this new horizon.

Characterizing a given conversion both by its kind and by its level creates a nine-cell matrix that can serve as a convenient heuristic structure for sorting out the various uses of the word "conversion" in theological, psychological, and even popular literature.

Foundational intellectual conversion occurs when a person first realizes that things are not what they seem to be, and that therefore knowing is not like seeing, but has structures and methods and a discipline of its own that must be adhered to if real knowledge is to be gained. The obligations to be attentive, be intelligent, and be reasonable are assumed by the knower, as Lonergan explains in *Insight*.

Revolutionary intellectual conversion occurs when an already responsible knower encounters a new intellectual perspective, a new framework that not only provides new answers, but asks new questions from a new point of view. Such a new intellectual horizon is the result of a vertical leap in intellectual self-transcendence that, while not as dramatic a change as fundamental intellectual conversion (which it in fact requires as a prerequisite), nonetheless deserves to be called a conversion. Revolutionary intellectual conversion is what is described in detail by T. S. Kuhn as a "paradigm shift." In physical science, an example would be the shift from Newtonian physics to quantum mechanics. In Catholic theology, an example would be the shift from the literal way of reading of Scripture that characterized the Pontifical Biblical Commission decisions of the early years of the 20th century to the critical way of reading that characterizes Vatican II's *Dei Verbum*.

Evolutionary intellectual conversion is the ongoing process of living up to the demands of the foundational and revolutionary conversions. Lonergan describes this when he talks about the need to identify and root out the individual, group, and general bias that can interfere with the process of knowing. Such biases are rarely completely obvious, and even more rarely totally eradicated, so this remains a lifelong process both for the individual and for the intellectual community. If even Einstein could refuse to accept the intellectual consequences of quantum mechanical theory because he could not believe that God shot dice with the universe, lesser mortals would be well advised not to neglect the task of ongoing intellectual conversion.

Fundamental moral conversion occurs when a person first realizes that satisfaction is not the same as value, that something can be a value in itself even when it is not a source of immediate or even delayed satisfaction to him, and chooses to base his actions on value rather than on satisfaction. This is sometimes called by moralists the "FUNDAMENTAL OPTION." Since the maturity necessary to distinguish between satisfaction and value is rarely achieved until sometime in middle to late adolescence, fundamental moral conversion is frequently experienced at this time, often in a religious context.

Revolutionary moral conversion is a vertical leap in moral self-transcendence that results in a new moral horizon. Such a new moral paradigm results, for example, when a person passes from a conventional moral framework, where the moral norms laid down by his or her society are uncritically accepted as values, to a postconventional moral framework, where these norms themselves are critically examined for bias and error, and where necessary rejected on the authority of conscience. A similar shift in moral paradigm results when a person passes from a strictly individual sense of morality to a moral framework that includes the social, economic, and political dimensions of our common existence. The move of Leo XIII to broaden the traditional notion of justice to include distributive as well as commutative justice, and the subsequent move of John Paul II to include contributive JUSTICE as well, represent revolutionary moral conversions in the Catholic community as a whole.

Evolutionary moral conversion is perhaps the one cell of this nine-cell matrix that most people are most familiar with in their lives, and perhaps most identify with being a good person: the everyday struggle to listen to the demands of reality and the values it presents instead of giving in to the easy temptation to choose satisfaction and call it value. If intellectual bias is insidious, moral bias is even more so. Calls to "continuing conversion" are often largely, if not exclusively, directed at this kind of ongoing moral conversion.

Fundamental religious conversion is the unconditional falling in love of which Lonergan spoke, the surrender to our inescapable orientation toward the mystery we call God of which Rahner spoke. It is experienced as gift, given us from without and yet freely accepted from within. It can also be spoken of as "operative" or "sanctifying" grace, or as *gratia increata*. This gift fundamentally reorients a person as a person unconditionally in love. This is the fundamental gift that empowers and sublates the fundamental option. Because this fundamental conversion is transcendental rather than thematic (to use Rahner's distinction between the two), it will not always occur in a recognizably religious context. It is this possibility of being in love with God without even knowing God explicitly, or even knowing that God exists, that creates the possibility for what an older theology called "baptism of desire," what Rahner called "ANONYMOUS CHRISTIANITY," and what is addressed by theologians under the rubric of Christianity and World Religions.

Revolutionary religious conversion is a vertical leap of self-transcendence that opens up a new horizon in one's relationship with the Absolute Mystery. This may be experienced primarily in terms of the Mystery, or primarily in terms of the relationship. A new horizon on the Mystery occurs when a person comes to a radically new experience of Who God is. A new image of God is frequently accompanied by a new self-image, a new religious community of reference, a new belief system, a new symbol system, a new form of spirituality. A person, for example, who was in love with a God seen primarily as the maker and enforcer of cosmic and moral law, and who comes to share in Jesus' experience of God as Abba, is undergoing a revolutionary religious conversion of this sort. A new horizon on the relationship occurs for a person who experiences the same God, but in a radically new way or with a radically different level of intensity. The three levels of monastic conversion found in JOHN CLIMACUS's Ladder of Divine Ascent, as explained by J. R. Price, are examples of revolutionary religious conversion of this sort, and each enables and is implemented by subsequent further intellectual and moral conversions.

Evolutionary religious conversion is the ongoing task of growing into the relationship to the Absolute established by fundamental and revolutionary religious conversion. Evolutionary religious conversion is the fruit of what Augustine called cooperative grace, and what later medieval theology called actual grace, the gradual movement toward a complete transformation of one's being and living. Greek theology calls this process theosis, literally, the process of divinization. As this process occurs, it will, at least in the paradigmatic case, both sublate and work itself out in intellectual and moral evolutionary conversion, gradually producing the whole human being, fully alive, whom Augustine called the glory of God. This is continuing conversion in its fullest form.

An understanding of the three kinds and three levels of conversion can help, not only to make sense of the various ways in which the word "conversion" is used by various authors and in various contexts, but also to diagnose and prescribe for our own conversion needs and those of others.

Such an understanding underlies, for example, the approach of the Rite of Christian Initiation for Adults (RCIA) developed since Vatican II and the new emphasis on ongoing adult religious education and formation in the Catholic Church. When conversion meant simply "becoming Catholic," the conversion process was essentially a one-size fits all phenomenon: the new "convert" studied the catechism under the tutelage of the parish priest until the latter was satisfied that enough doctrine had been learned and enough loyalty demonstrated, and then the new member was baptized, or "baptized conditionally" if previously baptized in some other denomination. Once people were received into the church, or after graduation from Catholic school if born into the church, it was assumed that they were fully prepared for life as good Catholics, and no further education or formation was deemed necessary for laypeople.

Today it is incumbent upon the ministers (priests, deacons, and lay catechists) conducting the RCIA and preparing a parish strategy for ongoing adult formation to assess the conversion status and conversion needs of each aspirant as an individual and of a parish as a whole. One seeker exploring the catechumenate may be a thoroughgoing American consumerist, whose life, dominated by the accumulation of things, has seemed emptier and emptier as his closets have gotten fuller and fuller, and who is seeking, perhaps rather vaguely, for some more enduring source of satisfaction. Such a person is in need of fundamental moral and religious conversion. The goals of the catechumenate for him will be to experience value as superior to satisfaction, and to abandon self-centeredness and fall in love with God.

A second aspirant may have already embraced a moral life based on value, and fallen in love with the Mystery, but have never seen the Mystery as a reality not less than personal, capable of infinite, personal loving as well as of being loved. Her moral conversion may only be evolutionary, but her religious conversion will be revolutionary. The goal of the catechumenate for her will be to experience the God of Jesus, to fall in love with that God, and to root herself in the community of faith that shares that love.

Still a third aspirant may have already experienced and fallen in love with Jesus' God, and been baptized and catechized in another Christian communion of a fundamentalist persuasion, but now finds himself drawn to the life of Word and Sacrament as these are lived in the local Catholic Church. Such a person is not a catechumen at all, but a candidate for full communion with the Church. The RCIA dictates that his baptism, and the fundamental conversion that first brought him to the font, be respected, not repeated. In the intellectual sphere, he may need to achieve a revolutionary conversion, learning the Catholic way of reading and interpreting scripture. But in the area of religious conversion, he needs probably only an evolutionary conversion, opening him up more and more to the fullness of Christian spiritual growth in our tradition.

A complacently middle-class parish may have a collective need for revolutionary moral conversion that becomes the highest priority in that parish's pastoral plan, in order to bring them to see the social, economic, and political dimensions of Christian morality. A parish in which most of the parishioners have deep roots in the Bible may have a greater need for evolutionary intellectual and religious conversion, which the parish will meet with a series of Bible study programs that helps them read and pray the Bible in a way that combines modern scholarship and traditional devotion.

Every person is different, and every community is different, at different levels of different kinds of conversion. Attention to these differences will be well repaid in pastoral practice as well as in understanding the literature on conversion.

Bibliography: W. J. CONN, ed., *Conversion: Perspectives on Personal and Social Transformation* (New York 1978). W. J. CONN, *Christian Conversion* (New York 1986). V. GREGSON, *The Desires of the Human Heart* (New York 1988). S. HAPPEL and J. WALTER, *Conversion and Discipleship* (Philadelphia 1986). JOHN PAUL II, "Ecclesia in America," *Origins* 27:28 (February 1999). B. LONERGAN, *Method in Theology* (New York 1972). J. M. MCDERMOTT, "Tensions in Lonergan's Theory of Conversion," *Gregorianum* 74:1 (1993) 101–140. J. R. PRICE, "Conversion and the Doctrine of Grace in Bernard Lonergan and John Climacus," *Anglican Theological Review* 62:4 (1980) 338–362. A. VEILLEUX, "The Monastic Way of Conversion," *American Benedictine Review* 37:1 (1986) 34–45.

[R. T. LAWRENCE]

CONVERSION, III (PSYCHOLOGY OF)

There has been a twofold movement in the psychology of conversion in recent decades: psychologists, primarily social psychologists, have continued to study the phenomenon of conversion, and theologians interested in conversion have begun to study psychology, primarily developmental psychology.

Social psychological studies on conversion have largely limited their scope to examining conversions which resulted in a change in religious identity, defined to include both radical change in one's self and change in one's professed religion, and have, in fact, often utilized a separate term, "intensification," for cases involving a new level of commitment to the religion in which one was born. Further, much of the research in the first half of the twentieth century centered on conversion as experienced in North American Protestantism, and much

research in recent years has examined conversions into and out of new religious movements, sometimes called sects or cults.

Examination of such research in light of the nine-cell matrix of types and levels of conversion suggested above (*see* CONVERSION, II [THEOLOGY OF]) reveals that type one, intellectual conversion, and level three, evolutionary conversion, will remain largely unobserved by these studies, as they fall outside of their definition of conversion. Further, the line between fundamental and revolutionary conversions will tend to escape notice on methodological criteria, since it would be difficult to establish empirical criteria for determining whether converts were basing their lives on values or were in love with the Mystery prior to their conversion processes. Even the distinction between moral and religious conversions will most frequently be blurred, leaving a single, undifferentiated phenomenon called simply "conversion" as the object of study.

Nonetheless, if these limitations are kept in mind, research done by sociologists and psychologists of religion can have considerable value in creating an interdisciplinary understanding of conversion in the broader sense in which the term is used in the contemporary Catholic tradition. Theologians studying conversion, as well as church leaders trying to plan effective evangelization and RCIA programs, for example, should take note of studies of the different characteristics of sudden and gradual conversions, of the interplay between change of belief and change of behavior in the conversion process, of the roles of social networks and advocates, and of the importance of helping an aspirant develop a master attribution scheme consonant with their new religious identity.

The second approach to the psychology of conversion in recent decades has been an effort to explore conversion in light of the insights of developmental psychology. The works of Piaget, Erikson, Kohlberg, Fowler, and Kegan, in particular, have been examined for their implications for religious development. An outline of religious development has been worked out, and the major transitions in that developmental process have been labeled "conversions."

A representative schema of this sort (Conn, 1986, 37) correlates moral conversion with Piaget's formal operations, Erikson's Identity stage, Kohlberg's conventional stages, Fowler's Synthetic-conventional stage, and Kegan's Interpersonal and Institutional stages. This correlation, if accepted, suggests that the earliest likely opportunity for a moral conversion, a decision to base one's life on value rather than satisfaction, occurs sometime during adolescence. This correlation would have explanatory value. For instance, it suggests that the reported age for the average evangelical "conversion experience," 15, invites us to understand this experience as perhaps primarily a conversion from satisfaction ("sin") to value ("God"). It would also have prescriptive value. For instance, religious education for pre-adolescents may well stress the content of moral norms, but the invitation to personally appropriate these norms rather than just follow them as laws would best be made a goal of programs for adolescents.

In the course of this work, more kinds of conversions have been proposed than Lonergan's intellectual, moral, and religious. An affective conversion is commonly added, and the moral and religious conversions are sometimes divided into moral and critical-moral and religious and critical-religious conversions, respectively. Further, there is as yet no agreement among authors about precisely how to correlate the stages outlined by the various developmentalists with the proposed schema of conversions. More research, both theoretical and experimental, is clearly needed.

In seeking to place the results of the work thus far in a context of Lonergan's original three-fold distinction of conversions, recourse to the nine-cell matrix of kinds and levels of conversion outlined in the previous article may serve a heuristic function. For instance, "moral conversion" can be seen as fundamental moral conversion, and "critical-moral conversion" can be seen as a species of revolutionary moral conversion.

As another example, "Religious conversion," variously placed by different authors as early as Kohlberg's Conventional stages and as late as his seventh, or Religious, stage, (corresponding to Erikson's final, Integrity stage), can be seen in either case as the capstone variety of revolutionary religious conversion, not to be equated with fundamental religious conversion. After all, if fundamental religious conversion can be equated by Lonergan with operative grace, surely that cannot be said to be usually absent before the mature years. On the other hand, it makes perfect sense to envision a final, radical gift of self and acceptance of God's love, yielding a radically new horizon for the summing up and handing over of one's life, as the culminating result of a life founded on a much earlier gift of love, lived out through one or more previous revolutionary conversions and a lifetime of evolutionary conversion.

Bibliography: M. C. BOYS, "Conversion as a Foundation of Religious Education," *Religious Education* 57 (1982) 211–224. J. W. CONN and W. E. CONN, "Discerning Conversion," *The Way Supplement*, 64 (1989) 63–79. R. W. HOOD, B. SPILKA, B. HUNSBERGER, and R. GORSUCH, *The Psychology of Religion: An Empirical Approach* (New York 1996). B. SPILKA and B. MCINTOSH, eds., *The Psychology of Religion: Theoretical Approaches* (Boulder 1997).

[R. T. LAWRENCE]

CONVERSION AND GRACE, CONTROVERSIES ON

A conversion is a turning toward God and away from SIN. Chrisian reflection on the nature of conversion derives largely from St. Paul. The need for conversion is expressed throughout his writings. He uses different terminology in speaking of different types of conversion. For the pagans, conversion consists in turning away from, leaving the service of, idols in order to be in God's service (Gal 4.9). Conversion is the fruit of divine initiative. God calls man to His kingdom and to His glory (1 Thes 2.12). One of the essential elements in every conversion to the life of grace is the knowledge of God, a knowledge that includes a total commitment of self to God. When turned away from God, one is unable to discern the things of God (cf. 1 Cor 2.14). As a result, one's moral judgments are perverted. Conversion effects a renewal of the mind so that one becomes capable of discerning all that is good, pleasing to God, perfect (Rom 12.2). The principal effect of conversion, according to Paul, is that one becomes a new creature (Gal 6.15), leaving off the old economy of the Law, which was sterile, and adopting the new economy brought by Christ. [*See* REBIRTH (IN THE BIBLE).] BAPTISM is, of course, the prime source of this new creaturehood. By it man is united to the death and RESURRECTION OF CHRIST, and is thus enabled to live a new life.

Pelagians and Semi-Pelagians. Through the centuries Catholic theology has elaborated upon the nature of and the requirements for this conversion to the life of grace. In the 5th century, against Pelagianism, which denied the absolute necessity of divine help in order to effect this conversion (*see* PELAGIUS AND PELAGIANISM), a Council of CARTHAGE anathematized anyone who denied that only through the grace of God is one enabled to know, desire, and do what he knows must be done for SALVATION (H. Denzinger, *Enchiridion symbolorum*, 226). Later, against SEMI-PELAGIANISM, a Council of ORANGE (529) settled the question concerning man's need of grace to dispose himself in a positive way for conversion (Denz 373–397). The Semi-Pelagians admitted against the Pelagians the absolute necessity of grace for salvation. They wished to save both the universal salvific WILL OF GOD, and the cooperation of man's free will in the matter of salvation. God's universal salvific will could not, they believed, be reconciled with His justice if He did not give the same grace to all in order that all might thereby be saved. On the other hand, it seemed impossible to explain the decisive cooperation of man's free will in his salvation unless there is at least one act that is attributable to that free will alone and in no way to the influence of grace. That one act they technically called "the beginning of faith'' (Denz 375; *See* FAITH, BEGINNING OF.) According to the Semi-Pelagians, just as the man who is sick and needs the doctor to cure him nevertheless retains the capacity to call him, so, too, without grace one cannot be saved, although he may positively prepare himself for the reception of grace by desiring it. If a man, according to the Semi-Pelagians, thus disposes himself to conversion, he will receive grace from God by which he is physically capable of being saved. Nevertheless, man's conversion to grace (and consequently his salvation) is in his own hands, just as his damnation is ultimately attributable to his free rejection of God's help. After ORIGINAL SIN man is not dead but only sick; he can still call the doctor, in order to be healed.

Before the time of the Pelagians and Semi-Pelagians, the Fathers did not methodically consider the problem of the necessity of grace for conversion, but much of what they wrote implicitly contained a condemnation of the two errors of these heretics. The Fathers indicated, at times, the need for grace even for the first steps toward salvation. The effects of the regeneration that takes place in conversion were described as totally surpassing man's natural capacities.

The principal opponent of Semi-Pelagianism was St. AUGUSTINE. Against its errors he wrote many works, among which was *De praedestinatione sanctorum,* in which he invites those who have erred as he once did to admit with him that even the beginning of faith is a gift of God.

Medieval Theologians. The decrees of the Council of Orange were practically forgotten until the middle of the 16th century. Medieval theologians did not consider explicitly the question of the need of grace for conversion, for the beginning of faith. It was only slowly that they came to the correct solution of this problem. In commenting upon St. Paul's Epistles medieval theologians frequently said that all good things, even the beginning of conversion, come from God. Paul had said: "For who singles thee out? Or what hast thou that thou hast not received?" (1 Cor 4.7); theologians began to affirm with St. Augustine and St. Paul that God singles the just from out of the mass of the damned by a gratuitous call. Man left to his own powers is the "sensual" man about whom Paul speaks (1 Cor 2.14–16), the man who cannot assent to the truths of faith or desire eternal life.

But when it came to further explanations the scholastics had difficulty. They admitted that grace is infused at the moment of JUSTIFICATION. They likewise held that before justification a man can and must prepare himself by his own acts for conversion. Some concluded: if he does everything he can without the aid of grace, God will not deny him that grace. They thought that man could by his own powers, and without grace, perform some acts that would in some way prepare him for the reception of grace. Until the second half of the 13th century scholastics tried to reconcile this conclusion with the doctrine of St. Paul and St. Augustine. Many held that man could prepare himself negatively for conversion by doing things that in no way placed an obstacle to grace. For example, if he were to observe the law of nature without grace, he would not be placing any impediments to grace, which would follow; the observance of the natural law would not be the positive reason for the reception of grace but only an occasion or condition for its reception. Finally, St. Thomas explained why the initiative must come from God. Every cause must direct its effects toward their proper end. Since the order of ends is according to the order of agents or movers, it is necessary that a man be converted to his ultimate end by the action of the first mover. Since God is the first mover, all things are converted to Him as to their last end by His own action (*Summa Theologiae* 1a2ae, 109.6).

Kind of Grace before Conversion. With regard to the nature of this grace, which precedes conversion and leads to it, there is discussion. Some theologians speak of it as an elevating actual grace by which a man performs an act of FAITH or HOPE or repentance. Infused habits of faith, hope, and CHARITY come in the moment of justification. Others insist that according to St. Thomas no act that is SUPERNATURAL can proceed other than from an infused HABIT. According to the *Summa theologiae,* conversion begins, strictly speaking, with faith, which is a prevenient grace, absolutely gratuitous. Divine motion does not add power to created being. It simply actuates those that it has already. The supernaturality of an act comes from its form; the divine motion only actuates the form. Therefore the divine motion toward conversion is always in relation to an infused habit, whether of faith, hope, fear, repentance, etc. This latter opinion seems to explain more coherently the texts of St. Thomas. An act that did not proceed from an infused habit would either be a natural act or it would not be accomplished actively by the subject. St. Thomas seems to admit that the habit of faith is sometimes infused before and without the virtue of charity or the moral VIRTUES.

On an exact opposite pole to the Pelagians are the reformers, who would not admit that a man could do anything to prepare himself for conversion since through original sin he has lost his freedom. Fiducial faith alone, which is a total casting of self into the arms of God, saves him. Even with this faith he does not MERIT conversion; it is rather an instrument by which man makes his own the justice of Christ.

In ch. 5 of its decree on justification, the Council of Trent repeats the doctrine of the earlier Council of Orange by establishing the divine initiative in conversion. Anyone who would say that without the prevenient inspiration and aid of the Holy Spirit a man could believe, hope, and love or repent as he must in order that he receive the grace of justification is condemned (Denz 1553). In ch. 6 the council enumerates the various human acts that individually, or at least implicitly, are present in the process of conversion. They are: dogmatic faith, filial fear of divine justice, hope, the "beginnings of love," and repentance. These shall not be considered here, but suffice it to say that with this declaration one has the perfect synthesis of revealed truths concerning this question of conversion. On the one hand, divine initiative is responsible for conversion to the life of grace. On the other hand, man himself, moved by this grace, freely cooperates in his own conversion.

See Also: JUSTIFICATION; CONVERSION, I (IN THE BIBLE); CONVERSION, II (PSYCHOLOGY OF); CONVERSION, III (THEOLOGY OF).

Bibliography: *Dictionnaire de théologie catholique,* ed. A. VACANT et al., (Paris 1903–50; Tables générales 1951–), Tables générales 1:811–812; 2:2782–96. R. SCHNACKENBURG et al., *Lexikon für Theologie und Kirche,* ed. J. HOFER and K. RAHNER (Freiburg 1957–65) 8:1033–50. H. BOUILLARD, *Conversion et grace chez s. Thomas d'Aquin* (Paris 1944). M. FLICK, *De gratia Christi* (Rome 1962) 140–176, 239–288. D. MOLLAT, "La Conversion," *Lumière et vie* 9.47 (Bruges, Belgium 1960) 1–114. M. FLICK and Z. ALSZEGHY, *Il vangelo della grazia* (Florence 1964).

[G. F. KIRWIN/EDS.]

CONVERTS AND CONVERSION

Among Roman Catholics the term "convert" properly applies to someone above the age of choice who, experiencing the grace of the Holy Spirit, accepts the person and teaching of Jesus Christ in the communion of the Church. Before the promulgation of the Rite of Christian Initiation for Adults in 1972, it was common to refer to anyone who joined the Catholic Church as a convert. Present usage, however, restricts the term to mean anyone who, not professing Christian faith and never having received baptism, joins the Catholic Church. Although the term "convert" is still loosely applied in practical usage to any adult who joins the church, the change in the formal vocabulary reflects better ecumenical understanding and appreciation of the traditions and practices of other Christian communions. It explicitly respects their baptism and Christian formation, which, in the past, were either not recognized or only "conditionally" accepted. In the context of the RCIA, individuals who have been previously baptized are referred to as candidates, while those who are seeking baptism are called catechumens.

Fuller notions of evangelization is treated below, but at the outset it is important to note that in the strict conception of the CATECHUMENATE, evangelization refers to the initial call and attraction of a person to faith. The 1997 *General Directory for Catechesis* refers specifically to "call" and "initiation" as two of five ministries of the Word of God (n. 51). Similarly, the process of being initially drawn to Christ and formed in his teaching can be specifically referred to as conversion, with catechetical formation building upon that. More generally, though, conversion refers to the whole process of entering the Church and not just the initial steps.

Individuals experience CONVERSION in variety and often mysterious ways. Catholics often use the term to describe intellectual and moral transformations that occur within the life of one who is already a believer. Sometimes these transformations are dramatic and sudden, but more commonly they are gradual and, in this latter case, are referred to as "ongoing conversion."

Proselytism. Inviting others to conversion is usually very carefully differentiated from proselytism, both in its conception and also its method. Because conversion involves a process of open discernment covering an extended period, it results from a free and mature decision. Proselytism, on the other hand, refers to a forced or manipulative approach to sharing faith, usually without respect for the past experience of the seeker and often restricting the contacts and experiences of the person and employing enticements of a non-religious nature.

The Roman Catholic-Pentecostal dialogue, held in Rome between 1990 and 1997, treated problems of proselytism in a very thorough way. This dialogue developed an initial working definition of proselytism as "a disrespectful, insensitive and uncharitable effort to transfer the allegiance of a Christian from one ecclesial body to another." It went on to specify particular unethical forms of proselytism, instructive for their nuance, which included: intellectually dishonest presentations of one's own faith community in disparagement of others; intellectual laziness in knowing the religious tradition of another; willful misrepresentations of the beliefs and practices of other Christian communities; any form of force or coercion; manipulation "including the exaggeration of biblical promises; abuse of mass media; judgments or actions which raise suspicions about the sincerity of others; and competitive evangelization focused against other Christian bodies. These amplifications of the meaning of proselytism were made while acknowledging that Christians have a right to bear witness to Christ, and that this witness "may legitimately involve the persuasive proclamation of the Gospel in such as way as to bring people to faith in Jesus Christ or to commit themselves more deeply to

Him within the context of their own church." If authentic witness leads people to freely choose to join a different Christian community, "it should not automatically be concluded that such a transfer is the result of proselytism."

Pastoral Dimensions. In the years after the Second Vatican Council, there evolved a movement from instructional classes for converts that focused on individuals to the wide-spread ministry of Christian initiation provided in virtually all parishes. The following changes have resulted from this transition: a formational notion of catechesis that extends beyond initial instruction; the establishment of adult initiation as the model for all initiation; the involvement of many laypersons in the conversion process; a clearer relating of converts to the local parish community.

The process whereby one joins the Church consists of a number of distinct elements. The Rite of Christian Initiation of Adults establishes discreet steps, each of which might vary in length depending on pastoral needs: 1) A period of inquiry presents the initial teaching of Jesus and the life of a believer; 2) then follows a period of more intense study and reflection called the catechumenate; 3) near the beginning of Lent those whose catechumenal experiences have led them to seek entrance into the Church become the elect and undergo a more intense spiritual preparation during the Lenten season; 4) the elect receive the three sacraments of initiation (baptism, confirmation and Eucharist) usually at the Easter Vigil, being referred to as "the enlightened"; and 5) they then begin a final period of formation called mystagogia.

The adoption of the catechumenal model was spearheaded primarily by the North American Forum on the Catechumenate which, through its workshops like "Beginnings and Beyond," that helped establish and dramatically shape the catechetical process in the United States and Canada. The practice of receiving adult converts into the Church at the Easter Vigil on Holy Saturday has become, in effect, the norm in most parishes; similarly, candidates, already baptized, are typically received at the Easter Vigil as well.

The catechumenal process has resulted in a substantial rise in the number of adults entering the Church, when one compares the number of converts in 1970 (92,670), in 1975 (75,123), in 1989 (82,406), in 1994 (163,351) and in 2000 (170,956). [Source: *National Catholic Directory*] However, despite this increase, the number of adults entering the Church at the turn of the millennium was just approaching the number of adults entering the church in 1950s, when the population of Catholics in the United States was much smaller. About 60% of those attracted to the catechumenal process have already been baptized in another Christian tradition; 25% have never been baptized, with the remaining 15% being baptized but uncatechized Catholics. (*Journey to the Fullness of Life: A Report on the Implementation of the Rite of Christian Initiation of Adults in the United States.*)

In November, 1977 Paulist Father Alvin Illig started an office of evangelization and served as the executive director of the bishops' committee on evangelization. Along with this, he also inaugurated the Paulist National Catholic Evangelization Association as a pastoral spearhead for the church, seeking to provide both materials and training in this field. In 1983, in an attempt to broaden participation in evangelization, the bishops' committee on Evangelization formed the National Council for Catholic Evangelization which serves as a wide network of people involved in evangelization; this organization has offered resources, training and nation-wide sharing of information concerning evangelization.

Pastoral practice to welcome and invite those who have no faith to experience Catholic faith varies tremendously from place to place. Evangelization efforts have often been buttressed by diocesan-wide renewal programs that seek to renew Catholic life; this renewal may become a resource for sharing faith as well. At the turn of the millennium, many dioceses involved themselves in programs like *Renew 2000, Disciples in Mission*, or *Follow Me*. These kinds of programs supplemented other world-wide renewal movements such as the Cursillo Movement, or the Charismatic Movement or Marriage Encounter which, in turn, built upon the renewed liturgy and interest in the Scriptures that were key pastoral fruits of the Second Vatican Council.

Research into the phenomenon of conversion shows the key role that contacts through marriage, family and friends play in attracting people to conversion and membership in a church. In addition, active parish outreach, a vital liturgy, welcoming clergy and general hospitality form important dimensions which supplement the human contacts which appear basic in the social dynamic of conversion. The attraction of the liturgical and spiritual richness of the Catholic tradition, along with its living authority and world-wide unity, also seems to motivate a good number of converts.

Bibliography: "Evangelization, Proselytism and Common Witness: the Report from the fourth Phase of the International Dialogue 1990–1997 between the Roman Catholic Church and Some Classical Pentecostal Churches and Leaders," *Information Service* # 97 (1998/I–II), 38–56. *Go and Make Disciples, A Pastoral Plan and Strategy for Catholic Evangelization in the United States* (USCCB, 1993). *Journey to the Fullness of Life: A Report on the Implementation of the Rite of Christian Initiation of Adults in the United States* (USCCB, 2000). K. BOYACK and F. P. DESIANO, *Creating the Evangelizing Parish* (New York/Mahwah, NJ 1993). F. P.

DESIANO, *The Evangelizing Catholic: A Practical Handbook for Reaching Out* (New York/Mahwah, NJ, 1999).

[F. P. DESIANO/R. J. O'DONNELL]

CONVOCATION OF THE ENGLISH CLERGY

The designation of two distinct but functionally related ecclesiastical assemblies associated in the past and at present with the government of the Archbishoprics of Canterbury and York. This entry covers the origins and historical developments of the Convocations of Canterbury and York.

Historically, there is an ecclesiastical assembly called the Convocation of Canterbury and another the Convocation of York. Both may be compared to provincial synods, but their involvement in English constitutional history has induced them to operate in areas not usually claimed by synods on a provincial level. Their development as an institution may be traced back to early Anglo-Saxon England. In form they have remained relatively stable since the Middle Ages, but the Reformation led to the loss of their power to act independently of the state. In the late 19th and 20th centuries they have functioned as the voice of the clergy of the Church of England, but their position and power have been overshadowed by the National Assembly created in 1919 by act of Parliament. Of the two, the Convocation of Canterbury has been considered the operational leader and the term "Convocation" is often used in reference to it alone. At times, members from both convocations have sat together in full synod to handle common problems.

Origins. English constitutional and ecclesiastical history constitutes the necessary background for a developmental study of convocation. Its history may be divided into six stages: (1) Anglo-Saxon England; (2) after the Norman Conquest to the 13th century; (3) the late Middle Ages; (4) the Reformation period; (5) the post-Reformation period; and (6) the late 19th and 20th centuries.

Ecclesiastical meetings were held in England as early as the time of Saint AUGUSTINE OF CANTERBURY. Under Saint THEODORE OF CANTERBURY, bishops were summoned to promote subscription to canons of the Church universal as well as to unify the Church in England. At a meeting in A.D. 680, the canons of the Lateran Council of 649 were adopted as well as the dogmas of the first five general councils. The 8th century witnessed the establishment of the Archbishopric of York as well as the continued development in the use of councils to help govern the Church. In the latter part of the 9th and 10th centuries and the first 60 years of the 11th, church councils as such were not fully utilized; the affairs of the Church were taken care of in a witan, a body in which ecclesiastics had a strong voice by virtue of their learning and territorial importance.

After LANFRANC was consecrated archbishop of Canterbury, the Church began to move away from governmental fusion with the state, a trend paralleling developments on the Continent. In the 12th century, papal legates presided over a number of ecclesiastical meetings. A mandate of the archbishop of Canterbury, summoning one for September 1125, contains the word *convocatio,* the first known use of this term to denote an ecclesiastical assembly in England.

The 13th century brought regular participation of the lower clergy in ecclesiastical gatherings, as the importance of the clergy as a class increased in relation to monarchical and papal assertions of authority and demands for financial aid. Clerics other than diocesan bishops were not given a decisive vote in the making of ecclesiastical constitutions, but it was recognized that they had a right to be heard on such matters, and if taxed, to consent in the determination of the amount of taxation. It became the practice of the lower clergy to attach conditions to their grants. The development of more refined procedure and greater organization for the summoning and conducting of ecclesiastical meetings accompanied this development.

In 1226, Stephen Langton, Archbishop of Canterbury, began the practice of distributing his mandate for a meeting through the bishop of London as dean of the province; this procedural step has been followed ever since for Canterbury. Representatives of the lower clergy also began in 1226 to participate in councils called to deal with the king's requests for money. In 1273, Robert Kilwardby, archbishop of Canterbury, summoned representatives of the lower clergy to a gathering designed primarily to handle ecclesiastical business. It was called and held independently of the king; abbots and priors did not attend. With the Convocation of Canterbury of May 1283, the system of having the diocesan clergy represented by two proctors from each diocese was inaugurated. The arrangement regarding representation was never embodied in a canon, but it was followed when the lower clergy were summoned to the Convocation of Canterbury. The Archbishopric of York's convocation was soon organized in the same manner except that two proctors were elected from each archdeaconry instead of each diocese. Until 1920 only beneficed clergy voted in an election for proctors.

In the autumn of 1295, Edward I summoned the diocesan clergy to Parliament. The form of the summons sent to the archbishop of Canterbury became the official form for summoning the clergy to Parliament in the future, except for occasional and slight changes. In the wording of the summons the word ''praemunientes'' appears for the first time, and it has since been used to describe the clause in question. The king asked for the same scale of representation as that of the 1283 Convocation of Canterbury.

The lower clergy resisted the attempt by the king to tax them through Parliament. Although proctors of the lower clergy appeared in Parliament, ecclesiastical meetings were needed to satisfy the king's financial demands as well as to provide for the government of the Church. The terms provincial council and convocation were both used to describe such meetings. In those meetings called to secure a grant, the participation of the lower clergy became formalized in representation according to precedent as well as in organization. After 1340, grants to the king by the lower clergy were determined in this type of meeting, the king usually ordering a meeting to be convoked at or near the time of a Parliament for such a purpose. Later, Convocation became the accepted designation for these gatherings. Clerical proctors continued to attend Parliament as observers or advisers into the 16th century.

When Convocation met, it became the custom for the archbishop to ask the lower clergy to deliberate separately. Out of this emerged the organizational division of Convocation into an Upper House for the archbishops and diocesan bishops and a Lower House for the rest of the clergy. Convocation usually opened with a joint session for a declaration of its authority and purpose and the two divisions then withdrew to deliberate as individual units. The decisions and grievances of the lower clergy came to be reported by an official called the prolocutor. In the 15th century the use of committees developed. Since 1429, the members of Convocation have had the same freedom from arrest as members of Parliament. In the pre-Reformation period Convocation was not controlled in its deliberations by the civil power.

Reformation. The independence of Convocation was lost by the Submission of the Clergy (1531), later given statutory force by Henry VIII in 1534. The king's writ became necessary for the assembling of any provincial meeting and his license had to be obtained for the enactment of any canon. After the passage of the Act of Supremacy (1559) and the Act of UNIFORMITY (1560), Convocation participated in the imposition of religious change upon England under the protection and supervision of the state. In character, it became the provincial assembly of the Church of England. Even with the king's permission, it was prohibited legally from enacting any canon contrary or inimical to the laws and customs of England.

With the Restoration, Convocation's right to act as the taxing authority for the clergy was abandoned to Parliament without a struggle. In the late 17th and early 18th century, it became an arena in which the religio-political questions of the day were debated. During the reign of Queen Anne, special ''Letters of Business'' were issued by the crown to Convocation for the purpose of securing consideration of certain specified matters. This procedure was followed at different times in the future. In 1717 the king prorogued Convocation against its will and, although it continued to be summoned before each Parliament, it was not allowed to operate beyond its formal opening ceremonies for the next 135 years. As part of the renewal of church life engendered by the OXFORD MOVEMENT, the Convocation of Canterbury was revived in 1852 and that of York in 1861. This revival made no change in the limitations placed upon Convocation by the Reformation, and historical precedents. Convocation deliberated and enacted canons with the king's permission, but it had no power to depart from its past relationships until the formation of the National Assembly established a body capable of sanctioning changes in its legal position. With the approval of the National Assembly, in 1921, both Convocations liberalized the use of the franchise and defined the membership arrangements of their lower house. Membership in the Convocation of Canterbury was reduced with the establishment of the province of Wales in 1920.

Bibliography: D. B. WESKE, *Convocation of the Clergy* (London 1937). E. BARKER, *The Dominican Order and Convocation* (Oxford 1913). J. T. DODD, *Convocation and Edward Dodd's Share in Its Revival* (London 1931). F. MAKOWER, *The Constitutional History and Constitution of the Church of England* (London 1895). T. LATHBURY, *A History of the Convocation of the Church of England* (London 1842). G. TREVOR, *The Convocation of the Two Provinces* (London 1852). J. W. JOYCE, *England's Sacred Synods* (London 1853). H. SPELMAN et al., eds., *Councils and Ecclesiastical Documents Relating to Great Britain and Ireland,* 3 v. (Oxford 1869–73). A. F. SMETHURST and H. R. WILSON, eds., *Acts of the Convocations of Canterbury and York* (London 1948). E. CARDWELL, ed., *Synodalia,* 2 v. (Oxford 1842). F. WARRE CORNISH, *The English Church in the Nineteenth Century,* 2 v. (London 1910). E. KEMP, ''The Origins of the Canterbury Convocation,'' *The Journal of Ecclesiastical History* 3 (1952) 132–43. F. M. POWICKE and C. R. CHENEY, *Councils and Synods,* v.2 (Oxford 1964).

[V. H. PONKO, JR./EDS.]

CONWAY, WILLIAM

Primate of Ireland; b. Jan. 22, 1913, Belfast; d. Apr. 17, 1977, Armagh. He studied in Belfast at St. Mary's Christian Brothers' School, St. Malachy's College, and Queen's University, receiving from the latter a B.A. in English literature in 1933. He then studied theology at St. Patrick's College, Maynooth, and was ordained there in

1937. He received a Doctor of Divinity degree from St. Patrick's in 1938, and a doctorate in canon law from the Gregorian University, Rome, in 1941. Returning to Maynooth, he served there as professor of moral theology from 1942 to 1958, the last year also as vice president. During this period he served on Government Commissions on Higher Education and on Income Tax. In 1958 Conway was consecrated titular bishop of Neve and named auxiliary to the archbishop of Armagh, Cardinal John D'Alton. In 1963 Conway was chosen to succeed D'Alton as Archbishop and Primate of All Ireland (the Republic and Northern Ireland), and held the post until his death. He was created cardinal in 1965 by Pope Paul VI, who also appointed him to be one of three chairmen for the 1967 Synod of Bishops and papal legate to the 1972 National Eucharistic Congress in Madras. Conway also served on the Sacred Congregation for Bishops, for the Clergy, for Catholic Education, and for the Evangelization of Peoples. He died of cancer at his residence.

Conway's service as primate covered a period of widespread violence in Northern Ireland that erupted in 1969 and continued with varying degrees of intensity throughout the rest of his life. Since the groups inflicting the violence were identified according to their association with the Catholic or Protestant communities, the conflict was commonly interpreted as a religious war. But Conway joined with the leadership of the Protestant churches to issue united appeals for peace. Some Protestants accused him of denouncing Protestant violence more strongly than Catholic. Some Catholic critics suggested that he should have moved more boldly to implement the new spirit of Vatican II and endorse the rights of Protestants to follow their own consciences in such areas as divorce and birth control. Also controversial was his continued support of separate schools for Catholic children, which many analysts thought served to continue the alienation between Catholics and Protestants. Virtually everyone agreed, nonetheless, that Conway was personally a man of peace who took significant strides toward improving the ecumenical climate in Ireland. His cautious style of leadership was also credited with maintaining a strong sense of Catholic unity and loyalty during the post-Vatican II years when bitter controversy and abandonment of the church were common in some other places. At the end of his tenure, surveys found nine out of ten Irish Catholics still attending Mass at least once a week. He was succeeded as archbishop by Msgr. Tomas O'Fiaich, a native of County Armagh and president of St. Patrick's College.

[T. EARLY]

CONWELL, HENRY

Second bishop of Philadelphia, Pa.; b. County Derry, Ireland, c. 1745; d. Philadelphia, April 22, 1842. He studied for the priesthood in the Irish College at Paris, where his family had a burse. After ordination, Conwell served in the Archdiocese of Armagh, Ireland, where he was vicar-general for 21 years. Normally he would have succeeded to that see, but the veto question, involving the alleged right of the civil government to veto papal appointments, was then being debated in Ireland. To ensure its choice for so crucial a post, the Holy See chose Dr. Patrick Curtis, who was uncommitted on this delicate issue. Conwell was offered a see in Madras, India, or that of Philadelphia in the U.S. Evidently unaware of the troubles then rife in Philadelphia, he accepted the latter appointment and was consecrated in London on Sept. 24, 1820.

Unacquainted with conditions in the U.S. and more than 70 years old, Conwell was installed in trustee-ridden Philadelphia, vacant for six years and previously refused by at least three candidates. The new bishop's most immediate problem was with Irish-born Rev. William HOGAN, who had entered Philadelphia without any dimissorial letters and had ingratiated himself with the trustees of St. Mary's Cathedral. When he was suspended, the trustees became his champions and caused a schism that continued even after Hogan, discredited by civil suits, left Philadelphia in August 1824.

Conwell's difficulties with trusteeism were aggravated when he invited back to Philadelphia William HAROLD, OP, whom his predecessor had dismissed for favoring the trustees. When Harold again proved recalcitrant, Conwell suspended him. Finally Rome intervened and had Harold transferred out of the diocese. The aged bishop also erred when he signed the notorious pact of Oct. 9, 1826, yielding to St. Mary's trustees the right of vetoing his appointment of pastors. When the agreement was rejected by both the Congregation for the Propagation of the Faith and Leo XII, the bishop humbly read his retraction in public.

Meanwhile, Conwell had been "invited" to Rome, but, alleging summer heat as an excuse, he did not sail. He was then ordered to Rome by Cardinal Bartolomeo Cappellari, Prefect of Propaganda, who arranged for the doting bishop to reside there permanently. However, the unstable bishop soon returned to the U.S. without permission, thereby incurring an automatic suspension. After the bishops attending the Provincial Council of Baltimore (1829) had interceded for him, Conwell was permitted to stay in Philadelphia, but his coadjutor, Bp. Francis Kenrick, was given full jurisdiction. For some years, the senile prelate made Kenrick's administration difficult, causing anxiety in Philadelphia and Rome. Conwell's last years were spent in total blindness and seclusion.

Bibliography: J. L. J. KIRLIN, *Catholicity in Philadelphia* (Philadelphia 1909). H. J. NOLAN, *The Most Reverend Francis Patrick Kenrick* (Catholic University of America, *Studies in American Church History* 37; Washington 1948). P. W. CAREY, *People, Priests, and Prelates: Ecclesiastical Demoncracy and the Tensions of Trusteeism* (Notre Dame 1987).

[H. J. NOLAN]

COOKE, TERENCE

Seventh archbishop of New York; b. New York City, March 1, 1921; d. there, Oct. 6, 1983. After graduation from St. Benedict's School in the Bronx and Cathedral College (the preparatory seminary of the archdiocese of New York), he entered St. Joseph's Seminary, Dunwoodie, in September of 1940, and was ordained to the priesthood on Dec. 1, 1945, by Francis Cardinal SPELLMAN in St. Patrick's Cathedral.

Immediately after ordination, he was sent to study for a degree in social work, first at the University of Chicago, and then at the National Catholic School of Social Service at the Catholic University of America, with brief assignments in between at St. Athanasius Parish in the Bronx and St. Agatha's Home in Nanuet, New York. Upon his return from Washington with a master's degree in June of 1949, he was assigned to the youth division of Catholic Charities, where he remained for the following four and a half years. From 1950 to 1956 he was also an instructor in the Fordham University School of Social Service. In January of 1954 Father Cooke was appointed procurator of St. Joseph's Seminary, Dunwoodie, a post that brought him into frequent contact with Cardinal Spellman. Three years later, the cardinal called him from Dunwoodie to become his secretary.

From that point on, advancement followed at regular intervals. In June of 1958, he became vice-chancellor; in June of 1961, chancellor; in February of 1965, vicar general; and in September of 1965, auxiliary bishop of New York (on the same day that John T. Maguire became Coadjutor Archbishop of New York without right of succession). The death of Cardinal Spellman on Dec. 2, 1967, touched off widespread speculation about his successor, but few people considered Bishop Cooke a serious contender. When his appointment as archbishop of New York was announced on March 8, 1968, the reaction was one of profound surprise. At the time, he was the youngest of the ten auxiliary bishops of New York and (with the exception of Archbishops HUGHES and CORRIGAN) the youngest ordinary ever appointed to the see.

Cooke assumed his new post during turbulent years of student protests, racial disturbances, and antiwar demonstrations. On April 4, 1968, he was installed as archbishop of New York and named Military Vicar for the Armed Forces. It was the day on which Martin Luther King, Jr., was assassinated in Memphis. That evening Archbishop Cooke left an ecumenical reception in his honor to visit a parish in Harlem and plead for racial peace. One year later, on April 28, 1969, he was elevated to the rank of cardinal, along with 32 other prelates, at one of the largest consistories in history.

Unlike his predecessor, Cardinal Cooke showed little interest in playing a prominent role in national and international affairs. The only important post to which he was elected by his fellow bishops was that of Chairman of the United States Bishops Pro-Life Activities Committee. In his own archdiocese, however, he won a reputation as a capable and energetic administrator with a prodigious memory and an enormous capacity for work. A naturally jovial and optimistic man, with a ready smile and a gift for small talk, he was adept at making friends and mingling easily on social occasions with people of every background and description. Both priests and laity found him approachable and unpretentious. Even during the most difficult years of his administration, at a time of unprecedented challenges to both Church and society, he preferred the ways of quiet diplomacy and persuasion over confrontation.

Years as Archbishop. During his 15 years as archbishop, the Catholic population remained approximately the same (1,800,000), but only because large numbers of Hispanic immigrants replenished the dwindling ranks of middle-class Catholics in New York City. Other statistics indicated a disquieting falling off in religious practice throughout the archdiocese. Between 1967 and 1983 the number of infant baptisms declined from 50,000 per year to 31,000 per year; the number of Church marriages, from 15,000 to 8,200 per year. For the first time in history there was a sharp drop in the number of diocesan priests (from 1,108 in 1967 to 777 in 1983) and an even more abrupt decline in the numbers of women religious (from 8,955 to 5,178) and diocesan seminarians (from 501 to 221).

Under such circumstances, the ambitious expansion programs of earlier eras were hardly feasible. Archbishop Corrigan had established 99 new parishes; Cardinal Spellman, 45; Cardinal Cooke, 4. Prudence now dictated a careful husbanding of available resources, and in meeting this challenge, Cardinal Cooke demonstrated exceptional expertise and a masterful command of the whole administrative structure of the archdiocese. At board meetings of Catholic institutions he regularly astonished bankers and businessmen with his encyclopedic knowledge of financial reports and balance sheets.

One of his first official acts as archbishop was to appoint a blue ribbon commission to study the future of

Catholic education in the archdiocese. The recommendations of this commission led directly to one of his most impressive achievements: the establishment of the Inter-Parish Finance Commission, which uses the surplus funds of more affluent parishes to subsidize churches and schools in disadvantaged neighborhoods. Thanks largely to this cooperative system, only 31 of the 305 Catholic elementary schools were forced to close during the Cooke years, despite a massive decline in enrollment (from 167,000 to 88,000) and the departure of three-quarters of the teaching sisters.

In 1979 Cardinal Cooke announced a major fund-raising campaign, the Cardinal's Archdiocesan Appeal, which proved so successful that it became an annual event. During his administration he also expanded the services of Catholic Charities, consolidated the archdiocesan offices in a new Catholic Center on the east side of Manhattan, established an Office of Pastoral Research, organized the Inner-City Scholarship Fund for needy youngsters, founded the Archdiocesan Catechetical Institute, and opened the St. John Neumann Residence for college-age seminarians. Sensitive to the needs of blacks and Hispanics, he created an Office of Black Catholics, supported the Northeast Center for Hispanics, and appointed the first black and Hispanic auxiliary bishops in the history of the archdiocese. As military vicar for the Armed Forces, he continued Cardinal Spellman's custom of frequent visits to American servicemen throughout the world. He also served as president of the Catholic Near East Welfare Association and took an active interest in the work of the organization.

Late in the summer of 1983, New Yorkers were shocked to hear the news that Cardinal Cooke was terminally ill with cancer. For the previous eight years he had been receiving medical treatment for a lymphoma condition, but in August of 1983 an acute leukemia suddenly aggravated the situation. On Aug. 24, 1983, he informed Pope JOHN PAUL II of his condition, and two days later he revealed the news to the general public. New Yorkers were moved by the announcement. During the next six weeks, as the cardinal remained secluded in his residence preparing for death, his faith and courage made a deep impression on the population of the city. After his death, early on the morning of Oct. 6, 1983, huge crowds filed past his bier, and over 900 priests attended his funeral. An editorial in the New York *Daily News* summarized the feelings of many Catholics and non-Catholics alike: "On Cardinal Cooke's final day a line from Shakespeare seems uniquely appropriate: 'Nothing in his life became him like the leaving of it.' This was a man who showed us all how to pass from time to eternity with courage and grace."

Bibliography: *Catholic New York* (Oct. 6, 1983). *New York Daily News* (Oct. 7, 1983). *New York Times* (Oct. 7, 1983).

[T. J. SHELLEY]

COOPER, JOHN MONTGOMERY

Anthropologist, educator; b. Rockville, MD, Oct. 28, 1881; d. Washington, DC, May 22, 1949. His parents were James Cooper, descendant of English Quakers who settled in Darby, PA, in 1684, and Lillie Tolou, of a Baltimore family of French origin. Cooper was sent from St. Charles College, Catonsville, MD, to the North American College in Rome, where he obtained doctorates in philosophy and theology. Following ordination in 1905, he was assigned to St. Matthew's Cathedral, Washington, DC, and appointed, in 1909, as a part-time instructor at The Catholic University of America. His interest in European archaeology broadened to include cultural anthropology, which later became his dominant intellectual interest. His first technical publication in the field appeared in 1917. After serving the National Catholic War Council during World War I, he became, in 1920, a full-time member of the faculty of Catholic University. There he organized the department of religion and pioneered in the effort to make religion courses correspond to the needs of the laity. Simultaneously, he taught anthropology in the Department of Sociology and advanced in rank as associate professor of sociology (1923) and professor of anthropology (1928). In 1934, he was appointed head of the newly inaugurated Department of Anthropology, the first such department under Catholic auspices in the United States. His reputation as scientist and teacher brought him invitations to serve as visiting professor at the University of California (1938) and the University of New Mexico (1948–49). He served on committees of several national research councils and held office in a number of anthropological societies, notably the American Anthropological Association, of which he was secretary from 1931 to 1937 and president during 1940. He was elevated to the ecclesiastical rank of domestic prelate in 1941.

Although Cooper contributed to social work, religious education, theology, and ethics, he was best known in the United States and abroad for his ethnological monographs and articles based on systematic field research among North American Indians and for his classification of the evidence of the indigenous cultures of South America. He was a principal collaborator with Robert Lowie and others on the *Handbook of South American Indians* (Washington 1949). A bibliography of his works was published in *Primitive Man* 23 (1950) 66–84. Cooper was a founder of the Catholic Anthropological Conference and founder and editor of its periodical, known from 1928 to 1953 as *Primitive Man* and subsequently as the *Anthropological Quarterly,* and of the Publications of the Conference, a series of monographs. He likewise inaugurated and edited the Anthropological Series of The Catholic University of America.

Bibliography: R. FLANNERY, ''John Montgomery Cooper,'' *American Anthropologist* 52 (1950) 64–74. P. H. FURFEY, ''John Montgomery Cooper,'' *Primitive Man* 23 (1950) 49–84. A. MÉTRAUX, ''The Contribution of Rev. Fr. Cooper to South American Ethnography,'' *ibid.* 39–48.

[R. FLANNERY]

COORNHERT, DIRCK VOLKERTSZOON

Dutch engraver, moralist, poet, and playwright; b. Amsterdam, 1522; d. Haarlem, Oct. 29, 1590. Although he was an artist, scientist, and civil servant (secretary to the states of Holland, 1572), he thought of himself as primarily a moralist. He translated Cicero (*De officiis*), Seneca (*De beneficiis*), Boethius (*De consolatione philosophiae*), the *Odyssey,* and Boccaccio's *Decameron* in order to perfect his style, and thus created modern Dutch prose at a time when rhetorical pomposity still held the field. His philosophical ideas were also an innovation: he was neither wedded to the old faith nor converted to the new learning of the Reformers (his motto was *Verkiezen doet verliezen:* preference causes loss), but was rather a protagonist of Christian STOICISM; this is evident in the philosophical and ethical ideas that color his translation of Boethius. His humanist treatise on morality, *Zedekunst dat is Wellevenskunste* (1586, The Art of Morality That Is the Art of Living Well), was the first work on ethics in Western vernacular literature. His thesis was that morality consists in a virtuous life under the guidance of reason. This view, a harbinger of modern individualism, roused the suspicion of his Catholic contemporaries and the enmity of the Calvinists, against whom he wrote many pamphlets. His moralizing leanings are manifest even in his adaptation of the *Odyssey* (*De Dolinghe van Ulysse*), the first Dutch classical epic. He produced some 145 works in verse and prose. His importance lies in his fusion of a rationally justified belief and a discernment acquired by self-knowledge with the old Dutch tradition of serious piety.

Bibliography: *Wercken,* 3 v. (Amsterdam 1630); *Zedekunst dat is wellevenskunste,* ed. B. BECKER (Leiden 1942). T. WEEVERS, *Coornhert's Dolinghe van Ulysse, De eerste Nederlandsche Odyssee* (Groningen 1934). B. BECKER, *Bronnen tot de kennis van het leven en de werken van D. V. Coornhert* (The Hague 1928).

[W. H. BEUKEN]

COPE, MARIANNE

Missionary to HAWAI'I, b. Heppenhein, a village in the German Grand Duchy of Hesse-Darmstadt, 1838; d. Molokai, Hawai'i, 1918, age 80. Two years after Barbara Koob was born in Germany, her family immigrated to Utica, New York. On arrival, they changed their name to Cope. Barbara joined the Sisters of St. Francis (O.S.F.) in Syracuse, New York, in 1862 and took the name in religion, Sister Marianne. After she taught and administered schools in New York, she became administrator of Syracuse's first hospital. Her leadership brought the Geneva Medical College to Syracuse for a successful development of medical practices between the hospital and the college.

Cope became the major superior of the Sisters in Syracuse in 1877. In 1883, after a letter and visit from Father Leonor Fouesnel, emissary from the Kingdom of Hawai'i, Mother Marianne and six sisters from her community went to the Kingdom of Hawai'i that year to work with lepers. Initially she was not sure how long she would remain there because of her responsibilities as the major superior, but she decided to remain permanently until her death. On arrival in 1883, they worked at the Kaka'ako Branch Hospital in O'ahu, where Hansen's disease patients were received and processed for shipment to Moloka'i. Two years later, Mother Marianne and her sisters established the Kapi'olani Home for the daughters of Hansen's disease patients who were quarantined in Moloka'i.

In 1888, Mother Marianne and two sisters, Srs. Leopoldina Burns and Vincentia McCormick accepted Father Damien's invitation to work with Hansen's disease patients on the island of Moloka'i, a ministry they continued after his death. Arriving on Nov. 14, 1888, they took charge of the Bishop Home for Girls in Kalaupapa. From 1888 to 1895, they also managed the Home for Boys at Kalawao that Father Damian had earlier founded. Her indefatigable spirit, unflagging optimism, and self-sacrificing devotion inspired her sisters to cope with the extremely heavy and punishing workload of caring for women and children with Hansen's disease. In 1918, at the age of 80, she passed away and her remains are buried on the grounds of her beloved Bishop Home for Girls, now a national park monument.

Mother Marianne led one of the earliest American Catholic women's congregations to establish missions outside the United States, when she set up homes for women and children with Hansen's disease in the Kingdom of Hawai'i. In doing so, she became the first U.S. Catholic woman missionary to minister to patients with Hansen's disease. She also practiced an ecumenism of good works, saying to her community: ''The charity of the good knows no creed, and is confined to no one placc.''

Bibliography: M. L. HANLEY and O. A. BUSHNELL, *A Song of Pilgrimage and Exile* (Chicago 1980). M. L. HANLEY and O. A. BUS-NELL, *Pilgrimage and Exile: Mother Marianne of Molokai* (Honolulu 1991). E. A. LENK, *Mother Marianne Cope (1838–1918): The Syracuse Franciscan Community and Molokai Lepers* (Ph.D. diss., Syracuse University, 1986).

[A. DRIES]

COPE AND HUMERAL VEIL

The cope is a liturgical cloak of semicircular form reaching to the feet; it is fastened at the breast but open below. Originally a hood was attached to the back, but in the 14th century a shield or decorated flap began to replace it.

Some historians (see Leclercq) hold that the cope was adopted for use in processions from the ancient civil raincoat, a more ample *lacerna* or *paenula*. However, most scholars are of the opinion that the cope came into liturgical use around the 9th century as an adaptation of the monastic choir cloak of the 8th century. It appears that the cope was originally bell-shaped and closed like the CHASUBLE but with openings cut in the front to allow the hands and arms to pass through. Soon the front of the cope was open all the way down and simply fastened at the top. By the end of the 11th century it was the vestment used for all liturgical functions except the Mass, and was worn not only by the officiant but by all the clergy on festive occasions.

There is no strict prescription that the cope be made of silk, but a rich material is in keeping with the solemn use to which the cope is put. Recent times have witnessed a return to attaching a hood to the back rather than a shield, for the former is more dignified. The cope follows the color of the feast.

The humeral veil (shoulder veil) is a long scarf eight to nine feet in length and two to three feet in width, worn over the neck, shoulders, and arms. It was known originally as a sindon and was used already in the 7th century to cover the hands out of reverence when holding sacred objects during liturgical ceremonies. It is still used for this purpose; e.g., the priest holds the monstrance with it when he blesses the people at Benediction. Its color varies with the feast, but white is always used at Benediction.

Bibliography: H. LECLERCQ and E. MOMBERT, *Dictionnaire d'archéologie chrétienne et de liturgie*, ed. F. CABROL, H. LECLERCQ, and H. I. MARROU, 15 v. (Paris 1907–53) 3.1:365–381. J. WAGNER, *Lexikon für Theologie und Kirche*, ed. J. HOFER and K.

Sketch of priest at Benediction of the Blessed Sacrament vested in cope and humeral veil. (The Catholic University of America)

RAHNER, 10 v. (2d, new ed. Freiburg 1957–65) 8:567–568. J. BRAUN, *Die liturgische Gewandung im Occident und Orient* (Freiburg 1907). E. BISHOP, *Liturgica historica* (Oxford 1918; reprint 1962) 260–275. M. RIGHETTI, *Manuale di storia liturgica*, 4 v. (Milan): v.1 (2d ed. 1950) 1:366.

[M. MCCANCE]

COPERNICUS, NICOLAUS

Polish scientist whose heliocentric theory upset the universally accepted notion that the earth was the center of the planetary system, physician, doctor of canon law, authority on money, soldier, and probably at the time of his death an ordained priest; b. Torún (then a Polish city), Feb. 19, 1473; d. Frauenberg, Polish Prussia, May 24, 1543. His father, also Nicolaus, was a prosperous merchant and municipal official of Torún. His mother, Barbara, was a sister of Lucas Watzelrode, who became bishop of Ermland in 1489.

Nicolaus Copernicus.

Education. Copernicus's early education was received at St. John's School in Torún, supplemented at home by the study of Latin and Greek. His parents died before he was 12 and he was entrusted to his uncle, the bishop. Copernicus attended the cathedral school at Wloclawek. In 1491, he matriculated at the University of Cracow, studying under Albert of Brudzewo.

Copernicus registered at the University of Bologna in 1496. Here, besides attending classes in canon law, he continued his astronomical studies under Dominicus Maria Novara. Through the instrumentality of Novara, Copernicus was named professor at the University of Rome in 1499. In 1501 Copernicus went north to Ermland for his formal installation as a canon in Frauenberg. He returned to Italy a few months later to finish his studies in medicine at the University of Padua. During this time he earned his doctor's degree in medicine from the University of Padua and in canon law from the University of Ferrara. Between 1504 and 1506 Copernicus returned to Frauenberg, and he never left the province of Ermland again.

He was not only physician and personal secretary to his uncle, but as canon of the cathedral he performed his part in divine service, and as doctor he ministered to the needs of his clerical friends and to the poor. The Teutonic

Order, under Albert of Hohenzollern, fomented disorders in Ermland. Copernicus, commissioned by the Cathedral Chapter, wrote a complaint to the king on July 22, 1516. When a war did break out with the TEUTONIC KNIGHTS in 1520, Copernicus became commander in chief of the defenses of Ermland. From the fortified but oppressed city of Allenstein he ably and successfully directed the defense.

Copernicus was chosen to be administrator of all Church property in Ermland. In connection with the currency reform of Ermland and neighboring provinces (1519), Copernicus wrote a treatise on coinage in which he formulated a theory that antedates by 40 years Gresham's law on the behavior of debased currency. As administrator he compiled a sliding scale of ceiling prices for bread based on the varying local prices of grain. He also normalized the weights and measures throughout the area under his jurisdiction.

The Heliocentric Theory. All the accomplishments of Copernicus as Churchman, physician, economist, and soldier, great as they were, are eclipsed by his work as an astronomer. The vastness of the mathematical problem in the heliocentric system as conceived by Copernicus required an unusual intellect. But in Copernicus intellect was sustained by moral heroism that, in humble pursuit of truth, dared to attack the problem and to challenge the scientific tradition of centuries, even though it was supported by the universal Church of which he was a loyal member. The greatness of Copernicus consists in his having framed and developed a new theory, not in his having provided astronomy with new facts. His system is based entirely on data then available, chiefly on that of PTOLEMY.

The *Letter Against Werner* and the *Commentariolus* are the minor astronomical works of Copernicus. The former is a critical essay on Werner's *De motu octavae spaericae tractatus primo*. Manuscript copies of this letter circulated for a time. The date of the *Commentariolus* cannot be determined. It expounds a heliocentric system independent of that in Copernicus's later work. It was never printed during his lifetime, but a manuscript copy found in Vienna was published by Maximilian Curtze (1878). The trigonometric portion of the great astronomical work of Copernicus was printed under the title *De lateribus et angulus triangulorum* at Wittenberg by Johann Luft (1542). The year 1543 witnessed the appearance of Copernicus's great work *De revolutionibus orbium coelestium*. This first edition was printed at Nüremberg. Other editions are: Basle (1566), Amsterdam (1567), Warsaw (1854) and Torún (1873).

Even though Copernicus persistently and obstinately opposed the publication of his works, he made no secret of his views. The *Commentariolus* seems to have circulated fairly widely. A member of the Roman Curia, Cardinal Nikolaus von Schönberg, wrote (1536) suggesting that he publish his discoveries. Tiedmann Giese, bishop of Kulm, insisted for a long time on publication, representing it to Copernicus as his duty to science and mankind. But when the young Lutheran scholar, George Joachim von Lauchen, universally known as Rheticus, desiring to learn more about the new theories that were slowly making their way into Central Europe, resigned his chair of mathematics at the University of Wittenberg and journeyed to Poland, he won the confidence and sympathy of Copernicus, who released his manuscripts to him and permitted a summary of their contents to be made. The summary took the form of a letter to the teacher of Rheticus, Johann Schöner. Schöner immediately had the letter printed in Danzig (1540). The letter was included in the second, fourth, and fifth editions of *De revolutionibus*. It was also included in the 1596 and 1621 editions of KEPLER's *Mysterium cosmographicum*. The publication of this summary made the withholding of *De revolutionibus* impossible. After he had supervised the publication of the trigonometric portion of this book at Nüremberg (1542), Rheticus was appointed professor at the University of Leipzig. He left the supervision of the printing of *De revolutionibus* to Andreas OSIANDER, a Lutheran theologian. Copernicus took very few, if any, precautions to disguise the directness of his views. To him it had been an error of the mathematicians to have made the earth the center of the world and the celestial movements. He joined to his book the letter he had received from Cardinal Schönberg some years before. He dedicated his work to Pope Paul III. In his own very noble foreword he insists upon the rights of science and philosophy. The boldness of Copernicus troubled Osiander. He replaced the introductory letter of Copernicus with an anonymous *Praefatiuncula* in which he put the whole theory on a hypothetical level. Copernicus never knew that his own introductory letter had been withheld from the first edition of his book, for he received the printed copy only a few hours before his death. The second edition (1566) also carried Osiander's preface. It was 60 years before Osiander's breach of confidence and his forgery became generally known.

The authority of the Bible, interpreted historically, weighed heavily against the heliocentric system and prevented its universal recognition until the 18th century. But in the time of Copernicus, and until GALILEO, and DESCARTES, the opposition of the Aristotelian philosophy and physics was at least as potent. In 1616 the Congregation of the Index forbade the reading of *De revolutionibus* until corrected. Thereupon nine sentences representing the heliocentric system as certain were changed. The complete and final vindication of Copernicus came when, in 1758, his work disappeared from the revised Index of Benedict XIV.

Bibliography: *Three Copernican Treatises,* ed. and tr. E. ROSEN (2d ed. rev. Gloucester, Mass. 1961). A. ARMITAGE, *Copernicus, the Founder of Modern Astronomy* (London 1957). H. BUTTERFIELD, *The Origins of Modern Science, 1300–1800* (New York 1960). A. C. CROMBIE, *Augustine to Galileo: The History of Science* A.D. *400–1650* (Cambridge, Mass. 1953). L. A. BIRKENMAJER, *Nikolaj Kopernik* (Krakow 1923); *Stromata Copernicana* (Krakow 1924). J. L. E. DRYER, *History of the Planetary Systems from Thales to Kepler* (Cambridge, Eng. 1906). T. S. KUHN, *Copernican Revolution* (Toronto 1959). L. PROWE, *Nicolaus Coppernicus,* 2 v. (Berlin 1883–84). M. C. ZELLER, *The Development of Trigonometry from Regiomontanus to Pitiscus* (Joliet, Ill. 1946). P. GASSENDI, *Vita Epicuri . . . Copernici . . . ,* in *Opera Omnia,* 6 v. (Paris 1658–75) 5.2.

[M. C. ZELLER]

COPLESTON, FREDERICK C.

Philosopher; b. near Taunton, Somerset, England, 1907; educated at Marlborough College (1920–25) and St. John's College, Oxford, graduating in classics and philosophy in 1929; became Catholic in 1925; entered the Society of Jesus in 1930; ordained priest in 1937; d. 1994.

Frederick Copleston was born into a very old West Country family with strong roots in the Indian Civil Service, in which his father was a senior judge, and in the Church of England, in which two of his ancestors had served as bishops. His move to the Roman Church led to his leaving school and to a certain amount of disapproval from his family.

Copleston's early years at Oxford, by his own account, were spent in acclimatizing himself to his new religious surroundings rather than in diligent study of the classics. His interest in philosophy was awakened, not by the modern developments in Oxford philosophy in the 1920s, but by those teachers who were still influenced by Hegel. Upon leaving Oxford, Copleston joined the Diocese of Clifton, in which Taunton lay, to study for the priesthood, but after a year in the seminary he decided to become a Jesuit.

He completed his studies for the priesthood without interruption at Heythrop College in Oxfordshire, which at that time was the main Jesuit house of studies in Britain. He abandoned plans to do a doctorate at the Gregorian University when war broke out in 1939. Instead, Copleston was appointed to lecture at Heythrop in the history of philosophy, which he continued to do until 1970. The college in Oxfordshire was closed then, and a new Heythrop College was founded by royal charter as a college of the University of London. Copleston became its first principal, a post which he held until his retirement in 1975. He continued to write and to lecture until within a year or two of his death.

His main achievement is his monumental *History of Philosophy*, whose nine volumes appeared between 1946 and 1975. A projected tenth volume on Russian philosophy was in fact published separately as *Philosophy in Russia: From Herzen to Lenin and Berdyaev* in 1986. The *History* was, at least at its inception, intended to be a three-volume work that would provide seminarians and especially his Jesuit students with a more accurate and broad-based view of the subject than was available in the rather impoverished and apologetically slanted manuals commonly in use at the time. However, the project grew in scope and in depth as it progressed. Copleston remained pleased with most of it, though in later years he considered the first volume "deplorable" and wished that he had time to rewrite it. Yet, the *History* as a whole is a model of clarity, objectivity, and scholarly accuracy, unsurpassed in its accessibility and balance. It has been translated into Italian, French, Spanish, Japanese, and Chinese.

Copleston's own philosophical interests are more readily found in the many other volumes that appeared over the 45 or so years of his teaching and writing career. His first books were monographs on Nietzsche (written to dissociate Nietzsche from the Nazis) and Schopenhauer; in 1956 he published a collection of essays, *Contemporary Philosophy,* in which he commented on various trends both in analytic and continental philosophy; *A History of Medieval Philosophy* (1972) functioned in part as a revision of volume 2 of the *History,* but it is evidence of his continuing interest, first avowed in his Oxford days, in metaphysics. Metaphysics received more direct and personal expression in his 1979 and 1980 Gifford Lectures at the University of Aberdeen, published as *Religion and the One.* The other topic that fascinated him was the relationship between the activity of philosophizing and the cultures in which that activity was variously pursued. He would have liked to have done a full-length study along those lines, but he came to believe that it was simply too large, though some of his thoughts on the topic can be found in his *Philosophy and Cultures,* a set of lectures he gave in Oxford in 1978.

Copleston was much in demand as a lecturer and broadcaster. He had a famous, if inconclusive, radio debate on the existence of God with Bertrand Russell in 1948 and made several appearances on radio and television with A. J. Ayer, who became a good friend. Despite, or perhaps even because of, the radical difference in their philosophical views, they both took the greatest pleasure in sparring with one another. Copleston was influential in dispelling the widespread prejudice that Catholics, and especially Catholic priests, cannot be expected to engage in intellectually honest philosophical debate. In 1970 he was elected a Fellow of the British Academy.

Bibliography: A full bibliography of all Copleston's books, articles, and reviews up to 1987 was compiled by Michael J. Walsh and published in the *Heythrop Journal* XXVIII (1987), 418–38.

[G. J. HUGHES]

COPTIC CHRISTIANITY

COPTIC ORTHODOX CHURCH (ORIENTAL ORTHODOX)

"Coptic" is ultimately derived from the Greek word Αἴγυπτος. The name is applied to the body of Egyptian Christians historically subject to the patriarch of Alexandria.

The patriarch of Alexandria at the time of the Council of CHALCEDON was DIOSCORUS (*c.* 454), who defended the MONOPHYSITE teaching, believing himself to be defending the orthodox teaching of St. CYRIL. When he refused to recant, Dioscorus was deposed from his patriarchal throne and died in exile. The vast majority of the Egyptian faithful looked upon their disgraced patriarch as a martyr to the true faith. The Council of Chalcedon was rejected.

The Byzantine emperors favored the decrees of Chalcedon, and their followers in Egypt were promptly labeled "King's followers," i.e., MELKITES. At times the Byzantine emperors maintained a Melkite on the Alexandrian patriarchal throne, though generally a Non-Chalcedonian patriarch occupied it. The desire for national and ecclesiastical autonomy played no small part in this struggle for ascendancy, the native Christian Egyptians firmly believing that they were defending the age-old rights of their venerable see against the inroads of the upstart, Constantinople. The century following the Council of Chalcedon was marked in Egypt by a religious civil war.

After Chalcedon, the bishops who grouped around Dioscorus, refused to recognize Proterius, the Chalcedonian Patriarch. After the death of Dioscorus, they elected Timotheus Aelurus, i.e., "the Cat." He, at the head of the rebels, invaded the cathedral where Proterius was celebrating the offices of Holy Week, slaughtered the patriarch as he hid in the baptistery, and occupied the vacant see. However, being excommunicated, he was sent first to Gangres and then Chersone, and was replaced by the Melkite Timotheus Salofaciakos, "the White," in 460. Timotheus could make no progress in bringing about peace, for he was harassed by the Anti-Chalcedonians, who were supported by the civil authorities.

Meanwhile, Timotheus Aelurus, having committed suicide (or so it was believed), was replaced by Peter Mongus, who at the death of Timotheus Salofaciakos became the sole patriarch.

John Talaya (d. 490) was recognized by the pope, but not by Acacius, the Ecumenical Patriarch of Constantinople. The divisions among the Copts led the Emperor ZENO in 482 to issue his HENOTIKON, hoping thus to unify the parties; but his attempts met with failure. Peter Mongus then occupied the See of Alexandria and was upheld by the emperor while John Talaya fled into exile to Rome. He died in Italy; soon after, Accius and Peter Mongus also died. However, the civil authorities continued to create trouble for one party or the other, depending on where their loyalties lay.

Finally, for the sake of peace, Emperor Justin II in 567 recognized two patriarchs of Alexandria: one Melkite, the other Non-Chalcedonian. From that day, the Coptic Church, embracing almost the entire native Egyptian population, became identified with the Non-Chalcedonian faction; its liturgy thenceforth was a modified form of the Alexandrian rite (*see* COPTIC LITURGY); and its liturgical language until the time of the Arab conquerors was Coptic. The Melkites followed Constantinople and gradually, by the 12th century, dropped their Alexandrian ecclesial and liturgical usages for Byzantine usages.

Before the Arab Conquest. St. JOHN THE ALMSGIVER became the Melkite patriarch in 610; by his charity he succeeded in partly unifying the population. Then came the Arab invasion; and although the Copts were glad to have done with the Byzantine Romans, who had repeatedly subjected the country to fire and the sword, their patriarch was forced to flee to Cyprus, where he died.

Benjamin, the Jacobite patriarch, occupied the See of St. Mark during the first Arab conquest. Having fled in turn, he did not reappear until the departure of the Romans in 644, having obtained a promise of safety from General Amrou. In 662, the year of his death, he became the leader of all the Egyptian Christians.

Cyrus, called by the Arabs *El Moukaukas,* the monothelite patriarch at the time, betrayed the Romans and delivered to the Arabs the great fortress of Babylon, the key to Upper Egypt.

Arab Period. Even before the Arab conquest, the Copts had tried several times to free themselves from Byzantine domination. They were bitter over the Council of Chalcedon, regarding it as the beginning of all their troubles.

Meanwhile Amrou was very generous to the Non-Chalcedonian patriarch, whom he recognized as the sole legitimate incumbent; he showed himself a sincere friend and ally during the conquest of Libya. But his tolerance, fraternity, and collaboration lasted only until the cost of the war depleted the treasury; then the Copts found themselves subject to taxes and tribute. Even the clergy and religious were not exempt. The Christians had to choose taxes, tribute, and possibly death . . . or Islam. So it was that Christians embraced Islam en masse, and many religious left their monasteries, which eventually fell to ruin.

Although all the caliphs did not manifest the same ferocity, none of them exempted the Copts from the onerous burden of tribute. Among these rulers was Abd'Allah ibn Marwan, who threw the Patriarch Alexandros II into prison and confiscated all his goods. Abd'el Malek forbade (705) the use of the Coptic language; from then on the Copts gradually lost their ancient tongue.

Assama ibn Zeid showed himself intransigent concerning tribute and taxes. He had churches demolished, crosses and icons smashed. The Copts revolted, but the rebellion was drowned in blood. North of the Delta, the Copts called *Bashmouri* continued to struggle ferociously for several years, but were finally conquered and either massacred or sold as slaves by the army of Ma'moun. The Copts never recovered from this defeat; they lost all prestige and have since then remained a minority among the population.

In 837, under Patriarch Eusebius, the Caliph El-Moutawakel ala Allah ordered Christians to wear a black turban and sash, to ride donkeys with wooden saddles, and to wear five-pound crosses around their necks. He had all new churches demolished and forbade Christian education and the solemn celebration of feasts.

The Fatimite caliphs and the Mamelukes were no less cruel. The worst was El-Hakem biamr Allah, who believed himself sent by God to rid the world of the Christian religion, which he considered pagan and polytheistic. He reportedly destroyed more than 30,000 churches and chapels, including the Holy Sepulcher in Jerusalem. This sacrilege was one of the causes of the Crusades. The Christians again had to choose between Islam and death, and many emigrated.

Outstanding Figures. Despite the ferocity of these continual persecutions, there were a number of great individuals among the Copts at this period. Severus ibn El Moukafa', Bishop of Ashmounein, wrote in Coptic the history of the patriarchs, basing himself on Eusebius of Caesarea; the work was completed by the Patriarch Michael in 1243.

Cyril III, surnamed Ibn Loklok (1235–43), was the author of the collection of canons that bears his name. These canons forbid simony and the acceptance of donations by judges; regulate marriage, inheritance, and wills; call for an annual synod of all the bishops on the third Sunday after Pentecost; forbid acceptance of accusations against a bishop or a religious without a previous investigation; declare the immunity of clerics, who are not to be judged by the laity; and forbid the suspension of bishops without three previous warnings.

The "Sons of Assal" were three brothers remarkable for their wisdom, zeal, piety, and influence with the Caliph. (1) Assad Abou-el-Farag Hebat-Allah was the author of several works on Scripture. (2) Saify Abi-el-Fadl el-Amgad compiled the canons known by his name (Ibn al-Assal), which govern the Coptic Church. (3) El mou'tamen ibn Ishaq composed a résumé for the teaching of the Coptic language, homilies for the feast of Our Lord, and an Arabic-Coptic dictionary.

Ibn Kabar (1319), secretary of Kohn-el-Dine Bibars El Mansour, abandoned his position to serve as a priest of the Moalaka Cathedral of Old Cairo, a church that had formerly served for the coronation of the patriarchs after their transfer to Cairo. He was a learned man and a physician, who composed homilies, sermons, and such works as *The Great Ladder* (Rome 1644) and *The Lamp of the Darkness,* an encyclopedia of ecclesiastical and liturgical knowledge. As an author he is known by the name El Kiss-el-Fadel, Shams-el-Rivaasa Abou El-Baraket ibn Kabar.

The Melkite faction of the Coptic Church was represented at the Council of Constantinople in 640, and likewise at the Seventh Council in 787, against the iconoclasts. At the time of Photius, in 1054, after the Great Schism, the Melkite Copts joined the Jacobites.

Turkish Period. The Turkish conquest of 1517 gave the Copts no respite. They were again hunted down without pity. Some scattered, and others were massacred. The Coptic Church suffered tremendously during this period.

18th Century Developments. The Copts by 1700 had lost almost all influence, especially in Cairo, although they were found in large numbers in Assiout and its environs, and also near Aswan. There were about 100,000 Oriental Orthodox Copts in a population of three million; they were divided into 12 dioceses, mostly in Upper Egypt, whereas, it is claimed, there had been 70 at the time of the Arab conquest. The few religious lived in four or five dilapidated monasteries. As for the priests, they had all married and were engrossed in making a living rather than in caring for souls. Their ignorance was abysmal, but they were pious and attached to the faith. However, religion, for them, had become reduced to prayer and fasting. The Turks despised them and considered them even lower on the social scale than they did the Jews.

And yet, during this period, several great Copts left their mark on history: Jacob Hanna (1745–1801), surnamed "the General," shone during the French conquest by his courage and victories against the Turks. He died at sea, after the departure of the French, having requested voluntary exile. Ibrahim El-Gohari (d. 1797) and Guiguis El-Gohari, his brother, succeeded in gaining the sympathy of the governor, Mohammed Aly, who revived the prestige of the Copts by retaining the services of Guiguis, and later of El-moalem Ghaly. Peter VII, known as El-Gawly, was the first patriarch consecrated and crowned in the church of Ezbekiyah. He himself later consecrated 25 bishops for the different dioceses and was the first to send a bishop to the Sudan. Cyril IV (1854–62) was called "the Reformer." He founded Coptic schools and the first school for girls, bought a printing plant for Coptic liturgical books, and lived in friendship with all the religious leaders. Demetrius II (1862–74) rejected the invitation of Pope Pius IX to attend Vatican Council I. Under the pontificate of Cyril V (1874–1927) the first religious tribunal (Maglis Melli) was erected. Its members did not agree with the patriarch, and the Khedive was forced to intervene and define their powers in 1883. The Tewfick society, which cared for the goods of the patriarchate, was instituted at this time.

In 1911, the Copts, feeling more powerful, met in a synod at Assiout and demanded their civil and religious rights. (1) The Christian religion should be taught to Christians in all schools. (2) Christian ecclesiastical tribunals should be subsidized by the state in the same manner as were the Muslim. (3) Sunday should be a free day for all Christian employees of the state. (4) Christians should have the right to promotion in all occupations. These decisions remained a dead letter, but they gave impetus to such Coptic works as schools, printing plants, and newspapers.

Throughout the 20th century, the Coptic Church was subjected to varying degrees of persecution. The rise of Islamic fundamentalism in Egypt caused much problems as Islamic fundamentalists attacked churches and harassed Christians. The Egyptian government was accused by Coptic Christians of discrimination at all levels. From 1981–1985, the Egyptian President Anwar Sadat placed Pope Shenouda III of the Coptic Church under house arrest. Notwithstanding these harassments, the Coptic Church has grown slowly but steadily. By the end of 2000, membership was estimated at about eight million, a figure many experts considered to be an undercount.

Canonical Sources. The Oriental Orthodox hierarchical lineage was begun in 567 with the elevation of Patriarch Peter of Alexandria. From that time on, there has been a continuous line of Coptic Oriental Orthodox bishops. However, they were constantly persecuted by the Byzantine emperors and from 639 by the Arab Muslims. The Copts accepted the early Church canonical documents common to all churches before the Council of Chalcedon. These included the pseudoapostolic writings such as the *Canons of the Holy Apostles,* the *Didascalia,* and the *Testamentum Domini Nostri Jesu Christi.* All of the canons of the Ecumenical Councils of NICAEA I (324), CONSTANTINOPLE I (381), and EPHESUS (431) were accepted. St. Athanasius had published the canons of the local Council of Sardis in 346 and accepted the canons from five other local synods of the East during the 4th century, i.e., Ancyra, Neocaesarea, Antioch, Gangres, and Laodicea. Other canonical sources were the recorded decisions of various bishops of Egypt during the 5th and 6th centuries. The most important collection is attributed to the Patriarch Timothy (381–384), who treated in 56 canons chiefly the liturgy and Sacraments.

Medieval Canonical Sources. Egypt's conquest by the Arabs had a double consequence for the Coptic Church. Since Muslim authority gradually recognized the Copts as a nation and permitted their religious leaders to judge their civil cases, they were forced to develop a code of civil law. Second, the Arab language began to supplant the dead language of Coptic, which explains how the translations of many Arabic canonical sources soon found their way into Coptic canonical sources. Christodoulos, Coptic Patriarch of Alexandria from 1047 to 1077, promulgated 31 canons that touched mostly ritual questions, administration of the Sacraments, and fasting customs. Babril II Ibn (1131–45) collected the most important series of canonical texts. One series touches regulations for the liturgical services in the Alexandrian churches; a second looks to the whole Coptic Church. At this time Arabic was substituted for Coptic, as seen in the nomocanon collection of Michael, Bishop of Damiette (d. c. 1180). The 13th century marked a literary renaissance in Egypt. Patriarch Cyril III ibn Laklak helped in bringing about the definitive nomocanons for the Coptic Church. He requested the priest Abul Fadail ibn Al Assal to compose in 1236 his *Collection of Canons (Kital al qawanin),* which contains the ecclesiastical canons of all the former Coptic sources as well as the civil law up to that time. Also deserving mention is Abul Barakat ibn Kabar for his *Lamp of Darkness,* which is an encyclopedia of Coptic canonical sources.

COPTIC CATHOLIC CHURCH (EASTERN CATHOLIC)

The first formal attempt to effect a union between the Copts and the See of Rome took place at the Council of FLORENCE (1439), the representative of the Coptic Church, in the name of the patriarch, signed the document of communion with Rome on Feb. 4, 1442. However, this act was not ratified by the church leaders in Egypt, and nothing came out of it.

At the end of the 16th century, the Holy See erected a vicariate apostolic for the Coptic Church under control of the Franciscans. At the same time, the Roman College of the Propagation of the Faith opened its doors to the Copts. Among its students were the seminarians Abou-el-Keir Bicharah, and Raphael el Toukhy. The latter had the Coptic liturgical books reprinted at Rome and composed a Coptic-Arabic dictionary in 1746.

Catholic Coptic Patriarchate. Efforts to reestablish unity among the three Christian Churches of Egypt—namely, the Oriental Orthodox Copts, the Byzantine Orthodox, and the Eastern Catholic Copts—have enjoyed little success through history. When, however, in 1741, the Coptic Patriarch of Jerusalem, Athanasius, recognized papal primacy, he was placed over the Coptic Catholics in Egypt, numbering at the time no more than 2,000. It was the first breath of the resurrecting Coptic Catholic Church, but Athanasius was not allowed to set foot in Egypt.

In the 19th Century, Eastern Catholicism was encouraged by Mohammed Aly, thanks to Prime Minister El-Moa'lem Ghaly, himself an Eastern Catholic Copt. The Holy See appointed as bishops Theodoros Abou-Karem in 1815, Maximos Gayed (apostolic administrator) in 1824, Athanasios Khousam in 1834, and Aghapios Bichay in 1866. In 1895 Leo XIII erected the Coptic Catholic Patriarchate and in 1899 appointed Cyril Makraios as Patriarch of the Catholic Copts. He was deposed in 1910 as a result of his having fallen into schism, but he submitted to Rome in 1921. However, the Catholic patriarchal see remained vacant from 1910 until 1947, when Pius XII named as patriarch Mark Khouzam, the patriarchal administrator, who died Feb. 2, 1958. His successor was his Beatitude Stephanos I Sidarous.

Coptic Catholics are found mainly in upper Egypt. The Coptic Catholic Patriarch, styled ''Patriarch of Alexandria of the Copts'' resides in Cairo.

Bibliography: MAKRIZI, *Geschichte der Copten,* ed. H. F. WUSTENFELD (Göttingen 1845), text in Arabic. J. MASPERO, *Histoire des patriarches d'Alexandrie* (Paris 1923). A. J. BUTLER, *The Arab Conquest of Egypt and the Last 30 Years of the Roman Dominion* (Oxford 1902); *The Ancient Coptic Churches of Egypt,* 2 v. (Oxford 1884). E. RENAUDOT, *Historia patriarcharum Alexandrinorum Jacobitarum* (Paris 1713). C. MACAIRE, *Histoire de l'Èglise d'Alexandrie* (Cairo 1894). J. TAGHER, *Aqbāt wa-Muslimūn* (Cairo 1951), Copts and Muslims. IBN AL 'ASSAL, *Kitâb al Qawanin,* ed. G. F. 'AOUWAD (1st ed. Cairo 1908). E. L. BUTCHER, *The Story of the Church of Egypt,* 2 v. (London 1897). W. RIEDEL, *Die Kirchenrechtsquellen des Patriarchats Alexandrien* (Leipzig 1900). F. J. CÖLN, ''The Nomocanonical Literature of the Copto-Arabic

Pope Shenouda III (center), head of the Egyptian Coptic Orthodox Church, blessing the congregation with incense during midnight Christmas Mass. (AP/Wide World Photos)

Church of Alexandria,'' *Ecclesiastical Review* 56 (1917) 113–141. R. ROBERSON, *The Eastern Christian Churches: A Brief Survey*, 6th ed (Rome 1999).

[A. H. SCANDAR/EDS]

COPTIC LITURGY

The Coptic liturgical forms, derived from the original Greek liturgy of Alexandria, have undergone much influence from monastic and Syrian circles. This article treats the Eucharistic Liturgy, buildings, vestments, Sacraments, and the Divine Office.

Eucharistic Liturgy. The Coptic Liturgy may be divided into two principal parts: the pre-Anaphora and the Anaphora. The pre-Anaphora includes a rite of preparation at which the gifts of bread and wine are made ready and then actually offered, and the reading service comprising the Epistle, the Trisagion, the Gospel, and various prayers of petition, followed by a profession of faith (the Nicene Creed in the plural form, i.e., ''We believe''). The Anaphora is divided into the Sacrifice Action and the Communion service. In the former are contained a prayer for peace, the Preface, Sanctus, Consecration, ANAMNESIS, and reading of the DIPTYCHS together with the Ostension, a ceremony in which the celebrant turns toward the congregation and points with his left hand to the Sacred Species as he imparts with his right hand the blessing of the Holy Gifts on the assembled faithful. The Communion service opens with a consignation: the celebrant dips his right index finger into the chalice and then moistens the Host with the Precious Blood, tracing upon it the form of a cross. Then follow the Fraction, the Lord's Prayer, an Elevation; the ceremony continues with a second consignation, the commingling of the two Species, a second Elevation, the Communion by the priest and the faithful, thanksgiving prayers, and a final blessing bringing the entire Liturgy to a close.

In general the Coptic Liturgy is a form of the original Liturgy of Alexandria. There are three Anaphoras of which that ''of St. Basil'' is the most frequently used. The rite of preparation used in the Coptic Liturgy is an importation from the Byzantine, no such ceremony being found in the early Alexandrian. Throughout the service incense is used profusely. Cymbals, triangles, and flutes are commonly used to set the rhythm of the chant, the congregation taking a very active part in the whole Liturgy. For some of the prayers, the celebrant holds small veils on his extended hands. After the offering of the gifts at the pre-Anaphora, the priest carries the bread, wrapped in a veil, around the altar, accompanied by a server carrying the wine. Importance is attached to the many veils used throughout the Liturgy as manifestations of reverence. Before receiving Communion, the priest kisses the consecrated bread. Before distributing Communion, the priest blesses the congregation with the consecrated Species saying at the same time ''Holy Things for the Holy.'' Arabic is used for the most part in the Divine Liturgy, though a few of the more familiar prayers, such as the Creed and the Lord's Prayer, may be said in Coptic. Remnants of the early Greek can still be found in the Trisagion and some of the shorter directives given by the deacon together with the short responses of the faithful.

Buildings. The older Coptic churches, rectangular in form, differ from the normal Christian church in that they have little to mark them off, exteriorly, as church edifices—a relic of the days of persecution. The interior, devoid of chairs and benches, is sometimes divided by three screens into four sections (sanctuary, choir, nave, narthex), though many have but one screen, often of open latticework, to set off the sanctuary.

Vestments. Except for the chasuble, which is open down the front like a cope, the vestments of the Copts are similar to the Byzantine vestments. Most of the altar vessels also are Byzantine in style. Ripidia, metal liturgical fans, are carried in procession and a Coptic hand-cross, having no corpus, is used to give the blessings during the Mass. Altar breads are leavened, thick, and round. Several veils, large and small, are used in the ceremony to cover the Holy Gifts, and at times, the hands of the celebrant.

Sacraments. Among the Copts, Baptism is a lengthy ceremony involving many prayers, many anointings, and professions of faith. Chrismation immediately follows and includes an additional 36 anointings. The Eucharist, as mentioned earlier, may be received in a variety of ways. In the Anointing of the Sick there is a very lengthy service administered by seven priests, though one is sufficient when seven are not available. Each of the seven lights an oil lamp after reading an Epistle, a Gospel, a psalm, and a prayer. This service, called the Office of the Lamp, is by no means restricted to the dying, but may be given to those with ordinary illnesses, and even to the healthy as a preventive. In Holy Orders a ceremony of investiture is climaxed by the imposition of the right hand of the bishop on the head of the ordinand. Two distinct ceremonies make up the administration of the Sacrament of Matrimony: the betrothal, during which the wedding garments are blessed; and the crowning, which includes an anointing on the head and wrists of those about to be wed. The Sacrament of Reconciliation contains a drawn–out formula of absolution, the first part of which is deprecatory in form, followed by a generic accusation of sin on the part of the penitent (''I have sinned.'') accompanied by a request for forgiveness (''Please forgive me.''), to which the priest responds ''God absolves you.''

Divine Office. The Office, called *al-Agbieh,* has seven hours: at sunset, at retiring, at midnight, at dawn, at nine, twelve, and three o'clock. The night service contains three nocturns with 12 psalms and a Gospel in each. The other hours also contain a large number of psalms— the dawn service, 19; each of the others, 12. Since 1906 Arabic has been used in almost the entire Office.

Bibliography: D. ATTWATER, *The Christian Churches of the East,* 2 v. (rev. ed. Milwaukee 1961) v. 1.

[E. E. FINN/EDS.]

COR ARCA LEGEM CONTINENS

An office hymn that was historically used for Lauds on the Feast of the Sacred Heart. Usually dated as an 18th-century composition, it is the work of an unknown author who is thought to have written also the hymns for Vespers and Matins of the same feast. In a series of types or figures, rather than in a fully developed allegory, stanzas one and two of the hymn represent the Sacred Heart as ark, temple, and—with reference to its open wounds— veil ''more profitable than the one rent asunder.'' For the thought and expression of the last three stanzas, the author is indebted to St. Bonaventure's *Vitis mystica* 3.4–6, read as the eighth and ninth lessons of the feast. Throughout the hymn a deeply personal note is blended with a more objective liturgical style.

Bibliography: J. JULIAN, ed., *A Dictionary of Hymnology* (New York 1957) 1:262. H. T. HERNY, *Eucharistica* (Philadelphia 1912) 164, 235. M. BRITT, ed., *The Hymns of the Breviary and Missal* (new ed. New York 1948). J. CONNELLY, *Hymns of the Roman Liturgy* (Westminster, MD 1957) 136–137, Eng. tr. H. LAUSBERG, *Lexikon für Theologie und Kirche*, ed. J. HOFER and K. RAHNER (Freiburg 1957–65) 3:53.

[M. I. J. ROUSSEAU]

CORBAN

Corban is a term used in the Hebrew Bible to signify literally ''the thing brought near,'' or ''offered to God.'' In general the Hebrew word *qorbān* refers to any kind of sacrifice or offering. The word appears in the Old Testament only in Leviticus, Numbers, and Ezekiel.

In the Septuagint the Greek term corban does not appear anywhere, the Hebrew equivalent being translated by a number of other words, such as gift, sacrifice, or offering.

In the New Testament, the term κορβᾶν appears only in Mk 7.11, where Jesus condemns an abuse of the practice of corban. In later Judaism, corban had acquired the meaning of consecration. But in the gradual evolution of the practice the invocation no longer meant that the objects had really been dedicated as an offering to God. The person invoking ''corban'' did not believe himself obliged to give it to the Temple. Rather, the sense is that the goods were now to be considered as if they had been dedicated. Thus, the invocation had the effect of a sacred oath isolating property from any claims, even those of filial piety. It was just such a situation that Our Lord condemned, probably referring to some contemporary *cause célèbre.*

Bibliography: *Encyclopedic Dictionary of the Bible,* tr. and adap. by L. HARTMAN (New York 1963), from A. VAN DEN BORN *Bijbels Woordenboek* 418. R. DE VAUX, *Ancient Israel, Its Life and Institutions,* tr. J. MC HUGH (New York 1961) 417.

[R. J. FLYNN]

CORBEIL, WILLIAM OF

Archbishop of Canterbury; b. Normandy, France, between 1060 and 1080; d. Canterbury, Kent, England, Nov. 21, 1136. First known as a clerk in the service of Ranulf Flambard (d. 1128), Bishop of Durham, he took Flambard's children to the schools at Laon perhaps between 1107 and 1109. He was a friend of ANSELM OF CANTERBURY and in 1116–17 accompanied Anselm's pupil and successor Ralph d'Escures on his disastrous journey to Rome in the attempt to settle the Canterbury-York dispute. In 1118 William became an AUGUSTINIAN CANON at the house of the Holy Trinity, Aldgate, London, possibly as a result of a vision described in the *Dicta Anselmi*. In 1119 he became first prior of St. Osyth's in Essex, and on Feb. 4, 1123, he was elected archbishop of CANTERBURY, to the great distress of the English black monks who had hoped for one of themselves, and after some controversy his election was confirmed by CALLISTUS II on the direct intervention of Emperor HENRY V. He refounded the houses of St. Gregory's, Canterbury, and Minster-in-Sheppey, Kent, and attempted to refound the house of secular canons in Dover as a house of regular canons, but in this he was defeated by the monks of Canterbury. He was appointed papal legate in 1126, held legatine councils in 1127 and 1129, and acted as judge delegate in the dispute concerning the See of LLANDAFF. In his time Canterbury effactually lost its claim to be supreme over YORK, and papal influence made considerable headway in England. He completed and dedicated the cathedral at Canterbury in 1130, and in 1135 he crowned STEPHEN as king. Thirty-three of his *acta* survive.

Bibliography: D. L. BETHELL, *The Archiepiscopate of William of Corbeil 1123–1136* (unpub. diss. Bodleian Library, Oxford). T. F. TOUT, *The Dictionary of National Biography from the Earliest Times to 1900,* 4:1120–23. K. LEYSER, "England and the Empire in the Early Twelfth Century," *Transactions of the Royal Historical Society,* ser. 5, 10 (1960) 61–85.

[D. L. BETHELL]

CORBIE, ABBEY OF

Also known as *Corbeia,* often confused with the daughter abbey *Corbeia nova* (Korvey, Saxony), abbey in northern France near Amiens. Founded by St. BATHILDIS, widow of Chlothar II, it was set up under the Benedictine Rule by monks from LUXEUIL, which had been founded by the Irish monk St. COLUMBAN. It reached its greatest fame in the 8th and 9th centuries and declined in the 16th. Taken over by MAURISTS in 1618, it was suppressed in 1790 after an existence of more than 1,100 years.

The abbey was renowned chiefly for its scriptorium, library, and school. Its SCRIPTORIUM contributed much to the movement away from the crabbed Merovingian hands into a clear and simple Carolingian script. In fact, it produced the first truly Carolingian writing during the abbacy of Maurdramnus (772–780). This shows traces of its Irish-Luxeuil background in its Insular *y* and perhaps in the heavy knobs in front of *f* and *s*. Among other Corbie types of writing was that called *ab* from the shapes of these letters.

Particularly prominent in the 9th century were Abbots ADALARD, who founded Korvey, and WALA. Their pupil PASCHASIUS RADBERTUS was a leading theologian. On request he wrote a commentary on St. Matthew's Gospel for the school. His disciple RATRAMNUS became famous chiefly by opposing Radbertus's views on the Eucharist (*see* EUCHARISTIC CONTROVERSIES). ANSGAR went to Scandinavia as a missionary. Indications are that from the 8th century, Corbie was much concerned with the seven liberal arts and caused the spread of various works, e.g., on surveying for the teaching of geometry. Possibly Corbie served as a bridge between antiquity and the modern world by preserving some of the classics.

The important library was transferred by the Maurists to SAINT-GERMAIN-DES-PRÉS in 1624. After 1790 about 20 valuable MSS came into the hands of the Russian ambassador and are now in Leningrad. The rest are chiefly in the collections of Bibliothèque Nationale, Paris, and the Amiens city library.

Bibliography: L. H. COTTINEAU, *Répertoire topobibliographique des abbayes et prieurés,* 2 v. (Mâcon 1935–39) 1:868–870. H. PELTIER, *Dictionnaire d'histoire et de géographie ecclésiastiques,* ed. A. BAUDRILLART et al. (Paris 1912–) 13:809–824. L. V. DELISLE, *Le Cabinet des manuscrits de la Bibliothèque nationale,* 3 v. (Paris 1868–81) 2:104–141. *Catalogue général des manuscrits des Bibliothèques publiques de France, Départements,* ed. U. L. L. ROBERT, v.19, E. COYECQUE, *Amiens* (Paris 1893). P. LAUER, "La Réforme carolingienne de l'écriture latine et l'école calligraphique de Corbie," *Mémoires présentés par divers savants à l'Académie des Inscriptions et Belles-Lettres* 13 (1924) 417–440. O. A. D. ROZHDESTVENSKAIA, *Histoire de l'atelier graphique de Corbie de 651 à 830 reflétée dans les Corbeienses Leninopolitani* (Leningrad 1934). L. W. JONES, "Scriptorium at Corbie," *Speculum. A Journal of Mediaeval Studies* 22 (1947) 191–204, 375–394. B. L. ULLMAN, "Geometry in the mediaeval Quadrivium," in *Studi in onore di Tammaro de Marinis* (Rome 1964).

[B. L. ULLMAN]

CORBINIAN OF FREISING, ST.

Missionary bishop; b. Châtres, near Melun, France, 670; d. Obermais, Bavaria, Germany, Sept. 8, *c.* 725. He became a recluse at an early age, but soon his fame for sanctity spread, and several persons came to live near him for spiritual guidance. To escape these distractions, he went to Rome and lived as a hermit near the tomb of St.

Peter. Pope Gregory II, hearing of his sanctity, consecrated him bishop and sent him to Bavaria. Duke Grimoald became his protector; but since the duke had contracted a marriage with his brother's widow Biltrudis without obtaining a dispensation, Corbinian upbraided the couple, and Grimoald repented. However, when Biltrudis conspired to have Corbinian murdered, he went into self-imposed exile. He returned to continue his missionary activities only after Grimoald had been killed in battle. When Corbinian died, he was buried in the monastery he had founded at Obermais; Arbeo, his second successor and biographer, brought his body to Freising in 769.

Feast: Sept. 8.

Bibliography: *Acta Sanctae Sedis* Sept. 3:261–296. *Vita in Monumenta Germaniae Historica: Scriptores rerum Merovingicarum* 6: 497–635. J. F. KENNEY, *The Sources for the Early History of Ireland* (New York 1929) 514. J. W. D. SKILES, *The Latinity of Arbeo's Vita. . .* (Chicago 1938).

[R. T. MEYER]

CORBISHLEY, THOMAS

English Jesuit, a foremost figure in England's Christian unity movement, author, journalist, and broadcaster; b. Preston, May 30, 1903; d. London, March 11, 1976. Corbishley studied philosophy and theology at St. Mary's Hall, Stonyhurst, and at Heythrop College (Oxon.); as an undergraduate at Campion Hall, Oxford, he received a first in Classical Mods and Greats. Ordained in 1936, he was prefect of Jesuit students 1938–45, then at Oxford, Master of Campion Hall, 1945–58. From 1958 he was Superior of the London Farm Street Church and Community until 1966 and spent the remainder of his life there with a reputation as "the Priest of London." Besides writing, broadcasting, lecturing, and caring for souls, he was active in groups concerned with ecumenism, relations with Jews, humanists, and Marxists, and with the promotion of the European Community ideal. One of his favorite roles was that of Chaplain to the Catholic Institute for International Relations. He was a frequent contributor to the Jesuit review *The Month* and served on its editorial board.

In addition to the many contributions he made to national and religious journals, he published many books, including: *Roman Catholicism* (1950), *Religion Is Reasonable* (1960), *Ronald Knox the Priest* (1964), *The Contemporary Christian* (1966), *The Spirituality of Teilhard de Chardin* (1971), and *The Prayer of Jesus* (1976); he also translated and edited the *Spiritual Exercises of St. Ignatius of Loyola* (1963).

Although he had the quality of a professional scholar, Corbishley's main contribution belongs to the realm

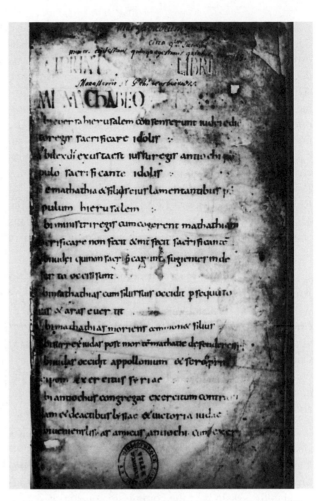

Folio from "Maurdramnus Bible," 8th century, written at Abbey of Corbie (Amiens MS11) (Bibliothèque Municipale, Amiens.)

of *haute vulgarisation*. It was first as a teacher that he revealed his Ignatian (and Teilhardian) vision in his awareness of continuity between the life of the spirit and natural creation—his understanding that the whole of creation is subsumed in Christ's redemptive dispensation, that the eternal Kingdom of God is to be quarried out of history. Many of those he taught learned the incarnational theology of Vatican Council II twenty years before it opened. His generous openness to the "separated brethren" prompted ice-breaking sermons at Westminster Abbey and St. Paul's Cathedral, yet was also manifest in his travels up and down the country, speaking to small audiences in church halls, students' societies, and local ecumenical groups.

[H. KAY]

CORCORAN, JAMES ANDREW

Theologian, editor, educator; b. Charleston, S.C., March 30, 1820; d. Philadelphia, Pa., July 16, 1889. He was the first native of South Carolina to become a priest. Sent to Rome in 1833 with Patrick N. Lynch (later bishop), he was ordained on Dec. 21, 1842, and received his doctorate in theology from the College of Propaganda. After his return to Charleston in 1843 he became a seminary professor, and later editor of the *United States Catholic Miscellany* (1848–61). Among the students he prepared for the priesthood was the former Episcopalian deacon (and later Paulist), Augustine F. HEWIT. With Hewit and Lynch, Corcoran edited *The Works of the Rt. Rev. John England,* published under the name of I. A. Reynolds (5 v. Baltimore 1849). His contributions to the *Miscellany* were in the polemical style of the era. This was particularly true of the treatment accorded Luther in the course of a long journalistic controversy.

In 1859 he declined the rectorship of the North American College at Rome, and from 1861 until 1868 was pastor at Wilmington, N.C., and vicar-general of Charleston. His work as secretary to the Baltimore Provincial Councils of 1855 and 1858, and to the Plenary Councils of 1866 and 1884, made him the American expert on conciliar legislation; his Latin style, evident in the decrees of the latter councils, won high praise at home and abroad.

In 1868, the U.S. archbishops were asked to send a single representative to assist in the preliminary work for Vatican Council I. Corcoran's learning and sound judgment made him an almost unanimous choice. He participated in the sessions of the commission on dogma for the first time on Dec. 30, 1868. Preparations for the Council had been under way for three years, and the U.S. representative disagreed with many of the decisions already made. He complained of a tendency to multiply definitions and reported to Abp. Martin SPALDING of Baltimore that some proposed canons would condemn "the fundamental principles of our [American and common-sense] political doctrine." Infallibility he accepted on faith, but he opposed its definition as inopportune. He also felt that too much attention was given to obscure German theories, and refused to draw up a list of contemporary American errors on the grounds that there were none except those that had been imported from Europe. By way of positive contribution, he assisted Klemens Schrader in preparing the draft of the decree on the Roman pontiff, revised the canons on church and state, and submitted two papers on matrimonial legislation. During the council, he aided Spalding in composing a compromise formula that would have defined papal infallibility indirectly.

While at the council, Corcoran accepted an invitation to teach theology at St. Charles Seminary, Philadelphia. He held that chair until his death and was for one year rector of the seminary. He was a founding editor of the *American Catholic Quarterly Review* (Philadelphia 1876–89), to which he contributed regularly. When the U.S. archbishops went to Rome in 1883 to plan the Third Plenary Council of Baltimore, he accompanied them as secretary. He was designated a domestic prelate in 1884. Advanced age forced him to decline a later invitation to join the first faculty of The Catholic University of America. Corcoran left no substantial published work, but he was for 40 years a valued consultant of the hierarchy on theological and canonical matters.

Bibliography: Archives of the Archdiocese of Baltimore, Corcoran-Spalding Correspondence. Archives of the Archdiocese of New York, Corcoran-McCloskey Correspondence. J. J. KEANE, "Monsignor Corcoran," *American Catholic Quarterly Review* 14 (1889) 738–747. G. E. O'DONNELL, *St. Charles Seminary, Overbrook,* 2 v. (Philadelphia 1943–53).

[J. J. HENNESEY]

CORDELL, CHARLES

English missionary priest and scholar; b. Oct. 5, 1720; d. Newcastle on Tyne, Jan. 26, 1791. Cordell, member of a prominent family of Scotney Castle and Calehill, Kent, received his early education at Dame Alice's school, Fernyhalgh, and began his studies for the priesthood at Douai in 1739. Following his ordination, he returned to England, June 10, 1748, where he first served as chaplain at Arundel, county seat of the Dukes of Norfolk. Between 1755 and 1791 Cordell labored as a missionary in Roundhay in Yorkshire, the Isle of Man, and Newcastle on Tyne. Cordell's superiors, regarding him as an effective preacher and sound scholar, offered him the post of president of the English College of Saint-Omer in 1778. He declined it. In addition to translating a number of devotional and controversial works, he wrote a refutation of an attack on Pope Clement XIV, *A Letter to the Author of a Book Called "A Candid and Impartial Sketch of the Life and Goverment of Clement XIV."* In this pamphlet he defended the pope's dealings with the Jesuits. In politics Cordell retained a sentimental attachment to the cause of the exiled Catholic Stuarts.

Bibliography: J. GILLOW, *A Literary and Biographical History or Bibliographical Dictionary of the English Catholics from 1534 to the Present Time,* 5 v. (London-New York 1885–1902; repr. New York 1961) 1:565–568. T. COOPER, *The Dictionary of National Biography from the Earliest Times to 1900,* 63 v. (London 1885–1900; repr. with corrections, 21 v., 1908–09, 1921–22, 1938; suppl. 1901–) 4:1138.

[H. F. GRETSCH]

CORDIER, JEAN-NICOLAS, BL.

Martyr and Jesuit priest; professor of theology; b. near Souilly, Lorraine, France, Dec. 3, 1710; d. Île Madame, La Rochelle, France, Sept. 30, 1794, (age 83). Cordier joined the Jesuits at Nancy (1728), and studied at the University of Pont-à-Mousson, where he received a doctorate in philosophy. He was a professor of theology at Dijon, Auxerre, Autun, Strasbourg, and Pont-à-Mousson. Later he was prefect of studies at Rheims (1757–61) and superior of the Saint-Mihiel community at Verdun (from 1761-62). Following the suppression of the Society until the suppression of all religious orders (1790), he acted as chaplain to a convent in Saint-Mihiel. The aged priest retired to Verdun, where he was arrested (Oct. 28, 1793). After a six-month imprisonment at Bar, he was taken to the prison ship *Washington* for deportation. He was the first of the prisoners to die on the Île Madame, which was used as a hospital. He was beatified by John Paul II, Oct. 1, 1995, together with other martyrs of La Rochelle.

Feast: Jan. 19 (Jesuits).

See Also: ROCHEFORT SHIPS, MARTYRS OF, BB.

Bibliography: I. GOBRY, *Les martyrs de la Révolution française* (Paris 1989). J. N. TYLENDA, *Jesuit Saints & Martyrs,* 2d ed. (Chicago 1998): 165–167. *Acta Apostolicae Sedis* (1995): 923–926. *L'Osservatore Romano,* no. 40 (1995): 3–5; Documentation Catholique 19 (1995): 923–26.

[K. I. RABENSTEIN]

CORDI-MARIAN MISSIONARY SISTERS

(MCM, Official Catholic Directory #0725); founded in Mexico City, Mexico, on March 19, 1921, by Mother Carmen Serrano and a Claretian priest, Julian Collell. Forced into exile by persecution, the sisters came to Martindale, Texas, in 1926. Six years later a novitiate was opened in San Antonio. Their apostolate consists of education, catechetics, and social work. The generalte is located in Toluca, Mexico. The United States provincialate is in San Antonio, Texas.

[M. E. RAMIREZ/EDS.]

CÓRDOBA

Capital of the province of Córdoba, on the right bank of the Guadalquivir River, in Andalusia, south Spain. Taken by Rome (152 B.C.), it was the capital (*Corduba*) of the *conventus* of Betica.

Early History. It was attacked without success by the Visigoth Agila (549), regained from the Byzantines by Leovigildus (572), and had to be reconquered when it sided with Hermenigild (583). Under the UMAYYADS (711–1031), it became an independent emirate (756) and a caliphate (929). As a petty kingdom, it was reconquered from the Moors by FERDINAND III (1236).

Córdoba, the birthplace of SENECA, became Romanized and Christianized very early. The martyr Acisclus may be of the third century. The first known bishop, Hosius (d. 357), persecuted under DIOCLETIAN (303), was a councilor of CONSTANTINE I and presided at the Council of NICAEA I. Prudentius praised other martyrs of Córdoba under Diocletian: Faustus, JANUARIUS, Martial and Zoilus. A ninth-century *passio* makes the legendary Victoria a companion martyr of Acisclus, but she is not mentioned by ninth-century authors in Córdoba. Bishop Higinius *c.* 380, with the metropolitan of MÉRIDA, acted against "abstainer" precursors of Priscillianism. According to WALAFRID STRABO, Emperor Theodosius I (379–395) praised Bishop Gregory for the pastoral and liturgical organization of the diocese; he commemorated the feasts of martyrs in Mass daily. Eight other bishops signed councils, from Stephen in Rome (503) to Zaccheus in Toledo (693).

The many Christians in Córdoba under Arab rule had freedom of cult with numerous basilicas and monasteries in the area and what must have been an outstanding school of Latin culture under Abbot Esperaindeo. An important Latin chronicle of 754 seems to have been written in Córdoba by a high ecclesiastic. But the Christians, later called Mozarabs, were molested, especially after Malachites arrived from the East in the late eighth century. They paid a high tribute, and whoever spoke ill of Muhammad or Islam paid the death penalty, as did the children of Christian-Muslim marriages who were known to practice the Christian faith. Molestations led to persecution and martyrdom. In 824 and 825 Adulfus and John, sons of Arab nobility, whose Christian mother Artemia later governed a monastery famous throughout the area, were martyred.

Arab Persecution. The great persecution that claimed some 50 victims (850–859) was provoked by Muslims who questioned the priest Perfectus, who knew Arabic, about his opinion of their prophet, promising not to prosecute him, but later making a public sacrifice of him at the end of Ramadan (850). The martyrdom created religious tension and led to a strong reaction on the part of Christians, many not natives of Córdoba. EULOGIUS, who was looked to for guidance on his return from a trip to north Spain, where he had seen a free and flourishing Christianity, reports the martyrdoms in detail and defends the martyrs in his writings. Some martyrs voluntarily came before the qadi and called Muhammad an imposter,

Exterior of Cordoba Cathedral, 8th–10th century, built as a mosque by the Moors on the site of a Roman temple, Córdoba, Andalusia, Spain. (© Vittoriano Rastelli/CORBIS)

identifying themselves with Perfectus: Isaac, a rich noble who knew Arabic and was a government official before becoming a monk; the merchant John; a group of six monks—in all, 13 martyrs in 851. Of 13 martyrs in 852 the most important were AURELIUS AND SABIGOTONA, martyred with George, a monk from Jerusalem and the subject of another Muslim ruler. Of seven martyrs in 853 COLUMBA and Pomposa are noteworthy. Of ten martyrs (854–856) ARGIMIR and AUREA are noteworthy because of their noble birth and high status among ruling Arabs. Some of the martyrs were rash: Emila and Jeremias, and Rogellus and Servus Dei, who entered the crowded mosque to preach Christ.

The martyrdom of Flora and Maria (851), innocent Christian daughters of a Muslim father, seems to have increased tension to such a point that in alarm officials convoked a council under Reccafred, metropolitan of Seville, who was opposed to a contest with Islam. The council in ambiguous terms discouraged future martyrdoms; but provocations, assertions and martyrdoms continued until Eulogius was slain (859) for having sheltered Leocritia, daughter of a Muslim father, from persecution by her brother. In 858 the martyrdoms drew USUARD and Odilard, monks of SAINT-GERMAIN-DES-PRES in Paris to Cór-

doba in search of relics. The emirs as a rule ordered the relics of the martyrs destroyed to prevent veneration by the Christians. Many Christians did not support the martyrs and after Eulogius there were but few, mostly in the tenth century.

Alcuin claimed that ADOPTIONISM, headed by ELIPANDUS OF TOLEDO and Felix of Urgel, was spawned in Córdoba. According to ALBAR, pupil of Esperaindeo and the author of a vita of Eulogius, it did infest Betica. Cassianist heretics were condemned at a council in Córdoba (839) attended by the three metropolitans of Spain (Toledo, Mérida and Seville). Anti-Trinitarian and anthropomorphic heresies also spread. The correspondence of Albar shows interest in and disputes about dogma and discipline. Saul, Córdoba's bishop during the persecution, seems to have been a venerable man. The lengthy *Apologeticus* of the Abbot Samson (864) is the last work of the Latin renaissance in Córdoba; but the activity of collecting and copying Latin texts may have had a more lasting influence.

The first caliph, 'Abd-ar-Raḥmān III, had the Christian Recemundus, head of his chancery, made bishop of Elvira for performing embassies to the Ottonian and Byzantine courts. Recemundus's calendar of Christian saints, compiled in Arabic and dedicated to Al Hakam II, offers much information on the Christian cult in Córdoba. With reputedly a library of 50,000 volumes, Córdoba was a major Arabic cultural center from which Eastern learning was transmitted to Europe. Neither the Almoravides nor the Almohades, however, made it a capital; and it declined in favor of Seville. MAIMONIDES and his family left Córdoba when it was taken by the Almohades (1148); AVERROËS (1126–98) became known to the Latin world *c.* 1230. The last known bishop of Córdoba before its reconquest by FERDINAND III in 1236 was John (988).

The episcopacy was restored with Lope de Fitero (1237–45), and the mosque became the cathedral of the Assumption. In 1241 the city received a special *fuero* based on the Visigothic *Forum iudicum.* Many monasteries were founded after the reconquest, and again in the 16th, 17th and 18th centuries. As in other places in Spain, there was a strong reaction against the Jews *c.* 1400. The Inquisition, established in 1482, had a fervent supporter in Diego Rodrigo Lucero *c.* 1500; and there were many autos-da-fé to *c.* 1750. Natives of Córdoba were Ambrosio de Morales, learned historian of the Renaissance, the poet Luis de Góngora and the artists Pablo de Cespedes (1538–1608) and Juan de Mesa. Blessed JOHN OF AVILA and Blessed DIEGO OF CÁDIZ carried on a great deal of their apostolate in Córdoba.

Art and Architecture. The cathedral, once a mosque, begun in 786, has 19 naves with more than 1,000 columns, many taken from Roman and Visigothic monuments. The cathedral proper, with a magnificent choir and an elegant bell tower, was built in the 16th century. Its treasures include a monstrance by the goldsmith Enrique de Arfe. S. Miguel has a tenth-century baptismal chapel. The 13th-century S. Pablo is built on an Almohad palace. S. Marina has a Moorish chapel (15th century). S. Bartolomé has a portico with Visigothic capitals. All the churches are rich in paintings. In 1548 the College of the Assumption was founded and in 1794 Ventura Rodríguez built the Santa Victoria school for children and San Pelayo seminary.

Bibliography: H. FLÓREZ et al., *España sagrada,* 54 v. (Madrid 1747–1957) v.10. J. GÓMEZ BRAVO, *Catálogo de los obispos de Córdoba,* 2 v. (Córdoba 1778). L. M. RAMÍREZ DE LAS CASAS DEZA, ''Anales de la Ciudad de Córdoba (1236–1850),'' *Boletín de la Real Academia de Ciencias, Bellas Letras y Nobles Artes de Córdoba* (Córdoba 1948). I. DE LAS CAGIGAS, *Los Mozárabes,* 2 v. (Madrid 1947–48). F. J. SIMONET, *Historia de los Mozárabes de España* (Madrid 1903). F. R. FRANKE, ''Die freiwilligen Märtyrer von Cordova . . . ,'' *Gesammelte Aufsätze zur Kulturgeschichte Spaniens,* 13 (Span. Aufsätze der Görresgesellschaft; Münster 1958) 1–170. E. P. COLBERT, *The Martyrs of Córdoba, 850–859: A Study of the Sources* (Washington 1962). C. M. SAGE, *Paul Albar of Córdoba: Studies in His Life and Writings* (Washington 1943). S. AL-COLEA, *Córdoba: Guías artísticas de España* (Barcelona 1951). L. TORRES BALBÁS, *La mezquita de Córdoba y las ruinas de Madinat al-Zahra* (Madrid 1952). F. PÉREZ, *Dictionnaire d'histoire et de géographie ecclésiastiques,* ed. A. BAUDRILLART et al. (Paris 1912–) 13:837–871.

[J. VIVES]

CÓRDOBA, ANTONIO DE

Franciscan moral theologian; b. Spain, 1485; d. Guadalajara, 1578. He was twice provincial minister in his order, and also took part in the Council of Trent at the request of Philip II. In his later years he declined the See of Piacenza and chose retirement instead. Among his numerous writings a commentary on the *Sentences* (Alcalá, 1569 or 1562) is often listed, but recent studies seem to disprove its existence (*see* Piatti, 22–24; Durán, 15–16). His major moral treatises were: *Quaestionarium theologicum* (Venice-Toledo 1569–70), under the general title *Opera Fr. Antonii Cordubensis. . . ,* and *Summa casuum* (Toledo 1582–83).

Bibliography: É. LONGPRÉ, *Catholicisme* 1:673. L. C. M. DURÁN, *Miguel de Palacios: Un gran teólogo desconocido* (Vigo 1958) 13–18. S. PIATTI, *Doctrina Antonii Cordubensis de conscientia cum speciali relatione ad probabilismum* (Trent 1952).

[R. A. COUTURE]

CÓRDOBA, PEDRO DE

Dominican missionary in the Caribbean; b. Córdoba, Spain, 1482; d. Santo Domingo, 1521. Las Casas described this man, who is credited with having induced him to give up his *encomiendas,* join the Dominican Order, and become the defender of the indigenous people, as being ''tall of stature and of a handsome appearance . . . of excellent judgment, prudent and by nature very discreet and very tranquil.'' Pedro joined the Order of Preachers early in life and received the habit in the convent of San Esteban de Salamanca. In 1510 he went to Santo Domingo, where, with other companions in religion, he founded the first convent of the order in the New World and the province of the Holy Cross, of which he was vice provincial. His mission work was not limited to the island of Española but extended to Cuba and to Cumaná on the mainland. With Bp. Alonso Manso he was inquisitor of the Indies. Córdoba, like other religious, envisioned the ideal of a native society converted to Catholicism with minimal colonization, in which the King of Spain would exercise nominal sovereignty and the government would be in the hands of the friars. He wrote memorials to the king, sermons, and instructions, etc., but they are as yet unpublished, and many have been lost. In

1544 his *Doctrina cristiana para instrucción e información de los indios, por manera de historia* was published posthumously in Mexico. It was reprinted in a bilingual edition (Spanish-Nahuatl) in 1548.

Bibliography: PEDRO DE CÓRDOBA, *Doctrina Cristiana,* ed. E. RODRIGUEZ DEMORIZI (Santo Domingo 1945). P. HENRÍQUEZ UREÑA, *La cultura y las letras coloniales en Santo Domingo* (Buenos Aires 1936).

[J. MALAGÓN BARCELÓ]

CÓRDOVA, MATÍAS DE

Dominican educator, poet, and social writer who introduced the first printing press into Chiapas, founded the first normal school there, and invented a phonetic language; b. Tapachula, Chiapas, April 20, 1768; d. Chiapas, 1828 or 1829. He studied at the Seminary de Ciudad Real de San Cristóbal Las Casas and then went to Guatemala. There he entered the Dominicans and was ordained in March 1790. He became a humanistic scholar and wrote poems, epigrams, and various humanistic studies. In 1801 he was a professor of theology at the Pontifical University of San Carlos. He went to Spain on business in 1803, and upon his return he lived not in Guatemala but at Ciudad Real in Chiapas. There he founded an economic society and the normal school. Córdova was a prolific writer. In 1797 he wrote "Utilidades de que todos los Indios y ladinos se vistan y calcen a la Española, y medios de conseguirlo sin violencia, coacción ni mandato," about the problems and aptitudes of the natives, and peaceful means of converting them. In 1801 Córdova published *Modo de leer con utilidad los auctores antiguos de elocuencia* and *Prelecciones a los libros de elocuencia.* Four of the writings in Gamboa's "Bibliografía," pertain to the normal school project. About 1824 Córdova published his *Método facil de enseñar a leer y escribir,* the purpose of which was to popularize primary education. He is the author of a moral fable-poem, "La Tentativa del León y el Exito de su Empresa."

Bibliography: J. FUENTE, *Los heraldos de la civilización centroamericana* (Vergara 1929). M. DE CÓRDOVA, "El Problema del Indio (1797)," *Ateneo de Ciencias y Artes de Chiapas* 2 (1951) 13–30. F. CASTAÑON GAMBOA, "Bibliografía de Fray M. de C.," *ibid.* 31–39.

[A. B. NIESER]

CÓRDOVA Y SALINAS, DIEGO DE

Franciscan historian; b. Lima, 1591; d. there, 1654. Fray Diego was a full brother of Fray Buenaventura Salinas y Córdova, a descendent of converted Jews, and a member of one of the prominent Peruvian families of colonial times. The studious and quiet Fray Diego was several times novice master as well as guardian of the Franciscan friary of Lima. His appointment in 1620 as historian of the Franciscan province of Peru marked the beginning of a new epoch in his life. He began his work by contacting as many old friars as possible and taking depositions of their reminiscences. However, the first work published by him was *Vida, virtudes y milagros del nuevo apóstol del Perú, el venerable P. Francisco Solano* (Lima 1630). Its chapters seem to be lectures to his novices rather than the life of a living person. After completing this work, Diego's main efforts were directed to fulfilling his commission as provincial historian. By 1638 he was able to send a synopsis to Tomóas Tamayo de Vargas, official royal historian of the Spanish Indies. Vargas never used the manuscript nor did his successor Gil González Dávila; but Diego incorporated the material in the Corónica. In 1642 a similar synopsis was sent to Luke Wadding. By 1646 Diego's main task was almost complete when he received a renewed appointment as chronicler of all Franciscan Peruvian provinces. The provincial history was so enlarged and changed that Diego himself could say with truth "that it seems a new history." However, at times, the more modest origins peek through in *Corónica franciscana de las provincias del Perú* (Lima 1651). The huge volume is a factual and objective narrative of the work and plans of the Franciscan provinces of almost all Spanish South America during the 1st century after Pizarro's conquest. The main emphasis, however, remains on Lima and its province. Diego obliged his friend Pedro Villagomez, Archbishop of Lima, by writing in 1650 a description of the Archdiocese: *Teatro de la Santa Iglesia Metropolitana de los Reyes* (Lima 1959).

Bibliography: D. DE CÓRDOBA Y SALINAS, *Corónica franciscana de las provincias del Perú,* ed. L. G. CANEDO (2d ed. Washington 1957).

[L. G. CANEDO]

CORELLI, ARCANGELO

Baroque composer, violinist, and teacher; b. Fusignano, Italy, Feb. 17, 1653; d. Rome, Jan. 8, 1713. From 1666 until 1670 he studied with Benvenuti, Gaïbara, and Brugnoli in Bologna, where he acquired the stylistic traits of the Bologna school. From 1675 until his death he was active mainly in Rome, where he moved in the most brilliant musical and literary circles, his principal patron being Cardinal Pietro Ottoboni, who gave him every opportunity to develop his talents. His compositions, in which the use of tonality and of a contrapuntal texture within a harmonic structure reveal the mentality of the late baroque era, influenced the history of baroque instrumental music enormously. His *sonate da chiesa* (church sonatas) are of special importance for baroque chamber music, since he standardized the four-movement form in which the first and third movements in slow tempo contrast with the second and fourth in a fast one. He wrote 30 such sonatas, all requiring organ continuo. Although designed to be performed during Mass and Vespers, when the liturgical action permitted incidental music, their use was not restricted to the church.

Bibliography: *Sämtliche Werke,* op. 1–6, ed. J. JOACHIM and F. CHRYSANDER, 5 v. (London 1888–91). *Sonate a tre,* op. 1–4, ed. W. WOEHL (Kassel 1933). There are a number of other modern eds. B. PAUMGARTNER, *Die Musik in Geschichte und Gegenwart,* ed. F. BLUME (Kassel-Basel 1949–) 2:1668–79. P. DAVID and H. C. COLLES, *Grove's Dictionary of Music and Musicians,* ed. E. BLOM, 9 v. (5th ed. London 1954) 2:438–440. M. F. BUKOFZER, *Music in the Baroque Era* (New York 1947). W. S. NEWMAN, *The Sonata in the Baroque Era* (Chapel Hill, N.C. 1959). P. ALLSOP, "*Da camera e da ballo-alla francese et all'italiana:* Functional and National Distinctions in Corelli's *sonata da camera,*" *Early Music* 26 (1998) 87–96. N. COOK, "At the Borders of Musical Identity: Schenker, Corelli and the Graces," *Music Analysis* 18 (1999) 179–233. W. CORTEN, "Fatto per la notte di Natale: *le Concerto* opus VI no. 8 de Corelli," *Analyse Musicale* 29 (1992) 5–17. L. DELLA LIBERA, "La musica nella basilica di Santa Maria Maggiore a Roma, 1676–1712: nuovi documenti su Corelli e sugli organici vocali e strumentali," *Recercare* 7 (1995) 87–161. L. U. MORTENSEN, "'Unerringly Tasteful'?: Harpsichord Continuo in Corelli's op. 5 Sonatas," *Early Music* 24 (1996) 665–679. R. PECMAN, "Corellis Concerti grossi als Vorboten des Klassizismus," *Sborník Prací Filosofické Fakulty Brnenské University* 3 (1968) 29–42. R. E. SELETSKY, "Eighteenth-Century Variations for Corelli's Sonatas, op. 5," *Early Music* 24 (1996) 119–130. N. ZASLAW, "Ornaments for Corelli's Violin Sonatas, op. 5," *Early Music* 24 (1996) 95–115.

[T. CULLEY]

CORINTHIANS, EPISTLES TO THE

First Corinthians. The longer of the two canonical letters to the "church of God at Corinth" appears in the canon of the New Testament immediately after Paul's letter to the Romans. PAUL, accompanied by Timothy, had visited Corinth for an 18-month period during 51–52 A.D.. He was in the city during the proconsulate of Gallio (Acts 18:12). The First Letter to the Corinthians, to which the Apostle added a personally signed a postscript (16:21–24), was written from Ephesus soon after Paul's visit to Corinth, probably as early as 53–54 A.D.

The variety of issues addressed in the letter led many 20th-century scholars, notably Johannes Weiss and Walter Schmithals, to claim that First Corinthians was not one letter but rather a composite text comprised of several

Arcangelo Corelli.

fragments of letters sent by Paul to the Corinthian Christians during the course of a relatively long correspondence. No manuscript evidence exists to suggest that the letter is a scribal composite. Insights derived from classical rhetoric allow the letter to be seen as a single composition whose theme is articulated in the plea "that all of you be in agreement and that there be no divisions among you, but that you are united in the same mind and the same purpose" (1:10). The appeal for harmony is a classical topos of Hellenistic rhetoric. From this perspective the body of the letter is a manifold plea for the unity of the church at Corinth as Paul successively addresses issues that had caused division within the community. Its structure is as follows:

1:1–9 Introduction
1:1–3 Epistolary Opening
1:4–9 Epistolary Thanksgiving
1:10–15:58 Body of the Letter
1:10–17 Theme and Occasion
1:18–4:21 First Rhetorical Demonstration: Wisdom and Power
5:1–7:40 Second Rhetorical Demonstration: Human Sexuality
8:1–11:1 Third Rhetorical Demonstration: Food Offered to Idols
11:2–34 Fourth Rhetorical Demonstration: The Christian Assembly

When writing the letter Paul was self-consciously aware that he was writing a letter and why he was writing it (4:14 5:11; 9:15; 14:37). Its length is such that many of its subunits are similar in form to one kind or another of a Hellenistic letter. Thus, the commendation of Timothy in 4:17–21 and of Stephanas and his companions in 16:15–18 are similar to the Hellenistic letter of recommendation while the admonition of 4:14–16 is similar to the Hellenistic letter of admonition. In many respects the letter in its entirety is similar to many of the *Moral Epistles* of Seneca, the Stoic philosopher and brother of the proconsul Gallio.

Paul had several sources of information regard the divisive issues, including a visit from people belonging to Chloe's household (1:11), a letter sent by the Corinthians (7:1), and a visit by Stephanas, Fortunatus, and Achaicus (16:17). If these three brought the Corinthians' letter to Paul, as is likely, they would have the opportunity to expand on and explain its contents. The length of Paul's own letter owes to the variety of topics addressed and Paul's various sources of information. It is not unlikely that Paul had already begun to address some of the issues dividing the community before the Corinthians' letter to him arrived.

The introduction to First Corinthians (1:1–9) anticipates the arguments that Paul develops in later sections of the letter. Paul introduces himself as an apostle, invoking the apostolic authority to which he will appeal in 7:12, 40; 9:1–27. He addresses the Corinthian Christians as "the church of God," a motif that recalls the unity of God's holy people and subtly challenges the Corinthians to serve God alone (cf. 8:1–11:1). Paul's thanksgiving reflects his gratitude for the gifts of speech and knowledge and many spiritual gifts given to the Corinthians. These are themes to which he returns at length in the first and fifth rhetorical demonstrations (1:18–4:21; 12:1–14:40). The introduction concludes on a note of anticipation of the PAROUSIA, an eschatological motif to which Paul returns in his final rhetorical demonstration (15:1–58).

The first rhetorical demonstration (1:18–4:21) addresses a claim to the possession of knowledge (γνώση)

by a group of puffed up Corinthians. Paul attempts to put them in their place by speaking about the power of the cross, "God's foolishness," and telling them that his proclamation of the Gospel did not rely on lofty words and rhetorical eloquence but on the power of the Spirit of God. Although Paul attributes the power of his proclamation to the demonstration of the Spirit (2:4), his letter is one in which he shows himself to be a master of Hellenistic rhetoric. The Spirit speaks through his rhetorical chiasms and the example that he offers of himself, the ethos appeal of Hellenistic orators. In his first demonstration Paul puts forth the imagery of a house and family. He appeals to the family ties that bind Christians to one another and uses the metaphor of the house, God's temple, to show that all have their role to play and that all will be judged on the quality of their work.

In the second rhetorical demonstration (5:1–7:40) Paul addresses a variety of issues that pertain to human sexuality. His starting point was a report that he had received concerning a member of the community who was involved in an incestuous relationship with his own father's wife. Paul scolds the community for not taking issue with this scandalous conduct. After a digression on Christians taking other Christians to court, presumably the rich and powerful taking the poor and powerless before secular judges instead of choosing a Christian arbitrator to help with the resolution of the dispute, Paul gets to the foundations of his understanding of sexuality, namely, the nature of human freedom and of the human body. As was customary in the Hellenistic world, Paul wrote about prostitution. Among Hellenistic moralists prostitution was the starting point for the discussion of sexual ethics. Thereafter, Paul describes a concern about which he had been informed by letter, namely, the claim by some that men should totally refrain from sexual relationships. Dividing the question, Paul writes about the sexuality of married people, widows and widowers, those contemplating divorce, mixed marriages, and those not yet married.

Food that had been offered to idols is the theme of Paul's third rhetorical demonstration (8:1–11:1). The matter was particularly problematic in a cosmopolitan city with temples devoted to the gods of various peoples and nations. The temple precincts often included halls that were used for festive banquets, particularly by people belonging to different guilds and brotherhoods. Compounding the urgency of the matter was that many Corinthian Christians were slaves or belonged to lower classes of society. These people rarely ate meat except if they benefited from the leftovers after a celebration that began with an invocation to the gods. Paul deftly wends his way through a variety of situations in which Christians might be inclined to eat food offered to idols. Throughout it all, his fundamental theme is "flee from the worship of idols." He undergirds the authority of his exhortation with an extensive digression on his own apostolic authority (9:1–27).

The fourth rhetorical demonstration (11:2–34) addresses two practical issues that must be resolved in a Christian fashion when the community assembles for worship. The first concerns the attire, specifically, the hair style of men and women. The issue was often addressed by the philosophic moralists of Paul's day. Paul's use of midrash makes it difficult for the modern reader to understand the precise meaning of his words but he certainly means that men and women are to be properly attired and coiffed when the Christian community comes together. Paul's second concern is more serious, namely, that some Christians have eviscerated the Eucharistic celebration itself by allowing their social divisions to separate Christians who gather to celebrate the Lord's Supper. Paul's response to them incorporates the oldest literary evidence of the institution of the Eucharist (12:23–26).

Spiritual gifts are the topic of Paul's fifth rhetorical demonstration (12:1–14:40). Some "charismatic" Christians who were able to speak in tongues considered themselves to be especially important within the community. Paul's censure of them began with a reminder that all Christians are charismatic; all possess some spiritual gifts. The Spirit allots these gifts to different individuals as the Spirit wills. What is crucial for the believer is that each and every believer use these gifts for the building up of the Church. The Church is the body of Christ in which each Christian has a role to play. Listing some of the gifts that are given to Christians, Paul deliberately places the gift of tongues at the end of the list. Doing so, he reminds the community that the gift of tongues is but one of the gifts of the Spirit. There follows a beautiful digression in which Paul speaks of love as the fundamental gift of the Spirit. Only thereafter does he come back to the gift of tongues, showing that it pales in comparison with the gift of prophecy that is so necessary for building up the Church.

The epistle's final rhetorical demonstration (15:1–58) considers the resurrection of the dead. The issue arose because some were saying that there is no resurrection of the dead (15:13). Paul begins his reflection by rehearsing an early Christian creed (15:3–7) in which the burial of Jesus attests to the reality of his death and his Resurrection appearances, beginning with his appearance to Cephas (Peter) and ending with the experience of Paul, witness to the reality of the Resurrection. Christians hold that the resurrection of the dead is a reality because they believe that Christ was raised from the dead. In God's eschatological plan, Christ's Resurrection is the first fruits of the resurrection of those who have died. Before the end comes, when the kingdom will be handed over to the Father, all those who belong to Christ will be raised.

Chapter 16 brings 1 Corinthians to a close. The letter began by recalling that the church of God in Corinth is "together with all those who in every place call on the name of our Lord Jesus Christ" (1:2). The epistle's final chapter articulates some elements of that togetherness. Paul gives directions for organizing a collection for Christians in Jerusalem, the mother church of Christianity, and offers the churches of Galatia as an example of how this is to be done. Paul's desire to go from Ephesus to Macedonia and then to Corinth speaks of his pastoral care for all the churches. The travels of Timothy, Apollos, Stephanas, Fortunatus, and Achaicus are a reminder of the interaction among members of the Christian community. Greetings sent from the Church that gathered in the house of Aquila and Prisca and from all the brothers and sisters attest to the bonds of affection that bound Christians in Asia to those in Achaia. The letter concludes with an expression of Paul's love for the community. No similar postscript is found in any of the other NT letters.

Distinguished by its length and the depth of Paul's theology, the First Letter to the Corinthians is particularly important insofar as it sheds light, as no other NT text does, on a 1st-century Christian community. Not only does it mention various people by name, but it also speaks of human problems and of the realities of human life in which the message of the gospel must be embodied—the use of one's mind and one's sexuality, concern for others and the sharing of wealth, social divisions within a community along with the Eucharistic celebration of its unity, and human death overshadowed by Christ's Resurrection.

Second Corinthians. Paul's Second Letter to the Corinthians is part of the extensive correspondence that took place between the Apostle and the community on the isthmus of Achaia, which he had evangelized. 1 Cor 5:9 mentions a letter that Paul had written to the Corinthians prior to the letter known as First Corinthians. 1 Cor 7:1 cites a letter that Paul had received. 2 Cor 2:3–4 mentions a "tearful" letter written prior to 2 Corinthians. The tearful letter can hardly be identified with 1 Corinthians, a challenging but loving piece of correspondence. Second Corinthians thus appears to have been at least the fourth of Paul's letters to the Corinthians. It is called the Second Letter to the Corinthians because it is shorter than the other Pauline letter to the Corinthians that is now part of the NT canon.

The fact that some of Paul's letters to the Corinthians are no longer extant, coupled with the harsh connections between some of the successive verses in 2 Corinthians, led the majority of late 20th-century interpreters of the epistle to consider it as a composite text compiled from fragments of Paul's ongoing correspondence with the Corinthians. On this hypothesis, articulated in Günther Bornkamm's seminal study (1961), extant 2 Corinthians consists of six fragments:

1. A letter of reconciliation, providing the extant text's epistolary framework (1:1–2:13; 7:5–16; 13:11–13).
2. A Pauline apology (2:14–6:13; 7:2–4).
3. A tearful letter (10:1–13:10).
4. A letter of recommendation of Titus (8:1–24).
5. An administrative letter to the churches of Achaia (9:1–15).
6. A non-Pauline interpolation (6:14–7:1).

Some less radical scholars (e.g., Victor Furnish) have proposed that the literary features of 2 Corinthians suggest that 2 Corinthians is a composite of but two previous texts, extant 2 Corinthians 1–9, and 2 Corinthians 10–13. Still others (e.g., Jan Lambrecht) hold that despite the harsh literary connections in the present text the epistle is one integral letter. On any theory the place of the exhortation in 2 Cor 6:14–7:1 must be given special consideration. Its Qumran-like language and the fact that 2 Cor 7:2 follows so readably after 2 Cor 6:10 make the origin of this passage and its place within the Pauline corpus an enigma.

In its extant state 2 Corinthians can be structured in this way:

1:1–11 Introduction
1:1–2 Epistolary Greeting
1:3–11 Praise of God
1:12–12:10 Body of the Letter
1:12–2:13 The Trustworthiness of the Apostle
2:14–7:4 Paul's Apostolate
7:5–16 The Return of Titus
8:1–9:15 The Collection for the Saints
10:1–13:10 A Pauline Apology
13:11–13 Epistolary Closing

The letter's epistolary greeting and closing are similar to those generally found in the Pauline letters. On the hypothesis that 2 Corinthians is a compilation, such epistolary features would have been taken into the composite text only once so as to avoid redundancy. The solemnity of the final greeting (13:13) has a liturgical ring such that it has been taken over into the Latin liturgy and suggests that extant 2 Corinthians was read to a community gathered for worship. This liturgical tone is also found in a prayer of praise (1:3–10) that resembles the Jewish běrakâ and takes the place of the thanksgiving typical in Paul's letters.

Apart from the two-chapter appeal on behalf of the collection for the saints, a classic reflection on the reality of love among Christians, the body of the letter is essentially apologetic. Paul is engaged in a task of self-defense against his opponents. Who those opponents are is a moot point among scholars. Various proposals have been advanced but none has gained a scholarly consensus. Among those considered to have been Paul's opponents are a group of Judaizers similar to those whom Paul confronted in Galatia, Jewish-Christian Gnostics, Hellenistic Christian preachers coming from Greece or Asia, Christians who oppose Paul and appeal to Jerusalem for support (cf. 11:5, 13; 12:1), and Hellenistic secularists who deem that Paul did not meet accepted social standards. There is no way to determine precisely who the troublemakers were. It may be that their christology led them to oppose Paul. In any case, it is well known that the Christian community at Corinth was rife with conflict and division at least from the time of Paul's first letter to the time of Clement's letter, and perhaps thereafter.

Paul's extensive apology had as its purpose the reconciliation of his opponents and the reconciliation of the community. Paul used a variety of rhetorical techniques to pursue his defense and foster reconciliation. Not only had he written a tearful letter to the Corinthians, but he also appeals to them as to his children and speaks of his intention to visit them for yet a third time (12:14; 13:1–2). The "fool's speech" (ch. 11) is a classic example of self-demeaning rhetoric in which Paul boasts of his own weakness and speaks of the many adversities that he had encountered; yet, he commends himself in 4:2 and 6:4. He speaks of his lack of rhetorical skill but proclaims his moral rectitude (2:17; 4:2; 6:4). He swears to his love for the Corinthians (11:11) and recalls that the signs of a true apostle had been present among them (12:12), thus recalling his own miraculous deeds. He uses the imagery of a triumphant procession led by Christ (2:14–17) whose herald is Paul (4:5). That Paul writes at such length and in so many different ways about his ministry leads many to conclude that 2 Corinthians is, in fact, the most personal of all Paul's extant letters.

Bibliography: R. BIERINGER, ed., "The Corinthian Correspondence," *Bibliotheca ephemeridum theologicarum Lovaniensium* 125 (Louvain 1996). J. LAMBRECHT, "Second Corinthians," *Sacra Pagina* 8 (Collegeville, Minn. 1999). V. P. FURNISH, "II Corinthians," *Anchor Bible* 32A (Garden City, N.Y. 1984). R. F. COLLINS, "First Corinthians," *Sacra Pagina* 7 (Collegeville, Minn. 1999). G. D. FEE, "The First Epistle to the Corinthians," *New International Commentary on the New Testament* (Grand Rapids, Mich. 1987). M. M. MITCHELL, *Paul and the Rhetoric of Reconciliation: An Exegetical Investigation of the Language and Composition of 1 Corinthians* (Louisville 1991). G. THEISSEN, *The Social Setting of Pauline Christianity: Essays on Corinth* (Philadelphia 1982).

[R. F. COLLINS]

CORKER, JAMES MAURUS

Benedictine monk; b. Featherstone, Yorkshire, 1636; d. Paddington, London, December 1715. His grandfather dissipated the family estates, and his father, Francis Corker, royalist vicar of Bradford, acted as a spy for the Cromwellian government. The consciousness of his father's treachery played a part in James's conversion and fidelity to the Catholic faith. He was admitted to the English Benedictine Abbey of Lambspring in Germany and was professed in 1656. In 1665 he went on the English mission. At the time of the Titus OATES PLOT he was arrested, tried for treason on July 18, 1679, and acquitted; but he was retried for his priesthood on Jan. 17, 1680, and condemned to death, but subsequently reprieved. In October 1681 the Privy Council ordered his transportation, with six other condemned priests, to the Isles of Scilly, but the sheriffs of London refused to release them from jail, and Corker remained there until the accession of James II (1685). While in Newgate jail, he acted as spiritual adviser to Abp. Oliver PLUNKET and gained many converts to Catholicism. He also edited the *Memoirs* (1679) of Richard Langhorne and wrote Stafford's *Memoirs* (1682), an account of the trial and execution of William Howard, Viscount Stafford (which included a statement of Roman Catholic principles on civil allegiance), and *A Remonstrance of Piety and Innocence* (1683), a collection of memorials of other Oates Plot victims. On his release, Corker established a chapel at Clerkenwell, London; his most celebrated convert at that time was John Dryden. At the revolution the Clerkenwell chapel was sacked by the mob; Corker retired to the Continent and in 1690 was elected Abbot of Lambspring. Probably in the same year he published *A Rational Account Given by a Young Gentleman . . . of the Motives and Reasons Why He Is Become a Roman Catholic,* an apologetic pamphlet similar in approach to that of François Veron. Corker was involved in quarrels with the community at Lambspring and resigned as abbot in 1696; he seems to have returned to England some time before that, as he was arrested for debt in 1694. He remained on the mission in London until his death.

Bibliography: *Publications of the Catholic Record Society* v.47–48 (1953–55). R. B. WELDON, *Collections,* and P. A. ALLANSON, *Collections,* in MSS at Downside Abbey, England. *Bradford Antiquary* (1940) 123–140. J. GILLOW, *A Literary and Biographical History or Bibliographical Dictionary of the English Catholics from 1534 to the Present Time* (New York 1961) 1:568–571. T. A. BIRRELL, *Catholic Allegiance and the Popish Plot* (Nijmegen 1950).

[T. A. BIRRELL]

CORMIER, HYACINTHE-MARIE, BL.

Baptized Henri Marie; master general of the Order of Preachers (DOMINICANS) and spiritual writer; b. Orleans, France, Dec. 8, 1832; d. Rome, Italy, Dec. 17, 1916. After the early death of Cormier's father, his mother took him and his brother Eugene to live near their uncle who was a priest. Both boys entered the junior seminary at Orleans, but Eugene died the following year. Shortly after Cormier was ordained a priest of the diocese of Orleans in 1856, he was received in the novitiate of the Order of Preachers at Flavigny by Father Henri LACORDAIRE and given the name Hyacinthe. The Dominican community hesitated to profess him because of his health, but in 1859 when Cormier fell seriously ill, he was anointed and allowed to make his profession in the belief he had only days to live. He recovered and served the Dominicans for another 50 years.

As a professor of theology, he demonstrated a firm grasp of the faith. During the years 1866–74, he was the first provincial of the restored province of Toulouse, and again from 1878–82, served intermittently as prior in various convents. Cormier's administrative competence helped solidify the Dominican restoration begun by Lacordaire.

Beginning in 1891 Cormier served in generalate of the Order, first as *socius* to Master General Frühwirth (1891–96), then as procurator general until 1904 when he was elected the 76th master general. As master general (1904–1916), Cormier restored many suppressed provinces and erected new ones, including one in Canada and another in California. His time as master general coincided with the difficult period of modernism in the Church, and he promulgated a new *ratio studiorum* for the Order. In 1909 he established the international Angelicum University (now the Pontifical University of St. Thomas) in Rome and lent his support to the theological faculty of the University of Fribourg in Switzerland. A noted spiritual director, Cormier was an esteemed confidant of St. PIUS X, prized for his intellectual honesty and compelling moral judgment.

Cormier practiced strict conformity to the Dominican Rule. Because he had been born on the Feast of the Immaculate Conception, he had a strong devotion to the Blessed Virgin Mary and the Rosary. Despite his heavy schedule of teaching, writing, administering, and spiritual direction, he spent hours daily before the Blessed Sacrament.

Cormier wrote his doctoral thesis on the biblical rationalism of David Straus. Among his 171 printed writings examined during the beatification process were encyclical letters, biographies, and spiritual books, including *Instruction des Novices* (Paris 1880) and *Quinze entretiens sur la liturgie dominicaine* (Rome 1913).

Cormier died quietly in Rome at the age of 84 and was buried in the church adjacent to the Pontifical University of St. Thomas. He was beatified by Pope John Paul II, Nov. 20, 1994.

Feast: May 21, the anniversary of his election as master general.

Bibliography: *Acta Capituli Generalis Ordinis Praedicatorum 1920* (Rome 1920): 60–67. B. MONTAGNES, ed., *Exégèse et obéissance: correspondance Cormier-Lagrange (1904–1916)* (Paris 1989). M. A. SALADINI, *Il p. Giacinto M. Cormier, maestro generale dei Frati predicatori* (Rome 1940). S. SZABÓ, *Hyacinth Marie Cormier,* translated by C. G. MOORE (New York 1938).

[A. B. WILLIAMS/K. I. RABENSTEIN]

CORNARO, ELENA LUCREZIA PISCOPIA

Poet and philosopher; b. Venice, June 5, 1646; d. Padua, July 26, 1684. Because she was born into the Cornaro Piscopia branch renowned for political and commercial affairs in Venice, Elena enjoyed the remarkable distinction, in contrast to many women of her day, of being formally educated. Besides classical Latin and Greek, she knew Hebrew, Arabic, and Spanish. Her family's influence and prestige gained her admission to the University of Padua, and she received the degree of doctor of philosophy in 1678. She also exhibited skill in mathematics and acquired a considerable reputation among her contemporaries as a poet. Much of her poetry dealt with ascetical or spiritual topics and was lauded for both its contents and its lyrical qualities. This high evaluation of her writing, however, has not persisted, and she may be regarded as of only minor importance in the field of ascetical literature. In 1688, the University of Padua published her works. Her personal fame was enhanced in her lifetime by many pious and charitable undertakings. She was received as an oblate of the Order of St. Benedict at 17, and at her early death, she was entombed in the Benedictine convent in Padua.

Bibliography: V. S. MARZOLO, *Elena Lucrezia Cornaro Piscopia* (Milan 1925). V. REDLICH, *Lexikon für Theologie und Kirche,* ed. J. HOFER and K. RAHNER, 10 v. (2d, new ed. Freiburg 1957–65) (1966)[2] 3:57.

[P. D. SMITH]

CORNELIUS, POPE, ST.

Pontificate: March 6 or 13, 251 to June 253. Cornelius, apparently a member of the distinguished Roman *gens Cornelia,* was elected pope (probably in March 251) when the Emperor Decius left Rome to repel the Goths. On the death of Fabian (250), it had been impossible to proceed at once to the election of a new bishop of Rome because of the Decian persecution. During the interval, the Roman Church was governed by a college of priests that included NOVATIAN. Abandoning his attitude of cautious reserve on the election of Cornelius, Novatian threw in his lot with the rigorist party and had himself consecrated rival bishop of Rome. His attempt to win over other bishops to his cause met with only partial success, thanks largely to the vigorous action of CYPRIAN OF CARTHAGE and of Cornelius. In October 251 the pope held a large synod at Rome, attended by 60 bishops and many priests and deacons. It excommunicated Novatian and his supporters and approved the decisions of a Carthaginian synod, ordering the restoration of the *LAPSI* ''with the medicines of repentance.'' The decisions of the Roman synod, together with a letter from Cyprian approving the condemnation of the Novatianists and the measures affecting the *lapsi,* were communicated by Cornelius to Fabius, Bishop of Antioch. Relations between Cornelius and Cyprian became strained (252) when Fortunatus, a rival of Cyprian, endeavored to poison the pope's mind concerning the African bishop, but Cyprian managed to regain the pope's confidence.

The letter of Cornelius to Fabius is historically interesting for the light it throws on the organization of the Roman Church at this time. According to the pope, it included 46 priests, 7 deacons, 7 subdeacons, 42 acolytes, 52 exorcists, readers, and doormen, and more than 1,500 widows. It has been estimated, on the basis of these figures, that the Roman community may have numbered 50,000 persons in the mid-third century.

The emperor Decius had died in battle, but his successor Gallus (251–253) continued to persecute, banishing Cornelius to Centumcellae (Civitavecchia) in June of 252. He ''died there gloriously,'' according to the Liberian Catalogue. He was not, it seems, officially regarded as a martyr at first, though Cyprian hailed him as such. He is not listed in the Fourth-century *Depositio Martyrum,* and a marble slab bearing the inscription Cornelius Martyr ep, found in the crypt of Lucina in the cemetery of St. Callistus, where Cornelius was buried, has the word *martyr* added by a later hand. The account of the alleged trial of Cornelius by Decius in the *Liber pontificalis* is taken from an apocryphal fifth-century *passio* of Cornelius. Three of his letters have survived, two to Cyprian (*Epist.* 49; 50) and one to Fabius of Antioch.

Feast: Sept. 16.

Bibliography: G. MERCATI, *Opere minore,* v.2 (*Studium* 77; 1937) 226–240, letters. *Liber pontificalis,* ed. L. DUCHESNE (Paris

1886–92) 1:150–152; 3.74. J. QUASTEN, *Patrology* (Westminster MD 1950) 2:236–237. G. BARDY, *Dictionnaire d'histoire et de géographie ecclésiastiques*, ed. A. BAUDRILLART et al. (Paris 1912) 13:891–894. G. SCHWEIGER, *Lexikon für Theologie und Kirche*, ed. J. HOFER and K. RAHNER (Freiburg 1957–65) 3:57–58. R. U. MONTINI, *Le tombe dei papi* (Rome 1957) 77–79. E. FERGUSON, ed. *Encyclopedia of Early Christianity* (New York 1997) 1.294. J. N. D. KELLY, *Oxford Dictionary of Popes* (New York 1986) 17–18.

[J. CHAPIN]

CORNELIUS, JOHN, BL.

Jesuit priest and martyr; baptised John Conor O'Mahony; *alias* Mohun; b. Bodmin, Cornwall, England, 1557; d. hanged, drawn, and quartered at Dorchester, Dorset, July 4, 1594. John was born to Irish immigrants on the estate of Sir John Arundell, who took an interest in the boy and provided for his education at Exeter College, Oxford. Seeking a Catholic education in theology, John transferred to the English College at Rheims (1579), then at Rome (1580), where he became acquainted with the Society of Jesus. Following his ordination (1583); he ministered for a decade at Lanherne, where he was chaplain to Lady Arundell. He requested entry into the Jesuits. Unable to leave his flock unattended to undertake his novitiate in Flanders, he kept in contact with the English superior, Henry Garnet, who sought permission for Cornelius to make his novitiate in England.

He was arrested April 14, 1594, at Chideock Castle, Dorsetshire. Bl. Thomas Bosgrave, a member of the Arundell family, met Cornelius as he was being taken away. Bosgrave offered the bareheaded priest his hat and was arrested for giving comfort to an illegal priest. Two Irish servants of the castle, John (or Terence) Carey and Patrick Salmon, were also arrested and suffered with Bosgrave and Cornelius. They were sent to the Marshalsea in London for examination. Even under torture the priest refused to divulge the names of other Catholics. He was returned to Dorchester, where he and his three companions were condemned, July 2, 1594. Cornelius pronounced his vows as a Jesuit before three witnesses during his imprisonment. The priest was the last of the four to suffer. Kissing the gallows and the feet of his three fellow martyrs, he uttered the words of St. Andrew: "O Cross, long desired." Then he prayed for his executioners and the queen. He was beatified by Pius XI on Dec. 15, 1929.

Feast of the English Martyrs: May 4 (England); July 4 (Diocese of Plymouth); Dec. 1 (Jesuits).

See Also: ENGLAND, SCOTLAND AND WALES, MARTYRS OF.

Bibliography: R. CHALLONER, *Memoirs of Missionary Priests*, ed. J. H. POLLEN (rev. ed. London 1924; repr. Farnborough 1969). J. H. POLLEN, *Acts of English Martyrs* (London 1891). J. N. TYLENDA, *Jesuit Saints & Martyrs* (Chicago 1998) 198–99.

[K. I. RABENSTEIN]

CORNERSTONE, CHURCH

The first stone laid in the construction of a church. The custom of blessing the site of a new church is of ancient origin. The sixth-century *Novellae* of Justinian (*Corpus iuris civilis, Novellae.* 131.7) says that the bishop shall say a prayer and fix a cross at the site; it is not clear if this involved a cornerstone. The 12th-century Decretal of Gratian, which in this matter draws on a sixth-century Council of Orleans, says that the bishop shall place a cross and designate the location of the atrium (*Corpus iuris caconici*, c.9). In the 13th century, Durandus makes clear mention of a "first stone." The Roman Pontificals of the same century give a simple blessing for this stone. The Pontifical of 1572 gives the ceremony essentially as it is today. Historically, the ceremony that was given in the Pontifical and the Ritual assumed that the foundation walls of the church were already in place. At the site of the future altar, a wooden cross was set up and blessed; the cornerstone was blessed and then set in place in a principal wall; and the foundation of the church was blessed. The prayers of blessing contain numerous scriptural references to Christ as the cornerstone.

Bibliography: J. NABUCO, *Pontificalis Romani expositio juridico-practica* (Paris 1962) 512.

[C. H. MEINBERG/EDS.]

CORONEL, JUAN

Franciscan missionary and linguist; b. Torija, Alcarria, Spain, 1569; d. Mérida, Yucatán, 1651. He studied humanities at the University of Alcalá de Henares and joined the Franciscan Order (1584). His biographers agree that he went to Yucatán prior to his ordination, but differ about the date of his arrival, placing it between 1580 and 1601. He mastered the Mayan language rapidly and taught it for many years. One of his pupils was the Franciscan historian Diego López de COGOLLUDO. Coronel was guardian of the convent of Ticax, Yucatán, and *definitor* in his province. Of his work *Arte en lengua de Maya* (Mexico 1620) only one volume is extant. In addition he wrote *Discursos predicables, con otras diversas materias Espirituales de la doctrina Xtna., y los Artículos de la Fe* (Mexico 1620) and *Doctrina christiana, en lengua Maya* (Mexico 1620). His linguistic publications were a revision of the work of his predecessors Villalpando, Landa, Solana, and Ciudad Real.

Bibliography: J. M. BERISTAIN DE SOUZA, *Biblioteca hispano americana septentrional,* 5 v. in 2 (3d ed. Mexico City 1947). MARCELLINO DA CIVEZZA, *Saggio di bibliografia geografica storica etnografica sanfrancescana* (Prato 1879). E. B. ADAMS, *A Bio-Bibliography of Franciscan Authors in Colonial Central America* (Washington 1953).

[E. GÓMEZ-TAGLE]

CORPUS ET SANGUIS CHRISTI, SOLEMNITY OF

The Solemnity of the Body and Blood of Christ, historically observed Thursday after Trinity Sunday where it is a holy day of obligation. In the United States and other parts of the world where the solemnity is not observed as a holy day of obligation, it is assigned to the Sunday after Trinity Sunday. This feast, still known popularly as *Corpus Christi*, celebrates the mystery of the enduring presence of the Body and Blood of Christ in the sacrament of the Holy Eucharist.

The name *Corpus Christi* ("the body of Christ") is an abbreviation of the name of the feast in the Missal of Pius V (1570), *festum sanctissimi corporis christi* ("the feast of the most holy body of Christ"). Older names for the feast include *Nova sollemnitas* and *Festa Domini*, the latter survives in the Romance languages as *Fête Dieu,* etc. The renewal of the name of the feast *Sollemnitas Corpus et Sanguinis Christi* ("Solemnity of the Body and Blood of Christ") correlates with the renewal of eucharistic theology and practice at Vatican II.

History. The history of the feast is inseparable from the social and political context of BELGIUM and medieval eucharistic devotion and practices. In response to debates about the Real Presence and infrequent communion, there was a great development of eucharistic devotion. The feast was established in 1246 in Liège (Luik), Belgium, by Bishop Robert of Turotte, in response to the call of Julianna of Cornillon (ca. 1193–1258) and Eve of St. Martin (ca. 1210–1265). In 1208 Julianna reported a vision through which she understood that Jesus lamented the absence of a particular feast in the Church's calendar focused on his sacramental presence on the altar. Her vision launched a campaign on the part of the Beguines for a feast centered on the presence of the Lord in the Blessed Sacrament, which met with reluctance on the part of some clergy. Inspired by the Beguine's piety and concern for orthodoxy, the other clergy soon promoted the feast. While it seemed to pass popularly with Julianna's death, her powerful confessors kept it alive in Liège and led to its reception in the schools of Paris. A key figure was the former archdeacon of Liège, Jacques Pantaléon, who later became Pope Urban IV (1261). He adopted the feast

. . . etc. (Aug. 11, 1264, is date of Transiturus; text in J. D. Mansi, *Sacrorum Conciliorum nova et amplissima collectio*; reprinted and continued by L. Petit and J. B. Martin, 23:1077f.) Noteworthy is the bull's call to communion on the feast, harkening back to a central motivation among the Beguines for its institution. Urban IV died before he could stir up Roman enthusiasm for a universal feast. However, it was repromulgated by Clement V (1305–1314) in his letter *Si Dominum,* and the feast spread more steadily through Europe.

The early office and texts for the feast composed by John of Cornillon and Julianna were replaced by Urban IV with new texts assembled by Thomas Aquinas, some of which he may have composed himself. Noteworthy is the sequence *Lauda Sion,* that remains part of the Mass in the revised Missal of Paul VI. There is no mention of eucharistic procession or exposition connected with the feast by its official promulgators. However, the procession came to be a hallmark of the feast for many local churches and contributed to the popularlity of the feast through the fourteenth century. Rome later adopted the practice. The eucharistic procession came to have great social and commerical signficance as well as an expression of popular religiosity.

Present-day Celebration. The 1969 sacramentary introduces new lections, while retaining the medieval sequence, *Lauda Sion.* Its euchology and antiphons express many facets of eucharistic theology: memorial, presence, and eschatological dimension. The liturgical guidelines for the procession long associated with the feast are found in the Ceremonial of Bishops, nos. 385 through 394 and Holy Communion and Worship of the Eucharistic Outside of Mass, nos. 101 through 108.

Bibliography: P. M. GY, "L'Office du Corpus Christi et Saint Thomas d'Aquin. Etat d'une recherche," *Revue des Sciences philosophiques et theologiques* 64 (1980) 491–507; reprinted in idem, *La Liturgie dans l'histoire* (Paris 1990). A. HAQUIN, ed., Fête-Dieu (1246–1996). Vol. 1, *Actes du colloque de Liège, 12–14 septembre 1996*; vol. 2, *Vie de sainte Julienne de Cornillon* (Louvain-la-Neuve 1999). J. LAMBERTS, "The Origin of the Corpus Christi Feast," *Worship* 71 (1996) 432–446. M. DUDLEY, "Liturgy and Doctrine: Corpus Christi," *Worship* 66 (1992) 417–426. M. RUBIN, *Corpus Christi: The Eucharist in Late Medieval Culture* (New York 1991). N. MITCHELL, *Cult and Controversy: The Worship of the Eucharist Outside Mass* (New York 1982). G. MACY, *Treasures from the Storeroom: Medieval Religion and the Eucharist* (Collegeville, Minn. 1999).

[M. F. CONNELL]

CORPUS IURIS CANONICI

Term used to indicate six compilations of CANON LAW, namely, (1) the Decretum of GRATIAN (c. 1140), (2)

the Decretals of GREGORY IX (1234), (3) the LIBER SEXTUS OF BONIFACE VIII (1298), (4) the CLEMENTINAE (1317), (5) the Extravagantes Ioannis XXII (1325), and (6) the Extravagantes communes (1500, 1503). These compilations served as the basis for Canon Law from the early 16th century up to the second decade of the 20th century. They were referred to as the *Corpus iuris canonici* by Pope GREGORY XIII when, in the brief *Cum pro munere pastorali* (1580), he approved as textually authentic an edition of them made by the *Correctores Romani.*

The content of the *Corpus iuris canonici* was determined by its being largely a revision of a three-volume collection of Church legislation entitled *Corpus iuris canonici,* that two Paris legists, Jean Chappuis and Vitalis de Thebes, had prepared between 1499 and 1502 for the Parisian printers Ulrich Guering and Berthold Rembolt. To the three authenticated collections (Decretals, Sext, Clementines) and the private collection of Gratian, Chappuis had added two sets of EXTRAVAGANTES, the first of which (namely, those of John XXII) had been circulating since 1325, and the second of which appears to have been put together by Chappuis himself. By the end of the Council of Trent, this arrangement was so well established that Pius IV decided in 1563 to revise and reissue officially the texts in the Chappuis *Corpus.* Subsequently, in 1566, a commission of cardinals was set up by Pius V to ascertain the authenticity of the texts in the Decretum, a work upon which some 28 experts were engaged until 1580. A perfunctory revision was made of the other parts of the *Corpus.*

In 1582 all six collections were issued, not as *Corpus iuris canonici,* but under their own separate titles, in three volumes (Decretum; Decretals; Sextus, Clementines, Extravagantes). Although later usage tended to restrict the term *Corpus* to the works found in this Roman edition, the body of Church law was in no way declared complete or closed by this promulgation and the papal use of the term *Corpus.* For one thing, the Roman *Corpus* did not go beyond the limit of 1484 set by Chappuis; for another, it took no account of conciliar legislation later than the Council of Vienne (1311–12).

Although attempts were made afterward to codify legislation enacted after 1484, for example, in an ill-fated Liber Septimus commissioned by Gregory XIII himself, the Roman edition of 1580 remained the only authenticated *Corpus* in the Western Church until the Code of Canon Law of 1917. It was reprinted often; the most recent edition is that of A. Friedberg, *Corpus iuris canonici. Editio Lipsiensis secunda post A. L. Richteri curas ad librorum manu scriptorum et editionis romanae fidem,* v.1. *Decretum Magistri Gratiani;* v.2. *Decretalium Collectiones* (Leipzig 1879–81).

Bibliography: P. TORQUEBIAU, *Dictionnaire de droit canonique,* ed. R. NAZ (Paris 1935–65) 4:610–664. P. CIMETIER, *Les Sources du droit ecclésiastique* (Paris 1930). A. M. STICKLER, *Lexikon für Theologie und Kirche,* ed. J. HOFER and K. RAHNER (Freiberg 1957–65) 3:65–69. A. M. STICKLER, *Historia iuris canonici latini: v.1, Historia fontium* (Turin 1950) 272–276. J. F. VON SCHULTE, *Die Geschichte der Quellen und der Literatur des kanonischen Rechts* (Graz 1956) 3:69–71. A. VAN HOVE, *Commentarium Lovaniense in Codicem iuris canonici 1* (Mechlin 1928–) 1:368.

[L. E. BOYLE]

CORREA MAGALLANES, MATEO, ST.

Martyr, pastor; b. July 22 or 23, 1866, Tepechitlán, Zacatecas, Diocese of Zacatecas, Mexico; d. Feb. 6, 1927, Durango, Jalisco, Diocese of Zacatecas. Fr. Correa was ministering in the parish at Valparaíso, Zacatecas, during the persecution, where he administered First Communion to another future martyr, (Bl.) Miguel Agustin PRO. Correa faithfully executed his sacerdotal duties, including evangelizing and serving the poor. He was continually harassed by the authorities, arrested and released. The last time he was administering the last rites. He was detained for several days at Fresnillo, Zacatecas, then taken to Durango. There General Eulogio Ortiz asked him to hear the confessions of some prisoners. Later he asked the priest to reveal the content of those confessions or be killed. When he refused, he was martyred outside Durango, where his relics are enshrined in the cathedral in the Chapel of Saint George the Martyr. He was both beatified (Nov. 22, 1992) and canonized (May 21, 2000) with Cristobal MAGALLANES [*see* MEXICO, MARTYRS OF, SS.] by Pope John Paul II.

Feast: May 25 (Mexico).

Bibliography: J. CARDOSO, *Los mártires mexicanos* (Mexico City 1953). J. DÍAZ ESTRELLA, *El movimiento cristero: sociedad y conflicto en los Altos de Jalisco* (México, D.F. 1979). V. GARCÍA JUÁREZ, *Los cristeros* (Fresnillo, Zac. 1990).

[K. I. RABENSTEIN]

CORRECTION, FRATERNAL

Fraternal correction is an admonition given to another to protect him from sin or to induce him to give up sin. It is called "fraternal" to distinguish it from paternal correction, which is administered by a superior in his capacity of father, and from judicial correction, which is given to a person after he has been proved guilty by a formal process of law. Fraternal correction is an act of charity and is numbered among the seven spiritual works of mercy, which are the effects of charity. Fraternal correction can sometimes be obligatory, for, just as one can at times be obliged to aid another in his bodily needs, as when he is seriously ill or wounded, so one can sometimes be bound to assist a fellow man in his spiritual needs, particularly when his soul is wounded or likely to be wounded by grave sin.

Jesus Christ explicitly commanded fraternal correction when He said: "If thy brother sin against thee, go and show him his fault between thee and him alone. If he listen to thee, thou hast won thy brother" (Mt 18.15). The phrase "against thee" might seem to limit the sin in question to a personal offense, but the common interpretation of Catholic theologians extends the meaning to every sin of another that has come to one's notice. Moreover, the phrase "against thee" does not appear in some of the earlier scriptural codices.

St. Paul also implied the duty of fraternal correction when he wrote to the Galatians: "Brethren, even if a person is caught doing something wrong, you who are spiritual instruct such a one in a spirit of meekness, considering thyself, lest thou also be tempted" (Gal 6.1).

Conditions for Fraternal Correction. Theologians generally require the fulfillment of five conditions before a person is gravely obliged to administer a fraternal correction: (1) It must be certain that a formal mortal sin has been committed or is likely to be committed by the other. (2) There must be good probability that the sinner will not amend on his own initiative or at the admonition of a third party. (3) There must be good probability that the culprit will listen to the correction and conform his conduct to it. Sometimes there is reason to fear that a correction will do more harm than good. (4) The person planning to give the correction must foresee that no serious harm will come to himself. For example, if he has reason to fear that the one corrected will calumniate him or even injure him physically as a result of his well-intended admonition, he has no obligation to attempt it; for fraternal correction is an act of charity, which does not bind a person when it is likely to involve serious inconvenience to himself. (5) The circumstances of time, place, etc., must be favorable to the administration of the correction. Thus, it would not be prudent to give an admonition to a person when he is in an angry mood.

Those who are inclined to scrupulosity sometimes worry whether or not they are bound to correct someone who is doing wrong or seems about to do something wrong. Such persons should bear in mind that it is only when all the conditions enumerated above are present that there is a grave obligation to make a correction. If they are in doubt as to the fulfillment of any of these conditions, it is better not to attempt the admonition; for in such circumstances they will probably do no good and will be denounced as busybodies. On the other hand, there are persons who, through timidity or indifference, refuse to correct an erring friend or relative when there is good reason to believe that a kindly admonition would effect much good.

Particular Points. It is commonly held by theologians that when another has committed or is about to commit a formal venial sin, there is a light obligation to correct him if the required conditions are present. There can be a grave obligation to make the correction if the venial sin is very likely to lead to mortal sin.

It is impossible to answer categorically the question of whether there is an obligation—at least a grave obligation—to enlighten one who is doing something wrong without realizing its malice. In any event, a distinction must be made between violations of human law and violations of divine law. Thus, if a Catholic sees another Catholic eating meat on Friday, evidently forgetting the day, there is no grave obligation to remind him, unless there would be scandal given to the bystanders; but if a young person is developing a habit of impurity without realizing the malice of his actions, he should be enlightened and admonished.

Normally a fraternal correction should first be administered privately, and then, as Christ prescribed, before two witnesses, if this be considered advisable. If the delinquent does not then amend, the matter should be brought to the attention of the proper superiors, at least if the common good is being injured. At times, it is better to omit the fraternal correction and report the case immediately to competent authority—for example, when a pupil in a school is secretly corrupting other students.

Bibliography: J. COSTELLO, *Moral Obligation of Fraternal Correction* (Washington 1949). H. DAVIS, *Moral and Pastoral Theology,* rev. and enl. ed. by L.W. GEDDES (New York 1958) 1:327–330. J. AERTNYS and C. A. DAMEN, *Theologia moralis,* 2 v. (16th ed. Turin 1950) 1:365–372. E. F. REGATILLO and M. ZALBA, *Theologiae moralis summa,* v.1 (*Biblioteca de autores cristianos* 93; Madrid 1952) 918–924. H. NOLDIN, *Summa theologiae moralis,* rev. A. SCHMITT and G. HEINZEL (Innsbruck 1961–62) 2:95–98. F. J. CONNELL, *Outlines of Moral Theology* (2d ed. Milwaukee 1964) 91–92.

[F. J. CONNELL]

CORRECTORIA

By *correctoria* are here meant, not the 13th-century Biblical correctories compiled in Paris by Dominicans and Franciscans for "correcting" the text of the Latin Vulgate, but those controversial writings exchanged between Franciscans and Dominicans in criticism or defense of St. THOMAS AQUINAS. These corrections are of two types, the anti-Thomist and the pro-Thomist.

Anti-Thomist Correctories. It was, perhaps, inevitable that the Aristotelian principles introduced by Aquinas into his synthesis of Catholic doctrine—in which "faith and reason, though distinct as of right, are joined together in the most intimate harmony of friendship" (Leo XIII, *Aeterni Patris*)—should rouse opposition from theologians brought up in a different tradition. The conflict became acute only after the Paris and Oxford syllabi of 1277.

Franciscan Correctorium. To render his fellow Franciscans immune from Thomist teaching, WILLIAM DE LA MARE wrote in 1278 a *Correctorium Fratris Thomae*, a correction of those theses he considered unsound, inasmuch as they were contrary to Scripture and the Fathers, and included, or at least implied, in the condemned errors. He censured 118 points drawn from the *Summa theologiae,* the *Quaestiones disputatae,* and *De quolibet* and from *In 1 sententiarum.* He systematically summarized Aquinas's doctrine, criticized it, and replied to his arguments. The censure falls mainly on philosophical matters: unicity of form, simplicity of spiritual beings, distinction of the powers of the soul, absolute potentiality of matter, eternity of the world, and similar topics regarded as opposed to the Augustinian school. About 1284 William meticulously undertook a revised edition, adding new criticism, enlarging his evidence, and improving it throughout, but without eliminating anything from his original. It is extant in Vat. lat. MS 4413, fol. 1–155r.

At the general chapter of Strasbourg in 1282, Bonagratia, Minister General, forbade the perusal of Thomas's *Summa theologiae* by the Franciscans, except by the more learned lectors; and even then it was to be accompanied by William's *Declarationes,* written not in the margins, but separately [G. Fussenegger, "Definitiones Capituli Generalis Argentinae celebrati anno 1282," *Archivum Franciscanum historicum* 26 (1933) 139]. Thus, by being made obligatory for students of the *Summa,* William's *Correctorium* became officially adopted by the Franciscans.

Ur-Correctorium. The so-called *Ur-Correctorium* [F. Pelster, *Recherches de théologie ancienne et médiévale* 3 (1931) 397–99; *Gregorianum* 38 (1947) 230–35], which for many years has unduly haunted scholars, need not be dwelt upon at length. Contrary to its editor's contention [F. Pelster, *Declarationes Magistri Guilelmi de la Mare, OFM, De variis Sententiis S. Thomae Aquinatis,* Opuscula et Textus 21 (Münster-i-W. 1956)] that it was the earliest *correctorium,* identical with the *Declarationes* of Bonagratia's decree, it has been conclusively shown that it is simply a later anonymous list of 60 propositions extracted from William's second recension [see D. A. Callus, *Bulletin Thomiste* (Paris 1924–) 9 (1954–56) 944–48; *Blackfriars* 40 (1959) 39–41].

Pro-Thomist Correctories. The Dominicans took up William de la Mare's challenge and riposted with their *Correctoria corruptorii Thomae.* Five replies have been preserved: three from Oxford and two from Paris, known by their *incipits* as: (1) *Correctorium Corruptorii "Quare"* (ed. P. Glorieux, *Bibliothèque Thomiste* 9, Le Saulchoir 1927); (2) *"Sciendum"* (ed. *idem, ibid.* 31, Paris 1956); (3) *"Quaestione"* (ed. J. P. Muller, *Studia anselmiana* 35); (4) *"Circa"* (ed. *idem, ibid.* 12–13, 1941); (5) *Apologeticum veritatis contra Corruptorium* (ed. *idem, Studi et Testi* 108). All the *correctoria* have in common that, rather than taking the offensive, they stood on the defensive; hence they also became known as *defensoria.* Their main purpose, strictly speaking, was not to attack, although some harsh words occur occasionally, but to demonstrate that William's critique sprang from an utter misunderstanding of Aquinas. From Aquinas's own writings they proved that his doctrine, correctly grasped, was neither against Scripture and the Fathers nor contrary to philosophy, but sound and Catholic. They endeavored to make Thomas speak for himself, *sui interpres,* by giving either his own words, or the gist of his argument.

Since the Franciscan attack had appeared in England, it was natural that the first defense should come from Oxford. Internal and external evidence shows that the three *correctoria "Quare," "Sciendum,"* and *"Quaestione"* were of Dominican and English provenance and that they were the first to arrive. However, owing to the prohibition of 1277 by ROBERT KILWARDBY, they were circulated anonymously, with the result that it is difficult to discover their authorship. The problem became further complicated by groundless conjectures. To proceed methodically one may, at the outset, eliminate such pretenders as GILES OF ROME, Hugh de Billom, Durandellus (DURANDUS OF AURILLAC), Bl. John of Parma, and HARVEY NEDELLEC, though they are tentatively suggested by great scholars. One is on firmer ground with the early catalogue of Dominican writers (*Tabula Stamsensis*), which attributes a *correctorium* to the Oxford masters RICHARD KNAPWELL and WILLIAM OF MACCLESFELD.

Correctorium Corruptorii "Quare." This is the earliest, the most complete, and the best known. It comprises the full text of the Franciscan "correction," and a thorough and complete answer to its criticism. It has come down in two recensions, which suggests that two writers collaborated on it. The revision consists chiefly in eliminating repetitions, in supplementing several additions, and in reducing the whole to firmer unity. On the authority of a late, and faulty, ascription (in MS Paris, Bibl. Nat. lat. 14549), it was printed under the name of the Italian Augustinian Giles of Rome (Strasbourg 1501; Venice 1508, 1516, etc.); but *"Quare"* is unquestionably of Dominican and Oxford origin. F. Pelster attributed it to

THOMAS OF SUTTON ["'Thomas von Sutton und das Corr
rectorium 'Quare detraxisti,'" *Mélanges A. Pelzer* (Louvain 1947) 441–66]. Almost all scholars, however, agree in ascribing it to Richard Knapwell, at least as to its principal author. Parallel passages between his *Quaestio disputata* on the unicity of form and *"Quare"* strengthen this conviction. It was written not later than 1282 or 1283, before the clash with JOHN PECKHAM. The *Dominus Cantuariensis* does not refer to Peckham, as has been assumed, but to Archbishop Kilwardby. The whole paragraph (p. 206, lines 22–34) is an allusion to the concluding sections of Kilwardby's letter to Peter of Conflans (ed. A. Birkenmajer, *Beiträge zur Geschichte der Philosophie und Theologie des Mittelalters* 20.5:60–64). Kilwardby dismissed the unicity tenet as absurd or as a figment of the imagination (*fatua positio, vel imaginatio phantastica*) against faith and philosophy (*see* FORMS, UNICITY AND PLURALITY OF). Knapwell ironically retorted that, lest it should seem to disparage the learned men (Kilwardby) who maintained an opposite opinion, he would not declare it contrary to faith and philosophy; he would not even reply to their arguments, lest he should be compelled to assert fancies and absurdities (*ficta et fatua*).

The author of this article tentatively suggests Thomas of Sutton as responsible for the second redaction of *"Quare."* Sutton wrote the *De unitate formae* to confute Kilwardby's letter [ed. F. Ehrle, *Archiv für Literatur und Kirchengeschichte des Mittelalters* 5 (1889) 614–32; Birkenmajer, *op. cit.*] and *De productione formae substantialis* against the *inchoationes formarum,* which is another aspect of the same question. On the other hand, most of William de la Mare's arguments against the unicity thesis are drawn from Kilwardby. Hence Sutton's confutation militates against both. Now it does not seem altogether inconceivable that Sutton and Knapwell, living in the same house and contemporaneously confuting the same adversaries, should communicate their findings to each other. If this conjecture is correct, it satisfactorily explains the borrowings from the *De unitate formae* and the *De productione formae substantialis.*

Correctorium "Sciendum." Like *"Quare,"* the *Correctorium "Sciendum"* contains an answer to all the points raised by the Franciscan critique; but unlike *"Quare,"* it omits William's text. The refutation, however, is wider, more vigorous, and sometimes aggressive. The redaction is somewhat hasty: the style is abrupt, the citations often unfilled; it gives the impression of a draft rather than of a finished version. Pressed, perhaps by the urgency of publishing his riposte, the author had no time to revise it. It was written shortly after *"Quare,"* yet before 1284. The *Tabula Stamsensis* assigns to the Oxford master ROBERT OF ORFORD a *Contra dicta Henrici* (HENRY

OF GHENT) and a *Contra primum Egidii* (Giles of Rome). The author appeals in both works to a *correctorium* of his own, which references fit well in *"Sciendum"* alone [see P. Bayerschmidt, *Divus Thomas* 17 (1939) 311–26]. He also cites his commentary *In 2 sententiarum,* of which there is a fragment (in MS Klosterneuburg 322) with the ascription *De Orforth.* The *Contra dicta Henrici* is attributed (in MS Vat. lat. 987, fol. 128v) to Robert de Colletorto, whereas the *Contra Egidium* in the only known MS (Oxford, Merton College 276) is anonymous, but cross references show that both works are by the same writer. In MS Todi 12, fol. 1 is noted explicitly "Inc. correct. corrupt. secundum collemtortum ordinis predicatorum"; but in MS Salamanca, University 1887 (*olim* Madrid, Bibl, Real VII.H.5) the author is called "William de Tortocollo." That Colletorto, or Tortocollo, is the author of *Contra dicta Henrici,* of *Contra Egidium,* and of *"Sciendum"* is unquestionable. The difficulty is whether his name was Robert or William. The editor of *"Sciendum,"* P. Glorieux, opting for William, unhesitatingly attributes it to William of Macclesfield, to whom the *Tabula Stamsensis* assigns a *correctorium* and a *Contra Henricum.* F. Pelster and others, on the contrary, identifying Colletorto with Robert of Orford, ascribe to him the *Correctorium "Sciendum."* The author of this article believes that Robert of Orford and Colletorto are the same person and suggests that the confusion arises from the omission of one line due to homography in the Salamanca MS. Similar omissions by copyists occur frequently, as all medievalists know [cf. an analogous instance in A. Dondaine, *Archivum Fratrum Praedicatorum* 17 (1947) 188–92]. The author's name, it seems, was inadvertently omitted, whereas *Guillermi* refers to the author of the *corruptorium,* not of the *correctorium.* In this case the colophon should read thus (or similarly):

> Explicit (correctorium) corruptorii Guillermi [de Mara anglici magistri in theologia,] de Torto collo anglici magistri in theologia ordinis fratrum predicatorum.

Correctorium "Quaestione." Unlike *"Sciendum"* and *"Circa,"* but like *"Quare,"* the *Correctorium "Quaestione"* first reproduces the Franciscan criticism in full, then vigorously refutes each of the arguments. But whereas William de la Mare's text is complete (except for the last nine *articuli*), the reply stops short at art. 30. That the author intended to continue his work is evident from several references (e.g., "hoc plenius ostendetur inferius; infra ad plenum improbabitur," etc.). It is anonymous in the only known manuscript. From internal evidence it is clear that the writer was an English Dominican and that it was written after *"Quare."* It has been attributed to Thomas of Sutton, Richard Knapwell, Hugh de Billom, and William of Macclesfield. Dom Muller, its editor, left the question open. Yet there is fairly circumstantial evidence pointing to Macclesfeld. According to the *Tabula Stamsensis* Macclesfeld wrote a *correctorium*. Now, of the three Oxford *correctoria*, "*Quare*" belongs to Richard Knapwell, and "*Sciendum*" very probably to Robert of Orford, or Colletorto; there remains "*Quaestione*," which one may tentatively assign to Macclesfeld. That he ceased abruptly at the point of treating the unicity thesis, which he had promised to discuss (p. 73), is telling. It seems to indicate that the interruption was due to a cogent reason, perhaps Peckham's intervention in the period between 1284 and 1286. Later he went to Paris to read the *Sentences* in preparation for his bachelorship in theology. He returned to Oxford to incept as master only after Peckham's death.

Correctorium "Circa." This correctory omits William's text, but gives the gist of his critique. It was written in Paris by JOHN (QUIDORT) OF PARIS [see M. Grabmann, *Revue néo-scolastique de philosophie* 19 (1912) 404–18] contemporaneously with his commentary on the *Sentences,* 1292 to 1294 [see J. P. Muller, *Angelicum* 36 (1959) 129–62]. It was left unfinished at the end of the criticism of *Summa theologiae* 1a2ae. Later hands supplemented some additions from "*Quare*" and "*Sciendum*" introduced by *secundum alios*. This correctory is remarkable for the large use of philosophical, particularly Arabic, sources.

Apologeticum veritatis contra Corruptorium. The last of the five Dominican correctories, the *Apologeticum veritatis contra Corruptorium,* was written in Paris by RAMBERT OF BOLOGNA, before 1299, when he left for home. It was interrupted at art. 16 in the middle of a sentence. Rambert followed the method of the earlier *correctoria;* and like John Quidort, he summarized William's text. The abrupt end of the *Apologeticum* is a grave loss to the history of the late 13th-century Paris theological speculation, for Rambert did not confine himself to the confutation of William de la Mare's attack, but riposted also against his contemporaries, the leading masters of the day—the *magni,* as he qualified them—Henry of Ghent, Giles of Rome, and RICHARD OF MIDDLETON (MEDIAVILLA). He borrowed tacitly from the *Correctorium "Circa,"* and referred to the "artists," SIGER OF BRABANT and others.

Finally, one may mention, to be complete, that *c.* 1315 to 1320 appeared a tardy reply to the Dominican *correctoria* by a German(?) Franciscan, which is extant (in Berlin MS 460, Theol. lat. qu. 13).

Significance of the Correctoria. Historically the *corruptorium* and *correctoria* are of considerable moment as witnesses of the first controversy between so-called Augustinianism and THOMISM. They are invaluable for ascertaining how far and how deeply St. Thomas's doctrine was understood by opponents and defenders. They show at a glance the primary equivocation under which many of the late 13th-century discussions labored: the disputants spoke a different language; they used the same terminology, but meant quite different things. Under the cloak of Augustine's authority, William de la Mare meticulously opposed Thomas's arguments and conclusions, without ever attempting to penetrate into the true meaning of the doctrine he was attacking. POTENCY AND ACT, MATTER AND FORM, PRIVATION and change, SEMINAL REASONS in matter, and other basic Aristotelian principles as interpreted by Aquinas have a totally different meaning in William and in Thomas. Hence the critique is based on an utter incomprehension of Thomism. The nature of BEING, the composition of ESSENCE AND EXISTENCE, and similar pertinent Thomistic theses were never discussed. The authors of the *correctoria,* on the other hand, knew Thomas well and generally interpreted him correctly, though occasionally they did not grasp his meaning fully. The depth and breadth of the Thomistic synthesis are so vast that it is not surprising that the first generation of Thomists should have failed to assimilate it completely. For example, the authors of "*Quare*" and "*Sciendum*" unequivocally asserted the composition of essence and existence; but one might, perhaps, have expected a fuller explanation of it, particularly when they dealt with the hylomorphic composition of spiritual beings.

Nevertheless the doctrinal value of the *correctoria,* though confined to points raised in the controversy and despite some defects, is indeed notable. The contribution they make to knowledge of the early Thomistic school is highly important. As an instance of the great profit that a serious study of the *correctoria* may yield, see A. Hufnagel, "Studien zur Entwicklung des thomistischen Erkenntnisbegriffes im Anschluss an das Correctorium 'Quare,'" *Beiträge zur Geschichte der Philosophie und Theologie des Mittelalters* 31.4 (Münster-i-W. 1935).

Bibliography: P. MANDONNET, "Premiers travaux de polémique thomiste," *Revue des sciences philosophiques et théologiques* 7 (1913) 46–70. F. EHRLE, "Der Kampf um die Lehre des hl. Thomas von Aquin in den ersten fünfzig Jahren nach seinem Tod," *Zeitschrift für katholische Theologie* 37 (1913) 266–318. P. GLORIEUX, "La Littérature des Correctoires: Simples notes," *Revue thomiste* 33 (1928) 69–96; "Les Correctoires: Essai de mise au point," *Recherches de théologie ancienne et médiévale* 14 (1947) 287–304; "Non in marginibus positis," *ibid.* 15 (1948) 182–84. F. PELSTER, "Zur Datierung der Correctoria und der Schriften des Johannes von Paris," *Divus Thomas* 3d series 30 (1952) 417–38. R. CREYTENS, "Autour de la littérature des Correctoires," *Archivum Fratrum Praedicatorum* 12 (1942) 313–30. A. VELLA, "Early Thomistic Controversies," *Melita Theologica* 3 (1950) 57–74; 4 (1951) 14–33. D. A. CALLUS, *Bulletin Thomiste* 9 (1954–56) 643–55. L. J. BATAILLON, *ibid.* 8 (1947–53) 1251–59; 10

Archbishop Michael Corrigan.

(1957–59) 583–94. F. J. ROENSCH, *Early Thomistic School* (Dubuque 1964).

[D. A. CALLUS]

CORRIGAN, MICHAEL AUGUSTINE

Sixth bishop and third archbishop of New York; b. Newark, N.J., Aug. 13, 1839; d. New York City, May 5, 1902. He was the fifth among nine children of Thomas and Mary (English) Corrigan, immigrants from Ireland. After attending a private school kept by his godfather, Bernard Kearney, and St. Mary's College in Wilmington, Del., he graduated from Mt. St. Mary's College, Emmitsburg, Md., in 1859. He wanted to become a priest and, as he already possessed some linguistic skill acquired in a year of European travel (1857), he was sent to Rome by his bishop, James Roosevelt Bayley of Newark, as one of the original 12 students with whom the North American College opened on Dec. 8, 1859. Upon completion of his course in theology at the College of Propaganda, he was ordained in the Basilica of St. John Lateran on Sept. 19, 1863.

Early Career. A year later, after earning his doctorate in theology at the College of Propaganda, he returned to the Newark diocese to become successively professor of dogmatic theology and Sacred Scripture, director of the seminary and vice-president of the collegiate department, and president of Seton Hall College (now University) and Seminary, South Orange, N.J. With his brothers, Fathers James and George and Dr. Joseph, he did much to ensure the prosperity of Seton Hall generally, and of its library in particular. In 1868 he was also named vicar-general; in this capacity he administered the diocese, coterminous with the state of New Jersey, during Bishop Bayley's attendance at Vatican Council I (1870) and upon the latter's translation to Baltimore (1872). Corrigan was then appointed to the See of Newark and consecrated on May 4, 1873, in St. Patrick's Cathedral, Newark, by Archbishop John McCloskey of New York.

For the next seven years, through diocesan synods, episcopal visitations, and annual parochial reports, he brought the spiritual and temporal affairs of his diocese into strict conformity with the decrees of the Plenary Councils of Baltimore. He devoted particular attention to the problems of Italian immigration. He also aided the Jesuit college, St. Peter's, in Jersey City; promoted the establishment of parochial schools, hospitals, orphanages, and other charitable institutions; encouraged the first pilgrimage of U.S. laymen to Rome (1874); and found time to pursue his favorite historical interests by beginning the systematization of the Baltimore archdiocesan archives.

Work in New York. On Oct. 1, 1880, Leo XIII appointed Corrigan titular archbishop of Petra and coadjutor, with right of succession, to Cardinal McCloskey of New York. Archbishop Corrigan was largely responsible for the preparation and conduct of the Fourth Provincial Council of New York (1883); he also visited Rome with other American archbishops to prepare the agenda of the Third Plenary Council of Baltimore (1884), at which he represented the cardinal. As McCloskey's agent, he succeeded, through President Chester Arthur and Secretary of State F. T. Frelinghuysen, in preventing confiscation by the Italian government of the North American College in Rome (1884). Upon the death of the cardinal (Oct. 10, 1885), he became archbishop of New York and was formally installed in St. Patrick's Cathedral on May 4, 1886. In November he summoned a diocesan synod to put into effect the legislation of the Third Plenary Council of Baltimore, one decree of which, concerning the necessity of establishing a church school in every American parish, formed part of the background of the severest trial of his episcopate.

Edward MCGLYNN, a fellow student of the archbishop in Rome and later rector of St. Stephen's Church in New York City, was an opponent of parochial schools. He had associated himself also with the land and tax theories of Henry George, whose candidacy for mayor of the city in 1886 he actively supported, despite the archbishop's prohibition. As a result of disobedience, McGlynn was repeatedly suspended and eventually removed from his pastorate. Subsequently summoned to Rome to account for his insubordination, McGlynn, upon the plea of ill health, refused to comply and incurred excommunication (July 4, 1887). Not until 1892, at a hearing in Washington before Archbishop Francesco Satolli, soon to become first apostolic delegate in the United States (1893), was the censure lifted; in 1895 Corrigan appointed McGlynn pastor of St. Mary's Church, Newburgh, N.Y.

The sensational aspects of the McGlynn affair, as well as the conservative stand of the archbishop on such issues as Irish nationalism, membership of Catholics in secret societies, the danger described in Europe as the heresy of AMERICANISM, and his lack of sympathy for Abp. John Ireland's FARIBAULT school experiment, overshadowed in the public mind, for a time, Corrigan's solid and lasting contributions to his archdiocese. He remodeled and brought efficiency into its various departments, from chancery to charities, and gave special care to the problems of the fast-mounting Italian immigration. He completed the towers and interior furnishings of St. Patrick's Cathedral and began construction of its Lady chapel. Stressing consistently the importance of education and scholarship, he reorganized the archdiocesan school system; fostered the generally neglected work of the pioneer historian of the American Church, John Gilmary Shea, and the infant fortunes of the U.S. Catholic Historical Society; made plans for a preparatory seminary; and erected what was for its time a model seminary, St. Joseph's in Dunwoodie, Yonkers, N.Y. He was buried beneath the high altar of St. Patrick's Cathedral.

Bibliography: *Memorial of the Most Rev. M. A. Corrigan,* J. M. FARLEY et al., comps. (New York 1902). F. J. ZWIERLEIN, *Letters of Archbishop Corrigan to Bishop McQuaid and Allied Documents* (Rochester 1946). J. T. ELLIS, *The Life of James Cardinal Gibbons,* 2 v. (Milwaukee 1952). A. J. SCANLAN, *St. Joseph's Seminary, Dunwoodie, New York, 1896–1921* (New York 1922). R. D. CROSS, *The Emergence of Liberal Catholicism in America* (Cambridge, Mass. 1958).

[J. A. REYNOLDS]

CORRIGAN, PATRICK

Controversialist; b. Longford, Ireland, Jan. 1, 1835; d. Hoboken, N.J., Jan. 9, 1894. He arrived at Jersey City, N.J., at the age of 13. After preparatory studies at St. Mary's College, Wilmington, Delaware, he studied theology at All Hallows College, Dublin, Ireland, and at St. Mary's Seminary, Baltimore, Maryland, where he was ordained on June 28, 1860. Corrigan filled several parochial assignments in the Diocese of Newark, New Jersey, concluding with the pastorate of Our Lady of Grace, Hoboken, New Jersey, which began in 1876. In 1883 he published a pamphlet, *Episcopal Nominations,* suggesting that another plenary council be convened and that experienced priests be given a voice in naming U.S. bishops. As a friend of Abp. John Ireland and an advocate of harmonizing the Church with the spirit of the United States, Corrigan was an outspoken foe of CAHENSLYISM. He denounced Bp. Winand M. WIGGER's connection with the sixth German Catholic Congress of 1892 so violently that he was subjected to an ecclesiastical trial and required to make an apology to Wigger. Claiming to have been the first priest in the United States publicly to advocate appointment of an apostolic delegate, Corrigan fêted Abp. Francesco Satolli at a banquet in his parish in May 1893. That same year, Corrigan was one of the sponsors of a bill to make New Jersey parochial schools part of the public school system with a share in state school funds. When the bill failed, he sought permission to rent his school to the public authorities. Bishop Wigger refused, and Corrigan closed the large school he had built, claiming straitened financial circumstances.

Bibliography: C. J. BARRY, *The Catholic Church and German Americans* (Milwaukee 1953).

[C. D. HINRICHSEN]

CORSINI

Mechant family of FLORENCE, prominent from the 13th to the 20th century, ennobled in 1629 by Pope URBAN VIII. St. ANDREW OF FIESOLE (d. 1373), a Carmelite, who became bishop of Fiesole, and Lorenzo Corsini, who became Pope CLEMENT XII (1730–40), were important religious figures in the family.

There were four Corsini cardinals (the first date given being that of their cardinalate). *Pietro* (1370), d. Avignon, 1405, a cousin of Andrew, served as bishop of Volterra (1362), of Florence (1363), and then of Porto (1374). A legate to Emperor Charles IV (1364), he received the title Prince of the Empire (1371). He wrote a tract on URBAN VI and the WESTERN SCHISM. *Neri* (1664), d. Florence, 1678, served as nuncio to France and in the papal camera before he was cardinal. Neri (1730), d. Rome, 1770, was the representative of Cosimo III de' Medici of Florence at The Hague, London, and Paris. After Cosimo's death (1723), Neri joined his uncle, Cardinal Lorenzo, who became Pope Clement XII, in Rome. About 1729 Neri bought the Riario palace, rebuilt it, and began adding to the books that his great-uncle, the first Cardinal Neri, and his uncle, the pope, had collected. In 1754 the library was opened to the public. In 1884 the family sold the palace to the Italian government and gave the library to the state. It is still housed in the Corsini palace in Rome. *Andrea* (1759), d. Rome, 1795, nephew of the younger Cardinal Neri, was interested in JANSENISM and opposed the JESUITS.

Lay members of the family have held many offices in the government of Florence since the 14th century. Their early residence was in the district of Santo Spirito and Santa Maria del Carmine. The present palace on Lung'Arno Corsini was built in the 17th century.

Bibliography: L. PASSERINI, *Genealogia e storia della famiglia Corsini* (Florence 1858). G. MORONI, *Dizionario de erudizione storico-ecclesiastica,* 103 v. in 53 (Venice 1840–61) 17:278–287. *Acta Sanctorum* 3 (Jan. 1863) 676–692. L. C. ÀLLARI, *I palazzi di Roma* (3d ed. Rome 1944) 425–428. P. O. SMERAGLIO, ''I C. a Roma e le origini della Biblioteca Corsiniana,'' *Atti della Accademia Nazionale dei Lincei,* ser. 8, 8.4 (1958) 291–331.

[M. L. SHAY]

CORTESE, GREGORIO

Monastic reformer, theologian, cardinal; b. Modena, 1483; d. Rome, Sept. 21, 1548. A brilliant student of the humanities and law, Giovanni Andrea Cortese graduated as doctor of laws at 17. After having served Cardinal Giovanni de' Medici and the Curia as a legal adviser, he turned to monastic life in 1507, entering San Benedetto in Polirone and assuming the name Gregorio. There he concentrated on the study of theology without, however, neglecting the humanities. Central to his thoughts was the conviction that the combined influence of the two branches of learning was best suited to achieve monastic reform. While congratulating Giovanni de' Medici on his elevation to the papal throne as LEO X in 1513, he also urged him to initiate the overdue reform of the Church. In 1522 he directed a similar missive to ADRIAN VI.

Cortese's monastic reform work began in 1516 at the monastery of Lérins, first as its prior and then as its abbot (1524). Subsequently, he served as a reforming abbot at the Benedictine monasteries in Modena and Perugia, at San Giorgio in Venice, in Praglia, and, coming full circle, in Polirone. Everywhere he raised not only the moral tone but also scholarship to a new height, stressing historical and philological studies side by side with theology. His extensive correspondence reveals his efforts to make the monasteries in his charge centers of learning. The academy that he founded at Lérins acted as a link in the transfer of Italian humanism to France, and to San Giorgio were attracted numerous prominent ecclesiastical and lay reformers.

The reform-minded cardinals Gasparo CONTARINI and Jacopo SADOLETO brought Cortese to the attention of

PAUL III. In 1536 the pope appointed him to the reform committee that drafted the epochal document *Consilium de emendanda Ecclesia* (1537), which combined a merciless indictment of the abuses of the Church with particulars for their removal. Cortese had been repeatedly visitor general of the Cassinese Congregation, and Pope Paul appointed him apostolic visitor for the whole of Italy. Upon the urging of Sadoleto, the pope created Cortese a cardinal (June 2, 1542) and named him administrator of the bishopric of Urbino (Nov. 6, 1542). On Nov. 19, 1544, he was appointed to the permanent committee of cardinals for conciliar affairs. This committee played an important part in preparing the Council of TRENT and, during its sessions, as an advisory board to the pope.

Cortese's reputation as a literary figure was high among his contemporaries, who warmly praised his pure Latin style and termed his poetry felicitous. He left a number of short works on a variety of subjects, most of which are of ecclesiastic nature.

Bibliography: *Opera,* ed. A. COMINO, with biog. G. A. GRADENIGO, 2 v. (Padua 1774). A. J. ANSART, *La Vie de Grégoire Cortez* (Paris 1786). E. GOTHEIN, *Rafael und der Abt Gregorio Cortese* (Heidelberg 1912). H. JEDIN, in *Lexikon für Theologie und Kirche,* ed. J. HOFER and K. RAHNER, 10 v. (2d, new edition Freiburg 1957–65).

[F. F. STRAUSS]

CORVEY, ABBEY OF

Former imperial BENEDICTINE monastery, on the Weser River, about 25 miles east of Paderborn, Westphalia, Germany, Diocese of Paderborn (Latin, *Corbeia nova*). It grew out of the original settlement of 815 at Hethi (Solling), which was moved to Corvey in 822 by the brothers ADALARD and WALA. The first monks, including ANSGAR, came from CORBIE; royal confirmation was received at the synod of Ingelheim (July 27, 823). Emperor Louis the Pious gave Corvey the relics of St. Stephen (hence, St. Stephen's church), and in 836 Abbot HILDUIN OF SAINT-DENIS gave it the relics of St. VITUS, who became the second patron of the church. It was from there that St. Vitus's cult spread over Saxony and north Germany. Corvey enjoyed a flourishing economic and intellectual life and numbered up to 300 monks. Outstanding men of Corvey included BRUNO of Cologne, the brother of Emperor Otto I, the archbishop of Cologne, and chancellor of the empire; the future Pope GREGORY V (996–999); and five monks who became archbishops of Bremen-Hamburg. Other monks became bishops of Halberstadt and Hildesheim, while still others were teachers in Bohemia, France, and Italy. In the days of Otto I, WIDUKIND OF CORVEY wrote a history of the Saxons. The *Annales Corbeienses*, the *Translatio s. Viti*, and certain letters of Abbot WIBALD OF STAVELOT are of Corvey provenance. Corvey's famous MS of Tacitus' *Annals*, rediscovered in 1517, is now in Rome. Corvey declined from the 14th century on (its bells were sold to Hildesheim), despite its membership in the Bursfeld Congregation (1505). It was pillaged five times in one year during the Thirty Years' War. The abbey dissolved by converting itself into a prince-bishopric (1794), since only noblemen could be received as monks and there were no new novices forthcoming. In 1803 the monastic domain was secularized and since then has known frequent changes of ownership. In 1825 the Diocese of Corvey was united with Paderborn.

Corvey's extant abbey church is a basilica whose outer crypt was finished in 844. The triple-storied, three-turreted west façade of the church was built from 873 to 885; the rest of the single-naved building is in baroque post-Gothic style and dates from 1667 to 1675. The monastery buildings date from 1699 to 1721. Corvey's picture gallery has 65 portraits of its abbots.

Bibliography: L. H. COTTINEAU, *Répertoire topobibliographique des abbayes et prieurés*, 2 v. (Mâcon 1935–39) 1:884–886. K. HALLINGER, *Gorze-Kluny*, 2 v. (*Studia anselmiana* 22–25; 1950–51) 1020. P. SCHMITZ, *Histoire de l'ordre de Saint-Benoît*, 7 v. (Maredsous, Bel. 1942–56). E. GALL, "Westwerkfragen," *Kunstchronik* 7 (1954) 274–276. A. FRANZEN, *Dictionnaire d'histoire et de géographie ecclésiastiques*, ed. A. BAUDRILLART et al. (Paris 1912–) 13:922–925. W. RAVE, *Corvey* (Münster 1958). E. LEHMANN, "Zum Buche von Wilhelm Rave über Corvey," *Westfalen* 38 (1960) 12–35.

[G. SPAHR]

COSGROVE, HENRY

Second bishop of Davenport, Iowa; b. Williamsport, Pa., Dec. 19, 1833; d. Davenport, Dec. 22, 1906. A few years after his birth, his parents, John and Bridget (Kane) Cosgrove, moved to Hollidaysburg, Pa., then in 1845 to Dubuque, Iowa. There he was educated by pioneer priests, one of whom, Joseph CRETIN, later first bishop of St. Paul, Minn., was his particular adviser. In 1852 Bp. J. M. P. LORAS of Dubuque sent Cosgrove to study philosophy at St. Mary's Seminary, The Barrens, near Cape Girardeau, Mo. After a year he returned to study theology at Mt. St. Bernard's Seminary at Table Mound near Dubuque, where he remained for two years. Subsequently he completed his studies at the St. Louis diocesan seminary, Carondelet, and was ordained (Aug. 27, 1857) in the old cathedral at Dubuque by Bp. Clement Smyth, OCSO.

First appointed to St. Margaret's Church in Davenport in September 1857, he became pastor of the same church in 1861. When the new Diocese of Davenport was created (1881), he remained as rector of the cathedral and vicar-general to the first bishop, John McMullen. On the death of McMullen (1883), Cosgrove administered the diocese until his own appointment (July 20, 1884) as second bishop of Davenport, the first American-born bishop appointed west of the Mississippi. He was consecrated at St. Margaret's Cathedral (Sept. 14, 1884) by Abp. P. A. Feehan of Chicago, Ill.

Cosgrove was distinguished as a pastor, preacher, and educator. He built the Cathedral of the Sacred Heart in Davenport (1890–91), where his remains are buried under the main vestibule. St. Ambrose College, founded in 1882, was incorporated and built at its present location in 1885. He founded St. Vincent's Diocesan Orphanage and numerous parishes and parochial schools in his diocese, which grew in Catholic population from about 45,000 with 79 priests in 1884 to about 70,000 with 135 priests in 1906. He was a leader in projects to settle Catholic immigrants in the Middle West and in organizing the Roman Catholic Mutual Protection Society of Iowa.

Bibliography: There is no full-scale work on Cosgrove, but information on him may be found in J. B. CODE, *Dictionary of American Hierarchy* (2d ed. New York 1964) 52. G. GIGLINGER, "Rt. Rev. Henry Cosgrove, D.D., Bishop of Davenport: A Biographical Sketch," *Acta et Dicta* 2 (1909–1910) 211–218. E. C. GREER, *Cork Hill Cathedral* (Davenport 1956).

[R. J. WELCH]

COSMAS THE MELODIAN

Called also Hagiopolites, Greek liturgical hymn writer; b. Jerusalem, *c.* 706; d. *c.* 760. Orphaned early in life, Cosmas was adopted by the father of JOHN DAMASCENE. Together with John, he studied under an Italian monk and poet also named Cosmas. This circumstance has caused confusion concerning the authenticity of some of the Melodian's poetry, and his career is occasionally confused with that of John Damascene. A *Vita* attributed to John VI, Patriarch of Jerusalem (*c.* end of 11th century) must be used with caution. Cosmas entered the LAURA of St. Sabas, near Jerusalem, *c.* 732 and in 743 was made bishop of Maiuma, near Gaza. He is famous in the Eastern Church for his hymns, especially his 14 canons (κανόνες), or chants, for the feasts of Easter, Christmas, and the Exaltation of the Holy Cross, which have been incorporated into the Byzantine liturgy. His knowledge of the Church's teaching is evident in his poetry, but he sacrifices clarity of thought for poetic form. He is regarded as the author of a prose commentary on the poems of GREGORY OF NAZIANZUS and is venerated as a saint in the East, where his cult spread along with his hymns.

Feast: Oct. 14 (Eastern Church).

Miniature detail of Cosmas and Damian from "Menologian of Basil II."

Bibliography: A. MAI, *Spicilegium Romanum* (Rome 1839–44) 2:1–306. *Patrologia Graeca* ed. J. P. MIGNE 38:339–680. W. VON CHRIST and M. K. PARANIKAS, eds., *Anthologia graeca carminum christianorum* (Leipzig 1871). T. E. DETORAKĒES, *Kosmas ho Melōdos, vios kai ergo* (Thessalonica 1979). H. J. W. TILLYARD, *Byzantinische Zeitschrift* 28 (1928) 25–37, music. G. CALIO, *Bibliotheca sanctorum* (Rome 1961) 4:219–221. J. PARGOIRE, *L'Église byzantine* (Paris 1905). B. ALTANER, *Patrology* (New York 1960) 635–636, 645. A. CHAPPET, *Dictionnaire d'archéologie chrétienne et de liturgie*, ed. F. CABROL, H. LECLERCQ, and H. I. MARROU (Paris 1907–53) 3.2:2993–97.

[F. DE SA]

COSMAS AND DAMIAN, SS.

Early Christian martyrs who are commemorated in the Canon of the Roman Mass. Despite numerous legends, nothing is known of their lives other than the fact that they suffered martyrdom at Cyr in Syria during the DIOCLETIAN persecution. A church erected at the site of their burial place was enlarged by the Emperor Justinian. The *Passio* describes them as being burnt, stoned, sawed in two, and finally decapitated, but it is pure legend. Their cult spread quickly in both the East and West and a famous basilica was erected in their honor in Constantinople, where the faithful repaired in search of medical cures. Pope Symmachus (498–514) dedicated an oratory in the Basilica of St. Mary Major in their honor, and Felix IV (526–530) joined two pagan temples in the Roman Forum to construct a basilica named after these saints. The Templum divi Romuli furnished the atrium, and the Templum sacrae Urbis was converted into the apse and decorated with a grandiose mosaic depicting the Apostles Peter and Paul presenting the two martyrs to Christ the Redeemer, with an inscription commemorating the event. It was probably at this time that their names were inserted in the Canon of the Mass. Six other Roman churches were dedicated in their honor. They are considered the patrons of doctors because they were reputed to be physicians who practiced medicine without taking payment from their patients.

Feast: Sep. 27.

Bibliography: A. BUTLER, *The Lives of the Saints,* rev. ed. H. THURSTON and D. ATTWATER (New York 1956) 3:659–661. A. J. FESTUGIÈRE, tr., *Sainte Thècle, saints Côme et Damien . . .* (Paris 1971), history of miracles. V. L. KENNEDY, *The Saints of the Canon of the Mass* (Vatican City 1938). R. KRAUTHEIMER, *Corpus Basilicarum Christianarum Romae* (Vatican City 1937–) v.1. H. SKROBUCHA, *Kosmos und Damian* (Recklinghausen 1965) tr. as *The Patrons of the Doctors*, tr. H. H. ROSENWALD (Recklinghausen

1965). D. VACCA, *Leggendo la vita dei santi medici Cosma e Damiano* (Bitonto 1973). A. WITTMANN, *Kosmas und Damian: Kultausbreitung und Volksdevotion* (Berlin 1967). J. ZURING, *De heilige genezers Cosmas en Damianus in Nederland* (Venlo 1989).

[E. G. RYAN]

COSMOGONY

The term employed to designate the oral or written response, on a pre-scientific and non-philosophical plane, that man gives to the questions that confront him regarding the origin and order of the universe around him. The word itself comes from the Greek κοσμογονία, cited first from Plutarch (A.D. 46–c. 120). Cosmogonies describe, under the form of a myth or myths, the creative action and the primordial events to which the world owes its existence. Their composition and complexity vary according to places, time, cultures, and the degree of their maturity. They are found among almost all primitive peoples, higher cultures, and civilizations. At a certain stage of their development, they also comprise a theogony that is inserted in a ''logical'' and indispensable fashion in the development of the given cosmogony and an anthropogony, the real importance of which depends on the degree of formal understanding that man has succeeded in attaining.

Despite the rich proliferation of cosmogonic myths, it is possible to single out a restricted number of basic elements whose particular content and numerous possibilities of combination give a special character to the various representations. At the same time, this special character bears witness to a tendency that is common to certain groups of cosmogonies. Thus, for example, in so far as the accent is placed on the acting subject in the personalistic cosmogonies, the High God is represented under an anthropomorphic form and is regarded as strictly supernatural. He acts alone or, after carrying out his work in partial manner, he makes use of other beings coming from himself by divine filiation or through his creative will (demiurges, the *Urmensch*). He derives the universe from nothing or, most frequently, from preexistent matter. He proceeds as an artisan or acts by the power of his word.

If the emphasis is placed on the object of the cosmogony, the existing universe may be considered to have originated not through one of the forms of creation mentioned, but through an emanation (which can have a highly spiritualized character, as in Neoplatonism) or through a spontaneous hatching (the Cosmic Egg, for example), the biological aspect of which does not necessarily exclude the acting will of a first cause.

The existing world is often connected in origin with a dark and formless chaos that in some way acquires a personal nature under the impact of cosmogonic events and constantly opposes the creating and ordering process. It remains vigorously active in the concrete reality of the universe, revealing its presence both at the divine level (in the various dualistic systems) and at the level of the human heart (torn between good and evil).

In the Greek world, where the concept of the *kosmos* as a universe harmoniously ordered had its origin and assumed definite shape, cosmogony found its classic expression in Hesiod's *Theogony* (*c.* 700 B.C.). While the Homeric cosmogony is confined merely to the mention of ''Oceanus, the father of the gods, and Tethys, their mother'' (*Iliad* 14:201), Hesiod presents an elaborate account that may be summarized as follows: First came Chaos, and next Earth, then Tartarus, and Eros. From Chaos came Erebus and Night, and of Night were born Aether and Day. Earth bore Heaven and the great sea, Pontus. Then, impelled by Eros, she united at one time with Heaven, at another with the sea, giving birth thus to different lines and generations of divine beings. Hesiod relates their theogonic conflicts in detail (*Theog.* 116 to the end).

According to Pherecydes of Syros (*c.* 550 B.C.), the three original gods, Zeus, Chronos, and Chthonius, always existed; the other gods descended from these three in five successive waves. Zeus, transforming himself into Eros, created the Earth and the Ocean, despite the opposition of the Titan Ophioneus.

The most original contribution of the cosmogonic myths of Orphism is their account of the origin of man. He was created from the ashes of the Titans who were destroyed by the thunderbolts of Zeus after they had devoured the infant Dionysos. Man, accordingly, bears within him the germs of evil as well as particles of divinity. The Cosmic Egg (mentioned by Epimenides of Crete, seventh century B.C.) is also an Orphic myth. From the Egg came Heaven and Earth, following the intervention of Phanes, the Orphic pendent of Hesiod's Eros.

The Ionian philosophers, in seeking to give a scientific explanation of the world's origin, replaced mythical forces by original physical principles (ἀρχαί), but did not thereby escape the influence of the old cosmogonies. Later, despite the attractive Platonic theory of the Demiurge responsible for transforming Chaos into Kosmos, the image of the scientific world, as it was projected by Aristotle and completed by Ptolemy the Geographer, imposed itself to such a degree that neither the conceptions of popular belief (see, e.g., Ovid's *Metam* 1:5–451) nor the mythical cosmogonies of the Hermetic writings (the speculations of the *Poimandres,* especially) and of Mithraism could prevail. Christianity alone, with its Biblical narrative of creation, introduced a permanent innovation in this respect.

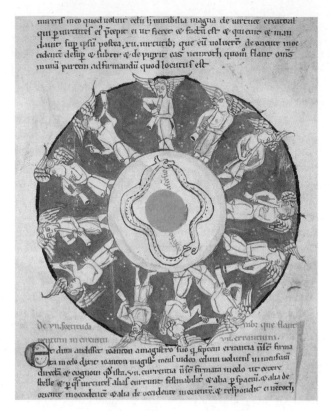

Astronomy treatise: sky cosmogony with angels. (©Archivo Iconografico, S.A./CORBIS)

Bibliography: J. SINT et al., *Lexikon für Theologie und Kirche*, ed. J. HOFER and K. RAHNER (Freiberg 1957–65) 6:567–574. C. M. EDSMAN, "Schöpfung I," *Die Religion in Geschichte und Gegenwart* (Tübingen 1957–65) 5:1469–1473, with bibliog. L. H. GRAY et al., J. HASTINGS, ed., *Encyclopedia of Religion and Ethics* (Edinburgh 1908–27) 4:125–179, old but still useful. H. SCHWABL and J. DUCHESNE-GUILLEMIN, "Weltschöpfung," *Paulys Realenzyklopädie der klassischen Altertumswissenschaft*, ed. G. WISSOWA et al. (1962) 1433–1589, comprehensive, systematic treatment. H. J. ROSE, *A Handbook of Greek Mythology* (6th ed. New York 1958) 17–42. U. BIANCHI, *Teogonie e cosmogonie* (Rome 1960). F. LAEMMLI, *Vom Chaos zum Kosmos,* 2 v. (Basel 1962). M. P. NILSSON, *Geschichte der griechischen Religion* (Munich 1955–61) v.1, 2, Indexes s.v. "Kosmogonie."

[G. SANDERS]

COSMOGONY (IN THE BIBLE)

This concept, which might more accurately be termed Biblical cosmography, is the Biblical concept of the physical world.

The Israelites borrowed their notions of the structure of the universe from their ancient Near Eastern neighbors. They conceived of the world as a sort of two-story edifice with a basement, i.e., the heavens and the earth as the two stories and nether world as the basement, the re-spective abodes of God, man, and the dead. This universe was most often referred to as "the heavens and the earth." The ground floor was the earth, thought to be a generally flat plane set upon the surface of the waters and supported by solid foundations sunk well into the subterranean depths [Ps 17(18).16; 23(24).2; 135 (136).6]. It is not clear whether the Israelites represented it to themselves as a disk or as a rectangular plane. (Is 11.12 speaks of the "four corners" of the earth.) The surrounding ocean and the subterranean waters that fed the earth's springs and streams were thought to be one body of water. Above the first-floor complex was spread the firmament, a solid vault whose main purpose was to support the heavenly waters that provided rain in due season. Upon these waters Yahweh had built Himself a palace, from which He ruled the world [Ps 103(104).3; 28(29).10]. Finally, in the nethermost regions of the universe (i.e., those most remote from Yahweh) lay SHEOL, the dark and uninviting land of the dead [Jb 11.8; *see* DEAD, THE (IN THE BIBLE)].

This image of the world, though quite ingenious, was based only on primitive observation. Much in it was deduced through analogy with human architecture, and some of it was postulated by theological beliefs (e.g., the existence of Sheol). Many of the Biblical passages that contribute to the reconstruction of this world image are poetic in nature, not always consistent with one another, and particularly vague in matters of detail. Israelite cosmogony is then a popular, unscientific concept of the universe, not essentially different from that shared by Israel's neighbors. If in time past the general tradition of the Church tended to accept these data as inspired for their own sake and, consequently, as sharing in the infallibility of divine truth, this was partly because of an imperfect understanding of the doctrine of inspiration, and partly because of the fact that the Biblical view was not seriously challenged until the 16th century. Unfortunately, by this time tradition had hardened and a generally stagnant scholasticism failed to appreciate the true value of empirical method and argumentation. The Galileo controversy is an example of such a failure (*see* GALILEI, GALILEO). Since, however, the Bible never intended to treat *ex professo* of cosmology or astronomy, it was without basis that Biblical concepts in these fields were utilized to combat scientifically established theories.

Bibliography: H. SCHWABL and J. DUCHESNE-GUILLEMIN, *Paulys Realenzyklopädie der klassischen Altertumswissenschaft*, ed. G. WISSOWA et al. (Stuttgart 1893–) suppl. 9 (1962) 1433–1589. A. KONRAD, *Das Weltbild in der Bibel* (Graz 1917). A. DEIMEL, *"Enuma elis" und Hexaëmeron* (Rome 1934). *Encyclopedic Dictionary of the Bible*, tr. and adap. by L. HARTMAN (New York 1963) 428–429.

[L. F. HARTMAN]

COSMOLOGICAL ARGUMENT

A term used to designate a type of argumentation whereby one reasons from observable aspects of the universe, or cosmos, to the existence of God. The reasoning process is a posteriori, from effects observable in the universe to a cause that do not fall directly under human experience, and in this respect is different from that employed in the ontological argument, which is a priori in that it argues from the concept or definition of God to His necessary existence. Although frequently used in the singular, the term actually refers to a number of arguments, depending on the particular observable aspect of the universe that is the starting point of the proof. Thus, of THOMAS AQUINAS's "five ways," the classical proofs for the existence of God, the first three are commonly regarded as cosmological insofar as they begin with the obvious facts of MOTION, EFFICIENT CAUSALITY, and CONTINGENCY in the universe, respectively, and from these rise to a knowledge of the Unmoved Mover, First Cause, and Necessary Being whom we call God. Some would also include the "fifth way" among the cosmological arguments, insofar as it argues from the fact of design in the cosmos to the existence of a Supreme Intelligence who has planned and guides the universe in its complex processes; others would make of this a special proof that invokes finality or teleology and so is more aptly designated as the teleological argument.

Kantian Origins. The practice of labeling rational proofs for God's existence as ontological, cosmological, and teleological takes its origin from Immanuel KANT's *Critique of Pure Reason* (1781), where this threefold division is first proposed. Kant's mentality was at root quite different from Aquinas's. Although much interested in rationalism's claim to provide systematic knowledge of God, and indeed conditioned by his university training to give a sympathetic hearing to G. W. F. LEIBNIZ and Christian WOLFF, Kant's own approach to God developed in a way that was predominantly affective and moral in character. Reacting in his early writings to Hume's skepticism with regard to demonstrations of God's existence, Kant at first hoped to recast the traditional proofs in such a way as to make them acceptable to the most critical thinker. As he worked out his own theory of knowledge, however, he became aware that according to its canons this would be no longer possible—not that he ever doubted God's existence himself, but because he had come to see the weaknesses involved in earlier speculative claims. Obviously unconvinced by, but still dependent upon, the rationalist metaphysics of Wolff, Kant reduced all previous proofs to three major types: the ontological argument, based on the idea of a most perfect being; the cosmological argument, based on the contingency found in the universe; and the teleological (or physicotheological)

argument, based on its order or design. Quite correctly, and here in company with Aquinas, Kant saw the impossibility of deducing anything about God's existence from the idea of His essence. He went on, however, to maintain further that attempts to reach God from an analysis of contingency being in the world, or from considerations of orderliness and design in the cosmos, also inevitably involve the use of the idea of a most perfect being. Thus he rejected, from the category of rigid proof, both the cosmological and the teleological argument as implicitly presupposing the ontological argument, and as being vitiated on that account.

Kant's rejection of the cosmological argument, according to Collins (pp. 162–86), is a logical consequence of the epistemological teachings that are central to the *Critique*. These effectively equate the requirements for all knowledge with those proper to the knowledge of Newtonian physics, which combines in its own distinctive way a rationalist conception of the use of reason and an empiricist theory of experience. Working within the narrow confines of this epistemology, Kant was unable to grasp sensible beings in their very act of existing, but instead he viewed them solely under the noetic conditions required for their becoming objects in classical physics. As a consequence, in speaking of contingency he could not begin with the existential act of things that come to be and pass away, but had to focus instead on the idea of contingency and so unwittingly placed himself in the purely ideal or possible order at the very outset of his projected proof. It is not in the later stages that the cosmological argument invokes the ideal order of essences; rather, as Kant formulates it in his synthetic a priori way, it does so at the very beginning because of the categorial view of existence it is forced to employ.

Other Alternatives. Those who continue to reject cosmological reasoning as a speculatively valid demonstration of God's existence usually do so either (1) because they remain captive to Kant's epistemology, with its rejection of metaphysics as a transcendental illusion and its consequent agnosticism with regard to God, or (2) because they subscribe to the Humean analysis of causation, with its substitution of temporal sequences among events for causal efficacy, and its resulting inability to rise above the phenomenal order to a transcendent cause. The rationale behind their rejection is also usually one of conforming with modern science and its methods, a motivation that was dominant for both Kant and HUME. Developments within science in recent years, however, and the associated growth of the philosophy of science movement, have provided other alternatives to those available to these philosophers of the 18th century, for whom science was perforce still in its infancy. The discovery of elementary particles, for example, and the ingenious proofs devised to reveal the existence of entities with properties that are not directly observable, and even unobservable in principle, suggest ways of transcending sense experience to arrive at deeper ontological explanations of the phenomena of the physical world. On the basis of the reasoning processes used to argue to the existence of electrons, positrons, and other "particles," one can now formulate canons of demonstrative inference for establishing the existence and attributes of entities quite unlike those of ordinary experience. Such canons are similar to those implicit in Aquinas's "five ways" and need only to be supplemented by his doctrine of analogy to provide adequate conceptual tools for arriving at knowledge of God's existence and His essential attributes.

Causality, of course, and this in its pre-Humean understanding of a knowable nexus between cause and effect, still remains the key concept on which cosmological argumentation must rest. Unfortunately, under the influence of Newtonian physics, there has been a tendency through the 18th and 19th centuries to identify causes with forces, and then further to equate causal explanation with complete determinism and predictability. This has fostered a concern with efficient causality alone, and a consequent neglect of other types of causal reasoning such as those based on material, formal, and final causality, which can serve as valid starting points for theistic proofs. In this connection it should perhaps be noted that one of the most powerful arguments advanced by Aristotle and Aquinas in support of a key premise in their cosmological argumentation, viz, the motor causality principle, "whatever is in movement is moved by another," is based not on efficient causality but on material causality. Again, concepts such as force and energy are far from transparent to philosophical analysis, particularly when used as vehicles to carry the causal inference required for arguments of the cosmological type. Those who would rely on them exclusively for this purpose thus expose themselves to the dangers of unwittingly terminating such arguments before they can be started, or of so insulating the phenomena under investigation from metaphysical inquiry as to nullify their value as starting points in any search for transcendence.

Difficulties. To turn now to more recent objections against the cosmological argument, these center around three difficulties that are commonly raised against this type of proof. The first is brought against it not so much by atheists and agnostics as by religious thinkers who, while themselves firmly convinced of God's existence, do not see such existence as a subject for rational inquiry. They would object to the proof on the grounds that it operates in virtue of a suppressed major premise to the effect that the universe is rationally explicable. Logically, however, as they see it, there seems to be no way of ruling

out the possibility that the world may be ultimately irrational or inexplicable; if one accepts the view that it is not, so their objection goes, he does so by virtue of his own individual belief and not from any objective necessity. This difficulty is likely to prove insurmountable for one imbued with a fideistic or pietistic spirit or who sees religion as ultimately an affair of man's heart or will and not of his intellect. It is not troublesome, on the other hand, to those to whom the cosmological argument is more likely to appeal in the first place, namely, scientists who daily use their intellects to come to a knowledge of nature and its underlying mechanisms. If the universe is ultimately irrational then science itself is radically impossible. Logic, of course, is powerless to solve this question on an a priori basis; the only way one can find out whether the universe is rational or not is by studying it and having its rationality revealed to him through the a posteriori process of discovery. It is this experience that makes a person a scientist; the same type of experience, pushed to metaphysical ultimates, can lend him to a rational knowledge of God's existence.

The second difficulty is somewhat akin to the first in that it too raises a logical question, and this relating to the type of necessity that attaches to the conclusion of the cosmological argument. The objection is that such type of argumentation does not conclude with logical necessity, since it is not concerned with a set of analytical propositions whose self-evidence can be made manifest, but rather speaks of contingent matters that could be otherwise and so at best can provide the basis for probable conclusions. So stated, the difficulty is connected with Leibniz's dichotomous division of "proofs" into two types; those concluding with strict logic to a self-evident necessity, and those based on probable occurrence that can never be reduced to self-evidence. Actually this objection is similar to that behind Kant's rejection of the cosmological argument, for it says, in essence, that anyone who pretends to reason a posteriori from a factual and contingent premise about the universe to God's necessary existence actually gets turned around in the process and draws his conclusion on definitional grounds, in a priori fashion. His reasoning process is thus equivalent to making the existence of a First Cause inconceivable, and so he implicitly invokes the ontological argument in his proof. This objection is particularly telling against those who conceive all of science on the model of mathematics, or who accept the rationalist ideal of formal logic as the only measure of necessary reasoning. The very possibility of natural science, however, is ruled out by the acceptance of this ideal. In the world of nature, as Aquinas pointed out centuries ago, nothing is so contingent that it does not have some element of necessity associated with it. The necessity of nature's operation is not that of mathematics or of logic; rather it is the conditional necessity that is characteristic of causes that attain their effects regularly and for the most part, even though occasionally, and on a contingency basis, they can be impeded. Once one learns how to achieve demonstration when dealing with subject matters that exhibit contingency of this type, he also becomes proficient in isolating the elements of necessity that can sustain the required inference to a First Cause. His demonstrations will then conclude with a real causal necessity that gives rise to true metaphysical knowledge, and not with the tautological necessity of self-evidence that characterizes the world of formal logic and pure mathematics.

The final difficulty is typical of a series of objections that have been raised by linguistic analysts and other analytical philosophers, who first were attracted to the ontological argument and subsequently have turned their attention to the cosmological argument as well. Such objections focus on the questions that the latter argument proposes to answer and raises doubts as to their being truly meaningful. Linguistic philosophers do not dispute that questions relating to the first cause of motion, etc., make grammatical sense or seem understandable on the basis of ordinary experience. They claim, however, that such questions turn out to be ultimately misleading, and the reason they urge is that the questions one may legitimately ask of a part of a system become inapplicable when applied to the system in its totality. Thus one may meaningfully ask where the earth is located with respect to the entire universe, but one may not ask where the universe as a whole is located, for to such a question there can be no answer. The objection is ingenious, and indeed is telling against some of the ways in which the cosmological argument has been articulated, notably by Duns Scotus in the Middle Ages and by Frederick Copleston in recent times. However, the argument need not be proposed in ways, for example, that allow the existence of an infinite series of contingent beings as a totality and then seek an extrinsic cause for it, on the grounds that such a series exists and whatever exists must have a cause. The arguments developed by Aquinas are not of this kind, nor are they vulnerable to the objection that the questions they raise are ultimately meaningless. They make no assumptions, in fact, about the universe in its totality, but rather show that the particular features of the cosmos they are examining require explanation, and yet are inexplicable in terms of the type of being of which the universe seems to be composed, whether finite or infinite in number, and so demand the existence of a transcendent being whom we call God.

See Also: GOD, PROOFS FOR THE EXISTENCE OF; ONTOLOGICAL ARGUMENT.

Bibliography: D. R. BURRILL, ed., *The Cosmological Arguments: A Spectrum of Opinion* (New York 1967). B. R. REICHENBACH, *The Cosmological Argument: A Reassessment* (Springfield, Ill. 1972). W. A. WALLACE, ''The Cosmological Argument: A Reappraisal,'' *American Catholic Philosophical Association. Proceedings of the Annual Meeting* 46 (1972) 43–57. J. D. COLLINS, *God in Modern Philosophy* (Chicago 1959). R. W, HEPBURN, ''Cosmological Argument for the Existence of God,'' *The Encyclopedia of Philosophy,* ed. P. EDWARDS, 8 v. (New York 1967), 2.232–37.

[W. A. WALLACE]

COSMOLOGY

From Gr. κόσμος, world, and λόγος, knowledge or science, cosmology means literally the science of the world. Christian WOLFF, introducing the term in 1730, classified cosmology as special metaphysics. Based on reason alone and deduced from notions previously defined and explained in general metaphysics, it applies the conclusions of ONTOLOGY to the consideration of the totality of existing things. In developing this metaphysics of bodies, Wolff was influenced more by LEIBNIZ than by ARISTOTLE. Leibniz's notion of ''a striving and a resisting substance'' led him to hold that there can be no body without motion and no substance without effort or force. For Wolff, however, matter and motor force are neither real beings nor distinct, substantial principles, but only ''substance phenomena'' whose common source are the elements from which bodies derive their substantiality. He regarded these elements as first principles containing the ultimate reasons for everything perceived in bodies, e.g., their composition, their apparent constituents, their changes, and their phenomena. Yet unlike Leibniz's MONAD, the elements have no power of representation and can influence one another in a physical way. Wolff's treatment strongly influenced the tradition of manuals in SCHOLASTIC PHILOSOPHY, with the result that the term cosmology came to be frequently used in SCHOLASTICISM to designate the philosophy of nature. In modern scientific usage, cosmology also specifies that discipline which concerns itself with theories pertaining to the origin and structure of the universe.

See Also: PHILOSOPHY OF NATURE; UNIVERSE, ORDER OF.

[J. V. BURNS]

COSTA BEN LUCA

Christian philosopher, Arabic name Qusṭā-ibn-Lūqā (other Latin forms: Constabulus, Constabulinus); b. Baalbek, Syria, 864; d. Armenia, 923. While he acquired some fame in the East by translating Aristotle's works into Arabic, the West knew him exclusively as the author (not absolutely established, according to Cheikho) of four chapters on the difference between soul and spirit (*De differentia animae et spiritus*). The work has professedly little originality, since it was meant to be nothing more than excerpts from PLATO, ARISTOTLE, Theophrastus, and GALEN. Following Galen, the author holds that spirit does not signify an incorporeal being higher than the soul, but ''a certain subtle body,'' almost liquid or gaseous in character, within the human body. Yet, whereas Galen explains the vital functions in man by means of three spirits—in the liver, heart, and brain respectively—Costa ben Luca unaccountably omits the first, and does not accurately summarize Galen's anatomical doctrines. Spirit for him is ''the proximate cause of life,'' while soul is ''the more remote or great cause.'' The translation from Arabic into Latin was made by JOHN OF SPAIN before 1143 (Alonso, 311). In the reorganization of the arts curriculum at Paris, 1255, the work became one of the required philosophical textbooks.

See Also: ARABIAN PHILOSOPHY.

Bibliography: A. ANGLICUS, *Excerpta e libro Alfredi Anglici de motu cordis: Item Costa-ben-Lucae De differentia animae et spiritus liber,* ed. C. S. BARACH, tr. J. HISPALENSI (Bibliotheca philosophorum mediae aetatis 2; Innsbruck 1878). M. ALONSO, *Temas filisóficos medievales (Ibn Dāwūd y Gundisalvo)* (Comillas 1959). L. CHEIKHO and L. MALOUF, *Traités inédits d'anciens philos. arabes musulmans et chrétiens* (2d ed. Beirut 1911).

[I. C. BRADY]

COSTA RICA, THE CATHOLIC CHURCH IN

The Central American Republic of Costa Rica is bound on the north by Nicaragua, on the east by the Caribbean Sea and Panama, and on the south and west by the Pacific Ocean. Encompassing the mountainous plateau region of the Continental Divide, the country is separated by a stretch of volcanic mountains into two fertile lowland regions with extensive coastlines. One of the few Central American nations to sustain long-term political stability, Costa Rica has developed a successful tourist industry to supplement an agricultural economy buoyed by its acclaimed coffee plantations and its banana and cocoa crops. Costa Ricans, who are predominately of European heritage, benefit from widespread employment opportunities and numerous social welfare programs. However along with increasing international traffic due to tourism has come problems with illegal drugs; in the 1990s Costa Rica became a transfer point for heroin and cocaine shipments from South America.

Early Christianization. The earliest appearance of the Christian religion in Costa Rica dates back to the

Capital: San José.
Size: 19,652 sq. miles.
Population: 3,710,558 in 2000.
Languages: Spanish.
Religions: 3,153,974 Catholics (85%), 519,472 Evangelical Protestants (14%), 37,100 other (1%).
Archdiocese: San José de Costa Rica, with suffragans Alajuela, Ciudad Quesada, Limón, Puntarenas, San Isidro de El General, and Tilarán.

fourth and final voyage of Christopher Columbus in 1502. Traveling with Columbus, Fray Alejandre was the first priest to set foot on the continent. After 1508, Christianity slowly spread along the coasts of the Pacific. The first diocese erected on the Central American isthmus was Nuestra Señora de Santa María de la Antigua del Darién (1513), with Franciscan Juan de Quevedo appointed bishop. Gil González Dávila and Diego de Agüero were the first to enter the area that would one day become Costa Rica and Nicaragua; their catechizing activity led to the baptism of 32,264 souls between 1522 and 1524. In 1526 the iconoclastic priest Diego de Escobar celebrated his first Holy Week in the New World with great pomp on the island of Chira. Because of his zeal in destroying the native idols, he created an animosity toward Christians that made later evangelizing difficult.

The establishment of the Diocese of León de Nicaragua, which included both Nicaragua and Costa Rica, heralded more peaceful times, and several churches were erected in the region. In 1550 Pedro de BETANZOS arrived in Costa Rica with two priests and was joined later by Lorenzo de Bienvenida. In 1560 Juan de Estrada Rávago founded the first churches on the Caribbean coast at Corotapa and Suerre. The consolidation and expansion of the faith in Costa Rica occurred after an embassy including Father Lorenzo traveled to Spain in 1565 to ask Philip II to aid in their missionary efforts.

In 1581 the zeal and bravery with which the early priests penetrated the hostile regions—usually with no more arms than a crucifix—produced the first martyr of Costa Rica, Juan Pizarro. Displeased by Pizarro's public admonishment because of his tribe's reversion to Dionysiac excesses, the Christianized chief Alonso de Alfaro ordered Pizzaro's death by flogging.

In 1564 Juan Vásquez de Coronado and a group of settlers founded the city of Cartago, their European populations replacing native populations killed by diseases to which they had no resistance. Other conquistadores and priests entered the territory of Talamanca, south-east of Costa Rica, lured by rumors of rich gold deposits and the great concentration of natives there. Unlike the events surrounding the establishment of Cartago, the city of San-

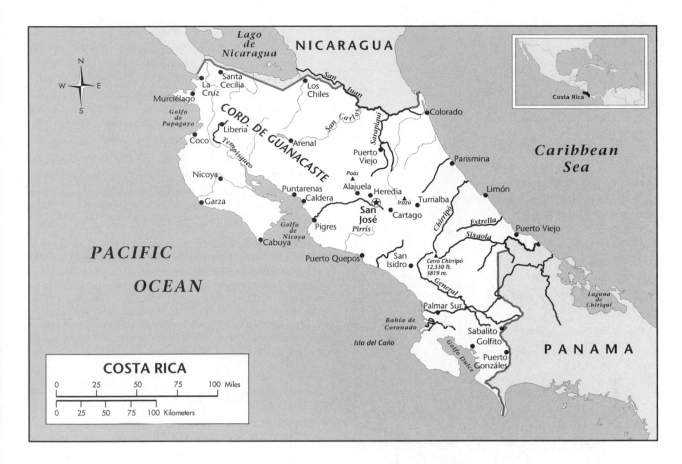

tiago de Talamanca, founded in 1605, was later destroyed by the natives, its inhabitants massacred. Rodrigo Arias Maldonado y Velazco (later known as Fray Rodrigo de la Cruz, cofounder of the Bethlehemites in Guatemala) and many others failed in their attempts to civilize these natives. However, as several Spanish icons became associated with circumstances considered miraculous by the native populations, evangelical efforts found increasing favor. In 1666, for example, natives attributed the departure of a group of marauding pirates to the Virgin of the Immaculate Conception, a century-old carved statue. The image was carried on a litter and the Mother of God invoked as a protectress as preparations were made to combat the invaders; she eventually became known as the Virgin of the Rescue. In 2000 a pilgrimage was made to Cartago, the city where Costa Rica's patron saint, the Virgin de los Angeles, once appeared, to pray that increasing frequent outbreaks of violent crime would end.

Consolidation and Organization. During the 17th and 18th centuries the real development of Costa Rica, both civil and ecclesiastical, began. Brotherhoods, religious associations and primary parochial schools were increased and consolidated. Renewed missionary visits to Talamanca Christianized almost all the natives, many of whom relocated to missions in the interior. Churches in the parishes of Nicoya, Orosi and Cartago acquired valuable ornaments and objects of gold and silver, some of them exquisitely made. Church architecture, however, remained modest.

In October of 1821 news reached Costa Rica of the region's bloodless political separation from Spain. Joining the Mexican Empire for a few years, it was eventually awarded independence in 1838. Political autonomy brought no noticeable changes with respect to the Church until 1850 when the bishopric of San José was created, independent of the Diocese of Nicaragua, which had governed Costa Rica for 319 years. The first bishop of San José was Anselmo Llorente y Lafuente, a native of Cartago, who defended with tenacity the ecclesiastical rights of the Church. After his death in 1871, the see remained vacant until the 1880 appointment of the German priest Bernardo Augusto THIEL. Thiel founded the *Mensajero del Clero,* made various visits to native groups whose language and customs he studied, and made valuable historical investigations. He was succeeded in 1901 by another German priest, Gaspar Stock, who continued the activities of his predecessor.

The Modern Church. The Bishopric of San José was elevated to an archdiocese in 1921. By mid-century Costa Ricans were considered strongly religious, and the

The National Theater of Costa Rica, San Jose. (©Dave G. Houser/CORBIS)

relations between Church and State were harmonious. Title VI of the modern constitution of Costa Rica, dated Nov. 7, 1948, made the Roman Catholic faith the country's national religion, adding that government would refrain from "impeding within the Republic the free exercise of other cults that do not oppose universal morality or good customs." Although political tensions grew during the 1970s due to economic problems, the nation managed to retain a democratic government which continued to value religion. By 2000 the country contained 241 parishes, with 510 secular and 236 religious priests, 46 brothers and 923 sisters administering to its predominately Roman Catholic population. In addition, the region's first Catholic television station, Telefides, proved successful in uniting Catholic families after its inception in 1996.

At the turn of the 21st century, because of its relative affluence Costa Rica faced problems more in line with technologically advanced European nations than with its Central American neighbors. The strong opposition given

by the nation's bishops to the adoption of in vitro fertilization procedures in 1997 was a major factor in at least one government agency's recommendation not to legalize such procedures. However, in 1999 equally vocal Church opposition to the legalization of sterilization procedures could not stop passage of such laws by an increasingly liberal government. Another symptom of modern times—an ever-increasing divorce rate—caused one member of the church hierarchy to comment on Costa Rica's "discard-after-use culture," while concerns were also aired over the sudden decline in church weddings in favor of civil marriage ceremonies that could more easily be undone.

Bibliography: V. SANABRIA MARTÍNEZ, *Episcopologio de la diócesis de Nicaragua y Costa Rica, 1531–1850* (San José 1943); *Documenta historica Beatae Virginis Angelorum* (San José 1945); *Anselmo Llorente y Lafuente* (San José 1933). R. BLANCO, *Historia eclesiástica de Costa Rica, 1502–1850* (San José 1960). M. DE LINES and J. A. LINE, *Costa Rica: Monumentos históricos y arqueológicos* (Mexico City 1964).

[J. A. LINES/EDS.]

COSTANTINI, CELSO

Cardinal, zealous promoter of the missions and of missionary art; b. Castion di Zoppola, Italy, April 3, 1876; d. Rome, Oct. 17, 1958. Costantini completed his ecclesiastical studies in Rome, taking degrees in both theology and philosophy; he was ordained on Dec. 26, 1899. Returning to his diocese (Concordia), he was engaged in the pastoral ministry until the outbreak of World War I, when he became a military chaplain. Because of the competence and energetic activity he displayed in saving precious works of sacred art in the war zone, he was made regent and conservator of the ancient basilica of Acquilea to work with the military authorities in protecting its treasures.

After the war Costantini became vicar-general of his diocese. He deepened his knowledge of the history of art and founded the society Amici dell'Arte Sacra and the illustrated review *Arte cristiana*, published at Milan. In 1920, during the development of the military and political events that turned upon the possession of Fiume, Costantini was made administrator apostolic of that diocese. He was promoted to the titular see of Geropolis on July 22, 1921, and was consecrated August 24 of that year. The following year he was named to the titular see of Theodosiopolis in Arcadia, given the rank of archbishop, and made apostolic delegate to China, the first to hold that office. While he was delegate, the Chinese hierarchy was established, the first plenary council of the Chinese Church was held in Shanghai in 1924, and six Chinese bishops were consecrated in 1926.

Costantini left the apostolic delegation in Beijing in 1933. He continued his literary activity. As delegate he had already begun to attract serious attention with his *La crisi cinese e il cattolicismo* and with numerous publications and conferences on missionary subjects and sacred art. He was strongly in favor of indigenous art for religious use in mission countries. His *L'arte cristiana nelle missioni* (Vatican City 1940) explains the principles of native art and argues for the reasonableness and desirability of indigenous, as opposed to foreign, aesthetic forms in Christian art and architecture.

In December of 1935 he was named secretary of the Congregation for the Propagation of the Faith, and he was also made *Rector Magnificus* of the Pontifical Urban Athenaeum in the same year. He was active and effective in promoting missionary work. He became known as an ardent proponent of the establishment of a local clergy in mission lands and of missionary adaptation. Many pontifical pronouncements and policies during these years may be attributed to his inspiration and incessant labors. Among other forms of missionary adaptation, Costantini is particularly recognized as an initiator, promoter, and theoretician of adaptation in art and architecture.

Costantini was created cardinal Jan. 12, 1953 and became chancellor of the Holy Roman Church on May 22, 1954.

Bibliography: A. CAMPS, "Celso Costantini, Apostolic Delegate in China (1922–1933): The Changing Role of the Foreign Missionary," in *Studies in Asian Mission 1956–1998* (Leiden 2000) 169–174. G. WEI-MING, M. SLOBODA, tr., "Costantini: Patron of Chinese Church Art" *Tripod* (1995) 40–46. R. SIMONATO, *Celso Costantini tra rinnovamento cattolico in Italia e le nuove missioni in Cina* (Pordenone 1985). C. SOETENS, "Celso Costantini et la Cina," *Revue d'histoire Ecclésiastique* 80, no. 2 (1985) 653–654.

[J. C. WILLKE]

COTON, PIERRE

Jesuit controversialist and spiritual writer; b. Néronde (Loire), France, March 7, 1564; d. Paris, March 19, 1626. He entered the Society of Jesus in 1583 at the novitiate of Arona, near Milan. He followed the course of philosophy and theology at Milan and then at Rome, where he studied under Gabriel VÁZQUEZ and Juan AZOR and enjoyed the spiritual direction of St. Robert Bellarmine. He completed his theology at Lyons and began his career as a preacher and controversialist. He was particularly occupied with the Huguenots of southern France and gained a considerable reputation for his defense of the Church and of the Jesuit position. In 1603 he was influential in determining the royal policy of reestablishing the Society of Jesus within France, and in 1608 he became confessor to Henry IV and to the future Louis XIII. His influence at court occasioned many and fierce attacks from the Calvinists. After the assassination of Henry IV, Coton had to defend himself and his order from charges of condoning regicide. Accusations and intrigue finally forced him to leave the court in 1617. He became rector of the college at Bordeaux and then provincial of the province of Aquitaine in 1622 and of the province of Paris in 1624.

Coton wrote many controversial works and apologetic tracts. His antagonists were so strong and numerous that they came to be called anti-Cotonists. Some of Coton's writings are *Institution catholique* (2 v. Paris 1610), *Lettre déclaratoire de la doctrine des Pères Jésuites* (Paris 1610), and *Responce apologétique à l'Anticoton* (Paris 1611).

Coton was also the friend of many spiritual leaders of his time, and he contributed significantly to the spiritual renaissance of the 17th century. His relationship with Pierre de BÉRULLE was particularly close. Coton's spirituality somewhat resembled that of St. Francis de Sales, and his *Intérieure occupation d'une âme dévote* (Paris 1608) seems to anticipate De Sales' *Introduction à la vie dévote*. Among Coton's other spiritual writings are *Méditations sur la vie de Notre Sauveur Jésus Christ* (Paris 1614) and *Sermons. . .en forme de méditations* (Paris 1617). His works went through numerous editions and were translated into various languages.

Bibliography: J. M. PRAT, *Recherches historiques et critiques sur la Compagnie de Jésus en France du temps du P. Coton, 1564–1626,* 5 v. (Lyons 1876–78). H. BREMOND, *Histiore littéraire du sentiment réligieux en France despuis la fin des guerres de religion jusqu'à nos jours,* 12 v. (Paris 1911–36). C. SOMMERVOGEL et al., *Bibliothèque de la Compagnie de Jésus,* 11 v. (Brussels-Paris 1890–1932 v. 12, supplement 1960). A POTTIER and M. J. PICAR, *Dictionnaire de spiritualité ascétique et mystique. Doctrine et histoire,* ed. M. VILLER et al. (Paris 1932–). Y. DE LA BRIÈRE, in *Dictionnaire de théologie catholique,* ed. A. VACANT et al., 15 v. (Paris 1903–50; Tables générales 1951–). G. WAGNER, in *Catholicisme. Hier, aujourd'hui et demain,* ed. G. JACQUEMET (Paris 1947–).

[J. C. WILLKE]

COTTAM, THOMAS, BL.

Jesuit martyr; b. 1549; d. London, May 1582. He was of an ancient family of some wealth whose seat was at Dilworth in Lancashire. Many of his relatives were Catholic, but his parents were Protestants. He was educated at Brasenose College, Oxford, and took his B.A. in 1568. He became a teacher in London where he met Thomas Pound, to whom he owed his conversion. He resigned his mastership, and crossed to Douai, arriving in May 1577. The following year, after a brief visit to England, Cottam returned to Douai by May 14, 1578, with five young converts from Oxford. He sought admission to the Society of Jesus, and in February 1579 left for Rome, where his health broke down. He was sent to Lyons for rest, but continuing poor health rendered him unfit for the hard life of the society. He returned to Douai, was ordained in May 1580, and left for the English mission the following June. Thanks to the information of Sledd, a noted English priest catcher, whom Cottam had met in Lyons, Cottam was a marked man, and he was arrested as soon as he landed at Dover. The mayor of Dover handed him over to a merchant, himself a secret Catholic, for delivery to Lord Cobham in London. With difficulty, the merchant persuaded him to escape, but when it appeared that the merchant would suffer for his action, Cottam surrendered himself to Lord Cobham. He was confined in the Marshal-sea and the Tower, and brutally tortured. In November 1581 he was tried and condemned with Edmund Campion and others. His execution was delayed until May 1582. While awaiting execution he was received into the Society of Jesus. With three others, he was hanged, drawn, and quartered at Tyburn. He was beatified by Leo XIII in 1886.

Bibliography: J. A. MYERSCOUGH, *A Procession of Lancashire Martyrs and Confessors* (Glasgow 1958).

[B. C. FISHER]

COTTOLENGO, GIUSEPPE BENEDETTO, ST.

Founder of the Piccola Casa and of several religious congregations; b. Bra, near Turin, Italy, May 3, 1786; d. Chieri, near Turin, April 30, 1842. Cottolengo, the eldest of 12 children, was ordained (1811), gained a doctorate in theology (1816), became a canon (1818), and devoted himself to pastoral work in Turin until 1827. Influenced by St. VINCENT DE PAUL, he spent the remainder of his life caring for the sick and unfortunate. In 1828 he organized the Brothers of St. Vincent, a pious association of laymen, and opened a small hospital in Turin. In 1832 the Piccola Casa della Divina Providenza (Little House of Divine Providence) moved to nearby Valdocco. Eventually it developed into a huge complex of institutions that still flourishes and includes a general hospital; homes for the mentally ill, the blind and crippled, deaf-mutes and orphans; a refuge for penitent women; and a nursing school for religious. To assist him in these diverse works, Cottolengo founded a number of religious congregations, each of which was intended to perform a separate function in the Piccola Casa. Best known of these congregations is that of the Sisters of St. Vincent de Paul, or *Cottolenghine*, founded in 1830 with the collaboration of Marianna Nasi. Cottolengo insisted on supporting his

Piccola Casa by private donations and refused to permit it to be endowed. Cottolengo was beatified on April 29, 1917, and canonized on May 19, 1934.

Feast: April 29.

Bibliography: P. GASTALDI, *San Guiseppe Benedetto Cottolengo* (new ed. Turin 1959), 1st pub. 1892, repr. in 3 v., 1910; *The Life of the Ven. Joseph Benedict Cottolengo*, tr. and abr. by a Jesuit Father (San Francisco–New York 1893–1897). B. LEJONNE, *Miracle à Turin: Saint Joseph Benoit Cottolengo, currier de la Providence* (Paris 1958). V. DI MEO, *La spiritualità di S. Cottolengo* (Pinerolo 1959). R. NASH, *God Is Our Banker* (London 1960). E. PILLA, *Un gigante della carità* (Siena 1964). G. BITELLI, *Il Santo degli infelici* (1964). G. BARRA, *Quando l'amore si fa pane* (Turin 1974). L. PIANO, *San Guiseppe Benedetto Cottolengo* (Turin 1996). A. BUTLER, *The Lives of the Saints*, ed. H. THURSTON and D. ATTWATER (New York 1956) 2:191–192.

[F. G. SOTTOCORNOLA]

COTTON, JOHN

Puritan clergyman; b. Derby, Derbyshire, England, Dec. 4, 1584; d. Boston, Mass., Dec. 23, 1652. Little is known of his early years. He received the degrees of B.A. (1603) and M.A. (1606) from Trinity College, Cambridge. He was awarded a fellowship to Emmanuel College, Cambridge, a school much inclined toward Puritanism, was ordained in 1610, and received his bachelor of divinity degree in 1613. For gradually adopting Puritan forms of worship, he was forced to flee to America when Abp. William Laud came to power in 1633. In Boston, Cotton was appointed teacher of the church, a post he held until his death. He believed the state should have the power of life and death to ensure conformity. His opinion was of such importance that whatever he preached soon became part of either civil law or church practice. Besides his controversial pamphlets, he wrote on prayer, church music, and the theory and methods of New England Congregationalism.

Bibliography: C. MATHER, *Magnalia Christi Americana: The Ecclesiastical History of New England . . . ,* (London 1702), 1st Amer. ed. 2 v. (Hartford, CT 1820). P. G. E. MILLER, *The New England Mind: From Colony to Province* (Cambridge, Mass. 1953). J. T. ADAMS, *Dictionary of American Biography,* ed. A. JOHNSON and D. MALONE, 20 v. (New York 1928–36; index 1937) 4:460–462.

[E. R. VOLLMAR]

COUDERC, MARIE VICTOIRE THÉRÈSE, BL.

Foundress of the Religious of the CENACLE; b. Sablières (Ardèche), France, Feb. 1, 1805; d. Lyons, France, Sept. 26, 1885 (feast, Sept. 26). In 1825 Marie Victoire returned from boarding school at Vans to attend a mission in her parish given by Abbé Jean Terme, a diocesan priest who had founded a religious teaching congregation at Aps, and who acted as its director. Influenced by him, Marie Victoire entered this congregation in 1826, taking the name Thérèse.

In 1827, she was sent with two other sisters to La Louvesc to open a hostel for women pilgrims to the tomb of St. John Francis REGIS. This community developed into the Congregation of the Cenacle. Thérèse, who became superior in 1828, arranged to restrict the house to women who wished to make retreats following the SPIRITUAL EXERCISES of St. IGNATIUS OF LOYOLA. The novitiate was soon transferred to La Louvesc under Thérèse's direction. After Terme's death (1834), supervision of the institute was entrusted to the Jesuits who had a decisive influence in the congregation's early years.

In 1836 the bishop of Viviers approved the rules, but obliged the Cenacle Sisters to separate from the Sisters of St. John Francis Regis who were dedicated to teaching. Thérèse, superior of her congregation, pronounced her perpetual vows in 1837 and made a special act of consecration in which she abdicated her authority.

At the suggestion of François Renault, the Jesuit provincial, Mme. Gallet, a wealthy widow 20 years old, became superior 15 days after joining the congregation as a postulant, but she died shortly afterward, leaving her fortune to the institute. Confusion followed, because her heirs contested her will and the Cenacle's incompetent treasurer grossly misrepresented the financial situation, which discredited Thérèse in the eyes of the local bishop. Countess de La Villeurnoy was designated superior general and foundress in 1838, but was removed from office in 1839 after her incompetence brought the congregation to the verge of ruin.

From 1839 until her death in 1852, Mother Contenet was superior general. In her endeavor to attract members from higher social stations, she dismissed all but one of the sisters accepted by Thérèse. The superior general, who had no confidence in the ability of the foundress, denied her all part in the direction of the institute and assigned her to lowly posts designed to keep her apart from the community, even during recreation periods. Internal dissension resulted from the election of a superior general in 1852, and as a result, Mother Anaïs, the superior general, quit the congregation in 1855. Thérèse was named local superior for short periods at Tournon and La Louvesc (1856–57), and later served as guardian at La Louvesc, Lyons, and Montpellier. The self-effacing foundress spent her remaining years from 1874 at Fourvières. She was beatified Nov. 1, 1951.

Feast: Sept. 26.

Pierre Marie Joseph Coudrin.

Bibliography: E. SURLES, *Surrender to the Spirit* (New York 1951). H. PERROY, *A Great and Humble Soul: Mother Thérèse Couderc,* tr. from French by J. J. Burke (pa. Westminster, Md. 1960). A. COMBES, *La Bienheureuse Thérèse Couderc* (Paris 1956).

[T. F. CASEY]

COUDRIN, PIERRE MARIE JOSEPH

Founder of the Fathers of the Sacred Hearts (Picpus Fathers) and Picpus Sisters; b. Coussay-les-Bois (Vienne), France, March 1, 1768; d. Paris, March 27, 1837. He was one of eight children of pious parents. After studies in the seminary and at the University of Poitiers he was ordained secretly during the FRENCH REVOLUTION (1792). Because of his refusal to subscribe to the CIVIL CONSTITUTION OF THE CLERGY, he had to exercise his ministry in secret to escape arrest. While in hiding (September 1792) he received an inspiration to found a missionary society for men and another for women. Together with Henriette AYMER DE LA CHEVALERIE, he founded a religious congregation for men (1792) and another for women (1797). Papal approval for both institutes came in 1817. Coudrin also established several colleges in France and served as vicar-general for the Dioceses of Rouen, Mende, Séez, and Troyes. His cause for beatification has been introduced in Rome.

Charles Edward Coughlin. (AP/Wide World Photos)

Bibliography: S. PERRON, *Vie du Très Révérend Père M.-J. Coudrin* (Paris 1900). A. LESTRA, *Le Père Coudrin* (Lyons 1952). W. H. HÜNERMANN, *Le Marquisard de Dieu,* tr. from German by G. D'ALMYS (Paris 1954). P. PIRIOU, *Dictionnaire de spiritualité ascétique et mystique. Doctrine et histoire,* ed., M. VILLER et al. (Paris 1932) 2:2433–43.

[P. HERAN]

COUGHLIN, CHARLES EDWARD

Priest, radio orator; b. Hamilton, Ontario, Oct. 25, 1891; d. Bloomfield Hills, Michigan, Oct. 27, 1979. The only child of Thomas and Amelia (Mahoney) Coughlin, young Coughlin graduated in 1911 from St. Michael's College, Toronto, receiving a degree in philosophy. In September 1911 he joined the Basilians (Congregation of Priests of St. Basil) in Toronto and was ordained on June 29, 1916, in St. Basil's Church, Toronto. From 1916 to 1923 Father Coughlin taught at Assumption College in Sandwich, Ontario, while also assisting at the college chapel and St. Agnes Church in Detroit. In 1923, he left the Basilians and was incardinated into the Diocese of Detroit under Bishop Michael J. Gallagher. In May 1926, he was assigned to Royal Oak, Michigan, to establish a new parish dedicated to St. Therese of the Child Jesus, the "Little Flower," who had been canonized in 1925.

In order to raise funds, Coughlin negotiated his first radio program, which was aired on Oct. 17, 1926 over WJR in Detroit.

WJR remained his sole outlet until the fall of 1929 when he added WMAQ, Chicago, and WLW, Cincinnati, and in 1930 the Columbia Broadcasting System (CBS) carried the program nationally. At first he confined himself to religious topics, but in 1930 he began to attack the injustices of American capitalism, using the encyclicals of Leo XIII and Pius XI to support his views. CBS officials soon became alarmed at the inflammatory nature of his talks and eased him off the air in April of 1931. Undaunted, Coughlin immediately formed his own network of stations. At the peak of his popularity he had a listening audience estimated at between 10 and 40 million. By 1934 he was employing 150 secretaries to handle mail and donations.

Deeply touched by the plight of the unemployed and angered that President Hoover did so little to help them, he supported Franklin D. Roosevelt in 1932. Coughlin became disenchanted with the New Deal in 1934 and formed the National Union for Social Justice with a 16-point program of social reform. In his Nov. 11, 1934 broadcast, he promoted the NUSJ as a group "to organize for action, if you will: to organize for social united action which will be founded on God-given social truths which belong to Catholic and Protestant, to Jew and Gentile, to blacks and whites, to rich and poor, to industrialist and laborer." He broke completely with Roosevelt in 1935 and organized the Union Party in 1936 with Congressman William Lemke as his candidate for President. He also launched a weekly newspaper, *Social Justice.*

After Bishop Gallagher died in 1937, Father Coughlin was frequently at odds with his new superior, Archbishop (and later Cardinal) Edward MOONEY. He became increasingly controversial, both over the air and in the pages of *Social Justice.* By 1938, he was openly anti-Semitic, going so far as to publish the discredited *Protocols of the Elders of Zion* in *Social Justice.* In that same year Father Coughlin came under the influence of Father Denis Fahey, CSS (1883–1954), an eccentric Irish theologian whose writings were openly anti-Semitic. Coughlin began a regular correspondence with Fahey and frequently quoted from Fahey's books on the radio and in the pages of *Social Justice.*

Father Coughlin was forced to give up broadcasting in 1940 when he refused to comply with the National Association of Broadcasters' new rule barring all "controversial" speakers unless they agreed to appear on a panel with speakers presenting divergent views. He continued to publish *Social Justice,* despite the opposition of Archbishop Mooney. Even after Pearl Harbor (1941) he consistently denounced the Roosevelt administration and America's ally, Great Britain. In the spring of 1942 a District of Columbia grand jury investigated *Social Justice* as a seditious publication. For the sake of wartime unity, President Roosevelt and his attorney general, Francis Biddle, arranged a behind-the-scenes deal with Archbishop Mooney: Father Coughlin would be silenced in return for the government dropping all legal action against him. Archbishop Mooney called in Coughlin on May 1, 1942 and ordered him to cease all public pronouncements on non-religious issues. Father Coughlin agreed and continued to serve as pastor of his large parish at Royal Oak until he retired in 1966. He faithfully kept his bargain with Archbishop Mooney and never again entered the public arena.

Bibliography: C. J. TULL, *Father Coughlin and the New Deal* (Syracuse 1965). S. MARCUS, *Father Charles E. Coughlin: The Tumultuous Life of the Priest of the Little Flower* (Boston 1973). A. BRINKLEY, *Voices of Protest: Huey Long, Father Coughlin and the Great Depression* (New York 1982). M. C. ATHANS, "A New Perspective on Father Charles E. Coughlin," *Church History* 56 (June 1987) 224–235.

[C. J. TULL]

COUGHLIN, MARY SAMUEL, MOTHER

Religious superior, educator; b. Faribault, Minn., April 7, 1868; d. Sinsinawa, Wis., Oct. 17, 1959. She was the daughter of Daniel and Ellen (O'Mahoney) Coughlin. After graduating in 1885 from Bethlehem Academy, Faribault, she entered the Congregation of the Most Holy Rosary and received the habit on Aug. 15, 1886. She taught for several years in parish schools and then was elected bursar general (1901) of the congregation, and prioress (1904) of St. Clara Convent, Sinsinawa. On the death of Mother Emily POWER in 1909, Sister Mary Samuel assumed the interim duties of superior general; she was elected mother general in August 1910. During the 39 years of her administration, 1,450 sisters made profession and 63 foundations were established. St. Clara College was transferred to River Forest, Ill., and incorporated (1918) as Rosary College. Edgewood College of the Sacred Heart, Madison, Wis., was established in 1927 to provide professional and liberal education for sisters and secular women. Villa des Fougères, Fribourg, Switzerland, was purchased in 1917 as a European house of studies and after 1924 provided facilities for the Rosary College Junior Year Abroad. In 1948 the Pius XII Institute, a graduate school of fine arts, was opened in Florence, Italy, at Villa Schifanoia, donated to the Holy See by Myron Taylor.

The diversity of Mother Samuel's interests was indicated by her cooperation in research projects conducted by the Institutum Divi Thomae, Cincinnati, Ohio, and by the Vatican Library, Rome. She also helped to prepare the curriculum, *Guiding Growth in Christian Social Living,* as part of the social action program of the Commission on American Citizenship of the Catholic University of America, Washington, D.C. She sent her sisters to American and European universities, fostered liturgical observance at the motherhouse and missions, and initiated (1924) vacation schools for religious instruction in the Diocese of Rockford, Ill. A catechetical center and five schools for African Americans and the reception of African-American applicants into the congregation testify to her racial attitude. Mother Samuel was granted (1932) an honorary degree of doctor of laws at Loyola University, Chicago, and served as first president of the American Dominican Mothers General Conference (1935–37).

Bibliography: M. E. MCCARTY, *The Sinsinawa Dominicans: Outlines of Twentieth Century Development, 1901–49* (Sinsinawa, Wis. 1952).

[M. G. KELLY]

COUNCIL OF CATHOLIC PATRIARCHS OF THE ORIENT (CPCO)

Better known by its French acronym CPCO (*Conseil des Patriarches Catholiques d'Orient*). The CPCO is a communion of all seven Catholic patriarchs in the Christian East that was formed in 1990 as a sign and instrument of patriarchal collegiality. These seven Catholic patriarchs, in order of precedence, dignity, and honor are: (1) the Patriarch of Antioch and all the East for the Maronite Church, (2) the Coptic Catholic Patriarch of Alexandria, (3) the Patriarch of Antioch and all the East, Alexandria, and Jerusalem for the Melkite Greek Catholic Church, (4) the Patriarch of Antioch and all the East for the Syrian Catholic Church, (5) the Patriarch of Babylon for the Chaldean Catholic Church, (6) the Patriarch (*Catholicos*) of Cilicia for the Armenian Catholic Church, and (7) the Latin Patriarch of Jerusalem. The seat of the CPCO is the Maronite Patriarchate at Bkerke, Lebanon. The CPCO meets once a year in regular session. Patriarchs preside at each session successively. The CPCO enjoys moral authority without any derogation to the rights and privileges of individual Patriarchs and synodal assemblies of each Patriarchal Church.

The objectives of the CPCO include: (i) to coordinate the pastoral activity of the Catholic Churches of the Orient, (ii) to strengthen the future of Christianity in the

NEW CATHOLIC ENCYCLOPEDIA

295

Orient, (iii) to consolidate the ties between the faithful of the Diaspora and their Churches, (iv) to foster ecumenical collaboration and interreligious dialogue, (v) to represent the Catholic Churches of the East in the Middle East Council of Churches (MECC), and (vi) to promote justice, peace, development and respect for human rights in the Middle East.

[K. ALWAN]

COUNCIL OF EUROPEAN BISHOPS' CONFERENCES (CCEE)

At Vatican Council II the bishops discovered the great value of collegiality. Toward the end of the council the presidents of 13 European episcopal conferences sought ways of continuing collegial cooperation. The result was the Council of European Bishops' Conferences (Consilium Conferentiarum Episcoporum Europae), founded in March 1971.

Composition and Purpose. The members of the CCEE are the Bishops' Conferences of Europe, numbering 33 as of 1994. Until 1993 the conferences were represented by a delegated bishop, but since April 1993, at the specific request of Pope John Paul II, the conferences are represented by their presidents. Normally, a general assembly is held every year.

The specific tasks that the CCEE has set itself are as follows: promotion of hierarchical communio; exchange of information; cooperation on common issues; the establishment of contact with episcopal conferences of other continents; ecumenical contact; and Christian witness within European society.

The presidents of the CCEE have been Cardinal Roger Etchegaray of France (1971–79); Cardinal Basil Hume of England (1979–86); Cardinal Carlo Maria Martini of Italy (1986–93); and Archbishop Miloslav Vlk of the Czech Republic (1993–). The secretary general of the conference until 1977 was Alois Sustar; since 1979 that position has been held by Ivo Fürer. The secretariat has been located in St. Gallen, Switzerland, since 1977.

Evangelization in Europe. The Councils of Bishops' Conferences that were set up in other continents were established to observe and monitor specific matters of concern and issues needing attention in those continents. For many centuries Europe and the universal Church had been identical. As a result it was only gradually that the CCEE discovered the problems that were of particular concern to the European continent. This growth in self-awareness occurred especially in a series of symposia organized by the European bishops.

A symposium has been held on average every three years. The different episcopal conferences are represented at these symposia by a number of bishops in proportion to the size of the conference. On each occasion roughly 80 bishops attend the symposium. Initially, the symposia were dedicated above all to following up issues raised at Vatican Council II: "Post-Conciliar Diocesan Structures" (1967); "The Life and Ministry of Priests" (1969); "The Mission of Bishops as Diakonia of the Faith" (1975). There followed a type of transitional symposium on "Youth and Faith" (1979). The remaining symposia have addressed various issues: "The Collegial Responsibility of the Bishops and of the Episcopal Conferences of Europe in the Evangelization of the Continent" (1982); "'Secularisation' as a Challenge and an Opportunity for the Gospel in Europe" (1985); "New Attitudes to Birth and Death as Opportunities for Evangelisation" (1989).

There has been a growing realization that the specific task of the CCEE is the evangelization of Europe. Europe has been shaped by the Christian faith and in turn Europe shaped Christianity. This mutual interpenetration, unchallenged from the earliest times, has been in steady decline for the past two centuries and had accelerated in recent times. This phenomenon is sometimes described as "secularization." The peculiar problem for Europe is that the continent finds itself at the close of a first, glorious age of evangelization, while also presiding over the transition to a totally new age in history.

Interaction Between East and West. Until 1989 the continent of Europe was sharply divided due to the isolation of those states in Central and Eastern Europe that were under communist domination. Whenever possible, contact between the different local churches was established within the context of the CCEE. The episcopal conferences of Poland, Hungary, Yugoslavia, Lithuania, Romania, and East Germany (the German Democratic Republic) also regularly worked together. The degree of cooperation on the two sides of the great European divide differed markedly.

This situation changed dramatically with the collapse of communism. In April 1990 the CCEE welcomed representatives of the episcopal conferences of Central and Eastern Europe to a discussion regarding the new situation on the continent. This discussion was continued and intensified at the special Synod for Europe held in December 1991. The new situation shaped the 1993 Symposium of European Bishops. Held in Prague in September, it brought together representatives of the laity, priests, and religious to address the theme, "The Gospel Lived in Freedom and Solidarity."

The totally contrasting patterns of society, one characterized by an atheistic state ideology and more or less public persecution of the Church, the other characterized by indifference and virtually unrestrained freedom, both in their own way shaped the Church in their separate regions. In the West, an attempt was made to explore the avenues opened up by this new situation, while in the communist countries constant opposition ruled out any form of experiment. It was during these years, when the two halves of the continent were so divided, that Vatican Council II took place. In its wake there were notable changes in the life of the Church and in theology in the West. In communist countries the tendency was to emphasize the immutability of Church teaching and thus to partially cut oneself off from developments in Western theology. At the CCEE plenary meeting held in January 1994, the two different patterns of development in East and West were quite evident. What is clearly needed on each side is a better knowledge of the other side and a recognition and exchange of the different gifts of East and West.

Thematic Meetings of the CCEE. The CCEE organizes meetings between bishops, who are entrusted with specific dossiers within their own episcopal conferences, and specialists in their particular field. When the CCEE was established, it was discovered that pastoral ministry to migrants and to tourists required a certain cooperation between episcopal conferences. At a meeting on migration held in December 1993, in addition to the question of pastoral care, the increasingly acute problems of racism and xenophobia came up for discussion.

Roughly every two years, a meeting has taken place in which the participants exchanged views on the question of catechesis. The principal matter of concern was the transmission of the faith in the contemporary world. Over the past few years in the West the question of religious instruction in the public school system has been an issue of contention, while in the countries that hitherto had been communist, religion is being reintroduced as a school subject.

A commission made up of six bishops, the same number of media specialists, and representatives of international Catholic media organizations deals with all issues related to mass media in the European context. Given the wide variety of languages and cultures represented on the European continent, the possibilities of exchanging religious programs between one country and another are very limited. There is urgent need for Western help in assisting the Church to gain access to the media in the formerly communist countries, and particularly to train Catholics to work in the media. A congress was held in Budapest in April 1994 on the subject, "The Value of the Gospel, Media Culture, and European Reconstruction." By way of making its contribution to the preparation of the Roman Synod on the Laity and on Priestly Formation, the CCEE invited the relevant bishops and representatives of the parties concerned from all of the countries of Europe to meet. This move enabled the participants to engage in discussions and thus helped give a clearer idea of which problems could best be solved at the national level and which required a solution at an international level.

Meetings have also been held for those bishops with special responsibility for ministry to youth, ecumenism, justice and peace, evangelization, pilgrimages, etc. Meetings are organized for those promoted to the episcopate in the previous five years. They meet with experienced bishops and discuss the fundamental question: How am I a bishop?

Ecumenical Cooperation. Pope John Paul II has repeatedly pointed out that the churches from the continent in which the separation of the churches originated have a special duty to promote the cause of unity. Since its foundation the CCEE has striven for ever closer cooperation with the Council of European Churches (KEK). This latter grouping represents some 120 churches and church communities from the Orthodox, Protestant, and Anglican families. A joint committee was set up in 1971, and the council has an annual meeting.

Especially significant are the European ecumenical meetings to which 40 representatives each from CCEE and KEK are invited. The themes of the meetings held to date have been: "One—That the World May Believe" (1978); "Called to One Hope—Ecumenical Fellowship in Prayer, Witness and Service" (1981); "Confessing the Faith Together—Source of Hope" (1984); "Your Kingdom Come!" (1988); "'At Thy Word': Mission and Evangelism in Europe Today" (1991). The CCEE and KEK have also mandated a joint committee to tackle the issue of "Islam in Europe."

Witness in the European Community/European Union (EC/EU). At a moment when the episcopal conferences in most communist countries enjoyed little possibility of influencing the socio-political life of their respective nations, more and more countries in the West were coming together in what is now known as the European Union. Given that many policy decisions are now being taken at the supranational level, the episcopal conferences of the nations concerned have found themselves obliged to get together and, in cooperation with the diplomatic representatives of the Holy See on the spot, make their views felt. This need for common action between conferences led to the setting up of the Commission of Episcopal Conferences of the European Community (COMECE) in March 1980. This latter body is made up of one delegate from each of the episcopal conferences of the European Union.

The enterprise with perhaps the greatest influence on society was the ecumenical meeting organized jointly by CCEE and KEK held in Basel in May 1989. There were 700 delegates from all the churches in Europe present, as well as thousands of visitors. The fact that this meeting immediately rode the crest of the European wave is quite remarkable. Discussions are under way at the moment regarding the convening of a second European ecumenical assembly to address the issue of reconciliation.

Exchange of Information. Cooperation between episcopal conferences requires that information be exchanged between conferences on a regular basis. It is precisely with the intention of keeping one another up to date that the secretaries of the national episcopal conferences have an annual meeting. Furthermore, the spokespersons of the conferences, i.e., their media officers, maintain regular contact. At irregular intervals the Secretariat of the CCEE issues a report on the principal issues dealt with by the individual bishops' conferences.

The CCEE has established multilateral contacts with a wide variety of European organizations and institutions, in particular the European Forum of National Councils of the Laity, the Council of Working Parties of the European Council of Priests, and the European Conference of National Major Superiors.

Bibliography: Conseil des Conférences Épiscopales d'Europe, *Les Évêques d'Europe et la nouvelle évangélisation* (Paris 1991). Conseil des Conférences Épiscopales d'Europe et Conférences des Églises Européennes, *Les Églises d'Europe: l'engagement œcuménique* (Paris 1993).

[I. FÜRER]

COUNCIL OF MAJOR SUPERIORS OF WOMEN RELIGIOUS

(CMSWR); established, 1992, to promote religious life in women religious orders in the United States, to encourage effective collaboration among those major superiors who desire it, and to cooperate closely with the hierarchy, the pope and bishops, of the Church. On June 13, 1992, the Congregation for Institutes of Consecrated Life and Societies of Apostolic Life officially erected the CMSWR and approved its statutes for an experimental period of five years. On Oct. 26, 1995, the congregation granted definitive approval to the statutes with some minor modifications.

As a canonical Conference of Major Superiors according to the Law of the Church (canons 708 and 709 of the *Code of Canon Law*), CMSWR brings major superiors together in collaboration and mutual support as they serve the Church and their individual institutes, transact common business, and coordinate active cooperation with UNITED STATES CONFERENCE OF CATHOLIC BISHOPS (USCCB). In connection with the USCCB, CMSWR members have been asked to serve in various capacities involving the National Religious Retirement Office (NRRO), the National Advisory Committee to Bishops, Bishops Health Care Committee, and the Bishops Committee on the Missions. By invitation, Board members have attended the Synod on Religious Life and the Synod on America.

The members of the council belong to communities of women that seek to promote the consecrated life as a radical way of life and calling of Christ. They are committed to a life of prayer, liturgical, communal and individual, as a means of deep union with Christ, their Spouse. The major superiors who are members of the Council share with one another both strengths and weaknesses arising from their common effort to serve the needs of the Church in each community's own unique way.

As of 2001, CMSWR had 160 members from 113 different institutes or provinces, representing over 6,000 sisters from across the United States. CMSWR holds national assemblies that provide opportunities for members to pray together, discuss common concerns and to participate in programs on various aspects of religious life. In addition to regional workshops and periodic courses that are offered to sisters for their continued formation, workshops are organized for those responsible for the formation of new sisters. In 1999, the CMSWR established the Domus Sanctae Mariae Guadalupe a residence in Rome, within a walking distance from the Vatican, for sister-students to pursue further studies at neighboring Catholic universities.

The CMSWR newsletter keeps readers informed about its activities, ecclesial publications and current happenings in Rome, especially those concerning religious life. A vocations directory is available at no charge to assist young women in the discernment of their vocation. A quarterly newsletter, *Consecrata,* is also distributed to over 5,000 individuals and agencies interested in supporting consecrated life through their prayers and funding.

[B. A. GOODING]

COUNCILS, GENERAL (ECUMENICAL), HISTORY OF

The precedent generally cited for Church councils was the assembly of the Apostles in Jerusalem *c.* A.D. 52 (Acts 15.28). Although it was not a representative gathering of leaders from all over the Church, it did discuss a doctrinal issue of lasting significance for Christians, namely, that Gentile converts were not bound to observe all the prescriptions of the Old Testament. Inspired by the example of the Apostles, bishops of different provinces used to gather during the first centuries in order to reach decisions on theological and disciplinary matters that required clarification or had disturbed the consciences of the faithful. The logical places for such meetings were the capitals (*metropoleis*) of the Roman provinces. The meetings were customarily convened by the bishops of the capitals.

Because of the adoption by the primitive Church of the system of accommodation to the political organization of the empire, the bishops of these cities gained a kind of superiority over the bishops of the provinces and were called metropolitans. Such assemblies are known to have taken place in the 2nd century against the errors of MONTANISM and during the EASTER CONTROVERSY. During the 3rd century conferences of bishops of different provinces took place regularly every year. A certain importance was ascribed to such gatherings in Carthage (*c.* 220), in Synnada and Iconium (*c.* 230), and in Antioch (264, 269). In the 4th century the assemblies of Carthage and Elvira (between 300 and 306), Arles and Ancyra (314), Alexandria (320), and Neocaesarea deserve special mention.

Early Conciliar Practice. CYPRIAN of Carthage supplies the most exhaustive information on the methods of organizing such assemblies. His letters show clearly that such gatherings modeled themselves on the rules of procedure for sessions of the Roman Senate. The presiding bishop assumed the role of the emperor or of his representative in the Senate. He used the same words for the convocation of the council as were used in the imperial summons for the convening of the Senate; and the conduct of debate, the interrogations of bishops, and their responses also imitated the procedure of the Senate.

The conciliar or synodal practice was already fully developed in the Church before the conversion of CONSTANTINE I. As a sincere convert he accepted the adaptation of Hellenistic political philosophy to the Christian creed, regarding himself as the representative of God on earth, who had been given by God supreme power in things material and spiritual. In the eyes of the first Christian political philosophers, the Christian emperor was a representative of the Eternal King, Jesus Christ, and his foremost duty was to lead men to God.

Constantine took his duties in religious matters very seriously, as he showed during the schism provoked by the African Donatists (*see* DONATISM). Invited by the bishops to intervene in their disputes, he followed first the Roman judicial procedure, appointing five bishops from Gaul, including the bishop of Rome, as judges. Pope Miltiades, however, following the current Church practice, transformed the court into a council (313). Constantine adopted this method; and when the Donatists repudiated the decision of the Roman synod presided over by the pope, the emperor summoned another council at Arles (314). He also regarded an episcopal conciliar decision as final and confirmed the decision of the Council of Arles against the Donatists.

The acceptance of a Christianized Hellenistic political philosophy by Constantine explains also his intervention against ARIUS, who denied the divine nature of the Second Person of the Trinity. Because the agitation of the Arians had spread and some other religious problems claimed attention, Constantine, mindful of his duty to promote the true worship of God and peace within the Church, decided to convoke a council of bishops from the whole empire, and so the first ecumenical council gathered in 325 in NICAEA.

The report of EUSEBIUS OF CAESAREA shows that the senatorial procedure, already in use in local councils, was followed also in Nicaea. The emperor convoked the bishops, giving them the senatorial privilege of the full use of the official stage post. Furthermore, he himself presided over sessions of the council, explained the reasons for its convocation and the subjects that the bishops should discuss, and directed the individual interrogation of the bishops. Instead of the statue of Victory, which stood in front of the imperial tribune in the Roman Senate, the Bible was placed between the bishops and the emperor. The prelates declared (about 300) that the term HOMOOUSIOS, which was proposed by the emperor after private discussions with bishops, best explained the Catholic doctrine that the Son was of the same nature as the Father. Clerical discipline was regulated in 20 canons; the celebration of Easter Sunday was fixed; and it was approved that Church organization should follow the civil division of the empire.

Although he played a prominent role in the council, the emperor had no right to vote. Voting was the privilege of senators in the Senate and of bishops in the council. Moreover, the place of the most important senator, the *princeps senatus,* was given in the councils to the representatives of the first bishop, the pope. Providentially this adaptation of senatorial procedure to ecumenical councils preserved the autonomy of the bishops in doctrinal matters and guaranteed to the Roman see the first and most important place in conciliar proceedings. This custom was observed in the convocation and direction of the ecumenical councils, especially from the third council on.

Eastern Ecumenical Councils. This section lists the first ecumenical councils of the Church and indicates briefly the main points about them.

Nicaea, held from May 20 or June 19 to *c.* Aug. 25, 325, was convoked by Emperor Constantine I, under Pope Sylvester I. The NICENE CREED was composed, defining the divine nature of the Son.

CONSTANTINOPLE I was convoked by Emperor Theodosius I (379–395) against the heresy of Macedonius, bishop of Constantinople. Pope Damasus I (366–384) was not represented because the council was intended to be a synod of the Eastern Church. The meetings took place between May and July of 381. Because it defined the divine nature of the Holy Spirit and made an addition to the Nicene Creed, it obtained ecumenical status; and this was recognized by the Council of Chalcedon (451). The third of the four canons voted by the Fathers gave the bishop of Constantinople precedence over all Eastern bishops.

The Council of EPHESUS was convoked by Emperor THEODOSIUS II (408–450) against Nestorius. CYRIL OF ALEXANDRIA represented Pope CELESTINE I (422–432). In five meetings from June 22 to July 17, 431, the 153 fathers defined the divine motherhood of the Virgin Mary and voted six canons.

The Council of CHALCEDON was convoked by Emperor MARCIAN (450–457), under Pope Leo I (440–461). In 17 sessions from Oct. 8 to Nov. 1, 451, the 600 bishops condemned the Robber Council of Ephesus (449), which was dominated by the Monophysite Patriarch DIOSCORUS of Alexandria; defined the person of Christ as having two natures, divine and human; and voted eight canons.

That of Constantinople II was convoked by Emperor JUSTINIAN I (527–565), under Pope VIGILIUS I (537–555). During the eight sessions from May 5 to June 2, 553, the 165 fathers condemned the "Three Chapters" of the Nestorians.

CONSTANTINOPLE III was convoked by Emperor CONSTANTINE IV (668–685), under Popes AGATHO (678–681) and LEO II (682–683), for the condemnation of MONOTHELITISM. The council is also called Trullanum because the 170 fathers held the 16 sessions, from Nov. 7, 680, to Sept. 16, 681, in the Cupola hall (Trullos) of the imperial palace. They defined the doctrine of two wills in the person of Christ and condemned Pope HONORIUS together with the promoters of Monothelitism. The synod of 692, called Synodus Quinisexta, convoked by Emperor JUSTINIAN II (685–695), is regarded by the Orthodox churches as the continuation of the sixth Ecumenical Council. The fathers voted 102 disciplinary canons, mostly concerning the Eastern Church.

NICAEA II was convoked (787) by Empress IRENE (797–802), under Pope ADRIAN I (772–795). The 338 fathers defined the legitimacy of the cult of images of the saints and voted 20 canons.

These seven great councils are regarded as ecumenical by both the Roman Catholic and Orthodox Churches. The so-called eighth Ecumenical Council was convoked by Emperor BASIL I (867–886) with the consent of Pope ADRIAN II (867–872) in order to condemn the Patriarch PHOTIUS. In six sessions from Oct. 5, 869, to Feb. 28, 870, the 102 fathers condemned Photius and approved 27 canons. Another synod, which the Orthodox called the Council of Union and was convoked by the same emperor, declared the previous council invalid during seven sessions from November of 879 to March 13, 880, and rehabilitated Photius. Pope JOHN VIII (872–882) accepted the decisions of this synod. Neither the first nor the second council is regarded by the Orthodox as ecumenical because neither of them made any dogmatic decisions. In the Western Church the Council of 869–870 was first called ecumenical by the canonists of Gregory VII at the end of the 11th century.

Western Ecumenical Councils. The practice of convoking ecumenical councils of the Western Church developed from the local synods that the popes convoked in Rome in order to make important decisions. Often, especially under Gregory VII and during the so-called INVESTITURE STRUGGLE, bishops from outside Italy attended these synods. When Rome was occupied by the antipope Clement III, URBAN II held synods in Piacenza and Clermont (1095).

10th to 14th Centuries. The first synod to acquire an ecumenical character in the later tradition was the Council convoked by CALLISTUS II (1119–24) in the Lateran from March 18 to April 6, 1123. It confirmed the Concordat of Worms, concluded in 1122, which marked the end of the first phase of the investiture struggle. More than 300 fathers assisted at the council and voted 25 canons. The Acts of the synod are not preserved. Western canonists call it the ninth Ecumenical Council.

The schisms provoked by the antipope Anacletus prompted Pope INNOCENT II (1130–43) to convoke a "general council" at the Lateran in April 1139. In three sessions the fathers, who numbered between 877 and 1,000, anathematized Anacletus and his adherents and voted 30 canons. It is counted as the 10th Ecumenical Council.

The Third Lateran Council was assembled by ALEXANDER III (1159–81) in 1179 in order to confirm the peace treaty with the Emperor FREDERICK BARBAROSSA concluded in Venice in 1177. In the three sessions from

March 5 to 19, 27 canons were voted. The most important was that requiring a two-thirds majority vote of the cardinals for the valid election of a pope. Another canon stipulated that no persons should be consecrated as bishop before reaching 30 years of age. In the West this is counted as the 11th Ecumenical Council.

INNOCENT III (1198–1216) convoked the Fourth LATERAN COUNCIL (12th Ecumenical Council) in 1215. In three sessions from November 11 to 30 the fathers voted 70 canons, condemned the CATHARI, defined the doctrine of transubstantiation, and obliged Catholics to go to confession and take Holy Communion at least once every year.

The First Council of LYONS, which is counted as the 13th Ecumenical Council, was convoked by INNOCENT IV (1243–54) in 1245. In three sessions from June 28 to July 17, the fathers voted 22 canons and confirmed the deposition of the Holy Roman Emperor FREDERICK II.

The Second Council of LYONS was convoked by GREGORY X (1271–76). In six sessions from May 7 to July 17, the fathers voted 31 canons and confirmed union with the Greeks, but the union did not last. It was decided that a new crusade should be organized, and regulations for a conclave for the papal election were approved. It is counted in the West as the 14th Ecumenical Council.

Pope CLEMENT V (1305–14) assembled in 1311 the Council of VIENNE, the 15th Ecumenical Council according to Western canonists. The fathers, 132 in number, held three sessions from Oct. 16, 1311, to May 6, 1312, confirmed the abolition of the Order of TEMPLARS, intervened in the quarrel of the Franciscans concerning the vow of poverty, and voted some decrees on Church reform.

The 15th to the 20th Century. The Council of CONSTANCE, called the 16th Ecumenical Council in the West, was convoked to end the schism in the Western Church. Forty-five sessions were held from Nov. 5, 1414, to April 22, 1418. The fathers accepted the abdication of the Roman Pope GREGORY XII and deposed John XXIII, who had been elected by the council, and BENEDICT XIII, the pope residing in Avignon. The conclave organized by the council elected MARTIN V (Nov. 11, 1417) as pope. The heretical doctrines of John WYCLIF were rejected, and his follower John HUS, who refused to recant the heresies of which he was accused, was condemned as an obstinate heretic and died at the stake on July 6, 1415. The council also confirmed the decree proclaiming the superiority of a general council over the pope and asked that councils be held at fixed intervals.

The Council of BASEL-Ferrara-Florence (17th Ecumenical Council) was convoked by Pope EUGENE IV (1431–47) in order to secure union with the Greeks. It held 25 sessions from July 1431 to May 4, 1437, in Basel, was transferred to Ferrara on Sept. 18, 1437, and from there to Florence in January 1439. The union with the Greeks was confirmed in Florence on July 6, 1439; with the Armenians on Nov. 22, 1439; and with the Jacobites on Feb. 4, 1442. On April 25, 1442, the council was transferred to Rome.

The Fifth LATERAN COUNCIL (18th Ecumenical Council) was held during the reign of Popes Julian II (1503–13) and Leo X (1513–21). The fathers held 12 meetings from May 3, 1512, to March 16, 1517. They condemned the schismatic synod of Pisa (1511–12) and voted some canons for the purpose of the reform of the Church.

The most important Western ecumenical council, the 19th Ecumenical Council, was the Council of TRENT, convoked by Pope PAUL III (1534–49) on May 22, 1542, for the condemnation of errors spread by the Protestants and for the reform of the Church. The first eight sessions were held in Trent from Dec. 13, 1545, to spring 1547. The 9th, 10th, and 11th sessions took place in Bologna in 1548. Under Pope JULIUS III (1550–55) the fathers met in Trent and held from the 12th to the 16th sessions there. The council continued its deliberations in Trent (17th session to the 25th and last session) under Pope PIUS IV (1559–65) in 1562 and 1563. The fathers voted dogmatic decisions concerning the authority of Holy Writ and tradition, original sin and justification, the seven Sacraments and the Mass, and the cult of the saints. Many decrees on Church reform were promulgated.

VATICAN COUNCIL I, convoked by Pope PIUS IX (1846–78), held four sessions from Dec. 8, 1869, to July 7, 1870, and was adjourned on Oct. 20, 1870. It defined doctrine on the faith and the Constitution of the Church, and on papal primacy and infallibility. This is held in the West to be the 20th Ecumenical Council.

VATICAN COUNCIL II was convoked by Pope JOHN XXIII (1958–63) and opened in St. Peter's basilica on Oct. 11, 1962. The first session dealt with liturgical problems, especially the use of vernacular languages in the liturgy. For the first time representatives of other churches, as well as laymen, attended the sessions as observers. The session closed on Dec. 8, 1962. Reassembled by Pope PAUL VI (1963–78) the second session (Sept. 29, 1963, to Dec. 4, 1963) promulgated decrees on the liturgy and communications media. The third session opened on Sept. 14, 1964. On the closing day, Nov. 21, 1964, the fathers promulgated the Constitution on the Church and the decrees on ecumenism and the Eastern Rite Churches. The fourth and final session opened on Sept. 14, 1965. On October 28, Pope Paul VI promulgated the decrees on the bishops and on Christian education, on religious life and priestly training, and the declaration of relations to non-Christian religions. On November 18 the decrees of the Constitution on Divine Revelation, and on the apostolate of the laity were promulgated. The council adjourned on Dec. 8, 1965, after the promulgation of the declaration on religious liberty, the decrees on the missions and on priestly life and ministry, and the document on the Church in the modern world.

The number of ecumenical councils—21 according to Western canon law—is not based on any official declaration of Church authority. Gregory I ordained that the first four ecumenical councils deserved the same respect as the Four Gospels. Gratian (*Dict.* 16.8) counted eight ecumenical councils, although there is some confusion in his work concerning the ecumenical character of the Ignatian Council of 869–870. Abraham of Crete, who translated the Greek Acts of the Council of Florence, with the permission of the Curia called this the eighth ecumenical council, following the Greek tradition. Cardinals Reginald POLE and CONTARINI also regarded this as the eighth ecumenical council. The 16th-century canonist Antonio Agustín, archbishop of Tarragona, although betraying some hesitation concerning the eighth council, said that both Churches recognized nine ecumenical councils—the ninth being the Council of Florence. He attributed an ecumenical character to only seven councils of the Western Church—the third, fourth, and fifth of the Lateran, the second of Lyons, and those of Vienne, Constance, and Trent.

In his edition of the Acts of Councils (1567), Laurence Surius, although not daring to suppress the figure "eighth" for the Florentine synod, warns the reader that "many important synods had followed the second of Nicaea, which is called the seventh." G. Bini, in his collection (1606), corrects Abraham of Crete and Surius, calling the Council of Florence the 16th ecumenical council. This designation was accepted by J. Sirmond, whose edition of the conciliar Acts (1608–12), published by order of Pope Paul V, was called *Collectio Romana;* his example was followed in other editions of the Acts: P. Labbe and G. Cossart (Paris 1671–72), I. Harduin (Paris 1715), Colletti (Venice 1728–33), D. Mansi (Florence and Venice 1759–98).

Local Councils (Concilia Particularia). The holding of local synods twice a year was recommended by canon five of the Council of Nicaea I. The patriarchs convoked bishops under their jurisdiction to deliberate on disciplinary and doctrinal questions. In the Patriarchate of Constantinople a so-called *synodos endemousa,* or permanent synod, developed, the patriarchs assembling bishops from the nearest dioceses and prelates who were visiting the capital for deliberation on current religious affairs. Such a synod had to select three candidates for the vacant patriarchal see and present them to the emperor for appointment. Similar practices existed in the East also for the election of bishops. In Germanic lands the synodal practice developed differently, under the influence of the idea that kings also had a priestly character that gave them a measure of control over the churches in their realms. The synods of the bishops were transformed into national assemblies presided over by the kings. Besides the bishops, the secular lords also participated, and not only Church affairs but also measures serving the interests of the state were debated. In the Frankish kingdom, the decisions were published as "orders of the ruler" (*capitularia*). The Visigothic kings, converted from Arianism, held 18 synods of this kind from 589 to 702 (*see* TOLEDO, COUNCILS OF).

Composition of the Councils. The first seven ecumenical councils of the West presented a similar pattern. Although convoked and directed by the popes, they admitted, besides the abbots and representatives of religious institutions (*procuratores*), princes and their ambassadors. Not only religious problems but also state affairs were discussed and decided, such as the truce of God, cessation of hostilities, and the organization of crusades. The Council of Constance even permitted persons without episcopal character to vote. The voting was carried out not according to the number of prelates present but according to the system adopted by medieval universities of the four nations: Germany, France, England, and Italy. A fifth vote was later given to Spain. Such a composition of a general council was a breach with tradition, and the proclamation of the superiority of a general council over the pope endangered the primatial right of the pope. This parliamentary system was even more fully developed by the Council of Basel, which ended in schism. The old tradition concerning the convocation and composition of general councils was firmly reestablished by the Council of Trent. The sessions were presided over by the representatives of the pope, and the right to vote was given only to bishops, to the generals of the orders, and to representatives of monastic congregations. Although princes were invited and were represented by their ambassadors, the council limited the discussions and decisions strictly to religious problems. This type of organization was further developed at Vatican Council I. No representatives of rulers were admitted. The pope maintained the right to propose the subject of debates. The preparation of the propositions (*schemata*) was entrusted to theologians of four deputations elected by the council. The right of vote was given only to bishops and to the heads of religious orders.

At Vatican Council II, major Christian bodies, Orthodox and Protestant, although not in communion with Rome, were invited to send delegates as observers. They were permitted to attend the public sessions and the general congregations, but they did not have the right to vote or speak. They could and did make their views known to the commissions through the Secretariate for Promoting Christian Unity. Before the opening of the third sessions (Sept. 8, 1964), Pope Paul VI announced that women auditors, eight religious and seven lay, had been invited to the council. By the end in 1965, the Second Vatican Council proved to be the most ecumenical council in the history of the Church both by reason of numbers in attendance and by broad representation of various Christian traditions.

Bibliography: R. BELLARMINE, *De conciliis et ecclesia* (Cologne 1633). F. X. FUNK, *Kirchengeschichtliche Abhandlungen und Untersuchungen,* 3 v. (Paderborn 1897–1907) 1:38–121, 498–508; 3:143–149, 406–439. C. J. VON HEFELE, *Histoire des conciles d'après les documents originaux,* tr. and continued by H. LECLERCQ 10 v. in 19 (Paris 1907–38). J. FORGET, *Dictionnaire de théologie catholique* (Paris 1903–50) 3.1:636–676. E. C. BUTLER, *The Vatican Council,* 2 v. (New York 1930). F. DVORNIK, *The Photian Schism* (Cambridge, Eng. 1948); *Emperors, Popes and General Councils,* Dumberton Oaks Papers 6 (1951) 1–23; *The Ecumenical Councils* (New York 1961). J. GILL, *The Council of Florence* (Cambridge, Eng. 1959). B. ROBERG, *Die Union zwischen der griechischen und lateinischen Kirche auf dem II. Konzil von Lyon* (Bonn 1964). H. JEDIN, *Ecumenical Councils of the Catholic Church,* tr. E. GRAF (New York 1960). H. JEDIN, *History of the Council of Trent,* tr. E. GRAF (St. Louis 1957–60). B. TIERNEY, *Foundations of the Conciliar Theory* (Cambridge, Eng. 1955). V. PERI, *I Concili et le Chiese* (Rome 1965). J. A. FITZMYER, *The Acts of the Apostles* (Anchor Bible 31 New York 1998).

[F. DVORNIK/EDS.]

COUNCILS, GENERAL (ECUMENICAL), THEOLOGY OF

By the theology of ecumenical councils is understood here both the exposition of the teaching of the Church on the subject and the reflection of the theologians on it. The substance of this teaching is to be found in the third chapter ("The Hierarchical Structure of the Church and the Episcopate") of VATICAN COUNCIL II's *Dogmatic Constitution on the Church, Lumen gentium;* the reflection of theologians is in a developing stage.

The constitution consolidates the points of doctrine that were clearly understood in the past, and at the same time it marks a new departure by its fresh approach and inspiration. It is not a formal definition, but it is the solemn expression of the mind of the Church on itself and its life; hence it is a document of the highest authority. A common theological NOTE (qualification) cannot be attached to the constitution as a whole: the theological value of each sentence should be determined by a careful analysis of the text, of its context, and of its historical background.

The constitution describes an ecumenical council as the solemn exercise of the full, supreme, and universal power of the episcopal college. The term "ecumenical" is here synonymous with "universal"; it means a council that represents the whole Church and that has full power over it.

Structure of an Ecumenical Council. The strongest manifestation of the unity of the episcopal college, of which it is the most important activity, an ecumenical council has a structure in substance identical with the structure of the college itself.

The episcopal college has to be understood as the community of bishops, united into one organic body (*see* BISHOP [IN THE CHURCH]). The structure of this communion is of divine origin; it has no parallel in civil corporations. It cannot be changed by any human power. Its head is the successor of PETER, the pope, who has in this structure a singular position that was given by Christ to Peter and has been transmitted by Peter to the bishops of Rome (*see* PRIMACY OF THE POPE). The pope is the principle and the foundation of the unity of the body: without him it could not exist at all. He is the universal bishop (a traditional name); he represents the UNITY OF THE CHURCH that transcends all diversity of peoples, nations, or persons. Without him there could not be a universal council; there would be only a meeting of individual bishops or the gathering of the local episcopate without the mark of supreme power. His power is the full power of keys to the exercise of the power of the episcopal college. It is his exclusive right to convoke, to preside over, and to confirm a council. The right of convocation is explicitly attributed to the pope by the constitution, although it is not necessary to conclude that it is so by divine law. In fact, some of the early councils were not convoked by the bishop of Rome. Also, it is the pope's prerogative to preside over an ecumenical council, either personally or through his legates. This right flows naturally from his office of being the head of the college, but it need not be exercised fully, nor has it always been exercised throughout the course of history.

The right to confirm the decisions of a council is again the pope's. This confirmation is so necessary that without it there can never be an ecumenical council: the final approval of the head is required by the law of God. Otherwise the acts of a council cannot be the acts of the whole body.

The primary members of an ecumenical council are all the consecrated residential bishops who are in hierarchical communion with the bishop of Rome. They are all shepherds of God's people in the fullest theological sense of the term. Their membership is of divine right. True members of it are also all the consecrated TITULAR BISHOPS, provided that they are in communion with the See of Rome. They have been incorporated into the episcopal college through their consecration, although they may not be in charge of a diocese. It is disputed whether or not they enter a council by divine right, since their share in the power of the episcopate is less than full. It is certain, however, that all bishops sitting in council are in possession of a power given to them by God and not by any human person. They are not the delegates of the pope; they are not simply dignitaries associated to the pope to help him in the supreme government of the Church. They are members of an organic body who have received their specific power and mission from God. They are not the delegates or representatives of their subjects in the modern parliamentary sense. They act as shepherds in the service of their flock and not as public servants to carry out the wishes of their people.

Persons who are not consecrated bishops have no native right to be active members of an ecumenical council, since they do not belong to the episcopal college. But a council itself or its head, the pope, may invite such persons and give them the right of speech and of vote, and thus enlarge a council's membership. Thus abbots of monasteries and heads of the greater religious orders or congregations were invited to sit at both Vatican Councils. There is no theological reason why laymen cannot take part in the proceedings, and in fact some of the lay auditors at Vatican II addressed the fathers. In this way the universality of a council is still more enhanced, and the presence of the Holy Spirit in those who are not bishops is honored.

An ecumenical, or universal, council is to be distinguished from a particular council. A universal council concerns and binds the whole Church; a particular council, only one part of the Church. The perfect definition of the term "ecumenical" does not exist. Theologians are divided about the essential elements. It is beyond doubt, however, that the distinction between universal and particular is not based on the larger or smaller number of bishops present, but on the particular structure of a council. Thus a council cannot be ecumenical without being acknowledged as such by the pope, the head of the episcopal college. The See of Rome could confer this universal character either expressly or by the tacit reception of the decrees of a council as binding on the universal Church. The presence of a certain number of bishops is required; but it is not necessary that the majority of bishops should be present. The doctrine formulated by them and proposed for approval to the pope ought to express the faith of the universal Church.

If the decisions of a local gathering of the bishops are not approved by the See of Rome as binding the whole Church, a council remains a particular one, regional, national, or provincial. It may have a high authority, but it is not an ecumenical council. The character of universality can be given to a council by the universal shepherd only, who is the pope.

Power of an Ecumenical Council. The episcopal college, whether sitting in council or dispersed, is in possession of a SUPERNATURAL power. The word "power" is of biblical origin, and traditionally it has the connotation of a divine gift in man that gives him strength to fulfill his mission and vocation. A divine power was present in Christ before, and more manifestly after, His RESURRECTION (Rom 1.4); He gave power to the APOSTLES individually and, in a different form, to their college. Each Apostle in his person and the TWELVE as a community became subjects of power. These powers substantially remained in the Church; every bishop receives it personally through his consecration, and the community of bishops has kept it without interruption since the time of the Apostles. To understand the power of the episcopal college and of an ecumenical council, one has to recognize precisely the distinction between the personal power of the bishops and the corporate power of their college. A bishop is exercising a personal power in governing his diocese; he is sharing a collective power when he is deliberating and deciding issues in an act done in common with his brother bishops under the presidency of the pope. The personal power of the bishop extends over his diocese; the collective power of the episcopate extends over the universal Church. When this collective power is exercised in a solemn way, there is an ecumenical council.

Since all episcopal power is supernatural, the council's power is supernatural. Its origin is in the mandate of Christ given to the Apostles to sanctify, to teach, and to rule God's people. Its permanent source is in the presence of the Holy Spirit among the bishops. It has to be distinguished from power as one understands it in a civil society; the analogy between the two is remote. Nevertheless, the manifestations of the supernatural power take form in a natural legal framework through decrees, decisions, constitutions, and other forms of juridical pronouncements. This blend of natural and supernatural reflects the divine and human in the character of the Church.

The power of an ecumenical council is a power to sanctify: not in the sense that the council as a collective body could distribute all the Sacraments, but in the sense that it could effectively regulate the worship of the

Church and the administration of the Sacraments and thus promote the sanctification of the faithful. It is also a power to teach. An ecumenical council is the most highly qualified witness of the word of God. It has the apostolic mission to declare the content of the faith to all nations and to every creature. It has the power to define what one has to believe. In other words, it has the charism of INFALLIBILITY in teaching. Nevertheless, to assess the theological significance of a conciliar statement, detailed study of the text and of the circumstances from which it was born has to be made. Further, it is a power to govern. A council is entitled to shepherd God's people toward God's kingdom through laws and commands that are binding on the consciences of the faithful (*see* PEOPLE OF GOD). A council is helped by the Holy Spirit to be wise in government, but it was not given by Christ the maximum degree of prudence. Therefore its disciplinary decrees have a permanent value only as far as they express some immutable truth. Otherwise they are subject to change by later councils or by the popes.

An ecumenical council has full power over the Church. Fullness here means all the power to sanctify, teach, and govern that the Church has received from Christ and that can be possessed by a community such as the episcopal college. There are powers in the Church that by nature have to be possessed by an individual person; they cannot be ascribed to a community. The power to baptize or to confirm has to be exercised personally; therefore a council cannot have it. The power to preach and to govern can be possessed by a community; therefore the ecumenical council has it.

The power of an ecumenical council is supreme in the Church. A council is not subject to any other authority, but all other authorities are subject to it. The power of a council is universal: it extends over all human persons who have received the Sacrament of Baptism and over all corporations that may exist in the Church.

The constitution states that the pope has the same full, supreme, and universal power in the Church as the council. This one has to believe with divine faith, since it has been defined at VATICAN COUNCIL I (H. Denzinger, *Enchiridion symbolorum,* ed. A. Schönmetzer [32d ed. Freiburg 1963] 3050–74). Theologians are debating whether or not the distinct attribution of power to an ecumenical council *and* to the pope implies two subjects of power (imperfectly distinguished, since without the pope there cannot be an ecumenical council), or two organs through which the power of a unique subject of power (the episcopal college) is expressed and exercised. Vatican II wanted to leave the question open; hence it can be freely discussed. It is certain, however, that on an empirical level there are two legal subjects exercising this su-

preme power, the pope and a council. On a deeper theological and ontological level, one probably has to say that the college of bishops forms a unity and is in permanent possession of the full, supreme, and universal power in the Church, but that this power is exercised either by the head alone or by the whole college through a corporate action. The solemn exercise of this corporate action is precisely the essence of an ecumenical council. In practice any conflict between the pope and an ecumenical council is excluded by the fact that the pope is the head of the council, and by carefully balanced legal provisions about the convocation, progress, and dissolution of a council. On a deeper level it is the Holy Spirit who preserves the divine structure of the Church in its integrity, since the danger of either the pope reducing the council to a shadowy existence or the bishops trying to weaken the authority of their head could not be excluded by any legal institution. The solemn exercise of power is here opposed to its ordinary use. The former means the exercise of their collective power by the bishops gathered under the presidency of the pope in one place deliberating and reaching decisions with a common effort. The latter signifies the use of the same power under the leadership of the pope by the bishops dispersed all over Earth. The specific difference is not in the extent of the power but in the way it is exercised.

An ecumenical council exercises its power in a collegiate way, which means that each bishop acting on the strength of the collective of the council contributes actively toward a final decision. The bishops share the same power as equal members of a body, except for the head, who retains his exceptional position throughout. It is, however, customary for him to keep out of the debates and to use his power only for the confirmation of the conclusions of the discussions. Further, it is of the essence of this power that the bishops are invested with it as God's trustees, the beneficiary being God's people, the whole Church. The power can be used only to build the Church in the service of the faithful. The competent authority to judge the right use of this power, however, is an ecumenical council itself and not any other person. There cannot be a judicial authority higher than the body possessing the power described.

Need for Ecumenical Councils. The constitution lays down that the collegiate character of the episcopate is of divine origin and that its permanence in the Church is of immutable divine right. It follows that it is of divine right too that the same college should have ways and means to exercise its power. To hear the voice of the episcopate is essential for the life and progress of the Church. This essential element may be present in the frequent consultations among the bishops themselves and between the bishops and the pope. Its solemn manifestation, however, remains the work of an ecumenical council. The judgment about its necessity is reserved to the pope; he is assisted by the Holy Spirit in carrying out his duty. The pope cannot be subject to any human tribunal. It can be said, however, that at the time of a crisis or great need in the life of the Church there may be a moral necessity for an ecumenical council.

When the whole Catholic episcopate is gathered together, it is easier to exchange information and to reach a decision; it is easier to share a common power and inspiration, and hence the importance and moment of ecumenical councils. They are the highest manifestations of the unity and diversity of the episcopal body.

Christ among the Bishops. An ecumenical council should not be considered as a body distinct from the Church. It is an organ of the Church; it is part of the greater unity that is the whole Church, the MYSTICAL BODY OF CHRIST. Through a council the faith of the Church is authentically expressed, and at the same time the teaching of Christ is made manifest for God's people. It is Catholic belief that Christ Himself is present among the bishops gathered together. He comforts them and helps them through His Spirit, so that in their turn the bishops should be able to comfort and help God's people. Ecumenical councils are great manifestations of the continuing gift of Redemption that God does not cease to offer mankind.

See Also: AUTHORITY, ECCLESIASTICAL; CONCILIARISM (THEOLOGICAL ASPECT); COUNCILS, GENERAL (ECUMENICAL), HISTORY OF; EPISCOPAL CONFERENCES.

Bibliography: Classical works: R. BELLARMINE, *De conciliis et ecclesia,* v. 2 of *Opera omnia,* ed. X. R. SFORZA, 8 v. (new ed. Naples 1872). L. THOMASSIN, *Dissertationes . . . in concilia tum generalia, tum particularia* (Paris 1667). C. PASSAGLIA, *De concili-is oecumenicis,* ed. H. SCHAUF (Rome 1961). Works pub. shortly before Vatican Council II: Y. M. J. CONGAR and B. D. DUPUY, eds., *L'Épiscopat et l'Église universelle* (Paris 1962). H. KÜNG, *Structures of the Church,* tr. S. ATTANASIO (New York 1964). K. RAHNER and J. RATZINGER, *The Episcopate and the Primacy,* tr. K. BARKER et al. (New York 1962). J. P. TORRELL, *La Théologie de l'épiscopat au premier concile du Vatican* (Paris 1961). *Conciliorum oecumenicorum decreta* (Bologna-Freiburg 1962). Reference works: J. FORGET, *Dictionnaire apologétique de la foi catholique,* ed. A. D'ALÈS, 4 v. (Paris 1911–22;) 1:588–628; *Dictionnaire de théologie catholique,* ed. A. VACANT et al., 15 v. (Paris 1903–50) 3.1:636–676. Y. M. J. CONGAR, *Catholicisme. Hier, aujourd'hui et demain,* ed. G. JACQUEMET (Paris 1947–) 2:1439–43. H. LAIS and H. JEDIN, *Lexikon für Theologie und Kirche,* ed. J. HOFER and K. RAHNER, 10 v. (2d, new ed. Freiburg 1957–65) 6:525–532.

[L. M. ÖRSY]

COUNSEL, GIFT OF

The gift of counsel is the gift of the Holy Spirit that perfects the acts of the infused virtue of prudence.

Through prudence elevated by grace, the soul reasons to the wisest course of action in a given situation. Counsel is concerned with the same practical issues as prudence, but it works with greater facility; it provides a quasi-instinctive solution to complex problems. Hence the person influenced by counsel is said to act by intuition. Reason is moved; it bypasses the usual acts in prudential decisions. But it also moves; it dictates action in the immediate issue. Because the end of counsel is a concrete act, it does not have its own beatitude, but it is related to the beatitude of mercy, since it directs the practical work of mercy. Counsel also lacks its own fruits because it ends in action.

See Also: HOLY SPIRIT, GIFTS OF.

Bibliography: B. FROGET, *The Indwelling of the Holy Spirit in the Souls of the Just,* tr. S. A. RAEMERS (Westminster, Md. 1950). A. ROYO, *The Theology of Christian Perfection,* ed. and tr. J. AUMANN (Dubuque 1962) 432–435. R. CESSARIO, *Christian Faith and the Theological Life* (Washington, D.C. 1996). S. PINCKAERS, *The Sources of Christian Ethics,* tr. M. T. NOBLE (Washington, D.C. 1995).

[P. F. MULHERN]

COUNSELS, EVANGELICAL

The advisory directives of Christ, as distinct from the moral precepts, given as guides to closer approximation to perfection and imitation of Christ Himself. Traditional Christianity has singled out poverty, chastity, and obedience from the whole complexus of such counsels, and these are the statements of Christ to which the term evangelical counsels usually refers.

New Testament Foundations. The evangelical counsels of poverty, chastity, and obedience receive varying degrees of support from the New Testament. Virginity receives the clearest and obedience the least. Regarding VIRGINITY, Mt 19.11–12 and 1 Cor 7.7, 25–40 indicate that it is a gift from God not granted to all Christians. Luke 18.29 speaks of leaving one's wife along with lands, etc., for the sake of the gospel, and another text, Lk 14.26, speaks of hating one's wife. Only the Matthean passage is relatively free from difficulties. The Corinthian text has for its context the concern for an imminent Parousia, and the motive for virginity or celibacy is undivided attention to the Lord while expecting His coming. The world is about to pass away (v. 29) and is therefore most irrelevant (v. 30, 31). In Lk 18.29 the text is found in a slightly different form from that of the earlier Gospel of Mark (10.29), where "wife" is not listed as one of the goods left for the sake of Christ. Mark's omission—if it is such—is supported by the actual apostolic practice referred to by Paul in 1 Cor 9.5–6. Peter, the brethren of the Lord, and the other Apostles are described as accompanied by their wives (Schnackenburg, *Die sittliche Botschaft des Neuen Testaments,* 146).

Poverty has traditionally found its support in the incident of the rich man recorded by Mk 10.17–22. "One thing is lacking to thee; go, sell whatever thou hast, and give to the poor, and thou shalt have treasure in heaven; and come, follow me." In the later and less original version of Matthew (J. Schmid, *Regensburg Neues Testament I,* 223) we have the basis for what has come to be the traditional distinction between counsels and commandments. Matthew gives the impression that the more perfect thing is to sell all, etc., but this is corrected by "You therefore are to be perfect, even as your heavenly Father is perfect" (Mt 5.48). That which was lacking in the rich man was something personal and not true of him as man, but only insofar as he was this man, i.e., with this disposition and call. Obedience is implicitly contained in the invitation to be associated with those who are to follow Christ in preaching and then later without Him to be members of the hierarchical Church in union with Peter. Passages such as "If any man wishes to be first, he shall be last of all and servant of all" (Mk 9.34) or ". . . the slave of all" (Mk 10.43) have provided motivation for "perfect" obedience (*Lexikon für Theologie und Kirche,* ed. J. Hofer and K. Rahner [Freiberg 1957–65] 3:1246), but do not record the institution of religious obedience.

Supererogation. Moralists usually consider that the counsels are works of SUPEREROGATION whose purpose is to aid more effectively the generous soul in its effort to attain the perfection of Christian life. They are the means to overcome the three great threats to that life, namely, concupiscence of the eyes, and of the flesh, and the pride of life. They are the means of gaining more merit and are pleasing to God because of the sacrifices they impose on the individual. Between the counsels as works of supererogation and the fulfillment of the basic commandment "Love the Lord thy God with thy whole heart" (Lk 10.27) there is a relationship of means to goal. Certainly this command is fulfilled by the blessed in heaven where the total capacity of the soul for love is fully involved. In this life, the totality of love is always a relative totality, dependent on the actual graces of the moment, but always excluding any created good as a more beloved object. St. Paul (Phil 1.9) prays that the charity of the Philippians may more and more abound in discernment so that they may approve the better things. Paul rather carefully expresses this as a desire rather than as a command, consistent with his theme of freedom and spontaneity in the love of God. However, moralists agree that the better good must be chosen with some frequency in life in order that the precept of charity be fulfilled. This interpretation does not exclude the circumstance where

the Holy Spirit has made it clear that here and now it is God's will that the Christian choose the better good. In this latter case, the option would be eliminated, and the objectively better good becomes the only good.

Love, as found in the context of supererogation, traditionally supposes no obligation, but rather signifies the desire to do more than the strictly obligatory. However, the possibility of supererogation ceases with the assumption that one must love according to the measure of grace given one and one's special awareness of the divine will. Perfect peace in love cannot obtain if mature invitations are rejected. The gifts (calls) of the Spirit, recognized by the virtue of prudence or the discerminent of spirits, are mature invitations. As such they are indications of what the invited must do under pain of some degree of disorder (loss of personal peace) and loss or postponement of some degree of maturity in his Christian life.

New Significance. The Second Vatican Council gave the evangelical counsels new significance for our time (*see Lumen gentium* 42–46; *Perfectae caritatis* 5, 12–14). Amidst the boredom of affluence, voluntary poverty witnesses to the joy that springs from needing less and being more grateful; celibacy proves that the loneliness of the "lonely crowd" can be turned into joyful solitude; obedience points toward the dimension of meaningfulness which lies beyond our preoccupation with purpose. These values are brought nearer to *all* human beings as the evangelical counsels are now seen as anchored not primarily in the Gospels, but in what Thomas Merton called an imperishable "instinct of the human heart," channeled and brought to its fulfilment when it finds its focus in Christ.

See Also: ASCETICISM (THEOLOGICAL ASPECT); CHASTITY; DISCERNMENT, SPIRITUAL; EXISTENTIAL ETHICS; OBEDIENCE; PAROUSIA; PRUDENCE.

Bibliography: E. DUBLANCHY, *Dictionnaire de théologie catholique,* ed. A. VACANT et al., (Paris 1903–50) 1.2:2037–77; 3.1:1176–82. In the *Lexikon für Theologie und Kirche,* ed. J. HOFER and K. RAHNER (Freiberg 1957–65), see J. SCHMID and L. HARDICK, 1:878–883; R. SCHNACKENBURG and B. HÄRING, 3:1245–50; F. BÖCKLE, 3:1301–04; L. NIEDER et al., 4:601–606; H. GROSS et al., 4:640–642; J. MICHL and L. M. WEBER, 5:1213–19. R. SCHNACKENBURG, *Die sittliche Botschaft des Neuen Testamentes* (Munich 1954). K. RAHNER, *Schriften zur Theologie* (Einsiedeln 1954–) 3:61–104. B. HÄRING, *The Law of Christ: Moral Theology for Priests and Laity,* tr. E. G. KAISER (Westminster, Md. 1961–). F. WULF, "Decree on the Appropriate Renewal of the Religious Life," *Commentary on the Documents of Vatican II,* H. VORGRIMLER et al., eds. (New York 1967–69) 2:301–370.

[J. D. GERKEN/D. F. K. STEINDL-RAST]

Saint Ignatius of Loyola, painting by Peter Paul Rubens.
(©Bettmann/CORBIS)

COUNTER REFORMATION

This designation for the great spiritual revival within the Church during the sixteenth and seventeenth centuries was used by Leopold von Ranke and gained a widely accepted reference value, being used both by Protestant and Catholic historians. Strictly speaking, however, the term remains a misnomer, since it implies that the undeniable revival of Catholicism that occurred in early modern Europe had its origin as a reaction to PROTESTANTISM and was entirely negative in aspect. Had the Catholic notion of reform been a counterreformation in this sense only, it could not have originated before the Protestant movement; and yet it did.

Analysis of the Term. Martin Luther was but one of many who cried for reform. The Oratory of DIVINE LOVE, for example, one of the most influential of the early reform groups, was initiated at Genoa in 1497 through the zeal of Ettore Vernazza and St. CATHERINE OF GENOA and spread to Rome (1515), Florence, Lucca, Vicenza, Naples, and elsewhere. Its origin was entirely independent of Luther and it was destined to remain an orthodox instrument of reform within the Church. Nor was this resurgence of Catholic spirit directed exclusively against or even connected with Protestantism. St. Teresa of Avila's holy life and mystical writings are not related in the usual sense of the term to the contemporary Protestant struggle with the Church, and yet she occupies an important place in the Catholic revival. Still reform efforts did touch doctrine. Protestantism championed beliefs devout Catholics judged erroneous, and the Protestant movements converted many to these beliefs. Thus, the Church declared these teachings false and actively sought to win back those who had adopted them. In this sense the term Counter Reformation retains a limited usefulness when used to describe those measures designed to combat Protestantism specifically. These negative dimensions of the movement, though, were only a small part of the whole. Consequently, scholars have more recently advocated the use of the term ''Catholic Reformation'' to describe the great international revival that occurred within the Church between the late fifteenth and early eighteenth centuries. This revival was not prompted by the appearance of Protestantism and was a phenomenon independent of the REFORMATION. The terms ''Counter Reformation'' or counterreformation continue to be used to describe the prohibitionary measures that appeared within the Catholic Church and Catholic states, particularly in the late sixteenth and early seventeenth century, that were designed to combat Protestantism specifically.

Elements of Catholic Renewal. Administrative abuse and corruption was common to the late-medieval Church, and had long been attacked by the institution's foremost spiritual leaders. The first signs of long-term renewal, though, can be traced to the resurgence of spirit within older religious orders, particularly in the fourteenth and fifteenth-century Observant movements. These movements strove to re-establish a disciplined observance of their order's primitive monastic rules. In addition, a number of new religious orders appeared, and an intensification of devotion, witnessed in a renewed commitment to ascetical and mystical life, is evident. New types of missionary organizations emerged as well; among these, the Jesuits (1540), were eventually to exercise the greatest influence upon Catholic renewal and upon the spread of Catholicism to new areas around the globe. The clarification of doctrine and disciplinary legislation effected by the Council of TRENT presented the Church with a clear program for institutional and doctrinal reform. Finally, in many states the support of temporal rulers was indispensable to the revitalization of the Church and the establishment of Tridentine discipline. The renewal that flowed from all these various sources were to leave their mark upon European culture, and through colonial contact, upon large areas of the globe. And they in turn influenced literature, scholarship, education, and the fine arts.

Condition of the Church. The Council of CON-STANCE (1414–18) had ended the Great WESTERN SCHISM (1387–1417) within Christendom but it did not accomplish its second great task, namely, that of reform. Long-standing abuses persisted. Authority, revenues, and the care of souls were held by autonomous groups and individuals whose jurisdictions often geographically overlapped and who were loosely held together only by their obedience to the pope. The result was confusion and corruption. Many parish appointments were in the hands of clerical patrons; in Lyons, a particularly notorious example, the archbishop controlled only 21 of the 392 parishes in his diocese. The plight of bishops was made more difficult by the exemptions from their jurisdiction often granted by the Holy See. Thus, within his diocese a bishop often lacked effective control over the cathedral chapters, collegiate churches, monasteries, religious orders, and clerical patrons. Furthermore, there was a fragmentation of jurisdiction among the monastic orders. This was illustrated in the unsuccessful attempts by the general chapters of Cluny, Cîteaux, and Prémontré to command their monasteries. Various national rulers regarded ecclesiastical positions in their realms as rewards for those who served them well and made appointments with disregard of spiritual qualifications. An office with its authority began to be regarded as a source of income, a piece of property. Money thus improperly channeled often led to financial privation. Clerical patrons, though collecting tithes, did not always provide for the needs of parish priests, and thus forced them to seek money through such practices as charging for the administration of the Sacraments. Moreover, the literacy of the lower clergy was poor since proper education was beyond their means. Monasteries that were held *incommendam* fell into ill repair because of inadequate funds. Since particular benefices yielded insufficient revenue, the practice of pluralism (necessarily involving absenteeism) became common. Moreover, bishops and even the papacy itself suffered financial want. For example, the pope was continually in debt from 1471 to 1520 and as a remedy sold offices and the privileges of religious exemption. The many jurisdictions caused an increasing emphasis upon nepotism as a means to protect and increase power. The papacy, surrounded by a tumultuous Italy, relied upon relatives for loyalty. As a further administrative complication, the papacy was surrounded by Catholic princes who, although religious subjects, were political enemies. This gave rise to yet another disedifying spectacle, the use of military force and diplomatic statecraft to ensure the security of those temporal papal possessions that in turn ensured the pope's spiritual independence. From the simony, pluralism, absenteeism, nepotism, and the lack of efficient discipline in the Church's structure moral decline often followed as in the reigns of the pontiffs INNOCENT VIII (1484–92) and ALEXANDER VI (1492–1503).

Martin Luther was officially excommunicated by the bull *Decet romanum pontificem* of Jan. 3, 1521, and throughout the 1520s and 1530s reform movements proliferated throughout Northern Europe. In 1525 the grand master of the Teutonic Knights, ALBRECHT OF BRANDENBURG, became Lutheran and secularized the territory of his jurisdiction. By 1528 areas won or nearly won for Protestantism in the empire were Brunswick-Lüneburg, Mansfeld, Silesia, Hesse, Brandenburg, and Electoral Saxony. In Switzerland Ulrich Zwingli fashioned a reform movement that was even more puritanical and extreme than the reforms advocated by Martin Luther. It soon was adopted at Zürich (1523), Bern (1528), Basel (1529), and Schaffhausen (1529), and would eventually spread throughout most of the German-speaking cantons. In Sweden Lutheranism triumphed at the Rikstag of Västerås in 1527. England broke from the Church through the Act of Supremacy in 1534. Denmark under King Christian III made Lutheranism its state religion in 1536 and imposed it upon conquered Norway the next year. Another of Denmark's subject areas, Iceland, would see its first Lutheran bishop, Gizzur Finarsson, elected in 1540. Livonia proclaimed Lutheranism in 1554. The same year Transylvania's national assembly decreed religious freedom for all faiths. In 1555 Sigismund II Augustus granted freedom of worship to all Protestants, the very year in which the Peace of AUGSBURG granted legality to Lutheran princedoms within the empire. In 1560 the parliament of Scotland rejected papal authority. France declared its first act of Protestant toleration by the edict of January 1562. The following series of religious wars ended in a more permanent act of toleration, the Edict of Nantes in 1598. The Dutch Netherlands secured its Calvinist religion by 1609. Also during this period Protestantism had made great strides in Austria, Hungary, and Bohemia. *See* REFORMATION, PROTESTANT (ON THE CONTINENT); REFORMATION, PROTESTANT (IN THE BRITISH ISLES); REFORMED CHURCHES; SCOTLAND, CHURCH OF; IRELAND, CHURCH OF.

First Signs of Revival in the Later Middle Ages. In the two centuries preceding the Reformation a number of new religious groups appeared, such as the Order of the Blessed Savior, inaugurated by St. BRIDGET OF SWEDEN in 1346, which established 80 houses within a century; the Alexians, originated in the Low Countries in 1348; the JESUATI, instituted in Italy by Bl. JOHN COLOMBINI *c.* 1366; the influential BRETHREN OF THE COMMON LIFE, established shortly before the death of their founder, Gerard GROOTE, in 1384 (*see* DEVOTIO MODERNA); the HIERONYMITES (LOS JERÓNIMOS) of Spain and Portugal organized by Pedro Fernandez Pecha and approved by Gregory XI in 1373; the Oblate Congregation of Tor de' Specchi, founded by St. FRANCES OF ROME in 1436. In the same year the Order of MINIMS was founded by St. FRANCIS OF PAOLA and was to spread to 450 houses in 100 years. Great devotional literature appeared, notably the *IMITATION OF CHRIST* and the work from which it borrowed material, the *Life of Christ* by the Carthusian LUDOLPH OF SAXONY. Among the numerous saints were VINCENT FERRER (1357–1418), JOHN CAPISTRAN (1393–1456), ANTONINUS (1389–1459), and Catherine of Genoa (1447–1510). Although these figures may not have given rise to reform movements as pervasive as those of Sts. Dominic or Francis, they demonstrated a spiritual continuity that would eventually produce extensive reform. This revival began through the combined influence of Christian humanists, reform-minded prelates, and new religious societies. Among the Christian humanists who kept the best of the classical past and used their learning to serve the cause of religion were Marsilio FICINO, Gasparo CONTARINI, Jacopo SADOLETO, Desiderius ERASMUS, and most notably St. Thomas More. Also the work and example of conscientious bishops encouraged this restoration. Thus the diocesan reform of Bb. Gian Matteo GIBERTI of Verona (1495–1543) became a model throughout Italy. Cardinal XIMÉNEZ DE CISNEROS, Primate of Spain (1495–1517), initiated a wide program that included monastic reform, the establishment of the University of ALCALÁ for the education of the clergy, attacks against absenteeism, and pressure on the clergy to care properly for souls under their charge. He also personally directed to completion the great Complutensian Polyglot Bible, a six-volume edition of the Scriptures. New religious societies came into being at the end of the fifteenth century, stemming from the influence of St. Catherine of Genoa. One of these was the Roman Oratory of Divine Love. Its membership, composed of laymen and clergy, sought as the first task the reform of their own lives through frequent Confession and Communion, works of charity, common prayer, meditation, and study. The Oratory is important because in its membership were effective Christian humanists and reformers, such as Sadoleto and Gian Pietro Carafa (PAUL IV).

Renewal within the Religious Orders. The religious orders, with their wide-ranging activities in education, prayer, scholarship, defense of the faith, charity, and pastoral care, had been in the past a mighty arm of the Church. However, they had suffered spiritual decline during the period of increasing darkness prior to the great resurgence within the soul of Catholicism. Their important role in the Church's apostolate made their revitalization valuable. At the same time it was symptomatic of the general transformation taking place elsewhere. The old orders were directed toward reform under the guidance of the Church, but their zeal was stimulated principally by numerous saintly members. Among the Camaldolese the movement began during the reign of Leo X (1513–21) through the efforts of Bl. Paolo GIUSTINIANI and his successor as superior general, Giustiniano da Bergamo. The Capuchins, inspired by Matteo Serafini da BASCIO, began as a reform within the Franciscans and date their foundation from the bull of Clement VII, *Religionis zelus,* July 3, 1528. This order was conspicuous in the years of struggle with Protestantism, and its reputation was brightened by Saints FELIX OF CANTALICE, LAWRENCE OF BRINDISI, and FIDELIS OF SIGMARINGEN, who was martyred by Calvinists in the Swiss Grisons in 1624. The revival of the Augustinians had begun prior to the time of Luther, in the person of the scholarly Giles of Viterbo, who was vicar-general from 1506, and in the thorough visitations ordered by the general Girolamo SERIPANDO in 1539. The Dominican Order was purged of heretical elements by visitations in 1543 and 1547 during the reign of Paul III. The saintly Dominican Antonio (Michele) Ghislieri, as commissary- general of the Roman Inquisition and later as PIUS V (1566–72), brought austerity and integrity to the Holy See in these crucial years. The outstanding reformers of the Carmelite Order were Saints Teresa of Avila (d. 1582) and JOHN OF THE CROSS (d. 1591). Their importance was derived not only from their organizational skill but also from their holiness and mystical writings.

New orders also developed and intensified the spiritual awakening. Out of the Oratory of Divine Love grew the THEATINES, founded by St. CAJETAN (Gaetano da Thiene) in 1524. These clerks regular, following the example of the Oratory, kept their membership small to act as a healthy cell in the body of the secular clergy. The Clerks Regular of SOMASCHI, founded *c.* 1532 by St. Jerome EMILIANI, devoted themselves especially to the aid of orphans and the poor. The BARNABITES, or Clerks Regular of St. Paul, owed their origin to St. Anthony ZACCARIA in 1530. As missionaries they spread throughout Italy, preaching, hearing confessions, and giving retreats; they quickly established themselves in France, Germany, and Bohemia. St. Angela MERICI founded the URSULINES for service to young girls in 1535. The Ursuline Order shared the Jesuit emphasis upon ''practicality'' in the field of education. All of these new orders adapted themselves to the needs of an active service outside the cloister.

The Society of Jesus. The JESUITS were among the most important organizations defending and propagating the Catholic faith. The society's many saints and martyrs testified to its dedication, and its enormous success demonstrated the suitability of its methods. St. IGNATIUS OF LOYOLA, wounded in 1521, had undergone a personal spiritual transformation during his convalescence. In

1534 Francis XAVIER, Peter FABER, Diego LAINEZ, Alfonso Salmeron, Nicolás de Bobadilla, and Simón Rodriquez joined him in solemn vows, thus forming the nucleus of the Jesuit Order. On Sept. 27, 1540, Paul III confirmed the order by his bull *Regimini militantis Ecclesiae.* The stated purpose of the order at its inception was the propagation of the faith; later the terminology was changed to *propagation* and *defense* of the faith. In this task it placed itself at the disposal of the pope in absolute obedience. The order's success was due to its flexibility and practicality. Thus, the Jesuits adopted the innovation of not saying the Office in choir, thereby freeing members to perform their active apostolate. St. Ignatius wrote the *Spiritual Exercises* (printed in 1548) as a practical guide by which the will could be trained to achieve complete dedication to God. The Jesuit *Constitutions* constantly stressed efficiency; they prohibited acceptance of benefices or episcopal office except at papal command; submitted its members, who were recruited with extreme care, to lengthy and thorough training; barred pious works that detracted from primary duties; and disapproved of extremes in mortification that might hinder health and competence. The order was structured to avoid controversy and delay and constantly stressed discipline and unhesitating obedience. Great power was given to the general; he was elected for life and nominated men to all important posts throughout the order. The general congregation made up of the order's elite was to be summoned only in exceptional cases. The growth of the Society of Jesus was remarkable: in the year of its foundation there were ten members; when St. Ignatius died (1566), there were 1,000; in 1580 the order had grown to 5,000. Seventy-six years after its foundation the Jesuits numbered 13,112 in 436 houses scattered through 37 provinces.

The activities of the order became diverse as it expanded but finally centered upon missions and education. In missionary work vigorous efforts were launched to hold and win back various areas of Europe for the Church. Inspired by St. Francis Xavier's example, the Society also spread the Catholic faith around the world. The *RATIO STUDIORUM* was issued during the generalate of Claudius ACQUAVIVA (1581–1615) to regulate a plan of studies and teaching method for the great number of Jesuit colleges scattered throughout Europe and in non-Christian lands. In the Holy Roman Empire alone 155 colleges were established between 1551 and 1650.

Devotional Revival. A renewal of Catholic piety took place in Europe even as religious unity was being shattered. Inspirational and mystical writings appeared, whose influence is still felt. St. John of the Cross wrote *The Ascent of Mount Carmel, The Dark Night of the Soul, The Spiritual Canticle,* and *The Living Flame of Love.* St.

FRANCIS DE SALES gave to Catholicism his *Introduction to the Devout Life* and *Treatise on the Love of God.* Pierre de BÉRULLE, founder of the French Oratory, is known for the *Brief Discourse of Christian Abnegation* but chiefly for *The Greatness of Jesus.* St. Teresa of Avila wrote her inspirational *Autobiography, The Way to Perfection,* and *The Interior Castle. The Spiritual Fight* is ascribed to Lorenzo SCUPOLI. John Baptist Carioni wrote *Concerning Knowledge and Victory over Oneself.*

The devotional revival manifested great variety. On the one hand, St. VINCENT DE PAUL emphasized asceticism; on the other, St. Teresa accented mysticism. St. Philip NERI's cheerfulness was in contrast to Pierre de Bérulle's somberness. The Italian devotional school differed from the Spanish by being less speculative, more tuned to action. St. John of the Cross's writings were directed especially to the cloistered and seemed severe by ordinary standards, while St. Francis de Sales's books were addressed particularly to the laity and were leavened with "spiritual sweetness."

Moreover, interest in St. Joseph was revived by Saints Teresa and Francis de Sales; perpetual adoration was originated by St. Anthony Zaccaria; devotion to the Child Jesus, the Sacred Heart, the Eucharist, the Holy Family, the angels and the guardian angels, and the Angelus were popularized.

Papal and Ecclesiastical Reformers. Because abuse and corruption had stemmed from faulty administration and unworthy administrators, thorough reform could not be achieved until the Church's hierarchy accepted corrective measures. Pope ADRIAN VI (1522–23) was the first pontiff vigorously to attempt such reform. Antagonism toward him as an "uncultured" northerner and the shortness of his reign prevented any appreciable results. PAUL III (1534–49) appointed to the cardinalate members of the reform party, Carafa, Pole, Giberti, and Sadoleto, and after two unsuccessful attempts succeeded in convening the Council of Trent. In the person of PAUL IV (1555–59) reform fervor reached flood tide. A strict moralist and a former inquisitor general, he personally undertook thorough reform, beginning with the Curia, from which unnecessary bishops were sent home to their dioceses. Fiscal abuses were prohibited. Life in Rome itself came under Paul's stern discipline. Under PIUS IV (1559–65) the Council of Trent was successfully concluded, and its measures began to be put into effect. Pope Pius practiced nepotism, but this was to issue in the Church's good fortune through the appointment of St. Charles BORROMEO to the Curia. PIUS V, the first pope in 272 years destined to be canonized, took many actions to strengthen the Church. For example, whereas Thomistic philosophy had been severely criticized by Protestant reformers, St. Pius upheld it by naming St. Thomas a Doctor of the Church. Moreover, Pius's personal holiness removed the stigma attached to the papacy by the religious secularism of the Renaissance popes. By the end of his reign, it was clear that the papacy was irrevocably committed to reform. After Pius V the popes followed the program laid down by the Council of Trent. In the hierarchy there were many eminent men, among them: St. Francis de Sales, Otto TRUCHSESS, St. Charles Borromeo, Stanislaus HOSIUS, David Rothe, Pierre de Bérulle, and William Damasus Lindanus. Of special significance was St. Robert BELLARMINE, who not only demonstrated the quality of Jesuit education and the moral caliber of the hierarchy, but by his great work, *Disputationes de controversiis Christianae fidei,* showed that Catholic polemicists could again defend doctrine with assurance.

The Council of Trent. Meeting at a time of crisis, the Council of Trent took up issues of moral, doctrinal, and administrative reform that had long plagued the Church. Moreover, through its doctrinal decrees, it cleared the theological atmosphere that had been clouded with confusion consequent to the many doctrinal assertions of Protestant leaders. Because of national interests, it was difficult to convene, to continue, and to implement the council. Emperor CHARLES V wished no interference with his own policies toward Protestants within the empire. Francis I, King of France, desired to maintain control over the Church within his state. Struggles between national rulers affected this international meeting. The unsuccessful attempts by Pope Paul III to convene the council and the fluctuation in the numbers of those present at the sessions are evidence of the national rivalries. There were at most 72 present at the first meeting (1545–48), 59 at the second (1551–52), and 235 at the third (1562–63). Nevertheless, in spite of difficulties, the council succeeded in reaffirming the traditional teaching of the Church and clarifying controversial points. Papal primacy was upheld: Trent submitted its decrees to the Pope for confirmation. The definition of the Catholic position on justification was approved during the very first meeting, thus giving the Church's position on the basic difference between itself and Protestantism. Protestant positions on such matters as the number and nature of the Sacraments were denied. The effect of Tridentine reforms was to strengthen the power of the bishop to combat abuse. The bishop was to have authority in granting benefices, in allowing preaching, in conducting visitations including those of religious houses not visited by the head of the order, in regulating women's convents by sending them confessors, in appointing parish priests to hear confessions. No longer were exemptions and appeals to Rome to interfere with the bishop's control, nor were benefices to be bequeathed. Also, action was taken against pluralities, provisions, expectancies, and the simoniacal acquisition of benefices. To safeguard the clerical office clerical dress was required, severe penalties were enacted against concubinage, and diocesan seminary education was to be provided for the priesthood. The laity was to be protected through prohibition of improper use of indulgences and by a revised INDEX OF FORBIDDEN BOOKS.

Pope Pius IV confirmed the Tridentine decrees in 1564, and the papacy fulfilled the council's wishes by issuing new editions of the Index (1564), a catechism (1566), a Breviary (1568), and the Missal (1570). Implementation of the council's decrees was handicapped by politics. Although Portugal and the Polish King Sigismund II Augustus accepted them in 1564, Spain would do so only after reserving rights previously held by the crown. The French government did not recognize the decrees, although they were accepted by the French clergy in 1615. In the empire they were received by Catholic princes in 1566 but never were approved by the Emperor. In spite of resistance, the council was a substantial advance toward spiritual and doctrinal reform. Still, the campaign against administrative abuse, clerical concubinage, and other corruption within the Church, while prescribed at Trent, required several generations of vigorous efforts upon the part of local bishops to accomplish. These reform efforts were, of course, most successful in those states in which the prince actively supported the cause of reform. But by 1700, the Tridentine program—with its emphasis on clerical discipline, sacramental religion, and diocesan authority—had achieved a degree of success throughout most of Catholic Europe.

Foreign Missions. The intensified zeal of Catholicism flowed from Catholic Europe to carry the Church's teachings around the world. Missionaries went also to those parts of Europe that had been lost to the Church and were thus now "foreign" to Catholic Christendom. St. Francis Xavier, only one year after the foundation of the Jesuit Order, traveled to India, Malaya, the East Indies, and Japan, and after converting hundreds of thousands, died as he prepared to evangelize China. Long before the official establishment of the Congregation for the PROPAGATION OF THE FAITH (1622) or any significant Protestant missionary effort, vast numbers were baptized. More people would be gained in distant parts of the world than were lost to Protestantism in Europe. In 1529 the Flemish Franciscan lay brother Peter of Ghent spoke of 14,000 daily Baptisms in the Mexican mission. By 1594 the saintly Turibio Alfonso de MOGROVEJO, Archbishop of Lima, had already confirmed 500,000 people. There were about two million conversions in the Philippines by 1620. Between 1647 and 1651 Felix de Viler baptized more than 600,000 in the Congo. Notable efforts would be made as well in Brazil, Paraguay, Japan (200,000 converts, 240 churches, and two Jesuit colleges by 1587), Canada, India, Indo- China, China, Constantinople, Syria, Ethiopia, Morocco, Persia, West Indies, and South Africa. In many of these places, though, indigenous elements of pre- Christian religions were to survive in tandem with Catholicism for many centuries to come. Sometimes new syncretic religions resulted from the contact with Catholic missionaries, too. Among the many other missionaries were Matteo RICCI, Jean de Brébeuf, Roberto de NOBILI, Alexandre de RHODES, José d'Anchieta, and Domingo de SALAZAR. In Europe many risked their lives to maintain or replant the faith in areas under Protestant control. Colleges were founded to train clerics for European mission fields. The English college, for example, founded at DOUAI by Cardinal William ALLEN, sent 488 priests to England prior to 1603. Between 1577 and 1603, there were 123 priests, in addition to about 60 of the laity who assisted them, put to death. (*See* ENGLAND, SCOTLAND AND WALES, MARTYRS OF.) Although England did not return to Catholic Christendom, the faith survived. Another example, one that could have had far-reaching consequences, was Sweden. Here Laurentius NIELSEN secretly began his work for the conversion of Sweden in 1576. Two years later Antonio POSSEVINO privately received King John III into the Church. The Swedish mission eventually failed, but the enterprise remained one of extraordinary daring.

Literary and Artistic Revival. Culture as a reflection of its times gave witness to Catholic revitalization. Writers, painters, sculptors, architects in many cases were personally affected by the new intensity of religious feeling. The musician Giovanni Pierluigi da PALESTRINA (1525–94) and the writer Luigi Tansillo demonstrate this in the change that took place between their earlier and later works. The painters Il Domenechino (Domenico Zampieri; 1581–1641), Jacques Callot, and Bartolomé Esteban MURILLO, who belonged to a religious brotherhood, were men of piety. The artistic demands of patrons and the popularity of such writers as Pierre Corneille show that public values had undergone transformation as well. This new cultural outlook sometimes recoiled from the worldliness of the Renaissance and concentrated on the spiritual. The simplicity and austerity that characterized the earlier period of this revival later ceded to the exuberance of the BAROQUE while still retaining its religious emphasis. The Council of Trent had indicated that art was to serve religion, and indeed one of the distinctive features of this cultural renewal was the emphasis upon religious purpose. Culture was not exclusively for culture's sake. Its religious use would extend to the field of apologetics. For example, in apparent defiance of the views held by Protestant leaders, Catholic artists frequently chose for their themes the most severely attacked Catholic beliefs and devotional subjects; the Real Presence, the Child Jesus, St. Joseph, the Blessed Virgin, St. Peter, Purgatory, and such contemporary figures as Charles Borromeo and Teresa of Ávila. The stress on religious utility also is seen in Church architecture. Churches were designed that could accommodate large congregations, provide good acoustics and be erected rapidly and inexpensively. Builders often dispensed with costly stained-glass windows.

In literature a choice of such themes as the repentant Saints Peter or Mary Magdalen was frequent; one of the greatest is Tansillo's *Lagrime di San Pietro*. Torquato Tasso believed that virtue must be stressed in poetry, and admirably carried out his idea in his epic poems *Gerusalemme liberta* (1575) and *Il mondo creato* (1590). In the field of drama the didactic drama produced by Jesuit colleges had a deep effect upon students as well as upon great writers, such as Corneille. In painting the foremost representative of reawakened Catholicism was the Bolognese school founded by the Carracci brothers. They were "eclectics" because of their combination of distinctive artistic techniques, but they chose religious themes that well illustrate the attempt of the Catholic revival to use the finest techniques in the service of religion. Their influence was widespread in Europe. In architecture the church of the Gesù built by Vignola (Giacomo Borozzi) in 1568 had a significant effect upon architectural style. The classical form of architecture accentuating horizontal lines was widely employed, but height was added to give the impression of soaring aspiration reminiscent of the Middle Ages. Giacomo della Porta achieved this in St. Peter's Basilica at Rome. In music the outstanding figure of this period was Palestrina, director of music at St. Peter's, whose services helped spiritualize church music. In sculpture less great work was done, but a worthy example of this age's ideals is Stefano Maderno's (1576–1636) St. Cecilia. (*See* CHURCH ARCHITECTURE, HISTORY OF; LITURGICAL MUSIC, HISTORY OF.)

Political Effects upon the Revival. The actions of secular rulers and political situations greatly influenced the results of Catholic religious fervor. The Council of Trent was temporarily hindered by French fears that, if it should be successful in ending Lutheranism within the empire, the Emperor would become too strong. Again, it was feared that there would be a loss of state control and of the use of the Church for the state's benefit. In England Queen Elizabeth's power, increased by a national dread of Spanish invasion, proved too great an obstacle for the missionaries. French support of the Swedish Protestant forces helped turn the tide against Catholic Hapsburgs in the THIRTY YEARS' WAR, which in 1648 concluded in a political stalemate. As a result, the principle *cujus regio,* *ejus religio* or "he who rules, his religion," was reapplied in the empire. Protestantism was upheld by the states in the north, but the gains made by St. Peter CANISIUS and others stabilized Catholicism in the south. In Poland the stanch loyalty of the peasants combined with the activity of the Jesuits had given determined resistance to the strong Protestant party. With the aid of Sigismund III, the battle was won in total victory for Catholicism. In France Catholics were aided by influence from Catholic Spain in preventing Calvinist control of their country. Calvinism gained the right of toleration, but it ceased to be a danger because of the continuing resurgence of French Catholicism. In Hungary the support of Hapsburg rulers favored Catholicism in its gains. Spain and Italy were two of the earliest areas to experience the Catholic revival. They needed but one ingredient to insure the faith, Catholic rule. Both lands were to have this during the Protestant movement. In Scandinavia Lutheranism gained ascendancy with governmental support. Except for the brief interlude of John III and his son, Sigismund, it would retain control with the same assistance.

Conclusion. The Catholic Church faced a severe test in the 16th and 17th centuries. Its corruption had long been criticized, but it was tolerated all the same. With the coming of the Reformation these faults became grist for Protestant attacks, and in the first generation after their appearance, vast areas of Northern and Central Europe were converted to the new religions. Even at this low point, though, the Catholic Church possessed great sources of spiritual renewal. In the century before Luther these forces had gathered strength, but they had been unable to achieve any long-standing reform of the Church. Now they gained momentum during the formation of Protestantism and helped to produce a great resurgence within Roman Catholicism. Though the episcopate and the papacy did not achieve any outstanding corporate reform in the century before Luther, evidence of inner dynamism for eventual restoration had appeared and would gain momentum during the formation of Protestantism.

Bibliography: P. JANELLE, *The Catholic Reformation* (Milwaukee 1949). H. JEDIN, *Katholische Reformation oder Gegenreformation? Ein Versuch zur Klärung der Begriffe* (Lucerne 1946); *History of the Council of Trent,* ed. E. GRAF, v.1–2 (St. Louis 1957–60), v.3 (in prep.); *Geschichte des Konzils von Trient,* 2 v. (Freiburg 1949–57; v.1, 2d ed. 1951). H. J. SCHROEDER, tr., *Council of Trent: Canons and Decrees, 1543–63* (St. Louis 1941). H. DANIEL-ROPS, *The Catholic Reformation,* tr. J. WARRINGTON (History of the Church 5; New York 1962). L. CRISTIANI, *L'Église à l'epoque du concile de Trente* (Paris 1948). P. TACCHIVENTURI, *Storia della Compagnia di Gesù in Italia,* 2 v. in 4 (2d ed. Rome 1930–51), v.5 by M. SCADUTO (1964). A. W. WARD, *The Counter-Reformation, 1550–1600* (London 1889). M. RITTER, *Deutsche Geschichte im Zeitalter der Gegenreformation und des dreissigjährigen Krieges,* 3 v. (Stuttgart 1889–1908). M. PETROCCHI, ed., *La Controriforma in Italia* (Rome 1947). O. BRUNNER, "Das konfessionelle Zeitalter," in *Deutsche Geschichte im Überblick,* ed. P. RASSOW (Stuttgart 1953). E. W. ZEEDEN, "Das Zeitalter der europäischen Glaubenskämpfe, Gegenreformation und katholische Reform," *Saeculum* 7 (1956) 321–368, bibliography; "Grundlagen und Wege der Konfessionsbildung in Deutschland im Zeitalter de Glaubenkämpfe," *Historische Zeitschrift* 185 (1958) 249–299; *Lexikon für Theologie und Kirche,* ed. J. HOFER and K. RAHNER, 10 v. (2d, new ed. Freiburg 1957–65) 4:585–588. A. FLICHE and V. MARTIN, eds., *Histoire de l'église depuis les origines jusqu'à nos jours* (Paris 1935–) v.17, 18. W. MAURENBRECHER, *Geschichte der kathotischen Reformation* (Nördlichen 1880–), only v.1 published. B. J. KIDD, *The Counter-Reformation, 1550–1600* (London 1933). P. IMBART DE LA TOUR, *Les Origines de la Réforme,* 2 v. (2d ed. Melun 1944–48). J. LORTZ, *Die Reformation in Deutschland,* 2 v. (4th ed. Freiburg 1962). P. HUGHES, *Rome and the Counter-Reformation in England* (London 1942). W. KAEGI, *Humanistische Kontinuität im konfessionellen Zeitalter* (Basel 1954). P. POURRAT, *Christian Spirituality,* 4 v. (Westminster, Maryland 1953–55). E. A. PEERS, *Studies of the Spanish Mystics,* 3 v. (v.1, 2d ed. Naperville, Illinois 1951; v.2–3, repr. 1st ed. 1960). É. MÂLE, *L'Art religieux de la fin du XVIe siècle* (2d ed. Paris 1951). G. GOYAU, *L'Église en marche,* 4 v. (Paris 1930–34). R. E. MCNALLY, "The Council of Trent and the German Protestants," *Theological Studies* 25 (1964) 1–22. O. GARSTEIN, *Rome and the Counter-Reformation in Scandinavia: Until the Establishment of the S. Congregatio de Propaganda Fide in 1622,* 2 v. (New York 1963–), v.1, *1539–83,* v.2 in preparation. W. MAURER, *Die Religion in Geschichte und Gegenwart,* 7 v. (3d ed. Tübingen 1957–65) 2:1254–62. J. DELUMEAU, *Catholicism between Luther and Voltaire* (London 1977). H. O. EVENETT, *The Spirit of the Counter-Reformation* (Notre Dame, Indiana 1970). M. FORSTER, *The Counter-Reformation in the Villages* (Ithaca 1992). P. HOFFMAN, *Church and Community in the Diocese of Lyon 1500–1789* (New Haven 1984). W. W. MEISSNER, SJ, *Ignatius of Loyola* (New Haven 1992). M. MULLETT, *The Catholic Reformation* (London, 1999). J. C. OLIN, *Catholic Reform* (New York 1990). J. W. O'MALLEY, SJ, ed., *Catholicism in Early Modern History* (St. Louis 1988). J. W. O'MALLEY, SJ, *The First Jesuits* (Cambridge, Massachusetts 1993). A. D. WRIGHT, *The Counter-Reformation: Catholic Europe and the Non-Christian World* (New York 1982).

[E. L. LAMPE/P. SOERGEL]

COUPERIN, FRANÇOIS

Illustrious baroque harpsichordist and composer (known as "Le Grand"); b. Paris, Nov. 10, 1668; d. Paris, Sept. 12, 1733. The greatest of a remarkable family of musicians, François had by 1690 been organist at Saint-Gervais for five years and published two organ Masses (for parish and convent use). From 1693 he was engaged at the Royal Chapel, first as harpsichord master to the royal princes (at the same time that FÉNELON was their tutor), and from 1717 as harpsichordist to the king. He received many honors, including the Lateran Order (1700). Although he composed church motets, *élévations,* secular songs, and occasional pieces, it is chiefly for his harpsichord and chamber music that he is remembered. The *Pièces de clavecin,* four books for harpsichord (1713–30), comprise 240 pieces arranged in suites. The trio sonatas and concertos, when sensitively edited and performed, may prove the equal of his harpsichord works. He produced also an important treatise on harpsichord technique, *L'Art de toucher le clavecin* (1717).

Bibliography: *Oeuvres complètes,* ed. M. CAUCHIE, 12 v. (Paris 1933); *L'Art de toucher le clavecin,* Eng. tr. M. ROBERTS (Leipzig 1933), *Pièces de clavecin,* ed. J. BRAHMS and K. F. CHRYSANDER (*Denkmäler der Tonkunst,* 4; Leipzig 1869–71), re-ed. T. DART (Paris 1959). W. MELLERS, *François Couperin and the French Classical Tradition* (London 1950); *Grove's Dictionary of Music and Musicians,* ed. E. BLOM, 9 v. (5th ed. London 1954) 2:484–498. C. BOUVET, *Une Dynastie de musiciens français: Les Couperin* (Paris 1919); *Nouveaux documents sur les Couperin* (Paris 1932). J. TIERSOT, *Les Couperin* (Paris 1926); ''Two Centuries of a French Musical Family: The Couperins,'' tr. T. BAKER, *Musical Quarterly* 12 (1926) 406–431. P. CITRON, *Histoire de la musique,* ed. ROLAND-MANUEL, 2 v. (Paris 1960–63); v. 9, 16 of *Encyclopédie de la Pléiade* 1:1634–39; *Couperin* (Paris 1956). C. ADDINGTON, ''Peace on Parnassus,'' *Recherches sur la Musique française classique* 23 (1985) 71–81. E. CORP, ''François Couperin and the Stuart Court at Saint-Germain-en- Laye, 1691–1712: A New Interpretation,'' *Early Music* 28 (2000) 445–453. E. HIGGINBOTTOM, ''François Couperin (ii) [*le grand*],'' in *The New Grove Dictionary of Music and Musicians,* ed. S. SADIE, v. 4 (New York 1980) 860–871. W. LANDOWSKA, ''French Music of the Past: François Couperin,'' in *Landowska on Music,* ed. and tr. D. RESTOUT (New York 1964) 259–267. D. M. RANDEL, ed., *The Harvard Biographical Dictionary of Music* (Cambridge, Mass. 1996) 181–182. N. SLONIMSKY, ed., *Baker's Biographical Dictionary of Musicians* (8th ed. New York 1992) 365–366.

[E. BORROFF]

COUPPÉ, LOUIS

Missioner in OCEANIA; b. Romorantin, France, Aug. 26, 1850; d. Douglas Park, Australia, July 20, 1926. After ordination (1874), he joined the SACRED HEART MISSIONARIES (1880), departed for Melanesia (1884), and established the office of mission procurator for his congregation at Sydney, Australia (1886). In 1887–88 he made several voyages of exploration in New Guinea, during which he discovered and named the St. Joseph River. Sent (1888) to New Britain, he founded and organized the mission at Rabaul and became its first vicar apostolic (1890–1923). As one of the first missioners in Oceania and an outstanding pioneer in the study of its culture, he began his apostolate among the tribes of the Guantana, concentrating his efforts on converting youths by creating schools, even for boarding students. At the same time he prepared for extending his work throughout New Britain by endowing the mission with such indispensable sources for material subsistence as plantations and woodwork shops. Despite his autocratic nature he left a great deal of liberty to his fellow missioners. An adept diplomat, he succeeded in obtaining from the German government full liberty for his mission. He founded a religious congregation for native women (1913). When he retired he be-

François Couperin. (Archive Photos)

queathed to his successor a mission with 23,498 Catholics, 6,205 catechumens, 36 priests, 33 brothers, and 76 sisters, of whom 37 were natives. In 1926, shortly before his death, he was made titular archbishop of Hierapolis.

Bibliography: R. STREIT and J. DINDINGER, *Bibliotheca missionum* (Freiburg 1916–) 21:288–291. *Pioniere der Südsee,* ed. J. HÜSKES (Hiltrup 1932).

[J. LAUWERS]

COURAGE

Courage is the emergency passion or emotion of the sensitive appetite directed toward a present evil, enabling one to stand firm in the face of danger or difficulty. Most often the word courage is used as a synonym for the natural or supernatural virtue of fortitude; seldom does it designate a simple sensitive reaction. Conduct designated as courageous has differed widely in human history, from place to place, from people to people, and from one age to another. What is common to every notion and kind of courage is the firm resistance to pain, danger, or difficulty, i.e., fearlessness in the face of that which threatens, and not a negative fearlessness that is the absence of fear, but rather the positive emotion that determines one to act unafraid, or to accept the fear and act reasonably in the face of it.

As an emotion, courage is psychosomatic—an affective feeling accompanied by bodily changes. Because it is so closely related to fear, hope, and love, the bodily changes involved in the exercise of courage are those of these emotions, in varying degrees.

Psychology. Courage is always related to FEAR, both as presupposing it and as its opposite. Courage can take on as many forms as the variety of objects that inspire fear. The courageous man is the one who conquers his fear; the coward is overcome by fear. In the discharge of duty and the pursuit of happiness, it is courage that makes a man firm in the difficult choices he is forced to make. (While daring is attributed also to animals, courage is possessed by man alone, since it implies knowledge of reasonable and unreasonable fears. Nor is the fearlessness of the ignorant and the drunkard rightly termed courage.)

Courage is related also to the emotion of HOPE, for it is with the hope of overcoming the threatening object feared that one attacks it boldly. Those things that make victory, success, or conquest possible strengthen hope and lead to courage—one's own power and bodily strength, previous experience of danger, abundance of possessions, loyal friends, and divine assistance.

Courage is related to LOVE, for one's courage is aroused when obstacles or dangers threaten that which one loves—e.g., life, reputation, family, friends, possessions, country, and God.

Morality. In itself, courage is morally neither good nor bad. However, as the emotion involved in the exercise of the virtue of fortitude, courage is good. Fortitude, natural or supernatural, is the mean between cowardice, by which a man is held back by fears that reason tells one could be overcome, and rashness, which is a reckless disregard for what should reasonably be feared. Thus courage is involved in the virtues that are parts of fortitude—magnanimity, magnificence, patience, and perseverance. Either it is lacking or the agent possesses a wrong concept of true courage in cases of cowardice, rashness, presumption, egotistic ambition, vainglory, pusillanimity, meanness, effeminacy or softness, and headstrongness or stubbornness.

Ordinarily, man needs physical courage to survive, but as a human person he also needs moral courage in the pursuit of truth and justice. The difficult choices of life demand courage, especially when one alternative seems to preserve principle and integrity, and the other alternative holds scorn and mockery, loss of friendship, ridicule, loss of possession, or even temporary ostracism.

See Also: VIRTUE; FORTITUDE, VIRTUE OF.

Bibliography: J. HASTINGS, ed., *Encyclopedia of Religion and Ethics,* 13 v. (Edinburgh 1908–27) 4:205–206. G. GARUTI, *Enciclopedia filosofica,* 4 v. (Venice-Rome 1957) 1:1239–40. THOMAS AQUINAS, *Summa theologiae,* 1a2ae, 45; 2a2ae, 123–140.

[M. W. HOLLENBACH]

COURNOT, ANTOINE AUGUSTINE

Mathematician, economist, educator, and philosopher; b. Gray (Haute-Saône), France, Aug. 28, 1801; d. Paris, March 30, 1877. Cournot taught at the academy of Paris from 1831 to 1834 before joining the faculty of science at Lyons for one year. An educational administrator, he served as inspector general of public instruction from 1835 to 1838, when he was made a member of the Legion of Honor. He was rector of the Academy of Dijon from 1854 to 1862 and wrote many outstanding works in mathematical economics and philosophy of science.

Cournot, the founder of mathematical economics, entered philosophy through the science of mathematics. His original views on economics, many of which are basic to contemporary theory, provided him with a key to a new philosophy of science. He fundamentally opposed the POSITIVISM of A. COMTE and the eclecticism of V. COUSIN in resolving the antinomies of science and philosophy. An ardent advocate of science and an enthusiastic admirer of I. KANT and G. W. LEIBNIZ, he proposed his theory of mathematical probabilities as a synthesis of idealism and positivism. Kant despised the non-certain, the logically non-rigorous, whereas science despaired of attaining certitude. The result was skepticism and agnosticism. Cournot answered this by saying that reality could be known with a probability that science progressively clarifies and philosophy progressively penetrates.

To Cournot, science without philosophy is blind; philosophy without science is empty. Philosophical truth is not a matter of positive fact beyond dispute, nor is reality merely reduced to statistical equations. Matter, life, reason, morals, and aesthetics are irreducible levels of developmental reality, which can be known with progressive clarity and depth, though not with certainty, by probability analysis. Order and disorder, law and chance are two unopposed phases of cosmic evolution, and as knowledge progresses, disorder and chance are reduced to law. Cournot applied his vitalistic, teleological EVOLUTIONISM and his mathematical methods to every area of science and art in an effort to unify science and philosophy and avoid skepticism and agnosticism.

Cournot contributed much to the 19th-century critical and epistemological idealism in France. He and Claude Bernard initiated the movement known as *Cri-*

tique de la science, which numbered such distinguished men as G. Tarde, H. Poincaré, P. Duhem, G. Milhaud, É. Meyerson, A. Hannequin, and A. Naville. However, his strength proved to be his weakness, for the uncertain knowledge provided by his mathematical probabilities neither attained the full reality of the cosmos nor avoided the skepticism and agnosticism he set out to refute.

Bibliography: J. A. SCHUMPETER, *History of Economic Analysis,* ed. E. B. SCHUMPETER (New York 1954). J. BENRUBI, *Les Sources et les courants de la philosophie contemporaine en France,* 2 v. (Paris 1933) v.1. T. V. CHARPENTIER, "Philosophes Contemporains: M. Cournot," *Revue Philosophique de la France et de l'Étranger* 11 (1881) 494–518. F. BARONE, *Enciclopedia filosofica.* (Venice-Rome 1957) 1:1305–06.

[R. J. NOGAR]

COURTENAY, PETER

Bishop of Winchester; b.*c.* 1432; d. Sept. 23, 1492. His knowledge of Canon and civil law, gained at Oxford, Cologne, and Padua, together with the influence of his family (he was a grandnephew of Richard COURTENAY), secured him appointment to an unusually large number of benefices and ecclesiastical offices. However, he gave little attention to pastoral responsibilities prior to his consecration as bishop of EXETER in 1478. Even then he continued an active interest in politics, having earlier served as secretary to both Henry VI and Edward IV. His episcopate is noted only for an extensive construction program, especially the addition at his own expense, of the north tower to the cathedral at Exeter. Here he placed the great "Peter bell." Shortly after Richard III seized power, Courtenay joined his kinsmen in organizing a revolt in Devon and Cornwall, but fled to Brittany when the effort collapsed. He returned to England with HENRY VII, who rewarded his loyalty and service by appointing him keeper of the privy seal in 1485 and arranging his translation to the see of WINCHESTER in 1487. Upon his consecration he resigned the keepership of the privy seal and withdrew from politics. He is probably buried in Winchester cathedral.

Bibliography: T. F. TOUT, *The Dictionary of National Biography from the Earliest Times to 1900,* 63 v. (London 1885–1900; repr. with corrections, 21 v., 1908–09, 1921–22, 1938; suppl. 1901–) 4:1264–65. A. B. EMDEN, *A Biographical Register of the Scholars of the University of Oxford to A.D. 1500,* 3 v. (Oxford 1957–59) 1:499–500. P. HUNT, *Fifteenth-Century England* (Pittsburgh 1962).

[J. DAHMUS]

COURTENAY, RICHARD

Bishop; b. *c.* 1381; d. Harfleur, France, Sept. 15, 1415. Richard was the son and heir of Sir Philip Cour-

tenay of Powderham, Devon, a grandson of the earl of Devon, nephew of Abp. William COURTENAY of Canterbury, and related by marrage to Henry IV. He studied law at Oxford and in 1406 was elected chancellor of the university. Although his uncle the archbishop had suppressed the teachings of WYCLIF at Oxford in 1382, Richard attempted to block the visitation of Abp. Thomas ARUNDEL, which had been prompted by the presence of Lollard sympathizers at the university. Henry IV supported Arundel, forcing Richard to resign (1411), although he was soon reelected. In recognition of his work in completing the university library and in increasing its collection of books, he was granted the privilege of free access. Most important of the many ecclesiastical preferments which Richard's influential connections assured him was Norwich, of which he was consecrated bishop in 1413 (*see* NORWICH, ANCIENT SEE OF). Political interests, however, continued to hold his attention. He became a member of the royal council, treasurer of the royal household, and in 1414 led a peace embassy to France. Its failure led to hostilities, and Richard died at the siege of Harfleur in the presence of Henry V, who ordered his body buried in Westminster.

Bibliography: T. F. TOUT, *The Dictionary of National Biography from the Earliest Times to 1900,* 63 v. (London 1885–1900; repr. with corrections, 21 v., 1908–09, 1921–22, 1938; suppl. 1901–) 4:1265–67. A. B. EMDEN, *A Biographical Register of the Scholars of the University of Oxford to A.D. 1500,* 3 v. (Oxford 1957–59) 1:500–502.

[J. DAHMUS]

COURTENAY, WILLIAM

Archbishop of Canterbury, opponent of John WYCLIF; b. near Exeter, *c.* 1341; d. Canterbury, July 31, 1396. William was the son of Hugh, Earl of Devon, and related through his mother to the Plantagenets. He studied law at OXFORD and in 1367 was chosen chancellor of the university despite difficulties with the Bishop of Lincoln over his election. Through the favor of the Black Prince and other influential patrons, Courtenay was richly provided with benefices, and climbed rapidly up the ecclesiastical ladder. In 1369 he was consecrated bishop of Hereford (*see* HEREFORD, ANCIENT SEE OF). In convocation three years later he made his entry into ecclesiastical-political affairs when he protested against papal exactions. In 1375 he was translated to London (*see* LONDON, ANCIENT SEE OF), where he accomplished what success the Church achieved in silencing Wyclif. The murder of Archbishop SIMON OF SUDBURY in the Peasant Revolt (1381) cleared the way for his translation to Canterbury (*see* CANTERBURY, ANCIENT SEE OF), where his first move was to convene a council of theologians and canon lawyers that condemned 24 of Wyclif's propositions (1382). This condemnation, supported by a royal ordinance, enabled him to suppress overt Wyclifitism at Oxford. Courtenay next undertook the visitation of his province, with which task he was occupied intermittently until his death. Because of his influence at Westminster and Rome, he was able to compel the recalcitrant bishops of EXETER and SALISBURY to acknowledge his right of visitation; his own death came in the midst of his dispute with the defiant bishop of HEREFORD. As primate of England he prevented RICHARD II from controlling the hierarchy by abuse of the CONVOCATION OF THE ENGLISH CLERGY. That Courtenay gave qualified acceptance to the Statutes of PROVISORS and PRAEMUNIRE when they were confirmed in the early nineties, suggests that these measures were not so sharply antipapal as frequently assumed. By order of the king, he was buried in Canterbury cathedral.

Bibliography: W. HUNT, *The Dictionary of National Biography from the Earliest Times to 1900,* 4:1267–72. J. H. DAHMUS, ed., *The Metropolitan Visitations of William Courteney: Archbishop of Canterbury, 1381–1396* (Urbana, Ill. 1950); *The Prosecution of John Wyclyf* (New Haven 1952). A. B. EMDEN, *A Biographical Register of the University of Oxford to A.D. 1500* 1:502–504.

[J. DAHMUS]

COURTESY

A moral VIRTUE annexed to justice and intimately associated, as are justice and all the virtues annexed to it, with charity. It is also called politeness, good manners, and, by moral theologians, affability. By it a man is disposed to conduct himself appropriately in his contact with his fellow man and to be ready to extend to each whatever considerate and gracious civility custom requires. It is related to MODESTY and decorum. As annexed to JUSTICE, it is an obligation flowing from man's social nature, because the satisfactory interrelationship of the members of society demand that the individual should conduct himself with thoughtful regard for the feelings of others. As a social virtue its importance for individuals and society is attested by both sacred and human authority. It is less than FRIENDSHIP, but to be truly virtuous it must be more than a false veneer covering contrary dispositions. As motivated by CHARITY, politeness is a good that the Christian is quick to show to others because they are created in the image and likeness of God and are— potentially, at least—temples of the Holy Spirit and members of the Mystical Body of Christ.

True courtesy is universal; that is, the courteous man is prepared to manifest it in appropriate circumstances to all men. Some marks of courtesy may without fault be withheld for a time from those who behave outrageously for the purpose of inducing them to mend their ways (*see* CORRECTION, FRATERNAL). Although a certain basic courtesy is due everyone, greater courtesy nevertheless is owed to some than to others because the claim of some is based not only upon the human dignity, which all share, but also upon special considerations of GRATITUDE, or special ties of blood or fellowship, or authority or other form of excellence (*see* RESPECT).

The opposite of courtesy, by way of defect, appears in discourtesy, incivility, rudeness, surliness, or other forms of offensive behavior. Acts of this kind are sinful. Generally the sin is considered a venial one, unless the offensiveness is great, or the acts, because of their frequency, make life difficult or very unpleasant for others.

By way of excess one can sin against courtesy by trying to please others more than he should. This can be done by praising others beyond their due, especially when this is done with a selfish end in view, or by hypocritical obsequiousness. Of itself flattery is only a venial sin, but circumstances could make it serious, e.g., if one were to praise a gravely sinful action, or if the flattery should cause notable harm to another.

The motivation by charity is important to keep courtesy sincere and unfailing. Moreover, it makes courtesy breathe with a spirit of Christlike love and gives even to small acts a significance and value far beyond what is superficially apparent (Mk 9.40).

Bibliography: THOMAS AQUINAS, *Summa Theologiae* 2a2ae, 114.1–2. M. J. GERLAUD, ''The Social Virtues,'' *The Virtues and States of Life,* ed. A. M. HENRY, tr. R. J. OLSEN and G. T. LENNON (Chicago 1957) 445–485. T. PÈGUES, *Commentaire français littéral de la Somme Théologique de Saint Thomas d'Aquin,* 21 v. (Paris 1922–33) 12:670–676.

[W. HERBST]

COURTLY LOVE

The term ''courtly love'' was invented in the late 19th century by Gaston Paris to designate the stylized attitudes of romantic love that appeared suddenly in the poetry of the troubadours in southern France at the beginning of the 12th century. The celebration of sexual love between men and women, and the poetic conventions developed to express it, became important elements in the literature of the West during the later Middle Ages and the Renaissance; indeed, the pervasive literary and social manifestations of this cultural innovation continue to play an important part in the sexual attitudes of modern times. The term ''courtly love'' is vague and complex because the kinds of behavior it is used to specify developed in different ways in many kinds of literature over a long

"Sacred and Profane Love," painting by Titian, from his early period (c. 1515).

period. It is, nevertheless, useful because we need a name for the whole complex phenomenon of romantic sexual behavior in all the variety of its literary manifestations.

CONVENTIONS OF COURTLY LOVE

The original form of courtly love and the point of departure for its later developments are found in the *chanson* of the troubadours. The following description of the phenomenon is a composite of the ''true love'' of the troubadours and the standard features of its later development in the literature of the 13th and 14th centuries.

The Lover. The courtly lover is characteristically a knight, though the poet himself is more often than not a man of more humble origin. The knight-lover sings the praises and seeks the favor of a lady according to a well-defined ritual. The lady is ordinarily his superior socially and is nearly always presented as a paragon of beauty and virtue. The knight offers his song and his service in the hope of winning his lady's regard, her ''grace,'' and perhaps ultimately her love. The mood of the lover begins in the melancholy of self-pity as he considers the difficulty of the enterprise and his own unworthiness. As the game progresses, he oscillates between hope and despair, as his suit is either encouraged or repelled by the lady.

Final success (or the promise of it) produces the perfect joy that the lover seeks. For the most part, however, the troubadour concentrates on this joy as a goal, not as an accomplished fact; it generates the excitement of the chase, the alternating hope and despair that are the psychological burden of the song.

The Beloved. The lady to whom the song, or suit, is addressed is a stereotype. Physically she is blond and fair, with stylized features and figure that vary little within the tradition. She may be addressed with the masculine *midons* (my lord); and the relation, in many of its formal aspects, between lover and lady is a highly conventional sexual version of the feudal relation between lord and vassal. The lady is almost invariably someone else's wife; and, if she is not, the love proposed by the knight is rarely directed explicitly toward marriage. In medieval religious terms, therefore, courtly love is nearly always illicit and usually adulterous. A major source of excitement in the songs is the threat of discovery by a jealous husband. Variations of this form, however, appear early in the tradition, and the nature of *fin amor* from this point of view is one of the most important aspects of its literary history.

"Nature with Venus, Juno and Pallas," manuscript painting from *"Le Livre des Echecs amoureux,"* 15th century, from the Bibliotheque Nationale, Paris. (Biblio. Nat. MS Fr. 143, fol. 198 v.)

The Suit. The process of love is also rigidly conventional. The lover is struck at first sight by the physical beauty of the lady. His passion is aroused at once and is further stimulated by dreams and fantasies in which she appears to him. He eventually declares his love, offers his service, and tries to prove his worthiness by his virtues, not the least of which is fortitude in dangerous ventures. He may or may not achieve the physical favors that are the ostensible object of his exertions. But, although his love is always sexual in origin, and sustained by desire for possession, it is rarely represented as lustful in a physical sense. The lover is restrained in his behavior, chaste in the sense that, for the time being at least, he loves no one else, and discreet in the conduct of his suit. Indeed, the highest form of courtly passion is so refined that it refuses ultimate physical fulfillment; the lover aspires to the joy of perpetual longing, a continuing erotic passion that is never satisfied and therefore can be sustained with-

out the risks of dishonor, exhaustion, or the potential absurdities of retrospection.

The Rewards. Since courtly love is an imitation, as its imagery and ritual show, of both divine love and its social manifestations in the feudal ideals of honor and friendship, it is assumed to produce virtue in those who practice it. The cardinal virtues of justice, wisdom, temperance, and fortitude are all increased by love and service, as are the social virtues of liberality, courtesy, and obedience.

Finally, the literature of true love and the later poetry that was influenced by its central theme employ a relatively constant pattern of images. The affair normally begins in April or May, and the stirrings in the lover are associated with the powers and demands of nature in springtime. Trees come to life, flowers bud, birds (especially nightingales, cuckoos, and larks) begin to sing and seek their mates, the whole Earth is warmed by breezes and quickened by rain. The lover is at once hunter and hunted, wounded by Love's arrows, stricken by the disease of love, driven to madness and despair, regarded as a slave, a prisoner, an exile, but always in hope of mercy, grace, and reward, which will compensate for his miseries and crown his service with unspeakable joy.

COURTLY LOVE AND CHRISTIAN DOCTRINE

Efforts to understand the poets' idealization of woman and their celebration of a rationalized and refined form of sexual desire have led to a careful examination of the points of similarity and difference between courtly love and the medieval doctrine of CHARITY, especially in the contemporary mysticism of divine love developed by St. BERNARD OF CLAIRVAUX. From most points of view, the cult of courtly love is the antithesis of the religious doctrine of the love of God for His own sake and the love of all other creatures, including love between men and women, for the sake of God. Courtly love, in Father Denomy's lucid description, is neither Christian nor Platonic, neither mystical nor lustful; it is desire for sexual possession in which desire is its own goal and the source of virtue in those who practice it. The beloved object of this desire becomes a substitute for God; the love itself is an indulgence of passion at the expense of reason; the virtues sought are social and natural rather than religious and supernatural. We must observe, of course, that the social virtues of the lovers were directed toward antisocial ends, as far as the norms of society were concerned; and the natural virtues of sexual desire were, in terms of ancient and medieval doctrines of the ordered supremacy of reason over the passions, "unnatural," as Alan of Lille made clear in his *De planctu Naturae.*

Amor* and *Caritas. Nevertheless, as Kenelm Foster, OP, has shown, there were affinities between *amor* and *caritas* that, in their recognition of potential moral and spiritual values in sexual love, made possible the mystical grandeur of Dante's love for Beatrice and point to recent developments in the theology of marriage. In addition to the general principle that *amor* is the source of all good in the world, in much the way that *caritas* was traditionally regarded as the principle of good, Foster notes the fidelity and restraint that courtly love ideally imposed on those who practiced it, the embodiment of the idea of love in a human person, love as a yearning that is never satisfied, a gift spontaneously given, by an act of grace, by the beloved; all of these suggest analogies with divine charity, or rather the transposition of a religious to a human ideal. Such similarities have led scholars to compare the rise of courtly love with the concurrent development of St. Bernard's theology of love in which the language of human passion drawn from the Song of Songs was made the appropriate means of expressing man's love for God. Others have pointed to the increase of devotion to the Blessed Virgin Mary expressed in the amatory language of human love, though the popularity of this devotion and the excesses that sometimes substituted Mary for her Son as the object of veneration belong more to the 13th and 14th centuries than to the 12th. If there is a relationship, literature of devotion to the Blessed Virgin, which freely and often daringly employs the language of human love, is more likely to have been influenced by the literature of courtly love than to have been among the causes of the secular phenomenon.

Status of Women. Courtly love may also be seen as a reaction against the generally humiliating position of women in medieval society and a theology of marriage that reflected the historical development of this social situation. Men were thought to be superior to women, not only socially and juridically, but even philosophically and theologically. Men regarded themselves as more rational, and therefore more human, than women. Interpretations of Genesis made woman's creation an indication of inferiority, and centuries of commentary on the Fall of man associated Eve and all subsequent women with sensuality, temptation, and the ruin of man. Monastic and sacerdotal celibacy encouraged a tradition of antifeminist attitudes and a literature that made women subhuman objects to be feared and scorned. Such distortions of woman's nature and role in society were balanced in some degree by Christian doctrines of the dignity of the human person, the creation of man *and* woman in the image of God, the honor paid to heroic women in Sacred Scripture, the veneration of female saints, and most of all the recognition of the unique prerogatives of the Mother of God. (*See* WOMAN.)

The consequences of the generally low view of women in the Middle Ages for the theology of marriage are in striking contrast to the exaltation of women and of sexual desire in the literature of courtly love. Father Foster writes: "A haunting fear of letting concupiscence into marriage was undoubtedly a powerful element in traditional marriage theology, and one backed by the greatest names, St. Augustine's, above all, and St. Jerome's. And with this fear went an implicit refusal to consider sex in any other than one of two ways: either as pleasant *and* procreative—and from this point of view the use of sex was justified, in marriage, by the intention to procreate; or as *merely* pleasant, and from this point of view its use was never justified whether in marriage or not." Foster therefore sees the possibility that the celebration of love freely sought and given between two autonomous personalities (and so necessarily outside the institution of marriage) may have arisen from a certain dissatisfaction with the restrictive, impersonal conditions of medieval marriage.

Philosophy of Nature. If the "true love" of the *chanson* and the romance may be regarded as an assertion of the rights and dignity of a universally felt natural appetite, which might, if properly governed and directed toward a worthy object, result in an increase in natural virtue, its rise in the 12th century may have some connection with a parallel phenomenon in the history of philosophy. Corresponding with the spread of the literary doctrines of courtly love are the rise of interest in the natural universe and the adoption of rational modes of inquiry in the pursuit of truth. It would be false to exaggerate the novelty of this attitude and to assume that it constituted a movement away from orthodoxy. The masters of Chartres, Bernard, WILLIAM OF CONCHES, THIERRY, BERNARD SILVESTRIS, and others associated with this movement, subordinated philosophical truth to the revealed truth of Scripture. Their Neoplatonic philosophy of nature proceeded on the assumption that the created universe could be studied rationally as a reality distinct from, but dependent on, its Creator. (*See* SCHOLASTICISM.)

In this natural theology and philosophy, nature was the instrument or servant of the Divine Maker, the sustaining and reproductive power inherent in created things. It was the principle by which divine love operated in the world, the *pulcherrimum involucrum* of the Holy Spirit. This operative principle of God's love found its most authoritative statement in Boethius's *Consolation of Philosophy* (2.8), where the harmonious order of the universe is said to be maintained by divine love. In addition to governing the macrocosm, "Love binds together people joined by a sacred bond; love binds sacred marriages by chaste affections; love makes the laws which join true friends. O how happy the human race would be, if that love which rules the heavens ruled also your souls!" But in the view of the 12th-century philosopher and theologian love did not preserve its original rule over the souls of men. In the disastrous exercise of freedom to rebel, man had, in original sin, wounded his nature. But this was the domain of biblical theology. The Platonism of Chartres and Poitiers, relying heavily on classical moral philosophy, particularly that of Cicero, took a more optimistic view of man's natural possibilities. Although this naturalism did not specifically encourage the view that sexual desire could be virtuous apart from its role in procreation, its general approach to ethical problems tended to broaden the medieval view of human love. At least it can be said that the stress on the naturalness of love in courtly literature is much closer to the moral philosophy developed in the 12th century than to the theologians' preoccupation with carnal concupiscence as the corrupting effect of original sin.

Bibliography: Best general introductions, with full bibliographies: R. R. BEZZOLA, *Les Origines de la Formation de la littérature courtoise en Occident, 500–1200* (Paris 1944–). M. J. VALENCY, *In Praise of Love* (New York 1958). F. SCHLÖSSER, *Andreas Capellanus: Seine Minnelehre und das christliche Weltbild um 1200* (Bonn 1960). Still useful for its extensive treatment and stimulating, if often unreliable, criticism is C. S. LEWIS, *The Allegory of Love* (Oxford 1936). For differing and influential points of view see A. JEANROY, *La Poésie lyrique des troubadours,* 2 v. (Paris 1934). G. ERRANTE, *Marcabru e le fonti sacre dell'antica lirica romanza* (Florence 1948). A. J. DENOMY, *The Heresy of Courtly Love* (New York 1947). C. H. DAWSON, *Medieval Essays* (New York 1954). ANDRÉ LE CHAPELAIN, *The Art of Courtly Love,* tr. J. J. PARRY (New York 1941). With the exceptions listed above, most scholarship concerned with the general problem of courtly love has appeared in periodicals. Some of the most important in English are: T. SILVERSTEIN, "Andreas, Plato, and the Arabs," *Modern Philology* 47 (1949–50) 117–126. A. J. DENOMY, "'Fin' Amors: The Pure Love of the Troubadors, Its Amorality, and Possible Sources," *Mediaeval Studies* 7 (1945) 139–207; "Courtly Love and Courtliness," *Speculum. A Journal of Mediaeval Studies* 28 (1953) 44–63. K. FOSTER, *Courtly Love and Christianity* (Aquinas Papers 39; London 1963). D. W. ROBERTSON, "The Subject of the 'De Amore' of Andreas Capellanus," *Modern Philology* 50 (1952–53) 145–161. For an excellent introduction to the philosophy and theology of the 12th century, see M. D. CHENU, *La Théologie au XIIe siècle* (Paris 1957).

[R. H. GREEN]

COUSIN, VICTOR

French philosopher and founder of ECLECTICISM: b. Paris, Nov. 28, 1792; d. Cannes, Jan. 13, 1867. Raised in a working-class family, Cousin completed his studies brilliantly at the secondary level before entering the École Normale (1810). Starting as an assistant to P. P. Royer-Collard (1763–1843) in the Faculty of Letters (1815), he later became titular professor (1830). The eloquence of his lectures and the novelty of his ideas brought him tremendous success.

At first (1815–16), Cousin sought inspiration from the SCOTTISH SCHOOL OF COMMON SENSE, as well as from

Victor Cousin. (Archive Photos, Inc.)

P. Laromiguière (1756–1837), Royer-Collard, and MAINE DE BIRAN. These thinkers had a long, lasting effect on him, and—along with Plotinus, Kant, Schelling, and Hegel, whom he also studied—helped him to untangle himself from the SENSISM of E. B. de CONDILLAC. In 1818 Cousin began teaching eclecticism, holding that there were in philosophy four opposing systems: idealism, materialism, skepticism, and mysticism—no one system being entirely true or entirely false. To arrive at the full truth, all four must be coordinated into a higher synthesis. Strongly influenced by Hegelianism, Cousin leaned toward PANTHEISM (*Fragments philosophiques,* 1826) while professedly disassociating himself from it.

The essential themes of his teaching are these: (1) the God of conscience is at once infinite and finite; (2) creation *ex nihilo* is unthinkable; creation is the necessary production of phenomena from the divine substance; (3) history is, therefore, the development of God in the world and in humanity (*Cours d'histoire de la philosophie moderne,* 5 v. 1841–46; *Études sur Pascal,* 1842; *Nouveaux fragments philosophiques,* 1847); and (4) thought arises from the "impersonal reason," immanent to the soul, the center of spontaneous inspiration, and the principle of all religion. Religion is a human work, stimulated by the divine within man.

Later, seeking to find a norm superior to individual inspiration, Cousin entrusted to history the duty of judging true doctrine from false: history saves what is valuable and eliminates what is not. This "judgment of history" is itself the effect of a certain idea of the true that is innate to conscience. From this time on, Cousin considered his teaching to be a type of SPIRITUALISM, that is, a doctrine propounding "the spirituality of the soul, the liberty and responsibility of human actions" and positing "beyond the limits of this world a God, author and type of humanity" (*Du vrai, du beau et du bien*, 1853).

A peer of France, director of the École Normale, minister of public education (1840), Cousin retired in 1851. Although the influence of his thought was at first considerable, its importance steadily declined after 1850 under pressure from POSITIVISM. From another quarter, Catholic philosophers decried the RATIONALISM that had inspired it and had made of revelation "an illusion and an impossibility." What primarily remains of Cousin's work is his historical contribution. This includes *Cours d'histoire de la philosophie morale au XVIIIe siècle*, 5 v. 1840–41; *Philosophie de Kant*, 1842; *Histoire générale de la philosophie*, 1863; and studies of scholastic philosophy contained in *Nouveaux fragments*, 1847.

See Also: ECLECTICISM.

Bibliography: C. ROSSO, *Encilclopedia filosofica* (Venice-Rome 1957) 1:1306–08.

[R. JOLIVET]

COUSSA, ACACIUS

Cardinal and canonist; b. Aleppo, Aug. 31, 1897; d. Rome, June 29, 1962. He entered the Order of Basilians in Aleppo and was ordained Dec. 20, 1920. He occupied several positions in the interests of the Oriental Church in the Roman CURIA. Among his positions were adviser to the Congregation for the Oriental Church and member of the commission for the revision of the Oriental Code.

He was nominated titular bishop of Gerapoli in Syria Feb. 26, 1961, and was consecrated April 16, 1961. He became prosecretary for the Congregation for the Oriental Church. On March 19, 1962, he was created a cardinal by Pope John XXIII. He was buried in the chapel of the Propaganda Fide al Verano in Rome.

He wrote the *Epitome praelectionum de iure ecclesiastico orientali*, two volumes (Venice 1921); and *E*

praelectionibus in librum secundum Codicis iuris canonici—De Personis: de clericis in specie (Grottaferrat 1953).

[L. R. KOZLOWSKI]

COUSTANT, PIERRE

Benedictine of the Congregation of Saint-Maur; b. in Compiègne, France, April 30, 1654; d. in Abbey of Saint-Germain-des-Prés, near Paris, Oct. 18, 1721. After he had been educated by the Jesuits at Compiègne, he entered the Benedictine Order at Saint-Remi in Reims. He made a new edition of the works of St. Hilary of Poitiers, published in 1693, worked on an edition of the Breviary and helped Claude Guesnie in making a general index to the works of St. AUGUSTINE. His greatest undertaking is the attempt to edit a collection of the letters of the popes from St. Clement I to Innocent III (*c.* 88–1216). Before his death he published only one volume, containing letters from 67 to 440, titled *Epistolae Romanorum Pontificium et quae ad eos scriptae sunt a S. Clemente I usque ad Innocentium III . . .* (Paris 1781). (*See* MAURISTS).

Bibliography: M. LALMANT, *Dictionnaire de droit canonique* 4:729–731. R. P. TASSIN, *Histoire littéraire de la congrégation de Saint–Maur* (Brussels 1770).

[L. R. KOZLOWSKI]

COUTURIER, PIERRE MARIE ALAIN

Pioneer of modern liturgical arts movement; b. Montbrison, central France, November 15, 1897; d. February 8, 1954. His father was a miller. Couturier received his education in various Catholic schools. In 1916 he went to war and the following year he returned, wounded and ill. In 1919 he went to Paris to study painting; there he joined M. Denis and Desvallières, who had just founded the "Ateliers d'Art Sacré." Couturier's special interest was stained glass.

In 1925 Couturier joined the Dominican Order and in 1930 was ordained priest. He executed frescoes and stained-glass windows in various houses of the order in Oslo, Paris, and Rome. He also painted, at Montbrison and at Namur, works in which his admiration for El Greco was apparent. In 1937 he became codirector of the review *Art Sacré*, which had been founded two years before by J. Pichard, OP. When war broke out, Couturier was in America, where he directed art at the College of Notre Dame, Baltimore, Md. He lectured frequently in Canada and the U.S. and published two short books, *Art et Catholicisme* (Montreal 1941) and *Chroniques* (Mon-

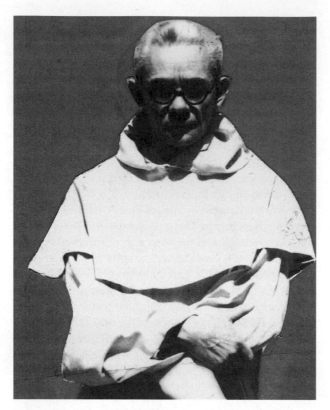

Pierre Marie Alain Couturier.

treal 1946). In 1946 he returned to France and resumed his work on *Art Sacré*. His articles aroused wide discussion, and he took a very active part in the building of the churches at ASSY, VENCE, Audincourt, and RONCHAMP, where he engaged some of the greatest artists and architects of the period.

Bibliography: *Art Sacré* (May–June 1954), memorial number. P. R. RÉGAMEY, *Catholicisme* 3:264–265.

[J. PICHARD]

COUX, CHARLES DE

19th-century precursor of social Catholicism and member of the circle of Félicité de LAMENNAIS; b. Paris, 1787; d. Guerande, Jan. 16, 1864. His father had emigrated to America in 1790 but returned to Paris in 1803. In 1830 Coux became one of the editors of *L'Avenir,* writing on economic and social questions. He traced the misery of the workers to the industrial system, which he condemned for its exploitation of labor. Reluctant to approve legislative interference with prices or wages, he supported the founding of workers' and masters' associations, anticipating in this the later goals of syndicalism. When *L'Avenir* was suspended in 1831, Coux and Philippe GERBET organized public conferences for young

students, asking Frédéric OZANAM, among others, to join this work. Coux's lectures were published as *Essais d'économie politique* (Paris 1832). In 1834 he accepted a post at the University of LOUVAIN, giving a *cours d'economie sociale* and a *cours d'economie politique.* Some of his lectures published in the review *L'Université catholique* reveal an increasingly timid critic compared to the outspoken contributor to *L'Avenir.* In 1845 Coux left Louvain and became editor of *L'Univers* until February 1848. After the revolution of that year he gradually withdrew from public affairs. His influence on Ozanam is considered great.

Bibliography: J. B. DUROSELLE, *Les Débuts du catholicisme social en France, 1822–1870* (Paris 1951). C. DE LADOUE, *Monseigneur Gerbet, sa vie, ses oeuvres et l'École Menaisienne,* 3 v. (Paris 1870).

[E. T. GARGAN]

COVENANT (IN THE BIBLE)

The biblical concept of *berît* (covenant) is so vast that this article can give only a brief survey. After a preliminary discussion of the meaning of the Hebrew term and the treaty form in the ancient Near East, details of the OT and NT covenant concept will be given.

Meaning of the Hebrew Term. Scholars are not agreed on the etymology of the Hebrew word *berît*. Various opinions derive the etymon from the Hebrew, or the Arabic, or the Akkadian (see G. da Fonseca, *Biblica* 8:31–50). But the Akkadian root *brt* (to bind) seems to be the most probable. Hence, the Hebrew word would reflect the idea of a binding tie (see D. J. McCarthy, *Treaty and Covenant* 54; hereafter cited as *TC*).

The term *berît* signifies primarily a contract agreement. This includes political alliances. But in the OT its use is mainly theological, to express the alliance between God and His people in the course of SALVATION HISTORY. Other variants of less consequence would be judicial decisions (Sir 38.33), contracts by oath (Hos 10.4; Is 33.8), marriage (Prv 2.17; Jer 31.32; Ez 16.8; Mal 2.14), and friendship (1 Sm 18.3; Ps 54[55].21). Metaphorically, *berît* could be an agreement made with eyes (Jb 31.1), animals (Hos 2.20), stones (Jb 5.23), death (Is 28.15), and day and night (Jer 33.20).

In a secondary sense, but not always sharply distinct from the former, *berît* signifies ordinance or law. Thus the Mosaic Law became the covenant (e.g., 1 Kgs 8.21; Jer 11.1), so much so that "to transgress the covenant" was to transgress the Law (Dt 4.13, 23; Jgs 2.20). In the last centuries before Christ, the Mosaic covenant was the cult of the true God, the true religion (Jdt 9.13; 1 Mc 1.15; 2 Mc 7.36).

Constitutive elements of *ber^et* are: (1) parties to the agreement, either two peoples or individuals of equal or unequal status, sometimes with a third party as proxy of YAHWEH (e.g., Jos 24.25); (2) stipulations; (3) oaths and imprecations; and (4) ritual enactment, at times in conjunction with sacrifice (Ex 24.5) and blood (Ex 24.8; Zec 9.11).

Primitive ritual form seems to have been the imbibing of blood, which gave way to such substitutes as a common meal (Gn 26.30), exchange of garments or weapons (1 Sm 18.3), or a simple handshake (Ez 17.18). The practice of literally "cutting a covenant" (the Hebrew expression for making a covenant) is exemplified in Gn 15.8–11, 17 and Jer 34.18. The phrase "covenant of salt" (Lv 2.13), associated with a common meal and theologically with Sinaitic covenant, expresses the durable trait of the pact. In some cases a covenantal stele (Heb. *maṣṣēbâ*) is associated with a pact (Gn 31.45, 51–52), but not as an object of worship (Lv 26.1). Not all of the above elements, however, are consistently verified in each and every covenantal situation. There are many published and unpublished analogies from the ancient and the modern Near East for the meaning and form of Biblical *b^erît*. Because of space limitation, treatment will be limited here to the covenant as an ancient form of treaty.

Covenant Treaty in the Ancient Near East. Since 1931 much evidence has accumulated to show that the covenant treaty was a widespread institution (see *TC* 13–106). The earliest texts, from the 3d millennium B.C., are in Sumerian and Akkadian. From the 2d millennium, however, the archives of Hattusa have provided more than 20 Hittite treaty texts (*c.* 17th–14th centuries B.C.).

These treaties are of two kinds: the parity treaty entered into by equals and involving perfect reciprocity, and the more common vassal treaty imposed by the more powerful Hittite king on an inferior in which the obligations were one-sided. A classic example of parity treaty is the one between Hattusili III and Ramses II. The vassal treaty was essentially a technique for imperial administration.

Formally, these treaties have constant elements (titulature, stipulations as case or apodictic law, oaths with divine witnesses, and curse and blessing formulas), and variables (historical prologues, document clauses, etc.). Because it is a literary form, chancellors could arrange the essential elements as circumstances warranted. Hence, there was "variety within a general uniformity" (*TC* 47, 50).

Treaties from Syria belong basically to the mainstream of treaty tradition, but depart principally from Hit-

Covenant stele carving.

tite tradition by using a new element, the *Drohritus* or curse rite, found also in West-Semitic covenant making and much developed in Assyrian texts of the 9th–8th centuries (see *TC* ch. 5–6). Herein lies a clue to the principal ideological difference between the two peoples. By the use of a historical prologue, the Hittite treaty appealed to historical experience as a basis for a plan of action. It did not deny that every event was the result of some god's will, but at the same time it remained at the level of the concept "what is, is right." The Syrian-Assyrian treaties, on the other hand, with their curse rites, appealed to a divinely willed order of events. Characteristic of these treaties is a gradual evolution toward a technical legal terminology, which is more probably of Babylonian rather than of Syrian-Assyrian origin.

Covenant in the Old Testament

The term *b^erît* occurs often in the OT and can be conveniently treated as the designation of an economic-political alliance and of a theological alliance.

Economic-Political Alliance. For the most part, the economic-political alliances mentioned in the OT are purely secular and profane in character. Nevertheless, by the fact that they were concluded by the leaders elect, they have a part to play in the gradual unfolding of salvation history. In some cases to separate the sacred from the profane does violence to the narrative, since both are usually intricately entwined.

In Patriarchal Times. ABRAHAM made an alliance with Canaanite chiefs that was instrumental in the rescue of Lot (Gn 14.13–16). He concluded a covenant with Abimelech (Gn 21.22–33), which Isaac renewed (Gn 26.26–31). In both instances, the contracting parties agreed on perpetual mutual loyalty. Jacob made an alliance only with Laban (Gn 31.43–55; see D. J. McCarthy, "Three Covenants in Genesis," *Catholic Biblical Quarterly* 26 [1964] 179–189).

From the Exodus to Saul. MOSES' marriage (a form of covenant) with Zipporah undoubtedly facilitated passage through Midianite territory; moreover, Jethro, Zipporah's father, offered sacrifice to God and counseled Moses on organized judicial affairs (Ex 2.21–22; 18.1–27). Joshua was fraudulently drawn into the Gibeonite covenant, which he nevertheless respected (Jos 9.3–27). In later times, Saul's descendants were punished for breaking this covenant (2 Sm 21.1–10). In the period of the Judges, the absence of central power and unity among the tribes prohibited the concluding of alliances with neighboring peoples. JEPHTHAH tried it with the Ammonites but without success (Jgs 11.12–28). Allusions in Jgs 1.16; 4.11, 17–22; 5.24; 1 Sm 15.6; 33.29 seem to indicate some alliance between the Israelites and the Kenites.

Period of the Kings. Once the kingdom was established, alliances proved to be advantageous and necessary for political and commercial reasons. Thus David depended on the friendship of various princes, e.g., Achish (1 Sm 27.2–12; 28.1–2) and the King of Moab (1 Sm 22.3–4); he married Maacah, daughter of the King of Geshur (2 Sm 3.3) and established better relations with Naas, King of the Ammonites (2 Sm 10.2). His most important alliance was with Hiram, King of Tyre (1 Kgs 5.15), who sent workers to construct David's palace (2 Sm 5.11). Solomon followed this covenant policy to obtain from Hiram materials and workers necessary for the construction of the Temple (1 Kgs 5.12). This Israelite-Phoenician alliance was long remembered, for in Am 1.9 divine punishment is announced for Tyre because it forgot the fraternal covenant. Finally, Solomon's covenants with Egypt and Sheba involved also commercial interests (1 Kgs 10.1–15, 28–29), and his many marriages to seal his covenants with foreign rulers led him to favor his wives' pagan cults (1 Kgs 11.1–8).

With the split between the North and the South, antagonism between the two kingdoms opened the door for offensive and defensive alliances. Such alliances in great part explain the events of the epoch. Thus, the Egyptian invasion of Judah was provoked by Jeroboam I, King of Israel, who found an ally in Egypt (1 Kgs 11.40; 14.25–26). The same antagonism between the successors of Jeroboam and Rehoboam, King of Judah, induced both the kings of Israel and the kings of Judah to seek alliances with the Syrian kings (1 Kgs 15.16–20). Such alliances, as well as the alliance of Judah with Israel against Syria, were condemned by Yahweh because they led to idolatry (1 Kgs 20.35–43; 2 Kgs 8.26). Despite divine disapproval the Judah-Israel alliance continued until the reign of Jehu (2 Kgs 9.27).

Antagonism between the two kingdoms resurrected under Jeroboam II of Israel and Amasiah of Judah (2 Kgs 14.8–14), leading at the time of Ahaz to alliances between Israel and Rezin, King of Damascus (2 Kgs 16.5) and between Judah and Tiglath-pileser, King of Assyria (2 Kgs 16.7–9). This intervention of Assyria in the international affairs of Judah and Israel marks a new period in the covenant history of the Israelites. Allusions are found both in the historical books (2 Kgs 17.4; 19.9; 23.29, 33–35; 24.1–2, 7; 25.1–21) and in the prophetical works (Is 30.2–4; Jer 46.2; Ez 17.13–19; etc.).

Maccabean Period. Judas Maccabeus established an alliance with the Romans against the Syrian kings (1 Mc 8.22–32), and it was renewed by Jonathan and Simon (1 Mc 12.1; 15.17). The Romans respected this alliance and accepted its renewal (1 Mc 15.16–23). In 1 Mc 12.2; 14.20 there is mention of an alliance between the Jews and the Lacedemonians. Hasmonean alliances, which proved to be fatal for the Jews, are known through Flavius Josephus (*Jewish Antiquities* 13.9.2; 14.4.4; 14.5).

Theological Alliance. Israel, in its sacred history, expressed its special relation with God by the term *berît*. Since it was a plastic human convention, sacred authors used *berît* rather freely to describe the mysteries of God's salvific acts in the history of man. Hence, the biblical concern is not so much with a contract as with a divinely guaranteed promise. Man's response must always be obedience to divine law. Naturally, the divine covenant involved partners of unequal status, wherein God always took the initiative and was the exclusive Lord of the covenant because He alone could and did save the people.

Covenant in the Pentateuch. The promises made to Noah and Abraham are called *berît*. In Gn 9.8–17 there is a *berît* between God and creation of which Noah, according to the YAHWIST (Gn 8.20–22), is the mediator because of his sacrifice. If the passage of the Pentateuchal PRIESTLY WRITERS (P) in Gn 9.1–7 properly belongs to this covenant, then the Noah covenant would also be a real contract besides a gratuitously given divine promise. The rainbow is the chosen sign of the alliance (Gn 9.13). In Is 54.9–10 (see also Sir 44.17–18) God's covenant with Noah is called a b⁻rît of peace.

God's covenant with Abraham consists of a twofold promise: numerous posterity and possession of the promised land (Gn 15.1–20). The parallel of P in Gn 17.1–14 prescribes both CIRCUMCISION as the sign of the covenant and the injunction to walk justly before God. The covenant is perpetual (17.13) and is extended in subsequent books to Isaac and Jacob (Ex 2.24; 6.4; etc.).

At Sinai, Israel became the people of God (Ex 6.7; Lv 26.12; often in Jeremiah and Ezekiel). This alliance is called the Decalogue in Ex 34.27, 38 and Lv 26.15 and a renewal of the patriarchal covenant in Ex 24.7–8. The sign of this alliance is the SABBATH (Ex 34.27–28). Recent studies concerning renewals of this covenant are those of N. Lohfink on Josiah's Covenant in 2 Kgs 23.3 and of J. L'Hour on Shechem Covenant in Jos 24.1–28. Possibly Dt 11.29–30; 27.1–26 is a tradition of the Shechem alliance independent of Jos 24.1–28. The latter passage contains elements of ancient covenant form and is more motivational than ritual or contractual (see *TC* ch. 11). In Exodus ch. 19–24 the treaty form is reflected only remotely, with emphasis on ritual (see *TC* ch. 12). The Book of Deuteronomy, on the other hand, has the complete treaty form (see *TC* ch. 9). Its theology is that of the heart, as it is in the prophetic and the wisdom traditions, leading the hearer to respond to the love of Yahweh.

Prophetic Covenant. The divine promise through Nathan to David (2 Sm 7.5–16), that Israel was the people of Yahweh and that David's dynasty would last forever, is expressed by later authors as a b⁻ rît (2 Sm 23.5; Ps 88 [89].40; Sir 45.25). In 2 Chr 13.5 its incorruptibility is stressed by calling it a covenant of salt (b⁻rît melah). The kingship now shared in the solidity of the Mosaic covenant, and sacred sonship culminated in the king of Israel. The Davidic covenant was bound up later with Temple tradition (Psalm 131 [132]), exemplified by the biblical CHRONICLER, who was intent on David and the Temple. In the prophetic books, this covenant was bound up with the prophetic-messianic expectation of the Davidic shoot (Is 11.1, 10; etc.). Hence, the people of God now had David as true shepherd (Jer 23.5; Ez 34.23–24; 37.24).

Moreover, the Prophets untiringly repeated the demands of Yahweh, His threats and His promises. Even though the word b⁻rît rarely occurred, the reality of the covenant found expression in such comparisons as betrothal (Hos 2.16–25) and paternal love (Hos 11.1–4), which Hosea attached to the Exodus, as Amos did with the idea of divine election (Am 3.1–2). Moreover, the re-

ality of God's covenant with Israel is presupposed in Hos 1.1–3.5 and Am 2.4–5. What all the Prophets, by reason of their vocation, were intent on was the application of the Mosaic Law to the existing circumstances.

Above all, there emerges the prophetic idea of a New Covenant, already described in Hos 2.18–25. It is not the same as the covenant of the fathers, but one written on hearts, and therefore spiritual (Jer 31.31–40; 32.38–42). Yet for Ezekiel the New Covenant is to be a renewal of the one made at the Exodus (Ez 20.34–38). Moreover, there is the covenantal guarantee concerning restoration of Temple cult and reestablishment of the priestly succession of Levi from Aaron and Phinehas to Zadok (Ez 44.15–31). After the Exile, the Levites make a formal covenant with God (Ezr 10.1–9; Nehemiah ch. 9–10). In Deutero-Isaiah, the first Exodus is both type and guarantee of the new Exodus from Babylon (Is 41.17–20; 43.16–21; 48.20–21); in the Songs of the SUFFERING SERVANT the servant becomes "a covenant of people, a light for nations" (Is 42.6). Finally, in Dn 9.4–6 the Law and the Prophets are united as b⁻rît.

Covenant in the New Testament

The NT uses the Septuagint term διαθήκη 33 times for b⁻rît, although in non-biblical Greek διαθήκη means last will and TESTAMENT. In the NT διαθήκη almost always means covenant. On the question of continuity or discontinuity between the OT and the NT, see R. Murphy, "The Relationship between the Testaments," *Catholic Biblical Quarterly* 26 (1964) 349–359, and J. Oesterreicher, *The Israel of God* (Englewood Cliffs, N.J. 1963).

In the Synoptics and Acts. The BENEDICTUS (CANTICLE OF ZECHARIAH) refers to God's covenants with David and Abraham (Lk 1.68–75); for Luke, διαθήκη is a sworn promise fulfilled in the Messiah whom God has sent, rather than a bilateral pact.

Regarding the meaning of the word διαθήκη in the institution of the Eucharistic consecration of wine (Mt 26.28; Mk 14.24; Lk 22.20; 1 Cor 11.25), there are three opinions: (1) last will and testament; (2) covenant, with allusions to Ex 24.8; and (3) both. The more probable opinion is the second. The first Old Covenant was made through Moses and ratified by sacrifice. The New Covenant is the Christian dispensation ratified by Christ's sacrifice on Calvary. In NT context, however, this New Covenant cannot be separated from the many promises that Christ gave to those who love Him (e.g., John ch. 14–17).

In Peter's discourse in the Temple, διαθήκη is the divine promise given to Abraham (Acts 3.25). The promised blessings are realized in Christ. For Stephen, διαθήκη is the precept of circumcision, and he calls "uncircumcised in heart and ear" those who reject and thus "do not keep the Law received as an ordinance of angels," i.e., the Sinai covenant (Acts 7.8, 51–53).

In the Pauline Epistles. In Rom 9.4 and Eph 2.12 διαθῆκαι includes all ancient pacts established by God. In Rom 11.27, however, the reference is specifically to the messianic covenant, the New Covenant foretold by the Prophets.

In terms of covenantal law, 2 Cor 3.6–18 presents the two διαθῆκαι as opposite orders. The old was a dispensation that condemned, whereas the new is a dispensation that justifies. The old was of the letter that killed, whereas the new is of the spirit that gives life, namely, Christ. The old was transient, whereas the new is permanent.

In Gal 3.15–18, 29 and 4.21–31 the two διαθῆκαι are presented as opposite orders in terms of slavery and freedom. As the slave girl HAGAR, the mother of Ishmael, represents the Sinai of Mosaic legislation, that is, the Jerusalem of Paul's time, so Sarah, mother of Isaac, the freeborn son of promise, represents the New Jerusalem, that is, the Church. Hence, for Paul the Abrahamitic covenant was superior to the Sinaitic covenant.

In Hebrews. The author reflects on all God's ancient covenants, e.g., with Noah (Heb 11.7), Abraham (6.13–20), Moses (3.1–6), David and the Prophets (11.32–33), and Levi (7.4–17), but especially on the New Covenant of the Messiah (ch. 8).

The Old Covenant was a shadow of the new (10.1), imperfect (9.7), and obsolete (8.13). On the other hand the New Covenant is superior, κρείττων (7.22), enacted on the basis of superior promises (8.6), faultless (8.7), a new and living way (10.20). Hebrews, in contrast to 2 Cor 3.6–18, speaks of insufficient-provisional and perfect-everlasting covenants.

Christ is the hope of the promise made to Abraham (6.19). He is the eternal High Priest superior to Levi because he is priest by divine oath (7.20–21), according to the order of Melchizedek (7.17), who was superior to both Abraham and Levi (7.1–10). As mediator, high priest, and victim, Christ enters the heavenly sanctuary only once to sacrifice Himself for the destruction of sin (8.1–5; 9.11, 26–28). Thus, the blood of Christ inaugurates the new διαθήκη (9.18–22). Although in Heb 9.16–17 διαθήκη is used juridically in the sense of last will and testament, in 9.15, 20 it has its usual biblical meaning of covenant—in v. 15 of the one sealed by the blood of Christ, in v. 20 of the other sealed by the blood of the Sinaitic sacrifice.

Conclusion. The theology of covenant in the Bible is consistently a theology of divine promise. Whether in a profane or sacred sense, the sacred authors use the conventional *berît* to trace the line of salvation history toward its divinely willed goal. For the NT authors, Christ is not only the culmination of OT covenants, but He also inaugurates the New Covenant that culminates in the apocalyptic heavenly Jerusalem, where the redeemed are God's people, and He is their God (Rv 21.3).

Bibliography: *Encyclopedic Dictionary of the Bible,* tr. and adap. by L. HARTMAN (New York 1963), from A. VAN DEN BORN, *Bijbels Woordenboek* 432–439. V. HAMP and J. SCHMID, *Lexikon für Theologie und Kirche,* ed. J. HOFER and K. RAHNER, 10 v. (2d, new ed. Freiburg 1957–65) 2:770–778. J. HEMPEL and L. GOPPELT, *Die Religion in Geschichte und Gegenwart,* 7 v. (3d ed. Tübingen 1957–65) 1: 1512–18. L. G. DA FONSECA, "Διαθήκη—foedus and testamentum?" *Biblica* 8 (1927) 31–50, 161–181, 290–319, 418–441; 9 (1928) 26–40, 143–160. D. J. MCCARTHY, *Treaty and Covenant* (Analecta orientalia 21; 1963). N. LOHFINK, "Die Bundesurkunde des Königs Josias," *Biblica* 44 (1963) 261–288, 461–498. J. L'HOUR, "L'Alliance de Sichem," *Revue biblique* 69 (1962) 5–36, 161–184, 350–368. G. E. MENDENHALL, "Covenant Forms in Israelite Tradition," *Biblical Archaeologist* 17 (1954) 50–76. E. F. SIEGMAN, "The Blood of the Covenant," *American Ecclesiastical Review* 136 (1957) 167–174.

[A. YONICK]

COVENANT THEOLOGY

Covenant, or federal, or puritan, theology was the dominant Calvinist theology in England and America throughout the 17th century. Its exponents were largely Non-Separatist Congregationalists resourceful enough to find contractual bases for their true Puritan church within the unruptured Church of England framework (*see* PURITANS). The Englishmen W. Ames, W. Perkins, J. Preston, and R. Sibbes at Cambridge elaborated this theology, but its full practical expression occurred only in the Massachusetts Puritan experiment—in the work of T. Shepherd, P. Bulkeley, J. Cotton, T. HOOKER, and the CAMBRIDGE PLATFORM of 1648. Covenant theology is best understood as a complex exfoliation of contracts designed to solve problems endemic to early CALVINISM.

Calvinist Problems. John Calvin's challenging legacy consisted of the doctrines of PREDESTINATION and of a transcendent God whose will lies outside human rational categories, and the ideal of a visible Church militant that would employ civil authority to purge itself gradually of the non-Elect. Covenant theologians epitomize one phase of the late Renaissance transition from feudalism to constitutional monarchy, from fixed status to contract. They had to fit an omnipotent voluntarist God into a universe daily proving more rationally tractable, reconcile irresistible grace with man's natural rights, and develop a church polity blending elements of Old Testament theocracy with contemporary theories of voluntary social origins. In the light of current SOCIAL CONTRACT theory, they reexamined the Biblical covenants of Yahweh with Noah, Abraham, and Moses, later renewed in the person of Christ, and discovered contractual relationships by which God freely imposed rational constitutional limitations on His whirlwind caprice, offered Himself as ready contractual partner to each believer, prescribed moral duties not brutally and irrationally but only with each Christian's reasonable and willing consent. Most viable in Puritan New England, the Israelites' new promised land, covenant theology declined as a meaningful rationale only when the age of common sense scoffed at fervid religious wars and Calvin's legacy, and turned to more immediate politicoeconomic problems for which secular contractual theories of T. HOBBES, J. LOCKE, and J. J. ROUSSEAU offered more pertinent solution.

Exfoliating Contracts. Covenant theologians viewed salvation history as a series of legal landlord-tenant, testator-heir contracts between God and man, freely initiated but perpetually binding. The first covenant of works between Adam and his Creator gave man life on condition that he obey the natural law within him, but Adam's fall broke this covenant and transmitted dread legal penalties to his descendants. A second covenant of works initiated by God on Sinai reaffirmed natural law in the Ten Commandments: God would heal His chosen people's depraved natural powers provided they would trust in a future Messiah. In Christ, the Father opened a covenant of Grace—foreshadowed progressively in conscience, the promise to Abraham, the Prophets, but now revealed to all believing Christians who were baptized and heard the ordinance of the preached Word. Here Puritan theologians proposed divergent liberal or strict Calvinist hypotheses: the Christian sinner as covenant-violator either manifests a predestined total absence of covenant or else reveals man's freedom to accept or reject covenant graces God always extends him. A fourth contract, the church covenant, gave visible realization to this invisible covenant of Grace—the saints covenanting together under Christ their head in separate Congregationalist communities, impatient of Anglican bishops and Presbyterian synods cluttering their direct relationship with God. Finally, there was the civil covenant, which fashioned a temporal state to serve the godly citizens of the churchcovenant.

Bibliography: H. C. BAKER, *The Wars of Truth: Studies in the Decay of Christian Humanism in the Earlier 17th Century* (Cambridge, MA 1952) 162–169, 203–214, 291–302. P. MILLER, "The Marrow of Puritan Divinity," *Errand into the Wilderness* (Cambridge, MA 1956); *The New England Mind: The 17th Century* (Cambridge, MA 1939). V. RULAND, "The Theology of New England Puritanism," *Heythropj* 5 (1964) 165–169.

[V. RULAND]

COVENANTERS

Scottish history in the 16th and 17th centuries presents many instances of covenants, or "bands," binding the signers to common action. The first specifically religious "band" was that signed in December 1557 by the nobles of the Reformation party, the Lords of the Congregation. Another "band," known as "the King's Confession," occasioned by a hysterical antipopery scare, was signed in 1581. The latter covenant was destined to become important in Scottish history because, in the widespread opposition stirred up against Charles I's effort in 1637 to impose a new liturgy on Scotland without the consent of Parliament or General Assembly, one of the leaders of the Presbyterian party proposed the revival of the "band" of 1581, with additions. This document, full of irrelevant but highly inflammatory phrases, was signed by a large number in the Greyfriars Kirkyard in Edinburgh, Feb. 28, 1638.

The document was known as the National Covenant; and its supporters, the Covenanters. Presbyterian elements in the Kirk gained control of the General Assembly held in Glasgow in November 1638, and episcopacy was abolished, despite the opposition of the royalist Duke of Hamilton. The Crown's attempt to suppress the Covenanters failed at Berwick, and Charles I agreed to withdraw the new service book and also to ratify the decision of the Assembly to be held on Aug. 12, 1639. This Assembly confirmed the abolition of episcopacy, and the Parliament, led by Argyll (Aug. 31, 1639), curtailed royal authority in Scotland. The Covenanter leaders decided to invade England in an effort to force the king to accept their demands (1640). They captured Newcastle, and Charles called a parliament that, as the famous Long Parliament, was to be the focal point of the great struggle against his rule in England.

The Covenanters and the English Parliamentarians eventually formed an antiroyalist alliance on the basis of the Solemn League and Covenant, signed on Aug. 17, 1743, which was to safeguard the "reformed religion in the Church of Scotland" and promote "the reformation of religion in the Kingdoms of England and Ireland according to the example of the best reformed churches." It was to the army of the Scots Covenanters that Charles I surrendered in May 1646, and on his refusal to subscribe to the Solemn League and Covenant, he was handed over to the commissioners of the English Parliament. Charles later sought to come to terms with the Covenanters by signing the "Engagement" (Dec. 26, 1647), but the subsequent Scottish intervention was rendered worthless by Cromwell's defeat of the Scottish army at Preston in 1648.

After the execution of Charles I, his less scrupulous son, Charles II, accommodated the Scots Covenanter leaders by accepting the Solemn League and Covenant; this availed him little, however, because the power of the Covenanters was largely destroyed by Cromwell's victory at Dunbar (1650). The ascendancy of the Covenanters was a time of great hardship for the Catholic minority in Scotland; the rigor of the penal laws was tightened and, in 1640, reinforced by complete economic boycott. In Scotland the advent of the Cromwellian regime was welcomed as a merciful release by Catholics. The restoration of King Charles II in 1660 was followed by the revocation of all acts passed since 1640 in favor of PRESBYTERIANISM; the Solemn League and Covenant was abrogated; patronage and episcopacy were restored.

These measures were accepted peacefully by the majority of Scotsmen. Fanatical Covenanters, however, held out in parts of southwest Scotland, and for a quarter of a century there was intermittent rebellion and repression by the government. Even when the Revolution Settlement of 1689 restored Presbyterian government in the national church, some extremists refused to conform on the ground that the covenants of 1638 and 1643 had not been renewed. The successors of this intransigent group still exist as the small Cameronian Church in Scotland to this day (*see* CAMERONIANS).

Bibliography: J. K. HEWISON, *The Covenanters,* 2 v. (Glasgow 1908). D. H. FLEMING, *The Story of the Scottish Covenants* (Edinburgh 1904). A. M. MACKENZIE, *The Passing of the Stewarts* (New York 1937). G. D. HENDERSON, *Religious Life in Seventeenth Century Scotland* (Cambridge, Eng. 1937). F. L. CROSS, *Oxford Dictionary of the Catholic Church,* 350.

[D. MCROBERTS]

COVENTRY AND LICHFIELD, ANCIENT SEE OF

See of Coventry and Lichfield, medieval diocese of England, a suffragan see of CANTERBURY (Latin, *Lichfeldensis*). The Anglo-Saxon Kingdom of Mercia was originally converted to Christianity by CEDD and his companions *c.* 652. When Cedd's brother CHAD was made bishop of the great Mercian diocese *c.* 669, he established his episcopal seat in Lichfield, west-central England (15 miles north-northeast of modern Birmingham). King Offa of Mercia received Pope ADRIAN I's sanction to constitute it an archiepiscopal see, and for a short time (786–803) Lichfield was England's third archdiocese. In 1075, after the Norman Conquest, the bishop's seat in the diocese was removed to CHESTER and then, perhaps because of the hostility of the Welsh, to Coventry (1102), where the monks of Coventry Abbey constituted the CATHEDRAL chapter. However, throughout the Middle Ages Lichfield retained its cathedral chapter of secular canons

as well as an episcopal palace and was the center of administration for the Coventry and Lichfield diocese. Pope GREGORY IX decreed that the two chapters alternate in the election of the bishop. Outstanding bishops included Walter Langton, Richard SCROPE, John CATRIK, and William BOOTH, while the last Catholic bishop was Ralph Bayne (d. 1559). Under King HENRY VIII (1541) the Anglican Diocese of Chester was carved out of the old medieval boundaries of Coventry-Lichfield and Lichfield replaced Coventry as the effective Anglican diocesan see, but in the 19th century it sank to the rank of a lesser diocese. The present Lichfield Cathedral is mainly 13th century. In 1895 the new Anglican Diocese of Coventry was constituted, and in 1918 this see was separated from Lichfield (*see* COVENTRY CATHEDRAL).

Bibliography: BEDE, *Eccl. hist.* 3:28, 4:2–3. THOMAS OF CHESTERFIELD, *Historia de episcopis coventrensibus et lichfeldensibus,* in v.1 of *Anglia sacra* (London 1691) 423–443 (to 1347), ed. H. WHARTON, 444–59 (continuation to 1575), ed. H. WHITLOCK. J. LE NVE, *Fasti Ecclesiae Anglicanae 1300–1541* (1716). Corr. and cont. from 1215 by T. D. HARDY, 3 v. (Oxford 1854); new ed. by H. P. F. KING et al. (London 1962–) v.10. W. DUGDALE, *Monasticon Anglicanum* (London 1655–73); best ed. by J. CALEY et al., 6 v. (1817–30) 6.3: 1238–1266. W. BOLTON, *Statutes of the Cathedral Church of L.* (Stafford 1871). *The Great Register of Lichfield Cathedral . . . ,* ed. H. E. SAVAGE (Kendal 1926). E. GORING, *Lichfield Cathedral* (Worcester 1954). A. J. KETTLE and D. A. JOHNSON, *A History of Lichfield Cathedral* (Stafford 1982). J. MADDISON, ed. *Medieval Archaeology and Architecture at Lichfield* (London 1993). G. DEMIDOWICZ, *Coventry's First Cathedral: The Cathedral and Priory of St. Mary: Papers from the 1993 Anniversary Symposium* (Stamford, Lincolnshire 1994).

[M. J. HAMILTON/EDS.]

COVENTRY CATHEDRAL

Coventry cathedral is the new cathedral of St. Michael, Coventry, England, consecrated on May 25, 1962. Its design by architect Sir Basil Spence was chosen in competition. It is the third cathedral at the same site; the first, built in 1043, was destroyed in 1538; the second, built as a parish church in 1326, became a cathedral in 1918 and was destroyed in the 11-hour Coventry air raid of November 1940. Ruins of the 14th-century church are still preserved as an integral part of the cathedral and contain the famous shrine of reconciliation, centered on the Charred Cross made of two burned beams from the roof of the old cathedral. The ancient church provides a superb parvis for the new; its sightless walls and roofless nave poignantly introduce the boldly stated contemporary building. The difficult juncture between the two has been particularly well handled. The interior of the new church, though too attenuated for current liturgical ideals, provides an impressive sweep that reaches a climax some 290 feet away in Graham Sutherland's wall-filling tapestry of "Christ in Glory," reportedly the largest ever woven in one piece. The nave, elegantly capped by a wood panel ceiling, provides a simple yet stately frame for the tapestry. However, the many elements at the chancel proper tend to be distracting: the spikey "Crown of Thorns" over the choir stalls and bishop's throne, the too-prominent organ pipes, and the disturbing geometric elements in the tapestry itself. The excellent nave illumination is highlighted by a lovely stained glass window by John Piper, bowed about the baptismal font. Other art, much of it superior, can be seen in the Chapel of Unity (the glass for it was appropriately given by Dr. Konrad Adenauer), the Chapel of Christ in Gethsemane, and in the exterior statue of "St. Michael Conquering the Devil" by Sir Jacob Epstein.

Bibliography: H. C. N. WILLIAMS, *The Latter Glory: The Story of Coventry Cathedral* (Manchester, England 1982). L. CAMPBELL, *To Build a Cathedral: Coventry Cathedral 1945–1962* (Warwick 1987). L. CAMPBELL, *Coventry Cathedral: Art and Architecture in Post-war Britain* (New York 1996).

[G. E. KIDDER SMITH/EDS.]

COVERDALE, MILES

Translator of the Bible; b. probably York, 1487 or 1488; d. London, Jan. 20, 1569. He took Holy Orders at Norwich in 1514 and joined the Augustinians at Cambridge, imbibing there the ideas of the prior, R. Barnes, who was tried for heresy in 1526. With T. Cromwell as patron, Coverdale preached against the Mass, auricular confession, and prayer before statues. Such views forced him into seven years' exile on the Continent, and at Antwerp he completed a translation of the Bible into English in 1534–35 with the financial aid of the merchant J. van Meteren. J. Mozley convincingly argues that E. Cervicorn and J. Soter printed this Bible at Cologne, and that Coverdale used five sources, W. Tyndale, M. Luther, the Vulgate, S. Pagninus, and the 1531 Zurich Bible. Coverdale produced at least five editions of the 1535 Bible, helped R. Grafton with the 1529 Great Bible, and translated minor works by D. Erasmus and Luther. From 1543 to 1547, and again as a Marian exile, Coverdale served Lutheran congregations at Bergzabern and elsewhere, returning to England in 1559. His reputation as a celebrated preacher grew during his term as bishop of Exeter (1551–53) and, after the Act of UNIFORMITY (1559) deprived him of a benefice, during his career as an itinerant preacher in London. His PURITAN ideas grew stronger from middle to later life, when he led the Puritan faction.

Bibliography: J. F. MOZLEY, *Coverdale and His Bibles* (London 1953). H. GUPPY, "Miles Coverdale and the English Bible," *The Bulletin of the John Rylands Library* 19 (1935) 300–328. J. and J. A. VENN, eds. *Alumni Cantabrigienses,* 4 v. (Cambridge, Eng.

1922–27) 1:406. H. R. TEDDER, *The Dictionary of National Biography from the Earliest Times to 1900,* 63 v. (London 1885–1900; repr. with corrections, 21 v., 1908–09, 1921–22, 1938; suppl. 1901–) 4:1289–97.

[M. J. HAVRAN]

COVINGTON, DIOCESE OF

Suffragan of the metropolitan See of LOUISVILLE, the diocese of Covington (*Covingtonensis*), Kentucky was established July 29, 1853, by Pius IX. Originally, it contained most of the eastern part of the state, including the sparsely populated mountains. At its inception, the Covington diocese was suffragan to the Archdiocese of Cincinnati; but in December, 1937, when Louisville was created a metropolitan see, Covington was translated to be one of its suffragans. When the Diocese of Lexington was created by Pope John Paul II in 1988, Covington's jurisdiction was reduced to the 14 counties lying largely along the Ohio River.

The first Bishop of Covington was Jesuit George Aloysius Carrell, who was consecrated Nov. 1, 1853, and died Sept. 25, 1868. When he assumed his post, he found within his jurisdiction six priests serving a scattered Catholic populace of 7,000. In all, there existed in the diocese six parishes, five missions, and nine stations. Successor prelates of the see have been: Augustus Maria Toebbe, consecrated 1870, died 1884; Camillus Paul Maes, consecrated 1885, died 1915; Ferdinand Brossart, consecrated 1916; resigned 1923. Francis William Howard, consecrated 1923, died 1944; William Theodore Mulloy, consecrated 1945, died 1959; Richard Henry Ackerman, transferred to Covington 1960, resigned 1978; William A. Hughes, appointed to Covington 1979. When Bishop Huges retired in 1995, he was succeeded in 1996 by Most Reverend Robert W. Muench, formerly auxiliary bishop in New Orleans.

Bishop Maes was largely responsible for the construction of the remarkable Cathedral Basilica of the Assumption, laying the cornerstone of the Gothic masterpiece in September, 1895. It was raised to the rank of a minor basilica by Pius XII in 1953. Covington is also home to Thomas More College, originally founded as Villa Madonna in 1921. In 2000 Covington had some 87,000 Catholics in 47 parishes.

Bibliography: Archives, Diocese of Covington. B. J. WEBB, *The Centenary of Catholicity in Kentucky* (Louisville 1884). P. E. RYAN, *History of the Diocese of Covington, Kentucky* (Covington 1954).

[P. E. RYAN/EDS.]

COWARDICE

Cowardice is a vice opposed to FORTITUDE or courage by way of defect. Fortitude, one of the moral VIRTUES, moderates the passions or emotions of fear and daring, i.e., those emotions concerned with an evil, difficult but possible to overcome. Some theologians argue that there are four vices opposed to fortitude: cowardice (*ignavia, vecordia*), which, taken most strictly, implies a lack of daring; FOOLHARDINESS, or audacity, which is an excess of daring; timidity, which is an excess of fear; and fearlessness, which is the absence of reasonable fear. Others, following St. THOMAS AQUINAS, argue that it is natural for man to have daring with regard to an object harmful to him, unless he is restrained by fear. In other words, a man does not lack daring except through excessive fear. Hence, timidity, or excessive fear, and cowardice, or lack of daring, are not distinct vices, but are two names or aspects of the same vice opposed to fortitude. Even those who hold that they are distinct vices would admit that the terms are often used interchangeably.

The fear involved in timidity or cowardice is not simply the emotion of fear, for the emotions as such are morally indifferent. Rather it is an inordinate fear. In every sinful act some element of fear is present: the miser fears the loss of money, the slothful man fears the effort required for spiritual progress, the envious man fears the good of his neighbor. Timidity or cowardice is concerned with the arduous good, but it shrinks from the effort. Just as fortitude is properly concerned with great dangers, especially the danger of death, so cowardice or timidity, properly speaking, is an excess of fear and a lack of daring with regard to these dangers. Cowardice is sometimes used, however, in a wider sense for excessive fears about lesser matters. To conquer cowardice does not mean the total exclusion of fear, but rather the control of fear so that it does not impede an individual from doing his duty.

Timidity or cowardice as such is venially sinful, but it becomes mortal, or is the cause of mortal sin, if it leads one to transgress the law of God in some serious way.

Since the opportunities for exercising fortitude in the strict sense are limited, one should accustom himself to acting courageously in small matters and thus prepare himself for greater tests in which he might otherwise be overcome by cowardice. Meditation on the greatness of divine gifts, on the Passion of Christ, and on the courageous action of Our Lady and the martyrs is a strong incentive to overcome temptations to cowardice.

Bibliography: THOMAS AQUINAS, *Summa Theologiae,* 2a2ae, 125, 127. F. DE VITORIA, *Comentarios a la Secunda secundae de Santo Tomás,* ed. V. BELTRAN DE HEREDIA, 5 v. (Salamanca 1932–35) 5:377–378. P. LUMBRERAS, *De fortitudine et temperantia* (Rome 1939) 34–37. J. PIEPER, *Fortitude and Temperance,* tr. D. F. COOGAN (New York 1954). R. A. GAUTHIER, "Fortitude," *The Virtues and States of Life,* ed. A. M. HENRY, tr. R. J. OLSEN and G. T. LENNON (Theology Library 4; Chicago 1956) 487–531.

[J. HENNESSEY]

COWL

From the Latin *cucullus* or *cuculla,* in contemporary English usage refers, in most cases, to the traditional monastic hood, which was adopted by the canons regular, friars, and religious of later institutions. In the English Benedictine Congregation, however, cowl historically referred to the large pleated choir robe that is worn by the monks during choral exercises. The other congregations of English-speaking monks called this garment by the Latin name *cuculla.* Both uses of the English word cowl are grounded in a long and complex history of monastic clothing and of the terminology by which it was designated. The *cuculla* referred to in the Rule of St. Benedict was probably a *birrus cuculatus* or hooded work-cloak of a kind worn outdoors especially by laborers in late imperial times. This hooded cloak continued to be used in a world of altered fashions and became the distinguishing characteristic of monastic dress. It took on a sacred significance comparable to that of the veil among the nuns; this significance was preserved by the Benedictines, among whom the cowl and the hood are given at the time of clothing. During the time of the monastic reforms of the 10th and 11th centuries, a large choir gown developed. This piece of clothing, which was often called a *casula,* was known also as a *cuculla* and was the prototype of the cowl or *cuculla* worn by choir monks. But the medieval use of the word *cuculla* was not uniform, and the meanings varied widely from place to place.

[A. DONAHUE/EDS.]

COWLEY FATHERS

A popular name for the Society of St. John the Evangelist (SSJE), the oldest male religious order in the Anglican Church. Its name was derived from the English town of Cowley, near Oxford, where the founder, Father Richard Meaux Benson (1824–1915), had been vicar. It was founded on Dec. 27, 1866 (St. John's Day), when Benson, in company with Father O'Neill and Father Grafton, who came from the U.S., pronounced vows of poverty, chastity, and obedience. With the permission of the bishop of Oxford, the three men had spent the previous year preparing to renew religious community life in England. The society's first foundation in the U.S. was in Boston (Nov. 1, 1870). In 1921 an independent congregation was established in the U.S. In the U.S., the Society has a monastery in Cambridge, Massachusetts, and a retreat center, Emery House, in West Newbury, Massachusetts. Members of the Society, who may be ordained priests or religious brothers, live under a Rule of Life and make the three vows of poverty, chastity and obedience. Principal ministries of the Society include retreats, spiritual direction and book publishing. In the U.S., the Society operates a publishing house, Cowley Publications.

Bibliography: P. F. ANSON, *The Call of the Cloister* (London 1955). A. M. ALLCHIN, *The Silent Rebellion: Anglican Religious Communities 1845–1900* (London 1958). M. V. WOODGATE, *Father Benson, Founder of the Cowley Fathers* (London 1953).

[T. F. CASEY/EDS.]

CRANMER, THOMAS

Archbishop of Canterbury, chief architect of the Book of Common Prayer, and Protestant martyr; b. Aslockton, Nottinghamshire, England, July 2, 1489; d. Oxford, March 21, 1556. His family, of Norman origin, had moved from Lincolnshire 60 years before his birth. His father was the squire of Aslockton. Thomas was educated at Jesus College, Cambridge, where he became a fellow, was ordained (before July 1520, when he was already a university preacher), and proceeded to the B.D. (1521) and D.D. (1526) degrees. His studies had included Erasmus, the Schoolmen, Latin, Greek, and Hebrew. He took no part in the Lutheran controversy at Cambridge but, characteristically, devoted himself to the study of Scripture and the Fathers to learn what they had to say on the matters in dispute. A chance meeting at Waltham, Essex, in 1529, with his old friends Stephen GARDINER and Edward Fox, in which Cranmer suggested forsaking the ecclesiastical courts and referring the matter of the king's divorce to qualified theologians in the universities, led to his rapid promotion. He was sent to Italy to attend the coronation of Charles V and was made ambassador at the emperor's court at Regensburg (1532). In Germany he encountered Lutheranism at first hand. He secretly married Margaret (August 1532), niece of the wife of Andreas OSIANDER, the German Lutheran theologian. He was consecrated archbishop of Canterbury at Westminster, March 30, 1533, Clement VII having issued the necessary bulls and sent the pallium. Before his consecration he made a declaration that he did not intend any oath to the pope to be binding if it was against the laws of God, of the king, or of the realm of England.

"All Christian princes have committed unto them immediately of God the whole cure of all their subjects, as well concerning the administration of God's word for the cure of souls, as concerning the ministration of things

Thomas Cranmer.

political and civil governance. And in both these ministrations they must have sundry ministers under them, to supply that which is appointed to their several offices.'' Thus wrote Cranmer in 1540, and so provided a key to his whole career as archbishop. As papal legate, in 1533 he annulled Catherine's marriage with Henry as contrary to the law of God and therefore invalid, and crowned Anne Boleyn. But in 1535 he pronounced her marriage invalid in turn. He was severe with Anabaptists and rebels, castigating the men of Devon in 1549 with the words, ''Is this the fashion of subjects to speak unto their Prince, 'We will have'?'' When the duty of obedience to the prince clashed with his conscience and the law of God (as he understood it), he withstood Edward VI's council over the spoliation of episcopal revenues and the publication of the ''Black Rubric'' to the 1552 Prayer Book, and finally went to the stake for his beliefs under Queen MARY TUDOR.

Cranmer took a leading part in the production of the ''Bishops Book'' (1537) and the ''King's Book'' (1543). He strongly supported the translation of the Bible into English; he himself translated the Litany (1544) and began the revision of the Breviary Offices. He was chiefly responsible for bringing to England the foreign reformers Martin BUCER, PETER MARTYR VERMIGLI, and Jan LASKI (A LASCO). The 1549 BOOK OF COMMON PRAYER was mainly his work, but there is no authentic record of those who compiled the second Prayer Book (1552). In common with all the English Reformers, Cranmer accepted the Lutheran doctrine of justification by faith, but he was never a Lutheran or a Zwinglian in his doctrine of the Eucharist. In 1538 he still held the official Roman doctrine, but in 1546 he ceased to believe in transubstantiation and was persuaded by Nicholas RIDLEY to embrace the doctrine taught by the monk RATRAMNUS OF CORBIE of Christ's spiritual, real presence, without any destruction of the substance of the bread and wine. At his final examination before James Brooks, Bishop of Gloucester (1554–60), in September 1555, Richard Martin accused him of having "taught in this high sacrament of the altar three contrary doctrines," to which Cranmer replied, "Nay, I taught but two contrary doctrines in the same," viz, transubstantiation and the doctrine that he had taken from Ratramus in 1546 and that was enshrined in his Prayer Book of 1549.

In the course of Cranmer's trial and following his official degradation, he signed a total of six recantations. These did not save him from the stake, and on March 21, he was executed at Oxford. While the fire was being lit, Cranmer denounced his recantations and placed his hand in the fire first to demonstrate his sorrow for having denied his Protestant faith. His dramatic execution was eventually to elevate him to the status of a martyr for English Protestanism, and with the accession of Elizabeth I in 1559 the restoration of his prayer book enshrined his theology as the dominant teaching of the English Church.

Bibliography: Works. *Remains of Thomas Cranmer,* ed. H. J. JENKYNS, 4 v. (Oxford 1833). *The Works of Thomas Cranmer,* ed. J. E. COX, 2 v. (Parker Society *Pub.* 15–16; Cambridge, England 1844–46). Literature. J. RIDLEY, *Thomas Cranmer* (Oxford 1962), bibliog. C. RATCLIFF, "The Liturgical Work of Archbishop Cranmer," *The Journal of Ecclesiastical History* 7 (1956) 189–203. C. W. DUGMORE, *The Mass and the English Reformers* (New York 1958); "The First Ten Years, 1549–59," *The English Prayer Book 1549–1662* (London 1963) 6–30. L. LOEVENBRUCK, *Dictionnaire de théologie catholique,* ed. A. VACANT, 15 v. (Paris 1903–50; Tables générales 1951–) 3.2:2026–31. P. HUGHES, *The Reformation in England,* 3 v. in 1 (5th, rev. ed. New York 1963) v. 1 and 2. L. B. SMITH, *Tudor Prelates and Politics, 1536–1558* (Princeton 1953). F. E. HUTCHINSON, *Cranmer and the English Reformation* (New York 1951). M. SCHMIDT, *Die Religion in Geschichte und Gegenwart,* 7 v. (3d ed. Tübingen 1957–65) 1:1878–79. P. N. BROOKS, *Cranmer in Context* (Minneapolis 1989). M. JOHNSON, ed. *Thomas Cranmer* (1990). D. LOADES *Thomas Cranmer and the English Reformation* (Gwynedd 1991). D. MACULLOCH, *Thomas Cranmer: A Life* (New Haven 1996).

[C. W. DUGMORE]

CRASSET, JEAN

Jesuit spiritual writer; b. Dieppe, France, Jan. 3, 1618; d. Paris, Jan. 4, 1692. He entered the Society of Jesus, Aug. 28, 1638, and first taught the humanities and philosophy but later gained fame as a preacher, especially against Jansenism. From Sept. 9, 1656, to Feb. 10, 1657, he was under an interdict imposed by Bishop d'Elbene of Orléans because in his preaching he had accused certain local churchmen of holding Jansenistic views similar to those condemned by Innocent X. He published retreat manuals adapting the Ignatian method of prayer for use by laymen. He catechized the young and directed groups of the poor, of the working class, and of servants. For 23 years, beginning in 1669, he directed the Congregation des Messieurs, a sodality of men at the Rue de Saint Antoine in Paris. Crasset's best known works are: *Méthode d'oraison avec une nouvelle forme de méditations* (Paris 1672); two retreat manuals, *Le Chrestien en solitude* (1674) and *Le Manne du désert* (1674); several books on death and *Considerations chrestiennes pour tous les jours de l'année* (3 v. Paris 1683); a biography of his spiritual charge, *Vie de Madame Helyot* (Paris 1683), which contains his own ideas on contemplation; *Histoire de l'église du Japon* (Paris 1689), a work largely dependent upon Solier (1627) and inferior to that of Charlevoix; the posthumous *La Foy victorieuse de l'infidélité et du libertinage* (Paris 1693); and *La Veritable devotion envers la sainte Vierge* (Paris 1679), which Antoine Arnauld tried unsuccessfully to have censured in Rome and which J. De Guibert described as one of the best books published by the Jesuits on Marian devotion. Crasset also composed classical religious poetry rich in rhythm and mystical symbolism.

Bibliography: *Bibliothèque de la Compagnie de Jésus* 2:1623–46; 9:146–148. *Histoire littéraire du sentiment réligieux en France depuis la fin des guerres de religion jusqu'à nos jours* 5:311–339; 8:289–309. J. BRUCKER, *Dictionnaire de théologie catholique* 3.2:2032–33. M. OLPHE-GALLIARD *Dictionnaire de spiritualité ascétique et mystique* 2.2:2511–20.

[M. A. FAHEY]

CRATHORN, JOHN

English Dominican; fl. Oxford, *c.* 1340. He lectured on the *Sentences* and on the Bible as a bachelor at Oxford before 1341. Questions raised by him "in prima lectione sua super bibliam" occasioned three responses from his confrere, ROBERT HOLCOT. These became known as *Sex articuli* and were appended to Holcot's commentary on the *Sentences.* Notwithstanding his deferential references to THOMAS AQUINAS, Crathorn frequently endorsed the fundamental views of NOMINALISM. In his *Quaestio de universalibus* (ed. J. Kraus, Münster 1937) he argued against the opinion of Aquinas, DUNS SCOTUS, and WILLIAM OF OCKHAM. He insisted that every reality is in itself singular and incapable of being rendered universal even by the mind. Further, he held that it is impossible for the real nature of anything to be abstracted; thus UNIVERSALS can neither be real nor represent the real nature of anything. The principle of INDIVIDUATION can be neither matter nor form, but is the final reality of a thing in itself. He represents a group of English Dominicans who tried to accommodate authentic THOMISM to nominalism and EMPIRICISM.

Bibliography: A. B. EMDEN, *A Biographical Register of the Scholars of the University of Oxford to A.D. 1500,* 3 v. (Oxford 1957–59) 1:511. P. ROTTA, *Enciclopedia filosofica,* 4 v. (Venice-Rome 1957) 1:1310–11. J. KRAUS, "Die Stellung des Oxforder Dominikanerlehrers Crathorn zu Thomas von Aquin," *Zeitschrift für katholische Theologie* 57 (1933) 66–88. F. PELSTER, *Scholastik* 9 (1934) 140–141, review.

[J. R. O'DONNELL]

CRAWLEY-BOEVEY, MATEO

Known popularly as Father Mateo, modern apostle of the Sacred Heart; b. Tingo, Peru, Nov. 18, 1875; d. Valparaiso, Chile, May 4, 1960. He was born of an English father and a Peruvian mother. In 1884 his parents moved to Valparaiso, where he was educated by priests of the Congregation of the Sacred Hearts (Picpus Fathers), whose novitiate he entered in 1891. He was ordained in 1898. He founded the Catholic University of Valparaiso in 1903. After the favor of a cure at Paray-le-Monial, France on Aug. 24, 1907, he established the crusade of the Enthronement of the Sacred Heart in the home. Upon presenting to St. PIUS X his program for the sanctification of the family through its dedication to the Sacred Heart, he was commanded by the pope to dedicate his life to that work. Faithful to this charge and encouraged by the successors of Pius X, he preached the cause in many places throughout the world, speaking, as circumstances required, in any of five languages. He exercised a great spiritual influence upon the clergy: through the retreats he preached to more than 100,000 priests. A pioneer in the lay apostolate, he preached Catholic Action throughout Italy at the request of PIUS XI. In 1917 he founded the Tarcisians, a society of youthful Enthronement apostles, and in 1927 he initiated a movement to promote night adoration in the home. The best-known of his published conferences are in *Jesus, King of Love* (1st Eng. ed. Fairhaven, Mass. 1933) and *Holy Hour* (Eng. ed. Fairhaven, Mass. 1943).

[F. LARKIN]

CREATED ACTUATION BY UNCREATED ACT

The formula used by M. DE LA TAILLE, SJ, to designate the central conception of his theory of supernatural reality. In the HYPOSTATIC UNION, divine INDWELLING, and BEATIFIC VISION, God is conceived as communicating Himself to created reality, which He immediately actuates and unites with Himself; the term of this self-communication is a created, supernatural actuation of the creatures's OBEDIENTIAL POTENCY by God, the uncreated Act.

Basic Conception. The theory is an effort at theological understanding of the three mysteries mentioned above, with the help of a metaphysics of act and potency. Whereas the notion of efficient causality suffices for the natural relationship of the created with the uncreated, supernatural union can be grasped in its uniqueness only by conceiving that God makes Himself, analogously, the act of a created POTENCY. As ACT communicates itself to, perfects, and actuates potency, so God supernaturally communicates Himself to, perfects, and actuates a created reality. Because of His transcendence, however, He does so without being limited by reception in the potency, so that actuation is not information in the technical sense (some proponents speak, however, of a quasi-formal causality). There is a term of the divine self-communication, the created actuation, distinct both from the uncreated act and from the potency being actuated. This real distinction of act and actuation has only one parallel in the natural order: the act of existence proper to the spiritual soul is the act whereby the body exists, but is not the body's actuation; for in death the latter ceases, while the former does not.

Applications. (1) The principal application is to the hypostatic union. The Son of God, according to His personal divine existence, is the uncreated act communicating Himself to His humanity as to a created potency. The term of this self-communication, the created actuation of the humanity, is identically the hypostatic union in its most formal aspect, the foundation of the real relation of union, the created grace of union (*see* HYPOSTATIC UNION, GRACE OF), the substantial sanctity of Christ as man, and a kind of secondary created EXISTENCE, whose presence, in place of the natural and proper existence had by other men, is the reason why the human nature of Christ belongs personally to the WORD. (2) Application is had also in the divine indwelling. The Triune God (or the Holy Spirit) indwelling is the uncreated act actuating the essence of the soul in the state of GRACE. The created actuation that is the term of this self-communication is sanctifying grace. Some proponents have explained how, according to the theory, sanctifying grace may be the foundation of proper and special relations to each of the Divine Persons. Others have extended the theory to the virtues of FAITH and CHARITY, as created actuations of man's intellect and will, and to the condign MERIT of the just man's good actions. (3) The beatific vision is another application of the theory. The Triune God as uncreated act known without objective medium actuates the human intellect through the LIGHT OF GLORY as created actuation. (4) The theory has been employed (by P. De Letter) to explain the role of the Holy Spirit as soul of the MYSTICAL BODY (see SOUL OF THE CHURCH). The Spirit, as immanent principle of life and unity, actuates men's sociability by giving them Himself as bond of unity. The created actuation that is the term of this self-communication is twofold: communal graces (or *gratiae gratis datae*), including both CHARISMS in the strict sense and graces associated with certain ecclesial functions, and *gratia gratum faciens* (principally sanctifying grace) in its social aspects.

Appraisal and Significance. Most theologians would agree that the theory represents a brilliant and important attempt at theological synthesis. It has been embraced, often in modified form, by some prominent Jesuits (K. Rahner, G. de Broglie, F. Malmberg, J. Alfaro, P. De Letter, F. Bourassa, R. Gleason, M. Donnelly) and other theologians, while meeting considerable opposition, not least from other Thomists. Critics generally feel that the central analogy with act-potency falls before the dilemma: either the created potency limits the divine act or the relationship is reduced to one of efficient causality. Other serious objections have been made (see Mullaney, Lonergan). Proponents maintain, however, that the soul-body relationship in man, which tradition has canonized as the most apt comparison with the mystery of the Incarnation [H. Denzinger, *Enchiridion symbolorum,* ed. A. Schönmetzer (Freiburg 1963) 76], already suggests the possibility of act retaining its transcendence while losing nothing of immediacy in its union with potency; this possibility is strengthened by the infinite transcendence of the divine act, and by the fact that potency is here the image of God, open to the infinite. The theory has been described as a metaphysical counterpart of the rich images (soul-body, glowing coal, etc.) used by the Greek Fathers to describe the mystery of man's divinization in the Incarnation and indwelling. From this point of view M. J. SCHEEBEN may be claimed as patron. Texts of St. Thomas have, unsurprisingly, been adduced both in support of and in opposition to the theory, which is Thomistic at least in maintaining a real distinction between essence and existence, and perhaps also in attributing to the existence of the formal principle of personality, in the line of L. BILLOT and, it is claimed, CAPREOLUS. Its synthetic sweep rather than the details of its analyses make it a major contribution to the theology of man's supernatural union with God.

See Also: HOMOOUSIOS; HYPOSTASIS; INCOMMUNICABILITY; NATURE; PERSON (IN THEOLOGY); SUBSISTENCE (IN CHRISTOLOGY).

Bibliography: M. DE LA TAILLE, *The Hypostatic Union and Created Actuation by Uncreated Act* (West Baden, Ind. 1952), the three basic essays. T. MULLANEY, "The Incarnation: De la Taille vs. Thomistic Tradition," *Thomist* 17 (1954) 1–42. P. DE LETTER, "Created Actuation by the Uncreated Act: Difficulties and Answers," *Theological Studies* 18 (1957) 60–92; "The Soul of the Mystical Body," *Sciences Ecclésiastiques* 14 (1962) 213–234. R. GLEASON, *Grace* (New York 1962). M. J. DONNELLY, "The Inhabitation of the Holy Spirit," *Catholic Theological Society of America. Proceedings* 4 (1949) 39–77. B. J. LONERGAN, *De Verbo Incarnato* (Rome 1964); *De constitutione Christi ontologica et psychologica* (Rome 1964).

[T. E. CLARKE]

CREATION, ARTICLES ON

Under "creation" fall several topics: the origin of the world, the relation between the world as created and God, the end for which the world was created, and the original condition of man. The principal article is CREATION, which treats of creation both in Scripture and in theology. The scriptural account is treated in GENESIS, BOOK OF; ADAM; EVE; and PARADISE. Several articles discuss the relation between Scripture and the scientific theories of the origin of the world: see EVOLUTION; CREATIONISM; MONOGENISM AND POLYGENISM. Philosophy contributes certain key concepts to the theological understanding of creation: see, e.g., MOTION, FIRST CAUSE OF; EFFICIENT CAUSALITY; FINAL CAUSALITY; SOUL, HUMAN, ORIGIN OF; MATTER, PHILOSOPHY OF (see also MATTER, THEOLOGY OF). On the original condition of man, see ORIGINAL JUSTICE; for further articles on this topic as well as on the place of man in creation, see MAN, ARTICLES ON. The end of God in creating is dealt with in GLORY OF GOD (END OF CREATION).

On the creation of spiritual beings other than man, see ANGELOLOGY; ANGELS.

[G. F. LANAVE]

CREATION

The scriptural presentation of creation is treated first in this article, prefaced, however, by some attention to the Near Eastern literary context. There follows a dogmatico-theological consideration of creation.

1. IN THE BIBLE

Israel's concept of creation as it is found in the Bible must be studied in its ancient Near Eastern setting; for it

The creation of the animals, detail of a 13th-century mosaic in the dome of the narthex of the Basilica of St. Mark at Venice, Italy.

borrowed, purified, elevated and added to the creation concepts of the ancient East. Therefore, this section describes the concept of creation outside Israel and the concept of creation in Israel in the preexilic, the exilic, and the postexilic writings of the Old Testament, followed by a brief treatment of the development of the creation concept in the New Testament and a discussion of the iconography of creation.

In the Ancient Near East. The Old Babylonian creation concept as it is found in the *ENUMA ELISH* (J. B. Pritchard, *Ancient Near Eastern Texts Relating to the Old Testament* 60–72) begins with Apsu and Tiamat, male and female deities, begetting other gods. Apsu is slain by his offspring Ea. Tiamat, after an epic battle, is slain by MARDUK, Ea's son, after he has been proclaimed chief god. From her remains Marduk fashions the world. Kingu, Tiamat's counselor, is slain; and from his blood mankind is fashioned.

According to the Egyptian theology of Heliopolis, Atum-Re, after being produced from Nun (waters of chaos), fertilized himself through masturbation and then sputtered out Shu (air) and Tefnut (moisture), putting his vital force, or *ka,* in them. They in turn produced Geb (earth), Nut (sky), and the other gods (*Ancient Near East-*

ern Texts Relating to the Old Testament 3–4, 6–7). The same account says that men came into being from the tears that came forth from the eye of RA (RE). At nearby Memphis the god Ptah was the creator, and all the living beings came into existence from what his heart thought and his tongue commanded (*Ancient Near Eastern Texts Relating to the Old Testament* 5). At Elephantine, near Aswan, it was said that all living beings were fashioned on a potter's wheel by the god Khnum.

In Canaan the god El bore the title of "creator of creatures" and also "father (i.e., creator) of men," and his consort, Asherah, "progenitress of the gods" (*Ancient Near Eastern Texts Relating to the Old Testament* 131–132). In some cases these gods fashioned things from matter; in others they produced them from their own being; but they themselves came from primordial matter. The Israelites were familiar with these and many other stories. J. L. McKenzie (77) says, after discussing the Mesopotamian myth: "Against this background, the Hebrew account of origins can scarcely be anything else but a counterstatement to the myth of creation." But it is a counterstatement clothed in familiar imagery.

In Genesis 1. "Creation account" is the name given to Gn 1.1–2.4a, which literary critics ascribe to the Pen-

Renaissance ceiling paintings of scenes from Genesis, Church of San Biagio, Italy. (©Archivo Iconografico, S.A./CORBIS)

tateuchal PRIESTLY WRITERS. By this story the SALVATION HISTORY of Israel is introduced in solemn and majestic tones, a veritable liturgy of the primordial manifestation of God's saving activity. An examination of its literary structure and an attempt to determine its literary genre in the light of modern discoveries of the ancient past will help one to see how modern exegesis has developed the traditional interpretation of the passage.

Structure. The account is characterized by a very schematic arrangement in which the same formulas, or their general equivalents, are successively repeated. This is particularly true of the HEXAEMERON, or six-day work of creation (Gn 1.3–31), although the seventh-day rest (Gn 2.2b–3) is an equally essential element of the story. The first verse seems to be a kind of title verse. It may have superseded, or even have been originally combined with, Gn 2.4a, a formula type introduction used ten times in Genesis. The introduction to the account (Gn 1.2) is a description of an emptiness that breathes a certain air of expectancy; God's spirit is poised for action. The words of 2.1–2a form a conclusion to the six-day work, but the grand climax is the seventh-day rest.

Eight distinct works are involved in the six-day period, two on the third and two on the sixth day. This may be a sign that a more ancient form of the account has been adapted to the six-day framework in order to express a new idea. There is also a parallelism between the first three days and the last three days. Various sections of the cosmos are first created, then they are adorned with moving objects. The literary elements of the "first day" (1.3–5) can be designated by letters: A—God's word (3a); B—The word creates (3b); C—God's complacency (3c); D—The work described (4); E—Naming, or blessing, E2 (5a); F—Day concluded (5b). The following pattern for the six-day narration then emerges: The text followed here is the Confraternity (CCD) translation, which is from the Hebrew Masoretic Text (MT) with some corrections from the SEPTUAGINT (LXX). The LXX has a tendency to fill out the pattern where elements seem to be lacking in the MT. However, one cannot say a priori that the original pattern must have been perfectly symmetrical (A B D E C F) throughout. Intentional variation of pattern, as well as expansion or alteration of literary formula, for the sake of literary effect or theological emphasis is part of the composer's artistry. The creation of the astral bodies (1.14) has a theological significance. The creation of man is a definite climax that is expressed by means of the deliberative form of command (1.26), by the repetition in poetic meter (1.27), and by the twofold blessing (1.28–30). The final note of divine complacency also is emphasized (1.31a).

Doctrine. The first chapter of Genesis presents certain teachings about God, about man, about the SABBATH, and about SALVATION HISTORY.

God. Genesis ch. 1 presents a somewhat developed idea of God's activity. It was written at a period when the original revelation granted to Israel had developed far beyond the primitive stage, after Israel had had experience of its God for many centuries. Because of the steady stream of prophetic clarification, the development of priestly zeal for the worship, and the deeper understanding of the ways of God through the reliving of the religious heritage of the past, the account conceives God no longer simply as the saving God of Israel, but as the God of all things and all men. Nevertheless, it would be incorrect to understand it as expressing concepts that derive from the perfection of Christian revelation or subsequent theological development. The foundations for such a development may be in the Genesis account, but one must distinguish what is expressly taught from what has been elaborated by later theological thinking. The polemic origins, as well as the main development of the story itself, point unmistakably to the central idea: instead of being the haphazard act of many gods, creation is the purposeful act of one God, the God of Israel. The gods of other peoples have no power over Israel, have no power over the world, because the world does not owe its origin to any act or conflict of theirs. The God of Israel is alone and completely independent in the formation of the world. True, it is but one step further to conclude that He is the only God, but this point is not developed. "In the beginning" implies God's preexistence, but the theological concept of eternity is still lacking.

The process of creation is pictured as drawing order and individual existence out of chaos, but this is not intended to mean that God formed the world out of some preexisting material. Chaos, an indistinguishable watery mass without order, form, or identity, completely undefinable, was an imaginative way of trying to describe nothingness, an abstract concept not yet developed in the

Jacopo della Quercia, "The Creation of Adam," relief sculpture on the doorjamb of the main portal of the Basilica of S. Petronio, Bologna, Italy, created between 1425 and 1438.

Hebrew mind. To personalize and deify nothingness was the pagan's error. It is the creation of the visible world that is being considered. Nothing is said about the spirit world, although its existence may be implied in 1.26. In spite of the anthropomorphic descriptions, God completely transcends this world. It is in no way a part of Him or any emanation from Him. It exists only because He wills it. Even light, often associated with the "glory" of God, is a distinct creation.

Man. The closest thing to God is man, "made in the image and likeness of God," the climax of His creative activity. Some exegetes interpret 1.26 as a picture of God addressing His heavenly court, implying the meaning: "Let us make man to the image of heavenly being." Whether this be correct or not, the divine likeness seems to consist in the fact of man's dominion over God's visible creation. This dominion, of course, requires something in man that is God-like, his powers of mind and will. Thus, as a theological conclusion, it may be correct to say that it is man's soul that is the image of God, but the Hebrew mind did not conceive man as a dichotomy of body and soul. It saw man only as a unified living being. The life that he has and can pass on to others and the dominion that he has over the rest of creation are spe-

The Creation of Adam and Eve, detail of the facade of the cathedral at Orvieto by Lorenzo Maitani, c. 1320.

cial blessings that make him more like God than anything God has made.

Sabbath. The arrangement, evidently artificial, of the picture of creation as six days of work (for eight works) with a seventh-day rest is simply an imaginative way of expressing the fact that the SABBATH observance also is willed by God. The origin of the Sabbath is not known, but it is vindicated in Genesis as the will of God, who has led His chosen people, through their hereditary customs and reasonable practices, to adopt this method of consecrating their lives to Him by regular worship. This is, in fact, the real climax of the story. All things must return to God, who made them. This is done by the Sabbath observance, which sets man apart for God alone. Sanctified by the will of God, it sanctifies man; and through him, all creation. Eschatological inference is not lacking. Man will enter into the joyous rest of the Lord when his work in this world is done. The author gives no conclusion to the 7th day. Finally, the whole of the account is permeat-

ed by the idea of goodness, which is of God. Evil has not yet appeared; but when it does, it will come from man.

Salvation History. The primordial activity of God is presented in the first pages of the Bible as the beginning of God's activity on behalf of His chosen ones. Because of man's sin, chaos threatens to return and destroy God's creation, but the Creator always remains active. His activity is then manifest as a saving activity, and this is recorded in the history of His chosen people, a salvation history that is the whole story of the Bible.

Elsewhere in the Old Testament. Israelite thought on creation naturally owed something to the cultures with which the Israelites were in daily contact, especially in its literary formulation. Their beliefs and teachings on creation, however, far transcended anything found in these other cultures because of the transcendent concept of God and His relation to the cosmos held by the Israelites.

Terminology. It is instructive to study the Hebrew verbs that describe the creative work of God. It is said that God founds (*yāsad*) the world, establishes (*kônēn*-polel of *kûn*) it, builds (*bānâ*), forms (*yāṣar*), and makes ('*āśâ*) His creatures. These verbs are not used exclusively of the activity of God. The verb *qānâ* however, when it means to make rather than to acquire, always has Yahweh as its subject. And the verb *bārā'*, used as a technical term by Deutero-Isaiah, always has as an object a product that is new, wonderful, astonishing; is reserved exclusively for God's works; and never has an accusative of material. Although seldom found in early writings, it is used frequently in exilic and postexilic writings.

Preexilic Writings. The creation story of the YAHWIST (Gn 2.4b–25) does not describe the production of the earth but speaks of the garden (*see* PARADISE) planted by God and then describes the formation of man. G. von Rad points out that here creation is expressly intended to be understood as a prologue and as a start of the divine saving work in Israel. Elsewhere in the preexilic writings Jeremia clearly speaks of Yahweh creating the world: "It was I who made the earth, and man and beast on the face of the earth, by my great power, with my outstretched arm" (Jer 27.5; see also 31.35). And Isaiah further pictures God as the one who fashions history, by bringing to pass His saving plan in history (Is 37.26; 22.11). The "Most High God" of Melchizedek (Gn 14.19; Heb. '*ēl* '*elyôn*), who is "creator of heaven and earth," is reminiscent of the Canaanite god El mentioned above; Abraham identifies Him with the God he worships (v. 22). The preexilic statements on creation are relatively few, but they are clear.

There is no reference to creation in the "cultic credo" of Jos 24.2–15; Dt 6.20–25; 26.5–9; 1 Sm 12.7–11. Von Rad suggests that Israel's first view of SALVATION HISTORY (*HEILSGESCHICHTE*) centered on the Exodus, and that it was not until much later that Israel recognized that saving history began with creation, the first saving event, the beginning of their history. Ps 18(19) and the passages mentioned above show that this connection was made quite early. The *Catechism of the Catholic Church* (CCC) speaks of the revelation of creation and the revelation of the covenant as inseparable: "Creation is revealed as the first step toward this covenant, the first and universal witness to God's all-powerful love" (CCC 288).

Exilic and Postexilic Writings. In the Psalms and in Job, creation is often depicted as a struggle or battle in which God vanquishes chaos, a primordial monster. For instance, in Ps 73(74).12–15 it is said, "Yet, O God, my king from of old, you doer of saving deeds on earth, you stirred up the sea by your might, you smashed the heads of the dragons in the waters. You crushed the heads of Leviathan, and made him food for the dolphins. You released the springs and torrents; you brought dry land out of the primeval waters." Here may be seen an echo of the battle of Marduk against the monster Tiamat in the *Enuma elish.* The monster is also called LEVIATHAN in Jb 3.8, but elsewhere its name is Rahab [Jb 9.13; Is 51.10; Ps 88(89).11]. Because these passages are late, there was no danger of a polytheistic interpretation; the monsters have no more substance than a desert mirage.

In the sapiential books God is sometimes presented as an architect and the builder of the heavens and the earth. He does this through personified Wisdom, as in Prv 8.27–31: "When he established the heavens . . . , then was I beside him as his craftsman . . . ." In Prv 3.19 it is said that "the Lord by wisdom founded the earth, established the heavens by understanding." This is reminiscent of the story of Ptah at Memphis. In Wis 7.22 the author refers to Wisdom as "the artificer of all."

It was Deutero-Isaiah (i.e., the author of Is ch. 40–55), however, who, toward the end of the Babylonian Exile, more fully developed the concept of Yahweh as creator and prepared the way for the profound theology of the Priestly account in Gn 1.1–2.4a. C. Stuhlmueller points out several major contributions to the concept of creation made by this anonymous author. For him, the Hebrew verb *bārā'* becomes a technical term referring only and always to the creative work of Yahweh. With him also the "word of God" is God's instrument of creation: it goes forth with irresistible power to create and to renew. It is personal, responsible, and effective: ". . . so shall my word be that goes forth from my mouth; it shall not return to me void, but shall do my will, achieving the end for which I sent it" (Is 55.11). It is also Deutero-Isaiah who so clearly marks off the "beginning" from the everlasting existence of God: "Who has performed these deeds? He who has called forth the generations since the beginning. I, the Lord, am the first, and with the last I will also be" (41.4). And finally Deutero-Isaiah presents creation as a saving event, an act of salvation, to be consummated by the second creation on the eschatological day of the Lord. Some other striking features of Deutero-Isaiah are the creation of darkness by Yahweh (45.7) and the creation of history effortlessly and irresistibly by Yahweh (41.20). And the power of Yahweh is eloquently contrasted with the powerlessness of idols made by men (40.18–28).

Few modern scholars hold that creation "out of nothing" is taught in the Old Testament. The abstract notion of nothing does not seem to have been reached by the Israelite mind at that time. The somewhat late statement of Wis 11.17 that God "had fashioned the universe from formless matter'' (ἐξ ἀμόρφου ὕλης) does not contradict this. It seems better to conclude that their silence on the subject of material used in creation made possible the later conclusion. Only in 2 Mc 7.28 is creation *ex nihilo* possibly stated, but the expression οὐκ ἐξ ὄντων ἐποίησεν may envision formless matter rather than nothingness as the starting point.

Summary. No generation of gods is found in the Old Testament. Yahweh has always existed and is utterly outside the cosmic process. The complete absence of sexuality in the God of Israel is in striking contrast to the crude creation stories of Egypt, Mesopotamia, and Canaan. Sources for the imagery used by the sacred writer may be found in these literatures, but not sources for his concepts. For Israel the polarity of the sexes belongs to creation alone, not to the Deity; this teaching acts as a strong counter-statement to the Canaanite fertility cult of Baal. There is no real struggle with monsters for Israel's God; they are vanquished or continually kept in subjection without effort. Finally, ''first creation'' is being continued through history and points to the great renewal of ''second creation,'' i.e., cosmic regeneration and REDEMPTION.

In the New Testament. The word used regularly in the New Testament to describe God's creative activity is κτίζω. It is equivalent to the Old Testament *bārā'*. There is a continuity and development of the Old Testament ideas in the New Testament. The world and time, in their totality, were brought into being by God (Rom 1.20; Heb 1.10; Rv 4.11). The LOGOS of Jn 1.1–18 is a profound development of the personified Wisdom of Prv 8.22–30 and the word of God of Is 55.10–11 especially. The linking of creation and redemption as two aspects of the same divine activity is carried forward from Deutero-Isaiah and the Wisdom literature (e.g., in Heb 1.2–3). The new creation of Is 65.17; 66.22 is earnestly yearned for in Rom 8.19–25 and is already here through Christ (cf. 2 Cor 5.17; Eph 2.10, 15).

Iconography. Needless to say, the representation of the work of creation in any medium of art is difficult. How can the artist depict in one picture the production of the cosmos from nothing? The difficulty is compounded by the fact that the Biblical account describes this as taking place in six separate acts, on the six days of creation, and not by any gesture of God but by His word. Yet because of the importance of the subject and its dramatic possibilities, the attempt has often been made, sometimes with considerable success. Since the New Testament depicts Christ as the Word of God and speaks of creation having been accomplished through Him, the Creator is sometimes represented with the Christnimbus. The various works of creation are sometimes represented as suc-cessive scenes, sometimes in a circle around the Deity. Two of the best-known creation scenes are those of Michelangelo in the Sistine Chapel (1508–12) and of Raphael in the Loge of the Vatican (1516–18).

Bibliography: *Encyclopedic Dictionary of the Bible*, tr. and adap. by L. HARTMAN (New York 1963), from A. VAN DEN BORN, *Bijbels Woordenboek* 442–449. H. JUNKER, *Lexikon für Theologie und Kirche*, ed. J. HOFER and K. RAHNER, 10 v. (2d, new ed. Freiburg 1957–65) 9:466–470. P. HEINISCH, *Theology of the Old Testament*, tr. W. G. HEIDT (Collegeville, Minnesota 1950). J. L. MCKENZIEZ, *The Two-Edged Sword* (Milwaukee 1956) 72–89, 90–108. H. FRANKFORT, *Ancient Egyptian Religion* (New York 1948; Torchbooks 1961). G. VON RAD, *Old Testament Theology*, tr. D. M. G. STALKER, (New York 1962–) 1:136–151, 446–453. T. MOUIREN, *The Creation*, tr. S. J. TESTER (New York 1962) 30–56. C. STUHLMUELLER, ''Theology of Creation in Second Isaias,'' *The Catholic Biblical Quarterly* 21 (1959) 429–467. R. W. GLEASON, ''Creation in the Old Testament,'' *Thought* 37 (1962) 527–542. L. LEGRAND, ''La Création, triomphe cosmique de Yahvé,'' *Nouvelle revue théologie* 83 (1961) 449–470. Iconography. L. RÉAU, *Iconographie de l'art chrétien*, 6 v. (Paris 1955–59) 2.1:65–76. F. CEUPPENS, *Quaestiones selectae ex historia primaeva* (3d ed. Rome 1953). H. RENCKENS, *Israel's Concept of the Beginning*, tr. C. NAPIER (New York 1964). C. HAURET, *Beginnings: Genesis and Modern Science*, tr. J. F. MCDONNELL (2d ed. Dubuque 1964). T. SCHWEGLER, *Die biblische Urgeschichte* (2d ed. Munich 1962).

[E. LOVELEY/H. J. SORENSON]

2. THEOLOGY OF

The understanding of creation has had a long and continuous evolution in the history of Christian dogma. Primitive patristic theology did little more than reflect the scriptural point of view: creation is a fundamental point of faith and of a religious world-picture. In the centuries that followed, Christian philosophers and theologians tried to penetrate more deeply the content of that truth. They gave their syntheses, depending on their concern, an apologetical, a philosophical, or a catechetical emphasis. For the truth of creation, standing as it does at the beginning of religious history, illuminates the very nature of God and the purpose of His interventions in time. It clarifies the fact that God is love and that from beginning to end, from creation through Redemption to the completion of all things in Christ, God continues to love all His creatures and the world freely, with abandon, simply because He is what He is. The Church's teaching on creation comprises the following theological truths [Vatican Council I: cap. 1, *De Deo rerum omnium creatore* (H. Denzinger, *Enchiridion symbolorum*, ed. A. Schönmetzer 3001–03, 3021–25)].

Distinct from Creator. It is a fundamental tenet in the Judaeo-Christian tradition that the world is totally distinct from God, its creator. God is not part of the world. He is not just the peak of reality. Between God and the world there is an abyss. What is not God is the work of God. In stating that there is no middle term between ''to create'' and ''to be created'' revelation puts God infinitely above his works.

God is the ''wholly other.'' The Church recalls this when it teaches that God is infinite, unique, simple, immutable; when it says that God is distinct from His creatures in a manner that allows each to keep its own complete proper reality, that which it is at its deepest point. Hence, it is necessary to reject all forms of PANTHEISM, of EMANATIONISM that would attempt to establish a continuity between God and creatures. One must deny all dualism that seeks to introduce a third being between Creator and creatures (*see* MANICHAEISM). One must eliminate preexisting matter. God alone is uncreated. He is absolutely apart, totally different from all reality, which exists only by the active presence of the transcendent God.

This distinction between God and His work—that between infinite and finite or pure act and composed being—is seen as singularly striking if one considers that the divine act of creating is absolutely free. The work of the Creator is in no way indispensable to Him.

Sacred Scripture expresses this distinction also by stressing God's sanctity in the face of man's blemishes and sins, His light in the face of man's darkness. Scripture notes especially the impressive stability of Him who had no beginning and remains the same, while man is changing and fragile. The distinction between Creator and creature leads one to the essential mystery of creation: one is dealing not with the activity of a God who, being of one body with the world, expands or degrades Himself in giving Himself, but with a perfect being who, autonomous with relation to His work as only the infinite can be, in the divine act of creating performs an act of pure liberality.

Produced from Nothing. Material realities and spiritual realities have been and are being produced from nothing by God according to the totality of their being. To be created is to be not of itself but from another. It is to be non-self-sufficient. This means that deep within itself it is in a condition of radical need, of total dependence. This is to be before God ''as though one were not,'' i.e., to stand before Him without autonomy. It means to accept the fact that the world has no reality except what the Creator thinks and wills. This becomes even more striking when one recalls that God had no recourse to previous matter nor to any instrument in creating. The world owes all to Him alone. This is what the expression *creatio ex nihilo* underscores. It is evidently only a way of talking; for ''nothing'' has no existence and never had. One cannot bring forth reality from the absence of reality. All the expression really does is to exclude any creature from escaping its creatural

dependence, and the world from emanating from God in a manner in which some systems of the past have misconstrued God's transcendence.

The created universe owes to God more than its mere existence; it owes to Him all that it is, its nature, its purpose as well as its origin. In God the universe finds its exemplary and final as well as its efficient cause.

The creature, which has its very existence from God, is in a state of total dependence that does not cease. Since it is entirely from Him, it would cease to be if it were in any way withdrawn from His dominion. At every moment God sustains his creature in being, enables it to act, and draws it toward its final end.

Out of Love. The world is the work of an inexpressibly wise and loving Creator, who produced all things by His omnipotence and with an absolutely free will. To believe in creation is to see Someone behind all things. It is to explain things themselves from an inner view—it is to see the world as a gift. One knows the inner life of God from the confidences He made to His chosen people and from the message of the Savior. The doctrine of creation is linked to what revelation tells of the complete spontaneity of the activity of Yahweh. As the election of Israel was completely free, so too is creation.

To create is above all to love. This love in no way depends on its object but rather brings it about completely. To know that God creates man is to know at that point that man does not have to be lovable to be loved. To know man is created is to know that man is loved by a love whose gratuitousness surpasses the most beautiful of human actions. In believing in creation man dares to affirm that all things rest on a ''heart.''

This absolutely initial spontaneity, which is the source of all reality existing outside it, is also what gives purpose to this reality. The universe receives its entire created reality from the solely efficacious intention of God, who has freely willed to communicate and show forth his glory (CCC 293).

This world is not the result of chance, but of God's love. It is not moving aimlessly, but toward God, to be with God, not for the increase of his beatitude but for the bestowal of his goodness on his creatures (*Dei Filius* 1). God is the source of being, the source of supernatural life through the Holy Spirit, and the source of bodily life to the dead through the resurrection (CCC 298). The doctrine of creation, therefore, and that of REDEMPTION mutually illuminate each other in clarifying all that glorifies God and manifests His all-powerful love.

Creation and Redemption. All things subsist ''in the Son,'' but they depend on the three Divine Persons as one sole creative principle. By linking the work of creation to that of SALVATION, the Old Testament prepared the way for the New, which introduced Christ and thus the Blessed Trinity into the total picture of the divine action in this world. Scripture compels one to say that it is essential to the Christian doctrine of creation to face the mystery of the Trinity. Christ is presented as mediator already in creation, and not only in the work of Redemption (*see* GOD (SON)).

The Old Testament tells about the liberality of the Creator of the world; and St. John characterizes Him simply: He is love. From the Old Testament one knows that the author of this world is Someone. But knowing that He is triune, one understands a little better what His personal life is. The Old Testament demonstrates His interest in His work; the INCARNATION and Redemption help one to see more and more the depth of that love.

The New Testament draws its inspiration from the manifestation of the all-powerful benevolence of God in the Person of Jesus. The Christian community understood that the divine self-giving, which is the principle of the inner life of God, is also the principle of the personal engagement of God in the destiny of His work. Thus when St. Paul and St. John speak of Him "in whom all was made," they are not thinking of an intermediary in the gnostic or Neoplatonic sense, but of Him who gathers both extremes in Himself.

The work of creation is common to all three Persons, and Christ is not mediator in it in the same way as in the Incarnation, where the Person of the WORD alone assumes the human nature. Between creation and Redemption there is a distinction, but the two are related. Each makes the other more intelligible. One comes to know better who the Creator is by knowing the Redeemer. One better understands the gratuitousness of the Redemption when he realizes that it has for its object all those things that God in His initial benevolence created out of nothing.

Secondary Causality, Providence, Time. God, the master of the universe, guides and governs all things by His providence. Things are not eternal, but had a beginning in time.

The world, brought about by the active presence of God, is not an inactive world. It was not made complete from the beginning. Along with existence each creature receives from God the ability to act, and it is because of Him that it actually does so. Through their activity beings endowed with the power to know and to love become more and more what they are; they become themselves by collaborating with the work of their Creator. Other creatures, endowed only with a transient activity, act upon each other in a common and immediate dependence on the creative action. The divine causality is not simply a point of departure in a series of causes. God is active at the heart of every action because He is not another created agent, but one who gives to each creature the power to act as well as the nature that is the principle of the action.

The universe, then, receives from God a dynamic structure, an intercausality behind which lies the Creator at every turn. The world constitutes a hierachy of beings that collaborate in an active way with the manifestations of the divine liberality revealed to men in a special way in the Lord Jesus.

The world at every moment of its existence is as much dependent on God as at the moment of its creation. It is constantly being created. The mystery of creation is just as rich in actual reality at the present moment as at the first moment of the world's origin. The essential point in the creature's condition is that it owes its whole reality to the goodness of God. The creature, whose reality is subject to duration, receives from the Creator in a continuing manner.

God not only gives duration to creatures. He intervenes actively in the orientation of the universe. He does not limit Himself only to conserving the universe; He also guides it by His PROVIDENCE. Faith in the active presence of Him on whom the universe radically depends leads one to conceive this universe as guided toward its goal by the One who never ceases to love it first. The universe, therefore, has direction; its path leads only one way. To accept the mystery of creation is to profess this optimistic view: the world, far from being absurd or unintelligible in its future, is good because it is moving toward a definite manifestation of Love. The revelation of the fact of Redemption, which unveils the extent of the creative goodness, teaches that the world is marked by the mystery of Jesus and that the eternal kingship of the Lord is in preparation.

Goodness of God. The purpose of the universe is the glory of God, i.e., the communication of His goodness, which is realized and will be ever more marvelously realized until the end of time through Christ Our Lord.

It is as impossible for man to grasp adequately the activity of God the Creator as it is for man to grasp God Himself. For the creative activity is identified with the Creator. The first result of human creativity is the completion of the human creator himself. God does not, however, complete Himself by acting. With a sovereign autonomy, He is, in fullness. He alone acts solely and directly by His existence, without any preexisting matter, without any instrument, without the intermediacy of faculties. His creative activity alone establishes the contact that is so profound and absolutely immediate between the being of Him who acts and the entire reality of that which receives.

The God who is Father, Son, and Spirit creates through the unity of the divine nature, but a nature that would not be what it is were it not the nature of a Triune God; and the same is true of the creative activity. God could not love His creatures from any other motive or design than those that come from Himself. He would not love His creatures as He does were He not Father, Son, and Spirit. He loves in such a way, in fact, that He brings about an encounter between the uncreated and the created in the ultimate realization of the unity of all things in Jesus the Lord. The divine action of creating will progress toward this definitive completion, this ultimate self-communication. From this fulfillment one might well begin His meditation on the Creator. With a better understanding of Jesus the Lord, one better discovers the dimensions of His kingdom, the final stage of God's glory. It is by contemplating the Lord Jesus at the term of creation as well as at its origin that one has a greater understanding of the liberty, might, and wisdom of Him who first loved it.

Creation and Evolution. The 19th and 20th centuries saw the rise to prominence of evolutionary world views, both physical (Darwin) and intellectual/spiritual (Hegel). Darwin's theory of evolution was generally regarded as challenging the Christian doctrine of creation on two points. First, it proposed an account of creation incompatible with a literal reading of the Book of Genesis. Second, it opposed the idea that God created fixed species, incapable of mutation into other species. The first challenge prompted the Church to articulate anew its understanding of the proper reading of Scripture. The truth given by God in revelation cannot conflict with the truth of things, known in part to scientific reason. Theologians thus began to emphasize the spiritual or theological meaning of Genesis 1, rather than insist on its historical accuracy. The Catholic response to Darwin's second challenge is enshrined in Pius XII's *Humani generis* (see also CCC 366). In terms of matter, man may have antecedents in lower forms of animal life. The human soul, however, cannot be explained in terms of such antecedents—or, indeed, in terms of any purely material cause. John Paul II likewise indicated that Catholic teaching does not object to the idea of evolution, but only to those evolutionary theories that attempt to explain man in material terms alone ("Discourse to the Pontifical Academy of Sciences," Oct. 22, 1996). Faced with the facts of physical evolution, the doctrine of creation proclaims that the ultimate origin of all things is God and that God is the immediate cause of all spiritual reality. The question of the relation between material and spiritual creation became prominent in the late twentieth century, in part through the work of Teilhard de Chardin.

A further challenge to the classical doctrine of creation came from various philosophical and historical theories of intellectual or spiritual evolution, inspired by HEGEL. In such views, evolution is the law not only of the material world but also of all distinctively human aspects of life. Human consciousness, human society, and human knowledge are all evolving. Thus to understand something one asks not what it is or where it came from, but what it is becoming. Catholic theologians did not in general accept such theories; however, they did begin to emphasize the teleological aspect of creation. The doctrine of creation concerns not only the origin of all things that are except God, but also the completion of the creation process. The Christian tradition frequently referred to Christ, the God-man, as the high point of creation. Thus the tradition offered clear warrant for connecting the doctrines of creation and Christology. Some theologians in the late twentieth century postulated a form of the Scotistic doctrine that God would have become man even if man had not sinned, because the Incarnation is necessary for the completion of creation. Others held to the Thomistic approach, and denied the absolute predestination of the Incarnation. But for both groups, the understanding of creation began to center around such Scripture texts as Col. 1:16: "all things were created through him and for him."

See Also: CAUSALITY; CAUSALITY, DIVINE; CONTINGENCY; GLORY OF GOD (END OF CREATION); TEMPORAL VALUES, THEOLOGY OF; TRINITY, HOLY; CREATION, ARTICLES ON; GOD, ARTICLES ON.

Bibliography: J. BRINKTRINE, *Die Lehre von der Schöpfung* (Paderborn 1956). M. FLICK and Z. ALSZEGHY, *Il creatore: L'inizio della salvezza* (2d ed. Florence 1961). R. GUELLUY, *La Création* (Paris 1963). T. L. HANDRICH, *Creation: Facts, Theories, and Faith* (Chicago 1953). H. E. HENGSTENBERG, *Sein und Ursprünglichkeit: Zur philosophischen Grundlegung der Schöpfungslehre* (Munich 1958). A. M. HENRY, ed., *God and His Creation*, tr. C. MILTNER (Chicago 1955). T. MOUIREN, *The Creation*, tr. S. J. TESTER (New York 1962). W. B. MURPHY et al., *God and His Creation* (Dubuque 1958). M. SCHMAUS, *Gott der Schöpfer* (his *Katholische Dogmatik* 2.1; 6th ed. Munich 1962). P. SCHOONENBERG, *God's World in the Making* (Pittsburg 1964). A. G. SERTILLANGES, *L'Idée de création et ses retentissements en philosophie* (Paris 1945). P. BOEHNER, "On the Production of Creatures," *Studia Theologica* Supplement (New York 1948) 3:3174–86. C. VOLLERT, "Creation," *ibid.* 3164–73. R. A. REDLON, "St. Thomas and the Freedom of the Creative Act," *Franciscan Studies* 20 (1960) 1–18. L. SCHEFFCZYK, *Creation and Providence*, tr. R. STRACHAN (London 1970). K. L. SCHMITZ, *The Gift: Creation* (Milwaukee 1982). C. E. GUNTON, *Christ and Creation* (Grand Rapids, Michigan 1992).

[D. J. EHR/EDS.]

Clarence Darrow (left), and William Jennings Bryan, during Scopes "Monkey" Trial, Dayton, Tennessee, 1925. (AP/Wide World Photos)

CREATIONISM

As the term has come to be understood in the United States, creationism is an ideological stance adopted by the fundamentalist movement in opposition to evolutionary theories of life that favors a literal reading of the book of Genesis. Creationists tend to insist on a literal six days of creation, the special creation of each major "kind" (not necessarily each current species) of life, and the direct creation of the first man and woman by God. Many creationists oppose the "day-age" compromise, wherein each "day" in the first chapter of Genesis is taken to mean an indeterminate eon in which God did part of the work of forming the universe and the Earth's species. They attribute many of the geological characteristics of the Earth to the great flood of Noah's time, and possibly to other catastrophes caused by God even when not mentioned in the Bible. Few are so literal-minded, however, as to accept such Biblical ideas as a hard firmament overhead, a flat Earth, or a geocentric universe.

Creationist beliefs have been a part of the fundamentalist reaction that began in the 19th century against liberal religion in general and evolutionary theories in particular. Creationists see the theory of evolution as a challenge to belief in God's creative and providential activity and to the special spiritual status and destiny of the human person. They hold that evolutionary theories are naturalistic, mechanistic, and reductionistic, that they seek to explain everything in terms of natural physical processes, thereby excluding a priori the possibility that supernatural agency might be at work in the world. Creationists view evolutionary theory as a manifestation of secular humanism and of unbelief in general, as an anti-Christian interpretation posing as neutral science, and as a theory that leads to disregard for the sacred character of human life and therefore to such evils as pornography, abortion, and totalitarianism.

In the 1920s in the U.S., creationist efforts produced laws against the teaching of evolution in public schools in several states, leading to the famous confrontation of William Jennings Bryan and Clarence Darrow in the Scopes "monkey trial" in Dayton, Tenn., in 1925. Following this controversy textbook publishers cautiously minimized any discussion of the topic. The result was a miseducation of a generation of students concerning the major organizing theory behind much of modern biology, including zoology, genetics, and paleontology.

When Sputnik's orbiting in 1957 provoked interest in improving science education in the U.S., new biology texts became more explicitly supportive of evolutionary theory, as well as of other ideas which many fundamentalists saw as part of naturalistic humanism. Attempts to oppose this change, in the name of belief in the Bible, were rebuffed on the grounds that religious belief had no place in determining public school curriculum.

Scientific Creationism. In response, Henry Morris, Duane Gish, and others of the Institute of Creation Research (ICR) at Christian Heritage College, San Diego, along with members of other creationist associations, began to develop a Biblical alternative to evolutionary theory, calling it "scientific creationism." A combination of Biblical ideas concerning creation and the great flood with some quasi-scientific theorizing. In certain cases this doctrine includes a micro-evolution of present day species from the basic "kinds" of life forms created originally by God and preserved in Noah's ark. A few creationists propose that there have been additional creations of new kinds or species by God that are not mentioned in the Bible, which do not contradict its teachings and account for the appearance of new kinds of fossils in certain geological strata.

Scientific creationists emphasize real as well as spurious difficulties with evolutionary interpretations of scientific data. They argue that evolution is a theory and not a fact, and that science is tentative and should be open to different theories. They note accurately that the actual processes whereby new species may arise are still in dispute (or in dispute once again) among biologists. They claim that the fossils, geological appearances, and other evidence do not require an evolutionary interpretation and are sometimes contrary to it. Their arguments, however, are often specious in spite of a scientific-sounding complexity, and tend to rest on attacks against some real or imagined weakness in a specific point in biology, paleontology, or other relevant field of science. They fail to review adequately, much less integrate into a coherent alternative explanation, the vast amounts of information and theories from the various fields of science that constitute the rather overwhelming evidence for the conclusion that there has in fact been a process of evolution of life on this planet over the last three and a half billion years or more, even though some aspects of the process are still not clear.

In recent years creationists have demanded that equal time be given in public school classes to scientific creationism wherever evolution was discussed. They have proposed laws to this effect in numerous states, winning in Arkansas and Louisiana. In a widely-reported trial in Arkansas, with leading theologians and representatives

of various Christian and Jewish traditions speaking against the state's law, the federal district judge, William Overton, ruled that scientitic creationism is not science but religion, and that the law requiring its presence in the curriculum was unconstitutional.

Creationists offer a religious justification for their belief, attributing it to their decision to accept the Bible as God's word. Social scientists, on the other hand, searching for the reason that only a minority of Christians are creationists, have advanced different theories, including resentment by creationists against modern science and other cultural influences that have disturbed traditional allegiances and security, as well as a general literal-mindedness among fundamentalists.

Official Catholic reactions to the Darwinian theory of EVOLUTION have been guardedly tolerant, although usually insistent that the human soul is created by God directly and that belief in the inheritance of original sin must be maintained. In the first part of this century the emphasis was on caution, represented by the warning from the Roman Biblical commission in 1910 against demythologizing the early chapters of Genesis, by the resistance of the Holy Office (now the Congregation for the Doctrine of the Faith) to the ideas of TEILHARD DE CHARDIN, and by the insistence of Pius XII in *Humani generis* on the importance of MONOGENISM (belief that all people have descended from one original set of parents). This has given way to an easier acceptance of evolutionary ideas. Catholic theologians now find themselves comfortable working with Teilhardian, Whiteheadian, and other evolutionary schemes to help them interpret Catholic tradition. In all of this, determining the correct relationship between traditional religious doctrines and changeable scientific theories has remained a friction point, although the Catholic practice has been to assume the reasonableness of faith and its compatibility with good science.

See Also: FUNDAMENTALISM.

Bibliography: R. M. FRYE, ed., *Is God a Creationist?* (New York 1983). L. GILKEY, *Creationism on Trial* (New York 1986). D. T. GISH, *Evolution, The Fossils Say No* (San Diego 1979). L. R. GODFREY, *Scientists Confront Creationism* (New York 1983). C. HYERS, *The Meaning of Creation* (Atlanta 1981). H. M. MORRIS, *The Scientific Case for Creation* (San Diego 1977). D. NELKIN, *The Creation Controversy* (New York 1982). P. P. T. PUN, *Evolution, Nature and Scripture in Conflict?* (Grand Rapids 1982).

[M. BARNES/EDS.]

CREATIVE IMAGINATION

In a broad sense the creativity of the IMAGINATION can be described according to its ability to combine and rearrange the different elements of the data gathered from sensory experience; this ability, an everyday phenomenon, has been noted by almost every philosopher. In discussing this function of the imagination, philosophers have tended to focus attention on the tricks that the imagination can play on man and on the danger of confusing the imaginary with the real that this ability poses. In short, speculation concerned with creative imagination in this sense has been chiefly concerned with mental chimeras, such as the illusion and the hallucination.

In a more restricted sense the creativity of the imagination relates to the unique function of the imagination in the production of a work of art, to the expression of the beautiful. Considered under this aspect, the creative imagination is of central importance to a philosophy of art, to a poetics. Philosophical speculation on this topic, although not entirely absent in ancient, medieval, and early modern philosophers, has been chiefly a topic of inquiry by contemporary philosophers.

Interrelation of Man's Powers. At times man is tempted to look on his varied powers and their acts—the imagination and its acts among them—as separate entities, almost as independent realities; and the work of analyzing these powers and distinguishing them one from the other perhaps fosters this temptation. To conceive them in this way is to rob them of their meaning as a living reality, for their nature and activities obey the laws of interiority, perfection, and self-construction, by which LIFE is defined. The acts of powers are not exterior to the powers themselves, and the powers are not exterior to one another or to the PERSON who is their source and end (Thomas Aquinas, *Summa theologiae* 1a, 77.5–7). The diversity of powers and acts within the human soul is not explained by the phenomenon of physical generation, but by a sort of emanation, of flowing from within, that has nothing to do with quantitative juxtaposition (*ibid.* 77.6 ad 3). Moreover, the more perfect powers emanate before the others, and in this procession one power or faculty proceeds from the essence of the soul through the medium or instrumentality of another that emanates beforehand. The more perfect powers, such as the INTELLECT, are the principle, or source, of others, such as the imagination, both as being their end and as being their active or efficacious source. The sensory powers of the soul, among them the imagination, exist for the sake of intelligence inasmuch as they are a "certain defective participation of the intellect" (*ibid.* 77.7). Imagination proceeds or flows from the essence of the soul through the intellect and the CENTRAL SENSE, both of which it serves, while the external senses, which exist to serve the imagination and intellect, proceed from the essence of the soul through the imagination. (*See* FACULTIES OF THE SOUL; SOUL.)

The imagination, in short, is not to be considered as something "outside" the intellect, competing with it, as it were, but rather as a vital instrument of intelligence serving it both in the realm of speculation and in the work of artistic creation.

Maritain's Analysis. It is against this backdrop that Jacques MARITAIN, a representative contemporary Thomist, presents his analysis of creative imagination. For Maritain, poetic intuition begins in the depths of the soul, "at the root of the soul's powers," where intellect, imagination, and external senses unite in the preconscious life of the spirit. According to Maritain, and here he is doubtlessly influenced by H. BERGSON, poetic intuition is born of the unconscious, not the Freudian unconscious of blood and flesh, instincts and complexes, but the spiritual unconscious that precedes rational discourse and conceptual thought. Moreover, poetic intuition has no conceptual expression but finds expression only in the artist's work, "in which the intellect exercises its activity at the single root of the soul's powers and conjointly with them."

In considering the imagination's role in the production of a work of art, Maritain first notes three possible states or existential conditions for the images born of the imagination. First, such images can be part of the "externals of the imagination," i.e., the images of daily life formed by the imagination as a response to sense perception and the needs of conscious daily life. Second, they can be part of what Maritain calls the "automatic or deaf unconscious." Here, cut off from intelligence, they lead a life more or less their own and give rise to dreams, illusions, hallucinations, etc. Third, they can be part of the "preconscious life of the intellect." Here, illumined by the intellect, they are used either in the genesis of concepts or by poetic intuition. In the production of works of art, images from the "preconceptual imagination" are used to make known and express what is totally singular and conceptually inexpressible. Such images Maritain terms "immediately illuminating images," illuminating because they are bathed in the light of intelligence and by poetic intuition. In this work, images are not compared with each other, but one thing that was unknown—contained only in the obscurity of an emotive intuition—is discovered and expressed through another already known. The ineffable, unique intuition of the poet is the reality that was previously unknown; and the poet, seizing an image already known but now elevated and transformed through the common activity of emotive intuition and the illuminating intellect, seeks to express what he has experienced through this transfigured image.

The use of images in creating works of art, thus, is no mechanical play. It is rather an act of transfiguring images present to the preconscious life of the intellect in order to express concretely what the artist has experienced in the depths of his being.

The creative work of the imagination has also been the subject of inquiry for philosophers such as B. CROCE, G. SANTAYANA, and J. P. Sartre. Maritain's position was chosen to illustrate the theme both because it is most consistent with a realistic philosophy wherein the paramount work of the intellect is recognized and because it reflects concretely how a philosopher in the tradition of THOMISM can bring to fruition the powerful insights of a Bergson, whose comments on the preconscious life of the spirit evidently contribute much to Maritain's own position.

See Also: ART (PHILOSOPHY); AESTHETICS; BEAUTY; POETICS (ARISTOTELIAN).

Bibliography: T. GILBY, *The Poetic Experience* (New York 1934). E. H. GILSON, *The Arts of the Beautiful* (New York 1965). J. MARITAIN, *Creative Intuition in Art and Poetry* (Bollingen Ser 35; New York 1953).

[W. E. MAY]

CREATOR ALME SIDERUM

An office hymn of five strophes in iambic dimeter traditionally sung at Vespers during Advent. It was extensively revised in the Roman Breviary of 1632 from an earlier—perhaps 7th-century—Ambrosian hymn, *Conditor alme siderum.* According to Britt (175), only one line was unaltered and 12 words left unchanged. The revisions resulted in a distortion of music, sense, and main idea, in the opinion of Connelly (51). The theme of this Advent hymn is Christ, who came in the flesh and in weakness in the past (lines 5–12) and whose coming now makes men tremble at His name (lines 13–16); in answer to prayer He will defend man from the enemy when, at the end of the world, He comes as Judge.

Bibliography: H. A. DANIEL, *Thesaurus hymnologicus,* 5 v. (Halle-Leipzig 1841–56) 1:74, text. *Analecta hymnica* 51:46. A. S. WALPOLE, ed., *Early Latin Hymns* (Cambridge, Eng. 1922) 299–302. M. BRITT, ed., *The Hymns of the Breviary and Missal* (new ed. New York 1948) 75. J. CONNELLY, *Hymns of the Roman Liturgy* (Westminster, MD 1957) 51, Eng. tr.

[M. M. BEYENKA]

CREED

The Latin *credo* ("I believe"), a compound of the Latin words *cor/cordis* ("heart") and *do/dere* ("put, place"), implies putting one's trust in someone or something. It is a profession of belief, an expression of faith and commitment, on the part of an individual (*credo*) or a group (*credimus*). In Christian tradition, the common declaration of beliefs on the part of the community became a password, a symbol (*symbolum* from the Greek *symballein*) whereby members recognized one another as belonging to the Church. A part of the baptismal rite whereby individuals were initiated into the Church was for the neophyte to declare publicly that he/she subscribed to the community's declaration of faith. The earliest form of the creed was a series of questions (interrogatory creed) that focused on the Holy TRINITY. This soon developed, for catechetical purposes, into a formal declaration (declaratory creed) that summarized the Church's belief in the saving work of the Father, Son, and Spirit. By the second century A.D., the declaratory creed was regarded as a "rule of faith" (*regula fidei*), a norm of fidelity to the teachings of the New Testament and apostolic Church.

Although they differed in wording and emphasis from place to place, the baptismal creeds were very similar in their Trinitarian structure and brevity. As controversies arose about points of doctrine, notably from the fourth century onwards, the formulas that had their origins in the liturgy began to be used more and more as tests of orthodoxy. Phrases were added and the wording was changed to define better the Church's faith and to safeguard the integrity of the traditional faith. The story of the development of Christian creeds from the primitive professions of faith made in apostolic preaching in the New Testament to the formalized declarations of Church councils and synodal statements is long and complicated. In the twentieth century the story took on new twists as the ecumenical movement sought a creedal formula that all Christians could profess as an expression of their common faith.

Baptismal Creed

The requirements of preaching, teaching, defending, and defining Christian doctrine dictated the gradual formulation of a series of statements embodying the basic beliefs of the Church. In the New Testament and the primitive Church documents, however, no creedal statement as such exists; but there is abundant evidence of certain basic truths that formed part of the apostolic preaching of KERYGMA. Beginning with the proclamation of a living God, the Apostles preached the birth, death, and Resurrection of Jesus Christ as the Son of God, and the coming of the Holy Spirit. The Epistle to the Hebrews urges its readers to "hold fast at whatever cost to Jesus, the pontiff of our confession" (3.1; 4.14) and, "in the fullness of faith . . . washed in the pure water, to the indefectible confession of our hope" (10.23). The Epistle of Jude recalls the "faith once delivered to the saints"

(3). St. Paul exhorts his hearers to "hold fast to the traditions which you have been taught" (2 Thes. 2.15) and insists on the "pattern of doctrine" (Rom. 6.17). He calls upon the Christian "to be established in the faith as you have been taught it" (Col. 2.7) and speaks of "one faith, one Lord, one baptism" (Eph. 4.5). All through the Gospels there are formulas of belief relative to God and His providence, to Christology and salvation, to the Trinity and other basic Christian teachings that reveal a pattern of belief but there is no established creed.

Several passages in Acts imply that a declaration of belief was required at Baptism. Thus before Philip baptized the Ethiopian eunuch, the latter declared: "I believe that Jesus Christ is the Son of God" in answer to the Apostle's question (8.36–38). After listening to Paul's preaching, Lydia was baptized on her declaration: "You judged me to believe in the Lord" (16.14–15). St. Paul's statement, "If you confess Jesus as the Lord with your mouth, and in your heart believe that God has raised him from the dead" (Rom. 10.9) is probably a fragment of a baptismal confession; and so is "In Whom, having believed, you were sealed with the Holy Spirit of promise" (Eph. 1.13).

In the 2d century JUSTIN MARTYR described the rite of Baptism, stating that those who received instruction and promised to live accordingly were admonished to fast and pray to God for forgiveness of past sins. They were then given a lustral washing in water in the name of the Father, the Lord of the universe; and of the Savior Jesus Christ, who was crucified under Pontius Pilate; and in the name of the Holy Spirit, who through the prophets announced beforehand things relating to Jesus (Rv. 1.61). TERTULLIAN (c. 195) testified to the threefold question used in the ceremony of Baptism: "Then we are three times immersed, making a somewhat fuller reply than the Lord laid down [Mt. 28.19] in his gospel" (Coron. 3); "For we are baptized not once but thrice into the three persons severally, in answer to their several names" (Adv. Prax. 26). Later he stated that the "soul is bound not by the washing, but by the candidate's answer" (Resur. 48).

Finally, the Apostolic Tradition of HIPPOLYTUS OF ROME (c. 217) described the baptismal process as including an interrogation that is very close to the Roman Creed. According to this document, the candidate goes down into the water, and the one baptizing lays his hand on him and asks:

Do you believe in God the Father Almighty?

Do you believe in Jesus Christ, the Son of God, born by the Holy Spirit of the Virgin Mary, who was crucified under Pontius Pilate and died [and was buried], and rose on the third day, alive from the dead, and ascended into heaven and sat down on the right hand of the Father, who will come to judge the living and the dead?

Do you believe in the Holy Spirit, and the holy Church, and the resurrection of the flesh?

And he who is being baptized shall say, "I believe." [Chapter 21]

ORIGEN in his Commentary (32.16) on the Gospel of John spoke of the "articles of faith, that in being believed, save the man who believes them"; and specified, "that there is one God, Who created and framed all things. . . . We must also believe that Jesus Christ is Lord; and all the true teaching concerning both His godhead and His manhood. And we must believe in the Holy Spirit; and that having freewill, we are punished for our misdeeds and rewarded for our good deeds." He makes similar summaries in his Contra Celsum (1.7); in his De principiis (1, praef.); and in his commentaries (in Ierem. hom. 5.13; in I Cor. hom. 4).

FIRMILLIAN OF CAESAREA in correspondence with Cyprian of Carthage spoke of an ecclesiastical rule of Baptism, and a "customary and established interrogation" (Cyprian, Epist. 75.10–11). Cyprian likewise gave an indication of the content of this interrogation and mentioned God the Father, Jesus Christ His son, and the Holy Spirit, as well as: "Do you believe in the remission of sins and everlasting life through the holy Church?" (Epist. 69.7). By the middle of the 3d century a formula of faith with minor variations had developed in all the main Churches, based upon the Trinitarian formula prescribed by Christ for Baptism (Mt. 28.19). Yet in all the available evidence, there is no indication of a declaratory creed connected with the baptismal ceremony.

Declaratory Creeds

Before the Council of Nicaea (325) EUSEBIUS OF CAESAREA said: "As we have received from the bishops before us, both in our catechetical training, and when we received the baptismal bath . . . so we now believe and bring our faith forward to you" (Eusebius, Letter to his Church, Patrologia Graeca, ed. J. P. Migne, 20:1535). IRENAEUS of Lyons (c. 200) referred to the "rule of faith . . . received through Baptism" (Adversus haereses 1.9.4); and in his Epideixis, or Proof of the Apostolic Preaching, he supplied examples of the catechetical summaries given by way of instruction in preparation for Baptism (chapters 6, 7, 100). These summaries expounded the three aspects of the Divine Being in whose triune name the Baptism was to be accomplished and they were evidently based on the baptismal interrogations.

Earlier still IGNATIUS OF ANTIOCH (c. 116) made quasi-creedal statements based on the primitive kerygma that gave evidence of the development of Christological doctrine in an anti-Doceticsense:

> Being fully persuaded as regards our Lord, that He was truly of David's stock after the flesh, Son of God by the Divine power and will, begotten truly of the Virgin, baptized by John that He might fulfil all righteousness, truly nailed in the flesh on our behalf under Pontius Pilate, and Herod the tetrarch, . . . that through His resurrection He might set up an ensign . . . in one body of His Church. [*Smyrn.* 1.1–2]

POLYCARP OF SMYRNA likewise presents a statement of doctrine built on phrases from 1 Pt. (1.21; 3.22; 4.5), which appears to have been a fragment of the teaching given to converts in the Smyrnaean Church (*Epist. ad Phil.* 2). Justin Martyr in both his *Apology* and *Dialogue with Trypho* echoed many quasi-creedal statements based on the apostolic kerygma that had a relationship to both the Trinitarian and Christological formulas used in preparation of candidates for Baptism. It thus seems apparent that, along with the baptismal interrogations, formulas of faith were gradually educed that were commented on in the catechetical instruction of converts and gradually built into a more or less fixed creedal statement.

Ancient Roman Creed. RUFINUS OF AQUILEIA in his *Commentary on the Apostles' Creed* (404) described the legendary origin of the creed of Aquileia, which he quoted as differing in only a word or two from the Roman Creed. He said that the Apostles, on the point of separating, first settled on an agreed norm for their preaching. They met together and, filled with the Holy Spirit, compiled a brief token (*symbolon*) of their future preaching, each making the contribution he thought fit, and decreed that it should be the standard teaching for believers (2; *Patrologia Latina*, ed. J. P. Migne, 21:337). The story reflected a tradition witnessed by the *Explanatio symboli ad initiandos* probably of St. Ambrose (*Patrologia Latina* 17:1193–96), and the 4th-century *Apostolic Constitutions* (6.14); it arose apparently in connection with the earlier conviction concerning the "rule of faith" that Justin Martyr, Irenaeus (*Adversus haereses* 1.10.1), and Tertullian (*Apol.* 47) claimed to have been handed down by the Apostles.

While there is no evidence to support the apostolic origin of the Roman Creed, there are indications that at the beginning of the 3d century a thorough reorganization of the catechetical system was in progress; and the *Apostolic Tradition* of Hippolytus contains evidence of the fact that at Rome a declaratory creed took shape that was handed over (*traditio*) to the catechumens by the bishop in the course of their instruction and given back (*redditio*) by the candidates as part of the immediate preparation for Baptism. The DISCIPLINE of the secret required that this creedal statement be memorized, and not betrayed to the uninitiated, since it contained the central mysteries of Christianity that had to be treated with great circumspection. There is evidence that indicates that the Roman Creed may have taken shape first in Greek before the pontificate of Pope Victor (189 to 199), for Greek was still current in Rome at the time, and the antiheretical bias of the creed seems directed against ADOPTIONISM, MONARCHIANISM, and DOCETISM, which were then bothering the Roman Church. As reported by Rufinus, the Roman Creed stated:

> I believe in God the Father Almighty; And in Christ Jesus His only Son, our Lord, Who was born from the Holy Spirit and the Virgin Mary, Who under Pontius Pilate was crucified, and buried; on the third day rose again from the dead, ascended to heaven, sits on the right hand of the Father, whence he will come to judge the living and the dead; and in the Holy Spirit, the holy Church, the remission of sins, the resurrection of the flesh.

The similarity between this creed and the interrogatory creed (quoted above) from the *Apostolic Tradition* of Hippolytus is striking, despite a number of significant differences. Further evidence for the Roman Creed is furnished by Tertullian (*De praescrip.* 36), who expressly alludes to the teaching that the Roman Church shared (*contesserarit*) with the African Churches. A substantially similar Greek text of the creed was submitted by MARCELLUS OF ANCYRA in Cappadocia to Pope JULIUS I at a synod in Rome in 340.

It would seem that the crystallization of the Roman Creed began toward the close of the 2d century and that several versions of the creed in both Latin and Greek were in circulation and that a standard version was achieved sometime during the 4th century, for Rufinus reports that at the recitation of the creed in the baptismal ceremony in Rome, the faithful listened carefully so that not a word would be changed (*Comm. in Symb.* 3). He testifies likewise that the same creed was in use in Jerusalem (*Apol. ad. Anast.* 8) and that "in other places, certain phrases are added to exclude the ideas of new doctrines because of heretics" (*Comm. in Symb.* 3).

Symbolon. The Greek word *symbolon* and its Latin transcription, *symbolum,* usually meant a seal or a signet ring or a legal bond or warrant. Thus Tertullian challenged MARCION, asking by what warrant (*symbolum*) of authority he took the Apostle Paul on board his vessel (*Adv. Marc.* 5.1). In the East, the customary description of the creed was the faith (*pistis*), or teaching (*mathema*). Cyprian of Carthage speaks of "baptizing with the symbol" (*Epist.* 69.7), by which he evidently means the creedal interrogation; and Firmilian of Caesarea mentions the *symbolum Trinitatis* in connection with Baptism (Cyprian, *Epist.* 75.10–11). Arnobius refers to the spoken symbols by which initiates in the rites of Eleusis recognized each other. Hence by the 4th century the word symbol was used in the sense of a creed; and the Council of Arles (314) directs that a heretic wishing to rejoin the Church should be interrogated regarding the symbol (*interrogent eum symbolum*); "if he does not answer with this Trinity [*non responderit hanc trinitatem*] he should be baptized" (J. D. Mansi, *Sacrorum Conciliorum nova et amplissima collectio* 2:472). Likewise the Council of Laodicea (353 or 380) used the expression "learn the symbols of the faith" (*Sacrorum Conciliorum nova et amplissima collectio* 2:563). Gradually in both East and West the word became synonymous with creed.

In explaining the origin of the word, Rufinus said it could mean either *collatio,* a whole made up of parts, and here he was following the erroneous legend and bad philology; or *indicium* or *signum,* a token or sign. In this sense he compared it to the password used by soldiers in battle to distinguish friend from foe (*Comm. in Symb.* 2). Augustine traced its meaning to the pacts or agreements made between businessmen (*Serm.* 212). Some modern authors believe that it signified a pact or contract between the person baptized and God. But the basic idea of a sign of belief in the triune God, in whose name Baptism was being enacted and with whom the Christian was being united, seems to have preserved the integrity of the word's original meaning and its connection with the primitive structure of the baptismal rite.

Eastern Creeds. No Eastern Church had an influence on the formation of creedal statements comparable to that of Rome. Eusebius of Caesarea gave evidence of the creed of his Church and indicated its longevity (*Patrologia Graeca* 20:1537). In 348 CYRIL OF JERUSALEM delivered a series of catechetical lectures explaining the articles of the creed (*Catech.* 7–18); and in 431 John CASSIAN wrote a treatise against NESTORIUS in which he quoted the creed of Antioch. The same creed is evident also in the Acts of the Council of EPHESUS (*Sacrorum Conciliorum nova et amplissima collectio* 4:1009). The Syrian version of the *Apostolic Constitutions* (end of 4th century) gave an account of the baptismal ritual, including a long creedal statement. The creed commented on by THEODORE OF MOPSUESTIA in his *Catechetical Lectures* betrayed a Syro-Palestine origin. Alexander of Alexandria echoed an Egyptian creed in his letter to Alexander of Constantinople (Theodoret, *Ecclesiastical History* 1.4.46, 53, 54); and there was another Egyptian creed connected with the so-called *Apophthegmata Macarii* (Kattenbusch, 2:242). While reflecting the basic articles of the Roman Creed, all these statements of faith manifested variations that pointed to independent but parallel development in the articulation of the statement of the faith. What is peculiar is that they did not manifest any considerable influence on the part of the Nicene Creed.

Conciliar Creeds

With the Council of NICAEA (325) the custom was established of ecclesiastics meeting in solemn conclave to frame formularies that were not merely epitomes of belief, but tests of orthodoxy for Christians in general. However, the change was not abrupt, for earlier creedal statements had been used as a challenge to the integrity of faith. But at Nicaea, while the basic structure of the baptismal creed was preserved, its articles were elaborated with the intention of excluding heretical interpretation and buttressed with anathemas or condemnations of whoever would not accept them in their literal signification.

Nicene Creed. Early in 325 a council had been held at Antioch in which the bishops of Palestine, Arabia, Phoenicia, Coele-Syria, and Cappadocia met to elect a metropolitan for the See of Antioch; but they used the occasion to publish a full statement of their faith in opposition to Arian teaching (Opitz, *Urkunden* 18). A few months later the Council of Nicaea opened (probably, June 19), having been called and presided over by the Emperor CONSTANTINE I.

Although the acts of the council have not been preserved, a glimpse of the proceedings is possible through a fragmentary reminiscence of EUSTATHIUS OF ANTIOCH, who possibly presided over the theological deliberations (Theodoret, *Ecclesiastical History* 1.8.1–5); recollections of ATHANASIUS of Alexandria (*De decret. Nic. syn.* chapters 19 and 20; *Patrologia Graeca* 25:448–52; 26:1036–40); and the letter of Eusebius of Caesarea to his Church (*Patrologia Graeca* 20:1535–44; Opitz, *Urkunden* 22). Eustathius stated that the Arians made the first attempt to formulate a creed and failed. Athanasius maintained that it was only after a vain effort had been made to use strictly scriptural terms in formulating the creed that recourse was had to clauses such as "from the substance of the Father" and "of one substance with the Father" (homoousios). Eusebius provided both a creed and a brief explanation of its clauses that he implied was a new formulation to which had been added the word homoousios (consubstantial). The text of the Nicene Creed that he produced was confirmed by Athanasius (*Epist. ad. Iov. imp.* 3), Socrates (*Ecclesiastical History* 1.8.29), and Basil of Caesarea (*Epist.* 125.2); it was also incorporated into the acts of the Councils of Ephesus (431) and CHALCEDON in 451 (*Acta conciliorum oeumenicorum* 2.1.2:79):

> We believe in one God, the Father almighty, maker of all things visible and invisible; and in

one Lord Jesus Christ, the Son of God, begotten from the Father, only-begotten, that is, from the substance of the Father, God from God, light from light, true God from true God, begotten not made, of one substance with the Father, through Whom all things came into being, things in heaven and things on earth, Who because of us men and because of our salvation, came down and became incarnate, becoming man, suffered and rose again on the third day, ascended into heaven, and will come to judge the living and the dead; And in the Holy Spirit.

But as for those who say, there was when He was not, and, before being born He was not, and that He came into existence out of nothing, or, who assert that the Son of God is of a different hypostasis or substance, or is created, or is subject to alteration or change—these the Catholic Church anathematizes.

Much confusion surrounds the harmonizing of the three sources of evidence. What seems most probable, however, is that Eusebius was not claiming that his creed of Caesarea is the Nicene Creed, but that he had read his creed at the council to clear himself of the charge of heresy. After that a committee of bishops worked out the new formula, which he said he scrutinized most carefully before accepting. St. Basil seems to have lent credence to this solution in his claim that a priest named Hermogenes, later bishop of Caesarea, was the leading spirit in composing the new creed (*Epist.* 81; 244.9; 263.3).

Homoousios. In the several phrases of the creed of Nicaea relating to the Son as "begotten of the Father" it was made unmistakable that the Son shared the divine essence to the full. That he was "true God of true God" was an answer to Arian misuse of Jn. 17.3. In insisting on Christ's divinity, the phrase "there was not when he was not" had been used by Origen (*De princip.* 4.4.1) and Dionysius of Rome (Athanasius, *De decret. Nic. syn.* 26). The word HOMOOUSIOS (consubstantial) met with much opposition because of the innumerable meanings given to *ousia,* or substance, in the current philosophies. The Arians sincerely understood it in a material sense. At the Council of Antioch in 268 Paul of Samosata's use of homoousios had been condemned; and it had been viewed with suspicion by Dionysius of Alexandria and the Origen tradition generally. The Meletians, Constantine, Hosius of Córdoba, and Eusebius of Nicomedia are each credited with having introduced the word. But whatever the true solution of the historical problem as to its origin at the council is, it is certain that it was accepted at the urging of the emperor and understood in various senses by the different factions, although the Western bishops, as well as Eustathius of Antioch and Marcellus of Ancyra, accepted it as giving expression to the identity of substance between Father and Son.

In the East the Nicene Creed was not fully reflected in the creeds of which we have texts that were used in catechetical instruction; nor did it greatly affect the series of synods or councils between Antioch (Dedication Council) in 341, Sardica in 342 or 343, and the first synod at Sirmium (351). However, at the second and third synods at Sirmium (357 and 359), Rimini (359), and Constantinople (360), the Homoean position triumphed and St. Jerome wrote: "the whole world groaned and wondered to find itself Arian" (*Dial. cum Lucif.* 19). The Nicene Creed was unknown in the West until HILARY OF POITIERS (*c.* 356), who confessed that he had not heard of it until leaving for exile.

The Constantinopolitan Creed. While not based directly on the creed of Nicaea, the doctrinal statement credited to the Council of CONSTANTINOPLE I (381) was a restatement of the faith of Nicaea, with its style emended by liturgical usage and its content adapted to the theological requirement of the council of 381. It probably reflected the "fuller statement of the faith" referred to in the synodal letter issued by the Synod of Constantinople assembled in 382 (Theodoret, *Ecclesiastical History* 5.13). Great obscurity surrounds its history, however. In the records of the council of 381 there is no direct reference to this creed, and when it was introduced by the imperial commissioners at Chalcedon in 451, it seems evident that the majority of fathers present had not heard of it before. Besides, a text very close to this creed was discovered in the *Ancoratus* (ch. 118) of Epiphanius of Salamis, certainly written in 374. This led modern scholars to claim that the creed of Constantinople was actually a reworking of a Palestinian creed; but, recently, the authenticity of the passage in Epiphanius has been challenged; and it is suggested that the original Epiphanian text actually contained the creed of Nicaea.

Origin and Text. The true solution as to the origin of the Creed of Constantinople seems to lie in the evidence of THEODORE OF MOPSUESTIA, who claimed that the so-called 150 fathers at Constantinople had merely endorsed the Nicene faith; they inserted "from the Holy Spirit and the Virgin Mary" to protect the doctrine concerning the divinity of the Third Person of the Trinity. This seems to have been the meaning of the Definition of Chalcedon when it decreed "that the creed of the 318 holy fathers [at Nicaea] should reman inviolate; and because of those who contend against the Holy Spirit, it ratifies the teaching subsequently set forth by the 150 holy fathers assembled in the royal city [Constantinople, 381] concerning the essence of the Spirit, not as adducing anything left lacking by their predecessors, but making distinct by Scriptural testimonies their conception concerning the Holy Spirit . . ." (*Acta conciliorum oecumenicorum* 2.1.2:128–29).

The text of the Creed of Constantinople was read in the fifth and sixth sessions of Chalcedon (October 22 and 25):

> We believe in one God, the Father almighty, maker of heaven and earth, of all things visible and invisible; and in one Lord Jesus Christ, the only begotten Son of God, begotten from the Father before all ages, light from light, true God from true God, begotten not made, of one substance with the Father, through Whom all things came into existence; Who because of our salvation came down from heaven, and was incarnate from the Holy Spirit and the Virgin Mary and became man, and was crucified for us under Pontius Pilate, and suffered and was buried, and rose again on the third day according to the Scriptures, and ascended to heaven, and sits on the right hand of the Father, and will come again with glory to judge living and dead, of Whose kingdom there will be no end; and in the Holy Spirit, the Lord and life-giver, Who proceeds from the Father, Who with the Father and the Son is together worshipped and together glorified, Who spoke through the prophets; in one holy Catholic and apostolic Church. We confess one baptism to the remission of sins; we look forward to the resurrection of the dead, and the life of the world to come. Amen.

Apollinarianism and Macedonianism. While possibly elaborated out of the Nicene Creed, this document could also reflect clauses of similar but more local creeds that had been modified in catechetical usage to repel heretical deviation. The inclusion of the words in the second article ''[Christ] became incarnate from the Holy Spirit and the Virgin Mary'' has been the subject of much discussion. At Chalcedon, Diogenes of Cyzicus claimed the words were added to refute APOLLINARIANISM (*Acta conciliorum oecumenicorum* 2.1.1:91). The clause itself was taken from the primitive kerygma and did not answer the explicit error of Apollinaris. However, confusion prevailed as to the true nature of his teaching, and it may be that he was thought to have denied that Christ had taken true flesh of Mary; and as the Council of Constantinople condemned the heretic himself, the phrase was adopted as a consequence. There is no doubt, however, that the inclusion in the same article of the phrase ''of whose Kingdom there shall be no end'' taken from Luke (1.33) was directed against Marcellus of Ancyra (d. 374), who maintained that the Incarnation would be dissolved at the end of time.

The development of the doctrine on the Holy Spirit in the third article was a refutation of the Pneumatomachians (opposers of the Spirit) or Macedonians. The language used was that of the Scripture. Paul had called the Spirit, Lord (2 Cor. 3.17–18), and spoke of the ''Spirit

of Life'' (Rom. 8.2). He had been designated as Life-giver in John (6.63); and Christ had described Him as ''The Spirit of truth, Who proceeds from the Father'' (Jn. 15.26); while ''Who spoke through the prophets'' was an adaptation of 2 Peter (1.21). The phrase ''Who with the Father and the Son is together worshipped, and together glorified'' reproduced the teaching of Athanasius (*Ad. Serap.* 1.31) and Basil of Caesarea (*Epist.* 90.2; 159.2; *De Spir. S.* ch. 9–24). Finally, the creed's statements of belief referring to the Church, Baptism, the remission of sins, the resurrection of the dead, and life in the world to come, while not in the Nicene Creed, are in keeping with the contents of almost all the contemporary baptismal formularies taught to catechumens.

Mildness of Statement. Scholars have been puzzled by the apparent mildness of expression on the part of this creed; its failure, for example, to use the word homoousios of the Holy Spirit as consubstantial with the Father and Son. But the historical situation evidently dictated that, while asserting the Godhood of the Holy Spirit, a great effort should be made to win over the Macedonians. This cautious approach had been the strategy of Basil (d. 379) and was apparently followed by the assembled fathers at the suggestion of Emperor THEODOSIUS I, who had summoned the council.

The Constantinopolitan Creed seems to have been established as a baptismal creed in the capital and its environs during the mid-5th century. Reaffirmed at Chalcedon, it was considered a complete and definitive form of the Nicene Creed by Emperor ZENO in his HENOTICON (482) and became the standard baptismal creed of the Eastern Churches. PHILOXENUS OF MABBUGH (d. 523) and SEVERUS OF ANTIOCH (d. 538) aided in the process of standardizing it. Finally it was reconfirmed at the Council of CONSTANTINOPLE II in 553.

In the West, however, a general silence seems to have prevailed with regard to Constantinople I and its creed, in good part because of the attempt of the council to elevate the See of Constantinople to a position second to that to Rome (c. 3). Pope LEO I, accepting the Definition of Chalcedon in 453, took no notice of the Constantinopolitan creed. Pope VIGILIUS I seems to have been the first Roman to make specific allusion to it in his encyclical of 552 written in Constantinople. However it was recognized by the Gelasian sacramentary and the Ordo Romanus VII as the declaratory creed in the baptismal ceremony recited before the interrogations and seems to have been adopted in Rome during the 7th century. It was certainly in use in Rome by 810, as the Abbot Smaragdus attested (*Patrologia Latina* 102:975).

Orthodox Churches. The Nicene and Constantinopolitan Creeds and the definitions of the first seven ecumenical councils are considered infallible statements of faith in the Orthodox Churches. In recent times the formulation of particular Orthodox confessions of faith were attempted in rejection of Catholic or Protestant tendencies. Thus the confession of GENNADIUS II, Patriarch of Constantinople (1455 to 1456), addressed to Sultan Mohammed II as a statement of Orthodox belief in the Trinity, Incarnation, immortality, and Resurrection, was directed against the reunion with Rome accomplished at Florence in 1439. Patriarch Jeremias II of Constantinople composed a confession directed against the Protestant theologians of Wittenberg and Tübingen in 1576, 1579, and 1581. The confession of faith composed by METROPHANES CRITOPOULOS of Alexandria in 1625 and 1636 sought to outline the Byzantine teaching, somewhat influenced by Protestantism. The Orthodox confession of Peter MOGHILA of Kiev (1640) against the Calvinist confession of Cyril LUCARIS, Patriarch of Constantinople (d. 1638), was approved by the Greek and Russian patriarchs (1643), but modified by the theologian Meletius Syrigos in keeping with an anti-Catholic position, departing from the doctrine in Moghila's small catechism of 1645.

The confession of the Patriarch Dositheus at the Synod of Jerusalem (1672) was directed against Cyril Lucaris and toward Catholicism. The catechism of the metropolitan FILARET of Moscow (ed. 1823, and 1827 under Protestant influence) went through more than 100 editions. The document of the patriarch Anthimus IV of Constantinople and the Eastern patriarchs rejecting the appeal of Pope Pius IX in 1848 and the answer of Anthimus VII to Leo XIII in 1895 also are looked upon as official statements of their belief.

Catholic Creeds. Over the centuries the Roman Catholic Church has formulated creedal statements to deal with specific doctrinal aberrations and schisms. These formularies include the basic statements of the ancient creeds, but are adapted to the situation dictating their application. They include the Symbol of Leo IX (1053); the Formula for the Waldenses (1208); the Confession of Michael Palaeologus (1267); the Decrees for the Greeks, Armenians (1439), and Jacobites (1442), resulting from the Council of Florence; the Creedal Confession of the Council of Trent (1564); the Maronite Formula (1743); and the Oath Against the Errors of Modernism (1910). By decree of Pope Pius X all clergy engaged in pastoral work and teaching of the sacred sciences were obliged to take the oath and affirm the Tridentine Confession of Faith. Bishops and other ecclesiastical officials took the Oath when assuming office, professors of theology took it at the opening of each school year, and candidates for the diaconate and priesthood took it before ordination In 1967 the Sacred Congregation of the Faith promulgated a new text. It suppressed the anti-Modernist Oath and appended a short formula to the Symbol of Constantinople that contained obvious references to the Councils of Trent, Vatican I and Vatican II. In June 1968, at the closing of the "year of faith" Pope Paul VI, taking note of the need for guidance felt by many faithful, promulgated the *'Credo' of the People of God*. He prefaced it saying,

> We shall accordingly make a profession of faith, pronounce a creed which, without being strictly speaking a dogmatic definition, repeats in substance, with some developments called for by the spiritual condition of our time, the creed of Nicea, the creed of the immortal tradition of the holy Church of God.

The 1983 Code of Canon Law requires a profession of faith of all ecclesiastics upon taking office as well as candidates for the diaconate. In 1989 the CDF replaced the 1967 formula with a new text that updated the profession of faith "as regards style and content," and to bring more in line with the teaching of the Second Vatican Council (PROFESSION OF FAITH).

A Common Confession of Faith. In 1927 the World Conference on Faith and Order addressed the issue of the Church's common confession of faith. In 1975 the Assembly of the WORLD COUNCIL OF CHURCHES meeting in Nairobi urged member churches "to undertake a common effort to receive, reappropriate and confess together, as contemporary occasion requires, the Christian truth and faith, delivered through the Apostles and handed down through the centuries." In response the Commission on Faith and Order initiated a project "Toward the Common Expression of the Apostolic Faith Today." It had three goals: 1) the common recognition of the apostolic faith as expressed in the Ecumenical Symbol of that faith, the Nicene Creed; 2) the common explication of this apostolic faith in contemporary situations of the churches; and 3) a common confession of the apostolic faith today.

The position of the World Council of Churches is that no creed, ancient or modern, is a complete summary of Christian belief and, therefore, no creed can be considered normative for every aspect of doctrine and practice. The number of creedal formulas promulgated by the Roman Catholic Church over the centuries to address particular needs seems to support this position. At the time that Lukas Vischer was director of the secretariat of the Faith and Order Commission, he wrote: Creeds must "be taken seriously as testimonies [of faith] because they were taken seriously by all the generation which preceded us, which means that a community through the ages is inconceivable without respect for the creeds."

Bibliography: J. N. D. KELLY, *Early Christian Creeds* (2d ed. New York 1960). J. DE GHELLINCK, *Patristique et moyen-âge:*

Études d'histoire littéraire et doctrinale v. 1 (2d ed. Paris 1949), bibliography. F. HORT, *Two Dissertations* (Cambridge, England 1876). F. LOOFS, *Symbolik* (Tübingen 1902); "Das Nicänum," *Festgabe . . . Karl Müller* (Tübingen 1922) 68–82. E. SCHWARTZ, *Zeitschrift für die neutestamentliche Wissenschaft und die Kund der älteren Kirche* 25 (Giessen-Berlin 1926) 38–88. J. LEBON, *Revue d'histoire ecclésiastique* 32 (1936) 809–77; 47 (1952) 485–529, consubstantial. F. J. DÖLGER, *Antike und Christentum* 4 (1934) 138–46. A. VON HARNACK, J. J. HERZOG and A. HAUCK, eds., *Realencyklopädi für protestantische Theologie*, 24 v. (3d ed. Leipzig 1896–1913) 1:741–55; 11:12–28. I. ORTIZ DE URBINA, *El símbolo niceno* (Madrid 1947); *Nicée et Constantinople* (Paris 1963); *Lexikon für Theologie und Kirche*, ed. J. HOFER and K. RAHNER, 10 v. (2d, new ed. Freiburg 1957–65) 7:938–40. P. T. CAMELOT, *Éphèse et Chalcédoine* (Paris 1962). H. ZELLER, *Lexikon für Theologie und Kirche* 2:144–46, 147–48. B. SCHULTZE, *ibid.* 148–49, Orthodox creeds. B. CAPELLE, *Revue Bénédictine* 39 (1927) 33–45; *Recherches de théologie ancienne et médiévale* 2 (1930) 5–20, Roman Creed. H. CARPENTER, *Journal of Theological Studies* 43 (1942) 1–11; 44 (1943) 1–11, Symbolum. D. VAN DEN EYNDE, *Les Normes de l'enseignement chrétien* (Paris 1933). F. KATTENBUSCH, *Das apostolische Symbol*, 2 v. (Leipzig 1894–1900). H. OPITZ, ed., *Urkunden zur Geschichte des arianischen Streites* (Berlin 1935). S. ZANKOW, *Das orthodoxe Christentum des Ostens* (Berlin 1928). M. JUGIE, *Échos d'Orient* 28 (1929) 423–30. M. GORDILLO, *Compendium theologiae orientalis* (3d ed. Rome 1950). Y. M. J. CONGAR, *Irénikon* 23 (1950) 3–36. P. SCHAFF, ed., *The Creeds of Christendom* 3 v., (New York 1931). C. POZO, *The Credo of the People of God* (Chicago 1980). J. NEUNER and J. DUPUIS, eds., *The Christian Faith in the Doctrinal Documents of the Catholic Church* rev. ed. (New York 1982). B. L. MARTHALER, *The Creed. The Apostolic Faith in Contemporary Theology*, rev. ed. (Mystic, Conn 1993). H. DENZINGER and A. SCHÖNMETZER, *Enchiridion Symbolorum* (36 ed. Herder 1976).

[F. X. MURPHY/EDS.]

CREED IN EUCHARISTIC LITURGY

This article reviews the history of the Creed in the Eucharistic Liturgy, and its musical use.

Eucharistic Liturgy. The Monophysite bishop of Antioch Peter the Fuller is credited with having first (*c.* 489) introduced the recitation of the Constantinopolitan Creed into the Eucharistic liturgy (Theodore Lector, *Ecclesiastical History*, 2 frag. 48). Peter evidently intended it as an attack on the Definition of Chalcedon to which he was violently opposed. In 511 Timothy of Constantinople, upon the deposition of his predecessor, Macedonius II, ordered the recitation of the creed in the liturgy every Sunday; it had previously been so used only on Good Friday (*ibid.* frag. 32). By 518 this recitation was considered customary (Mansi 8:1057–65); and in 568 Emperor Justin II ordered the creed to be sung in the liturgy everywhere before the Lord's Prayer.

In the West the Council of Toledo III (589) ordered that the creed be chanted aloud before the Lord's Prayer in all churches of Spain and Gaul, according to the usage of the Eastern Churches (c.2). The occasion was the conversion of King Reccared and his nation from Arianism; and the purpose was to strengthen the faith of the people before Communion. Relations between Byzantium and Spain were close as the presence of other Byzantine elements in the MOZARABIC liturgy demonstrates. Evidence supplied by the Stowe Missal (early 9th century) shows that the Irish Church had introduced the custom of singing this creed after the Gospel (fol. 20r), and the influence was from Spain rather than the Carolingian Empire. The custom seems to have passed from Ireland to England (Alcuin, *Epist. ad Felic.* 3; *Patrologia Latina,* 101: 121). The abbot Smaragdus, reporting a conference in 810 between Pope LEO III and three delegates from Charlemagne, states that while the pope had sanctioned the chanting of the creed in the Mass at Aachen and in Gaul, he refused to admit the word FILIOQUE into it (*Patrologia Latina,* 102:971–973). Walafrid Strabo of Reichenau (d. 849) witnessed to the spread of the custom of chanting the creed at Mass after the condemnation of the adoptionist Felix of Urgel at Aachen in 798 (*Patrologia Latina,* 114:947). Aeneas of Paris (d. 871) said the whole of Gaul chanted the creed at Mass on Sunday (*Adv. Graec.* 93). Paulinus of Aquileia in a synod at Cividale del Friuli (*c.* 797) ordered the learning of the creed by heart on the part of his clergy (*Monumenta Germaniae Concilia* 2.180, 189), and the text he supplied is almost identical with the Constantinopolitan Creed.

The *Ordo Missae of the Missale Ambrosianum* (1981) allows the option of reciting the Creed after the washing of the hands and before the eucharistic prayer. The Mozarabic *Novus Ordo* (1985) places it before the fraction and *Pater Noster*. Both the Episcopal BOOK OF COMMON PRAYER (1979) and the *Lutheran Book of Worship* (1978) used in North America call for the recitation of the Creed at the conclusion of the liturgy of the word. The Book of Common Prayer prescribes the Nicene Creed. The Lutheran Book of Worship directs that the Nicene Creed "be said on all festivals and on Sundays in the seasons of Advent, Christmas, Lent and Easter. The Apostles' Creed is said at other times."

Creed as Musical Chant. In the West it has been sung since Carolingian times. It is often spoken of as a congregational chant, but there must have been difficulties in such a performance. There is evidence that beginning in the 10th century the Credo was performed by the *chorus clericorum* or, occasionally, by the subdeacons or *basilicarii*. In various places in Germany, according to Berthold of Regensburg (d. 1272), the congregation joined in chanting the Credo in the vernacular, using a text that began "Ich glaube an den Vater." The Credo was sung not only in the Mass but also at baptisms. In the Roman *Ordo baptismi* an acolyte chanted the Credo first in Greek and then in Latin. This custom persisted into the 11th century, according to HONORIUS OF AUTUN; a melody with the Greek text πιστεύω εἰς ἕνα θεὸν is preserved in a 14th-century manuscript in Cologne.

Two melodic types are found in the oldest Credos. One is in recitative style; it is found in one Mozarabic [*Revue du chant grégorien* 38 (1934) 15] and two Ambrosian melodies (the first, *ibid.*, and also in *Antiphonale missarum Mediolanensis;* the second in *Paléographie musicale* 6:316–317 and in the most recent Solesmes editions of the Roman Gradual). The other is Credo I of the Vatican edition (for which there are manuscript sources as early as the 11th century) and its variants (among them Credos II, V, and VI of the Vatican edition). To this second group of related melodies belong (in addition to the melody referred to above, which is found with Greek text in a Cologne manuscript) a doubtless very old folk melody found in Flanders in the 19th century—the ballade of ''Halewijn''—and a French song of the Passion, *La passion de Jésus Christ.* This may suggest that Credo I of the Vatican edition itself originated as a folk melody. During the later Middle Ages the Credo was sung to another much-loved folk melody, as is shown by a regulation of a Basel synod of 1503: ''In Masses with music, let the Nicene Creed not be abbreviated but sung entire, at the appropriate time, and properly (especially in our cathedral, and in the collegiate churches) to the end; and that secular melody of the countryside, which pilgrims and tramps walking to St. James use, shall not be permitted.'' A 15th-century source from Siena sets the text of the Credo to the melody of the hymn *Vexilla regis prodeunt.* All this can be interpreted as resulting from an effort to have the congregation sing the Credo. Abbreviation of the Credo is found occasionally in late medieval manuscripts and printed sources; it may end, for example, ''. . . et homo factus est. Amen.''

It is noteworthy that new melodies were not composed for the Credo as they were for the other chants of the Ordinary of the Mass during the Middle Ages. On the contrary, apparently only variants of a single melody were used. A flourishing activity in the composition of new Credo melodies is not found until the 15th century. To this period belong Credos III and IV of the Vatican edition; in their early sources they are found generally not in chant notation but in mensural notation, and the second of them is often found in a two-voiced version. The Credo was the last of the sections of the Mass Ordinary to be set polyphonically, later even than the Sanctus. The earliest settings are from the 14th century. In the 15th century the polyphonic Credo became a section of the cyclic Mass Ordinary. In the development of this genre the Credo had a special place because of the opportunities for text expression and musical representation it offered. The

text of the Credo, relatively long in comparison to the other Mass chants, has always presented a problem to composers. This has led again to abbreviation of the text, or to the practice of singing the Credo in chant. The Credo retained a special position in the Roman Kyriale; Credo melodies were not part of the Mass Ordinaries but were found in a special section.

Bibliography: P. WAGNER, *Einführung in die gregorianischen Melodien* (Hildesheim 1962). A. MOCQUEREAU, ''Le Chant *authentique* du Credo,'' *Paléographie musicale* 10 (1909) 90–176, A. GASTOUÉ, ''Comment on chantait le *Credo* en certaines églises au XVe siècle,'' *Revue du chant grégorien* 36 (1932) 48–49; ''Les Chants du Credo,'' *ibid.* 37 (1933) 166–170. J. GAJARD and J. H. DESROQUETTES, ''Le Credo VI,'' *Revue Grégorienne* 9 (1924). *Deutsche Volkslieder mit ihren Melodien,* ed. J. MEIER et al. (Berlin 1935–), v.2.1 M. HUGLO, ''Origine de la melodie du Credo *authentique* de la Vaticane,'' *Revue Grégorienne* (Solesmes 1922–) 30 (1951) 68–78. B. STÄBLEIN, *Die Musik in Geschichte und Gegenwart,* ed. F. BLUME (Kassel-Basel 1949–) 2:1170–73. P. KAST, ''Messe, E: Mehrstimmige Messe bis 1600,'' *ibid.* 9:170–183. W. APPEL, *Gregorian Chant* (Bloomington, IN 1958). J. A. JUNGMANN, *The Eucharistic Prayer,* translated from the German by R. BATLEY (London 1966) 1:461–474.

[F. X. MURPHY/H. HUCKE/B. L. MARTHALER]

CREIGHTON

Family name of brothers who were businessmen and philanthropists. Their parents, James and Bridget (Hughes) Creighton, were Irish immigrants. The brothers were associated in business enterprises in the mining districts of the West and settled in Omaha in 1857. There they became interested in plans for a transcontinental telegraph system, completed on Oct. 24, 1861.

Edward, b. near Barnesville, Belmont County, Ohio, Aug. 31, 1820; d. Omaha, Nebr., Nov. 5, 1874. He surveyed the telegraph route and supervised construction of the line from Omaha to Salt Lake City, Utah. This portion of the telegraph was built at a cost of $147,000 by the Pacific Telegraph Company, in which Edward held an interest. Pacific Telegraph was soon absorbed by Western Union at the cost of $6 million in Western Union stock. Edward's fortune, later enlarged by stock raising and banking investments, was liberally expended on Catholic charities. Chief among his bequests was $200,000 left at his request in the will of his wife, Mary Lucretia (Wareham) Creighton, to found Creighton College (now University), Omaha.

John, b. Licking County, Ohio, Oct. 15, 1831; d. Omaha, Feb. 7, 1907. He inherited Edward's business interests, augmented his investments, and continued his philanthropies. John's benefactions built in Omaha the first two monasteries of the POOR CLARES in the U.S. and constructed St. Joseph-Creighton Hospital. His largest gifts went to Creighton University, which received more than $1 million for buildings and endowment. Leo XIII made John a Knight of St. Gregory and a papal count in 1895, and in 1904 Superior General Louis Martin made him a founder in the Society of Jesus. John's will left an additional $1¼ million to Creighton University.

Bibliography: V. ROSEWATER, *Dictionary of American Biography*, ed. A. JOHNSON and D. MALONE, 20 v. (New York 1928–36) (1928) 4:534–535. R. L. THOMPSON, *Wiring a Continent* (Princeton 1947). M. P. DOWLING, *Creighton University: Reminiscences of the First Twenty-Five Years* (Omaha 1903).

[H. W. CASPER]

CREIGHTON, MANDELL

Historian and Anglican bishop; b. Carlisle, England, July 5, 1843; d. London, Jan. 14, 1901. He was educated at Carlisle and Durham, received a B.A. degree from Merton College, Oxford (1867), and continued on as tutor. Creighton successfully pursued two vocations—clergyman and scholar. He received Anglican orders (1873) and administered a Northumbrian vicarage (1875–84). When he was appointed bishop of Peterborough (1891) and London (1897), he combined firm episcopal authority with tolerance for latitudinarian views. He was an urbane, talented administrator and a gifted speaker; among his many concerns, Creighton displayed a particular interest in English educational reforms at all levels.

Creighton is remembered chiefly as a historian. He was first to hold the Dixie Professorship of Ecclesiastical History at Cambridge (1884–90), first editor of the *English Historical Review* (1886–91), and first president of the Church Historical Society (1894–1901). His major writing was *History of the Papacy from the Great Schism to the Sack of Rome* (5 v., 1882–94; 2d ed. six v., 1897). Though lacking sufficient opportunity for archival research, Creighton skillfully utilized published sources to write a balanced, impartial account of the papacy from 1378 to 1527. Ironically, Catholic historian Lord John ACTON criticized Creighton for being too charitable in his moral judgments, particularly regarding certain Renaissance popes. *Cardinal Wolsey* (1888) and *Queen Elizabeth* (1896) are Creighton's best minor works.

Bibliography: L. CREIGHTON, *Life and Letters of Mandell Creighton,* 2 v. (New York 1904). G. L. STRACHEY, *Biographical Essays* (New York 1949). J. W. THOMPSON and B. J. HOLM, *History of Historical Writing,* 2 v. (New York 1942) 2:572–574. W. G. FALLOWS, *Mandell Creighton and the English Church* (London 1964).

[J. T. COVERT]

CREMATION

Cremation—that is, the reduction of dead bodies to ashes by burning—was and is widely practiced in some societies. In many cultures the practices of cremation and inhumation (burial in the earth) exist side by side. Among the ancient Greeks, ground burial was the more common practice, but the Greeks incinerated the corpses of warriors killed in battle in order more easily to transport their remains to the homeland for ceremonial entombment. Ancient writers reveal that cremation was the more common practice among the Romans in the centuries immediately preceding the birth of Christ. About the year A.D. 100 a noteworthy shift from cremation to inhumation took place in the Roman Empire that is said to have been caused by the shortage of wood for funeral pyres.

Another factor that contributed to the discontinuance of cremation was the development of ideas about afterlife in the dominant philosophies and religions that flourished across the Mediterranean basin. Cremation was never a common practice among the Egyptians, who expected departed souls to reenter the body. The Hebrew Scriptures witness to the fact that the Israelites buried their dead. The Gospel accounts describe how those who took Jesus' body from the cross were careful to observe Jewish burial practices as to time and manner of burial. Early Christians, even during the era of persecutions, maintained extensive cemeteries in Rome, North Africa, and elsewhere. Gradually Christian reverence for the body as a "temple of the Holy Spirit," together with their belief in life after death, resurrection, and the immortality of the soul, reinforced the practice of inhumation. Through the Middle Ages into modern times cremation remained the exception, surfacing from time to time in circumstances of mass deaths from plagues, war, and natural disasters.

New Interest and New Methods. When cremation returned to modern western culture in the 19th century, long gone was the ceremonial burning of the corpse on a pyre of wood. The development of the cremation chamber or retort, aided by ready availability of fossil fuels (coal and coke) and new technology, displaced the funeral pyre. The first successful cremation furnace and the remains of a cremated corpse displayed at the Vienna Exposition of 1873 mark the beginning of scientific cremation in the modern age. The following year, the practice gained more notoriety when Queen Victoria's personal surgeon, Sir Henry Thompson, one of the founders of the Cremation Society of England, published *Cremation: The Treatment of the Body after Death*. News of the Exposition and proliferation of cremation societies in Europe received wide coverage in the popular American press. In 1876 the first cremation in modern America took place in rural Washington, Pennsylvania.

In the 20th century cremation became the choice of rapidly increasing numbers in Great Britain and Europe. The move toward cremation was in part fueled by a reaction against the "American way of death" with embalming and cosmetic restoration of the corpse and funeral parlors where the deceased can be waked and viewed as life-like as possible. Opposition to the perceived ostentation and cost of funerals together with new ecological concerns about land use caused many in the United States, Catholics among them, to look for simpler alternatives. In the years between the 1960s and 1980s, cremations increased to some 13% in the United States and 25% in Canada. Catholics chose about 20% of the direct cremations reported, and Jews another 20%. By the year 2000, some 26% of Americans and 45% of Canadians opted for cremation, and by the middle of the third millennium, cremations are expected to overtake earth burials.

Modern cremation is a process of vaporization that reduces the human body to bone fragments by means of intense heat (1600–2400 °F). Ordinarily the bone fragments, weighing up to eight pounds, are then pulverized into a powder-like substance. In itself the end result of cremation is no different from that of natural decomposition in earth or sea. Although government documents and Catholic literature generally refer to them as "cremated remains" or simply by the colloquial term "ashes," the mortuary establishment has coined the neologism "cremains" to emphasize that the pulverized remains are not strictly speaking ashes.

The Church and Cremation. In the 19th century, proponents of cremation in Europe generally argued their case on the basis of public hygiene and land conservation, but the Church regarded the cremation societies as materialist and saw the practice as incompatible with the traditional burial customs of the Christian liturgy. In 1886 the Holy Office forbade Catholics from joining cremation societies and prohibited the practice of cremation. The 1917 Code of Canon Law did not address cremation as such but was sharply critical of the reasons used to justify it (c. 1203). The 1917 Code also prohibited ecclesiastical burial of bodies that were to be cremated (c. 1240). Directives to missionaries outside Europe, however, were milder in tone and allowed greater toleration of the practice [see Fonti (Fontes) CICO 4 n1189; 7n4905, Collectanea 2n1626]. Nonetheless, as late as 1926, an instruction of the Holy Office still characterized proponents of cremation as "enemies of Christianity" and warned of the dangers of deemphasizing the resurrection of the body (AAS 18.282). These societies were perceived to be sectarian, hateful, and contrary to Catholic doctrine (c. 1203).

Responding to the changing pastoral needs brought about by growth in the number of cremations, particularly in Great Britain and Europe, the Holy See lifted the ban on cremation. The penalties of canon 1240 were virtually repealed by an instruction of the Holy Office (*Piam et constantem*, July 5, 1963). The lifting of the prohibition reflected the reality that most proponents of cremation are not motivated by anti-Catholic sentiment. The reasons they give for cremation stress rather simplicity, sanitation, sound use of scarce land and, in North America, economic concerns.

Consequently, the option to select cremation as a means of final disposition was incorporated in the *Ordo Exsequiarum* for the universal Church of the Roman Rite (1969) and in funeral rites for English-speaking countries (The Rite of Funerals 1970–1989). The 1983 revision of the Code of Canon Law (*c. 1176*) codified the authorization and liturgical law. According to the revised law, good will among the faithful is presumed. Cremation and interment both are subject to the same criterion: that Catholic faith and liturgical practice guide and direct pastoral care at the time of death.

The bishops in Canada had secured permission from the Holy See to celebrate the full funeral liturgy with the ashes present. Thus, when the Canadian bishops published the funeral ritual for use in Canada (1990), it included a rite for "Funeral liturgy in the presence of ashes." Although the 1989 U.S. edition of the *Order of Christian Funerals* included prayers for cremated remains at the Rite of Committal (following the European model), it did not directly address the issue of funeral Mass with the cremated remains. By 1996, however, pastoral circumstances urged the National Conference of Catholic Bishops in the United States to request an "indult" to permit celebration of Catholic funeral liturgy with the cremated remains in place of the body. The Holy See authorized the permission on March 21, 1997, and an Appendix to the U.S. *Order of Christian Funerals* (411–438) appeared later that year.

The Funeral Liturgy and Disposal of the Remains. The 1997 Appendix for Cremation in the Order of Christian Funerals offers three options. *Cremation Following the Funeral Liturgy (OCF, 418–421).* The first option states the traditional preference that cremation follow the funeral while retaining reverent disposition of the cremated remains through burial or entombment in a cemetery. "The Church clearly prefers and urges that the body of the deceased be present for the funeral rites, since the presence of the human body better expresses the values which the Church affirms in those rites." *Cremation and Committal of the Remains before the Funeral Liturgy (OCF, 422–425).* This second option reverses the ordinary sequence of funeral rites by suggesting that the bereaved gather for the committal of the cremated remains at a cemetery first, and then proceed to the celebration of the Funeral Liturgy at church (OCF, 423). This option where cremation and committal both take place before the funeral Mass implicitly acknowledges the distinction between the body and cremated remains as two different forms of mortal remains. That is, it identifies the Rite of Committal as the existing service already designated for use with cremated remains and invites the bereaved to adapt Prayers after Death and the Vigil for the Deceased to the new circumstances (OCF, 422). *Funeral Liturgy with the Cremated Remains Present (OCF, 426–431).* This third option responds to the practical realities of direct or immediate cremation in the United States and Canada. This includes the understanding that the Rite of Committal will mark the burial or entombment of the remains at an appropriate time following the Funeral Liturgy.

Finally, a word about the manner of disposing of cremated remains. Liturgical tradition and the role the Catholic cemetery plays in preserving the memory of Christians profess explicit belief in the promise of resurrection. The cremation Appendix to the OCF expresses the clear preference for preserving the remains of loved ones by interment in a tomb or preservation in a columbarium. ''The practice of scattering cremated remains on the sea, from the air, or on the ground, or keeping cremated remains in the home of a relative or friend of the deceased, are not the reverent disposition that the Church requires'' (OCF, 417). Burial at sea, however, whether marking the final disposition of a corpse in a coffin or cremated remains in an urn or appropriate vessel, is acceptable.

The resurrection of the body. The *Catechism of the Catholic Church,* citing canon 1176, makes the simple statement, ''The Church permits cremation, provided that it does not demonstrate a denial of faith in the resurrection of the body'' (n. 2301). Christian belief in the resurrection of the dead is in no way affected by the state of the corporeal remains. This has been the clearly articulated teaching of the Catholic Church throughout the history of the cremation controversy in the 19th century. Whatever their form, the mortal remains of the dead—whether lost at sea, destroyed by fire, naturally decomposed, or cremated—function in faith and liturgy in relation to the person whose living flesh and blood they once were.

The faith claims expressed in the historic rites of the Order of Christian Funerals are grounded in the symbol of the mortal remains, attended to liturgically through symbols related to the person. That is, we invest the mortal remains with what we believe about the person. Chris-

tians have always treated the body with reverence and kept its resting place sacred because they believe it has been one with the soul in life's spiritual journey. In the funeral the Church addresses the person, reflected in the body or cremated remains, who, in Christian hope, is believed to be participating now in the victory of Jesus' death and resurrection, carried by angels to the heavenly Jerusalem, and welcomed triumphantly by the martyrs and all the saints even as the corpse is carried in procession to the church (the earthly symbol of that heavenly court) for a final farewell.

The symbolic motif of procession to Christ (*ire ad Christum*) captures the religious imagination of the bereaved church, as do the references to the sacramental life of the deceased expressed in baptismal water, white pall, paschal candle, and, above all, the Eucharistic celebration itself. For ancient Christians, belief in the mystery of the incarnation and the promise of resurrection in the likeness of the risen Christ transformed superstitious concerns about the lot of the dead. What emerged was the traditional heritage that informs Catholic funeral liturgy today. The body that participated integrally in all the expressions of Catholic sacramental life is the primary object of liturgical attention in funeral liturgy. Yet, whatever form human remains take, they are due Christian respect as the final form of the flesh and blood person who lived and died and will rise in relationship with God.

Bibliography: NATIONAL CONFERENCE OF CATHOLIC BISHOPS, *Order of Christian Funerals* (1989), including Appendix on Cremation; available from three publishers: Catholic Book Publishing Co., The Liturgical Press, and Liturgical Training Publications. COMMITTEE ON THE LITURGY, NATIONAL CONFERENCE OF CATHOLIC BISHOPS, *Reflections on the Body, Cremation and Catholic Funeral Rites* (Washington, DC 1997). M. E. CUNNINGHAM, ''Cremation in Catechesis and the Funeral Liturgy,'' *Living Light* 34 (1998) 19–29. J. D. DAVIES, *Cremation Today and Tomorrow* (Nottingham 1990). M. J. HENCHAL, ''Cremation: Canonical Issues,'' *The Jurist* 55 (1995) 281–298. J. MITFORD, *The American Way of Death Revisited* (New York 1998). S. R. PROTHERO, *Purified by Fire: A History of Cremation in America* (Berkeley, CA 2001). H. R. RUTHERFORD, ''Cremation American style: A Change for the Better?'' in: T. FITZGERALD and M. F. CONNELL, eds., *The Changing Face of the Church* (Chicago 1998) 159–175. ''Different Symbols—Different Rites: Funeral Liturgy with Cremated Remains,'' *Liturgical Ministry* 4 (1995) 36–44. *Honoring the Dead: Catholics and Cremation Today* (Collegeville, MN 2001). J. M. C. TOYNBEE, *Death and Burial in the Roman World* (London 1971).

[R. RUTHERFORD/EDS.]

CRESCAS, ḤASDAI BEN ABRAHAM

Religious philosopher and statesman; b. Barcelona, Spain, 1340; d. Saragossa, Spain, 1410. He was the first Jewish thinker to challenge the fundamentals of Aristotelianism, the system that had influenced Jewish thought since the days of Gaon SA'ADIA BEN JOSEPH (882–942) and had reached its culmination in the writings of Abraham ibn Daud (RABaD, c. 1110–c. 1180), MAIMONIDES (RaMBaM, 1135–1204), and LEVI BEN GERSON (RaLBaG, 1288–1344). He belonged to an illustrious, scholarly, and wealthy family and was held in high esteem by Jew and non-Jew alike. As a man of sterling character and wisdom he rose above the prevailing mediocrity of his time and soon came to the attention of Pedro IV, King of Aragon (1336–87), who frequently employed him on diplomatic missions and consulted him on important matters of state. Crescas, who had been a disciple of the distinguished Talmudist Nissim ben Reuben Gerondi (RaN, d. c. 1380), was the teacher of Joseph ALBO (c. 1380–c. 1435), the author of Ikkarim (Principles), a well-known work on the fundamentals of Judaism.

Despite his close relations with the court, Crescas was not spared the sufferings of his coreligionists. In 1367, as a result of a conspiracy, the nature of which was never made known, he and his close colleague the celebrated respondent (see RESPONSA, JEWISH) Isaac ben Sheshet (RIBaSH, 1326–1408) and the aged Nissim Gerondi, among others, were denounced before Pedro IV and cast into prison. Although ben Sheshet gave assurances that they were innocent of any crime, they were released after several months in prison only after the payment of a considerable amount of bail. After this indignity Crescas settled in Saragossa. He never occupied any official rabbinical position. Nevertheless his counsel on legal and ritual matters was frequently invoked, and his decisions were accepted as law by many Jewish communities. He was referred to at the time even as the "Rab of Saragossa." But additional personal tragedy was in store for him. The infamous persecution and massacre of the Jews in 1391 robbed him not only of his entire fortune but also of his only son, who was martyred on the eve of his marriage in Barcelona.

Of his literary contributions, Crescas's magnum opus was his Or Adonai (The Light of the Lord), which he completed in 1410, the year of his death. It was first printed at Ferrara in 1555. In this work he endeavored, by logical analysis and argumentation, to disprove the Stagirite's position that had been basically accepted by Maimonides in his Môrēh Nᵉbûkîm and by RaLBaG in his Milḥamot Adonai, and he sharply criticized these two for "reducing the doctrinal contents of Judaism to a surrogate of Aristotelian concepts." According to M. Joel the Or Adonai had a stimulating influence on the philosophy of Baruch SPINOZA; from Crescas Spinoza derived his views on the love of God, on free will and creation, and on the distinction between attributes and properties.

Crescas's work is divided into four parts, which deal respectively with (1) the existence and nature of God; (2)

the fundamental doctrines of the faith without which Judaism would fall, i.e., God's omniscience, providence, and omnipotence, and belief in prophecy, freedom of the will, and the purpose of creation; (3) other doctrines that, without being fundamental and essential to Judaism, it would be heresy to deny, i.e., creatio ex nihilo, immortality, divine retribution, the resurrection of the body, the irrevocability of and eternal obligation to the Torah, the supremacy of Moses as a prophet, the value of the URIM AND THUMMIM, and messianic redemption; and (4) traditional doctrines that are not binding and are open to philosophical interpretation (13 opinions, among them questions that are concerned with amulets, the dissolution of the world, and metempsychosis).

Crescas attacked the Aristotelian propositions that Maimonides had generally accepted as axiomatic, and he thereby demolished the arguments that Maimonides had used as the basis for his concept of God. Furthermore, he rejected the theory that man can comprehend God through intellectual speculation and human cognition. According to Crescas it is not reason but love for God, reverence, and goodness of character that bring men closer to and in communion with God. Whereas Maimonides could not explain the ultimate purpose of the world and the reason for existence and considered futile every inquiry concerning these questions, Crescas posited that the world had come into being in order to fulfill God's law and thereby assure the happiness of the soul. Man's fulfillment of the Commandments strengthens the mutual love between God and the soul and causes (as in natural things) an inevitable fusion between the two. This unity, Crescas maintained, surely leads to happiness and immortality.

In addition to Or Adonai two other writings of Crescas are extant. One is a mournful letter to the Jewish communities of Avignon, written on Oct. 19, 1391, in which he recapitulated the story of the persecutions of that year and mentioned the many who were martyred (including his son), as well as those who were spared by accepting Christianity. The other work is a Refutation of the Main Doctrines of Christianity, written in 1398. The Spanish original is no longer available, but a partial Hebrew translation by Joseph ibn Shem-Tov (1451) has been preserved. It has been surmised that Crescas prepared this paper in an effort to stem the tide of the many conversions to Christianity that were taking place at that time.

Bibliography: E. G. HIRSCH, The Jewish Encyclopedia, ed. J. SINGER, 13 v. (New York 1901–06) 4:350–353. A. KAMINKA, Universal Jewish Encyclopedia, 10 v. (New York 1939–44) 3:408–409. F. BAER and J. GORDIN, Encyclopedia Judaica: Das Judentum in Geschichte und Gegenwart, 10 v. (Berlin 1928–34) incomplete, 5:696–708. I. HUSIK, A History of Medieval Jewish Philosophy (2d ed. New York 1930; pa. 1958) 388–405. M. JOEL,

Zur Genesis der Lehre Spinozas (Breslau 1871). H. A. WOLFSON, *Crescas' Critique of Aristotle* (Cambridge, Mass. 1929). H. H. GRAETZ, *History of the Jews*, ed. and tr. B. LÖWY, 6 v. (Philadelphia 1945) 4:145–155. M. WAXMAN, *Philosophy of Don Ḥasdai Crescas* (New York 1920).

[N. J. COHEN]

CRESCENTII

Italian family that ruled Rome late in the 10th century. Its founder is generally agreed to be Crescentius, one of the *iudices Romani* in 902; a nobleman of the same name, possibly his son, was a member of the court of Alberic, Prince of Rome. The family first attained prominence in 963 when Crescentiux de Caballo Marmoreo took a leading part in the synod convened by Emperor OTTO I to depose Pope JOHN XII. When there was a revolt in Rome (966) against Otto I's nominee, Pope JOHN XIII, Crescentius' son John killed Count Roffredus, the rebel leader, and in return for this support, Crescentius' daughter, Theodoranda, was allowed to marry the pope's nephew, Benedict, Count of the Sabina. It is generally agreed that this Crescentius de Caballo Marmoreo was a kinsman of Crescentius de Theodora, who in 974 led a revolt against Pope BENEDICT VI, imprisoned him in the CASTEL SANT' ANGELO, and set up as antipope the cardinal deacon Franco, who took the name of Boniface VII. The antipope procured the murder of Benedict VI, but was ejected from Rome by the emperor's representative and fled to Constantinople. Pope BENEDICT VII was then elected, and he granted Crescentius de Theodora full pardon. Some time after 977 Crescentius was professed a monk at SS. Boniface and Alexius, Rome; he died there in 984.

In that year Boniface VII returned from exile and seized power in Rome with the help of John and Crescentius II, the sons of Crescentius de Theodora. Boniface VII imprisoned the lawful pope, JOHN XIV, starved him to death, and reigned in his stead. He created John, son of Crescentius de Theodora, PATRICIUS ROMANORUM to assist in governing. When Boniface VII died in 985, John the patrician was responsible for choosing his successor, Pope JOHN XV, formerly cardinal priest of San Vitale. The patrician conducted the temporal government of Rome until his death *c.* 990; his brother, Crescentius II, then took the title of *consul Romanorum,* and ruled in Rome, keeping the pope a virtual prisoner at the Lateran. Pope John appealed for help to Emperor OTTO III (995), but he died before Otto could reach Rome; the emperor then appointed as John's successor his own cousin, Bruno, who became Pope GREGORY V in 996. At Gregory V's request Otto pardoned Crescentius II; but when the emperor left Rome in the summer of 996 Crescentius rebelled and drove Gregory from the city. He appointed John Phila-

gathos, the Greek-speaking archbishop of Piacenza as antipope (with the title of John XVI), possibly hoping thus to secure Byzantine support. In 998 Otto III again marched on Rome, deposed the antipope, and restored Gregory V. Crescentius II took refuge in the Castel Sant' Angelo, but the fortress was taken by treachery, and the rebel was executed on the battlements and buried in the church of San Pancrazio. In the 11th and 12th centuries the Castel Sant' Angelo became known as the *Turris Crescentii.*

In 1002 Crescentius II's son, John, was made *patricius Romanorum* by Pope SYLVESTER II, and he remained powerful during the pontificates of JOHN XVII (1003) and JOHN XVIII (1004–09). He died in the reign of Pope SERGIUS IV (1009–12), and political power in Rome then passed to the Tusculani family.

A cadet branch of the Crescentii remained in office as counts of the Sabina and supported John, Bishop of Sabina, when he became antipope with the title of Sylvester III in 1045. In 1060 Pope NICHOLAS II deprived the Crescentii of the countship of the Sabina, and from then they ceased to influence the history of Rome.

Bibliography: F. A. GREGOROVIUS, *History of the City of Rome in the Middle Ages,* tr. G. W. HAMILTON, 8 v. (v.1–6 2d ed., 7–8 1st ed. London 1900–09), v.3, 4. G. BOSSI, ''I Crescenzi: Contributo alla storia di Roma dall 900 al 1012,'' *Archivio della società romana di storia patria* 38 (1915) 389–399; ''I Crescenzi di Sabina stefaniani e ottaviani,'' *ibid.* 41 (1918) 111–170. W. KÖLMEL, *Rom und der Kirchenstaat im 10. und 11. Jahrhundert* (Berlin 1935). O. GERSTENBERG, ''Studien zur Geschichte des römischen Adels im Ausgange des 10 Jahrhunderts,'' *Historische Vierteljahrschrift* 31 (1937) 1–26. C. CECCHELLI, *I Crescenzi, i Savelli, i Cenci* (Rome 1942). P. BREZZI, *Roma e l'Impero medioevale* (Bologna 1947).

[B. HAMILTON]

CRETAN-MYCENAEAN RELIGION

In the Minoan period, the chalkstone caves of Crete served as places of worship, as is evidenced by the votive offerings found in them. The strange limestone formations, when viewed in the dim light or darkness of the caves, suggested the work and presence of divinities. The Little Palace at Cnossos has revealed fetishes of the same nature. The Cretan idols imitate the rock ''statues.'' The pillar represents the natural column resulting from the meeting of a stalactite and stalagmite. The Labyrinth recalls the mazes of the caves rather than those of the palace. Homer (*Od.* 19.188), Callimachus (*Jov.* 45), and Nonnus (*Dionys.* 8.115; 13.250) were familiar with the grotto of Eileithya at Amnisus; Hesiod (*Theog.* 483), with the grotto of Zeus (Psykhro, Arkalaphon, or St. Photinus); and Diogenes Laertius (8.44), with the cave of Ida. Pythagoras was initiated in one of these grottoes, the typical arrangement of which was perhaps copied in the *Telesterion,* or Hall of the Mysteries, at Eleusis. Certain trees surrounded by an enclosure bear witness to a cult in the open air. The palaces had chapels for their cult statues and paved spaces for ritual dances. On the other hand, Crete shows no trace of temples proper or public sanctuaries.

Paraphernalia of worship. The paraphernalia employed in worship were: tripodal portable altars; offering tables; libation vases—the *rhyton* or horn-shaped cup, the *kantheros,* a cup with two handles and narrow spout, the *kernos,* a small earthenware dish, with small pots affixed, intended to receive the first fruits of the harvest; the double ax symbolizing lightning—already found in the hand of the Mesopotamian or Syro-Anatolian god Hadad-Teshup, the lord of the thunderbolt; the "horns of consecration," a schematic adaptation of the horns of the bull and a symbol of power and fertility; and, finally, the bilobed shield, the emblem of divine protection.

Conduct of worship. Women conducted worship as priestesses, attendants, or dancers. Originally, men were excluded, unless they are to be recognized as concealed under the dress and masks of the figures in animal form who present offerings to the god. The costume of the officiating personnel is often a tunic of skin or an imbricated cloak, or sometimes a long robe. In addition to vegetable offerings, the Minoans sacrificed animals, namely, goats, sheep, pigs, and bulls. However, terracotta figurines could serve as substitutes. The instruments of sacred music were the Egyptian sistrum and the marine shell played by the Tritons (Moschus 2.123–124). The flower dance was intended to produce fructification, and the crane dance, to attract the birds that were the harbingers of the sowing season. The bullfights and performances of acrobats enhanced the brilliance of the ceremonies and gave them a magic value.

The dead were venerated, and the offerings placed beside their bodies served as provisions for their journey to the land beyond the grave (Homer, *Od.* 4.561).

The Minoans regarded divinity as the principle of universal fertility. Its symbol was a woman with bared breasts, the mother who nurses her child. But since the fertility of the soil depends on rain, the divinity is probably to be recognized under the form of a woman wielding the double ax, the symbol of the rainstorm (cf. Nauck, TGF A.44). The goddess may be identified as Ariadne, Britomartis, Dictynna, or Eileithya.

Mycenaean Religion. The Mycenaeans gave an anthropomorphic form to the Minoan symbols. Thus, they had Zeus and Di-u-ja, the Magna Mater of the Pamphylians, and Poseidon and his feminine counterpart. The Cretan goddess was addressed as Hera, Athana, Lady, and Lady of the fawns. These avatars and the Winds, Enyalius, Hermes, Pacan, and perhaps Hephaestus and Dionysus, constituted a pantheon and were the recipients of the first fruits at Cnossos. Religion moved from the caves to the acropolis where the double ax was set up. The priest-king received the divinity into his palace (Homer *Od.* 7.81), which thus became a temple (Homer *Il.* 2.549). The dead were buried within the enclosure of the fortress and protected the living.

Bibliography: M. P. NILSSON, *The Oxford Classical Dictionary,* ed. M. CARY et al. (Oxford 1949) 762–763; *The Minoan-Mycenaean Religion and Its Survival in Greek Religion* (2nd ed. rev. Lund 1950). A. W. PERSSON, *The Religion of Greece in Prehistoric Times* (Berkeley 1942). T. B. WEBSTER, *From Mycenae to Homer* (London 1958).

[J. B. DUMORTIER]

CRÉTIN, JOSEPH

First bishop of ST. PAUL, Minn.; b. Montluel, Ain, France, Dec. 10, 1799; d. St. Paul, Feb. 22, 1857. He was one of four children of Joseph and Mary Jane (Mery) Crétin, both members of families distinguished for their heroic practice of the Catholic faith during the French Revolution. Joseph attended the presbyteral schools at Montluel (1812) and Courcieux (1813), made his classical studies at the preparatory seminary of Meximieux, and studied philosophy at L'Argentière and Alix. He entered the grand seminary of Saint-Sulpice in Paris on Oct. 20, 1820, was ordained for the Diocese of Belley on Dec. 20, 1823, and then served as curate (1823–31) and pastor (1831–38) at the parish of Ferney, where he founded a presbyteral school in 1826. During this period he received the degree of bachelor of letters from the University of France (1829) and became a close friend of the Curé of Ars, (St.) John VIANNEY.

In August 1838 Mathias Loras, first bishop of Dubuque, Iowa, returned to France to secure priests for his new diocese. While visiting Ferney, he invited Crétin, his former pupil at Meximieux, to work in the U.S. Crétin, with his own bishop's permission, left France on Aug. 27, 1838, arriving in Dubuque on April 18, 1839, where he was immediately named vicar-general of the diocese. During the 11 years he held this post, he also devoted himself to pastoral care among the Winnebago of upper Iowa and the French settlers and Canadian *voyageurs* at Prairie du Chien, Wis. When, on July 19, 1850, Pius IX created the Diocese of St. Paul in Minnesota, Crétin was chosen first bishop; he was consecrated in France by Bp. Alexander Devie of Belley on Jan. 26, 1851. While in France, Crétin recruited two priests, three subdeacons, and one cleric in minor orders to serve in his diocese. He was canonically installed July 2, 1851.

During his 6-year episcopate, Crétin brought the Sisters of St. Joseph of Carondelet and the Sisters of St. Benedict to the diocese. He also secured the services of Francis PIERZ, the celebrated missionary to the Chippewa. Letters written by Crétin and Pierz, and published in U.S. and German newspapers, attracted hundreds of Catholic immigrants to Minnesota. Through Pierz, Crétin invited to Minnesota the Benedictine priests, whose Abbey of St. John, now in the Diocese of St. Cloud, constitutes (1963) the largest Benedictine community in the world.

Bibliography: "The Letters and Papers of Bishop Joseph Cretin," Archives, Catholic Historical Society of St. Paul, St. Paul Seminary, St. Paul, Minn. Excerpts appear as "The Cretin Collection," *Acta et Dicta,* 1.1 (July 1907) 34–38; 2.1 (1909) 1–41; 2.2 (July 1910) 183–204; 3.1 (July 1911) 1–20; 3.2 (July 1914) 226–234. J. IRELAND, "Life of the Rt. Rev. Joseph Cretin . . . ," *ibid.,* 4.2 (July 1916) 187–218; 5.1 (July 1917) 3–66; 5.2 (July 1918) 170–205. J. M. REARDON, *The Catholic Church in the Diocese of St. Paul* (St. Paul 1952) 61–121.

[J. P. SHANNON]

CRIB, CHRISTMAS

St. Jerome (d. 420) believed that the manger-crib of Christ was molded in clay [Christmas homily, *Anecdota Maredsolana* (Maredsous-Oxford 1897) 3.2:393]. It is more likely it was carved into the rock of the stable-cave of BETHLEHEM. The Roman basilica of St. Mary Major has five small boards of Levantine sycamore venerated as the crib of Christ. If the actual crib was of clay or stone, these would have formed a subsidiary part. The basilica has possessed the boards, supposedly, since the 7th century, but John the Deacon the Younger, writing about 1169, was the first to attest to their presence at the basilica (*Liber de Ecclesia Lateranense* 15; *Patrologia Latina* 194:1543–50).

A century before the presumed acquisition of the relics, and perhaps as early as the 5th century, when Sixtus III reconstructed St. Mary Major, the basilica had a small oratory built like the cave of Bethlehem. Hence the basilica's secondary title, applied at least by the mid-6th century, *S. Maria ad Praesepe* or *ad Praesepem.* Hence also the designation of the chapel, at least by the 7th century, as the station for the first papal Mass at Christmas.

The "crib" as a synonym for the whole nativity scene is normally restricted to plastic representations. The scene was often depicted in Roman Christian sarcophagal sculptures; and the earliest datable Roman relief (343) already pictures the ox and the ass, following the faulty interpretation of Is 1.3, which ch. 15 of Pseudo-Matthew popularized. Our oldest devotional crib is the marble group carved by Arnolfo di Cambio (1232?–1302), when he remodeled the oratory of the crib in St. Mary Major. (Since the 17th century, both crib and oratory have occupied the crypt in the church's Sistine Chapel).

However, it was St. FRANCIS OF ASSISI who really launched the crib devotion with his *presepio* at Greccio in 1223. Promoted by the Franciscans and other religious, the custom spread widely on the Continent after the 14th century. By the dawn of the baroque era, the crib setting had become an intricate scenic landscape, and numerous secular figures were now added to those of the Holy Family, shepherds, and Magi. Crib-making thus developed into an important folk art, especially in Portugal, in the Tyrol, and most of all in the Kingdom of the Two Sicilies, where it was actively patronized by Charles III de Bourbon (d. 1788).

The home crib became popular in Catholic Europe after 1600, owing, it is said, to the efforts of the Capuchins. Except for the crib (the "putz") of the pietist Moravians, manger-building was not originally adopted by Protestants. Pre-Reformation England had had its own crib custom, that of baking the Christmas mince pie in an oblong manger shape to cradle an image of the Child. The British Puritans, therefore, in outlawing Christmas, declared particular war on mince pie as "idolatrie in crust."

Finally, missionaries to the natives and immigrants from various European countries also brought their crib customs to the Americas.

Bibliography: N. DE ROBECK, *The Christmas Crib* (Milwaukee 1956). D. J. FOLEY, *Little Saints of Christmas: The Santons of Provence* (Boston 1959). F. X. WEISER, *The Christmas Book* (New York 1952).

[R. F. MCNAMARA/EDS.]

CRIMINALI, ANTONIO, VEN.

Protomartyr of the Society of Jesus; b. Sissa (Parma, Italy), Feb. 7, 1520; d. Vêdâlai (South India), May or June, 1549. A meeting with J. Laínez and Peter Faber in Parma (1539–40) inspired him to join the Jesuits in Rome, where he pronounced his first vows April 9, 1542. IGNATIUS LOYOLA sent him to Coimbra for further study. An abortive effort to reach India was followed by a successful voyage to Goa in 1545. As a missionary along the Fishery Coast, Criminali was confirmed as superior of the mission by St. FRANCIS XAVIER. He was an indefatigable apostle, learning Tamil and organizing the catechists in the villages. Xavier called him "a saintly man, born to be a missionary for these countries." During an attack by the Vadagar, while he was trying to save Christian children and women in Vêdâlai (Ramnâd, Madras), he was killed, probably by a Muslim.

Bibliography: L. VALMERANA, *Vita del B. Antonio Criminale,* ed. G. SCHURHAMMER, *Archivum Historicum Societatis Jesu* 5 (1936) 235–267. J. CASTETS, *The Venerable Anthony Criminali* (Trichinopoly 1926). R. STREIT and J. DINDINGER, *Bibliotheca missionum* 4:127–128.

[J. WICKI]

CRISOGÓNO DE JESÚS SACRAMENTADO

Lawrence Garrachón, Discalced Carmelite writer and lecturer; b. Villamorisca, Leon, Spain; d. Usúrbil, Guipuzcoa, Mar. 5, 1945. After completing his studies in the humanities in the minor seminary of the Discalced CARMELITES at Medina del Campo, he was professed in the monastery of Segovia, Dec. 5, 1920. When he had finished his philosophical studies at Avila, and theology at Toledo, he was ordained in Toledo, April 2, 1927. He was professor of philosophy at the Discalced Carmelite college in Avila until 1931, when he was absent from Spain for a time taking supplementary philosophical courses at Louvain. During the Spanish Civil War he took refuge in France, but returned to Spain at the end of the war. In 1941 he founded the journal *Rivista de Espiritualidad* that he edited until his premature death, which occurred while he was conducting a retreat. Despite his early death, his writings are numerous, some very controversial. Among his better known works are: *San Juan de la Cruz: Su Obra Científica y Su Obra Literaria* (2 v. Avila 1929); *La Escuela Mistica Carmelitana* (Avila 1930; tr. French, Lyon 1936); *Compendio de Asetica y Mistica* (Avila 1933; tr. Latin, Turin 1936); *Biography of St. John of the Cross* (Madrid, B.A.C., 1946; tr. English, 1951).

Bibliography: ALBERTO DE LA VIRGEN DEL CARMEN, "Silueta científica del P. Crosógono de J. S." *El Monte Carmelo* 49 (1945) 292–303. SILVERIO DE SANTA TERESA, *Historia del Carmen Descalzo en España, Portugal y América,* 15 v. (Burgos 1935–49) v.14. E. A. PEERS, *St. Teresa of Jesus and Other Addresses* (London 1953) 198–200.

[O. RODRIGUEZ]

CRISPIN OF VITERBO, ST.

Also known as *Il Santorello* in Viterbo; Capuchin lay brother, questor, and apostle of the poor; b. Nov. 13, 1668, Viterbo, Italy; d. May 19, 1750, at Rome. After receiving his early education from the Jesuits, Pietro Fioretti followed the trade of shoemaker until he joined the Roman province of the Capuchins on July 22, 1693, and became Brother Crispin. He was cook, gardener, and infirmarian. For 46 years he acted as questor, the chief financial officer. From his early days as a Capuchin until

"The Adoration of the Shepherds," tempera painting on wood panel by Taddeo Gaddi, 14th century, in the Galleria dell' Accademia, Florence.

his death, he was blessed with the gift of miracles and an infectious joy and cheerfulness. Both laity and ecclesiastics sought him for encouragement. In his many years of questing in Orvieto, he not only became the provider for his Capuchin family, but begged for all the poor. Throughout his life Crispin's spirituality was based on his trust in Mary Immaculate. In 1748, because of ill health, Crispin was sent to the infirmary in Rome, where he died of pneumonia two years later. The incorrupt body of St. Crispin, who was beatified in 1806, now rests under a side altar in the Capuchin church at Rome. His was the first canonization presided over by Pope John Paul II on June 20, 1982.

Feast: May 21 (Capuchins).

Bibliography: *Acta Apostolicae Sedis,* 75 (1983): 789–795. *Analecta Ordinis Fratrum Minorum Cappucinorum,* v. 1–70, see general index. "Epistola exhortativa nunc primum edita," *Analecta Ordinis Fratrum Minorum Cappucinorum,* 27 (1911): 19. *Bibliotheca Sanctorum IV* (Rome 1964) 312 f. *Bullarium Ordinis Fratrum Minorum Cappuccinorum* (Innsbruck 1883–84) v. 10. R. BRANCA, *Un frate allegro* (Cagliari 1971). C. HAMMER, "Our Lady's Favorite," *Round Table of Franciscan Research,* 23 (1958): 17–21. *L'Osservatore Romano,* Eng. ed., no. 26 (1982): 1–2. GIORGIO DA RIANO, ed., *Massime e preghiere,* 3d ed. (Rome 1950).

[T. O'ROURKE]

CRISPINA, CRISPIN, AND CRISPINIAN, SS.

Martyrs whose deaths are connected with the Diocletian persecutions.

Crispina, born in Thagora, Numidia, was married and had several children. She was tried before the proconsul of Africa, Anulinus, for refusing to obey an edict commanding sacrifice to the Roman gods and was beheaded at Theveste (Tebessa) on December 5, 304. The acts that record the final hearing of her trial are accepted as authentic. A cult in her honor was quickly established in North Africa. St. AUGUSTINE celebrated her sanctity in two sermons (286 and 354) and in his *Enarrationes in Psalmos* (120 and 137) giving details of her family, social condition, and martyrdom. There is doubt about the location of her grave in the remains of the Basilica of Theveste.

Feast: Dec. 5.

Crispin and Crispinian were allegedly beheaded in Gaul in 287 by the Emperor Maximian. According to an unreliable, ninth-century *Passio* recounting their martyrdom, this followed a trial by the legendary persecutor Rectorianus. They seem to have been authentic Roman martyrs, however, whose bones were early transferred to Soissons in Gaul, and later (ninth century) brought back to Osnabrück in Germany. The Roman martyrology claims that their bodies were transferred from Soissons and located in the church of San Lorenzo in Panisperna. They were considered examples of industrious virtue who supported themselves as shoemakers, and they were held up as models in sermons during the Middle Ages. Their fame in England stems in part from a passage in Shakespeare's *Henry V* (Act 4, scene 3). They are the patrons of shoemakers, saddlers, and tanners.

Feast: Oct. 25.

Bibliography: *Acta Sanctae Sedis* Oct. 11:495–540. L. JULLIAN, "Le Cycle de Rectorianus," *Revue des Études anciennes* 25 (1923) 367–378. H. DELEHAYE, *Étude sur le légendier romain* (Brussels 1936). L. DUCHESNE, *Fastes Épiscopaux de l'ancienne Gaule* (Paris 1907–15) 3: 141–152.

[E. G. RYAN]

CRISPOLTI, FILIPPO

Journalist and senator; b. Rieti, Italy, May 25, 1857; d. Rome, March 2, 1942. Crispolti was copy editor of the *Corriere nazionale* of Turin as a young man, and subsequently (1886) of the OSSERVATORE ROMANO, edited by his uncle Cesare Crispolti, for whom he sometimes substituted. In 1887 he began to contribute to the *Cittadino* of Genoa under the pseudonym "Fuscolino"; in 1896 he left the *Osservatore Romano,* and at Bologna founded *Avvenire,* later *Avvenire d'Italia.* In 1919 he returned to *Cittadino* as political editor and remained there until 1924. From 1927 to 1930 he was co-editor of *Momento* at Turin and continued to contribute to *Corriere d'Italia* and to the weekly *Pro familia,* for which he wrote for 40 years. Crispolti wrote numerous articles for other Catholic dailies and magazines and published books of poetry, novels, lives of saints, literary studies (especially on Manzoni), polemics, and memoirs.

Crispolti was among the earliest members of the Italian Catholic movement, participating in all the congresses and serving as chairman for several of them. He was communal counselor at Rome and Turin, and in 1919 was elected deputy by the Italian Popular Party (the first political party of Italian Catholics). He was elected senator in 1922. He was extremely loyal to the Holy See and was a member of the Noble Pontifical Guard. Crispolti directed all his public activity so as to provide liaison between the papal aristocracy and the middle class of the RISORGIMENTO, keeping a certain aloofness toward the more popular elements in the Catholic movement, both social and political. In 1924, during the most severe clash between POPULARISM and FASCISM, when many thought the Holy See wished to see the end of the Catholic political movement, Crispolti promulgated a manifesto against the Popularists that they considered a betrayal. Among his published works—besides the Manzoni studies—the following deserve to be remembered: *Il laicato cattolico italiano* (Rome 1890), *Questioni vitali* (Rome 1908), *Il rinnovamento dell'educazione* (Rome 1919), *Ricordi personali: Pio IX, Leone XIII, Pio X, Benedetto XV* (Milan, Rome 1932), and *Corone e porpore* (Milan 1936).

Bibliography: E. A. MARTIRE, *Filippo Crispolti: Note biografiche* (Milan 1943). A. GIANNINI, *Tre cattolici* (Milan 1943).

[E. LUCATELLO]

CRITERION (CRITERIOLOGY)

In philosophic inquiry about the validity of KNOWLEDGE, some rule or standard, called a criterion (Gr. κριτήριον), by which TRUTH can be known and distinguished from ERROR is usually sought and applied. The fact that men hold different opinions about things, or that sometimes one finds that he has been mistaken in a previous judgment, urges a consideration of how to distinguish between valid knowledge or truth and mere thought or OPINION. The very fact that one does distinguish between truth and error indicates that some criterion exists for judging the validity of knowledge. The study of such a criterion is sometimes called criteriology.

Early History. In the history of GREEK PHILOSOPHY, the conflicting views of the Ionians, who admitted change in things, and of the Eleatics, who denied it, brought forth the problem of the relationship between sense knowledge and intellectual understanding. SOCRATES was unable to solve questions concerning the nature of changing things and turned more hopefully to the study of moral problems. These he tried to elucidate by processes of induction and definition that, when successfully brought to term, he accepted as genuine knowing, not mere opinion. PLATO likewise thought that man cannot have genuine knowledge of the sensible world but only more or less probable opinions about it; he held that the realities that are the objects of philosophical inquiry exist in a world of Forms, or Ideas, apart from sensible things.

Aristotle tried to close the gap between the sensible and the intelligible by admitting that intelligible forms are in sensible things and are not separated from them save by the operation of man's understanding. Sensible things are themselves intelligible, but they are known in different ways by the SENSES and by the INTELLECT. By sense man apprehends the particular and the changing, whereas by intellect he understands the necessary and universal aspects of things. His intellect, working with the data of sense, grasps the intelligible aspect of being and proceeds to understand by distinguishing being from nonbeing, this from that, one from many, whole from part, and cause from effect. The validity of all knowledge can be judged with truth and certitude by the intellect's reflecting on the various kinds of knowledge and evaluating these in the light of the principle of CONTRADICTION, which it applies with the help of experience and logical analysis. The chief root of error in man is not the senses but rather the PHANTASM, which exhibits to the intellect things that are absent as if they were present, and things that are different as if they were alike.

The Stoic philosophers, both Greek and Roman, did not maintain a distinction between sense and intellect, and in effect reduced all knowledge to sensation, with all its vagaries and uncertainties. The Skeptics went a step further and admitted only internal phenomena. They denied all intelligible essences and necessary truths and held that there is no criterion by which one can distinguish between contradictory views, so that man cannot know whether he possesses truth or not.

Scholasticism. Scholastic philosophers admitted a distinction between sense and intellect and held that man is already in possession of many truths, which he attains not only from ordinary experience and the various scientific disciplines but also through faith in the Christian teachings. For the scholastics the chief epistemological problem was to account for the validity of abstract or uni-versal knowledge in relation to the singulars that exist in nature. Some held that the universal is only a word or name (NOMINALISM); others maintained that it expresses something apart from sensible things, either entirely apart (Platonic REALISM) or separated from sensible matter by the abstractive action of the mind (moderate realism). According to the account of moderate realism, the nature, or essence, that is known by the intellect is really in the singulars that exist in the world of things; but the abstract or universal manner in which it is known depends upon the mind of the knower. (*See* UNIVERSALS.)

Modern Thought. The modern critical problem arose with the philosophy of R. DESCARTES; it came from his method of universal doubt and from his starting point in thought (*cogito ergo sum*). This approach brought up the question whether and how one knows the external world or anything that is real and distinct from one's knowledge of it. Descartes tried to solve this problem with the criterion of clear and distinct ideas, passing from the idea of a limited and imperfect self and the idea of something unlimited and perfect to the assertion of God and His goodness and then to the general veracity of the created mind and the validity of its ideas. G. W. LEIBNIZ likewise wished to proceed from thought to things and employed the postulate that each mind mirrors the universe more or less adequately according to a harmony preestablished by God.

I. Kant also acknowledged a gap between thought and things, which he declared unbridgeable in theory, although in practice he maintained that man ought to live as if he possessed valid knowledge of moral duty and its practical implications of freedom, justice, God, and immortality. Kant held that whereas sensible phenomena are particular and contingent, yet they are understood in ways that are determined by the structure and laws of the mind, which molds and shapes sensory experience according to its own patterns. These a priori patterns give universality and necessity to experimental knowledge, and suffice, Kant thought, to account for the scientific character of mathematics and physics. But one has no assurance that things are as he understands them. Indeed things in themselves are unknowable, and man has no valid knowledge of essences or necessary reasons of being. (*See* CRITICISM, PHILOSOPHICAL; NOUMENA; PHENOMENA.)

The Problem. In summary, philosophers who admit only sense knowledge and neglect or deny intellectual knowledge propose no criterion other than SENSATION by which to distinguish between truth and error, and they acknowledge the uncertainties and limitations of this criterion. On the other hand, philosophers who admit intellectual knowledge as distinct from sense knowledge find difficulty in relating sense and intellect. Some deny that the sensible is intelligible and assert either that the intelligible is something real and apart from the sensible or that the intelligible is merely the mold or pattern according to which the mind understands sensible phenomena. Others advance in the direction of SUBJECTIVISM and IDEALISM and deny the distinction between knowledge and its object, that is, between knowledge and things, and maintain that the mind actively constitutes or constructs or posits all its objects, without question of truth or of a criterion of truth.

A Realist Solution. According to natural or moderate realism, the sensible is also intelligible and is understood by the intellect in the light of the apprehension of its own object, namely, BEING, and the evident FIRST PRINCIPLES and laws of being. For valid knowledge there must be a starting point or principle that is evident and unshakable, and this is found to be the principle of contradiction: it is impossible to affirm and deny at once the same of the same. This principle is so evidently valid that no one can be mistaken about it. Moreover, it is not a supposition or postulate, or a dogmatic affirmation, but something that the mind must and naturally does embrace. Thus equipped with the principle of contradiction, and proceeding on the basis of sense EXPERIENCE, man gradually builds up his understanding of things, distinguishing between one and many, being in nature and being in knowledge, whole and part, cause and effect, etc. By reflecting on his knowledge of things in the light of intelligible being, that is, of objective evidence, which is the universal criterion of truth, he can know the conformity between the intellect judging and the thing judged. Thus he can distinguish between truth and error, and can determine the reasons or causes of truth.

See Also: EPISTEMOLOGY; GNOSEOLOGY; KNOWLEDGE, THEORIES OF.

Bibliography: V. SAINATI, *Enciclopedia filosofica*, 4 v. (Venice-Rome 1957) 1:1347–48. J. OWENS, *An Elementary Christian Metaphysics* (Milwaukee 1963). R. F. O'NEILL, ed., *Readings in Epistemology* (pa; Englewood Cliffs, N.J. 1962).

[W. H. KANE]

CRITICISM, PHILOSOPHICAL

A term used primarily to designate the philosophy of Immanuel KANT; in a more general sense, it applies to any philosophical doctrine that adopts a critical attitude, i.e., that systematically questions whatever appears to be true and yet is capable of being doubted. In EPISTEMOLOGY, criticism is opposed to DOGMATISM; its aim there is to make evident the postulational character of KNOWL-

EDGE or its decisive presuppositions and fundamental premises. This article is concerned with criticism in the Kantian sense, treating of its basic notion and its development into the critical idealism of J. G. FICHTE.

Kantian criticism. Criticism, according to KANT, is an investigation of the nature and the limits of reason and knowledge pursued in such a manner that both SKEPTICISM and dogmatism are avoided. Kantian criticism arose out of a dissatisfaction with the RATIONALISM of the 17th century and the EMPIRICISM of the 18th century, both of which had failed, in Kant's eyes, to deal adequately with the problem of knowledge. Whereas rationalism, for him, sought first to preserve necessity and universality in knowledge, and, second, to bring that knowledge into contact with the existential real, empiricism reversed the epistemological process; it started with sensations of things and attempted to raise these, through experience, to a knowledge that was necessary and universal. Yet Kant's work was more than a critical investigation of these epistemological theories. It consisted surely in this, but Kant's principal undertaking was to offer a critique of the faculty for acquiring knowledge itself. To criticize such a faculty, for Kant, is not only to expose sources of error, but also to discover and examine elements in knowledge and stipulate conditions that are necessary for its acquisition.

Transcendental Philosophy. Kantian philosophy of criticism is also called transcendental philosophy, an expression that has a proper meaning for Kant. The transcendental method of argument is opposed to classical ontology, which seeks to explain in some rational way the existence of particular objects given in knowledge; the transcendental method, on the other hand, is primarily concerned with the very possibility of knowledge. Philosophies that consider concepts and principles relating to the existence of objects were regarded by Kant as metaphysical and, as such, opposed to his transcendental philosophy. The latter considers concepts and principles as conditions for the very possibility of knowledge and shows these conditions to be sufficient and necessary. *See* TRANSCENDENTAL (KANTIAN).

Analysis and Deduction. Kant's critical reflection upon the functioning of knowledge and the validity of its affirmations may be considered under the two aspects of critical analysis and critical deduction. The purpose of the first is to examine the elements and laws that operate in the formation of a true judgment. This aspect of criticism is concerned with the parts of judgment and the conditions under which judgment is true. It attempts to determine the constitutive elements of judgment by examining the conditions for its validity. This first aspect of critical analysis, or "transcendental analysis," as Kant called it, is complemented by the aspect of critical deduction. Here the philosopher shows the absolute necessity of those conditions in the act of knowledge on which truth and thought are grounded.

Critical idealism. Out of Kantian critical philosophy came other philosophical currents, some leading to developments within Kantianism and NEO-KANTIANISM, others more significantly prompting the growth of German speculative idealism. Thus J. G. Fichte (1762–1814), who had deeply immersed himself in the works of Kant, set into operation a series of philosophical movements that owe much to the critical attitude of Kant. Fichte called his own position a critical idealism, which he distinguished from Kant's philosophy and from the dogmatism of some forms of realism.

Whereas Kant had taken a variety of objects for critical study, Fichte made man the sole object of study and made man's ego the source of the being of the world. Fichte's main departure from Kant, however, was on the notion of the thing-in-itself. Fichte criticized this notion because on Kantian premises there was no reason to assert the existence of any entity that is unknowable. This led him to transform critical philosophy into a consistent critical idealism, which taught that things had to be considered in their totality as products of thought.

Fichte further converted Kant's transcendental ego into a metaphysical or ontological principle. The ego of Fichte became, not the individual finite ego, but the Absolute Ego. Hegel later made the ultimate principle Infinite Reason or Infinite Spirit. Critical idealism thereupon became a metaphysical idealism in which reality is the process of the self-expression or the self-manifestation of Infinite Reason.

See Also: IDEALISM; KANTIANISM; KNOWLEDGE, THEORIES OF.

Bibliography: F. C. COPLESTON, *History of Philosophy* (Westminster, Md. 1946—) v. 6, 7. V. SAINATI, *Enciclopedia filosofica* (Venice-Rome 1957) 1:1352–55. R. EISLER, *Wörterbuch der philosophischen Begriffe* (4th ed. Berlin 1927–30) 1:877–880. H. W. CASSIRER, *Kant's First Critique* (New York 1954); *A Commentary on Kant's Critique of Judgment* (London 1938). A. C. EWING, *A Short Commentary on Kant's Critique of Pure Reason* (Chicago, Ill. 1950).

[T. A. WASSMER]

CROAGH PATRICK

An isolated peak rising from the shore beside Clew Bay, five miles from Westport, Mayo County, West Ireland. It has long been known as Cruach Phádraig (St. Patrick's Ridge), and in St. PATRICK's day was called

Immanuel Kant, engraving. (©Bettmann/CORBIS)

Cruachan Aigli. Tírechín (late 7th century) reports that Patrick fasted and prayed for 40 days and 40 nights on the peak, after the example of Moses and Christ, and was comforted in seeing as the fruit of his labors all the saints of Ireland to the end of time, so numerous that they obscured the sky from view. The report is elaborated in the 10th-century Tripartite Life of St. Patrick. Croagh Patrick from an early date was a place of pilgrimage, originally for the feast of St. Patrick; but because of wind, rain, and cold, the date was changed to the last Sunday of July. In the days of the PENAL LAWS, when Catholics had to hold divine services in secret, the pilgrimage to the bare mountain top flourished. Modern transportation has brought many pilgrims. The pilgrim path begins at 1,000 feet and covers 1,500 feet of stony terrain to the summit, where an oratory was built in 1905.

Bibliography: *Liber Ardmachanus: The Book of Armagh,* ed. J. GWYNN (Dublin 1913). W. STOKES, ed. and tr., *The Tripartite Life of Patrick,* 2 v. (*Rerum Brittanicarum medii aevi scriptores* 89; 1887). J. B. BURY, *The Life of St. Patrick* (New York 1905). J. HEALY, *The Life and Writings of St. Patrick* (Dublin 1905).

O'MADDEN, *Cruach Phádraig, St. Patrick's Holy Mountain* (Dublin 1929).

[J. RYAN]

CROATIA, THE CATHOLIC CHURCH IN

The Republic of Croatia is located in southeastern Europe, on the Balkan Peninsula, and is bordered on the north by Slovenia and Hungary, on the east by Serbia, on the southeast by Bosnia and Herzegovina, and on the southwest by the Adriatic Sea. The southern region is alpine, falling to level, fertile plains in the north. Natural resources include petroleum and natural gas reserves, bauxite, iron ore and calcium, while agricultural products consist mainly of grain, sugar beets, potatoes and grapes, the last of which are cultivated on the islands off the western coast.

A wealthy, industrialized constituent republic of the former Yugoslavia, Croatia comprises Croatia proper, Slavonia, Dalmatia and Istria. Gaining independence in 1991, the region quickly became involved in ethnic warfare, both on its own soil and in neighboring Bosnia-Herzegovina. By 1995 a peace had been reached in both nations, leaving Croatia to resolve its remaining land disputes by 1998. Communist mismanagement of the Croatian economy, as well as damage caused by years of fighting, were among the issues confronting the country's newly elected government in 2000, as Croatia attempted to privatize its industrial base and reform its banking system. Ethnic Croats, who lived in Bosnia-Herzegovina as well as in Srijem (Syrmia) and Voivodina, remained overwhelmingly Catholics at the start of the 21st century; their faith distinguished them from the Serbs, who were Orthodox.

Early History. The Croats, who were believed to be migrants from Ukraine, settled in Pannonia, Istria and Dalmatia *c.* 600. In 615 they destroyed Salona (now Solin), capital of Byzantine Dalmatia, but were unable to seize the fortified cities on the Adriatic, in which the Roman population had taken refuge, until much later. When the Croats migrated into this territory, which had long been Christian, they came into contact with Catholicism. In 641 Pope John IV sent legates to Croatia to ransom Christian captives held by the Croats and to obtain for Rome relics of the Christian martyrs. So rapidly did Christianity penetrate the region that by 679 a treaty with Pope St. Agatho declared that the Croats would not undertake an aggressive war against Roman forces, signaling their orientation to the Western, rather than Eastern Orthodox, Church. Pope John X in 925 called them *spe-

cialissimi filii Sanctae Romanae Ecclesiae.* Pope Gregory VII further accentuated this Western and Catholic tendency of the Croats by sending in 1076 a royal crown to Zvonimir, *Rex Croatiae Dalmatiaeque.*

When the 812 treaty of Aachen returned the cities along the Dalmatian coast to Byzantine rule, attempts were made to convert the nearby Croats to Byzantine policy and to the schism of PHOTIUS. The Croats, however, refused to submit to the jurisdiction of pro-Byzantine Dalmatian bishops and in 864 established in Nin (Nona) their own bishopric, immediately subject to the Holy See until 928, when changed circumstances caused it to be abolished.

St. Methodius, the apostle of the Slavs, obtained from John VIII the bull *Industriae Tuae* (880), which approved, as had Adrian II, the Roman-Slavonic or Glagolitic, liturgy. On his way from Rome Methodius probably passed through Croatia and effected the adoption of this liturgy in the See of Nin. Soon it spread over all the Croatian lands near the Adriatic, and for centuries was distinctive in Croatian Catholicism. Because of this liturgy, understood by the people, Protestantism had slight success among the Croats, who clung to their traditional faith. Such was not the case in Dalmatia, where, under Venetian, Austrian and Italian domination, the Glagolitic liturgy continually waned. After 1918 it started to spread, and eventually was incorporated into a number of Dalmatian dioceses.

Hungary extended its sovereignty over Pannonian Croatia in 1093, and Hungary and the Croatian Kingdom of Dalmatia were joined in dynastic union by the *pacta conventa* of 1102. In 1094 St. Ladislaus founded the Diocese of Zagreb, which became an archdiocese and metropolitan see in 1852. Croatia was largely instrumental in saving the Church in the West by its heroic resistance against the Tatars in 1242, and later against centuries of Turkish incursions. For this they earned the title *scutum solidissimum et antemurale christianitatis* from Pope Leo X in 1519.

That part of Croatia not seized by the Turks suffered national and religious erosion because of an influx of Orthodox Serb refugees who entered Croatia in search of refuge from the Ottomans. The bishops of Zagreb labored zealously among these Serbs, with little success. The Church suffered further erosion during the 16th century as Protestantism spread among the nobility in Zagreb, although the action of Bishop Bratulić (1603–11) and a 1604 decree of banishment enacted by the Croatian *Sabor* (parliament) saved the Catholic faith in the region. The Orthodox Bishop of Marča, Simeon Vretanja, visited Rome in 1611 and made his profession of the Catholic faith, while a small group of Catholics from the district of Žumberak also joined with Rome, leading to a small Eastern Catholic population in Croatia by the 20th century.

The Illyrian movement initiated by Napoleon Bonaparte during the first years of the 19th century aroused Croatian nationalism, promoted solidarity with other southern Slavs and resulted in short periods of national autonomy, first from Austria during the 1848 revolution and then from Hungary in 1868. The Diocese of Zagreb was made a metropolitan archdiocese in 1852, and its first two archbishops became cardinals. The Society of St. Jerome was established in Zagreb during this period.

The Formation of Yugoslavia. In 1918 Croatia again asserted its political independence, joining Slovenia and Serbia in forming the kingdom that after 1929 became known as Yugoslavia (South Slavia). Although the constitution of this new nation guaranteed religious equality, Serbs who aligned state interests with those of the Serbian Orthodox Church controlled the government. In 1922 the Yugoslavian government began negotiations with the Holy See for a concordat. They reached agreement in 1935, but the Yugoslavian parliament heeded the opposition of the Orthodox Church and refused ratification. This concordat would have regularized the Catholic Church's organization so that diocesan and state borders would correspond. Belgrade was to be the metropolitan see for Serbia; Ljubljana for Slovenia; and Split for Dalmatia. The Roman-Slavonic liturgy was to prevail in all parts of Yugoslavia where Catholics so desired.

Dissatisfied with the government's preference for one church over another, Croatian Catholics began to support the idea of an independent Croatian state. During World War II Germany invaded the country and caused it to be divided, whereupon Croatia proclaimed its independence. Led by fascist Ante Pavelíc, this new state aided the Catholic Church by promoting religious instruction in schools, although it also injured the Church morally by involving it in the forced conversion of Orthodox Serbians over the objection of Church leaders.

Pavelíc's brutal regime ended in 1945, when Communists seized power and in a constitution dated Nov. 30, 1946, established the Federal People's Republic of Yugoslavia, comprised of six federal republics: Slovenia, Croatia, Serbia (with the two autonomous territories of Voivodina and Kosovo-Metohia), Bosnia-Herzegovina, Montenegro and Macedonia. Although religious freedom was guaranteed under the constitution, under the leadership of communist Marshall Josip Broz Tito the state did its best to break Church power in Croatia, condemning Zagreb Archbishop Alojzije STEPINAC (d. 1960) to 16 years imprisonment in 1946 for refusing to set up a puppet Croatian Catholic Church that would be controlled by

Capital: Zagreb.
Size: 21,829 sq. miles.
Population: 4,282,216 in 2000.
Languages: Croatian.
Religions: 3,639,884 Catholics (85%), 256,932 Orthodox (6%), 41,950 Muslims (1%), 343,450 other or unknown.

Tito. Catholic schools closed, their buildings confiscated, while all religious instruction in state schools ceased.

A clash of ideology between Tito and the Soviet Union that started in 1948 forced Yugoslavia to court Western powers and caused a lessening of religious persecution. By the mid-1950s the state's policy toward the Church had been liberalized to the point where the Holy See could appoint new bishops and Stepinac was released from prison; in 1962 bishops from Croatia were in attendance at Vatican Council II.

A nationalist movement begun in 1966 played on Croatian fears of Serbian dominance and sought political reforms that would substantially increase Croatian autonomy. However, this movement threatened the unity of the Yugoslav federation, prompting the eradication of nationalist elements from the Croatian party by 1972. Still, nationalist sentiments remained and, following Tito's death in 1980, became more openly expressed as the Yugoslav economy faltered and inflation took its toll. In 1988 Croats refused to support Yugoslav leader Slobodan Milosevic's manipulation of politics in Vojvodina and the Serbian enclave of Knin, where Serbian minority populations were agitating for the creation of self-governing provinces within the country.

In 1989 Croatia legalized opposition parties and established multiparty elections, while a new constitution was drafted in December of 1990 that provided for freedom of religion. On June 25, 1991 Franjo Tudjman won the election to form the first postwar noncommunist government in Yugoslavia. Scattered fighting followed, as Croats and Serbs fought in the region, bombing the city of Dubrovnik in 1992. In the region of Krajina, which declared itself a Serbian enclave, heavy fighting continued and the 1994 Croat offensive that led to the ultimate Serbian withdrawal from the area was marked by extreme violence that forced 150,000 ethnic Serbs from their Croatian homes. Following the peace of 1995, when Croatian bishops addressed the animosity between Catholic Croats and Orthodox Serbs and encouraged a resolution to the country's history of ethnic violence, they were criticized for overlooking Croat abuses in Krajina. Other issues confronting both the Church and the Croatian government into the 21st century included aiding returning Serbian refugees, making restitution for Church lands

Archdioceses	Suffragans
Rijeka-Senj	Gospić-Senj Krk, Poreć-Pula
Split-Makarska	Dubrovnik, Hvar, Šibenik, Kotor (in Serbia-Montenegro)
Zagreb	Djakovo-Srijem, Požega, Varaždin

The archdiocese of Zadar is immediately subject to the Holy See. The diocese of Križevci serves the Byzantine rite church. In addition, there is a military ordinariate in the country.

confiscated by the communist government of Yugoslavia, dealing with accusations of war crimes, strengthening the economy and putting an end to further ethnic discrimination. In 1996 the Vatican made a pact with the Croatian government to reaffirm the Church's rights to teach, worship and engage in the sacrament of marriage; a further accord two years later provided for "reparations for the injustices to the Catholic Church caused in the past by the confiscation of ecclesiastical properties."

By 2000 Croatia had 1,521 parishes tended by 1,440 diocesan and 800 religious priests, while approximately 90 brothers and 3,600 sisters worked in the region. The Church ran primary and secondary schools, as well as hospitals and other humanitarian institutions. In addition, the Church operated the nation's sole privately owned radio station, Radio Marija. Unlike members of other faiths, beginning in 1991 all Catholic religious received pensions from the government, although by 2000, under Zagreb Archbishop Josip Bozanic, the Church became increasingly independent of such favoritism. In October of 1998, during a visit to Croatia, Pope John Paul II beatified Cardinal Stepinac, although Serbs who believed the Cardinal to have been a Nazi sympathizer during World War II criticized this move. In addition to a Roman Catholic population, Croatia retained a small community of Old Catholics.

Bibliography: *Monumenta spectantia historiam Slavorum meridionalium* (Zagreb 1868–). M. SPINKA, *A History of Christianity in the Balkans* (Chicago, IL 1933). R. RISTELHUEBER, *Histoire des peuples balkaniques* (Paris 1950). P. D. OSTROVÍC, *The Truth about Yugoslavia* (New York 1952). W. MARKERT, *Jugoslawien* (Cologne 1954). F. DVORNIK, *The Slavs: Their Early History and Civilization* (Boston 1956); *The Slavs in European History and Civilization* (New Brunswick, NJ 1962). K. S. LATOURETTE, *Christianity in a Revolutionary Age: A History of Christianity in the Nineteenth and Twentieth Centuries*, 5 v. (New York 1958–62) v.1, 2, 4. F. MACLEAN, *The Heretic: The Life and Times of Josip Broz-Tito* (New York 1957). V. KLAIĆ, *Povijest Hrvata*, 6 v. (Zagreb 1899–1919). *The Croatian Nation in Its Struggle for Freedom and Independence: A Symposium*, eds., A. BONIFAČIĆ and C. S. MIHANOVICH (Chicago 1955). R. KISZLING, *Die Kroaten* (Graz 1956). *Croatia: Land, People, Culture*, eds., F. H. ETEROVICH and C.

SPALATIN v.1 (Toronto 1964). S. P. RAMET, *Nihil Obstat: Religion, Politics, and Social Change in East-Central Europe and Russia* (Durham, NC 1998). J. MATL, *Lexikon für Theologie und Kirche²*, eds., J. HOFER and K. RAHNER, 10 v. (2d, new ed. Freiburg 1957–65) 5:1191–94. B. SPULER and H. KOCH, *Die Religion in Geschichte und Gegenwart³*, 7 v. (3d ed. Tübingen 1957–65) 3:1054–60. *Bilan du Monde*, 2:914–928. *Annuario Pontificio* has annual data on all dioceses.

[P. SHELTON]

CROCE, BENEDETTO

Italian idealist philosopher, statesman, historian, and literary critic; b. Pescasseroli, Feb. 25, 1866; d. Naples, Nov. 20, 1952. In 1902 he founded the journal *La Critica*, through which, for 50 years, he wielded a wide cultural influence in Italy and throughout Europe. A most effective critic of the paraconstitutionalism of fascism, after World War II he dominated the constituent assembly from which the Italian Republic eventually emerged.

Eschewing systematic philosophy, Croce yet achieved an articulated position, absolute historicism, which effectively shaped his activity as historian, critic, and statesman. For him, the controlling principle of absolute historicism is IMMANENCE, excluding all TRANSCENDENCE. Immanence is the concrete inwardness of spirit to its own processes. Spirit is immanent to human presence, temporally diffused through individual existents but transcendentally synthesized in "expression." Expression as first isolated in the aesthetic moment, art, is intuitive, lyrical, and cosmic. Extended to all its moments—logical, economic and ethical—expression becomes the transcendental principle of spirit itself. Fullness of expression and the concrete reality of spirit are achieved in the dialectical movement of history, wherein these moments are concretely synthesized in a "unity of distincts." History, concrete expressive unity in diversity, is the supreme mode of presence of spirit; all significant discourse is constructed and interpreted on historical canons. Historical presence is the eternal present, the contemporaneity of all history, and completes the absolute immanence of spirit. Past and present are projective interpolations within the eternal present and are immanent to it.

Absolute historicism holds the clue to Croce's activity as a historian, pursued at two mutually immanent levels, the theoretical and the practical. The theoretical problem of history is to determine the transcendental principles of historical presence and discourse. Historiography is the interpretation of human documents on the basis of transcendental principles projected in narration. These transcendental principles cannot be fixed a priori but must emerge from the documents. Philosophy and

history are concretely united in the activity of the historian; yet the transcendental principles thus determined are not ontological but methodological. History thus is the self-constituting act of human presence in its pure generation. The supreme transcendental principle of history and of the unity of thought and action in human presence is the canon of "history as the history of freedom." The freedom here intended is not an empirical fact, but a transcendental principle in the sense that on its basis alone the human documents can be significantly construed and the rational unification of thought and action achieved. History constitutes a unique transcendentally constructed system of discourse. This conception of history is the key

to the reading of Croce's own historical works. They all attest to the transcendental principle of history as the history of freedom. They extend this principle in an everwidening circle of concern from the *Rivoluzione napoletana del' 99* (3d ed. 1912) to the now-classic *Storia d'Europa nel secolo XIX* (1932), properly construed as the primary document of the historiography of ethical liberalism.

Croce thought of himself primarily as a literary critic. The vast body of his critical writings, touching all the important literatures of Europe as well as the classics, contains an inexhaustible wealth of special insights. Its greatest interest, however, lies in the manner in which it

Benedetto Croce.

illustrates Croce's philosophical principles. Two concerns permeate this criticism: just evaluation of the particular work and the discovery of the transcendental principle of artistic expression, i.e., the principle that would render the work universally significant. Croce first formulated the theory of expression as pure intuition. While establishing the work of art as an autonomous moment of the human spirit, this principle left it in isolation from the universal consciousness of spirit. Croce then moved on to the conception of the lyricity of art. This constituted a step toward the recognition of the transcendentality of art, because the notion of lyricity already contains the notion of human universality. The final step is taken in the notion of the cosmicity of art. Cosmicity is the pure principle of the transcendentality of art and the guarantee of its human significance. With its discovery Croce achieves the complete unification of his critical and his philosophical efforts. This movement toward the discovery of the transcendental principle of art, philosophical in its nature, is richly documented by the critical works from which it emerges. These are highlighted by the great studies of Dante, Shakespeare, Carducci, and Manzoni, but richly textured with perceptive studies of minor figures.

See Also: IDEALISM; HISTORY, PHILOSOPHY OF, HEGELIANISM.

Bibliography: A comprehensive edition of Croce's works, ed. F. NICOLINI (Bari; in prep.). ISTITUTIO DI STUDIA FILOSOFICI, *Bibliografia filosofica Italiana,* 4 v. (Rome 1950–56) 1:314–334. E. CHIOCCHETTI, *La filosofia di Benedetto Croce* (3d ed. Milan 1924). U. SPIRITO et al., *Benedetto Croce* (Rome 1929). D. FAUCCI, *Storicismo e metafisica nel pensiero crociano* (Florence 1950). C. CARBONARA, *Sviluppo e problemi dell'estetica crociana* (Naples 1947). A. CARACCIOLO, *L'estetica di Benedetto Croce nel suo svolgimento e nel suoi limiti* (Turin 1948). A. MAUTINO, *La formazione della filosofia politica di Benedetto Croce,* ed. N. BOBBIO (3d ed. Bari 1953). A. R. CAPONIGRI, *History and Liberty: The Historical Writings of Benedetto Croce* (London 1955). G. N. ORSINI, *Benedetto Croce, Philosopher of Art and Literary Critic* (Carbondale, Ill. 1961). V. MATHIEU, *Enciclopedia filosofica,* 4 v. (Venice-Rome 1957) 1:1356–64. ISTITUTO ITALIANO PER GLI STUDI STORICI, *L'Opera di Benedetto Croce: Bibliografia,* ed. S. BORSARI (Naples 1964).

[A. R. CAPONIGRI]

CROCKAERT, PETER

Belgian Dominican scholastic; b. Brussels, second half of the 15th century; d. probably Paris, 1514. He studied arts at the Collège de Montaigu in Paris, where he had the Scottish Ockhamist John Major (1469–1550) as one of his professors. As a young man he defended NOMINALISM but later whole-heartedly embraced THOMISM. In 1503 he became a Dominican at the reformed priory of Saint-Jacques in Paris, where he lectured in theology the rest of his life. He ardently defended Thomism against nominalism and SCOTISM. His deep appreciation of HUMANISM and his humanistic elegance in style revolutionized scholastic theology and inaugurated a "second Thomism." In 1509 he began lecturing on the *Summa theologiae* of St. Thomas Aquinas instead of the *Sentences* of Peter Lombard. He greatly inspired his disciples, notably Francisco de VITORIA, with whom he coedited the *Summa theologiae* 2a2ae (Paris 1512). His writings were greatly esteemed in his day, particularly his commentaries on the *Summa theologiae* and on the *De ente* of Aquinas, on the *De anima* and other physical and logical works of Aristotle, and on the *Summulae logicales* of Peter of Spain.

Bibliography: E. M. FILTHAUT, *Lexikon für Theologie und Kirche,* ed. J. HOFER and K. RAHNER (Freiburg 1957–65) 3:98. *Biographie nationale de Belgique* 4:511–512. M. GRABMANN, *Mittelalterliches Geistesleben,* 3 v. (Munich 1926–56) 1:320. R. G. VILLOSLADA, "La Universidad de Paris durante los estudios de Francisco de Vitoria, 1507–1922," *Analecta Gregoriana* 17 (1938) 229–270.

[J. F. HINNEBUSCH]

CROCKETT, RALPH, BL.

Priest, martyr; b. Barton-on-the-Hill, near Farndon, Cheshire, England; hanged, drawn, and quartered at

Broyle Heath, Chichester, Oct. 1, 1588. Having completed his education at Cambridge, Crockett was a schoolmaster in East Anglia until he discerned a call to the priesthood. He studied and was ordained at Rheims (1585). En route to his assignment in the English mission, he was captured on board ship at Littlehampton, Sussex, April 19, 1586, together with Frs. Thomas Bramston, George Potter, and Bl. Edward James. The following week they were transferred to a London prison. On Sept. 30, 1588, he was tried and condemned under 27 Eliz. c. 2 at Chichester with Frs. Edward James, John Oven, and Francis Edwardes. Oven took the Oath of Supremacy after the trial and Edwardes recanted at the gallows. Both were reprieved. James and Crockett absolved one another before execution. He was beatified by Pius XI on Dec. 15, 1929.

Feast of the English Martyrs: May 4 (England).

See Also: ENGLAND, SCOTLAND AND WALES, MARTYRS OF.

Bibliography: R. CHALLONER, *Memoirs of Missionary Priests,* ed. J. H. POLLEN (rev. ed. London 1924; repr. Farnborough 1969). J. H. POLLEN, *Acts of English Martyrs* (London 1891).

[K. I. RABENSTEIN]

CROKE, THOMAS WILLIAM

Archbishop, Irish patriot; b. Castlecor, County Cork, Ireland, January 1823; d. Thurles, County Tipperary, Ireland, July 22, 1902. Croke was the son of William and Isabelle (Plummer) Croke; his mother was a Protestant who converted to Catholicism four years before her death. After studies at the Irish ecclesiastical colleges in Paris (1840–44) and Rome, Croke was ordained (1847). He then taught theology at Carlow and Paris (1847–49), did mission work in the Diocese of Cloyne (1849–58), served as the first president of St. Colman's College, Fermoy (1858–65), and as pastor at Doneraile (1865–70). At Vatican Council I he was theologian to Bishop Keane of Cloyne. In 1870 he was appointed bishop of Auckland, New Zealand. When he returned to Ireland in 1875 for a rest, he was promoted to the Archdiocese of Cashel and Emly. As bishop in Auckland and in Cashel, Croke initiated extensive building programs for churches, schools, and rectories. He enlarged St. Patrick's College in Thurles and completed the cathedral there. He supported the temperance movement and also the Gaelic League, formed in 1891 to revive the Irish language and culture. Croke's greatest prominence, however, was in Irish national affairs.

During the repeal agitation of the 1840s he was an enthusiastic follower of Daniel O'CONNELL; later he turned to the Young Ireland party. Through the 1850s he associated himself closely with the Irish Tenant League. After his return to Ireland he was an outspoken advocate of home rule, and he backed the Land League and the leadership of Charles Parnell in Parliament. But his nationalism, intense and often imprudently expressed, roused the suspicion and hostility of successive British governments. A letter of his to the *Freeman's Journal* of Dublin, which attacked the use of Irish tax revenues to finance police repression and which seemed to encourage nonpayment of taxes, was denounced to Rome by English Catholics (1887). At this juncture Abp. William WALSH of Dublin served as a moderating influence, and Croke's friendship with Cardinal Manning of Westminster kept him in good standing. The scandal that involved Parnell in a divorce suit (1891) disenchanted Croke with the Irish Parliamentary party. More and more he disagreed with its program until finally he withdrew from political controversy.

Bibliography: P. J. WALSH, *Life of William J. Walsh: Archbishop of Dublin* (Dublin 1928).

[A. O'DONNELL]

CROMWELL, OLIVER

Revolutionary English Puritan general and head of state; b. Huntington, April 25, 1599; d. London, Sept. 3, 1658. Cromwell, a minor member of the Long Parliament opposition, rose by 1646 to command the cavalry of the New Model army and was Lord Protector of England from 1653 to 1658. It was mostly presumed in the past that he was, whatever his theories of religious toleration, the inveterate persecutor of English Catholics. Modern study of his religious policy is modifying that view, although critical evaluation of his cruel policy toward the Irish Catholics has not been substantially changed. Here Cromwell was inspired by national and religious policy and vengeance. The Irish were dealt with as rebels and papists. Theologically he was always far removed from Catholicism. Politically, a large section of the English Catholic gentry was firmly Royalist and a real danger to his regime. Nevertheless he had solid reasons for sincerely wanting to grant freedom of worship and some relief from discriminatory financial levies to many Catholics. In his letter to Cardinal Mazarin of Dec. 26, 1656, he admitted that persecution "tyrannised over" the consciences of Catholics and that much in the penal financial sequestrations of papists by the Commonwealth was "an arbitrariness of power." It was therefore, he said, his purpose gradually to ease the lot of nondelinquent papists. There is solid evidence of his determination here. He received at his house and table moderate Catholic leaders,

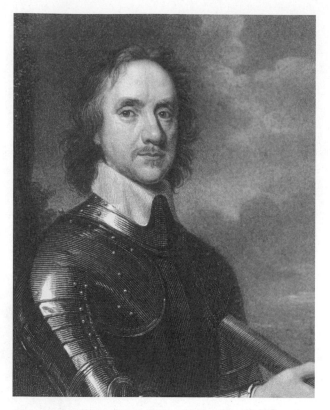

Oliver Cromwell, portrait by Robert Walker. (Archive Photos)

such as the Lords ARUNDEL, Montague, and Worcester, and Sir Kenelm Digby, with whom he negotiated as representatives of that large minority of Catholics who either had been neutral in the wars or had now become prepared to give a degree of loyalty to his government. In 1655 he even dispatched two Catholic agents to Rome—a convert, Thomas Bayly, and William Metham, a former student of the English College there. We know little of this very amateurish mission, except that it was a failure. The political divisions among English Catholics, Cromwell's hankering after a Protestant crusading foreign policy, and the suspicion with which many Puritans regarded his negotiations with Catholics, all combined to prevent any formal declaration of toleration for Catholics. However, in practice, the remarkably severe system of Parliamentary sequestrations of Catholics' property instituted by the Commonwealth was appreciably relaxed—though it is hard to determine how much part in this relaxation was played by Cromwell and how much by the class-solidarity of the gentry. Most of the active Royalist Catholic gentry, who had been forcibly deprived of their estates as traitors, were in fact able to buy them back through agents; and John Rushworth, the attorney, historian, and former secretary of Cromwell, played a massive part in this agency. Ordinary delinquent papists were mostly able either to get the sequestrations of their estates

lifted in return for a composition payment or to become themselves state farmers of the sequestered lands. It seems also certain that Cromwell himself acted discreetly to blunt the practical effect of various anti-Catholic measures that he could not openly resist in Parliament or the Council of State, for instance, the application to Catholics of the very anti-Catholic Oath of Abjuration by Statute in June 1657.

Bibliography: *Writings and Speeches,* ed. W. C. ABBOTT, 4 v. (Cambridge, MA 1937–47). P. H. HARDACRE, *The Royalists During the Puritan Revolution* (The Hague 1956). C. H. FIRTH, *Oliver Cromwell and the Rule of the Puritans in England* (New York 1953), best scholarly work on Cromwell. E. CURTIS, *History of Ireland* (6th ed. London 1950), for Cromwell's Irish policy. A. H. WOOLRYCH, *Oliver Cromwell* (London 1964). C. HILL, *Intellectual Origins of the English Revolution* (Oxford 1965). D. L. SMITH, *Oliver Cromwell: Politics and Religion in the English Revolution, 1640–1658* (Cambridge 1992). D. A. WILSON, *The King and the Gentleman: Charles Stuart and Oliver Cromwell, 1559–1649* (New York 1999). P. GAUNT, *Oliver Cromwell* (Oxford 1997).

[H. AVELING]

CROMWELL, THOMAS

Earl of Essex and chief agent of HENRY VIII in establishing the King's position as Supreme Head of the English Church and in organizing the dissolution of religious houses; b. Putney, England, 1485?; d. Tower Hill, London, July 28, 1540. Cromwell was the son of Walter Cromwell, a tradesman. In his youth Thomas served as a soldier with the French in Italy; became accountant to a Venetian merchant; and returning to England about 1512–13, began to practice law in London. In this capacity he was employed by Cardinal Thomas WOLSEY in the dissolution of some small monasteries and in supervising the new educational foundations to be built from their revenues.

Upon Wolsey's fall (1529), Cromwell attracted the favorable notice of the King by his ability and wit. He was soon given high office, including vicar-general in things spiritual and visitor general of the monasteries. He was ambitious, skillful, grasping of power, and prudent in affairs, knowing his own advance to be dependent on his capacity for increasing the King's power and wealth. His ideal was a popular one among the intelligentsia of the Renaissance world—the ideal of a prince whose despotism was benevolent, making for order and prosperity by the imposition of his own will. The concentration of all authority, religious and civil, in the hands of the reigning prince was an alternative to the papacy and an expression of this ideal. The *Defensor Pacis* by Marsilius of Padua, a 14th-century Italian humanist, was an exposition of this thesis; Cromwell had caused it to be translated for

Henry's benefit. It is known too that Cromwell was a student of Niccolò Machiavelli's treatise *Il Principe*. This manual of statecraft advises unscrupulous action, when necessary, provided it succeeds, and every kind of dissimulation used to ensure success. These principles certainly underlay much of the policy of Henry and his ministers, notably in the achievement of the dissolution of the monasteries and the suppression of the PILGRIMAGE OF GRACE.

Bibliography: R. B. MERRIMAN, *Life and Letters of Thomas Cromwell,* 2 v. (Oxford 1902). P. WILDING, *Thomas Cromwell* (London 1935). A. G. DICKENS, *Thomas Cromwell and the English Reformation* (New York 1960), with bibliog. G. BASKERVILLE, *English Monks and the Suppression of the Monasteries* (New Haven 1937). G. R. ELTON, *The Tudor Revolution in Government* (Cambridge, England 1953). P. HUGHES, *The Reformation in England,* 3 v. in 1 (5th, rev. ed. New York 1963) v.1, 2. J. GAIRDNER, *The Dictionary of National Biography from the Earliest Times to 1900,* 63 v. (London 1885–1900; repr. With corrections, 21 v., 1908–09, 1921–22, 1938; suppl. 1901–) 5:192–202. G. R. ELTON *Policy and Police* (Cambridge 1972). G. R. ELTON *Reform and Renewal* (Cambidge 1973). A. J. SLAVIN, *Thomas Cromwell on Church and Commonwealth* (New York 1969).

[H. ST. JOHN]

CROSIER FATHERS

The Canons Regular of the Order of the Holy Cross, commonly known as the Crosier Fathers, were founded, according to their tradition, by Theodore of Celles about 1210. The name Crosier is derived from the French *croisès* (Latin *crucisignati*); the literal medieval English rendering of the word was CRUTCHED (crossed) Friars. The designation refers to the spirituality of the order and, in particular, to the distinctive mark of the Crosier habit, namely, the crusader's cross worn on the scapular. The history of the order may be divided into three periods: the medieval period when ascendancy was shared by the houses at Huy (Belgium) and Paris; the period following 1410 when the newer monasteries of the Low Countries, especially the monastery of St. Agatha, spearheaded a general reform; and the modern period of revival, which is dated from the year 1840.

Medieval Period. The early period of the founding and first growth is represented in history by only fragmentary evidence. Theodore is known to have come from Liège, Belgium, the city of prince-bishops and numerous canonries. There is a tradition that as a young cleric he had accompanied his bishop on the Third Crusade. Disillusioned by the military adventure, Theodore joined the spiritual crusade against the ALBIGENSES. He preached in and around Toulouse, France, where (the tradition continues) he met and worked closely with St. DOMINIC. The best history of the early period, the *Chronicon Crucifer-*

Thomas Cromwell, portrait by Hans Holbein, 1533, oil on wood.

orum by H. Russelius (Cologne 1635), is all too brief and uncritical in its account of the founding, but recent research has shown that on the whole it is trustworthy.

Theodore and four companions, desiring to live a common life according to the Rule of St. Augustine, withdrew to a country place called Clairlieu. This was located not at Huy, as previously thought, but near the village of Seyl (of which Celles is a derivative), seven and a half miles from Huy on the Meuse River in Belgium. They were soon joined by dedicated laymen and laywomen (BEGUINES) in their apostolate of liturgical prayer and hospitality (running of hospices). In 1248, when full approbation was granted by Innocent IV, five Crosier houses were already in existence, including one in England. The decisive establishment, however, quite different from that of Clairlieu, was made at Huy (1248) under the direction of Peter of Walcourt. He drew up a set of constitutions modeled in part on those of the Dominican Order. The apostolate of preaching was given more stress but, unlike the Dominicans, Peter retained as primary the traditional concern of canons regular for the liturgy and laid little emphasis on scholarship or attendance at the universities. By 1270 the community at Clairlieu had broken up, while the foundation at Huy prospered and became the motherhouse. Important houses were founded in Paris and Toulouse (which grew into quasi-provinces), as well as in the Rhineland and in England.

Fifteenth-century Reform. The reform of 1410 marks one of the decisive turning points in the order's long history. The newer monasteries of the Low Countries had become centers of the spiritual movement known as the DEVOTIO MODERNA, which inspired a new development in Crosier spirituality. It was typified by a personal devotional faith such as is found in the IMITATION OF CHRIST and the *Vestis Nuptialis*. This new feature remained the dominant one for centuries; only recently have the order's spiritual writers reemphasized the role of the liturgy and the mystery of the triumphant cross. The centuries of religious conflict, that began with the Reformation and terminated in the general persecution of religious orders during and after the French Revolution, swept away most groups of canons regular. Those houses that remained to the Crosier Order in the Rhineland, France, and Belgium were confiscated or destroyed during the Napoleonic occupancy. For a time only St. Agatha and Uden (in Holland) remained, empty monasteries awaiting the repeal of the law forbidding the acceptance of novices. Four old Crosiers acted as caretakers; the order was, in truth, on the verge of extinction.

Modern Period. When the law was finally repealed in 1840, a surprisingly large number of diocesan clergy and seminarians joined the four Crosier fathers who still held the thread of a continued tradition. The former rector of the Latin School at Gemert (Holland), Henricus van den Wijmelenberg, was the first to receive the habit. Shortly afterward he was appointed a superior, and then elected master general (1853–81) of the revitalized order. While reestablishing houses in Holland and Belgium, Van den Wijmelenberg looked also to the mission field. He sent priests to England, the West Indies, and, in 1850, to Wisconsin at the invitation of Bp. John Henni, of Milwaukee. In all, nine Crosier priests and brothers accompanied various groups of Belgian and Dutch immigrants that settled around Green Bay, Wis. Edward Daems attempted to establish a monastic community at Bay Settlement. At the start of the Civil War, several of the fathers and brothers returned to Holland, and the attempt was abandoned. Daems founded a group of religious sisters, the Franciscan Sisters of the Holy Cross, and served as the first vicar-general of the Green Bay Diocese.

The order did not sustain its effort under Van den Wijmelenberg or succeeding master generals. It was not until Henricus Hollmann became master general (1899–1927) that Crosier communities began to flourish once again. Besides establishing new houses in Europe, Hollmann successfully undertook mission ventures in the U.S. (1910), the Belgian Congo (1920), and Java (1926).

Despite disastrous setbacks in Minnesota—caused largely by the drought of 1910—the Crosiers remained to serve scattered parishes in the northern dioceses. In 1922 a small monastery was built at Onamia, Minn., and a minor seminary was opened for the reception of seven candidates. From this unpretentious beginning, the order has spread in the U.S. In 1957 the U.S. Province of St. Odilia was created. The Crosier Fathers are located chiefly in Europe and the U.S., with a growing presence in Africa (Congo) and Asia (Indonesia and Japan).

Bibliography: OSC, Official Catholic Directory #0400. H. VAN ROOIJEN, *De Oorsprong van de Orde der Kruisbroeders of Kruisheren* (Diest, Belg. 1961). J. W. RAUSCH, *The Crosier Story: A History of the Crosier Fathers in the U.S.* (Onamia, Minn. 1960). M. VINKEN, *Lectures on Crosier Spirituality*, tr. J. FICHTNER (Wawasee, Ind. 1957); *The Spirituality of the Crosier Fathers*, tr. J. FICHTNER (Wawasee, Ind. 1958). A. RAMAEKERS, *The Crosier Indulgence*, tr. B. VAN GILS (Huntington 1950). J. M. HAYDEN, ''The Crosiers in England and France,'' *Clairlieu* 22 (1964) 91–109.

[J. W. RAUSCH/EDS.]

CROSS

This article treats both the cross and the sign of the cross. It discusses: the history, forms, uses and blessing of the cross, the history and ways of making the sign of the cross and devotion to the cross.

History. The cross is found in both pre-Christian and non-Christian cultures, where it has largely a cosmic or natural signification. Two crossed lines of equal length signify the four dimensions of the universe. The swastika cross symbolizes the whirling sun, the source of light and power, or the power of the elements, especially of lightning, or, in some cultures, the power of generation. Such symbols with the same basic meaning occur in primitive and advanced civilizations, in areas as widely separated as India, Etruria and Peru. These natural significations of the cross are not abrogated, but rather deepened and purified by the development of Christian symbolism. Apparently unrelated to such symbolic meaning is the use of the cross in non-Christian cultures as a means of punishment.

The early Christians generally avoided representing the body of Christ on the cross, for the first evidence of such representation comes from the fifth century. In fact, until the fourth century, even the simple cross rarely appeared in public. The reasons given for this twofold phenomenon have been many.

Both pagans and Jews saw an irreconcilable contradiction in the belief of Christians that a crucified man could also be God. The opprobrium associated with crucifixion lasted for some time even among Christians. There was a certain reluctance, in some quarters, to admit the reality of Christ's death in proportion as His humanity was eclipsed. The Councils of Ephesus (431) and Chalcedon (451) marked the most intense period of the Christological controversy. Though MONOPHYSITISM was condemned at Chalcedon, its adherents could see the Crucifixion only as the crucifixion of God. Hence they refused to portray the body of the crucified, and limited themselves to displaying the bare cross.

Furthermore, during the age of persecution there was fear both of being identified as Christian by the authorities because of this symbol and of its profanation at the hands of nonbelievers. An eloquent witness to the pagan mentality of these times is the second-century cartoon scratched on one of the Roman Palatine buildings. In this a man with an ass's head is shown on a cross while another man stands nearby in adoration. The words "Alexamenos adores his God" are scratched in the plaster.

There is also historical evidence to the effect that Christians showed an unwillingness to contemplate the Savior's ignominy on the cross, particularly His nudity. They preferred to see in the cross a symbol of His victory, a source of life, just as it was His means of passing to the divine glory that was His by nature.

The cross, occasionally even the crucifix, was used for private devotion in the first three centuries. In the fourth century, however, a change occurred. Peace came to the Church; the cross need no longer be hidden. Constantine claimed to have seen the cross in the heavens and had it inscribed on the shields of his soldiers. He subsequently abolished crucifixion as a death penalty. In time the cross appeared everywhere in public places.

But the event that had the most profound effect on the history of the cross was the finding of the true cross (Jerusalem, 326; *see* CROSS, FINDING OF THE HOLY). It was venerated as the most precious relic remaining from Our Lord's earthly life. Its wood was divided in several parts; the first step in what soon became a great dispersal of relics of the cross had been taken. Major portions of the cross were brought to Rome and later, to Constantinople. Many further divisions were made until now the individual relics are very small.

The fifth and sixth centuries were the high time of the glorified cross, although this concept continued to appear through the early Middle Ages. This type of cross was heavily studded with large jewels. In the earliest cases the jewels were represented by rich mosaic, as at Santa Pudentiana, Rome (fifth century), or San Apollinare in Classe, Ravenna (sixth century). Also from the sixth century is the gold cross of Justin, the jewels of which are semiprecious stones; a small relic of the true cross is enshrined in it. In all these cases the evident in-

Cross surmounted by a Chi-Rho crowned with laurel, central panel on front of a 4th-century sarcophagus found in the Cemetery of Domitilla at Rome, now in the Lateran Museum, Rome. The two sleeping soldiers clearly indicate that this device is a symbol of the victorious, Risen Christ. (Alinari-Art Reference/Art Resource, NY)

tention was to portray the glorification of the cross, splendid and regal, the antithesis of the opprobrium-laden image of the first centuries.

Related concepts of glorification, victory and life are to be seen in the images of the Agnus Dei and the living tree. In the former a lamb is shown carrying a cross; this is an apocalyptic symbol of Christ's triumph. In the latter, two vine like branches bearing leaves arise from the foot of the cross; in this case the obvious intent is to contrast the tree of life (the cross) and the tree of death (the tree of good and evil in Paradise).

In the early Middle Ages IRISH CROSSES tended to be intricately geometrical. They were usually carved in stone and were sometimes of great size. Representation, even when the human figure was involved, was ordinarily highly abstract. Irish manuscripts, for example the "Cross Page" of the Book of Kells, show similar tendencies.

While sculptured crosses were abundant all over medieval Europe, with the late Middle Ages the use of the bare cross became less frequent. The age of "passion

A priest blesses while the faithful make the sign of the cross with three fingers, 12th-century relief on the portal, Cathedral in Modena, Italy. (Alinari-Art Reference/Art Resource, NY)

mysticism'' led to the predominance of the CRUCIFIX as emphasis on the *suffering* Savior increased.

Forms. Since the cross plays a very large part in HERALDRY, most of the forms of the cross are subject to the variations of heraldry. The majority of the heraldic variations occur at the ends of the arms of the cross; thus the Greek cross with forked terminations is known as the Cross Moline, while if rectangular feet are used instead it becomes the Cross Potent.

There is no rule for the relative slenderness or heaviness of the cross. This has varied according to the materials employed and the designer's concept. Nor are there any fixed proportions other than those shown in the diagram.

Uses. The cross is beyond doubt the widest used of all Christian signs. A cross was placed on the altar during Mass as early as the fifth century in Syria, but there is no proof of a similar custom in the West until much later.

It would seem that the use of a processional cross goes back at least to the late sixth century when Venantius Fortunatus composed the hymn *VEXILLA REGIS PRODEUNT.* In 800 Charlemagne gave a processional

cross to the pope; the use of such a cross was common for stational processions in Rome. When the procession arrived at the church where Mass was to be celebrated the processional cross was set up at, but at first not on, the altar. A ninth century fresco in St. Clement's in Rome shows four such processional crosses. In the 13th century Innocent III prescribed that the cross was to be placed on the altar, but it was not until the following century that this cross became a crucifix.

During the Middle Ages up to the 16th century there was commonly a rood beam over the division of presbytery and nave; this was a large cross or crucifix, not to be confused with the altar crucifix.

Sometime in the Middle Ages the custom of painting 12 crosses on the walls of a church arose; these were the consecration crosses, places at which the church was anointed in the consecration ceremony. The oldest extant example of this seems to be the Carolingian chapel at Nijmegen, Holland. Also of a dedicatory character are the customs of placing the cross on the walls of buildings other than churches, for example, of homes and schools; of erecting cemetery crosses; and of sewing the cross on vestments and linens.

"Alexamenos worships his God," graffito of the 2d century, Museo Nazionale delle Terme, Rome. This blasphemous caricature by a pagan is probably the oldest representation of the Crucified Christ.

Blessing of Cross and Crucifix. The Roman Ritual gives three blessings of the cross. The first of these is the blessing of a cross to be placed in the fields. The other two, solemn blessings of the cross or crucifix, are reserved to the bishop; however, any priest may be delegated to impart them. Since 1840 the cross or crucifix may be blessed by means of a simple sign of the cross. The indulgences that may be put on a cross or crucifix are the Apostolic indulgences, the indulgence of the Stations of the Cross, the indulgence for a happy death (*see* INDULGENCES).

Sign of the Cross. Tracing the cross on one's forehead with the thumb or index finger was already customary in the second century as a private devotion. In the fourth century it came into wide use in the liturgy. We find a signing of the breast as well as the forehead toward the end of the fourth century. The same century yields evidence for signing forehead and eyes with the Eucharistic species. Finally a signing of the lips is mentioned in the eighth century.

In the East the practice of making the sign of the cross with two or three fingers was introduced in the sixth century to combat the Monophysites. In this case the emphasis was on number—the numbers signifying the two natures of Christ or the Trinity, etc. The custom passed over into the West and in the ninth century we find a synod directing the priest to make the sign of the cross with the thumb and two fingers over the oblation at Mass. This gesture remains to this day in the Eastern rites and also in the papal rite of blessing.

The large sign of the cross made on forehead, breast and shoulders, though used in private devotion as early as the fifth century, seems to have been introduced into the monasteries first in the tenth century, although it may be more ancient. In the 13th century we find Innocent III directing that the sign is to be made with three fingers from forehead to breast and from right to left shoulder. Later the whole hand with fingers extended was used and the direction changed from left to right.

The sign of the cross was usually accompanied with a verbal formula. The most ancient of these is still used frequently: "In the name of the Father, and of the Son, and of the Holy Spirit." In the Eastern rites one of the formulas is "O Holy God, O Holy Strong One, O Holy Immortal One, have mercy on us."

The sign of the cross is used in many ways during liturgical functions, thus expressing different meanings. Sometimes it is the sign of Christ impressed like a seal on the body of the catechumen indicating that the person signed belongs wholly to Christ, or a profession of unswerving faith in Christ, or an affirmation of the sovereign power of Christ against the evil spirits. It may be an invocation of God's grace, efficaciously imploring the infinite merits of Christ's cross (the meaning in all the Sacraments). It can be used as a blessing of a person or of a thing and a way of consecrating that person or thing to God, in a way analogous to the consecration of the Christian effected by Baptism. But sometimes, it is only a demonstrative sign to point out a person or a thing; the first three signs of the cross in the Canon of the Mass and perhaps those signs after the consecration have this character.

Devotion to the Cross. It was quite natural and logical that the instrument of salvation should become an object of special respect and veneration. It is clear that devotion to the cross, beginning already with St. Paul (1 Cor 1.17; Eph 2.16; Col 1.20; Gal 6.14), was not chiefly concentrated on the negative aspect of mere physical suffering and death; uppermost in the Christian mentality was the cross' saving role in the divine plan. As Christ through His Passion was a triumphant victor over death and sin, so the cross, the means of suffering, became the source of life. Thus it was looked upon as the throne and standard of the King of Glory.

Not only were the walls of homes and edifices used by Christians marked with this sacred sign in one or another of its forms, but stones and various objects carried on the person were engraved with it. With the discovery of the true cross, devotion increased. Though relics of it were gradually distributed throughout the world, pilgrimages to the holy places to adore the sacred wood became frequent.

Because of the danger of misunderstanding, the Council of Nicaea II (787) decreed that the veneration of the faithful was due the cross and images of Christ and the saints [H. Denzinger, *Enchiridion symbolorum,* ed. A. Schönmetzer (Freiburg 1963) 600], for he who adores the images, adores the person it represents (*ibid.* 601). Theologians are commonly agreed that the cult of *relative latria* is due to the cross. Hence the Church calls for a genuflection before the cross on Good Friday, and a special part of the liturgical service for that day is dedicated to veneration of the cross, the faithful being invited to kiss it. It should be noted, once again, that the motif of this GOOD FRIDAY, unveiling and veneration of the cross is one of glorious triumph.

Liturgical feast. A liturgical feast in honor of the cross is of early origin. It was connected from the very beginning with the finding of the true cross and the dedication of churches at the sites of the Holy Sepulcher and Calvary in Jerusalem, the *Anastasis* and *Martyrion*. In 325 the dedication of these churches was celebrated with great solemnity on September 13 and 14. The annual commemoration of this event was equally solemn and spread quickly to other Eastern churches. Though the feast was originally known as the *Encaenia,* the name "Exaltation of the Cross," given to it by Alexander of Cyprus in the sixth century, has remained. While Rome adopted the feast sometime in the seventh century and called it the "Feast of the Exaltation of the Holy Cross," Gallican churches introduced a "Feast of the Invention of the Holy Cross" on May 3 sometime in the first half of the eighth century. May 3 was apparently chosen to commemorate Heraclius's recovery of the true cross from the Persians and its solemn return to Jerusalem on that day. The Gallican feast was added to the Roman calendar in Gaul and thus returned to Rome. Although Benedict XIV's commission for the reform of the Breviary tried in vain to drop the feast of May 3, John XXIII omitted it from his reformed calendar in 1960. The 1969 reform of the liturgical calendar recovered the historical feast of the Exaltation (or Triumph) of the Cross for the Roman Catholic Church. The Greek Church observes a feast of the Apparition of the Cross to St. Cyril of Jerusalem on May 7 and one of the Adoration of the Cross on August 1 and on the third Sunday of Lent. The Armenians celebrate a feast of the cross as one of their seven principal feasts, in the autumn near the time of the feast of the Assumption.

Bibliography: R. GUARDINI, *Sacred Signs* (St. Louis 1956). A. K. PORTER, *The Crosses and Culture of Ireland* (New Haven 1931). J. GRETSER, *De Sancta Cruce,* v. 1–3 of *Opera Omnia* (Ratisbon 1734). J. B. O'CONNELL, *Church Building and Furnishing* (Notre Dame, Ind. 1955) 105–106, 205–208. F. J. DÖLGER, "Beiträge zur Geschichte des Kreuzzeichens," *Jahrbuch Für Antike und Christentum,* 1 (1958) 5–19; 2 (1959) 15–29; 3 (1960) 5–16; 4 (1961) 5–17; 5 (1962) 5–22. O. MARUCCHI, *The Catholic Encyclopedia,* ed. C. G. HERBERMANN et al., 16 v. (New York 1907–14; suppl. 1922) 4:517–539. N. LALIBERTÉ and E. N. WEST, *The History of the Cross* (New York 1960). P. THOBY, *Le Crucifix des origines au Concile de Trente: Étude iconographique* (Nantes 1959).

[C. MEINBERG/EDS.]

CROSS, FINDING OF THE HOLY

The New Testament writers do not mention what became of the cross of Christ or the disposition of the crosses of the thieves crucified with Him. Justin Martyr and Origen, who both lived in Palestine before 350 and transmitted information concerning the Holy Land, say nothing about the cross.

Constantine. The Emperor CONSTANTINE I in a letter of congratulation to Bishop Macarius of Jerusalem offers to adorn the newly discovered tomb of Christ with a splendid church, but says nothing about the cross (Eusebius of Caesarea, *Vita Const.* 3.30–32). The Pilgrim of Bordeaux, who visited the "hill of Golgotha" in 333 and described the Constantinian church with its lateral reservoirs, is equally silent about the cross [*Corpus scriptorum ecclesiasticorum latinorum* (Vienna 1866–) 39:22–23].

EUSEBIUS likewise says nothing of it in his Panegyric for Constantine's 30th anniversary (July 25, 335) where he praises the emperor's munificent adornment of the place of Christ's burial. The same silence prevails even in his *Life of Constantine,* where he describes the buildings marking the site of Christ's Resurrection (3.25–40) and St. HELENA's pilgrimage to the holy places (3.42–45).

Cyril of Jerusalem. In the course of a catechetical lecture in Lent of 350, St. CYRIL OF JERUSALEM assures the candidates for Baptism that the cross of Christ has been in the Church's possession at Jerusalem for some time and that pieces broken off by Christians motivated by faith "had already been scattered throughout the land" (*Cat.* 4.10; 10.19; 13.4). In a letter to the Emperor CONSTANTIUS II reporting the apparition of a luminous cross in the heavens over Jerusalem on May 7, 351, Cyril mentions the salvific wood of the cross discovered in the city during the reign of Constantine (*Patrologia Graeca,* 33:1167]. The conviction that the cross of Christ had been found spread widely in the Christian world of the second half of the fourth century and pieces of the cross were said to be in various places.

Cyril of Jerusalem's assertions were not fictional. An inscription found at Tixter near Setif in Algeria mentions a relic *de ligno crucis* in 359. But the statement of JULIAN THE APOSTATE in his *Contra Galileos* accusing the Christians of "adoring the Cross" does not refer to the cross of Christ, but rather to the sign of the cross, which the faithful traced on their foreheads or with which they adorned the façade of their homes (Cyril of Alexandria, *Cont.* Jul. 6). There were pieces of the true cross in Cappadocia in the late 370s during the lifetime of St. MACRINA (Gregory of Nyssa, *Patrologia Graeca,* 46:489); at Antioch in 386 or 387 (John Chrysostom, *Quod Chr.* 10; *Patrologia Graeca,* 48:826); and in Italy and Gaul in 403 (Paulinus of Nola, *Epist.* 31.1; 32.11).

Aetheria (Egeria). Soon after the pilgrim Aetheria who assisted at the Veneration of the Cross in the Good Friday liturgy at Jerusalem, records the care exercised by two deacons to ensure that no one kissing the cross should bite into it in order to obtain a relic (*Itinerarium* 37.2). The prohibition of taking pieces of the cross must have been laid down by the bishop of Jerusalem after the first sojourn there of MELANIA THE ELDER, for on her return to Italy *c.* 400 she spoke about the cross to Paulinus of Nola; and it was doubtless on her testimony that in 403 Paulinus described the cross as remaining intact despite the removal of small particles (*Epist.* 31.6).

Aetheria is understood to have said that on the feast of the Dedication (*Encaenia*) of the Basilica or Martyrium at Golgotha and in the nearly circular church of the Resurrection (*Anastasis*), the anniversary of the finding of the cross of Christ was celebrated annually (*Itin.* 48). Thus the finding of the cross must have taken place on September 13 between 325 and 334; but it is surprising that Eusebius of Caesarea gives no positive support for this belief then current at Jerusalem. The seventh century Constantinopolitan *Chronicon Paschale* gives Sept. 14, 320, as the precise date for the discovery.

While Aetheria provides chronological information, she says nothing of the circumstances surrounding the finding of the cross; one would wish to have proof that more circumspection was shown in this matter than for the discovery of the "Ring of Solomon" or the "Cruet employed in the anointing of the kings of Israel," two relics offered at Jerusalem on Good Friday for the veneration of the faithful along with the cross and Pilate's inscription connected with it (*Itin.* 37.3). Mention of this custom is made about 530 in the *Breviarius Hierosolymae* and by the archdeacon Theodosius (*Corpus scriptorum ecclesiasticorum latinorum,* 39:154, 174).

The Legends. Four versions of the legend give the circumstances of the reappearance of the cross. In three of them, St. Helena, the mother of Constantine, leads the way to the excavations either on her own volition (Ambrose in 395, followed by Sozomen), or by divine inspiration (Paulinus of Nola in 403, *Epist.* 31.4; Rufinus of Aquileia, *Hist. eccl.* 1.7; Socrates, *Hist. eccl.* 1.17; George the Monk, *Patrologia Graeca,* 110:620), or at the request of Constantine (Malalas 13; Theophanes 1.25, 28; Cedrenus, *Patrologia Graeca,* 121:544).

St. AMBROSE is the first known author to mention this role of the empress (*De ob. Theod.* 40–48), but his citation of Zechariah (14.20) in this connection concerning the nails of the crucifixion, with the same interpretation as that given by Sozomen, Cyril of Alexandria (*Patrologia Graeca,* 72:272 A) and Gregory of Tours (*De glor. mart.* 6), gives the impression that, as so often, he is here dependent on a Greek text. Jerome ridicules this interpretation of Zacharias's verse (*Patrologia Latina,* 25:1615 B).

Paulinus of Nola. Following Melania, Paulinus of Nola gives details unmentioned by Ambrose concerning St. Helena's activities: the empress engaged in her own investigations, then called wise Jews and Christians to Jerusalem for consultation and finally found herself embarrassed by the discovery of three crosses. She prayed for guidance and was inspired to bring each of the crosses into contact with the body of a dead man; the cross that restored life to the body could then be identified as the

cross of Christ. SULPICIUS SEVERUS, relying on the narrative of Paulinus, does not credit Helena alone with this idea. The inspiration, he says, was received by all those who were puzzled by the difficulty of distinguishing the true cross from those of the thieves (*Chron.* 2.34.4).

Two other forms of the legend in which Helena is the principal actor mention a man as counseling the application of the cross to a person in death agony (Rufinus, etc.) or to a dead man (the legend of Judas-Cyriacus). According to Rufinus and the Byzantine chroniclers, it is Bishop Macarius who is said to have suggested the solution to Helena.

The Syrian legend. During the first half of the fifth century, there were three forms of the Helena legend in Syriac, which were known at least orally to Sozomen who questioned their reliability (*Hist. eccl.* 2.1.4). In these, not only did the emperor's mother consult the Jews she brought to Jerusalem, but she was given effective counsel by a certain Jew called Judas, who is thought to be the fifth and last Judeo-Christian bishop mentioned by Eusebius (*Hist. eccl.* 4.5.3). This strange person, capable of calling on a peculiar family tradition as witness to the messiahship of Christ, made known Golgotha, discovered the cross and applied it to a dead man who was being transported to be buried.

After Judas was baptized, Helena had him consecrated a bishop by Eusebius of Rome in the Holy City, and gave him the name of Cyriacus. In his new dignity, he was able to satisfy a further wish of the empress. By a Hebrew prayer he obtained a luminous sign from heaven that led to the discovery of the nails of the Crucifixion. This legend was preserved in Syriac, Greek and Latin.

The Latin recension found in an eighth century codex, which could have come from a Syrian colony established in the West, seems close to the Syrian version preserved in a seventh century manuscript; but its dependence on a Greek text is not completely excluded [J. Straubinger, *Analecta Bollandiana,* 32 (1910) 303]. The redaction of the notice devoted to Pope Eusebius in the LIBER pontificalis has retained from the Latin text the date of May 3 for the finding of the cross; but the date given in the Greek version is September 14. A Coptic fragment published by W. Spiegelberg likewise associates the Jew Judas with Helena in the discovery of the cross.

A fourth form of the legend, which does not mention Helena, Bishop Macarius or Judas Cyriacus, puts the Empress Protonica, the wife of the Emperor Claudius (41–54), on the scene. She had, according to the legend, abandoned paganism in Rome after seeing miracles worked by St. Peter, and then departed with her two sons for Jerusalem, where St. James showed her the hill of

Golgotha, which she forced the Jews to hand over to the Christians. Then her daughter died suddenly; the event was hailed as providential by her eldest son, for when the true cross was applied to the girl's body, life was restored.

This story, supposed to have been written by St. James and sent to the Apostles, is preserved as an appendix in the Preaching of Addai. Composed in Syriac, it was received by the Nestorians and Jacobites and was taken over by the Armenians and translated into their language. It apparently goes back to Eastern Syria (*c.* 390 or 400) and precedes the legend of Judas Cyriacus (*see* ADDAI AND MARI, SS).

Actually the Syrian manuscripts juxtapose the Judas Cyriacus version to this fourth form of the legend or present the original Helena version as the narrative of the second finding of the cross. Furthermore, in the Greek, Syriac and Latin version, Judas tells Helena: "Behold more or less two hundred years the cross has been hidden"; these words refer to a burial of the cross under Trajan after its discovery by Protonica. St. CYRIL OF ALEXANDRIA had knowledge of this story of the first finding of the cross, since he remarks: "It has been said at different times that the Wood of the Cross has been discovered" (*In Zach.* 14.20).

John Chrysostom. These four versions of the legend were contradicted by St. Chrysostom in 386 or 387 (*Patrologia Graeca,* 48:826) and in 391 (*Hom. in Joh.* 85.1); he declared that "the Savior did not leave his Cross on earth, but took it with him into heaven, since he is to appear with his Cross in the second and glorious coming" (*Patrologia Graeca,* 49:403). This text repeats many similar ancient statements concerning the eschatological cross and applied to the figures of the cross traced on the apses of churches. A like opinion is stated in an interpolation in the recital of the pilgrimage of the archdeacon Theodosius in 530: the part of the cross that touched the body of Christ and was stained with His blood was taken up into heaven, and will appear in the Last Judgment (*Itin. Hier.* 1.64).

It has been said that the cross was concealed and found in the grotto that goes down 13 paces in one of the apses of the chapel of St. Helena, in the present church of the Holy Sepulcher. In this cavity, whose original purpose is disputed, but which is frequently filled with rainwater, the preservation of wood for two or three centuries would have been impossible.

Between at least 530, as the Breviarius of Jerusalem attests (*Corpus scriptorum ecclesiasticorum latinorum,* 39:153) and the episcopate of Sophronius of Jerusalem (*Anacreontic Ode* 20; *Patrologia Graeca,* 87: 3820), it was said that the three crosses had been found under the apse of the Martyrium of Constantine. The discovery of the nails followed that of the cross according to St. Ambrose, the Legend of St. Helena and that of Judas Cyriacus. Other discoveries followed: the Anonymous of Plaisance in 570 shows the sponge and the hyssop stalk mentioned in John 19.29 (*Corpus scriptorum ecclesiasticorum latinorum,* 39:173).

Jewish literature. The legend of Helena has an echo in Jewish literature. A recension of the *Toledot Yeshu* reports that the Rabbi Juda, chosen by the Jews of Jerusalem to be a wise man for the mother of Constantine, counseled the Jewish elders to bury three pieces of wood. After three days of fasting and prayer, Juda satisfied the empress by leading her to the hiding place. Asked to make known the cross of Jesus, he had a dead man brought and put in contact with each of the three crosses; and by the power of the name of God (*Shem ha-Mephorash*) of which Juda possessed the secret, the dead man began to move at being touched by the first cross; at contact with the second, he lifted himself; and on contact with the third he was fully restored. Rabbi Juda thus showed himself devoted to his brethren, delivering them from vexations without apostatizing. With Alcimus, the man brought back to life, he showed himself an apostle "as Peter and Paul," acting for the good of his brethren without changing his religion. The redactor desired to deny the conversion of Judas Cyriacus as well as that of the Apostles Peter and Paul, while expressing his dislike for Christ and for the Christian veneration of the relics of the cross.

H. Vincent and F. Abel [*Jerusalem,* 2 (Paris 1914) 190] and D. Baldi [*Enchiridion locorum sanctorum* (Jerusalem 1955) 624, n.1.] interpret Eusebius's *Laudes Constantini* (9.6; *Die griechischen christlichen Schriftsteller der ersten drei Jahrhunderte,* Eusebius 1.221.16) as mentioning the cross; so does E. Richardson in his translation of the Post-Nicene Fathers [2d Ser. 1 (New York 1890) 594]. But there is no justification for this interpretation. H. Goussen has challenged the authenticity of the passages in Cyril of Jerusalem's *Catechesis* and Letter to Constantius, basing his complaint on the Armenian version [*Über georgische Drücke und Handschriften die Festordnung und Hieligenkalender betreffend* (München-Gladbach 1923) 32], but his objections are without substantial proof. The Feast of the Finding of the Cross on May 3 was suppressed for the Latin rite in 1960.

Bibliography: H. LECLERCQ, *Dictionnaire d'archéologie chrétienne et de liturgie,* ed. F. CABROL, H. LECLERCQ and H. I. MARROU, 15 v. (Paris 1907–53) 3.2:3131–39. H. QUILLIET, *Dictionnaire de théologie catholique,* ed. A. VACANT et al., 15 v. (Paris 1903–50) 3.2:2342–63. G. JACQUEMET et al., *Catholicisme,* 3:321–329. G. RÖMER and D. SCHAEFERS, *Lexikon für Theologie und Kirche,* ed.

J. HOFER and K. RAHNER, 10 v. (2d, new ed. Freiburg 1957–65) 6:614–615. *Acta Apostolicae Sedis,* 52 (1960) 707. *Bibliotheca hagiographica Graeca,* ed. F. HALKIN, 3 (1957) 396–413. J. STRAUBINGER, *Die Kreuzauffindungslegende* (Paderborn 1913), Cyriacus and Protonica legends. W. SPIEGELBERG, "Koptische Kreuzlegenden," *Recueil de travaux relatifs à la philologie et à l'archéologie égyptiennes et assyriennes,* 23 (1901) 206–211. E. NESTLE, *Byzantinische Zeitschrift,* 4 (1895) 319–345, text of Cyriacus legend; ed., *De sancta cruce* (Berlin 1889), 2 Syriac texts. L. DUCHESNE, *Fastes épiscopaux de l'ancienne Gaule,* 3 v. (2d ed. Paris 1907–15) 1:cvii–cix; 3:56–57. J. RAUCH, "Die Limburger Staurothek," *Münster,* 8 (1955) 201–218. A. AUDOLLENT, *Mélanges d'archéologie et d'histoire de l'École Française de Rome,* 10 (1890) 452, the Tixter inscription.

[H. CHIRAT]

CROTUS RUBIANUS (JOHANNES JÄGER)

German humanist; b. Dornheim (near Arnstadt, Thuringia), *c.* 1480; d. Halle, Saxony, *c.* 1545. At the University of Erfurt (B.A. 1500, M.A. 1507) he at first accepted scholastic teachings, but came in touch with humanist circles and soon became an outspoken advocate of the new learning. He knew Martin Luther before Luther's entry into the Augustinian Order and met Ulrich von Hutten at Fulda, Hesse-Nassau (1505) and was his fellow student at Cologne and Erfurt. He associated also with the anticlerical humanistic circle of Mutianus Rufus at Gotha in Thuringia. In 1510 he became head of the monastery school at Fulda. His humanist sympathies and anticlerical tendencies made him an enthusiastic supporter of Johann REUCHLIN in his controversy with the Cologne scholastics. He probably originated the idea of producing a series of satirical letters supposedly written by the enemies of Reuchlin. The result was *Epistolae obscurorum virorum* (1515), and although Hutten was active from the beginning, Crotus produced most of the original collection. In 1517 Crotus went to Italy and remained there three years, studying at Bologna and taking a doctorate in theology. At first he was indifferent to news of Luther's teachings, but eventually he became a warm partisan and while accompanying Eobanus Hessus to Rome (1519), he spoke out for Luther. In Germany in 1520 he was elected rector of the University of Erfurt, and gave a warm official welcome to Luther, en route to the Diet of Worms (1521). In subsequent years, increasingly dismayed by the popular violence and narrow fanaticism that accompanied the Reformation, he (like many humanists) gradually retreated. He was still friendly to Luther and Melanchthon in 1524, when he went to serve Duke Albrecht of Prussia in Königsberg. His duties there included authorship of treatises defending the secularization of this ecclesiastical principality and the introduction of Lutheranism. But his letters expressed growing distaste for the Reformation. In 1530 he went to Halle, where the archbishop-elector of Mainz, Albrecht of Brandenburg, made him canon (1531). That same year he published *Apologia,* which publicly affirmed his return to Catholicism and rebutted Lutheran charges that he had been bought. His later years were darkened by such slanders, but after his *Apologia* he refused to be dragged back into public controversy. His silence stemmed partly from his awkward position: his ultimate decision to stick by the Roman church did not make him any less painfully aware of its need for true reform. His later years are obscure.

Bibliography: A. H. HORAWITZ, *Allgemeine deutsche Biographie,* (Leipzig 1875–1910) 4:612–614. F. W. KAMPSCHULTE, *De J. Croto Rubiano commentatio* (Bonn 1862). W. REINDELL, *Luther, Crotus und Hutten . . .* (Marburg 1890). U. VON HUTTEN et al., *On the Eve of the Reformation . . . ,* tr. F. G. STOKES (New York 1964), introd. H. HOLBORN. R. KLAUSER, *Lexikon für Theologie und Kirche,* ed. J. HOFER and K. RAHNER, 10 v. (2d, new ed. Freiburg 1957–65) 3:100–101.

[C. G. NAUERT, JR.]

CROW, ALEXANDER, BL.

Priest, martyr; b. ca. 1550 at Howden, Yorkshire, England; d. Nov. 30 (or 13), 1586, hanged, drawn, and quartered at York. He was a cobbler for some years before beginning his seminary studies at Rheims, where he was ordained ca. 1583. Returning to the English Mission in 1584, he began his work in Yorkshire, where he was arrested at Duffield on his way to a baptism. Crow, condemned for priesthood, was beatified by Pope John Paul II on Nov. 22, 1987 with George Haydock and Companions.

Feast of the English Martyrs: May 4 (England).

See Also: ENGLAND, SCOTLAND AND WALES, MARTYRS OF.

Bibliography: R. CHALLONER, *Memoirs of Missionary Priests,* ed. J. H. POLLEN (rev. ed. London 1924). J. H. POLLEN, *Acts of English Martyrs* (London 1891).

[K. I. RABENSTEIN]

CROWLAND, ABBEY OF

Former Benedictine monastery, known also as Croyland, dedicated to St. Mary, St. BARTHOLOMEW, and St. GUTHLAC in the county and Diocese of LINCOLN, England. Tradition claims it was founded by Ethelbald of Mercia (*c.* 716) in the fens near St. Guthlac's hermitage, piles having to be driven to provide a firm site. In 870 the abbey was destroyed by the Danes and was not restored until *c.* 970, when a rich clerk, Turketyl, became abbot and provided ample endowment. Following a disastrous fire, Abbot Godfrey rebuilt the church *c.* 1110. Building continued during the 13th century, and a fine tower in perpendicular Gothic (*see* CHURCH ARCHITECTURE) was added *c.* 1460. The successful farming of the rich fenlands led to frequent attempts at encroachment by neighbors and to lawsuits to protect the abbey's interests. These disputes fostered a strong community spirit among the 40 monks, a solidarity that was reflected in the high standard reported at visitations. Among artistic productions the Guthlac Roll reached the high-water mark of English outline drawing. Literature flourished during the 13th century, when William of Ramsey wrote metrical lives of SS. Guthlac, NEOT, and Waldef, whose shrine was in the abbey. The best-known work was the abbey chronicle compiled *c.* 1360, though ascribed to Ingulf (appointed abbot in 1085). It was continued during the 15th century. John Bridges, an unpopular and arbitrary abbot, surrendered the house in December 1539 [*see* REFORMATION, PROTESTANT (IN THE BRITISH ISLES)]. The monks were pensioned.

Bibliography: W. FULMAN, ed. *Ingulfi Croylandensis historia* and *Historiae Croylandensis continuatio in Rerum Anglicarum scriptores veteres,* 3 v. (Oxford 1684–91) v.1. *The Victoria History of the County of Lincoln,* ed. W. PAGE (London 1906) v.2. D. KNOWLES, *The Monastic Order in England* (2d ed. Cambridge; Eng. 1962). D. KNOWLES and R. N. HADCOCK, *Medieval Religious Houses: England and Wales* (New York 1953).

[F. R. JOHNSTON]

Crowland Abbey and Cemetery. (©Michael S. Yamashita/ CORBIS)

CROWN, FRANCISCAN

A seven-decade rosary, each decade consisting of an Our Father and 10 Hail Marys, with two additional Hail Marys at the end of the seventh decade followed by an Our Father and a Hail Mary for the pope. The seven decades honor the Seven Joys of Mary: the Annunciation, Visitation, Nativity, Adoration of the Magi, Finding of Jesus in the Temple, Resurrection and Appearance to Mary, and Assumption. Although probably of Cistercian origin (cf. Wilmart, *Auteurs spirituels et textes dévotes au moyen âge latin* [Paris 1932] 339–352), devotion to the Joys of Mary flourished in crowns of many forms among the Friars Minor. L. Bracaloni describes: (1) a crown of Five Joys attributed to St. Bonaventure; (2) a crown of six decades propagated by Bl. Cherubin of Spoleto (d. 1484); and (3) a crown proposed by St. John Capistran with seven meditations. Another seven-decade crown appeared *c.* 1500, according to B. Bughetti, but with different meditations. D. Van Wely mentions that Pelbart of Temesvár (d. 1504), author of *Stellarum coroenae B. Virginis* (*c.* 1483), knew a crown of Seven

Joys corresponding to the present form, and Mariano of Florence, whose unpublished treatise on the crowns (1503) is described and excerpted by C. Cannarozzi, also knew the same crown, but without the two additional Hail Marys. The crown of St. Joan of France (d. 1515) and another propagated by her Annunciades, was widely used in France but was not connected with the Seven Joys. The two traditions, the one known to Pelbart and that of the Annunciades, seem to have merged to form the crown now in use. There is a legend that Our Lady appeared to a Franciscan novice and taught him the crown. Mariano of Florence refers to a similar vision of a Cistercian novice. The confused history of the crown makes it difficult to determine the indulgences that have been attached to it. The present surety of indulgences attached to the crown goes back to St. Pius X.

Bibliography: C. CANNAROZZI, "La *Corona B. Mariae Virginis* e la *Corona Domini Nostri Jesu Christi,* in due opere inedite di Fr. Mariano da Firenze," *Studi Francescani* 28 (1931) 14–32. L. BRACALONI, "Origine, evoluzione ed affermazione della Corona

Reliquary made in 1862 for the crown of thorns, Treasury of the Cathedral of Notre Dame, Paris. (Alinari-Art Reference/Art Resource, NY)

Francescana Mariana,'' *ibid.* 29 (1932) 257–295. B. BUGHETTI, ''Descriptio rarissimae editionis quae tractatus continet de Corona septem B.V.M. Gaudiorum,'' *Archivum Franciscanum historicum* 4 (1911) 366–371. J. CAPISTRAN, ''Letter to Puchelbach,'' *Analecta Franciscana* 2 (1886) 342. D. VAN WELY, *Het kransje der twaalf sterren in de Geschiedenis van de rozenkrans* (Collectanea franciscana neerlandica 6; Boisle-duc 1941). J. CAMBELL, *De indulgentiis Seraphici Ordinis hodie vigentibus . . .* (Compostella 1958) 192, 305–308. R. HUSER, ''How to Recite the Franciscan Crown,'' *Provincial Chronicle* 35 (1962–63) 33–34; ''The Franciscan Crown Recited in Common,'' *ibid.* 444–445.

[M. F. LAUGHLIN]

CROWN OF THORNS (RELIC)

According to some authorities it is likely that the Christ's crown of thorns was helmetlike in form, rather than a circlet. The type of thorn used was the jujube, now known as the *zizyphus spina Christi,* abundant in the Jerusalem area, producing both straight and curved spines,

similar to existing relics. The relic of the crown of thorns was venerated at Jerusalem for many centuries. Individual thorns were dispersed as relics elsewhere. The relic was taken to Byzantium about 1063. In 1238, Baldwin II gave it to St. Louis of France. The famous Sainte-Chapelle in Paris was erected in 1248 to conserve this relic. Besides thorns from the actual crown at authentic shrines, there are also many thorns venerated that have merely touched the alleged originals.

Bibliography: F. D. DE MÉLY, *La Croix des premiers croisés; La Sainte Lance; La Sainte Couronne,* v.3 of P. E. RIANT, *Exuviae sacrae Constantinopolitanae,* 3 v. (Geneva 1877–1904). C. ROHAULT DE FLEURY, *Mémoire sur les instruments de la Passion* (Paris 1869). R. GORMAN, *The Last Hours of Jesus* (New York 1960).

[J. MEAD/EDS.]

CRUCIFIX

A CROSS on which there is an image of Christ Crucified. Although the custom of portraying the Redeemer on the cross reaches as far back as the 6th century, it was not until the 13th century that complete realism characterized sculpture accentuating Christ's Passion. Before this time the representation of the living, triumphant Christ appeared on the cross, thus stressing the theological significance of Good Friday as essentially a paschal event: through His sufferings Christ conquered sin and death. This was often brought out by the adornment with jewels instead of the image of the Crucified. In the 20th century there has been a return to this theological emphasis in the crucifix in that the image of the Crucified appears vested in royal and priestly garments.

The cross first appeared on the altar table during the 13th century; soon after it was replaced by a crucifix. Only with the Roman Missal of Pius V in 1570 is there any mention of an obligation to have a crucifix on the altar. This did not mean that the crucifix must actually rest on the altar. It may be suspended above it, or placed near it in the form of a processional cross.

Bibliography: G. RIMINGTON, ''The Cross and the Crucifixion in Christian Art,'' *Areopagus* 4:4 (1991) 41–46. E. DUFFY, ''Devotion to the crucifix and related images in England on the eve of the Reformation,'' in *Bilder und Bildersturm im Spätmittelalter und in der frühen Neuzeit,* ed. R.W. SCRIBNER (Wiesbaden 1990) 21–36.

[J. H. MILLER/EDS.]

CRUCIFIXION

Crucifixion was a method of capital punishment commonly used among the ancient peoples surrounding the Mediterranean basin from approximately the 6th century B.C. to the 4th century A.D.. Crucifixion was finally banned by Constantine the Great, the first Christian emperor, in A. D. 337 as a token of respect for Jesus Christ, who chose to redeem the world through death on a cross. This article discusses crucifixion in the ancient world, the Crucifixion of Christ, and the significance of the cross.

Crucifixion Among the Ancients. Because of its cruelty, crucifixion was intended as both a severe punishment of the victim and a frightful deterrent to others. Crucifixion developed from a method of execution by which the victim was fastened to an upright stake either by impaling him on it or by tying him to it with thongs. Impalement inflicted extreme pain but brought death in a short time. When the victim was merely fastened to the stake, he suffered much longer and finally died of exhaustion, exposure, or torments inflicted on him by passersby and even wild animals, if he was sufficiently close to the ground. From this form of execution was developed crucifixion in the strict sense, whereby the outstretched arms of the victim were tied or nailed to a crossbeam (*patibulum*), which was then laid in a groove across the top or suspended by means of a notch in the side of an upright stake that was always left in position at the site of execution.

The oldest known written reference to impalement is in the Code of Hammurabi [par. 153; J. B. Pritchard, *Ancient Near Eastern Texts Relating to the Old Testament*[2] (Princeton 1955) 172] dating from about 1700 B.C. Mention of impaling prisoners of war is frequent in the inscriptions of the kings of the Neo-Assyrian Empire (10th to 7th centuries B.C.), and portrayals of such impalements are common in their bas-reliefs. The earliest historical record of crucifixion as such dates back, on the authority of Herodotus (Hist. 9.20), to the beginning of the Persian period (6th century B.C.). Later Persian history is replete with stories of crucifixions. From the Persians this method of execution spread to other peoples, the Phoenicians, the Egyptians, the Grecian colonies (though it seems it was never practiced in Greece itself), the Carthaginians, and the Romans. Among the last, crucifixion was practiced with great abandon whenever the occasion seemed to warrant it.

The Romans considered crucifixion so shameful a penalty that it could not be inflicted on Roman citizens. Roman crucifixion was always preceded by a scourging of the victim at the place of judgment. Then the criminal, still naked after the scourging, was made to carry his own cross (i.e., the crossbeam) to the place of execution, where he was exposed to public ridicule and death. On the top of the upright stake was fastened a placard with the culprit's name and a statement of the crime for which

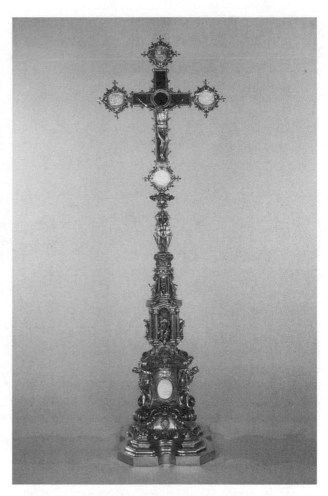

Silver gilt crucifix, by Antonio Gentili. (©David Lees/CORBIS)

he was being put to death. The full weight of a body hanging by the arms would prevent the functioning of the lung muscles and so cause death by asphyxiation after not too long a time. Therefore, to prolong the agony of the victim, support was given to his body by a kind of seat block and by binding or nailing his feet to the cross. Death could later be hastened by breaking the victim's legs (*crurifragium*), so that shock and asphyxiation soon ended his life. Sometimes, however, the side and heart would be pierced by a spear to cause immediate death. After death the body was left to rot on the cross as an additional sign of disgrace and as a warning to the passersby.

Although among the Israelites stoning was the common form of capital punishment, the Old Testament sometimes speaks of hanging the condemned on a tree (Dt 21.22–23; Jos 8.29, 10.26). In these cases, however, the culprit was first killed by other means and was then "hanged on a tree" as a token of further disgrace and warning. Another instance of hanging on a tree is given in 2 Sm 21.6–9 (possibly also in Nm 25.4), where it is

"Crucifixion," part of the San Zeno Altarpiece by Andrea Mantegna, Musee du Louvre, Paris, France. (©Archivo Iconografico, S.A./ CORBIS)

not certain whether suspension was the means of execution or whether the victims were dead before they were hanged. But crucifixion was always something foreign to Jewish law.

Crucifixion of Christ. Jesus suffered crucifixion at the hand of the Roman authorities then ruling in Palestine (Lk 3.1, 23.1). The account of His execution as narrated by the Evangelists agrees entirely with what is known about the Roman method of crucifixion and their way of dealing with their subjected peoples. Thus, Jesus was scourged (Mk 15.15 and parallels) before He was led forth to the place of execution carrying His cross (Jn 19.17). The Jews, however, with their sense of public decency, objected to a man going about naked in public, and as a concession to their feelings the Romans in Palestine allowed the condemned criminal to put his clothes on again after he had been scourged instead of being driven naked through the street. Thus Jesus, too, was given back his clothes after His scourging (Mk 15,20; Mt 27.31). *See* FLAGELLATION (IN THE BIBLE)). As usual, the execution was also to serve as a warning to the public, and so, to prevent Jesus from dying on the way, He was given aid in carrying his cross (Mk 15.21 and parallels). When He had arrived at the place of execution, Jesus was offered

a drink of spiced wine to numb the pain, but He refused to drink it (Mk 15.23; Mt 27.34). Such a drink was another concession made by the Romans to the more humane feelings of the Jews. After this, Jesus was stripped of His garments (Mk 15.24 and parallels) and nailed to the cross, at least by His hands (Jn 20.25).

On the top of the cross was placed the customary placard with His name and, at Pilate's insistence, the statement of His "crime," that He was actually the King of the Jews (Mk 15.26; Mt 27.37; Lk 23.38; Jn 19.19). The four Evangelists differ slightly in the wording of the inscription, which shows that they were citing from memory and hearsay evidence; but all agree that it was in three languages, "Hebrew" (i.e., Aramaic), Greek, and Latin. As was their custom with more notorious criminals, the Romans raised Jesus on a rather high stake, so that He could be seen by everyone; it was in fact so high that, when the soldiers wanted to put a sponge soaked in wine to His lips, they first had to put it on the end of a stick (Mk 15.26; Mt 27.48; Jn 19.29).

Because of the Jewish law that the body of an executed criminal should "not remain on the tree overnight" but had to be buried the same day (Dt 21.23), the Romans, at the request of the Jewish authorities, decided to hasten death by breaking the legs of the Crucified; since Jesus, however, was already dead, His legs were not broken, but "one of the soldiers opened his side with a lance" (Jn 19.31–34). Again because of the Jewish law, the dead bodies were not to be left on the cross to rot but were taken down before sunset of the same day and given decent burial (Mk 15.42 and parallels).

Significance of the Cross. The significance of Christ's death on the cross can be learned from the many references made to it throughout the New Testament. All of them, however, can be reduced to one single idea, God's great love for man. Among the Jews and the Romans death on the cross was a sign of shame and ignominy (1 Cor 1.18, 23; Heb 12.2). Yet Jesus did not shrink from this extreme manifestation of His love for man (Phil 2.8). For the Jews a man hanging on a tree was cursed, an object of reprobation (Dt 21.23). Christ chose to do just this, to redeem man from the malediction of the Law that imposed obligations but was unable to save (Gal 3.10–13).

Through Jesus the cross became a means of reconciling fallen and sinful mankind with the holy God (Eph 2.16; Col 1.20, 2.14). The cross is, therefore, the instrument of man's liberation from slavery to this world and to sin (Rom 6.6) and the means of his renewal (Gal 3.1, 6.14). Through the cross the redeemed become new creatures, new men, to be coheirs with the God-man in the kingdom of Heaven (Gal 6.15–16).

The cross is thus a symbol of complete union with Christ. To take up one's cross means to turn away from the service of the world and the flesh (Gal 5.24), and thus to be a true disciple (Lk 14.27), a follower of Christ (Mk 8.34; Mt 16.24). Anyone who refuses to take up the cross is unworthy of Jesus (Mt 10.38); the true disciple takes up his cross daily to follow the Master (Lk 9.23). As a follower of Jesus he is willing to deny himself many things (Mt 10.34–39) and even to make the supreme sacrifice of his life for the sake of Christ and the gospel (Mk 8.35).

The Crucifixion is ultimately a mystical event representing the whole redemptive work of Christ and its proclamation throughout the world. It is the fulfillment of all the salvific deeds of Yahweh in the Old Testament, prefigured by the bronze serpent made by Moses at the Lord's behest and raised on a pole (Nm 21.4–9) and prefigured by the Hebrew letter *tau* (at that time shaped like a "T" or an "X") marked on the forehead of the citizens of Jerusalem who were not to be struck down because of abominations of the city (Ez 9.4–6). It is a total commitment to the way of life as it was lived for us by God's own Son. The cross is the pivotal point of history from which all history, prior and subsequent, derives its meaning.

Bibliography: H. F. HITZIG, *Paulys Realenzyklopädie der klassischen Altertumswissenschaft,* ed. G. WISSOWA et al. 4.2 (1901) 1728–31. *Encyclopedic Dictionary of the Bible,* tr. and adap. by L. HARTMAN (New York 1963) from A. VAN DEN BORN, *Bijbels Woordenboek* 462–465. H. MARUCCHI, *Dictionnaire de la Bible,* ed. F. VIGOUROUX, 5 v. (Paris 1895–1912) 2:1127–34. R. DE VAUX, *Ancient Israel, Its Life and Institutions,* tr. J. MC HUGH (New York 1961) 158–160. J. BLINZLER, *Lexikon für Theologie und Kirche²,* ed. J. HOFER and K. RAHNER, 10 v. (Freiburg 1957–65) 6:621–622; *The Trial of Jesus,* tr. I. and F. MC HUGH (Westminster, Md. 1959). N. LALIBERTÉ and E. WEST, *The History of the Cross* (New York 1960). W. BULST, *The Shroud of Turin,* tr. S. MCKENNA and J. J. GALVIN (Milwaukee 1957) 44–52, 106. P. BARBET, *A Doctor at Calvary* (New York 1954) 41–67.

[M. W. SCHOENBERG]

CRUCIFIXION (IN ART)

The representation of Christ's redemptive death on Golgotha does not occur in the symbolic art of the first Christian centuries. The early Christians, influenced by the Old Testament prohibition of graven images, were reluctant to depict even the instrument of the Lord's Passion. When the cross comes to be represented in the time of Constantine, it is seen both as the trophy of the victorious Christ of Easter and as the sign in the sky preceding the Second Coming of the Son of Man. The scene of the crucifixion, however, is still absent from the early Passion cycles; even in the 6th-century mosaic sequence of S. Apollinare Nuovo in Ravenna, the Golgotha scene is left out. This article treats the historical development of literal and symbolic representation of the crucifixion.

Early Examples. The only two crucifixion scenes that antedate the 6th century show the artist's hesitation in front of this new theme. On the ivory casket of the British Museum as on the doors of S. Sabina in Rome, both of the early 5th century, Christ appears covered only with the narrow *subligaculum,* his eyes open and his hands nailed to the cross. While the beardless Christ of the ivory seems to hover on the cross, the bearded Christ of the wooden panel seems to stand on the ground, his arms extended in the manner of the ORANS. In the ivory scene, on Christ's left Longinus is about to stab the Lord's side; on Christ's right Mary and John stand in silent grief; in the left corner, Judas is hanged on a tree.

Eastern Art. Dogmatic reasons alone, that is, the reduced fear of Arian and Apollinarist misinterpretation or the apologetic efforts against Monophysitism, cannot explain the sudden popularity of crucifixion scenes in the later 6th century. At this time, the faithful increasingly demanded images of Christ and the saints for their private devotion.

Cover of a wooden reliquary casket from Palestine, showing the Crucifixion, 6th century.

Syrian and Palestinian. Piety was nowhere directed so strongly toward Christ's Passion as in Syria from the time of St. Ephrem. The first datable image of the crucifixion of this new age is found in the Syriac Gospel Book, written by Rabbula in 586 (Laurentian Library, Florence). A bearded Christ in a sleeveless tunic, the *colobium,* is crucified between the thieves, with Mary and John framing the scene on Christ's right and the three women on his left. Three soldiers gamble for the cloak below, the lance-bearer and the sponge-bearer fill out the center of the scene, and the sun and moon above show the event in its cosmic dimension. The open eyes of Christ indicate that the Logos, divine nature, remains in the dead body. His wound is on the side of honor as is that of the good thief, and thus it is indicative of the life-giving source from which the Church is born.

The crucifixions on the late 6th-century Monza and Bobbio ampullae from Palestine show a mixture of historical reference and symbol. Christ's head appears nearly always above, or in the middle of, the empty central cross. When Christ is represented in the colobium, extending his arms like an *orans,* the cross is missing (Monza 12, 13). The presence of Longinus and Stephaton next to an empty cross (Bobbio 6) shows the continuance

of the mingling of the historical and the symbolic. The two pilgrims kneeling at the foot of the holy cross symbolize its liturgical veneration (Dumbarton Oaks, Washington, D.C.). On a contemporary Palestinian reliquary box from the Sancta Sanctorum (Vatican Museum) Mary and John stand on opposite sides, and both thieves look to their left as on the pilgrim's flasks. John holds the Gospel Book and raises his right hand in testimony. Here, however, the scene is not framed by Mary and John, but by the thieves. Christ stands erect on the footrest in hieratic solemnity. The next step, that of eliminating the marginal figures of the thieves, is accomplished in the mid-8th-century fresco in S. Maria Antiqua in Rome. More than in any previous example, the symbolic gradation of size gives Christ in the colobium a supra-human majesty, while his inclined head suggests a deep spiritual communication between the figures of this timeless, sacramental mystery. Here the devotional image is achieved.

Unlike the Rabbula type with its synchronic representation of John 19.24, 29, 39, some reliquaries and pectoral crosses depict the moment when Christ entrusted Mary and John to each other (Jn 19.26–27; Rhode Island School of Design). Another type, not yet sufficiently studied, presents Christ on a Maltese cross ending in medallions with saints' busts. On the oldest of these (*c.* 600, Dumbarton Oaks), the Lord appears without a cross, but with the titulus and with his hands lowered as though to show his wounds. A *parousia* seems superimposed on the sign of Christ's Passion. A transformation of this type leads to the first crucifixes proper, a group of 7th-century pectoral crosses found in Hungary.

Transitional Types. The use of a lamb as symbol for Christ, as seen in a crucifixion on a column in St. Marks, Venice, was forbidden by the Quinisext Council of Constantinople (692); He was to be represented thereafter "in human form." This decision not only reflects the extent to which realistic images came to be acceptable but also indicates that resistance against such representations continued. Consequently, the iconoclasts attacked the crucifixion scene with particular vehemence and employed the simple cross of glory as a symbol of their faith.

Their opponents, the monastic party, multiplied crucifixion scenes in their psalters; these reveal a number of iconographic innovations. Christ is seen dead, with closed eyes, in the mid-9th century Chludoff Psalter in Moscow, as on an 8th- or 9th-century icon of Mount Sinai. The same psalter from Moscow shows the centurion and the crowd of Jews; the latter appear as early as the 8th century in the ruined fresco in the main apse of S. Maria Antiqua, where for the first time angels typical of Byzantine crucifixions appear. The freedom of monastic art in arranging the main figures, the grouping of women, soldiers, and Jews, and the dead rising from their tombs (11th century, BN gr. 74; Bibl. Nat., Paris) contrasts markedly with the strict symmetry and restrained attitude of the few figures contained in crucifixions of the aristocratic school. In the most famous work of the latter group, the Gregory of Nazianzus of Paris (*c.* 880, Bibliothèque Nationale manuscript gr. 510), a colobium painted over the original loincloth provides the earliest Eastern example of the *perizonium.*

The frescoes of the Cappadocian rock churches (9th to 13th centuries) follow in their early phase the archaic Syrian iconography, showing the three crosses several times. They reflect popular piety in the importance given to the Passion (11 scenes in Tokali Kilisse, late 10th century) and in the use of the apocryphal sources (Jesus crowned with thorns, carrying the cross, in Elmali Kilisse, late 11th century). The old restraint gives way to a dramatic expression of grief in the symmetrical gestures of Mary and John raising one hand to the cheek.

Byzantine. In the 11th century, the representation of the event on Golgotha, which hitherto had been remarkably free, was reduced to a few types. As one of the 12 festival images of the liturgical cycle in the church nave, it received a prominent place in the transept or narthex.

Crucifixion of Christ, 8th-century fresco, Santa Maria Antiqua, Rome.

Just as in Byzantine liturgy the death of Christ remains always a phase in the work of Redemption, so the crucifixion, though it has an important position, remains within the framework of the liturgical cycle without assuming the preeminent place that it attained in the late Middle Ages in the West.

The classical form of Byzantine representation of the crucifixion was established in the mosaic cycles of the 11th century in Greece. Christ stands between Mary and John on the suppedaneum, clothed only in the loincloth; two angels above and Adam's skull below the cross complete the scene. At Hosios Lukas in Phocis (early 11th century), the dead Christ with closed eyes is given a place for the first time in monumental art. The violent linear design of the curving body speaks the language of monastic art, while the delicate organic movement of the slender Christ of Daphni (late 11th century) incorporates the best of both traditions. Here Christ's eyes are open and they look toward Mary in sad tenderness, while the Disciple's eyes seek the viewer's in order to draw him into the mystery to which he gives witness with his raised hand. The iconic dignity and liturgical significance of this crucifixion make it an image of prayer rather than a historical representation. This spirit is to prevail throughout Byzantine art.

Fourteenth-century French ivory of the crucifixion of Christ. (©Burstein Collection/CORBIS)

The addition of one holy woman and the centurion to the three main figures is peculiar to Eastern iconography. The composition appears mostly in the minor arts (11th-century enamel of Queen Gisela, Munich) and is often found on Russian icons. More common is the iconography showing groups of women behind Mary and soldiers and Jews behind John (11th-century ivory triptych, Kaiser Friedrich Museum, Berlin; 12th-century mosaic in St. Mark's, Venice, where the gambling soldiers and eight half-figures of angels add to the crowding of the scene). To heighten the dramatic effect of the crucifixion, the artists of the Paleologan renaissance in the 14th century turned to the latter type, sometimes even representing the two thiefs. The later 15th-century icon of Cardinal Bessarion (Academy, Florence) illustrates the qualities of this art: the use as scenic background of the walls of Jerusalem, the compact grouping of the figures, and above all the depth of grief expressed by the heavy curve of John contrasted with the restraint of the Lord's Mother.

Western Art. The first representations of the crucifixion in Western art were made in Ireland. In the 8th-century Irish Gospel Book of St. Gall (Manuscript 51) a beardless, open-eyed Christ is clothed in a colobium stylized into strange bindings coiled about His body. Two half-figures of angels above and Longinus and Stephaton below fill the remaining space. On Christ's left, Longinus is healed of his blindness by the blood flowing into his eyes, in accordance with apocryphal legend (cf. bronze plaque of Athlone). The crucifixion carvings on the Irish high crosses (9th to 11th centuries) usually show the St. Gall and Athlone type. The presence of related Old and New Testament scenes may be attributed to Eastern models of the minor arts, e.g., the Holy Land ampullae (Monza 2v, New Testament cycle; Monza 13v, Apostles' busts).

The most complex crucifixion scenes are to be found on Carolingian ivories, such as the book cover in the state library of Munich (c. 870, clm 4452). At the top the hand of God appears between the figures of the sun and moon in chariots. Christ in the loincloth is flanked on the right by Mary and the holy women, Longinus, and the Church with a fanion receiving Christ's blood into a chalice. On the left appear Stephaton, John, and a seated figure of the Church taking the shield from the Synagogue. Three angels hover above the cross, and the serpent is crushed below. The lower half represents the holy women at the sepulcher, the resurrection of the dead, and enlarged personifications of Earth, Sea, and Rome. The cosmic dimension of Redemption, the victory over the Prince of this World, the transition from the age of the Law to that of Grace, the unity of redemptive death and resurrection, and the sacramental oneness of Golgotha and the Mass have been organized by the Carolingian artist into an image for meditation in which the regal and triumphant character prevails according to contemporary theology. In later Carolingian art the tendency is toward clearer, more rigid structure. The four Evangelists are introduced, and sometimes Adam and Eve are shown rising from their tombs.

The crucifixions in book illuminations are close to the traditional types. The colobium, which is rarely seen in ivories, occurs frequently, especially in Ottonian manuscripts where the three crosses are sometimes shown. The most important innovation in Anglo-Saxon and Ottonian miniatures was the representation of the dead Christ, his eyes closed, his head falling to his shoulder, and his body beginning to arch (c. 980, Harley 2094; British Museum). This development heralds a trend that was to become general only two centuries later.

At this time also, the crucifix with separate body appears, as in Bernward's cross (c. 1000, Hildesheim). In the later 10th century, a fillet or crown is to be seen in God's hand above the cross. In the early 11th century it appears on Christ's head, where it signifies the crown of thorns as a token of glory. In the 12th century, Christ is frequently depicted with a royal crown (Spanish crucifix; The Cloisters, New York). The *Volto Santo* of Lucca (11th century) and a group of 12th- to 13th-century Catalan crucifixes showing a bearded Christ with inclined head and dressed in a long tunic with sleeves, translate into monumental sculpture an iconographic type going back to the 7th and 8th centuries (7th-century golden pectoral cross, British Museum, London; Hungarian pectoral crosses). Christ in the loincloth remains, however, the normal type in medieval crucifixions.

The dead Christ appears more often in the later 12th century, but it is not until the mid-13th century that he replaces the triumphant Christ. The crown of thorns remains infrequent until the late 13th and the 14th century. The two nails holding Christ's feet are replaced by one (1149, baptismal font from Thienen, Brussels). In the 13th century, when this type begins to prevail, the suppedaneum disappears and Christ's legs are crossed. Mary is represented as being overpowered by her suffering. The first representations of the faltering strength of Mary are Byzantine (late 12th century, Monreale); there she does not swoon, but is supported by holy women, or John, who reappears at her side. The fainting of Our Lady is combined during the 13th century with the piercing of her heart by a sword. While in Romanesque art the scene was reduced to the three-figure image of prayer with two angels or with the sun and moon above, in the 13th century the composition again had numerous figures, a type that predominated throughout the late Middle Ages.

In Italy the transition from the triumphant Christ of the earlier centuries to the suffering Christ of the later

Middle Ages was made through the medium of painting on cruciform panels. The earliest extant examples come from Tuscany (1138, Sarzana) and Umbria (1187, Spoleto). The works of the Umbrian school show only Mary and John on either side of Christ, while Passion scenes accompany the mourning figures in Lucca and appear alone on the central panel in Pisa. On all early crosses, the wide-eyed Christ stands upright, with two nails in his feet, a hieratic image of the victor on the cross. This type is replaced by the dead Christ in the work of Giunta Pisano in 1236 and after; by 1260, the living Christ has disappeared completely. On Giunta's crosses, the agony just ended remains engraved on Christ's face in the deep-cut lines of mouth, eyes, and eyebrows (*c.* 1250; S. Domenico, Bologna). In GIOTTO the panel cross transcends itself; the traditional frame created to enshrine a sacred idea cannot hold in its plane the spatial life of the heavily hanging body with its forward thrust of the angular knees (end of 13th century; S. Maria Novella, Florence).

The historical crucifixion scene found its way from Byzantine into Italian art in the sculpture of Niccolò Pisano, who showed the violent motion of Mary's fainting and first represented Christ crucified with three nails in the northern manner. By unifying the groups on either side of the cross through a common emotion, grief or fear, he initiated a tradition of the utmost importance (1266 to 1269, pulpit, Siena Cathedral). His son Giovanni introduced the vertical dynamism of Gothic art into the scene, raising the three crosses high above the spectators (after 1300, pulpit, Pisa Cathedral). In Duccio's *Maestà* the two groups of people move apart, leaving the center open for the vertical axis of Christ's cross (1308 to 1311; Cathedral Museum, Siena). Giotto shows fewer figures and no thieves; the spectators below the cross are bathed in the solemn stillness of death (*c.* 1305; Scrovegni Chapel, Padua). Pietro Lorenzetti deepens the setting, filling it with numerous horses and people (*c.* 1355; S. Francesco, Assisi). In Andrea da Firenze's crucifixion, the mass of people watching the drama enhances the solitude of Christ and of his mother (*c.* 1355; Spanish Chapel, S. Maria Novella, Florence). Through Simone Martini, Italian elements such as Mary lying unconscious on the ground, the grieving angels flying around the cross, and Mary Magdalen embracing it or throwing up her arms in the gesture of distress, penetrated into northern art.

Late Medieval. In the late 14th and early 15th centuries, Italian art moved toward the devotional image showing saints or donors. The meditative quality draws the onlooker into the emotions of the figures under the cross, as in the great crucifixion scene picturing many saints by Fra Angelico (*c.* 1440 to 1445; S. Marco, Florence) or in Sano di Pietro's small canvas (National Gallery, Washington), where Mary and John sit on the ground, meditating in an ancient attitude of mourning, a true "image for worship by empathy" (E. Panofsky).

During the transition period of the 13th century, the North depicted Christ in a Gothic manner, on a slender cross without a footrest, and hanging low between straining arms with knees bent at a sharp angle. A group of 14th-century Rhenish crucifixes presents this type in its extreme form. On the forked, treelike cross in St. Maria im Kapitol in Cologne (1304), Christ's suffering is strikingly told in his emaciated body covered with wounds and his face distorted by pain. In the iconography toward the end of the century, a less agitated body of Christ reflects the calm of death; but the crown of thorns, now become general, begins to lie as a heavy weight on Christ's head. The 14th-century crucifixions with numerous figures rarely have more than eight or ten persons on each side of the cross. But in the 15th century, the artists began to exploit all the narrative details of the Gospel. They depict the thieves tied to T-shaped crosses; Christ's cross generally bears the abbreviated titulus INRI. They multiply Scribes and Pharisees, soldiers and Jews, bringing in also a number of horses, and delighting in genre elements. Yet in the strong individual expression of prominent figures or in the unified attitude of the astonished or the mourning, the doubtful or the mocking, there is meaning upon which to meditate (1533, painting by Lucas Cranach the Elder; Art Institute of Chicago).

The composition becomes even more complex in the later 15th century, expecially in northern Germany, by the addition of scenes not simultaneous with the crucifixion, such as the carrying of the cross, the descent from the cross, and the entombment. These are shown either as small background scenes or an integrated part of the spectacle of Golgotha. But the tendency was soon checked in southern Germany by the influence of the Flemish, who, like the Italians, preferred the devotional image and represented only the holy figures of the Biblical text in a wide landscape. In Roger van der Weyden, the historical event is transformed into a suprahistorical mystery, a completely interior drama transpiring in the dreamlike space of an open landscape (Kunsthistorisches Museum, Vienna), in the liturgical space of a Gothic church (Museum of Fine Arts, Antwerp), or in an ideal space enclosed by a high wall (Philadelphia Museum of Fine Arts).

In the late Middle Ages, the thoughts of the faithful were absorbed increasingly by the humanity of Christ. The unbridled realism found in the figures of the thieves and the executioners generally stopped short of Christ on the cross. GRÜNEWALD offers a remarkable exception. The emotions of the holy women, all interior in the Washington crucifixion (National Gallery; *see* GRÜNE-

WALD, MATTHIAS), have overpowered them on the Isenheim altarpiece (*c.* 1515; Unterlinden Museum, Colmar); the body of Christ hanging above them is filled with the abysmal horrors of a violent death. Still, John the Baptist and the lamb whose blood flows into a chalice reveal in this unspeakable suffering the immeasurable redemptive love of Christ.

Renaissance to Modern. The paintings of the crucifixion in the Italian High Renaissance continued in the direction indicated by the early 15th century, presenting but few figures of a statuesque freedom in a wide landscape. The solemn stillness of Christ, whose body betrays no suffering, and of Mary and John, Jerome and Mary Magdalen meditating upon the mystery, is enhanced by the harmony of the landscape (1502 to 1503, Raphael; National Gallery, London). The symmetry of the Renaissance crucifixion was abandoned in Germany by Lucas Cranach the Elder (1503; Alte Pinakothek, Munich). Though the thieves' crosses had been represented diagonally since the early 15th century, Christ's cross appears here for the first time on the right, so that Christ is seen almost in profile and the two thieves face each other on the left. Thus a strong diagonal relationship is established between Christ and His Mother in the center of the scene. Through Tintoretto the diagonal or lateral position of Christ's cross becomes a frequent feature in baroque art (1508; S. Cassiano, Venice). Tintoretto also gives a new impetus to the historical crucifixion (*c.* 1565; Scuola di San Rocco, Venice). The dramatic agitation of the many groups under the dark, storm-swept sky enhances the isolation of Christ and the group of his friends at the foot of the cross. Rembrandt far surpasses the Venetian in his etching of 1660 (or 1661), where a cosmic struggle between light and darkness reflects the agony of Christ.

Baroque art, which was remarkably free in the choice of iconographic elements, represented both the dead Christ and the living Christ on the cross. In 17th-century Spain and France, Christ was more frequently shown alone, usually in front of a dark, storm-filled sky. Nothing was allowed to distract from the solitude of the victim on the cross. The stillness of the accomplished sacrifice speaks from Velázquez's famous crucifix (*c.* 1630; Prado, Madrid). The most striking type of baroque crucifixion, first found in a painting in Dresden formerly attributed to Dürer, became common after El GRECO. It shows the suffering Christ with His head cast back, His eyes turned upward to heaven, and His mouth open in agony (Cleveland Museum). This search for the most dramatic moment to represent the fullness of Christ's Passion is evident in Rubens's crucifixion (1612; Musée Royal des Beaux-Arts, Antwerp) depicting the piercing of Christ's side. It explains the importance assigned to the raising of the cross in both Rubens's and Rembrandt's

work. A second crucifixion by Rubens (The Johnson Collection, Philadelphia) helped to establish the type of the living Christ with steeply raised arms, a type frequently found in ivory crucifixes.

The 18th century produced dramatic images of the crucifixion, but it did not add to the developed iconography. The 19th-century representations, when not drawing on the popular traditions of the 18th century, were rarely more than academic exercises in the effects of light and in the anatomy of the nude. Gaugin sought to translate the spiritual message of Golgotha in his "Yellow Crucifixion." In the prayerful night of his "Guerre et Miserere," Rouault has created the 20th century's profoundest image of Christ's great suffering and love. In Chagall's "White Crucifixion" (1938, The Art Institute of Chicago), man's, that is Jewry's, unending suffering becomes one with Christ's timeless Passion. Germaine Richier leaves the figurative behind in her crucifix in Assy to speak of the shapeless victim of the cross. Manessier, the spiritual heir of Rouault, lyrically expresses the mystery of Christ's death and Resurrection in abstract compositions.

See Also: JESUS CHRIST, ICONOGRAPHY OF

Bibliography: J. REIL, *Die frühchristlichen Darstellungen der Kreuzigung Christi* (Leipzig 1904); *Christus am Kreuz in der bildenden Kunst der Karolingerzeit* (Leipzig 1930). L. BRÉHIER, *Les Origines du crucifix dans l'art religieux* (3d ed. Paris 1908); *L'Art chrétien, son développement iconographique des origines à nos jours* (2d ed. Paris 1928). G. SCHÖNERMARK, *Der Kruzifixus in der bildenden Kunst* (Strasbourg 1908). B. LAZAR, *Die beiden Wurzeln der Kruzifixdarstellung* (Strasbourg 1912). G. MILLET, *Recherches sur l'iconographie de l'Évangile aux XIV*ᵉ *et XVI*ᵉ *siècles* (Paris 1916). E. PANOFSKY, "Imago pietatis," in *Festschrift für Max J. Friedländer* (Leipzig 1927) 261–308. K. KÜNSTLE, *Ikonographie der christlichen Kunst*, 2 v. (Freiburg 1926–28) 1:446–76. É. MÂLE, *L'Art religieux du XII*ᵉ *siècle en France* (5th ed. Paris 1947); *The Gothic Image: Religious Art in France of the 13th Century*, tr. D. NUSSEY (New York 1958); *L'Art religieux de la fin du moyen-âge en France* (5th ed. Paris 1949); *L'Art religieux de la fin du XVI*ᵉ *siècle, du XVII*ᵉ *siècle et du XVIII*ᵉ *siècle* (2d ed. Paris 1951) 267–79. E. SANDBERG Vavalà, *La croce dipinta italiana e l'iconografia della passione* (Verona 1929). G. DE JERPHANION, "La Représentation de la croix et du crucifix aux origines de l'art chrétien," in *La Voix des monuments: Études d'archéologie*, new series 1 (Rome 1938) 138–64. A. K. PORTER, *The Crosses and Culture of Ireland* (New Haven 1931). E. DUMOUTET, *Le Christ selon la chair et la vie liturgique au moyen-âge* (Paris 1932). G. SCHNÜRER and J. M. RITZ, *Sankt Kümmernis und Volto santo* (Düsseldorf 1934). G. DE FRANCOVICH, "L'origine e la diffusione del crocifisso gotico doloroso," *Römisches Jahrbuch für Kunstgeschichte 2* (1938) 143–261. L. H. GRONDIJS, *L'Iconographie byzantine du Crucifié mort sur la croix* (2d ed. Brussels 1947). P. DONCOEUR, *Le Christ dans l'art français*, 2 v. in 1 (Paris 1939–48) v.2. E. KITZINGER, "The Cult of Images in the Age before Iconoclasm," *Dumbarton Oaks Papers* 8 (1954) 83–150. E. LANKHEIT, "Egell-Studien," *Münchner Jahrbuch der bildenden Kunst*, 3d series, 6 (1955) 243–53. R. FÜGLISTER, *Das lebende Krenz* (Einsiedeln 1964). A. M. AMMANN, "Eine neue Variante der Darstellung des bekleideten Christus am Kreuz," *Orientalia Christiana periodica*

21 (1955) 21–35. A. GRILLMEIER, *Der Logos am Kreuz: Zur christologischen Symbolik der älteren Kreuzigungsdarstellung* (Munich 1956), the best presentation of one period, bibliography; see review of H. RAHNER, *Scholastik* 32 (1957) 410–16. L. RÉAU, *Iconographie de l'art chrétien,* 6 v. (Paris 1955–59) 2.2:462–512. V. GUREWICH, "Observations on the Iconography of the Wound in Christ's Side," *Journal of the Warburg and Courtauld Institutes* 20 (1957) 358–62. A. GRABAR, *Les Ampoules de Terre Sainte* (Paris 1958). E. ROTH, *Der volkreiche Kalvarienberg in Literatur und Kunst des Spätmittelalters* (Berlin 1958), very useful for the late Middle Ages, bibliography. P. THOBY, *Le Crucifix des origines au Concile de Trente: Étude iconographique* (Nantes 1959), bibliography. W. MESSERER, *Byzantinische Zeitschrift* 52 (1959) 48–51. K. WESSEL, "Frühbyzantinische Darstellung der Kreuzigung Christi," *Revista di archeologia cristiana* 36 (1960) 45–71; "Die Entstehung des Kruzifixus," *Byzantinische Zeitschrift* 53 (1960) 95–111. E. LUCCHESI-PALLI, *Lexikon für Theologie und Kirche,* ed. J. HOFER and K. RAHNER, 10 v. (2d, new ed. Freiburg 1957–65) 6:610–14, 622–25.

[A. A. SCHACHER]

CRUCIFIXION, THEOLOGICAL SIGNIFICANCE OF

The theological significance of the CRUCIFIXION and death of Jesus forms an essential element in the primitive KERYGMA or apostolic preaching. This is clear from 1 Cor 15.3, where, stressing his dependence on the traditional gospel, Paul insists. "For I delivered to you first of all, what I also received, that Christ died for our sins according to the Scriptures." This oft-repeated formula heralds the saving value of the Crucifixion as a vicarious SACRIFICE (2 Cor 5.14–15; 1 Thes 5.10; Jn 11.50–52; 1 Pt 3.18; Hebrews ch. 9).

The early Christian community characteristically interpreted the salvation event of the Lord's Crucifixion and death in terms of the Old Testament Scriptures. The suffering victim of Psalm 21(22) and the bronze serpent of Nm 21.9 are among the Old Testament images applied to the Passion and death of Jesus. Moses' lifting up of the serpent to heal the diseased Israelites foreshadows the lifting up of the Son of Man (Jn 3.14–15) in death (Jn 12.32–33) for the healing of God's people.

The Isaian suffering servant, who gave his life as an offering for sin, is recognized in Jesus who came not "to be served but to serve, and to give his life as a ransom for many" (Mk 10.45; cf. Acts 8.32; 1 Tm 2.5–6; Rom 8.32; Eph 5.2). The death of Jesus is not the destruction of a victim against his will, but the heroic sacrifice of a life freely given for the SALVATION of men (Jn 10.17–18; 18.4–8; 19.11; Phil 2.8). Likewise, the exaltation of Jesus echoes the servant of God theology in Is 52.13; 53.11–12.

For John and Paul, the sacrifice of Jesus was a paschal sacrifice (1 Cor 5.7), a sacrifice by which Christ

Himself returned to His Father and opened the way for the return of sinners. Jesus passed out of this world to the Father (Jn 13.1) by the redemptive journey of His death, RESURRECTION, and ASCENSION at the very time of the Jewish Passover Feast, of which He was the true paschal lamb that year (Jn 19.33–36).

Jesus' death constituted a covenant sacrifice (cf. Genesis ch. 15; Ex 24.8; Mk 14.24) by which He acquired for the Father a new people purified in His blood, united to God as His blood relatives. The crucified Jesus shed His blood not to appease an angry God, but to restore men to kinship with the Father. *See* PRECIOUS BLOOD, II (THEOLOGY OF).

Over this new family, a kingdom purchased by His blood (Ti 2.14), Jesus began to rule from the cross-throne as messiah-king (Pius XII MysCorp 35). Mocked as a king by the soldiers (Jn 19.2–3), enthroned symbolically by Pilate, according to some exegetes, in royal judgment over His people (Jn 19.13–15), Jesus, having proclaimed His true kingship to Pilate (Jn 18.33–38), is crucified under the title of His universal sovereignty (Jn 19.19–20). The Christ of Calvary appears, then, as the true suffering servant of God, the high priest returning to His Father in paschal sacrifice, the mediator of a new covenant, the messiah-king reigning over the new priestly kingdom of the Church.

See Also: SACRIFICE OF THE CROSS.

Bibliography: P. CLAUDEL, *Dictionnaire de théologie catholique,* ed. A. VACANT, 15 v. (Paris 1903–50), Tables générales 2:2614–39. M. OLPHE-GALLIARD, *Dictionnaire de spiritualité ascétique et mystique. Doctrine et histoire,* ed., M. VILLER et al. (Paris 1932) 2.2:2607–23. J. BONSIRVEN, *The Theology of the New Testament,* tr. S. F. L. TYE (Westminster, MD 1963). L. CERFAUX, *Christ in the Theology of St. Paul,* tr. G. WEBB and A. WALKER (New York 1959). S. LYONNET, *De peccato et redemptione* (Rome 1957–), 4 v. planned; "Conception paulinienne de la rédemption," *Lumière et vie* 7 (Bruges Belgium 1958) 35–66. R. SCHMITTLEIN, *Umstände und Ursache von Jesu Tod* (Mainz 1951). I. DE LA POTTERIE, "Jesus King and Judge according to Jn 19.13," *Scripture* 13 (1961) 97–111.

[J. P. SCHANZ]

CRUMPE, HENRY

Irish Cistercian monk involved in the Wyclifite controversy; fl. 1376–1401. Crumpe joined the CISTERCIANS at Baltinglass Abbey, Co. Wicklow, Ireland. At Oxford, where he became a doctor of theology, he gave a sermon opposing WYCLIF's views on subjecting both clergy and Church property to secular control (*c.* 1376), and in 1380 he was one of 12 doctors who condemned Wyclif's doctrine of the Eucharist. In 1382 Crumpe was named regent

"Crucifixion with The Virgin and St. John," panel of the triptych "Crucifixion with Saints," painting by Perugino, 1485, The National Gallery of Art, Washington, D.C. (©Francis G. Mayer/CORBIS)

master of the Cistercian students at Oxford, but in June of the same year he was suspended from "scholastic acts" because of opposition from the pro-Wyclif faction in the University—opposition aroused especially by Crumpe's calling Wyclif's followers LOLLARDS at the Black Friars council of Abp. William COURTENAY. In the following month he appealed to the archbishop and the king's council and was reinstated.

Returning to Ireland, Crumpe attacked the mendicants for hearing confessions of parishioners and was himself condemned for heresy by the bishop of Meath (March 1385). By 1391 Crumpe was back at Oxford, where his continued opposition to the mendicants and his opinions on the Eucharist—which were then dangerously close to Wyclif's—led to his denunciation before the king's council and his condemnation in 1392 by the archbishops of Canterbury, York, and Dublin. He abjured any heresy and returned to Ireland. In 1401 he was condemned to silence by the pope for opposing the PORTIUNCULA indulgence extended to the DOMINICANS of Drogheda. His works include *Determinationes scholasticae, Contra religiosos mendicantes, Responsiones ad objecta, De fundatione monasteriorum in Anglia, Vita s. Edithe,* and *Vita s. Ethelrede.*

Bibliography: *Fasciculi zizaniorum magistri Johannis Wyclif cum tritico,* ed. W. W. SHIRLEY (*Rerum Britanicarum medii aevi scriptores* 5; 1858) 113, 289, 311–312, 314, 343, 346, 348–356, 358. D. KNOWLES, *The Religious Orders in England* (Cambridge, Eng. 1948–60) 2:89–92. A. B. EMDEN, *A Biographical Register of the University of Oxford to A. D. 1500* (Oxford 1957–59) 1:524–525.

[B. F. BYERLY]

CRUSADE LITERATURE

Specifically literary, as opposed to homiletic, writing related to the CRUSADES survives from around the time of the Second Crusade, in the form of crusade songs composed by Occitan troubadours and French *trouvéres.* For literary accounts of the First Crusade we have to wait for the Old French Crusade Cycle, a series of epics almost all composed in the 13th and 14th centuries.

Crusade epic. This material exists in three forms: a cycle with individual epics arranged in chronological order; a form in which an attempt has been made to produce a continuous, homogenous narrative and a much shorter prose version. The most developed form of this cycle includes twelve poems, most of which deal with Godefroi de Bouillon (*La Naissance du Chevalier au Cygne, Les Enfances Godefroi,* for example) and with major events of the expedition and the founding of the crusader kingdom (*La Chanson de Jérusalem, La Prise d'Acre*). It is generally agreed that *La Chanson d'Antioche,* in its original form, is the closest in date of these epics to the events it describes and that, it may well have been the work of an eyewitness. However, it has only survived in a 12th-century redaction by Graindor de Douai.

The *chanson de geste* which is closest to, indeed more or less contemporary with the events which it relates is the Occitan *Canso de la Crotzada* (the title is modern), an account of the Albigensian Crusade by two poets, the first half by one Guilhem de Tudela who writes from the viewpoint of the French crusaders and the second by an anonymous author, closely associated with the Occitan defenders of the domains of Count Raimon of Toulouse.

Crusade songs and poetry. The earliest crusade songs, by the troubadours Marcabru and Cercamon, written at or just before the time of the Second Crusade, are among the most remarkable of the genre and effectively prescribe the themes for their successors. Marcabru's "Vers del lavador" was perhaps the most famous of all troubadour songs. It criticizes those who fail to support God's enterprise or who do so in a spirit which is less than totally committed and generous and reminds his listeners of the need to support the *Reconquista* as well as the *Outremer* crusade. In 1188–89, Gaucelm Faidit applauds Richard Coeur de Lion's decision to take the cross but points out that it is actually *going* that counts, and Peirol, in 1221, warns the Emperor Frederick II of the consequences should he fail to undertake his promised expedition. Later songs, by French leaders such as Conon de Béthune (Fourth Crusade) and Thibaut de Champagne (Crusade of 1238) continue to use participation in the crusade as a touchstone for *courtoisie* and *chevalerie.* The image of the beloved left behind lamenting her absent crusader is frequently exploited but rarely with such lyrical and erotic force as in Guiot de Dijon's "Chanterai por mon corage" (early 13th century). The Parisian poet, Rutebeuf, writing at the time of the expeditions of Saint Louis produced twelve poems in which he eloquently argued the case for enthusiastic participation in the crusades by knights and barons. In Germany, *Minnesinger,* such as Walther von der Vogelweide and Hartmann von Aue, wrote in much the same vein, while Neidhart von Reuental, in 'Ez gruonet wol diu heide' provides a graphic account of the hardships and political in-fighting associated with Frederick II's expedition of 1228–29.

Histories and chronicles. The Third Crusade saw the earliest surviving histories. The *Chronique d'Ernoul et de Bernard le Trésorier* recounts the events of 1187, including the defeat at Hattin, and the *Histoire de la guerre sainte* by Ambroise provides an account of the crusade in 12,000 lines of verse. The major histories in French are those of the Fourth Crusade by Robert de Clari, a simple knight, and the *Conqueste de Costentinoble* by Geoffroi de Villehardouin, an important official, closely involved in the planning of the expedition. Joinville's *Vie de saint Louis* is not so much an official history of Louis IX's crusades as an almost hagiographical portrait of the king combined with an often picturesque and anecdotal account of the expeditions of 1248 and 1270. German histories are of much later date: the two most interesting, *Die Kreuzfahrt des Landgrafen Ludwigs des Frommen von Thüringen* and Ottokar's *Österreichische Reimchronik* appear in the early 14th century and deal respectively with the Third Crusade and with the loss of Acre in 1291. In Spain, *La gran conquista de ultramar* was composed for the King of Castile, Alfonso el Sabio in the late 13th century.

Romances. Few romances have crusades as their primary subject or setting. The most notable exceptions are Jean d'Arras's *Mélusine* (1382–94), which deals with the legendary ancestry of the Lusignan family, and the Catalan Joanot Martorell's *Tirant lo Blanc* (1460–68), a gripping adventure story set primarily in Rhodes. However, the crusades are an important and recurrent motif in many romances well into the Renaissance. The most striking innovation is provided by Wolfram von Eschenbach's *Parzival* (c. 1200) in which the quest for the Grail is identified with the quest for the Holy City and, it has been argued, with major political questions concerning succession to the Empire and the throne of Jerusalem.

Theatre. The crusades even find a reflection in contemporary theatre. The earliest full-length miracle play in French, Jehan Bodel's *Le Jeu de saint Nicolas* (1200–02), places the familiar story of St Nicholas's protection of an unbeliever's treasure in the context of a war between a Saracen king and his Christian neighbors. When St Nicholas restores the treasure, all but one of the Saracens convert to Christianity.

Italy. A 15th-century Italian history of the crusades provides a good illustration of the continuity of the tradition. This general survey, by Benedetto and Leonardo Accolti, *De Bello a Christianis contra Barbaros gesto pro Christi sepulcro et Judfa recuperandis libri tres* (Venice, 1452) derives principally from William of Tyre's chronicle (written before 1184) but served as the source for Torquato Tasso's epic masterpiece about the First Crusade, *Gerusalemme liberata* (1574–75), one of the most influential works of the Renaissance period.

Bibliography: F. W. WENTZLAFF-EGGEBERT, *Kreuzzugsdichtung des Mittelalters* (Berlin 1960). J. A. NELSON and E. J. MICKEL eds., *The Old French Crusade Cycle* (Tuscaloosa-London 1977–95). S. DUPARC-QUIOC, *Le Cycle de la Croisade* (Paris 1956). M. ROUTLEDGE, ''Songs,'' in *The Oxford Illustrated History of the Crusades,* ed. J. RILEY-SMITH (Oxford 1995). H. J. NICHOLSON, *Love, War and the Grail. Templars, Hospitallers and Teutonic Knights in Medieval Epic and Romance, 1150–1500* (Leiden 2001).

[M. J. ROUTLEDGE]

CRUSADERS' STATES

States founded in the Levant by the Franks (i.e., Westerners, Latin settlers), in the aftermath of the CRUSADES.

Foundation and Settlement. When the First Crusade (1095–99), conquered the Holy Land the FRANKS took control of an area of considerable cultural, political, and religious complexity. After the capture of JERUSALEM in 1099, many of the crusaders returned home, leaving those leaders who had planned to settle in the Levant to impose their authority and to give each of the four Crusader states a particular character, based on a combination of their own background and that of the native populace. The county of Edessa was founded in 1097 by Baldwin of Boulogne who was invited to join the local Armenian Christians in their struggle against the surrounding Muslim rulers. Baldwin soon took control of the area for himself and created a large and wealthy county astride the River Euphrates. The Franks intermarried with the Armenian nobility although the inland location of the county meant that it was particularly vulnerable to pressure from the northern Muslim cities of Aleppo and Mosul.

The principality of ANTIOCH was set up by Bohemond of Taranto (a Norman from southern Italy) in particularly controversial circumstances. As the leaders of the First Crusade had traveled to the Levant they had, in return for military help, promised the Byzantine emperor, Alexius Comnenus, to restore lands that had formerly belonged to him. Antioch had been held by the Greeks until 1085 and was the seat of an Orthodox patriarch; it was, therefore, of particular significance to the Byzantines. Bohemond, however, was an old adversary of the Greeks and when he captured the city in June 1098 he refused to hand it over to Alexius. This dispute would develop further and the status of Antioch would be a cause of considerable tension between the settlers and the Greeks in future decades. The native population of Antioch was largely Greek Orthodox, although areas of Armenian Christian and Sunni Muslim farmers also existed.

When the First Crusade conquered Jerusalem in July 1099 GODFREY OF BOUILLON was chosen to rule the city, and he took the title *advocatus,* because he did not wish to be called a king in Christ's city. Godfrey died in 1100 and his successor, Baldwin of Edessa (Godfrey's brother) took a more pragmatic view and adopted a royal title, probably for reasons of status on both the local and international political stages. The population of the kingdom was particularly diverse, with many Muslims in rural areas and also regions of Greek Orthodox villages as well. The selection of Godfrey as ruler of Jerusalem had frustrated the rival candidacy of Raymond of St. Gilles, count of Toulouse. He retired northwards to create the county of Tripoli, although it was not until after his death that the city itself fell (1109) and the fourth and final Crusader State effectively came into being. Tripoli had a large native Christian population, with a particularly strong MARONITE community in the inland mountains. It also had an enclave of Nizaris, a renegade Shi'i sect, known popularly as the Assassins. At times, military campaigns meant there was the possibility of further Frankish states being created, particularly at Damascus (1148) and Shaizar (1157), but tensions over whom should rule these lands—Western newcomers or the existing settlers—led to the failure of these campaigns.

Throughout the territory that they settled the Franks had to establish their authority, starting with the imposition of military strength. They then had to set up their own political and religious hierarchies (see below), as well as the organs of administration, justice, and taxation. In all their actions, however, the Franks were constrained by their limited numbers. After the capture of Jerusalem only a few hundred knights remained and while there was a significant level of immigration over subsequent decades (farmers were offered highly attractive terms to hold land), the Franks were always in a minority. This meant that they needed to form a modus operandi with the native populace, of whatever faith, to ensure that the day-to-day practicalities of food production, trade, and taxation could continue.

Other than the massacres that followed the sieges of Jerusalem, Acre, and Sidon, the native population was generally treated with restraint. In 1110, for example, Tancred of Antioch urged the wives of Muslim farmers to return to their lands from Aleppo where they had fled to for safety from the Christians. In other words, Tancred appreciated the importance of a settled and content labor force. For that reason the Franks also imposed a relatively light burden of taxation on their Muslim subjects— lighter, in fact, than that in many Muslim lands, which was another way of ensuring security and productivity. Furthermore, the indigenous populace was permitted to practice the Islamic faith, although public prayers on Fridays were not allowed.

The rulers of the Frankish states granted nobles land or privileges (such as rights to tax trade, or the use of mills, baths, and ovens), in return for homage and military service. Other landowners, such as religious institutions, also had to contribute knights to the defense of the Holy Land. There were rebellions against the crown of Jerusalem in 1134 and in 1187, but these reflected disquiet at the actions of particular kings, rather than the system of government itself.

Two other key features of the Latin states were the prominence of the Latin Church and the emergence of the MILITARY ORDERS. The settlers established a Catholic hierarchy in the Frankish east with the patriarchates of Antioch and Jerusalem at its head. The Latins took over many of the lands of the Orthodox Church, particularly in the north, although a Greek presence remained highly visible at the great shrine churches of the Holy Sepulchre (rebuilt by the Franks in the form we see today and reconsecrated in 1149), Bethlehem, and Nazareth. Latin Churches such as the Holy Sepulchre had considerable landholdings in the Levant and were also heavily endowed by Western pilgrims. Latin monasteries and nunneries were founded, often in urban areas, although again this was frequently at the expense of Orthodox institutions. The EASTERN CHURCHES also survived and there were attempts to bring them into the Catholic fold with the Maronites of the Lebanon recognizing papal authority in 1181.

The Military Orders emerged in the second quarter of the 12th century and soon became important and enormously wealthy institutions. As well as providing protection and shelter for pilgrims they owned considerable areas of land and numerous castles. In northern Antioch the Templars ruled an area around Baghras as, effectively, a sovereign territory, and in northern Tripoli, the Hospitallers held similar sway over the region around Krak des Chevaliers.

In 1191 Richard the Lionheart conquered the island of Cyprus from the renegade Byzantine ruler Isaac Comnenus. Richard soon sold the island to the Templars, whose harsh treatment of the native populace made the Templars unsuitable rulers. Through Richard's intervention the island then came into the possession of the displaced king of Jerusalem, Guy of Lusignan, who set up a dynasty that was to rule Cyprus until the 16th century. At first, as the Catholics tried to impose their religious authority on the island, the Orthodox Church was dealt with harshly, but promises of allegiance to the Latin bishops and the continued presence of Orthodox priests (to minister to the majority of the population), resulted in compromise in the *Constitutia Cypria* of 1260.

The Fourth Crusade created the Latin empire of CONSTANTINOPLE after the capture of the city by the crusaders in 1204. These lands covered much of mainland Greece and the islands with some areas under the control of Western lords and others, such as Crete, under Venetian authority.

Relations between the Crusader States and with Byzantium. The four Frankish states were, on their foundation, independent of one another. The complex effects of political and military needs, and the realities of their relative strengths would soon change this. From the early 12th century the counties of Tripoli and Edessa were vassals of the kingdom of Jerusalem, although the nature of this was not one of especially strict dependence. The princes of Antioch managed to impose their authority on Edessa at times, but the counts were reluctant to acknowledge this. Antioch itself was independent of Jerusalem, although the political crises of 1119 (after the Battle of the Field of Blood) and 1130 (the succession to Count Bohemond II), meant that the king of Jerusalem was obliged to journey north; in the first case, to establish order in the principality and to act as regent, and in the second, to choose a new prince.

During the 12th century it was relations with the BYZANTINE EMPIRE that dominated the affairs of Antioch. As we saw above, Bohemond rejected the Greek claim to the principality. When the prince tried to invade Byzantium in 1108 his defeat led to the Treaty of Devol in which he acknowledged imperial overlordship, although his successors sought to evade this by arguing Bohemond's oaths were personal and did not tie subsequent rulers. Distractions elsewhere in the Byzantine Empire prevented the Greeks from pursuing their claims until 1137–38 when Emperor John Comnenus (1118–43) brought a large army to northern Syria. The Antiochenes wanted to preserve their independence and the Latin Church hierarchy was determined to avoid the imposition of an Orthodox patriarch. Nevertheless, John's presence forced a nominal acceptance of Byzantine authority, although so plain was the Antiochenes' hostility to this that 1138, 1142–43 and 1145 saw the need for further threats to the Franks. After this final episode Prince Raymond (1136–49) was compelled to travel in person to Constantinople and to swear homage to the emperor.

Raymond's successor, Reynald of Châtillon, rashly attacked the Byzantine-controlled island of Cyprus in 1156, and Emperor Manuel Comnenus (1143–80) chose to march down to Antioch to bring him to heel. It was agreed that a Byzantine patriarch should be restored, although when Patriarch Athanasius perished in an earthquake in 1170 the Franks rather smugly regarded this as God's judgment on the issue. On this occasion, Manuel's assertion of authority over Antioch was supported by the kings of Jerusalem who, for reasons of military necessity, sought a close rapprochement with the Greeks.

The failure of the Second Crusade (1145–49) had caused a rift between the Latin settlers and Western Europe: each blamed the other for the collapse of the expedition. The Franks still had to face the growing power of the Muslims and, in light of their shared faith, their relative geographical proximity, and interest in the Eastern Mediterranean a more positive relationship with the Greeks was prudent. King Baldwin III of Jerusalem (1143–63) took a Byzantine bride and Manuel Comnenus married an Antiochene princess. Amalric of Jerusalem (1163–74) also had a Greek wife. Such was the pressure on the settlers after the Syrian Muslims took control of Egypt (1169), thereby surrounding the Christians on land, that Amalric took the unprecedented step on journeying to Constantinople in 1171 to swear homage to Manuel in return for military support. Little was achieved, however, before the arrival of an anti-Latin regime in Constantinople in 1182 marked the end of this rapprochement for both Antioch and Jerusalem.

Antioch and Jerusalem remained independent of one another, although in 1187 Prince Bohemond IV took control of the county of Tripoli, while his father, Prince Bohemond III remained prince of Antioch. In 1201, however, when Bohemond senior died, claimants from Armenia disputed the succession and years of conflict followed (1201–18) before Bohemond IV (d.1233) triumphed. Cyprus became a kingdom in 1195 when Guy of Lusignan's successor, Aimery, acknowledged the overlordship of Emperor Henry VI of Germany. Cyprus was a fief of the empire, leading to imperial involvement in the island from the early 1230s. Jerusalem moved into the imperial orbit in 1225 when Emperor Frederick married Isabella, the heiress to the kingdom, but when she died he acted as regent for their son, Conrad. After 1229 Frederick was not present in the Holy Land in person and in 1243 Queen Alice of Cyprus was appointed regent for Conrad. In 1247 the pope absolved King Henry I of Cyprus of his imperial vassalage and took the island under the protection of the Holy See with the Lusignan dynasty recognized as the lords, if not the formally titled kings, of Jerusalem—the imperial connection was, therefore, ended. Charles of Anjou, the ruler of Sicily, tried to buy the royal title in the late 1270s and this provoked considerable unrest in the kingdom before finally, in 1286, King Henry II of Cyprus took Acre and was crowned king of Jerusalem.

Territorial History (1097–1188). After the capture of Jerusalem in 1099 the Franks had to consolidate and expand the land under their control and the period down to 1144 was generally one of positive achievement for the settlers. As the First Crusade hurried south to besiege the holy city, it had bypassed many Muslim towns and castles and these had to be persuaded to surrender peacefully, or to be taken by siege. The most important settlements were on the coast and it was essential that the Franks take these places to facilitate trade and the flow of pilgrim traffic and immigrants. In 1101 Arsuf and Caesarea were captured, in 1104 Acre and Haifa, in 1110, Sidon and Beirut, and in 1124, Tyre. These successes were usually achieved in conjunction with crusading expeditions from Western Europe and with the assistance of the Italian mercantile communities of Genoa, Pisa, and Venice who provided naval support for the settlers in return for extensive trading and property privileges. In addition to their successes on the coast they also moved inland into Galilee and Samaria and then, in 1115, based at the castle of Montreal, into the Transjordan region.

One of the key reasons for the settlers' expansion during this period was the fragmented nature of the Muslim world. One index of the relative strength of the Franks to the Muslims was the fact that down to 1144 there were only four appeals to the West for new crusades (1101, 1106–08, 1120–24, 1127–29), compared to at least 15 for the period 1144 to 1186. The disunity between Sunni and Shi'i Muslims (the latter ruled Egypt), and the dissent amongst the Sunni rulers of northern Syria had been of great benefit to the First Crusade and this situation continued down to 1144 when Zengi, the *atabeg* of Aleppo and Mosul, captured the Christian city of Edessa. For the Muslims of northern Syria this marked their first major territorial success against the Franks, and it was hailed as a turning point in the *jihad* against the Christians. The settlers appealed to the West, but in spite of the efforts of the Second Crusade (which actually tried to capture Damascus in 1148), the threat posed by Islam began to grow.

In 1149 Zengi's successor, Nur ad-Din, killed Prince Raymond of Antioch at the Battle of Inab and in 1150 the remnants of the county of Edessa fell to him as well. While the Franks captured the remaining Muslim-held port of Ascalon in 1153 this success was negated the following year by Nur ad-Din's seizure of power in Damascus, which meant that the two most important cities of Muslim Syria were under the control of the same man for the first time.

The Franks remained an extremely potent force, however, and the 1160s were dominated by an intense rivalry between Nur ad-Din and King Amalric of Jerusalem as they both tried to conquer Egypt. The Fatimid regime in Cairo was on the verge of collapse and both the settlers and the Syrian Muslims desired the strategic and economic benefits of taking the country. In 1169 Nur ad-Din captured Egypt and the Franks were surrounded by a single Muslim power for the first time. Frantic efforts to persuade Western Europe to send out a new crusade

were unsuccessful and, as noted above Amalric was forced to look to Constantinople for protection. In 1174 Amalric and Nur ad-Din died. The former was succeeded by the young leper-king, Baldwin IV (1174–85), the latter by Saladin (d.1193). The final stages of Baldwin's reign saw deep divisions amongst the nobility of Jerusalem as factions struggled to assert their claim to the succession.

Saladin, meanwhile worked hard to reassemble the Muslims of the Middle East and used both military force and the message of the *jihad* to gather his strength, first in his power base in Egypt, then at Damascus and finally in Aleppo and Mosul. The Franks had defeated him in battles in 1177 and 1179, and had resisted invasion in 1183—he needed, therefore, as strong a force as possible to invade. In June 1187 the attack began and on July 4, at the Battle of Hattin the Christian army was routed. The Frankish lands were almost defenseless and in the next few months Saladin swept through their lands, taking Jerusalem itself in September. Parts of Antioch and Tripoli survived, but in the south, only the port of Tyre resisted and this would be a crucial bridgehead for the Third Crusade.

After the Third Crusade (1192 Onwards). The Third Crusade (1189–92) allowed the Christians to regain control over the coastal strip of the Mediterranean, with the kingdom of Jerusalem now based around Tyre, Acre, and Jaffa. Antioch and Tripoli were somewhat reduced as well, although those nobles dispossessed after the Battle of Hattin were able to find new and safer lands on Cyprus. A German-led crusade in 1197 succeeded in recapturing Beirut and the settlers began to strengthen their hold on the coast. Given their reduced numbers the construction or redevelopment of castles led to hugely sophisticated fortifications such as Krak des Chevaliers in northern Tripoli, Margat (in southern Antioch), and Chastel Pelerin (near Acre).

The early years of the 13th century were a time of relative peace and prosperity in the Levant. Acre was the wealthiest port in the region, while the Muslim world was again riven by internal divisions in the wake of Saladin's death in 1193. The Fifth Crusade (1217–22) failed to capture Egypt, but progress was made in 1229 when the Holy Roman Emperor Frederick II persuaded Sultan al-Kamil to concede Jerusalem, Nazareth, and Sidon to him in return for peace. Frederick had become involved in the affairs of the kingdom through his marriage to Isabella, the heiress to the throne in 1225. The kingdom was drawn toward the orbit of the Holy Roman Empire, but Frederick's representatives in the Holy Land and Cyprus were opposed by many of the local nobles, particularly the powerful Ibelin clan, and there was considerable tension, exacerbated by the emperor's political struggles with the papacy.

The end of a period of truce with the Muslims brought a crusade in 1240–41, but in 1244, the Khwarizmians, a group of fierce tribesmen who had been pushed west by the Mongol invasions of Persia, joined with the Egyptians to capture and sack Jerusalem. The Christian army was decimated at the Battle of La Forbie (July 1244) and this precipitated a new crusade. Louis IX's expedition (1248–54) failed to capture Egypt, but managed to consolidate and strengthen the fortifications along the coast. Louis also left a regiment of French knights to serve in the East—a belated form of permanent support that the settlers would have benefited from decades before.

In c. 1250 the Mongols began to appear in northern Syria. As they grew in influence after the sack of Baghdad (1258), Prince Bohemond IV of Antioch submitted to them, but the kingdom of Jerusalem chose to resist. The latter group of Franks offered limited support to the Mamluks of Egypt who defeated the Mongols at the Battle of Ain Jalut (1260), to end the nomads' incursions into the Holy Land. The Mamluk sultan Baibars emerged from this episode with his power enhanced and his ruthless military efficiency made significant progress against the Franks. Antioch, Jaffa, and Caesarea fell to him before 1271 and over the next two decades the settlers' lands were remorselessly eroded. Acre itself fell in May 1291 to mark the end of the Christian rule in the Levant, although Cyprus remained in Frankish hands and was a base for possible counterattacks onto the mainland.

The kingdom of Cyprus took the ports of Adalia (1361–78) and Gorgios (1359–1448) in southern Asia Minor, and participated in crusades against the Turks and Egypt. In 1373 the Genoese took Famagusta and in 1426 the Egyptians attacked and forced the king to become a tributary. In 1489 the kingdom was ceded to Venice, until, in 1571 the Turks took Famagusta after a lengthy siege.

Bibliography: T. S. ASBRIDGE, *The Creation of the Principality of Antioch, 1098–1130* (Woodbridge 2000). P. W. EDBURY, *The Kingdom of Cyprus and the Crusades, 1191–1374* (Cambridge 1991). R. ELLENBLUM, *Frankish Rural Settlement in the Latin Kingdom of Jerusalem* (Cambridge 1998). J. FOLDA, *The Art of the Crusaders in the Holy Land, 1098–1187* (Cambridge 1995). B. HAMILTON, *The Latin Church in the Crusader States* (London 1980); *The Leper King and His Heirs: Baldwin IV and the Crusader Kingdom of Jerusalem* (Cambridge 2000). C. HILLENBRAND, *The Crusades: Islamic Perspectives* (Edinburgh 2000). A. JOTISCHKY, *The Perfection of Solitude: Monks and Hermits in the Crusader States* (Philadelphia 1995). R.-J. LILIE, *Byzantium and the Crusader States, 1096–1204* (Oxford 1994). C. J. MARSHALL, *Warfare in the Latin East, c.1187–1291* (Cambridge 1990). J. P. PHILLIPS, *Defenders of the Holy Land: Relations between the Latin East and the West, 1119–1187* (Oxford 1996). J. RICHARD, *The Crusades, c.1071–1291* (Cambridge 1999). J. RILEY-SMITH, *The Feudal Nobility and the Kingdom of Jerusalem, 1174–1277* (London 1973); *The Crusades. A Short History* (London 1987); ed., *The Oxford Illustrated History of the Crusades* (Oxford 1995). R. C. SMAIL, *Crusading Warfare, 1097–1193* (Cambridge 1956).

[J. P. PHILLIPS]

Ruins of Crusader castle, 1228, Sidon, Lebanon. (©Michael Nicholson/CORBIS)

CRUSADES

I. THE INSTITUTION OF THE CRUSADE

Origins. The roots of the institution of the crusade are to be found in the political, cultural and theological developments that shaped Western European society during the eleventh century. Throughout the medieval West the political fragmentation following the break up of the Carolingian empire led to a decentralization and diffusion of political power both in terms of geography and social hierarchy. As a result of these long term developments a substantial share of the execution and administration of political and economic power passed to a new knightly elite which had emerged by the eleventh century. These knights, called *milites* (singular *miles*), did not only claim an important position in the social hierarchy, they also developed the means to defend and enlarge their political and economic power. The typical knight of the eleventh century distinguished himself by his military prowess as a mounted soldier, his social connections with other knights and his close association with ecclesiastical insti-

Richard the Lionheart (left) in combat with Saladin, manuscript painting, 14th century.

tutions, in particular local monasteries. Political life was dominated by violent conflicts between smaller or larger groups of knights who were increasingly capable and willing to co-ordinate and apply the military force supplied by mounted combat troops and vested in fortified strongholds that became the centre of knightly power. At the same time, the association with ecclesiastical institutions was an important element of knightly identity and group solidarity. There was an acute awareness that life in all its aspects was to a great extent dependent on a favourable disposition of God's grace. The patronage of monastic institutions and the veneration of saints by way of pilgrimages, prayers and donations was high on the agenda of knights seeking to confirm and consolidate their power and identity. It was this new knightly elite of the eleventh century that was targeted and who responded most enthusiastically when Pope Urban II proclaimed the First Crusade in 1095. The knights' military expertise and experience, their desire to acquire power and honour and their religious orientation made them the ideal candidates to embrace crusading as a means of fulfilling their personal, political and religious ambitions.

The second factor which made the emergence of the institution of the crusade possible consisted in the far-reaching changes that affected the Catholic Church in the century preceding the First Crusade. The so-called Gregorian Reform, which made itself felt from about the 1140s, was an attempt by religious leaders, and in particular the papacy, fundamentally to reorganise the Church both in terms of religious practice and administrative or-

ganisation. The first main element of these reforms concerned a variety of aspects of the Church's internal conduct and government ranging from moral issues such as sexual behaviour to measures aimed at improving clerical education and ensuring the independence of individual churches and ecclesiastical offices. The aim was to ensure that the Church could fulfil its pastoral and intercessionary roles in a responsible and efficient manner. The second main element of the reform programme was to assert the moral and political leadership of the papacy in an attempt to guarantee ecclesiastical independence and foster the collective institutional identity of the Church throughout Europe. This involved the organisation and support of military ventures aimed at guaranteeing the integrity of the possessions of the papacy and the defence of the Church against attacks by lay people as well as heretics and non-Christians. In Italy the popes even staged their own military campaigns for this purpose. In order to overcome the traditional notion of warfare and the use of violence as intrinsically sinful, the popes of the second half of the eleventh century, in particular Pope GREGORY VII (1073–1085), began to view and promote warfare in the service of the Church as an acceptable form of violence. By focussing on the motivation of the individual participants and the underlying cause of wars fought in defence of the Church and faith, Pope Gregory VII even formulated the theory that military service could in such conditions be seen as penitential. Although revolutionary, the idea of penitential warfare in the service of the Church could be incorporated into a long tradition of patristic thought about the legitimate use of violence in the context of just or holy wars. The ideological foundations for these intellectual developments went back to St. AUGUSTINE of Hippo, whose works were studied in scholarly circles close to the papacy. It was the idea and practice of penitential warfare in the service of the Church, developed in the Gregorian reform movement, which made it possible for Pope URBAN II (1088–1099) to formulate the idea of crusade and institute the practice of crusading in 1095.

It would thus be wrong to seek the origins of the crusade as an institution solely in a reflex to the call for aid issued by the Byzantine Emperor ALEXIUS I (1081–1118), who asked Western Christians for military assistance in repelling the Muslim advances in Asia Minor. People in the West had for some time been developing a renewed interest in the Levant, most noticeable in the revival of large scale organised pilgrimages to Jerusalem, and they were aware of the growing domination of Muslim forces in the Near East. Already in 1074 Pope Gregory VII entertained plans to launch a military expedition under papal leadership to come to the aid of the Eastern Christians, but nothing came of this initiative. It was not until 20 years later that Urban II was able to formulate and propagate a project for a military expedition to Palestine, which met with an overwhelming and unexpected response from thousands of men and women across Europe. In planning the First Crusade Urban managed to amalgamate a number of elements developed by his predecessors which caught people's imagination and played to their ambitions. He primarily called upon knights to abandon their violent conflicts with their neighbours and exercise their military prowess in the service of the Church. Rather than fighting for the pope and his patron St. Peter, which had been the appeal of previous papal campaigns, Urban now asked people to fight in God's name for the good of the whole Church by defending the honour of the Christian religion against the Muslims and recapturing the most holy sites of Christianity in Jerusalem. In terms of ideology and propaganda, this was a new departure. The idea of becoming a soldier of Christ (Latin *miles Christi*) and fighting a military campaign to restore God's honour where it mattered most, i.e. the Holy Land where Christ had lived and saved humankind, was a powerful propaganda concept to which people responded enthusiastically. At the same time Urban defined service on crusade as an obligation towards God following from a voluntary vow the crusaders took similar to the well-known vow taken by pilgrims. In addition, the pope promised the participants the remission of all their penitential obligations for the sins that they confessed. The crusade thus offered a way of dealing with the terrifying consequence of sin both before and after death. By defin-

ing the First Crusade in the way he did, Pope Urban II played both to the military ambition and the religious sensibilities of many of his contemporaries, in particular the arms-bearing knights, but also many other lay people and members of the clergy. Guibert of Nogent (ca. 1055 to 1125), a monk and contemporary observer, described the effect of the crusade as follows: ''In our time God instituted holy warfare, so that the arms-bearers and the wandering populace, who after the fashion of the ancient pagans were engaged in mutual slaughters, should find a new way of attaining salvation; so that they might not be obliged to abandon the world completely, as used to be the case, by adopting the monastic way of life or any other form of professed calling, but might obtain God's grace to some extent while enjoying their accustomed freedom and dress, and in a way consistent with their own station.'' Although the institution of the crusade was triggered by events taking place in the Near East and had its first powerful military impact far away from the European heartland, the crusade grew out of the social, religious and cultural conditions of Western European society in the eleventh century. As the subsequent history of the crusades shows, the crusade was fundamentally an institution of Western Latin Christendom, having a strong impact on the way in which internal and external conflicts with other Christians and other religious groups, in particular the Muslims, were conducted throughout the late middle ages and beyond.

Definition. The defining elements of the institution of the crusade were already integral to the First Crusade of 1095 to 1099. Although the exact juridical formulation of all aspects of the crusade was not completed until the first half of the thirteenth century, Pope Urban II laid down the institutional foundations of the crusade which were pivotal for its initial success and its long and varied history. The crusade was thought of as a war called upon and authorised by God himself through his first vicar on earth, the pope. It was directed against enemies of the Catholic faith and the Church and was aimed at restoring God's honour on earth. Because of this, and because of its primarily defensive character, the crusade was considered legitimate warfare in accordance with the medieval theory of just and holy wars. Following from the representation of the crusade as God's war, the participants were considered to be God's soldiers or soldiers of Christ (Latin *milites Dei, milites Christi*). Their task and their status was defined by the act of taking the cross, which meant that the crusaders made a binding vow to participate in the crusade on the conditions set for each campaign. This vow had to be taken in the presence of a bishop or a representative of the pope, such as a crusade preacher or a papal legate, and the sign of the cross had to be displayed on the crusader's garments as public confirmation from the moment of taking the vow to the end of the crusading campaign. Hence the Latin word *cruce-signatus,* meaning "the one signed with the cross," used to designate a crusader from the end of the twelfth century. A crusade vow was binding and could only be dispensed by papal authority if it was commuted to other forms of penance or redeemed by sending a substitute on crusade or paying money in aid of the crusade. In return for his or her service on crusade, a crusader was granted a number of privileges by the pope. Like the crusade vow the privileges accompanying the participation in a crusade were derived from the model of pilgrimage, although they went beyond what pilgrims were generally offered. Most important among these privileges was the plenary INDULGENCE for the remission of all the penalties affecting people on account of their sins, in their lifetime or after death. Although the theological concepts underlying the indulgence changed considerably throughout the twelfth and thirteenth centuries, the majority of people at the time understood the indulgence as a way of escaping punishment for their sins imposed by the Church or directly by God either on earth or in purgatory. In short people conceived of the plenary indulgence as a "remission of all sins" (Latin *remissio peccatorum*) that they confessed to a priest when they took their crusading vows. The belief that by participating in the crusade it was possible through the plenary indulgence to wash away the taint of sin and dispense with any further penance to a large extent accounted for the unexpected initial response and the enormous appeal of the crusades throughout the later middle ages. In addition to the indulgence, crusaders were granted a number of legal privileges aimed at encouraging them to take the cross and to facilitate their absence from home. For the duration of the crusade, the Church through their courts granted legal protection to the crusaders, their families and dependants and their possessions. This also meant that law suits pending against crusaders were postponed until after the crusade. Crusaders were also freed from feudal duties, tolls and taxes as well as interest payments and repayment of any debts they had incurred. Lay people were also permitted to dispose of property which was under normal circumstances considered inalienable, while clerics were given the right to use the income of their benefices during their absence on crusade. Given the enormous cost of a crusade and the great danger of not returning alive from an expedition, the privileges regulating financial and legal matters were crucial in attracting potential crusaders, who had their families and finance to consider when deciding whether to take the cross. The crusade campaigns as a whole also profited from propaganda, financial and liturgical support, which became regular elements of the institution of the crusade. The pope proclaimed a crusade by issuing a papal bull detail-

ing the causes and conditions of each expedition, which would be sent to potential military leaders and chosen propagandists. Crusade propaganda usually took the form of organised preaching campaigns, in which people were directly encouraged to take the cross. Whereas at the beginning crusade propaganda was most forcefully conducted by individual, and often charismatic, preachers such as BERNARD OF CLAIRVAUX, from about the 1230s the bulk of the propaganda activity passed over to the preaching orders of the Dominicans and Franciscans, whose vast resources of trained preachers made the spread of crusade propaganda particularly effective. Crusade preaching went hand in hand with the collection of voluntary donations and vow redemption payments, volunteered by or enforced from those incapable of joining a crusade army, as well as taxes imposed on clerical incomes in support of the crusade. These moneys were often passed directly onto prominent crusaders to help finance their large contingents of retainers and mercenaries. At the same time, the popes organised the liturgical back-up on the home front for crusaders in the field. During crusade campaigns prayers were to be said and processions held regularly throughout the churches of Christendom with even more elaborate liturgical exercises to be performed by monks. These intercessionary liturgies were believed to sway God's favour in support of the crusade and were therefore considered to be crucial to a successful outcome. In sum a crusade was a war authorised by the pope and fought in order to defend and protect the honour of the Catholic Church and faith. It was represented as a war conducted on God's behalf by people who thought of themselves as God's soldiers. The participants of a crusade took a binding vow and enjoyed a number of spiritual and temporal privileges, most importantly the plenary indulgence. At the same time crusades benefited from financial, liturgical and propaganda support centrally organised by the papacy and its agents.

Scope. The history of the institution of the crusade began in the late eleventh century and continued until the sixteenth century, while the idea of crusading, embodied for example in the military alliances of the Holy Leagues and the military orders, lasted even longer into the modern era. Crusading in medieval Europe and the Near East underwent periods of varying intensity. The First Crusade (1095–1099), attracting perhaps as many as 120,000 men and women, arguably produced the largest single crusade expedition ever, but the intensity of overall crusading activity was probably never higher than in the first half of the thirteenth century, when many crusades were operating in different parts of Europe and its border regions: against Muslims in Egypt, Palestine and in the Iberian Peninsula, against Byzantine Christians in Greece, against heretics in southern France, Germany and Hungary, against the Mongols, against the non-Christian peoples of the Baltic and against the political enemies of the papacy in the Empire. There was never a lack of crusading initiatives from popes and other religious and political leaders throughout the later middle ages. But the realisation and success of crusade campaigns very much depended on the actual threats posed and the willingness and ability of political leaders to organise crusades effectively. Thus crusade expeditions to the Levant lost their force with the fall of the Latin establishments in Palestine at the end of the thirteenth century as people realised that it would take an enormous effort to dislodge the Muslim domination in the Eastern Mediterranean. Nevertheless numerous small crusading projects to the area were promoted throughout the fourteenth and fifteenth centuries, often in collaboration with the military orders. The steady advance of the Turkish empire in the Balkans and the fall of Constantinople in 1453 were responsible for a number of new crusade projects to the East at the end of the middle ages. In other theatres, the crusades against political enemies flourished during the time of the Great Schism in the fourteenth century, while the growth of the Hussite heresy in the first half of the fifteenth century gave rise to five successive crusades between 1420 and 1431. The most extensive and from a military perspective most successful crusading campaigns were fought in the Iberian Peninsula from the twelfth to the fifteenth centuries and in the lands along the Baltic in the thirteenth and fourteenth. In both these areas the crusades were bound up with colonising projects and missionary activities and were thus part of a continual process of conquest which was systematically promoted by political leaders eager to extend the frontiers of Christian Europe.

With the crusade being an institution of the whole Church universally proclaimed by the pope, participation was in theory open to all members of society. Although most crusading centred around an élite of military leaders who recruited their followers from particular social circles and geographical areas, most of the larger crusade armies, especially in the first centuries of crusading history, comprised participants from across the social scale and from many different countries. This accounted for the sometimes huge size of crusading armies, which proved problematic in terms of organisation, logistics and military strategy. Regarding their material resources, their particular motivation and their military ability, crusaders often differed considerably from each other. With popular enthusiasm powered by eschatological expectations at one end of the scale and keen military leadership geared at individual glory and political profit at the other, it could prove difficult to wage effective warfare. Largely due to Pope Innocent III's reforms, embodied in the constitution "Ad liberandam" at the Fourth LATERAN COUN-

CIL in 1215, the crusades were set on a new footing in the thirteenth century in terms of propaganda, finance and logistics. By calling upon the mendicant orders of the Franciscans and Dominicans to preach the cross, thirteenth century popes managed to increase and target crusade propaganda. By introducing crusade taxes on clerical income and allowing the redemption of crusade vows in return for financial subsidies the financial requirements of crusaders could be met more readily. Attempts were also made to prevent those who could make no proper military contribution to the crusade from joining the armies. Women, old people and the sick were encouraged to stay at home, redeem their vows for money and support the crusade armies with prayers. From this there developed a vision of Christian society as a whole engaged in and organised for the crusade. While the clergy and the religious orders were involved in propagating and financing the crusade as well as organising liturgical support at home, lay members of society were expected to contribute to the best of their means and abilities as leaders and fighters in the actual armies or by financial contributions and prayers. The papacy thus also responded to more general developments in warfare which demanded better trained and more professional, and thereby more expensive armies, often including a mercenary element of considerable size. At the same time an upsurge in popular religious sentiment and devotion caused many people to respond eagerly to the offer of a plenary indulgence as a reward for their financial and intercessionary contributions to the crusades. Nevertheless, crusade armies never lost their popular elements altogether and occasionally spontaneous "popular crusades" were started without papal authorisation, such as the Children's Crusade of 1212 and the Crusades of the Shepherds in 1254, 1309 and 1320. Pope Innocent III's initiative paired with his rigorous leadership provided the crusade with a solid institutional foundation and explains the enormous popularity of the crusades in the first half of the thirteenth century. Nevertheless his reforms also sowed the seeds of structural weaknesses in the institution of the crusade that were to be felt throughout the later middle ages. While the downsizing and professionalisation of crusade armies was aimed at making the crusade a more effective instrument of warfare, crusading still demanded enormous organisational and financial resources. These often proved too difficult to provide and meant this that many crusade projects could never be realised as planned. Especially the crusades for the recovery of the Holy Land after the end of the thirteenth century fell victim to the unwillingness of the leading rulers of Europe to cooperate and their inability to set aside the military force and finance necessary for such a large scale enterprise. But even if the far-reaching aims of many crusade projects were never reached, religiously powered enthusiasm for the crusade never abated in the late middle ages and affected all sections of society. This does not of course mean that crusading went unopposed in medieval society. Criticism of crusading was almost as old as the crusade itself. Although fundamental opposition to the institution of the crusade and its aims was relatively rare, single aspects of the institution provoked frequent criticism. Crusades against heretics and other fellow Christians, for example, were not universally approved of. But the sharpest criticism was levelled against the misappropriation of crusading funds for other purposes and also against the practice of granting crusade indulgences in return for money payments, which became increasingly common in the later Middle Ages.

With the REFORMATION and the COUNTER-REFORMATION of the sixteenth century the institution of the crusade came to an end in most parts of Europe. The unity of Western Christianity and the papacy's effective political leadership—two important factors upon which the crusade was built—had ceased to exist. Remnants of crusading were to be found in the Holy Leagues created at the end of the seventeenth century to repel the last Turkish attacks on the Habsburg Empire and the military orders who were engaged in anti-Muslim warfare until the late eighteenth century. The crusade, however, left its imprint on Western European society. In the early modern era elements of crusade ideology appeared in the propaganda and warfare of many of the budding dynastic nation-states and marked the confrontation of Catholic forces with non-Christian cultures in the process of the European expansion overseas. More generally speaking, "the ideas, iconography, and language associated with crusading survived, to fertilise the thinking and behaviour of all Christians engaged in military struggles which they considered to be inseparable from their religious beliefs, spanning time and space from Early Modern Europe to contemporary Latin America" (N. Housley).

II. CRUSADES AGAINST MUSLIMS

Near East. Pope Urban II proclaimed the First Crusade on Nov. 27, 1095, at the Council of Clermont. In response to a request for military assistance from the Byzantine Emperor Alexius I, Urban called upon Westerners to help their fellow Christians in the Near East to free themselves from Muslim rule and liberate the Christian holy sites in Palestine, in particular Jerusalem. Thanks to the promise of spiritual and temporal privileges for the participants and owing to the religious fervour stirred up by Urban's appeal, a large number of people, probably as many as 120,000 men and women from all walks of life, took the cross. They joined one of the armies that left Europe in three big waves between 1096 and 1101, marching to Palestine through the Balkans and Asia Minor. In military terms, the First Crusade was an overwhelming success, which ultimately led to the establishment of the so-called Crusader states in the Levant. On July 15, 1099, the crusaders conquered Jerusalem, having previously defeated a number of Muslim armies along the way and taken Antioch as well as Edessa. These unexpected results helped cement the view that the crusade was willed and supported by God, which from then onwards became a pivotal element of crusade ideology. Despite being a military and for many of the participants also a personal success—those who died on the way were considered martyrs, those who returned home heroes—victory came at a price. Not only did many of the crusaders and their families make enormous sacrifices to finance their participation, many also died in the cruel conditions of the long journey and on the battlefields. This was particularly true for the popular contingents led by the charismatic priest Peter the Hermit. Those who found riches and power in the newly established states, notably a number of French and Italian knights, were few and far between. There were also numerous tensions among the leaders of the crusade armies and the collaboration with the Byzantine Greeks at times turned into open hostility. The religious fervour of many of the participants, fuelled by eschatological and revivalist tendencies, was also responsible for the cruel attacks on Jewish communities in France and Germany perpetrated by crusaders along the way. Considered to be enemies of the Christian religion, Jews were again and again seen as legitimate targets of crusader aggression throughout the later middle ages, despite attempts by the Church hierarchy to stop such attacks.

Throughout the twelfth century a succession of large and small scale crusades to the Near East took place, aimed first at enlarging and later defending the Latin establishments in the Levant. During the first half of the century, smaller crusades took place such as the one led by King Sigurd of Norway in 1107 to 1110 and a crusade proclaimed by Pope Calixtus II resulted in expeditions in 1123 to 1124 and 1125 to 1126. After the re-conquest of Edessa by Muslim forces in 1144 Pope Eugene III issued the earliest extant crusade bull (*Quantum praedecessores*) launching the Second Crusade. This expedition, led by King Louis VII of France, who was later joined by King Conrad III of Germany, was part of a major crusading effort on several Christian frontiers in Spain, Eastern Europe and the Levant. The German and French crusade armies in the East failed to secure northern Syria and were beaten in 1147 and 1148 respectively. The unexpected defeat of two royal armies provoked massive criticism of the crusade as an institution, much of which was aimed at Bernard of Clairvaux, the chief ideologue and propagandist of the Second Crusade. Despite the need of the Latin establishments for military assistance, crusade activity to the Levant was low until the very end of the twelfth century. The frequent calls for crusades by the papacy went largely unheeded, with the exception of a small crusade force led by Philipp of Flanders in 1177. It was not until the victory of Saladin's Muslim forces over the army of the crusader states at Hattin and the subsequent loss of Jerusalem in 1187 that crusading to the Levant resumed on a large scale. Pope Gregory VIII's bull *Audita tremendi* issued in October of that same year triggered what was perhaps the greatest crusading effort in aid of the Holy Land ever to occur, known as the Third Crusade. Between 1190 and 1197 two German emperors and the kings of France and England took the cross and organised major crusade campaigns heading for Palestine. While neither Emperor FREDERICK I nor his successor Henry VI reached the crusader states—Frederick drowned on route in Asia Minor and Henry died prior to departure—their respective armies played an important part in recapturing Acre, Sidon and Beirut for the Latins. The crusade armies of King Philipp II of France and King Richard I of England also failed to regain Jerusalem in 1191 to 1192, but their victories over the Muslims crucially helped to secure and consolidate the survival of the crusader states in the coastal regions of Palestine for another one hundred years and also put Cyprus under Latin rule, which lasted until the sixteenth century. The Fourth Crusade (see below), proclaimed by Pope Innocent III in 1198, was famously diverted to Constantinople and only a few elements of its army ever reached Palestine.

The thirteenth century marked the heyday of crusading to the Eastern Mediterranean. Until the 1270s major crusade armies left for the Holy Land every decade, while numerous smaller expeditions took place in between; these included the unauthorised and ill-fated expeditions known as the Children's Crusade of 1212 and the Crusade of the Shepherds of 1251, which despite their utter failure in military terms bore witness to the fanaticism of crusaders from the lower echelons of society. However, internal strife, wars between the leading powers in the West and competition from other crusades meant that the large-scale effort necessary to re-conquer Jerusalem and save the crusader states from succumbing to the mounting pressure from Muslim forces never took place. Nevertheless, temporary military success was provided and, here as in other crusade theatres, individual participants could fulfil their religious vocation and gain their spiritual rewards independent of the outcome of each crusade. The Fifth Crusade, proclaimed in 1213 and lasting until 1221, constituted an ultimately futile attempt at breaking the Muslim domination in the Levant by attacking Egypt. Bogged down in the Nile delta, the crusaders hoped for

help from Emperor Frederick II, who had taken the cross in 1215 but again and again delayed his departure until he was excommunicated by the pope in 1227 for his failure to fulfil his vow. Nevertheless, having married Isabella of Brienne, the heiress to the Latin Kingdom of Jerusalem, the emperor was eager to impose his domination in the East and went on crusade in 1228. His excommunication prevented Frederick from gathering enough military support to wage a war, but he managed to negotiate a ten-year-truce with the Muslims and the return of Jerusalem to the Latins in 1229. In view of the end of the truce, two sizeable crusade armies sailed to Palestine in 1239 to 1240 led by Theobald IV of Champagne and Richard of Cornwall respectively. Having regained territories previously lost to Christian control and negotiated a new truce, this crusade was successful on the whole, even though its military achievements did not last long. By 1244 Muslim forces had retaken Jerusalem and some of the territories secured by the recent crusade. In reaction, King Louis IX of France committed himself to a grand crusading project which he organised with unprecedented care. In 1248 his crusade left from the port of Aigues Mortes, specifically built for the use of the royal army, reaching Cyprus and finally Damietta in Egypt in June 1249. Once again and despite the enormous efforts put into this expedition the strategy of attacking the Muslim forces from the Nile turned out a failure. Louis himself was taken prisoner and had to be redeemed for a large sum of money, while the ambitious military aims of his crusade were all but abandoned. Nevertheless, the French king stayed in Palestine until 1254, once more negotiating a truce and assisting the crusader states in strengthening their defences. He also established a permanent French garrison, which stayed until 1286. More than any other medieval ruler, Louis IX was personally committed to the crusade. But his second attempt at bringing aid to the Holy Land in the late 1260s also failed. Planned in conjunction with King James of Aragon, his brother King Charles of Sicily and Prince Edward, son of King Henry III of England, Louis IX's second crusade only got as far as Tunis, where the crusade army was ravaged by plague, with the king himself dying on Aug. 25, 1270. Only Edward's army reached Palestine where it fought a number of battles before returning to Europe in 1272. The remainder of the thirteenth century was marked by unsuccessful attempts to stop the continuous Muslim conquest of the Latin establishments in Palestine which was finally completed when Acre fell in 1291. At the Second Council of Lyon in 1276 Pope Gregory X, one of the most fervent supporters of the crusade to the Holy Land, once again tried to launch a pan-European expedition, but his death in the same year meant that his high-flown plans bore no fruit.

Crusading to the East from the fourteenth to the sixteenth century was fuelled by the continuing enthusiasm in Europe for the recovery of the Holy Land, but its scope was checked by the political situation and the military conditions in the Levant. First the Mamluk and later the Turkish empire proved too potent for the limited crusade efforts the European powers were ready to commit to the East. Most crusade projects were relatively small expeditions undertaken in conjunction with the Italian city states, the kings of Cyprus or the Order of St. John (later Order of Malta), who all had tangible economic and political interest in the area. The main aims of these various crusades were either the recovery of Jerusalem via Egypt or the defence of Latin Greece from Turkish pirate action. Thus, for example, Dauphin Humbert II of Viennois gathered a crusade force to attack Smyrna in 1345 to 1347 and King Peter I of Cyprus led a crusade in 1365, which temporarily conquered Alexandria. The steady advance of the Turkish empire in the late fourteenth and the fifteenth centuries met with a renewed crusade response from Europe, which ultimately remained limited, despite numerous initiatives by the papacy. In 1396 a crusade army was beaten at Nicopolis in Bulgaria, failing to halt the Turkish progress through the Balkans. Similarly a large crusade force led by the king of Hungary was defeated at Varna on the Black Sea fifty years later in 1444. Following the Turkish conquest of Constantinople in 1453, a crusade mainly made up of Hungarian participants was gathered and led by the charismatic preacher John of Capistrano. This played a major part in successfully defending Belgrade and thus contributed towards stopping the Turkish advance. But despite further forceful initiatives by popes like, for example, Pius II and despite the ambitious plans by political rules like Emperor Maximilian I, the crusades to the Eastern Mediterranean were not revived after the fifteenth century even though the ideology and to some extent also the practice of crusading continued to play a part in the Holy Leagues and the military activities of the Order of Malta.

Iberian Peninsula. Crusading against the Muslims in the Iberian Peninsula was an integral part of the Reconquista, which began long before the institution of the crusade was born. Shortly after the First Crusade, at the beginning of the twelfth century, the popes began to assign crusade status to the military campaigns for the reconquest of Muslim territories organised by Iberian kings and noblemen. The crusade and its ideology thus became part of the ongoing process of Christian colonisation of the Iberian Peninsula which lasted until the very end of the fifteenth century. Whereas much of the Reconquista was fought by feudal armies and urban militias, crusaders from Spain and elsewhere played an important part in supplying additional military support when it was most needed. In terms of men, money and ideology the institution of the crusade thus made an indispensable contribution towards the Reconquista. The first major crusade campaign in the Iberian Peninsula was fought in Andalucia in 1125 to 1126 by King Alfonso I of Aragon, closely followed by the campaigns in the context of the Second Crusade in the 1140s, during which Almeria, Santarem, Lisbon and the remaining Muslim territories of Catalonia were conquered. Like in other crusading theatres, the first half of the thirteenth century was a period of intensive crusading in the Iberian Peninsula. A large army made up of French, Spanish and Portuguese crusaders defeated the Muslims at Las Navas de Tolosa in July 1212, a victory which marked the turning point of the Reconquista and broke the Muslim dominance in Spain. Both King James I of Aragon's conquest of Majorca in 1229 to 1231 and Valencia 1232 to 1253 and King Ferdinand III of Castile's conquest of Badajoz in 1230, Jérez in 1231, Córdoba in 1236 and Seville in 1248 were achieved with massive assistance by crusaders. In the second half of the thirteenth century, the Spanish rulers even made attempts to attack Muslim strongholds across the Straits of Gibraltar, drawing on crusading support readily granted by the papacy. With the exception of the conquest of Algeciras in 1344 the Reconquista came to a temporary halt between 1275 and the final decades of the fifteenth century. The Muslim presence in the Iberian Peninsula was finally ended with the conquest of Granada in 1492. The conflict with the Muslims in the Western Mediterranean, however, did not stop after the end of the fifteenth century, with the crusade playing an important part in the Spanish and Portuguese kings' wars against the Muslims in Northern Africa in the sixteenth century. But the crusades to Morocco and later against the advancing Turkish empire in Northern Africa, fought amongst others by Emperor Charles V and King Sebastian of Portugal, were largely unsuccessful and came to an end in the late 1570s. Throughout the later middle ages the Reconquista not only relied on the military support of crusaders, but also on the important financial contribution the crusade was able to provide through the systematic sale of indulgences (*cruzadas*) and the frequent imposition of crusade taxes.

III. CRUSADES AGAINST CHRISTIANS

Heretics. Canon 27 of the Third LATERAN COUNCIL of 1179 provided limited military support for bishops fighting heretics in their dioceses, while offering a limited indulgence for those participating in these campaigns. This prepared the ground for full-scale crusades to be directed against heretical Christians. The use of military force to combat heresy was justified by arguing that heretics disregarded doctrine and disobeyed the ecclesiastical hierarchy, thus threatening the unity and integrity of the Catholic Church. In connection with the Inquisition, the crusades against heretics were part of the brutal suppression of dissident Christian communities by the medieval Church. It was in fact Pope INNOCENT III who proclaimed the first anti-heretical crusade against the dualist Albigensian heretics of southwestern France in 1208, granting participants a plenary indulgence in return for 40 days service in the crusade armies. The crusades against the Albigensians intermittently operated between 1208 and 1226 with several campaigns led by the Northern French nobility, most notably Count Simon of Montfort and King Louis VIII. But although the crusade campaigns ended in military defeat for the heretics, the Albigensian faith survived into the early fourteenth century, when it was finally eradicated by the Inquisition.

Small scale crusades were fought against the heretical Bosnian church and also against the Drenther and the Stedinger peasants in the Netherlands and in Northern Germany between 1227 and 1234. The cross was also preached against small groups of heretics in Northern Italy in the 1250s, and in 1306 to 1307 a crusade was launched against the followers of Fra DOLCINO in Piedmont. In Eastern Europe crusades against heretical groups survived into the fourteenth and fifteenth centuries, with the cross being preached against Cathars in Hungary in 1327 and a crusade army fighting against heretical movements in Bohemia in the 1340s.

The five crusades fought against the HUSSITES between 1420 and 1431 arose from a combination of religious and political developments in Bohemia. King Sigismund of Hungary fought these crusades with the assistance of a number of German princes in the hope of imposing his political authority by suppressing the religious unorthodoxy of the Hussites, who also entertained strong anti-Imperial sentiments. Despite its initial success the five crusades against the Hussites failed to eradicate the heretical movement in Bohemia. The wars against the Hussites were the last crusades against heretics of the late Middle Ages. But with the sale of crusade indulgences and the use of crusade rhetoric, elements of the anti-heretical crusades surfaced again in the Catholic response to the Reformation in the sixteenth century as well as in the Thirty-Years' War of 1618 to 1648.

Schismatics. Crusades against schismatics were proclaimed against exponents of the Greek and Russian Orthodox Church as well as against opponent Catholic factions during the Great Schism of the fourteenth century. As early as 1107 to 1108 Bohemund of Taranto led a crusade force against Byzantines in Northern Greece, albeit without tangible military results. The first full scale crusade against the Byzantine Empire came in the course of the Fourth Crusade. Proclaimed by Pope Innocent III in 1199, this expedition was originally planned as a crusade to the Holy Land led by the Counts of Champagne, Blois and Flanders. When the crusaders gathered at Venice in 1202, it soon became clear that they did not possess the financial means to pay for transport to the Levant. In a deal, the Venetians offered their fleet in return for military assistance first in attacking the Christian city of Zara in Croatia and later the Byzantine capital of Constantinople. The Venetians were eager to promote their own interests by helping Alexius IV, who had fled to the West and promised to support the crusaders, to regain the Byzantine throne. After the conquest of Constantinople, relations with the new Byzantine emperor, however, turned sour and the crusaders ended up ousting the new ruler. After three days of terrible pillaging, the crusaders installed Baldwin of Flanders as the first Latin emperor. Pope Innocent III reluctantly accepted the diversion of the Fourth Crusade, justifying the attacks on the Greeks as schismatics. With the creation of the Latin Greek empire a new crusade theatre was in fact established. The survival of the Latin empire and the Latin principalities of Southern Greece heavily depended on military assistance from the West. From the 1230s to the 1250s a large number of French crusaders were involved in repelling Byzantine attempts to re-conquer Constantinople. The massive crusading support for the Latin empire planned by Pope Urban IV in the 1260s came too late, however. In 1261 Michael Paleologus recaptured Constantinople. Although Urban IV immediately renewed his call for a crusade, it was not until the beginning of the fourteenth century that a last unsuccessful attempt was made to re-establish the Latin empire of Constantinople.

Other wars against Orthodox Christians on the frontiers of Catholic Europe in the fourteenth century were also assigned the status of crusades. Thus King Amadeus IV of Savoy led crusaders to Bulgaria in 1366 to 1367 and several crusading campaigns were fought by the Scandinavian kings against the Russian rulers of Novgorod between 1348 and 1351.

The Great Schism of 1378 to 1417 also produced two crusades, which both originated in England and were fought by supporters of the Roman faction against adherents of the Avignon popes. In 1383 Henry Despenser, bishop of Norwich, led a crusade force across the English Channel to fight the count of Flanders and in 1386 to 1387 John of Gaunt invaded Castile. Both crusades were limited in scope and did not achieve any lasting results.

Political Enemies of the Papacy. The crusades against political enemies of the papacy grew out of a long tradition of armed conflicts between the papacy and its political opponents in Italy in the eleventh century. In

1135 the Council of Pisa for the first time granted a crusade indulgence to those supporting the papal cause in Italy. The first political crusade to be preached in Italy was directed against Markward of Anweiler, a German ministerial eager to assert his power in Southern Italy after the death of Emperor Henry VI and thus acting against papal claims of overlordship. This crusade, however, never got off the ground properly and became redundant after Markward's death in 1203. By the middle of the thirteenth century political crusading had come into its own. From 1239 the cross was preached in Italy, Germany and Hungary against the excommunicate Emperor Frederick II and his followers. After the emperor's death in 1250 the crusade was renewed against his heirs Manfred and Conradin. In Germany the anti-king William of Holland was the main beneficiary of the crusading contingents recruited by the papal propagandist. In Italy a number of papal armies were operating in the 1250s, but the final success for the anti-Hohenstaufen crusade was provided by the leadership of Charles of Anjou, brother of King Louis IX of France. Charles led his crusaders on a triumphal crusade through Italy, beating Manfred at Benevento in 1266, Conradin at Tagliacozzo in 1268 and finally conquering the last Hohenstaufen outpost, the Muslim colony of Lucera, in 1269. The establishment of Angevin rule in the kingdom of Sicily did not, however, put an end to political crusading in Italy. After the Aragonese conquest of Sicily in 1282, the papacy launched a number of crusades for its return to the Angevins. These crusades came to an end in 1302 when the papacy finally accepted Aragonese rule on the island of Sicily. In northern Italy, however, the crusade against papal enemies, fuelled by the popes' exile at Avignon, operated intermittently until the 1360s in the attempt to restore the papal states to Guelf rule.

In another context, it has been argued that the political conflicts in England in the 1210s and the 1260s showed elements of political crusading, with the popes supporting King Henry IIII against their internal opponents.

IV. CRUSADES AGAINST OTHER ENEMIES OF THE CHURCH

Northeastern Europe. There is evidence from as early as 1108 that the wars fought by the German nobility against the non-Christian Wends east of the river Elbe were viewed in terms of crusading. In the context of the Second Crusade the Wendish wars were explicitly granted the status of a crusade by Pope Eugene III. The Wendish crusades were closely bound up with the colonising and missionary activities in North-Eastern Germany. In the late 1140s four crusade armies were led against the Wends made up of Danish, German and Polish partici-

pants with the archbishop of Bremen and the duke of Saxony as their principal leaders. The conquest of Dobin, Demmin and Stettin as well as the Danish occupation of Rügen in 1168 foreshadowed the Christian expansion along the Baltic coast between the late twelfth and the late fourteenth centuries, which heavily relied on crusading support. The main protagonists of these colonising and missionary wars were the archbishops of Bremen, the northern German, Danish and Swedish nobility and the military orders of the Swordbrothers and the Teutonic Knights. The first wave of colonisation between the late 1190s and the 1230s led to the occupation of Western Pommerania, Livonia and Estonia. This was supported by regular crusade propaganda in Germany and Scandinavia principally organised by the mendicant orders. Whereas Swedish crusaders continued their activities in the second half of the thirteenth century by conquering large parts of Finland, the long drawn out struggle for the occupation of Prussia and Lithuania was directed and controlled by the Teutonic Knights from the 1230s onwards, sometimes in competition with the Polish nobility. While they initially drew on crusaders recruited by the mendicant orders, the organisation of crusade support was granted directly to the Knights in the second half of the thirteenth century. Until the end of the fourteenth century, by which time most of Lithuania was christianized, a steady influx of knightly crusaders from across Europe supported the Teutonic Order in their colonizing activities.

Mongols. Although no crusade army ever confronted the Mongols in the field, the crusade machinery was set in motion against them several times. When a huge Mongol army, after having devastated parts of Poland and Hungary, threatened to invade Germany in 1241, the German bishops proclaimed a crusade, which was later confirmed by the pope. King Conrad IV agreed to lead the crusade and a great number of crusaders were recruited and large sums of money collected. But the Mongols did not cross the Danube after all and the crusade never took place. Similarly a crusade was preached in the late 1250s when another Mongol invasion of Christian Europe seemed a possibility. But once again the Mongols did not move towards Central Europe and the crusade never materialized.

Bibliography: *The Atlas of the Crusades,* ed. J. S. C. RILEY-SMITH (London 1991). *A History of the Crusades,* 6 v., ed. K. M. SETTON, (2d ed. Madison, Wisconsin, 1969–89). *The Oxford Illustrated History of the Crusades,* ed. J. S. C. RILEY-SMITH (Oxford 1995). P. ALPHANDÉRY et A. DUPRONT, *La chrétienté et l'idée de croisade,* 2 v. (Paris, 1954–59, reprint 1995). J. A. BRUNDAGE, *Medieval Canon Law and the Crusader,* (Madison, Wisconsin and London, 1969). M. G. BULL, ''Knightly Piety and the Lay Response to the First Crusade,'' *The Limousin and Gascony, c. 970–c. 1130* (Oxford, 1993). R. CHAZAN, *European Jewry and the First Crusade* (Berkeley 1987). E. CHRISTIANSEN, *The Northern Crusades: The Baltic and the Catholic Frontier 1100–1525* (London 1980). P. J.

COLE, *The Preaching of the Crusades to the Holy Land, 1095–1270* (Cambridge, Massachusetts, 1991). P. W. EDBURY, *The Kingdom of Cyprus and the Crusades, 1191–1374* (Cambridge 1991). K. ERDMANN, *The Origin of the Idea of Crusade,* tr. M. W. BALDWIN and W. GOFFART (Princeton 1977). J. FLORI, *La première croisade. L'occident chrétien contre l'Islam* (Brussels 1992). J. FRANCE, *Victory in the East: A Military History of the First Crusade* (Cambridge 1994). N. J. HOUSLEY, *The Italian Crusades: The Papal-Angevin Alliance and the Crusades against Christian Lay Powers, 1254–1343* (Oxford 1982); *The Avignon Papacy and the Crusades, 1305–1378* (Oxford 1986); *The Later Crusades, 1274–1580. From Lyons to Alcazar* (Oxford 1992). W. C. JORDAN, *Louis IX and the Challenge of the Crusade: A Study in Rulership* (Princeton, New Jersey, 1979). B. Z. KEDAR, *Crusade and Mission: European Approaches towards the Muslims* (Princeton 1984). S. D. LLOYD, *English Society and the Crusade, 1216–1307* (Oxford 1988). D. M. LOMAX, *The Reconquest of Spain* (London 1978). A. MACQUARRIE, *Scotland and the Crusades 1095–1560* (Edinburgh 1985). C. T. MAIER, *Preaching the Crusades: Mendicant Friars and the Cross in the Thirteenth Century* (Cambridge 1994). H. E. MAYER, *The Crusades,* tr. J. GILLINGHAM (2d ed. Oxford 1988). J. PHILLIPS, *Defenders of the Holy Land: Relations Between the Latin East and the West, 1119–1187* (Oxford 1996). J. M. POWELL, *Anatomy of a Crusade, 1213–1221* (Philadelphia 1986). M. PURCELL, *Papal Crusading Policy, 1244–1291* (Leiden 1975). D. E. QUELLER and T. F. MADDEN, *The Fourth Crusade: The Conquest of Constantinople* (2d ed. Philadelphia 1997). J. RICHARD, *The Crusades, c.1071–c.1291,* tr. J. BIRELL (Cambridge 1999). J. S. C. RILEY-SMITH, *The Crusades: A Short History* (London 1987); *The First Crusade and the Idea of Crusading* (London 1986); *What Were the Crusades,* (2d ed. London 1992); *The First Crusaders, 1095–1131* (Cambridge 1997). M. ROQUEBERT, *L'épopée Cathare,* 5 v. (Toulouse, 1970–98). H. ROSCHER, *Papst Innocenz III: und die Kreuzzüge* (Göttingen, 1969). P. ROUSSET, *Histoire d'une idéologie: La croisade* (Lausanne 1983). F. H. RUSSELL, *The Just War in the Middle Ages* (Oxford 1985). S. SCHEIN, *Fideles Crucis: The Papacy and the Recovery of the Holy Land, 1274–1314* (Oxford 1991). E. SIBERRY, *Criticism of Crusading, 1095–1274* (Oxford 1985). J. R. STRAYER, *The Albigensian Crusade* (New York 1971). C. J. TYERMAN, *England and the Crusades, 1095–1588* (Chicago 1988); *The Invention of the Crusades* (London 1998).

[C. MAIER]

CRUTCHED FRIARS (FRIARS OF THE CROSS)

The name "crutched," "crouched," or "crossed" friars was applied in medieval England to a number of orders: KNIGHTS OF MALTA, TEMPLARS, TRINITARIANS, probably BETHLEHEMITES, and particulary to the Order of the Holy Cross (*the Kruisherren* of the Netherlands, the *Croisiers* of France, known in English-speaking lands as CROSIER FATHERS). It would presumably have been applied also to the Italian Order of the *Cruciferi* (which grew up in 12th-century Italy, centered at Bologna, and was abolished in 1656 by Alexander VII) had that Order ever reached England.

According to tradition, the order of the Holy Cross was founded in 1211 at Huy (Belgium) by Theodore de Celles, a canon of Liège. There is, however, no documentary evidence for the order before 1247, when it was approved by INNOCENT IV. There were then two houses: the motherhouse at Huy and a second at Whaplode in Lincolnshire. The order adopted the Rule of St. AUGUSTINE along with constitutions borrowed from the DOMINICANS; the habit consisted of a white cassock with a black scapular bearing a red and white cross. In the 13th century the order showed the characteristics of the MENDICANT ORDERS, but it subsequently evolved into an order of canons regular. Although some of the early foundations were unsuccessful, by 1300 the order had about a dozen establishments, confined to Belgium, France, and England. In the 14th and 15th centuries it grew to about 60 houses— more than half of them in Holland and the Rhineland—all subject to a prior general at Huy. The English, German, and most of the Dutch houses were lost to Protestantism in the 16th century, while the French and Belgian foundations did not survive the 18th. By 1840 only two small houses in Holland remained, and from these the modern Crosier Fathers grew.

See Also: BRETHREN OF THE CROSS.

Bibliography: R. W. EMERY, "The Second Council of Lyons and the Mendicant Orders," *American Catholic Historical Review* 39 (1953) 262–264 H. F. CHETTLE, "The Friars of the Holy Cross in England," *History* 34 (1949) 204–220. R. HAASS, *Die Kreuzherren in den Rheinlanden* (Bonn 1932). E. BECK, "The Order of Holy Cross (Crutched Friars) in England," *Transactions of the Royal Historical Society* 3d. ser., 7 (1913) 191–208. C. R. HERMANS., *Annales canonicorum regularium s. Augustini ordinis s. Crucis,* 3 v. ('s Hertogenbosch 1858).

[R. W. EMERY]

CRUZ, GASPAR DA

First Dominican missionary to China; b. place and date unknown; d. Setuval, Portugal, 1570. With Father Diogo Bermúdes he left the Dominican Convent of Azeitão (Portugal) for India, founded the first convent in Goa (1548), and opened a convent in Malacca. At the invitation of the native king, Cruz traveled to Cambodia in 1555; he learned the language, but met with great resistance from the natives. In 1556 he left for China where the Portuguese had settled in 1554. He went to Canton with merchants from the newly founded Macau colony, but like his predecessor Melchior Nunes Barreto, SJ, he was forced to leave. Cruz resolved to seek permission from the Portuguese king to lead a mission to Beijing. After returning via India and Ormuz to Portugal, he published a description of China based on his own experiences and the writings of Galeotto Pereira, who had been a prisoner for 14 years in Fujian. Cruz, after ministering to the sick in Lisbon (1569), succumbed to the plague

(1570). He was buried in Azeitão. Gaspar was to have been named bishop of Malacca, a bishopric established in 1557.

Bibliography: B. M. BIERMANN, *Die Anfänge der neueren Dominikanermission in China* (Münster 1927). H. BERNARD, *Aux Portes de la Chine* . . . (Tientsin 1933). R. STREIT and J. DINDINGER, *Bibliotheca missionum* (Freiburg 1916–) 4:518. M. TEIXEIRA, *Macau e a sua Diocese,* v.6 (Lisbon 1963).

[B. M. BIERMANN]

CRUZ ALVARADO, ATILANO, ST.

Martyr, priest, b. Oct. 5, 1901, Ahuetita de Abajo (parish of Teocaltiche), Jalisco, Diocese of Aguascalientes, Mexico; d. July 1, 1928, Las Cruces Ranch, Cuquío, Guadalajara. Atilano herded cattle until his Native parents sent him to Teocaltiche for schooling. He began his seminary studies there (1918), continued in Guadalajara (1920), and was ordained (July 24, 1927) at the height of the religious persecution when it was a felony to be a priest. Thereafter he was sent to replace St. Toribio ROMO, another martyr, in the parish of Cuquío, Jalisco, but hidden on the ranch of Ponciano Jiménez called Las Cruces. Eleven months after his ordination, forty soldiers arrived in the dead of night with civilian authorities. When Atilano heard them killing his superior, Justino Orona, he knelt in prayer to await them. His naked body, deposited by the soldiers in the city square, was retrieved and buried by the faithful at the parish church of Cuquío, where it is venerated today. He was both beatified (Nov. 22, 1992) and canonized (May 21, 2000) with Cristobal MAGALLANES [*see* GUADALAJARA (MEXICO), MARTYRS OF, SS.] by Pope John Paul II.

Feast: May 25 (Mexico).

Bibliography: J. CARDOSO, *Los mártires mexicanos* (Mexico City 1953). J. DÍAZ ESTRELLA, *El movimiento cristero: sociedad y conflicto en los Altos de Jalisco* (México, D.F. 1979). Y. PADILLA RANGEL, *El Catolicismo social y el movimiento Cristero en Aguascalientes* (Aguascalientes 1992).

[K. I. RABENSTEIN]

CRYPTO-CALVINISM

Crypto-Calvinism is a term used by the exponents of GNESIOLUTHERANISM (genuine or strict Lutheranism) to describe a slant in the moderate or conciliatory theology of Philipp MELANCHTHON (*see* PHILIPPISM) away from orthodox Lutheranism and toward Calvinism, especially in the doctrine of the Lord's Supper. A lively controversy ensued between the orthodox Lutheran party, led by Matthias FLACIUS ILLYRICUS, and the liberals, whom they called Crypto(secret)-Calvinists. In its progress occurred the Consensus Tigurinus (1549), an attempt at compromise by John CALVIN and Heinrich BULLINGER; the sharp polemic of Calvin against Joachim Westphal's *Farrago confusanearum* (1552); and the protection of Philippism by electoral Saxony when it officially approved the *Corpus doctrinae Philippicum* (1564). In 1574 M. E. Vögelin, a Leipzig book dealer, published the *Exegesis perspicua* by the Philippist Joachim Curaeus (1532–73), in which Philippism's view of the Lord's Supper was frankly conceded to be in essentials Calvinistic. This led to the imprisonment or exile of leading Philippists. The harshness and bitterness that marked the disputes on such questions as ubiquity and the *communicatio idiomatum* (*see* COMMUNICATION OF IDIOMS) was augmented by a political factor, namely, the fear of the German princes that Crypto-Calvinism tended to draw their creedally based regional power into the orbit of Calvinism, which had become politically international. Among the leading Crypto-Calvinists were: Georg MAJOR, Paul Eber (1511–69), Caspar Cruciger (1525–97), Nicolaus Crell (1550–1601), Caspar Peucer (1525–1602), Victorinus Strigel (1524–69), Joachim Camerarius, Johann Pfegginger (1493–1573), and Christoph Pezel (1539–1604).

See Also: CONFESSIONS OF FAITH, PROTESTANT.

Bibliography: R. CALINICH, *Kampf und Untergang des Melanchthonismus in Kursachsen in den Jahren 1570–74.* . . (Leipzig 1866). O. RITSCHL, *Dogmengeschichte des Protestantismus,* 4 v. (Göttingen 1908–27) 4:1–106. H. W. GENSICHEN, *Damnamus: Die Verwerfung von Irrlehre bei Luther und im Luthertum des 16 Jahrhunderts* (Berlin 1955). T. DIESTELMANN, *Die letzte Unterredung Luthers mit Melanchthon über den Abendmahlsstreit* (Göttingen 1874). L. LOEVENBRUCK, *Dictionnaire de théologie catholique,* ed. A. VACANT et al., 15 v. (Paris 1903–50: Tables générales 1951–) 3.2:2396–98. K. ALGERMISSEN, *Lexikon für Theologie und Kirche,* ed. J. HOFER and K. RAHNER, 10 v. (2d, new ed. Freiburg 1957–65) 6:653–654.

[Q. BREEN]

CUBA, THE CATHOLIC CHURCH IN

Cuba is the largest and most populated of the numerous West Indian islands that form the archipelago of the Greater Antilles. The position of Cuba just south of Florida between the Gulf of Mexico and the Caribbean Sea has given the island strategic and commercial advantages that have been evident throughout its history. The landscape is characterized by rolling plains in the northwest, rising to rugged mountains in the southeast. Cuba's natural resources include cobalt, nickel, iron ore, and petroleum; agriculture—primarily sugar production—accounts for 25 percent of its export. During the late 20th century the government also began to encourage tourism as a way to draw money into the socialist Cuban economy.

Subject to Spain until 1902 and a communist state since 1961, Cuba suffered the loss of Soviet economic subsidies following the demise of the USSR. The resulting economic downturn, fueled as well by the trade embargo imposed by the United States beginning in 1962, forced dictator Fidel Castro to loosen price restrictions and encourage productive labor within his centralized economy. Most Cubans are of European heritage, while a small number are of African decent, mixed race, or Asian.

Following its adoption of a communist platform, the government of Cuba tolerated religious expression only within the confines of church premises, although this policy relaxed somewhat during the late 1990s. Ecclesiastically, Cuba is divided between three archdiocese: Camagüey has suffragans Ciego de Avila, Cinefuegos, and Santa Clara; San Cristóbal de Habana has suffragans Matanzas and Pinar del Río; and Santiago de Cuba has suffragans Guantánamo-Baracoa (1997), Holguín, and Santísimo Salvador de Bayamo-Manzanillo.

Early Christianization. Cuba was originally the home of hunter-gatherer tribes from South America who were joined by Arawak Indians c. 1000 B.C. The first religious to set foot on Cuban soil was a Mercedarian friar, and in the indigenous regions of Macaca and Cueiba rustic altars erected to Our Lady were venerated by the native peoples. During the late 15th century Dominican friars from Española endeavored to give religious instruction to the natives, but the subsequent conduct of the conquistadores over the next half-century negated their achievements. Christopher Columbus arrived in Cuba on Oct. 27, 1492; less than two decades later the island was conquered by a group of 300 Spaniards led by Diego Velázquez de Cuéllar, a wealthy settler from Santo Domingo who founded the city of Havana in 1511. Four religious came with Velázquez, one the Franciscan lay brother Juan de Tesin. The most notable missionary figure was undoubtedly Fray Bartolomé de LAS CASAS, whose apostleship of more than 50 years began in Cuba around 1514. The great example of Las Casas moved the Franciscan Provincial Pedro Mexía de Trillo to try the so-called "experiment plan" with the Cuban natives around 1526. Unfortunately, as was the case throughout much of the Americas, European-introduced disease and exploitation caused the extinction of the Arawak people by the end of the 1500s. Beginning in 1526 slaves from Africa were imported to replace the declining Arawak populations on the island's many sugar and tobacco plantations. Slavery would continue on Cuba until it was outlawed in 1886.

Religious Orders. Dominicans (1524) and Franciscans (1529) quickly established religious communities in

Capital: Havana.
Size: 44,218 sq. miles.
Population: 11,141,997 in 2000.
Languages: Spanish.
Religions: 4,902,480 Catholics (44%; formerly 80% prior to communist takeover), 1,114,200 nominally Protestants, Jews, Jehovah's Witnesses, or Santeria (15%), 5,125,317 atheists or without religious affiliation.

Cuba, and were joined several decades later by the Society of Jesus (1566) and other orders. Some communities, such as the Hospitallers of St. John of God (1603) and the Bethlehemites (1704), gave their full attention to hospitals; others, including the Jesuits, Piarists (1857), Augustinians from North America (1898), Marists (1903), and Christian Brothers (1905), founded centers of learning; while still others, Franciscans, Paulists (1862), and Barnabites (1953), specialized in journalism and editorial work. By the 18th century native vocations flourished in all the orders.

Communities of women religious arrived in Cuba much later than the male religious orders. The Poor Clares arrived in 1644, and the Catalinas in 1688, leading the way for Discalced Carmelites, Ursulines, Sisters of Charity, Religious of the Sacred Heart, Dominicans, the Company of Mary, and many others. They established and maintained schools, cared for inmates of asylums, sanitariums, jails, and reform schools, and rendered valuable assistance in catechesis and social welfare. Five communities were dedicated to the contemplative life. Five female communities were founded in Cuba: Claretians (1853), Sisters of Cardinal Sancha (1869), Apostolines (1891), Messengers of the Heart of Mary (1957), and Diocesan Cooperators (1960).

From the 16th century onward, Cuba remained for the most part under the control of Spain, despite efforts by British, and then U.S. economic interests to liberate it. During the colonial period, the Church devoted careful attention to educating Cuban citizens. The Catholic religion was the religion of the state, and the teaching of Catholic dogma was obligatory in the schools. The Royal and Pontifical University of St. Jerome, founded in Havana in 1728 by the Dominicans and secularized in 1842, was for many years the only center of higher learning in all Cuba. The Royal College of St. Charles and St. Ambrose, college *ad instar* of the conciliar seminaries, established for "the general utility of the country and not for that of one of its classes," became the birthplace of Cubano nationalism during the early decades of the 19th century. This desire for independence fueled the failed first War of Independence of 1868–78, a revolt encour-

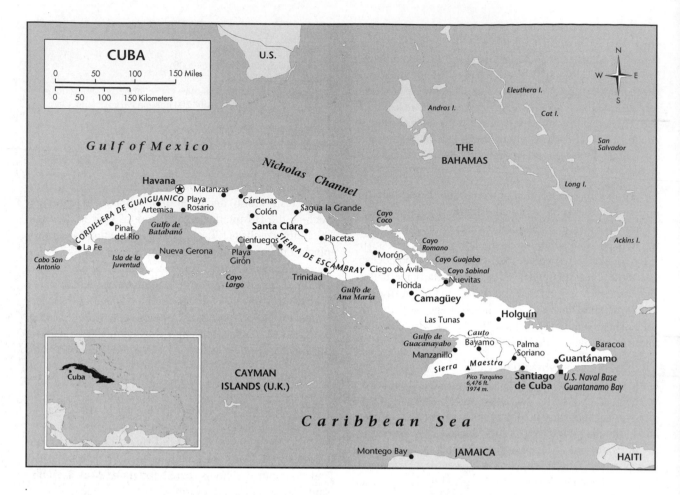

aged by imperialist-leaning interests within the United States.

Cuba Becomes a Republic. After Cuba's second War of Independence flared in 1895, the United States finally found justification to declare war on Spain after the U.S. battleship *Maine* mysteriously blew up in Havana's harbor. A result of the Spanish-American War of 1898 was the occupation of the Central American region by U.S. troops in 1899, in defense of the United States' significant investment in the Cuban sugar industry. Cuba ultimately achieved independence from Spain on May 20, 1902.

The problem of ownership of Church properties that arose following the withdrawal of Spain's colonial government was first addressed during the U.S. military occupation in favor of the claims of the Church, with the payment of a five-percent revenue on the total value of the properties. However, after the first republican government took power, it gained the preemptive right to acquire these properties. The ownership of mission properties was ultimately solved, a result of the prudent intercession of Bishop González Estrada, first Cuban bishop of Havana, at the time of the second U.S. interven-

tion in 1907. The Church in Cuba would thereafter be supported by stipends and the alms of the faithful. While the republic adopted the policy of secularism in education, during the first half of the 20th century many accredited Catholic schools were founded and flourished.

The newly independent Cuba was wracked by a series of ineffective civilian governments, including the brutal authoritarian regime of Geraldo Machado (1925–33). Cuba again endured dictatorship when, in 1940, Colonel Fulgencio Batista came to power. Batista jockeyed for power, with U.S. support, until January 1959 when a successful revolution was led against his dictatorship by 32-year-old Fidel Castro. Under the new communist regime Catholics could take heart in the words of their new pope, John XXIII, who had reversed the position of Pius XII that all communists should be excommunicated from the Church. During his short reign, Pope John attempted a dialogue with communist leaders around the world, including Castro. Catholics struggling to follow their faith under communist dictatorships would be further supported by Vatican II.

Prior to Castro's revolution there were over 250 Church institutes devoted to social work in Cuba, 181 of

Menoyo Gutierrez (left), William Cardinal Keeler (center) and Jaime Cardinal Ortega, before Mass at Old Havana Cathedral, Havana, January 1, 1997. (AP/Wide World Photos)

those organized within the previous 50 years. Over 300 schools enrolled 61,000 primary- and secondary-school students. In 1946 the North American Augustinian Fathers had founded the Catholic University of St. Thomas of Villanova, the first private university in the history of the republic, and by 1959 it had 1,200 students. Two useful institutions, the Catholic University Group, established in 1931 by the Jesuit Felipe Rey de Castro, and the Catholic University Home (1946), the special project of Brother Victorino of the La Salle School, rendered assistance to the Catholic students of the official University of Havana. Catholic teachers in Cuba, united in a strong association (with almost 5,000 members), played a significant role in the religious instruction in the country.

The Church under Communism. First taking power as Cuba's prime minister, Castro quickly proclaimed his Marxist-Leninist agenda through a series of laws. His law of June 6, 1961, which stated that education

was to be public and free, nationalized all schools and other learning centers then in private or Church hands, as well as placing under control of the state "all properties, rights and stocks included in the assets of those centers." This law resulted in the emigration of hundreds of religious who had dedicated themselves to education and other social services within Cuba. The 53 religious communities of women in Cuba were reduced to 13, all confined to charitable works. By the mid-1990s there were only 280 priests remaining in Cuba.

After December 1976 Castro ruled Cuba as president, the office of prime minister having been abolished under the country's new constitution. His regime would face several crises in the coming decades, both economic and social in nature. Lacking was the moral and religious structure given by the Church, as religious services remained restricted, the distribution of religious literature was forbidden, and affiliation with the Church discour-

The Cathedral of Havana c. 1900. (©CORBIS)

aged. Of particular interest to the Church was the decline in the birth rate to .72 children per woman by 1996, a consequence of the free birth control and abortion services made available as a means to maximize the supply of full-time laborers.

In the early 1990s relations between Castro and Pope JOHN PAUL II improved, the result of an effort on the part of the Cuban dictator to rebuild international relations following the demise of Cuba's Soviet support system. In November 1994 Pope John Paul II celebrated the investiture of Cardinal Jaime Ortega y Alamino as Archbishop of Havana during an address to the Vatican. Two years later, Castro traveled to the Vatican for an audience and extended to the pontiff a formal invitation to visit Cuba in 1997. Castro's efforts to relax restrictions on the Church were acknowledged during a conversation focusing on the role of the Church in Cuban life. In advance of the pope's historic visit, the government breached its ban on the dissemination of religious information through

the media by allowing the schedule of the papal visit to be published. The Church began an international outreach, launching an internet website featuring news about its activities, including the upcoming papal visit. Although the site was not accessible to residents of Cuba, who still lacked internet access, it was hoped that it would counter the dearth of information provided by the government-controlled Cuban media. Castro also allowed Catholics from the United States entry into Cuba to witness the first papal visit to Cuba. In response to the pope's impending visit, an unprecedented number of both adults and teens requested baptism or reentry into the Church in Cuba.

From January 21 to January 25, 1998, the Pope traveled throughout Cuba, preaching a message of reconciliation. "The state, while distancing itself from all forms of fanaticism or secularism, should encourage a harmonious social climate and a suitable legislation which enables every person and every religious confession to live his

Pope John Paul II posing with a group of Cuban bishops during a private audience at the Vatican. Photograph by Arturo Mari. (©AP/Wide World Photos)

faith freely,'' John Paul II told millions of Cuban faithful at his final mass in Havana. His plea that the world reopen dialogue with Cuba prompted Guatemala to reestablish diplomatic relations with Cuba shortly after the pope's visit.

Hopes that the pope's visit might prompt a more liberal government policy with regard to the Church were further heightened by the Cuban government's approval, in November 1998, of visas for 19 foreign priests to take up residence in the country, and the subsequent decision to allow several religious-run humanitarian groups to once again operate outside the confines of church walls. A publication by the Archdiocese of Havana was permitted distribution to that city's parishes for the first time in several years. And in 1997 public religious processions celebrating the birth of Christ, and in 1998 Holy Week, traveled Cuban streets for the first time in three decades. However, by 2000 such liberal attitudes had been over-

shadowed by renewed repression, as Church officials were accused of conspiring against the revolution, Church-run social services were harassed by government officials, and educated professionals entering religious communities were banned from practicing in their field. Despite assurances to the contrary during the pontiff's visit, the Cuban government remained wary of Church efforts at increased involvement in Cuban society, fearing that social unrest would cause such involvement to filter into the political sphere.

Bibliography: J. M. LEISECA, *Apuntes para la historia eclesiástica de Cuba* (Havana 1938). G. AMIGÓ, *La iglesia católica en Cuba* (Havana 1949). F. ZAPATA, *Primer catálogo de las obras sociales católicas de Cuba* (Havana 1953). A. PÉREZ CARREÑO, *Extensión y eficacia de la educación religiosa en los colegios católicos de La Habana* (Havana 1960).

[J. M. PÉREZ CABRERA/EDS.]

CUERO Y CAICEDO, JOSÉ DE

Ecuadorean bishop and political leader; b. Cali, 1734; d. Lima, Peru, Oct. 9, 1815. In Quito he received the doctorate in philosophy in 1762; the licentiate, in 1765; and the title of lawyer, on June 20, 1768; he was already a cleric. Because of his illustrious lineage he quickly obtained high ecclesiastical posts in Quito and Popayán. He was dean of Popayán when his appointment as the second bishop of Cuenca was confirmed; he took possession by proxy on Aug. 13, 1799. Before going to this diocese, however, he received notice of his promotion to the See of Quito. He was a founding member of the Patriotic Society of Friends of the Country.

When he was 74, the first call for independence occurred (Aug. 10, 1809), an event that plunged him into bitter uncertainty as to whether he should abandon his flock or remain in the rebellious city. He chose the second course, but the fear of reprisals caused him to make secret protestations of his loyalty to the king. He was appointed vice president of the junta, but new events forced him to withdraw the following September 7. During the assassination of the Grandees (Aug. 2, 1810) he acted with admirable boldness and was a peacemaker and defender of his people against the military. With the arrival of the Royal Commissioner, Montúfar, the situation changed. Shortly afterward a new junta was set up as a symbol of the union of all social elements. On December 11 a congress, with Cuero y Caicedo as president, met and prepared the Pact of Union among the provinces that made up the State of Quito. When the monarchic reaction set in, the bishop renounced the presidency, but he invited the clergy to the defense of the country. He did not hesitate to force the regalistic clergy, through the most severe measures, to support the independence movement. However, when the royalist armies drew near the capital, the bishop fled. He was allowed to return to Quito until the judgment of the king was issued. Then he was transferred to Lima, where Archbishop Las Heras charitably received him.

Bibliography: J. TOBAR DONOSO, *La iglesia ecuatoriana en el siglo XIX* (Quito 1934); *La iglesia modeladora de la nacionalidad* (Quito 1953). J. M. VARGAS, *Historia de la iglesia en el Ecuador durante el patronato español* (Quito 1962). R. VARGAS UGARTE, *El episcopado en los tiempos de la emancipación sudamericana* (Buenos Aires 1945).

[J. TOBAR DONOSO]

CUEVAS, MARIANO

Mexican Jesuit and outstanding historian; b. Mexico City, Feb. 18, 1879; d. Mexico City, March 31, 1949. In 1893, Cuevas went to Spain, where, on September 24, he entered the novitiate of the Society of Jesus at Loyola in the Basque province of Guipúzcoa. His studies were extensive: Latin and the humanities at Loyola; rhetoric in Burgos; philosophy in Oña; theology at St. Louis University, Missouri; history at the Gregorian University, Rome, and the University of Louvain, Belgium, where he received the Ph.D. in 1912. He was ordained on Aug. 24, 1909. From 1913 to his death, with the exception of eight years spent in teaching and in other occupations, such as being the director of Our Lady's Sodality at the military garrison in Toledo, Spain, Cuevas dedicated himself mainly to research in the archives and libraries of Spain, England, Italy, the United States, various countries of South America, and his native Mexico.

He wrote more than 15 major works in 23 volumes. Too numerous to mention are minor works and articles that appeared in newspapers and magazines both in Mexico and abroad. Of all Cuevas's books, the outstanding is his five-volume history of the Church in Mexico, *Historia de la iglesia en Mexico* (Mexico City and El Paso 1921–28). It has been printed in five editions and is still the only work of its kind. Besides this, his *Historia de la nación mexicana* has appeared in two editions, the first in 1940. His *Monje y marino,* published in 1943, tells of the life and times of Fray Andrés de URDANETA, who accompanied Legazpi (1564) on the successful voyage from Mexico to the Philippine Islands and who, by discovering a northerly return route, made possible the establishment of a flourishing trade route between Acapulco and Manila. The editing of various books of significant documents adds to the contribution that Cuevas made to the history of Mexico. The more important were: *Documentos inéditos del siglo XVI; Testamento de Hernán Cortés; Descripción de la Nueva España en et siglo XVII por el Padre Fray Antonio Vázquez de Espinosa y otros documentos; Historia antigua de Mexico del Padre Francisco Javier Clavijero.* He ranks among the foremost historians of Mexico and all Latin America.

Bibliography: J. BRAVO UGARTE, "El P. Mariano Cuevas, S.J., 1879–1949," *Revista de historia de América* 27 (1949) 103–107.

[N. F. MARTIN]

CULDEES

A group of Celtic religious recluses found mainly in Ireland and Scotland throughout the Middle Ages. A collection of documents dating from *c.* 800 gives rules for such a group of religious, which it refers to as Céli Dé (hence the name Culdees). The life prescribed in these documents is one of extreme rigor, with the religious obviously living in community. The teaching and practices of several saints and holy men are cited, but the central figure throughout these documents is Máel-Ruain (d. 792) of Tamlachta or TALLAGHT (an abbey three miles southwest of Dublin), much of whose teaching is given in the form of answers to questions put by various persons, especially Máiel-Díthruib. In these documents—which did not emanate from Tallaght—superstitious practices are found side by side with high asceticism; and it may well be doubted if Máel-Díthruib could have elicited the information given, for according to the annals he was an anchorite of Tír-DaGlas or Terryglas (County Tipperary) who died in 840, forty-eight years after Máel-Ruain. On the other hand, Dub-Litter, Abbot of Finglas (north of Dublin), also appears but in a secondary role. He is described in the *Annals of Ulster* for 780 as being the chief (*dux*) of the anchorites and scribes. As will be seen, this may be the equivalent of calling him chief of the Culdees. The explanation for Máel-Ruain's central role in these Culdee documents may well be that Máel-Ruain quickly became a legend; material showing the growth of this legend is not wanting. In any event, the Culdees—followers of Máel-Ruain or not—were to be found throughout much of Scotland and Ireland by the ninth century. The native annals seldom speak of the Culdees by name—and some of the few entries mentioning them derive obviously from legendary sources—but an examination of the annals shows a remarkable rise in the number of obits of anchorites and scribes at this period. Among those so styled are to be found the names of men elsewhere called Culdees. It would seem, then, that many, if not all, of the "anchorites" mentioned in the annals were in fact Culdees.

There is another noteworthy fact: in point of numbers of such anchorites, Armagh ranks highest, followed closely by CLONMACNOIS and GLENDALOUGH. By contrast, Tallaght and those monasteries closely associated with it in the Culdee documents have least of all. Hence the commonly held opinion that Máel-Ruain was the founder of the Culdees is not based on incontrovertible evidence. On the other hand, it is to be noted that the number of obits for anchorites and scribes is highest during the first half of the ninth century, suggesting that the anchoritic movement reached its peak during the lifetime of Máel-Ruain. The various reform laws introduced among the Culdees were nearly all promulgated at the beginning of the eighth century.

Apart from the literature on the monastic life, the Culdees produced two martyrologies (that of Tallaght and one of Oengus Céle Dé) and the Stowe Missal. Their extensive use of the vernacular in dealing with religious and ecclesiastical subjects is a noteworthy innovation in their work; but illiteracy on the part of some of their num-

bers does not seem to have been the chief reason for this practice. In this connection it is significant that personal lyrics in the vernacular make their appearance for the first time at this period, and nearly all are obviously of monastic or eremitic origin.

Yet it is not known exactly to what type of religious the Culdees belonged. Though called hermits, they were not such in the accepted meaning of the word, for in general they do not seem to have cut themselves off from the older foundations, of which they were a reform element, but rather to have maintained association with them, directed as they were by their own superior, who was subject to the abbot. Some Culdees (as at Armagh) seem to have lived within the old monastic enclosure; others occupied a separate, dependent site as at Monahincha, dependent on Roscrea. Tallaght, on the other hand, seems to have been composed entirely of Culdees. And it was Tallaght and Finglas that succeeded in escaping destruction by the Norse marauders, seemingly on account of the extreme poverty of their members. Complete renunciation of worldly goods and utter dependence on Providence seem to have been the guiding principles of Culdees, as is to be inferred from incidental references in anecdotes dealing with them. They survived in Ireland and Scotland till the time of the dissolution of the monasteries under King HENRY VIII, but many centuries before that they had lost all contact with their original idealism, even abandoning celibacy.

Bibliography: Works of Culdee Provenance. D. A. BINCHY, *Old-Irish Penitential* (8th century), in *The Irish Penitentials,* ed. L. BIELER (Dublin 1963) 258–277. D. A. BINCHY, *The Old-Irish Table of Commutations* (8th century), *op. cit.,* 277–283. *Customs of Tallaght* (9th century), "The Monastery of Tallaght," *Proceedings of the Royal Irish Academy,* eds., E. J. GWYNN and W. J. PURTON, 29, Section C (1911) 113–179; cf. "The Rule of Tallaght," *Hermathena,* ed. E. J. GWYNN, 44 (1927) suppl. 2:104–109; cf. P. GROSJEAN, "Extraits de la règle de Tallaght," *Études Celtiques,* 2 (1937) 301–303. *Rule of the Céli Dé* (9th century), ed. and tr., E. J. GWYNN, *op. cit.,* 65–87, 97–103. *Rule of Tallaght,* later ed. of *Customs,* ed. E. J. GWYNN, *op. cit.,* 2–63. *Rule of Fothad no Canóine or of Mochutu* (9th century), J. F. KENNEY, *The Sources for the Early History of Ireland: v.1, Ecclesiastical* (New York 1929) 1:473–474 for this rule treating of the duties of all believers; the section dealing with the Céli Dé (written in the first person plural) may be a later insertion into the other material (written in the second person singular). *Early Irish Lyrics: Eighth to Twelfth Centuries,* ed. G. MURPHY, (Oxford 1956) 2–71, for Culdee monastic poems. Literature. W. REEVES, "On the Céli Dé, Commonly Called Culdees," in *Transactions of the Royal Irish Academy,* 24 (1873) 119–264, most detailed account, but with imperfections. L. GOUGAUD, *Dictionnaire d'archéologie chrétienne et de liturgie,* eds., F. CABROL, H. LECLERCQ and H. I. MARROU, 15 v. (Paris 1907–53) 3.2:3186–90, with comments on the Stowe Missal. *Early Sources of Scottish History, A.D. 500–1286,* ed. and tr., A. O. ANDERSON, 2 v. (Edinburgh 1922). J. F. KENNEY, *The Sources for the Early History of Ireland: v.1, Ecclesiastical* (New York 1929) 1:468–482. R. FLOWER, "The Two Eyes of Ireland," in *The Church of Ireland, A.D. 432–1932: The Report of the Church of Ireland Conference Held in Dublin,*

11th–14th October, 1932, eds., W. BELL and N. D. EMERSON (Dublin 1932). *The Irish Tradition* (Oxford 1947) 24–66. F. O. BRIAIN, *Dictionnaire d'histoire et de géographie ecclésiastiques,* ed. A. BAUDRILLART et al., (Paris 1912–) 13:1099–1100. D. A. BINCHY, *op. cit.,* 47–51.

[C. MCGRATH]

CULLEN, PAUL

Cardinal, archbishop of Dublin; b. Ballitore, County Kildare, Ireland, April 29, 1803; d. Dublin, Oct. 24, 1878. After studying at a local Quaker school and at Carlow College, he entered (1820) the College of Propaganda in Rome, where he was ordained (1829) and then appointed professor of Sacred Scripture and Hebrew. Named rector of the Irish College, Rome (1832), he acted until 1850 as agent of the Irish and Australian bishops and worked to counteract British influence at the Vatican.

In 1840 the Holy See commissioned Cullen to examine the Irish national school system, which was occasioning serious division among the Irish bishops. Rome followed his recommendation and dispatched a rescript that left each bishop free to accept or disallow these schools in his diocese. The hierarchy was also at variance concerning the Queen's colleges, which Cullen strongly opposed. Rome condemned these colleges and urged the bishops to establish a Catholic university (1847). From Rome Cullen organized help for his starving countrymen during the great famine (1847). When the Roman Republic set itself up and replaced the papal government (February 1849), Cullen became rector of the College of Propaganda at the request of the Sacred Congregation of Propaganda. When the revolutionary triumvirate ordered the college dissolved, Cullen appealed to the United States minister for protection of the American students and thereby saved the institution.

Cullen succeeded William Crolly as archbishop of Armagh (1850), an appointment designed to strengthen the unity of the Irish hierarchy. Following his consecration in Rome, Cullen was appointed apostolic delegate to Ireland and ordered to convene a national council, the first since the 12th century. The Synod of Thurles, which resulted, convened on Aug. 22, 1850.

Memory of the Irish Rebellion of 1798 and the Roman Revolution of 1848, as well as theological considerations, nurtured Cullen's hatred of revolution and secret societies. He regarded the Young Ireland and Fenian leaders as sowers of dissension and enemies of Ireland, although he sympathized with their sufferings and saved Thomas F. Burke, the Fenian leader, from hanging. Cullen advocated constitutional action as the best remedy for Ireland's grievances and pleaded for national unity. He was a defender of the rights of tenants, a champion of poorhouse reform, and an advocate of industrial schools. His testimony before the Poor Law Commission in 1861 and the Powis Commission on education in 1869 helped to produce substantial improvements.

The appointment of John Henry NEWMAN (1854) as first rector of the Catholic University of Ireland, founded in 1854, was a result of Cullen's influence. Because of the government's refusal to grant a charter, the university led a struggling existence; but the medical school founded by Newman and Cullen was eminently successful, and their educational ideals were substantially realized when the National University was founded in 1908.

Cullen labored to improve the morale and preparation of the Irish clergy, opening a diocesan seminary at Clonliffe in 1859. In 1866 he became Ireland's first cardinal, and he took a leading part in VATICAN COUNCIL I as a framer of the definition of papal infallibility. He is buried at Clonliffe.

Bibliography: P. CULLEN, *Pastoral Letters and Other Writings,* ed. P. F. MORAN, 3 v. (Dublin 1882). P. J. CORISH, "Cardinal Cullen and Archbishop MacHale," *The Irish Ecclesiastical Record* 91 (1959) 393–408. J. F. WHYTE, "Fresh Light on Archbishop Cullen and the Tenant League," *ibid.* 99 (1963) 170–176. P. MACSUIBHNE, *Paul Cullen and His Contemporaries* (Naas, Ire. 1961–).

[P. MAC SUIBHNE]

CULTS

There is no clear consensus in the published literature as to which religious groups should appropriately be designated "cults" and which should not. The term can be considered generic, however, and need not pertain exclusively to religious phenomena. Broad fields such as politics, popular culture, psychotherapy, and personal development have produced associations with cult-like characteristics.

In reference to religious groups, the term "cult" has been linked with some or all of the following characteristics: a focus on individual concerns, indifference to the world, privatized and/or ecstatic religious experience, syncretistic doctrines of a mystical, esoteric, or psychic nature, or doctrines that draw inspiration from other than the religion of the tradition in which they exist. Cults are also held to have a charismatic leader, to lack formal criteria for membership, to have weak organizational structure, and to eschew rigorous ethical demands on members. Cults are more tolerant toward other religious groups and are likely to have a transitory or short-lived existence.

Recent scholarship distinguishes types of cults on the following basis: Audience cults generally lack formal

Hundreds of members of the People's Temple committed suicide on the order of cult leader Jim Jones, Guyana, November 1978.
(©Bettmann/CORBIS)

organizations. They give expression to parallelisms of spontaneities in which individuals with common interests, ideas, and experience gather informally for sharing and providing mutual support. Client cults are more formally organized. They promulgate doctrines and services and resemble consultant/client relationships in their organizational structure. Cults of this type often emphasize pragmatic considerations related to self-adjustment and self-mastery.

Cult movements are more explicitly religious and are concerned with meeting the need for various religious rewards and compensations. While sects are potentially schismatic groups seeking to purify or refurbish an established religious tradition, cult movements are a type of religious innovation that rearrange familiar cultural and symbolic patterns, or that import new ones. By so doing, cult movements signal a break with the general pattern of established religious tradition in society.

Why cults form and what factors are conducive to their spread has been the subject of long-standing discussion. Anthropological and psychoanalytic perspectives associate cult formation with charismatic leaders and with messianic, millenarian, or nativistic religious move-

ments that arise where traditional social structures and cultural patterns have broken down and where values, norms and myths from an alien culture have been introduced.

Sociological perspectives have linked cult formation to the presence of entrepreneurial personalities who are adept at developing various spiritual, social, and psychological products by assembling components of pre-existing religious systems into new configurations. Sociologists have also linked cult formation with urban areas undergoing rapid social and demographic change, with wide-spread alienation and anomie (especially among the middle-class), with weak established institutional churches, and where individuals are adrift from conventional religious organizations.

In the 1960s and 1970s, the term "cult" came to be associated with a proliferation of non-conventional religions, many of which were of Eastern derivation. In the U.S., the growth of such movements among an affluent, college-educated, youth constituency coupled with dramatic changes in the participant's values, life-styles, and controversies surrounding cult proselytizing strategies and organizational characteristics gave rise to considerable opposition in the form of a loose coalition of anti-cult groups.

Although the term "cult" is still widely used in public parlance to refer to groups that are small, unorthodox, and culturally anomalous, many scholars consider the term obsolete because of its pejorative connotation and lack of empirical clarity. Academic treatment of marginalized or non-conventional religion has moved in the direction of theories and methodologies derived from resource mobilization and social movement perspectives. Within these frameworks, cults are viewed as movements concerned with transformations in religious meaning, symbolism, and innovation.

See Also: SECT.

Bibliography: L. VON WIESE & H. BECKER, *Systematic Sociology* (New York 1932) 621–628. A. WALLACE, "Revitalization Movements," *American Anthropologist* 58 (1956) 264–281, P. WORSLEY, *The Trumpet Shall Sound: A Study of Cargo Cults in Melanesia* (New York 1968). B. CAMPBELL, "A Typology of Cults," *Sociological Analysis* 39, 3 (1978) 228–240. G. K. NELSON, "The Concept of Cult," *Sociological Review* 16, 3 (November, 1968) 351–362. R. STARK & W. S. BAINBRIDGE. *The Future of Religion: Secularization and Cult Formation* (Berkeley 1985).

[W. D. DINGES]

CULT (WORSHIP)

In general, the recognition of the excellence and superiority of another, together with a manifestation of the reverence and esteem in which that recognition is expressed. Cult, understood in this broad sense, is exercised in the practice of the virtues of RELIGION, PIETY, and observance. But the term is more commonly used in reference to the latria that the virtue of religion gives to God alone, or the hyperdulia and dulia accorded, respectively, to the Blessed Virgin and the saints, or the veneration of sacred images, relics, etc. (*See* WORSHIP; SAINTS, DEVOTION TO THE; IMAGES, VENERATION OF.)

The 1917 Code of Canon Law distinguished between public and private cult; it is public if it is carried on in the name of the Church by persons legitimately designated to do so and by the performance of acts that, according to the institution of the Church, are referable only to God, the saints, and the beatified; otherwise it is private (1917 CIC c.1256). Since the time of Urban VIII the Church has insisted that no public cult be given to anyone except those who have a rightful place on the list of the saints or the beatified. Indeed one of the steps in the existing procedure in causes of beatification and canonization consists of processes *de non cultu,* or investigations aimed at proving that the prohibition by Urban VIII of public cult before beatification has been observed.

[P. K. MEAGHER]

CULTURE

The term culture has become central and of primary importance to the social sciences; it is difficult, however, to encompass in a single definition all the meanings attached to it. After surveying and analyzing more than 160 definitions, A. L. Kroeber and Clyde Kluckhohn have summarized the basic ideas as follows: "Culture consists of patterns, explicit and implicit, of and for behavior acquired and transmitted by symbols, constituting the distinctive achievement of human groups, including their embodiments in artifacts; the essential core of culture consists of traditional (i.e., historically derived and selected) ideas and especially their attached values; culture systems may, on the one hand, be considered as products of action, on the other as conditioning elements of further action" (*Culture: A Critical Review of Concepts and Definitions* 357).

Concept

In Latin and in languages that have borrowed from Latin, the term culture implies cultivation, or becoming cultured, and is used to refer to individuals rather than to groups. This meaning has been retained in both popular and literary English, especially within the humanistic tradition. Similarly, the German word *Kultur* is equated with the idea of "higher" values and the enlightenment of society. Matthew Arnold elaborated this meaning, proposing that culture is, or ought to be the "study of perfection," consisting in "an inward condition of the mind and spirit, not in an outward set of circumstances" [*Culture and Anarchy,* ed. J. D. Wilson (Cambridge, England 1960) 48].

Introduction in the Social Sciences. The concept as used in the social sciences was introduced into English by E. B. Tylor [*Primitive Culture* (London 1871)] but did not become established as a key concept in English anthropology until its use by Sir James Frazer in 1885. Even then the older term custom continued to be preferred. British social anthropologists, principally concerned with social structure, were reluctant to use the newer term widely. Recent writers have reintroduced it in order to describe the part of a people's behavior that cannot be subsumed under social structure, since "no account of social relationships . . . can be complete unless it includes reference to what it means to the people who have it . . . for human beings have cultures, systems of beliefs and values" [J. Beattie, *Other Cultures* (New York 1964) 13]. Nevertheless the term custom is frequently used in place of culture. There is an awareness that culture is more inclusive, whereas custom refers to "habits" and usages, usually of a nontechnical sort, learned by the individual and shared by a group.

Culture has sometimes been used as a substitute for or in opposition to civilization. In England and France, the term civilization was used in preference to culture in regard to complex societies, ancient and modern. Civilization implied a "high" culture characterized by writing and a highly developed political organization, i.e., a state administered from cities and exercising dominance over others. As in America, culture and civilization were also used interchangeably by European writers.

The culture concept has had a longer history in Germany. Kroeber and Kluckhohn have traced it back to the end of the 18th century. At first the idea as it appeared in general histories had an almost modern ring. Culture implied progress in cultivation toward enlightenment, but there was already an interest in comparing cultures. During a second phase of development, from Kant to Hegel, the emphasis shifted more to the idea of spirit (*Geist*) and its ennoblement. *Kultur* was opposed to crude nature. In a third phase, beginning with the ethnographer Gustav Friedrich Klemm [*Allgemeine Culturgeschichte der Menschheit,* 10 v. (Leipzig 1843–52)], the more modern and technical meaning came into use. Klemm suggested a definition that in its enumerative aspects (i.e., the study of customs, arts, skills, domestic and public life in peace and war, religion, science, and art) foreshadowed the now classic definition by Tylor. Indeed, Tylor was influenced by Klemm and decided to use the term culture instead of his earlier term civilization because it was more inclusive and descriptive. Thus, among social scientists culture began to denote the characteristic modes of human existence.

Principal Emphases. The precise meaning that is given to the concept in modern social science tends to vary according to the interests and purposes of anthropologists and sociologists, both of whom use the term most frequently, and of psychologists, psychiatrists, and other social scientists and humanistic scholars. Kroeber and Kluckhohn have identified six major emphases.

First, one view emphasizes the comprehensive totality of culture and the enumeration of aspects of cultural content. Customs characterizing group behavior and habits characterizing individual behavior, as well as the products of both, comprise the content of culture. Culture is based on the life of a group or a SOCIETY and is learned. The learning of culture is implied or explicitly stated by most authors. The role of symbolism, especially in language, is stressed as an aspect of culture, as is the idea that culture has historical depth.

Second, other conceptions tend to emphasize history, or the idea of a social heritage or a tradition. Ralph Linton notes that "as a general term, *culture* means the total social heredity of mankind, while as a specific term, *a cul-*

ture means a particular strain of social heredity" [*The Study of Man* (New York 1936) 78].

Third, still others emphasize a distinctive way of life; or normative ideas and their consequences; or culture as a "design for living" or as "that whole 'way of life' which is determined by the social environment" [O. Klineberg, *Race Differences* (New York 1935) 255]. Some, such as the sociologist P. A. Sorokin, emphasize values and ideals: "The cultural aspect of the superorganic universe consists of meanings, values, norms, their action and relationships, their integrated and unintegrated groups . . . as they are objectified through overt actions and other vehicles in the empirical and sociocultural universe" [*Society, Culture and Personality* (New York 1947) 313].

Fourth, emphasis may be placed on the psychological aspects of culture insofar as they point to such processes as adjustment, learning, and habit formation. Culture becomes a means for solving problems, for satisfying needs, and for adjusting to the environment as well as to other men. This view is somewhat widely held by followers of Bronislaw Malinowski.

Fifth, the structural and hence also the systematic nature of culture may be stressed. This implies that the elements of culture are related and linked. Culture becomes abstract, a conceptual model of behavior, but not behavior itself. Parts of culture are functionally interrelated. Terms such as cultural system, cultural configuration, and cultural organization become key terms in this approach.

Finally, culture may be conceived as a product of human action. This results from attempts to answer the question of how culture comes to exist. Culture is seen on the one hand as the result of the interaction of individuals and their environment; on the other, as "the summation of all the ideas for standardized types of behavior" (C. Kluckhohn and W. H. Kelly, "The Concept of Culture" in Linton, ed., *The Science of Man* 97), and as dependent on the use of systems of symbols by man.

Component Elements

Most social scientists note that although each culture is unique, all cultures can be analyzed from the point of view of (1) *abstract* qualities, categorized according to standard anthropological concepts; (2) the substantive aspects, or *content,* of culture, which can be variously classified; and (3) the organization of this content into systems and subsystems that are to some extent *integrated.*

Analysis of Abstract Qualities. Basic to any consideration is the behavioral reference of culture. Behavior ultimately provides the basic data from which culture is abstracted. Not all behavior provides such data, however; it must be repetitive and show some degree of structuring, which implies standardization. In short, behavioral units form patterns. Wherever behavioral elements form a pattern, the emphasis is on the relationships between the elements, rather than on content. Kroeber distinguishes three kinds of patterns: the universal, manifest in speech, art, knowledge, religion, etc.; the systematic, the whole-culture pattern that reveals the coherence of an entire cultural system; and the style, a characteristic mode of doing or expressing things (*Anthropology* 311–43). Since behavior is more or less continuous, forming a behavioral stream, patterns may be recognized and distinguished from one another through the identification of discontinuities that produce sets of behaviors. Not all patterns are evenly distributed in a society. In Linton's terms, when they are common to all members of a society, they are universal, in contrast to specialties, which are restricted to selected individuals (such as doctors, lawyers, scientists), and to alternatives, which suggest that there are several equally legitimate ways of thinking, doing, knowing (*The Study of Man* 272–74).

Social scientists frequently begin their work through observation of human aggregates; the behavioral patterns they describe constitute the *overt culture*. This includes socially standardized motor activities readily understood by the members of the subject people, e.g., houses, books, canoes, speech forms, clothing, and appropriate postures for particular situations. But no description would be complete without *covert culture*. It is not directly observable because sentiments, beliefs, values, and fears may only be inferred from what people say about their own subjective states. It may be necessary to use psychological depth techniques to obtain data on this dimension of culture.

There is a closely related distinction between *explicit* and *implicit* cultural patterns. Explicit patterns are readily verbalized by members of a group. This implies that the pattern is recognized and defined by the people being studied. The reference is to the cognitive ''map'' by which people orient their behavior more or less rationally. Most Americans can readily describe at least part of a school system, the manner of staffing it, the norms controlling it, and how they have to behave in relation to it. Implicit cultural patterns, in contrast, are forms of behavior about which no coherent account can be given, even though they have the same compelling force. In the U.S., social relationships between friends or between husband and wife are in large measure controlled by implicit canons of appropriateness, rather than by explicit norms; one ''knows'' how to behave. Most users of any language speak grammatically although they may not know the rules of the grammar. Implicit culture may also refer to assumptions, postulates, and themes never made explicit.

When people in a society give expression to the appropriate mode of behaving, that is, make statements about the way they should behave, the way they would like to behave, or the way they believe they behave, they are describing the *ideal culture*. The term refers to the perceptual, cognitive, and evaluative behavior of a people. Cultural ideals do not imply desirability. For example, if a member of a community asserts that delinquency is getting out of hand and if this sentiment is shared by a large proportion of the community, the members are making ''ideal'' statements that may have no basis in fact. Only careful social studies of the actual behavior of juveniles can reveal the real culture (sometimes called manifest culture). Empirical evidence alone can establish the difference or concordance between ideal and real patterns. If the discrepancy between the ideal and the real is appreciated in a society, this may provide the occasion for the introduction of change.

Cultural patterns and their arrangements may be said to be facilitating insofar as they extend man's control over his environment and society. Machines that allow man to harness and convert energy and social arrangements and organizations with the associated values, norms, beliefs, and knowledge allow man to increase and extend his activities. On the other hand, every culture includes rules and limitations on man's behavior; there are patterned ways of *restraining* man. Every culture has not only systems of prescription but also systems of proscription manifest in rules against aggression, the control of the sexual impulse illustrated in the universal prohibition of incest, etc. The specific and concrete content and structure of these patterns varies considerably from culture to culture.

Man's culture, ideas, beliefs, norms, and the products of his activities tend to outlive particular individuals and generations. Culture is the nongenetic social heritage (Linton) that is not entirely based on a particular human organism; individuals are born into a culture, and often the culture outlives them. In this sense, culture becomes superorganic (Kroeber). All the same, without the biological organism in which thinking, feeling, and acting take place, culture would cease to exist. Culture is man-made; it is also dependent on man's normal constitution. Much, if not all, cultural activity centers on biological needs. For this reason, there is an organic base for culture.

Analysis of Content. The culture *trait* or *element* refers to an identifiable unit of a culture. How small or how large a trait is is determined by the purpose of the analysis. Pattern and trait are sometimes used interchangeably; however, methodologically, this is not altogether accurate, because a pattern is a more abstract derivation of observed behavior that is regular and recurring, whereas a trait relates more directly to observed behavior, a cultural artifact, or other feature. Thus, fishing, hunting, or agriculture may be considered cultural traits when they have diagnostic value for establishing relationships between cultures. For an archeologist, the tempering of clay used for pottery or the technique used for making a pot (e.g., using a wheel, or coiling the clay and molding it with an anvil paddle) may be diagnostic traits that differentiate and relate culture.

Combinations of traits that are organized or related to one another so that they form an organic unity are called culture *complexes.* The traits persist in certain fixed relationships. Thus if any one trait considered vital for the complex is removed, the complex has become another thing. The plow complex, for instance, is comprised of a draft animal, a harness, a plow, and a male operator. After making its first appearance in Mesopotamia more than 5,500 years ago, it reached nearly every part of the world. Archeologists and at least one cultural anthropologist have also used the term *assemblage,* ''a cluster or associated body of ideas, symbols, artifacts and behavior called into play by a culturally significant event.'' The various parts of an assemblage are *components.* Assemblages, unlike complexes, are clusters of traits that appear only in certain situations, such as initiation rites [M. E. Opler, ''Component, Assemblage, and Theme in Cultural Integration and Differentiation,'' *American Anthropologist* 61 (1959) 955–64].

Interest in the geographic distribution of cultural traits and complexes, that is, the spatial classification of cultures, gave rise to the concept of the *culture area.* It was suggested by museum presentations of ethnological specimens (traits of material culture) according to geographical areas (rather than some evolutionary or other taxonomic scheme). Clark Wissler recalled, ''We saw that the natives of the New World could be grouped according to single culture traits, giving us food areas, textile areas, ceramic areas, etc. If, however, we take all the traits into simultaneous consideration and shift our view to the social, or tribal units, we are able to form fairly definite groups. This will give us culture areas, or classification of culture groups according to their culture traits'' [*The American Indian* (2d ed. New York 1922) 217–18].

Kroeber not only expanded this new research and drew some new boundaries for the more than 15 culture areas in the New World, but was interested also in the degree to which there was concordance between them and natural areas. In some instances, as in California, the northwest coast, and the plains, there was considerable concordance; elsewhere there was little or none, suggesting the interdependence of culture and environment, but no direct causal relationship. There is no agreement on criteria for classifying culture areas, and authors tend to draw boundaries differently. An attempt to classify ethnic units as cult units met considerable criticism, partially because it did not resolve the problem of the relatively impressionistic way in which traits, complexes, etc., are selected for classification [R. Narroll et al., ''On Ethnic Unit Classification,'' *Current Anthropology* 5 (1964) 283–312].

Although cultural content is presented variously according to problems under consideration and methodology, it is generally agreed that all cultures share some broad, descriptive qualities. Detailed catalogues of cultural elements have been designed for field workers and analysts, e.g., British Association for Advancement of Science, *Notes and Queries on Anthropology* (6th ed. London 1951), and Human Relations Area Files, *Outline of Cultural Materials* (New Haven, Connecticut 1961). These descriptive outlines attempt to group cultural findings under headings that are general enough to be labeled cultural universals since they apply to all cultures of mankind, viz: (1) Technology, the utilization of natural resources to secure food and manufacture tools, weapons, clothing, shelters, containers, and other artifacts necessary to life. (2) Economic organization, comprising the patterns of behavior and the resultant organization of society relative to production, distribution, and consumption of goods and services. (3) Social organization, comprising the social institutions that determine the positions of men and women in a society and thus channel their personal relationships into two major classes, those that derive from KINSHIP and those that derive from the more or less free association of individuals. (4) Political organization, frequently included under social organization but more recently the focus of special attention as pertaining to social relationships involving leadership and its administrative apparatus, recognized legal machinery, police, armies, and the form and control of social conflict on local and national levels. (5) Education, viewed broadly as comprising all the ways through which the individual learns the appropriate ways of behaving in his cultural milieu, including not only the conscious transmission of culture to the individual, but also the ways in which the culture subtly molds the individual to become an acceptable member of his group or the other groups he joins during his life cycle. (6) Religion, that behavior relative to man's relations to unknown forces and the concomitant systems of belief and ritual associated with such forces. *See* RELIGION (IN PRIMITIVE CULTURE). (7) Symbolic culture, encompassing ''systems of symbols and the techniques of using them relative to the acquisition, ordering, transferring of knowledge,'' especially through language, which becomes an intricate part of culture if not the most important part of the system of symbols, and also through the arts, folklore, drama, and music [R. R. Beals and H. Hoijer, *An Introduction to Anthropology* (2d ed. New York 1965) 287–88].

Integration of Culture. It is a widely accepted assumption in the social sciences that cultures differ not only in content but also in the *integration* or organization of their components. In this view cultures form systems with limits that are more or less open.

Uniqueness. The idea that a culture is more than the sum of its parts is expressed in a variety of ways. Ruth Benedict was a pioneer in illustrating integration in terms of a unified plan, a *Leitmotiv*, or configuration. She wrote that "a culture, like an individual, is a more or less consistent pattern of thought and action. Within each culture there comes into being characteristic purposes not necessarily shared by other types of society. In obedience to these purposes, each people further and further consolidates its experience, and in proportion to the urgency of these drives, the heterogeneous items of behavior take more and more congruous shape" [*Patterns of Culture* (New York 1934) 42]. Not all cultures succeed equally well in integrating these heterogeneous items. Benedict isolated and described two major motifs, the Apollonian among the Pueblo peoples and the Dionysian among the Plains peoples: "The desire of the Dionysian, in personal experience or in ritual, is to press through it toward a certain psychological state, to achieve access. . . . He values the illuminations of frenzy. . . . The Apollonian distrusts all this and has often little idea of the nature of such experiences. . . . He keeps the middle of the road, stays within the known map, does not meddle with disruptive psychological states" (72).

A psychological emphasis is also reflected in the concept of ethos, a general term designating the affective character of a culture. For some, however, it is less inclusive and differentiates between the major values, implicit premises, acquired drives, etc., that underlie behavior. J. Honigmann describes the ethos of the Kaska of British Columbia in terms of ego-centricity, utilitarianism, deference, flexibility, dependence, and emotional isolation; these emotional qualities "explain" their behavior in different situations [*Culture and Ethos of Kaska Society* (New Haven 1949)]. As Kroeber remarks, the concept of ethos emphasizes cultural goals and purposes and refers "not so much to the specific ethics or moral code of the culture as to its total quality, to what would constitute disposition or character in an individual; to the system of ideals and values that dominate the culture and so tend to control the type of behavior of its members" (*Anthropology* 294).

Continuity. Emphasizing the historical continuity of cultures, and viewing a culture as a historically derived system, Kroeber has sought cultural climaxes in the major culture areas of the world, on the assumption that the accumulation of cultural traits "seems to have corresponded essentially with a period of successful organization of culture content—organization in part into a conscious system of ideas but especially into an integrated nexus of styles, standards and values" ["Cultural Intensity and Climax" in *The Nature of Culture* (Chicago 1952) 340]. In recognition of the diachronic integration of culture, Robert Redfield has referred to the relation of historical events to one another and to the central purposes of the small community. Large complex societies (e.g., civilizations) are composed of cities *and* villages, urbanites *and* peasants that form societies within societies (part-societies) and have corresponding great and little traditions. The great tradition cultivated in schools or temples is the tradition of the philosopher, theologian, and literary man that is handed down from generation to generation. "The little tradition works itself out and keeps itself going in the lives of the unlettered" in the small community and among the great majority of little people. But "the two traditions are interdependent. Great and little traditions have long affected each other and continue to do so" through the interchange of personnel. The priests in the village, for instance, as carriers of the great tradition, have to modify their approach to villagers, and the urbanite is dependent upon the services and products of the peasant (*Peasant Society and Culture* 70–71). Characteristic of Redfield's approach is his use of tradition as an over-arching principle that integrates apparent opposites that are themselves historically derived.

Functional Integration. Another approach to the problem of cultural integration derives from the recognition that elements in culture may be functionally related to one another or to a cultural whole. Functional integration in the past has stressed pattern maintenance and need satisfaction. The functional interpretations of Malinowski and A. R. Radcliffe-Brown were both concerned with whole cultural systems, but with important differences. According to Malinowski, functional integration is achieved when cultural traits, complexes, and institutions serve individual needs in a society. To the extent that cultural elements promote adaptation to the social and natural environment, to that extent the culture is more, rather than less, integrated. Radcliffe-Brown was concerned with how the relation of sociocultural arrangements to one another helps to maintain the system rather than the individual. The family, for example, in addition to its obvious reproductive function, contributes to the continuity of the society through all its associated behavior patterns, be they economic, religious, legal, or political. Such functional integration presumably contributes to social cohesion, social stability, and group solidarity.

Themes. Linton also stressed the interrelationships of parts in the concept of cultural interest: "Every culture has several interests which are of primary importance and which together constitute an integrated system. To select even two or three of these as the focal points for the whole culture configuration probably involves a distortion of the actual condition, but such distortion is requisite to any comprehensible descriptive account" (*The Study of Man* 443). So too, when members of a society show much concern about a particular cultural feature, such as success in American culture, this can be called a cultural focus (Herskovits) since apparently unrelated behavioral elements come to a focus at this point and integrate or relate diverse patterns of behavior. Recognizing the contradictions as well as the relationships in culture, Opler has suggested that culture patterns may be integrated around several themes, since most cultures appear not to have as total an integration as Benedict's work suggests. A theme is "a postulate or position, declared or implied, and usually controlling behavior or stimulating activity, which is tacitly approved or openly promoted in a society" ["Some Recently Developed Concepts Relating to Culture," *Southwestern Journal of Anthropology* 4 (1948) 120]. Analysis recognizes the interplay of themes and dynamic qualities. Similarly the notion of postulates of culture (Hoebel) calls attention to the logical integration in all societies. Sorokin speaks of the logico-meaningful integration that "has its own common denominator of all relevant phenomena: it is the identity (or similarity) of central meaning, idea, or mental bias that permeates all logically related fragments" [*Social and Cultural Dynamics* 4 v. (New York 1937–41) 1.24]. Thus, the apparent irrationality of exotic peoples can be explained away if the observer is able to isolate basic assumptions of their cultures. Contradictions can be understood either in terms of compartmentalization—where the people under study do not perceive any connection between two sets of behavior—or of an underlying assumption about life in general that explains the relationships between apparently divergent phenomena.

Values. In an attempt to bring sociological, psychological, and philosophical ideas pertaining to the ideational realm of culture into a more general frame of reference, the Harvard department of social relations has investigated problems of cultural values. Clyde Kluckhohn has defined a value as a conceptualization "explicit, or implicit, distinctive of an individual or characteristic of a group, of the desirable which influences the selection from available modes, means, and ends of action," and value orientations as "complex, but definitely patterned (rank ordered) principles, resulting from the transactional interplay of three analytically distinguishable elements of the evaluative process—the cognitive, the affective, and the directive elements-which give order and direction to the ever-flowing stream of human acts and thoughts as these relate to the solution of common human problems" ["Values and Value Orientations in the Theory of Action" in T. Parsons et al., *Toward a General Theory of Action* (Cambridge, Massachusetts 1951) 395, 411]. An important contribution of this effort is the stress on the valuation process and the attempt to move beyond the static description of structural integration of culture. This approach tries not only to emphasize the rational (logical) and purely subjective (affective) modes through which individuals in a culture orient themselves, but recognizes also that "there would be no ordered, no systematic, value system without a directive tendency which both aids in the selection among possible value systems and also serves to give continuity to the total system" [F. R. Kluckhohn and F. L. Strodtbeck, *Variations in Value Orientations* (Evanston, Illinois 1961) 8].

Culture, Society, and Individual

As Kroeber and Kluckhohn have explained, "culture is produced and changed, concretely, by individuals. . . each distinctive life-way is also the product of a group. Yet culture is not necessarily tied throughout time to a particular society. Islamic culture, as we know it today, cuts across communities, societies, and nations. Roman society ceased to exist as such more than a millennium ago, but Roman culture was a vital force throughout the Middle Ages and, in certain aspects, is still alive today" (*op. cit.* 367). For analytical purposes at least, concrete behavior and its products may be conceptualized in social, cultural, and psychological dimensions. These dimensions are not empirically but analytically distinct. There is, however, no unified theory of human behavior, and what is social or cultural or psychological is not always agreed upon.

Culture and Personality. The individual is born into a human group (usually the social subsystem called the family) composed of culturally defined social roles that assure the helpless infant's reaching maturity. Unlike other animals, the human child depends for a long time on other members of his society to satisfy and meet his many needs in the maturation process. This dependency varies in length of time, however; in American society, for example, as compared with many others, it is extended considerably beyond puberty. At first the needs of the infant are met within the basic or extended family, but the modes in which they are met vary in accordance with customary ways of raising babies (i.e., with cultural systems). By the time the individual reaches maturity (also variable according to cultural prescriptions, but usually defined as the time when he can provide for his own needs), he has well established habits. This is not to say that the habits may not be changed, that new ones cannot be learned or some old ones be displaced. The processes of socialization (learning the appropriate social responses) and enculturation (learning the appropriate cultural responses in terms of symbols, etc.) are never-ending. This human capability also makes possible cultural change.

The individual learns his social and cultural system and those of others (if he travels or is forced to live in another system) both through formal and informal means. These include schools or their equivalents in nonliterate societies (e.g., initiation rites) and habituation; that is, cultural and social behaviors are learned without being explicitly taught—they are "just picked up"—and in this there is little conscious learning but rather unconscious imitation. Nevertheless, even in relatively small communities, no person ever acquires the whole inventory of all behavioral responses appropriate to his culture. In part this is related to the various ways in which people organize themselves to educate their children. The system of social interaction may bring individuals in close association in schools, with grandparents, with organized groups of older children who teach younger ones (as in age-graded societies), or with the community as a whole. Learning occurs when appropriate behavior is rewarded or approval is withheld. Even when the socializing and enculturating processes fail, and when the individual may be said to be socially or mentally ill, rebellion is manifested in terms of his own culture and society.

The individual acquires his culture within the ever-expanding network of social relationships. Culture may be thought of as the medium in which the personality develops. Thus the techniques and ideas that individuals learn have a lasting effect on the adult person; yet these cultural behaviors differ between groups, communities, and societies. It is possible to say that different norms and social institutions produce different personality structures; and if they are widely shared in a population, the result is referred to as basic personality, i.e., "a structure of articulated personality characteristics and processes attributable, non-statistically, to almost all members of some culturally bounded population" (A. F. C. Wallace, *Culture and Personality* 106). The statistical distribution of personality traits determined by certain psychological tests (Thematic Apperception or Rorschach tests, for instance) discloses modal personality. The significance of personality variation lies in the fact that different societies and cultures may emphasize or reward some types more than others. Consequences for the direction of culture change may result through suppression of those who do not have the requisite personality traits or of those whose personalities are not malleable enough to change.

Culture and Social Relations. Social relationships as elements of the social system are greatly influenced by culture. In the process of maturation the individual learns cultural obligations, first from interacting with his mother, later with other members of his family, and eventually with individuals outside the family. Each person met affects the individual in some way, but the relationships are reciprocal; that is, all individuals involved in interaction have certain expectations of each other. To the extent that an individual learns to meet these expectations, others in his interactive network of social relationships will reward him according to the standards set by the culture. Although the expectations of two or more interacting individuals must in some degree be complementary, they need not be identical and indeed rarely are. It is the regularity of expectations that allows social life, for it ensures a necessary minimum of predictability among individuals. Learning a culture may be said to involve meeting expectations and holding them in the mind and using the appropriate ones in the appropriate situations.

The social system can be conceived in terms of reciprocal social relationships and mutually adjusted expectations and their controlling norms; this pattern is called a system of social roles (analogous to but not identical with theatrical roles). Social roles are performed by actors—the term calls attention to the interchangeability of individuals in the role. Not everyone performs a role according to culturally standardized expectations; nevertheless role performance is socially controlled and involves positive and negative sanctions in conformity with cultural norms. An individual who does not meet the standards or who violates the norms associated with the role must relinquish the role. For example, a man who does not meet the socially and culturally defined role expectations of the father may lose this role by having his children placed in foster homes. Legal sanctions are brought against him. It is useful, however, to distinguish between the individual personality, sometimes referred to by the individual as the "real me," and the social personality, which reflects the capacity and the quality of the individual in performing his role, the "social me." Although one affects the other, it is the individual style with which roles are performed that gives considerable variation in role performance. The latitude allowed in role performance is, however, a matter determined largely by the cultural norms.

It is easy to reduce personality to cultural and social explanations or to equate personality traits with cultural traits (cf. Benedict). In regard to homogeneous cultures, there appears to be much concordance between culture and personality. But the "fit" is not precise in complex heterogeneous cultures, and consequently the ideas of modal personality extended to national character have been challenged. There is currently no satisfactory theory to account for the recognized empirical interrelationships between culture, society, and the individual.

Theories of Culture Growth

Man in nearly all cultures has been concerned about his origins, development, and differences and has proposed many different explanations in myth, fantasy, and theory. By the beginning of the 19th century there was a strong tendency to formulate evolutionary theories. A hundred years later there was a decided reaction against such sweeping explanations and a new interest in detailed, historically descriptive studies. More recently, evolutionary schemes have again become important in social science. It is convenient to discuss these theories under three headings: (1) evolutionary approaches, old and new, (2) historical explanations, and (3) diffusionism. Recent views of cultural change are presented in a final section.

Evolutionary Theories. Underlying most ideas of cultural growth is the observation that for mankind as a whole culture has expanded in time and space. The ever-increasing finds of archeology and human paleontology have suggested that man's culture began simply and increased in content and complexity through the ages. Levels of cultural growth are recognized: the life of the earliest men was concerned principally with food gathering and was followed by the slow acquisition of additional knowledge and techniques leading to food production prior to the development of urban centers and the rise of states. Evidence for these levels or stages has been accumulated from the Middle East, Asia, and the Americas.

The early accumulation of evidence from history and prehistory led to increased speculation on the origin and growth of "high" cultures. Klemm tried to show in his early work how mankind had passed through successive stages of savagery, tameness, and freedom. August COMTE, sometimes referred to as the father of sociology, had man advancing from the theological to the metaphysical to the positive, or scientific, stage. Herbert SPENCER, although less optimistic about the advances of mankind, nevertheless had man pass through fixed stages dictated by "natural law." By 1860, which marks a turning point in thinking about man's development, explanations of cultural growth were given a distinct evolutionary turn by the influence of Charles DARWIN's Origin of Species (1859).

Analogies with Biological Evolution. The presumed analogy between biological evolution and cultural evolu-

tion stimulated much research, leading investigators into a number of blind alleys yet increasing the yield of data through field investigations. Evolutionary theories assumed that elements of culture appearing among the simplest contemporary societies were "survivals" from the past and that the evolutionary process moved from simplicity in the direction of increasing complexity and heterogeneity. Thus, the customs of man could be arranged in a series, or in stages, generally divided into savagery, barbarism, and civilization. The comprehensive approaches of the British anthropologist Tylor and the American Lewis Henry Morgan ordered the numerous ethnographic data on "a rough scale of civilization [representing] a transition from the savage state to our own" (Tylor, *Primitive Culture,* 1.24). Morgan divided the stages of mankind into smaller subdivisions, noting the appearance of diagnostic cultural traits to mark the "necessary sequences of progress" (*Ancient Society,* New York 1877).

Unilinear evolutionary thought of the 19th century proposed theories of progress rather than empirical formulations of what actually happened. It was based on faulty evidence, did not take into account regional variations, and underplayed the effects of cultural borrowing. Differences in the various conditions of mankind were explained in terms of climate, soil, race, and other factors; yet the mainspring for this progress was attributed to a never-defined psychic unity characteristic of all mankind. Major limitations of 19th-century evolutionary explanations may be traced to uncritical comparisons of cultural traits without recognition of the importance of their functional integration and the contexts in which they appeared.

Neoevolutionary Theories. Current theories of cultural growth are considerably more sophisticated, largely because better and more extensive archeological and ethnographic data have become available. Even modern sociology has reintroduced the problem of social evolution. The major difference between the older approaches and the more recent ones is the development of criteria for the assessment of evolutionary change. Leslie A. White has had considerable influence on contemporary thought by suggesting as an objective measure of progress the increasingly efficient use of human effort through technological control. This index is based on the assumption that "cultures are dynamic systems; they require energy for their activation. The history of civilization is the story of the control over forces of nature by cultural means" (362). In his view, the cultural system is "a series of three horizontal strata: the technological layer on the bottom, the philosophical on the top, the sociological stratum in between," but "the technological system is basic and primary" (366). As technology changes, especially through its ability to convert energy ever more efficiently, so also culture as a whole is transformed. The social and philosophical strata are admitted to have a conditioning but not a determining influence upon technology. White's cultural determinism has been criticized by a number of contemporary anthropologists, especially by those who give primary or at least equal weight to the important influence of ideas, values, and social relationships.

Concern for the causes underlying the development and evolution of culture has led J. H. Steward to look at the relationship of technology and environment as a problem of adjustment. Varying adjustment patterns give rise to different successive "levels of sociocultural integration" (43–63). Changes occurring in any part of the sociocultural system may become basic adjustments. The ecological adjustments made in simple hunting and gathering cultures constitute a cultural core around which family, religion, and other cultural activities are integrated to form cultural types. But through any shift in the relationships of cultural patterns (resulting from either innovation or cultural contact) the core may take on a new structure; and as population and other factors also change, a new level of sociocultural integration is achieved. Steward made a tentative test of this hypothesis by comparing the development of five early cultures culminating in civilizations in Mesopotamia, Egypt, North China, northern Peru, and Meso-America. All developed from a hunting and gathering base in a semiarid environment and followed similar sequences through incipient agriculture, a formative stage, regional florescence, an initial empire, dark ages, to cyclical conquests.

Although Steward's formulations lack precision, they have nevertheless given rise to new interpretations, especially by Robert J. Braidwood and G. R. Willey. These theories of multilinear evolutionism are cognizant of the complexity of the problems of diverse sequences of cultural development in different parts of the world. Thus Steward and other neoevolutionists, in proceeding carefully, have begun to establish sequences of development that are not as all-encompassing as those of the universal evolutionists, but account more adequately for processes in cultural development.

Change and the Moral Order. Although not in the stream of cultural evolutionism, Redfield was also concerned with long-term change. Much of his early work was devoted to the integration of the folk society in contrast to the urban society. The folk society is a characteristically small, isolated, close-knit, homogeneous entity. Its social relationships are principally patterned around kinship; its members have a supernaturalistic world view; and its values are more implicit than explicit. Civilization, in contrast, consists not only of things added to soci-

ety—such as cities, writing, public works, the state, the market—but also of increased heterogeneity, increased division of labor, partial displacement of personal ties by impersonal ones, replacement of family connections by political affiliation and contract, and increased reflective and systematic thought. Redfield was mainly concerned about the role of the moral order in transforming the folk society and the role of the individual in changing this moral order. Going back to the preurbanized folk society and tracing changing ethical judgments through to the present, he found that even the earliest evidence suggested that moral behavior was strongly sanctioned and that at no time did man in his history behave selfishly without restraint. Historically speaking, the major transformations of the primitive world have involved an increase and widening of humane standards. But from the start, the nexus for holding human groups together, no matter how primitive or civilized, was the moral order and the ideas on which it is based. Redfield's views provide a balance to the materialistic interpretation of culture and history by White, V. G. Childe, and others. According to Redfield, "it is not enough to say that the technical order is destroyer of the moral order, it is not enough to identify civilization with development in the technical order alone. It is also to be recognized that the effects of the technical order include the creation of new moral orders. . . . Through civilization also people are stimulated to moral creativeness. Civilization is also ideas in history. It is new vision, fresh and bold insights, perceptions and teachings of religious and ethical truth which could not have come about had there not been the expansion of the technical order" [*The Primitive World and its Transformation* (New York 1953) 77].

This implies that standards of evaluation can be applied to different societies, and in this Redfield agreed with Kroeber, who suggested some indices to measure progress, viz, the decline of magic and superstition; the "decline of infantile obsession with the outstanding physiological events in human life"; and finally technology, mechanics, and science, which show most clearly the cumulative effect in culture. But Redfield pointed out that, even in evaluating the development of mankind, judgments among social scientists have changed as well. The relativism that was characteristic of much of the social science of the first half of the 20th century, in which all cultures were considered to be equally valid, has given way to a critical reappraisal of the development of mankind as a whole. Although the canons of social science involve nonjudgmental statements, contemporary evaluations of societies lay special stress on the degree to which these societies achieve their own goals and aspirations.

Historical Explanations. Historical explanations of the growth of culture may be said to have been particularistic because they avoided broad generalizations and emphasized description and the uniqueness of cultural systems and events in any historical period. Many of the cultural studies of the early 20th century were reactions to the unilinear explanations that were criticized as impressionistic and premature.

American Historical School. The German-born anthropologist Franz Boas reacted strongly against the evolutionary trend in theory, and his opinions influenced social science for at least a generation. In his attack on the comparative method (identified with evolutionism), he pointed out that similarities between cultural traits did not necessarily prove historical connections and common origins. Instead he called for a detailed study of customs in particular cultures in relation to the natural environment and the neighboring cultural and social groups. Through minute studies of this sort the historical causes of the formation of individual customs or whole cultures could be ascertained. Such detailed studies would also illumine the psychological processes contributing to the development of culture. In this view the growth of culture results from the creative abilities of the members of a society and from borrowing from neighboring cultures. This so-called American historical school thus proceeded pragmatically and showed the fallacy of other broad generalizations, especially those of the racial, geographic, and economic determinists.

Boas and his students made important contributions to the study of cultural processes and encouraged many field studies of Native Americans. But they also initiated a trend toward reification of cultural traits; that is, traits were taken out of their context and handled statistically. Culture then became an object *sui generis* that frequently was unrelated to the individuals who manifested it. The active element was culture; the individual was passive. In this extreme form, cultural determinism was, however, somewhat limited. The approach nevertheless imposed critical rules for historical reconstruction; isolated principles of order, especially those pertaining to time and space distributions and to the recognition of cultural patterning; traced concrete events of diffusion and invention when possible; and presented the broad unity of the biocultural potential of all mankind.

Many anthropologists used the framework of the culture area. In the absence of written histories they borrowed the age-area hypotheses from the biologists when they needed a device for introducing a time dimension into their distributional studies. The implication of the hypothesis is that the traits most widely distributed in an area also have the greatest antiquity. But such traits and complexes as Buddhism, though widely distributed in Asia, do not represent the oldest religious forms. Although this hypothesis has proved valuable in areas where cultures have been diffused at a slow pace and by word of mouth, it is not valid in other culture areas.

Cyclical Theories. Among culture historians another trend is in evidence. Impressed by the rise and decline of specific civilizations, they have developed analogies with the human life cycle. Unlike the evolutionists, who postulated the inevitability of progress and perfection, these theorists postulated the inevitability of the cycle. Oswald SPENGLER's *Der Untergang des Abendlandes* (2 v. Munich 1919–22) was perhaps the most influential of works of its kind, although in modified form others less pessimistic also dwelt on the apparent cyclical nature of historical events. Spengler maintained that the West, which had created industrial society, was losing to the awakening Orient, a view that received some support from events after World War I. The difficulty with this and other cyclical interpretations of history is the tendency to focus principally on political and military domination as criteria of ascendancy. Historians such as A. J. Toynbee [*A Study of History,* 12 v. (London 1948–61)], although considerably more moderate, hold to the idea that cultures rise and grow in response to a challenge. The manner in which Toynbee has selected his data to support his thesis has brought doubt upon his formulations. Furthermore, it is not clear that he has unambiguously identified and connected challenges with responses, a task of doubtful validity in any case. For the investigator who is dependent on documentary evidence, incomplete as it is, this becomes an extremely difficult undertaking.

Diffusionism. Although the American approach was concerned with diffusion, it was limited in scope. Studies of actual diffusion were confined to local and regional reconstructions, the interrelations of tribal and cultural areas, and the distribution of cultural elements over larger or smaller segments of the world. The focal interest was in relationships among cultures in the New World and the development of New World cultures in relative isolation from those of the Old World.

Extreme diffusionism had its sources in England and on the Continent. In England, E. G. Smith, for example, held that all cultures were ultimately traceable to one center, the valley of the Nile, and that after a technological spurt with concomitant cultural development, the culture had spread to the Mediterranean and hence to the rest of the world [*The Migrants of Early Culture* (Manchester 1915)]. The basic assumption underlying this approach is man's basic uninventiveness. Trade and other forms of travel and communication are considered to be the only means by which culture can develop and spread. This was supposed to have taken place all across Asia and even to Middle America via the Pacific Ocean. This approach discounted the formidable obstacles of oceans and land and magnified superficial similarities of form to the exclusion of function and meaning (e.g., in comparing Mayan and Egyptian pyramids). Furthermore, there is no evidence in intervening areas of any movement of either people or cultural traits from the postulated Egyptian center. The theory was not accepted in England, on the Continent, or in America.

A more scholarly and scientific approach to the spread of culture took the form of the German-Austrian Kulturkreis Theory that emanated from the Vienna school of Wilhelm SCHMIDT, SVD. In spite of the tremendous scholarly effort of the followers of this approach, it was eventually considered inadequate, at least as a unified theoretical approach, even by its former proponents.

Culture Change

Older views in the study of culture change tended to focus on cultural elements themselves. The emphasis has shifted to the study of the changing relationships between elements; change between groups of individuals, sharing a common or different culture; change between segments of a society; and adjustments of individual personalities to their changing culture (see Wolf, 53–86, for a partial review of changes in anthropological thinking after World War II).

Culture change is viewed in terms of the modification of the cultural system and subsystems, not merely as the addition, loss, or modification of cultural elements. Processes of culture change are only now being classified and involve such ideas as integration, adaptation, and isolation—all operating on social, cultural, and psychological levels. There is currently no unified theory of culture change, but many hypotheses and propositions have been put forward to explain the large body of empirical observations.

Bibliography: D. BIDNEY, *Theoretical Anthropology* (New York 1953). F. BOAS, *The Mind of Primitive Man* (New York 1938); *Race, Language and Culture* (New York 1940). R. J. BRAIDWOOD and G. R. WILLEY, eds., *Courses toward Urban Life* (Chicago 1962). T. G. HARDING et al., *Evolution and Culture,* ed. M. D. SAHLINS and E. R. SERVICE (Ann Arbor, Michigan 1960). M. J. HERSKOVITS, *Man and His Works: the Science of Cultural Anthropology* (New York 1949). J. J. HONIGMANN, *Culture and Personality* (New York 1954). A. L. KROEBER, *Anthropology* (new ed. New York 1948); *Cultural and Natural Areas of Native North America* (Berkeley 1954); ed., *Anthropology Today* (Chicago 1953). A. L. KROEBER and C. KLUCKHOHN, *Culture: a Critical Review of Concepts and Definitions* (Cambridge, Massachusetts 1952; repr. pa. New York 1963). R. LINTON, *The Study of Man* (New York 1936); ed., *The Science of Man in the World Crisis* (New York 1945). B. MALINOWSKI, *A Scientific Theory of Culture, and Other Essays* (Chapel Hill, North Carolina 1944). W. E. MOORE, *Social Change* (Englewood Cliffs, New Jersey 1963). A. R. RADCLIFFE-BROWN, *A Natural Science of Society* (New York 1957). R. REDFIELD, *The Little Community: Viewpoints for the Study of a Human Whole* (Chicago 1955); *Peasant Society and Culture: An Anthropological Approach to Civilization* (Chicago 1956). N.J. and W. T. SMELSER, *Personality and Social Systems* (New York 1963). J. H. STEWARD, *Theory of Cultural Change* (Urbana, Illinois 1955). A. F. C. WALLACE, *Culture and Personality* (pa. New York 1961). L. A. WHITE, *The Science of Culture* (New York 1949). E. R. WOLF, *Anthropology* (Englewood Cliffs, New Jersey 1964).

[G. O. LANG]

CUM OCCASIONE

A bull of INNOCENT X dated May 31, 1653, that condemned the five propositions attributed to C. JANSEN in his work entitled *AUGUSTINUS*. These five propositions, formulated for the first time by the trustee of the Sorbonne, Nicolas Cornet, in July of 1649, had been delated to the Holy See at the beginning of 1651 by the bishop of Vabres, Isaac Habert, with whom 78 other bishops joined. This bull had been written after long discussions at Rome in the commissions of the cardinals and later of the theologians named by the pope, at which the deputies sent by the French Jansenist group had been authorized to present their various writings in the defense of Jansen. Besides, within the commission itself, this defense was remarkably strengthened by the Franciscan Luke Wadding. In the bull the five propositions were separately classified: the first four were declared heretical; and the fifth, false and capable of becoming heretical in a special sense. It was declared at the beginning that the propositions were condemned in connection with the book by Jansen, but they were not altogether clearly attributed to it; this fact later gave rise to complicated discussions to find out if Jansen had really sustained them, and in what sense. Moreover, Innocent X later declared verbally that in publishing this bull he wished to give full protection to the doctrine of St. AUGUSTINE.

Bibliography: H. DENZINGER, *Enchiridion symbolorum,* ed. A. SCHÖNMETZER (Freiburg 1963) 2001–07. L. CEYSSENS, "La cinquième des propositions condamnées de Jansenius: sa portée théologique papal bull *Cum Occasione,*" in *Jansenius et le jansenisme dans les Pays-Bas* (Leuven 1982) 39–53.

[L. J. COGNET]

CUMMINGS, JEREMIAH WILLIAMS

Parish priest, writer; b. Washington, D.C., April 15, 1814; d. New York City, Jan. 4, 1866. His family were Northern Irish Protestants, who had immigrated to the U.S. and settled (*c.* 1782) in Washington; his maternal granduncle, Capt. Worthy Stephenson, was one of the founders of the city of Washington, and was grand marshal when Gen. George Washington laid the cornerstone of the Capitol. His mother's conversion to the Catholic Church, shortly after his birth, led to an estrangement from her family and, later, to her removal to New York. There Cummings was one of the few students in Bp. John Dubois's short-lived seminary at Nyack; later he attended the College of the Propaganda, Rome, Italy, where he was ordained Jan. 3, 1847. On his return to New York he served first as curate at old St. Patrick's Cathedral, and in November 1848 was appointed first pastor of St. Stephen's parish, where he spent the rest of his life. He made it one of the most prominent parishes in New York, well-known for the excellence of the liturgical ceremonies and music. An accomplished linguist, writer, and speaker, he was a friend of Orestes BROWNSON and contributed to his *Review.* When Cummings criticized the prevailing system of Catholic education and seminary training, a bitter controversy ensued during which New York's Abp. John Hughes replied in his noted essay "Reflections on the Catholic Press." Besides contributing to *Brownson's Review,* Cummings also wrote for *Appleton's Encyclopedia* and published *Italian Legends* (1859), *Songs for Catholic Schools* (1862), and *Spiritual Progress* (1865).

Bibliography: *Historical Records and Studies of the U.S. Catholic Historical Society of New York* 4 (1906) 100. J. G. SHEA, *The Catholic Churches of New York* (New York 1878). L. J. HUNT, *History of St. Stephen's Parish, 1848–1948* (New York 1948).

[F. D. COHALAN]

CUMMINS, PATRICK

Scripture scholar and humanist; b. Burlington Junction, Mo., April 19, 1880; d. Conception, Feb. 14, 1968. In 1899 he joined the Benedictine community of Conception Abbey, changing his name from John Thomas Benedict to Patrick; he was professed in 1900. From 1902 to 1906 he studied in Europe, first at Sant'Anselmo in Rome (where he received the S.T.D. in 1905), then at Maximilian University in Munich.

He returned to Conception, where he filled the office of novice master and taught languages and philosophy in the seminary. In 1921 he was called back to Sant'Anselmo to be rector and professor of dogmatic theology, posts he held until 1925. In that year he presented proposals for revising the program of studies to the Congress of Abbots; although his proposals brought him into disfavor and forced his return to Conception, they became, 40 years later, the basis of a new Ratio Studiorum for Sant'Anselmo. Most of the rest of his life was passed at Conception in study, teaching, and faithful observance of the monastic life.

His interest in liturgical life was intense and he advocated many elements of liturgical reform long before

their time had come; his translation of the hymns for the Breviary anticipated the vernacular movement, and he contributed a column and many articles to the liturgical publication *Caecilia.* Four areas of his special interest were the PSALMS, DANTE, THOMAS AQUINAS, and G. K. CHESTERTON. His *Dante Theologian* was a translation of and commentary on the *Divine Comedy.* He was president of the Catholic Biblical Association in 1947–48 and contributed many articles and reviews of high quality to the *Catholic Biblical Quarterly* between 1940 and 1950.

In 1941 he proposed that the Catholic Biblical Association, which was then engaged in revising the Douay Old Testament on the basis of the Vulgate, ought rather to undertake a translation from the original languages. When, after the appearance of *Divine Afflante Spiritu* (1943), the Association began a new translation (which reached completion in 1970 as the *New American Bible*), Cummins produced the first draft of Jeremiah. His principle in this work (and in a translation of the Psalms unrelated to the NAB) was to reproduce in English the same number of syllables and the same rhythm as the Hebrew. Although the starkness of his Jeremiah translation was somewhat mitigated in the final version, his pioneer work in rhythm remains significant.

Bibliography: P. CUMMINS, *Dante Theologian: The Divine Comedy* (New York 1948); "A Test Case in Transmission: Jeremias 33:14–26," *The Catholic Biblical Quarterly* 2 (1940) 15–27; "Rhythm, Hebrew and English," 3 (1941) 27–42; "Jerome against Jerome: A Study of Jeremias 3:1," 6 (1944) 85—90; "Semantic Terminilogy: Presidential Address," 11 (1949) 9–13; "Jeremias Orator," 11 (1949) 191–201.

[J. JENSEN]

CUMONT, FRANZ

Belgian archeologist and historian of ancient religions; b. Alost, Belgium, Jan. 3, 1868; d. Brussels, Aug. 19, 1947. He was a professor at the University of Ghent from 1896 to 1910 and curator of the museum at Brussels from 1899 to 1913. He spent the rest of his life as a private scholar in Rome and Paris. His major contributions were made in the field of Oriental religions, and on the afterlife in Greco-Roman paganism. He maintained that there was a marked influence of Iranian religion on the Jewish and Greco-Roman worlds. While he exaggerated the influence of the Oriental mystery religions on Christianity, he recognized the unique and different character of the latter in its essential features. Among his principal works may be mentioned: *Textes et monuments figurés relatifs aux mystères de Mithra* (2 v. Brussels 1896–99); *Astrology and Religion among the Greeks and Romans* (New York and London 1912); *Les Religions orientales dans le paganisme romain* (3d rev. ed., Paris 1929); with J. Bidez, *Les Mages hellénisés* (2 v. Paris 1938); *Recherches sur le symbolisme funéraire des Romains* (Paris 1942); *Lux perpetua* (Paris 1949).

Bibliography: *Mélanges Franz Cumont* (Brussels 1936). F. MAYENCE, *Franz Cumont* (Brussels 1956).

[A. LAURAS]

CUNIALATI, FULGENZIO

Theologian, writer [pseudonym Mariano (degli) Amatori]; b. Venice, Feb. 22, 1685; d. there, Oct. 9, 1759. He entered the Order of Preachers at Conegliano in 1700 and later taught philosophy and theology there. In the probabilist dispute, he favored PROBABILIORISM. His principal work, *Universae theologiae moralis accurate complexio*, 2 v. (Venice 1752), gives moral solutions according to the principles of St. Thomas. He also wrote other ascetical and historical works.

Bibliography: J. F. B. DE RUBEIS, *De rebus congregationis . . . B. Jacobi Salomonii* (Venice 1751) 463, 479–480. R. COULON, *Dictionnaire de théologie catholique*, ed. A. VACANT et al., 15 v. (Paris 1903–50; Tables générales 1951–) 3.2: 2427–28.

[J. F. QUIGLEY]

CUNIBERT OF COLOGNE, ST.

Bishop; b. Moselle region of France, late sixth century; d. *c.* 663. He was educated at the court of Chlotaire II (d. 628) in Metz and at the cathedral school of TRIER, where he later became archdeacon. Consecrated bishop of COLOGNE on Sept. 25, 623, he participated in the synods of Clichy (626–627) and Reims (627–630). Cunibert was a counselor to the mayor of the palace, (Bl.) Pepin of Landen (d. 640), and to King Dagobert I (d. 639). He was also made tutor of Dagobert's young son, SIGEBERT III, and in 634, one of his ministers in Austrasia. During his episcopate, he organized an apparently unsuccessful missionary endeavor among the Frisians, with its center at Utrecht, and founded convents, charitable institutions, and churches, among them St. Clement, later renamed St. Cunibert, in Cologne, where he was buried. His cult has been popular since the ninth century. The medieval lives of the saint, dating probably from the tenth century, are unreliable. In iconography he is represented as a bishop holding a church model with a dove hovering over him.

Feast: Nov. 12.

Bibliography: W. NEUSS, ed., *Geschichte des Erzbistums Köln* (Cologne 1964—) 1:127–131. A. FRANZEN, *Dictionnaire d'histoire et de géographie ecclésiastiques*, ed. A. BAUDRILLART et al. (Paris 1912) 13:1111–12, good bibliog. R. AIGRAIN, *Catholicisme* 3:375. M. COENS, "Les Vies de s. Cunibert de Cologne et la tradition manuscrite," *Analecta Bollandiana* 47 (1929) 338–367.

[M. F. MCCARTHY]

CURIA, ROMAN

The Curia is that complexus of bureaus that the pope uses to implement his judicial, legislative, and executive office as head of the Church. Although it really exists and acts only insofar as he wishes it to, its specific powers are set out in the Code of Canon Law and post-Code documents. By force of tradition and practice, moreover, it has assumed a powerful position in day-to-day Church operations.

History. The history of the Curia can be traced through three periods. From the first to the 11th century, the popes exercised their rule through synods—the *presbyterium apostolicae sedis*—composed of the clergy of Rome. At first priests and deacons were consulted at these gatherings. Later on, from about the sixth century, the priests of principal churches or titles (the first cardinals) and the seven regional deacons of the city composed the synod together with the pope.

During the 11th century the authority of the Roman synod and presbyterium was transferred gradually to the CONSISTORY, made up exclusively of CARDINALS. Alexander III, in 1170, laid down specific rules governing consistorial meetings, and other popes, notably Innocent III, further regulated their power. In later centuries the complexities of papal administration necessitated further modifications. By his celebrated bull *Immensa* (Jan. 22, 1588), Sixtus V both created and regulated all those bureaus that, in one form or another, are still in existence today.

Organization. On June 28, 1988, Pope John Paul II promulgated the apostolic constitution *Pastor Bonus*, to take effect on March 1, 1989, modifying the organization and competencies of the Roman Curia which had been regulated by the norms of the Aug. 15, 1967, apostolic constitution *Regimini ecclesiae universae* issued by Pope Paul VI. The introduction to the new norms highlights the nature of the Curia as an aid to the Petrine ministry in service to the universal Church (n. 3) as well as to the bishops throughout the world (n. 9), and suggests that this reorganization of the Curia makes it conform more closely to the needs of the post-conciliar Church as well as to the exigencies of modern times (n. 13).

The dicasteries, as the various agencies of the Curia are called, include the Secretariat of State (arts. 39–47), nine Congregations (arts. 48–116), three Tribunals (arts.

117–130), 12 PONTIFICAL COUNCILS (arts. 131–170), and three Offices (arts. 171–179), all of which are juridically equal. Other institutes attached to the Curia or related to the Holy See include the Prefecture of the Pontifical Household (arts. 180–181), the Office of Liturgical Celebrations of the Pope (art.182), the Advocates for various tribunals and dicasteries (arts. 183–185), and other important entities such as the Vatican secret archives, the Vatican libraries, press and radio and television (arts. 186–192).

Cardinals and bishops, some residing in Rome and others in various parts of the world, comprise the actual membership of the different congregations (arts. 3–7). They are assisted in their work by secretaries, consultors, administrators and other officials, from both clergy and laity (arts. 8–9, 12). All Curia members and officials are named for five-year terms (art. 5). The dicasteries of the Curia deal with matters beyond the competence of bishops or groups of bishops, as well as with items reserved to the Holy See or committed to them by the Pope (art. 13). No general decrees issued by dicasteries have the force of law or derogate laws unless given specific approbation by the Pope, and no extraordinary business is to be handled by dicasteries without his cognizance (art.18). All of the dicasteries are to foster good relationships with individual dioceses by communicating with the bishop of a diocese before issuing documents that concern matters therein and by responding expeditiously to requests made of them (art. 26). AD LIMINA VISITS are presented as a prime opportunity for fostering good functional relationships between Bishops and the dicasteries of the Curia (arts. 28–32). Each dicastery has its own special norms for handling business (arts. 37–38), while a Central Labor Office handles all questions connected with employment in the Curia (art. 36).

Secretariat of State and the Congregations. The Secretariat of State, consisting of two sections, directly assists the Pope in expediting governance of the universal Church (arts. 41–44) and in relating with sovereign nations and international organizations (art. 45–47). A special group of 15 cardinals offers advice to the Secratariat of State in financial matters related to the Vatican (arts. 24–25).

The Congregation for the Doctrine of the Faith (CDF) is responsible for protecting all matters of doctrine relating to faith and morals (art. 48), and documents of other dicasteries which relate to faith and morals are subject to prior judgment by this congregation (art. 54). Attached to the CDF are the PONTIFICAL BIBLICAL COMMISSION (17:523a) and the INTERNATIONAL THEOLOGICAL COMMISSION (art. 55). The Congregation for the Oriental Churches has competence in all that concerns the faithful of Eastern Catholic Churches, except for those matters reserved to other dicasteries (arts. 58–59). The Congregation for Divine Worship and Discipline of the Sacraments oversees, fosters, and protects the valid celebration of liturgy and Sacraments and has responsibility for liturgical texts and missals (arts. 63–64), as well as for cases concerning non-consummation of Marriage and the nullity of Orders (arts. 67–68).

The Congregation for Causes of Saints deals with processes for canonizations and authentication of relics (arts. 71–74). The Congregation for Bishops is competent in all matters concerning particular churches, bishops, and groups of bishops, as well as personal prelatures (arts. 75–82). Attached to this congregation is the Pontifical Commission for Latin America (arts. 83–83). The Congregation for Evangelization of Peoples is responsible for moderating and coordinating all missionary activity, including erecting missionary institutes of consecrated life, regulating missionary organizations and overseeing finances for the missions (arts. 85–92). The Congregation for the Clergy has competence in all matters concerning the discipline, rights, and obligations of clergy, as well as what pertains to the clerical state (arts. 95–97). It also oversees religious education and catechical instruction (art. 94), and is responsible for major actions in the administration of temporal goods belonging to the Holy See throughout the world (art. 98). To this congregation is attached the Pontifical Commission for Preservation of Artistic and Historical Heritage (arts. 99–104). The Congregation for Institutes of Consecrated Life and Societies of Apostolic Life has competence over these entities its well as over associations of the faithful formed with a view to becoming such institutes or societies (arts. 105–111). The Congregation for Seminaries and Institutes of Studies has competence over seminaries, issues norms for Catholic schools, and ratifies statutes for ecclesiastical institutions and universities (arts. 112–116).

Tribunals and Pontifical Councils. The Tribunals of the Curia include the Apostolic Penitentiary, the Apostolic Signatura, and the Roman Rota. The Apostolic Penitentiary deals with all internal forum matters, as well as with indulgences (arts. 117–120). The Signatura cares for the proper administration of justice in various grades of tribunals in the Church and deals with complaints of nullity, recourse, exceptions, conflicts of competence among dicasteries, and actions impugned due to alleged violations of law or of procedure (arts. 121–125). The Rota, to which judges from all parts of the world are assigned by the Pope, is the tribunal of the Apostolic See for protecting rights in the Church, developing jurisprudence, and aiding other ecclesiastical tribunals (arts. 126–130).

The most notable change effected by *Pastor Bonus* was the formation of 12 Pontifical Councils. Formerly categorized as secretariats, commissions or councils, these new Councils are: 1) the Pontifical Council for the Laity (arts. 131–134); 2) the Pontifical Council for Promoting Christian Unity (arts. 135–138); 3) the Pontifical Council for the Family (arts. 139–141); 4) the Pontifical Council for Justice and Peace (arts. 142–144); 5) the Pontifical Council ''Cor Unum'' [for the promotion of humanitarian endeavors] (arts.145–148); 6) the Pontifical Council for Spiritual Care of Migrants and Travelers (arts. 149–151); 7) the Pontifical Council for the Apostolate of Hospital Workers (arts. 152–153); 8) the Pontifical Council for Interpreting the Texts of Laws (arts. 154–158); 9) the Pontifical Council for Dialogue among Religions (arts. 159–162); 10) the Pontifical Council for Dialogue with Non-Believers (arts. 163–165); 11) the Pontifical Council for Culture (arts. 166–168); and 12) the Pontifical Council for Social Communications (arts. 169–170).

Offices of the Curia include the Apostolic Camera, which operates especially during the vacancy of the Apostolic See (art. 171), the Administration of the Patrimony of the Apostolic See, which handles administration of goods related to the Curia (arts. 172–175), and the Prefecture of the Economic Affairs of the Holy See, which is responsible for the actual financial administration of the Holy See in general (arts. 176–179). Finally, there are two addendas to the apostolic constitution, one concerning guidelines for *ad limina* visits, as treated in articles 28–32, and another concerning those who work for the Apostolic See, as treated in articles 33–36.

Bibliography: *L'Osservatore Romano,* Italian Edition (June 29, 1988)

[J. J. MARKHAM/E. MCDONOUGH]

CURIOSITY

As here understood, curiosity is a culpably excessive desire to know. When the human mind is confronted with a question, it is naturally moved to make inquiry. Normally the mind does not rest until it is decided that the matter does not merit the trouble of investigation, or that investigation would be fruitless, or until adequate evidence for a judgment is obtained. Moralists consider curiosity as a VICE opposed to STUDIOUSNESS. The subject matter for this VIRTUE is not knowledge in itself, but rather the desire to know. This desire is capable of both excess and defect, and hence a particular virtue is required to moderate it according to the norms of right reason. To this virtue curiosity is opposed by way of excess. Though knowledge is a good thing in itself, the desire for it is immoderate and unreasonable when its pursuit involves evil motivation (e.g., pride), or an inordinate waste of time,

or injustice to another (e.g., when what one seeks to know is another's rightful secret), or the use of illegitimate means (e.g., divination or traffic with evil spirits), or when the knowledge would be likely to constitute a serious occasion of sin (e.g., for ordinary people and under ordinary circumstances, knowledge of the contents of a truly pornographic book). Curiosity in its common occurrences is not a grave sin, but it can be serious by reason of circumstances, as when it leads to the unjust exploration of the secrets of others or the invasion of their privacy, or when it causes one to commit grave sin of other kinds.

Bibliography: THOMAS AQUINAS, *Summa Theologiae,* 2a2ae, 167. F. L. B. CUNNINGHAM, ed., *The Christian Life* (Dubuque 1959).

[T. C. KANE]

CURLEY, MICHAEL JOSEPH

Archbishop, educator; b. Athlone, County Westmeath, Ireland, Oct. 12, 1879; d. Baltimore, Maryland, May 16, 1947. Michael, first of ten children born to Michael and Maria (Ward) Curley, attended the Marist brothers' school before enrolling in the seminary division of Mungret College, Limerick, at the age of 16. After U.S. Bp. John Moore, of St. Augustine, Florida, visited Mungret, Curley chose Florida as his future mission field. He received his B.A. from the Royal University of Dublin at age 20, then entered Propaganda College at Rome where he earned the S.T.L. degree. Nervous strain forced him to discontinue his studies for some months, but he was at length ordained at the Church of St. John Lateran, Rome, on March 19, 1904.

Curley arrived in Florida in November of 1904, and after some months was named the first resident pastor of the city of De Land with a parish embracing 7,200 square miles. While there, Curley became a U.S. citizen. He built for the parish a rectory and several mission churches, as well as renovating the main church.

Curley's preaching talents influenced Theodore Basselin to endow a seminarians' foundation at The Catholic University of America in Washington, D.C., for specialized training in sacred eloquence. At Bp. William John Kenny's death, Curley, at 34, was appointed ordinary of ST. AUGUSTINE; he was consecrated on June 30, 1914. During the next seven years, nearly 40 churches were built in the diocese as the Catholic population increased from 39,000 to 51,000.

When a convent-inspection bill was proposed in the state legislature, Curley announced that all convents in the diocese were open to all visitors. The bill failed to pass, but another was enacted forbidding white women to teach black children. The bishop refused to enforce the law and invited the authorities to arrest the offending nuns. He led the fight contesting the law and rejoiced to see it declared unconstitutional.

Five months after Cardinal James Gibbons of BALTIMORE, Maryland, died, Michael Curley was named his successor and installed in Baltimore's Basilica of the Assumption on Nov. 30, 1921—the youngest archbishop in the U.S. As a supporter of Catholic education, he insisted that if the choice lay between a new church and a needed school, the latter was to take precedence. During his episcopate in Baltimore, 66 new schools were established and an estimated $25 to $30 million expended on educational growth. He sponsored the new St. Mary's Seminary in Baltimore, and helped to complete St. Charles College in Catonsville, Maryland. He also gave active attention to his role as chancellor of Catholic University.

During Curley's episcopate the Bureau of Catholic Charities was incorporated and various fund-raising devices employed, including the formation of the Confraternity of the Laity. He was an outspoken critic of the anti-Catholic forces in Mexico and Spain during the 1920s and 1930s. To build a militant laity, he promoted the lay retreat movement and endorsed numerous rallies of Catholic organizations. On July 22, 1939, he became the first archbishop of WASHINGTON, D.C., remaining as archbishop of Baltimore and governing with a single curia. He was installed on March 25, 1940, in St. Matthew's Cathedral. His later years were burdened with a growing blindness and failing health. He died of a stroke and was buried in the Basilica of the Assumption.

Bibliography: V. DE P. FITZPATRICK, *Life of Archbishop Curley* (Baltimore 1929).

[J. J. GALLAGHER]

CURRIER, CHARLES WARREN

Bishop, writer; b. Saint Thomas, West Indies, March 22, 1857; d. Baltimore, Md., Sept. 23, 1918. He was the son of Warren Green and Deborah (Heyliger) Currier. Charles, taken to Europe in 1871, studied at the Redemptorist Preparatory College of the Assumption at Roermond, Holland. Professed a Redemptorist in 1875, he attended the seminary at Wittem, Holland, and was ordained in Amsterdam on Nov. 24, 1880, by Bp. Henri Schaap, Vicar Apostolic of Surinam, Dutch Guiana. He returned with that prelate to Surinam in January 1881, but recurrence of a nervous indisposition forced him to go to the U.S. in February 1882 to recover his health. For nine years, while stationed in Annapolis and Baltimore, Md., Boston, Mass., and New York City, he labored as a home

missionary and retreat master in the eastern U.S. A new onset of his illness forced him to request a dispensation from his vows as a Redemptorist; this was granted in November 1891. For the next 21 years, Currier was attached to the Archdiocese of Baltimore, serving as pastor of St. Mary's parish, Washington, D.C., after 1900. In 1905 he became assistant director and field lecturer of the Bureau of Catholic Indian Missions.

In 1913 Currier was elected to the new See of Matanzas, Cuba, and was consecrated in Rome by Cardinal Diomede Falconio, OFM, on July 6. He held the first synod in his diocese in January 1915, but because of ill health he resigned his see shortly afterward and was appointed to the Titular See of Etalonia. His remaining days were spent in the Archdiocese of Baltimore.

Currier traveled widely in Europe and in North and South America. A director of the Spanish-American Athenaeum of Washington, D.C., he was recognized as one of the most learned of the country's Hispanists. From 1892 to 1915 he attended International Congresses of Americanists, reading papers on Spanish-American history and serving as official U.S. government representative at the congresses in Stuttgart, Germany (1904), Buenos Aires, Argentina (1910), and Mexico City, Mexico (1910). Currier was steadily engaged in writing after 1890. His best known work was *History of Religious Orders* (1894). His other books include *Carmel in America* (1890), *The Rose of Alhambra* (1897), *Church and Saints* (1897), *Mission Memories* (1898), and *Lands of the Southern Cross* (1911).

Bibliography: Archives, Redemptorist Fathers, Brooklyn, N.Y. Archives, Archdiocese of Baltimore.

[M. J. CURLEY]

CURSE

The possibility of a curse is present whenever man stands in any relation whatever to the Absolute and the Transcendent. Cursing presupposes this reality, at least in principle. According to the forms of relation to the Holy—as the reality of the Absolute and the Transcendent may be designated—two kinds of curse can be distinguished and defined. With respect to other persons, the curse, in contrast to blessing, signifies the calling down of misfortune upon persons or objects, or it is this misfortune itself. With respect to the curser, the curse is the consciously irreverent act—and proclaimed as such—of hostility toward the world of the Holy (misuse of the name of God, or of holy persons and things). In both cases, magic attitudes and practices are often in evidence.

In respect to others, the curse, on the one hand, belongs to prayer, so far as the curser maintains an attitude

Christ cursing the barren fig tree, from an Armenian Gospel, illuminated in Cilicia in 1262.

which I have enacted. . . , may mighty Anum, the father of the gods, who proclaimed my reign, deprive him of the glory of sovereignty, may he break his scepter, may he curse his fate!'' (J. B. Pritchard, *Ancient Near Eastern Texts Relating to the Old Testament* [2d, rev. ed. Princeton, N.J., 1955] 30–31).

In this general category should be placed as well the elaborate curse formulas associated with the execution of a judgment against an individual, such as to involve exclusion from the community. There is a widespread idea that the curse of a dying person, and particularly of a mother, has special efficacy (see, e.g., *Odyssey* 2.134; Sir 3.9). Conversely, the removal of the curse by ritual purification, or its warding off, e.g., by making the sign of the cross, may be cited as ambivalent phenomena.

In the second sense, the curse is made against the world of the Holy itself. God is blasphemed in order by this means to take vengeance on Him and on the lot given by Him. This is done by the blasphemous utterance of sacred or tabooed names. The names are often given a changed meaning (euphemism) or are mutilated, so that the curse may not turn against the curser himself. Emotions of revenge, pride, despair, defense, or unjust anger, therefore, operate together, so that it is necessary in a given case only to determine which of these emotions specifies the curse. Here, too, the transition from curse and violent expression is easy, and especially because the custom and practice of daily speech no longer make it possible to recognize the original sense of many curses.

Curse in the religion of Israel. Israel's faith in the sovereign power of Yahweh transformed the curse, once thought to possess independent and inexorable efficacy, into an expression of God's justice, which operated only to punish the guilty. The ORDEAL rite prescribed for a wife suspected of adultery (Nm 5.11–29) had its origin in magical practice. However, it was now no longer the words of imprecation washed off into the holy water that was to bring punishment upon the guilty wife but rather the Lord who would execute the curse (Nm 5.21). Formulas that previously might have been employed to invoke a curse upon the enemy appear in the Psalter as prayers to God for vindication (Ps 82–83).

Particularly important from the viewpoint of orientation toward the NT was the covenant curse. Yahweh was the guardian of all covenants (Gn 21.22–23; 31.44), and especially the covenant between Himself and Israel. Guilty Israel had merited the incurring of all the covenant curses (Dt 27.14–26; 28.15–68). The Deuteronomist could only hold out the hope that, should they still repent, ''all those curses the Lord, your God, will assign to your enemies'' (Dt 30.7). Jeremiah (31.31–34) and Ezekiel (16.62; 34.25) held out the more radical promise of a new covenant.

of reverence and affirms the holy in relation to divine commands and norms, as in the OT. On the other hand, the curse belongs to magic. Yet in concrete instances the transition to prayer can be easy. A definite effect (the onset of misfortune or its averting) is thought to be accomplished by the employment of harmful expressions or signs. In Egypt vessels on which curse formulas were written were broken. In Athens and Rome too, curse tablets were in frequent use.

The occasion for the curse may be anger and fear, but it may also be hate and envy. In the latter case, there is often question of the use of witchcraft and sorcery, which may also be called black magic. Examples of transitional forms of the curse are cursing motivated by a more or less justified anger, or the cursing of desecrators of graves or of sacred objects. The following words are found on the great stele of Hammurabi and may have helped to preserve it: ''If that man did not heed my words which I wrote on my stele, and disregarded my curses, and did not fear the curses of the gods, but has abolished the law

Curse in the New Testament. Christ warns His disciples against recourse to imprecatory oaths (Mt 5.33–37). He threatens with woe the Pharisees (Mt 23.13–31) and the incredulous (Mt 11.21), but, apart from His symbolic cursing of the barren fig tree, He pronounces a proper malediction only once: "Depart from me, accursed ones" (Mt 25.41). It is the common theology of the NT that redemption in Christ has taken away the force of all curses, except for the final curse of a freely chosen damnation. St. Paul says that Christ became "a curse for us" to redeem us from the curse of the law (Gal 3.13), so that for those who are in Christ Jesus, "there is now no condemnation" (Rom 8.1); and creation itself, which had been put under a curse because of man (Gn 3.17), "also will be delivered from its slavery to corruption into the freedom of the glory of the sons of God" (Rom 8.21). Revelation teaches the same doctrine under the figure of the Heavenly City, where "there shall be no more any accursed thing" (Rv 22.3). Christ comes as the AMEN to the covenant promises of blessing (2 Cor 1.20; *see also Lk 24.50–53*), and not as the Amen to the curses of the old covenant (Dt 27.15–26).

See Also: MAGIC; BLESSING (IN THE BIBLE).

Bibliography: S. EITREM, *The Oxford Classical Dictionary,* ed. M. CARY et al. (Oxford 1949) 246. A. E. CRAWLEY, *Encyclopedia of Religion and Ethics,* ed. J. HASTINGS (Edinburgh 1908–27) 4:367–374. R. THURNWALD, "Fluch," *Reallexikon der Vorgeschichte,* ed. M. EBERT (Berlin 1924–32) 3:391–398. J. A. WILSON, in J. B. PRITCHARD, *Ancient Near Eastern Texts Relating to the Old Testament* (2d, rev. ed. Princeton, N.J., 1955) 328. A. AUDOLLENT, *Defixionum tabellae* (Paris 1904). G. VAN DER LEEUW, *Religion in Essence and Manifestation,* tr. J. E. TURNER (London 1938). H. C. BRICHTO, *The Problem of "Curse" in the Hebrew Bible* (*Journal of Biblical Literature* monograph ser. 13; Philadelphia, Pa. 1963). S. H. BLANK, "The Curse, Blasphemy, the Spell, and the Oath," *Hebrew Union College Annual* 23 (1950–51) 73–95. J. SCHARBERT, *Solidarität in Segen und Fluch im A.T. und in seiner Umwelt* (Bonn 1958). S. O. MOWINCKEL, *Segen und Fluch in Israels Kult und Psalm-endichtung* (Kristiana 1923; repr. Amsterdam 1961).

[W. DUPRÉ/J. V. MORRIS]

CURSILLO MOVEMENT

The Cursillo Movement is a movement of the Church in the area of the apostolate of the laity that has as its purpose the Christianization of the world through the apostolic action of Christian leaders in all the areas of human activity. The Movement's purpose is achieved by means of a strategy and a method. The strategy involves seeking out (the precursillo stage) the key people in the different environments, converting them to a deeper relationship with God by having them accept their role as lay apostles and then linking them together for their mutual support and apostolic effectiveness (the postcursillo stage).

The *cursillo de cristianidad* or "little course in Christianity" is a three-day period of spiritual renewal or of spiritual awakening that attempts to convey a new sense of the dynamic and personalistic aspects of the Christian faith. The weekend is an intensive experience in Christian community living centered on Christ and built around 15 talks (ten by laymen, five by priests), active participation in the discussions and related activities, and the celebration of the Liturgy. The follow-up program focuses on small weekly reunions of three to five persons and larger group reunions, called *ultreyas*, in which participants share experiences and insights derived from their prayer life, study, and apostolic action.

The name most often mentioned in connection with the development of the cursillo is that of Juan Hervas, Bishop of Ciudad Real, Spain. However, in his own writing Bp. Hervas disclaimed the idea that the final product was the work of any one person. He said that the cursillos were produced by a team of clergy and laymen working under the encouragement and direction of their bishop and that the individual contributors prefer to remain anonymous. The available evidence indicates also that the development of the cursillo was a gradual process and that the final product was the result of much experimentation and revision.

The cursillo seems to have been in use in its present form in Spain about 1949. It first made its appearance in the U.S. among the Spanish-speaking people of the Southwest, particularly Texas. Cursillos in Spanish spread from this area to the far extremities of the nation, New York and San Francisco, and north into Michigan and surrounding areas.

The Movement operates within the framework of diocesan and parish pastoral plans, and functions autonomously in each diocese (120 in the U.S.) under the direction of the bishop. Responsibility for growth and effectiveness rests with a diocesan secretariat and a diocesan leaders' school, or both. By 1977, when Spain was celebrating the twenty-eighth anniversary of the first cursillo, the Movement was operative on five continents, in nearly fifty countries, with a total of 857 dioceses; there are two and one half million *cursillistas*, of whom nearly 500,000 are in the U.S.

Stability and acceptability of the Cursillo Movement by the hierarchy would not have been possible without its being accepted and encouraged by the Holy See. Paul VI was the first pope to speak about the Movement. In 1963, he named St. Paul its patron. Later in an allocution on May 28, 1966, on the occasion of the first World *Ultreya* in Rome, he noted that the Christian life contains many riches of which Christians are unaware and commended Cursillo for making it possible to recall these riches to a conscious level and its ability to enrich *cursillistas* with a *sensus ecclesiae.* He reminded the *cursillistas* that they should take the lead in renewing the world for Christ by implementing the documents of Vatican Council II.

The U.S. Movement is overseen by a national board of 24 priests and laity and Bishop Joseph Green of Adrian, Mich., who is National Episcopal Advisor to the Movement and the liaison with the National Conference of Catholic Bishops. A National Center is staffed and located in Dallas, Texas, and provides the local movements with Cursillo literature and educational material, including a monthly magazine, *Ultreya.* The modern thrust of Cursillo in the U.S. is in terms of evangelization. It sees itself as an instrument of evangelization for the Church in the world. The last two National Encounters (1973 and 1977) have focused on this theme and the challenge of meeting today's need for a Catholic laity that will respond individually and collectively to their vocation to be evangelizers in the world.

Bibliography: J. HERVAS Y BENET, "The *Cursillos de cristianidad:* A Magnificent Instrument of Christian Renewal and of Apostolic Conquest," *Christ to the World* 7 (1962) 161–178, 312–324.

[G. P. HUGHES/J. F. BYRON]

CURSUS

A system of Latin accentual prose rhythm widely employed in late antiquity and in the later Middle Ages. Greek rhetoricians of the classical and Hellenistic periods had developed a system of prose rhythm based on quantity that was adapted to Latin use by Cicero. Special attention was given to the rhythm before strong pauses. Since word combination played a significant role in metrical prose rhythm or *clausulae,* the word accent could not be ignored entirely. As this Latin stress accent became pronounced, word accent became more important, particularly in the last word in metrical *clausulae.* Thus from the late 2d century to CASSIODORUS and GREGORY THE GREAT, writers were shifting from a system of *clausulae* based on quantity to one based on accent called *cursus,* although better prose writers retained a feeling for quantity in their prose rhythm to the end of antiquity. In this period of transition, three favorite forms of the cursus emerged: *cursus planus* (e.g., in English, "All's well that ends well"), based on the cretic-spondee *clausula;* the *cursus tardus* (e.g., "happy and glorious"), based on the double cretic; and the *cursus velox* ("varsity education"), based on the cretic-dichoree. Word combinations found in the ancient accentual prose rhythm never conformed fully to the strict rules of the medieval *cursus,*

which excluded monosyllables and any word of more than five syllables (according to Buoncompagno).

The ancient *cursus* was used by the Fathers of the Church in the ancient prayers of the Church and in the imperial and papal chanceries. The common name for the *cursus,* the *cursus leoninus,* took its name from Pope Leo the Great.

The *cursus* fell into disuse after Gregory but was revived by the *dictatores* of Monte Cassino. Its use was promoted by Pope Urban II in the papal chancery, where it become stereotyped as the *Cursus Curiae Romanae,* a rhythmical style utilizing only the three above-mentioned kinds of *cursus,* out of the many possible forms. With the spread of papal influence, the *Cursus Curiae Romanae* was adopted by all the chanceries of western Europe. It is to be noted that the School of Orléans differed from that of the Roman Curia only in matters of terminology, for the *cursus* (e.g., John of Garland and Peter of Blois) of Orléans preserved a classical terminology of dactyls and spondees.

The *Cursus Curiae Romanae* was also favored by writers outside the chanceries. Many chroniclers in England used it, though not Matthew Paris, whose rhythmical usages were markedly idiosyncratic. The best use of the *Cursus Curiae Romanae* in medieval literature was in the *Philobiblon* ascribed to RICHARD OF BURY (d. 1345), in which every clause was laced together in a concatenation of some 19,000 accented *clausulae.*

The *Cursus Curiae Romanae* dominated the writing of official Latin prose for many centuries and found an analogue in the Collects of the BOOK OF COMMON PRAYER as translated by Cranmer, and, in another key, probably in the prose of Gibbon's *Decline and Fall of the Roman Empire.*

In addition to the *Cursus Curiae Romanae* as used by the papal chancery and writers such as Richard of Bury, there is a much-used *cursus* that is named (seemingly only by modern scholars) the *cursus trispondaicus.* It is an ending consisting of a word of six syllables accented on the penultimate. Some think that there is also a singular rhythmic form of this, by extension, to include a word of eight syllables (or seven syllables followed by a monosyllable), i.e., four spondees (e.g., *excommunicationis* or *a communicatione*), but this is questionable.

The earliest treatise on the use of the medieval *cursus* is said to be preserved in the work of Transmondus (late 12th century; in Paris Bibliothèque nationale, Lat. 2820, fol. 59ᵛ and 13688, fol. 127).

Bibliography: N. DENHOLM-YOUNG, "The Cursus in England," *Oxford Essays in Medieval History Presented to H. E. Salter* (Oxford 1934), for general history and bibliog. to 1930. K.

POLHEIM, *Die lateinische Reimprosa* (Berlin 1925). L. LAURAND, *Études sur le style des discours de Cicéron,* 3 v. in 1 (v.1, 3d ed.; v.2 and 3, 2d ed; Paris 1926–28). M. G. NICOLAU, *L'Origine du "cursus" rhythmique et les débuts de l'accent d'intensité en Latin* (Paris 1930). H. LAUSBERG, *Handbuch der literarischen Rhetorik* (Munich 1960). G. LINDHOLM, *Studien zum mittellateinischen Prosarhythmus* (Stockholm 1963), with excellent bibliog.; use of *cursus* as weapon of textual criticism is not developed here. For Matthew Paris, see R. A. BROWNE, ed., *British Latin Selections, A. D. 500–1400* (Oxford 1954). M. E. MANN, *The Clausulae of St. Hilary of Poitiers* (Catholic University of America Patristic Studies 48; Washington 1936). M. J. SUELZER, *The Clausulae in Cassiodorus* (Washington 1944).

[N. DENHOLM-YOUNG]

CURTIS, ALFRED ALLEN

Second bishop of Wilmington, Del.; b. Rehoboth Del., July 4, 1831; d. Baltimore, Md., July 11, 1908. His father, an Episcopalian, conducted a country school, where Curtis received his only formal education. Curtis taught school at Princess Anne, Md., from 1849 to 1855, when he began to study for the Episcopal ministry. William Rollinson Whittingham, Episcopal bishop of Maryland, ordained him in 1859, and he was given assignments in Baltimore, Frederick, and Chestertown, Md. In 1862 he became rector of Mt. Calvary Church, Baltimore, where he abolished the system of pew rent and founded St. Philip's, a mission for African Americans. He began to lead an ascetical life and to make a close study of Scripture and the Church Fathers. In December 1871 he resigned as rector and went to England, where, unswayed by the arguments of leading Anglican divines, he was received into the Catholic Church by Cardinal John Henry Newman on April 18, 1872. Acting on Newman's advice, Curtis returned to Baltimore and entered St. Mary's Seminary in the fall of 1872. He was ordained on Dec. 19, 1874, by Abp. James Roosevelt Bayley. While assigned to the cathedral staff, he served as secretary to Bayley and his successor, Cardinal James Gibbons. Curtis helped to organize the Third Plenary Council of Baltimore (1884), during which he was secretary and theologian to Abp. Charles John Seghars of Oregon City.

In June 1886 Curtis was chosen to succeed Thomas A. Becker as bishop of Wilmington. He was consecrated in Baltimore by Cardinal Gibbons on Nov. 14, 1886. Curtis journeyed regularly to every section of his diocese, preaching, giving missions, and lecturing in hired halls. He built churches in a dozen country towns and founded parishes and six parochial schools in his see city. Pleading ill health, Curtis resigned on June 10, 1896, becoming titular bishop of Echinus. He remained as administrator apostolic until the arrival of his successor, John J. Monaghan, on May 10, 1897. Curtis then retired to Baltimore,

taking up residence with Cardinal Gibbons and acting as his vicar-general.

Bibliography: Sisters of the Visitation, Wilmington, Del., *Characteristics of Right Reverend Alfred A. Curtis* (New York 1913). J. T. ELLIS, *The Life of James Cardinal Gibbons,* 2 v. (Milwaukee 1952). Archives, Diocese of Wilmington.

[E. B. CARLEY]

CUSACK, MARGARET ANNA

Also known as Mother Clare and/or "the Nun of Kenmare," b. Dublin, Ireland, May 6, 1829, d. Lemington, England, June 5, 1899. Born to Anglo-Irish parents, Sarah Stoney and Dr. Samuel Cusack, and was christened in the Anglican Church of Ireland. She received an excellent education and showed talent in creative writing, languages and music. After her parents separated she moved with her mother to Exeter, England. There she became involved in the OXFORD MOVEMENT and joined and Anglican religious community, founded by Dr. Edward PUSEY, and while a member worked with the poor. After five years, she left, disillusioned with internal conflicts in the convent.

Margaret Anna was received into the Roman Catholic Church in 1858 and was confirmed by Cardinal WISEMAN, Archbishop of Westminster, who encouraged her to devote her life to Catholic literature. A year later she entered the Irish POOR CLARE Community in Newry, Co. Down and was given the name Sister Mary Francis Clare. In October 1861 she was among a group of Sisters sent to form a new foundation in Kenmare, Co. Kerry. With the approval of the Bishop of Kerry she was put in charge of the convent's Kenmare Publications. Her remarkable literary output included local histories, lives of saints, biographies, books and pamphlets on social issues, and letters to the press. While doing all she could to feed the hungry she also campaigned vigorously, through her writings, against the abuses of absentee landlords, lack of education for the poor and a legal system which oppressed a whole section of society, especially women. Income from her books was distributed throughout Ireland especially in Co. Kerry.

Cusack moved to Knock, Co. Mayo in 1881 with the intent of expanding the ministry of the Poor Clares. She started an industrial school for young women and evening classes for land workers. After two years in Knock, she believed she was called by God to found a new religious Order. Conflict in Knock led her to seek support in England, and it was there in the diocese of Edward G. Bagshawe, Bishop of Nottingham, that the SISTERS OF ST. Joseph of Peace were founded. The purpose of the new foundation was to promote the peace of the Church both by word and work'' as well as ''devotion to ameliorating the conditions of the homes of the poor.'' Mother Francis Clare had a private audience with Pope LEO XIII in May 1884. She wrote to the young community, ''His Holiness is pleased on this occasion to congratulate me on the favor which God had granted me in being Foundress of a new religious order.'' Two houses were established in 1884: a school in Grimsby and mother house and novitiate in Nottingham.

In November 1884 Mother Clare came to the United States to raise money to support the young community's works in England and to explore the possibility of establishing a home for young women immigrants there. Rebuffed in the archdiocese of New York, she was welcomed by Bishop Winard Michael WIGGER of Newark, New Jersey in 1885. A house was established in downtown Jersey City in 1885 and the following year property atop the Palisades in Englewood Cliffs, NJ, was acquired as a summer vacation place for working women.

In 1887, she became embroiled in a political controversy surrounding the mayoral candidacy of the social reformer Henry George. Bishop Wigger judged that she had made an unwarranted and scandalous attack on Archbishop Corrigan of New York. Bishop Wigger would not allow the Sisters of Peace to admit more women into the congregation and denied permission for novices to pronounce vows. Physically and emotionally exhausted, she decided in 1888 to withdraw from the congregation she founded in order to save it. She wrote to the community, July 1888, ''You must make a decided and determined position and save the Order for God and the Church, and I may say for me, though I say this only because it will have weight with you . . . the interests of the Order are very dear to me and I want these interests provided for and protected first.'' Shortly after writing her autobiography, *The Nun of Kenmare* (1889), she returned to England and to her Anglican roots. In later years she tried to keep in touch with the Sisters and showed a loving concern for them. She died June 5, 1899, and is buried in that portion of the cemetery reserved for the Church of England in Lemington, England.

Bibliography: I. EAGAR, *Margaret Anna Cusack: One Woman's Campaign for Women's Rights, a Biography,* rev. ed. (Dublin 1979). D. VIDULICH, *Peace Pays a Price: A Study of Margaret Anna Cusack, the Nun of Kenmare,* rev. ed. (Washington, DC 1990).

[C. O'CONNOR]

CUSACK, THOMAS FRANCIS

Bishop; b. New York City, Feb. 22, 1862; d. Albany, NY, July 12, 1918. After study at St. James School and St. Francis Xavier College in New York City and St. Joseph's Seminary, Troy, NY, he was ordained May 30, 1885. He was consecrated titular bishop of Themiscyra and auxiliary for the Archdiocese of New York on April 25, 1904, and transferred to Albany July 5, 1915, where he was enthroned Sept. 9, 1915. His lifelong interests included convert work and missions for Catholics. Convinced that these apostolates should be the concern of the diocesan clergy, he established a diocesan mission band and personally conducted ''A Question Box'' in the cathedral on Sundays during Lent. Among the other accomplishments of his short episcopate were the establishment of the diocesan offices of Catholic charities and the Propagation of the Faith, the convocation of the 13th synod (January 1916), and the organization of the diocese to assist in meeting the spiritual needs of soldiers during World War I.

Bibliography: *A Short Sketch of the Life of Bishop Cusack: America's Uncanonized Saint* (Washington 1934) an anonymous compilation of newspaper articles. J. B. CODE, *Dictionary of American Hierarchy* 2nd ed. (New York 1964).

[J. P. CONWAY]

CUSHING, RICHARD

Cardinal, archbishop of Boston; b. Boston, Aug. 24, 1895; d. Boston, Nov. 2, 1970. The son of a blacksmith, he received his elementary education in local public schools and secondary education at Boston College High School. He then attended Boston College for two years before entering St. John's Seminary, Brighton. He was ordained a priest on May 26, 1921.

After about a year in parish work, Cushing was selected for work with the Boston office of the Society for the Propagation of the Faith. He was named director of the office in 1928. During his 23 years' association with the Boston office, it became the foremost unit of the Propagation in the United States. He inaugurated a variety of mission organizations which raised funds and supplied information concerning the missions.

In April 1939 Cushing was named domestic prelate, and on June 29 he was consecrated auxiliary to Cardinal William O'Connell of Boston. After the death of O'Connell in 1944, Cushing was appointed archbishop of Boston by Pope Pius XII. On Dec. 15, 1958 he was created a cardinal by Pope John XXIII.

Cushing's immense energy sparked wide programs of youth activity, the construction of secondary schools throughout the Boston archdiocese, the establishment of six hospitals, and the chartering of three colleges. He also erected at Weston, Massachusetts, a national seminary for men in their mature years for the priesthood. Soon after World War II, he inaugurated a "lend-lease" system, whereby clergy of the archdiocese volunteered to work in less fortunate American dioceses, either permanently or on a temporary basis. In 1958 the program was enlarged when the cardinal established the Missionary Society of St. James the Apostle for work in Latin America. In five years almost 100 priests from Boston and eight other American dioceses, as well as from England and Ireland, were actively at work in missions in Peru, Bolivia, and Ecuador.

Another area to which the cardinal gave his special attention is to the care of handicapped children. In 1947 he established the St. Coletta School in Hanover, Massachusetts, for the education of mentally retarded youngsters. A day school of the same name was set up in Braintree, Massachusetts, ten years later. Cushing's devotion to the handicapped prompted him to lead a pilgrimage to Lourdes, France (1957), during which he personally helped care for the 100 young patients he had invited to attend.

Cushing was interested in the promotion of broad religious understanding among Catholics, Protestants, and Jews. At the Massachusetts Institute of Technology he encouraged the establishment of an interdenominational chapel.

His close friendship with the Kennedy family led to his offering the prayer of invocation at the inauguration of President Kennedy. In November 1963 he presided at the funeral rites in St. Mathew's cathedral in Washington, D.C., following the President's assassination.

Cushing, a man of large stature and commanding presence, for the last two decades of his life was ravaged by internal cancer. In addition to this illness, he had suffered from asthma for many years; and he was forced for some periods to give up public appearances for even weeks at a time. He never ceased an active life in his office, however, and received visitors on an almost daily basis. A popular and forceful speaker, he continued to address large gatherings within and without his archdiocese. In September 1970 he resigned from his see.

[F. J. LALLY]

Richard Cardinal Cushing. (©Bettmann/CORBIS)

CUSMANO, GIACOMO, BL.

Physician, priest, founder of the Servants of the Poor and the Congregation of the Missionary Servants of the Poor (MSP); b. March 15, 1834, Palermo, Italy; d. there, March 14, 1888. Giacomo (in English, Jacob or James) was born into a bourgeois family. Following the death of his mother, Maddalena Patti, in 1837, her older sister Vincenzina Patti cared for the Cusmano children. His pious aunt instilled in Giacomo the sense of charity for which he became known, and his Jesuit teachers at Palermo reinforced this virtue. Although he contemplated becoming a missionary, he studied and practiced medicine at Palermo, offering his services to the poor free of charge. Under the spiritual direction of Monsignor Turano, he followed his vocation to the priesthood and was ordained (Dec. 22, 1860). Cusmano used his wealth to buy land, buildings, and factories to provide employment, housing, and training. With the blessing of Archbishop Naselli and the approval of Pope Pius IX, Cusmano founded (Aug. 5, 1868) the first *Boccone del Povero* ("Morsels of the Poor"), which spread throughout Sicily to provide for orphans, the aged, and the sick. He also founded two congregations to serve these people. The first Servants of the Poor brothers received their habit on Oct. 4, 1884; the Missionary Servants, Nov. 21, 1887. When the first Sister Servants were veiled (May 23, 1880), his aunt Vincenzina Patti was appointed superior. After exhausting his own resources, he begged in the streets of Palermo and relied on God to provide the rest. Many miracles are attributed to his intercession. He is noted for his courage in working among the impoverished during a cholera epidemic in 1888, which led to his death at age 54. Cusmano was beatified by John Paul II, on Oct. 30, 1983.

Feast: March 13.

Bibliography: *Lettere del servo di Dio p. Giacomo Cusmano fondatore del Boccone del povero* (Palermo 1970). G. CIVILETTO and M. T. FALZONE, eds., *L'eredità spirituale e sociale di Giacomo Cusmano*, proceedings of the 3d congress, Palermo 17–20 November 1988 (Rome 1990). F. CONIGLIARO, L'evento-Cristo nell'esistenza del povero: la profezia ecclesiale di Giacomo Cusmano, in AA. VV., La "Chiesa" del Cusmano (Palermo 1995) 50–178. M. T. FALZONE, *Giacomo Cusmano: poveri chiesa e società* (Palermo 1986). G. LENTINI, *Un santo a Palermo* (Rome 1985); *Beato Giacomo Cusmano: medico e prete dei poveri* (Turin 1989). *Acta Apostolicae Sedis* 77 (1985): 112–14. *L'Osservatore Romano,* Eng. ed. 47 (1983): 6–7.

[K. I. RABENSTEIN]

CUSTODES HOMINUM PSALLIMUS ANGELOS

An office hymn historically assigned for Matins and Vespers on the feast of the Guardian Angels. It has sometimes been ascribed to Robert Bellarmine, but more recently (Connelly, 229) it is credited to an unknown author of his era. The four strophes each contain three Asclepiads and a Glyconic. In the first two stanzas the author praises the angels whom God has given for additional help to man, who is always under the attack of enemies. Lucifer, the fallen angel, enviously strives to draw to destruction those whom God invites to heaven. In the third stanza the Guardian Angel is implored to protect his charges from spiritual illness (perhaps heresy) and all that deprives man of peace of soul. The doxology mentions *machina triplex,* the threefold fabric made up of heaven, earth, and purgatory or hell. The author has summarized in this hymn the traditional role of the angels as guardians of nations (Ex 23.20; Dan 10.13) and of individuals (Tob 5–12; Mt 18.10).

Bibliography: H. A. DANIEL, *Thesaurus hymnologicus,* 5 v. (Halle-Leipzig 1841–56) 2:375, text. J. H. NEWMAN, ed., *Hymni ecclesiae* (London 1865) 157–158, text. P. GUÉRANGER, *L'Année liturgique,* 7 v. in 12 (Paris 1878–1901) 5:364–372. J. CONNELLY, *Hymns of the Roman Liturgy* (Westminster, MD 1957) 229–231, Eng. tr.

[M. M. BEYENKA]

CUSTODY OF THE SENSES

The deliberate effort of the Christian to correct, train, and discipline his five external senses and the internal senses of memory and imagination. The Christian is aware that human nature, with its senses, is good, but that it has been weakened by original and personal sin. There are inordinate tendencies in our bodies and our senses that seek pleasures to the detriment of our life in Christ. There is need, then, for every Christian to guard and discipline his senses. Custody of the senses becomes all the more urgent in the light of their deep and abiding influence on the emotions, intellect, and will. The senses play an important and powerful role in the attraction and inclination to evil. The senses must not only be deterred from evil (e.g., evil talk, evil touches) but they must be controlled also in seeking what is licit. Experience teaches that mortification in what is licit is necessary if one is to achieve the control needed to avoid what is sinful. But prudence and guidance are necessary, so as to avoid extravagant and ridiculous extremes.

Bibliography: A. ROYO, *The Theology of Christian Perfection,* tr. and ed. J. AUMANN (Dubuque 1962). A. TANQUEREY, *The Spiritual Life* (Westminster, MD 1945).

[N. LOHKAMP]

CUTHBERT OF CANTERBURY

Archbishop of Canterbury; d. 758. Of noble parentage, he was abbot of Lyminge, Kent, until consecrated bishop of Hereford by Abp. Nothelm of Canterbury in 736. He was translated to Canterbury in 740, receiving the PALLIUM from Pope Gregory III. In 742 he was present at the council of Clovesho when Ethelbald, king of Mercia and overlord of Kent, confirmed the privileges granted to the Kentish monasteries and churches by Wihtred, the former king. Cuthbert was a friend of St. BONIFACE, and it was to him that Boniface wrote, warning against allowing women to go on pilgrimage to Rome because so many succumbed to the moral temptations along the way. Boniface also urged Cuthbert to warn his people against drunkenness, the besetting vice of the English, and to avoid vanity in dress. In 747 Cuthbert called a provincial synod of the English Church at Clovesho. There 30 canons were enacted concerning the duties of monks, bishops, and priests, and confirming the observance of certain feasts, especially rogation days and the feasts of Gregory the Great and St. Augustine. On hearing of Boniface's martyrdom (754), Cuthbert ordained the celebration of his feast on June 5. Cuthbert was the first archbishop of Canterbury to be buried, not in SAINT AUGUSTINE'S ABBEY, but in his own cathedral church, where all succeeding archbishops have been buried.

Bibliography: A. W. HADDAN and W. STUBBS, eds., *Councils and Ecclesiastical Documents Relating to Great Britain and Ireland,* 3 v. in 4 (Oxford 1869–78) 3:340–396. *Die Briefe des heiligen Bonifatius und Lullus,* ed. M. TANGL, *Monumenta Germaniae Epistolae selectae* 1 (1916) nn. 73, 78, 111; Boniface's letter to Cuthbert, in *The Anglo-Saxon Missionaries in Germany,* ed. and tr. C.

H. TALBOT (New York 1954) 129–134. W. HUNT, *The Dictionary of National Biography from the Earliest Times to 1900*, 63 v. (London 1885–1900; repr. with corrections, 21 v., 1908–09, 1921–22, 1938; suppl. 1901–) 5:362–363.

[B. COLGRAVE]

CUTHBERT OF LINDISFARNE, ST.

Monk, hermit, bishop, one of the most popular of the English saints; d. Farne Island, Northumberland, England, 687. Of unknown parentage, he was brought up by a foster mother named Kenswith. Many incidents in his biographies illustrate his youthful piety. A vision, experienced reputedly as he was keeping sheep on the night of St. AIDAN's death in 651, led him to enter a monastery at MELROSE, where Eata, one of Aidan's disciples, was abbot. Boisil (Boswell), the prior, became Cuthbert's teacher. Cuthbert soon distinguished himself by his zeal and devotion. When Eata established a new monastery at RIPON, Cuthbert went as guest master; however, the brethren were compelled to leave, and they returned to Melrose. Not long afterward Boisil died of the plague; Cuthbert was also a victim, but he survived and became prior, occupying himself with evangelizing journeys in the neighborhood, often performing miracles and winning many souls. After the Council of WHITBY, Cuthbert and Eata accepted the Roman discipline. But the Celtic Bp. Colman of Lindisfarne resigned, and Eata was given his monastery of LINDISFARNE. Cuthbert took charge as prior and instituted a stern rule that the monks sometimes found difficult to bear. After about 12 years (676) he became a hermit and built himself a little oratory and dwelling place on a tiny island, the largest of the FARNE group, about nine miles from Lindisfarne. There he lived a life of great austerity, making friends with the seabirds for which the island is still famous and growing some of his own food. People came from afar to seek his advice. He remained there until 685, when he was finally compelled to leave to become bishop of Lindisfarne, succeeding Eata. After less than two years of devoted activity, he retired to Farne Island to die. His body was buried in the church at Lindisfarne; after 11 years it was found incorrupt and placed in a new coffin, of which portions are still extant. Owing to Viking raids, the body was translated to Chester-le-Street in 875, after having been carried from place to place for seven years, and in 995 to DURHAM, where his relics remain. The chief sources for the life of Cuthbert are the biography by an unknown monk of Lindisfarne, written *c.* 720, and the prose and verse lives by BEDE.

Feast: March 20.

Bibliography: *Two Lives of St. Cuthbert,* ed. and tr. B. COLGRAVE (Cambridge, Eng. 1940, rep. 1985). C. EYRE, *The History of St. Cuthbert* (3d ed. New York 1887). H. COLGRAVE, *St. Cuthbert of Durham* (Gateshead on Tyne 1955). *The Relics of St. Cuthbert,* ed. C. F. BATTISCOMBE (Oxford 1956). *The Age of Bede,* tr. J. F. WEBB, ed. D. H. FARMER (Harmondsworth, Middlesex, England 1983). G. BONNER, *Church and Faith in the Patristic Tradition: Augustine, Pelagianism, and Early Christian Northumbria* (Brookfield, Vt. 1996). W. M. AIRD, *St. Cuthbert and the Normans* (Woodbridge, Suffolk, UK 1998).

[B. COLGRAVE]

CUTHBERT OF WEARMOUTH

Anglo-Saxon abbot, student of Bede. He entered the abbey of JARROW in 718 and there was taught by BEDE. He became abbot of the twin Benedictine abbeys of WEARMOUTH-JARROW sometime after 747. He is remembered chiefly as the writer of a touching letter to Cuthwine, his fellow disciple, describing the deathbed of their master Bede. He corresponded also with St. BONIFACE and Bp. LULL OF MAINZ, sending them copies of Bede's works. In one letter to Lull he apologized for not having sent more, saying that the terrible winter of 763–764 had prevented work in the Jarrow scriptorium. He also asked Lull to send him a glassmaker and a harpist, for they had a harp at Jarrow that no one could play. He added that he had used Lull's present of an elaborate coverlet not as a protection against the cold, but as an altar cloth. The date of his death is unknown.

Bibliography: BEDE, *Eccl. hist.* 1:lxxi–lxxviii, clx–clxiv. BONIFACE, *Briefe,* ed. M. TANGL, *Monumenta Germaniae Historica: Epistolae selectae* 1 (1916), nos. 116, 117, 126, 127. J. RAINE, *A Dictionary of Christian Biography,* ed. W. SMITH and H. WACE 1:730.

[B. COLGRAVE]

CUTHBURGA, ST.

Anglo-Saxon queen and abbess; d. after 724. She was the daughter of Coenred, a member of the West Saxon royal house, and sister to King INE; she married King Aldfrith of Northumbria, who died in 705. She then became a nun at BARKING under Abbess HILDELIDE; she later founded WIMBORNE ABBEY. It is not clear whether she was the sole foundress or whether the cost was shared by her sister Tetta as some traditions maintain. Cuthburga became first abbess; she unfortunately never had a contemporary biographer.

Feast: Aug. 31; Sept. 3 with St. Hildelitha in the Diocese of Brentwood.

Bibliography: *Acta Sanctae Sedis* Aug. 6:696–700. A. M. ZIMMERMANN, *Kalendarium Benedictinum,* (Metten 1933–38) 2:641–643. J. WARRILOW, *Dictionnaire d'histoire et de géographie* *ecclésiastiques*, ed. A. BAUDRILLART et al. (Paris 1912) 13:1120–21.

[E. JOHN]

CUXA, ABBEY OF

Former BENEDICTINE monastery; present-day Cistercian monastery, in the Pyrenees at Prades, Pyrénées-Orientales, France; Diocese of Perpignan, former Diocese of Elne, France (Latin, *Cuxanense, de Coxano*). This monastery, originally dedicated to St. Germanus and later to St. Michael (953), grew out of the modest monastery of Saint-André d'Exalada, known to have existed in 840–841 and enlarged in 845 by the arrival of rich clerks from the Diocese of Urgel (Catalonia). Emperor Charles the Bald (871) granted the abbey EXEMPTION and allowed the monks free election of their superiors. In 878 a landslide destroyed the Exalada buildings, and Abbot Protase (one of the Urgel priests) transferred the monks to the church of Saint-Germain in Cuxa, thanks to the largesse of the local Count Myron and his son, Seniofred. In the 10th century Pope AGAPETUS II (950) and the Carolingian kings confirmed the privileges of the monastery, which by then controlled 22 parishes and had holdings in the Conflent, Roussillon, and Cerdagne. Abbot Guarinus (962–997), a friend of Gerbert (the future Pope SYLVESTER II), introduced the CLUNIAC REFORM, and under him Cuxa attained its apogee. In Rome he obtained the relics of St. VALENTINE. From Jerusalem he brought back the alleged manger in which Christ was laid, whence Cuxa's name, *Monasterium praesepii Domini*. Doge Peter Orseolo of Venice returned with him to become a novice at Cuxa (the Prades church preserves his body), as did the hermits, Marinus and ROMUALD, who lived in the forest near Cuxa for seven years; later Romuald founded CAMALDOLI in Italy. Guarinus built the new church of St. Michael, consecrated Sept. 28, 974. He was succeeded by Guasfred (997–1008), the son of Count Seniofred, and then by Oliba (1008–46), who was simultaneously abbot of Cuxa and RIPOLL and bishop of Vich. As abbot he extended Cuxa's holdings, developed the SCRIPTORIUM, obtained a confirmation of the rights and possessions of the monastery from Pope SERGIUS IV, and added two bell towers to the abbey church. The immense holdings of Cuxa excited the greed of the noble families who provided the abbots after the late 11th century, while a series of grave crises shook the abbey. In 1203 the pope deposed Abbot Arnold for squandering the goods of the abbey; twice Cuxa was united to Saint-Martin of Canigou; in 1293 King John I of Aragon intervened to stop scandals. In 1473 King Louis XI of France introduced COMMENDATION. From 1592 to the French Revolution, Cuxa belonged to the cloistered Congregation of Tarragona. The monks successfully opposed secularization (1694 and 1701–02), but evaded the reforms prescribed for French Benedictines by Pope Clement XIV (1772). In 1790 the Revolution dispersed the remaining eight monks, and on Jan. 27, 1793, the abbey was destroyed.

CISTERCIANS of the Congregation of Sénanque-Lérins restored monastic life at Cuxa in 1919. Remains of the old monastery include the church of St. Michael, an original specimen of Mozarabic art (10th–11th century); one of the two square towers (11th century); the circular crypt called "Church of the Manger" with Trinity Chapel above (11th century); nine cloister arcades with superb capitals (12th century), though most of the Cuxa capitals are at The Cloisters of the Metropolitan Museum, New York.

Bibliography: C. F. FONT, *Histoire de l'abbaye royale de Saint-Michel de Cuxa* (Perpignan 1881). L. H. COTTINEAU, *Répertoire topo-bibliographique des abbayes et prieurés* 1:937–938. M. SAHLER, *Les Grands ordres monastiques* (Auch 1949–), v.1, *Les Abbayes de France* 88–91. M. DURLIAT, *Roussillon roman* (La-Pierre-Qui-Vire 1958) 29–69. M. B. BRARD, *Catholicisme* 3:391–392. C. M. BARAUT, *Dictionnaire d'histoire et de géographie ecclésiastiques* 13:1121–42.

[J. DAOUST]

CYBELE

Cybele was the great mother-goddess of Asia Minor. Primarily a goddess of fertility, but also a source of cures and oracles and a protector of her people in war, she was worshipped along with her lover, Attis, a god of vegetation, at Pessinus in Phrygia. The cult was introduced into the Greek world by the end of the 6th century B.C. and was brought to Rome near the end of the Second Punic War (205–204 B.C.). Cybele, under her Latin name, Magna Mater deorum, was worshipped by an elaborate ritual, her chief festival being celebrated in the last part of March. Eunuch priests or attendants, the Galli, had an important place in her cult.

Under the Roman Empire, the ritual of the TAUROBOLIUM, a form of initiation, was required; the candidate was placed in a pit and bathed in the blood flowing from a bull killed above the pit. The cult of Cybele and Attis, including the rite of Taurobolium, spread throughout the West, and was especially popular in Gaul and Africa. In some respects, it resembled the contemporary cults of Mithras and Isis.

See Also: MYSTERY RELIGIONS, GRECO-ORIENTAL.

Bibliography: F. R. WALTON, *The Oxford Classical Dictionary*, ed. M. CARY et al. (Oxford 1949) 246–247. F. CUMONT, *The Oriental Religions in Roman Paganism* (Chicago 1911) ch. 3. K.

Kidnapping of Cybele, statue. (©Cuchi White/CORBIS)

PRÜMM, *Religionsgeschichtliches Handbuch für den Raum der altchristlichen Umwelt* (2d ed. Rome 1954) 255–263.

[T. A. BRADY]

CYBERNETICS

A term coined by Norbert Wiener (1894 to 1964) from the Greek, κυβερνήτης (steersman), to designate the science of control and communication in both animals and machines. It supplies novel instruments for investigating life and mental processes that open up new avenues of research in the study of organisms, nerve impulses, sensation, memory, and even mind. Yet it also gives rise to philosophical problems by suggesting that mental processes, hitherto regarded as distinctive of man's higher faculties, can ultimately be performed by a machine. What follows is concerned with the ways in which such problems may be resolved to the mutual benefit of the cybernetician and the philosopher.

Basic Difficulties. Confusions over the implications of cybernetics can usually be traced to one of two sources. The first is an uncritical acceptance of the assumptions that underlie cybernetics and make it feasible, while the second is the analogous terminology that is employed in work on control and communications.

Suppositions. The cybernetician is committed to a program of research in which animal and human means of communication are studied through the use of electronic and mechanical devices. Even superficial examination, however, reveals vast differences between organisms and machines, including machines of the most complicated types. In order to bridge the gap, the researcher in this area must "down-grade" living phenomena until they approach the level of the nonliving, and "up-grade" mechanical and electrical phenomena to confer on them the status of vital activities.

Thus the suppositions on which the cybernetician works commit him to a monist view of reality. He may be aware of profound differences between the living and

Norbert Wiener, founder of cybernetics.

the nonliving in his ordinary experience, but when carrying out his research he must abstract from these differences. Following a procedure that is typically scientific, he first simplifies the phenomena he is studying in order to arrive at some type of idealized generalization; then, by various approximations, he attempts to reproduce the complexity found in nature by adding new elements to his simplified model. Although simplification thus becomes an integral part of his method, it need be no cause for concern if the investigator is aware that he is so simplifying.

Terminology. The second source of confusion is closely associated with the first. It concerns the use of terms hitherto reserved exclusively for animal or human activity but now applied somewhat indiscriminately to machines. Cybernetic devices are described as ''learning,'' ''adapting,'' ''self-correcting,'' and ''thinking.'' Such usage leads those who are philosophically naïve to imagine that these devices eliminate the need for distinction between living and nonliving or between the mental and the purely material.

Such an inference, admittedly alarming, fails to take account of the primitive state of cybernetics as a science. In the early stages of any scientific development, the investigator is forced to employ terms that are generally used in quite different contexts. For example, early theories of momentum had to employ the concept of IMPETUS, which immediately implied a reference to the efficient cause of inertial motion. Similarly, when Newton first arrived at the notion of mass, he had to designate it by the expression *quantitas materiae,* or quantity of matter, because no other term was available. So also, in the beginnings of cybernetic research, it seems inevitable that analogy or equivocation be employed until a proper scientific terminology is developed.

The scientific mind cannot rest content with analogy or equivocation; scientists typically attach univocal meanings to the terms they employ. Thus, as cybernetics moves into its more advanced stages, it develops its own terminology—already the term programming illustrates this development. As this process continues, early confusions disappear, a precise vocabulary is adopted, and distinctions become available that can be used with profit by philosophers as well as by cyberneticians.

Particular Problems. An indication of how this may be done is given by an analysis of problems presented to the philosopher by the concepts of perception, memory, and abstraction when these concepts are applied to the machine.

Perception. When a machine ''perceives,'' in the sense of recognizing a pattern, it compares a pattern presented to it with certain test features that serve to identify this pattern as one of several possibilities. The comparison is more than one of mere juxtaposition, such as is done, for example, when two patterns are placed one on top of the other and viewed toward a light source. Rather there is an indeterminacy in the standard pattern that is resolved on a probabilistic basis and subsequently corrected whenever the result is found wrong. By trial and error, the machine advances toward more and more perfect identification of the pattern.

Yet this process is not the mechanism whereby a man perceives an object or a pattern. Human perception involves more than comparison with a standard pattern. It does presuppose identification of the pattern, but above and beyond this it involves an element of signification or INTENTIONALITY not found in machine perception. For example, when the eye sees a coin at a distance, the pattern presented to it is generally oval, or elliptical, because the coin is usually seen from an angle. But the coin, when perceived, is not perceived as elliptical or oval, but as a circular disc. Similarly, a square may be presented to the eye as a rhombus, but it is perceived as a square. Spatial perception is thus self-corrective for the effects of perspective, for the angle of vision, for distortions introduced by the medium, and so forth.

Human perception, on this account, involves more than pattern recognition. The additional factor is what enables man to recognize the identity of an object perceived when it is sensed in different orientations. Man perceives because he is capable of grasping the signification of a particular representation, of knowing it in an intentional way. Signification or intentionality is the synthesizing factor that unifies many possible representations and enables the perceiver to identify a particular content through any one of them. Machine perception reaches the first stage of comparing representations, but the machine is not capable of grasping the signification associated with individual representations as is the human being.

Memory. Computers are said to have memory when they store information and make it available for future use. They do this by mechanically or electronically locating "bits" of information that are present and recorded in the machine. Machine memory is thus limited to recording the past as present, i.e., it re-presents information in the present. This operation is much like that of mechanically locating an object present in a filing system.

Human memory involves more than this. It does not consist merely in recalling a representation received in the past as it is now present, but rather in perceiving the past as past, i.e., as temporally situated in a bygone present. The person who remembers filing an object does something different from another who merely locates the same object present in the file. The remembering does not concentrate on the present action, i.e., locating the material, but rather on identifying a past action, i.e., placing the matter in the file, precisely as a past action, i.e., as done several days, weeks, or months ago.

Abstraction. If machines cannot perceive and remember in the same way as human beings, even less can they form a CONCEPT that is univocally the same as the product of the mental process of ABSTRACTION. A concept is a universal idea that expresses a nature or a QUIDDITY without including the specific characteristics that determine "this" or "that" particular realization of the idea in matter. Thus the concept is essentially immaterial, and in this respect differs from the PHANTASM. The concept is the product of the INTELLECT; the phantasm is the product of the IMAGINATION.

When machines attempt to simulate abstraction and concept formation, they substitute a minimal representation for the complexity of all the different representations that might exemplify a particular concept. This minimal representation, however, remains at the level of a material symbol, and thus lacks the immateriality and universality of the concept. The machine's method of "concept formation" consists in constructing complex representations, or drawing more and more complicated pictures, with the elements present in its simplest representation. It does not form a concept in the human sense, since it cannot grasp a meaning or a universal idea in an immaterial way.

Closely related to this topic is the subject of mechanical translation. Actually, when a machine is said to "translate," the process employed is not so much translation as it is deciphering or decoding. Decipherment is concerned with the manipulation of symbols, whereas translation deals with the meaning behind these symbols. Being concerned with meaning, translation requires intelligence and cannot be performed at a merely mechanical level. Where questions of meaning are involved, a deciphering machine is only as valuable as a translator or interpreter who does not understand what he is saying in either language. This is not meant to imply that the highly complex operations performed by such machines are valueless. They have their uses, but these can be called "concept formation" or "translation" only at the risk of equivocation.

Critique. While the computing machines used in cybernetic research are marvels of human ingenuity, they are not human and as such cannot be a proper subject of predication for human attributes. If men do not commonly attribute their own personal skills to the instruments they employ, even less should they attribute their basically human powers to machines. To do so is similar to imagining, in Aristotle's words, "not only the forms of gods, but their ways of life, to be like their own" (*Pol.* 1252b). Rather they should recognize computers for what they are, namely, powerful instruments for research and technology, and use them to investigate the material phenomena that underlie vital and cognitional processes.

See Also: SOUL, HUMAN; SPIRIT; SENSATION; KNOWLEDGE; UNIVERSALS.

Bibliography: N. MORAY, *Cybernetics* (New York 1963). D. DUBARLE, *Scientific Humanism and Christian Thought,* tr. R. TREVETT (New York 1956). W. A. WALLACE, "Cybernetics and a Christian Philosophy of Man," *Philosophy in a Technological Culture,* ed. G. F. MCLEAN (Washington 1965); "A Thomist Looks at Teaching Machines," *Dominican Educational Bulletin* 4 (1963) 13–23. M. A. BUNGE, *Metascientific Queries* (Springfield, Illinois 1959).

[W. A. WALLACE/R. S. LEDLEY]

CYDONES, DEMETRIUS

Byzantine scholar and statesman; b. Thessalonica, *c.* 1324; d. Crete, winter of 1397–98. As a student at the school of Nilus CABASILAS, he joined the party of the future John VI Cantacuzenus who brought him to Constantinople; but after Cantacuzenus fell from power in 1354,

Demetrius departed for Italy. In 1369 he became imperial secretary and accompanied John V Palaeologus to Rome; upon his return he lived privately until MANUEL II PALAEOLOGUS (1391–1425), his former pupil, had him return to court. He was in Venice with Manuel Chrysoloras (c. 1390), then in Milan and Crete. His epitaph was written by MANUEL CALECAS, who had been his disciple. Demetrius played an important role in politics, encouraging a Byzantine-Occidental alliance against the Turks. As friend of the humanists, he spread Oriental culture in the West and with his brother Prochorus CYDONES opposed Palamitism (see PALAMAS, GREGORY). Before 1365 he was converted to Catholicism, and he translated Latin theological works into Greek, including writings of St. AUGUSTINE, FULGENTIUS OF RUSPE, St. Anselm of Canterbury, Ricoldo of Monte Croce, and the *Summa contra Gentiles* and the *Summa theologiae* (1a, 1a2ae, and 2a2ae) of St. Thomas Aquinas.

Bibliography: Works. *Patrologia Graeca*, ed. J. P. MIGNE, 161 v. (Paris 1857–66), 109:637–652; 151:1283–1301; 154:836–1212; *Correspondance*, ed. R. J. LOENERTZ, 2 v. (*Studi e Testi* 186, 208; Rome 1956–60); *Correspondance*, ed. and tr. G. CAMMELLI (Paris 1930). G. MERCATI, *Notizie . . . Demetrio Cidone* (*Studi e Testi* 56; Rome 1931). Literature. R. J. LOENERTZ, *Les Recueils de lettres de Démétrius Cydonès* (*Studi e Testi* 131; Rome 1947). B. KOTTER, *Lexikon für Theologie und Kirche,* ed. J. HOFER and K. RAHNER, 10 v. (2d, new ed. Freiburg 1957–65); suppl. *Das Zweite Vatikanische Konzil: Dokumente und Kommentare,* ed. H. S. BRECHTER et al., pt. 1 (1966), 3:217. V. LAURENT, *Dictionnaire d'histoire et de géographie ecclésiastiques,* ed. A. BAUDRILLART et al. (Paris 1912–), 14:205–208; "La Correspondance de Démétrius Cydonès," *Échos d'Orient* (Paris 1897–) 30 (1931) 339–354. M. CALECAS, *Correspondance,* ed. R. J. LOENERTZ (*Studi e Testi* (Rome 152; (Rome 1950). C. BUDA, *Byzantinische Zeitschrift* 49 (1956), 318–331. Thomism. M. GRABMANN, "De rationibus fidei contra Saracenos . . . des hl. Thomas von Aquin," *Scholastik* 17 (1942) 187–216. H. G. BECK, *Kirche und theologische Literatur im byzantinischen Reich,* (Munich 1959), 731–737.

[P. JOANNOU]

CYDONES, PROCHORUS

Byzantine monk and theologian; b. Thessalonica, c. 1330; d. 1368 or 1369. Prochorus, a brother of Demetrius CYDONES, became a monk in the Laura on Mt. Athos; he was ordained a priest and left the monastery solely to visit his brother. He was attracted by scholastic thought. Strenuously opposed to Gregory PALAMAS and HESYCHASM, he translated into Greek, works of Augustine, Boethius, Herveus Natalis, and Thomas Aquinas (*Summa theologiae* 3a), and directed an anti-Hesychast study (*De essentia et operatione*) to Philotheus Coccinus. He was excommunicated and degraded by the Synod of 1368, which canonized Gregory Palamas. It is probable that he had become a Catholic in secret. His brother Demetrius's eulogy of him was also his defense.

Bibliography: G. PALAMAS, *Contra Prochorum Cydonium, Patrologia Graeca* 151:693–716. G. ACINDYNI, *De essentia et operatione Dei, Patrologia Graeca* 1191–1242. B. KOTTER, *Lexikon für Theologie und Kirche*[2] 8:781. M. CANDAL, "El libro VI de Prócoro Cidonio," *Orientalia Christiana periodica* 20 (1954) 247–297. G. MERCATI, ed., *Notizie di Procoro e Demetrio Cidone Studi e Testi* 56 (1931) 1–6, 285–355. H. G. BECK, *Kirche und theologische Literatur im byzantinischen Reich* 60, 737–739.

[P. JOANNOU]

CYNEBURG, ST.

Name also spelled Kyneburg(a) or Cyniburg; Benedictine abbess, one of the remarkable progeny of Penda, pagan king of Mercia, all zealous propagators of the faith among whom are several saints; d. c. 680. Before 653 she married Alcfrith, son of King Oswy of Northumbria, himself sub-King of Deira. Probably upon his death, after 664, or possibly, as Florence of Worcester says, "renouncing a marriage of fleshly connection for love of God," she became abbess of the house called after her, Cyneburgecaestre, now Castor, Northamptonshire (where there is still a path called Lady Connyburrow's Way). A doubtful PETERBOROUGH tradition records her participation in the original endowment of that abbey. In the mid-tenth century her remains were translated there from Castor. Her name occurs with Alcfrith's in runic on the Bewcastle Cross.

Feast: March 6.

Bibliography: *Acta Sanctae Sedis* March 1:440–446. BEDE, *Ecclesiastical History* 3.21. FLORENCE OF WORCESTER, *The Chronicle . . . with the Two Continuations,* tr. T. FORESTER (London 1854) 37. J. EARLE and C. PLUMMER, eds., *Two of the Saxon Chronicles Parallel,* 2 v. (Oxford 1892–99) years 656, 675, 963, with notes. A. M. ZIMMERMANN, *Kalendarium Benedictinum* (Metten 1933–38) 1:293–294.

[R. D. WARE]

CYNEWULF

A name signed in runes to four Old English religious poems. The passages in which the runes are incorporated give biographical details of a very general nature, e.g., that the author was a sinner and in need of prayer. The original dialect of the poems was, apparently, northern. The runic spellings of the name indicate a 9th-century date. Attempts to identify the poet with historical Cynewulfs have not proved convincing. Of the four poems, two, *Elene* and *Juliana,* are legends of saints; one, the second part of the composite poem *Christ,* is based on a homily on the Ascension by St. Gregory the Great (c. 540–604). The fourth, *The Fates of the Apostles,* is a relatively brief mnemonic poem. All the poems are technically very competent work; *Elene,* an account of the finding of the true cross, is poetically the most successful.

Besides the signed work there are a considerable number of poems that are religious but not, like the Caedmonian poems, of direct scriptural inspiration (*see* CAEDMON); they are probably of northern origin and may be of the 9th century. Many of these poems have been attributed to Cynewulf, but in no case is the evidence conclusive. Their existence, however, makes it convenient to speak of the school of Cynewulf. Of the poems of the school, the first part of *Christ* and one of two poems on St. Guthlac (673–714), *Guthlac B,* seem to be closest in manner to the signed work. *Phoenix,* an adaptation of LACTANTIUS's *De Ave Phoenice, Guthlac A, Christ III* (on the Day of Judgment), and *Andreas,* a vigorous handling of a legend of SS. Andrew and Matthew, are more remotely connected with the school.

Bibliography: CYNEWULF, *The Poems of . . .,* tr. C. W. KENNEDY (New York 1910). *The Vercelli Book,* ed. G. P. KRAPP (New York 1932), contains texts of *Elene, The Fates of the Apostles,* and *Andreas. The Exeter Book,* ed. G. P. KRAPP and E. V. K. DOBBIE (New York 1936), contains other texts mentioned. C. SCHAAR, *Critical Studies in the Cynewulf Group* (Lund, Sweden 1949). K. SISAM, *Studies in the History of Old English Literature* (Oxford 1953).

[C. J. DONAHUE]

Old English Script, folio of "The Exeter Book of Old English Poetry," containing Cynewulf's runic signature.

CYNICS

Ascetical philosophers who appeared first in Athens in the 4th century, B.C.; their name (οἱ κυνικοί), derived from the Greek for dog (κύων), was applied to them chiefly for their vulgar and often shameless public behavior. Reliable testimony about the origins of the movement is lacking, and different hypotheses have been proposed regarding the first Cynic and originator of Cynicism. Recent research favors Diogenes of Sinope rather than Antisthenes or Crates.

Antisthenes. While he had listened to Gorgias of Leontini (*c.* 483–375), Antisthenes (*c.* 445–*c.* 365) was a faithful disciple of SOCRATES and was present at his death (*Phaedo* 59B). He was a prolific writer in rhetoric and philosophy and had interests in politics as well. There seems to be a considerable difference between the doctrines of Antisthenes and the tenets of the Cynics. The chief sources—namely, Xenophon, Aristotle, and Cicero—do not speak of him as a Cynic. Both the historians of the successions of the philosophers and the Stoics traced the lines of descent from Socrates to the Stoics through Antisthenes, conceiving him as the founder of Cynicism. This genealogy seems to be without solid basis.

Diogenes of Sinope. Exiled from his native city of Sinope in Pontus, Diogenes (*c.* 410–*c.* 320) went to Athens in about 350 B.C., where he was named Diogenes the Dog (ὁ κύων), as Aristotle reports (*Rhet.* 1411a 24). Unfortunately the Diogenes of history is little known, whereas the Diogenes of legend and anecdote is a familiar character the world over. Both the historians of the successions of philosophers and the Stoics make him a disciple of Antisthenes, though there is scant justification for the relationship. Indeed, if modern chronology is even approximately correct, it would seem impossible. Nevertheless it is most likely that Diogenes was the first Cynic, the one who gave the movement its essential characteristics, namely, asceticism and individual freedom (ἐλευθερία). Though Diogenes Laertius attributes both dialogues and tragedies to him, none have survived. Some scholars believe he wrote nothing. The disciples of Diogenes are traditionally said to have been Onesicratus, Monimus, and Crates.

Crates. A native of Thebes, Crates (fl. 328 B.C.) contributed to the development of Cynicism by introducing the element of concern for mankind (φιλανθρωπία). He is regarded as the link between the Cynics and the Stoics since he was the master of Zeno of Citium, the founder of STOICISM. Crates was considered the Cynic par excel-

Diogenes, (holding lantern).

lence in antiquity, along with Diogenes. His strange marriage (κυνογαμία) with Hipparchia was discussed widely by ancient writers. Only fragments of his literary works remain, but these are of a fairly high order and brought Cynic literary genres into Greek literature. It is he who first wrote of the Cynic paradise, the Isle of Pera. Besides Crates other early Cynics who contributed to the tradition were Bion of Borysthenes, Menippus, Teles, and perhaps Cercidas, all of whom belong to the 3d century B.C.

Cynic Teachings. There is no systematic Cynic doctrine, for the Cynics purposely avoided speculation and imparted a way of life (κυνικὸς βίος) instead. At no time in their long history did they form a school in the strict sense, for their extreme individualism and mobile existence made this impossible. The Cynic life varied with different personalities and from age to age; yet a family resemblance existed in their extremely individualistic and ascetical tendencies. As a rule the Cynics spurned human conventions and artificial institutions; they advocated life according to nature and an overturning of the prevailing structure of civilization. Rejecting political boundaries, they considered themselves citizens of the world with unlimited freedom to criticize political authorities. They strove also to develop complete self-sufficiency, spurning material possessions and training themselves to endure pain and hardship. Though ambi-

tioning complete indifference, they did not deny themselves gross sensual indulgence and on occasion practiced sexual immorality in public. Such conduct notwithstanding, the individual Cynic became convinced that he was a preacher of morality to the common people and characterized his vocation as scout of God (ἐπισκόπος), as teacher (παιδαγωγός), and as doctor of souls (ἴατρος). The mendicant Cynic preacher was a familiar figure in the ancient world, recognizable by his cloak, wallet, and staff.

Revival in Roman Empire. From about 200 B.C. to the 1st century A.D., Cynicism exerted little influence; Rome, for example, was unconcerned with the movement until it became popularly identified with Stoicism. The Stoics all revered Diogenes, and the Stoic EPICTETUS heaped eloquent praise on the Cynic ideal. Both movements rose in opposition to the luxury and moral decay of the empire. The Stoics appealed to the aristocrats, while the Cynics preached to the masses—though Lucian excoriated the Cynics for their ignorance and vulgarity. While there were charlatans and imposters among them, Dio Chrysostom (b. A.D. 40), the celebrated preacher, was an admirable character who became a friend and adviser to Trajan (A.D. 53–117). Other important Cynics were Demonax (*c.* A.D. 50–150), who was revered in Athens, and Oenomaus of Gadara.

Cynics and Christianity. Only fragmentary evidence remains concerning the relations between Cynics and Christians. Peregrinus presents the first clear case of a Christian who embraced Cynicism. He was born at Parium on the Propontis at the end of the 1st century A.D. and joined the Christian community in Palestine. Imprisoned by the Romans, he was then released and lived as a Cynic; he was accepted by Christian society until expelled some years later for a misdeed. In A.D. 167 he sensationally burned himself to death during the Olympic festival. Tatian, the famous author of the *Diatesseron* born in Syria *c.* A.D. 120, was a convert and disciple of St. Justin. Later he became a Gnostic and founded the heretical Encratite (Gr. ἐγκρατερία, self-restraint) sect, which was similar to that of the Cynics in mode of life. In the 4th century another Christian, Maximus of Alexandria, who became a trusted friend of GREGORY OF NAZIANZUS, lived as a Cynic. Gregory publicly praised Maximus for both his Christianity and his noble Cynic life. Later he had cause to regret his words, for Maximus was clandestinely consecrated bishop in Constantinople. After unsuccessfully trying to gain support of various groups, Maximus disappeared from history. In addition to St. Gregory, other Christian leaders entertained a high regard of Cynic asceticism, among them St. BASIL, who admired what he took to be the virtues of Diogenes of Sinope. The Cynic qualities of endurance and indifference, in stark contrast to the luxury and dissipation of the other pagans, were held up as models for Christians. Perhaps the development of Christian asceticism was somewhat influenced by the Cynic ideal, even though the obvious vices of the Cynics were continually being condemned.

See Also: GREEK PHILOSOPHY; ASCETICISM

Bibliography: F. C. COPLESTON, *History of Philosophy* (Westminster, Md. 1946–) v. 1., *Greece and Rome* (1946; 2d ed. 1950). A. H. ARMSTRONG, *An Introduction to Ancient Philosophy* (3d ed. London 1957). J. OWENS, *A History of Ancient Western Philosophy* (New York 1959). D. R. DUDLEY, *A History of Cynicism from Diogenes to the 6th Century A.D.* (London 1937). F. SAYRE, *Diogenes of Sinope: A Study of Greek Cynicism* (Baltimore 1938); ''Greek Cynicism,'' *Journal of the History of Ideas* 6 (1945) 113–18.

[L. A. BARTH]

CYPRIAN, ST.

Bishop of Carthage 249 to 258 and martyr; d. Carthage, Sept. 14, 258.

Life. Before his conversion (246) Cyprian (Caecilius Cyprianus) had the best education of the day and made his mark as a master of eloquence. In his account of the transformation effected by his baptism (*Ad Donatum*), he paints his early life in dark colors but without significant detail. His style is stilted and affected, but the sincerity of his response to grace is shown by his distribution of his abundant wealth to the poor and by his dedication to chastity—as also, thereafter, by the almost complete absence of artificiality in his speech and writing.

Cyprian's newly found devotion to Christ led him to the Scriptures as a practical guide to his thought and life, and he profited by and added to an already existing collection of proof texts in his TESTIMONIA. He read TERTULLIAN and used him freely, but with discrimination: though he called Tertullian ''the Master,'' he often disagreed with him radically. His early election to the episcopate is proof of the influence he exercised in Carthage, though it gained him a few lifelong clerical enemies.

Decian Persecution (250–251). Cyprian went ''underground'' during the persecution of Decius, directing and encouraging his clergy and faithful from his place of hiding and resisting the insubordination of some of the priests and of the confessors who were pandering to the lapsed. On his return he addressed his people about these last (*De lapsis*), and with the other African bishops in concert with Rome drew up equitable measures, exacting further penance only from the Christians who had sacrificed to the pagan gods (*sacrificati*). As the liberal opposition persisted in its schism and a contrary rigorist schism under NOVATIAN broke out in Rome, Cyprian de-

Woodcut of St. Cyprian. (The Library of Congress)

livered his famous address, *De ecclesiae catholicae unitate*. The threat of a fresh persecution under Gallus (252) led to the restoration of Communion to the penitents, and the same year Cyprian had to appeal to the courage of his people during a devastating plague, urging them to self-sacrificing charity toward Christian and pagan sufferers alike (*De mortalitrate*).

The spread and persistence of the Novatianist schism raised the question whether those who had received Novatianist baptism should, on reconciliation with the Church, be baptized anew. This led to the baptismal controversy (255–257). It was the practice of the African Church (as of many Oriental churches) to ignore all heretical baptisms, and Cyprian himself maintained that no baptism, or any sacrament administered outside the Church, had any value. He felt that the unity of the Church was at stake, and by his correspondence and in three successive synods hc succeeded in rallying the whole African episcopate to his view, as is proved by the unanimous votes of the third synod, Sept. 1, 256 (*Sententiae episcoporum numero LXXXVII*).

The very length of the controversy indicates that Cyprian's view was not so obvious as he tried to make out and that, in fact, it was not the universal practice of the Church. Indeed Stephen, bishop of Rome, appealed to traditional practice when he exacted that reconciliation should be effected without fresh Baptism. Cyprian vehemently repudiated this recognition of heretical baptism as a betrayal of the Church's unity and refused to be intimidated by Stephen's threat of excommunication. Cyprian was supported in this attitude by a vehement denunciation of Pope Stephen that he received from FIRMILIAN, bishop of Caesarea in Cappadocia. However, Cyprian may well have been distressed about it, for it was at this time that he wrote his treatise *De bono patientiae*.

Valerian Persecution. Cyprian was exiled to Curubis on the coast (Aug. 30, 257), and a year later, by reason of more stringent imperial orders, he was returned to be tried in Carthage, where he was permitted to wait quietly in his villa. He ignored the proconsul's summons to Utica, determined, as he said, not to deprive his own people of the witness of their bishop's martyrdom. The plain records of his trial and of his last moments before beheading show him treating it all as a matter of course, with no call for rhetoric. Martyrdom spoke louder than words. Of Christ himself he had written: *Dei Sermo ad crucem tacens ducitur* (The Word of God was led, wordless, to the cross).

Cyprianic Corpus. Cyprian's writings are generally divided into treatises, letters, and *spuria,* among which the last are a few contemporary significant writings. Besides the treatises already mentioned, the *Ad Demetrianum* is a vigorous defense of Christianity against pagan calumnies; but most of the treatises are addresses to his flock: an exhortation to those expecting martyrdom, *Ad Fortunatum,* a commentary on the Our Father; *De dominica oratione,* a conference to consecrated virgins; *De habitu virginum;* and the last two, on charity and on jealousy, *De opere et eleemosynis* and *De zelo et livore.* The *Quod idola dii non sint* is almost certainly spurious.

The standard collection of 81 letters includes a few by his correspondents or by other contemporaries. Altogether they give a vivid picture of Christian life in Carthage, especially during the persecutions, and throw light on the organization of the Church not only in Africa from Mauretania to Tripolitania, but also in Spain, Gaul, and Rome itself. At the same time they reveal the character and activities of Cyprian, a bishop often in peril of his life but totally dedicated to his flock, and while a leader of men, beloved and respected by Christian and pagan alike, yet the object of slander and opposition from a handful of his clergy. He could be sympathetic yet firm, just as he could be lyrical in his praises and mordant in his irony. He was a man of prayer who drew his strength from his faith in Christ and the Holy Spirit dwelling in the Church, at one with the sufferings of those whom he encouraged to martyrdom, and training his people to be at one with

him in his own. His writings reveal his practical faith and his humanity far better than does the stilted eulogy of his *Vita* (written soon after his martyrdom, apparently by his deacon, Pontius) or even the so-called *Acta proconsularia,* though both these records have preserved factual details that complete the portrait. These, too, form part of the corpus.

Ecclesiology. Cyprian's conception of the Church manifests itself in his treatment of Baptism, the Eucharist, PENANCE, and the ministry, as also in his relations with the laity (parents and children, virgins, etc.), with his clergy, and with his fellow bishops. He had a keen sense of the unity of the Church which was shown in his own church of Carthage, not only by the assertion of his episcopal authority over the faithful, but also by his normal practice of making no clerical appointment without first consulting his clergy and people. All alike had committed themselves to Christ; and their union with him, which had begun with the remission of sin in Baptism, was fostered and strengthened by the Eucharist and repaired or restored by almsdeeds or by the official Penance in which bishop, clergy, and faithful cooperated with the repenting sinner.

The Universal Church. The Carthaginian Church was only part of a greater unity: the unity, first, of the African Churches, whose bishops met in frequent synods, and then of all the rightful bishops of the *ecclesia catholica,* whose common faith and concord were inspired by the Holy Spirit. Hence HERESY and SCHISM were equally abhorrent to Cyprian as breaches of the one faith and of the charity that the unity of the Church demanded. Anyone who broke with his bishop put himself outside the Church; and a bishop who broke away from the consortium of his fellow bishops not only put himself outside the Church, but forfeited all his episcopal powers, as did a bishop who betrayed the faith under persecution or who led a scandalous life.

In reaction, perhaps, to Tertullian's MONTANISM, Cyprian believed that the Spirit was not active save through the legitimate bishops of the Church; hence his stand against heretical baptism and orders. He did not allow for any uncovenanted action of the Spirit, and while he was wont to quote ''He that is not with Me is against Me'' (Lk 11.23), he never quoted ''He that is not against you is for you'' (Lk 9.50). His attitude was later explicitly adopted by the DONATISTS. St. AUGUSTINE, while refuting them, rightly excused Cyprian's mistake as a result of the incomplete understanding, in earlier times, of the complexities of sacramental efficacy. In the interval the Church's practice had been defined on the lines laid down by Pope Stephen, against Cyprian's intransigence, but with qualifications that met some of Cyprian's criticisms.

The Roman Primacy. The dispute between Pope Stephen and the African bishops raises the question of Cyprian's attitude to the PAPACY, which has given rise to much barren controversy in the past. This was partly a result of the so-called interpolations in Cyprian's *De unitate* but chiefly because of the mistaken assumption, common to both sides, that if the papal primacy was of divine origin, Cyprian would have recognized it on the baptismal issue and bowed before it. Catholics strove to prove that he did, others that he did not. But it is now generally recognized that in the first centuries the position of the bishop of Rome was not so clear-cut as to constitute a doctrine explicitly believed by every part of the Church, but was the subject of a development analogous to that of many other elements of the faith.

Cyprian's attitude (of which his dispute with Stephen was only a short, if violent, phase) represents one of the stages of that development in the African area. If he based the unity of the Church on the concord of bishops—the "collegiality of the episcopate"—it was because they all derived their responsibilities and powers in the Church from Peter "on whom the Church was built." He argued that Christ had first entrusted them to that *one* man alone (Peter) to show that all the shepherds of the Church should act *as one,* that is, in harmony with one another. But this theory, true as far as it went, put all bishops on the same level and left vague the position of the bishop of Rome in spite of his having inherited, in a more special way, the *Cathedra Petri.*

In practice Cyprian generally showed the greatest regard toward Rome and recognized his obligation to inform its bishop of any important development in his own Church. Even when he thought that Pope Stephen was imperiling the unity of the Church by recognizing heretical baptism, he never considered that Stephen should be deposed, as he had Marcianus of Arles for his Novatianism. In fact, he showed by his conduct a certain consciousness of elements in the mystery of the Church that he did not allow for in this *theory* of its unity. Thus if each bishop was free to "rebaptize" or not (as Cyprian's second council assured the pope), what would Cyprian do when heretics reconciled by Stephen visited Carthage? According to him they had never been baptized and, logically, he would have to refuse them communion. Without being aware of it, he was undermining that very unity of the Church that he had so much at heart.

Whether Cyprian ever came to see the ambiguity of his position is not known; but even if Stephen excommunicated him (which is quite uncertain), after Stephen's death Cyprian's relations with Rome seem to have been renewed. Rome must have soon forgotten the brush with Cyprian, since it included the day of his martyrdom among the very few feasts of its earliest calendar, that of the CHRONOGRAPHER OF 354, and set his name permanently among the martyrs selected for special mention in the canon of its liturgy.

Influence and Memory. Cyprian's influence in subsequent ages may be gauged by the number of manuscripts of his works that have survived, perhaps surpassed only by those of the four great Latin DOCTORS OF THE CHURCH. Already highly esteemed by Augustine, he was one of the few authorities quoted as decisive at the Council of EPHESUS (431) against NESTORIANISM, and his name heads the list of orthodox Fathers in the *Decretum Gelasianum.* He was used by both sides in the INVESTITURE controversy and also provided material for GRATIAN's *Decretum,* through which the great scholastics chiefly quoted him.

Diligently transcribed during the RENAISSANCE, his writings were freely drawn upon for proof texts during the century of the Reformation by Cardinal FISHER, John CALVIN, Robert BELLARMINE, and many other writers.

In modern times a number of authors specify the contrasting ecclesiologies that allow or refuse validity to sacraments conferred outside the Church as being, respectively, Augustinian or Cyprianic, but this is an oversimplification. Cyprian's ecclesiology contained much more than do many such "Cyprianic" theories today, and except for that one point, Augustine's ecclesiology was but a development of Cyprian's.

By the time of St. Augustine there were in Carthage three churches dedicated to St. Cyprian, one of which stood over his tomb. At Moissac, in the south of France, what purport to be his relics have been venerated since 1122, having been transferred there from Lyons, where, according to FLORUS the deacon, they were brought from Carthage in the time of Charlemagne.

Feast: Sept. 16.

Bibliography: Works. *Opera omnia,* ed. G. HARTEL, 3 v. (*Corpus scriptorum ecclesiasticorum latinorum* (Vienna 1866–) 3.1–3.3; 1868–71); *Patrologiae cursus completus, series latina;* suppl., ed. A. HAMMAN (Paris 1957–) 1:34–71; "De ecclesiae catholicae unitate," critical ed. in M. BÉVENOT, *The Tradition of Manuscripts* (Oxford 1961) 96–123; *Select Epistles,* ed. T. A. LACEY, tr. N. MARSHALL (Society for Promoting Christian Knowledge; London; 1922); *"The Lapsed"* and *"The Unity of the Catholic Church,"* ed. and tr. M. BÉVENOT (*Ancient Christian Writers,* ed. J. QUASTEN et al. 25; Westminster, Md.-London 1957). Literature. M. BÉVENOT, "St. Cyprian and Moissac: A 13th–Century Sequence," *Traditio* 19 (1963) 147–166; *St. Cyprian's "De Unitate" Chapter 4 in the Light of the Manuscripts* (Analecta Gregoriana 11; Rome 1937); *"Primatus Petro datur," Journal of Theological Studies* 5 (1954) 19–35. J. LE MOYNE, ". . . De Unitate chapitre 4," *Revue Bénédictine* 63 (1953) 70–115. *Latinitas christianorum primaeva* 5, 6, 8, 9 (Nijmegen 1936–39). A. D'ALÉS, *La Théologie de saint Cyprien* (2d ed. Paris 1922). H. KOCH, *Cyprianische Unter-*

suchungen (Bonn 1926); *Cathedra Petri* (Giessen 1930). B. POSCH-MANN, *Ecclesia Principalis . . . zur Frage des Primats bei Cyprian* (Breslau 1933). J. QUASTEN, *Patrology*, 3 v. (Westminster, Md. 1950–53), 2:340–383. B. ALTANER, *Patrology*, tr. H. GRAF from 5th German ed. (New York 1960) 193–205. *Clavis Patrum latinorum*, ed. E. DEKKERS (2d ed. Streenbrugge 1961) 38–79. P. GODET, *Dictionnaire de théologie catholique*, ed. A. VACANT et al., 15 v. (Paris 1903–50; Tables générales 1951–) 3.2:2459–70. O. BARDEN-HEWER, *Geschichte der altkirchlichen Literatur*, 5 v. (Freiburg 1913–32) 2:442–517. E. W. BENSON, *Cyprian: His Life, His Times, His Work* (London 1897). J. J. SEBASTIAN, *Baptisma Unum in Ecclesia Sancta . . .: A Theological Appraisal of the Baptismal Controversy in the Work and Writings of Cyprian of Carthage* (Delhi 1997). J. P. BURNS, "Social Context in the Controversy Between Cyprian and Stephen," *Studia Patristica* 24 (Louvain 1993) 38–44. M. M. SAGE, *Cyprian* (Cambridge, Mass. 1975). P. B. HINCHCLIFF, *Cyprian of Carthage and the Unity of the Christian Church* (London 1974). *Letters of St. Cyprian of Carthage*, 4 v., ed. G. W. CLARKE (New York 1984). P. MONCEAUX, *Histoire littéraire de l'Afrique chrétienne*, 7 v. (Paris 1901–23; repr. Brussels 1963) v.2. J. LUDWIG, *Der heilige Märtyrerbischof Cyprian von Karthago* (Munich 1951).

[M. BÉVENOT]

CYPRIAN OF TOULON, ST.

Bishop; d. Toulon, France, *c.* 543–49. CAESARIUS OF ARLES consecrated Cyprian bishop of Toulon (before 517). His signature is recorded for a number of synods: the first, Arles (524), and the last, Orléans (541). At the synods of Orange (529) and Valence (*c.* 529), SEMI-PELAGIANISM found in him a vigorous opponent. Disciple, friend, and stanch supporter of Caesarius, he is the principal author (among several collaborators) of the *Vita s. Caesarii*, accepted by critics of medieval hagiography as "an exceedingly precious monument of history." Also extant is a letter, dated 530, from Cyprian to Bp. Maximus of Geneva that gives evidence of Cyprian's orthodoxy on certain moot theological questions of the day.

Feast: Oct. 3.

Bibliography: *Vita s. Caesarii*, in *Monumenta Germaniae Historica: Scriptores rerum Merovingicarum* 3:457–501. *Letter to Maximus*, in *Monumenta Germaniae Historica: Epistolae* 3:434–436. *Monumenta Germaniae Historica: Concilia* 1:38, 42, 53, 58, 59, 61, 96. *Acta Sanctae Sedis* Oct. 2:164–178. O. BARDEN-HEWER, *Geschichte der altkirchlichen Literatur* (Freiburg 1913–32) 5:356. J. L. BAUDOT and L. CHAUSSIN, *Vies des saints et des bienheureux selon l'ordre du calendrier avec l'historique des fêtes* (Paris 1935–56) 10:53–54.

[G. M. COOK]

CYPRUS, THE CATHOLIC CHURCH IN

The largest island in the eastern Mediterranean Sea, located approximately 60 miles south of the Turkish coastline and west of Syria, Cyprus has a long and important political and cultural history, owing to its geographical position. The island's central treeless plains rise to mountains in the north, with Mt. Olympus dominating the range at over 6,400 feet. Mountains rise in the southern part of the island, worn by heavy winter rains. There are few rivers and no significant inland lakes. The island's name derives from the Latin "cuprum" or copper, and Cyprus was one of the chief sources of that metal in the ancient world. Other natural resources include pyrites, asbestos, timber, salt and marble. Agricultural production, which occurs mainly in the north and which is restricted by the lack of fresh water, includes potatoes, citrus, vegetables, barley, grapes and olives.

Under the political sway of Turkey until the region became part of the British Empire in the late 19th century, Cyprus attained political independence in 1960. Armed rebellion between southern Greeks and northern minority Turkish factions followed a Greek Cypriot effort to take control of the government in 1974, resulting in the intervention of Turkish troops and proclamation of a Turkish Republic of Northern Cyprus in 1983. Settlement talks remained underway in 2000. While Cyprus was invited to join the European Union, the political stalemate threatened that opportunity.

Ecclesiastically, the autocephalous Greek Orthodox Church has its archdiocese in Nicosia, as does the Latin vicariate under the patriarch of Jerusalem, which has five parishes. The Maronite archdiocese of Cyprus is also located in Nicosia, and has ten parishes administered by six diocesan and 11 religious priests, while seven brothers and 43 sisters attend to the parishioners' educational and humanitarian needs. Cyprus' Christian churches belong to the Middle East Council of Churches, which meets regularly to promote unity in the conflict-ridden Middle East.

The Early Church

Cyprus was the center of a flourishing culture during the Bronze Age, and relations with Syria and Asia Minor were particularly close and constant. From the city of Salamis, Mycenaean influences spread rapidly from *c.* 1400 B.C. and coincided with an increasing exploitation of the island's copper deposits. Greek immigration increased due to the influx of refugees from central and southern Greece following the Dorian migration, and Greek culture eventually dominated the island. Kingship was the normal form of government among Cypriot cities.

Beginning *c.* 1000 B.C., Phoenicians established themselves on the island, establishing the city of Citium (Larnaca). From 709 to 350 B.C. the island fell in turn under the domination of Assyria, Egypt and Persia. In

333 B.C. Cyprus supported Alexander the Great, and in 295 B.C. it became one of the prized possessions of the Ptolemies, kings of Egypt, who exploited its timber, copper and other resources. In 58 B.C. Cyprus, with its ten city kingdoms, was annexed by Rome and became a senatorial province.

Pagan cults flourished on the island from the earliest times. The religious institutions that followed were predominantly Greek, but reflected influences of the eastern Mediterranean from Asia Minor to Egypt. Paphos, associated with the birth of Aphrodite, was the center of one of the most important cults of that goddess in the Greek world. Beginning in the early Ptolemaic period, a steady influx of Jews immigrated to Cyprus. In A.D. 115–116 Jews revolted throughout the island under the rule of Trajan; the destruction of life and property was enormous and the revolt was put down with corresponding severity, culminating in the expulsion of the remaining Jews from Cyprus and their future exclusion.

Cyprus was one of the first regions to hear the Gospel outside of Palestine. Barnabas and Mnason were Cypriots (Acts 4.36; 21.16), and the Gospel was first preached in Antioch by men from Cyrene and Cyprus who had fled from Jerusalem after the stoning of Stephen (11.19). Saints PAUL and BARNABAS preached throughout the island on Paul's first missionary journey, and evidence of his presence has been uncovered near an ancient Greek temple in the town of Paphos. Barnabas, with Mark as his companion, returned to Cyprus at a later date (15.39). Apart from what is related in Acts there is no reliable information on the Church of Cyprus until the early 4th century.

Under Byzantium and Islam. Following the reorganization of the Roman Empire by Diocletian and Constantine the Great, Cyprus was included in the Diocese of the Orient, under the jurisdiction of the *Comes Orientis.* Under Justinian the Great, it was placed under the control of the *Quaestor Exercitus* (quaestor of the army), and from the 7th century it became one of the Byzantine themes.

Cypriot bishops are known to have signed the acts of the Council of Nicaea in 325 and the letter of the Council of Sardica in 343–344, and at least four were present at the Council of Constantinople in 381. The most distinguished representative of the Church of Cyprus in this period was the scholar EPIPHANIUS OF SALAMIS-Constantia (d. 403). During the 5th century the Church engaged in a heated struggle with the Patriarchate of Antioch, and ultimately secured recognition of its independence on the ground that St. Barnabas founded it. The archbishop of Constantia henceforth had the right to consecrate his suffragans, summon them to council and assume the title of Beatitude.

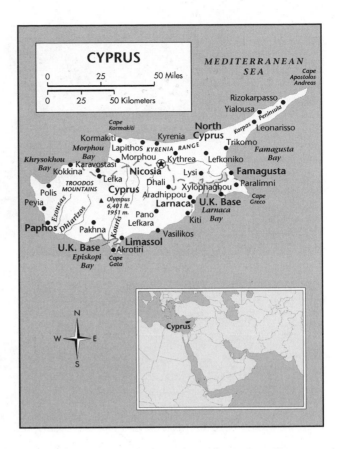

From the 5th to the 9th century the Church of Cyprus took an active part in religious affairs in the East. Three Cypriot bishops participated in the Council of Chalcedon (451) and at the Second Council of Nicaea (787), which condemned the ICONOCLASM of the Byzantine emperor; the archbishop of Constantia took a leadership role.

As early as 632, Cyprus had begun to suffer from Arab attacks, and in 647 it was conquered and briefly held by Muslim invaders. In 802 it was occupied by the Arabs, who remained until they were driven out under Nicephorus II Phocas (963–969). The patriarchs of Constantinople seized the opportunity provided by the Islamic incursions to interfere in internal Church affairs, resulting in revolts against the Church under emperors Michael IV (1034–47) and Alexius Comnenus (1081–1118). The brutal reigns of later emperors would prepare the way for Latin domination.

Under the Crusaders and the Venetians. Richard I, of England, called Cœur de Lion, seized Cyprus in 1191, and the island soon found its way to French crusader Guy de Lusignan, titular king of Jerusalem. On Guy's death in 1194 his brother Amaury assumed the title of king of Cyprus and established a dynasty which ruled the island until 1489, when Catarina Cornaro, widow of King James II, abdicated the throne in favor of the Italian trad-

Boats moored in the harbor at Kyrenia, Cyprus. (©Chris Hellier/CORBIS)

ing state of Venice. Transformed into a Western feudal state by its new Venetian rulers, a Latin Church hierarchy was established beside the Greek. The Latin hierarchy eventually gained dominance, reducing the 15 Greek sees to four. A number of Western monastic orders were also established on the island, and there occurred the confiscation of much Greek ecclesiastical property by the Latin-rite Church. Tension and frequent violence erupted between Greeks and Latins of all ranks during the schism, and papal interventions supported the subordination of the Greek hierarchy to the Latin, although some attempts were made to ameliorate the general situation. The Council of Florence, despite its efforts at reunion, could not reduce tension in Cyprus. The attempt of Helen Palaeologus, wife of King John II, to appoint a Greek archbishop independent of Rome led Pope Nicholas V (1447) to order his legate, Archbishop Andrew of Nicosia, to work actively for the conversion of the Greeks using such civil authority as was necessary. The Venetians treated Greek Cypriots harshly, forcing many to flee to Asia Minor. Those who remained looked forward to the island's imminent conquest by the Ottoman Turks.

Under Turkish Domination (1571–1878). The Turkish conquerors who routed the Venetians in 1571 did little to stabilize the Greek Orthodox Church. Instead, Greeks and Latins alike were massacred, including bishops and heads of monasteries; churches were profaned and turned into mosques, monasteries into stables. After Ottoman rule was firmly established, Greeks were permitted to restore their hierarchy and buy back some of their monasteries, although old sees were not re-erected and the Church was limited to the four the Latins had not abolished. Nicosia became the archepiscopal see, and the three bishops took the title of metropolitans under the jurisdiction of the archbishop.

Under Turkish administration, the members of the Greek hierarchy functioned as civil as well as ecclesiastical heads of their people. Perhaps because of this extended power, a continuous scramble for high ecclesiastical office continued through the early 19th century, and numerous abuses and quarrels arose, particularly between the archbishop and his metropolitans. Revolution was soon in the wind, and on July 9, 1821 a meeting of all Christian religious and lay leaders was convoked at Nicosia. The gates of the city were closed, and the Turkish garrison massacred all who were assembled there, including the archbishop, his three metropolitans and the heads of monasteries. The Turks then requested the Christians to select new bishops. Failing in their appeal to the Patriarch of Constantinople, they turned to the Patriarch of Antioch, who sent three archbishops as consecrators. Joachim, the econome of the church of St. Barnabas, was made archbishop of Cyprus, in part because of his knowledge of Turkish. He and his successors worked tirelessly to prevent further persecutions. While they were unable to alleviate the heavy burden of taxation on their flocks, they succeeded to some extent in restoring educational training, which had been suppressed following the massacre.

The Modern Era

Cyprus remained part of the Ottoman Empire until the late 19th century, when it reverted to British control. Since that time the region has suffered from strong social, cultural and religious barriers between Cyprians of Greek and Turkish descent.

Ethnic Violence Characterizes 20th Century. In 1878 Great Britain leased Cyprus from Turkey and took over its administration. It annexed the island in 1914 and 11 years later made it a crown colony. The long agitation by many for union with Greece entered a new stage following World War II, marked by violence, guerilla warfare, terrorism and increasingly bitter relations and strife between Greek and Turkish Cypriots. Both Christian and Muslim religious leaders were heavily involved in political affairs, and repressive measures taken by the British, including the exile of bishops, failed to quell the growing violence.

In 1959, following a conference in Zürich, the prime ministers of Great Britain, Greece and Turkey signed an agreement accepted by both the Greek and the Turkish representatives from Cyprus. The agreement, which established Cyprus as an independent republic, went into effect on Aug. 16, 1960, and His Beatitude, Archbishop Makarios III, was elected the country's first president. The treaty precluded both union with Greece and partition, but brought little peace to the island.

Violence continued between Greeks and Turks in the island, resulting in heavy loss of life and destruction of property. In 1963 British troops were sent to Cyprus at the president's request, followed a year later by a U.N. peacekeeping force. Following an attempt by Greek Cypriots to take control of the government, Turkish military invaded the island, and the government temporarily collapsed. Ultimately, Makarios regained the presidency, although the location of a British Air Force base at Akrotiri and the establishment of a Turkish Federated State over more than 30 percent of northern Cyprus engendered political conflicts. Appointing its own president, the Turkish region proclaimed itself the Turkish Republic of North-

ern Cyprus in 1983; despite continued negotiations between the two governments there was little movement toward unity by 2000.

Greek Church Gains Independence. Dissension in the Cypriot Greek Orthodox Church reached a crisis following the death of Archbishop Sophronios in 1900, and the quarrel over his successor was ultimately settled by British recognition of one of the candidates in 1909. A charter for the Orthodox Church of Cyprus, containing 138 articles, was adopted in 1914, with some additions made in 1917 and 1918. The independence of the Church of Cyprus was again proclaimed, to be governed by a Holy Synod composed of the archbishop of Nicosia and the metropolis of Kyrenia, Citium and Paphos.

The exile of the bishops in 1931 created a new crisis. With the cooperation of the Patriarchate of Constantinople, the Church of Greece and the British government, the bishoprics were filled and a new archbishop was elected in 1947. The constitution of 1960 extended to the Greek Orthodox Church, as well as to the Muslim Vakf, and the Armenian Orthodox, Maronite and Latin-rite churches, the exclusive right to regulate its affairs and holdings. Both religious groups remained exempt from all state taxes. In the northern, Turkish-controlled area, only the Vakf was recognized by the government.

In 2000 the Greek Orthodox Church had one seminary and some 600 priests, and operated fewer than ten monasteries. The Franciscans of Jerusalem, who despite hazards had reestablished themselves in Cyprus in 1572, conducted the parishes of the Latin Catholics. Catholic sisters operated a hospital and several schools, supplementing the state-sanctioned teaching of the Greek Orthodox religion in all government-controlled schools. Other Catholic churches included Armenian, Byzantine and Maronite. There were several other orthodox groups, all small in the number of their respective adherents. There were also small groups; of Anglicans and Presbyterians as well as three schools under U.S. Protestant missionary control.

The forced emigration of Orthodox faithful and the loss of over 500 churches to the Muslims in the north continued to be a cause for distress among the island's Greek Orthodox community. In a speech before the Middle East Council of Churches convened in Cyprus in 1996, Orthodox Archbishop Chrysostomos called upon representatives of the assembled churches to ''not forget us in your prayers. . . . pray for us too and . . . we too will be praying for our brothers going through trials in the Middle Eastern region.'' In early 2000 borders between the two regions opened on religious holidays to allow the free passage of Greek pilgrims, north to the Apostolos Andreas monastery and Turkish faithful, south to the Hala Sultan mosque.

Bibliography: E. KIRSTEN, *Reallexikon für Antike und Christentum,* ed. T. KLAUSER [Stuttgart 1941 (1950)–] 3:481–499. H. LECLERCQ, *Dictionnaire d'archéologie chrétienne et de liturgie,* eds., F. CABROL, H. LECLERCQ and H. I. MARROU, 15 v. (Paris 1907–53) 3.1:1568–84. R. JANIN, *Dictionnaire d'histoire et de géographie ecclésiastiques,* ed. A. BAUDRILLART et al. (Paris 1912–) 12:791–820. G. HILL, *A History of Cyprus,* 4 v. (Cambridge, Eng. 1940–52). *Bilan du Monde. Encyclopédie Catholique du monde Chrétien,* 2 v. (Tournai 1964).

[M. R. P. MCGUIRE/EDS.]

CYRENAICS

A group of ancient Greek hedonists of the third and fourth centuries B.C., so named because Cyrene was the native city of the chief personalities. Reliable testimony from antiquity is scant; the main sources are Xenophon, Aristotle, Plutarch, Eusebius, and especially Cicero, Diogenes Laertius, and Sextus Empiricus. The Cyrenaics represented a tendency (αἵρεσις) rather than a school (σχολή).

Aristippus the Elder. The originator of the movement was Aristippus the Elder whose central notion was that pleasure is the *summum bonum* (*see* HEDONISM). Born in Cyrene *c.* 435 B.C., he arrived in Athens *c.* 416 and became a close follower of SOCRATES. Plato reports that he was absent from Athens in 399 at Socrates's death (*Phaedo* 59C). He seems to have taught the single Socratic doctrine that happiness is the end of the ethical life. Although Aristotle calls him a Sophist (*Meta.* 996a 33), he was not a disciple of Protagoras or other Sophists. Antiquity credits him with a long list of works, none of which are extant.

Aristippus the Younger. The son of Aristippus the Elder's daughter Arete, by whom he was instructed in hedonism, Aristippus the Younger was known on this account as Μητροδίδακτος (Mother-taught). The younger Aristippus developed and expanded the leading principles of the Cyrenaic movement, though many of his elaborations were attributed to the older man. It is likely that he was influenced by Pyrrho in his skeptical conception of knowledge (*see* PYRRHONISM).

Doctrines. Cyrenaic teaching is in effect an uncomplicated hedonism integrated with a thoroughgoing skeptical phenomenalism. Philosophy was conceived as a way of life rather than a scientific enterprise; consequently, philosophy of nature and logic were purposely neglected. The Cyrenaics used only a modicum of theory in order to rationalize their position.

Knowledge. The basic assumption is that the individual knows only his own sensations, which somehow arise from things in themselves that are not known [Sextus Empiricus, *Against the Logicians,* tr. R. G. Bury (*Loeb Classical Library* 1957) 1:191]. When one has the sensation of sweet or white, he does not know whether the object is sweet or white. His feelings are infallible, however, and thus whatever he perceives is true for him. No two perceivers have the same sensations, so that there is no knowledge common to different knowers. While it is true that men use words in common, the terms do not have a common referent. From this view, true communication would seem to be impossible. Sextus Empiricus carefully distinguished this theory of knowledge from that of the skeptics, while admitting a strong similarity between them [*Outlines of Pyrrhonism,* tr. R. G. Bury (*Loeb Classical Library;* 1955) 1:215].

Ethics. Cyrenaic morality is an ethic only in the sense that it deals with conceptions of good and evil; it lacks a recognition of obligation and duty. The basic principle is that the end (τέλος) of life and action is pleasure (ἡδονή), i.e., the pleasure of the present moment (μονοχρόνος ἡδονή) and not the sum of those of a lifetime (εὐδαιμονία). Accordingly actions are judged as good or evil, or indifferent, insofar as they afford pleasure or cause pain, or bring neither pleasure nor pain. Bodily pleasures are more intense than those of the mind. However, the wise man will always exercise prudence (φρόνησις) in assessing the consequences of actions in order to experience the most desirable effects. One must remain master of himself while seeking the maximum of pleasure. He should possess the pleasures and not they him [see Diogenes Laertius, *Lives of Eminent Philosophers,* tr. R. D. Hicks (New York 1925) 2:75, 87–88].

Further Developments. Ancient sources discuss other personalities of the third century B.C. indifferently as Cyrenaics, even though they introduced distinctive innovations and had their own disciples. Theodore the Atheist placed true pleasure in contentment rather than in present gratification. A wise man would perform religiously and socially unacceptable actions if the circumstances made them advisable. He stressed the independence of man and denied the existence of the gods. Hegesias considered individual acts of pleasure indifferent, and the τέλος to be a negative one, namely, the absence of pain (ἀπονία). If suicide were a means to this end, he recommended it; thus he was named Πεισι Θάνατος (Death-persuader) by the doxographers. Anniceris restored the primitive Cyrenaic conceptions situating pleasure in momentary feelings, but he also advocated a social consciousness for the wise man. Antiquity has indiscriminately fused his doctrines with those of the two Aristippuses.

Influence. The Cyrenaics had a short-lived influence in ancient Greece. By the end of the third century B.C. they were supplanted by the more powerful Epicurean hedonists who subsumed, where possible, the Cyrenaic views under their own. EPICURUS himself seems to have been influenced by them, and there were probably some controversies between Anniceris and the Epicureans.

See Also: EPICUREANISM; SKEPTICISM; GREEK PHILOSOPHY.

Bibliography: F. C. COPLESTON, *History of Philosophy* (Westminster, Maryland 1946–) v.1. J. OWENS, *A History of Ancient Western Philosophy* (New York 1959). G. GIANNANTONI, *I Cirenaici* (Florence 1958). ARISTIPPUS, *Aristippi et Cyrenaicorum fragmenta*, ed. E. MANNEBACH (Leiden 1961).

[L. A. BARTH]

CYRIL OF ALEXANDRIA, ST.

Bishop, theologian, Father and Doctor of the Church; b. Egypt, second half of the 4th century; d. Alexandria, June 27, 444.

Relatively little is known of Cyril's life and activity before 429. Nephew of Patriarch THEOPHILUS OF ALEXANDRIA, he received a comprehensive classical and theological education in that cultured city and was received by Theophilus into the ranks of the clergy. A monastic formation, though often asserted, is difficult to establish. Some personal and epistolary contact with monks of the desert in his formative period is likely, but an extended stay in the desert is open to serious objection.

Episcopate. The first clear date in Cyril's life is 403, when he accompanied Theophilus to Constantinople and, apparently convinced of the guilt of St. JOHN CHRYSOSTOM, was present at his deposition by the Synod of the OAK (Chalcedon). Elected to succeed Theophilus despite fierce opposition (Oct. 18, 412), he revealed affinities to his impetuous, highhanded uncle, especially in the early years of his episcopate (Socrates, *Hist. eccl.* 7.7, 13–15). Until 417, or even later, he refused to include Chrysostom's name in the diptychs of the Alexandrian Church. He pillaged and closed the churches of the NOVATIANS.

In retaliation for Jewish attacks on Christians, possibly perturbed as well by the attractive power of Judaism and its proselytizing activity, he expropriated the Jews and expelled them from Alexandria. Serious animosity severed him from the imperial urban prefect Orestes. For a time he honored as a martyr the Nitrian monk Ammonius, who had been fatally tortured not for his faith but for violence done to Orestes. The persistent tradition, based unjustifiably on Socrates' account (*Hist. eccl.* 7.15) of the incident, that Cyril provoked or was otherwise responsible for the murder of the famous Neoplatonist philosopher Hypatia, torn to pieces by a fanatical Christian mob in March of 415, lacks genuine foundation.

St. Cyril of Alexandria.

The regrettable violence of these early years was followed by a decade or more of peace, marked by much exegetical and theological writing, directed in part against 4th-century Arianism (cf. *Ep. pasch.* 12.3–6, for the year 424).

Nestorianism. Cyril's significance for theology and Church history stems from his opposition to NESTORIANISM. NESTORIUS, enthroned as patriarch of Constantinople on April 10, 428, found the expression Theotokos (God-bearing) difficult to harmonize with his conception of the relationship between the divine and the human in Christ. He preferred Christotokos (Christ-bearing) for its seeming lack of ambiguity and as a *via media* between Theotokos and anthrōpotokos (man-bearing). His intemperate language in this regard roused violent opposition in Egypt, Constantinople, and Rome. Cyril, with his Alexandrian background, found in Nestorius's position the 4th-century Christological error of two sons linked by a sheerly moral union, thus making the Incarnation an illusion, undermining the redemption, and reducing Communion to cannibalism. To the refutation of this doctrine Cyril devoted a special letter to the Egyptian monks (*Ep.* 1) and his pastoral letter for Easter 429 (*Ep. pasch.* 17), in which he declared that to deny or even abandon Theotokos would be equivalent to denial of the Council of Nicaea.

A sharp exchange of letters between Cyril (*Ep.* 2 and 4) and Nestorius (Loofs, *Nestoriana* 168–169, 173–180) only confirmed their opposition. To counteract Nestorian influence at the imperial court, Cyril wrote three memorials in 430 *On Correct Belief in Christ,* the first addressed to THEODOSIUS II, the second to his younger sisters, Arcadia and Marina, the third to his elder sister, PULCHERIA, and his wife, Eudocia. In the same year both patriarchs presented their case to Pope Celestine I (*Ep.* 11; Loofs, 165–172), who held a synod at Rome (August 430) that pronounced in favor of Theotokos and condemned Nestorius, "the denier of God's birth." Celestine warned Nestorius that unless he retracted his doctrine in writing within ten days of receiving this notification and adopted the doctrine "of Rome, Alexandria, and the whole Catholic Church" (Celestine, *Ep.* 13.11), he would be considered excommunicate.

Council of Ephesus. Cyril, delegated to act for Celestine, held a synod in Alexandria in November, then sent a letter to Nestorius (*Ep.* 17), appending for his acceptance 12 anathemas couched in uncompromisingly Alexandrian terms that carried to Antiochene ears Apollinarian overtones. On Nov. 19, 430, Theodosius, persuaded by Nestorius (who did not learn of his Roman condemnation until December 7), summoned a general council to meet at Ephesus on June 7, 431 [J. D. Mansi, *Sacrorum Concilliorum nova et amplissima collectio,* 31 v. (Florence-Venice 1757–98); repr. and cont. by L. Petit and J. B. Martin 53 v. in 60 (Paris 1889–1927; repr. Graz 1960–) 4: 1112–16]. The council thus convoked was accepted by Celestine [see letters written in May of 431 to the court and to Cyril; P. Jaffé, *Regesta pontificum romanorum ab condita ecclesia ad annum post Christum natum 1198,* ed. S. Löwenfeld et al., 2 v. (2d ed. Leipzig 1881–88; repr. Graz 1956) 1.377], but he still regarded Nestorius as condemned; his three legates were to conform in all respects to Cyril's views (*ibid.* 1.378–379).

Cyril opened the council on June 22, though the Oriental bishops (in large measure supporters of Nestorius) and the papal legates had not arrived. In these circumstances Nestorius understandably refused to appear, despite the three canonical citations. That first day, the council declared Cyril's second letter to Nestorius (*Ep.* 4) in full accord with Nicaea, condemned Nestorius as a heretic and deposed him, and proclaimed Mary Theotokos. The same evening, Nestorius was notified of the council's action in a document that began, "To Nestorius, the new Judas."

John of Antioch. Four or five days later, John of Antioch and the Oriental bishops arrived in Ephesus, held a synod (43 or 53 participants), denounced the condemnation of Nestorius, and deposed Cyril and the local bishop,

Memnon (Mansi 4:1372–73). On July 11 the papal legates approved what the council had done before their arrival and confirmed the deposition of Nestorius. Theodosius, on his part, approved the depositions of Cyril, Memnon, and Nestorius, had them imprisoned, and reproved the council for not heeding his instructions. Cyril, under guard for almost three months, was released in mid-October and returned to Alexandria, where he was welcomed on October 30 as a second Athanasius. Nestorius retired to a monastery in Antioch.

Sequel of Ephesus. The rupture between Cyril and the Orientals was not healed until 433. The chief obstacles were the 12 anathemas of Cyril and the condemnation of Nestorius. Thanks in great part to the mediation of Acacius of Beroea and to legitimate compromise on both sides, an accord was reached. Cyril, still suspected of Apollinarian tendencies, provided explanations of his doctrine (e.g., *Ep.* 33, to Acacius), especially to refute the charge of change or confusion of the two natures in Christ. These explanations were found acceptable, and the leading Antiochenes were persuaded, reluctantly, to abandon Nestorius.

Symbol of Union. The instrument of agreement, the Symbol of Union, was contained in a letter from John to Cyril (*Ep.* 38, in the correspondence of Cyril). Apart from the closing sentence, it reproduced a formula, drafted by THEODORET OF CYR, that the Oriental bishops had approved at Ephesus in August 431 and had sent to Theodosius. Cyril welcomed this formula with enthusiasm (*Ep.* 39).

Cyril's reaction to the Symbol of Union reveals a remarkable maturing on his part. As with Athanasius after Nicaea, so here too terminology was seen as secondary and deceptive. He made concessions: the 12 anathemas were played down; such favorite expressions as "one nature" and "hypostatic union" were dropped; Antiochene language such as "one *prosōpon*" and "union of two natures" was accepted; safeguards were appended to Theotokos; the Antiochene description of Christ's humanity as the Word's "temple" was recognized as legitimate; Cyril's far-reaching *communicatio idiomatum* had limits placed on it. But in substance he was vindicated: Nestorius's condemnation was accepted; Theotokos, properly understood, was pronounced orthodox; the "two sons" doctrine was clearly rejected; the identification of the subject in the God-man with the eternal Word was indisputably recognized; all talk of "conjunction" of the two natures had given place to *henōsis* (union).

Policy of Moderation. Tragically but understandably, the Symbol of Union did not achieve more than a partial, fragile unity. Cyril's own allies were not altogether convinced that he had sacrificed language only, and not orthodoxy. Especially outside Egypt, he was obliged time and again to defend his position on the "two natures": in answer to Acacius of Melitine (*Ep.* 40), Eulogius of Constantinople (*Ep.* 44), Valerianus of Iconium (*Ep.* 50), and Successus of Diocaesarea in Isauria (*Ep.* 45, 46). He had to write to Maximus, a deacon of Antioch (*Ep.* 57, 58), to urge continued communion with Bishop John.

For a large number of the Oriental bishops, e.g., Theodoret of Cyr, Nestorius had been illegitimately deposed and his doctrine unjustifiably condemned. The bishops of Cilicia Secunda severed Cyril from their fellowship until such time as he should retract his anathemas. Until his death, however, Cyril's policy of moderation kept his extreme partisans under reasonable control; on his deathbed he refused, despite personal inclination and uncommon pressure, to condemn THEODORE OF MOPSUESTIA, the teacher of Nestorius. With his death were unleashed the forces that brought MONOPHYSITISM to a head and led to the Council of CHALCEDON.

Writings. Cyril's extant works fill 10 volumes of J. P. Migne's *Patrologia Graeca.* Diffuse and ornate save in polemics, they are rich in ideas, sometimes profound in their development, often penetrating in argumentation. His literary activity is divided by the Nestorian controversy: until 428 he concentrated on exegesis and anti-Arian polemics; from 429, he was all but exclusively concerned with Nestorianism.

Scriptural Exegesis. Cyril's exegetical works form the major, but not the more impressive, portion of his literary production. His Old Testament exegesis was highly influenced by Alexandrian allegory and typology, though he insisted that not all the details of the Old Testament have a spiritual meaning. His New Testament exegesis was more literal, particularly in doctrinal controversy, but the historical-philological approach is still not the hermeneutic of his predilection. His Old Testament commentaries include: *Adoration and Worship in Spirit and Truth* (after 412, before 429), 17 books proving from texts of the Pentateuch that the Law was abrogated only in its letter; 13 books of *Elegant Comments* or *Polished Explanations* (*Glaphyra;* same period), exegeting select passages of the Pentateuch in their proper sequence; *Commentary on Isaia* (after *Adoration* and *Glaphyra,* but before 429), five extensive books in 12 main sections.

Extant in catenae are numerous fragments from other Old Testament commentaries: Kings, Psalms, Song of Songs, Proverbs, Jeremiah, Ezekiel, and Daniel. New Testament exegesis includes: *Commentary on John* (before 429, but *terminus a quo* strongly disputed), 12 books (7 and 8 not extant) of a dogmatic-polemic tendency—e.g., against Arianism, Eunomianism, and Antiochene Christology; *Commentary on Luke,* actually a series of

homilies (perhaps from 430 on), practical rather than dogmatic, with anti-Nestorian polemic (only three complete sermons in Greek, though a Syriac version gives 156 homilies); *Commentary on Matthew* (after 428), fragmentary, but covering all 28 chapters of Matthew. Extant in catenae are fragments from lost commentaries on Romans, 1 and 2 Corinthians, and Hebrews.

Dogmatic and Polemic Works. The earliest of Cyril's dogmatic-polemic works were directed against the Arians. The more important is the *Thesaurus on the Holy and Consubstantial Trinity* (early in his episcopal career, or 423–425), a summa of Arian objections and their refutation, almost a third of it a reproduction of Athanasius, *C. Arianos* 3; the other, *On the Holy and Consubstantial Trinity* (shortly after *Thesaurus*), is in the form of seven dialogues: one to six on the consubstantiality of the Son; the seventh on that of the Spirit.

Anti-Nestorian Writings. Against the Nestorians Cyril wrote *Five Tomes against the Blasphemies of Nestorius* (spring 430), a critical examination of sermons published by Nestorius in 429; *On Correct Belief in Christ* (430), three memorials to the imperial court; three apologies (431) defending the 12 anathemas (cf. *Ep.* 17), viz, *Against the Oriental Bishops* (answering charges of Andrew of Samosata), *Letter to Euoptius* (answering accusations of Theodoret of Cyr), and *Explanation at Ephesus* (written while in prison, August or September 431); *Apology to the Emperor* (immediately after release and return to Alexandria), justifying his actions before and during the council; *Scholia on the Incarnation* (after 431), explaining the names Christ, Emmanuel, and Jesus, and defining the hypostatic union as opposed to a mixture or external relationship only; *Against Those Who Refuse to Acknowledge the Holy Virgin to Be Mother of God* (between 435–440?), insisting that to reject Theotokos is to oppose Scripture; *Against Diodore* [of Tarsus] *and Theodore* [of Mopsuestia], teachers of Nestorius (*c.* 438), extant in considerable Greek and Syriac fragments; and *On the Unity of Christ,* a dialogue on the union of divine and human in Christ so mature in thought and expression that it seems to be one of Cyril's last anti-Nestorian writings.

The *Apology against Julian* (between 433 and 441) is an effort to refute Julian the Apostate's three books *Against the Galileans* (363); the first ten books are extant in their entirety in Greek, books 11 to 20 only in Greek and Syriac fragments. The work suggests that paganism was still very much alive in 5th-century Egypt.

Letters, Sermons. There have survived 29 of Cyril's annual *Paschal Letters* to the churches of Egypt (years 414–442), announcing the date of Easter and the preceding fast, and exhorting to fast and abstinence, vigilance and prayer, almsgiving and works of mercy, with some polemic against paganism, Judaism, and heresy. Of the *Sermons,* no more than 22 survive (called *Homiliae diversae* in the editions), some of them fragmentary; most of them demand careful investigation for authenticity, even the famous Marian homily (*Hom.* 4) supposedly delivered at Ephesus between June 23 and 27, 431. Cyril's *Letters* (71 in Migne, five more published by Schwartz), mostly of dogmatic importance (cf. the three "ecumenical" letters to Nestorius: 4, 17, and 39), have also some significance for the history of church-state problems, East-West relations, episcopal sees, and theological schools.

Doctrinal Significance. Cyril was primarily a dogmatic theologian. Although in the course of his prolific production he touched most of the important areas of theology (creation, sin, grace, Church, Sacraments, eschatology, faith), systematically and *ex professo* he dealt only with the Trinity (the first 15 years of his episcopate) and the Incarnation (from 429). His Trinitarian doctrine gathers up the Eastern heritage of the 4th century (especially Athanasius and the Cappadocians) and is rich and suggestive on the Holy Spirit, not only within the Trinity but in His mission to men.

Christology. Cyril's claim to theological immortality rests on his role in the development of Christology, for the Council of Ephesus, the controversies that raged around Theotokos, and even Cyril's Mariology were basically Christological issues, primarily an effort to plumb the meaning of St. John's "The Word was made flesh." Cyril's principal preoccupation here was to preserve the unity of Christ, which he felt was compromised by Nestorius and other Antiochenes. In the Incarnation, he insisted, the eternal Word took to Himself, and made His own, human flesh animated by a rational soul. The union between the Word and this humanity is a true, real union, as opposed to a merely moral or accidental union, or a union by sharing the same honor or adoration.

One Hypostasis. Because the union is so intimate, one may and must say not simply that the Word is in a man as in a temple, or that the Word assumed a man, but that the Word *is* man. In Christ there is only one Son of God, namely, the eternal Word who is both God and man. There is only one "hypostasis" or "nature" existing independently in the real order, the Word Incarnate; therefore there is only one incarnate "nature" of the Word of God. Consequently, He who was conceived and born of Mary, He who suffered, died, and was buried, is identically He who was eternally begotten of the Father. For the same reason Mary is truly and properly Theotokos. Nevertheless the flesh of Christ does not cease to be human. It is the Word's flesh, but it is not the Word. There is no mixing of humanity and divinity, no conversion of one into the other; each retains its properties. Though the Word of God actually suffered, He did so in His humanity, not in His divinity.

The fact is that the Nestorian question need not have developed so acrimoniously or ended so tragically. The tragedy was born of the two protagonists, different in theological background, in approaches to the Christological problem, and in personal defects and mistakes.

Complicating Factors. The different theological backgrounds are understandable: Cyril's thinking is rooted in the School of ALEXANDRIA; Nestorius's in that of ANTIOCH. In approach, as Grillmeier has shown, Nestorius stressed the distinction in Christ; his insight lay in seeking the unity and the distinction on different levels: unity on the level of the *prosōpon,* distinction on the level of the natures. Cyril stressed the unity of Christ, without being able to explain the distinction adequately, and he sought a solution not on different levels but in the *mia physis* (one "nature") and the picture of Christ that this produces. Especially contributory were the defects of each man. Nestorius's faults were imprudence on the pastoral level: he had publicly attacked a key word in the Church's preaching of the Incarnation; and confusion on the theological: he did not really understand the *communicatio idiomatum.* Cyril's deficiencies lay in the area of the interpersonal: e.g., his designation of Nestorius as "the new Judas"; the political: e.g., his refusal to wait for the Oriental bishops before opening the Council of Ephesus; and the philological: his terminology lent credence to the charges of APOLLINARIANISM; e.g., the famous *mia physis tou theou Logou sesarkōmenē* (one incarnate nature of God the Word) derived not, as he thought, from Athanasius but from Apollinaris.

An unemotional discussion, aimed at clarity and informed by charity, might well have found the two in substantial agreement. Cyril's effort to draw out of Nestorius's rejection of Theotokos all its abstract objective consequences resulted in an impersonal heresy, which was then attributed to Nestorius as its progenitor. The fact is that Nestorius, for all his theological inadequacy, repudiated any theory of "two sons." He was seriously concerned with maintaining the traditional unity in Christ and wanted very much to provide a clear distinction of the natures in the face of apparent heresy.

The problem was further complicated in that Rome was not in a position to provide a *via media* between Constantinople and Alexandria, did not have the philological and theological equipment to play the role of mediator, and did not even recognize the real significance of the Christological problem raised by Nestorius. Cyril's own deeper recognition of the Nestorian issues came too late. Ironically, the whirlwind of MONOPHYSITISM reaped by Alexandria was sown in Cyril's terminology.

Redemption. For Cyril, Christology was not an abstract, isolated issue: on the solution of the Nestorian question hung the reality of man's redemption. Only if it is one and the same Christ who is consubstantial with the Father and with men can He save us (*Monumenta Germanie Historica* 75: 1288; 76:144), for the meeting ground between God and man is the flesh of Christ. Only if this is God's own flesh can man come into contact with Christ's divinity through His humanity, and through His divinity come into contact with the Trinity. In consequence of our kinship with the enfleshed Word we are sons of God in imitation of and participation in the relation of filiation that the Son bears to the Father: we are sons in the Son. This redemptive relationship of men with God the logic of Nestorianism seemed to threaten.

Similarly for the Eucharist, by which we participate in the flesh of Christ in a fashion that is quasi-physical: through this contact with the life-giving body of Christ, we participate in His divinity. For Cyril, the Eucharist consummated our kinship with the Word, our communion with the Father, our participation in the divine nature, by adding to these supernatural relations that already exist what Janssens calls "a special nuance and a superlatively intimate character, because it realizes them by means of a very real contact between our body and that of the Word."

Spirituality. Preoccupation with Cyril's polemics slights his rich spirituality. This spiritual doctrine, nowhere presented systematically, pervades much of his writing. Flowing from dogma and theology, it is Christocentric: Christians, solidary with the Christ who is consubstantial with God and with men, must reproduce mystically and communally, especially through the Eucharist, the mysteries of Christ. But this Christocentrism has a Trinitarian framework: it is through the Spirit of Christ that the Christian is conformed to Christ, and so to the Father, whose Image the Son is.

Spirituality. Perhaps here is the focal point of Cyril's spirituality: his doctrine of the image of God in man. For here lies man's dignity (*Monumenta Germaniae Historica* 75:740) and his happiness (*ibid.* 75:808). Six facets of the Cyrillan image can be isolated: reason, freedom, dominion, holiness, incorruptibility, and sonship—splendidly present in man's creation. Sin marred the beauty of this primeval image. Adam, and humanity in him, remained essentially rational but lost a certain perfection of intelligence, of wisdom; remained essentially free, but did not preserve the original unreserved response to grace; was stripped of sovereignty over earth; lost ontological and dynamic holiness, i.e., participation in God's nature and conscious imitation of God; became subject to passions and corruption; and, remaining a child of God, ceased to be His son.

Restoration of the image comes through Christ. It is achieved radically in the Incarnation, Resurrection, and Ascension of Christ, with His death as a central facet; it is achieved individually in Baptism, where the image is recovered because man receives the Spirit of Christ. Concretely, reason is perfected by faith; freedom is consummated by grace; dominion is recovered, though it will not be actualized until the next life; man shares in the divine nature, and virtuous activity is once again possible; unending life is restored, to be made definitive at the resurrection, and man is freed from slavery to passion; adoptive sonship is given through the indwelling Spirit of adoption, the Spirit of Christ.

Feast: June 27 (Western Church); June 9 (Eastern Church).

Bibliography: Sources. *Patrologia Graeca,* ed. J. P. MIGNE, 161 v. (Paris 1857–66) v.68–77. More recent critical edition of certain treatises (esp. *Minor Prophets, John,* and anti-Nestorian works) by P. E. PUSEY, 7 v. (Oxford 1868–77). Critical text of many anti-Nestorian works in E. SCHWARTZ, *Acta conciliorum oecumenicorum* (Berlin 1914–). For details on editions, see J. QUASTEN, *Patrology,* 3 v. (Westminster, Md. 1950–53), 3:116–142. Studies. *Kyrilliana: Spicilegia edita sancti Cyrilli Alexandrini XV recurrente saeculo* (Cairo 1947). J. N. HEBENSBERGER, *Die Denkwelt des hl. Cyrill von Alexandrien* (Augsburg 1927). G. JOUASSARD, in *Mélanges E. Podechard* (Lyons 1945) 159–174; *Studia Patristica* 6 (*Texte und Untersuchungen zur Geschichte der altchristlichen Literatur* 81; Berlin 1962) 112–121. H. DU MANOIR DE JUAYE, *Dogme et spiritualité chez saint Cyrille d'Alexandrie* (Paris 1944). A. KERRIGAN, *St. Cyril of Alexandria: Interpreter of the Old Testament* (Rome 1952). J. VAN DEN DRIES, *The Formula of St. Cyril of Alexandria* μία φύσις τοῦ θεοῦ λόγου σεσαρκωμένη (Rome 1939). J. LIÉBAERT, *La Doctrine christologique de saint Cyrille d'Alexandrie avant la querelle nestorienne* (Lille 1951). P. GALTIER, "Saint Cyrille et Apollinaire," *Gregorianum* 37 (1956) 584–609. H. M. DIEPEN, *Aux origines de l'anthropologie de saint Cyrille d'Alexandrie* (Bruges 1957). E. WEIGL, *Die Heilslehre des hl. Cyrill von Alexandrien* (Mainz 1905). O. BLANCHETTE, *Sciences ecclésiastiques* 16 (1964) 455–480. A. EBERLE, *Die Mariologie des hl. Cyrillus von Alexandrien* (Freiburg 1921). L. JANSSENS, "Notre filiation divine d'après saint Cyrille d'Alexandrie," *Ephemerides theologicae Lovanienses* 15 (1938) 233–278. A. STRUCKMANN, *Die Eucharistielehre des hl. Cyrill von Alexandrien* (Paderborn 1910). J. B. WOLF, *Commentationes in S. Cyrilli Alexandrini de Spiritu Sancto doctrinam* (Würzburg 1934). L. MALEVEZ, *Recherches de science religieuse* 25 (1935) 257–291, 418–440, ecclesiology. W. J. BURGHARDT, *The Image of God in Man according to Cyril of Alexandria* (Washington 1957). N. M. HARING, *Mediaeval Studies* 12 (1950) 1–19, influence on Latin theology (430–1260). L. WELCH, *Christology and Eucharist in the Early Thought of Cyril of Alexandria* (San Francisco 1994). J. HOUDEK, *Contemplation in the Life and Works of Saint Cyril of Alexandria* (Los Angeles, 1979). R. L. WILKEN, *Judaism and the Early Christian Mind; A Study of Cyril of Alexandria's Exegesis and Theology* (New Haven 1971). J. A. MCGUCKIN, *St. Cyril of Alexandria: The Christological Controversy: Its History, Theology, and Texts* (Leiden 1994). S. A. MCKINION, *Words, Imagery, and the Mystery of Christ: A Reconstruction of Cyril of Alexandria's Christology* (Leiden 2000). R. A. NORRIS,

"Christological Models in Cyril of Alexandria," *Studia Patristica* 13 (Berlin 1975) 255–268.

[W. J. BURGHARDT]

CYRIL OF CONSTANTINOPLE, ST.

Erroneously considered a CARMELITE prior general; b. *c.* 1138; d. May 7, 1234. What are apparently the earliest accounts describe him only as a Greek who was a priest and hermit of Mount Carmel. His title, doctor, cannot be justified. Writings incorrectly assigned to him are *Oraculum angelicum s. Cyrilli,* a Joachimite tract (*see* JOACHIM OF FIORE), and *Epistola ad Eusebium,* a fanciful history of the Carmelites up to the early thirteenth century, actually an integral part of the collection of Philip Ribot, OCarm, who toward the end of the fourteenth century edited or probably wrote all the parts of this collection.

Feast: March 6.

Bibliography: G. MESTERS, *Lexikon für Theologie und Kirche,* ed. J. HOFER and K. RAHNER (Freiburg 1957–65) 6:710. R. BAUMER, *ibid.* 7:1186. G. WESSELS, ed., "Epistola s. Cyrilli," *Analecta Ordinis Carmelitarum Calceatorum* 3 (1914–16) 279–286.

[K. J. EGAN]

CYRIL OF JERUSALEM, ST.

Bishop (*c.* to 387) and doctor of the universal Church; d. Jerusalem, 387. Cyril was the author of the famous *Catecheses,* at least of the Lenten, prebaptismal, catechetical lectures, which contain a fine exposition of the ancient CREED of Jerusalem, as well as a notable statement of the principles of the apophatic or nondialectical theological tradition.

While nothing is known about Cyril's early life, it is possible that his family had Caesarean connections. He became a cleric in the Church of Jerusalem, and was raised to the diaconate by MACARIUS OF JERUSALEM. In or after 342 he was certainly ordained a presbyter by Bishop Maximus, famous as a confessor in the persecution of DIOCLETIAN.

In the ARIAN controversy, which had broken out while Cyril was still a boy, the Church of Jerusalem under Macarius and Maximus had been stanchly Nicaean and pro-Athanasian. The neighboring Church of Caesarea, the Metropolis of Palestine, had anti-Athanasian bishops, first in the moderate and traditionalist though somewhat minimizing EUSEBIUS OF CAESAREA and, from 337, in Acacius, who very probably later became an Arian. In July 335, under pressure from CONSTANTINE I,

who greatly desired the union of Christendom and had come to think that ARIUS was orthodox and ATHANASIUS of Alexandria the troublemaker, a packed council at Tyre deposed Athanasius. It then proceeded to Jerusalem to dedicate Constantine's magnificent new church and solemnly readmit the Arian leaders to communion. At some of these proceedings in Jerusalem, over which Eusebius presided, Cyril was no doubt present.

At Sardica in 342 or 343 Maximus of Jerusalem sat with Athanasius and the Western bishops when that council deposed a number of anti-Nicaean, Eastern bishops, including Acacius of Caesarea, Maximus's own metropolitan. Though repudiated in the East, the decrees of SARDICA meant ecclesiastical civil war in Palestine; and perhaps they also divided the Church of Jerusalem. Acacius apparently retaliated by excommunicating and deposing Maximus. Cyril, by then a senior presbyter, was no doubt again present when in 346, with Maximus presiding, a council of 16 bishops met at Jerusalem for the purpose of giving a resounding welcome to Athanasius when the great exile was returning to his see.

Bishop of Jerusalem. In 348 Maximus died, and probably in late 350 Cyril succeeded him in the see, but not without a struggle. According to the well-informed St. Jerome (*Chron.,* at the 11th year of the sons of Constantine, *Patrologia Latina,* ed. J. P. Migne, 217 v., indexes 4 v. (Paris 1878–90) 27:501–502), Maximus, when he saw death approaching, presumed to ordain a certain Heraclius as his successor, to prevent the see from falling into the hands of an Arian. Cyril, after submitting to reordination, was consecrated bishop of Jerusalem by Acacius and his Arian allies in Palestine. Although Jerome's stigmatization of Cyril as an Arian is utterly unjust, his account of the facts must be, in the main, correct, for the story is repeated, with minor variations, by Socrates (*Hist. Eccl.* 2.38) and Sozomen (*Hist. Eccl.* 4.20): "The Arian bishops of Palestine expelled Maximus and constituted Cyril an anti-bishop."

Jerome's account is apparently admitted also by the not unfriendly RUFINUS OF AQUILEIA (*Hist. Eccl.* 1.23). Moreover it fits perfectly the whole pattern of Jerusalem-Caesarea relations. Jerusalem had a tradition of high-handedness in the appointment of its own bishops, and Maximus had owed his own appointment and consecration to his predecessor, Macarius. Jerome's account does not contradict the statement addressed to a Roman synod by the ecumenical Council of CONSTANTINOPLE I (381) that Cyril was the lawful bishop of "the Mother of all the Churches," having been "canonically ordained by the bishops of the province" (Theodoret, *Hist. Eccl.* 5.9).

The circumstances of his election reflect no discredit upon Cyril. Most Eastern canonists, even if they had not, as Cyril probably did, regarded Acacius' deposition of Maximus as valid, would have considered Maximus's appointment of his own successor as a flagrant violation of the canons of Nicaea and Antioch. Cyril's acceptance of the bishopric, therefore, was in the interest of law, order, and peace, and he knew that it would tend to the continuance of a sound theological tradition worthy of the Holy City. Probably in 351 Cyril, for the first time, conducted the Lenten and Easter catechizing and then (May 7, 351) wrote to Emperor Constantius II his triumphant letter on the occasion of the appearance of a luminous cross over Jerusalem.

If the Metropolitan of Caesarea Acacius counted on finding in Cyril a pliant tool, he was mistaken. In 355 Cyril was arraigned by Acacius for a breach of the canons in that he had sold Church property to feed the starving poor of his diocese. But the cause of the dispute lay deeper. Perhaps Acacius was by then displaying pronounced Arian tendencies, and the true issue was doctrinal. But also, probably since the strengthening of metropolitan jurisdiction at Nicaea, certainly since the rediscovery of the Holy Sepulchre in 326, rivalry had developed between Jerusalem and Caesarea. For two years Cyril apparently disputed Acacius' jurisdiction over Jerusalem and refused to appear before the metropolitan court; but in 357 Acacius "with the aid of his allies among the bishops of the province got his blow in first and deposed him" (Sozomen, 4.25; Socrates, 2.40; Theodoret, 2.25). Cyril gave notice of appeal, which was sanctioned by the emperor.

Meanwhile, the See of Antioch being vacant, Cyril found refuge with Silvanus of Tarsus, where he won the hearts of the people by his preaching (Theodoret, 2.26). Cyril then associated, or renewed his association, with the other leaders of the moderate, traditionalist, or Homoousian party, including Basil of Ancyra and George of Laodicea, who in 358 issued their historic manifesto against the Anomoean Arians. In September 359, under the wing of Silvanus, Cyril attended the preponderantly Homoiousian council of Seleucia, which after the withdrawal of the Acacians deposed the Acacian and Anomoean leaders, reinstated Cyril, and adopted the moderate second creed of the Dedication Council at Antioch of 341. Envoys of the three parties represented at Seleucia proceeded to Constantinople to gain the ear of the emperor. If, as is probable, Cyril was among the ten envoys of the moderate party, he did not regain his see at that time, for it was the Acacians who won over Constantius, and the Homoean council of Constantinople (January 360) deposed Basil, Eustathius, Silvanus, and Cyril.

Thereafter Cyril shared the fortunes of so many other orthodox bishops. On the accession of JULIAN THE APOSTATE, who revoked sentences of episcopal banishment passed under Constantius, Cyril was recalled from exile. He retained his see during the short reign of Julian and of the orthodox Jovian and, on the death of Bishop Acacius in 366, he secured, against Arian opposition, the appointment of his nephew GELASIUS to the Metropolitan See of Caesarea. Gelasius was banished by the Arian-influenced Valens (c. 367), but returned finally to his see shortly before or after Valens' death (Aug. 9, 378).

Orthodox Faith. Cyril never wavered in adherence to the orthodox and Catholic faith, for which, as the second ecumenical council observed, he suffered several times as a confessor. He steadfastly refused all complicity with the Arianism enforced by the heretical emperors and was among those divided from the Nicaeans, as Athanasius remarked of Basil of Caesarea, not by a difference of doctrine but only by a word. But when did Cyril accept the "consubstantial" (HOMOOUSIOS) and achieve formal Nicene orthodoxy? Socrates (5.8), followed by Sozomen (7.7), represented Cyril as a recent convert to the homoousian concept in 381.

It would seem that Cyril's acceptance of the term dated from the time when THEODOSIUS I became the Eastern Augustus (January 379) and made subscription to the Nicene formula obligatory and that Cyril accepted it only in the interests of unity. L. de TILLEMONT conjectured that Cyril accepted the term homoousios in 362 or 364, and F. Hort adopted this view, alleging an alliance between Cyril and Meletius of Antioch, who presided (363) at a synod that sent to Emperor Jovian a Nicene profession of faith.

It is certain, however, that the signatories of this memorial did not include Cyril, while they did include his implacable enemies Acacius and Eutychius (Socrates, 3.25). Cyril seems to have been a member of a group of theologians led by Silvanus and Eustathius who accepted the term homoousios after much debate and who, when persecuted by Emperor Valens, sent deputies to the Western Emperor and bishops. This group accepted the "consubstantial," glossing it as the equivalent of "very God" and "like the Father in all things" (exactly Cyril's formula: *Cat.* 4.7; 11.4, 9, 18; cf. 11.17); they were received into communion by Pope Liberius (Socrates, 4.12; but of. 5.4).

While the records of the second ecumenical council (Constantinople I, 381) have almost entirely perished, it appears that Cyril played a leading role in its deliberations. Socrates names him second, Sozomen third, among the chiefs of the Homoousian party. Cyril's influence probably was especially great during the later sessions when Meletius had died and GREGORY OF NAZIANZUS had left the assembly.

Writings. One homily (before 348) survives, *The Healing of the Paralytic* (*John,* 5.1–15). An example of the "contemplative exposition" of the Scriptures (*theoria: Cat.* 13.9), it catches the tone and temper—spiritual, dramatic, eschatological—of the Fourth Gospel. While the evidence slightly favors his successor, JOHN OF JERUSALEM, as the author of the celebrated *Mystagogical Catecheses,* these may well be the work of Cyril, to whom they have been traditionally ascribed; if John's, they are probably his revision of Cyril's lectures, so that in any case they represent the traditional sacramental teaching of the Church of Jerusalem.

The Catecheses. Cyril's fame will rest on his great Lenten, prebaptismal *Catecheses.* Though Asianic influence appears in his rather frequent use of anaphora and, rarely, other tropes, the style of exposition, or rather, demonstration, of the creed is plain, noble, eloquent, sometimes poetic, and always highly Biblical. Rather surprisingly in spite of the strong historical links between the two Churches of Jerusalem and Alexandria, the *Catecheses* reproduce—though in a very different way, for Cyril strictly bars any kind of philosophical speculation—the Alexandrine *pistis-gnosis* (faith to knowledge) pattern. The purpose of the instruction given to the candidates for illumination (Baptism) is the imparting of gnosis: esoteric, transcendent, and supernatural knowledge, though less mystical and personal than in the *Sermon.* In the *Procatechesis,* Cyril states: "We bring you the stones of gnosis"; and, in the key passage (5.12), that the creed "embraces all the *gnosis* of the religion of the Old and New Testaments" (5.12), just as CLEMENT OF ALEXANDRIA taught that the whole gnosis from A to Z is contained in the Old and New Testaments (*Strom.* 7.16, 95). This pattern explains why in Cyril's Jerusalem the candidates for Baptism were no longer called catechumens, but believers or faithful (*Procat.* 6.12; *Cat.* 1.4; 6.29).

The "illumination" given in these *Catecheses* consists in the imparting of the revealed doctrine or gnosis; i.e., in the conversion of the candidates' simple faith (*pistis*) into grounded knowledge or theological science through the demonstration from Scripture (*see* 4.17; 5.12; 12.5) of the creed (*pistis*), itself viewed (5.12) as a posy or daisy chain (συλλεχθέντα) culled from Scripture. The scriptural demonstration both verified the creed and illuminated its individual articles by relating them to the whole scriptural *Heilsgeschichte* or salvation history. While in the earlier APOLOGISTS the demonstration from Scripture, especially from miracle and prophecy, was concerned to establish the credentials of the Gospel against the criticisms of the pagans, the *Catecheses* are more in the Alexandrine tradition, in which the Scriptures are regarded as in some sense self-authenticating. The movement is thus, "from faith to faith," and gnosis is regarded both as a higher, spiritual knowledge and as a scientific elaboration of the dogmas of faith through the study of Scripture. The *Catecheses* are primarily a work of systematic and dogmatic, rather than apologetic, theology.

The Homoousios. Since the *Catecheses* are a monumental example of that apophatic theological tradition that emphasizes the mysterious and transcendent character of revelation and shrinks from the use of human or philosophical analogies to find assured responses for questions not answered in revelation, the question arises whether Cyril's hesitation about the homoousios may not have been due partly to his theological principles.

There are many possible reasons for this hesitation, including reluctance to accept an unscriptural term into the creed: the term's reputed connection with PAUL OF SAMOSATA; its suspected Sabellian implications; and its high degree of ambiguity in the 4th century, especially after Nicaea's equiparation of *ousia* and *hypostasis.* It is possible that Cyril delayed acceptance of the term so long as he understood it as asserting more than the Son's eternal generation and equality in nature with the Father, and as trespassing upon the mystery of the Divine Being by purporting to "solve the problem" of the Trinity-in-Unity, perhaps by offering an explanation of the *manner* of the Son's generation (*Cat.* 11.8–14). Evidently he finally achieved the conviction that it was no more than a summary expression of the scriptural data and the traditional faith of the Church.

Feast: March 18.

Bibliography: *Opera,* ed. and tr. A. A. TOUTTÉE [Paris 1720; repr. *Patrologia Graeca,* ed. J. P. MIGNE, 161 v. (Paris 1857–66) 33:331–1182]; *Opera,* ed. W. K. REISCHL and J. RUPP, 2 v. (Munich 1848–60). W. TELFER, *Cyril of Jerusalem and Nemesius of Emesa* (Philadelphia 1955). H. LECLERCQ, *Dictionnaire d'archéologie chrétienne et de liturgie,* ed. F. CABROL, H. LECLERCQ, and H. I. MARROU, 15 v. (Paris 1907–53) 7.2:2374–92. J. QUASTEN, *Patrology,* 3 v. (Westminster, Md. 1950–53) 3:362–377. A. A. STEPHENSON, *Theological Studies* 15 (1954) 103–116, 573–593, creed; *Studia patristica,* v.1 (*Texte und Untersuchungen zur Geschichte der altchristlichen Literatur* 63; 1957) 142–156, gnosis. J. VOGT, *Mélanges Henri Grégoire,* v.1 (Brussels 1949) 593–606, cross. H. A. WOLFSON, *Dumbarton Oaks Papers,* Harvard Univ. 11 (1957) 1–19, homoousios. N. J. TORCHIA, "The Significance of Charismation in the Mystagogical Lectures of Cyril of Jerusalem," *Diakonia* 32, no. 2 (1999): 128–144. R. L. MULLEN, *The New Testament Text of Cyril of Jerusalem* (Atlanta 1997). R. C. GREGG, "Cyril of Jerusalem and the Arians," *Arianism* (Philadelphia 1985), 85–109.

[A. A. STEPHENSON]

CYRIL OF SCYTHOPOLIS

The biographer of St. Sabas, who made a penitential prostration (*metanoia*) before the saint at the age of seven, influenced by his father, John, who had met Sabas in 518 at Scythopolis and as a result of a miracle performed by the saint, resolved to follow him (*Vita Sabbae* 63). Sabas had frequently visited the home of John and blessed his wife; and on his return in 532, the couple resolved to live a continent life. John was employed in the metropolitan tribunal and given lodging in the episcopal residence. At the urging of St. Sabas he taught his son Cyril the *Psalter*. The family was occasionally visited by monks from the Great Laura (Mar Saba) and each year sent a gift to the monastery and to St. John the Solitary.

Under this influence Cyril at 18 (in 543) entered clerical orders as a lector, and visited the monastery of Beella (Ain Bala), where he was clothed with the monastic habit by the Hegoumen or Abbot George, who later ordered him to write the *Lives* of Sabas and of Euthymius. Cyril then departed for the desert of Juda between Jerusalem and the Dead Sea to carry out his vocation as a disciple of Sabas. When passing through Jerusalem (Nov. 21), he assisted at the dedication of the new church of St. Mary and, in accord with his mother's instructions, paid a visit of consultation to John the Solitary in the Great Laura. Despite this non-agenarian's advice, he entered the Laura of Calamon (Qasr-Hadjla) near the Jordan. The physical and moral hardships proved too difficult for his youth, and in a dream he was encouraged to follow a guide who led him to the Laura of St. Euthymius. There he decided to write the lives of the more remarkable ascetics in the Judean desert. He was one of the more fervent orthodox monks chosen to repopulate the New Laura after its Origenistic community was dispersed (Feb. 555). Two years later he was admitted to the Great Laura and began to gather the sayings of St. Sabas and the counsels of George of Beella. He also found the opportunity to visit John the Solitary. After John's death (Jan. 8, 559), Cyril completed his life of John with an account of his death. The signature of three of Cyril's compositions claim that he was a priest; but the incomplete state of the manuscripts indicates that he never had time to form a single, finished corpus for his biographies.

E. Schwartz has published the seven biographies written by Cyril in what appears to be their chronological order: the lives of Saints Euthymius, Sabas, John the Solitary, Cyriacus, Theodosius, Theognius, and Abraham of Crete. The life of Theodosius was taken from a panegyric by Bp. Theodore of Petra pronounced on Jan. 11, 529; that of Theognius from a panegyric written by Paul Helladius, the Solitary of Elousa. The complete text of the Life of Abramius is preserved in an Arabic version translated into German by E. Graf [Byzantinische Zeitschrift 14 (1905) 509–518] and Latin by P. Peeters [*Analecta Bollandiana* 24 (1905) 349–366], and G. Garitte has pub-

lished 17 lines of the life of John the Solitary narrating his death scene [*Analecta Bollandiana* 72 (1954) 75–84].

One of the better Greek hagiographers, Cyril does not employ a blatant rhetoric but a simple style that reveals his faith and narrational facility; his work is based on the information of his own experiences and the traditions he collected from the monasteries and coenobia. His mention of persons and places gave his contemporaries opportunity to control his statements. Modern scholars who do not appreciate the apparent credulity of his epoch and the theological interests and prejudices of his milieu are nevertheless provided with numerous precious chronological indications.

Bibliography: E. SCHWARTZ, ed., *Kyrillos von Skythopolis* (*Texte und Untersuchungen zur Geschichte der altchristlichen Literatur* 49.2; 1939). E. STEIN, *Analecta Bollandiana* 62 (1944) 169–186. F. DÖLGER, *Byzantinische Zeitschrift* 40 (1940) 474–484. A. J. FESTUGIÈRE, ed., *Les Moines d'Orient* (Paris 1961–) v.3. F. DIEKAMP, *Die origenistischen Streitigkeiten im sechsten Jahrhundert* (Münster 1899); "Zur Chronologie der origenistischen Streitigkeiten im 6. Jahrhundert," *Historisches Jahrbuch der Görres-Gesellschaft* 21 (1900) 743–757. H. G. BECK, *Kirche und theologische Literatur im byzantinischen Reich* (Munich 1959) 408–410. K. BAUS, *Lexikon für Theologie und Kirche*, ed. J. HOFER and K. RAHNER, 10 v. (2d, new ed. Freiburg 1957–65) 6:711. I. HAUSHERR, *Dictionnaire de spiritualité ascétique et mystique. Doctrine et histoire*, ed. M. VILLIER et al. (Paris 1932–) 2:2687–90.

[H. CHIRAT]

CYRIL OF TURIV

Sometimes Turov, bishop of the princedom of Turiv (a principality of the Kievan Rus'), preacher, writer, and poet; b. *c.* 1130; d. 1182. A scion of an old patrician family, Cyril entered the monastery at an early age, already as an established writer. He was very popular among his contemporaries and was consecrated bishop in the second half of the 12th century, upon the request of the citizens of Turiv. His extant works include eight collections of sermons written for various Church feasts, two parables, 22 prayers, and a Canon of the Mass. His works abound with metaphors, similes, antitheses, and other literary devices. The rhythmic language and the dramatic style of his works characterized by the use of dialogues carried an appeal both to the mind and to the heart. Many of his works are strongly influenced by the writings of Byzantine theologians, whom he was able to read in the original. Cyril's writings exerted considerable influence on Russian, Ukrainian, and Byelorussian literatures, and on the literatures of the Balkan nations.

Bibliography: D. CISEVSKY, *Istoriia Ukrainskoi literatury* (New York 1956); *Geschichte der altrussischen Literatur* (Frankfurt 1948). C. A. MANNING, *Ukrainian Literature* (Jersey City, NJ 1944). O. OHONOVSKYI, *Istoriia literatury rus'koï*, 3 v. in 4 (Lvov

Christ blessing SS. Cyril and Methodius, flanked by angels and saints, in a 9th-century fresco in S. Clemente, Rome.

1887–93). A. N. PYPIN and V. D. SPASOVICH, *Geschichte der slawischen Literaturen,* v.1 (Leipzig 1880). V. P. VINOGRADOV, *V pamjat' stoletija Moskovskoj Duchovnoj,* 2 v. (Moscow 1915).

[G. LUZNYCKY]

CYRIL (CONSTANTINE) AND METHODIUS, SS.

Doctors of the Slavs, both outstanding figures of the ninth century Church. Constantine (Cyril was to be his name in religion), the youngest of seven children, was b. Thessalonica (Saloniki), Greece, *c.* 826–7; d. Rome, Feb. 14, 869. His brother Methodius (known only by his religious name), d. April 6, 885. Their father, Leo, was *drungarios* or officer under the *strategos* commanding the theme of Thessalonica, a Byzantine province peopled by numerous Macedonian Slavs, whose language Constantine and Methodius spoke at an early age. His father died when Constantine was 14 years old and shortly afterward he left for Constantinople. There he was cared for by the Logothete Theoctistos, chief minister of THEODORA (842–856), widow of Emperor THEOPHILUS I (829–842) and regent of the Byzantine Empire during the minority of Emperor MICHAEL III (d. 867). Constantine pursued a brilliant course of studies at the imperial university, where his teachers included Leo the Mathematician and PHOTIUS, the future patriarch (858–867; 877–888). GREGORY OF NAZIANZUS and PSEUDO-DIONYSIUS were among his favorite authors. His talent for philosophy earned for him, both at Byzantium and at Rome, the appellation of "the Philosopher." At the close of his studies, he refused a governorship of a district, such as Methodius had accepted among a Slavonic-speaking population. When ordained a priest, he was nominated patriarchal librarian (*chartophylax*) of Hagia Sophia, under Patriarch IGNATIUS (847–858; 867–877). After a six-month retreat to a monastery on the Bosporus, he returned to become a professor of philosophy in the imperial university. He was victorious in a debate on the veneration of IMAGES against the former iconoclast Patriarch JOHN VII GRAMMATICUS, who had been deposed in 843. At the age of 24, as a member of a delegation to the Arabs, he had further discussions on the Trinity at the caliph's court at Samarra on the Tigris. Perhaps as a consequence of the assassination of his protector Theoctistos (d. Nov. 20, 855) by Bardas, Theodora's brother, he withdrew first into solitude, then to a monastery on Mount Olympus in Bithynia (Asia Minor), where Methodius had become a monk after spending many years at his governmental post.

Mission to the Khazars. Toward the close of 860 both brothers were included in a delegation that took them as far as the boundaries of the Caspian Sea and Caucasia, a delegation to the KHAZARS, a people hesitating between Judaism, Islam, and Christianity. On both the outward and the return journeys, they halted at Cherson (in southwest Crimea), where on Jan. 30, 861, an expedition led by Constantine discovered what were held to be the relics of Pope St. CLEMENT I of Rome. An account of this discovery, a sermon on the subject and a hymn, composed in Greek by Constantine, have not survived apart from a free Slavonic version; also lost is the account of the controversy with the Khazars, both in the Greek version of Constantine and in the Slavonic translation by Methodius. On their return Constantine was professor at the patriarchal academy in the church of the Holy Apostles for a few months, while Methodius became abbot of the monastery of Polychronion on the Hellespont (Asia Minor).

Mission to the Slavs. Their life underwent a fresh and decisive modification with the request presented in 862 to Emperor Michael III by Rastislav (846–870), duke of Greater Moravia (present-day Moravia and Slovakia), who wished to secure for his country ecclesiastical autonomy as well as political independence from the Franks under King Louis the German. For his people—already partly converted, first by Iro-Scottish monks, then by Bavarian missionaries—he sought to obtain a bishop capable of embodying this autonomy, a teacher able to instruct the Slavs in their own tongue. The first task of Constantine, to whom the Emperor delegated this mission with Methodius as his adjutant, was to invent a Slavonic alphabet (the Glagolitic script, not the Cyrillic one, as was long believed). Before setting out, Constantine and Methodius, with a few companions, composed an Old Church Slavonic translation of the Gospels, beginning with St. John. In 863 they brought this alphabet and translation to the Moravian court (whose exact location is still unknown). Straightaway there followed, amid other apostolic and cultural tasks, the translation of the liturgical books into Slavonic. This made possible the boldest innovation of Constantine and Methodius: the introduction of a Slavonic liturgy. But this project swiftly brought them face to face with the hostility of the Western clergy in Moravia, in particular of the Bavarian priests who were dependent on the Diocese of Passau. It was these that Constantine styled "trilinguists" or "Pilatians," as they only accepted the three languages used by Pilate in his inscription as sacred, namely, Hebrew, Greek and Latin.

In Moravia, Constantine and Methodius busied themselves especially in training disciples and some of these, who they hoped would be consecrated bishops,

they took to Rome with them, for Moravia lay directly under Rome's jurisdiction. On their journey they stayed some time in Pannonia, to the south of the Danube, at Blatensk Kostel on Lake Balaton, where the chieftain Kocel (861–874), also a Slav, entrusted to them 50 young men for training in Slavonic. They also stopped at Venice, where fresh discussions with the "trilinguists" took place. Bearing the relics of St. Clement, which had accompanied them in all their wanderings, they reached Rome shortly after Pope ADRIAN II had mounted the papal throne (Dec. 14, 867); Pope NICHOLAS I, who had originally invited them, had died a month earlier. At St. Mary, Major Adrian solemnly approved the Slavonic liturgy, ordained Methodius (for he had only been tonsured as yet) and had three of their disciples raised to the priesthood by Cardinal Bishops FORMOSUS of Porto (the future pope) and GAUDERICH OF VELLETRI. The new priests celebrated the Slavonic liturgy at St. Peter's, St. Petronilla's, St. Andrew's and St. Paul's, assisted by Arsenius, cardinal bishop of Orte and by his nephew ANASTASIUS THE LIBRARIAN, who became a friend of Constantine. Having long been an invalid and having grown weaker, Constantine died at Rome 50 days after taking the monastic habit with the name of Cyril. He was 42 years of age. Methodius had at first desired Constantine's body to be transferred to their monastery in Asia Minor; but it was finally buried at San Clemente in Rome. One of the last episodes in the complicated story of the relics of Constantine concerns the solemn restoration to this same basilica on Nov. 17, 1963, of a few fragments of his bones that had been recovered.

Methodius alone. Methodius continued the work of Constantine for another 16 years. At Kocel's pleading he went first to Pannonia as papal legate for all the Slavic peoples. At the same time Pope Adrian addressed to Rastislav, to his nephew Svatopluk (870–894) and to Kocel the important bull *Gloria in excelsis* (the text of which is known only through the Slavonic Life of Methodius), in which the liturgy in Slavonic was authorized on certain conditions (at Mass the Epistle and Gospel were to be read first in Latin and then in Slavonic). Then with an escort of 20 nobles Methodius was sent back to Rome by Kocel to be consecrated bishop. On this occasion in 869, Adrian II restored the ancient archiepiscopal See of SIRMIUM (in Pannonia, today Sremska Motrovica in Yugoslavia) and conferred it on Methodius. Thus, Pannonia, together with Greater Moravia, was subtracted from the jurisdiction of the Bavarian bishops who retaliated with a violent storm of accusation against Archbishop Methodius in the presence of Louis the German. As a result Methodius was exiled for about three years to Swabia, probably confined to ELLWANGEN, the former abbey of Bishop ERMENRICH OF PASSAU (d. Dec. 26, 874), the leading opponent of Methodius after Adalwin of Salzburg (d. May 14, 873) and Anno of Freising (d. Oct. 9, 875). Through his legate Paul of Ancona, Pope JOHN VIII (Dec. 872–Dec. 882) secured Methodius's liberation in 873 and his installation in the See of Greater Moravia. In addition, this same Paul of Ancona seems to have been given the task of informing Methodius at least of restrictions concerning the Slavonic liturgy, if not its prohibition. The apostolic activity of Methodius and his disciples prospered in spite of the difficulties caused either by the Frankish clergy, including Wiching, or by Svatopluk, the disreputable successor of Rastislav whose conduct Methodius had often been obliged to rebuke and whose personal preferences were for the Latin liturgy. In 879, at the request of Svatopluk's emissary, a priest named John, Methodius was ordered to appear at Rome and answer a double accusation made against him, the first concerning the orthodoxy of his doctrine —no doubt because of his refusal to insert the FILIOQUE into the Creed as the Franks insisted—the other about his course of action regarding the Slavonic liturgy. Methodius appeared and completely justified himself, perhaps with the help of the Life of Constantine, the composition of which, in Slavonic and inspired by Methodius, dates back to that time. John VIII's subsequent bull, *Industriae tuae,* dated June of 880, unreservedly praised both the orthodoxy and conduct of Methodius, confirmed the privilege of his independence in jurisdiction from all except the Holy See itself and expressly authorized the Mass in Slavonic. Unfortunately, Wiching, who had meanwhile been consecrated bishop of Nitra (today in Slovakia), was made a suffragan of Archbishop Methodius. He forthwith indulged in various deceitful activities against Methodius's authority, thus planting in the mind of the archbishop certain doubts that he poured out in a letter (now lost) to Pope John, who completely reassured him in his reply *Pastoralis sollicitudinis* of March 23, 881.

The last four years of Methodius were not destined to be any less painful and he had to go as far as threatening Wiching with excommunication. It is in these years that one must place a journey to Constantinople, where Methodius met Emperor BASIL I (867–886), who had invited him and Photius, patriarch for the second time and then in communion with Rome. A period of intense literary activity followed his return. With the help of two disciples, Methodius translated the whole Bible (except Maccabees) in eight months; Constantine and he had already translated the Psalter, the Gospels and St. Paul. He also composed codes of both civil and ecclesiastical law, as well as works bearing on the Fathers based on the pattern of the Byzantine NOMOCANON. He died on Tuesday in Holy Week, surrounded by his disciples, in his cathedral church, the site of which has still not been deter-

mined. None of his relics have so far been recovered. Before his death he chose as his successor Gorazd, a native of those parts. But the intrigues of Wiching at Rome and the position taken by Pope STEPHEN V (885–891) prevented this succession from being put into effect. Similarily, through the hostility of Svatopluk, the work of the two brothers in Moravia was brought to a halt. In 886 Methodius' disciples of were driven out of the country; these included Gorazd, CLEMENT THE BULGARIAN, Constantine of Přeslav, Naum the Bulgarian, Angelar, Sabas and Lawrence. This expulsion, however, had the beneficial effect of forcing these disciples to spread the spiritual, liturgical and cultural work of their masters among the neighboring Bulgars, Bohemians and southern Poles. One of them compiled the Slavonic Life of Methodius immediately after his death. A native hierarchy was reinstalled in Moravia only in 898 and 899. Then in 907 the Moravian Empire fell victim to the onslaughts of the Hungarians.

The "ecumenical" bearing of the two brothers continues to increase in importance, for, though born and educated in the Byzantine Empire, they devoted their lives (from the first patriarchate of Photius and at a time when he was in conflict with Pope Nicholas I) to promoting the Christianization of the Slavs, remaining in complete and at times meritorious, union with Rome.

Feast: Feb. 14 (formerly March 9 or July 7); May 11(Eastern Church).

Bibliography: F. PASTRNEK, *Dějiny slovanských apoštolů Cyrilla a Methoda, s rozborem a otiskem hlavních pramenů* (Prague 1902). P. A. LAVROV, *Materialy po istorii vozniknovenija drevnejšej slavjanskoj pismennosti* (Leningrad 1930). G. A. IL'INSKIJ, *Opyt sistematičeskoj Kirillo-Mefodïevskoj bibliografii* (Sofia 1934). F. DVORNIK, *Les Slaves, Byzance et Rome au IXᵉ siècle* (Paris 1926); *Les Légendes de Constantin et de Méthode vues de Byzance* (Prague 1933; 2d. ed. Hattiesburg, Ms. 1969); *The Slavs: Their Early History and Civilization* (Boston 1956); *Byzantine Missions among the Slavs* (New Brunswick, N.J. 1970). *Der Streit um Methodius,* ed., H. LÖWE, (Cologne 1948). P. MEYVAERT and P. DEVOS, "Trois énigmes cyrillo-méthodiennes de la *Légende italique* résolues grâce à un document inédit," *Analecta Bollandiana,* 73 (1955) 375–461; "Autour de Léod'Ostie et de sa *Translatio s. Clementis,*" *ibid.* 74 (1956) 189–240; "La *Légende morave* des ss. Cyrille et Méthode et ses sources," *ibid.* 441–469. *Zwischen Rom und Byzanz,* ed. and tr., J. BUJNOCH, (Graz 1958). F. GRIVEC, *Konstantin und Method: Lehrer der Slaven* (Wiesbaden 1960). F. GRIVEC and F. TOMŠIČ, *Constantinus et Methodius Thessalonicenses: Fontes* (Zagreb 1960). J. CIBULKA, *Velkomoravský kostel v Modré u Velehradu a začcátky křest'anství na Moravé* (Prague 1958); "Grossmährische Kirchenbauten," in *Sancti Cyrillus et Methodius, Leben und Wirken* (Prague 1963) 49–117. Z. R. DITTRICH, *Christianity in Great-Moravia* (Groningen 1962). I. DUJČEV, *Kiril i Metodij: Bibliografija na bŭlgarskata literatura, 1944–1963* (Sofia 1963). L. BOYLE, "The Fate of the Remains of St. Cyril," in *Cirillo e Metodio* (Rome 1963) 159–194. *The Work of Constantine-Cyril the Philosopher* (Sofia 1969). *The Vita of Constantine and the Vita of Methodius,* tr., M. KANTOR and R. S. WHITE (Ann

Arbor 1976). A. BOZHKOV, *The San Clemente Basilica in Rome and the Portrayals of Cyril and Methodius in Old Bulgarian Art* (Sofia 1977). *Cirillo e Metodio, le biografie paleoslave*, ed. and tr., V. PERI (Milan 1981). *Kiril and Methodius: Founders of Slavonic Writing: A Collection of Sources and Critical Studies*, ed., I. DUICHEV, tr., S. NIKOLOV (Boulder, Colo. 1985). JOHN PAUL II, *Slavorum apostoli* (Vatican City 1985). D. OBOLENSKY, *Byzantium and the Slavs* (Crestwood, N.Y. 1994). M. EGGERS, *Das Erzbistum des Method* (Munich 1996). *Christianity Among the Slavs: The Heritage of Saints Cyril & Methodius: Acts, Pont Orntl Inst Rome, O 1985*, ed., E. G. FARRUGIA and R. F. TAFT (Rome 1988). *The Legacy of Saints Cyril and Methodius to Kiev and Moscow: Proceedings of the International Congress of the Millenium of the Conversion of Rus' to Christianity, Thessaloniki 26–28 November 1988*, ed., A. E. N. TACHIAOS (Thessalonike 1992). *SS. Cyril and Methodius Among the Slovaks: Observing the 1,000th Anniversary of Saint Methodius' Death*, ed., I. KRUZLIAK and F. L. MIZENKO (S. I. 1985) *Acta Sanctorum* Dec. (Propylaeum) 63, 274.

[P. DEVOS]

CYRION (KYRION)

Catholicos of Iberia, East Georgia, *c.* 598 to after 609; d. after 609. Iberia had adhered to the Emperor ZENO's pro-Monophysite policy and had in recompense the rank of a catholicos for its primate (486–488). In 505 or 506, together with Armenia and Caucasian Albania, it had accepted the *HENOTICON*. In 519 the empire, later followed by Iberia and Lazica (West Georgia), was reconciled with Rome, while Armenia drifted toward MONOPHYSITISM; thus Cyrion on accession to the catholicate was still in communion with the Monophysite Church of Armenia. But in 600 he returned to the Catholic faith and entertained direct relations with Rome (Pope GREGORY I's letter of June or July 601 was written in reply to Cyrion's message). This caused a clash between the Iberian and the Armenian Monophysite Churches, which began in 602 and was complicated by the Georgian-Armenian rivalry in the South Iberian Diocese of Tsurtavi. Finally, in 608 or 609 Abraham, Catholicos of Monophysite Armenia, excommunicated Cyrion and the Catholic Iberians, and the seeds of discord were sown between the two Christian Caucasian nations.

Bibliography: Gregory I, *Monumenta Germaniae Epistolae* (Berlin 1825–) 2.2:52. P. GOUBERT, *Byzance avant l'Islam*, 2 v. (Paris 1951–55). C. TOUMANOFF, "Christian Caucasia between Byzantium and Iran," *Traditio* 10 (1954) 109–189. N. AKINIAN, *Kiwrion Kat'olikos Vrac'* (Vienna 1910), in Armenian. I. A. DZHAVAKHOV, "Istorīa tserkovnago razryva mezhdy Gruzīeĭ i Armenīeĭ v nachalī̆e VII vī̆eka," *Bulletin de l'Académie des Sciences de St. Pétersbourg* 6 (1908) 433–446.

[C. TOUMANOFF]

Tomb of Cyrus, king of Persia, Pasargadae, Iran.

CYRUS, KING OF PERSIA

Reigned 559 to 530 B.C., the second of three Achaemenid kings to bear this throne name (Persian *kuruš*, Akkadian *kuraš*, Greek Κῦρος, Hebrew and Aramaic *kōreš*), which is probably of Elamite origin. He is rightly known as Cyrus the Great. The ancient sources of information concerning Cyrus are (1) among the cuneiform inscriptions: the Cyrus Cylinder [J. B. Pritchard, *Ancient Near Eastern Texts Relating to the Old Testament* 315–316], the Verse Account of Nabonidus (*ibid.* 312–314), and the Nabonidus Chronicle (*ibid.* 305–306); (2) among the Greek historians: Herodotus, Xenophon, Ctesis, and BEROSSUS; (3) in the OT: Is 41.2–4; 44.28; 45.1; 46.11; Ez 1.1–11; 4.3–5; 5.13–17; 6.3–5; 2 Chr 36.22–23. The references to Cyrus in Dn 1.21; 6.28; 10.1 are of no historical value.

In 559 B.C. he succeeded his father, Cambyses I, on the throne of Anshan, a district of northwestern Elam. At that time Elam was under the control of the Achaemenide kingdom of Anshan and Parsa (southwest of Elam), which was in turn part of the empire of the MEDES, then ruled by Astyages. (There is probably no truth in the later legend that the daughter of Astyages was the mother of Cyrus.) In 553 Cyrus rebelled against his Median overlord, King Astyages, with the encouragement of Nabuna'id (Nabonidus), King of Babylon (555–538). The latter saw in this local rebellion a weakening of his archrival, Media. By 550, however, Cyrus had captured Ecbatana, dethroned Astyages, and been proclaimed king of the Medes and Persians. In a futile attempt to stop this advance, a defensive alliance was formed by Babylon, Egypt, Lydia, and Sparta. In 546 King Croesus of Lydia alone attacked Cyrus. After an indecisive battle Croesus retired and disbanded his mercenaries for the winter. In a surprise move Cyrus counterattacked in midwinter and burned Croesus' capital, Sardis. Leaving a lieutenant, Harpagus, to take over the rest of Asia Minor, Cyrus marched eastward, occupying the territory probably as far as the Jaxartes River.

As Babylon helplessly awaited its downfall, the voice of an unknown prophet (now commonly called Deutero-Isaiah) arose among the Jewish exiles there (*c.* 540). This man saw Cyrus as God's chosen ''shepherd'' and ''anointed one'' who would free His people from Babylonian bondage (Is 44.28; 45.1; 46.11). Cyrus is referred to in Is 41.2, which is part of the first of the Songs of the SUFFERING SERVANT (42.1–9).

The Persian army captured Sippar on Oct. 10, 539, and Babylon two days later. The Babylonian populace had become dissatisfied with Nabonidus, especially because of his religious innovations. When Cyrus made his triumphal entry a little later (Oct. 29, 539), he was welcomed as a great liberator by both citizen and exile alike.

The realm of the neo-Babylonian kings, comprising all of Mesopotamia, Syria, and Palestine, was thus incorporated by Cyrus into his vast empire that later extended from the Aegean Sea to the Indian frontier. Its administration centers were in SUSA, Ecbatana, BABYLON, and Pasargadae (in Parsa, 30 miles northeast of the later capital Persepolis). As the foundation of this empire Cyrus established a *pax orientalis,* a policy contrasting sharply with the actions of his predecessors. While he held firm control by placing Medes and Persians in highest local offices, by establishing an efficient communications system, and by his armies, he respected the indigenous religious and cultural sensibilities. In keeping with these enlightened policies, he issued an edict in 538 allowing the Jewish exiles to return to their homeland and rebuild their Temple, for which he returned to them the treasures that had been plundered by Nebuchadnezzar (Ez 1.1–4; 6.3–5; 2 Chr 36.22–23).

In 530 Cyrus lost his life in battle against the nomads on his northeastern frontier in central Asia. He was buried in Pasargadae, where his empty tomb still stands. He was succeeded by his son Cambyses II (530-522), the last of the elder line of the Achaemenids, who in turn was succeeded by DARIUS I, of the younger Achaemenid line.

See Also: PERSIA.

Bibliography: J. BUCHANAN, *The Cambridge Ancient History*, 12 v. (London and New York 1923–39) 4:1–15. A. T. E. OLMSTEAD, *History of the Persian Empire: Achaemenid Period* (Chicago 1948). F. H. WEISSBACH, *Paulys Realenzyklopädie der klassischen Altertumswissenschaft,* ed. G. WISSOWA et al. suppl. 4 (Stuttgart 1924) 1129–66. R. MAYER, *Lexikon für Theologie und Kirche,* ed. J. HOFER and K. RAHNER, 10 v. (2d, new ed. Freiburg 1957–65) 6:715–716. *Encyclopedic Dictionary of the Bible,* tr. and adap. by L. HARTMAN (New York 1963), from A. VAN DEN BORN, *Bijbels Woordenboek* 477–478.

[E. A. BALLMANN]

CZECH REPUBLIC, THE CATHOLIC CHURCH IN THE

Formerly a part of Czechoslovakia, the Czech Republic is a landlocked nation located in eastern Europe. It borders Germany on the west and northwest, Poland on the northeast, Slovakia on the southeast and Austria on the south. Made up of the former kingdoms of Bohemia and Moravia, the Czech Republic contains numerous mineral springs and fertile soil lines its many rivers. The landscape features rolling plains and hills in the west, which rise to hilly regions in the east. Natural resources include coal, copper, zinc and some gold. Containing one of the most stable economies of any of the eastern European communist states during the mid- to late 20th century, the region suffered from a financial setback in 1997. However, restructuring efforts and increased exports of machinery and other manufactured goods led the way to recovery by 2000.

Together with the neighboring kingdom of Slovakia to the southeast, the lands of the Czechs in Bohemia (to the west) and Moravia (to the east) were provinces of the Empire of Austria-Hungary through the 19th century. Sharing a common language and culture, these three regions joined after World War I, and in 1918 the Republic of Czechoslovakia was formed. When the Communists seized power in 1948, the Slovakian region of Carpethian Ruthenia was ceded to the USSR and the rest of Czechoslovakia was termed a People's Republic. In 1960 it became the Czechoslovak Socialist Republic. Prompted by a strong internal desire for independence, Slovakia separated from the Czech Republic in 1993; the dissolution of the union between the two countries was so peaceful that it was sometimes referred to as the ''velvet divorce.'' The Republic entered NATO in March of 1999, and looked forward to acceptance in the European Union.

The following essay is in two parts: Part I focuses on the early church to World War II, while Part II covers the Church from 1948 through the fall of communism into the present day.

Czechs and Christianity to 1918

Joining Celtic and Germanic tribes that had inhabited the region since the 4th century B.C., the West Slavic immigration into the present-day Czech Republic reached its zenith by the 6th century, and within 300 years fortified towns had developed in the region encompassing southern Moravia and western Slovakia, near the modern localities of Staré Město, Velehrad, Mikulčice, Devín and Nitra. This political center controlled the region of Great Moravia, situated on the border of two cultural worlds, the Latino-Germanic to the west and the Byzantine to the east. The region came under Roman conquest near the decline of the empire.

Origins among West Slavs. Christianity spread from the Germanic west and began to take roots in the region soon after the defeat of the Turkish AVARS (796). The bishop of Regensburg considered Bohemia as his mission field, and the bishop of Passau claimed Moravia as part of his diocese. Fear of German expansion led Rastislav, of the ruling Mojmirid dynasty, to seek missionaries from Constantinople. In reply the imperial city sent Saints CYRIL (CONSTANTINE) AND METHODIUS. These two missionaries celebrated the Christian mysteries in Slavonic and with their disciples created a rich Slavic literature. Their missionary methods proved very successful and received the full approval of the Roman See. Great Moravia was made a separate ecclesiastical province subject to Rome, but was destroyed in 970 due to internal divisions, pressure from the Germans, and finally the invasion of the pagan Magyars.

Czech Lands to 15th Century. After the collapse of Great Moravia, a new political nucleus was formed during the 10th century in the heart of Bohemia (which owes its name to the Celtic *Boii* who inhabited it from the 4th century B.C.) and under the Přemyslid dynasty. Christianity continued to penetrate Czech lands from the west, but the Cyrillo-Methodian form did not disappear. The Slavic liturgy even experienced a brief revival, thanks to the monastery of Sázava, founded by Procopius (d. 1053), whom the Holy See added to the list of saints in 1204. By the 12th century the Přemyslid state was within the orbit of Latin culture.

Christian missionaries met opposition at first. A pagan reaction led to the martyrdom of St. Ludmilla in 921 and her grandson, the young Duke St. WENCESLAS I (Václav), in 929, although the effect of the latter's martyrdom was to speed the process of Christianization and seemingly to convince contemporaries of the legitimacy of the Czech state. The victory of the new faith was

---

Capital: Prague.
Size: 30,442 sq. miles.
Population: 10,272,179 in 2000.
Languages: Czech.
Religions: 4,006,149 Roman Catholics (39%), 308,165 Eastern Orthodox (3%), 513,609 Protestants (Hussite) (5%), 1,129,940 other (11%), 4,314,316 without religious affiliation.
Archdioceses: Prague, in Bohemia, with suffragans Litoměřice, Hradec Králové, České Budějovice, and Plzeň; Olomouc, in Moravia, with suffragans Brno and Ostrava-Opava. Catholics of the Byzantine Rite are organized around the apostolic exarchate in Prague, which is directly subject to the Holy See.

---

sealed by the construction of the Diocese of PRAGUE (973) and by the renewal of the Moravian hierarchy with the establishment of the See of Olomouc (1063). The second bishop of Prague, St. ADALBERT (Vojtěch, d. 997), an ardent admirer of the current Western reform movement, brought the BENEDICTINES into Bohemia to Břevnov (992–993). Princess Mlada founded a monastery for women at St. George in Hradčany (971).

The GREGORIAN REFORM reached Bohemia and Moravia a century after the rest of Europe, introduced by the CISTERCIANS from the Abbey of MORIMOND who settled at Sedlec, near Kutná Hora (1142), and at Velehrad in Moravia (1205). The soul of the reform of the clergy was the Bishop of Olomouc, Henry Zdík (d. 1150), who welcomed the PREMONSTRATENSIANS to Strahov in 1142. Only after the popes triumphed over the German kings and contact between Central Europe and the Latin countries became more frequent, did Gregorian reform ideals truly take root in Czech lands. The 13th century saw parishes replacing the former system of PROPRIETARY CHURCHES.

When the MENDICANT ORDERS began ministering to the spiritual welfare of the rising towns, Bohemia became more closely linked to the Latin countries. St. CLARE OF ASSISI found a kindred spirit in St. AGNES OF BOHEMIA (d. 1280), daughter of King Přemysl Ottokar I, who served as the superior of the first monastery of POOR CLARES in Prague. After the death of Wenceslas III (1306), the last of the Přemyslids, the Cistercian abbots were primarily responsible for establishing the Luxemburg family on the throne of Bohemia. In 1212 the Czech rulers won the confirmation of their royal title in perpetuity from FREDERICK II. While the kingdom was a part of the HOLY ROMAN EMPIRE, feudal links between the two were weak. The King of Bohemia invested the bishops of Prague and Olomouc. Bohemia experienced its golden age under the second Luxemburg king, Charles IV (1346–78).

In 1344 Prague became an archbishopric, with Olomouc and Litomyšl as suffragans. It was soon among the

Empire's leading cultural and artistic centers and became the home of Charles University, the first in central Europe, founded in 1348. HUMANISM was introduced to Bohemia by John Dražic (1301–42), bishop of Prague, and merged with the genuine desire for Christian renewal in the Czech DEVOTIO MODERNA, whose nurseries were the Carthusian monastery in Prague and the house of the Canons Regular of St. Augustine in Roudnice. Among the leaders of this movement were Adalbert Ranconis (d. 1388), rector of the University of Paris, and Matthias Janov (d. 1399), who in the spirit of the Devotio Moderna recommended frequent Holy Communion. Another leader was Thomas Štítný (d. 1401), a member of the Czech gentry whose writing in the vernacular instructed members of his social class in the genuine imitation of Christ. John Milíč of Kroměříž (d. 1374) and Konrad Waldhauser (d. 1369), an Austrian Canon Regular of St. Augustine, tried by their preaching to correct abuses among the clergy, who formed a numerous and wealthy group.

St. JOHN OF NEPOMUC, the vicar-general of Prague, was martyred (1393) during the troubled reign of Wenceslas IV (1378–1419).

Hussitism. Although the partisans of the Devotio Moderna were guilty of certain exaggerations, they were respectful of ecclesiastical authority. Some reformers of the second generation, however, fell under the spell of the heretical writings of John WYCLIF. Best known among them were JEROME OF PRAGUE (d. 1415), James of Stříbro (Jacobellus, d. 1429), Nicholas of Dresden (d. 1416) and above all, John HUS, the fiery preacher of the Bethlehem Chapel in Prague. Rumors that heterodox teachings were spreading in Bohemia moved the Council of CONSTANCE to summon Hus to answer charges of heresy. In 1415, after being convicted of errors concerning the nature of the Church, the papal primacy and other doctrines, the Czech reformer was burned at the stake as a relapsed heretic. This ignominious death of a beloved

Protest after the Soviet invasion of Prague, 1968. (AP/Wide World Photos)

leader aroused the indignation of Bohemia and marked the beginning of the Hussite wars.

The program of the HUSSITES did not always agree with that of Hus himself. In Prague, Jacobellus began (1414) to distribute Communion under both species, a practice approved by Hus in a letter from Constance, but strongly disavowed by the hierarchy. The chalice for the laity became the symbol of the Hussites, who were for that reason called UTRAQUISTS or Calixtines. The Hussite League, formed in 1415, decided to introduce Hussitism throughout Bohemia, but discord developed between its moderate wing, represented by the people of Prague, and the radical sectarians, who were adherents of Wyclif and the WALDENSES, who were influenced by the chiliastic notions of JOACHIM OF FIORE. One of the radical groups became known as TÁBORITES because its center was the city of Tábor in southern Bohemia.

The Hussite movement was fostered by national and social issues as well as religious ones. It voiced the ani-mosity of the Czech peasants and gentry against the German element in the higher clergy, in the monasteries, and in the cities. A leading Hussite motivation was an eagerness to strip the clergy of their property under the pretext of conforming them to the spirit of the gospel. Despite their internal discords, Hussite factions united whenever external danger required. Between 1419 and 1431 they thwarted several military campaigns conducted by Emperor SIGISMUND, heir to the Czech throne, and the Crusaders. The Council of BASEL settled the Bohemian question by issuing the Compactata, which ratified in modified form the Four Prague Articles of the Hussites, including the privilege of Communion under two species for the laity in Bohemia and Moravia. The Compactata never received papal approval, because medieval Christianity acquiesced reluctantly in national particularities of this kind, and Pope PAUL II eventually proclaimed the Czech King George of Poděbrady (1458–71) a heretic for observing them. In their wrath the Hussites caused a

Buildings line the Vltava River in Prague, Czech Republic.
(©David Cumming; Eye Ubiquitous/CORBIS)

cleavage between Bohemia and the other territories belonging to the Czech crown. It also ruined the kingdom economically, isolated it culturally and permanently divided it religiously.

In addition to sewing discord, Hussitism gave birth to the BOHEMIAN BRETHREN (*Unitas Fratrum*), a peaceful movement originating after 1450 that drew its inspiration from the Czech squire Peter Chelčický (d. 1460), whose writings were influenced by Wyclif and the Waldenses. By 1500 the Brethren formed a small but active minority group of about 100,000 members. JAGIEŁŁO (Władisław II, 1471–1516) tried vainly by special laws to check their advance.

While Catholicism survived the Hussite disturbances it declined to minority status, less so in Moravia than in Bohemia. Church property was confiscated, monastic communities were massacred or dispersed, and ecclesiastical organization was destroyed. Hussitism also interrupted the promising development of humanism in the region; after 1450 the Czech kingdom renewed its contacts with the Italian centers of the RENAISSANCE at the urging of Czech Catholics.

Reformation and Catholic Restoration. After the death of Louis Jagełłon in 1526 at the battle of Mohács,

the Bohemian estates elected the Hapsburg Emperor Ferdinand I as king, prompted in their choice by the danger of Turkish invasion and by existing agreements concerning the succession to the throne. The HAPSBURGS, who provided a succession of Holy Roman emperors during 1438–1806, united the Czech and Hungarian territories to its Austrian possessions and remained in Bohemia until 1918.

The Hussites, who were falling into decadence for lack of able priests, listened eagerly to the teachings of Martin LUTHER and for the most part adopted LUTHERANISM. Under the leadership of Bishop John Augusta (d. 1572) the Bohemian Brethren also inclined toward the doctrines of Luther and MELANCHTHON and, in 1547, became involved in the halfhearted and unsuccessful rebellion of the Czech estates against Ferdinand I. The Brethren paid dearly for this involvement; only their Moravian branch, which took no part in the uprising, was spared.

Meanwhile, the region's Catholic minority was strengthened by the vigorous COUNTER REFORMATION that originated in the Latin countries. In 1566 the JESUITS opened a college in Prague, and in 1600 the Capuchins extended their activity to Bohemia (*see* FRANCISCANS, FIRST ORDER). In 1564 Pope Pius IV granted the king's request and permitted the laity in the ecclesiastical provinces of Prague and Salzburg to receive Communion under two species, but this concession came too late to bear the expected fruit. The extent to which Protestant innovations had infiltrated the Lutheranized Hussites was manifested in the *Confessio Bohemica* (1575), which was based to some extent on Hussite traditions, primarily on the AUGSBURG CONFESSION (1530).

The *Confessio Bohemica* was intended to embody a creed common to all non-Catholic Christians of the realm, but it was unable to satisfy all Protestant groups. When the estates asked Maximilian II (1564–75) to approve this creed, they received no more than a verbal assurance of religious tolerance. Written guarantees of religious liberty arrived from Rudolph II (1576–1612) in his Letter of Majesty (1609). A few years later, the Protestant estates claimed that this royal charter had been violated and, relying on the solidarity of the Protestant world, rebelled against Rudolph's successor. In 1619 they elected Frederick, the Calvinist Elector of the Palatinate, as king of Bohemia. This selfish oligarchy ended at the brief battle at the White Mountain near Prague on Nov. 8, 1620, when Frederick, the "Winter King," was eliminated as a claimant to the throne.

The victorious FERDINAND II (1618–37), ruling according to the Spanish pattern of absolutism, curtailed the powers of the diet and the privileges of the estates. German became an official language along with Czech. Convinced he could best attain his political aims in an entirely Catholic realm, Ferdinand II set out to reconquer Bohemia by applying the principle, *cuius regio, ejus religio,* and revoking the Letter of Majesty. Thereafter he permitted only the Catholic religion in the kingdom and exiled those who refused to return to the old faith. As a result, about 30,000 families left the country. Properties of religious recalcitrants were confiscated on a vast scale, and passed into the hands of the foreign nobles and adventurers who filled the kingdom. Bohemia's misery was consummated by the horrors of the THIRTY YEARS' WAR.

Nominally Catholic Bohemia received better ecclesiastical organization after construction of sees at Litoměřice (1655) and Hradec Králové (1660), but a shortage of priests handicapped the progress of religious life by permitting only a third of the 1,000 parishes to be staffed. The opening of Jesuit colleges did much to gain converts to Catholicism, as did missionaries such as Albert Chanovský (d. 1643) and Adam Kravařský (d. 1660). Many other priests went on foreign missions and helped spread the faith in South America and China. Regenerated Catholicism created a new literature and left many monuments of BAROQUE art.

Despite the brilliance of baroque culture, there were shadows. The hand of the absolutist Hapsburg state lay heavy on Church and State. To multiply conversions, force and military intervention were used, despite opposition from Church leaders who realized that such measures of compulsion by the government injured the Church by association. National individuality was on the whole disregarded, although it found one stanch defender in Bohuslav Balbin, SJ (d. 1688). The preservation of both the traditional Catholic faith and a national consciousness was due to the efforts of the educated priesthood. The great national awakening of later times was built on the foundations set during the Catholic Restoration.

Enlightenment and Liberalism. The ENLIGHTENMENT of the 18th century deeply affected ecclesiastical life. Some Catholic disciples of the Aufklärung disavowed only the excesses of baroque religiosity, but others, even among the clergy, shared the current optimism in the omnicompetence of human reason. Catholic philosophy proved unable to compete in popularity with the original approach of Christian WOLFF (d. 1754), who found supporters even among the Jesuits of Prague. The arbitrary interference of Holy Roman Empress MARIA THERESA (1740–80) in ecclesiastical affairs differed only in method from that of her son JOSEPH II (1780–90). Joseph II dissolved 71 monasteries in Bohemia and 31 in Moravia, and was responsible for the destruction of

Women praying in front of local shrine, Stradznice, Czech Republic. (©Hulton-Deutsch Collection/CORBIS)

countless artistic and literary treasures. In pursuance of his policy of JOSEPHINISM he removed clerical training from episcopal control and entrusted it to general seminaries created by him in Prague and Olomouc with the intent of educating priests to be trustworthy civil servants more than mediators between God and man. Leopold II (1790–92) restored the seminaries to the bishops, but the spirit of Josephinism survived beyond 1850. Ecclesiastical divisions remained unchanged except for the creation of the Diocese of Brno (1777) and the elevation of Olomouc to the status of a metropolitan see. The government caused new parishes to be formed without previous consultation with Church authorities.

The grant of tolerance in 1781 affected the REFORMED CHURCHES, those which subscribed to the Augsburg Confession, Hussites and Orthodox. Between 1781 and 1787 about 78,000 of the four million inhabitants of Bohemia and Moravia became Protestants.

Catholic Revival. The rise of ROMANTICISM *c.* 1800 stimulated a Catholic revival. In part the government sponsored the Catholic restoration, but this restoration, based on the union of throne and altar, harbored many tenets of the Austrian Enlightenment. There was also a more genuine revival, whose leading figure was St. Clement HOFBAUER (d. 1820), a native of southern Moravia. Romanticism was also responsible for a lively re-awakening of nationalism in Czech territories.

Liberalism, jealous of any encroachment upon human liberty, opposed state absolutism and the Austrian Church which was closely linked with it. The controversies concerning ULTRAMONTANISM and the growing power of the PAPACY affected the German element in the population more than the Czech. This was true also of the LOS-VON-ROM movement. At VATICAN COUNCIL I Cardinal SCHWARZENBERG of Prague was among those who opposed as inopportune the definition of papal primacy and infallibility.

Political leadership among the Czechs was exercised at first by the conservative Old Czech party, whose ideals were those of the historian Francis Palacký (d. 1876). During the 1890s this party ceded leadership to the Young Czechs, who were openly anti-Catholic and devoted to Hussite traditions. However, they subordinated the religious aspects of Hussitism to secondary ones. The notion of Slavic solidarity inherent in the Czech revival from the very beginning roused their enthusiasm. This idea appeared in the scholarly works of Joseph Dobrovský (d. 1829), a priest who began the scientific study of Slavic philology. Slavic solidarity inspired the Pan-Slav Congress in Prague (1848). One effect of this sentiment in Catholic circles was the growth in devotion to Saints Cyril and Methodius. From the same roots grew the movement for the religious unification of all Slavs, the most tangible results of which were the unionist congresses held at Velehrad from 1907–36.

The Catholic awakening *c.* 1900 had strength enough only to assume a defensive position in the face of rising liberalism, materialism and the anti-Catholic interpretation of Czech history as propounded by Tomáš Masaryk. Pope Leo XIII, who was deeply interested in the development of Czech Catholicism, founded (1890) in Rome the *Bohemicum* for seminarians from Czech lands. In 1929 this college became the *Collegium Nepomucenum,* intended for students of theology from the whole of Czechoslovakia.

The Period of the World Wars

On Oct. 28, 1918, after the capitulation of the Hapsburgs' Austro-Hungarian Empire in World War I, the lands of the Czech crown and Slovakia regained their freedom and together organized a new republic. Despite the Czechoslovakian government's professions of democracy, the Catholic Church had to fight for its existence during the first years of the new regime. Strong anti-Catholic prejudices existed throughout the region, caused by the widespread belief that the Vatican had supported Austria-Hungary in its oppressive policy, as well as from religious indifferentism among a citizenry exposed to liberal and socialist slogans.

Rival Faiths, Apathy, Preface War. During the critical postwar years (1919–21), Catholics were left without bishops to provide leadership, and this proved fatal. In this crucial period, along with a lack of bishops, a reform movement started among the Catholic clergy that demanded the liturgy in the vernacular and a married priesthood. Open revolt occurred in 1920 when the national Czechoslovak Church was proclaimed in Prague, and before long some of its radical leaders had brought their sect to the margins of Christianity. Official government circles favored anti-Catholic propaganda, which disseminated slogans such as: "Settling accounts with both, Vienna and Rome."

Flux within the Church ultimately led to a mass apostasy, and in the Czech lands about 20 percent defected. Although a few became Protestants, far more joined the Czechoslovak Church, which numbered close to 750,000 members by 1930. Many others severed all religious affiliations. Upholders of the Augsburg and Helvetic confessions merged to form the Evangelical Church of Czech Brethren, which accepted the Czech confession of 1575. With almost 300,000 members by 1930, it was the largest Protestant Czech group. Little support for the struggling Church was gained from the State: Tomáš Masaryk, Czechoslovakia's first president, publicly commented that Catholics "would enjoy as many rights as they would be able to gain." Fortunately, the Church did have its defenders, among them Monsignor John Šrámek, head of the Czech Catholic People's Party. Šrámek could not stop the passage of anti-Catholic legislation on marriage and education, but he did forestall the planned separation of Church and State in a manner hostile to the Church.

Eventually passions subsided, and more moderate elements replaced the Socialists in positions of power. Beginning in the late 1920s the zealous and patient work of diocesan and religious priests rejuvenated Catholicism. This new vitality was noticeable during the celebration of the millennium of St. Wenceslas (1929), during the Pribina festivities in Nitra (1933), and especially during the general convention in Prague of all Catholics of Czechoslovakia, with Cardinal Verdier present as papal legate (1935).

Diplomatic relations were established between Czechoslovakia and the Holy See in 1920, although a temporary interruption occurred in 1925 due to the actions of the papal nuncio. A *modus vivendi* was signed in 1928 by the papal secretary of state and the minister of foreign affairs that provided, among other things, that diocesan boundaries should be adjusted so that no part of the country would be under the jurisdiction of foreign dioceses. It further stipulated that religious houses should not be subject to provincial superiors resident outside Czechoslovakia. Residential bishops were to be named by the Holy See, after the government was given the opportunity to raise objections of a political nature concerning any appointments. Prior to assuming office, new bishops would be required to take an oath of fidelity to the state. However, such things as the status of the Czecho-Slovak districts previously belonging to the Polish Archdiocese of Wrocław (Breslau) and now forming the Apostolic Administration of Český Těšín remained undecided due to the onset of World War II.

Church Confronts National Socialism. The international crisis caused by the expansion of National Socialism during the late 1930s directly affected Czechoslovakia. Under the terms of the Munich Pact signed with German Chancellor Adolf Hitler in September of 1938 all Czech lands were deprived of their border territories, including the Sudetenland to the northwest, while Slovakia lost its southern districts. Changed to a federated state on Oct. 6, 1938, the republic of Czechoslovakia was forcibly dissolved six months later, on March 14, 1939.

By 1939 the Nazis had occupied the Sudetenland, which was annexed to the Third Reich as the Protectorate of Bohemia and Moravia. Czechs living in that region were kept in a state of constant terror because of ever-increasing violence until 1945. Universities were closed, along with their theological faculties. Catholic publications and organizations ceased. Of the 370 priests arrested by the Nazis, eight were executed, 70 died in prison, 58 died in concentration camps, seven perished from tortures and two died from unknown causes. Ecclesiastical administration also suffered; to avoid placing German candidates in vacant sees the Holy See named no new bishops. Even the Archdiocese of Prague remained vacant after the death of Cardinal Charles Kašpar in 1941.

Bibliography: P. DAVID, *Dictionnaire d'histoire et de géographie ecclésiastiques,* ed. A. BAUDRILLART et al. (Paris 1912–) 9:418–479. E. WINTER, *Tausend Jahre Geisteskampf im Sudetenraum* (Salzburg 1938). K. KROFTA, *Československé dějiny* (Prague 1946). B. RÁČEK, *Československé dějiny* (Prague 1929). V. NOVOTNY et al., *České dějiny,* 12 v. (Prague 1912–48). D. PERMAN, *The Shaping of the Czechoslovak State* (Leiden 1962). K. KROFTA, *Dějiny československé* (Prague 1946). F. CINEK, *Knáboženské otázce v prvních letech našl samostatnosti, 1918–1925* (Olomouc 1926). *Katolicke Slovensko* (Trnava 1933). E. BENEŠ, *Czechoslovak Policy for Victory and Peace* (London 1944). K. GLASER, *Czecho-Slovakia: A Critical History* (Caldwell ID 1961). H. RIPKA, *Le Coup de Prague: Une Révolution préfabriquée* (Paris 1949). J. KORBEL, *The Communist Subversion of Czechoslovakia, 1938–1948* (Princeton NJ 1959). E. J. TÁBORSKÝ, *Communism in Czechoslovakia, 1948–1960* (Princeton NJ 1961). L. NEMEC, *Church and State in Czechoslovakia* (New York 1955). K. S. LATOURETTE, *Christianity in a Revolutionary Age: A History of Christianity in the Nineteenth and Twentieth Centuries,* 5 v. (New York 1958–62) v.1, 2, 4. *Bilan du Monde,* 2:837–846. *Annuario Pontificio* (Rome 1912–).

[J. KRAJCAR]

The Church since 1945

On May 8, 1945, Czechoslovakia was reestablished and it regained its pre-war boundaries, save for the 4,500-square-mile region of southeast Slovakia known as Carpathian Ruthenia, which joined the USSR as the Transcarpathian Oblast. While the restored Republic professed democratic principles, in accordance with the Potsdam agreement it was considered an area of Soviet influence. Communists quickly occupied key political positions and by February of 1948 had gained control of the government.

Church-State Relationship Falters. Soon after World War II new bishops were appointed to the vacant sees, an effort of the Holy See to secure the Church in advance of political upheavals. Josef BERAN (1888–1969; bishop 1946, cardinal 1965) became archbishop of Prague in 1946; he had been rector of the seminary there and had survived the concentration camp in Dachau. Josef Matocha was named archbishop of Olomouc. His consecration of the bishops of Trnava and Rožnava in August of 1949 was the first public episcopal consecration in Czechoslovakia.

As in most of eastern Europe following Soviet intervention, the Church did not fare well under communism. The internuncio to the Czechoslovak government was forced to leave the country in 1948, and open conflict broke out between the Church hierarchy and the Communist regime of Klement Gottwald later that year, following a decision by the bishops that priests were barred from taking an active part in political life. Despite this prohibition, Czech priest Josef Plojhar accepted a government appointment as minister of health and was consequently suspended from his priestly functions. The government did not view this action as conciliatory on the part of the Church, and a systematic persecution of the Catholic Church began shortly thereafter. Diplomatic relations between Prague and the Vatican would terminate on March 18, 1950.

During the four decades of Communist rule that followed, the Czech Church suffered restrictions and harassments while its leaders were persecuted. Deprived of property, buildings and land, it was robbed of its economic base. Monasteries were transformed into state offices and warehouses; church schools were abolished. The government Ministry of Internal Affairs occupied the seminary building in Prague.

A law nationalizing education (April 21, 1948) resulted in the seizure of all Catholic schools, including minor seminaries. Another law aimed at the complete control of the Church by the state caused a special ministry for Church affairs to be organized. All diocesan seminaries were closed on June 14, 1950. In their stead the government opened one seminary for the Czech lands, located in Prague (soon moved to Litoměřice) and another in Bratislava for Slovakia. Both of these state-controlled institutions were termed theological faculties. Students, who needed government permission to study for the priesthood, generally suspected the seminary professors to be collaborators to one degree or another. Theological books and journals from abroad were banned and, as of 1974, so were radios.

By the end of 1948 three influential Catholic weeklies had been shut down, and soon the free Catholic press had ceased to exist except for one weekly and one monthly for the clergy, published in both the Czech and Slovak languages and government-controlled. The charity CATHOLIC ACTION was also dissolved late in 1948. Within a few months the government, with the help of some "patriotic" priests, sought to found its own spurious version of Catholic Action, but this attempt was quickly condemned by the bishops and by the Holy See. The so-called Peace Committee of the Catholic Clergy was formed in 1951. The Czechoslovak Society for the Spreading of Scientific and Political Knowledge, started in 1955, had as its real purpose the organized spread of atheism.

The Communist government acknowledged a legal obligation to support the needs of the Church and to pay the salaries of priests. In return, priests were allowed to carry on their ministry only with a state permit. Article 178 of the criminal code regulated the activities of anyone involved in pastoral work. Clergy were able to carry out their ministry only with "the prior approval of the state." According to Article 178 priests were "licensed" as employees of the state. A priest whose license was revoked could no longer function publicly and had to seek some other form of employment. Sees vacated through Article 178 were placed under the control of vicars-capitular who cooperated with the Communist regime. Eleven prominent religious priests were placed on trial in order to justify the invasion of religious houses during the night of April 13, 1950. All religious men were sent to "concentration monasteries." A few months later religious women suffered the same fate, and their work at schools and hospitals reverted to secular staff. Several years later all religious were dispersed.

The Czechoslovakian government allowed three bishops from both the Czech lands and Slovakia to attend Vatican II in 1962, and four to attend the sessions in 1963. By 1964, however, no diocese in Czech lands was administered by an ordinary approved by Rome. The Communist regime placed Archbishop Beran under confinement in June of 1949; 15 years later, at the personal request of Pope Paul VI, Beran was allowed to leave the country to live in Rome where he died in 1969. The only state-acknowledged bishop in that time was František Tomášek (d. 1992) who had been consecrated auxiliary bishop of Olomouc in 1949, but was not allowed to carry out his office. In 1965 Tomášek was appointed apostolic chancellor in Prague. In 1977 he was named a cardinal and, subsequently, archbishop of Prague. Another noted victim of Communist persecution was Štepán Trochta (d. 1974), bishop of Litoměřice (1947–74), who was interned in 1950 and resumed his office only in 1968. Pope Paul VI named Trochta a cardinal in 1971.

During the era of communist suppression, the Church was able to minister to its faithful only by going "underground," as discrimination in areas of employment and housing existed for practicing Catholics. The clandestine bishop Felix Davidek, who himself had been consecrated by a clandestine bishop early in the communist era, felt that it was necessary for the underground to have its own bishops. Beginning in 1968 and with the help of Bishop Jan Blaha, Davidek consecrated fifteen bishops and ordained uncounted married men to the priesthood. These married men, ordained in both the Latin and Greek Catholic rites, were less likely to be suspected by the police than unmarried men. Davidek also ordained one woman, Ludmilla Javorova. Unlike his own ordination, Davidek's consecrations were done without the approval of the Holy See.

Country moves toward Liberation. A brief respite of repressive government policies—the so-called "Prague Spring"— occurred in 1968 under the rule of Czechoslovakian President Alexander Dubček. However, it quickly ended via a military invasion from the Soviet bloc, leaving in its wake Gustav Husák. Husák was chosen first secretary of the Czechoslovakian Communist party in April of 1969 with a promise of "normalization." During the 20 years of Husákian normalization, repression of the Church continued, and the relentless pressure of the state police took its toll.

During the Husák years, an organization of priests called *Pacem in terris* provided a front for priests who, for one reason or another, collaborated with the government. Well-intentioned members thought that it was only way of saving the Church for the future. The organization served the purposes of the regime by legitimating its policies, and dividing the presbyterate. At the same time the government offered inducements to parents and teachers to discourage their children from attending religious education classes.

Success of the Velvet Revolution. Efforts on the part of the Holy See to reach some sort of accommodation with the Communist regime began under Dubček. Finally in 1973 the government permitted the Holy See to appoint four residential bishops. Two of them, Josef Vrána and Josef Feranec, who had been prominent members of *Pacem in terris*, were received coldly by the Catholic laity. No other bishops were appointed until 1989, even though ten of the 13 dioceses in Czechoslovakia were soon without a residential bishop.

The election of Karol Wojtyła as Pope John Paul II in 1978 marked a turn in the Church's policy and fortune. While archbishop of Krakow, Wojtyła had assisted the underground church in Czechoslovakia. Václav Benda and other Catholic activists who had a part in promulgating Charter 77, a manifesto denouncing oppression and proclaiming human dignity and rights based on moral principles, found encouragement. In 1983 the Czechoslovakian foreign minister met with the Pope, the first such meeting since relations between the Holy See and the Czech government ended in 1950. Meanwhile, the 1982 instruction of the Congregation for the Clergy banning priests' involvement with partisan politics led to a decline in the numbers and influence of *Pacem in Terris*. Cardinal Tomášek surrounded himself with priest advisors committed to an activist role for the Church and began more and more to support Catholic resistance.

The 1985 commemoration of the 1,100th anniversary of the death of St. Methodius demonstrated to Czechoslovakian Catholics a reason for renewed hope. Between 150,000 and 200,00 pilgrims made their way to the Cistercian monastery at Velehrad in Moravia for the occasion. Three years later a Moravian peasant named Augustin Navrátil began circulating a petition for religious freedom that sought redress for the multiple grievances of Czech and Slovak Catholics. Its 31 points spelling out the implications for Czechoslovakia of the fundamental principle of separation of church and state gave the signatories the opportunity to affirm publicly the basic human rights of freedom of speech, assembly and habeas corpus. Cardinal Tomášek told Catholics it was their duty to sign the Navrátil petition, and many Protestants and nonbelievers joined in registering their support.

The end of communist rule came swiftly and smoothly—thus it was named the "Velvet Revolution." The 1980s, which had begun as a decade of growing resistance, ended in open rebellion on Nov. 17, 1989 after a non-violent student demonstration was attacked by riot police. Following six weeks of mass demonstrations, strikes and negotiations between the communist regime and resistance groups, Václav Havel was duly installed as president of Czechoslovakia in June of 1991. His first action was to dissolve the Warsaw Pact. On Jan. 1, 1993 the "velvet divorce" was achieved and the Czech Republic came into being, a consequence of rising Slovakian nationalism.

Restoration of the Faith. The freedom attained by the Church brought with it a complex web of administrative, economic and pastoral problems. When restored to Church ownership in 1990, many schools and other buildings were found to be damaged and in need of repair. In all, 175 monasteries and similar buildings reverted back to the church under the 1991 Law on Restitution. However, the law only applied to property confiscated after 1948, and the government's Social Democratic party stalled some claims for restitution by claiming that certain property had reverted to the State. By 2000 there were still outstanding claims for Church property taken by local government bodies, some of which included farmlands, 430,000 acres of forest and income-producing property.

Because religion was not taught in state-run schools, the Church hurried to reopen schools and train teachers. In the first years after the revolution, hundreds of laity studied theology and catechetics to become religion teachers. Religion was taught in the state-run elementary schools and, when demanded, in the secondary schools.

Religious orders played an important part in the restoration and re-evangelization of the country, a task that was encouraged further by the Pope. By the mid-1990s 33 religious orders of men worked within the Czech Republic, while women's religious orders, which had seen their numbers shrink and age under Communist rule, benefited from a resurgence of interest in the consecrated life. Religious sisters were soon back at work in public health care, homes for the elderly, disabled and sick, and in schools. The responsibility for evangelical efforts extended to the laity, noted Pope John Paul during a visit with Czech bishops in 1998.

Church Looks to 21st Century. By 2000 the Church in the Czech Republic oversaw 3,150 parishes, and benefited from the ministrations of 1,301 secular and 555 religious priests, 110 brothers and 2,484 sisters. Despite the country's Catholic history, only 39 percent of the population claimed membership in the Church, and informal polling revealed that over 60 percent of citizens felt themselves to be atheists. Among the biggest problems facing the Church in the new millennium was the religious indifference created by 41 years of secularism, a need to tend to the families of the faithful and the proliferation of questionable religious sects throughout Eastern Europe. In an effort to resolve more material issues related to the future of the Church, Pope John Paul II hoped to establish a joint committee of Church leaders and government officials that could handle Church-State matters.

In 1951 the Czechoslovakian Orthodox Church had formed an autocephalous metropolis with four dioceses. When the Greek Catholic Diocese of Prešov was suppressed on April 28, 1950, all of its 305,000 members were declared members of the Orthodox Church and subjected to the patriarch of Moscow. The Greek Catholic Church was reestablished in 1968, and 147 parishes across the region soon required priests. For this reason the Greek Church would be helpful in resolving one pastoral problem of the Roman Catholic Church that required special attention in the mid-1990s: How to assimilate the married priests of the former ''underground clergy'' into the life of the Church? Questions were raised regarding the legitimacy of Davidek's clandestine ordinations of married men, all of which had been performed without papal approval. After some debate, in 1997 it was decided that each case would be examined individually. By answering the Vatican's call to come forth, most clandestine priests would be re-ordained *sub conditione* in the Greek Catholic church, which had a tradition of married clergy. By 2000 over 50 of these priests had come forth, accepted the directives of the Pope, and were working within the Czech Republic, some even in Latin communities where their presence was needed.

In April of 1997 the Pope visited the Czech Republic, and spoke of the importance of Christian values to a nation that had become secularized by decades of communist rule. Recalling the heroic actions of many of the country's religious, he added that pardons must be granted, forgiveness given and divisions healed in the ''hour of charity.'' Cardinal Miloslav Vlk, Archbishop of Prague, suffered much during the Communist era. In the early 1990s he also looked back into the century almost past, in search of positive effects on the Catholic Church in Czech lands. Christians learned to practice their religion in small communities and to survive in adversity without outside support, concluded Vlk. It would be with this legacy to support them that the Church in the Czech Republic would build its future.

Bibliography: G. ASH, *We the People: The Revolution of '89 Witnessed in Warsaw, Budapest, Berlin & Prague* (Cambridge UK 1990). J. BROUN, *Conscience and Captivity: Religion in Eastern Europe* (Washington DC 1988). *Církevní komise ÚV KSČ 1949–1951, Edice dokumentů,* 1 (Prague/Brno 1994—). B. J. FREI, *Staat und Kirche in der Tschechoslowakei, 1948–1968,* 5 vols. (Munich 1989–91). K. KAPLAN, *Staat und Kirche in der Tschechoslowakei 1948–1953* (Munich 1990); *Stát a církev v Českoslvensku v letech 1948–1953* (Brno 1993) with English summary and texts of the official Communist documents. V. VAŠKO, *Neumlčená,* 1 (Prague 1990–). G. WEIGEL, *The Final Revolution. The Resistance Church and the Collapse of Communism* (New York 1992).

[M. FIALA/EDS.]

CZERSKI, JOHANN

Apostate priest, sectarian leader; b. Warlubien, East Prussia, May 12, 1815; d. Schneidemühl, Germany, Dec. 22, 1893. After ordination at Posen (1842) he was a curate at the cathedral there, but was transferred to Schneidemühl (1844) after twice being suspended for concubinage. In August 1844 he left the Church and founded the Christian Apostolic Catholic Community, a small group that rejected papal primacy, veneration of saints, fasting, celibacy, indulgences, and remission of sins; he also introduced Communion under two species and the vernacular in the liturgy. Four days after his degradation from the priesthood and excommunication (Feb. 17, 1845) he married Mary Gutowska before a Protestant minister. After 1846 he became involved in the German Catholic movement (*Deutschkatholizismus*), which he helped Johann RONGE to found. Czerski's followers were few in number, consisting chiefly of Catholics discontented with Catholic teachings on mixed marriage. His religious conceptions were moderate at first, but after 1860 he abandoned Christianity and became a roving preacher of the Religious Society of Free Congregations. As a religious leader he lacked theological and moral integrity.

Bibliography: J. J. HERZOG and A. HAUCK, eds., *Realencyklopädie für protestantische Theologie* 4:583–589. *Wetzer und Welte's Kirchenlexikon,* 13 v. (2d ed. Freiburg 1882–1903) 3:1603–15.

[V. CONZEMIUS]

CZĘSTOCHOWA

Capital city of province of same name in south central Poland on the Warta River in the Kraków-Częstochowa upland, 220 km from Warsaw. It is famed for its possession since 1382 of an icon of the Blessed Virgin Mary, venerated under the titles ''Our Lady of Częstochowa,'' ''Our Lady of Jasna Góra,'' and the ''Black Madonna,'' the most famous icon in the country. The icon is housed in a basilica on a limestone hill known as the Jasna Góra (Bright Mountain) above the city. The complex of sacred buildings surrounding the icon constitutes one of the major shrines and pilgrimage centers in Christendom. The spire of the basilica church on Jasna Góra is the highest in Poland, 106.3 km, visible from a distance of several kilometers.

Legends abound regarding the origins of the icon of Our Lady of Częstochowa, the most popular of which attributes the painting to St. Luke, who worked on wood from the table of the Holy Family. Historians date it to the Byzantine period, sixth or seventh century, from the region around Constantinople. Measuring 122.2 cm (48.11 inches) high, 82.2 cm (32.36 inches) wide, and 3.5

Pope John Paul II (left) praying in front of the image of the Black Madonna on the Jasna Góra hill in the town of Częstochowa, Poland, 1999. (AP/Wide World Photos; photo by Diether Endlicher)

cm (1.38 inches) thick, the holy image was painted on wood covered by a tightly woven canvas. The Blessed Virgin Mary is represented in the *hodegetria* pose, pointing to the Christ Child, who sits erect not like a suckling infant but as the Christ-Emmanuel full of wisdom. After 500 years at the Castle of Selz in Ukraine, the icon was brought to Poland in 1382 by Prince Ladislaus of Opole, who entrusted it to the care of the Pauline Hermits at the monastery he had built for them atop Jasna Góra in Częstochowa. The same order of hermits remains its custodian today. In 1430, the icon was vandalized and desecrated by robbers, whom some historians believe were Polish nobles associated with the Hussite movement. The scars on Mary's cheek date from these events. Two large parallel scars slash vertically, while a third wider scar cuts horizontally across them. The darkened skin tone derives from a chemical reaction to fire, aging of the pigment, and centuries of votive candle smoke.

After the Swedish invasion of Poland was repulsed at Częstochowa in 1655, King Casimir proclaimed Our Lady of Częstochowa "Queen of the Realm of Poland," and from this dedication the icon attained a new status as the symbol of Polish nationalism, unity, and liberty. Through subsequent centuries of invasion, partition, Nazi occupation, and communist oppression, Poles regarded Częstochowa as the touchstone of their national identity. As part of the Great Novena of nine year's spiritual preparation for the millennium of Christianity in Poland in 1966, Cardinal Stefan WYSZYŃSKI circulated a special copy of the icon throughout Poland. In the 1980s, the leaders of the Solidarity movement wore small icons of the Częstochowa Virgin on their lapels. Solidarity's founder Lech Wałęsa donated his 1983 Nobel Peace Prize to Częstochowa, where it remains enshrined.

Votive offerings fill the treasury of the Jasna Góra monastery. The icon itself is heavily decorated with bejeweled attire and crowned with diadems that date to the official papal coronation of the icon in 1717. Pope Paul VI sent a golden rose to the shrine at the conclusion of the Second Vatican Council in honor of the millennium of Poland's Christianity celebrated in 1966. Pope John Paul II sent his white sash, bloodstained from the 1981 assassination attempt. It is kept in a sealed box near the icon.

The most famous tradition associated with Częstochowa is the "Walking Pilgrimage" that dates from 1711. About 50 pilgrimage routes throughout Poland converge on Częstochowa. The walk from Warsaw takes nine days, from Kraków six days, from Gdansk 13 days. For the feasts of the Assumption (August 15) and Our Lady of Częstochowa (August 26), more than one million pilgrims walk, and this religious movement grew throughout the 1990s in conjunction with several visits of Pope John Paul II to the shrine. Six million visitors a year visit Częstochowa.

Bibliography: A. GIEYSZTOR, S. HERBST, and B. LESNOCORSKI, *Millenium: A Thousand Years of the Polish State* (Warsaw 1961). M. HELM-PIRGO, *Virgin Mary, Queen of Poland* (New York 1957); OUR LADY OF CZĘSTOCHOWA FOUNDATION, ed., *The Glories of Częstochowa and Jasna Góra* (Stockbridge, Mass. 1981). Z. ROZNOW and E. SMULIKOWSKA, *The Cultural Heritage of Jasna Góra* (Warsaw 1974). J. ST. PASIERB, J. SAMEK, et al., *The Shrine of the Black Madonna at Częstochowa* (Warsaw 1980). M. ZALECKI, *Theology of a Marian Shrine: Our Lady of Częstochowa* (*Marian Library Studies,* n.s. 8, Dayton, Ohio 1976).

[J. E. MCCURRY]

D

DABLON, CLAUDE

Missionary; b. Dieppe, France, *c.* 1618; d. Quebec, Canada, May 3, 1697. After entering the Society of Jesus he was sent to Canada in 1655 and with Pierre Chaumonot, SJ, was charged with establishing a mission among the Iroquois at Lake Ganentaa (Syracuse, N.Y.). In 1661 he accompanied Gabriel Druillettes, SJ, on an unsuccessful expedition to find the ''Northern Sea.'' In collaboration with Claude Allouez, SJ, he drew up the map of all the posts visited by the two missionaries on Lake Superior. This ''Map of the Jesuits'' was considered a masterpiece in its time and has rendered valuable service to many researchers. Dablon served as superior general of the Jesuit missions of New France (1671–80, 1686–93), was the editor of the *Relations* (1672–79), and wrote a description (1678) of Jacques MARQUETTE's expedition down the Mississippi River.

Bibliography: T. J. CAMPBELL, *Pioneer Priests of North America, 1642–1710* (New York 1908–19) 1:110–133. J. DE-LANGLEZ, *Frontenac and the Jesuits* (Chicago 1939); ''Claude Dablon, 1619–1697,'' *Mid-America* 26 (1944) 91–110. SISTER MARIE DE SAINT-JEAN-D'ARS, *Claude Dablon et la Nouvelle France,* 1655–1697 (Doctoral diss. unpub. U. of Montreal).

[L. POULIOT]

DABROWSKI, JOSEPH

Priest, educator who influenced the growth of Polish Catholic parishes and schools in the U.S.; b. Zoltańce, Russian-held Poland, Jan. 27, 1842; d. Detroit, Mich., Feb. 15, 1903. The first of five children of Jozef Teodor Konstanty and Karolina (Borucka) Dabrowski, he was baptized Jan Jozef Henryk. From the Lublin *gimnazjum* he went to the University of Warsaw, which he left to fight under Gen. Ludwik Mieroslawski in the unsuccessful Polish uprising of January 1863 against czarist Russia. After living as a refugee in Saxony, Switzerland, and the Papal States, he was among the first six students admitted to the new Pontificio Collegio Polacco founded at Rome (1866) by Pius IX, who entrusted its care to the RESURRECTIONISTS. Dabrowski completed his philosophical and theological studies at the Gregorian University and was ordained Aug. 8, 1869, in Rome. At the suggestion of Rev. Leopold Moczygemba, OFM Conv, and with the help of Bp. Joseph Melcher of Green Bay, Wis., Dabrowski immigrated to the United States in December of 1869 to work among Polish Catholics in Wisconsin. During 11 years as parish priest, he built two churches, a mission chapel, parochial school, convent, and rectory. At his insistence, the Felician sisters arrived in the United States (1874) to staff the parochial school in Polonia, Wis., whence they spread elsewhere. He assisted the sisters in establishing a novitiate and in setting up a printing shop, which published Polish textbooks for elementary grades. In 1882 he transferred his activities to Detroit, where during the remaining two decades of his life he continued to guide the expansion of the Felician sisterhood and its schools and publications. He also collaborated in establishing SS. Cyril and Methodius Seminary and St. Mary's High School in 1885 for the training of bilingual Polish-American priests. As rector of the Polish seminary (1885–1903) and director of the Felicians (1874–1903), he helped to provide Polish parishes with priests and parochial schools with teachers, contributing more than any other single individual to their development.

Bibliography: J. V. SWASTEK, ''The Formative Years of the Polish Seminary in the U.S.'' in *The Contribution of the Poles to the Growth of Catholicism in the United States,* ed. F. DOMAŃSKI et al. (Rome 1959) 29–150. M. J. STUDNIEWSKA, ''Father Dabrowski and the Felicians,'' *Polish American Studies* 16 (1959) 12–23. B. KOLAT, ''Father J. D.: Educator,'' *ibid.* 9 (1952) 11–16. E. BOZEK, ''The Founder of the Polish Seminary,'' *ibid.* 8 (1951) 21–28.

[J. V. SWASTEK]

DACHERIANA COLLECTIO

The *Dacheriana collectio* is a systematic Gallic canonical collection dating from the Carolingian Reform at the end of the 8th century. Originally entitled *Excerpta de canonibus or canonum,* it was later named *Dacheriania,* after Jean Luc d'Achéry, who published it in 1672 on the basis of two manuscripts. Except in a few manuscripts, it is preceded by a preface consisting first of a treatise "de utilitate paenitentiae," and then a brief explanation of the grouping into three books of authentic excerpts from the councils and decretals.

The success of the collection resulted from its divisions and choice of materials. The first book is a treatment "de paenitentia et paenitentibus, criminibus atque iudiciis"; the second, "de accusatis et de accusatoribus, iudicibus atque iudiciis"; the third, "de sacris ordinibus." Four manuscripts contain also a dogmatic table of 36 titles, only nine of which were transcribed, without numbering, in a fifth manuscript. There is no fourth book in the collection.

The *Dacheriana* is one of the principal sources of the material to be found in collections of the 9th and 10th centuries. It contributed to the regulation of ecclesiastical discipline from the reign of Charlemagne until the time of the Decree of Gratian. The 40 extant manuscripts bear witness to the authority it enjoyed until the 12th century.

It was subjected to modifications whose extreme forms are described as: Form A, the most widely disseminated, free from extraneous additions; and Form B, influenced by the FALSE DECRETALS (Pseudo–Isidorian forgeries). The B form is represented by five manuscripts and by the corrections of three others. D'Achéry's edition makes use of Form B. A comparison of the two forms shows several textual revisions, as well as additions or omissions that justify the classification of the manuscripts into several distinct families. The *Dacheriana* derives from the *HADRIANA COLLECTIO* and from the *HISPANA COLLECTIO,* but the absence of critical editions does not permit its identification with a specific stage in their evolution. However, in the case of the *Hispana,* the textual criticism demonstrates the dependence of the *Dacheriana* upon the systematic nature of its form, and beyond this, the dependence of its composition upon that of the *Excerpta hispanica.*

Bibliography: A. VAN HOVE, *Commentarium Lovaniense in Codicem iuris canonici 1,* v. 1–5 (Mechlin 1928–); v. 1, Prolegomena (2d ed. 1945) 1:293–294. F. MAASSEN, *Geschichte der Quellen und der Literatur des canonischen Rechts im Abendlande bis dem Ausgang des Mittelalters* (Graz 1870; repr. Graz 1956) 848–852. G. HAENNI, "La Dacheriana mérite–t–elle une réédition?" *Revue historique de droit français et étranger* 33 (1956) 376–390.

[G. HAENNI]

DACIA

Originally the name of a province of the Roman Empire north of the Danube, was erroneously used during the Middle Ages as the Latin name for Denmark. This mistake was first observed *c.* 1020 in the Chronicle of Dudo of SAINT-QUENTIN, but penetrated into Scandinavia *c.* 1100. When the MENDICANTS during the 13th century (e.g., the DOMINICANS in 1228, the Franciscans before 1239) organized their Scandinavian territories— Denmark, Norway, and Sweden (with Finland)—the provinces were named for that country which was nearest the rest of the Continent. The Scandinavian Dominicans were often called *de Dacia* (from Denmark) no matter what their native land. During the late Middle Ages a *provincia Daciae* was organized also in the other orders (CARMELITES and KNIGHTS OF MALTA). The work of the Dominicans and Franciscans in the evangelization of the Scandinavian area was complemented by that of several other religious orders (CISTERCIANS, PREMONSTRATENSIANS) and of diocesan clergy. Archbishoprics were established in Nidaros (Norway), which had four suffragan sees, and in Uppsala (Sweden), with five bishoprics. In Denmark, Lund was an archbishopric with six sees; along the eastern shores of the Baltic, Riga was the only archbishopric in that area with six suffragan sees. The hierarchy were principally drawn from the mendicant orders. Houses of the Dominicans were usually in the larger cities, and those of the Franciscans, in smaller settlements.

Bibliography: J. GALLÉN, *La Province de Dacia de l'ordre des frères prêcheurs* (Helsinki 1946). *Kulturhistorisk leksikon for nordisk middelalder,* v. 2 (Copenhagen 1957).

[C. M. AHERNE]

DAĒVAS

A term applied to certain Persian divinities. The Iranian opposition between *ahuras* and *daēvas* is ancient since it is paralleled in India, although with different values for the *asuras* and the *devas*. The *asuras,* as opposed to the gods who were mere gods (*devas,* "celestial beings"), had a more moral, abstract quality. This contrast developed in India and in Iran but in two different directions. In India, the moral quality became occult, evil, and the *asuras,* in the classical period, became demons, leaving the *devas* as the only gods. In Iran the opposite took place; the *ahuras* monopolized divinity at the expense of the *daēvas* who sank to the level of demons. Thus Indra is a god in India, but a demon in Iran. Zoroaster opposed the cult of the *daēvas,* as did Xerxes, according to a recently discovered inscription.

Mazdaean propaganda never was able to stamp out the cult of Ahriman and the other *daēvas,* which is still attested, e.g., in the Latin Mithraic inscriptions *Deo Arimanio* (e.g., *Corpus inscriptionum latinarum* (Berlin 1863–) 3.3415).

For bibliography, *see* AMESHA SPENTA; PERSIAN RELIGION, ANCIENT.

[J. DUCHESNE-GUILLEMIN]

DAGOBERT II, KING OF AUSTRASIA, ST.

Martyr; b. *c.* 652; d. Stenay, Dec. 23, 679. An infant at the death of his father, Sigebert III (656), Dagobert was exiled to Ireland by the palace mayor Grimoald and replaced by Grimoald's son, Childebert. After Childeric II's murder (675), some Austrasians, helped by WILFRID OF YORK, repatriated Dagobert and proclaimed him king (spring of 676). Opposed by Ebroïn, the Neustrian palace mayor, and too energetic for his magnates' liking, Dagobert was murdered and buried at Stenay (near Verdun). The violent nature of his death earned him the title of martyr and a limited cult in Lorraine.

Feast: Dec. 23.

Bibliography: *Liber historiae Francorum,* ch. 43, ed. B. KRUSCH, *Monumenta Germaniae Historica: Scriptores rerum Merovingicarum* 2:316. E. STEPHANUS, *Vita Wilfridi Eboracensis* 25, 28, 33, ed. B. KRUSCH and W. LEVISON, *ibid.* 6: 219–221, 227–228. L. LEVILLAIN, "Encore la succession d'Austrasie au VIIᵉ siècle," *Bibliothèque de l'École des Chartes* 106 (1946) 296–306. J. M. WALLACE-HADRILL, *The Long-Haired Kings and Other Studies in Frankish History* (New York 1962) 234–235, 238. R. BORDES, *Les Mérovingiens à Rennes-le-Château, mythes ou réalités* (Rennes-le-Château, France 1984). R. FOLZ, "Tradition hagiographique et culte de saint Dagobert, roi des Francs," *Moyen-âge* 69, 4th ser., 18 (1963) 17–35. L. VAZART, *Dagobert II et le mystère de la cité royale de Stenay* (Paris 1983). R. AIGRAIN, *Catholicisme* 3:421–423. L. DUPRAZ, *Le Royaume des Francs et l'ascension politique des maires du palais au déclin du VIIᵉ siècle* . . . (Fribourg 1948).

[W. GOFFART]

DAGON

Weather- and vegetation-god of ancient Mesopotamia, whence his cult spread to Syria and Palestine. There was a temple of Dagon at MARI in the 18th century B.C. In the tablets from UGARIT, BAAL is termed Dagon's son (see J. B. Pritchard, *Ancient Near Eastern Texts Relating to the Old Testament* 142), and gradually Dagon's functions as a vegetation-god were transferred to Baal. That the Canaanites venerated Dagon as a vegetation-god can be seen in the fact that in Hebrew, a Canaanite dialect, the word for grain, *dāgān*, is connected with the name

(dāgôn) of this god. As the national god of the Philistines, Dagon had temples at Gaza in Samson's time (Jgs 16.21–23), at Azotus (Ashdod), where the ark of the covenant was brought after its capture from the Israelites (1 Sm 5.1–7; see also 1 Mc 10.83–84, where mention is made of the destruction of this temple by Jonathan), and apparently also at Beth-san, where Saul's cut-off head was displayed (1 Chr 10.10; but cf. 1 Sm 31.10). Dagon's cult in Palestine is attested by the place name Beth-Dagon in Juda (Jos 15.41) and in Aser (Jos 19.27). The erroneous idea of Dagon as a fish-god, suggested by St. Jerome and clearly stated by David Kimchi, goes back to popular etymology (Heb. *dāg*, fish) and to Kimchi's proposed reading of 1 Sm 5.4: "Only his [Dagon's] fishy part *(dāgô)* was left on him," where according to the versions, the reading should be "only his trunk *(gēwô)* was left on him." The fishtailed deity on coins from Arad and Ascalon should not be connected with Dagon.

Bibliography: F. J. MONTALBANO, "Canaanite Dagon: Origin, Nature," *The Catholic Biblical Quarterly* 13 (Washington DC 1951) 381–397.

[H. MUELLER]

DAHLMANN, JOSEPH

Jesuit Orientalist, whose writings on Indian culture and religion, Chinese literature, and comparative linguistics furthered the field of missiology in the early 20th century; b. Coblenz, Germany, Oct. 14, 1861; d. Tokyo, June 23, 1930. After entering the Society of Jesus in 1878, and teaching briefly in Bombay, he studied philology and comparative linguistics in Holland and England, and archeology in Vienna from 1891 to 1893. He received the doctorate (1902) at Berlin, and was made a staff member of the periodical *Stimmen aus Maria Laach,* from which resulted his *Indische Fahrten* (2 v., 1908, 1927). In China, Japan, and India for the next three years, at the request of the general of the Jesuits, he began investigation regarding the return of the society to the Japanese Missions. Through his knowledge of Far Eastern conditions, he was a principal authority for the foundation of Sophia University in Tokyo. When PIUS X founded the Catholic College in Tokyo, Dahlmann went, in 1908, as the first German Jesuit sent to Japan. There, from 1913 to 1930, he was professor of Indology and German literature. He held the same chairs, besides that of Greek, at the Imperial Japanese University from 1914 to 1924. From this period date his works on the earliest Christian missions to the Far East and on the Far East's historic relations with Western Europe.

Bibliography: J. DAHLMANN, *Der Auslandsdeutsche* 13 (1930) 522–524, a brief autobiography. L. KOCH, *Jesuiten-Lexikon*

Die Gesellschaft Jesu einst und jetzt (Paderborn 1934); photoduplicated with revisions and supplements (Louvain-Heverlee 1962), 1:373–374.

[J. FLYNN]

DAIG MACCAIRILL, ST.

Irish bishop; d. 586–7. He is known as Daig MacCairill (Daig the son of Cairell), Dagaeus, and Daganus, and is said to have been a pupil of FINNIAN OF CLONARD. The early, and largely legendary, accounts of his life state that he was a scribe and a worker in metal. It is highly questionable, however, whether Kieran of Clonmacnois (d. 549) was his patron, and it is extremely doubtful whether he was ever consecrated a bishop. He is the patron of Iniskeen, a parish on the borders of Counties Louth and Monaghan that belonged to the *paruchia* of Kieran. His genealogy was apparently composed only later in order to link his church with the Úi Néill.

Feast: Aug. 18.

Bibliography: *Annals of Inisfallen,* ed. and tr. SEÁN MACAIRT (Dublin 1951), give his obit under year 589 and make him, through a scribal error, grandson of Colmán Bec. *Annals of Ulster,* ed. W. M. HENNESSY and B. MACCARTHY, 4 v. (Dublin 1887–1901), under year 586. E. KNOTT, ed., "A Poem of Prophecies," *Ériu* 18 (1958) 65, 79. TALLAGHT ABBEY, *Martyrology of Tallaght,* ed. and tr. R. I. BEST and H. J. LAWLOR (Henry Bradshaw Society 68; 1931) 126. *Martyrology of Oengus,* ed. and tr. W. STOKES (*ibid.* 29; 1905) 186. Kenney 383–384.

[C. MCGRATH]

DAILLÉ, JEAN

French Protestant preacher and scholar; b. Châtellerault, France, Jan. 6, 1594; d. Charenton, France, April 15, 1670. Daillé was born of a devotedly Protestant family; he studied philosophy and theology at Saumur, and became a protégé of Philippe DUPLESSIS-MORNAY, then the most prominent lay leader of French Protestantism. As tutor to Mornay's grandchildren, Daillé toured Italy and other countries (1619–21). When a newly ordained Protestant minister, he became Mornay's castle preacher (1623). Soon thereafter Mornay died, however, and Daillé was named minister first in Saumur (1625), then in the important Paris suburb of Charenton (1626–70). He gradually rose to national prominence as a spokesman for Protestantism, and in 1659 presided over the Loudun national synod of the French Reformed Church, the last permitted by the government of LOUIS XIV. Daillé published many volumes of sermons, most of them exegetical, and he was widely praised as a master of French style. He was also widely respected as a student of patristics, but he argued against placing great reliance on the authority of the Church Fathers, a position that provoked attacks by both Catholic and Anglican scholars. Within his own Calvinist theological camp, Daillé tended to side with Moïse AMYRAUT and others who softened the rigors of extreme predestinarianism by introducing a doctrine of conditional universal grace.

Bibliography: E. and E. HAAG, *La France protestante,* ed. H. BORDIER (2d ed. Paris 1877–88) 5:23–36. A. RÉBELLIAU, *Bossuet: Historien du protestantisme* (3d ed. Paris 1909). H. R. GUGGISBERG, *Die Religion in Geschichte und Gegenwart* (3d ed. Tübingen 1957–65), 2:20. F. STEGMÜLLER, *Lexikon für Theologie und Kirche,* ed. J. HOFER and K. RAHNER (2d, new ed. Freiburg 1957–65) 3:124.

[R. M. KINGDON]

DAIMIEL, MARTYRS OF, BB.

Also known as Nicéforo Diez Tejerina and Companions, 26 religious from the Passionist house of studies, Christ of the Light, outside the city of Daimiel, about 80 miles south of Madrid, Spain; they were Nicefero Diez Tejerina, 43; Ildefonso García Nozal, 38; Pedro Largo Redondo, 29; Justiniano Cuesta Redondo, 26; Eufrasio de Celis Santos, 21; Maurilio Macho Rodríquez, 21; Jose Estalayo García, 21; Julio Mediavilla Concejero, 21; Fulgencio Calvo Sánchez,19; Honorino Carracedo Ramos, 19; Laurino Proaño Cuesta, 20; Epifanio Sierra Conde, 20; Abilio Ramos Ramos, 19; Anacario Benito Nozal, 30; Felipe Ruiz Fraile, 21; Jose Osés Sáinz, 21; Felix Ugalde Irurzun, 21; Jose Maria Ruiz Martínez, 20; Zacarias Fernández Crespo, 19; Pablo Maria Lopez Portillo, 54; Benito Solana Ruiz, 38; Tomas Cuartero Gascón, 21; Jose Maria Cuartero Gascón, 18; German Pérez Jiménez, 38; Juan Pedro Bengoa Aranguren, 46; Felipe Valcobado Granado, 62; beatified Oct. 1, 1989 by John Paul II.

Born in 1893 in Spain, Nicéfero Tejerina responded to God's call to embrace religious life in the Passionist Congregation. He studied in Toluca, Mexico, but because of the persecution of the Church there during the presidency of Plutarco Calles, he was arrested and later exiled to the United States, where he finished his studies in Chicago. He was ordained by Archbishop George Mundelein in 1916. After ministering in the United States, Mexico, and Cuba, he returned to Spain in 1932 to assume responsibilities as provincial superior of the order there. An antireligious climate swept Spain after the proclamation of the republic in 1931.

In 1936 Nicéforo went to visit the young religious studying for ordination and missionary work, the priests who taught them, and the brothers who served in the community at Daimiel. On the night of July 21, 1936, militiamen entered the Passionist house and ordered the thirty-one religious to leave in one hour. The militiamen ordered the group to the cemetery and told them to flee. At the same time, they alerted companions in the surrounding areas to shoot the religious on sight. The Passionists split into five groups. The first group of nine was captured and shot to death outside the train station of Carabanchel in Madrid on July 22, 1936.

The second group of twelve, Father Nicéforo among them, was taken at the station at Manzanares and shot by a firing squad. Nicéforo and four others died immediately; seven were taken to the hospital where one later died. Six of them recovered, only to be shot to death later on October 23, 1936. Three other religious, traveling together, were executed at the train station of Urda (Toledo) on July 25. Two gave their lives at Carrion de Calatrave on September 25. Only five of the thirty-one religious were spared. Numerous eyewitnesses testified afterwards to the brave faith and courage shown by the Daimiel community in their final moments, especially the signs of forgiveness they gave their executioners. Today their bodies are interred in the Passionist house at Daimiel.

At their beatification John Paul II said of them: "None of the religious of the community of Daimiel was involved in political matters. Nonetheless, within the climate of the historical period in which they lived, they were arrested because of the tempest of religious persecution, generously shedding their blood, faithful to their religious state of life, and emulating, in the twentieth century, the heroism of the Church's first martyrs" (Homily, Oct. 1, 1989).

Feast: July 23.

[V. HOAGLAND]

DAIMON

This article deals with the concept, and the development of the concept, of *daimon* (Greek δαίμων), and the influence of demonism in non-Christian religion, mythology, and folklore.

Concept and Development

The word occurs first in Homer, and the concept itself had a complex development in Greek literature, mythology, religion, and philosophy. However, the concept is likewise found fully developed in numerous other cultures and civilizations.

In Homer and Hesiod. In Homer it is applied to one of the great deities, e.g., Aphrodite (*Iliad* 3.420), and thus is used almost synonymously with θεός, θεά "god, goddess." More frequently, however, it denotes the occa-

sional manifestation of some indistinct supernatural or divine power; e.g., *Il.* 11.792: σὺν δαίμονι "by the grace of divine power"; *ibid.* 17.98: πρὸς δαίμονα, "defying divine power." *Daimon* may also refer to the power controlling the destiny of an individual and thus come near the significance of a man's "lot" or "fate," e.g., *Iliad* 8.66: πάρος τοι δαίμονα δώσω, "first I will give you your lot," that is, I will kill you.

In Hesiod (*Op.* 121–126; cf. 252–255) the souls of the men of the Golden Age have "by the will of Zeus" become "benevolent *daimones* on earth (δαίμονες ἐπιχθόνιοι), watchers of mortal men," invisibly roaming the earth, dispensing riches like kings and taking note of right and wrong. They are powers working among men "on earth"; hence they are called ἐπιχθόνιοι, in contrast to the ἐπουράνιοι, "celestial," gods whose sphere of activity extends to the inaccessible realms beyond this world. Because of their lofty state—they have raised from human mortality to godlike immortality—Hesiod describes them as *daimones*, a name that otherwise he and Homer apply to the gods. In the same sense, Hesiod (*Theogony* 991) refers to Phaethon who, after his ill-starred attempt to drive the chariot of the sun, was snatched up by Aphrodite, raised to immortality, and installed as her "nightly temple-keeper," δαίμονα δῖον, "a godlike *daimon*."

The Hesiodic conception of "earthly" *daimones* as a kind of agent or minister of the gods—a conception no doubt older than the Boeotian poet and inherited by him from tradition—opened the way to later speculation according to which the *daimones* form a separate class of beings standing midway between divine completeness and human incompleteness. There are both good and evil *daimones*. Plato (*Apology* 27D) refers to a general belief of his day, when he defines the *daimones* as second-rank supernatural powers, "illegitimate children of the gods either by nymphs or by some other mothers."

To this class belong the δαίμονες πρόπολοι of the gods, a term that Plato (*Leg.* 848D) explains by describing them as "the *daimones* attending the gods." In literature there appear a great number of such *daimones* forming the entourage of a god, e.g., the Satyrs and *Sileni* of Dionysus, the Curetes of the Cretan child-Zeus, the Corybantes of Rhea Cybele, the *daimones* around Demeter, and the ghostly hosts of Hecate. Mention must be made also of the demonic personifications of abstract or poetic ideas, such as Aidos (Shame), Ate (Blind Folly), Dike (Justice), Eris (Strife), Thanatos (Death), and others. They are divinized demonic powers to whom worship is paid on altars and in shrines. It is worthy of note that the "attendant" *daimones* are especially numerous in the company of chthonic deities with their gloomy

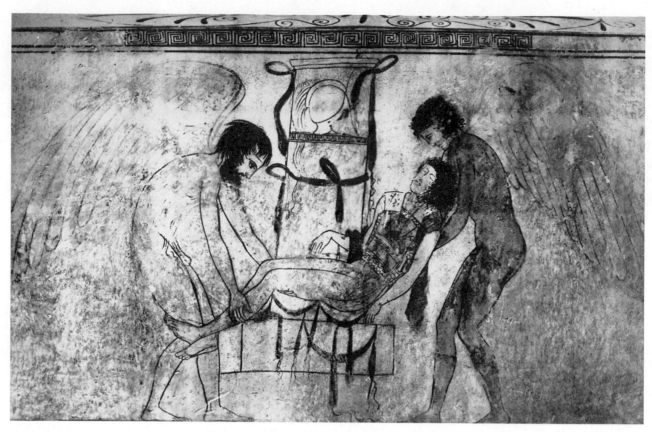

The Daimons Sleep (Hypnos) and Death (Thanatos) carrying the body of a warrior, c. 440 B.C.

cults. Moreover, as a result of the steadily increasing number of such lesser supernatural beings, the word *daimon*, if occurrences in magic papyri are excepted, is less frequently employed to denote one of the great gods.

Bringers of calamities and spirits of the dead. The tendency develops as well to ascribe to the *daimones* all the various kinds of calamities that may befall man in his earthly career. While the gods are generally looked upon as benevolent powers, the word *daimon*, though in itself not denoting an evil force, is actually used in this pejorative sense because of a certain awe against putting the blame for misfortunes on the gods. This marks the beginning of a depreciation of the word *daimon*. Since the *daimones* are thought to be in charge of human fate, they are especially associated with ill luck and distress. An examination of the tragic poets shows that the passages in which the *daimon* brings upon an individual suffering, disease, death, and other misfortunes, that is, something that is contrary to his will and expectations, are far more numerous than those in which the word *daimon* signifies a happy fate.

Repeatedly the spirits of the dead also are called *daimones* by the tragic poets. Thus, after their death, King Darius and Alcestis are referred to as *daimones* (Aeschy-

lus, *Persians* 641–646; Euripides, *Alcestis* 1002f). The word *daimon* is then quite commonly employed to denote the dead spirit of a particular person (e.g., Pausanias 6.6.8). As a rule, however, not the singular, but the plural word is used somewhat illogically of the single spirit (Philo, *Leg. Ad Gaium* 65; Lucian, *De luctu* 24; *Inscriptiones graecae* [Berlin—] 14:1683, Δαίμοσιν εὐσεβέσιν Γαίου Ἰουλίου Καρακουττίου, corresponding to the common Roman form of epitaph on the tombs from the early empire, "*Dis Manibus* of so-and-so").

Daimon and the individual. From the narrower conception of divine power surrounding man and controlling his destiny, there develops the belief that a special *daimon* is associated with the individual from birth, ruling over him through his life and guiding his soul as he departs for Hades. This idea, already found in Plato (*Phaedo* 107D) and Aristotle (frg. 193, ed. V. Rose), comes to full fruition in the Hellenistic period with its conscious individualism. It finds expression, e.g., in the well-known fragment of the comic poet Menander (frg. 714, eds. Koerte, Thierfelder): "A *daimon* stands by every man, straightway from his birth, a beneficent guide initiating him into the mysteries of life, for it is unthinkable that there is an evil *daimon* doing harm to upright life.'' In this passage, Menander obviously rejects a belief widespread at that time, according to which the good aspirations and accomplishments of an individual were ascribed to his good *daimon*, while the evil desires and deeds were attributed to the evil *daimon* within him. In this way the struggle between conscience and evil desires could be represented as a contest between these two *daimones* in man. This dualistic conception of the *daimon* also explains such compound as εὐδαίμων, ''a person who is guided by a good *daimon*'' κακοδαίμων, ''a person who is under the influence of an evil *daimon*''; and cognate words.

In this connection Socrates described his *daimonion* as a voice of divine origin which he heard within him, dissuading him from doing something, but never inciting him to action. On the other hand, Xenophon (*Memorials of Socrates* 1.1.2–4) represents Socrates' *daimonion* as a constructive, creative force, both constraining and impelling him. However Socrates himself may have conceived this *daimonion*; not a few among its contemporaries were convinced that there was a sort of higher being within him that acted through this voice.

In the later Hellenistic period these various meanings of the word *daimon* are less prominently employed in general usage. The exception is the one that designates *daimonions* as beings that, though below the gods in rank and power, are nonetheless above men and intervene in human life and fortune. Normal everyday usage, and popular belief, can be seen clearly in the magic papyri and curse-tablets (*tabellae defixionum*).

Influence in Religion, Mythology, and Folklore

The belief in demonic being as forming an intermediate realm between the gods and men has played an important part in the religions, mythologies, and popular traditions of all peoples the world over. These mysterious beings vary in character from the simply playful and mockingly mischievous to the ghastly and terrifying. Often they are invisible, though not incorporeal. They appear in human or animal or half-human, half-animal shapes. Having the power to change form in the twinkling of an eye, they are active in unusual places, at particular times, and in uncommon events in nature and human life.

Nature daimones or demons. Nature demons form the most numerous group. Popular belief peopled the mountains and forests of ancient Greece with goat-like Satyrs and horse-shaped *Sileni*. There was Arcadian Pan, at the outset simply a generative demon of flocks and herds, haunting the summer pastures in the mountains and playing his syrinx at noontide when the flocks grazed peacefully, but also causing a sudden panic when the animals, seized for some unknown reason by fright broke away in a stampede. At many places, especially in caves and at springs, there were believed to be nymphs— beautiful, young, fairylike women, fond of music and dancing, usually amorous and benevolent, but also dangerous and threatening: if a man lost his mind, it was said that he had been ''caught by the nymphs'' (νυμφόληπτος).

In ancient Italy Faunus, the native *numen* of the woods, was identified with Pan and was represented, like Pan, with horns and goats' feet. The mythology and folklore of northern Europe include a large number of similar spirits to whom the varied appearances of nature, terrifying or attractive, have given form and character: trolls, pixies, mermen, mermaids, nixes, and dwarfs, many of them dangerous, some with alluring beauty. Ancient Semitic demonology likewise recognized a great number of nature demons haunting lonely places. Reference to them is made in the OT prophecies against Babylon (Is 13.21) and Edom (*ibid.* 34.14): both will be laid waste and become lurking-places of desert animals, satyrs, and other demons.

Heat, night, and other demons. The strange sensations caused by the scorching heat in summer and the languor then falling upon the landscapes of southern Europe and Oriental desert countries created the mid-day demon. The feeling of the eerie, experienced in the dark hours of the night and strengthened by other night fears, such as unexplained sounds in the midst of darkness and silence, gave birth to the Norse *gandreid*, ''the spirits' ride,'' and *Aasgaardsreia,* ''Asgard's chase,'' to Holla's troop and Perchta's host in German folklore, and to Hecate's swarm of ghosts haunting the crossroads after nightfall in Greek mythology. The lonely traveler in the desert at night is confronted by the *gul*, a generic Arabic name for any sort of specter. It changes its shape and appearance, and men faint at the sight of it. Rabbinical literature was acquainted with demons of morning and midday, evening and night.

Other demons owe their existence to sensations experienced in sleep. Nightmare demons (*incubi*) were supposed to ride or press people during sleep, the sleeper's feelings varying from great pain or oppression to mild or even voluptuous sensation. Among these are the Greek Ephialtes (ἐφιάλτης, ''one who leaps upon''), the Old Norse *Mara* (cf. The Danish *Mare*, the German *Mahr*, English ''nightmare,'' and the French *cauchemar*). In upper Germany the nightmare demon was known as Alp, Schrat, or Trude. The Greeks also knew a number of other uncanny specters, e.g., Lamia (akin to the Jewish Lilith), a hideous monster that abducted children and attacked women in childbed. Other demonic beings of this kind were Alphito, Akko, Empusa, called also Onoskelis (donkey-footed), Gello, Karko, and Momo, which drank the blood of men and ate their flesh. They belonged to such fables as imprudent nurses were wont to tell to small children, both to frighten them into good behavior and also to entertain them.

As bringers of disease. Finally, the source of a disease was supposed to be the direct influence of a demon. Especially mental disorders and those diseases whose natural causes were unknown were associated with the world of demons. If a man lay wasting of disease or became mentally deranged, it was thought that a demon was surely within him, manifesting malevolence. Because there could be no recovery until the demon was exorcised, it was to the exorcising of demons that such a large part of Babylonian religious literature was devoted. Even today, it is the office of the sorcerer or medicine man among primitive peoples to detect and expel the malign influence of a demon thought to be the source of a malady.

Various theories have been advanced to explain demonism. It has been regarded as a development of an original belief in impersonal powers (dynamism), of animism, and of earlier polydemonism evolving through polytheistic or other routes to monotheism. Each of these theories is one-sided because the phenomena are independent of each other and defy arrangement in successive stages.

Bibliography: J. HENNINGER and B. KOTTING, *Lexikon für Theologie und Kirche*, ed. J. HOFER and K. RAHNER (Freiburg 1957–65) 3:139–141, 144–145. A. SCHIMMEL and H. RINGGREN, *Die Religion in Geschichte und Gegenwart* (3d ed. Tübingen 1957–65) 2:1298–1304. L. H. GRAY et al. *Encyclopedia of Religion and Ethics,* ed. J. HASTINGS (Edinburgh 1908–27) 4:565–636. O. WASER, *Paulys Realenzyklopädie der klassischen Altertumswissenschaft,* ed. G. WISSOWA et al. (Stuttgart 1901) 4.2:2010–12. F. ANDRES, *ibid.* Suppl. 3 (Stuttgart 1918) 267–322. F. PFISTER, *ibid.* Suppl. 7 (Stuttgart 1940) 100–114. W. FOERSTER, *Theologisches Wörterbuch zum Neuen Testament* (Stuttgart 1935–) 2:1–16. I. BROYDE, *The Jewish Encyclopedia,* ed. J. SINGER (New York 1901–06) 4:514–521. P. TILLICH, *Das Dämonishe* (Tübingen 1926). G. VAN DER LEEIW, *Religion in Essence and Manifestation,* tr. J. E. TURNER (London 1938) 134–140. M. P. NILSSON, *Greek Popular Religion* (New York 1940) 10–21. E. RHODE, *Psyche,* tr. W. B. HILLIS (New York 1925) index, s.v. "Daemonium meridianum," "Daimones Deities of the Second Rank," etc. J. TAMBORNINO, *De antiquorum daemonismo* (Giessen 1909).

[R. ARBESMANN]

DALBERG

A noble family of the Rhineland, many of whose members have appeared as ecclesiastics, particularly in the service of the bishop of Worms as early as the middle of the 12th century. The following are notable in the history of the family.

Johann von. Bishop of Worms, chancellor of the University of Heidelberg, and humanist; b. Oppenheim, Aug. 14, 1455; d. Heidelberg, July 27, 1503. As a result of his studies at Erfurt and throughout Italy he developed a lasting interest in classical literature and became a champion of the Christian humanism of his time. He became chancellor of the University of Heidelberg (1481) and through the influence of the Elector of the Palatinate, was appointed bishop of Worms in 1482. He showed skill as a diplomat in various missions of the Elector and Emperor Frederick III (reigned 1440–93), while not neglecting the administration of his diocese. Through his wholehearted support Worms and Heidelberg became centers for humanistic pursuits, and to the "Sodalitas litteraria Rhenana" came such scholars as Johann REUCHLIN, Johannes TRITHEMIUS, Conrad Celtis, Sebastian BRANT, Willibald PIRKHEIMER, and Dalberg's great friend, Rudolphus Agricola. He also gathered rare books and MSS into a valuable library.

Wolfgang von. Elector and archbishop of Mainz; b. 1537; d. Mainz, April 5, 1601. On April 20, 1582, he was elected to the archbishopric of Mainz over Julius ECHTER VON MESPELBRUNN, bishop of Würzburg, a leading figure in the Catholic Counter Reformation. Dalberg was chosen because of his tendency toward compromise, and during the first part of his tenure he appeared weak-willed and compliant in his attitude toward the Protestants. Concentrating his efforts on maintaining a neutral position in the religious strife of the period, he refused, for example, to promulgate the reform bull *In coena Domini* (1584) of Gregory XIII. As the radical aspects of the Reformation became more evident, and in the light of the pronouncements of the Council of Trent, he drew away from this position, and cooperated with a program of diocesan reform under pressure of the papal legate, Ludovico Madruzzo.

Adolf von. Prince-abbot of Fulda; b. May 29, 1678; d. Hammelburg on the Saale, Lower Franconia, Nov. 3, 1737. Elected prince-abbot of the Benedictine monastery of Fulda (1724), Dalberg, in virtue of his quasi-episcopal powers, held a diocesan synod in 1729. He hoped to make Fulda the seat of learning it had been in the Middle Ages, and founded there a university that was later named after him, the "Alma Adolphina." Here he formed the faculties of philosophy and theology by uniting the already existing schools of the Jesuits and Benedictines, and also set up departments of law and medicine. A charter of foundation was granted (1732) and confirmed by Emperor Charles VI in 1733. The university was inaugurated on Sept. 19, 1733. The suppression of the Jesuits caused the university to pass into the hands of the Benedictines. They were forced to abandon it in 1805 because of the secularization of the monastery three years earlier.

Johann Friedrich Hugo Nepomuk Eckenbrecht von. Ecclesiastic, pianist, composer; b. Herrnsheim, May 17, 1752; d. Aschaffenburg, July 26, 1812. After his theological studies he served as a canon in the cathedrals of Trier, Worms, and Speyer. His wide interests are seen in two early works on meteorology and penal law (1782). Soon, however, he gave his entire attention to musical theory and aesthetics, and published *Blicke eines Tonkünstlers in die Musik der Geister* (Mannaheim 1787), *Untersuchen über den Ursprung der Harmonie,* and *Die Äolsharfe, ein allegorischer Traum* (Erfurt 1801). His works show the influence of Jean Jacques Rousseau and Johann Herder. His compositions are much in the style of Wolfgang Mozart. Dalberg gave concerts as a pianist, wrote several vocal works, and set to music Johann Schiller's *Ode an die Freude* (1799).

Bibliography: Johann. K. MORNEWEG, *Johann von Dalberg, ein deutscher Humanist und Bischof* (Heidelberg 1887). G. RITTER, *Die Heidelberger Universität, I: Des Mittelalter, 1386–1508* (Heidelberg 1936–). H. RAAB, *Lexikon für Theologie und Kirche,* ed. J. HOFER and K. RAHNER (2d, new ed. Freiburg 1957–65) 3:124. R. AUBERT, *Dictionnaire d'histoire et de géographie ecclésiastiques,* ed. A. BAUDRILLART et al. (Paris 1912–) 14:19–20. Wolfgang. H. E. HEIM, *Wolfgang, Erzbischof und Kurfürst von Mainz* (Mainz 1789). L. A. VEIT, *Kirche und Kirchenreform in der Erzdiözese Mainz* (Freiburg 1920). R. AUBERT, *Dictionnaire d'histoire et de géographie ecclésiastiques,* 14:22–23. L. LENHART, *Neue deutsche Biographie* (Berlin 1953–) 3:490. Adolf. G. RICHTER and L. PRALLE, eds., *Quellen und Abhandlungen zur Geschichte der Abtei und Diözese Fulda* (Fulda 1904–). Johann Friedrich. K. M. KOMMA, *Neue deutsche Biographie* (Berlin 1953–) 3:488–489. *Die Musik in Geschichte und Gegenwart,* ed. F. BLUME (Kassel-Bassel 1949–) 2:1869–71. *Baker's Biographical Dictionary of Musicians,* ed. N. SLONIMSKY (5th, rev. ed. New York 1958) 341–342.

[G. J. DONNELLY]

Adolf von Dalberg.

DALBERG, KARL THEODOR VON

Archbishop of Mainz, prince-elector and archchancellor of the HOLY ROMAN EMPIRE, prince-primate of Germany, grand duke of Frankfort, president of the Confederation of the Rhine; b. Herrnsheim, near Worms, Germany, Feb. 8, 1744; d. Regensburg, Feb. 10, 1817. Attracted by ambition to the ecclesiastical state, to which his parents early destined him, he studied in the Protestant faculties of law at Göttingen and Heidelberg from 1759, and gained a doctorate in civil and Canon Law (1761), but studied little theology. Travels through neighboring countries to complete his studies placed him in close, sympathetic touch with contemporary trends in FEBRONIANISM, GALLICANISM, and the ENLIGHTENMENT whose humanistic ideals particularly attracted him. In 1754 he became a benefice holder in WÜRZBURG and Mainz, and in 1762 entered the service of the Elector of Mainz, where he was preoccupied with educational problems, as he was from 1772 as governor of Erfurt. He was dean of the cathedral chapter in Würzburg and Mainz (1779–86), and soon after at Worms and Constance. After being chosen coadjutor to the archbishop of Mainz and Constance (1787), he ceased to be a Freemason and was ordained (Feb. 2, 1788) and consecrated bishop (Aug. 31, 1788). He became coadjutor bishop (June 1788) and then bishop of Constance (1800), archbishop of Mainz and Worms (1802), and bishop of Regensburg (1802). Dalberg appointed as vicar-general (1802) and coadjutor bishop (1814) of Constance Ignaz von WESSENBERG, with whom he shared many views on Canon Law, pedagogy, liturgy, and other subjects.

With the help of Napoleon I, Dalberg emerged from the vast ecclesiastical secularizations in Germany (1803) with increased jurisdiction and dignities. By obtaining the See of Regensburg (1802), which became a metropolitan see (1805), he became elector and archchancellor of the Empire, and primate of Germany (although not recognized as such by Rome). When the Confederation of the Rhine was proclaimed, Dalberg became its president (1806). Napoleon named him Grand Duke of Frankfort, but ceded Regensburg to Bavaria (1810). Napoleon's downfall (1814) ended the secular power of Dalberg, who henceforth lived modestly and piously at Regensburg. His attempt to create a German national church along Febronian lines largely independent of Rome was forestalled when Pius VII concluded concordats with individual German states instead of a single one for all Germany.

Dalberg was a capable administrator, generous and interested in liturgical and pastoral reforms, science, and literature. He was highly regarded by Goethe, Schiller, and Wilhelm von Humboldt. He served as chancellor of the University of Erfurt and rector of the University of Würzburg, founded Karls University in Aschaffenburg (1808), and tried to restore the University of Mainz after the ravages of the French Revolution. Dalberg remains a controversial figure, but recent judgments on him have been more favorable.

Bibliography: H. BASTGEN, *Dalbergs und Napoleons Kirchenpolitik in Deutschland* (Paderborn 1917). G. SCHWAIGER, "Die Kirchenpläne des Fürstprimas K. Th. von Dalberg," *Münchener theologische Zeitschrift* 9 (1958) 186–204. L. LENHART, *Neue deutsche Biographie* (Berlin 1953–) 3:489–490. H. RAAB, *Lexikon für Theologie und Kirche*, ed. J. HOFER and K. RAHNER (2d, new ed. Freiburg 1957–65) 3:125–126. A. FRANZEN, *Dictionnaire d'histoire et de géographie ecclésiasitques*, ed. A. BAUDRILLART et al. (Paris 1912–) 14:20–22.

[L. LENHART]

DALGAIRNS, JOHN DOBREE

Theologian; b. Guernsey, Oct. 21, 1818; d. Burgess Hill, Sussex, April 6, 1876. He took a second class in humane letters at Exeter College, Oxford, in 1839. Already an ardent disciple of NEWMAN, his letter of 1838 to the Paris *Univers* on the OXFORD MOVEMENT led to correspondence with the Passionist Dominic Barberi. The first to join Newman at Littlemore in 1842, he wrote scholarly lives of saints for the series of early English saints edited by Newman, and manifested in them a profound grasp of medieval history. Feeling drawn ever closer to Catholicism through his studies, he invited Barberi to Littlemore with Newman's consent and was received into the Church in September 1845. Ordained in December 1846, he joined the London Oratory in 1849, and after several assignments succeeded Frederich H. Faber as superior in 1863. An eminent preacher, confessor, and member of the Metaphysical Society, he was the most gifted of the London Oratorians. His knowledge of philosophy and acquaintance with the writings of German scientists enabled him to meet Thomas Huxley successfully on his own grounds. Unfortunately, he suffered from chronic restlessness, laying too much stress on interior perfection, and making excessive demands upon his own zeal. Overstrain brought on paralysis and, after a year's mental illness, death. His chief Catholic writings are: *The Devotion to the Sacred Heart of Jesus* (London 1853; latest edition

1920 with an introduction on the history of Jansenism); *The Holy Communion, its Philosophy, Theology and Practice* (Dublin 1861); the editor of the latest edition (1911), A. Ross, notes that one chapter needs revision because of Pius X's decree of 1905.

Bibliography: J. GILLOW, *A Literary and Biographical History or Bibliographical Dictionary of the English Catholics from 1534 to the Present Time* (London-New York 1885–1902; repr. New York 1961), 2:3–5. F. L. CROSS, *The Oxford Dictionary of the Christian Church* (London 1957) 369.

[H. E. ROPE]

DALÍ, SALVADOR

Artist renowned for both technical innovations in the advance of surrealism and the breadth of artistic interests from painting to cinema; b. Figueras, Spain, March 11, 1904; d. Figueras, January 23, 1989. Dalí attended the Marist Brothers School (1914–18) and the Municipal School of Drawing in Figueras. At San Fernando Academy of Fine Arts in Madrid (1922–26), he befriended Luis Buñuel and Frederico Garcia Lorca. Dalí's artistic vision was initially influenced by nineteenth-century Spanish genre painters, the British Pre-Raphaelites, and the great baroque masters, Velázquez and Vermeer. In 1928 Dalí encountered the French surrealists (Max Ernst, Yves Tanguy, and André Bréton) whose artistic philosophy shaped the young Spaniard's mature artistic vision. Dalí's greatest influences were the texts of Sigmund Freud, the poetic-philosophical vision of the Italian metaphysical painter Giorgio de Chirico, and cubism. Dalí created the style of painting identified as "paranoiaccritical method" in order to free the visions of the subconscious through meticulous images of the fantastic merged with reality through a juxtaposition of brightly-colored small objects against expanses of dull colors in a unique perspectival space.

Contribution to Modern Culture. From his first exhibitions in Paris (1929) and in New York (1933), Dalí captivated the public with his visualizations of the modern subconscious—sexual anxiety, the eminent destruction of civilization, the fear of war, and the recognition of violence as both a plague and an irremediable element of modern society—as evidenced in his masterpiece, *Persistence of Memory* (1931). Some cultural commentators find Dalí's greater contribution to modern culture to be his literary and cinematic productions. A prolific writer, he collaborated with Buñuel in the development of modern cinema, thereby expanding the boundaries of high art to include photography and film. Critical consensus affirms Dalí's period of artistic innovations and influence as being between 1929 and 1939. His initial public embrace of Roman Catholicism occurred during the Spanish Civil War when he supported the Monarchy; for him to be Spanish was to be simultaneously Catholic and Monarchist.

His religiosity became both more public and more profound as a result of personal crises that shifted his thinking towards traditional Christian subject matter in his painting during the late 1940s and 1950s, e.g., *Madonna of Port Lligat* (1950), *Christ of St. John of the Cross* (1951), and *The Sacrament of the Last Supper* (1955). These large-scale meticulous presentations effected a traditional aura of religious devotion through the artist's emphasis on dramatic lighting and spatiality and concentration on singular iconographic elements. His late works garnered Dalí a large new public audience and the critical cynicism of the artistic community that categorized them as sentimental popularizations or devotional illustrations.

Bibliography: D. ABADIE, *Dalí: Retrospective 1920–1980* (Paris 1979). D. ADES, *Dalí* (London 1983). A. BOSQUET, *Entretiens avec Dalí* (Paris 1966) [ET 1969]. W. CHADWICK, *Myth in Surrealist Paintings, 1929–1939* (Ann Arbor 1980). R. CREVEL, *Dalí, o el anti-oscurantismo* (Barcelona 1978). S. DALÍ, *L'Amour et la mémoire* (Paris 1931); *Babaou* (Paris 1932); *Comment on devient Dalí* with J. PARINAUD (Paris 1973) [ET 1976]; *Dalí par Dalí de Draeger* (Paris 1970) [ET 1971]; *Dalí on Modern Art, the Cuckolds of Antiquated Modern Art* (New York 1957); *Dalí's Moustache* with P. HALSMANN (New York 1954); *Declaration of the Independence of the Imagination and the Rights of Man to His Own Madness* (New York 1938); *Dix recettes d'immortalité* (Paris 1973); *Hidden Faces* (New York 1944); *La Conquete de l'irrationnel* (Paris 1935) [ET 1935]; *Les Diners de Gala* (New York 1963); *La Femme Visible* (Paris 1930); *Fifty Secrets of Magic Craftsmanship* (New York 1948); *Journal d'un génie* (Paris 1964) [ET 1964]; *Lettre ouverte à Dalí* (Paris 1996) [ET 1967]; *Manifeste mystique* (Paris 1951) [ET 1951]; *Métamorphose de Narcisse* (Paris 1937) [ET 1937]; *Oui: Méthode paranoiaque: Critique et autres textes* (Paris 1971); *The Passion According to Dalí* with L. PAUWALS (St. Petersburg FL 1985); *Procès en diffamation* (Paris 1971); *Ma révolution culturelle* (Paris 1968); *The Secret Life of Dalí* (London 1961). M. GERARD, ed., *Dalí de Draeger* (Paris 1968) [ET 1970]. M. DEL ARCO, *Dalí in the Nude* (St. Petersburg FL 1984). R. DESCHARNES, *The World of Dalí* (London and New York 1972). J. DOPAGNE, *Dalí* (Paris 1974; New York 1976) I. GOMEZ DE LIAÑO, *Dalí* (London 1987). R. GOMEZ DE LA SERNA, *Dalí* (Madrid 1977; London 1984). R. GUARDIOLA ROVIRA, *Dalí y su museo* (Figueras 1984). C. LAKE, *In Quest of Dalí* (New York 1969); L. LIVINGSTONE, ed., *Dalí* (Greenwich CT 1959). C. MADDOX, *Dalí* (London and New York 1979). K. VON MAUR, *Salvador Dalí, 1904–1989* (Stuttgart 1989). G. MAX, ed., *Dalí* (New York 1968). M. MERLINO, *Diccionario privado* (Madrid 1980). A. R. MORSE, *Dalí: A Study of His Life and Work* (Greenwich CT 1958); *Catalogue of Works by Dalí* (Cleveland 1956); ed., A DALÍ *Journal: Impressions and Private Memoirs of Dalí* (Cleveland 1962); *A New Introduction to Dalí* (Cleveland 1960); *The Dalí Museum* (Cleveland 1962); *A Dalí Primer* (Cleveland 1970); *Dalí: The Masterworks* (Cleveland 1971); *Dalí: A Guide to His Works in Public Museums* (Cleveland 1974); *Salvador Dalí, Pablo Picasso; A Preliminary Study in Their Similarities and Contrasts* (Cleveland 1973). R. PASSERON, *Dalí* (Paris 1978). J. PLE, *Dli, Guardi, Nonell, tres artistes catalanes*

Salvador Dalí, with his painting "The Madonna," 1949. (AP/ Wide World Photos)

(Barcelona 1986). C. ROJAS, *El mundo mitico y magico de Salvador Dalí* (Barcelona 1985) [ET 1993]. L. ROMEO, *Dalí* (Secaucus 1979). M. SECREST, *Dalí: The Surrealist Jester* (London 1986). J. T. SOBY, *Dalí* (New York 1969 [1946]); P. WALTON, *Dalí, Miro* (New York 1967). **Collections:** Stedelijk Museen, Amsterdam; Neue Nationalgalerie, Berlin; Cleveland Museum of Art, Cleveland; Dalí Museum, Figueras; Glasgow Art Gallery, Glasgow; The Tate Gallery, London; The Metropolitan Museum of Art, New York; The Museum of Modern Art, New York; The Solomon R. Guggenheim Museum, New York; Musée Nationale d'Art Moderne, Centre Georges Pompidou, Paris; Philadelphia Museum of Art, Philadelphia; Dalí Museum, St. Petersburg, FL; Hirshhorn Museum and Sculpture Garden, Smithsonian Institute, Washington, DC; The National Gallery of Art, Washington, DC; Kunsthaus, Zurich.

[D. APOSTOLOS-CAPPADONA]

DALMATIC

A liturgical garment proper to the deacon, worn over all other vestments. It was originally a garment imported from Dalmatia and worn by the noble class of Roman society. In its primitive form it was a gown reaching to the feet and made of white wool, linen, and even silk, ornamented with two red or purple stripes running from the shoulders to the hem in front and back. The more common opinion holds that at first only the Pope wore it; he gradually allowed others (the Roman deacons first of all in the 4th century) to wear it as a privilege. By the 12th century it had become the proper outer vesture for all deacons, while bishops wore it beneath the chasuble. In the same century the dalmatic was made in the liturgical colors. By the 9th century outside Rome there had begun a process of shortening it to the knees. It was opened on either side to give freedom of movement to the wearer. Heavy velvets, damasks, brocaded silks, brocatelles, and silks with gold and silver threads made the dalmatic a splendid but heavy and unmanageable garment; it was soon opened all the way to the arms with the sleeves themselves slit and held in place by ribbons or cords with tassels. The ribbons in turn disappeared, and the sleeves became short flaps. Modern light and flexible fabrics together with a growth in better taste led to a gradual restoration of the original simplicity of the vestment. With the restoration of the permanent deaconate the dalmatic is frequently worn. Being a garment of nobility, it offers dignity and solemnity to ceremonies.

Bibliography: H. NORRIS, *Church Vestments* (London 1948). E.A. ROULIN, *Vestments and Vesture*, tr. J. MCCANN (Westminster, MD 1950). J. BRAUN, *Die liturgische Gewandung im Occident und Orient* (Freiburg, 1907). J. MAYO, *A History of Ecclesiastical Dress* (London: B.T. Batsford, 1984). D. HINES, *Dressing for Worship: A Fresh Look at What Christians Wear in Church* (Cambridge 1996). D. PHILIPPART, ed., *Clothed in Glory: Vesting the Church* (Chicago 1997).

[M. MCCANCE]

D'ALTON, EDWARD ALFRED

Irish historian; b. Lavallyroe, Ballyhaunis, Co. Mayo, Nov. 5?, 1859; d. Ballinrobe, Co. Mayo, Jan. 25, 1941. His parents, John and Ellen (Reynolds) D'Alton, were farmers. He studied at St. Jarlath's College, Tuam, and then at St. Patrick's College, Maynooth, where he matriculated in 1881 without receiving a degree. He was ordained in 1887. He applied unsuccessfully for the chairs of history in Cork and in University College, Dublin (1909). After serving as a curate in five parishes, he became, in 1911, pastor in Ballinrobe, cathedral canon, and vicar forane; and in 1912, a domestic prelate. In 1930 he became dean and vicar-general of the Archdiocese of TUAM. D'Alton's writings on Irish history include articles on the Cromwellian and Restoration periods that appeared in the *Dublin Review* (1904–05) and several articles in the *Catholic Encyclopedia*. His best-known work was his *History of Ireland,* the first edition of which, in three volumes (1903–10), went to 1908; and the third edition, in eight half-volumes (1920–25), to 1925. He published also a *History of the Archdiocese of Tuam* (2 v., 1928). D'Alton's earlier writings were marked by open-

mindedness, sober and objective judgments, and avoidance of dogmatism on controversial issues. His later publications, however, tended to take sides in disputed matters. His views approximated those of the "faith and fatherland" school that succeeded the "loyal Catholic" school of the preceding generation. Thus D'Alton was uncritical in his acceptance of writers of the Young Ireland movement against Cardinal Paul Cullen and in his treatment of the period subsequent to Parnell's condemnation. D'Alton's histories also lacked precision, originality, and familiarity with original sources.

Bibliography: For critiques of his *History of Ireland,* see *The Irish Eccesiastical Record*, 4th series, 15 (1904) 91–93; 28 (1910) 557–559. For a review of his *History of the Archdiocese of Tuam,* see *Studies* 18 (1929) 152–157.

[R. D. EDWARDS]

D' ALZON, EMMANUEL

Founder of two religious congregations; b. Vigan (Gard), France, Aug. 30, 1810; d. Nîmes (Gard), France, Nov. 21, 1880. Emmanuel Marie Joseph Maurice d'Alzon was born of an aristocratic family. Influenced by Hugues Félicité de LAMENNAIS, he studied for the priesthood at Montpellier and Rome, and was ordained (Dec. 26, 1834). He became vicar-general of the Diocese of Nîmes (1835), preached extensively, and became responsible (January 1844) for the administration of the College of the Assumption, a secondary school that he sought to raise to university status to break the state monopoly on higher education. Until his death he continued to serve as college president and vicar-general. After taking the vows of religion privately (June 1844), he received episcopal permission to do so publicly, along with five teachers from his college, thereby inaugurating the ASSUMPTIONISTS (Dec. 27, 1850), whose superior general he remained during his lifetime. In 1865 he was cofounder of the Oblate Sisters of the Assumption. Upon the suggestion of Pius IX he oriented his activities after 1862 toward Catholics of the Byzantine rite. D'Alzon was a friend of MONTALEMBERT, OZANAM, and VEUILLOT. His interest in Catholic journalism was evidenced by his collaboration in several publications. He attended VATICAN COUNCIL I as theologian to Bp. Claude Plantier and labored vigorously for the definition of papal infallibility. As a spiritual director d'Alzon was very influential. His letters to Mother Marie Eugénie de Jésus, foundress of the Congregation of the ASSUMPTION, are esteemed for their literary and spiritual excellence. An immense amount of d'Alzon's personal correspondence and many manuscripts of sermons and meditations survived him; some of them have since been published.

Bibliography: S. VAILHÉ, *Vie du P. Emmanuel d'Alzon,* 2 v. (Paris 1927–34). S. PEITAVI, *Dictionnaire d'histoire et de géographie ecclésiastiques,* ed. A. BAUDRILLART et al. (Paris 1912–) 2:908–913. S. SALAVILLE, *Dictionnaire de spiritualité ascétique et mystique. Doctrine et histoire,* ed. M. VILLER et al. (Paris 1932–) 1:411–421. M. H. LAURENT, *Dictionnaire de biographie française* (Paris 1929–) 2:370–371.

[G. H. TAVARD]

DAMASCUS, MARTYRS OF

A group of eleven martyrs, eight Franciscans and three laymen, put to death for their faith during the night of July 9–10, 1860, at DAMASCUS, Syria (then part of Turkey in Asia), and beatified Oct. 10, 1926. Of the six priests, Engelbert Kolland, aged 33, was Austrian; the others were Spaniards—Emmanuel Ruiz, the superior, 56; Nicholas Alberca, 30; Nicanor Ascanio, 46; Peter Soler, 33; and Carmel Volta, 57. Two were Spanish lay brothers—John James Fernandez, 52, and Francis Pinazo, 58. The three laymen, natives of Damascus, belonging to the Maronite rite, were Francis Massabki, an important silk merchant, aged over 70; and his two brothers slightly younger—'Abd-al-Mūti (Servant of God who gives), and Raphael. The first two were fathers of large families; the last was unmarried.

The Sultan's proclamation (1856) at the end of the Crimean War guaranteeing equality between his Christian and Muslim subjects irritated many Muslims. When news reached Damascus that the DRUZES of Lebanon had attacked many Christian localities and perpetrated massacres with the complicity of the Ottoman authorities, the populace, roused by government agents and leading citizens, attacked, burned, and pillaged the wealthy Christian quarter, killing about 4,000.

The Franciscans were assailed either in church, where their superior had the opportunity to consume the Sacred Species reserved there, or on the convent terrace, or in the street. After their refusal to apostatize, they were slaughtered. The Massabki brothers, who had taken refuge with them, had received Holy Communion and were praying at the foot of the altar. A Muslim notable who owed Francis 8,000 napoleons proposed to spare all three if only they would embrace Islam. Francis told the Muslim to keep the money, but that he would give his soul to no one. The brothers, thereupon, were martyred.

Feast: July 10.

Bibliography: A. BUTLER, *The Lives of the Saints,* ed. H. THURSTON and D. ATTWATER 3:68–70.

[H. JALABERT]

DAMASUS

A native of Hungary, not of Bohemia or Italy as has been frequently asserted; fl. beginning of 13th century. He taught Canon Law and wrote his works at Bologna. Little else is known of his life. The following works are known: (1) Glosses on the Decretum of GRATIAN, not enough to constitute a formal apparatus. (2) Apparatus to the first two *Compilationes Antiquae,* with two recensions, one before and the other after the *Compilatio* IV; they include a great number of Tancred's glosses. (3) Apparatus to *Compilatio* III, which has not yet been found. (4) Apparatus to the constitutions of the Fourth Lateran Council (1215), which is subsequent to that of VINCENT OF SPAIN. (5) Glosses on the tree of consanguinity. (6) *Quaestiones,* written probably before the Fourth Lateran Council. (7) *Summa titulorum,* prior, perhaps, to the same council. (8) *Brocarda* or *Brocardica,* the only printed work (ed. Lyons 1519, Milan 1516–21, Cologne 1564, Venice 1584 in the *Tractatus Universi Iuris* v.18 fol. 506–512). Works (4) and (5) will appear in *Monumenta Iuris Canonici* of the Gratian Institute. A *Historiae super librum decretorum* and an *Ordo Iudiciarius* were attributed to him, but with very little probability. Although Damasus is an important author, little research has been done on his writings.

Bibliography: J. F. VON SCHULTE, *Die Geschichte der Quellen und der Literatur des kanonischen Rechts,* 3 v. in 4 pts (Stuttgart 1875–80, repr. Graz 1956) 1:194–197. H. KANTOROWICZ, *Zeitschrift der Savigny-Stiftung für Rechtsgeschichte, Kanonistische Abteilung,* (Weimar 1863–) 16 (1927) 332–340. S. KUTTNER, "Damasus als Glossator," *ibid.* 23 (1934) 380–390. S. KUTTNER, *Repertorium der Kanonistik,* (Rome 1937) 378, 393–394, 426–427, and *passim.* C. LEFEBVRE, *Dictionnaire de droit canonique,* ed. R. NAZ, 7 v. (Paris 1935–65) 4:1014–19, with bibliog. A. GARCÍA, "Observaciones sobre los apparatus de Dámaso Húngaro a las tres primeras Complilaciones antiguas," *Traditio* 18 (New York 1962) 469–471. R. WEIGAND, *Die bedingte Eheschliessung im kanonischen Recht* (Munich 1963).

[A. GARCÍA]

DAMASUS I, POPE, ST.

Pontificate: Oct. 1, 366, to Dec. 11, 384; born in Rome, c. 304/5; died Rome.

Very little is known about Damasus before he became pope, and the early history of his pontificate has to be based largely on documents that emanated from his opponents. His father, Antonius, may have been from Spain, but it is clear from Damasus's own testimony (*Epigram* 57) that Antonius rose through the ecclesiastical grades to become a priest of the titulus of Lucina—later the basilica of San Lorenzo—at Rome; where it seems Damasus also served. His mother's name was Laurentia, and he had a sister, Irene. He was a deacon under Pope Liberius (352–366) and accompanied him into exile (355). After his return to Rome, however, Damasus supported the antipope Felix II. On the death of Felix (Nov. 22, 365), he became reconciled with Liberius. Following the death of Liberius less than a year later (Sept. 24, 366), a violent controversy broke out over the choice of his successor. A small but powerful faction, supporters of Felix who had not become reconciled with Liberius, assembled at once in the Julian Basilica of S. Maria in Trastevere with their candidate, the deacon Ursinus, and had him irregularly consecrated by Paul, bishop of Tibur. The great majority of the clergy and people elected Damasus, who was consecrated on October 1 in the Lateran Basilica by the bishop of Ostia.

Opposition of Ursinus. Before his consecration, Damasus and his followers had routed the Ursinians, with heavy loss of life, from the Julian Basilica. Late in October another bloody battle took place at the Liberian Basilica on the Esquiline in which the Ursinians had installed themselves. Viventius, the prefect of the city, supported Damasus, and in the interests of public order sent Ursinus and his deacons, Amantius and Lupus, into exile. With imperial permission (Valentinian), however, they returned to Rome (September 367), and violence broke out anew. By the end of the year, Ursinus was again in exile in Gaul, his adherents lost the Liberian Basilica, and all supporters of Ursinus among the Roman clergy were driven from Rome. The bishops of Italy were scandalized at this exhibition of violence. When Damasus asked them, on the occasion of the synod held in honor of his *natale* (September 368) to approve his action, he received the sharp answer: *Nos ad natale convenimus, non ut inauditum damnemus* (We assembled for a birthday, not to condemn a man unheard; *Avellana Collectio* ep. 1).

Ursinus and his followers continued their agitation. In 370–372 they were permitted to return to Italy, provided that they kept away from Rome and its environs. They established themselves at Milan, the capital of the empire in the West. In their opposition to Damasus they received Arian support and were able to prevail upon the convert Jew Isaac to accuse Damasus of a grave crime—probably adultery—and to have him brought to trial. With Van Roey, it would seem better to put these events in the early 370s, and not in 378 as is usually done. The confirmation of the exoneration by the Council of Rome in 378 implies that the civil exoneration had taken place some time before. Damasus was exonerated; Ursinus was exiled to Cologne, and Isaac to Spain. Ursinus is last mentioned as being engaged in an intrigue against Damasus in a letter addressed by the Council of Aquileia to the emperors in 381.

Struggle against Heresy. The pontificate of Damasus was a troubled period in the history of the universal Church. From the outset he had to combat Arians of various shades of doctrine, who were especially strong through their occupancy of important sees, and the support given by the emperor, Valens, and the empress, Justina. He had to deal also with adherents of other heresies, with schismatics, and with the efforts of influential pagans to maintain their institutions. In 369 he deposed the Arian bishops of Illyricum, Ursacius and Valens, and, about the same time, seems to have taken some action against Auxentius, the Arian bishop of Milan. In any event, Auxentius remained in his see until his death in 374, when he was replaced by Ambrose, the great bishop destined to play a larger role in the suppression of Arianism in the West than Damasus himself. Damasus took strong measures against the adherents of Lucifer of Cagliari, sending their clerical leaders into exile. At the Council of Rome held in 378, one of the most significant decrees was to the effect that henceforth bishops should be tried by a court of fellow bishops and not be subjected to trial in civil courts, and that this policy should be followed, above all, in the case of the bishop of Rome. The imperial rescript of 378 dealing with the recommendations of the council did not exempt even the pope in principle from imperial jurisdiction in the instance of criminal charges, but the exemption, in practice, was permanently observed.

The religious situation in the East was extremely complex, and Damasus had little more than moderate success in establishing peace and unity. His long negotiations with Basil of Caesarea were clouded by Basil's misunderstanding of the Trinitarian terminology as employed by Rome, and vice versa. After Basil's death, the Council of Antioch (379) accepted the formulas of Damasus, but its president, Meletius, was obviously not well disposed to a pope who had favored his rival, Paulinus. Damasus continued to support Paulinus after the death of Meletius (381) and refused to recognize Flavianus as Meletius's successor. The controversy raised by the Trinitarian heresy of Marcellus of Ancyra was largely abated by his death (374), and the heretical Christology of Apollinaris of Laodicea was formally condemned in 375.

Damasus did not participate in the Council of Constantinople I (381). The third canon of that council, which based the second preeminence of the bishop of New Rome on a political principle, was not acceptable to Rome. In the Roman Council of 382, Damasus, without formal mention of the canon in question, emphasized in unmistakable terms that the bishop of Rome's claim to supremacy was based exclusively on the succession of St.

Peter. He was the first of the popes to call the See of Rome the Apostolic See.

Liturgical Reforms and Restoration of the Catacombs. Damasus took a special interest in preserving papal records and in developing the papal chancery. He carried out some liturgical reforms, and it was under his pontificate that Latin became the principal liturgical language at Rome. Jerome became his secretary in 377 and, because of his knowledge of Scripture, was commissioned to revise the Latin translations of the New Testament on the basis of the original Greek. Jerome was responsible also for the official canon of the Scriptures approved by the Roman Council of 382. In addition to other building activities, as an ardent promoter of the cult of the martyrs he restored and redecorated the tombs of the martyrs in the catacombs and composed epigrams that were inscribed on marble slabs in the beautiful letters created by Furius Dionysius Filocalus. Despite the violence associated with his election and the beginning of his pontificate, Damasus must be regarded as one of the great popes of the fourth century.

Feast: Dec. 11.

Bibliography: F. L. CROSS, *The Oxford Dictionary of the Christian Church* (London 1957) 370–371. O. PERLER, *Lexikon für Theologie und Kirche,* ed. J. HOFER and K. RAHNER (Freiburg 1957–65) 3:136–137. G. BARDY, *Catholicisme* 3:429–431. A. VAN ROEY, *Dictionnaire d'histoire et de géographie ecclésiastiques,* ed. A. BAUDRILLART et al. (Paris 1912–) 14:48–53. O. BARDENHEWER, *Geschichte der altkirchlichen Literatur* (Freiburg 1913–32) 3:503–507, 588–591. F. X. SEPPELT, *Geschichte der Päpste von den Anfängen bis zur Mitte des 20. Jh.* (Munich 1954) 1:109–126. E. CASPAR, *Geschichte de Papsttums von den Anfängen bis zur Höhe der Weltherrschaft* (Tübingen 1930–33) 1:196–256. E. AMAND-DE-MENDIETA, ''Basile de Cesaree et Damase de Rome: Les causes de l'echec de leurs negociations,'' in *Biblical and Patristic Studies in Memory of Robert Pierce Casey* (Freiburg 1963) 122–66. L. ANDRE-DELASTRE, *Saint Damase I, defenseur e la doctrine de la primaute Pierre, des Saint Ecritures et patron des archeologues* (Paris 1965). G. BARDY, ''L'Église romaine, de Silvestre à Damase,'' H. CHADWICK, ''Pope Damasus and the Peculiar Claim of Rome to St. Peter and St. Paul,'' *Neotestamentica et Patristica* (Leiden 1962) 313–8. M. R. GREEN, ''Supporters of the Antipope Ursinus,'' *Journal of Theological Studies* 22 (1971) 531–8. C. PIETRI, ''Damase et Theodose: communion orthodoxe et geographie politique,'' *Epektasis* (Paris 1972) 627–34. PONTIFICIO INSTITUTO DI ARCHEOLOGIA CRISTIANA, *Secularia Damasiana: atti del Convegno internazionale per il XVI centenario della morte di papa Damaso I* (Rome 1986). M. H. SHEPHERD, ''The Liturgical Reforms of Damasus I,'' *Kyriakon* (1970) 847–63. J. TAYLOR, ''St. Basil the Great and Pope St. Damasus I,'' *Downside Review* 91 (1973) 186–203, 262–74. A. FLICHE and V. MARTIN, eds. *Histoire de l'église depuis les origines jusqu' à nos jours* (Paris 1935–) 3:228–236. C. J. VON HEFELE, *Histoire des conciles d'après les documents originaux,* tr. and continued by H. LECLERCQ (Paris 1907–38) 1.2:825–1045; 2.1:1–65.

[M. R. P. MCGUIRE]

DAMASUS II, POPE

Pontificate: July 17, 1048 to Aug. 9, 1048. b. Poppo; d. at Palestrina. A Bavarian, he owed his bishopric of Brixen to Emperor HENRY III. He rose to prominence in the reform synods of 1046. When Pope CLEMENT II died on Oct. 9, 1047, the deposed Pope BENEDICT IX again seized Rome. At Poehlde an anti-Tuscan delegation waited on Emperor Henry, who by virtue of his title, *PATRICIUS ROMANORUM,* gave them Poppo to be pope. Margrave Boniface of Tuscany forcibly cleared Rome for the papal coronation on July 17, 1048, but within 23 days Damasus died of malaria.

Bibliography: *Liber Pontificalis,* ed. L. DUCHESNE (Paris 1886–1958) 2. H. K. MANN, *The Lives of the Popes in the Early Middle Ages from 590 to 1304* (London 1902–32) 6. A. HAUCK, *Kirchengeschichte Deutschlands* (Berlin-Leipzig 1958) 3. A. FLICHE, *La Réforme Grégorienne,* v.8 of *Histoire de l'église depuis les origines jusqu'à nos jours* (Paris 1935). F. X. SEPPELT, *Geschichte der Päpste von den Anfängen bis zur Mitte des 20. Jr.* (Munich 1954–59) 3. A. VAN ROEY, *Dictionnaire d'histoire et de géographie ecclésiastiques,* ed. A. BAUDRILLART et al. (Paris 1912) 14:53–54. P. BERTOLINI, *Dizionario biografico delgi italiani* 32 (Rome 1995). G. SCHWAIGER, *Lexikon für Theologie und Kirche,* 3d. ed., (1994). J. N. D. KELLY, *Oxford Dictionary of Popes* (New York 1986) 146–147.

[V. GELLHAUS]

DAMIAN OF FINARIO, BL.

Dominican; b. near Finario (Genoa), Italy, *c.* 1400; d. Reggio (near Modena), 1484. Very little is recorded of Damian. He is said to have been kidnapped as an infant by a lunatic and to have had his hiding place revealed by a miraculous light. He entered the Dominican order, probably at Finario, and became renowned as a preacher in Lombardy and Liguria. In 1441 he was at the convent of San Marco, Florence. His writings include collections of sermons and meditations. After his death many miracles were attributed to his intercession. Pius IX confirmed his cultus in 1848.

Feast: Oct. 26.

Bibliography: J. QUÉTIF and J. ÉCHARD, *Scriptores Ordinis Praedicatorum* 1.2:808. *Année Dominicaine,* 23 v. (Lyons 1883–1909) Oct. 2:735–738. A. MERCATI and A. PELZER, *Dizionario ecclesiastico* 1:805. A. BUTLER, *The Lives of the Saints* 4:207. V. KOUDELKA, *Lexikon für Theologie und Kirche*[2] 3:138.

[M. J. FINNEGAN]

DAMIAN OF PAVIA, ST.

Bishop; d. Pavia, April 4, *c.* 715. The son of a noble family, he early achieved a reputation for learning and piety. As a priest he vigorously opposed MONOTHELITISM at the Synod of Milan (680). He composed the letter sent in the name of the synod by Bishop Mansuetus to Emperor CONSTANTINE IV Pogonatus. The letter, read at the Council of CONSTANTINOPLE III, contained a profession of faith that affirmed two natural wills and two natural operations in Christ. When elected bishop of Pavia (*c.* 685), he played the role of peacemaker between the Byzantine emperor and the LOMBARDS. Shortly before his death he visited Constantinople.

Feast: April 12.

Bibliography: *Acta Sanctorum Sedis* April 2:91–92. DAMIAN, ''Epistola,'' *Patrologia Latina* 87:1259–68. J. L. BAUDOT and L. CHAUSSIN, *Vies des saints et des bienhereux selon l'ordre du calendrier avec l'historique des fêtes* (Paris 1935–56) 4:276. R. VAN DOREN, *Dictionnaire d'histoire et de géographie ecclésiastiques,* ed. A. BAUDRILLART et al. (Paris 1912) 14:54.

[J. E. LYNCH]

DAMNATION

In theological discourse, ''damnation'' is one of the terms, ''HELLFIRE'' being the other, used in connection with the punishment of the demons and the damned. It signifies the technical concept of punishment of loss (*poena damni*), the concept used to interpret the primary element in the punishment of the damned.

This concept of punishment of loss is the important contribution to the theology of hell made by the scholastics, but its value is apparent only when set within their thought pattern. There, its content is the punishment due for the loss of God, and this content is objective in the measure that it is meaningful to speak of the loss of God. Loss of the vision of God occurs in the letter *Majores* (H. Denzinger, *Enchiridion symbolorum,* ed. A. Schönmetzer [32d ed. Freiburg 1963] 780) of Innocent III as the punishment for original sin (for the problem of this punishment *see* LIMBO). Loss of God in the context of damnation has another meaning.

The last end is a major idea in the thought pattern of scholastic theology, where God is seen as the last end. Loss of God in this context means the loss of the last end. The concept of mortal sin when analyzed in reference to the last end is seen to involve the loss of the last end (*Summa contra gentiles* 3.143). Punishment for this loss is also worked out in terms of the last end. Because of the special relation between SIN and punishment to the will (*Compendium theologiae ad fratrem Reginaldum socium suum carissimum* 121), it is seen to involve the sinner in deprivation of the divine illumination (*Summa theologiae* 1a, 64.1) by which God is effectively appre-

hended as the last end. This privation implies that the sinner, on his own determination and obstinately, is turned away from the goodness of God (*Comp. theol.* 174), a situation spoken of in scriptural statements as hatred (Jn 15.24). Elaborated in this way, punishment for the loss of God is understood as something more than the full unfolding of the devastation sin produces in the person and in personal relations (Gal 5.17–21). It is a punishment supposing the exercise of supreme authority (*Comp. theol.* 121) and is measured according to the fault it punishes. So the doctrinal statement (H. Denzinger, *Enchiridion symbolorum,* 858, 1306) about the disparity in the punishment of the damned is intellectually justified. The concrete setting the concept of punishment of loss or damnation is used to interpret is, in scriptural statements, associated with the appearance of the Son of God (1 Jn 3.8) and the Holy Spirit the Advocate (Jn 16.8). And the effect this punishment produces in the sinner, spoken of in scriptural statements as the humiliation that is the contrary to the exaltation inseparably associated with the KINGDOM OF GOD, is expressed in the concept of punishment of loss as the misery that is the contrary to the happiness entailed in the concept of the last end (*Comp. theol.* 174).

See Also: ESCHATOLOGY, ARTICLES ON; FIRE OF JUDGMENT; HELL (THEOLOGY OF); JUDGMENT, DIVINE (IN THEOLOGY); SANCTION; SANCTION, DIVINE.

Bibliography: T. ORTOLAN, *Dictionnaire de théologie catholique,* ed. A. VACANT et al., 15 v. (Paris 1903–50; Tables générales 1951–) 4.1:6–25. M. J. SCHEEBEN, *The Mysteries of Christianity,* tr. C. VOLLERT (St. Louis 1946) 684–694.

[E. G. HARDWICK]

DANCE OF DEATH

The German expression for dance of death is *Totentanz,* meaning a dance of the dead, not of personified Death. The bizarre French term *danse macabre,* or *danse de Macabré,* is of uncertain origin, though there is a traditional interpretation as ''dance of the Machabees.'' The gruesome story recorded in 2 Mc 7 fits in neatly with the idea and could quite well be associated in some way with the dance of death, for such it was.

The so-called ''dance'' is not a dance at all but a motif that found expression in prose and poetry, in painting and sculpture, in music, in sermon, and on the stage. Some writers have developed the theory that it arose from the succession of terrible plagues and disasters that struck Europe in the 14th century, the most devastating being the Black Death (1348–50). Others consider it a deriva-

Tormented souls in Hell, engraving by B. Picart, 18th century. (©Historical Picture Archive/CORBIS)

tion from the motif of "the three living and the three dead" that began to appear in French literature as early as the 13th century, wherein three young men are suddenly confronted by three decomposing dead men who warn them of their approaching death. There is still another possibility that the dance was an elaboration of superstition and folklore about ghostly dancing in graveyards or the dance of preternatural creatures luring men to their doom. This cannot be demonstrated in exact citations, but there are intimations of it in the many accounts of visits to the underworld (Vergil, Dante, and a host of lesser writers). Thus there are at least four possible concepts (perhaps many more) that account for the appearance and widespread popularity of the dance of death in the 15th century.

The "dance" is a representation of a horrible corpse leading a living man by the hand, the corpse being the man as he will be after death. The portrayal (whether in art or in literature) was therefore a pictorial exhortation that could have religious, moral, or satirical import and sometimes had all three at once. It was also an attempt to teach at least the equality of all men before the leveling hand of death. In attenuated form it persisted into the 18th century in the phrase (and its representations) "Et in Arcadia ego," and indeed the motif has not entirely disappeared. It survives in Halloween customs, tombstone epitaphs, mystery magazines, and popular radio and television programs, especially those with musical background, and in particular with the familiar composition by Camille Saint-Saëns, *La Danse Macabre.*

No doubt the best known "Dance of Death" is the series of woodcuts by Hans Holbein the Younger (1497?–1543), printed in Lyons in 1538. From that date to 1562, ten more authentic editions were published. Later copies and imitations have been estimated at more than 100. In these pictures Death confronts pope, emperor, cardinal, empress, duke, abbot, judge, senator, preacher, nun, old woman, physician, astrologer, merchant, rich man, seaman, knight, countess, peddler, plowman, child, drunkard, fool, beggar, bride, and many others. Here is found the culmination of the genre: all classes of society are equal in the presence of the Grim Reaper.

Bibliography: J. M. CLARK, *The Dance of Death by Hans Holbein* (London 1947); *The Dance of Death in the Middle Ages and the Renaissance* (Glasgow 1950). J. HUIZINGA, *The Waning of the Middle Ages,* tr. F. HOPMAN (Garden City, N.Y. 1954). E. PANOFSKY, *Meaning in the Visual Arts* (Garden City, N.Y. 1955) 295–320. L. P. KURTZ, *The Dance of Death and the Macabre Spirit in European Literature* (New York 1934). E. K. STAHL, *Lexikon für Theologie und Kirche*[1], ed. M. BUCHBERGER, 10 v. (Freiburg 1930–38) 10: unnumbered insert p. between cols. 228 and 229. F. EICHENBERG, *The Dance of Death: A Graphic Commentary on the Danse Macabre Through the Centuries* (New York 1983).

[A. CABANISS]

DANDOY, GEORGE

Important figure in the Catholic press of India; b. Hemptinne, Belgium, Feb. 5, 1882; d. Calcutta, India, June 11, 1962. He entered the Society of Jesus in 1899, and graduated from Oxford University (1909) in Sanskrit and Indian philosophy in preparation for missionary work in Bengal, India, where he arrived the same year. Ordained in 1914, he taught theology at St. Mary's College, Kurseong, until 1922 when he went to Calcutta and launched the *Light of the East,* a monthly magazine. An editorial of September 1924 enunciated the guiding principles of the publication:

> We have no intention of attacking Hinduism or any other religion. . . . All we wish to do is to expose our own religion, propose its proofs, manifest its beauty, and show how well it answers the deepest longings of the Indian heart, and solves the eternal problems of the Indian intelligence.

Although the *Light of the East* failed to build the circulation it desired among a non-Christian intelligentsia (it was 3,000 at its highest), it was still a notable achievement in the history of the Catholic press in India. It exerted a lasting influence on missionary thought and method; from it the clergy learned to give Eastern religions and mentality the respect, sympathy, and serious study they merit. Even those who did not subscribe wholeheartedly to its policy caught its spirit of avoiding harsh polemics or an un-Christian arrogance toward non-Christian religions. Publication was suspended in 1946.

From 1946 to 1962, Dandoy was stationed at St. Xavier's College, Calcutta, lecturing in apologetics; his pioneer work has been carried on in a modified form by the publication of *The Light of the East* series of apologetic works in English and Bengali.

[H. ROZARIO]

DANIEL

Legendary protagonist of the Book of Daniel. He is known only from this book. According to the story told in it, he, with three other Jewish youths who had been taken as captives from Jerusalem to Babylon in 605 B.C., was given special training in the palace school at Babylon, where he remained faithful to the Jewish dietary laws (Daniel ch. 1). According to the deuterocanonical ch. 13, even as a young boy in Babylonia he had saved the life of the chaste SUSANNA by his wise judgment. In the 2d year of NEBUCHADNEZZAR he interpreted a dream that had disturbed the king and was therefore promoted to power in Babylon (ch. 2). He later interpreted another dream for Nebuchadnezzar (ch. 4) and read the writing on the wall for Belshazzar, the last Babylonian king (ch. 5). King Darius "the Mede" wished to place Daniel over his entire kingdom, but a plot, born of envy, resulted in Daniel's being thrown into a den of lions, from which God rescued him (ch. 6). A similar story of Daniel's rescue from the lions' den is told in the deuterocanonical ch. 14, where, however, the reason for Daniel's being thrown to the lions was his destroying the statue of the god Bel and his killing the dragon that the Babylonians worshiped. He was favored with apocalyptic visions in the 1st and 3d years of Belshazzar (7.1; 8.1), in the 1st year of Darius (9.1), and in the 3d year of Cyrus (10.1–536 B.C.). His rescue from the lions' den is referred to in 1 Mc 2.60; otherwise he is not mentioned in the Bible. On the historicity of his story, *see* DANIEL, BOOK OF.

The name Daniel (Heb. *dāniyyē'l,* for *dānî-'el,* "my judge is God") was borne also by a postexilic priest of Jerusalem (Ezr 8.2; Neh 10.6). However, the Daniel of Ez 14.14, 20; 28.3 is an entirely different man; even his name is different in the Hebrew consonantal text: *dān'el* (God judges). This man is mentioned with Noah and Job as a figure of hoary antiquity, not as an exilic Prophet. He is probably to be connected with the wise judge Dan-el of the Ugaritic *Tale of Aqhat* (see Pritchard ANET 149–155). The Akkadian name *Dan-ilu* (God judges) is attested from *c.* 2000 B.C. [see J. de Fraine, *Verbum Domini* 25 (Rome 1947) 127]. The Babylonian name given to Daniel (Dn 1.7), Belteshazzar (Heb. *bēlṭeša'ṣṣar*), represents the Akkadian *balaṭšu-uṣur* (protect his life!); by Hebrew folk etymology the name of the Babylonian god Bel was read into it (5.4).

In Christian iconography scenes from the Book of Daniel fall into three main types: (1) the story of Susanna and the elders—a favorite of painters from the Renaissance on because of the bathing scene; (2) the story of the three youths in the furnace; and (3) the story of Daniel in the lions' den. The last is by far the oldest, going back perhaps to Jewish models. Daniel as an *orans* between two or more lions is sculptured on several sarcophagi from the 4th century as a symbol of the salvation of the departed soul from the terrors of the realm of death. The same scene is shown on catacomb frescoes, terra cotta lamps, and other early objects of art. The rescue of the three youths from the furnace was depicted likewise for its symbolic reference to the resurrection of the dead.

Bibliography: *Encyclopedic Dictionary of the Bible,* tr. and adap. by L. HARTMAN (New York 1963) from A. VAN DEN BORN, *Bijbels Woordenboek,* 483–484. P. JOÜON, *Biblica* 19 (1938) 283–285. M. NOTH, "Noah, Daniel, und Hiob in Ezechiel XIV," *Vestus Testamentum* 1 (Leiden 1951) 251–260. B. MARIANI, *Danel "il partriarca sapiente" nella Bibbia, nella tradizione, nella leggenda* (Rome 1945). Iconography. L. RÉAU, *Iconographie de l'art chrétien* (Paris 1955–59) 2.1:391–410. V. H. ELBERN, *Lexikon für Theologie und Kirche,* ed. J. HOFER and K. RAHNER (Freiburg 1957–65) 3:153.

[M. MCNAMARA]

DANIEL, BOOK OF

A book of the Old Testament that is named after its protagonist. In the Masoretic Text (MT) it is placed in the Writings, the third section of the Hebrew canon, after Esther and before Ezra and Nehemiah. In Christian Bibles, following the example of the Septuagint (LXX), "Theodotion-Daniel" (see below), and the Vulgate (Vulg), it is ranked as the last of the four Major Prophets (*see* PROPHETIC BOOKS OF THE OLD TESTAMENT). This article will treat of the book's deuterocanonical sections, language, protocanonical sections, interpretation, composition, and literary genre.

Deuterocanonical Sections. Certain parts of the Book of Daniel are not in the MT (containing the protocanonical sections) but are in the two Greek versions, Vulg, and all Catholic Bibles and are known therefore as deuterocanonical. These parts are: (1) the prayers and hymns connected with the story of the three Jews in the furnace inserted in the LXX and the Vulg between 3.23 and 3.24 of the MT and reckoned as 3.24–90 of the Greek versions and Vulg, so that 3.25–33 of the MT is counted as 3.91–100 of the Vulg (Greek versions 3.91–97); this section was apparently inserted into the text to supply the seeming lacuna in the MT of 3.24–25; (2) the story of Susanna (ch. 13 of the LXX and the Vulg, but before ch. 1 in "Theodotion-Daniel"); and (3) the stories of Bel and of the Dragon (ch. 14 of the LXX and the Vulg). The Catholic Church has always accepted these sections as canonical Scripture. The other additions are from a cycle of traditional stories about Daniel; for other similar tales preserved in fragments among the DEAD SEA SCROLLS, see discussion by J. T. Milik, *Revue biblique* 63 (1956) 407–415.

Language. The Book of Daniel is unique in that it is preserved in the three languages of the Bible: Hebrew, Aramaic, and Greek. The deuterocanonical additions are extant only in Greek, which is probably a translation from Hebrew or Aramaic originals. There are two distinct Greek forms of the book: LXX-Daniel and "Theodotion-Daniel," the latter being a misnomer, for it is not related to the historical Theodotion of the 2d century A.D. (see A. A. Di Lella, "The Textual History of Septuagint-Daniel and Theodotion-Daniel," in *The Book of Daniel: Composition and Reception* [ed. J. J. Collins and P. W. Flint] 2. 586–607. Of the protocanonical text, section 1.1–2.4a and section 8.1–12.13 are in Hebrew. The text changes to Aramaic at 2.4b and continues to 7.28, revert-

"Daniel in the Den of the Lions," engraving by Gustave Dore from "The Bible," 1866. (©Chris Hellier/CORBIS)

ing to Hebrew at 8.1. No satisfactory explanation of this phenomenon has been given. The Aramaic section is certainly in its original language. Some scholars (e.g., H. L. Ginsburg) hold that the Hebrew is a translation from Aramaic (except 9.4–20, which is original Hebrew). Others take the two languages to be original, the change in 2.4b coinciding with the reply of the Chaldeans (presumed to have spoken in Aramaic), or take the two languages to be due to the sources used by the final editor(s) or to indicate that the author(s) first published the work in parts for a bilingual audience and later edited these in book form. If not original, this bilingual nature of the book is at least very old, since it is attested, as in MT, in the Qumran Daniel fragments from the end of the 2d century B.C. to A.D. c. 50.

Protocanonical Sections. These sections consist of two distinct parts, which, however, do not coincide with the division between the Hebrew and the Aramaic parts of the book.

First Part: Chapters 1–6. This section consists of episodes from the life of Daniel and his companions: the food test (ch. 1), the king's dream (ch. 2), the fiery furnace (3.1–97), the king's vision of the great tree and his madness (3.98–4.34), the writing on the wall (5.1–6.1), and Daniel in the lions' den (6.2–29).

Second Part: Chapters 7–12. This section sets forth the visions seen by Daniel and the revelations received by him during his exile. The first vision (ch. 7), from the first year of Belshazzar, tells of four monstrous beasts arising from the deep, the fourth being the fiercest, from which comes forth a "little horn" that acts and speaks arrogantly; the beasts are deprived of their power; then comes with the clouds of heaven "one like a SON OF MAN," i.e., "one in human likeness," symbol of "the people of the holy ones of the Most High" (7.27) who receive everlasting dominion; an angel explains that the monsters represent four kingdoms, and the "little horn" an individual king. The next vision (ch. 8), from the third year of Belshazzar, details further the persecution and arrogance of the "little horn." In the third vision (ch. 9), from the first year of Darius, an angel explains that Jeremiah's 70 years of exile are to be understood as SEVENTY WEEKS OF YEARS, i.e., 490 years. The final vision (ch. 10–12) gives the history of the Persian and Greek Empires, in particular the reigns of Antiochus III and IV and their relations with the Jews. The vision ends with a reference to the resurrection and final retribution.

Interpretation. A correct understanding of the book depends on a right interpretation of the "four kingdoms" with which the book is largely concerned.

In 2.31–35 four world empires are symbolized by the metals gold, silver, bronze, and iron (or iron plus clay),

which are destroyed and replaced by a fifth kingdom, symbolized by a stone. The dream of ch. 2 is paralleled by the vision of ch. 7, which tells of four kingdoms inimical to God, symbolized by four monstrous beasts, whose rule is replaced by a divine reign. In ch. 8 the he-goat that overcomes the ram is identified with the fourth kingdom of ch. 7 (cf. 8.8–9 with 7.8).

The four kingdoms of ch. 2 and ch. 7 are evidently the same. The first empire of ch. 2 is identified in 2.37–38 as the Neo-Babylonian, represented by NEBUCHADNEZZAR. The fourth empire of ch. 7 and the last one of ch. 8 has as its most important king the "little horn," i.e., ANTIOCHUS IV EPIPHANES, and this empire is identified as the Greek in 8.21. The fourth empire is, then, the Greek one of Alexander and his successors. The second and third kingdoms must be empires intermediate between the Neo-Babylonian and Greek. The third (2.39: 7.6) can be identified from history and Dn 8.20–21 as the Persian, defeated by Alexander. The second insignificant empire, mentioned in ch. 2 and ch. 7, must be that of the Medes, which, according to the chronology peculiar to the book (5.30–31: 9.1; see also 8.1), followed on the Neo-Babylonian Empire.

History admits no such Median Empire between the Neo-Babylonian and the Persian, for the latter succeeded the former at the fall of Babylon (539 B.C.). The author(s) of Daniel adopted either a historically false chronology, or a purely fictitious one. Possibly, ch. 2 is dependent on a view of world history considered to be growing increasingly worse. In Hesiod (*Works and Days* 109–201) four ages of such history are symbolized by the same four metals as in Daniel ch. 2. The true historical sequence is Assyria, Media, Persia, and Greece. It is quite possible that the book's chronology is due to the replacement of Assyria by the more relevant Babylon. On both questions see J. S. Swain, *Classical Philology* 35 (1940) 1–21. True chronology is secondary for the author(s) of Daniel, since the four empires are more important as symbols of world power before the inauguration of God's kingdom than as historical realities.

The identification of the empires given above appears most in keeping with the book and is the one now generally accepted.

Composition. The traditional view that the book is an exilic production about Daniel encounters serious difficulties. The earliest reference to the Book of Daniel is in 1 Mc 2.59–60, written after the Maccabean persecution. Not even Ben Sira (c. 180 B.C.) refers to Daniel where he would be expected to do so (Sir 49.6–10). The book's place in the Jewish canon indicates a late date. The historical inaccuracies (a siege of Jerusalem in 605 B.C. [Dn 1.1–2]; Darius "the Mede" [6.1]; Belshazzar, the "son" of Nebuchadnezzar and "king" of Babylon, etc.) are scarcely conceivable in an exilic writer. The language and religious concepts of the book are postexilic and, in part, Maccabean. The perspective of ch. 7–12 is clearly Maccabean, and a revelation of the detailed course of history found there cannot easily be postulated. For these and other reasons, ch. 7–12 and the publication of the entire work as it now stands are now generally ascribed to the Maccabean age, *c.* 165 B.C., a date advocated by the pagan Neo-Platonist Porphyry (d. A.D. 304; see Jerome, *Com. in Dan.: Corpus Christianorum. Series latina* 75A.771).

The book shows signs both of unity and of plurality of authorship for its two parts. On the one hand, both parts show the same doctrine, similar phrases, and the same peculiar chronology. On the other hand, the background of ch. 1–6 is Babylonian, whereas the perspective in ch. 7–12 is Maccabean. This has led most authors to claim a pre-Maccabean (*c.* 300 B.C.) age for ch. 1–6, while they place the composition of ch. 7–12 *c.* 166 B.C. Some scholars (e.g., Ginsburg) postulate separate authors for each of the four visions in ch.7–12. In contrast, H. H. Rowley considers ch. 1–12 a unity, composed entirely by a Maccabean author, who, however, used earlier sources for ch. 1–6. (See Hartman and Di Lella, ch. III.)

Concerning ch. 4, similarities with the history of Nabonidus led P. Riessler (*Das Buch Daniel* [Vienna 1902] 43), F. Hommel (*Theol. Litteraturblatt* 23 [1902] 145–147), and E. Dhorme (*Revue biblique* 8 [1912] 37–38) to surmise that the episode recounted of Nebuchadnezzar in ch. 4 is based on the history of King Nabonidus and his withdrawal from Babylon to the desert oasis of Tema in Arabia. That such is the case is clear from a Qumran parallel to ch. 4 (4QOrNab, published by J. T. Milik, *Revue biblique* 63 [1956] 407–411), which recounts the cure of Nabonidus by an anonymous Jew at Tema. This 10-year desert sojourn is described in detail by Nabonidus himself in his Harran inscriptions, published and studied by C. H. Gadd (*Anatolian Studies* 8 [1958] 35–39). The Harran inscriptions of Nabonidus bear a remarkable similarity (e.g., in dreams and "fixed times") to Daniel ch. 4 and other chapters.

Belshazzar, who is called the son of Nebuchadnezzar in Daniel ch. 5, was really son of Nabonidus.

Chapters 2–3 are also probably based on traditions connected with Nabonidus, a point already noted by Riessler, 14–15, 27–28. This king was worried by dreams he thought came from the moon-god Sin. He felt called to rebuild Sin's temple at Harran, which he did, probably in his 3d regnal year (see E. Vogt, *Biblica* 40 [1959] 57). The king's attention to Sin, his neglect of Marduk and a statue he made (presumably for the Harran temple, there-

fore in his 2d or 3d regnal year—cf. Dn 3.1) infuriated the Marduk clergy and estranged them from him; hence his withdrawal to Tema. In the history of Nabonidus there is the same sequence as in Daniel ch. 2–4.

The probable history of the book's composition may be stated as follows: ch. 1–6 are stories that once circulated independently, the Jewish protagonists being perhaps originally anonymous (cf. 4QOrNab), ch. 2–4 being connected with the reign of Nabonidus, ch. 6 with that of Darius. These stories probably originated in Babylon and were brought to Palestine in the 2d century B.C. (see D. N. Freedman, *Bulletin of the American Schools of Oriental Research* 145 [1957] 31). The Maccabean author(s), *c.* 165 B.C., who composed ch. 7–12 (or ch. 8–12) to strengthen the faith of the persecuted Jews, probably rewrote the earlier stories of ch. 1–6, substituting Nebuchadnezzar for (the less known) Nabonidus and placing the entire work within the book's peculiar chronology. Other stories about Daniel also circulated, and from among them the Greek translators added the deuterocanonical sections, which had been composed some time between the 3d and 1st centuries B.C.

Literary Genre. Chapters 1–6 are stories, perhaps well-known, which are composed or recast for the sake of teaching some moral—in the present case, for the purpose of reminding the persecuted Jews of God's providence toward the loyal adherent of the true religion.

Chapters 7–12 are apocalypses in which Israel's past history is presented as if it were prophecy—in the present case, the postexilic history of Israel up to the tenth year of Antiochus IV Epiphanes (165 B.C.). The lesson intended here is the same as in ch. 1–6, namely, God's command of the course of human events.

Bibliography: Commentaries. S. R. DRIVER (Cambridge, Eng. 1901; repr. 1922). J. A. MONTGOMERY (*International Critical Commentary*, 22, ed. S. R. DRIVER et al.; Edinburgh 1927). R. H. CHARLES (Oxford 1929). G. RINALDI (4th ed. Milan 1962). F. NÖTSCHER (2d ed. *Echter Bibel: Die Hl. Schrift in deutscher Übersetzung* [Würzburg 1947] 3; 1958). L. F. HARTMAN and A. A. DI LELLA (Anchor Bible 23; Garden City, N.Y. 1978). A. LACOCQUE (Atlanta 1979). P. GRELOT (Paris 1992). J. J. COLLINS (Hermeneia; Minneapolis 1993). D. BAUER (Neuer Stuttgarter Kommentar Altes Testament 22; 1996). A. A. DI LELLA (Hyde Park, N.Y. 1997). Studies. H. L. GINSBURG, *Studies in Daniel* (New York 1948); "The Composition of the B. of D.," *Vetus Testamentum* 4 (1954) 246–275. W. DOMMERSCHAUSEN, *Nabonid im Buche D.* (Mainz 1964). O. EISSFELDT, *The Old Testament: An Introduction*, tr. P. R. ACKROYD (New York 1965) 512–529. W. BAUMGARTNER, *Die Religion in Geschichte und Gegenwart*, 7 v. (3d ed. Tübingen 1957–65) 2:26–31; "Ein Vierteljahrhundert Danielforschung," *Theologische Rundschau* 11 (1939) 59–83, 125–144, 201–228. H. O. THOMPSON, *The Book of Daniel: An Annotated Bibliography* (Books of the Bible 1; Garland Reference Library of the Humanities 1310; New York/London 1993). T. M. MEADOWCROFT, *Aramaic Daniel and Greek Daniel: A Literary Comparison* (Journal for the Study of the Old Testament Supple-

ment Series 198; Sheffield 1995). T. MCLAY, *The OG and Th Versions of Daniel* (SBL Septuagint and Cognate Studies 43; Atlanta 1996). P. W. FLINT, "The Daniel Tradition at Qumran," in *Eschatology, Messianism, and the Dead Sea Scrolls,* ed. C. A. EVANS and P. W. FLINT (Grand Rapids 1997) 41–60. J. J. COLLINS and P. W. FLINT, eds., *The Book of Daniel: Composition and Reception* (2 v.; Formation and Interpretation of Old Testament Literature; Vetus Testamentum Supplementum Series 83.2; Leiden 2001).

[M. MCNAMARA/A. A. DI LELLA]

DANIEL OF BELVEDERE, ST.

Martyr; d. Ceuta, North Africa, Oct. 10, 1227. Daniel was the FRANCISCAN provincial of Calabria, who with six companions—Samuel, Agnellus (Angelus or Angeluccio), Domnus, Leo, Nicholas, and Hugolinus—had the permission of Brother ELIAS OF CORTONA, the successor of FRANCIS OF ASSISI, to embark for Morocco from a port in Tuscany. They spent a few days outside Ceuta, in the *fondouq,* or compound, of Christian merchants from Genoa, Pisa, and Marseille. Prepared by confession, Communion, and *mandatum* (the washing of feet) and after a night spent in prayer and pious ejaculations, they entered Ceuta on the morning of Sunday, Oct. 3, 1227. Although there is no evidence that they knew any Arabic, they preached the gospel publicly and were arrested and brought before the Moslem authorities. They were imprisoned as fools and eight days later, when deaf to promise or threat, they refused to renounce their faith, they were sentenced and beheaded. The Christians were allowed to bury the remains in their own *fondouq.* In 1516 the cult was approved for the Franciscan Order by LEO X, and their names were inscribed in the Roman Martyrology.

Feast: Oct. 10.

Bibliography: *Acta Sanctae Sedis* Oct. 6:384–392, *Propylaeum Decembris* 451–452. C. M. DE WITTE, *Dictionnaire d'histoire et de géographie ecclésiastiques,* ed. A. BAUDRILLART et al. (Paris 1912) 14:68. F. DELORME, "Pour l'histoire des martyrs du Maroc," *La France franciscaine* 7 (1924) 111–135. L. WADDING, *Scriptores Ordinis Minorum* (3d ed. Quaracchi-Florence 1931—) 2:29–35. *Bibliotheca hagiograpica latina antiquae et mediae aetatis* (Brussels 1898–1901) 1:2093–94.

[T. C. CROWLEY]

DANIEL PALOMNIK

Russian abbot and pilgrim; b. probably in the Province of Chernigov, Little Russia, *c.* mid-11th century; d. possibly Tartu, Estonia, Sept. 9, 1122. He was a contemporary of the chronicler Nestor, but the few facts known about him come almost entirely from internal references in his famous account of his pilgrimage to the Holy Land, the *Puteshestvie igumena Daniila,* which survives in a number of manuscript copies, the earliest of which dates from *c.* 1475. He set out for PALESTINE in the reign of the Russian Grand Duke Michael Sviatopolk II of KIEV (d. 1113). His account begins with his departure from Constantinople and describes his stopover in Cyprus before he landed at Jaffa. He traveled extensively in Palestine west of the JORDAN River and visited most of the important Biblical sites, leaving a careful description of all that he saw. He accompanied Baldwin I, King of Jerusalem after the First Crusade (*see* JERUSALEM, KINGDOM OF), on an expedition against DAMASCUS, undertaken probably in 1106 or 1108. While in Jerusalem Daniel stayed at the Greek monastery or LAURA of Mar Saba and an elderly monk of this foundation served as his guide. The pilgrim spent Easter in the city and his description of the descent of the holy fire in the church of the Holy Sepulcher might well be compared with that of FULCHER OF CHARTRES for the year 1101 in his *Historia Hierosolymitana.* Daniel's work reflects the cooperation and mutual respect still prevalent between the Greek and Latin clergy in the Holy Land at that time, and he himself was welcomed in foundations of both rites. After more than a year in Palestine the abbot returned to Russia, where he wrote an account of his journey. As a literary production, the *Pilgrimage of the Abbot Daniel* is important, for its language closely resembled the spoken Russian of the day, and it became popular with the Russian people who were intrigued with the idea of pilgrimage (*see* PILGRIMAGES, 3). The author is probably the same Abbot Daniel who in 1115 was made bishop of Yurev (present day Tartu in Estonia), which was then under Russian rule. Earlier Russian historians, owing to the use of erroneous dates for Daniel's sojourn in the Holy Land, found it difficult to identify the abbot with the bishop.

Bibliography: Definitive Russ. text *Puteshestvie igumena Daniila,* ed. A. S. NOROVA (St. Petersburg 1864). *Itinéraires russes en Orient,* Fr. tr. S. DE KHITROW (Geneva 1889) 3–83. *The Pilgrimage of the Russian Abbot Daniel in the Holy Land 1106–1107,* tr. and annotated C. W. WILSON (Palestine Pilgrims Text Society; London 1888), based on Fr. tr. of DE KHITROW. M. A. VENEVITINOV, "Khozhdenie igumena Danilla v sviatuiu zemliu v nachalie XII vieka," *Lietopis' zaniatii arkheograficheskoi kommissii* 7 (St. Petersburg 1884) 1–138. *Russkii biograficheskii slovar* 6 (St. Petersburg 1905) 95–96. B. LEIB, *Rome, Kiev et Byzance à la fin du XIe siècle* (Paris 1924) 276–285. N. K. GUDZII, *History of Early Russian Literature,* tr. S. W. JONES (New York 1949) 114–117. V. LAURENT, *Dictionnaire d'histoire et de géographie ecclésiastiques,* ed. A. BAUDRILLART et al. (Paris 1912–) 14:67–68. A. LIASHCHENKO, *Bol'shaia sovetskataîa entsiklopediia* 19:90. A. VETELEV, "Palomnik Daniila mnikha," *Zhurnal Moskovskoi patriarkhi* 10 (1958) 48–57.

[B. J. COMASKEY]

DANIEL-ROPS, HENRI

French ecclesiastical historian, essayist, novelist, editor; b. Epinal (Vosges), Jan. 19, 1901; d. Chambéry (Savoie), July 27, 1965. Henri, whose family name was Petiot, was the son of an artillery officer. After attending the Lycée Champollion in Grenoble, he made his higher studies in the faculties of letters and of law at the University of Grenoble. In 1922 he obtained his degree (*agrégé*) in history after working under Henri Foçillon and Léon Homo. From then until 1946 he taught history in secondary schools (*lycées*) in Chambéry, Amiens, and Neuilly-sur-Seine. When his writings began to appear he adopted the pseudonym Daniel-Rops, the name of a character in one of his short stories; he did so to avoid the difficulties of obtaining the permission from the ministry of education required of public school teachers who wished to publish. During the four decades preceding his sudden death from a cerebral hemorrhage, his literary output was enormous. Besides numerous short stories, essays, and articles, he published about 70 books, 20 of them novels. Several of his works have been translated into English.

Notre inquiétude (1926) was an appropriate title for his first book, a series of essays, which revealed an unrest characteristic of those who approached maturity during World War I and the disturbed period following it. Although he was reared as a Catholic, his adherence to his faith was for some years nominal. Later he became a devout, zealous Catholic. His next books, *La vent dans la nuit* (1927), *Carte d'Europe* (1929), *L'âme obscure* (1929), *Edouard Estain* (1931), and *Péguy* (1933), demonstrated his intelligence and literary skill.

In 1932 he joined a movement, called the New Order, started by three young intellectuals, Arbaud Dandieu, Denis de Rougement, and Robert Aron. Its aim was to supply young Frenchmen, faced with dictatorships, with a political doctrine based on democratic humanism. Daniel-Rops was the principal author of the movement's manifesto in 1934: "Against the declining powers, against absurd and criminal economic regimes, the necessary protestations no longer suffice. A constructive will is required. We want a revolution in the present order."

Soon he passed beyond the small circle of the New Order. In 1934 he asserted himself as a Catholic author with his best-known novel, *Mort où est ta victoire?* (*Death, Where Is Thy Victory?* 1946), which was immensely popular and was made into a moving picture. In 1937 appeared *Tournant de la France* and *Ce qui meurt et ce qui naît,* two collections of essays whose thesis was that Christianity is the safeguard of the world. *L'Épée de feu* (1939), his second most famous novel, maintained that the anguish of individuals and of society throughout the course of history makes sense only if one accepts the gospel message. Daniel-Rops was thus clearly outside the ACTION FRANÇAISE movement but very close to *Esprit,* a more radical movement, and also to the Popular Republicans, the spiritual heirs of Marc SANGNIER and Sillon. Daniel-Rops became the voice of thoughtful, right-minded persons. He maintained a balance that relied above all on Christian values.

In 1941 Octave Aubry asked Daniel-Rops to contribute a volume for the collection *Grandes Études historiques,* published by the Parisian firm of Fayard, and thereby enabled Daniel-Rops to discover the role best suited to him as a Catholic thinker by returning to his profession as an historian. The volume, entitled *Le Peuple de la Bible,* appeared July 1, 1943. The Gestapo confiscated and suppressed the book on July 20; but it proved to be the first of 12 volumes on Biblical and ecclesiastical history, completed only on the eve of the author's death, that made its author world famous. It was soon translated into English and other languages. In English this first volume was translated in 1949 as *Sacred History* (or as *Israel and the Ancient World*); it was followed by the enormously popular, *Jesus and His Times* (1954) and by the ten-volume *History of the Church of Christ* (1957–).

Meanwhile Daniel-Rops had become editor of the popular periodical *Ecclesia* (1949) and of the collection of texts entitled *Textes pour l'histoire sacrée.* He drew up plans for and then acted as editor for the 150-volume series, *Je sais, je crois* (1956–), translated as *Twentieth Century Encyclopedia of Catholicism* (1958–). In addition he wrote numerous hagiographical, devotional, and other religious books, illustrated volumes, and essays intended for wide popular consumption. He also delivered many lectures. In 1955 he was elected to the French Academy.

The historical synthesis by Daniel-Rops was not an original one, but it had the merit of placing at the disposal of a vast audience a very readable work whose contents and judgments were sound. The long narrative revealed a Catholic optimist who found in the course of ecclesiastical history much less reason for scandal than for admiration.

[E. JARRY]

DANIÉLOU, JEAN

Jesuit theologian, patristics scholar, spiritual writer, bishop, and cardinal; b. May 14, 1905, Neuilly-sur-Seine near Paris; d. May 20, 1974, Paris. His father, Charles Daniélou, was a deputy and minister during the Third Republic; his mother, Madeleine Clamorgan, was a woman of great spiritual and intellectual caliber. Daniélou obtained his degree in classical letters from the Sorbonne and passed the competitive teaching examination in the section of classical philology (*agrégation de grammaire*) in 1927. He was then introduced to political life by his father, and at the same time briefly engaged in the brilliant Parisian life of that era, translating into Latin Jean Cocteau's *Oedipus Rex.* On Nov. 20, 1929, answering a call he had felt since childhood, he entered the novitiate of the Society of Jesus (*see* JESUITS) at Laval. After making his profession of first vows on Nov. 21, 1931, he took his course in philosophy at Jersey (1931–34). He served as professor of rhetoric at the Collège St. Joseph in Poitiers (1934–36), then took his theological studies at the theologate of Lyon-Fourvière (1936–39). At Fourvière, where the Fathers of the Church were held in great esteem, and where plans were maturing for the collection *Sources Chrétiennes,* his elders, Victor Fontoynont (1880–1958) and Henri de LUBAC, introduced Daniélou, along with his fellow scholastic Hans Urs von BALTHASAR, to patristic studies (*see* PATRISTIC THEOLOGY). He was ordained to the priesthood on Aug. 24, 1938. He was mobilized into military service in 1939 and performed his "Third Year" (the Jesuit tertianship) from 1940 to 1941. He pronounced his solemn vows in Paris, Feb. 2, 1946. The personal notes he took during this long formative period, published posthumously as *Carnets spirituels* (1993), witness the seriousness of his spiritual training.

In 1941 Fr. Daniélou was assigned to Paris, where he spent the rest of his life. His background made him a fitting apostle to intellectuals, who accepted him as one of their own. In 1942 he published *Le Signe du Temple ou de la Présence de Dieu,* which contained the whole of his thought in embryonic form. Characteristic of the personality of its author, it shows a contemplative attitude, a taste for symbolic theology, a use of the exegetical methods of the Fathers, and a care to impart in a simple way to a vast public the riches of his spiritual life, scholarly work, and highly cultivated mind. His doctoral dissertation dealt with the spiritual doctrine of St. GREGORY OF NYSSA. He defended it successfully in 1943 at the Institut Catholique in Paris, and in 1944 at the Sorbonne. For the secondary thesis at the Sorbonne he translated Gregory of Nyssa's *Life of Moses,* which formed the first volume of *Sources Chrétiennes.* The rapid development as well as the high scholarly quality of this collection owes much to the personal initiative of Daniélou, who was its codirector along with de Lubac. In 1943 he was given the status of writer (scriptor) for the Jesuit review *Études* and succeeded Jules LEBRETON (1873–1956) as professor of the history of Christian origins in the faculty of theology of the Institut Catholique in Paris. He served as dean of this faculty from 1961 until 1969.

Daniélou's substantial professional achievement opened several new areas in the academic and broader Christian world. Parallel to Walther Volker and Balthasar, he was the chief instrument of a Gregory of Nyssa renaissance, dedicating numerous articles to the subject. The most important ones are collected in *L'être et le temps chez Grégoire de Nysse* (1970). He prepared an anthology of Gregory's mystical texts (Eng. trans. H. Musurillo, *From Glory to Glory,* 1961). As an intellectual sensitive to the problems raised by secular culture for the Christian, he applied himself to the study of how Gregory reworked and Christianized the philosophical ideas of his day.

With Lubac, Daniélou was the principal artisan of a rediscovery of patristic exegesis, which, like the liturgy to which it is closely bound, explores the symbolic dimension of Scripture in order to draw therefrom an understanding of the Christian revelation. In particular he illuminated the notion of typology, tying history and symbolism together in a specifically Christian way. Salvation history is marked by such interventions of God that the events of the Old Testament announce those of the New. They, in turn, are spread out across the ages of the Church in the sacramental and mystical life of the Christian people in anticipation of full eschatological realization. Here Daniélou's pertinent works are *Sacramentum futuri/Étude sur les origines de la typologie biblique* (1950); *Bible et liturgie; La théologie biblique des sacrements et des fêtes d'après les Pères de l'Église* (1951), which resulted from courses given at the University of Notre Dame in 1950; *Les symboles chrétiens primitifs* (1961); and *Études d'exégèse judéo-chrétienne: Les Testimonia* (1966).

In his *Histoire des doctrines chrétiennes avant Nicée* (3 vols.: *Théologie du judéo–christianisme* [1958], *Message évangélique et culture hellénistique aux IIe et IIIe siècles* [1961], and *Les origines du christianisme latin* [1978]), Daniélou sketched a history of Christian culture, showing how it tested, purified, or adopted the surrounding cultures. He became one of the most outstanding specialists of a rediscovered "Judaeo–Christianity." With the same care for cultural roots, he dedicated a monograph to each of the two Alexandrians, *Origène* (1948) and *Philon d'Alexandrie* (1958), as well as the first part of the first volume of the *Nouvelle histoire de l'Église: Des origines à Grégoire le grand* (1963). Daniélou exerted a notable influence in the scientific life of his time by producing yearly from 1946 his "Bulletin d'histoire des origines chrétiennes" in the Jesuit review *Recherches de Science Religieuse.*

Professionally, Daniélou was a historian of the early Church. However, by family heritage, the Jesuit tradition, and his own temperament, he was intellectually alive to every contemporary current of thought and open to every kind of dialogue. Thus he was, along with Marcel Moré (1887–1969) and the Islamic scholar Louis Massignon (1883–1962), the soul of the short-lived review *Dieu Vivant/Perspectives religieuses et philosophiques* (1945–55). *Dieu Vivant* had as its fundamental concern to recall to a secularizing world the transcendence of God and the ultimate eschatological effect which that transcendence imposes on human destiny.

Daniélou cofounded the Cercle Saint–Jean Baptiste, a group of young people dedicated to the missionary vocation, and served as its chaplain. He proposed that Christianity in non-Christian cultures should be formed not of individuals torn from their own culture and uprooted from their natural environment, but of Christians who were part and parcel of their actual culture. He tried to develop a theological vision flexible enough to embrace these principles, but especially to draw out all the implications related to Christian spirituality. The essential teaching which he gave to the Cercle Saint Jean–Baptiste is contained in: *Le mystère du salut des nations* (1945); *Le mystère de l'Avent* (1948); *L'essai sur le mystère de l'histoire* (1953); *Les saints païens de l'Ancien Testament* (1956); *Jean-Baptiste témoin de l'Agneau* (1964); and *L'Église des apôtres* (1970). Two retreats given to the Cercle have also been published: *La Trinité et le mystère de l'existence* (1968) and *Contemplation, croissance de l'Église* (1977). They show us the true stature of Daniélou as a spiritual theologian. Father Daniélou exerted a great and lasting influence as chaplain upon the Catholic students at the Sorbonne, and especially beginning in 1941 upon the young women of the École Normale Supérieure (Sèvres). Out of this apostolate came *Dieu et nous* (1956) and *Approches du Christ* (1960).

In 1962, Daniélou was nominated as a *peritus* to the Second Vatican Council (*see* VATICAN COUNCIL II) by Pope JOHN XXIII. The preparation of the first part of the constitution *Gaudium et spes* owes much to him. He was consecrated bishop in Paris on April 21, 1969, and created cardinal deacon by Pope PAUL VI during the consistory of April 28. Increasingly, he spoke out on issues of the day and warned against a reductionist reading of the council. This struggle alienated him from the most influential part of the Catholic intelligentsia and clergy. His burning zeal expressed itself through his talent as a polemicist. He who in the past was an "avant-gardist" was now rebuked for having gone over to the "integralist" or reactionary side. Concerning this struggle see: *L'oraison, problème politique* (1965); *L'avenir de la religion* (1968); *Christianisme de masse ou d'élite?* (1968); *Tests* (1968); *La foi de toujours et l'homme d'aujourd'hui* (1969); *Nouveaux tests* (1970); *La culture trahie par les siens* (1972); and *Pourquoi l'Église* (1972).

Bibliography: A complete bibliography is available in Fr. Frei, *Médiation unique et transfiguration universelle: Thèmes christologiques et leurs perspectives missionnaires dans la pensée de J. Daniélou* (Bern and Frankfurt 1984). For patristic writings see *Epektasis: Mélanges offerts au cardinal Jean Daniélou* (Paris 1972). For works on Judaeo-Christianity see *Judéo-christianisne. Recherches historiques offertes au cardinal Daniélou*, special issue of *Recherches de Science Religieuse* 60 (1972). A bio-bibliography by M. SALES is in M.-J. RONDEAU, ed., *Jean Daniélou 1905–1974* (Paris 1975). J. DANIÉLOU, *Et qui est mon prochain?/Mémoires* (Paris 1974). P. LEBEAU, *Jean Daniélou* (Paris 1967). The collection *Jean Daniélou, 1905–1974* gathers memoirs about the man himself together with introductions to the principal aspects of his activity and thought. Works in English: *The Salvation of the Nations*, tr. A. BOUCHARD (London 1949); *Advent*, tr. R. SHEED (London 1950); *Origen*, tr. W. MITCHELL (New York 1955); *Bible and Liturgy* (Notre Dame, Ind. 1956); *The Angels and Their Mission according to the Fathers of the Church*, tr. D. HELMANN (Westminster, Md. 1957); *God and Us*, tr. W. ROBERTS (London 1957); *Holy Pagans of the Old Testament*, tr. F. FABER (London 1957); *The Lord of History*, tr. N. ABERCROMBIE (Chicago 1958); *The Dead Sea Scrolls and Primitive Christianity*, tr. S. ATTANASIO (Baltimore 1958); *The Presence of God*, tr. W. ROBERTS, (Baltimore 1960); *From Shadows to Reality: Studies in the Biblical Typology of the Fathers*, tr. W. HIBBERD (Westminster, Md. 1960); *The Christian Today*, tr. K. SULLIVAN (New York 1960); *Christ and Us*, tr. W. ROBERTS (New York 1961); *From Glory to Glory: Texts from Gregory of Nyssa's Mystical Writings*, introd. J. DANIÉLOU, tr. H. MUSURILLO (New York 1961); *The Scandal of the Truth*, tr. W. J. KERRIGAN (Baltimore 1962); *Primitive Christian Symbols*, tr. D. ATTWATER (London and Baltimore 1964); *History of Early Christian Doctrines*, tr. J. A. BAKER: v. 1, *Theology of Jewish Christianity* (London and Chicago 1964); v. 2, *The Gospel Message and Hellenistic Culture* (London 1973); v. 3, *Origins of Latin Christianity* (London and Philadelphia 1977); *In the Beginning*, tr. J. L. RANDOLF (Baltimore 1965); *The Work of John the Baptist*, tr. J. A. HORN (Baltimore 1966); *Prayer as a Political Problem*, tr. J. R. KIRWAN (New York 1967); *The Infancy Narratives*, tr. R. SHEED (New York 1968); *Myth and Mystery*, tr. P. J. HEPBURNE–SCOTT (New York 1968); *Dialogue with Israel*, tr. J. M. ROTH (Baltimore 1968); *God's Life in Us* (Denville, N.J. 1969); *The Faith Eternal and the Man of Today*, tr. P. J. OLIGNY (Chicago 1970); "The Crisis in Intelligence," in *The Media of Communication: Art and Morals*, intro. and tr. M. DOMINIC (Slough 1970); *Why the Church?* tr. M. F. DE LANGE (Chicago 1975); *Prayer: The Mission of the Church*, tr. D. SCHINDLER (Grand Rapids, Mich. 1996). J. DANIÉLOU, J. BOSC, and J. GUITTON, *The Catholic–Protestant Dialogue*, tr. R. J. OLSEN (Baltimore 1960). J. DANIÉLOU and H.–I. MARROU, *The Christian Centuries*, vol. 1, *The First Six Hundred Years*, tr. V. CRONIN (New York 1964); J. DANIÉLOU and A. CHOURAQUI, *The Jews: Views and Counterviews, a Dialogue* (Westminster, Md. 1967).

[M. J. RONDEAU/B. VAN HOVE]

DANTE ALIGHIERI

The Poet (as Italians call him); b. Florence, May 1265; d. Ravenna, Sept. 13 or 14, 1321. He was the most learned layman of his time and deeply versed in theology.

But he was first of all a man of action, an ardent combatant for the cause of justice and piety. His work is, for this reason, closely interwoven with the events of his life.

Early Influences. In his youth Dante seemed concerned exclusively with pure literature. As early as his 15th or 16th year, he took part in the game of exchanging with the Tuscan poets sonnets on the nature of love and its effects. These poets, the representatives of the new learned class, were proudly shaping the literature of the new free states. The old themes of the Provençal tradition, in being transplanted into a new middle-class environment, were losing their romantic tone and giving way to dry reasoning on the essence of love. Dante, however, soon discovered CAVALCANTI's poetry, considered him his ''first friend,'' and listened with him to the sweet harmony and wisdom that came from Bologna. At first it was the smoothness of Guido Guinizelli's (1230 or 1240–76) poetry that appealed to him, but his friendship with Cavalcanti aroused his interest in Aristotelian philosophy. Several of his sonnets and *canzoni* reflect Cavalcanti's conceptions about the disastrous results of love and express Dante's own feeling of mortal distress at the approach of his beloved. However, his love for Beatrice, a girl whom he had known since his early youth, was connected more with sensations of devotion and exaltation than of fear. Thus he turned more confidently to Guinizelli's theories about the ennobling effects of love and drew a new feeling of mystic adoration from the corroboration they gave to his personal experience. From this stemmed some of his most inspired sonnets in praise of Beatrice as a living miracle and a supernatural appearance in the world. At the same time his verses reached the highest degree of smoothness and softness of language characteristic of the ''new style'' of the school. But then, when the poet was 25, Beatrice died.

Spiritual Crisis. At first Dante seemed to cling to an inner revelation that Beatrice was a saint, but this kind of rapture for the dead beloved did not last, and Dante soon gave himself over to despair, disordered life, and unbelief. Some sonnets exchanged with Forese Donati give testimony to this spiritual crisis, which lasted for some years. Toward the end of 1293, searching for a solution of this crisis, Dante began to attend lectures on philosophy and theology and found more than he was looking for. His struggle with philosophy was hard, but in 30 months he found himself regaining his lost faith. Beatrice appeared to him in a vision, and all his thoughts were recalled to the pure devotion of his youth. Overwhelmed by the conviction that he had experienced a miracle, he started (*c.* 1296) to write the *Vita Nuova,* the account of his youthful life and the miraculous influence of Beatrice. It was like a *legenda* of St. Beatrice. The *dolce stil nuovo,* with all its pagan philosophy of love,

''Dante Alighieri,'' detail of a fresco of paradise by Giotto (1267–1337), in the Bargello, Capella del Podesta, Florence.

was now a thing of the past. The *Vita Nuova* includes the poems after the manner of Guinizelli or Cavalcanti that on various occasions Dante had written about Beatrice; but clearly they are testimonies of the past and not expressions of his thought when he wrote the prose of *Vita Nuova,* which is several years later than the poems and reflects a thoroughly religious vision. However, this phase of mysticism did not long endure. The poet returned to his struggle with philosophy and wrote (*c.* 1296) the *Rime petrose,* which speaks of a lady (Philosophy) who is his Pietra (rock), unyielding to his passionate love. A little later these studies also were put aside.

Political Activities. In the last years of the century, Dante was prompted by his ardent temperament and also by religious zeal to take an active role in the political life of his town. Florence, as a result of a split in the dominant Guelf party, was divided into two factions: the Blacks, inclined to accept the influence of the pope, and the Whites, jealous defenders of the autonomy of the town. (*See* GUELFS AND GHIBELLINES.) Dante soon became one of the rigorous supporters of the Whites. He was at this time probably under the influence of Petrus Olivi, a Spiritual Franciscan strongly opposed to the temporal power of the Church. In 1300 Dante was elected one of the *priori* (the highest office in the commune) and, in an attempt

Dante's Purgatorio, Dante and Pope Adrian V, illustration by Gustave Dore. (Corbis-Bettmann)

for him the path to salvation. Substantially it is a compilation based mainly on Aristotle's *Nicomachean Ethics,* but Dante's intention was clearly to offer a body of edifying doctrine. The noble lady who is the symbol of philosophy is a friend dearer even than Beatrice, since philosophy by itself is able to bring most people to salvation. Dante followed Aristotle so confidently that he accepted even the principle that man's desire for knowledge can be entirely fulfilled in this life: an obvious denial of the Christian teaching that only in heaven can the human thirst for knowledge be quenched.

At this time, Dante thought also that there was an order of reason completely independent of revealed truth, and that the emperor's authority, based on the light of reason, was sufficient to itself and needed no guidance or control from the Church. Yet, despite these doctrines, the *Convivio* is far from representing a phase of rationalism in Dante's spiritual evolution, as is often said, for the work is pervaded with mysticism: Philosophy is Wisdom itself, "the very beloved daughter of God." While working on the *Convivio,* Dante must have acquired a more solid knowledge of the relationship between reason and revelation, but he did not complete the work. In the fourth and last book composed, "good brother Thomas" (Aquinas) is quoted. It was no longer possible for Dante to rest on the rather crude mixture of Aristotelianism and Christian truth of the first books. Above all, as a man of action, or rather as a reformer stirred by the urge to find a solution for the evils of Italy (and of Florence), Dante was at this time profoundly concerned with the concrete political problems of the Christian world.

The *Monarchia.* The long debate between the advocates of the sovereign authority of the emperor and the supporters of the hierocratic views of the popes had been renewed by the bull UNAM SANCTAM of BONIFACE VIII (1302), and the subsequent *Annominatio.* During the hard-fought conflict between Philip II of France and Boniface, many treatises appeared on both sides. In his fight against those who had exiled him, Dante had progressively approached the views of the Ghibellines, or the imperial party, and had become the guest of the Della Scala, the most powerful Ghibelline family in Italy. Dante's treatise *Monarchia* (*c.* 1309) was a rigorous reassessment of the contrasting views and a firm assertion of the independent sovereignty of the emperor. His position in the conflict, however, was fundamentally different from that of the lay supporters of the empire.

Dante's assumption was that the empire was itself a sacred institution proceeding directly from God's will, "from the very sources of religion," and, as such, needed no counsel from the Church. There were two distinct ends, earthly happiness to be provided by the emperor,

to restore peace, agreed to the banishment of his friend Cavalcanti together with other leaders of the two conflicting factions. The following year, Pope Boniface VIII sent to Florence Charles of Valois, a member of the Angevin family, apparently as a peacemaker, but actually with the mission of helping the Blacks to seize power. Dante led an embassy to Rome to persuade the Pope to recall Charles. It seems that Boniface calculatedly detained him in Rome in order to give the Blacks in Florence time to assume control and issue decrees of condemnation against Dante and others. First the poet was condemned to pay a large fine; then, since he did not return to Florence to make the payment, he was condemned (1302) to be burned alive should he ever come under the power of the commune.

The *Convivio.* Thus began the exile that was to last until Dante's death. There followed years of wandering, poverty, and humiliation. For all his pride, Dante gives unmistakable somber hints of what he had to undergo. At first he took part in armed attempts of his party to reenter Florence, but then he forsook his companions. In order to restore his fame, but also to give his fellow men "the bread of the angels" he had found, he wrote a treatise on the virtues, the *Convivio* (1305), an allegorical "banquet" of the same philosophical wisdom that had been and heavenly bliss to be attained through the Church. The biblical ''render to Caesar what is Caesar's,'' and other sources seemingly asserting the total disjunction and independence of the temporal order from spiritual authority, were naturally utilized to the full to corroborate the principle of the separation of the two powers. Dante even used the Averroistic principle of the unity of the human intellect to defend the theory that there must exist only one emperor for all mankind. The idea of two separate orders was also closely linked to the doctrine of two independent orders of reason and revelation. Dante later rejected this idea in the composition of the *Divina Commedia.*

However, what then distinguished his conception from both the secular doctrine of the state and that of the religious, Franciscan opponents of the temporal power of the Church was his deep persuasion that the empire was sacred and that nature was itself divine (''Deus vult quod natura vult''). The emperor was for him ''the Anointed,'' and those who elected him were directly inspired by the Holy Spirit. The history of the Roman Empire was to Dante a kind of revelation parallel to the history of Israel. Accordingly, when Emperor Henry VII came to Italy (1310) to assert his authority over the Italian states, Dante took part in the expedition with the deepest religious sense of hope and faith. In fervent letters exhorting the lords of Italy to welcome the emperor, he pointed to him as *Agnus Dei.* Dante's whole life, centered on the hope of returning to Florence, as well as the theories he held, his aspiration for peace and justice, and his faith in God, were all at stake in these fateful hours.

By 1313 everything had failed. The hope of returning to Florence that had given deep personal meaning to the mystical anticipation of the renovation of the world was extinguished. Dante had to revise all his views, all the projects of his life. From no earthly authority, it was now clear to him, could a remedy for the cupidity prevailing throughout Christendom be expected. Only a messenger from heaven was to be hoped for. Dante dreamed that he himself—having already experienced the miraculous help of Beatrice and having discovered the truth about the situation of mankind—had been chosen to announce the next Coming.

The Shaping Vision of the *Divina Commedia.* A vision came to him. He was persuaded that his mind had been elevated by God's grace to a supernatural vision of himself going through hell, purgatory, and paradise for the salvation of his own soul and of all mankind. He was able to be extremely precise about the details of that supernatural journey—and he happened to be the most gifted poet, perhaps, of all times. His poem was to be a combined work of heaven and earth (''Whereto both

Dante Alighieri.

heaven and earth have set a hand''): God's vision and his human skill.

There is no conclusive proof, of course, that the vision was real, but there is no ground for not accepting the poet's claim of having *seen* certain things. In his *Letter to Cangrande* he refers those who do not believe him to the works of St. Augustine, St. Bernard, and Richard of St. Victor, wherein the possibility of such supernatural experiences is explicitly stated. Without doubt, the poem he began to write after the failure of Henry VII had the feeling of reality, the impressiveness, the dramatic, concrete sense of a great epic. The allegories of the vices and virtues, philosophy, reason, love, friendship, and the arts, which had crowded so many pages of medieval literature, were left far behind. Dante spoke of historical sacred events in the same way (he pointed out) as the Bible had done.

Analysis of the *Divina Commedia.* Vergil was the guide given him for his journey to hell and purgatory. Vergil had spoken of a similar journey, a descent to the underworld, which in Dante's mind was somehow willed by God and contained truth. First of all Vergil had revealed to Dante the divine mission of Rome and the providential plan of human history. On this basis, Dante was able to reject the Averroistic doctrines of the eternity of the world and man's subjection to astrological influences. In the history of mankind leading to the coming of Christ, Vergil had been closest to Christian thought, almost foretelling the new age. No one but he was entitled to be the guide for a journey that was the symbol of man's historical pilgrimage to the height of revelation.

By the time the poet began the *Divina Commedia,* he had also reached a more consistent view of the relationship between reason and faith. Accordingly, there was in the work a transition from Vergil, the symbol of the *lumen naturale,* to Beatrice, who was to lead the pilgrim through heaven and was the symbol of the *lumen gratiae:* one was the complement of the other. The poem, however, does not deal with abstract figures. Just as the biblical account in Exodus (Dante himself makes the comparison) reports historical events that carry a moral or spiritual meaning, so the *Divina Commedia* deals with concrete facts and real historical figures, which, being ordered by God, also have a spiritual meaning.

Going through the circles of hell—a kind of funnel that plunges to the center of the earth—the pilgrim meets many historical personages, mostly from his own time or from antiquity: a very concrete, real world, the opposite of the allegorical construction of *Le roman de la rose.* The personages are distributed on the various levels of the realm of damnation so that the account of Dante's journey is also a kind of universal judgment and illumination of human vices and virtues. As the poet himself says in his dedicatory letter of the *Paradiso* to Cangrade della Scala, the subject of the work "is man, liable to the reward or punishment of Justice, according as through the freedom of the will he is deserving or undeserving" (tr. C. S. Latham).

The Pilgrim and the Poet. The poem has to be, however, primarily the story of a man, Dante, passing through and suffering the various levels of hell. The grace of the journey has been granted to him so that he can have "full experience" of sin. In order to be saved he has to see and above all feel in the depths of his being the error of his own sins and those of his fellow men. Going through hell cannot be just a sightseeing trip; it is going into darkness and being affected by it. Sin is contagious. And the pilgrim with all his weakness and blindness is taken there. Only at the summit of purgatory will Vergil announce to him that his free will has been restored and his intellect is sane. But before that he must sympathize with the denizens of hell. He faints out of pity for Francesca da Rimini, a lady who had yielded to the illusions of COURTLY LOVE, become enamored of her brother-in-law, and met death at the hands of her husband. His answer to Farinata, the great Ghibelline leader who had made politics the supreme end of life in substitution for God,

betrays a fierce political pride, deep as the sinner's. In no case does the pilgrim manifest any awareness of the terrifying chasm between those dead souls and God; rather he sympathizes with them. He expresses his willingness to sit for a while with Brunetto, his former teacher, punished as a sodomite; he even says that if it were in his power Brunetto would still be among the living— a way of blaspheming against God's will. The pilgrim is so deeply attracted by Ulysses, the personification of vain curiosity, that he almost plunges into the valley where the sinner is transformed into a wandering flame. Such representation is most suitable to the task of describing the meetings of an infirm soul with the creatures of evil. These creatures speak, act according to their sinful nature, express in all their words the sin that for eternity has taken possession of their lives.

Errors in Interpretation. Unfortunately, much Dante criticism that has been rooted in secular culture has been unable to perceive the sinful character of the personages of Hell. Francesca da Rimini, Farinata, and Ulysses have been seen in a light of beauty and greatness very different from the light in which the poet really saw them. Further, such criticism has mistaken the reactions of Dante, the character of the drama, for the reactions and feelings of sympathy and pity of the poet himself. The general belief is that, while writing his poem, Dante was still entangled with the passions, hopes, and hatreds of the world and inevitably gave expression to these deep impulses of his soul. Francesca, Farinata, Brunetto, and Ulysses, it is said, were persons and symbols dear to his heart despite the fact that they were under God's condemnation. Because of these preconceptions, the *Divina Commedia* has been read rather as a representation of this life and the exaltation of all its passionate, heroic, worldly attachments than as a vision of supernatural reality. To F. de Sanctis, the greatest Italian critic of the 19th century, as well as to C. H. Grandgent and all contemporary Italian critics, Dante appeared and still appears much more excited by the "heroic" suicides of the ancient world than by the martyrdoms of the early Christians.

Such a view of Dante's work is entirely distorted. The sentiments of sympathy, admiration, and devotion expressed by Dante in presence of those in Hell, all the emotions he reveals, belong to the *character* Dante, the infirm, blind soul who is reexperiencing the sinful inclinations of earthly life and is unable to perceive the evil nature of the damned. The *poet* Dante has portrayed past meetings of his own weak and blind soul with the various figures of human perdition. His greatness as a poet consists precisely in the objectivity of this representation and the profundity of his perception of the terrible, often hidden aspects of human wickedness. Francesca, one sees, is the symbol and, at the same time, the victim of the subtle enthrallment of courtly love and the theories of the *dolce stil nuovo;* the man Dante who expresses his deepest pity to her is a person who has passed through the same delusions and now surrenders to the contagious presence of that sin. Farinata is clearly the exponent of a political commitment blind to all the superior values of the soul. Ulysses is the personification of a reason perverted by a vain curiosity directed to a false knowledge. The poet could not be more effective in revealing through the gestures, the words, often very few words, of the personages, and of the pilgrim among them, the sinful situation in which they are.

For one extraordinary moment the characters come forth on the stage of hell, revealing their prides, their stubborn, blind minds, their delusions, and the pilgrim who summoned them forth is with them on their own spiritual level, sharing their evil or unable to understand their depravity. Accordingly, he staggers when he approaches the terrace of sloth in purgatory; he is unable to see in the place of blind anger. Similarly, he will be filled with light and love in paradise. The *Divina Commedia* is the objective, coherent narrative of the ascent of a man from darkness to God; it is something very different from a work in which the author gives voice through his own character to his actual conflicting impulses of vengeance or love, tenderness or hatred.

Theological "Interpolations." From all this it is clear that the passages, especially in the *Paradiso,* that appear to be theological discussions inserted by the poet to communicate to the reader some of the truths that Dante himself had accepted, are by no means interpolations that reveal the poet's personal views. They too belong to the story. It is the personages who reveal in these passages their own understanding of truth and thus help the ascent of the pilgrim. Marco Lombardo's speech in purgatory on the relationship between the empire and the Church, which is always mistaken for the expression of Dante's own ideas and for a philosophical digression, is most evidently the utterance of a Ghibelline spirit, still blinded by worldly political passions and regretting the times of his emperor, Frederick II, still far from the truth that will be revealed in paradise. There is no break in the consistent line of the narrative.

One must look at the whole rigorously unitarian world the poet has represented in order to understand Dante's own vision of the world. With the characteristic medieval love for correspondences, Dante has also made use of some kind of recurring signs in order to direct our attention and to make us understand his point of view. The third canto of the *Inferno* treats of those who were pusillanimous; the third canto of the *Purgatorio* deals with those outside the Church who were courageous; the third canto of *Paradiso* speaks of those who had Christian fortitude. The sixth canto of the *Inferno* depicts citizens prone to greed, gluttony, and civil discord; the sixth canto of the *Purgatorio* speaks of princes who neglected the universal good; the sixth canto of the *Paradiso* presents those who were truly magnanimous and searched for the common good. To Farinata's total blindness correspond the vice of pride in purgatory and the love of wisdom in paradise.

Once the ordering mind behind the work is grasped and account taken of the views expressed in the *Paradiso,* it is clear that Dante's views and sentiments about the moral world, or the relationship between nature and Grace, reason and faith, are entirely consistent with those of St. Thomas.

An Allegorical Poem? It must be made clear, however, that the *Divina Commedia* is far from being a kind of *Summa* put in verse or translated into allegory. There is no more false way of describing Dante's work than to call it an allegorical didactic poem. At the basis of the poem's vision there is indeed a system that matches St. Thomas's in sweep and profundity, but Dante's mentality was not a theologian's. He was concerned with the concrete problems of the world, with persons, with Florence and Italy, with ways to restore the empire. He had rather the mind of a pastor, of a prophet. He judged people, not ideas; he portrayed the life of the Church, and denounced the deficiencies of the leaders of the world; when he did introduce St. Thomas, it was not to have him speak of theology but to deliver a panegyric on St. Francis of Assisi. First of all it must be realized that Dante's vision is essentially a profound and consistent vision of history rivaling St. Augustine's and Vico's; and a vision is not speculative theology. For Dante, God operates through history and in contemplation of the historical process His will can be seen and understood. The development of Rome was clearly in Dante's thought the central line of this divine operation, the mainstream of mankind's salvation. Before and after the Advent, Rome is the place and the temporal institution where the City of God can be built on earth. This emphasis on secular history and politics as an essential foundation of God's kingdom is the most important characteristic of Dante's vision.

The Goal of Christian Unity. In an age when many irrepressible intellectual, political, and economic forces were undermining the universalistic structures on which the civilization of the Middle Ages had rested, Dante was driven by a deep prophetic urge to renew the empire as man's only hope, under God, for salvation. His was the last attempt, or, at least, the final flowering of hope in the possibility of rebuilding, without denying the new autonomous forces of the world, the unity of Christianity as a temporal body directed to the divine goal.

From the point of view of literature, the *Divine Comedy* was the ultimate expression of Gothic aesthetics, and its very characteristics tend toward the multiplicity of elements, the search for correspondences, elevation, difficulty, subtlety, and extreme refinement. Only two decades later PETRARCH was to begin a completely new style, the style of RENAISSANCE.

Bibliography: *Opere: Testo critico della Società dantesca italiana,* ed. M. BARBI et al. (Florence 1921); *La vita nuova,* ed. M. BARBI (Florence 1932), v.1 of Edizione nazionale; *Il convivio,* ed. M. BARBI (new ed. Florence 1934–37), v. 4–5 of *Opere; Rime,* ed. G. CONTINI (Turin 1939); *Divina commedia,* ed. N. SAPEGNO, 3 v. (Milan 1958), ed. G. H. GRANDGENT (rev. ed. Boston 1933). N. ZIN-GARELLI, *La vita, i tempi e le opere di Dante,* 2 v. (Milan 1931). M. APOLLONIO, *Dante: Storia della "Commedia,"* 2 v. (Milan 1950–51). S. A. CHIMENZ, in *Letteratura italiana: I maggiori* (Milan 1956). D. MATTALIA, in *I classici italiani nella storia della critica,* ed. W. BINNI, 2 v. (2d ed. Florence 1960–61). N. D. EVOLA, *Bibliografia dantesca (1920–1930)* (Florence 1932). F. DE SANCTIS, *Saggi critici* (Naples 1866; 3 v., Bari 1952). G. E. PARODI, *Poesia e storia nella Divina commedia* (Naples 1920). B. CROCE, *La poesia di Dante* (2d ed. Bari 1921), Eng. D. AINSLIE (New York 1922). M. BARBI, *Problemi di critica dantesca,* 2 v. (Florence 1934–41). B. NARDI, *Dante e la cultura medievale* (Bari 1942; 2d ed. 1949); *Nel mondo di Dante* (Rome 1944). R. MONTANO, *Suggerimenti per una lettura di Dante* (Naples,1956); *Storia della poesia di Dante,* 2 v. (Naples 1962–63). G. GETTO, ed., *Letture dantesche,* 3 v. (Florence 1958–61). L. MALAGOLI, *Saggio sulla Divina commedia* (Florence 1962). *Studi danteschi* (Florence 1920–). *L'Alighieri* (Rome 1960–). *Annual Report of the Dante Society* (Cambridge, Mass. 1881/82–). *Nuova lectura Dantis* (Rome 1950–) a ser. of individual titles pub. Signorelli. *Lectura Dantis Scaligera* (Florence 1960–) a similar ser. pub. Le Monnier. E. K. RAND and E. H. WIL-KINS, *Dantis Alagherii operum latinorum concordantiae* (Oxford 1912). E. MOORE, *Studies in Dante,* 4 v. (London 1896–1917). P. H. WICKSTEED, *Dante and Aquinas* (New York 1913). C. H. GRAND-GENT, *Dante* (New York 1916). E. G. GARDNER, *Dante* (London 1923). K. VOSSLER, *Medieval Culture,* tr. W. C. LAWTON (New York 1929). J. E. SHAW, *Essays on the Vita nuova* (Princeton, N.J. 1929). C. WILLIAMS, *The Figure of Beatrice* (London 1943). É. H. GILSON, *Dante the Philosopher,* tr. D. MOORE (New York 1949). C. S. SIN-GLETON, *An Essay on the Vita nuova* (Cambridge, Mass. 1949); *Dante Studies,* 2 v. (Cambridge, Mass. 1954–58). A. PASSERIN D'ENTRÈVES, *Dante as a Political Thinker* (Oxford 1952). F. FER-GUSSON, *Dante's Drama of the Mind* (Princeton, N.J. 1953). D. L. SAYERS, *Introductory Papers on Dante* (New York 1954); *Further Paper on Dante* (New York 1957). M. BARBI, *Life of Dante,* ed. and tr. P. RUGGIERS (Berkeley, Calif. 1954). C. T. DAVIS, *Dante and the Idea of Rome* (Oxford 1957). K. FOSTER, *God's Tree* (London 1957). J. A. MAZZEO, *Structure and Thought in the Paradiso* (Ithaca, N.Y. 1957). I. BRANDEIS, *The Ladder of Vision* (Garden City, N.Y. 1960). E. AUERBACH, *Dante, Poet of the Secular World,* tr. R. MAN-HEIM (Chicago 1961). T. K. SWING, *The Fragile Leaves of the Sybil* (Westminster, Md. 1962). A. H. GILBERT, *Dante and His Comedy* (New York 1963). P. J. TOYNBEE, *Dante in English Literature From Chaucer to Cary* (London 1909). T. N. PAGE, *Dante and His Influence* (New York 1922). A. LA PIANA, *Dante's American Pilgrimage* (New Haven 1948). A. L. SELLS, *The Italian Influence in English Poetry from Chaucer to Southwell* (Bloomington, Ind. 1955). W. P. FRIEDERICH, *Dante's Fame Abroad, 1350–1850* (Chapel Hill 1956). Tr. include: *Divine Comedy,* ed. and tr. J. D. SINCLAIR, 3 v. (London 1939–46); *ibid.* tr. L. HOW, 3 v. (New York 1934–40); *ibid.* ed. and tr. H. R. HUSE (New York 1954); *ibid.* ed. and tr. T. G. BER-GIN, 3 v. (pa. New York 1948–54); *ibid.* tr. D. L. SAYERS and B. REY-NOLDS, 3 v. (New York 1962, 1959–62); *Purgatorio,* tr. J. CIARDI (pa. New York 1961); *Inferno,* tr. J. CIARDI (New Brunswick, N.J. 1954); *ibid.* tr. W. CHIPMAN (London 1961); *Monarchy,* tr. D. NICHOLL (New York 1955); *ibid.* tr. H. W. SCHNEIDER (2d ed. New York 1957); *Epistolae,* ed. and tr. P. TOYNBEE (Oxford 1920); *La Vita nuova,* tr. D. G. ROSSETTI, in *The Early Italian Poets* (London 1861) 223–309; *ibid.* tr. M. MUSA (New Brunswick, N.J. 1957); *ibid.* tr. R. W. EMERSON, and ed. J. C. MATHEWS (Chapel Hill 1960); *The Vita nuova and Canzoniere,* tr. T. OKEY and P. H. WICKSTEED (London 1906; repr. 1911); *Odes,* tr. H. S. VERE–HODGE (Oxford 1963).

[R. MONTANO]

DAOISM (TAOISM)

Indigenous Chinese philosophical-religious system that emerged in the dying years of the Zhou (Chou) dynasty; subsequently evolving into diverse schools and sects; significantly influenced Chinese BUDDHISM and Neo-Confucianism. The Chinese generally classify the diverse variations of Daoism within two broad categories: *Daojia* (Philosophical Daoism) and *Daojiao* (Religious Daoism). *Daojia* and *Daojiao* are closely intertwined and do not represent incompatible alternatives, as early 20th century Western scholars once thought.

FOUNDATIONAL PRINCIPLES OF DAOISM

Dao (Tao). Within Chinese cosmology, the *Dao* may be defined as the matrix of all dynamic actualities and potentialities. It encompasses all actualities that are existing and all possibilities that could happen, but exclude all impossibilities. It is a dynamic ontology which simultaneously embodies both "being" and "non-being" in constant, cyclical and evolutionary flux of production and destruction, rather than a static, once-for-all production. Daoists understand the *Dao* as the unnameable ultimate reality that defies all attempts at categorization. It is the source for everything that existed, exists and will exist.

Yin-yang. In Chinese cosmology, yin-yang are two opposite but complementary energies that make manifest and differentiate the "myriad things" (*wan wu*) that emerge into existence from the undifferentiated, primordial *Dao.* The popular symbol of *yin-yang* reveals the cyclical nature of the Chinese worldview—life undergoes cycles of production and destruction. The dynamic interaction of yin and yang give rise to cycles of production and destruction, from which the universe and its diverse forms of life (*wan wu*) emerge. At the height of the cycle of production of one phase, and before the cycle of destruction begins, the seeds for the next cycle of production of the complementary phase emerge. From the constant intermingling of yin and yang, the "Five Elements" (*wu xing*) of water, fire, wood, metal and earth emerge, which in turn gives rise to myriads of forms, history and time. Chinese-Daoist cosmological thought maps all phenomena in pairs of bipolar complementary opposites according to the yin-yang matrix, e.g., male-female, odd-even, active-passive, sun-moon, hot-cool, production-destruction, etc.

Reversion. Daoists also emphasize *reversion,* viz., all things ultimately revert to their primordial, original tranquil state of equilibrium—the *Dao* itself. In Daoist cosmology, once the potentiality of the *Dao* is realized into actuality in various forms of "myriad things" (*wan wu*), it cuts off other potentialities. Therefore, reversion to the *Dao* means to break free of the mundane world to enjoy the unbounded freedom that *Dao* affords. In *Daojiao* (religious Daoism), this unbounded freedom would be understood as immortality.

Meditation. Daoist meditation seeks to break free of all categories of "myriad things" (*wan wu*) to identify one's body and mind with the unbounded freedom of the primordial *Dao*. Daoist meditational practices aim to deconstruct the body and mind from reified actuality back to the fluidity of the potentiality that has yet to reify itself. Deconstruction of one's body and mind is not the end-goal of Daoist meditation. Rather, deconstruction should lead to the construction of an ideal, embryonic self that embodies a perfected body and mind. For this purpose, meditational techniques are often combined with special breathing techniques that regulate the *qi* to refine and nurture this embryonic self, where new potentialities from the *Dao* are being shaped and brought together. When the embryonic self is ready to burst forth, the present physical body (which is perceived as the husk of the embryo) dies, and the embryo is released to travel to the stars, ride the clouds, go through walls, and so forth.

Many Daoist popular sects have popularized meditational practices that visualize different parts of the human body as interior landscapes, paths and parts of countries. Each point of the human body is mentally visualized as being inhabited by a deity, spirit, immortal or demon, all of whom have their own independent existence. According to Daoist cosmology, death is seen as the release and dispersal of these beings from the human body. Hence, meditational techniques are used to recruit them to serve oneself, to use them to obtain revelations, scriptures, talismans, or even to bribe them or kill them (in the case of the "Three Corpses" or *san shi*—see Daoist Alchemy below).

PHILOSOPHICAL DAOIM (*DAOJIA*)

Philosophical Daoism (*Daojia*) emerged during the period of the Hundred Schools (*Bai jia*) as an advocate of a naturalistic philosophy that emphasized the artificiality of human institutions, and promoted the abandonment of worldly pursuits in favor of an accommodation with the natural flow of things in the world. Although its principal goal is the attainment of *wuwei* ("non-action"), which it shared in common with Legalism, Daoist philosophers interpreted *wuwei* as the mode of being and action that seeks to flow with the grain of the *Dao* (Tao, "Way") in bringing manifest forms into actuality from primordial flux. *Wuwei* was understood not as the total lack of activity, but rather active inactivity that would allow the *Dao* (Tao) to run its course and unveil all potentialities to their fullest without any human interference. Thus, *wuwei* is the opposite of "calculated or intentional action" that limits the fullest range of potentialities. While it is true that some Daoists were attracted to the eremitical lifestyle of permanent contemplation of nature of the type that the Daoist philosopher ZHUANGZI (CHUANG-TZU) had advocated, many Chinese intellectuals found in philosophical Daoism (*Daojia*) a source of spiritual comfort and renewal in the stressful pressures of Confucian officialdom, especially in the midst of sociopolitical upheavals.

Principal canonical texts of *Daojia*. The three principal texts of *Daojia* are the *Daodejing* (Tao Te Ching), attributed by tradition to the mythical LAOZI (LAO-TZU) the *Zhuangzi* (Chuang-Tzu), written by the Daoist philosopher ZHUANGZI (CHUANG-TZU) and *Huainanzi* (Huainan Tzu), a 2nd century B.C. work written by Daoist philosophers at the court of Liu An (circa 179–122 B.C.), the king of Huainan.

***Daodejing* (Tao Te Ching).** Some scholars have questioned the attribution of the great Han dynasty historian Sima Qian (Ssu-ma Ch'ien) of the authorship of the *Daodejing* (Tao Te Ching) to Laozi, as there is no mention of an author in all extant versions of the *Daodejing*. Sima Qian had recounted a legend in which Laozi, weary of living and heading westward in search of wisdom, penned down his philosophy in a work that would be later known as the *Daodejing* (Tao Te Ching) at request of the "Keeper of the Pass" (i.e., frontier guard). Contemporary textual analysis of the received text points to the existence of several redactional layers. Although the received text is traditionally divided into 81 chapters of 5,000 characters, the earliest extant manuscripts—the *Guodian* text (circa 300 B.C.) and the *Mawangdui*, (*Mawang Tui*) texts (168 B.C.), while preserving the contents of the work albeit in an inverted order, suggest that the original was probably a continuous work of some 5,400 characters, in all likelihood written or edited by a single author.

The *Daodejing* presents the *Dao* (*Tao*) as a nameless, undefinable, spontaneous, eternal, cyclical and ever-changing cosmological essence. It advocates that one engages in "non-action" (*wu-wei*) to be in harmony with the *Dao*. The utopian society which the *Daodejing* presents is one of harmony between ruler-and-ruled, in which the Sage-Ruler embodies "*wu-wei*" as a way of governing, viz., governing behind the scenes in a manner that the subjects are not even aware that they are being governed. The remarkable similarities of the *Daodejing*'s political philosophy to the Legalists' position, shorn of its autocratic leanings, has led many scholars to speculate a link between the two. Such an interpretation appears to be supported by the *Mawangdui*, and *Guodian* manuscripts that invert the traditional order of the received text, beginning with the section on political philosophy rather than the metaphysical section.

Zhuangzi (**Chuang-tzu**). An important *Daojia* text written by Zhuangzi (Chuang-Tzu, circa 370–286 B.C.). While the text of Zhuangzi shares much in common with the *Daodejing* on the cosmological and metaphysical frameworks of *Daojia*, Zhuangzi differs from *Daodejing* in one significant area—he champions an anarchistic, spontaneous and subversive approach to life and statecraft that rejects participation in politics in favor of a withdrawal to an eremitical and naturalistic lifestyle of harmony with the *Dao*. Zhuangzi highlights the relativity and impermanence of "myriad things" (*wan wu*), and therefore the insignificance of all human action in the world. Rather than wasting time on statecraft and politics, one should focus instead on the harmony of oneself with the *Dao*. Indeed, Zhuangzi claimed that he would rather be "a living tortoise dragging its tail in the mud, than a gilded but dead tortoise venerated in the ancestral shrine of the King of Chu." This illustration dispels the typical misconception of Zhuangzi as an advocate for hedonism and selfishness. Zhuangzi was more concerned with the freedom to do what came most naturally within the natural ordering of things in the *Dao,* and a tortoise dragging its tail in the mud best exemplified that natural ordering.

Huainanzi (**Huai-nan Tzu**). This 2nd century B.C. *Daojia* text is important for giving its readers a glimpse into the swirling, intellectual debates during the later years of the Hundred Schools (*Baijia*). It is primarily an apologetical work that seeks to present *Daojia* as superior over the other schools such as Confucianism, Legalism, Moism, etc. It originally comprised 54 chapters—21 inner chapters on the superior *Daojia* and 33 outer chapters on inferior rival schools, the latter chapters no longer extant today. Its principal significance lies in its advocacy of an alternative philosophical framework for social ordering and statecraft based on *Daojia*.

RELIGIOUS DAOISM (*DAOJIAO*)

Daojiao is a broad category encompassing diverse Daoist popular sects that emerged from the Han Dynasty onwards. In contrast to the focus of *Daojia* (philosophical Daoism) on individualistic introspection and contemplation, the diverse religious sects of *Daojiao* are generally institutional in structure, replete with a hierarchically ordered priesthood, scriptural texts, liturgical ceremonies, purification and exorcism rituals, talismans, divination, as well as pantheons of greater and lesser deities.

Celestial Masters Sect. The oldest and most prominent Daoist popular sect is the Celestial Masters Sect that was founded in 142 A.D. by Zhang Daoling (Chang Taoling), who claimed to have received a revelation of the Dao from *Taishang Laojun,* the Highest Venerable Lord who was also the deified Laozi (Lao-Tzu). The Celestial Masters sect continues to be the largest Daoist popular sect in the 21st century, with a huge following in Taiwan, Hong Kong and in the many Chinese diasporas scattered throughout the world.

Shangqing (*Shang Ching*) **Sect.** The second Daoist sect that emerged was the *Shangqing* (*Shang Ching*, "Highest Clarity") sect that emerged from a series of apparitions of the immortalized Lady Wei (251–334 A.D.) to the medium *Yang Xi* (*Yang Hsi*) in the period 364–370 A.D. In these apparitions, Lady Wei was reputed to have dictated the scriptures that would later form the core of the *Shangqing* corpus of canonical texts. The *Shangqing* sect gained many adherents among the Chinese intelligentsia and aristocracy, in contrast to the Celestial Masters sect's popularity among the masses. *Shangqing* scriptures played a major role in developing the classical artistic and literary conventions, especially in Tang China (618–906 A.D.), when the sect reached the zenith of its influence.

Quest for Immortality. The common thread running through the diverse Daoist popular sects is the quest for immortality within the *Dao*. Within *Daojiao*, immortality means more than a mere indefinite prolongation of one's mundane life. It is also a yearning for a better life that is commonly described in terms of an achievement of complete and unfettered freedom to move in harmony with the *Dao*. In this regard, classical Daoist metaphors speak of the ability to ride the clouds, breathe under water, go through walls, etc. Immortality also encompasses a transformation of one's mind to be always attuned to, and completely engaged with, the present. Various Daoist sects emphasized a diverse range of techniques for attaining immortality, understood either literally or metaphorically, or as a prolonging of life. These techniques include: internal and external alchemic practices (see below, under "Daoist Alchemy"), the dietary practice of grain avoidance, gymnastic or sexual exercises, meditation and breathing exercises to regulate the flow of *qi,* and revelations from immortals, i.e., humans who transcended the limitations of human mortality.

Daoist Alchemy. Among the diverse Daoist techniques for attaining immortality, alchemy is perhaps the most significant. Within the many Daoist popular sects, alchemy was practiced in an attempt to transform the Daoist adept into an immortal through the ingestion of the "elixir of immortality" (*dan*). Within *Daojiao* (religious Daoism), two types of alchemic practices may be distinguished: *wai dan* ("external alchemy") and *nei dan* ("internal alchemy"). *Wai dan* seeks to concoct elixirs of immortality in specially constructed laboratories for ingestion by the Daoist adept, while *nei dan* seeks to achieve the same through the adept's *inner* practices of meditation and strict ascetical lifestyle that manipulate what is already present in the adept's body. Both *wai dan* and *nei dan* presupposes the adept's faith (i.e., it is going to work), purity (i.e., moral and ritual cleansing) and consecration (i.e., a wholehearted dedication to the quest for immortality).

Wai dan ("external alchemy") was developed by *fangshi* (*fang-shih*, "prescription masters"), the heirs to the ancient shamans, metallurgists, smelters and magicians. Its theoretical foundations emerged from a combination of the yin-yang cosmological matrix with the "Five Elements" (*wu xing*). Physical immortality of the body was the primary goal of the practitioners of *wai dan*, who had hoped to transmute the highly toxic cinnabar (mercuric sulphide or red ochre) into the elixir of immortality. The use of cinnabar in Daoist alchemy arose out of homological thinking that sought to connect the cinnabar's red color with blood, and its transformation into liquid mercury "quicksilver" with the vitality of human semen, the source of new life. The outstanding Daoist *wai dan* master, Ge Hong (Ko Hung, 261–341 A.D.) wrote the 4th century Daoist classical *wai dan* alchemical text called *Baopuzi* (*Pao-p'u tzu*, "Book of the Master who embraces simplicity"), a work which provides recipes on the transmutation of alchemical cinnabar into the elixir of immortality. By the end of the Tang dynasty, *wai dan* had declined and died out, as Daoist adepts began to realize the extreme toxicity of the metals they were experimenting with.

Nei dan ("internal alchemy") gained popularity towards the end of the Tang Dynasty, when *wai dan* fell into disuse. Attention shifted to applying alchemical theories to the body using homological thinking and using techniques of meditation, breathing, dieting, body and sexual exercises. During this period, the texts of *wai dan* were reinterpreted to refer to the interior of the human body. The raw materials of external alchemy were substituted, using homologous thinking, by the three treasures of semen, vital and spirit energy. The body became the laboratory where the elixir of immortality was produced. The *dan tian* ("fields of cinnabar") was identified with the three regions of the human body—head, heart and abdomen. These three regions were the center of life, but they were also inhabited by the three corpses (*san shi*) whose principal goal was to hasten death. Popular Daoist thought held that at birth, a person is allotted a limited lifespan, which could be extended or subtracted. The three corpses were three celestial spies who lived in the three "fields of cinnabar" (*dan tian*) in the human body. They leave their human host on the completion of every sixty-day cycle to report to the Jade Emperor on the moral conduct of their human hosts. Based upon their reports, the Jade Emperor would either extend their human hosts' lives for good deeds, or subtract years for evil deeds. Popular Daoist piety evolved three ways of dealing with the three corpses: (i) do good deeds, so that the three corpses have nothing but good things to report, (ii) kill the three corpses by the dietary practice of grain avoidance, and (iii) keeping awake on the sixtieth night, so that the three corpses would be unable to escape to make their reports.

See Also: CHINESE PHILOSOPHY; CHINESE RELIGIONS; CONFUCIANISM AND NEO-CONFUCIANISM.

Bibliography: W. T. CHAN, *A Source Book in Chinese Philosophy* (Princeton 1964). T. CLEARY, *Vitality, Energy, Spirit: A Taoist Sourcebook* (Boston 1991). K. DEWOSKIN, *Doctors, Diviners, and Magicians of Ancient China: Biographies of Fang-shih* (New York 1983). A. C. GRAHAM, *Disputers of the Tao: Philosophical Argument in Ancient China* (La Salle, IL 1989). L. KOHN, ed., *Taoist Meditation and Longevity Techniques* (Ann Arbor 1989). L. KOHN, *Early Chinese Mysticism: Philosophy and Soteriology in the Taoist Tradition* (Princeton 1992); *The Taoist Experience: An Anthology* (Albany, NY 1993). J. LAGERWAY, *Taoist Ritual in Chinese Society and History* (New York 1987). M. LOEWE, *Ways to Paradise: The Chinese Quests for Immortality* (London 1979). H. MASPERO, *Taoism and Chinese Religion* (Amherst 1981). I. ROBINET, *Taoist Meditation* (Albany, NY 1993). K. SCHIPPER, *The Taoist Body* (Berkeley, CA 1993). B. I. SCHWARTZ, *The World of Thought in Ancient China* (Cambridge, MA 1985). N. SIVIN, *Chinese Alchemy: Preliminary Studies* (Cambridge, MA 1968). H. WELCH, and A. SEIDEL, eds. *Facets of Taoism: Essays in Chinese Religion* (New Haven 1979). E. WONG, *Seven Taoist Masters* (Boston 1990); *The Shambhala Guide to Taoism* (Boston 1997).

[J. Y. TAN]

DAQUIN, LOUIS CLAUDE

Popular keyboard composer of the late French baroque; b. Paris, July 4, 1694; d. there, July 15, 1772. The family was of Jewish ancestry and took its surname from Aquino, where one of its members, a rabbi of Avignon, was baptized. During the 17th century, this family contributed several distinguished men to French public life. Louis Claude was a godson of Elisabeth Jacquet de La Guerre, who probably instructed him. At six he played before Louis XIV, and at eight he studied with Marchand. Like Marchand, Daquin became a master of improvisation and was praised by his rival RAMEAU as well as by Bédos de Celles. Always associated with Parisian churches, Daquin was appointed to the royal chapel in 1739 and to Notre Dame a few years later. In 1735 he published his *Piéces de clavecin*, which includes a number of descriptive or programmatic pieces such as the rondeau "The Swallow." His second collection, *Livre de Noëls*, contains variations on popular Christmas tunes for organ or harpsichord with instruments. As was the custom with French rococo organists, Daquin depended on his instrument for expressive effects, and hence indicated precise registration.

Bibliography: Works. *Livre de clavecin* (Paris 1735), ed. P. BRUNOLD and H. EXPERT; *Livre de noëls in Archives des maîtres de l'orgue*, ed. A. GUILMANT, v.3 (Paris 1900). Literature. N. DOUFOURCQ, *La Musique d'orgue française de Jehan Titelouze à Jehan Alain* (2d ed. Paris 1949). F. RAUGEL, *Die Musik in Geschichte und Gegenwart*, ed. F. BLUME (Kassel-Basel 1949–) 3:1–2; *Les Organistes* (Paris 1923). A. PIRRO, *Les Clavecinistes* (Paris 1924). *Histoire de la musique*, ed. ROLAND-MANUEL 2 v. (Paris 1960–63) v.1. K. G. FELLERER, *The History of Catholic Church Music*, tr. F. A. BRUNNER (Baltimore 1961). M. F. BUKOFZER, *Music in the Baroque Era* (New York 1947). E. HIGGINBOTTOM, "Louis-Claude Daquin" *The New Grove Dictionary of Music and Musicians, vol. 5*, ed. S. SADIE (New York 1980) 238–239. J.-P. MONTAGNIER, *La Vie et L'Œuvre de Louis-Claude Daquin (1694–1772)* (Lyon 1992). D. M. RANDEL, ed., *The Harvard Biographical Dictionary of Music* 196 (Cambridge, Massachusetts 1996). N. SLONIMSKY, ed., *Baker's Biographical Dictionary of Musicians, Eighth Edition* (New York 1992) 391.

[D. BEIKMAN]

DARBOY, GEORGES

Archbishop of Paris, author; b. Fays-Billot (Haute-Marne), France, Jan. 16, 1813; d. Paris, May 24, 1871. Of humble birth, he was ordained (1836), became curate at St. Dizier (1837) and professor at the major seminary in Langres (1839–45), chaplain at the Lycée Henri IV, Paris (1845), honorary vicar-general of Paris (1852), and prothonotary apostolic and archdeacon of St. Denis (1855). In addition to his ecclesiastical duties in Paris, he translated (1845) the works of the Pseudo-Dionysius the Areopagite whose authenticity he accepted, and the *Imitation of Christ,* with reflections (1852). He composed *Les Femmes de la Bible* (1846–49) and *Les Saintes femmes* (1851), which went through several editions, and also *Vie de Saint Thomas Becket* (1858), and other works. He became bishop of Nancy (1859) and archbishop of Paris (Jan. 16, 1863). Darboy was a pious and dedicated bishop, but in the tradition of GALLICANISM, an upholder of episcopal independence of Rome. His unwarranted attempt to make canonical visitations of the houses of the

Jesuits and Capuchins in his diocese drew a severe letter from Rome (1865).

At VATICAN COUNCIL I Darboy was one of the most influential members of the minority group opposed to the definition of papal infallibility. He spoke against its opportuneness, and appeared to oppose it also on doctrinal grounds. Together with Bishop DUPANLOUP he sought unsuccessfully the aid of the French Emperor Napoleon III to block the discussion in the Council. Darboy joined the group that left Rome on the eve of the final vote (July 18, 1871) to avoid participation in it. After the definition was approved, he subscribed to it. Darboy conducted himself with heroism during the Prussian siege of Paris (1870–71) and refused to exile himself when the communards gained control of the city. He was arrested, held as a hostage, and shot in the prison yard of La Roquette while blessing his executioners.

Bibliography: J. A. GUILLERMIN, *Vie de Mgr. Darboy* (Paris 1888). J. A. FOULON, *Histoire de la vie et des oeuvres de Mgr. Darboy* (Paris 1889). C. BUTLER, *The Vatican Council,* 2 v. (New York 1930). A. DANSETTE, *Religious History of Modern France,* tr. J. DINGLE, 2 v. (New York 1961). A. LARGENT, *Dictionnaire de théologie catholique,* ed. A. VACANT et al. (Paris 1903–50) 4.1:141–144. F. GUÉDON, *Dictionnaire d'histoire et de géographie ecclésiastiques,* ed. A. BAUDRILLART et al. (Paris 1912–) 14:84–86.

[R. W. REICHERT]

DARBY, JOHN NELSON

Chief organizer of the PLYMOUTH BRETHREN; b. London, Nov. 18, 1800; d. Bournemouth, April 29, 1882. A graduate of Trinity College, Dublin (1819), he was admitted to the Irish bar (1822), and ordained as a priest in the Church of ENGLAND (*c.* 1826). He served briefly as a curate but left this body because of his objections to denominational differences, creeds, and a regular ministry. In Dublin he joined with a group of Christians (1828) to study the Bible and to meet for prayer and a weekly communion service. Another such brotherhood met at Plymouth and from that city the movement took the name Plymouth Brethren. In 1838 Darby left for Switzerland and France to spread his ideas; he did not return to England until 1845. His return split the Plymouth Brethren in England into two factions and began the fragmentation that has since characterized this movement. The first two groups were the Darbyites or Exclusive Brethren, and the Bethesda or Open Brethren. Darby served the movement as evangelist, editor, and writer until his death. He visited Germany, the U.S., Canada, Italy, New Zealand, and the West Indies on preaching missions. For many years he edited the *Christian Witness,* the main organ of the Brethren. The Plymouth Brethren disagreed among themselves on various positions but they did agree that all

Christians have the right to preach the Gospel and to administer the sacraments. They constantly urged a return to New Testament practices and rejected denominationalism, creeds, a paid ministry, and church titles.

In addition to his role in the organization of the Plymouth Brethren, Darby was the first to systematize and promote DISPENSATIONAL THEOLOGY. Among the features of dispensationalism that he popularized were the division of history into several time frames or dispensations, the separation of God's plan for his people into two different programs, one for Israel and one the Church, and the anticipation of a secret RAPTURE or a snatching away of all true Christians from the earth prior to the great tribulation and second coming of Christ. As a result of Darby's travels to North America from 1862 to 1877, dispensationalism became a mainstay of the teaching of many evangelical and fundamentalist pastors.

Bibliography: J. N. DARBY, *Collected Writings*, ed. W. KELLY, 34 v. (London 1867–1900), plus Index (1902). G. C. BOASE, *The Dictionary of National Biography from the Earliest Times to 1900*, 63 v. (London 1885–1900; repr. with corrections, 21 v., 1908–09, 1921–22, 1938; suppl. 1901–) 5:493–494. W. G. TURNER, *John Nelson Darby* (London 1926). L. V. CRUTCHFIELD, *The Doctrine of Ages and Dispensations* (Ph.D. diss. Drew University, 1985).

[W. J. WHALEN/W. T. STANCIL]

D'ARCY, MARTIN CYRIL

English Jesuit lecturer and author; b. Bath, 1888; d. London, Nov. 20, 1976. He was educated at Stonyhurst and joined the Society of Jesus in 1906. He read for a classical degree at Oxford (1912–16), taught at Stonyhurst (1916–19), and was ordained in 1921. Later he went to Rome for a biennium in philosophy. From 1927 he was at Oxford as researcher and lecturer, then as Master of Campion Hall (1933). D'Arcy succeeded Fr. Cyril Martindale as the dominant Catholic radio speaker on BBC. During World War II he lectured in the U.S. and in Portugal at the request of the British government. In 1945 he was appointed provincial of the English Jesuits and took up residence at Farm Street, London, where he remained for the rest of his life. His term of office ended in 1950. In 1953 he lectured in the Far East (some of his works have been translated into Japanese) and from 1956 until the early 1970s lectured annually for some months in the U.S.

D'Arcy's outstanding books include: *The Mass and the Redemption* (1926); *Catholicism* (1927); *Christ as Priest and Redeemer* (1928); *The Spirit of Charity* (1929); *Thomas Aquinas* (1930); *Christ and the Modern Mind* (1930); *The Nature of Belief* (1931); *Mirage and Truth* (1935); *Death and Life* (1942); *The Mind and Heart of Love* (1945); *Communism and Christianity* (1956); *The Problem of Evil* (1957); *The Sense of History, Secular and Sacred* (1959); *No Absent God* (1962); *Facing God* (1966); *Facing the People* (1968); *Facing the Truth* (1969); and *Humanism and Christianity* (1971).

D'Arcy's originality lay in his gift for integrating the beliefs and experiences of others into a new enlightenment, his refusal, as one critic put it, to leave them scattered on the ground for the birds to pick at. The essential D'Arcy appeared in *The Mind and Heart of Love* in which he sought a clue to the working of the human spirit in the duality running through creation and experience: the active and passive, egoism and sacrifice, the classical and the romantic, life and death, masculine and feminine, the dominant and the recessive, Eros and Agapē, the lion and the unicorn: *animus,* the reason dominating passion, *anima,* the great longing, the breakaway of desire from self.

In *The Sense of History* D'Arcy rejected the cruder forms of the providential theory and did not attempt to verify the rise and fall of historic societies against theology. He argued, however, that out of God's Revelation and man's relation with God something could be garnered to illuminate man and his development through the ages, and to enlarge the vision of human effort and achievement. Bringing sacred and profane wisdom together, he saw human history working towards a communal fulfilment in Christ. His position was that Christians could see more in history than others and point to its destination. The historian or philosopher equipped with Christian insight could dig deeper into the evidence.

[H. KAY]

DARIUS I, KING OF PERSIA

Reigned 522 to 486 B.C., known as "the Great"; b. 550. Darius (Old Persian *dārayavahuš,* Hebrew and Aramaic *dārᵉyāweš,* Greek Δαρεῖος) was a son of the satrap of Persia, Hystaspes, an Achaemenian prince distantly related to CYRUS the Great and Cambyses II. The principal sources for his reign are his own inscriptions, especially the great trilingual (Old Persian, Elamite, and Akkadian) Behistun Inscription. As a member of the royal bodyguard he accompanied Cambyses II on his conquest of Egypt (525–522). In spring or summer of 522, as the Persian army was returning from Egypt, the King died under mysterious circumstances (accident or suicide), and his throne was occupied by a man who claimed to be Bardiya (Smerdis), the son of Cyrus and brother of Cambyses. Darius hurried to Media, killed the new King, and seized the throne. He justified his action by claiming that the

Darius I. (©Gianni Dagli Orti/CORBIS)

man was not Bardiya, whom he said had been secretly murdered by Cambyses before the Egyptian campaign, but one Gaumata, a member of the powerful Magian priesthood. Darius spent the next two years putting down uncoordinated revolts that rocked the sprawling empire.

Even though Judah was apparently not directly involved in these disturbances, its dormant messianic hopes were awakened, and it believed that the present upheaval of the kingdom of this world was heralding the future kingdom of God, and that Zerubbabel, King Jehoiachin's grandson, who was then governor of Judah, would restore the Kingdom of Israel (Zec 6.9–15). The Prophets Haggai and Zechariah used these hopes as a stimulus to spur the people to resume the rebuilding of the Temple destroyed by Nebuchadnezzar in 587. Judah was one of many small political units within the fifth satrapy [*ăbar-nahărā*, beyond (i.e., west of) the (Euphrates) River]. Obstructionist elements within the satrapy forced the satrap Thathanai (Tattcnai) to obtain proof of Darius's approval of the construction; in 519 Darius reaffirmed the earlier decree of Cyrus, encouraging the construction to continue (Ezra ch. 5–6). This, as well as other indications, show that Darius, although an ardent Zoroastrian [*see* ZOROASTER (ZARATHUSHTRA)] continued the enlightened religious policies of Cyrus.

Darius was also, like Cyrus, a highly successful administrator and legislator. His law code (''the irrevocable laws of the Medes and the Persians'': Dn 6.9, 13, 16) laid the basis on which his empire survived for almost two centuries. He was less successful as a military leader, and every schoolboy knows of the defeat that the Greeks inflicted on him at Marathon in 491. He was succeeded by his son Xerxes I (486–464).

The ''Darius the Persian'' mentioned in Neh 12.22 is probably Darius II Nothus (423–404). In 1 Mc 1.1 mention is made of Darius III (335–330), whom Alexander the Great overthrew. The historically impossible figure of ''Darius the Mede'' of the Book of DANIEL is essentially based on the character of Darius I, even though he is regarded as the predecessor of Cyrus the Great (Dn 5.1) and called ''the son of Xerxes'' (Dn 9.1).

Bibliography: A. T. E. OLMSTEAD, *History of the Persian Empire: Achaemenid Period* (Chicago 1948). J. BUCHANAN, *The Cambridge Ancient History* (London and New York 1923–39) 4:20–25. L. W. KING and R. C. THOMPSON, *The Sculptures and Inscription of Darius the Great on the Rock of Behistûn in Persia* (London 1907). R. MAYER, *Lexikon für Theologie und Kirche*, ed. J. HOFER and K. RAHNER (2d, new ed. Freiburg 1957–65) 3:165–166. *Encyclopedia Dictionary of the Bible*, tr. and adap. by L. HARTMAN (New York 1963) from A. VAN DEN BORN, *Bijbels Woordenboek* 490–493.

[E. A. BALLMANN]

DARK AGES

The Dark Ages is a designation for the medieval period, usually in a derogatory sense. In its widest application the term embraces the epoch from the 6th to the 15th centuries. Renaissance humanists were responsible for the concept of a *medium aevum* (e.g., Flavio BIONDO), by which they understood a negligible interval during which classical literature was totally neglected. They contrasted their own passionate interest in man as man with the occasionally vain speculations of late medieval philosophy, their own anthropocentrism with the alleged theocentrism—unfortunately, to the medievalist usually more apparent than real—of medieval man. Even Martin LUTHER considered the MIDDLE AGES of no value to Christianity itself, insisting on the need for a return to its sources, free of medieval adulterations.

The 17th and 18th centuries continued the attack on the Middle Ages as part of the religious controversy, intensified by the Enlightenment, Modernism, and nationalistic movements, such as the Risorgimento and the Kulturkampf. Romanticism, with its insistence on the return to national origins, helped to open up the medieval period to serious study with the happiest results. Scientific historical research uncovered the rich developments of the Middle Ages in the fields of technology (e.g., the wheeled plow, the horse collar and shoe, crank motion, and soap); philosophy (SCHOLASTICISM); literature, both Latin and vernacular; art (Romanesque and Gothic); and music (GREGORIAN CHANT, organum, and counterpoint). Evidence of the development in the high Middle Ages of enduring political, educational, and economic institutions of such apparent modernity as constitutional government, the jury system, university education, and banking have caused some scholars to reset the boundaries of the Dark Ages (e.g., 5th to 11th centuries in F. L. Cross, *The Oxford Dictionary of the Christian Church* [London 1957] 373), and have led others to say that ''the six centuries following the collapse of the Roman Empire are . . . dark through the insufficiency of historical evidence'' (F. M. Stenton). The term could be less inappropriately applied to the chaotic period following the Germanic invasions (376–568), which accentuated a sharp economic, social, and cultural decline already begun in the third century. Even so, M. L. W. Laistner's study of the years 500 to 900 reveals a period of ceaseless, if not universal, intellectual activity.

Bibliography: A. DOVE, ''Der Streit um das Mittelalter,'' *Historische Zeitschrift* 116 (1916) 209–230. P. LEHMANN, *Vom Mittelalter und von der lateinischen Philologie des Mittelalters* (Munich 1914); *Erforschung des Mittelalters*, 4 v. (2d ed. Stuttgart 1959–61). M. L. W. LAISTNER, *Thought and Letters in Western Europe, A.D. 500 to 900* (2d ed. New York 1957), *passim.* H. WOLTER,

Lexikon für Theologie und Kirche, ed. J. HOFER and K. RAHNER, 10 v. (d, new ed. Freiburg 1957–65) 9:206–207.

[C. M. AHERNE]

DARK NIGHT OF THE SOUL

St. John of the Cross, taking the expression "dark night" from his poem of that name uses it as a literary figure of the journey toward divine union that he expounds in his works the *Ascent of Mount Carmel* and *Dark Night of the Soul.* He employs the term, according to his explicit testimony, as a metaphor, likening this journey to a dark night, and thus builds his systematic exposition of the development of the spiritual life upon this likeness. As night involves the privation of light, the journey to union entails the privation of everything contrary to perfect love of God. Through a synecdoche that has become common, however, he often calls the particular periods of passive purification "the dark night of the soul." But in the poem itself, the dark night, in the opinion of many commentators, is a symbol of the saint's mystical experience within the period of his ultimate purification, an experience that cannot be adequately expressed through concepts.

See Also: PURIFICATION, SPIRITUAL.

[K. KAVANAUGH]

DAROWSKA, MARCELINA KOTOWICZ, BL.

In religion Maria Marcelina; widow, cofounder of the Sisters of the Immaculate Conception of Mary (*Niepokalanki*); b. Jan. 16, 1827, Szulaki, Podolia, Ukraine; d. Jan. 5, 1911, Jazłowiec, Ukraine. Although Marcelina Kotowicz expressed a desire to enter religious life, her dying father made her promise that she would marry. She fulfilled her pledge in 1849 by marrying Karol Darowski and bore him two children before his death three years later. Her son died the next year. In 1854, Marcelina traveled to Rome, where she met Resurrectionist Father Hieronim Kajsiewicz, who became her spiritual director, and through him met Josephine Karska, with whom she founded (1857) the Congregation of the Sisters of the Immaculate Conception of the Blessed Virgin Mary. After Josephine's death in 1860, Marcelina moved her four sisters to Jazłowiec (Archdiocese of Lviv [now Ukraine]), where the congregation opened its first school for girls (Nov. 1, 1863) without the approbation of the state. Dissatisfied with the quality of available textbooks, Mother Marcelina purchased a printing press in

1901 and began publishing books written by the sisters. When government authorities attempted to regulate the subjects taught, Marcelina threatened to close the schools and alter the 1867 constitutions to create a contemplative order. Despite these problems and other difficulties with governmental authorities, at the time of her death the Sisters of the Immaculate Conception had seven convents, each of which ran a school for girls. In 1882, Marcelina commissioned Tomasz Oskar Sosnowski to sculpt an image of the Immaculate Conception, which became famous as "Our Lady of Jazłowiec," an object of national veneration. More than 200 sisters continue Marcelina's work of forming Christian women in Poland, the Ukraine, and Belarus. She was beatified by Pope John Paul II on Oct. 6, 1996.

Feast: Jan. 6 (Lviv).

Bibliography: E. JABLONSKA–DEPTULA, *Marcelina Darowska niepokalanka* (Lublin 1996). M. A. SOLTAN, *Czlowiek wielkich pragnien: matka Marcelina Darowska* (Szymanów 1978).

[K. I. RABENSTEIN]

DARWIN, CHARLES ROBERT

Naturalist and evolutionist; b. Shrewsbury, England, Feb. 12, 1809; d. Down, England, April 19, 1882. Darwin's father, Robert, and grandfather, Erasmus (1731–1802), were prominent physicians, the latter a minor writer on evolution; his maternal grandfather, Josiah Wedgwood (1730–95), was the famous porcelain manufacturer. Background and wealth predisposed Charles to become a physician. He had no formal training in the sciences and never held a salaried position in them, yet his fame rests on his scientific writings; he rarely appeared in public, yet he became both well known and controversial; he was a semi-invalid, yet his scholarly output was phenomenal. Uniquely, his inheritance of wealth and his chronic illness granted him valuable independence and isolation.

Voyage of the *Beagle*. Darwin, after his preliminary schooling at Shrewsbury, was sent (1825) to the University of Edinburgh to study medicine; thoroughly disliking the program, he transferred to Cambridge (1828–31) to prepare for the ministry. Neither institution trained him in science because at the time the sciences were considered unimportant components of the curriculum and were not even included in the university examinations. Darwin's penchant for natural history was satisfied by personal contacts with scientists, especially geologist Adam Sedgwick (1785–1873) and botanist John Henslow (1796–1861), both of whom invited him on their field excursions.

Native interest fashioned Darwin into a self-made scientist. From his youth he had been an ardent beetle collector and an avid hunter of small game. His major exposure to nature was, however, a completely fortuitous event. After his Cambridge studies he was offered the post of naturalist aboard the *Beagle,* a government-sponsored cartographic ship, but only after two older scientists had refused.

The *Beagle's* assignment to the South American coastline required five years (1831–36). Darwin's experiences, especially his visits to such islands as the Galápagos and Tierra del Fuego, were startlingly new. Official duties provided many port calls and other delays that allowed him to travel inland to observe and collect varied data and specimens. His notes included perspicacious details on the flora, fauna, geology, and ecology of this new world. Here, according to his diary, his tenets on special creation of species were first shaken by the array of organic modification and adaptation and by the ensuing taxonomic confusion of species. That each of several islands had a unique species of birds created especially for it seemed incredible.

The *Beagle* returned to England in October 1836. Darwin soon married (1839) his first cousin, Emma Wedgwood, and settled in London, moving later (1842) to Down, where he spent the remainder of his life. In a spacious home surrounded by gardens and orchards, he occupied his days in methodical study, experiment, and extensive correspondence. Routine was frequently interrupted, however, by long periods of physical wretchedness, probably psychogenic.

Zoological Works. Contributions to serial publications, forwarded to England from the *Beagle,* had already gained respect for Darwin. Publication of *The Voyage of the Beagle* (1840), a well-received account of his observations, comments, analyses, and opinions, further identified him favorably with natural sciences. The mere arrangement of his *Beagle* notes and the disposition of the specimens collected to appropriate institutions required several additional years. Within this unwieldy project he met the problem of barnacle taxonomy. His exacting standards drew him into a detailed study of these Crustacea (1846–54) and led to the publication of *A Monograph of the Cirripedia* (1851, 1854). During these years, known only to a few colleagues, e.g., J. D. Hooker (1817–1911) and Charles Lyell (1797–1875), he had been gathering data to support his rising contention that species are mutable, and that in their mutability some are favored to better survive the rigors of environment.

Although as a student he had readily accepted the theology of fundamentalist William Paley (1743–1805) and had skeptically read Erasmus Darwin's allusions to

Charles Darwin.

evolution and Lamarck's ideas on "the tendency to progression," further reading influenced him differently. Aboard the *Beagle* he had been deeply impressed by Charles Lyell's new departure in his *Principles of Geology* (3 v. 1830–33). Lyell believed that the world, in its formation, had been subjected to the same laws now in operation and that these laws usually produced changes gradually and continuously. In fact, he held that these changes are even now imperceptibly taking place. Gradual change, Lyell emphasized, is the hallmark of nature.

In 1838 Darwin read T. MALTHUS's *An Essay on the Principle of Population* (5th ed. 1817), which advanced the proposition that all species produce more living offspring than can be supported by the economy of nature. Hence there is unending natural attrition, the reward of survival going only to the best-suited individuals. These two theses Darwin combined and furtively formulated into his incipient natural selection theory. The "raw materials" of his theory were the variability in organisms together with sweeping, but gradual, changes in environment. As time progressed, the better adapted, newly modified forms survived to reproduce their advantageous features in offspring. By reviving the ancient and invalid theory of pangenesis he tried vainly to disclose the biological mechanism involved. Gregor MENDEL'S laws of heredity (1866) and Hugo DeVries's (1848–1935) mutation data ultimately supplied the answers, but in Darwin's time the former was not understood and the latter not available.

Natural Selection. In 1842 Darwin first sketched his theory of natural selection in a few pages of cryptic notes. Two years later he expanded it to 231 pages. In 1854 he began seriously to write the theory into book form. He drew not only upon his *Beagle* experiences, but also upon the results of man's selection in domestic organisms. Here were races and varieties manifestly produced on the experimental level within a brief time. Extensive correspondence with breeders, farmers, fanciers, and collectors, together with his own work with pigeons, formed this supporting pillar.

In 1858, after about two decades of assembling data for his giant premise and the completion of about half of his book, he was jolted into an accelerated pace. Alfred Russell Wallace (1823–1913), an English naturalist, writing from the East Indian Archipelago, asked for appraisal of his own briefly sketched-out theory to explain organic EVOLUTION. In essence it was identical with Darwin's secret thesis. Magnanimously Darwin proposed to Lyell and Hooker that Wallace be allowed to announce the theory of natural selection. They persuaded Darwin to collaborate with Wallace in a brief, dual announcement (1858). Then Darwin resolved to publish as soon as possible his own version, an abstract in book form. The book (over 500 pages) appeared in December 1859, titled *On the Origin of Species by Means of Natural Selection, or the Preservation of Favoured Races in the Struggle for Life.* Although ponderous and data-laden, it was sold out the day of publication.

Impact of the Theory. The immediate effect of the *Origin* was to advance the cause of organic evolution by offering a credible and tangible *modus operandi,* stating the dimensions of available testimony. Countless examples of evidence set evolution and its plausibility in bold relief, no longer to be ignored. The book stimulated a general participation by intellectuals of varied casts and backgrounds, some of whom were poorly qualified to join the battle. Philosophers, theologians, biologists, geologists, anthropologists, sociologists, even politicians and men of letters, joined in the melee, with victors and vanquished almost indistinguishable.

The natural selection theory (survival of the fittest) persists, and Darwin's importance seems assured. His theory's centennial (1959) caused worldwide academic pause and celebration.

Darwin's genius lay in his use of broad perspective; in his obsession to find and draw support from such diverse fields as taxonomy, geography, geology, morpholo-

gy, paleontology, and anatomy; in his infinite patience and tenacity; and in his painstaking data-gathering. He was less than brilliant, always a mediocre student. Writing was, by his own admission, "a wretched chore." His several other books include works on botany, psychology, breeding, geology, and anthropology [*The Descent of Man* (London 1871) incited further controversy], but none of these was as significant as his *Origin.*

His letters disclose his sensitivity to criticism, as well as his patience and restraint in making reply. Despite his lyrical declaration of faith in the closing paragraph of later editions of his *Origin,* his letters proclaim an undisguised agnosticism. Darwin was mild, gentle, retiring, devoid of animosity, greed, and ambition. His real friends were few but steadfast, especially compatriots Henslow, Hooker, Wallace, and later T. H. Huxley, who belatedly accepted evolution and became its chief protagonist. Darwin's wife administered cheerfully to his chronic illnesses, read to him, and joined him in cards. She restrained her husband somewhat in his quiet rebellion against religion; even after his death she prevented publication of some acerbic passages in his letters.

Darwin was both esteemed and denounced during his productive lifetime and was honored almost everywhere in his old age. His body rests in Westminster Abbey. Although such eminent men as Asa Gray (1810–88) in America and Ernst Haeckel in Germany endorsed his ideas, equally prominent biologists such as Richard Owen (1804–92) and St. George MIVART in England and Louis Agassiz in America strongly opposed him. His sustaining influence on biology and on most other disciplines, however, cannot be denied.

See Also: EVOLUTION.

Bibliography: *Life and Letters,* ed. F. DARWIN, 2 v. (New York 1911). G. R. DE BEER, *Charles Darwin* (New York 1958). G. HIMMELFARB, *Darwin and the Darwinian Revolution* (Garden City, N.Y. 1962).

[L. P. COONEN]

DAUDET, LÉON

Writer, politician, codirector of ACTION FRANÇAISE; b. Paris, Nov. 16, 1867; d. St.-Rémy-de-Provence, July 2, 1942. He was the son of Alphonse Daudet, the writer. He studied medicine at the University of Paris (1885–91), and then abandoned this profession for literature and journalism, publishing essays and novels, and contributing to various newspapers. His civil marriage with the granddaughter of Victor Hugo (1891) ended in divorce (1895). In 1903 he became for life a practicing Catholic, and entered a sacramental marriage with Marthe Allard.

He succeeded his father as a member of the Académie Goncourt (1897). Daudet, known as a sociable, sophisticated *bon vivant* who frequented Parisian literary and political *salons,* with Charles MAURRAS, a man of very different temperament, founded Action Française (1908). He led campaigns against Jews, Dreyfus, anti-clericals, Freemasonry, members of parliament, Catholic supporters of the Third Republic or the RALLIEMENT, and defeatists during World War I. He was elected to the Chamber of Deputies (1919–24). When his 14-year-old son Philippe was found in a taxi dead of bullet wounds (1923), possibly self-inflicted, Daudet accused the police of murder, and the taxi driver of complicity in the crime. The latter individual caused Daudet to receive a five-month prison sentence for defamation; but he fled to Belgium for three years until pardoned (1930). Like Maurras he rebelled in 1927 against the condemnation of Action Française by Pius XI, and did not submit until 1939.

Daudet's literary output of some 100 books and numerous articles (sometimes under the pseudonym Rivarol) included almost daily contributions for years to *L'Action française.* These writings dealt with medicine, psychology, politics, and literary criticism; they also comprised novels, essays, and personal reminiscences. Pius XI once declared: "His criticisms are more valuable than his novels, and his literary reminiscences are more valuable than his criticisms, but he does not know how to separate the pure from the impure." *Le Voyage de Shakespeare* was placed on the Index (Dec. 14, 1927), as was *Les Bacchantes* (Feb. 17, 1932). Other works of his also caused scandal. His writings are not of enduring interest save for his reminiscences, which were written in a sparkling style and abounded in truculent phrases and unforgettable word portraits. Daudet was devoid of charity, critical spirit, and sound theological or philosophical judgment; but his genius with words, violent, satirical, and Rabelaisian, and his talent for polemics made him the leading French pamphleteer of his time.

Bibliography: P. DRESSE, *Léon Daudet vivant* (Paris 1948). J. MORIENVAL, *Catholicisme. Hier, aujourd'hui et demain,* ed. G. JACQUEMET (Paris 1947–) 3:475–477. H. TEMERSON, *Dictionnaire de biographie française* (Paris 1929–) 10:262–265.

[A. DANSETTE]

DAUGHTERS OF ISABELLA

The Daughters of Isabella (DOI) is a beneficent society incorporated in 1907 under the laws of the state of Connecticut to unite Catholic women in the interests of the Church and society, and in their own religious, intellectual, and social needs. The society had its origin in the Russell Circle instituted in New Haven, Connecticut,

May 14, 1897, as an auxiliary to Russell Council No. 65 of the Knights of Columbus. Named for the Reverend John Russell, pastor of St. Patrick's church in New Haven, the circle secured a charter under the name of National Circle, Daughters of Isabella by a special act of the General Assembly of Connecticut in July 1907. In May 1963, the name was legally changed to Daughters of Isabella. Like the Knights, initiation rituals of the DOI are secret and the members continue to use a secret password to verify membership at meetings.

The international circle includes the episcopal advisor, the liaison bishop, the international officers and directors, one delegate from each local circle, and the state regents. In 1929 the national convention of the DOI authorized formation of state circles, with four circles required to form a state circle. This group meets biennially in August for legislative purposes and for the election of officers and directors.

The society is composed of international officers, a board of directors, state circles and local circles located in the United States and Canada. Membership grew from the initial 67 charter members in 1897 to peak at 133,000 in 1959. By June of 2000 the DOI had 70,000 members who met in 691 circles, 348 in Canada and 343 in the United States. Introduced in Montreal, Quebec, Canada in March 1925, the society at one point numbered more than 240 circles throughout the provinces of Manitoba, New Brunswick, Ontario, Nova Scotia, and Quebec. In May 1951, three circles began in the Philippines and soon increased to 38. However, because the Philippine government did not allow members to send money out of the country, the circles had to be abandoned.

The DOI has been benefactor to the orphan, the missionary, the refugee and religious communities, as well as Catholic educational institutions and foundations. The society established a memorial in 1943 in the form of the Queen Isabella Foundation in the National Catholic School of Social Service at the Catholic University of America. The foundation provides graduate fellowships, many of which have gone to students from the Far East and Latin America. From 1941 to 1992 the order helped finance the Confraternity of Christian Doctrine home study service to provide religious instruction for men and women in the armed forces of the United States. Scholarship grants have also been provided for training religious sisters in methods of teaching the handicapped, and for catechists and seminarians. Memorials established by the society include the statue of Mary Immaculate over the south balcony entrance of the National Shrine of the Immaculate Conception in Washington, D.C. The society also has given assistance to Catholic radio and television.

Between 1961 and 1963 the order published the *Isabellan,* a magazine for Catholic women that included editorials, Catholic news stories, and activities of the circles. *The Daughters of Isabella Newsletter,* published periodically, replaced the magazine.

Bibliography: Archives of the Daughters of Isabella (New Haven, Conn.)

[F. SHELTRA]

DAUGHTERS OF MARY AND JOSEPH

(DMJ; Official Catholic Directory #0880), also called Ladies of Mary, a pontifical institute founded in Belgium in 1817 by the priest educator Canon Constant G. Van Crombrugghe, minister of education in the Belgian National Congress. The rule of the congregation received papal approbation in 1891. From Belgium the community spread to England and thence to the United States, coming to Los Angeles, California, in 1926 at the request of Bishop John J. Cantwell. In addition to the work of education, the sisters have undertaken catechetical work, youth clubs, and retreats, as well as missionary activities in Africa. The motherhouse, hitherto in Belgium, was transferred to Rome; the United States provincialate is in Rancho Palos Verdes, California.

[M. C. COTTER/EDS.]

DAUGHTERS OF OUR LADY OF MERCY

(DM, Official Catholic Directory #0890), a pontifical institute founded in Savona, Italy, in 1837 by (Saint) Maria Giuseppa ROSSELLO. The congregation began at the request of the bishop of Savona, Agostino De Mari. The foundress, herself of a poor family, answered his plea for help in the education of youth, especially the underprivileged. The congregation soon spread through northern Italy. In 1875 it extended to South America when the sisters were invited to take care of cholera victims in Buenos Aires, Argentina. In 1919 the sisters came to the United States to open a school and parish center in Springfield, Massachusetts. Later they accepted work in New Jersey and Pennsylvania. They expanded their work to include hospice, healthcare, parochial ministries, and education on the preschool, elementary and high school levels. The generalate is in Rome; the United States provincialate is in Newfield, New Jersey.

[K. BURTON/EDS.]

DAUGHTERS OF ST. MARY OF PROVIDENCE

(DSMP, Official Catholic Directory #0940), a pontifical institute that originated in the work of a group of young women in a small country parish in northern Italy about 1872. Under their pastor's direction they opened a hospice to care for the aged and to offer instruction to young girls. In 1881 the Reverend Luigi Guanella (d. 1915) organized the group as a formal religious community, and Sister Marcellina Bosatta, the foundress (d. 1934), became the first superior general. The Holy See gave final approval to their rule in 1917. The sisters arrived in Chicago, Illinois, in 1913 to assist Italian immigrants, and in 1925 they opened a residential school for mentally retarded girls. Since then, their ministries expanded to include care facilities for the disabled and aged. The general motherhouse is in Rome, Italy; the United States provincialate is in Chicago, Illinois.

[M. MAURI/EDS.]

DAUGHTERS OF THE CROSS

(DC, Official Catholic Directory #0770), a diocesan congregation whose motherhouse is in Shreveport, Louisiana. It stems from the Daughters of the Cross who were founded in Paris about 1640 by Marie l'Huillier de Villeneuve (1597 to 1650) with the guidance and assistance of St. Vincent de Paul. In its early history the congregation experienced many difficulties and vicissitudes. Not until the 19th century was the community reorganized in its modern form, and in 1853 the initial approval of the Holy See was granted.

Two years later Mother Marie Hyacinthe Conniat led a group of ten sisters to Louisiana. They established their headquarters in Shreveport, where their principal foundation, St. Vincent's Academy, eventually became the motherhouse when in 1902 the sisters in the United States separated themselves from the congregation in France. In 1958 the United States community revised its constitutions and adopted a spiritual directory based on the teachings of St. Francis de Sales. The sisters are engaged in conducting elementary and secondary schools, schools of Christian doctrine, and women's retreat houses, all of which are located in the Diocese of Shreveport.

Bibliography: K. HOFMANN, *Lexikon für Theologie und Kirche,* ed. J. HOFER and K. RAHNER, 10 v. (2d, new ed. Freiburg 1957–65) 6:616.

[M. B. RILEY/EDS.]

DAUGHTERS OF THE CROSS OF LIÈGE

Filiae Crucis Leodiensis (FC, Official Catholic Directory #0780), a religious congregation with papal approval (1845), founded at Liège, Belgium, in 1833 by Maria Theresia Haze and Jean Habets (d. 1876), a pastor in Liège. The apostolate includes educational work and care of the sick and aged. During the lifetime of the foundress the Daughters spread to Germany (1851), India (1862), and England (1863). Foundations have since been made in the Netherlands, Italy, Ireland, Brazil, and the United States. The congregation's United States headquarters is in Tracy, California.

[M. B. BLISS/EDS.]

DAVENPORT, DIOCESE OF

Suffragan of the metropolitan See of DUBUQUE, the Diocese of Davenport *(Davenportensis)*, was erected May 8, 1881, and embraced 22 counties in southeast Iowa, an area of 11,438 square miles. Approximately 15 percent of its population is Catholic. Prior to 1911, when the original diocese was divided to form the Des Moines diocese, Davenport included the four southern tiers of Iowa counties.

History. As part of the Diocese (now Archdiocese) of Dubuque from 1837, the Church in southern Iowa grew rapidly. In 1881 the new Davenport diocese included 70 priests, 56 churches with resident pastors, and a Catholic population of approximately 45,000. By 1911, when the diocese was divided, there were 151 priests, 117 churches with resident pastors, and a Catholic population of 75,997.

John McMullen, formerly vicar-general of Chicago, Ill., was consecrated first bishop of Davenport, July 25, 1881, and served until his death, July 4, 1883. A lasting achievement of his tenure was the establishment of St. Ambrose Preparatory Seminary and School of Commerce for young men in 1882. (In 1908, the seminary and school became St. Ambrose College, and in 1987, St. Ambrose University.) Henry Cosgrove, rector of St. Margaret's Cathedral, Davenport, succeeded him in 1884, thereby becoming the first American-born bishop west of the Mississippi. During his 22-year episcopate, Cosgrove directed the building of a new cathedral, Sacred Heart, and St. Vincent's orphanage. At his death, Dec. 22, 1906, he was succeeded by his coadjutor, Bp. James Davis, formerly a priest of the diocese. During the last two years of Davis's 20-year episcopate, which ended with his death, Dec. 2, 1926, auxiliary Bishop Edward D. Howard

Tower of Christ the King Chapel, St. Ambrose University, Davenport, Iowa.

assisted him. On July 25, 1927, Henry P. Rohlman was consecrated Davenport's fourth bishop and served until June 15, 1944, when he was appointed coadjutor-archbishop of Dubuque. Ralph L. Hayes, formerly bishop of Helena, Mont., and rector of the North American College, Rome, became bishop of Davenport Nov. 16, 1944. Bishop Gerald F. O'Keefe became the next bishop of Davenport in 1966, following the retirement of Bishop Hayes. Upon his retirement, Bishop O'Keefe was succeeded by Bishop William Franklin, Auxiliary Bishop of Dubuque, who was transferred to Davenport in 1994.

Bibliography: J. J. MCGOVERN, *The Life and Writings of the Right Reverend John McMullen, D.D.* (Chicago 1889). E. C. GREER, *Cork Hill Cathedral* (Davenport 1957). M. M. SCHMIDT, *Seasons of Growth: History of the Diocese of Davenport, 1881–1981* (Davenport, Iowa 1981).

[W. F. DAWSON/EDS.]

DAVENTRY, PRIORY OF

Former Cluniac monastery dedicated to St. Augustine, in Daventry, Northamptonshire, England, ancient See of LINCOLN. It was founded before 1109 by Hugh of Leicester, first at Preston Capes and then near the parish church of Daventry. An earlier endowment of four canons was appropriated for the foundation, and four BENEDICTINE monks—as at nearby Saint Andrews, Northampton—were brought from the Abbey of La CHARITÉ-SUR-LOIRE. In 1221 the bishop, acting under papal instructions, took charge of the priory, and from that time La Charité exercised no control over it. The founder's family continued to act as patrons and allowed free election of priors after 1331. Daventry was well endowed with churches and continued to add to its possessions in the 14th century, when there were regularly 18 monks there. The priory was dissolved by papal authority in 1525 to form part of Wolsey's college at Oxford, subsequently Christ Church.

Bibliography: *Victoria History of the County of Northampton,* ed. W. R. D. ADKINS et al., v. 2 (London 1906). N. DENHOLM-YOUNG, ed., *Cartulary of the Medieval Archives of Christ Church* (Oxford 1931). H. DAUPHIN, *Dictionnaire d'histoire et de géographie ecclésiastiques,* ed. A. BAUDRILLART et al. (Paris 1912–) 14:111–113. D. KNOWLES, *The Monastic Order in England, 943–1216* (2d ed. Cambridge, Eng. 1962) 155. D. KNOWLES, *The Religious Orders in England,* 3 v. (Cambridge, Eng. 1948–60) 210–211. D. KNOWLES and R. N. HADCOCK, *Medieval Religious Houses: England and Wales* (New York 1953) 96.

[D. J. A. MATTHEW]

DAVID

Traditionally Israel's greatest king, David (Heb. *dāwīd,* beloved or prince) was a man after God's heart, a central figure in Israel both historically and theologically; he successfully united the tribes in an acceptable monarchy and became the kingly type of the Messiah, Israel's hope of salvation. This article treats in order David's early life, his service under Saul, his life as a fugitive, his life as king, significance of his reign, and finally, iconography of David.

Early Life. David was the youngest son of Isai (or Jesse), who was an Ephrathite from Bethlehem in Judah (1 Sm 17.12) and a grandson of Ruth the Moabitess (Ru 4.18–22), though the latter relationship is questioned (see Eissfeldt, 590–591). One tradition (1 Chr 2.13–16) gives David at least six brothers and two sisters, while another tradition (1 Sm 17.12) supposes eight sons (or children?) of Isai. David was an attractive youth (1 Sm 16.12; 17.42), a courageous shepherd (1 Sm 16.11; 17.34–36), and a skillful player of the harp (1 Sm 16.18). At God's command Samuel came to Bethlehem to anoint one of the sons of Isai as SAUL's successor; the purpose and true significance of the anointing, as the subsequent history shows, remained hidden to those who witnessed it, even to Isai and David (1 Sm 16.1–13). Of the two traditions, one in 1 Sm 16.14–23 and one in 1 Sm 17.1–18.5 [*see* SAM-

UEL, BOOK(S) OF], that explain how David came to the court of Saul, the former, telling how David had been invited to dispel Saul's melancholy by his music, appears more plausible (see Driver, 179–180).

His Service under Saul. Saul appreciated David's music and appointed him one of his armor bearers (1 Sm 16.15–23). The youth's bravery, however, and his popularity for slaying Goliath aroused Saul's jealousy (1 Sm 17.12–58; 18.5–9). Saul attempted to slay David (1 Sm 18.10–11) and persisted in this intent (1 Sm 19.1), although his son Jonathan had become David's best friend and his daughter Michal was in love with him (1 Sm 18.1–4, 17–27). Saul's repeated attempts to dispose of David indicated also that he considered him a strong prospect for the throne, a threat to the succession of his son Jonathan (see Morgenstern's hypothesis of *beena* marriage, 323).

The Fugitive. Aware of Saul's jealousy and enmity, David fled and sought refuge in the desert of southern Judah. His visit at Nob (1 Sm 21.2–10) occasioned, through the treachery of Doeg, the slaughter of the priests by Saul (1 Sm 22.9–19); Abiathar, the only survivor of the priests, fled to David (1 Sm 22.20–23). Kinsmen, fugitives, and malcontents rallied to David. By bravery and craftiness David managed not only to escape again and again the clutches of Saul (1 Sm 23.19–24.22; 26.1–25), but also to gain the good will of many (cf. 1 Sm 23.5; 25.7–17; 30.26 31). Yet distrusting some of the Judeans (1 Sm 23.12; 25.10; 26.1), David sought protection with the Philistines at Geth (1 Sm 27.1–12); when informed of Israel's defeat at Mt. Gilboa, he mourned in a celebrated dirge the fate of Jonathan and Saul (2 Sm 1.19–27; see Smith, 257–265, for a detailed analysis of the dirge).

King at Hebron and Jerusalem. About the year 1000 B.C., David, 30 years old, became the king over Judah in Hebron (2 Sm 2.1–4). The other tribes followed Saul's general, Abner, and recognized Saul's son, Ishbaal, as their king (2 Sm 2.8–10). The ensuing civil war came to an end with the assassination, sorely against David's will, of Abner and Ishbaal (2 Sm 2.12–4.12). After a reign of seven years in Hebron, David was proclaimed king over all Israel (2 Sm 5.1–5). Having conquered the Jebusite stronghold of JERUSALEM (2 Sm 5.6–10), he made it his royal city. With the intention of making it also the religious capital, he brought the ark there from Cariath-Jarim (2 Sm 6) and appointed Zadok and Abiathar his high priests (2 Sm 8.17). According to 2 Sm 7.1–17, when David was deterred from building a temple by a divine oracle, the prophet NATHAN assured him of a perpetual dynasty. Many details of zeal for the future temple and the organization of its liturgy are attributed to David in 1 Chr 22.2–26.32, but probably this largely represents the liturgy and personnel of the postexilic Temple projected retrospectively by the Chronicler to the time of David. Little is known of the King's administration except two lists of his chief officers (2 Sm 8.15–18; 20.23–26). Perhaps the census (2 Sm 24.1–9) was taken up for administrative purposes, to prepare systematic taxation and conscription. Justice was ministered locally. Although subjects could appeal to the King (2 Sm 14.1–24), there was dissatisfaction with this method (2 Sm 15.1–6). Regarding David's military strength, a picked body guard (2 Sm 23.8–39), foreign mercenaries (2 Sm 20.23), and a standing army (1 Chr 27.1–15) are mentioned. David's outstanding, though self-willed, commander was JOAB. David's court was modest, but his harem of considerable size; eight wives are named (1 Sm 18.27; 25.42, 43; 1 Chr 3.2, 3, 5), and their number may have been greater (2 Sm 5.13–16). Of his sons six are listed as born in Hebron (2 Sm 3.2–5) and thirteen as born in Jerusalem (2 Sm 5.14; 1 Chr 3.5–9). For the safety of the kingdom, David had to contend with various revolts (2 Sm 15.1–18.33; 20.1–22) and wage war against the Philistines (2 Sm 5.17–25; 23.9–17), the Ammonites (2 Sm 10.1–14; 12.26–31), the Aramaeans (2 Sm 10.15–19), Moab and Edom (2 Sm 8.2, 13–14; 1 Kgs 11.15–18), and Damascus and Zobah (2 Sm 8.3–12). With Hiram, King of Tyre, David negotiated a lasting treaty (2 Sm 5.11–12; see also 1 Kgs 5.12). In Israel's history David's empire had the greatest extension, stretching from the River of Egypt to Kadesh on the Orontes (emended reading of 1 Sm 24.6).

A shadow is cast over David's life and work by his adultery with Bathsheba and his murder of her husband, Uriah the Hittite (2 Sm 11.1–27). Although David confessed his sin (2 Sm 12.1–14), his bad example unleashed the worst passions within his family. Amnon's rape of his half sister Tamar led to his assassination by ABSALOM (2 Sm 13.1–33), followed by the latter's flight, revolt, and death (2 Sm 13.34–18.33). Intrigues of disastrous consequences were carried on for the succession to the throne, which was ultimately gained by SOLOMON (1 Kgs 1.1–53). David died c. 961 B.C. after a reign of 40 years. The location of his tomb was still known at the time of Nehemiah (Neh 3.16) and even in the days of Christ (Acts 2.29); but since it was in "The City of David," i.e., on Ophel, it is certainly not to be identified with the modern "Tomb of David," which is located on so-called Christian Sion.

The Significance of His Reign. David was "a man after God's own heart" (1 Sm 13.14; Acts 13.22). This judgment does not imply that David was sinless, but refers to his docile and sincere heart. Sirach gives a more detailed description of David's qualities (47.1–12). Although David was without doubt a great king, later writ-

King David. (Archive Photos)

ers idealized him considerably, holding him up as the model for subsequent kings (1 Kgs 14.8) and especially as the type of the coming Messiah (see T. Vriezen, 48–49, 53, for Deuteronomist view of David). The Prophets see the Messianic King as a descendant of David (Is 11.1, 10; Jer 23.5; 33.15; Mt 9.27; etc.) or even a David *redivivus* (Hos 3.5; Jer 30.9; Ez 37.24). A unanimous tradition praises David also as poet and musician (2 Sm 1.19–27; 3.33–34; 22.1–51; 23.1–7; Sir 47.9), and numerous Psalms have been attributed to him (*see* PSALMS, BOOK OF).

Iconography. The themes that in the course of the centuries seem to have especially impressed the artistic minds of men are David's fight against Goliath (fresco in Dura-Europos, painting in the catacomb of Domitilla and in S. Maria Antiqua, Rome, 4th century) and David as musician and composer of Psalms (the Paris Psalter, Gr. 139, Bibl. Nationale, Paris, 9th century). The best-known sculptures showing a youthful and athletic David are the works of Donatello, Michelangelo, and Bernini. The most outstanding artist who painted various scenes of David's life was Rembrandt; also to be mentioned are A. F. Maulbertsch, D. Rossetti, A. Böcklin, and M. Chagall.

Bibliography: L. PIROT, *Dictionnaire de la Bible,* suppl. ed. L. PIROT, et al. (Paris 1928) 2:287–330. R. DE VAUX, *ibid.*

4:743–745. *Encyclopedic Dictionary of the Bible,* tr. and adap. by L. HARTMAN (New York 1963) 494–497. H. SMITH, *A Critical and Exegetical Commentary of the Books of Samuel (International Critical Commentary,* ed. S. R. DRIVER, et al. New York 1904). S. R. DRIVER, *An Introduction to the Literature of the Old Testament* (11th ed. New York 1905). J. L. MCKENZIE, "The Dynastic Oracle: 2 Sam 7," *Theological Studies* 8 (1947) 187–218. P. HEINISCH, *History of the Old Testament,* tr. W. G. HEIDT (Collegeville, Minn. 1952) 175–191. O. EISSFELDT, *Einleitung in das Alte Testament* (3rd ed. Tübingen 1964). T. VRIEZEN, *An Outline of Old Testament Theology,* tr. S. NEUIJEN (Newton Centre, Mass. 1958) 48–49, 53. J. MORGENSTERN, "David and Jonathan," *Journal of Biblical Literature* 78 (1959) 322–325.

[F. BUCK]

DAVID, ARMAND

Lazarist missionary, naturalist; b. Espelette (Basses Pyrenees), France, Sept. 7, 1826; d. Paris, Nov. 10, 1900. He taught in Italy from 1851 to 1861. After his ordination in 1862 he was sent to China; he soon published *Quelques observations sur les productions naturelles de la Chine.* He explored Mongolia in 1866, Tibet from 1868 to 1870, and central China from 1872 to 1874. As a result, he greatly enriched the zoological and botanical collections of the Museum d'Histoire Naturele of Paris, and was elected a member of the Academy of Sciences (1872). His publications include: *Voyage en Mongolie* (1875); *Second voyage d'exploration de l'ouest de la Chine* (1876); *Journal de mon troisieme voyage d'exploration dans l'Empire chinois* (1875); *Les oiseaux de la Chine* (1877); *Plantae Davidianae* (catalogue of his plant collections, 1884–86); *Notice sur quelques services rendus aux sciences naturelles par les missionnaires d'Extreme-Orient* (1888); and contributions to the journals *Bulletin de la Société de Géographie, Missions Catholiques,* and *Annales de philosophie chrétienne.*

Bibliography: P. FOURNIER, *Voyages et découvertes scientifiques des missionnaires naturalistes français à travers le monde* (Paris 1932) 67–91, with bibliog. A. TRIN, *Dictionnaire de biographie francçaise* (Paris 1929–) 10:340.

[M. F. DUROZOY]

DÁVID, FRANZ

Chief figure in the founding and forming of the Unitarian church of Transylvania; b. Kolozsvár (Cluj), Transylvania, *c.* 1510; d. Déva, Transylvania, Nov. 15, 1579. He was born of a Saxon father and a Hungarian mother. After preliminary studies in the local Franciscan school, Dávid studied in Wittenberg (1545–48) and became the superintendent successively of the Hungarian Evangelical (Lutheran) Church (1557), of the Calvinist Reformed Church (1564), and of the separated antitrinitarian Reformed Church (1566). Court preacher under the Unitarian King John Sigismund, he debated at the diet and in synod for religious toleration. By 1571 the Unitarian Church itself was dividing into two factions. Dávid, the leader of the more radical party, opposed prayer to Christ and sought the restoration of certain Jewish views and practices. In 1579 he was imprisoned for innovations, and he died there. He was later revered as the fountainhead of Hungarian-speaking Unitarianism.

Bibliography: E. JAKAB, *Dávid Ferencz Emléke,* 2 v. (Budapest 1879). E. M. WILBUR, *A History of Unitarianism,* 2 v. (Cambridge, Mass. 1945–52), v.2 *In Transylvania, England, and America,* 16–80.

[G. H. WILLIAMS]

DAVID, JOHN BAPTIST MARY

Frontier missionary, bishop of Bardstown, Ky., diocese (now LOUISVILLE Archdiocese); b. Couëron, France, June 4, 1761; d. Nazareth, Ky., July 12, 1841. He received his early education at the Oratorian college in Nantes, France, and prepared for the priesthood at the Nantes seminary. After two years in the Sulpician novitiate at Issy, he was ordained on Sept. 24, 1785, and was admitted to the Society of the Priests of St. Sulpice. Under Benedict Flaget, he taught philosophy, theology, and Scripture, and served as *écome* (bursar) of the Angers seminary until it was attacked by revolutionaries in 1790. He sailed for America in November 1791 with Flaget, Jean Baptiste Chicoisneau, and seminarians Stephen Badin and N. Barrett, and reached the U.S. in March 1792. He was first sent by Bp. John Carroll to serve the Catholics of southern Maryland in Bryantown and its missions in Charles County. From 1803 to 1804 he taught philosophy at Georgetown College, Washington, D.C. At the request of Jacques André Émery, the Sulpician superior, he was transferred to St. Mary's Seminary in Baltimore and was temporary president (1810–11) and chaplain to Charles Carroll of Carrollton, Md. After a short term as superior and spiritual director of the Sisters of Charity at Emmitsburg, Md., he accompanied the newly consecrated Bishop Flaget to Kentucky, arriving at Louisville on June 4, 1811. He served at St. Thomas Seminary, Bardstown, for years as superior and professor as well as missionary to the surrounding territory. In 1812 he founded the Sisters of Charity of Nazareth and later gave them the rule of St. Vincent de Paul. On Aug. 15, 1819, he was consecrated by Flaget as titular bishop of Mauricastro and coadjutor of Bardstown. Although he had been suggested for the sees of Cincinnati, New Orleans, and Philadelphia, he was appointed the second bishop of Bardstown in 1832. He resigned, however, in 1833 to allow Flaget to resume the administration. A retiring, bookish, prayerful man, David served as pastor, organist, choirmaster, composer of church music, superior of the Sisters of Charity of Nazareth, pastor of the cathedral, rector of the seminary, and confessor and advisor to Flaget. He attended the Second Provincial Council of Baltimore in 1833.

Bibliography: C. FOX, *The Life of the Right Reverend John Baptist Mary David, 1761–1841* (U.S. Catholic Historical Society 9; New York 1925). M. R. MATTINGLY, *The Catholic Church on the Kentucky Frontier, 1785–1812* (Catholic University of America, Studies in Medieval and Renaissance Latin, Language and Literature 25; Washington 1936). J. H. SCHAUINGER, *Cathedrals in the Wilderness* (Milwaukee 1952). M. J. SPALDING, *Sketches of the Early Catholic Missions of Kentucky, 1787–1827* (Louisville, Ky. 1844); *Sketches of the Life, Times, and Character of the Rt. Rev. Benedict Joseph Flaget, First Bishop of Louisville* (Louisville, Ky. 1852). B. J. WEBB, *The Centenary of Catholicity in Kentucky* (Louisville, 1884). R. J. PURCELL, *Dictionary of American Biography*, ed. A. JOHNSON and D. MALONE (New York, 1928–36) 5:89–91.

[V. MC MURRY]

DAVID I, KING OF SCOTLAND

Reigned 1124 to May 24, 1153; b. *c.* 1080; d. Carlisle. The sixth son of Malcolm III and St. MARGARET OF SCOTLAND, David succeeded to the crown in 1124 just when his country was ready to enter into the mainstream of ecclesiastical reform then invigorating Western Christendom. His mother and brother had already introduced Anglo-Norman religious communities into the country in an attempt to break down the prevailing Celtic parochialism of church life. David's greatness lay in peaceably completing their policy. He founded at least 12 of the major BENEDICTINE, CISTERCIAN, and AUGUSTINIAN abbeys of Scotland, reorganized six of the ten dioceses, successfully resisted the encroachments of YORK, and forged the independence of the Scottish Church. A just and saintly ruler, he was popularly venerated as a saint after his death.

Feast: May 24.

Bibliography: *Acta Sanctorum* May 5:274. J. DE FORDUN, *Scotichronicon,* ed. W. GOODALL, 2 v. (Edinburgh 1759) 1:292–313. A. C. LAWRIE, ed. *Early Scottish Charters* (Glasgow 1905). A. O. ANDERSON, ed. and tr., *Early Sources of Scottish History,* A.D. *500–1286,* 2 v. (Edinburgh 1922). G. W. S. BARROW, *The Acts of Malcolm IV, King of Scots, 1153–1165* (Edinburgh 1960); *Feudal Britain* (London 1956) 134–145; ed., *The Charters of King David I* (Rochester, NY 1999). R. L. G. RITCHIE, *The Normans in Scotland* (Edinburgh 1954). Easson. W. DANIEL, *The Life of Ailred of Rievaulx,* tr. F. M. POWICKE (London 1950).

[L. MACFARLANE]

John Baptist Mary David.

DAVID OF AUGSBURG

Franciscan ascetical-mystical theologian; b. Augsburg, *c.* 1200; d. there, Nov. 19, 1272. He probably joined the Friars Minor in Regensburg, and studied and taught at the studium generale in Magdeburg; from 1235 to 1250 he was master of novices in Regensburg. In 1246 he was named visitator together with Berthold of Regensburg, and from about 1250 accompanied Berthold on his preaching missions. He also served as inquisitor against the Waldensians. As a spiritual writer, he ranks among the greatest of his time, both for the quality of his German and Latin prose and for his sober and circumspect mystical theology. His influence on the *Schwabenspiegel* (1268), DEVOTIO MODERNA, the Spanish Franciscan mystics, and the German mystics of the 14th century has been noted, although he has nothing in common with the extravagances of the last mentioned. His most important work, *De exterioris et interioris hominis compositione libri III* (Quaracchi 1899), appeared in more than 370 editions after 1240. His other Latin works include: *Tractatus de oratione* and *Expositio Regulae OFM, Zeitschrift für Kirchengeschicte* 19 (1898) 341–359; *De haeresi pauperum de Lugduno, Abhandlungen des Bayerischen Akademie der Wissenschaften* (Munich 1835–) 14 (1878) 181– ; *De septem gradibus orationis, Revue d'ascétique et de mystique* 14 (1933) 146–170. Pfeiffer attributed

Kings David I (left) and Malcolm IV of Scotland. (Hulton-Deutsch Collection/CORBIS)

eight German works to him: *Die sieben Vorregeln der Tugend; Der Spiegel der Tugend; Christi Leben unser Vorbild; Die vier Fittiche geistlicher Betrachtung; Von der Anschauung Gottes; Von der Erkenntnis der Wahrheit; Von der unergründlichen Fülle Gottes;* and *Betrachtungen und Gebete.*

Bibliography: F. PFEIFFER, *Deutsche Mystiker des vierzehnten Jahrhunderts* (Leipzig 1845). F. HECKER, *Kritische Beiträge zu David von Augsburg: Persönlichkeit und Schriften* (Göttingen 1905). D. STÖCKERL, *Bruder D. von A., ein deutscher Mystiker aus dem Franziskanerorden* (Munich 1914). M. BIHL, "Survey of Scholarship on D. of A.," *Archivum Franciscanum historicum* 7 (1914) 765–769; 18 (1925) 143–147; 26 (1933) 527–531. V. DE PERALTA, "Mistocos Franciscanos," *Estudios Franciscanos* 24 (1920) 275–283. C. SMITS, "D. van A. en le invloed van zijn Profectus op de moderne Devotie," *Collectanea Franciscana Neerlandica* 1 (1927) 171–203. J. HEERINCKX, "Theologica mystica in scriptis D. ab A.," *Antonianum* 8 (1933) 49–83. A. RAYEZ, *Dictionnaire de spiritualité ascétique et mystique. Doctrine et histoire*, ed. M. VILLER et al. (Paris 1932–) 3:42–44.

[M. F. LAUGHLIN]

DAVID OF DINANT

Scholastic philosopher; b. Dinant, Belgium (or Dinan, Brittany?), second half of 12th century; d. after 1206. Like AMALRIC OF BÈNE, his senior contemporary, David lectured in Paris *c.* 1200 on Aristotle, interpreting him with the help of *De divisione naturae* of JOHN SCOTUS ERIUGENA. The doctrine developed was a materialistic PANTHEISM in which God was identified with Aristotle's primary matter. The Council of Sens, held in Paris in 1210, ordered that all copies of David's *Quaternuli* be sent immediately to the bishop of Paris to be burned. Anyone possessing a copy after Dec. 25 was to be considered a heretic (*Chartularium universitatis Parisiensis*, ed. H. Denifle and E. Chatelain, 1:11). In August 1215 ROBERT OF COURÇON proscribed the reading of certain books of Aristotle at Paris and all summaries (*summae*) of the doctrine of David of Dinant (*ibid.* 1:20). He himself was exiled from France as a heretic (*ibid.* 1:11 n.17).

Only fragments of his writings survive, notably his natural questions (ed. M. Kurdziałek). Some of his teaching can be reconstructed from quotations and paraphrases preserved by ALBERT THE GREAT, THOMAS AQUINAS, and NICHOLAS OF CUSA. Albert attributed to him a work described as *De tomis, hoc est de divisionibus,* which might be related to the *Quaternuli* condemned in 1210. According to Aquinas, "He divided reality into three categories: bodies, souls, and eternal separated substances; the first indivisible from which bodies are constituted he called *hyle;* the first indivisible from which souls are constituted he called *nous* or mind; however the first indivisible among eternal substances he called *God;* and these three are one and the same. From this it also follows that all things are essentially one" (*In 2 sent.* 17.1.1). Discussing pantheism, Aquinas says that the third type of error was that of David of Dinant, "who stupidly (*stultissime*) maintained that God is primary matter" (*Summa theologiae* 1a, 3.8). According to Albert the Great, David argued that every analysis must terminate in a unique, absolutely simple principle of being beyond which analysis is impossible. By reason of this unique, absolutely simple principle, there is no differentiation of beings. Differentiation is due to accidental forms (*Summa theologiae* 1a, 6.29.1.2; 2a, 12.72.4.2).

Bibliography: É. H. GILSON, *History of Christian Philosophy in the Middle Ages* (New York 1955) 241–243, 654. G. BONAFEDE, *Enciclopedia filosofica* (Venice-Rome 1957) 1:1408–09. R. ARNOU, "Quelques idées néoplatoniciennes de David de Dinant," *Philosophia perennis: Festgabe J. Geyser* (Regensburg 1930) 1:115–127. G. THÉRY, *Autour de Décret de 1210: I. David de Dinant* (Bibliothèque Thomiste, Le Saulchoir 1921– 6; 1925). M. KURDZIALEK, "Fragments des Questions naturelles de David de Dinant," *Mediaevalia philosophica polonorum* 2 (Warsaw 1958) 3–5; "Davidus de Dinanto quaternulorum fragmenta," *Studia Mediewistyczne* 3 (Warsaw 1963).

[A. J. HEIMAN]

DAVID OF HIMMEROD, BL.

Cistercian mystic; b. Florence, Italy, *c.* 1100; d. Himmerod, Eifel, Germany, Dec. 11, 1179. He studied in Paris and entered CLAIRVAUX in 1131. St. BERNARD sent him in 1134 to the abbey at HIMMEROD in the Diocese of Trèves (Trier), where he became noted for mysticism and miracles. He was venerated immediately after death. The Benedictine, Peter of St. Eucharius, in Trier, *c.* 1204 composed his vita, one of the first pieces of Cistercian hagiography, emphasizing interior sanctity rather than miracles. David was buried first in the chapter room, and translated to a marble altar in the cloister in 1204, and to a chapel in the cloister church in 1692 for public veneration. A Cistercian general chapter confirmed his cult as immemorial in 1699. After Himmerod's secularization in

1802, the relics were taken to Trier, to Jupille, Belgium, in 1913, and back to Himmerod in 1930. David is the patron of mothers.

Feast: Dec. 11.

Bibliography: A. SCHNEIDER, "Der Kult des sel. David," *Cistercienser-Chronik* 50 (1938) 97–102, 135–143, 170–176; "Vita B. Davidis monachi Hemmenrodensis," *Analecta Sacri Ordinis Cisterciensis* 11 (1955) 27–44. C. HONTOIR, *Dictionnaire de spiritualité ascétique et mystique. Doctrine et histoire,* ed., M. VILLER et al. (Paris 1932) 3:44–46. K. SPAHR, *Lexikon für Theologie und Kirche,* ed. J. HOFER and K. RAHNER, 10 v. (2d, new ed. Freiburg 1957–65) 3:178–179.

[A. SCHNEIDER]

DAVID OF VÄSTMANLAND, ST.

One of the chief patrons of the Diocese of Västerås, Sweden, believed to have lived in the eleventh century. He is known also as David of Munktorp, of Väasteräss, or of Snävringe härad, and is often called "abbot," although no monastery can be traced to his region at his time. He is connected with St. SIGFRID, especially Sigfrid's murdered nephews. According to a popular legend, David hung his glove on a sunbeam. There are numerous paintings of him in Swedish churches. A rhythmical Office by an unknown author and two Sequences have been written for David. The sources for his cult date from the fifteenth century.

Feast: July 15.

Bibliography: *Scriptores rerum Suecicarum,* ed. E. M. FANT, 3 v. (Uppsala 1818–76) v. 2. *Analecta hymnica* 25:234–236; 42:191–193; 43:115–116. G. EKSTRÖM, "St. David av Munktorp," *Västmanlands fornminnesförening Arsskrift* 41 (1958–59) 54–. O. ODENIUS, "En legend om S. David av Munktorp," *Fornvännen* 57 (1962) 26–40. T. SCHMID, "Eskil, Botvid och David, Tre sevenska helgon," *Scandia* 4 (1931) 102–114.

[T. SCHMID]

DAVIDIANS

The Davidians, a small ADVENTIST reform movement, was established by Victor T. Houteff in 1929. In 1955, under Ben Roden, it gave rise to the Branch Davidians. Both groups were created to prepare for the second advent of Christ, and both movements survive in small but active communities chiefly in the United States. The Branch Davidians achieved international notoriety in 1993 when their leader, David Koresh, and 80 followers perished by fire while surrounded by U.S. government personnel.

Houteff, a Bulgarian immigrant, settled in Rockford, Illinois, where in 1918 he adopted Seventh-day Adventist teaching. He moved to California and taught in the weekly Sabbath school. During his study, Houteff began to publish his teachings in a series of small tracts that he called *The Shepherd's Rod*. In these writings, he advanced the idea that the General Conference of Seventh-day Adventists had gone astray. He believed that it was his task to call the mother church back to the true teaching of the faith. Houteff's relationship with the parent denomination was ambivalent. He taught that although Adventism needed reforming, it was the only denomination that had the doctrinal framework to understand his teachings regarding Christ's second coming. Houteff shared central Adventist teachings: the imminent return of Christ, observance of the Sabbath rather than Sunday, dietary regulations encouraging vegetarianism, and pacifism in time of war.

Houteff's Vision. Houteff's core idea was the second advent of Christ. William Miller had set the date of Christ's return twice: first for 1843, then for 1844. Both Miller and Houteff keenly anticipated the second advent. Houteff was also indebted to Ellen White, whose prolific writings elaborated Adventist thought. Houteff cited her opinions constantly.

Houteff produced hundreds of pages of biblical interpretations. His view of scripture was governed by the notion of prophecy and fulfillment. He looked for predictions in the Bible in order to correlate them with contemporary events, thereby fulfilling biblical prediction. Millennialists, seeking to determine the date of Christ's return, have long looked for their clue in Daniel's 2,300 days. Adventists have traditionally taught that in scripture one "day" is to be equated with one year. Miller and later Adventists worked out a scheme whereby 2,300 years is added to a late biblical event so that Christ's return is predicted for the near future. Houteff worked diligently to provide his readers with new knowledge about Christ's return; he called his new interpretations "present truth." Followers looked on him as a prophet because only he had these new insights. The precedent persists, and Davidian leaders carry much authority in their communities.

In Houteff's view, Christ would delay his return until he had a pure church to receive him. Therefore, Houteff's message to the parent Adventist Church was urgent: it must be reformed, and he cited particulars. It had become captive to worldly pursuits, including worldly dress and idle waste of time in entertainment when the end of the world was near. Furthermore, the clergy relied on seminary training, but did not know true prophecy. He believed that the true people of God would form the pure church of 144,000.

The parent Seventh-day Adventist Church rejected Houteff's teaching, and in 1935 he and 37 followers moved to Mount Carmel, Texas, convinced that Isaiah 11 had directed him to a site "in the midst of the land." Houteff not only set forth a reform proposal in his teaching; he also provided a model community for Adventists to follow. His Mount Carmel community, which soon grew to about 70 members, separated themselves from the rest of society, built housing, dining, and meeting facilities, lived simply, and devoted themselves to worship and study. They created a viable economy, established a printing press, and produced and distributed thousands of copies of Houteff's tracts, which served as the principle means of communicating their message. Recently, these tracts have been collected and published as the Shepherd's Rod and Symbolic Code. In 1942 Houteff changed the name of his movement from "Shepherd's Rod" to "Davidian Seventh-day Adventists" in a successful effort to achieve conscientious objector status for young Davidians.

Houteff's unexpected death in 1955 shocked the community; they thought that he was the new Elijah appointed to announce the new age. His wife Florence succeeded him. In 1957 she sold the old property and moved ten miles east of Waco. Houteff never set the date of Christ's return; Florence announced it for April 22, 1959. About 900 followers gathered from Adventist churches all over the United States and Canada, having sold businesses and homes. When no sign of the new age occurred, many suffered devastating disappointment.

Branch Davidians. The death of Houteff and the debacle of 1959 provided the occasion for the organization of several Davidian splinter groups, including the Branch Davidians, organized by Ben Roden in 1955 near Waco, Texas. Like other Davidians, Roden shared Seventh-day Adventist teachings regarding the imminent return of Christ, Sabbath observance, and attention to dietary regulations. Roden also embraced Houteff's central notion of a purified church. Roden's own teaching emphasized the significance of the state of Israel. He believed that the 1967 Israeli-Arab War made possible the proclamation of the word of God from Jerusalem, thereby fulfilling biblical prophecy of the end of the present age. After Roden's death in 1978, his wife Lois led the group. Her distinctive contribution was the notion of a female Holy Spirit. She also advocated the ordination of women.

The Rodens' son, George, who assumed leadership in 1985, claimed to be the Messiah. A rival faction soon emerged led by Vernon Howell, a persuasive Bible teacher. Roden expelled his opponents at gun point in 1985. Howell and his followers moved to Palestine, Texas, but returned to exchange gunfire with Roden in 1987. The two Davidian groups were brought to trial. Roden was jailed; the Howell faction occupied Mt. Carmel.

Howell inherited the Davidian tradition of the authoritarian leader, built a large centralized living complex, and recruited followers from Adventist centers around the world. He accepted most Davidian doctrine and also introduced new teachings during the period of his leadership from 1987 to 1993. The millennial expectation remained central in his thought, but he heightened its intensity. First, he changed his name to David, suggesting his messianic role, and Koresh, suggesting that he would destroy God's enemies as Cyrus had freed the Jews from the Babylonians. Second, whereas the Adventist-Houteff tradition had been pacifist, Koresh stockpiled weapons and ammunition. Third, Koresh fathered many of the children of the coming age. DNA evidence established that he was the father of 13 of the Davidian children by seven separate mothers. He taught that members of the new kingdom should be the children of the new messiah.

The Bureau of Alcohol, Tobacco, and Firearms raided the Davidians at Mt. Carmel in February of 1993 for illegal arms possession and subsequently surrounded their residence for 51 days. When the government moved to destroy their building, fire engulfed it and killed 81 Davidians, including Koresh. The event received extensive media coverage and raised heated debate over several issues, including church-state relations, the tenacity of religious belief, the nature of religious authority, arms accumulation, responsibility for the fire, and the structure and interpretation of apocalyptic biblical images.

Davidians flourish in small communities located in South Carolina, Missouri, New York, and the Caribbean. Branch Davidians have followers scattered throughout the United States. In the fall of 1991, a group of Jamaican Davidians purchased the old Mt. Carmel. It thrives today as a Davidian center that actively publishes many of the tracts of Houteff. It claims complete separation from the Branch Davidian movement. On November 22, 1994 a Branch Davidian remnant returned to new Mount Carmel, determined to reestablish a center for Bible study and to recreate their life together.

Bibliography: The primary sources for the writings of Victor Houteff are *The Shepherd's Rod Series* (reprint, Salem, SC 1990); *The Symbolic Code Series* (reprint, Tamassee, SC 1992). For background and current developments, see: J. LEWIS, ed., *From the Ashes: Making Sense of Waco* (Lanham 1994). W. PITTS, ''The Davidian Tradition,'' *Council of Societies for the Study of Religion Bulletin* 22 (1993) 99–101; ''Letter from Waco: Millennial Spirituality and the Branch Davidians,'' *Christian Spirituality Bulletin* 1 (1993) 19–20; ''The Mount Carmel Davidians: Adventist Reformers, 1935–1959,'' *Syzygy* 2 (1993) 39–54; ''Davidians and Branch Davidians: 1929–1987,'' in *Armageddon in Waco*, ed. S. WRIGHT (Chicago 1995).

[W. PITTS]

DAVIDSON, RANDALL THOMAS

Archbishop of Canterbury; b. Edinburgh, April 7, 1848; d. London, May 25, 1930. Although he came of Scottish Presbyterian ancestry, Davidson received confirmation in ANGLICANISM while attending school at Harrow. At Trinity College, Oxford, he took his degree in law and modern history. After ordination (1875) he became a curate at Dartford in Kent, and then (1877–83) resident chaplain to the Archbishop of Canterbury, Archibald Tait, whose daughter he married (1878). Largely because of Queen Victoria's favor, he became dean of Windsor (1883). After being named bishop of Rochester (1891), he associated himself with the efforts of his friend Abp. Edward Benson to prevent Viscount HALIFAX from negotiating with the Holy See over the recognition of ANGLICAN ORDERS. Davidson moved to the See of Winchester (1895), and then to that of Canterbury (1903–28). He gave no more than a certain ''friendly cognizance'' to the MALINES CONVERSATIONS between Anglicans and Roman Catholics; yet his churchmanship was broad and diplomatically comprehensive. His statesmanship, able administration, and simplicity of character increased the prestige of the primatial see, but his last years were saddened by failure when Parliament rejected the Revised Anglican Prayer-Book in 1927, and again in 1928. He retired from Canterbury in 1928 and was created Baron of Lambeth.

Bibliography: G. K. A. BELL, *Randall Davidson: Archbishop of Canterbury* (2d ed. Oxford 1938). *The Dictionary of National Biography from the Earliest Times to 1900*, Supplement (London 1922–30) 240–248.

[W. HANNAH]

DAVIES, WILLIAM, BL.

Priest, martyr; b. in North Wales, possibly in Crois in Yris, Denbighshire, or at Colwyn Bay, Wales; d. July 21, 1593, hanged, drawn, and quartered at Beaumaris, Anglesey, North Wales. He arrived at the English College in Rheims, April 6, 1582, just in time to assist the first Mass of the Bl. Nicholas GARLICK. Following his own ordination in April 1585, he labored zealously in Wales and succeeded in reclaiming many Catholics.

In 1591–92, he was arrested at Holyhead with four students whom he was sending via Ireland to the English College at Valladolid. Davies was thrown into the dungeon in Beaumaris Castle and separated from his companions. Later he was able to join the students for an hour daily and even to celebrate Mass. An indulgent judge allowed Catholics from all parts to consult him, and Protestant ministers came to dispute with him.

When the death sentence was pronounced at the assizes, Davies intoned the *Te Deum,* which the others took up. To still the murmurs of the people against the injustice of the sentence, the judge reprieved the condemned until the queen's pleasure be known.

Davies was sent to Ludlow to be examined by the Council of the Marches. He was transferred to various prisons until he was sent back to Beaumaris, where his young companions were being held. For some six months they lived the life of a religious community, dividing their time between prayer and study, "with so much comfort to themselves that they seemed to be rather in heaven than in prison."

At the summer assizes it was decided that the priest must die as a traitor. Eventually his young companions escaped from prison and the youngest made his way to Valladolid, where he recounted the whole story to Bishop Yepes, who recorded it.

There is now a chapel in Anglesey, built as a memorial to the martyr, who was declared venerable by Leo XIII in 1886 and beatified by Pope John Paul II on Nov. 22, 1987 with George Haydock and Companions.

Feast: July 27; May 4 (Feast of the English Martyrs in England).

See Also: ENGLAND, SCOTLAND, AND WALES MARTYRS OF.

Bibliography: R. CHALLONER, *Memoirs of Missionary Priests,* ed. J. H. POLLEN (rev. ed. London 1924). J. H. POLLEN, *Acts of English Martyrs* (London 1891). D. DE YEPES, *Historia Particular de la persecución de Inglaterra* (Madrid 1599).

[K. I. RABENSTEIN]

DÁVILA Y PADILLA, AGUSTÍN

Archbishop of Santo Domingo and chronicler; b. Mexico City, 1562; d. Santo Domingo, 1604. He was the son of Pedro Dávila and Isabel Padilla. After receiving a master's in arts at the University of Mexico in 1578, he entered the Dominican Order the next year and was professed Nov. 13, 1580. He was also a master in philosophy and theology and an excellent Latinist. In his order he held a number of positions: prior of the convent of Puebla, censor, definitor of the general chapter in Rome, procurator before the courts of Madrid and Rome. In 1589 he was named chronicler of the Indies. He was preacher to Philip III and was one of the most famous orators of his time. He was presented for the archbishopric of Santo Domingo by Philip III in 1599 and arrived in his see in 1601. There he became involved in a controversy with the royal *audiencia* so severe that it was a partial cause

of his death. Many Lutheran Bibles had been clandestinely introduced into the northeastern area of the island, and the *audiencia* had decided to depopulate various centers there as punishment. Dávila authorized the confiscation and burning of the Bibles, but moved by concern for the natives and for the future of the island, he refused to sanction more and sought the support of the king. The king instructed the president of the *audiencia* that he could proceed with his plans only if he could secure the consent of the archbishop. However, by the time the royal decision reached Santo Domingo, Dávila was already dead. The natives were deported; raids by pirates were made easier; and Santo Domingo lost its eastern territory. Dávila wrote "Historia de las antigüedades de los Indios," the manuscript of which has been lost, and *Historia de la fundación y Discurso de la Provincia de Santiago de México de la Orden de Predicadores* (Madrid 1596; Brussels 1625; spurious ed. Brussels 1648).

Bibliography: A. M. CARREÑO, "El arzobispo cronista Fray Agustín Dávila Padilla," *Memorias de la Academia mexicana de la historia* 10 (1951) 245–260.

[E. GOMÉZ TAGLE]

DAVIS, HENRY

Jesuit moral theologian; b. Liverpool, England, Dec. 1, 1866; d. Heythrop College, Jan. 4, 1952. Educated at St. Francis Xavier's College, he entered the Jesuit novitiate in 1883; and after the usual course of training, during which he took a bachelor's degree in classics at London University, he became prefect of studies at Stonyhurst in 1903. In 1911 he began his life's work—40 years as professor of moral theology, first at St. Beuno's College and then at Heythrop. In addition to lecturing regularly during the years when he was training successive generations of Jesuit priests, he wrote numerous articles and small books on topical and moral problems, e.g., birth control, eugenics, artificial insemination, and sterilization. But his major production remains his *Moral and Pastoral Theology* (4 v. London 1935), which he personally revised and brought up to date in five subsequent editions.

The most industrious and fruitful years of Davis's life were passed at a time when the moral theologian was required to train both clergy and laity (but especially the clergy) in a traditional body of doctrine, based on the Fathers and the great classical moralists. His four volumes bear witness to this attitude of mind. Reliable, even cautious, in their approach to pastoral problems, they form a complete compendium of the Church's official teaching, before the word *aggiornamento* had been given currency.

Yet it would be wrong to give the impression that Davis merely repeated the views of others, with no additions of his own. Certainly, in his lectures and in private discussions, he manifested a genuine independence of outlook and a truly pastoral solicitude based on a lengthy experience of the confessional and a profound sympathy with the difficulties of the ordinary Catholic layman.

That his interests were not confined to the technicalities of moral theology is shown by the work he put into revising the edition of Suárez's *De legibus* (1944), published by the Clarendon Press as one of the Classics of International Law. His last important work was an edition of St. Gregory's *Pastoral Care* (1950).

As a man, he combined intelligence and erudition with a natural simplicity and modesty that won him the affection, no less than the respect, of his many pupils. He was certainly one of the outstanding Catholic moral theologians in the English-speaking world in the second quarter of the 20th century.

[T. CORBISHLEY]

DAWSON, CHRISTOPHER

Historian; b. Hay Castle, Wales, Oct. 12, 1889; d. Budleigh Salterton, Devon, England, May 25, 1970. The son of a military, landowning Anglican family, Dawson was educated at Winchester and Trinity College, Oxford. In 1914 he became a Roman Catholic. From 1930 to 1936 he lectured in University College, Exeter. In 1934 he was Forwood Lecturer in the University of Liverpool and in 1947 and 1948 he delivered the Gifford lectures at the University of Edinburgh. In 1958 he became the first Chauncey Stillman Professor of Roman Catholic Studies in Harvard University, where he lectured until 1962.

Dawson's first book, *The Age of the Gods* (1928), reflected his conviction, supported by his study of pre-Christian cultures, that religion formed the basis of every culture. For the rest of his scholarly life he evaluated religion's place in the evolution of Europe.

In 1929 Dawson's *Progress and Religion,* an analysis of the historical implications of the evolution of the idea of progress, described modern Europe as tempted by various secularist alternatives to her true Christian culture. He found the belief in the inevitability of progress, central to these aberrations, unacceptable for a Christian. His numerous writings fostered a critical examination of the secular origins of current values and a new appreciation for the distinctively Christian values which had been central to Western culture, and which remained, he thought, essential to its survival.

For Dawson, Christianity, which was the creator of Europe, could be seen to have found its full form only in the Roman Catholic Church. He thought himself neither a theologian nor a philosopher but rather a "metahistorian"—a historian who asked large questions and drew far-reaching conclusions. At the source of his creative power was what he called "a universal metahistorical vision . . . partaking more of religious contemplation than of scientific generalization."

Dawson was an early ecumenicist, but in the last decades of his life ill health prevented him from confronting the evolution of contemporary Catholicism. His works include *The Making of Europe* (London 1932); *Religion and the Modern State* (London 1935); *Christian Freedom* (London 1943); *Religion and Culture* (London 1948); *Understanding Europe* (London, New York 1952); *The Revolt of Asia* (London 1957).

Bibliography: C. SCOTT *A Historian and His World: A Life of Christopher Dawson* (New Brunswick, NJ 1992).

[J. HELLMAN]

DAY, DOROTHY

Social activist, author and lecturer; b. Bath Beach, Brooklyn, Nov. 8, 1897; d. Nov. 27, 1980. The third in a family of five children, her father, John Day, was a newspaper reporter from Cleveland, Tenn., who attempted to impose on Dorothy a rigid Victorianism in manners and values, much of which she resisted. He did, however, introduce her to good reading, an occupation that remained a passion with her throughout her life. Her mother, Grace, with whom she was always close, was from New England.

In her autobiography, *The Long Loneliness*, Day divides her life into two parts. "The first 25 years," she writes, "were floundering, years of joy and sorrow . . . with a sense of that insecurity one hears so much about these days." Dorothy's girlhood in Chicago was spent in the performance of household chores and in reading. At the age of 15 she won a scholarship to the University of Illinois, where she remained for two years. Because of poverty and her youth, it was a difficult time for her, but also one of satisfaction because, as she later said, she found that she could live by her own resources.

In 1916 she moved with her family to New York City and there, following her own bent, she worked as a journalist for the Socialist *Call* and otherwise pursued a precarious and bohemian-like existence, living on the Lower East Side and in Greenwich Village. In 1919 she became enamored of a swashbuckling journalist, Lionel Moise. When pregnancy occurred, she, at his insistence, had an abortion. The consequences of this for her was a four-year period of delirium-type wandering, pursuing Moise in the hope that she might again become pregnant by him.

Sometime about 1925, her wandering ended when she was able to buy a small beach cottage at the west end of Staten Island. Living there with an amateur marine biologist, Forster Batterham, she bore a daughter, Tamar Therese, in March, 1926. Such was her joy, and such had been the healing effect of her quiet life on the beach, that she turned to God in gratitude. In December 1928, she was baptized in the Catholic Church at Tottenville, Staten Island.

Five years after her entrance into the Catholic Church, she met the saintly French peasant, Peter MAURIN, whom Dorothy described as her master. It was through Maurin's teaching that she came to see how her faith related to the social order. It was in personal action and not state action that those vexing and ever-growing problems of history—war, poverty, and the depersonalization of life—could be reduced. This was, for her, *the* real revolution and she immediately gave it substance by opening a house of hospitality for the poor and publishing *The Catholic Worker*. For the next half century, her voice, in the paper and on her speaking tours, was heard supporting the personalist revolution. The name of Dorothy Day became synonymous with that of a social order that was voluntaristic, communal, and open to creative work. She abhorred modern warfare and all of the instruments with which it was waged. Her pacifism was absolute.

But Dorothy Day was more than a voice for a cause. During the 40s, in a series of religious retreats held by Father John Hugo and others of the diocese of Pittsburgh, she was given what she called "the bread of the strong." Because of her early history with Marxists and anarchists, and because of her pacifist beliefs, especially during World War II, she was viewed with suspicion in the early years of her Catholic life by many who thought she had never completely broken with her radical past. But in her later life few who knew her could doubt that she had become a woman of prayer. As she herself said, she wished to be thought of only as a "daughter of the Church." She died at Maryhouse, a Catholic settlement house for homeless women in New York City's Lower East Side.

Dorothy Day was a significant figure both for her revolutionary vision and for the passion and singular steadfastness with which she pursued it. At a time, beginning with the first World War, when the friction of the historical process began to mount rapidly, and human destiny was increasingly placed at the disposal of the Caesars of the world, she wrote, spoke, and lived for a social order in which the freedom and creativity of Christ would be restored to all persons. She was a figure who moved out of the social encyclicals of the popes and who then underwrote them in the thought and action of her life.

Bibliography: D. DAY, *The Long Loneliness* (San Francisco 1952; rev. ed. 1982); *Loaves and Fishes* (San Francisco 1963). J. FOREST, *Love is the Measure. A Biography of Dorothy Day* (New York 1986). W. D. MILLER, *A Harsh and Dreadful Love. Dorothy Day and the Catholic Worker Movement* (New York 1972); *Dorothy Day* (San Francisco 1980); *All is Grace. The Spirituality of Dorothy Day* (New York 1987).

[W. D. MILLER]

DAY, GEORGE

Bishop of Chichester, prelate in the reign of Henry VIII; b. probably at Newport, Shropshire, 1501; d. London, Aug. 2, 1556. After being educated at Cambridge (D.D. in 1537), he became chaplain to Bishop Fisher of Rochester, master of St. John's, and (1537) vice chancellor of Cambridge. In 1540 Day helped in revising the Bishops' Book, which emerged as the King's Book in 1543. In the latter year he became bishop of Chichester. His religious conservatism manifested itself in 1547, when he severely rebuked the Fellows of King's College, Cambridge, for discontinuing the traditional practice of saying private Masses. He was noted for his eloquence, and in Edward VI's reign preached against the destruction of altars, was summoned before the Council, imprisoned, and deprived of his bishopric. He was released in Mary's reign and restored to his see. Day is said to have confessed that his earlier religious adherence to Henry was against his conscience.

Bibliography: P. HUGHES, *The Reformation in England*, 3 v. in 1 (5th, rev. ed. New York 1963). R. W. DIXON, *The Dictionary of National Biography from the Earliest Times to 1900* (London 1885–1900) 5:681–682.

[J. E. PAUL]

DAY, VICTOR

Diocesan administrator; b. Desselghem, Belgium, March 29, 1866; d. Helena, Mont., Nov. 7, 1946. He was the son of Henry and Fébronie (De Brabandère) Day. He was educated in Belgium at the college of Saint-Amand, Courtrai; the minor seminary of Roulers; and the major seminary of Bruges. Day was ordained on May 23, 1891, and spent two years in Bruges before leaving for the Diocese of Helena where he was to spend the remainder of his life. In 1894, he was appointed rector of the Cathedral of the Sacred Hearts by John B. Brondel, first bishop of Helena. Brondel also named him vicar-general of the diocese, an office he held for 45 years under five bishops. Day had the further distinction of acting four times as administrator of the diocese during periods when the See of Helena was vacant. He also helped to plan and build the Gothic-style Cathedral of St. Helena, begun in 1908 and completed in 1914. On June 19, 1911, he was made a domestic prelate by Pius X. Among Day's published works were his translations of Gottfried Kurth's *The Church at the Turning Points of History* (1918) and *What Are the Middle Ages?* (1921). He also compiled *An Explanation of the Catechism* (1924) and translated part two of Jacques B. Bousset's *Discourse on Universal History* (1928). He was an occasional contributor to journals and periodicals, and a life member of the American Catholic Historical Association and a member of the Medieval Academy of America.

[T. M. O'DONNELL]

DAY OF THE LORD (ESCHATOLOGY)

One concept in a cluster of ideas that center on the theme of divine JUDGMENT under its two aspects of condemnation and salvation. The word LORD in the phrase comes from the custom of substituting this term for the divine name YAHWEH toward the end of the OT period. The actual content of the expression differs according to the view taken of the object and extent of the judgment. This article treats the origin and development of the concept in the OT, the use made of the term in the apocryphal writings of the intertestamental period, and the teaching embodied in the use of the term in the NT.

In the Old Testament. The phrase ''the Day of Yahweh'' seems to find its natural setting in the cultic context of a holy war, evidence for which may be found in both biblical and extra-biblical documents. There is no direct evidence, however, that the day of battle in a holy war was called the Day of Yahweh, but one may point to the imagery employed by later prophetic texts (see below) and to the fact that such terms as ''the day of Madian'' (Is 9.3), ''the day of Jerusalem'' [Ps 136(137).7], and ''the day of Egypt'' (Ez 30.9) refer to a disaster that overtook these peoples or places in a situation otherwise viewed as a holy war.

The contrast between what the Israelite traditions presented as the messianic promises of the KINGDOM OF GOD and Israel's actual situation in the world led people to expect an imminent event in which Yahweh would destroy His enemies and make good His promises. Faith impelled these people to view this act as something required by God's justice.

It was in such a context that Amos, in the earliest use of the term ''the day of Yahweh'' in the OT (Am 5.18–20), threatened that the looked-for day of ''light'' would not automatically ensure for Israel an untroubled

possession of its land. God would act in judgment against His enemies, but these would include Israel itself, since its infidelity to the COVENANT had made it even more guilty than its neighbors (Am 3.2). The same prophetic irony is found in Isaiah (2.5–22), while in another passage (Is 22.5) the terminology of the Day of Yahweh is applied in retrospect to the humiliating events of the siege of Jerusalem (701 B.C.). The actual destruction of Jerusalem in 587 B.C. was considered in the Book of Lamentations (2.21–22; 1.21) to be the Day of Yahweh, and the same designation *post eventum* is found in Ez 13.5 (see also Ez 34.12; Jer 46.10). Such Semitic totality-thinking enabled the Prophets to characterize as the Day of Yahweh any event in which they perceived some of its component factors to be present and operative. A Western mind would be inclined to speak of analogy and would hesitate to transfer images from one event to another; but to a more imaginative mind such careful distinctions only obscure the force of the identification. This factor of totality-thinking, when added to the Israelite conviction that there was yet to be a definitive act of God sometime in the future, helps to explain the Prophets' expectancy of some one act of judgment even while they continued to characterize any similar event, whether past or future, in terms of this ultimate.

Many other expressions that include ''day'' were either coined in descriptions of the Day of Yahweh or drawn, because of some verbal similarity, into its circle of associations. The phrase ''in that day'' may be taken as an instance of the latter process. Though it is often nothing more than an editorial link binding together previously disparate oracles, it gradually took on the nature of a quasi-technical formula. In Zep 1.15 are six descriptive words occurring in sonorous cadence that repeat well-established terminology and that are repeated in turn by later Prophets (see Jl 2.2; 1.15). This process, by which a literary image became traditional and in which the aura of its meaning became fixed and almost technical, must be borne in mind in any discussion of the cosmic imagery found in connection with the Day of Yahweh. Given the constant concatenation of the forensic and martial elements that have been noted, it also may be regarded as highly unlikely that the origin of this concept is to be found in a liturgical feast of Yahweh's kingship or enthronement as S. Mowinckel and others hold, though there may be some interpenetration of thought and imagery in relation to the human king as possibly in Ps 109(110).3, 5 (*see* KINGSHIP IN THE ANCIENT NEAR EAST).

The theme of judgment, especially when applied to Israel, brought with it the notion of salvation. This is already implied in Am 5.15, and the terms connected with the concept Day of the Lord and used in this sense are found throughout the prophetic writings (see Is 2.2; 4.2–6; 11.11; Am 9.11; Jer 31.31; etc.). Both aspects of judgment are apparent in the postexilic period, and along with them is the theme of the holy war regaining its power to influence the prophetic imagery. In Is 13.1–22 one can trace all the events of this war as the Prophet imagined it to be coming upon Babylon; Obadiah employed the same concept in relation to the Edomites, who had connived at Jerusalem's fall (Ob 15). Joel, in a passage inspired by a then-recent plague of locusts (2.1–22), used the holy war imagery to create a scene of devastation and avenging fury; and still later Deutero-Zechariah (Zec 14.1–21) portrayed the final destruction of Jerusalem's enemies in terms of the great war first described in Ez 38.1–39.20. The cosmic imagery of Joel's poem can be found in connection with the holy war theme as early as the Canticle of Deborah (e.g., Jgs 5.20; Jos 10.11–15) and is alluded to in the narratives relating the Exodus events (Ex 14.19–20; 19.16–21). Cosmic upheavals are a feature of the Day of Yahweh in its first literary description (Am 5.18–20) and are found with increasing frequency (Zep 1.1–18; Is 13.1–22, and 24.1–23). The theme of salvation also continues in this later period, as can be seen from Zec 13.1; Mal 3.17; etc., and from the glosses inserted into the writings of the earlier Prophets, e.g., Am 9.11–15.

In the Apocryphal Writings. The eschatological and apocalyptic potential of the elements that composed the concept of the Day of the Lord were well exploited by the writers of the intertestamental period, who began to calculate the exact moment when the day would come and to accentuate its cosmic aspect. They described the Day of the Lord, which they designated also by all the terms used in the prophetic literature, according to their theories regarding the events that would take place at "the end" (2 Baruch 85.20). The Day of the Lord was predominantly a day of judgment (Enoch 19.1; 94.9; 100.4; Jubilees 5.10; 23.4; Testament of Levi 3.3; etc.), although the nature of this judgment became more and more individualistic. For some authors the Day of the Lord was an event in which God, either Himself or through His MESSIAH, would destroy His enemies and usher in a new period of peace and prosperity in this world (Enoch 22.10). For most writers, however, there was a real distinction between this age and the "age to come," and they based their reasoning on a more cosmic outlook regarding the nature of the coming struggle. Again, the protagonist was to be either God Himself or the Messiah, and the final Day was either to come suddenly or to be preceded by an earthly reign of God (*see* 4 Esdras 7.112–114; Assumption of Moses 10.1–7; Enoch 93.1–10; 51.1–3; 54.1–3; Jubilees 1.29; 1QpHab 7.16; etc.).

In the New Testament. The concept of the Day of the Lord in the NT reflects the profound transposition that affected all OT teaching. The fundamental context of definitive judgment is preserved, though there the judge is Christ or God through Christ (Acts 17.31; Rom 2.16). There are texts that employ the familiar phrase "Day of Judgment" (Mt 11.22, 24; 1 Jn 4.17), and these sometimes include the notion, characteristic of late Jewish thought, that men and angels are being held for some future moment of universal judgment (2 Pt 2.9; 3.7; Jude 6). When the name of Christ is substituted in the formula, usually the context is likewise one of judgment. Such phrases are: "the day of Our Lord Jesus Christ" (1 Cor 1.8), "the day of the Lord Jesus" (1 Cor 5.5; 2 Cor 1.14), "the day of Christ" (Phil 1.10). In the same context are found such phrases as "the day" (1 Cor 3.13; Heb 10.25), "that day" (2 Tm 1.12, 18; 4.8), "day of visitation" (1 Pt 2.12), "day of redemption" (Eph 4.30), "day of salvation" (2 Cor 6.2).

There is also a rather large number of passages in which one finds overt allusion to the NT teaching regarding the "passing away" of this world. A complete scenario of the Day of the Lord is provided by St. Paul in his earlier writings (1 Thes 4.13–5.3; 2 Thes 2.1–12; 1 Cor 15.24–28, 51–55), and this bears many resemblances to the Synoptic tradition regarding Our Lord's eschatological discourse (Mt 24.1–51; Mk 13.1–35; Lk 21.5–36); the most explicit description, however, is found in Mt 26.31–46. Since these texts reflect not only the doctrine but also the standardized imagery of the prophetic writings, it is difficult to determine the exact nature of the event that is described, but there is no doubt that it centers on Christ. Thus the forensic and cosmic aspects of the Day of the Lord blend in with the theme of Our Lord's PAROUSIA.

The prophetic totality-thinking that described the fall of Jerusalem in 587 B.C. as the Day of the Lord, either immediately before (Zep 1.1–18) or after (Ez 34.12) the event, seems also to be operative in the predictions and *post factum* descriptions of the destruction of Jerusalem in A.D. 70. There are also passages that speak of the day or days of the SON OF MAN in such a way as to include the present Christian era as well as the future (Lk 17.22, 26, 30; see also Jn 8.56). This sort of anticipated ESCHATOLOGY can be seen also in the use of the term "the last day" or "the last days" (Jn 6.39, 40; 2 Pt 3.3), while there are other texts that describe post-Resurrection salvation history as "the day" or "that day" (Mk 2.20; Jn 14.20; 16.23); St. Peter is quoted in Acts 2.14–36 as applying the oracle about the "last days" of Jl 3.1–4 to the events of Pentecost. Other places in the NT seem to use the term "Day of the Lord" in a less integrated manner

(2 Pt 3.10–12) or merely to repeat pre-Christian images (Rv 16.14).

It might be observed here that the patristic use of biblical imagery reflects all the many facets of the inspired text itself and continues the sacred tradition, though sometimes it is too dependent on the thought-world that gave rise to the apocalyptic literature of late Judaism and to the cosmic speculations of Hellenism.

The OT teaching concerning the Day of the Lord was transposed into the new context of the Christ-event, preserving its analogous qualities as an act of judgment present, imminent, yet still to achieve definitive realization. So too the ancient concept of the holy war, with the cosmic imagery it inspired, has been transposed and linked with the notion of Parousia so as to become the symbol of this event, which marks the cessation of all those cosmic and human forces now resisting God's merciful designs to bring about this Day of the Lord on which all things are summed up in Christ.

See Also: RESURRECTION OF THE DEAD.

Bibliography: G. VON RAD, "The Origin of the Concept of the Day of Yahweh," *Journal of Semitic Studies* 4 (1959) 97–108. L. ČERNÝ, *The Day of Yahweh and Some Relevant Problems* (Prague 1948). K. D. SCHUNCK, "Strukturlinien in der Entwicklung der Vorstellung vom *Tag Jahwes*," *Vetus Testamentum* 14 (1964) 319–330. F. PRAT, *The Theology of St. Paul,* tr. J. L. STODDARD, 2 v. (London 1926–27; repr. Westminster, Md. 1958) 2:352–476. D. S. RUSSELL, *The Method and Message of Jewish Apocalyptic* (Philadelphia 1964). H. W. ROBINSON, *Inspiration and Revelation in the O.T.,* rev. L. H. BROCKINGTON and E. A. PAYNE (Oxford 1946) 135–147. J. SCHMID, *Lexikon für Theologie und Kirche,* (Freiburg, 1957–66) 9:1273–75. For additional bibliography, *see* ESCHATOLOGY (IN THE BIBLE).

[F. MARTIN]

DAYTON, UNIVERSITY OF

Originally known as St. Mary's School for Boys (1850), also as St. Mary's Institute (1850), St. Mary's College (1912), and under its present name (1920), the University of Dayton was one of the first and now is the largest institution of the Society of Mary (MARIANISTS) in the United States. Founded as a school for boys by the Alsatian Marianist, Rev. Leo Meyer, it had its beginning on a 125-acre farm that he purchased shortly after his arrival. As enrollment increased, the curriculum was gradually extended until in 1882 the state of Ohio empowered the institution to confer collegiate degrees. A preparatory division was maintained along with the college program until 1936; since then all facilities have been used exclusively for higher educational purposes.

The direction of the University (2000) is set by a two-tiered board, the Corporation (7 members, the major-ity of whom are Marianists) and a board of trustees (34 members, nine of whom are Marianists). The president of the University is a member of both bodies. Full-time faculty number 400, 94 percent of whom are lay people, 89 percent holding doctorates. For administrative purposes, the University is operated through a series of councils; academic policies are set by the Academic Senate. Its four professional schools (Business, Education, Engineering, and Law) are accredited, as well as are several programs in the College of Arts and Sciences, which enrolls one half of the 6,500 full time undergraduate students. These major academic divisions comprise 33 departments and offer 37 different degrees on the bachelor, master, and doctoral levels. Besides the regular day session, the University also conducts evening and summer sessions and offers short-term credit courses, conferences, and institutes through the Continuing Education and Summer Programming division.

In 2000 its library housed 1,353,366 volumes, subscribed to 5,985 periodicals, and its Marian Library houses the largest collection of Marian publications in the world and provides academic sources for the International Marian Research Institution. This institution, affiliated with the Marianum in Rome, offers STLs and STDs in MARIOLOGY.

The university pioneered in Catholic coeducation with the introduction of women students in 1935, who now constitute one half the undergraduate population. In keeping with its special spirit, the University grants the yearly Marianist Award (since 1949) for outstanding scholarship for the Mother of God, and since 1986 for an outstanding contribution to the intellectual life by a Catholic.

From a total of only 171 students in 1920, the total enrollment has risen with increasing momentum since World War II to 10,318 in 2000. First in size among private institutions of higher learning in the state of Ohio, the University is 11th among the nation's Catholic colleges, and seventh in the size of its endowment. To provide the necessary facilities to accommodate the postwar student influx, the addition of 76 acres in 1960 doubled the campus; 95% of its undergraduate population, drawn from 44 states and over 30 countries, are residential.

Celebrating its 150th anniversary in 2000, the University's undergraduate program features an integrated general education program, an extensive and innovative set of courses that links liberal education and professional learning, and a philosophy of education that focuses on learning for leadership and service. Its seven doctoral programs, including most recently one in theology, positions the University of Dayton as a leader in Catholic higher education.

[J. HEFT]

DE HERETICO COMBURENDO

De heretico comburendo is the act of the English parliament passed in 1401 for the suppression of the LOL-LARDS. The spread of the ideas of John WYCLIF by this heretical group was a cause of great alarm to the Church, but the accession of the strictly orthodox Lancastrian Henry IV in 1399 marked the inception of a new phase in the constraint of HERESY in England. William Sawtre was burned at Smithfield in early 1401, and the statute *De heretico comburendo* was passed before the dissolution of parliament on March 10 that same year. The act condemned the preaching and teaching of "wicked, heretical and erroneous opinions" and forbade unlicensed preaching, the teaching or writing of doctrines contrary to the Catholic faith, and the holding of heretical conventicles and schools. The initiative lay with the bishops, who could call in the support of the secular arm. The penalties imposed by the Church courts included imprisonment and fines, and, for refusal to abjure or for relapsing, condemned heretics were to be abandoned to the secular court for public burning in order to strike fear into the minds of others so that false doctrines would be neither sustained nor tolerated. Despite its official sanction and powerful support, the act provoked resentment. Possibly in response to such feelings, as well as to minimize the role of the Church and thus disarm opposition, an attempt was made in 1406 to transfer responsibility for the prosecution of heretics from the bishops to secular officers. The Lollards in parliament requested modifications of the act in 1410, and the Commons, alleging the act's clerical origins, sought a safeguard against oppressive arrests. These efforts were unsuccessful, but a compromise was reached by the statute of 1414, which entrusted the arrest of heretics to secular officers, while preserving the Church's jurisdiction in the resulting trial. But the problem of heresy remained in England and was not permanently settled by these measures. The act was later repealed by HENRY VIII and again by ELIZABETH I after it had been restored in the reign of MARY TUDOR.

Bibliography: K. B. MCFARLANE, *John Wycliffe and the Beginnings of English Nonconformity* (New York 1953) 149–156. F. L. CROSS, *The Oxford Dictionary of the Christian Chruch* (London 1957) 384, 819. E. F. JACOB, *The Fifteenth Century, 1399–1485* (Oxford 1961) 94–96. H. S. BETTENSON, ed., *Documents of the Christian Church* (2d ed. New York 1963) 251–255. B. WILKINSON, *Constitutional History of England in the Fifteenth Century* (London 1964) 379–381, 388–389. F. D. LOGAN, *Excommunication and the Secular Arm in Medieval England* (Toronto 1966).

[C. DUGGAN]

DEACON

The English word "deacon" is derived from the Greek διάκονος, which means originally "servant," and then "helper." The term was also used among pagan Greeks to designate the holder of a cultic office, but in the Christian community it acquired a new significance. This article first treats the role and nature of the deacon's office in the early Church, then provides a brief survey of its development as a transitional stage in preparation for presbyteral ordination and, finally discusses the renewal of the order of deacons in the wake of the Second Vatican Council. This last section includes a summary of theological reflections, canon law, and norms that guide the formation and life of deacons.

Early Church. The earliest certain written use of διάκονος as the title of a specific office in the Church is found in Phil 1.1, where from the context it is clear that the special meaning of the term was already known.

Origin. This office apparently arose in the earliest days of the Church in Jerusalem. As the number of Christians in Jerusalem increased, the Greek-speaking Christians, or HELLENISTS, began to complain against the "Hebrews," or Aramaic-speaking Christians, "that their widows were being neglected in the daily ministration." The Apostles, not wishing to "forsake the word of God and serve at tables," selected seven men "of good reputation, full of the Spirit and of wisdom," to attend to this less important task. After the Apostles "had prayed, they laid their hands upon them." The seven bore Greek names, and probably the title given them, "deacons," was also Greek in origin (Acts 6.1–7). Philip, one of the seven, who later lived in Caesarea of Palestine, was also known as "the Evangelist" (Acts 21.8), a title that is also mentioned in Eph 4.11 and 2 Tm 4.5. In the latter passage the work of Timothy (not one of the seven) as an "evangelist" is called his διακονία. Another of the seven, Stephen, was soon arrested and put to death by the Jews because of the success of his wonder-working and preaching among the Jews who came from the DIASPORA, in other words, among those who at least in great part were Greek-speaking (Acts 6.8–13; 7.5460). Philip preached and baptized (Acts 8.4–14, 26–40), but "the laying on of hands" was reserved to the Apostles (Acts 8.14–17).

It is disputed whether the term διάκονος, as used in Acts 6, designates exactly the same thing as the later ecclesiastical office of deacon. The nature of the work of Stephen and Philip would seem to indicate that it did; yet the confinement of their activity to those who were not Palestinian Jews by origin, at least in Jerusalem, would appear to militate against the interpretation of the term in its technical sense; nevertheless, Philip preached to other than Hellenistic Jews in Samaria (Acts 8.5). Deacons are mentioned together with the BISHOPS, but after them in Phil 1.1 and 1 Tim 3.1–13. While the qualities expected in a deacon were superior to those of laymen, they were of a lesser order than those desired in a bishop or presbyter (cf. 1 Tm 3.8–13 with 1 Tm 3.1–7 and Ti 1.5–9). Their office was that of serving (1 Tm 3.10); yet it is implied that they shared in the power of ruling the Church (1 Tm 3.12). From the PASTORAL EPISTLES it appears that the deacons together with the bishop and the PRESBYTERS made up the hierarchy of the local churches in which Timothy and Titus labored; from these epistles it is clear that the deacons were subject to the other officials, and this also seems to be taught elsewhere (Phil 1.1).

Functions and duties. As the Church became organized administratively, deacons emerged as a distinct class. The patristic writings of the first few centuries indicate that deacons had achieved a recognized status within the hierarchy of the Church. St. Clement of Rome, when writing to the church at Corinth (42.4.) in A.D.. 96, speaks of bishops and deacons as first fruits of the Apostles. Throughout the letters of St. Ignatius of Antioch, deacons are presented as constituting the lowest order of a three-fold hierarchy, subordinate to bishops and priests. The same role is assigned to deacons by St. Polycarp (d. 156) in his letter to the Philippians (5.2–3). As he notes the qualities required in deacons, Polycarp says that they are servants of God and Christ, not of men.

Over the centuries the duties and privileges varied and at times were very extensive. In early centuries, not only did the deacon assist the priest at Mass and other liturgical services, but also kept order and gave signals for the conduct of the faithful during services, and pronounced the dismissal (as our *Ite, missa est*) for various categories of people at Mass. According to Cyprian (*Epist.* 18.1) and several ecclesiastical synods, deacons were empowered to reconcile with the Church sinners at the point of death. Whether this involved sacramental absolution or not is still controverted (see Miller FundLit 461–463). The protection and care of the poor, originally entrusted to deacons, developed in later times to wider responsibilities in the government of the Church. In some places they had more or less complete control over the goods of the Church. They served as official inspectors for the local bishop, counselors of popes and bishops, and papal emissaries to kings and councils. Until the promulgation of the Code of Canon Law in 1917, a deacon could hold the position of pastor.

Imposition of hands and sacramental character. That the order of deacon is of divine institution is clearly implied in the teaching of the Council of Trent, which condemns those who deny that in the Catholic Church there is a hierarchy, instituted by divine ordination, consisting of bishops, priests, and ministers (H. Denzinger, *Enchiridion symbolorum* 1776). The word "ministers" has reference at least to deacons, though some theologians have held that the subdiaconate and some, if not all, of the minor orders represent a division of the order of diaconate. The apostolic constitution *Sacramentum Ordinis* of Pius XII (Nov. 30, 1947) teaches clearly that deacons, no less than priests and bishops, receive the Sacrament of Holy Orders by the IMPOSITION OF HANDS (*ibid.*3859).

Essential Ceremony. The same constitution *Sacramentum Ordinis* (*ibid.* 3860) settled a controversy regarding the rite necessary for the diaconate, as well as that for priestly ordination and episcopal consecration. Formerly it was held by some that not only the imposition of hands, but also the presenting and accepting of the book of Gospels was necessary for the validity of the diaconate. The *Sacramentum Ordinis* clearly states, however, that for ordination to the diaconate the matter is the single imposition of the hand of the bishop that occurs in the rite of ordination. The formula for this Order is the Preface, the words essential for validity being the words *Emitte in eum* [or *eos*], *quaesumus Domine, . . . roboretur,* which are to be spoken not sung. Words of similar meaning have always been found in association with the imposition of hands. On the other hand, the words *Accipe Spiritum Sanctum, ad robur,* which in the present ritual accompany the imposition of the bishop's hand, represent a more recent addition to the ceremony of ordination.

At one time theologians questioned whether or not ordination to the diaconate conveyed the sacramental character. Once they reached a common consensus that the diaconate is a Sacrament, they followed with corresponding unanimity the opinion that it also imprints the sacramental character, by which the deacon becomes associated with Christ in His ministry and receives special sacred powers in his own right.

Renewal of the diaconate. The Council of Nicea (325 A.D.) in restricting the role of deacons in the eucharistic celebration stated that "they are the ministers of the bishop and the inferiors of the presbyters" (c. 18). Similarly, in 692 the Council in Trullo (c. 7) stressed the inferior place of deacons in the hierarchy, as did the Council of Toledo in the West (633 A.D.). In medieval times their influence continue to diminish to the point that the diaconate came to be considered merely a transitional stage in preparation for ordination to the priesthood. From time to time, efforts were made to restore the order of deacons to its original role. A proposal to this end was made at the Council of Trent, but it came to naught. In Germany in the 19th century the matter continued to be discussed, but it was only in the 20th century that the efforts began to bear fruit. Following the experience of many church leaders in the Dachau concentration camp during World War II, a vigorous movement got underway to renew the Church to meet the pastoral needs of the contemporary world. The diaconate was seen as an opportunity to provide a sacramental recognition of *diakonia* as a constitutive element of Church. When in 1957 Pope Pius XII responded publicly that "the time is not yet ripe" for the restoration, he declared that deacons with priests and bishops formed the Church's hierarchy and asked bishops and theologians to continue their investigations into the possibilities for a renewal of the order [*Acta Apostolicae Sedis* 49 (1957) 924–925].

In the preparatory stages before Vatican II, 90 specific proposals, many signed *en bloc*, were submitted to the Vatican, representing the desires of hundreds of bishops from many parts of the world for the restoration of the diaconate as a permanent order. In September of 1964 the council voted to revive the diaconate, including the possibility of ordaining mature married men. The council echoed the Church's ancient practice by describing the deacon as a special minister of Christ and the Church in liturgy, word, and charity. Specifically the council stated, "Strengthened by sacramental grace, deacons are dedicated to the People of God, in conjunction with the bishop and his body of priests, in the service of the liturgy, of the Gospel and of works of charity" (*Lumen gentium* 29). The council allowed for the specific roles and theology of the diaconate to be discerned as pastoral experience was gained. The *Dogmatic Constitution on the Church* endorsed the teaching of Pius XII and the majority of theologians that the diaconate was sacramental and that deacons belonged properly to the Church's hierarchy. "The diaconate can in the future be restored as a proper and permanent rank of the hierarchy. It pertains to the proper territorial bodies of bishops to decide with the approval of the supreme Pontiff whether and where it is opportune for such deacons to be appointed for the care of souls." Pope Paul VI implemented the council's decision through his *motu proprio Sacrum Diaconatus Ordinem*, which provided "certain and definite norms" for the restoration [*AAS* 59 (1967) 697–704].

The United States bishops were among the first to respond. In April of 1968 the National Conference of Catholic Bishops petitioned the Holy See for permission to revive the permanent diaconate in the United States; in August of 1968 that permission was received. Since that time more than 13,000 deacons have been ordained in the United States, with more than 2,600 candidates in formation. Approximately 93% are married. As of 1998, there were approximately 26,000 deacons serving in 129 countries around the world.

Toward a theology of the diaconate. In recognizing *diakonia* as a constitute element in the Church, Vatican II gave the diaconate new significance as a permanent order within a broader context of a renewal of all ministry in the church. No longer is it seen as a transitional stage en route to ordination to the presbyterate. The implications, however, of Vatican II's emphasis on the sacramental nature of the Church, the nature and role of all the baptized in the life of the Church and the world, and the relationship between local churches and the universal Church need further exploration. "The almost total disappearance of the permanent diaconate from the Church of the West for more than a millennium has certainly made it more difficult to understand the profound reality of this ministry" [Congregation for Catholic Education, *Basic Norms for the Formation of Permanent Deacons* (Vatican City 1998) 3.] Nonetheless, several essential elements toward a theology of the diaconate have emerged.

First, the deacon participates in the apostolic ministry of the bishop, reflecting the ancient teaching that the deacon is ordained "not unto the priesthood, but to the ministry of the bishop." This is evidenced in the deacon's ordination, in which the bishop alone lays hands upon the ordinand. Just as the bishop enjoys a unique relationship with his presbyters, who share in priestly ministry with him, so too the bishop enjoys a unique sacramental bond with his deacons, who share in his diaconate. Second, since ordination is a participation in the apostolic ministry, diaconal ordination involves a permanent and public commitment to servant-leadership. The ordination of a deacon recognizes the diaconal nature of the church herself, and the deacon sacramentalizes this reality. Third, the *diakonia* of the Church is a three-fold function of Word, Sacrament, and Charity. There is a fundamental unity in this tripartite function; this expects and demands a balanced approach to ministry on the part of the deacon, and all of it – Word, Sacrament, and Charity—is to be permeated by a commitment to charity and justice. In the words of Pope Paul VI, echoed repeatedly in official statements ever since, the deacon is to be "a driving force (*animatore*) for the Church's service or *diakonia* toward local Christian communities, and as a sign or sacrament of the Lord Christ himself, who 'came not to be served but to serve'" [Paul VI, *Ad Pascendum* (Aug. 15, 1972), Introduction].

In summary, the theology of the diaconate is concerned less with what the deacon does than with who he is, with his special relationship to the Church and world. In the person of Christ and the Church, the deacon sacramentalizes the inherent link between the worship of God and the loving care of others, thereby binding the Church's service to all people more visibly and more closely to the Gospel and the Eucharist. Through his ordination, the deacon is a sign to all God's people of what all Christians are called to be: leaders of God's people in their service to their neighbors. The deacon, because he is an ordained minister in the very midst of the world, brings the Church's ordained ministry to every dimension of human life—from the workplace and marketplace, to home and school, and to hospital, nursing home and prison.

The 1983 Code of Canon Law. The 1983 Code of Canon Law incorporated the norms established by Pope Paul VI in his *motu proprio Sacrum Diaconatus Ordinem* (1967) and *Ad Pascendum* (1972). The revised code includes deacons in the ranks of the clergy (c. 1008, c. 1009). They serve as ministers of the word (cc. 757, 764, 776), as ordinary ministers of Baptism (c. 861 §1), and as an assisting minister in the Eucharistic celebration (c. 835 §3). He is an ordinary minister for the distribution of communion (c. 910 §1), for exposition and benediction of the Blessed Sacrament (c. 943), and those blessings expressly permitted him by law (cc. 1168, 1169 §3). He may be delegated by the local ordinary or pastor to assist at and bless marriages (c. 1108). When expressly empowered to do so, the deacon my dispense from universal or particular laws (c. 89); he may also, under very strict conditions, dispense from some matrimonial impediments (cc. 1079–1081). Deacons may officiate at funeral rites (cc. 1176–1185), preside at the celebration of the liturgy of the hours, at services of the Word, at services for Sundays and feast days, where no Mass is possible (cc. 1173, 1248 §2). The deacon may be assigned the pastoral care of a parish, under the direction of a canonical pastor (c. 517 §2). Deacons may serve as judges (c. 1421), promoters of justice, defenders of the bond, and auditors or relators (cc. 1428 §2, 1435). The deacon may also serve as chancellor since that office is not restricted to priests [William H. Woestman, OMI, *The Sacrament of Orders and the Clerical State* (Ottawa 1999), 387–388].

Formation and life of deacons. In 1998, the Congregation for Catholic Education and the Congregation for Clergy issued two documents on the diaconate. *Basic Norms for the Formation of Permanent Deacons* and the *Directory for the Ministry and Life of Permanent Deacons* "are intended as a response to a widely felt need to clarify and regulate the diversity of approaches adopted in experiments conducted up to now, whether at the level of discernment and training or at that of active ministry and ongoing formation. In this way it will be possible to ensure a certain stability of approach. . . ." [Congregation for Catholic Education and Congregation for the Clergy, *Joint Declaration and Introduction* (Vatican City 1998)]. Regional conferences of bishops are to use these documents in the preparation of their own regional or national standards for the formation, ministry, and life of permanent deacons in their jurisdictions.

Throughout both documents, there is emphasis on the sacramental identity of the deacon from which specific diaconal functions flow. In many areas, since practical experience with the diaconate was lacking, the local church had focused, sometimes exclusively, on what deacons were supposed to do, rather than on who deacons were supposed to be. The Vatican documents, as well as other recent statements from Pope John Paul II, attempt to reverse that tendency. While the functions of deacons described in these documents are consistent with previous canonical and theological statements, this greater appreciation of the sacramental nature and identity of the diaconate prior to its functionality is a significant development.

Based on this sacramental identity, "it is important that deacons fully exercise their ministry, in preaching, in the liturgy, and in charity to the extent that circumstances permit. They should not be relegated to marginal duties, be made merely to act as substitutes, nor discharge duties normally entrusted to non-ordained members of the faithful" [Congregation for the Clergy, *Directory* 40]. Particular emphasis is placed on the various dimensions of formation for diaconal ministry, from the discernment and selection process for candidates, through candidate formation and ongoing formation following ordination.

The only distinction made between unmarried and married candidates for ordination to the permanent diaconate is in the promise of celibacy made by unmarried candidates during the ordination rite. In the 1990 *Roman Pontifical*, this promise is included with a number of other promises that all the ordinands (married and unmarried) make prior to the ordination itself. The ongoing development of a theology of diaconate will have to be sensitive to the states of life of the ordinand. In the vast majority of cases, the deacon will live and minister within the framework of marriage and family, speaking to the mutuality of the sacraments of matrimony and order. On the other hand, the theology of diaconate must also address the situation of celibate permanent deacons who, while sharing in the charism of celibacy with most in the presbyterate, nonetheless share in a vastly different order than presbyters. In addition, should a married deacon's wife die, the normative practice is for the deacon to remain celibate thereafter. The question of adequate formation of married candidates for the eventual possibility of living a celibate state of life is a continuing challenge.

In June of 2000, the United States Conference of Catholic Bishops (USCCB) approved a *National Direc-*

tory for the Formation, Ministry and Life of Permanent Deacons in the United States. This comprehensive document replaced the *Guidelines for the Formation of Permanent Deacons in the United States* published in 1984. The new document applies the concerns of the *Basic Norms* and the *Directory* provided by the Vatican to the unique requirements and pastoral needs of the United States. It offers a systematic review of all aspects of the diaconal ministry, from discernment through post-ordination issues, including a series of basic standards for formation for every level and dimension of the formation process.

Bibliography: PIUS XII, "Sacramentum Ordinis" (Apostolic Constitution, Nov. 30, 1947) *Acta Apostolicae Sedis* 40 (1948) 5–7. H. LECLERCQ, *Dictionnaire d'archéologie chrétienne* (Paris 1907–53) 4.1:738–746. T. KLAUSER, *Reallexikon für Antike und Christentum*, ed. T. KLAUSER (Stuttgart 1941) 3:888–909. N. MITCHELL, *Mission and Ministry: History and Theology in the Sacrament of Order* (Wilmington, Del. 1982). J. M. BARNETT, *The Diaconate: A Full and Equal Order* (2d ed.; New York 1995) J. A. KOMONCHAK, "The Permanent Diaconate and the Variety of Ministries in the Church," *Diaconal Quarterly* 3, no. 3 (1977) 15–23; 3, no. 4 (1977) 29–40; 4, no. 1 (1978) 13–25.

[J. J. O'ROURKE/T. J. RILEY/W. T. DITEWIG]

DEACONESS

The office of woman deacon belongs to the earliest stratum of Christianity and may originate with the Galilean women who ministered to Jesus (Lk 8.1–3, Conzelmann) and/or the official widows mentioned in 1 Tm 5.3–16 (Viteau). It is uncertain whether 1 Tm 3.11 refers to the wives of deacons or to deaconesses, but the majority of scholars favor the latter interpretation. In Rom 16.1–2 the woman Phoebe is described as a *diakonos* (*diakonissa* does not occur in the NT) of the church of Cenchreae, 15 miles from Corinth. She must have been an important and authoritative personage as she is said to be the *prostatis* (the feminine form of *prostates,* signifying governor, patroness, or defender) of many including St. Paul (cf. 1 Chr 27.31, 29.6; 2 Chr 8.10, 24.11, etc., and Josephus *Bible de Jérusalem,* 43 v., each with intro. by the tr. [Paris 1948–54]; single v. ed. of the complete Bible [Paris 1956] 1.385 and *Ant.* 7.380). Phoebe may have been the bearer of Paul's letter to the Romans.

We hear consistently of women deacons in the West until about the 5th century, and of isolated cases until the 10th. They obtained longer in the East. The church of St. Sophia allowed 100 male deacons and 40 female deacons (*Patrologia Latina,* ed. J. P. Migne, 271 v., indexes 4 v. [Paris 1878–90] lxxii, 924). We know the names of at least 25 women deacons (*Church Quarterly Review* 48.314, 319). *Didascalia 17* commands the bishop to ap-

point deacons and deaconesses, and the Apostolic *Constitutions 20* gives the prayers recited over both (A.N.F. 8.492). The Council of Nicaea (c. 19) and the Council of Chalcedon (c. 15) speak of the ordination of deaconesses and the imposition of hands, respectively. The Council of Trullo (cc. 14, 48) also mentions the imposition of hands upon women.

The *Pontificale Romano-Germanicum* of the 10th century contains rites for the ordination of deaconesses; these are variously called *De Benedictione* or *De Ordinatione* or *Ad faciendam diaconam.* The deaconess receives the orarium (diaconal stole) and authority to proclaim the Gospel and read the homily. The duties of deaconesses have included baptizing and anointing women candidates; instructing newly baptized women; being a liaison "officer" between the bishop and women; ministering to the poor, sick, and imprisoned; presiding over women entering into Church; caring for widows and orphans; and taking the Eucharist to sick women. They may also have administered the Sacrament of the Sick.

Modern Movements. In the 19th century there was a movement in some Protestant churches to revive the office of the deaconess. In 1833 Theodor Fliedner founded a community of deaconesses in Kaiserwerth, Germany, for the purpose of training women for hospital work and other charitable ministrations. The Church of England in 1871 sanctioned a limited revival of the office and instituted a ceremony for the ordaining of deaconesses. In 1888 deaconesses were admitted in both the Church of Scotland and the Methodist Church. The principal work of the deaconesses, ministering to the sick and the needy, recalls the memory of the charitable women whom St. Paul praised as his faithful coworkers.

The restoration of the diaconate as a permanent order in the Catholic Church fueled the discussion as to whether women could be ordained deacons. In 1992 a committee was established to study the question. The committee relied on existing studies that dealt with the biblical and historical background of the order. Its report, published in 1995, concluded women in times past were ordained deacons and it would be possible for the Church to determine to do so again. It stated that "only a few derogations would be required from current church law," all within the authority of the Apostolic See to make, to open the diaconate to women.

Bibliography: ANON., "The Early History and Modern Revival of Deaconesses," *Church Quarterly Review* 48 (1898, 1899) 302–341. J. M. FORD, "Biblical Material Relevant to the Ordination of Women," *Journal of Ecumenical Studies* 10 (1973) 669–694; "Women Deacons Past and Present," *Sister Today* (1974). R. GRYSON, *The Ministry of Women in the Early Church* (Collegeville, Minn. 1976). A. G. MARTIMORT, *Deaconesses: An Historical Study,* tr. K. D. WHITEHEAD (San Francisco 1986). C. VAGAGGINI,

"L'ordinazione delle diaconesse nella tradizione greca e bizan-tina," *Orientalia christiana periodica* 40 (1974) 146–189. REPORT OF AN AD HOC COMMITTEE OF THE CANON LAW SOCIETY OF AMERI-CA, *The Canonical Implications of Ordaining Women to the Perma-nent Diaconate* (Washington, D.C. 1995).

[J. M. FORD/T. J. RILEY/EDS.]

DEAD, PRAYERS FOR THE

This article surveys briefly the history of prayers for the dead and then gives the theological foundation under-lying this practice.

History. The earliest mention of prayers for the dead in the Judaeo-Christian tradition is found in 2 Mc 12.39–45. After a battle in 163 B.C., Judas Maccabee, the Jewish leader, directed that the bodies of the slain Jews be gathered from the battlefield for burial. They found under the tunic of each of the fallen men a valuable amu-let taken as booty from a pagan temple at Jamnia. This was in violation of the prescription of Dt 7.25 that such objects should be destroyed by fire. Judas and his men at once besought God in prayer that He would forgive the sin of these men, who had fought for His cause. More-over, Judas took up a collection to send to Jerusalem for a sacrifice of EXPIATION for SIN on behalf of the dead. The inspired author praises the action of Judas as based on faith in the resurrection of the dead. The sin of these fall-en men now stood between them and a share in that resur-rection. The prayer and sacrifice offered by the living could serve to free the dead from the condition brought on by their offense.

The promptness with which they undertook to pray for these men, the generous collection taken up by Judas from his whole army, the presumed acceptance of the priests at Jerusalem, the praise of the inspired writer—all these point to the fact that this was not an innovation but an accepted part of Jewish religious life at this time.

The only passage in the New Testament that can be adduced as evidence of prayers for the dead is Paul's prayer for Onesiphorus in 2 Tm 1.18: "May the Lord grant him to find mercy from the Lord on that day." From the context it seems clear that Onesiphorus is dead and the Apostle begs God's mercy on him.

Patristic Period. Although the references to liturgi-cal practice that have survived from the subapostolic pe-riod (e.g., in the Didache and Clement's *Letter to the Corinthians*) contain no indication of prayers for the dead, the custom of Christians praying for their departed in the 2nd century is clear from inscriptions on tombs, no-tably in the Roman catacombs. Likewise, the epitaph of ABERCIUS (d. *c.* 180), Bishop of Hieropolis in Phrygia,

concludes by asking those who understand and agree with it to pray for him (cf. H. Leclercq, *Dictionnaire d'éologie chrétienne et de liturgie,* 1:68–75).

The earliest mention of prayers for the dead in public Christian worship is found in Tertullian in 211 (*Coron.* 3.3; CorpChrist 2:1043). He speaks of Christians observ-ing the anniversary day of their departed, and he express-es himself as if he were describing a long-standing custom and not something newly introduced (cf. also *Monog.* 10.4; CorpChrist 2:1243). The *Canons of Hip-polytus* [33.1.169; H. Achelis, *Texte und Untersuchungen zur Geschichte der altchristlichen Literatur* 6.4 (Leipzig 1891) 106], which almost certainly reflect 3rd-century usage, explicitly mention prayers for the dead in the cele-bration of the Eucharist. Arnobius (*Nat.* 4.36; *Corpus scriptorum ecclesiasticorum latinorum* 4:171) toward the end of the 3rd century describes how peace and pardon are asked for all in Christian assemblies, both for those still living and for those freed from the bond of the body.

By the 4th century the evidence is universal and abundant. A few examples may suffice. Eusebius re-counts (*Life of Constantine* 4.71; *Die griechischen chris-tlichen Schriftsteller der ersten drei Jahrhunderte* 7:147) how after the death of Constantine in 337 the Emperor's body was placed before the altar and the people together with the priests prayed for his soul. St. Cyril of Jerusalem in a catechetical discourse in 348 [*Catech.* 23 (*Mystag.* 5) 9–10; *Florilegium Patristicum* 7.2:102–103] told the newly baptized that in the Eucharistic sacrifice, after the living are prayed for, the dead are also remembered. He then explained how Christ, offered in sacrifice on behalf of sinners living and dead, will be of great value before the merciful God. St. Epiphanius (*c.* 375) defends the usefulness of prayers for the dead against Aerius, a pres-byter of Pontus (*Panarion* 75.7.1–5; *Die griechischen christlichen Schriftsteller der ersten drei Jahrhunderte* 37:338–339). St. Ambrose, Bishop of Milan, writing in 379 about the death of his brother, refers to the solemn anniversary celebration of the Eucharist for the departed [*Exc. Sat.* 1.80; 2.5 (*Patrologia Latina* 16:1315–16)]. St. John Chrysostom in the last decade of the 4th century re-gards the practice of praying for the dead, especially in the Eucharistic sacrifice, and of almsgiving to implore the divine mercy for the departed as established by the Apos-tles (*Home. 3 in Phil.* 4; Field 5.37).

St. Augustine in the first part of the 5th century re-sumes the whole of the previous tradition. He cites the testimony of 2 Mc 12.43 in favor of prayers for the dead, but appeals even more strongly to the custom of the Church (*Cur. mort.* 1.3). He stresses the fact that prayers for the dead will benefit only those who have so lived as to be able to receive benefit from them (*Enchir.* 110; *Civ.*

21; 24.2). Prayer in general, but especially the Holy Sacrifice, and almsgiving are of help to the departed (*Serm.* 172.2.2).

Succeeding Centuries. The same custom was received and confirmed in the times subsequent, but it was not until the 13th century that this became the object of a solemn magisterial pronouncement in an ecumenical council, Lyons II (1274), when there was question of a reunion with the Greek church. Then, in connection with the doctrine on PURGATORY, it was declared that souls undergoing purification after death could be assisted by the suffrages (i.e., the intercessory prayers) of the living faithful, namely, by Masses, almsgiving, prayers in general, and other devout practices according to the custom of the Church (H. Denzinger, *Enchiridion symbolorum* 856). The matter was repeated in almost identical language at another Council of reunion, Florence (1439), in the *Decree for the Greeks* (ibid. 1304).

With the development of the doctrine on INDULGENCES a new element was added to the assistance the living could provide for the dead. In 1476 Pope Sixtus IV granted the first plenary indulgence applicable to the souls in purgatory (ibid. 1398). Since this caused some misunderstanding, the following year he issued a document explaining that this indulgence was of avail to the departed in the same way as other prayers and almsgiving, though in a higher degree (ibid. 1407). Against doubts raised by the reformers, the Council of Trent defined that "purgatory exists and that the souls detained there are helped by the suffrages of the faithful, but especially by the acceptable sacrifice of the altar" (*Decree on Purgatory,* Dec. 3, 1563; *Enchiridion symbolorum* 1820). The Sacred Congregation of Indulgences in 1840 made clear an important distinction between an indulgence as it is offered to God as a suffrage by the Church and its actual effect for the soul for whom it is offered (ibid. 2750). What is offered to God in the case of a plenary indulgence is fully sufficient to free the soul at once from purgatory, but what is actually effected will depend on the acceptance and the good pleasure of God.

Theological Foundations. The practice of praying for the dead rests upon two principal foundations. The proximate foundation is the COMMUNION OF SAINTS. The remote foundation is the meaning of creaturely activity within the plan of God.

Communion of Saints. Pope Leo XIII (encycl. *Mirae caritatis,* May 28, 1902; *Enchiridion symbolorum* 3363) explained in the following way the first of these foundations:

> The grace of mutual love among the living, strengthened and increased by the Sacrament of the Eucharist, flows, especially by virtue of the Sacrifice [of the Mass], to all who belong to the communion of saints. For the communion of saints is simply . . . the mutual sharing of help, atonement, prayers, and benefits among the faithful, those already in the heavenly fatherland, those consigned to the purifying fire, and those still making their pilgrim way here on earth. These all form together one city, whose head is Christ, and whose vital principle is love. Faith teaches that although the august Sacrifice can be offered to God alone, it can nevertheless be celebrated in honor of the saints now reigning in heaven with God, who has crowned them, to obtain their intercession for us, and also, according to apostolic tradition, to wash away the stains of those brethren who died in the Lord but without yet being wholly purified.

This communion of saints is rooted in the creative intention of God. For He intends to communicate His goodness not to many isolated individual beings unrelated to one another in any significant way, but to one family that He establishes in Christ, His Son. He intends to achieve a social result: the heavenly Jerusalem, the City of God, the glorified Body of Christ. And men's acceptance of God's self-giving love is fundamentally their willingness to be members of this society. Whatever anyone in this communion freely and lovingly does is not simply his own possession and achievement, but belongs to the whole society, and to each within it according to his capacity to receive.

Creaturely Activity in the Plan of God. The second or remote foundation of prayers for the dead concerns the meaning of creaturely activity within the plan of God. God does not produce the heavenly Jerusalem by a simple *Fiat!* (Let it be made!), but through the efforts and toil of His creatures, so that it is their city as well as His. God never acts in the world as if the actions of creatures counted for nothing.

However, He does at times produce extraordinary results that are like a new creation, as when He first justifies a sinner in Baptism. In this case God in an instant fits a soul for immediate entrance into heaven, provided only it is willing and accepts His grace in faith. One who dies directly after Baptism goes at once to heaven. Yet even here God is not acting without taking created activity into account. For this result is due to the merits of Christ, to His loving, free obedience unto death whereby He passed to glory. The sinner in Baptism is buried with Christ in death and rises to a new life in Him (cf. Rom 6.4).

But once a person has been incorporated into Christ he must bear the responsibility for his actions in his new condition, whether these be good or bad (*see* INCORPORATION IN CHRIST). The Church has always recognized that the justification of one who sins grievously after Baptism does not necessarily fit him for immediate entrance into heaven. His own deeds of life in the Spirit must put to death the sinful deeds of the flesh. He must act in the power of Christ to destroy the evil effects of his sin and to purify himself through works of penance, a task that may still remain to he done even after the actual guilt of sin is removed and he is once more restored to God's friendship. To suppose that God deals otherwise with man is to regard a man's acts as ultimately irrelevant. It is to affirm that God alone does everything and creatures even under divine GRACE do nothing. One who dies in the friendship of God but has not done full penance for the sins he has committed (unless he dies immediately after Baptism) is still in some sense bound by his sin. Purification remains to be done. God could effect this in an instant without any punishment being undergone by the sinner, as He does for the newly baptized. But this would be to disregard the intrinsic meaning of created action. Or He can exact full punishment so that the reshaping of the created will and of its disposition within the harmony of the divine plan be experienced as something painful, something against the selfishness of the will that committed sin.

But there is a third possibility that flows from the communion of saints. God can look upon the prayers, the almsgiving, the penances, and other good works done by the living, especially as united in worship to Christ's sacrifice in the Mass and offered on behalf of the departed, and in view of this remit their debt of punishment in whole or in part. For this both safeguards the meaning of created activity and recognizes the bond of union that joins all together in the love of Christ. It should be noted that it is more a work of the pilgrim Church than of the triumphant Church to intercede on behalf of the departed, for the saints in heaven are no longer in a position to merit or to do deeds of penance. Still their prayers also are no doubt of great assistance to those in purgatory.

See Also: INTERCESSION; POOR SOULS; SAINTS, INTERCESSION OF.

Bibliography: A. MICHEL, *Dictionnaire de théologie catholique,* ed. A. VACANT et al., 15 v. (Paris 1903–50; Tables générales 1951–) 13.1:1197–98, 1204–12,123037, 1301–10. A. J. MACLEAN, J. HASTINGS, ed. *Encyclopedia of Religion and Ethics,* 13 v. (Edinburgh 1908–27) 10:209b–213b. C. V. HERIS, "Théologie des suffrages pour les morts," *Maison-Dieu* 44 (1955) 58–67. H. RONDET, "La Prière pour les morts," in *Le Purgatoire profond mystère* (Paris 1957) 48–56. Y. M. J. CONGAR, "Le Purgatoire," in *Le Mystère de la mort et sa célébration* (Lex Orandi 12; Paris 1956) 279–336. B. BARTMANN, *Purgatory* (London 1936) 160–182. M. JUGIE, *Purgatory and the Means to Avoid It,* tr. M. G. CARROLL (Westminster, Md. 1949) 88–103. E. O'BRIEN, "The Scriptural Proof for the Existence of Purgatory from 2 Mac. 12:43–45," *Sciences ecclésiastiques* 2 (1949) 80–108.

[J. H. WRIGHT]

DEAD, WORSHIP OF THE

The primitives' customs and practices connected with the dead often evoke a feeling of revulsion in modern minds, even though they were frequently carried out in a reverential attitude. Again, much that to moderns appears as worship was done to avert dangers that people fear can come from the dead. The casting out of the corpses in Iran to carnivorous animals was motivated by the desire to get the skeleton stripped of decayed flesh as soon as possible. The bones themselves, however, were held in high honor. Through the eating of parents, a practice that was found in some parts of Australia, the survivors wished to bury their parents in their own bodies. This action was regarded as so proper that family groups often carried these dead with them in their wanderings as long as possible, and often under great difficulties. On the other hand, grave offerings were often given only to restrain the dead from acts of vengeance; and the closing of the eyes and mouth and the avoidance of touching the threshold in carrying out the corpse were likewise thought of as measures of protection.

From a loving attitude toward the dead came the rites for laying out the corpse and the laments for the dead among some cultures of the world; platform burial facing the light; deposition of the body in the fruitful earth, often in a facing and standing position—interpreted by some as an indication of expected rebirth; the painting of the corpse with red ocher, the color of blood; the preservation of the corpse through a process of desiccation or mummification and embalming; the placement of the body in a stone grave chamber (stone itself being a symbol of permanence); and the practice of erecting megaliths—all bear witness to a loving and pious activity, the purpose of which was to assure the dead an "eternal dwelling." This concern culminated in the building of the pyramids.

Most offerings to the dead, funeral rites (including joint burial of living beings and funeral games), and the hospitable celebration of anniversaries—all point in the same direction. In the Urabon Festival in Japan, little lighted boats are put in the rivers to accompany the departed guests to the other world. The honoring of the dead also explains the custom of engraving the family tree on the grave monument and on a tablet in the home, and of making announcements of departures and returns and important family events before this shrine.

The disposal of the corpse by fire (cremation) did not necessarily presuppose an attitude of fear toward the dead. It could give quicker freedom of the spirit from the corpse and an earlier passage to a happier and brighter existence in the other world. The acceleration of the process of reincarnation is also a factor to be considered. The reverential rites of the dead, a cult of the dead in the strict

A Dani village chief displays the mummified body of a village elder, preserved in a sitting position to be honored after death, Irian Jaya, Indonesia, c. 1990. (©Chris Rainier/CORBIS)

sense, reached their culmination in ancestor worship and in ruler worship.

See Also: ANCESTOR WORSHIP.

Bibliography: C. M. EDSMAN, *Die Religion in Geschichte und Gegenwart* (Tübingen 1957–65) 6:959–961 with good bibliog. G. ECKERT, *Totenkult und Lebensglaube im Caucatal* (Braunschweig 1948). J. G. FRAZER, *Belief in Immortality and the Worship of the Dead* (London 1913–14). F. HERRMANN, *Symbolik der Naturvölker* (Stuttgart 1961) 188–202. H. BÄCHTOLD-STÄUBLI, ed., *Handwörterbuch des deutschen Aberglaubens,* 10 v. (Leipzig 1927–42) 1:976–997; 5:1023–1167.

[A. CLOSS/EDS.]

DEAD SEA

A body of water in Palestine at the southern end of the Jordan Valley. The Dead Sea, whose surface lies 1,286 feet below sea level, is the lowest point on the surface of Earth. Its name is well chosen, since the excessive chemical content of the lake, including potassium, sodium, and magnesium chlorides, prevents all forms of vegetation and sea life from existing there. It resembles the Great Salt Lake of Utah in that both have a salt concentration of more than 20 percent, almost six times that of ordinary sea water. The Israelites called it the Salt Sea. The OT refers to it also as the Sea of the Arabah, i.e., of the desert. The Greeks were fascinated by the chunks of bitumen that were occasionally found floating on its surface, and therefore they referred to it as the Asphalt Lake. In modern Arabic it is the Bahr Lūt (Lot's Sea), recalling Gn 19.1–29.

In its northern sector the waters of the Dead Sea reach down to depths of about 1,300 feet. The warm and dry climate causes heavy evaporation and leaves a bluish haze hanging perpetually over the lake; thus although it has no outlet, a natural balance with the incoming waters of the JORDAN River is maintained, so that the level of the Dead Sea from year to year is fairly constant; but the minerals carried into it remain. In recent years, however, the inflow has been greatly reduced by the increased use of the waters of the Jordan for irrigation.

The lake, 48 miles long and 8 miles wide, is surrounded on both its east and west sides by barren highlands that break off unevenly as they descend to the water's edge. The hills on the eastern side are for the most part very precipitous, often plunging directly into the

Shoreline of the Dead Sea. (©Richard T. Nowitz/CORBIS)

depths of the lake and making travel along the shoreline impossible. At best, travel is hazardous even on the high plateau, which is broken by deep canyons leading down to the lake. The most treacherous of these are the Arnon (Wâdī el-Môjib) and the Zared Valley (Wâdī el-Ḥesā), both providing an abundant source of water for the Dead Sea during the winter rainy season.

A broad marl peninsula, called the Lisân (tongue), extends from the southeastern shore of the Dead Sea to within two miles of the opposite shore. It helps to form the large shallow bay, averaging about three feet in depth, at the southern extremity of the lake. According to biblical tradition, this area was the inhabited plain of the Five Cities, or Pentapolis, among which were the sinful cities of Sodom and Gomorrah. On the western corner of the bay there is a sizable natural mountain of salt (Jebel Usdum), which, with its contorted cliffs and dunes, easily evokes the image of Lot's wife.

Because of the lack of rainfall on the Desert of Judah, no rivers flow into the Dead Sea from the west, although a few wadies (e.g., Wadi Qumran) may have small streams in the winter. Nevertheless, two important springs form little oases along the western shore. One, called 'Ain Feshkha, is located close to the Dead Sea near the site of the former QUMRAN COMMUNITY, where the DEAD SEA SCROLLS were found. Farther south, another spring, that of Engedi (modern Arabic 'Ain Jidi), which lies on a plateau, provides sufficient water for rather extensive irrigation.

Symbolic of desolation and destruction, the wrath of nature and of God, the Dead Sea somewhat surprisingly figures but little in the pages of the Bible. The single account, however, of the punishment of the sinful cities of Sodom and Gomorrah in Gn 19.1–29 leaves mankind with an interpretative history that is not easily erased. Tradition has also placed the imprisonment and behead-

Dead Sea Scrolls, on display at the Special Museum, House of the Book in Jerusalem. (CORBIS/Bettman)

ing of John the Baptist at Herod's fortress of Machaerus overlooking the northeastern end of the Dead Sea.

Bibliography: *Encyclopedic Dictionary of the Bible,* tr. and adap. by L. HARTMAN (New York 1963), from A. VAN DEN BORN, *Bijbels Woordenboek* 513–514. D. BALY, *The Geography of the Bible* (New York 1957) 202–210. F. M. ABEL, ''Notes complémentaires sur la Mer Morte,'' *Revue biblique* 38 (1929) 237–260; *Géographie de la Palestine,* 2 v. (Paris 1933–38) 1:498–505. E. G. KRAELING, *Rand McNally Bible Atlas* (2d ed. New York 1962) 25–26. W. SMITH, *Dictionary of Greek and Roman Geography,* 2 v. (London 1873–78).

[J. W. RAUSCH]

DEAD SEA SCROLLS

Dead Sea Scrolls (DSS) is the generic title for six groups of documents discovered between 1947 and 1956 in caves and sites of the Judean Desert in several wadies (torrent-beds) that empty into the western side of the Dead Sea; two other groups found elsewhere are related to them. Altogether they constitute one of the major archaeological discoveries of the twentieth century.

Definition. The most important group of these documents was found in eleven caves near the Wadi Qumran, and they are often called ''Qumran Scrolls'' (QS) or

''DSS'' (in the specific sense). The first Qumran cave was discovered by Bedouin shepherd boys in 1947, when the West Bank was part of the British Mandate of Palestine. Between 1952 and 1956 ten further caves were discovered, either by Bedouins or archaeologists, in the Jordanian-controlled West Bank. From these eleven caves came scrolls and fragments, dating roughly from the end of the third century B.C. to A.D. 68, written mostly in Hebrew, although many were in Aramaic, and a few in Greek. All told, they number today about 820 texts, usually divided into three classes: biblical, sectarian, and intertestamental Jewish writings.

Related to the QS are two groups of documents coming from elsewhere. One group was found in the genizah (hiding-place) of the Synagogue of Ezra in Old Cairo (Egypt) in 1896. Among the thousands of texts discovered there by Solomon Schechter were copies of two texts little understood at the time (Damascus Document [CD] and Testament of Levi [CTL]), both of which are now recognized as copies of or related to Qumran texts. The other group was found in 1963 by Israeli archaeologists at Masada, the remains of a Herodian fortress south of Qumran, to which Jews had fled after the destruction of Jerusalem (A.D. 70) and the Qumran community (A.D. 68). These were fragmentary documents, some biblical, but most nonbiblical, yet related to the QS.

Four other groups of documents, not related to the QS, were found, at first by Bedouins and later by archaeologists, in caves of Wadi Murabba'āt, Wadi Ḥabra (called in Hebrew Naḥal Ḥever), Wadi Mahras (Naḥal Mishmar), and allegedly in Wadi Seiyal (Naḥal Ṣe'ĕlîm). Apart from the last mentioned, these caves are situated in torrent-beds south of and parallel to Wadi Qumran, mostly in Israel. Wadi Seiyal was said by the Bedouin finders of a Greek Minor Prophets scroll to be the site of its discovery, when it was brought to the Palestine Archaeological Museum in East Jerusalem, which was under Jordanian control at the time. Later it was learned that ''Seiyal'' was used to disguise the scroll's real provenience, Israeli Naḥal Ḥever. The fragments coming from these sites have a few biblical texts among them, but are mostly domestic documents (letters, contracts deeds of sale). Some are dated and come from the period A.D. 70–135; most are related to the Second Jewish Revolt against the Romans (A.D. 132–135).

The eighth group of documents was found in 1952 at Khirbet Mird, the ruins of a Byzantine Greek monastery, Kastellion, built on the site of an older Herodian fortress, Hyrcanium near Wadi en-Nār, nine miles southeast of Jerusalem (not near the Dead Sea). Some are biblical documents (NT) written in Greek and Christian Palestinian Aramaic, but 100 are in Arabic, dating from the 6th-to-10th centuries A.D. Among the Greek texts, one is even a fragment of Euripides' *Andromache*. These texts are unrelated to the seven other groups; they have been called "DSS" simply because they were discovered about the same time as the QS and initially were thought to be related to them. These eight groups of documents from the Judean Desert make up the "DSS" in the generic sense. The rest of this article will be devoted to the QS or "DSS" in the specific sense.

Discovery and excavation of Qumran. Prior to 1947, little attention had been paid to Khirbet Qumran, the Roman-period stone ruins on a plateau immediately north of Wadi Qumran and a half mile south of Cave 1. A suspected connection between them was confirmed by the subsequent excavation of Kh. Qumran by G. L. Harding (Jordanian Department of Antiquities) and R. De Vaux, OP (École Biblique) from 1951 to 1956. The excavation revealed a community center belonging to an ascetic pre-Christian Jewish group (*see* QUMRAN COMMUNITY). When in February of 1952 the Bedouins found Cave 2, three archaeological institutions of Jerusalem sent out an investigating party to scour the area about Qumran. They searched 267 caves or holes in the cliffs lining the northwest shore of the Dead Sea and found artifacts and evidence of human habitation in 37 of them, but only 25 caves yielded material related to Kh. Qumran. These were places where individuals of the community lived, who used the center for common activities (meals, meetings, study, baths, work areas). The numbered caves are those that yielded written material; some of them were also habitats. Cave 1 had been a genizah-like storage cave, and Cave 4, hollowed out artificially in antiquity, became the place where the community deposited its library of scrolls for safekeeping when it learned of the advance of a Roman legion against it in A.D. 68.

The community center had been built on the ruins of an earlier site, probably the Judean fortress, "Salt City" (Jos 15.62). Sometime prior to 135 B.C., they constructed the first stage of their building, which was later expanded, and more strongly rebuilt after an earthquake of 31 B.C., mentioned by Josephus (*Ant.* 15.5.2 §121). The community center is divided by a corridor separating its two main parts: the eastern part containing a large dining hall, kitchen, pantry, laundry, dyeing area, pottery kiln, defense tower, and second-floor scriptorium; the western part a storage and work area with stable, forge, bake ovens, cisterns, and a long aqueduct bringing water from the wadi to baths, a circular Iron Age cistern, and six rectangular cisterns constructed in Roman-period style. The community center finally was destroyed by fire, as a stratum of ash with Roman arrowheads reveals, suggesting that it was razed by the Roman *Legio X Fretensis*, which

was in the Jordan Valley before it went up to the siege of Jerusalem (Josephus, *Bell. Jud.* 5.2.3. §70).

Publication of Scrolls. In 1947 seven major scrolls and fragments of some seventy other texts were retrieved from Qumran Cave 1. The seven scrolls were sold by the Bedouins in two batches. Four of the them (Isaiah A, Manual of Discipline, Pesher on Habakkuk, and Genesis Apocryphon) were acquired initially by the Syrian Orthodox Metropolitan of St. Mark's Monastery in Jerusalem, who allowed three of them to be published almost immediately by the American Schools of Oriental Research (editor M. Burrows, 1950–51). The other three (War Scroll, Thanksgiving Psalms, Isaiah B) were acquired by E. L. Sukenik, professor of the Hebrew University in Jerusalem, and published by him (1954–55). The fragments of Cave 1 were published by Clarendon Press (Oxford) in 1955 as volume 1 of Discoveries in the Judaean Desert (DJD), which is the series of official publication for the vast majority of the DSS.

The scrolls and fragments from Qumran caves 1–3, 5–11, the texts of Murabba'ât and most of those of Naḥal Ḥever were published with reasonable dispatch. The big problem was the Cave 4 material, discovered in 1952. From that cave came no full scroll, but more than 15,000 fragments, which had to be assembled like a giant jigsaw puzzle. In 1954 an international and interconfessional team of seven scholars was set up to work on these fragments housed in the Palestine Archaeological Museum (Jordanian-controlled East Jerusalem, to which no Jew was allowed to come, which explains why no Jewish scholar was on the team). By 1960 most of the jigsaw puzzle was complete, and publication of the fragments should have ensued; but for one reason or another delay set in (procrastination; desire to write full commentaries on assembled texts, joined with theories that were unconvincing; sickness and death of team members). By 1985 only a small portion of these important fragmentary texts had been released by these scholars to the public domain; then outcries began, becoming vociferous across the world. Eventually, the Israel Antiquities Authority moved in and reconstituted the leadership of the editorial team and expanded it. In the 1990s, volumes of DJD began to appear regularly, with the vast majority of the Cave 4 texts being officially published by 2001.

Dating of scrolls. Once the scrolls were recognized as genuinely ancient documents, scholars began to work out a way of dating them palaeographically (according to the handwriting). In general, four stages are recognized: (a) *Archaic*, 250–150 B.C.; (b) *Hasmonean*, 150–30 B.C.; (c) *Herodian*, 30 B.C.–A.D. 70; (d) *Post-Herodian/Ornamental*, after A.D. 70. Some of the biblical texts were written in archaic script, but the vast majority of the QS were inscribed in either Hasmonean or Herodian scripts. Palaeographers often further distinguish both cursive and formal hands within these classes. Palaeographical dates always have to be understood as within 50 years. To some critics, this mode of palaeographical dating seemed subjective and suspect, but no one would have expected the confirmation of the dates, which came with the use of radiocarbon dating. In 1991 fourteen documents (QS and texts from Murabba'ât, Seiyal, and Mird) were subjected in Zurich, Switzerland, to radiocarbon dating, which likewise has its own range. To the surprise of all, it confirmed the palaeographical dating, with one exception, to which it gave an even earlier dating. Again in 1995, still other texts were subjected to this testing in Tucson, Arizona, and the result was no different.

Sigla of Scrolls. Because the titles of QS are often lengthy and there are multiple copies of them, sometimes coming from different caves, a system of *sigla* (abbreviated signs) was worked out for them. The usual scheme follows this order: material (often omitted), place of discovery, title, copy, and language. Thus pap = papyrus; cu = copper; o = ostracon; 1Q = Cave 1 of Qumran; 4Q = Cave 4 of Qumran; Hev = Hever; Mas = Masada; Mur = Murabba'ât; C = Cairo (Genizah texts). Titles of OT books are those usually used; those of nonbiblical books have to be learned (e.g. S = Serek Hayyah ad [Community Rule]; D = Damascus Document; M = *Milhamah* [War Scroll]). Before such titles one uses other notations that must be learned: p = *pesher* (commentary); ap = apocryphon. A superscript letter denotes the copy of a given text: [a, b, c]. Finally, the language of the text is given: heb = Hebrew (usually omitted); ar = Aramaic; nab = Nabatean; gr = Greek. Thus 1QIsa[a] = first copy of Isaiah from Qumran Cave 1; CD = Damascus Document from Cairo Genizah; 4QD[a] = first copy of same from Qumran Cave 4. Instead of a title, many nonbiblical texts are referred to by number (all texts published in DJD have a number). Thus cu3Q15 = copper text numbered 15 from Qumran Cave 3 (= so-called Copper Scroll). After such sigla one usually finds numbers: 9.11, which can mean fragment 9, line 11, or (in continuous texts) column 9, line 11. When a lower-case roman numeral appears between two arabic numbers, then the first number = fragment, the roman numeral = column, and the last number = line(s). Thus 4QpNah 3–4 ii 5–10 = *pesher* (commentary) on Nahum from Qumran Cave 4, joined fragments 3–4, column ii, lines 5–10.

Lists of Scrolls. The complete list of the DSS is too long to reproduce here, but the reader will find lists in the following (see bibliography below): *Encyclopedia of the DSS*, 2.1013–1049 (Qumran, Masada, Murabba'ât, H ever-Seiyal, Mishmar-Nar, Mird); F. García Martínez, *Dead Sea Scrolls Translated*, 465–519 (Qumran only);

García Martínez and Tigchelaar, *DSS: Study Edition*, 2.1311–1361.

Biblical Texts. Of the 820 QS, about a quarter are copies of OT books. Among the 127 biblical texts from Cave 4 alone, every protocanonical book is represented except Esther and Nehemiah. Since in antiquity Ezra and Nehemiah formed one book (as in the Septuagint, called *Esdras B*) and since Ezra is represented by a fragment, Esther is the only one missing. No one knows why; it may be sheer chance that no fragment has survived. All 66 chapters of Isaiah are preserved in 1QIsa[a], which is dated both palaeographically and by radiocarbon to 125–100 B.C. Prior to its discovery the oldest known copy of Isaiah was dated A.D. 895 (in M. ben Asher Codex of the Prophets). Consequently, this Qumran Isaiah text takes one back over 1000 years and testifies in general to the care with which Jewish scribes copied this book throughout the centuries. Some biblical fragments are even older, dated to the end of the third century B.C. Such texts would not have been copied in the community scriptorium; rather, they had been brought to Qumran by sectarians who came there.

The Qumran biblical texts, however, brought some surprises. One is that fragments of 1 Samuel and Jeremiah reveal a Hebrew form of those books that differs from the medieval Masoretic text, but agrees with the Septuagint. Sometimes it had been thought that the Septuagint of such a book was a poor translation that deliberately abridged the Hebrew text. The Septuagint of Jeremiah is about 1/8 shorter than the Hebrew text. 4QJer[b], however, having a Hebrew text that corresponds to the Greek of the Septuagint, has a form of Jer 10:3–11 without vv. 6–8, 10 of the Hebrew. It thus shows that the Septuagint was an accurate translation of a different Hebrew recension of Jeremiah, which coexisted in Palestinian Judaism along with the Masoretic recension. The same is true of 4QSam[a], which has a form of 1 Samuel 17 with only 33 verses of the 58 in the Masoretic Hebrew.

Another surprise is that 4QExod[m], dating from the early 2nd century B.C., contains the repetitious, expanded form of Exodus, previously known from the Samaritan Pentateuch. Hence such discoveries show that some OT books did not have a fixed text tradition such as we have been assuming on the basis of the known Hebrew text of the Masoretic tradition. Qumran phylacteries and mezuzot also contain OT passages that have noteworthy variants (DJD 6.31–85).

Semitic forms of certain deuterocanonical books of the OT have turned up in the QS. For centuries Catholic Bibles depended on the Greek and Latin versions of Sirach, until 1896 when Hebrew fragments of Sirach were recovered in the Cairo Genizah. In addition to these six texts, older Hebrew fragments of Sirach were retrieved from Qumran Cave 2 (2Q18 [= Sir 6.14–15; 6.20–31]), Cave 11 (11QPsᵃ [11Q15] 21.11–17; 22.1 [= Sir 51.13–20b; 51.30b]), and Masada (Mas1h [= Sir 39.27–43.30]). Similarly, Catholic Bibles used the Book of Tobit in the short Latin form of Jerome's Vulgate, which corresponded somewhat to the short Greek recension of Tobit (MSS Vaticanus and Alexandrinus). In 1844 Constantin von Tischendorf discovered Codex Sinaiticus with its long Greek recension of Tobit, remarkably close to the neglected Vetus Latina. Now from Cave 4 have come four fragmentary Aramaic texts of Tobit (4QTobᵃ⁻ᵈ ar [4Q196–4Q199]) and one Hebrew (4QTobᵉ [4Q200]; see DJD 19.1–80). These fragments supply about 1/5 of Tobit not only in the original Aramaic form, but also in a Hebrew translation. This Semitic form of the story is sometimes longer than the so-called long form.

Because copies of such non-protocanonical writings have turned up at Qumran, they raise the question about the canon among such Jews. "Canon," however, is a Christian term, which would have meant nothing to ancient Jews; a Christian anachronism is involved. Yet the Jews of Qumran considered the Law and the Prophets to be God's commands given to them "through Moses and all his servants the Prophets" (1QS 1.2). Whether other writings (such as Sirach, Tobit, 11QTemple) would have had the same authority for this community as the Law and the Prophets is a question no one can answer.

Finally, three ancient targums have been recovered from Qumran. A fairly extensive Aramaic translation of the Book of Job is found in the fragments of 11QtgJob (11Q10), and a tiny fragment of it is 4QtgJob (4Q157 [= Job 3.5–9; 4.16–5.4]). Two small fragments of an Aramaic translation of Leviticus 16 are found in 4QtgLev (4Q156 [= Lev 16.12–15; 16.18–21]; in DJD 6. 86–90).

Sectarian Texts. As important as the biblical texts are among the QS, the sectarian texts may be even more important, because they supply us with so much evidence about the history of ancient Palestinian Judaism that was unknown prior to 1947. These sectarian texts were composed explicitly for use by members of the Qumran community: 1QS (Community Rule [often called "Manual of Discipline"] and its ten 4Qcopies [4QSᵃ⁻ʲ], and 5QS [5Q11]); CD (Damascus Document and its eight 4Q copies [4QDᵃ⁻ʰ], possibly composed for community members not living at Qumran); the various *pesharim* (commentaries on OT prophets and psalms) from different caves; 1QHᵃ (Thanksgiving Psalms); 1QM (War Scroll), 4QMMT (*Miqṣat Ma'ăśê hat-Tôrāh*, "Some Deeds of the Law" [4Q394–399]); and possibly 11QTempleᵃ⁻ᵇ (11Q19–20). Whereas previously we knew a little about such Jews from information supplied

by Pliny, Josephus, Philo, and Hippolytus (*see* QUMRAN COMMUNITY), now we have not only the biblical texts that they read, but also the rulebooks and theological treatises that guided their way of life.

The sectarian literature gives firsthand evidence of the regulations governing their communal ascetic life and reveals how they dealt with purity and defilement in ways different from later regulations formulated in the Mishnah and rabbinic writings. Although they deal with some of the same problems, they often supply a slightly different solution to them, based on this community's esoteric interpretation of Scripture.

This category of writings is striking in that practically all of it is composed in Hebrew, which reflects an important aspect of the Jews of Qumran, who made an effort to use the "language of the sanctuary" in their communal life, when the vast majority of their contemporaries were speaking Aramaic.

Intertestamental Jewish Literary Texts. "Intertestamental" is a Christian misnomer for the third kind of documents found among the QS, but it is the conventional term. It refers to Qumran copies of writings composed in the time between the final redaction of Daniel, the latest OT book, and the first of the NT compositions. It includes such writings as *Jubilees, 1 Enoch*, and the forerunners of the *Testaments of the Twelve Patriarchs*. To these well-known writings one must add many other literary, liturgical, and sapiential texts previously unknown, especially the Aramaic writings, which Qumran Jews read, but undoubtedly did not compose.

DSS and Early Christianity. In the DSS there is no mention of John the Baptist, Jesus of Nazareth, his apostles and disciples, or anything Christian. In the early 1970s, José O'Callaghan attempted to identify Greek fragments of Cave 7 as bits of NT writings. He has, however, convinced no more than a half-dozen followers. More recently 7Q5, which he claimed was a fragment of Mark 6.52–53, has been shown to be a fragment of *Enoch* in Greek. Although the Australian Barbara Thiering and American Robert H. Eisenman have maintained that the DSS are Jewish Christian writings, their claims have fallen on deaf ears among scholars.

Nevertheless, there is no doubt that the discovery of the QS has shed much light on the Palestinian Jewish matrix of early Christianity. Anyone who studies the QS and the NT cannot help but detect familiar parallels and literary contacts. How does one account for the mysterious silence in the NT about the Jews of Qumran? Did Jesus of Nazareth know of them? Presumably he did, but the Gospels never depict him in controversy with them, as they do with Pharisees, Sadducees, and Jewish leaders.

Does Jesus ever refer indirectly to Qumran Jews? Perhaps in the Sermon on the Mount, when he mentions what has been said to people of old, "You shall love your neighbor and hate your enemy" (Mt 5.43). Love of the neighbor is found in Lv 19.18, but one looks in vain for hatred of enemies in the OT. From QS, however, we learn that members of the Qumran community were "to love all the sons of light . . . and hate all the sons of darkness" (1QS 1.9–10). "Sons of light" is a designation for fellow members, whereas all others were "sons of darkness." Moreover, Jesus' prohibition of divorce (Mk 10.2–9) may echo the prohibition of it among the Jews of Qumran (11QTemple 57.17–19; CD 4.12b–5.14a). So such Jews may not be mentioned in the NT because they never figured as Jesus' important opponents; and the similarity one finds in NT writings to some of their tenets may explain that mysterious silence.

Some of that similarity is seen in the Pauline teaching about justification and the NT use of significant christological titles. Paul speaks of "the righteousness of God" (*dikaiosynē theou*, Rom 1:17). That phrase is not found verbatim in the OT, which otherwise calls God "righteous" and mentions his "righteousness." The phrase, however, has turned up verbatim as ṣedeq 'ēl (1QM 4.6) or ṣideq 'ēl (1QS 10.25; 11.12). Paul's idea of justification is derived from the OT, but he insists that one cannot be justified by doing "works of the law" (Gal 2.16). Again, that phrase is found in neither the OT nor rabbinic literature, but it occurs in a significant context discussing "righteousness" in 4QMMT C 26–32: "We have written to you (about) some of the works of the law, which we consider for your welfare and that of your people . . . it will be reckoned to you as righteousness." This shows that Paul knew whereof he was speaking when he wrote about this matter. The Jews of Qumran similarly wrote about human righteousness: "As for me, I know that righteousness belongs not to a human being, nor perfection of way to a son of man. To God Most High belong all the deeds of righteousness. . . . I have based myself on Your graces and on the abundance of Your mercy. For You expiate iniquity to clean[se a human be]ing from guilt by Your righteousness" (1QHᵃ 4.30–38).

Moreover, the use of titles such as "Lord," "Son of God," and "Messiah," in the QS sheds light on the NT usage of them. Rudolf Bultmann once maintained that it was "unthinkable" for a Palestinian Jew to speak of God as "(the) Lord" (without any modifiers). Hence the title *Kyrios*, as used of Christ in the NT, could not have imitated Jewish usage, but would have emerged when Christian heralds carried the gospel outside of Judea and borrowed it from the eastern Mediterranean Hellenistic world, where *Kyrios* was often used of gods or Roman rulers.

Now, however, the absolute use of "Lord" has turned up in Aramaic texts of Qumran. In the Hebrew text of Job 34:12, Elihu says to Job, "God indeed will not act wickedly; the Almighty will not pervert justice!" That statement becomes a question in the targum of Job: "Now will God really prove faithless, and [will] the Lord [distort justice]?" Here Aramaic mārê', "Lord," stands in parallelism to 'ĕlāhā', "God." (See also māryā' in 4QEnochᵇ 1 iv 5.) Still more striking is the Qumran use of "Son of God" for a human being. The first extrabiblical attestation of this title is found in 4Q246 1.7–2.1, which speaks of an unnamed coming royal figure thus: "[X] shall be great upon the earth, [O King! All sha]ll make [peace], and all shall serve [him, and he] shall be called [son of] the [gr]eat [God], and by his name shall he be named. He shall be hailed the Son of God, and they shall call him Son of the Most High." No one who reads those lines fails to see how Lk 1.32, 35 echoes such contemporary Jewish terminology. The NT often calls Jesus "Messiah" (*Christos*). Hebrew māšîaḥ in the sense of an expected Anointed One occurs in the OT only in Dn 9.25; but the QS reveal how lively was the expectation of a Messiah or Messiahs among the Qumran Jews: "until the coming of a prophet and the Messiahs of Aaron and Israel" (1QS 9.11).

Many more items in the QS could be mentioned here, but it will suffice to conclude with the dualistic references: Christians are called "sons of light" (Jn 12.36; Lk 16.8; 1 Thes 5.5; Eph 5.8), using a phrase never found in the OT, but now abundantly attested in Qumran sectarian writings (1QS 1.9–10; 1QM 1.1). "Sons of darkness," used in QS, is not found in the NT, but rather "sons of disobedience" (Eph 2.2; 5.6) and "son of perdition" (Jn 17.12; 2 Thes 2.3); compare Qumran bĕnê 'awel (1QS 3.21); bĕnê 'ašmāh (1QH 5.7; 6.30). This dualism is especially prominent in John's Gospel (1:4–5; 3:19–21; 12:35–36); the struggle between them is also found in QS (e.g. 1QS 3:20–25; 1QM 13.5,10).

Bibliography: Archaeology. R. DE VAUX, *Archaeology and the Dead Sea Scrolls* (Schweich Lectures of the British Academy 1959; London 1973). J.-B. HUMBERT and A. CHAMBON, *Fouilles de Khirbet Qumran et de Ain Feshkha* (Novum Testamentum et Orbis Antiquus, Series archaeologica 1; Fribourg/Göttingen 1994). J. MAGNESS, "Qumran Archaeology: Past Perspectives and Future Prospects," *Dead Sea Scrolls after Fifty Years: A Comprehensive Statement* (see below), 1. 47–77. Scrolls and Translations. *Discoveries in the Judaean Desert* (35 vols.; Oxford 1955–). F. GARCÍA MARTÍNEZ and W. G. E. WATSON, *The Dead Sea Scrolls Translated: The Qumran Texts in English* (2d ed.; Leiden/Grand Rapids, MI 1996). F. GARCÍA MARTÍNEZ and E. J. C. TIGCHELAAR, *The Dead Sea Scrolls: Study Edition* (2 vols.; Leiden/Grand Rapids, MI 1997, 1998). M. ABEGG, P. FLINT, and E. ULRICH, *The Dead Sea Scrolls Bible: The Oldest Known Bible Translated for the First Time into English* (San Francisco 1999). G. VERMES, *The Complete Dead Sea Scrolls in English* (London/New York 1997). Secondary Literature. L. H. SCHIFFMAN and J. C. VANDERKAM, eds., *Encyclopedia of the*

Dead Sea Scrolls (2 v.; Oxford/New York 2000). J. A. FITZMYER, *The Dead Sea Scrolls: Major Publications and Tools for Study: Revised Edition* (SBL Resources for Biblical Study 20; Atlanta, GA 1990); *Responses to 101 Questions on the Dead Sea Scrolls* (New York/Mahwah, NJ 1992). F. M. CROSS, *The Ancient Library of Qumran: Third Edition* (Minneapolis 1995). P. W. FLINT and J. C. VANDERKAM, eds., *The Dead Sea Scrolls after Fifty Years: A Comprehensive Assessment,* 2 v. (Leiden 1998, 1999).

[J. A. FITZMYER]

DEADLY SINS

Also called "capital sins," they are those vices that by their particular attractiveness are likely to lead to additional sins. Although the lists of such sins vary, they have been reckoned since the Middle Ages to include pride, greed, lust, gluttony, envy, anger, and sloth.

History of the Tradition. Scripture, while it contains lists of sins and mentions all those sins that were later called capital, is not the actual source of the tradition. Moreover, scholarly efforts to trace its beginning to Oriental astrology, mythical soul-journeying, demonology, and even Stoic Philosophy are largely inconclusive. It seems certain that the general cultural milieu of Hellenistic syncretism formed the matrix in which the Christian experience of monastic asceticism developed the idea. When, in 383, Evagrius Ponticus wrote of eight evil thoughts (*Patrologia Graeca* 40:1271–73), the theme was already common in the Egyptian desert. John Cassian, after a visit to monastic centers in Egypt (385–403), brought the tradition to the West in his *Conferences* (*Patrologia Latina* 49:609–642) and *Institutes* 5–12 (*Patrologia Latina* 49:201–476). Although arranged in different order, Cassian's list contains the same eight sins as that of Evagrius: gluttony, lust, avarice, anger, melancholy, sloth, vainglory, and pride. Gregory the Great, in his commentary on Job (*Moralia* 31.45; *Patrologia Latina* 76:621), gives a slightly different rendition (seven instead of eight, leaving pride out, adding envy, and subsuming sloth under melancholy). Following the Vulgate, where pride is called "the root of all evil" (Sir 10:13), Gregory pictures the root, pride, producing seven branches he considers "leaders of wicked armies," and identifies offspring of each. A modification of the Gregorian classification eventually prevailed in the Western Church.

The theme enjoyed enormous popularity in the medieval period. Together with the Creed and the Decalogue, the deadly sins were the staple of sermon topics, and often received more attention than the virtues with which they were sometimes pictured as battling. In 1236 Guillaume Perrault wrote a *Summa vitiorum* that inspired imitation not only in other sermon books and confessors'

"Psychomachia," depicting faith offering the crown of Victory to martyrs and Modesty combating Lust, 9th-century manuscript by Prudentius.

manuals but in literature and art. The sins appear in allegorized drama and gargoyles; they form the structure of Dante's *Purgatorio* and the concluding sermon in Chaucer's *Persoun's Tale.* Notwithstanding this popular interest, St. Thomas Aquinas did not grant the capital sins (*vitia capitalia*) a predominant place in his doctrine of sin. In the *Summa,* for example, the deadly sins as causes of other sins are treated in two brief articles (*Summa theologiae* 1a2ae, 84.3–4), although the sins are considered separately in their opposition to the virtues throughout the *Secunda Secundae.* Renaissance classicism, Reformation emphasis on sin rather than sins, and fading interest in allegory weakened the popularity of the tradition, although the theme has recurred persistently.

Theology. Both titles, "the deadly sins" and "the capital sins" are misnomers in that their referents are not necessarily either mortal sins or capital crimes. Following St. Thomas, Catholics have long preferred the designation "capital sins," since the term "capital," when understood as chief or head of a class, indicates that these sins are important not because they are the worst sins but because they lead to other sins. Thomas's designation of them as "vices" or habits of evil as opposed to "sins" or evil acts has received less consideration.

"The Table of the Seven Deadly Sins," painting by Hieronymous Bosch, c. 1480–1490, Prado Museum, Madrid, Spain. (©Archivo Iconografico, S.A./CORBIS)

Although much of the appeal of the concept lies in its succinct formulation, the emphasis on a list of "seven deadly sins" contributes to their trivialization. That there are seven, a number that biblically connotes totality, fullness, and completion, may lead to the erroneous conclusion that eliminating the deadly sins and eradicating evil are equivalent. The classical list has also been deemed problematic by theologians who criticize its excessive attention to individual sins, to the exclusion of any consideration of social sin. Other theologians argue that the classical list manifests a cultural bias, and obscures the fact that other sins might rightly be called "capital."

Inasmuch as sin is a reality that dissipates and disorganizes human life, the tradition of the deadly sins has value in tracing patterns of that dissipation and disorganization. In spiritual direction the device can be used to diagnose spiritual diseases manifest in apparently unrelated symptoms. Contemporary efforts along these lines include texts that guide readers through a process of reading about the sins and reflecting on their expressions in life. A more thorough revision of the tradition attempts to correlate personality types, with their particular weaknesses, with the sins. In light of the history of the tradition, such revisions seem appropriate and testify to the continuing vitality of Christian asceticism in general and the theme of the deadly sins in particular.

Bibliography: M. W. BLOOMFIELD, *The Seven Deadly Sins: An Introduction to the History of a Religious Concept, with Special Reference to Medieval English Literature* (East Lansing, Mich. 1956; repr., 1967). M. DUNNAM and K. D. REISMAN, *The Workbook on the Seven Deadly Sins* (Nashville 1997). R. C. SOLOMON, ed., *Wicked Pleasures: Meditations on the Seven "Deadly" Sins* (Lanham, Md. 1999). S. SCHIMMEL, *The Seven Deadly Sins: Jewish, Christian and Classical Reflections on Human Nature* (New York 1992). F. J. VAN BEECK, "Fantasy, the Capital Sins, the Enneagram, and Self-Acceptance," *Pro Ecclesia* 3 (1994) 179–196. G. P.

WEBER, *The Capital Sins: Seven Obstacles to Life and Love* (Cincinnati 1997).

[U. VOLL/S. A. KENEL]

DEAN, WILLIAM, BL.

Priest, martyr; b. Linton-in-Craven, Yorkshire, England; hanged at Mile End Green, London, Aug. 28, 1588. William Dean was a Protestant minister prior to his conversion to Catholicism. Thereafter, he studied at the English College of Rheims and was ordained at Soissons, France, Dec. 21, 1581, with fellow martyrs BB. George HAYDOCK and Robert NUTTER. The following month he left for the English mission. He ministered successfully for several years until he was captured in 1585 and exiled in Normandy. Although he knew that certain death awaited him in England, he quickly returned. He was arrested, tried, and condemned for his priesthood, Aug. 22, 1588. He was among the 27 Catholics executed in retribution for the failure of the Spanish Armada, despite the loyalty of English Catholics manifested during the crisis. At the time of the execution, Dean tried to speak to the people, "but his mouth was stopped by some that were in the cart, in such a violent manner that they were like to have prevented the hangman of his wages." He was beatified by Pius XI on Dec. 15, 1929.

Feast of the English Martyrs: May 4 (England).

See Also: ENGLAND, SCOTLAND, AND WALES, MARTYRS OF.

Bibliography: R. CHALLONER, *Memoirs of Missionary Priests*, ed. J. H. POLLEN (rev. ed. London 1924; repr. Farnborough 1969), I, 209. J. MORRIS, ed., *The Troubles of Our Catholic Forefathers Related by Themselves* (London 1872–77), II, 72, 156, 157. J. H. POLLEN, *Acts of English Martyrs* (London 1891).

[K. I. RABENSTEIN]

DE ANDREA, MIGUEL

Argentine bishop and social leader; b. Navarro, Buenos Aires, 1877; d. Buenos Aires, 1960. He was ordained in Rome in 1899, and held various posts in his native city, including that of rector of the Catholic University of Buenos Aires. His chief position from 1912 until his death was parish priest of San Miguel. He was consecrated titular bishop of Temnos in 1919, and served as founder and adviser of the Argentine Popular Union and of his favorite project, the House of Working Women, which has not declined in importance since his death. In 1923, following the death of Archbishop Espinosa, the president of Argentina, Marcelo T. de Alvear, urged the Holy See to appoint De Andrea as his successor. For very confidential reasons that were never divulged, the Holy See refused to do so. The scandal was great and caused shock and disunity among the Catholics. The nuncio, Beda Cardinale, was dismissed by the government, and the Jesuits were considered enemies of the country since they did not adhere to the regalist traditions that the country had inherited from Spain. The anti-Catholic elements played an important part in augmenting the schism between the Catholics of both factions. Three bishops—Alberti, of La Plata; Orzali, of San Juan; and De Andrea—were not as prudent as they should have been in such compromising circumstances.

Both before and after that unpleasant event, from 1911 until his death, De Andrea was not only a spokesman for the social encyclicals, but a man of action, who worked ceaselessly to implement their directives in factories, shops, and all kinds of undertakings, promoting and obtaining laws on accidents that occurred at work, repression of alcoholism, employee retirement, construction of low–cost housing, regulations for piecework at home, healthful conditions in factories, etc. In 1919 he organized a memorable campaign to build low–cost housing developments for workers. It was very successful, and resulted in the construction of some 400 homes in suitable locations within the city limits of Buenos Aires. He was a great preacher and an excellent speaker. Far from being strident, his words fell slowly, gently, on the ears of those who listened to him and encouraged them to think. He knew how to descend to the level of children, whose catechism classes in his own parish he himself directed.

Bibliography: A. ROMERO CARRANZA, *Itinerario de monseñor de Andrea* (Buenos Aires 1957).

[G. FURLONG]

DEANE, HENRY

Archbishop of Canterbury, chancellor of Ireland; d. Lambeth Palace, Feb. 15, 1503. He appeared as a scholar in 1457, probably at Oxford, although there is no record of his having graduated. A CANON REGULAR OF ST. AUGUSTINE, he was prior of Llanthony, near Gloucester, from 1467 to 1501. He restored its buildings and finances and merged its endowments with those of the original priory of LLANTHONY in Breconshire. After he was papally provided to the See of Bangor on July 4, 1494, he did much to rebuild the cathedral. He was translated to the Diocese of SALISBURY by papal bull Jan. 8, 1500, and he became archbishop of Canterbury May 26, 1501. His Canterbury register survives. He was chancellor of Ireland from September 1494 to August 1496 and deputy governor and justiciar in 1496. From Oct. 13, 1500, to

July 27, 1502, he was Keeper of the Great Seal, and he was chief commissioner in the negotiations for the marriage of Princess Margaret and James IV of Scotland, Nov. 28, 1501, to Jan. 24, 1502.

Bibliography: T. F. TOUT, *The Dictionary of National Biography from the Earliest Times to 1900* (London 1885–1900) 5:702–704. A. E. CONWAY, *Henry VII's Relations with Scotland and Ireland* (Cambridge, Eng. 1932). A. B. EMDEN, *A Biographical Register of the University of Oxford to A.D. 1500* (Oxford 1957–59) 1:554.

[G. WILLIAMS]

DEARDEN, JOHN FRANCIS

Second archbishop and sixth bishop of DETROIT, cardinal; b. Valley Falls, Rhode Island, Oct. 15, 1907; d. Detroit, Michigan, Aug. 1, 1988. John Dearden was the first of five children born to John S. and Agnes (Gregory) Dearden. After graduation from Cathedral Latin School in Cleveland, Ohio, in 1925, Dearden entered St. Mary's Seminary. He also studied theology at the North American College in Rome, Italy, and was ordained to the priesthood on Dec. 8, 1932. He completed his doctorate in theology in 1934, and after serving as assistant pastor at St. Mary's Parish, Painesville, Ohio (1934–37), Dearden taught philosophy at St. Mary's Seminary (1937–44), being named rector there in 1944. His strictness in the position and subsequently in Pittsburgh, Pennsylvania, earned him the sobriquet "Iron John."

Dearden was appointed titular bishop of Sarepta in 1945, and co-adjutor bishop of Pittsburgh *cum jure successionis* in 1948, and chose *Servio in evangelio* as his motto. Dearden succeeded to the See of Pittsburgh as its seventh bishop in 1950. Promoted to the Archdiocese of Detroit on Dec. 18, 1958, he was installed by Cardinal O'Hara of Philadelphia on Jan. 29, 1959.

Dearden attended all sessions of Vatican II. From 1962 through 1965 he was a member of the Secretariat for the Promotion of Christian Unity and of the Vatican II Doctrinal Commission for Faith and Morals (the Theological Commission). Dearden worked on the chapter of *Lumen Gentium* dealing with the People of God, reported to the Council Fathers on the chapter on family life, *Gaudium et Spes* 47–52, and helped promote the teaching that conjugal love and procreation are equally ends of marriage and that married couples have the duty to determine family size. He was also instrumental in avoiding language that would have prejudiced the discussion about birth control by the commission of Paul VI.

His fellow bishops chose him as the first president (1966–72) of the newly reorganized National Conference of Catholic Bishops (NCCB). Under his leadership, the NCCB made several innovations, including a due process procedure; creation of the United States Advisory Council, to allow clerical, religious, and lay collaboration; better relationships with other hierarchies; and the Campaign for Human Development. The bishops elected him to the 1967, 1969, 1971, 1974, and 1977 Synods of Bishops. Pope John Paul II appointed him to the 1985 synod.

His leadership in the Archdiocese of Detroit was also widely admired, as he sought to implement conciliar teaching on a pastoral level in Detroit. Dearden ascribed this change, which did not affect his shy and reticent demeanor, to the activity of the Holy Spirit.

The bishop's primary mode of renewal was education. As early as 1959 he had helped establish the Pius XII Center to train catechists. He summoned a diocesan synod in 1966 and established the Institute for Continuing Education, under lay leadership, to organize the parish, regional, and diocesan input of 80,000 participants. This institute also began what was to be one of the longest sustained adult education efforts in the church on the teachings of Vatican II. Dearden expressed his rationale in these words:

> The people must be educated first so they are not offering recommendations for the future of the Archdiocese out of the bag of old theologies and misunderstandings they have carried for years. I know it will be slower, but the people will have a more profound grasp of what it means to be Church.

After the Synod of 1969, Dearden continued the educational thrust with "Church, World, and Kingdom," a program involving nearly 40,000 adults.

For Dearden, the heart of Vatican II was its teaching on the Church as the People of God. Since the new focus was on the persons who constitute the Church, authority had to be exercised pastorally. He saw herein a call for the laity to assume their proper role in the church, within "a new style of democratic administration," as one writer put it. Dearden thus promoted liturgical renewal, though he opposed those who would press the Church to "do something that is contrary to the mind of the Church." He instituted parish councils, diocesan subunits called vicariates, and a diocesan pastoral council, urging clergy and laity to collaborate and to reach consensus. He relied on a diocesan-wide commission to respond to the Michigan electoral ban on aid to parochial schools and closed one-fifth of the Catholic schools in 1969. Dearden organized the Michigan Catholic Conference for the Province of Detroit, which utilized lay talents to work with state government and agencies. His new pastoral style led him to be quite tolerant; as one Detroit priest put it: "Even some relative irresponsibility, especially if marked by sincerity, is at least tolerated." This allowed for creativity, but also some abuses in the liturgical and pastoral life, something he personally opposed but did not address.

Soon after his arrival in Detroit, Dearden spoke to the Detroit Economic Club on respect for the dignity of the human person, the foundation of his lifelong concern for social justice. He began Project Commitment to inform Detroit Catholics about the Church's social teachings. After the 1967 Detroit race riots, he addressed the Church's role in education and health care in the city and challenged all peoples to promote justice. His pledge of one million dollars of the annual archdiocesan appeal to urban grant projects earned him the enmity of many Catholics. These efforts, combined with his leadership in diocesan-wide education, led the American bishops to entrust to Dearden a primary role in organizing the Church's American Bicentennial celebration, which concluded with the CALL TO ACTION CONFERENCE. He viewed as a success the conference's process of hearing many Catholics nationwide on justice issues, but he also recognized the limits of many untenable proposals and the domination of the process by special interest groups.

Dearden was created a cardinal on April 18, 1969, and assigned the titular church of St. Pius X near Monte Mario. He was appointed to the Sacred Congregations for the Discipline of the Sacraments and for Divine Worship and to the Secretariat for Non-Christians. A heart attack prevented his attendance at the 1977 synod, although he later participated in the two papal conclaves of 1978. In 1980, Pope John Paul II accepted his resignation due to poor health, and Dearden was named administrator until the installation of his successor, Edmund Szoka.

Dearden received numerous awards: Notre Dame honored him with the Laetare Medal (1982) for being an "outspoken advocate of increased recognition and development in lay ministries," and the Catholic University of America granted him an Honorary Doctorate of Laws (1983), for being "a man committed to the fullest measure of justice in our own time."

Dearden is buried in the Bishops' Plot at Holy Sepulchre Cemetery, Southfield, Michigan; his papers are equally divided between the Archives of the University of Notre Dame (his NCCB papers) and the Archives of the Archdiocese of Detroit.

Bibliography: J. B. HEHIR, "Going Forward: The Leadership of Cardinal Dearden," *Commonweal* 115 (1988) 553–54. J. WOLFORD HUGHES, "In Memoriam. Cardinal John F. Dearden: Teacher," *Living Light* 25 (1989) 308–16. E. KENNEDY, "Two for Detroit. I. Cardinal Dearden," *The Critic* 32 (1974) 40–57.

[E. BOYEA]

DEASE, MARY TERESA, MOTHER

Missionary; b. Dublin, Ireland, May 7, 1820; d. Toronto, Canada, July 1, 1889. She was the eldest child of Oliver and Ann Dease and was baptized Ellen. In 1847, immediately after profession at the Irish motherhouse of the Institute of the Blessed Virgin Mary, Rathfarnham, she became a pioneer missionary to Toronto, Canada, new episcopal see of Bp. Michael Power, who died within a week of the sisters' arrival. The sisters were harassed by the severity of the climate, poverty, and insecurity; within two years, three of them died. In 1851, youthful Mother Mary Teresa, as superior, accepted responsibility for the first convent of her institute in America. She was superior general until death, at which time Loretto schools flourished in many cities of Ontario and in Illinois. A simple monument marks her grave in the gardens of Loretto Academy, Niagara Falls, Ontario.

[M. F. MADIGAN]

DEATH (IN THE BIBLE)

Because ancient Semitic anthropology, or concept of man's composition, differs so strikingly from the Greek dichotomistic view of man widely held today, it would be incorrect to define death in Biblical thought simply as the separation of the soul from the body. An adequate explanation requires an investigation of the Biblical data. This article discusses the Bible's teaching on death first from a physiological, then from a theological point of view; finally it discusses the metaphorical uses of the term.

Physiologically Considered. For the man of the ancient Orient, life and death were not two abstract entities, but two opposing spheres. Death (Heb. *māwet*) was experienced not only spatially as the realm of the dead, but also dynamically through its power (Hos 13.14). The Israelite did not meditate on death as a physiological process, neither did he describe death as a separation of body and soul in the Greek manner. Rather, he viewed death as the ultimate and undesired weakening and loss of vitality. Only in advanced age did death become acceptable as something natural [Ps 89(90).10]. The emptying out of man in death was concretely pictured as a going out of the *nepeš*, the soul or vital force (Gn 35.18; 2 Sm 1.9; 1 Kgs 17.21). [*See* SOUL, (IN THE BIBLE).] Man lost his vital force with the last breath that he exhaled (Jb 11.20; Jer 15.9). On the basis of the empirical observation that life manifests itself in breath, the death of man or beast was described as the departure of the breath (Heb. *rûaḥ*) from the body, as in Ps 145(146).4; 103(104).29; Jb 12.10; Eccl 8.8; 12.7.

The prophet Zechariah is stoned to death by the order of King Joash, scene from 2 Chronicles, chapter 24. (©Historical Picture Archive/CORBIS)

In a somewhat later conception, the blood received primary consideration as the vitalizing element. [*See* BLOOD, RELIGIOUS SIGNIFICANCE OF.] Blood was called the seat of life; when the blood was poured out, life also flowed away (Lv 17.11; Dt 12.23).

The NT described the physiological phenomenon of death (θάνατος) in a similar fashion. Here too, the principle of life was the spirit or breath (πνεῦμα) given by God (Acts 17.25). Death is the giving up of the spirit (Mt 27.50; Lk 23.46; Jn 19.30) or of the soul (ψυχή; see Jn 10.11; 15.17; 13.37). Without the spirit, the body is dead (Jas 2.26); if a dead person comes back to life, his spirit returns (Lk 8.55).

Theologically Considered. There is a continuity in the teaching on death in the OT and in the NT. In each case death is seen to be the ultimate consequence of sin. Yet in the NT, because of the victory of Christ over sin and the kingdom of Satan and the Christian's conforma-tion to His death and Resurrection, death takes on a new, less terrible meaning.

In the Old Testament. Since the violence of death is such a terrible evil, man naturally connected its origin with primeval transgression and consequent punishment. It could not have been intended by an all-good God who had indeed destined man for life (Gn 2.9; 3.22); only by breaking God's command was man to die (Gn 2.17; 3.3; see also Rom 5.12–21). Death is an inescapable necessi-ty, yet those are praised who die "after a full life" (Gn 25.8) or "at a good old age" (Gn 15.15; Jgs 8.32).

For the Israelite, death was thought not only to affect the body, but also to mark the end of all religious activity. God's relationship to SHEOL (abode of the dead—the nether world) is difficult to define (see Is 38.11). It was subject to His limitless power [Am 9.2; Is 7.11; Ps 138(139).8; Jb 26.6], but He seemed to have no concern about the dead [Ps 87(88).6]. Similarly after death man thought no more of Yahweh or of His wonderful deeds [Ps 6.6; 87(88).13]. He no longer praised God's goodness and fidelity [Ps 29(30).10; 87(88).12; 114(115).17; Is 38.18], or rendered honor to the Lord, or extolled His righteousness (Bar 2.17). This is the most decisive as well as the most crushing statement on the dead in the OT. It naturally engendered a horror of death that could be lightened only by a long life, which was the most tangible proof of God's lasting favor. The apocalyptic world concept that became familiar in late Judaism broke the ground for the decisive change of attitude toward death in the NT. (*See* RESURRECTION OF THE DEAD, 1; AFTERLIFE, 2.) From this point on, it was believed that God would conquer death, at least for a portion of mankind, through the eschatological salvific resuscitation and the inauguration of a new era.

In the OT, death is viewed as the climax of all pain and sorrow, the final estrangement from God that flowed from God's wrath and was provoked by primeval as well as personal sins (Prv 2.18; 7.27; 21.16; 22.23; Is 5.14). A long life is looked upon as a reward for virtue and for faithfulness to Yahweh's law (Dt 30.15–20; 32.47; Bar 3.14). By committing sins, the Israelite brings a premature death upon himself [Ps 54(55).24; Jb 15.32; 22.16]. By the practice of virtue, good deeds, and almsgiving, man could make reparation for his sins and thus save himself from an early death (Prv 10.2; 11.4; Tb 4.11; 12.9). Vigorous opposition to any generalization of this doctrine is found in Wis 4.7–20; this reflects a more mature attitude to the problem of RETRIBUTION.

In the New Testament. The dominating concern in the NT is not death, but life in Christ. The core of the apostolic kerygma is the death and Resurrection of Christ that bring salvation for all men and ensure man's resurrection. Christ "destroyed death" (2 Tm 1.10) by suffering it Himself and by atoning for sin. By His death, He annihilated the one who held the empire of death, the devil (Heb 2.14–15). Death now has no effective power over the redeemed. Finally, in apocalyptic terminology, death will be "cast into the pool of fire" (Rv 20.14), and by virtue of Christ's victory, "death shall be no more" (Rv 21.4).

In Metaphorical Sense. Often death designates not so much the separation of the body from the soul, as the privation of everything that can contribute to true happiness in this world or in the next; e.g., sin deprives man of God's friendship and brings about death (Prv 11.19). Further, the winding roads of lies and other vices lead to death (Prv 12.28; 14.12; 16.25; Wis 1.12). In the NT, the word death is frequently used to refer to the eternal death, i.e., damnation, that results from disbelief and sin (Jn 5.24; 8.51; Rom 7.9–11; Jas 1.15; 1 Jn 3.14; 5.16); Reve-lation uses the term "second death" for this (2.11; 20.6, 14; 21.8). Spiritual death is overcome by spiritual resurrection, i.e., by repentance and conversion (Acts 11.18). Finally, the word death is used figuratively by St. Paul for the passage from the state of sin to the state of grace through baptism: the believer "dies" to sin (Rom 6.2–11; 1 Pt 2.24), is buried with Christ (Rom 6.4, 8), so that he may rise with Christ to a new life in God (Rom 6.5; Col 3.1–4). St. John, too, describes man's justification as the transition from death to life (1 Jn 3.14). He who possesses the Son, i.e., is united with Him in faith and love, enjoys the new spiritual life of divine adoption that will find its ultimate completion in heavenly glory (Jn 3.15).

Bibliography: *Encyclopedic Dictionary of the Bible,* tr. and adap. by L. HARTMAN (New York 1963) from A. VAN DEN BORN, *Bijbels Woordenboek,* 532–536. H. SCHMID and B. RIECKE, *Die Religion in Geschichte und Gegenwart,* 7 v. (3d ed. Tübingen 1957–65) 6:912–914. H. LESÈTRE, *Dictionaire de la Bible,* ed. F. VIGOUROUX, 5 v. (Paris 1895–1912) 4.2:1285–89. R. K. BULTMANN et al., G. KITTEL, *Theologisches Wörterbuch zum Neuen Testament* (Stuttgart 1935–) 2:833–877; 3:7–21. J. A. FISCHER, *Studien zum Todesgedanken in der alten Kirche* (Munich 1954). E. C. RUST, *Nature and Man in Biblical Thought* (London 1953). R. K. BULTMANN, *Theology of the NT,* tr. K. GROBEL, 2 v. (New York 1951–55). G. VON RAD, *OT Theology,* tr. D. STALKER (New York 1962–), *passim.*

[H. KÖSTER]

DEATH (THEOLOGY OF)

The theology of death will be considered under three main headings: (1) the problem of death, i.e., the apparent contradictions that arise when man tries to understand the phenomenon of human death; (2) the mystery of death, i.e., the answer to this problem as it is contained in divine revelation (this will have two main aspects, death a consequence of sin and death transformed by the dying and rising of Christ); (3) theological understanding of the mystery of death, i.e., an endeavor to penetrate the meaning of the answer supplied by revelation to the problem of death.

PROBLEM OF DEATH

Man's knowledge of death on the human level comes only from external observation. No one has experienced death and then explained to other men the nature and meaning of this experience. As one observes this phenomenon of death, two apparently contradictory judgments concerning it force themselves upon the mind, and this is what constitutes the problem of death. On the one hand, death for man seems entirely natural and in keeping with what he is. On the other, death seems completely absurd, in flat contradiction to the special characteristics that distinguish man from all other creatures in the material universe.

Naturalness of Death. Death seems perfectly natural when one considers the obvious affinity man has with the material life of the universe. He possesses a complex organic structure that has been modified and perfected through many centuries of development and adaptation. This organic structure draws its support from the environment that surrounds it, an environment that everywhere manifests the cycle of birth, growth, decline, and death. It is characteristic of all plant and animal life that the individual goes through a maturing process, during which it is benefited by its surroundings and at the same time contributes some benefit to these same surroundings. When the maturing process is complete and the individual's function realized, it yields in death to other individuals of its kind to continue the process. So the human individual passes naturally through the same phases of life to find his normal and fitting end in death. In ancient Israel, it was only sudden death cutting a man off in the midst of his youth or mature years that was regarded as unfitting. The early Hebrews gave little thought to an existence beyond the grave and accepted with serenity the prospect of death at the end of a full life, of a death that meant the end of all truly meaningful existence, as far as they knew. Life was a gift of God. It was not less truly a gift of God because it had an end [see LIFE, CONCEPT OF (IN THE BIBLE); DEATH (IN THE BIBLE)].

Absurdity of Death. However, this serene acceptance of death as a natural, normal part of human existence is greatly disturbed when one considers the special characteristics of human life. For every living being except man, death at the end of the completed aging process is a reasonable conclusion to a life in which all the individual's potentialities have been realized. The plant has flowered and produced fruit and seed. The bird has grown to beauty, learned to fly and sing, has produced offspring able to do these same things. Each of the lower animals comes to the normal end of its life having achieved completely, or very nearly so, everything it was capable of achieving. But death always finds man in some very real and significant sense incomplete, his potentialities unrealized, the full resources of his personality hardly tapped. The capacity of the human spirit for friendship, truth, the creation and appreciation of beauty, the enlightenment of others and the spreading of happiness, for technological development, moral advance, new and enriching experiences, and for innumerable other things—all this capacity passes from this world in death only partially fulfilled. And paradoxically, the more the human personality has been developed, the more abrupt and absurd does death seem when it makes its appearance; for this development always holds the promise of much more. If Einstein had lived longer, perhaps he would have been able to formulate the theory for expressing the fundamental unity of all material phenomena. If Beethoven had not been taken by death, the beauty of other symphonies would have come from the resources of his spirit. If Thomas Aquinas had lived longer, his contribution to man's accumulation of wisdom would have been proportionately greater.

This absurdity of death manifests itself also in the special human fear of death. This fear in man is something more than the biological instinct of bodily self-preservation. Because man is reflexively and explicitly aware of his own personal life and activity, death appears as a threat to what he is at his deepest level. Man's self-possession in knowledge and his self-giving in love all appear to be awaiting destruction in death. Death seems the supreme evil for himself as a person.

The philosophical reflections on the special nature of the human soul do little to relieve this fearful apprehension. It is true that in man the phenomena of full conscious reflection upon himself and his activity, of abstract, universal, and necessary knowledge, of free self-determination in deliberate choice, all point to the fact that the inner source of this activity is not matter nor essentially dependent upon matter for existing and acting; the human soul can be and operate even apart from the body (see IMMORTALITY). But such a state of separation must appear violent and unnatural. There is nothing that man now does, no relation he has with the material world or with other persons, that does not have a fundamental bodily component. The prospect of being and acting in a way that totally relinquishes this connection with matter can well seem abhorrent, futile, and illusory.

Points of View. In the face of this problem of death there are two attitudes possible: one atheistic, the other religious. The atheist accepts the absurdity of human death as a manifestation of the total absurdity of existence. Just as human life must finally be said to have no reasonable purpose or destiny, so the entire structure of reality is without explanation or meaning. There is no need to look for a supreme principle or cause to account for what one experiences, because what one experiences is absurd, irrational, incapable of being accounted for. Indeed, from man's point of view there is no room for God. For the human spirit can live with absurdity only if it can create values where none now exist. But the existence of God would stand in the way of creating these values. The existence of God would deny the full freedom of man to establish goals and strive for them, to give himself an essence that can make the anguish of this absurd existence tolerable. Such is the position of the modern atheistic existentialist.

The religious man accepts the absurdity of death as evidence of the incompleteness of his knowledge of the whole. He recognizes that a detail or part, no matter how important and central, can well seem absurd if considered apart from the totality to which it belongs. His acknowledged inability to grapple successfully with the problem of death on his own resources prepares him to accept from divine revelation a solution to this problem that will unite meaningfully all the aspects of life and death that he observes.

MYSTERY OF DEATH

Divine revelation makes known to men that death in general and the particular death of each individual fall within the plan of God's ordering wisdom and His self-giving love. In the light of this revelation death becomes a mystery instead of a problem. That is, it no longer seems a combination of contradictions, but a reality whose full meaning touches the infinite and in this way escapes man's total comprehension. The emphasis here is not upon darkness and hiddenness, but upon light and the richness of what has been made known to man by God [see MYSTERY (IN THEOLOGY)].

Viewed in this way death as a natural phenomenon not only manifests man's affinity with the material universe, it also illuminates his essential relationship to God. Before the necessity of dying all of man's pretense to self-sufficiency crumbles. He recognizes his radical difference from God and his complete dependence on Him. God alone is absolutely immortal; man is mortal. God has in freedom given life to man. In freedom likewise He takes this life away. He is the lord of man's essential being. This freedom and lordship do not imply capriciousness or tyranny, but they do emphasize the fact that man's destiny is not ultimately in his own hands but in God's.

This has special relevance for the question of the survival of man's soul after bodily death. Although the specifically human activity noted above manifests a radical capacity of the human principle of life to exist and act apart from the body, any attempt to conceive how this activity can be carried on apart from the conditions of time and space deriving from the body meet with very little success. Here man must be willing to trust his death to God even as he trusts his life to Him. This confidence in the face of darkness and obscurity is the earliest religious attitude of the Hebrews toward death.

But, in the actual historical order of things, man's reaction to death as something absurd and out of place is well founded. "Because God did not make death," as the Book of Wisdom informs man, "nor does he delight in the destruction of the living. . . . God formed man to be imperishable; the image of His own nature he made him. But by the envy of the devil, death entered the world" (1.13; 2.23–24). Death is a consequence of sin, of man's

free acceptance of the temptation to evil. God permitted this sin and its consequence, and in His loving wisdom draws good from it.

Death a Consequence of Sin. The story of man's creation and fall in Genesis ch. 2–3 belongs to the most ancient religious traditions of Israel. The sacred writer is endeavoring to explain the universal phenomenon of sin and death in the world. God is the living and holy Lord, how can death and wickedness have place in His work? These things cannot belong to His original plan and intention. God is therefore shown as taking special care in the creation of man, breathing life into him, extending to him, in a condition of primitive innocence, a life of close union with Himself. To live is to share what belongs by right and in its fullness to the living God alone. So long as man maintains his union with the living God, he shall never lose the gift of life. But if he turns from God in disobedience, then loss of life is inevitable. The spirit of wickedness tempted man to independence of God and man yielded to this illusion and estranged himself from God. As a result, man is cut off from the living God and made subject to corruption and death.

This disorder belongs to the primordial condition of man. It affects the whole race of mankind, because it affected the very beginnings of the race. Human nature as it is passed on to mankind from the first parents of all men is deprived of that link with God which would have guaranteed incorruption and life. The necessity of dying that lies upon everyone who is born manifests historically not simply man's affinity with the material world, but his failure to cling to Him who is life. And, apart from any remedy that God might provide, the experience of bodily death itself must seal man's alienation from God.

Death is thus not simply an arbitrary punishment for sin, one of several possible ways of exacting justice. Death is intrinsically connected with separation from God. It is true that if man had not been called to the special intimacy with God that constitutes the SUPERNATURAL ORDER, then death, as a natural phenomenon, would not have bespoken any moral deviation from the divine will. But, in the present order of things, human immortality could not remain where sin severed the root of that immortality in man's relationship to God; nor could immortality have been lost so long as that root remained.

This also explains a deeper dimension of the human shrinking from death. By sin man never lost his ordination to a SUPERNATURAL goal, though he lost the inner resources that would lead him to that goal. Hence, man always retained a basic ordination to immortality even in his body. The fear of death, then, is a reaction aroused by an instinctive awareness of an immortal destiny that may be lost to him.

Death, as experienced by the sinner unredeemed by Christ, is a punishment not only for ORIGINAL SIN, but for his own actual sins as well. It is not just a concrete human nature that is dying, but a unique human person. If that person by his own deliberate choices has ratified the alienation from God that his nature inherited from Adam, then he lives out his freely chosen separation from God in the moment of death as his own personal experience, the fruit of his own rejection of life in God.

The punishment that death contains is twofold. It is the destruction of the body and the isolation of the soul. Man's well-being cannot be found apart from his own inner unity and harmony, nor apart from his community with the rest of the universe. Death destroys both of these in the sinner. Through the separation of body and soul and the consequent disintegration of the body, the inner unity and harmony of man is lost. Furthermore, the soul of man is naturally inserted into the universe only by its union with a body, by organizing matter as the instrument of its experience, development, and expression. With its loss of a body, its existence is in isolation from everything else, left inescapably alone in its own incompleteness and unrealized potentiality.

The death of a sinner is his final submission to the empire of Satan. Sin always bears some relationship to diabolic influence; not that every temptation is directly from the devil, but man's original infidelity and loss of internal wholeness did result from the devil's suggestion, and it is this loss that continues to manifest itself in some way in all subsequent rebellion. Each individual sin is a further extension of the devil's disorder, and the sinner's death makes this a stable and permanent condition. One would, of course, be wrong in imagining the rule of Satan as a power he has to direct persons or events to his own purposes; Satan rules only in the sense of withdrawing something from the immediate purpose God intends for it. The death of the sinner withdraws him finally from the way in which God first wished to manifest Himself in him and to him, the way of SALVATION. Thus, this death is the ultimate achievement of diabolic power.

Death Transformed by Christ. Sacred Scripture describes man's need of salvation in many ways. He is said to be in captivity or bondage, to be a slave, to be wandering astray, to be in debt, to be living according to the flesh (in the Pauline sense of creaturely weakness cut off from the divine strength), to be sick, to be in darkness, to be subject to futility. But all these ways and many others are summed up in saying that sinful man is mortal, dwelling in the shadow of death, is, in fact, dead in sin. Death in these expressions does not mean exclusively either the material death of the body or the spiritual death of the soul, but total death as it afflicts man's entire per-

son. Salvation, then, must mean a transformation of man's mortal condition, a changing of death into life.

God's determination to save man did not mean that He would erase death and pretend that man's sin had never happened. God's respect for created freedom and activity never allows Him to act as if some actual event had not occurred. The fact of man's sin remains and the consequences of that fact remain also. But God can change the internal meaning of those consequences, and, provided only man is willing, thereby make those consequences work for man's ultimate well being, instead of for his ultimate destruction. This change cannot be simply a different way of looking at death from the outside, nor an arbitrary connection of death with certain beneficent effects to which it bears in itself no inner relationship. Rather, the very nature of death must be changed so that it leads to God and life, rather than away from Him to everlasting ruin.

The Death of Christ. To effect this inner transformation of death and the human condition, God sent His Son into the world "in the likeness of sinful flesh" (Rom 8.3). The Son of God became a mortal man; sinless in Himself, He assumed a nature made subject to suffering and death by man's sin. When the selfishness, ignorance, and malice of His contemporaries forced death upon Him, He freely and willingly accepted it in a spirit of loving dedication to His Father's will. Death, whose inner nature had been filled with disobedience and rejection, was now in Christ suffused by love and submission. It became a sacrificial act, manifesting in the highest fashion His total self-giving and surrender. This adoring love, belonging as it did to a Divine Person, had within it the power to transfer Christ in His human nature into the divine sphere of immortal life and glory. The gift of Himself in death was accepted by the Father, who raised Him from the dead and filled Him with the undying life of the Holy Spirit. Death is swallowed up in victory. In Christ its meaning has been totally transformed. It no longer means simply man's rebellion against God; it is also now a sign of the presence of God's saving love in the world.

It is important to note that in His sacrificial activity Christ was not acting as a private individual but as the divinely constituted high priest of the human race. He underwent death on man's account, not in the sense of suffering the punishment man deserved to suffer and in this way satisfying the impersonal demands of a violated law, but in the sense of sharing with His fellow men the triumph He achieved through death. As the new Adam, founder of a new humanity, summing up in Himself the race of mankind, one with man in flesh and blood, He was for man's sake obedient unto death. Therefore He was exalted by the Father and brought to a position of consummated perfection at the Father's right hand. Thus perfected, Christ is the source of man's salvation, the principle of the life-giving Spirit who leads men as the children of God through suffering and death to an eternal inheritance with Christ Our Lord. This means that the total situation of fallen man has been changed. He no longer dwells simply in the shadow of death, but the light of life shines upon him. For within the human race, in one of its members who has triumphed over death and sin, there exists the efficacious and imperishable source of eternal life.

The Death of a Christian. The death of one who is in Christ, the death of a Christian, is thus immeasurably different from the death of a sinner, who dies in Adam. It is true that death as he approaches it still appears dark and forbidding, for it is still a consequence of sin. Only now, death may not be considered a punishment for sin, for there is nothing in the Christian who is alive in Christ that falls under the condemning judgment of God (cf. Rom 8.1). Since death is radically natural to man, God may leave it as part of human existence without thereby implying any rejection or lack of forgiving love, in spite of the fact that its presence historically manifests the fact of man's fall, for death now manifests also God's redemptive purpose, and it becomes for the Christian, as it was for Christ, an object of humble acceptance. It becomes the occasion for the exercise of the divine life with an intensity and purity it would not otherwise achieve.

The transformation of death in the case of the individual Christian is not just an automatic consequence of the dying and rising of Christ. It is the culminating result of the whole supernatural and sacramental life of the Christian whereby during life he opened himself to the divine power that was at work throughout all of Christ's life, death, and Resurrection, and continues to operate in His glorious humanity. This can be seen specifically in the development of the theological virtues, faith, hope, and charity, which constitute the essential activity of the supernatural life, and in the effect of all the Sacraments, with the possible exception of Holy Orders and Matrimony, which as Sacraments of vocation are more directly related to the manner of Christian living in this world.

Death: Fulfillment of the Life of Grace. Faith is the basic activity of the supernatural life, the life of GRACE. Here man opens himself to the saving revelation which God has made in and through His Son, Jesus Christ. By FAITH man responds to this revelation by an act of total acceptance and total dedication, accepting from God the ultimate meaning of his life in a destiny that exceeds his understanding and his own internal powers of achievement, and dedicating himself to walk toward the realization of that destiny. By faith, then, man orients himself

toward a goal that lies beyond the visible confines of this mortal life. Faith thus necessarily bespeaks an attitude toward bodily death. For the believer, approaching death is the veil that conceals the goal to which he has committed himself. Death is not defeat, nor destruction, nor final estrangement from God. The experience of death, precisely because it takes place in one whose mind is turned in faith toward the eternal truth of God manifested as savior, means the unveiling of the face of God. Faith is transformed into vision. It is true that lesser unforgiven sins or an unpaid debt of punishment for forgiven sins can delay the full effect of this final transformation until purification is achieved; but in death it is radically and essentially accomplished. If the soul in purgatory does not yet see face to face, neither does it still behold as in a glass darkly. The radiance of the divine splendor has already begun to shine upon it unmistakably, and the promise of clarity to come is experientially realized, not taken upon external testimony (*see* PURGATORY). The same thing holds proportionately for what is to be said about hope and charity and the Sacraments.

Hope is the developing activity of the supernatural life. Here man meets the challenge of difficulty and his own internal weakness with an ever greater reliance on the divine goodness, power, and wisdom. This reliance in trial draws him continuously closer to God and causes the divine life to flourish with greater intensity and purity. But all the hardships that man must endure and all the inner weakness that he experiences in life are concentrated in the event of bodily death. Without hope man can undergo death only in despair; there is no middle ground. For the one whose entire trust and power is in God, death changes the assured confidence of hope into the joy of possession.

Love, finally, is the perfect, mature activity of the supernatural life. Here man responds to the loving initiative of God with an act of complete self-giving and affective identification. He no longer lives to himself but to God, and to Him who for his sake died and rose again. The process of the dispossession of self whereby a man endeavors to love God with his whole heart and mind and strength and will reaches its perfect realization in the unselfing event of bodily death. For one who loves, this moment of dissolution is the moment of final consummation, in which with Christ he delivers his spirit into the hands of God his Father.

Death: Completion of the Sacraments. It is through the Sacraments that man most thoroughly enters into the transforming power of Christ's Passion, death, and Resurrection. In each case (except for Orders and Matrimony, as was indicated) what is begun in the reception of the Sacrament is perfected in the experience of

Christian death. Baptism is supernatural rebirth; it is a passing from death to life by being buried and raised with Christ [see REBIRTH (IN THE BIBLE)]. The paschal mystery that was accomplished in Christ is applied to the offspring of Adam infected by original sin; it transports him from darkness into the kingdom of God's beloved Son. The Holy Spirit is given as the pledge, the actual beginning of the eternal life to come. This is the start of the journey whose end is reached through the experience of death. Man's incorporation into Christ's death through Baptism is a preparation for his own death wherein that incorporation is made perfect and enduring.

Confirmation is the Sacrament of Christian maturity. The Spirit of Christ is given not simply as to a child but as to a developed member of the MYSTICAL BODY OF CHRIST. Through this Gift of the risen Lord the Christian is empowered to bear witness in word and deed to the present reality of the kingdom of Christ in the world. But nowhere is this witness more fully given than in death. For this reason those who undergo death for their loyalty to Christ are called martyrs, ''witnesses'' par excellence. But the same witness that the martyrs give so strikingly in suffering the loss of all things for Christ is given more prosaically but no less truly in the day-to-day living of the Christian life, and especially, in the confident acceptance of death at the end of life. In the end, every Christian who dies in Christ gives his life for the faith; and the mission he was entrusted with at Confirmation is thereby perfectly fulfilled.

The celebration of the Eucharist in the Mass is the reality of Christ's sacrificial act of dying and rising made present and operative in the midst of men enabling them day by day to join the motion of their lives with His. The reception of the Eucharist in Holy Communion is a sharing in the life of the glorified Victim, making men to dwell in Him and Him in them and directing their mortal natures to the future triumph of the Resurrection. Through the Eucharist, then, men both continually renew the dedication of their lives to God in union with Christ and are nourished by His glorified humanity for the daily living out of this dedication. In their actual experience of death this dedication is at length perfectly achieved. For this reason, the Holy Eucharist more than any other Sacrament has in the tradition of the Church been the Sacrament of the dying. Viaticum traditionally has been the food for the journey through death to eternal life in a spirit of obedience and adoring love.

Although popular piety since the Middle Ages has considered the Anointing of the Sick the special Sacrament for the dying, in the longer perspective of Christian tradition its scope is broader than this, though it comes to a focus of special meaning in the hour of death. Sick-ness is evidence of Satan's dominion over mankind as a result of the Fall. The NT reflects this point of view, especially in the narration of Christ's miracles of healing. Hence it happens that sickness, especially serious sickness, can be a time of great spiritual trial, when the forces of wickedness act upon men in their weakened condition to cause them to grow slack in their exercise of love, to become self-centered and demanding, to become anxious and lose confidence in the abiding love of God for them. In this time of special need, Christ comes to them in the Anointing of the Sick to raise up their hearts and to strengthen them. It is clear, then, that their last sickness is a time of particular trial. The Fathers of the Church and the Council of Trent teach that the hour of death is the time of man's last great struggle with the devil. If a Christian has led a life of faithful devotion to God, Satan endeavors to withdraw him from his complete dedication to God as savior. If he has led a remiss and sinful life, the devil tries to confirm him in his estrangement from God by tempting him to despair or to harden his heart in pride. In this hour Christ comes to him to arm him for this conflict and to encourage him through the Sacrament of the Anointing of the Sick. Death thereby becomes the moment of final, triumphant rejection of all of Satan's power over men.

Penance, the Sacrament of the forgiveness of sins committed after Baptism, was given to the Church by Christ on the day of His Resurrection from the dead. Through it Christians regain the life they have lost through personal grave sin committed after their rebirth in Christ. It is the special function of the Sacrament of Penance to render efficacious before God both the Christian's sorrow for these sins, and the works he does in union with Christ to make up for them. This Sacrament, as its effects are prolonged in the Christian's daily life, not only protects him from future sins but transforms the sufferings and works of life into a power of renewal that effectively compensates for the disorder and offense of personal sin. This makes death itself in a special way a work of satisfaction and penance for past sins. Indeed, death perfectly accepted in union with Christ can mean the perfect appropriation of His dying in oneself through the Sacrament of Penance. This will complete the purification from sin and render purgatory unnecessary. All self-love and disordered attachments will disappear, and God's redemptive love will produce its full effect in the immediate gift of the splendor of the BEATIFIC VISION. This perfect acceptance of death in a spirit of repentance is not primarily men's work, but God's work in men, produced through the Sacrament of Penance received either actually or in the sincere desire to submit themselves to His economy of forgiveness and purification.

Finally, although it does not seem that the Sacraments of vocation, Matrimony and Orders, produce an effect which is directly consummated in death, still the commitment to God for a life of service in His Church which these Sacraments consecrate is brought to a close by Christian death and is succeeded by a still more universal concern for the whole COMMUNION OF SAINTS.

Death: The Coming of God's Kingdom. Just as the death of a sinner is an extension of the empire of Satan, so the death of a Christian is a step toward the universal coming of the KINGDOM OF GOD. By this death in union with Christ an area of creation is forever rescued from the power of evil and prepared for insertion into the eschatological kingdom of God's love. For the individual himself eternal life is definitively begun. The incorporation into Christ's death and Resurrection during the preceding period was only inchoative. The Spirit was received and possessed as the first fruits, the pledge of eternal life. All this, from man's point of view, was fragile and provisional. Now death has rendered this incorporation definitive; the Holy Spirit is possessed beyond all possibility of loss. Furthermore, the event looks beyond the individual himself to the final, total, unfailing realization of God's wisdom, power, and love in the city of the blessed, the eternal kingdom of Our Lord and Savior Jesus Christ. One by one the living stones of the heavenly Jerusalem are being made ready until the end comes and the Son delivers the kingdom to God the Father.

For this reason, too, the separation effected by death is not so total and absolute as it would otherwise be. It is true that death, even in the case of a Christian, breaks all accustomed relationships with other persons. But this is not that terrible isolation implied in death as a punishment for sin. Since death in Christ deepens and confirms the supernatural life, it likewise deepens and confirms the relationships the Christian has with all others who are in Christ. Christian death is the beginning of ultimate union with Christ, of intimate presence to Christ, in whom all are made one. This means a union of mutual knowledge and love with all those who have already died in Christ. It means a new relationship in love to all those whose lives are still being tried, whose moment of final commitment in death is still to be realized.

Christian death, finally, is already linked to the resurrection of the body. For the disintegration of bodily union in love and obedience has already opened the soul to the fullness of the Spirit of Christ. It is this indwelling Spirit, now fully energizing the soul, who will extend His power even to the body in the resurrection. The soul transformed by glory is already the apt instrument of Christ's power for raising the body from the dead. It awaits only the word of command, the word that God's work has been achieved, the end is reached, the kingdom of heaven has come.

The phenomenon of death is thus the visible manifestation of one side of the paschal mystery of Christ being reproduced in the life of the Christian. The other side, to which it is intrinsically linked, is the bodily RESURRECTION OF THE DEAD, the transformation accomplished by Christ conforming men's lowly bodies to His glorious body by the power that enables Him to subdue all things to Himself in sending the life-giving Spirit.

THEOLOGICAL UNDERSTANDING OF THE MYSTERY OF DEATH

From the above description of death as a consequence of sin and as an event of salvation through the dying and rising of Christ, two things become abundantly clear. First, death is the decisive moment in every man's life; it ends the period of probation or trial, during which a man may freely avert himself from God as his last end or turn himself toward Him. After death a man's condition is eternally fixed either for joy or for misery, depending on whether he died in Christ or in Adam. Second, the natural essence of death must be such that it is open either to a meaning of loss or a meaning of salvation. In itself bodily death cannot naturally and essentially be either of these, otherwise it could not be one thing for some men and another thing for others. The question for theological understanding is therefore: why is death the decisive event in human existence? What is death in itself that it can be either the seal of one's doom in separation from God, or the definitive beginning of eternal life in union with Him?

Question of God's Will. Some theologians have been of the opinion that death is decisive simply and solely because God wills it to be. It is clear that if man is finally to be in an eternal and unchangeable state, some moment in his existence must designate the end of the time of trial and the beginning of the state of eternal reward or punishment. The period of trial cannot be indefinitely prolonged, otherwise the final state would never be achieved. In itself, no moment of human existence is naturally and necessarily this decisive moment, they affirm. It could be some moment during one's adult life, or the moment of death, or some moment after death. That it is the moment of death, as revelation clearly shows, is due merely to the fact that God decided it should be. From this moment onward God no longer wills to give to sinners the grace to be converted to Him, though He could if He wanted to. From this moment onward, He no longer allows the just to be tempted and He sustains their otherwise weak and fallible wills in unfailing love toward Himself, though, again, if He chose to, He could permit them to sin and turn away from Him. This decision of

God is rescued from pure arbitrariness on the grounds that death is at least an appropriate time for ending the period of trial. Man's mode of existence changes so radically at death that it is fitting to make death the dividing point between endeavor and achievement, between labor and reward, between crime and punishment. Still, they say, it could have been otherwise.

First Critique. It is not possible to say that this explanation is certainly erroneous, though there are very good reasons for rejecting it. First of all, any explanation that finally and ultimately rests on a free decision of God alone is suspect, unless some reason is given why this must be the case. Creation, for example, and supernatural elevation have their ultimate explanations in purely free and gratuitous divine decrees defining that this shall be so and not otherwise, though God in His wisdom could have decreed the opposite. The appropriateness and fittingness of these decrees can be shown, but the final explanation is God's free determination to act in this way. In these cases, too, it can be shown why this must be the final explanation; for otherwise God becomes dependent on His creation for His own completeness and essential life. But, where no such reason as this is in evidence, one must seek some intrinsic reason guiding the divine will in wisdom and justice. One could not, for example, say that God rewards the good and punishes the wicked merely because He chooses to do things that way, that He might possibly or conceivably have chosen to punish the good and reward the wicked. The ultimate explanation of God's acting as He does in this matter is not His freedom, but His wisdom and His justice. His wisdom establishes an intelligible order in things, an order fundamentally rooted in the natures of the things that make up the universe, and His justice acts to conserve that order. Speculative theology seeks, wherever possible, to discover this intelligible order of divine wisdom and not to rest content in arbitrary decrees without clearly sufficient reason for doing so. Hence, a theological explanation that says in effect, God wants it that way and that's all there is to it, can often be simply a refuge from the exacting work of thinking. In the present instance, there is no reason that explains why the divine freedom must alone be the final answer to why death is the decisive moment in human existence. Hence, one must endeavor to find such a reason in death itself.

Second Critique. Furthermore, not only is this appeal to divine freedom suspect, there is also good reason for considering it erroneous. The economy of Redemption is revealed to men in Scripture as rooted in love, in the love that God is. Of Christ Our Lord it is said that He did not break the bruised reed nor quench the smoking wick. It is strangely inconsistent with this revelation of divine mercy to affirm that God refuses the grace of forgiveness

and repentance to persons who are still intrinsically capable of accepting it. Hence it is quite unsatisfactory to say that sinners who have died are confirmed in their sinfulness only because God is no longer willing to have mercy on them. Death itself must somehow confirm sinners in their aversion from God in such wise that God's mercy no longer reaches them not because He is unwilling to give them grace, but because He is unable to, on account of the intrinsic situation itself. What this intrinsic situation is remains to be investigated. Furthermore, even in the case of the good, it is strange that God would restrict their period of growth in merit to these short years of mortal life, if really nothing objectively stands in the way of lengthening that period beyond the grave. Why should the degree of union with God be irrevocably determined at death, if the objective possibility exists of achieving a still greater degree of union through meritorious activity beyond the grave? This difficulty can be urged with still more force in the case of both sinners and just when it is recalled that death would inevitably give them a deeper insight into a true standard of values and in this way would render more likely a fuller realization of God's basic intention to communicate His goodness and life to rational creatures. Hence, it must be the nature of death itself, and not merely an extrinsic free decision of God, that makes this moment irrevocably decisive for the eternal destiny of each man. This is the teaching of St. Thomas Aquinas and, after him, the majority of theologians writing on this subject.

Condition of Spiritual Human Activity. To discover why death by its nature is the finally critical event in human existence, one must analyze the condition of spiritual human activity in the present state of the union of body and soul and then see what follows from a separation of that union. The human spiritual activity of which there is question is free, deliberate activity.

Body and Soul United. In man's condition of mortal life all his vegetative, sensitive, and intellectual processes are integrated into a life of choice, whereby he selects goals and directs himself toward them. So long as man makes his choice as a spirit-matter composite, his most solemn and total dedication to a goal lacks perfect interior stability. No matter how thoroughly good he is, his moral character is not absolutely incorruptible; and no matter how evil he may become, he is not utterly irredeemable. Thus, even in his commitment to what he deems his highest good, his choice remains intrinsically reformable. This reformability comes from the conditions that matter introduces into man's life of choice. His intellectual and volitional life is directly dependent in its functioning upon his sense life, which is in continual contact with ever-changing material reality. This contact makes man's imagination shift frequently from one thing to another.

This shift in imagination introduces a shift in intellectual attention, and this in turn makes possible a shift in the intention of the will, in man's dedication to a goal. This shift in the will need not take place, but it is always possible so long as man's dedication depends on a kind of knowledge which is continually changing its point of view and is hence able to consider various choices and ways of acting in other terms than their relationship to the goal a man has already dedicated himself to. Hence, so long as man's spirit is directly subject to the conditions of time and space in its activity, he may always revise his judgment about what is supremely important and his determination about the goal of his life.

State of Separation. But once separated from matter, the human spirit is no longer subject to the mutability that material conditions introduce into its activity. The goal that it has freely determined on as its last end remains unchangeably the first principle of all subsequent choice and activity. This goal has become for the soul the supreme GOOD to which it has dedicated itself with the full force of its personality, with full intellectual clarity and total attention. The commitment to the end is now from within irreformable. This end is now willed entirely for its own sake alone, and whatever else may be later willed, must be willed for the sake of this end in some way. This choice could be changed only if it were possible to change the past, to make that which has been done not to have happened. The soul has now determined forever, from within, its essential and fundamental orientation in activity.

Moment of Transition. But there remains to be examined the actual moment of transition from the one way of acting to the other, the moment of death. It is at this moment of separation from the body that the soul ceases to act in a fundamentally changeable way and begins to act with an intrinsically unchangeable intention of some concrete last end. If the man has died in Christ, this intention is forever directed toward God in love and submission and joy. If the man has died rejecting Christ, this intention is forever directed toward oneself in hatred of God and rebellion and unending misery. How is this intention finally arrived at? How does man at the moment of death finally fix his immutable direction toward the end?

Free Option. Theologians are not in perfect agreement about the answer to this question. Some will give to this act made in the instant of separation of soul from body all the qualities of a perfectly free act. Man, after shaping himself partially by a myriad of choices that could never completely commit him to a definite goal, now, bearing all the history of those choices, definitively, irrevocably, freely opts either to ratify the life that he has

led or to reject it. It is the supreme human act, supremely free, choosing finally between God and created goodness, closing the time of probation and trial and joining it to its everlasting consequence. It must be insisted that this act, though free, does not take place without any relation to and dependence on the life that preceded it. It is theoretically possible, according to these theologians, that a person could live a thoroughly sinful and selfish life and then in this last moment submit to God's saving grace; but, they add, it is extremely unlikely. It is as if a man had to walk a tightrope over a bottomless abyss to safety on the other side. If he has never before seriously concerned himself about how to walk a tightrope (when there was always a net there to catch him), there is not much hope that this final effort will succeed. Habits formed during the course of life lose nothing of their power to influence choice in this moment of final decision. A person whose whole life has been one of self-gratification would almost certainly at this moment be more concerned about himself than anything else, and would be willing to think of God only as a means to his own happiness, not as the end to be worshipped in adoring love. He would simply choose freely to pass eternity as he had freely chosen to pass time.

Critique of Free Option. Various arguments are advanced in support of this theory of a free option at the moment of death. No mortal sin committed during life seems sufficiently malicious to justify the eternal punishment of hell; but an act against God placed with a completely clear understanding of the issues involved would concentrate in itself all the evil necessarily presupposed in the just infliction of so terrifying a penalty. This act of fully deliberate rejection of God would of itself extinguish the habits of supernatural faith and hope in those sinners who die possessing them, though lacking charity; for it seems unfitting that God should Himself be somehow the direct cause of their cessation, and yet they must cease when the soul is forever cut off from God in hell. Such an option could explain how God's saving grace can touch and rescue infants who die without Baptism; they are enabled at this moment to choose God as their last end and achieve thereby eternal happiness with Him. Finally, it would appear strange, they say, that the act upon which everything in human existence depends should not be in the fullest sense of the term a human act, that is, a free, deliberate act.

These arguments, while suasive, are far from conclusive, and they lack any real support in Scripture and tradition. Scripture everywhere seems to suppose that a man is finally judged and his eternal lot is determined by the deeds and choices accomplished during his mortal life, while the soul is still united to the body and functioning in dependence on it. Nowhere is provision made for a determining choice made by the soul in the instant of being separated from the body and without dependence on it. St. Paul, for example, writes: "We must all appear before the tribunal of Christ in order to receive good or evil, according to what each has done in the body" (2 Cor 5.10). The Fathers manifestly suppose that the time of probation and the state of union are identified. This is especially clear in their exhortations to penance, where they warn Christians that there is no opportunity for repentance once they have left this world (cf. Pseudo-Clement, *Cor.* 8.2–3). Furthermore, it is a matter of defined Catholic faith that *all* infants who die after Baptism are saved. Yet, if they freely choose their final destiny at the instant of death there seems no explanation why some of them do not choose to reject God, just as some of the angels did in their trial. Furthermore, the visible Church, the Mystical Body of Christ, is presented in revelation as the ark of salvation, the one means of attaining eternal life. It would seem then that man's definitive activity for reaching everlasting union with Christ should take place while he is still a member of the visible Church (*see* VISIBILITY OF THE CHURCH). Finally, when it is recalled how much the literature of the early Gnostics abounds in tales of trials and temptations to be overcome when the soul was no longer in union with the body, it is remarkable, indeed unintelligible, that the whole of Christian revelation has maintained a deep silence about just such a trial upon which everything supposedly depends. For these reasons, many theologians do not accept the theory of a free option at the instant of death and explain somewhat differently this activity of the soul that inaugurates man's unchangeable state at the moment of death.

Summation of Many Free Acts. For these theologians, then, the act of the soul in the moment of death, in which the liberty of man is thereafter forever fixed upon a particular last end, is not free in the sense that it could be otherwise, given the concrete history of the individual who is placing the act. It is free in the sense of being wholly spontaneous, not constrained or determined by anything outside the soul, but springing totally from what the soul has become during life and expressing perfectly the character that has been formed by the many free choices that have preceded it. This act is free in the sense that it totally sums up all the free acts that have been placed during one's mortal life. It embodies especially the radical orientation of the will that was last freely adopted by the person in an act occurring before the moment of death, a free act that falls in a special way under the loving and wise providence of God. The appeal of grace in this moment may be extraordinarily strong, but the free act made before death is qualitatively the same as any free orientation made in the course of life. Thus the actual moment of death for each one is a matter of

special concern for God's care of men. This does not mean that death always occurs in circumstances positively willed by God—some die at a particular time because of the malice or negligence of others, which God does not positively will. But it does mean that God's grace is certainly there to make death a salvific event, unless a person by his previous choices has so hardened his heart as to place himself beyond the reach of the divine mercy as God in His wisdom extends this to all men. The act of the will, then, that emerges in the precise moment of death as the first instant of the soul's permanent state is the necessary fruit of all man's free responses to divine grace, especially to that last grace intended by God to bring him finally to Himself.

These theologians reply to the arguments for a free option in the moment of death by saying first that what individual free choices made during life lack in total, full responsibility is made up for by the very number and interconnection of these choices. Man, unlike the angel, does not decide his destiny in a single instant of total comprehension and commitment, but as a being of space and time whose life of free decision only cumulatively mounts toward the permanent dimensions of a definite personality. The act, then, that emerges as the intrinsically necessary consequence of this process reasonably explains the sinner's just exclusion from God's presence, and also the extinction of the habits of faith and hope. For every unrepented sin tends naturally to erode faith and hope; here that tendency is finally effective. The lot of infants dying without Baptism is, they say, far too obscure a point to be used to clarify something else. And finally, they insist, this last free act, as described by the proponents of a final option at death, is not a human act at all but an angelic act, reflecting a hidden Platonic persuasion of mind.

Points of Similarity. Although there is a real difference of opinion between these groups of theologians on the nature of the act of the soul in the moment of death, it would be a mistake to exaggerate this difference. Both agree that this act depends profoundly and inescapably upon the prior choices made while the soul is in the state of union with the body. If one position says that these prior choices do not wholly and necessarily determine this act from within, this is not said to encourage sinners to put off their repentance and plan to fix things up at that last instant of freedom, but to make a man unequivocally assume full responsibility for the answer he makes to God's grace. Both agree, too, that in this act man becomes definitively himself, and that in this moment his preparation is joined intrinsically to divine fulfillment or to the awful emptiness of sin that remains forever. Both agree, finally, that the state that follows death does not derive its essential immutability from an extrinsic, free decree of God, but from the very nature of death and the activity elicited by the soul in this moment. Death and eternity hang upon mortal life and time.

Anticipation. But it is also true that because mortal life and its choices are all directed toward the fulfillment of death, life hangs upon death. The soul's activity in the moment of death is already present by anticipation and intrinsic purpose in all the deliberate free activity of life. It is this which gives to all human events an aspect of irrevocability. These events are not caught up in a cycle that is endlessly repeating itself, where things if they are done one way this time may be done another way next time; for in the profoundest sense of the term, there never is a next time. Whatever is done is done once and for all because it bears upon a single, definite climactic event in the future. The influence of a particular free choice, is not, of course, isolated and determinative all by itself; but it is irrevocably inserted into a person's life to emerge as finally accepted or rejected at the moment of death by reason of the attitudes subsequently assumed toward it in the movement toward death.

This anticipated presence of the activity of the moment of death in all free choices during life gives also the fully human experiences of life a quality of anticipated realization as well. It means that all the sufferings and trials of life form part of that redemptive unselfing that death perfects. It means that all the unselfish joys of life, whereby the happiness of others is one's own and the victories of God's mercy through Christ are also one's own victories—that these joys are the beginnings of the full glory that will be revealed in men. One sees that this was true in the case of Christ Himself, that all His willing acceptance of privation and anguish was an anticipation of His acceptance of death, and that Thabor and other manifestations of the coming of the kingdom of God were anticipated experiences of the triumph of His Resurrection.

Essential Consummation. This article may conclude by noting briefly how the essentially consummating quality of the experience of death also helps explain the special aspects of the mystery of death considered earlier. Although death as a natural event is not determinately an event of condemnation or of salvation, its first appearance in human history was the manifestation of God's adverse judgment on sinful man. This outward loss of bodily life symbolized and secured in the case of the rebellious sinner his irreversible separation from God. For in the activity of the moment of death the sinner fully expressed the movement of his life away from God and discovered only the terrible isolation of his own being in the choice that set him at odds with the universe. Hell thereafter is essentially the continuation of this moment throughout eternity.

It becomes clear, too, how the transformation of human existence can only be accomplished by the transformation of death; for all of human life tends toward death, and the activity of death is anticipated in all the choices of life. This means then that if Christ is to redeem mankind by being the intrinsic source within the human race of the transforming glory of God, He will fully become this by undergoing Himself the experience of death. In a sense, of course, Christ was from the beginning already essentially perfect even in His human nature; He was already as man in possession of the vision of God beyond all possibility of loss. But the condition of His human nature as He assumed it was not perfectly consummated; it was subject to suffering, rejection, loneliness, and the darkness of death. It was not yet the glorified source of the giving of the Spirit. It became this by the consummating experience of death, wherein all the love and obedience of His mortal life concentrated themselves in the perfect act of self-giving to the Father and achieved the total transferal of His human nature into the realm of the divine glory, a transferal completed in the Resurrection.

So, too, for the Christian as he gradually becomes more and more assimilated to Christ—as the paschal mystery of the Lord becomes more and more fully expressed in his life—death, because it fully captures the completeness of his response to God, becomes the moment of his final appropriation of Christ's life and death and a straining toward the resurrection of the body. Faith, hope, and love, and all the worship of the sacramental life of the Church reach full maturity in this moment of complete submission with Christ. This activity, which places the Christian forever beyond the possibility of succumbing to the deceits of Satan, joins him to the company of the saints, who will rise to meet Christ at the end, when he comes in glory to hand over the kingdom to God the Father that He may be all in all.

See Also: ESCHATOLOGY, ARTICLES ON; SACRAMENTS, ARTICLES ON; FREE WILL; JUDGMENT, DIVINE (IN THEOLOGY); MAN, 3; RESURRECTION OF CHRIST; WILL OF GOD.

Bibliography: M. and L. BECQUÉ, *Life after Death,* tr. P. HEPBURNE-SCOTT (New York 1960). R. GARRIGOU-LAGRANGE, *Life Everlasting,* tr. P. CUMMINS (St. Louis 1952). R. W. GLEASON, *The World to Come* (New York 1958). R. GUARDINI, *The Last Things,* tr. C. E. FORSYTH and G. B. BRANHAM (New York 1954). E. H. SCHILLEBEECKX, "The Death of a Christian," in his *The Layman in the Church and Other Essays,* tr. from the Dutch (New York 1963). A. WINKLHOFER, *The Coming of His Kingdom,* tr. A. V. LITTLEDALE (New York 1963). L. BOROS, *The Mystery of Death,* tr. G. BAINBRIDGE (New York 1965). H. M. CARGAS and A. WHITE, eds., *Death and Hope* (New York 1970). B. J. COLLOPY, "Theology and Death," *Theological Studies* 39 (1978) 22–54. M. MCC. GATCH, *Death: Meaning and Mortality in Christian Thought and Contem-*

Pope St. Boniface I conducting the last rites for St. Alexius, detail of an 11th-century fresco in the Basilica of S. Clemente at Rome. The meeting of the two saints is a legend that grew out of the dedicating of a church on the Aventine in both their names. (Alinari-Art Reference/Art Resource, NY)

porary Culture (New York 1969). K. RAHNER, *On the Theology of Death,* tr. C. H. HENKEY, *Quaestiones Disputatae* 2 (New York 1961). R. TROISFONTAINES, *I Do Not Die,* tr. F. E. ALBERT (New York 1963). J. WAGNER, ed., *Reforming the Rites of Death, Concilium* 32 (New York 1968).

[J. H. WRIGHT]

DEATH, PREPARATION FOR

Death from the natural point of view is a fearful and terrifying event, for it is the dissolution of the human personality. To grasp its full meaning, however, one must turn to faith and see death as the result of sin (Rom 5.12; H. Denzinger, *Enchiridion symbolorum* [Freiburg 1963] 1511–12). It is of man's making, not God's. Wisdom expresses the profound and consoling truth: "God did not make death, nor does he rejoice in the destruction of the living" (Wis 1.13; cf.2.23–24). Moreover, the power of Satan (Jn 8.44; Heb 2.14) and death was broken by its paradoxical overthrow by death. The Word made flesh took on even that which is most terrifying to man and "Death is swallowed up in victory" (1 Cor 15.54).

"Dying, he destroyed our death and rising he restored our life" (Preface for Easter).

One's own death now takes on new meaning: it is to be in union with Christ. When and how death may come are God's to determine, but the individual chooses how he is to accept it. He can freely accept God's will, for indeed the most important preparation for death is its willing acceptance. This begins with humble, hopeful, and loving faith, with praying and living the petition "Thy will be done." This requires a spirit of contrition and self-denial. Death is a sacrificial act, one's last; hence a spirit of sacrifice is essential in preparing for it.

There is no better way to prepare for death's sacrifice than association with Christ's Passion, which is "applied to man through the Sacraments" (Aquinas, *Summa theologiae* 3a, 61.1, ad 3). Each of the Sacraments helps, in a special way, to prepare one to face death without fear. This is best appreciated and applied by participation in the liturgy, teacher of "the true Christian spirit" (Vatican Council II, *Constitution on the Liturgy* 14). "The liturgy . . . moves the faithful, filled with 'the paschal sacraments,' to be 'one in holiness'. . . . The Eucharist

. . . draws the faithful in the compelling love of Christ and sets them on fire'' (*ibid.* 11).

"By Baptism men are plunged into the paschal mystery of Christ" (*ibid.* 6). Sacramentally, we have died, been buried, and have risen with Christ (see Rom 6.3–4; Col 3.3; 2 Tm 2.11). Physical death holds no fears; it only effects a fuller sharing in Christ's glory. To face life's daily way of the cross, one has a fuller share in Christ's priesthood and the Spirit of Love. Confirmation gives "the fullness of the Holy Ghost . . . for the spiritual strength which belongs to the perfect age" (*Summa theologiae* 3a, 72.2). Here is a constant source of strength to face death's ordeal. In the Eucharist, Christians "proclaim the death of the Lord, until he comes" (1 Cor 11.26). It is not just recalling, it is "re-presenting" His death: "The victory and triumph of his death are again made present" (*Constitution on the Liturgy*, 6). Sharing His priesthood, Christians offer Christ and are also victims who suffer and die with Him. The Eucharist is death to self. Every Communion should prepare for death's eternal union with Christ. Sins make man fearful of divine judgment. Graciously, however, divine mercy is available in Penance. The mercy of the Passion is applied to man. Each confession is a fuller sharing in the paschal mystery. Marriage is to be a constant reflection of the love between Christ and His Church (Eph 5). This Sacrament effecting death to selfishness is a constant preparation for actual death. Sacred Orders makes of man another Christ. Sacrifice and sharing heavenly gifts is his vocation: it is death to self. When sickness takes its toll, as death is near, a man is at his weakest. His is singularly associated with Christ's death; so too, Christ's strength is shared. Even as he goes down into the valley of death, the Anointing of the Sick effects a paradox: "the Lord will raise him up" (Jas 5.15). Incarnate mercy would even accompany him into eternity through Viaticum. He is already prepared for glory. Compline, the Church's night prayer, is a preparation for sleep, so symbolic of death. Indeed every prayer a man says unites his will to God's will, thus preparing him to do so at death. Mary's rosary teaches this in a practical way. Such prayers, liturgical and private, as prelude to heavenly prayer, are effective preparations for a happy death.

Bibliography: A. LIGOURI, *Preparation for Death* (New York 1885). M. C. D'ARCY, *Death and Life* (London 1942). J. C. DIDIER, *Death and the Christian,* tr. P. J. HEPBURNE-SCOTT (New York 1961). F. C. HOUSELANDER, *The Way of the Cross* (New York 1955). B. JARRETT, *No Abiding City* (Westminster, Md. 1949). J. H. NEWMAN, *The Dream of Gerontius* (New York 1926). K. RAHNER, *On the Theology of Death,* tr. C. H. HENKEY (*Quaestiones disputatae* 2; New York 1961). A. S. PERRET, *Toward Our Father's House,* tr. R. N. ALBRIGHT (St. Louis 1958). E. H. SCHILLEBEECKX, "The Death of a Christian," in his *Layman in the Church and Other Essays,* tr. from Dutch (New York 1963). B. ULANOV, comp., *Death* (New York 1959). H. VAN ZELLER, *Death in Other Words* (Springfield, Ill. 1963).

[P. J. KELLY]

DEATH OF GOD THEOLOGY

Death of God theology was the generic title given to a movement in American theology during the 1960s. Although there were echoes of the death of God theme in the writings of Jewish theologians, especially Richard L. Rubenstein, and Catholic thinkers were influenced by it, the death of God movement remained a primarily Protestant one.

Notion of God and Christianity. Reflecting on Martin LUTHER's famous phrase, "God is dead," which Friedrich NIETZSCHE had transformed into a striking expression of modern man's total rejection of Christianity, the death of God theologians endeavored to elucidate the theological significance of the precipitous decline of religious faith and practice in contemporary society. They were agreed that this startling decline should not be treated simply as a problem in pastoral sociology. The widespread rejection of traditional religion, which is one of the marks of modern society, cannot be attributed solely to social and cultural changes. Contemporary science and philosophy have exposed fundamental deficiencies in the notion of God proposed by traditional theology that have rendered the traditional God meaningless to men whose minds have been formed by contemporary culture. Consequently, unless these deficiencies are removed by a radical revision of our notion of God, God will continue to be meaningless to modern man.

An important consequence of this necessary revision of the notion of God would be an equally radical reconstruction of the meaning of Christianity. "Otherworldly" Christianity, centered on the Incarnate Word of Chalcedonian theology and focused on the Church as the source of supernatural salvation through her rites and preaching, is incompatible with the revision of the notion of God demanded by contemporary science and philosophy. The revised notion of God would call for a secular, "Churchless" Christianity, whose primary expression would be social involvement. This new Christianity would be focused on the human Christ. Christ's religious function would be to give modern man through the Gospels the inspiring example of a truly human life lived totally for others.

The death of God theologians not only shared a number of common preoccupations; they had also undergone a number of common influences. Like many theologians of their generation, they had been influenced by the debate between Karl BARTH and liberal Protestantism during their theological formation. They had also been influenced by Rudolf BULTMANN's DEMYTHOLOGIZING approach to exegesis and a radical—and disputed—interpretation of Dietrich Bonhoeffer's "religionless Christianity," based largely on the latter's *Letters and Papers from Prison*. As a result of these theological influences, and the influence of a variety of contemporary philosophies, the death of God theologians manifested a strong distrust of the traditional metaphysical approach to Christianity. Modern man, in their view, can no longer accept the notion of an infinite, immutable, transcendent God who gives witness to His nature through His creation and to His revealed word by signs and miracles. This immutable, transcendent God is the God who has died because the purely immanent intelligibility of our secular, scientific world no longer speaks of Him. Metaphysical notions, such as the hypostatic union, the Trinity, grace, and sacrament have lost all significance for modern man. Whether personal survival has any factual basis or not, it has ceased to be a matter of pressing concern to the socially involved Christian. For the death of God theologians prayer no longer figured as a central element in a religious life.

Hamilton. Despite these common characteristics, the death of God theologians remained too diverse in their philosophical and theological thinking to create a clearly definable theological school. Indeed, William HAMILTON, one of the more radical among them, preferred to use the method of shorter essays, "theological fragments," to express his thought rather than work out a consistent large-scale synthesis. Writing in a highly autobiographical style, Hamilton described the lack of faith that besets even the theologian today. The immensity of human suffering in the world today has destroyed man's faith in the providential God who watched over man and cared for his needs. The collapse of metaphysics has eroded modern man's belief in the God of paradise whose enjoyment alone could satisfy the inborn drive of the human spirit. Since the strictly immanent intelligibility of the contemporary scientific world excludes any knowledge of a transcendent divine nature, and there is no void in the human soul that calls for God to fill it, not even the theologian today can maintain any interest in dogmatic statements about God. Therefore the time has now come for contemporary Christians to radicalize the movement initiated by the Protestant Reformers. All Christians, including the theologians, must leave the Church and move out into the world. They must give up their concern for personal supernatural salvation and abandon their preoccupation with rites and dogmatic statements. Instead, they must devote themselves wholeheartedly to the contemporary struggle for the improvement of man, stirred

on in their new intraworldly religious work by the inspiring example of Christ.

Van Buren. Hamilton's conviction that metaphysical or dogmatic statements about God were no longer possible was reiterated in a more systematic way by Paul van Buren. Using the verification principle of the logical positivists, according to which only tautologies and empirically verifiable statements can be called meaningful, van Buren drastically reduced the meaningful content of the New Testament. Statements about the divine nature, the divinity of Christ, the supernatural life, etc., are clearly neither tautologies nor empirically verifiable statements. Thus the meaningful Christ who emerges from van Buren's New Testament is the man who was "free" to give Himself for others, and the meaningful content of the Easter message is the "contagion" of Christ's freedom that His disciples caught from Him. The contagion of Christ's freedom transformed the lives of His immediate disciples and they in their turn transmitted it to others through their preaching. Borrowing the term from R. M. Hare, van Buren describes Christianity as a "blik," a sound though nonverifiable worldview. Because of his Christian blik, the Christian looks on the world through the optic of Christ's freedom. Thus, in the manner described by R. R. Braithwaite, the Christian can devote himself to a life of generous social interaction with his neighbor under the inspiration of the Christ of the Gospels.

Van Buren was the most philosophically unified and coherent of the death of God theologians. His *Secular Meaning of the Gospel* was a consistent application to the New Testament of a rather narrow logical empiricism. Van Buren's consistency, however, was also his weakness. The narrowness of logical empiricism, especially in relation to the verification principle, has been severely criticized by other linguistic philosophers. Many of the criticisms leveled against logical empiricism can also be leveled against van Buren's theology, which is largely dependent on it.

Hamilton and van Buren proclaimed themselves theologians who were content to go about their work without any affirmable knowledge of a transcendent God. Hamilton indeed asserted that the contemporary theologian must be willing to dispense with even religious faith in a transcendent divinity. As a result of their skepticism, Hamilton and van Buren reduced Christianity to a fundamentally ethical enterprise. The Christian is distinguished from the secular humanist because he has chosen to perform his human work for the world under the inspiration of Christ. Neither the intelligibility of the world, the exigencies of human nature, nor religious experience provide any compelling evidence for God's existence.

Biblical revelation can solve no problems that the unbeliever cannot cope with just as effectively as the Christian. Since our modern age has reached adulthood, it now realizes that the world no longer needs God to solve its problems. Christianity has become simply one of many possible ways in which modern man can live a rich human life. The Christian is distinguished from other men because he has chosen the Christian option for his own.

Altizer. Thomas J. J. Altizer approached the death of God in a much more metaphysical and theological manner than either Hamilton or van Buren. He agreed with them that the widespread rejection of traditional Christianity is a social fact. He also saw in it a challenge to Christians to revise radically their notion of God and embrace a secular Christianity characterized by its strong affirmation of the value of worldly reality. Altizer, however, did not regard the decline in religious faith as the result of epistemological and cosmological advances that had undermined the credibility of the traditional conception of God. He saw it rather as the reflection in human society of a progressive ontological change that is taking place within God Himself. The death of God, the effect of which has now become visible in modern society, is the ontological process of God's KENOSIS. God "emptied Himself" ontologically when His Word became flesh in Christ. The Incarnation marks the inception of an ongoing metaphysical identification of God with the finite universe. This self-identification of God with His finite universe is an irreversible movement of God into the world. For, through the "self-emptying" of the Incarnation, God definitively abandoned His state of isolated transcendence in order to unite Himself inseparably with the temporal process of His worldly creation. Since this progressive identification of God with His creation is the true meaning of the Incarnation, the Christian's fidelity to the Incarnation does not mean that the Christian must define his faith in the traditional way by looking back upon the life, death, and Resurrection of Christ as past events that have left the transcendent God fundamentally unchanged. On the contrary, fidelity to the Incarnation means that the Christian must identify himself with the God who has united Himself through His Incarnate Word with the evolutionary process of creation and human society.

Since God is identified with the world, revelation has not closed with the last Apostle. Therefore the Christian will hear God's revealing word addressed to him through successive prophetic voices in the course of history. According to Altizer, three of the great revealing voices through which God speaks to contemporary Christians are those of G. W. F. HEGEL, William BLAKE, and Nietzsche. Hegel has revealed that God truly becomes Himself only by identifying Himself with His manifestations in finite being. Blake has revealed that the God who is worshiped in the traditional Christian churches is not the true God. Nietzsche has forced Christians to admit that saving truth can be found only in their powerful affirmation of the worth of worldly reality.

The progressive revelation of God through His prophetic voices in modern history requires a transformation of the Christian's understanding of the sacred and the profane. Primitive man, as Mircea ELIADE has shown, considered that worldly being, "the profane," was unreal in comparison with the sacred, the changeless transcendent God. Profane being was given its true value only when it was denied, i.e., reduced to the status of an "unreal" manifestation of true being, the sacred transcendent God. Once Christians have come to realize that the death of God means God's irreversible identification of Himself with the process of His creation, their understanding of the relation of the sacred and the profane must be reversed. Sacred, "real" being is no longer found above the world in a transcendent God. The sacred, real, divine being is found in the only place in which it can exist after the death of God, in the ongoing secular process of the world itself.

If the practical conclusions of Altizer's death of God theology were very similar to those of Hamilton and van Buren, its philosophical foundations were completely different. Although Altizer's writings contained the germ of a powerful philosophical theology, he never worked out the implications of his major metaphysical assertions. Consequently the many ambiguities of his system, e.g., the immanence or transcendence of God, the relation of creation to the Incarnation, the relation of grace to nature, the precise significance of the Word of God, remained unresolved. As a result Altizer's death of God theology remained a series of provocative suggestions. It never became a coherent theological synthesis capable of exerting a lasting influence.

Robinson and Vahanian. Although the theology of the Anglican bishop of Woolwich, John A. T. Robinson, resembled the theology of the death of God movement in many respects, Robinson was not a member of the movement. Like the American death of God theologians, Robinson rejected the notion of a transcendent God described in personal categories. Under the influence of Bultmann he refused to accept the concept of a God who worked within our empirical world through signs and miracles. He found Paul TILLICH's conception of God as the unobjective ground of being more satisfactory than the traditional notion of a transcendent God standing over against the human subject as a sort of superperson. Nevertheless Robinson did not draw the radical conclusions that the death of God theologians drew from his revised understanding of God and God's relation to the world. A radical revision and updating of religious practice to make the Church more significant to modern man rather than an abandonment of the institutional Church was the theme of Robinson's much discussed *Honest to God.*

Similarly, Gabriel Vahanian, whose name was often linked to the death of God movement, was not a death of God theologian. Vahanian was concerned with the death of God, the general decline of religious belief and practice, as a historical fact. Since he was an orthodox Protestant theologian in the Barthian tradition, however, he looked on this cultural death of God as a call to return to a purer and more biblical conception of God.

Bibliography: T. J. J. ALTIZER, *The Gospel of Christian Atheism* (Philadelphia 1966); ed., *Toward a New Christianity: Readings in the Death of God Theology* (New York 1967); T. J. J. ALTIZER and W. HAMILTON, *Radical Theology and the Death of God* (Indianapolis, Ind. 1966). W. HAMILTON, *The New Essence of Christianity* (New York 1961); ''Thursday's Child: The Theologian Today and Tomorrow,'' *Theology Today* 20 (January 1964) 487–495; ''The Death of God Theology,'' *Christian Scholar* 48 (Spring 1965) 27–48; ''The Shape of Radical Theology,'' *Christian Century* 82 (Spring 1965) 1219–22. J. A. T. ROBINSON, *Honest to God* (Philadelphia 1963); *Exploration into God* (Palo Alto, Calif. 1967). G. VAHANIAN, *The Death of God* (New York 1961); *No Other God* (New York 1966); ed., *The God Is Dead Debate* (New York 1967). P. VAN BUREN, *The Secular Meaning of the Gospel* (New York 1963); *Theological Explorations* (New York 1968). Secondary sources. L. GILKIE, *Naming the Whirlwind: The Renewal of God Language* (Indianapolis, Ind. 1969) esp. 107–145. V. MEHTA, *The New Theologians* (New York 1966). T. W. OGLETREE, *The Death of God Controversy* (Nashville 1966).

[G. A. MCCOOL]

DEBUSSY, ACHILLE CLAUDE

Impressionist composer; b. Saint-Germain-en-Laye, Aug. 22, 1862; d. Paris, March 25, 1918. Eldest of five children, Claude was baptized two years after his birth, at the suggestion of his godmother aunt, Clémentine de Bussy, who also arranged for his first music lessons. At ten he began his training at the Paris Conservatory, and soon revealed a disposition for composition and the piano. His music was more secular than sacred; yet often its apparent archaism, particularly in its modality, might be a reflection of his visit to Solesmes and his knowledge of early French folk songs. His incidental music for Gabriele d'Annunzio's mystery play, *Le Martyre de Saint Sébastien,* was proscribed for Catholics by the archbishop of Paris because a woman portrayed the martyr, not because d'Annunzio's text was placed on the Index in the same year (1911). Debussy protested that he had written it as though commanded by a church. Yet the play contains profane as well as sacred elements, and the music, though often elevated and infiltrated with modal color, is uneven. Essentially a poet and a miniaturist of music, Debussy created evanescent atmospheres through his sensitivity to the vocal inflection, scales, and instrumentation of exotic regions. In his search for iridescent and sonorous color he created not only a personal style marked by ingenious evasions of tonality and sensuous sonorities that shocked his contemporaries, but also a harmonic vocabulary that heralded a new era in music.

Bibliography: E. LOCKSPEISER, *Debussy: His Life and Mind* 2 v. (New York 1962–65). M. DIETSCHY, ''The Family and Childhood of Debussy,'' tr. E. LOCKSPEISER, *Musical Quarterly* 46 (1960) 301–314. A. LIESS, *Die Musik in Geschichte und Gegenwart,* ed. F. BLUME (Kassel-Basel 1949–) 3:62–77. E. WEBER, ed. *Debussy et l'evolution de la musique aux XXe siècle* (Paris 1965). J. D'ALMENDRA, *Les Modes grégoriens dans l'oeuvre de Claude Debussy* (Paris 1950). J. BRAUNER, ''Anmerkungen zu späten Klavieretüden von Debussy und Skrjabin,'' *Die Musikforschung* 53 (2000) 254–271. T. DAVIDIAN, ''Debussy, D'Indy and the Société Nationale,'' *Journal of Musicological Research* 11 (1991) 285–301. A. FORTE, ''Debussy and the Octatonic,'' *Music Analysis* 10 (1991) 125–169. D. KOPP, ''Pentatonic Organization in Two Piano Pieces of Debussy,'' *Journal of Music Theory* 41 (1997) 261–287. F. LESURE, ''Debussy et les Transcriptions,'' *Revue Belge de Musicology* 52 (1998) 85–90. T. MALENGREAU, ''Du *Pelléas* de Maeterlinck au *Pelléas* de Debussy,'' *Analyse Musicale* 31 (1993) 31–39. R. S. PARKS, ''A Viennese Arrangement of Debussy's *Prélude à l'après-midi d'un faune:* Orchestration and Musical Structure,'' *Music and Letters* 80 (1999) 50–73. S. RUMPH, ''Debussy's *Trois Chansons de Bilitis:* Song, Opera, and the Death of the Subject,'' *Journal of Musicology* 12 (1994) 464–490.

[V. RAAD]

DECADI, CULT OF

One of the naturalistic, patriotic religious cults concocted during the FRENCH REVOLUTION as a substitute for Christianity. The Second Directory promulgated the Decadi as the nation's official cult (1797–99) and organized it so that the *décadi,* recurring every tenth day in the French Revolutionary calendar, would be soleminized in such a manner as to replace the services of the Christian Sunday. Although the majority of Frenchmen had refused since 1793 to exchange 36 *décadi* per year for 52 Sundays as days of rest and religious observance, the Directory in 1797 passed penal legislation insisting on the suspension of work in courts, government offices, schools, factories and shops on the *décadi* and nullifying contracts and deeds of sale on that date, while requiring the performance of marriage ceremonies on that day alone. Local governments were required to solemnize publicly the official cult, and persons who observed Sundays were threatened with fines and imprisonment lasting one *décade* (ten days). All the bishops and most of the constitutional clergy as well as the nonjuring priests opposed the suppression of the Lord's Day and demanded the restoration of Christian marriage. Many of them paid for their recalcitrance with imprisonment, transportation to Cayenne, or death on the guillotine.

Marie Joseph Chénier (1764–1811) was the cult's theorist. François de Neufchâteau (1750–1828), poet and minister of the interior, was its liturgist; he originated the elaborate ceremonial with its garlanded ploughs, bonfires, chants, imprecations and oaths prescribed for each of the seven major feasts commemorating youth, age, knowledge, agriculture, etc. Ceremonies for ordinary feasts on the *décadi,* as instituted by the decree of Aug. 30, 1798, were held before an altar dedicated to the fatherland, where a municipal official proclaimed the public enactments of the past ten days, read selections from the *Décadaire Bulletin* concerning civic virtue, agriculture, the mechanical arts and reported on current events. The congregation then sang some patriotic song; marriages were performed and births were recorded; and school children, who were present with their teachers, were quizzed. All churches were locked on Sundays. On the *décadi* in Paris, Notre Dame cathedral and 14 other churches were opened for ceremonies. Government officials, teachers, students and persons attending marriages were present perforce, but the mass of the population was indifferent to the cult and absented itself, aware of the powerlessness of the Directory to enforce its will on the entire nation. When Napoleon gained power after the *coup d'état* of 18th Brumaire (Nov. 9, 1799), he reopened the churches on Sundays. In 1800 the cult ceased to be obligatory. Napoleon officially dissolved it in 1805.

See Also: REASON, CULT OF GODDESS OF; SUPREME BEING, CULT OF THE; THEOPHILANTHROPY.

Bibliography: A. MATHIEZ, *La Théophilanthropie et le culte décadaire, 1796–1801* (Paris 1904). A. LATREILLE, *L'Église catholique et la révolution française,* 2 v. (Paris 1946–50). J. LEFLON, *Catholicisme,* 3:499.

[M. LAWLOR]

DECAPOLIS

Region in northeastern Palestine in the Greco-Roman period. The term means ''The Ten Cities,'' and it is thus referred to as αἱ δέκα πόλεις in Josephus's *Vita* (341–342), but it is mentioned more commonly by the compound noun ἡ Δεκάπολις, from which the English term is derived; so it is used in the New Testament (Mt 4.25; Mk 5.20; 7.31), in Josephus (*Bell. Jud.* 1.7.7; 3.9.7; *Ant.* 12.3.3; 14.4.4), in Pliny (*Hist. Nat.* 5.16.74), and in a few other places. At different periods the term had vary-

Achille Claude Debussy. (Archive Photos, Inc.)

ing geographical limits, but it always meant the area east both of Perea and lower Galilee. Its northernmost city was Damascus, its southernmost one Philadelphia (Ammân), and its easternmost one Canatha; but in New Testament times, Damascus and Canatha were considered outside the Decapolis proper, the northern boundary of which was drawn above Abila and Hippos east of the lower half of the Sea of Galilee. All the cities of the Decapolis lay east of the Jordan river, except Scythopolis, which was a few miles west of this natural boundary. The area embraced ancient Galaad (except the part of it in upper Perea) and the territory to the north and west.

A distinctive feature of the Decapolis was its political status as a loose confederation of essentially independent cities that were mostly Greco-Roman in tradition and outlook. Most of the Ten Cities were of Greek origin, founded or taken over and made important by veterans of Alexander's army at the end of the fourth century B.C. or established by the Seleucid dynasty somewhat later. Their Hellenistic spirit and population made them a counterbalance to Jewish nationalism and centers of opposition to the Maccabean revolt and subsequent HASMONAEAN rule in the second and first centuries B.C. Several of these cities were conquered and destroyed by the Jewish militants of that period, but when Pompey subdued Palestine, his reorganization of the area in 63

Ruined colonnades of Decapolis, near Jaresh, in northern Jordan. (©Adam Woolfitt/CORBIS)

B.C. reestablished these essentially non-Jewish cities as autonomous states in a common federation loosely attached to the Roman Province of Syria. The cities paid taxes to Rome, but were basically independent. The peak of their prosperity occurred in the second Christian century, especially between 138 and 193, when Roman power was at its height.

According to Pliny (*c.* A.D. 75), the Ten Cities of the Decapolis were the following: (1) Gadara (modern Muqeis), considered the capital, about 8 miles southeast of the Sea of Galilee; (2) Scythopolis (Old Testament Bethsan, modern Beisan), west of the Jordan, about 25 miles southwest of the Sea of Galilee, guarding the main road from the Plain of Jezreel to the Jordan fords, called the largest city of the Decapolis by Josephus; (3) Pella (modern Khirbet Fahil), east of the Jordan, seven miles southeast of Scythopolis, the place where the Christians of Jerusalem sought refuge during the siege of 66–70; (4) Hippos (Sousitha, modern Qala'at el-Husn near Fîq), on the slopes of the lower east shore of the Sea of Galilee;

(5) Rephana (the Raphon of 1 Mc 5.37, modern er-Râfeh), about 35 miles south of Damascus; (6) Dion (modern Tell el-Ash'arī), about 12 miles southwest of Rephana; (7) Gerasa (modern Jerash), the best preserved of the ancient cities of the Decapolis; (8) Philadelphia (the Old Testament Rabbah of the Ammonites, modern Ammân, capital of the Hashemite Kingdom of JORDAN); (9) Canatha (the Canath or Kenath of Nm 32.42, modern Qanawât), in Auranitis near the edge of the Syrian Desert; and (10) DAMASCUS, well-known from the Old Testament.

The geographer Ptolemy (Claudius Ptolemaeus), in his second-century list (*Geogr.* 5.14.18), replaced Rephana by Abila (modern Tell Abil), about midway between Dion and Gadara. In late antiquity other cities also were counted as belonging to the Decapolis, such as Edrei (modern Der'ā, border post between Syria and Jordan), Capitolias (modern Beit Ras, about two miles north of Irbid), and another Gadara (or Gadora; modern Tell Jadūr, near es-Salt).

Jesus seldom entered this essentially non-Jewish region, but He passed through the northern part of it on His way from Phoenicia to the eastern side of the Sea of Galilee (Mk 7.31). In this section of the Decapolis, but on another occasion, He cured a man possessed by a legion of demons (Mk 5.1–20). According to Mt 4.25, among the crowds that followed Jesus, some came even from the Decapolis.

Bibliography: F. M. ABEL, *Histoire de la Palestine depuis la conquête d'Alexandre jusqu'à l'invasion Arabe*, 2 v. (Paris 1952) 1:263–264. F. M. ABEL, *Géographie de la Palestine* (Paris 1933–38) 2:145–146, 230. K. HÖPF, *Lexikon für Theologie und Kirche*, ed. J. HOFER and K. RAHNER (Freiburg 1957–65) 3:204–205. *Encyclopedic Dictionary of the Bible*, tr. and adap. by L. HARTMAN (New York 1963) 537–538, with map.

[R. V. SCHODER]

DECEIT

The malice added to lying, by which one, in addition to uttering an untruth, attempts to make another believe it. A lie, strictly, consists of the intention to say what is contrary to one's thoughts; deceit adds the intention of getting another to accept the expressed falsehood as the truth. Thus, one testifying in court may know that everyone understands his words to be false but, for the record, on which alone he may be judged, he utters a falsehood. Thus, deceit involves more than a lie. It is more than a falsification in words; it is also an attempt, by word or deed, to have the falsification accepted as true.

It should be noted, however, that deceit can be present even when there is no lie or simulation. Indeed, one can deceive by telling the truth. For instance, if an inveterate and notorious liar wishes to deceive another, he might find the way easier and surer by telling the truth rather than a lie. Knowing that people are inclined to believe the opposite of what he says, he can tell the truth and thereby secure that they will believe what is false. His intention is to deceive, and so his very act of telling the truth becomes an act of deception.

In itself deceit, like lying in general, is a venial sin. However, where it causes serious harm to another, or in any case in which truthfulness is urgently and desperately needed, it becomes gravely sinful.

Bibliography: J. A. MCHUGH and C. J. CALLAN, *Moral Theology,* rev. E. P. FARRELL, 2 v. (New York 1958) 2:2403–04.

[S. F. PARMISANO]

DECHAMPS, VICTOR AUGUSTE

Theologian; b. Melle near Ghent, Dec. 6, 1810; d. Mechlin, Sept. 29, 1883. When he was 12 the family moved to the Castle of Scailmont near Manage; he and his brother studied philosophy and letters under their father's supervision. They shared a preference for the writings of Lamennais. When the Brabançonnic revolution broke out in 1830, they published their "lamennaisien" opinions in the *Journal des Flandres* as well as in *L'Emancipation.*

Victor Dechamps entered the seminary at Tournai in 1832, attended Louvain University, and was ordained in 1835. Feeling himself called to religious life, Dechamps left the University for the Redemptorist novitiate at Saint-Trond. In 1836 he became professor of dogma and Scripture at the Redemptorist scholasticate in Wittem. It was here that he conceived his apologetic method. He later developed this in his great works, especially in *Entretiens sur la Démonstration de la Foi* (1856); *Lettres Théologiques* (1861); and in two volumes entitled *La Question Religieuse* (1861).

This method, called the "method of Providence," contrary to those in the texts of the day, was founded on two factors: man himself in his desire and need for the living divine word (internal factor) and the Church who alone responds to this human desire and proves from within herself that she comes from God by her "subsistent miracle" of unity, universality, indefectibility, and holiness (external factor). This method was the fruit not only of Dechamps's years at Wittem, but also of the rich experiences of his apostolic life.

He left Wittem in 1840. In his own religious community he was several times rector, and became provincial superior from 1851 to 1854. A frequent visitor to Rome on matters of his congregation, he did everything in his power to establish the generalate of the Redemptorists there. In 1855 at the Redemptorist general chapter in Rome he supported those seeking a more strict form of religious poverty. Since they were not a majority he fell into disfavor with his new religious superiors.

The Belgian bishops considered naming him rector of Louvain University. Because his writings were somewhat opposed to the semitraditionalism of the professors of Louvain, his nomination would have been welcomed by Pius IX. But Dechamps refused it. He became bishop of Namur in 1865 and two years later bishop of Malines. At VATICAN COUNCIL I (1869–70), with Cardinal H. E. MANNING, he led the "Infallibilists." He did not assume doctrinal leadership, but his letters to F. A. P. DUPANLOUP and A. J. A. GRATRY are famous. His apologetic views on revelation and the credibility of the Church were used in the constitution *De Fide.* Although esteemed by the pope, he was not made a cardinal until 1875.

Leo XIII asked him to name a professor of Thomistic philosophy for Louvain. He chose Désiré MERCIER, the future Cardinal Archbishop of Malines. The pope intervened in the Belgian school question, asking Cardinal Dechamps and his suffragans who had condemned severely the "Loi de Malheur" (1879–80) to be more moderate. Dechamps died a year before the victory of the Catholic party.

Bibliography: *Oeuvres complètes,* 17 v. (Mechlin 1874–83). M. BECQUÉ, *L'Apologétique du cardinal Dechamps* (Paris 1949); *Le cardinal Dechamps,* 2 v. (Louvain 1956). R. ARCHAMBAULT, *Catholicisme. Hier, aujourd'hui et demain,* ed. G. JACQUEMET (Paris 1947–) 3:508–509. A. LARGENT, *Dictionnaire de théologie catholique,* ed. A. VACANT et al. (Paris 1903–50) 4.1:171–182.

[M. BECQUÉ]

DECIUS, PHILLIPUS (PHILIPPE DE DEXIO)

Professor of Canon and civil law; b. Milan, 1454; d. Siena, 1536. At 20 he taught law in Paris; he later taught law in Siena (1490). In 1502 he was auditor of the Roman Rota. While teaching at Siena in 1505, he instigated a meeting of cardinals opposing Julius II in favor of Louis XII. For this he was excommunicated. He fled to France, where he taught at Valence. His former pupil, Leo IX, Julius's successor, summoned Decius to Rome. Francis I recalled him to France, but he returned to Italy to reside in Pisa. His important works include the *Commentaria in Decretales;* the *Repetitiones,* edited in Pisa in 1490; and the *Consilia* (Lyons 1565, with notes by C. Dumoulin). His writings on the authority of the general councils and the Council of Pisa appear in Goldast's *Monarchia S. Romani Imperii* (Frankfurt 1614–21).

Bibliography: R. NAZ, *Dictionnaire de droit canonique*, ed. R. NAZ (Paris 1935–65) 4:1059. A. VAN HOVE, *Commentarium Lovaniense in Codicem iuris canonici 1*, v.1–5 (Mechlin 1928–1945) 1:499.

[H. A. LARROQUE]

DECIUS, ROMAN EMPEROR

Reigned 249 to 251; b. Budalia, near Sirmium (in modern Yugoslavia), *c.* 201; d. Abrittus in the Dobruja, June 251. He was of Etruscan descent and probably of a senatorial family. He was prefect of Rome before Emperor Philip the Arab sent him to command the armies on the Danube. After his troops proclaimed him emperor in the summer of 249, he defeated and slew Philip near Verona in September. He spent his brief reign fighting the GOTHS and being betrayed by his generals. In hopes of restoring the ancient religious traditions of Rome, he began a systematic persecution of Christians. His decree, which is not extant, required everyone in the empire to appear before special commissions and perform some act of public worship to the Roman gods. Compliance with the decree was attested to by *libelli* (certificates), more than 40 of which, dated June 12 to July 15, 250, have been discovered in Egypt. Many Christians, including bishops and other clergy, apostatized, and others went into hiding. Among those who suffered in the persecution were: SS. CYPRIAN of Carthage, DIONYSIUS OF ALEXANDRIA, and GREGORY THAUMATURGUS (who wrote of the persecution); Pope FABIAN, whose martyrdom left the See of Rome vacant for some time; ORIGEN, who survived tortures; Bishops ALEXANDER OF JERUSALEM and Babylas of Antioch; Pionius, Asclepiades, and Sabina of Smyrna; the SEVEN SLEEPERS OF EPHESUS; Carpus, Papylus, and Agathonice in Pergamum; Melitenus and Polyeuctus in Armenia; Mappalicus and his companions and Celerinus in Africa; the priest Moses in Rome; and Bishop Nestor of Magydus.

After Decius died in battle against the Goths, the persecution, which had not been renewed at the beginning of 251, came to an end. The Church then took up the problem of dealing with *LAPSI* (apostates) who wished to return to their faith. *LIBELLATICI*, those who had purchased *libelli* without sacrificing to the gods, were readmitted after penance. Those who had sacrificed willingly were not absolved until the moment of death. So strong was the impression made on Christians by the persecution of Decius that in later times martyrdoms about which

little or nothing was known were described in terms of the persecution of Decius. The persecution has been interpreted as a manifestation of the growing state absolutism that would not tolerate a rival in the conscience of its subjects.

Bibliography: J. WITTIG, *Paulys Realenzyklopädie der klassischen Altertumswissenschaft*, ed. G. WISSOWA et al. 15.1 (1931) 1244–84. L. FRONZA, *Studi sull'imperatore Decio*, 2 v. (Trieste 1951–53). G. BARDY, *Catholicisme. Hier, aujourd'hui et demain*, ed. G. JACQUEMET (Paris 1947–) 3:506–507. K. GROSS, *Lexikon für Theologie und Kirche*, ed. J. HOFER and K. RAHNER (2d, new ed. Freiburg 1957–65), 3:184–185; *Reallexikon für Antike und Christentum*, ed. T. KLAUSER (Stuttgart 1950) 3:611–629.

[M. J. COSTELLOE]

DECLARATION OF RIGHTS OF 1689

This declaration, thrashed out by the Houses of Lords and Commons in the preceding fortnight and accepted by William and Mary on Feb. 13, 1689, formed the basis of the Bill of Rights enacted later in the same year as "an Act Declaring the Rights and Liberties of the Subject and Setleing the Succession of the Crowne." The terms of the declaration were designed to prevent the perpetration by future monarchs of acts such as those by which James II had precipitated the Revolution (*see* REVOLUTION OF 1688). Having first enumerated James's misdeeds, it goes on to lay down limitations to which all monarchs shall henceforth be subject; viz, "the pretended power of suspending laws . . . without consent of Parlyament is illegal," as was the royal power of exempting individuals from the operation of the law, "as it hath beene assumed and exercised of late" (in the subsequent Bill of Rights this "dispensing power" was, in effect, abolished altogether). The court of ecclesiastical commission was abolished and such bodies were henceforth illegal; no money could be raised by the crown without Parliament's consent; all subjects could petition the monarch; there was to be no standing army without parliamentary approval; Protestant subjects could keep weapons for their defense; parliamentary elections and the speeches and proceedings of members were to be free, and "Parlyaments ought to be held frequently." Further clauses concerned the impanelling of jurors and the imposition of bail, fines, and other penalties. When embodied in the Bill of Rights, this declaration was supplemented by a ban on the accession of any Catholic or person married to one (*see* ROYAL DECLARATION).

Bibliography: G. N. CLARK, *The Later Stuarts* (2d ed. Oxford 1955). D. OGG, *England in the Reigns of James II and William III* (Oxford 1955). D. L. KEIR, *The Constitutional History of Modern Britain since 1485* (6th ed. London 1960). D. C. DOUGLAS, ed., *English Historical Documents* (London 1953–) v.8 *1660–1714*, ed.

A. BROWNING. W. C. COSTIN and J. S. WATSON, comps., *The Law and Working of the Constitution: Documents,* 2 v. (London 1952) v. 1 1660–1783.

[J. A. WILLIAMS]

DECLARATION OF THE FRENCH CLERGY

Also known as the "Four Articles" or the "Gallican Articles," the high-water mark of Old Regime Gallicanism, promulgated in March 1682. Relations had steadily deteriorated between LOUIS XIV and INNOCENT XI because of the affair of the *régale,* the controversy over the appointment of a new abbess for the convent of Charonne, the papal condemnation of a book by Jean Gerbais previously sanctioned by the French clergy and other incidents. Thus Louis XIV convoked a general assembly of the clergy in June 1681, to achieve a settlement of the *régale* with or without the approval of the Pope and to issue a new statement defining the power of the papacy in French ecclesiastical affairs. That Louis XIV exercised considerable pressure in the selection of at least the lower order of deputies is indubitable. Most of the preparatory work was in the hands of the Archbishop of Paris, Harlay Chanvallon, a powerful influence on the King and an extreme Gallican. In 1680 in answer to papal threats of the excommunication of Louis XIV, Harlay had written for the French clergy a statement that "nothing would separate them from him." Nevertheless, the extremists were not in full control of the Assembly, since Louis XIV did not want a complete rupture with Rome. The moderate Bishop of Meaux, Bossuet, was chosen for the opening address, and delivered a masterpiece of conciliation. Praising both the Gallicans and Rome, he appealed for the unity of the Church. All sides applauded, although it was apparent that accord on general principles was far easier than on the hard and immediate issues. An attempt was made to reach accord on the *régale* by drawing a distinction between the spiritual and temporal regalia, but Innocent XI disdained the entire proceedings and refused a reply.

The skill of the moderates, led by Bossuet, avoided a peremptory repudiation of papal infallibility. In the end, Bossuet was chosen to draft a statement of the Gallican doctrine. In four short articles, the Declaration maintained that: (1) Kings were not subject to any ecclesiastical power in temporal matters; (2) the reservations of the Council of Constance with regard to the spiritual supremacy of the pope still applied; (3) in exercising his functions, the pope must heed the customs and rules of the Gallican Church; (4) while it was acknowledged that the pope had the "principal part in matters of faith," his decisions were not final unless they had been "confirmed by the judgment of the whole Church."

Bad as this statement was from the point of view of the orthodox upholders of papal infallibility, it did prevent an even bolder pronouncement. There was in the document much ambiguity and hedging that reduced its effectiveness. Innocent XI wisely refrained from an outright condemnation, fearing to do anything that might lead to national schism. He contented himself with withholding institution to bishoprics for all participants in the Assembly, and was gratified to observe surprising opposition to the Declaration among the French clergy, particularly among the Sorbonne faculty. In 1692 his successor, Innocent XII, received from the King a communication that the Declaration would not be taught in French seminaries. Shortly thereafter, the Pope received a letter of apology from each participant in the Assembly. For the rest of the Old Regime the Declaration remained a dead letter.

Bibliography: *New Cambridge Modern History* (2d ed. London–New York 1957–) v.5. J. ORCIBAL, *Louis XIV contre Innocent XI* (Paris 1949). J. T. LOYSON, *L'Assemblée du clergé de France de 1682* (Paris 1870). C. CONSTANTIN, *Dictionnaire de théologie catholique,* ed. A. VACANT et al., 15 v. (Paris 1903–50) 4.1:185–205. J. DEDIEU, *Dictionnaire d'histoire et de géographie ecclésiastiques,* ed. A. BAUDRILLART et al., (Paris 1912–) 4:1098–1103.

[L. L. BERNARD]

DE CONCILIO, JANUARIUS VINCENT

Theologian, author; b. Naples, Italy, July 6, 1836; d. Jersey City, N.J., March 22, 1898. Beginning his studies in Naples, he completed his theology at Brignole Sale seminary, Genoa, Italy, where he was ordained for the Diocese of Newark, N.J., on March 9, 1860. He served as an assistant at Our Lady of Grace parish, Hoboken, N.J.; as chaplain and professor of philosophy and theology at Seton Hall College and Seminary, South Orange, N.J.; and as assistant at St. Mary's parish in Jersey City. In 1865 he became the first pastor of St. Michael's in Jersey City, where he built the church, rectory, and school, and constructed an orphanage and academy. He was a member of Bp. Michael A. Corrigan's council and of Bp. Winand Wigger's during the first years of his administration. De Concilio attended the Third Plenary Council of Baltimore and was appointed to the subcommittee that compiled the Baltimore Catechism for presentation to the council. He was made a papal chamberlain in 1886, and the following year was named a domestic prelate. In 1892 he was given the degree of doctor of divinity by Georgetown University, Washington, D.C.

De Concilio was treasurer of the St. Raphael Italian Benevolent Society and maintained that every parish should have a priest who understood the language of the people. He wrote pamphlets deploring the religious condition of Italians in America, as well as frequent articles for the *Freeman's Journal*. He opposed the theory of theistic evolution suggested by Rev. John A. Zahm's *Evolution and Dogma* (1896). Among De Concilio's works were *Catholicity and Pantheism* (1873), *The Knowledge of Mary* (1878), *The Elements of Intellectual Philosophy* (1878), *The Doctrine of Saint Thomas on the Right of Property and Its Use* (1887), *The Harmony Between Science and Revelation* (1889), and *Child of Mary* (1891). He also wrote two plays, *The Irish Heroine* and *Woman's Rights*.

Bibliography: C. D. HINRICHSEN, *The Diocese of Newark, 1873–1901* (Doctoral diss. unpub., Catholic University of America 1962).

[C. D. HINRICHSEN]

DECONSTRUCTIONISM

Deconstruction analyzes the ontotheological, metaphysical presuppositions of written texts and argues that all texts subvert their own internal structures when they claim a fully systematic, coherent frame of reference. Primarily the product of the French thinker Jacques Derrida (b. 1930), deconstructionism follows upon the perceived inadequacies of the structuralist approach and derives inspiration from the post-Kantian thinkers Sigmund Freud, Martin HEIDEGGER, and Friedrich NIETZSCHE. The deconstructionist maintains that every classical text tries to construct or propose a metaphysical presence to hide the inherent absences and gaps in the human psyche, the history of freedom and power, or the fully gracious presence of God/Being. Deconstruction notes the linguistic sutures that try to sew these spaces together and unravels their positive meaning.

Derrida. In 1967 Jacques Derrida published three volumes of philosophical essays (*Le Voix et Le Phénomene* [*Speech and Phenomena* 1973]; *De la Grammatologie* [*Of Grammatology* 1974]; and *L'écriture et la différence* [*Writing and Difference* 1978]) and established himself as a critical voice in contemporary French philosophy. In a stream of articles and books since 1959, Derrida's publications inaugurated a movement that has been called deconstructionism. This philosophical method of reading has affected disciplines as widely disparate as literary criticism, law, medicine, and theology. The interpretation of deconstruction that follows will treat the background of Derrida's philosophical positions, his characteristic terms and strategies for interpreting texts as well as its linkages to theology.

Born of Sephardic Jewish parents in Algiers, Derrida came to France for military service and continued work at the École Normale with Jean Hippolyte, the translator and commentator on G. W. F. HEGEL. In the 1960s he helped maintain the journal *Tel Quel*. During his tenure as *maître-assistant* of philosophy at the École Normale Supérieure in Paris, was also visiting professor at Johns Hopkins University and Yale University. His early work in philosophy focused upon Edmund Husserl's understanding of the production of meaning.

Philosophical Context. Immanuel KANT's (1724–1804) philosophical project to ground Newtonian science was issued in *The Critique of Pure Reason*. His analysis focused upon the conditions in the subject for the possibility of knowing any object whatsoever. Objects in the world were known through a combination of human sensibility, imagination, and understanding. Subjects engaged in knowing themselves knew only their own empirical inner sense, not the transcendental unity of apperception that Kant postulated as the subjective presence that actively preceded the process of objectification. Even objects that had been traditionally the province of philosophy (God, freedom in the world, and the soul) were suspect because they escaped perception. Kant argued that these topics were ideas of pure reason, regulative of our ways of acting, but not constitutive, i.e., content filled, in themselves. Reason could both prove and disprove with convincing clarity that the theological, cosmological and psychological ideas did and did not exist. Classical metaphysics died in a violent war of contradictory antinomies. Human beings should act ''as if'' God existed, as if the world were free and not determined, as if there were a continuous human subject—but there was no way to provide certainty for these assumed ideas.

Philosophies of the 19th and 20th centuries have promoted solutions to Kant's antinomies and also carried his program of suspicion farther. Deconstruction as a movement has had as its partners in conversation the figures most allied with the tradition of suspicion: Nietzsche (1844–1900), Heidegger (1889–1976), and Freud (1856–1939). Derrida has reinterpreted all three figures and his remarks framing all three will help the understanding of deconstruction as a project.

Derrida notes that Freud has described the way in which human subjects are never present to themselves completely. Not only is the subject ''broken up'' in itself as an id, an ego, and a superego, but the unconscious, following Jacques Lacan's (1901–81) reading of Freud, can never be objectified. Human beings are forever involved in an otherness over which they have no control. Psychoanalysis is, therefore, not a discipline to be confined to a small range of data, but a way of reading all of human experience. The signs that emerge from the unconscious can never be anything but suspect; they will never be deciphered completely. Indeed, all human beings have are the signs that appear; there is no permanent personal presence that generates the signs. They come from the unconscious nowhere. There is no constituting subjectivity. Kant's psychological idea annihilates itself through its own internal conflicts.

Heidegger argues that there is a precomprehended question of Being (*Sein*) that is asked and answered in every statement or position taken. Since it is always prior to thinking itself, it cannot be formulated in a propositional form if someone asks "What is being?" *Dasein* (human being) is that reality where the disclosure of *Sein* can appear. Being is thus not a being among other beings, like plants, trees, chairs, or even people. Being is both absence and presence, and is, according to Derrida, written ~~Being~~.

For Heidegger, this de-structs Western metaphysics. The age of metaphysics extending from Plato (428–347 B.C.) to at least Hegel (1770–1831) was a tradition that believed that a fully constituted presence of positive ground supported phenomena. Being was the ultimate foundation of all that is, including that which is not. Heidegger argued that the unholy wedding of this concept of being with the divine produced an ontotheology in which ~~Being~~ was not itself in radical difference, but a supreme being related to all other beings. Contemporary confusion in this regard is simply nostalgia for lost presence.

Derrida speaks of Being, this deleted and present word, as "under erasure" (*sous rature*) and agrees with Heidegger's argument that metaphysics cannot survive, but he maintains that even Heidegger's Being might direct thinking toward a mystical presence. Derrida points to the absence, the lack that is the condition of life and thinking. The attempt to understand never allows a coincidence of word, thought, and thing. Instead, Derrida marks the present absence as a trace, the way in which the radically other appears in the midst of human attempts to signify anything. A trace points to the ineradicable nonidentity that conditions the motion of discourse. There can therefore be no full presence—whether Being or God. Kant's theological idea is unavailable for saving the appearances.

From Nietzsche, Derrida learns a style of philosophizing. The perpetual creativity of the artist continually invents metaphors, tropes that ironically subvert the received pieties. For Nietzsche, metaphors, not concepts, are the process of truth telling. The fragmentation of Nietzsche's prose, the rapid reconfiguration of his texts from aphorisms to fables to lengthy conceptual commentary reveal the multifaceted play of the writing that is the creative force of the inscribed author. The reader's "access" to the thinker is only through the pathways of the prose. The subjects' freedom (in the Kantian framework) has become the power to write, undoing one position by espousing another. And this process has no end.

Remaining oneself therefore requires playing in the differences, not attempting to master one metaphoric appearance by another. The movement has neither origin (and hence no "original" sign) nor a specific ending (and hence no probable or improbable dénoument). Eternally creative subjects, by noting the otherness within their own psyches, allow the signs to appear.

Characteristic Terms. Derrida uses the term *différance* to mark the reality of absent otherness that is always present in the traditional notions of self, Being/God, and the power of freedom. The word is spelled with an "a" to show its relationship in French to both "difference" and "deferral." *Différance* is the structure of the human psyche, never possessed of itself, always dispersed in its specific signs. The psyche is never quite there, never completely perceived. This *différance* is always what marks the human nostalgia for being and the Power of Freedom. Each is radically absent from its attempts at self-identification.

This *différance* appears in *writing*. Writing is at once the ordinary notion of having marks on paper and a psychic space, a metaphoric sense of the word in which the subject is always distanced from itself in its objectifications. Words therefore are always rifled by their own ambiguity, leading down labyrinthine paths to other terms, not back to a primordial presence either human or divine. The subject "knows" itself only in the play of different signs, the marks that it traces throughout time and space. The continuity of time and space is abolished in a constant stream of differences. The economy of understanding these signs requires maintaining their nonidentities, not overcoming them.

Any attempt to turn the deconstructionist project into a positive avowal of presence destroys its operative motifs and returns to what Derrida calls *logocentrism* or rational, logos-focused discourse. Deconstruction does not claim that the negative reading is the whole; that would turn the nonidentity into a positive presence and misconstrue the project. There is in deconstructive analysis a constant postponement of complete meaning. The unconscious is not a hidden or potential self-presence; it is simply not—only to be read in its traces. To recognize that the self is available only in its differences and deferrals is sufficient. There are no similarities, only differents.

Strategies for Interpretation. What does it mean to deconstruct a particular text? What difference does deconstructive writing make to reading? First, it ignores the absolute authority of the text. It is not what the author may have said that is important, but what the subject matter has achieved in the writing itself. Second, texts are always made up of other texts; no writing is pristine. Rather it is always plagiarized, borrowed unconsciously from previous discourse. Inter-textuality is the discovery of the dependences in the text, the blocks of writing sewn together to look like a whole. Third, readers actively unmake the constructs of the text. They look for the moments in the text that transgress or subvert the system of values that the text is consciously presenting. This strategy focuses upon the double-edged words, the crucial metaphors that disclose the collapse of the systemic order. Fourth, this process discloses the dyadic either/ors that the text hopes to conceal. Invariably, one member of these differences is promoted to mastery over the other. By searching for the structures of concealment and radical indecipherability, readers isolate the general structures of human activity, discover the fundamental spaces that establish the network of signs.

This process produces a counter-reading of the texts themselves. The interpretations are not protected by a neutral commentary, but allowed to deconstruct their proper selves. Deconstructive readings of texts regularly toy with texts, drawing from them the metaphoric playfulness that marks their primordial antinomous moments. Deconstructive interpretations are expressed in a further metaphoric game in which the differences appear as tolerable, even invited chaos. Just as the text was disseminated by the writer, so the seeds of its polysemy are scattered through the work of the reader. Deconstructive prose regularly espouses opposite positions in the same text and switches perspectives by changing stylistic devices and levels of discourse. Prose, poetry, scholarly commentary, typographic displays, etc., may all be found in the same writing. There is no suppression of one reading by another; there are only differing interpretations. Any choice of one reading over another would be oppression. It is precisely the differences of genres that disclose the burden and joy of reading.

Influences on Theology. Following the influence of Derrida on literary criticism (Paul de Man, Harold Bloom, J. Hillis Miller), Protestant biblical critics and theologians have recently made use of the style, strategies, and underlying program of deconstructionism. They have seen in it some continuity with the Protestant critique of metaphysics and natural theology. The radical disjuncture between the human and divine in the early neo-orthodox theology of Karl BARTH (1886–1968) and his arguments against the analogy of being have certainly been in the theological background of these theological uses of deconstruction. Paul TILLICH's (1886–1965) "God beyond God" and Rudolph Bultmann's (1884–1976) program of demythologization also may

have provided a context for its inclusion in contemporary discussions. The radically negative Hegelianism of Thomas J. J. Altizer, especially in his extension of William Blake's (1757–1827) dialectical vision, has developed a metaphoric, radically incarnational reading of the Christian universe, establishing a matrix for later deconstructionist writing.

Mark C. Taylor, recognizing the avowedly atheistic motifs of deconstruction, has taken up its strategies more than any other single figure. He argues for the death of God, the disappearance of the self, the end of history and the closing of the book. Each is deconstructed within its own exclusive dyadic formulations (infinity-finitude, time-eternity, self-other, speaking-writing, etc.), especially in its ability to deny its own otherness. The completely enclosed, identically self-present God who is wholly other dies through its own refusal to include the very creation it invents. This God simply alienates the self, establishes its hegemony over all subjects and destroys human self-agency. The autonomous self disappears for the same reasons; its attempts at total self-making deconstruct in its refusal to face death. Taylor argues that human meaning is possible only by non-self-possession, by spacing the self through writing. History-writing is the attempt to control death by filling in the holes. By coding the events, the writer tries to repress the gaps, turning history into a colonial enterprise. But there is no plot at the heart of history, only different irreducible elements with no explanatory nexus. The matter has no plot. Books are irredeemably ontotheological, since they presume that what is known can be enclosed in a whole. The belief that coherence can be maintained grants certain works classic status, but every masterpiece subverts itself, disclosing its own incompletion, its need for interpreters to keep its memory alive. Rather, interpreters are left with no promise of total stability, a refusal to close the book, a constant dissemination of ideas, and the uneasy joy of being open to *différance*.

For Taylor, this way of reading the Bible, providential history, saving grace, and divine identity is "truer" to the original faith of the Cross. The experience of the Cross is paradoxical and open-ended. It refuses to avoid death, indeed embraces it as the way to salvation. Jesus is the disappearance of the Being of total self-presence into the signified, where neither identity nor difference can be seen as prior. The divine milieu includes both the finite and the infinite, time and eternity in such a way that neither can claim priority. With Derrida, Taylor maintains that there is no transcendental signified. The fundamental kenotic character of the mystery of God is a/ presented. Human beings live in the irreducible generative multiplicity of the signs that disclose the play of a god who is not God, who is only dispossession.

The experience of God is also the experience of the self and the way that the self can experience grace. The Christian subject is ever in exile, an undomesticated drifter who is in ceaseless transgression, in an unavoidable purposelessness. Living always at this margin, the Christian is ever the threshold person, experiencing the gratuity of the divine milieu. Transcience is what the ritualizing, religio-secular clown celebrates in comedy.

In Catholic theology, little use has been made of deconstruction as a program. Derrida's work, however, has been recognized as a significant challenge to classical formulations of philosophy and theology. Theologians recognize the ways in which systems are not closed except through their refusal to account for the alterity that exists within their own proposals. Theologies that do not listen to deconstruction fail to meet the negative questions of the gaps in human narratives, the oppressive violence that marks human relationships, and the illusory character of the autonomous self-making self. Deconstructive analyses, in their powerful ironies, can function as a critical linguistic therapy, requiring clarity of argument, specification of metaphors, and nonsuppressive proposals for future religious discourse.

Questions. Derridean deconstructionism and its variants raise the most fundamental questions for traditional philosophers and theologians. How is being to be understood? Does the finite character of human knowing prohibit an understanding of absolute transcendence? Is there a positive relationship between the patterning in events and the stories that human beings write? What is the relationship between conceptual and metaphoric or symbolic discourse? What can account for the difference between what one writer calls the "terrifying and exhilarating vertigo" of deconstructionist interpretations and a stoically repressive, relativistic nihilism?

What are the consequences of using deconstructionist discourse in theology as an ironic therapy for smug complacency? In the religious acceptance of deconstructionist strategies of interpretation, how does one tell the difference among events if they all disclose the divine milieu or grace? Is there a difference in choosing one path over another? Are specific choices of evil, such as murder of the innocent, malice toward the charitable, the degradation of the poor, oppression of the powerless, all paths to the world of grace? While deconstructionist readings can intrigue the mind and even tease the heart, they fail to discriminate the differences among the silences (solitude, narcissism, and sin) and they deny a transformative teleology to the Cross. It makes a difference which action one chooses in the present such that one might anticipate some future more valuable than the past. That there might be a nondominative victory of the Cross and Resurrection

where a true discipleship of equals could emerge seems justifiably utopian when the ironic subtext of deconstructionist theology commands the same thing, but refuses to enter discussion on the appropriate paths to arrive at the disclosure.

Bibliography: T. J. J. ALTIZER et al., *Deconstruction and Theology* (New York 1982). J. DERRIDA, *Speech and Phenomena: And Other Essays on Husserl's Theory of Signs,* tr. D. B. ALLISON (Evanston 1973); *Of Grammatology,* tr. G. CHAKRAVORTY (Baltimore 1974); *Writing and Difference,* tr. A. BASS (Chicago 1978). J. V. HARARI, ed., *Textual Strategies: Perspective in Post-Structuralist Criticism* (Ithaca, N.Y. 1979). R. MACKSEY, ed., *Velocities of Change* (Baltimore 1974). M. C. TAYLOR, *Erring: A Post-Modern A/theology* (Chicago 1984); *Altarity* (Chicago 1988). D. TRACY, *Plurality and Ambiguity: Hermeneutics, Religion, Hope* (San Francisco 1987).

[S. HAPPEL]

DECORA LUX AETERNITATIS

An office hymn, sections of which were formerly sung on various feasts in honor of SS. Peter and Paul, the divisions beginning with *Beate pastor Petre* and *Egregie doctor Paule.* It is made up of 6 four-line stanzas (iambic trimeter) without regular rhyme. The present text arose from a 17th-century revision of the hymn *Aurea luce et decore roseo* (*Analecta hymnica* [Leipzig 1886–1922] 51:216), which was earlier attributed incorrectly to a certain Elpis (wife?) but which is in fact a Carolingian poem. This hymn originally had 5 five-line stanzas, but since the period from 1568 to 1629 it has been arranged as 5 four-line stanzas plus doxology. The second stanza of *Decora lux* names the Apostles *Romae parentes,* using an idea employed by Leo I (in Sermon 82). The fourth stanza comprises the brief hymn *Egregie doctor Paule* used on feasts of St. Paul. The fifth stanza is borrowed from another Carolingian hymn, *Felix per omnes* (ascribed to Paulinus of Aquileia), which in 1629 completely replaced the original fifth stanza of the *Aurea.*

Bibliography: J. CONNELLY, *Hymns of the Roman Liturgy* (Westminster, MD 1957) 168–170. J. SZÖVÉRFFY, *Die Annalen der lateinischen Hymnendichtung* (Berlin 1964–65) 1:122–124. H. LAUSBERG, *Lexikon für Theologie und Kirche,* ed. J. HOFER and K. RAHNER (Freiburg 1957–65) 3:186. P. PARIS, *Dictionnaire pratique des connaissances religieuses,* ed. J. BRIOOUT, 6 v. (Paris 1925–28) 3:836–838, esp. 836.

[J. SZÖVÉRFFY]

DECORATIONS, PAPAL

The supreme pontiff, like other sovereigns, can confer outward signs of benevolence or appreciation. Recognized as such by all when conferred by the pope on lay people of any country, these signs are decorations officially called pontifical equestrian orders. They are bestowed according to merit, protocol, or courtesy. There are five orders, or degrees of conferment, three of which are additionally divided into classes. Clergy and women are traditionally excluded from these honors, the first because specific honorary ranks may be bestowed upon them, the second because by ancient usage only the GOLDEN ROSE and the Cross *Pro Ecclesia et Pontifice,* as well as personal titles of nobility, are granted to deserving ladies, although strictly speaking these are not considered decorations. In recent times, however, more women have been created Ladies of the Holy Sepulcher, a group closely linked with the Holy See (*see* KNIGHTS OF THE HOLY SEPULCHER).

The Order of Christ, the highest distinction that the Holy Father can confer, is rarely given, and then only to Catholic heads of state of great countries. By tradition it is also given, after some years of service, to the prince commandant of the papal Noble Guards. It dates from the time of Pope John XXII (1319). A Spanish branch of the same order exists, although for several centuries it has been entirely separate from the papal order of the same name.

The Golden Spur, or Golden Militia, is the honor (but seldom given) for non-Catholic heads of state of great nations. It consists, like the former order, of one class, ancient date of origin unknown. The insignia of both these orders are beautifully designed wide gold and enamel chains to be worn around the neck and over the shoulders.

The Piano Order, although rare, is better known than the first two and consists of four (or five) classes: (1) Knights with Chain (for heads of state), (2) Knights Grand Cross (for heads of government and ambassadors to the Holy See), (3) Knights Commander with Star, (4) the same without Star, and (5) Knights. It owes its name to Pope Pius IX, who instituted the order in 1847.

The Order of St. Gregory the Great, perhaps the best-known, consists of three (or four) classes: (1) Knights Grand Cross, (2) Knights Commander with Star, (3) the same without Star, (4) Knights. The order has a civil as well as a military division, the latter being reserved for military personnel who receive the order in that capacity. It was founded in 1831 by Gregory XVI.

The Order of St. Sylvester Pope possesses the same classes as the preceding order. It was constituted as such, being formerly part of the Order of the Golden Spur, in 1841, by Pope Gregory XVI.

Gentlemen who belong to the different orders rank *inter se* and *unus post alium;* e.g., a Knight of the Piano Order precedes one of St. Gregory; and he in turn one of St. Sylvester. However, a Knight of the Piano Order would be preceded only by a Knight Commander of St. Gregory or a Knight Commander with Star of St. Sylvester, etc.

The orders are conferred by the pope on such as have been recommended by their bishops or by the papal representatives in their countries. Diplomats, as well as members of official delegations (on the occasion of papal coronations, etc.) receive one of the orders as a mark of courtesy to the country they represent. Although in former times the Piano Order was generally reserved for Catholics, the distinction was dropped long ago, as was the automatic nobility of rank that came with the Piano Order—hereditary in its first classes, personal in the lower ones. Each order has its own uniform. The classes can be clearly distinguished by variations in the elaborateness of dress as well as by the insignia of the order worn with the uniform.

[P. C. VAN LIERDE]

DE COURCY, HENRY

Historian, foreign correspondent; b. Brest, France, Sept. 11, 1820; d. Lawrence, Mass., May 14, 1861. He was born of a family famed for soldiers and seamen; he came to New York in 1845 as the business agent of the Paris glass company of Saint-Gobain. Here he also acted until 1856 as correspondent for the Paris publication *L'Univers* of Louis Veuillot. His writings on Catholic affairs in North America influenced French opinion, but in America he was best known for his work, translated by John Gilmary Shea in 1856, on *The Catholic Church in the United States; a Sketch of its Ecclesiastical History.* This book, one of the earliest histories of the American Church, was characterized by ultramontanism, stress on the Irish character of American Catholicism and on the exploits of French missionaries, and distrust of Protestants. These qualities caused Orestes Brownson, a convert and a Yankee, to attack the book. Because much of his writing was polemical, De Courcy, for business reasons, adopted the pen name C. de Laroche-Héron. As Laroche-Héron he wrote *Les Servantes de Dieu en Canada* (1855); as De Courcy he published *Lettres inédites de J.-M. et F. de La Mennais adressées à Mgr. Bruté, de Rennes, ancien évêque de Vincennes* (1862). He wrote also four short works.

Bibliography: R. SYLVAIN, *La Vie et l'oevre de Henry de Courcy, 1820–1861* (Quebec 1955).

[B. R. WEITEKAMP]

DECRETALISTS

A decretalist is a canonist in the history of Canon Law whose main object of study was papal DECRETALS (*epistolae decretales*, papal replies or mandates of a canonical nature). The term is particularly applicable in the formative stages of canonistic science *c.* 1200–34 (*see* CANON LAW, HISTORY OF, 4). Decretalists are distinguished from DECRETISTS, whose primary object of study was the legal tradition of the Church as contained in the *Decretum* of GRATIAN. The decretalists of the Middle Ages had a twofold concern: the searching out and collecting of decretals (*see* DECRETALS, COLLECTIONS OF) and the systematic and scientific exposition of the Canon Law contained in the decretals. There are three main periods of decretalist activity: the first period (*c.* 1160–1200) is primarily concerned with the collection of decretals; the second period (*c.* 1200–34) is marked by the development in the nature and organization of the decretal collections, as well as by the beginning of decretal exegesis; and the third period (1234–1348) is almost solely concerned with decretal exegesis.

Collection Decretalists (*c.* 1160–*c.* 1200). For most of this period canonists were preoccupied with assimilating and presenting the legal tradition of the Church as conveyed by Gratian's *Decretum*. Decretalist scholarship, in contrast to widespread decretal research, was negligible. Decretals were employed, of course, from SIMON OF BISIGNANO (*c.* 1177) onward in decretist glosses, *summae,* and *quaestiones,* at Bologna and Paris, but there were no explicit commentaries on decretals as such. In fact, all major systematic collections of decretals before the *Breviarium extravagantium* (*Compilation prima*) of Bernard of Pavia (1191–92) were ignored by Bolognese glossators, though Bernard naturally used his own earlier *Parisiensis II.* This was not quite the case in England, where almost half of the more than 30 collections before the *Breviarium* were compiled. Thus the *Appendix concilii lateranensis* (1181–85), which played a formative role in late 12th-century collections that reached, by way of the French *Bambergensis,* to Bernard's *Compilatio* itself, was used by Anglo-Norman decretists in their *summae* (possibly also in their glosses), notably in *In nomine* and *De iure canonico tractaturus* (1180–90) and in the *Summa decretalium quaestionum* of HONORIUS MAGISTER (1186–90). Even after the *Breviarium* had been made a subject of teaching at Bologna (*c.* 1196), Anglo-Norman, and to a lesser extent Franco-Rhenish, schools continued to cling to their own systematic collections: the ''Tanner'' collection succeeded the *Appendix* between 1190 and 1200; the *Collectio Sangermanensis* (*c.* 1198) possibly represents an attempt to rival Bernard's *Compilatio.* More importantly, Anglo-Norman decretists composed glosses on the *Appendix* as such. This pointed

Folio from decree Breviarium extravagantium (Compilation prima) and apparatus of Tancred, 13th century, by Bernard of Pavia (Cod. Vat. Lat. 1377, fol. 2r).

the way, possibly, to the great era of decretalist scholarship that, with the participation of canonists of Anglo-Norman background, such as RICHARD DE MORES, and centering around Bernard's *Compilatio prima,* flourished at Bologna from about 1200.

Compilation Decretalists (*c.* 1200–34). In the first 30 years of the 13th century many collections of decretals were made at Bologna to supplement the *Compilatio prima,* four of which were accepted by the schools as basic texts (*compilationes*): the *Tertia antiqua* of PETRUS COLLIVACCINUS, authorized by Innocent III (1210); the *Secunda antiqua* of JOHN OF WALES (1210–12); the *Quarta antiqua* of JOANNES TEUTONICUS (1215–16); and the *Quinta antiqua,* commissioned from Tancred by Honorius III and published in 1226 (*see* QUINQUE COMPILATIONES ANTIQUAE). To these years belong both the first true period of decretalist scholarship as such and the great, classic moment of decretist exegesis. These and lesser collections (e.g., of GILBERTUS ANGLICUS,

1202–03; Alanus Anglicus, *c.* 1206; BERNARD OF COMPOSTELLA THE ELDER, *Compilatio romana,* 1208) occasioned a flow of decretalist writing that appeared for a moment to paralyze decretist activity, but that in fact served to stimulate it in an extraordinary manner; indeed, more often than not the decretalist pioneer was also a consummate decretist, e.g., Alanus Anglicus, Joannes Teutonicus. It was in these years that the most advanced and characteristic glossatorial technique of all, the *apparatus glossarum* or systematic, continuous gloss, was adopted. Each compilation in turn, as well as the *Collectio* of canons of Fourth Lateran Council (1215), excited decretalist attention, chiefly at Bologna, and many decretalists commented on more than one compilation.

The following are the principal decretalist commentaries on the important canonical compilations of this period: (1) *Compilatio prima:* besides the *Casus decretalium* of Richard de Mores (1192–98) and a *Summa* of Bernard of Pavia himself (1192–98), there are *glossae* from Bernard, Pelagius of Spain (*c.* 1206), Bernard of Compostella the Elder (1205–06), Martin of Zamora (*c.* 1217), and William Vasco of Gascony (*c.* 1220), and *apparatus* from Richard de Mores (1194–98, outstanding), Peter of Spain the Elder (*c.* 1198), the anonymous *Militant siquidem patroni* (1203–10, French), LAWRENCE OF SPAIN (*c.* 1210), VINCENT OF SPAIN (*c.* 1210), Tancred (1210–15; revised forms 1216–20: *glossa ordinaria*), and Damasus of Hungary (*c.* 1215; *Recens, c.* 1215). (2) *Compilatio secunda:* glosses from Alanus Anglicus (*c.* 1210–12), Vincent of Spain (1210–15), and Damasus (*c.* 1215); *apparatus* from Albertus (1210–15), Lawrence of Spain (1210), and Tancred (two forms, 1210–15 and 1215–20; *ordinaria*). (3) *Compilatio tertia:* *apparatus* from John of Wales (1210–15), Lawrence, Vincent (1210–15), Joannes Teutonicus (*c.* 1217), Tancred (lecture notes, *c.* 1216; personal recension, 1220: *ordinaria*), and Damasus (unidentified); *casus* from Vincent. (4) *Canons of Fourth Lateran Council:* *apparatus* from Vincent of Spain (two recensions, 1216–20), Joannes Teutonicus (*c.* 1216–17), Damasus, Lawrence(?), and the anonymous *Quoniam omnes quaestionum articuli.* (5) *Compilatio quarta:* Joannes Teutonicus (1215–17, *glossa ordinaria*), Peter of Spain the Younger (*notabilia*), and William Vasco (glosses). (6) *Compilatio quinta: apparatus* of JAMES OF ALBENGA (*c.* 1230; chief glossator) and Zoën, and glosses of Tancred, Lawrence of Spain, and Joannes Teutonicus. Other writings included glosses by Gilbertus Anglicus on his own collection, the *Quaestiones* of Bernard of Compostella, Damasus, and Joannes Teutonicus, a *Summa iuris canonici* of RAYMOND OF PEÑAFORT (*c.* 1220), monographic treatises, e.g., Tancred's *de matrimonio* and *ordo iudiciarius.*

Gregorian and Post-Gregorian Decretalists (1234–1348). With the definitive collection of decretal letters made by Raymond of Peñafort for Gregory IX (*see* GREGORY IX, DECRETALS OF), the age of decretal research came to a close. Though they did not fail to draw upon the decretist-decretalists who had wrestled with the old superseded collections and compilations, canonists were now free to concentrate on scholarship and interpretation. Bologna continued to hold its place, and with some exceptions the literary techniques were those established by the decretists (*glossa, summa, quaestio*) and decretalists (*apparatus*).

Decretals of Gregory IX. The following productions are based on the *Decretals* of Gregory IX: (1) *apparatus:* Vincent of Spain (*c.* 1234–35), Godfrey of Trani (*c.* 1245), BERNARD OF PARMA (*glossa ordinaria,* 1241; revised 1263–66), INNOCENT IV (Sinibaldus Fieschi; 1246–51, 1253); (2) *summae:* Joannes de Petesella (*c.* 1235–36), Godfrey of Trani (1241–43), Henry of Merseburg (*c.* 1245), HOSTIENSIS (HENRY OF SEGUSIO), the *Summa aurea* or *copiosa* (exhaustive and influential, begun 1239, completed 1253), and Baldwin of Brandenburg (*c.* 1270); (3) *Lecturae:* William Naso (*c.* 1234), Peter of Sampson (*c.* 1246–53), JOANNES DE DEO (*c.* 1248), Abbas antiquus (BERNARD OF MONTMIRAT; 1259–66), BERNARD OF COMPOSTELLA THE YOUNGER (1261–67), Hostiensis (1270–71), Boatinus of Mantua, and many others down to Joannes Andreae (*novella, c.* 1338). Other productions based on the *Decretals* of Gregory IX include *Casus, Distinctiones, Notabilia, Ordines Iudiciarii, Quaestiones, Repertoria, Reportationes, Specula, Tabulae,* and a unique *Summa summarum* from the now listless English schools (WILLIAM OF PAGULA, Oxford 1319–21).

Post-Gregorian Decretalists (1245–1348). The volume of commentary on post-Gregorian collections of decretals, constitutions, and conciliar legislation is no less impressive: (1) *Novellae* of Innocent IV (1243–54): *apparatus* from Godfrey of Trani (*c.* 1245) and Innocent IV (*c.* 1251); the *glossa ordinaria* from Bernard of Compostella the Younger (*c.* 1254); *lecturae* from Peter of Sampson (1250–55), Bernard of Montmirat (*c.* 1260), Hostiensis (*c.* 1253), and Boatinus of Mantua (*c.* 1274). (2) *Novissimae* of Gregory X (1274; 2 Lyons): *apparatus* from Joannes Garsias (*c.* 1280); *lecturae* from Joannes de Anguissola, William DURANTI the Elder, Franciscus de Albano, and Boatinus of Mantua (all *c.* 1274–84). (3) *LIBER SEXTUS* of Boniface VIII (1298): *apparatus* from JOHN LE MOINE (1301), JOANNES ANDREAE (1301; *ordinaria*), and GUIDO DE BAYSIO (1306–11); *lecturae* from William of Mont Lauzun (1306–16), Joannes de Borbonio (1308–17), Zenzelinus de Cassanis (*c.* 1317), Lapus Tactus (*c.* 1320), Pierre BERTRAND (combined *lec-*

tura on *Sextus, Clementinas,* and *Extravagantes,* after 1334), Joannes Andreae (1338–42), ALBERIC OF ROSATE (*c.* 1340). (4) *CLEMENTINAE* (1317): *apparatus* from Joannes Andreae (1322; *ordinaria*) and Zenzelinus de Cassanis (1323); *lecturae* from William of Mont Lauzun (1319), Stephanus Hugoneti (1324–30), Lapus Tactus (*c.* 1320), Mattheus of Rome (*c.* 1320), PAULUS DE LIAZARI-IS (before 1330), and Joannes Calderini (*c.* 1335). (5) EX-TRAVAGANTES (1317–25) of John XXII: *apparatus* from William of Mont Lauzun (1319, three constitutions) and Zenzelinus de Cassanis (1325, 20 constitutions).

Bibliography: J. F. VON SCHULTE, *Die Geschichte der Quellen und der Literatur des kanonischen Rechts,* 3 v. in 4 pts. (Stuttgart 1875–80; repr. Graz 1956) v. 1–2. S. KUTTNER, *Repertorium der Kanonistik (Studi et Test*; Rome 1937) 71. A. VAN HOVE, *Commentarium Lovaniense in Codicem iuris canonici 1,* v.1–5 (Mechlin 1928–); v.1 Prolegomena (2d ed. 1945) 1:352–77, 428–36. A. M. STICKLER, *Historia iuris canonici latini:* v.1 *Historia fontium* (Turin 1950) 217–72. A. M. STICKLER, *Lexikon für Theologie und Kirche,* ed. J. HOFER and K. RAHNER, 10 v. (2d, new ed. Freiburg 1957–65) 5:1289–1362. S. KUTTNER, "Bernardus Compostellanus Antiquus," *Traditio* 1 (1943) 277–340; "Notes on a Projected Corpus of 12th Century Decretal Letters," *ibid.* 6 (1948) 345–51. S. KUTTNER and E. RATHBONE, "Anglo-Norman Canonists of the 12th Century," *ibid.* 7 (1949–51) 279–358. A. GARCÍA GARCÍA, "El Concilo IV de Letrán y sus commentarios," *ibid.* 14 (1958) 493–98. W. HOLTZMANN, "Zu der Dekretalen bei Simon von Bisignano," *ibid.* 18 (1962) 450–59. C. DUGGAN, "English Canonists and the 'Appendix Concilii Lateranensis,'" *ibid.* 459–68. T. P. MCLAUGHLIN, "The Extravagantes in the *Summa* of Simon of Bisignano," *Mediaeval Studies* 20 (1958) 167–76. See bibliography and notes in the *Bulletin of the Institute of Research and Study in Medieval Canon Law* in *Traditio* 11 (1955–). G. LE BRAS et al., *L'Âge classique, 1140–1378. Sources et théorie du droit* (Histoire du droit et des institutions de l'Église en Occident 7; Paris 1965).

[L. E. BOYLE]

DECRETALS

The term decretal, *epistola decretalis* or *littera decretalis,* is used very generally to describe a letter containing a papal ruling, more specifically one relating to matters of canonical discipline, and most precisely a papal rescript in response to an appeal. The decretal is distinguished from the solemn *privilegia,* confirming rights or jurisdiction, and from other *litterae* touching on matters of political or nonjuristic interest. A given decretal may have universal or limited application, or indeed be restricted to its single immediate context. In practice, mandates and commissions relating to judicial or administrative matters are often considered decretals, although they are not strictly so, and are frequently found in decretal collections.

Nature and History. The earliest decretals were *litterae praeceptoriae,* issued with emphatic and conscious mandatory force and modeled on the judicial formulae of Roman law. It is debated whether the first known papal decretal was issued by Damasus (d. 384) or Siricius (d. 399), although the latter asserted that such *litterae* were issued by Liberius (d. 366). Their use is clear from Siricius' pontificate, in the incorporation of such authoritative phrases as *volumus et mandamus,* and in the following centuries they were widely used in matters of canonical discipline. The growth of papal centralization from the mid-11th century led to a striking increase in the number of decretals issued, as a result both of the rising number of appeals to the Curia from all parts of the Western Church and of the need to resolve numerous doubtful questions that the evolving doctrines and judicial practices of the period provoked. The *Decretum* of GRATIAN (*c.* 1140–41) marked a major turning point in the history of canonical codification. Following the general acceptance of Gratian's work as an adequate summary of *ius antiquum,* decretals now formed increasingly the principal element in collections, composed predominantly of new law enunciated for the most part in the numerous contemporary or recent decretals mentioned above (*see* DECRETALS, COLLECTIONS OF). Simultaneously, reflecting the new scientific spirit of Canon Law, the decretals became the subject of more precise definition and analytical classification in decretist commentaries.

A classical definition of the decretal was provided by STEPHEN OF TOURNAI (1160–70), for whom it was a papal rescript to a bishop or ecclesiastical judge on any doubtful point of law, *super aliqua causa dubitante,* or for resolving some difficult question of procedure arising in the Church courts. He distinguished it as a species of law from a canon (the decision of a general or provincial council) and from a decree (a decision reached by the pope in consultation with his advisers and set down in writing, but not in response to a particular enquiry). Meanwhile, the scientific method applied in decretist commentaries by Stephen's contemporaries to the problem of the various species of decretals and their individual sanctions produced the following more complex classification: general and special. General decretals are sent to all or many provinces; special decretals are sent to individuals. Special decretals are in turn subdivided into several kinds. Some define or limit a point of law and are important even outside their immediate context, unless specifically limited to time or person. Some mandate a course of action, but do not require immediate compliance unless questions of faith are involved. Some prohibit action, but do not require immediate compliance unless the matter forbidden is altogether illegal. Others, finally, grant indulgence or dispensation by virtue of the pope's discretionary powers, and these have no importance outside their special circumstances. This was a satisfactory basic classification, and later canonists had little need of further elaboration. In practice, from the mid-12th century, decretals were often described as *extravagantes,* that is, *extra Decretum Gratiani vagantes,* and were sometimes referred to also as *sententiae,* or even as *decreta.* After the medieval period the use of the term decretal was narrowed, being limited to solemn documents dealing with such matters as dogmatic definitions and canonizations.

Legal Authority. The legal force of decretals was discussed by popes from the time of their earliest known use: on specific points by Siricius (385), Innocent I (405), and Zosimus (418); and as a general principle by Leo I in 443. Gregory I, Nicholas I, and Gregory VII are among later popes known to have repeated and defined this principle, in demanding obedience to apostolic precepts expressed in decretal letters. The 19th distinction of Gratian's *Decretum* provides a useful retrospective summary of earlier pontifical statements on decretal authority and an insight into the growing perception of the problem in a period when the decretals were increasing numerically beyond all previous practice and widening in the scope of their applications. Gratian here declares that decretals have the same authority as *canones* and *decreta,* even if they are not incorporated in canonical collections, although they may not conflict with scriptural precepts or previously existing papal statutes. In the 20th distinction, he proceeds to place them likewise above scriptural writings of the Fathers, such as Augustine and Jerome, since, although the Fathers may have greater *scientia,* they have not the papal *potestas.* Gratian further asserts in the 25th *causa* that the *prima sedes* has the power to make laws binding to others without itself being subject to them; it may grant special privileges and concessions beyond the general rules, but as *mater iustitiae* it should observe equity in all things.

Although Gratian was not dealing specifically with decretals in the 25th *causa,* the decretists swiftly developed his thesis and applied it to them. The most radical elaboration is found in Huguccio's *Summa* (*c.* 1188–90). For HUGUCCIO, so great is the authority of the papal decretal that, in the event of conflict with previously existing law, the decretal has the greater force, since the pope can exercise his discretionary power; he has the right of laying down canons and interpreting them, and in practice he does so in dogmatic, moral, administrative, and other matters. In support of this argument, Huguccio instances decretals of Alexander III (1159–81) and proceeds to analyze the essential basis of papal power, resting on the Petrine foundation of the Roman See: to resist the apostolic precepts savors of heresy and schism, and persons guilty of such an offense should be excom-

municated as heretics. It was not possible to take the theory of decretal authority much farther than this.

Form and Pattern. The pattern of decretal composition evolved to reflect the general diplomatic developments of the papal chancery. The earliest decretals already imitated the mature practice of Roman imperial forms of legal instruments; the later letters in general passed through many stages of growth, with high points of achievement under the chancellors John of Gaeta (from 1089) and Albert de Morisa (from 1178), attaining a marked distinction in the pontificate of Innocent III. In their fully matured forms of the 12th and 13th centuries, decretals, like most forms of simple *litterae,* were less lavishly drafted than solemn *privilegia,* which were noted for their generosity of spacing and elaboration of detail, rotas, monograms, crosses, subscriptions, and so forth. The decretals were simpler in form and smaller in size, with an economy of parchment and script alike. Both kinds were sealed with the two-faced bulla. The *privilegia* and *litterae gratiosae* had their seals attached by silken cord; those of the decretal letters were attached by hempen cord. Conventions of internal structure and transcription had become stabilized by the late 12th century. The diplomatic formulae and cursive traditions were now well established, and the overall pattern had become uniform. Every decretal, as well as every privilege, was drawn up in three main parts: protocol, *contextus* (or text), and eschatocol. The protocol included the inscription with identification of pope and recipients, conventional phrases, and greetings. The *contextus* comprised the *arenga, narratio,* and other elements peculiar to the matter in hand, and included a *pars historica* (or *species facti*) and a *pars dispositiva,* dealing with the strictly juridical matter of the case. The eschatocol was composed of the terminal elements, including date. The convention in the late 12th century was to state the place of issue, the date according to the Roman style, and the pope's pontifical year. Within these sections, common form phrases were devised to meet frequently recurring situations, as with the *Sane si his exequendis* and *Sane si uterque vestrorum* in letters to judges delegate. Large numbers of 12th–century decretals survive in canonical collections only, greatly distorted as a result of the loss of nonjuridical elements. In these the protocol was drastically abbreviated, at times with the corruption of historical details. The *species facti* of the text was sometimes eliminated. The eschatocol was often omitted entirely, with the resulting loss of the date.

The incidence of forgery raises a further question of much importance. In Alexander III's pontificate, canonists already included in their decretal collections sections dealing with the forging of papal letters. Lucius III, Urban III, Celestine III, and Innocent III are known to have been concerned with this problem. Decretist commentators likewise dealt with the question, throwing incidental light on the circumstances of the issue and composition of decretals. Huguccio on this point refers to the chancery records, the bullation, parchment, thread, script and so forth, indicating lines of detection of decretal forgeries.

Place in History. The importance of decretals in the history of canonical collections and in the science of Canon Law is self-evident. Not only were the significance and authority of the individual letters recognized from very early times, but canonical interest in their codification was hardly less ancient. The collection of DIONYSIUS EXIGUUS in the early sixth century was among the first, and exercised wide and lasting influence on later works, including the *Dionysio-Hadriana* in the Carolingian Empire and the Pseudo-Isidorian collection of Frankish provenance in the mid-ninth century (*see* FALSE DECRETALS). The pseudo-Isidorian collection included many supposititious decretals from the earliest Christian centuries and established an important canonical tradition stressing papal authority and clerical privilege; many of its decretals were transmitted through the great collections of later times and of the Gregorian Reform, into Gratian's *Decretum*. It was in the post-Gratian period, above all, that decretals both individually and collectively rose to a position of dominance in canonical evolution. Starting from very rudimentary beginnings in the mid-1170s the compilers swiftly transformed their decretal collections into a highly systematic pattern of composition best expressed in Bernard of Pavia's *Breviarium extravagantium* (*c.* 1192). Bernard's work was the culmination of a creative and individualistic phase of decretal codification, but it also formed a classical model for most later works (*see* QUINQUE COMPILATIONES ANTIQUAE).

The rise to importance of decretal collections coincided with the scientific evolution of Canon Law, and both factors were interlocking elements of a single whole. The individual decretals provided the principal instrument whereby the papacy controlled the development of doctrinal, moral, jurisdictional, and administrative policies, while the decretal collections provided a continuously revised corpus of law both for legal administration and academic instruction. Contemporaneously with the growth of the collections, decretists, at least from the time of SIMON OF BISIGNANO (*c.* 1177–79), drew on the most recent decretals to illustrate their expositions. In due course the main focus of glossatorial interest was transferred from the *Decretum* to the now more important decretal collections, until from the mid-13th century the collections and their commentaries provided almost the

total bulk of canonical sources (*see* CORPUS IURIS CANONICI).

Bibliography: S. KUTTNER, *Repertorium der Kanonistik* (Rome 1937). A. VAN HOVE, *Commentarium Lovaniense in Codicem iuris canonici 1* (Mechlin 1928–) v.1. C. DUGGAN, *Twelfth-Century Decretal Collections and Their Importance in English History* (London 1963). R. L. POOLE, *Lectures on the History of the Papal Chancery to the Time of Innocent III* (Cambridge, Eng. 1915). H. BRESSLAU, *Handbuch der Urkundenlehre für Deutschland und Italien,* ed. H. W. KLEWITZ, 2 v. (2d ed. Leipzig 1912–31). INNOCENT III, *Selected Letters of Pope Innocent III concerning England,* ed. C. R. CHENEY and W. H. SEMPLE (London 1953). E. C. BABUT, *La plus ancienne décrétale* (Paris 1904). H. WURM, *Studien und Texte zur Dekretalensammlung des Dionysius Exiguus* (Bonn 1939). G. LE BRAS et al., eds., *Histoire du droit et des institutions de L'Église en Occident* (Paris 1955–), v.7 *L'Age classique, 1140–1378: Sources et théorie du droit* (1965).

[C. DUGGAN]

DECRETALS, COLLECTIONS OF

A decretal letter is a papal RESCRIPT of canonical significance, in contrast with *privilegia* and nonjuristic letters, on the one hand, and with conciliar canons and papal decrees, on the other. The earliest authentic DECRETALS date from the late 4th century and are preserved in canonical collections, papal registers, episcopal archives, cartularies, chronicle records and many other sources. Original letters survive occasionally, but the extant decretals are mostly found in transcript only.

Collections before Gratian. Canonical collections antedate the first decretal letters: the *Collectio Romana,* containing the canons of the Councils of Nicaea and Sardica, was completed not later than 352; but the importance of papal decretals was soon attested by their inclusion in canonical collections, either those of decretal letters exclusively or of ecclesiastical laws of all kinds.

Early Collections. Among the earliest decretal collections were the *Canones urbicani,* dating probably from the pontificate of Sixtus III (432–40), and the slightly later Epistolae decretales. The so-called QUESNELLIANA COLLECTIO, comprising both decretals and conciliar canons, and the *Collectio Frisingensis* date from the closing years of the 5th century or from the beginning of the 6th. All these bear the imprint of Roman, or at least Italian, origins, though the *Canones urbicani* and the Quesnelliana were made possibly in Gaul.

Of outstanding importance were the translations and collections of the Scythian monk DIONYSIUS EXIGUUS (d. post 525), whose canonical works, known collectively as the DIONYSIANA COLLECTIO, included the Apostolic Canons; the canons of Greek councils and of Chalcedon, Sardica, and Carthage; and a group of 38 decretals, ranging in time from the pontificate of Siricius (384–99) to that of Anastasius II (496–98). The decretals, arranged in roughly chronological order, deal mostly with matters of ecclesiastical discipline, including also decisions on the date of Easter and on the precedence of Antioch in the Eastern Church. The collection was made at Rome about the end of the pontificate of Symmachus in 514. The *Dionysiana* achieved a widespread and lasting influence on canonical collections, passing through the principal lines of transmission down to the *Decretum* of Gratian in the mid-12th century.

The regional collections of Africa, Italy, and the Frankish kingdom revealed an assimilation of Dionysian material together with continuing fresh accessions. In Italy, collections were assembled of decretals solely, of decretals and conciliar canons, and exclusively of canons: the Collectio AVELLANA (*c.* 555) and the early 7th-century *Codex Mutinensis* (including some apocryphal matter) are examples of the first; the 6th-century *Colbertina,* the *Dionysiana Bobiensis* (with decretals to Boniface IV, d. 615), and the celebrated HADRIANA COLLECTIO, sent by Adrian I to Charles the Great in 774, are examples of the second. Many collections made in Frankish lands, such as the *Collectio Corbeiensis* (post 524), incorporated large or small numbers of decretals, and the systematic *Collectio Andegavensis* (post *c.* 670), though composed primarily of canons, included some decretals. The HISPANA COLLECTIO of the late 6th century, associated with Isidore of Seville (d. 636), was the most important of the Spanish collections; it included 104 papal letters to the time of Gregory I (d. 604).

8th to 12th Century. The centralized direction of the Church reform in the Carolingian period had its canonical counterpart in the heightened importance attached to particular collections, above all in the tradition of the *Dionysiana* or the *Hispana;* the *Hadriana Collectio,* though lacking exclusive authority, became the *liber canonum* for the Frankish realm. But a point of departure was reached with the production of Pseudo-Isidore, the FALSE DECRETALS, assembled at Reims or Le Mans or in the royal chapel of Charles the Bald, between 847 and 852. Together with numerous perfectly genuine texts, the author or authors inserted 60 apocryphal papal letters for the period from Clement I (d. 97) to Melchiades (d. 314), and interpolated 30 or more false decretals for that from Sylvester I (d. 335) to Gregory II (d. 731). These spurious texts are uniquely significant in revealing the forger's motives, which were preeminently the preservation of clerical status and privilege in Christian society, the consolidation of papal authority and jurisdiction throughout the Church, and the curtailment of metropolitan powers over suffragan bishops. From the Pseudo-Isidorian collection, the false decretals, as well as the genuine texts,

were transmitted into many of the most important later collections, until the mid-12th century, and thus played a vital part in sustaining the doctrines of clerical and papal superiority, which received an ever more confident expression.

The numerous well-known collections between the Pseudo-Isidorian decretals and Gratian's *Decretum* were rarely composed of decretal letters predominantly, but decretals formed a highly significant part of their content. Among these works must be mentioned the Italian ANSELMO DEDICATA COLLECTIO (882–96), the Frankish *Collectio Abbonis Floriacensis* (988–96), the German collection by Regino of Prüm (*c.* 906) and the *Decretum* of BURCHARD OF WORMS (*c.* 1012). The long-term effects of the Pseudo-Isidorian decretals are evident in the Italian collections of the Gregorian reform period and in their successors: the *Diversorum sententiae Patrum* (the Collection in SEVENTY-FOUR TITLES, *c.* 1050); the *Collection of* ATTO (ante-1084); the important collection of ANSELM OF LUCCA (*c.* 1083); that of DEUSDEDIT (1083–87); Bonizo of Sutri's *Liber de vita Christiana* (1089–95); the *Collectio Britannica* (*c.* 1090), which included many papal letters; and Cardinal Gregory's POLYCARPUS (1104–06). In France, the collections of IVO OF CHARTRES (d. 1116), BERNOLD OF CONSTANCE (d. 1100), and ALGER OF LIÈGE (d. 1131) played a distinguished part in the development of a scientific treatment of canonical codification, their works including numerous decretal letters. Alger's *Liber de misericordia et iustitia* contained 125 papal decretals and fragments of papal letters.

The Period of the Corpus Iuris Canonici. The *Decretum* of GRATIAN, dating in its vulgate form from *c.* 1140 to 1141, marked a decisive turning point in the history of Canon Law. (*See* CORPUS IURIS CANONICI.) It effected the transition from *ius antiquum* to *ius novum,* summarizing the best of existing traditions and expressing them in the new scholastic method; it became the standard text in the schools and the principal work of reference in the courts. It marks the end of the old style of collections, whose broad historical sweep in time and whose varied canonical sources it reflected; it provided a foundation for the classical period of decretal codification, whose origins can be traced from the mid-1170s in the pontificate of Alexander III (1159–81). Whereas Gratian's collection incorporated many decretals, genuine and apocryphal, from the earliest centuries down to the period of its own conception, intermingled with *canones* of all kinds, the dominant source of canonical compilation was now found in contemporary or nearly contemporary decretals, together with the canons of the most important recent councils. These new collections record the gradual accumulation and systematization of ecclesiastical case law, based on the most up-to-date authoritative rulings, and are known as *libri extravagantium* or *libri decretalium*. Beginning simply as brief appendices to Gratian's work, they swiftly grew in content and juristic maturity of style to become the most influential law books in their own right, achieving their final form in Bernard of Pavia's *Breviarium extravagantium*, or *Compilatio Prima* (c. 1192). (*See* QUINQUE COMPILATIONES ANTIQUAE.)

Primitive Collections. More than 50 decretal collections survive from the closing decades of the 12th century, together incorporating more than 1,000 papal letters for the period from the pontificate of Alexander III to that of Celestine III (d. 1198). Numerous other collections have been lost, and many collections are still known in manuscript only. All these works are unofficial in character and can be classified as primitive or systematic according to technical style. The primitive group includes the most rudimentary collections, consisting in some instances of merely a few decretals transcribed in order of acquisition. But the best of this class, containing several hundred letters, are divided and subdivided on the basis of subject matter. The systematic collections reveal, in addition to subject classification, a juristic treatment of their contents: the dissection of individual long decretals dealing with several diverse topics within a single letter, the redistribution of the resulting component chapters, and the excision of nonjuridical matter. A majority of the extant primitive collections are of English provenance and make up the English, Bridlington, and Worcester families, spanning the years from c. 1175 to 1194 or later. The Continental primitive collections can be similarly grouped into the French, Italian, and Roman (or "Tortosa") families. A notable feature of the English collections is their dependence on the archives of English judges delegate, especially at Canterbury, Worcester, and Exeter. It is evident that they played a part in shaping many of the earliest collections assembled on the Continent. The influence of the Roman Curia in stimulating the evolution of decretal compilation has been much discussed, and excerpts from the papal registers can be identified in certain instances. There was undoubtedly a rapid exchange of material and expertise among the schools, whether English or Continental, by the late 1170s.

Systematic Collections. The systematic collections played the more significant part in the history of decretal codification; their influence can be traced from their earliest surviving exemplars in the Italian *Parisiensis II* (c. 1179) and in the *Appendix Concilii Lateranensis* (c. 1181–85), a most important collection, though not certainly of Anglo-Norman authorship. From the *Appendix* were derived several strands of development with many interconnections, most notably in the Bamberg-Leipzig group, including the Bamberg (1181–85), Amiens, Com-piègne, Leipzig, and Cassel collections. The *Appendix* Bamberg transmission led finally to *Compilatio Prima* (c. 1192), with its fivefold division of material under the headings *iudex, iudicium, clerus, connubium,* and *crimen,* which set the pattern for all of the more important subsequent collections. Meanwhile, among the numerous systematic compilations of the period were the French *Brugensis* (c. 1191), the Anglo-Norman *Tanner,* and the members of the German "Frankfurt" family. The five most decisive collections before the publication of the official *Decretales* of Gregory IX in 1234 were the celebrated QUINQUE COMPILATIONES ANTIQUAE; among them, Peter of Benevento's *Compilatio Tertia* (1209–10), composed of decretals of Innocent III, is remarkable for being the first officially promulgated collection of Canon Law. But the continuation of decretal codification was not confined to these famous works: there were also the Anglo-Norman St. Germain and Avranches collections; that of RAINERIUS OF POMPOSA (1201–02); those of the Englishmen GILBERTUS ANGLICUS (1202–03) and ALANUS ANGLICUS (1206 or shortly after); and the collection of BERNARD OF COMPOSTELLA, THE ELDER, composed of decretals from the first ten years of Innocent III's pontificate with a single addition from the 11th. The collections of Gilbert and Alan formed the basis of JOHN OF WALES's *Compilatio Secunda* (1210–15). In practice the *Quinque Compilationes* effectively superseded all other decretal collections, as they themselves were to be superseded by the Gregorian collection of 1234.

It is clear that decretal codification had become the central interest of collectors by the late 12th century; and parallel with this development can be traced the literary expositions of Canon Law by the commentators, at first on the *Decretum,* from mid-12th century (*see* DECRETISTS), and later on the decretals (*see* DECRETALISTS). Now the Gregorian *Decretales,* based in substance and style on the *Quinque Compilationes* with some recent supplements, rendered obsolete all previous collections, either authentic or private, and provided a definitive corpus of Canon Law. In the course of the following decades five further authentic collections were published: the constitutions from three authentic collections of Innocent IV (1243–54) were inserted in some manuscripts of the *Decretals of* GREGORY IX, but the collections of Gregory X (1271–76) and Nicholas III (1277–80) were simply appended to the Gregorian codices. Still further collections were made by Innocent IV, Alexander IV (1254–61), and Clement IV (1265–68) and during the pontificate of Boniface VIII (1294–1303); but these collections were not officially promulgated.

The *LIBER SEXTUS* (1298) of Boniface VIII was designed to supplement the *Decretals of Gregory IX,* and therefore superseded the intervening collections: in addition to revising and correcting texts, it incorporated 108 decretals of the period from Gregory IX to Nicholas III, the canons of the Councils of Lyons (1245 and 1274), and 251 chapters of Boniface VIII. It was followed by the *Constitutiones Clementinae* of Clement V (1305–14), promulgated by John XXII (1316–34) in 1317. The *Liber Sextus* and the CLEMENTINAE were designed on the same pattern as the *Decretales,* and these three works together complete the official *CORPUS IURIS CANONICI.*

The *EXTRAVAGANTES* of John XXII, in 14 titles, and the *Extravagantes communes* of papal decisions for the period from Urban IV (1261–64) to Sixtus IV (1471–84), are conventionally included in editions of the *Corpus Iuris;* but they were never officially issued. The *Liber septimus decretalium* (1590) of Petrus Matthaeus had little influence; the *Decretales Clementis VIII* (1598) were not authenticated; and the various other attempts to supplement the official *Corpus Iuris,* down to the 19th century, were not of lasting importance.

Papal Registers. As mentioned above, canonical collections are not the only records of decretals: the papal registers provide a further important source of supply. Most of the registers before Innocent III's pontificate are lost; but transcripts, excerpts, or fragments survive from the registers of Gregory I (590–604), John VIII (872–882), Stephen V (885–891), Gregory VII (1073–85), the antipope Anacletus II (1130–38), and Alexander III (1159–81). From and after the pontificate of Innocent III, the registers survive, though they do not record every letter. They are classified according to Curial or non-Curial subject matter from the time of Urban IV (1261–64), with further specialization from the reigns of Clement V and John XXII.

Papal letters are found also in the increasingly specialized departmental records of chancery, Apostolic Camera, papal *secreta,* and penitentiary. More precisely, the important accumulations of letters include: the *Regesta Vaticana,* from Innocent III to Pius V (1566–72), with some material to Clement VIII (1592–1605); the *Regesta Avenionensia,* from John XXII to the anti-pope Benedict XIII (1394–1423); the *Regesta Lateranensia,* from Boniface IX (1389–1404) to Pius VII (1800–23) and later material to Leo XIII (to 1897); and the *Regesta Brevium,* from Martin V (1417–31) to Gregory XV (1621–23).

Bibliography: P. FOURNIER and G. LEBRAS, *Histoire des collections canoniques en occident depuis les fausses décrétales jusqu'au Décret de Gratien,* 2 v. (Paris 1931–32). S. KUTTNER, *Repertorium der Kanonistik* (Rome 1937). H. WURM, *Studien und Texte zur Dekretalensammlung des Dionysius Exiguus* (Bonn 1939). A. VAN HOVE, *Commentarium Lovaniense in Codicem iuris canonici 1,* v.1–5 (Mechlin 1928–); v.1, *Prolegomena* (2d ed. 1945). W. HOLTZMANN, ''Über eine Ausgabe der päpstlichen Dek-

retalen des 12. Jahrhunderts,'' *Nachrichten von der Akademie der Wissenschaften in Göttingen, Phil.-hist. Klasse* (1945) 15–36; W. HOLTZMANN and E. W. KEMP, eds., *Papal Decretals relating to the Diocese of Lincoln in the 12th Century* (Hereford 1954). A. VETULANI, ''L'Origine des collections primitives de décrétales à la fin du XIIe siècle,'' *Actes du Congrès de droit canonique médiéval,* Louvain et Bruxelles, 1958 (Louvain 1959) 64–72. C. DUGGAN, *Twelfth-Century Decretal Collections and Their Importance in English History* (London 1963). G. LE BRAS et al., *L'Âge classique, 1140–1378. Sources et théorie du droit* (Histoire du droit et des institutions de l'Église en Occident 7; Paris 1965). For additional bibliographies, see CORPUS IURIS CANONICI; DECRETALS; FALSE DECRETALS; QUINQUE COMPILATIONES ANTIQUAE.

[C. DUGGAN]

DECRETISTS

The term decretists refers in general to civil and ecclesiastical jurists of the Middle Ages whose main object of study was the laws of the Church (*decreta*), in contrast to secular laws (*leges*). More specifically the term designates that group of canonists of the period between the *Decretum* of GRATIAN (*c.* 1140) and the *Decretals* of GREGORY IX (1234), whose primary interest was the *Decretum* of Gratian. The publication of the *Decretum* of Gratian was followed by almost a century of intense exegesis of the legal tradition of the Church as set out by Gratian in more than 4,000 texts. Bologna was the hub of all this activity, but great centers also arose in France (Paris), the Rhineland (Cologne), and England (Oxford) after STEPHEN OF TOURNAI had introduced the methods of Bologna to Paris *c.* 1160. This period of decretist activity, which overlaps the era of the first DECRETALISTS, had two distinct phases: a time (*c.* 1140–1200) that concentrated on the *Decretum* and was productive of cumulative rather than coherent glosses; and a less prolific, but more incisive time (*c.* 1200–20) that, together with the stimulus provided by new decretal collections and decretalist writing, fathered great systematic commentaries of glosses (*apparatus glossarum*).

First Decretist Phase (*c.* 1140–1200). During the early period, the principal methods that were to dominate the history of scientific canon law were evolved: *glossa, summa, quaestio.*

Glossa. A *glossa* is a marginal or interlinear annotation of a word, phrase, or passage in the *Decretum,* and it is the basis of all other exegetical techniques. It began in an elementary fashion, sometimes consisting of no more than a cross reference or a marginal underlining (*argumentum, nota, ita habes,* etc.) of noteworthy points (*notabilia*), generally rules of law, legal norms, and doctrinal commonplaces. From about 1150, however, the glossators became more venturesome: the techniques of civil law (explanation of conflicting references, citations from non-*Decretum* sources) were adopted under the influence of RUFINUS (*Summa* and glosses, before 1160); the use of *extravagantes* (i.e., legislation, etc., not found in, or coming after, the *Decretum*) became common from the time of SIMON OF BISIGNANO (*Summa* and glosses before 1180). A wealth of glosses of this period survive; they are chiefly in the form of mixed glosses, i.e., selections from oral or published glosses of the masters of Bologna and elsewhere. As decretist succeeded decretist these glosses were added to, layer upon layer; there are extant almost 200 copies of the *Decretum* glossed in this way, and the variety is astonishing. From these mixed or cumulative glosses, and from the personal writings of masters of Bologna and elsewhere, the names of many glossators are known. From Bologna there are, before 1150, PAUCAPALEA (Gratian's disciple and collaborator) and Rolandus Bandinelli (ALEXANDER III); Rufinus (before 1160); JOANNES FAVENTINUS (of Faenza); PETER OF SPAIN; Albert of Benevento (Gregory VIII, 1187); Cardinalis (Gratianus); Gandulphus (all *c.* 1160–70); David of London(?); Melendus, and BAZIANUS (1180–90). From the Franco-Rhenish school there are Gerard Pucelle (*c.* 1155–70), Godfrey of Cologne (*c.* 1170), SICARDUS OF CREMONA, and Rodoicus Modicipassus (1175–85). From the Anglo-Norman school come HONORIUS MAGISTER (mainly Paris, 1180–90), John of Tynemouth, Nicholas de Aquila, Simon of Southwell, Simon of Apulia, John of Kent, Simon of Derby, and Gregory of London (all *c.* 1188–98).

Summa. A *summa* is a composition that presents a concise, ordered rendering of and commentary upon the principal contents of the *Decretum*. The first *summae* were hardly more than summaries or lists of contents of the *Decretum*. From about 1160, however, they became progressively more systematic and more aware of non-*Decretum* sources (e.g., Rufinus, before 1160, and Simon of Bisignano, before 1180), less tied to the formal divisions (e.g., Sicardus, 1179–81) and order (e.g., Peter of Blois, *Distinctiones*, *c.* 1180; Honorius, *Summa*, 1186–90) of the *Decretum*, and more inventive (e.g., the *quaestiones* of Sicardus and Honorius). As a literary genre the *summa* is really a continuous gloss that has detached itself from its *Decretum* moorings. It allowed a greater freedom of movement than the *glossa* and attracted a large number of decretists—from Bologna: Paucapalea (1140–48), Rolandus Bandinelli (*Stroma, c.* 1148), OMNIBONUS (*Abbreviatio, c.* 1157), RUFINUS (before 1160), STEPHEN OF TOURNAI (*c.* 1160), Joannes Faventinus (*c.* 1171), SIMON OF BISIGNANO, HUGUCCIO (1188–90), RICHARD DE MORES (Paris 1186–87; Bologna 1196–98), and *Summa Reginensis* (Peter of Benevento? *c.* 1191); from the Franco-Rhenish schools: *Coloniensis*

(1169, Godfrey of Cologne?), *Monacensis* (*c.* 1175), *Tractaturus magister* (1175–78) SUMMA PARISIENSIS (*c.* 1160–70), *Permissio quaedam* (1178–87), Sicardus (1179–81), *Reverentia sacrorum canonum* (*c.* 1185–90), and Everard of Ypres (*c.* 1185); from the Anglo-Norman school: *De multiplici iuris divisione,* Odo of Dover, *Decreta minora* (both 1160–70), *De iure naturali* (1171–79), *Omnis qui iuste* (*Lipsiensis,* the most elaborate commentary before that of Huguccio), *In nomine, De iure canonico tractaturus* (Honorius, at Paris), *Duacensis* (all *c.* 1186–90), *Prima primi uxor Adae,* and *Quamvis leges saeculares* (both *c.* 1192).

Quaestio. A *quaestio* is a method of interpreting, clarifying or propounding the content of the *Decretum* by means of dialectical techniques. Although the *quaestio* owes something to the civil law *quaestiones legitimae* (problems illustrating laws), its more immediate inspiration was the dialectical framework of the *Decretum* itself. Originating in Franco-Rhenish circles between 1160 and 1170, it was popularized to some extent by Sicardus and his imitator, Everard of Ypres.

One basic form of the canonical *quaestio* was the *quaestio decretalis,* a gloss consisting of a dialectical examination of a question arising out of, or suggested by, a Decretum in order to arrive at a clearer idea of the implications of that decretum. A question is proposed ("Utrum. . ."), then contrary approaches are outlined ("Quod videtur. . . Sed contra videtur posse probari. . .") that deploy relevant parts of the whole decretum and thus make possible a balanced *solutio* of the question. A variant on this exegetical type of *quaestio* was used widely for purposes of teaching, but the *quaestio* or query in this case did not spring from a decretum as such, but from a *thema* or "problem" in which a real or fictitious legal situation was presented in the manner of a mathematical problem or a moral *casus.* Very many collections of the "problem" *questio* are extant, and often the same stock problems and queries recur from collection to collection. Another version of the canonical *quaestio* was the *quaestio disputata:* a classroom exercise, akin to the better-known *quaestiones disputatae* of the civilian and theological schools, in which two students demonstrated their knowledge of the *Decretum* by taking opposite sides on a question before their professor, who at the end provided the definitive *solutio* on the basis of the arguments presented *pro* and *contra.*

The *quaestio* was also employed in systematic expositions (*summae*) of the *Decretum*. These *summae quaestionum* originated probably among Anglo-Norman masters [e.g., Honorius, *summa quaestionum decretalium* (Paris 1186–90)], and may have been introduced to Bologna by the Englishman Richard de Mores [*Summa,*

"Circa ius naturale" (Paris 1186–87); *Summa brevis* (Bologna *c.* 1196–98)]. The *Summae quaestionum decretalium,* however, are not, as such, collections of *quaestiones decretales* or *quaestiones disputatae,* but rather textbooks of the *Decretum* in the form of a series of *quaestiones decretales.* They are also quite distinct from the *Casus decretorum,* a form of reference work in which the main content of each text in the *Decretum* is briefly reported (e.g., that of Benencasa of Arezzo at Bologna *c.* 1190–1200). A more refined literary genre is that of *Distinctiones,* a technique whereby a conclusion from, or a Summary of, some text or series of texts in the *Decretum* was tested by arguments "Sed contra" based on general dialectic principles (e.g., the *Distinctiones* of Peter of Blois, *c.* 1180); or whereby concepts or doctrines were analyzed in diagrammatic condensations (e.g., *Distinctiones* of Richard of Mores, *c.* 1196–98). Other forms of decretist activity before *c.* 1200 include rearrangements of the *Decretum (Transformationes),* e.g., that by Laborans (*c.* 1182); and monographic tracts, e.g., the *Summae de matrimonio* (1173–1179) and *De electione* (1177–79) of Bernard of Pavia, the *Summa De ordine iudiciario* of Richard de Mores (1196–98), or the anonymous *De presumptionibus* ("Perpendiculum," *c.* 1180).

Second Decretist Phase (c. 1200–20). The exhaustive *Summa* of Huguccio (Bologna, 1188–90) crowned fifty years of "summarist" activity. On the other hand, glossator scholarship, for all its industry, had not achieved by 1190 anything more than amalgamations of mixed glosses—not even in the great composite gloss *Ordinaturus magister* (*c.* 1180). However, when Bolognese glossators, after a slight pause, turned once more (*c.* 1200) to the *Decretum,* their method was now tight and controlled. Two factors conditioned, if they did not inspire, this new, and in fact final, decretist phase: the publication in 1191–92 of the great collection of decretals (*Breviarium extravagantium,* the *Compilatio prima* of the *QUINQUE COMPILATIONES ANTIQUAE*) of Bernard of Pavia; and the coherent, systematic glosses (*apparatus glossarum*) in which a fresh breed of canonists (Decretalists) were to cast their exegesis of the texts. This new literary form (in use among Bolognese civilians, and possibly among French decretists, e.g., the *apparatus, Ecce vicit leo* and *Animal est substantia; c.* 1202–10) clearly showed up the shapelessness of mixed-gloss compositions.

There now followed at Bologna a burst of decretist activity (largely decretalist-decretist) that resulted in four splendid *apparatus* between 1200 and 1220, including the overdue *glossa ordinaria:* the *Ius naturale* of ALANUS ANGLICUS (*c.* 1202, a revision of an earlier effort, *c.* 1192); the *apparatus* of LAWRENCE OF SPAIN (1210–15); the *Glossa Palatina* (1210–15), which leaned heavily on

Lawrence; and finally, the *apparatus* of JOANNES TEUTONICUS (1216), a revised form of which was received at Bologna as the *glossa ordinaria c.* 1220. Side by side with these *apparatus,* and in the midst of intense decretal research and scholarship, there were many other decretalist-decretist and decretist productions: the *Summa Posnaniensis* (1204–09); glosses from BERNARD OF COMPOSTELLA, THE ELDER (1210–15), Martin of Zamora, Damasus of Hungary, VINCENT and Pelagius of Spain, RAYMOND OF PEÑAFORT, William of Gascony, Peter of Brittany, JAMES OF ALBENGA; *apparatus-glossae* on the *De poenitentia* and *De consecratione* (1210–12); *summae titulorum decreti* from Bernard of Pavia (1198), Ambrosius (after 1215), and Damasus (*c.* 1215); collections of *quaestiones disputatae* of Bernard of Compostella, the Elder (1204–09, Vicenza?), Damasus, TANCRED and Joannes Teutonicus; *notabilia* of Bernard of Pavia, Richard de Mores, Paul of Hungary; *brocarda* of de Mores and Damasus.

The *glossa ordinaria* of Joannes Teutonicus marks the end of the decretist era as such, but although the study of decretals took place primarily after 1234 (*see* GREGORY IX, DECRETALS OF), the *Decretum* continued to evoke writings from generation after generation of decretalists, e.g., BARTHOLOMEW OF BRESCIA (*Quaestiones, c.* 1234; revision of *casus* and of *glossa ordinaria,* 1240–45), the Irishman Joannes de Phintona, to whom is due the division of the *Decretum* into parts and paragraphs (*Lecturae,* after 1240), Petrus de Salines (*Lectura, c.* 1250), and GUIDO DE BAYSIO (*Rosarium,* 1300, supplementing B. of Brescia's revision of the *ordinaria,* particularly important for incorporating much from the decretists who preceded the *glossa ordinaria*), not to mention the various authors of *Flores Decreti, Breviaria,* etc., such as Martin of Poland (*c.* 1279) and his popular *Tabula Decreti (Margarita).*

Bibliography: J. F. VON SCHULTE, *Die Geschichte der Quellen und der Literatur des kanonischen Rechts* (Stuttgart 1875–80) v.1–2. J. JUNCKER, "Summen und Glossen," *Zietschrift der Savigny-Stiftung für Rechtsgeschichte, Kanonistische Abteilung* 14 (1925) 384–474. S. KUTTNER, *Repertorium der Kanonistik* (Rome 1937). H. KANTOROWICZ, "The *Quaestiones disputatae* of the Glossators," *Tijdschrift voor rechtsgeschiedenis* 16 (1939) 1–67. S. KUTTNER, "Les Débuts de l'école canoniste française," *Pontificio instituto utrisque iuris, Studia et documenta historiae et iuris* (1938) 193–204; "Bernardus Compostellanus Antiquus," *Traditio* 1 (1943) 277–340; "Some Gratian Manuscripts with Early Glosses," *ibid.* 19 (1963) 532–536; ed., "Notes on Manuscripts," *Bulletin of the Institute of Research and Study in Medieval Cannon Law, ibid.* v.11–14, 16–17 (1955–58, 1960–61). S. KUTTNER and E. RATHBONE, "Anglo-Norman Canonists of the 12th Century," *ibid.* 7 (1949–51) 279–358. G. FRANSEN, "Les *Quaestiones* des canonistes," *ibid.* 12 (1956) 566–592; 13 (1957) 481–501; 19 (1963) 516–531; 20 (1964) 495–502. A. VAN HOVE, *Commentatium Lovaniense in Codicem iuris canonici 1* (Mechlin 1928–) 1:412–427. A. M. STICKLER, "Sacerdotium et regnum nei decretisti e primi decretalisti,'' *Salesianum* 15 (1953) 575–612; ''Decretisti Bolognesi dementicati,'' *Studia Gratiana* 3 (1955) 375–410; *Lexikon für Theologie und Kirche*, ed. J. HOFER and K. RAHNER (Freiberg 1957–65) 5:1289–1302. H. E. FEINE, *Kirchliche Rechtsgeschichte* (3d ed. Weimar 1955) 247–251. C. LEFEBVRE and G. FRANSEN, *Dictionnaire de droit canonique*, ed. R. NAZ (Paris 1935–65) 7:409–418. G. LE BRAS et al., *L'Âge classique, 1140–1378. Sources et théorie du droit* (Histoire du droit et des institutions de l'Église en Occident 7; Paris 1965).

[L. E. BOYLE]

DEDICATION OF THE TEMPLE, FEAST OF

The Jewish Feast of the Dedication, called in Greek τὰ ἐγκαίνια and in Hebrew *ḥănukkâ* (hence the modern Jewish name Hanukkah), is celebrated for eight days, beginning on the 25th of Kislev (early December). Its origin is related in 1 Mc 4.36–59. On the 25th of Kislev, 167 B.C., the Syrian monarch ANTIOCHUS IV EPIPHANES had desecrated the Temple by sacrificing to Zeus Olympios on a pagan altar erected in its sanctuary. Three years later the successful revolutionary leader Judas Maccabee rededicated the altar of the Temple in a joyous ceremony and decreed the annual observance of the feast. (*See* MACCABEES, HISTORY OF THE.)

Ancient Customs. In addition to this account, 2 Mc 1.1–10.8 has, as its main purpose, the historical justification of the feast and the imposition of it upon the Jewish world. Here the feast is called ''the Feast of Booths of the month of Kislev'' (2 Mc 1.9; see also 10.6), and the similarity to the ancient festival is stressed. [*See* BOOTHS (TABERNACLES), FEAST OF.] The comparison may be an afterthought because of some similar rites—duration of eight days, a procession with palms, the joyous atmosphere—or it may have been thus intended by its founders. The Jewish historian Josephus mentions the feast (*Ant.* 12.323–325), calling it ''the Feast of Lights,'' after the most distinctive rite, which consisted of lighting lamps before each house, an additional one for each day of the feast. Hanukkah is also mentioned in the New Testament in Jn 10.22, where Jesus is said to have attended it at the Temple. The MISHNAH mentions it several times, but only in passing.

The most ancient sources do not describe the rites of the feast, except to mention sacrifices and rejoicing and the duration of the festival. The use of lights in the earlier period is rightly inferred from Josephus and from 2 Mc 1.8. The suggestion that Hanukkah embodies features of some ancient pagan feast, such as the Dionysiac festival or the celebration of the winter solstice, must be judged improbable in the light of the precise information that is given in the Books of Maccabees.

Modern Customs. The theme of joy persisted as the keynote of the feast long after the destruction of the Jerusalem Temple. It is symbolized by the lighting, especially within the house, of the Hanukkah lamp, the modern form of the ancient lamps that were lighted before homes. A Talmudic legend (*Sabb* 21b) traces the custom to the miraculous burning of one day's supply of oil for eight days in the Temple lamp when the feast was instituted. The Hanukkah lamp is an eightbranched candlestick (or MENORAH), often very ornate. The custom of lighting first one candle, then an additional one each successive night, prescribed by the rabbinical teacher Hillel, prevailed over the opposite practice of the rival school of Shammai of beginning with eight lamps and extinguishing one each night. The lamps are meant only for display and hence are placed in windows or near doors; sometimes as many lamps are lit as there are persons in the house. The original practice is extended to lighting lamps in the synagogues as well. Two benedictions are prescribed before the lighting each night: ''Blessed be the Lord our God, King of the Universe, who has sanctified us by His commandments and enjoined us to kindle the Hanukkah lamp''; and ''Blessed . . . who has worked miracles for our Fathers in days of old at this season'' (*Sabb* 23a).

In addition to the lamp ceremony the synagogue services for these eight days prescribe the reading of Nm 7.1–8.4, describing the gifts of the tribal leaders at the dedication of the altar in the wilderness and the installation of the lamps in the TENT OF MEETING. The Hallel [Ps 112(113)–117(118)] is recited each day of the feast. Special hymns have been composed for Hanukkah to praise God as the deliverer of Israel. The most popular of these is the *Mā'ôz sûr*, ''The Rock of Ages,'' probably composed by a 13th-century poet named Mordecai. Also, Psalm 29(30) is recited during the feast, as stated already in its superscription.

Popular custom has associated family feasting with the Hanukkah season. It was not thought proper that work should be done by the light of the festive lamp, and, as a result, games, riddles, puzzles, etc., became a common feature of the earlier celebrations. The *Hanukkah Trendel*, a four-sided top, was a famous Jewish toy of medieval origin. Hanukkah has also become a time for gift-giving, especially within the family circle. The custom of giving coins to the children of the family has long prevailed. Since this feast was of post-Biblical origin (the Books of Maccabees not being included in the Jewish canon), it has always been reckoned a minor festival, and therefore business and manual labor are not forbidden during its celebration. In modern times, however, it has grown to be one of the more popular festive occasions in the Jewish calendar.

Bibliography: *Encyclopedic Dictionary of the Bible*, tr. and adap. by L. HARTMAN (New York 1963) 539–540. R. DE VAUX, *Ancient Israel, Its Life and Institutions*, tr. J. MCHUGH (New York 1961) 510–514. D. SCHÖTZ, *Lexikon für Theologie und Kirche*, ed. J. HOFER and K. RAHNER (Freiburg 1957–65) 2:1014–15. K. KOHLER, *The Jewish Encyclopedia*, ed. J. SINGER (New York 1901–06) 6:223–226. O. S. RANKIN, *The Origins of the Festival of Hanukkah* (Edinburgh 1930). S. ZEITLIN, ''Hanukkah: Its Origins and Its Significance,'' *Jewish Quarterly Review* 29 (1938–39) 1–36. J. MORGENSTERN, ''The Chanukkah Festival and the Calendar of Ancient Israel,'' *Hebrew Union College Annual* 20 (1947) 1–136. T. H. GASTER, *Purim and Hanukkah in Custom and Tradition* (New York 1950).

[G. W. MACRAE]

DEDUCTION

Deduction is a type of REASONING whereby a person concludes from one or more given premises to a proposition that is their necessary and logical consequent (*see* ARGUMENTATION; SYLLOGISM). The term is of recent origin in the history of logic, its French equivalent appearing only in the last edition (1835) of the *Dictionnaire de l'Académie française*. ARISTOTLE characterizes a certain type of argument as ἀπαγωγή, which is rendered into Latin as *deductio* but is better translated into English as reduction; the argument known as *reductio ad impossibile* is of this type (*Anal. pr.* 29b 6; see also *ibid.* 69a 20). Again, THOMAS AQUINAS uses the term *deductio* in at least four different senses, none of which has the precise modern signification [*see* L. Schütz, *Thomas–Lexikon* (2d ed. Paderborn 1895; repr. Stuttgart 1958) 203]. I. KANT speaks too of a transcendental deduction as part of his transcendental method. *See* TRANSCENDENTAL (KANTIAN). Modern logicians sometimes oppose deduction to INDUCTION on the basis that the first concludes from the general to the particular, whereas the second concludes from the particular to the general; this characterization is inaccurate, however, since deduction need not conclude to the particular and its process is far from being the logical inverse of the inductive procedure (*see* INDUCTION; DEMONSTRATION). For specific teachings on deduction, *see* R. eisler, *Wörterbuch der philosophischen Begriffe*, 3 v. (4th ed. Berlin 1927–30) 1:245–247.

See Also: LOGIC, SYMBOLIC.

[R. HOUDE]

DEER, ABBEY OF

Former Cistercian abbey, in the county and Diocese of Aberdeen, Scotland. Deer (Dér, Deir) was founded by William Comyn, Earl of Buchan, in 1219 and colonized by monks from KINLOSS. It is clear from the Book of Deer, a 9th-century Celtic MS now in the possession of the University of Cambridge, that a CULDEE monastery had been established in the vicinity of Deer for centuries before the arrival of the CISTERCIANS. Then with the reorganization of the parish system following the reforms of King DAVID I, it would seem that it had either decayed or had been suppressed, and that its lands had passed into the possession of the earls of Buchan, who used them to found the Cistercian abbey nearby. The abbey suffered badly in the Scottish wars of independence. In 1537 the monastery was visited by the abbots of Glenluce and Kinloss and by 1543 there were only 14 monks left in the abbey. In 1587 its lands were erected into a temporal lordship for Robert Keith. Only the foundations of the abbey remain.

Bibliography: J. STUART, ed., *The Book of Deer* (Aberdeen Spalding Club; Edinburgh 1869). A. O. ANDERSON, ed. and tr., *Early Sources of Scottish History*, 2 v. (Edinburgh 1922) 2:181, 439–440. W. D. SIMPSON, *The Abbey of Deer* (Edinburgh 1952). D. E. EASSON, *Medieval Religious Houses: Scotland* (London 1957) 63. J. M. CANIVEZ, *Dictionnaire d'histoire et de géographie ecclésiastiques*, ed. A. BAUDRILLART et al. (Paris 1912–) 14:157–158.

[L. MACFARLANE]

DEFAMATION

Defamation is an action whereby one blackens the good name of an absent person. A good name or reputation is the esteem in which a person is held by his fellowmen, and it confers a certain luster on a person. Defamation blackens, tarnishes, or even destroys this luster. There are two sinful extremes of defamatory speech, namely, the unadorned lie and unreserved truthfulness. The second extreme consists in revealing hidden blackening truths about another without necessity. These two extremes are called calumny and detraction, respectively. Between the two extremes there are defamatory methods that contain some truth as well as some falsity.

One method of defamation, containing some truth and some falsity, is exaggerating another's fault or ''making mountains out of molehills.'' A particularly insidious exaggerator is the one who begins to speak about another and then stops, saying ''. . . I better not tell you all I know about him.'' Such a remark can have a devastating effect, because the listener's imagination is left free to roam through the entire territory of possible sins. Another method is diminishing what is good in another or ''damning with faint praise.'' One of the most destructive forms of defamatory speech is found in what is known as ''the sinister interpretation.'' A person admits another's good action but wonders why he did it. ''What is he going to get out of it?'' These expressions can cause others to question not only the present action but make suspect any future good action of the person.

Defamation is more than uncharitable speech. It is an act of injustice. The defamer has harmed another's possession. The extent of the harm can be gauged from the evaluation of a good name. Defamation obliges one to restore another to the esteem in which he was formerly held. Needless to say, once a person's good name has been blackened, it is impossible to undo the damage. The realization of this fact is an added incentive for one to exercise control over his tongue.

See Also: REPUTATION, MORAL RIGHT TO; DETRACTION; CALUMNY.

Bibliography: A. THOUVENIN, *Dictionnaire de théologie catholique,* ed. A. VACANT et al., 15 v. (Paris 1903–50; Tables générales 1951–) 10:487–494. H. DAVIS, *Moral and Pastoral Theology,* rev. and enl. ed. by L. W. GEDDES (New York 1958). F. J. CONNELL, *Outlines of Moral Theology* (2d ed. Milwaukee 1964). K. B. MOORE, *The Moral Principles Governing the Sin of Detraction . . .* (Washington 1950).

[K. B. MOORE]

DEFENDER OF THE FAITH

A title conferred on HENRY VIII by Pope LEO X in 1521 and still retained as part of the style of the English crown, appearing on all royal instruments, e.g., English coins. Henry VIII had been pressing for years for a papal title—to match those enjoyed by the French and Spanish kings. In 1512, 1515, and 1516 various formulae were proposed, including "Defender of the Holy See," "Apostolic King," and "Defender of the Faith," but none succeeded. In 1521, having produced his work against Martin LUTHER and thinking that his claim was thus strengthened, he resumed the quest. A presentation copy of his work was sent to Rome and, after considerable dilly-dallying, Leo X conferred on its author the title of his choice, viz, "Defender of the Faith."

This somewhat grudging grant was probably intended as a personal gift to Henry but was converted into a permanent addition to the royal style. Despite England's repudiation of Rome and the fact that the faith concerned was that of the popes and scarcely that of the Church of which the English monarch is supreme head, it has remained. Of the many extra titles acquired by the English crown, this one has fared best.

Bibliography: M. BROWN, "Henry VIII's Book *Assertio Septem Sacramentorum* and the Royal Title of *Defender of the Faith*" in *Transactions of the Royal Historical Society* 1st ser. 8 (1880) 242–262. M. CREIGHTON, *History of the Papacy . . . ,* 6 v. (New York 1897) 6:374–375. F. L. CROSS, *The Oxford Dictionary of the Christian Church* (London 1957) 384.

[J. J. SCARISBRICK]

DEFENSOR CIVITATIS

The term applied to the official created in the later Roman Empire as the defender of the city or people. Valentinian I, in 364, created the office of *defensor civitatis* principally to defend the powerless against the privileged in minor litigations. He was appointed for life by the praetorian prefect, and was to have easy access, in the cause of justice, to the praetorian prefect and the emperor himself. Under THEODOSIUS I (387) the office became elective, and its powers were enlarged to deal with criminal and religious affairs. By 428 the *defensor civitatis* had become a municipal magistrate with wide administrative powers. JUSTINIAN I, in 535, strengthened the institution, which had become corrupt and ineffective, by putting it into the hands of the first citizens of the city, who would take turns holding it for two years. With increased powers of administration and jurisdiction, the *defensor civitatis* became a lieutenant governor, to whom the city officials and provincial officials dwelling within the city owed obedience. As the office became almost completely transformed from its original character, the *defensor civitatis* became more a ruler than the defender of the ruled. In the 9th century the office was abolished. In the meantime the defense of the powerless had fallen more and more to the bishops.

Bibliography: H. LECLERCQ, *Dictionnaire d'archéologie chrétienneet de liturgie,* ed. F. CABROL, H. LECLERCQ and H. I. MARROU, 15 v. (Paris 1907–53) 4.1:406–427. J. B. BURY, *A History of the Later Roman Empire from the Death of Theodosius I to the Death of Justinian A.D. 395–565,* 2 v. (London 1923; repr. pa. New York 1957) 1:60–61.

[E. DAY]

DEFINITION

A mental process, namely, one of clarifying the meaning of a TERM by analyzing and relating the elements involved in it; or, alternatively, the product of a mental process, viz, an expression explaining the use of the term or its meaning. Definition is the opposite of DIVISION, which separates the elements involved in the meaning of a term or in the thing it signifies.

Notion. As a mental process, definition arises not only from simple APPREHENSION, but also from JUDGMENT and REASONING, and, in the latter case, through both DEDUCTION and INDUCTION. Thus intellectual apprehension of one's experiences with individual human beings can lead one to realize that "animal in whom instinct is replaced by reason" is what is meant by "man." The process here is often one of defining through division, as exemplified in Plato's *Sophist* (218D–221C). Or, one may judge it true to say, "Man is an animal," and so utilize the notion of "animal" as a clarification of "man." Finally, one may argue to the conclusion, "Man is meant to live in society," from the findings of psychological tests, and then employ "social" as a clarification of "man." This method is often used by St. THOMAS AQUINAS in his *Summa theologiae,* as when he formulates the full definition of a virtue only at the end of its treatment (for example, that of charity, ST 2a2ae, 23). Definitions can thus be said to grow or expand as one's knowledge is increased and is related consciously to what was previously known. As the product of a mental process, definition is distinguished from the term or thing defined, which is often labeled "the definitum," or "the definiendum." In the examples cited above, "man" is the definitum. Furthermore, definition is not a sentence or PROPOSITION, but an expression that merely juxtaposes the definitum and the definition; this can be signified by means of a colon—"man: social being." For this reason, definitions are not true and false, but good and bad or adequate and inadequate. For it is generally agreed that definition, as the product of a mental process, is related only to the first act of the mind, that is, to simple apprehension.

Kinds. There are two major groups of definitions. The first includes expressions that explain the use of a term; these are called nominal definitions because the definitum is a term usually in the noun form (Lat. *nomen*). There are four classes of nominal definition. The first makes use of a synonym or of the corresponding word in another language, as in "man: human being," or "man: *hombre.*" Such a definition is of value only when the definition is clearly more known than the definitum. The second employs the etymology of a term—"man: from the Anglo-Saxon *mann,*" or "magnolia: from Magnol, its discoverer's name." The third is based on the history of a term's use throughout the ages; thus one may study the usage of "man" in Chaucer, Shakespeare, Restoration drama, etc. The fourth is based on an imposed or stipulated use of a term, as is done when proving theorems in mathematics and symbolic logic.

The second major group of definitions includes all expressions that explain the meaning of the term and of the CONCEPT it signifies. Aristotle explains it as a phrase signifying a thing's ESSENCE (*Topics,* A 101b). This kind of definition is often called "real," not because the nominal definition is fictional, but because the definitum of the second group is taken as referring more directly to reality (Lat. *res*).

There are many varieties of real definition. First, a thing may be defined in terms of its efficient causes, or its origins, as in "man: one born of rational parents," or "water: a product of oxygen and hydrogen." Second, one may define something in terms of its end or purpose,

as in "man: a being whose destiny it is to rule the universe," or "watch: an instrument for telling time." Third, a thing may be defined in terms of its intrinsic principles, as in "body: a composite of primary matter and substantial form," or "man: a composite of organic body and intellectual soul." This is sometimes labeled a physical definition. Fourth, a definition may be given through a thing's properties and accidents, as in "man: a being capable of enjoying a joke," or "water: a substance with a boiling point of 100°C." This is often called a descriptive definition. Finally, a thing may be defined in terms of its GENUS and difference, as in "man: rational animal." This is called a metaphysical definition.

These definitions are not all of equal value. The ordinary man tends to define in terms of synonyms, purposes and accidents. The mathematician finds use only for stipulated definitions. The philosopher and the scientist employ all forms of real definition, together with the results of etymological and historical studies, often combining these into one definition that completely expresses the essence of the definitum, as in "man: one born of rational parents, composed of organic body and intellectual soul, made to dominate the universe, meant to live in society, etc."

Rules. In order to bring order and accuracy to the work of defining, logicians have developed several rules for formulating definitions. These may be summarized as follows. First, the definition should be coextensive with the definitum. Thus to define man as "two-legged" is bad form, for other things besides man are two-legged. Second, the definitum should never be found in the definition, as in "man: creature composed of organic body and *human* soul;" here "human" is equivalent to "man." This is perhaps the most common form of bad definition. Third, whenever possible the definition should be in univocal terms, so as to avoid ambiguity. Fourth, whenever possible the definition should be in positive, affirmative terms, since negative terms do not tell what a thing is but only what it is not. Thus, to define man as "a non-feathered creature" is to say little about him. Finally, every definition should contain a genus and a difference, the genus expressing what the definitum has in common with other things or words, and the difference expressing what is peculiar to the definitum. It may be noted that, while all definitions should indicate a genus and a difference, the best definition will specify the proximate genus and the specific difference, for it is this kind of definition that fulfills perfectly the logical rules cited above. But such a perfect definition is rare (the standard example, "man: rational animal," may well be unique), presupposing, as it does, extensive investigation of its subject matter.

Real definitions that comply with all the rules for definition are difficult to obtain in theology since analogical and negative terms are the best available for defining supernatural entities. Nor do existentialist philosophers feel at home with the notion of a real definition that is oriented to essence. Nevertheless, scientists and philosophers recognize in definition a valid mode of attaining SCIENCE through continued clarification of terms and their meanings.

See Also: QUIDDITY; SPECIES; DISTINCTION, KINDS OF.

Bibliography: *The Material Logic of John of St. Thomas,* tr. Y. R. SIMON et al. (Chicago 1955). F. H. PARKER and H. B. VEATCH, *Logic as a Human Instrument* (New York 1959). J. A. OESTERLE, *Logic: The Art of Defining and Reasoning* (2d ed. Englewood Cliffs, N.J. 1963). V. E. SMITH, *The Elements of Logic* (Milwaukee 1957); "Definitions," in *From an Abundant Spring* (New York 1952), The Walter Farrell Memorial v. of *The Thomist,* 337–362. J. A. MOURANT, *Formal Logic* (New York 1963). E. D. SIMMONS, *The Scientific Art of Logic* (Milwaukee 1961).

[E. BONDI]

DEFINITION, DOGMATIC

In the language of Catholicism, dogmatic definition is a technical expression used in connection with the object of FAITH either to signify that an object of faith is a DOGMA, revealed by God and proclaimed as such by the Church (e.g., the dogmatic definition of papal infallibility, H. Denzinger, *Enchiridion symbolorum,* ed. A. Schönmetzer [Freiburg 1963] 3074), or to give precision to the formularization of a dogma (e.g., Chalcedon's definition of the Christological dogma, *Enchiridion symbolorum* 301–303); dogmatic definition falls within the wider expression of the RULE OF FAITH (*regula fidei*). This article deals with (1) the act by which a dogmatic definition comes into being, and (2) the nature of a dogmatic definition.

Act. A dogmatic definition is an act of the Church as the living instrument through which the WORD OF GOD is operative in human history from the time when that Word became flesh in Jesus Christ until its final revelation in the PAROUSIA of the Lord Jesus. To enable the Church to function as the living instrument of the Word of God, there is within the Church the institution of the magisterium (the teaching authority of the Church). Through this institution the Church is the prophetic instrument of the Word of God in that it gives testimony to that Word (*see* WITNESS, CHRISTIAN).

By teaching this institution the Church is the pastoral instrument of the Word of God, and through this same institution the Church is the judicial instrument of the Word of God, proclaiming in an authoritative manner what must be believed as the Word of God. A dogmatic definition is an act of the Church through the institution of the magisterium acting in its judicial capacity; as such, it is an act of the supreme AUTHORITY within the Church. This judicial act of the supreme authority of the Church is seen first in the ordinary functioning of the institution of the magisterium, the handing on of the APOSTOLIC TRADITION by the successors of the APOSTLES. For in this preaching and teaching of the apostolic Church, there is not only the transmission of the Word of God but also the definition of dogma, of what is revealed by God.

Thus Origen writes [*De prin.* 4, 5 (praef.); *Patrologia Graeca* ed. J. P. Migne (Paris 1857–66) 11:118]: "quod manifestissime in ecclesiis praedicatur. . . . Est et illud definitum in ecclesiastica praedicatione omnem animam rationabilem esse liberi arbitrii . . . ." Here the act of supreme authority by which dogmatic definition comes into being has the form of traditional or customary law (Scheeben, *Handbuch der Katholischen Dogmatik* 1:190). The various creeds and confessions of faith (*Enchiridion symbolorum* 1, 2, 75–76,125–126, 150, 525–541, 680–686, 800–802) used by the Church, together with the PROFESSIONS OF FAITH (*Enchiridion symbolorum* 1862–70, 1985–87, 3537–50), are the objectivization of this form of dogmatic definition representing a formulation of the Church's belief.

The judicial act of the supreme authority of the Church by which dogmatic definition comes into being also takes the form of statutory law. This involves the extraordinary intervention of the institution of the magisterium, a formal judgment of the supreme tribunal of the Church. Since this supreme tribunal has two juridical forms—the pope as head and representative of the apostolic college, and the pope together with the apostolic college—dogmatic definition in this form comes into being through an EX CATHEDRA judgment of the pope (*judicium plenum*) or through a judgment of a general council (*judicium plenissimum*). Although on occasions, such as the Council of Trent, these judgments cover a wide area of dogma, the history of dogma shows that for the most part they are concerned with particular dogmas. They are expressed in various ways: by the condemnation, appended to the statement of creeds, of heretical belief (*Enchiridion symbolorum* 126, 151); by anathema (*Enchiridion symbolorum* 153); by canons (*Enchiridion symbolorum* 222,371); by dogmatic letters (*Enchiridion symbolorum* 546–548); or by decrees (*Enchiridion symbolorum* 178–180).

Whether it comes into being as an act of the ordinary or extraordinary intervention of the institution of the magisterium, dogmatic definition is to be interpreted according to the rules used in the interpretation of law. Concerning the act by which a dogmatic definition comes into being, the doctrinal statement of Vatican Council I (*Enchiridion symbolorum* 3011) is normative: "Furthermore, by divine and Catholic faith all must be believed that is contained in the written word of God or in tradition and that is set forth by the Church as a divinely revealed object of belief either in solemn decree or in ordinary, universal teaching."

Nature. The theological determination of the nature of dogmatic definition depends on a theology of the Word of God and on the scientific understanding of the phenomenon of human speech. Using modern developments in the field of speech-theory, theologians such as Edmund Schlink have begun to investigate the peculiarities of theological statements, the Church's response in faith to the actuality of the Word of God. This investigation shows that dogmatic definition is a form of theological statement rooted in the primary theological statement, the Church's confession of faith. In this confession (cf. *Enchiridion symbolorum* 265–266) the Church, together with the Holy Spirit, testifies that response to the Word of God is the obedience of faith (Rom 1.5). Dogmatic definition, therefore, is not a rationalization of divine truth but the manifestation of the Church's faith as normative for the belief of members of the Church. Where other norms, such as the objectivization of the faith of the primitive Church in the corpus of New Testament writings, are concerned with the formation of dogma, dogmatic definition is concerned primarily with the formularization of dogma. The temporal and so changing character of the Church's human speech in which the Word of God is embodied postulates this normative role of the Church's faith. However, because it is the expression of the Church's faith, the content of dogmatic definition is divine truth, and in relation to this content dogmatic definition is irreformable. The thought patterns used to conceptualize this content and the words in which it is expressed are conditioned by factors, cultural and anthropological, subject to change.

See Also: ARTICLE OF FAITH; DEPOSIT OF FAITH; DOCTRINE; DOCTRINE, DEVELOPMENT OF; FAITH AND MORALS; INFALLIBILITY.

Bibliography: A. MICHEL, *Dictionnaire de théologie catholique,* ed. A. VACANT et al., (Paris 1903–50) Tables générales 1:916–917. M. J. SCHEEBEN, *Handbuch der katholischen Dogmatik,* v.1 (Freiburg 1948) 187–283. C. DAVIS, "The Living Word," *Theology for Today* (New York 1962) 100–113. W. PANNENBERG, "Was ist eine dogmatische Aussage?" *Kerygma und Dogma* 8 (1962) 81–99. K. RAHNER, "Was ist eine dogmatische Aussage?" *Schriften zur Theologie,* v.5 (Einsiedeln 1962) 54–81. E. SCHLINK, "Die Struktur der dogmatischen Aussage als oekumenisches Problem," *Kerygma and Dogma* 3 (1957) 251–306.

[E. G. HARDWICK]

DEFINITOR, RELIGIOUS

A religious deputed or elected to participate authoritatively in the government of a religious institute. In the history of monasticism the office of definitor originated in the 11th and 12th centuries in an effort to ameliorate the excessive authoritarianism of the Cluniac structure, and it was adopted and developed further by the mendicant orders during the 13th century.

Two types of definitor may be distinguished: capitular, or those having a voice in the affairs of a chapter, general or provincial, and who are also electors in an elective chapter (*see* CHAPTERS, RELIGIOUS); and consultive definitors, or those who pertain to the permanent council of the superior. Capitular definitors as a body, the *definitorium,* usually enjoy complete general or provincial authority while a chapter remains in session. Consultive definitors serve only as a consensual or advisory body to the general or provincial superior, who, according to the constitutions, must obtain their consent or advice for the validity of his administrative acts (1917 *Codex iuris canonici* cc.105n1, 516.1; PostApost c.48.1). The manner of deputing or electing definitors is determined by the constitutions of an institute.

Bibliography: M. J. GRAJEWSKI, *The Supreme Moderator of Clerical Exempt Religious Institutes* (Catholic University of America, CLS 369; Washington 1957). G. LEWIS, *Chapters in Religious Institutes* (Catholic University of America CLS 181; Washington 1943).

[W. B. RYAN]

DEHARBE, JOSEPH

Jesuit catechist and theologian; b. Strassburg, April 1, 1800; d. Maria-Laach, Nov. 8, 1871. He entered the Society of Jesus in 1817; and, after teaching for 11 years at the Jesuit College in Brieg, Switzerland, he became a missionary and catechist at Cöthen in 1840. He and Peter Roh, SJ, established the Academy of St. Charles Borromeo at Lucerne in 1845. Two years later, when persecution broke out in Switzerland, he barely escaped alive. The rest of his life was spent chiefly in giving missions in Germany and in revising his catechism. This work, *Katholischer Katechismus oder Lehrbegriff* (Zurich 1847; Ratisbon 1848), was modeled on the Mainz Canisius catechism of 1843, although other texts were utilized also, notably Bossuet's catechism. Although Deharbe wrote the book only under obedience to his superior, feeling himself incompetent for the task, it won immediate acclaim, and was adopted within a year by the bishops of seven dioceses. In 1853, it was introduced officially throughout the whole kingdom of Bavaria. Within the next 15 years, it was used in the dioceses of Cologne, Mainz, Paderborn, Fulda, Ermland, Culm, and Gnesen-Posen, as well as in several dioceses of Switzerland, Austria-Hungary, and the U.S. It was first translated into Magyar in 1851, and before long translations were made into most European languages, including English (1863). The book or its revisions continued in widespread use into the 20th century, the Linden version being adopted throughout Germany in 1925. Introduced into America in 1850 by Bishop Purcell of Cincinnati, and first published there in 1869, it became the catechism most frequently employed in the U.S. until past the turn of the century, and in some places into the 1930s.

Although based on the Canisius catechism, Deharbe's text introduced a new arrangement of matter into sections on faith, the Commandments, and the means of grace, a division that most subsequent catechists followed. Recently, however, this order has been abandoned because it was said to lead children to think that the Commandments and Sacraments are not matter for faith. Later revisions allayed much of the criticism against the work for having too many questions and definitions, and because its abstract theological formulas were unintelligible to children. The book has received praise for its theological correctness, brevity of sentences, preciseness of expression, clearness, and arrangement. Deharbe's other works include four extracts of his first book, all published at Ratisbon: *Katholischer Katechismus* (1847), *Kleiner katholischer Katechismus* (1847), *Anfangsgründe der katholischen Lehre für die kleinen Schüler* (1847), *Kleiner katholischer Katechismus* (1849–50). Also published at Ratisbon were: *Die vollkommene Liebe Gottes* (1855), *Erklärung des katholischen Katechismus* (4 v. 1857–64), *Kürzeres Handbuch zum Religionsunterrichte* (1865–68), *Handbuch zum Religionsbuch in den Elementarschulen* (1868).

Bibliography: C. SOMMERVOGEL, et al., *Bibliothèque de la Compagnie de Jésus* (Brussels-Paris 1890–1932) 2:1875–84; 9:182–184. A. N. FUERST, *The Systematic Teaching of Religion,* 2 v. (New York 1939–46). F. SPIRAGO, *Spirago's Method of Christian Doctrine,* ed. S. G. MESSMER (New York 1901). K. SCHREMS, *Lexikon für Theologie und Kirche,* ed. J. HOFER and K. RAHNER (2d, new ed. Freiburg 1957–65) 3:195, bibliography. F. L. KERZE, *The Catholic Encyclopedia,* ed. C. G. HERBERMANN et al. (New York 1907–14) 4:678.

[J. E. KOEHLER]

DEHON, LÉON GUSTAVE, VEN.

Founder of the Priests of the Sacred Heart of Jesus; b. March 14, 1843, La Capelle (Aisne), France; d. Aug. 12, 1925, Brussels, Belgium. After gaining a doctorate in civil law at the Sorbonne (1864), he entered the French seminary in Rome, where he was ordained (1868) and was granted doctorates in philosophy, theology, and canon law after attending the Gregorian University and the Apollinaris. At Vatican Council I he was one of four French priests who acted as stenographers. His record of the proceedings has been published as *Diario del Concilio Vaticano I,* edited by V. Carbone (Vatican City 1962). When he returned to his native Diocese of Soissons (1871), he became a curate in Saint-Quentin. Between 1871 and 1877 Dehon was active in the social apostolate in Saint-Quentin, where he associated himself with the *Oeuvre des cercles* recently started by Albert de MUN, opened centers for social studies, organized a society for young workers, and sought to instill in employers a sense of their Christian responsibilities. In 1877 Canon (since 1876) Dehon founded the Oblates of the Sacred Heart as a diocesan congregation, and in 1878 he pronounced his first vows, taking as his name in religion John of the Heart of Jesus. The purpose of the institute was to spread the reign of the Sacred Heart by means of the sacred ministry, by education, and especially by social works. In 1878 Dehon allied with his congregation a pious association dedicated to reparation and open to priests and laymen. The early years of the Oblates proved very difficult, especially because of certain errors concerning spirituality within the group. This led to a Roman decision pronouncing the congregation's dissolution (December of 1883). As a result of the intervention of the bishop of Soissons, this decision was quickly withdrawn and the organization was permitted in March of 1884 to continue under the new name of Priests of the SACRED HEART OF JESUS. In 1884 Leo XIII gave papal recognition to the congregation, which then had 78 members in eight houses. Definitive approval of the Holy See came in 1923. In 1886 Dehon was elected superior general for life, meanwhile continuing his social apostolate. In 1897 he was named a consultor of the Congregation of the Index. Dehon wrote numerous articles for newspapers and periodicals, and published several books on social problems, on various current questions, and on devotional topics, designed especially to spread devotion to the Sacred Heart. When France outlawed religious institutes in 1901, Dehon was forced into exile. The mother-house of the congregation was transferred in 1906 to Brussels, where Dehon lived until his death. His cause for beatification was introduced in Rome in 1960. On March 8, 1997, Pope John Paul II declared him venerable.

Bibliography: E. B. CAPORALE, *Leone Dehon scrittore* (Bologna 1979). J. CHRISTEN, *Le Père Dehon* (Clermont-Ferrand 1944). H. DORRESTEIJN, *Leven en persoonlijkeid van Pater Dehon* (Maastricht 1949); *Dictionnaire de spiritualité ascétique et mystique. Doctrine et histoire,* ed. M. VILLER et al. (Paris 1932) 3:105–115. A. DUCAMP, *Le Père Dehon et son oeuvre* (Bruges 1936). C. KANTERS, *Le T. R. P. Léon Dehon* (2d ed. Bruges 1932). G. MANZONI,

Leone Dehon e il suo (Bologna 1989). *Nuove mete dell'azione sociale: la "Rerum novarum" tra passato e futuro*, ed. A. CAVAGNA (Bologna 1992). J. F. DE OLIVEIRA, *Por causa de um certo reino: história de Leão João Dehon e sua incrível paz inquieta* (São Paulo 1978). R. PRELOT, *L'Oeuvre sociale du chanoine Dehon* (Paris 1936). *Rerum Novarum en France: le père Dehon et l'engagement social de l'Église*, ed. Y. LEDURE (Paris 1991). R. AUBERT, *Dictionnaire d'histoire et de géographie ecclésiastiques*, ed. A. BAUDRILLART et al. (Paris 1912) 14:162–165. G. FREDIANI, *Un apostolo dei tempi nuovi: P. Leone G. Dehon* (Rome 1960).

[J. T. O'CONNOR]

DE HUECK DOHERTY, CATHERINE

Pioneer among the Catholic laity in North America in implementing the social doctrine of the Church; b. Nijni-Novgorod (present Gorki), Russia, Aug. 15, 1896; d. Combermere, Ontario, Canada, Dec. 14, 1985. Foundress of Madonna House Apostolate, Combermere, and of FRIENDSHIP HOUSE in Canada and the United States in the 1930s and 1940s.

The family lived in Ekaterinoslav (Russia), Alexandria (Egypt), India, and Paris before finally settling down in St. Petersburg. Catherine's mother communicated to her an extraordinary faith in the presence of Christ in the poor. Though a communicant in the RUSSIAN ORTHODOX CHURCH, Catherine studied in the convent schools of the Sisters of Sion in both Alexandria and Paris. In 1912 Catherine married Boris de Hueck. World War I found them both with the 130th Division on the Western Front. As a nurse she was decorated on several occasions for bravery. Escaping to Finland after the Revolution, she and Boris ran into Bolshevik sympathizers who almost succeeded in starving them to death. Catherine made a promise to God that if she survived she would give Him her life.

The couple made their way to Scotland and then to England, where Catherine de Hueck was received into the Catholic Church. In 1921 they emigrated to Toronto, Canada, where a son, George, was born to them in July of that year.

De Hueck eventually joined the Chatauqua circuit as a lecturer on Russia and communism. Such activities brought her again into wealth. But the promise made in Finland would not leave her. She kept hearing the words of the Gospel: "Go, sell all you possess." Meanwhile her marriage to Boris had been under strain due to the revolution, differing personalities, and a growing divergence in goals. In the early 1930s they separated, eventually obtaining an ecclesiastical annulment.

Friendship House. The baroness believed living the gospel without compromise was the only answer to the social problems of the time and the appeal of communism. She opened Friendship House, a settlement house in the slum area of Toronto where she and a small band of followers served meals, handed out clothes, and conducted classes in the social teachings of the Church. Under the spiritual guidance of Father Paul of Graymoor they formed themselves into a dedicated band with promises and a simple rule of life.

Soon opposition developed: a rumor spread that de Hueck herself was a communist. Misunderstandings also developed on the parochial level. The archbishop of Toronto supported her, but unable to work in a climate of suspicion, she moved to the United States. At the suggestion of Father John LAFARGE, SJ, in 1938 she opened Friendship House in Harlem, N.Y. As in Toronto, others were attracted by her life, and a dedicated laity formed into a small movement around her. In 1943, Catherine married Eddie Doherty, a well known newspaperman of the time.

Madonna House. Eventually problems also arose in the Friendship House in Harlem. In addition to disagreements about practices and structures, a deeper rift opened when some members wanted to focus completely on interracial work. De Hueck Doherty always believed her vocation was broader, "to restore all things to Christ." At a painful convention in Chicago in 1946, she retained nominal status as foundress. But on May 17, 1847, she went with Eddie Doherty to Combermere in the rural areas of Ontario where she established Madonna House and where the culmination of her life's work was to begin.

Canonically Madonna House is a Public Association of the Faithful under the bishop of Pembroke, Ontario. In actuality, it is an evangelical community, inspired by Catherine's vision and imbued with her spirit. By the time of her death in 1985, the Madonna House community had about 150 Catholic laymen, laywomen, and priests. Small mission houses were opened, mostly in North America, but eventually in the West Indies, England, France, and Africa. By 1987 there were 22 missions. In addition there were about 70 associate priests, and several associate bishops and deacons.

As her own spiritual life matured, she was better able to communicate to the West the treasures of holy Russia. Her spiritual classic, *Poustinia*, is a call to prayer and the "desert" of the heart. *Sobornost* describes a unity in the Holy Spirit beyond any human effort or model. *The People of the Towel and the Water* reveals the gospel dimensions of the ordinary life.

During her lifetime de Hueck Doherty influenced millions of people and received many awards, among them the pontifical medal "Pro Ecclesia et Pontifice" and, in 1977, the Order of Canada, the country's highest civilian honor. Her deeper personal life with God, found in her diaries and private writings, is still to be made known. She had an extraordinary love for the Church as the radiant Bride of Christ. She insisted that all the baptized were called to love with God and to become icons of His presence in their everyday lives. Many consider her a truly prophetic voice, one of the authentic teachers of the gospel in the twentieth century.

Bibliography: C. DE HUECK DOHERTY, *Fragments of My Life* (Notre Dame 1979); *My Russian Yesterdays* (Milwaukee 1951); *Friendship House* (New York 1946). E. DOHERTY, *Tumbleweed* (Milwaukee 1948). R. WILD, *Journey to the Lonely Christ* (New York 1987); "A Visit to Madonna House and Mrs. Doherty," *Crux of Prayer* (Albany, N.Y. 1976). O. TANGHE, *As I Have Loved You* (Dublin 1987); "Catherine de Hueck Doherty: A Twentieth-Century Spirituality," *The Canadian Catholic Review* (Saskatoon Sept. 1987).

[R. WILD]

DEICOLUS OF LURE, ST.

One of the famous Irish *peregrini minores;* d. c. 625. Deicolus (Deel, Deicola, Delle, Deille, Desle, or the Irish, Dichul) accompanied COLUMBAN to LUXEUIL in France. When Columban was expelled in 610, Deicolus went with him but became too ill to continue. He built a hermitage in the vale of Orignon in the Vosges mountains in Burgundy, and in time he was joined by others. This became the great Abbey of Lure (later united to MURBACH), and a monk of this abbey wrote his life some 300 years after Deicolus died at an advanced age.

Feast: Jan. 18.

Bibliography: J. COLGAN, *Acta Sanctorum Hiberniae*, ed. B. JENNINGS (Louvain 1645; repr. Dublin 1948) 115–127. *Acta Sanctae Sedis* Jan. 2:564–574. *Monumenta Germaniae Historica: Scriptores* 15.2:674–682. L. BESSON, *Mémoire historique sur l'abbaye et la ville de Lure* (Besançon 1846). W. WATTENBACH, *Deutschlands Geschichtsquelen im Mittelalter bis zur Mitte des 13. Jh.* (Stuttgart-Berlin 1904) 1:116, n. 2. J. F. KENNEY, *The Sources for the Early History of Ireland*, v. 1: *Ecclesiastical* (New York 1929) 208. L. GOUGAUD, *Gaelic Pioneers of Christianity*, tr. V. COLLINS (Dublin 1923) 134–135. J. M. B. CLAUSS, *Die Heiligen des Elsass* (Düsseldorf 1935). J. GIRARDOT, *La Vie de saint Desle. . .* (Lure 1946). R. AIGRAIN, *Catholicisme* 3:545–546.

[R. T. MEYER]

DEISM

Until the 19th century the terms "deism" and "theism," one with a Latin root *(deus)* and the other with a Greek root (θεός), were used interchangeably. Since that

Lord Herbert of Cherbury, the Father of Deism. (The Library of Congress)

time, however, the custom has been to use the words in a mutually exclusive sense. A number of quite divergent theological and philosophical positions are now indicated by the term "deism," but they resemble one another in that all reject one or more of the traditional Christian theses concerning the relationship that exists between God and the universe.

Kinds of Deism. One form of deism holds that God created this universe, either *ex nihilo* or from a preexisting "chaos"; that all things in the universe, including man, are directed by divine providence; and that there is a life-after-death in which God will reward the good and punish the wicked. Divine revelation is rejected, however, and it is maintained that man must depend upon his reason alone to give him some knowledge of the existence and nature of God and of man's moral duties.

A second form of deism differs from the first only by asserting that there is no future life, that man is rewarded or punished in this life. A third and more radical form claims that divine providence does not extend to the moral actions of man, but only to nature. It asserts that whatever happiness or sorrow man experiences before his final annihilation in death has no relation to divine judgments; virtue is its own reward.

The most extreme form of deism retains from Christianity only the notions that an intelligent and powerful God brought this world into being, though by imposing order on preexisting matter, and that He devised the natural laws according to which the universe functions; however, this God does not intervene at all in the functioning of the universe. There are no exceptions to natural laws; there are no miracles; and God is not concerned at all with the individual human being. Nevertheless, man's own happiness requires that he recognize and admire the Creator and that he deal justly with his fellow men. But experience led certain deists, notably VOLTAIRE, to maintain that such a view of the universe is suitable only for the well educated. Ordinary men, if they are to be kept in order, must be told that an eternity of damnation awaits them if they do not conform to the traditional standards of truth and honesty.

Besides this division of deism into types characterized by the degree to which Christian doctrine is rejected, deists can be classified according to the general trend of their writings. Deism that concentrates on attacking Christianity (the historicity of Scripture, the possibility of miracles, the efficacy of the Sacraments, etc.) is termed "critical," while deism that concerns itself principally with attaining to a knowledge of the existence and nature of God and to an understanding of natural morality is called "constructive." In many deistic writings, of course, there are both "critical" and "constructive" elements. In general, the arguments of critical deists would be thought naïve today, for they are directed against a fundamentalist interpretation of Scripture, an uncritical taste for the miraculous and quite a mechanical view of the Sacraments. That is, they are opposed to a caricature of Christianity, though Christians who resembled the caricature were all too numerous, among both the laity and the clergy, when such deism was developing.

Historical origins. A number of important factors contributed to the rise of deism in the 17th century. The Protestant view that Scripture interpreted in isolation from ecclesiastical tradition is the ultimate guide to faith had by this time presented Englishmen with innumerable scriptural problems that seemed incapable of reasonable solution. It appeared that men of a critical turn of mind could no longer accept the notion that God had truly revealed Himself in the Old and New Testaments. These books, it seemed, were simply compilations of ancient literary works bearing the scientific inaccuracies, cultural oddities, and sapient insights characteristic of other classical writings. The conclusion drawn was that man must depend upon himself, his experience and reason, to attain to a knowledge of God. The popularity of the doctrine of John Locke, that ideas are not prenatally impressed upon the mind by God (a repudiation of Descartes's widely accepted INNATISM), but have their origin in sense experience, served to weaken further the notion of any special bond existing between God and human knowledge.

Scientific Revolution. Perhaps the strongest element contributing to the development of deistic thought was the rise of the new sciences. Discoveries of the 16th and 17th centuries made it imperative for Europeans to change their basic ideas of the universe; and since traditional theology had made extensive use of the old thought patterns, theological revisions were needed. However, it was extremely difficult for most theologians to separate the many layers of centuries-old scientific accretions from the deposit of faith. The result was that large numbers of intellectuals were needlessly presented with the necessity of repudiating either the new sciences or the old religion.

This was particularly the case where theology and physics had become intertwined. The old Christianized Aristotelian physics had supposed a certain relationship of the universe to God that was completely overthrown by the physics of Galileo and Newton. According to the Aristotelian conception, celestial bodies traveling about the earth in perfect circles were directly dependent upon a First Unmoved Mover to conserve them in motion. Gradually, through the work of Copernicus, Kepler, Galileo and Newton, the view became prevalent that two forces, gravitational attraction and inertia, were adequate to account for their movement and its mathematical regularity. Thus it was no longer necessary to posit the existence of God on this account. Although Newton thought divine intervention was still periodically necessary to set things aright after planets had strayed slightly from their orbits, later calculations showed that more refined laws of mechanics could account for the seeming perturbations, without God's special causality. It became, in fact, common to assert that a perfect workman, as God was taken to be, would produce a world machine so perfectly balanced that no adjustments need ever be made. All of this encouraged the form of deism that assigned to God only the role of original architect and initial mover; it seemed that traditional notions of divine providence could not be reconciled with a universe whose actions were all determined by physical laws.

Travel and non-Christian cultures. A less important factor contributing to the development of deism was the impact of the many written accounts of travels to hitherto unknown lands. Explorers and travelers had come upon peoples who had had no contact with Christianity, but who seemed nonetheless to have highly developed systems of morality and admirable religious principles. The deists argued from this that human reason was sufficient to establish religion and morality; man did not need

God's revelation of a "divine positive law." Moreover, some deists asserted, recently discovered non-Christian cultures often exhibited a morality superior to that practiced in Christian Europe. It must be noted, however, that much of this travel literature contained gross exaggerations and exhibited none of the cautious scholarship characteristic of present-day anthropology.

The net result of this religious, scientific, and cultural ferment in Europe was that large numbers of educated men were inclined to reject traditional religious principles as guides to life; instead, they turned to the new sciences, to human reason, to the spirit of the ENLIGHTENMENT.

British Deists. In England the first important deistic work, the *De Veritate, prout distinguitur a Revelatione, a Verisimili, Possibili, et a Falso,* by Lord HERBERT OF CHERBURY, was published in 1624. It won Cherbury the title of Father of Deism, and was followed in 1696 by John Toland's *Christianity not Mysterious, or, a treatise shewing, That there is nothing in the Gospel contrary to Reason, nor above it: and that no Christian Doctrine can be properly call'd a Mystery.* Toland attempted to demonstrate that true religion and natural morality are synonymous. Notions that transcend reason, such as the Trinity, the Incarnation and grace, ought to be set aside as superstitions. In 1713, Anthony Collins' *Discourse of Free-Thinking, occasion'd by the rise and growth of a sect call'd Free-Thinkers* called for a rejection of the Christian doctrines of divine judgment and future retribution. Collins asserted that men would be more truly moral if they were presented with a purely natural system of ethics. In 1724 Collins published, in his *Discourse of the Grounds and Reasons of the Christian Religion,* an extensive criticism of the prophecies of the Old Testament and the miracles of the New.

Another attack on tradition was made by Matthew Tindal in his *Christianity as old as the Creation: or, the Gospel a republication of the Religion of Nature* (1730), which came to be called "the deists' Bible." As the title indicates, Tindal claimed that the Gospels, if interpreted correctly, taught only a natural religion, a natural ethics. His conclusion was:

> Nothing can be requisite to discover true Christianity and to preserve it in its native purity free from all superstition, but after a strict scrutiny to admit nothing to belong to it except what our reason tells us is worthy of having God for its author. And if it be evident that we cannot discern whether any instituted religion contains everything worthy, and nothing unworthy, of a Divine original, except we can antecedently by our reason discern what is or is not worthy of having God for its author, it necessarily follows that natural and re-vealed religion can't differ, because what reason shows to be worthy of having God for its author must belong to natural religion, and whatever reason tells us is unworthy of having God for its author can never belong to the true revealed religion.

It would be difficult to state more clearly what is essential to all the various forms of deism.

Deism on the Continent. In France, early in the 18th century, a number of deistic works circulated clandestinely in manuscript form. One of them, first published about 1750, was the anonymous *Pensées sur la religion dont on cherche de bonne foy l'éclaircissement,* also known as *Doutes sur la religion* and *Examen de la religion.* The deism found in this work is principally of the critical type, with attacks on the historicity of Scripture and such doctrines as the Trinity, original sin and redemption. It maintained that true religion is founded on reason and on the "golden rule." A similar work, *Analyse de la religion chrétienne,* attributed to Dumarsais, was also passed about secretly during the same period. However, French deism attained its full growth only with the ENCYCLOPEDISTS, notably Voltaire and Jean Jacques Rousseau.

In France deism took on some characteristics that are not to be found to the same extent in the English variety; that is, French deism was bound up with an intense anti-clericalism and a strong opposition to the royal government. Moreover, in France the introduction of deistic thought led more quickly and more often to a full-fledged ATHEISM, as exemplified in the later writings of Denis DIDEROT, the principal author and the editor of the *Encyclopédie;* in the *Système de la Nature* of HOLBACH; and in *L'homme machine* of LaMettrie.

In Germany, the growth of deistic thought enjoyed the patronage of Frederick II, the "philosopher king," at whose court several of the French Encyclopedists lived for various periods of time. Gotthold Ephraim LESSING popularized the deists' opposition to revealed dogma, particularly in his *Nathan der Weise* (1779) and *Die Erziehung des Menschengeschlechts* (1780). Moses Mendelssohn, a lifelong friend of Lessing and the inspiration for *Nathan der Weise,* was influential in the Jewish "enlightenment," the HASKALAH. Reform Judaism stems in large part from Mendelssohn's work.

American Deists. While German deism had little or no effect on American thought in the 18th century, British and French enunciations of deistic ideas had echoes in writings of several Americans, notably in *Reason, the only Oracle of Man, or a compenduous system of natural religion* by Ethan Allen (1784), and *The Age of Reason* by Thomas PAINE (1794), the latter work unjustly called "the atheists' Bible." Many passages in the works of

Benjamin Franklin and Thomas Jefferson indicate that these men also were deists. For Americans the attraction toward deism was largely what it had been for their British and French predecessors, namely, that in the spirit of the Enlightenment it favored science and reason over revealed religion and faith. Also, it was simpler to maintain that whatever happens in this universe results exclusively from empirically verifiable physical and psychological laws than to be faced with the problem of how to reconcile these laws with the Christian doctrine of divine providence.

In America, moreover, still another factor favored the growth of deistic ideas. The widespread Calvinistic doctrine of PREDESTINATION was scarcely compatible with the developing optimistic temper of the American people. One obvious alternative was the deistic system, which assured man that his efforts toward a better life would not be frustrated by any arbitrary divine decree of reprobation. However, in America, as in England and France, deism was never a position consciously assumed by the masses; its appeal was restricted in large part to those with some degree of scientific learning. Deism survives today principally as a theory in certain branches of freemasonry and as the point of view of some members of the Unitarian and Universalist Churches (*see* UNITARIANS; UNIVERSALISTS).

See Also: THEISM; FREETHINKERS; AGNOSTICISM.

Bibliography: C. L. BECKER, *The Heavenly City of the Eighteenth Century Philosophers* (New Haven 1932). C. M. CRIST, *The Dictionnaire philosophique portatif and the Early French Deists* (Brooklyn 1934). P. HAZARD, *European Thought in the Eighteenth Century: From Montesquieu to Lessing,* tr., J. L. MAY (New Haven 1954). R. Z. LAUER, *The Mind of Voltaire: A Study in His 'Constructive Deism'* (Westminster, Md. 1961). F. R. MANUEL, *The Eighteenth Century Confronts the Gods* (Cambridge, Mass. 1954). H. M. MORAIS, *Deism in Eighteenth Century America* (New York 1960). R. R. PALMER, *Catholics and Unbelievers in Eighteenth Century France* (Princeton 1939).

[R. Z. LAUER]

DE KONINCK, CHARLES

Philosopher and theologian who exerted profound influence on Catholic philosophy in North America; b. Thourout, Belgium, July 29, 1906; d. Rome, Feb. 13, 1965. De Koninck went to Detroit with his parents as a child but returned to Belgium in 1917 to attend the College at Ostend. He entered the Dominican Order, but was dispensed from his vows for reasons of health. He pursued graduate studies at Louvain, receiving the Ph.D. in 1934; subsequently he received the S.T.D. from Laval, where he was professor of natural philosophy from 1934 until his death. He married Zoe Decruydt in 1933; they had 12 children.

De Koninck was dean of the faculty of philosophy at Laval from 1939 to 1956 and was reappointed to that post in June 1964. From 1957 to 1963 he was visiting professor in the fall semester at the University of Notre Dame. He held similar posts at the University of Mexico (1944), McMaster University, Ontario (1959), and Purdue University (1960). He was a member of the Third Order of St. Dominic, the Royal Society of Canada, the Roman Academy of Saint Thomas, the Canadian Association of Philosophy, and the American Catholic Philosophical Association; the last-named organization awarded him the Cardinal Spellman-Aquinas medal in 1964. He was a Commander of the Order of St. Gregory.

The key to De Koninck's thought is found in his lifelong devotion to the doctrine of Thomas Aquinas. This devotion manifested itself in writings that range from painstaking textual commentaries to daring extensions of Thomistic doctrine in an effort to cope with 20th-century issues. The latter type of writing involved De Koninck in many controversies; from the outset of his writing career he inspired vigorous attack and impassioned defense.

His work on the common good was directed against those he called personalists, men who, seeing that neither the family nor political community could constitute man's ultimate good, were led to assert that the good of the individual takes precedence over the common good. De Koninck argued that the inadequacy of lesser common goods can be read only in terms of a more comprehensive good, that the common good always takes primacy over the merely private good.

De Koninck's most influential tenet was the claim that traditional natural philosophy and recent natural science, though dramatically different in method, are essentially one SCIENCE in the Thomistic sense. Throughout his career, De Koninck made more precise and nuanced this fundamentally unchanged position (*see* PHILOSOPHY AND SCIENCE).

In theology his principal interest was Mariology. Before the promulgation (1950) of the Apostolic Constitution on the Assumption, he published many articles in favor of that doctrine. At the time of his death, as *theologus* of Cardinal Maurice Roy at Vatican Council II, the only layman in such a position, he was concerned with the morality of pills that aid nature in ensuring periods of infertility in women. He had developed a complex but clear argument in favor of the use of such pills that insisted on the traditional doctrine of the primary end of marriage, the *bonum prolis*.

De Koninck's principal works are *De la primauté du bien commun* (Quebec 1943), *Ego Sapientia. La sagesse qui est Marie* (Quebec 1943), *La Piété du Fils. Etudes sur l'Assomption* (Quebec 1954), *The Hollow Universe* (London 1960), *Le Scandale de la Médiation* (Paris 1962), and numerous articles in *Laval théologique et philosophique* (1945–65).

[R. M. MCINERNY]

DE LA CROIX, CHARLES

Missionary; b. Hoorebeke-Saint-Corneille, Flanders, Oct. 28, 1792; d. Ghent, Belgium, Aug. 20, 1869. As a seminarian in Ghent, he met Charles Nerinckx, already a missionary in Kentucky, who influenced him to serve in America. Ordained a priest in 1817 by Bp. Louis W. Dubourg, of Louisiana, he and other clerical recruits sailed that year for America with the prelate. By May 1818, De la Croix was acting as architect and supervisor for the first seminary building at "The Barrens," Perry County, Mo. He later superintended the "Bishop's Farm" at Florissant, ministered to the pioneer group of Religious of the Sacred Heart headed by (Bl.) Philippine Duchesne, served as missionary among the natives on the Gasconade and Osage Rivers, and collaborated with the early Jesuits, Vincentians, and Brothers of the Christian Schools in Missouri. In 1823 he became pastor of St. Michael's, Convent, La., where he built a new church in 1832. He also temporarily administered the neighboring church of St. James, Cabahanoce, and laid the groundwork for the future St. John the Evangelist Cathedral parish in Vermilionville, now Lafayette, La. In 1834 he returned to Belgium, and in 1849 became a canon of the Cathedral of St. Bavo, Ghent.

Bibliography: *American Catholic Historical Researches* 24 (1907) 59–61.

[H. C. BEZOU]

DELANOUE, JEANNE (JOAN), ST.

Known in religion as Joan of the Cross (Jeanne de la Croix); founder of the Sisters of Saint Anne of the Providence of Samur; b. June 18, 1666 at Samur, Anjou, France; d. Aug. 17, 1736 at Fencet, France.

The youngest of 12 children, Joan's early years were not edifying: she was small, coquettish, avaricious, and quick tempered. When her widowed mother's death left her proprietress of the family's religious goods store, Jeanne planned to enrich herself on pilgrims to the shrine of Our Lady of Ardilliers. Intent upon making money, she scandalized her neighbors by keeping the shop open on Sundays. Her miserly nature is revealed in her refusal to keep food on hand so that she could tell beggars that she

had nothing to give them. The Holy Spirit spoke to her through two different individuals in 1698. One was a dubious visionary named Françoise Suchet, whose pious exhortation stirred Joan. The other was Abbé Genetau, whose conversations caused her to reform her life. After performing severe penance she was granted an ecstasy in which her vocation to help the poor was revealed. She began this at once by giving away her goods to the poor and living a life of austerity and penance. Her home, known as "Providence House," in which she cared for orphans, was destroyed in an earthquake in 1703. She started over, closed her shop in order to devote herself full–time to charity, and gathered like–minded women, including her niece, to found formally the Sisters of St. Anne (later called the Sisters of Providence) in 1704. The sisters cared for single mothers, prostitutes—anyone in distress. Jeanne had a devotion to the Christ Child, which led her to her particular work with orphans. Her rigorous personal life drew criticism from the local bishop, from Jansenists, and from Louis de Montfort until her sincerity was proved. The congregation received diocesan approval in 1709. When she died peacefully at the age of 70, the people of Saumur praised her goodness. She was beatified in 1947, and canonized by John Paul II on Oct. 31, 1982.

Feast: Aug. 17.

Bibliography: *Acta Apostolicae Sedis* 40 (1948): 314–19; 79 (1987): 233–37. J. L. BAUDOT and L. CHAUSSIN, *Vies des saints et des bienheureux selon l'ordre du calendrier avec l'historique des fêtes,* ed. by the Benedictines of Paris, 12 v. (Paris 1935–56) 8:311–317. *L'Osservatore Romano,* English edition, no. 45 (1982):1, 2, 12. M.–C. GUILLERAND–CHAMPENIER, *Les Servantes des pauvres de la Providence de Saumur* (Chambray 1985). M. LAIGLE, *La Mère des pauvres* (Saint–Hilaire–Saint–Florent, France 1968). J. NICODÈME, *Quand souffle l'Esprit: itinéraire spirituel de Jeanne Delanoue* (Saint–Hilaire–Saint–Florent 1970). F. TROCHU, *La Bienheureuse Jeanne Delanoue,* new ed. (Paris 1950).

[K. I. RABENSTEIN]

DELANY, SELDEN PEABODY

Author; b. Fond du Lac, Wis., June 24, 1874; d. Highland Mills, N.Y., July 5, 1935. He was the son of Edmund and Evelyn (Peabody) Delany. In 1896 he graduated from Harvard University, where he was converted from Presbyterianism to High Church Episcopalianism. Three years later, after study at Western Theological Seminary, Chicago, Ill., he was ordained to the Episcopal ministry. After serving as curate at Fond du Lac, Wis.; Boston, Mass.; and Menasha and Appleton, Wis., he became dean (1907–15) of the Episcopal cathedral in Milwaukee, Wis.; from 1915 to 1929 he was curate at the Church of St. Mary the Virgin, New York City, where he edited the *American Church Monthly;* he was promoted to rector in 1930. He resigned his rectorship and received conditional baptism on June 24, 1930, at Our Lady of Lourdes Church, New York City. Following study at the Beda College in Rome (1930–34) he was ordained on March 17, 1934. On his return to New York, he became chaplain at Thevenet Hall, Highland Mills, N.Y., where he remained until his death.

Delany had long been a leader of the High Church movement in America, and some 200 Episcopalians, including a dozen members of the clergy, followed him into the Catholic Church. He described the process of his conversion in *Why Rome?* (1930), where he stated that the primacy of the papacy was the chief obstacle to his conversion. He revealed, too, that he had not previously read *Apostolicae curae,* Leo XIII's encyclical declaring Anglican orders null and void, having accepted as adequate the reply of the Anglican archbishops to the encyclical. Delany was also the author of *Rome from Within* (1935) and *Married Saints* (1935).

[F. D. COHALAN]

DE LA SALLE, JOHN BAPTIST, ST.

Founder of the Institute of the Brothers of the Christian Schools, religious educator; b. Reims, Apr. 30, 1651; d. Saint-Yon, Rouen, Apr. 7, 1719.

John Baptist, the eldest son of a well-to-do bourgeois family, was appointed canon of the cathedral chapter at Reims at age 16. After obtaining a master of arts degree from the Collège des Bons Enfants, he entered the Seminary of Saint-Sulpice and attended courses at the Sorbonne. When his studies were interrupted by the death of his parents, he enrolled in the University of Reims, was ordained in 1678, and received the degree of doctor of theology in 1680. Despite the unsuitability of his upbringing for the work and the social gulf separating the rich and the poor in 17th-century France, he became interested, through a meeting with M. Nyel from Rouen, in assisting the poorly prepared schoolteachers Nyel had recruited to open schools for the poor. The idea of devoting himself completely to this enterprise had never occurred to him and, on his own testimony, the association with the uncouth schoolteachers was distasteful in the extreme. Once he became convinced that his divinely appointed mission was to conduct these schools for the poor, he threw himself wholeheartedly into the work, left home and family, resigned his canonry, gave away his personal fortune and reduced himself to the level of the poor to whom he henceforth consecrated his life.

Founding of the Brothers. His first concern was to train the teachers Nyel had recruited. He brought them into his home, taught them good manners and self-discipline, provided them with religious motivation for their work, and discussed with them the best method of coping with the large number of poor boys in their classes. As Nyel faded from the scene, De La Salle took over the supervision of the teachers in three schools in Reims and three more in the surrounding towns of Rethel, Guise, and Laon. Discouraged by the hard and unrewarding life, the first teachers gave up the work, but other young men of even better quality replaced them. It was at this point in 1682 that De La Salle left his own home, moved with them to a rented house in a poor neighborhood, and gradually formed them into a community of celibate laymen living a religious lifestyle.

On Trinity Sunday, 1686, after lengthy deliberation, De La Salle and 12 of the teachers bound themselves by a vow of obedience for three years, renewable annually, formalized the adoption of a distinctive habit that was neither clerical nor secular and the title BROTHERS OF THE CHRISTIAN SCHOOLS. The drawing up of a rule, however, was postponed until further experience had been gained. Neither the founder nor the brothers wanted to conform to any of the forms of religious life then prevalent in the church. They were not to be cloistered monks, medicant friars, or clerks regular, but dedicated teaching brothers with a religious lifestyle, derived to some extent from other traditions, but modified to suit their distinctive mission. Realizing that the success of the first schools was due to the teamwork of the brothers, so different from the isolated schoolmasters of the time, the brothers established a policy that schools would be conducted "together and by association," never assigning only one brother alone to a school. When De La Salle was unable to accommodate requests for a single brother for country parishes, he established in Reims a sort of normal school, the first of its kind, to train lay teachers for the country parishes. In later years, two more such schools would be established in the outskirts of Paris.

Up until this time, with a few notable exceptions, the parish charity schools for poor boys were marked by incompetent and poorly motivated teachers, lack of organization, inefficient methods, and the students unkempt, unruly, and frequently absent. Religious instruction was rarely provided or inadequate at best. If the poor were not to be permanently abandoned to ignorance, squalor, and degradation, there was needed a community of religiously dedicated men committed to this apostolate. In his view of faith, De La Salle saw the discrepancy between God's will that "all should be saved and come to the knowledge of the truth," and the situation of the poor youngsters who had little hope of salvation either in this world or the next. The term "Christian Schools" was adopted to indicate that they would be characterized by quality education provided by dedicated teachers free of charge, religious instruction, a practical curriculum, and good discipline. Eventually the schools became so efficient that they attracted boys without charge from families that could afford the fees charged by the schoolmaster of the "little schools" as they were called. This would later lead to trouble.

When the Archbishop of Reims offered to sponsor and finance the work of the brothers, provided that they restrict their activity to the archdiocese, in 1688 De La Salle accepted an offer from the Sulpicians to open a school and center his activity in Paris. After initial success in the capital the enterprise began to fall apart. Morale was low with some brothers leaving, many sick, and all of them overworked. De La Salle himself fell ill, recovering only after a close brush with death. The prospects seemed so discouraging at this point that he and two companions vowed never to abandon the work even if only they remained and had to beg for bread to survive. Eventually he was able to restore morale, open a novitiate and, after extensive consultation with the brothers, develop a rule combining inspiration and specific practices of religious living with policies and procedures relating to the conduct of the schools. In 1694, a general chapter was held that elected De la Salle as superior with the stipulation that thenceforth the society would remain exclusively lay and that no one in Holy Orders would be accepted as superior. On that occasion, De La Salle and 12 of the principal brothers bound themselves by vows of association to conduct gratuitous schools with stability and obedience, an important step in establishing the new society on a firm basis.

Spread of the Institute. In the closing years of the 17th century, schools were opened in Chartres and Calais, while in Paris there were several new ventures: a new center to train lay teachers for the country parishes, a Sunday academy providing working teenagers with either the elementary education they never had or classes in more advanced subjects combined with suitable religious instruction, and a new house for the novitiate. King James II of England, living in exile, confided to De La Salle 50 Irish youths, sons of his faithful followers. The king visited the novitiate house in Paris where the lads were housed and educated, probably in advanced subjects, encouraging the brothers in the work they were doing. In Calais a second school was opened near the seaport where courses in navigation were added to the curriculum for the children of mariners.

The first decade of the 18th century saw the beginning of a series of persecutions directed primarily at the person of the founder rather than the work of the brothers. It began out of a conflict with the pastors of Saint-Sul-

pice, upon whom De La Salle depended to be allowed to conduct the schools, but who wanted also to have some control over the internal affairs of the society. At one point the cardinal was persuaded to appoint another superior to replace De La Salle, but the brothers obstinately refused to accept anyone but De La Salle as superior. A compromise of sorts was worked out, but the relationship between De La Salle and the local ecclesiastical authorities remained strained. Without the strong support of the parish priest, De La Salle then became the target of the writing masters who brought him to court for violating their monopoly granted by the king for teaching writing, especially teaching teachers of writing in the novitiate and the teacher- training center. At the same time the guild of schoolmasters accused De La Salle of infringing on their franchises granted by the archdiocese by accepting without charge students who could afford to pay. In the system of the time, parish charity schools were restricted to the certified poor. De La Salle eventually lost the court cases, was fined, and forbidden to assign teachers, or to post any signs using a corporate title without "letters patent" from the king. The brothers continued to teach in the schools under the authority of the pastor, but the teacher-training center had to be closed.

In the face of these difficulties De La Salle remained calm, trusting in the providence of God and the work of the institute which he saw as God's work. He did not remain idle, but continued to open schools throughout France beyond the bounds of Paris. In 1702, he sent two brothers to Rome, only one of whom, Br. Gabriel Drolin, remained to keep a presence of the institute in the eternal city. In the following years there were new foundations in Avignon, Dijon, Troyes, Marseilles, Grenoble, Mende and the towns that were centers of Protestant resistance in the southwest, Versailles, and Boulogne.

In 1705, De La Salle took over several new schools in Rouen and then rented an extensive property in Saint-Yon just outside the city where he made his headquarters and reestablished the novitiate. To support the novitiate and to supplement the meager salaries of the brothers, he opened a boarding school. Unlike the colleges in France conducted by other religious congregations intended to cater to the upper classes, Saint-Yon offered a more practical course of studies which excluded the classics and was designed to meet a growing demand of the bourgeoisie for a more vocational-oriented alternative to the traditional curriculum in liberal arts. A separate division was established for delinquent youngsters to provide for the needs of children in need of correction and rehabilitation. A third program was designed for older men, many of them sons of well-known families who had been imprisoned under lettres de cachet. On arrival they had to be kept locked up until they gradually became tractable and in some cases gave proof of genuine conversion. The work of the brothers in such programs became well known and served as models and precedent for similar institutions in the subsequent history of the institute.

The cross followed De La Salle wherever he went and his final years were no exception. The victim of a trumped-up charge of taking advantage of a young ecclesiastic who offered to help establish a new training college for teachers, the founder was condemned in criminal court and forced to flee to the south. At first he was well received, but in Marseilles there soon developed opposition to his person and his policies. His bold anti-Jansenist stance and loyalty to the Holy See was part of it, but so also were his refusal have the brothers tonsured, his insistence that the school brothers live in the newly established novitiate, and his plans to assign brothers wherever they were most needed. Convinced that even some the brothers had abandoned him and that he was becoming an obstacle to the work, he fled to the grotto of the Sainte-Baume where he underwent a devastating experience of "the dark night of the soul." Thinking that perhaps he should leave the brothers to their own devices, he retired to the hermitage of Parmenie outside Grenoble and sought the advice of a Sister Louise, renowned for her gift of spiritual direction. But at that juncture, the principal brothers in Paris, learning of his whereabouts and fearful for the independent future of the institute, wrote a forceful letter commanding him to return in virtue of the vow he had made to obey the body of the society. Priest though he was, on the advice of Sister Louise he accepted the summons from the brothers. He returned to steady the situation in Paris, but gradually handed over the day-to-day operations to Brother Bartholomew who, at a general chapter in 1717, was elected to succeed him as superior, thus averting any danger that the ecclesiastical authorities would impose a priest as superior after his death. He spent the last years of his life at Saint-Yon, counseling the novices, writing meditations for the brothers and his *Method of Interior Prayer,* and revising the rule according to the suggestions from the brothers at the general chapter.

De La Salle died at Saint-Yon on Good Friday, Apr. 7, 1719. Though he had always shunned notoriety and lived in seclusion, the news of his death was followed by a manifestation of public sympathy and veneration. "All Rouen regrets him and looks upon him as a saint," wrote brother Bartholomew to Br. Gabriel Drolin in Rome. De La Salle's nephew, Dom Elie Maillefer OSB, in his biography described him as "kindhearted, generous and sincere," with "a peculiar gift for bringing back to God the most hardened sinners, whose conversion he never undertook in vain." Maillefer went on to explain that "by nature he was resolute and intrepid; he took his stand

after mature reflection, held to it when he thought it was conformable to the will of God, and was always ready to undertake the most difficult things for God's sake." The earliest biography to be published was that by Canon J. B. Blain which appeared in two volumes divided into four books in 1733: *La vie de M. Jean-Baptiste de La Salle, instituteur des Frères des Ecoles chrétiennes.*

After the death of De La Salle, the brothers were successful on obtaining letters patent from King Louis XV in 1724 and approval as a lay institute of pontifical right by the Bull of approbation granted by Pope Benedict XIII in 1725. During the century following the institute expanded throughout France numbering just about 1,000 brothers at the beginning of the French Revolution. All but suppressed during the revolution, the reorganization during the nineteenth century was accompanied by extraordinary growth both in numbers and in missionary activity. By the end of Vatican Council II in 1965 there were more than 16,000 brothers conducting schools in 80 countries on all six continents. In the aftermath of the ensuing changes in church and religious life, the numbers declined, until at the turn of the millennium there were just over 6,000 brothers, less than half of them still active in educational ministry. On the other hand there were new initiatives in favor of direct service of the poor and numerical growth in third world countries. It was also seen as a grace that the Lasallian mission and spirituality were riches to be shared between brothers and lay associates everywhere. Meanwhile, there was a new interest in the life, achievement and vision of John Baptist De La Salle due to the extensive research undertaken by Lasallian scholars, published in the 60 volumes of *Cahiers lasalliens,* and propagated through workshops and formation programs for brothers and lay partners alike with a view to keeping the Lasallian tradition alive and effective in the educational world.

Religious Educator. De La Salle's teaching method is found principally in the *Conduct of Schools,* continually revised during his lifetime in collaboration with the brothers in the light of their experience, and first published in 1720. He was not a theorist; his method of education was strictly practical. Because his schools were always filled to capacity and the classes large, he discarded the tutorial model in use in the charity schools of the time in favor of a simultaneous method, training his teachers to control large groups of pupils by maintaining strict discipline and sub- dividing the classes according to the ability and progress of the pupils. He also discarded the use of Latin, hitherto considered the vehicle for learning to read, and used the vernacular instead. In these matters, which are today taken for granted, he was a pioneer and met with considerable opposition. It was in response to new needs as he met them that led him to establish the schools for training lay teachers, schools for delinquents, and boarding schools with offerings in advanced technical or pre-professional courses, unavailable and unheard of in the colleges and universities at the time.

Convinced that religion was the sound basis of true education, he considered the teaching of religion the most important duty of those entrusted with the training of the young, and the primary reason why the schools were established. He organized the school schedule with a view to maintaining a religious atmosphere, especially by recalling the presence of God at intervals during the day. He regarded the religion lesson as the most important and outlined in detail the method to be used, with emphasis on fundamentals and a level of understanding suitable to the age ability of the students. He published a manual of prayers for use in the schools and a booklet of prayers to be said during Mass. His three-volume work entitled *The Duties of a Christian,* contains a comprehensive exposition of Christian doctrine for the theological education of the teachers and a catechism for use in the schools. The catechism subsequently went through 250 editions, an indication of its enduring value beyond the schools of the brothers. In teaching catechism, De La Salle urged the teachers not to be satisfied with rote memorization and external observance, but ''by touching hearts'' to form their students into convinced disciples of Jesus Christ. In his *16 Meditations for the Time of Retreat* he tells the teachers that they are ''ambassadors and ministers of Jesus Christ,'' so that students would learn from the teacher's love and example what it means to encounter the living Christ. De La Salle had no interest in catechetical teaching apart from the school. He felt that religious education should be integrated with learning the skills needed to succeed in this world. By reason of the importance that he placed on the person of the teacher, he succeeded in raising the hitherto despised function of teaching school to the level not only of a profession but a vocation in the theological sense.

De La Salle was beatified in 1888 and canonized in 1900. During the French Revolution, his tomb was violated but the relics were left intact. They were enshrined at first in Rouen, then at the motherhouse in Lembecq in Belgium until they were moved in 1937 to the generalate in Rome where they are presently venerated. St. John Baptist De La Salle was declared the heavenly patron of all teachers of Christian youth by Pope Pius XII in 1950.

Feast: Apr. 7 (formerly May 15).

Bibliography: For the reproduction of original texts and documents relating to St. John Baptist De La Salle, see *Cahiers lasalliens: Textes-études documents* (Rome 1959) v. 60 to date. J. B. DE LA SALLE, *Oeuvres complètes* (Rome, 1993). Lasallian sources. *The complete works of Saint John Baptist de La Salle,* 6 v. (Romeoville, IL 1988–1990, Landover, MD 1993–2001): *Letters* (v.1), tr. C. MOLLOY, ed. A. LOES; *The Rules of Christian Decorum and Civility* (v. 2), tr. R. ARNANDEZ, ed. G. WRIGHT; Collection of various short treatises (v. 3), tr. W. BATTERSBY, ed. D. BURKE; *Meditations* (v. 4), tr. R. ARNANDEZ and A. LOES, ed. A. LOES and F. HUETHER; *Explanation of the Method of Interior Prayer* (v. 5), tr. R. ARNANDEZ, rev. tr. and ed., D.C. MOUTON; *The Conduct of the Christian Schools* (v. 6), tr. F. DE LA FONTAINERIE and R. ARNANDEZ, ed., W. MANN. In Preparation: the Rule and foundational documents, Instructions and school prayers, duties of a Christian towards God. Lasallian resources; F.E. MAILLEFER and BROTHER BERNARD,*John Baptist de La Salle: Two early Biographies,* tr. W. J. QUINN, rev. tr. of Reims MS of 1740 D.C. MOUTON, ed. P. GRASS (Landover, MD 1996). J. B. BLAIN, *The Life of John Baptist de La Salle, Founder of the Institute of the Brothers of the Christian Schools. A Biography in Three Books,* tr. R. ARNANSEZ, ed. L. SALM (Landover, MD 2000). E. BANNON, The Mind and Heart of St. John Baptist de La Salle (Oxford, nd). W. J. BATTERSBY, De La Salle: A Pioneer of Modern Education (New York, 1949); St. John Baptist de La Salle (London 1957). R.C. BERGER, ed. *Spirituality in the Time of John Baptist de La Salle* (Landover, MD 1999). L. BURKHARD, *Encounters, De La Salle at Parmenie* (Romeoville, IL 1983); *Beyond the Boundaries* (Landover, MD 1994). A. CALCUTT, *De La Salle, a City Saint* (Oxford nd). L. J. COLHOCKER, ed. *So Favored by Grace: Education in the Time of John Baptist de La Salle* (Romeoville, IL 1991). S. GALLEGO, *Vida y Pensiamento de San Juan Bautista De La Salle* (Madrid 1986). W. MANN, ed. *John Baptist de La Salle Today* (Manila 1992). J. PUNGIER, *John Baptist de La Salle: The Message of his Catechism* (Landover, MD 1999). L. SALM, *John Baptist de La Salle: The Formative Years* (Romeoveille, IL 1989; *The Work is Yours* (2d ed. Landover, MD 1996). M. SAUVAGE and M. CAMPOS, *St. John Baptist de La Salle: Announcing the Gospel to the Poor,* tr. M.J. O'CONNELL (Romeoville, IL 1981). L.VARELLA, *Sacred Scripture in the Spirituality of Saint John Baptist de La Salle,* tr. F. VESSEL, ed. D. C. MOUTON (Landover, MD 1999). O. WÜRTH, *John Baptist de La Salle and Special Education: A Study of Saint Yon,* tr. A. LOES, ed. F. HUETHER and B. MINER (Romeoville, IL 1988).

[W. J. BATTERSBY/L. SALM]

DE LA TAILLE, MAURICE

Theologian; b. Semblancy (Indre-et-Loire), France, Nov. 30, 1872; d. Paris, Oct. 23, 1933. After secondary schooling in England under the exiled French JESUITS, he entered the society there in 1890; two of his ten brothers also became Jesuits: a younger, Arthur, who died as a novice, and an older, Timoléon, who survived him as a missionary in China. Maurice studied philosophy at Jersey and theology at Lyon and was ordained at Tours in 1901. From 1905 he taught theology at Angers, and from 1919, at the Gregorian University, Rome. De la Taille interrupted his professorial work in order to serve as a military chaplain during World War I.

The work *Mysterium fidei de augustissimo Corporis et Sanguinis Christi sacrificio et sacramento: Elucidationes L in tres libros distinctae* grew out of de la Taille's study of the Epistle to the Hebrews while he was a young priest. He developed and wrote it during the years at Angers and completed it in 1915, but the war delayed its publication until 1921. A second improved edition appeared in 1924; a third, in 1931, included *Vindiciarum liber unus,* in which de la Taille took issue with the major, persistent objections to his work.

The priority given to sacrifice over Sacrament was more than a superficial pedagogical departure from the usual treatises of the time; the specific novelty of de la Taille's work centered precisely on sacrifice. Cardinal Billot, in returning to St. THOMAS AQUINAS's theology of transubstantiation, had prepared the way for de la Taille's strong rejection of the post-Tridentine theories of the Eucharistic Sacrifice (Billot and others had, of course, also rejected them, but without giving thorough attention to the true idea of sacrifice itself). However, de la Taille did not think it sufficient, as did Billot, to have an "immolation" (regarded as a necessary part of any sacrifice offered by fallen man) that remained purely in the order of sign. He evolved his own distinctive thesis: that the Last Supper and the cross complemented each other as oblation and immolation to form the one redemptive sacrifice and that each Mass is an oblation of the once immolated Christ, now permanently in the state of victimhood (thus the cross is, equivalently, the one immolation with many ritual oblations). This thesis evoked great enthusiasm for its speculative simplicity and the stimulus it gave to solid Eucharistic piety by centering the worshiper's attention strongly on the glorified victim of the cross; however, it also aroused strenuous opposition. De la Taille devoted not only the lengthy *Vindiciarum liber* of the third edition of *Mysterium fidei,* but also numerous articles in periodicals to a defense of this basic thesis; a collection of these appeared as *Esquisse du mystère de la foi suivie de quelques éclaircissements* (Paris 1925) and was translated in 1930 to form, along with further papers written in the intervening years, *The Mystery of Faith and Human Opinion Contrasted and Defined* (London 1930).

De la Taille's principal thesis is today abandoned by the majority of theologians on the grounds that it does not have the basis in the Epistle to the Hebrews and the Church Fathers that de la Taille claimed for it, and that it is inconsistent with the doctrine of the Council of TRENT on the Mass. But even after this rejection, *Mysterium fidei* remains probably the greatest theological work produced since that of M. SCHEEBEN, not only as marking the decisive return to a sound conception of sacrifice nor simply for its ample scope and breadth of vision, but for its permanent contributions to Eucharistic theology in all its aspects and to the integration of this with the rest of dogmatic theology. To these virtues must be added de la Taille's erudition, dialectical skill, and elegant Latin style; his combination of speculative thought with piety, not in artificial juxtaposition but in genuine fusion, his piety emerging organically from his speculative thought.

The fostering of the one was the goal of the other according to de la Taille's own ideal (see *Mysterium fidei* viii).

After *Mysterium fidei,* de la Taille's major theological contribution consisted of three seminal articles on "created actuation by uncreated Act," providing a speculative theory of the supernatural union of God with man in the three pivotal arenas of the Incarnation, sanctifying grace, and the beatific vision. This theory has been adopted and developed by numerous theologians; and though attacked by others, especially of the Thomist school, it seems to have won a permanent place as a synthesizing explanation of the supernatural. De la Taille was supposedly working on a major treatise on grace that would rival his *Mysterium fidei,* but nothing further is known of it.

Other articles of de la Taille touched, though in less original fashion, on problems of mystical prayer and of God's knowledge.

Bibliography: "In Memoriam [P. Mauritius de la Taille]," *Gregorianum* 14 (1933) 635–637. E. HOCEDEZ, "Laudem eorum nuntiet ecclesia (*Eccli.* 44, 15): S. É. le Cardinal Ehrle et le R. P. de la Taille," *Nouvelle revue théologique,* 61 (1934) 595–603. J. LEBRETON, "Le Père Maurice de la Taille: In Memoriam," *Recherches de science religieuse* 24 (1934) 5–11. B. LEEMING, "A Master Theologian: Father Maurice de la Taille," *The Month* 163 (1934) 31–40.

[M. J. O'CONNELL]

DELAWARE, CATHOLIC CHURCH IN

Delaware, named after Thomas West, Lord De la Warr, colonial governor of Virginia, was discovered in 1609 by Henry Hudson in Dutch employ. After an initial unsuccessful settlement by the Dutch West India Company at present Lewes (1632), a permanent establishment was made (1638) by the Swedes at Christianaham, the present Wilmington. The colony was named New Sweden. In 1655 the Dutch regained control of their colony, calling it New Netherlands, and established themselves at New Amstel, present New Castle. In 1664, however, the Dutch in turn were forced to acknowledge the prior claims of the British, and in 1682 Delaware was included in the grant made to William Penn by Charles II. It then became known as "the Three Lower Counties on Delaware" and from 1704 was permitted to have its own legislative assembly at Dover. On Dec. 7, 1789, Delaware, the first colony to ratify the U.S. Constitution, became the first state. During the Civil War Delaware officially sided with the Union cause; but Kent and Sussex were Confederate in their sympathies. Delaware had the smallest slave population of the slave states.

Catholics in Delaware were not tolerated under the Swedes or the Dutch. After it became an English colony, they were theoretically under the same legal and civil disabilities as their coreligionists in England; but, as part of Penn's grant they benefited by his *de facto* toleration. However, this did not extend to their enjoyment of full civil rights for they could not qualify to vote or to hold office without first taking the heretical Test Oath. The legal and teaching professions were closed to them. Possibly because of their small numbers, no outstanding incidents of friction or open hostility are recorded. Throughout the colonial period the Catholic communities at Lewes, Laurel, Murderkill, Dover, Appoquinimink (Odessa), New Castle, and Mt. Cuba were served by the Jesuits from the nearby Maryland missions.

The largest concentration of Catholics during the colonial period developed in the southwest corner of present-day New Castle County. The Jesuits from Cecil County, Maryland, founded a mission there in the Forest of Appoquinimink (now Blackbird) in 1740. Joseph Weldon began this chiefly Irish community in 1701. A second Jesuit mission was established south of Dover in 1747 in the area known as Willow Grove. This community consisted mainly of the Cain, Reynolds, and Lowber families, and was served by the Jesuits until 1785. A third Jesuit mission was established in 1747 in upper New Castle County at Cuba Rock, where Mass was first offered in the home of Con Hollahan, and then at White Clay Creek, where the Jesuits purchased property in 1772.

Early National Catholic Background. The first Catholic church in Delaware was named in honor of St. Mary of the Assumption and was completed at White Clay Creek by 1788. In the 1790s numerous French exiles settled in the city of Wilmington. Two French priests, the first priests to live in Wilmington, offered Masses there on French Street at the home of Colonel John Keating. Two Augustinians, John Rosseter and Matthew Carr, and a Capuchin, Charles Whelan, ministered to the French and Irish in upper Delaware until 1804, when Patrick Kenny, a diocesan priest from Dublin, arrived to begin a thirty-six year long ministry. His church and home were at Coffee Run at White Clay Creek in Mill Creek Hundred. From Coffee Run he served Catholics in Wilmington, New Castle, and some missions in Pennsylvania.

In 1808 Delaware became part of the newly established diocese of Philadelphia. Kenny had laid the cornerstone for a church in New Castle the previous year, and in 1816 he laid the cornerstone for the first Catholic church in Wilmington that was to become a transept of the Cathedral of St. Peter. In 1829 the Rev. George Carrell was assigned to Wilmington, and by 1830 he had promoted the completion of the church of St. Peter in New Castle, and had secured the services of the Daughters of Charity from Emmitsburg, Maryland, to found an orphanage for children of victims of the Du Pont Company explosions. They also began an academy for girls and a parochial school at St. Peter Church in Wilmington. Father Carrell was replaced by Father Patrick Reilly in 1834. In 1839 Father Reilly opened a school for boys at St. Peter, which was so successful that it developed into St. Mary College in 1847. The college prospered until the Civil War and was forced to close in 1866. Father Reilly was appointed pastor of a new parish, St. Mary of the Immaculate Conception on the eastside of Wilmington, in 1858. On Dec. 24,1841, a new church was dedicated near the Du Pont mills on the Brandywine River that was named in honor of St. Joseph. Reverend Bernard McCabe was its first pastor.

Diocese of Wilmington. On March 3, 1868, Pope Pius IX established the Diocese of Wilmington as a suffragan see of the Archdiocese of Baltimore. The new diocese encompassed the entire Delmarva Peninsula: Delaware and the Eastern Shore counties of Maryland and Virginia. In 1972 when the Bay Bridge and Tunnel were completed, the two counties of Virginia were returned to the Richmond diocese.

The first Bishop of Wilmington, Thomas Andrew Becker, was consecrated on Aug. 16, 1868. In 1878 Bishop Becker in a published reply refuted the accusations made against the Church by Alfred Lee, the Episcoplian bishop of Delaware. During his 18 years as bishop of Wilmington, the number of churches doubled and the number of priests in the diocese almost tripled. Despite the noticeable advances of the church in Delaware, Becker asked to be transferred because of what he considered a lack of progess. When in 1896 Becker moved to Savannah, he was succeeded by Alfred Allen Curtis who ministered to the Catholics of Delaware until 1887.

The next two bishops of Wilmington, John J. Monaghan (1897–1925) and Edmond J. Fitzmaurice (1925–1969) guided the church in Delaware for more than 60 years—through two world wars, a depression and great expansion into the suburbs. Both built churches and schools to serve the immigrant population that continued to grow. Bishop Michael W. Hyle, who had been consecrated coadjutor-bishop in 1958, took over leadership of the diocese in 1959. He supported the civil rights movement and attended the first three sessions of the Second Vatican Council, but it was largely left to his successors, Bishops Thomas J. Mardaga (1969–1985), Robert E. Mulvee (1985–1995) and Michael A. Saltarelli (1995–) to implement the renewal called for by the council.

The people of Delaware are predominantly Anglo-Saxon and Celtic in origin, together with considerable numbers of Germans, Italians, Poles, and African-

Americans. In 2000 the population of Delaware was 783,600 of which 18% (205,000) was Catholic. Most of those who identify themselves as Protestants are Methodists, Episcopalians and Presbyterians. There are also many Lutherans, Baptists, Friends, and Jews, with Greek and Russian Orthodox in fewer numbers. Wilmington was once called a Quaker town.

Bibliography: H. C. CONRAD, *History of the State of Delaware from the Earliest Settlement to the Year 1907*, 3 v. (Wilmington 1908). A. F. DIMICHELE, comp., *Coffee Run 1772–1960: The Story of the Beginnings of the Catholic Faith in Delaware* (Wilmington 1960). D. DEVINE, ''Beginnings of the Catholic Church of Wilmington, Delaware'' *Delaware History* 28(1999–2000): 323–344. C. A. H. ESLING, ''Catholicity in the Three Lower Counties, or Planting of the Church in Delaware.'' *Records of the American Catholic Historical Society 1* (March 1886): 117–60. T. J. PETERMAN, *Catholics in Colonial Delmarva* (Devon, Pennsylvania 1996). *The Cutting Edge of Life of Thomas Andrew Becker, the First Catholic Bishop of Wilmington, Delaware and Sixth Bishop of Savannah, Georgia, 1831–1899* (Devon, Pennsylvania 1982). *Catholic Priests of the Diocese of Wilmington, A Jubilee Year 2000 Commemoration,* (Devon, Pennsylvania 2000). R. E. QUIGLEY, ''Catholic Beginnings of the Delaware Valley.'' *History of the Archdiocese of Philadelphia,* J. E. CONNELLY, ed. (Philadelphia 1976). P. J. SCHIERSE, *Laws of the State of Delaware Affecting Church Property* (Washington, D.C. 1963).

[E. B. CARLEY/T.J. PETERMAN]

DELEHAYE, HIPPOLYTE

Hagiographer and Bollandist; b. Anvers, Aug. 19, 1859; d. Brussels, April 1, 1941. Having entered the Society of Jesus in 1876, he joined the BOLLANDISTS in 1891 and became president of the group in 1912, serving as the great master of hagiography until his death. His 50 years of activity in this institution were interrupted only by the war, during which he wrote the life of St. JOHN BERCHMANS from memory. Studying the more ancient martyrs and the saints of the Greek Church, he conducted projects that required indefatigable labor, perspicacious judgment, and rigorous method. In the *Acta Sanctorum* he left three masterpieces: his edition of the *Synaxarium Ecclesiae Constantinopolitanae* (*see* SYNAXARY); a historical commentary of the MARTYROLOGY OF ST. JEROME based on the text established by Dom H. Quentin; and a commentary on the ROMAN MARTYROLOGY discussing its sources and historical value. He compiled catalogues of hagiographical manuscripts, of which the model remains the *Bibliotheca hagiographica graeca* [ed. F. Halkin, 3 v. (Brussels 1957)] and edited either in the *Analecta Bollandiana* or in separate volumes a number of texts: *Saints de Chypre* [*Analecta Bollandiana* 26 (1907) 161–301]; *Les Légendes grecques des saints militaires* (Paris 1909); *Les Saints stylites* (Brussels 1923); *Étude sur le légendier romain: les saints de novembre et décembre* (Brussels

1936). A series of works of historical criticism offering a condensation of its thought and method have become classics of hagiography: *Les Légendes hagiographiques* (3d ed. Brussels 1927); *Les Origines du culte des martyrs* (2d ed. Brussels 1933); *Les Passions des martyrs et les genres littéraires* (Brussels 1921); *Sanctus. Essai sur le culte des Saints dans l'antiquité* (Brussels 1927); *Cinq leçons sur la méthode hagiographique* (Brussels 1934). While new numbers of the *Acta Sanctorum* were not published with the regularity one might have expected under H. Delehaye, his own investigations brought about a fundamental renewal in the methods and substance of hagiography. He untangled problems considered inextricable, such as the evolution of the Martyrology of St. Jerome [*Acta Sanctorum* (November 2) Brussels 1931], and provided scholars with new tools for hagiographical research. His vigorous enthusiasm, extreme competence as a scholar, and the disinterested aid he gave and received from collaborators made him the equal of D. PAPEBROCH, if not the greatest of the Bollandists.

Bibliography: P. PEETERS, *Analecta Bollandiana* 60 (1942) i–lii, list of works; *L'Oeuvre des Bollandistes* (new ed. Brussels 1961). R. AIGRAIN, *L'Hagiographie* (Paris 1953). B. DE GAIFFIER, *Lexikon für Theologie und Kirche,* ed. J. HOFER and K. RAHNER (2d, new ed. Freiburg 1957–65), 3:208. É. DE STRYCKER, *L'Année théologique* 3 (1942) 265–283; *Catholicisme. Hier, aujourd'hui et demain,* ed. G. JACQUEMET (Paris 1947–) 3:562–563.

[P. ROCHE]

DELFINI, JOHN ANTHONY

Theologian; b. Pomponesco, near Cremona, March 26, 1507; d. Bologna, Sept. 5, 1561. He studied at Cremona and Bologna, taught metaphysics in Padua, later at the University of Bologna. He was elected provincial of the Bologna province of the Conventual Franciscans (1548), served as inquisitor of Bologna and Romagna (1550–59), and was elected vicar-general of his order (1559–61). His most important theological works were written in connection with his activities at the Council of Trent: *De Potestate Ecclesiastica* (Venice 1549), *Universale fere Negotium de Ecclesia* (Venice 1552), *De salutari omnium rerum et praesertim hominum progressu* (Camerino 1553), *De tractandis in Concilio Oecumenico* (Rome 1561), *Commentarii in Evangelium Joannis et in Epistolam Pauli ad Hebraeos* (Rome 1587). Delfini was leading Scotist at the Council; his views on almost every important question discussed in the first and second periods are to be found in the volumes of *Concilium Tridentinum: Diariorum, Actorum . . . nova collectio* (Freiburg im Br. 1901 ss.). In general he followed the common teaching of the schools, but to this he brought a knack for clarity of exposition, apparent especially in his important works on justification and on the Church.

Bibliography: V. HEYNCK, *Lexikon für Theologie und Kirche*, ed. J. HOFER and K. RAHNER (2d, new ed. Freiburg 1957–65) 3:209. A. GARANI, *De Ecclesiae Natura et Constitutione Doctrina J. A. Delphini* (Padua 1942) 11–35. F. LAUCHERT, *Die italienischen literarischen Gegner Luthers* (Freiburg 1912).

[P. FEHLNER]

DELFINO

A noble Venetian family of which the following members are prominent.

Pietro, humanist, Camaldolese abbot; b. Venice, 1444; d. Venice, Jan. 16, 1529. He entered the Monastery of San Michele at Murano and in 1480 was elected abbot of the community and made general of the Camaldolese Order. He held the office of general until 1513, when he resigned in favor of Paolo Giustiniani; he was the last abbot elected for life. In 1488 he was designated by his countrymen as cardinal but refused to accept the honor from Innocent VIII. He was named vicar in 1514 by Leo X. His letters are valuable for the light they throw upon events and personalities of his day. An opponent of Savonorola, he is known for his *Dialogus in Hieronymum Ferrariensem*.

Zaccaria, cardinal; b. Venice, May 29, 1527; d. Rome, Dec. 19, 1583. He was named bishop of Lesina in 1553, and was nuncio to Vienna to the courts of Ferdinand I (1554–56) and Maximilian II (1556–65). He tried to obtain Ferdinand's consent for the reopening of the Council of Trent. After much criticism of his efforts, he finally achieved accord with Ferdinand. At Ferdinand's wish he attended the Protestant reunion at Naumburg, where he was able to do nothing. He promised Ferdinand concessions of the use of the chalice for the laity and the marriage of the clergy, but only the first of these was approved by the pope. Zaccaria was named cardinal on March 12, 1565, by Pius V.

Giovanni, papal nuncio; b. Venice, March 1528; d. Brescia, May 1, 1584. He was named bishop of Torcello in 1563, and bishop of Brescia in 1579. From 1571 to 1578 he served as nuncio to the imperial court.

Giovanni, cardinal; b. Venice, 1545; d. Venice, Nov. 25, 1622. He served as bishop of Vicenza and was named cardinal by Clement VIII June 6, 1604.

Giovanni, cardinal; b. Venice, April 22, 1617; d. Udine, July 19, 1699. Great-nephew of Cardinal Giovanni Delfino, he was named bishop coadjutor of Ende (1556), and patriarch of Aquileia (1657). Named cardinal in 1667, he was considered a papal candidate in the conclave that elected Innocent XII (1691).

Daniello, archbishop; b. Venice, 1688; d. Udine, March 13, 1743. He was named coadjutor archbishop of

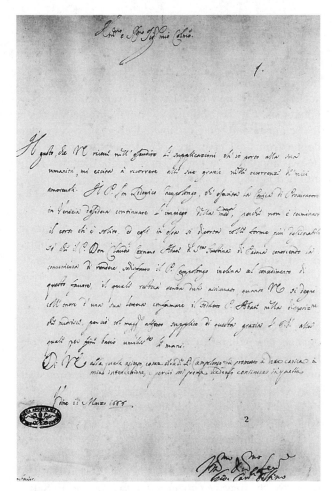

Personal letter from Cardinal Giovanni Delfino to Cardinal Francisco Barberini, March 11, 1668.

Aquileia in 1714, and patriarch in 1734. In the partition of the patriarchate he became the first archbishop of Udine in 1751.

Bibliography: B. G. DOLFIN, *I Dolfin, patrizi veneziani . . . 452–1923* (2d ed. Milan 1924). J. LECLERCQ, *Un Humaniste ermite; Le Bienheureux Paul Giustiniani, 1476–1528* (Rome 1951). L. PASTOR, *The History of the Popes from the Close of the Middle Ages* (London-St. Louis 1938–61): v. 13-40 from 1st German ed. *Geschichte des Päpste seit dem Ausgang des Mittelalters* (Freiburg 1885–1933 repr. 1955–) v. 20, *passim*. F. D. RAGNI, *Il Giovanni Delfino patriarca aquileise drammaturgo* (Udine 1940). J. WODKA, *Lexikon für Theologie und Kirche*, ed. J. HOFER and K. RAHNER (2d, new ed. Freiburg 1957–65) 3:208–209. R. AUBERT and J. RUYSSCHAERT, *Dictionnaire d'histoire et de géographie ecclésiastiques*, ed. A. BAUDRILLART et al. (Paris 1912–) 14:178–180, with bibliog.

[R. L. FOLEY]

DELGADO, JOSÉ MATÍAS

Churchman and political leader who played an important and controversial role in the independence movement of El Salvador and in the organization of the Church in that region; b. San Salvador, El Salvador, Feb. 24, 1767; d. there, Nov. 12, 1832. Delgado belonged to an aristocratic family that had contributed to the initial conquest of Guatemala. At an early age he was granted a scholarship by the archbishop of Guatemala to study in Guatemala City. In addition to completing his studies at the seminary and being ordained, Delgado received a law degree from the University of Guatemala. In August 1797 he was appointed pastor of San Salvador. During a difficult period when El Salvadore suffered from earthquakes and economic problems, Delgado came to be admired for the zeal and integrity with which he fulfilled his priestly duties. In the independence movement in Central America, Delgado headed the region's first revolutionary uprising of Nov. 5, 1811. When this movement collapsed, he was recalled to Guatemala, where he remained for the next ten years, except for occasional visits to San Salvador under the close supervision of royal authorities. On Sept. 15, 1821, when Central America established its independence without having to resort to warfare, among the signers of the declaration of independence was Delgado. Together with fellow Liberal Manuel José Arce, Delgado served on a governing junta in San Salvador under the jurisdiction of the federal government of Central America in Guatemala. When Mexico tried to annex all of the Central American provinces, only El Salvador protested. Preferring annexation to the U.S. to absorption by Mexico, Delgado framed the futile request (Jan. 5, 1823) to the North American government to take over El Salvador. When Central America reasserted its independence, Delgado was overwhelmingly elected president of the First National Constituent Assembly of Central America.

For many years before the end of the colonial period, El Salvador had vainly sought establishment of a diocese. When El Salvador began its existence as a semi-autonomous province within the Central American confederation and convened a joint congress and constituent assembly, that body on April 27, 1824, created a diocese and appointed Delgado as bishop. Delgado was invested in his new office on May 5. The following month the Spanish-born archbishop of Guatemala Ramón Casaús y Torres published an edict declaring null and void the actions of the Salvadorean congress in creating a diocese and appointing Delgado bishop. The Federal Assembly in Guatemala City likewise declared illegal El Salvador's controversial ecclesiastical decrees. Though lacking papal confirmation, Delgado refused to renounce episcopal powers. The Salvadorean government dispatched a representative to seek confirmation in Rome, but Leo XII on Dec. 1, 1826, fully backed Archbishop Casaús. Delgado was instructed to renounce his office within 50 days, under pain of being branded a schismatic. By the end of

the following year Delgado had relinquished all claims on the disputed bishopric. Meantime, however, the Salvadorean government had exiled many ecclesiastics who opposed the Delgado cause.

The controversy over the Diocese of El Salvador produced political ramifications throughout Central America. Liberals supported Delgado, while the Conservatives or ''Serviles'' backed the Guatemalan archbishop. By 1829 liberals under Francisco Morazán had gained control of the Central American federal government in Guatemala and shortly began to promulgate the most anticlerical series of laws that had appeared in Latin America up to that time. With liberalism ascendant, Delgado was more popular than ever in El Salvador. In 1832 a new Salvadorean assembly elected Delgado its presiding officer. Throughout his life he had thought it possible to defend both liberal political principles and the Catholic faith. In the last moments of his life Delgado is reported to have said: ''I hereby declare that I have lived and die happily in the religion of Christ, the only true one, in communion with the Roman Apostolic Catholic Church; that my conscience is at peace regarding the ecclesiastical matters of this state and that before the Divine Presence we shall see who is the one at fault . . . .''

Bibliography: R. LÓPEZ JIMÉNEZ, *José Matías Delgado y de León: Ensayo histórico* (San Salvador 1962). R. BARÓN CASTRO, *José Matías Delgado y el Movimiento insurgente de 1811* (San Salvador 1962).

[P. TENNANT PIKE]

D'ELIA, PASQUALE

Jesuit missionary and Orientalist, most noted for his writings on the early history of the Society of Jesus in China; b. Pietra Catella, Campo Basso, April 2, 1890; d. Rome, May 18, 1963. He entered the society in 1904 and studied theology at Woodstock College, Md., from 1917 to 1920, when he was ordained; he taught theology in Jesuit houses of study in Shanghai from 1921 to 1934. During this period he edited the original Chinese classics together with a European vernacular commentary. He returned to Rome in 1934 as professor on the faculty of missiology at the Gregorian University, where he remained until his death. His writings during this period dealt mainly with the contemporary political conditions in China and with the early history of the Jesuits in China. His summary, the *History of the Catholic Church in China* [*Studia missionalia* (Rome 1950) 1–68], is considered the briefest and most authoritative statement on the matter.

Bibliography: R. STREIT and J. DINDINGER, *Bibliotheca missionum* (Freiburg 1916–), v.14, pts. 1, 3.

[J. FLYNN]

DELIBERATION AND MORALITY

In ordinary speech the word deliberation means any weighing or examining of reasons for or against a given choice. In moral philosophy and theology it defines more narrowly the scope of human reasoning required by the matter in question and by the facts of a situation (circumstances) to arrive at a judgment or conclusion that is final and decisive concerning the choice of particular means to some end already intended.

The task of deliberation is compounded of several factors and is related to certain antecedent and subsequent steps in the process of choosing and acting as well as to certain important concepts of morality. Therefore it will be helpful to discuss deliberation first in itself, then in relation to other steps in the process of arriving at human action, and finally in relation to other important moral concepts.

The free or HUMAN ACT of man proceeds from deliberate will, i.e., from the will determined to this act through previous deliberation (Thomas Aquinas, *Summa theologiae* 1a2ae, 1.1). Over such an act man exercises dominion; it is his own, because by deliberation he makes it such. Therefore, it is imputable to him. He is its free cause through deliberation and his will-act determined by the judgment flowing from deliberation. Deliberation is moral, because it and the concluding dictate of reason include a consideration of good and evil as objects of choice conforming or not to man's nature and END. Such conformity exists if the choice is in accordance with LAW, including that which is intrinsic because derived from man's own nature and that which is extrinsic because derived from the positive will of legitimate authority.

In the analytical process of the human act, deliberation is simply "taking counsel" with oneself or "the enquiry of reason preceding the judgment of choice" (ST 1a2ae, 14.1). This part of the total process is necessary because once one has set himself a goal to be achieved, one still must find a suitable way to realize it. Sometimes the way to a goal is predetermined by circumstances. More often there are several different choices. To act effectively one must settle upon a single way to realize his purpose. Hence, he will deliberate; he will consider or weigh the various possibilities open to him to achieve his purpose. If he is decisive, he will come to a definite conclusion as to how he should act, or perhaps whether he should act at all, given the facts and morality of the possibilities. This deliberative process can only concern means, i.e., those things that are ordered to an end (*ea quae sunt ad finem*) according to St. Thomas (ST 1a2ae, 14.2), although one must recognize that all inferior or subordinate ends or goals require deliberation, since in respect to higher goals they are themselves means. Delib-

eration is not required for the goal that is absolutely final by innate and necessary tendency of human nature (happiness in general), nor is further deliberation required for means that are obviously seen as conforming and indispensable to the final goal.

In the analytical process of the free act, deliberation is closely related to the judgment of choice. This judgment refers to the precise means that one takes to realize the goal he has in mind. Together with the will-act of choice that makes such judgment decisive and controlling, it constitutes the interior free act, which, when carried out by the powers and organs necessary realizes in a human way the goal first intended.

The deliberative process is clearly rational. It is also discursive. Though it should be strictly logical and orderly, the very contingency of its objects renders it less than certain in the speculative sense. It can result only in the practical certainty that contingent reality allows, a degree of probability proportionate for the concrete situation. Further, the appetitive powers, both sensible and volitional, have a part to play. If rightly developed and exercised, they do not hinder, but rather promote, deliberation and right judgment. If they are disordered and incline to goods not in keeping with man's nature, dignity, and supernatural destiny, emotions will tend to distort or sidetrack the logical process of practical reason and lead to judgments of choice that are morally wrong or evil.

Deliberation as described here fits into the pattern of prudential reasoning. Since deliberation is a function of intellect, it is subject to an evolution toward the perfection of the habit of PRUDENCE or toward the distortions of imprudence. In the context of prudence, deliberation is closely related to those integral parts of prudence that prepare for the prudential judgment: memory, understanding, docility, sagacity, and rational thought (ST 2a2ae, 49). There is similarly a relation to the habit of *eubulia*.

A more significant relation exists between deliberation and CONSCIENCE. This latter is the personal and subjective judgment of morality that terminates moral reasoning. Since ends and means concern the good, they have a moral value that the mind should not fail to consider. Deliberation therefore deals with means as conducive to ends, and precisely as moral. Morality, a quality of goodness or evil, characterizes every free act.

Finally, a word should be said about the supernatural. Man shares the triune life of God on earth by grace and by the infused virtues of faith, hope, and charity. These virtues illuminate man's mind and inspire his will to realize his supernatural destiny by all those means that God places at man's disposal. Obviously the deliberation of the child of God and member of Christ will be affected accordingly. The Christian will guide his reasoning by the truths revealed by God and enjoy the gifts of the HOLY SPIRIT, one of which is counsel.

Bibliography: V. J. BOURKE, *Ethics* (New York 1953). M. CRONIN, *The Science of Ethics,* 2 v. (Dublin 1939) v. 1. O. LOTTIN, *Morale fondamentale* (Tournai 1954). A. G. SERTILLANGES, *La Philosophie morale de saint Thomas d'Aquin* (rev. ed. Paris 1946). H. RENARD, ''The Functions of Intellect and Will in the Act of Free Choice,'' *The Modern Schoolman* 24 (Jan. 1947) 85–92. J. PIEPER, *Prudence,* tr. R. and C. WINSTON (New York 1959). H. D. NOBLE, *Dictionnaire de théologie catholique,* ed. A. VACANT et al., (Paris 1903–50) 13.1:1023–76. THOMAS AQUINAS, *La Prudence* (*Summa theologiae* 2a2ae, 47–56), tr. and ed. T. H. DEMAN (2d ed. Paris 1949).

[F. J. HUNNEFELD]

DE LISLE, AMBROSE LISLE MARCH PHILLIPPS

Philanthropist, writer; b. Garendon Park, Leicestershire, England, March 17, 1809; d. there, March 5, 1878. The son of Charles Phillipps, he assumed the name De Lisle upon inheriting the family property (1862). His early education was at a private school near Gloucester. There, his friendship with a French priest, one of the French Revolutionary EMIGRÉS, led to his secret conversion to Catholicism at the age of 16. At Trinity College, Cambridge, he became friendly with Kenelm Digby. Bronchial illness compelled him to leave the University (1828) after two years. In 1833 he married into the old Catholic family of the Cliffords of Chudleigh. His wife, Mary, had 16 children, of whom 11 survived their father. De Lisle established the CISTERCIANS in Leicestershire, introduced the ROSMINIANS into the country, and initiated a revival in plainchant. Together with Rev. George Spencer (who owed his own conversion to De Lisle), he founded the Association of Universal Prayer for the Conversion of England, which enjoyed notable success and was approved by Cardinal WISEMAN. Later, in the excitement engendered by the OXFORD MOVEMENT and the restoration of the hierarchy (1850), De Lisle established the Association for Promoting the Unity of Christendom, whose 14 original members included only three Catholics. Rome disapproved of this association, whose aim was corporate reunion.

Bibliography: E. S. PURCELL, *Life and Letters of Ambrose Phillipps de Lisle,* 2 v. (London 1900). J. GILLOW, *A Literary and Biographical History or Bibliographical Dictionary of the English Catholics from 1534 to the Present Time* (London-New York 1885–1902; repr. New York 1961) 2:38–47.

[V. A. MC CLELLAND]

DELLA CHIESA, BERNARDINO

Bishop and vicar apostolic; b. Venice, May 8, 1664; d. Linqing, China, Dec. 21, 1721. He was sent by the Holy See to China to enforce the subjection of all missionaries to the vicars and to terminate the Portuguese and Spanish patronage. He sailed in October 1680 with Basilio BROLLO and three other confreres, spent two years in Siam (Thailand), and entered China by Guangzhou on Aug. 27, 1684. Upon Bp. François PALLU's death on October 29, he succeeded him as vicar apostolic of Fujian vicariate and general administrator of all China missions despite Charles Maigrot's pretensions. In 1685 he named Brollo his provicar and made a partial visit of several provinces. During 1686, accompanied by Brollo, he revisited these missions, confirming many. In 1689 he at once published the decree he obtained from Propaganda revoking the oath of subjection to the vicars that had been responsible for the self-suspension and departure of missionaries. Rumors of the division of China into three dioceses under Portuguese patronage made his position uncertain. Thereupon in 1691 he bought a house in Nanjing, and exercised the authority of vicar apostolic, but refrained from visitations pending clarification. Finally, in 1700 armed with the bull naming him bishop of the newly set diocese of Beijing, he reached his see, made a pastoral visit, and settled at Linqing, Shandong. In November 1705 he welcomed there Patriarch Carlo T. Maillard de TOURNON, apostolic legate to China, on his way to court. In January 1706 he joined the sick legate and assisted him to the end of his ill-fated legation, returning to Linqing with the legate on October 4. The next day, before seeing the legate off, he deeded his house to the Propaganda.

In force of the imperial decree of Dec. 17, 1706, he requested and was granted the imperial certificate on an affidavit to follow Matteo RICCI, SJ, and remain in China for life, and asked his missionaries to do likewise. Obedient servant of the Holy See, he carried out its policies as well as he could. Aging and laboring under great difficulties, he could not take part in the legation of Patriarch Carlo A. MEZZABARBA (1720), and died the following year. His greatest merit was to have established the hierarchical Church and to have fostered peace and harmony among missionaries in China under most trying circumstances (*see* CHINESE RITES CONTROVERSY).

Bibliography: *Sinica franciscana,* ed. A. VAN DEN WYNGAERT, 5 v. (Quaracchi-Florence 1929–54); v.6, ed. G. MENSAERT (Rome 1961). A. S. ROSSO, *Apostolic Legations to China of the Eighteenth Century* (South Pasadena, Calif. 1948). G. MENSAERT, ''L'Établissment de la hiérarchie catholique en Chine de 1684 à 1721,'' *Archivum Franciscanum historicum* 48 (1953) 369–416.

[A. S. ROSSO]

DELLA ROBBIA

Family name of three important Italian Renaissance sculptor-artists.

Luca, sculptor included by Alberti among the founders of the Italian Renaissance; b. Florence, 1399 or 1400; d. Florence, Feb. 22, 1482. He received important commissions for reliefs in marble and bronze, but is best known for his Madonnas, religious scenes, and coats-of-arms in glazed terra cotta, a technique that he invented. Nothing is known of his early work, but his later style suggests that Luca was probably trained by Nanni di Banco and perhaps took over the direction of the workshop when Nanni died in 1421. Luca's first dated work is the beautiful marble *cantoria* or music-loft (1431–38; Cathedral Museum, Florence). Its ten reliefs with *putti* singing and playing instruments illustrate Psalm 150. Not only the epigraphy and architectural framework but the style of the reliefs themselves bears remarkable resemblances to the antique. A change in style toward a deeper undercutting and more vigorous movement that occurred in those of the reliefs done after 1434–35 may be due to the influence of Donatello, who in 1433 began to contribute to the project. In contrast to Donatello's boisterous dancers who fill a frieze running behind projecting columns, Luca della Robbia's children are calmer, and the verticals and horizontals of the compositions are in perfect harmony with the frame that clearly separates the panels. The superb bronze door of Florence Cathedral (1464–69) is Luca's last surviving work in metal; each of the reliefs contains three figures in a quietly arranged composition. After 1440 Luca worked chiefly in the medium of enameled terra cotta. His first dated work, a marble tabernacle at Peretola (1441–43), contains only small sections done in terra cotta, which the artist used here for its coloristic effects. In his well-known Madonnas, Luca's invention was inexhaustible; the compositions never repeat themselves, though the palette is limited to white and blues. A greater range of color is found in his architectural decorations, e.g., the roundels with figures of Apostles in the Pazzi Chapel (*c.* 1440–50; S. Croce, Florence) and the lunettes of the "Resurrection and Ascension" (1442–51; Cathedral Museum, Florence).

Andrea, Luca's nephew, continued the workshop tradition; b. 1435; d. 1525. His ten medallions of children on the arcade of the Ospedale degli Innocenti (1463–66) are remarkable works, though they show a trend toward sentimentality. Under Andrea the mass production of terra-cotta Madonnas for private devotional use resulted in a decorative art of lower quality.

Giovanni, the most important artist among Andrea's five sons; b. 1469; d. 1529. In his works, such as the "Temptation" (1515; Walters Art Gallery, Baltimore), a greater naturalism is combined with a wider range of color.

Bibliography: L. PLANISCIG, *Luca della Robbia* (Florence 1948). G. BRUNETTI, *Encyclopedia of World Art* (New York 1959) 4:295–302. J. POPE-HENNESSEY, *Italian Renaissance Sculpture* (New York 1958). C. SEYMOUR, "Young Luca della Robbia," *Bulletin of the Dudley Peter Allen Memorial Art Museum of Oberlin College* 20 (1963) 92–119. A. MARQUAND, *Andrea della Robbia and His Atelier*, 2 v. (Princeton 1922); *Giovanni della Robbia* (Princeton 1920).

[M. M. SCHAEFER]

DELLA ROVERE

A family prominent in Italian ecclesiastical and political history from the mid-15th to the early 17th century. The family was of humble origin and originated near Savona. Its rise began with *Francesco* (b. 1414), son of *Leonardo*. As Pope SIXTUS IV, Francesco arranged marriages, benefices, and feudal grants for his relatives. The children of *Rafaello* (brother of Sixtus IV) included: *Giuliano,* who became cardinal and later Pope JULIUS II; *Giovanni,* made Lord of Senigaglia and Mondavio, who wed on equal terms Giovanni di Montefeltro, daughter of Federico, Duke of Urbino; *Leonardo,* who married a natural daughter of Ferrante, King of Sicily, and became Duke of Sora (1472) but had no issue; *Bartolomeo* (d. 1494), bishop of Massa (1472) and of Ferrara (1474), and governor of CASTEL SANT' ANGELO (1487); and *Luchinetta,* who was mother of *Galeotto* (d. 1508) and *Sisto* (d. 1517) by her second husband Gian Francesco Franciotti of Lucca. Galeotto became bishop of Vicenza and bishop of Lucca, was made cardinal in 1503, and was a papal vice chancellor. Sisto also became bishop of Lucca, was made cardinal in 1507, and became vice chancellor. From another line came *Girolamo* and *Antonio,* sons of Basso Della Rovere, Marquis of Bistagno and of Monastero, and his wife Luchina. Girolamo became bishop of Recanati in 1476, and cardinal in 1477; he was favored by Julius II. After his death in 1507, he was buried in a splendid tomb designed by Sanseverino. Antonio married the niece of the King of Naples but this line died out.

Also connected with the Savona line were *Clemente Grosso* Della Rovere (d. 1504) and his brother *Leonardo Grosso* (d. 1520). Clemente was made cardinal in 1503. Leonardo was made cardinal in 1505, and was legate in Viterbo in September 1506, legate in Perugia in 1507, papal confessor, and one of the executors of the will of Julius II.

From a separate family, that of Turin, came *Cristofero* (d. 1478), the archbishop of Tarantasia, who became cardinal in 1477. His brother *Domenico* (d. 1501) was made cardinal in 1478.

Guilio (1533–78), son of Francesco Maria, Duke of Urbino, became archbishop of Ravenna and cardinal. *Girolamo* (d. 1592), made archbishop of Turin (1564), became cardinal in December 1586 at the intercession of the Duke of Savoy. Girolamo sought to dissuade Sixtus V from publishing a bull concerning the Sixtine text of the Bible (1590); he served on the Congregation of the Index.

The ducal line of Urbino began with Francesco Maria I (1490–1538), a Venetian general, succeeded by his son Guidobaldo II (1514–74); the latter was much hated for his harsh rule. Guidobaldo's son Francesco Maria II (1548–1631) was a better ruler, although morose. He fought at Lepanto on the flagship of Savoy. His son, Federico Ubaldo, a dissolute man, died before his father. The direct line ended in 1631, and the Urbino holdings reverted to the papacy.

Bibliography: P. LITTA et al., *Famiglie celebri italiane* (Milan 1819–1923) v.10. F. UGOLINI, *Storia dei conti e duchi di Urbino* (Florence 1859) v.2. C. MARCOLINI, *Notizie storiche della provincia di Pesaro e Urbino* (Pesaro 1868). L. DE VILLENEUVE, *Récherches sur la famille de la Rovère* (Rome 1887). O. VARALDO, *Sulla famiglia Della Rovere* (Savona 1888). R. REPOSATI, *Della zecca di Gubbio, e delle geste de, conti e duchi di Urbino*, 2 v. (Bologna 1772–73).

[D. R. CAMPBELL]

DELLA SOMAGLIA, GIULIO MARIA

Cardinal, papal secretary of state; b. Piacenza, Italy, July 28, 1744; d. Rome, March 30, 1830. Of noble birth, he became secretary of the Congregation of Indulgences and Relics (1774) and of the Congregation of Rites (1784). After being created cardinal (1795) he suffered imprisonment during the French occupation of Rome, and later departed from the city. He attended the conclave at Venice (1800), after which he was sent as legate by Pius VII to discuss with the governor of Rome the pope's arrival in the Eternal City. Della Somaglia was one of 13 cardinals, out of 27 invited, who refused to attend the nuptials (April 2, 1810) of NAPOLEON I and Archduchess Marie Louise of Austria, because of the way in which the annulment of the emperor's marriage to Josephine Beauharnais had been maneuvered. As a result he and the other cardinals were deprived of their benefices and exiled, Della Somaglia being sent to Mazières and then to Charleville. Upon Napoleon's downfall, Della Somaglia governed Rome (March–June 1815), until the return of Pius VII. He became bishop of Frascati (1814), secretary of the Holy Office (1814) and bishop of Ostia and Velletri (1820). LEO XII named him secretary of state (1823–28), but handled most negotiations himself. Despite the widespread urge for self-determination of peoples, the pope and his secretary of state labored to maintain royalty in its traditional role and made every effort to restrain republican forces throughout Italy and elsewhere.

Bibliography: J. LEFLON, *La Crise révolutionnaire 1789–1846* (*Histoire de l'église depuis les origines jusqu'à nos jours* 20; 1949). E. E. Y. HALES, *Revolution and Papacy* (New York 1960). W. SANDFUCHS, *Die Aussenminister der Päpste* (Munich 1962).

[T. F. CASEY]

DELPHI, ORACLE OF

The Oracle of Delphi, or the oracle of Apollo situated at Delphi, north of the gulf of Corinth, and a site that was regarded as the navel or center of the earth, was the oldest and most influential of Greek sanctuaries.

Its role as a kind of international court of reference in political as well as religious affairs, public and private, was important especially in the period from the 8th to the early 5th century B.C. It gave sound advice that was usually couched, however, in obscure or ambiguous language. Well informed as an international center on conditions in the Mediterranean world, it could indicate good sites for Greek colonies and could help to settle disputes between Greek states. In the religious sphere, it promoted the hero-cult, the healing cult of Asclepius, and the worship of Dionysus—but in a tempered form. On the moral side it gave the Greeks the basic precepts "Know thyself" and "Nothing too much."

Politically, it never regained the prestige it lost when it advised against resistance to Persia, but it continued to be consulted on religious and moral questions during the Hellenistic and Roman periods. The oracle announced its own decline to the Emperor Julian, and it was suppressed by Theodosius the Great in A.D. 390. The inquirers, after a purification and sacrifice, approached the oracle in an order normally determined by lot. A male prophet or priest then presented the question of the inquirer to the Pythia, or medium, at first a young woman, but later an elderly one, seated on a tripod and in a state of trance. He interpreted the utterance of the Pythia and delivered the answer, ordinarily in hexameter verse, to the inquirer. There are various theories on how the trance was induced; but, apart from the Pythia's unquestioned belief in the power of Apollo and strong emotional suggestion, no other explanations are completely satisfactory. The traditional view that it was produced by inhaling vapors at the site has been disproved by archeology.

See Also: ORACLE; DIVINATION.

Bibliography: W. K. C. GUTHRIE, *The Oxford Classical Dictionary,* ed. M. CARY et al. (Oxford 1949) 261–262. H. W. PARKE, *A*

History of the Delphic Oracle (Oxford 1939). H. W. PARKE and D. E. W. WORMELL, *The Delphic Oracle*, 2 v. (Oxford 1956). K. PRÜM-MER, *Religionsgeschichtliches Handbuch für den Raum der altchristlichen Umweld* (2d ed. Rome 1954) 415–419.

[T. A. BRADY]

DELPHINA OF SIGNE, BL.

Franciscan tertiary; b. Puy-Michel (Provence), 1283 or 1284; d. Apt, France, Nov. 26, 1358 or 1360. In 1299 Delphina, daughter of Count William of Glandèves, was married to ELZÉAR OF SABRAN, with whom she lived in continence. In 1317 Elzéar was summoned to the court of King Robert of Naples, where Delphina formed a life-long friendship with Queen Sanchia. After the death of Elzéar (1323), she returned to Provence and lived as a re-cluse in absolute poverty, devoting herself to works of mercy. After many sufferings and a long last illness, she was buried beside Elzéar in Apt. Her iconography shows the symbols of her noble rank and Franciscan affiliation. In 1694 Innocent XII confirmed her cult, which had been introduced under Urban V.

Feast: Sept. 26; in order, Dec. 9.

Bibliography: *Acta Sanctorum,* Sept. 7:50l–519. L. WAD-DING, *Scriptores Ordinis Minorum*, 86 v. (Lyons 1625–54) 6:280–289; 8:172. G. DUHAMELET, *Saint Elzéar et la b. Delphine* (Paris 1944). B. DE GAIFFIER, *Analecta Bollandiana* 65 (1947) 179–180. A. BUTLER, *The Lives of the Saints*, rev. ed. H. THURSTON and D. ATTWATER (New York, 1956) 3:661–662. T. DE MOREM-BERT, *Dictionnaire d'histoire et de géographie ecclésiastiques*, ed. A. BAUDRILLART et al. (Paris 1912–) 15:366–368.

[M. F. LAUGHLIN]

DELUIL-MARTINY, MARIE OF JÉSUS, BL.

Baptized Marie Caroline Philomène; founder of the Daughters of the Sacred Heart of Jesus; b. May 28, 1841, Marseilles, France; d. Feb. 27, 1884, La Servianne Con-vent, Marseilles. Educated by the Visitation nuns in Lyons, Marie became a member of the Guard of Honor of the Sacred Heart of Jesus. Under the guidance of Jean Colage, S.J., in 1873 she founded in Belgium a contem-plative congregation of women to make reparation to the Sacred Hearts of Jesus and Mary and to pray for priests. She took the name Marie de Jésus. The Institute's consti-tutions were definitively approved by the Holy See in 1902. As a model for the institute the founder chose the Blessed Virgin under the aspect of victim and associate of Christ in the Passion. She adopted from Msgr. O. Van den Berghe the devotion to Mary as "virgin and priest."

Ruins on the site of ancient Delphi, on the slopes of Mount Parnassos in Greece. (©Paul Almasy/CORBIS)

In 1916, the Holy Office published a decree forbidding representations of Mary in priestly vestments; and in 1927 it prohibited the spread of this devotion among the faithful, but permitted the daughters to practice the devo-tion within the confines of the congregation. During the lifetime of the founder, the congregation spread in France and into Belgium. It has since established houses in Aus-tria, Italy, Switzerland, and the Netherlands. Marie De-luil-Martiny was shot to death by an anarchist employed at the motherhouse. Her remains rest in the Basilica of the Sacred Heart at Berschem (near Antwerp), Belgium. Her cause was introduced in 1921 and completed with her beatification by Pope John Paul II on Oct. 27, 1998.

Feast: Oct. 27.

Bibliography: *Acta Apostolicae Sedis* (1989): 1079. L. LA-PLACE, *Immolation: Life of Mother Mary of Jesus*, tr. J. F. NEWCOMB (New York 1926). R. GARRIGOU–LAGRANGE, *La Vita interióre della Madre Maria di Gesù* (Milan 1939). On the cult of the "Virgin and priest," see: R. LAURENTIN, *Marie, l'église et le sacerdoce*, 2 v. (Paris 1952–53). A. DE BONHOME, *"Dévotions prohibées," Dic-tionnaire de Spiritualité Ascétique et Mystique*, ed. M. VILLIER et al. (Paris 1932) 3:786–788.

[M. H. QUINLAN]

DE MEESTER, MARIE LOUISE, MOTHER

Foundress of the Missionary Sisters of St. Augus-tine; b. Roulers, Belgium, April 8, 1857; d. Heverle, Belgium, Oct. 10, 1928. Her desire to devote herself to the conversion of the heathen became a reality when she was sent to Travancore, India, in 1897. While wishing to extend her missionary activities beyond a single country, she was unable to recruit for her new community, the Missionary Sisters of St. Augustine, until a novitiate was established in Belgium in 1908. In 1910 Pius X authorized her to found missions in the Philippines, and Belgian Redemptorist Fathers in the Caribbean requested two foundations in the Virgin Islands also. In the U.S., where she obtained the assistance of Abp. Denis Dougherty of Philadelphia, Pa., she opened (1919) the congregation's first American house in New York City. This foundation later served as a procuratorial center for the Caribbean missions. After returning to Belgium in October 1919, she accepted further missions in the Congo and China and also directed the construction of a new motherhouse in Heverle, near the University of Louvain, Belgium. Her international apostolate was carried on by her congregation in nine countries. In the U.S. the novitiate for the Missionary Sisters of St. Augustine was established at Mount St. Augustine, Albany, N.Y.

[J. CALBRECHT]

DE MELLO, ANTHONY

Spiritual writer, retreat master, priest, member of the Society of Jesus; b. Sept. 4, 1931; d. June 2, 1987. De Mello was raised in an old Catholic family in Bombay, India, and eventually took degrees in philosophy (Barcelona), psychology (Loyola University, Chicago), and spiritual theology (Gregorian University, Rome). He entered the Society of Jesus in Bombay in 1947. De Mello was the founder and director of the Sadhana Institute of Pastoral Counseling near Poona, India. He sought the integration of Eastern prayer methods into classical Christian forms, particularly the Ignatian Exercises. His most famous work *Sadhana* was translated into 40 languages and was the distillation of scattered notes used in retreats or prayer workshops. It helped gain a wide readership for nine other books that he saw through publication in his lifetime. De Mello died while giving conferences at Fordham University.

De Mello's spirituality, while not anti-intellectual, gives priority to sensate or body centered modes of spiritual awareness. Stillness and breathing techniques in De Mello's system are reminiscent of the hesychist. Imagination or fantasy permits a kind of self-displacement into a new historical moment. A new story emerges, such as when a person imagines walking with Jesus along the Via Dolorosa or witnessing the miracle at Cana as if at the wedding party. Feelings and intuitions are key; devotions

are more secondary. Meditation is the pathway to love, not necessarily greater knowledge or cognition of some tangible reality. True cognition emerges when love is engaged. Here De Mello echoes Teresa of Avila: "The important thing is not to think much but to love." In offering spiritual counsel De Mello exhibited a self-deprecating wit and never forced his positions on his retreatants, choosing rather to teach by suggestion.

De Mello left a large body of unpublished work, some of which he edited before his death, though he never authorized their publication. Motivated in part by these later, posthumous writings, the Congregation for the Doctrine of the Faith issued a notification that some of De Mello's ideas were "incompatible with the Catholic faith and can cause harm." The principal issue was the charge of indifferentism. The Congregation called for bishops to see to the withdrawal of De Mello's works and the cessation of further reprinting. Friends and Jesuit colleagues, particularly in India, publicly protested this move, seeing it as inhibiting Christian encounters and dialogue with Eastern traditions and beliefs.

Bibliography: A. DE MELLO, *Sadhana: A Way to God: Christian Exercises in Eastern Form* (St. Louis 1978); *Praying Body and Soul: Methods and Practices of Anthony De Mello* (New York 1997). P. DIVARKAR, "The Enigma of Anthony De Mello," *America* 179, no. 14 (1998): 8–13. W. DYCH, ed., *Anthony De Mello: Writings* (Maryknoll, N.Y. 1999).

[P. J. HAYES]

DEMETRIAN OF KHYTRI, ST.

Bishop and national saint of Cyprus; b. village of Sykai, Diocese of Khytri, Cyprus, *c.* 830; d. *c.* 911. He was married very young, and after the death of his bride he took the monastic habit at the age of 16 in the monastery of St. Anthony in his native town. He was ordained by Eustathios, bishop of Khytri, a see in central CYPRUS, the exact location of which is uncertain today. The bishop would have kept him in his service, but Demetrian, scorning worldly pursuits, begged leave to return to his cloister, where he remained for 40 years leading an exemplary life and where he was eventually elected abbot. When Eustathios was translated to the metropolitan See of Salamis (*c.* 885), he named Demetrian to succeed him at Khytri. The monk felt compelled to accept, and he served as bishop for the next 25 years. The last days of his episcopate were clouded by one of the periodic Arab invasions of Cyprus, which resulted in the sack of Khytri, and the 80-year-old bishop himself undertook a journey to BAGHDAD to seek the ransom of some of his people from the caliph. There is a nearly contemporary life of the saint in Greek by a cleric of his diocese.

Feast: Nov. 6.

Bibliography: Greek vita, ed. H. GRÉGOIRE in *Byzantinische Zeitschrift* 16 (1907) 204–240. *Acta Sanctae Sedis* Nov. 3:298–308. R. JENKINS, *Mélanges Henri Grégoire* (Brussels 1949) 1:267–275. H. DELEHAYE, ''Saints de Chypre,'' *Analecta Bollandiana* 26 (1907) 243, 249, 253, 267.

[B. J. COMASKEY]

DEMETRIAS, ST.

Fifth-century virgin and ascetic; b. *c.* 398, Rome; d. 460. She came of the illustrious *gens Anicia.* Demetrias escaped to Africa with her mother Juliana and her grandmother Faltonia Proba after Alaric's siege of Rome in 410. In 413 or 414 she received the veil of the consecrated virgin from Aurelius, Bishop of Carthage. Congratulations, addressed to Proba and Juliana, came from Pope INNOCENT I (*Patrologia Latina* 20:518–519) and St. AUGUSTINE (*Ep.* 150). Demetrias received carefully composed letters of direction from St. JEROME (*Ep.* 130) and from PELAGIUS (*Patrologia Latina* 33:1099–1120). In *Ep.* 188, Augustine warned her against Pelagius's letter, criticizing its ambiguous position on grace. Later, after returning to Rome, she received another letter, written probably by St. PROSPER OF AQUITAINE (*Patrologia Latina* 55:161–180). During the pontificate of St. LEO I (440–61) she arranged to have a church in honor of St. Stephen built on her estate on the Via Latina. Excavation of the ruins in 1858 brought to light the dedicatory inscription (E. Diehl, *Inscriptiones Christianae latinae veteres* 1765). Until the 1960 revision of the Roman Breviary, her name was mentioned in the Divine Office for the feast of St. Leo (April 11).

Feast: Feb. 24.

Bibliography: M. GONSETTE, ''Les Directeurs spirituels de Démétriade,'' *Nouvelle revue théologique* 60 (1933) 783–801. G. BARDY, *Dictionnaire de spiritualité ascétique et mystique. Doctrine et histoire,* ed. M. VILLER et al. (Paris 1932) 3:133–137. K. C. KRABBE, *Epistula ad Demetriadem de vera humilitate* (Catholic University of America, *Patristic Studies* 97; 1965).

[K. C. KRABBE]

DEMETRIUS, SS.

Demetrius of Alexandria, bishop (189–231), patron of Origen, and first bishop of that see of whom there is certain knowledge. While the catechetical school of ALEXANDRIA flourished during his episcopate, it is most probable that neither CLEMENT nor ORIGEN were connected with that institution despite the generally accepted stories based on the Church history of Eusebius (*Historia Ecclesiastica,* 6.2–3, 8, 14, 19, 26) and St. Jerome's *De viris illustribus* (ch. 54). He defended Origen after his

Saint Demetrius the Megalomartyr on horseback spearing an enemy, fresco, c.19th century, Backovo, Bulgaria. (© Paul Almasy/CORBIS)

rash self-mutilation, but reacted unfavorably when he learned that Origen, though still a layman, had preached in churches in Palestine. When still later (*c.* 230) Origen was ordained by the Bishop of Caesarea without permission of his own bishop, hence against the Church's law, Demetrius held local synods that condemned Origen and deposed him from the priesthood. Letters concerning the EASTER CONTROVERSY ascribed to Demetrius are not authentic; nor is Jerome's statement that Demetrius sent St. PANTAENUS as a missionary to Yemen and Ethiopia.

Feast: Oct. 9.

Demetrius (or Dimitri) the Megalomartyr, honored as ''the Great Martyr'' especially among the Slavs, martyred probably in Sirmium (Mitrovica) in the early fourth century, during the persecution of Maximian. His cult was established in Salonika, where in the fifth century a great basilica was erected in his honor, probably by Leontius, Prefect of Illyricum. His protection was invoked against evil spirits, and as his cult spread through both the East and the West, he was looked upon as a never failing helper in all necessities. During the Middle Ages his presumed tomb in Salonika became a pilgrimage center where holy oil was connected with his relics, hence his title *Myrobletes* (oil-dripping). His feast day, *ta Demetria,* is specially marked with festivities and processions in the Balkan countries, where more than 200 churches are dedicated in his name. Both the lives and the collection of miracles (*Miracula S. Demetrii*) are legendary; but the accusation that the cult grew out of pagan practice is no longer tenable. He is considered a patron of military men.

Feast: Oct. 8; Oct. 26 (Eastern Church).

Bibliography: M. GRIGORIOU-IOANNIDOU, *Une remarque sur le récit des miracles de Saint Démétrius* (Athens 1987). J. C. SKEDROS, *Saint Demetrios of Thessaloniki* (Harrisburg, PA 1999). V. GRUMEL, *Dictionnaire d'histoire et de géographie ecclésiastiques*, ed. A. BAUDRILLART et al. (Paris 1912) 4:198–199. R. AUBERT, *ibid* 14 suppl.:1493–99. *Acta Sanctorum* Oct. 4:50–209; 855–864. O. BARDENHEWER, *Geschichte der altkirchlichen Literatur*, 5 v. (Freiburg 1913–32) 2:194–195. *Corpus scriptorum Christanorum orientalium* (Paris-Louvain 1903) 78:64–66. H. DELEHAYE, *Les Légendes grecques des saints militaires* (Paris 1909). A. BUTLER, *The Lives of the Saints*, ed. H. THURSTON and D. ATTWATER (New York 1956) 4:63.

[E. G. RYAN]

DEMETRIUS CHOMATIANUS

Archbishop and Greek canonist of the 13th century. He possessed the See of Ochrida from 1217 to 1234. He is noted for his letter to (St.) Sabas, Archbishop of Serbia, which dealt with the jurisdictions of the Churches of Ochrida and Ipek (A.D. 1220); the coronation of the despot Theodore Ducas (A.D. 1223); and his correspondence with the patriarch of Nicaea German II, in relation to the consecration of the bishop of Serbia, which Demetrius did not consider canonical. These exchanges of letters are important for the history of Byzantine Canon Law of that epoch. His works were printed by Cardinal Pitra in *Analecta sacra et classica Spicilegio Solesmensi Parata* (Paris 1891), volume eight.

Bibliography: L. PETIT, *Dictionnaire de théologie catholique*, ed. A. VACANT et al. (Paris 1903–50) 4:263–264. L. STIERNON, *Dictionnaire d'histoire et de géographie ecclésiastiques*, ed. A. BAUDRILLART et al. (Paris 1912–) 14:199–205. G. MORAVCSIK, *Byzantinoturcica* (2d ed. Berlin 1958) 1:244.

[L. R. KOZLOWSKI]

DEMOCRACY

Modern democracy is the outgrowth of many ancient theories and more recent practices. In its ancient form, characterized by direct participation of all citizens in legislation, it is found in some of the Swiss cantons and in New England town meetings. In its modern form as a representative system, it is not more than a century and a half old. Many of the theories underlying democracy have been used in other times and under other systems in which democracy itself has been rejected; but as both the political responsibility of men and the vital functions of GOVERNMENT have increased, the demand for govern-

mental responsibility to the popular will has been irresistible. Faith in majority rule under a regime of universal suffrage has spread throughout the Western world since the English revolutions of the 17th century. Whatever religious practices may have been, religious thought has supplied many of the fundamental principles upon which the democratic order is built: the dignity of man, the equality of men in the sight of God, the responsibility of man for his acts, the rights of the human person; all of these have been fundamental in the long struggle for popular government. Pius XII went so far as to say, "If, then, we consider the extent and nature of the sacrifices demanded of all citizens, especially in our day when the activity of the state is so vast and decisive, the democratic form of government appears to many as a postulate of nature imposed by reason itself" [*Benignitas et humanitas*; *Acta Apostolicae Sedis* 37 (1945) 13].

Democracy has come to prevail not alone because of the inadequacies of alternatives, but also through the ever-expanding numbers of educated citizens and the facilities offered by modern communications. Although these causes have also served the interests of totalitarianism, it is certain that without them the democratic order could not flourish. Medieval men knew and espoused most of the theories on which democratic polity is built, but they lacked an educated electorate and the material means of making the theories effective.

Greek Beginnings. The development of democratic theory involves the whole history of political philosophy; and without some understanding of that development, the theory of democracy can be only partially comprehended. "As for democracy," said the brilliant but traitorous Alcibiades, toward the end of the Peloponnesian War, "why should we discuss acknowledged madness?" He was expressing a point of view that Plato (c. 427–347 B.C.) must have held. According to Plato, under a democratic regime insolence is termed breeding; anarchy, liberty; waste, magnificence; and impudence, courage:

> The teacher in such case fears and fawns upon the pupils and the pupils pay no heed to the teacher or to their overseers either. And in general the young ape their elders and vie with them in speech and action, while the old, accommodating themselves to the young, are full of pleasantry and graciousness, imitating the young for fear they may be thought disagreeable and authoritative. . . . Without experience of it no one would believe how much freer the very beasts subject to men are in such a city than elsewhere. The dogs literally verify the adage and "like their mistresses become." And likewise the horses and asses are wont to hold on their way with the utmost freedom and dignity, bumping into everyone who meets them and who does not step aside. And so all

things everywhere are just bursting with the spirit of liberty. . . . And do you note that the sum total of all these items when footed up is that they render the souls of the citizens so sensitive that they chafe at the slightest suggestion of servitude and will not endure it? For you are aware that they finally pay no heed even to the laws written or unwritten, so that forsooth they may have no master anywhere over them. . . . This, then, my friend . . . is the fine and vigorous root from which tyranny grows. [*Republic* 563.]

Although for Plato democracy ranked next to the lowest political phenomenon (tyranny), for Pericles (d. 429 B.C.) it was the best of all forms. According to Thucydides, Pericles gave, in the famous funeral oration, the reverse point of view on democracy when he said:

We live under a form of government which does not emulate the institutions of our neighbours; on the contrary, we are ourselves a model which some follow, rather than the imitators of other peoples. It is true that our government is called a democracy, because its administration is in the hands, not of the few, but of the many; yet while as regards the law all men are on an equality for the settlement of their private disputes, as regards the value set on them it is as each man is in any way distinguished that he is preferred to public honours, not because he belongs to a particular class, but because of personal merits; nor, again, on the ground of poverty is a man barred from a public career by obscurity of rank if he but has it in him to do the state a service. And not only in our public life are we liberal, but also as regards our freedom from suspicion of one another in the pursuits of every-day life; for we do not feel resentment at our neighbour if he does as he likes, nor yet do we put on sour looks which, though harmless, are painful to behold. But while we thus avoid giving offence in our private intercourse, in our public life we are restrained from lawlessness chiefly through reverent fear for we render obedience to those in authority and to the laws, and especially to those laws which are ordained for the succour of the oppressed and those which, though unwritten, bring upon the transgressor a disgrace which all men recognize. [*Thucy.* 2.37.]

Classification of Governments. To Plato is owed the classic threefold division of constitutions: MONARCHY, a rule of one in accordance with law; ARISTOCRACY, a rule of a few in accordance with law; polity, a rule of the many in accordance with law. The opposite forms are TYRANNY, the lawless rule of one; oligarchy, the lawless rule of a few; democracy, the lawless rule of the many. Plato departed from this order, however, in his description of the degeneration of forms of government. His ideal best is an aristocracy, a rule by philosophers in

Chinese students rally for democracy, 1989. (©UPI/CORBIS)

which justice is the aim of the rulers. This form degenerates into a timocracy, a rule of a few with honor and glory being the motivating principle. The next stage is oligarchy, in which money and material wealth determine the goal of the rulers. This is followed by democracy, where no one standard guides either the rulers or society. Out of this develops the arbitrary rule of one man, tyranny. Thus each form of government has a guiding principle, and each in departing from that principle degenerates into a lower form. It seems that to the Greeks, with their cyclical idea of history, no form of government could be lasting, and change lurked behind every political institution. Each form contained the seed of its own destruction.

Aristotle (384–322 B.C.) appears less dogmatic than either Plato or Pericles. Though asserting that monarchy is ideally the best form of government, he believed that a mixture of the three possible forms is best practically, i.e., a combination of monarchy, aristocracy, and democracy; and he even granted that the people as a whole possess a political wisdom in judging their rulers that may not be lightly put aside. His preference was for a middle-

DEMOCRACY

class polity uncontrolled by forces of great wealth or military power.

Greek Practice. To all Greeks democracy meant a form of direct government and control by free citizens, obviously excluding foreigners and slaves. Thus the Greek citizen took part in the deliberations of the assembly and activities of the courts, and much of his time was taken up by these. Plato's attitude toward the democratic order may be explained by his feeling that the misfortunes of Athens in the Peloponnesian War were due largely to the absence of strong leadership and the mistakes of popular direction in the area of military requirements. Added to this, the condemnation of his mentor, SOCRATES (c. 470–399 B.C.), by one of the popular courts caused him to have little faith in the judgments of the populace. Democracy in Athens suffered as much from the loss of prestige resulting from its humiliating defeat at the hands of oligarchic Sparta as it did from the internal weaknesses of its system of government.

From Greek times until the present era, Pericles had far less influence in shaping the reputation of democracy than Plato and the cautious Aristotle. Democracy was commonly regarded as rule by the mob, or the least worthy and the least prepared for sober rule. Even when, in succeeding centuries, democracy was seriously advocated as a partial element in a stable regime, it was understood that democracy would be checked by monarchical and aristocratic forms. Thus the ideal regime that Polybius recognized in the Roman Republic was composed of the monarchical element (two consuls), the aristocratic (the Senate), and the democratic (the assembly of the plebeians). The prevalence of any one form meant the early destruction of the regime. So monarchy degenerated into tyranny, aristocracy into oligarchy, and democracy into irresponsible mob rule.

Roman Theory. The Romans devoted themselves more to jurisprudence than to philosophy, either pure or practical, and contented themselves with liberal borrowing from the Greeks. Their forms of government were largely *ad hoc* arrangements that met special situations as they arose. Political structures that no longer served a purpose very often continued to exist theoretically although effective power no longer inhered in them. The political history of Rome suggests gradual development rather than periodic wholesale renovations. Yet the legal basis of these forms remained.

Even under the most tyrannical emperors the theory in law remained that ultimate power inhered in the populace. At some time, in some form, the power of the emperors was conferred by the Senate and the people. This was historically true, whatever the existing situation, and despite the inadequate way in which power was con-

ferred. However dimly realized at times, the Roman maxim "Salus populi, suprema lex" (the welfare of the people is the supreme law) remained firmly set in Roman law. The standards carried into battle with SPQR ("Senatus populusque Romanus") emblazoned on them meant that even conquest had popular approval. Even the phrase frequently quoted in later centuries in defense of absolute royal power has reference to a popular grant: "quod principi placuit, legis habet vigorem: cum lege regia, quae de eius imperio lata est, populus ei, et in eum, omne imperium suum et potestatem concedat" (the ordinance of the prince hath also the force of a law; for the people, by the *lex regia,* make a concession to him of their whole power—*Dig.* 1.2.6).

Although it is not to be assumed that in strict practice democratic procedure in the modern sense operated at all times in the making of law, the theory always held in Rome that in some manner law emanated from the people or with their approval. Whether enunciated by Gaius ("law is what the people orders") or by CICERO ("power is in the people") or by JUSTINIAN, it is always accepted that the people are the source of law. Accepted by authorities in the Middle Ages, this principle has come to form a basic standard of the democratic order in modern times. It forms a fundamental part of constitutionalism restrictive of arbitrary governmental action for all time.

Medieval Developments. The Middle Ages provided many of the theories on which later defenders of democracy built their philosophy. Theories of individual rights, political and juridical; theories of limited executive power; theories of representative government; and theories of constitutional government developed during this period. Absence of institutional arrangements and sanctions prevented a full realization of the theories in universal practice. Few questioned the doctrine, inherited from Roman law, that law and governmental power stem from the people. How to apply this theory, and who were the people, were questions on which the medievals found no uniform agreement.

Influence of the Church. The recurring crises between the Church and the political order tended in the main to restrict governmental operation. Earlier medieval theories held that the political order was a device for the restriction of evil and a retribution for man's sins. As contrasted with the Church, it was not a holy order. Some went so far as to call political power an invention of the devil. The tendency was to restrict political operation and particularly the power of kings. At the same time the necessity of curbing the disorders of the time called forth other theories that, referring to certain scriptural passages, required the recognition of the king as worthy of respect and obedience. Passages from St. Paul were most frequently used: "he who resists the authority, resists the ordinance of God" (Rom 13.2). Kings were referred to as God's vicars and as holding a "priestly office." Contemporary paintings of Charlemagne showed him clothed in priestly vestments.

From the earliest period of the Middle Ages, however, the king was held to be bound by his coronation oath, by custom, by Scripture, and by the natural law. No king was absolute, and no responsible teaching of the Middle Ages held him to be so. Violation by a king of any of the rules that bound him placed him in the position of an outlaw against whom penalties both of excommunication by the Church and of rebellion by his subjects might be used. The general lack of institutions (outside of the Church) for judging the king's conduct left open to the king's opponents no course other than military action.

Feudal System. From FEUDALISM the idea of a contractual relationship between king and subject arose. Under this complicated system of interrelationships, kings were generally bound in some form of service to overlords or other monarchs or popes. The feudal world was one of contractual agreements. Under these circumstances, the theory of agreement by contract readily entered the realm of political theory.

Rise of Representative Government. From a principle of Roman private law medieval thinkers drew a theory of responsible government that in future years was to play a large part in struggles against ABSOLUTISM: "quod omnes tanget debet ab omnibus approbari" (what touches all should be approved by all—*Corpus iuris civilis, Codex Iustinianus*, ed. P. Krueger 5.59.5). In no sense was this applied in the broad meaning that the phrase might imply. Nevertheless, the constant use of the phrase and its actual application in the religious orders gave the theory a lasting prominence and importance in the development of representative government. Because of this principle, Henry III of England in 1254 could "cause to come before the King's Council two good and discreet Knights of the Shire, whom the men of the country shall have chosen for this purpose instead of all and each of them, to consider along with the Knights of other shires what aid they will grant to the King." While such assemblies were meeting in England to form the first Parliaments, similar assemblies were meeting in Spain and France. The feudal system itself strengthened the representative idea in that overlords in council represented their tenants to such a degree that unanimity was required in some cases in the proceedings of such assemblies. This was especially the case when one lord might represent such military power that he could not be controlled by a majority vote.

The class structure of medieval society prevented any overall egalitarian idea of representation. According to the medieval notion, not only quantity, but also quality, formed the basis of representation. Even MARSILIUS OF PADUA (c. 1290–1343)—erroneously held by some to be the forerunner of modern democracy—held to the notion of a representation of "the wiser and better part," a phrase common in the Middle Ages. A man's equality consisted in his equality with his peers by birth and status. A knight was not equal to a prince; nor could he be judged by a prince. Early, however, in England the interests of the nobility came to diverge to such a degree from those of people of lower status that two groups of representatives came to form two separate houses in the Parliament. By the 16th and 17th centuries the expanding economy of Europe and the rise of a new merchant class gave the lower house a power first equal to and then greater than that of the house representative of the peerage.

Contribution of St. Thomas Aquinas. St. THOMAS AQUINAS (c. 1225–74) has frequently been interpreted as a partisan of popular government. A thorough examination of his writings, however, fails to show that he was much in advance of his time in propounding theories basic to democratic thinking. Much is made of his use of a quotation from St. Augustine (*Lib. arb.* 1.6) in one paragraph of the *Summa:* "If a people have a sense of moderation and responsibility, and are most careful guardians of the common weal, it is right to enact a law allowing such a people to choose their own magistrates for the government of the commonwealth. But if, as time goes on, the same people become so corrupt as to sell their votes, and entrust government to scoundrels and criminals, then the right of selecting their public officials is rightly forfeit to such a people, and the choice devolves to a few good men" (*Summa theologiae* 1a2ae, 97). He even discusses, without in any sense condemning, the three classical forms of constitutions—monarchy, aristocracy, and democracy—and a regime composed of the three. His preference throughout, however, is for "pure monarchy"—the beneficent rule of one man holding absolute power, who holds himself bound by natural, divine, and customary laws. If he holds with most medievals that the king is in some way the choice of the people, this in no way signifies popular election, even though he prefers elective monarchy to hereditary monarchy. So in *De regimine principuum* he remarks that "the common natural rule is by one" (1.2). St. Thomas shows no preference for self-government. His conception of a ruler is one of great power. He does consider that a ruler might be checked by public authority in unusual cases, if, obviously, such an authority exists; however, he does not look upon this as a case likely to arise. If, unhappily, an unjust tyrant rules, the sinfulness of the people has brought this about. Tyrannicide is not permissible.

If one contribution to later democratic thought is provided in St. Thomas, it is in his discussion of LAW, particularly in his consideration of natural law as an unwritten check on all human action, whether public or private. Natural reason supplies the end and goal of the political order, which is the common good toward which men are directed by the natural law. Following Aristotle, St. Thomas asserts that the political order is a good (not a necessary evil or primarily a divine remedy for sin) and that it has a positive end of protection of citizens and the promotion of their welfare. The natural-law theory not only provides the ends and limits of government, but gives the basis for the obligations and rights of the people that come to form a part of the democratic theory of later years.

Early Modern Developments. The RENAISSANCE and the Protestant REFORMATION had varying effects on the relation of the individual to governing authorities. For the most part, the Renaissance with its secular leanings gave little heed to the restriction on rulership provided by divine law, and its general disregard of the philosophical found no bar to tyranny in natural law. The general attitude of Renaissance man was one of lack of concern for things either religious or political. He desired a regime of peace, no matter how absolute, that afforded opportunity to pursue the new learning. So far as politics was concerned, the grandeur of imperial Rome was his ideal. The Renaissance world has its typical representative in Niccolò MACHIAVELLI (1469–1527). A pure pragmatist in advancing the test of workability as the standard for judging all institutions, he nevertheless in the *Discourses* shows a distinct preference for a republic as against a princedom. Freedom of discussion, freedom of choosing officials by the people, and freedom for wide participation of the citizenry in affairs of state are characteristics of a republic, which is the reward of a brave, patriotic, and self-sacrificing people. The ancient republic of Rome is the ideal, but most people are not worthy of it.

Opposition to Absolutism. The immediate effect of the Reformation, despite the emphasis of the reformers on religious individualism, was to strengthen the power of kings in both Catholic and Protestant lands and to give emphasis to the Roman concept that the monarch is outside the law (*legibus solutus*). The period of absolutism gave rise to a whole literature challenging the concept of absolute rulership. The challenge arose mainly from an attempt on the part of rulers to impose their religious views on dissenting groups. Foremost among the critics of absolute kingly power were the Calvinists and the Jesuits. The older idea of government as a contract between ruler and people had a rebirth and was used as an argument against arbitrary divine-right rule. Disregard of divine or natural law on the part of the ruler gave a right to withdrawal of obedience on the part of subjects and might justify rebellion and overthrow of a regime. Recourse was had to the older concept of power arising in the people. Among the Catholic controversialists, St. Robert BELLARMINE (1542–1621) asserted that power comes from God to the people who in turn may set up any kind of lawful regime that serves the purpose of the common good. Among the religious opponents of kingly power, however, there was no defense of religious toleration.

Religious Toleration. Toleration appeared more frequently as a thesis defended among secular writers such as Jean Bodin (1530–96), who, though asserting the rights of monarchs and their limitations, lays down the rule that religious uniformity is desirable, but that if the attempt to enforce it endangers the foundations of the political order, then toleration of religious dissent is to be preferred.

Social Contract Theories. The SOCIAL CONTRACT theory itself played an ever-increasing role in the defense of limited government. In one case, however, it was used by Thomas HOBBES (1588–1679) in his *Leviathan* to strengthen a defense of royal absolutism. It was significant in the theories of the American colonists in defense of their own revolution against the English Crown. In the case of the Americans, the theory was taken from John LOCKE (1632–1704), who in his *Two Treatises on Government* made use of the theory to defend limited monarchy. In brief, his theory of contract held that in the condition before the existence of civil society, man living in a state of nature had certain natural rights (life, liberty, and property) that were not conferred by government, but protected by government when political society came into being. The main purpose of government was the protection of rights, a protection guaranteed by contract between governors and governed. American revolutionists seeking justification for their revolt from the mother country found it—outside the British constitution itself—in Locke's theory of natural rights. Locke, however, was no defender of republican or democratic regimes; his ideal state was a middle-class constitutional monarchy of property holders. However, his theory of popular change of government, peaceful or revolutionary, came to be firmly established as part of the democratic philosophy of government.

Classical Republicans. Previous to Locke, in the 17th century a group of theorists defending the Puritan Revolution in England and the overthrow of the monarchy had written works that profoundly influenced the American revolutionists. This group, sometimes referred to as the Classical Republicans, defended not only revolutionary change, but also the substitution of republican government for monarchy. The best-known among them are John MILTON (1608–74), James Harrington (1611–77), and Algernon Sidney (1622–83). Their theories were based on the historical experience of republican Rome and the Republic of Venice. In addition, they made free use of Machiavelli's theory of republican government as constituting the best form of political regime. Before their time, the term republic was used to designate any type of regime; it simply meant a commonwealth, whether monarchical or non-monarchical. Plato's *Republic* described an aristocracy as an ideal form, but it also included variations from the ideal. In the 16th century, Bodin's *Six Books of the Republic* advocated consititutional monarchy as the best form of republic. The Classical Republicans, however, made a distinct differentiation between a regime, constitutional or otherwise, ruled by a lifelong monarch and a regime with an elective executive head, which to them was known as a republic. This differentiation has come down to contemporary times. The founders of the American Republic generally thought of a republic in these terms, the influence of Harrington being especially great among them, and they held the age-long prejudices against democracies, used in the sense of direct rule by the populace.

American Views. In the *Federalist Papers* (No. 10) James Madison wrote:

> It may be concluded that a pure democracy, by which I mean a society consisting of a small number of citizens, who assemble and administer the government in person, can admit of no cure for the mischiefs of faction. . . . A republic, by which I mean a government in which the scheme of representation takes place, opens a different prospect, and promises the cure for which we are seeking. . . . The two great points of difference between a democracy and a republic are: first, the delegation of the government, in the latter, to a small number of citizens elected by the rest; secondly, the greater number of citizens, and greater sphere of country, over which the latter may be extended.

The Classical Republicans of England and their followers in America thought in terms of a suffrage restricted by property qualifications, since ownership of property in some way represented civic virtue, and also in terms of representation of property holders similarly restricted by property qualifications. Even while the authors of the Constitution of the United States deliberated, there were stirrings among the populace for a broader suffrage base, and the term democracy was beginning to lose its tarnished reputation. Vermont came into the Union in 1791 without property restrictions, and Delaware gave the ballot to all white men who paid taxes. During George Washington's administration, the country was shaken by

news of the French Revolution, and the agricultural forces of the American frontier, heavily in debt to the powers of the East, were demanding greater political control of their government. In the cities along the Atlantic seaboard, mass meetings of workingmen demanded a vote in government. President Washington was warning that "the tumultous populace of large cities are ever to be dreaded." Even Thomas Jefferson referred to "the mobs of great cities" as "sores" on the body politic (*Notes on the State of Virginia,* Query 19). Jefferson thought that any orderly government of large cities was impossible. With the pressure for a universal manhood suffrage, the term democracy found more frequent usage as applied to the operation of government in America. This was particularly so with the sweep of the Jacksonian movement through the country. Thus in the 1830s Alexis de Tocqueville adopted *The American Democracy* as the title of his classic work on politics and society in the United States. The party of Jefferson took the name of the Democratic-Republican party, but by the Jacksonian period it had become the Democratic party. As the suffrage base was broadened, the term democracy came to be the usual designation for the form of government that existed in the United States.

Principle of Representation. In the thinking of the people of the time, the chief touchstone of a democracy was representative government. Not only was great faith placed in representative assemblies, but in the elective process itself more and more names of administrative and executive offices found their places on the ballot. Faith in the legislative process was accompanied by a fear of executive power, so that mayors and governors found themselves surrounded by innumerable checks in the exercise of their functions. In Europe, too, political reform emphasized the importance of suffrage for the agricultural and laboring classes, and more favorable representation of these groups. Influenced by the theories of the French Revolution, a strong emphasis on egalitarianism characterized all the democratic movements. Tocqueville feared that there was a tendency to overemphasize this in the America of the 1830s. It would have been difficult, however, in the America of that day, with its strong frontier attitudes, to find or defend any class divisions in society.

Democratic Ideology. Democracy both in the United States and abroad ceased to have either the form or the reputation that had characterized it in preceding centuries. It became the aim of all political reform both in the United States and in the Western world. The principal test of democracy came to be universal manhood suffrage and equal representation for all classes in the legislature. Basic to all theoretical defenses of democracy were the ancient theories of political power emanating from the people, the medieval doctrine of "what touches all must be approved by all," the limitation of political power by unchanging laws of God and of nature, the determination of consent by majority, and the inherent worth of the individual soul derived from the ancient Judeo-Christian heritage. Some saw democracy as inevitable in a world built upon these principles.

Both in the United States and in England democratic movements had a strong evangelistic religious impetus. Although in America church attendance and adherence to religious groups fell to a low level during and immediately after the Revolution, a strong revivalist movement in the early 19th century brought religion to the forefront in American society. Religious groups, such as the Baptists and the Methodists, and a variety of splinter Protestant groups that followed the democratic form in the management of their churches combined their religious and egalitarian principles in advocating ever-increasing popular control. The same influences were at work in England, where the backbone of the democratic movement was found in the members of the so-called Free Churches. Much of the evangelistic fervor that spurred on the Jacksonians in the United States and the Chartists in England came from this source. On the Continent of Europe democratic movements had been influenced to a large degree by the theories of the French Revolution and were most frequently secular in tone and often inspired by anti-religious aims.

Growth of Executive Power. By mid-19th century faith in legislative bodies as representing the ideals and aspirations of the people suffered a reverse with the awareness that legislators were corrupted and election practices were a scandal. The belief came to be held that executives armed with proper authority, far from being a danger to the democratic form, constituted effective agents of the people's will. One governor or one president, it was recognized, more often represented the will of the electorate than scores of legislators, whether in a state capital or in Washington. Throughout the whole Western world the move toward concentration of greater powers in the hands of executives finds firm support even today among the most liberal defenders of democracy. The flexible provisions of the United States Constitution have lent themselves to an interpretation consistent with this demand for executive power and responsibility, particularly under strong presidents.

Economic Democracy. Out of the Renaissance and Reformation periods there had developed a strong theory of individualism that affected religious, political, and economic life. The theory that man's unaided reason or divine illumination could lead him to his proper end— and in the political and economic spheres, to the best life for society—captured the minds of the 17th, 18th, and early 19th centuries. This blind faith in the infallible instinct of man in following his own interests was highlighted by a disregard of societal or communal obligations. If a man starved or failed in any sense, he had himself to blame, for within him existed all the necessary physical strength or natural reason for success. In the political sphere, governments were necessary, but necessary evils, for protection of life and limb alone. Leaders of democratic movements sought first the suffrage for the middle- and lower-middle-class groups, and then for the larger masses of the laboring people. It should be remembered that the early exponents of democracy had little faith in the masses and sought only a bourgeois commonwealth. By reason of their own theory of man's rational nature, however, they had to face the necessity of extending the rights of citizens to an ever-increasing number of people.

The older theory of natural law with its emphasis on rights as proceeding from obligations had, following the theories of Locke and Hobbes, become largely a theory of rights alone. This attitude characterized particularly the economic life of the rapidly expanding industrial society. In exploitation not only of natural resources, but of men, the economically successful interpreted the doctrine of natural rights as complete, unhindered freedom in the pursuit of wealth. The great economic advance of the Western world was paid for in a frightening wastage of health and lives.

Pragmatic Trends. In recognition of a prevailing economic anarchy, there arose not only a demand for a greater voice of the working class in government, but also a demand for governmental regulation of economic activity. The use of the natural-rights doctrine in defense of economic exploitation gave place in democratic demands to a doctrine of social rights. The obviously just reminder that society too had rights was accompanied by the more dangerous doctrine that society, through organized government, conferred rights. The feeling existed that since the bulk of the male population controlled the action of government through suffrage and representation, fear of an overpowering or tyrannical political order was baseless. The amazing advances of science and the scientific method had the effect of reducing philosophy to a crude pragmatism that saw in immediate effects the justification of public activity. The cure for the ills of democracy was, it was claimed, more democracy. Speculative philosophy and theoretical justification of the system itself found little support among the intellectual leaders of the new industrial era. Use of a corrupted natural-rights doctrine in defense of the glaring evils of the industrial revolution had discredited philosophy itself.

Marxism. In the 19th and early 20th centuries certain schools of thought pointed out the weakness in political democracy and turned their attention to the operation of the economic system itself. The followers of Karl MARX (1818–83) based much of their philosophy on an ancient theory. Plato, Aristotle, and medieval and later theorists had pointed to the corrupting influences on stable forms of government of great accumulations of wealth in private hands. Machiavelli had written that under a good form of government, only the government should be rich. Plato would have had his rulers divested of all wealth, and the possessor of wealth debarred from active citizenship. Aristotle desired a middle-class regime with a wide dispersion of wealth. That the owners of vast economic power could control the possession of political power was not an original discovery of Marx. Nevertheless, Marxist thought turned in the direction of economic democracy as opposed to political democracy. The thoroughgoing Marxist renounced politics, warned against suffrage and reforms in representation, and condemned socialist participation in any government existing side by side with the capitalistic order. He believed that all political forms existing under capitalism were mere shams and agencies of exploitation by the owners of the means of production. Only where the workers owned and governed the means of production would genuine—or economic—democracy prevail.

Divergent Theories. Other schools of thought had turned their attentions in the same direction. Some, such as syndicalism and ANARCHISM, advocated violent revolution for the purpose of setting up self-governing federations of industrial groups. Others, such as guild socialism and various schools of political pluralism, advocated guild associations of workers and employers with special parliaments representing trades and professions; but these were to be accomplished by peaceful means. Support for corporativist and pluralist ideas was found in the encyclicals of LEO XIII, PIUS XI, and PIUS XII. Unlike Fascism, which looked upon the state as the creator of economic associations, the encyclicals emphasized the necessity of the free formation of guilds, with the state as the general overseer of guild obligations and rights.

New Problems. The Marxist still considers the true socialist regime a democracy, and the term has been freely appropriated by Communist regimes. The challenges offered by the emphasis on economic democracy, the catastrophic effects of the world Depression of the early 1930s, and the rise of totalitarian regimes of the right and left, offering both "security" and "freedom," caused the leaders of established democracies to reevaluate democracy in both its forms and its effects. The older democracies of the West had successfully withstood the assaults of the turbulent 20th century, but something more than

a pragmatic defense of the system was called for. The Fascist and the National Socialist revolutions had themselves been called the pragmatic revolt in politics. Their leaders claimed that they offered new systems that "worked," whereas the democracies had failed in practice. More attention to an underlying philosophy of democracy was called for.

More serious attention, too, had to be given to the practical questions of the role of government, the practice of planning, the existence of poverty and slums, the problems of health and old age, the injustice of racial discrimination, the causes and cures of fluctuations in the economic order, and, after World War II, the adequate popular control of the vast scientific discoveries that spelled life or annihilation for large masses of people. A great number of new nations, only recently freed from colonial control, came into existence, each looking for the freedom that democracy promised, but lacking both economic resources and generations of politically educated populations on which to build stable governments. These people desired democracy, but held in low esteem its association with the capitalistic order, under which they believed they had until recently been exploited. Communism, because of its declared enmity to capitalism and its influence on economic democracy, seemingly held out greater promise to these people than did the established democracies. Some leaders of the Western world have advocated the use of the term welfare democracy and a playing down of the capitalist element in democracies of the past and present, in order to guard these new nations from Communist inroads. It is argued that, because of the complexity of modern economic life and the need for immediate relief from poverty, the individualism that in the span of centuries brought the Western world to its material eminence may not be counted on to solve the urgent problems of the new nations. Greater need, therefore, calls for more socialized forms of economic life.

A Catholic Appraisal. Recognized today as essential elements in democracy are universal adult suffrage; representation in a legislative body of a fair proportion of the electorate; decision by majority vote of the electorate in determination of major questions of policy; equality before the law; equality of opportunity; freedom of speech, press, and assembly; freedom from arbitrary arrest and punishment; freedom in the exercise of religion; and the largest possible exercise of individual activity consonant with social requirements. Catholic defenders of the democratic order point out that although by natural or divine law there is no one required form of government for all times and places, democracy best meets the requirements of the modern age and best fulfills the underlying principles inherent in Catholic teaching.

Catholic teaching incorporates certain basic principles underlying political relationships. Among these are: recognition of the political order as natural and necessary (not only a necessary evil); the common good as the end of that order; and the recognition of the dignity of the individual person, with respect for his rights and obligations as man and citizen. Defenders of the democratic system point out that since it is a form of government requiring the assumption by the citizen of the most important public decisions, it is therefore a system that has led to the steady broadening of educational opportunities for all. They would insist that the practice of the political art makes possible, although not inevitable, political maturity and political virtue. In no other form is the medieval principle that what touches all must be approved by all better realized.

The Catholic political theorist, however, would reject the purely relativistic theory held by some modern apologists for democracy that no natural-law standards exist to guide both the government and the governed or that decision by popular vote constitutes a guarantee of moral rectitude. Yet in the field of politics, the determination of right and wrong is rarely as clear as the distinction between true and false in mathematics or metaphysics. Government involves the application of objective principles to practical situations, and PRUDENCE plays the leading role. It is therefore essential that full discussion and deliberation, which democracy allows for, should precede all decisions. Defenders of democracy are aware that it has not yet realized its full promise and that the complexities of modern life place before it awe-inspiring problems to which answers must be given. Democracy is not a thing of perfection; but, to paraphrase a statement of Sir Winston Churchill, the alternatives to it are too horrible to contemplate.

See Also: GOVERNMENT; STATE, THE.

Bibliography: Y. SIMON, *Philosophy of Democratic Government* (Chicago 1951). J. MARITAIN, *Man and the State* (Chicago 1951); *The Rights of Man and Natural Law,* tr. D. C. ANSON (New York 1943); *Reflections on America* (New York 1958). H. A. ROMMEN, *The State in Catholic Thought* (St. Louis 1945). C. H. MCILWAIN, *Constitutionalism: Ancient and Modern* (rev. ed. Ithaca, New York 1958). H. LASKI, *The American Democracy* (New York 1948). W. LIPPMANN, *Essays in the Public Philosophy* (Boston 1955). J. MESSNER, *Social Ethics,* tr. J. J. DOHERTY (new ed. St. Louis 1964). C. V. SHIELDS, *Democracy and Catholicism in America* (New York 1958). J. H. HALLOWELL, *The Moral Foundation of Democracy* (Chicago 1954). M. P. FOGARTY, *Christian Democracy in Western Europe, 1820–1953* (Notre Dame, Indiana 1957). A. C. DE TOCQUEVILLE, *Democracy in America,* tr. H. REEVE, 4 v. (London 1835–40); ed. P. BRADLEY, 2 v. (New York 1960). T. E. UTLEY and J. S. MACLURE, *Documents of Modern Political Thought* (Cambridge, England 1957), pt. 1. C. E. MERRIAM, *The New Democracy and the New Despotism* (New York 1939). J. S. MILL, *On Liberty and Considerations on Representative Government,* ed. R. B. MCCALLUM (Oxford 1946). O. F. VON GIERKE, *The Development of Political Theory* (New York 1939) pt. 2. E. LEWIS, *Medieval Political Ideas,* 2 v. (New York 1954), v.1.

[J. G. KERWIN]

DEMOCRITUS

Greek cosmologist and moralist, disciple of Leucippus, the father of ancient ATOMISM. His native city was Abdera on the northern coast of the Aegean Sea. He lived to a very old age, and although his exact dates are unknown, his life spanned virtually the entire 5th century B.C. He traveled widely and may have visited Athens. Encyclopedic in his interests, Democritus further developed the cosmology of atomism, but was best known among the ancients as a moralist. Although several works have been attributed to him, only fragments remain. The best known work of his school was entitled *The Great Diakosmos,* although the authorship and manner of composition cannot be determined.

Greek atomism developed in the spirit of the earlier Milesian tradition and as a response to the Eleatic objections against the possibility of motion. The whole of reality was reduced to atoms, infinite in number, imperceptible to the senses, and possessing only the properties of solidity, size, and varying shapes. The early atomists did not attribute weight to their atoms, an addition made later by EPICURUS. Moving at random in a void the atoms coagulated into the larger and familiar objects of experience. Unlike EMPEDOCLES and ANAXAGORAS, the atomists felt no need to posit a moving force; the atoms were simply "given" in motion. The soul was understood as composed of spherical atoms of fire.

In the latter half of the 5th century B.C. the attention of Greek philosophers shifted to epistemological and moral problems, and Democritus shared these interests. He taught that sensation is produced by groups of atoms from external objects entering into the pores of the sensory organs. But sense knowledge for Democritus was subjective and did not provide true insight into the atomic structure of reality. This doctrine has been interpreted as an anticipation of the distinction between primary and secondary sense qualities.

Most of the extant fragments of Democritus are moral maxims. He taught that the moral ideal is the life of cheerfulness, unperturbed by chance occurrences and by excess or defect in human action. The sign of this ideal life is pleasure; he was not a sensualist, however, since he extolled the values of rational truth and the life of reason. He counseled moderation as the safeguard of true and lasting pleasure, and emphasized the values of law

Christ driving a demon out of mute man. (©Historical Picture Archive/CORBIS)

and ordered civil society in assisting the individual to attain the life of cheerfulness.

See Also: GREEK PHILOSOPHY; MATERIALISM

Bibliography: H. DIELS, *Die Fragmente der Vorsokratiker Griechisch und Deutsch*, ed. W. KRANZ, 3 v. (8th ed. Berlin 1956); v.1 (10th ed. Berlin 1960–61). English. K. FREEMAN, tr., *Ancilla to the Pre-Socratic Philosophers* (Cambridge, Mass. 1948). Secondary Studies. F. C. COPLESTON, *History of Philosophy: Greece and Rome* (Westminster, Md. 1946; 2d ed. 1950) 1:72–75, 124–126. C. BAILEY, *The Greek Atomists and Epicurus* (Oxford 1928). M. SOLOVINE, tr., *Démocrite: Doctrines philosophiques et réflexions morales* (Paris 1928).

[R. J. BLACKWELL]

DEMON (IN THE BIBLE)

As used in the Bible, the word demon designates an evil spirit. Originally, however, the Greek word δαίμων, from which the English word demon is ultimately derived, meant a divine being, normally regarded as good; thus, the term οἱ δαίμονες is used in Homer in the meaning of "the gods." Later this word and, more commonly, its neuter adjective δαιμόνιον, like the Latin word *genius*, were frequently used of lesser spirits, demigods, especially men's guardian spirits or spirits that influenced men's characters. Still later, the word δαιμόνιον (borrowed into Latin as *daemonium*) was applied to evil spirits, spirits that tormented men or caused them harm.

In the Old Testament and Judaism. Although belief in demons as evil spirits was widespread in the ancient Near East, DEMONOLOGY played an insignificant role in the older books of the Old Testament. For the Israelite, evil as well as good was sent by Yahweh or by His (good) messengers (*mal'ākîm*, angels) who were commissioned by Him to punish men (e.g., 2 Sm 24.16–17; cf. Ex 12.23). Even SATAN was originally thought of as Yahweh's obedient servant sent to test men (Jb 1.6–12;

2.1–7) or to accuse them of wrongdoing before His tribunal (Zec 3.1–2). Popular Israelite religion, however, laid more stress on the power of evil spirits (*šēdîm*), whom orthodox Yahwism identified with pagan gods [Dt 32.17; Ps 105(106).36–37]. The ghosts of the dead (called *'ĕlōhîm*, gods, in 1 Sm 28.13) were apparently regarded as quasi demons, with whom converse was strictly forbidden (1 Sm 28.9; Lv 20.27; Dt 18.11; *see* NECROMANCY). The word *śā'îr* (hairy?), which probably designated originally a species of desert owl (Is 13.21; 34.14), as did the word *lîlît* (Is 34.14), was used in postexilic times as a name for certain demons, traditionally translated as satyrs (Lv 17.7; 2 Chr 11.15). Perhaps also postexilic was the concept of Azazel as a desert-dwelling demon to whom the SCAPEGOAT was sent on the Day of Atonement (Lv 16.8, 10, 26).

However, in the late books of the Old Testament, the Old Testament apocrypha, and the rabbinical writings of the time of Christ, demons became much more important and were known by various names, especially unclean spirits. They were regarded not only as causing men physical harm, but also as seducing them to moral evil, and they were therefore considered God's enemies (e.g., Enoch, Ethiopic 9.8; 10.8; 64.2; Jubilees 7.27; 10.1; 11.4). According to Jewish speculation, the demons were fallen angels whose fall consisted either (as in Enoch, Ethiopic ch. 15; Jubilees 5.1; 10.5) in having sexual intercourse with women (the "sons of God" and the "daughters of men" of Gn 6.4) or (as in Enoch, Slavic ch. 7; *Vita Adam* ch. 15) in rebelling, under the leadership of Satan, against God. These concepts had probably been influenced by Iranian DUALISM, with which the Jews in the Babylonian Diaspora came in contact. Such influence can scarcely be doubted in the case of Asmodaeus, the evil demon of the Book of Tobit (Tb 3.8; 8.3), who even had an Iranian name.

In the New Testament. The term οἱ δαίμονες (the demons) occurs only in Mt 8.31, but the terms (τὸ) δαιμόνιον and τά δαιμόνια are of frequent occurrence in the New Testament. Naturally the New Testament reflects largely the ideas about the demons that were current among the Jews of the time; this is especially true in the vivid imagery of the Apocalypse (Rv 16.13–14; 18.2). St. Paul alludes to the Old Testament idea that the demons are the pagan gods (1 Cor 10.20–21), but the concept of the demons and unclean spirits as causing men physical harm is not stressed in the New Testament (2 Cor 12.7), apart from the many references to demoniacs. [*See* DIABOLICAL POSSESSION (IN THE BIBLE).] The New Testament is concerned primarily with the moral aspect of demons as hostile to man's spiritual good (Eph 6.12; 1 Jn 4.1–3), and Christ's power to overcome the physical harm that the demons can do is really symbolic of His conquest of spiritual evil and His establishment of the kingdom of God (Mt 12.28; Mk 3.22–26; Lk 11.20). The New Testament words on the demons should not be discarded as empty mythology. While it may be granted that they are colored by the folklore of the time (e.g., in Mk 5.12–13; Lk 11.24–26), they contain theological truths of great value.

Iconography. Representations of demons in the art of the Christian West did not begin until the 12th century, but from then on they are very common. In the Middle Ages demons were portrayed in the most horrible and frightening forms the artists could imagine, especially as tormenting the damned in hell. From the 14th to the 16th century a common theme was St. ANTHONY OF EGYPT being tempted by demons; well known are such paintings in the museums of Lisbon and the Prado by Hieronymus Bosch. Also, the fall of the rebellious angels from heaven was a favorite theme of the artists, e.g., the painting by Pieter Brueghel the Elder in the Royal Museum of Brussels. In folk art, demons were commonly portrayed with bat wings, horns, a pointed tail, and birdlike claws.

Bibliography: *Encyclopedic Dictionary of the Bible*, tr. and adap. by L. HARTMAN (New York 1963) 545–548. R. SCHNACKENBURG, *Lexikon für Theologie und Kirche*, ed. J. HOFER and K. RAHNER (Freiburg 1957–65) 3:141–142. M. GRUENTHANER, "The Demonology of the O.T.," *The Catholic Biblical Quarterly*, 6 (1944) 6–27. D. SABBATUCCI et al., *Encyclopedia of World Art* (New York 1959–) 4:306–335.

[L. F. HARTMAN]

DEMON (THEOLOGY OF)

It is clear that anything like a developed demonology among the Jews arose during the intertestamental period. An exception must be made for the Book of Tobit, which is, however, late and probably reflects the impetus given to this area of speculation by Persian ideas after the Exile. The detailed demonology of the apocryphal Book of Enoch—so important because of the allusions to it in the New Testament (1 Cor 10.19–22; Jude 6–7; 2 Pt 2.4)—is based on an interpretation of Gn 6.1–4, rather than on any extraneous material. For this reason it won acceptance among the Jews and remained normative both for them and for the Christians of the first few centuries.

Fathers. The most elaborate presentation of this misunderstanding of Gn 6.1–4 in a Christian document appears in the *Clementine Homilies* (*Hom.* 8), which are assigned by some scholars to the second century and by others to the fourth. There is no question, however, that the doctrine it teaches was widely held. Tertullian accepted it in the West (*De virg. vel.* 7), as did Athenagoras in the East (*Leg.* 24). St John Chrysostom rejected it (*Hom.*

Demons tormenting the damned in hell, detail of a 13th-century mosaic in the Baptistery vault, Florence, Italy.

22 in Gen. 2), but St. Augustine hesitated to do so (*Quaest. hept.* 1.3). Interestingly, St. Augustine came very close to a correct understanding of Gn 6.1–4 in his *City of God* (3.5), for he compared that account to the Greco-Roman legend of Venus and Anchises begetting Aeneas; had he known of the Sumero-Babylonian heroes such as GILGAMESH, who were half human and half divine, he would have been able to cite the apparent source of the curious tale of Genesis.

According to the Clementine account, the giants born of intercourse between the lustful angels and women did not survive the flood, but their souls did, and these disembodied souls became nothing less than the gods of the pagan world. God commanded them through an angel to ''trouble no one, unless anyone of his own accord subject himself to you, worshipping you, and sacrificing and pouring libations, and partaking of your table . . . .'' The belief that idols were inhabited by demons was, of course, a commonplace among the Christians of the first

five centuries, and one can see in the Clementine exposition an attempt to attribute a superhuman reality to the gods of the pagans without straying from the revelation of the Bible and without acknowledging any need to worship them. This made discussion with their idolatrous neighbors possible.

If what one may call the Clementine explanation of who the demons were and how they came into being (remembering always that this explanation is founded on the book of Enoch's misinterpretation of Gn 6.1–4) was widespread in antiquity, it was not the only one. Justin Martyr assumed that the DEVIL fell from grace when he tempted Eve (*Dial.* 124), and in another passage he identified the LEVIATHAN of Is 27.1 with SATAN (*Dial.* 112). This latter interpretation is not without interest for the modern theologian, who knows that Leviathan was the Canaanite monster of primordial chaos. Such an identification suggests a line of development worthy of pursuit. Similarly, Athenagoras, though he accepted the general view that demons are angels who fell through lust, seems not to have implicated their leader in this action. Satan, rather, became "heedless and wicked in the administration of his charge," and that charge was "the regulation of matter and its patterns" (*Leg.* 24). This too has more relevance for contemporary theological speculation than most patristic contributions to demonology.

As might be expected, Origen had some original ideas in this area; he initiated a trend in the exegesis of certain Biblical texts that was to dominate Christian demonology for more than 17 centuries. In the Lucifer of Is 14.12–15 and in the king of Tyre of Ez 28.12–19, he saw a supernatural being who could be none other than Satan. Accordingly, the fall of the devil was due to pride (as indicated in these texts) and not to any lustful cravings. Origen was correct in judging that these texts use language applicable to superhuman beings. What he could not know, but what one does now, is that the Prophets both borrowed from Canaanite mythology and poetically applied what they took to the human kings to whom these oracles were addressed. The original material (Canaanite) did indeed speak of gods or demigods but not, obviously, of the devil.

The extent of patristic literature precludes a more detailed analysis than has been given, but the teaching presented is representative, and no other significant schools of thought in this matter existed. One may conclude by noting, once again, that the impact of the apocryphal book of Enoch on early Christian demonology cannot be overestimated. Even though the views of Chrysostom and Origen ultimately prevailed, the Clementine exposition was responsible for the unfortunate and unhealthy medieval speculations about incubi and succubi and for the yet present readiness to attribute sins of the flesh to diabolical activity.

As to the authority of patristic teaching on this subject, it is of utmost importance to remember that there was no unanimity regarding the time and manner of the fall of the angels. In point of fact the Fathers, where they did attempt to answer these questions on the basis of Biblical texts, were in error. On the other hand, unanimity did exist as to the existence of evil spirits who tempt man and otherwise create disturbance in the cosmos.

Later Thought. During the Middle Ages philosophical speculation supplied the need, previously met by the fictitious tales of the apocrypha, to satisfy the curiosity of the faithful about those matters that had not been clearly revealed. Such speculation used the Scriptures as a starting point, however, and as indicated previously, the cited texts from Ezekiel and Isaiah were generally regarded as relevant to the fall of Satan and his followers.

It is not surprising, consequently, that one finds more or less general agreement as to the nature of the sin of the angels as well, namely, pride. Duns Scotus is characteristically original in this respect, however, and describes Satan's sin as one of inordinate self-love, a kind of narcissistic lewdness. This would be, of course, a kind of pride, but Scotus classifies it as *luxuria*. The sin of pride envisioned by the other scholastics, of whom St. Thomas Aquinas is representative, consisted in wishing to be entirely independent of God; Satan wished, that is, either to attain supernatural beatitude by his own power or to enjoy a natural beatitude and reject the supernatural beatitude given by God (*Summa theologiae* 1a, 63.2–3). There is unanimity about the idea that God did not create the demons evil (inasmuch as, had He done so, He would have been directly responsible for evil), and Scotus maintains that even after his fall Satan is capable of willing some good although, through malice, he probably does not do so. St. Thomas affirms that Satan was created in grace, but sinned from the first instant of his creation. The Angelic Doctor admits, however, the possibility of an interval of time having elapsed between creation and fall, and this is definitely the view propounded by Scotus.

The demons were conceived of as spiritual beings, although this did not preclude the possession of a *corpus subtile* as Cajetan called it, but the lingering influence of the misinterpreted text in Genesis ch. 6 prevented medieval theologians from ruling out sexual activity on their part. This was supposed to have been possible through the temporary assumption of human bodies; a demon who performed the male role was called an incubus, while the demon who assumed the female role was called a succubus (Peter Comestor, St. Albert the Great). It was taken for granted that anyone might be the prey of such lustful demons. Ordinarily, the demons were thought to inhabit the stormy, dark, and cloudy regions of the atmosphere (author of the *Summa sententiarum,* St. Bonaventure, St. Albert the Great, etc.). In this respect medieval opinion merely reflected man's ageless fears and superstitions. It was their residence in the atmosphere, moreover, that made it possible for them to tempt man.

Toward the very end of the scholastic period, F. Suárez explained that these demons, removed though they are from the site of hell, suffer the pain of fire by "virtual contact." Moreover, he continued, the demons in the atmosphere take turns of duty in the underworld, being replaced by those who act as tormentors there. Suárez is also to be credited with the suggestion that Satan's sin of pride lay in this, that he wished his own angelic nature to be hypostatically united to the divine Word rather than that God should, as He had determined, choose a human nature for this union. This can only be classified as extravagant speculation, although it enjoyed a vogue in popular theology for many centuries—simply because it gave a detailed answer to a question that is inevitably raised.

Magisterium. The official teaching of the Church on demons is far from being extensive. The earliest documents were negative in character, refuting (1) Origen's theory of APOCATASTASIS (final restitution, i.e., salvation), according to which Satan and his angels would be restored to grace and admitted into glory, and (2) the Manichaean doctrine that Satan was not originally an angel, good by nature and created by God, but an independent, evil principle who emanated from primordial darkness. The first condemnation was contained in the canons of the synod held at Constantinople (543 A.D.), and these were, according to Cassiodorus, approved by Pope Vigilius. The second was formulated by the Council of Braga (561 A.D.) and expressed the view of Pope Leo the Great as his letter to Turibius, Bishop of Astorga, reveals. Certainly both of these errors may be said to stand condemned implicitly in the many definitions affirming the eternity of hell and the attribution of everything apart from God to His creative power (e.g., Vatican I; H. Denzinger, *Enchiridion symbolorum* 3025) so that the dogmatic value of these early documents—which is difficult to evaluate—is not crucial in this matter. By contrast, the solemn profession of faith drawn up by the Fourth Lateran Council (1215 A.D.) is of prime importance. In it one finds the following sentence concerning demonology: "For the devil and the other demons were created good by nature, by God, but of their own doing they became evil" (*Enchiridion symbolorum* 428). In this document one also finds it stated that after the resurrection the good will achieve eternal glory with Christ whereas the wicked will be allotted "perpetual punishment together with the devil" (*Enchiridion symbolorum* 429). The Church has, then, defined only those truths that are contained implicitly or explicitly in the Scriptures. Nothing is stated regarding the nature of the sin committed by Satan and the other demons, nor is the time of its commission specified, although the wording of the decree issued by the Fourth Lateran Council assumes that these angels had fallen before the creation of man. Neither are the demons said to dwell in any place or region other than hell. The Council of Trent declared, *in obliquo,* that the devil rules the kingdom of death (*Enchiridion symbolorum* 1511), which means that he is responsible for it—a teaching found in both Old and New Testaments (Wis 2.24; Jn 8.44). In his encyclical HUMANI GENERIS Pius XII listed as an error the view that angels may not be "personal beings" (*Enchiridion symbolorum* 3891), from which it certainly follows that demons, too, are personal beings.

Contemporary Appraisals. The demonology of the Middle Ages remained standard until fairly recent times.

The advances made in the natural sciences have, however, considerably altered this state of affairs. The present, more detailed knowledge of the universe has forever destroyed the crude concept of a three-storied world in which angels and demons materialize with ingenuous frequency. Psychiatry, moreover, has shown that the workings of the subconscious explain many, if not most, of the abnormal conditions that earlier generations had attributed to diabolical activity. For these reasons and because the need to reorient theology along more positive lines has been recognized, demonology has not been the object of very much serious study in the 20th century.

Yet the need for such study is apparent. The Church is committed to a belief in angels and demons, but the meaning of this belief in terms that are both comprehensible and relevant to modern man has not been adequately presented. K. Rahner has written that the angels belong to the world "in a permanent and continuous fashion . . . . They are in fact principles . . . of the world. To be somewhat more specific, they are the ultimate foundations of the natural order of things, determining the right order of events in this world because of their essential relationship to the universe" [*On the Theology of Death,* tr. C. H. Henkey (New York 1961) 32]. Conversely, it might be said that demons determine the disorder of events in the world. This is really nothing more than a restatement of the view of Athenagoras or a development of Justin Martyr's identification of Satan with the monster of chaos. The appeal of such an interpretation rests in the fact that it can be integrated with the evolutionary view of the universe that is all but universally accepted today. There is a regressive factor in evolution, and at the close of his *Phenomenon of Man* P. Teilhard de Chardin asks: "is it really sure that, for an eye trained and sensitised by light other than that of pure science, the quantity and the malice of evil *hic et nunc,* spread through the world, does not betray a certain *excess,* inexplicable to our reason, if to *the normal effect of evolution* is not added the *extra-ordinary* effect of some catastrophe or primordial deviation?" [tr. B. Wall (New York 1959) 311].

See Also: ANGELS; DIABOLICAL POSSESSION (THEOLOGY OF); DIABOLICAL OBSESSION; EXORCISM.

Bibliography: E. MANGENOT and T. ORTOLAN, *Dictionnaire de théologie catholique,* ed. A. VACANT et al., (Paris 1903–50) 4.1:399–409. A. DARLAPP, *Lexikon für Theologie und Kirche,* ed. J. HOFER and K. RAHNER (Freiburg 1957–65) 3:142–143. F. NAU, *Dictionnaire apologétique de la foi catholique,* ed. A. D'ALÈS (Paris 1911–12) 1:923–928. G. ROTUREAU, *Catholicisme* 3:599–601. S. LYONNET et al., *Dictionnaire de spiritualité ascétique et mystique. Doctrine et histoire,* ed. M. VILLER et al. (Paris 1932–) 3:141–238. J. MICHL, H. FRIES, ed., *Handbuch theologischer Grundbegriffe* (Munich 1962–63) 2:469–478. *Satan,* ed. B. DE JÉSUS-MARIE, tr. M. CARROLL et al. (New York 1952). N. CORTE (L. CHRISTIANI), *Who*

"De Spectris, Lemuribus, Variisque Praesagitionibus," 17th-century Latin manuscript by Ludovici Lavateri, 1659. (©CORBIS)

is the Devil? tr. D. K. PRYCE (New York 1958). L. CHRISTIANI, *Evidence of Satan in the Modern World,* tr. C. ROWLAND (New York 1962). E. J. MONTANO, *The Sin of the Angels* (Washington 1955).

[L. J. ELMER]

DEMONOLOGY

Here the term "demonology" is taken to mean the occult and superstitious lore that has grown up about the subject of evil spirits, and especially the art and practice of seeking their intervention in human affairs. The term could signify the science concerned with demons or evil spirits. In this sense the subject is dealt with in the article DEMON (THEOLOGY OF).

There are two ways of seeking the help of evil spirits: to attempt to obtain preternatural knowledge from them; and to seek their aid in producing effects that are above human capabilities. The seeking of assistance from evil spirits may be either formal or explicit. It is formal when Satan (or any other evil spirit) is expressly called upon for help; when a formal pact is made with the devil, in which the petitioner promises his soul or certain services if his request is granted; or when religious homage is paid to evil spirits in the form of genuflections or other ceremonies in order to obtain some favor. It is implicit when a person does not expressly ask the devil for a favor, but from the nature of the thing sought or the way in which it is to be obtained, it can only be concluded that the devil is tacitly invited to grant the request. In such a case, a kind of knowledge, or the performance of a kind of deed, is sought that could not be achieved by human powers alone. Supposing it to be evident that the favor is not sought from God, we presume that the petitioner is invoking the aid of a superhuman power of evil.

In genuine religion, we recognize God to be all good and all holy. Therefore, the only attitude of man confronted with an all good, all holy God is one of reverence, gratitude, and submission; but throughout history there have been those who rebel at their obligation of subjection to God, and who are impatient because God will not gratify their every whim and caprice. In their pride, they do not want to fit into the plans of Divine Providence; rather, they expect God to be at their beck and call.

The moral appraisal of particular cases of the invocation of evil spirits is complicated, so far as subjective responsibility is concerned, by the fact that a willingness to traffic with evil spirits suggests the possibility of paranoid delusions and hallucinations. Where a person is a responsible human agent and knows what he is doing, theologians are agreed that any pact with an evil spirit is a mortal sin. The same is true of any attempt to elicit enlightenment or aid from the devil. Even to ask for a small favor would be a mortal sin, for the reason that the evil spirits are the enemies of God and of mankind, and to invoke their help would involve grave dishonor to God.

Objectively, even the implicit invocation of the devil is gravely sinful; but there is more probability, where the invocation is tacit or implicit, that the act is less deliberate, or that it is not performed with a clear awareness that one is really calling upon the evil spirits for assistance.

A question can be raised about the permissibility of performing an experiment in which there is a possibility of diabolical intervention. Must such experiments be avoided? The more common answer to this is that if there is only a possibility of diabolical intervention, it is permissible, for a just cause, to conduct such experiments; but prudence would seem to require the experimenter to disavow any intention of seeking diabolical aid, and to state that he positively does not want it. However, in cases in which, instead of a possibility, there is a notable probability of diabolical intervention, it is evident that there is no moral justification for such experimentation.

Bibliography: B. DE JÉSUS-MARIE, ed., *Satan* (New York 1952). B. J. KELLY, *God, Man and Satan* (Westminster, MD 1950). L. CRISTIANI, *Who Is the Devil?,* tr. D. K. PRYCE (New York 1958);

Evidence of Satan in the Modern World, tr. C. ROWLAND (New York 1962). E. A. GRILLOT DE GIVRY, *Picture Museum of Sorcery, Magic and Alchemy* (New Hyde Park, NY 1963). S. LYONNET et al., *Dictionnaire de spiritualité ascétique et mystique. Doctrine et histoire,* ed. M. VILLER et al. (Paris 1932–) 4:141–238. L. RULAND, *Foundations of Morality,* tr. T. A. RATTLER, ed. N. THOMPSON (St. Louis 1936). L. GARDETTE, *Dictionnaire de théologie catholique,* ed. A. VACANT et al., (Paris 1903–50) 9.2:1510–50. P. SÉJOURNÉ, *Dictionnaire de théologie catholique,* ed. A. VACANT et al., (Paris 1903–50) 14.2:2763–2824.

[M. D. GRIFFIN]

DEMONSTRATION

As used in philosophy and theology, demonstration is a logical and methodological term first employed by Aristotle (Gr. ἀπόδειξις, apodictic) to designate REASONING or PROOF that is necessarily true and absolutely certain. It was adopted by medieval scholastics (Lat. *demonstratio*), notably by St. ALBERT THE GREAT and St. THOMAS AQUINAS, whose commentaries on Aristotle's *Posterior Analytics* and Boethius's *De Trinitate* give significant insights into the concept. Later scholastics also used the notion, modifying it according to their particular views concerning KNOWLEDGE and SCIENCE. In modern and contemporary thought, demonstration is commonly equated with any kind of proof that yields CERTITUDE.

This article explains the definition of demonstration in the context of Aristotle's theory of scientific reasoning, lists the various types of demonstration, and notes the knowledge prerequisite to it. It then details the usage of demonstration in different scholastic disciplines, and concludes with appraisals of demonstration in the thought of modern philosophers.

Science and Demonstration. The theory of demonstration presupposes Aristotle's notion of scientific knowledge. He says: "We suppose ourselves to possess unqualified scientific knowledge of a thing . . . when we think that we know the cause on which the fact depends, as the cause of that fact and of no other, and, further, that the fact could not be other than it is" (*Anal. post.* 71b 8–11). He speaks of unqualified scientific knowledge as edge ἐπιστήμη, the same word that Plato had used for the contemplation of subsistent ideas. The characteristics of such knowledge are the certitude and necessity of some fact through assignment of its proper cause (*see* CAUSALITY). Such a requirement is more stringent than that associated with science in modern thought. Aristotle points out that this concept of scientific knowledge is evident, since men do actually desire and claim it (*ibid.* 71b 12). The logical vehicle for attaining such knowledge is called demonstration. "By demonstration I mean a syllogism productive of scientific knowledge, a syllogism, that

is, the grasp of which is *eo ipso* such knowledge" (*ibid.* 71b 17–19).

As an instrument of scientific knowledge, demonstration can be defined in terms of its conditions: "The premises of demonstrated knowledge must be true, primary, immediate, better known than and prior to the conclusion, which is further related to them as effect to cause" (*ibid.* 71b 20–22). The premises must be known as "true," since doubtful or false premises cannot generate a true and certain conclusion. These premises must be "primary," that is, they are not themselves the result of demonstration, but they are indemonstrable propositions into which a demonstration can be resolved. In a series of demonstrations, the conclusion of one may serve as a premise of the following one, but there must be a first that does not have to be demonstrated. Such a premise is "immediate," that is, no middle term is needed to join subject and predicate, because the mind is able to grasp their mutual implication directly from the meanings of the terms, once these latter have been understood by induction from sensory experience. The premises must also "cause" the conclusion, and this in two ways: (1) as causes of one's knowledge of the conclusion, or the instruments used by the mind in inferring the new truth of the conclusion and (2) as causes, in the ontological order, of the attribute asserted of the subject in the conclusion. As causes, the premises are known "prior to" the conclusion; they are also "better known," as being immediately evident.

Types of Demonstration. A demonstration is had whenever a statement is given together with the reason for its truth, that is, whenever the question "why" is answered. Because there are different senses of "why," there are different kinds of demonstration. Since the reason "why" is expressed by the middle term of the demonstrative SYLLOGISM, it can be equivalently said that the types of demonstration correspond to the condition of the middle term that links the subject and predicate of a scientific conclusion. Thus, the general division of demonstration according to Aristotle (*ibid.* 78a 22–79a 16) is into knowledge of the fact (ὅτι, *quia*) and knowledge of the reasoned fact (διότι, *propter quid*). Only demonstration of the reasoned fact fulfills all the requirements stated in Aristotle's definition of demonstration. Knowledge of fact is called demonstration analogously by reason of its similarity with, and ordination to, demonstration *propter quid.*

Propter Quid. Demonstration *propter quid* assigns the proper ontological cause of an attribute's inherence in a subject. Thus, the human soul is immortal because it is incorruptible. In the most perfect type of *propter quid* demonstration, all the terms of the syllogism are convertible, or commensurately universal. However, as long as the middle term and the attribute are convertible, there is *propter quid* demonstration, even though the subject of the given demonstration is only a subjective part of the proper subject of the attribute; e.g., every isoceles has three angles equal to two right angles because it is a triangle. What is essential to this sort of demonstration is that the cause of the attribute be proper. This type is sometimes called *demonstratio propter quid particularis*, or particular demonstration.

Quia. Demonstration *quia* is had whenever the middle term is not the proper cause of the attribute. This demonstration can be a priori or causal when a remote cause is assigned; e.g., A wall does not breathe because it is not living (the proper cause is that it has no lungs). Demonstration is a posteriori when the middle term is not a cause at all, but an effect of the attribute. If the effect is not adequate or convertible with the cause, the demonstration yields knowledge of the existence of the cause and some of its conditions, e.g., God as known from His creation (St. Thomas Aquinas, *In Boeth. de Trin.* 6.4 ad 2). If, however, the cause and effect are of commensurate universality, e.g., the intellect as the cause of abstract reasoning, then the demonstration makes known the proper cause, and hence the terms may without circularity be recast as a *propter quid* demonstration (*Anal. post.* 78a 39b 10).

Subalternation. When the middle term is a commensurate cause and is defined with principles of the same nature as the major and minor terms (e.g., with sensible matter), then there is proper knowledge of the reasoned fact. If the middle term is defined with other principles (e.g., mathematical or metaphysical), then the conclusion is said to be factual or *quia* knowledge in its own order, and causal only as subalternated to principles of a higher order. Thus, the practical science of medicine is subalternated to natural science. Physicomathematical sciences demonstrate through remote causes, i.e., mathematical principles, that are formal causes, although Aristotle does refer to them as being in a broad sense demonstrations διότι (*Anal. post* 79a 3, 12; cf. St. Thomas, *In 1 anal. post.* 25.6)

Prerequisite Knowledge. All the formal logic of the syllogism is presupposed for demonstration. But only the first figure of the syllogism in the mood of *Barbara* is perfectly adequate, since it alone concludes to a universal affirmative proposition (*see* SYLLOGISM).

The truth of the premises must be solidly established. The minor premise contains the term that serves as subject of the conclusion; to this term is predicated the middle term, thereby constituting a DEFINITION of it. Such a premise, in which a definition is predicated of a subject, is self-evident. The major premise in every demonstra-

tion connects a cause and an effect, the nature of the demonstration depending on whether the cause or the effect is the middle term. This premise becomes known through a process of INDUCTION (*Anal. post.* 100b 4), which terminates not merely in empirical correlation, but in UNDERSTANDING of, or INSIGHT into, the nature of cause and effect and their necessary bond.

Some foreknowledge is required of the terms of the demonstrative syllogism. Usually the existence of the subject, or minor term, must be known in order that attributes may be joined to it. However, in an a posteriori demonstration that establishes the existence of the subject, e.g., proofs for the existence of God, only the nominal meaning of the subject-term can be had. A definition of the subject is necessary as the predicate of the minor premise; this definition represents either a cause in a priori demonstration, or an effect in a posteriori demonstration; in this latter case it is only a nominal definition.

In the process preparatory to *propter quid* demonstration, some knowledge is already had of the conclusion of the demonstration. For the existence and definition of the subject are known. At least the nominal definition of the predicate is known in the very asking of a question to be demonstrated, e.g., Why is the sky blue on a cloudless day? The fact of the conclusion may be known by observation, as in the example given. Even a definition of the predicate as an ACCIDENT may be known, but not a definition of the predicate as a PROPERTY. The definition of a property as such presupposes knowledge of its necessary connection with its proper subject; this is precisely what has to be demonstrated. Therefore, the foreknowledge of the predicate as a property can be only a nominal definition. There is no foreknowledge of the middle term as such; the finding of the middle term is the demonstrative process.

The self-evident premises of demonstration are called the principles. They deal with definitions and insight into causal connections, and thus their self-evidence becomes apparent only after a careful and sometimes extended investigation. The principles must be proper for *propter quid* demonstration. There are other more general self-evident principles involved in demonstration, such as the principle of CONTRADICTION, the principle of agreement and disagreement, and the principle of the syllogism (*dictum de omni* and *dictum de nullo*). These higher principles, or axioms, are implicit in every demonstration, but they do not function as the content of premises from which conclusions are deduced. (*See* FIRST PRINCIPLES.)

Demonstration in Various Disciplines. LOGIC, besides being the art of reasoning, is also a science. It establishes true laws of thought and demonstrates them through universal and necessary reasons. Since the subject matter of logic is relations of reason, the definitions used in logical demonstrations will be in the order of formal cause. These are obtained through ABSTRACTION by the intellect reflecting on its own operations.

Mathematics. Long considered the perfect model of *propter quid* demonstrative science, mathematics is similar to logic in that it usually demonstrates from formal cause. In Aristotelian theory mathematical definitions were considered to be obtained through abstraction from sensory matter. Modern theory emphasizes the postulational nature of the principles of mathematics. When principles are only postulated, the conclusions of demonstration share the unproved status of the principles and the proofs reduce to mere formal inference. (*See* MATHEMATICS, PHILOSOPHY OF.)

Philosophy of Nature. Aristotelian natural philosophy demonstrates according to all four causes (*Phys.* 194b 16–195b 30). The middle terms are defined with sensory matter and in abstraction from individual things, which are contingent. The necessary bond linking the terms in the conclusions of such demonstrations is called conditional. The reason for such necessity rests in natures and essential relations, but the existence of these natures is always contingent and the perfect realization and operation of the natures may be hindered. But *if* the truth of the conclusion is to be in reality, the cause assigned in the premises will be necessarily involved.

For Aristotle and his medieval followers, philosophy of nature did not stop at general considerations of mobile being, but pursued its investigation to the specific level. At this level demonstrations must be given through efficient and final causes, or by definitions of specific natures in terms of properties, which are signs of the specific nature. A posteriori demonstrations also have a fundamental place in the science of nature, since sensible effects are better known to man than their causes. Modern sciences of nature share this Aristotelian demonstrative method to the extent that they assign proper causes.

Mathematical Physics. Modern sciences of nature that employ mathematical reasoning can in principle give factual demonstration of physical realities, but cannot assign proper causes, which have to be of the physical order. The validity of the demonstrations of these hybrid sciences depends in each case upon the status of the premises, and particularly on whether they have an admixture of constructional or hypothetical matter in them.

Metaphysics. In scholasticism METAPHYSICS has been traditionally considered a science. St. Thomas calls it *maxime scientia* (*In 1 anal. post.* 17.5). It treats of ''being, its parts, and its passions'' (*ibid.* 20.5) *per modum demonstrationis* (*ibid.* 20.6). The subject is *ens*

commune, conceived in abstraction from all matter, but able to exist either in matter or immaterially, therefore excluding God and separated substances (*In Boeth. de Trin.* 5.4). Whenever one can ask a question about such BEING, in general or of any of its parts, and can assign a proper reason for it, one has a *propter quid* demonstration. For example: Why is being contingent? Because it is composed of essence and existence, as two principles really distinct. Note that the reason need not be a physical cause, but can be a prior reason only virtually distinct from the attribute that it explains; e.g., the immutability of God is the reason for His eternity. A posteriori demonstrations are relevant to metaphysics, especially in proving the existence and attributes of God.

Moral Science. Demonstration in ETHICS and MORAL THEOLOGY provides special difficulties, for as practical sciences they have subjects and ends that differ from those of speculative sciences. The subject of moral science generally is human acts, and the end is not knowledge but the morally good operation. There is, however, a phase of such science in which the truth of moral principles is sought in a universal way, and here demonstration is used. If it is asked, for instance, whether a certain medical practice is moral, the answer must apply a proper reason to the case. This will be the proper final cause, which itself is either immediately or mediately connected with the final end of man, the first principle of moral science. The universal truth, however, is not altogether sufficient for moral action; it is in the prudential judgment that the final truth is attained regarding an individual action to be performed in all its contingency.

Sacred Theology. There are demonstrations in sacred theology, insofar as statements are made and proper reasons given for their truth. Thus, the answers to many of the questions asked by St. Thomas in his *Summa Theologiae* are demonstrations. If the two premises are revealed, then demonstration explicates what was implicit in revelation. Likewise, one premise can be a truth of faith, while the other is a self-evident or demonstrated truth of human science. The middle term is therefore once illuminated by a divine light of faith and once by human intelligence. These middle terms may be causes or effects, proper or remote. Such demonstrated conclusions are said to be virtually contained in the deposit of revelation (*see* THEOLOGICAL CONCLUSION).

Demonstration and Modern Philosophy. Modern philosophy takes an attitude to demonstration corresponding to its acceptance, limitation, or rejection of UNIVERSALS, SUBSTANCE, and causality. Galileo GALILEI, T. HOBBES, F. BACON, and many of their successors restricted causal explanation to the material and efficient causes, or to mechanical causes. Hobbes interpreted all rational discourse in a nominalistic spirit, so that science is knowledge, not of the consequences of one thing to another, but of one name of a thing to another name of the same thing (*Leviathan*, 1.7).

Cartesian Proof. The value of demonstration depends on the status accorded the premises. René DESCARTES could not admit the validity of intuitions based on sensory experience, but sought clear and distinct conceptions that sprang from the light of reason alone. Such a starting point for deductive reasoning assured him of results of the same order as arithmetic and geometry, the only two sciences that he admitted as free from any taint of falsity or uncertainty (*Rules for the Direction of the Mind*, 2–3). For him, the method of proof is two-fold: analytic, or from causes; and synthetic, or from effect to cause. Descartes preferred analysis as the best and truest method; synthesis he considered as not conveniently applicable in metaphysical matters (*Objections Urged by Certain Men of Learning Against the Preceding Meditations*, Reply to Second Objections, n. 7). Even when a posteriori demonstrations are used, they proceed from effects present within experience, not from effects existing in an objective world. Cartesian demonstration remains more in the realm of ideas and pure essences than in the world of existent things. The triumph of the method can be found in B. SPINOZA, whose *Ethics* is evolved *more geometrico*.

Locke's Theory. John LOCKE resolutely denied the existence of innate ideas. Ideas enter the mind through sensation, yet it is the ideas, not things responsible for producing the ideas, that constitute the object of knowledge. Intuition is immediate perception of the agreement or disagreement among ideas. Demonstration is knowledge of agreement or disagreement among ideas through the mediation of other ideas (*Essay Concerning Human Understanding*, 4.2.2–). The necessary connections are only relations among ideas, not relations of things with their attributes. Locke rigidly restricted the extent of demonstration. While admitting the validity of mathematical demonstration, he denied the possibility of a demonstrative science of the physical world, because the middle terms he sought as causes are unknown motions of minute particles. The existence of God can be demonstrated, but only by starting from intuitive awareness of one's own existence. He admitted in principle the possibility of demonstration in moral matters, but he did not himself elaborate such a demonstrative science (*ibid.* 3.11.16). Since Locke's doctrine of causality was weak and ambiguous, his concept of demonstration is little more than that of an explicative syllogism, and of the syllogism itself he made little account. Hume's further development of Locke's philosophy and his relegation of

causality and universality to mental habits effectively destroyed demonstration.

Kant's Compromise. Immanuel Kant tried to save the prerogatives of reason from the attack of Hume. But the conditions of knowledge necessary to validate demonstration were supplied by Kant through a priori categories of the understanding. Thus, the concepts of substance and accident, existence, universality, causality, and necessity were not conditions of extramental things, but were a priori and constitutive of experience. Reasoning serves merely to unify the manifold knowledge of the understanding. It thus takes on a subjective character, yielding no universal and necessary knowledge of things, or NOUMENA. In fact, Kant limits the use both of definitions and of demonstration to mathematics. He requires that demonstration be intuitive; this is not possible of empirical objects, because no necessity in them can be grasped through intuition, but only subsequently through application of a category of the understanding (*Critique of Pure Reason*, Transcendental Doctrine of Method, chapter 1, section 1, B756, 762–63). Rather than yield the eternal truth claimed by Aristotelian demonstration, Kant's system falls back into the skepticism it attempted to avoid.

Positivism. A. COMTE and subsequent positivists abandoned the ideal of causal explanation and settled for a notion of science as the laws of relations of PHENOMENA. This noncausal and nonsubstantial PHENOMENALISM constitutes the philosophy that has most influenced modern science. Aristotelian demonstration would henceforth be an alien concept to modern thought, for only in a context of moderate REALISM does the doctrine of demonstration have relevance.

See Also: ARGUMENTATION; DEDUCTION; DIALECTICS; METHODOLOGY (PHILOSOPHY).

Bibliography: ARISTOTLE, *Anal. post.*, tr. G. R. G. MURE, *The Basic Works of Aristotle*, ed. R. MCKEON (New York 1941). THOMAS AQUINAS, *Exposition of the Posterior Analytics of Aristotle*, tr. P. CONWAY (Quebec 1956). M. A. GLUTZ, *The Manner of Demonstrating in Natural Philosophy* (River Forest, Ill. 1956). W. A. WALLACE, *The Role of Demonstration in Moral Theology* (Washington 1962); ''Some Demonstrations in the Science of Nature,'' *Thomist Reader* 1 (1957) 90–118. P. COFFEY, *The Science of Logic*, 2 v. (New York 1912; reprint 1938). E. D. SIMMONS, ''Demonstration and Self-Evidence,'' *Thomist* 24 (1961) 139–62. W. BAUMGAERTNER, ''Metaphysics and the Second Analytics,'' *The New Scholasticism* 29 (1955) 403–26. J. F. ANDERSON, ''On Demonstration in Thomistic Metaphysics,'' *ibid.* 32 (1958) 476–94. M. J. ADLER, ed., *The Great Ideas: A Syntopicon of Great Books of the Western World*, 2 v. (Chicago 1952) 2:546–68. C. FILIASI CARCANO, *Enciclopedia filosofica*, 4 v. (Venice-Rome 1957) 1:1578–80.

[M. A. GLUTZ]

DE MORGAN, AUGUSTUS

English logician, the first modern philosopher to develop a clear idea of logical form; b. Madura, India, June 27, 1806; d. London, March 18, 1871. His greatest achievement is to have initiated serious research into the logic of relations. Regarded by C. S. PEIRCE as "one of the best logicians who ever lived," he undertook the considerable task of broadening and generalizing Aristotle's syllogistics. In particular, he held that the theory of the syllogism is only a special case of a more general theory of relations; this conception was later to be developed by Peirce in algebraic form similar to that used by G. Boole in the logic of classes, and was finally systematized by E. SCHRÖDER. De Morgan's name is attached to two laws earlier known to WILLIAM OF OCKHAM (*Summa totius logicae* 2.32), but which De Morgan rediscovered: *ENKpqANpNq* and *ENApqKNpNq*. Another notable achievement of De Morgan is his introduction of the theory of probability into logic, in connection with the study of modalities.

Bibliography: Works. *Formal Logic* (London 1847); *Essays on the Life and Works of Newton,* ed. P. E. B. JOURDAIN (Chicago 1914); *A Budget of Paradoxes* (2d ed. Chicago 1915). Literature. S. E. DE MORGAN, *Memoir of Augustus De Morgan* (London 1882). I. M. BOCHEŃSKI, *A History of Formal Logic,* ed. and tr. I. THOMAS (Notre Dame, Ind. 1961). A. N. PRIOR, *Formal Logic* (2d ed. Oxford 1962).

[G. L. FARRE]

DEMPSEY, MARY JOSEPH, SISTER

Hospital superintendent; b. Salamanca, N.Y., May 14, 1856; d. Rochester, Minn., March 29, 1939. During childhood she moved to Rochester, Minn., where she entered the Third Order Regular of St. Francis of the Congregation of Our Lady of Lourdes in 1878, one year after its foundation. She was teaching in a parochial school in Ohio in 1889 when St. Mary's Hospital was opened in Rochester by Mother Alfred. Sister Mary Joseph was assigned to the new hospital, and was soon made head nurse. In 1892 she was appointed superintendent, a position she held until her death. Under her direction, the institution grew, through a series of six additions, into a modern 600-bed hospital. This expansion was a result not only of her leadership, but of the efforts of Drs. William W., Charles H., and William J. Mayo, who directed its staff and later organized the Mayo Clinic. From 1890 to 1915, Sister Mary Joseph, in addition to directing the hospital's operations, served as first surgical assistant to Dr. W. J. Mayo. She founded (1906) St. Mary's School of Nursing. In 1915 she participated in the organization of the Catholic Hospital Association of the U.S. and Canada, serving as its first vice president. Although her activities were chiefly confined to St. Mary's, her reputation in medicine was international.

Bibliography: H. CLAPESATTLE, *The Doctors Mayo* (Minneapolis 1941).

[M. B. CASSIDY]

DEMPSEY, TIMOTHY

Founder of charitable institutions; b. Cadamstown, Offaly County, Ireland, Oct. 21, 1867; d. St. Louis, Mo., April 6, 1936. He was the eldest of 11 children of Thomas H. and Bridget (Ryan) Dempsey. He studied for the priesthood at St. Mary's Seminary, Mullingar and St. Patrick's Foreign Mission College, Carlow. On June 14, 1891, he was ordained for the U.S. After seven years as a curate in Missouri—at Indian Creek, Moberly, and St. Louis—he was appointed pastor of St. Patrick's in St. Louis in 1898, and in 1923 was made a domestic prelate.

Early in his career he became active in the rehabilitation of paroled convicts and then in other areas of social work. He established low-fee hotels for workingmen (1906) and women (1911); a free labor agency (1906); "Exiles' Rest," a burial plot in Calvary Cemetery for the indigent (1909); a nursery and emergency home (1910); a White Cross Crusade to gather discarded articles for resale (1922); and a short-lived home for African Americans (1922). In 1924 he added a convalescent home to the women's hotel, and in 1931 he opened a free lunchroom to meet depression needs.

"Father Tim's" rich personality and sympathy for the unfortunate made him a popular counselor and aided in his success as a peacemaker in industrial disputes and gang wars. He is buried in the "Exiles' Rest," which he established.

Bibliography: H. J. MCAULIFFE, *Father Tim* (Milwaukee 1944).

[H. J. MCAULIFFE]

DEMYTHOLOGIZING

Demythologizing refers to a hermeneutical method that takes the position that much of Scripture is mythological, and that it is necessary to take account of this fact in perceiving the religious significance of Scripture. The prominence of this method in the second half of the twentieth century was due to Rudolf BULTMANN (1884–1976), particularly to his essay of 1941 titled "The New Testament and Mythology; The Problem of Demythologizing the New Testament Preaching.'' Bultmann proposed that a thorough demythologizing is the key to interpreting the mythological statements in the NT, the means to recover the deeper meaning of myth, and the process to clarify and restore the challenge and call of the Word of God.

To understand demythologizing one must consider myth first and then HERMENEUTICS. After considering the characteristics of mythology and the relationship between myth and the NT, this article will treat of the relationship between hermeneutics and mythology in Bultmann's thought and present a critique thereof. It will then discuss the rehabilitation of the category of myth in Catholic thought.

Mythological Thought. No one definition of myth is completely satisfactory. Bultmann's methodology considers myth an unscientific and primitive manner of conceiving and expressing thought in which imagery is used to express the otherworldly in terms of this world and the divine in terms of the human. Thus the TRANSCENDENCE of God is expressed by spatial distance. Because myth concretizes, HELL and HEAVEN are localized. As a primitive and uncritical way of reasoning, myth attributes disease to demons, the current state of evil to a primeval war among gods, and cosmic phenomena to the activity of spirits.

Characteristics. The essence of mythological thought appears in opposition to the developed, scientific, objective, and critical thought best exemplified in the empirical sciences and the modern scientific world. While scientific thought seeks intelligibility from within phenomena, mythical thought postulates otherworldly causes. Scientific thought proposes a closed world; mythical thought, an open world. Mythical thought further presents human existence itself as open and susceptible to outside influence. Thus myth really expresses the enigma and mystery of human existence, its dependence on otherworldly powers. Since mythical thought manifests purpose and intention, the possibility of demythologizing lies in the relatively modern discovery of a controlled hermeneutics that seeks to reach the intention and meaning of myth.

Myth and the New Testament. Before proceeding to hermeneutics as a method of understanding myth, the broad structure of myth in the NT must be considered. In the obsolete cosmology of the NT the world is spatially conceived in three layers: heaven, earth, the underworld. Earth is capable of influence from above and below. Before the Redemption man is under the hegemony of the lower world and is so influenced that Satan, sin, and death dominate him. In the redemptive process God's Son is sent from above to overcome the lower forces. Thus there is continual conflict of the upper and lower forces.

Aptly taken from GNOSTICISM and the Jewish apocalyptic, myth permeates the presentation of the SALVATION HISTORY. JESUS CHRIST is the preexistent SON OF GOD. He is born of a virgin and performs miracles. His death expiates the sins of others and His Resurrection precipitates a cosmic catastrophe. He descends into hell and ascends into heaven, whence He shall return on the clouds to judge. Soon a RESURRECTION OF THE DEAD will signify the final defeat of powers from the nether world. Believers united by faith in the saving events portrayed in mythical terms are bound to Christ by Baptism [*see* BAPTISM (IN THE BIBLE)] and the EUCHARIST, which work like purely physical forces. Hermeneutics must distill the meaning of myth and at the same time preserve the Gospel as KERYGMA.

Hermeneutics and Mythology. If the genre of myth was a stage of expression in a civilization of limited science and fewer literary forms and was found in literature contemporaneous with the Bible, then hermeneutics could expect to find and hope to interpret myth in the Bible. With relative ease and certainty one could locate myth in Genesis. J. G. Eichhorn (1752–1827), who had introduced C. G. Heyne's concept of myth into Biblical criticism, further applied the theory to the TEMPTATIONS OF JESUS, the apparition of the angels, the pouring out of the Holy Spirit. In 1835 D. F. STRAUSS applied the theory of myth to the entire NT. Scholars of mythological tendencies sought an apologetic significance—some religious or theological purpose—in the newly discovered mythology. Their problem was to eliminate myth and to retain a significant religious truth capable of independent existence.

Existentialist Hermeneutics. From his earliest days Bultmann had been occupied with the problem of interpreting documents. He rejected solutions of the liberal theologians and those of the History of Religions School (*see* RELIGIONS, COMPARATIVE STUDY OF). He based his own hermeneutical method on a viewpoint large enough to interpret myth and to retain the NT as kerygma. Bultmann's teacher, Wilhelm Herrmann, had said that to say something about God is to affirm something about man, and that understanding history is understanding one's own existence. Wilhelm DILTHEY had asserted that all understanding and interpretation involves a prior relation, that is, the relation of the interpreter in his life to the subject or text at hand. Thus Bultmann was to say later that there is no such thing as presuppositionless interpretation; the perspective and interests of the interpreter govern all interpretation. The precise basis for interpreting Scripture is the question about God at the heart of human existence.

Given the relation of man to the text, it was partially Martin Kähler's influence that suggested that human existence as described in the NT is historical, *geschichtlich,* for salvation history too is the field of human decisions. Both Kähler and Bultmann saw in the NT, especially in St. PAUL the Apostle, history absorbed into ESCHATOLOGY, so that historical significance is in the human choice, the now of accepting or rejecting God (Rom 7.7–25). Salvation history is the history of the man who is freed from sin and death to live under grace (Rom 6.14). And human existence receives its historical and eschatological character through a willed encounter with Christ in the preached word. Strictly human history, therefore, is distinguished from and goes beyond what is commonly called world history or the study of nature because man's history is constituted by actions, decisions, and choices based on man's own understanding of himself. Inquiry into man's existence, therefore, cannot be neutral because man lacks the distance required for neutral observation. Thus man's existence is historical and must be understood and interpreted in this historical sense.

Application to the New Testament. The kerygma of the Church proclaims that in Scripture man will receive a decisive understanding of his existence. But the saving events are not recovered by strictly neutral or disinterested historiography but rather by personal engagement. Hence the question about God (which is really the question about human existence) comes face to face with a particular understanding of God and human existence. This interested, involved, existential question about existence—answered in the NT—is not answered by objectifying processes that would offer an illusory security but rather by faith. Thus is the relation of man to the NT resolved.

At this point Heideggerian philosophy has provided the concepts and terms by which human existence may be understood, interpreted, and explained. This philosophy correctly assumes that being can speak to man. The reflective analysis of existence seeks the meaning of existence. Faith, on the other hand, shows that this question is really the question about God. While philosophy cannot give man the power to achieve authentic existence, it can put man in a position where he is capable of meeting God. Philosophy can further provide the theoretic structure capable of articulating the understanding of existence found in the NT.

All the above aspects focus on the one major element of the NT—the possibility of a new understanding of existence given to man in the supreme events of salvation. Myth, therefore, is interpreted in terms of what God says about human existence through the mythological accounts. Thus the expiatory death of the preexisting Son of God intends to convey the eschatological character of God's activity in Christ so far as this event is decisive for man. The purpose of the Resurrection narratives is didactic, not historical. The Resurrection accounts inform man that Christ's death was not an ordinary death but the judgment and salvation of the world. Cross and Resurrection together are the judgment of the world and the possibility of a new and authentic existence for man. In the preached Word man is asked to understand himself as crucified and risen with Christ. The intention of the mythological portrayal is to present a reality beyond the objectifiable and observable in its decisive significance.

Critique. Bultmann's basic hermeneutics have the merit of attempting to make revelation relevant for modern man through a systematized theology and a pertinent interpretation of modern significance. The concomitant presuppositions of this kind of demythologizing intelligently stress what James M. Robinson has called the heuristic involvement of the scholar in the work of interpretation. Demythologizing further emphasizes that God speaks to every aspect of the human condition. Thus demythologizing intends to preserve the vertical perspective of the Bible by reaching the Lord as Lord here and now and by demanding authentic Christian witness here and now. At the same time demythologizing seeks to preserve seeming opposites—the transcendence of God as well as the dimension of God as the God-for-us, an idea so congenial to the Greek Fathers.

However, there are evident difficulties to Bultmann's posture of demythologizing. Many scholars have noted that demythologizing tends (despite Bultmann's emphasis on the fact that self-understanding depends on events outside of man's consciousness) to minimize or eliminate the objective reality of the saving events. It is difficult to see how demythologizing avoids turning Christ into a symbol where inward faith is almost the sole determining constituent of saving reality.

Secondly, admitting God's activity in history, as demythologizing certainly does, the difficulty of distinguishing myth from events that are nonmythical yet beyond the range of normal occurrence must make one cautious in calling too much of the NT myth. Nor are mythical extra-Biblical parallels apodictic proof that similar Gospel incidents are mythological because of a so-called scientific world view. Arguments here must be treated with the complexity and finesse they deserve.

Thirdly, Bultmann's opposition between myth and empirical scientific thought is perhaps too rigid and does not allow for the polymorphism of human cognition on all levels and the complementary dialectic rather than contradictory opposition of various modes of cognition. More work is required to appreciate the analogous nature of understanding and insight.

Contemporary Catholic Thought. Modern studies in the field of depth psychology and the history of religions have brought about a far-reaching rehabilitation of myth. Myth is rather commonly regarded by Catholic scholars as a distinct mode of knowledge that can never be adequately reduced to rational discourse and as a mode essential to religious expression. If religion is understood as a dialogue between God and man, and if Revelation is viewed as the total process by which God draws near to man and manifests his presence, then assuredly the possibility that the divine presence might be apprehended and registered in mythical thought and symbolism must be kept open.

Among Catholic biblical scholars the thought of Mircea ELIADE and Paul RICOEUR on myth has been influential in recent years. Eliade describes myth as the narration of a sacred history, relating an event that took place in primordial time, the sacred time of the beginning. Myth narrates how through the deeds of supernatural beings a reality came into existence. Myth can be known, experienced, and lived by means of recitation and ritual. The myth is lived in the sense that one is seized by the sacred, exalting power of the events recollected or reenacted. The relevance of such a description for a deeper understanding of both the Jewish Passover and the Christian Eucharist has been grasped by Catholic biblical scholars.

In his work, Paul Ricoeur has analyzed the process whereby a primal experience finds a language, assembles that language into a myth, and subsequently generates reflection on the myth, which reflection, in turn, becomes a theology. Myth, secondary symbolism according to Ricoeur, emerges from primary symbolism and develops into an elaborate, tertiary symbolic system. In the NT are found the primary symbols of sin and redemption from sin. The NT theologies accept the myth of the rebellion of the primal man, Adam, as the narrative account of the origin of the primary symbol, "sin," and accept the symbol "sin" as corresponding to a fundamental aspect of reality experienced in the world (e.g. Rom 5.12). But there is also in the NT the corresponding primary symbol of redemption from sin (e.g. Rom 5.18–21), which is based upon the death of Jesus interpreted as redemption by means of the symbolic language deriving from the suffering servant passages in Isaiah 53, and expressing the fundamental view of mankind's situation in the light of resurrection faith. From these examples it may be seen that the type of myth or mythical symbol that is the concern of the NT and scholars is the existential myth.

The existential myth or mythical symbol comes into existence so that man can live meaningfully in the tension of his unlimited desire to know, his orientation toward the transcendent, and his finite capacity both to know and to achieve. Against man's permanent horizon of mystery, transcendence and the unknown, mythical symbolism provides both a necessary and realistic orientation; it provides some realistic sense of balance in the tension at the heart of all human existence, and as such is permanently a legitimate vehicle of human meaning and cognition. The existential mythical symbol is found not only in the creation myth involving Adam and the vicarious redemption found in Second Isaiah, but is also biblically expressed in the concept of cosmic salvation found in the prologue of John's Gospel and in such similar NT hymns as Philippians 2.6–11; Colossians 1.15–20; 1 Timothy 3.16; Hebrews 1.2–5 and 1 Peter 3.18–22. And certainly the eschatological and apocalyptic presentation of both the OT and NT fulfill the criteria of existential mythical symbolism.

The most common function of the mythical symbol in the NT is that of interpreting history. In the crucifixion narrative for example, Mark presents details taken from Psalms 69 and 22, which are concerned with the righteous sufferer and God's vindication of him: Mark 15.23, the offering of wine mingled with myrrh from Psalms 69.21; 15.24, the dividing of the garments from Psalms 22.18; and 15.29, the mocking from Psalms 22.7. These narrative details are not true at the level of factual history but are included because the crucifixion of Jesus is interpreted by Mark as the death of the righteous sufferer whom God vindicated and hence as the fulfilment of Psalms 69 and 22. In an interpreted sense, however, they are true and their use illustrates how the NT narrative through the mythical symbol interprets the event. In much of the NT history (*Historie*) is presented as historic (*Geschichte*), and that history as historic involves history as historical and the historical as interpreted by the mythical symbol.

See Also: HERMENEUTICS, BIBLICAL; MYTH AND MYTHOLOGY (IN THE BIBLE).

Bibliography: H. FRIES, *Lexikon für Theologie und Kirche,* ed. J. HOFER and K. RAHNER, 10 v. (2d, new ed. Freiburg 1957–65) 3:898–904. H.OTT, *Die Religion in Geschichte und Gegenwart,* 7 v. (3d ed. Tübingen 1957–65) 2:496–499. R. K. BULTMANN, *Existence and Faith,* tr. and ed. S. M. OGDEN (New York 1960); *Jesus Christ and Mythology* (New York 1958); "On the Problem of Demythologizing," *Journal of Religion* 42 (1962) 96–102. K. JASPERS and R. BULTMANN, *Myth and Christianity* (New York 1958). H. W. BARTSCH, ed., *Kerygma und Mythos,* with contributions by R. BULTMANN et al., 5 v. (Hamburg 1955–60); Eng. tr. of selected articles: *Kerygma and Myth,* tr. R. H. FULLER, 2 v. (London 1960–62) G. BORNKAMM, "Die Theologie Rudolf Bultmanns in der neueren Diskussion," *Theologische Rundschau* 29 (1963) 33–141, good bibliography. I. HENDERSON, *Myth in the New Testament* (London 1952). F. GOGARTEN, *Demythologizing and History,* tr. N. H. SMITH (New York 1955). H. P. OWEN, *Revelation and Existence* (Cardiff 1957). L. MALEVEZ, *The Christian Message and Myth,* tr. O. WYON

(London 1960). J. MACQUARRIE, *The Scope of Demythologizing* (New York 1960). G. MIEGGE, *Gospel and Myth in the Thought of Rudolf Bultmann,* tr. S. NEILL (Richmond 1960). O. CULLMANN, "Rudolf Bultmann's Concept of Myth and the New Testament," *Concordia Theological Monthly* 27 (1956) 13–24. C. K. BARRETT, "Myth and the New Testament," *Expository Times* 68 (1956–57) 345–348, 359–362. P. J. CAHILL, "The Scope of Demythologizing," *Theological Studies* 23 (1962) 79–92. C. HARTLICH and W. SACHS, *Der Ursprung des Mythosbegriffes in der modernen Bibelwissenschaft* (Tübingen 1952). R. BULTMANN, "The Primitive Christian Kerygma and the Historical Jesus," in C. BRAATEN and R. H. HARRISVILLE, eds., *The Historical Jesus and the Kerygmatic Christ* (Nashville 1964) 15–42. P. J. CAHILL, "Myth and Meaning," in J. W. FLANAGIN and A. W. ROBINSON, eds., *No Famine in the Land* (Missoula, Mont. 1975) 275–291. M. ELIADE, *The Quest: History and Meaning in Religion* (Chicago 1969); *Myth and Reality,* tr. W. R. TRASK (New York 1963). H. FRIES, *Bultmann, Bank, and Catholic Theology,* tr. L. SWIDLER (Pittsburgh 1967). B. J. F. LONERGAN, *Insight: A Study of Human Understanding* (London 1958). J. L. MODENZIE, *Myths and Realities* (Milwaukee 1963). N. PERRIN, *The Promise of Bultmann* (Philadelphia 1969); *The New Testament: An Introduction* (New York 1974). P. RICOEUR, *The Symbolism of Evil,* tr. E. BUCHANAN (Boston 1969); *Freud and Philosophy: An Essay in Interpretation,* tr. D. SAVAGE (New Haven 1970). W. SCHMITHALS, *An Introduction to the Theology of Rudolph Bultmann* (Minneapolis 1968).

[P. J. CAHILL/J. RYAN]

DE NEVE, JOHN

Seminary rector; b. Evergem, Belgium, July 5, 1821; d. Lierre, Belgium, April 11, 1898. He was educated at St. Nicholas College and at the major seminary in Ghent, Belgium. After his ordination on March 20, 1847, he was assistant pastor at Renaix and Waerschoot, Belgium, until he left for Detroit, Mich., in October 1856. In 1857 he was appointed the first resident pastor at Niles, Mich., where he remained until Bp. Peter Paul Lefevere chose him in 1859 to succeed Rev. Peter Kindekens as rector of the American College of Louvain, Belgium. During the first period of his rectorship, he gained benefactors and patrons for the college, especially among the American bishops; purchased or rehabilitated most of its property; increased the number of students; and sent 132 missionaries to America. Incapacitated by mental illness in 1871, he was relieved of his duties and cared for by the Alexian Brothers at Diest, Belgium, until his recovery in 1878. Then, convinced that the college had declined during his absence, and eager to be reinstated, De Neve traveled to the U.S. in 1880 to obtain the consent of the bishop patrons of the seminary. The decision was finally left to the Belgian bishops, and De Neve was rector again from 1881 to 1891. During these years he not only saved the seminary from closing, but stabilized it economically and administratively for the future. After resigning his office in 1891, he lived in retirement at the priests' home in Lierre.

Bibliography: J. D. SAUTER, *The American College of Louvain, 1857–1898* (Louvain 1959), bibliog. 282–284. G. W. PARÉ, *The Catholic Church in Detroit, 1701–1888* (Detroit 1951).

[J. D. SAUTER]

DENGEL, ANNA

Medical missionary, foundress, physician; b. Steeg, Austria, March 16, 1892; d. Rome, Italy, April 17, 1980. The oldest of nine children, she developed an early interest in the missions. After graduating from secondary school and briefly teaching in Lyons, France, she heard that Dr. Agnes McLaren, a Scotswoman, was recruiting women doctors for poor Muslim women in India. Their customs of "purdah" prevented medical attention by men, placing them outside available health care.

Dengel responded immediately and quickly began further studies: first, at Ursuline Colleges in Innsbruck, Austria, and Cork, Ireland, then at Cork's University College. In 1919 she graduated from medical school. After a nine-month residency in Claycross, England, she left for St. Catherine's Hospital in Rawalpindi, India.

For four years she served as the only doctor to 10,000 sick and dying women and children. She became convinced that numbers of professionally trained women were needed to effect real healing among the people. At the same time she felt called to a religious vocation. Entering an existing congregation, however, meant abandoning medicine, as canon law forbade sisters to practice medicine, surgery, or obstetrics.

An Austrian priest, Rochus Rimml, SJ, persuaded her to establish a new congregation to respond fully to medical mission needs. In 1924 Dengel traveled to the United States to make her cause known. Michael A. Mathis, CSC, helped her write a constitution, and Michael Curley, archbishop of Baltimore, gave permission to begin the new foundation.

Four women gathered in Washington, D.C. on Sept. 30, 1925 to begin the MEDICAL MISSION SISTERS. Originally classified a "pious society" because of the canon law restriction, the congregation was granted full canonical status on Feb. 11, 1936, when Pope Pius XI lifted the ban on sisters being doctors.

Superior general of the Medical Mission Sisters (1925–67), Dengel spearheaded their growth to over 700 members serving in 50 health facilities in 33 countries. Under her leadership thousands of indigenous people were trained in the health professions. Government officials were persuaded to make health a priority for their people.

Author of *Mission For Samaritans* and numerous articles on medical mission work, she received many

Heinrich Seuse Denifle.

awards, including Austria's "Golden Cross of Merit" (1967), Tyrol's "Ehrenring" (1968), and the Church's "Pro Ecclesia et Pontifice" (1967).

Dengel is remembered for making medical mission work not only acceptable but essential to the mission of the Catholic Church. Her concern for the plight of women and for professionalism in religious health care remain examples for many.

Bibliography: M. M. MCGINLEY, "Mother Anna Dengel, M.D.—A Pioneer Medical Missionary," *Worldmission* 31 (New York 1980) 26–31. Medical Mission Sisters, "In Memory of Mother Anna Dengel, M.D.," *Medical Mission Sisters News* 10 (Philadelphia 1980) 1–4.

[M. M. MCGINLEY]

DENIFLE, HEINRICH SEUSE

Dominican historian of the Middle Ages; b. Imst (Tirol), Jan. 16, 1844; d. Munich, June 10, 1905. While a student at Brixen, Denifle (baptismal name, Josef Anton) decided to enter the Dominican Order in Graz. As a cleric he was especially influenced by his confrères, Franz Brentano (professor of philosophy), Bernard Zeno (friend of Emperor Maximilian of Mexico), and Andreas Frühwirt (later general of the order). From 1870 to 1880

Denifle devoted himself exclusively to his order's work as a teacher and preacher in Graz. When Pope Leo XIII commissioned a new edition of the works of THOMAS AQUINAS, Cardinal T. ZIGLIARA, the chairman of the commission, brought Denifle to Rome as his collaborator in 1880. In 1883 Leo appointed him one of the three assistant papal archivists. This position determined Denifle's subsequent research labors as a historian. In an effort to make Vatican source materials accessible to research, he cultivated ties with the directors of the various historical institutes in Rome (Theodor Sickel, Ludwig von PASTOR, Johann Peter KIRSCH, and Paul Fridolin KEHR). Upon conclusion of his work on the history of the University of PARIS, Denifle returned to Rome (1899), thereafter devoting all his time to visiting Austrian and German archives and libraries to collect material for his work on Luther. He died in Munich on his way to Cambridge.

Denifle's merit as a historian lies chiefly in his investigation of the history of late medieval thought. Besides studies and editions on the history of mysticism and scholasticism, his writings include pioneer works on the history of the universities in the Middle Ages. His study on Luther, which was neither his chief work nor his specialization, became his best-known writing and the object of the most violent criticism. In this work Luther is presented as the product of a decadent age. Of lasting value for research on Luther was Denifle's discovery of a copy of the hitherto unknown Luther commentary on the Epistle to the Romans, dating from 1515 to 1516.

Bibliography: Works. *Die Universitäten des Mittelalters bis 1400* (Berlin 1885; repr. Graz 1956), only v. 1 pub.; *La Désolation des églises, monastères et hôpitaux en France pendant la guerre de cent ans,* 2 v. (Paris 1897–99); *Luther und Luthertum,* 2 v. (Mainz 1904–09); É. L. M. CHATELAIN, *Chartularium universitatis parisiensis,* ed. H. DENIFLE and E. CHATELAIN, 4 v. (Paris 1889–97). Literature. M. GRABMANN, *P. Heinrich Denifle* (Mainz 1905). G. P. GOOCH, *History and Historians in the Nineteenth Century* (2d ed. New York 1952; pa. Boston 1952). A. WALZ, *Andreas Kardinal Frühwirth* (Vienna 1950); *Analecta Denifleana* (Rome 1955); *Dictionnaire d'histoire et de géographie ecclésiastiques,* ed. A. BAUDRILLART et al. (Paris 1912–) 14:221–245; *Lexikon für Theologie und Kirche,* ed. J. HOFER and K. RAHNER (2d, new ed. Freiburg 1957–65) 3:227–228.

[H. RUMPLER]

DENIS OF PARIS, ST.

Alleged to have been the first bishop of Paris, a martyr and patron of France. He owes his great popularity to a series of legends connecting him with SS. Eleutherius and Rusticus (*Mart. Hier.* 203 and 548), with PSEUDO-DIONYSIUS, and with the founding of the great abbey church of St. Denis. GREGORY OF TOURS (*Hist. Francorum* 1.30) calls him the first bishop of Paris, and the

Episcopal List (published by L. Duchesne, *Listes Episco-paux* 2. 469) begins with a St. Dionysius (Denis). The best hypothesis contends that Denis was sent to Gaul from Rome in the third century and that he was behcaded in the Valerian persecution of 258. Excavations beneath the abbey church at St. Denis, conducted in 1957 by E. Salin, indicate that he was buried in a pagan cemetery. A ninth century *Passio* describes the legend of his beheading on Montmartre (the mountain of martyrs) in Paris, after which he carried his head to a village (Vicus Catulliacus) northeast of the city, where the great cult of St. Denis began. The cult is first mentioned in the *Vita* of St. GENEVIÈVE (*c.* 500), based on an ancient Passio; she built a basilica over the saint's tomb. Venantius Fortunatus speaks of a basilica built in Bordeaux by Bishop Amelius toward 520 in honor of the great saint of Paris (*Carm.* 8.3, v. 159). In 624 King Dagobert founded an abbey next to the Basilica of St. Denis; and Abbot Hilduin in 827 translated the works of Pseudo-Dionysius sent to King Louis the Pious by the Byzantine Emperor Michael II, identifying the Parisian patron with the Athenian disciple of St. Paul to whom these books of mystical theology were attributed. In the ninth century ANASTASIUS the papal librarian accepted this legend and the Roman Breviary lessons still reflect the legendary *Vita* of St. Denis composed by Hilduin, which eventually, though not without the resistance of scholars, found its way into the Greek synaxaries and the Church's hagiographic tradition.

Feast: Oct. 9.

Bibliography: R. AUBERT, *Dictionnaire d'histoire et de géographie ecclésiastiques,* ed. A. BAUDRILLART et al. (Paris 1912–) 14:263–265. S. LE NAIN DE TILLEMONT, *Mémoires pour serviv à l'histoire ecclésiastique des six premiers siècles,* 16 v. (Paris 1693–1712) 4:442–451. I. BÄHR, *Saint Denis und seine Vita im Spiegel der Bildüberlieferung der französischen Kunst des Mittelalters* (Worms 1984). H. DELEHAYE, *Les Origines du culte des martyrs* (2d ed. Brussels 1933). A. KRAUS, *Die translatio S. Dionysii Areopagitae von St. Emmeram in Regensburg* (Munich 1971). R. J. LOENERTZ, "La Légende Parisienne de S. Denys l'Aréopagite," *Analecta Bollandiana* 69 (1951) 217–237. A. BUTLER, *The Lives of the Saints,* rev. ed. H. THURSTON and D. ATTWATER, 4 v. (New York 1956) 4:67–68.

[E. G. RYAN]

DENIS THE CARTHUSIAN

Theologian and mystical writer, called the Ecstatic Doctor; b. 1402 or 1403 at Ryckel, Belgium; d. Roermond, Holland, March 12, 1471. After leaving the university at Cologne as a master of arts in 1424, in that or the following year he became a Carthusian at Roermond. From 1432 until 1434 he held the office of procurator.

NICHOLAS OF CUSA insisted upon having him as assistant during his reform visitations in the Rhineland in 1451 and 1452. Denis was put in charge of a Carthusian foundation at Bois-le-Duc in 1465, but in 1469 he resigned because of failing health and returned to Roermond.

Denis was a prolific writer. His works fill 42 volumes in quarto, with two index volumes, in the Montreuil-Tournai-Parkminster edition (1896–1935). There are 14 volumes of commentaries on the Scripture, and commentaries on Pseudo-Dionysius, Peter Lombard, Boethius, and John Climacus. He wrote a compendium of the *Summa* of St. Thomas Aquinas. Among his minor works are 21 treatises aimed at the reformation of the Church and of Christian society. There are also some letters written to princes on this topic, and others about a crusade against the Turks. In consequence of several revelations he had a premonition of the calamities threatening the Christian world if a reformation did not take place in time.

Although an eclectic, Denis was no mere compiler. He sifted critically and organized his diverse sources with a powerful analytic and synthetic mind. The many editions of his commentaries and spiritual treatises in the 16th century testify to their popularity. SS. Ignatius Loyola, Francis de Sales, and Alphonsus Liguori read and quoted him often. In recent years an increasing number of monographs have been devoted to the study of his many-sided work.

Denis was much concerned to lead souls to contemplation. His most important work on the subject is his *De contemplatione* (*Opera omnia* 41.135–289). He thought contemplation in the highest sense to be a negative knowledge of God, by which the soul, inflamed by love, aided by the gift of wisdom and a special illumination, arrives at ecstatic union with Him. This negative knowledge of God supposes a positive one, which attributes in an infinite degree to the Creator every perfection found in creation. The positive knowledge of God, through the operation of the gift of wisdom and special illumination, sometimes becomes "savory" (wisdom is *sapientia,* which is derived from *sapere,* to savor) and produces an experience of contact of loving knowledge with God. This experience in itself deserves to be called true mystical contemplation. But the contemplative may progress further, that is, to an awareness that the perfections of creatures, however purified his concept of them may be, fall infinitely short of God's excellence. Therefore, drawn on by illuminating graces, the contemplative turns away from the contemplation of God in the mirror of creation and tries the "negative way." He now sees God as *not* good, *not* wise, and so on, because these attributes, the concept of which is derived from creatures, are incapable of expressing what God really is. Denis sometimes referred to God as *superbonissimus, supersapientissimus,* i.e., more than supremely good, or more than supremely wise. Realizing this, the contemplative prefers to remain in silent adoration before the Inconceivable One, "smiting with a sharp dart of longing love upon that thick cloud of unknowing" (see *Cloud of Unknowing,* ch. 6). When the soul's love is sufficiently purified and intensified, it may, by a special grace and for a short time "enter and penetrate an inner keep, outside of which knowledge must remain." No one can understand such things unless he has experienced them.

The influence of Pseudo-Dionysius on the mystical doctrine of Denis is prominent, as it was also on the older Carthusian authors, HUGH OF BALMA and GUIGO DE PONTE. Denis, however, did not limit himself to a treatment of the sublime. His *Opuscula* deal also with such topics as the devout recitation of the Psalms, meditation, the combatting of inconstancy of heart, mortification, the reformation of the inner man, progress, and the custody of the heart.

Bibliography: A. STOELEN, *Dictionnaire de spiritualité ascétique et mystique. Doctrine et histoire,* ed. M. VILLER et al. (Paris 1932–) 3:430–449. *Theologisch Woordenboek,* ed. H. BRINK (Roermond 1952–58) 1:105–62; *Month* 26 (1961) 218–230. F. VANDEN-BROUCKE, "Nouveaux milieux, nouveaux problèmes du XIIᵉ au XIVᵉ siècle," J. LECLERCQ et al., *La Spiritualité du moyen âge,* v.2 of L. BOUYER et al., *Histoire de la spiritualité chrétienne* (Paris 1960–).

[B. DU MOUSTIER]

DENMARK, THE CATHOLIC CHURCH IN

The Kingdom of Denmark, located in northwest Europe on the Jutland Peninsula, is separated from Norway to its north by the Skagerrak channel, and from Sweden to its east by the Kattegat channel, the Øresund and the Baltic Sea. It borders Germany on its south, and its western shore edges the North Sea. A number of surrounding islands, among them Sjaelland, Fyn and Bornholm, are also under Danish rule, while Greenland and the Faeroe Islands have been sovereign territories of Denmark since the 14th century.

Predominately lowlands and rolling plains, Denmark has an extensive shoreline indented by fjords and lagoons. The country's highly developed agricultural base includes wheat and other grains, sugar beets, dairy and meat products, making food one of its main exports. Denmark's primary economic strength lies in the areas of machinery and instrumentation, fuel, ships, fish and chemicals. A member of the European Union, it ab-

---

Capital: Copenhagen.
Size: 16,629 sq. miles.
Population: 5,336,394 in 2000.
Languages: Danish; Faroese, Turkish, Greenlandic (Inuit dialect), and German are spoken in various regions; English is the predominant second language.
Religions: 37,500 Catholics (.7%), 4,589,298 Evangelical Lutherans (86%), 106,728 Muslims (2%), 122,737 Protestants (2.3%); 480,131 without religious affiliation.
Diocese: Copenhagen, immediately subject to the Holy See. The diocese includes Denmark, the Faeroe Islands, and Greenland. In 1960 an apostolic delegation for all Scandinavia was established, with headquarters in Vedbäk, near Copenhagen.

---

stained from adopting the euro in 1999 and was involved in fishing disputes with several of its North Sea neighbors.

Early History: 800 to the Reformation

Christian Origins, 826–960. Inhabited by Teutonic Danes by the 6th century, Denmark was the launching point for many Viking long ships, as these Scandinavian explorer-pirates raided much of Great Britain, France and western Europe through the 8th and 9th centuries. Nothing was sacred, even the wealth of the Church, and many monasteries and other Church lands were pillaged. Viking long ships even threatened the distant city of Constantinople, while Viking settlements were established as far away as Greenland and even Newfoundland. Although initially pagans, the Viking raiders became receptive to the teachings of the Church after repeated exposure to it during their explorations, and many returned home as Christians.

Denmark's first contact with Christianity came in the 7th century via Frisian merchants from Dorstad who traded with Danish merchants at Ribe, in Jutland, and Hedeby, in Schleswig. Christian missionaries soon followed these merchants. The first known missionary bishop was St. WILLIBRORD OF UTRECHT, who reached the court of the Danish King Agantyr *c.* 710. When he returned home, he took with him 30 young Danes to be instructed in the Christian faith. In 823 Archbishop EBBO OF REIMS undertook a brief missionary journey to Denmark as papal envoy. A turning point in the region's missionary history occurred in 826, when St. ANSGAR, a Frankish Benedictine, received a commission to evangelize Denmark with the political support of Emperor Louis the Pious. Together with the newly converted Danish King Harald Klak, he traveled to Hedeby, where he preached for two years. In 831 the Diocese of Hamburg was created with Ansgar as its first bishop; a year later Pope Gregory IV appointed

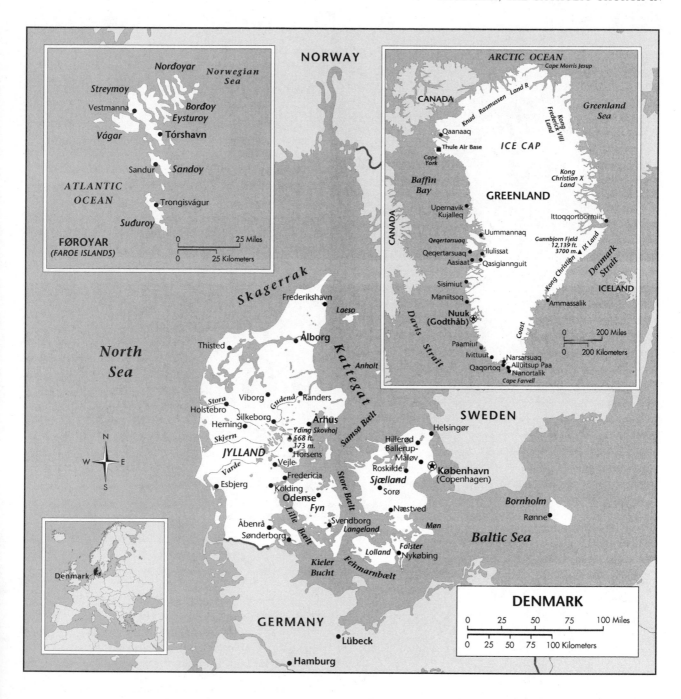

him archbishop of Hamburg and papal legate for the North. After the destruction of Hamburg in 845 by the Dane Wikinger, the seat was transferred to Bremen, which was united with Hamburg. Before his death in 865 Ansgar built missionary churches in Hedeby and Ribe. St. Ansgar is justly considered the founder of the Danish mission and the apostle of the North. Under his successors in the archiepiscopal See of Bremen-Hamburg, missionary work came to a temporary standstill until the conversion, *c*. 960, of the Danish King Harald Blaastand (''Bluetooth''), who vigorously promoted Christianity.

To this day a huge runic stone in Jutland contains the oldest Nordic picture of Christ; it is inscribed: ''King Harald erected this stone. . . . Harald, who conquered all of Denmark and Norway and converted the Danes to Christianity.''

Establishment of the Church, 960–1104. The first Danish sees were established by 948 in Schleswig, Ribe and Aarhus, under Archbishop ADALDAG OF Bremen-Hamburg. However, the actual conversion of the Danish people was undertaken only from 960–1060. Promoting Christian culture and ecclesiastical and monastic life, Ca-

The Stroget, a mile-long pedestrian street along the harbor in Copenhagen, Denmark. (©Steve Raymer/CORBIS)

nute II (1018–35) invited to Denmark bishops and priests closely associated with the CLUNIAC REFORM. During Canute II's reign, relations between Anglo-Saxon and Danish churches were close, and under his successor, King Svend Estridson, Denmark was organized into eight sees: Schleswig (created in 948), Ribe (948), Aarhus (948), Odense (956), Roskilde (1022), Lund-Dalby (1048), Viborg (1065) and Vestervig (1065; later Börglum). Adam of Bremen, the historian of the Nordic Church, counted approximately 300 churches in Skaane, 150 on the Sjaelland islands and 100 on the island of Fyn during his journey to Denmark *c.* 1070. St. CANUTE IV, king from 1080–86 and a son of Svend Estridsen, increased respect for the clergy while aiding the construction of churches, advocating the observance of Church laws and the practice of tithing. While the severity of his measures led to his murder in St. Alban's Church at Odense, Canute IV was later venerated as a martyr and the patron saint of Denmark. His brother Eric I (''Evergood''; 1095–1103)

successfully urged Pope Urban II to establish an independent ecclesiastical province in the North, and in 1104 the North became a province with Lund as the metropolitan see. In 1152 NORWAY became an independent Church province, with Trondheim as metropolitan, as did SWEDEN in 1164, with Uppsala as metropolitan.

West of Denmark, in Greenland, Catholicism was introduced *c.* 1000, and a diocese established there in 1124. From the work of modern archeologists, it is known that Greenland was home to the first known church buildings in the Western Hemisphere, 19 of which have been determined by scholars to date from the 11th century.

The Golden Age: 1104–1340. Under the first two archbishops of Lund, Asger (1104–37) and ESKIL (1138–77), the Danish Church successfully negotiated its independence from Bremen-Hamburg, sought to free itself from state control and put into effect the Gregorian reform ideas. After the 1131 murder of Duke Canute the

Saint, civil war weakened the country until the golden age of Catholic Denmark was ushered in with Waldemar I, the Great, king from 1157 to 1182. At the head of the Church were such notable men as Eskil, who was completely loyal to Rome; ABSALON (1177–1201), an exemplary statesman and ecclesiastic; and Anders Sunesen (1201–24), whose poem *Hexaemeron* condensed the philosophy and theology of his time into 8,040 Latin hexameters. Saxo Grammaticus wrote his *Gesta Danorum,* an outstanding contribution to the historical literature of the Middle Ages. Monasteries produced a wealth of annals, chronicles and biographies which would later be useful historical documents.

During the 12th century approximately 2,000 stone churches were erected in Denmark, many of them with valuable altars and frescoes that are still extant. The cathedrals of Lund, Viborg, Ribe, Roskilde, Odense and Aarhus continue to bear monumental witness to their Catholic past. Danish youths studied at the University of Paris, whose professors included Martin of Denmark, a logician, and Boethius of Denmark, a philosopher. Peter of Denmark composed learned works on astronomy and mathematics, which were widely read and acclaimed in Europe. The country's 12 Benedictine, 11 Cistercian and three Praemonstratensian monasteries were centers of Christian culture and piety. Later, 25 Franciscan and 23 Dominican houses became centers for pastoral work in the towns.

Harmony between Church and State brought Denmark to its most flourishing state (1160–1240). Zeal for the Crusades rallied Danish knights under Waldemar the Great, Archbishop Absalon, King Waldemar Sejr and Archbishop Anders Sunesen to aid in the realization of a goal at once ecclesiastical and political: the conquest and evangelization of the territory of the Wends (West Pomerania and Rügen, 1169) and of Estonia (1219). The crusaders' white cross with red background has since been the Danish national flag. From this political and cultural peak, the years 1241–1340 witnessed a temporary decline, as internal decay was experienced by both Church and State. The stubborn struggle between them, especially under the brave defender of ecclesiastical independence and freedom Archbishop Jakob Erlandsen (1254–74) and the adamant Archbishop Jens Grand (1290–1302), drained the energies of the nation and stifled prosperity and progress.

Gradual Decline: 1340–1523. Under the politically talented King Waldemar Atterdag (1340–75) and his devout daughter, Queen Margrete (1387–1412), prosperity returned and Church life improved externally. The rise of pious foundations and brotherhoods, the splendid presentation of divine services and the increase of religious in-

struction through more frequent sermons and edifying literature (DEVOTIO MODERNA) in the second half of the 15th century were evidence of a higher standard of piety among the populace. The increase of Marian devotion found an outlet in the poetry of Peder Raff Lille and Michael Nicolai of Odense, a priest. The reform program of the Council of Basel (1431–37) was carried out in most Danish monasteries. Several Benedictine monasteries joined the Bursfeld Congregation and a few Augustinian monasteries entered the Windesheim Congregation. The Order of the Knights of St. John was also reformed, while between 1470 and 1517 numerous Franciscan houses joined the strict observance. Monasteries of the Bridgettines in Maribo and in Mariager were centers for the production of devotional literature and the 11 Carmelite monasteries stimulated the study of the Bible and Marian devotion. New trends in theology at the University of Copenhagen (founded 1479) had as their chief representatives the Thomist Peder Skotte and the Biblical humanist Povl HELGESEN.

Abuses among the higher and lower clergy nevertheless existed. Almost without exception, episcopal sees and higher ecclesiastical positions in cathedral chapters were held by nobles. Ecclesiastical and political cooperation between the Roman Curia and the Danish king weakened the position of the bishops and the independence of the Church. The poverty of the lower clergy created a spiritual proletariat who later joined the Lutheran Reformation without hesitation. The last Catholic king, Christian II (1513–23), adhered to the reform ideas of Wittenberg. Resisted by bishops and nobles in his attempts to establish a National Church independent of Rome, Christian II was forced to flee the country. His successor, King Frederick I (1523–33), was well disposed toward Martin Luther and prepared the way gradually for the transition to Lutheranism.

From the Lutheran Reformation to World War I: 1536–1914

Despite his oath at the beginning of his reign to defend the Catholic Church against the reformers, Frederick I secretly supported Lutheranism. At the Diet in Odense in 1527 he placed Luther's adherents on a parity with Catholics, a catastrophe the episcopate was incapable of preventing. Of the eight Danish bishops, five had not been consecrated at that time, three lacked papal confirmation and four had promised not to resist the Reformation. Helgesen attempted vainly, by preaching and writing, to defend the Church against Lutheran attacks and to introduce reforms in the Catholic sense. The Diet of Copenhagen (1530) rejected these reform proposals. In the same year began the seizure of monasteries and a wave of iconoclasm. The 1534 election of the Lutheran-minded King Christian III sealed the fate of the Catholic Church in Denmark. On the recommendation of his German advisers, on Aug. 12, 1536 the King deposed and imprisoned the Catholic bishops and ordered ecclesiastical property to be confiscated. In Greenland, the Church was eradicated entirely after 1537, Catholic priests not returning to that island until the 1930s [see REFORMATION, PROTESTANT (ON THE CONTINENT)].

The Growth of Lutheranism. The Lutheran Church Discipline, formulated in 1537 by Luther's friend Johann BUGENHAGEN with the cooperation of Danish preachers, led to a complete break with the Catholic Church. The apostolic succession was intentionally broken when Bugenhagen, only a priest, "consecrated" Denmark's first seven Lutheran bishops. The king was the highest ecclesiastical authority; the bishops were royal officials who administrated the Church. To facilitate the conversion of the people, most of whom still adhered to Catholic customs, much of the exterior cult of the Catholic Church was retained for a while. Certain of the Catholic-minded clergy, especially in the cathedral chapters, recognized the new discipline with the reservation that they would submit to the decisions of the coming general council. The freedom of conscience that had been promised was soon abolished. In 1569 a law concerning the supervision of immigrants (Article 25) hermetically sealed the country from all outside Catholic influences.

Contact with the Catholic Church could not, however, be completely prevented. Toward the end of the 16th century Danish students attended by preference Jesuit colleges in Braunsberg, Vilna, Olmütz, Vienna and Augsburg. To prevent a Catholic reaction, King Christian IV forbade Jesuit students to hold public offices, fined their families and in 1604 expelled them from the country. After the founding of the Congregation for the Propagation of the Faith (1622), Dominicans and Jesuits secretly entered Denmark to investigate the possibilities of founding a mission, but such plans were dismissed after a 1624 law prohibited, under penalty of death, the residence of Catholic priests within the country. When the Spanish, French and German embassies were erected in Copenhagen at the end of the Thirty Years' War, Catholic ambassadors received special permission to erect private chapels and to have chaplains, who were almost exclusively Jesuits. Embassy personnel, and as a rule, foreign Catholics were thereby enabled to attend divine services. These were the beginnings of a Catholic community for foreigners in Copenhagen. A second Catholic community, also restricted to foreigners, was established at Fredericia in Jutland (1674); it was made possible by the presence of numerous Catholic mercenaries in the Danish army. Its central location made the garrison city

of Fredericia the center of the military care of souls in Jutland and on the island of Fyn. When foreigners residing in Fredericia were granted freedom of worship within the city in 1682, a small Catholic community soon developed, receiving permission in 1686 to build a chapel and a school. A small baroque chapel, built in 1767, is still in use. Small Catholic communities also grew in Altona, Friedrichstadt, Nordstrand, Glückstadt and Rendsborg, places that then belonged to Denmark. The immigration of Catholic artisans, merchants and artists considerably increased the number of foreign Catholics in Copenhagen and Fredericia.

Because the conversion of a native Dane involved loss of property and expulsion from the country, Danes entered the Catholic Church only in foreign countries. Much comment followed the conversions of the natural scientist, anatomist and saintly bishop Niels STENSEN (1667); of the professor of anatomy and surgery Jacob Benignus Winsløw (1669); and of the archeologist George Zoega (1783). Following the suppression of the Society of Jesus (1773), secular priests took charge of pastoral work in Copenhagen and Fredericia after 1800. The census of 1841 recorded 865 Catholics in Denmark proper, 550 of whom were in Copenhagen and 58 in Fredericia. The mission stations in the Kingdom of Denmark were first under the jurisdiction of the nuncio in Brussels until 1678, when they were placed under the vicar apostolic of the Northern Missions.

Constitution Brings Religious Freedom. In 1849 a constitutional hereditary monarchy and a democratic constitution replaced Denmark's former absolutist government and Lutheranism was declared the state religion. The constitution of June 5, 1849 granted civil equality to all, regardless of religious belief, and thus extended to Catholics complete freedom of worship. Gradually Danes began to join the Church and began to play an important part in Catholic communities. The first prayer book in Danish appeared in 1852. The Ansgar Union, founded in 1853, began its activity with the printing of the *Scandinavian Church Journal for Catholic Christians*. This publication, eventually renamed the *Catholic Weekly,* remained in print through the 20th century. In 1854 the Sisters of St. Joseph of Chambery became Denmark's first congregation of religious women. The first Catholic hospitals were founded by the Sisters in Copenhagen (1875) and in Fredericia (1879).

After 1861 attempts were made to join the Danish mission with the Prefecture Apostolic of the North Pole, established in 1855. It was to the advantage of the Danish mission that this plan be abandoned; in its place the Prefecture Apostolic of Denmark was created in 1869, encompassing the Kingdom of Denmark, the Faeroe Islands and ICELAND. Hermann Grüder, a convert, became the first prefect apostolic (1869–83) and under his care the mission thrived. The number of Catholics rose from 865 to 3,000. New parishes were established in Horsens (1869), Aarhus (1873), Kolding (1882) and Svendborg (1883), in addition to those founded in 1867 in Randers (Jutland) and in Odense on the island of Fyn. In 1872 Grüder invited to Denmark Jesuits who had been expelled from Germany during the *Kulturkampf.* One of the schools started by the Jesuits was the College of St. Andrew, a secondary boarding school located in Ordrup, that developed into an intellectual stronghold of Catholic life before closing in 1920 for financial reasons.

Vicariate Apostolic of Denmark Established. In 1892 Pope Leo XIII raised the status of the Prefecture Apostolic of Denmark to that of vicariate apostolic, and Johannes von Euch became the first vicar apostolic. Owing to Bishop Von Euch's energy, optimism and organizational ability, the Church expanded and flourished. With the financial support of the German St. Boniface Society and the Society for the Propagation of the Faith in Lyons, 18 new mission parishes, 19 elementary schools and 17 hospitals were erected. Missionary work in Iceland, which had continued from 1859 to 1875, was renewed in 1895. Nine religious institutes of men and ten of women entered Denmark. Their efforts in pastoral work, teaching and nursing were of great apostolic value. Marian congregations, brotherhoods, St. Vincent de Paul societies, workers guilds and other Catholic associations increased greatly. A society for Catholic university graduates, founded in 1896, debated contemporary problems from a Catholic viewpoint in its meetings. Johannes Jørgensen published a weekly, the *Catholic* (1898–1903), while the Catholic monthly journal *Varden* (1903–13) added its voice to Church-related issues. The first Catholic translation of the New Testament into Danish appeared in 1893.

The Modern Era: World War I and Beyond

Despite the climate of rising political unrest felt throughout Europe at the turn of the 20th century, the Catholic Church in Denmark continued to expand its evangelical activities. During von Euch's years as bishop the number of Catholics grew from 3,000 to 15,000. There were also 14,000 Polish temporary farm workers before World War I, although these numbers would decrease to 8,000 by 1918. A Danish *Messenger of the Sacred Heart* was established in 1913. After World War I— during which Denmark declared itself a neutral party— the youth movement received special attention. The Catholic Youth Organization of Denmark, started in 1919, published a biweekly journal, *Catholic Youth,* which became popular among the country's youth. And

the convert movement was rewarded by an average annual total of 100 to 150 conversions.

In 1922 the Belgian Praemonstratensian Josef Brems succeeded von Euch. During his years as vicar apostolic (1923–38), 30 churches and chapels were built, five new parishes were founded, and seven schools and nine hospitals were opened. To promote the publication and dissemination of religious literature, Knud Ballin, a pastor, founded the publishing house St. Paul's Circle in 1933. On the occasion of Cardinal Willem van Rossum's visit to Scandinavia in 1923, the Church in ICELAND was made a prefecture apostolic (1929, vicariate apostolic). The mission in the Faeroe Islands was revived in 1930 and in 1934 a parish and a school were started in Thorshavn. The first Scandinavian Eucharistic Congress met in Copenhagen in 1932. In 1938, when Bishop Brems resigned because of ill health, the number of Catholics had increased to 22,000.

Theodore Suhr, OSB, a native Dane and convert, succeeded Brems and set about systematically reorganizing the internal workings of the Church. However, war soon broke out in Europe again. This time Denmark would not be able to maintain a peaceful state of neutrality; the country's occupation by Nazi Germany resulted in grave financial difficulties because of the discontinuance of all support from Catholic sources outside the country. To finance the vicariate, Guilds of St. Canute were founded in 1941; their weekly collections covered one-fifth of the Church's expenses. Financial considerations caused the *Catholic Church Weekly* to be combined with the *Youth Journal* in 1939, and the three Catholic schools in Copenhagen were merged into one central school a year later. An institute to supply parish workers, founded in 1946 and directed by the Sisters of St. Lioba, handled most of the social and charitable works in the vicariate.

Apart from its horrors, World War II awakened great public interest in the spiritual and moral strength and significance of the Church and of the papacy. Literary works by Catholic authors such as Robert Hugh Benson, Karl Adam, Georges Bernanos, G. K. Chesterton, Christopher Dawson, Jacques Maritain, François Mauriac, Graham Greene, Bruce Marshall, Daniel-Rops, Sigrid Undset and Evelyn Waugh were translated during the war years and read widely by a Danish public searching for meaning in the face of a war that shattered their moral sphere.

At the end of World War II, the Church was faced with the unusual task of ministering to numerous refugees. Among the 250,000 German and 24,000 allied refugees were 51,000 Catholics. Following the war the Catholic Bureau for German and Non-German Refugees was established in close cooperation with the State's refugee administration. In 1947 Father Ballin founded "Caritas Denmark" a Catholic organization to aid war-stricken countries. During his lecture tour of the United States in 1947, Bishop Suhr obtained financial help for his Church and established contacts with ST. ANSGAR'S SCANDINAVIAN CATHOLIC LEAGUE. The Church's commitment to help refugees continued into the 21st century, as reflected by Pope John Paul II's words of encouragement to the Danish ambassador in 1999. "People should have the right to immigrate freely in search of freedom, security, or a better way of life," the Pope noted.

Church Moves into 21st Century. The Danish Church was the only Catholic Church in Scandinavia that did not experience a rapid population increase following World War II, a consequence of both the small number of immigrants to Denmark and to the static number of Danish Catholics. Administering to the country's 50 parishes by 2000 were 99 priests (down from 131 in 1964; 46 secular, 53 religious) affiliated with Jesuit, Redemptorist, Oblates of Mary Immaculate, Premonstratensian, Franciscan, Lazarist, Benedictine and Montfort orders. A small Trappist monastery was founded in 1966. In 2000 there were 240 religious sisters from 15 congregations, more than half of which were aged 65 or older. Although Catholic hospitals were closed, the Church continued to operate 23 primary and secondary schools, many around Copenhagen. Three Catholic publishing houses remained in operation and the diocesan newspaper *Katolsk Orientering* was delivered *gratis* to all Catholic households.

Despite the decreasing numbers of Church clergy, ecumenical work continued to take place in Denmark, in large part because of the efforts of Bishop Martensen. A recognized Luther scholar, Martensen was a member of the Secretariat for the Promotion of the Unity of Christians and former co-chairman of the international Lutheran-Roman Catholic Theological Commission. In 1997, during a meeting with Scandinavian bishops, Pope John Paul II encouraged a continued effort toward the ecumenical efforts promoted by Denmark's bishop.

Bibliography: *Den danske kirkes historie,* eds., H. KOCH and B. KORNERUP, v.1–5 (Copenhagen 1950–65), 8 v. planned. J. O. ANDERSEN, *Survey of the History of the Church in Denmark* (Copenhagen 1930). P. G. LINDHARDT, *Den nordiske kirkes historie* (Copenhagen 1945). E. H. DUNKLEY, *The Reformation in Denmark* (Society for Promoting Christian Knowledge, London 1948). G. SCHWAIGER, *Die Reformation in den nordischen Ländern* (Munich 1962). J. METZLER, *Die apostolischen Vikariate des Nordens* (Paderborn 1919); *Biskop Johannes von Euch* (Copenhagen 1910). H. HOLZAPFEL, *Unter nordischen Fahnen* (Paderborn 1955). K. S. LATOURETTE, *Christianity in a Revolutionary Age: A History of Christianity in the Nineteenth and Twentieth Centuries,* 5 v. (New York 1958–62) v.1–2, 4. K. HARMER, *Biskop Josef Brems* (Copenhagen 1945). *Scandinavian Churches,* ed. L. S. HUNTER, (London 1965). A. RAULIN, *Dictionnaire d'histoire et de géographie ecclésiastiques,* ed. A. BAUDRILLART et al., (Paris 1912–) 14:57–67. H. KOCH et al., *Die Religion in Geschichte und Gegenwart,* 7 v. (3d ed. Tübingen 1957–65) 2:5–18. A. OTTO, *Lexikon für Theologie und Kirche,* eds., J. HOFER and K. RAHNER, 10 v. (2d, new ed. Freiburg 1957–65) 3:148–150. *Bilan du Monde,* 2 (1964) 303–308. *Annuario Pontificio* (1965) 218. *St. Ansgar's Bulletin* (St. Ansgar's Scandinavian Catholic League; New York 1915–).

[A. J. OTTO/EDS.]

DENVER, ARCHDIOCESE OF

Metropolitan see comprising 24 counties in the northern part of the state of Colorado, the Archdiocese of Denver (*Denveriensis*) in 2000 ministers to about 363,000 Catholics in a total population of 2.7 million. Erected as a diocese Aug. 16, 1887, it was raised to the status of an archdiocese Nov. 15, 1941. Its suffragan sees are Pueblo, Colorado Springs, and Cheyenne, Wyoming.

Early History. The permanent settlements in northern Colorado that developed as a result of the discoveries of gold in 1858 and 1859 were under the jurisdiction of Bp. John B. Miège, SJ, Vicar Apostolic of Kansas. In 1860, after his visitation to the Catholics of Auraria, Denver City, and the mining camps in the Rockies, the bishop secured the transfer of the Colorado district to the jurisdiction of the New Mexico diocese. Bp. John B. Lamy sent Fathers Joseph Machebeuf and John B. Raverdy to the Pikes Peak region where they worked until their deaths in 1889, laying the foundation for the Church in Denver.

Diocese. A rapid growth in population led to the establishment (1868) of a vicariate apostolic at Denver for Colorado and Utah. Machebeuf was named to it and consecrated titular bishop of Epiphania at Cincinnati, Ohio, on Aug. 16, 1868. Three years later Utah was transferred to the jurisdiction of the Diocese of San Francisco. Denver was erected a diocese on Aug. 16, 1887, with Machebeuf as first bishop. In spite of financial difficulties in the state and the diocese, the westward migration continued and the Church grew. When Machebeuf died in 1889, Catholics numbered more than 40,000, and schools under Catholic auspices were educating more than 4,000 pupils.

Matz. Nicholas Chrysostom Matz, a native of Munster, Lorraine, and missionary to Colorado after his ordination in 1874, was consecrated coadjutor of Denver on its erection as a diocese in 1887; he succeeded to the see at Machebeuf's death on July 10, 1889. During Matz's 28-year rule, the Church in Colorado made notable progress. He conducted the first synod for the diocese in 1890, erected a cathedral in honor of Our Lady of the Immaculate Conception, and stressed the importance of a Catholic education for the young. Matz proved a capable administrator, although his episcopate was plagued by fi-

Denver, Colorado. (Denver Metro Convention & Visitors Bureau)

nancial problems caused in part by the fluctuating mining economy of the state, and by difficulties stemming from the growing animosity toward Catholics and from the German-Irish conflict within the Catholic body itself. By 1917 there were 174 priests caring for 110,000 Catholics in 188 churches and 133 missions. The diocese had 31 parish schools and five academies, educating 7,584 pupils; two colleges and preparatory schools for young men (one initiated by the Benedictines in Pueblo; the other, Jesuit-run Sacred Heart College and High School that was renamed Regis in 1921 in Denver). The Vincentian Fathers had opened St. Thomas Seminary in Denver (1908) for the diocese and the surrounding area.

Tihen. The third ordinary was John Henry Tihen; he was bishop of Lincoln, Nebraska when he was transferred to Denver to succeed Matz, who died on Aug. 9, 1917. After Tihen was installed on Nov. 28, 1917, he had to counter the attacks of the KU KLUX KLAN, which grew in power following World War I, until discredited in the mid-1920s. In the developing field of Catholic journalism, Tihen gave financial and moral upport to Matthew Smith (d. 1960), editor of the *Denver Catholic Register*; he encouraged him to establish a national weekly edition of the *Register* as well as local editions for other dioceses.

Tihen's 14-year episcopate was notable also for a successful campaign to enlarge St. Thomas Seminary, the establishment in 1918 by the Sisters of Loretto of a Catholic college for girls, the unification of charitable works in the diocese under a centralized Catholic Charities (1927), the inauguration of vacation schools for rural public school pupils, and the consecration of the cathedral in 1921. When age and infirmity led Tihen to resign on Jan. 2, 1931, the Catholic population had increased to 135,258, the number of priests to 229, and the number of parish schools to 49, with a student body increase of 11,981. Three new hospitals, an orphanage, and the J. K. Mullen Home for the Aged also were well established. Tihen died Jan. 13, 1940.

Vehr. Urban J. Vehr was installed as fourth bishop of Denver on July 16, 1931. Born in suburban Cincinnati on May 30, 1891, Vehr had been ordained in 1915 and served as rector of Mt. St. Mary Seminary, Cincinnati. Despite the problems of the Depression years, the new bishop promoted the Church's growth, particularly in education and the press. The school system for the diocese was unified under a diocesan superintendent, while the *Register* system of newspapers was further expanded. Cordial relations with non-Catholic groups also marked the bishop's approach.

Archdiocese. By 1941 the Catholic population of the state had increased to 147,217, and the Holy See separated the southern counties of Colorado to form the new Diocese of Pueblo. At the same time (Nov. 15, 1941), Denver was made a metropolitan see, with the Dioceses of Pueblo and Cheyenne, Wyoming, as suffragans.

Casey. When Archbishop Vehr retired in February of 1967, James V. Casey, bishop of Lincoln, Nebraska, was named his successor. It was Archbishop Casey's lot to steer the Church of Denver through the years of change that followed Vatican Council II. Archbishop Casey created many new offices and agencies to administer and coordinate parish programs, ministries to Hispanic Catholics, family life, and social services. He made a conscious effort to encourage laymen and lay women to become actively involved in parish and diocesan programs. On the downside, he found that the *Denver Register* was floundering and deeply in debt because of dwindling circulation and increased competition. Shortly after Casey's arrival the archdiocese sold the *Register* to the Twin Circle Publishing of Culver City, California. In preparation for the centennial celebration of the diocese in 1997, Archbishop Casey commissioned Tom Noel to write a history that appeared under the title *Colorado Catholicism,* but Casey did not live to celebrate the centenary. He died March 14, 1986.

Stafford. Casey's successor, J. Francis Stafford, a native of Baltimore and formerly bishop of Memphis, served the archdiocese for ten years, from the time he was installed as archbishop July 30, 1986 to his resignation in 1996 when Pope John Paul II named him president of the Pontifical Council on the Laity. The high point of Stafford's episcopate occurred in August 1993 when Denver hosted World Youth Day that was attended by some 450,000 young people and Pope John Paul II. The pope named Stafford a cardinal in 1998. One of his last acts as archbishop of Denver was to establish the Redemptoris Mater Archdiocesan Mission Seminary of Denver (March 25, 1996) under the aegis of the Neocatechumenal Way. Like other missionary seminaries in the network, Redemptoris Mater prepares presbyters for the work of evangelization both in the archdiocese of Denver and in mission lands.

Chaput. Charles J. Chaput, O.F.M. Cap., was bishop of Rapid City, South Dakota when he was transferred to Denver to replace Archbishop Stafford in February 1997. Chaput, by reason of his Potawatomi ancestry, was the first Native American to head a metropolitan see in the U.S. Chaput moved swiftly to consolidate the administrative offices of the archdiocese, moving the chancery to a 40-acre site officially known as the John Paul II Center for the New Evangelization. It is also the site of the New

Advent Theological Institute established in 1999 to consolidate the work of evangelization in the archdiocese. The Institute has four divisions: St. John Vianney Theological Seminary, established by Archbishop Chaput in 1999; Redemptoris Mater Missionary Seminary; the archdiocesan program for permanent deacons; and the division of Lay Formation.

Bibliography: Archives of the Archdiocese of Denver, Chancery Office. W. H. JONES, *The History of Catholic Education in the State of Colorado* (Washington 1955). W. O'RYAN and T. H. MALONE, *History of the Catholic Church in Colorado* (Denver 1889). H. L. MCMENAMIN, *The Pinnacled Glory of the West* (Denver 1912); *Diamond Jubilee of the Cathedral Parish* (Denver 1935). T. J. NOEL, *Colorado Catholicism* (Denver 1989).

[T. M. FEELY/EDS.]

DENZINGER

The name "Denzinger" is synonymous with a Catholic "handbook of creeds, definitions and declarations on matters of faith and morals" (*Enchiridion Symbolorum Definitionum et Declarationum de Rebus Fidei et Morum*) which has appeared in 37 editions from 1854 to 1991. The current Denzinger collection contains two main parts: first, a collection of "symbols" or professions of faith from early apostolic times up through the fifth century; and second, a chronological compilation of "Documents of the Church's Magisterium" beginning with Pope Clement of Rome (c. 92–101 A.D.) and continuing up through the pontificate of John Paul II.

The original 1854 edition of the *Enchiridion* was the idea of Heinrich Denzinger (1819–83), a priest and professor of dogmatic theology in Wurzburg, Germany. Denzinger was distressed by what he perceived as a neglect of the positive documents on faith and morals promulgated by the authority of the Church. Thus, in his first edition, he compiled some 100 ecclesiastical documents in Latin translation that included symbols or professions of the faith, decrees and declarations of councils (both provincial and ecumenical) and papal decrees up to the pontificate of Pius IX. Denzinger oversaw a total of five editions during his lifetime, and he expanded the selections to include excerpts from Pius IX's 1865 encyclical, *Quanta cura* (along with his "Syllabus") as well as passages from Vatican I. Curiously, he did not include any of the texts of the Council of Trent.

The sixth through the ninth editions (1888–1900) of Denzinger were overseen by Ignaz Stahl, a *privatdozent* and honorary professor at the University of Wurzburg. Under Stahl, the number of documents increased to 155 with the inclusion of documents from Trent, the constitutions of Vatican I and more papal encyclicals. After

Stahl's death in 1905, the Herder Publishing Company took over the production of all subsequent editions. The first nine editions had been produced by Oskar Stahel of Wurzburg.

The tenth through thirteenth editions (1908–21) were overseen by Clemens Bannwart, S.J. and his assistant, Johannes B. Umberg, S.J. Making use of the best research of his day, Bannwart completely revised the first part of Denzinger on the creeds. In addition, he reworked the systematic index according to ten main categories, an arrangement that figured largely in the handbooks of dogmatic theology up until Vatican II. A special concern with the dangers of Modernism is evidenced by Bannwart's inclusion of 34 pages of documentation from Pius X's 1907 encyclical, *Pascendi dominici gregis.*

Johannes B. Umberg, S.J. is listed as the editor for the fourteenth through the twenty-seventh editions of Denzinger (1922–1951). Umberg was a specialist in sacramental theology, and he included more documents in that area as well as references to the 1917 Code of Canon Law. He also reintroduced a section on moral theology into the Index, arranging it according to the decalogue.

The twenty-eighth through the thirty-first editions (1952–57) were overseen by Karl Rahner, S.J. In the twenty-eight edition, Rahner asked for suggestions for a revised edition of "Denzinger." In anticipation of the revision project, only minor changes were made in the editions of this period.

The revisions foreseen by Rahner were undertaken by Adolf Schonmetzer, S.J., who is listed as the editor for the thirty-second through the thirty-sixth editions (1963–76). In thirty-second edition of 1963, Schonmetzer included close to 150 more documents and expanded about 100 others. He revised the section on the creeds as well as the introductions, the numbering system and the Index. In the thirty-third and thirty-fourth editions, Schonmetzer included excerpts from the encyclicals of John XXIII and documents of Paul VI. However, he did not include any of the documents of Vatican II since he planned to publish these in a separate volume that also would include other recent magisterial documents. Schonmetzer did not see this project to completion.

In 1981, Professor Peter Hunermann of the University of Tubingen began work on a new bilingual edition of Denzinger. The idea was to completely update the *Enchiridion* with the addition of key texts of Vatican II and postconciliar documents. Among those who provided suggestions for the new documents was Bishop Walter Kaspar of Rottenburg-Stuttgart, now the Cardinal-Prefect of the Pontifical Council for Promoting Christian Unity.

Hunermann and his assistants likewise revised the original texts according to the most recent critical editions and provided changes and additions to the introductions and Index as needed.

Hunermann decided to provide German translations on pages opposite to the original texts in Greek, Latin and other languages. The numbering system of Schonmetzer was retained but expanded. In the 37th edition which appeared in 1991, the creeds of the ancient Church comprised *1 to 76 (as in Schonmetzer), but the documents of the Church's Magisterium now went from 101 to 4858 with the last entry being John Paul II's 1988 apostolic exhortation, *Christifideles laici.* The numbering of the texts up to 3997 corresponds to that of Schonmetzer's thirty-sixth edition, but a new system from 4001 onwards was devised to include the texts from Vatican II through the pontificate of John Paul II. In 1997, a CD-ROM version of the thirty-seventh edition was produced that extended the texts up to 5041, ending with the Dec. 11, 1995. Response of the Congregation for the Doctrine of the Faith regarding the doctrinal authority of John Paul II's 1994 Apostolic Letter, *Ordinatio sacerdotalis.*

An Italian bilingual version of the 1991 edition appeared in 1995, and a second Italian version was produced in 1996. An English bilingual edition by Ignatius Press of San Francisco will include the supplemental texts provided by the 1997 CD-ROM version. This will be the first English translation of Denzinger to appear since that of the thirtieth edition produced by Roy J. Deferrari in 1957.

Neuner & Dupuis. A handbook in English that serves the same purpose as Denzinger in many respects is the volume edited by J. Neuner and J. Dupuis entitled *The Christian Faith in the Doctrinal Documents of the Catholic Church* which appeared in its sixth edition in 1996. Whereas the documents in Denzinger are arranged chronologically, those in Neuner and Dupuis are arranged topically according to headings such as "Revelation and Faith," "Tradition and Scripture," etc. The documentation in Neuner and Dupuis is not as extensive as that of Denzinger, but it does have the advantage of topical arrangement for those who are interested in documents pertaining to a certain subject.

While prominent theologians such as Karl Rahner and Yves Congar have warned about the dangers of "Denzinger theology," there is no doubt that the *Enchiridion* is an important resource for students, theologians, teachers and pastors. The citing of creeds and Magisterial statements by references to Denzinger continues in the *Catechism of the Catholic Church* and in the writings of Pope John Paul II.

Bibliography: H. DENZINGER and P. HUNERMANN, *Enchiridion symbolorum definitionum et declarationum de rebus fidei et* *morum* 37th ed. (Freiburg, Basel, Rome and Vienna 1991) Einleitung [Introduction] 3–13. Y. CONGAR, "Du bon usage de 'Denzinger,'" *Situations et taches presentes de la theologie* (Paris 1967) 111–13. J. SCHUHMACHER, *Der "Denzinger" : Geschichte und Bedeutung eines Buches in der Praxis der neueren Theologie* (Freiburg 1974). J. NEUNER, S.J. and J. DUPUIS, S.J., eds., *The Christian Faith in the Doctrinal Documents of the Catholic Church*, 6th edition (New York 1996).

[R. FASTIGGI]

DENZINGER, HEINRICH JOSEPH

Theologian; b. Liège, Belgium, Oct. 10, 1819; d. Würzburg, Germany, June 19, 1883. Ordained in 1844, he began teaching theology at Würzburg in 1848. He contributed to the renewal of sacred science in the 19th century by his many theological works of a positive-historical orientation. Chief among them were: *Vier Bücher von der religiösen Erkenntnis* (Würzburg 1856–1857); *Ritus Orientalium, Coptorum, Syrorum et Armenorum* (Würzburg 1863–1864). His best–known work, used by all theologians, is the *Enchiridion Symbolorum et Definitionum*. First published at Würzburg in 1854, it has passed through 36 editions, the most recent undertaken by A. Schönmetzer (Barcelona 1976).

Bibliography: J. HASENFUSS, *Lexikon für Theologie und Kirche* (Freiburg 1965) 3:233–234. E. MANGENOT, *Dictionnaire de Théologie Catholique* (Paris 1950) 4.1:450–451. L. STACHEL, *Vernunft und Offenbarung bei H. Denzinger* (dissertation; Munich 1950).

[J. BEUMER]

DEOCHAR, ST.

Benedictine abbot (known also as Theotker, Theutger, Dietker, Gottlieb); d. *c.* 832. Having been a monk at FULDA, then a disciple of ALCUIN at the court of CHARLEMAGNE, Deochar retired to solitude in Haserode (later Herrieden) in Franconia. There Charlemagne built a small chapel and later a Benedictine monastery of which Deochar became the first abbot, *c.* 795. An authority on Scripture and the monastic rule, Deochar acted as *missus regis* in Regensburg (*c.* 800–04) and participated in the translation of the relics of St. BONIFACE to Fulda (November of 819). He headed the list of signatories to the synod of Mainz. He died at an advanced age. Most of his relics were solemnly enshrined in the church of St. Lawrence, Nuremberg, in 1316 and were brought to Eichstätt in 1854.

Feast: June 7.

Bibliography: *Acta Sanctorum* June 2:38. F. GELDNER, *Lexikon für Theologie und Kirche*, ed. J. HOFER and K. RAHNER (Freiburg 1957–65) 3:234. H. HEIDINGSFELDER, *Regesten der Bischöfe von Eichstätt*, 1 (Erlangen 1938). M. ADAMSKI, *Herrieden: Kloster, Stift und Stadt im Mittelalter bis zur Eroberung durch Ludwig den Bayern im Jahre 1316* (Kallmünz 1954). F. H. HUNDT, *Die Urkunden des Bisthums Freising aus der Zeit der Karolinger* (*Abhandlungen der Bayerischen Akademie der Wissenschaften* 13.1; 1877) 69–72.

[M. B. RYAN]

DEODATUS OF BLOIS, ST.

Hermit or abbot in Blois; lived in the sixth or seventh century. The three lives from the late ninth century are completely legendary. One account describes him as born and educated at Bordeaux; with the priest Baudemire he entered the monastery at nearby Iccio under St. Phaletro. Envious of Abbot Phaletro's praise of his virtue, the monks made life so miserable for Deodatus that he sought and received permission to retire to a life of solitude in Bordeaux. King CLOVIS reputedly visited him to seek support for his expedition against the Goths. Convinced that Deodatus's prayers had been a great help in his victory, Clovis reported back to him, gave him gifts for the poor, and presented himself to St. REMIGIUS for baptism. Eventually about 40 men joined Deodatus, and subsequently he established the monastery of St.-Dyé-sur-Loire on land given him by Clovis. A church erected in his honor was burned during a local skirmish but was restored by Abbot Aurelius and Charles the Bald.

Feast: April 24.

Bibliography: *Acta Sanctae Sedis* April 3:275–279. *Bibliotheca hagiograpica latina antiquae et mediae aetatis* (Brussels 1898–1901) 1:2128–30. A. M. ZIMMERMANN, *Kalendarium Benedictinum* (Metten 1933–38) 2:104. J. L. BAUDOT and L. CHAUSSIN, *Vies des saints et des bienhereux selon l'ordre du calendrier avec l'historique des fêtes* (Paris 1935–56) 4:613–614.

[B. CAVANAUGH]

DEODATUS OF NEVERS, ST.

Bishop (known also as Dié, Didier), probably Irish; d. probably June 18, 679. He is the founder (669) of the monastery of Jointures in the Vosges named Val de Galilée. From King Childeric II (660–73) he obtained, for the monastery, part of the valley of the Meurthe and exemption from the jurisdiction of the bishop of Toul. His monastic constitutions were drawn from the rules of St. Benedict and St. Colomban. The abbey and the town that grew around it were named for him. In the past his cult was very active, as indicated by the many translations of his relics (e.g., 1003, 1648, 1679, 1735, 1766, 1792, 1808, 1851). The few relics remaining after the destruction of the church in 1944 were placed in a ceramic reliquary blessed in 1950. The *Vita Deodati* written in 1048 by HUMBERT OF SILVA CANDIDA, a monk of the neighboring monastery of MOYENMOUTIER, adds much information, some of which is legendary: for instance, that Deodatus was bishop of Nevers, that he traveled to Alsace, and that he knew HIDULF (d. 707), who was the founder of Moyenmoutier.

Feast: June 19.

Bibliography: Sources. J. M. PARDESSUS, ed., *Diplomata . . . ad res gallo-francicas spectantia*, 2 v. (Paris 1843–49) 2:147. "Vita . . . Deodati," *Richeri Gesta Senoniensis ecclesiae, Monumenta Germaniae Historica: Scriptores* 25:259–262, 276–277. J. B. E. L'HÔTE, ed., "Praefatio in vitam S. Deodati," *Analecta Bollandiana* 6 (1887) 151–160. Literature. C. PFISTER, "Les Légendes de S. Dié et de S. Hidulphe," *Annales de l'Est* 3 (1889) 377–408, 536–588. J. B. E. L'HÔTE, "Les Reliques de Saint Dié," *Analecta Bollandiana* 11 (1892) 75–99. G. BAUMONT and A. PIERROT, *Iconographie de Saint-Dié* (Mulhouse-Dornach 1936).

[P. COUSIN]

DEONTOLOGISM

Deontologism is an ethics of duty. While some great systems, especially the Stoic and the Kantian, put duty at the heart of morality, modern deontologism is a species of British intuitionism. Intuitionists are divided on two questions. Whereas G. E. Moore held that good is the fundamental concept of morality, that the right act is the one that will produce the most intrinsic good, the deontologists held that right or duty is the fundamental notion, that the rightness of an act depends on its nature, not on its consequences. The term deontologist (from δέον, it is necessary) originated with J. BENTHAM, who claimed that duty is the prime ethical concept. The older deontologists held that man has an intuition of moral principles; present-day deontologists say that man intuits only the rightness of particular acts.

Basic Notions. According to Ross, the right act is the one that a man "ought" to choose. Right is what is fitting, wrong is what is inappropriate. While moral suitability may resemble utilitarian suitability for the production of good consequences, it is not identified with it, but it is akin to aesthetic rightness. Rightness may be analyzed to the extent of saying that it is suitability, but beyond that the concept cannot be analyzed. Again, the ground of right is those characteristics in an act that make it morally suitable. This is certainly not capacity to produce the greatest good. There is, moreover, no single principle underlying all moral rightness: morality is pluralistic.

There are *prima facie* duties and proper duties. The former are acts that at first sight tend to be morally obligatory. They result from a partial view of the situation, whereas one's proper duty is that which fits the entire situation. Proper duty is left to the immediate insight of the agent.

How does man know that any act is a duty? Prichard says that no one can prove by reasoning that any act is obligatory. To know that an act is obligatory (say, payment of a debt), all that one can do is to put himself in the situation in which he owes a debt; there, he immediately perceives the right thing to do. However, any ultimate basis of obligation is unknown, for "obligation," like "good," is unanalyzable. One can only say that certain actions are to be done or not to be done; their obligatory character is seen immediately. If, however, someone does not see a particular obligation, he cannot be proved to be wrong. For example, in the case of someone who gets the wrong answer to a simple arithmetic problem, all that can be done is to tell him to look again. Can anyone give reasons why he should be moral? The answer is no, and if ethics is looked upon as the attempt to answer this question, ethics is based upon a mistake.

Some deontologists hold that good is of secondary importance, that unless one acts from a sense of duty, one's act is immoral and that morality and virtue are absolutely distinct. They argue that to be virtuous an act must be done willingly and from a good motive, but motive is not always within a person's control.

All deontologists say that right is independent of good, that the assertion that an act is right or wrong is not the same as saying that it is good or bad. Just as the right road need not be a good road and a good road may be the wrong road, so an act good in itself may not be right and a bad act may not be wrong. Moreover, when one acts from a sense of duty, one has no purpose, for the moral act is done neither for the sake of itself nor for anything to be got out of the act; duty alone explains it.

Critique. The deontologist makes such statements about motive because if he should admit that the moral act proceeds from a motive, he would have to admit that right is based on good—a thesis he attempts to deny. Yet modern deontologism has something in common with scholastic ethics in the sense that its proper duties are common Christian principles. Moreover, it evokes sympathy for its effort to keep close to common sense; the adult, particularly, has easy insight into his duties in obvious cases, but all cases are not obvious, and some require very close reasoning. Nor is it true that one is unable to give reasons for being moral and doing one's duty; it is the task of the moralist to elucidate these reasons. Deontologism fails to make a good case for its claim that right is independent of good; if right were independent of good, man would sometimes be obliged to do evil. It is mistaken also about motive and its influence on the moral act. Again, while making much of right and duty, it fails to give an ultimate account of moral obligation; it confuses SYNDERESIS with INTUITION and does not completely explain the role of either in establishing norms of morality.

See Also: CATEGORICAL IMPERATIVE; STOICISM; GOOD; OBLIGATION, MORAL; ETHICS, HISTORY OF.

Bibliography: W. D. ROSS, *Foundations of Ethics* (Oxford 1939); *The Right and the Good* (Oxford 1930). A. C. EWING, *The Definition of Good* (New York 1947); "A Suggested Non-Naturalistic Analysis of Good," *Mind* 48 (1939) 1–22. C. D. BROAD, *Five Types of Ethical Theory* (New York 1930). E. F. CARRITT, *The Theory of Morals* (London 1928). A. A. PRICHARD, "Does Moral Philosophy Rest on a Mistake?" *Mind* 21 (1912) 21–37.

[T. J. HIGGINS]

DEPORTATION (IN THE BIBLE)

Although deportation of conquered people did not originate with Tiglath-Pileser III (745–727 B.C.), he was the first to institute it as a fixed policy of state. This transplanting of influential citizens, their families, and transportable goods to far off areas in the Assyrian Empire eliminated the possibility of rallying points for intrigue and rebellion. The deportations were apparently effected not by one mass movement, but by a series of movements extending over a period of time. The land was then resettled by foreign colonists and incorporated into the system of Assyrian provinces. Authorities differ concerning the number of deportees given in the Biblical and Assyro-Babylonian sources. At most the figures given are rough estimates, perhaps including many who died on the journey. The tendency of scholars today is to admit lower figures than those listed. However, it must be noted that women and children were not usually counted. As depicted by Assyrian monuments, the deportees had their hands bound and were marched in columns. The women usually were not bound, and so could minister to the needs of the prisoners and care for their possessions. Those who could not bear up under the cruel, exhausting journey were left to perish. Deportations from both the Northern and Southern Hebrew kingdoms are treated below.

Deportations from the Northern Kingdom. The Northern kingdom of Israel, which in part was organized as the province of Samaria under an Assyrian governor after its fall in 721 B.C., was the first of the Hebrew kingdoms to experience deportation.

The first deportation of Israel took place in 732 B.C. Pekah, King of Israel (737–732 B.C.), joined with Damascus in a coalition against ASSYRIA. Tiglath-Pileser utterly destroyed the coalition, striking Israel with full force. The Israelite lands in Galilee and Transjordan were overrun and numerous cities destroyed. A portion of the inhabitants of these areas was deported (2 Kgs 15.29–30). At least the deportees from Transjordan were settled in northern Mesopotamia and in Media (see 1 Chr 5.26).

The second deportation of Israel occurred in 721 B.C. After the death of Tiglath-Pileser, HOSEA, who had succeeded Pekah on the throne, withheld the tribute due to SALMANASAR V. The Assyrians invaded Israel and captured Hosea. After a resistance of more than two years, the city of Samaria fell. Salmanasar's successor, Sargon II, gave 27,290 as the number deported. These were settled in the same regions as the deportees of 732, and if the geographical data of the book of Tobit are correct, some found their way to NINEVEH (see Tb 1.3, 10).

Deportations from the Southern Kingdom. With the rise of the Chaldean or Neo-Babylonian Empire, Judah became a vassal of NEBUCHADNEZZAR who followed the policy of deportation instituted by the Assyrians.

The first deportation of Juda took place in 597 B.C. King Joakim of Judah rebelled against Nebuchadnezzar but died before full retaliation could be effected (4 Kgs 24.1–2). Joakim's 18-year-old son Joachin was placed on the throne, and within three months the city surrendered. Joachin was deported to Babylon with the queen mother, many nobles, and leading artisans (2 Kgs 24.6–16). According to the prophet EZEKIEL, who was among the deportees (Ez 1.1–3; 3.15), one of the settlements of the exiles was at Tell-abib (probably near Nippur). Biblical records of their numbers differ: 10,000 in 2 Kgs 24.14; 8,000 in 2 Kgs 24.16; 3,023 in Jer 52.28. The last figure appears to have been taken from an official list.

The second deportation of Juda occurred in 587 B.C. Zedekiah, who succeeded Joachin, rebelled against Babylon in 589 B.C. Nebuchadnezzar besieged Jerusalem, and the city fell in 587 B.C. (2 Kgs 25.1–3; Jer 52.4–5). Some prisoners were put to death; Sedecia was blinded and with others taken to Babylon (4 Kgs 25.4–7, 18–21; Jer 52.7–11, 24–27). The torch was put to Jerusalem and its walls leveled. Jeremiah gives the number of deportees as 832 (Jer 52.29), probably referring to adult males.

The third deportation of Judah happened in 582 B.C. This deportation of 745 Jews is mentioned only by Jeremiah (Jer 52.30). It may have been a reprisal for the disturbances that arose during the governorship of Godolia.

Bibliography: J. BRIGHT, *A History of Israel* (Philadelphia, PA 1959). P. HEINISCH, *History of the Old Testament*, tr. W. G. HEIDT (Collegeville, MN 1955). M. NOTH, *The History of Israel*, tr. S. GODMAN (London 1958). E. R. THIELE, "New Evidence on the Chronology of the Last Kings of Judah,'' *The Bulletin of the American Schools of Oriental Research* 143 22–27. J. M. WILKIE, ''Nabonidus and the later Jewish Exiles,'' *Journal of Theological Studies* 2 36–44. W. F. ALBRIGHT, ''An Ostracon from Calah and the North-Israelite Diaspora,'' *The Bulletin of the American Schools of Oriental Research* (New Haven 1958) 149 33–36.

[J. P. WEISENGOFF]

DEPOSIT OF FAITH

In Jewish, Grecian, and Roman law a deposit was a contract by which the depositor freely entrusted something to the guardianship of another. The Greek word for deposit (παραθήκη) is used three times in the New Testament (1 Tm 6.20; 2 Tm 1.12, 14). In each case it refers to the spiritual heritage entrusted to the author of the Epistles or to their recipient. The term was not unknown to the Fathers; Vincent of Lérins used it in speaking of the unchanging teachings that the Church ever preserves. Not in use in the Middle Ages, the word came into the theological vocabulary at the end of the 16th century, and it was canonized by Vatican Council I (H. Denziger, *Enchiridion symbolorum* 3070, cf. 3020), which identified the deposit of faith with the revelation made known by God and handed down to the Church through the Apostles.

Meaning. The deposit of faith can be considered as an ensemble of truths entrusted by Christ to the Apostles and now guarded as a sacred trust by the Church, which can neither subtract nor add to it. This notion is valid but incomplete, for the deposit of faith is first of all a reality given to the Church and only subsequently an apprehension of that reality. The deposit of faith includes all that God has entrusted to the Church—His great acts in history (in the OT the acts by which God saved Israel; in the NT the activity, the Passion, and death of Christ) in their enduring salvific efficacy and in their divinely revealed meaning, and the prolongation of that reality and meaning in the Church by means of the divinely given Sacraments, Scriptures, hierarchical institution, and the continuous interpretative assistance of the Holy Spirit in the whole body of the faithful. Thus, in the integral sense, the deposit of faith is a divinely given reality whose salvific efficacy and divinely assigned meaning is preserved in the Church.

The deposit of faith and the church. Vatican I and the two Epistles to Timothy (see citations above) stress that the Church has the duty to preserve and interpret the deposit of faith, neither adding to it nor subtracting from it. This must not be taken to mean that the Church keeps the deposit rigid and immobile as a buried treasure. Rather, because the deposit of faith is meant to be a living and efficient salvific reality for every age, the Church preserves it by proclaiming it in such a way as to make present and meaningful its salvific efficacy. In short, the Church guards the deposit by making it relevant to every age and mentality. Hence, in the apostolic age the Twelve made relevant the deposit to the needs and problems of the various communities they encountered. (This ultimately led to four forms of the one gospel.) *See* GOSPELS, THE HOLY. In subsequent ages the Church refuted erroneous interpretations of the deposit and gradually unfolded some of its inexhaustibly rich significance in accordance with the needs of the times.

The existence of a deposit of faith forcefully impresses upon the Church that it is God's servant. The divine goods with which the Church is enriched are not its own but God's. Over these it has not an unlimited control. It is a faithful servant, a depositary, a guardian—not a master of these goods. The Church may act in regard to them only in the service of God.

Related realities. Revelation, Scripture, tradition, and Church are closely related to the deposit of faith. Revelation is the deposit of faith insofar as this deposit makes known or reveals the God who gives it to the Church. The Church is the divinely instituted community within which the deposit of faith is preserved in the Scriptures and in divinely guided traditional activity (e.g., oral tradition, liturgy, ecclesiastical practices, and attitudes passed on from generation to generation).

See Also: DOCTRINE, DEVELOPMENT OF; ORTHODOXY; REVELATION, FONTS OF; REVELATION, THEOLOGY OF; RULE OF FAITH; TRADITION (IN THEOLOGY); WITNESS, CHRISTIAN.

Bibliography: E. DUBLANCHY, *Dictionnaire de théologie catholique,* (Paris 1903–50) 4.1:526–531. J. R. GEISELMANN, *Lexikon für Theologie und Kirche* (Freiburg, 1957–66) 3:236–238. P. MÉDEBIELLE, *Dictionnaire de la Bible,* suppl. ed. L. PIROT et al. (Paris 1928) 2:374–395. Y. M. J. CONGAR, *La Tradition et les traditions,* 2 v. (Paris 1960–63). R. LATOURELLE, *Théologie de la révélation* (Bruges 1963). C. SPICQ, ''S. Paul et la loi des dépôts,'' *Revue biblique* 40 (1931) 481–502.

[P. F. CHIRICO]

DEPOSITIO MARTYRUM

The oldest list of Roman martyrs, forming, together with the Depositio Episcoporum, the so-called Philocalian Calendar. The two lists are found along with other documents in the CHRONOGRAPHER OF A.D. 354, written perhaps by Furius Dionysius Philocalus, the calligrapher of Pope DAMASUS I (d. 384). By means of these *depositiones* the faithful of Rome were informed concerning the day and place of liturgical worship. Both lists were probably fixed by 336 since the Depositio Martyrum names no one after this date, and the Depositio Episcoporum maintains an orderly arrangement of feasts from January to December, in which the name of Pope SYLVESTER I (d. 335) is the last recorded; and two popes, Mark I (d. 336) and Julius I (d. 352), are evident additions. Their feasts fall on October 7 and April 12.

In both *depositiones* the indications are kept to a minimum: the day of month, the name of the pope or martyr, and location of his tomb. When two notices are given under one and the same heading in the Depositio Martyrum, the order is inverted; the indication of the cemetery precedes the name of the martyr. No information is given to identify individuals, nor are there indications of the kind of death suffered by the saint.

The earliest name in the Depositio Episcoporum is Pope Lucius I (d. 254). With the exception of the Apostles Peter and Paul, none of the 52 martyrs recorded in the Depositio Martyrum is prior to the 3d century; the earliest African martyrs are PERPETUA AND FELICITY (d. 203), and the earliest Roman martyr of certain date is Pope Callistus (d. 222). Notations are made for the celebration of Christmas on December 25, *Natus Christus in Bethleem Iudaeae*; and on February 22, the *Natale Petri de cathedra.*

The Philocalian Calendar underwent subsequent revisions, two of which are attributed respectively to the time of INNOCENT I (401–417) and BONIFACE I (418–422); and at a later date both *depositiones,* enlarged in the course of years, were used in the compilation of the MARTYROLOGY OF ST. JEROME at the beginning of the 5th century. Archeological investigation has confirmed the reliability of the two lists of saints. In the Depositio Martyrum the names of the cemeteries and related topographical indications have been verified by findings of inscriptions and *graffiti* such as those concerning St. Fabian, and findings of inscriptions in the cemetery of St. Callistus have confirmed the exactness of the Depositio Episcoporum.

Bibliography: R. VALENTINI and G. ZUCCHETTI, eds., *Codice topografico della città di Roma,* 4 v. (Rome 1940–53) 1:1–28. H. LIETZMANN, ed., *Die drei ältesten Martyrologien* (2d ed. Bonn 1911). *Liber Pontificalis,* ed. L. DUCHESNE (Paris 1886–92) v. 1. J. P. KIRSCH, *Der stadtrömische christliche Festkalender im Altertum* (Münster 1924). W. H. FRERE, *Studies in Early Roman Liturgy,* 3 v. (Oxford 1930–35) v.1. R. STIEGER, *Lexikon für Theologie und Kirche,* ed. J. HOFER and K. RAHNER, 10 v. (2d, new ed. Freiburg 1957–65); suppl., *Das Zweite Vatikanische Konzil: Dokumente und kommentare,* ed. H. S. BRECHTER et al., pt. 1 (1966) 7:138–140.

[R. BRYAN]

DE RAEYMAEKER, LOUIS

Philosopher; b. Nov. 18, 1895, Sint-Pietres Roda, Belgium; d. Feb. 25, 1970, Louvain.

He received his doctorate in philosophy (1920) and in theology (1927). From 1927 to 1935, he was professor of philosophy at the Seminary of Malines, Belgium. From 1934 to 1965 he was professor at the Catholic University of Louvain, Belgium, where he taught psychology, introduction to philosophy, and metaphysics. In 1948, De Raeymaeker became president of the Institut Supérieur de Philosophie of Louvain; in 1957, counselor of the "rector magnificus;" and in 1962, prorector of the Flemish section of the university (since then an autonomous university under the denomination Katholieke Universiteit te Leuven). He retired in 1966. From 1935 to 1948, he was president of the Seminary of Leo XIII, Louvain.

His main works are an *Introduction to Philosophy,* which is one of the best-known works of this kind (published for the first time in French, in 1938, last edition in 1964; published in Flemish 1946, English translation in 1948), and a work of metaphysics, *The Philosophy of Being* (first published in Flemish, *De metaphysiek van het zijn,* 1944, then in French, *Philosophie de l'être,* 1946, 2d edition in 1947, English translation in 1954). This book can be considered as one of the most important contributions to metaphysics in the Neothomistic school. Based upon a very personal meditation of the texts of St. Thomas, it undertakes an original reconstruction of a doctrine of the absolute and of creation, starting from the "Ego," conceived as the human person, which is free and autonomous, but limited by the non-Ego, and must be understood as related to a transcendent Absolute. De Raeymaeker also wrote an interesting history of the Institut Supéreiur de Philosophie of Louvain, and numerous articles and contributions to collective works.

Bibliography: L. DE RAEYMAKER, *Introduction to Philosophy,* tr. H. MCNEILL (New York, London 1948); *The Philosophy of Being* (New York, London 1954); *Le Cardinal Mercier et l'Institut Superieur de Philosophie de Louvain* (Louvain 1952).

[J. LADRIERE]

DERISION

Derision is the vice by which one wrongly causes shame or embarrassment in another because of his defects either of body or soul or of the conditions of his life. It may be carried out by words or derisive sounds (Mt 27.41–44; Lk 23.36), by mocking gestures or grimaces (Mt 27.40), or by other acts (Mt 26.68; 27.29; Lk 22.63). These different modes, however, do not constitute distinct species of the sin of derision.

This vice, directly opposed to commutative justice, may be opposed also to other virtues. For example, to deride one's parents or a cleric would be opposed also to piety or to religion.

Theologians dispute about its precise relationship to CONTUMELY. Many modern theologians argue that it is opposed to the HONOR of another and therefore is essentially the same as contumely. The opinion of St. Thomas Aquinas that derision and contumely differ specifically is held by many contemporary theologians. They argue that the specific objects of the vices differ. Contumely is opposed to another's honor, while derision is ordered to his embarrassment, which is more a fear of dishonor than a dishonor in itself. Aquinas explains that good works not only enhance the fame and glory in which one is held by others but also give their doer serenity or tranquillity of conscience. By contumely and detraction a man loses his honor; by derision he is disturbed and embarrassed, thus losing this serenity or tranquillity.

Derision or mockery is a grave sin of its nature, although it is frequently venial because of lightness of matter. In judging the gravity of the matter the condition of both the one deriding and the one derided should be considered. In some circumstances, such as in correction or in recreation, derisive or mocking words or acts are not sinful, but great care should be taken that no unjust harm is done to another by such actions, however well intentioned they may be.

One guilty of derision must make satisfaction for the harm that he has caused. Those derided should bear this wrong patiently, although in certain circumstances they can or should resist derisive actions, especially when the good of others is at stake.

Bibliography: THOMAS AQUINAS *Summa theologiae,* 2a2ae, 79. I. RINALDI, *Dictionarium morale et canonicum,* ed. P. PALAZZINI (Rome 1962–) 2:815–818. D. M. PRÜMMER, *Manuale theologiae moralis,* ed. E. M. MÜNCH, 3 v. (12th ed. Freiburg–Barcelona 1955) 2:183–186.

[J. HENNESSEY]

DERVISHES

Members of one of the mystic Islamic orders practicing austerity and poverty and living in special quarters or wandering as mendicants are known as dervishes. The word "dervish," as commonly explained, comes from the Persian *darvīš,* "beggar" (one at the *dar* or city gate), written in Arabic script as *darwīš.* In Arabic-speaking countries a dervish is called a *faqīr* (poor man) or *sūfī* (*see* SUFISM). From the prolonged repetition of strange bodily movements or of shouted religious formulas that some of the dervish groups use for the sake of inducing a sort of trance or ecstasy, these groups are commonly known as dancing (or whirling) or howling dervishes.

In the early centuries of ISLAM, small groups of pious men would gather around a shaykh (*muršid,* guide) seeking religious instruction and guidance and would later either return to the world or continue to live with him. They were usually men who found no spiritual satisfaction through intellectual knowledge and sought it by striving for a closer personal approach to God through inner light and emotional processes. In the 12th century, no doubt influenced by early Christian monasticism, they were organized into several religious fraternities (*see* ISLAMIC CONFRATERNITIES). Their technical vocabulary has several words of Syriac origin.

Bibliography: J. P. BROWN, *The Darvishes,* ed. H. A. ROSE (New York 1927). D. B. MACDONALD, *Encyclopedia of Islam,* ed., M. T. HOUTSMA et al., 4 v. (Leiden 1913–38) 1:975–976.

[P. K. HITTI]

DESCARTES, RENÉ

French philosopher, also called Cartesius; b. La Haye, Touraine, March 31, 1596; d. Stockholm, Feb. 11, 1650. The philosophy of Descartes has been described as a turning point or watershed in European thought. Descartes himself has been called the father of modern philosophy and said to mark the intellectual transition from the Middle Ages to the modern world. These descriptions are acceptable provided it is understood, as modern scholars have emphasized, that while there is much that is genuinely new in his philosophy, there is also a continuity with the SCHOLASTICISM that preceded it.

Life and Works. Descartes, the son of a family of minor nobility, was a pupil at the famous Jesuit college of La Flèche from 1604 to 1612. His studies included the usual classics, philosophy (physics, logic, and metaphysics, which may be roughly described as Suarezian in tendency), and mathematics. The last subject made a deep impression on the boy "because of the certainty of its proofs and the evidence of its reasonings." He completed his studies at Poitiers by taking a licentiate in law. A brief period of military service, and a voyage in Italy, were followed by a two-year stay in Paris where he met Cardinal Bérulle and Marin Mersenne, who became his lifelong friend and correspondent. In 1628 Descartes went to Holland where, in various towns, he spent the rest of his life and wrote his major works. The *Discourse on Method* was published in 1637. The Latin edition of the *Metaphysical Meditations* was published in 1641 (French translation in 1647). The *Principles of Philosophy* ap-

Whirling dervishes, wash drawing. (CORBIS-Bettmann)

peared in Latin in 1644, the French translation in 1647; and finally the *Passions of the Soul* in 1649. Both the *Regulae,* probably composed in 1628, and the two treatises *Man* and the *World* are posthumous publications. Descartes was called to Sweden by Queen Christina and after only six months there, he died, fortified by the rites of the Church.

Cartesian Method. Descartes's preoccupation with methodology can be seen from his earliest works, the unpublished and incomplete *Regulae* and the *Discourse,* and he asserts repeatedly that the supreme question for philosophy is that of method. At the basis of this assertion is his view that the human mind, in its natural and unperverted state and insofar as it functions in accordance with its nature, cannot fail to think truly. The rules by which one is to search, that is, the method, are to be found by a careful reflection upon the human mind, by a study of its procedure when it functions purely and when its natural power of grasping truth is not corrupted or hampered

by "prejudices." Method is not merely an instrument for constructing knowledge; it expresses the very nature of mind. Thus the problem of method is identical with the problem of the nature and limits of human knowledge.

Influence of Mathematics. The Cartesian conception of method was derived, as Descartes himself tells us in the autobiographical passages of the *Discourse,* from a personal dissatisfaction with the philosophical and scientific doctrines he was taught and, more positively, from a reflection on, and practice of, the procedure of the mathematical sciences. Impressed, as Immanuel Kant was to be, by the striking achievements of these sciences, he attempted to formulate their methodological principles in most general terms and, in so doing, thought he could constitute a general theory of method.

If, he argued, one reflects upon the certainty of mathematical demonstration, he finds that it depends upon fulfilling two main conditions: (1) one must start from self-evident data, and (2) every step in the progress from the self-evident data must be self-evident. No conclusion must be affirmed unless it follows from an uninterrupted sequence of self-evident data. To these two conditions of the certainty of demonstration correspond two functions of the intellect: (1) intellectual intuition (*intuitus*), the power of apprehending the self-evident data, and (2) deduction, the power of moving, by an uninterrupted sequence of self-evident steps, from the data to their consequents. These two operations of the intellect are the primary conditions of all knowledge and express the very nature of the intellect. No theory of method can teach the intellect to perform them, for they are presupposed in all learning. A theory of method can do no more than facilitate their right use.

Intuition. By intellectual intuition is meant a conception of "a pure and attentive mind," such that no doubt whatever can remain as to what it is one conceives. The objects conceived are "simple natures," simple ideas, or two elements of an idea in immediate and necessary connection. Two conditions are required: the data must be conceived "clearly and distinctly" and they must be apprehended all at once and not successively. To apprehend the elements of a self-evident proposition "clearly" means to have the apprehended content present to the mind that is "attending" to it; to apprehend it "distinctly" means to have before the mind precisely the relevant content, neither more nor less.

Deduction. The second primary operation of the intellect is deduction, which involves the use of intellectual intuition in all its stages and is, as it were, a process by which intuition extends itself so as to comprehend within itself a complex of intuitions. It differs from the traditional subsumptive syllogism of formal logic, but is akin to the ἀποδεικτικὸς συλλογισμός of Aristotle. The movement of thought is deduction. Insofar as the mind could retain, in a single undivided vision, all the single steps of the whole process, the completed deduction would be an intellectual intuition, and would possess the self-evidence of immediate presence, the *praesens evidentia* that is essential to the mind's certainty.

Where the demonstration must depend to some extent on memory, and accordingly, in the more complex cases where the data do not form a single chain of linear deductions but many interconnected groups of linear deductions, or what, Descartes calls, a network of chains, a second form of deduction called enumeration is required. Its function is to assist, and in a sense eliminate as far as possible, memory by arranging and preparing the data and by introducing and ordering them so as to facilitate the unbroken movement of illation.

Applications of the Method. The four "easy and certain rules" of the *Discourse* are the somewhat simpli-

René Descartes.

fied, almost dangerously simplified, expression of the methodological doctrine summarized above, omitting many important details. It should also be noted that the *Discourse* itself is only a preface to a volume containing three "exercises in method," that is, three applications of the method to various problems: the *Dioptric,* in which Descartes discusses and lays down the laws of refraction; the *Meteors,* in which he discusses the nature of light and the rainbow and approaches Newton's discovery of the composite nature of white light; and the *Geometry,* which is the basis of most of his fame as a mathematician and which won him his title as the founder of analytic geometry.

Analytic Geometry. This last work reproduces the fundamental characteristic of the method and illustrates the reduction of a problem to its most general and simple form. The representation of a curve is simplified by relating it, by putting it "into proportion" with the lengths of two straight lines—than which, says Descartes, one can find in the field of continuous magnitudes, no other objects "more capable of being distinctly represented," since "straightness" is a simple nature or idea. Then curved lines can be expressed algebraically in terms of an equation involving the perpendicular distance of a point to two perpendicular lines of reference. A point in a plane can be uniquely determined when its distances (usually designated x and y) from the lines of reference (the coordinates, as G. W. LEIBNIZ was to name them) are known. With this knowledge, an equation can be formulated, $F(xy) = 0$, that expresses a property true of every point of the curve. For every curve, some relationship can be shown to exist between the coordinates of a point anywhere on it. A curve may also be defined in terms of an equation involving x and y. And when two or more curves have the same coordinates, their points of intersection may also be found by the common solution of their equations. A curve has been simplified by reduction to an equation that is ultimately soluble by two straight lines: simple ideas that are the proper objects of intellectual intuition. The rest of the *Geometry* is a continuation of the procedure of analytical simplification, linked to the solution of the problem of Pappus and the required locus of a point set therein.

Transition to Metaphysics. Despite Descartes's admiration for the mathematical sciences, on which he based his method, his enthusiasm for his own demonstrations and their use in the *Geometry* is limited. In the course of his life after 1637 he showed a singular lack of interest in possible developments of the geometry that was to be a fertile source of inspiration to succeeding generations of mathematicians. The rest of the *Discourse,* the *Meditations,* and part of the *Principles* are devoted to his philosophical doctrines. But the transition from methodological problems to the study of metaphysics is not a mere accidental one. For, as is clear from the argument of the *Meditations* (which constitute the most elaborate of his philosophical expositions), to metaphysics falls the responsibility of conferring validity on the method, and, by implication, on the natural sciences. When Descartes, in the *Principles* (1.13), makes the strange statement that an atheist cannot possess knowledge in the strict sense, he means by atheist someone whose knowledge is not based on a suitable metaphysic.

Methodical Doubt. What one needs for a sound metaphysics is some apprehension that is clear and distinct, that refers to some existent, and that can be known with certainty. The first rule of the method is to rid the mind of prejudices. This is Descartes's starting point: the application of methodical doubt, a universal doubt applied to all accepted ideas, opinions, and beliefs. It may be noted that Descartes excepts from this universality the moral axioms, as a practical expediency, and the beliefs of his faith. His is not, like the skeptic's, a mere passive state of wavering indecision; it is a free and deliberate action pursued to its logical limit.

When one analyzes "the things which can be doubted," it is not necessary "to show that the whole of these are false." A preliminary classification of the sources and kinds of belief enables one to group them and test typical members, not for their falsity but for their doubtfulness. In replying to Father Bourdin, Descartes uses a homely metaphor: "Supposing a man had a basket of apples and feared that some might be rotten . . . would he not first tip out the whole lot . . . then having chosen those which he saw not to be rotten, he would place them again in the basket" (*Oeuvres* 7:481). Thus, the phenomena of illusions, hallucinations, etc., show that the senses are untrustworthy, and the doubt applies to common beliefs based on sense-experience, even to the existence of the external world and one's own body. Psychologically, one may not be able to doubt them; logically, there are no grounds for asserting their certainty.

Even the conclusions of the exact sciences of mathematics, apparently indubitable, may be subject to a systematic defect of human minds or, possibly, a systematic deception of a "malignant demon," all-powerful. This last hypothesis, a literary device, is a hypothetical reformulation of his methodological principle, reversed into the proposition that the human mind cannot attain truth. If a single belief can be asserted in this "deep water" of universal uncertainty, then one can find a starting point, for that which destroys the strongest possible doubt must be itself, *ipso facto,* the greatest possible certitude.

Cogito Ergo Sum. This single assertion Descartes finds in the famous *Cogito ergo sum,* "I think, therefore I am." Even if I am deceived, there must exist an "I" who is deceived. It is impossible that I should doubt or be deceived, and yet not exist at the moment of doubting or being deceived. It should be noted that "thought," at the time of Descartes, had a wider connotation than now: it embraced not only thought but all mental data, will, feeling, perception, etc. "I am" is an immediate consequence, not an inference (despite the *ergo*) of "I think," and it establishes a starting point because it is clear and distinct, it essentially refers to an existent, and it can be seen to be indubitably certain. But, it should also be noted, at this point in the argument all that has been established is the existence of a self as a thinking being, as and insofar as it thinks; in other words, not as a being possessing a body, senses, etc.

God's Existence. The next major step in the argument is to prove the existence of God, which is needed, according to Descartes, to extend the universality of the criterion of evidence beyond the privileged instance of the *Cogito.* This step is, as it were, the reflection of the hyperbolic "malignant demon." Descartes offers three proofs that all tend to demonstrate God, not as First Cause, but as a Perfect Being whose veracity will be the guarantee of man's clear and distinct ideas. It is impossible here to analyze the logical structure of these arguments. The general tenor is that a being that thinks, that doubts, errs, etc., knows that it is imperfect and finite; yet it could not be clearly aware of its own essential finitude and imperfection, if it did not also have in itself the idea of something infinite and perfect. The mind does not build the negative idea of infinitude by negating the limitations: it forms the idea of finitude by introducing a limit, which is a negation, into the idea of infinitude. The mind that produces an idea must at least be at the same level of perfection as the idea it produces, and therefore only an infinite being, that is God, can produce the idea of God.

Cartesian Dualism. The veracity of God establishes for Descartes the possibility of attaining knowledge of innumerable other propositions whose truth is certain. It is also the veracity of God that explains the presence in man's mind of clear and distinct innate ideas, and justifies his assertion of their validity and their conformity with the real world created by God. Man has two clear and distinct ideas, of soul and of body. The nature of the soul, as described in the *Cogito,* is to think, to be conscious. Conversely, the idea of body or matter does not include consciousness; it excludes it. When one thinks of body or matter, he may think of color, weight, hardness, shape, and other secondary qualities. But analysis shows that the essential nature of matter is spatial extension, figure and movement being regarded as modifications or modes of extension.

The consequences of this definition are radical, both for Cartesian doctrine and the future of the physical sciences. An obvious dualism of mind and matter is thereby created, and, given the nature of matter, the physical sciences assume a purely quantitative basis. An immediate problem for Descartes's doctrine was that of the unity of the human being, for he has rejected the hylomorphic solution. He asserts, somewhat inconsistently, that there is one idea that, although unclear and indistinct, is nevertheless certain, that is, the idea of the substantial union of the body and soul. But he offers no further solution as to how the two "substances" can and do unite, leaving the field open to the not very satisfactory solutions of OCCASIONALISM, as proposed by N. MALEBRANCHE and Leibniz (*see* MIND-BODY PROBLEM). It can, however, be seen that the radical separation of thought and extension leads to a purely mechanistic conception of the physical sciences.

Physical Sciences. One direct consequence of this aspect of Cartesian doctrine is that all terrestrial and celestial phenomena, chemical as well as physical, are reduced fundamentally to the one science of what one should call physics, itself ideally to be formulated in mathematical formulas (*see* PHILOSOPHY AND SCIENCE;

MECHANISM). Descartes goes further, logically so in his own terms, by including also the biological sciences within the mechanistic scheme. There is no difference of principle in the explanation of the organic and the inorganic, since they are only modes of "matter." Hence, the well-known theory of "animal-machines"; the same can be said of the human body, which is merely differentiated from inanimate matter by a greater complexity. The simile often used of the body is that of a watch; a simile used by many later Cartesians, e.g., A. GEULINCX and Leibniz. Animals, not having the power of thought, are pure automata.

The physical theories of Descartes were originally set forth in the *World,* which was not completed or published in his lifetime, and in the third part of the *Principles.* They rest upon the metaphysical conclusions of the *Meditations.* The greater part of his scientific theories have long been discarded; they form part of the history of science. Descartes's theory of vortexes was shown by Newton to be impossible as a dynamical system; its chief merit was that it was a brilliant attempt to present a theory in which all the celestial phenomena could be rationally explained by mechanical processes. Descartes enunciates three primary laws of motion (or laws of nature, as he calls them) and seven secondary laws of "impact," the latter to a large extent incorrect. The fixed amount of motion in the universe is based on the immutability of God. Descartes's main achievement was in the field of optics, where he established the law of the refraction of light and adumbrated the undulatory theory of light. The *Principles* contains, in the latter parts, mainly obsolete scientific speculation.

Psychology and Free Will. Descartes did not elaborate a system of ethics. The *Passions of the Soul* and the correspondence with Princess Elizabeth of Bohemia are more a psychophysical theory of the emotions, presupposing the fundamental doctrine of the complete separation of the body and soul and the paradox, for Cartesian philosophy, of their "substantial union." It is therefore a theory of interaction, wherein what is "a passion" in the soul is "an action" of the body, the one being caused by the other. The perception of passions is, of course, different and must be distinguished from them. The problem then is how one can control this interaction. The stress on self-control and the various rules, adopted from the four rules of the method, have much in common with Stoic doctrine, and Descartes, contrary to his usual habit, quotes Seneca in his letters.

There is no discussion of free will as such in these writings. The reason for this omission is that for Descartes, free will is self-evident, a primary datum, an innate idea, logically implicit in *Cogito ergo sum,* since the hyperbolical doubt implies the possibility of choosing to doubt even such things as the existence of the external world, the truths of mathematics, etc. The nature and extent of human freedom, once the existence of God is established, does involve further problems, problems that in the 17th century were the subjects of the great controversies of JANSENISM and MOLINISM. It is possible to find, in the works of Descartes, expressions of his views that tend toward both positions, although the expressions of his latter writings tend away from the extremist views of Jansenism. On the whole, his major interest was in the epistemological problem of error and the role of the will therein. He was chary of theological disputes and was generally content to assert both the freedom of will and the omnipotence of God and assert that the problem transcends the human mind.

Critique and Evaluation. The position of Descartes in the history of philosophy is a puzzling one. Certain facts are clear. His contributions to experimental science were without great value; his physical theories were discarded within 100 years; only his mathematical discoveries had permanent value. On the purely metaphysical side, he has not the wider brilliance of Leibniz or the depth of B. SPINOZA, the other two "rationalists" of the 17th century. Yet his work constitutes a nodal point in the history of thought; he is rightly considered the father of modern thought, for he gathered together previously unconnected strands of thought into a single train of thought and gave new impetus and direction to all subsequent inquiry. He set men thinking in new directions and, in this sense, was the most influential philosopher since Plato.

Merits and Defects. In a certain sense, the merits and defects of Descartes's philosophy have prolonged its influence in the varying emphases placed on the different, and not too consistent, aspects by thinkers of subsequent generations. It should be noted that even in the task of exegesis of Descartes's own doctrine, as the vast literature of commentary testifies, there is far from unanimity. Descartes has been variously identified as a skeptic, a phenomenalist, a realist, and a subjective idealist; even the modern school of PHENOMENOLOGY would claim descent from Descartes. The apparent simplicity and the economy of his writing hide what is often a heroic attempt to maintain his system through a series of improvisations. These were revealed by his own intellectual probity when he attempted to answer the objections raised by his contemporaries, especially the sharp critic Arnauld. Some of the subtle and insidious mistakes made by Descartes sent generations of philosophers on a wild-goose chase that still continues. To this extent only, can one accept J. Maritain's statement that "Descartes [or Cartesianism] has been the great French sin in modern history." Moreover, Descartes used an existent terminology and often could

not escape entanglement in its content and implications. The new wine was too strong for the old bottles.

Theory of Knowledge. Modern epistemology, or the problem of knowledge, which has occupied most philosophers since the time of Descartes, may be said to have grown from the Cartesian use of the word "idea," in other words, from his theory of "representative ideas," in which ideas are regarded as objects of mind. This theory, a direct consequence of his dualism, was later accepted by Leibniz and John LOCKE. If what is perceived is in the mind, the obvious question arises as to the nature of what it is supposed to represent. If the mind of spirit and the material world are in absolute separation and antagonism, how is the fact of knowledge, which involves their interrelation, to be accounted for? Descartes is able to assert the reality of matter by the veracity of God. Insofar as he asserts a causality of interaction between body and mind, he breaks down his theory of innate ideas and opens the door to other kinds of ideas. To localize the point of contact in the "pineal gland" merely pushes the problem one stage further back.

General Influence. The *Cogito* itself has been the subject of controversy and criticism, ranging from the atomistic views of David HUME and the logical analysts, to the criticisms of Kant, G. W. Hegel and J. P. Sartre. The great protagonist of "clear and distinct ideas" has led many historians of philosophy to different, and even opposed, interpretations of his doctrine. There are many loose ends, many inconsistent improvisations in his thought. The claim that he is the father of modern philosophy cannot be based on any general acceptance of his most cherished views; they have all been partially or totally rejected.

It has been said that the history of philosophy consists of footnotes to Plato. Modern philosophy, in a similar fashion, consists in an endeavor to solve, or dissolve, problems raised in an original manner by the vision and genius of Descartes. One point of controversy at least can be settled. It was fashionable at one time to throw doubt on the sincerity of Descartes's religious convictions. He was and died a Catholic, in "the faith of his nurse."

See Also: CARTESIANISM; DUALISM; INNATISM; SUBJECTIVISM; RATIONALISM; PHILOSOPHY, HISTORY OF.

Bibliography: Works. *Oeuvres,* ed. C. ADAM and P. TANNERY, 12 v. (Paris 1897–1910); *Correspondance,* ed. C. ADAM and G. MILHAUD, 8 v. (Paris 1956–63); *Philosophical Works,* tr. E. S. HALDANE and G. R. T. ROSS, 2 v. (Cambridge, Eng. 1931–34; reprint New York 1955); *Philosophical Writings,* tr. N. K. SMITH (New York 1958); *Philosophical Writings,* ed. E. ANSCOMBE and P. T. GEACH (Edinburgh 1961); *Selections,* ed. R. M. EATON (New York 1927); *Essential Works,* tr. L. BAIR (New York 1961); *Discours de la méthode,* ed. É. H. GILSON (Paris 1955); *Geometry,* tr. D. E. SMITH

"Descent of Christ into Hell," 14th-century fresco by Andrea da Firenze.

and M. L. LATHAM (New York 1954). Studies. F. ALQUIÉ, *Descartes: L'homme et l'oeuvre* (Paris 1956); *La Découverte métaphysique de l'homme chez Descartes* (Paris 1950). A. G. A. BALZ, *Descartes and the Modern Mind* (New Haven 1952). L. J. BECK, *The Method of Descartes* (Oxford 1952). J. CHEVALIER, *Descartes* (new ed. Paris 1949). J. DE FINANCE, *Cogito cartésien et réflexion thomiste* (Paris 1946). A. B. GIBSON, *The Philosophy of Descartes* (London 1932). É. H. GILSON, *Études sur le rôle de la pensée médiévale dans la formation du système cartésien* (Paris 1930). H. G. GOUHIER, *La Pensée métaphysique de Descartes* (Paris 1962). M. GUÉROULT, *Descartes, selon l'ordre des raisons,* 2 v. (Paris 1953). E. S. HALDANE, *Descartes: His Life and Times* (New York 1905). O. HAMELIN, *La Système de Descartes* (2d ed. Paris (1921). H. H. JOACHIM, *Descartes's Rules for the Direction of the Mind* (London 1957). S. V. KEELING, *Descartes* (London 1934). J. M. F. LAPORTE, *Le Rationalisme de Descartes* (Paris 1945). J. MARITAIN, *The Dream of Descartes,* tr. M. L. ANDISON (New York 1944). G. RODIS–LEWIS, *La Morale de Descartes* (2d ed. Paris 1962). N. K. SMITH, *New Studies in the Philosophy of Descartes* (London 1952). L. J. BECK, *The Metaphysics of Descartes* (Oxford 1965).

[L. J. BECK]

DESCENT OF CHRIST INTO HELL

The descent of Christ into hell denotes the belief that His soul, separated from His body but remaining united to His Divine Person, passed into the abode of the dead and stayed there as long as His body, likewise remaining united to His Divine Person, reposed in the tomb, that is, until the Resurrection. The English word "hell" in this context corresponds to the Hebrew *še'ōl* (SHEOL), the Greek Ἅιδης (HADES), and the Latin *inferus,* or *infernus,* and therefore means the abode of souls after death. The ancients thought and spoke of this abode as being in the underworld. Although the notion of the structure of the universe has changed, the ancient terminology persists.

In the New Testament. The apostolic KERYGMA proclaimed, as did the works and words of Jesus, that His power dominated the metahistorical sphere of the dead (Mt 11.5; Lk 7.22). The oldest documentary witness to the kerygma states "that Christ died . . . and that he was buried and that he was raised on the third day" (1 Cor 15.3–4). The abrupt, archaic formula was within a few years rephrased to affirm that Jesus was raised "from the dead" (1 Thes 1.10 and *passim*). Emphasis thus moved from the verifiable fact of burial to the belief in Jesus' continuing but metahistorical life between His death and His Resurrection.

The formula was rooted in the Jerusalem kerygma (Acts 3.15; 4.10; 10.41), in which Old Testament terms and images for the afterlife were early employed to expound what it meant to have returned "from the dead." The Lord's burial, like His death and Resurrection, must be "according to the Scriptures" [1 Cor 15.3–4; see also Acts 2.24–31, where Peter cites Ps 15(16).8–11 and Ps 17(18).6 as foretelling Christ's burial and Resurrection].

The baptized believed that Jesus had risen "from the dead," and now a phrase that described a *terminus a quo* became itself the object of further explication. The believer asked, "Where were the dead? Why did Jesus go to them? Who were they?" To these questions the New Testament didache addressed itself. Like the kerygma, this inquiry worked the mine of the Old Testament. Thus one sees the mysterious Jonah logion developing from Mt 16.4; Lk 11.29 (both from the "Q" source) to Mt 12.39–40 (*see* JONAH, SIGN OF). Popular images and terms describing the afterlife also were taken up into the New Testament; note the "Hades" of Mt 11.23; Lk 10.15 (both from the "Q" source); the parabolic didache on a man's rising from the dead (Lk 16.19–31); the "PARADISE" logion of Lk 23.43; and the account of the dead rising at Christ's Resurrection in Mt 27.52–53.

Paul in Rom 10.6–9 paraphrased Deuteronomy 30.11–14 and the Septuagint (LXX) reading of Ps 70(71).20 (cf. Mt 12.40b, which alludes to the latter passage according to the Hebrew reading) to show that rising "from the dead" was equivalent to the LXX's phrase "from the abyss." In Phil 2.10 the implied three-story spatial image is referred to in the statement that "those in heaven and on earth and under the earth" must acknowledge Jesus as Lord (see also Is 45.23; Rom 10.9; 14.9–12). Thus Jesus' passage into the abyss of those under the earth was an epiphany of His victory over the realm of death. A like conviction underlies Rv 1.18; Mt 16.18 (and perhaps Col 1.18; Rv 1.5).

The New Testament demurs to identify specifically the dead from whom Jesus rose. Demons can be visualized as living not only in the abyss (Lk 8.31 and Revelation, passim) but also in the air above the earth (Eph 2.2; 6.12). In 1 Pt 3.18–20 an Ascension victory over such spirits is described (note "he went," not "he descended"). The dead to whom the gospel was proclaimed, according to 1 Pt 4.6, are deceased Christians who, when alive, had believed in Christ. In Heb 11.39–40; 12.22–23 it is implied that the just of the Old Testament awaited the victory of Jesus for their reward, but no descent to a place of detainment is noted; compare the single reference to Jesus rising "from the dead" in Heb 13.20.

Earlier Fathers. As the 2d century opened, Ignatius of Antioch reaffirmed the apostolic kerygma that Jesus "was really raised from the dead" (*Trall.* 9). He was the first to identify the dead as the Old Testament Prophets: "when He [Christ] came He raised them from the dead"

(*Magn.* 9.2; cf. Mt 27.52 and the Jeremiah Apocryphon cited by Irenaeus, *Haer.* 3.20.4; 4.22.1, and Justin, *Dial.* 72). Where previous age had seen in the descent of Jesus a victorious epiphany, Ignatius saw its soteriological function for the righteous dead. The 2d-century Apocrypha, especially those of Syrian provenance that inherited the interests and methods of Jewish Christian theology, further developed this doctrine. In the West, Justin, Hermas, and Irenaeus (not to mention Marcion) took this soteriological aspect of the descent for granted. The 2d-century Paschal homily of Melito of Sardis also develops the dramatic imagery of the conquering of Hades by Jesus.

Tertullian spoke of the descent clearly, especially in *De anima* 55, where he understands the descent as the ultimate term of the incarnation. Clement of Alexandria first linked 1 Pt 3.19 with Jesus' descent, and he averred that Christ converted the souls of even the pagan dead at this time. Origen continued this exegesis. In general the early fathers used the theme of the descent to hell to speak of two aspects of salvation in Christ. In temporal terms, Christ came to save all people, even the patriarchs of the Old Testament. In spatial terms, Christ came even to the deepest realm of the earth. This teaching was upheld against the Marcionites and Gnostics.

[J. D. QUINN/EDS.]

Later Fathers. After the 4th century nearly all the Fathers of both East and West mentioned the descent of Christ into hell. Cyril of Alexandria continued the specific exegesis of Clement and Origen. And Saint Augustine, for instance, asked the rhetorical question: "Who but an unbeliever would deny the fact that Christ descended to the underworld" (*Epist.* 164).

The descent theme found a lively development in the third part of the apocryphal Gospel of Nicodemus (ch. 17–27), which comes down in two Latin recensions and was perhaps composed as early as the 5th century (cf. J. Quasten, *Patrology* 1:116), is called *Descensus Christi ad inferos* and tells in very dramatic style how Christ after His death entered hell, set free the Old Testament saints, and took them to heaven, whereas He cast Satan into Tartarus. The apocryphal Gospel of Bartholomew also describes the descent of Christ in detail (*ibid.* 127). These dramatic accounts of Christ trampling the gates of Hell inspired medieval representations of the scene. In English, the tradition came to be known as the "harrowing" of hell by Christ, from the verb whose root means "to raid." Alois Grillmeier has suggested a linear development of Latin and Greek theological interpretation of the descent with the confluence of three distinct motifs. He argued that the descent of Christ took a soteriological and then later christological trajectory. Three ways of conceiving the descent, according to a baptismal motif, a preaching motif, and a battle motif, emerge from the original soteriological focus of the descent teaching. The christological development reflects the questions put to the tradition by the growing precision in doctrinal and theological language concerning the relationship of the humanity and divinity of Christ.

The descent began to appear in the creeds in the 5th century. According to the testimony of Rufinus *c.* 400, it was mentioned in the recension of the Apostles' Creed being used by the Church of Aquileia (H. Denzinger, *Enchiridion symbolorum*, 16). An assembly of Semi-Arian bishops included the descent in a formula that they promulgated in 369 at Sirmium in Pannonia. Gradually Churches in other localities, including Rome, inserted it (*Enchiridion symbolorum* 23, 27–30, 62, 63). The present form of the Apostles' Creed and the so-called Athanasian Creed, composed about the middle of the 5th century and accepted by both East and West, include it (*Enchiridion symbolorum* 76).

An important development of the descent tradition occurs after the fourth century in the West in conjunction with the development of a theology of hell as the place of eternal punishment for the damned. Among the early fathers, Christ's descent was placed with the horizon of universal salvation of the just who predeceased Christ. Christ descended to the dead or place of the dead, grasped like the shadowy postmortem existence in Sheol or Hades. It was not the Gehenna of fire and brimstone or the punishment of Tartarus. Gradually the moral dimensions coalesce with the more neutral image of the place of the dead in the Latin concept of hell. When Christ was understood to descend to hell, the descent motif becomes allied with the forgiveness of sin of those who had died.

Ecclesiastical Documents. Lateran Council IV in 1215 mentioned the descent (*Enchiridion symbolorum* 801), as did the profession of faith by Emperor Michael Palaeologus approved by the Second Council of Lyons in 1274 (*Enchiridion symbolorum* 852). In the meantime the Council of Sens in 1141 had condemned a view of Abelard, who held that the soul of Christ did not descend into hell in its essence, but only produced effects there by its power (*Enchiridion symbolorum* 738). During these centuries the imagery and theology of the the descent also developed strongly in the Byzantine and Syriac liturgical traditions, each with different accents in the development of the theme.

Teaching of Western Theologians. The fact of Christ's descent into hell is certainly an article of faith. His activity while there is not clearly defined. Thomas Aquinas addressed the descent in *Summa theologiae* 3, 52.1–8. Since by His death and Resurrection Christ gained the victory, not only over death, but also over sin and Satan, His descent must be interpreted in the light of that victory. Before His Passion no one could enter heaven (*Summa theologiae* 3, 49.5 ad 1). Now the Redeemer brought deliverance to those who before their death were united to His Passion through faith quickened by charity whereby sins are taken away. He did not descend in order to suffer there, or to convert unbelievers or those lacking charity, but to put them to shame for their unbelief and wickedness. To those lost souls His descent brought no deliverance from the debt of punishment. To the just and holy souls of the Patriarchs, those who had died with faith and charity and were now free from all sin and debt of punishment, Christ imparted the fruit of His Passion. He delivered them from the penalty whereby they had hitherto been excluded from the light of glory. He did not lead them at once from the confines of hell, but enlightened them with the light of glory in hell itself (*Summa theologiae* 3, 52.4 ad 1). He took them to heaven when He ascended (*Summa theologiae* 3, 57.6). According to the imagery of the day, Christ descended into all the sections of the underworld, insofar as by His power He produced the effects mentioned, but into the Limbo of the Patriarchs His soul itself united to His Divine Person descended and remained till the resurrection on Easter morning.

Contemporary Teaching. The descent of Christ to hell was retrieved in 20th-century theology in conjunction with by a number of exegetical and patristic studies. The outstanding figure is Hans Urs von Balthasar who developed the descent as a trinitarian event in the drama of salvation where the descent is the "deployment of the effects of the Cross in the abyss of deadly perdition." He emphasized the descent of Christ to hell as the "final consequence of the redemptive mission." Herbert Vorgrimler also presented the descent to hell as a decisive juncture for vital theological issues like theological anthropology, questions of the universality of salvation, and soteriological implications of Jesus' descent. The *Catechism of the Catholic Church* (nos. 631–35) gives brief consideration to the doctrine. It emphasizes that Jesus "did not descend into hell to deliver the damned, nor to destroy the hell of damnation, but to free the just who had gone before him."

The Roman Rite Liturgy of the Hours for Holy Saturday gives poetic expression to the descent. In the office of readings, for example, the antiphons emphasize rest imagery, a divine Sabbath. The third psalm, Ps 24, has long been associated in the tradition of medieval liturgical drama, where its dialogue, "Lift high your heads, ancient doors," etc., was used to depict Christ at the gates of hell. The second reading is taken from an anonymous Greek homily (*Patrologia Graeca*, 43, 439, 451,

462–63). It gives vivid narrative development to the descent, drawing on a variety of stock motifs like the silence of earth, the trembling of hell, the rescue of the First Adam, the rousing of the sleepers in hell, the trophy of the cross, and the opening of paradise. The dramatic imagery of epiphany, proclamation, and struggle find ample expression in the paschal liturgies of the Byzantine and Syriac churches where Christ's trampling Death by his death and descent is a consitutive metaphor for proclamation of the resurrection.

Bibliography: A. BERSTEIN, *The Formation of Hell* (Ithaca 1993). A. GRILLMEIER, *Mit Ihm und in Ihm: Christologische Forschungen und Perspektiven* (Freiburg 1975) 76–174. H. QUILLIET, *Dictionnaire de théologie catholique*, ed. A. VACANT et al., 15 v. (Paris 1903–50) 4.1:565–619. W. J. DALTON, *Christ's Proclamation to the Spirits* (*Analecta biblica* 1965). J. DANIÉLOU, *The Theology of Jewish Christianity,* ed. and tr. J. A. BAKER (Chicago 1964). J. N. D. KELLY, *Early Christian Creeds* (3d ed. New York 1972). A. T. HANSON, *The New Testament Interpretation of Scripture* (London 1980). W. HALL HARRIS III, "The Descent of Christ: Ephesians 4:7–11 and Traditional Hebrew Imagery," *Arbeiten zur Geschichte des antiken Judentums und des Urchristentums 32* (Leiden 1996). M. HERZOG, "Descensus ad Inferos" "Eine religionsphilosophische Untersuchung der Motive und Interpretationen mit besonderer Berücksichtigung der monographischen Literatur seit dem 16. Jahrhundert," *Frankfurter theologische Studien 53* (1997). Z. IZYDORCZYK, "The Medieval Gospel of Nicodemus: Texts, Intertexts, and Contexts in Western Europe," *Medieval and Renaissance Texts and Studies 158* (Tempe, Ariz. 1997). O. ROUSSEAU, "La Descente aux enfers dans le cadre des liturgies chrétiennes," *LMD 43* (1955) 104–23. H.-J VOGELS, *Christi Abstieg ins Totenreich und das Läuterungsgericht an den Toten: Eine bibeltheologisch-dogmatische Untersuchung zum Glaubensartikel "descendit ad inferos,"* *Freiburger theologische Studien 102* (1976). H. URS VON BALTHASAR, *Mysterium Paschale: The Mystery of Easter* (Edinburgh 1990); "Eschatologie," *Fragen der Theologie Heute,* eds. J. FEINER, J. TRÜTSCH, and F. BÖCKLE, (3d ed. Einsiedeln 1960). H. VORGRIMLER, "The Significance of Christ's Descent into Hell," *Concilium 11* (1966); *Geschichte der Hölle* (Munich 1993).

[J. H. ROHLING/EDS.]

DESERT FATHERS

The hermits and cenobites of Egypt, *c.* 250 to 500, who through their way of life and spiritual teachings developed the institution of MONASTICISM. They made three Egyptian desert areas famous: the THEBAID, the Nitrian Desert or Valley (also called Scete), and Middle Egypt, between the Nile and the Red Sea, where ANTHONY OF EGYPT directed colonies of hermits. Paul of Thebes (*c.* 227–340) is the first hermit of whom there exists an account that clearly identifies him as an inaugurator in the Desert tradition (JEROME, *Patrologia Latina* 23:17–28). Anthony of Egypt (*c.* 250–356) is usually regarded as the prototype of the Desert Fathers because of the widespread influence of his vita by St. ATHANASIUS of Alexandria. PACHOMIUS from the Thebaid, a younger

contemporary, ranks among the first of the Fathers as the founder of CENOBITISM (*c.* 320). Ammon was the founder of the cenobitic settlements in Nitria (*c.* 320); Macarius, Paphnutius, and Pambo were some of their most noted Fathers. From the end of the third century, increasing numbers of Fathers, many of them simple Coptic peasants, drew thousands to permanent discipleship in their desert retreats through the force of their single-minded search for God and the freshness and vigor of their teachings. As these teachings came to be recorded in ascetical treatises, monastic rules, sermons, and above all in collections, of spiritual sayings or apophthegmata, they created a distinct literary type. When studied with the reports of pilgrims from other parts of the Christian world, including those of RUFINUS OF AQUILEIA, JEROME, John CASSIAN, and PALLADIUS OF HELENOPOLIS, these writings attest that the first hermits and cenobites of Egypt form a distinct and important group among the FATHERS OF THE CHURCH and for their influence on ascetical and mystical doctrine, and in the institution of monasticism.

Bibliography: J. QUASTEN, *Patrology*, 3 v. (Westminster, Md. 1950–) 3:146–189. P. DE LABRIOLLE, *Histoire de l' église depuis les origines jusqu' à nos jours*, eds. A. FLICHE and V. MARTIN (Paris 1935–) 3:299–369. H. ROSWEYDE, ed., *Vitae Patrum*, 2 v. (Antwerp 1628; repr. *Patrologia Latina* 73–74). H. WADDELL, tr., *The Desert Fathers* (New York 1936). R. DRAGUET, ed., *Les Pères du désert* (Paris 1949). E. A. W. BUDGE, ed. and tr., *The Paradise or Garden of the Holy Fathers*, 2 v. (London 1907). ATHANASIUS, *The Life of Saint Anthony*, ed. and tr., R. T. MEYER, *Ancient Christian Writers*, ed. J. QUASTEN et al., 10 (Westminster, Md. 1950). G. M. COLOMBÁS, "The Ancient Concept of Monastic Life," *Monastic Studies* 2 (1964) 65–117. G. GOULD, *The Desert Fathers on Monastic Community* (Oxford 1993). A. G. ELLIOT, *Roads to Paradise: Reading the Lives of the Early Saints* (London 1987). M. GALLI, ed., "St. Antony and the Desert Fathers: Extreme Faith in the Early Church," *Christian History* 64 (1999) 8–45. D. E. LINGE, "Asceticism and 'Singleness of Mind' in the Desert Fathers," in *Monastic Life in the Christian and Hindu Traditions*, ed. A. B. CREEL and V. NARAYANAN (Lewiston, N.Y. 1990) 37–70.

[M. C. MCCARTHY]

DESHAYES, GABRIEL

Religious founder; b. Beignon (Morbihan), France, Dec. 6, 1767; d. Saint-Laurent-sur-Sèvre (Vendée), France, Dec. 28, 1841. He was a deacon when the French Revolution forced him to flee in exile to Jersey in the Channel Islands, where he was ordained (1792). He returned then to France and exercised his ministry amid the perils of the Reign of Terror. In 1805 he became pastor in Auray (Morbihan) and began reestablishing parish missions, recalling religious orders, providing welfare agencies, and opening schools. In conjunction with Michelle Guillaume he founded the Sisters of Christian Instruction of Saint-Gildas-des-Bois (1807). In the rectory he organized (1816) a community of teaching brothers that merged (1820) with another group established by Jean de LA MENNAIS to form the BROTHERS OF CHRISTIAN INSTRUCTION OF PLOËRMEL. His role in the foundation of the BROTHERS OF CHRISTIAN INSTRUCTION OF ST. GABRIEL began in 1821 [see *Acta Apostolicae Sedis* 39 (1947) 240–241]. In 1839 Deshayes founded the Brothers of St. Francis of Assisi to conduct agricultural schools. This group fused in 1899 with the Salesians. After joining the MONTFORT FATHERS in 1820, Deshayes served (1821–41) as superior general of this institute and of the Daughters of WISDOM, both being foundations of St. Louis GRIGNION DE MONTFORT. Deshayes also organized special institutions for the care of the deaf and mute. After his death an endeavor was made to establish a link between the first schools founded by St. Louis Grignion de Montfort in 1705 and the Brothers of St. Gabriel organized by Deshayes at Saint-Laurent-sur-Sèvre in 1821, thus making Deshayes the restorer rather than the founder of the Brothers. The Historical Commission of the Congregation of Rites studied the matter and in 1947 recognized Deshayes as the founder.

Bibliography: A. CROSNIER, *L'Homme de la Divine Providence, Gabriel Deshayes*, 2 v. (Paris 1917). A. LAVEILLE, *Gabriel Deshayes et ses familles religieuses* (Brussels 1924). Crosnier presents Deshayes as founder of the Brothers of St. Gabriel; Laveille, as restorer of the congregation.

[E. G. DROUIN]

DESHON, GEORGE

Missionary, author; b. New London, Conn., Jan. 30, 1823; d. New York, N.Y., Dec. 30, 1903. A descendant of French Huguenots on his father's side and of a Mayflower settler on his mother's, Deshon was raised as an Episcopalian. After his sixteenth birthday, he entered the U.S. Military Academy at West Point where he was a roommate of Ulysses S. Grant. Graduating second in his class, Deshon remained at the academy to teach mathematics and ethics. Under the influence of Gen. William S. Rosecrans, he became a Catholic in 1850. He resigned his captaincy to enter the Redemptorist community and was ordained on Oct. 28, 1855. With three other Redemptorist converts, Isaac HECKER, Augustine HEWIT, and Clarence WALWORTH, he gave missions throughout the Eastern seaboard. In 1858, Pius IX released him and his missionary companions from their Redemptorist vows and he joined Hecker, Hewit, and Francis BAKER in forming the Paulist Fathers (*see* PAULISTS). To the new community he brought a practical business sense and considerable organizing ability, serving as assistant superior, novice master, and superintendent of the construction of the Church of St. Paul the Apostle, New York

Gabriel Deshayes. (The Catholic University of America)

City. In 1873, at the request of the bishops of the U.S., Deshon interceded with President Grant on behalf of the Catholic natives of the United States. On Sept. 9, 1897, he was elected third superior general of the Paulist Fathers and continued in that office until his death. In addition to writing for the *Catholic World,* he published *Parochial Sermons* (New York 1901), and the *Guide for Catholic Young Women* (New York 1860), which ran to 25 editions and had a larger sale than any other Catholic book of its day.

Bibliography: J. MCSORLEY, *Father Hecker and His Friends* (2d ed. St. Louis 1953). P. J. RAHILL, *The Catholic Indian Missions and Grant's Peace Policy 1870–1884* (Washington 1953).

[V. F. HOLDEN]

DESIDERATUS OF BOURGES, ST.

Bishop; d. May 8, 550. Together with his brother Deodatus, he was a valued councilor of King Chlotar I (d. 561) and keeper of his seal. Giving up his inclination to the monastic life at the request of the king and the magnates, as his vita relates, he succeeded Archadius (d. 543), becoming 23d bishop of Bourges in 543. After a pilgrimage to Rome, he was present in 549 at the synod of Orléans held under King Childebert I (d. 558). He is held to be the founder of the church of St. Symphorien, later called St. Ursin, in Bourges. He was succeeded in office by St. Probianus (d. 568). A late vita, suspiciously similar to that of St. OUEN, may be found in *Acta Sanctorum* May 2:303–305.

Feast: May 8.

Bibliography: R. AUBERT, *Dictionnaire d'histoire et de géographie ecclésiastiques*, ed. A. BAUDRILLART et al. (Paris 1912) 14:343. A. BUTLER, *The Lives of the Saints*, ed. H. THURSTON and D. ATTWATER (New York 1956) 2:251–252. R. AIGRAIN, *Catholicisme* 3:674.

[V. I. J. FLINT]

DESIDERIUS, KING OF THE LOMBARDS

Duke of Tuscany, reigned 756 to 774; date of death unknown. Desiderius secured papal support for his election by recognizing papal rule over the territory conferred on STEPHEN III by the ''donation of Pepin,'' but his position was difficult. The existence of a strip of papal territory extending from Rome to Ravenna cut the Lombard kingdom into two parts—the main kingdom in the north and the duchies of Spoleto and Benevento in the south. Although the Lombard nobility normally sought independence, that same nobility favored Lombard expansion under royal leadership and, in order to consolidate the Lombard state, urged Desiderius to take those lands claimed by the papacy. In answer to an appeal from ADRIAN I, CHARLEMAGNE, Desiderius's son-in-law, led a Frankish invasion into Italy in 773–774. The Lombard nobility failed to cooperate with the crown and the Lombard kingdom fell to the Franks. Desiderius was deposed and spent the rest of his life in a Frankish monastery.

Bibliography: T. HODGKIN, *Italy and her Invaders,* 8 v. in 9 (Oxford 1892–99) v.7. L. M. O. DUCHESNE, *The Beginnings of the Temporal Sovereignty of the Popes, A. D. 754–1073,* tr. A. H. MATHEW (London 1908). F. LOT et al., *Les Destinées de l'empire en Occident de 395 à 888,* 2 v. (new ed. Paris 1940). W. K. WILLIAMS, *The Communes of Lombardy from the VI to the X Century* (Baltimore 1891). T. SCHIEFFER, *Lexikon für Theologie und Kirche,* ed. J. HOFER and K. RAHNER (2d, new ed. Freiburg 1957–65) 3:250.

[K. F. DREW]

DESIDERIUS OF CAHORS, ST.

Merovingian bishop of Cahors (known also as Didier, Géry); b. Obroge, France; d. Milhac, Nov. 15, 655. Desiderius was a member of a wealthy Gallo-Roman family. Upon coming of age, he and his brothers, Syagrius and St. Rusticus, took their places in the court of the Merovingian Chlotar II (d. 623). Rusticus received an ecclesiastical post as bishop of Cahors. Syagrius became count of Albi and, perhaps, prefect of Marseilles, though this is not certain. Desiderius, a court favorite, was made royal treasurer in 608. Upon the murder of Rusticus, Desiderius was consecrated bishop of Cahors in 630 by SULPICIUS OF BOURGES. His vita states that he was faithful to king and Church. Some 16 of his letters and 20 received by him survive in good Latin. This correspondence includes letters of King Sigebert III and Grimoald, Sigebert's mayor of the palace. Desiderius is credited with writing a rule, holding regular synods, building a number of churches, and establishing monasteries.

Feast: Nov. 15.

Bibliography: *Acta Sanctae Sedis* Feb. 3:172. *Patrologia Latina* ed. J. P. MIGNE (Paris 1878–90) 87:239–246. *Corpus Christianorum. Series latina* 117:309–401. A. BUTLER, *The Lives of the Saints,* ed. H. THURSTON and D. ATTWATER (New York 1956) 11:476–482. H. PLATELLE, *Catholicisme* 4:1900–01. R. VAN DOREN, *Dictionnaire d'histoire et de géographie ecclésiastiques,* ed. A. BAUDRILLART et al. (Paris 1912) 14:399.

[B. F. SCHERER]

DESIDERIUS OF LANGRES, ST.

Listed as third bishop of Langres, France; d. Langres, *c.* 407–11. According to Warnacher, his seventh-century biographer, Desiderius suffered martyrdom with many of his people, though he begged mercy for them from the VANDALS in 407 or 411, or possibly in some earlier invasion. His feast was February 11 in the Hieronymian martyrology but he was later confused, possibly because of errors in MS copying, with Bp. DESIDERIUS OF VIENNE, and took the latter's feast in the Roman martyrology. His name has been given to several churches in France and to the city of Saint-Dizier, of which he is patron.

Feast: May 23.

Bibliography: *Acta Sanctae Sedis* May 5:244–249. *Bibliotheca hagiograpica latina antiquae et mediae aetatis* (Brussels 1898–1901) 1:2145–46. L. DUCHESNE, *Fastes épiscopaux de l'ancienne Gaule* (Paris 1907–15) v. 2. É. GRIFFE, *La Gaule chrétienne à l'époque romaine* (Paris 1947—) 1:226. R. AIGRAIN, *Catholicisme* 3:753–754. R. VAN DOREN, *Dictionnaire d'histoire et de géographie ecclésiastiques,* ed. A. BAUDRILLART et al. (Paris 1912) 14:405.

[L. M. COFFEY]

DESIDERIUS OF VIENNE, ST.

Desiderius (French, Didier) is the name of a number of early sainted bishops of cities in France: Auxerre

(605–27), Cahors (630–55), Langres (fl. 343), Rennes (eighth century), and Vienne (595–606). Desiderius of Vienne was born of Christian parents. He devoted himself to grammatical and religious studies and, after refusing a number of bishoprics, was persuaded to become bishop of Vienne in 595. He received many letters from Pope St. GREGORY I (590–604), who recommended St. AUGUSTINE OF CANTERBURY to his hospitality on the latter's way to evangelize England; but at the Council of Chalon-sur-Saône in 602 and 603, Desiderius was deposed on a morals charge at the instigation of Queen Brunhilde. Four years later he was recalled from exile and restored. Because he continued to reprove the queen and her son, Theodoric II, he was arrested in his church and eventually assassinated. Details of his life are given in an early *Passio* and a *Vita* written by the Visigothic King Sisebut. The church of Saint-Didier-sur-Charlaronne was erected over his tomb.

Feast: May 23.

Bibliography: R. VAN DOREN, *Dictionnaire d'histoire et de géographie ecclésiastiques*, ed. A. BAUDRILLART et al. (Paris 1912) 14:410–411. B. KRUSCH, ed., ''Vita Desiderii Episcopi Viennensis.'' *Monumenta Germaniae Historica: Scriptores rerum Merovingicarum* 3:620–648. A. BUTLER, *The Lives of the Saints*, ed. H. THURSTON and D. ATTWATER (New York 1956) 2:374–375.

[E. G. RYAN]

DESIDERIUS RHODONENSIS, ST.

Martyr; d. near Belfort, Alsace, France, Sept. 17 *c.* 670–3. According to the ninth-century vita, he was a bishop, and as he was returning from a pilgrimage to Rome, he was killed *tempore Childerici regis* together with his companion, the deacon Raginfridus, by brigands. The king referred to is probably Childeric II (d. 673). Desiderius was buried at the place of his murder in an oratory dedicated to St. Martin, and this chapel was later known as Saint-Dizier-l'Evêque. The building at his tomb of a church, given *c.* 735–7 by Count Everard of Alsace to the Abbey of MURBACH, is evidence that his cult existed in the eighth century. His relics were translated to the abbey before 1041, and he is honored as a martyr in Alsace. No early tradition associates this St. Desiderius with Rennes.

Feast: Sept. 18.

Bibliography: *Acta Sanctae Sedis* 5 Sept. (1863) 788–792. *Monumenta Germaniae Historica: Scriptores rerum Merovingicarum* 6:55–63. R. AUBERT, *Dictionnaire d'histoire et de géographie ecclésiastiques*, ed. A. BAUDRILLART et al. (Paris 1912) 14:409–410. R. AIGRAIN, *Catholicisme* 3:751–752. J. CLAUSS, *Die Heiligen des Elsass* (Düsseldorf 1935) 52–53, 199.

[V. I. J. FLINT]

DESIRE

Any internal movement of body or spirit toward the possession and enjoyment of some object seen as good. Though it is commonly identified with love (becoming what in fact is a special kind of love: love of eros, or erotic love), actually it is a tendency consequent upon love. First there is the love—a kind of perceived harmony between the one loving and the person or object loved. Then there is the reaching out, or desire, for the object. Finally there is rest, and so joy or delight, in the object possessed.

Desire may be purely physical, mere appetite for that which sustains the individual or the race: food and drink, warmth, coolness, exercise, sleep, sex. As such it is blunt and undiscriminating, as when a man starving simply wants food with little or no consideration as to kind or quality. On the other hand, it may be ''psychical,'' as when thought and imagination discover or create various shades of object for the one physical appetite (e.g., the connoisseur of fine wines wants at a given moment this particular vintage and no other). Finally, it may be purely spiritual, as when the object loved is of the spiritual or intellectual order—e.g., wisdom or science, art or justice or the kingdom of God—such that while the body is calm and at rest, the spirit yearns for its beloved.

However in man desire is rarely, if ever, merely physical or merely spiritual, for man himself is neither one nor the other, but both, in substantial and vital union. Even the man who is starving finds his desire altered or alterable by his thought and imagination; and the man who deeply and seriously loves justice finds his very body involved in his desire, finds himself wanting justice with a passion.

The worth of desire depends upon the worth of its object. If the object desired is morally good, the desire itself is good; if the object is bad, then the desire is evil. The question here is one of moral goodness and evil. Desire, as defined above, is always toward some perceived good, but not necessarily toward what is perceived as morally good. A man, for instance, may see a woman as good from many different points of view—personality, beauty, wealth, charm—and so feel his desire stirred: he wants her for his very own. However, if he or she happens already to be married, then the desire becomes a morally evil one, since the object, namely, this-woman-as-my-wife, is morally evil.

Yet in a larger sense, desire can be spoken of as having a kind of moral value independent of its ''visual'' objects; for in reality desire moves not so much toward such objects as through them to the infinite, unseen goal of the human heart. A woman loves and wants her children; but more deeply still, in and through that very desire she is loving and wanting God. St. Augustine and his famed description of all human restlessness in terms of ultimate rest is another illustration; still another is the beautiful temptress in Claudel's play whose ''special grace'' was to stir men's desire and, in their inevitable disappointment with her, leave them with God.

This is not, of course, to condone any and every desire, whether good or evil. Indeed, a desire that continually feeds off evil dies precisely for that reason, but it is to point up the positive value of desire in man's life vis-à-vis with his God. Control, direction, purification—not the suppression—of desire is the ideal of Christian spirituality. In addition, the pseudospirituality of quietism and Oriental indifferentism, which suggest that all desire is evil, have always been as foreign to orthodox Christianity as the death of desire—the despair, ennui, and boredom—of the extremes of present-day existentialist thinking and living. Desire in its deepest heart is man's movement toward God. The proper grace is to recognize it as such and to help it reach its goal.

Bibliography: J. RICKABY, *Moral Philosophy* (London 1918). D. VON HILDEBRAND, *Christian Ethics* (New York 1953). M. C. D'ARCY, *The Mind and Heart of Love* (New York 1947).

[S. F. PARMISANO]

DESIRE TO SEE GOD, NATURAL

The problem of the natural desire of the vision of GOD did not arise among Catholic theologians until the time of the scholastics, when the notion of NATURE had been philosophically perfected and the distinction between the natural and the SUPERNATURAL clarified. In the 13th century the problem was treated as one of the elements of the more general questions of man's knowledge of God and of beatitude. In modern times it is discussed on it own merits as a means of showing that the supernatural is not something alien to human nature. The bridge, it is sometimes said, between nature and supernature is the desire for God, and more specifically the desire to see God, to know by intuition His very essence.

St. Thomas Aquinas. Since the early years of the 20th century the treatment of the natural desire of the vision of God has centered mainly around St. Thomas and his 16th-century commentators. To begin with, it is admitted on all sides that to see God face to face is for St. Thomas something strictly supernatural, that it is above the natural capacities of man and in no way due to his nature as such. A typical text in which the Angelic Doctor affirms the natural desire of this supernatural vision and explains its meaning is his response to the question whether man's beatitude consists in seeing the divine essence. He says:

Final and perfect happiness can consist only in the vision of the essence of God. The evidence for this lies in two considerations. First of all, man is not perfectly happy so long as there remains something for him to desire and look for. Secondly, the perfection of every power is to be judged from its object. But the object of the intellect is *what a thing is,* that is, its essence, as Aristotle says in the third book *On the Soul.* Hence the perfection to which the intellect attains is to be gauged by its knowledge of the essence of a thing. If, therefore, an intellect cognizes the essence of an effect in such a way that it does not know the essence of the cause, that is, in such a way as to know what the cause is in itself, it is not said to reach the cause in every possible way, even though it knows through the effect that the cause exists. And hence when a man cognizes an effect and knows it has a cause there naturally remains in him the desire to know the quiddity of the cause, that is *what it is.* And the desire is one of wonder, and it causes a search, as is said in the beginning of the *Metaphysics.* For example, if a person has knowledge of an eclipse of the sun, he considers that it comes from a cause, and since he does not know what this is he wonders about it and in his wonder he sets up an inquiry. This inquiry does not end until he comes to know the very essence of the cause.

So it is that if the human intellect cognizing the essence of some created effect knows only this of God that *He is,* its knowledge of the first cause is not yet simply perfect. Rather there still remains the natural desire of inquiring about the cause, and hence the man is not yet perfectly happy. For perfect happiness, therefore, it is necessary that the intellect should reach to the very essence of the first cause. And so it will have its perfection through union with God as the object in which alone man's beatitude consists. [*Summa Theologiae* 1a2ae, 3.8.]

The phenomenological character of St. Thomas's reasoning is quite evident: the natural curiosity of the human mind cannot be completely satisfied this side of the vision of God's essence. It follows quite simply that final and perfect HAPPINESS can be found only in the contemplation of God face to face. Is one to conclude, then, that if God creates an intellectual creature He *must* make it possible for that creature to come to the vision, which is entirely above nature and not due to it? In other words can God leave man's natural desire perpetually frustrated, or rather has not man a right to that which, given the supernaturality of the vision, is in no way due to him? Strange to say, St. Thomas never explicitly faced up to this inherent paradox in man's situation. His interest never went beyond trying to show that the fact of the vision of God, known from REVELATION, is perfectly in accord with reason. But he never concluded to the *fact* from his reasonings about the natural desire, nor did he ever hold that man's elevation to the vision is a necessity. If in some places of his writings he seems to be proving the *fact* from reason alone, the context will always show that such is not his intention. All that he wishes to establish through rational discourse is that the intuitive vision of God is *possible* to man. To select one example from many, we read:

> But since it is impossible for natural desire to be in vain, which it would be if it were not possible to attain to that intuition of the divine substance which all minds naturally desire, it is necessary to say that it is *possible* for all intellects to see the substance of God, both those of separated intellectual substances and our souls. [*C. gent.* 3.51]

The possibility of which St. Thomas is speaking can become an actual fact, as he expressly holds, only by the gratuitous elevation of intellect to an order of existence above its own natural powers and exigencies. The natural desire manifests man's capacity for receiving such a supernatural elevation but does not demand that it be given.

Interpretations. Many and diverse have been the interpretations of St. Thomas's teaching on the natural desire. Cardinal CAJETAN (TOMMASO DE VIO), OP, thought that he was speaking of a desire of rational nature in the supposition that this nature possesses knowledge of the existence of the vision of God through revelation. Even in that supposition God is desired only under the aspect of first cause, God the creator, governor of the universe. Domingo de SOTO, OP, considered Cajetan's opinion to be a distortion of St. Thomas's texts. Soto believed that for the Angelic Doctor the natural desire is innate, a bent or inclination in the will, a *pondus naturae,* prior to all cognition. If one looks merely at the tendency, which is in every human being, the end (that is, the vision of God) is natural; if one looks to the attainment of that end, it is supernatural. In this position Soto professes to be, as he really is, a follower of John DUNS SCOTUS, OFM.

Another great Thomist, Sylvester of Ferrara, OP [*see* FERRARIENSIS (FRANCESCO SILVESTRI)], rejects the supposition of revelation as a prerequisite to the natural desire. He holds this to be an elicited act of the will which supposes and follows that cognition of God by which we know that *God is.* It is the desire of the vision of God *as first cause,* not as the object of supernatural beatitude. But Sylvester's limitation of man's natural desire to see God as the author of nature is in turn rejected by Domingo Báñez, OP (*see* BÁÑEZ AND BAÑEZIANISM). This renowned theologian also refuses to accept the mere innate tendency of Soto and Scotus. For him the desire is *elicited* because, he says, according to St. Thomas's texts it arises from the knowledge of created effects. This elicited desire is natural; but it remains with regard to its object, the vision of God as He is in Himself, *conditional* (if the vision is possible) and *inefficacious* (in itself of no avail for the attainment of the supernatural end). Finally, Báñez insists, the power of rational nature to see God is merely obediential; that is, man is made in the image of God, and therefore his intellectual nature is such that it can be elevated to the divine vision. The common opinion of Thomists even today is said to be a combination of elements from the positions of Báñez and Sylvester: the natural desire is elicited, conditioned, inefficacious; its object is God the author of nature (cf. Garrigou-Lagrange).

Dominating the theological discussion of the problem until the end of the 19th century were the classic opinions outlined above. Since that time a more literal exegesis of St. Thomas's texts has been essayed by theologians. The years preceding the publication of *HUMANI GENERIS* in 1950 witnessed the proposal of the opinion that the intellectual creature by virtue of its creation is necessarily destined to the vision of God as its end, even though this end remains supernatural. The encyclical identified such a position as untenable; Pope Pius XII warned all Catholics against the novel speculations of those who "corrupt the true gratuitous character of the supernatural order when they assert that God cannot create beings endowed with intellect without ordaining them for the beatific vision and calling them to it" (Denz 3891). Another hypothesis endeavoring to explain the natural desire, but not attributable to St. Thomas, is that of the "supernatural existential." This means that every human soul in its creation is endowed with an ontological supernatural reality added to its nature and destining it to the vision of God as its end. This reality, which is said to be the desire for God, is not GRACE as we know it but a prerequisite for grace.

See Also: BEATIFIC VISION; DESTINY, SUPERNATURAL; ELEVATION OF MAN; GOD, INTUITION OF; GRACE AND NATURE; HEAVEN; LIGHT OF GLORY; MAN, 3; NATURAL ORDER; OBEDIENTIAL POTENCY; PURE NATURE, STATE OF.

Bibliography: A. GARDEIL, *Dictionnaire de théologie catholique,* ed. A. VACANT et al., (Paris 1903–50; Tables générales 1951–) 1.2:1696–1700. A. MICHEL, *ibid.* 14.2:2854–59. F. TAYMANS D'EYPERNON, *Dictionaire de spiritualité ascétique et mystique. Doctrine et histoire,* ed. M. VILLER et al, (Paris 1932–) 3:929–947. J. ALFARO, *Lexikon für Theologie und Kirche,* ed. J. HOFER and K. RAHNER (Freiburg 1957–65) 3:248–250; *Lo natural y lo sobrenatural desde Santo Tomás hasta Cayetano* (Madrid 1952). V. DE BROGLIE, *De fine ultimo humanae vitae* (Paris 1948). R. GARRIGOU-LAGRANGE, *De revelatione,* 2 v. (Rome 1929–31) 1:208. W. R. O'CONNOR, *The Eternal Quest* (New York 1947).

[T. J. MOTHERWAY/EDS.]

DESMAISIÈRES, MARÍA MIGUELA OF THE BLESSED SACRAMENT, ST.

Foundress of the HANDMAIDS OF THE BLESSED SACRAMENT AND OF CHARITY, Sisters Adorers; b. Madrid, Spain, Jan. 1, 1809; d. Valencia, Aug. 24, 1865. María de la Soledad Miguela Desmaisières Lopez de Dicastillo, viscountess of Jorbalán, displayed from an early age zeal for the ascetical life and for charitable works. During a cholera epidemic in Madrid, she attended the plague-stricken (1834) and set up home assistance boards to aid them. In 1845 she established a home to rehabilitate fallen or endangered young women. To perpetuate this work she founded her religious congregation (1859) and acted as its superior general until her death. Papal approval came in 1866. Men who had preyed on the recipients of this charity caused the foundress to be slandered, but by 1865 the institute numbered seven houses. María died after contracting cholera while attending her own religious during an epidemic. She was beatified on June 7, 1925 and canonized on March 4, 1934 by Pope Pius XI.

Feast: Aug. 25.

Bibliography: *Autobiografía*, ed. M. M. TOFFOLI MOYANO (Madrid 1981). T. J. CÁMARA, *Vida de la ven. M. Sacramento*, 2 v. (Madrid 1908). A. ROMANO DI SANTA TERESA, *La beata Maria Michelina del Sacramento* (new ed. Rome 1934). E. BARRAQUER Y CERERO, *La siempre calumnida* (2d ed. Madrid 1955). A. CABRÉ RUFATT, *Micaela, entre cardos y espigas* (Santiago 1984). *Acta Apostolicae Sedis* 17 (1925) 292–296; 26 (1934) 160–164.

[I. BASTARRIKA]

DE SMET, PIERRE JEAN

Founder of Native American missions; b. Termonde, Belgium, Jan. 30, 1801; d. St. Louis, Mo., May 23, 1873. De Smet was of Flemish-Walloon stock and the fifth of nine children. After meeting Charles Nerinckx, early Kentucky missioner, he came to the U.S. in 1821, entered the Society of Jesus, and was ordained at Florissant, Mo., on Sept. 23, 1827. He then became treasurer of St. Louis College (later University). Returning to Belgium because of ill health, he remained there for four years, two of which he spent outside the Society. In 1837 he returned to Missouri, was readmitted to the Jesuits, and a few months later set out for the mission at Council Bluffs, Iowa, where he remained until 1839. The same year he visited native tribes along the middle Missouri River and encountered two Flathead natives en route to St. Louis to ask for priests to instruct their nation. This visit was to prove the turning point of his life.

De Smet visited the Rocky Mountain area in 1840. Returning in 1841 with five companions, he founded St. Mary's Mission (near Missoula, Mont.), visited Fts. Colville and Vancouver in the far Northwest, and with missionaries F. N. BLANCHET and Modeste DEMERS (both future bishops) planned the expansion of the Church in the Oregon country. In 1843 he sailed to Europe, recruited five Jesuits and six Sisters of Notre Dame de Namur, chartered a vessel in Antwerp, Belgium, and returned to the United States on July 31, 1844. After founding a central mission on the Willamette River (near St. Paul, Ore.), De Smet revisited the natives in the mountains and journeyed to Ft. Edmonton, Alberta, Canada, to bring the Blackfoot confederacy to peaceful ways.

On his return he was notified of his removal from the office of superior and of his recall to St. Louis. Arriving there he was made provincial treasurer and secretary; his formal missionary career in the Far West had come to an end. During the 1850s and 1860s, however, he visited the Great Plains and the Rocky Mountains seven times as an agent of the federal government. In 1864 he alone could enter the camp of Sitting Bull; and his last journey West (1870) was to establish a mission among the Sioux. De Smet was not so much a missionary as he was a promoter and procurator of missions; in their interest, he made repeated journeys to the mountains and crossed the Atlantic Ocean 16 times. His principal published works include *Letters and Sketches* (Philadelphia 1843), *Oregon Missions and Travels* (New York 1847), *Western Missions and Missionaries* (New York 1863), and *New Indian Sketches* (New York 1865).

Bibliography: H. M. CHITTENDEN and A. T. RICHARDSON, *Life, Letters and Travels of Father Pierre Jean De Smet, S.J.*, 4 v. (New York 1905). G. J. GARRAGHAN, *Jesuits in the Middle United States*, 3 v. (New York 1938). E. LAVEILLE, *Life of Father de Smet, S.J.*, tr. M. LINDSAY (New York 1915). H. MARGARET, *Father De Smet, Pioneer Priest of the Rockies* (Milwaukee 1940). J. SCHAFER, *Dictionary of American Biography*, ed. A. JOHNSON and D. MALONE (New York 1928–36) 5:255–256.

[W. L. DAVIS]

DESPENSER, HENRY

Bishop; b. *c.* 1343; d. Aug. 23, 1406. He studied civil law at Oxford and received a licentiate in civil law in 1370. In that year, because of the prominence of his family, he was made bishop of Norwich by papal PROVISION; he received a papal dispensation since he was only 27. He suppressed the Peasants' Rebellion of June 1381 in East Anglia, delivering PETERBOROUGH and its monks from the rebels and hanging three captive rebels at Wymondham on his own authority. In 1382 Pope URBAN VI commissioned him to raise and conduct an English crusade against the French supporters of the Avignon antipope CLEMENT VII in Flanders (*see* WESTERN SCHISM).

The INDULGENCES, with absolution from punishment and guilt, which were conceded to him for the crusade by Pope Urban VI, stimulated the project but also provided an occasion for John WYCLIF to attack the Church in general and the crusade in particular. Parliament, which at the time was weighing the value of an English expedition to Spain under John of Gaunt's leadership against the crusade to Flanders, opted—with the support of the Commons and the Church—for the bishop's crusade. But the crusade ended in disaster, and on his return Despenser was impeached by the Commons for the misconduct of the war, found guilty by the Lords, and condemned to lose the temporalities of the see (1383). However, these were restored in 1385. A steadfast supporter of Richard II, he only reluctantly accepted Henry IV (1399). He is buried in Norwich cathedral.

Bibliography: T. F. TOUT, *Chapters in the Administrative History of Mediaeval England,* 6 v. (Manchester, Eng. 1920–33). E. POWELL, *The Rising in East Anglia in 1381* (Cambridge, Eng. 1896). A. B. EMDEN, *A Biographical Register of the University of Oxford to A.D. 1500* (Oxford 1957–59) 2169–70. R. L. POOLE, *The Dictionary of National Biography from the Earliest Times to 1900* (London 1885–1900; repr. with corrections, 1908–09, 1921–22, 1938) 14:410–412. A. B. STEELE, *Richard II* (Cambridge, Eng. 1941; repr. 1963).

[V. MUDROCH]

DESPREZ, JOSQUIN

Illustrious Renaissance composer of Franco-Flemish style (also des Prez, Jodocus Pratensis); b. Picardie or Hainaut *c.* 1440; d. Condé-sur-l'Escaut, Aug. 27, 1521. He is considered, on vague evidence, to have been a pupil of OKEGHEM. He was a singer at Milan cathedral (1459–72), then in the ducal chapel until *c.* 1479. He served as singer, then choirmaster, in the papal chapel from 1486 to at least 1494 and choirmaster to Duke Ercole I d'Este at Ferrara (for whom he wrote *Missa Hercules*) *c.* 1496 to 1505. He was probably associated with the court of Margaret of Austria at Malines *c.* 1507 and with that of Louis XII of France *c.* 1512 or 1515. Toward the end of his life he was provost of the chapter of Notre Dame at Condé-sur-l'Escaut, while maintaining ties with the imperial court at Brussels. He was universally regarded as the finest composer of his era. In a music MS written in Paris *c.* 1520 (St. Gall MS 463) he is designated *omnium princeps.* C. Bartoli, in his *Ragionamenti accademici* (Venice 1567), likens his importance in music to that of MICHELANGELO in visual arts. Glareanus in his *Dodecachordon* (Basel 1547) repeatedly praises him as the preeminent musician of his time.

Josquin's works include 20 Masses, nearly 100 motets, and about 60 secular works with texts in French, Italian, and Latin. Petrucci published three books of Masses by him, the only composer so honored. Josquin brought to a point of perfection the Franco-Flemish polyphonic style, combining elaborate *cantus firmus* treatment with pervasive imitation. His Masses, notably *L'Homme armé* (2), *Hercules,* and *Pange lingua,* provide abundant illustration of his fluent technique. This Northern heritage was subtly remolded under the influence of Italian humanism, which led Josquin to conceive of music as a means for the communication of a text. His motets offer many fine examples: the stark, imploring *Miserere,* the mournful *Absalon fili mi,* and the serene *Ave Maria* are among his best.

Bibliography: *Werken,* ed. A. SMIJERS (Amsterdam 1925–), continued by M. ANTONOWYTCH. H. OSTHOFF, *Josquin Desprez* (Tutzing 1962–); *Die Musik in Geschichte und Gegenwart,* ed. F. BLUME (Kassel-Basel 1949–) 7:190–214. W. WIORA, "Der religiöse Grundzug im neuen Stil und Weg Josquins des Prez," *Die Musikforschung* 6 (1953) 23–37. M. ANTONOWYTCH, "The Present State of Josquin Research," *International Musicological Soc., Report of the 8th Congress,* 2 v. (Kassel 1961) 1:53–64. E. H. SPARKS, *Cantus Firmus in Mass and Motet* (Berkeley 1963). G. REESE, *Music in the Renaissance* (rev. ed. New York 1959) 228–260. G. G. ALLAIRE, "Some Overlooked Modulations in the Works of Josquin Des Prés?," *Revue Belge de Musicologie,* 46 (1992) 33–51. L. F. BERNSTEIN, "*Ma bouche rit et mon cueur pleure:* A Chanson a 5 Attributed to Josquin des Prez," *Journal of Musicology,* 12 (1994) 253–286. L. D. BROTHERS, "On Music and Meditation in the Renaissance: Contemplative Prayer and Josquin's *Miserere,*" *Journal of Musicological Research,* 12 (1992) 157–187. A.-E. CEULEMANS, "A Stylistic Investigation of *Missa Une mousse de Biscaye,* in the Light of Its Attribution to Josquin des Prez," *Tidschrift van de Koninklijke Vereniging voor Nederlandse Muziekgeschiedenis,* 48 (1998) 30–50. N. DAVISON, "*Absalom fili mi* Reconsidered," *Tidschrift van de Koninklijke Vereniging voor Nederlandse Muziekgeschiedenis,* 46 (1996) 42–56. C. C. JUDD, "Some Problems of Pre-Baroque Analysis: An Examination of Josquin's *Ave Maria . . . Virgo Serena,*" *Music Analysis,* 4 (1985) 201–239. P. MACEY, "Galeazzo Maria Sforza and Musical Patronage in Milan: Compere, Weerbeke, and Josquin," in *Early Music History 15: Studies in Medieval and Early Modern Music,* ed. I. FENLON (Cambridge, Eng. 1996) 147–204. L. MATTHEWS and P. L. MERKLEY, "Josquin Desprez and His Milanese Patrons," *Journal of Musicology,* 12 (1994) 434–463. P. F. STARR, "Josquin, Rome, and a Case of Mistaken Identity," *Journal of Musicology,* 15 (1997) 43–65.

[M. PICKER]

DESTINY, SUPERNATURAL

The final goal or end that God establishes for men (and angels) and to which He leads them; in that this destiny surpasses the powers and exigencies of their natures, it is SUPERNATURAL.

Scripture. The rich and varied biblical vision of man's destiny implies that this destiny is supernatural. God Himself, alpha and omega, is the beginning and end of all (Rv 21.5–6; Heb 2.10). At the origin of man's destiny is God's plan, or mystery (Eph 1.9–10), hidden since the foundation of the world (Mt 13.34–35), the mystery of the KINGDOM OF GOD (Mk 4.11), the mystery of Christ, revealed in the Spirit (Eph 3.4–5). God's mysterious, hidden wisdom (1 Cor 2.7), grace (Eph 1.6–9), love (Rom 8.37–39), and justice (Rom 3.21–22) establish and accomplish this destiny in a measure far beyond what man can ask or conceive (Eph 3.20): those whom God has foreknown He pre-*destines,* calls and justifies (Rom 8.29–30); these gifts are gratuitous and undeserved (Rom 11.6; Gal 2.21). Man cannot conceive what God has prepared for those who love Him, but He reveals it through His Spirit (1 Cor 2.9–10). This destiny is both personal and social: men are destined to holiness in Christ (Eph 1.4–5); the Church is to be holy and glorious through Christ (Eph 5.27). In Christ men are to be perfect (Col 1.28), to be a new creation (2 Cor 5.17). The whole of creation will share this renewal in Christ (cf. Eph 1.9–10; Col 1.15–20; 1 Cor 15.25–28) and will become a new heaven and a new earth (Rv 21.1, 5; 2 Pt 3.13; cf. Rom 8.19–22). God destines men to glory (Rom 8.18, 30; 1 Pt 5.10), a glory now unseen but eternal (2 Cor 4.17–18); this is a sharing in Christ's glory (Rom 8.17; Col 3.4; cf. Jn 17.10, 24), in His reign (2 Tm 2.12), His heavenly state (Eph 2.6), His divine sonship and inheritance (Rom 8.14–17, 29). In the New Jerusalem God will dwell with men (Rv 21.2–3; cf. 1 Thes 4.17), who will know Him as He knows them, seeing Him face to face (1 Cor 13.12; Ap 22.4) just as He is (1 Jn 3.2; cf. Mt 5.8). In this everlasting life (Jn 17.2–3) God will be all in all (1 Cor 15.28), and in the liturgy of the heavenly temple (Rv 21.22–27) all creation will join in the praise of the glory that is to be revealed in time to come (Eph 1.6; cf. 1.12, 14; 1 Pt 5.1).

Magisterium. The biblical teaching on man's destiny has been gradually made explicit in the Church's teaching. Although the second Council of Orange's assertion that eternal life is open to man only through the Holy Spirit's influence (Denz 377) can be strictly referred only to man's historical state, the later condemnations of the BEGUINES AND BEGHARDS (Denz 895) and of the Ontologists (Denz 2841, 2844) show that man's destiny is above the powers of his nature in any state, while the condemnations of BAIUS, Quesnel, and the Jansenists (Denz 1921, 1923, 1926, 2435, 2616) make it further clear that man's ELEVATION is also not due to his nature in any state and so surpasses its exigencies; thus his destiny appears as supernatural. Vatican Council I made it explicit: "God . . . ordained man to a supernatural end" or destiny (Denz 3005; cf. 2854); the Council also stated the possibility of man's being raised by God "to a knowledge and perfection surpassing the natural" (Denz 3028; cf.

Denz[31] 2103). Successive papal statements have reaffirmed this supernatural destiny of all men, e.g., John XXIII's in *Pacem in terris* [*Acta Apostolicae Sedis* 55 (Rome 1963) 289].

Theological Debates. Several doctrinal currents led theologians in the last few centuries to contrast man's supernatural destiny with a natural destiny thought of as corresponding to man's nature in a hypothetical state of PURE NATURE. Also, in reply to 19th-century RATIONALISM and NATURALISM, great stress was laid on a sharp distinction between the NATURAL ORDER and the SUPERNATURAL ORDER. More recently, however, fears arose that such views made man's supernatural destiny appear to be extrinsic and without resonance in man's being. To counteract this, some authors sought to show that man's supernatural destiny is so inscribed in his nature that he can have no other destiny or end. Thus H. de Lubac, in his influential study *Surnaturel,* held that God's creation of intellectual beings with a natural DESIRE to see Him is itself a destination of them to the BEATIFIC VISION, which alone can fulfill them. In this view man neither has nor could have any other end, so that a state of pure nature is impossible in fact and is theologically misleading as a concept; man's destiny would nevertheless be gratuitous and supernatural because, like creation, it is an undeserved, unexacted gift of God's free love and because the one so destined needs God's grace as means to reach it. Many theologians objected that such a theory fails to guarantee the gratuity and supernaturality of man's destiny: it would, they said, reduce man's supernatural destiny to the same order as creation, make it an exigency of his nature, and make only the means supernatural but not the destiny itself. Amid the ensuing debates Pius XII warned against destroying the gratuity of the supernatural order through holding that God could not create intellectual creatures without ordering and calling them to the beatific vision (Denz 3891). Many theologians exaggerated the force of this statement, saying it implies necessarily that another destiny than the beatific vision was possible for men and angels: this possibility they held to be the only way to maintain the distinction of the natural and the supernatural. Most modern theologians nevertheless agree in rejecting views that make the supernatural appear extrinsic and juxtaposed to nature and in insisting on the positive openness of intellectual creatures to a supernatural destiny. Many would say further that, although men and angels could either have received another destiny or have been left with no truly final destiny at all, God actually created them only for the sake of the supernatural destiny He freely gives them. For the various attempts within such positions to relate man's nature positively to his supernatural destiny, *see* OBEDIENTIAL POTENCY.

In two later volumes [*Augustinisme et théologie moderne* (Paris 1965) and *Le Mystère du surnaturel* (Paris 1965)] De Lubac greatly clarifies the conclusion of his *Surnaturel* (admittedly an "esquisse . . . trop rapide": *Mystère* 76): he clearly states that God could have created men and still not called them to see Him (*ibid.* 110; cf. 289, 252); he also modifies other earlier judgments, such as that concerning Thomas Aquinas's role in this question. At the same time he points out certain misrepresentations of his own thought made by others and reaffirms with new developments several of his basic positions. Thus he insists, with abundant appeals to patristic and theological tradition, that the truly final destiny of actually existing men is and should be conceived to be only the beatific vision (had God not called man to this, as He was free not to do even after creating him, man would have had no truly final destiny but only an unconscious natural attraction for God: *ibid.* 252; cf. 247–248); the sign or expression of this unique supernatural destiny is man's natural and absolute desire to see God, a desire itself clearly known only in the light of faith; the hypothesis of a state of pure nature and a natural final end, however useful it may have been for its relatively recent originators, betrays the sound tradition of the Fathers and great medieval theologians and fails, moreover, to account for the supernatural character of the destiny and vocation actually given the men we are in our concrete historical situation. These volumes and the views they express undoubtedly provide a starting point for renewed debates on the topic.

Society, Evolution, and Supernatural Destiny. According to papal social theology, the supernatural destiny of individuals is one important source of their personal rights and the most fundamental guarantee of their freedom from total subjection to civil society. As for the Church as a whole, its supernatural destiny gives it both rights and apostolic duties in human society and history. Because of the harmony between the natural and the supernatural, the Church's insistence on and concern for man's supernatural destiny contribute to the progress of society itself without interfering with its legitimate ends.

In the theology of TEMPORAL VALUES and in ESCHATOLOGY theologians are examining the interrelationship between the natural evolution of the universe (including man) and man's supernatural destiny. Material creation is seen as somehow involved in man's supernatural destiny.

See Also: GRACE, ARTICLES ON; JANSENISM; MAN; MYSTERY (IN THE BIBLE); ONTOLOGISM; SALVATION; SECULARISM; SUPERNATURAL EXISTENTIAL.

Bibliography: *Encyclopedic Dictionary of the Bible,* tr. and adap. by L. HARTMAN (New York 1963) from A. VAN DEN BORN, *Bijbels Woordenboek,* esp. "Eschatology," 677–686;"Glory," 867–871; "Grace," 897–903; "Mystery," 1578–84; "Predestination," 1909–10. X. LÉON-DUFOUR, ed., *Vocabulaire de théologie biblique* (Paris 1962), esp. "Dessein de Dieu," 208–215; "Gloire," 412–419; "Grâce," 420–424; "Mystère," 664–670. R. FOLLET and K. PRÜMM, *Dictionaire de la Bible,* suppl. ed. L. PIROT, et al. (Paris 1928–) 6:1–225, esp. 173–225. Vatican Council II, *Lumen gentium, Acta Apostolicae Sedis* 57 (Rome 1965) 5–67, esp. ch. 1, 2, 7. JOHN XXIII, "Mater et Magistra," *Acta Apostolicae Sedis* 53 (1961) 401–464 encyclical. PAUL VI, "Ecclesiam suam" (encyclical, Aug. 6, 1964) in *Acta Apostolicae Sedis* 56 (1964) 609–659. H. DE LUBAC, *Surnaturel: Études historiques* (Paris 1946); "Le Mystère du surnaturel," *Rechershes de science religieuse* 36 (Rome 1949) 80–121. J. MARITAIN, *True Humanism,* tr. M. R. ADAMSON (6th ed. New York 1954). M. SECKLER, *Instinkt und Glaubenswille nach Thomas von Aquin* (Mainz 1961). P. J. DONNELLY, "Discussions on the Supernatural Order," *Theological Studies* 9 (1948) 213–249; "The Gratuity of the Beatific Vision and the Possibility of a Natural Destiny," *Theological Studies* 11 (1950) 374–404. É. H. GILSON, "Sur la problématique thomiste de la vision béatifique," *Archives d'histoire doctrinale et littéraire du moyenâge* 31 (Paris 1964) 67–88. A. MICHEL, "Nature et surnaturel," *Ami du Clergé* 67 (Langres 1957) 435–440, doctrine of Pius XII. T. J. MOTHERWAY, "Supernatural Existential," *Chicago Studies* 4 (1965) 79–103. L. RENWART, "La 'Nature pure' à la lumière de l'encyclique *Humani generis,"* *Nouvelle revue théologique* 74 (Tournai-Louvain-Paris 1952) 337–354. E. SCHILLEBEECKX, "L'Instinct de la foi selon S. Thomas d'Aquin," *Revue des sciences philosophiques et théologiques* 48 (Paris 1964) 377–408.

[W. H. PRINCIPE]

DESURMONT, ACHILLE

Redemptorist ascetical writer; b. Tourcoing, France, Dec. 23, 1828; d. Thury-en-Valois, July 23, 1898. Professed as a Redemptorist in 1851 and ordained in 1853, he became successively prefect of seminarians, professor of theology, provincial of the French province of his congregation from 1865 to 1887, and again in 1898. In spite of his administrative and pastoral activities, he made a considerable contribution to spiritual literature. The contents of his *Rapports de Notre Règle avec la fin de Notre Institut* (1854) are evident from the title. His principles of pastoral practice are found in his posthumous work, *La Charité sacerdotale* (Paris 1899). He founded the periodical *La Sainte Famille* and contributed to it more than 300 articles. Retreats, essays, meditations, prayers, hymns, apologetic dialogues, histories of devotions, and biographies of saints were published in his *Oeuvres Complètes* (12 v. Paris 1906–13). He was steeped in the ascetical spirit of St. ALPHONSUS LIGUORI, and his works represent an expression and adaptation of that spirit to contemporary needs.

Bibliography: A. GEORGES, *Le T. R. P. Achille Desurmont,* (Paris 1924). J. BOUBÉE, "Les Oeuvres du T. R. P. Desurmont," *Études* 120 (1909) 563–574. G. LIÉVIN, *Dictionnaire de spiritualité ascétique et mystique. Doctrine et histoire,* ed. M. VILLER et al.

(Paris 1932–) 3:648–651. P. P. POURRAT, *Christian Spirituality*, tr. W. MITCHELL and S. JACQUES (Westminster, Md. 1953–55) 4:389–391.

[J. M. COLLERAN]

DETRACTION

An act whereby a person takes something from the reputation or worth of another with a view of lessening him in the estimation of others, depreciating another from envy or malice, or representing his merit as less than it really is. The theological significance of the term detraction has varied during the centuries. Early theologians used the term in practically the same way as it is preserved in modern English, but with the added notion of the act's taking place in the person's absence or "secretly." Currently theologians make a different distinction, namely, between statements that reveal damaging truths about another unnecessarily and those that are deliberate lies. The former is called detraction, the latter is called calumny. Hence, detraction is the blackening of an absent person's good name by unnecessarily revealing a true but hidden crime, sin, or defect. "Blackening" is used to express the effect of detraction, namely, dulling or obscuring the luster of a good name.

Scripture points out that a good name ". . . is more desirable than great riches" (Prv 22.1). Blackening another's good name is more than an uncharitable act; it is a sin of injustice. That the detracting statements are true is not a justification for their being made. The hidden truth about another that would damage his reputation may not be revealed without necessity.

Morality. The sinfulness of detraction depends on the detractor's intentions and the realization of the damaging effect that his words will have. The actual harm to reputation depends on the nature of the fact revealed, the reputation of the person wronged, the credibility of the detracting person, etc. A detractor who cannot gain an attentive audience is harmless. Eager listeners, on the other hand, encourage the detractor; and hence share in the malice of the sinful act. Moreover, one who deliberately initiates or prolongs the detracting conversation by questioning also participates to some extent in the sinful action.

The detractor is obliged to repair the damage done to the person's reputation. If other harm, e.g., monetary, has been caused and was foreseen by the detractor, this must also be repaired. The detractor can make partial reparation of the harm done by speaking in a friendly way about the person wronged, by showing him deference, etc. The impossibility of adequately restoring the lost reputation should serve as an added deterrent to a detracting tongue.

Exceptions. The virtue of veracity forbids lying at all times, but it does not demand that a person reveal the truth at all times. There are occasions when a person is obliged in conscience to hide the truth. On the other hand, a person may sometimes licitly reveal the truth, even though this may result in harm to another's reputation. Examples of this occur when there is a conflict between the rights of the person about whom something discreditable is known and moral rights of equal or greater urgency. Thus, when the continued ignorance of a blackening truth will cause harm to the common good, to an innocent third party, to the one about whom the truth is known, or to the one who knows the truth, the facts need not be kept secret. For example, one who knows that an innocent person will be sent to prison may licitly reveal the identity of the true criminal. For the manifestation of a blackening truth to be licit, it must be a necessary means to avoid harm, and the manifestation must be made with as little injury to the person's reputation as possible.

The view of earlier theologians in regard to the good name of one who had been sentenced to prison were based on the court's intention to deprive the criminal of his reputation, to safeguard society against criminals, etc. The civil law today does not intend the perpetual deprivation of the good name of the criminal. Present-day rehabilitation procedures confirm this view. Hence, contemporary moralists incline to the view that the forgotten past of one who has changed his name, moved to a different section of the country, and is now living as a respected citizen cannot be legitimately divulged.

Bibliography: D. M. PRÜMMER, *Manuale theologiae moralis*, ed. E. M. MÜNCH (12th ed. Freiburg-Barcelona 1955) 2:165–201. B. H. MERKELBACH, *Summa theologiae moralis* (8th ed. Paris 1949) 2:423–432. THOMAS AQUINAS, *Summa theologiae* 2a2ae, 73–74. A. THOUVENIN, *Dictionnaire de théologie catholique*, (Paris 1903–50) 10.1:487–494. K. MOORE, *The Moral Principles Governing the Sin of Detraction . . .* (Washington 1950).

[K. B. MOORE]

DETROIT, ARCHDIOCESE OF

The Archdiocese of Detroit is a metropolitan see comprised of six counties of southeastern Michigan: Lapeer, Macomb, Monroe, Oakland, St. Clair, and Wayne (3901 square miles), with a total population of more than 4,260,000, predominantly of English, German, Polish, Irish, and African-American extraction, including about 1,430,000 Catholics (34 percent). In 2001 they were served by 485 diocesan priests and 294 religious order priests, 146 permanent deacons, 130 brothers, and 1,900 sisters, in 308 parishes and 4 missions, with 34 Catholic high schools and 134 Catholic grade schools.

Adam Cardinal Maida of the Archdiocese of Detroit. (AP/Wide World Photos)

The diocese was established on March 8, 1833; the archdiocese, on Aug. 3, 1937. Gaylord, Grand Rapids, Kalamazoo, Lansing, Marquette, and Saginaw dioceses in Michigan are suffragans of Detroit.

Catholicism in Michigan began in the northern area of the state due to pressures from the Iroquois confederation which kept both Native Americans and missionaries from the southeastern part of the lower peninsula. The first known priest in the Detroit area was Fr. François Dollier who was accompanied by Deacon René de Galine (1670). A stable ecclesial settlement, however, had to await the founding of a French fort at Detroit in 1701 and its parish of Ste. Anne. The entire area was turned over to the British in 1763. Bishop John Carroll of Baltimore added the area to his diocese in 1796 when the British left. Carroll sent two former Sulpicians, Michael LEVA-DOUX and GABRIEL RICHARD to pasture the Catholics in the present area of Michigan and Wisconsin. Richard proved to be a heroic leader of the community, helping it recover from the devastating fire of 1805, representing the Territory of Michigan in Congress, and dying ministering to cholera victims in 1832.

The first bishop of Detroit, Frederic Résé (1833–1871), arrived with high hopes but eventually was forced to retire to Europe in 1840 due to a series of conflicts. His coadjutor bishop, Peter Paul Lefevere (1841–1868) never actually became the bishop of Detroit, dying prior to Résé. Lefevere brought order and discipline to the diocese and helped it recover from his predecessor's misdeeds. Wisconsin was taken from the diocese in 1843 and the upper peninsula was also removed from Lefevere's jurisdiction in 1853. Caspar Henry Borgess served as coadjutor from 1870 to Résé's death and then as ordinary until his own retirement in 1887. In 1882 a large portion of the western half of the state was removed from Detroit to form the Diocese of Grand Rapids.

John Samuel Foley (1833–1918), a close friend of Cardinal James Gibbons of Baltimore and an Americanist, was ordained the third bishop of Detroit in 1888. His ineptness as a leader in his early years and poor health in the latter ones left the diocese without strong leadership for many years. This was more than alleviated by his successor, Michael Gallagher (1866–1937), who began an energetic term in 1918. He built many diocesan buildings, recruited clergy, centralized offices, and tightened the administration. The greatest memory of Gallagher, however, is his tolerance of the Rev. Charles Coughlin, the "Radio Priest." Gallagher steadfastly refused to silence the man and it is this that most likely explains the Vatican's decision not to raise Detroit to archepiscopal status in Gallagher's lifetime.

Archdiocese. When Edward F. MOONEY, Bishop of Rochester, N.Y., was installed as successor to Gallagher on Aug. 3, 1937, Detroit was made an archdiocese with the suffragan sees of Grand Rapids, Marquette, and the newly established Diocese of Lansing. In early 1938, 16 counties in the Saginaw Bay area and in the northeastern section of the state were assigned to a newly formed diocese with Saginaw as the see city. In the same year Blessed Sacrament Church was named the cathedral of Detroit.

Mooney. The new archbishop faced serious financial problems resulting from the Depression and the heavy archdiocesan debt incurred during the extensive building program of the 1920s. Within a few years Mooney refinanced the debt, and with the institution of the yearly Archdiocesan Development Fund he was able to embark on programs such as the building of St. John's Provincial Seminary; the erection of Boysville, the Catholic Youth Organization Home for Boys; the purchase of a Catholic Charities building; the extensive program of Catholic Family Centers and other social welfare services; Kundig Center and Carmel Hall for the aging; and Our Lady of Providence School for retarded girls. Parish planning was facilitated by the purchase of more than 100 sites for future development. The fund also made possible summer camps, community centers, convents for home-visiting and catechizing sisters. The Gabriel Richard Building in downtown Detroit was purchased to house additional diocesan offices.

When Mooney was appointed to Detroit, the great automotive unions were just beginning. He organized study and training centers to impart the social message of the Church, fostered the work of the Association of Catholic Trade Unionists, and initiated the Archdiocesan Labor Institute to sponsor management-labor forums and discussion meetings on the Church's social doctrine. He also united the many lay groups of women into the Detroit Archdiocesan Council of Catholic Women.

On Feb. 21, 1946, Pius XII conferred on Mooney the honor of cardinal priest. During World War II, the population of the archdiocese had expanded; with peacetime prosperity there was a great exodus to the suburbs of Detroit leaving the "inner city" to underprivileged and minority groups. Missionary efforts were expended to reach the people left in the older parishes of the city, while new parishes sprang up throughout the archdiocese, especially in the environs of Detroit. Educational facilities kept pace. The Mercy Sisters opened Mercy College in 1941 and the Felician Sisters, Madonna College, Livonia, in 1947. The number of Catholic elementary and high schools more than doubled, making the Detroit parochial school system the second largest in Michigan. The Confraternity of Christian Doctrine provides instruction to over 100,000 Catholic children in public schools, through 1,500 sisters and 1,800 laymen and women teaching in 381 centers; in addition it operates summer religious vacation schools and special classes for the deaf.

During the 20 years of Mooney's administration, the Marianhill Mission Society, Irish Pallottine Fathers, Missionaries of SS. Peter and Paul, and the Bernardine Sisters established headquarters in the archdiocese; the Jesuits erected a Detroit province. Two diocesan sisterhoods were founded: the Catholic Mission Sisters of St. Francis Xavier, for work in Japan and India; and the Home Visitors of Mary, for work among converts and lapsed Catholics, especially African Americans. Besides, there was the rich influx of religious to staff parishes, to teach in parochial and central schools, to engage in social service, catechetics, and the home missionary apostolate. Four new hospitals were built: The Mercy Sisters erected Mt. Carmel Mercy in Detroit and Mercy Hospital in Port Huron, the Sisters of St. Francis built Holy Cross, and the Sisters of St. Joseph established St. John Hospital in Detroit. When Cardinal Mooney died on Oct. 25, 1958, Detroit ranked seventh among all the dioceses in the U.S.

Dearden. John Francis DEARDEN, who had been bishop of Pittsburgh, Pa., was transferred to Detroit on Dec. 18, 1958, and installed there Jan. 29, 1959. Dearden retired on July 15, 1980, and died on Aug. 1, 1988. Under Dearden, the Cardinal Mooney Latin School (closed in 1970) was built on the campus of Sacred Heart Seminary to provide additional accommodations for high school students preparing for the diocesan priesthood. Day school programs for retarded children were doubled and the St. Louis School for retarded boys was built. Facilities for the aging were increased by the erection of a 25-unit building for low income pensioners. A student exchange program with Latin America was accelerated and further emphasis was placed on religious and social welfare services for the migrant laborers in southeastern Michigan. In the fall of 1960, the Archbishop's Committee on

Human Relations was organized with priests and laymen to disseminate the Church's teaching on interracial relations. Within two years the Felician Sisters had opened St. Mary's Hospital in Livonia.

During the course of Vatican Council II, Dearden adopted a change in administrative style, becoming much more open and tolerant of diverging views and new ideas. He sought to bring this same openness to the diocese by emphasizing adult education. This was epitomized in the Archdiocesan Synod of 1969, which included a grassroots process of 250,000 responses and was exhortatory rather than prescriptive, and the national Call to Action (1976) gathering in Detroit which celebrated the American Bicentennial. Dearden restructured the archdiocese into subunits called vicariates, urging greater dialogue and collaboration in the Church. After the 1967 race riots in Detroit, Dearden promoted racial harmony. He was created a cardinal on April 18, 1969.

Dearden was well-loved by many in the archdiocese, but his tolerance of creativity led to some liturgical and pastoral abuses. These were addressed by his successor, Edmund Szoka (b. Sept. 14, 1927, Grand Rapids, Mi.). Szoka was ordained the first bishop of Gaylord on July 20, 1971 by Archbishop Luigi Raimondi. On March 28, 1981, after meeting with the Holy Father to discuss the needs of the Church of the Archdiocese of Detroit, Szoka was announced as the new archbishop. His decade of service saw a great deal of controversy: the closing of the Poletown parish (process begun by Cardinal Dearden) and then 31 other parishes in 1989; restructuring of the Tribunal; handling the personnel issues of Fr. Anthony Kosnik and Sr. Mary Agnes Mansour; banning the use of General Absolution; establishing a local Catholic television station; mounting a major Vocations campaign, ''We invite, God calls;'' hosting Pope John Paul II's visit (Sept. 18–19, 1987); closing St. John's Provincial Seminary and opening a theological seminary at Sacred Heart Seminary in 1988; completing major renovation projects of the Chancery buildings and the seminary; substantially raising the annual income of the Catholic Services Appeal (begun in 1982); and making a statement about racial integration when he sponsored Mayor Coleman Young's membership in the all-white Detroit Boat Club (1985). On June 28, 1988, he was elevated to the cardinalate. When Pope John Paul II named him president of the Prefecture of the Economic Affairs of the Holy See in April, 1990, he resigned his see.

His successor, Adam Maida, was born in East Vandergrift, Pa., March 18, 1931. Ordained the bishop of Green Bay on Jan.15, 1984, he was transferred to Detroit on April 28, 1990. He was created a cardinal on Nov. 26, 1994. He established the St. John's Family and Youth Retreat Center at the former provincial theologate.

The archdiocese is fiscally very solvent due to the actions taken by Cardinals Szoka and Maida. Cardinal Maida's diocesan endowment campaign raised over $100 million. In addition, both men brought greater order and discipline to the diocese. As the diocese faced problems stemming a priest shortage and an aging clergy, they furthered programs for the formation of lay ecclesial ministers.

The auxiliary bishops of Detroit have been: Edward Kelly, ordained a bishop on Jan. 26, 1911, and transferred to Grand Rapids on Jan. 16, 1919; Joseph Casimir Plagens, ordained a bishop on Sept. 30, 1924, and transferred to Marquette on Nov. 16, 1935; Stephen Woznicki, ordained a bishop on Jan. 24, 1938, and transferred to Saginaw on March 28, 1950; Allen Babcock, ordained a bishop on March 25, 1947, and transferred to Grand Rapids on March 23, 1954; Alexander Zaleski, ordained a bishop on May 23, 1950, and transferred to Lansing on Oct. 7, 1964; Henry Donnelly, ordained a bishop on Oct. 26, 1954; John Donovan, ordained a bishop on Oct. 26, 1954, and transferred to Toledo on Feb. 25, 1967; Joseph Breitenbeck, ordained a bishop on Dec. 20, 1965, and transferred to Grand Rapids on Oct. 6, 1969; Thomas Gumbleton and Walter Schoenherr, both ordained bishops on May 1, 1968; Arthur Krawczak, ordained bishop on April 3, 1973, and transferred to Joliet on June 30, 1979; Moses Anderson, ordained a bishop on Jan. 27, 1983; Patrick Cooney, ordained a bishop on Jan. 27, 1983, and transferred to Gaylord on Nov. 6, 1989; Dale Melczek, ordained a bishop on Jan. 27, 1983, and transferred to Gary, Aug. 19, 1992, as administrator and later as ordinary; Bernard Harrington, ordained a bishop on Jan. 6, 1994, and transferred to Winona on Nov. 6, 1998; Kevin Britt, ordained a bishop on Jan. 6, 1994; John Nienstedt, ordained a bishop on July 9, 1996, and transferred to New Ulm on June 12, 2001; Allen Vigneron, ordained a bishop on July 9, 1996; and Leonard Blair, ordained a bishop on Aug. 24, 1998.

Bibliography: G. B. CATLIN, *The Story of Detroit* (Detroit 1926). J. K. JAMISON, *By Cross and Anchor: The Story of Frederic Baraga* (Paterson 1946). P. L. JOHNSON, *Stuffed Saddlebags: The Life of Martin Kundig, Priest* (Milwaukee 1942). G. W. PARÉ, *The Catholic Church in Detroit, 1701–1888* (Detroit 1951). F. B. WOODFORD and A. HYMA, *Gabriel Richard: Frontier Ambassador* (Detroit 1958). S. AGER, ''Through the Eye of a Needle [:Archbishop Edmund Szoka].'' *Detroit 10–25*. E. BOYEA, ''Father Kolasinski and the Church of Detroit.'' *Catholic Historical Review* 74:420–39. L. TENTLER, *Seasons of Grace: A History of the Catholic Archdiocese of Detroit* (Detroit 1990). R. F. TRISCO, *The Holy See and the Nascent Church in the Middle Western United States, 1826–1850* (Rome 1962). J. WYLIE, *Poletown: Community Betrayed* (Urbana 1989).

[F.X. CANFIELD/E. B. BOYEA]

DEUS SCIENTIARUM DOMINUS

The apostolic constitution *Deus scientiarum dominus,* issued on Pentecost, May 24, 1931, was promulgated in *Acta Apostolicae Sedis* in July together with the *Ordinationes* for its implementation, which were issued by the Congregation of Seminaries and Universities on June 12, 1931.

Purpose. The purpose of the constitution was to foster perfection in ecclesiastical studies by the establishing of uniformity of ends, methods, and forms of instruction in all faculties and universities; by providing a broad, solid base for primary theological training; and by ensuring constant value to the doctorate.

The desired uniformity was to be achieved by (1) extending the Congregation's control to matters academic and economic in all institutes granting pontifical degrees; (2) ensuring responsible direction of the institutes, and requiring adequate and qualified personnel, proper physical installations, and financial stability; (3) establishing minimum requirements for admission and for conferring degrees; and (4) increasing the basic requirements for the doctorate to include original scientific research and specialization, as well as a sound general formation.

Legislation. The introduction, after detailing the history of the interest of the Church in education, states that the contemporary needs of the Church for profound, scholarly work in the sacred sciences prompted a study of ecclesiastical faculties and universities, by an appointed group of experts, from which issued the present legislation.

Title I. General Norms (1–12). Universities and Faculties of Ecclesiastical Studies are those that are established by the authority of the Holy See with the right to confer academic degrees. The purpose of these institutes is to form students to a profound knowledge of the sacred sciences. The institutes concerned are those that teach philosophy, theology, or Canon Law, and the five Roman Pontifical Institutes. The canonical erection and the direction of all faculties is reserved to the Congregation, which approves the institutes and empowers them to confer degrees.

Title II. Academic Officers, Professors, Students (13–28). The rector is named or confirmed by the Congregation, whereas the university names the other officers and determines their functions. The university also establishes the number, duties, rights, nomination, promotion, etc., of the professors whose quality as ordinary, extraordinary, or temporary are here indicated. The *Ordinationes* set the conditions for the admission of students to the institute, for conferral of degrees, and for transfer to another institute, in more detail.

Title III. Programs and Methods of Study (29–34). The study of positive theology and the scholastic method, according to the principles and doctrine of St. Thomas, are prescribed for theology. In philosophy, a study of the methods and principles of St. Thomas is to precede the examination and appreciation of the various philosophical systems. Besides the regular courses, there are to be seminars to teach scientific research and the written exposition thereof.

Title IV. The Granting of Degrees (35–40). The requirements are, in general, regular attendance at courses, the profession of faith, and a regular cycle of studies. For the doctorate, there are required, besides five years in theology, four in philosophy, three in canon law, etc., (1) a dissertation, published in part, which is useful for the progress of the science and proves the aptness of the candidate for scientific research and writing; (2) a public defense of the dissertation; and (3) some other public specimen of the candidate's capability.

Title V. Teaching Adjuncts and Economic Matters (47–52). Buildings must be ample, functional, and well-equipped for scholarly work. The salaries, pensions, etc., of the personnel must provide them a living consonant with their state in life. Fees for students are to be established by the institute.

Title VI. Transitory Norms (53–58). By the effective date, the academic year 1932 and 1933, all contrary prescriptions and privileges are revoked.

Bibliography: C. BOYER, "Annotationes," *Periodica de re morali canonica liturgica* 20 (1931) 298–312, J. DE GHELLINCK, "La Nouvelle constitution sur les études," *Nouvelle revue théologique* 58 (1931) 769–785.

[V. M. BURNS]

DEUS, TUORUM MILITUM

An Ambrosian hymn historically assigned for Matins and Vespers for the common feast of a martyr in the Roman BREVIARY. It dates probably from the sixth century and is attributed to the unknown author of *REX GLORIOSE MARTYRUM* and *JESU, REDEMPTOR OMNIUM.* The hymn exists in a longer version of eight strophes and a shorter one of four, which is probably earlier. The Vatican antiphonary provided two different melodies for use in the paschal season and during the octave of the Nativity, during which the feast of STEPHEN THE PROTOMARTYR occurs. The hymn is a prayer of the Christian assembly asking God to forgive the sins of His servants on the day of the martyr's triumph over the pleasures of the world and the torture of persecution.

Bibliography: *Analecta hymnica* 51:130–131, text. R. GAZEAU, *Catholicisme* 3:698. J. CONNELLY, *Hymns of the Roman*

Liturgy (Westminster, MD 1957) 140–143, Eng. tr. J. SZÖVÉRFFY, *Die Annalen der lateinischen Hymnendichtung* (Berlin 1964–65) 1:65, 96.

[M. M. BEYENKA]

DEUSDEDIT, COLLECTION OF

The Collection of Deusdedit is the second major canonical work under Pope Gregory VII, after that of ANSELM II OF LUCCA, compiled between 1083 and 1087 and dedicated to Pope Victor III. Few facts are known of the author's life. By his own report, he was an only child and already cardinal priest of St. Peter in Chains (*in Eudoxia*) in his early 30s; he is first mentioned by this title in 1078 by BERENGARIUS OF TOURS, who further identified him as a monk of Tulle (*Tudelensis:* Benedictine Abbey of St. Martin, Diocese of Limoges). Dates and details of his Roman career are unknown. He spent some time in Germany, perhaps on a papal mission, where he found material for his collection. A most strenuous promoter of the full GREGORIAN reform program, he wrote in its defense against the adherents of antipope Clement III his *Libellus contra invasores,* completed in 1097 under Pope Urban II. He died in 1100.

The primary purpose of his *Collectio canonum* was to buttress the privileged status and universal rights and responsibilities of the Roman primacy in the Universal Church, as a basis for achieving the ends of the reform. It was planned systematically in four books: 1, the Roman Church's authority; 2, the Roman clergy; 3, the Roman Church's temporalities; 4, the liberty of the Church in its personnel and properties. Its mass of texts (1,173 items) includes many disciplinary norms of general utility. Four tables of rubrics (*capitulationes*) provide an index to facilitate use. In addition to the collections already in use (DIONYSIUS Exiguus, HISPANA COLLECTIO, FALSE DECRETALS, BURCHARD'S *Decretum,* Collection in SEVENTY-FOUR Titles, ATTO'S Collection), he drew upon sources newly exploited by contemporary compilers in the *LIBER DIURNUS, Ordines Romani,* LIBER Pontificalis, Roman civil law, and the papal archives. Although of limited influence, the collection of Deusdedit provides valuable evidence of the aims and methods of the 11th–century papal reform, and of the obligation of the secular arm to enforce them.

See Also: CANONICAL COLLECTIONS BEFORE GRATIAN.

Bibliography: Editions. V. WOLF VON GLANVELL, ed., *Die Kanonessammlung des Kardinals Deusdedit: Die Kanonessammlung, selbst* (Paderborn 1905), all published. E. SACKUR, ed., *Libellus contra invasores et symoniacos et reliquos scismaticos,* in *Monumenta Germaniae Historica: Libelli de lite* (Berlin 1826–) (1892) 292–365. Literature. P. FOURNIER and G. LE BRAS, *Histoire des collections canoniques en occident depuis les fausses décrétales jusqu'au Décret de Gratien,* 2 v. (Paris 1931–32) 2:37–54. P. FOURNIER, "Les Collections canoniques romaines de l'époque de Grégoire VII," *Mémoires' de l'Académie des inscriptions et belles–lettres* 41 (1918) 271–395, also separate. W. HOLTZMANN, "Kardinal Deusdedit als Dichter," *Historisches Jahrbuch der Görres–Gesellschaft* 57 (1937) 217–232 with biog. details. C. LÉFEBVRE, *Dictionnaire de droit canonique,* ed. R. NAZ, 7 v. (Paris 1935–65) 4:1186–91.

[J. J. RYAN]

DEUSDEDIT I (ADEODATUS), POPE, ST.

Pontificate: Oct. 19, 615 to Nov. 8, 618; b. Rome. The successor of BONIFACE IV, Deusdedit had been a priest in Rome for 40 years when he began his three-year pontificate. At the time Italy was a battleground for the LOMBARDS, despite the attempts of the exarchs in Ravenna to control the peninsula in the name of the Byzantine Emperor. (*See* RAVENNA.) Following an uprising in which the exarch John and his officials were killed, the emperor HERACLIUS sent Eleutherius as exarch to Ravenna to restore order. The exarch put to death the murderers of John and marched to Naples to subdue other revolutionists. The pope remained loyal to the emperor and the exarch in these dim conflicts. Deusdedit also had to contend with an earthquake and a plague in Rome itself. Legend records that the pope restored a sufferer to instant health with a kiss. He was esteemed for his love of the diocesan clergy as contrasted with Gregory the Great's favoring of monks. He was buried in St. Peter's.

Feast: Nov. 8.

Bibliography: *Liber pontificalis,* ed. L. DUCHESNE (Paris 1886–1958) 1:319–320. P. JAFFÉ, *Regesta pontificum romanorum ab condita ecclesia ad annum post Christum natum 1198* (Graz 1956) 1:222; 2:698,739. H. K. MANN, *The Lives of the Popes in the Early Middle Ages from 590 to 1304* (London 1902–32) 1:280–293. O. BERTOLINI, *Roma di fronte a Bisanzio e ai Longobardi* (Bologna 1941). B. BOTTE, *Dictionnaire d'histoire et de géographie ecclésiastiques,* ed. A. BAUDRILLART et al. (Paris 1912) 14:356–357. J. N. D. KELLY, *Oxford Dictionary of Popes* (New York 1986) 69.

[C. E. SHEEDY]

DEUSDEDIT OF MONTE CASSINO, ST.

Abbot and martyr; d. 834. He became abbot of the BENEDICTINE foundation at MONTE CASSINO in 828. After the death of Sicon (833), prince of Benevento, with whom he was on friendly terms, Deusdedit was taken captive by Sicon's son Sicard (d. 839) who wished to appropriate the property of the abbey; Deusdedit was allowed to die in prison. Many miracles are reported to have been worked at his tomb, but the exact location of his remains is not now certain, and sometimes they have been erroneously confused with those of Pope St. DEUS-DEDIT I, venerated in S. Giovanni di Valle Roveto in the Diocese of Sora.

Feast: October 9.

Bibliography: LEO MARSICANUS and PETER THE DEACON, *Chronica monasterii Casinensis,* ed. W. WATTENBACH, *Monumenta Germaniae Historica: Scriptores* 7:596. PETER THE DEACON, *De ortu et obitu justorum coenobii Casinensis,* ch. 27, *Patrologia Latina* ed. J. P. MIGNE (Paris 1878–90) 173:1090. J. MABILLON, *Acta sanctorum ordinis S. Benedicti* (Venice 1733–40) 6:472. E. GATTOLA, *Historia abbatiae Cassinensis,* 2 v. (Venice 1733). L. TOSTI, *Storia della badia di Montecassino,* 4 v. (Rome 1888–90). G. FALCO, "Lineamenti di storia Cassinese nei secoli VIII e IX," *Casinensia,* v. 2 (Monte Cassino 1929) 512. A. M. ZIMMERMANN, *Kalendarium Benedictinum,* (Metten 1933–38) 3:155–158.

[A. LENTINI]

DEUTERONOMISTS

A term applied to the school of writers responsible for the great historical work contained in Deuteronomy to 2 Kings inclusive. The traditional division into the Pentateuch and the historical books was made late in the postexilic period and was based on religious, not literary, analysis; the Pentateuch contains the normative Torah, or Law, for Judaism. Literary analysis, however, indicates that the Deuteronomistic vocabulary, style, and especially theology are found in the following historical books in the form of editorial comments and judgments on the period in question. This suggests that the book of Deuteronomy was drawn up in its present form as an introduction to the history that follows and that the history itself is a collection of ancient material, now given a literary unity by the Deuteronomists (D). In this view the significance of a HEXATEUCH would be greatly lessened. The fate of the supposed YAHWIST (J), ELOHIST (E), and Priestly (P; *see* PRIESTLY WRITERS, PENTATEUCHAL) accounts of the Israelite conquest of Canaan in the later editorial work is now extremely difficult to assess. The Deuteronomistic history was seemingly concluded some time during the Exile; the last reference is to the release of Jehoiakim, king of Judah, from prison by the Babylonian king Evil-Merodach (2 Kgs 25.27–30), which probably reflects the author's hope for the end of the Exile.

The theology of D is based principally on the conception of the covenant as expressing God's free loving choice of Israel (Dt 7.8; 23.6; etc.) and of the Law as Israel's loving response to that choice (Dt 6.5–9; 11.1; 19.9; etc.). From this flows the conviction that prosperity and divine blessings are the rewards of loving service (Dt 6.1–3; 11.1–25; 28.1–14; etc.), while disobedience brings punishment (Dt 11.26–28; 28.15–69; etc.). These same ideas, expressed in much the same vocabulary, are found in the historical books that follow and are the basis of the Deuteronomistic judgment on history. The four principles of disobedience, punishment, prayer, and deliverance, contained in the book of Deuteronomy, are succinctly presented in Jgs 2.11–19. The identification of the authors responsible for this work is impossible. Deuteronomistic ideas and terminology are found elsewhere in the OT, particularly in Hosea and Jeremiah. This would indicate that a Deuteronomistic theology and literary style were not confined to one period or to one kingdom. Because of the emphasis on the covenant, an emphasis found also in the northern E tradition, there are those who would trace the origin of D's theology, vocabulary, and style to the North. These elements would have been greatly developed in the South after the destruction of Israel in 721 B.C. The ideas, developed by a "school of D" and by men such as Jeremiah, would have provided the basis for Josiah's reform about a century later.

Bibliography: M. NOTH, *Überlieferungsgeschichtliche Studien* (Halle 1943–). G. VON RAD, *Studies in Deuteronomy,* tr. D. STALKER (Chicago 1953).

[E. H. MALY]

DEUTERONOMY, BOOK OF

The fifth and last book of the Pentateuch, Deuteronomy is presented as a second legislation of Moses given the nation just before it entered the Promised Land. This article treats in order the book's name, division, contents, and date of composition.

Name. The English name Deuteronomy is based on a transliteration of the Septuagint title τὸ δευτερονόμιον (the second law), itself an incorrect Greek rendering of the Hebrew term *mišnê hattôrâ* (Dt 17.18), more correctly translated as the copy or duplicate of the law.

Division. The book lends itself to a sixfold division. In the first section (Dt 1.1–4.43) the journey from Mt. Horeb to Baal Phogar is related in historical retrospect by Moses. In the second section (4.44–11.32) Moses explains with repeated exhortations that the nation's life and prosperity depend on observance of the covenant. The third section (12.1–26.19), technically known as the Deuteronomic Code, contains laws of religious cult, national and religious institutions, family life, and personal ethics. In the fourth section (27.1–28.69) Moses, with the elders of Israel, exhorts the people to fidelity to the Law;

curses are pronounced against the nation if it should be disobedient, while blessings are promised the nation if it is faithful to Yahweh. The fifth section (29.1–30.20) contains a fresh exhortation to observe the covenant. The sixth and final section (31.1–34.12) contains the final events of Moses' life. He commissions Joshua as the new leader, warns the nation against apostasy in a didactic song known as the Canticle of Moses (32.1–32.43), and alludes to the nation's tribal history in a prophetic-styled song called Moses' Oracles (33.2–29). The last chapter of Deuteronomy narrates Moses' death and burial.

Contents. Above all, Deuteronomy contains a long section of legislation (ch. 12–26), most notable for its hortative framework, concern for centralization of cult, solicitude for the underprivileged, and insistence on Israel's separation from other peoples. The covenant-inspired legislation, instead of imposing itself on the people by authority, attempts to persuade them to obey the Law for the nation's welfare and thus for their own.

A version of the Ten Commandments, almost synonymous for the COVENANT in the mind of the author, appears in the book (5.6–18); so, too, does the great commandment of love of God, the ethical center of religion (6.5; cf. Mk 12.29–30 and parallels). It is much emphasized and repeated in the book that the children must be instructed in the Law by their parents (Dt 6.27; 11.29; 31.13), since the nation's future in the land depends on their obedience to the Law (5.26; 11.21).

Separation from the religious practices of other peoples is a recurrent theme of the book (7.25; 12.29–31; 18.9; 20.16–18). The Israelites must never forget they are God's chosen people, a holy people, His inheritance (4.20), and peculiar property (sᵉgûlâ, 7.6; 14.2), a people apart, who must avoid contamination from corrupt religions of other peoples. Although the stranger (gēr) in their midst is to be loved (1.16; 10.19; 24.14; 27.19), still the ban (anathema, Heb. ḥerem) is sanctioned against the idolatrous Canaanites (7.2), the stubborn enemy in war (20.16), and even the Israelite city that would harbor apostates (13.16). Deuteronomy is colored by a nationalistic sentiment (see Manley, 31–33); in its teaching on RETRIBUTION attention is focused on national solidarity.

Date of Composition. It is now commonly agreed that Deuteronomy in its present form is connected with the religious reform of Josiah. In 2 Kings it is narrated how Hilkiah the high priest, while engaged in taking money from the Temple treasury to pay the workmen, found a hitherto unknown "book of the Law" whence Josiah inaugurated a religious reform (2 Kgs 22.3–13). The main reform of Josiah was centralization of cult in agreement with the "reform" prescription of Deuteronomy ch. 12. Modern exegetes interpret the centralization

Intermingled with stones and earth are fragments of ancient scroll Deuteronomy, which pertains to the 33rd chapter of the Book of Deuteronomy discovered in Masada, Israel. (©Bettmann/CORBIS)

of cult, so strongly emphasized in Deuteronomy (12.5, 14, 18; 14.23–24; 15.20; 16.2, 6, 11; 26.2) as a reform of the previous Pentateuchal legislation (Ex 20.24) that permitted worship in many sanctuaries scattered throughout Israel (see Driver, *Introduction,* 85; Eissfeldt, 263). Other reform moves of Josiah (2 Kgs 23.4–24), designed to prevent contamination with foreign cults, coincide with the laws and spirit of Deuteronomy. From these reform laws, 19th-century criticism, beginning with M. L. De Wette in 1805 and climaxed by the Graf-Wellhausen hypothesis in the latter part of the 19th century, maintained that the Law found in the Temple must have contained the substance of present Deuteronomy. This is still the reigning hypothesis, and a date of the 7th century B.C. is generally ascribed to Deuteronomy. However, criticism and resistance to this hypothesis have grown during the last 30 years (see Manley, 9–22). The 7th-century date does not mean that Deuteronomy is a totally new creation of this period; its sources, written and oral, go back, at least in its central message, to much older legislation in the spirit of Moses. Since it was the practice in Israel to modify, reinterpret, and make additions to existing documents according to religious and social exigencies of later times, it is not surprising that Deuteronomy took on its peculiar emphasis and style from a redaction in the 7th century B.C. of a document written a century before perhaps in the Northern Kingdom of Israel.

Bibliography: S. R. DRIVER, *Deuteronomy* (*International Critical Commentary*; New York 1906); *An Introduction to the Literature of the Old Testament* (11th ed. New York 1905) 69–103. A. C. WELCH, *Deuteronomy: The Framework to the Code* (London 1932). G. R. BERRY, "The Date of Deuteronomy," *Journal of Biblical Literature* (Boston 1881–) 59 (1940) 133–139. J. P. HYATT, "Jeremiah and Deuteronomy," *Journal of Near Eastern Studies* 1 (1942) 156–173. O. EISSFELDT, *Einleitung in das A.T.* (2d ed.Tübingen 1956), 202–206, 262–278. C. R. NORTH, "Pentateuchal Criticism," *The Old Testament and Modern Study,* ed. H. H. ROWLEY (Oxford 1951) 48–82. G. T. MANLEY, *The Book of the Law: Studies in the Date of Deuteronomy* (Grand Rapids 1957). G. VON RAD, *Studies in Deuteronomy,* tr. D. M. G. STALKER (Chicago 1953); *Old Testament Theology,* tr. D. M. G. STALKER (New York 1962–) 1:71–80, 99, 219–231. W. L. MORAN, "The Ancient Near Eastern Background of the Love of God in Deuteronomy," *The Catholic Biblical Quarterly* 35 (1963) 77–87.

[B. VEROSTKO]

Untersuchung zum Kolosserbrief als Beitrag zur Methodik von Sprachvergleichen (Göttingen 1973). G. B. CAIRD, *Paul's Letters from Prison* (London 1976). J. E. CROUCH, *The Origin and Intention of the Colossian Haustafel* (Göttingen 1973). N. A. DAHL, "Interpreting Ephesians: Then and Now." *Theology Digest* 25 (1977) 305–315. R. DEICHGRÄBER, *Gotteshymnus und Christushymnus in der frühen Christenheit* (Göttingen 1967). K.G. ECKART, "Der Zweite echte Brief des Apostel Paulus an die Thessalonicher," *Zeitschrift für Theologie und Kirche* 58 (1961) 30–44. K.-M. FISCHER, *Tendenz und Absicht des Epheserbriefes* (Göttingen 1973). C. H. GIBLIN, *The Threat to Faith: An Exegetical and Theological Re-examination of 2 Thessalonians 2* (Rome 1967). J. GNILKA, *Der Epheserbrief* (3rd ed. Freiburg 1982). E. J. GOODSPEED, *The Meaning of Ephesians* (Chicago 1933). L. E. KECK and V. P. FURNISH, *The Pauline Letters: Interpreting Biblical Texts* (Nashville 1984). E. LOHSE, *Colossians and Philemon* (Philadelphia 1971). R. P. MARTIN, *Colossians and Philemon* (London 1981). W. A. MEEKS, *The First Urban Christians: The Social World of the Apostle Paul* (New Haven and London 1983). B. RIGAUX, *Saint Paul: Les Epîtres aur Thessaloniciens* (Paris 1956). A. VAN ROON, *The Authenticity of Ephesians* (Leiden 1974).

[M. P. HORGAN]

DEUTERO-PAULINE LITERATURE

The term "Deutero-Pauline" refers to New Testament letters that are included in the Pauline corpus but are now viewed by most critical scholars as products, not of the apostle Paul, but of Paul's followers or perhaps of a Pauline school. The letters thus designated are 2 Thessalonians, Colossians, Ephesians, and the Pastoral Epistles—1 and 2 Timothy and Titus. In previous volumes they are treated under individual headings (q.v.), but in this article they are dealt with as a group. For 1 and 2 Timothy and Titus, however, *see* PASTORAL EPISTLES.

In the New Testament, 2 Thessalonians, Colossians, and Ephesians purport to be from the hand of Paul (2 Thes 1:1; 2:17; Col 1:1; 4:18; Eph 1:1), and the tradition has regarded them as authentic Pauline writings (e.g., Polycarp, Justin, Marcion, Irenaeus, Muratorian Canon, Hippolytus of Rome, and Tertullian). Modern scholars have challenged the authenticity of these letters chiefly for the following reasons: the letters show differences in style, vocabulary, and theology from the undisputed Pauline letters, and they address issues and situations that do not correspond to those of Paul's lifetime, but seem to reflect a later period. Some scholars have seen in the Deutero-Pauline letters, especially in Colossians and Ephesians, evidence for a Pauline school, perhaps centered in Ephesus, that preserved, developed, and applied the Pauline teachings.

Bibliography: J. A. BAILEY, "Who Wrote II Thessalonians?" *New Testament Studies* 25 (1979) 131–45. M. BARTH, *Ephesians* (Garden City, N.Y. 1974). E. BEST. *The First and Second Epistles to the Thessalonians* (New York 1972). W. BUJARD, *Stilanalytische*

DEVIL

The supreme evil spirit. The term devil is derived from the Greek word διάβολος, which etymologically means an accuser, a slanderer. In classical Greek the word διάβολος was applied, as a noun or an adjective ("slanderous"), only to men, and in this way it is used also in 1 Tm 3.11; 2 Tm 3.3; Ti 2.3. The Septuagint, however, used the term ὁ διάβολος to translate the Hebrew term *haśśāṭān* (the accuser, the adversary), and so also in the New Testament ὁ διάβολος (the devil) is a common synonym for the somewhat less frequently used term ὁ σατάν or ὁ σατανᾶς (Satan). Other New Testament synonyms for the devil are BEELZEBUL, Belial, the Evil One (ὁ πονηρός: Mt 13.19, 38; Jn 17.15; Eph 6.16; etc., and most likely Mt 5.37; 6.13), the Accuser (ὁ κατήγωρ: Rv 12.10), the Tempter (Mt 4.3), the Great Dragon and the Ancient Serpent (Rv 12.9), the Prince of This World (Jn 12.31; 14.30; 16.11), and the God of This World (2 Cor 4.4). The only New Testament occurrence of the term "a devil" (without the definite article in Greek) is in Jn 6.70, where Jesus speaks of Judas Iscariot as a devil, no doubt because Judas was already in the power of the devil (Jn 13.2, 27). Although strictly speaking there is only one devil, just as there is only one Satan, the term is often used broadly in the plural (devils) as a synonym for demons (though never thus in the Bible). *See* DEMON (IN THE BIBLE). For the teaching of the Bible on the devil and for the treatment of the devil in Christian art, *see* SATAN.

Bibliography: *Encyclopedic Dictionary of the Bible,* translated and adapted by L. HARTMAN (New York, 1963) 564–565. F. HORST, *Die Religion in Geschichte und Gegenwart,* 7 v. (3d ed. Tübingen 1957–65) 6:705–707. E. KREBS, *Lexikon für Theologie und Kirche,* ed. M. BUCHBERGER, 10 v. (Freiburg 1930–38) 10:10–17.

[L. F. HARTMAN]

DEVIL WORSHIP

Cultic practices of homage paid to Satan, frequently developed from the doctrine that there are two supreme beings, the one all good, the other all evil. Devil-worshipers have argued that since the God of all the good things receives his homage from many, it is only fitting that the god of wickedness should also have cult and worship paid to him.

The chief liturgical service of the Satanists, or Luciferians, as they are called, was the celebration of the Sabbath. They also possessed a service called the Black Mass, over which they believed Satan himself personally presided. In devious ways they obtained Hosts that were truly consecrated, or, whenever possible, they invited apostate priests for the purpose of consecrating the sacred species so that they could be desecrated and profaned.

Devil worship maintained this manner of cult whenever it was practiced by those acquainted with the Judeo-Christian history and the story of the fall of Lucifer.

There are others, like the Kurd Yezidis who still exist today in Upper Mesopotamia, worshiping Satan under the name of Iblis. They do not believe in dualism, but profess the belief that Satan rebelled against God, and that at a later time he was forgiven and given the government of this world and the administration of the transmigration of souls.

Devil worship is obviously a grievous offense against the virtues of charity and religion for all Christians and in most major religions.

Bibliography: E. A. GRILLOT DE GIVRY, *Picture Museum of Sorcery, Magic and Alchemy* (New Hyde Park, NY 1963). L. CRISTIANI, *Evidence of Satan in the Modern World,* tr. C. ROWLAND (New York 1962). N. CORTE, *Who Is the Devil?,* tr. D. K. PRYCE (New York 1958). H. T. F. RHODES, *The Satanic Mass* (New York 1955).

[M. D. GRIFFIN]

DEVIL'S ADVOCATE

The general promoter of the faith (formerly and popularly called the devil's advocate) is that official of the Congregation of RITES whose duties consist in safeguarding the rights of the faith and the observance of the ecclesiastical laws in processes of beatification and CANONIZATION OF SAINTS. Before the reform of the pro-

"Knight, Death and The Devil," by Albrecht Durer. (AP/Wide World Photos)

cess of canonization by John Paul II's apostolic constitution *Divinus perfectionis magister* (1983), the promoter of the faith took on a legal adversarial role. He was entrusted with opposing the claims of the patrons of the cause and those of the "saint's advocate," thereby earning for himself the easily misunderstood title of "devil's" advocate. In actual fact, he was rather the advocate of the Church, which must be extremely severe in the investigation directed to establish whether or not a baptized person is truly qualified to be beatified or canonized. Statistical data on such causes clearly show that several processes, apparently very promising at the beginning, had to be abandoned later because of difficulties, raised by the promoter of the faith, that could not be satisfactorily answered. In these cases, the critical and seemingly negative work of the promoter of the faith undoubtedly had a great positive value, inasmuch as it prevented the Church from pronouncing a certain and favorable judgment on the life and works of a person without possessing unquestionable proof. The function of the promoter of the faith proved itself most useful in the processes that were successfully concluded. Not only did he guarantee that the proceedings were conducted according to law, but the objections raised by him (*animadversiones*) compelled the patrons of the cause to perform an ever more profound and complete examination of the person in question. Consequently, his activity contributed to the effort of presenting the servant of God in his true image, so that the faithful may come to know the Christian richness of his soul and look on him as a person selected by God for the Church and worthy of beatification and canonization.

Historical Background. A definite juridical structure has been given to processes of beatification and canonization only in relatively recent times. The first mention of the office of promoter of the faith was made at the time of Leo X (1513–21), and the office was united with that of the fiscal advocate. In 1708 Clement XI decreed that these two functions had to be separated; he selected a distinguished jurist, Prospero Lambertini, to discharge the duties of general promoter of the faith. During 20 years of research and study Lambertini established the definitive foundation of the present legislation and outlined, in a clear form, the various rights and duties of the *promotor fidei.* Lambertini, who was elected pope and took the name of Benedict XIV, declared that the offices of promoter of the faith and fiscal advocate were incompatible and decreed that the office of general promoter of the faith had to be autonomous. John Paul II reformed the office so that the promoter of the faith, while still having oversight over the canonization process, no longer acts as a legal adversary.

Bibliography: BENEDICT XIV, *De servorum Dei beatificatione et beatorum canonizatione,* ed. N. and M. PALEARINI, v. 1–4 (3d ed. Rome 1747–49), esp. 1:147–156. A. M. SANTARELLI, ed., *Codex pro Postulatoribus Causarum Beatificationis et Canonizationis* (4th ed. Rome 1929), *passim,* esp. 37–42. JOHN PAUL II, *Divinus perfectionis magister* (Vatican City 1983).

[P. MOLINARI/EDS.]

DEVINE, ARTHUR

Theologian and devotional writer; b. Kilmactiege, Sligo, Ireland, Dec. 1, 1849; d. St. Paul's Retreat, Mount Argus, Dublin, April 20, 1919. Devine entered the Passionist Order in 1865 and was ordained in 1872. He was lector of theology for almost 30 years at St. Joseph's, Highgate Hill, London. From 1884 to 1887 he was consultor to the provincial of his order. During the last 12 years of his life, he taught theology, Scripture, and Canon Law at Mount Argus. While in England he followed the developments of the Oxford Movement with great interest, and through his preaching and direction led many Anglicans into the Catholic Church. He was also interested in the revival of the Gaelic language and preached frequently to his Irish parishioners in that tongue. His chief works are *Auxilium Praedicatorum, a Short Gloss upon the Gospels* (3 v. Dublin 1884); *History of the Passion*

(London 1890); *A Manual of Ascetical Theology* (1903); *The Sacraments Explained* (1918); *The Creed Explained* (1923); and articles for the *Catholic Encyclopedia* and for Catholic magazines.

Bibliography: E. DONOVAN, *The Catholic Encyclopedia,* ed. C. G. HERBERMANN et al. (New York; suppl. 1922) 1:257.

[M. M. BARRY]

DEVOLUTION, RIGHT OF

The right of collation (*COLLATIO*) of an ecclesiastical benefice that an extraordinary collator exercises by default of the ordinary collator. The concept has its origins in steps taken by the General Councils of the 12th and 13th centuries to ensure that benefices, particularly those with a pastoral care attached, were not collated casually or allowed to remain vacant for too long. Thus, when the Third LATERAN COUNCIL in 1179 determined the qualities required in clerics collated to deaneries, parish churches, etc., it added that if a bishop in a given case failed to observe these conditions, then a fresh collation was to be made by his chapter, or, in the event of a similar failure on the part of the chapter, by the metropolitan (c.3: *Conciliorum oecumenicorum decreta* (Bologna-Freiburg 1962) 188–189; *Corpus iurus canonici,* ed. E. Friedberg (Leipzig 1879–81; repr. Graz 1955) X 1.6.7). Further, the council legislated for protracted vacancies (c.8: *ibid.* 191; *Corpus iurus canonici,* X 3.8.2): should a bishop neglect to collate someone within six months to any benefice of which he was patron, his right in that case passed to his chapter; if, on the other hand, a similar situation occurred with respect to a collation belonging to the chapter, then the bishop was to step in; finally, when both bishop and chapter failed in either case to fill the benefice, their metropolitan had to take over the collation (for a later refinement see the decree *Postulasti* of Innocent III in 1212: *Corpus iurus canonici,* X 3.8.15). Reiterating previous legislation on the accumulation of dignities and parochial churches, this same council also ordained (c.13: *ibid.* 194; *Corpus iurus canonici,* X 3.4.3) that any patron collating a cleric who already possessed a dignity or a parochial church was thereby deprived of the right to the collation in question; and that if lay founders of churches or their heirs could not agree within three months of a vacancy upon whom to collate to a particular church of lay foundation, the local bishop was to make the collation (c.17: *ibid.* 196; *Corpus iurus canonici,* X 3.38.3). A generation later the Fourth Lateran Council (1215) made further provision for devolution, decreeing that an ordinary collator of any benefice forfeited by a pluralist had to make a new collation within three months, otherwise his right of collation would "devolve" to another collator (c.29: *ibid.* 224; *Corpus iurus canonici,* X 3.5.28). More importantly, the council ordered that a failure on the part of the clergy of a cathedral church, whether secular or regular, to elect a new bishop within three months of a vacancy, entailed the transference of "the power of electing" to the immediate ecclesiastical superior, who in turn had three months in which to act (c.23: *ibid.* 222; *Corpus iurus canonici* X 1.6.41). Apart from this constitution, the regulations of the Third and Fourth Lateran Councils on collation did not affect benefices in the collation of monastic (i.e., regular) establishments until the Council of VIENNE in 1311 (*Conciliorum oecumenicorum decreta* (Bologna-Freiburg 1962) 338–339. Nowhere in conciliar legislation was a right of devolution granted to the papacy, but in practice there are many instances of the papacy's exercising such a power, e.g., in the pontificate of Pope Innocent III.

Bibliography: G. J. EBERS, *Das Devolutionsrecht vornehmlich nach katholischem Kirchenrecht* (Stuttgart 1906). T. ORTOLAN, *Dictionnaire de théologie catholique,* ed. A. VACANT et al., 15 v. (Paris 1903–50; Tables générales 1951–) 4.1:674–678. G. MOLLAT, *La Collation des bénéfices ecclésiastiques sous les papes d'Avignon* (Paris 1921); *Dictionnaire de droit canonique,* ed. R. NAZ, 7 v. (Paris 1935–65) 2: 414–415. É. JOMBART, *Catholicisme* 3:708–710. W. M. PLÖCHL, *Geschichte des Kirchenrechts,* v.2 (Vienna 1954) 178.

[L. E. BOYLE]

DEVOTIO MODERNA

Devotio Moderna is a school and trend of spirituality that originated in the Netherlands at the end of the 14th century and spread during the 15th century through that region and through the Rhineland, Saxony (J. Busch), Northern France (J. MOMBAER, J. Standonch), Spain (Montserrat), and possibly Italy (L. Barbo).

Origin. Gerard GROOTE (1340–84) was the father and founder of the Devotio Moderna. He was a deacon and a fervent preacher in Deventer. H. Pomerius called him *Fons et origo modernae devotionis* (*c.* 1420). Groote's principal disciple was FLORENTIUS RADEWIJNS (1350–1400), founder of the BRETHREN OF THE COMMON LIFE and of the Canons Regular of WINDESHEIM. In these two institutions the Devotio Moderna acquired a canonical status that enabled it to contribute to western spirituality and to the reform of the Church. It was called "modern" in opposition to the "old" spirituality of the 13th and 14th centuries, which was highly speculative and scholastic in character. The nominalism of Ockham had been hailed as a *via moderna* compared with the *via antiqua* of the Thomists and Scotists; similarly, Groote and his disciples introduced a *devotio moderna* in contrast to the mysticism of ECKHART and TAULER.

Characteristics. The principal features which, taken together, distinguish the Devotio Moderna from other schools and trends of Christian spirituality can be reduced to the following: 1. Christocentrism. The disciples of Groote and Radewijns did not meditate upon the divine nature and attributes, but rather upon Christ's humanity, the virtues of which they sought to imitate (cf. *The Imitation of Christ*). 2. Affectivity. In their attitude toward emotion they followed the Cistercians, Franciscans, and Carthusians, their affectivity tending to be more rational than "enthusiastic." They had a preference for devotion to the Eucharist and to the Passion of Christ. 3. Technique. They introduced method in meditation as well as in the other exercises of life. A complicated example of the method for meditation is to be found in Mombaer's *Scala meditatoria.* 4. Moralism. The Devotio Moderna claimed that the basis of perfection is self-knowledge and the fulfillment of obligations, i.e., the practice of virtue and the avoidance of vice. 5. Asceticism. Without excluding mysticism they nevertheless insisted more upon self-abnegation and the effort of the will. "The more constraint you put on yourself, the more progress you will make; that is certain" (*Imitation of Christ,* 1.25). 6. Antispeculative tendency. The place of learning in their system is clear from their question "What does it profit you to talk learnedly about the Trinity. . . . Of what value is knowledge without the fear of God?" (*ibid.,* 1.1.) 7. Interiority and subjectivism. They tended to attach little importance to external works and ritual; only intention, reflection and fervor counted. The ideal of Thomas à Kempis was *homo compunctus, internus et devotus.* Probably because it was born in the dark days of the Western Schism, the Devotio Moderna was wanting in an appreciation of the Church and the hierarchy. 8. Retirement from the world. They commended solitude and silence; in dealings with men they saw only danger and temptation; they showed little love or concern for the apostolate. 9. Devotional reading of the Scriptures. They were much given to reading the Bible, but only for edification and devotion, not for scientific research. They recommended the translation of the Bible into the vernacular tongues. 10. Antihumanism. From what has been said it is evident that this school of spirituality had nothing in common with the humanistic tendencies that were beginning to be felt in those times. They despised culture and knowledge and had no use for purely human values.

Writers. After G. Groote and F. Radewijns, the most important author among the Brethren of the Common Life was Geert Zerbolt v. Zutphen (1367–98), who wrote two significant treatises, *De reformatione virium animae* and *De spiritualibus ascensionibus.* Among the Canons Regular of Windesheim the following authors deserve mention: Gerlac Peters (1378–1411), author of a small ascetical work, *Breviloquium,* and of the *Soliloquium,* which has a more mystical character and was probably inspired by Ruysbroeck; Joannes Vos de Heusden (1391–1424), who, although he did not write the treatise once attributed to him, *Epistola de vita et passione D. N. Jesuchristi et aliis devotis exercitiis,* nevertheless used to recommend it to his disciples; Hendrik Mande (1360–1431), the greatest mystic of the school, and author of *Een boecskijn van drien staten (Liber de tribus statibus hominis), Eene claghe of enighe sprake der mynnender Sielen (Amorosa querela amantis animae)* and about 10 other small books that are held in great esteem by modern Dutch philologists and writers; THOMAS À KEMPIS (1380–1471), universally known figure and greatest representative of Devotio Moderna, whose treatise, *The IMITATION OF CHRIST,* ranks among the greatest of the classics of Catholic spirituality; and Joannes Mauburnus (Mombaer, 1460–1501), whose *Rosetum exercitiorum* is like an encyclopedia of the spirituality of the Devotio Moderna. Thomas à Kempis wrote a number of other small works also, e.g., *Soliloquium animae, De elevatione mentis ad inquirendum Summum Bonum* (of Augustinian inspiration), *Dialogus novitiorum* (pious biographies of the founders of the Devotio Moderna), *Hortulus rosarum, Vaillis liliorum, Sermones de vita et passione D. N. Jesu Christi.*

The Devotio Moderna flourished through the 15th century, and during the 16th century it influenced other schools of spirituality, such as the Erasmian, Ignatian, and even the Benedictine, Franciscan, and Dominican. In the end it was absorbed by these. It almost disappeared when the Protestant revolution destroyed many houses of the Brethren of the Common Life and convents of the Canons Regular.

Bibliography: Sources. A. HYMA, ed., ''The Original Constitution of the Brethren of the Common Life at Deventer,'' *The Christian Renaissance* (New York 1925) Appendix C: 440–474. J. BUSCH, *Chronicon Windeshemense,* ed. K. GRUBE (Geschichtsquellen der Provinz Sachsen 19; Halle 1886). THOMAS À KEMPIS, *Opera omnia,* ed. J. POHL, 7 v. (Freiburg 1902–22) v.7 ''Vita Gerardi Magni,'' 31–115, ''Vita Domini Florentii,'' 116–210, ''Chronica Montis Sanctae Agnetis,'' 333–478. J. MAUBURNUS, *Rosetum exercitiorum spiritualium et sacrarum meditationum* (Paris 1510). General. R. R. POST, *De Moderne devotie* (Amsterdam 1950), best general work. A. HYMA, *The Christian Renaissance* (New York 1925). E. DE SCHAEPDRIJVER, ''La Dévotion moderne,'' *Nouvelle revue théologique* 54 (1927) 742–772. M. DITCHE, ''Zur Herkunft und Bedeutung des Begriffes 'Devotio Moderna','' *Historisches Jahrbuch der Görres-Gesellschaft* 79 (1960) 124–145. K. C. L. M. DE BEER, *Studie over de spiritualiteit van Geert Groote* (Brussels 1938). S. AXTERS, *Geschiedenis van de vroomheid in de Nederlanden* (Antwerp 1950) v.3 *De Moderne devotie 1380–1550* (1956), with extensive bibliog., 416–456. P. DEBONGNIE, *Jean Mombaer de Bruxelles, abbé de Livry, ses écrits et ses réformes* (Louvain 1927); *Dictionnaire de spiritualité ascétique et mystique. Doctrine et histoire,* ed. M. VILLER et al. (Paris 1932) 3:727–747. J. M. E. DOLS, *Bibliographie der Moderne devotie,* 2 v. (Nijmegen 1936–37), an incomplete work. More useful is the logical exposition of W. J. ALBERTS, ''Zur Historiographie der 'Devotio Moderna' und ihrer Erforschung,'' *Westfälische Forschungen* 11 (1958) 51–67. Complementary bibliography in the articles: GROOTE; BRETHREN OF THE COMMON LIFE; THOMAS À KEMPIS.

[R. GARCÍA-VILLOSLADA]

DEVOTION

A word from the Latin signifying total dedication. In pagan usage that man was devout who vowed to suffer death in the defense of his country. Christian writers consequently found in the word ''devotion'' an ideal expression of what man's proper disposition toward God should be. St. Thomas Aquinas, without departing from the traditional teaching of the Fathers and Doctors of the Church, made precise and clear what had been obscurely understood in earlier periods (*Summa theologiae* 2a2ae, 81.9; 82).

According to him, devotion is an act of the habit or virtue of religion, that virtue by which man is inclined to pay to God the worship to which He is entitled by right. The virtue of religion subjects man to God, the source of man's perfection. By religion man is inclined to render to God the reasonable service of creature to Creator including everything the creature is or has. Man is composed of a body and a soul, and the soul acts through the faculties of will and intellect. These are offered to God in service by devotion and prayer. By adoration the body is offered to God. By sacrifice, oblation, first-fruits, and tithes, external things belonging to man are offered to God. By vows, things are promised to God in worship. In the reception of the seven Sacraments and in the use of God's name (by the taking of oaths, by adjuration, and by praising God) man uses things belonging to God to worship God. These 11 acts, namely, devotion, prayer, adoration, sacrifice, oblation, first-fruits, tithes, vows, the Sacraments, oaths, adjuration, and praise, constitute the perfect worship of God so far as the creature is capable of giving to God His due. Each offers to God a different thing—something that man is, or something that man in some way dominates or uses.

Devotion is the first act of the virtue of religion and is defined as: promptness or readiness of will in the service of God. Concretely, this means the perfect offering of the will itself to God, for readiness of the will in the service of God is the will offered to God in worship. Just as by adoration the body of man is offered to God, so by devotion the will of man is offered to God. Devotion, besides being the first, is also the principal act of the virtue of religion. Religion is a virtue of the will, so its first and principal act is the offering of the will itself. Since devotion is the first and principal act of the virtue of religion, it must appear in every other act of religion. Devotion is in this respect like the first and principal act of the virtue of charity, which is love. Almsgiving, a secondary act of charity, must flow from love or it is not an act of charity at all. So also every other act of religion must flow from devotion, or it fails to be an act of religion. It is in this sense that prayer, sacrifice, adoration, and all the rest must be devout to be truly acts of religion.

Feeling or emotion is not to be mistaken for devotion. While devotion is an act of the will, feelings or emotions are activities of the sense appetite. Ordinarily these are aroused by concrete, material objects. Devotion moves toward an object of which the senses know nothing. Consequently, the feelings that are based upon sense knowledge have of themselves no place in the act of devotion. Yet it is obvious that feelings or emotions do play an important part in man's worship of God. The explanation of this is found in the substantial unity of the human being. Although man has many diverse principles of activity corresponding with the diverse elements of his nature, matter and spirit, yet he is one thing substantially. If the will is set in motion toward an object proper to it, a corresponding movement of feeling or emotion is to be expected, for man is substantially one principle of operation. Likewise, if feeling or emotions are aroused by an object proper to the senses, a corresponding movement of the will, making due allowance for the will's freedom, is to be expected. Especially, therefore, when the act of devotion is intense, it is to be expected that such feelings as love, desire, pleasure, and hope will be aroused. Feelings, then, may and normally do accompany devotion but the truth and reality of devotion, the reality of the prompt and generous offering of the will itself, is not to be tested or measured by feelings. The only test and measure of the reality of devotion is its expression in other acts of religion, especially prayer, sacrifice, the continuation of Christ's supreme sacrifice of the Mass, the use of the Sacraments, praise of God, and the vows—particularly, the vows of religion.

Since St. Thomas speaks of the infused virtue of religion, he assigns as the principal cause of devotion the activity of God in man. Only God can be the cause of a virtue that is an essentially supernatural principle of human activity. There is, however, another cause of devotion to be found in man's own activity. This is meditation or contemplation. Devotion is aroused by meditation; first, on the goodness and loving-kindness of God, the Father and Creator of man; second, by a realization of man's own shortcomings, his sinfulness, his need to lean upon God as the source of whatever perfection is possible to him. As is evident, devotion has an important place in the plan of Christian perfection. St. Thomas does not hesitate to say that the virtue of religion, of which devotion is the first and principal act, is identical with sanctity. By this he does not mean to deny that Christian perfection consists formally and essentially in the act of charity. In this context he means by sanctity two things: detachment from what would impede union with God, and firmness and stability in being attached to God. Both of these are accomplished by the virtue of religion and the act of devotion. Religion, as the highest of the moral virtues, directs all the actions of the other moral virtues to the worship of God. Thus, acts of justice, or temperance, or modesty, for example, become in addition, by reason of the influence of religion and devotion upon them, acts of worship of God. By detachment from what would impede his union with God, by attachment to God as creature to his Creator, man is prepared in some measure for the union of friendship with God that the theological virtue of charity accomplishes.

Bibliography: THOMAS AQUINAS, *Summa theologiae* 2a2ae, 82–85. BONAVENTURE, *De sex alis Seraphim*, ch. 7 in *Opera omnia*, 10 v. (Quaracchi-Florence 1882–1902) 8:147–151. F. SUAREZ, *De oratione, devotione, et horis canonicis*, 2:6–8 in *Opera omnia*, 28 v. (Vives, Paris 1856–78) v.14. FRANCIS DE SALES, *Introduction to the Devout Life*, tr. M. DAY (Westminster, Md. 1959). J. N. GROU, *Marks of True Devotion* (Springfield, Ill. 1963). J. W. CURRAN, "Thomistic Concept of Devotion," *Thomist* 2 (1940) 410–443, 546–580.

[J. W. CURRAN]

DEVOTIONS, POPULAR

The term "devotion" here has two related meanings. (1) It means exercises of piety (*pia* or *sacra exercitia*): public prayers, worship services, or church ceremonies—but somehow other than the official church liturgy in the strictest sense. Thus, for example, the Way of the Cross is considered a popular devotion; but the veneration of the cross on Good Friday is part of the official liturgy. (2) "Devotion" is also the general term for themes characteristic of some of these exercises of piety, even when these have been assumed into the official liturgy. Thus, for example, the devotion to the Sacred Heart of Jesus. These devotions are called "popular" for several reasons. (1) They were designed for and practiced by ordinary people in the Church, and not mainly by religious professionals. (2) At some periods in history they have appealed to a relatively large proportion of church members. (3) They are capable of communal celebration and were often so celebrated: they are the prayer of structured groups of Christians and not only of individuals.

Counter-Reformation Origins. There are phenomena analogous to popular devotions in some Eastern and

Reformation Churches, and some of what later came to be considered popular devotions can be traced to origins in the medieval West. But the category of popular devotion is above all a creation of the Counter Reformation in the Latin West. Popular devotions arose as a consequence of the codification of the Roman liturgy following the Council of Trent. The limits and content of the official liturgy were quite precisely prescribed, with a two-fold result. (1) The spontaneous evolution of the rites now for the first time defined as part of the official liturgy was almost completely stifled. Thus much of the creative response of the Counter-Reformation Church to the needs of its worshipers had to be embodied in forms which supplemented or paralleled the official liturgy, now regarded as a given and not to be tampered with. (2) In time specific papal authorization came to be considered an indispensable element in constituting a form of worship as part of the official liturgy. Popular devotions, no matter how expressive of the actual worshiping consciousness of the Christian people, had to be something other than—and in a legal sense less than—the official liturgy of the Church.

This left compilers and practitioners of the devotions relatively free from official control. But many of the devotions were forced to the edges of the central mysteries of Christian worship. And some of them were couched in a literary and conceptual style too tied to the religious fashions of the moment. Conversely the official liturgy tended to become more and more remote from the living religious consciousness of Catholic worshipers.

Devotions and Vatican II. Official Roman Catholic church discipline has maintained the distinction between popular devotions and the official liturgy. The Constitution on the Liturgy of Vatican II warmly recommends popular devotions that conform to church norms and laws; the devotions form part of the actual, though extraliturgical, spiritual life of the Church. They should in every way be oriented toward the official liturgy, which is said to be by its very nature superior to any of them. Devotions, especially those celebrated in common as part of the public life of the Church, should harmonize with the seasons of the liturgical year. They are in some way derived from the liturgy, and should in turn lead people to the liturgy (*Sacrosanctum Concilium* 13).

In fact, at least in the U.S., the devotions, while they are still important in the individual prayer lives of many Catholics, have almost disappeared from the public life of the Church. Probably the hardiest survivor, the STATIONS OF THE CROSS, has traditionally been celebrated publicly only during Lent, and thus thoroughly accords with the church year. And the actual celebration of the official Liturgy of the Eucharist and other Sacraments has assumed many of the characteristics—like the use of the vernacular language, light music, and a generally more colloquial style—formerly associated almost exclusively with the popular devotions.

Liturgical Origins of Devotions. There is general agreement that most of the popular devotions can be traced to some kind of origin in the classical liturgy. The complete ROSARY, for example, parallels the liturgical Psalter, with one Hail Mary for each of the 150 Psalms. Until about the middle of the 16th century, the devotions tended to be patterned directly on the existing liturgy. The LITTLE OFFICE OF THE BLESSED VIRGIN MARY, for example, until very recently the most widely used nonclerical Liturgy of the Hours, follows quite exactly the shape of the canonical Office. There are the usual hours, each with its complement of Psalms and canticles, readings, hymns, and collects. But there is only one Office, to be repeated each day of the week. Probably the next most widely distributed medieval devotion, the Hours of the Cross or Passion, is composed as a commemoration (antiphon, versicle-response, collect) to be added to each hour of the canonical Office. The commemoration relates each hour of the occurring canonical Office with a time and an event in the history of the Passion.

After the middle of the 16th century, other forms began to appear. Generally they are an adaptation for communal recitation of a form of written meditation or reflection first designed for private and individual use. Probably even these more recent forms could be shown to have some connection, even if remote, with the classical liturgy.

The basic afternoon devotion in honor of the Blessed Sacrament, prominent in the public worship life of the American Church in the 19th and early 20th century, originally began as a festive conclusion to the canonical hour of VESPERS. In some places the final Marian antiphon (usually *Salve Regina*) was enriched with additional prayers and songs, called "Salve devotions." In other places the Blessed Sacrament was sometimes exposed at Vespers; Eucharistic songs were sung, and the people were blessed with the reserved Sacrament. These two traditions combined and the splendid result began to rival canonical Vespers in importance and came to be celebrated independently.

Richness of Continental Devotion Forms. The international treasury of popular devotions is very rich. In some countries the devotions formed a local, episcopally approved supplement to the Roman liturgy. Polish and Hungarian diocesan rituals, for example, provided additional services to fill out the Roman program for Holy Week and Easter. Before the reform of the official Roman services, at a time when the Easter Vigil, for example, was anticipated very early on Holy Saturday morning, these colorful, obvious, and well-timed vigils and processions were far more prominent in the popular mind and at the parochial level than the relatively opaque and difficult liturgical services for the TRIDUUM. From some points of view these local devotions were better vehicles of Christian worship than the adjacent rites in the Roman books. In some local Churches, most notably the dioceses of Germany, a complete cycle of popular devotions has grown up to parallel the Roman liturgy throughout the whole church year. The texts of these devotions, of a kind almost unknown in the U.S., are edited and printed with great care and have enjoyed the most solemn episcopal approval. Local devotions of this sort, with deep roots in the traditions of a region or institute, are said by the Vatican II Constitution on the Liturgy to have a special dignity (ibid.). Postconciliar legislation directs that such devotions, provided they are in accord with the official liturgy and the liturgical seasons, are to be treated with reverence in the formation of the clergy (*Inter oecumenici* 17; see bibliog.).

The United States. American Catholics had to be satisfied with a plainer devotional diet. The Roman Catholic Church in the U.S. assumed much of its style from the Church in England and especially in Ireland. There during the Counter-Reformation centuries, when devotion-making flourished on the Continent, the public worship life of the Church had to be kept to the bare and unobtrusive minimum because of the English penal laws.

In America the principal devotion was to the Lord present in the reserved Sacrament. Exposition of and benediction with the Blessed Sacrament typically formed the celebrational context of other devotions. Whether directed to the Lord himself or to a saint, the devotional prayers were usually recited consciously and specifically in the presence of the Lord in the Blessed Sacrament; and most of the devotions concluded with Eucharistic benediction. In a typical American Roman Catholic parish in the second quarter of this century the regular round of public common worship consisted of Mass every morning, with some form of popular devotion for Sunday afternoon and perhaps one evening during the week. The Sunday service, which earlier American church legislation had determined ought ideally to have been canonical Vespers, might consist of a Holy Hour or the Rosary during the plain seasons, prayers to the Mother of God during May (with no reference to Eastertide) and October, to Saint Joseph during March (with no reference to Lent), and to the Sacred Heart of Jesus during June. The week-night service was often an unchanging perennial novena. Benediction would inevitably conclude all of these services. Once a year the FORTY HOURS DEVOTION, a three-day solemnity in honor of the Blessed Sacrament, would be observed. There was little tie-in to the official church

year, though Lent was and is usually marked by the public celebration of the Stations of the Cross.

In the U.S. the principal reason for the demise of the devotions, which were almost exclusively afternoon functions, was the rise of the evening Mass, a development that was made possible by the reduction of the eucharistic fast to one hour. Church legislation has constantly emphasized the importance of corporate prayer other than the Eucharist, usually in terms of a kind of Liturgy of the Hours pastorally unfeasible for non-professionals. But there is no popular theological conviction that would lead clergy and people to choose any non-sacramental (and thus seemingly somehow "non-effective") prayer service in preference to the Mass. Once it became possible and easy to celebrate afternoon and evening Masses, the afternoon and evening devotions disappeared from parish schedules. Other reasons for the extinction of the devotions were associated with socio-economic or ethnic groupings which were dissolving or at least becoming unfashionable. There was more competition for leisure time. The official services could incorporate many appealing features of the devotions. Finally, the widespread Catholic charismatic movement responds to the need for warmth of expression and religious experience that was formerly met almost exclusively—to speak of worship services—through the devotions.

The Values in Popular Devotions. Popular devotions are a powerful and authentic expression of the prayer life of the Church. It is appropriate to suggest perennial values that devotions have and that should continue in future forms of prayer intended for ordinary people in the Church.

(1) Popular devotions represent the continuance in the Latin West of the *cathedral* style of public prayer—the style of common worship for ordinary Christians, as distinct from the *monastic* style—the style developed among religious professionals (clerics, monks, religious, laity with a special religious interest). The cathedral style of worship did not find a place in the post-Tridentine Roman Liturgy of the Hours, which is a thoroughly monastic prayer form. Since ordinary Christians could not accommodate themselves to the official Liturgy of the Hours, their style of public prayer had to appear in other less official and seemingly peripheral forms. Though the devotions are legally less than liturgical, they embody a tradition of popular liturgical prayer that dates back to the patristic age and is a precious, if not essential, part of the patrimony of the praying Church.

(2) The devotions tend to be an expression of religious experience rather than a statement about religious experience. The deep-seated bias of the Roman liturgy is to conceive and experience public worship as a concise,

abstract, external, and relatively superficial statement about the way things are between God and human beings. The devotions do not suffer from that impoverishment: they are an embodiment or a way of experiencing the relationship between God and his people.

(3) The devotions are conceived as a way of enabling the worshiper to do something rather than as a way of something being done to the worshiper. They are expression rather than education: they regard the Christian as a privileged person rather than as an object of instruction.

(4) The devotions, relative to the standard official liturgy of their time, are highly ceremonialized. They are thus simultaneously available to people of a wide range in age, educational background, and degree of religious interest.

(5) The devotions are almost unvarying in form and repetition of parts is frequent even within a given service. Although they were rightly criticized for not reflecting the seasons of the liturgical year, the devotions bear witness to the principle—so fundamental in the tradition of individual, private prayer—that variety is not the spice of prayer. The devotions are a reminder that rhythm of public and private prayer is similar and that norms for the composition of public prayers are appropriately found within the experience of those who pray.

See Also: POPULAR PIETY, HISPANIC, IN THE UNITED STATES; POPULAR PIETY, POLISH, IN THE UNITED STATES.

Bibliography: Congregation of Rites, *Inter oecumenici, Acta Apostolicae Sedis* 56 (1964) 877–900; tr. *Instruction for the Proper Implementation of the Constitution on the Sacred Liturgy* (Washington, D.C. 1964), C. DEHNE, ''Roman Catholic Popular Devotions,'' *Worship* 49 (1975) 446–460. This article includes a basic bibliography on the subject of popular devotions, esp. notable are the works on ''cathedral'' and ''monastic'' forms of liturgy, 447. R. W. SCRIBNER, ''Ritual and Popular Religion in Catholic Germany at the Time of the Reformation,'' *Journal of Ecclesiastical History* 35 (1984) 47–77. T. MATOVINA, ''Liturgy, Popular Rites, and Popular Spirituality,'' *Worship* 63 (1989) 351–361. O. O. ESPÍN, ''Popular Catholicism among Latinos,'' in *Hispanic Catholic Culture in the US*, eds. J. P. DOLAN and A. F. DECK (Notre Dame, Ind. 1994) 308–359. V. ELIZONDO, ''Popular Religions as Support of Identity—Based on the Mexican-American Experience in the United States,'' in *Spirituality of the Third World*, eds. K. C. ABRAHAM and B. MBUY-BEYA (Maryknoll, NY 1994) 55–63. M. E. ENGH, ''Companion of the Immigrants: Devotion to Our Lady of Guadalupe among Mexicans in the Los Angeles Area, 1900–1940,'' *Journal of Hispanic/Latino Theology* 5 (1997) 37–47. P. L. MALLOY, ''The Re-Emergence of Popular Religion Among Non-Hispanic American Catholics,'' *Worship* 72 (Ja 1998), p. 2–25.

[C. DEHNE/EDS.]

DE WULF, MAURICE

Historian of medieval philosophy; b. Poperinge, Belgium, April 6, 1867; d. there, Dec. 23, 1947. As a student at the University of Louvain, De Wulf followed the courses given by D. MERCIER on the philosophy of St. Thomas Aquinas, during the years from 1885 to 1891. Following the suggestion of Mercier he wrote a thesis on Henry of Ghent; he received the title ''docteur en philosophic selon saint Thomas'' (1893), and was immediately named professor at the ''Institut supérieur de Philosophie'' at Louvain (1893–1939).

In 1900, De Wulf published the *Histoire de la philosophie médiévale,* which promoted the scholastic revival by pointing out the essence of scholasticism, and not just by providing a collection of facts about scholastic philosophy. By scholasticism, De Wulf meant a body of original doctrine of a metaphysical nature, arrived at by reason; despite secondary divergences, this was common to the great thinkers of the Middle Ages and found its most adequate expression in the works of St. Thomas Aquinas. De Wulf devoted particular studies to some of the medieval philosophers who came from his own country: Henry of Ghent, Giles of Lessines, and Godfrey of Fontaines. In 1910 he published a *Histoire de la philosophie en Belgique.* Following upon his wartime conferences in the U.S. and Canada, De Wulf held a chair of the history of medieval philosophy at Harvard, which he occupied from 1920 until 1927. Through these courses and his lectures at other universities (Princeton, etc.) he played an important role in the development of medieval studies in America.

See Also: SCHOLASTICISM; SCHOLASTIC PHILOSOPHY; NEOSCHOLASTICISM AND NEOTHOMISM

Bibliography: L. NOËL, ''L'Oeuvre de Monsieur de Wulf,'' *Revue néo-scolastique de philosophie* 36 (1934) 11–38. P. HARMIGNIE, ''La Carrière scientifique de Monsieur le Professeur de Wulf,'' *ibid.* 39–66. F. VAN STEENBERGHEN, ''Les 'Beiträge' dans la tourmente,'' *Revue philosophique de Louvain* 46 (1948) 481–490.

[A. WYLLEMAN]

DEXIOS, THEODORE

Fourteenth-century Byzantine monk and anti-Palamite theologian; d. *c.* 1360. A spiritual son of Matthew of Ephesus, Theodore received his habit as a monk from Nicephorus Gregoras. He joined Gregory Akindynos in his propaganda against Palamism in Thessalonika and repudiated the use of the dialectical method in theology. He wrote a four-part work against JOHN VI CANTACUZENUS and the Tome of the synod of 1351. He expressed an agnostic attitude in regard to the essence of the Light of Mt. Tabor, and he claimed that as the divine essence was incomprehensible, theologians who attempted to discuss it were temerarious. For Dexios, the Light of Mt. Tabor was the Word of God, the Second Person of the Trinity, who manifested Himself to the Apostles not as He is in heaven, but with His humanity shining like the sun. This opinion brought him into conflict with his anti-Palamite friend Isaac Argyros (d. 1375), and he wrote three short apologies to justify his position. While he favored the mystical elements in Palamism, he maintained it was both foolish and impossible to give any explanation beyond that which was furnished by the Gospels.

Bibliography: H. G. BECK, *Kirche und theologische Literatur im byzantinischen Reich* (Munich 1959) 330, 716, 729. M. JUGIE, *Dictionnaire de théologie catholique*, ed. A. VACANT et al. (Paris 1903–50) 11.2:1804–05. G. MERCATI, *Notizie di Procoro e Demetrio Cidone* (*Studi e Testi* 56; 1931) 225–229. E. CANDAL, "Argiro contro Dexio," *Orientalia Christiana periodica* 23 (1957) 80–113.

[F. X. MURPHY]

DEYMANN, CLEMENTINE

First commissary provincial of the California FRANCISCANS; b. Klein Stavern, Diocese of Osnabrück, Hanover, Germany, June 24, 1844; d. Phoenix, Ariz., Dec. 4, 1896. He was christened John Henry, receiving the name Clementine after he immigrated to America (1864) and entered the Franciscan Order in Illinois (1867). He was ordained in 1872 and served the Sacred Heart Province of his order in the Middle West for 13 years. In 1886 he was assigned to Watsonville, Calif., where he spent most of the remainder of his life. Because of the distance between the provincial headquarters in St. Louis, Mo., and the West coast houses of his order, Deymann was appointed provincial visitor for the California area. He served two terms as definitor (councilor) for his province and was instrumental in obtaining Franciscan parishes in Los Angeles, San Francisco, Oakland, and Sacramento. Shortly before his death the Far West was made into a partially self-governing division of the province (1896), and Deymann was named first commissary provincial. He is buried in Santa Barbara, Calif. His works include lives of St. Francis Solanus, Crescentia Hoess, Junípero Serra, and Magín Catalá. A number of devotional works, most of which were written during the 1880s, are also ascribed to him.

Bibliography: M. A. HABIG, *Heralds of the King: Franciscans of the St. Louis-Chicago Province 1858–1958* (Chicago 1959).

[E. BURNETT]

DEZZA, PAOLO

Jesuit, university rector, cardinal; b. Dec. 13, 1901, Parma; d. Dec. 17, 1999, Rome. His life was dedicated to higher education, teaching philosophy, administration in the Society of Jesus, and service to the Holy See. He entered the Society of Jesus in 1918, studied philosophy in Spain and theology at Naples, and was ordained a priest on March 25, 1928. In 1929, Dezza began a long career at the Pontifical Gregorian University in Rome, where he taught metaphysics intermittently for more than 35 years. From 1935 to 1939 he served as provincial of the Veneto-Milanese province. He was rector at several institutions: the Jesuit philosophy scholasticate in Gallarate, Italy (1939–1941), Gregorian University (1941–1951), and St. Robert Bellarmine College (1951–1965). His *Metaphysica* became a classic textbook in many universities and seminaries. Young Karol Wojtyła attended his lectures in Rome.

In 1965 Fr. Dezza was elected assistant general of the Jesuits and began to take on various roles within the Vatican. He was a *peritus* at the Second Vatican Council, contributing particularly to the commission that wrote the Declaration on Christian Education (*Gravissimum educationis*); he published a commentary on this document in 1965. He served as consultor at several posts of the Holy See: namely, the congregations for evangelization, religious, divine worship and sacraments, and education. He was a highly regarded adviser for the Congregation of Catholic Education, helping with the reform of the Catholic universities. He conducted the Spiritual Exercises for Popes Pius XII and John Paul I, and was confessor to Paul VI and John Paul I.

In 1981, Fr. Dezza was an assistant general when, on August 7, Fr. General Pedro Arrupe suffered a stroke that disabled him severely. On Oct. 5, 1981, the pope named Fr. Dezza his pontifical delegate for the Society of Jesus. This appointment suspended the Jesuit constitutions until the election of a new general. With prudence, calm, and fidelity to the pope, Fr. Dezza prepared the order for a new General Congregation. In a series of conferences and meetings, he informed the Fathers of the concerns and hopes of the pope for the society. The special mission of Fr. Dezza lasted until Sept. 13, 1983, when the 33d General Congregation elected Fr. Peter-Hans Kolvenbach as superior general.

On June 28, 1991, Fr. Dezza was created cardinal with the title of Deacon of Saint Ignatius Loyola in Campo Marzio. It meant much for him, since the church of St. Ignatius is the church of the Gregorian University. He requested, and was granted, an exemption from the requirement of episcopal consecration. He died on Dec. 17,

Paolo Dezza. (AP/Wide World Photos)

1999, at the age of 98, and was buried in the church of St. Ignatius.

[H. CARRIER]

DHARMA

In Pāli, *dhamma,* a word derived from *dhara* (to hold, bear, or possess), meaning anything right, something that is to be held fast or kept; a law, statute, usage, or practice. In HINDUISM, *dharma* signifies the cosmic ordering of universe and life, and the conduct needed for the maintenance of that order. What is commonly understood as ''Hinduism'' in Western thought is referred to as *sanātana dharma* (''Everlasting Dharma'') by Hindu adherents. Hence, in Hinduism, *dharma* is the religion-inspired moral ideal, the moral law that sustains the world, human society, and the individual. In the Upanisads, *dharma* is presented as ways for attaining the BRAH-MAN. In Jainism, *dharma* may be understood as the all-pervading notion of activity or motion, making movement possible; the teachings of the *Jinas*; and the universal rule of nonviolence.

Within BUDDHISM, the term *dharma* took on several meanings. One of the core teachings of Buddhism from the start was the radical impermanence and insubstantiality of things, and one way of accounting for this state was to posit ''dharmas,'' which functioned much like ''atoms'' in ancient Greek thought. That is to say, they were infinitesimal building blocks of reality. Eternal and permanent in themselves, they combined and recombined with each other to form the phenomena of the world, thus accounting for the arising and decay of things. Thus, dharma in Buddhist thought came to be used as a reference to constituents of reality. In Abhidharma philosophy, *dharma* are fundamental building blocks of reality, rather like the atoms of ancient Greek philosophy. In popular Buddhist literature, *dharma* is identified as ''phe-

Golden dharma wheel, Lhasa, Tibet. (©Brian Vikander/CORBIS)

nomenon.'' Another use of *dharma* is in reference to the teachings of Sakyamuni Buddha, who is himself seen as a manifestation of *dharma* (truth), as well as the practice of that truth (*patipatti*). The central role of *dharma* within Buddhism can also be seen in the the traditional Buddhist formulation of the ''Three Jewels'' (*Triratna*), i.e., taking refuge in the *Buddha*, the *Dharma*, and the *Sangha*.

Bibliography: T. SHCHERBATSKY, *The Central Conception of Buddhism and the Meaning of the Word ''Dharma''* (London 1923). R. C. HAZRA, ''Dharma: Its Early Meaning and Scope,'' *Our Heritage* 7 (Calcutta 1959) 15–35; 8 (1960) 7–34. W. T. DE BARY, ed., *Introduction to Oriental Civilizations*, 3 v. (Records of Civilization 54–56; New York 1958–60).

[A. S. ROSSO/C. B. JONES]

DHIMMI

A relative noun from the Arabic *dhimma,* which is a contraction of *Ahl al-dhimma,* the people with whom a compact or covenant has been made. *Dhimma* is the status conferred by Islamic law on the ''people of the (revealed) scripture'' (*Ahl al-kitāb*); and *dhimmī* refers to a person who possesses that status. Through payment of a poll tax (*jizya*), the Jews, Christians, and Sabaeans were promised security of life, liberty, and property. The levy of the *jizya* is mandated by the *Qur'ān*: ''Fight against those who have been given the Scriptures (but) believe not in Allāh and the Last Day . . . and follow not the Religion of the Truth (i.e., *Islām*), until they pay the jizya.'' Unlike the pagans (*mushrikūn*) who were prohibited from practicing their religion, *dhimmīs* were generally permitted to practice their religions, subject to strict legal and socio-economic restrictions. Under Islamic (*Shari'a*) law, *dhimmīs* are not citizens of an Islamic state, but remained under the jurisdiction of their respective religious leaders. Because of their talents and skills, many *dhimmīs* were employed as court officials, city administrators, teachers or physicians. Nevertheless, numerous restrictions reinforced the second-class status of *dhimmī* communities and forced them into ghettos. For instance, they must distinguish themselves from their Muslim neighbors by their dress. They were not permitted to build new churches or synagogues, but only to repair old ones. A Muslim man may marry a *dhimmī* woman of the *ahl al-kitāb*, who may keep her own religion, but a Muslim woman cannot marry a *dhimmī* man unless he embraces the Islamic faith. *Dhimmīs* are prohibited from converting Muslims under severe penalties, while Muslims are encouraged to convert *dhimmīs*. The historical ''millet'' system that governed the Jewish and Christian communities in the Ottoman empire is an example of the *ahl al-Dhimma*.

Bibliography: A. S. TRITTON, *The Caliphs and Their Non-Muslim Subjects: A Critical Study of the Covenant of 'Umar* (New York 1930). A. R. I. DOI, *Non-Muslims Under Shari'ah* (London 1983).

[G. MAKDISI/EDS.]

DHŪ-NUWĀS MASRUḲ

King (*c.* 523–*c.* 525) of pre-Islamic South Arabia, known especially for his ferocious persecution of the Christians. In the Arabic chronicles he is known generally under the name of Zur'at ben Tibbān As'ad; in the Syriac sources (*The Book of the Ḥimyarites*), under that of Dhū-Nuwās Masruḳ. His real name, however, as the South-Arabic epigraphical sources testify, was Yūsuf 'As'ar Yat'ar. According to the Syriac sources he had been indoctrinated in Judaism by his mother, who was from Nisibis in Syria, and he reigned after the death of his father. The Arabic writers state, on the contrary, that he was converted to Judaism and that he deposed King Lahay'a ben Yanūf. Actually, according to the contemporary epigraphical sources, he succeeded King Ma'adīkarib Ya'fur *c.* 522 to 523, and from the beginning his reign was marked by an irreconcilable antipathy toward Christians, caused perhaps by the hostile attitude of the Christian negus (king) of Ethiopia and his disastrous attempt to invade Yemen from motives of religious zeal.

Be that as it may, as soon as Dhū-Nuwās gained the royal power the persecution of the Christians spread throughout the region of the Ḥimyarites (a people of South Arabia). Moreover, Dhū-Nuwās enticed al-Mundhir, the king of Ḥira (in North Arabia), who was then engaged in war against the Byzantines in the Syrian Desert, to follow his example and exterminate all the Christians who would not deny Christ. Dhū-Nuwās's bloody persecution of the Christians had begun in Ẓafar, where he burned down the church that had still belonged to the Ethiopians. But soon he turned his fury against the Christians of the tribe of al-'Aš'ar, and finally he attacked Mukhā. In these quasi wars of extermination he slew 14,000 people and took 11,000 prisoners. Before long (November 523) he sent his forces against the Christians of Naǧrān.

The actions of Dhū-Nuwās aroused the Byzantine Emperor JUSTINIAN I (518–527), who urged the negus of Ethiopia to intervene once more. So the Negus 'Ellā 'Asbeha (known also as Kālēb) again invaded Yemen (525), this time with a strong fleet and an army of 120,000 warriors. According to the Syriac sources Dhū-Nuwās was assassinated and succeeded on the throne of Ḥimyar by the Christian King Abramos (whose real name, according to the epigraphical sources, was 'Abraha). But the fall of Dhū-Nuwās was perhaps due, at least in part, to deep dissensions within the ranks of his followers and to the treachery of some of them. In fact, the epigraphical sources place, between the end of Dhū-Nuwās's reign and the beginning of 'Abraha's (*c.* 530), the short reign of the Christian King Sumyafa' 'Ašwa', who has been identified as one of the early followers of Dhū-Nuwās.

Bibliography: A. MOBERG, *The Book of the Himyarites* (Lund 1921). J. RYCKMANS, *La Persécution des chrétiens himyarites au sixième siècle* (Istanbul 1956); *Le Christianisme en Arabie du Sud préislamique* (Rome 1964) 413–453. H. ST. J. B. PHILBY, *The Background of Islam* (Alexandria 1947). M. R. AL-ASSOUAD, *Encyclopedia of Islam*, ed. B. LEWIS et al. (2d ed. Leiden 1954–) s.v. Dhū Nūwas 1:985. R. GEIS, *Lexikon für Theologie und Kirche*, ed. J. HOFER and K. RAHNER (2d, new ed. Freiburg 1957–65) 3:317. A. JAMME, *Research on Sabaean Rock Inscriptions from Southwestern Saudi Arabia* (Washington 1965) 28–39.

[J. M. SOLA-SOLE]

DIABOLICAL OBSESSION

As distinguished from DIABOLICAL POSSESSION, diabolical obsession refers to hostile action of the devil or an evil spirit besetting anyone from without.

Examples of this phenomenon in the Scriptures are rare and difficult to evaluate. The misfortunes that overtake Job's family and possessions are all ascribed to Satan (Jb 1.12), as are the severe boils that ultimately cover Job himself (Jb 2.6–7), but all these calamities are actually described as natural events not recognizable as anything but the result of God's providence (Jb 2.10). Moreover, the Satan of Job is not the Satan of later Judeo-Christian theology; he is one of the "sons of God," although, in a real sense, man's adversary (or inquisitor). Finally, the story of Job is didactic, not historical, even though the hero of the poem probably lived in remote times.

A clearer instance of diabolical obsession can be found in the Book of Tobit (3.8; 6.14). The seven husbands of the innocent young Sara were believed to have been slain by the demon Asmodaeus, who looked after the frustrated bride himself. Here again, however, one is dealing with didactic fiction in all probability, but at least these texts presuppose Jewish belief in the reality of diabolical obsession. In the New Testament the only possible reference to this phenomenon is 2 Cor 12.7–8, where Paul tells his readers that "lest the greatness of the revelations should puff me up, there was given me a thorn for the flesh, a messenger of Satan to buffet me. Concerning this I thrice besought the Lord that it might leave me.'' The precise meaning of this text has, however, been widely disputed and it would be rash to cite it as an example of true diabolical obsession.

Cases involving the molestation and bombarding of individuals, houses, and animals were recorded during the Middle Ages. St. Augustine tells such a story (*Civ* 22.8), as do St. Cyprian (*Life of St. Caesarius of Arles*) and Alcuin (*Life of St. Willibrand*). In modern times the phenomenon has been widely reported and with great frequency, although the general tendency is to find some natural rather than preternatural explanation for it—psychokinetic energy, for instance. Even Catholic theologians are prepared to admit this. The late Herbert Thurston, SJ, who was an authority in occult phenomena, wrote: ''That there may be something diabolical, or at any rate evil, in them I do not deny, but, on the other hand, it is also possible that there may be natural forces involved which are so far as little known to us as the latent forces of electricity were known to the Greeks. It is possibly the complication of these two elements which forms the heart of the mystery'' (p. VI). Cases in which the devil or devils are said to have appeared (e.g., to the Curé d'Ars) on such occasions are not necessarily more certain as to cause; the psychology of the individual involved would have to be analyzed in each instance.

See Also: DEMON (IN THE BIBLE); DEMON (THEOLOGY OF); EXORCISM.

Bibliography: T. ORTOLAN, *Dictionnaire de théologie catholique,* ed. A. VACANT et al., (Paris 1903–50) 4.1:409–414. B. THUM et al., *Lexikon für Theologie und Kirche,* ed. J. HOFER and K. RAHNER (Freiberg 1957–65) 2:294–300. H. THURSTON, *Ghosts and Poltergeists,* ed. J. H. CREHAN (Chicago 1954). A. WIESINGER, *Occult Phenomena in the Light of Theology,* tr. B. BATTERSHAW (Westminster, Md. 1957).

[L. J. ELMER]

DIABOLICAL POSSESSION (IN THE BIBLE)

Strictly defined, diabolical possession is the state of a person whose body has fallen under the control of the DEVIL or a DEMON. Although the Old Testament was familiar with demons (e.g., the goat offered annually to Azazel and their attempts to harm man, exemplified especially in the case of Asmodaeus in the Book of TOBIT (Tobias), it would seem that it describes no true cases of possession. The ''evil spirit from the Lord'' that troubled Saul (1 Sm 16.14, 23; 18.10) can hardly be classed as a demon; in any case, Saul's symptoms point to pathological depression rather than to diabolical possession.

In the New Testament, on the other hand, many cases of possession are described. The possessed person may display superhuman strength (Mk 5.3–4; Acts 19.16) or knowledge (Mk 1.23–24; Acts 16.16). It is clear that the New Testament often attributed to diabolical possession some purely natural afflictions, such as epilepsy (Mk 9.13–28) and blindness and dumbness (Mk 12.22). Of such it may be said indifferently that they are cured or that the spirits are driven out (Mt 12.22; 17.15, 18; Lk 6.18). Part of the reason for these attributions was the lack of knowledge in those days (and even much later) necessary for scientific diagnosis of nervous and mental disorders. This does not provide a basis, however, for a rationalistic denial of the possibility or fact of possession. The indifference with which the New Testament writers often attribute disorders to demons or to more natural causes springs from their theological view of the relationship existing between the devil and his minions, sin, human ills of all sorts, and the mission of Jesus. God created all things good and established man free of every affliction (Gn 1.1–2.25); death and other human ills entered the world through the sin of man (Gn 3.16–19; Rom 5.12–14), instigated by the serpent that later tradition identified with the devil or SATAN (Wis 2.24; Rv 12.9). Thus the presence of death and other human ills were a continuing sign of the dominion of Satan in the world. Jesus, coming to establish the kingdom of God, enters into immediate conflict with the satanic powers that have dominion over men. His triumph is seen at the very outset in His personal conquest of temptation (*see* TEMPTATIONS OF JESUS) and throughout His ministry in His MIRACLES, especially in raising the dead, in cures, and in exorcisms. So closely are these three types of miracles related in releasing man from the power that held him captive that St. Peter could recapitulate the miracles of Jesus' ministry by saying, ''He went about doing good and healing all who were in the power of the devil'' (Acts 10.38); Jesus Himself summed it up in a similar way in saying, ''Behold, I cast out devils and perform cures today and tomorrow, and the third day I am to end my course'' (Lk 13.32). His exorcisms are done by the power of God and are a sign that ''the kingdom of God has come upon you'' (Mt 12.28); they signify that one stronger than Satan has entered his house, bound him, and seized his spoils (Lk 11.22). The dominion of Satan was radically overcome in the ministry of Jesus, by the conquest of sin in the obedience of His death, and by the conquest of death in His Resurrection, but Satan's efforts will continue until the parousia; for this reason Jesus gave to His disciples and to His Church the power to continue to triumph through exorcism (Mk 6.7, 13; 16.18; Acts 5.16; 8.7;16.16–18; 19.12).

Bibliography: *Encyclopedic Dictionary of the Bible,* tr. and adap. by L. HARTMAN (New York 1963), from A. VAN DEN BORN,

Bijbels Woordenboek, 565–567. R. E. BROWN, "The Gospel Miracles," *The Bible in Current Catholic Thought,* ed. J. L. MCKENZIE (New York 1962) 184–201. F. M. CATHERINET, *Les Démoniaques de l'Evangile: Satan* (Paris 1952). W. FOERSTER, in G. KITTEL, *Theologisches Wörterbuch zum Neuen Testament* (Stuttgart 1935) 2:19.

[J. JENSEN]

DIABOLICAL POSSESSION (THEOLOGY OF)

The theological problems raised by the phenomenon of diabolical possession are both empirical and speculative: how may a true case of possession be detected, and how is possession compatible with the radical freedom of the human will and with divine justice? A satisfactory answer to the first question was necessarily delayed by the general ignorance about the organic causes of various neurasthenic disorders. Possession was thought to exist where, perhaps most often, it did not. The speculative question did not present the same difficulty. As spirits, the demons are capable of penetrating and manipulating matter of any sort. Hence, according to both St. Thomas Aquinas and St. Bonaventure, what occurs in instances of possession is the entrance of a demon into a human body, the faculties (physical) of which he proceeds to control. The soul, however, cannot be entered or overcome and thus remains free, although its functions in respect to the body it informs are, as it were, suspended. Estius described possession in terms of a ship: the demon assumes the role of the pilot who steers the vessel. The 17th-century French divine, Surin, actually compared the demon's role to that of the soul. Probably the most authoritative statement in this matter is that of Benedict XIV in his *De servorum Dei beatificatione, et beatorum canonizatione* (4.1.29.2). This is not in any sense a dogmatic definition, since it was issued in his capacity as a private theologian, not as pope, but it is clear and succinct: "Demons, in the individuals whom they possess, are like motors within the bodies which they move, but in such a way that they impress no quality on the human body nor do they give it any new mode of existence nor, strictly speaking, do they constitute, together with the possessed person, a single being."

Credit for distinguishing among the apparent signs of possession must be given to the 17th-century theologian P. Thyräus, SJ. In his judgment the physical or corporeal indications of possession—spastic movements or hysterical convulsions, etc.—were not to be considered in any way decisive. The true criteria, he asserted, are a knowledge of secret things and a knowledge of languages never learned (by the possessed individual). Even these criteria leave something to be desired, since one is aware today of the very real probability that telepathic communications between human beings exist, but at least Thyräus relegated the popular signs to the minimal significance they should have.

All writers on the subject of possession have insisted that the possessed person's lack of memory as to what he did or said during the seizure also be recognized as another fundamental criterion. Possession, in other words, precludes normal human consciousness. In this respect cases of possession resemble those pathological states known to modern clinical psychology in which the patient projects two or more wholly different personalities none of which is conscious of the other. The parallel here illustrates again the caution that must be preserved in attempting to determine an authentic case of possession. Perhaps only the effect of an EXORCISM upon the person possessed can really be said to settle the question.

One cannot hope to understand in every—if in any—case, why God permits possession. It is, however, a consequence of the fact that He has not annihilated the evil spirits, who remain, therefore, capable of disturbing the normal processes of created matter. The Council of Trent noted that man had become subject to Satanic influence as a result of the Fall (H. Denzinger, *Enchiridion symbolorum* 1511), and although man has been "rescued . . . from the power of darkness" by Jesus Christ (Col 1.13), he has not been relieved of the necessity of struggling against the continued attacks of that power (Eph 6.12). In exorcism, however, he possesses the ultimate weapon against these inroads of Satan, which are not, in any case, as frequent as once imagined.

See Also: DIABOLICAL OBSESSION; DEMON (THEOLOGY OF).

Bibliography: L. ROURE, *Dictionnaire de théologie catholique,* ed. A. VACANT et al., (Paris 1903–50) 12.2:2640–47. B. THUM et al., *Lexikon für Theologie und Kirche,* ed. J. HOFER and K. RAHNER (Freiburg 1957–65) 2:294–300. *Satan,* ed. B. DE JÉSUS-MARIE, tr. M. CARROLL et al., (New York 1952). L. CRISTANI, *Evidence of Satan in the Modern World,* tr. C. ROWLAND (New York 1962). T. K. OESTERREICH, *Possession, Demoniacal and Other,* tr. D. IBBERSON (New York 1930). J. LHERMITTE, *True and False Possession,* tr. P. J. HEPBURNE-SCOTT (New York 1963). J. DE TONQUÉDEC, *Les Maladies nerveuses ou mentales et les manifestations diaboliques* (Paris 1938).

[L. J. ELMER]

DIACONIA

A service particularly of the poor, widows, orphans, pilgrims, and strangers, organized by the Church in a systematic fashion. The term "diaconia" has special reference to established centers, particularly in Rome and Italy from the 8th century. Almsgiving, together with prayer and fasting, had been a primary function of Christian life from the beginning. The Acts of the Apostles described the selection of deacons to care for the economic needs of the Hellenistic widows and orphans in the primitive Christian community at Jerusalem (6.1–7). The early Church documents indicate that the deacon assisted the bishop in the administration of the Church's goods and the care of the poor, as well as in certain liturgical functions (*Shepherd of Hermas, Vis.* 3.5.1; *Trad. Ap.* 16). In the 2d and 3d centuries the deacon cared for the sick, widows, orphans, catechumens, sinners, the imprisoned, and strangers, as well as the discipline of the church services (*Test. Dom.* 1.34; Cyprian, *Epistolae* 15.1; 50; 52). In the 3d century in Rome, Pope Fabian divided the city into seven regions for administrative purposes and put a deacon in charge of each (*Lib. pont.* 5), and CORNELIUS (251–253) spoke of caring for 1,500 widows and indigents in his letter to Fabius of Antioch (Eusebius, *Hist. eccl.* 6.43.2). The Church in Carthage was likewise divided into regions presided over by deacons (*Dictionnaire d'archéologie chrétienne et de liturgie,* ed. F. Cabrol, H. Leclercq, and H. I. Marrou, 15 v. (Paris 1907–53) 2.2:2270–71); there is evidence for a similar development in other Churches (Elvira, c.77).

John CASSIAN described the diaconia or service of the poor rendered by the monks of Egypt, who applied gifts of the faithful or their own earnings in alms (*Coll.* 21.8; 18.7). There is evidence that during the 5th and 6th centuries there was a gradual changeover from the state-supplied *annona* or food distribution in both the Orient and the West; and in the East the care for the poor was associated with the Metanoia monasteries, usually outside the city, which provided for cleanliness as well as for feeding the needy. In 5th-century Egypt, the diaconia of Komos Apollonopolis Heptakomias received its supplies from the local bishop, and there were diaconiae connected with monasteries in the Thebaid and the Metanoia at Alexandria (522–585), as is indicated by papyri recently discovered at Aphroditopolis.

The popes took charge of providing for the poor and abandoned in Rome long before they were forced to assume political power. Pope GELASIUS I (492–496) liberated the city from the peril of famine (*Lib. pont.* 1:255); Boniface II (530–532) likewise fed the population (InscripLatChristVet 987), and the people of Rome cried after VIGILIUS I was abducted by the Byzantine soldiers: "May the famine go with you" (*Lib. pont.* 1:297). In 554, with the Pragmatic Sanction of JUSTINIAN I, provision for the *annona* at Rome included the sending of grain in October each year by the governor of Sicily and its reception in the public granary (*sitoricium*). Under

BENEDICT I (575–579), Emperor Justin II sent supply ships from Egypt to Rome because of the famine (*Lib. pont.* 1:308).

GREGORY I (590–604) suggested that the rich make testamentary provision for the poor by contributing to the diaconia at Pesaro (*Epistolae* 5.25) and blamed the pretorian prefect of Italy for failing to provide the customary *annona* or supplies for the diaconiae of Naples (*Epistolae* 10.8). He appointed a certain Johannes Religiosus as overseer of the tables of the poor and put him in charge of the diaconia (*Epistolae* 11.17). Church, state and citizenry were involved in this religious work, and at Rome the Lateran was the center. The pope used the revenues of the papal patrimony for this.

Under popes Benedict II (684–685), John V (685–686), Conon (686–687), and Gregory II (715–731), monasteries of Greek monks fleeing iconoclastic persecution were introduced into Rome and given charge of the diaconiae (*Lib. pont.* 1:364, 367, 369, 465). Under Adrian I (772–795) there were 16 such posts (*ibid.* 1:504); and with the founding of those of St. Adrian and of SS. Cosmas and Damian, the pope increased the number to 18. In the vita of Leo III (795–816) a catalogue of these diaconiae is supplied (*ibid.* 2:18).

The Eustathius inscription in the church of S. Maria in Cosmedin indicated that a priest said daily Mass and received three *solidi* for this service in the diaconia (*Ord. Rom.* 1.4). The diaconate churches were turned over to the diaconia, and oratories connected with the monastic diaconiae were turned into churches to which Pope PAUL I (757–767) allowed the bones of the martyrs to be brought from the catacombs (*Lib. pont.* 1:465). Pope Adrian closed the gap between the ancient diaconate and the diaconia. In each monastery a *dispensator* or *pater* was in charge, and he used the personnel of the monastery for the care of the poor. Abandoned buildings were reemployed. S. Maria in Cosmedin occupied the porticus of an ancient grain depot or *statio annonae;* St. Theodore's was located in the ancient granary of Agrippina.

The diaconia itself consisted of an oratory or church where the poor were gathered for religious services, a monastery of monks in charge, and a depot or granary where the monks (*diaconitae*) distributed food and alms. On certain days the poor formed in procession and sang hymns on their way to the baths. The city's revenue, as well as papal patrimony, was turned to this use. Benedict II distributed to each cleric, each monastery of the diaconia, and each *mansoniarius,* 30 *librae* of gold; and JOHN V (685) gave a similar sum for religious cult, the poor, and the sanctuaries. When the supply of grains from Egypt was cut off by the Saracen invaders, Popes Martin I and Adeodatus (672–676) obtained fiscal exemptions from Constantinople for the papal patrimonies in Lucania, Sicily, and Calabria. The Byzantine emperor LEO III took revenge on Pope GREGORY III for his anti-iconoclast stand by occupying Calabria (*Lib. pont.* 1:442); and ZACHARY I demanded compensation from the emperor (*ibid.* 1:433). Meanwhile the popes had organized the supply of the city from Formia, Anzio, and the confines of Etruria. In a prosperous year, Eugene II (824–827) ordered a general distribution of food to all his subjects.

In Naples, S. Andrea ad Nidum served as a diaconia under Pope Gregory II; and S. Januarius ad ulmum was used as a center of distribution by Bishop Agnellus of Naples at the end of the 7th century. He delegated 210 *tritici mediorum* and 210 *hornas* of wine annually for distribution by the monastery and ordered soap to be given out at Christmas and Easter [*Monumenta Germaniae Historica: Scriptores rerum Langobardicarum* (Berlin 1826–) 418]. There is a record that in 721 or 736 a church of SS. John and Paul was being used as a diaconia. At Cremona in 686 the archpriest of St. Mary's, with his brethren, constructed an oratory (*oratorium*) and a hospital (*xenodochium*) for the sick and pilgrims, as well as for the care of the poor. At Lucca in 729 the Archpriest Sigismund also built an oratory and hospital for strangers and the distribution of alms. This custom carried on into the Middle Ages and is noted both in the ITINERARIA and in the records of PILGRIMAGES.

Bibliography: A. KALSBACH, *Scientia sacra: Theologische Festgabe . . . Kardinal Schulte,* ed. C. FECKES (Cologne 1935) 71–84; *Reallexikon für Antike und Christentum,* ed. T. KLAUSER [Stuttgart 1941 (1950)–] 3:909–917. J. LESTOCQUOY, *Revista di archeologia cristiana* 7 (1930) 261–298. H. I. MARROU, *Mélanges d'archéologie et d'histoire* 57 (1940) 95–142, Oriental origin. O. BERTOLINI, *Archivio della società romana di storia patria* 70 (1947) 1–145. R. VIELLIARD, *Recherches sur les origines de la Rome chrétienne* (Mâcon 1941; repr. Rome 1959) 116–128.

[F. X. MURPHY/EDS.]

DIACONICUM

From Greek διακονικόν (service room), one of the side rooms found frequently in the early Christian basilica, serving many of the functions of today's sacristy in the Latin Church. The diaconicum was more common in the Christian East and was generally located just south of the apse. Although it served principally as a vesting place and "treasury" (σκευοφυλάκιον or κειμηλιαρχεῖον) where the liturgical books and vessels, as well as relics, might be kept, it served also as a place for preparing the bread and wine and for reserving the Eucharist (whence its other names, πρόθεσις and παστοφόριον). Since the 7th century, the two functions were differentiated, and two rooms, the prothesis and the dia-

conicum, balance one another on either side of the apse of church buildings in the Christian East.

Bibliography: G. BANDMANN, ''Über Pastophorien und verwandte Nebenräume im mittelalterlichen Kirchenbau,'' *Kunstgeschichtliche Studien für Hans Kauffmann,* ed. W. BRAUNFELS (Berlin 1956) 19–58.

[T. F. MATHEWS/EDS.]

DIADOCHUS OF PHOTICE

Fifth-century bishop and anti-Monophysite theologian; d. before 486. Nothing is known of the life of Diadochus other than that he signed the response of the bishops of Epirus in Greece to the encyclical letter of Emperor LEO I in 457 (J. D. Mansi, *Scaorum Conciliorum nova et amplissima collectio* 7.619; *Acta conciliorum oecumenicorum* 2.5.95), thus indicating his adherence to the Council of CHALCEDON. He is mentioned as an adversary of MONOPHYSITISM by Photius (*Bibl. cod.* 231); and his death is recorded in the prologue to Victor of Vita's history of the Vandal persecution. The main work of Diadochus is the *Capita centum de perfectione spirituali,* or 100 chapters on spiritual perfection. It is a treatise that begins with ten definitions of virtues, following a common literary genre for such compositions. It deals with the discernment of spirits (ch. 26–35), the difficulties of contemplation (ch. 69–75), the theology of grace (ch. 76–89), the two stages of spiritual desolation (ch. 86–87), and the doctrine of man's creation in the image and likeness of God (ch. 89). Diadochus is also considered the author of the sermon for the Ascension, and a collection of questions and answers concerning the spiritual life under the title *The Vision of John the Baptist.*

In his ascetical doctrine Diadochus stressed the practice of the presence of God and the JESUS PRAYER, following the tradition of EVAGRIUS PONTICUS. He is also thought to have opposed the Messalians, using the pseudo-Macarian homilies as a source. Certain difficulties have been encountered in his concepts, for he seems at times to use the technical language of the Messalians when referring to the supernatural. This gave rise to a confusion between grace as a theological concept and its consequence in the psychological order. His work on spiritual perfection had an influence on MAXIMUS THE CONFESSOR, SYMEON THE NEW THEOLOGIAN, TERESA OF AVILA, and IGNATIUS OF LOYOLA, as well as on the 18th-century Oriental collection of spiritual writers known as the *Philocalia.*

Bibliography: *Oeuvres spirituelles,* ed. and tr. É. DES PLACES (*Sources Chrétiennes* 5; 1955). F. DÖRR, *Diadochus von Photike und die Messalianer* (Freiburg 1937). H. MARROU, *Revue des études anciennes* 45 (1943) 225–232, Victor de Vita. E. HONIGMANN, *Pa-*

tristic Studies (Studi e Testi 173; 1953) 174–184. B. ALTANER, *Patrology*, tr. H. GRAEF from 5th German ed. (New York 1960) 391. H. G. BECK, *Kirche und theologische Literatur im byzantinischen Reich* (Munich 1959) 360–361.

[É. DES PLACES]

DIALECTICAL THEOLOGY

Coming as a reaction to Protestant liberalism, dialectical theology, sometimes called the theology of crisis, appeared as a movement among European Protestant theologians right after World War I. It is represented in the works of K. Barth, F. Gogarten, E. Thurneysen, E. Brunner, and R. Bultmann. Initially, all the members of the group employed the pages of the review *Zwischen den Zeiten* to echo the message Barth proclaimed in the second edition of his *Römerbrief* (1922): God's absolute transcendence, the sovereignty of His revelation in Jesus Christ, the authority of the Scriptures, and the emptiness of man, *simul justus et peccator*, before God.

Barth's starting point was God's "critical negation" (hence the movement's alternate designation) of all man's endeavors to be religious. God remains totally other even in His revelation, for His eternity and the temporality of human existence are altogether disparate. He does not enter into history in order to be captured by time. Rather, in SALVATION HISTORY the sovereign action of God touches man's world somewhat as a tangent brushes the circumference of a circle. The Word of God in Jesus Christ is, however, not merely a negation. In Him God also accepts man, so that Christ at one and the same time reveals God's wrath and His mercy.

About 1927 Barth appears to have modified his view of the dialectical situation of man. Especially in the *Kirchliche Dogmatik* (1932–67) he substitutes the positive notion of God's fidelity for the critical negation. Thus his theory merits the designation "dialectical" less than previously.

The other representatives named above supported Barth's affirmation that revelation and faith transcend all historical information and religious experience. Seeds of disagreement were present even initially, however, for Gogarten, Bultmann, and Brunner could not accept without reservation what Barth said of the radical opposition between time and eternity. From 1926 on it was evident that each of them had a peculiar and personal understanding of what dialectical theology is.

For Gogarten its basis is our recognition that we have no knowledge of God which is not, at the same time, knowledge of ourselves. Bultmann, in his own manner, thinks of the existential situation (historicity) of man and his speech concerning God (*see* EXISTENTIAL THEOLOGY). Brunner makes much of the "formal" opposition between man's being a sinner and, at the same time, made in the image of God.

These are obviously different approaches; but they have in common the consciousness of the necessity of a simultaneous "yes" and "no" concerning man before God—the dialectics of human existence. Barth would seem to go a step further in saying that nothing at all can be known about this existence of man save in the Word of God.

These theologians did a great service to Protestant Christianity by calling attention to the errors of liberalism. They did not escape ambiguity, however, especially when they discussed created existence, temporality, and how these are affected by the gracious love of God.

Bibliography: H. BOUILLARD, *Karl Barth*, 3 v. (Paris 1957), v. 1 *Genèse et évolution de la théologie dialectique*. H. U. VON BALTHASAR, *Karl Barth: Darstellung und Deutung seiner Theologie* (Cologne 1962). J. FEHR, *Das Offenbarungs-Problem in der dialektischen und thomistischen Theologie* (Freiburg 1939).

[M. B. SCHEPERS]

DIALECTICS

Basically a method for establishing the TRUTH of man's beliefs; varying estimates of its value for this purpose have been given in the history of thought. This article is concerned mainly with the nature and estimate of dialectics in Aristotle, who considered it capable of rendering beliefs only probable. His position is explained in contrast to that of Plato, who regarded dialectics as yielding the surest kind of knowledge. Since a method is determined by the subject matter on which it is used, the difference between the two is accounted for in terms of their different views of the real. The value of dialectics in modern thought is then briefly indicated.

Plato. One of the earliest extended treatments of dialectics occurs in PLATO as part of his general opposition to the SOPHISTS. It is to the credit of the Sophists that, as a consequence of their interest in truth and its grounding, especially in the moral and political spheres, they helped launch Western man into the life of reason. In Plato's judgment, that life, as they conducted it, lacked proper control, and reason's function of "cutting at the joints" of the real world was not achieved. The Sophists either relativized truth to particular, changeable circumstances, or denied the possibility of the attainment of truth, or made allowance for the presence of truth on both sides of an argument.

According to Plato, the truth about a question was determinate because the being about which any argument concerned itself was determinate (*Rep.* 478A–480). Unreconciled opposition and irrational contradiction applied to appearances, not to the really intelligible; to OPINION, not to KNOWLEDGE. Truth dealt with the eternal, real unity over the many and changing appearances of it. In fact, man is able to organize the changing images of experience only to the extent that he can recognize the stable, intelligible models they reflect, just as one can organize various pictures of different people because he knows those who posed for them (*ibid.* 514A–518).

Having this conviction about the character of truth and its object, Plato developed a method by which it became determinable. It was a method of approximation, and he traced out the various stages of approximation in a divided line of knowledge (*ibid.* 509E–514). Truth is approached by stabilizing sense knowledge through postulated intelligible hypotheses. Through deduction from such hypotheses empirical knowledge is given a universality, necessity, and rational connection it does not have in itself. As merely postulated, however, hypotheses have no more justification than what the deduced empirical knowledge can afford them. Although modern empirical philosophers take this limitation as a virtue, Plato did not so regard it (*ibid.* 529A–530).

To justify hypotheses requires the highest stage in knowledge—dialectics (*ibid.* 511). As practiced by Plato, dialectics consist of a search for the unique meanings of the terms entering the hypothesis that make their synthesis as stated by the hypothesis necessary (*ibid.* 338C). Whatever is intelligibly necessary in this way must then be true, as the intelligible is the real and the real is the intelligible.

Discrimination of meanings for terms is not a conventional matter settled only by the pragmatic results for the user, as the Sophists would have it with their *homo mensura* doctrine. Any term taken in isolation signifies merely a mode in which the things man experiences can be alike. Before it has an unambiguous sense a mode of differing must be fixed with that likeness, since definition is by way of likeness and difference. Plato, however, held that the differences that can be thought along with any given likeness to obtain a definition is a matter of intelligibility itself, not merely of an operational success in practice. It is determined by a more comprehensive concept that can embrace both the given term and its contrary in its own meaning. Thinking the given term in the context of this more comprehensive concept fixes the mode of difference that can be thought along with it. This difference then consistently opposes its contrary and makes for an unambiguous discrimination in experience. A similar reconciliation of the comprehensive term with its contrary in a yet higher and richer term then becomes necessary.

Since things are determinately defined, and so have being, only as moments of an organically intelligible whole, the search in dialectics is for the ultimate whole that gives intelligibility and, therefore, being to all things. Dialectics culminates asymptotically in the vision of the GOOD (*ibid.* 509A–510). The success of the method is guaranteed because this ultimate comprehensive whole cannot be confused with anything else, since there is nothing more with which it can be confused. PARMENIDES was basically right, except that the whole has an internal relational structure that makes rational discourse possible. Dialectics is the technique by which man explores this internal relational structure.

When Christian thinkers later speculated on revelation, seeking to give their faith an understanding, they found in PLATONISM, with its notions of transcendence, imitation, and rational model for the world, a powerful ally (*see* DIALECTICS IN THE MIDDLE AGES).

Aristotle. With ARISTOTLE dialectics became a second-best method. This change in valuation is a consequence of his changed view about the real that is to be methodically explored. An intelligible is not stabilized as a transcendent form by its rational relations of sameness and difference to all other forms in one rational whole. It is stabilized by its being this way rather than not. For man's concepts express diverse modes of BEING, and not a common, formal mode above the many of experience. They express, moreover, not a transcendent mode above the many of experience but the diverse modes in which the many are.

The basic and diverse modes are Aristotle's CATEGORIES of being. What man experiences is stabilized within a category by means of a difference specific to that mode of being and no other (*see* SPECIES). This difference, with the generic trait it specifies, is given to the thing by an efficient cause acting for some purpose; both genus and difference assume the role of definitory, actualizing form in relation to the thing's underlying matter (*see* MATTER AND FORM). The mind's search is, therefore, for these definitory components as well as for the extrinsic causes responsible for the thing's coming under their determination, since all of these necessitate its being. Differences pertinent to another mode and their causes can be ignored since they are not necessary for the mode in question.

Repeated experience makes manifest differences that are specific; but once they are made manifest to the mind by experience, their connection with the categorical trait is then directly known. Such differences are recognized as a difference of one particular category and of no other, as being three-sided is immediately recognized as a mode of being a plane figure and not a mode of being a color.

No dialectical search is required to fix these differences with a likeness, since the structure of being itself determines what differences make a difference and repeated experience of this stabilized structure leads to direct insight into it. Hypotheses are justified neither by dialectical search into meanings of terms, which could necessitate their synthesis in the hypothesis, nor by deduced empirical consequences, which could make them probably true. They are justified because the intellect intuitively recognizes that they state the causes of the thing, of that thing and no other, and that the thing could not, consequently, be other than it is (*see* CAUSALITY).

Once specific differences and the causes responsible for their presence in the composite are discovered, they can be used as middle terms in arguments or syllogisms that show or demonstrate the necessity of the thing. Since such arguments proceed from middles that signify proper and constitutive causes, they are strictly scientific arguments (*see* DEMONSTRATION).

Dialectical Reasoning. When the intellect, however, confronts an area of contingent beings or when it has not yet seized upon the proper and intrinsic causes of necessary things, it cannot argue scientifically. But, in Aristotle's view, inability to argue in this way does not mean complete inability to reason at all (*Topica* 100a 25–101a 18). To be sure, any inferential process requires a middle term to join subject and predicate in the conclusion. But in lieu of the objective causes that show the objective necessity of their connection, a trace or SIGN of their connection can function as a middle for at least probable knowledge of their juncture. A sign cannot cause the being of the thing, but it can cause a probable knowledge of the thing. One such trace or sign of the thing's being is the logical order caused in the mind as it thinks about it. For Aristotle, the technique of establishing probable truth through a sign of this type is dialectical reasoning.

The problem of grounding the truth is not merely a question of looking to see whether things are the way one states them to be in propositions. Truths can be universal; and, therefore, some knowable principle must be used to establish them universally. In science this principle is the objective cause, which grounds the truth universally through the necessity it produces in the thing itself. In dialectics this principle is the kind of order of predicating UNIVERSALS that one can establish in his thought about things. For, in knowing, one knows universally and then relates universals to particulars in PREDICATION. Since the mode of predicating a universal is merely a logical order, it is impotent in the real. But since man's ability to predicate the universal according to a given mode is controlled by things, such predication can be taken as an intelligible sign of things. Being an intelligible sign in-

volving a universal, it points to a connection in things that transcends, with some probability, the particulars immediately given in experience.

Because dialectics considers only the mode of predicating the universal and not the nature expressed in it, it is not limited to any one subject matter as is SCIENCE (*scientia*) in the strict sense (*ibid.* 104b 1–13). It becomes, therefore, a counterpart to RHETORIC—the ability to persuade on almost any subject that is presented (*Rhet.* 1354a 1–5). The problem of rhetoric, however, is more complicated, since there it is not merely a question of establishing the probability of a belief, but of establishing it for a given audience. The principles that a rhetorician uses, accordingly, are not simply the commonplaces of dialectics, but also whatever is includable in argument that will dispose the audience to accept it. They include, therefore, his own character and the emotional dispositions of his audience as well.

Dialectical Problems. Ability to reason dialectically turns, in part, on a knowledge of the possible kinds of problems that can occur for a universal predicate is attributed to a subject, regardless of the peculiar natures they signify. Aristotle distinguishes four such problems based on a combination of convertibility with, and essentiality to, the subject. A universal predicated convertibly and essentially of the subject constitutes the problem of DEFINITION; predicated convertibly but not essentially, the dialectical problem of PROPERTY; predicated essentially but not convertibly, the dialectical problem of GENUS; predicated nonessentially and nonconvertibly, the dialectical problem of ACCIDENT (*Topica* 101b 18–25, 101b 38–102b 26, 103b 2–20).

An actual dialectical problem arises only when a universal is predicated of a subject in one of the above modes, not from the universal by itself. To ask, "Is 'an animal that walks on two feet' a definition of man or not?," raises a dialectical problem (*ibid.* 101b 26–29). These problems form the subjects on which reasonings take place. If one changes the turn of the phrase and says, "'An animal that walks on two feet' is the definition of man, is it not?," he forms a dialectical proposition. These propositions are the materials with which arguments start; and since they differ from problems only in phraseology, they are equal in number to them. In either case, a grasp of the kinds of problems or propositions is requisite for dialectical skill.

Although a mode of predication accompanies every proposition and question, appeal to the mode of predication as a principle for grounding the truth is superfluous in those cases in which certainty is possible. Accordingly, not every proposition or every problem can be set down as dialectical. About things that are evident to everyone, no dialectical problem can be formed, since the truth about them is already known. Conversely, about things that no one would accept, no dialectical proposition can be formed, since they are evidently false (*ibid.* 104a 3–8). In dialectics the mind is dealing with the order it itself creates while judging about things. In evident things it does not advert to that order to make the judgment. In nonaccepted things no order is formed to which it could advert.

Techniques and Rules. Besides this formal knowledge of kinds of problems and propositions, dialectical skill, for its exercise, requires that one become well supplied with a stock of them. Aristotle organizes the acquisition of such a stock around four techniques: the securing of propositions; the distinction of senses of particular expressions; the discovery of the differences of things; and the investigation of their likenesses (*ibid.* 105a 20–33). In the case of the last three, since it is always possible to make a proposition corresponding to each of them, one has techniques for securing propositions not yet formed, whereas the first systematically collects those already in existence.

In the discovering of the differences of things, care should be taken to preserve the dialectical character of the inquiry. If the things one examines are very far apart, the differences between them will be entirely obvious. No dialectical proposition is made about the obvious. A similar precaution should be observed with investigating likenesses. In things very close, the likeness is obvious. In securing propositions, they too should be selected in ways that correspond to distinctions drawn regarding their dialectical character. They should be about something having common agreement or the agreement of the experts. Since dialectics is not limited to any one objective subject matter, the propositions should further be organized according to their ethical, logical, or physical content. Distinction of meanings of terms can proceed also by the common dialectical technique of examining the senses of opposed terms. If the opposite has more than one sense, then the original has also (*ibid.* 105a 34–108a 17).

With these techniques for supplying propositions and problems, it becomes possible to apply the commonplace rules that govern the four different modes of predication. Given the proposition "'animal' is the genus of man, is it not?," then "animal" should be true in every instance of man, applicable to other things as well, and predicated in the same category as "man." It would be possible to defend the proposition by showing that everyone agrees or that the experts agree in applying the term universally to men; that, in cases in which it is denied of man, the sense of the term that is denied is different from its asserted sense; that men are like tigers, which are conceded to be animals; or that men are radically different from the things an opponent would allege as constituting the class to which men belong. Most of Aristotle's treatise on dialectics is given over to delineating these commonplace rules for each of the modes of predication.

The value of dialectics becomes apparent from its nature (*ibid.* 101a 25–101b 4). That it is useful as an intellectual training follows from the orderly plan of inquiry based on the modes of predication one is able to bring to bear on a subject; he is thus able to argue more easily about it. It also has a value in disputes with people on contingent matters. One can meet them on commonly accepted grounds or oppose them with authorities more expert than the ones they cite. In regard to matters necessary in themselves, but for which one does not yet know the proximate principles of the scientific proof, it disposes the mind to those principles by establishing the facts for which they must account. The more one can establish as probably true of a subject, the better his chances of inducing the indemonstrable premise from which genuine science can start. Finally, it defends the principles themselves when they come under attack. Principles cannot be scientifically proved, being the condition for all proof in a field; they can only be dialectically defended.

Moderns. Science, as that term is understood in modern thought, does not search for causes in the sense in which Aristotle deemed necessary for certain knowledge of the world. Hence, his account of the general nature of scientific method does not generally receive a favorable hearing. Modern investigators into nature are content to discover and confirm empirical hypotheses that merely give a probable rule for the anticipation of future experience [A. J. Ayer, *Language, Truth and Logic* (2d ed. London 1946) 41]. Empirical hypotheses, however, have two dimensions to them: a formal structure supplied by the scientist's logical system and a material content supplied by experience. Empirical confirmation, through examination of likenesses and differences, of one's ability to think the data in the formal mode of organization given to them by the hypothesis is then taken as an indication of the probable truth of the hypothesis. The procedure is much like what Aristotle would call dialectics. Although the Aristotelian logical modes of definition, genus, property, and accident are not explicitly in the forefront of discussion of logical frameworks (being based on the subject-predicate formal relation), the dialectical techniques for accumulating a supply of problems and propositions and for applying the commonplace rules of whatever logical modes are used are still valued. Consensus of the experts, distinction in meanings of terms, and discovery of likenesses and differences are still carried on, albeit at a more sophisticated level.

Modern theoreticians of science are also inclined to classify problems on the basis of the subject dealt with, in the dialectical fashion that Aristotle recognized. Problems of determining the formal structure of hypotheses are logical problems; those dealing with the predictable empirical content of hypotheses are problems of physics in the broad sense; and those dealing with emotional expression relative to what one experiences are ethical problems. Although Aristotle recognized such a dialectical division of problems, he complemented it with a scientific division into theoretical, practical, and productive.

In the history of philosophy subsequent to Aristotle's time, dialectics has often been elevated, as with Plato, to the primary method for examining the real. The character of the real and the character of the principles by which the dialectical method can be brought to bear on the real have not, however, been the same as Plato's. At times the method is conceived on an idealist base, as with G. W. F. HEGEL, in which, through the dialectical process, Spirit reflexively realizes itself in ever more encompassing totalities (see HEGELIANISM AND NEO-HEGELIANISM). At others, it is conceived on a materialist base, as with K. MARX, in which, through the dialectical process, man actionally overcomes class antagonisms in ameliorating his social world into a classless society. Dialectics is calculated, however, to reconcile just such oppositions as that between spirit and matter (see MATERIALISM, DIALECTICAL AND HISTORICAL).

See Also: ARGUMENTATION; METHODOLOGY (PHILOSOPHY); REASONING.

Bibliography: M. J. ADLER, *Dialectic* (New York 1927). M. J. ADLER, ed. *The Great Ideas: A Syntopicon of Great Books of the Western World,* 2 v. (Chicago 1952) 1:345–357. C. CAPONE BRAGA, *Enciclopedia filosofica,* 4 v. (Venice-Rome 1957) 1:1539–1559, complete bibliog.; *Della dialettica* (Turin 1953). R. EISLER, *Wörterbuch der philosophischen Begriffe,* 3 v. (4th ed. Berlin 1927–30) 1:268–272. T. GILBY, *Barbara Celarent: A Description of Scholastic Dialectic* (New York 1949). L. M. RÈGIS, *L'Opinion selon Aristote* (Ottawa 1935). B. LAKEBRINK, *Hegels dialektische Ontologie und die Thomistische Analektik* (Cologne 1955).

[J. J. ZIEGLER]

DIALECTICS IN THE MIDDLE AGES

From the patristic period to the end of the 12th century, dialectics was synonymous with LOGIC and considered one of the LIBERAL ARTS of the trivium. The central problem was the validity of using rational dialectics in the domain of divine revelation, a domain that can be entered only by supernatural faith. Certain ecclesiastical writers, such as TATIAN and TERTULLIAN, rejected dialectics as the father of heresy. Others, notably St. AUGUSTINE, ap-

proved the use of dialectics in Christian doctrine as a means to a deeper appreciation of revelation and as a means of recognizing and refuting heresy (*Ordine* 2.3; *Civ.* 8.10). This controversy reached its peak in the 11th and 12th centuries. In the 11th century the tension was between dialecticians and grammarians in the Eucharistic controversy, and in the 12th century, between dialecticians and the monks in the Trinitarian controversies. By 1200 the legitimacy of using dialectics in theology was assured, thus opening the way to the full development of the scholastic method in *quaestiones disputatae, quodlibetales, summae* and commentaries, in which new scholastic syntheses were achieved. The excessive, futile use of dialectics, both in philosophy and in theology, finally led to its decline during the late period of medieval scholasticism.

Growth. Before the end of classical antiquity BOETHIUS had translated the major logical works of Aristotle, commented on several of them and composed logical treatises of his own. These works described a theory of reasoning, called logic that was included in early medieval education. CASSIODORUS and St. ISIDORE OF SEVILLE transmitted the essentials of dialectics in their discussion of the seven liberal arts. In the Carolingian revival of learning, masters such as ALCUIN and RABANUS MAURUS stressed the importance of both dialectics and grammar, even though their own works were devoid of originality. Both grammarians and dialecticians applied their art to theological questions. Thus GOTTSCHALK OF ORBAIS, a grammarian, successfully discussed problems of predestination and free will, while JOHN SCOTUS ERIUGENA, the dialectician, was condemned for his refutation of Gottschalk. RATRAMNUS OF CORBIE, a dialectician, successfully criticized the views of Macarius Scotus in his *De anima* and *De quantitate animae* (see M. Manitius, *Geschichte der lateinischen Literatur des Mittelalters,* 1:414–417). Despite Erigena's great genius, his *De divisione naturae* was not wholly conformable to orthodox teaching. The tentative efforts of these thinkers indicate the great difficulty of trying to give a rational explanation of the world. Toward the end of the tenth century, Gerbert, later SYLVESTER II, emphasized the importance of definition and classification in his *De rationali et de ratione uti;* this was a prelude to the development of dialectics in the 11th century.

Professional Dialecticians. In the 11th century professional dialecticians such as Anselm of Besata (Milan), known as the Peripatetic (fl. *c.* 1048) and BERENGARIUS OF TOURS appeared, who were frequently imprudent in their application of dialectics to the doctrine of the Eucharist. Berengarius, believing the Eucharistic treatise of Ratramnus of Corbie to be the work of John Scotus Erigena, defended it with dialectical acumen against the doctrine of St. PASCHASIUS RADBERTUS. Berengarius, insisting on the Augustinian distinction between *sacramentum* and *res,* declared that the external, visible sacrament of the altar is not the real Body and Blood of Christ, but only a symbol. LANFRANC THE GRAMMARIAN, refusing to limit the meaning of the word sacrament to the external, visible materials, reproached Berengarius for denying the Real Presence of the true Body and Blood of Christ: "By seeking refuge in dialectics you have abandoned the holy writers." Berengarius's view, as understood by his contemporaries, was condemned by many synods between 1050 and his formal profession of faith at the Council of Rome in 1059 (Denzinger, *Enchiridion symbolorum* 690).

The case of Berengarius was only one example of the use of dialectics in the 11th century. But the numerous condemnations of his Eucharistic doctrine gave strength to vociferous antidialecticians, who feared the use of dialectics in matters of faith. St. PETER DAMIAN violently opposed the use of dialectics in the sacred sciences, as did MANEGOLD OF LAUTENBACH and GERARD OF CSANÁD, who insisted that "philosophy is only the handmaid of theology."

Early Scholasticism. At the Abbey of Bec, Lanfranc's disciple, St. ANSELM OF CANTERBURY, achieved the first successful synthesis of dialectics and faith: "I do not seek to understand in order to believe, but I believe in order to understand" (*Proslog.* 1.227). The spirit motivating Anselm's dialectics is aptly expressed in the rule, *FIDES QUAERENS INTELLECTUM* (faith seeking understanding). Although Anselm refused to subordinate, as some dialecticians had done, Holy Scripture to dialectics, he took sides against the adversaries of dialectics, insisting on the need to strive toward rational understanding of what one believes. For this reason Anselm tried to find "necessary reasons" within faith for the truths of belief. He opened the way to a fruitful collaboration between faith and rational investigation.

Pure dialectics and applied dialectics were cultivated to an intense degree by the *scholares,* or schoolmen, of the early 12th century (*see* SCHOLASTICISM, 1). Already St. IVO OF CHARTRES had collected the legislative texts of the Church and used dialectics to harmonize divergent provisions of the law (*see* IVO OF CHARTRES, COLLECTION OF). At the cathedral school of Laon, the first collections of *sentences* were made by Anselm, Ralph and their students (*see* SENTENCES AND SUMMAE). These orderly, systematic collections of reconciled patristic texts were accomplished by the careful use of dialectics, defining terms, distinguishing aspects and reasoning from sound principles. The use of dialectics in the cathedral schools of the early 12th century initiated the SCHOLASTIC METH-

OD. This use of dialectics, however, did not displace the Bible, the Fathers of the Church, or the humanities. The schools of the 12th century, despite certain excesses, tried to cultivate a harmony between dialectics and Christian humanism.

Between 1115 and 1140 Peter ABELARD made a strong effort to increase the role of dialectics in its pure form of scientific logic and in its applied form in theology (*see* LOGIC, HISTORY OF; UNIVERSALS). He firmly believed in the ability of reason to clarify even the profoundest mysteries of faith. The list of pro and con texts dealing with 158 theological problems, which were collected by Abelard and his school in *Sic et non,* indicates the kind of problem commonly discussed by the dialecticians. Abelard's boldness in applying dialectics to the Trinity aroused the hostility of St. BERNARD OF CLAIRVAUX, WILLIAM OF SAINT-THIERRY and other Cistercians against dialectics and scholasticism: "God cannot be imprisoned in a syllogism." Although Abelard was condemned in 1121 and in 1140 for his misuse of dialectics in Trinitarian doctrine, and although GILBERT DE LA PORRÉE, Bishop of Poitiers, was condemned in 1147 for a similar misuse, dialectics became an essential feature in scholastic education. GRATIAN used it in the compilation of the *Decretum* (before 1140); PETER LOMBARD used it to compile his *Sentences* (*c.* 1150); PETER OF POITIERS used it in his commentaries and Peter Helias used it in grammar in the second half of the 12th century. The use of dialectics in theology was still opposed by GERHOH OF REICHERSBERG, so that in 1164 Alexander III forbade "all figures of speech and inordinate questions (*indisciplinatas*) in theology." Although the Canons Regular of Saint-Victor had been founded early in the century to bridge the chasm that had developed between the *scholares* (schoolmen) and *claustrales* (monks), WALTER OF SAINT-VICTOR asserted (*c.* 1170) that every dialectician was a heretic. Nevertheless, the schools of Paris flourished under STEPHEN LANGTON, PETER CANTOR, SIMON OF TOURNAI and PHILIP THE CHANCELLOR, who not only studied dialectics, but developed the scholastic commentaries and the scholastic disputation.

Maturity. Dialectics, in the sense of logic, reached its full maturity in the 13th century. Although the new books of Aristotle's logic (*logica nova*) and Arabic treatises and commentaries in logic were translated by the end of the 12th century, time was needed to assimilate the new learning. With the new learning came the distinction between LOGIC in the broad sense of the entire *Organon* of ARISTOTLE and DIALECTICS in the narrow sense of tentative and probable reasoning. The new Aristotelian books, particularly the *Posterior Analytics,* helped the schoolmen understand the meaning of SCIENCE (*scientia*) as the knowledge of a stated truth through principles that are demonstratively causes of that stated truth. The schoolmen could then distinguish between demonstrative (scientific) reasoning, probable (dialectical) reasoning, and sophistical (false) reasoning. The schoolmen of the 13th century, although desirous of true demonstrations, did not underestimate the value of dialectical arguments. But, for them, it was important to distinguish between the two.

Scholastic Disputations. The new Aristotelian learning, culminating in the development of dialectics in the earlier period, contributed to the perfecting of scholastic *quaestiones disputatae* in medieval universities. In every faculty, masters were obliged to hold scholastic disputations on fixed days of the academic year. The rules of this technique were learned in the faculty of arts; the art was acquired in the same faculty through disputations *de sophismatibus.* In the lower faculty of arts it was important for the student to recognize false or sophistical arguments and to distinguish logical terms in proper form. The rigid form of scholastic disputations prevented the one objecting (*obiiciens*) from straying afield and forced the one responding (*respondens*) to answer to the point. This dialectic between student objectors and a bachelor respondent was resolved by the determination of the master who presided over the disputation. Under the stimulus of scholastic disputations, the art of dialectics reached a new high, unparalleled in history. The schoolmen of the 13th century did not dispute for the sake of disputing, but for the sake of reaching truths with certitude. By the middle of the century, courageous masters in theology were willing to hold special disputations, during Advent and Lent, called *de quolibet.* In these, anyone could pose any question for discussion by the group; the master was bound to respond to difficulties and to resolve the problem.

Scholastic Summae and Commentaries. The form of the disputation was so much a part of scholastic education that when the great commentaries and *summae* were written in the 13th century, they naturally took the form of dialectical debate. An outstanding example of this is the *Summa theologiae* of St. THOMAS AQUINAS, each article of which is like a finished version of a disputed question. However, not every question is resolved by a demonstration in the Aristotelian sense; many questions are resolved dialectically, in the strict sense of the term. This is also true of the great commentaries on the *Sentences,* such as those by St. Thomas Aquinas, St. BONAVENTURE, RICHARD FISHACRE, St. ALBERT THE GREAT and RICHARD OF MIDDLETON. In the *Summa contra gentiles,* St. Thomas presented one argument after the other in proof of a Catholic truth without designating those that are demonstrative and those that are only persuasive, or dialectical.

Thus, by the end of the 13th century, the word dialectics was used in three senses: (1) the use of reason to investigate even revealed truths; (2) the logical art of disputing questions in all faculties of the university; and (3) the restricted sense of a probable, or persuasive, argument.

Decline. Some historians consider the decay of dialectics to begin with John DUNS SCOTUS or, at least, with WILLIAM OF OCKHAM. Others, considering Scotus and Ockham as belonging to the full bloom of scholastic dialectics, believe that the decline should be dated after 1350. Actually, the decline of scholasticism was a result of many factors, of which the subtleties of Scotus and the nominalism of Ockham are only symptomatic. By 1300 dialectics in the Middle Ages had lost its Biblical, patristic and humanist moorings. Scholastics, preferring to dispute subtle questions rather than to comment on the Bible, made dialectics an end in itself, divorced even from patristic sources. Neither Scotus nor Ockham wrote commentaries on Scripture. Secular masters in particular were conspicuous for their reluctance to comment on Scripture, preferring instead the subtleties of dialectics. This is evident both from the dearth of such commentaries by seculars and from the controversy between the University of Oxford and the Dominicans in the early 14th century. Most important of all was the influence of the *calculationes,* or "letter calculus," that developed in the faculty of arts at Oxford. The enthusiasm of philosophers and *sophistae* for the *calculationes* was normal, even though humanists, such as Giovanni Pico and Luis VIVES, were horrified. Before the middle of the century, however, the *calculationes* were freely employed in commentaries on the *Sentences.*

The arid sterility of such dialectics ultimately provoked two reactions, namely, the humanist revival in philosophy and the Biblical and patristic revival in theology. It was largely responsible also for the preference of RHETORIC over dialectics as a pedagogical method among the followers of Peter RAMUS.

See Also: DIALECTICS; FAITH AND REASON; METHODOLOGY (PHILOSOPHY).

Bibliography: E. GILSON, *History of Christian Philosophy* (New York 1955). F. C. COPLESTON, *History of Philosophy* (Westminster, Md 1946–) v.2. C. E. SHEEDY, *The Eucharistic Controversy of the Eleventh Century against the Background of Prescholastic Philosophy* (Washington 1947). J. DE GHELLINCK, *Le Mouvement théologique du XIIIᵉ siècle* (2d ed. Bruges 1948). J. DE GHELLINCK, "Dialectique, théologie et dogme aux IXᵉ–XIIᵉ siècles," *Festgabe Clemens Bäumker* (*Beiträge zur Geschichte der Philosophie und Theologie des Mittelalters* Suppl.1; 1913) 79–99. G. PARÉ et al., *La Renaissance du XIIᵉ siècle: Les Écoles et l'enseignement* (Ottawa 1933) 125–131, 197–201, 275–306. A. VAN DE VYVER, "Les Étapes du développement philosophique du haut moyen-âge," *Revue belge de philologie et d'histoire,* 8 (1929) 425–453. T. HEITZ, *Essai* *historique sur les rapports entre la philosophie et la foi de Bérenger de Tours à s. Thomas d'Aquin* (Paris 1909). E. GARIN, "La dialettica dal secolo XII al principio dell'età moderna," *Rivista di filosofia neoscolastica,* 49 (1958) 228–253. M. GRABMANN, *Die Geschichte der scholastischen Methode,* 2 v. (Freiburg 1909–11). J. A. ENDRES, *Forschungen zur Geschichte der frühmittelalterlichen Philosophie* (*Beiträge zur Geschichte der Philosophie und Theologie des Mittelalters,* 17.2–3; 1915). J. A. WEISHEIPL, "The Evolution of Scientific Method," *The Logic of Science,* ed., V. E. SMITH (New York 1964) 59–86. M. MANITIUS, *Geschichte der lateinischen Literatur des Mittelalters,* 3 v. (Munich 1911–31).

[P. MICHAUD-QUANTIN/J. A. WEISHEIPL]

DIALOGUE (LITERARY GENRE)

Dialogue was a medium of instruction before the Academy, a teaching technique of Socrates that was perfected by Plato as a literary form. There are four main forms: the dialogue-report, a stenographic account of a conversation; the dramatic dialogue, which transforms a historical dialogue for literary effect; the fictional dialogue; and the didactic discourse, where the dialogue is only a framework. Plato's dialogues, dramatic and fictional, were probably influenced by the mimes of Sophron (*Athenaeus* 11.504b; Plato, *Rep.* 5.451C), but their total meaning emerges only through the subtle dialectic and the resolution of opposing points of view. This concept of the dialogue was not fully grasped by Cicero or Tacitus, or by Christian imitators of Plato who used the dialogue as a vehicle of instruction. Examples of the dialogue–report are Augustine's *On the Happy Life* and Gregory of Nyssa's *On Fate;* of the didactic discourse, the *Symposium* of Methodius of Olympus.

Bibliography: R. HIRZEL, *Der Dialog,* 2 v. (Leipzig 1895). R. HACKFORTH and R. M. HENRY, *The Oxford Classical Dictionary,* ed. M. CARY et al. (Oxford 1949) 273–274. A. HERMANN and G. BARDY, *Reallexikon für Antike und Christentum,* ed. T. KLAUSER [Stuttgart 1941 (1950)–] 3:928–955.

[H. MUSURILLO]

DIAMOND, CHARLES

Journalist; b. Maghera, Ireland, Nov. 17, 1858; d. London, Feb. 19, 1934. Early in life Diamond migrated to England and settled among the large working-class population of Irish immigrants in Newcastle-upon-Tyne. In this environment he grew deeply interested in Irish nationalist politics. He was elected Member of Parliament for North Monaghan (1892), but the absorbing interest of his life was Catholic journalism. He founded the *Irish Tribune* (1884) to champion the cause of the immigrants in industrial Tyneside and developed the New Catholic Press Ltd. In 1887 he was invited to Glasgow to help the

group of Irish immigrants who had launched the *Glasgow Observer.* He bought the paper in 1894 and established the Scottish Catholic Printing Co. Ltd., which published local editions of the paper in other parts of Scotland, such as the *Edinburgh Catholic Herald,* the *Lanarkshire Catholic Herald,* and the *Clydesdale Catholic Herald.* He adopted the same policy in England, where the parent paper was the *London Catholic Herald.*

In addition to these newspapers, Diamond sponsored weekly and monthly journals and is reputed to have controlled more than 40 publications, covering all the areas of Scotland and England where Irish immigrants had settled in large numbers. He was a vigorous writer in the cause of Irish nationalism; the policies of his newspapers won the sympathies of the expatriated Irish of Great Britain and, in particular, they encouraged the flow of money and material from the Irish immigrants in southwest Scotland to make possible the success of the Sinn Fein campaign in Ireland. An article he wrote in December 1919 on the ethics of tyrannicide brought him a six-month jail sentence. His benefactions toward the social and educational improvement of Catholics increased with advancing years, and his journalistic activities continued until his death.

[D. MCROBERTS]

DIAMPER, SYNOD OF

Convoked by Alexis de Menezes (Alexio de Meneses), the Latin Archbishop of Goa, the Synod of Diamper was held in the parish church of Diamper (Udayamperoor) near Ernakulam, Kerala, from June 20 to 26, 1599. A total of 153 priests and 660 lay representatives attended the Synod, as it was the custom of the *Yogam* of the Malabar Church to include the laity. Many clergy refused to attend the synod as a mark of displeasure and protest at Menezes' interference. According to Francis Roz, a Jesuit and Menezes' assistant who was present at Diamper and who subsequently became the first Latin Bishop of Angamaly, the synod was not in proper form, nor was there any discussion. Through decrees which had been prepared in advance and translated into the vernacular, and which were neither accurate nor objective, Menezes attempted to correct supposed "errors" and to latinize the St. Thomas Christians. Roz conceded that members of the synod did not understand the proceedings, but were forced to put their signature under duress and pain of excommunication. He further admitted that Menezes modified the synodal acts and unilaterally added new ones.

The earliest authoritative report on Diamper, and its acts and decrees is given by the Portuguese writer Gouvea (*Jornada do Arcebispo de Goa Dom Frey Alexio de Menezes,* Coimbra, 1606). The official acts of the synod comprised the profession of faith and decrees on the sacraments, especially the Eucharist, corrections of "errors" in liturgical books, the reduction of the juridical status of the ancient Metropolitan See of Angamaly to that of a Latin suffragan see under the *Padroado* Metropolitan of Goa, and the expurgation of supposed "errors" in the customs and traditions of the St. Thomas Christians.

Looking back, many contemporary historians argue that the synod was invalid on the grounds that it was convoked without authority, because Menezes' authority as the Latin Primate of the East did not extend beyond the Latin sees into the Oriental churches. The synod was not conducted in accordance with ecclesial canons, and it was neither canonically approved nor ratified by Rome, which had merely authorized Archbishop Menezes to investigate the situation of the St. Thomas Christians and to appoint a successor to Mar Abraham should he die without consecrating a successor. Scholars agree that Menezes never received any authorization from Rome to convoke a synod to reform the ecclesial life and traditions of the St. Thomas Christians.

The Synod of Diamper resulted in the latinization of the St. Thomas Christian communities. The synodal decrees condemned many of the ancient indigenous customs and traditions and latinized their East Syrian (Chaldean) liturgy, prayers and devotions. It also resulted in the destruction of a significant number of valuable Syriac manuscripts and books on the suspicion of heresy. Historians are unanimous in concluding that the Synod of Diamper almost destroyed the unique identity and ancient heritage of the St. Thomas Christians in India.

See Also: INDIA, CHRISTIANITY IN.

[K. PATHIL]

DIANA, ANTONINO

Theatine moral theologian who strongly influenced the development of CASUISTRY in 17th and 18th centuries; b. Palermo, Sicily, *c.* 1585; d. Rome, July 20, 1663. Even before taking his vows in the Theatine Order (1630), he had become famous as a counselor in moral matters. URBAN VIII, INNOCENT X, and ALEXANDER VII esteemed him highly and named him examiner of bishops. In 1629 Diana published at Palermo a first series of cases, entitled *Resolutiones morales.* The work's immediate success compelled him to make repeated additions to it; when completed (1659), the 12-volume collection contained 6,000 cases. During the following century it was republished frequently, either in original form or in abridged versions. But when RIGORISM set in at the end of the 18th century, Diana's reputation waned quickly. Theologians now agree that he had laxist tendencies, and often relied too much on extrinsic proofs to the neglect of moral principles. But his name still exemplifies an epoch in modern casuistry.

Bibliography: A. INGOLD, *Dictionnaire de théologie catholique,* ed. A. VACANT, et al. (Paris 1903–50) 4.1:734. H. HURTER, *Nomenclator literarius theologiae catholicae* (3d ed. Innsbruck 1903–13) 3:1191–93. R. BROUILLARD, *Catholicisme. Hier, aujourd'hui et demain,* ed. G. JACQUEMET (Paris 1947–) 3:739–740.

[R. A. COUTURE]

DIANA (ARTEMIS) OF THE EPHESIANS

The Latin name Diana was adopted by the Old Latin and the Vulgate as the equivalent of the Greek Artemis (Acts 19:24–40). The Artemis of Ephesus had or was given certain Greek traits characteristic of Artemis on the mainland of Greece, but she was essentially a Greek adaptation of the Great Mother-Goddess of Asia Minor. She was at once a mother-goddess and a virgin-goddess of the woods and hills. Her temple at Ephesus was regarded as one of the Seven Wonders of the World. In the Hellenistic and early Roman period her worship was the most important of the cults of Asia Minor, and she was venerated throughout the whole Mediterranean area. The chief priest in her worship was a eunuch, but she was served also by maiden priestesses who held office for a fixed time and were then free to marry. Sacrifices of food, libations, incense, and, more rarely, animal victims were made to her. Her main festival, the *Artemision,* was celebrated with great pomp in the month Artemisios (March 24–April 24). Her temple was widely recognized as an asylum for fugitives and, in particular, for runaway slaves.

The goddess herself, who was called "the great Ephesian goddess Artemis" and "Artemis of the Ephesians," among other titles, was originally represented as nude or draped, sitting or standing, with accompanying symbols. Before the 4th century B.C., there is no trace of the representation of the goddess as a multibreasted standing figure. The earliest dated examples of this type come from Ephesus and Tralles (133 B.C.). The headdress, the numerous breasts, the animals and birds depicted among the bands covering the lower part of her body all point to the Oriental character of her cult and to her identification as a syncretistic divinity of fertility.

The cult of Artemis played a major role in the economic life of Ephesus as well as in its religious life. Her rich temple served not only as a center of cult and pilgrimage but also as an important bank. Accordingly, it is easy to understand the hostility that St. Paul's successful preaching aroused among craftsmen and others deriving their livelihoods from her cult.

Bibliography: L. R. TAYLOR, "Artemis of Ephesus," F. J. FOAKES JACKSON and K. LAKE, eds., *The Beginnings of Christianity: pt. 1, Acts of the Apostles,* 5 v. (London 1920–33), Part 1, v.5 (London 1933) 251–256. P. ANTOINE, *Dictionnaire de la Bible,* supp. ed. L. PIROT, et al. (Paris 1928–) 2:1076–1104. F. MILTNER, *Ephesos, Stadt der Artemis und des Johannes* (Vienna 1958).

[M. R. P. MCGUIRE]

DIASPORA, JEWISH

The word "diaspora" is a transliteration of the Greek word διασπορά "dispersion." In historical writing the word is used to designate the diffusion of Jews through the Greek and Roman world in the Hellenistic and early Christian eras. This diffusion is here treated in its origin and extent, and in its influences on Judaism and early Christianity.

Origin and Extent. The diffusion of the people of Israel outside Palestine began late in the eighth century B.C. When the northern kingdom, Israel, was destroyed by the Assyrians (734–721 B.C.) and its territory incorporated into the Assyrian empire, much of the population was deported to other parts of the empire. These, "the Lost Ten Tribes" of popular tradition, lost their distinct ethnic and religious identity by assimilation with the foreign peoples among whom they lived. Similar removals were made from Judah in the Babylonian campaigns that ended that kingdom (598–587 B.C.). There were migrations, voluntary or forced, to other regions, especially to Egypt; a Jewish military colony was stationed under Persian rule at the frontier post of Elephantine on the Nile (near the modern Aswan) before 525 B.C. A migration to Egypt is related in Jeremia, ch. 42 to 43. The colony from Juda in Babylon, however, was the most notable and historically significant group of exiles; it retained its ethnic and religious identity, and when the Persians conquered Babylon in 539 B.C., it furnished wealth and people for the restoration in Palestine. The Babylonian community was also largely responsible for the beginning of the collection of sacred books that became the Old Testament.

The conquest of the Persian empire by Alexander (d. 323 B.C.) effected a cultural revolution in the Near East. Along with Greek rule, Greek culture flooded the area. A great development of trade and commerce resulted, and migration was encouraged in the kingdoms of Alexander's successors. In this movement the Jews were very active. There is no history of their migrations, but under the Ptolemies Jews could easily migrate to Egypt, and many Jewish communities appear by the end of the 1st century B.C. in Syria, Egypt, Asia Minor, Mesopotamia, Greece, and Italy. In Acts 2.9–10, Jews who are Parthians, Medes, Elamites, residents of Mesopotamia, Cappadocia, Pontus, Asia, Phrygia, Pamphylia, Egypt, Cyrene, Rome, Crete, and Arabia are mentioned. The largest Jewish centers of the Diaspora were in Rome, Alexandria, and Antioch, the three largest cities of the Roman Empire. Jews probably did not reach Antioch before 150 B.C., and Rome later. Alexandria's Jewish population was the largest, richest, and most influential. They dwelt in their own quarter and enjoyed municipal autonomy under their own ethnarch. The number of Jews of the Diaspora is estimated in the millions, possibly 8 to 10 per cent of the Roman Empire's population.

Influences on Judaism and Early Christianity. Jews of the Diaspora were much more open to Greek culture than the Palestinian Jews. They spoke Greek, and only a few were acquainted with Hebrew or Aramaic. They often had Greek names or deliberately altered a Hebrew name to an assonant Greek name (Joshua-Jason, Eliakim-Alcimus). Most of them were engaged in trade and the crafts, in many cases having migrated because of better opportunities presented in the Hellenistic cities. As a group they had a higher income than Palestinian Jews. Their commercial importance normally brought them privileges from royal and local governments. Their position at Alexandria was better than that of the natives. Because of their religious scruples about military emblems, which they considered idols, the Romans exempted them from military service. When the Romans began to extend Roman citizenship throughout the empire, Paul was one of many Jews who acquired it.

Because they lived surrounded by Greek culture, the Hellenistic Jews did not exhibit as much hostility to it as was shown by Pharisaic Judaism. As a result, Alexandria, the great center of Greek scholarship, also became a center of Jewish Hellenistic learning. The Jews of Alexandria very likely produced the Greek translation of the Old Testament, the Septuagint, and thus performed a work of incalculable importance for Christianity. Scholars and authors appeared among them, of whom PHILO Judaeus is the most renowned.

In spite of immersion in Greek civilization, Jews looked to Palestine for spiritual leadership. Their contributions were essential for support of the temple and the priests. A network of communications knit them with Jerusalem and with each other; thus, the exiles remained solidly Jewish. Since sacrifice could be offered only in Jerusalem, the synagogue was instituted by the Diaspora and spread into Palestine itself. Through synagogical worship Judaism survived after Jerusalem, its spiritual home, was destroyed. The network of synagogues was a path for Paul on his missionary journeys.

Among the Disapora anti-Judaism first appeared. The exclusiveness of Jews, their prosperity and privileges, aroused a harsh xenophobia in many great cities. Anti-Jewish riots occurred at Antioch, Alexandria, and Caesarea, and charges were frequently laid against them in courts. At Alexandria a nearly perpetual feud developed into a brief but genuine persecution under Caligula; a Jewish delegation headed by Philo presented the Jewish case at Rome, but Caligula's assassination ended his oppressive measures. Jews were expelled from Rome more than once, and elsewhere their privileges were temporarily revoked. Anti-Jewish prejudice was expressed by such figures of Roman literature as Cicero, Seneca, Persius, Quintilian, Statius, Juvenal, and Tacitus. Flavius Josephus composed an apology for Judaism in response to an attack by a certain Apion.

Bibliography: W. O. E. OESTERLEY, *The Jews and Judaism During the Greek Period* (New York 1941). S. W. BARON, *A Social and Religious History of the Jews,* 8 v. (2d ed. rev. and enl. New York 1952). E. SCHÜRER, *A History of the Jewish People in the Time of Christ,* 5 v. (Edinburgh 1897–98).

[J. L. MCKENZIE]

DIATESSARON

An early recension of the Gospel text. The Diatessaron (lit. "out of four [gospels]," as it was known to Greek-speaking Christians; *Euangelion da-meḥallēṭē,* "the Gospel, the mixed ones," as it was known to the Syrians) is not a synopsis in the modern sense. It is rather a composite within which the threads of the narrative of the four Gospels were dexterously interwoven. It was composed by TATIAN, a Syrian, shortly after the middle of the 2d century (Eusebius, *Ecclesiastical History* 4.29.6). This most important monument is lost in the original. The loss has created historical and literary problems. Many have argued that its original language was Greek. Analysis of the few extant Greek fragments, however, supports the probability that Tatian wrote it in Syriac. The Diatessaron played an extraordinary role among the Syrian Christians. Of the factors to which its success was due, nationalist fervor must have been a primary one that promoted its immediate spread: it was a Syriac gospel, created by a Syrian. Moreover, it arrived on the scene in Mesopotamia at a time appropriate for its adoption as the Gospel of the Syriac-speaking communities.

It continued to be of central importance down into the 4th century, when St. EPHREM THE SYRIAN (d. 373) used this text and wrote a commentary on it. In his dio-

cese of Cyrrhus, in the second quarter of the 5th century, Theodoret found more than 200 copies still in use in the churches and had them destroyed (*Haeret. fabul. comp., Patrologia Graeca,* ed. J. P. Migne, 161 v. [Paris 1857–66] 83:372). The fact that no copy in Syriac has survived indicates that drastic measures were employed to achieve this end. Quotations in Syriac patristic literature do survive; in particular, a large part of St. Ephrem's commentary on the Diatessaron, formerly available only in Armenian translation, has recently come to light and has been edited from a unique Syriac manuscript; it includes many textual citations.

The success of the Diatessaron was not merely local; it followed the spread of Christianity throughout the world. The vestiges of its influence from Armenia to Abyssinia and from Persia to the British Isles present us with a grandiose concept of the circulation of this document. Its popularity prompted translation into many languages, and these versions constitute the material for a modern reconstruction of the lost original. From the East we have several Arabic manuscripts and a Persian one at our disposal; from the West, manuscripts in Latin, Italian dialects, medieval German dialects, Dutch, French, and English. That these are in many cases adaptations rather than straight translations makes their evaluation difficult. Yet the reconstruction of the lost Diatessaron is urgently desired by textual critics. Not only does it stand near the beginning of the Syrian textual tradition for the Gospels; it was a factor in the transmission of the Greek text itself.

Bibliography: H. VOGELS, *Beiträge zur Geschichte des Diatessarons im Abendland* (Münster 1919). C. PETERS, *Das Diatessaron Tatians* (*Orientalia Christiana Analecta* 123; Rome 1939). A. VÖÖBUS, *Studies in the History of the Gospel Text in Syriac* (*Corpus scriptorum Christianorum orientalium* 128; Louvain 1951) 10–24; *Early Versions of the New Testament* (Stockholm 1954) 1–31. L. LELOIR, ed., *Le Témoignage d'Éphrem sur le Diatessaron* (*Corpus scriptorum Christianorum orientalium* 227; Louvain 1962); ed. and tr., *Saint Éphrem, Commentaire de l'Évangile Concordant: Texte syriaque* (*MS Chester Beatty 709;* Dublin 1963).

[A. VÖÖBUS]

DÍAZ, MANUEL

Missionary to China and astronomer; b. Castello Branco, Portugal, 1574; d. Hangzhou, China, March 4, 1659. He is called "junior" to distinguish him from Manuel Díaz, SJ (1559–1639), who was a Portuguese missionary in Eastern India and a figure in the early disputes on the INDIAN RITES CONTROVERSY. Díaz entered the Society of Jesus in 1592 and sailed for the Indies in 1601. He arrived in China in 1610 and taught theology for six years at Macau. He worked also in the missionary fields of Fujian and Zhejiang in South China, and, as the first vice provincial of China for 18 years, traveled extensively throughout the Orient. He published several works in Chinese on ascetical theology and on astronomy; they include *Tai i luen* (dissertation on the Incarnation), *Cheng king tche kiai* (commentary on the Gospels), and *Tien wen lio* (explanation of the celestial spheres).

Bibliography: C. SOMMERVOGEL et al., *Bibliothèque de la Compagnie de Jésus* (Brussels-Paris 1890–1932) 3:44–45. R. STREIT and J. DINDINGER, *Bibliotheca missionum* (Freiburg 1916–) 5:710–711, 738, 743–745. G. H. DUNNE, *Generation of Giants: The Story of the Jesuits in China in the Last Decades of the Ming Dynasty* (Notre Dame, Ind. 1962).

[E. D. MCSHANE]

DÍAZ DEL RINCÓN, FRANCISCO, ST.

Dominican priest, martyr; b. Oct. 2, 1713, Ecija, Spain; d. Oct. 28, 1748, Fujian (Fuzhou), China. Son of a wealthy family, Francisco's father tried to persuade him to accept the benefice that belonged to the family rather than joining the mendicant Dominicans. Nevertheless, he was professed a Dominican at Ecija, Spain in 1731. Five years later (1736), he was in Manila, where he studied Chinese in preparation for the mission he had desired from childhood. Finally in 1738 he arrived in the Fujian mission in China, where he labored in secret for eight years. Because his health was frail, when persecution followed the publication of a libel against the Christians of Fujian, he was given permission to return to Manila. He refused to abandon his persecuted flock. He was captured (June 29, 1746) and imprisoned at Fuzhou. He, Francisco Serrano, and Juan ALCOBER were tortured to betray the location of Bishop Pedro SANZ. Fr. Joachim Royo Pérez turned himself in to authorities to spare them further torment. All were sentenced to death in December 1746 and branded on the face as criminals. He was strangled one night in his prison cell together with Juan Alcober, Joachim Royo Pérez, and Francisco Serrano to prevent them from converting their jailors. Local Christians collected and preserved their relics. He was beatified May 14, 1893 and canonized (Oct. 1, 2000) by Pope John Paul II with Augustine Zhao Rong and companions.

Feast: June 5.

Bibliography: M. J. SAVIGNOL, *Les Martyrs dominicains de la Chine au XVIIIe siècle* (Paris 1893). H. I. IWEINS, *Le Bx Pierre Sanz et ses quatre compagnons* (Ostende 1893). J. M. GONZÁLEZ, *Misiones dominicanas en China, 1700–1750* (Madrid 1952). M. J. DORCY, *Saint Dominic's Family* (Dubuque 1963), 484–87.

[K. I. RABENSTEIN]

DÍAZ GANDÍA, CARLOS, BL.

Lay martyr; b. Dec. 25, 1907, Ontinyent (Onteniente), Valencia, Spain; d. Aug. 11, 1936 Agullent, Valencia. Cándido Díaz and Vicenta Gandía baptized their son Carlos (Charles) in St. Mary's Church, Onteniente, the day after his birth and ensured he received formation in the faith leading to his confirmation, April 23, 1911. Carlos attended both public and parochial schools. On Nov. 3, 1934, he married Luisa Torró Perdeguer. Their only daughter, María Luisa Díaz Torró, was born eight months before her father's death.

Carlos was known as an authentic Christian, who lived out his vocation as a husband, father, and worker. He is described as energetic, serious-minded, joyful, and possessing a strong personality. Deeply religious, he received the Eucharist frequently, and prayed the rosary at dawn. He enjoyed the fellowship of other Catholics in Christian associations, including the Nocturnal Adoration Society, School of Christ, Society of St. Vincent de Paul, and Apostleship of Prayer. He joined the Youth of Catholic Action at age 14, and later the Men of Catholic Action, of which he became president. Although his charity extended to everyone in need, he had a special love of youth and assiduously visited the sick.

Díaz founded catechetical centers in four locations, at which he served as catechist every Sunday throughout the year, despite the weather and having to walk or ride a bicycle for three hours to travel among them. He especially enjoyed organizing theatrical productions at the centers to present moral plays.

He was aware that his activities would attract the attention of the militant anti-Catholics who attained power during the Second Republic. Nevertheless, he fearlessly continued his apostolates and added to them the guarding of the churches, especially Santa María and the Carmelite convent chapel, where the Youth of Catholic Action met nightly. On July 24 during nocturnal Adoration of the Blessed Sacrament, he and others offered their lives to God for the salvation of Spain.

When the systematic sacking of the churches began on July 28, 1936, he ran to the church and took the reserved Blessed Sacrament to prevent sacrilege. Thereafter the churches were burned and many Catholics imprisoned. On August 4 the militiamen arrived at the Díaz home, pistols pointed, to arrest him. Initially he was held in a side chapel of San Francisco.

Later he was imprisoned with Fr. Juan Belda, Bl. Rafaél Alonso Gutierrez, Eduardo Latonda Puig, Juan and Vicente Mico Penadés, Gonzalo Gironés Plá, and Luis Mompó Delgado de Molina in the converted church of San Carlos. During his incarceration he suffered maltreatment, but Carlos remained prayerful and serene throughout. On August 6, Díaz, Gutierrez, and Latonda were taken to the neighboring town of Ayelo. There they were subjected to various tortures and beaten before being returned to Onteniente.

During the night of August 11, José María García Marcos, Rafaél Alonso Gutierrez, and Carlos Díaz Gandía were taken by taxi to a place near the village of Agullent for execution. Each shouted "Long live Christ the King!", prior to being shot. Their bodies were left at the site of execution. Díaz and García died immediately from shots in the head. Gutierrez lived for several hours. Díaz's mortal remains were placed in a niche in the cemetery of Agullent. All three martyrs were beatified by Pope John Paul II with José Aparicio Sanz and 232 companions on March 11, 2001.

Feast: Sept. 22.

See Also: SPANISH CIVIL WAR, MARTYRS OF, BB; GUTIÉRREZ, RAFAEL AND COMPANIONS, BB.

Bibliography: V. CÁRCEL ORTÍ, *Martires españoles del siglo XX* (Madrid 1995). W. H. CARROLL, *The Last Crusade* (Front Royal, Va. 1996). J. PÉREZ DE URBEL, *Catholic Martyrs of the Spanish Civil War,* tr. M. F. INGRAMS (Kansas City, Mo. 1993). R. ROYAL, *The Catholic Martyrs of the Twentieth Century* (New York 2000). Consejo Archidiocesano de los Hombres de la Acióón Católica de Valencia. *Possumus,* no. 100 (1960). *L'Osservatore Romano,* Eng. no. 11 (March 14, 2001) 1–4, 12.

[K. I. RABENSTEIN]

DÍAZ Y BARRETO, PASCUAL

Mexican archbishop; b. Zapopan, Jalisco, June 22, 1875; d. Mexico City, May 19, 1936. He studied at the Tridentine Seminary of Guadalajara and was ordained Sept. 17, 1899. He entered the Society of Jesus in 1903 and was sent to the Colegio Máximo in Oña, Spain, to perfect his philosophical studies and then to Enghien, Belgium, for further theology; at the latter institution he received the doctorate. On his return to Mexico he taught logic at Tepozotlán for a time, was prefect of the Colegio de Mascarones in 1913 and chaplain in the Holy Family Church from 1915 to 1922. He was consecrated bishop of Tabasco in 1923, but lived only a short time in his see. During the rebellion there he saved the life of Tomás Garrido Canabal, but when Garrido Canabal recovered the governorship, he expelled the bishop. Díaz y Barreto went to Mexico City, where he served as secretary for the Episcopal Committee organized to unify measures taken to protect the Church from the persecution under Pres. Plutarco Elías CALLES. He was exiled in January 1927. Much of his exile was spent in the U.S. In 1929 he accompanied Abp. RUÍZ Y FLORES to Mexico for the meet-

ing with Pres. Portes Gil at which a *modus vivendi* was arranged. In June of that year the Holy See appointed Diáz y Barreto archbishop of Mexico, a heavy responsibility in that period of internal and external difficulties for the Church. Persecution increased; the state restricted severely the number of churches and the number of clergy in his diocese. He himself had to perform all sorts of activities. Eventually these weakened his health. His funeral was marked by a moving demonstration of grief on the part of the Catholic population, which continued through the procession that accompanied his remains to their burial at Tepeyac.

Bibliography: A.M. CARREÑO, *El Exmo. Sr. Dr. Pascual Díaz y Barreto* (Mexico City 1936). E. J. CORREA, *Pascual Díaz, S.J. el Arzobispo Mártir* (Mexico City 1945).

[D. OLMEDO]

DIBDALE, ROBERT, BL.

Priest and martyr; b. Shottery, Warwickshire (or Worcestershire), England, *c.* 1558; d. hanged, drawn, and quartered at Tyburn, Oct. 8, 1586. Dibdale studied and was ordained at Douai or Rheims (1584), then returned to England to work in the London area. He practiced exorcisms at the home of Sir George Peckham in Denham, where he had been chaplain until a raid in June of 1586. Dibdale then served as chaplain to Richard Bold, who had just settled at Harlesford in order to withdraw from the anti-Catholic life at Elizabeth's Court. Dibdale was tracked down, arrested, tried in the company of Bl. John AMIAS, and condemned for his priesthood. Anthony (Dean) Champney, an eyewitness to his execution, left an account of his martyrdom. Dibdale was beatified by Pope John Paul II on Nov. 22, 1987 with George Haydock and Companions.

Feast of the English Martyrs: May 4 (England).

See Also: ENGLAND, SCOTLAND, AND WALES, MARTYRS OF.

Bibliography: R. CHALLONER, *Memoirs of Missionary Priests,* ed. J. H. POLLEN (rev. ed. London 1924). J. H. POLLEN, *Acts of English Martyrs* (London 1891). D. DE YEPES, *Historia Particular de la persecución de Inglaterra* (Madrid 1599).

[K. I. RABENSTEIN]

DIBELIUS, MARTIN

NT scholar who was one of the leaders in the movement of Biblical form criticism; b. Dresden, Germany, Sept. 14, 1883; d. Heidelberg, Nov. 11, 1947. He studied at Neuchâtel, Leipzig, Berlin, and Tübingen and taught at Berlin (1910–15) and Heidelberg (1915–47). As a student of A. von HARNACK and H. GUNKEL, he applied to the NT the principles of the history-of-religions school and the investigation of *Gattungen* (literary genres) for the formation of the *Formgeschichte* (form criticism) school (together with K. L. Schmidt, R. Bultmann, M. Albertz, and G. Bertram). He approached the critical investigation of the evolution of oral tradition in the primitive Christian community by a study of the history of the forms in the Gospels and the Acts. The main categories that he established were paradigm, *Novelle* (short story), exhortation, legend, and myth. By a determination of these categories he sought to attain to their *Sitz im Leben* (life situation). [See *Die Formgeschichte des Evangeliun* (Tübingen 1919), Eng. tr. *From Tradition to Gospel* (London 1934); and *Botschaft und Geschichte* (2 v. 1952–53), a posthumous collection of special studies on form criticism.] The theory of the undeniable influence of the needs of the community on the development of the Gospels was vitiated by rationalistic principles and conclusions. However, the valid conclusions of this school have given a vigorous impulse to modern Gospel criticism in both Protestant and Catholic circles. In his numerous commentaries, which have passed through many editions, Dibelius stressed the origin and history of the ethical statements of the NT. He also endeavored to resolve the tension between the eschatological hopes and the permanent validity of NT ethics.

See Also: FORM CRITICISM, BIBLICAL

Bibliography: W. G. KÜMMEL, *Theologische Literaturzeitung* 74 (1949) 129–140; *Die Religion in Geschichte und Gegenwart* (3d ed. Tübingen 1957–65) 2:181. A. FRIDRICHSEN, ed., ''Bibliographia Dibeliana atque Bultmaniana'' in *Coniectanea neotestamentica* 8 (1944) 1–22. R. RUSCHE, *Lexikon für Theologie und Kirche*, ed. J. HOFER and K. RAHNER (2d, new ed. Freiburg 1957–65) 3:350.

[L. A. BUSHINSKI]

DIBELIUS, OTTO

Lutheran bishop of Berlin and Brandenberg (1945–67) and courageous opponent of Nazism and communism; b. May 15, 1880 in Berlin; d. there on Jan. 31, 1967. Dibelius earned a Ph.D. in theology at the University of Berlin (1901), and during several pastoral positions wrote a number of historical and theological studies. He rose quickly in the German Protestant hierarchy, and in 1925 became bishop of the East Prussia (Berlin) diocese. When Hitler came into power in 1933, Bishop Dibelius was suspended from his office for refusing to concur in Nazi racial theories. Though he was arrested three times and forbidden to speak or publish, he was never convicted of any crime. Throughout World War II, he was an active member of the Confessing Church and joined in drafting the Barmen Declaration.

Soon after the war, he was appointed bishop of the divided city of Berlin, a position which he held until a year before his death. Again, Dibelius found himself laboring to build the church under a totalitarian regime, this time in the form of communism. He worked indefatigably not only to reunite the church in Germany but world wide. In 1948 he participated in the formation of the World Council of Churches and was instrumental in the formation of Germany's Evangelical Church (E.K.i.D.). He subsequently served as chairman of the E.K.i.D. (1949–61) and President of the World Council of Churches (1954–61).

Bibliography: O. DIBELIUS, *In the Service of the Lord* (New York 1964). W. J. SMART, *Walking With God* (London 1955). J. E. WAGNER, *Day Is Dawning: The Story of Bishop Otto Dibelius* (Philadelphia 1956).

[J. K. LUOMA]

DICCONSON, EDWARD

Professor of theology, vicar apostolic of the (English) Northern district (1740–52); b. Wrightington Hall, Lancashire, 1670; d. Finch Mill, Wrightington, 1752. The third son of Hugh Dicconson of Wrightington, he was educated at Douay College, ordained there in 1700, and the following year became procurator, and later vice president. He was largely instrumental in getting Douay cleared of charges of JANSENISM. After 20 years as professor and official at Douay he was sent to the English mission (1720) and, though his name was frequently put forward for a bishopric, it was not until he was past 70 that he was appointed to the Northern district. Meanwhile, he had been chaplain to Peter Giffard at Chillington and grand vicar to his close friend, Bishop John Stoner of the Midland district. In 1736 the vicar apostolic sent him to Rome to urge the Franciscan observance of the decree of Innocent XII concerning the relations between the regular orders and the bishops, and also to remove the Jesuits from their charge over the English College in Rome. In the latter he was successful.

On March 19, 1740, he was consecrated at Ghent as titular bishop of Malla for the Northern district, and as such was instrumental (with Bishops John Stoner and Francis Petre) in obtaining from Benedict XIV the *Apostolicum Ministerium* laying down the rules for the government of the English mission. He was afflicted with a stammer that prevented him from preaching. In his last years he wrote a detailed account of his agency in Rome in four volumes.

Bibliography: J. GILLOW, *A Literary and Biographical History or Bibliographical Dictionary of the English Catholics from 1534 to the Present Time* (London-New York 1885–1902; repr.

New York 1961) 2:56–59. W. M. BRADY, *The Episcopal Succession in England, Scotland, and Ireland, A.D. 1400 to 1875* (Rome 1876–77) v.3 *passim.* J. KIRK, *Biographies of English Catholics in the Eighteenth Century,* ed. J. POLLEN and E. BURTON (New York 1909). *The Dictionary of National Biography from the Earliest Times to 1900* (London 1885–1900; repr. with corrections, 1908–09, 1921–22, 1938) 5:916–917. B. HEMPHILL, (pseud. for B. WHELAN) *The Early Vicars Apostolic of England, 1685–1750* (London 1954).

[B. WHELAN]

DICKENSON, ROGER, BL.

Priest, martyr; b. Lincoln, England; hanged, drawn, and quartered at Winchester, July 7, 1591. Following his seminary studies at the English College of Rheims, Dickenson was ordained (1583) and returned to England to minister to the spiritual needs of a persecuted flock that was scattered throughout the countryside. He was arrested with Bl. Ralph MILNER, who acted as his escort as he traveled between villages. They were imprisoned in Winchester jail until their trial and execution. Dickenson was beatified by Pius XI on Dec. 15, 1929.

Feast of the English Martyrs: May 4 (England).

See Also: ENGLAND, SCOTLAND, AND WALES, MARTYRS OF.

Bibliography: R. CHALLONER, *Memoirs of Missionary Priests,* ed. J. H. POLLEN (rev. ed. London 1924; repr. Farnborough 1969). J. H. POLLEN, *Acts of English Martyrs* (London 1891).

[K. I. RABENSTEIN]

DICTATUS PAPAE

A term in diplomatics that designates a letter or memorandum dictated or drafted by the pope himself rather than by officers of the papal chancery. In common scholarly usage, it refers specifically to one entry in the Register of Gregory VII (1073–85) consisting of 27 titles or propositions that affirm the spiritual headship of the bishop of Rome over all Christians and his official dominance over all other clergy and temporal princes. Three letters in the Register also bear the title *Dictatus Papae* (Register II, 31, 37, 43), but the term has become permanently attached only to this list (Register II, 55a).

Of the propositions, 24 treat of ecclesiological matters, particularly of the special position of the Church and bishop of Rome in the universal Church. The first title affirms "that the Roman Church was founded by the Lord alone"; subsequent titles elaborate upon the sanctity of this institution and deal with the specific ways in which the pope's supreme juridical, legislative, and administra-

tive powers in the Church may be exercised. Only three propositions are directly related to the powers of the bishop of Rome over temporal princes. According to them, only the Roman pontiff may use the imperial insignia (no. 8), only his feet are kissed by all princes (no. 9), and the pope may depose emperors (no. 12). Scholars tend to associate with these titles those dealing with the accusation of superiors by their subjects on papal warrant (no. 24), and with the power of the pope to absolve subjects from their allegiance to their superiors (no. 27); Gregory's actions indicate that he himself applied these principles to dealings with secular rulers as well as with ecclesiastical princes.

The interpretation of these 27 titles is highly problematical, since the purpose for which they were written is unclear. The list was written into the original manuscript of the Register, which still exists, between a letter dated March 3, 1075, and one dated March 4, 1075; the first is to the clergy of Laon and the second to Archbishop Manasses of Reims. Both letters concern the reform of ecclesiastical abuses. The *Dictatus* certainly grew out of Gregory's effort to vindicate his principles of reform, and it is likely that they derived at least in part from Gregory's struggle with Henry IV, which began in earnest during March 1075. Some scholars have proposed that the *Dictatus* were crisp statements of principle, complete in themselves, and others have held the similar opinion that they comprised a sort of *aide-mémoire.* It has since been cogently argued that they were simply chapter headings for a short collection of canonical authorities reflecting the revival of the study of Canon Law that Gregory VII encouraged. In any case, one can not assess the *Dictatus* as indications of Gregory's thought or relate them to his policies toward spiritual and temporal princes until their precise purpose and character has been ascertained.

The influence of the *Dictatus* on the development of Canon Law is negligible. But in the second half of the 12th century there was written another list conceptually similar to the *Dictatus* of Gregory VII. This second list, the so-called *Dictatus of Avranches,* is of an uncertain provenance. Apparently independent of the *Dictatus Papae,* it has no textual affinity to the Gregorian propositions, and indeed it contains no statements related to *Dictatus Papae* nos. 1, 4, 6, 9, 10, 11, 14, 15, 21, 22, 23, and 27.

Bibliography: Eds. of the *Dictatus Papae:* E. CASPAR, ed., "Das Register Gregors VII," *Monumenta Germaniae Historica, Epistolae selectae* (Berlin 1826) 2.55a:201–208 (best ed.). J. D. MANSI, *Sacrorum Conciliorum nova et amplissima collectio* (Paris 1889–1927; repr. Graz 1960) 20:168. *Patrologia Latina,* ed. J. P. MIGNE (Paris 1878–90) 148:407. P. JAFFÉ, *Bibliotheca Gregoriana* (Berlin 1865) 174. *Dictatus of Avranches:* S. LÖWENFELD, ed., "Der Dictatus Papae Gregors VII. und eine Überarbeitung desselben im 12. Jh.," 16 (1890) 193–202. Recent interpretations of the

Dictatus Papae: J. BERNHARD, *La Collection en deux livres* (Strasbourg 1962) v.1 *La Forme primitive.* . . . K. HOFMANN, *Der 'Dictatus Papae' Gregors VII* (Paderborn 1933); "Der Dictatus Papae Gregors VII, als Index einer Kanonessammlung?" *Studi gregoriani* 1 (1947) 531–537. S. KUTTNER, "Liber Canonicus: A Note on Dictatus Papae c. 17," *Studi gregoriani* 2 (1947) 387–401. R. MORGHEN, "Richerche sulla formazione del Registro di Gregorio VII," *Annalli di Storia del Diritto,* 3–4 (1959–60) 35–63.

[K. F. MORRISON]

DIDACHE

Also known as *The Teaching of the (Twelve) Apostles.* Surviving from the late first or early second century, the *Didache* is often regarded as the oldest extant manual of church order. Previously known only by name from passing patristic references, the Greek text was discovered in 1873 by Archbishop Philotheos Bryennios, metropolitan of Nicomedia, in the library of the patriarch at Constantinople and published a decade later. Further fragments of Greek, Coptic, Ethiopic, and Georgian versions have subsequently been found. Examination of the document reveals a close relationship between portions of the *Didache* and later canonistic works such as the Latin/Syriac *Didascalia* and the Latin *Doctrina apostolorum.* The compiler of the seventh book of the *Apostolic Constitutions* incorporated the entire *Didache* into his work in a modified recension.

The *Didache* may be divided into four main sections. These are (1) an opening catechesis on the "two ways" (1:1–6:3); (2) a liturgical section dealing with baptism, fasting, prayer, and the Eucharist (7:1–10:7); (3) regulations for church order, especially the reception of itinerants (11:1–15:4); and (4) an apocalyptic conclusion (16:1–8).

Early scholarship on the "two ways" section focused on the relationship between this passage and its parallel in the *Epistle of Barnabas* (18–20). The current consensus is that both works depend upon a common (or similar) source, which was incorporated into numerous canonistic works. The liturgical section reproduces a version of the Lord's Prayer (8:2) that resembles its Matthean form (Matt 6:9–13) and includes the later doxological appendix. There are eucharistic prayers for the cup (9:2), the bread (9:3–4), and a concluding thanksgiving prayer (10:2–6). These three prayers follow a common substructure, which reads, "We thank you Father . . . for the [vine / name / life / knowledge / faith / immortality] which you have made known to us through Jesus your servant; to you be the glory forever." The regulations in 11:1–15:4 reflect a time when itinerant prophets and teachers were still common. Guidelines are simple and pragmatic: anyone who stays more than one

or two days, or asks for money, is a false prophet (11:5–6). Others who come "in the name of the Lord" may stay three days at most; if they wish to stay longer they must work (12:1–5). However, genuine prophets and teachers who settle in the community are entitled to communal support (13:1–7). Instructions are given to appoint bishops and deacons, who are to be esteemed on par with the prophets and teachers (15:1–2). One of the more notable features of the apocalyptic conclusion (16:1–8) is that it reserves bodily resurrection for the righteous only, at the Lord's return—an expectation it defends by citing Zech 14:5. The explanation of this event ends abruptly, and many speculate that a description of the judgment of the world has been lost. The *Apostolic Constitutions* and the Georgian version both supply such an ending, though they diverge significantly.

The provenance of the *Didache* remains uncertain though both Syria and Egypt have frequently been proposed. Scholars disagree whether the Didachist knew the Gospel of Matthew or used precanonical forms of the Synoptic tradition.

Bibliography: *Anchor Bible Dictionary* 2.197–98. J. A. DRAPER, *The Didache in Modern Research: Arbeiten zur Geschichte des antiken Judentums und des Urchristentums* 37 (Leiden 1996). C. N. JEFFORD, ed., *The Didache in Context: Essays on Its Text, History, and Transmission* Supplements to Novum Testamentum, 77 (Leiden 1995). R. A. KRAFT, *Barnabas and the Didache*, vol. 3 of *The Apostolic Fathers: A Translation and Commentary* (New York 1965). K. NIEDERWIMMER, *The Didache* (Hermeneia; Minneapolis, 1998).

[J. N. RHODES]

DIDACUS OF ALCALÁ, ST.

In Spanish, Diego; Franciscan lay brother and ascetic; b. S. Nicolás del Puerto, near Seville; d. at advanced age in Alcalá, Nov. 12, 1463. He was at first a mendicant hermit, but he later entered the monastery of Arizafa in Córdoba and was an exemplar of virtue, especially of humility and simplicity. He was sent to the Canaries (1441–49) and became guardian of the Franciscan mission and converted many pagans. In 1450 while in Rome for the canonization of BERNARDINE OF SIENA, he served the sick in the convent of Aracoeli. In 1456 he was sent from Salicetum in Castile to a new monastery in Alcalá, where he was revered for penances, miracles, and a divinely infused knowledge of theology. After death his severely mortified body did not suffer *rigor mortis* or corruption. Miraculous cures were reported immediately. In 1562 his body was taken to the bedside of Carlos, son of PHILIP II, to effect his cure. His canonization, requested by Philip in 1564, was obtained in 1588.

Feast: Nov. 13.

Bibliography: P. E. SPALDING, *San Diego and Santiago* (Claremont, Calif. 1934). L. WADDING, *Scriptores Ordinis Minorum,* 11:157–164; 12:75, 512–513;13:323–373. G. FUSSENEGGER, *Lexikon für Theologie und Kirche,* ed. J. HOFER and K. RAHNER, 10v. (Freiburg 1957–65) 3:370.

[E. P. COLBERT]

DIDACUS OF AZEVEDO, BL.

Bishop of Osma, Old Castile; d. Dec. 30, 1207. As prior, Didacus (Diego de Acebes) collaborated with Bp. Martin Bazan in transforming the cathedral chapter of Osma into a chapter of canons regular; St. DOMINIC was elected his subprior. Didacus was chosen bishop of Osma in 1201. In 1203, and again in 1205, with Dominic as companion, he went to Denmark to negotiate the marriage of Ferdinand, son of Alphonsus VIII. In 1206, after INNOCENT III had refused him permission to resign his bishopric to preach to the Cumans, he reorganized the preaching against the ALBIGENSES on the pattern of Christ and the Apostles, a plan that was later fully realized in the Order of Preachers (*see* DOMINICANS). He established a community of women at Prouille, which later became the order's first monastery.

Feast: Feb. 6.

Bibliography: JORDAN OF SAXONY, *Libellus de principiis ordinis Praedicatorum,* ed. H. C. SCHEEBEN, *Monumenta Ordinis Fratrum Praedicatorum historica* 16 (1935) 31–40. A. LAMBERT, *Dictionnaire d'histoire et de géographie ecclésiastiques* 5:1343. G. GIERATHS, *Lexikon für Theologie und Kirche*[2] 3:370.

[J. F. QUIGLEY]

DIDASCALIA APOSTOLORUM

A Church order, written originally in Greek. The complete text survives only in a Syriac version under the title *The Catholic Teaching of the Twelve Apostles and Holy Disciples of Our Saviour.* It must have been composed in the first part of the third century in northern Syria. Much of the Greek text can be reconstructed from the first six books of the *APOSTOLIC CONSTITUTIONS,* which embodied the *Didascalia.* The work is modeled on the DIDACHE, the prototype of all Church orders. The arrangement of the content is unmethodical. The author seems to have been a physician and a convert from Judaism. He betrays considerable medical knowledge, but a lack of theological training.

The first chapters are addressed to husbands and wives, and warn against pagan literature and promiscuous bathing (ch. 1–2). There follows canonical legislation for the election of bishops, the ordination of priests and

A statue of Saint Didacus (Diego) stands in the garden at Mission San Diego de Alcalá, which bears his name. (©Cummins/CORBIS)

deacons, and the instruction of catechumens (ch. 3). Lenient treatment of the sinner and care for the poor are especially emphasized among the duties of a bishop (ch. 5–8). Chapter 12 describes liturgical meetings and the place of worship: "Let a place be reserved for the presbyters in the midst of the eastern part of the house; and let the throne of the bishop be placed amongst them. Let the presbyters sit with him; but also at the other eastern side of the house let the laymen sit; for thus it is required . . . that when you stand to pray the rulers may stand first, afterwards the laymen, and then the women; for towards the East it is required that you should pray."

It cautions the Christian not to neglect attendance at the eucharistic service for work or shows. Regulations for widows, deacons, and deaconesses, and Christian charity are followed by an exhortation to bishops to take care of those who are persecuted or imprisoned for the name of Christ. The regular fastdays are set for Wednesday and Friday, but another fast is set from Monday to Saturday preceding Easter. The *Didascalia* contains more moral instruction and canonical legislation than dogma, though it deals in detail with penance. It teaches, against all rigoristic tendencies, that every sin, even that of heresy, can be forgiven. The writer explicitly numbers adultery and apostasy among the offenses that can be forgiven. There is a well-developed liturgy of public penance, but no private penance. Wherever the author enters into a doctrinal discussion, it is in refutation of Judaism, and especially its ceremonial law. He claims that the *Didascalia* was written by the Apostles: "When therefore a danger arose that heresies should be in all the Church, we, the twelve Apostles, assembled together in Jerusalem, and considered about what was to be. It pleased us all with one mind, to write the Catholic Didascalia for the assurance of all" (ch. 25).

Bibliography: P. DE LAGARDE, ed., *Didascalia apostolorum syriace* (Leipzig 1854). M. D. GIBSON, ed. and tr., *Horae Semiticae* (London 1903), v.1 *The Didascalia Apostolorum in Syriac*, v.2 *The Didascalia Apostolorum in English* (London 1903). R. H. CONNOLLY, *Didascalia apostolorum* (Oxford 1929). F. X. FUNK, ed., *Didascalia et constitutiones apostolorum* (Paderborn 1905) 1:1–384. J. HARDEN, tr., *The Ethiopic Didascalia* (Society for Promoting Christian Knowledge 1920). J. QUASTEN, ed. *Monumenta eucharista et liturgica vetustissima* (Bonn 1935–37) 34–36, liturgical parts. E. TIDNER, *Sprachlicher Kommentar zur lateinischen Didascalia Apostolorum* (Stockholm 1938). P. GALTIER, *Revue d'histoire ecclésiastique* 42 (Louvain 1947) 315–351, date. K. RAHNER, *Zeitschrift für katholische Theologie* 72 (Vienna 1950) 257–281. J. QUASTEN, *Patrology* (Westminster, Md. 1950–) 2:147–152. W. H. C. FREND, "Mission, Monasticism and Worship (337–361)," in *L'Eglise et l'empire au IVe siècle: Sept exposés suivis de discussions*, ed. A. DIHLE (Genève 1989), ch. 3. M. METZGER, "The Didascalia and Constitutiones apostolorum," in *The Eucharist of the Early Christians*, ed. W. RORDORF (New York 1986), 194–219.

[J. QUASTEN]

DIDYMUS THE BLIND

Alexandrian theologian; b. *c.* 313; d. Alexandria, between 395 and 399. PALLADIUS states that Didymus was blind from the age of four or five and that he remained a layman whose considerable theological learning and asceticism amazed his contemporaries. ATHANASIUS entrusted him with the leadership of the Catechetical School, and his theological lectures were frequented by scholars such as JEROME, who calls him his master (*Epist.* 50.1; 84.3); RUFINUS OF AQUILEIA (*Apol. In hier.* 2.25); and Palladius (*Hist. Lausiac.* 4). Many of Didymus's writings were inculpated with the condemnation of Origen as favoring the preexistence and apocatastasis of human souls at the Council of CONSTANTINOPLE II in 553 and consequently disappeared. Some of his works have been recovered, however, in the manuscripts discovered in the excavations at Tura in 1941, but questions regarding authenticity have proved most difficult.

His dogmatic writings include a tract against the Manichees, a treatise in three books on the Holy Spirit (used by St. Ambrose), which Jerome translated into Latin, and three books on the Trinity composed between 381 and 392 and considered orthodox by Jerome (*Lib. 2 Adv. Rufin.* 16). Extant in Greek are 18 chapters of a tract against the Manichees that is almost certainly authentic.

A commentary on the *De Principiis* of Origen, a *Sectarum volumen,* and a short work *On the Death of Infants* have been lost. Other works such as an *Ad philosophum* and a *De Incorporeo* have been attributed to him by JOHN DAMASCENE; and modern scholars suggest that he is the author of the *Adversus Arium et Sabellium* found among the works of Gregory of Nyssa, of the seven Pseudo-Athanasian Dialogues, and of a treatise *On the Vision of the Seraphim.*

Didymus is credited with composing a commentary on almost every book of the Old and New Testaments; however, these commentaries are witnessed to only in fragments of the Biblical chains, or excerpts, found among the papyri at Toura. Jerome credits Didymus with commentaries on the Psalms, Job, Isaiah, Hosea, and Zechariah. Cassiodorus mentions a commentary on Proverbs (*Inst. div. litt.* 5), and among the papyri is evidence of commentaries on Genesis. Both the commentary on the Psalms and the one on Isaiahs were monumental works, the latter running to 18 books although it dealt only with chapters 40 to 66, which Didymus considered a book by itself (Jerome, *De vir. ill.* 109; *Prolog. Comm. in Is. Proph.; Epist.* 112.20).

Didymus provided commentaries on Matthew, John, the Acts of the Apostles, 1 and 2 Corinthians, Galatians, and Ephesians as well as a *Brevis enarratio in Epistolas canonicas.* Jerome used the Commentary on Matthew as well as those on Galatians and Ephesians, and Theophylactus cites *catenae* from the Commentary on Acts; Epiphanius the Scholastic translated the *Expositio septem canonicarum* (*Catholic Epistles*) into Latin for CASSIODORUS (*Inst. div. litt.* 8).

Didymus's Biblical thought is more extensive than profound, and is in keeping with the theological thinking of his age. Although he follows Nicene orthodoxy on the Trinity, he accepts ORIGEN's hypotheses regarding the preexistence of souls and the final apocatastasis. His scriptural works betray his addiction to a mystique in the Word of God. The reading of the Bible is a purificatory experience and should lead to an intimate comprehension of the Word, which is an introduction to contemplation. Thence, likewise, the Christian is inspired to spread the Word of God among his contemporaries.

Bibliography: *Patrologia Graeca,* ed. J. P. MIGNE (Paris 1857–66) 39:131–1818. L. DOUTRELEAU, ed. and tr., *Sur Zacharie,* 3 v. (Paris 1962). W. J. GAUCHE, *Didymus the Blind, an Educator of the 4th Century* (Washington 1934). E. L. HESTON, *The Spiritual Life . . . in the Works of Didymus of Alexandria* (St. Meinrad, Ind.

1938). W. C. LINSS, *The Four Gospel Text of Didymus the Blind* (Doctoral diss. microfilm; Boston U. 1955). T. BARROSSE, *Theological Studies* 15 (1954) 355–388. A. GESCHE, *La Christologie du "Commentaire sur les Psaumes" découvert à Toura* (Gembloux 1962).

[P. ROCHE]

DIEGO OF CÁDIZ, BL.

Spanish Capuchin preacher; b. Cádiz, March 30, 1743; d. Ronda (Malaga), March 24, 1801. José Francisco López Camoño took the name Diego after joining the Capuchins (1759). After ordination (1766) he dedicated his religious life largely to preaching missions in Spain, Portugal, and the Levant, but he won his greatest renown in Andalusia. He delivered more than 20,000 sermons, sometimes as many as 15 a day, to audiences that often numbered 15,000 to 20,000. His most common themes were the Holy Trinity and the Blessed Virgin under the title of Shepherdess of Souls and of Peace. Diego was in great demand as a confessor and impressed people as much by his asceticism as by his eloquence. He enjoyed also a reputation as a thaumaturge (miracle-worker). Diego led the resistance to the influence of French ENLIGHTENMENT in the Spanish court, but he met opposition there from anticlerical officials such as José Moniño (Count Florida Blanca), Pedro Campomanés, and the favorite in the court of Charles IV, Manuel de Godoy. When the armies of the French Revolution invaded Spain, Diego crusaded for national independence. The published volumes of his sermons fail to reveal the qualities that made him the most popular Spanish preacher of his century. A valuable source for knowledge of his life and spirituality is contained in his published correspondence. Diego was beatified on April 23, 1894.

Feast: March 24.

Bibliography: S. DE UBRIQUE, *Vida del beato Diego J. de Cádiz,* 2 v. (Seville 1926). C. C. CASTRO, *Beato Diego Jose de Cadiz: capuchino, misionero y santo* (Cordoba 1990). A. ZAWART, *The History of Franciscan Preaching and of Franciscan Preachers, 1209–1927* (New York 1928). S. DE AUSEJO, *Reseña bibliográfica de las obras impresas del beato Diego J. de Cádiz* (Madrid 1947). F. DE ROS, *Dictionnaire de spiritualité ascétique et mystique. Doctrine et histoire* (Paris 1932—) 3:875–878, with good bibliog.

[I. BASTARRIKA]

DIEGO OF ESTELLA

Franciscan ascetical-mystical theologian (known also as Diego de San Cristóbal); b. Estella, Navarre, 1524; d. Salamanca, Aug. 1, 1578.

He was a nephew of St. Francis XAVIER and studied probably at the University of Toulouse, returning to Spain to join the Friars Minor in Salamanca. In 1552 he accompanied Ruy Gómez da Silva to Portugal; by 1561 he was again in Spain, writing and preaching with enormous success, serving as court preacher and theological adviser to Philip II. As one of the official preachers of his province, he preached, at the request of St. Teresa, for the opening of her convent in Salamanca. His most noted works are the ascetical *Libro de la vanidad del mundo* (Toledo 1562) and the mystical *Meditaciones devotísimas del amor de Dios* (Salamanca 1576). Both these works are strongly Augustinian and have appeared in many editions and languages up to the present. He wrote with unusual power and persuasive beauty, appealing to all Christians, for he held that all are called to the life of contemplation. His commentary on St. Luke was censured by the Inquisition, but he died before trial. His order defended him for several years until the case was finally dropped. Other of his works are: *Tratado de la vida, loores, y excelencias del glorioso apóstol y bienaventurado evangelista San Juan, el más amado y querido discipulo de Christo nuestro Salvador* (Lisbon 1554); *In sacrosanctum Jesu Christi Domini Nostri evangelium secundum Lucam enarrationes* (2 v. Salamanca 1574–75); *Modo de predicar: Modus concionandi* (Salamanca 1570–76); *Explanationes in Ps 136 Super flumina Babylonis* (Salamanca 1576).

Bibliography: "Estudio histórico-crítico sobre la vida y obras de Fr. Diego de Estella" and "Bibliografia," in *Archivo Ibero-Americano* (centenary issue) 22 (1924) 5–278, 384–388; 24 (1925) 383–386; 2d series, 13 (1953) 110–112. A. ANDRÉS, "Fray D. de E.: Causas, incidentes y fin de un proceso," *ibid.,* 2d series, 2 (1942) 145–158. E. A. PEERS, *Studies of the Spanish Mystics,* v.2 (London 1930) 220–249. M. MENÉNDEZ Y PELAYO, *Historia de las ideas estéticas en España,* v.2 (rev. ed. Santander 1940) ch. 7. J. B. C. GOMIS, ed., *Místicos Franciscanos españoles,* v.3 (*Biblioteca de autores cristianos* 1949) 41–54, introd.; 59–367, *Meditaciones.* P. SAGÜÉS AZCONA, ed., *Modo de predicar: Fray Diego de Estella, 1524–1578,* 2 v. (Madrid 1951), critical biog. and analysis of style. DONAT DE MONLERAS, *Dictionnaire de spiritualité ascétique et mystique. Doctrine et histoire,* ed. M. VILLER et al. (Paris 1932–) 4.2:1366–70.

[M. F. LAUGHLIN]

DIEKAMP, FRANZ

Theologian; b. Geldern, Rhineland, Nov. 8, 1864; d. Münster, Oct. 10, 1943. After his ordination in 1887 he spent some time in parish work. In 1889 he taught at the Münster theological seminary, and in 1898 was a lecturer at the University of Münster. In 1904 he was named professor, and until 1933 taught patrology, history of dogma, Church history, and dogmatic theology. Diekamp advanced the science of patrology and history of dogma by his editions of and commentaries on the Fathers. His works are distinguished by an extraordinary accuracy, thoroughness, and clarity. In 1902 he founded the *Theologische Revue,* and in 1923 he became editor of the *Münsterische Beiträge zur Theologie.* Of his numerous writings the following are especially important: *Die Gotteslehre des hl. Gregor v. Nyssa* (Münster 1896), *Die origenistischen Streitigkeiten im 6. Jahrhundert u. das 5. allg. Konzil* (Münster 1899), *Doctrina Patrum de incarnatione Verbi* (Münster 1907), *Über den Ursprung des Trinitätsbekenntnisses* (Münster 1911). His best-known work, representing the most important German effort in a Thomistic direction, is *Katholische Dogmatik nach den Grundsätzen des hl. Thomas,* 3 v. (Münster 1912–14); new edition by K. Jüssen (Münster 1958–62); Latin version by A. Hoffmann, *Theologiae dogmaticae Manuale,* 4 v. (Paris-Tournai-Rome 1932–34).

Bibliography: B. ALTANER, *Historisches Jahrbuch des Görres-Gesellschaft* 62–69 (1942–49) 916–919. M. SCHMAUS, *Neue deutsche Biographie* (Berlin 1953–) 3:645.

[K. JÜSSEN]

DIEKMANN, GODFREY

Benedictine monk, liturgist; b. April 7, 1908, Roscoe, Minn.; d. Feb. 22, 2002, Collegeville, Minn. The sixth of eight children of German emigrés from Westphalia, John Conrad and Rosalie (Loxterkamp) Diekmann, he was baptized Leo. After his education at St. John's Preparatory School and two years at St. John's University in Collegeville, Minn., he joined the Benedictine Order there in 1925. This was the same year that Virgil MICHEL, just back from his European studies and thoroughly inspired by Lambert BEAUDUIN, began to promote an American LITURGICAL MOVEMENT. During Diekmann's first year in the abbey, *Orate Fratres* (later renamed *Worship*) was founded and the Liturgical Press began publication of its Popular Liturgical Library. He also learned of the theology of the MYSTICAL BODY OF CHRIST, which was for him the discovery of a new ecclesiology with profound liturgical ramifications.

In 1928 Diekmann was sent to Rome to pursue a Doctorate in Sacred Theology at Sant' Anselmo. There Dom Anselm Stolz introduced him to the Church Fathers, particularly Tertullian, whose writings became the focus of his dissertation. Diekmann was ordained to the priesthood on June 28, 1931. He returned from Europe in 1933, and became a professor of theology at St. John's University, where he taught for 62 years. Also in 1933, he was appointed assistant editor of *Orate Fratres.* Upon Virgil Michel's sudden death in 1938, Diekmann succeeded him as editor and began soliciting regular contributions from a circle of young scholars including Hans Ansgar

Reinhold, Kathryn Sullivan, Frederick McManus, and Gerard Sloyan.

Diekmann's association with the annual Liturgical Weeks secured his role as a key leader and spokesperson of the liturgical movement in the 1940s and 1950s. These Weeks were launched under the auspices of the Benedictines in 1940 and were sustained by the creation of the Liturgical Conference in 1943. His gift to the movement was to provide a vision of sacramental life solidly grounded in patristic sources and always oriented to the church's pastoral life.

By the 1950s Diekmann was a regular participant in study weeks and conferences in Europe. At Lugano (1953), Louvain (1954), Assisi (1956), and Monserrat (1958), he heard scholars and pastors together with representatives from the Sacred Congregation of Rites openly debate a wide range of pastoral liturgical reforms, including Holy Week reforms, readings in the vernacular, a three- or four-year cycle of Scripture readings, concelebration, vernacular recitation of the breviary, and restoration of the catechumenate. Diekmann was invited to serve as a consultant to the Pontifical Liturgical Preparatory Commission of the Second Vatican Council. His work on the commission included drafting the articles on the cultural adaptation of the liturgy (*Sacrosanctum Concilium* 37–40), articles that he judged, in retrospect, not nearly bold enough in promoting diversity of rite and adaptation to given cultural structures. He also lobbied for permission to recite the breviary in the vernacular.

Diekmann was nominated by Archbishop Paul Hallinan as a *peritus* to the council for its second, third, and fourth sessions. He was instrumental in the founding of the INTERNATIONAL COMMISSION ON ENGLISH IN THE LITURGY (ICEL), and served on its advisory committee from the beginning. With the close of the council, Diekmann became one of the most sought-after interpreters of its content and implications. His interest in ecumenism was manifest in his membership in the National Lutheran-Catholic Dialogue and his positions as founding fellow and professor at the Ecumenical Institute for Advanced Theological Studies at Tantur, Israel, and co-founder of the Ecumenical Institute of Spirituality.

He retired from teaching in 1995 and continued to reside at St. John's Abbey until his death on Feb. 22, 2002.

Bibliography: K. HUGHES, *The Monk's Tale: A Biography of Godfrey Diekmann* (Collegeville 1991); includes comprehensive bibliography of the works of Godfrey Diekmann, 345–365.

[K. HUGHES/EDS.]

DIEPENBROCK, MELCHIOR VON

German cardinal, theologian; b. Bocholt, Westphalia, Jan. 6, 1798; d. Johannesburg Castle, Jan. 20, 1853. The son of a merchant and counselor to the Prince of Salm-Anholt, he studied at the minor seminary at Wikinghege, near Münster, and at the French academy in Bonn, which he left for disciplinary reasons. During the campaign against France (1814–15) he served as a lieutenant in a Prussian regiment. Influenced by Johann Michael SAILER, he reformed his life, studied political science at the University of Landshut, and prepared for the priesthood at Mainz, Münster, and Regensburg. He was ordained in 1823 by Sailer, who had become coadjutor bishop of Regensburg, then served his friend as secretary and shared in his activities to promote Christian unity. In 1845 Diepenbrock became prince-bishop of Breslau (Wrocław), where he resisted the encroachments of the Prussian and Austrian governments on the rights of the Church. He succeeded also in his opposition to *Deutschkatholizismus,* a religious movement with pronounced rationalistic tendencies, led by Johann CZERSKI and Johann RONGE. He reinvigorated parish life throughout his huge diocese by his visitations, and established a minor seminary and a theological faculty at the University of Breslau. Although he remained loyal to his Prussian rulers, he looked to the Hapsburgs to unite Germany. In 1850 he was created cardinal. Diepenbrock's sermons and pastoral letters were highly esteemed and continued Sailer's irenic and ecumenical tone. His interest in mysticism led him to write *Heinrich Suso's Leben und Schriften* (1829, 4th ed. 1884). His *Geistlicher Blumenstrauss aus spanischen und deutschen Dichtergärten* (1829, 4th ed. 1862) contains translations of Spanish and German mystics.

Bibliography: F. VIGENER, *Drei Gestalten aus dem modernen Katholizismus: Möhler, Diepenbrock, Döllinger* (Munich 1926). H. RAAB, *Dictionnaire d'histoire et de géographie ecclésiasitques*, ed. A. BAUDRILLART et al. (Paris 1912–) 14:1509–11. F. LAUCHERT, *Lexikon für Theologie und Kirche*, ed. J. HOFER and K. RAHNER (2d, new ed. Freiburg 1957–65) 3:379.

[S. J. TONSOR]

DIERINGER, FRANZ XAVER

Theologian; b. Rangeningen, Germany, Aug. 22, 1811; d. Veringendorf, Sept. 8, 1876. He studied at Tübingen and was ordained at Freiburg im Breisgau in 1835. After teaching in seminaries he was called to the chair of dogma and homiletics at the University of Bonn, where HERMESIANISM had all but destroyed the reputation of the theological faculty. Dieringer founded and edited a journal, *Katholische Zeitschrift für Wissenschaft*

und Kunst (Cologne 1844–49; since 1849 called *Katholische Vierteljahrschrift*), to provide a forum for orthodoxy; and for many years his writing and teaching did much to restore balance to theological thought in Germany. Among many other writings he is noted for his *Lehrbuch der katholischen Dogmatik* (Mainz 1847), which long remained a widely used manual, and for his *Laienkatechismus* (Mainz 1865), which presented theology in popular form. He also wrote against A. GÜNTHER. He was a founder and for many years president of the *Verein vom hl. Karl Borromäus.* In 1853 he was named a canon of Cologne, though permitted to retain his chair at Bonn. Three times he was proposed for the episcopacy, but he was vetoed twice by the Prussian government and in 1874 by the government of Baden, whose terms he was unwilling to meet. Though he had taught papal infallibility, when the question came up in connection with VATICAN COUNCIL I, he at first opposed its definition as inopportune and later as wrong in itself. After it was defined, he accepted it but resigned his professorship and his dignities to become a parish priest.

Bibliography: E. MANGENOT, *Dictionnaire de théologie catholique*, ed. A. VACANT et al. (Paris 1903–50) 4.1:755. A. FRANZEN, *Lexikon für Theologie und Kirche*, ed. J. HOFER and K. RAHNER (2d, new ed. Freiburg 1957–65) 3:380.

[A. ROCK]

DIERKX, ANNE CATHERINE, ST.

In religion Marie Adolphine; martyr, religious of the Franciscan Missionaries of Mary; b. March 8, 1866, in the Netherlands; d. July 9, 1900, Taiyüan, China. Upon the death of her mother, Anne and her five siblings were adopted by poor neighbors. When she was old enough to work she packed coffee to help support her adoptive family. Later she was a household servant nearby, then in Antwerp. There she joined the Franciscan Missionaries of Mary (1893), where she was known for her compliance and willingness to undertake the most menial chores. In 1898, she was sent to China, where she was martyred during the Boxer Rebellion. Sr. Marie Adolphine was beatified with her religious sisters by Pope Pius XII, Nov. 24, 1946, and canonized, Oct. 2000, by Pope John Paul II with Augustine Zhao Rong and companions.

Feast: July 4.

Bibliography: G. GOYAU, *Valiant Women: Mother Mary of the Passion and the Franciscan Missionaries of Mary*, tr. G. TELFORD (London 1936). M. T. DE BLARER, *Les Bse Marie Hermine de Jésus et ses compagnes, franciscaines missionaires de Marie, massacrées le 9 juillet 1900 à Tai-Yuan-Fou, Chine* (Paris 1947). L. M. BALCONI, *Le Martiri di Taiyuen* (Milan 1945). *Acta Apostolicae Sedis* 47 (1955) 381–388. *L'Osservatore Romano,* Eng. Ed. 40 (2000): 1–2, 10.

[K. I. RABENSTEIN]

DIES IRAE

Sequence that was assigned in the Tridentine Missal to All Souls' Day and Mass for the Dead. Its composition is commonly ascribed to THOMAS OF CELANO, but it was probably not written by him. Though found in manuscripts of the 13th century, the *Dies irae,* according to Inguanez, belongs perhaps to the 12th century (*cf.* Cod. VII D 36, Bibl. Naz. of Naples), a view opposed by Lampen. Some portions of the text (such as *Lacrimosa dies illa:* see Mone 1:408) antedate the 13th century. The initial words *Dies irae* have biblical background (Soph 1.14–16) and appear in several hymns and liturgical texts (Strecker), including the famous Irish hymn *Altus prosator* (of the 6th century). As Strecker and Ermini demonstrated, many motifs are drawn from earlier hymns and poems; accordingly, Gazeau suggests that Thomas of Celano only reworked an earlier text already in use. Thomas's authorship is a late attribution (Bartolomeo degli Albizzi, d. 1401, and *Liber conformitatum,* 1385). The *Dies irae* was not designed originally to be used as a Sequence (Blume: *Libera trope*). It was used as a sequence only in the Tridentine Missal (1570). In its text unusually forceful language and vivid images of the Last Judgment are interwoven with subjective tones. Apart from a general biblical background deriving from passages in the Gospel referring to the Last Judgment, the first verse (*teste David cum Sibylla*) reflects the medieval "Sibyll" tradition as well as a liturgical Christmas ceremony (*Ordo prophetarum:* K. Young). At the same time, there are other classical reminiscences (Vergil's *Georgics,* especially the Orpheus episode: Savage). Some ascribe the general mood of the poem to the atmosphere of the age, created by Abbot JOACHIM OF FIORE. A. Kaminka pointed to similarities between the *Dies irae* and a Jewish *piyyut* called *Unethane toquef.* Werner and Deutschmann associate the latter with a *Kontakion* by ROMANUS MELODUS—a theory rejected by L. Kunz. Manuscripts show three different groups of versions, among which is the "Mantuan text" once recorded on a marble tablet in the Franciscan church in Mantua.

The common text consists of 17 three-line verses to which four 12th-century lines (beginning *Lacrimosa dies illa*) and a two-line prayer (*Pie Jesu Domine*) are added. The form is trochaic dimeter acatalectic, accentual, with two-syllabled rhyme (*a a a*). The text falls into two parts, which differ greatly from each other. The first part (verses 1–7) is an economically worded, majestic, and objective description of the Last Judgment, a summary of Christian ESCHATOLOGY in microcosm. The second part (verses 9–17) is a passionate appeal to Christ's mercy, with reference to MARY MAGDALENE and the Good Thief (exemplars of the divine mercy). The two parts are joined together with the exclamation, "In such a plight what can I plead?" The melody is tripartite, using identical formulas.

Bibliography: Text. *Analecta hymnica* 54:269. J. CONNELLY, *Hymns of the Roman Liturgy* (Westminster, MD 1957) 252–256. Literature. K. STRECKER, "Dies irae," *Zeitschrift für deutsches Altertum und Literatur* 50 (1909) 227–255. F. ERMINI, *Il Dies irae* (Geneva 1928). M. INGUANEZ, "Il Dies irae in un codice del secolo XII," *Revista liturgica* 18 (1931) 277–282; *Miscellanea Cassinese* 9 (1931) 5–11. K. YOUNG, *The Drama of the Medieval Church,* 2 v. (Oxford 1933) 1:125–171, *Ordo prophetarum.* W. LAMPEN, "Losse Aren X," *Tijdschrift voor liturgie* 16 (1935) 263–268. B. CAPELLE, "Le *Dies irae*: Chant d'espérance?" *Questions liturgiques et paroissiales* 22 (1937) 217–224. L. KUNZ, "Ist die Sequenz *Dies irae* von dem *Kontakion* des Romanos vom letzten Gericht abhängig?" *Der Christliche Orient* 5 (1940) 43–46. R. GAZEAU, *Catholicisme* 3:764–765. F. J. E. RABY, *A History of Christian-Latin Poetry from the Beginnings to the Close of the Middle Ages* (Oxford 1953) 443–452. A. M. KURFESS, *Historisches Jahrbuch der Görres-Gesellschaft* 77 (1957) 328–338. L. KUNZ, *Lexikon für Theologie und Kirche,* ed. J. HOFER and K. RAHNER (Freiburg 1957–65) 3:380–381. E. WERNER, *Sacred Bridge* (New York 1959) 252–255. J. SZÖVÉRFFY, *Die Annalen der lateinischen Hymnendichtung* (Berlin 1964–65) 2:220–224.

[J. SZÖVÉRFFY]

DIETARY LAWS, HEBREW

The existence of Hebrew dietary laws is a natural consequence of the classification of things into pure and impure, clean and unclean, that has always been present in the Israelite religion (*see* PURE AND IMPURE). The full expression of these laws is found in the rabbinical writings, principally in the Talmudic tract Hullin. These writings represent the elaboration of biblical elements found in such sections of the Bible as Dt 14.3–21 and Lv 11.2–23. Both of these sections pertain to the Priestly tradition (*see* PRIESTLY WRITERS, PENTATEUCHAL); no laws on the subject are found in the traditions of the YAHWIST or the ELOHIST. It is generally recognized, however, that such legislation is not merely a postexilic development fostered to achieve a sense of separation or national identity. These motives were present and served to increase the importance of these practices in postexilic times, but they were not responsible for their existence. Their origin is pre-Israelitic, for these practices were known to the ancient Babylonians, Egyptians, and Hindus.

The dietary laws, called *kashrut* in Hebrew, indicate what foods may or may not be eaten. Only food that is kosher (Ashkenazic pronunciation of Heb. *kāšēr,* fit) may be eaten; anything that is not kosher is to be avoided. The uncleanness of food derives from several sources. The principal source is the characterization of certain animals as unclean by nature. Thus, any land animal that is not cloven-hoofed and does not chew its cud is unclean; any fish or other water creature that does not have scales and fins is unclean; and all birds of prey and most insects are also unclean. The reason these animals are so regarded is not known with certainty. There is, most probably, a connection with ancient religious sacrificial practices and taboos. Thus, anything that was connected with an alien god or cult was considered to be unclean. It is known that the pig was a Canaanite domestic and sacrificial animal. Mice, serpents, and hares were regarded as effective media of demonic power. The opinion that the origin of the classification is to be found in hygienic or psychological motives is not considered to be correct.

Other sources of uncleanness are such prohibitions as those against eating any animal that died a natural death (Dt 14.21), or against eating the blood or certain parts of the fat of an animal (Lv 17.10–14). These biblical prohibitions were developed at great length by the rabbis, who set down minute rules for the inspection and slaughter of animals as well as for the preparation of food. The prohibition in Ex 23.19; 34.26 against boiling a kid in its mother's milk is the origin of the absolute distinction between meat and milk dishes that forbids the eating of both at the same meal and requires even the use of separate sets of dishes.

Dietary laws as a means of separation and of establishing religious identity are rejected in the NT. In the episode of St. Peter's dealing with Cornelius, the centurion, at Caesarea (Acts 10.1–43) and his subsequent report to the Church in Jerusalem (Acts 11.1–18), this rejection is based on divine instruction and serves to guarantee for the Gentile converts equality in the Church. This teaching probably influenced the account in Mk 7.14–23 and Mt 15.10, 15–20 of the saying of Jesus concerning the consequence of eating with unwashed hands. For, to this account of a particular case common to both Mark and Matthew, there is added in Mk 7.19b ("Thus he declared all foods clean") a universal rejection of dietary laws. This editorial comment clearly points out the Christian attitude toward these laws. Such a rejection, however, was not put into practice without some difficulty, as is seen from the concession given to scrupulous Judeo-Christians in Acts 15.29 and Rom 14.14–16.

The dietary laws are still strictly observed today by Orthodox Jews, who regard rejection of them as heresy. In case of illness or emergency, however, these laws may be relaxed. Reform Jews no longer see a need for these laws. They consider them to be intended as a means of separation from a hostile and idolatrous world. Since, in the judgment of these Jews, these conditions no longer exist, the laws are without further purpose and are to be discarded. They do, however, retain some of the prohibitions, such as avoiding the eating of blood or animals that have died a natural death. Conservative Jews theoretical-

ly uphold the observance of these laws, but, in practice, many follow the Reform Jews in disregarding them.

Bibliography: S. I. LEVIN and E. A. BOYDEN, *The Kosher Code of the Orthodox Jew* (Minneapolis 1940). B. D. COHON, *Judaism in Theory and Practice* (New York 1954) 149–151. W. H. GISPEN, "The Distinction between Clean and Unclean," *Oudtestamentische Studiën* 5 (1948) 190–196. K. KOHLER, *The Jewish Encyclopedia,* ed. J. SINGER, 13 v. (New York 1901–0) 4:596–600. S. COHEN, *Universal Jewish Encyclopedia,* 10 v. (New York 1939–44) 3:564. R. RENDTORFF, *Die Religion in Geschichte und Gegenwart,* 7 v. (3d ed. Tübingen 1957–65) 6:231–232; 5:942–944. W. KORNFELD, *Lexikon für Theologie und Kirche,* ed. J. HOFER and K. RAHNER, 10 v. (2d, new ed. Freiburg 1957–65) 8:1150–51.

[S. M. POLAN]

DIETZ, PETER ERNEST

Labor priest, journalist; b. New York, N.Y., July 10, 1878; d. Milwaukee, Wis., Oct. 11, 1947. His father, Frederick Dietz, was a native of the Palatinate, Germany; his mother, Eva Kern Dietz, came from Bavaria. In 1900, after his early education at Holy Redeemer School, New York City, Peter entered the novitiate of the Society of the Divine Word in Moedling, Germany. Three years later he returned to the U.S. and was ordained a diocesan priest by Cardinal James Gibbons on Dec. 17, 1904.

Dietz early displayed interest in social questions; his desire to apply the principles of Leo XIII's RERUM NOVARUM was an essential part of his vocation to the priesthood. Associated with Fathers John A. RYAN and William KERBY, he pioneered for labor legislation, for a bishops' pastoral on the labor question, for a unification of Catholic social agencies, and for an effective Catholic press. He edited the English section of the German Catholic Central Verein's organ, *Central Blatt and Social Justice,* and organized the Verein's first social studies institute. As secretary of the Social Service Commission of the American Federation of Catholic Societies, he edited the *Bulletin* and a weekly *Newsletter,* which circulated among 100 Catholic and labor papers. His American Academy for Christian Democracy in Hot Springs, N.C., prepared young women for a wide range of social service. This academy, later moved to Cincinnati, Ohio, became the first labor college in the country.

Dietz defended trade unionism. He was a personal friend of labor leaders John Mitchell, Matthew Woll, and Philip Murray, whom he greatly influenced. His Militia of Christ for Social Service, an organization of Catholic trade unionists, effectively combated the influence of socialism, especially at the national conventions of the American Federation of Labor, which Dietz attended and frequently addressed from 1909 to 1922. He pioneered in setting up an industrial council plan among the building trades in Cincinnati during the 1920s.

Dietz's public career ended abruptly in 1923 when Catholic members of the Chamber of Commerce protested to Abp. J. T. McNicholas that his influence on labor had interfered with their business. Dietz, forced to close his academy at Ault Park, withdrew from the Archdiocese of Cincinnati and spent the next 24 years building St. Monica's, Milwaukee, into a large and important parish.

Bibliography: A. I. ABELL, *American Catholicism and Social Action: A Search for Social Justice, 1865–1950* (New York 1960). M. H. FOX, *Peter E. Dietz, Labor Priest* (Notre Dame, Ind. 1953).

[H. FOX]

DÍEZ LAUREL, BARTOLOMÉ, BL.

Franciscan martyr; b. Puerto de Santa María, Spain, date unknown; d. Nagasaki, Japan, Aug. 17, 1627. His real name was Díaz Laruel. He was a sailor, and while living in Acapulco, Mexico, he requested permission to enter the Franciscan Order. He took the habit of a lay brother (May 13, 1615) in Valladolid (Morelia), Mexico, but he did not persevere. He again took the habit (Oct. 17, 1616) in the same convent, where he was professed (Oct. 18, 1617) as a lay brother. At the end of 1618 he was in the convent of San Francisco del Monte in Manila. There he learned and practiced medicine in a hospital. In 1623 he went to perform missionary work in Japan, where he disguised himself as a physician. At Pentecost in 1627 he was imprisoned in Nagasaki, and in August of the same year he was martyred. His cause of beatification was included with that of many other martyrs of his time: "the 205 marytrs of Japan." This process underwent various irregularities of a legal nature, and it lacked many biographical data. Pius IX corrected the irregularities and conceded that the servants of God in question could be called Blessed and that an Office and Mass belonging to them could be prayed in certain places. In Mexico there is a special Office and Mass (August 18) for Bl. Bartolomé but the biographical data of the Breviary and the popular hagiographies do not seem to be correct [cf. J. G. Gutiérrez, *Vida del Beato Padre Fray Bartolomé Gutiérrez* (Mexico City 1932), on another of the 205 martyrs].

Feast: Aug. 18.

[E. GÓMEZ TAGLE]

DIEZ Y BUSTOS DE MOLINA, VITORIA, BL.

Martyr, teacher, Carmelite of the Teresian Institute; b. Nov. 11, 1903, Seville, Spain; d. Aug. 12, 1936, Rincón at Hornachuelos near Cordoba, Spain. Vitoria, the only child of a devout, middle class couple, wanted to become a missionary and an artist, but bowed to her parents' wish that she teach. She studied pedagogy while also taking art classes in her hometown. Seeing an opportunity to combine teaching with evangelization, she became a member of the Teresian Institute, founded by Blessed Pedro Poveda Castroverde (1874–1936). Vitoria was assigned to teach first in Cheles near the Portuguese border. The following year she was transferred to an Andalusian country school in Hornachuelos. There she was active in the life of the parish and in charitable ministries. In addition to the charism of teaching, Vitoria possessed a profound joy that attracted others to her words. At the start of the Spanish Civil War, when many abandoned the faith, Vitoria used her position to influence her charges and their families to remain faithful. She was arrested together with 17 men by the revolutionaries on Aug. 11, 1936. The next day they were executed and their bodies thrown into a mine shaft. The declaration of her martyrdom was signed on July 6, 1993, leading to her beatification by John Paul II on Oct. 10, 1993.

Bibliography: G. MARTINA, "To Become a Saint," *Sanctity Today* (Rome 1998–1999).

[K. I. RABENSTEIN]

DIGAMY

Or remarriage, is the state of being married after the dissolution of a previous marriage by death. It thus differs from BIGAMY, the condition of a person who has contracted a second marriage while he still has an existing marriage. The acceptability of digamy depends on social, religious, and ethical considerations connected with attitudes toward the nature of marriage itself. In a society that looks upon marriage exclusively as the method for the propagation of mankind, digamy is permitted without disqualification, and can even be obligatory, e.g., the Levirate law (Dt 25.5–10; Mt 22.25–27), observed not only by the Hebrews but also by the Arabs, Persians, Mongols, etc. In the early Christian dispensation digamy was excluded neither for the man (1 Cor 7.27) nor for the woman (Rom 7.2; 1 Cor 7.8, 39), but because marriage could be considered as a certain handicap to a total love of God (1 Cor 7.32–34) digamy was not encouraged (1 Cor 7.8, 40) except as a remedy for incontinence (1 Cor 7.9; 1 Tim 5.14). Bishops, deacons, and members of the official widowhood could not be digamists (Tit 1.6; 1 Tim 3.2, 12; 4.9) and this prescription has been inserted in the present Code of Canon Law (c.984.4). Many Fathers of the Church, basing their attitude on St. Paul's doctrine of marriage as a symbol of the union between

Christ and the Church, discountenanced digamy, but the Church followed the Biblical moderation and resisted the errors of the Montanists, and particularly of TERTULLIAN, by legitimizing digamy.

Bibliography: L. GODEFROY, *Dictionnaire de théologie catholique,* ed. A. VACANT, 15 v. (Paris 1903–50; Tables générales 1951–) 9.2:2063–64, 2077–2101. B. KÖTTING, *Reallexikon für Antike und Christentum,* ed. T. KLAUSER [Stuttgart 1941 (1950)–] 3:1016–24. A. OEPKE, *ibid.* 4:655–661. E. G. PARRINDER, *The Bible and Polygamy* (London 1958). TERTULLIAN, *Treatises on Marriage and Remarriage,* tr. W. P. LE SAINT (*Ancient Christian Writers* 13; 1951).

[J. VAN PAASSEN]

DIGBY, EVERARD, SIR

Courtier and Gunpowder Plot conspirator; b. Stoke Dry, Rutland, May 16, 1578; d. London, Jan. 30, 1606. On the death of his father, Everard Digby (1592), he became a page at court, and as a ward of the crown was brought up a Protestant. The large estates he had inherited were augmented by his marriage to Mary Mulso of Gothurst (now Gayhurst), Buckinghamshire, in 1596. Both he and his wife were converted to Catholicism by John GERARD, SJ, who remained a close friend. Support for James's accession won him a knighthood on April 23, 1603. In May 1605 he unsuccessfully offered himself to Robert Cecil as an intermediary between the English government and the pope. The following October, disaffected by James's attitude toward Catholicism, he was easily recruited by Robert Catesby, the ringleader of the Gunpowder Plot, and although never fully admitted to the inner circle of the conspiracy, he agreed to provide money and arms to organize a rising in the Midlands immediately after the main blow had been struck. When the plot miscarried, the conspirators fled to Holbeach House in Staffordshire to make a desperate stand. Digby broke away with two attendants but was soon apprehended. He stood trial in Westminster Hall Jan. 27, 1606. Conducting himself with dignity, he pleaded guilty and suffered a traitor's death three days later. Of a noble but weak character, Digby was skilled in the arts. He left two sons, Kenelm, the author and diplomat, and John, a Cavalier General.

Bibliography: H. ROSS WILIAMSON, *The Gunpowder Plot* (New York 1952). T. LONGUEVILLE, *A Life of a Conspirator* (London 1895). J. GERARD, *The Condition of Catholics under James I . . .,* ed. J. MORRIS (2d ed. London 1872); *The Autobiography of a Hunted Priest,* tr. P. CARAMAN (London 1951). V. GABRIELI, *Sir Kenelm Digby* (Rome 1957). A. JESSOPP, *The Dictionary of National Biography from the Earliest Times to 1900* (London 1885–1900; repr. with corrections, 1908–09, 1921–22, 1938) 5:956–957. J. GILLOW, *A Literary and Biographical History or Bibliographical Dictionary of the English Catholics from 1534 to the Present Time* (London–New York 1885–1902; repr. New York 1961) 2:62–65.

Sir Everard Digby.

[A. G. PETTI]

DIGNITY/USA

"An organization of gay and lesbian Roman Catholics and their friends" was formally established September 1973 in Los Angeles, and is now incorporated as a nonprofit organization under the laws of the District of Columbia, where it has its national headquarters. Dignity believes homosexuals "can express their sexuality in a manner . . . consonant with Christ's teaching." Local chapters serve as support groups for their members, establishing an environment that affirms their sexual orientation and provides opportunities for spiritual growth. Chapters also sponsor a variety of educational programs, including the dissemination of information and publications designed to defend the rights of gays and lesbians, and to inform Catholics about the accord that Dignity perceives between HOMOSEXUALITY and Christian faith. The Dignity/USA organization has no official ecclesiastical standing; and in the wake of the instruction "On the Pastoral Care of Homosexual Persons" promulgated by the Congregation of the Doctrine of the Faith (Oct. 1, 1986), many dioceses have banned Eucharistic liturgies sponsored by Dignity and closed church facilities to its local meetings and social activities.

[T. J. SENA]

DILTHEY, WILHELM

German philosopher and historian famed for his work in the cultural and historical sciences (*Geisteswissenschaften*); b. Biebrich on the Rhine, Nov. 19, 1833; d. Seis on the Schlern, Oct. 1, 1911. The son of a Protestant clergyman, Dilthey studied at Berlin; he taught successively at Berlin (1865), Basel (1867), Kiel (1868), and Breslau (1871), and finally was recalled to Berlin (1882) to succeed R. H. LOTZE. He ranks as one of the great representatives of the German historical school.

Thought. The breadth and versatility of Dilthey's inquiries and the often tentative and fragmentary character of his works belie the strong inner unity of his thought. Everything he wrote expresses an undeviating concern with the problem of historical consciousness. History, he said, would not hold his interest were it not a way to understand the universe and man. He conceived his life's work as one of providing a critique of historical reason comparable and complementary to the *Critique of Pure Reason* of I. KANT. This interest was occasioned by the rapid development and proliferation of the historical and cultural sciences in the early 19th century, which he felt were threatened by the imposition of unsuitable methods from the sciences of nature (*Naturwissenschaften*) and by innovations in metaphysics. The historical and cultural sciences therefore required a philosophical foundation if they were to avoid complete relativism and skepticism.

In its first formulation Dilthey's problem appeared, in Kantian guise, as the critical foundation of the *Geisteswissenschaften;* or, with positivist overtones, as their organization and unification; or along empiricist lines, as a need for a profounder psychological understanding of man. Dilthey saw all historical phenomena as an expression (*Ausdruck*) of man's ongoing vital experience (*Erlebnis*), which he inevitably understands (*Verste-hen*) before he analyzes them scientifically. At this level there is a vital connaturality of knower and known, in contrast to the alien externality of physical nature and the abstractions of the natural sciences.

On the second level of inquiry Dilthey's theory of the *Geisteswissenschaften* became his "philosophy of life" (*Lebensphilosophie*), which culminated in a "new" historical concept of philosophy (*Weltanschauungslehre*), a "philosophy of philosophy." This affirms the historical relativity of every philosophical system, the impossibility of absolute, perennially valid formulas, and a limited acceptance of philosophy, not as a science but as a "metaphysical consciousness." Unable to escape the positivist dilemma, Dilthey continued to search for a methodic secret that would deliver him from skeptical relativism.

On a third restless round of inquiry he undertook a critical analysis of his method of "*Verstehen*," i.e., the spontaneous, empathic, intuitive structuring of life-experience that precedes reflective concept formation. In this patient process Dilthey enlarged the "historical method" into a basic method for all philosophy.

Critique. Growing contemporary interest in Dilthey still concentrates too narrowly on his *Weltanschauungslehre* as a contribution to the philosophy of history. M. Heidegger has recognized Dilthey's philosophical importance by presenting his own profound analysis of historicity as simply assisting later generations to understand and to assimilate the work of Dilthey. Catholic scholars welcome Dilthey's exposé of a false RATIONALISM and abstractionism, but deplore his rejection of the supernatural and his failure to see that Kant's refutation of a deductive, Cartesian type of metaphysics was no refutation of metaphysics itself. By his painful inability to break out of the positivist prison, Dilthey bears witness to the power of his own "historical situation."

See Also: HISTORY, PHILOSOPHY OF

Bibliography: Works. *Gesammelte Schriften,* 12 v. (Berlin 1914–36; repr. Göttingen 1957–60); *Das Leben Schleiermachers,* 2d ed. H. MULERT (Berlin 1922); *Das Erlebnis und die Dichtung* (Berlin 1913); *Grundriss der allgemeinen Geschichte der Philosophie,* ed. H. G. GADAMER (Frankfurt 1949); *Die grosse Phantasiedichtung und andere Studien zur vergleichenden Literaturgeschichte* (Göttingen 1954); *Der junge Dilthey: Ein Lebensbild in Briefen und Tagebüchern, 1852–1870,* ed. C. MISCH (Berlin 1933); *The Essence of Philosophy,* tr. S. A. and W. T. EMERY (Chapel Hill, N.C. 1954), tr. of *Das Wesen der Philosophie* (1907). Literature. H. HOLBORN, "Dilthey and the Critique of Historical Reason," *Journal of the History of Ideas* 11 (1950) 93–118. H. A. HODGES, *Wilhelm Dilthey: An Introduction* (New York 1945); *The Philosophy of Wilhelm Dilthey* (London 1952). W. KLUBACK, *Wilhelm Dilthey's Philosophy of History* (New York 1956). W. KLUBACK and M. WEINBAUM, *Dilthey's Philosophy of Existence* (New York 1957). H. P. RICKMAN, ed., *Wilhelm Dilthey: Pattern and Meaning* *in History* (New York 1962). H. DIWALD, *Wilhelm Dilthey: Erkenntnistheorie und Philosophie der Geschichte* (Göttingen 1963). J. F. SUTER, *Philosophie et histoire chez Wilhelm Dilthey* (Basel 1960).

[P. L. HUG]

DIMISSORIAL LETTERS

Dimissorial letters are the authorization a bishop or other competent ordinary gives to another bishop to confer Orders on his subject. Ecclesiastical law has traditionally required that ordination be received from one's proper bishop or upon his authorization [cf. *Codex iuris canonici* (repr. Graz 1955) *c.* 1015 §1, *Codex canonum ecclesiarium orientalium, c.* 747]. The present legislation concerning dimissorials is basically that of the Council of Trent.

For the ordination of diocesans, dimissorials may be granted by the proper bishop after he has taken possession of his diocese. The diocesan administrator of a vacant diocese, with the consent of the diocesan college of consultors, may also grant dimissorial letters [*Codex iuris canonici* (Graz 1955) *c.* 1018, *Codex canonum ecclesiarium orientalium, c.* 750]. Usually these letters are sent to a designated bishop, although they may be given in such a manner that the candidate may be ordained by any bishop of the same church *sui iuris* who is in communion with the Holy See. Exceptionally, the Eastern code allows for an ordinand's proper bishop to send dimissorials to a bishop of another church *sui iuris*, with the condition that the bishop obtain certain permissions before issuing the letters (*Codex canonum ecclesiarium orientalium, cc.* 752, 748 §2).

Latin religious who are members of clerical institutes or societies of pontifical right cannot be licitly ordained by any bishop without dimissorial letters from their own major superiors. Superiors of such institutes or societies can never issue dimissorials for major orders on behalf of their subjects who are not definitively incorporated [*Codex iuris canonici* (Graz 1955) c. 1019]. The superiors of Eastern monasteries *sui iuris* and major superiors of Eastern orders, congregations, and societies of common life according to the manner of religious may issue dimissorial letters in accord with their proper law (*Codex canonum ecclesiarium orientalium, cc.* 472; 537 §1; 560 §1).

In the case of both diocesans and religious, dimissorials must be issued for the ordination of a definite subject to certain specific orders. They should also include mention of the fact that the testimonials required according to *Codex iuris canonici, cc.* 1050 and 1051 or *Codex*

canonum ecclesiarium orientalium, c. 769 have been obtained [*Codex iuris canonici, c.* 1020, *Codexcanonum ecclesiaarium orientalium, c.* 751]. Ordinarily, dimissorial letters are granted in writing, but oral concession is possible.

Bibliography: F. CLAEYS BOUUAERT, *Dictionnaire de droit canonique*, ed. R. NAZ, 7 v. (Paris 1935–65) 4:1244–50. J. J. QUINN, *Documents Required for the Reception of Orders* (Catholic University of America Canon Law Studies 266; Washington 1948).

[D. BONNER]

DINTILHAC, JORGE (LOUIS EUGENE)

Peruvian educator; b. Provins, France, Nov. 13, 1878; d. Lima, Peru, April 13, 1947. He entered the Congregation of Sacred Hearts (Picpus Fathers) in October 1895 and pursued ecclesiastical studies in France, Spain, Chile, and Peru, where he received a doctorate in theology from the University of San Marcos.

As a university student in Lima, Dintilhac became interested in the education of boys. The school conducted by the Picpus fathers in Lima, called La Recoleta, had opened in March 1893 with 22 students. Among the first students were José de la Riva-Agüero, Francisco and Ventura García Calderón, and later such men as Luis Alberto Sánchez, Raúl Porras Barrenechea, and Jorge Basadre. For such students, Dintilhac began a youth club with its own library, sporting events, and such academic activities as a review, discussions, debates, and a free night school for workers, staffed in part by former students. Through the students, Dintilhac became aware of the confusion at the University of San Marcos, which most of the graduates of the Recoleta attended.

Florentino Prat, head of the Recoleta, in 1916 received permission from his religious superiors to begin a law course leading to a degree. Dintilhac was appointed head of the course and authorized to apply to the Ministry of Education for permission to begin the Catholic University of Peru. The permission was granted on March 24, 1917, and the new university, with only a law faculty, began classes April 15, 1917, with ten students and with Dintilhac as rector. Later it was designated a pontifical university by the Holy See. During the 30-year rectorship of Dintilhac the University developed five faculties and, with its affiliated institutions, grew to a student body of more than 4,000.

[G. HABERSPERGER]

DIOCLETIAN, PERSECUTION OF

Diocletian's persecution of Christians ceased with his retirement in 305, but his policy had inaugurated the severest repressive measures against Christianity. This article deals with (1) the religious policy of Diocletian, (2) the Edicts of 303, (3) the persecutions to 311 and the Edict of Toleration, and (4) the final persecution under Licinius.

Religious Policy of Diocletian. Of peasant stock and naturally religious if not superstitious, Diocletian at first tolerated Christianity along with the Oriental mystery religions, the Egyptian, Mithraic, and other cults then flourishing in the empire. In an attempt to bring external security and internal peace to his realm, he had spent the first 20 years of his reign reorganizing the frontier defenses and civil administration. He then attempted to restore the religious practices of the old Roman cults as a stabilizing factor in the everyday life of the empire, and in this he was influenced by the revival of religiosity that marked the end of the 3d century among all classes of Roman society. Nevertheless, in introducing the tetrarchy as a means of controlling the vast expanse of the empire and defending its frontiers, Diocletian had recourse to the mechanism of the ruler-cult; he proclaimed himself and GALERIUS, his Caesar in the East, as the sons or representatives of Jupiter, and his colleague Maximian, with Constantius Chlorus, his Caesar in the West, as sons of Hercules.

Christian Reaction. This move was bound to cause difficulty for the Christians, who by the end of the 3d century formed a large and ubiquitous group, well represented in the army, the imperial household, and civil administration, with well-organized communities and notable churches in the greater cities of the empire. Christians were suspected of atheism because of their refusal to participate in many phases of civic life, and in the pagan religious ceremonies, which they maintained were dominated by demons. They were accused of moral turpitude because of the secrecy with which they generally surrounded their religious rites. In 295 Diocletian had issued an edict on marriage designed to strengthen its moral force, and in 297 he inaugurated a savage persecution of the Manichees (*see* MANICHAEISM) as disruptors of the public peace and morality because of the dualistic attitude they had toward marriage.

As a result of strong anti-Christian propaganda on the part of intellectuals, such as Porphyry and particularly Sossianus Hierocles (250–308), who opposed the exclusive monotheistic claims of the Christians, as well as of popular prejudices based on the ascetical and antipagan attitudes of many Christians, Diocletian finally decided upon a policy of extermination. In this he was encouraged by the Caesar Galerius whose mother, a pagan priestess, was fanatically anti-Christian. The thesis, however, advanced by Eusebius and Lactantius blaming Galerius as the principal instigator of the persecution does not seem tenable.

The Army. The first difficulties arising from the renewal of the ruler-cult were experienced in the army. Hitherto, Christian soldiers had not refused to participate in the *adoratio* of the emperor as *Dominus,* nor had they refused to take the oath of loyalty on the royal standards; and no attempt had been made to have them participate in the sacrifice to the gods. But with the emperors proclaimed as gods or the sons of gods, difficulties began. In Numidia in 295 a Christian recruit named Maximilian refused to accept the leaden tag signifying his dedication to military service because it contained the image of the emperor as god; and on July 21, 298, during the ceremony commemorating the epiphany or appearance of the emperors as Jupiter and Hercules, the centurion Marcellus threw down his sword before the standards, stating that he could acknowledge only one "sacramentum," or religious oath, that binding him to Christ. The veterans Tipasius, in 298, and Julius, at Durostorum in 302, refused to accept the imperial *donativum* because the coins depicted the emperors as gods; there were instances of similar insubordination on the frontiers in Africa and on the Danube between 295 and 298. Hence, the following year Diocletian instituted a purge of the military, giving soldiers and officers the choice between offering sacrifice or resigning from the army.

Finally, influenced by a pamphlet of anti-Christian propaganda emanating from the imperial circle, and encouraged by the priests and soothsayers, Diocletian instituted a purge of the imperial household, extending evidently even to his wife Prisca, his daughter Valeria, and several high officials in the fiscal section, all of whom were Christians or Christian-sympathizers.

Edicts of 303. On Feb. 23, 303, an imperial edict bearing the signature of the two emperors and the two Caesars was promulgated. It ordered the destruction of Christian churches and books, prohibited gatherings of Christians for worship, and deprived Christians generally of their civil rights. This ordinance was executed with severity in the East; at Nicomedia a Christian who mutilated a copy of the edict was burned alive, and the church that bordered on the imperial palace was destroyed. When uprisings broke out in Mytilene and Syria, two more edicts were published, one ordering the imprisonment of all Christian clerics, the other stating that a cleric who offered sacrifice would be freed, while any who refused should be tortured and put to death. Toward the end of 303, Diocletian celebrated the 20th anniversary of his reign in Rome, exacting a profession of loyalty to the gods as part of the religious ceremony; and in 304, after recovering from a critical illness at Nicomedia, he released a fourth edict ordering death for all Christians who refused to offer sacrifice.

It is difficult to assess the results of these edicts despite the evidence supplied by the ACTS OF THE MARTYRS; eyewitnesses, such as LACTANTIUS and EUSEBIUS OF CAESAREA; and later Christian writers, including Optatus of Milevis, PRUDENTIUS, St. Basil, and John Chrysostom. Diocletian and Maximian retired in May 305, but in the Orient Galerius and Maximinus Daia pursued the persecution with passion, and there were numerous martyrs in Illyria, Asia Minor, and Egypt.

Persecutions to 311 and Edict of Toleration. In Cappadocia and Pontus the persecutors distinguished themselves by their cruelty, and in Phrygia a small, totally Christian village was burned to the ground. In Syria, Phoenicia, and Palestine, despite the large number of martyrs, there were apostates and *traditores*—those who handed over the sacred books—even among the clergy. Egypt, where the Christians were particularly numerous, suffered most under the anti-Christian polemicist Hierocles, whose aides employed refinements of cruelty. Eusebius testifies that on many days from 10 or 20, or even 60 to 100, Christians were condemned to death or to the mines, to have an eye plucked out or a foot hacked off. Nevertheless, many judges and officials attempted to protect Christian relatives and friends, and to reduce the severity of the persecution.

In the West. Constantius and later his son Constantine seem to have put the first edict into effect in Britain and Gaul, but not to have implemented the others, perhaps because of the relatively small number of Christians there. Martyrs were numerous in Spain, Africa, and Numidia where Maximian saw to the execution of the imperial edicts. In Rome, Pope MARCELLINUS was put to death in 304, and it was impossible to provide a successor until 307. The difficulties that broke out among the Christians because of apostates and *traditores* caused so much trouble that the Caesar Maxentius continued repressive measures, although he was apparently not a convinced persecutor. In fact, after peace was restored in 312, he returned Church properties to the Christians.

Edict of Toleration. In 311 Galerius acknowledged the uselessness of the persecution; and at Sardica, in April, in the name of the regents he promulgated an Edict of Toleration that acknowledged the right of Christians to exist (*ut denuo sint christiani*), allowed them to assemble for worship, and urged them to pray for the empire and their rulers. In the West this ordinance merely legitimized a situation that already prevailed; in the East it re-

stored Christianity as a *religio licita* among others tolerated by the state. Prisoners were freed; exiles were returned from the mines, and religious ceremonies were jubilantly restored. Licinius, who took control of the Danube and Balkans after the death of Galerius, continued this policy, and Maximinus Daia was forced to comply with it in Asia Minor. In Syria and Egypt, however, Maximinus made a final attempt to suppress the Church in 311 and 312, making martyrs of bishops and other Christians, and attempting to organize pagan churches and develop a defamation campaign against Christians.

In 312 Constantine attacked Maxentius, and after the victory of the Milvian Bridge turned to the support of Christianity. At Milan in February 313, he achieved a far-reaching agreement with Licinius that has been erroneously referred to as the Edict of MILAN, but which was rather a series of stipulations whereby Christians were to be gradually given back confiscated properties and restored their civil rights. As upholder of Christian rights, Licinius attacked Maximinus at Adrianople (April 30, 313), and shortly before he died, Maximinus promulgated an edict of toleration for Christians. When Licinius became master of the East he supplemented the Milan agreement.

Final Persecution. In the West, Constantine had actually favored the Christian cause, gradually making Christianity the religion of the state. Hence, when war broke out between the two emperors in 321, Licinius returned to a policy of persecution of the Christians whom he rightly suspected of favoring the Constantinian cause. He drove Christians from his court, forced civil officials and soldiers to sacrifice to the gods, forbade the holding of synods, and curtailed religious assemblies. Some of his subordinates burned churches, imprisoned confessors, and gave the impression that a large persecution had begun. Thus, the Licinian revolt took on the proportions of a religious war that ended with Constantine's victory in 324 at Chrysopolis.

Recent historical investigation tends to reduce greatly the number of martyrs in comparison with traditional estimates. The authority of many of the legends of the saints (*see* SAINTS, LEGENDS OF THE) connected with the persecutions has been challenged also. Modern scholarship, however, has ascertained the reliability of many of the Acts of the Martyrs and the basic records of both Lactantius and Eusebius without denying their natural bias and exaggerations. Of Diocletian it must be said that he was fully responsible for the persecutions perpetrated during his reign; but that he embarked on this policy in good faith.

Bibliography: N. H. BAYNES, *The Cambridge Ancient History,* 12 v. (London and New York 1923–39) 12:646–677. H. GRÉGOIRE et al., *Les Persécutions dans l'Empire romain* (Brussels 1950). W. SESTON, *Dioclétien et la tétrarchie* (Paris 1946); *Reallexikon für Antike und Christentum,* ed. T. KLAUSER (Stuttgart 1941 [1950]–) 3:1045–53.

[E. G. RYAN]

DIOCLETIAN, ROMAN EMPEROR

Reigned Nov. 20, 284, to Jan. 5, 305; b. Gaius Aurelius, Dalmatia, *c.* 245; d. Salona in Dalmatia, Dec. 3, 316. He reorganized the administration of the Empire and inaugurated the last and most severe Roman persecution of Christians. Like many Illyrians, Diocletian was a career soldier who eventually became the *comes domesticorum,* or commander of the imperial guard. When the Emperor Carus died during the Persian campaign of 283 and his sons were assassinated, the legions supported Diocletian, who subsequently became emperor. The new emperor, gifted with an orderly mind and the equanimity and religious sense of his peasant ancestry, stemmed the anarchy that had racked the Empire for 92 years, and set about restructuring its organization. He instituted stringent measures regarding coinage and price control and strengthened the frontiers, especially against the Persians. In 286 he selected Maximian Hercules as coemperor for the West, and in 293 he associated in the government GALERIUS for the East and Constantius Chlorus for the West as *Augusti,* or Caesars, with the right of succeeding their respective coemperors. This tetrarchy was given a religious foundation with Diocletian as representative of the god Jupiter and Maximian of Hercules. At first Diocletian tolerated Christianity, particularly since his wife Prisca and his daughter Valeria took an interest in that religion, but once the frontiers of the Empire were secured, he decided to strengthen the ancient pagan religion. He published regulations regarding marriage (295) and an edict against the Manichees (297). That same year he ordered the dismissal from the army of all who would not participate in the pagan rites. By 303 he was convinced that an extermination of Christians was the only certain way of restoring to the Empire internal unity based on religious uniformity. LACTANTIUS blames Galerius for this decision (*De mortibus persecutorum* 11–14), but his judgment is prejudiced. An edict of Feb. 23, 303, ordered the destruction of Christian places of worship, the surrender of Christian books, and the social degradation of Christian office-holders; the second and third edicts directed the imprisonment and execution of clerics who refused to offer sacrifice; and a fourth commanded exile in the mines or death for nonsacrificing Christians. Although in Rome, Spain, and Africa there were martyrs, the Caesar, Constantius Chlorus, seems to have put only the first edict into effect in the northwest;

but in the Orient and particularly in Egypt, great numbers of Christians were martyred. On May 1, 305, Diocletian and Maximian retired, whereupon the two Caesars succeeded as coemperors and the persecution died out. In 308 Diocletian attempted to save the tetrarchy whose efficiency was impaired by rivalry between Galerius and Constantius Chlorus. He died in his villa near Salona.

Bibliography: W. ENSSLIN, *Paulys Realenzyklopädie der klassischen Altertumswissenschaft,* ed. G. WISSOWA et al. 7A.1:2419–95. W. SESTON, *Dioclétien et la tétrarchie* (Paris 1946); *Reallexikon für Antike und Christentum,* ed. T. KLAUSER [Stuttgart 1941] 3:1036–53. LACTANTIUS, *De la Mort des persécuteurs,* ed. J. MOREAU (*Sources Chrétiennes* 39; 1954) 2:231–320.

[E. G. RYAN]

DIODORE OF TARSUS

Bishop, theologian, and exegete of the School of ANTIOCH; b. Antioch; d. Tarsus, before 394. After receiving a secular education at Athens, Diodore studied Scripture and theology under Silvanus of Tarsus and EUSEBIUS OF EMESA. He entered and later presided over the monastic school near Antioch, where St. JOHN CHRYSOSTOM and THEODORE OF MOPSUESTIA were his pupils. After being ordained by Meletius of Antioch between 361 and 365, he shared his bishop's exile under the Arian Roman Emperor VALENS from 372 to 378. Then Meletius consecrated him bishop of Tarsus, in which capacity he took part in the Council of CONSTANTINOPLE I (381). In an edict confirming this Council, Theodosius named Diodore as a standard of orthodoxy (*Codex Theodosianus* 16.1.3). He maintained this reputation until his death; but about 40 years later CYRIL OF ALEXANDRIA, in his tract *Against Diodore and Theodore,* accused Diodore of NESTORIANISM. Cyril's judgment was sanctioned by a synod held in Constantinople in 499. Diodore's condemnation by this synod led to the destruction of most of his writings.

The many titles listed by Suidas and the Syrian Ebedjesu show Diodore to have been a prolific writer whose interests included cosmology, astronomy, and chronology, as well as exegesis and theology. His commentary on the Psalms, discovered by Mariés and edited by Olivier, is now generally recognized to be genuine. *Catenae* have yielded fragments of his extensive writings on other parts of Scripture. Fifty–three fragments of his anti-Apollinarist tract *Against the Synousiasts* have come down to us, all but one of which are in florilegia that were gathered by his adversaries.

Diodore's criticism of Apollinaris was directed not at the latter's denial that Christ had a human soul, but at the threat to the divinity of the Word that Diodore rightly saw in the idea of a mixture of Word and flesh in one composite being. Diodore differed from later exponents of Antiochene theology, in his occasional use of the "Word–flesh" formula, and in the fact that he did not attribute to the soul of Christ the theological significance which others such as Theodore of Mopsuestia would give to it. In order to safeguard the divinity of the Word, which he saw as compromised by the predication of human attributes to the Divine Person, Diodore insisted on the distinction between the eternal Son of God and the son of Mary in whom the Word dwelt. To the charge that he divided Christ into two Sons, he replied that although one is the Son of God by nature and the other son of God by grace, Christ is rightly adored as one Son of God. He refused to speak of "one hypostasis," because he took that to mean a natural unity of Word and flesh, which he saw as incompatible with the divinity of the Word. In Grillmeier's judgment, Diodore was unable to construct an effective christology with a "Word–man" framework, but he prepared the ground for another Antiochene who was to carry on the task, Theodore of Mopsuestia.

Bibliography: *Patrologia Graeca* (Paris 1966) 33:1559–1628. P. GODET, *Dictionnaire de Théologie Catholique* (Paris 1950) 4:1363–1366. M. BRIÈRE, "Fragments syriaques de Diodore de Tarse," *Revue de l'Orient chrétien*, 30 (1946) 231–283. M. RICHARD, "Les Traités de Cyrille d'Alexandrie contre Diodore et Théodore et les Fragments dogmatiques de Diodore de Tarse," *Mélanges F. Grat* (Paris 1946) 1:99–116. J. M. OLIVIER, *Diodori Tarsensis Commentarii in Psalmos*, CCG 6 (Louvain 1980). G. BARDY, *Dictionnaire de spiritualité ascétique et mystique* (Paris 1932) 3:986–993. L. ABRAMOWSKI, *Dictionnaire d'histoire catholique* 14:496–504. R. ABRAMOWSKI, "Untersuchungen zu Diodor von Tarsus," *Zeitschrift für die neutestamentliche Wissenschaft und die Kunde der äteren Kirche* 30 (1931) 234–261; "Der theologische Nachlass des Diodors von Tarsus," *Zeitschrift für die neutestamentliche Wissenschaft und die Kunde der äteren Kirche* 42 (1949) 19–69. M. JUGIE, "La doctrine christologique de Diodore de Tarse d'après les fragments de ses oeuvres," *Euntes Docete* 2 (1949) 171–191. L. ABRAMOWSKI, "Der Streit um Diodor und Theodor zwischen den beiden ephesinischen Konzilien," *Zeitschrift für Kirchengeschichte* 67 (Stuttgart 1955–56) 252–282. F. A. SULLIVAN, *The Christology of Theodore of Mopsuestia* (Rome 1956) 172–196. R. A. GREER, "The Antiochene Christology of Diodore of Tarsus," *Journal of Theological Studies* 17 (1966) 327–341. M. J. RONDEAU, "Le Commentaire des Psaumes de Diodore de Tarse I–III," *Revue d'histoire et de philosophie religieuses* 176: 5–33, 153–188; 177: 5–33. A. GRILLMEIER, *Christ in Christian Tradition* (London/Oxford 1975) 1:352–360.

[F. A. SULLIVAN]

DIOGNETUS, EPISTLE TO

Mid-2nd-century apology that followed five treatises attributed to St. JUSTIN MARTYR and was assigned to the same author in the Codex Argentoratensis, destroyed at Strassburg in 1872. It is not mentioned by any ancient or medieval author, and there is no conclusive internal evidence as to its date, the identity of Diognetus, or authorship of the epistle. Because the author calls himself a "disciple of the Apostles," it has commonly been published along with the APOSTOLIC FATHERS but is really an apology, now generally assigned to the middle or latter half of the 2nd century. The letter proper encompasses the first ten chapters and may have lost its ending. Although addressed to an individual, it is clearly directed toward a wider public but it lacks the quasi-official justificatory attitude toward authority of such apologetic as Justin's. The author sets himself to answer three questions posed by Diognetus: (1) Who is the Christian God? (2) What is this affection that Christians feel for one another? (3) Why has this new race and new way of life entered into the world now?

In simple, lucid, and graceful language, epigrammatic at times, he first treats of the variety and nature of heathen gods and the folly of worshiping them. He then trounces the Jews just as roundly and stigmatizes their sacrifices as foolish and their religious customs as absurd. He gives a moving description of Christians, "who are in the world what the soul is in the body," and in a series of vivid antitheses marks the differences between their way of life and that of their neighbors. Their religion was not discovered by man's intellect but revealed through God's Son and is apprehended by God-given faith. The Son is the agent of salvation, an atonement that is essentially moral, though "ransom" and "substitution" are also used. He came at this time because of the loving purpose of God, who wished men to recognize their inability to work out their own salvation. Finally Christian faith is seen as an imitation of God, and its character and fruits are described. There is no mention of institutional religion or developing heresies regarding the Holy Spirit.

An Appendix (cc.11–12) contains an allegory of the six days of Creation and the Garden of Eden to illustrate the indissoluble union between knowledge and life. The florid style and allegorical treatment are quite alien to the foregoing text and more akin to Melito or Hippolytus.

Bibliography: Editions. J. B. LIGHTFOOT and J. HARMER, eds. and trs., *The Apostolic Fathers* (New York 1891). K. BIHLMEYER, ed., *Die Apostolischen Väter* (2d ed. Tübingen 1956–), new rev. of F. X. FUNK ed., 2 v. (Tübingen 1881–87). K. LAKE, ed. and tr., *The Apostolic Fathers* 2 v. (*Loeb Classical Library*; London-New York-Cambridge, Mass 1917–19). G. G. WALSH, tr., in *The Apostolic Fathers* (*The Fathers of the Church: A New Translation* 1; 1948) 355–369. J. KLEIST, ed. and tr., *Ancient Christian Writers* 6 (1948) 125–147. H. I. MARROU, ed. and tr., *Sources Chrétiennes* 33 (1951). M. MEECHAM, *The Epistle to Diognetus* (Manchester 1949). B. ALTANER, *Patrology*, tr. H. GRAEF from 5th German ed. (New York 1960) 135–136. J. QUASTEN, *Patrology,* 3 v. (Westminster, Md. 1950–53) 1:248–253. J. T. LIENHARD, "The Christology of the Epistle to Diognetus," *Vigiliae Christianae* 24 (1970): 280–289. R. BRÄNDLE, *Die Ethik der "Schrift an Diognet": eine Wiederauf-

nahme paulinischer und johanneischer Theologie am Ausgang des zweiten Jahrhunderts (Zürich 1975).

[M. WHITTAKER]

DIONIGI DA PIACENZA

Missionary, whose writings contributed greatly to European knowledge of distant peoples and places in the modern era of discovery and exploration; b. Piacenza, Italy, 1637; d. Venice, Italy, 1695. In 1652, at the age of 15, Dionigi Carli entered the Bologna province of the Capuchin Order. Dionigi, destined to become one of the most traveled missionaries up to his time, labored in the Congo from 1667 to 1671, after which he went to Brazil. After returning to Italy, he was sent in 1678 to the missions of Asia Minor, Persia, and Russian Georgia. In Georgia he served as proprefect of the mission. He spent his last years in Venice. Dionigi's two books of narration of his experiences caused a sensation among his European contemporaries. His narratives were widely distributed, and even during his lifetime appeared in French and German translations, and were incorporated in monumental collections of works on foreign travel, for example, the English rendering by J. Pinkerton in *A General Collection of the Best and Most Interesting Voyages and Travels* (v. 16 London 1808).

Bibliography: *Lexicon Capuccinum* (Rome 1951) 507–508.

[T. MACVICAR]

DIONYSIANA COLLECTIO

The *Dionysiana* is a canonical collection, written in the first half of the sixth century. Of the eight extant manuscripts, the earliest dates from the seventh century. It is believed that three versions existed. The first, dedicated to *Petronius episcopus,* is found in the single manuscript of the Vatican (Pal. lat. 577) and includes the Canons of the Apostles and the Councils of Nicaea, Ancyra, Neocaesarea, Gangra, Antioch, Laodicea, Constantinople, Sardica, Carthage, and Chalcedon. The second, which is most widely disseminated, is dedicated to *Stephanus episcopus* and includes the same Councils, but Chalcedon is placed between Constantinople and Sardica instead of being relegated to the end. Two MSS contain an additional series of decretals from Pope Siricius (384–399) to Pope Anastasius II (496–498) that are dedicated to Julian, Cardinal-priest of St. Anastasius. All that remains of the third version, in the MSS Novara XXX (66), is the dedicatory epistle to Hormisdas that announces a juxtalinear translation of the Greek Councils.

It is not impossible that Petronius and Stephanus were one and the same person. The texts of the two letters addressed to them differ only in that the one to Stephanus enumerates the texts included in the collection. Both texts announce, in the same terms, the same reasons that induced Dionysius to compile his collection. He was asked to translate the Greek ecclesiastical regulations by his beloved brother Lawrence, who was particularly disturbed by the "ignorance" of the ancient translations. In the *Dionysiana,* therefore, we find only rigorously authentic texts, with the exception of the Canons of the Apostles; Dionysius always considered them suspect, but retained them because they had been widely used in the dioceses to draw up local discipline. The *Dionysiana* is a work adapted to the needs of the time. It prepared the way for that reconciliation of the Churches of the Orient and of the West, the goal always pursued by Dionysius.

Concerning dogma, Dionysius stressed the inviolability of the Canons of Nicaea that all succeeding Councils affirmed. He took care not to reproduce the four professions of faith of the Council of Antioch that accused the doctrine of Nicaea of Sabellianism. Concerning discipline, he strove to establish definitively the supremacy of Rome. He reproduced the sixth canon of Nicaea confirming the primacy of Alexandria and Antioch in the Church of the Orient modeled after the Church of Rome. He also gave the third canon of Constantinople that instituted the patriarchates of Alexandria, Antioch, Ephesus, Pontus, and Thrace, while granting a primacy of honor to Constantinople immediately after Rome. However, he carefully refrained from translating canon 28 of Chalcedon that gave the bishop of Constantinople powers equal to those of the bishop of Rome.

It is probable that the *Dionysiana* was prepared at Rome under the pontificate of Pope Hormisdas (514–523). From the time of the pontificate of John II (533–535), the *Dionysiana* became the preferred collection of the Roman Church. At the end of the sixth and beginning of the seventh century, many additions were made to it, and it served as the point of departure for new collections, such as the *Dionysiana* of Bobbio, continued until the pontificate of Boniface IV (608–615). Above all, it served as the basis for the HADRIANA COLLECTIO.

Bibliography: DIONYSIUS EXIGUUS, *Die Canonessammlung des Dionysius Exiguus in der ersten Redaktion,* ed. A. STREWE (Berlin 1931); "Codex canonum ecclesiasticorum," and "Collectio decretorum Pontificarum romanorum," ed. C. JUSTEL, *Patrologia Latina,* ed. J. P. MIGNE (Paris 1878–90) 67:93–316. F. MAASSEN *Geschichte der Quellen und der Literatur des canonischen Rechts im Abendlande bis dem Ausgang des Mittelalters* (Graz 1870) 425–436. H. WURM, *Studien und Texte zur Dekretalensammlung des Dionysius Exiguus* (Bonn 1939); "Decretales selectae ex antiquissimis romanorum Pontificum epistulis decretalibus," *Appollinaris* 12 (1939) 40–93. M. CAPPUYNS, "L'Origine des Capitula pseudo-célestiniens contre le semi-pélagianisme," *Revue Bénédictine* 41

(1929) 156–170. J. RAMBAUD-BUHOT, *Dictionnaire de droit canonique*, ed. R. NAZ (Paris 1935–65) 4:1131–52.

[J. RAMBAUD-BUHOT]

DIONYSUS, CULT OF

Dionysus was a god of the mysterious, uncontrollable powers in nature, and became associated with wine only by a later specialization. The Greeks generally supposed that his worship spread from Thrace southward to Boeotia, where he is said to have been born, and eastward with those Thracians who became the Phrygians. His cult took two forms: (1) In Asia Minor the rites were generally held in spring and were based upon the belief that Dionysus, as a vegetation god, died in winter and was reborn in spring as a child. Rites of this type spread in Asia Minor and are represented at Athens by the Anthesteria. (2) Greek literature and art were more concerned, however, with the orgiastic cult, which spread rapidly like a type of mass hysteria. Of these rites Euripides' *Bacchae* is the most impressive account.

The orgiastic cult was limited almost exclusively to women, who went, dressed in animal skins and carrying thyrsi or torches, to the woods and mountains, where they danced until exhausted and sometimes devoured wild animals that they had caught and dismembered. Dionysus was regarded as being present at times in snakes, lions, goats, bulls, and other animals. Hence, when his votaries dressed in animal skins and devoured the flesh of animals, they were practicing a form of communion with their god. The Greeks usually approached their gods through a priest as intermediary, but, in the ecstatic cult of Dionysus, the god was believed to be personally present among, and even within, men.

The orgiastic cult was taken up into the official religion of various Greek states, being regulated and tamed in the process, especially under the influence of the Oracle of Delphi. The phallic procession was a typical form of the rites of Dionysus and was intended to promote fertility. At Athens his official worship was orderly, with emphasis on music and drama. It is to the cult of Dionysus that we owe the origins of the drama that produced the plays of Aeschylus, Sophocles, Euripides, and Aristophanes. There were also private Bacchic mysteries, and Dionysus was introduced into the Orphic mysteries by identification with Zagreus.

See Also: MYSTERY RELIGIONS, GRECO-ORIENTAL.

Bibliography: M. P. NILSSON and H. J. ROSE, *The Oxford Classical Dictionary*, ed. M. CARY et al. (Oxford 1949) 288–289. M. P. NILSSON, *Geschichte der griechischen Religion*, 2 v. (2d ed. Munich 1955–61) 1:532–568. O. KERN, "Dionysus (2)," *Paulys Realenzklopädie der klassischen Altertumswissenschaft*, ed. G. WISSOWA et al. 5.1 (1903) 1010–46. F. A. VOIGT and E. THRAEMER, "Dionysos," W. H. ROSCHER, ed. *Ausführliches Lixikon der griechischen und römischen Mythologie*, 6 v. (Leipzig 1884–1937); suppl., 3 v. in 2 (1893, 1902, 1921) 1:1029–1153. EURIPIDES, *Bacchae*, ed. E. R. DODDS (2d ed. New York 1960), esp. xi–xxv.

[H. S. LONG]

DIONYSIUS, POPE, ST.

Pontificate: July 22, 259 to Dec. 26, 268. Both Eusebius and Jerome gave these dates for his pontificate, while E. Caspar and modern authors give 260 to 267. His origin is unknown. Dionysius (Denis), while still a Roman priest, received an appeal from Dionysius of Alexandria for aid in reconciling Eastern practice, condemned by Pope Stephen I, with the Roman bishops' stand on the validity of Baptism performed by heretics (Eusebius, *Ecclesiastical History* 7.5). Athanasius cites two of his letters as pope to Dionysius of Alexandria in which he condemned Sabellianism and Subordinationism. Reports reached Rome from Egypt that, in his denunciation of the Sabellian heresy among the monks, the Alexandrian bishop used expressions that emphasized the distinction between Father and Son so as to approach the subordinationist teaching attributed to Origen. Dionysius then held a Roman Synod in 260, issued a summary of the Church's Christological teaching (Athanasius, *De decretis Nic. Syn.* 26), and respectfully requested information concerning the Alexandrian bishop's orthodoxy. He received in reply a *Refutation and Apology* in which Dionysius of Alexandria used the HOMOOUSIOS formula and demonstrated that any charges of Tritheism against him were untrue (Athanasius, *De Sent. Dion.* 13). In 340 Pope Julius I referred to this interchange as a precedent for Roman supervision over Alexandrian doctrine.

In 261 the Emperor Gallienus emancipated the Christian community and restored its confiscated property (Eusebius, *Ecclesiastical History* 7.13). The *Liber pontificalis* records that Dionysius reorganized the Roman Church, assigned cemeteries to different parishes, and arranged new episcopal administrative units in the metropolitan area, which were necessary after the dislocation of the emperor Valerian's persecution and particuarly after the martyrdom of Pope Sixtus II and his deacons.

St. Basil (*Ep.* 70) praised the orthodoxy of Dionysius and his charity in sending funds to redeem Christian captives in Cappodocia. Eusebius related that a Council of Antioch (*c.* 268) addressed a circular letter to Dionysius and Maximus of Alexandria; the letter announced the deposition of Paul of Samosata for his adoptionist leanings.

This report reached Rome about the time of Dionysius's death (Eusebius, *Ecclesiastical History* 7.7). He was buried in the cemetery of St. Callistus.

Feast: Dec. 30.

Bibliography: EUSEBIUS, *Ecclesiastical History* 7.5, 26, 27, 30. A. CLERVAL, *Dictionnaire de théology catholique*, ed. A. VACANT et al. (Paris 1903–50) 4.1:423–425. J. SHOTWELL and L. LOOMIS, *The See of Peter* (New York 1927) 429–438. L. ABRAMOWSKI, "Dionys von Rom (d. 258) und Dionys von Alexandria (d. 264/5) in den arianischen Streitigkeiten des 4. Jahrhunderts," *Zeitschrift für Kirchengeschichte* 93 (1982), 240–272. J. N. D. KELLY, *Oxford Dictionary of Popes* (New York 1986) 22–23. E. FERGUSON, *Encyclopedia of Early Christianity* (New York 1997) 1:334. L. ABRAMOWSKY, "Dionysius of Rome (d. 268) and Dionysius of Alexandria (d. 264/5) in the Arian Controversies of the Fourth Century," in *Formula and Context: Studies in Early Christian Thought* (London 1992). G. SCHWAIGER, *Lexikon für Theologie und Kirche*, 3d. ed. (Freiburg 1995). B. SODARO, *Santi e beati di Calabria* (Rosarno 1996) 29–37.

[E. G. WELTIN]

DIONYSIUS, EXIGUUS

Also known as Denis the Little, canonist, monk; lived in Rome at the end of the 5th century and in the first half of the 6th century. Internal criticism of the works of Dionysius has made it possible to add a few facts to this sketchy biography, A. van Hove writes that Dionysius was taken in and brought up by Gothic monks, became a monk, arrived in Rome after the death of Pope Gelasius (Nov. 21, 496), and died there after 525. The date of Dionysius's death is controversial. According to L. Duchesne, no trace of him was found in Rome after 526. A. Amelli claims he could not have died before 534, the date when Pastor Felicianus (to whom the "Tome to the Armenians" is dedicated) succeeded Fulgentius of Ruspe. Gelasius called Dionysius to his side in 496 to classify the pontifical archives and to compile a collection of texts of incontestable worth and authenticity. By then Dionysius was already of mature years, and could not have lived beyond 527. The entire work of Dionysius had but one purpose: the reconciliation of the Churches of the Orient and the West.

Dionysius's perfect knowledge of Greek and Latin is proved by his many translations: "The Penance of St. Thaïs" [Ambrosian MS D. 525, in-folio ed. from the *prol. et incipit ds. Analecta bibleca* 11 (1892) 298–299]; *Life of St. Pachomius* (*Patrologia Latina*, ed. J. P. Migne, 72:227–282) addressed to a Roman lady who may have been Galla, daughter of the patrician Symmachus and sister-in-law of Boethius; *De inventione capitis s. Johannis Baptistae* (*Patrologia Latina* 67:417–431). We have only one translation of a philosophical work by him: the *De opificio hominis* of Gregory of Nyssa, published under the title *De creatione hominis liber* (*Patrologia Latina* 67:347–408).

Three of his translations were concerned with the fight against Nestorius: "St. Cyril of Alexandria, letter to Nestorius and anathematizations" (*Patrologia Latina* 67:9–18), a translation that may be merely a new edition of that by Marius Mercator; *Oratio la de Deipara* of Dec. 23, 428, in which he proclaimed the divine maternity of Mary; and "Tome to the Armenians," addressed to Patriarch John, which refutes the arguments of Theodore of Mopsuestia and of the partisans of Nestorius. The *Oratio* and the "Tome" were works of Proclus, bishop, to whom the Emperor Theodosius preferred Nestorius in 427.

The Orient and the West were divided on the question of the way to determine the date of Easter. The Council of NICAEA had commanded the adoption of the Alexandrine rule, based on the 19-year cycle. At Rome, a tradition had been adopted that declared Easter should not be celebrated before March 25 or after April 21, and the basis for calculation was the old 84-year cycle. Tables for the dates of Easter had been prepared in the Orient by Theophilus of Alexandria, and St. Cyril had continued his work. In the West tables were drawn up by Victorius of Aquitaine. They terminated with the year A.D. 531, and had as their respective points of departure the reign of Diocletian, for the Orient; and the Passion, for the West. In the *Liber de Paschate* (*Patrologia Latina* 67:483–508), Dionysius recommended the adoption of the Alexandrine cycle, as required by the Council of Nicaea, whose decisions were universally respected. He established a table of Paschal dates up to the year 626, which was a continuation of the table of Cyril of Alexandria, but used the year of the Incarnation as the point of departure. He was the first to date the Christian era by the birth of Christ, but he made a four- to seven-year error.

Dionysius is best known as a canonist. We owe to his ability as a translator and compiler the first canonical collection worthy of the name, the *DIONYSIANA*.

Bibliography: L. DUCHESNE, *L'Église au VIᵉ siècle* (Paris 1925). A. VAN HOVE, *Commentarium Lovaniense in Codicem iuris canonici 1*, v.1–5 (Mechlin 1928–1945) 1:157–158. A. VAN DE VYVER, "Cassiodore et son oeuvre," *Speculum. A Journal of Mediaeval Studies* 6 (1931) 244–292; "Les Institutions de Cassiodore et sa fondation à Vivarium," *Revue Bénédictine* 53 (1941) 59–88. W. M. PEITZ, "Dionisio el exiguo como canonista: Nuevas soluciones de antiguos problemas de la investigación," *Revista españ de derecho canónico* 2 (1947) 9–32. J. RAMBAUD-BUHOT, *Dictionnaire de droit canonique*, ed. R. NAZ (Paris 1935–65) 4:1131–52. J. LENZENWEGER, *Lexikon für Theologie und Kirche*, ed. J. HOFER and K. RAHNER (2d, new ed. Freiburg 1957–65) 3:406.

[J. RAMBAUD-BUHOT]

DIONYSIUS OF ALEXANDRIA, ST.

Bishop of Alexandria, 247–265, disciple of ORIGEN, and FATHER OF THE CHURCH; b. *c.* 190; d. Alexandria, 265. Dionysius, a convert who had studied literature and philosophy at ALEXANDRIA, succeeded Heraclas in 232 as head of the Didascaleion, or catechetical school, and in 247 followed him as bishop of Alexandria. During the Decian persecution (250) Dionysius went into hiding, but he returned to Alexandria in 251. In the Valerian persecution of 257, Dionysius was exiled to Libya after making a public profession of faith. He participated in the doctrinal disputes caused by the TRINITARIAN controversies, NOVATIANISM, CHILIASM, and the rebaptism of heretics. His writings have been preserved only in fragments but include a book *On Nature* written for his son, *Refutations and Defense, On the Promises* in which he denied the Johannine authorship of the Apocalypse, and two letters (Eusebius, *Hist. Eccl.* 4.45).

Feast: Nov. 17.

Bibliography: DIONYSIUS, *The Letters and Other Remains of Dionysius of Alexandria,* ed. C. L. FELTOE (Cambridge, Eng. 1904); *Das erhaltene Werk. Dionysiou leipsana,* tr. W. A. BIENERT (Stuttgart 1972). F. C. CONYBEARE, ''Newly Discovered Letters of Dionysius of Alexandria,'' *English Historical Review* 25 (1910) 111–114. U. HEIL, *Athanasius von Alexandrien: De sententia Dionysii* (Berlin 1999). J. QUASTEN, *Patrology* (Westminster, MD 1950) 2:101–109.

[E. G. RYAN]

DIONYSIUS OF CORINTH, ST.

An outstanding writer among the non-Romans who corresponded with Pope SOTER *c.* 170. He was bishop of Corinth under Emperor Marcus Aurelius and was one of the most holy and zealous pastors of the Church in the second century. Eusebius gives us an account of the letters of Dionysius (*Histoire ecclesiastique* 4.23). Since none of the original letters are extant, the report of Eusebius is important.

In his letter to Soter, Dionysius thanked the bishop of Rome for his generosity in sending alms to the needy throughout the empire. This same letter mentions the letter of Pope St. CLEMENT to the Christians of Corinth. It is interesting to note in what esteem the letter of Clement was held. Dionysius' letter to the Lacedaemonians is an instruction in orthodoxy on the subject of peace and unity. Another letter to the Nicomedians combats the heresy of MARCION. Dionysius wrote also to the Church while sojourning in Amastris, together with the churches in Pontus, adducing interpretations of the Scriptures and giving them many exhortations about marriage and chastity. In this same letter he also orders the faithful to receive those who are converted from any backsliding, whether of conduct or of heretical error.

From the account of Eusebius it appears that the letters of Dionysius must have been extant in one volume, which could have been completed while the writer was still living. It is also evident that his letters were held in high esteem by the different Christian communities, because he himself reported that the heretics tried to falsify them.

Feast: April 8 (Western Church); Nov. 29 (Eastern Church).

Bibliography: EUSEBIUS, *Histoire ecclesiastique* 4.23. J. QUASTEN, *Patrology,* 3 v. (Westminster, MD 1950–) 1:280–282. I. TSAVARĒ, *Concordantia in Dionysii Periegetae descriptionem orbis terrarum* (Hildesheim 1992), in Greek with an Eng. preface. P. NAUTIN, *Dictionnaire d'histoire et de géographie ecclésiastiques* (Paris 1912–), 14:261–262. B. ALTANER, *Patrology,* tr. H. GRAEF (New York 1960) 148.

[D. P. KELLEHER]

DIONYSIUS OF THE NATIVITY (PIERRE BERTHOLET), BL.

Baptized Pierre Bertholet; missionary and protomartyr of the Discalced Carmelite reform; b. Honfleur, France, Dec. 12, 1600; d. Sumatra, Nov. 27, 1638. He was a professional navigator and cartographer, captured by Dutch pirates and imprisoned at Java on his first expedition to the Indies. After his release he settled in Malacca and worked for the Portuguese, assuming command of a ship. His voyages brought him into contact with the recently founded Discalced Carmelite monastery at Goa, and in 1634 he entered the order. After his ordination in 1638, his superiors assigned him, at the request of the Portuguese viceroy, as the chaplain of an expedition to Sumatra and appointed a lay brother, Blessed Redemptus of the Cross (Thomas Rodriguez da Cunha), as his companion. When the expedition arrived at Sumatra, both men were captured by the natives and martyred when they refused to apostatize to Islam. LEO XIII beatified them in 1900. Some of Dionysius's cartographic work is in the British Museum.

Feast: Nov. 29.

Bibliography: R. AIGRAIN, *Catholicisme* (Paris 1947–) 3:617–618. M. PREVOST, *Dictionnaire de biographie française* (Paris 1929–) 6:200–201.

[P. T. ROHRBACH]

DIOSCORUS, ANTIPOPE

Pontificate: September 20 or 22 to Oct. 14, 530. Following the death of Pope Felix IV (III), the majority of the Roman clergy elected the Alexandrian deacon Dioscorus, who had fled to Rome from the Monophysites and had long resided there. He was consecrated in the Lateran basilica, apparently on the day of Felix's death. Dioscorus had taken a leading part in the negotiations under Popes SYMMACHUS and HORMISDAS that brought the ACACIAN schism to an end, and Hormisdas had attempted to persuade Emperor JUSTIN I to appoint Dioscorus Patriarch of Alexandria. A minority of the clergy had voted for BONIFACE II, in accordance with the wishes of Pope Felix. The fact that no biography of Dioscorus was included in the *Liber pontificalis* appears to have been decisive in excluding him from the list of popes. His early death and the rallying of the clergy to Boniface II, whose chancery would not permit acknowledgment of a rival, were undoubtedly the ultimate determining factors. The *Annuario Pontificio 2001* considers him an antipope, but with the qualification that "perhaps the legitimacy of Dioscorus can be sustained." If one judges by the Canon Law of the time, he could be regarded as a legitimate pope. The burial place of Dioscorus is unknown.

Bibliography: L. DUCHESNE, *Liber pontificalis*, 1:46, 108, 273, 282, 287; 3:91. H. MAROT, *Dictionnaire d'histoire et de géographie ecclésiastiques*, ed. A. BAUDRILLART, et al. (Paris 1912–) 14:507–508. *Annuario Pontificio* (1964) 10*. H. JEDIN, *History of the Church* (New York 1980), 2:626. J. N. D. KELLY, *Oxford Dictionary of Popes* (New York 1986), 56–57. J. RICHARDS, *Popes and Papacy the Early Middle Ages* (London 1979), 123–125. G. BRAGA, *Dictionnaire de biographie française,* 40 (Paris 1990–91). G. SCHWAIGER, *Lexikon für Theologie und Kirche,* 3d. ed. (Freiburg 1995).

[J. CHAPIN/EDS.]

DIOSCORUS, PATRIARCH OF ALEXANDRIA

Reigned 444 to 451; b. Alexandria; d. in exile, Gangra, Paphlagonia, Sept. 4, 454. Dioscorus, successor of CYRIL OF ALEXANDRIA as patriarch of Egypt, was an archdeacon of strong convictions who accompanied Cyril to the Council of EPHESUS (431) and shared his theological ideas concerning CHRISTOLOGY and the THEOTOKOS. He followed Cyril as patriarch in 444. Dioscorus did not hesitate to use violent means in ousting the relatives of Cyril from ecclesiastical and administrative positions; and he forced them to restore what they had inherited from Cyril. He deposed the priest Athanasius and the deacons Theodore and Ischyrion, who had been favored by his predecessor.

When the Constantinopolitan Archmandrite EUTYCHES was condemned by a local synod (448) under FLAVIAN OF CONSTANTINOPLE for his ideas on the union of natures in Christ, Dioscorus came to the aid of Eutyches.

He presided at the Robber Synod of EPHESUS in August 449, prevented the reading of the Tome of Pope LEO I, and condemned Flavian and the representatives of the Antiochene theology. He was supported by Emperor THEODOSIUS II. When Theodosius died (July 28, 450), however, MARCIAN and Pulcheria summoned the Council of CHALCEDON (451), which deposed Dioscorus in its third session (October 13), after he had defied Pope Leo and the council. It did not condemn Dioscorus as a heretic, however; and, despite the fact that he was given a successor in Proterius, on the death of Emperor Marcian (Jan. 26, 457) the Egyptian Church was taken over by the Monophysites (*see* MONOPHYSITISM).

Dioscorus adhered strictly to the theological thought and expressions of Cyril, giving his Christology an apparently Monophysitic interpretation; but he left no writings of a specific doctrinal nature. His panegyric was written by the deacon Theopistus (455), and he is venerated as a saint in the Coptic Church.

Bibliography: S. LE NAIN DE TILLEMONT, *Mémoires pour servir à l'histoire ecclésiastique des six premiers siècles* (Paris 1693–1712) v.15. F. HAASE, "Patriarch Dioskur I," in *Kirchengeschichtliche Abhandlungen,* ed. M. SDRALEK (Breslau 1902–11) 6:141–236. F. NAU, *Journal asiatique* 10.1 (1903) 5–108, 241–310, panegyric. G. BARDY, *Catholicisme. Hier, aujourd'hui et demain,* ed. G. JACQUEMET (Paris 1947–) 3:857–858. J. LEBON, *Le Monophysisme Sévérien* (Louvain 1909) 84–93, writings; *Le Muséon* 59 (1946) 515–528, condemnation. A. FLICHE and V. MARTIN, eds., *Histoire de l'église depuis les origines jusqu'à nos jours* (Paris 1935–) 4:211–240, 271–272. *Dictionnaire de théologie catholique: Tables générales,* ed. A. VACANT et al. (Paris 1951–) 1:999–1000. N. CHARLIER, *Dictionnaire d'histoire et de géographie ecclésiastiques,* ed. A. BAUDRILLART et al. (Paris 1912–) 14:508–514. B. L. DENDAKIS, *Lexikon für Theologie und Kirche,* ed. J. HOFER and K. RAHNER (2d, new ed. Freiburg 1957–65) 3:409–410.

[F. X. MURPHY]

DIPLOMATICS, ECCLESIASTICAL

Diplomatics is the systematic critical study of historical sources, such as charters, public and private acts, judicial records, and related written documents. Ecclesiastical diplomatics is concerned with papal and other Church records of the same basic character but with emphasis on their special distinguishing features.

History. The Romans first used the word *diploma,* a word borrowed from the Greek, to indicate a double or folded sheet, or two sheets hinged together like the bronze plates employed in military discharges. Subsequently they used the term to designate a certificate or license to travel by the *cursus publicus,* or public post, and then for official grants or privileges in general. The word passed on to the Middle Ages and, in the Renaissance, came to be used as a designation for public, especially royal, acts and privileges and for medieval documents in general. The adjective *diplomaticus* is a coinage of Renaissance Latin. *Res diplomatica* was employed to designate the study of medieval documents in particular. Hence it was only natural that J. MABILLON should choose the term as the title of his epoch-making work, *De re diplomatica* (1681), in which he founded the twin sciences of paleography and diplomatics. It remained for his confrere B. de MONTFAUCON to coin the word *palaeographia* in his *Palaeographia Graeca* (1708). Mabillon's work was further elaborated by the MAURISTS Toustain and Tassin, in their *Nouveau traité de diplomatique* (1750–65). The modern science of diplomatics, however, was developed especially at the École des Chartes in Paris (founded 1821), and at the Institut für Österreichische Geschichtsforschung in Vienna (founded 1854 and reorganized 1878).

Types of Documents. There are three major groups of documents: papal, imperial, and private. By private documents are meant all documents that are neither papal nor imperial. Ecclesiastical diplomatics is strictly speaking papal diplomatics; all documents originating outside the Roman CURIA in the episcopal curias, in abbeys, and in other ecclesiastical institutions are to be considered private documents. In form, style, and material, ecclesiastical documents usually follow contemporary developments in the various countries of origin. Aside from originals, they are found chiefly in special collections as in the *libri traditionum* of old monasteries. Generally speaking the documents were drawn up by notaries according to certain formularies in the chanceries of secular or ecclesiastical rulers. Seals were appended or attached, and the names of witnesses were inserted in the documents.

Notaries. The institution of ecclesiastical notaries most probably dates back to the times of the primitive Church. During the persecution clerics were employed particularly in Rome to draw up the acts of the martyrs. During the reign of Pope JULIUS I (337–352) notaries had an important position at the Roman Curia. Fifth-century sources mention the notaries of the apostolic see. Even before the time of GREGORY I THE GREAT (590–604), a college (*schola*) of notaries had been established, headed by the *primicerius notariorum*. Most probably notaries were the first officials of the apostolic chancery. The first signs of an organization can be found during the pontificate of Pope ADRIAN I (772–795). The *primicerius* or *secundicerius notariorum* signed the papal documents.

Epistles. During the time of the primitive Church and in the first centuries afterward, the form of an epistle (*litterae encyclicae*) was used, first by the Apostles, and later by popes and bishops.

Formularies. In the 7th century, collections of formularies came into use not only to improve the style, but also to give uniformity to the legal contents. Among the most important collections of formularies were the two volumes collected by the monk Marculf. They were composed *c.* 660 and contained ecclesiastical as well as secular formularies, and were employed generally in the chanceries of Europe. The Roman Curia also used formularies. The most important curial formulary was the *LIBER DIURNUS*, composed between the 7th and the 9th century. During the time of GREGORY VII (1073–85) the use of the *Liber diurnus* was discontinued.

Summae Dictaminis. By 1228 there were several *summae dictaminis*. Some kind of official collection, called *Liber provincialis,* later *Provinciale cancellariae,* was in use in the Roman Curia. In Avignon an addition was made, the *Quaternus albus,* used together with the *Liber provincialis* until 1560. The most important collections were the so-called Rules of the Papal Chancery, which came into existence some time during the 12th century, taking over several rules from the *Liber diurnus.* These rules underwent changes and modifications from time to time. The most modern rules were approved by Pope PIUS X (1910). It must be added that all these collections, besides being used as formularies in the strict sense, also contained administrative and procedural law to be used in composing papal documents. The same is true of collections and formularies used by bishops.

Privilegia and Litterae. Since the time of Pope Hadrian I, two kinds of papal documents can be distinguished: *privilegia* and *litterae*. *Privilegia* are more formal documents, usually containing dispositions of permanent character. The *litterae* were less elaborate, concerning political, administrative, and jurisdictional matters. To those that were of a judicial character, a leaden seal was attached with silken laces. From the 12th century on, documents containing mostly administrative matters (*gratiae*) were distinguished from those concerned with judicial matters (*mandata*). The seal for *gratiae* was appended with silken laces; for *mandata,* with hempen laces (*see* SIGILLOGRAPHY). *Bulls.* Since INNOCENT IV (1243–54) the bull has become the usual form for more important documents. It was written in a formal curial style (*see* PALEOGRAPHY, LATIN), which had been preceded by the so-called Lombard hand; under the influence of AVIGNON (*see* AVIGNON PAPACY), Gallic characters were introduced. From the time of ADRIAN VI (1522–23), Gothic characters were used, the so-called *litterae sancti Petri* or *Bullaticum Teutonicum,* to be replaced during the 19th century with modern typeface. The bull was reserved for matters of great importance. Its seal, usually made of lead, bore on one side a representation of the heads of SS. Peter and Paul, separated by a

Latin cross with the initials S.P.-S.P. beneath. On the obverse the name of the reigning pontiff was inscribed. The document was written with red or black ink upon a rectangle of parchment, made usually of sheepskin. The name of the pope without the number was given first, followed by the words *servus servorum Dei*. The place of issuance was mentioned at the end of the document. Finally the date was given in this order: year, day, month, and the year of the pontificate. Until the time of Pope Pius X, bulls were dated by the years of Incarnation reckoned from March 25. The days were also reckoned originally in the Roman fashion, by calends, nones, and ides (*see* CHRONOLOGY, MEDIEVAL, 2).

Modern Papal Documents. Beginning with 1908 the dates of papal documents have been reckoned by the regular civil calendar. Bulls concerning matters of great importance, given in the papal consistory, are signed by the pope and by all the cardinals of the Curia. These bulls are called consistorial bulls. In other cases bulls are signed by the cardinal chancellor and other officials of the apostolic chancery or by the chancellor together with the cardinal prefect of a Roman congregation. The name "bull" stems from the Latin *bulla* (capsule or disk) wherein the seal is embedded. Usually these capsules were made of lead. In rare cases they were of silver or gold. Golden bulls usually were those confirming the election of a Roman emperor. In 1878 LEO XIII had ordered that only in the most solemn circumstances was a leaden bull to be appended to a papal document. In all other cases a red, waxen seal was to be appended or a red rubber seal stamped on the documents.

Briefs. In the time of MARTIN V (1417–31) the ancient form of *litterae* was replaced by *brevia* or apostolic briefs. They are simpler in style and deal with matters of relatively minor importance. They are sealed with the fisherman's seal, representing St. Peter seated in a boat and drawing his net from the sea. Originally the impression was made on the document in red wax with the fisherman's ring. Now they are in red varnish. The brief is written on thin white parchment, oblong in shape; its method of dating follows that for bulls. It is signed by the cardinal secretary of state or by the secretary of briefs.

Motu Proprio. This document came into use during the pontificate of INNOCENT VIII (1484–92). Originally it was issued in all cases concerning the Roman Curia and the temporal affairs of the Holy See. It is signed by the pope personally, without seal. From the legal point of view a motu proprio is a papal ordinance originating directly from the sovereign pontiff.

Rescript. In contrast to the motu proprio, the simple rescript is generally an answer to a petition made by someone to the Roman Curia or to the pope himself. The papal rescript has two identifying characteristics: it is signed by the cardinal prefect and the secretary of the congregation to which the case belongs, and bears the seal of that congregation. Decrees of congregations containing matters of general importance may also be issued in the form of a motu proprio.

Chirographa. Chirographa are personal letters written by the pope.

Bibliography: T. SICKEL, "Beiträge zur Diplomatik," *Sitzungsberichte der Akademie der Wissenschaften in Wien* 36 (1861) 329–402, continued in v. 39–101 (1862–82) *passim.* R. L. POOLE, *Lectures on the History of the Papal Chancery down to the Time of Innocent III* (Cambridge, Eng. 1915). J. FICKER, *Beiträge zur Urkundenlehre,* 2 v. (Innsbruck 1877–78). F. PHILIPPI, *Einführung in die Urkundenlehre des deutschen Mittelalters* (Bonn 1920). A. G. CICOGNANI, *Canon Law,* tr. J. M. O'HARA and F. J. BRENNAN (rev. ed. Westminster, Md. 1947). A. M. STICKLER, *Historia iuris canonici latini,* v. 1: *Historia fontium* (Turin 1950). A. DE BOÜARD, *Manuel de diplomatique française et pontificale,* 2 v. (Paris 1929–54). G. TESSIER, "Diplomatique," in *L'Histoire et ses méthodes,* ed. C. SAMARAN (Paris 1961) 633–676.

[W. M. PLÖCHL]

DIPTYCHS, LITURGICAL USE OF

Small folding tablets used for writing notes, letters, appointments, or lists of names. The Latin word *diptychum* was borrowed from the Greek δίπτυχον (δις, twice, and πτύσσειν, to fold) and originally meant anything folded in two. The Greek word designated an ornamented or simple, usually square, set of folding tablets made of wood, ivory, metal, silver, or gold and bound together on one side with rings; each tablet had a plain or ornamented outer surface, and usually a waxed inner surface. In Latin they were known also as *tabellae duplices.* The blank surface of wooden or ivory diptychs was written on with ink; metal diptychs were covered with resin or wax, and a stylus was used for writing on them. They were employed as gifts by emperors and consuls for recording titles, offices, and other official texts.

Christians adapted these diptych tablets to liturgical use, inscribing on them the names of martyrs or of bishops or faithful to be remembered by name in liturgical functions. After 313 they were also used for recording the names of catechumens, baptismal candidates, and the clergy. In the third century CYPRIAN OF CARTHAGE supplies evidence that, even in his day, calling out the names of the living and the dead at Mass was an ancient and established custom (*Epist. 1*). The first known use of the diptychs for this purpose was late in the fourth century. The custom played a special role in the Eastern and Byzantine Church.

In the West there developed fairly early the convention of reading the names of all those who had offered the holy gifts (elements) for the Eucharistic liturgy; in the East there is no trace of such a list, and even the custom of the laity offering the elements was abolished very early. After the names were read, an oration called the *Post nomina* or *super dipticia* was said, and this apparently developed into the *memento vivorum* in the Roman Canon. Gradually the names of the bishop of the diocese, the metropolitan, the pope, and the emperor were added.

The diptych tablets were used to record three different sorts of lists of names: those of the newly baptized (Cyril of Jer., *Procatech.* 1.4.13, Gregory of Nyssa, *De bapt.*), those of a certain number of the living who were to be remembered at the altar, and those of the faithful departed.

The correspondence of Cyril of Alexandria with Patriarch Atticus of Constantinople (406–425) proves that the diptychs were in use in Antioch and Constantinople in the early fifth century and that already there were separate tablets for the lists of the living and the dead. In the Byzantine Church the diptychs contained the list of the succession of bishops; in the main Churches, the names of the metropolitans and patriarchs were added gradually to signify religious community and union between the Churches. In the fifth century, a heretic's name was "struck from the diptychs"; and this became a particular weapon in the controversies between Rome and the Eastern Churches. It played a critical part in the settlement of the ACACIAN SCHISM (482–519) and before the Council of NICAEA II. JUSTINIAN I ordered an inquiry at Cyr to see whether the name of Theodoret had been retained in the diptychs. During the Council of Nicaea he announced that the name of the Council of CHALCEDON had been added to the diptychs at Constantinople and had the name of Pope VIGILIUS I struck from the diptychs when the Pope refused to attend the council (Nicaea II, seventh session).

In the diptychs of the dead, customary commemorations were made for the martyrs, deceased local ordinaries, founders, and benefactors of the local Church. In the East the recitation of the names of the dead came to be the important thing, and St. Cyril mentions such a list, divided into patriarchs, Prophets, Apostles, and martyrs, who are begged to pray for the congregation, and the holy fathers, bishops, and deceased faithful in general, for whom the congregation prays. An interesting Fulda diptych has the names of deceased kings on the left and those of deceased bishops at the right [A. Gori, *Thesaurus diptychorum veterum* 2 (Florence 1759) 198].

The diptychs were read aloud by the deacon in the Greek Church, sometimes near the altar, sometimes on the ambo; in the Latin West the subdeacon read them in a low voice, sometimes near the priest, sometimes behind the altar. The rapid multiplication of names soon precluded the diaconal recitation, which by the time of ISIDORE OF SEVILLE (*c.* 560–633) was a thing of the past (*Patrologia Latina.* ed. J. P. Migne [Paris 1878–90.] 83:895). Then began the practice of a simple global commemoration of all whose names were on the diptych exposed on the altar.

The diptychs came to be touchstones of orthodoxy: the inscription of Chrysostom's name occasioned protracted controversy (*Patrologia Graeca.* ed J. P. MIGNE [Paris 1857–66] 145:1137–49); the long pre-Photian, and more especially, the post-Photian period abounded in instances of temporary deletions of the name of the pope from the diptychs of Eastern Churches, preeminently those of the Constantinopolitan patriarchate, and retaliatory deletions ordered in the West by Rome. Diptychs fell into disuse in the West about the 12th century and in the East around the 14th century.

Bibliography: E. MELIA, ''Les diptyques liturgiques et leur signification ecclésiologique,'' in *L'église dans la liturgie* (Rome 1980) 209–229. W. J. GRISBROOKE, ''Intercession at the Eucharist,'' *Studia Liturgica* 4 (1965) 129–155 [Pt. 1], 5 (1966) 20–44 [Pt. 2], 5 (1966) 87–103 [Pt. 3]. R. F. TAFT, *A History of the Liturgy of St John Chrysostom, Vol. 4: The Diptychs* (Rome 1991).

[A. J. GIBSON/EDS.]

DIRECTION, SPIRITUAL

The guiding of a Christian soul in the path of perfection. On the part of the guide, or spiritual director, it demands knowledge of the general and more specific principles of Christian action as well as insight into the state of soul of the one directed. This requires that the director have considerable theological science and at least some degree of experience in spiritual matters to give him an understanding of the spiritual condition of the person whom he directs. Without such experience he could hardly have the penetrating perception classically known as DISCERNMENT of spirits. Since he must have this, the spiritual director is ordinarily a man not only of theological learning, but also possessed of a degree of holiness. Direction itself supposes some lack of these qualities in the soul under direction, a deficiency that justifies the counseling in the sense that it makes counseling necessary or at least useful. This judicious counseling is the essence of spiritual direction.

In Catholic theology, especially during the last two centuries, the term has usually been taken to mean the counseling of individuals within the framework of sacramental confession. Historically the Christian tradition concerning it seems to have arisen from the same context, that is to say, as an extension of sacramental confession and revelation of conscience for absolution from sins. But since sacramental confession is connected with the total sacramental and hierarchical action of the Church, the extrasacramental counseling of individuals or groups, or hierarchical action, or other activities aimed at promoting the advance of souls in perfection can be included under the term. The more restricted meaning of the counseling of individual souls, however, has become common and is the accepted meaning today.

Understood in this way it is a peculiarly Christian phenomenon because of the special goal to which Christian counseling is directed. Something generically similar to it, however, has existed from time immemorial, even outside of the Christian tradition. The pagans of Western antiquity practiced a sort of moral guidance. Men put themselves under learned masters to develop in virtue. Socrates was a famous example of such a master and was thought to have genius in the area of moral decision. In the Buddhist tradition, a sort of psychological counseling has been used as a fundamental technique for the advancement of its disciples. In recent years this has become better known to the West through its growing acquaintance with Zen BUDDHISM. In brief, these and other examples make it clear that some generic form of spiritual direction seems to be a nearly universal phenomenon.

Early Eastern Christianity. In early Oriental Christianity spiritual direction seems to have developed chiefly because of its utility in the formation of monks, although it had broader roots. Indirect evidence suggests that bishops must have exercised it with respect to groups of Christians in their communities who sought a more perfect way of life in the practice of continence and prayer. At all events, it was a much-honored practice and Oriental Christianity gave tribute to it in the names it applied to spiritual directors, e.g., the honorable name of father. The spiritual director was conceived of as the progenitor of the one directed in the life of perfection. This was a peculiarly Christian conception that apparently arose from the community awareness that Our Lord had never codified His doctrine and made explicit all of its principles. Neither had the disciples and apostles done this. The major portion of these principles was therefore implicit, and it was the work of the spiritual father to make them explicit.

Early Western Christianity. Evidence of such spiritual direction in early times in the West is obscure and indirect. It seems reasonable to believe that the ascetics among the community in the early Church, particularly the holy virgins, were the object of special instruction by the bishops and that this instruction had of necessity to take something of the form of spiritual direction. Many early works hint at this. Tertullian and St. Cyprian wrote at considerable length about the guidance of virgins. Unambiguous evidence is meager, however, and when it first appears it is chiefly in the form of letters and of legislative texts for monasteries, in which sources it is difficult to distinguish individual counseling from group direction.

St. Ambrose. This is not the case in the writings coming down from St. AMBROSE. They contain a clearly identifiable example of the practice of spiritual direction aimed at the perfecting of particular souls. It was not the advanced sort of guidance associated with the higher stages of the spiritual life and with mysticism. St. Ambrose restricted himself to the stage of the beginner and encouraged those whom he directed to practice the fundamental Christian virtues, particularly those connected with the state of virginity. His accentuation of virginity gained for him the reputation of being a determined opponent of marriage, and his basic attitude toward the moral life has often been pointed to as indicative of his debt to the Stoics. Although his spiritual treatises, compiled from his sermons, concentrated on virginity, his letters manifested a much wider range of interest. Some of them show him to have been a true master of the art of spiritual direction.

St. Jerome. St. JEROME too was a talented counselor of souls as the term is now commonly understood. While in the East, he studied the ascetical practices of the monasteries. When he returned to Rome in 382, he was therefore well equipped to teach and to counsel the pious souls, particularly women, who sought him out. He was an excellent teacher, but an even more adept director of souls. From his writings it is clear that the moment he began to practice this art he became more at ease, more open, and more confident of himself. He did not hesitate to give orders and expected them to be obeyed. He was particularly at home in counseling concerning the life of virginity and of monastic perfection.

St. Augustine. The busy life of St. AUGUSTINE made it impossible for him to dedicate much time to the direction of particular souls. Nevertheless, he is important in the history of spiritual direction because of his efforts to set up and sustain monastic communities. This was the milieu in which he lived his own personal life from the time of his conversion, and it was particularly dear to him. His counseling therefore tended to concentrate on it, but he replied also to particular requests for help from individuals in every station of life. These replies gained him his reputation as an authority in spiritual direction.

5th and 6th Centuries. During the 5th and 6th centuries the major portion of spiritual counseling was devoted to the formation of novices to the monastic life. CASSIAN enjoyed a widespread reputation for this. His counseling was based on his youthful experience in the Near East, particularly in Egypt, where he received his own spiritual formation. He applied the fruits of this experience to the formation of novices in the monastic life of southern France. He put every novice under the guidance of an older member of the community, and the young monk was encouraged to reveal his conscience and the movements of his heart to the older monk assigned to direct him. Without his advice no spiritual enterprise was to be undertaken. Cassian warned that great care should be taken in choosing responsible directors. Any imprudence on the part of the director would cause the novice to lose confidence in the value of revealing his conscience. This work of Cassian was furthered and stabilized by the Rule of St. Benedict (*c.* 580). This stressed the importance of the spiritual director for the monastery, because the maintenance and conservation of community life depended on the formation of the new generation of its members (*see* BENEDICTINE RULE).

7th to 11th Centuries. This tradition of spiritual direction, once firmly established by Cassian and St. BENE-DICT, continued in effect during the period from the 7th to the 12th centuries. But its vigor varied with the decline and the revitalization of society at large. During the period of cultural decay preceding the Carolingian renaissance and following it, spiritual direction fell into decline. No doubt there were souls during this time who attempted a high level of spirituality and who sought out directors to aid them, but they could not have been very numerous, for the evidence of their existence is scanty. What direction remained took place, for the most part, within the monasteries. There is scarcely any evidence from the 10th and 11th centuries of spiritual direction as it is now understood.

12th to 15th Centuries. With the 12th century, however, it began to rise to a high level with St. ANSELM OF CANTERBURY. Anselm's efforts were directed primarily to the formation of the monks who were under his charge, but he also provided counsel for others in every walk of life. In his instruction he was gentle and kind, but at the same time forceful. He insisted on unceasing effort and continuing progress. He taught that the primary goal was not the negative one of avoiding sins, small and great, but the positive one of union with God. The high level of spiritual counseling as practiced by Anselm continued in vigor during the period from the 12th to the 15th centuries. For the most part it maintained its traditional purpose of forming novices to the monastic life, a direction given it by St. Benedict and generally followed in the newly emerging orders. An exception must be made for the Dominicans. Because of the specific purpose of their foundation, spiritual direction became one of their prima-

ry activities; and because the souls toward whom their apostolate was directed were primarily the laymen of the emerging medieval cities, their spiritual direction became oriented toward them. Even so, it still maintained some connection with the past in that it attempted to impart to laymen the maximum of the benefits of monastic experience that were compatible with their lives. The Third Order was the favorite vehicle for this, but the type of monasticism that could be adapted to this purpose was more primitive in form than that which derived from St. Benedict. This explains, in part, the spiritual direction given by St. Catherine of Siena, which was outside the hierarchical structure and fundamentally charismatic.

Other noted directors, such as St. BERNARD OF CLAIRVAUX, in the 12th century, had exercised a strictly ecclesiastical direction. They were concerned with the diminishing authority of the Church, and therefore made submission to it a prime object of their counseling. St. Bernard preached, above everything else, the necessity of obedience. Since this was to be given to a spiritual director acting in the name of the Church, it placed enormous responsibility on him. St. Bernard, recognizing this, attempted to achieve the necessary balance by stressing the importance of choosing for this function only a person of recognized ability in the discernment of spirits.

In the Franciscan school the work of St. BONAVEN-TURE merits special attention. His spirituality was totally oriented toward the mystical, but his attitude toward the necessity of spiritual direction for this end was not rigid. He thought that those who had themselves the gift of discernment of spirits did not need it. He was convinced, however, that there were few such souls and that most individuals needed spiritual guidance at least in the initial stages of their advance to perfection.

During the last centuries of the Middle Ages, the Dominicans exercised a great influence through their spiritual direction. This was a natural consequence of their specific mission in the Church. Teaching and preaching Christian doctrine naturally led them to the counseling of individual souls. St. DOMINIC had given the example of it by his own apostolic activity. He had also made it part of the legal structure of the order in abbreviating the office, exempting the friars from manual labor, and granting dispensations liberally for the needs of study. All of this inevitably gave rise to increased activity in the area of spiritual direction. The *cura animarum* thus became primarily counseling of souls in the way of perfection. A striking case of this occurred when the Dominican friars took over the spiritual direction of the convents of Dominican sisters in the Rhineland. This particular apostolate gave rise to the remarkable school of Rhineland mysticism in which both directors and directed reached a high level of mystical perfection (*see* SPIRITUALITY, RHENISH). In England Richard ROLLE DE HAMPOLE, an independent spirit living an eremitical life, hardly insisted on spiritual direction at all. But the author of the celebrated *CLOUD OF UNKNOWING* thought it necessary. Humble submission to a spiritual director is needed for spiritual progress. Among the Lowland writers, Jan van RUYSBROECK, who depended on the Rhineland mystics for many of his teachings, stressed the possession of the discernment of spirits on the part of the soul seeking perfection, as more necessary for progress than submission to a director. For this reason, although he consented to advise many souls on particular problems, he refused to do it in the continuous way ordinarily understood as spiritual direction. Gerard GROOTE followed Ruysbroeck's principles and stressed obedience to superiors as fundamental for the monk. The deplorable condition of many convents in his time, however, led him to put limits to this. THOMAS À KEMPIS, author or definitive editor of the *IMITATION OF CHRIST,* placed great importance on spiritual direction as one of the four ways to obtain deep peace of soul.

Modern Period. With the 16th century, the character of spiritual direction changed. It became institutionalized and empirical. In large part this was the result of the great success of the *Exercises* of St. IGNATIUS, which encouraged the practice of individual and group retreats. It was due also to a heightened appreciation of the necessity for the interior life to counter the forces that culminated in the Reformation. With respect to this, spiritual direction of a more institutionalized form had an obviously important role to play. The Dominicans of Florence, whose attention was drawn to it by the example of Girolamo Savonarola, were among the initiators of the new movement. At Rome, the Oratory in the church of S. Girolamo gave it great impetus through the work of St. PHILIP NERI. In his apostolate, spiritual direction was essential. He gave it with profound perception, being at the same time paternal and firm. The primitive form of the Oratory, with its considerable liberty of action, aided him in this work.

St. Philip Neri was only one of many who began at this time to practice spiritual direction intensely. Others too saw it as a necessary correction for the neglect of this sort of apostolate in the preceding period. To this neglect they attributed a large part of the spiritual decline of the Church. The absence of an intense sacramental life was felt to be a contributing cause. Spiritual directors therefore began to counsel an intense life of sacramental activity and of prayer. Through the influence of Savonarola and others of his brethren, the prayer took the special form of meditation on the Passion of Christ. Louis of Granada, in Spain, was one of the leading advocates of this form of meditation.

In Spain also the great works of TERESA OF ÁVILA and JOHN OF THE CROSS inculcated the necessity of spiritual direction for the renewal of the Church. St. Teresa took care to provide her convents with good confessors. Because many of the difficulties she encountered came from her failure to find them, she developed a great respect for theological learning and regarded it as a fundamental qualification in a spiritual director no less necessary than a personal experience of spiritual things. In his writings, St. John of the Cross aimed at illuminating not only souls seeking perfection, but also spiritual directors. He was severe against ignorant and timid guides. The role of the director as he saw it was that of an instrument of the Church who provided a vital sense of the Church's presence at each step in the advancement toward perfection. The director was not a master imperiously intervening in the affairs of the soul and limiting its progress by the standard of his own spiritual gifts, but an instrument to maintain contact with the Church in the soul as it developed through the operations of the Holy Spirit.

Another classical source for spiritual direction was provided by the *Exercises* of St. Ignatius. Although these were not properly a manual of direction, they constituted a standard framework of reference. This was particularly true for the doctrine of discernment of spirits. The *Exercises* taught that by this knowledge a prudent director can safely lead the soul into the first steps of the spiritual life. But he should do this, according to St. Ignatius, as a witness of God and should carefully avoid involving himself in any way except as one who mediates a divine action. The detailed revelations of the soul of the one whom he guides permit him to accomplish this, as long as he can truly perceive the spirits involved.

17th Century. The 17th century has been called the golden age of spiritual direction. During this period a rich literature arose on the subject. The general tendency was to regard it as continuous with sacramental confession. In the beginning this led to the mixing of matters of internal and external forum in the government of convents. Consequently there were many works of that time bearing on the external forum, but containing much excellent advice on the direction of souls. The leading director of the period was St. FRANCIS DE SALES. His passage in the *Introduction to the Devout Life* on the necessity of spiritual direction became classic. The ancient religious orders also occupied themselves extensively with spiritual direction during this period as did the secular clergy. Bishops J. B. BOSSUET and F. FÉNELON, MARIE DE L'INCARNATION, and several lay men and women gained fame by their achievement in the apostolate of spiritual direction.

18th Century. The 17th century condemnation of the errors of Miguel de MOLINOS and of Fénelon's *Maximes des Saints* tempered enthusiasm for the publication of spiritual writings and for the apostolate of spiritual direction. In some circles this gave rise to a spirit of obstinate resistance, as among the Jansenists. The result was an impoverishment of doctrine and a paucity of spiritual directors. Some outstanding examples of men skilled in the art of direction did emerge, however, such as the Jesuit Jean Pierre de CAUSSADE, whose name is commonly associated with the doctrine of abandonment to divine providence. But even Caussade's estimation of the need of a director was much tempered by his experience. He once characterized a director of conscience as more an embarrassment than an aid. In this censure, however, he criticized certain faults in the relationship of director and directed, rather than the essence of the practice itself.

19th Century. With the end of the French Revolution and the termination of the Napoleonic Wars, Europe experienced a renewed interest in religion and therefore in spiritual direction. The basis for this was less theological than had previously been the case, but the charity animating it was undoubtedly genuine. Some founders of religious congregations made important contributions. G. J. CHAMINADE, founder of the Marianists; John BOSCO, founder of the SALESIANS; and Charles de FOUCAULD, founder of the Little Brothers and Sisters of the Sacred Heart are only a few. The Dominican LACORDAIRE, and J. N. GROU, SJ, also made important contributions to the reviving spirituality. The REDEMPTORISTS, preachers by vocation and therefore naturally inclined to carry this forward into direct counseling of individual souls, made comparable contributions, as did various bishops and secular priests who distinguished themselves in this apostolate.

20th Century. All of this activity in the 19th century, but particularly the work of editing spiritual texts and the publication of studies in numerous spiritual periodicals, as well as the promulgation of a number of important papal documents, led to a flourishing of direction in the 20th century. The discouraging effects of the condemnation of quietism have been removed and directors have been freed to resume this important ministry now on a solid and authoritative basis, for the Holy See has given the movement considerable encouragement, although it has insisted on certain qualities in those who occupy themselves in giving direction.

The advancing knowledge of depth psychology has both aided and hindered spiritual direction. Although it is popularly surmised that a crisis is imminent in the apostolate of the director as a result of depth psychology, the demand for direction is greater than ever before.

Depth psychology and guidance in the life of grace are different things. Neither need be a hindrance to the other, but both may gain by mutual confrontation if the possibilities and the limitations on both sides are properly understood.

Bibliography: FRANCIS DE SALES, *Introduction to the Devout Life,* tr. M. DAY (Westminster, Md. 1959); *Spiritual Directory for People Living in the World,* ed. J. E. WOODS (Westminster, Md. 1959). JOHN OF THE CROSS, *The Dark Night of the Soul, in Collected Works,* tr. K. KAVANAUGH and O. RODRIGUEZ (Garden City, N.Y. 1964) bk. 1, ch. 2, 3, 6. TERESA OF ÁVILA, *The Way of Perfection* in v. 2 of *Complete Works,* ed. SILVERIO DE SANTA TERESA and E. A. PEERS, 3 v. (New York 1964) ch. 5; *Interior Castle, ibid.* 6th Mansions, ch. 8; *Life,* tr. D. LEWIS (Westminster, Md. 1962) ch. 5. IGNATIUS OF LOYOLA, *Spiritual Exercises,* tr. L. J. PUHL (Westminster, Md. 1951). L. SCUPOLI, *The Spiritual Combat* (London 1935), tr. from It. F. W. FABER, *Growth in Holiness* (Westminster, Md. 1960) ch. 18. L. LALLEMANT, *The Spiritual Doctrine,* ed. A. G. MC-DOUGALL (Westminster, Md. 1946), tr. from Fr. A. TANQUEREY, *The Spiritual Life,* tr. H. BRANDERIS (2d ed. Tournai 1930; repr. Westminster, Md. 1945) ch. 5.2. C. MARMION, *The English Letters of Abbot Marmion 1858–1923* (Baltimore 1962). R. GARRIGOU-LAGRANGE, *The Three Ways of the Spiritual Life* (London 1938; repr. Westminster, Md. 1950) v. 1, ch. 17. LEO XII, "Testem benevolentiae" (letter to Cardinal James Gibbons, Jan. 22, 1899), *Acta Sanctae Sedis* 31 (1898–99) 470–479, Eng. J. T. ELLIS, ed., *Documents of American Catholic History* (Milwaukee 1956) 553–562. PIUS XII, "Menti nostrae" (Apostolic exhortation, Sept. 23, 1950) *Acta Apostolicae Sedis* 42 (1950) 657–702, Eng. *Catholic Mind* 49 (1951) 37–64. P. P. PARENTE, *Spiritual Direction* (rev. ed. New York 1961). *Workshop on Spiritual Formation and Guidance-Counseling in the CCD Program, 1961,* Catholic University of America (Washington, D.C. 1962). E. DES PLACES et al., *Dictionnaire de spiritualité ascétique et mystique. Doctrine et histoire,* ed. M. VILLER et al. (Paris 1932–) 3:1002–1214. F. WULF, *Lexikon für Theologie und Kirche,* ed. J. HOFER and K. RAHNER, 10 v. (2d, new ed. Freiburg 1957–65) 574–575. P. POURRAT and M. GAUCHERON, *Catholicisme. Hier, aujourd'hui et demain,* ed. G. JACQUEMET 3:864–873.

[K. A. WALL]

DIRECTORY FOR THE MINISTRY AND LIFE OF PRIESTS (1994)

The Second Vatican Council called for a *Directory for the Ministry and Life of Priests* (*Christus Dominus,* no. 44). A long time in the making, the Directory was approved by Pope John Paul II, Jan. 31, 1994 and authorized for publication by the Congregation for the Clergy. The directory does not replace canon law, but rather addresses the principal questions of a doctrinal, disciplinary, and pastoral nature faced by priests of the Latin rite, especially diocesan priests.

The *Directory for the Ministry and Life of Priests* is divided into three almost equal chapters: The Identity of the Priest, Priestly Spirituality, and Ongoing Formation. The identity of the priest is described in terms of four dimensions of his life: the Trinitarian, Christological, pneumatological, and ecclesial. These dimensions form the basis for his relationship with God, with the hierarchy, and with all the Christian faithful. The chapter on priestly spirituality is a more practical exposition of the priest's life of prayer, ministry, relationship to the Word of God and the sacraments, celibacy, and obedience. The third chapter acknowledges the rapid rate of change in the modern world and calls for a spiritual, intellectual, and pastoral education that is continuous, systematic, and personal. In addition to suggesting practical means to achieve this goal, the directory recognizes that responsibility for those programs belongs to the entire community and that the special circumstances of new priests and those of advanced age must be taken into account.

The directory is related to the teaching of the Second Vatican Council and relies heavily on Pope John Paul II's apostolic exhortation *Pastores dabo vobis,* published after the eighth assembly of the Synod of Bishops.

Bibliography: D. GOERGEN, ed., *Being a Priest Today* (Collegeville, Minn. 1992). R. SCHWARTZ, *Servant Leaders and the People of God* (New York 1989).

[E. PFNAUSCH]

DI ROSA, MARIA CROCIFISSA, ST.

Foundress of the HANDMAIDS OF CHARITY; b. Brescia, Italy, Nov. 6, 1813; d. there, Dec. 15, 1855. She was the sixth of nine children of a wealthy nobleman and landowner who occupied important posts in Brescia. After her mother's death (1824), Paolina Francesca Maria (her name at baptism) was entrusted for her education to the Visitandines (1824–30). Then she took charge of her father's household and developed a talent for organization and supervision. Her father's active Catholicism urged her to engage in a variety of good works. Monsignor Faustino Pinzoni, archpriest of the cathedral in Brescia, who was her spiritual director and later cofounder of her congregation, gave explicit direction to her charitable endeavors. During a devastating cholera epidemic (1836), Paola and her companion Gabriella Bornati won wide admiration by caring for the sick. To Paola, Brescia owes its first three Sunday school groups, its first school for deaf mutes, its first home for the rehabilitation of girls, and also the enactment of reforms to aid indigent women, popular missions, and diverse forms of spiritual, catechetical, and material aid. Her chief accomplishment was the foundation in 1840 of her religious congregation, popularly called at first the Hospitable Adorers. Her timely intervention with an unruly mob saved the Jesuits of the College of St. Christopher, who took refuge in her house before the college was sacked (1848). That year she also intervened in defense of the Daughters of the Sacred Heart and sent her Handmaids to assist the wounded at the Battle of Valeggio.

In 1849 she was responsible for saving the hospital in Brescia from destruction by the Austrian troops. Maria Crocifissa went to Rome in 1850 and obtained approval of her institute's rule. Basic to her spirituality was the imitation of Christ's sorrowful life; this led her to infused contemplation and inspired her with the idea of aiding the sick and the poor, the sorrowful members of Christ's Church. The chapel in the motherhouse at Brescia is her burial place. She was beatified on May 26, 1940, and canonized June 12, 1954.

Feast: Dec. 15.

Bibliography: S. CABIBBO and M. MODICA, *La santa dei Tomasi: storia di suor Maria Crocifissa* (Turin 1989). L. FOSSATI, *Beata Maria Crocifissa Di Rosa* (Brescia 1940). A. BUTLER, *The Lives of the Saints*, ed. H. THURSTON and D. ATTWATER (New York 1956) 4:566–569.

[L. FOSSATI]

DISCALCED ORDERS

Discalced orders signifies religious orders in the Christian Church whose members, both men and women, are barefooted or who wear sandals with or without covering for the feet (Lat., *Discalceati;* It., *Scalzi;* Fr., *Déchaussés;* Ger., *Barfüsserden*). In the Old Testament bare feet symbolized reverence for the divine presence (Ex 3.5), humiliation (Dt 25.9), poverty and shame (Is 20.24), penance and supplication (2 Sm 15.30). The significance of bare feet in the mystery religions of antiquity seems to have been similar, and perhaps influenced the early Christian barefooted ascetics of the desert as much as did the Hebrew tradition. The Egyptian monks removed their shoes before receiving the Holy Eucharist, and in the Coptic (Ethiopian) rite priests still celebrate Mass in bare feet. Western monasticism did not follow the tradition of the East, as much perhaps by reason of temperament as of rigorous climate. Not until the 12th century did monks of the West appear unshod, JOACHIM OF FIORE and St. Norbert being among the earliest. The discalced order *par excellence,* however, is the Order of Friars Minor, founded by St. FRANCIS OF ASSISI, who saw in bare feet a symbol of the imitation of Christ and of the apostolic life, as well as penance, poverty, and humble social status. St. CLARE and her nuns at San Damiano at first went barefooted, but later adopted sandals. Many of the religious institutes founded during the 16th century and the reformed branches of the older orders were discalced. The Franciscan Friars of the Alcantarine Reform (1590) were completely barefooted. Of the three branches of the

Order of Friars Minor now in existence, the Conventuals wear shoes and stockings and the Franciscans and Capuchins wear sandals on bare feet. Among the discalced religious that have survived to the present time are the Minims (1493), the Camaldolese monks (1522), the Augustinians of St. Thomas of Jesus (1532), the Servites (1593), the Discalced Carmelites (1568), the Feuillants (1575), the Trinitarians (1594), the Reformed Mercedarians (1604), and the Passionists (1741). Modern usage, which is based more on expediency than symbolism, permits members of discalced orders to wear shoes, especially when appearing in clerical garb rather than the religious habit.

Bibliography: BONAVENTURE, *De sandaliis Apostolorum* in *Opera omnia,* ed. D. FLEMING, 10 v. (Quaracchi–Florence 1882–1902) 8:386–390. L. GOUGAUD, "Anciennes traditions ascétiques," *Revue d'ascétique et de mystique* 4 (1923) 140–156. M. BIHL, "De Tertio ordine S. Francisci in provincia Germaniae superioris sive argentinensi syntagma," *Archivum Franciscanum historicum* 17 (1924) 237–265. F. J. DÖLGER, "Das Lösen der Schuhriemen in der Taufsymbolik des Klemens von Alexandrien," *Antike und Christentum* 5 (1936) 87–94; "Das Schuh–Ausziehen in der altchristlichen Taufliturgie," *ibid.* 95–108; "Das Verbot des Barfussgenhens und der kultisch reine Schuh der Täuflinge in der Oktav nach der Taufe," *ibid.* 109–115. W. LAMPEN, *Lexikon für Theologie und Kirche,* ed. J. HOFER and K. RAHNER, 10 v. (2d, new ed. Freiburg 1957–65) 1:1244.

[P. F. MULHERN]

DISCERNMENT, SPIRITUAL

Christian ascetical tradition has adopted from two places in the NT (1 Cor 12.10; 1 Jn 4.1) the formulas "discernment of spirits, to discern spirits." In Jewish literature such formulas do not appear until the QUMRAN period, when they are applied uniquely to the testing of candidates for the monastic community: "Each year their spirit and actions shall be examined to promote each candidate, should his formation and the perfection of his conduct warrant it, or, to demote him in view of his faults." (*Manual of Discipline,* 5, 24). This discernment supposes the principle that two spirits may possess man, the spirit of good and the spirit of evil; its purpose is the community's good order; its execution is by an "expert" invested with an official duty; its norm is conformity to a set of rules. There is no question yet of a spiritual experience as a source of one's own conduct. The spirit is not conceived as a power one invokes or with whom one communes, but as an asset from which one may profit.

Scripture. By the time of St. Paul and St. John, each Christian is invited to be guided personally: ". . . be reformed in the newness of your mind, that you may prove what is the good and the acceptable and the perfect will of God." (Rom 12.1, 2); ". . . proving what is well

pleasing to God. And have no fellowship with the unfruitful works of darkness . . ." (Eph 5.10, 11); "And this I pray: That your charity may more and more abound in knowledge and in all understanding: that you may approve the better things . . ." (Phil 1.9, 10). Paul is describing an interior experience of God's spirit, whose results are light, peace, charity, and acknowledgment of Jesus as the Lord. "But the fruit of the Spirit is charity, joy, peace, patience, benignity, goodness, longanimity, mildness, faith, modesty, continency, chastity" (Gal 5.22, 23). St. John adds that the experience of the Spirit has to be the same as the teaching received from the Apostles (1 Jn 2.24; 4.6). He insists upon the confidence that this experience gives for the day of judgment (*ibid.,* 4.17, 18). John and Paul, then, appear less preoccupied with determining the symptoms of an evil spirit than with indicating the signs of a good spirit. Their purpose is primarily positive. Moreover, they apply to "the spirits" the Gospel recommendation for discerning true and false prophets: "By their fruits you shall know them" (Mk 7.16). It is by the fruit a tree is judged, not conversely. In this way the Pharisaic attitude of judging the fruit by the tree is condemned, i.e., judging in the name of an external criterion established a priori: Since Jesus does not observe the Sabbath, His miracles could come only from the devil.

The Fathers. In the patristic period, the word διάκρις, in Latin *discretio,* is used to transmit this tradition from Paul and John. The key texts are the 2nd conference of CASSIAN and the 26th step of the *Scala Paradisi* of JOHN CLIMACUS. They become much more preoccupied with unmasking diabolical illusions than with discerning the divine Spirit. They also speak especially of the origin of motions or phenomena, not of their orientation. This leads to a recurring confusion between two questions that are quite distinct today: that of the "goodness" or "malice" of an interior movement, and that of its natural or preternatural origin.

The Scholastic Period. In the Middle Ages, St. THOMAS AQUINAS introduces an important distinction between simple *discretio,* which he rarely treats, and the charism of *discretio spirituum,* an extraordinary gift allowing a man who enjoys it to know future contingents or secrets of hearts (*Summa theologiae* 1a2ae, 111.4). Simple discernment becomes, then, a potential part of the virtue of prudence. It intervenes when duty is not clearly indicated by the ordinary norms for acting. The Christian should then be guided by more elevated and more interior principles. By the virtue of prudence, grace grants him a habitual skill in judging, by which he discerns the divine will behind the common rules of Christian living. Thus, St. Thomas avoids using the word "discernment" and attributes to the "virtue of prudence" the task of perpetuating the constant teaching of spiritual authors (ibid. 2a2ae, 51.4).

Nevertheless, a number of authors, even Thomists, continue to utilize the classical term. The better known are Cardinal Bona (*De discretione spirituum liber unus*), and the Jesuit Scaramelli, whose *Discernimento degli spiriti* (1753) is well known through its numerous editions and translations. They are certainly subject to the influence of St. IGNATIUS OF LOYOLA, whose *Spiritual Exercises,* without ever mentioning the virtue of prudence, attempts a forthright education with regard to spiritual discernment. In the normal development of Christian life there comes a stage when the Christian is no longer content to rule his conduct by laws and exterior norms that he has accepted without having interiorly assimilated and loved them. He becomes fully conscious then of two influences that are at war within him, mixed together like the weeds and wheat of the parable: the power of grace and the power of sin. He proposes to himself true cases of personal conscience. As St. Thomas said, he is above and beyond the *communes regulas agendorum* (the general norms of behavior). There is no longer any question of conforming to an objective and general law, but of deciding to follow a vocation, as John, alone of all the Apostles, decided to follow his Master to the foot of the cross. Didactic treatises do not invite the conscience itself to undertake this work of formation, but are preoccupied with giving spiritual directors a catalogue of signs that can be used by them to counsel others on the states of prayer, inspirations, and spiritual endeavors.

Ignatian Use. St. Ignatius of Loyola is one of those rare teachers who makes one enter into one's own conscience with a dynamic discernment, by means of a series of personal exercises. Basically, the alternating experience of states of consolation and desolation, normal to the spiritual life, teaches the Christian to stop opposing the difficulty, and to stop relaxing in the moments of euphoria. These fluctuations are only transitory situations, "creatures" to be utilized by the believer for God's glory. Behind them, the conscience experiences the unshakable certitude of faith and the unique peace it brings. Then "temptation under the appearance of good," the illusion of generosity, must be controlled by its relation to this certitude and peace. For example, in the development of an authentic missionary vocation, if the Christian is confronted with an alteration of his previous interior equilibrium, which "takes away from him his peace, tranquillity and repose and makes him fall from the spiritual sweetness and joy to which he had been accustomed," this is a clear symptom of the evil spirit's effort to lead him astray, imperceptibly, from his vocation or his spiritual endeavor. Only a man who has experienced

that "peace of God, which surpasseth all understanding," and which ought to "keep your hearts and minds in Christ Jesus" (Phil 4.7), can diagnose such a malady. Otherwise, one may as well describe colors to a blind man. Hence, St. Ignatius insists that the exercises that have to do with this discernment of illusion be not given to everyone. But there is no doubt that he invites the retreatant to an experience of discernment that a spiritual director could guide by counseling, without ever seeking to be a substitute for it.

Contemporary Developments. Building on the long history of the discernment of spirits in the Christian tradition contemporary discussions approach the topic through an assessment of inspirations, intuitions, impulses and affective states in general, combined with an examination of the sources of these experiences, and an appraisal of their congruity with the overall direction of a person's life. The process of discernment, with its focus on God's action in life and man's appropriate response to that action, allows an individual to become more aware of the elements involved in personal decision making. Discernment results in a better knowledge of the self and a better knowledge of the various influences which affect the self in its movement toward God. In addition to an ongoing appreciation of the importance of discernment in spirituality and spiritual direction, contemporary authors explore such topics as a foundational structure for Christian discernment, the relationship of interpretation and discernment, and the role of discernment in moral life.

Foundational Structure. Jon Sobrino has noted that the Gospels present Jesus in a state of constant conversion to the will of the Father, coupled with an equally constant process of discernment. For Jesus, in His human consciousness, discerning the will of God involved first clarifying for Himself who God really is. Ongoing conversion meant discerning the ever greater reality of God. Discernment of who the Father is served as a foundation upon which all of Jesus's particular discernments could be based. Jesus presented discernment as a radical choice between alternatives. People were to choose between God and mammon, life and death. They were to say "yes" to what God affirms in history and "no" to what God refutes as a world of sin. These choices flowed from preliminary or foundational discernments of who God is and who the people are in relation to God. For Sobrino, the discernment of Jesus draws attention to the importance of a foundational discernment regarding both God and self. Such foundational discernments develop over the course of a lifetime in which a person is actively seeking the ever greater God.

Interpretation and Judgment. Both in traditional and recent theology, discernment has been integrally connected with making judgments. In reference to the complex reality of discernment, S. Schneiders has spoken of three distinct but related types of judgment. The first is an evaluative judgment in which some determination is made as to the truth or falsity of a phenomenon, such as the perception of a call to change. Evaluation is followed by a second judgment, a hermeneutical one, which arrives at some interpretation of the phenomenon. Finally there is a practical judgment in which the appropriate response is formulated. Through interpretation deeper levels of meaning in a person's life are exposed. One's life story stands as a text which can yield new interpretations in the light of Scripture and a belief in God intimately tied to life. Discernment, as an exercise in interpretation, can uncover inadequate or foreclosed understandings of the self and God and lead to new images of both.

Contemporary psychology makes its contribution to the exercise of discernment by illuminating distortions of the self and God which have their roots in the vicissitudes of human development. Spiritual discernment in its honest interpretation of one's past, its deficiencies as well as its positive experiences, opens the way to a new interpretation of one's life as redeemed in Christ and opened to future grace.

Moral Decision-Making. Discernment is occasionally discussed in both contemporary Protestant and Roman Catholic moral theology where it assumes a prominent role in moral decision-making. The attention to discernment in moral theology is an instance of a movement that seeks to go beyond logic and deductive methodologies in understanding the complexities of moral life. It recognizes the role of imagination and creativity in the exercise of moral responsibility. For criteria in evaluating appropriate moral choices discernment makes use of the central symbols of the Christian tradition and basic affections or virtues of the Christian life, such as radical dependence on God and repentance. The moral agent is a self who responds to a God who is active in personal and social life. The symbols and stories of the Scriptures influence the moral imagination and give rise to a moral vision. With the aid of scriptural paradigms the person sees more clearly the action of God in personal history and the events of his time. The Biblical narratives (*see* NARRATIVE THEOLOGY) and symbols provide normative guidance so that an appropriate moral response to God's activity may be taken.

Discernment engages the heart of a person where feelings, memories, and imaginings are found. The discerning moral agent seeks to follow a course of action which is in harmony with the affections and virtues supported by the scriptural narratives. An aesthetic judgment is made about the appropriateness of a particular action

Saint Andrew the Apostle. (©Archive Photos)

in the light of affective convictions rooted in the gospel. Discernment based on both affective and symbolic criteria drawn from the Christian tradition operates within the framework of general moral principles.

Bibliography: The most complete bibliography is found in J. PEGON, et al., *Discernment of Spirits,* tr. I. RICHARDS (Collegeville, Minn. 1970). J. J. TONER, *A Commentary on St. Ignatius' Rules for the Discernment of Spirits* (St. Louis 1982). J. GUSTAFSON, *Ethics from a Theocentric Perspective,* v. 1 *Theology and Ethics* (Chicago 1981). P. KEANE, *Christian Ethics and Imagination: A Theological Inquiry* (New York 1984). S. SCHNEIDERS, ''Spiritual Discernment in *The Dialogue* of Saint Catherine of Siena,'' *Horizons. Journal of the College Theology Society* 9 (1982) 47–59. J. SOBRINO, ''Following Jesus as Discernment,'' *Concilium* 119 (1978) 14–24. W. SPOHN, ''The Reasoning Heart: An American Approach to Christian Discernment,'' *Theological Studies* 44 (1983) 30–52. *Discernment of the Spirit and of Spirits,* C. FLORISTAN and C. DUQUOC, eds. (New York 1979). E. E. LARKIN, *Silent Presence, Discernment as Process and Problem* (1981).

[J. PEGON/R. STUDZINSKI]

DISCIPLES

Introduction. ''Disciple,'' from the Latin *discipulus,* translates the New Testament μαθητής (*mathētēs*), which at its root means ''learner,'' or ''apprentice.'' The word is used 261 times in the New Testament, all of which appear in the Gospels and Acts of the Apostles (72, 46, 37, 78, 28, respectively). In addition, the word for "fellow disciple," συμμαθητής (*summathētēs*), is used in Jn 11:16, so as to show the closeness of the disciples with Jesus, "and on this basis their fellowship with one another" (Rengstorff, 460). The feminine form μαθητρία (*mathētria*) is used once, in Acts 9:36 (cf. below). In addition, related verbs fill out the rich disciple-related vocabulary (see, e.g., Rengstorff): μανθάνω (*manthanō*), "to learn" or "to direct one's mind to something"; καταμανθάνω (*katamanthanō*), "to examine closely," "to learn"; μαθητεύω (*mathēteuō*), "make a disciple," or, in the passive, "become a disciple." After treating possible background for the term μαθητής (*mathētēs*), its New Testament usage, related terminology and distinctiveness will be investigated. Finally, some reference to the employment of μαθητής (*mathētēs*) in Jewish and early nonbiblical Christian writers of the first and second centuries A.D. will be offered.

Background. The New Testament word for "disciple," μαθητής (*mathētēs*), which can also be understood as "adherent," "student," "learner," or "follower (of a master/teacher)," is related to the Hebrew terms *talmîd* and *limmûd*, and the Aramaic, *talmîdā'*, "disciple" or "student," which may have been chosen "during the pubic ministry, either [by] Jesus himself or [by] his immediate followers," and which had not yet become "a technical term in the later rabbinic use" (Meier, 3.44; cf. below on the rabbinic use). The Hebrew terms, however, are rather rare in the Old Testament. The former term is used only in 1 Chr 25:8, in reference to one whom is studying music. As rare as *talmîd* is in the Old Testament, it is "absent from the nonbiblical writings discovered at Qumran" (Meier, 3.42). The latter Hebrew term, *limmûd*, is used of those who are in the process of learning from Isaiah (8:16; 50:4 [*bis*]) and from the Lord (54:13). In none of these instances, however, is the term μαθητής (*mathētēs*) used by Septuagint (LXX) as the Greek translation of *talmîd* or *limmûd*.

Despite the lack of the specific terminology—whether in Aramaic, Hebrew or Greek—in the Old Testament, the relationships between ELIJAH and ELISHA and those learning from Isaiah, provide background for the New Testament understanding of Jesus and his disciples. Only Elijah was "(1) an itinerant miracle working prophet, active in northern Israel, who (2) issues a peremptory call to another individual (Elisha) to leave home, family, and ordinary work in order to follow, serve, and ultimately succeed Elijah in the ministry of prophet" (Meier, 3.48, cf. 48–49 and 91–92 nn. 25–26; see below, for the presentation of Elijah and Elisha by Josephus). There are, however, some distinctive characteristics of the relation-

ship between Jesus and his disciples (see below) when compared to the models in the Old Testament and the Greek exemplars among the philosophers.

Greek Usage. In classical Greek literature μαθητής (*mathētēs*) was used generally of any "learner," but more technically of an "adherent" to a particular philosopher or master, i.e., a teacher (διδάσκαλος— *didaskalos*) who was engaged in teaching pupils his thought, way of life, and/or religious beliefs. The SOPHISTS restricted the term even more, namely, to "institutional pupil" (Wilkins, "Disciples," 176). SOCRATES, in the writings of PLATO, used the word in the general sense, but avoided the technical use of the term, probably so as not to be associated with the Sophists (cf. Rengstorff, 418).

During the Hellenistic period, which includes the time of Jesus, μαθητής (*mathētēs*) was used both in the general sense as well as the more technical sense of "adherent," with the "type of adherence . . . determined by the master." One could be a "follower of a great thinker and master of the past," or a "pupil of a philosopher," or a "devotee of a religious master" (Wilkins, "Disciples," 176). The disciples were to imitate, i.e., be the imitators (μιμηταί— *mimētai*), of their master, so as to be recognized as a disciple of the master, but also to learn the master's teaching and then pass it on, but with some development, as the former disciples might now be considered teachers with their own disciples (cf. Weder, 209). Although the Pauline and other New Testament letters do not use the term "disciple," the language of imitation is found: "imitators" in 1 Thes 1:6; 2:14; Phil 3:17; 1 Cor 4:16; 11:1 and in Eph 5:1; Heb 6:12; verb form in 2 Thes 3:7, 9; 3 Jn 11; Heb 13:7. This usage may reflect the Greek background, but certainly for PAUL, to be imitators of him, who is an imitator of the Lord, was not so that the imitators would be carbon copies of the original, but rather, so that they would "incorporate certain specific aspects of his [Paul's/Lord's] life into their own lives." In addition, for Paul to urge others to imitate him is not arrogance, as modern individualists might assume, but rather reflects "the notion of imitating some sort of moral exemplar [which] was quite common in the ancient world" (cf., e.g., 2 Mc 6:27–28 (4) Mc 9:23). Finally, this language implies that those who have recently come to faith in Christ "need both instruction in their new faith and concrete examples of how to embody their faith in the various contexts in which they find themselves" (see Fowl, esp. 430 for quotations; see below on Mt 10:24–25).

Disciples of John the Baptist. Another possible background for the use of "disciples" of those associated with Jesus, may have been the use of the term, probably in Aramaic, for the disciples of JOHN THE BAPTIST, among whom Jesus may have been counted for a time (cf. Meier, 2.119–129 and 3.45–46). Two of John's disciples, Andrew and an anonymous disciple (probably not "the beloved disciple"; cf. Neirynck) are presented as among the first to follow Jesus (Jn 1:35–40); like the PHARISEES (or their "disciples," Lk 5:33), John's disciples fast (Mk 2:18 ‖ Mt 9:14 ‖ Lk 5:33); they confront "a Jew" on purification (Jn 3:25) and are outnumbered by Jesus' disciples (Jn 4:1–2); some of them were sent by John to query Jesus in Lk 7:18–23 ‖ Mt 11:2–6; they had learned to pray from John, according to Lk 11:1; after John's beheading, Mk 6:29 notes that they buried their master's body, and, according to the parallel in Mt 14:12, reported this to Jesus; finally, Paul encounters about Twelve "disciples" in Ephesus, presumably of John, who had received John's baptism of repentance (cf. 18:24–26 on Apollos), but not the Holy Spirit, and who, after being baptized into the name of the Lord Jesus and receiving the spirit through the laying on of hands, are taken from there by Paul after some stubborn members of the synagogue refused to believe (Acts 19:1–10). Disciples of John, even after the ministry, death and resurrection of Jesus, were also known to Josephus (*Ant.* 18.5.2 §117–18; Meier, 3.46; for more on Josephus, cf. below).

New Testament Use. As noted, μαθητής (*mathētēs*) is only used in the Gospels and Acts of the Apostles, and in addition to disciples of Jesus, the term is used of disciples of the Pharisees, John the Baptist (cf. above), and of Moses (Jn 9:28). No doubt, a rather common understanding, especially of "the/his disciples," οἱ/αὐτοῦ μαθητάς (*hoi/autou mathētas*), is to equate this group with "the Twelve" (οἱ δωδέκα— *hoi dōdeka*). Mark uses "(one of) the Twelve" absolutely, though Mk 3:14 (see the parallels in Mt 10:1–2 and Lk 6:13) notes that when Jesus appointed Twelve from among those he summoned, he named them "apostles," ἀπόστολοι (*apostoloi*), that is, "sent ones" (cf. too, the 70[-two] who are sent out in Lk 10:1ff). In their redactions of Mark, Matthew and Luke occasionally either add "disciples" or "apostles" to (noted by +d or +a, respectively) or change the absolute use of "the Twelve"; the following list offers a synoptic comparison: Mk 3:14 ‖ Mt 10:1+d ‖ Lk 6:13; Mk 3:16 ‖ Mt 10:2+a; Mk 4:10 ‖ Mt 13:10 ("the disciples") ‖ Lk 8:9 ("his disciples"); Mk 6:7 ‖ Mt 10:1+d ‖ Lk 9:1; Mk 9:35 ‖ Mt 18:1 ("the disciples"); Mk 10:32 ‖ Mt 20:17[+d textually uncertain] ‖ Lk 18:31; Mk 11:11; Mk 14:10 ‖ Mt 26:14 ‖ Lk 22:3; Mk 14:17 ‖ Mt 26:20 ‖ Lk 22:14 ("the apostles"); Mk 14:20; Mk 14:43 ‖ Mt 26:47 ‖ Lk 22:47. In addition, see: Mt 11:1 ("his twelve disciples") and 28:19 ("the eleven disciples"); Lk 8:1; 9:12; 18:31 and Acts 6:2 for "(one of) the Twelve"; Jn 6:67, 70, 71; 20:24 for "(one of) the Twelve"; and 1 Cor 15:5, "the Twelve." From the above, it is clear that Matthew,

more than any other evangelist, has a tendency to identify "the disciples" with "the Twelve," especially from Mt 10:1–4 on.

It goes without saying that each of the TWELVE apostles is a disciple, but to reduce the use of "disciple(s)," even in Matthew, to "(one of) the Twelve" limits the richness of the term. As already noted, John the Baptist had disciples, among whom Jesus may have been counted for a time. Moreover, Jesus has disciples before he names "the Twelve." Early on Jesus calls four fishermen, Simon, Andrew, James and John (Mk 1:16–20 ‖ Mt 4:18–22; cf. Lk 5:1–11), to follow him, and although they are not immediately called "disciples," they will be counted among the Twelve. But Jesus also calls Levi, who worked in a tax office, in Mk 2:13–14 (‖ Lk 5:27–32). Like the fishermen, Levi left his employ and followed Jesus, and thus Mark and Luke probably consider him a disciple, even though they do not apply the term to him and even though they will not count Levi among the Twelve (note, however, that Mt 9:9 changes the name to Matthew, thereby including him among the Twelve, and using a name for which there is no other specific call story; the name also serves the gospel well because of its Jewishness, Hebrew for "gift from the Lord," as well as its assonance with μαθητής [*mathētēs*]; cf. Davies and Allison, 2.98–99). Later, at dinner in Levi's house, Mark uses the term "disciples" of those with Jesus for the first time, and these "disciples" are questioned about the company that Jesus keeps (Mk 2:15–16 ‖ Mt 9:10–11 ‖ Lk 5:29–30). But to the first indication of "disciples," Mark adds a grammatically clumsy, but probably explanatory, phrase, "for there were many who followed him," thereby indicating more disciples than the four fishermen (cf. Meier, 3.51 and 93–94 n. 32). As for the parallels, Mt 9:10 mentions "disciples" but omits the problematic phrase, while Lk 5:29 omits "disciples" and recasts the phrase as "and others were at table with them." Nevertheless, in the subsequent verse Luke writes, "The Pharisees and their scribes complained to his disciples . . ." In addition, it seems difficult to limit to or include in "disciples" only the few who had been called and would eventually be among the Twelve in some other early uses of "disciples," for example: those who hear the Sermon on the Mount (Mt 5:1); the one who wishes to bury his father (Mt 8:21); those who pluck and eat grain on the Sabbath (Mk 2:23 ‖ Lk 6:1; note that the parallel in Mt 12:1 takes place after choosing the Twelve); those who are with Jesus when he heals a multitude by the sea (Mk 3:7–12; the parallel in Lk 6:17–19 has been transposed to take place immediately after choosing the Twelve, rather than just before as in Mark). In addition, John does not mention the Twelve until 6:67–71, but he does note that a large crowd is already following Jesus in 6:2, and then Jesus goes up a mountain and sits "down with his disciples" (6:3), without any clear distinction, though another large crowd, clearly not part of the disciples, approach Jesus (6:5). Later in Jn 6, after the Bread of Life Discourse, "many of his disciples who were listening" (6:60) found Jesus' teaching more than they could take, and thus left him and "returned to their former way of life" (6:66), leaving at the very minimum the Twelve (6:67).

Luke offers the clearest indications that the term "disciples" includes more than just those for whom there is a specific call story and/or named among the Twelve, for it is already from a larger group of disciples that the Twelve are selected (Lk 6:13), and "a great crowd of his disciples" (Lk 6:17) are among an even larger number of people who come to hear and be healed by Jesus. In Lk 6:20, "raising his eyes toward his disciples" (is the number of disciples now even larger than it was in 6:17?), Jesus preaches his Sermon on the Plain. In Lk 9:52, messengers are sent ahead of Jesus to prepare a Samaritan village for his visit, which is similar to the seventy[-two] whom Jesus "sent ahead of him in pairs to every town and place he intended to visit" (Lk 10:1). In neither case are those sent specifically called "disciples," but it is hard to imagine that the evangelist thought of them otherwise. Finally, later in Luke's narrative, as Jesus "was approaching the slope of the Mount of Olives, the whole multitude of his disciples began to praise God" (19:27).

These larger groups of people following Jesus and/or sent out by him raise the question of whether or not women were considered to be disciples of Jesus. The Gospels use neither μαθητής (*mathētēs*) of a woman nor its feminine form, μαθητρία (*mathētria*; only use is of Tabitha in Acts 9:36). This may be due (cf. Meier, 3.73–80) in large part to the lack of call stories of women and to the general androcentrism of the gospel narratives. But also, the fact is that the masculine term would have been the one used to include both men and women disciples. Moreover, the evangelists may not have had a feminine form available to them due to the recentness of the phenomenon of female disciples (for an analogous situation, note that Paul does not use a feminine form of "deacon" for Phoebe, in Rom 16:1; see too, 1 Tim 3:8–12). It seems clear that women had accompanied Jesus and can be counted among the disciples, for at least some of the women are presented as doing what disciples do— even doing what many of the male disciples fail to do: they had followed him and ministered to him and/or the other disciples from the time of Jesus ministry in Galilee (Mk 15:41 and parallels; cp. Lk 8:1–3); they witnessed his death from afar (Mk 15:40 and parallels; Jn 19:24–27); they saw where Jesus was buried (Mk 15:47 and parallels); they returned to find the grave empty (Mk

16:1–8 and parallels; Jn 20:1–13); they are commissioned with a message for the other disciples at the tomb (Mk 16:7 and parallels) and/or by the risen Lord (Mt 28:9–10; Jn 20:17); they report what they have seen (Lk 24:10–11; Jn 20:2, 18); they see the resurrected Lord (Mt 28:9–10; Jn 20:14–18).

Another group of persons to whom μαθητής (*mathētēs*) is not applied are those who strongly believed in Jesus and were committed to him, but did not accompany Jesus on his itinerant ministry, i.e., they seem to have remained in their homes (cf. Meier, 3.80–82), for example: Martha and Mary (Lk 10:38–42; Jn 11:1–12:2); Zacchaeus (Lk 19:1–10); Nicodemus (Jn 3:1–9; 7:50; 19:39); Lazarus (Jn 12:1–2); Simon the leper (Mk 14:3); the anonymous host of the Last Supper (Mk 14:13–15); Joseph of Arimathea (Mk 15:43 and parallels; Jn 19:38).

A final extension of the term μαθητής (*mathētēs*) is seen in its use in Acts of the Apostles: in Jerusalem, 6:1, 2, 7; 9:26 (*bis*); 15:10 (Peter's speech at the council); in Damascus 9:1, 10 (Ananias), 19 (in 9:25 "his disciples" refers to Paul's disciples); near Joppa, 9:36 (Tabitha; feminine form), 38; in Antioch, 11:26, 29; 13:52; 14:28; in Lystra, 14:20; 16:1 (Timothy); in Derbe, 14:21 (μαθητεύω— *mathēteuō*; cf. below); cities throughout Lycaonia, 14:22; in Galatia and Phrygia, 18:23; in Achaia, 18:27; in Ephesus, 19:2; 20:1, 30; in Tyre, 21:4; from Caesarea and Cyprus, 21:16 (*bis*). Except for the reference to John's disciples (cf. above), the meaning Luke essentially seems to intend for "disciple(s)" in Acts is one/those who believe in Jesus Christ, i.e., "Christian(s)," which is most clear in 11:26b: "it was in Antioch that the disciples were first called Christians." In addition, except for 15:10, the use of "disciple(s)" to refer to those who now believe in Jesus Christ, but had not physically followed him during his public ministry, "always occurs in Luke's narrative," by which Luke provides "links between the time of Jesus and the time of the church" (Meier, 3.41), even though this usage in Acts demonstrates a willingness to employ the term in a way that it is not often applied in later Christian writings (cf. below).

Certainly "the Twelve" had important symbolic function in that they represented the Twelve Tribes of Israel, the New Israel (the number seems more significant than the names, on which the lists of the Twelve do not agree; cp. Mk 3:16–19; Mt 10:2–4; Lk 6:13–16; Acts 1:13; see Wilkins, "Disciples," 179, for a comparison of the lists and brief biographical sketches). But given that there are multiple sources for the existence of the Twelve and that the use of μαθητής (*mathētēs*) is not much used in later Christian writings (see below), it would seem unwise to deny the historicity of this inner group of disciples (Meier, 3.45, 47; cf. too Nepper-Christiansen, 373).

But as much as the Twelve played a symbolic function, the expansion of the notion of "disciples" to include the many men and women who followed Jesus, as well as those faithful who remained in their homes, symbolizes the universality of Jesus'—and the Christian community's—message and ministry. Again, however, because the same criteria used to establish the historicity of the Twelve could be applied to this more expanded understanding of disciples, it would also be unwise to deny the historicity of the larger circle of Jesus' disciples.

Related Vocabulary in the New Testament. Although μανθάνω (*manthanō*), "to learn" or "to direct one's mind to something," due to its similar root, would be a natural word to employ for the learning process of Jesus' disciples, of the 25 times it is used in the New Testament, it is only rarely used for that purpose. To those who murmur about Jesus eating with tax collectors and sinners, Jesus says, "Go and learn the meaning of the words, 'I desire mercy, not sacrifice'" (Mt 9:13a; cf. Hos 6:6). Jesus invites all "who labor and are burdened" to come to him, and encourages them: "Take my yoke upon you and learn from me" (Mt 11:28, 29, respectively). Jesus urges the disciples to "learn a lesson from the fig tree" (Mk 13:28 ‖ Mt 24:32 ‖ Lk 21:29, who uses "consider"[ἴδετε— *idete*] instead of "learn"), as a way to discern the import of events leading up to the coming of the Son of Man. In Jn 6:45b, an interpretation of Is 54:13, the focus is on the Father: "Everyone who listens to my Father and learns from him comes to me." The term is also on the lips of "the Jews" for the technical, academic study of the Scriptures, which Jesus had not done (Jn 7:15). Paul uses μανθάνω (*manthanō*) to indicate how prophecy ought to be given "so that all may learn" (1 Cor 14:31). According to Heb 5:8, even Christ "learned obedience from what he suffered." In general, then, with the use μανθάνω (*manthanō*), "if not always with equal clarity, an intellectual process is always implied and this always has external effects" (Rengstorff, 392; cf. Nebe, 384).

Despite the rare use of μανθάνω (*manthanō*), the basic educational relationship between a disciple and his mentor is certainly evident in the proverb of Mt 10:24–25: "No disciple is above his teacher [διδάσκαλος—*didaskalos*], no slave above his master [κύριος— *kurios*]. It is enough for the disciple that he become like his teacher, for the slave that he become like his master" (cp. the briefer parallel in Lk 6:40). As a result, the disciples, as well as other persons who know of Jesus and his disciples, call Jesus by titles appropriate to his teaching role: *rabbi/rabbouni* (ῥαββι—Mk 9:5; 11:21; 14:45; Mt 26:25, 49; Jn 1:38, "which translated means Teacher"; 1:49; 3:2, 26; 4:31; 6:25; 9:2; 11:8/ ῥαββουνι—Jn 20:16, "which means Teacher"; cf. too

Mt 23:8); teacher (διδάσκαλος— *didaskalos*; Mk 4:38; Mk 9:17 ‖ Lk 9:38; Mk 9:38; Mk 10:17 ‖ Mt 19:16 ‖ Lk 18:18; Mk 10:20, 35; Mk 12:14 ‖ Mt 22:16 ‖ Lk 20:21; Mk 12:19 ‖ Mt 22:24 ‖ Lk 20:28; Mk 12:32; 13:1; Mk 14:14 ‖ Mt 26:18 ‖ Lk 22:11; Mt 8:19; 12:38; 22:36; Lk 7:40; 9:38; 10:25; 11:45; 12:13; 19:34; 20:39; 21:7 [note that John the Baptist is addressed as "Teacher" in Lk 3:12]); master (ἐπιστάτα— *epistata*; Lk 5:5; 8:24 [*bis*], 45; 9:33, 49; 17:13); and, of course, Lord/Master/ir (κύριος— *kurios*; Mk 11:3 ‖ Mt 21:3 ‖ Lk 19:31, 34; Mt 8:2, 8, 21, 25; 9:28; 14:28, 30; 15:22, 27; 16:22; 17:4, 15; 18:21; 20:30, 31, 33; Lk 5:8, 12; 6:46; 7:6, 19; 9:54, 59; 10:17, 40; 12:41; 13:23; 17:37; 18:41; 19:8; 22:38, 49; 24:34; Jn 6:68; 8:4; 9:38; 11:3, 12, 27, 28, 32, 34, 39; 13:6, 9, 13–14 [twice, "Teacher and Lord"], 25, 36, 37; 14:5, 8, 22; 20:2, 13, 18, 20, 25, 28; 21:7, 12, 15–17, 20–21). Of course, the Gospels also have numerous examples of Jesus teaching (διδάσκω— *didaskō*) or giving a teaching (διδαχή— *didachē*, e.g.: Mk 1:22, 27; 4:2; 6:2, 6b, 34; 11:18; 12:14; 14:49 and parallels; Mk 4:1; 8:31; 9:31; 12:35). The post-Easter mission of the disciples involves teaching "all the nations" what Jesus had commanded them (Mt 28:20).

All of these titles put Jesus within the sphere of other Jewish teachers, e.g., the scribes (see above on the Baptist and the Pharisees), who had their *talmîdîm*, (pl. of *talmîd*), "whom they instructed in the Scripture and in the traditions of the fathers" (Nepper-Christiansen, 372). And although "to learn," μανθάνω (*manthanō*), would be an appropriate way to speak of the disciples relationship to Jesus, the primary New Testament vehicle to speak of the basic relationship is "to follow," ἀκολουθέω (*akoloutheō*; cf. below).

Καταμανθάνω (*katamanthanō*), is "in some sense the intensive of μανθάνω [*manthanō*] in the sense of 'to examine closely,' 'to learn,' 'to grasp,' 'to note'" (Rengstorff, 414). Mt 6:28 is the only New Testament occurrence of this term: "Why are you anxious about clothes? Learn from the way the wild flowers grow" (the parallel in Lk 12:27 has κατανοήσατε—*katanoēsate*, "notice"; cp. this to the variance noted above in another lesson from nature, Mk 13:28 ‖ Mt 24:32 ‖ Lk 21:29).

Finally, μαθητεύω (*mathēteuō*) is used four times in the New Testament. It is "constructed from μαθητής [*mathētēs*], . . . means intrans. 'to be (a.) or to become (b.) a pupil'" (Rengstorff, 461). Joseph of Arimathea "was himself a disciple of Jesus" (Mt 27:57). The other uses are transitive, "to make disciples." According to Mt 13:52, ". . . every scribe who has been instructed in [or "who has been made a disciple of"] the kingdom of heaven is like the head of a household who brings from his storeroom the new and the old." The 11 disciples are commissioned by the risen Lord to "Go . . . and make disciples of all nations" (Mt 28:19) by baptizing and teaching them. Finally, Barnabas and Paul have great success in Derbe: "After they had proclaimed the good news to that city and made a considerable number of disciples, they returned to Lystra and to Iconium and to Antioch" (Acts 14:21). "Behind this peculiar New Testament [transitive] use there possibly stands the insight that one can become a disciple of Jesus — this also stands behind Mt 13:52 — only on the basis of a call which leads to discipleship" (Rengstorff, 461; for this distinctive aspect, see below).

Distinctiveness of the Disciple in the New Testament. Although Greek and Jewish understandings of discipleship provide some background for the New Testament understanding, to be a disciple of Jesus is not equivocated with the earlier understandings, but rather, appears to have some rather distinctive elements. "To be sure, rabbinical students shared their master's life, imitated his conduct, and memorized his words. But this did not involve imitating a prophetic and healing ministry in an eschatological context" (Meier, 3.71). This context seems to contribute to some distinctive characteristics of being a disciple of Jesus.

First, it seems that the Greek and Jewish norm was for the would-be disciple to seek out the master under whom he wished to study (cf. Meier, 3.53). In the Gospels, however, most especially in the call and healing stories (cf. examples above), it is clear that to be a disciple of Jesus was initiated by Jesus (cf. Meier, 3.50–54). Moreover, Jesus' call was often given to "those 'outside the pale'" (Meier, 3.73), e.g. tax collectors, the poor, women. In the rare instances when someone sought permission to follow Jesus as a disciple, there seems to be less than full understanding and/or commitment; for example, see the scribe's request in Mt 8:19–20 (‖ Lk 9:57–58), another person's verbal application in Lk 9:61–62, and the desire of the former demoniac in Mk 5:18–20 (‖ Lk 8:38–39).

Second, the Greek or Jewish disciple would certainly leave home during the course of instruction, but eventually return. To be a disciple of Jesus, however, can imply a life-long commitment which requires giving up home and family (e.g., Mk 10:28–30 and parallels), even to the point that families will be torn apart over commitment to Jesus (Mt 10:34–37 ‖ Lk 12:51–53; 14:26) and that basic familial duties, such as burying the dead, are relativized (Mt 8:21–22 ‖ Lk 9:59–60). The disciples of Jesus are now his—and, presumably, the disciples'—true family (e.g., Mk 3:34 and parallels). By the second century A.D., one can see more similarities between Jesus' disciples and rabbinic disciples on this point (cf. Meier, 3.48).

In connection with this aspect of discipleship, the primary metaphor for accompanying Jesus as a disciple is "to follow" (ἀκολουθέω— *akoloutheō*) Him. The imperative invitation, ἀκολούθει μοι (*akolouthei moi*), "Follow me," is found in Mk 2:14 ‖ Mt 9:9 ‖ Lk 5:27; Mk 10:21 ‖ Mt 19:21 ‖ Lk 18:22; Mt 8:22 ‖ Lk 9:59; Jn 1:43; 21:19, 22. Similarly, see the imperative δεῦτε ὀπίσω μοι (*deute opisō moi*), "come after me," in Mk 1:17 ‖ Mt 4:19.

In other sayings, Jesus speaks of 'following' and/or 'coming/following after' him: Mk 8:34 ‖ Mt 16:24 ‖ Lk 9:23; Mt 10:38 ‖ Lk 14:27; Mt 19:28; Lk 21:8 (disciples are not to go after those who falsely come in Jesus' name). Others also speak or ask about following Jesus: Peter (Mk 10:28 ‖ Mt 19:27 ‖ Lk 18:28); a scribe (Mt 8:19 ‖ Lk 9:57, "someone"); John (Mk 9:38 ‖ Lk 9:49, concerning an exorcist who does not follow Jesus); "another" (Lk 9:61).

Particular persons or groups are following Jesus in Mk 1:18 ‖ Mt 4:20; Mk 2:14 ‖ Mt 9:9 ‖ Lk 5:28; Mk 2:15; Mk 3:7 ‖ Mt 4:25 (cp. 12:1); Mk 5:24 ‖ Mt 9:19; Mk 5:37; 6:1; 10:32; Mk 10:52 ‖ Mt 20:34 ‖ Lk 18:43; Mk 15:41 ‖ Mt 27:55 ‖ Lk 23:49; Mt 8:10 ‖ Lk 7:9; Mt 8:1, 23; 9:27 (cp. 20:29); 14:13; 19:2; Lk 9:11; 22:39; 23:27; Jn 1:37, 40; 10:4–5 and 27 (of sheep as an image for disciples); 13:36; 18:15; 21:19, 22. The sons of Zebedee "went after" Jesus, Mk 1:20 (the parallels in Mt 4:22 and Lk 5:11 have "followed him").

Third, in addition to the radical denial of family, discipleship required a break with one's former life and livelihood (cf. above on Mk 1:16–20; 2:13–14 and parallels; cp. Jn 6:66), and the paradox that the disciple can only save his or her life by losing it (Mk 8:35 ‖ Mt 16:25 ‖ Lk 9:24; cp. Lk 17:33 ‖ Mt 10:39 and Jn 12:25). The disciple must be willing to follow Jesus even to taking up the cross (e.g., Mk 8:34 and parallels; Mt 10:38 ‖ Lk 14:27), and to face persecution (e.g., Mk 4:17; Mt 5:1, 44; 10:23; Lk 11:49; 21:12; Jn 15:20; 16:33), suffering (e.g. Mk 13:19 and parallels) and even death (e.g., Mk 13:12 and parallels; Mk 10:35–39 ‖ Mt 20:20–23; Jn 16:2). There are, however, promises associated with the perseverance and endurance of the disciple (e.g., see Mk 10:30; 13:13 and parallels; Mt 10:22; cp. Jn 6:68), as well as dire consequences for those who deny or are ashamed of Jesus (e.g., see Mk 8:38 ‖ Lk 9:26; Mt 10:33 ‖ Lk 12:9)—even though Simon Peter denied Jesus three times (Mk 14:29–31, 66–72 and parallels; Jn 13:36–38; 18:15–18, 25–27), he is rehabilitated, most especially in Jn 21:15–19.

Fourth, the goal of the Greek or Jewish disciple was to one day become a master who would be sought out by those who wish to be his disciples. To be a disciple of

Jesus, however, is to always be his disciple. Jesus remains the teacher, the master, and the disciple, regardless how long he or she is a follower of Jesus, remains a disciple. For example, in Mt 10, the Twelve are presented as learners, that is, "disciples," who by necessity will experience what their teacher has. Usually a disciple him/herself becomes a teacher, but verses 24–25 (‖ Lk 6:40; cf. above) indicate that in relationship to Jesus Christ, the disciple is "to be a life-long learner. . . . This means that for the believer Jesus is not only a teacher but also an abiding lord" (Viviano, 651; cf. Meier, 3.55). This enduring relationship with Jesus means that the disciples are representatives of Jesus, such that to welcome a disciple is to welcome Jesus (Mt 10:40; cp. Lk 10:16 and Jn 13:20).

Finally, Greek and Jewish disciples were to be solid and true representatives of their masters, but the narrative use of the disciples in the Gospels is far from ideal. Jesus' disciples are rather mixed characters, so that the reader not only learns from their example, but also from their mistakes. The presentation in Mark is more negative than in the other Gospels, but even after recognizing the difference in degree, all the Gospels show that the disciples often fail to understand (e.g., Mk 4:13; 6:52; 7:18; 8:17, 21; 9:32 and parallels), experience fear (Mk 4:40; 6:50; 9:32; 10:32 and parallels) and doubt (e.g., Mt 14:31; 28:17), and, except for Jn 19:25–27, abandon Jesus so that he dies on the cross with only some women disciples looking on from afar (Mk 15:40 ‖ Mt 27:55 ‖ Lk 23:49). Perhaps the closest the Gospels come to an idealize disciple is found in John's presentation of the "disciple whom Jesus loved," the so-called "beloved disciple," who first appears at the Last Supper (cf. above on the "anonymous disciple" of Jn 1:35–40) and whose testimony is foundational for the Johannine community (Jn 13:23; 19:26–27; 20:2; 21:7, 20; see too references to "this/(an)other disciple" in Jn 18:15–16; 20:3–8; 21:23–24). Although this disciple was traditionally identified with John, the Son of Zebedee, the Fourth Evangelist, "the disciple whom Jesus loved" seems more likely to be a literary device which draws the reader into the narrative and gives a solid foundation for the faith of the community/-ies out of which the gospel comes and to whom it is addressed (cf. Meier, 3.114–115 n. 110).

Jewish Writings and the Apostolic Fathers. The Jewish author, Philo of Alexandria (*c.* 25 B.C.–50 A.D.) uses "disciple" only 14 times in his extensive writings. Although he does use "the word at times in the general sense of a learner or one receiving instruction from a teacher, he typically uses *mathētēs* within the context of his mystical views about the 'perfect' person who is directly taught by God" (Meier, 3.42; cf. above on Jn 6:45b). Likewise, the nearly as extensive writings of Jo-

sephus (*c.* 37–100+ A.D.) witness only 15 uses of *mathētēs*, "scattered throughout *The Jewish Antiquities* and *Against Apion*" from *c.* 93 to 94 and 100 to 105 A.D., respectively. Besides its general use for "one who learns from another's example (*Ant.* 1.11.3 §200)" or "to describe persons or groups who follow the philosophical teachings of some other person or group that is notably distant from the learners in time and space (*Ag. Ap.* 1.2 §14; 1.22 §176; 2.41 §295)," Josephus uses *mathētēs* of a number of Old Testament relationships of disciples to their masters: Joshua to Moses (*Ant.* 6.5.4 §84); Elisha to Elijah (*Ant.* 8.13.7 §354); Baruch to Jeremiah (*Ant.* 10.9.1 §158). These examples show how Josephus "interprets these biblical heroes in the milieu of Hellenistic Judaism" (Meier, 3.42–43).

Josephus offers more detail with respect to Elisha: *Ant.* 9.2.4 §68 finds Elisha in his house with his disciples; in *Ant.* 9.6.1 §106 Elisha sends a disciple on a mission. These presentations can be contrasted with "the elders" and "one of the guild prophets" in 2 Kgs 6:32; 9:1, respectively. "Here Josephus may be rereading biblical passages in the light of the Pharisaic and nascent rabbinic movements with their schools—a phenomenon that in turn reflects Hellenistic cultural influence" (Meier, 3.43, cf. 92 n. 26).

Josephus, who "claimed that he had been a Pharisee from early adulthood onwards," presents the Hasmonean ethnarch, John Hyrcanus (63–40 B.C.), as a disciple of the Pharisees (*Ant.* 13.10.5 §289). "In context, the passage probably means that Hyrcanus flattered the Pharisees by insisting how much he was influenced by their teachings" (Meier, 3.43). The strict sense of a true disciple, Samaias, of a Pharisaic teacher, Pollion, is found in *Ant.* 15.1.1 §3, and both of them had "constant followers" (*Ant.* 15.10.4 §370). "Here the Greek idea of a master-disciple relationship within a philosophical school has clearly sunk roots in a Jewish Palestinian setting . . . ," which provides "the closest 1st-century Jewish parallel we can find to the Gospels' use of *mathētēs* for the disciples of Jesus. . . . Prior to the lifetime of the historical Jesus, there is no Jewish author we can point to who speaks of disciples who are at least in some ways similar to the disciples Jesus gathers around himself" (Meier, 3.43–44).

Despite the writings of Philo and Josephus, and more importantly the frequency of the use of μαθητής (*mathētēs*) in the Gospels and especially of "Christian(s)" in Acts, it "was not the ordinary way Christians of the first and second Christian generations spoke to or about one [an] other" (Meier, 3.41). This "discontinuity" between the Gospels and later Christian writings further substantiates "the historicity of a group of disciples around Jesus during his lifetime,'' rather than some ''anachronistic retrojection of the early church's way of speaking of its members into the time of Jesus' public ministry'' (Meier, 3.41, see too, 3.44; cf. above for more on historicity). Μαθητής (*mathētēs*) is not found in 1 and 2 Clement (*c.* 96 and 150 A.D.), The Epistle of Barnabas (*c.* 130 A.D.), Polycarp's letter to the Philippians (pre-130 A.D.), The Shepherd of Hermas (*c.* 140 A.D.), and The Didache (pre-150 A.D.). Moreover, although Ignatius uses μαθητής (*mathētēs*) nine times in his letters of 108 to 117 A.D., for him, ''the true disciple is the martyr,'' toward which Ignatius himself is moving. He also refers to the Old Testament prophets ''as spiritual disciples of Jesus Christ (*Magnesians* 9:2),'' and uses the term similarly to Acts of the Apostles (to Polycarp 2:1 and *Magnesians* 10:1), but never in reference to the disciples of the Gospel narratives. In the context of some of the names of the Twelve, ''the disciples of the Lord'' are twice mentioned in the fragments of *Interpretations of the Sayings of the Lord* by Papias of Hierapolis (from about 130 A.D.) preserved by Eusebius' Ecclesiastical History. *The Martyrdom of Polycarp* 17:3 ''reflects the Ignatian usage of describing martyrs'' as disciples, and ''contains the only occurrence in the Apostolic Fathers of 'fellow disciple,''' συμμαθητής (*summathētēs*). The Epistle to Diognetus (an apologist, probably from the second or third century A.D.) uses μαθητής (*mathētēs*) ''once of the author, once of those becoming Christian, and twice of the original disciples of Jesus.'' ''In sum, most of the Apostolic Fathers never use *mathētēs*. Ignatius, who accounts for the vast majority of occurrences, uses it mostly of martyrs, rarely of contemporary Christians in general, and never of the original disciples of Jesus'' (Meier, 3.84–85 n. 6).

The possible background as well as the use of μαθητής (*mathētēs*) and related vocabulary in the Gospels and Acts and in later Christian writings pose more complexity than one might first expect. In the Gospels, ''disciple(s)'' can refer to those among the Twelve, a wider circle of male and female followers of Jesus, and even committed persons who did not accompany Jesus on his public (cf. the summary in Meier, 3.627–632). In Acts, ''disciples'' usually designates believers, that is, ''Christians,'' even though this was not the common way for early Christians to refer to one another. Therefore, those preachers and writers who want to extend ''pulpit oratory and theological musings to employ the word 'disciple' in as many meanings or in as broad a sense as possible . . . might appeal to Luke as their patron saint'' (Meier, 3.49).

Bibliography: E. BEST, *Disciples and Discipleship. Studies in the Gospel according to Mark* (Edinburgh 1986). R. E. BROWN, *The Community of the Beloved Disciple* (Mahwah, New Jersey 1979). W. D. DAVIES and D. C. ALLISON, JR., *A Critical and Exegetical Commentary on the Gospel according to Saint Matthew in Three Volumes*: Vol. I: *Introduction and Commentary on Matthew I–VII*; Vol. II: *Commentary on Matthew VIII–XVIII*; Vol. III: *Commentary on Matthew XIX–XXVIII* (International Critical Commentary, Edinburgh 1988; 1991 and 1997). P. NEPPER-CHRISTENSEN, ''μαθητής'' in H. BALZ and G. SCHNEIDER, eds., *Exegetical Dictionary of the New Testament*, 3 v. (Grand Rapids, Michigan 1990) v. 2, 372–74. S. E. FOWL, ''Imitation of Paul/of Christ,'' in G. F. HAWTHORNE, R. P. MARTIN and D. G. REID, eds., *Dictionary of Paul and His Letters. A Compendium of Contemporary Biblical Scholarship* (Downers Grove, Illinois 1993). W. S. KURZ, *Following Jesus. A Disciple's Guide to Luke and Acts* (Ann Arbor, 1984). U. LUZ, ''The Disciples in the Gospel according to Matthew'' (tr. R. MORGAN), in *The Interpretation of Matthew, Issues in Religion and Theology*, 3, ed. by G. STANTON (Philadelphia 1983), 98–128. J. P. MEIER, *A Marginal Jew. Rethinking the Historical Jesus*: Vol. 1: *The Roots of the Problem and the Person*; Vol. 2: *Mentor, Message, and Miracles*; Vol. 3: *Companions and Competitors* (The Anchor Bible Reference Library, New York 1991; 1994; 2001, respectively). F. J. MOLONEY, ''The Vocation of the Disciples in the Gospel of Mark,'' *Sal* 43 (1981) 487–516. G. NEBE, ''μανθάνω'' in H. BALZ and G. SCHNEIDER, eds., *Exegetical Dictionary of the New Testament*, 3 v. (Grand Rapids, Michigan 1990) v. 2, 383–84. F. NEIRYNCK, ''The Anonymous Disciple in John 1,'' *ETL* 66 (1990) 5–37; reprinted in *Evangelica II: 1982–1991 Collected Essays*, ed. by F. VAN SEGBROECK (Leuven 1991), 617–49, with an additional note, 649. P. NEPPER-CHRISTENSEN, ''μαθητής, ου, ὁ . . . μαθητεύω,'' in H. BALZ and G. SCHNEIDER, eds., *Exegetical Dictionary of the New Testament*, 3 v. (Grand Rapids, Michigan 1990) v. 2, 372–74. J. A. OVERMAN, ''Disciple,'' in *The Oxford Companion to the Bible*, ed. by B.M. METZGER and M.D. COOGAN (New York 1993) 168–69. K.H. RENGSTORFF, ''μανθάνω, καταμανθάνω, μαθητής, συμμαθητής, μαθητρία, μαθητεύω,'' in G. KITTEL, ed., *Theological Dictionary of the New Testament* (tr. and ed., G. W. BROMILEY), 10 v. (Grand Rapids, Michigan 1964–1976), v. IV, 390–461. F. SEGOVIA, ed., *Discipleship in the New Testament* (Philadelphia 1985). J. J. VINCENT, *Disciple and Lord. The Historical and Theological Significance of Discipleship in the Synoptic Gospels* (Sheffield 1976). B. T. VIVIANO, ''The Gospel according to Matthew'' in R. E. BROWN, et al., eds., *NJBC* (Englewood Cliffs, New Jersey 1990) 630–74. H. WEDER, ''Disciple, Discipleship'' (tr. by D. MARTIN) in *Anchor Bible Dictionary*, 6 v., ed. by D. N. FREEDMAN (New York 1992), v. II, 207–10. M. J. WILKINS, *The Concept of Disciple in Matthew's Gospel. As Reflected in the Use of the Term* Μαθητής, *Novum Testamentum Supplment* 59 (Leiden 1988). M. J. WILKINS, ''Disciples'' and ''Discipleship,'' in J. B. GREEN, S. MCKNIGHT, and I. H. MARSHALL, *Dictionary of Jesus and the Gospels. A Compendium of Contemporary Biblical Scholarship* (Downers Grove, Illinois 1992) 176–82 and 182–89.

[T. A. FRIEDRICHSEN]

DISCIPLINE, THE

The discipline was a whip used to inflict chastisement on the body as a means of mortification. Although it was originally an instrument of punishment, its use came to have a place among the common works of supererogation.

In its penal use, the discipline had a place in monastic life from its beginnings. The rule of St. Pachomius listed faults and the number of stripes with which each was to be punished. St. Benedict, too, decreed punishment by the discipline and for this reason is often pictured holding a bundle of switches. Monastic codes contained an elaborate ritual to accompany the imposition of penances. The punishment was not merely symbolic; offenders often were beaten until the blood flowed. The rule of St. Columban, however, limited the number of lashes at any one time to 25.

The employment of the discipline as a penal practice was replaced about the 12th century by its use for personal mortification. St. Peter Damian (d. 1072) was chiefly responsible for this. In his preaching and writing (e.g., *De laude flagellorum,* in *Patrologia Latina,* ed. J. P. Migne, 145:679–686), he urged on monasteries the use of the discipline as a way of imitating Christ. In the 12th and 13th centuries, voluntary flagellation became part of the penitential fabric of the religious life. Early ascetics used thorny branches, iron chains, leather straps tipped with metal or bone. Contemporary disciplines are generally made of several strands of rope bound together and knotted at the ends. Each community developed its own ceremonial accompaniment to the taking of the discipline. In some groups the flagellation was self–administered; in others, the superior or hebdomadary administered it. Generally, it was the practice to take the discipline in the church during the recitation of the *Miserere* or other Psalms.

The zeal for FLAGELLATION, so common in the Middle Ages, has declined in modern times. It remains in some religious communities as one of the religious observances inherited from the past. In such cases it is used with moderation, and spiritual authorities are generally slow to recommend its use.

Bibliography: L. GOUGAUD, *Devotions et pratiques ascetiques du moyen âge* (Paris–Maredsous 1925) 175–199. D. GAZEAU, *Catholicisme* 3:880. É. BERTAUD, *Dictionnaire de spiritualité ascétique et mystique. Doctrine et histoire,* ed. M. VILLER et al. (Paris 1932) 3:1302–11.

[P. F. MULHERN]

DISCURSIVE POWER

In general, any power of KNOWLEDGE that acts discursively is a discursive power. A discursive action is one that moves from one point to another because it is unable to grasp a complex whole in a single act (*see* REASONING). In ARISTOTELIANISM, the ''deliberative imagination'' is often called ''the discursive power,'' e.g., by AVERROËS. As a technical term in THOMISM, discursive power is a variant phrase used to translate *vis cogitativa.* This term is more commonly translated as cogitative power or cogitative sense.

See Also: COGITATIVE POWER; CREATIVE IMAGINATION; INTELLECT.

[G. P. KLUBERTANZ]

DISENTIS, ABBEY OF

Benedictine abbey at the source of the Rhine, Graübunden, Diocese of Chur, Switzerland. Disentis is the German equivalent of the Romansh Mustér. Both names derive from the ''cell'' of St. Sigisbert (*c.* 720), a Frankish disciple of St. COLUMBAN. The Rhaetian noble St. Placidus, co-founder of the hermitage, was slain to prevent the founding of a monastery, which was achieved by Bishop Ursicinus *c.* 750. Bishop Tello of Chur granted many lands and privileges (765), and Disentis flourished as an imperial abbey in Carolingian times. After its destruction by Saracens (940) it revived, thanks to the Ottos and especially Frederic I Barbarossa, who favored it with grants as far away as Milan because of its strategic location on the Lucmagn Pass between Germany and Italy. St. ADALGOTT brought reform and a liturgical movement from EINSIEDELN *c.* 1000. Abbots Gion II (1367–1401) and Pieder de Pultengia (1402–38) helped found the Gray League Republic. Three monks and the abbot joined the Reformation, but the abbey remained Catholic. Christian de Castelberg (1566–84), friend of St. Charles BORROMEO, raised the level of religious life. In the 17th century Disentis devoted itself to the apostolate and to the spread of Romansh spiritual literature through its press. The abbey prospered under Adalbert II de Medell (1655–96) and Bernard Frank de Frankenberg (1742–63) before it was burned by the French (1799). The monks returned (1804), but the abbey declined after another fire (1846). It was restored from Muri-Gries (1880).

The 8th-century reliquary crypt grew to three churches: St. Peter, Our Lady (*c.* 750), and St. Martin (*c.* 800). The present baroque St. Martin (rebuilt 1695–1712 after plans by Caspar Moosbrugger) is a landmark of the Upper Rhine. The monk Placia Spescha (1752–1833) was an encyclopedist and geographer; Maurus Carnot (1865–1935) was a Romansh poet and dramatist; Notker Curti (1880–1948) was a historian of folk art. Disentis, with 40 monks and 25 lay brothers (1964), has a Gymnasium with 200 students, a Romansh library, and a museum of folk art.

Bibliography: I. MÜLLER, *Disentiser Klostergeschichte,* v.1 (720–1512) (Einsiedeln 1942); *Die Abtei Disentis* (Fribourg 1952–), 4 v. pub. to 1960; *Dictionnaire d'histoire et de géographie ecclésiastiques,* ed. A. BAUDRILLART et al. (Paris 1912–) 14:516–519; *Lexikon für Theologie und Kirche,* ed. J. HOFER and K. RAHNER, 10 v. (2d, new ed. Freiburg 1957–65) 3:417–418. F. PIETH and K. HAGER, *Pater Placidus Spescha, sein Leben und seine Schriften* (Bern 1913). O. ZURKINDEN, *Pater Maurus Carnot* (Glion,

Switz. 1945). L. H. COTTINEAU, *Répertoire topobibliographique des abbayes et prieurés*, 2 v. (Mâcon 1935–39) 1:972–974. O. L. KAPSNER, *A Benedictine Bibliography: An Author-Subject Union List*, 2 v. (2d ed. Collegeville, Minn. 1962) 2:203.

[A. MAISSEN]

DISHYPATOS, DAVID

Fourteenth-century Byzantine Hesychast and theological polemicist. David presumably belonged to the Dishypatoi family of Constantinople. He was a monk and apparently worked in close contact with Gregory PALAMAS. He wrote (*c.* 1347) a short but important account of the controversy between Palamas and BARLAAM OF CALABRIA for Empress Anne of Savoy. He is credited with a diatribe (*logos*) against Barlaam and GREGORIUS AKINDYNOS addressed to Nicolas CABASILAS; and a polemic poem in 468 verses against Akindynos. These works have remained unedited. To Dishypatos is attributed also a Canon of the Mass dedicated to St. George, the martyr, but he is no longer credited with the section of the patristic florilegium.

Bibliography: H. G. BECK, *Kirche und theologische Literatur im byzantinischen Reich* (Munich 1959) 730–732. B. KOTTER, *Lexikon für Theologie und Kirche*, ed. J. HOFER and K. RAHNER (2d new ed. Freiburg 1957–65) 3:178. V. LAURENT, *Dictionnaire d'histoire et de géographie ecclésiastiques*, ed. A. BAUDRILLART et al. (Paris 1912–) 14:115–116.

[G. LUZNYCKY]

DISPENSATIONAL THEOLOGY

A system of ESCHATOLOGY characterized by three central ideas. First, history is divided into time frames or dispensations. Each dispensation represents a specific form of revelation given by God to humanity, with a corresponding covenant delineating God's expectations of humans and God's judgments when humans inevitably fail. The most widely held divisions of history are those of C. I. SCOFIELD (1843–1921), who outlined seven dispensations between creation and the millennium. Second, with few exceptions dispensationalism insists on a literal interpretation of Scripture. This literalism is grounded in a commitment to biblical inerrancy and a belief that prophecy is prewritten history. Third, dispensationalism draws a sharp distinction between Israel and the Church. Since all prophecy must be fulfilled literally, the 1948 establishment of Israel as a nation is considered by dispensationalists to be the fulfillment of prophecy concerning the regathering of God's people. Thus, when Christ returns he will set up an actual kingdom in Jerusalem and reign for 1,000 years. For dispensationalism the restored nation of Israel is the staging ground for the impending eschatological events.

The following features are typical of the dispensational system: the RAPTURE of the church, a seven-year tribulation period, the battle of Armageddon, the rise of the antichrist, the imposition of the mark of the beast, the mass conversion of Jews to Christianity in the end times, the return of Christ, the establishing of the millennial kingdom on earth, the defeat of Satan, and the last JUDGMENT with rewards in heaven and punishments in hell.

Though belief in a literal thousand-year reign of Christ on earth can be found in several pre-Augustinian church fathers, dispensationalism as a system of theology has its origins in the nineteenth century with John Nelson DARBY (1800–1882). Darby, an Irish cleric in the Church of England, broke with Anglicanism in 1827. Darby made several trips to Canada and the United States between 1862 and 1877 and found eager audiences for his dispensational system. The dissemination of dispensational thought was greatly aided by the publication of the *Scofield Reference Bible* in 1909. In the 1920s Clarence Larkin (1850–1924), an engineer turned Baptist minister, visually depicted the dispensational system through his hand-drawn and intricately detailed charts, which were published in books and in wall-sized reproductions. In 1924 Lewis Sperry Chafer (1871–1952), a student of Scofield, founded Dallas Theological Seminary, the theological center of dispensationalism and the teaching post for two of the most important dispensational theologians of the latter half of the twentieth century, John F. Walvoord (b. 1910) and Charles C. Ryrie (b. 1925). A newer generation of dispensational theologians has advocated a "progressive dispensationalism," a modified and more mainstream system of eschatology. Traditional dispensationalism continues to be a force for shaping popular views on eschatology.

Bibliography: C. BASS, *Backgrounds to Dispensationalism* (Grand Rapids 1960). C. A. BLAISING and D. L. BOCK, *Progressive Dispensationalism* (Wheaton, Ill. 1993). L. S. CHAFER, *Systematic Theology,* 8 v. (Dallas 1948). N. C. KRAUS, *Dispensationalism in America* (Richmond 1958). C. C. RYRIE, *Dispensationalism Today* (Chicago 1965).

[W. T. STANCIL]

DISPOSITION

The term disposition, as used in scholastic writings, always implies an ORDER among the parts of a thing having parts. Although this is a simple notion, it has widespread application in philosophy and theology, for the concept of a "thing having parts" can be taken very broadly.

Disposition of Parts in a Whole. In its most concrete application, disposition is the same as the category of SITUATION (*situs*), which defines the order in PLACE that the physical parts of a body might have, e.g., the arrangement of its limbs by which an animal is said to be standing or sitting or lying down. Disposition is used also to denote the order of bodies or of any kind of units within an aggregate, as the disposition of an army or the disposition of funds. In this acceptation, disposition can be taken in an active sense to denote the ordinance by which the units are arranged, e.g., the disposition of the army that the general effects; or it can be taken passively, as the positions occupied by the troops in virtue of the ordinance. In all these instances, disposition refers to the ordering of parts in a whole. It can, however, be extended to include the ordering of things to an END or purpose; in fact, many orderings of parts in a whole include an ordering to a purpose. (*See* WHOLE; PART.)

Disposition as a Quality. Perhaps the most important use of disposition in scholastic writings is the sense in which it designates a QUALITY. The category of quality is divided into four species, of which the first includes habit and disposition. A HABIT is a quality by which a thing is well or badly disposed either in itself or in relation to its operations. What is implied in this definition is that a thing has parts, that these parts can be variously organized among themselves, and that in virtue of diverse organizations the thing is well constituted or badly constituted, and operates well or badly. If the organization of the parts is by its very nature firm and stable, it is called a habit. If it is labile and easily disrupted, it is called a disposition. Thus scientific knowledge constitutes a habit of accepting one truth and rejecting its opposite, because the truth is certified, but knowledge based on rumor or hearsay constitutes only a disposition to accept an opinion, because by its very nature it is subject to easy disproof. A disposition, therefore, though it is like a habit is weaker by nature. In this acceptation of the term, disposition is something distinguishable from habit. However, the term disposition is sometimes used interchangeably with the term habit, and at other times it is used to designate a general category that includes both habit and disposition.

As used in connection with the concept of habit, disposition is subject to the same divisions as habit. Thus there are entitative habits and operative habits, and entitative dispositions and operative dispositions. As there are habits of intellect, will, and passions, so there are dispositions of intellect, will, and passions, and so on. Thus we can speak of dispositions to illness, benign dispositions, cruel dispositions, irascible dispositions, etc.

Insofar as dispositions are tendencies that can develop into habits if they become firm and stable, there can be a threefold relationship of disposition to habit. Disposition and habit can be, first of all, of the same nature and in the same subject, as a disposition to face dangers can be developed into a habit of courage. The disposition is of the nature of courage from the beginning, and in the same subject, i.e., the irascible appetite. Secondly, the disposition can be of a different nature but in the same subject, as the disposition to react violently to dangers can lead to physical illness. The violent reaction is not of the same nature as the illness, but it is in the same subject, namely, the organs that respond in strong emotions. And finally the disposition can be of a different nature and in a different subject, as the ability to remember well, which is a disposition toward acquiring science, is not of the essence of science, nor is it in the intellect, where science resides.

Dispositions of Matter in Relation to Form. According to HYLOMORPHISM, matter is the element of a thing that is potential and of itself without any characteristics, and form is what makes a thing be what it is, determining all its characteristics (*see* MATTER AND FORM). Nevertheless, matter is spoken of as having dispositions to form. This means, on the one hand, that matter is by its very nature susceptible to being formed by form. Again, it means that in any given thing, the characteristics given by the form and received by the matter are those that are appropriate to the form. Thus the scholastics would say that matter must be organized to receive a living form, for life is exercised through organs, and the higher the grade of the living thing, the more complex its organization must be. These various grades of organization are material dispositions to various grades of living forms, although they are also, more strictly speaking, the formal effects of the forms.

In the case of SUBSTANTIAL CHANGE in nature, when some agent acts on a body and changes it to a different kind of thing, the agent operates by changing the accidental features of the patient until the patient is no longer capable of retaining its substantial form, whereupon that form returns to the potentiality of the matter and a new substantial form takes its place. Thus when wood is burnt, the gradual heating of the wood to the point at which it ignites is an accidental change, which leads finally to the substantial change, from wood to ashes. The accidental changes in a body leading to substantial changes are called dispositions of its matter. The last accidents inhering in a subject before its substantial change are called the previous dispositions. The first accidents in the new subject produced in a substantial change are called the proximate dispositions of the substantial form of that subject. They are the characteristics of the body that make it proportioned to the new substantial form, although strictly speaking, they depend on that form for their own being.

Disposition in Theology. This concept of disposition as a preparation for a change is used also in theology. For example, the profound difference between the natural and supernatural orders makes it necessary to deny that there could be any natural dispositions to supernatural gifts, in the sense of preparatory acts or states that by their nature are proportioned to effects of the supernatural order. On the other hand, since the supernatural order does not operate without reference to the natural order, it is defensible to speak of natural dispositions to FAITH, GRACE, SACRAMENTS, and the like. Natural virtues and natural truths can be considered as remote dispositions to grace, at least insofar as they remove impediments to grace, although they cannot be conceived as eliciting or demanding grace. The proximate disposition to supernatural grace is the act of free will accepting this grace; but this act itself is prompted and caused by a supernatural movement divinely bestowed (see St. Thomas Aquinas, ST 1a2ae, 109.6).

See Also: TEMPERAMENT; VIRTUE.

Bibliography: R. J. DEFERRARI et al., *A Lexicon of St. Thomas Aquinas* (Washington 1948–53). V. E. SMITH, *The General Science of Nature* (Milwaukee 1958). J. GREDT, *Elementa philosophiae Aristotelico-Thomisticae,* 2 v. (12th ed. Freiburg 1958). P. H. J. HOENEN, *Cosmologia* (5th ed. Rome 1956). JOHN OF ST. THOMAS, *Cursus philosophicus,* ed. B. REISER, 3 v. (new ed. Turin 1930–37). R. EISLER, *Wörterbuch der philosophischen Begriffe,* 3 v. (4th ed. Berlin 1927–30) 1:287–89.

[M. STOCK]

DISSIMULATION

As understood here, dissimulation is the concealment or cloaking of the truth. The term is applicable not only to culpable deception and want of candor, but also to the legitimate defense of a secret against those who have no right to share it, as in the case of smiling when in much pain, or being friendly to those whom we naturally abhor, not that we might deceive, but that our natural state might for good reason remain unnoticed. Dissimulation must be practiced to some degree by everyone, but most especially by those whose profession requires that they be wards of SECRETS and confidential matters; for example, priests and doctors. In order to avoid the slightest betrayal they must not only be silent before the probing questions of the curious, but they must prevent those very questions from arising. This can often best be accomplished by timely dissimulation.

Bibliography: J. A. MCHUGH and C. J. CALLAN, *Moral Theology,* rev. E. P. FARRELL, 2 v. (New York 1958) 2:2403–04.

[S. F. PARMISANO]

DISTICHA CATONIS

Disticha catonis is a collection of moral maxims in four books of 306 hexameters (18 in prefaces, 288 in distichs), of unknown origin, perhaps from the 2nd or 3rd century A.D., attributed to Cato the Elder (*c.* 200 B.C.). It is a curious mixture of pagan and Christian injunctions, some with a Machiavellian slant. The manuscripts also contain 56 short prose *sententiae.* A prose preface to Book I may have been added in a Carolingian recension of the collection. In the Middle Ages it was used as a schoolbook from which students learned moral precepts as well as Latin grammar. It was translated into Greek by Maximus PLANUDES (d. 1310), into German by NOTKER LABEO (d. 1022), and into other Western vernaculars in the late Middle Ages. Almost every medieval library catalogue lists a copy. It was frequently imitated and parodied, and was one of the first books printed.

Bibliography: M. BOAS, ed., *Disticha Catonis* (Amsterdam 1952). J. W. and A. M. DUFF, eds. and trs., *Minor Latin Poets (Loeb Classical Library*; London 1934). F. SKUTSCH, *Paulys Realenzyklopädie der klassischen Altertumswissenschaft,* ed. G. WISSOWA et al. (Stuttgart 1893–) 5:358–370. M. SCHANZ, C. HOSIUS, and G. KRÜGER, *Geschichte der römischen Literatur,* 4 v. in 5 (Munich 1914–35) 3:34–41. H. HELD, *Lexikon für Theologie und Kirche,* ed. J. HOFER and K. RAHNER 10 v. (2d, new ed. Freiburg 1957–65) 2:980–981.

[R. T. MEYER]

DISTINCTION, KINDS OF

Distinction is opposed to IDENTITY and to confusion. Objectively, a distinction is any degree or kind of nonidentity or nonlikeness by which one thing or aspect is not another (Thomas Aquinas, *C. gent.* 1.71). Operationally, it is the act of distinguishing, i.e., the act or state of the mind discerning a nonidentity or dispelling the confusion in a precedent act that fell short of such discernment. The foundation of this twofold usage is itself twofold: the plurality of things and of conditions and aspects of things, both static and in process; and the stages and conditions in the development of the mind as it passes from potency to act. Whether there is a one-to-one correspondence between the distinctions operationally drawn by the mind and the ontological perfections of things in themselves anterior to the mind's attention to them has historically been a divisive question in SCHOLASTICISM. Thomists and Aristotelians generally maintain the negative; Scotists and Suarezians, the affirmative (*see* ARISTOTELIANISM; SCOTISM; SUAREZIANISM; THOMISM).

Related Terms and Classical Sources. Distinction may be said to bear to DEFINITION a relation somewhat the inverse of the relation that collection bears to DIVI-

SION. For just as definition is a summary or synthesis of the comprehension of a concept and collection is a like synthesis of the extension of a concept, so distinction is an analysis or breakdown of concepts on the basis of the nonidentity in whole or in part of their contents and division is an analysis of their extension. Accordingly, just as ''plant'' and ''animal'' must be divided in order to be united in the collection or universalization of ''body,'' so ''living body'' and ''sentient'' must be distinguished in order to be united in the definition of ''animal.'' Note from the example that this proportion holds particularly for the essential definition and for the distinction of reason (see below).

Distinction is related also to both of these sets of opposites: (1) the identical or same and the diverse or other and (2) the like or similar and the unlike or different. Distinction obtains between the different as well as between the diverse. Hence it is opposed to likeness, or SIMILARITY, as well as to identity in the strict sense, and, consequently, to confusion based on nondiscernment of either difference or diversity.

The statements of ARISTOTLE on this topic, as is often the case, give verbal indication of various kinds and shades of distinction that later were canonized and profoundly elaborated upon by the scholastics. Apart from discrimination (διάκρισις in the *De anima*, bk. 3) there seems to be no one technical term for distinction in his writings or in those of PLATO. The more metalogical words used for distinction also serve more properly and significantly for division and ABSTRACTION (διαιρεῖν; ἀφαιρεῖν, χωρίζειν). There is, however, the direct way of expressing distinction by denying identity: μὴ τὸ αὐτὸ εἶναι (not to be the same); ἄλλο καὶ ἄλλο εἶναι, ἄλλως ἔχειν (to be other, to be otherwise). Discussions of distinction are mostly incidental to discussions of definition, as in bk. 7 of the *Metaphysics*. It should be noted that when Aristotle says that two things, though one in being, are diverse κατὰ λόγον (*secundum rationem*), the implied distinction is more the ancestor of the scholastic modal distinction than of the scholastic distinction of reason. The classical source for the scholastics' theories of distinction of reason, virtual distinction, and actual formal distinction lies more probably in the Stoic theory of the λεκτόν (*see* STOICISM), which came to them mainly through BOETHIUS. An indirect but special source of the Scotistic formal distinction is Plato's *Sophist*. The influence of this came westward via NEOPLATONISM and ARABIAN PHILOSOPHY.

Thomistic Distinctions. For St. THOMAS AQUINAS, the term distinction is often almost synonymous with diversity and difference; when he wishes, however, not to impute diversity or difference to the ESSENCE under con-

sideration and yet to indicate that meaningful distinctions can be drawn that have bearing on it, he resorts to the term distinction (*Summa theologiae* 1a, 31.2).

Formal and Material Distinction. Distinction is either formal or material, i.e., numerical; the former indicates a difference of species or FORM, a difference properly so called, and the latter, a difference in number, i.e., a diversity (*De pot.* 2.4, 9.8 ad 2; ST 1a, 47.2). This basic but often slighted Thomistic division partially overlaps with the more famous division of distinction into real and rational; it subdivides the real distinction but not the rational distinction, all of whose subtypes are formal in some extended sense.

Real Distinction. Objects distinct according to a real distinction are nonidentical as things in their own right, prior to and independent of any objectifying insight or construction elicited by the human reason. The ultimate case of this would be two individuals of the same atomic SPECIES: they are not at all formally distinct but are distinct from each other by a real, absolute, material or numerical (and entitative) distinction. They are diverse as beings, though altogether alike in essential form. If the two individuals differ also in species, then they are distinct by a real, absolute distinction that is both material and formal. They are diverse and different. If one abstracts from the individuals as such and considers their essences either as natures in themselves or as so-called metaphysical UNIVERSALS, then these essences are distinct from each other by a real, absolute, formal distinction.

The real distinction may be either absolute, as in the three ways just enumerated, or modal. The modal distinction seems to have been employed by St. Thomas but is not fully discussed by him or even by his commentators. The question of modal distinction in Thomism requires further study, if only because of the multiplicity of meanings associated with the term MODE. Briefly, whereas the unqualified or real absolute distinction, as has been seen, obtains, for example, between Peter and Paul in the same species and between Peter and Fido in different species, the modal distinction, of which there are two types, holds (1) between a thing and its mode of being or acting or (2) between two modes of the same thing (ST 1a, 85.4; 1a, 5.5; 1a2ae, 27.6; *C. gent.* 3.97, 100). To illustrate the two types of modal distinction Thomists give examples such as (1) the distinction between Socrates and his being seated and (2) that between his being seated and his being in prison (JOHN OF ST. THOMAS, *Ars logica*, 2.2.3).

More significantly, the distinction, drawn in natural philosophy, between a CONTINUUM and its actual indivisibles is a modal distinction and, analogously, the distinction, drawn in metaphysics, between an essence and its act of SUBSISTENCE is also modal. In each case the latter term is in its own way an intrinsic term and not a part. The actual INDIVISIBLE, not being itself a continuum, is not a part of the continuum; yet it is the point of both continuance and termination of any such continuous part with respect to the next part; thus it renders each part unmixed with and impenetrable by the next (Aristotle, *Phys.* 527a 10–16; Aquinas, *In 6 phys.* 1.5). The distinction between an essence and subsistence as its intrinsic term is a real modal distinction, whereas the distinction between an essence and its act of EXISTENCE, which in some sense can be called a real extrinsic term or completion outside the line of essence, is a real absolute distinction.

In the Thomistic theory of real distinction, the separation of two objects is a sufficient but not a necessary sign that a real distinction obtains between those objects. An object may be a PRINCIPLE rather than a THING. Real principles, e.g., primary matter and merely informing substantial form (*forma informans*), are really distinct, though neither can exist apart from the other (*see* MATTER AND FORM). As a cardinal example, the essence of a creature and its existence are really distinct for St. Thomas; yet this does not mean that they can be separated, even by the absolute power of God, so that, absurdly, the essence would somehow be without existence and the existence would somehow be without its being the existence of something. Clearly, then, St. Thomas does not mean that essence and existence are two things (*De ver.* 27.1 ad 8; *De pot.* 7.7).

GILES OF ROME, however, in placing a real distinction between the creature's essence and its existence, goes so far as to say that they are distinct "as two things" (*In 1 sent.* 4.4.1; *Theoremata de esse et essentia* 9–). F. SUÁREZ, in reaction (*Disp. meta.* 31), rejects any real distinction between the essence and the existence of a creature, insisting that there is not even a modal distinction between them, as he reports Scotus, HENRY OF GHENT, and Domingo de SOTO to have held (*Disp. meta.* 31.1.11; 31.6; 31.10.2). There is only a distinction of reason with a foundation in reality (31.6.23, 24).

Distinction of Reason. The rational distinction, or distinction of reason, is of two sorts: the lesser of the two is titled the distinction of the reason reasoning, because it originates exclusively in the mind that understands or reasons; hence it is called also the distinction of reason without a foundation in reality. The greater is titled the distinction of the reason (or object) reasoned about, because it has a double foundation, viz, in the reasoning mind and in the thing affording rational analysis. It is to be noted that the word reason (*ratio*) does not mean quite the same in the titles of the two rational distinctions: in the former case it has the more usual formal or mental

sense; in the latter, the more peculiarly scholastic usage of object or objective content.

Thomistic scholarship bases its division of the distinction of reason on St. Thomas, who, treating of God (*De pot.* 7.6; *C. gent.* 1.35), insists that the names for His attributes are not synonyms. Though signifying the one Being, they signify different intelligible contents (*non secundum eandem rationem*)—hence the distinction of reason reasoned about; but, since the divine intellect is always in act, the distinction between God's intellect and His act of intellection is merely one between ways of signifying (ST 1a, 41.4 ad 3)—hence the distinction of reason reasoning.

The foundation of the distinction of reason reasoning is extrinsic to the thing being distinguished. Yet it seems to be more than the illusion of a distinction, caused by the mere repetition of a verbal or mental term (formal concept), as G. VÁZQUEZ and Suárez maintain. For example, there is a distinction of reason reasoning between the object that is subject and the object that is predicate in either of the following two propositions, "Man is man" and "Man is a rational animal," but this posits not the least nonidentity intrinsic to the object or objective concept "man." Yet that object, precisely as an object of the reason, presents to the reason a duality or distinction resulting from its extrinsic comparison to the two moments of the reason itself in taking that same object materially as subject and formally as predicate. Thus the intellect sees the object "man" as subject to be extrinsically affected by the rational condition of being subject, and sees the same object as predicate to be extrinsically affected by the rational condition of being predicate. This is an objective duality, not a mere doubling of formal concepts, and it is enough to find between "man" and "man" both the distinction of reason reasoning and the radical relation of reason, that of identity. Accordingly, neither distinction nor relation of reason posits in the object any intrinsic difference in intelligibility. The distinction of reason reasoning is not a distinction between objective contents intrinsically taken as such.

The distinction of reason reasoned about, however, is just such a distinction. Its mental foundation is the mind's passage from potency to act through a series of concepts such that not all the features revealed in one objective concept are revealed in the other. Thus the successive essential predicates of one and the same subject reveal progressively more actuality about the subject. For example, in the PORPHYRIAN TREE, for Socrates the predicates "body," "living," "animal," and "man" are all distinct from each other and from Socrates—whom they, in act, are—by a distinction of reason reasoned about (ST 1a, 85.3). Because they all indeed are Socrates in point of fact, there is no real distinction between them. Or, even when the objective concepts cannot be thus ordered in a categorical or predicational series of mental progress, so long as each brings out features that the other does not, they are in diverse respects in a potency-act relationship to each other.

Later Thomists speak of two sorts of distinction of reason reasoned about, the major and the minor. The distinction just given between the predicates or so-called metaphysical grades of the same being illustrates the major distinction. It obtains between two objective concepts, i.e., objective contents or reasons, one of which necessarily implies the other, but not vice versa; e.g., all instances of man are instances of animal, but not conversely. The minor distinction of reason reasoned about holds between two objective contents, each of which necessarily implies the other without simply being intelligibly the other, e.g., 5 + 7 and 12.

Analogously, some contemporary Thomists see degrees even within the distinction of reason reasoning. Between subject and predicate in the proposition "Man is man" they see a minor distinction of reason reasoning, but between *definitum* and *definiens* in the definitional proposition "Man is a rational animal" they see a major distinction of reason reasoning. The former would thus be of more rhetorical, the latter of more logical, significance (*Material Logic of John of St. Thomas* 618, n.14).

Scotistic Formal Distinction. Speaking doxographically, Suárez places the famous Scotistic "actual formal distinction from the nature of the thing" as midway between the lesser real or modal distinction and the greater distinction of reason, that of reason reasoned about. Hence it is frequently called the intermediate distinction. It was surely one of the features of his teaching that earned for John DUNS SCOTUS the title of Subtle Doctor. He was not the originator but the perfecter of the "formal distinction from the nature of the thing" or "on the side of the thing (*a parte rei*)." Like the Thomistic distinction of reason reasoned about, it seems to have arisen first in theological contexts out of an epistemological need to safeguard the objectivity of human concepts that express partial insights into a nature rich in intelligibility, such as that of God. These two distinctions in fact seem to have a common origin in GILBERT DE LA PORRÉE; but by the time of Henry of Ghent (*Quodl.* 5.6 L), a "distinction of intention" is spoken of as obtaining between two intentions or conceptual contents by reason of the fact that the thing, though unaffected by any actual distinction or composition, has the capacity or "virtue by its very nature" of giving rise to these concepts of formally different content (*see* INTENTIONALITY; SPECIES, INTENTIONAL).

It is to be noted that Thomists also commonly speak of a virtual distinction in the thing as grounding the objectivity of the distinction of reason reasoned about. The difference is precisely the virtuality and nonactuality of the distinction in the thing and its having been rendered actual by the mind in the act of drawing the distinction between those aspects that the thing affords (*In 1 sent.* 2.1.3; *De ente* ch. 3; Cajetan, *In ST* 1a, 39.1). This part of the Thomistic theory of distinction parallels the Thomistic theory of the universal; i.e., the nature as in a plurality of individuals is not actually but virtually one, and it is rendered positively and actually one by the abstractive power of the mind. In both areas the mind has a more existentially actualizing, unifying role in the school of St. Thomas than in the school of Duns Scotus.

In controversy with Henry of Ghent, Scotus does not deny Henry's intentional distinction but attempts, by means of the doctrine of objective intentions that he borrowed from AVICENNA and that he calls "formalities" or "real reasons," to ground Henry's actual distinction between intentions in an actual distinction or distinctness between these formalities or "somethings" (*In 7 meta.* 19.5), viz, one that already obtains between them in the thing anterior to the mind's attending to them. There is a one-to-one correspondence between the essential perfections of the thing and the mind's intentions of them. Because of its actuality on the part of the thing, the Scotistic distinction is not the virtual distinction of Thomists and of other scholastics; nor is it the consequent distinction of reason reasoned about, rendered actual only in the mind; nor is it a modal distinction, since the distinction is formal, i.e., obtains between two formal perfections, not between a form and its mode or intrinsic term. Being both actual and formal, the distinction falls between the real modal distinction and the distinction of reason reasoned about. It is closer to the real distinction in being actual in the thing, though the formalities are said to be neither things nor parts of things, but closer to the rational distinction in being intended, like the virtual distinction, to supply a foundation for it.

Scotus sees this as the only way to avoid rendering the predicate concepts all synonymous (or, what is the same thing, fictitious) in their claim to supply any advance in knowledge one over the other in the categorical series or Porphyrian tree. It is also the only way of avoiding what would be worse, i.e., rendering the predicates expressive of the divine attributes as fictions too (*Op. Oxon.* 1.8.4.18). The actuality in reality of this distinction between formalities is thus, for Scotus, the ultimate bulwark against NOMINALISM and hence the only guarantee of the mind's possibility of developing a SCIENCE (*SCIENTIA*) of metaphysics and of theology. From the standpoint of doxography and doctrinal coherence, the reason for this stand is Scotus's necessary coupling (in the Platonic tradition) of perfection and positive unity: if an ontological PERFECTION, be it a metaphysical grade of the essence of Socrates or an attribute of God, were not to have a degree of positive UNITY within its essence, then that perfection would simply not be in the essence. Consequently, the fullness and integrity of the essence would be destroyed. These formalities, it is asserted, are actually distinct from each other as metaphysical perfections, because each of them in itself has a "positive unity less than numeric" (*In 7 Meta.* 19.5). This position in metaphysics closely parallels the doctrine of the plurality of forms in the philosophy of nature (*see* FORMS, UNICITY AND PLURALITY OF).

Thomists distinguish between the substance, as it were, of a unit, or something positive on the part of an entity that is one, and something negative on the part of the formal element that unity adds to the entity, i.e., the negation of division (*De ver.* 1.1). Now there may be many ways of negating division without there corresponding to each such negation a positive entitative unit (*In 1 sent.* 19.4.1 ad 2; 24.1.3; ST 1a, 11.1 ad 2; John of St. Thomas, *Ars logica* 2.3.3). Hence there does not have to correspond to each of the mind's units of thought, or intentions—formed as they are implicitly or explicitly by negation of division (i.e., by abstraction or by precision)—something positively one in the nature of the thing.

Among Scotus's most able early disciples, Francis of Meyronnes elaborated the theory still further and extended its application, whereas WILLIAM OF ALNWICK rejected it in its radical testing ground, the realm of the divine ideas. Many modern Scotists tend to accommodate the actual formal distinction to the virtual distinction.

Bibliography: Thomistic. THOMAS AQUINAS, ST, ed. T. GILBY et al. (New York 1964–) 1:113–119; 2:220–221, notes on distinction. JOHN OF ST. THOMAS, *The Material Logic,* tr. Y. R. SIMON et al. (Chicago 1955) 2.3, "On the Distinctions of Reasoned and Reasoning Reason, and on the Corresponding Unities," 76–88; 3.3, "Whether Formal Unity, as Distinct from Singular Unity, Belongs to the Nature Prior to the Operation of the Intellect," 102–114; 3.6, "Whether in any Nature Whatsoever Metaphysical Degrees are Distinguished only according to a Distinction of Reason, or Whether Their Distinction Results from the Nature of the Thing," 130–140; and 618, n. 14. R. GARRIGOU-LAGRANGE, *God: His Existence and His Nature,* tr. B. ROSE, 2 v. (St. Louis 1934–36) 2:21–32; ch. 2; epilogue, 548–558. J. GREDT, *Elementa philosophiae Aristotelico-Thomisticae,* ed. E. ZENZEN, 2 v. (13th ed. Freiburg 1961). B. S. LLAMAZON, "Suppositional and Accidental Esse: A Study in Bañez," *The New Scholasticism* 39 (1965), esp. 184–187. B. MILLER, *The Range of Intellect* (London 1961), app. Scotistic and Suarezian. M. J. GRAJEWSKI, *The Formal Distinction of Duns Scotus* (Washington 1944). B. JANSENS, "Beiträge zur geschichtlichen Entwicklung der Distinctio Formalis," *Zeitschrift für katholische Theologie* 53 (1929) 317–344, 517–544. A. B. WOLTER, *The Transcendentals and Their Function in the Metaphysics of Duns Scotus* (Washington 1946); "The Realism of Scotus," *Journal of Philosophy* 59 (1962) 725–736. F. SUÁREZ, *On the Various Kinds of Distinctions,* tr. with introd. C. VOLLERT (Milwaukee 1947), disp. 7 of *Disputationes Metaphysicae.* A. B. WOLTER, "The Formal Distinction," in *John Duns Scotus, 1265–1965,* ed. J. K. RYAN and B. M. BONANSEA (Studies in Philosophy and the History of Philosophy; Washington 1965) 45–60.

[J. J. GLANVILLE]

DISTRIBUTISM

The theory that personal freedom belongs to man by his nature and that this freedom, especially in the political and economic fields, can be safeguarded only if there is widespread personal ownership of all forms of property, particularly of productive property. In this form distributism has special links with Catholic social thought, and in the main, its principal English adherents were Catholics, although it was supported also by a few non-Catholics headed by A. J. Penty. As an organized force it was represented by the Distributist League under G. C. Heseltine. In the U.S., non-Catholics such as Herbert Agar, Ralph Borsodi, and O. E. Baker were its best-known advocates. Among American Catholics, distributist ideas had only limited influence within other movements such as the CATHOLIC WORKER and the National Catholic Rural Life Conference.

The main objects of the distributist attack were large concentrations of wealth; capitalism, which was seen as the rule of the moneylender; and industrialism, seen as the rule of the machine. To combat these evils, the distributists urged the revival of small-scale family farming, small units in trade and industry, and the encouragement of the craftsman. They attracted many who were shocked by the mass unemployment of the 1920s and 1930s, alarmed at the growth of monopoly, or fearful of the depersonalizing influence of the modern factory.

The origins of the movement were varied. In order of time, the first proponent was Hilaire BELLOC, who held that modern politics were of their nature corrupt and that modern political practice would lead inevitably to the "servile state." In such a state peoples' lives would be controlled by a clique of wealthy men. Belloc held that industrial capitalism was a direct product of the Protestant revolt and could be defeated by Catholic principles linked with the agrarian way of life. G. K. CHESTERTON's writings introduced these ideas to a large number of readers. The emphasis on the importance of the person and of the small unit is found throughout his works. His own contribution was an attack on the materialism of the 19th century. Eric GILL brought to the movement a hatred of mass production and a love for the craftsman who could develop his personality through his work. Under his influence there were founded communities of craftsmen and farmers, which in time either failed or adopted modern methods. Only one group, a farming group at Laxton, survived World War II. Vincent MCNABB, OP, emphasized the social evil of poverty and the love of ordinary people. His solution was to take the poor out of the slums and give them the opportunity of a full life on the land, thus using untilled acres to solve the problems of unemployment, overcrowded cities, and slum life.

In addition to the practical aspect of the movement represented by the communities of craftsmen, a back-to-the-land movement was launched by the debate over distributism. In the 1930s this was a much needed movement, although it was unfortunate that it was a return to primitive agriculture. Of those who went back to the land, few survived for long, and most of those who did developed into modern farmers using the very techniques so often attacked by the agricultural wing of the distributists. The distributists attacked many real evils and played a part in making public opinion aware of the need for social reform. But it must be recorded, too, that their distrust of central government and their hatred of party politics diverted part of a generation of intelligent people into a dream-world and kept them out of politics and government. Moreover, distributism presented an interpretation of Catholic social doctrine that was alien to the outlook of the times and became a barrier between the faith and the masses. It could be argued that the British Catholic community has only begun to free itself from restrictions imposed by the brilliant work of Chesterton and Belloc.

Bibliography: J. M. CLEARY, *Catholic Social Action in Britain: 1909–1959* (Oxford 1961). G. P. MCENTEE, *The Social Catholic Movement in Great Britain* (New York 1927). *The Cross and the Plough*, ed. H. ROBBINS, (Sutton Coldfield, Eng. 1934–39). J. F. CRONIN, *Catholic Social Principles* (Milwaukee 1950). The chief periodical of the movement appeared successively as *Eye Witness* (London 1911–13), *New Witness* (1912–23), *G. K.'s Weekly* (1925–38), and *Weekly Review* (1938–46).

[R. P. WALSH]

DITCHLING, GUILD OF ST. JOSEPH AND ST. DOMINIC

The Guild of St. Joseph and St. Dominic Ditchling was comprised of a group of professional artists and craftsmen who left London between 1912 and 1914 to start fresh in Ditchling, an Old World village ten miles north of Brighton, Sussex. They attempted to counteract what they considered the dehumanizing influence of industrialism. Led by the sculptor Eric Gill, who had become a Catholic earlier; the poet-handprinter Hilary

Pepler, who was guided to Catholicism by Vincent MCNABB, OP; and the calligrapher Edward Johnston, who remained an Anglican and later withdrew from Ditchling. The community was organized under the rules of the Dominican Third Order and of the guild of craftsmen they had formulated. A farm was bought, and in one field a chapel, where the Dominican Little Office was sung daily, and workshops, where sculptor, woodcarver, weaver, carpenter, printer, silversmith, and others plied their crafts, were built. Each family remained independent and had its own house, but the craftsmen assisted each other in their work. Ideally they were to be self–sustaining and independent of the industrial world, but in effect they depended largely on selling their work to those who could afford hand–made goods. Their economic resources became confused, and in 1924, when Gill decided, against McNabb's advice, to depart for Wales with half the community, misunderstanding inevitably arose. A few years later, when Pepler partially mechanized St. Dominic's Press and took on a non–Catholic apprentice, he was expelled from the guild, though he remained on the Common and on friendly terms with the members.

At its height the guild's membership included David Jones, Desmond Chute, Valentine Kilbride, Dunstan Pruden, and Philip Hagreen—all well-known artists. Ditchling was visited by BELLOC, CHESTERTON, and other leading Catholic thinkers who together with the members articulated the social principles of THOMAS AQUINAS, LEO XIII, Maritain, and others, and made Ditchling an important center of Catholic social theory and practice for several decades. The guild was disbanded in 1989.

Bibliography: C. PEPLER, "H.D.C.P.," *Catholic World* 178 (March 1954) 445–450. H. D. C. PEPLER, *The Hand Press* (Ditchling 1953). *The Aylesford Review* (Spring 1965), H. D. C. PEPLER commemorative No., with articles by B. SEWELL et al.

[C. PEPLER]

DIVES IN MISERICORDIA

Pope John Paul II's second encyclical was issued November 30, 1980. *Dives in misericordia* (DM), "Rich in Mercy," is properly read as a continuation of the first encyclical, *Redemptor Hominis* (RH). While RH is devoted to Jesus Christ as the one who "fully reveals man to himself," DM turns to Christ as the one who makes known the Father, who reveals to humans "the countenance of the 'Father of mercies and God of all comfort'" (DM 1). Christ is at once the New Adam and the icon of the Father, fully human and fully divine. The perspectives of "anthropocentrism" and "theocentrism" are not at all antithetical; rather, "the Church, following Christ, seeks to link them up in human history, in a deep and organic way'' (DM 1). For John Paul this connection is ''perhaps the most important'' of the teachings of Vatican II. And because ''in the present phase of the Church's history we put before ourselves as our primary task the implementation of the doctrine of the great Council'' (DM 1), we readily see how RH and DM, standing together at the beginning of the pontificate, signal John Paul's intent to extend the reception of the council.

Dives in misericordia unfolds the revelation of divine mercy in salvation history through eight chapters, beginning with the biblical message of compassion and moving toward the mission of the contemporary Church to put mercy into practice. Chapter 4 is an extended reflection upon the parable of the prodigal son, and represents perhaps the symbolic heart of the text. The younger son ''in a certain sense is the man of every period'' (DM 5), and the human father of the story of course reflects the divine Father, whose ''readiness to receive the prodigal children who return to His home'' is ''infinite'' and ''inexhaustible'' (DM 13). Mary the mother of Jesus represents a special biblical manifestation of divine mercy in action, as she sings in the Magnificat of God's mercy that is ''from generation to generation.'' These words of hers ''have a prophetic content that concerns not only the past of Israel but also the whole future of the People of God on earth'' (DM 10). Mary and the other figures of salvation history all point to Christ, who ''by becoming the incarnation of the love that is manifested with particular force with regard to the suffering, the unfortunate, and sinners, makes present and thus more fully reveals the Father, who is God 'rich in mercy''' (DM 3).

Following Christ, who taught, ''Blessed are the merciful, for they shall obtain mercy,'' the Church is called to show that humans not only receive and experience the mercy of God but are likewise to practice mercy toward others. It is not enough for personal and social relationships to be governed solely by the measure of justice; ''mercy becomes an indispensable element for shaping mutual relationships between people'' (DM 14). Only through the exchange of mercy and compassion can the essential value and dignity of the person be preserved and more deeply experienced. The very mission of the Church is to be an effective sign (''sacrament,'' according to Vatican II) in the world of the compassion and love of God the Father. ''The Church herself must be constantly guided by the full consciousness that in this work it is not permissible for her, for any reason, to withdraw into herself. The reason for her existence is, in fact, to reveal God, that Father who allows us to 'see' Him in Christ'' (DM 15).

Bibliography: For the text of *Dives in misericordia*, see: *Acta Apostolicae Sedis* 72 (1980) 1176–1232 (Latin); *Origins* 10, no. 26 (December 11, 1980): 401, 403–416 (English); *The Pope Speaks* 26 (1981): 20–58 (English). For a commentary on *Dives in misericordia*, see: A. DULLES, *The Splendor of Faith: The Theological Vision of Pope John Paul II* (New York 1999).

[M. PELZEL]

DIVINATION

The art or practice of foreseeing or foretelling future events or of discovering hidden or secret knowledge. Divination goes back to prehistoric times and in numerous and various forms has worldwide distribution. At all cultural levels, some kinds of divination, such as astrology, crystal gazing, and palmistry, continue to flourish even in mature modern civilizations. It is convenient, following the example of Cicero (*De divinatione* 1.1i and 2.26) to distinguish two main categories in divination, the natural or intuitive and the artificial or inductive. In practice, however, there is considerable overlapping in this division.

Natural Divination. Among its various forms, divination based on dreams (oneiromancy) and that based on oracles (chresmology) are especially important. An elaborate system of interpretation of dreams was developed among the ancient Greeks in which time, place, and content all entered as factors in the symbolical explanation. The extant treatise of Artemidorus of Daldis (late 2d cent. A.D.) on the interpretation of dreams (*Oneirocritica*) is an example of this kind of literature. Ordinary dreams all had meaning, but particular weight was given to dreams occurring in temple incubation.

Oracles in the strict sense were the utterances of a seer, prophet, or prophetess in a state of trance or ecstasy; therefore, under divine influence or possession. The utterances, in fact, were regarded as coming directly from the invoked divinity. Since many, if not most of these utterances, were unintelligible, or at least vague and ambiguous, skilled interpreters of oracles became necessary and formed an influential class of specialists in religion. The oracles of Delphi given by the Pythia or priestess of Apollo were especially significant, as were also the utterances ascribed to the legendary sibyls, the Sibyl of Erythrae in Asia Minor and the Sibyl of Cumae near Naples being the most famous. Collections of such oracles were made and were consulted in times of crisis under the direction of expert diviners. The *Sibylline Books* mentioned by Vergil and others—not to be identified with the extant work of the same name—constituted such a collection.

Artificial, or Inductive, Divination. This kind of divination, which assumes a number of different forms, is based primarily on the observation and interpretation of certain actions of men, animals, or other living beings, and on human contacts with or employment of certain inanimate objects. The following list is not exhaustive, but includes the more significant and characteristic types. In some instances the term alone is sufficient, as it is self-explanatory.

Ornithomancy. Divination based on the flight, cries, and eating of various species of birds, and especially on deviations from the habitual in such cases, was a very important and influential type. Among the Romans, it was made an official part of the state religion. The College of Augurs was one of the oldest and most significant of Roman religious institutions. No public act was undertaken without consulting the auspices. Besides ornithomancy, there are methods of divination based also on the actions of fish, reptiles, and bees.

Cledonomancy. Divination by observation of human signs, actions, or utterances, is also a very significant type. Special importance was attached to sneezing, twitching of the hands or other members, and chance utterances or exclamations. The utterances of children, quite unconscious of deeper implications of what they said, were solemnly interpreted. Chiromancy or palmistry may be included under this general class of signs or omens.

Extispicy. Divination based on the examination of the entrails of animals was a widespread type, familiar through the liver divination (hepatoscopy) borrowed by the Romans from the Etruscans, who brought it to Italy from the Orient. It was a common form of divination in ancient Mesopotamia. Frequent animal sacrifices made this type of divination easily possible and at the same time led to its elaboration. The Romans always regarded the Etruscans as experts in hepatoscopy.

Pyromancy, or Empyromancy. This is divination based on the observation of the actions of wood, bone, eggs, flour, or incense when thrown on a sacrificial fire, or less formally, on any fire, and also on the shape of the flame, curling of the smoke, and similar phenomena. Omoplatoscopy or scapulimancy involved the observation and interpretation of changes in color, especially in the white shoulder blade of a sheep or other animal when placed above a fire.

Hydromancy. This is divination by water. The actions of springs and fountains were observed as offerings were thrown into them. If the offerings did not sink, this was regarded as a very bad sign. Hydromancy was more commonly practiced with a dish or a basin (lecanomancy) in which the actions of globules of oil or the eddies produced by dropping a pebble in the water were carefully observed. Catoptromancy, or mirror divination, is closely related. It was often used as a substitute for hydromancy. It was employed also, especially with the accompaniment of magic formulas, in necromancy.

Cleromancy. Divination by lots has a very wide distribution and assumes many forms. In addition to the casting of dice, one finds astragalomancy (divination with knuckle bones), axinomancy (observation of vibrations of an ax hurled into a post), sphondulomancy (divination by spindles), rhabdomancy (divination by rods or arrows), divination by oscillation of a suspended ring, rotation of a ball or sphere, and similar means. Geomancy can be included here also. It is a form of divination mentioned in antiquity, but especially common among the Arabs and medieval Latin writers under Arabic influence, in which points were marked off and lines or figures drawn, originally in sand, which were then interpreted according to definite rules. The drawing of lots inscribed with letters or formulas was very common, as was also the related practice of placing one's finger at random at a verse in Homer or Vergil (rhapsodomancy), and applying its apparent message to the question at issue (*see* SORTES HOMERICAE, VERGILIANAE, BIBLICAE).

Meteorological Divination. This was concerned with the interpretation of lightning flashes and strokes, shooting stars, meteorites, and earthquakes, as also with monstrous human or animal births, all these phenomena being regarded as portents of evil or major change, especially in the state.

Astrology. Mathematical divination as applied to the planets and the stars and their supposed influence on the lives of men had been developed in the Near East and spread throughout the Greco-Roman world with further elaboration after the conquests of Alexander the Great. Because of its special character and importance, it is treated in separate articles (*see* ASTROLOGY; HOROSCOPES).

In Judaism. The religion of Yahweh could not countenance divination. Hence throughout the OT there are stern prohibitions against it and denunciations of it as an evil (cf., Dt 18.9–14; Lv 19.26; Is 44.25; Jer 14.14; 27.8; Ez 13.6, 9, 23). The whole Biblical milieu, however, from Egypt to Babylonia practiced divination in numerous and elaborate forms, and the prophets, especially, found it necessary to fulminate against it not only among the masses but also at the courts of the kings of Juda and Israel. The lots involved in the mysterious URIM AND THUMMIM were always regarded as being permitted by and under the control of Yahweh. Postbiblical Judaism did not look with favor on divination, at least in strictly orthodox circles. Biblical sanction was claimed for divination from the cup, as it is called, and also for the rare and solemn divination by the sacred name of Yahweh. In cabalistic and popular Judaism under the influence of non-Jewish environment, however, certain forms of divination were practiced that were not originally or characteristically Jewish in any way.

Christianity and Divination. Like Judaism, Christianity could not tolerate divination, yet in its mission to the Gentiles as well as to the Jews it found itself in a world steeped in all phases of polytheism, divination, and other forms of superstition. Hence from the time of the New Testament on, the Church had to combat divination in public and private life, in both of which divination was inextricably connected with every kind of activity. The Fathers of the Church found it necessary to attack divination in all its forms and to warn converts against slipping into their old ways, especially in times of crisis. The opposition ranges from the learned expositions of Clement of Alexandria and St. Augustine to popular sermons. Pagan emperors had repeatedly condemned many aspects of divination that they regarded as dangerous to the state. But, beginning with Constantine the Great, Christian emperors were much more severe, and Theodosius the Great, at the end of the 4th century, forbade divination and attached heavy penalties to its practice. Certain Greco-Roman practices, as well as Celtic and Germanic ones, were eradicated slowly only by persistent ecclesiastical legislation and preaching; and a few Christian usages, adopted under pagan influence, such as the biblical *sortes,* lasted until very recently, despite ecclesiastical prohibition. A Christianized form of astrology had a vogue even as late as the Renaissance, but disappeared with the rise of modern astronomy.

In Islam and Other Living Religions. Ibn Khaldun (A.D. 1332–1406) listed the forms of divination employed in Islam, the most important being geomancy and gematria. Islam, however, shows considerable diversity in divination, owing to the influences of the institutions of peoples converted to Islam or to the general environment of the Islamic groups. Buddhism, Hinduism, and other religions of the Middle and Far East give an important place to divination. With these religions, however, much more than in the case of Islam, there is an intimate connection between divination in its various forms and astrology. Finally, divination is found among the existing primitive cultures, but its range is limited, and, ordinarily, magic plays the dominant role.

See Also: DELPHI, ORACLE OF; MAGIC; SIBYLLINE ORACLES.

Bibliography: A. S. PEASE, *The Oxford Classical Dictionary,* ed. M. CARY et al. (Oxford 1949) 292–293, with good bibliog. P. COURCELLE, *Reallexikon für Antike und Christentum,* ed. T. KLAUSER (Stuttgart 1941 [1950]–) 3:1235–51, an excellent article, with copious bibliog. R. BROUILLARD and H. CAZELLES, *Catholicisme. Hier, aujourd'hui et demain,* ed. G. JACQUEMET (Paris 1947) 3:905–910, with bibliog. H. J. ROSE et al., *Encyclopedia of Religion and Ethics,* ed. J. HASTINGS, 13 v. (Edinburgh 1908–27) 4:775–830, a series of articles giving worldwide coverage. T. HOPFNER, ''Mantike,'' *Paulys Realenzyklopädie der klassischen Altertumswissenschaft,* ed. G. WISSOWA et al. (Stuttgart 1893–) 14.1 (1928) 1258–88. A. BOUCHÉ-LECLERCQ, C. DAREMBERG, and E. SAGLIO, *Dictionnaire des antiquités grecques et romaines d'après les textes et les monuments,* 5 v. in 9 (Paris 1877–1919; repr. Graz 1962–63) 2.1:292–319, old, but excellent. T. ORTALAN, *Dictionnaire de théologie catholique,* ed. A. VACANT et al., 15 v. (Paris 1903–50; Tables générales 1951–) 4.2:1441–55, with bibliog. *Encyclopedic Dictionary of the Bible,* tr. and adap. by L. HARTMAN (New York 1963), from A. VAN DEN BORN, *Bijbels Woordenboek* 176–177. J. P. HYATT, ''Magic, Divination, and Sorcery,'' *Dictionary of the Bible,* J. HASTINGS and J. A. SELBIA, eds., 5 v. (Edinburgh 1963) 607–611. H. LECLERCQ, *Dictionnaire d'archéologie chrétienne et de liturgie,* ed. F. CABROL, H. LECLERCQ, and H. I. MARROU, 15 v. (Paris 1907–53) 4.1:1198–1212. R. LA ROCHE, *La Divination: Avec un supplément sur la superstition en Afrique Centrale* (Washington 1957).

[M. R. P. MCGUIRE]

DIVINE CHARITY, DAUGHTERS OF

(FDC, Official Catholic Directory #0790), a congregation with papal approbation founded in Vienna, Austria, in 1868 by Mother Franziska Lechner (1833 to 1894) for the purpose of engaging in educational and welfare work. Growing rapidly, the community soon spread into many countries in Europe and the Americas. In 1913 a small band of sisters went to the United States and established St. Mary's, a residence for business and professional women in New York City's mid-Manhattan area. In 1919 Arrochar Park, Staten Island, New York, became the site of the first American provincial house, academy, and novitiate. The sisters are engaged in education, nursing, catechetical centers, ministry to the homeless, and residences for women. The generalate is in Rome; the United States provincialate is in Staten Island, New York.

Bibliography: K. BURTON, *One Thing Needful: The Biography of Mother Franziska Lechner* (New York 1960).

[C. POCH/EDS.]

DIVINE COMPASSION, SISTERS OF THE

(Abbreviation: RDC, Official Catholic Directory #0970), founded in the Archdiocese of New York by Mother Mary Veronica Starr and Thomas S. Preston, vicar-general of the diocese, on July 2, 1886. Both the founders were prominent converts who for the previous 17 years had been collaborators, along with Catholic lay women and men, in a charitable organization known as The Association for Befriending Children and Young

Girls and in the supervision of its home, The House of the Holy Family, in New York City. In 1890 the sisters bought property in White Plains, N.Y. for a motherhouse and novitiate that became known as Good Counsel. There, in an expansion of their ministry of education with children and young girls, the sisters established an elementary school, high school and college (1923–1975). In 2001 the congregation numbers about 115 members and 50 lay associates and sponsors two high schools, an elementary school, a spiritual renewal center, a counseling center, a ministry with migrant workers and a ministry with the rural poor, all in the Archdiocese of New York. In addition, sisters serve in other elementary schools, high schools and colleges as well as hospitals, social service agencies and religious education programs.

[M. T. BRADY/A. V. FEELEY]

DIVINE LOVE, ORATORY OF

The source of a significant pre-Tridentine reform movement that originated in Genoa at the end of the 15th century. The oratory (Fraternita del divino amore sotto la protezione di San Girolamo) was founded by a jurisconsult, Ettore Vernazza, together with three other Genoese citizens, Giovanni Battista Salvago, Nicolo Grimaldi, and Benedetto Lomellino, and with the advice and inspiration of St. CATHERINE OF GENOA. According to its rule, approved by Leo X on March 24, 1514, membership was restricted to 36 laymen and four priests. The rule prescribed a fixed program of prayers, a weekly fast, monthly confession, and Communion four times a year (St. Catherine favored daily Communion; Vernazza and his wife, Bartolomea, received the Sacrament weekly). The objective of the oratory, however, was not restricted to self-sanctification, but included an energetic apostolate of charity. Members cared for orphans and delinquents, helped the poor, consoled imprisoned criminals, and attended the sick in hospitals. To facilitate their work throughout all classes of society, the names of the members of the oratory and its program were kept secret from others.

In 1499 Vernazza founded a hospital for incurables (Societas reductus incurabilium), the first of its kind in Italy. It was approved by the senate on Nov. 27, 1500, and privileged by Julius II and Leo X. Vernazza's part in its origin and organization is attested to by his daughter, Ven. Battista (1497–1587), in her "Lettera del padre e della madre" [Opere spirituali (Verona 1602) 4:1–14]. Two affiliate reform groups, La compagnia del Mandiletto and La compagnia di Gesù e Maria, were organized at Genoa by Vernazza and St. Catherine.

Similar oratories were founded at Milan, Florence, Verona, Lucca, Vicenza, Brescia, Faenza, Padua, Rome, and Naples. Though the Roman oratory, established in the Trastevere before 1515, was disbanded at the sack of Rome (1527), its spirit survived in the hospital for incurables of S. Giacomo in Augusta and in the reform measures championed by its members, such as Gian Matteo GIBERTI, reform bishop of Verona, St. CAJETAN (Gaetano da Thiene) and Gian Pietro Carafa (PAUL IV), founders of the Theatines, and Jacopo SADOLETO, Luigi Lippomano, and Gasparo CONTARINI.

Bibliography: P. PASCHINI, La beneficenza in Italia e le compagnie del divino amore . . . (Rome 1925); Tre ricerche sulla storia della chiesa nel cinquecento (Rome 1945). Dictionnaire de spiritualité ascétique et mystique. Doctrine et histoire, ed. M. VILLER et al. (Paris 1932–) 1:531–533, 2:316–325. P. TACCHI-VENTURI, Storia della Compagnia di Gesù in Italia, 2 v. in 4 (2d ed. Rome 1930–51) 1.2:25–42, contains the "Capitula fraternitatis Divini Amoris." CASSIANO DA LANGASCO, Gli ospedali degli incurabili (Genoa 1938). A. CISTELLINI, Figure della riforma pretridentina (Brescia 1948). A. BIANCONI, L'opere della compagnie del Divino Amore nella riforma cattolica (Città di Castello 1914). F. VON HÜGEL, The Mystical Element of Religion, 2 v. 2d ed. (New York 1923).

[E. D. MCSHANE]

DIVINE REDEEMER, SISTERS OF THE

(SDR, Official Catholic Directory #1020), a congregation with papal approbation founded in Niederbronn, Alsace, in 1849 by Elisabeth EPPINGER (Mother Alphonsa) to nurse the sick in their homes and to care for the poor. The community eventually spread through France, Germany, and Austria. By 1863 it was established in Hungary, and from that foundation the United States province of the Sisters of the Divine Redeemer later emerged. The community broadened its apostolate to include the education of youth and the care of orphans, the aged, and the infirm in charitable institutions. The congregation came to the United States in 1912 when four sisters from Sopron, Hungary, responded to the invitation of the Reverend Colman Kovats to work among the Hungarians of the Monongahela Valley in Pennsylvania. In the United States 170 sisters were engaged in teaching, healthcare, nursing, parish ministries and catechetical instruction. The general motherhouse is in Rome, Italy; the provincial headquarters, in Elizabeth, Pennsylvania.

Bibliography: W. FREISCHLAG, Lexikon für Theologie und Kirche, ed. J. HOFER and K. RAHNER, 10 v. (2d, new ed. Freiburg 1957–65) 7:951–52.

[M. A. VARGA/EDS.]

Coronation of King Mathias (Corvinus) by two angels, relief sculpture, Budapest, Hungary. (©Paul Almasy/CORBIS)

DIVINE RIGHT OF KINGS

A theory that flourished in the 16th and 17th centuries to explain and justify the source of political authority in the state. The divine right theory did not treat primarily of the nature or character of political authority. Rather, it maintained that the king possessed and exercised an authority granted directly by God to his person, not, as in medieval ideas, through the office of kingship or through a grant of the people. It came by the laws of God and of nature directly to the person of the king because he was born into the kingly succession.

The office of kingship in the Middle Ages had already been invested with a sacral character. Now this sacral character was transferred to the person of the king. The idea flourished in 17th-century England, where it was used by the Tory party in reaction against the execution of Charles I and as a defense of the king after the Restoration. On the Continent, it was used to defend the rapidly developing national monarchies. For if the king in his person had authority from the laws of God and nature, there could be no question of a right of the people to resist or to disobey that authority. The denial of any right of disobedience was essential to a monarchy presented with both internal religious divisions and dynastic aspirations. Also, at a time when the pope was exerting a universal spiritual and even temporal power over the heads of states, the idea of divine right put the kings of national states in a position to justify their authority as being equally divine with that of the pope.

The most fully developed and best known theories of divine right were those of James I of England and Sir Robert Filmer. James based his theory of the origin of authority on the conquest of William I. Robert Filmer traced the grant of authority back from the kings of England to the Hebrew patriarchs. But, for both, the source of authority was a direct grant by God to the person of the king.

The theory of divine right was vigorously opposed by the theologians BELLARMINE and SUÀREZ, who claimed that, though God was the ultimate source, the people were the proximate source of political authority. This idea of the people as the source of authority was supported by the vast majority of the Catholic theologians of the 17th century.

See Also: ABSOLUTISM; MONARCHY.

Bibliography: J. N. FIGGIS, *The Divine Right of Kings* (2d ed. Cambridge, Eng. 1914). J. W. ALLEN, *History of Political Thought in the Sixteenth Century* (3d rev. ed. New York 1957). C. H. MCILWAIN, *Encyclopaedia of the Social Sciences,* ed. E. R. SELIGMAN and A. JOHNSON, 15 v. (New York 1930–35) 5:176. R. FILMER, *Patriarcha and Other Political Works,* ed. P. LASLETT (Oxford 1949). JAMES I, ''The Trew Law of Free Monarchies,'' *Political Works* (Harvard Political Classics 1; Cambridge, Mass. 1918) 53–70.

[D. WOLF]

DIVINE SAVIOR, SISTERS OF THE

(SDS, Official Catholic Directory #1030), also known as the Salvatorian Sisters, a religious community with papal approbation, founded at Tivoli, outside Rome, Italy, in 1888. The founders were Franziskus Maria JORDAN (also founder of the SALVATORIAN fathers) and Baroness Theresia von Wüllenweber (later Mother Mary of the Apostles). Their purpose was to establish a missionary society to work in all parts of the world. In 1890 three sisters set out to begin a mission in India, and three years later others went to Ecuador. In 1894 the motherhouse was moved to Rome. Four sisters came to the United States in 1895 at the invitation of Archbishop Frederick Katzer of Milwaukee, Wisconsin. They took up nursing, caring for the sick and aged in their homes. As their numbers grew, the sisters were able to engage in other works and to conduct their own hospitals and schools. In the United States, the congregation is engaged in education, pastoral ministries, healthcare and care facilities for the aged. The United States provincial headquarters and novitiate are in Milwaukee, Wisconsin.

[M. C. VAN DE KAMP/EDS.]

DIVINE WORD, SOCIETY OF THE

(SVD, Official Catholic Directory #0420); a religious congregation founded, 1875 at Steyl, Holland, by Arnold JANSSEN, a priest of the German Diocese of Muenster. His original plan was for an institute of German secular priests to labor in the foreign missions; lay brothers, however, were soon included and even outnumbered the clerics for many years. At first the members took private vows and followed the rule of Dominican tertiaries. After the first general chapter (1884), a new rule recast the Steyl enterprise into a religious congregation with public vows; it was approved by the local ordinary (1889) and the Holy See (1905). The congregation then numbered 2,000 members and students and was established on five continents and the island of New Guinea. Foundations were made in South America (Argentina) in 1889; in West Africa (Togo) in 1892; in the United States, 1895; in New Guinea, 1896; in Japan, 1907; and in the Philippines, 1909. At the time of the founder's death in 1909, his society had been entrusted with mission territories containing 14 million persons.

Activities. Among the works of the society, mission and evangelization hold the chief place; to this work every member must feel himself called. Schools of all kinds are maintained. Special emphasis is placed on the training of a native clergy. From its earliest years, the society accepted recruits from its missions. In the field of science, the most notable achievements have been in anthropology, under the leadership of the world famous ethnologist, Wilhelm SCHMIDT. His work continues to be carried on by the priest-scientists who form the Anthropos Institute, which has international headquarters in Switzerland and publishes a quarterly journal, *Anthropos*. Divine Word missionaries have traditionally furthered the apostolate of the press; they maintain their own printing plants to disseminate Catholic literature, chiefly magazines and pamphlets. In this effort, major contributions have been made by the brothers, who are invaluable for their many technical skills.

Work in the United States. The first Divine Word missionaries to the United States were two brothers who were sent to solicit subscriptions for the society's publications. When others joined them (1897), the community settled on a farm near Shermerville (now Northbrook), just north of Chicago, Illinois. Here they opened St. Joseph's Technical School (Techny), which on Feb. 2, 1909, became the first Catholic foreign mission seminary in the United States. It was also the cradle of the nationwide CATHOLIC STUDENTS MISSION CRUSADE (CSMC), founded in 1918 by Clifford King, SVD. In the United States, the SVD houses are grouped into three provinces: Chicago (headquartered in Techny, Illinois), Southern (headquartered in St. Louis) and Western (headquartered in Los Angeles). The generalate is in Rome.

Bibliography: H. FISCHER, *Life of Arnold Janssen*, tr. P. M. LYNK (Techny, Ill. 1925).

[V. J. FECHER/EDS.]

DIVINE WORSHIP AND THE DISCIPLINE OF THE SACRAMENTS, CONGREGATION FOR

The Congregation for Divine Worship and the Discipline of the Sacraments, is the successor to two previously autonomous congregations: the Congregation of Rites and the Congregation for the Discipline of the Sacraments (established by Pius X on June 29, 1908) (for historical information, *see* RITES, CONGREGATION OF).

The general reform of the Roman Curia by Pope Paul VI in 1967 left the Congregation of Rites, founded in 1588, relatively unaffected. It retained its competence over the ordering of divine worship, in its pastoral and ritual aspects, for the Roman and other Latin rites. As a temporary arrangement, the revision of liturgical books and the carrying out of liturgical renewal, together with relations with episcopal conferences, were to be handled primarily by the still distinct CONSILIUM for the Implementation of the Constitution on the Sacred Liturgy.

A further step in reform was taken by the Pope on May 8, 1969, in the apostolic constitution *Sacra Rituum*. The original Congregation was divided into two congregations: the Congregation for Divine Worship, corresponding largely to the existing section for worship, and the Congregation for the Causes of Saints, which succeeded to the Congregation's competence over beatification and canonization, that is, what had been called since 1969 the judicial section.

The new Congregation for Divine Worship thus succeeded to the liturgical competence of the Congregation of Rites. In effect, however, it succeeded the Consilium, the actual work of which far out shadowed the section for worship within the Congregation of Rites. The membership of the Congregation for Divine Worship (and in large part its personnel) was derived from the Consilium: the cardinal members of the Consilium became members of the Congregation; the bishop members of the Consilium, for this occasion only, elected the seven bishop members of the Congregation from their number. The president of the Consilium, Cardinal Benno Gut, was named as the first prefect of the Congregation; Father (later Archbishop) Annibale Bugnini, the secretary of the Consilium, became the secretary of the Congregation. In 1970 the first body of consultors was appointed.

On July 11, 1975, Paul VI established a new Congregation for the Sacraments and Divine Worship by the apostolic constitution, *Constans nobis*. This was done by formally suppressing the two existing congregations, the Congregation for the Discipline of the Sacraments and the Congregation for Divine Worship, and uniting their functions. On April 5, 1984, John Paul II separated the congregation into two: Congregation for the Sacraments and Congregation for Divine Worship. Pursuant to the reorganization of the Roman Curia by John Paul II under the apostolic constitution, *Pastor Bonus* dated June 28, 1988, these two congregations were reconstituted as one under its present name, the Congregation for Divine Worship and the Discipline of the Sacraments.

The congregation's purview encompasses the regulation of the liturgy and the sacraments. In the area of liturgy, it is responsible for the preparation of typical editions of liturgical texts, and it works closely with episcopal conferences to ensure the accuracy of translations and adaptations. In the area of sacraments, it is principally concerned with resolving disciplinary and administrative questions, without prejudice to the right of the Congregation for the Doctrine of Faith to resolve doctrinal issues. Specifically, the congregation is concerned with questions of irregularities, impediments and validity in the administration of the sacraments of matrimony and holy orders. Where justified, it is authorized to grant indults and exemptions. The official publication of the congregation is a bimonthly journal, *Notitiae*.

[F. MCMANUS/EDS.]

DIVINI REDEMPTORIS

Divini Redemptoris, an encyclical of Pope PIUS XI dated March 19, 1937, establishes by its superscription *De communismo atheistico* and by its contents that the most fundamental objection of the Church to communism is its atheism. In the first part, after citing earlier papal pronouncements on communism beginning with a passage in the first encyclical of Pius IX, *Qui pluribus,* in 1846, and noting his own previous protests against persecutions in Russia, Mexico, and Spain, the pope justifies another solemn document on the subject with the observation that "the crisis, brought about by the cunning of revolutionaries, daily becomes more and more serious" (par. 6). Warnings against the deceit of communist leaders are repeated throughout the encyclical, which contains the injunction, "Since Communism is intrinsically evil, whoever wants to save Christianity and civilization from destruction must refrain from aiding it in the prosecution of any project whatever" (par. 60). In the immediate background was the success of European communists in winning the support of non-communist workers as a result of the united front policy ordered at the Seventh Congress of the Communist International in July of 1935. Their doctrine, "in the guise of a message of redemption for the poor" (par.8), was gaining hearers because of the world-wide economic depression of the time. The second part of the encyclical summarizes and condemns the communist system and movement but expresses paternal charity for the peoples of the Union of Soviet Socialist Republics.

More than half of the encyclical, which is the only one to treat comprehensively both the theory and tactics of communism, is devoted to a restatement of Christian social principles and an urgent exhortation to various groups to rebuild Western society on them. The central ideas of *Rerum novarum* and *Quadragesimo anno* are recalled in the third part, while the fourth part insists that an effective anti-communist program must be founded upon reasonable detachment from earthly goods, the precept of charity, and the application of commutative and social justice in the solution of economic and social problems. These virtues are emphasized as correctives for the evils brought about by the unrestricted competition of international finance capitalism deplored in other social encyclicals. The exposition of social justice as demanding from the individual "everything that is necessary for the common good" (par. 52) elucidates significantly this concept, employed earlier in *Quadragesimo anno*. In the final part of the encyclical, Catholics in various categories are given specific advice, warned against division, and urged to cooperate with one another; further, an appeal is addressed to all who believe in God and especially to heads of governments to join with the Church under the guardianship of St. Joseph in active opposition to atheistic communism and in social reforms to prevent its spread.

Bibliography: J. P. LERHINAN, *A Sociological Commentary on "Divini Redemptoris"* (Catholic University of America *Studies in Sociology* 17; Washington 1946). R. CALDERA, "International Social Justice in the Pontifical Documents," in *Pro Fide et Iustitia* (Berlin 1984) 795–808.

[J. LERHINAN]

DIVINO AFFLANTE SPIRITU

Encyclical of Pope PIUS XII concerning the advancement of biblical studies. The document is dated Sept. 30, 1943, feast of St. Jerome, patron of studies of the Bible. The present article treats of the contents of the encyclical, the circumstances leading to the document, its characteristics, and its effects.

Contents. The introduction states that the occasion of the encyclical is the 50th anniversary of the biblical encyclical of Pope Leo XIII, *PROVIDENTISSIMUS DEUS*, and declares that the purpose of the document is to encourage in the most opportune way further developments in biblical studies.

The first section is devoted to a historical summary of the teachings and activities of Leo XIII and succeeding popes concerning the study of the Bible. Emphasis is placed on the teaching of Leo XIII on the inerrancy of the Bible with reference to problems arising from the physical sciences and history, and on his establishment of the Biblical Commission. The remainder deals with the founding of the Pontifical Biblical Institute by Pius X, with the encyclical *SPIRITUS PARACLITUS* by Benedict XV, and with progress made during the previous half century in Catholic Biblical studies.

The second and more important part of the encyclical sets down a scientific program for biblical studies. It first cites recent discoveries in archeology, ancient history, linguistics, and other technical sciences contributing to a better understanding of the Bible. The pope encourages the furtherance of the scientific study of the Bible through the investigation and translation of the biblical texts in their original languages rather than in the traditional Latin Vulgate, and insists upon the importance of textual criticism to obtain the most accurate biblical texts. He defines the prime task of the biblical interpreter as the discovery of the literal sense of the Word of God, as intended by the inspired human author.

Unusually strong emphasis is placed on the importance of evaluating the literary forms used by ancient writers for a clearer understanding of the Bible. The Catholic commentator is warned that the study of the ancient literary forms "cannot be neglected without serious detriment to Catholic EXEGESIS." The pope urges the use of archeology, ancient history, and ancient literature as subsidiary sciences contributing to a better understanding of the Bible. The doctrinal section concludes on the positive note that the scientific method in Scripture studies, having already solved many difficulties of long standing and demonstrated the historical nature of the Bible, still affords promise of the solution of remaining difficulties.

The encyclical concludes with an assurance of liberty to Catholic Scripture scholars and with a request that the scholars be judged by all with the utmost charity. In conclusion the Holy Father exhorts bishops, priests, laity, and seminarians to use the Holy Bible for spiritual profit.

Circumstances. As the document itself states, the remote occasion for this encyclical was the considerable development in archeological, historical, and other technical fields during the decades preceding 1943. The encyclical lists (without further explanation) six areas of

scientific progress in biblical studies. An analysis of these six areas demonstrates why, in 1943, it was clear that the traditional fundamentalist approach to biblical study was insufficient and why a new and scientific approach to Bible study was necessary: (1) Archeology in Egypt, Mesopotamia, and in Palestine itself had developed with unparalleled rapidity after 1918 and had succeeded in rewriting in considerable detail the history of Egypt, of the Mesopotamian civilizations, and of Palestine itself. Excavations at Ur, Nippur, Nineveh, Babylon, Mari, Ras-Shamra, Byblos, Jericho, and Samaria, among other sites, had yielded much new information relating to the Bible. (2) The numerous monuments and written documents from the ancient Near East had shown parallels between the Bible and the literature of other ancient peoples. Other documents had greatly increased our knowledge of the history, the daily life, and the religious thought of the ancient world. (3) The discovery of papyri in Egypt had revealed much information concerning the daily life and language of the Egyptians in the first centuries of Christianity, and had led to the discovery of numerous biblical texts from as early as the 2d and 3d centuries after Christ. (4) The discovery and publication of new manuscripts of the Bible and of improved critical texts of the Greek New Testament had given scholars a closer approximation of the original texts of the Bible than had been available 50 years before. (5) An increasingly extensive and thorough study of patristic exegesis during the preceding 50 years had led to better knowledge of the texts and the intellectual characteristics of early exegetical schools in the Church. (6) The establishment (from many examples) of how ancient peoples spoke, narrated, and wrote had led to a greater appreciation (by modern students) of the concrete ways in which the writers of antiquity expressed their thoughts, and of the literary forms by which the Bible should be interpreted.

The progress in knowledge in these six areas in particular had already resulted in an increasing use, before 1943, of the scientific method by many Catholic exegetes, but at the same time had caused hesitation on the part of some concerning the propriety of using scientific means to interpret Sacred Scripture.

The opposition between traditional and scientific approaches to Bible studies was epitomized in a pamphlet written by an Italian priest, Dolindo Ruotolo (using the pseudonym Dain Cohenel), protesting strongly against the use of scientific, historical, and critical methods in the study and interpretation of Holy Scripture, particularly by the Pontifical Biblical Institute. This pamphlet was answered in a letter of the Biblical Commission dated Aug. 20, 1941, which, by its vindication of a scientific approach to biblical studies and its insistence on the primacy of the literal sense, was a significant antecedent of the *Divino afflante Spiritu.*

Characteristics. This encyclical can be described as positive in tone and liberalizing in effect. Its historical section does not dwell on the serious controversies over rationalism and modernism. They are treated as past issues, and Pius XII dwells upon the positive contributions of scientific research towards the solution of biblical difficulties. In this attitude the *Divino afflante Spiritu* differs from the previous Scriptural encyclicals of Leo XIII and Benedict XV. The encyclical is likewise liberalizing in that it removed the requirement that official Catholic Bible translations be from the Vulgate, stressed the fact that only a few biblical texts had been officially interpreted by the Catholic Church, and encouraged Scripture scholars to make full use of scientific means in studying and interpreting the Holy Bible.

Effects. Catholic exegetes received the *Divino afflante Spiritu* with profound gratitude. During the preceding 50 years they had been gradually improving their methods and principles. This encyclical was a vindication of the persevering work of the Dominican Father M. J. LAGRANGE in the employment of critical and historical approaches to biblical interpretation.

There was a significant return in the Church to the scientific study of the Bible. Although started by the Catholic Oratorian priest Richard Simon in 1678 and continued by the Catholic doctor Jean Astruc in 1753, this scientific approach had been the domain for nearly a century, almost exclusively, of rationalist scholars such as those of the Tübingen school. The encyclical put a decisive end to the crisis of Catholic exegetes who had been encountering difficulties in presenting an exegesis at the same time scientific and orthodox.

Modern Catholic biblical exegesis, which is both scientific and religious, was greatly furthered by this encyclical. The satisfaction of Pius XII with the new directions given by the *Divino afflante Spiritu* was demonstrated shortly before his death. On July 28, 1958, he sent a message to the first Catholic International Biblical Congress at Brussels. In that message Pius XII referred with gratification to the beneficial results of his encyclical of 15 years before.

Bibliography: POPE PIUS XII, "Divino afflante Spiritu," (Encyclical, Sept. 30, 1943) *Acta Apostolicae Sedis* 35 (1943) 297–326; English translation, *Rome and the Study of Scripture* (5th ed. rev. St. Meinrad, Ind. 1953) 79–107. A. BEA, "Divino afflante Spiritu," *Biblica* 24 (1943) 313–322. H. LEVIE, *The Bible, Word of God in Words of Men* (New York 1962) 3–199. R. B. ROBINSON, *Roman Catholic Exegesis since Divino Afflante Spiritu* (Decatur, GA, 1988). J. R. DONAHUE, "The Bible in Roman Catholicism since Divino Afflante Spiritu," *Word & World* 13 (1993) 404–13.

[J. F. WHEALON]

DIVINUM ILLUD MUNUS

An encyclical on the HOLY SPIRIT by LEO XIII, issued on May 9, 1897. It begins by emphasizing the unity of the three Divine Persons, who are not to be honored separately in divine worship, nor to be considered as acting separately in the work of sanctification. Accordingly, it treats of the mission of the Holy Spirit: His part in the Incarnation, His role as the soul of the Mystical Body of Christ (the Church), and His personal presence in the souls of the just. In those who will respond by a love of conformity to His divine operations, the Holy Spirit, the "life-giving Love," will perfect their "wonderful union" with God. The sequel to this encyclical is the *MYSTICI CORPORIS* of Pius XII.

Bibliography: LEO XIII, "Divinum illud munus" (encyclical, May 9, 1897), *Acta Sanctae Sedis* 29 (1896–97) 644–658, Eng. *Catholic Mind* 36 (May 8, 1938) 161–181.

[G. M. GREENEWALD]

DIVISION (LOGIC)

The name (Gr. διαίρεσις, Lat. *divisio*) for various mental operations or their expressions that have in common the consideration apart from each other of the several parts as a whole. As such the idea of division is analogical, having as many meanings as there are senses of WHOLE and PART. This analogicity is consequent not only upon the diversity of objective wholes, but also on the three types of mental act: simple APPREHENSION, JUDGMENT, and REASONING. The auxiliary or instrumental operations of division have a somewhat different sense according as they play their clarificatory role in conjunction with each of these mental acts.

Historically, division first appeared among the Greeks either as itself a mode of reasoning to a DEFINITION (PLATO) or as an operation preparatory to definition and to reasoning from the definition so obtained (ARISTOTLE). The scholastics elaborated with special care the nature and kinds of division as a clarification of the terms and contents of the concepts formed by simple apprehension.

Notion. What is usually meant by the word "division" is a kind of clarification of terms and concepts. The objective CONCEPT, i.e., the content of the concept, may be taken as a whole in several "physical" or natural senses of whole, or in the more properly logical sense of a universal. An illustration of the former class is the integral whole, man, as composed of the parts: head, trunk, and members. A natural division of this kind is, in a broad sense, logical because it is the consideration (and not the physical cutting) apart from each other of the several parts of a real or natural whole. But UNIVERSALS as such are properly logical wholes, and as such are divided into subjective parts, i.e., the potential subjects of which they are potentially the predicates, e.g., the division of triangle into equilateral, isosceles, and scalene, and the division of animal into man and brute. Dialectically or nominally, such a scientific division of a conceptual content is imitated or approximated by the division of a linguistic term into the several senses in which it is used. Such a preliminary investigative division that exploits the riches of a given language may be called a nominal division; it is usually taken as preparatory to the scientific division; but it often resembles and anticipates the sapiential division of an analogical universal whole, which does not have the unity of one objective meaning (*ratio*), into its several only proportionally unified meanings. The terminological divisions drawn from ordinary language and previous philosophical usage that constitute Aristotle's dictionary (*Metaphysics* bk. 5) anticipate such analogical divisions. The division of division is itself an analogical division.

With respect to extension and comprehension, in the light of a general theory of ANALYSIS AND SYNTHESIS, division in the strict sense of that of a logical whole, or universal concept, is the analysis of the extension of a concept. It is thus contrasted to collection (συναγωγή; see Plato, *Phaedrus* 265D–266B) or universalization, i.e., the synthesis of the extension of a concept, as when one consciously returns in distinct virtual knowledge to the recognition that animal is the universal including man and brute. The two are in turn contrasted with distinction and definition, which are the analysis and synthesis, respectively, of the comprehension of a concept.

In the domain of judgment, division is contrasted to composition (σύνθεσις); they are, respectively, the negative and the affirmative categorical judgments (see Aristotle, *Interp.* 16a 12, *Meta.* 1027b 19–1028a 5, 1051b 1–35, *Anim.* 430a 26–b 31), in which the mind either divides one object from another or composes one object with another. If one considers the act rather than the object of judgment, however, this is always a composition, since it is always a comparison of one simple objective concept with another (St. Thomas Aquinas, *In 1 perih.* 3.4; *De ver.* 1.3, 9; *Summa theologiae* 1a, 16.2).

Kinds. Excluding division *per accidens,* i.e., the division of an accidental whole, six species of division are generally recognized among the scholastics: (1) Nominal division is the distinction of the meanings of a term with respect to the various objects it signifies. (2) Integral division is the division of a quantified whole into component parts that are continuous but lie outside each other; it is also called partition. (3) Physical division, in the strict sense, is the division of a natural whole into its proper constitutive physical principles, its matter and form, e.g., the division of man into a rational soul and an organized body of such and such specifications. In both integral and physical division the parts are really distinct from each other and therefore really compose the whole. (4) Essential division. e.g., of man into rational and animal, is a division into parts that are not really distinct and compositive, being differentiated only by a distinction of reason. Between rational and animal as understood of man there obtains, according to St. Thomas, only a distinction of reasoned reason. According to Duns Scotus, these are in reality actually distinct metaphysical grades or formalities that together constitute man's essence. The essential whole and its division are sometimes referred to as metaphysical. This usage of Scotists and Suarezians was widely shared by Thomists of the second SCHOLASTICISM; it is infelicitous, however, in that it misleadingly suggests that the parts or grades being distinguished are metaphysically (i.e., really) distinct from each other. (5) Logical division, in the proper sense, is the division of the universal, or extensive whole, into the parts of its extension, which are called its subjective parts. Such division usually refers to a univocal whole; analogical division is sometimes termed unequal division (*per prius et posterius*), whereas univocal division is referred to as equal division (*ex aequo,* see *De malo* 7.1 ad 1). (6) Dynamic, or potestative, division is the division of a functional whole into its functional parts or powers, e.g., the soul into rational, animal, and vegetative. Both logical and dynamic division have in common that their members are in a broad sense subjective, or subordinated to the whole. Accordingly, as both St. ALBERT THE GREAT (*In 1 sent.* 3.34) and Thomas (*Summa theologiae* 1a, 77.1 ad 1) remark, the dynamic whole may be called a potential whole since it may be predicated distributively of its several parts. Thus the dynamic whole mediates in a certain sense between the integral whole and the universal or logical whole, and consequently its mode of division also mediates between their modes of division.

Rules. The conditions or rules for good division are framed in view of the logical division of a univocal whole, just as the rules of definition are framed in view of the real physical definition, but each set of rules is applicable analogically to the other forms of division or definition. The rules of division are: (1) that the members taken singly be inferiors, i.e., less than the thing divided, since every whole is greater than its part; (2) that all the members that divide the whole taken together fill up or equal the whole divided, the reason being that the whole is equivalent to all its parts taken together; and (3) that the members that divide the whole be opposed, at least formally, to each other. If they had no OPPOSITION, they would not have distinction, but rather identity; and therefore they would not be diverse.

A corollary of the first rule is that the genus is not divided into differences but, through the differences, into the several species. A fourth rule is sometimes added, namely, that the opposition between the members should be one of contradiction; actually, however, since this opposition fails within the genus to be divided, it amounts to one of contrariety, and thus this rule is reducible to the third. The fourth rule is sometimes referred to as the rule of dichotomous division, which insists that each division have only two members. A better, and more general, rule is that "a division have only two dividing members, or at least as few as possible" (John of St. Thomas, *Summulae* 2.4). In his *Parts of Animals* (624b 5–664a 11, esp. 643a 24–27) Aristotle criticizes dyadic division as allowing only a single *differentia* to each species, whereas what is often needed to distinguish the several biological species of a genus is a set of *differentiae* or properties that can uniquely define a species.

A set of topics or sources (Gr. τόποι Lat. *loci*) for arguing, or rules of consequences, can be framed in accordance with these three (or four) rules of division. They are (1) the rule of equivalence or substitution of the dividendum for the division, and vice versa—of use for materially converting the minor premise in INDUCTION; (2) the rule of negating one alternate and then affirming the other, i.e., *modus tollendo ponens,* for the so-called weak disjunctive or alternative; (3) the rule of affirming one disjunct and then negating the other, i.e., *modus ponendo tollens,* for the strong or strict disjunctive—see John of St. Thomas, *loc. cit.*; (4) the rules of subalternation and categorical seriality or transitivity, e.g., if *a* is a subjective part of *b,* and *b* of *c,* then *a* is a subjective part of *c.* This is of importance as the *dictum de omni* of the SYLLOGISM, formulated either according to extension ("to be in the whole of") or comprehension ("to belong to"); it has also a negative formulation, the *dictum de nullo.*

See Also: DISTINCTION, KINDS OF; LOGIC.

Bibliography: JOHN OF ST. THOMAS, *Cursus philosophicus thomisticus,* ed. B. REISER, 3 v. (new ed. Turin 1930–37), v. 1 *Ars Logica,* pt. 1 *Summulae* 2.4, 20b 42–22a 41; Eng. *Outlines of Formal Logic,* tr. F. C. WADE (Milwaukee 1955) 49–51; *The Material Logic,* tr. Y. R. SIMON et al. (Chicago 1955). J. A. OESTERLE, *Logic: The Art of Defining and Reasoning* (2nd ed. Englewood Cliffs, N.J. 1963). V. E. SMITH, *The Elements of Logic* (Milwaukee 1957). J. A. MOURANT, *Formal Logic* (New York 1963). F. H. PARKER and H. B. VEATCH, *Logic as a Human Instrument* (New York 1959). E. D. SIMMONS, *The Scientific Art of Logic* (Milwaukee 1961). H. F. CHERNISS, *Aristotle's Criticism of Plato and the Academy* (Baltimore 1944).

[J. J. GLANVILLE]

DIX, GREGORY

Historian and liturgist; b. Oct. 4, 1901; d. May 12, 1952. He was educated at Westminster and Merton College, Oxford, and ordained to the Anglican ministry in 1924. He joined the Anglican Benedictine communion of Nashdom in 1926, and became its prior in 1948. Dix's main interest was the study of Christian thought and its manifestation in the liturgical usages of Western and Eastern churches. He published *The Treatise on the Apostolic Tradition of Hippolytus* (London 1937). His book, *A Detection of Aumbries* (Westminster 1942), about the history of Eucharistic reservation, aroused much interest, but his scholarship was shown to be somewhat defective by the critical study of S. J. P. Van Dijk and J. H. Walker, *The Myth of the Aumbry* (London 1957). Dix's best work, *The Shape of the Liturgy* (Westminster 1944), analyzes and compares the texts and actions that go to make up several of the early liturgical rites. Discussing these in the light of Scripture and tradition, Dix produces a vivid picture of the Eucharistic rites of the primitive Church. He shows a rare ability for opening up new and exciting lines of approach, and evaluating the religious and theological factors influencing early liturgical developments.

Bibliography: F. L. CROSS, *The Oxford Dictionary of the Christian Church* (London 1957) 409.

[C. W. HOWELL]

DJIBOUTI, THE CATHOLIC CHURCH IN

The Republic of Djibouti is located in East Africa and borders Eritrea on its north, the Gulf of Aden on its east, Somalia on its southeast and Ethiopia on its south and west. Located in the Great Rift Valley, the region is predominately desert, with a harsh and dry climate; earthquakes, drought and flash floods are not uncommon. With little agriculture and few natural resources, Djibouti derives much of its income from its status as a free trade zone and its location near one of the world's major shipping lanes. Djibouti City is part of a major trade route to Ethiopia and surrounding nations. Chief exports include hides and cattle raised by the region's nomadic population, as well as salt. Djibouti has been heavily reliant upon foreign aid, and its economy burdened by heavy debt repayments. Forty percent of the population was unemployed in 2000.

Formerly known as the French Territory of the Afars and Issas, a part of Somaliland, Djibouti was an overseas territory of the French Republic until 1977 when it became the last of those territories to gain independence. The population is predominately Somali and includes

Issa, Gadaboursi, Issaq, Afar and Arabs, as well as Europeans, many of whom are French military personnel and their families.

History. Part of the Ethiopian Empire, the region was Christianized until the Arab invasion in 1200. A French protectorate was established near the coastal city of Obock in 1884, and the seat of the colonial government was later transferred to Djibouti. Modern evangelization began late in the 19th century by Capuchins, to whom the mission remained entrusted through the 20th century. As part of Somaliland, Djibouti was originally part of the Vicariate Apostolic of Galla (erected in 1846). After 1914 it fell under the Prefecture Apostolic of Djibouti, which became a diocese directly subject to the Holy See in 1955. Bishop George Perron OFM, a Capuchin, administers the affairs of the diocese.

A railroad constructed between Djibouti and Addis Ababa, Ethiopia, during World War I expedited trade through the country's ports and boosted its economy. The region became a territory in the French Union in 1946, and was granted membership in the French Community as the Territory of the Afars and Issas in 1958. Djibouti was granted political independence on June 27, 1977, with Islam as the state religion. Armed fighting erupted in the west in 1991, sparked by Afars desire for independence and disagreements over the nation's constitution. Government reprisals were harsh, but ultimately a ceasefire was called and constitutional reforms enacted in 1992. Diplomatic relations were established with the Vatican in May of 2000.

Famine and regional wars negatively affected the nation for much of the late 20th century as refugees from neighboring Somalia and Ethiopia settled in Djibouti and put stresses upon its fragile economy. In 1981 alone the country gave refuge to over 50,000 Ethiopians fleeing the fighting in the Ethiopian province of the Ogaden; the continued stream of refugees prompted calls for humanitarian support from both the Holy See and the region's papal nuncios. In 2000 Djibouti was home to 12,000 Catholics, the majority of whom lived in the capital city. The country's five parishes were administered to by one diocesan and six religious priests, seven brothers and 19 sisters. The 11 Catholic elementary, high schools and trade schools provided education to the several hundred Catholic students in the country, many of whom were of European ancestry. As a minority faith in a predominately Muslim country, missionary activity remained focused on humanitarian endeavors rather than evangelization. An annual celebration held by Djibouti's Catholic population was open to all the nation's Christians.

Bibliography: *Annuaire des Diocèses d'Expression Françaises . . . pour l'Afrique . . . et Madagascar* (Paris 1955—). *Annuario Pontificio* has further information.

[T. A. WHITE/EDS.]

DŁUGOSZ, JAN

Priest, educator, and influential Polish historian (known also as Iohannes Longinus); b. Brzeznica, Poland, 1415; d. Cracow, Poland, May 19,1480. After early schooling at Nowy Korczyn and higher studies at the University of Cracow, he was ordained in 1440. He was appointed secretary to Cardinal Zbigniew Olesnicki, Bishop of Cracow, and he later became a canon of the cathedral. He was one of the Polish delegates to the Council of BASEL. As special envoy of Polish Church authorities to Pope EUGENE IV, with whom he reconciled the University of Cracow, he returned with the cardinal's hat for

Olesnicki. Shortly before his death Długosz was named archbishop of Lvov, but he was never consecrated. Well educated and in close contact with various humanists, he could not bring himself to accept the ideology of the new movement. His works, especially the outstanding *Annales seu chronicae inclyti regni Poloniae, libri XII,* a 12-volume history of Poland written in classical Latin between 1455 and 1480, removed much prejudice toward that nation among the learned of Europe and inspired the Poles with patriotism and respect for their heritage. Długosz also emphasized the importance and advantages of the traditional role of the Catholic Church in Poland. Through his many charities he founded a home for university students and built monasteries and churches, beneath the most beautiful of which, Na Skalce (upon rock) in Cracow, he lies buried.

Bibliography: Works. *Ioannis Dlugosii senioris canonici Cracoviensis opera,* ed. A. PRZEZDZIECKI, 14 v. (Cracow 1863–87). Literature. E. PERJECKIJ, *L'Histoire polonaise de Jan Dlugosz et les Annales Lusses* (Prague 1932). T. SINKO, ''De Dlugosii praefatione Historiae Polonorum,'' *Studja z dziejów kultury Polskiej,* ed. H. BARACZ and J. HULEWICZ (Warsaw 1949) 105–145. K. LEPSZY, ed., *Dzieje Uniwersytetu Jagiellońskiego w Latach 1364–1764,* v.1 (Cracow 1964). A. BRÜCKNER, *Tysiac lat kultury Polskiej,* 2 v. (3d ed. Paris 1955) 1:440–443, 455–456, 484, 500. *The Cambridge History of Poland,* ed. W. F. REDDAWAY et al. (Cambridge, Eng. 1941–50) 1:163–165, 241, 275. A. STRZELECKA, ''Długosz w Świetle Nowych Badań,'' *Nasza Przesłość* 8 (1958) 497–504. B. STASIEWSKI, *Lexikon für Theologie und Kirche,* ed. J. HOFER and K. RAHNER (2d, new ed. Freiburg 1957–65) 5:1028. P. URBAN, *Dictionnaire d'histoire et de géographie ecclésiastiques,* ed. A. BAUDRILLART et al. (Paris 1912–) 14:530–531.

[L. SIEKANIEC]

DOANE, GEORGE HOBART

Diocesan administrator; b. Boston, Mass., Sept. 5, 1830; d. Newark, N.J., Jan. 20, 1905. Although he graduated in 1852 from Jefferson Medical College, Philadelphia, Pa., he decided to enter the ministry and was ordained a deacon in the Protestant Episcopal Church, New Jersey, of which his father, George Washington Doane, was bishop. In 1855 he became a Catholic; and after study at the Seminary of St. Sulpice, Paris, and the Collegio Pio, Rome, he was ordained for the Diocese of Newark by Bp. James Roosevelt Bayley on Sept. 13, 1857. Under Bayley he became pastor of the Newark cathedral, secretary to the bishop, and chancellor of the diocese. He served briefly as chaplain in the 1st New Jersey Brigade during the Civil War. Afterward (1868–69) he was instrumental in collecting funds to save the North American College in Rome. Under Bp. Michael Corrigan, Doane became a domestic prelate and vicar-general of the diocese, first president (1875) of the Catholic

Young Men's National Union, and diocesan administrator (1876–77, 1880–81). Misunderstandings arose between Doane and Corrigan's successor, Bp. Winand Wigger, over the administration of the diocese and the rights of the pastor of the cathedral; but these were settled, and Doane was named prothonotary apostolic in 1889. In 1884 he declined the presidency of Mt. St. Mary's College, Emmitsburg, Md., and was appointed theologian for Bp. John Salpointe at the Third Plenary Council of Baltimore. After attending the council, he was named to the diocesan posts of consultor, dean, and member of the cathedral committee. In honor of his contributions to Newark for more than half a century, a statue was erected by public subscription in 1908.

Bibliography: C. D. HINRICHSEN, *The History of the Diocese of Newark: 1873–1901* (Doctoral diss. unpub. Catholic U. 1962).

[C. D. HINRICHSEN]

DOBRIZHOFFER, MARTIN

Jesuit missionary and author; b. Friedberg, Bohemia, Sept. 7, 1718; d. Vienna, July 17, 1791. He entered the Austrian province of the Jesuits Oct. 19, 1736. He was already ordained when he arrived in Buenos Aires as a member of the expedition of Father Orosz on Jan. 1, 1749. For 18 years he worked among the Abipon natives in Gran Chaco and among the northern tribes of the Guarani. After the expulsion of the Jesuits (1768), he returned to Austria and lived in Vienna until his death. From 1773 he was preacher at the court and Empress Maria Theresa frequently invited him to tell his experiences as a missionary. His excellent, objective work on this subject, the *Historia de Abiponibus* (3 v., Vienna 1783–84), was immediately translated into German by A. Krail (Vienna 1783–84), and into English by S. Coleridge (London 1822). This still-valuable book puts Dobrizhoffer among the pioneers of ethnology.

Bibliography: M. A. BLANKENBURG, ''German Missionary Writers in Paraguay,'' *Mid-America* 29 (1947) 122–131, J. V. JACOBSEN, ''Dobrizhoffer: Abipón Missionary,'' *ibid.* 139–184. E. CARDOZO, *Historiografía paraguaya* (Mexico City 1959–) 1:344–351.

[H. STORNI]

DOCETISM

The theological error of those who denied the material reality of the body of Christ. The word probably comes from the Greek δοκεῖν, referring to appearance or representation of something not existing in reality (Tertullian, *De carne Christi* 1). According to the Docetists, Christ did not have a true body during His earthly existence, but merely a bodily appearance. The origins of Docetism are obscure. The heresy could have taken its rise from diverse causes such as the opinion current in the first century that material in itself is evil; or the scandal given by the bodily weaknesses exhibited by Christ while on earth, and more particularly his ignominious death on the cross. The earliest evidence of the existence of this heresy is probably that of the first two Epistles of St. John (1 John 4.2–3; 2 John 7). At the start of the second century, IGNATIUS OF ANTIOCH explicitly condemned this doctrine (*Smyr.* 1–3; 7.1; *Tral.* 9–10). Ignatius saw clearly that to deny the reality of the body of Christ was to destroy the reality of Christianity and the CHRISTIAN way of life.

In the course of the second and third centuries, Docetism found an ally in GNOSTICISM. Beginning with the principle that the flesh is evil and that salvation consists in evading the consequence of having a body, the various expressions of Gnosticism, even though differing in modalities, were united in claiming that Christ had assumed only a bodily appearance. According to Basilides, Simon of Cyrene was miraculously substituted for Christ and crucified in His place, while Jesus Himself returned to heaven (Irenaeus, *Adv. haer.* 1.24.4). According to Valentinian, Christ had passed through Mary as water passes through a channel; and His body had not known any physical necessities (*ibid.* 1.7.2). Outside the Gnostic circles, Docetism exercised a more or less profound influence on the early Christian world. Traces of it are to be found in some of the apocryphal books, such as the Gospel of Peter, the Acts of Peter, the Ascension of Isaiah and certain expressions used by Clement of Alexandria (*Stromateis* 6.9.71) and Origen (*In Matt.* 13.2) that, if detached from their context, have a Docetist connotation.

Among the adversaries of Docetism, along with Ignatius of Antioch, were POLYCARP OF SMYRNA (*Philip.* 7.1), Irenaeus (*Adv. haer.* 4.23.1–5; 5.1.2; 5.2.2), Serapion of Antioch (Eusebius, *Hist. Eccl.* 6.12.6) and particularly TERTULLIAN (*Adv. Marcionem* 3; *Adv. Valent.; De carne Christi*). With Tertullian the history of Docetism, properly so-called, ceases. While Docetism in its radical form was a heresy of the first centuries of Christianity, certain Docetist tendencies and mentalities continued to make themselves manifest within Christianity both in the sphere of doctrine and in the moral and ascetical sphere, particularly as a consequence of Pelagianism. Docetism is a danger for all who do not admit that the Son of God became man in everything similar to all men, except sin, and refuse to draw the practical conclusions from this fact (*see* PELAGIUS AND PELAGIANISM).

Bibliography: G. BARDY, *Dictionnaire de spiritualité ascétique et mystique. Doctrine et histoire,* ed. M. VILLER et al., (Paris 1932–) 3:1461–68. A. GRILLMEIER, *Lexikon für Theologie und Kirche,* eds., J. HOFER and K. RAHNER, 10 v. (2d, new ed. Freiburg 1957–65) 3:470–471. R. SCHNACKENBURG, *Die Johannesbriefe* (2d ed. Freiburg 1963) 20–22. L. VAGANAY, *L'Évangile de Pierre* (2d ed. Paris 1930) 188–122. *Les Actes de Pierre,* ed. and tr. I. VOUAUX (Paris 1922) 66–73. *Ascension d'Isaie,* ed. and tr. E. TISSERANT (Paris 1909). G. BAREILLE, *Dictionnaire de théologie catholique,* ed. A. VACANT et al., 15 v. (Paris 1903–50) 4.2:1480–1501.

[A. HUMBERT]

DOCILITY

Docility is a moral quality by which a person is apt, ready to learn, take instruction, or accept intellectual discipline. In his lexicon, St. Isidore (d. 636) wrote: "One is docile, not because he is learned, but because he can be taught; for he is capable and apt for learning" (*Patrologia Latina,* ed. J. P. Migne, 82:374). Docility has consistently been related to the virtue of prudence. St. Thomas Aquinas regarded docility as one of the eight integral parts of prudence—forming with memory, reasoning, understanding, shrewdness, and foresight, the cognoscitive aspect of that virtue (ST. THOMAS, *Summa theologiae,* 2a2ae, 48). Some docility is evidently needed for acquiring knowledge in one not expert in some field of learning. Most properly, docility pertains to the relationship of pupil to teacher in the classroom, of student to professor in the lecture hall. From this point of view, docility may be fittingly regarded as a special virtue, and defined as that moral virtue connected with justice through observance, whereby one renders the honor and attention due to another whose excellence in learning merits respect and reverence. Moreover, docility is invaluable in the area of moral training, but again under the aspect of knowledge wherein the untutored accepts the direction of those in authority. Progress in holiness ultimately depends on docility to the inspirations of the Holy Spirit. As with other moral virtues, two extremes are possible, and hence two vices are opposed to docility. Indocility means an unwillingness to accept the superior intellectual authority of a competent teacher. At the other extreme, the mind can yield to human authority a slavish subservience that bars all critical judgment. The happy medium is docility, which is a common sense willingness to learn from others.

Bibliography: M. J. ADLER, "Docility and Authority," *Commonweal,* 31 (April 5, 1940) 504–507; "Docility and History," *ibid.* 32 (April 26, 1940) 4–8. R. SMITH, "The Virtue of Docility," *Thomist* 15 (1952) 572–623.

[R. SMITH]

DOCTA IGNORANTIA

Docta ignorantia, or learned ignorance, is a Latin expression designating the limitations of human knowledge. Man knows and affirms what is true but in an incomplete and partial manner. As a consequence, he should be constantly aware of personal limitations and discover in this consciousness the beginning of true WISDOM. The phrase itself comes from St. Augustine (*Epist.* 130.28; *Patrologia Latina,* ed. J. P. Migne, 33:505) and was used by St. Bonaventure to describe an aspect of mystical knowledge (*Brevil.* 5.6.7). NICHOLAS OF CUSA, in the light of St. Paul's teaching (1 Cor 1.18–31; 13.9–12), stressed the incompleteness and imperfection of man's knowledge. Although the principle of *docta ignorantia* permeated medieval philosophical and theological thinking, it received particular elaboration in Cusa's major work, *De docta ignorantia* (1440). His epistemological idea of limitation pervades modern philosophy.

Bibliography: E. VANSTEENBERGHE, *Dictionnaire de théologie catholique,* ed. A. VACANT et al., 15 v. (Paris 1903–50; Tables générales 1951–) 11.1:601–612; *Autour de la docte ignorance* (Münster 1915). R. HAUBST, *Lexikon für Theologie und Kirche,* ed. J. HOFER and K. RAHNER, 10 v. (2d, new ed. Freiburg 1957–65) 3:435. F. L. CROSS, *The Oxford Dictionary of the Christian Church* (London 1957) 955–956. É. H. GILSON, *History of Christian Philosophy in the Middle Ages* (New York 1955) 534–540. J. MARÉCHAL, *Le Point de départ de la métaphysique,* v. 2 (Paris 1944) 15–35. V. MARTIN, "The Dialectical Process in the Philosophy of Nicholas of Cusa," *Laval théologique et philosophique* 5 (1949) 213–268.

[N. SHARKEY]

DOCTOR (SCHOLASTIC TITLE)

In the Middle Ages the titles of doctor and master were synonymous in theology, law, medicine, and arts. In the early Middle Ages any learned scholar who attracted students desirous of learning was called a master, much after the Hebrew manner of calling teachers rabbi, lord, master, or doctor (see Dt 29.10, 31.28; Lk 2.46; 2 Cor 12.28; Eph 4.11). When the medieval universities were organized under papal protection, it was more common to call approved teachers of theology *magistri sacrae paginae* (i.e., of the Bible) or *magistri sacrae theologiae,* while others were called masters of civil law (*magistri legum*), canon law (*magistri decretum*), medicine (*magistri medicinae*), or arts (*magistri artium*). As early as the 12th century the lawyers of Bologna preferred to be called doctor. Writing to the masters of Paris in 1208 or 1209, Innocent III addressed them as "doctors of the sacred page, canon law, and arts" (*Chartularium universitatis Parisiensis,* ed. H. Denifle and E. Chatelain, 4 v. [Paris 1889–97] 1.67). It was not until the early 16th century, however, that master theologians, lawyers, and physicians were commonly addressed as doctor, and that masters in arts ceased to be addressed as master.

The official function of a doctor in the Middle Ages was to teach (Lat. *docere*). For this he was constituted by the guild of masters (*universitas*) and the chancellor acting in the name of pope or emperor. At the time of his installation (*inceptio*) the young master had to take an oath that he would teach for at least two years, and he was considered a perjurer until this oath was fulfilled, unless a dispensation was obtained. A master actually fulfilling his duty was called *magister regens,* exercising full responsibility in the class room (*schola*) and in the university or studium. A master who had ceded his chair to another was called *non regens,* but he retained certain privileges in the university (*see* OXFORD, UNIVERSITY OF; PARIS, UNIVERSITY OF).

Honorific titles were given to outstanding masters by contemporaries and posterity to do them honor and to preserve academic impersonality. Just as Aristotle was commonly referred to as "the Philosopher," Averroës as "the Commentator," and St. PAUL as *Doctor gentium,* so too, frequently quoted masters were referred to under an honorific title, not officially conferred by any university or decree, but by contemporaries. The medieval penchant for honorific titles extended beyond the university to founders of religious orders: *Pater apostolicus* (St. DOMINIC), *Pater seraphicus* (St. FRANCIS OF ASSISI), and others. But it was principally outstanding theologians and lawyers who were known to contemporaries and posterity by honorific titles. The custom of assigning such titles continued throughout the period known as the second scholasticism, and the titles of more eminent thinkers are still employed among scholastic writers (*see* SCHOLASTICISM).

The following list of honorific titles gives the principal surnames, the religious order affiliations (where known), and the date of death (where known). It is divided into two parts, the first giving titles associated with the appellation *Doctor,* the second those associated with other designations such as *Magister.*

Scholastic Doctors

Abstractionum: Francis of Meyronnes, OFM
Acutissimus: Pope SIXTUS IV, OFM
Acutus: WILLIAM OF WARE, OFM; Francis of Meyronnes, OFM; GREGORY OF RIMINI, OESA; Nicolas de Orbellis, OFM, *c.* 1472; Gabriel VÁZQUEZ, SJ
(Ad)mirabilis: ROGER BACON, OFM
A doctoribus: Anthony François, 1528
Amoenus: ROBERT COWTON, OFM
Angelicus: THOMAS AQUINAS, OP; Richard Brinkel, OFM, *c.* 1350
Armatus: Matthias Döring, OFM, 1469
Authenticus: RICHARD OF MIDDLETON; Gregory of Rimi-

ni, OESA
Authoratus: Richard of Middleton
Beatus: Thomas Aquinas, OP; GILES OF ROME, OESA
Bonus: Walter Brinkley (Brinkell), OFM, *c.* 1310
Breviloquus: Gui Terreni of Perpignan, OCarm, 1342
Brevis: WILLIAM OF VAUROUILLON, OFM
Bullatus: Roberto Caracciolo, OFM
Cherubinus: Thomas Aquinas, OP
Christianissimus: Jean GERSON
Christianus: NICHOLAS OF CUSA
Clarus: Peter of Aquila, OFM; Denis of Montina, OESA, 1371 or 1372; Thomas Doctius, 1441; Luis de Montesinos
Collectivus: Landolf CARACCIOLO, OFM
Communis: Thomas Aquinas, OP; Richard of Middleton
Consummatus: Dominic of St. Theresa, OCarm, 1654
Contradictionum: Johannes Wessel GANSFORT
Copiosus: Richard of Middleton
Correctivus: William de la Mare, OFM
Curialis: PETER AUREOLI, OFM
Decretalium: Bonagratia of Bergamo, OFM, 1347
Decretistarum: Peter Quaesuet
Devotus: BONAVENTURE, OFM
Difficilis: JOHN OF RIPA, OFM
Digressivus: HENRY OF GHENT
Divinus: Jan van RUYSBROECK
Doctorum: ANSELM OF LAON; ALEXANDER OF HALES, OFM
Dulcifluus: ANTONIUS ANDREAS, OFM
Dulcis: Humbert of Garda
Egregius: Thomas Aquinas, OP
Egregius . . . in saeculorum fine doctissimus: ISIDORE OF SEVILLE
Elegans: Peter Aureoli, OFM
Eminens: JOHN OF MATHA
Eucharisticus: Thomas Aquinas, OP
Evangelicus: ANTHONY OF PADUA, OFM; Philip of Montecalerio, OFM, *c.* 1335; John WYCLIF
Excellentissimus: Anthony Corsetto, 1503
Eximius: Thomas Aquinas, OP; Richard of Middleton; Peter Aureoli, OFM; John Tissier, *c.* 1564
Expertus: ALBERT THE GREAT, OP
Exstaticus: Jan van Ruysbroeck; DENIS THE CARTHUSIAN
Facundus: Peter Aureoli, OFM
Famosissimus: Peter Alberti, 1426
Famosus: Peter of Tarentaise (Pope INNOCENT V), OP; Bertrand de la Tour, OFM, 1332
Fertilis: Francis of Candia, OFM, 15th century
Firmus et indefatigabilis: ROBERT HOLCOT
Fructuosus: PETER OF LA PALU, OP
Fundamentalis: John Faber (Le Fèvre) of Bordeaux, 1340
Fundatissimus: Richard of Middleton; Giles of Rome, OESA

Fundatus: William of Ware, OFM; DURANDUS OF SAINT-POURÇAIN, OP; Peter of Navarra
Generosus: Peter de Turre
Gratiae: AUGUSTINE
Gratiosus: JAMES OF VITERBO, OESA; Durandus of Saint-Pourçain, OP
Hispaniae: Isidore of Seville
Illibatus: Alexander Alamannicus, *c.* 1400
Illuminatissimus: Thomas Aquinas, OP; Francis of Meyronnes, OFM
Illuminatus: Raymond LULL, OFM; Francis of Meyronnes, OFM; Johannes TAULER, OP
Illustratus: ADAM MARSH, OFM; Francis of Marchia, OFM
Illustris: Adam Marsh, OFM
In expondis sacris scripturis: JEROME *Inclytus:* WILLIAM OF MACCLESFIELD, OP
Inflammatus: Luke of Padua, OFM, 14th century
Ingeniosissimus: Andrew of Novocastro, OFM, 14th century
Ingeniosus: JOHN PECKHAM, OFM; Peter Aureoli, OFM
Inter aristotelicos aristotelicissimus: HAYMO OF FAVERSHAM, OFM
Inventivus: James of Viterbo, OESA
Invincibilis: WILLIAM OF OCKHAM, OFM; PETER THOMAE, OFM
Irradiatissimus: Thomas Aquinas, OP
Irrefragabilis: Alexander of Hales, OFM
Lucidus: Pope ALEXANDER III
Magnificus: Pope Sixtus IV, OFM
Magnus: Gilbert the Cistercian, 1168; ALAN OF LILLE
Marianus: ANSELM OF CANTERBURY; John DUNS SCOTUS, OFM
Maximus: Jerome; John Duns Scotus, OFM
Mellifluus: BERNARD OF CLAIRVAUX
Mellifluus alter: AELRED
Memorialis: BARTHOLOMAEUS ANGLICUS, OFMv
Memoriosissimus: Ludovicus PONTANUS ROMANUS
Mirabilis: Anthony Perez, SJ, 1649
Modernus: Durandus of Saint-Pourçain, OP
Moralis: Gerald Odonis, OFM, 1349
Navarrus: Martin ASPILCUETA
Nominatissimus: STEPHEN LANGTON
Noster: Thomas Aquinas, OP; THOMAS BRADWARDINE
Notabilis: Peter de Insula (d'Isle), OFM, 14th century
Novus: Peter Aureoli, OFM
Ordinatissimus: John of Bassols, OFM, 1333
Ornatissimus: John of Bassols, OFM, 1333; Peter of Aquila, OFM
Ornatus: Antonius Andreas, OFM
Pacificus: Nicholas BONET, OFM
Panormitanus: Nicolaus de TUDESCHIS
Parisiennsis: Gui Terreni of Perpignan, OCarm, 1342
Perplexus: Francis of Marchia, OFM

Perspicacissimus: John Faber (Le Fèvre) of Bordeaux, 1340

Perspicuus: Jerome of Ascoli (Pope Nicholas IV), OFM; WALTER BURLEY

Planus: Walter Burley; Nicholas of Lyra, OFM

Praecellentissimus philosophiae: SIGER OF BRABANT

Praeclarus: William of Ware, OFM; Peter of Kaiserslautern, OPraem, 1330

Praefulgidus: Francis of Marchia, OFM

Praestantissimus: Thomas NETTER

Primus: Alexander of Hales, OFM

Proficuus: Peter Thomae, OFM; Nicholas Bonet, OFM

Profitabilis: Nicholas Bonet, OFM

Profundissimus: Paolo VENETO; Gabriel BIEL; Juan Alonso Curiel

Profundus: James of Ascoli, OFM; Francis of Marchia, OFM; Thomas Bradwardine

Rarus: HARVEY NEDELLEC (HERVAEUS NATALIS), OP

Recollectus: Landolph Caracciolo, OFM

Refulgens: Peter of Candia (Alexander V, antipope)

Refulgidus: PETER OF CANDIA (ALEXANDER V, ANTIPOPE)

Relucens: Francis of Marchia, OFM

Resolutissimus: Durandus of Saint-Pourçain, OP

Resolutus: JOHN BACONTHORP, OCarm

Reverendus: Henry of Ghent; GODFREY OF FONTAINES

Sanctissimus: Anthony of Padua, OFM

Sanctus: Thomas Aquinas, OP

Satisfaciens: Astesanus, *c.* 1330

Scholasticus: Anselm of Laon; Peter ABELARD; GILBERT DE LA PORRÉE; PETER LOMBARD; PETER OF POITIERS; HUGH OF NEWCASTLE

Securus: Peter Reginaldeti

Seraphicus: Bonaventure, OFM

Serenus: Peter Thomae, OFM

Singularis: William of Ockham, OFM

Solemnis: Henry of Ghent

Solidus: Richard de Paribilla

Sollers: Peter Thomae, OFM

Spectabilis: Peter of Tarentaise (Pope Innocent V), OP

Speculativus: James of Viterbo, OESA

Strenuus: Peter Thomae, OFM

Sublimis: Johannes Tauler, OP; Francis BACON, OCarm; Jean Courtecuisse (BREVICOXA)

Subtilior inter omnes: Durandus of Saint-Pourçain, OP

Subtilis: John Duns Scotus, OFM; John Faber (Le Fèvre) of Bordeaux, 1340; Denis of Montina, OESA, 1371 or 1372; Joannes Calderini; Benedict Raymundus, 1440; Philip Corneo, 1462

Subtilissimus: Peter of Mantova, 14th century

Succinctus: Francis of Marchia, OFM

Sufficiens: Peter of Aquila, OFM

Summus: Francis of Perusio (Paris?), 14th century

Supersubtilis: John of Ripa, OFM

Universalis: Alan of Lille; Thomas Aquinas, OP; Albert the Great, OP

Utilis: Nicolas of Lyra, OFM; Nicholas Bonet, OFM

Venerabilis: Thomas Aquinas, OP; Albert the Great, OP; Jean Gerson

Venerandus: Godfrey of Fontaines

Verbalis: Francis of Candia, OFM, 15th century

Verbosus: Giles of Rome, OESA

Other Titles

Abbas modernus: Nicolaus de Tudeschis

Abbas siculus: Nicolaus de Tudeschis

Antoninus consiliorum: ANTONINUS, OP

Arca testamenti: Anthony of Padua, OFM

Aristoteles lusitanus: Peter da FONSECA, SJ

Aristotelis anima: John Dondus, 1380

Averroista: Urban of Bologna, OSM, 1403

Chrysologus minorita: FRANCIS OF OSUNA, OFM

Columna doctorum: WILLIAM OF CHAMPEAUX

Conciliator: Peter of Abano, *c.* 1315

Dialogus: Pope GREGORY I (THE GREAT)

Divus Thomas: Thomas Aquinas, OP

Doctoris sancti viae archicursor et sancti doctoris doctrinae armarium refertissimum: Peter Piscatoris, OP, 1508

Dominus legum: Azzo dei Porri, 13th century

Egregius versificator: HILDEBERT OF LAVARDIN

Emporium theologiae: Laurent Gervasi, OP

Eucharistiae praeco et vates maximus: Thomas Aquinas, OP

Eximius et pius: Francisco SUÁREZ, SJ

Facundus apollo: Ralph of Rodington, OFM, 14th century

Famosus expositor: Thomas Aquinas, OP

Flos mundi: Maurice O'FIHELY, OFM

Flos omnium artistarum: William of Ockham, OFM

Flos omnium modernorum: Roger Bacon, OFM

Fons canonum: Joannes Andreae

Fons doctorum: Thomas Aquinas, OP

Fons vitae: Alexander of Hales, OFM

Gilbertus universalis: Gilbert of London, 1134

Gregorius Novellus: Gregory of Rimini, OESA

Inceptor profundus: William of Ware, OFM

Lector exiguus: JOHN OF FREIBURG, OP

Lucerna iuris: IRNERIUS; Baldus de Ubaldis

Lucerna iuris pontificii: Nicolaus de Tudeschis

Lumen iuris: Pope Clement IV

Lumen legum: Irnerius

Lumen magistrorum: Augustine

Lumen mundi: Thomas Aquinas, OP

Lux mundi: Johannes Wessel Gansfort

Magister: Augustine

Magister de proprietatibus: Bartholomaeus Anglicus, OFM

Magister Hieronymus: Jerome of Ascoli (Pope Nicholas IV), OFM

Magister historiarum: PETER COMESTOR

Magister Scott: William of Ware, OFM

Magister sententiarum: Peter Lombard

Magnus: Albert the Great, OP; Siger of Brabant

Malleus: BERNARD OF AUVERGNE, OP

Malleus haereticorum: Francis Coster

Modernorum magister magistrorum: MANEGOLD OF LAUTENBACH

Monarcha iuris: Bartholomew of Saliceto, 1412

Monarcha theologorum: Alexander of Hales, OFM

Mundi probatus magister: Augustine

Nemo bonus iurista nisi sit Bartolista: BARTOLO OF SASSOFERRATO

Normaque morum: Joannes Andreae

Os aureum: Bulgarus, *c.* 1166

Pater decretalium: Pope GREGORY IX

Pater et organum veritatis: Pope INNOCENT IV

Pater et tuba iuris canonici: Joannes Andreae

Pater iuris: Pope INNOCENT III

Pater peritorum: Peter of Belle-Perche, 1308

Peripateticus palatinus: Peter Abelard

Philosophiae parens: Urban of Bologna, OSM, 1403

Phoenix theologorum: John Baptist of Asti

Praeceptor germaniae: RABANUS MAURUS

Princeps averroistarum: John Baconthorp, OCarm

Princeps scotistarum: Bartholomaeus MASTRIUS, OFM

Princeps subtilitatum: Francis de Accoltis, 1485?

Princeps thomistarum (in philosophia): DOMINIC OF FLANDERS, OP

Princeps thomistarum (in theologia): John Capreolus, OP

Rabbi censor: Joannes Andreae

Rabbi doctorum: Joannes Andreae

Rabbi lux: Joannes Andreae

Scotellus: Peter of Aquila, OFM

Scotulus: Antonius Andreas, OFM

Speculator: William DURANTI THE ELDER

Speculum et lumen iuris canonici: Joannes Andreae

Speculum iuris: Bartolo of Sassoferrato

Studiorum ducem: Thomas Aquinas, OP

Summus doctorum: Henry of Ghent; Peter of Belle-Perche, 1308

Tortor parvulorum: Gregory of Rimini, OESA

Venerabilis inceptor: William of Ockham, OFM

Vir trilinguis: Jerome

Vitae arbor: John of Wales, OFM

Bibliography: F. EHRLE, *Die Ehrenfitel der scholastichen Lehrer des Mittelalters (Sitzungsberichte der Bayerischen Akademie der Wissenschaften zu München;* 1919). F. PELSTER, "Die Ehrentitel der scholastischen Lehrer des Mittelalters," *Theologische Quartalschrift* 103 (1922) 37–56. P. LEHMANN, "Mittelalterliche Beinamen und Ehrentitel," *Historical Journal* 49 (1929) 215–239. L. MEIER "De anecdoto titulorum scholasticorum elencho," *Antonianum* 25 (1950) 153–157; "De quodam elencho titulorum scholasticorum denuo invento," *ibid.* 27 (1952) 367–376.

[J. C. VANSTEENKISTE]

DOCTOR OF THE CHURCH

Title given to certain ecclesiastical writers on account of the great advantage the Church has gained from their doctrine.

Requirements. Three requirements are demanded: great sanctity, eminent learning, and proclamation as a Doctor of the Church by a pope or ecumenical council. Only canonized saints receive this title. There have been ecclesiastical writers of great influence who are not Doctors of the Church, e.g., Origen, because they are uncanonized. This requirement indicates that the title is not concerned exclusively with a person's ability to expound the faith. It is by the gifts of the Holy Spirit that one both savors and enables others to savor the things of God, that therefore one's exposition of the faith is effective in radiating the supernatural character of the faith that draws man to God. Hence the need for sanctity in a Doctor of the Church.

The requirement of eminent learning indicates the importance that the Church attaches to the knowledge of God and of divine things. It has sometimes been necessary for the Church to condemn systems that regard knowledge as the only way of salvation. There is, however, a sense in which the word of God enshrines the Word of God and the life that He makes available through the Church: "this is eternal life, that they may know thee, the only true God, and Jesus Christ, whom thou hast sent" (Jn 17.3). Hence this respect shown to the great teachers of the faith.

The third requirement is that the Church, either by a pope or by an ecumenical council, proclaim a man of learning and sanctity a Doctor of the Church. Benedict XIV mentions that a council may do this, but in fact the most a council has done is acclaim the writings and influence of various Doctors. Apart from the great Doctors of the first six centuries—four Western and four Eastern— all subsequent Doctors have been proclaimed since the Reformation. The procedure has been to extend to the universal Church the Office and Mass of a saint to whom this title is applied, after consulting the Congregation of Rites, which will first, if necessary, have had his writings carefully examined.

Original Doctors. The original four Western Doctors are AMBROSE, AUGUSTINE, JEROME, and GREGORY the Great, whose feasts were imposed by Boniface VIII in 1298. The original Eastern Doctors were JOHN CHRYSOSTOM, BASIL THE GREAT, and GREGORY OF NAZIANZUS, to whom ATHANASIUS was later added; Pius V recognized all four in 1568. All these Doctors lived after the era of the great persecutions; consequently none were martyrs, nor have any martyrs since then been nominated Doctors. Many of the early martyrs, however, did contribute greatly to the Church's understanding of the faith. It may be that the historical fact of martyrdom's being the only officially recognized form of sanctity was deemed to make it unnecessary to apply other encomia to martyrs who were learned, or it may be that the title martyr sufficiently demonstrated their having witnessed to Christ and His teaching; at any rate, the fact that the liturgical office of a confessor is used for Doctors is surely the consequence rather than the cause of martyrs' not being proclaimed Doctors.

The common teaching of theologians that a special reward in heaven is given to Doctors does not imply that only Doctors of the Church receive this reward; it would seem to be the right of all who distinguish themselves by their contribution to Christ's cause as teachers of the faith. Similarly many of the scholastic theologians were dignified with the general title doctor.

Doctors Proclaimed Later. The original eight Doctors were not added to until the Dominican Pius V recognized THOMAS AQUINAS along with the original four Eastern Doctors (1568). The Franciscan Sixtus V added BONAVENTURE (1588). The number stayed at 10 until Clement XI nominated ANSELM (1720); Innocent XIII named ISIDORE OF SEVILLE (1722); Benedict XIII, PETER CHRYSOLOGUS (1729). Benedict XIV gave belated recognition to LEO THE GREAT (1754). Leo XII named PETER DAMIAN (1828); Pius VIII, BERNARD OF CLAIRVAUX (1830); Pius IX, HILARY OF POITIERS (1851), ALPHONSUS LIGUORI (1871), and Francis de Sales (1877). Leo XIII took the number beyond 20 in nominating the three Easterners CYRIL OF ALEXANDRIA, CYRIL OF JERUSALEM (1882), and JOHN DAMASCENE (1890) and the English BEDE THE VENERABLE (1899). Benedict XV recognized EPHREM THE SYRIAN deacon (1920); Pius XI: PETER CANISIUS (1925), JOHN OF THE CROSS (1926), ROBERT BELLARMINE (1931), and ALBERT THE GREAT (1932). Pius XII named the Franciscan ANTHONY OF PADUA (1946), and John XXIII brought the number to 30 in nominating the Capuchin LAWRENCE OF BRINDISI (1959). Paul VI named the first two women doctors, TERESA OF ÁVILA (1970) and CATHERINE OF SIENA (1970). John Paul II followed by nominating THÉRÈSE OF LISIEUX (1997). There are 25 Westerners and 8 Easterners, 14 secular priests and 16 regulars, including 2 popes, 18 bishops, 9 priests, and 1 deacon.

See Also: DOCTRINE.

Bibliography: E. VALTON, *Dictionnaire de théologie catholique,* ed. A. VACANT et al., 15 v. (Paris 1903–50; Tables générales 1951–) 4.2:1509–10. *Sacrae theologiae summa,* ed. FATHERS OF THE SOCIETY OF JESUS, PROFESSORS OF THE THEOLOGICAL FACULTIES IN SPAIN, 4 v. (Madrid), v. 1 (5th ed. 1962) 1.3: 822–823.

[B. FORSHAW/EDS.]

DOCTRINE

The word doctrine comes from the Latin *doctrina,* the Vulgate translation for διδασκαλία and διδαχή. It means teaching or instruction and is closely associated with the words CATECHESIS and KERYGMA. It is used both in the active sense of the imparting of knowledge and in the passive sense of what is taught.

Christ was a teacher, and His teaching was what He had received from the Father (Jn 3.13; 5.17; 8.25–27). This teaching had continuity with that of Moses and the Prophets, but it completed and added to it. Christ taught with power and authority (Mt 7.29), and man's eternal SALVATION depended on the way this teaching was accepted (Lk 9.26). After Christ's Resurrection and Ascension the APOSTLES saw their task as that of handing on faithfully what they had received from Christ (Rom 16.17; Gal 1.8; Eph 4.14; Col 2.6–8; 1 Tm 1.3; 2 Timothy 1.13–14; 2.2; 3.14; Titus 1.9). The word doctrine was used not only of their teaching (1 Tm 4.6, 16) but also of the content of their preaching (Acts 2.42). It was the good news, the gospel, and from it stemmed the new way of life of the Christian. It was the message of salvation, the kerygma. Although acceptance of the good news was required before enrollment into the Church, and although the teaching of Christ soon became formulated into PROFESSIONS OF FAITH, it was never merely a theoretical communication of knowledge or information about certain salvific events. It was always directed beyond knowledge to a change of heart; it became effective in action. Just as the Apostles became changed men after Pentecost and proclaimed their belief in Christ, so were their hearers expected to change their lives and hand on the message they had received [*see* CONVERSION II (THEOLOGY OF)]. From the beginning the Church was a teaching Church that looked back to certain historical happenings but also forward to the future transformation of the world that these events heralded.

Preaching and Catechesis. This teaching office of the Church was exercised chiefly through preaching and instruction, or catechesis. Preaching was closely associated with the liturgy and was addressed to believers throughout the year as occasioned by the season or feast. Catechesis was a basic introduction to the faith and so gave a more general picture, but in both cases Christian teaching never considered knowledge as an end in itself. That was more the tendency among the Gnostics. Knowledge was a practical knowledge, a means of closer union with God. This is seen very clearly in the development of the CATECHUMENATE, the instruction given before reception into the Church. This consisted of an explanation of the creed and an instruction in the Bible—often in the form of a narration of SALVATION history from the Fall to the Last Judgment. This was accompanied by a period of probation so that it was a moral as well as an intellectual preparation for Baptism. St. Augustine in his *De catechizandis rudibus* gives an account of the method to be adopted, and in St. Cyril of Jerusalem's *Catecheses,* written in 348, one has examples of the instructions given. In the ceremonies that took place during Lent one can see how in fact the catechumenate was closely associated with the liturgical worship of the Church.

Accommodation and Systematization. The Christian message cannot be proclaimed in isolation from human experience and thought. Indeed, the earliest statements of Christian doctrine were formulated in Semitic and Greek thought forms, for together with the task of preaching and catechizing there is the need to speak the message to man in the condition in which he is found (*see* ACCOMMODATION). For this task a certain amount of reflection and systematization is necessary. In order to safeguard the kerygma and avoid the excesses and deficiencies of HERESY, ideas have to be further clarified, and in order to appeal to the educated, revealed truths have to be related to those known naturally. Thus one has the work of such men as Origen, whose systematization arose from the needs of the catechetical school of Alexandria. Whenever the Church is confronted with a new situation, there is a need to re-present the Christian teaching. The Holy Spirit has been given to the Church to guide it in this so that it never departs from the message of Christ and hands on what is merely a human fabrication. A systematic exposition of Christianity is consequently demanded by the needs of instruction and preaching. Theological science deals with revelation primarily from the standpoint of truth, whereas catechetics stresses the goodness of the teaching, but the two cannot be divorced, and the theoretical has to be associated with the practical since there is a danger that doctrine may become isolated from vital problems [*see* METHODOLOGY (THEOLOGY)].

At some periods of history this has been the case. The Council of Trent realized the need for a greater instruction of the faithful, and the catechisms of the Counter Reform of Canisius, Bellarmine and others were marked by the way in which they set out a summary of Christian belief in all its fullness. The need for a better knowledge of the faith can also be seen in the widespread establishment of the Confraternity of Christian Doctrine,

whose purpose is to deepen the knowledge of the ordinary faithful. This stress on the objective content of revelation was continued as a reaction against the excessive subjectivism of the Modernists, for whom doctrine was simply a way of expressing a religious sense with dogma differing from age to age. Consequently, since the Reformation, Catholics have more often understood the word doctrine of a body of truths and used other words to express the active teaching of the faith. But the liturgical movement and modern catechetics have helped to restore the balance, and once more the practical takes precedence over the theoretical aspect of doctrine.

Concerning the system of Christian doctrine, early summaries and creeds soon coalesced into the present form of the creed, where there is expressed: first, belief in God the Father of all; then belief in Christ the Redeemer, involving an account of salvation history especially as seen in the mysteries of His Passion, death, Resurrection, and Ascension; and finally, belief in the Holy Spirit and His work of sanctification in the Church, which will continue until the end of the world.

See Also: DOCTOR OF THE CHURCH; DOCTRINE, DEVELOPMENT OF; DOGMA; DOGMATIC THEOLOGY; NOTES, THEOLOGICAL; TEACHING AUTHORITY OF THE CHURCH (MAGISTERIUM); THEOLOGY.

Bibliography: *Dictionnaire de théologie catholique,* ed. A. VACANT et al., 15 v. (Paris 1903–50) Tables générales 1:1012. Y. M. J. CONGAR, "*Traditio* und *Sacra Doctrina* bei Thomas von Aquin," in *Kirche und Überlieferung,* eds., J. BETZ and H. FRIES (Freiburg 1960) 170–210. J. A. JUNGMANN, *Handing on the Faith,* tr. and rev. A. N. FUERST (New York 1959). V. SCHÜRR, in *Concilium,* 3.1 (1965) 78–81. G. VAN ACKEREN, *Sacra doctrina: The Subject of the First Question of the Summa theologica of St. Thomas Aquinas* (Rome 1952).

[M. E. WILLIAMS]

DOCTRINE, DEVELOPMENT OF

Although the development of DOGMA is closely connected with the development of THEOLOGY (the first is usually elaborated in the second), "doctrine," when it is used in the phrase "development of doctrine," is not understood in a generic sense, as including theology, but in a specific sense, as the objective correlative of FAITH. However, it is preferable not to define doctrinal development at the beginning of a discussion on the subject, for it is about the very nature of development that the discussion must turn. It is necessary, nevertheless, to indicate the elements of the problem.

(1) The objective correlative of faith, if not exclusively, then at least in an essential aspect, is understandable TRUTH, which can be communicated in human

language. (2) The historical revelation of that truth was given in a definite epoch, closed, as is generally admitted by orthodox Christianity, at the end of the apostolic generation. (3) Since that moment points of doctrine that were not explicit in the primitive DEPOSIT OF FAITH have, nevertheless, emerged in dogmatic tradition. Thus defined, the problem is posed for all forms of Christianity that accept its terms: the Roman Catholic and the Eastern Orthodox as well as those forms of Protestantism and Anglicanism which allow that in the CREED there may be points of doctrine which, although agreeing with Scripture, are not explicit in it.

General History of the Problem. The Fathers of the 4th century, engaged in elucidating the central dogmas of Christian faith, were clearly aware of the fact of development. In a letter concerning the admission into the Church of those who denied the divinity of the Holy Ghost, St. Basil declared that, according to Athanasius and the practice of many bishops, they were to be admitted if they held the true Nicene faith (*Epist.* 204.6; *Patrologia Graeca*, ed. J. P. Migne, 32:753). And Gregory of Nazianzus asked that the divinity of the Holy Ghost not be affirmed in the presence of the weak because that point of doctrine was still beyond their power (*Or.* 41.6–8; *Patrologia Graeca* 36:437–39). He justifies this attitude by a theory of development: in His manifestation of truth God does not proceed by violence but by conviction, gradually integrating truth up to its fullness. Mankind first had to realize the divinity of the Father, next that of the Son, and now that of the Spirit (*Or.* 31.25–26; *Patrologia Graeca* 36:160–64). Such attitudes and utterings are unthinkable if the Fathers had in their minds that an explicit statement of the Trinity did belong to the deposit of faith.

Later, however, after the great dogmas of Christian doctrine had been firmly established and commonly accepted, awareness of development began to wane. The idea prevailed that the Church was to differentiate between true and false traditions by means of the triple test of VINCENT OF LERINS' canon: "*quod ubique, quod semper, quod ab omnibus creditum est*—what has been believed everywhere, always, and by all" (*Commonitorium* 1.2; *Patrologia Latina*, ed. J. P. Migne, 50:640). In the controversies of the 17th century between Catholics and Protestants, the Vincentian rule was still admitted by both parties without qualification. Bossuet only voiced the general sentiment of his age when he wrote: "if at any time someone says that the faith includes something which yesterday was not said to be of the faith, it is always heterodoxy.There is no difficulty about recognizing false doctrine. It is recognized at once, whenever it appears, merely because it is new" ["Instruction pastorale sur les promesses de l'Eglise," *Oeuvres completes* (Paris

1828) 30:419–20]. Of course heresies often compelled the Church to express her truths in clear technical language. But these explanations declare only what the Church has always explicitly and consciously believed.

Soon after Bossuet the problem of development became topical, and by the end of the 19th century it had become the most urgent and difficult problem posed for Catholic apologetics. The reasons for this change are various. From LEIBNIZ on, German thought elaborated the idea of development and progress as the inner meaning of history. In addition, the success of DARWIN's theory of evolution led to its acceptance as a general hypothesis to explain the origin of things and ideas. More particularly, modern historical investigation set forth with increasing evidence the fact and range of development. Finally the dogmatic definitions of the 19th century were beset by special difficulties.

Types of Solution. Doctrinal development is explained in three ways: as a process of logical unfolding (logical theories), historical transmutation (transformistic theories), or supernaturally guided continuity (theological theories). The second is considered as heretical by all orthodox Christians. It does not accept the elements or terms of the problem (see above), but it has to be carefully examined if one is to grasp the all-important difference between it and the theological theory. Each of the three solutions is connected with a different conception of the nature of revelation and faith.

Logical Theories. The logical explanation of doctrinal development supposes an exclusively propositional conception of faith and revelation. Through His Prophets God has publicly communicated to mankind a set of truths about Himself and SALVATION. Divine faith is an assent to these propositions because of the authority of God, who has revealed them. If so, development itself cannot but be propositional, i.e., logical. Logic provides at the same time the way and the test of true development.

Most of the logical theories were already elaborated by the scholastics of the 16th and 17th century in order to answer the question whether and how one could accept a theological conclusion with an assent of faith. After the Modernist crisis, contemporary scholastics took refuge in these theories in order to solve the problem of development. In order to understand the different shades of logical theory some distinctions must be grasped. (1) Propositions are formally revealed when they are contained in the verbal expression of primitive faith, either explicitly or implicitly. Implicitly revealed propositions are those that follow from a logical comparison of propositions that are explicitly revealed. The reasoning by which the implicitly revealed becomes explicit is said to be a mere explanatory syllogism, and the conclusion is not properly an inference. (2) Propositions are only virtually revealed when a premise of natural reason has to intervene in order to deduce them from a revealed proposition. In this case one has to do with inferential syllogisms and real theological conclusions. (3) Some theological conclusions produce a necessary quality of revealed truth, and then their inclusion in revealed truth is said to be "virtual-identical"; others produce only something connected with revealed truth by reason of historical contingent facts, e.g., that this person is a saint on account of an infallible declaration of the Church, and then the inclusion is said to be "virtual-connected" (*see* REVELATION, VIRTUAL).

One group of theologians (Cardinal Franzelin, R. Schultes, R. Garrigou-Lagrange), considering that true inference leads to new insight, excluded the virtually revealed from the deposit. The Church cannot define it as dogma, to be held by divine faith, but only as truth, to be held by ecclesiastical faith. Others, considering that the foregoing theory does not cover the facts, extended the range of possible dogmatic development to the virtually revealed: either without any limitation (M. Tuyaerts), so that theological conclusions of all kinds may be defined as divine truth and ought individually to be held by divine faith even before the definition, if one sees the logical sequence; or with the limitation that only conclusions that are virtual-identical can be defined, thus excluding virtual-connected conclusions and leaving room for a kind of ecclesiastical belief; or with the limitation that theological conclusions become objects of divine faith only in virtue of ecclesiastical definition (F. Marin-Sola). Many early twentieth-century writers admitted that the logical connection between the new definition and the formally revealed doctrine need only be probable, but then they already inclined to the theological theory.

Transformistic Theories. All transformistic theories profess that unchangeable doctrine is not of the essence of Christianity. They draw a sharp distinction between doctrine that is nonessential and something else that they consider to be the essence: the Bible, freely to be interpreted according to the general evolution of thought (LATITUDINARIANISM); religious experience, general or specifically Christian [liberal theology (*see* LIBERALISM, THEOLOGICAL)]; faith as an existential decision (*see* EXISTENTIAL THEOLOGY). Since this article is not considering transformistic theories for their own sake, it may dispense with the treatment of all of them except that based on religious experience.

General Structure. This theory supposes an exclusively experiential conception of revelation and faith. Revelation is always at work in human experience, slowly creating, purifying, and clarifying a consciousness of

communion with God in the individual and in humanity. Faith is an inner disponibility for that revelation, leading to a growth of intimate conviction, self-surrender to God, reformation of all sentiments and attitudes. Propositional doctrines are no more than creations of the mind, inspired by faith, but by no means containing the truth of revelation, which by its necessary in order to guide one's religious reflection. They change with the general evolution of culture. The identity of contemporary faith with that of the Apostolic age is an identity not of doctrine but only of inspiration.

German Proponents. The origin of this theory lies in German PIETISM. According to P. J. SPENER (1635–1705) one is not a Christian by virtue of his acceptance of orthodox doctrine but by virtue of the inner disposition of his heart. J. S. Semler (1725–1791) already sees an opposition between private religion, which is true religion, and public religion, which is but a condition of the historical continuation of private religion. Public religion must create a uniform doctrine for the use of the community, and this inevitably leads to different confessions, degrading compromises, and historical transmutations according to the evolution of culture. According to SCHLEIERMACHER (1768–1834), Christianity is a spirit, the spirit of Christ, who through the Holy Ghost bestows upon Christians a participation in His perfect experiences of the redeeming love of the Father and this unites them into one invisible community. This intimate participation leads to a slow transformation of the public norm of doctrine and behavior. The Church is "a whole in motion, capable of progress and development," but this may never be thought of as directed "towards a perfection beyond that which is established in Christ" [F. Schleiermacher, *Samtliche Werke* (Berlin 1884) 12.1:72]. It is a genuine development because the perfection at which it aims is not implicitly given in the apostolic doctrine, but only in the Person of Christ Himself, who continually inspires His Church with His living spirit. Throughout history, the Church expresses with increasing fullness and purity the spirit of the Lord. This conception, according to Schleiermacher, is specifically Protestant, because the Catholic Church does not admit any evolution in doctrine itself but only in its formulation.

Schleiermacher, and after him A. RITSCHL and his school, hold to a specifically Christian experience and present one with a rather optimistic view of doctrinal history. Not so A. VON HARNACK (1851–1930): he reduces true religion to an interior experience and attitude that, although they reached their purest expression in Christ, are as old as religious humanity. True interior religion is a matter of the heart. In this essential respect Christianity is beyond history or development. But religion cannot live without a body: a visible society with creeds and social norms. It creates, then, according to its needs and to historical circumstances, the forms of life that it cannot dispense with. On that level it is subject to development and successive transformations, in which, however, the essence of Christianity is not at stake. All historical forms, Protestant as well as Catholic, are in part failures. They are respectable only insofar as they convey the Gospel message and foster the interior life of religious experience. They are not objects of any science of faith, but only of historical investigation.

Loisy, Tyrrell. Modernism in the Catholic Church was born from an ambiguous reaction against liberal Protestantism. A. LOISY presented his first essays as a refutation of Harnack, but at the same time he was deeply influenced by liberal ideas. He rejected the individualism and dualism of Harnack. There is nothing in Christianity that is not historical and social. Its essence is to be found in the fullness of its social and historical life. The Church is not opposed to the Gospel but is its continuation. If the kingdom of God is not the Church, it is to become the Church. In the development of its organization, doctrine, and cult, the essence of Christianity manifests itself with increasing clearness. But the historian can only describe the outward appearance and historical sequence of doctrines and cultural forms in which the mystery of a supernatural intuition clothes itself in accordance with the general development of human consciousness. That intuition, however, has not a separate life in souls. It lives and thrives in its historical forms. For each age the divine authority of the Church gives the sole genuine interpretation of the gospel. The error of Loisy seems to have been that the norm of development is exclusively conceived by him as a mysterious intuition. Doctrine is not the translation of the truth of that intuition into human concepts, but a mere symbol, pointing to it and changing according to its cultural surroundings. The identity of doctrine through its manifold development is not so much of a problem, because the identity of Christianity does not lie on that level. Liberal dualism persists, but the relation between its two terms is conceived otherwise. Apart from his Catholic stress on church and authority, Loisy is nearer to Schleiermacher than to Harnack, but in his acceptance of Christ as an absolute norm, Schleiermacher was a more genuine Christian than Harnack or Loisy.

The clearest statement of the Modernist theory was given by G. TYRRELL (1861–1909). One is to choose between old and new theology. According to the first, the Church speaks from memory of a revealed truth once given in the past; then identity of doctrine can only be warranted by logical reduction of present doctrine to antiquity. According to the second, the Church speaks from an always present vision that defies conceptual translation. That vision works as "a spiritual force or impetus."

It creates an intellectual embodiment varying with the history of human consciousness. Tyrrell identified that vision or spiritual force with "the mystical element in religion" analyzed by his friend F. von HÜGEL.

Theological Theory. The third theory is called theological because it introduces in the process of development and in the guarantee of its faithfulness a SUPERNATURAL factor that can only be accepted by faith and elucidated by theology.

General Structure. It supposes a conception of revelation and faith that combines intimately a propositional and a nonpropositional moment. God not only gives to His Church a doctrine of salvation, expressed in human words, but also a light to enter into living communion with the reality of the saving God. This inner light does not make Christians see or know explicitly anything independent from the message but enables them to attain in the message itself the mystery about which it speaks. The integral concept of revelation, then, not only comprises the public prophetical revelation, given and closed in a definite epoch (revelation in the strict theological sense), but also the inner unveiling of its truth by the light of faith. Faith, in consequences, is an assent to propositional doctrine; but through these propositions it is in touch with the ineffable reality of divine mystery, so that, according to Thomas Aquinas, the propositions are not so much the object of faith as "the means through which faith tends to its object" (*De ver.* 14.8 ad 11). The starting point of development, then, is an imperfect and partial verbal expression of the divine mystery of salvation together with an abiding supernatural grasp of the mystery as a whole. If a few words may introduce a man into the inner world of someone who speaks to him, why should the imperfect utterances of primitive doctrine not introduce men into the inner world of God, if He speaks to men through His Prophets and enlightens men through His Spirit?

It follows that the deposit of faith is not only a set of propositions about God but the divine mystery as communicated through a partial expression to the mind of the Church, enlightened and guided by the indwelling Spirit. As the mystery of God and salvation is a coherent whole in which all aspects are intimately connected, the implicit aspects are already indicated in the explicit. Doctrinal development, then, is a process of explication, historically conditioned but guided by the light of the Spirit. In that process new aspects emerge from the depths of the mystery into the consciousness of the Church, but always in connection with what is explicitly believed. The Church, consulting that ripening consciousness, declares from time to time, under the pressure of circumstances, that some point or other, which formerly was not explicitly believed, belongs to the original treasure of revelation.

The process partakes of the mysterious character of its object. Hence it is often impossible to show in an entirely satisfactory way by means of history and reasoning that the new is included in the old. Therefore ecclesiastical definition is not only the instrument by which a development becomes objective, i.e., imposing itself on all believers, but it is also the conclusive guarantee that it is divinely true, i.e., that its content belongs to the original revelation (*see* DEFINITION, DOGMATIC).

Beginnings. The first traces of this theory are to be found in the works of two Catholics theologians of Tåbingen, J. S. von DREY (1777–1853) and J. A. MÖHLER (1796–1838). They are greatly influenced by contemporary idealistic philosophy. Their central idea is a conception of the Church as an organic whole, animated by the Holy Ghost and subject therefore to growth in all respects, doctrine being one of them. The history of the Church is the reality of that growth. Sometimes their conception is called "organistic." Indeed, the metaphor of the organism enhances the unity of the starting point of development (against logicism) and the identity of doctrine throughout the process (against transformism). Drey and Möhler think that the KINGDOM OF GOD is the all-inclusive idea of Christian dogma. Möhler describes how, through the activity of the Spirit, the Christian message sinks into the Church so as to become there the inmost foundation of conscious life (*intimus conscientiae fundus*) in which the object of faith is rather lived as a whole and directly contemplated than reflected upon or analyzed. Under the pressure of heresy that living whole becomes an object of reflection, and in this way the unconscious focus of faith is gradually broken down as it were by refraction into its various aspects, and its riches become more distinct and explicit. Möhler does not, however, analyze the process of development itself, nor does he verify his idea by a careful study of the facts. He is rather vague in his statement of the nature and the range of development.

Solov'ev. The thought of V. SOLOV'EV (1853–1900) betrays the same influences of German philosophy. He too has a predilection for organistic imagery. He likewise stresses the extrinsic influence of HERESY and the inner character of wholeness. But in accordance with the main idea of his Christian philosophy, he considers the INCARNATION as the all-inclusive revealed reality. The Incarnation is the point at which God inserts Himself in mankind, and the universal Church is the historical reality of that progressive Incarnation. Development takes place on the human level of that incarnational reality but under the influence of the divine principle, which contains the whole of truth in an unchangeable way. There is always a logical link between the new dogmas and the all-inclusive idea. Development is an objective process because truths that

formerly were not to be professed explicitly by the Christian community become obligatory dogmas by virtue of the legitimate exercise of the infallible teaching authority of the Church.

Cardinal Newman. The contribution of J. H. NEWMAN (1808–1890) is unique owing to his originality, his minute knowledge of facts, and his comprehensiveness. To him development is a necessary characteristic of all living truth in human society. If revelation is entrusted to historical mankind, it can only conserve its living identity by faithful development. The deposit is no mere list of articles, but a rich idea "all parts of which are connected together so that he who really knows one part, may be said to know all" [letter to J. S. Flanagan (Feb. 15, 1868), *Gregorianum* 39 (1958) 5941]. The Apostles perceived the whole *per modum unius* through a knowledge that was only partly explicit. Tradition is a handing over of a creed but with the supernatural gift, bestowed upon the Church, of knowing its true and full meaning. Together with the historical continuity of the message, divine GRACE "fosters in the bosom of intuition" (*Fifteen Sermons*), "an intimate sense" (Newman-Perrone paper), a "real apprehension" (*A Grammar of Assent*) of the divine mystery. Development, then, is a historical process: all that makes the history of the Church conditions the process of development.

Newman analyzes the different roles of heresy, theology, the FAITHFUL, ecclesiastical government, dogmatic authority, national pluralism. The process that results from all this is a supernaturally guided unfolding: new aspects of the mystery emerge from the unconscious (not reflectively conscious) idea or vision of faith, but apprehended in connection with explicit doctrine. The transition is not an act of logical deduction but rather a perception of how the new point fits within the total pattern, synthetically apprehended as a whole in its explicit and implicit fullness (ANALOGY OF FAITH). An analysis of the process would bring to light a multitude of convergent logical relations between the new points and other doctrines, but the new points do not "become logical, because theologians afterwards can reduce them to their relations to other doctrines" (letter to Flanagan, *op. cit.* 596).

That later dogmas are original parts of the deposit that can only be finally warranted by a supernatural organ of the supernaturally enlivened body of the Church: infallible authority. It is possible however to defend the general consistency of the Catholic doctrine throughout its history on a broad rational basis: the general notes of healthy development. Newman sets down seven of them: "There is no corruption if it retains one and the same type, the same principles, the same organization; if its beginnings anticipate its subsequent phases, and if later phenomena protect and subserve its earlier; if it has a power of assimilation and revival, and a vigorous action from first to last'' (*Essay on the Development*). It is significant that the notes regard at the same time the whole and the parts of the process.

Blondel. In his ''Histoire et dogme'' (1904) the French philosopher M. BLONDEL (1861–1949) supplied another original contribution to a theological understanding of development. What nexus is there, he asks, between the facts of primitive Christianity and present doctrine? He repudiates two solutions: extrinsicism, which simply admits that all present dogmas must be primitive, because the Church is admittedly infallible on the ground of her being divine, as may be demonstrated by external miraculous facts; historicism (Loisy), which reduces the reality of Christianity to its historical appearances and ignores its organic unity and its supernatural experience, nourished by the love for Christ and the efforts of sanctification. The object of that experience is Christian truth as a whole, concentrated in the reality of Christ. Although partly expressed, it is entirely possessed and acted upon from the beginning. There is much in it that is only ''subconscious, unreflected, provisionally and partly irreducible to explicit thought'' (210). Development is a passage from ''implicitly lived'' (*implicite vecu*) to ''explicitly known'' (*explicite connu*). The whole life of the Church enters into the process. There are definite connections between recent dogma and previous doctrine, but they are not reducible to Aristotelian syllogisms. ''Infallible authority is the superior and truly supernatural guarantee'' (216).

20th Century. For a long time the theological solution did not make its way in ecclesiastical circles. In the times of the Modernist crisis, the ideas of Möhler, Newman, and Blondel were confounded with those of the Modernists. Of course, there were theologians, such as M. de la Barre, who fully grasped and prudently adopted the theological solution. But on the whole they found but little understanding. Later, theologians such as Marin-Sola tried to interpret Newman's thought in the sense of their own logical conception. The cause of that misunderstanding was clearly the deep-seated, exclusively propositioned conception of revelation and faith, and the general influence of RATIONALISM on theology since the beginning of the modern era. Rationalism, which separates reason from the living whole of human personality, is by its very nature unable to understand any legitimate progress of knowledge that is not reducible to formal deductive inference.

Two factors contributed to the general change of intellectual climate: for one thing, the historical evidence that an exclusively propositional conception of revelation and faith was entirely alien to antiquity and to the great theologians of the Middle Ages; and second, the predominance of personalist and existential trends in contemporary thought. According to PERSONALISM, ''man moves as a whole,'' as Newman said, and as embedded in the wider totality of historical and contemporary mankind. Rationalism is an illusion. Reason should not and simply cannot cut itself off from the total movement of conscious life. Man should critically take into account the personal and social roots that secretly help to determine his viewpoints and his first principles. This is the only way of freeing reason and attaining to true rationality. Existential thinking stresses the fact that all reflection is reflection upon a prereflective self-conscious existence and a spontaneous experiential thought, thriving upon a direct, unexpressed and subconscious awareness, the riches of which cannot be exhausted by reflective analysis and objectivation (*see* EXISTENTIALISM). It is clear that such views fit in with the presuppositions of the theological theory.

Since Vatican Council II, two movements have developed: one toward relativism, another toward a reconciliation of relativity and irreformable truth. The former has been influenced by the first generation of the philosophers of linguistic analysis. Paul Van Buren, for instance, applied to the question the so-called principle of verification to religious doctrine and concluded from this that no theoretical propositions about an extramundane reality could have any meaning. Christ for example was no more than the purest realization of man ''existing for others'' and His Resurrection means only that the contagious power of His example continues after His death. Theologians such as P. Tillich were also influential. According to him, dogmas are symbols that as logical propositions do not enounce a truth about God but are occasions for a personal revelation of the divine in ecstatic experience. Such symbols, as accepted by the community, are valuable as long as they work; but they may die and be replaced by others.

The encounter with contemporary hermeneutics is very important for this question. The problem with the development of dogma is now seen to be the way in which the hermeneutical question was asked within traditional Catholic theology. Hermeneutic interpretation, as Hans-Georg Gadamer explained in his now classic *Truth and Method,* demands that the text to be interpreted be confronted within the horizon of worldview of both the ancient writer and the contemporary critic (fusion of horizons).

The advances in analytical philosophy are also important. According to these developments, different "languages" or methods of conveying meaning, each with its own logic, co-exist and sometimes overlap. As applied to theology, this theory would hold that dogmatic and theological statements belong to a different "language." Acceptable change in theology, therefore, would not be limited by dogmatic formulations which, according to this perspective, would be written in terms of such elementary, common sense concepts that their obvious meaning would remain unchanged and unchangeable even in the midst of theological evolution.

In *Mysterium Ecclesiae* (1973) the Congregation for the Doctrine of Faith made a distinction between the meaning of a dogma, which always remains true, and the dogmatic formulas of the Church, which also are simply true for those who understand them but are perfectible and replaceable when changed historical conceptions make it desirable or necessary.

It is the merit of contemporary theology to have revalued the ancient conception of revelation and faith as the supernatural focus from which development of doctrine proceeds.

See Also: DOGMATIC THEOLOGY; METHODOLOGY (THEOLOGY); REASONING, THEOLOGICAL; RELATIVISM; REVELATION, THEOLOGY OF; SYMBOL IN REVELATION; THEOLOGICAL TERMINOLOGY; TRADITION (IN THEOLOGY).

Bibliography: General surveys. *Dictionnaire de théologie catholique*, ed. A. VACANT et al. (Tables générales 1951–) 1:1016–21. K. RAHNER, *Lexikon für Theologie und Kirche*, ed. J. HOFER and K. RAHNER, 10 v. (Freiburg 1930–38) 3:457–63. P. A. LIEGE, *Catholicisme. Hier, aujourd'hui et demain,* ed. G. JACQUEMET 3:957–62. E. H. SCHILLEBEECKX *Theologisch woordenboek*, ed. H. BRINK, 3 v. (Roermond 1952–58) 1:1087–1106. M. SCHMAUS, *Katholische Dogmatik*, 5 v. in 8 (5th ed. Munich 1953–59; 6th ed. 1960–) 1 (1960) 84–101. **Historical studies.** E. HOCEDEZ, *Histoire de la théologie au XIXe siècle*, 3 v. (Brussels-Paris): v. 1 (1800–31) (1948); v. 2, 1831–78 (1952); v. 3, 1878–1903 (1947). O. CHADWICK, *From Bossuet to Newman* (Cambridge, England 1957). A. MINON, "L'Attitude de Jean Adam Moehler dans la question du developpement du dogme," *Ephemerides theologicae Lovanienses* 16 (1939) 328–82. J. H. WALGRAVE, *Newmann the Theologian*, tr. A. D. LITTLEDALE (New York 1960). E. POULAT, *Histoire, dogme et critique dans la crise moderniste* (Paris 1962). **Sources.** J. H. NEWMAN, *Fifteen Sermons Preached before the University of Oxford Between 1826 and 1843* (3d ed. London 1872; New York 1918); *An Essay on the Development of Christian Doctrine*, ed. C. F. HARROLD (New York 1949); "The Newman-Perrone Paper on Development of Doctrine," *ibid.* 39 (1958) 585–96, a letter to J. S. Flanagan with some historical background, also appears in *The Letters and Diaries of John Henry Newman*, ed. C. S. DESSAIN (New York 1961–). M. BLONDEL, "Histoire et dogme" (1904) in *Les Premiers écrits de Maurice Blondel* (Paris 1956). V. S. SOLOV'EV *History and Future of Theocracy* (1885–87) in *Works* (St. Peterburg 1901–07) 3:270–382, the main work of Solov'ev on this question. M. M. TUYAERTS, *L'Évolution du dogme* (Louvain 1919). F. SCHULTES, *Introductio in historiam dogmatum* (Paris 1922). F. MARIN–SOLA, *L'Évolution homogene du dogme catholique*, 2 v. (2d ed. Fribourg 1924). R. DRAGUET, "L'Évolution des dogmes," in M. BRILLANT and M. NEDONCELLE et al., *Apologétique* (Paris 1948) 1097–1122. H. D. SIMONIN, "'Implicite' et 'explicite' dans le developpment du dogme," *Angelicum* 14 (1937) 126–45. H. DE LUBAC, "Le Problème du développement du dogme," *Recherches de science religieuse* 35 (1948) 130–60. F. TAYMANS, "Le Progrès du dogme," *Nouvelle revue théologique* 71 (1949) 687–700. J. DUHR, L'Évolution du dogme de l'Immaculée Conception," *ibid.* 73 (1951) 1013–32. E. DHANIS, "Revelation explicite et implicite," *Gregorianum* 34 (1953) 187–237. K. RAHNER, "Überlegungen zur Dogmenentwicklung," *Schriften zur Theologie* 4 (1960) 11–50. H. HAMMANS, *Die neueren katholischen Erklarungen der Dogmentwicklung* (Essen 1965). "Recent Views in the Development of Dogma," ed. E. SCHILLEBEECKX, *Concilium* 21 (1967) 109–31. J. RATZINGER, *Das Problem der Dogmengeschichte in der Sicht der katholischen Theologie* (Cologne, Opladen 1966). Z. ALSZEGHY and M. FLICK, *Lo sviluppo del dogma cattolico* (Brescia 1967). D. CONNELL, "Professor Dewart and Dogmatic Development," *The Irish Theological Quarterly* 34 (1967) 309–28; 35 (1968) 33–57, 117–40. W. C. HUNT, *Intuition: The Key to Newman's Theory of Doctrinal Development* (Washington 1967). J. STERN, *Bible et tradition chez Newman: Aux origines de la théorie du développement* (Paris 1967). M. WILES, *The Making of the Christian Dogma: Study in the Principles of Early Doctrinal Development* (Cambridge 1967). W. SCHULZ, *Dogmenentwicklung als Problem der Geschichtlichkeit der Wahrheitserkenntnis* (Rome 1969). J. H. WALGRAVE, *Unfolding Revelation* (London, Philadelphia 1972); "Change in Christian Dogmatic Language," *Louvain Studies* 4 (1973) 245–53. H. H. PRICE, *Belief* (New York 1969).

[J. H. WALGRAVE]

DODD, CHARLES HAROLD

New Testament scholar; b. Wrexham, Wales, April 7, 1884; d. Goring, England, Sept. 22, 1973. After receiving a B.A. from University College, Oxford, in 1906 and then studying at Berlin, Dodd pursued theological studies at Mansfield College, Oxford, from 1908 to 1911 and was ordained as a Congregational minister in 1912. He served as pastor of Warwick Congregational Church until 1915, when he was appointed New Testament lecturer, later professor, at Mansfield. In 1930 he became Rylands Professor at Manchester and in 1935 the first non-Anglican Norris Hulse Professor at Cambridge, holding the post until 1949.

The author of numerous scholarly works, he was particularly known for the concept of "realized eschatology" set forth in *Parables of the Kingdom* (1935) and *History and the Gospel* (1938). This theory emphasized the presence of the kingdom of God in the ministry of Christ and placed less emphasis on eschatology as having to do with future events. Dodd was also known for his theory of the New Testament KERYGMA (proclamation, preaching) set forth in *The Apostolic Preaching and Its Developments* (1936). Another area of special interest for him was the Gospel of John, treated in *Interpretation of the Fourth Gospel* (1953) and *Historical Tradition in the*

Fourth Gospel (1963). In 1950 he was appointed director of the ecumenical group of scholars that produced the translation of the Bible published in 1970 as the New English Bible (NT 1961). A participant in the ecumenical movement, Dodd addressed the 1948 founding assembly of the World Council of Churches on the biblical basis for Christian unity.

Bibliography: W. D. DAVIES and D. DAUBE, eds., *The Background of the New Testament and Its Eschatology: In Honour of C. H. Dodd* (Cambridge 1956) contains a bibliography of Dodd's writings.

[T. EARLY]

DODGE CITY, DIOCESE OF

Established May 19, 1951, as the fourth diocese in Kansas, the Diocese of Dodge City *(Dodgepolis)* comprises an area of 23,000 square miles in the southwestern part of the state. A suffragan of the Metropolitan See of Kansas City, approximately 20 percent of its total population is Catholic, distributed among 50 parishes.

The area was in turn under the jurisdiction of the Vicariate Apostolic of Kansas (1850–77) and the Dioceses of Leavenworth (1877–87) and Wichita (1887–1951). Philip Colleton, SJ, traveled from the Osage Native American Mission to minister to soldiers stationed at Fts. Larned and Dodge in 1868–69. Felix Swenberg, pastor in Wichita, was placed in charge of missions in the southwestern part of the state and was a prime promoter of Catholic colonization to the West; he served as president of St Dominic's Colonization Society, wrote articles for eastern publications, and worked assiduously for the Santa Fe Railroad to encourage Catholic colonies to locate in western Kansas. Irish, Germans, German-Russians populated the section in the 1870s and 1880s. The building of the Santa Fe and Rock Island railroads hastened settlement.

The first bishop of the See of Dodge City was John B. Franz, who was installed Sept. 12, 1951, and later transferred to the Diocese of Peoria, Aug. 8, 1959. The second bishop was Marion F. Forst, who was consecrated March 24, 1960, and installed April 5. He resigned from the see and was appointed auxiliary bishop of Kansas City in Kansas on Oct. 16, 1976. The third bishop was Eugene J. Gerber, who was appointed Bishop of Dodge City on Oct. 16, 1976, installed on Dec. 15, 1976, and later transferred to the Diocese of Wichita on Nov. 23, 1982. The fourth bishop was Stanley G. Schlarman, who was appointed Bishop of Dodge City in March of 1983, installed on May 4, 1983, and named Bishop Emeritus of Dodge City on May 11, 1998. The fifth bishop is Ronald M. Gilmore, who was appointed Bishop of Dodge City on May 11, 1998, and installed on July 16, 1998.

A new cathedral, named for the patroness of the diocese, Our Lady of Guadalupe, was dedicated on Dec. 9, 2001.

Bibliography: P. BECKMAN, *The Catholic Church on the Kansas Frontier, 1850–1877* (Washington 1943). R. J. BOLLIG, *History of Catholic Education in Kansas, 1836–1932* (Washington 1933). *Kansas: The First Century,* 4 v. (New York 1956) 2:300–326, 327–347. G. J. GARRAGHAN, *Jesuits of the Middle United States,* 3 v. (New York 1938). M. E. THOMAS, *Foot-prints on the Frontier* (Westminster, Md. 1948). T. F. WENZL, *A History of the Diocese of Dodge City* (Newton, KS 2001).

[M. E. THOMAS/B. MOORE]

DODO OF ASCH, BL.

Premonstratensian hermit; d. Asch, Friesland, Mar. 30, 1231. After several years of a marriage reluctantly contracted, he became a Premonstratensian canon of Mariengaard, and his wife entered a convent. Permitted to live as a hermit in a cell at Bakkeveen, Dodo practiced extraordinary austerities for many years. About five years before his death he moved to a sanctuary at Asch. His reputation for sanctity and wonder-working attracted the sick of every kind, and many were cured. Stigmata were found on his body when he died, but they may have been caused by the falling wall that killed him. His feast has been celebrated by the PREMONSTRATENSIANS in Spain at least since 1636.

Feast: March 30.

Bibliography: *Acta Sanctorum* March 3:847–849. H. THURSTON, "Some Physical Phenomena of Mysticism," *Month* 134 (1919) 45–46.

[J. J. JOHN]

DOGMA

The Greek word dogma, also used in English, is found among classical authors. It is derived from the Greek δοκεῖν, to seem. It can mean (1) a private opinion: what seems good to the individual; (2) a decree: what seems good to public authority; (3) the teaching of a philosopher, which was considered authoritative by his followers. In the Septuagint and New Testament the word is used of a decree of the state (Dn 2.13; 3.10; Lk 2.1). The ordinances of Moses (Eph 2.15; Col 2.14) are called dogmas, as also the decrees of the Council of Jerusalem (Acts 16.4).

However, it is a derivation of the third sense indicated above that finds general acceptance among the Fathers and theologians. Dogma is used either of a particular belief, a tenet—for example, the Christian teaching on the immortality of the soul or on the unity of God—or it is used of the whole system of belief, i.e., Christian dogma as distinct from pagan dogma. In the first three centuries among Latin and Greek writers nearly everything related to Christian belief and practice is called dogma. With Saints Basil and John Chrysostom it takes on a more fully developed meaning, viz, a truth above reason but revealed by Christ to His Church. The scholastics did not use the term often; St. Thomas Aquinas preferred the expression ARTICLE OF FAITH.

Contemporary Usage. Today dogma is widely used in a strict sense, for all and only those truths that have been revealed by God and proposed as such by the Church for belief by the FAITHFUL, that is, those things that Vatican Council I (H. Denzinger, *Enchiridion symbolorum* 3011) maintains have to be believed on divine and Catholic FAITH. Thus, denial of a dogma is HERESY. To be a dogma in this strict technical sense, the truth in question has to be part of the public revelation. (Thus, truths privately revealed are not dogmas.) Moreover, it has to be declared by the Church's authority to be believed as revealed. Since dogma is proposed for men's belief as revealed, it is the object of divine faith and is to be distinguished from those other truths that the Church proposes but not precisely as revealed.

Development. As revelation ceased with the death of the last Apostle, in enunciating a new dogma the Church does not add to revelation but simply declares or defines what has been revealed. The Church's task is to guard the DEPOSIT OF FAITH; this involves expounding it to different ages so that it always remains a living thing. The Church does not create a new thing; it merely states what has been revealed. Many factors contribute to the development of dogma.

Controversy can help to a better formulation of what the faith demands, and the devotional life and piety of the faithful is a constant means of deeper penetration into the truths of the Catholic religion. However, dogma is to be found not only in the solemn definitions of pope or council but in the ordinary day-to-day teaching of the Church. Under the guidance of the Holy Spirit the Church is continually uncovering the meaning and the riches of what has been revealed. This is the true meaning of the progress of dogma.

See Also: DOCTRINE; DEFINITION, DOGMATIC; DOGMATIC THEOLOGY, ARTICLES ON; FREEDOM, INTELLECTUAL; NOTES, THEOLOGICAL; RELATIVISM (THEOLOGICAL ASPECT); RULE OF FAITH.

Bibliography: *Dictionnaire de théologie catholique*, ed. A. VACANT et al., (Paris 1903–50) 1:1013–21. H. VORGRIMLER et al., *Lexikon für Theologie und Kirche*, ed. M. BUCHBERGER (Freiburg 1930–38) 3:438–446. G. W. H. LAMPE, ed., *A Patristic Greek Lexicon* (Oxford 1961—). P. A. LIÉGÉ, *Catholicisme* 3:951–962. J. R. GEISELMANN, *Handbuch theologischer Grundbegriffe*, ed. H. FRIES, (Munich 1962–63) 1:225–241. K. RAHNER and H. VORGRIMLER, *Kleines theologisches Wörterbuch* (Freiburg 1961) 73–74. C. JOURNET, *What is Dogma?* tr. M. PONTIFEX (New York 1964). H. RONDET, *Do Dogmas Change?* tr. M. PONTIFEX (New York 1961).

[M. E. WILLIAMS]

DOGMATIC FACT

A judgment of fact by which the deposit of revealed truth is applied to contingent realities, i.e., to particular persons, objects, and occurrences: e.g., the reigning pontiff is the authentic successor to St. Peter; Vatican II was an ecumenical council; the Canon of the Mass is free from doctrinal error; the propositions contained in a particular book concerning the faith are in error; this version of the Bible faithfully reproduces the sacred writings.

The magisterium may define infallibly such propositions, since it falls within its competence infallibly to guard as well as to explain the revealed deposit for the whole church. Those facts that are necessarily connected with the fulfillment of this office may be infallibly declared as true.

A dogmatic fact is distinguished from a particular fact. The latter is a proposition of a religious truth that does not involve or demand the faith of the whole church: e.g., this host is consecrated; this marriage is valid. In judging such facts the church may be mistaken, since a judgment depends upon fallible elements: e.g., one party to the marriage may have falsified his intention. For such facts the church does not demand an act of faith from all its members.

Bibliography: H. BACHT, *Lexikon für Theologie und Kirche*, ed. J. HOFER and K. RAHNER, 10 v. (2d, new ed. Freiburg 1957–65) 3:456–457. C. JOURNET, *The Church of the Word Incarnate*, v.1, tr. A. H. C. DOWNES (New York 1955) 341. I. SALAVERRI, *Sacrae theologiae summa*, ed. FATHERS OF THE SOCIETY OF JESUS, PROFESSORS OF THE THEOLOGICAL FACULTIES IN SPAIN, 4 v. (Madrid) 1.3: 702.

[A. E. GREEN]

DOGMATIC THEOLOGY, ARTICLES ON

In the late twentieth century, the term "dogmatic theology" generally gave way, in the English-speaking world, to the term "systematic theology." Here the former term is retained to signify systematic reflection on the subjects enunciated in the dogmas of the Church. The principal article is DOGMATIC THEOLOGY; see also THE-

OLOGY and THEOLOGY, HISTORY OF. Each of the major areas of dogmatic theology is outlined in a separate subject-area article: GOD, ARTICLES ON; TRINITY, HOLY, ARTICLES ON; CREATION, ARTICLES ON; MAN, ARTICLES ON; JESUS CHRIST, ARTICLES ON; GRACE, ARTICLES ON; MARY, BLESSED VIRGIN, ARTICLES ON; CHURCH, ARTICLES ON; SACRAMENTS, ARTICLES ON; ESCHATOLOGY, ARTICLES ON. Key elements in the formulation of dogmatic theology—as based in dogma—are treated in separate articles: DOGMA; DOGMATIC FACT; DEFINTION, DOGMATIC; DEPOSIT OF FAITH; DOCTRINE; DOCTRINE, DEVELOPMENT OF; ARTICLE OF FAITH; HIERARCHY OF TRUTHS; NOTES, THEOLOGICAL.

[G. F. LANAVE]

DOGMATIC THEOLOGY

The term dogmatic theology seems to have been used first by the Lutheran humanist Georg CALIXTUS (1586–1656). However, by the end of the 17th century it was in fairly common use among Catholic theologians even though the connotations of the term dogmatic were varied. The term is widely used by modern Catholic theologians to describe the branch of THEOLOGY that concerns itself with setting forth and explaining the DOGMAS received by Catholic faith.

The term is also common to Protestant theologians in the sense of a scientifically elaborated interpretation of the Christian religion. In the 20th century, the term was given considerable currency in the Protestant world through the *Church Dogmatics* of Karl Barth (*see* BARTH, KARL). By this term he meant the theological task of ensuring that the content of the preaching of the Church conforms to the Word of God (Christ). This conformity is achieved through adherence to the written word of the Bible.

HISTORY

In the patristic and medieval eras, dogmatic theology was not conceived as a separate theological discipline. Behind the modern Catholic usage lies a history that offers considerable insight into the development of the Catholic theological enterprise itself, as well as a much deeper understanding of the term.

Positive Theology. The opening stage in the development of dogmatic theology as a distinct theological discipline was the beginning of a consciously conceived positive theology. There was, first of all, the humanistic reaction of the 15th century against the scholastic form of theology and the effort to replace it by returning to the Bible in its original languages. To this was added an emphasis on the FATHERS OF THE CHURCH as being closer to the Bible and so possessing a deeper insight into its meaning. Giving impetus and immediacy to this emphasis on Scripture and the sources was the polemic with Protestantism. Here the controversy over the principle *sola scriptura* obviously gave force to the humanistic demands; but because it would make Scripture the sole theological criterion, it evoked a whole new order of critical reflection on theological METHODOLOGY. Out this would come the first stages of a theology of the sources, or what came to be called positive theology.

In this development the major figure was Melchior CANO, a Spanish Dominican theologian (1509–60). Essentially humanistic in temperament and outlook, he was also a modern who wanted to formulate a theology more suitable to his age. The result was the theological classic *De locis theologicis*. In this work Cano set into clear relief the essential role of what he called the *auctoritates*, i.e., the positive sources, in the work of theology. It is from these authorities, such as Scripture, the Fathers, and the councils, that theology takes its principles. The quality of the conclusions of theology is in direct proportion to the quality and certitude of these principles or sources. It is these sources that he called "theological places." His work looked to formulating these sources, to setting up the norms that determine their value, and to positing the conditions under which they will best serve their purpose. The work was a pioneering effort and created a theological methodology and tradition that was decisive in the development of a dogmatic theology (*see* LOCI THEOLOGICI).

Moral Theology. The next stage in the evolution of a dogmatic theology was the conception of MORAL THEOLOGY as a distinct branch of theology. From the early Middle Ages on moral theology as the practice of the Christian life was enshrined in small practical handbooks for confessors. Discussions of the principles of human nature and action came to be located in the *summae* of the masters, where they were part of the integral view of the whole of theology. The distinct moral theology of the late 16th century abstracts these principles, thus producing separate tracts dealing with the last end of man, the morality of human acts, natural and positive law, and ecclesiastical sanctions. Something of the practical manuals of the earlier period is retained, but understood within the elaboration of the theoretical principles. The reasons for this change are not easy to discern, and there is no agreement as to its causes. It does represent, however, an important step in the process of specialization that will bring about a whole series of divisions in the science of theology.

First Dogmatic Theology. It is in the last decade of the 17th century that the modern forms into which theology is divided begin to appear, and among these is dogmatic theology. To understand the particular character of these first efforts at a dogmatic theology something of the age itself must be understood. By the last quarter of the 17th century empirical science was beginning to dominate the intellectual world. The movement of defense stemming out of Trent has taken a distinctive shape. Particularly to be noted is the fact that the theology of the university world is no longer a creative theology. The university faculty is involved in the enervating quarrels over JANSENISM, GALLICANISM, and eventually JOSEPHINISM, as well as the effects of the controversy over efficacious grace (*see* CONGREGATIO DE AUXILIIS). Out of all this arises the felt need to give to the student, and specifically to the seminarian, an organized body of common doctrine as received by the Church, a body of doctrine not obscured by the controversy of the schools. It is this need, joined with the concern for the sources, and the strong sense of dogma deriving from Trent, that constitutes the first stage of a recognizable dogmatic theology, or, as it will be widely called in the beginning, *theologia dogmatica-scholastica.*

As the usage *dogmatica-scholastica* indicates, it is an attempt to join the positive elements with the scholastic tradition of speculative theology. The first concern is the presentation of the actual teaching of the Church together with the theological NOTE proper to it. Then comes the scholastic exposition of that teaching. It is basically a manual theology, having as its fundamental concern the pedagogical rather than the dialectical. Accordingly, a new method of presentation takes over. The traditional *quaestio* and *lectio* disappear, and the fundamental point of departure becomes the *thesis* together with a *status quaestionis,* proof from the sources, theological reasons, and, finally, practical corollaries. It is this pedagogical and largely manual form of dogmatic theology that dominates the development down to Vatican II.

19th Century. The next major step in this development takes place in the middle of the 19th century. After almost a century of decadence, Catholic theology begins to renew itself. This renewal derives first of all from the extraordinary development of historical and critical sources. With Egyptology the whole ancient world with which the Bible has been the primary contact now begins to be known in its own right. Study of the Babylonian and Assyrian civilizations and Palestinian archeology all set the Bible into an immense framework that calls for profound reevaluations of long-held positions and explanations. At the same time, particularly in Germany, the study of the history and the philosophy of religion (*see* RELIGION, PHILOSOPHY OF), together with critical studies of the history of dogmas, open up a world whose full challenge will not be realized until the eve of the Modernist

crisis (E. Hocedez, *Histoire de la théologie au XIXe siècle* 3:53–161). Theologians such as J. FRANZELIN are aware of these developments and make use of the sources on a considerable scale. Yet, by and large, their usage is uncritical and subordinated to the "proof text" approach.

Along with this historical development is the neoscholastic revival [*ibid.* 2:319–328; B. M. Bonansea, "Pioneers of the 19th-Century Scholastic Revival in Italy," *The New Scholasticism* 28 (1954) 1–37]. The first stage of this renewal runs from about 1825 to the issuance of Leo XIII's encyclical *AETERNI PATRIS* on Aug. 4, 1879. Prominent in this stage would be men such as J. KLEUTGEN, G. PERRONE, J. Franzelin, C. PASSAGLIA, M. LIBERATORE, G. SANSEVERINO, L. TAPARELLI D'AZEGLIO. Their work is often eclectic and by no means represents a really profound insight into the thought of St. Thomas. One exception should be mentioned here—the work of M. J. SCHEEBEN, whom M. GRABMANN calls the greatest speculative theologian of the 19th century. In his work one finds a genuine effort to plumb the thought of St. Thomas and make his fundamental intuitions the personal reflection of the author himself. He also incorporates into his speculation the light cast on the thought of St. Thomas by the current medieval study. Equally to be noted are his studies in the history of dogma and his establishment of his speculative endeavor on a sound patristic and scriptural foundation. If his usage is not always strictly critical, it is well advanced for his time, and the whole work is a significant example of a truly developing dogmatic theology [M. J. Scheeben, *The Mysteries of Christianity,* tr. C. Vollert (St. Louis 1946)].

With the appearance of Leo XIII's *Aeterni Patris* there begins renewed effort to develop the philosophical resources of speculative theology. Although there is opposition on the part of some Catholics, historical studies and a more profound study of St. Thomas's own thought set in motion a revival that will be strongly influential throughout all Catholic theology for the next century. The speculative element in the manuals of dogmatic theology is only very slowly touched by this renewal. It takes a very extensive popularization of Thomism before the speculative depths of St. Thomas really begin to penetrate into seminary teaching with power and effectiveness. Prescinding from this, however, a considerable body of speculative work does create a whole new dimension for dogmatic theology in the present time.

20th Century. Contemporary with the beginnings of this speculative renewal comes the initial stages of what will be the crisis of Modernism. It raises far-reaching questions for theology in general, and the resolution of the issues has a decisive influence on the work and structure of modern dogmatic theology. Modernism poses for theology two fundamental issues: first, the question of the homogeneity of what the Church teaches now and the primary sources of all Christian doctrine; second, the questions raised when the Bible and ancient traditions and institutions are examined in the light of modern critical and historical methods. The first involves the question of the relation between tradition and the teaching authority of the Church. (See Louis Billot, *De immutabilitate traditionis* [Rome 1904], where he clearly delineates the role of the magisterium as the proximate RULE OF FAITH.) The second issue is concerned with the nature of the theological method itself. It stems from the need to show the distinction between theology and dogma, between theological development and revelation (*see* REVELATION, THEOLOGY OF); the relation between positive and speculative theology and the criteria that make of them a genuinely scientific effort. Especially to be noted here is A. Gardeil's *Le donné révélé et la théologie* (Paris 1910). The last concern and the slowest to take form is, in fact, the central one. It is the whole question of the development of both dogma and doctrine. Though Franzelin recognizes the fact, and Cardinal J. H. NEWMAN makes a decisive contribution to its understanding, it is not until F. Marín-Sola publishes his *L'Évolution homogène du dogme catholique* (2d ed. Fribourg 1924) that it begins to take its full place in theological debate and reflection.

Essentially the history of theology and, therefore, of the resources of theology between Vatican I and Vatican II is the continuation and development of studies along these three lines: (1) tradition and the magisterium; (2) the nature, function, and method of theology; (3) the development of doctrine.

All these developments are very closely related, and while they do not deeply influence the seminary theology in the late 1920s, still in the 1930s they begin to influence the theologians themselves. Discussion, articles, and meetings at congresses bring all this to the fore. By the end of World War II, there is a good deal of ferment and very extensive discussion over the nature and function of theology as well as the methods proper to dogmatic theology. In the United States it is possible to see much of this development in the *Proceedings of the Catholic Theological Society of America,* which were first published in 1946.

Following Vatican II, "dogmatic theology" quickly gives way to "systematic theology" as the name of that branch of theology that deals principally with the intellectual understanding of the things of faith. By the end of the 20th century, very few non-pontifical theology departments offer programs in dogmatic theology. The questions of the early 20th century persist, particularly those concerning the nature and method of theology, but they are joined by questions about the very nature of dogma. Whereas previously theologians regarded dogmas, known with certitude in faith, as sure starting points for theology, they now turn their attention to the dogmas themselves, asking whether the dogmatic formulation or something else in the dogma is to be regarded as normative. Confrontation with contemporary hermeneutical theory is an important element of this shift. Theologians are increasingly unwilling to take the propositional content of dogmatic statements as a given, without consideration of the context—social, cultural, intellectual—in which the dogmas were originally formulated. The 1973 document of the Congregation for the Doctrine of the Faith, *Mysterium Ecclesiae,* acknowledges the importance of such contextual considerations. However, it also maintains that dogmatic statements are not only approximations of the truth, but determinate affirmations of truth. Its limitations notwithstanding, dogmatic theology is a legitimate and necessary theological enterprise.

Biblical Studies. One last area should be included in this necessarily limited presentation of the history of the development of dogmatic theology—the correlative development of biblical studies. Beginning with the establishment of the Pontifical Biblical Institute in Rome (1909), there comes into being a large corps of Catholic biblical specialists formed in the very best of modern techniques. Gradually, through biblical periodicals and discussions, this work takes on an increasingly important role in the discussion of the function of dogmatic theology. As might be expected, it also involves an increasing number of debates and discussions on the validity and legitimacy of the methodology of biblical study. Much of this is resolved, at least in principle, with the publication by Pius XII of his encyclical *DIVINO AFFLANTE SPIRITU* in 1943.

Most important for the understanding of this movement in the United States and its wide influence is the *Catholic Biblical Quarterly,* published by the Catholic Biblical Association since 1939. Of the whole biblical development it must be said that it is an indispensable resource for the dogmatic theologian who would carry out his function soundly and effectively in modern times.

WORK OF DOGMATIC THEOLOGY

As a brief history of this branch of theology shows, it has, as all intellectual disciplines have, undergone much development. While its purpose has remained substantially the same, the resources available to it have been both multiplied and perfected. Likewise, as is proper to any maturing intellectual work, there has come a broadening and deepening vision of the purposes and the role of this discipline in the service of the Church. In the light of these premises, this section of the article treats of the work of dogmatic theology as it is modernly formulated by a large number of theologians.

Point of Departure. As its specification indicates, dogmatic theology centers its effort on the dogmas of the Church. Perhaps it might be better to say that in its search for intelligibility, dogmatic theology takes the dogmas of the Church as its point of departure. By dogma here is meant a truth of revelation that has been formulated and infallibly proposed by the Catholic Church. It is this formulation so proposed that the Catholic accepts on divine FAITH as an accurate expression of the reality contained in revelation. Strictly speaking, these dogmas are not coextensive with Catholic doctrine. Catholic doctrine includes not only these dogmas but other truths and positions taught by the Church but not as revealed, even though the assent of Catholics is or may be called for. Dogmatic theology will also be concerned with this corpus of Catholic teaching since it is part of the process of intelligibility, but dogmatic theology begins with dogma. It is for this reason that this theological effort must also begin with divine faith. For the precise role of faith in this context is to guarantee that the truths as formulated in these dogmas have been revealed by God and transmitted to the faithful by the Church. Neither science nor experience is able to refute or verify these truths. It is faith that enables the faithful to hold them as unshakably certain. Theology, however, subject to faith and the light of faith, adds a distinct element, since it considers these dogmas as objects of a properly intellectual process. The theological endeavor is to bring to bear the resources of human intelligence in order to explicate as fully as possible the intelligibility of these dogmas and through them to arrive at something of the intelligible structure of revelation itself. Theology is thus the response of a living mind to what, through the grace of faith, it believes. This response is not only an assent but, in the theological order, an effort to understand and to come to what Vatican Council I called a most fruitful intelligence of the revealed mysteries (H. Denzinger, *Enchiridion symbolorum*, ed. A. Schönmetzer 3016). It is this theological effort that in modern times has been commonly divided, in accord with the function involved, into positive and speculative theology. Positive theology would employ largely the historical and evidential resources of human intelligence. Speculative theology would bring to bear philosophic intelligence, but it is not limited to that alone. The distinction tends to be descriptive rather than definitive.

Role of Positive Theology. Since theology is an effort to elaborate in a scientific manner revelation as it is proposed by the Church, it is an intellectual process. Hence in fulfilling theology's purpose of scientific elaboration, the exercise of critical intelligence is essential. If it is to be a genuinely scientific process, it is obliged to verify its data. This it does by determining accurately what has been revealed and how it has been proposed by the Church. A bare fact is not a scientific fact. A fact concerns a science only when it is viewed in its own proper light and is subjected to its proper critique. So the data must be verified even though the assent is by faith, and faith itself is an organic part of the light of theology. It is the work of positive theology to undertake this work of verification. This work of verification and the examination of the sources does not primarily involve proving the data, but looks directly to intelligibility and understanding. Positive theology looks not only to ascertaining that these dogmas are revealed, but to how they are revealed and the relation of the formulation to its revealed source. What it seeks is a living communion with the totality of revelation as it has been constituted and transmitted down to the present day. To do this, it must employ the resources of historical reason as speculative theology draws upon the philosophical intelligence of the Church. Thus positive theology draws upon BIBLICAL THEOLOGY, patristic theology, conciliar theology, the history of dogma, and history itself in order to carry out its function. Only by drawing upon them to the fullest, and doing so in an intellectual and scientific way, is objective contact with the sources maintained.

What the first step of positive theology should be in its study of the dogma was the object of considerable debate during the theological renewal of the mid-20th century. During the course of its development, controlled as it was by pedagogical purposes, it generally formulated the dogma into a thesis giving the ecclesiastical source for its definition, some explanation of the terms as well as the errors involved, a presentation of texts from Scripture and the Fathers, and finally the relevant speculative theology. In relation to this presentation there was a demand that dogmatic theology begin its work with the Bible and the KERYGMA. However, dogmatic theology is neither biblical theology nor KERYGMATIC THEOLOGY, but has its own proper function to perform. It is the dogmas that constitute its first principles and that it attempts to explain and render as fully intelligible as possible. Dogmatic theology, by reason of its purpose, comes to Scripture in order to penetrate more deeply into dogma and at the same time to vitalize, enrich, and balance the theological synthesis that it is its office to develop, shape, and communicate. Hence, while in certain cases a general survey of the biblical theology of the subject of a tract such as GRACE may serve as an introduction to the work of dogmatic theology, still, normally, the specific first step will concern the dogma itself. This would also seem to be a legitimate application of the statement of Pius XII in *Humani generis* that ". . . the sacred office of teacher in matters of faith and morals must be the proximate and universal criterion of truth for all theologians, since to it has been entrusted by Christ the Lord the whole deposit of faith, both Sacred Scripture and divine tradition, to be preserved, guarded, and interpreted . . ." [*Acta Apostolicae Sedis* 42 (1950) 567].

The first step, therefore, in the work of positive theology will be a study of the dogma in the historical action of the Church that formulated the dogma. This means an understanding of the concrete historical situation in which it was formulated, the historical stages that led up to the moment, the various aspects of the issue itself, and how it came to be. Finally, it involves an understanding of precisely what question the conciliar fathers or the pope intended to consider and what limitations they imposed on the answer. This careful historical process is essential to the work of dogmatic theology because it sets in proper perspective the limitations as well as the potentialities of intelligibility and understanding. It is important to emphasize here that this carefully done historical effort is absolutely necessary also if a genuine ecumenical perspective is to be maintained and a sound insight into dogmatic development is to be acquired.

Positive Theology and Scripture. It would be well to give an extensive treatment of the use of Sacred Scripture as a theological resource. In this regard the work of dogmatic theology must be carefully distinguished from that of both exegesis and biblical theology. Between the generalizations and abstractions in word and concept represented by the dogma, and the insights, concrete, personal, spontaneous, and often highly individual given by the inspired writer in Scripture, there is a definite gap. It is a gap at once historical and theological, and with regard to this problematic the dogmatic theologian and the exegete have two distinct functions. The exegete must endeavor to determine what the text manifests as to the degree of awareness that the inspired author had of the doctrine given, that is, the literal sense. The theologian has for his function to illumine the relationships between dogma and its source, between divine truth and its scriptural place. By reason of his faith he is sure that there is a legitimate and necessary bond between the two: legitimate because the Church that defines the dogmas is the same Church as that to which has been entrusted the deposit of revelation to be transmitted and explained; necessary because the Catholic theological endeavor affirms that a dogma presupposes homogeneity and indefectible transmission. By reason of this, positive theology not only penetrates the dogma more fully but, in the light of that dogma, searches for a fuller understanding of the divine message communicated through Scripture. This work presumes and must depend on the work of exegesis and biblical theology if the effort is to be soundly theological. Yet its purpose remains theological, seeking to illumine the divine message and draw out its intelligibility and ultimately to synthesize it, order it, and organize it. Scripture, therefore, is a basic resource of dogmatic theology but not its only one.

Dogmatic Development. How, then, does dogmatic theology show the homogeneity between dogma and its Scriptural sources? The basic instrument is an understanding and proper application of the principle of doctrinal development. Without a viable and workable conception of dogmatic development, it is not possible for the theologian to make full theological use of Scripture as a theological place. It is only through the medium of dogmatic development that one can see, for example, how the definition of the HYPOSTATIC UNION at the Council of CHALCEDON is prepared for, given a foundation, and rendered possible by the inspired text. For between the literal sense and the full theological content and context lies precisely the fact of dogmatic development. It is clear that since God knows the whole saving design down to its least detail, then Scripture will be engorged with senses and meanings known only to God. The inspired author can only be a deficient instrument as regards the totality of the divine thought. Further, too, the inspired book passes beyond its immediate audience, the author's contemporaries, and is destined for the Church of Christ, which will continue until the consummation of the world. It is this fact above all others that necessitates the instrumentality of dogmatic development.

The concept of dogmatic development is not, as Newman saw, something introduced to meet a historical problem; rather it is inherent in the very nature of revelation itself. The Christian revelation is a fact transmitted as an idea. The divine message incarnated in human thought cannot completely express itself (or ever reach a real coextension with the truth as it is in the mind of God) save by a continuing historical development. But this development, because it is a development of ideas, is a dynamic thing—a thing of meaning and understanding. It is, in short, a homogeneous development between the revealed idea and the understanding of it as it is in the mind of God [see J. H. Newman, *An Essay on the Development of Christian Doctrine* (New York 1890) 55–75]. Exactly how this development takes place has, of course, been heatedly debated (*see* DOCTRINE, DEVELOPMENT OF).

Analogy of Faith from the Scriptures. This and the following section are inferred from the usage of Pope Leo XIII in his encyclical *Providentissimus Deus*. There is here, of course, all that is available in the work of biblical theology. Also of relevance is the theological synthesis that underlies the writings of the inspired authors, particularly of the New Testament. In addition, this article maintains that there is incorporated the various senses that the Church, illumined by the Holy Spirit, has come to see in the divine message. It involves all that is encompassed under the term "spiritual sense." By this is meant the whole area that, while it may have escaped the inspired author himself, is nonetheless willed by the primary author, God, and is part of the formal element of the divine message. This usage must, of course, depend on the primacy of the literal sense and is authentic only when it does no violence to that literal sense. It must flow from the literal sense and be discernible in the light of the religious and doctrinal context proper to the Sacred Books. This spiritual sense represents a deeper penetration of the message under the guidance of the Church and its historical experience. As such, it looks to being an enrichment of the literal sense through clarification and exploitation of the nuances and resonances present only obscurely. Before these analogies may be used, however, assurance must be had from the liturgical and patristic teaching of the Church that they are integral to the total historical development [see J. Levie, *The Bible, Word of God in Words of Men,* tr. S. H. Treman (New York 1961) 252–264].

Analogy of Faith Drawn from Catholic Teaching. By Catholic teaching or doctrine here is meant not only dogma but also other truths that call upon Catholics for assent as certain. There must also be taken into account, though not as normative, theological positions quite generally held. For while the Church has not authentically interpreted many texts, there are nonetheless a large number of doctrinal affirmations born of Scripture in which the Church has continued and completed the scriptural interpretation. So, for example, the Church draws dogmatic conclusions from the text of St. Paul. The exegete may not be able to show that they are explicitly in the consciousness of the inspired author, but since it is the Church that judges the total idea, then in its present doctrinal synthesis the conclusions become clear. It is this body of Catholic teaching as it is here and now that forms the necessary context for Catholic interpretation of Scripture. The office of the Church is not simply to reject a particular interpretation or to interpret a particular text infallibly. Rather it is to make a living and continuing effort to develop the totality of its theological implications and content.

Positive Theology and the Fathers. The modern developments in patrology and PATRISTIC THEOLOGY have considerably enlarged the use of the Fathers in dogmatic theology. Yet from fairly early in the history of the Church their importance has been underscored by the Church itself—and this a number of times, as for example, at the Council of Ephesus in 431 or the Roman Council in 680. For the medievals down to the 15th century, the single source of Christian doctrine was Scripture as

authoritatively interpreted by the Fathers. Both the Council of Trent and Vatican Council I insist that Scripture must not be interpreted against the unanimous consent of the Fathers. Since mid-nineteenth century a considerable body of theological writing has been done on the Fathers as witnesses to the teaching of the Church. As a result of this work, it would certainly be common teaching among modern theologians that the morally unanimous teaching of the Fathers can be an unerring witness to the teaching of the Church in matters of faith and morals. While it is true that a good deal of this usage has tended to be by way of proof text, nonetheless the renewal of emphasis on the homogeneity between dogma and Scripture has brought about a change of emphasis. By studying the Fathers the dogmatic theologian is able to see through their witness to the actual state of Catholic teaching in its first preaching as well as in the stages of its doctrinal development. Through their writings he sees the actual issues and problematics as they are called forth, and the process by which the Church came, for instance, to the HOMOOUSIOS, or the hypostatic union. The concern is not to set up a history of dogma but to see what the Church taught at a given moment in definite historical circumstances and in the face of specific questions and specific difficulties that were raised. This whole use, however, is a theological use and not a historical one. Dogmatic theology employs a set of criteria different from those of purely historical use. For the implicit is explained and clarified by the explicit (i.e., what the Church teaches today) because there is a homogeneity and indefectible transmission. The theological judgment is not soundly excercised without an equally sound patrology.

This emphasis on biblical theology and history represents one of the important contemporary stresses in dogmatic theology. It is a conviction of very many theologians that it is not possible to have a sound and fruitful theologizing about the dogmas of the Church without an extensive and intensive study of the Bible and the tradition of the Church. More and more, too, it is evident that the idea and the context in which it came to birth belong together. Likewise, between the history of the Church and the history of the Church's reflection on the deposit of faith there is an interrelation that can be broken only at the risk of a deep misunderstanding. By reason of its purpose, dogmatic theology itself will have certain limitations in its employment. It is not biblical theology or exegesis or history, though there is nothing to prevent the theologian from being deeply imbued with all three. Yet, only when speculative theology is vitally and organically related to the sources through positive theology and continually renewing itself in those sources is it open and relevant and vital. These two functions, positive and speculative, cannot be separated from one another, in fact, without devitalizing each of them.

Speculative Theology. Theological manuals, histories of theology, and popular usage have tended to identify speculative theology and scholastic theology. Justification of this equation lies in the fact that 17th-century SCHOLASTICISM, with its emphasis on theology as a science of certain conclusions, did become the accepted form of speculative theology. It is also true, however, that this is basically a scholastic method and a particular adaptation of it, and not the integral scholastic tradition. As Chenu has made clear in the study of the 13th-century scholasticism, this limned approach is not truly representative of the flowering period of scholasticism (M. D. Chenu, *La Théologie comme science au XIIIᵉ siècle* (3d ed. Paris 1957). Yet even this limited 17th-century concept of speculation is deformed under the influence of CARTESIANISM and the Enlightenment (*Histoire de la théologie au XIXᵉ siècle* 1 *passim*). Aware of this historical situation many contemporary theologians have given voice to the need for a dynamic concept of speculative theology. In the many-faceted intellectual developments of the last half of the 20th century, represented by such things as psychology, sociology, and philosophy of religion, these theologians would see a call for a dynamic and vital speculative theology. Included, therefore, under this term would be the use of every form of systematic and ordered reflection on matters of faith. Rooted in a sound positive theology and living in the light of faith, speculative intelligence ought to call on any intellectual resource that offers a fruitful possibility of reflecting on the truths entrusted to the Church through revelation.

It is, of course, a matter of history that the speculative efforts of Catholic theology have often given rise to suspicion on the part of some Catholics. Its purposes have been attacked in the name of the Bible or Christian piety or spiritual simplicity. Underlying these charges is the conviction or feeling that this speculative approach somehow detracts from the MYSTERY or the TRANSCENDENCE or the spiritual character of revelation. Some Christians object to it because they see it as an attempt to submit God to man's limited human categories and, therefore, as simply a manifestation of human pride. Against these positions stands a long and strongly encouraged speculative tradition in the Church itself. The Church has always been aware that speculative theology is a vital exigency of a living mind illumined by faith and receptive of revelation. To do away with a sound speculative theology will, as history shows, force the introduction of an unsound or inadequate one, or inhibit the use of intelligence altogether. It is not the only way of applying the mind to God's Word, but to criticize it for not undertaking the other ways is as futile as it is unwarranted [J. Daniélou, *God and the Ways of Knowing,* tr. W. Roberts (New York) 1957].

Work of Speculative Theology. Speculative theology seeks to accomplish its role in the theological enterprise by two fundamentally related activities that may be described as exposition and theological reflection.

Exposition. This work comprises two elements, namely, the organization of the theological work, and what are traditionally called the arguments from fitness.

Concerning organization, it may be said that one of the deepest exigencies of the intelligence is the search for order. The history of theology bears this out by showing that this matter of organization and the search for organizational principles becomes a primary concern of speculative theology almost as soon as it becomes conscious of being a distinct effort. Some great theologians, because of temperament or genius or time, were not concerned to construct a systematic organization of their theological work. Many others, however, made the inner plan the very heart of their theological reflection. For St. Thomas the plan of his *Summa* is a manifestation of his personal vision of the whole range of theology, a vision that affects every part of his work. Different theologians emphasize various elements of revelation or make a personal perspective with regard to revelation, the keystone to their systematization. Commonly, the organizational pattern dominating theology between Vatican I and Vatican II arose from the development on a major scale of positive theology. The very quantity of the material made to bear on the theological effort as well as its increasing importance forced into existence a new approach to organization. This was a division of the material of dogmatic theology into tracts or treatises that incorporate and unify both the positive and speculative theologies with regard to GOD, the TRINITY, the INCARNATION, and REDEMPTION, the SACRAMENTS, and the CHURCH. Each of these tracts had a logical unity, with many of them retaining the inner unity worked out for each of these areas in the *Summa* of St. Thomas. In the years 1935 to 1965 there was much discussion, and a number of tentative proposals were advanced to systematize this dogmatic theology. Such principles as the kerygma or the *totus Christus* were advanced. None of these proposals received widespread acceptance among theologians. Subsequent years saw a trend to broaden the Thomistic organizational principle of *Deus sub ratione deitatis* in order to incorporate the specifics proper to Christian revelation. This would make the object of theology God as He reveals Himself in JESUS CHRIST and the Church. This was seen as enabling the theologian to develop more dynamically the inner logic of dogmatic theology but at the same time to integrate more directly the positive theology by basing his work more directly upon it.

The argument from fitness is sometimes described as the analogy of faith, i.e., the comparison of the revealed mysteries among themselves and with the last end of man. As the history of theology shows, it is not only a fruitful way of theologizing but a readily available one. It has its roots deep in the Fathers as well as in the scholastic tradition and is recommended by Vatican Council I as an exceedingly fruitful source of understanding (*Enchiridion symbolorum* 3016). It takes its rise from the fact that the whole saving design and thus the whole history of SALVATION is a unique act of God's love toward man and, on God's part, a unitary action. While recognizing that the inner unity of this action is known totally only to God, still, what is believed and experienced brings to the fore indications that enable the believer to discern aspects of this unity. So, seeing the relation between the redemptive death of Christ and His RESURRECTION brings out dimensions of meaning that could not otherwise be achieved. Likewise, any fuller penetration of the doctrine of justification means the relating of it to the redemptive Incarnation, the Resurrection, man's last end, and the term of the justified man's engraced life, the divine IN-DWELLING. Vatican II spoke of this interconnection of doctrines as a "hierarchy of truths" (*Unitatis redintegratio* 11), thus highlighting not only the relationship of the doctrines but their order of priority.

Supplementing these analogies of faith would be the natural analogues taken from the created order, or what St. Thomas calls "true similitudes" (*C. gent.* 1.9). These are employed as instruments of exposition in order to show that the revealed doctrine is in harmony with the things one knows naturally. Just as nature is preparatory for grace and is perfected by grace, so from the created world one can obtain expository insights into the meaning of revelation. These insights are not intended to be demonstrative arguments but illuminative, and they presuppose the light of faith. It is in this light and in the perspective of the Church's understanding of revelation and its intelligibility that the theologian employs as far as possible his knowledge and appreciation of the world in which he lives (*see* REASONING, THEOLOGICAL; CONVENIENTIA, ARGUMENTUM EX).

Theological Reflection. As the history of Christian thought makes ineluctably evident, divine faith is compelled to seek understanding, and this impulse is an exigency of the believing intelligence. Hence, the believing intelligence brings to bear on the Christian message, as it must, historical experience, psychological insight, philosophical perspectives, and ontological reflection. To these basic resources will be added whatever rational and scientific achievements are germane to this exigency. This form of theological effort is nothing else than the law of a mind that by its very nature must strive to search out the intelligible structure of its experience. "Thinkers try to see the truth from a standpoint higher than its initial setting, if possible from a standpoint that is universal, one valid for all human thought, and, in doing so, they search for more general concepts of permanent validity in which to formulate it. To the extent that they succeed, they reach a new understanding of the truth. This new understanding makes it possible not merely to keep the truth in relation to its first expression, but also to express it for new audiences. The higher the standpoint from which the truth is seen, the more easily can it be related to the contents of different mentalities and the more surely can the discrimination of what is true and false in these be effected" [C. Davis, *Theology for Today* (New York 1962) 20–21].

The first and most basic form of this theological reflection is by way of psychological insight and description. This is nothing else than the exploitation of that area of reality of which one has direct and immediate experience. This is one's own psychological life as it is refracted through one's own continuing consciousness of oneself. It is this life that every human being uses to probe into the mysteries of life and so generalize about them and ultimately come to the most universal of all languages—the symbolic. This psychological description and its ordinarily achieved symbolic expression is, as a rule, readily grasped and valuable for pedagogical as well as for theological purposes. It is one of the fundamental forms of theologizing among the Fathers; in fact Augustine is one of the masters of it. It is also a richly rewarding element of medieval theology as is borne witness to by Bernard of Clairvaux, Hugh of Saint-Victor, and in a profound fashion by St. Thomas Aquinas. Contemporarily, it has come to the fore as one of the means by which the religious phenomenon as manifested in social and cultural anthropology and history finds effective understanding. By its very nature, however, the psychological and the symbolic isolated from the philosophical do not and cannot encompass all the aspects of theological reflection. Left to themselves they cannot directly and cogently confront or controvert error that has been formulated in rationalistic terms.

The second form of theological reflection may be described as metaphysical. Some would prefer the term ontological, others would call it "essential analysis," but in view of the history of theology and the nature of this form of reflection the term metaphysical seems to be a more accurate description. It means that, among the ways in which man unfolds his desire to know, is asking and answering questions and in so doing operating in the intellectual pattern of experience. It is out of this intellectual pattern that in turn comes the metaphysical pattern natural to the human mind, that is, what is generally termed the *philosophia perennis*. In order to come to the universal viewpoint that is an integral element of any full interpretation of reality, the Church makes use of the *philosophia perennis* to develop under faith its own proper philosophic intelligence. It is this, in turn, that its theologians expand into one of the essential elements of speculative theology and so enrich the Catholic understanding of God's revealed word [B. Lonergan, *Insight: A Study of Human Understanding* (New York 1957) 736–748.] As already noted, since the 19th century, under Pope Leo XIII and his successors, this metaphysical form of theological reflection has been done primarily in accord with the mind and principles of Thomas Aquinas (as the first to construct a metaphysical instrument precisely for this purpose).

In essence, this way of theological reflection draws upon and elaborates a metaphysical pattern in order to discover, as far as it can, the intelligible structure of revealed truths and their relationship to each other as well as to the whole corpus of revealed truth. Through the systematic development and application of this metaphysical pattern it seeks to illumine and formulate the ontological unity that relates all the facets and aspects of revealed doctrine. By careful, patient, extensive philosophizing and metaphysical reflection made in the light of faith the theologian arrives at analogies. These analogies enable him to state accurately the universal content of a truth of revelation, for instance, regarding "person" or "nature" or "generation" in Christology or Trinitarian theology (*see* ANALOGY, THEOLOGICAL USE OF). It is this universal, not the singular and the concrete, that is the object of the theologian's concern. So the speculative theologian is concerned with and employs the principles of contradiction and identity, the meaning of the act of existence, the bearing of sense experience on man's understanding, and the necessary relevance of the Catholic propositions, because these are affirmed by the Church as a part of the *philosophia perennis*. Through all these and in accord with the system he formulates or accepts, the speculative theologian reflects metaphysically, but this reflection is always illumined by faith. Modernly, as has been said, special approval has been given to the *Summa* of St. Thomas, even though a variety of syntheses and interpretations has been present.

Beginning the 1950s, a third manner of theological reflection arose that recognized the need for the objective and analytical approach of the metaphysical way, but insisted that in view of contemporary needs this metaphysical approach should be supplemented and enlarged. These enlargements would involve a much more vital integration into theological reflection of the dynamic and operational aspects of human existence and human thought.

There two prominent varieties of this method. The first is generally called "existential." The term as used here means a centering of reflected concern on personal responsibility seen in relation to the actualities of the material and human world. It looks to describing and analyzing the phenomenology of the actual world as it is: concrete, present, immediate—the world in which the individual exercises his personal responsibility and concern. This draws in part on the phenomenology of the human personality endeavoring to elaborate the interrelation of this to God's saving design. Here, too, is the recognition of the value given to religion and religious experience by EXISTENTIALISM, for which it is a proper theme; hence the effort to integrate the descriptive treatment of religious experience with the Christian philosophical tradition. This would set into a constructive relationship this phenomenology and the knowledge gained about God and man through causal inference and the analogical predications employed in such inferences. Yet at the same time there is stressed the value of setting forth a philosophical-psychological description of the actual, basic attitudes of man and so seeking out their meaning in the personal and existential structure of religious experience.

Since Vatican II, the new "theologies of liberation" came to represent a second kind of distinctively contemporary theological reflection. The existential method was critiqued as being too individualistic. Liberation theologians maintain that a foundational factor, long overlooked, in theological reflection is the social dimension of the gospel. The sociology of knowledge enters as an important philosophical discipline. Such theologies, though they speak at length about the need for genuine Christian praxis, do not understand themselves as being confined to the practical: they seek as well to address the adequacy of the speculative formulations of theology. Theological reflection is grounded in an honest apprehension of the causes of suffering and oppression in the world and a hope for liberation. This method of speculation recurs more to the use of religious symbols—retrieving those that are most liberating—than metaphysical reflection.

See Also: DOGMATIC THEOLOGY, ARTICLES ON

Bibliography: E. DUBLANCHY, *Dictionnaire de théologie catholique,* ed. A. VACANT et al. (Paris 1903–50) 4.2:1522–74. Y. M. J. CONGAR, *ibid.* 15.1:341–502; *Catholicisme* 3:949–951. K. RAHNER, *Lexikon für Theologie und Kirche,* ed. J. HOFER and K. RAHNER (Freiburg 1957–65) 3:446–454. J. R. GEISELMANN, *Handbuch theologischer Grundbegriffe,* ed. H. FRIES (Munich 1962–63) 1:225–241. H. FRIES, *ibid.* 2:641–654. G. GLOEGE, *Die Religion in Geschichte und Gegenwart* (Tübingen 1957–65) 2:221–230. K. ALAND, *ibid.* 230–234. G. EBELING et al., *ibid.* 6:754–782. M. D. CHENU, *Is Theology a Science?,* tr. A. H. N. GREEN-ARMYTAGE (New York 1959). P. FRANSEN, "Three Ways of Dogmatic Thought," *Heythrop Journal* 4 (1963) 3–24. A. HAYEN, "La Théologie aux XIIe, XIIIe et XXe siècles," *Nouvelle Revue Théologique* 79 (1957)

1009–28; 80 (1958) 113–132. C. JOURNET, *The Wisdom of the Faith,* tr. R. F. SMITH (Westminster, Maryland 1952). E.G. KAISER, *Sacred Doctrine: An Introduction to Theology* (Westminster Maryland 1958). A. M. LANDGRAF, *Dogmengeschichte der Frühscholastic* (Regensburg 1952–56). B. M. XIBERTA Y ROQUETA, *Introductio in sacram theologiam* (Madrid 1949). A. DULLES, *The Survival of Dogma: Faith, Authority, and Dogma in a Changing World* (New York 1982, c.1971). F. S. FIORENZA and J. P. GALVIN, eds., *Systematic Theology: Roman Catholic Perspectives* (Minneapolis 1991). W. KASPER, *The Methods of Dogmatic Theology* (New York 1969). G. A. LINDBECK, *The Nature of Doctrine: Religion and Theology in a Postliberal Age* (Philadelphia 1984). Ú. O'NEILL, *The Function of Doctrines: A Study of Selected, Contemporary Roman Catholic Theologians* (Ph. D. Thesis, Catholic University of America, 1982). W. PANNENBURG, *An Introduction to Systematic Theology* (Grand Rapids, Michigan 1991). J. MACQUARRIE, *Principles of Christian Theology* (2d ed. New York 1977). K. RAHNER, *Foundations of Christian Faith,* tr. W. V. DYCH (New York 1978). E. FARLEY, *Theologia: The Fragmentation and Unity of Theological Education* (Philadelphia 1983). K. RAHNER and K. LEHMANN, *Kerygma and Dogma* (New York 1969).

[E. M. BURKE/EDS.]

DOGMATISM

In general, the positive assertion of opinion or belief; it frequently connotes authoritativeness or arrogance in such assertion, as well as lack of argument or evidence in its support.

The term has its historical origin in Hellenistic times. In that period the first dogmatists were a group of physicians, following the tradition of HIPPOCRATES, who practiced their profession with definite assertions about the causes and cures of disease. They established themselves in opposition to the methodists, another group of physicians who practiced medicine with definite theories about, and emphasis on, the method to be followed in the treatment of disease. Further opposition came from the empirics, a third group who excluded theory altogether in their practice.

Immanuel KANT (1724–1804) applied the term dogmatist to any previous philosophers who had neglected to examine critically the nature and limitations of the human mind in the acquisition of knowledge. Seeking to unite RATIONALISM, which he equivalently identified with dogmatism, and EMPIRICISM, which he equivalently identified with SKEPTICISM, he intended his philosophy to rectify the errors of both. (*See* CRITICISM, PHILOSOPHICAL).

In defense of Christian thinkers who are often charged with dogmatism, it should be emphasized that the positive statement of objective and certain TRUTH is not dogmatism. The human mind unconditionally assents to what has been divinely revealed, once it has intellectu-al conviction of the divine origin of the truth. Again, as regards the truth of reason, the mind's assent to what can be demonstrated or conclusively proved, and therefore held with natural CERTITUDE, is not dogmatism.

See Also: DEMONSTRATION; DOGMA; EVIDENCE.

Bibliography: G. DI NAPOLI, *Enciclopedia filosofica,* 4 v. (Venice-Rome 1957) 1:1704–06. R. EISLER, *Wörterbuch der philosophischen Begriffe,* 3 v. (4th ed. Berlin 1927–30) 1:291–293.

[M. W. HOLLENBACH]

DOLCINO, FRA

Heretical leader of the Apostolici; b. Diocese of Novara, Italy; d. Vercelli, June 1, 1307. The son of a priest or hermit, he was raised by a priest from Vercelli who obtained a good education for him. Dolcino ran away in 1291 and joined the sect of the APOSTOLICI or Pseudo-Apostles founded by Segalelli. Upon the latter's execution (July 18, 1300), Dolcino succeeded as leader. His eloquence, agreeable manners, and skillful interpretation of Scripture won him nearly 4,000 disciples. Assuring provisions for his followers, who practiced strict poverty, became a great problem. He was forced to seek refuge in the mountains to escape the pursuers organized by the bishop of Vercelli. The sect's plundering led Pope CLEMENT V to assist the people of Novara to organize a crusade, and on March 23, 1307, Dolcino was captured by the crusaders. He was executed by the civil authority, and his body was cut into pieces and burned. The Pseudo-Apostles practiced absolute poverty and obeyed God alone, allowing the Roman Church no authority because of the wickedness of its prelates. Two of Dolcino's letters (August 1300 and December 1303) outlined his doctrines. He awaited the return of the Church to evangelical poverty and to virtue under the leadership of his disciples. He predicted that after the inevitable extermination of contemporary popes and cardinals, God would then choose the sovereign pontiff.

Bibliography: BERNARD GUI, *Manuel de l'inquisiteur,* ed. and tr. G. MOLLAT (Paris 1926–27) 1:84–107; 2:75–103, for letters. S. D. SKAZKIN, *Le condizioni storiche della rivolta di Dolcino* (Moscow 1955), a biased account. *Dictionnaire d'histoire et de géographie ecclésiastiques,* ed. A. BAUDRILLART et al. (Paris 1912–) 14:574.

[G. MOLLAT]

DOLD, ALBAN

Liturgist and historian; b. Villingen (Baden), July 7, 1882; d. Munderkingen (Württemberg), Sept. 27, 1960. After secondary studies at Freiburg im Breisgau and

Seckau in the Steiermark he entered Beuron in 1902, making his profession Oct. 5, 1903. Upon completing studies in philosophy at Maria Laach and theology at Beuron, he was ordained Sep. 22, 1908. In 1917, having served as a field chaplain in World War I, he took over the Palimpsest Institute founded in 1912 at Beuron. Dold improved the method developed by R. Kögel, OSB, of St. André near Bruges, for fluorescence-photography of parchment codices that had been used twice for writing. As an organ for publication he founded the series, "Texte und Arbeiten: Beiträge zur Ergründung des älteren lateinischen und christlichen Schrifttums und Gottesdienstes," in which he himself edited 22 works, partly with co-workers. All told, his life's scholarship embraces 133 contributions, the greater part of which were articles in different scholarly periodicals. Dold mastered what he had begun as a self-taught man; in recognition of his learning he was presented with an honorary doctorate in philosophy from the University of Fribourg (Switzerland), and one in theology from the University of Tübingen. Having been gifted with a knack for practicality, untiring endurance, and the enthusiasm of a self-made scholar, he dedicated his energy to reproducing and commenting on liturgical and scriptural palimpsests and fragments.

Bibliography: S. MAYER, *Beuroner Bibliographie, 1863–1963* (Beuron 1963) 38–50.

[V. FIALA]

DÖLGER, FRANZ JOSEPH

Church historian, archeologist, educator; b. Sulzbach, Germany, Oct. 18, 1879; d. Schweinfurt, Oct. 17, 1940. After ordination in 1902, he served in parishes at Amorbach im Odenwald, then resumed his studies at the University of Würzburg, where he obtained a doctorate in theology in 1904. Subsequent travels in Italy and North Africa deepened his interest in the history of the adaptation of the early Church to its cultural environment. He was the first Catholic scholar to devote himself wholly to this subject, and he trained many students in an exact, scientific study of the field.

Dölger began his teaching career as a *Privatdocent* at Würzburg, went to Rome for five years of research, and in 1912 became professor of comparative history of religion, ancient Church history, and Christian archeology at the University of Münster, Westphalia. He later held professorships at Breslau (1926–29) and Bonn (1929–40). His studies, which reveal an astonishing knowledge of classical and patristic literature, reflect at the same time his scientific development and sober judgment.

His earliest work, *Das Sakrament der Firmung historisch-dogmatisch dargestellt* (1906), represents his starting point, the history of dogma. His later works elucidate the influence of ancient culture on Christian faith, liturgy, and art: *Der Exorzismus im altchristlichen Taufritual* (1909); *Sphragis: Eine altchristliche Taufbezeichung in ihren Beziehungen zur profanen und religiösen Kultur des Altertums* (1911); *Die Sonne der Gerechtigkeit und der Schwarze* (1916); *Sol salutis, Gebet und Gesang in christlichen Altertum* (1920). His principal work is a monumental history of the sacred symbol of the fish, ΙΧΘΥΣ (5 v., 1910–43).

In 1929 he founded the periodical *Antike und Christentum,* of which he was editor and sole contributor of more than 150 articles in its five volumes (1929–50). He also edited the commemorative volume for the jubilee year of Constantine the Great, *Konstantin der Grosse und seine Zeit* (1913), and was joint editor of *Liturgiegeschichtliche Forschungen* (1918–27), a series of studies in the history of the liturgy.

Bibliography: T. KLAUSER and A. RÜCKER, eds., *Pisciculi:. . . F. J. Dölger zum 60. Geburtstage* (Münster 1939), with complete bibliog. E. STOMMEL, *Aschaffenburger Jahrbuch* 3 (1956) 412–414. T. KLAUSER, *F. J. Dölger: Leben und Werk* (Münster 1956), with bibliog. J. QUASTEN, *American Catholic Historical Review* 27 (1941) 112–114.

[J. QUASTEN]

DÖLLINGER, JOHANNES JOSEPH IGNAZ VON

Ecclesiastical historian, theologian; b. Bamberg, Germany, Feb. 28, 1799; d. Munich, Jan. 10, 1890.

Early Career. His father was a distinguished anatomist and embryologist whose studies of animal growth and of *Naturphilosophie* had an important influence on the son's theological development. His pious mother counterbalanced his anticlerical father. After studying at the University of Würzburg and the seminary in Bamberg, Döllinger was ordained (1822) and served briefly as curate to Markt Scheinfeld. In 1823 he began to teach Canon Law and Church history in Aschaffenburg. In 1836 he was awarded a doctorate from the University of Landshut for his dissertation, *Die Lehre der Eucharistie in den ersten drei Jahrhunderten,* which drew heavily from Antoine ARNAULD'S *Perpetuité de la foi de l'Eglise catholique sur l'Eucharistie.* Upon the recommendation of Johann Michael SAILER, he was appointed to the chair of Church history in the University of Munich (1826).

Döllinger's memory and linguistic ability were phenomenal, and his erudition vast. As a historian, however, he was for the most part unoriginal and derivative in his thought. Thus his inaugural address at Munich, *Über die*

Ausbreitung des Christentums in den ersten Jahrhunderten (1826), was in good part borrowed from Hugues Felicité de LAMENNAIS'S *Essai sur l'indifférence* (1818). He joined the Catholic circle in Munich led by Franz von BAADER and Joseph von GÖRRES, and collaborated with them in publishing the review *Eos* (1825–32). This circle was influenced by contemporary Romanticism and was politically conservative, anticapitalistic, monarchist, and mildly ultramontane. It sought to restore social and religious life on Catholic principles, much as did the French movement of liberal Catholicism. Döllinger stressed the importance of public opinion and engaged in public affairs because he believed theologians should guide the public. He defended Archbishop DROSTE ZU VISCHERING in the COLOGNE MIXED MARRIAGE DISPUTE, represented the university in the Landtag (1845–47, 1849–51) and Lower Bavaria in the Congress of Frankfort (1848–49), organized the *Katholischer Verein* (after 1849), encouraged the growth of a Catholic press, and convinced the German bishops that they should meet regularly (1848). After a dispute with King Ludwig I of Bavaria concerning the dismissal of four professors, Döllinger himself was dismissed in 1847 but was restored in 1850.

Historian. Döllinger used his historical knowledge to argue that Protestantism, liberalism, and rationalism marked breaks with the historic past. He collaborated in founding the *Historisch-politische Blätter* (1838) and contributed to it articles attacking the writings of Leopold von RANKE and other Protestant or liberal historians. ''Organic growth'' and ''consistent development'' were his key expressions. The concept of tradition played an important role in his thinking, as it did in that of Johann Adam MÖHLER, the Tübingen school of Catholic theologians, and Joseph de MAISTRE. Döllinger published two works on the Reformation: *Die Reformation, ihre innere Entwicklung und ihre Wirkungen im Umfange des Lutherischen Bekenntnisses* (3 v. 1846–48) and *Luther* (1850; Eng. tr. 1853). In both he tried to demonstrate that Protestantism represented a break in historical continuity and development. His other works on Catholic history, which won international renown through many translations, included: *Lehrbuch der Kirchengeschichte* (2 v. 1836; Eng. tr. 1840–42); *Hippolytus und Callistus oder die römische Kirche in der ersten Hälfte des dritten Jahrhunderts* (1853; Eng. tr. 1876); *Heidentum und Judentum, Vorhalle zur Geschichte des Christentums* (1857; Eng. tr. 2 v. 1862); *Christentum und Kirche in der Zeit der Grundlegung* (1860; Eng. tr 1862); *Die Papstfabeln des Mittelalters* (1863; Eng. tr. 1871–72).

Growing Anti-Romanism. By 1850 a subtle but detectable tincture of nationalism affected Döllinger's work, and in a spirit not unlike the FEBRONIANISM of the 18th century he began to call for episcopal independence

Johannes Joseph Ignaz Von Döllinger.

of Rome, a Catholic Church in Germany headed by a German metropolitan, and education for the priesthood in universities rather than in seminaries. He became so disturbed by what he considered growing papal absolutism that he delivered lectures questioning the further usefulness of the STATES OF THE CHURCH and criticizing their current administration. He published these lectures as *Kirche und Kirchen. Papsttum und Kirchenstaat. Historischpolitische Betrachtungen* (1861; Eng. tr. 1862) to contradict a report that his talks were overtures to CAVOUR. This book was poorly received in Rome. More fundamental, however, was Döllinger's hostility to the revival of SCHOLASTIC THEOLOGY, particularly by Roman Jesuits. Döllinger preferred the study of historical theology, and feared the tendency of some scholastics to label as heretical opinions contrary to their own and to suppress them by means of the INDEX OF FORBIDDEN BOOKS. Döllinger minimized Roman scholarship but extolled German accomplishments in history and theology. He argued that scholars in their research must be free from arbitrary interference by Church authorities. His fears seemed to him to be confirmed by the definition of the IMMACULATE CONCEPTION (1854) and then by the publication of the SYLLABUS OF ERRORS (1864). He expressed his sentiments in a speech published as *Die Universtäten sonst und jetzt* (1867; Eng. tr. 1867).

Vatican Council I. Döllinger was not asked to participate in VATICAN COUNCIL I, but he was drawn into the central controversy concerning papal primacy and infallibility. In his attack upon the Jesuits of *La Città Cattolica*, which appeared originally in the *Allgemeine Zeitung* of Augsburg under the pseudonym Janus, he opposed the doctrines themselves, whereas the minority group in the Council merely held that a definition would be inopportune. The book by Janus, *Der Papst und das Concil* (1869; Eng. tr. 1870–73), was placed on the Index on Nov. 26, 1869, shortly before the Council opened. During the sessions he kept in correspondence with Bishop DU-PANLOUP of Orléans and other minority leaders. His friends Lord ACTON (John Emerich Edward Dalberg), Johann FRIEDRICH, and the Bavarian ambassador supplied him with information and impressions about conciliar proceedings. Again in the *Allgemeine Zeitung* under the pseudonym Quirinus appeared 69 Roman letters in which Döllinger attacked the conduct of the leaders of the majority group and complained that bishops of the minority were not entirely free to speak their minds. These letters appeared in book form as *Römische Briefe vom Concil* (1870; Eng. tr. 1870), but their intemperance injured the inopportunist cause.

Late Career. When Döllinger refused to subscribe to the definitions of papal prerogatives, he was excommunicated by the archbishop of Munich (1871) and lost his professorship (1872), but King Ludwig II of Bavaria befriended him. He considered his excommunication unjust. Although he participated in discussions with the leaders who were organizing the OLD CATHOLICS, he refused to identify himself with this schismatic sect. His subsequent historical work has become somewhat outdated. Promotion of Christian unity engaged him. His most notable efforts in this regard were his lectures of 1872, published as *Über die Wiedervereinigung der christlichen Kirchen* (1888). After his excommunication, he no longer celebrated Mass or participated in the Church's sacramental life, but he regularly attended Mass. He received the last rites from Johann Friedrich, an Old Catholic priest.

Döllinger had many contacts with leaders of the Catholic revival in Germany, France, and England; but many of his ecclesiological concepts derived from 18th-century thinkers imbued with GALLICANISM and Febronianism. He exerted considerable influence by impressing on Catholic scholars the necessity of developing a historical as well as a speculative approach to theology. Also he did much to promote among Catholics an interest in scientific research and study of ecclesiastical history.

Bibliography: S. LÖSCH, *Döllinger und Frankreich* (Munich 1955), with complete biblig. of Döllinger's writings, including Eng. and other tr. V. CONZEMIUS, ed., *Ignaz von Döllinger: Brief-wechsel* 1820–90 (Munich 1963). J. E. E. ACTON, ''Doellinger's Historical Work,'' *English Historical Review* 5 (1890) 700–744. J. FRIEDRICH, *Ignaz von Döllinger,* 3 v. (Munich 1899–1901), by an Old Catholic and close friend of Döllinger. F. VIGENER, *Drei Gestalten aus dem modernen Katholizismus: Möhler, Diepenbrock, Döllinger* (Munich 1926). S. TONSOR, ''Lord Acton on Döllinger's Historical Theology,'' *Journal of the History of Ideas* 20 (1959) 329–352. V. CONZEMIUS, ''Aspects ecclésiologiques de l'évolution de Döllinger et du Vieux Catholicisme,'' *Revue des sciences religieuses* 34 (1960) 247–279. P. GODET, *Dictionnaire de théologie catholique,* ed. A. VACANT et al. (Paris 1903–50) 4.2:1512–22. Y. M. J. CONGAR, *Catholicisme* 3:972–974. W. MÜLLER, *Dictionnaire d'histoire et de géographie ecclésiastiques,* ed. A. BAUDRILLART et al. (Paris 1912) 14:553–563. A. SCHWARZ, *Lexikon für Theologie und Kirche,* ed. J. HOFER and K. RAHNER (Freiburg 1957–65) 3:475.

[S. J. TONSOR]

DOMENEC, MICHAEL

Second bishop of PITTSBURGH, Pa.; b. Ruez, Tarragona, Spain, Dec. 27, 1816; d. Tarragona, Jan. 7, 1878. His education at Madrid was interrupted by the failure of the Carlist movement, and at 15 he fled with his father to Paris, where he joined the Congregation of the Mission (Vincentians). John TIMON, then Vincentian visitor general, persuaded him to finish his studies in the U.S., where he was ordained at the seminary in Barrens, Mo., June 29, 1839. Domenec was assigned to the seminary faculty, but he engaged also in missionary activities in Missouri. In 1845 he went to Philadelphia, Pa., to teach at St. Charles, the diocesan seminary; in addition, he served as pastor in Nicetown and later founded St. Vincent's parish in Germantown. He was notably successful as a preacher and lecturer. He was named second bishop of Pittsburgh and consecrated on Dec. 9, 1860.

Some of the bishop's policies, especially regarding the seminary and the diocesan newspaper, the *Pittsburgh Catholic,* were unpopular. They appear to have led to the resignations of James O'Connor, rector of the seminary; Rev. J. Keogh, editor of the paper, who went to Philadelphia; and others. Domenec's rule was handicapped also by financial difficulties and by the Civil War. Domenec was a staunch Unionist in a city torn by internal strife; he traveled to his native Spain on behalf of the Union. According to his contemporary, Abp. John Hughes of New York, Domenec was the most successful of all the ecclesiastic ambassadors during the Civil War. His administration was marked also by an increase in the number of Catholics from 50,000 to 200,000. To provide for the new Catholics, many of them immigrants, ten churches, including one for emancipated slaves, were erected in the city alone. In all, 60 churches were dedicated and the cathedral was enlarged. Two orphanages were built for war orphans, and the Sisters of St. Francis, Ursuline

Nuns, Carmelites, Little Sisters of the Poor, Sisters of the Good Shepherd, Sisters of St. Joseph, and Sisters of Charity, as well as the Oblate Fathers, Capuchins, and Holy Ghost Fathers, were brought into the diocese. In 1870 Domenec attended Vatican Council I; he originally voted *non placet* on the question of papal infallibility, but later changed his vote.

The rapid growth in population and serious financial problems resulting from the 1873 depression led Domenec to petition Rome to divide the diocese; on Jan. 11, 1876, he was transferred to the new Diocese of Allegheny (suppressed in 1889 and reunited with Pittsburgh). But the division aggravated the financial situation, and, broken in health, Domenec resigned on July 27, 1877, and returned to Spain, where he died six months later.

Bibliography: W. P. PURCELL, *Catholic Pittsburgh's One Hundred Years* (Chicago 1943).

[H. J. NOLAN]

DOMENECH, EMMANUEL

Missionary, writer; b. Lyons, France, Nov. 4, 1824?; d. France, June 1886. At the invitation of Bp. John Odin of Texas, Domenech left the seminary in Lyons (March 1846) for the U.S., where he completed his studies at the seminary in Barrens, Mo.; he was ordained in 1848, and was assigned to Castroville, Texas, and surrounding areas. In 1850 Domenech, ill and exhausted, was granted leave of absence for a visit to France. On his return to Texas in the spring of 1851, he was sent to Brownsville as pastor, and he remained there until October 1852. Ill health again necessitated his return to France, where he remained until his death, devoting himself primarily to writing. He is known for his works on Mexico, Native Americans, missionary life in America, the Franco-Prussian War, and particularly for his *Journal d'un Missionnaire au Texas et au Mexique* (Paris 1857; Eng. tr. London 1858).

Bibliography: R. BAYARD, *Lone-Star Vanguard: The Catholic Reoccupation of Texas, 1838–1848* (St. Louis 1945). M. G. CALLAHAN, *The History of the Sisters of Divine Providence, San Antonio, Texas* (Milwaukee 1955). B. DOYON, *The Cavalry of Christ on the Rio Grande, 1849–1883* (Milwaukee 1956).

[M. G. CALLAHAN]

DOMESDAY BOOK

At Christmas of 1085, King WILLIAM I THE CONQUEROR held "deep speech" with his great men at Gloucester "about this land and how it was peopled and with what sort of men," as the *Anglo-Saxon Chronicle* reports. The results of this inquiry are the two great volumes preserved in the Public Record Office in London and known as the Domesday Book. The relationship between this inquiry and the finished product has been and still is controversial, but the outlines of the making of the Domesday Book are clear enough.

England was divided into circuits, except for the devastated north, and commissioners, many of them bishops and all of them trusted advisers of the king, were sent to conduct the inquiry. They were assigned to parts of the country where they did not themselves hold land. They probably sat in the county courts and received the reports of local juries, who would be mostly English, and probably also statements from the baronage, who would be mostly French. The information was then arranged county by county and barony by barony. A fair copy of these reports was sent to the treasury at Winchester where the information was further digested, and the Domesday Book as we have it was the result.

It is unlikely that this was quite finished when William died late in 1087. The existing volumes show signs of work under great pressure suddenly relaxed. In particular the second volume, the so-called Little Domesday, looks like the fair copy sent in from East Anglia that arrived late and was never incorporated into the main volume as were the rest of the counties.

There is no agreement about the purpose of this quite unprecedented act of government. It was a fantastic effort for an 11th-century government to undertake. It caused comment and great resentment at the time, but such was the power and prestige of William that it was done. Unfortunately, his untimely death meant that we cannot be sure that it was ever used for the purpose he had in mind. It was certainly an invaluable tool of reference to his immediate successors. They knew the approximate wealth of their greater subjects, and this knowledge must have been useful for assessing what we call death duties and estate duty (inheritance tax). Further, the book was so laid out that it was possible to see in which county each lord held estates. Since the county was the main unit of local government, the value of the information is obvious. Domesday Book might also be consulted in lawsuits about land titles. The older views, however, that it was really intended to be the basis of reassessment of the traditional tax, called the geld, which was too unpopular for the Conqueror's successor to attempt, still has something to be said for it. The Domesday Book contains also information about parish churches and the ecclesiastical economy in general that is useful for the church historian.

Bibliography: J. H. ROUND, *Feudal England* (London 1895). F. W. MAITLAND, *Domesday Book and Beyond* (Cambridge, Eng.

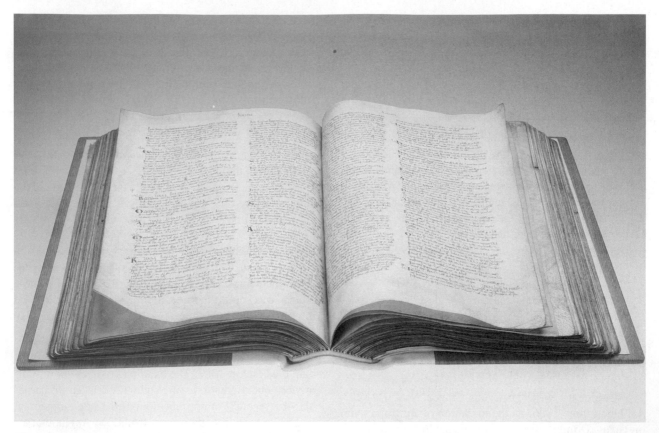

The Domesday Book associated with William the Conqueror, c. 1085–1086, housed in the Public Record Office, London, England. (©Michael Freeman/CORBIS)

1897). R. W. FINN, *Domesday Inquest* (London 1961). V. H. GAL-BRAITH, *The Making of Domesday Book* (Oxford 1961). The *Victoria County Histories* contain abstracts of Domesday Book in translation; those for Norfolk and Wiltshire have esp. valuable introductions.

[E. JOHN]

DOMESTIC PRELATE

The basic honor of the papal household. Clerics appointed to this dignity, by diploma, retain the rank for life, even if later promoted to higher dignities such as prothonotary apostolic or BISHOP. Their title *praelatus domesticus* or *antistes urbanus* carries with it the mode of address Right Reverend Monsignor, and they rank between prothonotaries apostolic and papal chamberlains. They may wear silk robes during the warm season and woolen ones during wintertime, i.e., violet cassock, rochet, and mantelletta. If performing liturgical functions without sacred vestments (assisting bishops or conferring the Sacraments), they wear a surplice instead of the mantelletta over their rochet. Their nonliturgical ceremonial dress consists of black cassock with crimson buttons and lining and violet *ferraiolone,* as well as violet socks. Their coat of arms is surmounted by a violet prelatial hat with six violet tassels pending on each side of the crest.

Most domestic prelates are named directly because of merit or because of their position in authority (e.g., most are vicars-general); but for some the dignity comes automatically, e.g., for assistants at the pontifical throne, participating and supernumerary prothonotaries apostolic, certain canons, and auditors of the Sacred Roman Rota. They stand *in cornu epistolae* in the *capella papalis* and enjoy several liturgical, as well as ceremonial, privileges; of these they are notified at the time of nomination.

[P. C. VAN LIERDE]

DOMINGO DE LA CALZADA, ST.

Hermit; d. May 12, 1109. Domingo (Dominic), a native of Viloria in the Basque country, was first a shepherd. He was drawn to the religious life, and sought admittance to a Benedictine monastery; he was rejected because of his ignorance and his uncouth appearance. However, he was ordained by GREGORY OF OSTIA, and became his companion. Upon Gregory's death (1044), he became a hermit in a forbidding forest near the Oja River. The presence of numerous CLUNIAC REFORM monasteries in Spain and the lure of the *Reconquista* in the closing decades of the 11th century enhanced the reputation of the shrine of SANTIAGO DE COMPOSTELA. Pilgrims en route to the Galician holy place had to pass through Dominic's wilderness of Bureba, and for their convenience and safety he constructed a hospice, a bridge, and a road (*calzada*). King Alfonso VI of León-Castile admired and aided him.

Feast: May 12.

Bibliography: *Acta Sanctorum* (Paris 1863–), May 3: 167–179. J. DE ENTRAMBASAGUAS Y PEÑA, *Santo Domingo de la Calzada, el ingeniero del cielo* (Madrid 1940). A. BUTLER, *The Lives of the Saints* (New York 1956), 2:289–290, K. LECHNER, *Lexicon für Theologie und Kirche* (1957–), 2 3:479–480. C. M. MOLAS, *Dictionnaire d'histoire et de géographie ecclésiastiques* (Paris 1912–), 14:609–610.

[A. G. BIGGS]

DOMINGO Y SOL, MANUEL, BL.

Priest, founder of the Fraternity of Diocesan Worker Priests; b. April 1, 1836, Tortosa, Tarragona, Spain; d. there, Jan. 25, 1909. Son of Francisco Domingo Ferré and Josefa Sol Cid, Manuel received his early education at local schools and from a tutor before undertaking the study of philosophy in the diocesan minor seminary (1851–52) and theology in the major seminary. He was ordained deacon by the bishop of Vich (1859) and priest at Tortosa (1860). After another year of study, he began his ministry by concentrating on catechesis and giving missions in towns surrounding Tortosa. On March 7, 1862, he took possession of the parish at La Aldea, 13 kilometers from Tortosa. While serving his parish he completed further study in theology at the University of Valencia and began teaching at Tortosa's seminary. Among his many pastoral works were the founding of Catholic Youth of Tortosa (1869), an evening school for workers and artisans, the publication *El Congregante* to foster Christian ideals among youth, a theater complex, and a recreational center. He became known as a great confessor and a spiritual director for the discernment of vocations. In 1872 to 1873, Domingo established the College of Church Vocations of St. Joseph in Tortosa in order to allow poor seminarians to continue their study of philosophy and theology. Later he founded similar schools at Almería, Burgos, Lisbon, Murcia, Orihuela, Plasencia, Rome (Pontifical Spanish College), Toledo, and Valencia. With six other priests, Domingo founded the Fraternity of Diocesan Worker Priests (1883) to fur-

ther foster vocations. Manuel Domingo, whose cause was opened in 1946, was declared venerable by Paul VI (May 4, 1970) and beatified by John Paul II (March 29, 1987), who called him "the holy apostle of priestly vocations."

Bibliography: J. M. JAVIERRE, *Reportaje a Mosén Sol: un hombre bueno y audaz* (Madrid 1987). F. MARTÍN HERNÁNDEZ, *Mosen Sol: vida de Manuel Domingo y Sol, fundador de la Hermandad de Sacerdotes Operarios Diocesanos* (Salamanca 1978). *L'Osservatore Romano,* English edition, no. 14 (1987): 1–2.

[K. I. RABENSTEIN]

DOMÍNGUEZ, ISIDORO

Spanish Caraccioline, last colonial archbishop of Santa Fe de Bogotá, Colombia; b. Galaroza, Huelva Province, Spain, April 1762; d. Burgos, April 1822. He studied at the seminary in Málaga. In 1806 he was appointed administrator of Gibraltar (a part of the diocese of Cádiz although a British possession), with the title of apostolic vicar-general dependent on the Congregatio de Propaganda Fide. He served successfully in this delicate position until August 1816. In December 1818, Ferdinand VII nominated him archbishop of Santa Fe. There were some difficulties over the approval in Rome, and the pontifical appointment was not made until August 1819. But on August 7 the battle of Boyacá took place, and General Bolívar entered Santa Fe and began to govern the area as president of the republic. The Spanish officials had to flee. Bishop Domínguez was consecrated in January 1820 by Bishop Luis López Castrilló, but for two reasons he could not leave for his diocese: no Spanish ships were leaving for Cartagena, and the republican government would not have received him. He spent the next two years in Spain in serious financial difficulty. In 1821 he was appointed vicar-general in the archbishopric of Burgos.

[J. RESTREPO POSADA]

DOMINGUITO OF SARAGOSSA, ST.

Also called Dominic of Val; reputed martyr; d. Saragossa, Aragon, Spain, 1250. Seven-year-old Dominguito was an altar boy at Saragossa cathedral. He is among the many Medieval boy martyrs whose death was ascribed to Jews without evidence to support the claim. Little Dominic was allegedly kidnapped and nailed against a wall by Jews in hatred of the faith. Pope Pius VII approved (Nov. 24, 1805) the continuation of the de facto cultus for Saragossa.

Feast: formerly Aug. 31 (Aragon).

See Also: MEDIEVAL BOY MARTYRS.

[K. I. RABENSTEIN]

"Rosary Madonna Altarpiece," by Gaspare Narvesa, shows Madonna and Child handing a rosary to St. Dominic and St. Catherine of Siena, Cathedral of Aviano, Italy, 1617. (©Elio Ciol/CORBIS)

DOMINIC, ST.

Founder of the Friars Preachers, or DOMINICANS; b. Caleruega (Diocese of Osma, Old Castile) after 1170; d. Bologna, Italy, Aug. 6, 1221.

Early Career. Dominic was trained for the clerical state by an uncle who was an archpriest, and he studied arts and theology at Palencia. About 1196 he became a canon in the chapter of the cathedral of Osma, which in 1199 had fully revived the regular common or apostolic life in accord with Acts 4.32–33. He was elected subprior *c.* 1201. In 1203 and again from 1205 to 1206, two journeys on a royal embassy to northern Europe with his bishop, Didacus of Acebes, drew him from the contemplative life, revealing to him the state and needs of the Church, especially the threat posed by heresy in Languedoc; and at that time he visited Rome and Cîteaux. At Montpellier (June 1206) a meeting with three Cistercian legates sent against the ALBIGENSES (WALDENSES), and especially the CATHARI, led to his being commissioned for the papal mission under the authority of the legates. With the Cistercians and, after 1207, with a few companions, he engaged in itinerant mendicant preaching according to the gospel ideal (Lk 9.1–6; 10.1–12) This ministry had been proposed by the bishop of Osma and adopted by the legates, and it was confirmed by the pope (bull of Nov. 17, 1206). Dominic pursued this apostolate until the end of 1217, despite the obstacles created after 1209 by the Albigensian Crusade. Toward the end of 1206, he founded

at Prouille a convent of women for the purpose of receiving converts from Albigensianism. This convent served thenceforth as a base for his preaching.

Founding of the Friars Preachers. About 1214, his band of preachers was in the process of becoming a community, and in 1215 Dominic took them to Toulouse, then recently conquered by the Crusade. There he founded a religious house, with the consent of the legate and the approval of Bp. Fulk of Toulouse, who accepted his regular program, conferred on him half the diocesan tithes reserved for the poor, and entrusted to him and to his confreres the preaching and defense of faith and morals in the entire diocese. This preaching was conducted according to the gospel style already practiced by the group. At the time of the Fourth LATERAN COUNCIL (October 1215) Dominic solicited INNOCENT III for confirmation of his order, i.e., of his regular purpose, of the revenues accorded to his brethren, of their ministry, and even of their name, the Preachers. He was granted all these requests the following year (bulls of Dec. 22, 1216, and Jan. 21, 1217) by HONORIUS III, but only after he and his confreres had adopted the rule of St. AUGUSTINE and the strict observances borrowed from PRÉMONTRÉ. The latter prescription was made to satisfy the requirements of canon 13 of the Council, forbidding new orders.

Development of the Order. From 1217 to 1221, Dominic worked simultaneously on three levels: (1) He completed the organization of his order, which he expanded by distributing his friars among Toulouse, Paris, Bologna, Madrid, and Rome (Aug. 15, 1217). The Universities of PARIS for Theology and BOLOGNA for Canon Law became the pivots of the order. At the first general chapter, held in Bologna on May 17, 1220, he achieved the adoption of conventual mendicancy that, by complementing the mendicancy of the friar during his ministry, assured the homogeneity of his evangelical program. At this chapter he also drafted the order's constitutional legislation, completed at the next chapter (Bologna, May 30, 1221). (2) During his stay in Rome, where he spent each winter except that of 1219, the pope and curia gave him vigorous support. He was in Bologna in the summer of 1219 and in the spring of 1220 and 1221. In Rome and Bologna, as well as during his journeys, especially the great swing from Rome to Madrid, Toulouse, Paris, and Bologna from 1218 to 1219, he was busy at setting his brothers everywhere studying and preaching, and at establishing new houses. In four years, six priories were founded in Lombardy, four in Provence, four in France, three in Tuscany and Rome, and two in Spain; bands of preachers also left for England, Germany, Hungary, and Scandinavia. He founded also convents for women, especially that of St. Sixtus in Rome, whose rule exerted influence even outside the order. (3) Dominic devoted himself personally to a strenuous ministry of preaching. He even dreamed of evangelizing the savage Cumans in Eastern Europe. With Cardinal Hugolino, he undertook a vast mission in northern Italy (1220–21), almost a replica of his Albigensian mission. But these exertions were too much for him and, exhausted, he died at Bologna.

Sanctity. The dominant traits of Dominic's personality were attachment to truth, a quick grasp of situations, maturity of reflection aided by long periods of prayer, and firmness in decision. Joined to these were a great capacity for instant rapport, sympathy, and enthusiasm, a great heart quickly moved to mercy, an attachment to confreres and friends, and courage. Three heroic virtues were especially evidenced throughout his entire life: mortification, in vigils, fasts, corporal penances, and the privations of mendicant poverty; prayer, often for whole nights in the church with intervals of sleep taken on the ground; above all, his love of neighbor, which he never separated from his love of the Church. As a cleric, he had a keen sense of the needs of the Church, of her hierarchy, of her resources for action, and he was completely dedicated in accepting and bearing the totality of her anxieties and burdens. He had, in addition, a taste for community living and a genius for synthesis. If he created the prototype of apostolic orders, it was because he was the first to succeed in linking organically a life with God, impelling him to study and prayer in all its forms, with the ministry of salvation of his fellowman by the word of God, which ministry he assigned as the specific goal of his order and to which he subordinated all else. Everything he thought and said and did was rooted in a strong and poignant love of the Savior, which often made him weep while preaching or celebrating Mass. It was in the constant contact with the Christ of the Gospel that he discovered the point of convergence of all the traditions of "imitation of the Apostles," which he gathered together: "to speak only of God or with God."

Cultus. From the start, his tomb became the site of public veneration. After his canonization by Gregory IX on July 3, 1234, a new monument was erected by Nicola Pisano (1265), finished by Nicolò d'Antonio (1473), with a detail added by Michelangelo (1495). Confraternities of St. Dominic were organized from 1244 on. Development of the ROSARY devotion and confraternities of the rosary at the end of the 15th century further advanced his cultus.

There is no authentic portrait of St. Dominic. The 13th-century paintings are symbolic and Byzantine-inspired. But there is a description of him by Sister Cécile (Lehner, 183–), who saw him in 1221. The scientific examination of the relics in 1943 made it possible to check on the accuracy of this description and to make an anatomically accurate effigy, which measures 5 feet 5 1/2 inches.

His iconographic symbols, drawn from his work or the legends about him, are the book of the constitutions, the dog running with a burning torch in its mouth, the star on his forehead, and the lily and the rosary. He is portrayed wearing the black and white habit of the Preachers and often with a short beard.

Feast: Aug. 4.

Bibliography: M. H. LAURENT, ed., *Monumenta Ordinis Fratrum Praedicatorum histoica* 15 (1933). JORDAN OF SAXONY, *Libellus de principiis ordinis praedicatorum*, ed. H. C. SCHEEBEN ibid. 16 (1935). GERARD DE FRACHET, *The Vitae fratrum*, ed. B. M. REICHERT, pt. 2 ibid. 1 (1896). STEPHEN OF SALAGNAC, *De quatuor in quibus*, ed. T. KÄPPELI ibid. 22 (1949). P. MOTHON, "Constitutions primitives," *Analecta Sacri Ordinis Praedicatorum* 2 (1895) 619–648. Eng. tr. of the principal sources in F. C. LEHNER, ed., *Saint Dominic: Biographical Documents* (Washington 1964). V. J. KOUDELKA, "Notes sur le cartulaire de S. Dominique," *Archivum Fratrum Praedicatorum* 28 (1958) 92–114; 33 (1963) 89–120; 34 (1964) 5–44. *Bibliotheca sanctorum* 4:692–727. Biographies. B. JARRETT, *Life of St. Dominic* (2d ed. London 1934). H. C. SCHEEBEN, *Der heilige Dominikus* (Freiburg 1927). P. MANDONNET, *Saint Dominique: L'Idée, l'homme et l'oeuvre*, ed. M. H. VICAIRE and R. LADNER, 2 v. (Paris 1938); Eng. tr. M. B. LARKIN (St. Louis 1944). M. H. VICAIRE, *Histoire de saint Dominique*, 2 v. (Paris 1957); Eng. tr., *Saint Dominic and His Times*, tr. K. POND (New York 1964). Spirituality. H. CLÉRISSAC, *The Spirit of Saint Dominic*, ed. B. DELANY (London 1939). M. H. VICAIRE, *Dictionnaire de spiritualité ascétique et mystique. Doctrine et histoire*, ed. M. VILLER et. al 3:1519–32; *L'Imitation des apôtres* (Paris 1963). Iconography. P. A. D'AMATO et al., *Le Reliquie di S. Domenico* (Bologna 1946). G. BAZIN, *Saint Dominique* (Paris 1937). M. H. VICAIRE and L. VON MATT, *St. Dominic, a Pictorial Biography*, tr. G. MEATH (Chicago 1957) M. C. CELLETTI, *Bibliotheca sanctorum* 4:727–734.

[M. H. VICAIRE]

DOMINIC GUNDISALVI (GUNDISSALINUS)

Twelfth-century philosopher who worked in Spain and there translated numerous Arabic philosophical works into Latin. He is mentioned as an archdeacon residing in Toledo in the prefatory letter of the translation of Avicenna's *De anima*, dedicated to the Archbishop of Toledo, John (1151–66). He was associated with a learned Jew (*israelita philosophus*) named Avendauth (Ibn Daud), who translated verbatim the Arabic text into Castilian, leaving Gundisalvi to translate the Romanic into Latin. The archdeacon Don Domingo Gonzalbo appears again in two Toledan charters dated 1178 and 1181 (C. A. González Palencia). He signed a charter in 1190 as a member of the chapter of Segovia (D. Mansilla). According to these documents, it seems that Gundisalvi's ecclesiastical and literary activities took place during the second half of the 12th century. Possibly he studied in France *c.* 1140; he was acquainted with the teachings of

THIERRY OF CHARTRES, Master Helias, WILLIAM OF CONCHES, and HUGH OF SAINT-VICTOR; and two of his works (*De anima* and *De immortalitate animae*) show close parallels with the treatise *De essentiis,* written in 1143 by Hermann of Carinthia, who was a disciple of Thierry.

According to the custom generally used for translations from the Arabic, Gundisalvi worked with an Arabicist and retranslated into Latin. From manuscript evidence the following translations can be positively ascribed to him: (1) Avicenna's *De anima,* translated with Avendauth; (2) Avicenna's *Metaphysica;* (3) Algazel's *Summa theoricae philosophiae* (including logic, metaphysics, and physics), translated with ''Magister Johannes''; and (4) Avicebron's *Fons vitae,* translated with ''Johannes.'' Possibly he translated Avicenna's *Logica* (the *Isagoge* only), the *Physica,* and the Pseudo-Avicennian *De caelo.* Probably he translated Avicenna's commentary on the *Analytica posteriora* 2.7, which is included in his own *De divisione philosophiae.* It is likely that he translated also the *De ortu scientiarum* attributed to ALFARABI, and revised and adapted Gerard of Cremona's literal translation of *De scientiis,* since both of these treatises are used in *De divisione philosophiae.* He may have translated and revised other philosophical works, but precise data are lacking.

Gundisalvi was not an original thinker, but it would be unfair to qualify him as a mere compiler. He tried earnestly to adapt the teachings of Avicenna and Avicebron to the use of Latin Christians in the West. He showed strong Neoplatonic tendencies, and his favorite authority was BOETHIUS; he knew St. AUGUSTINE too, and quoted Scripture with ease. He seems to have recognized the importance of Avicenna's psychology, and was the first to combine it with the traditional Augustinian doctrine of the divine ILLUMINATION of the soul. His translations are not always easy to understand, but his vocabulary is more precise and adequate and his style more fluent than that of most of his predecessors and contemporaries.

See Also: SCHOLASTICISM.

Bibliography: Works. *De anima,* complete ed. J. T. MUCKLE in ''The Treatise *De anima* of Dominicus Gundissalinus,'' *Mediaeval Studies* (1940) 23–103; *De unitate et uno,* ed. P. CORRENS in ''Die dem Boethius fälschlich zugeschriebene Abhandlung des Dominicus Gundissalinus *De unitate,*'' *Beiträge zur Geschichte der Philosophie und Theologie des Mittelalters* 1.1 (1891); *De immortalitate animae,* ed. G. BÜLOW in ''Des Dominicus Gundissalinus Schrift von der Unsterblichkeit der Seele,'' *ibid.* 2.3 (1897); *De divisione philosophiae,* ed. L. BAUR in ''Dominicus Gundissalinus' *De divisione philosophiae,*'' *ibid.* 4.2–3 (1903); *De processione mundi,* ed. G. BÜLOW in ''Des Dominicus Gundissalinus Schrift . . . *De processione mundi,*'' *ibid.* 24.3 (1925). M. MENÉNDEZ Y PELAYO, *Historia de los heterodoxos españoles,* ed. E. SÁNCHEZ REYES (*Edición nacional* 35–42; Santander 1946–48) 2:173–186. DOMINIC GUNDISALVI, *De scientiis,* ed. M. ALONSO (Madrid 1954). Studies. É. H. GILSON, *History of Christian Philosophy in the Middle Ages* (New York 1955) 652–653. M. T. D'ALVERNY, ''Notes sur les traductions médiévales d'Avicenne,'' *Archives d'histoire doctrinale et litéraire du moyen-âge* 27 (1952) 337–358; ''Avendauth? (=Abraham ibn David),'' *Homenaje a Millás-Vallicrosa,* 2 v. (Barcelona 1954–56) 1:19–43. M. ALONSO, ''Notas sobre los traductores toledanos Domingo Gundisalvo y Juan Hispano,'' *Al-Andalus* 8 (1943) 115–188; ''Traducciones del arcediano Domingo Gundisalvo,'' *ibid.* 12 (1947) 295–338; ''Gundisalvo y el *Tractatus De anima,*'' *Pensamiento* 4 (1948) 71–77. É. H. GILSON, ''Les Sources grécoarabes de l'augustinisme avicennisant,'' *Archives d'histoire doctrinale et litéraire du moyen-âge* 4 (1929–30) 5–107 A. H. CHROUST, ''The Definitions of Philosophy in *De divisione philosophiae* of Dominicus Gundissalinus,'' *The New Scholasticism* 25 (1951) 253–281. R. W. HUNT, ''The Introduction to the 'Artes' in the Twelfth Century,'' *Studia mediaevalia in honorem . . . R. J. Martin, OP* (Bruges 1948). R. MCKEON, ''Rhetoric in the Middle Ages,'' *Speculum* 17 (1942) 1–32, also in *Critics and Criticism: Ancient and Modern,* ed. R. S. CRANE (Chicago 1952). D. MANSILLA, ''La documentacion pontificia del Archivo de la Catedral de Burgos,'' *Hispania sacra* 1 (1948) 161. C. A. GONZÁLEZ PALENCIA, *Los Mozárabes de Toledo en los siglos XII y XIII,* 4 v. (Madrid 1926–30) 2:141, 154.

[M. T. D'ALVERNY]

DOMINIC LORICATUS, ST.

Benedictine hermit; place and date of birth unknown; d. Oct. 14, 1060. He considered his parents' gift to the bishop who ordained him simoniacal, and on this account he determined to do the strictest penance and to resign from the practice of his priestly functions. For some time he lived as a hermit near Sitria. But soon after 1040 he joined the group of hermits around PETER DAMIAN at FONTE AVELLANA, and later became the prior at Suavicinum near Frontale. Dominic Loricatus (i.e., the Armored One, so-called from the metal breastplate he wore about his chest) can be considered as a prominent representative of those Italian hermits of the 10th and 11th centuries who practiced extraordinary penance. Peter Damian described Dominic's penitential practices in a letter to Pope ALEXANDER II (*Patrologia Latina,* 144:1012–24). Dominic's remains are in Frontale.

Feast: Oct. 14 (observed by the CAMALDOLESE and in the Dioceses of Gubbio, San Severino, and Pergola, Italy).

Bibliography: PETER DAMIAN, *Vita, Patrologia Latina,* ed. J. P. MIGNE, 217 v. (Paris 1878–90)144:945–952. *Bibliotheca hagiographica latina antiquae cr mediae aetatis* (Brussels 1898–1901), 2239. A. POTHAST, *Bibliotheca historica medii aevi* (Graz 1957), 1272. A. M. ZIMMERMANN, *Kalendarium Benedictinum* (Metten 1933–37) 3:178, 180. J. L. BAUDOT and L. CHAUSSIN, *Vies des saints et des bienheureux selon l'ordre du calendrier avec l'historique des fêtes, by the Benedictines of Paris* (1959) 10:451–455. A. BUTLER, *The Lives of the Saints* (New York 1956) 4:110–111.

[F. DRESSLER]

DOMINIC OF FLANDERS

Belgian Dominican, professor of philosophy in Italy; b. Merris, Diocese of Tirouane, *c.* 1425; d. Florence, July 16, 1479. After studying philosophy and some theology at the University of Paris, he entered the order at Bologna on Sept. 7, 1461. An ardent disciple of St. THOMAS AQUINAS, he became one of the most celebrated philosophers in the Thomistic school. He taught in the *studium* in Bologna (1462–70) and in Florence (1471–72). At the request of Lorenzo de' Medici, he taught physics at the new Accademia of Pisa (1472–73). Then he returned to Florence, where he taught in the *studium* until he died of the plague. His extremely popular writings were printed many times. His *Summa divinae philosophiae* (ed. Venice 1499) is said to present the best synopsis of Thomism before the work of JOHN OF ST. THOMAS. His writings are marked by great subtlety and clarity, although they are not notably original. Among his more important works are *In 12 libros metaphysicae Aristotelis secundum expositionem angelici doctoris* (ed. Venice 1496); *Quaestiones 49 in 1 posteriorum et 20 in 2 posteriorum* (ed. Venice 1496); *Quaestiones et annotationes in 1–3 de anima* (ed. Venice 1503); *Quaestiones quodlibetales* (ed. Venice 1500); and commentaries on all the Aristotelian books of natural science, which apparently have not survived.

Bibliography: J. QUÉTIF and J. ÉCHARD, *Scriptores Ordinis Praedicatorum* (New York 1959) 1.2:894. G. MEERSSEMAN, "Dominicus de Flandria: Sein Leben, seine Schriften, seine Bedeutung," *Archivum Fratrum Praedicatorum* 10 (1940) 169–221; "Dominicus von Vlaanderen," *Tomistisch Tijdschrift von Katholischen Kulturleven* 1 (1930) 385–400, 590–592. L. MATHIEU, *Lexikon für Theologie und Kirche*, ed. J. HOFER and K. RAHNER (Freiburg 1957–65) 3:480; *Dominique de Flandre et sa métaphysique* (*Bibliothèque Thomiste* 24; 1942).

[J. F. HINNEBUSCH]

DOMINIC OF PRUSSIA

Carthusian spiritual writer (known also as Dominicus Prutenus, or Rutenus; Dominic of Trier); b. East Prussia, 1384; d. Trier, 1460. He entered the Carthusians at Trier in 1409, served as vicar and novice master at Sierk, Mainz, and finally at Trier. None of his writings have been edited. He is memorable for the interest he took in the devotion to the Sacred Heart, and even more conspicuously as a propagator of a rosary devotion. Indeed, some attribute the belief that the rosary began with St. Dominic, founder of the Friars Preachers, to a confusion between the two Dominics. (See H. Thurston, *Dictionnaire d'archéologie chrétienne et de liturgie*, ed. F. Cabrol, H. Leclerq, and H. I. Marrou, 3.1:399–406.) A rosary of 50 Ave Marias was in use at St. Alban's in Trier in the time of Dominic of Prussia. His prior, Adolph of Essen, was devoted to its recitation, as was another monk mentioned by Dominic, who can probably be identified as James of Meisenberg (d. 1427). It has also been suggested that the "D. Dominicus" on ancient pictures of Dominic receiving the rosary contributed to the confusion, the "D." being mistaken for "Divus" (Saint), instead of "Domnus" (Dom), which was intended. We do know for certain that Dominic of Prussia made a point of associating meditation with the recitation of the Ave Marias. A volume of meditations on the life of Christ, which his prior, Adolph, had extracted from Ludolph of Saxony's *Vita Christi,* appears to have suggested this to him. He also composed 50 formulas to be added to the Ave Marias. The Dominican propagator of the rosary, Alan de la Roche, seems to have been familiar with this method of recitation.

Bibliography: A. STOELEN, *Dictionnaire de spiritualité ascétique et mystique. Doctrine et histoire*, ed. M. VILLER et al. (Paris 1932–) 3:1539–42. Y. GOURDEL, "Le Culte de la très sainte Vierge dans l'Ordre des Chartreux: Le Rosaire de Dominique le Chartreux," *Maria: Études sur la Sainte Vierge* (Paris 1949–) v.2.

[B. DU MOUSTIER]

DOMINIC OF SILOS, ST.

One of four famous 11th-century Benedictine abbots in Castile; b. Cañas, Navarre (now Rioja), *c.* 1000; d. Silos, *c.* 1076, in the monastery that he refounded in 1041. He left San Millán de la Cogolla in Navarre because of difficulties with King Garcia I. His monastic revival at Silos preserved the Visigothic script and elements of the MOZARABIC RITE, before the Roman liturgy was imposed in Castile in 1081. His cult began in 1076 and spread widely. Reports of captives miraculously redeemed from Muslim hands in the 13th century through his aid are fantastic. Biographies, beginning in 1653, are restatements of a vita attributed to a Grimaldus, *c.* 1088, published in 1736, and of the vernacular verse of Gonzalo de Berceo, *c.* 1225 (ed. A. Andres, Madrid 1958).

Feast: Dec. 20.

Bibliography: L. SERRANO, *El real monasterio de Santo Domingo de Silos* (Burgos 1926); *El obispado de Burgos,* 3 v. (Madrid 1935). J. DEL ALAMO, *Vida histórico-crítica del taumaturgo* (Madrid 1953). P. C. GUTIÉRREZ, *Vida y milagros de Santo Domingo de Silos* (3d. ed. Silos 1973). A. GUTIÉRREZ BERNARDO, *Santo Domingo de Silos* (Madrid 1973). R. ALCOCER, *Santo Domingo de Silos* (2d ed. Burgos 1974). GRIMALDO, *La "Vita Dominici Siliensis" de Grimaldo*, ed. and tr. V. VALCÁRCEL (Logroño 1982). E. SANTOS ELOLA, *Domingo de Silos* (Almeria, Spain 1991).

[E. P. COLBERT]

DOMINIC OF SORA, ST.

Abbot; b. Foligno, Italy, 951; d. Sora, Campania, Italy, Jan. 22, 1031. As a child he was educated in the monastery of San Silvestro at Foligno, and later he was ordained there. He lived both as a hermit and as a cenobite: he was a monk at Pietra Dèmone, and then a hermit on a nearby mountain. He founded the monastery of San Salvatore at Scandriglia in 986, then retired to Mount Pizzi and built two other monasteries. Dominic sought solitude at Prato Cardoso, and at the request of the Counts of Valva, he founded San Pietro del Lago and San Pietro di Avellana, both of which shortly afterward passed under the jurisdiction of MONTE CASSINO. Dominic transferred his activity to the area of the lower Lazio and there built monasteries at Trisulti and at SORA, where he became abbot. A famous wonderworker and devoted to the monastic ideal, he combated energetically the vices of clergy and people. He is buried at Sora, and canonical recognition of his relics was granted in 1951.

Feast: Jan. 22.

Bibliography: *Bibliotheca hagiographica latina antiquae et mediae aetatis* (Brussels 1898–1901), 1:2241–46. *Chronica monasterii casinensis* 2.59, *Monumenta Germaniae Scriptores* (Berlin 1825–), 7:667–668. L. JACOBILLI, *Vita di S. Domenico da Foligno* (Foligno 1645). L. TOSTI, *Della vita di S. Domenico abate* (Sora 1877). A. LENTINI, "La *Vita S. Dominici* di Alberico Cassinese," *Benedictina* 5 (1951) 57–77; "S. D. S. e Montecassino: Su tre inni di S. D. abate," *ibid.*, 185–199. A. M. ZIMMERMANN, *Kalendarium Benedictinum: Die Heiligen und Seligen des Benediktinerorderns und seiner Zweige*, 4 v. (Metten 1933–38) 1:114–117; 4:13. J. M. HOWE, *Church Reform and Social Change in Eleventh-Century Italy: Dominic of Sora and His Patrons* (Philadelphia 1997).

[A. LENTINI]

DOMINICAL LETTER

The letter used in liturgical calendars to denote the Sundays in a particular year. Since to determine the date of Easter one must know the sequence of the days of the week following the paschal full moon, the early Christians devised special tables, basing these on existing Greco-Roman computations of the seven possible relationships of the days of the week to the calendar of the year. Thus, in the time of Augustus the Romans had allotted the letters A to G of the alphabet to the seven days of any of the 52 seven-day cycles of the full year, beginning from January 1. In Christian usage, therefore, the Dominical or Sunday letter for any given year is the letter that occurs on the first Sunday of the first cycle; and in a normal year the date of all the other Sundays will follow automatically, as the Dominical letter recurs in each of the 52 cycles. In the sequence of years, however, the Dominical letters run in a retrograde series (G–A), since a year that begins, for example, on a Monday (yielding on Sunday, January 7, the Dominical letter G) is commonly succeeded by a year beginning on a Tuesday (giving the Dominical letter F on January 6). Thus, since Jan. 1, 1962, fell on a Monday and the first Sunday of 1962 on January 7, the Dominical letter for 1962 was the seventh letter, i.e., G. In 1963, however, January 1 was on a Tuesday, so the first Sunday fell on January 6, and the Dominical letter for 1963 was therefore F. Again, Jan. 1, 1965, was on a Friday, so the first Sunday was on the third day of 1965, giving C as the Dominical letter for that year. The year 1964, however, is more complicated since it is a leap year. In a leap year (*annus bissextilis*) there is an extra day in February, and this was denominated *dies bissextus* from the fact that VI Kal. Mar. (February 24) was the day selected for doubling (in the modern system the extra day is added after February 28). The insertion of this doubled day in February means that there is a change in the seven-day cycle of letters at this point, so that the Dominical letter for the period after the extra day (February 24 or 28) must differ from that governing the Sundays from January 1.

The Dominical letter does not seem to have been familiar to BEDE in his *De temporum ratione* (c. 725), but in its place he adopts a similar device of Greek origin that uses seven numbers (1–7), called *concurrentes* by Bede; these denote the day of the week on which March 24 falls in the successive years of the solar cycle, one standing for Sunday, two for Monday (*feria secunda*), three for Tuesday (*feria tertia*), etc. A table coordinating the Dominical letter with *concurrentes* and other reckonings of the year is conveniently included at the beginning of every BREVIARY and MISSAL under the heading *Tabula paschalis nova reformata*.

Bibliography: BEDE, *Patrologia Latina: De ratione temporum*, ed. J. P. MIGNE, (Paris 1878–90) 90. G. DURANDUS, *Rationale divinorum officiorum* (Lyons 1560, Venice 1568). C. CLAVIUS, *Romani calendarii a Gregorio XIII restituti explicatio* (Rome 1603). J. LACAU and P. CALOT, *Dictionnaire de droit canonique*, ed. R. NAZ (Paris 1935–65) 2:1243–46. C. R. CHENEY, *A Handbook of Dates for Students of English History* (London 1945).

[L. E. BOYLE/EDS.]

DOMINICAN NUNS (NUNS OF THE ORDER OF PREACHERS) [1050]

The Dominican nuns were founded by St. DOMINIC in 1206 at the Monastery of Notre Dame at Prouille, near Carcassonne, in southern France. They are juridically members of the Dominican Order, professing obedience to the Master and submitting their constitutions to him for approval.

The original community, which was made up of converts from the ALBIGENSES, constituted a corps of auxiliaries in the apostolic preaching of Dominic and his brethren. Their contribution was significant, since among the heretics, women were an effective means of propagating their errors. Though cloistered, the nuns, who were referred to as Sister Preacheresses, participated in the ministry of preaching by their prayers, by their rigorous ascetical life, and by the instruction of young women. As his order grew, Dominic established monasteries of nuns at Madrid in 1218 and at Rome (St. Sixtus) in 1219. Another monastery that he had planned for Bologna, Italy, did not come into existence until shortly after his death (1221). As with the Dominican friars, the nuns followed the Rule of St. Augustine and were governed by constitutions framed by Dominic. The primitive rule of the nuns at Prouille, preserved in part in the extant *Institutions* of the Nuns of St. Sixtus, was subsequently completed by borrowing from the constitutions of the friars.

As early as 1226 opposition arose among the friars to the government of monasteries of nuns, lest the office of preaching suffer because too many friars were engaged in looking after both the spiritual and the temporal affairs of the nuns. The persistence and effectiveness of the opposition may be seen in the fact that, while at the end of the 13th century there were in 18 provinces nearly 600 priories of friars, there were fewer than 140 monasteries of nuns incorporated into the order. There were many others that were left to, or passed under, the jurisdiction of bishops. To some extent, however, the nuns (and the ideas of Dominic) prevailed, for in 1259, at the instance of Alexander IV, the general chapter of Valencia approved the definitive *Constitutions of the Nuns of the Order of Preachers.* With only minor changes, these constitutions prescribed the rule of life for Dominican nuns until modern times, though the Council of Trent placed all monasteries of women under the jurisdiction of bishops, unless the Holy See otherwise provided for their government.

Despite the vicissitudes of the centuries, and especially the antireligious and destructive forces let loose or engendered by the French Revolution, the Dominican nuns survived. In 2001 there were worldwide nearly 3,800 Dominican nuns in 235 monasteries. They are governed by their Constitutions, approved by the Holy See in 1987. The nuns observe papal enclosure in their monasteries, which are autonomous, though they may form federations or associations in accordance with the provisions of the Apostolic Instruction *Verbi Sponsa (1999).*

The nuns are to strive after their own personal sanctification and the salvation of all people, interceding for the needs of the Church and the preaching mission of the friars, sisters, and laity of the Dominican Order. They make solemn profession of the evangelical counsels of poverty, chastity and obedience, leading a life in community, which is fostered through the solemn celebration of the liturgy (notably the Divine Office), private prayer, the study of sacred truth, enclosure, silence, the habit, work, and penitential practices.

In the U.S. in 2001 there were 18 monasteries of cloistered Dominican nuns. All of them derive ultimately from Prouille, through Nay, France, which was the first monastery to revive (1807) in that country after the French Revolution, and from which Prouille itself was reestablished in 1880. They originate from two groups: the Dominican Nuns of the Second Order of Perpetual Adoration, growing out of Nay through Oullins, France; and the Dominican Sisters of the Perpetual Rosary. The latter began as an institute of third order contemplatives, established in Belgium (1880) by Dominican Father Damien M. Saintourens, in collaboration with Mother Rose de Ste. Marie, who was chosen from the second order monastery in France at Mauleon (which derived from Nay) to form and govern the community. Although originally of the third order, most of the monasteries have been incorporated into the Order during the course of the 20th century.

A number of these monasteries still continue the traditions of Perpetual Adoration of the Blessed Sacrament, or Perpetual Rosary, i.e. recitation of the rosary before the Blessed Sacrament. In 2001, there were 18 monasteries with 390 nuns in the U.S.: Marbury, Ala. (1944); Los Angeles, Calif. (1924); Menlo Park, Calif. (1921); North Guilford, Conn. (1947); Washington, D.C. (1909); Camden, N.J. (1900); Newark, N.J. (1880); Union City, N.J. (1891); Summit, N.J. (1919); Bronx, N.Y. (1889); Buffalo, N.Y. (1905); Elmira, N.Y. (1944); Syracuse, N.Y. (1924); West Springfield, Mass. (1922); Farmington Hills, Mich. (1906); Lancaster, Pa. (1925); Lufkin, Tex. (1945); and Milwaukee, Wis. (1897). The U. S. monasteries have made foundations in Fatima, Portugal (1954); Karachi, Pakistan (1959); Nairobi, Kenya, (1965); Cainta, Rizal (1977) and Bocaue, Bulacan, Philippines (1977); and Surrey, B.C., Canada (2000).

[J. B. WALKER/J. MIRYAM OF THE TRINITY]

DOMINICAN REPUBLIC, THE CATHOLIC CHURCH IN

Located in the eastern two-thirds of the island of Hispañola, the Dominican Republic borders Haiti on the west. To the north and east is the North Atlantic, while

Capital: Santo Domingo.
Size: 18,704 sq. miles.
Population: 8,442,533 in 2000.
Languages: Spanish.
Religions: 6,909,800 Catholics (70%), 928,678 Protestants (11%), 604,055 follow vodun or are without religious affiliation.
Archdioceses: Santiago de los Caballeros, with suffragans La Vega, Mao-Monte Cristi, Puerto Plata, and San Francisco de Macorís; Santo Domingo, with suffragans Baní, Barahona, Nuestra Señora de la Altagracia en Higüey, San Juan de la Maguana, and San Pedro de Macorís. A military ordinariate is also established. The country is notable as the territory in which the first civil and ecclesiastical government in America was established, the first schools and universities founded, the first churches and the first cathedral built.

to the south is the Caribbean Sea. The region is characterized by rocky highlands rising to mountains and cut through by fertile valleys that supply the region with its agricultural base. The tropical climate is marked by annual hurricanes that strike the island during the summer months. Natural resources include nickel, bauxite, gold and silver; among the country's chief agricultural exports are coffee, sugar and cocoa.

Early History. The island of Hispañola—known by its native peoples as Quisqueya, Bohío, Bebeque and Haiti— was discovered on Dec. 5, 1492, by Christopher Columbus, who dubbed it Hispañola. Columbus erected on the island the first building in the New World, the Fuerte de la Navidad. On his second trip in 1493 he founded the first city, La Isabela, which was abandoned after a few years when Bartolomé Columbus established Santo Domingo, the oldest city of America. Christopher Columbus, who established the first government of the Indies, was also the island's first governor. With him began a series of rulers that would later include some of the great figures of the Dominican Church.

As the civil government of the Indies was exercised in Santo Domingo through the first governors and the royal *audiencia,* ecclesiastical government extended its jurisdiction to the same dominions. The island's civil governments alternated between periods of progress and decadence, and its policies resulted in the virtual extinction of native peoples and their replacement by African slaves. In 1586 British explorer Sir Francis Drake invaded Hispañola, sacking and burning the city of Santo Domingo.

Development of the Church. In 1493 Father BUYL arrived in Santo Domingo, and within 15 years established several bishoprics, churches and convents. By the 16th century the cathedral of Santo Domingo was the center of the faith, overseeing a house of Jesuits as well

as convents in San Francisco, Santo Domingo, Mercedes, Santa Catalina de Sena, Santa Clara and the Ermita del Carmen. The life of the colony centered on the Church, which established schools, universities and hospitals, housed in great examples of colonial architecture. Many of these buildings were still standing at the close of the 20th century.

The Church's tradition was enriched by the bishops and archbishops of Hispañola, many of whom exercised their sacred ministry in other parts of the Indies, thus creating a spiritual tie between the most distant regions: the men of the Church were true forgers of Hispanic unity. Among them were the humanist Bishop Alejandro GERALDINI; Bishop Sebastián Ramírez de Fuenleal, later president of the *audiencia* in Mexico; Alonso de Fuenmayor, first archbishop of Santo Domingo; the preacher Nicolás Ramos, who took part in the controversies over the translations of the Bible in Spain; the archeologist and historian Agustín DÁVILA Y PADILLA; Domingo de Valderrama, theologian and famed preacher, who had been professor at the University of Lima; Domingo de Navarrete, missionary in China; and many other great figures of the Church, letters and government in the New World and in Spain.

Area Becomes Focus of Competing Colonial Interests. Because of Spain's monopoly on commerce within her colonies, pirates sponsored by other governments attacked settlements in the north and west of Hispañola. On the nearby island of Tortuga and thence to the Dominican coast, French, English and Dutch forces fought until France finally won control of the western part of the island. Despite taking violent measures against the intruders, after 1630 Spain's control of the eastern part of the island was constantly threatened. However, in 1655 the Spanish-Dominicans successfully repelled invading forces sent by British ruler Oliver Cromwell. Although the Ryswick Treaty of 1697 divided the island into two colonies, Spanish and French, a perpetual state of war existed because of French aggressions. The Treaty of Aranjuez in 1777 did little to reduce the French and Spanish hostilities, although it set a boundary line between the two colonies. Finally, in 1795 through the Treaty of Basel, Spain ceded her half of the island to France, an action rooted in economic necessity. While slaves from Africa had been imported by the French— more than 30,000 per year from 1750 to 1789—to farm western lands, the section of Hispañola under Spanish control, where cattle ranches predominated, suffered continual labor shortages due to emigration. In 1789, the year Spain relinquished its rights to the island, there were only 125,000 people living in the east under Spanish rule, whereas at least 450,000 slaves occupied the French region to the west. Political boundaries aside, this situation

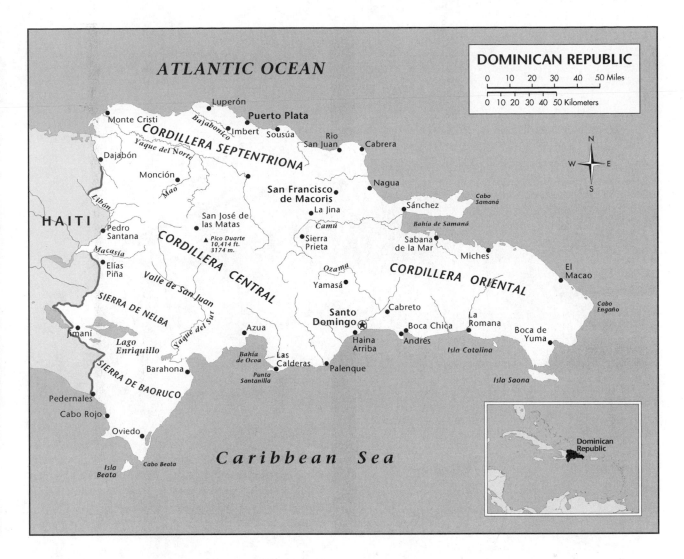

would ultimately result in an island divided along ethnic lines: in the west, Haiti developed a homogenous French-speaking European/African society which became prosperous, while in the Dominican Republic people of predominately Spanish origin, who spoke a purely Spanish language, suffered under relative poverty.

The Church in the 18th Century. Although many of the island's Christian monuments were erected during the 16th and 17th centuries, an enterprising spirit still remained by 1700. New churches were constructed and centers of culture and charitable refuges founded. The intellectual life of the island during the 18th century was dominated by Francisco Rincón, archbishop of Santo Domingo, then Bogotá; Domingo Pantaleón Alvarez de Abreu, educator, organizer, author and archbishop of the island in 1738 and then in Puebla de los Angeles; the Mexican Augustinian Ignacio de PADILLA Y ESTRADA, who was archbishop of Guatemala and Yucatán; from 1789 to 1798; and the Dominican Fernando Portillo y Torres, later archbishop of Bogotá (d. 1804).

Formation of Modern Republic. During the French era, both Church and country weathered several hazards. Revolutionary leaders Toussaint L'Ouverture in 1801 and Dessalines in 1805 invaded the Spanish part of Hispañola and decimated the remnants of the old Spanish colony. In 1804 a slave uprising against France resulted in the formation of the state of Haiti, and in 1808 the Dominicans reconquered the eastern part for Spain. Inspired by revolutions in South America, on Dec. 1, 1821, Dominicans led by José Nuñez de Cáceres created the ephemeral independent state of Spanish Haiti under the protecting flag of Gran Colombia. The reconquest and expulsion of the French gave rise to the period of España Boba, and the prestige of the Dominican Church was, in part, reestablished. For the first time, a native of the island, Pedro Valera y Jiménez, occupied the archbishop's throne.

In 1822 Haiti invaded the new nation to the east, sparking a second wave of nationalism that resulted in the

Cathedral de Santa Maria La Menor, Dominican Republic. Photograph by Abbie Enock. (©Travel Ink/CORBIS)

independent state of the Dominican Republic. Brought about through the efforts of such Spaniards as Juan Pablo Duarte and General Pedro Santana, the creation of the Dominican Republic on Feb. 27, 1844 was the culmination of the heroism and persistence of the region's Hispanic culture, fueled by the same spirit that had led to the first Spanish establishment in the New World. Two notable leaders of the Dominican Church would become presidents of the new republic: Archbishop Meriño in 1880 and Archbishop A. A. Nouel in 1913.

The constitution of the First Republic went into effect on Nov. 6, 1844, with Pedro Santana as president. Unable to maintain order due to persistent aggression from Haiti, in 1861 Santana asked Spain to resume control over the area. Under the leadership of Buenaventura Báez independence was achieved again four years later and the Second Republic was proclaimed. It, too, had a history checkered with violence and U.S. intervention was requested *c.* 1905 due to a bankrupt economy. In 1916 the United States took over full control of the Dominican Republic, installing a military government for almost eight years as a means of curbing internal violence. General Rafael Leónidas Trujillo Molina became president in 1930 after overthrowing a constitutional government established in 1924; he retained control of the country until he was assassinated in 1961, his death forestalling a planned mass arrest of the nation's bishops. The political unrest of the 1960s resulted in the return of U.S. Marines, and a new constitution was implemented on Nov. 28, 1966, after which time the country established a stable democratic government under the Partido Reformista. In 1996 power reverted to the Liberation Party, a moderate government that began instituting a market-oriented economy.

Although Catholicism was not made the state religion through the constitution of 1844, in 1954 the Vatican signed a concordat with the state that extended to it preferential treatment as the majority faith. The state subsidized certain Church expenses and waived all applicable customs duties. In addition, members of the National Police were required to attend Catholic Mass. During the Trujillo administration Church leaders remained apolitical, the result of a policy of government harassment provoked by a pastoral letter against mass political arrests. The role of the Church had altered by the late 1990s, as Church leaders advocated for human rights issues and involved themselves with trade unions, peasant leagues, student groups and other local secular associations. In 1963 the government legalized divorce and began sponsoring family planning four years later, despite opposition from the Church, which was unable to rally members against these measures.

By 2000 there were 410 parishes within the Dominican Republic, tended by 300 diocesan and 394 religious priests, while 79 brothers and 1,500 sisters administered to Dominicans in areas of health care, education and other humanitarian concerns. The Church operated 190 primary schools in the country, as well as more than 100 secondary schools. In 1992, Pope John Paul II visited the Dominican Republic as part of a celebration of the discovery of the New World by Columbus.

See Also: SANTO DOMINGO.

Bibliography: B. PICARDO, *Resúmen de la historia de Santo Domingo* (Santo Domingo 1964).

[E. RODRÍGUEZ DEMORIZI/EDS.]

DOMINICAN RITE

The Dominican Order began early on to feel the need for a unified rite like the Cistercians or Premontre. Some have argued that St. DOMINIC, who was very concerned about the liturgy, desired this and they profess as evidence the annotations in his Breviary, now at the Cloister of Monte Mario in Rome. Gleason thinks that this Breviary was St. Dominic's and some think that it was probably a Cistercian book edited by him. There is evidence of a pre-Humbert rite in that Breviary, the Copenhagen Choir book, the Missal of Paris, the Diurnal of Engelberg (for Nuns), the Breviary of the Four Friars, and the Rau Missal. The fact that the 1228 Constitutions state that no friar was to change the day or night offices suggests a somewhat uniform rite. The general chapter of 1244 under the Master of the Order, John the Teuton, directed delegates to bring the rubrics of the Breviary, Missal, and Gradual (proper and ordinary chants of the Mass) to be corrected at the next chapter. A year later the chapter commissioned four friars to revise and unify the diversity of rites, chants, books, etc. which suggests that there was still no uniform Dominican Rite. The work of the four friars was not well received suggesting perhaps the Order was too attached to elements of local rites. In 1254 Blessed Humbert was elected Master and was authorized to correct the liturgical books used by his brethren. It seems that he accepted and simplified the work of the four friars. In 1256 the chapter approved his work which he enjoined on the Order. This was formally approved by Clement IV for the order in the bull *Consurget In Nobis* of July 7, 1267. The *Codex Humberti* at the Angelicum in Rome is Humbert's typical edition of the Gradual, Missal for Community Mass, the Epistle book, Gospel book, side altar Missal, the Martyrology, book of Collects, Psalter, Breviary, Lectionary, Antiphonary, Ordinary, Pulpit book, and Processional, from which all copies of these books were to be made.

Sources. The sources of the Dominican Rite are complex. The only pre-Humbert books we have are St. Dominic's Breviary, as well as the five books described above. The early Dominican Constitutions and Humbert's Breviary shows the influence of Premontre; the chant seems to be a simplified version of CITEAUX and there seems to be influences of the CISTERCIAN RITE as well. This is not surprising since for his constitutions St. Dominic took from both the Norbertines and Cistercians *quod arduum* (whatever was strict), *quod decorum* (whatever was beautiful), and *quod discretum* (whatever was balanced). Some have also thought they detected influences not only of Rome, but also traces of Paris, Salisbury, Hereford, and Exeter.

Characteristics. The sobriety, simplicity and beauty of the Dominican Rite exercised great appeal. Many orders and dioceses adopted it. It was widespread in Scandinavia, the Baltic area, Italy, and even Armenia. The Low Mass featured the preparation of the chalice at the beginning of the rite, not unlike the Eastern rites or the Sarum use. The *Confiteor* was shorter and there was no psalm in the prayers at the foot of the altar. At the preparation of the gifts, host and chalice were offered in a single oblation and a candle was lit at the *Sanctus* on the epistle side of the altar. Solemn Mass featured the preparation of the chalice at the sedila by the celebrant, deacon, and subdeacon in between the Epistle and Gospel. The latter was chanted facing "liturgical north," where lived the pagans who needed conversion, and facing the processional cross which was held by the cross bearer flanked by two candle bearers. When the office was chanted in choir the unusual custom was maintained of one side of choir standing and chanting to the other side which sat and chanted back. Then both sides rose and bowed for the *Gloria Patri* and the pattern was reversed. Standing represented the active life of preaching while sitting represented listening and therefore the contemplative life. This custom is often still followed.

Current Status. The Dominican Mass changed little until Vatican II, although revisions in the Roman Breviary in 1920 changed the Dominican Breviary substantially. Still the Rite continued with its own books accepting new feasts and rubrics from the Church, issuing a missal in 1965 and a Breviary in 1962. The extraordinary chapter of River Forest in 1968 commissioned the Master of the Order to adopt the Roman Rite after its full conciliar reform. This was so that people in Dominican churches might better participate. This was requested of the Holy See and conceded by the Church on June 2, 1969, although the Master could grant individual friars (especially the old) permission to celebrate Mass in the Dominican Rite. Although some had wanted to keep the rite and adapt it to the new reforms (as did the Milanese Rite),

nonetheless when the missal of Paul VI, with its offertory procession, was adopted as well as the new lectionary, distinctive Dominican elements in the Mass were few and far between. The same held true for the Breviary, for most wanted the new distribution of psalms, the new plan of readings from Scripture, and the complementary patristic readings. When all of this was accepted, little that was distinctively Dominican remained except for the feasts of the Order. In 1970 the pre-chapter commission on liturgy asked for reactions to the current liturgical situation as well as particular feasts for the universal Dominican calendar. Out of this process, the Chapter of Tallaught in 1971 commissioned *periti* to consult the friars and gather peculiar elements (both ceremonies and texts) so that venerable Dominican traditions could be passed on to the Dominican family and thus foster devotion. This was done and a liturgical directory was published in 1977 suggesting ways that former Dominican customs might be incorporated as options into the Roman rite Mass of Paul VI and into the reformed Liturgy of the Hours as well. In 1983 the Order issued its own supplement to the Liturgy of the Hours with Dominican texts for the feasts of the Order culled from the old Breviary, but also chose readings from other writings of Dominican saints and *beati*. In 1985 the order issued its own Missal and Lectionary with traditional texts for Dominican feasts. Both of these were issued in Latin and have been or are being translated into modern languages. In summary, one could say the Dominican Rite is no more, but preservation of traditional Dominican elements in celebrating Mass and the Liturgy of the Hours is an option and might be said to perhaps to be a usage or use in the Roman Rite.

See Also: DOMINICANS.

Bibliography: D. A. MORTIER, *La liturgie dominicaine,* 9 v. (Bruges 1921–24). A. A. KING, *Liturgies of Religious Orders* (Milwaukee 1955). W. R. BONNIWELL, *History of the Dominican Liturgy 1215–1945,* 2d ed. (New York 1945). A. DIRKS, "De Novo Ordine Missae," *Analecta Sacri Ordinis Fratrum Praedicatorum* 39 (1970) 572–74; "De Orationibus Sanctorim," *Analecta Sacri Ordinis Fratrum Praedicatorum* 40 (1972) 514–25; "De evolutione liturgiae Dominicanae," *Archivum Fratrum Predaicatorum* 50 (1980) 5–21; 52 (1982) 5–76; 53 (1983) 53–145; 54 (1984) 39–82; 55 (1985) 5–47; 57 (1987) 25–30. P. GLEASON, "Dominican Liturgical Documents from before 1254," *Archivum Fratrum Praedicatorum* 42 (1972) 80–135. D. DYE, "Le rit dominicain a la suite de la reforme liturgique de Vatican II," *Analecta Sacri Ordinis Fratrum Praedicatorum* 42 (1977) 193–306.

[G. R. DIMOCK]

DOMINICAN SISTERS

Congregation of Our Lady of the Rosary (Sparkhill, N.Y.) [1070–11] A diocesan community founded on May 6, 1876, in New York City by Mother Catharine Antoninus Thorpe, a convert from the Anglican Church. The first work of the Congregation was the care of the sick in their homes as well as providing a refuge for indigent women. From this developed the necessity of caring for destitute children. Property was purchased in Sparkill, N.Y., and the motherhouse and novitiate were moved there in 1895. By 1900 the sisters' work included teaching in elementary and high school, and that same year their ministry was extended to Missouri. Eventually education became the congregation's principal ministry. In 1958 the sisters responded to an appeal to serve in Pakistan. Since 1980 Associate members have shared actively in the mission and charism of the Congregation. Today, the ministries of the sisters have expanded in response to the needs of contemporary society to bring about a more just and peaceful world. They are child-care workers, educators, parish ministers, social workers, nurses, chaplains, artists, spiritual directors, housing managers, campus ministers and counselors.

[M. HARRISON]

Congregation of Our Lady of the Sacred Heart (Grand Rapids, Mich.) [1070–14]. This community is a daughter community of the community in Newburgh, N.Y., and began in 1877 when five sisters came from New York to Traverse City in northern Michigan for the purpose of establishing Catholic schools. By 1885 personnel and schools had increased so much that the Michigan foundations were organized into the province of St. Joseph, with its central house at Holy Angels Convent, Traverse City. In 1894 Henry Joseph Richter, first bishop (1883–1916) of the Diocese of Grand Rapids, which embraced the western and northern two-thirds of Michigan, suggested that the sisters sever connections with distant New York and form a separate community. The present congregation with its motherhouse at Marywood in Grand Rapids thus came into existence. The sisters who were outside the diocese continued their affiliation with the New York group, but later formed an independent community, the Dominican Sisters of Adrian, Mich.

The congregation's Novitiate Normal School eventually evolved into Aquinas College in 1940, though the college is no longer owned by the congregation. Besides education, the sisters minister health care, pastoral services and the foreign missions.

[M. G. UDELL]

Congregation of St. Catherine de Ricci (Elkins Park, Penn.) [1070–17] A community with papal approbation (1938) founded in Glens Falls, N.Y., in 1880 by an American convert, Lucy Eaton Smith, to meet the spiritual needs of women. By 1883, Lucy Smith (Mother

Motherhouse and St. Clara Academy of the Dominican Sisters of Sinsinawa, Wis. (a) as it appeared prior to 1963 and (b) the motherhouse extension erected between 1963 and 1965.

Maria Catherine de'Ricci) and her small community established the first retreat house for women in the United States on the Albany-Troy Road. The first motherhouse was built in Albany in 1887. The ministry spread south and west, and included religious education and the residence apostolate as companion ministries. Three academies in Cuba (1899 to 1961) were confiscated by the Castro government; ministry to the Cuban refugees continued in Miami until 1971. A second outreach for various mission involvements operated in Cali, Columbia, from 1965 to 1980. The sisters continue their ministry in retreat centers, parish work, faith formation, campus ministry, and areas of women's needs.

[C. KREBS]

Congregation of St. Catharine of Siena (St. Catharine, Ky.) [1070–01] Founded in 1822, this congregation of Dominican Sisters is the oldest Dominican congregation in the United States. The founder was a Dominican priest, Samuel Wilson, who had come to Kentucky with several confreres in 1806. Unable to obtain help from convents in Europe, he decided to meet the need for sisters by establishing a new community. A beginning was made in 1822 with nine candidates, young women from Kentucky and Maryland. One of these,

Mother Angela Sansbury, was chosen the first superior. With teaching as its chief work, the congregation expanded into many areas of the U.S., and eventually to Puerto Rico. The sisters continue to minister in education at all levels and sponsor St. Catharine College in St. Catharine, Kentucky. They also minister as pastoral associates, social justice advocates, and health care workers.

Two other congregations in the U.S. have stemmed from St. Catharine, Kentucky—the Dominican Sisters of Columbus, Ohio, and Springfield, Illinois.

Bibliography: A. C. MINOGUE, *Pages from a Hundred Years of Dominican History* (New York 1921). V. F. O'DANIEL, *A Light of the Church in Kentucky . . . Samuel Thomas Wilson, O.P.* (Washington 1932). P. NOONAN, *Signadou: History of the Dominican Sisters.*

[M. A. MARTIN]

Congregation of St. Catherine of Siena (Racine, Wis.) [1070–09]

In 1862 Mother Benedicta Bauer and Sister Thomasina Ginker went to Racine from the Dominican convent in Ratisbon, Germany. This was the same community that had begun its first U.S. mission in Brooklyn, New York, in 1853 (the Dominican Sisters of Amityville, N.Y.). The sisters staffed parochial schools, and in 1864 they opened an academy that was the forerunner of St. Catherine's High School in Racine. The sisters continue their ministry in education and pastoral ministry, as well as health care, social justice ministry, and other outreaches to the poor and disenfranchised

Bibliography: M. H. KOHLER, *The Life and Works of Mother Benedicta Bauer* (Milwaukee 1937); *Rooted in Hope* (Milwaukee 1962).

[M. H. KOHLER]

Congregation of the Dominican Sisters of St. Catherine of Siena of Kenosha (Kenosha, Wis.) [1070–25]

These sisters, who formed an independent community in 1952, stem from the Irish Dominican Sisters by way of Portugal. The Portuguese branch began in 1865 under the leadership of a noblewoman named Thereza Salhdana. Four years later, six sisters who were trained in Ireland came to Portugal. The work of the congregation, mainly in education, flourished until 1910, when the anticlerical government suppressed religious communities. From the dispersal of the sisters there developed new ventures in the U.S. and Brazil. Six sisters, who had been deported to their native Ireland, were invited in 1911 by the bishop of Baker City, Ore., to open a convent in his diocese. They first established themselves in Ontario, Ore., and then, in 1915, in Hanford, Calif. In 1917 the novitiate (and later the motherhouse) was located in Kenosha, Wis. Until 1952 the U.S. foundation continued to be subject to the Portuguese congregation.

[M. D. GRADY]

Congregation of St Cecilia (Nashville, Tenn.) [1070–07]

A community with papal approbation, begun in 1860 as a branch of the Dominican Sisters of Columbus, Ohio. Four sisters from Somerset, Ohio, came to Tennessee in 1860 to open an academy for girls at the invitation of the bishop of Nashville, James Whaleen (1859–63). Although threatened with financial and other difficulties during and after the Civil War, the sisters succeeded in opening a novitiate in 1867. Several years later (1873) the sisters rendered valuable service by nursing the victims of cholera and yellow fever. The congregation, engaged mainly in teaching, has houses in Tennessee, Alabama, Ohio, and Virginia. In 1929 the sisters opened their own normal school, the first of its kind to be affiliated with The Catholic University of America. The sisters continue their ministry in education and sponsor Aquinas Junior College in Nashville.

[M. R. SCHAEFER]

Congregation of St. Dominic (Blauvelt, N.Y.) [1070–15]

A diocesan community with the title Congregation of Saint Dominic. Originated in New York City from the Ratisbon (Germany) Dominican Foundation in 1859. Mother Mary Ann Sammon and six other sisters established an orphanage for children in 1878 in Blauvelt (Rockland County), N.Y. An independent Dominican Congregation for women under the archbishop of New York was formally established in 1891.

The Congregation is actively involved in education at all levels, as well as ministries that serve the poor and disenfranchised. The Congregation is served by a president and three councilors.

[R. A. CAIMANO/EDS.]

Congregation of St. Mary (New Orleans, La.) [1070–08]

A congregation with papal approbation (1946), begun in 1860 by a group of the Irish Dominican Sisters. Mother Mary John Flanagan and five other sisters from Dublin, Ireland, arrived in New Orleans on Nov. 5, 1860, to staff a parochial school at the request of Rev. Jeremiah Moynihan, pastor of the church of St. John the Baptist. From 1910 to 1985 they sponsored St. Mary's Dominican College in New Orleans. The sisters minister in education, retreats and social work.

[M. DE R. ALBRECHT/EDS.]

Congregation of the Queen of the Holy Rosary (Mission San Jose, Calif.) [1070–12]

A community with papal approbation (1922) that stemmed from the Dominican Sisters of Amityville, N.Y. In 1876 Mother Maria Pia Backes, accompanied by Mother Mary Amanda Bednartz and Mother Mary Salesia Fichtner, came at the request of Joseph Sadoc Alemany, O.P., first archbishop of San Francisco, Calif., who was seeking religious teachers for the Catholic children of the West. In 1888 the autonomy of the California foundation was effected. The new motherhouse was established in San Francisco, and Mother Maria Pia was elected the first superior general. The motherhouse was transferred in 1906 to Mission San Jose in the Diocese of Oakland, Calif. The sisters continue to minister in education and other areas of pastoral ministry with a special outreach to the poor.

[E. BALDE]

Congregation of St. Rose of Lima (Oxford, Mich.) [1070–26].

The community began in 1923 with the founding of the convent of SS. Cyril and Methodius in Windber, Pennsylvania., by Sister M. de Sales Zavodnik, a member of the Dominican Sisters of Olomouc, Czechoslovakia. A notiviate was established on June 9, 1923, with the investiture of three American postulants by the bishop of Altoona, Pennsyvlania, John J. McCort (1920–36). In 1927, with the approval of the bishop of Detroit, Mich., Michael J. Gallagher (1918–37), the motherhouse and novitiate were canonically founded at Warren, Mich. Twelve years later, the Menscola Manor in Pontiac, Mich., was given to the sisters to house their increasing membership. In 1948 the motherhouse was transferred to Oxford, and in 1950 the U.S. community separated from the European motherhouse.

The sisters minister in health care, retreats, and education.

[M. G. WOYTKO]

Congregation of St. Rose of Lima (The Servants of Relief for Incurable Cancer in the U.S., Hawthorne, N.Y.) [1070–23].

A diocesan community of Dominican Sisters founded in 1896 by Rose Hawthorne Lathrop (Mother Alphonsa LATHROP), the younger daughter of Nathaniel Hawthorne. A convert of five years and a widow, she undertook in September of 1896 the work of caring for the cancerous poor on New York City's lower East Side. From the earliest days she was aided by a young associate, Alice Huber, from Louisville, Ky. On Dec. 8, 1900, they took religious vows as Third Order Dominicans. When Mother Alphonsa died in 1926, she was succeeded by Miss Huber (Mother Rose) who was superior until her death in 1942. The sisters continue to minister individuals who suffer from incurable cancer.

Bibliography: K. BURTON, *Sorrow Built a Bridge: A Daughter of Hawthorne* (New York 1937). T. MAYNARD, *A Fire Was Lighted: The Life of Rose Hawthorne Lathrop* (Milwaukee 1948). See also G. GIERATHS, *Lexikon für Theologie und Kirche,* (Freiburg 1957–65) 3:491–493. M. HEIMBUCHER, *Die Orden und Kongregationen der katholischen Kirche* (Paderborn 1932–34) 1:524–536.

[J. T. CLUNE]

Congregation of St. Thomas Aquinas (Tacoma, Wash.) [1070–20].

A community with papal approbation which stemmed from the Dominican Sisters of Caldwell, N.J. The community was begun at Pomeroy, in the Diocese of Nesqually (now Seattle), Washington Territory, on Oct. 24, 1888, when three sisters arrived from Jersey City, N.J. In 1893 property was acquired in Tacoma and the motherhouse and novitiate were moved there from Pomeroy. In response to Vatican II the sisters initiated many changes in structure, ministry and lifestyles.

[M. R. HURLEY]

Congregation of the Holy Cross (Amityville, N.Y.) [1070–05].

The community originated in 1853 when four sisters came to Williamsburg in Brooklyn, N.Y., from the Dominican convent in Ratisbon, Germany. Led by Sister M. Josepha Witzlhofer, these sisters, who traced their history in Germany back to the early 13th century, became the forerunners of numerous Dominican congregations in the U.S. Three of these stem directly from the Brooklyn community—the Dominican Sisters of Newburgh, N.Y.; Mission San Jose, Calif.; and Great Bend, Kans.

The sisters in Brooklyn became an independent congregation probably in 1857. Nearly a century later, in 1947, the motherhouse was transferred to the same location as the novitiate in Amityville, now in the Diocese of Rockville Centre, N.Y. The sisters minister in education and pastoral work, as well as social work and spiritual direction.

Bibliography: E. J. CRAWFORD, *The Daughters of Dominic on Long Island,* 2 v. (New York 1938–53).

[R. M. CONNOLLY]

Congregation of the Most Holy Name (San Rafael, Calif.) [1070–04].

The Congregation was founded in 1850 by Joseph Sadoc Alemany, O.P., who, while in Rome, was named bishop of Monterey, Calif. On his return to the United States he stopped in Paris seeking help for his diocese. Sister Mary of the Cross Goemaere of the Monastery of the Cross volunteered to accompany him. She obtained two novices as companions and set out for California with Bishop Alemany. The novices were left at the Dominican convent in Somerset, Ohio, and in their place two professed Somerset sisters came to California. Bishop Alemany and Sister Mary Goemaere arrived in San Francisco on Dec. 6, 1850. On July 18, 1851, the first foundation, a convent and school, was canonically erected in Monterey. In 1854 the motherhouse was moved to Benicia, Calif., and in 1889, to San Rafael, Calif. The Congregation received papal approval of its constitutions in 1931.

Since the beginning, the sisters have ministered in United States in the fields of education and health care.

The Congregation is credited with having established the first convent in California.

[M. SAGUES]

Congregation of the Most Holy Rosary (Adrian, Mich.) [070–13]. A community that traces its roots to the Dominican Sisters of Newburgh, N.Y. In 1879 four sisters came from New York to Adrian, Mich., to teach at St. Mary School. In 1880, four more sisters came to St. Joseph parish to teach, and in 1884 six sisters from Rosary Convent in New York established St. Joseph Hospital and Home for the Aged in a farmhouse on the outskirts of Adrian.

In 1892 the Adrian community became a province of the New York Dominicans and Mother Mary Camilla Madden was appointed the first provincial. In 1923 the community became a separate congregation and Mother Mary Camilla became the first superior general. Following her death on Jan. 8, 1924, she was succeeded by Mother Mary Augustine Walsh, who served until she died on Jan. 8, 1933. During her term of office the sisters, who ministered mainly in teaching, undertook social work in the Archdiocese of Cincinnati, Ohio.

Mother Gerald BARRY, elected third superior general in 1933 and reelected in 1939, remained in office, with the permission of the Holy See, until her death on Nov. 20, 1961. Under Mother Gerald vocations increased notably and many new foundations, including hospitals, were made. In 1960 a five-province plan of government was inaugurated, the generalate headquarters and novitiate remaining at Adrian. Mother Mary Genevieve Weber was elected fourth superior general in June of 1962. Her first official acts included the establishment of a poor parish in Lima, Peru, and the drawing up of plans for Maria Hall, a sisters' infirmary and retirement center at the Adrian motherhouse.

In the wake of Vatican II, the sisters entered into a variety of new ministries besides education and hospital ministry. They adopted a participatory form of government and have adapted community life to new forms. The sisters sponsor Barry University in Miami Shores, Fla., and Siena Heights University in Adrian, Mich.

[M. P. MCKEOUGH]

Congregation of the Sisters of St. Dominic of the Immaculate Heart of Mary (Akron, Ohio) [1070–28]. A diocesan community founded in 1929 that stems from the Dominican Sisters of Caldwell, N.J. Early in 1887 the sisters came from New Jersey to found a mission in Ravenna, Ohio, and then in Akron six years later. In 1923 Joseph SCHREMBS, Bishop of Cleveland, urged the purchase of the present motherhouse at Our Lady of the Elms

in Akron. Mother M. Beda Schmid became the first superior general in 1929. The sisters minister in education, pastoral ministry and a variety of other apostolates.

[M. R. PAULUS]

Dominican Rural Missionaries [1130]. A congregation of women religious with papal approbation. The community was founded in France in 1932 by Mother Marie de St. Jean Beauté to assist priests in rural parishes. The motherhouse is at Flavigny, Côte d'Or, France. The sisters came to the U.S. in 1951 and founded a convent in Abbeville, La., to work among the French-speaking people in the southwest portion of the state.

[M. DE P. REHKOPF]

Dominican Sisters of Charity of the Presentation of the Blessed Virgin Mary (Dighton, Mass.) [1100]. Founded in 1696 in Sainville, France, by Bl. Marie Poussepin, who gathered women for prayer and works of mercy. Keeping with the spirit inherited from their foundress, the sisters observe the Third Order Rule of St Dominic, pray the Dominican Office of the Hours, and set aside quality time for meditation and other daily prayers.

The Congregation had twenty houses in France at the time of the foundress' death in 1744 and subsequently spread out to 36 countries in North, South, and Central America, and France, England, Italy, and Spain, West, East, and North Africa, Iraq, Lebanon, Jerusalem, India, and Korea. It received pontifical status in 1887 and official Dominican recognition in 1897.

In North America the activities of the sisters extend from the pastoral ministry in the local parish to education at all levels, and various forms of social work in order to respond to the calls of the time and to the urgency of evangelization.

Bibliography: G. THÉRY, *Recueil des actes de la Vénérable M. Marie Poussepin: 1653–1744,* 2 v. (Tours 1938). T. MAINAGE, *Mère Marie Poussepin* (Paris 1914).

[M. W. LAPOINTE]

Dominican Sisters Congregation of Holy Cross (Edmonds, Wash.) [1070–21]. This group stems from the Dominican Sisters of Newburgh, N.Y. (now the Dominican Sisters of Hope), who established a western province at Aberdeen, Wash., in 1890. The sisters in the Far West were governed from the eastern motherhouse until 1923, when they formed an independent congregation. The sisters minister in education at all levels as well as health care, community service, peace and justice ministry and advocacy for women and children.

[M. A. LOGAN]

Dominican Sisters of Great Bend (Great Bend, Kans.) [1070–24]. A community with papal approbation

(1954) which began in 1902 as an offshoot of the Dominican Sisters of Amityville, N.Y., founded by Mother Antonina Fischer. The sisters' ministries include preaching; education; healthcare; housing for the elderly, handicapped, and poor; domestic work; parish ministry; Hispanic ministry; work in peace and justice; and foreign missionary work. The congregation has an international Rosary Shrine prayer ministry. A daughter foundation, the Dominican Sisters of St. Catherine of Siena of Nigeria, has also been established.

[M. T. TOCKERT]

Dominican Sisters of Hope [1105]. A Papal Congregation formed from three former congregations of Dominican Sisters: the Congregation of St. Catherine of Siena, Fall River, Mass.; the Dominican Sisters of the Most Holy Rosary, Newburgh, N.Y., and the Dominican Sisters of the Immaculate Conception of the Sick Poor, Ossining, N.Y. The Congregation was begun on July 20, 1995. Rooted in the charism of St. Dominic, the sisters, through work and prayer, seek to be givers of hope in their ministries in education, spiritual direction, retreats, and parish ministry, especially in low-income areas.

[J. MEYER]

Dominican Sisters of Houston, Texas (Congregation of the Sacred Heart) [1070–19]. The congregation began when 20 sisters from Somerset, Ohio, arrived in Galveston, Tex., on Sept. 29, 1882, in response to an appeal from Bp. Nicholas A. Gallagher (1882–1918). Mother M. Agnes Magevny governed the group until her death in 1891. Her successor, Mother Pauline Gannon (1891–1921), recognizing the need for teacher certification, began sending the sisters to study at the University of Texas. In order to accommodate them and other young women she built a residence, Newman Hall, near the campus in 1918. The next superior general, Mother Catherine Kenny (1922–34), moved the motherhouse of the community to Houston in 1926.

The congregation has provided leadership for Project Head Start, the Montessori method of education, and the accreditation of schools in the Diocese of Galveston-Houston. St. Agnes Academy and St. Pius X High School, both in Houston, are operated by the Dominican Sisters of Houston. Sacred Heart Dominican College, later Dominican College, operated on the motherhouse grounds from 1945 to 1974, providing an opportunity for the sisters to earn degrees and teacher certification. Following Vatican Council II, the congregation began to serve in campus ministry, parish religious education, social work, and a Guatemala mission.

[H. CRUZAT]

Dominican Sisters of Our Lady of the Rosary and of St. Catherine of Siena, Cabra [1110]. A congregation with papal approbation founded in Cabra, Dublin, Ireland, in 1644 founded in Galway, and confirmed by Giovanni Battista Rinuccini (1592–1653), Archbishop of Fermo and papal nuncio to Ireland. Temporarily dispersed by religious persecution early in the 18th century, the sisters established a central house in Dublin in 1717. From this community several new congregations were founded in the 19th century in the United States (the Dominican Sisters of New Orleans, La., founded in 1860), South Africa, Australia, and New Zealand.

The sisters are engaged in education, social work, parish and retreat ministry.

From the original Galway community there is also a group of cloistered nuns at the convent of St. Catherine of Siena, founded in Drogheda in the 18th century.

[M. G. MURPHY]

Dominican Sisters, St. Mary of the Springs (Columbus, Ohio) [1070–02]. A Dominican congregation established in 1830 in Somerset, Ohio, by Sister Benvin Sansbury and three other Sisters from the St. Catharine's Kentucky Dominican community. The sisters minister in education at all levels as well as pastoral ministry, peace and justice ministry, and spiritual renewal.

[M. MCINTYRE]

Dominican Sisters of Springfield in Illinois [1070–10]. Founded in Jacksonville, Ill., in 1873 by Sister Mary Josephine Meagher and five sisters, who traveled from the motherhouse of the Dominican Sisters of St. Catharine, Ky., at the request of Peter J. Baltes, Bishop (1870–86) of the Diocese of Alton, now Springfield, Ill. The community of 45 sisters moved to Springfield in 1893. The congregation is committed to preaching the gospel through education, pastoral, and healthcare ministries. In 1964, the sisters opened a mission in Peru.

Bibliography: T. A. WINTERBAUER *Lest We Forget: The First Hundred Years of the Dominican Sisters, Springfield, Ill.* (Chicago).

[M. K. WALSH]

Eucharistic Missionaries of St. Dominic (OP, Official Catholic Directory #1140), until 1956 known as Missionary Servants of the Most Holy Eucharist, a modern American congregation of religious women of diocesan jurisdiction founded in Amite, La., in 1927. The founders, Catharine Bostick (Mother Catharine, first mother general) and Zoe Grouchy (Mother Margaret), received the approval of Abp. John W. Shaw of New Orleans, La.; his successor Joseph Francis Rummel promoted aggregation to the Order of Preachers in 1956 (*see* DOMINICANS). The sisters are engaged in a diverse range of ministries, including catechesis, parish and diocesan services, healthcare, outreach to the homeless and immigrants, counseling, chaplaincies and parish administration. The generalate is in New Orleans, LA.

Bibliography: M. F. EVERETT, "Nuns of the Bayou," *Ave Maria* 86 (Aug. 17, 1957) 15–18.

[M. M. GROUCHY/EDS.]

Sinsinawa Dominican Congregation of the Most Holy Rosary (Sinsinawa, Wis.) [1070–03]. The community was founded by famed Italian missionary, Samuel Mazzuchelli, in 1847, when he received the religious profession of four sisters at Sinsinawa. For this and other efforts to spread the Catholic faith in the Upper Mississippi Valley, 1835–65, Fr. Samuel, "pioneer priest," was declared "venerable" by Pope John Paul II in 1993. With their central mission "to proclaim the Gospel through the ministry of preaching and teaching," the sisters taught in rural and small-town schools and in St. Clara Academy. Transfer of the motherhouse and academy from Benton, Wis., to Sinsinawa in 1867 made this the site of the sisters' permanent home. As the congregation grew, it attained the status of a pontifical institute: final approval of the Holy See was given in 1889. From that year until 2000, the superiors general/prioresses general were: Emily Power, Samuel Coughlin, Evelyn Murphy, Benedicta Larkin, Marie Amanda Allard, Cecilia Carey, Kaye Ashe, Jean McSweeney, and Antoinette Harris. In 1901 St. Clara Academy became a college and the forerunner of Rosary College, River Forest, Ill. In 1997 the name was changed to Dominican University. Edgewood College of the Sacred Heart, Madison, Wis., was founded in 1927. Study of music and art in European centers began during the first decade of the 20th century. To further advance the education of the community, the sisters acquired an institute of higher studies in Fribourg, Switzerland, in 1917, and also opened Villa Schifanoia, a graduate school of fine arts, in Florence, Italy, in 1946. Foreign missions were established in Bolivia in 1960, Trinidad in 1979, and Guatemala in 1994. In 1995 the congregation merged with the Spokane Washington Dominicans (Poor School Sisters of Penance), a diocesan Dominican congregation founded in 1852 in Speyer, Germany. Since Vatican II, the Sinsinawa Dominicans have branched out from teaching into other ministries including peace and justice issues.

Bibliography: M. E. MCCARTY, *The Sinsinawa Dominicans: Outlines of Twentieth Century Development, 1901–49* (Sinsinawa, Wis. 1952).

[S. GOERDT]

Sisters of St. Dominic of the American Congregation of the Sacred Heart of Jesus (Dominican Sisters of Caldwell, NJ) [1070–18]. A diocesan community with the title Congregation of the Sacred Heart of Jesus, stemming from the foundations made in the area of New York City by Dominican sisters who came from Germany in 1853. The central house of the Caldwell group was first established in 1881 at the convent of St. Dominic in Jersey City, N.J. In 1912 the motherhouse was transferred to Caldwell (Archdiocese of Newark, N.J.). From this congregation two other congregations later developed— the Dominican Sisters Congregation of St. Thomas Aquinas, of Tacoma, Wash. [1070–20], and the Congregation of the Sisters of St. Dominic of the Immaculate Virgin Mary, of Akron, Ohio [1070–28]. The Caldwell Dominicans work in diverse ministries, including education at all levels. They also conduct Caldwell College, Caldwell, N.J.

[M. R. MCENTEE]

The Vietnamese Dominican Sisters of St. Catherine of Siena (Mary Immaculate Province, Houston, Tex.). The Vietnamese Dominican Sisters trace their foundation to the endeavors of the Dominican Friars of the Most Holy Rosary Province (Philippines) in the 18th century. According to Fr. Angelo Walz, the first Dominican House in Trung Linh, Bui Chu (located in northern Vietnam) was founded by a Fr. Bustamante in 1715. This center was called "Nha Phuoc" (Blessing House), indicating that women who lived in this house practiced virtues and performed good works. From 1757 onward, the Dominican Friars established many "Nha Phuoc" in their parishes. These communities of women were independent organizations; the women made private vows and observed the Rule of the Third Order of Abstinence (Penance) of St. Dominic (Dong Ba Ham Minh Thanh Daminh).

The Vietnamese Dominican Sisters in Vietnam. In the 20th century, the Holy See directed that all the "Nha Phuoc" had to be reorganized according to the norms of 1917 Code of Canon Law. Bishop Pham Ngoc Chi of Bui Chu reorganized the Vietnamese Dominican Sisters from seven "Nha Phuoc" into religious congregations. On March 21, 1951, by a decree of the Congregation of the PROPAGATION OF THE FAITH, the first congregation of the Vietnamese Dominican Sisters of St. Catherine of Siena was officially established in Bui Chu. In the years that followed, congregations of Vietnamese Dominican Sisters were established in various dioceses: Hai Phong, Bac Ninh, Lang Son, and Thai, all located in northern Vietnam.

With the Geneva Conference of July 20, 1954, which partitioned the country into the communist north and non-communist south, many communities of Vietnamese Dominican Sisters joined the massive refugee trek southward. On April 10, 1956, the Congregation for the Propagation of the Faith granted permission for the Vietnamese Dominican Sisters to establish new communities in the south using the Constitution of the Congregation of Bui Chu, and to operate a common novitiate at Ho Nai, Bien Hoa. The Ordinaries chose Thanh Tam, Ho Nai, as the Center of Formation for the Dominican Sisters. In April of 1956 about 83 postulants members from various "Nha Phuoc" received their first Dominican habit as novices. On Jan. 21, 1858, the second Congregation of the Vietnamese Dominican Sisters of St. Catherine of Siena was erected through the support of Bishop Simon Hoa Nguyen Van Hien of Saigon. Its Mother House was constructed at Thanh Tam, Ho Nai, Bien Hoa under the bishop's jurisdiction.

Several months later, the Vicar of Bui Chu and the Vicar of Lang Son withdrew their novices and postulants from the Mother House in Ho Nai. A third congregation was formed at Lang Son that was independent of the earlier two congregations. Efforts to unite the three congregations of Lang Son, Bui Chu, and Ho Nai were unsuccessful. On Jan. 1, 1973, three groups of sisters from Hai Phong, Thai Binh, and Bac Ninh decided to form their own congregations with the intention of observing and preserving their own traditions and origins, and carrying out their missionary endeavors without hindrance. These three groups of sisters became known as the Dominican Sisters of St. Rose of Lima at Thu Duc.

The fall of Saigon in 1975 resulted in the seizure of the schools, centers for social services and formation houses of the Vietnamese Dominican Sisters by the communist authorities. The Sisters survived by working in farms. Their religious lifestyle had to be adjusted to the harsh living conditions. Many sisters lost their lives under such conditions, while others returned to their families. Improved conditions in the 1990s allowed the Sisters to rebuild their communities and gain new members. By the year 2000, there were twelve convents in Dong Nai Province, Ba Ria Province, and Ho Chi Minh City with 142 sisters with perpetual vows, 41 sisters with temporal vows, 23 novices, and 80 postulants. The postulancy and the novitiate were reopened at the Mother House in Ho Nai. The sisters have established mission centers in Dong Lach (Dong Nai), Bao Ham (Dong Nai), Hon Dat (An Giang), and Ca Mau (Can Tho). Barred from running schools, the Sisters have turned to the parishes, where they are engaged in catechetical, missionary, educational, social, healthcare, and other pastoral activities.

The Vietnamese Dominican Sisters in the U.S. The Vietnamese Dominican Sisters trace their U.S. foundation to a group of seven Vietnamese Dominican Sisters of St. Catherine of Siena, who fled Vietnam in two fishing boats in the aftermath of the 1975 fall of Saigon. Res-

cued by the U.S. Navy, they were split into two groups and resettled in Arkansas and Florida. Two sisters who were sent to study nursing in the United States in 1970 heard about these sisters, and they brought them to Waterbury, Conn., after obtaining permission from their local ordinary.

Adapting to the cold weather of Connecticut was a struggle for the sisters, especially for the older sisters. A decision was made to move the community to Houston, where there was already a community of the Vietnamese Dominican Fathers. On Sept. 8, 1978, Bishop John Morkowsky officially erected the Religious House of the Congregation of the Dominican Sisters of St. Catherine of Siena in Houston, in accordance with CIC canons 496 and 497. In 1978 several young women sought admission, and a fledging community was established in Milwaukee.

After surviving many years of uncertainty, a turning point was reached in 1986, when land was acquired and a new convent constructed with through the generosity of the Scanlan Foundation, the Kennedy Foundation of Corpus Christi, and donations from well-wishers. St. Catherine Convent was officially opened on Aug. 15, 1987. This turning point has led to a period of growth in number of new sisters and new ministries. By the end of 2000, the initial community of nine sisters in 1975 had grown to 54 sisters with final vows, 34 with temporal vows, eight novices, and 15 postulants in seven convents. Four convents are located in the Diocese of Galveston-Houston, Tex., one in Beaumont-Tex., one in Victoria, Tex., and one in Milwaukee, Wis. In addition to teaching at day schools, the sisters are engaged in catechetical and missionary endeavors, nursing, child care, youth ministry, and social work.

Bibliography: PHAM THI HUY, *A Proposed Continuing Formation Program for the Vietnamese Dominican Sisters of St. Catherine of Siena, Thanh Tam, Xuan Loc* (Manila 1999).

[C. T. NGUYEN]

DOMINICAN SPIRITUALITY

The form of Christian spirituality proper to the Dominican Order (*see* DOMINICANS). The spirituality taught by St. DOMINIC combines elements common to that of all Christians, of the clergy, of other orders, and of the medieval evangelical movements; but St. Dominic united and oriented these elements in an original, balanced, and unique way. Dominican spirituality is theocentric, Christological, contemplative, monastic, priestly, apostolic, and doctrinal. Its first five qualities are common and generic; its apostolic doctrinal character is specific, setting it apart from others. Dominican contemplation seeks to sanctify the friar and also to bear fruit in the apostolate, especially through preaching, teaching, and writing. The constitutions clearly indicate this twofold purpose:

> The principal reason why we are gathered together is that we might dwell together in harmony and have one mind and one heart in God, that is to say, that we might be found perfect in charity. . . . Our Order is known to have been founded from the beginning expressly for preaching and the salvation of souls. . . . This end we ought to pursue, preaching and teaching from the abundance and fullness of contemplation in imitation of our most holy Father Dominic, who spoke only with God or of God for the benefit of souls.

Monastic Element. The contemplative character of Dominican spirituality is clearly marked, especially in its monastic and priestly elements. The constitutions prescribe ''the three solemn vows of obedience, chastity, and poverty, the regular life with its monastic observances, the solemn chanting of the Divine Office'' as essential means (which can never be radically altered) for achieving the end of the order. Through these means, traditional in the religious life, the Dominican breaks with the world, commits himself to God, and promises to live a contemplative, penitential life seeking Christian perfection. The chanting of the DIVINE OFFICE, especially, prepares the friar for contemplation by pivoting his life around the liturgy. After Matins and Compline the early friars stayed in church for ''secret prayers,'' i.e., mental prayer that prolonged the sentiments of the liturgy. Mental prayer is obligatory in the modern order. Imitating St. Dominic, the friars enjoyed great freedom of spirit and movement, reciting psalms and Aves, visiting altars, making abundant use of gestures, genuflections, and prostrations. Dominic taught the friars to contemplate even on the highway, saying to them: ''Let us think of our Savior.'' He sang the *Ave Maris Stella* or the *Veni Creator* as he walked. His *Nine Ways of Prayer* manifest a variety of methods and postures. Constantly he urged his friars ''to speak only with God or of God'' and put this mandate into the constitutions. The 1963 text urges the master of novices

> to teach and earnestly recommend to them that they carry out fully the precept concerning the love of God and neighbor placed at the head of the Rule. . . . Along with the nature and general end of the religious life—the personal sanctification of each member—let the novices be taught the special end of our Order, namely, to communicate to others the things they contemplate in prayer and study.

Dominican spirituality is penitential. The order borrowed its regular observances from the PREMONSTRATEN-SIANS, but they are, basically, those of the austere Cistercian discipline (*see* CISTERCIANS). They included Matins and Lauds at midnight, fasting and abstinence, use of the discipline, poverty of wardrobe and housing, strict silence, and constant purification of conscience through the chapter of faults. To these practices St. Dominic added the severe deprivations of mendicant poverty, abandoning fixed revenues to rely solely on Divine Providence. St. Dominic so valued the monastic part of the order's life that he carried it into his apostolate.

> Almost always when he was outside the priory, on hearing the first stroke of the matins bell from the monasteries, he used to arise and arouse the friars. With great devotion he celebrated the night and day Office at the prescribed hours so that he omitted nothing. And after compline, when traveling, he kept and had his companions keep silence just as though they were in the priory. Then in the morning, while en route, he had them remain silent every day almost until tierce.

Dominican community life and observances seek to form the friar and prepare him for contemplation. They impose on him self-control, constant scrutiny of conscience, and obedience to rule and authority. They subject him to a ceaseless exercise of the virtues, restraining the impetuosity of his emotions and passions; establishing peace in his soul; and nourishing in him the fraternal charity that is prerequisite for contemplation, community life, and the apostolate. Bl. JORDAN OF SAXONY recommended only one thing to the Paris Dominicans on Easter Day, 1233: ''have a constant mutual charity among yourselves, for it cannot be that Jesus will appear to those who have cut themselves off from the community: Thomas, for not being with the others when Jesus came, did not merit to see him.''

Priestly Element. Dominican spirituality is theocentric, Christological, and priestly because it is canonical (Dominicans were, in origin, CANONS REGULAR). Praising God through the liturgy is the essential duty of the Canon Regular. St. Dominic, who constantly urged the friars to sing the Office well, began the constitutions with detailed rubrics for the Office and made the conventual Mass the pivot of the day. The constitutions (1963) consider the choral Office as an essential means for achieving the aims of the Dominican spirituality and apostolate. The order's concern for the liturgy caused it to develop the so-called DOMINICAN RITE.

Dominican priestly spirituality accents loyalty to the Church, the pope, and the truths of faith; it focuses attention on God, the beginning and end of all things; on Christ, the way of return to God; on the Mass and Sacraments, especially the Eucharist. Even when traveling, St. Dominic celebrated Mass almost every day, singing it by preference, and invariably weeping during the Canon. St. VINCENT FERRER, for 40 years an itinerant apostle, chanted Mass and Office daily. St. THOMAS AQUINAS celebrated every day.

Particular Devotions to Christ. Dominican love of Christ centers on the Crucified, the Sacred Heart, the Precious Blood, and the Holy Name. Bl. HENRY SUSO, seeking mystical union with the Divinity, was told by his beloved Eternal Wisdom: "No one can arrive at divine heights or taste mystical sweetness without passing through my human bitterness." Henry Suso made a Way of the Cross of 100 stations, "so that Christ's every pain, from beginning to end, was individually recalled." He particularly venerated the pierced heart of Christ. St. ALBERT THE GREAT and Meister ECKHART emphasized the Eucharistic presence of the divine Heart. SS. CATHERINE OF SIENA and CATHERINE DE' RICCI experienced an "exchange of hearts" with Christ (*see* MYSTICAL PHENOMENA), while St. ROSE OF LIMA heard Him saying to her, "Rose of my heart, be thou my spouse." French Dominican tertiaries suggested the building of Montmartre basilica, Paris, as a national act of reparation to the Sacred Heart.

Fra Angelico painted St. Dominic contemplating the Scriptural account of the Passion and bathed in the blood from the side of Christ, and pictured St. Thomas intently contemplating the Crucified. St. Catherine of Siena constantly spoke of "the Blood." She and St. Martin de PORRES drank mystically from the pierced side of Christ. She and St. Catherine de Ricci, and, it is estimated, 83 other Dominicans experienced the stigmata. (*See* STIGMATIZATION.)

Bl. JOHN OF VERCELLI, commissioned by GREGORY X in 1274 to implement the decree of the Second Council of LYONS, organized the friars to teach the people to venerate the Holy Name of Jesus and bow their heads when it is mentioned.

Marian Devotion. Devotion to the Mother of God flowed from devotion to Christ. Convinced that the order owed its foundation to her intercession, the friars put Mary's name in the profession formula, daily recited the Little Office, celebrated her Saturday Office and feasts, solemnly chanted the *Salve Regina* at the end of Compline, visited her altars, saluted her images, recited hundreds of daily Aves. They gave the ROSARY, the most excellent of Marian devotions, to the Church, especially through the Confraternity. An epitome of spirituality, the rosary summarizes the liturgical cycle, combines affective devotion with strict theology, leads to contemplation, and is a kind of preaching that expresses itself in praise.

Apostolic Element. St. Dominic went beyond all tradition and made Dominican spirituality apostolic. He

himself was preeminently an apostle. His friend GREGORY IX said, "In him, I knew a man who lived the rule of the apostles in its totality." "He was filled," testified John of Spain, at the process of canonization, "with compassion for his neighbors and most ardently desired their salvation. He himself constantly and frequently preached and, in every way he could, urged the friars to preach, begging and advising them to be solicitous for the salvation of souls and sending them to preach."

Perfection for the Dominican consists in imitating the poor Christ of the Gospel, the Preacher, who having formed his Apostles spiritually, sent them out two by two to preach. St. Dominic clearly established the evangelical spirit of Dominican spirituality when he inserted these instructions for preachers in the constitutions:

> Receiving a blessing, they shall then go forth as men wanting their own salvation and that of others. Let them act with religious decorum as men of the Gospel, following in the footsteps of their Savior, speaking with God or about God to themselves and their neighbor. . . . Furthermore, those going out to exercise the office of preaching or traveling for any other reason shall neither receive nor carry with them any gold, silver, money or gifts, but only food, clothing, books, and other necessities."

Dominicans must be apostles who converse with God, or, in the classic phrase of St. Thomas, "contemplate and give to others the fruit of their contemplation." Fraternal charity, sustained by the penitential exercises of the common life, and cloistered contemplation, nourished on the truths of faith, reach out to souls, make reparation for them, permit the preacher to testify both "by word and example," and merit for his sermons many graces.

Doctrinal Element. Dominican apostolic spirituality is, therefore, doctrinal. The Dominican cannot neglect the study of sacred truth without jeopardizing his vocation. The "assiduous study of sacred truth" is an essential means for realizing the order's ends. St. Dominic "often admonished and exhorted the friars . . . by word and letter to study constantly in the Old and the New Testament." The primitive constitutions required every priory to have a professor as well as a prior; incorporated an academic code; permitted friars in their cells to "read, write, pray, sleep, and also, those who wish, to stay up at night to study"; and instructed the novice-master to teach them "how they ought to be so intent on study that day and night, at home or on the road, they read or meditate something."

The most representative Dominican theologians, SS. Albert and Thomas, gave primacy to contemplation. "The method for one who teaches things divine," wrote

Albert, "is to gain by grace the truth of the divine doctrine he must hand on to others, because in every theological undertaking one ought to start off with prayer" (*De myst. theol.* 1). Reginald of Priverno, the companion of St. Thomas, testified that the saint's

> knowledge, which was amazing beyond that of others, was not the result of human genius but of prayer. For always before he studied, disputed, lectured, wrote, or dictated, he would have recourse to the help of prayer, begging with tears to be shown the truth about the divine things he had to investigate.

Only through such contemplative study can the friar gain the mastery he needs to preach the supernatural truths of faith with charity and zeal.

> The religious state is a state of contemplation [wrote Humbert of Romans] but things that are preached are gathered in contemplation, according to the words of Bl. Gregory, who says: "In contemplation they drink in what later they pour out in preaching." Therefore, it would seem that the religious state would have more that ought to be preached than the secular state, since it is more contemplative. Thus preaching befits it more because, not just by way of instruction but by way of contemplation as well, it possesses in abundance what it preaches.

Blending of Elements. There is no dichotomy in Dominican spirituality. Its monastic, contemplative, and priestly constituents, focusing on love of God, fructify in the apostolate, centering on love of neighbor. The evangelical vocation vitalizes the priestly and contemplative vocations, directing them to their logical and highest development, exemplified by Christ and the Apostles. St. Dominic restored the evangelical vocation by imbuing it with the riches of sacerdotal and sacramental spirituality that the would-be lay apostles of the 12th and 13th centuries (e.g., WALDENSES and HUMILIATI) had scorned.

Dominican spirituality is delicately balanced and hard to live. If thrown off center, its constituents will defeat themselves—the priestly element will become "clerical," mired in "parochial" interests; the monastic will become "monkish," considering religious observance an end and the apostolate a distraction; the apostolic will become "activistic," spending itself in feverish activity. To escape these extremes the Dominican must nourish his zeal with a burning love for Christ. In his life, contemplation must be primary and redemptive, centering on Christ and engendering the apostolate.

The members of the second and third orders also profess a spirituality that is priestly and apostolic, thirsting for souls. By baptism and confirmation they are marked with the imprint of Christ's priesthood; they have the power and duty to profess and defend the faith.

Bibliography: P. LIPPINI, *La spiritualità domenicana* (2d ed. Bologna 1958). R. SPIAZZI, *Via Dominici, lo spirito e la regola di San Domenico* (Rome 1961). M. H. VICAIRE, *Dictionnaire de spiritualité ascétique et mystique. Doctrine et histoire,* ed. M. VILLER et al. (Paris 1932–) 3:1522–32. W. A. HINNEBUSCH, *Dominican Spirituality, Principles and Practice* (Washington 1965). P. RÉGAMEY, "Principles of Dominican Spirituality," *Some Schools of Catholic Spirituality,* ed. J. GAUTHIER, tr. K. SULLIVAN (New York 1959) 76–109.

[W. A. HINNEBUSCH]

DOMINICANS

The Order of Friars Preachers (OP), commonly known as the Dominicans, comprises: the First Order, fathers and laybrothers; the Second Order, contemplative nuns; and the Third Order. The last includes: (1) the conventual third order and (2) lay tertiaries. The habit of the fathers consists of a white robe, scapular, and cowl, with a black open mantle and cowl. Lay brothers wear a black scapular and cowl. Sisters of the second and third orders replace the cowl with a veil. All fasten the robe at the waist with a leather belt from which is suspended a rosary. The Dominicans in England have been called Blackfriars because of the black mantle, and the French Dominicans are sometimes referred to as Jacobins after their priory of Saint-Jacques in Paris.

Foundation, Spirit, and Organization. The First Order is a clerical, religious institute of mendicant friars with solemn vows, living under the Rule of St. Augustine and its own constitutions, and subject only to its own superiors and the Holy See. The preaching mission among the ALBIGENSES of southern France in the early 13th century was the occasion for the beginning of the Dominican Order. St. DOMINIC was the director of this preaching from 1207 onward. To combat the pretensions of the heretics, the preachers practiced evangelical poverty. In April 1215 Dominic transformed this voluntary association into a permanent institute with the approval of Fulk of Marseilles, Bishop of Toulouse (d. 1231). After consultation with Pope Innocent III, Dominic and his companions, meeting in a founding chapter in 1216, adopted the Rule of St. Augustine and drew up the first part of the constitutions. Although they abandoned ownership of property, they temporarily retained income from rents granted to them. On Dec. 22, 1216, Honorius III gave papal confirmation to the order and, on Jan. 17, 1217, approved its name and preaching mission.

The order is a synthesis of the contemplative life and the apostolic ministry. The contemplative element includes the vows of poverty, chastity, and obedience; the chanting of the Divine Office; community life; monastic observances; and the assiduous study of sacred truth

(*Constitutions*, 1932, no. 4). The apostolic element, conceived as an imitation of the evangelical life of Christ, embraces the teaching and defense of Catholic truth primarily through preaching. The two elements are so blended that contemplation not only sanctifies the friar but prepares him for the apostolate. The Dominican motto, "To contemplate and to give others the fruits of contemplation," neatly sums up these concepts. Dominic resolved the apparent contradiction between the two elements by widening the scope of dispensation to favor students and preachers when monastic observances impeded their work. On Aug. 15, 1217, he inaugurated the universal mission of the order by sending his friars away to found new centers, notably in the university cities of Paris (1217) and Bologna (1218). In 1220, when a dozen or so houses existed, Dominic convened the first general chapter at Bologna. Under his presidency the chapter shaped the core of the second part of the constitutions, regulating the order's government, preaching, and study. Absolute poverty, which prohibited the holding of both property and revenues, and made the order dependent on free-will offerings and the quest for alms by the friars, was adopted. The second general chapter, Bologna, 1221, divided the order into provinces and determined their government.

The government of the order, by Dominic's desire, is democratic. It preserves a careful balance between democratically constituted chapters and strong, but elected, superiors. The composition of successive general chapters gives a preponderance of power to elected definitors (representatives) chosen by the provinces, rather than to provincials. Delegates from the priories sit on equal terms with their priors in the provincial chapter. Professed friars who are clerics form the chapter of the priory. The provinces, composed of both priories and nonpriorial houses, enjoy a considerable degree of autonomy. Congregations or vicariates, consisting of houses under a vicar, have been common since the 15th century. They do not possess all the rights of provinces and occasionally have no fixed territory. Only the general chapter, the supreme Dominican authority, may modify the constitutions, provided three successive chapters approve. It shares with provincial chapters and superiors the power to issue executive orders. Until 1370 it met annually; thereafter, every two or three years; since 1561, triennially. Successive chapters rotate among the major cities. In 1949, in Washington, DC, the chapter convened for the first time outside Europe. Except that they have not the lawmaking power, provincial chapters hold authority in the provinces paralleling that of the general chapter in the entire order. They met annually until 1410, biennially until 1629, and quadrennially thereafter. The master general is the major superior over the entire order; the provincial,

over his province; and a prior, over his priory. All superiors, except vicars, are elected by the chapters of their respective jurisdictions. Terms of office, which in the medieval period perdured until terminated by higher authority, are now restricted to 12 years for the general; four for the provincial; and three for priors and vicars. The curia of the master general is made up of eight associates (1945) and the procurator general, the order's liaison officer with the Holy See.

Dominicans vow to obey their superiors according to the rule and constitutions, rather than to obey the statutes themselves. This makes obedience the keystone of Dominican life and gives flexibility to administration. The order's law, apart from vows, precepts, and laws derived from higher authority, does not bind under sin but obliges only to the acceptance of penalties for violations. This regulation affords great liberty of spirit. The novelty and perfection of the Dominican constitutions led to their imitation by other mendicant orders.

The primitive version of the constitutions was superseded in 1241 by a text cast in improved juridical form by (St.) RAYMOND OF PEÑAFORT. Subsequently, major revisions were made in 1518, 1566, 1871, and 1932. The first printed edition appeared in 1505. The Dominican Order has its own liturgical rite with distinctive Missal, Breviary, rubrics, and liturgical calendar. Among its members the order has 18 saints and about 312 blesseds.

First Three Centuries, 1215 to 1500. Under their founder, the Dominicans made establishments in all the western countries of Europe, including Hungary and Scandinavia. Dominic's death in 1221 did not halt the order's rapid progress, for his five immediate successors (Bl.) JORDAN OF SAXONY, Raymond of Peñafort, John of Wildeshausen (d. 1252), HUMBERT OF ROMANS, and (Bl.) JOHN OF VERCELLI, were conspicuously able men of saintly character. Under their government, which extended over a period of 60 years, the order developed its characteristic apostolate and activities, founded many new priories, and increased its membership. In 1221 eight provinces existed or were being formed: Spain, Provence, France, Lombardy, Rome, Hungary, England, and Germany. Poland, Scandinavia, Greece, and the Holy Land joined them before 1228. Except for mission territory, these divisions marked the area of activity until 1510, but the number of provinces increased by subdivision, so that in 1303 there were 18; in 1500, 22. In 1277 the order counted 404 priories; in 1303, 590; in 1358, 635. Membership was approximately 13,000 in 1256, and was probably above 21,000 in 1347 at the beginning of the Black Death, which greatly reduced the order's numbers.

Scholarship. Dominic laid the foundation of the Dominican educational system and intellectual excellence.

He did this at the first general chapter when he included provisions in the constitutions that regulated and encouraged study and stipulated that no priory might be erected without a professor. He established the school at Paris and secured its incorporation into the university, where, in 1229, the order obtained its first chair of theology; in 1230, its second. The English Dominicans had a chair at Oxford before 1248. The order's curriculum of studies, completed in 1259, ranged upward through priory schools, provincial schools of arts, philosophy, and theology, to a general house of studies at Paris, where the order promoted friars to the mastership in theology. In 1248 additional general houses opened at Oxford, Cologne, Montpellier, and Bologna. After the 13th century all the major provinces established general houses of studies.

The friars at Paris, under the direction of HUGH OF SAINT-CHER, undertook major scientific works such as the correction of the Vulgate text of the Bible and the compilation of Biblical commentaries and concordances. By the middle of the 13th century (St.) ALBERT THE GREAT and (St.) THOMAS AQUINAS, ROBERT KILWARDBY and (Bl.) Peter of Tarentaise (INNOCENT V), had carried the order to preeminence in the scientific and theological fields. The Thomistic philosophico-theological system, a profoundly unifying and cohesive factor in the order, was transmitted and developed by a constant succession of commentators and theologians.

Only a few of the host of friars who wrote in the scholastic and other cultural fields can be mentioned here. WILLIAM OF MOERBEKE's translations of the works of Aristotle and other Greek writers powerfully aided the speculations of the scholastics. Raymond of Peñafort, with his compilation of the *Decretals* and his *Summa de poenitentia*, achieved eminence as a canonist and moralist. The treatises of Cardinals Juan de TORQUEMADA and John Stojkovic of RAGUSA in ecclesiology, and the *Summa moralium* of St. ANTONINUS in moral theology, pioneered new fields of theological research. The *Golden Legend* of JAMES OF VORAGINE was universally read and loved. The directories for inquisitors by BERNARD GUI and Nicholas Eymeric (d. 1399), and the exposition of the tenets of the Cathari and Waldenses by Moneta of Cremona (d. *c.* 1260), strengthened the Catholic apostolate among the heretics. VINCENT OF BEAUVAIS in his *Speculum majus* provided an encyclopedic work that aimed to give a compendium of contemporary knowledge. The humanist Francis Colonna (d. 1527) later attempted a similar feat regarding the knowledge of antiquity in his celebrated romance, *The Dream of Poliphilus*. Jerome of Moravia (fl. *c.* 1250) wrote the most important 13th-century work on liturgical chant. The *Catholicon* of John Balbus (d. *c.* 1298) was a pioneer treatise on, and etymological dictionary of, the Latin language. Bernard Gui, Ptolemy of Lucca, NICHOLAS TREVET, MARTIN OF TROPPAU, and Antoninus rank as historians.

Apostolic Activities. Preaching, the primary work of the order, absorbed the energies of the greater number of Dominicans. Their priories, erected by preference in the cities, became centers of an organized ministry. Each priory subdivided its territory and assigned friars to preach systematically in the rural parishes of individual districts. In remote areas ''preaching homes'' were built so the friars could stay for long periods of intense evangelization. The so-called penitential preachers, proclaiming penance and reform of life, developed roving apostolates over a wide area. John of Vicenza led a crusade for peace in Lombardy and the Marches in 1233. VENTURINO OF BERGAMO preached penance in the 14th century; (St.) VINCENT FERRER, Manfred of Vercelli (d. *c.* 1431), and SAVONAROLA did the same in the 15th.

Dominicans constructed spacious churches to accommodate large congregations. They preached sermons in their churches as often as 250 times a year, speaking morning and evening on Sundays, and daily during Advent and Lent. To prepare preachers, they stocked large libraries, collected sermons, wrote preaching manuals, and compiled books of illustrative materials, such as John Bromyard's (d. *c.* 1352) great *Summa for Preachers*. Except for sermons to clerical audiences, they used the vernacular languages. The opposition that arose from the secular clergy bears witness to the scope of the friars' preaching and ministry. Pastors challenged the right of the mendicant orders to preach, hear confessions, and bury. The resulting quarrel, which simmered throughout the 13th century, was partially allayed when Boniface VIII in 1300 restricted, but did not destroy, mendicant privileges with the bull *Super cathedram.*

Many other Dominican activities developed from preaching. The rapid growth of the Second Order indicates the order's contribution to the development of the contemplative life of religious women. Another facet of this apostolate was the directing of BEGUINES in the Rhineland and the Netherlands. The Dominican Third Order was an offshoot of preaching to the laity. The confraternities founded in the order's churches provided congregations for the preachers and perpetuated the fruit of their sermons. In 1274 Gregory X, at the instance of the Second Council of Lyons, commissioned the order to preach devotion to the Holy Name of Jesus. From this preaching, the Holy Name Society was to develop. The Rosary Confraternity, founded by ALAN DE LA ROCHE about 1470 at Douai, made the rosary the most popular nonliturgical devotion in the Western Church.

The popes drew on the experience of the friars by enlisting them to reform monasteries and dioceses; to administer convents of nuns; to serve as masters of the Sacred Palace, papal penitentiaries, preachers of the crusade, collectors of crusading levies; and to carry out diplomatic missions. Dominicans habitually, though not exclusively, staffed the INQUISITION, a task for which their doctrinal training made them especially suited. The order gave two popes, 28 cardinals, and hundreds of bishops to the Church before 1500. The kings of France, England, Spain, and Portugal, as well as many princes, often had Dominican confessors.

Missions. Dominic, desiring to evangelize the pagans, had sent friars to the frontiers of Europe. By 1225 the friars in Spain had contacted the Arabs and Jews of the peninsula and had moved into Africa. Under Raymond of Peñafort's direction the Spanish province pioneered schools for Oriental languages. RAYMOND MARTINI, the finest Orientalist before the modern age, supplied his brethren with treatises, especially his *Pugio fidei* and *Capistrum Judaeorum,* for their controversies, and Pablo Cristiani (d. *c.* 1265), a converted Jew, achieved fame as a polemicist. Dominicans of Scandinavia, Poland, and Germany worked among the Baltic peoples, the Lithuanians, and the Russians. St. HYACINTH, founder of the Polish province, pushed as far east as Kiev in 1222. Hungarian Dominicans built a flourishing church among the Cumans of the Russian steppes until the Mongol invasions of 1241 destroyed it.

The province of Greece and the Holy Land worked in the Latin Empire of Constantinople and in the crusader states, evangelizing Western Christians, dissident Christians, Muslims, Jews, and Mongols. Friar polemicists through their treatises and friar diplomats through their negotiations worked for the reunion of the dissidents with Rome. WILLIAM OF TRIPOLI, a friar in Palestine, claimed to have baptized 1,000 Arabs, while RICOLDUS da Monte i Croce learned Arabic and preached to Nestorians, Jews, and Muslims in the Khanate of Persia. William's *On the State of the Saracens,* Ricoldo's *Itinerary* and *Refutation of the Koran,* and Burchard of Mount Sion's (fl. 1290) *Description of the Holy Land,* gave Europe new knowledge of Islam and the western Asiatic peoples. With the fall of the crusader states, the provinces of Greece and the Holy Land had to retreat to the islands of the Mediterranean.

The Congregation of Friars Pilgrims for Christ among the Gentiles opened a new mission phase about 1300, founding residences eastward from Pera (Constantinople) through the Black Sea area into India. Its members supplied the bishops for the ecclesiastical province of Sultanieh, erected by John XXII in 1318. Its most striking achievement was the conversion of the monks of Qrna (1331), who founded the Order of Friars Unitors of St. Gregory the Illuminator, subject to Dominican jurisdiction, to work for the cause of reunion. Great initial success, radiating from 50 monasteries, was dissipated when excessive zeal provoked a nationalistic reaction after 1380. Although Tamerlane's invasions closed the East to all but the most intrepid friars, Portuguese Dominicans heralded a new mission era when they penetrated into the heart of the Congo after 1480.

Decline and Reform. Early idealism carried Dominicans through their golden age, the 13th century. About 1290 the order began to experience a decline of fervor and relaxation of discipline. The observance of poverty had brought even earlier embarrassment. Free-will offerings and the quest for alms did not keep pace with the order's expansion of priories, personnel, and apostolate. Seeking security, priories began to sign over property offered to them by benefactors to a monastery or confraternity with the obligation of providing a regular quota of consumer goods in return. Individual friars received permission to seek funds through their own industry or from friends, first for books, later for clothing. Concurrently, strict observance, no longer buttressed by early fervor, weakened under the impact of interpretation and compromise. The Black Death, beginning in 1347, sharpened these trends and brought a widespread collapse of observance and life in common, particularly neglect of choral obligations and attendance in refectory. Unwise recruiting, looking more to numbers than to quality, compounded the damage.

Friars in Tuscany made the first attempt to bolster discipline in about 1300. Though nicknamed "spirituals," because of their similarities to the Franciscan FRATICELLI, they avoided the doctrinal errors and excessive emphasis on poverty of the latter. The Black Death dissipated the strength of this movement, but its remnants supported a more official attempt at reform begun in 1369 by Stephen Lacombe (d. *c.* 1416), provincial of Tuscany and Italian vicar of the master general. His adherence to the Avignon Obedience when the Western Schism began in 1378 nullified his efforts. The reform then turned to (Bl.) RAYMOND OF CAPUA, the confessor of (St.) CATHERINE OF SIENA, and secured his election as master general in the Roman Obedience in 1380. With papal support he put reform on a solid footing by creating vicars of observance and founding priories where primitive observance, including that of strict poverty, was introduced.

Reformed priories were grouped in congregations of observants. The congregations of Holland and Lombardy were outstanding in influence and extent; the latter produced many saints and blesseds during the 15th century. Reform did not lead to schism in the order; although the observant congregations enjoyed considerable autonomy,

Dominican emphasis on obedience kept them loyal to the master general. Strict poverty soon proved impossible even for the observants, forcing Master General Bartholomew Texier (d. 1449), an exponent of reform, to seek from Martin V, in 1425, authority to permit priories, according to need, to own possessions and fixed revenues. Sixtus IV in 1475 granted all mendicant orders, save the Franciscans, the right to own property, thus lifting the insupportable yoke of absolute poverty and aiding the Dominican revival of the 16th century. This mitigation was accompanied among the observants by a lessening of severity that prepared for a rapprochement with nonreformed Dominicans who had meanwhile tightened their discipline.

The Modern Period, 1500 to 1850. The order entered the 16th century with 22 provinces and a new strength gained when observant congregations took control of the provinces of Germany, Spain, Lombardy, Central Italy, and Holland. The decrees of the Council of Trent and of Pius V gave additional strength.

Scholarship. This vitality was especially evident in a vigorous renewal of theological studies in France, Spain, and Italy, under Peter CROCKAERT, Francisco de VITORIA, and CAJETAN (Tommaso de Vio). Under the impact of Protestantism, the Dominicans broadened their curriculum and concentrated education in larger houses of study. General houses of study increased until there were 27 to 1551. In addition, Thomistic studies flourished in the colleges of St. Gregory in Valladolid, 1488; St. Thomas in Seville, 1515; and the two Roman colleges—St. Thomas at the Minerva, 1577, and the Cassanata, 1700. Overseas the order opened at least 12 colleges and universities, such as San Domingo, 1538; Santa Fé de Bogotá, 1612; Manila, 1645; and Havana, 1721.

The *Summa theologiae* became the theological text, and great commentators—Cajetan, FERRARIENSIS (Francesco Silvestri), and members of the Spanish school—developed the Thomistic synthesis. The participation of approximately 130 Dominican bishops and theologians at the Council of Trent made THOMISM an important influence in the discussions and decrees of the Council. Controversies over grace, the doctrine of the Immaculate Conception, and probabilism, engaged the attention of Dominican theologians. Outstanding scholars appeared also in fields other than theology and philosophy: Santes PAGNINI and Sixtus of Siena in Biblical science, Jacques GOAR and Michael le Quien (1661–1733) in Oriental studies, Francis Combefis (1605–79) in patristics, Noel ALEXANDRE in history, and Nicholas COEFFETEAU in linguistics. Dominican historians established the general archives of the order in Rome and published the *Bullarium*

ordinis Praedicatorum and the *Scriptores ordinis Praedicatorum.*

Two Dominican Popes, St. PIUS V (1566–72) and BENEDICT XIII (1724–30), 41 cardinals, and more than 1,000 archbishops and bishops served the Church. By privilege Dominicans permanently held the offices of commissary of the Holy Office and Secretary of the Index (abolished in 1917). The master general and the master of the Sacred Palace are also ex officio consultors to the Holy Office.

Dominicans and the Protestant Reformation. Protestantism did great damage to the Dominican order. The provinces of Scotland, Scandinavia, and Saxony disappeared, while England, Holland, Germany, and Ireland were crippled for several centuries. Poland, Bohemia, and the four French provinces experienced great losses. At the same time, Hungary and Dalmatia suffered from the attacks of the Turks. This weakening in northern Europe concentrated Dominican strength until the 20th century in the Latin countries. Protestantism faced numerous Dominican opponents in the pulpit, in controversy, and in writing. The order ran well ahead of other Catholic defenders in point of time, numbers, and excellence of doctrine [P. Tacchi-Venturi, SJ, *Storia della Compagnia di Gesù in Italia* (2d ed. Rome 1950) 1.113]. In Germany "no other religious organization produced so many and such outstanding literary champions as the Order of St. Dominic" [N. Paulus, *Die deutschen Dominikaner im Kampf gegen Luther, 1518–63* (Freiburg im Breisgau 1903) vi].

Expansion. Losses during the Reformation were compensated for by overseas expansion and the development of new provinces in Europe; by 1789 the provinces numbered 45. Membership had reached a peak in the 17th century, when there were an estimated 30,000 to 40,000 friars and nuns. In 1720 there were 1,200 priories and houses, and 200 monasteries. Dominicans entered America in 1510 and founded the province of the West Indies in 1530. By 1724 there were 11 provinces in the Spanish colonies and the Congregation of the Holy Cross (1551) in Portuguese possessions. Dominicans, especially Bartolomé de LAS CASAS, author of the *Historia de las Indias,* championed the natives against the exploitation of the Spanish settlers. St. Louis BERTRAND, Apostle of New Granada (1562–69) was noted for his numerous conversions, the gift of tongues, and many miracles. The Philippine province, created in 1592, evangelized in China, Formosa, Tonkin China, and Japan. These missions suffered many persecutions: Ignacio Delgado (1761–1838), Jerónimo Hermosilla (1800–61), Díaz Sanjurjo (1818–57), and their respective companions have been beatified as martyrs. The French Fathers established missions in Guadaloupe and Martinique. Italian Dominicans worked in the Near East, Mesopotamia, and Kurdistan.

Conflicts and Suppressions. The government of the order in the modern period remained structurally the same, with refinement of details, but the administration suffered greatly from political and religious changes. The Holy See, through the cardinal protector, intervened frequently in the government, forcing the resignation of two masters general—Sixtus Fabri in 1589, and Nicholas Ridolfi in 1644. After 1650, political conditions kept general chapters from convening, for the most part, except for elections to the generalship. This fact gave relatively more importance to the position of the masters general, who were obliged to govern for long periods without help from the chapters. The order lost most of its political influence in a world of absolutist rulers who had little sympathy for religious orders, though in Spain Dominicans continued to serve as royal confessors until 1700. After 1765 the courts of Vienna, Naples, and Madrid prohibited recourse to the master general. In Austria, the Sicilies, Russia, and France, the sovereigns suppressed many houses. This tyranny and the spirit of the Enlightenment impeded vocations, diminished religious fervor, and again made reform necessary.

From 1789 to 1850, a series of calamities disrupted the order's government; destroyed or weakened its priories, monasteries, and provinces; crippled its foreign missions; scattered its members; and brought it close to extinction. No general chapter convened between 1777 and 1832. Between 1790 and 1819 the houses of France, Belgium, and Germany were suppressed. In Italy only 105 of 750 houses survived. After 1808 the wars of independence destroyed most of the Latin American provinces. Suppression of the Portuguese and Spanish provinces followed in 1834 and 1837, respectively. Russia gradually smothered the Lithuanian, Russian, and Polish houses under its dominion after 1842. But the provinces of Ireland, England, Holland, Dalmatia, Ecuador, Chile, Argentina, the Philippines, and the U.S. continued without interruption. Of these only the Philippine province was strong in membership. In 1804 Charles IV of Spain, with papal consent, separated the provinces in his dominions from the jurisdiction of the master general, a separation that lasted legally until 1872.

Contemporary Period, 1850–1963. From 1850 the Dominican Order experienced gradual recovery. Most significant for the future was the establishment of the province of St. Joseph in the U.S. in 1805. Steady restoration began in 1850 with the reestablishment of the province of France with strict observance under the leadership of Jean Baptiste Henri LACORDAIRE, who received the habit in 1839. Vincent Jandel, his disciple, as vicar gener-

al and then as master general (1850–72), marshaled the order's internal forces and gave the restoration consistency and strength. He established a province in the Austrian Empire in 1857 and restored the provinces of Spain and Belgium in 1860, Lyons in 1862, and Toulouse in 1865. He visited the provinces, held three important general chapters, issued new editions of the liturgical books and of the constitutions, opened new mission fields, and restored the Spanish-speaking provinces to the order's jurisdiction.

Jandel's regime was troubled by repeated persecutions of the Italian provinces during the unification of Italy. European conditions remained so disturbed that his successor, Joseph M. Larroca, had to be chosen in 1879 by the unprecedented procedure of sending ballots through the mail. The French Dominicans were expelled from France in 1881, while in Germany the friars suffered exile during the Kulturkampf under Otto von Bismarck. Nevertheless, important progress was made in the intellectual field. Dominicans became the collaborators of Leo XIII in his revival of Thomistic studies and took over the theological faculty at the University of Fribourg, Switzerland. In 1890 Joseph Lagrange began his pioneer work in Biblical studies and founded St. Stephen's Biblical School (ÉCOLE BIBLIQUE).

While French anticlerical laws kept the theological faculty of the French province in exile (in Corbora, Corsica, and then in Kain, Belgium) until 1937, it was reestablished on French soil then near Paris at Ètiolles. This faculty of theology, called "Le Saulchoir," became famous for its extraordinary output of academic production in books and periodicals and for the notable figures who taught there. All these persons, significant in Neo-Thomism, were connected to "La Saulchoir" for at least some time: Mandonnet, Gardeil, Sertillanges, Roland-Gosselin, Chenu, and Congar. In particular, this school became the center for a Dominican reading of Aquinas rooted in history, culture, and social context that would influence Dominican scholars around the world.

At the time of the Second Vatican Council, Yves CONGAR (who would end his days as a cardinal of the Roman Church) was appointed a member of the Theological Preparatory Commission of the Council and had great influence on the preparation of several Council documents, most notably *Lumen gentium.* M.-D. CHENU, a *peritus* for an African bishop, generated the idea of a "Message to the World" from the Council as it inaugurated its work. Another French Dominican, J. L. Lebret, the founder of the Center Èconomie et Humanisme (near Lyons), played an important role in the evolution of *Gaudium et spes.*

Progress in the 20th Century. Under the masters general of the 20th century the order continued its restoration, developing works in many new fields. Internal life gained strength from the regular convening of chapters after 1891, from the periodic visitation of the provinces, and from the splendid encyclical letters of the masters general. The foundations of Dominican life were reinforced by revisions of the liturgy (1923; 1961–65), the constitutions (1932), the rule for the Third Order (1932; 1964), and by creation of the Historical Institute (1929), the Liturgical Commission (1934), and the school for the training of novice and student masters (1938).

This development took place despite suppression in France (1903), expulsion from Mexico (1910), and heavy losses during the Spanish Civil War. The two World Wars severely affected the European provinces and saw the mobilization of the friars as chaplains and soldiers. More than 100 Dominicans lost their lives in World War II. After the war, the Communists suppressed the provinces of Hungary and Bohemia.

In the intellectual field, new norms for the curriculum of studies were published (1907; 1935; 1965). The "Angelicum," founded (1910) by Hyacinth CORMIER, with faculties in theology, philosophy, and Canon Law, was raised by John XXIII to university rank, March 7, 1963, under the title Pontifical University of St. Thomas Aquinas in Rome. Pontifical institutes were erected also in various provinces, e.g., the pontifical faculty of theology at the House of Studies, Washington, D.C., and the pontifical philosophical faculty at River Forest, IL. The English Dominicans returned, after 400 years, to Oxford in 1929 and to Cambridge in 1939. The order has established important special institutes, such as the Instina Study Center at Paris for Russian studies and the Institute of Oriental Studies in Cairo for Islamic studies. The various provinces publish about 320 popular, cultural, and scientific periodicals and sponsor series of learned works, such as the *Études bibliques* and the *Studia Friburgensia*.

The traditional works of the order have taken diversified forms since 1919. Preaching, while continuing in the traditional forms of domestic missions and retreats, has also entered the fields of film, radio, and television. The fathers of the French, Belgian, German, and Canadian provinces have been active in the field of social action and labor. Henry Pire, the Belgian Dominican, won the Nobel prize for peace in 1958 for his humanitarian work for refugees.

In 1922 Dominicans worked in 20 mission countries; in 1957, in 40. To develop native provinces, novitiates were founded in 1951 at Hanoi in Vietnam, Sendai in Japan, and Viadana in the Congo, where 51 African novices took the habit at the inception. The rise of Communism in China interrupted the work of the Chinese missions after 1946.

The Order in the U.S.A. The story of the Dominican Friars in the United States may be divided roughly into three periods. The first period would include individual Dominican Friars who either accompanied early explorations of the North American continent, such as Pedro de Cancer, who was martyred in Florida in 1549, or came to this country on their own and ministered as individuals. The second period could be seen as beginning in the early 19th century with the efforts of Edward Dominic Fenwick, OP (1768–1832), who was born in the American colonies and educated in Europe, entering the Order there. He obtained permission to move to the United States with some companions (1804) and they were assigned by Bishop John Carroll to missions in Kentucky at Springfield near Bardstown. After considerable hardship, Fenwick (subsequently appointed Bishop of Cincinnati) and his companions were able to establish in 1828 the Province of St. Joseph (also called the Eastern Province). From this province were formed the Provinces of the Holy Name of Jesus in 1912 (Western Province), the Province of St. Albert the Great in 1939 (Central Province) and the Province of St. Martin de Porres in 1979 (Southern Province, formed from states in St. Joseph and St. Albert Provinces). Of note in the 19th century was the individual missionary work of Fr. Samuel Mazzuchelli in Wisconsin and Michigan. Spanish Dominican friars ministered in New Orleans from 1903 till 1939 and in South Texas from 1925 till the present. Small numbers of Spanish Friars ministered in the Archdiocese of Miami, FL (Beticia Province) and French (Lyons Province) and French-Canadian Friars (Canadian Province) in the Diocese of Portland, ME, and Fall River, MA.

Until the beginning of the 20th century, the Province of St. Joseph remained relatively small (about 100 members) but during the 20th century, it experienced the general expansion of Catholic population, especially through immigration, and vocations multiplied, making a division of territory feasible. The principal ministries that characterized the Friars in the United States in this second period were parish ministry (reflecting the priorities of the American hierarchy), educational (campus ministry at secular and Catholic universities and teaching philosophy and theology in Catholic colleges and high schools) and devotional (groups of preachers who specialized in parish missions, retreats, novenas, etc.). The Province of St. Joseph continues to sponsor and staff Providence College (f. 1917) in Providence, RI, and the Province of St. Albert the Great sponsors and staffs Fenwick High School in Oak Park, IL. Foreign Missions were also established by St. Joseph Province (Pakistan and Kenya), St. Albert the Great (Nigeria and Bolivia), and Holy Name (Mexico). Each of the three provinces formed in this period also established their own *studia generalis* to educate and form

Dominican priests. These are now located in Berkeley, CA at the Graduate Theological Union (Western Province), St. Louis, MO, at Aquinas Institute (serving both the Central and Southern Provinces) and Washington, DC (Eastern Province). In addition, each of these studia have served or continue to serve as the location for preaching formation programs or theological journals (e.g. D. Min. in Preaching at Aquinas Institute, *The Thomist* at Washington, DC) and other theological and philosophical programs.

The third period of Dominican history in the United States may be said to have begun with the General Chapter of 1968 in River Forest, IL. This chapter responded to the call of the Second Vatican Council (1962–65) to reform constitutions and customs to more accurately reflect the original founding charism of the particular religious order. In the case of Dominicans (officially titled ''Order of Preachers''), this meant a return to a focus on preaching as the primary charism and mission of the Order. The elaborate constitutions were simplified to bring out the essential characteristics of Dominican life (prayer, study, vowed community and ministry) as ordered to the mission of preaching. The democratic governmental structure (a unique characteristic of the order from its beginning) was simplified to eliminate *ex officio* or privileged voting that had grown up over the centuries. A new document, *The Fundamental Constitution*, was added at the beginning to give voice to the basic purposes and values of the Order. The term of the Master of the Order was shortened from twelve to nine years and the unique cycle of General Chapters meeting every three years, each giving representation to either leadership or grassroots membership, was retained. In 1979, a new province (St. Martin De Porres) was established in the southern states with the hope of generating a ''new birth in hope'' and a renewed identity for all the provinces in the United States. During this period, the four provinces of Friars experienced, along with all other religious orders, the difficult years of adjustment following the second Vatican Council. The departure of members and the diminishment of numbers entering meant that some ministries were discontinued and others cut back. At the beginning of the third millennium a gradual increase in new membership is offering hope. A new era of collaboration with the Dominican sisters' congregations has been manifested through the Dominican Leadership Conference, representing the leaders of the provinces and congregations of Dominican men and women, and the Parable Conference of Dominican Life and Mission which sponsors retreats, pilgrimages and conferences featuring teams of Friars and Sisters and Dominican Laity. New collaborative ventures include an annual meeting of Dominican artists and a project called OPUS which is working on a comprehensive history of Dominicans in the United States.

Bibliography: A. M. WALZ, *Compendium historiae ordinis Praedicatorum* (2d ed. Rome 1948). W. R. BONNIWELL, *A History of the Dominican Liturgy,* 1215–1945 (2d ed. New York 1945). R. DEVAS, *Dominican Revival in the Nineteenth Century* (London 1913). G. R. GALBRAITH, *The Constitutions of the Dominican Order, 1216–1360* (Manchester 1925). W. A. HINNEBUSCH, *Early English Friars Preachers* (Rome 1951). B. JARRETT, *The English Dominicans,* rev. and abr. W. GRUMBLEY (2d ed. London 1938). V. F. O'DANIEL, *The Dominican Province of St. Joseph* (New York 1942). D. D. C. POCHIN MOULD, *The Irish Dominicans* (Dublin 1957). J. B. REEVES, *The Dominicans* (reprint, Dubuque 1959).

[W. A. HINNEBUSCH/P. PHILIBERT/R. B. WILLIAMS]

DOMINICI, JOHN, BL.

Writer, reformer, cardinal; b. Florence, *c.* 1356; d. Buda, Hungary, June 10, 1419. He took his name after his father, Domenico Banchini (or Bacchini); his mother was Paola Zorsi. He became a DOMINICAN *c.* 1373; studied at Florence, Pisa, and Paris (1377–80); and was subprior at S. Maria Novella, Florence (1381), then prior there (1385–87), and finally lector at SS. John and Paul, Venice (1388). He came under the spiritual influence of CATHERINE OF SIENA, who cured him of stammering (1381). An ardent follower of RAYMOND OF CAPUA in the reform of his order, he personally reformed the priories of S. Domenico di Castello, Venice (1390), Chioggia (1392), and Città di Castello (1393); finally he was made vicar-general over all the reformed priories in Italy. At Venice he founded Corpus Christi (1393), a monastery of nuns, where his mother, Sister Paola, lived for 20 years, and at Fiesole he founded the priory of S. Domenico (1406). As a great popular preacher, he attracted many disciples, especially at Florence and Venice, where he promoted the movement of penance, and the accompanying *processione dei bianchi,* for which he was banished (1399) from the Venetian territories for five years. Carlo Malatesta of Rimini sent him on embassies to Venice (1404) and from Venice to Rome concerning the election of GREGORY XII. Having worked vigorously for the extinction of the WESTERN SCHISM, he was held in great esteem by Gregory, who made him the archbishop of Ragusa July 29, 1407, and cardinal April 23, 1408, and then legate to Hungary and Poland (1409) and to the Council of CONSTANCE, where he represented Gregory and read his resignation (1415). MARTIN V sent him as legate to Hungary and Bohemia against the HUSSITES (1418). The author of many theological, Biblical, and ascetical treatises, he took part in the controversy against the paganizing humanists and wrote the *Lucula noctis* (ed. E. Hunt, Notre Dame, Ind. 1940), in which he insisted on the Christian basis of education and the careful use of pagan authors, leaving out what is lascivious and tempting in them, especially for the young. In the *Regola del governo di cura familiare* (ed. D. Salvi, Florence 1860) he improved his Christian pedagogical system. He died while on embassy at Buda. His cultus was approved in 1832.

Feast: June 10.

Bibliography: J. QUÉTIF and J. ÉCHARD, *Scriptores Ordinis Praedicatorum* (New York 1959) 1.2:768–771. A. RÖSLER, *Kardinal Johannes Dominicis Erziehungslehre* (Freiburg 1894). A. GALLETTI, "Una raccolta di prediche volgari inedite del card. G. D.," *Miscellanea di studi critici pubblicati in onore di Guido Mazzoni,* ed. A. DELLA TORRE and P. L. RAMBALDI, 2 v. (Florence 1907) 1:253–278. L. SANTAMARIA, "Il concetto di cultura e di educazione nel b. G. D., O.P.," *Memorie Domenicane* 47 (1930), *passim*. S. M. BERTUCCI, *Bibliotheca Sanctorum* (Rome 1961), 4:748–756. S. ORLANDI, *Necrologio di S. Maria Novella,* 2 v. (Florence 1955) 2:77–126. I. COLOSIO, *Giovanni Dominici + 1419 saggi e inediti* (Pistoia 1970). C. MÉSONIAT, *Poetica theologia: la "Lucula noctis" di Giovanni Dominici e le dispute letterarie tra '300 e '400* (Rome 1984).

[S. L. FORTE]

DOMINICUS GERMANUS

Missionary, lexicographer, and Orientalist; b. Schurgast, Silesia, 1588; d. El Escorial, Spain, Sept. 26, 1670. He entered the Franciscan Order in 1624 and devoted himself to the study of Arabic and other Oriental languages under Friar Thomas Obicini at the Missionary College of St. Peter in Montorio, Rome. After a period of special study in Palestine, he returned there and taught Arabic from 1636 until 1640. During those years he published an Arabic grammar, *Fabrica ovvero Dittionario della lingua volgare arabica ed italiani* (Rome 1636), and an apologetical treatise, *Antithesis fidei* (Rome 1638); he also compiled a dictionary in Arabic, Latin, and Italian, *Fabrica linguae arabicae* (Rome 1639), widely used in Italy and Palestine until the middle of the 19th century. He also collaborated on an Arabic version of the Bible (Rome 1671). In 1640 he returned to Palestine, and in 1645 was made prefect of the mission of Samarkand, Tatary. At the request of King PHILIP IV of Spain, he was sent in 1652 to El Escorial, where he taught Arabic and left in still unpublished MSS several apologetical treatises against the Muslims. His Latin version of the Qur'ān, *Interpretatio Alcorani* [*Journal asiatique* 8 Series 1 (1883) 343–406] is the best Latin translation and confutation of the Qur'ān written up to that time.

Bibliography: R. AUBERT, *Dictionnaire d'histoire et de géographie ecclésiastiques*, ed. A. BAUDRILLART et al. (Paris 1912–) 14:608. B. ZIMOLONG, *Dominicus Germanus de Silesia* (Breslau 1928).

[D. A. MCGUCKIN]

DOMINIS, MARCANTONIO DE

Italian ecclesiastic, scientist, and apostate; b. island of Arbe (now Rab, Croatia), 1566; d. Castel Sant' Angelo, Rome, 1624. He entered the Society of Jesus at an early age and on leaving the Society in 1596, was appointed bishop of Segni (Senj). In 1602 he was elevated to the archbishopric of Spalato (Split), and later to the primatial See of Dalmatia, which he held until 1616. He was also professor of mathematics at Padua, where he published *De radii visus et lucis in vitris perspectivis et iride tractatus* (1611), a scientific explanation of the rainbow, according to Sir Isaac Newton. He became involved in the quarrel between the papacy and Venice, and in 1616 went to England, where he was appointed dean of Windsor and master of the Savoy by JAMES I. In 1617 he published the first part of his *De republica ecclesiastica,* a work in which he asserted that the pope had no jurisdiction over bishops, but was only *primus inter pares.* Two years later he published, without authority, Paolo Sarpi's *Istoria del Concilio di Trento* with a dedication to James I. At the accession of Gregory XV, a relative and fellow countryman, Dominis returned to Rome. There he attacked the Church of England in *Sui reditus ex Anglia consilium* (1623). After Gregory XV's death, Dominis was seized by the Inquisition and confined to the Castel Sant' Angelo as a relapsed heretic, where he died. His body and books were burned on Dec. 21, 1624.

Bibliography: H. NEWLAND, *The Life and Contemporaneous Church History of Antonio de Dominis, Archbishop of Spalato* (Oxford 1859). D. CANTIMORI, "Sua M. A. DeDominis," *Archiv für Reformationsgeschichte* 49 (1958) 245–258. *The Dictionary of National Biography from the Earliest Times to 1900* (London 1885–1900; repr. with corrections, 1908–09, 1921–22, 1938) 5:1106–08. V. GABRIELI, "Bacon: La reforma e Roma," *English Miscellany* 8 (1957) 226–233.

[V. LUCIANI]

DOMINUM ET VIVIFICANTEM

Pope John Paul II's fifth encyclical, issued on May 18, 1986. *Dominum et vivificantem* (DV), "The Lord and Giver of Life," deals with the Holy Spirit "in the Life of the Church and the World." The introduction makes clear that DV stands with the first two encyclicals of John Paul, *Redemptor hominis* (RH) and *Dives in misericordia* (DM) to form a textual triptych, with each document highlighting a specific person of the Trinity. After recalling the doxology of St. Paul, "The grace of our Lord Jesus Christ and the love of God and the fellowship of the Holy Spirit be with you all" (2 Cor 3.13), John Paul continues: "In a certain sense, my previous encyclicals *Redemptor hominis* and *Dives in misericordia* took their origin and inspiration from this exhortation. . . . From this exhortation now comes the present Encyclical on the Holy Spirit'' (DV 2).

DV is closely linked and makes frequent reference to the Second Vatican Council: "The Encyclical has been drawn from the heart of the heritage of the Council. For the Conciliar texts, thanks to their teaching on the Church in herself and the Church in the world, move us to penetrate ever deeper into the Trinitarian mystery of God himself . . . to the Father, through Christ, in the Holy Spirit'' (DV 2). Again, as with the previous, the impending approach of the third Christian millennium forms a crucial horizon within which the present reflection on the Holy Spirit takes place. Of special importance in this context is the role of the Spirit "as the one who points out the ways leading to the union of Christians'' (DV 2); Christian ecumenism is an especially prominent dimension of the millennial commemoration.

The text of DV moves in three main parts: (1) "The Spirit of the Father and the Son, Given to the Church''; (2) "The Spirit Who Convinces the World Concerning Sin''; and (3) "The Spirit Who Gives Life.'' Four scenes from the "Upper Room'' form the framework of the encyclical's theological vision. First, there is the farewell discourse of Jesus at his final meal with his disciples (John 14:17). In this scene "the highest point of the revelation of the Trinity is reached'' (DV 9). Here Jesus begins to disclose the personal role that the Spirit will play in communicating the Gospel to the world: "All that the Father has is mine; therefore I said that he [the Holy Spirit] will take what is mine and declare it to you'' (Jn 16:15). John Paul then makes the obvious point: "By the very fact of taking what is 'mine', he will draw from 'what is the Father's''' (DV 7).

The second Upper Room scene takes place on the evening of the first Easter Sunday, according to John (20:19–22). Jesus breathes on his disciples and says to them, "Receive the Holy Spirit.'' Here "there is fulfilled the principal prediction of the farewell discourse: the Risen Christ . . . 'brings' to the Apostles the Holy Spirit'' (DV 24). The further giving of the Holy Spirit to the world takes place in the third Upper Room scene, on the day of Pentecost. "This event constitutes the definitive manifestation of what had already been accomplished in the same Upper Room on Easter Sunday'' (DV 25). Thus the era of the Church begins, and the Holy Spirit is precisely the soul of this new body. The fourth evocation of the Upper Room concerns the Church's fidelity to its mission, which requires it always to be attentive to the circumstances of its beginning. "While it is an historical fact that the Church came forth from the Upper Room on the day of Pentecost, in a certain sense one can say that she has never left it. Spiritually the event of Pentecost does not belong only to the past; the Church is always in the Upper Room that she bears in her heart'' (DV 66).

DV explores the "double rhythm'' of salvation history, the "rhythm of the mission of the Son'' and the "rhythm of the mission of the Holy Spirit,'' both sent into the world by the Father (DV 63). The articulation of this crucial principle of Trinitarian theology reflects a recovered attention to pneumatology, especially in the self-understanding of Western Christianity. The missions of the Son and the Spirit are intimately co-related; the Spirit's role is precisely to make the Son more fully known in the world. And the role of the Son, as RH and DM had already emphasized, is itself twofold: to reveal humans to themselves and to reveal God as the Father of mercy. The Spirit helps us to ponder the total gift that Christ made of himself for our sake; on this basis, then, people are called, with the help of the same Spirit, to find themselves fully through a sincere gift of self. This idea, often cited by John Paul from *Gaudium et spes,* "can be said to sum up the whole of Christian anthropology'' (DV 60). The theme of gift, of mutual giving and receiving among persons, aptly sums up Christian anthropology precisely because it is also definitive of God's very life. "It can be said that in the Holy Spirit the intimate life of the Triune God becomes totally gift, an exchange of mutual love between the divine Persons and that through the Holy Spirit God exists in the mode of gift. It is the Holy Spirit who is the personal expression of this self-giving, of this being-love'' (DV 10).

Bibliography: For the text of *Dominum et vivificantem,* see: *Acta Apostolicae Sedis* 78 (1986) 809–900 (Latin); *Origins* 16, no. 4 (June 12, 1986): 77, 79–102 (English); *The Pope Speaks* 31 (1986): 199–263 (English). For a commentary on *Dominum et vivificantem,* see: A. DULLES, *The Splendor of Faith: The Theological Vision of Pope John Paul II* (New York 1999).

[M. PELZEL]

DOMITIAN, ROMAN EMPEROR

Reigned 81 to 96; b. Titus Flavius Domitianus, Oct. 24, 51; d. Sept. 18, 96. As the son of the Emperor Vespasian, Domitian was named caesar by the praetorians upon the death of his father's rival, Vitellius. In 73 and 80 he held ordinary consulships, but no power under Vespasian or Titus. He succeeded the latter as emperor in 81. Like Augustus, Domitian attempted a renewal of religion and of public morality despite the sensuality of his private life. He built a number of imposing temples. In 83 three Vestal Virgins were executed for having failed to preserve their chastity, and in 90 the *Vestalis Maxima* Cornelia was buried alive on a similar charge. He checked

Domitian, contemporary marble sculpture from the Vatican Museum. (Alinari-Art Reference/Art Resource, NY)

theatrical license, prohibited castration, and revived the *Lex Scantinia* against unnatural vice. Though he took the title of imperator more than 20 times, his military achievements were not significant. Domitian chose good administrators and checked abuses in the administration of justice and the collection of taxes. Until the rebellion of L. Antonius Saturninus in 88 or 89 he ruled with a strong but equitable hand. Afterward, a victim of suspicion, he was ruthless in suppressing opposition. Among the many nobles he sentenced to death were his cousin Flavius Clemens, consul in 95, and M. Acilius Glabrio, consul in 91, on a charge of "atheism," an accusation employed against "many other citizens who had adopted Jewish [probably to be understood as Christian] ways" (Dio Cassius 67.14). Domitian is cited by Christians in antiquity as the author of the second persecution. His insistence upon the cult of the emperors and his title "Lord and God" were bound to bring him into conflict with the Church. St. JOHN mentions martyrdoms in Pergamum and Smyrna (Rv 1.9; 2.9–13), and Pope CLEMENT I seems to have died for the faith at this time. In 96, Domitia, the emperor's wife, joined a conspiracy that ended with the emperor's death at the hands of Stephanus, a freedman of Clemens. Domitian's reign marks a definite advance toward the absolutism of the emperors of succeeding centuries.

Bibliography: R. WEYNARD, *Paulys Realenzyklopädie der klassischen Altertumswissenschaft,* ed. G. WISSOWA et al. 6.2 (Stuttgart 1909) 2541–96. S. GSELL, *Essai sur le règne de l'empereur Domitien* (Paris 1893). M. P. CHARLESWORTH, *The Cambridge Ancient History* (London and New York 1923–39) 11:22–45.

[M. J. COSTELLOE]

DOMITIAN OF ANCYRA

6th-century Byzantine bishop. A learned Origenistic monk, he was an intimate friend of THEODORE ASCIDAS; together they helped spread "Origenism" among their fellow monks in Palestine. St. SABAS, their superior, appealed to Emperor JUSTINIAN I to have the Origenists expelled from Palestine (*c.* 530) but died before any action was taken. Domitian gained the favor of the emperor and was named bishop of Ancyra in Galatia (*c.* 537), but remained in residence in Constantinople. In his treatise *On the Origenian Controversy* (*c.* 545), addressed to Pope VIGILIUS, Domitian admitted that the Origenists disputed the THREE CHAPTERS in order to divert public opinion from their own teachings; FACUNDUS OF HERMIANE quotes this treatise in his *Defense of the Three Chapters* (1.2; 4.4).

Bibliography: E. VENABLES, *A Dictionary of Christian Biography,* ed. W. SMITH and H. WACE (London 1877–87) 1:875. H. G. BECK, *Kirche und theologische Literatur im byzantinschen Reich* (Munich 1959) 384. F. DIEKAMP, *Die origenistischen Streitigkeiten im 6. Jahrhundert* (Münster 1899). O. BARDENHEWER, *Geschichte der altkirchlichen Literatur* (Freiburg 1913–32) 5:25.

[R. K. POETZEL]

DOMITIAN OF MAASTRICHT, ST.

Bishop; b. France; d. Maastricht, Netherlands, *c.* 560. As bishop of Tongeren when the see was transferred to Maastricht, Domitian was present at the Councils of Clermont (535) and Orléans (549). He evangelized the valley of the Meuse, founding churches and hospitals and caring for the poor. His cult was fostered by an annual procession at Huy, Belgium, where according to tradition he slew a dragon that was poisoning the drinking water. He is the patron of Huy, and his relics are preserved in the church of Notre Dame. Only his finger is preserved at Maastricht. He is invoked against fever.

Feast: May 7; June 15 (translation at Huy).

Bibliography: *Bibliotheca hagiographica latina antiquae et mediae aetatis* (Brussels 1898–1901), 1:2251–56. *Monumenta Germaniae Scriptores* (Berlin 1825–), 7:176; 25:26–27,109–110, 112. J. P. MIGNE, *Patrologia latina* (Paris 1878–1890) 139:1033–34. *Acta Sanctorum* (Paris 1863–), May 2:145–153. É. DE MOREAU, *Histoire de l'Église en Belgique* (2d ed. Brussels 1945–) 1:54, 60,

104, 288. M. COENS, "Les Saints vénérés à Huy," *Analecta Bollandiana* 76 (1958) 316–335.

[C. P. LOUGHRAN]

DOMITILLA, FLAVIA, SS.

The name of two famous Christian women whose history stems from the obscure period of the Church at the close of the first century. The first and most famous was a niece of the Emperors DOMITIAN and Titus and the wife of Flavius Clemens, consul in 95. Domitian is reputed to have executed him for embracing Christianity, and to have exiled Flavia Domitilla to the island of Pandataria, outside the Gulf of Gaeta. The pagan historians Suetonius (*In Domit.* 15.1) and Dion Cassius (*Hist.Roman* 67.14) stated that both husband and wife were condemned for the crime of atheism or sacrilege, which later historians presume to be a reference to Christianity since in Roman legal terminology the crime meant refusal to honor the gods of the empire. According to Eusebius (*Histoire ecclesiastique* 3.18.4), their niece, also named Flavia Domitilla, was exiled to the isle of Pontia, some 25 miles north of Pandataria. Jerome speaks of this exile "as a long martyrdom" (*Epistolae* 108 *Ad Eust.; Corpus scriptorum ecclasiasticorum latinorum* 552:312), and it has been suggested that there was only one Flavia Domitilla, mention of a second being due to the martyrology of FLORUS.

The identification of the catacomb excavated by G. B. de Rossi in 1864 on the Via Ardeatina as that of Domitilla stems from two pagan inscriptions found above the underground cemetery attributing sepulchers "to the indulgence of Flavia Domitilla" (*Corpus inscriptionum latinarum* 6.16246, 8942), a fifth-century *passio,* and a late Roman *Index of Cemeteries,* all of which associate Domitilla with the martyrs Nereus and Achilleus (d. *c.* 100).

Feast: May 7.

Bibliography: C. J. HEFELE, *Histoire des conciles d'après les documents originaux* tr. H. LECLERCQ (Paris 1907–), 4.2:1404–06. U. FASOLA, *Dictionnaire d'histoire et de géographie ecclésiastiques* (Paris 1912–), 14:630–634. J. KNUDSEN, "The Lady and the Emperor: A Study of the Domitian Persecution," *Church History* 14 (1945) 17–32. E. KIRSCHBAUM and L. HERTLING, *The Roman Catacombs and Their Martyrs,* tr. M. J. COSTELLOE (Milwaukee 1956). E. VACCHINA, *Flavia Domitilla* (Genoa 1969).

[E. G. RYAN]

DOMNOLUS OF LE MANS, ST.

Abbot, bishop; d. Dec. 1, 581. He was at first abbot of Saint-Laurent in Paris. Having declined the bishopric of Avignon he was later (559) appointed bishop of Le Mans. In 567 he attended the Synod of Tours. He built several churches and a hospice for pilgrims on the Sarthe River. GREGORY OF TOURS (*Historia Francorum* 6.9; 9.39) relates that Domnolus was a saintly man who worked many miracles.

Feast: May 16.

Bibliography: *Acta Sanctorum* May 3:600–609. A. PONCELET, *Analecta Bollandiana* 24 (1905) 515–516. J.L. BAUDOT and L. CHAUSSIN, *Vies des saints et des bienheureux selon l'ordre du calendrier avec l'historique des fêtes* (Paris 1935–1936), 5:326. A. BUTLER, *The Lives of the Saints* (New York 1956), 2:329. L. CELIER, "Les Anciennes vies de Domnole," *Revue Historique et Archéologique du Maine* 55 (1904) 375–391. L. DUCHESNE, *Fastes épiscopaux de l'ancienne Gaule,* 3 v. (2d. ed. Paris 1907–15) 2:333–334. R. AIGRAIN, *Catholicisme* 3:1012–13.

[O. L. KAPSNER]

DOMNUS OF ANTIOCH

The name of two early bishops of Antioch in Syria.

Domnus, bishop of Antioch from 268 to 271, was the son of Bishop Demetrianus (253–260), who had been taken captive by the Persians. After Antioch had been freed by the Palmyran Kingdom, Domnus, then a priest, joined the priest Malchion in opposition to the heresies and scandalous behavior of Bp. PAUL OF SAMOSATA, his father's successor. A council held in Antioch (268) excommunicated Paul and chose Domnus as his successor, declaring that he had "all the necessary qualities to become a bishop." Since the election of Domnus was supported by bishops from the Roman Empire party, Zenobia, Queen Regent of Palmyra, protected Paul and acknowledged his right to the Church possessions; and many continued to consider Paul as local bishop. This difficult situation lasted until 272, when Emperor Aurelian decreed that the Church possessions belonged to the legal bishop in communion with Rome. But by then Domnus had probably died and been succeeded by Timeas.

Domnus, patriarch of Antioch from 441 to 449, was the nephew of JOHN OF ANTIOCH, his predecessor. The Act of Union signed by Cyril of Alexandria and John of Antioch in 433 had brought ecclesiastical peace. But in 447 EUTYCHES, the Constantinopolitan Archimandrite, started the theological dispute surrounding MONOPHYSITISM by an exaggerated adherence to the Incarnational teaching of Cyril of Alexandria. Domnus, together with THEODORET OF CYR, was among the first to denounce the doctrine of Eutyches as Monophysite in tendency. Emperor Theodosius II sided with the Archimandrite, and the Syrian monk Barsumas, a follower of Cyril, attacked

Domnus in Antioch itself. Meanwhile, the Patriarch of Alexandria, DIOSCORUS, supported Eutyches and accused Domnus of having aided bishops of his patriarchate, such as Ibas of Edessa, who were allegedly guilty of Nestorian leanings. In 449 by order of the emperor, partly at the instigation of Dioscorus, the Eutychian affair was brought before a synod later branded by Pope LEO I as the ''brigandage of Ephesus.'' Under pressure, Domnus exonerated Eutyches and signed or approved acts of deposition of bishops who had condemned Eutyches, such as Flavian of Constantinople, Eusebius of Doryleum, and Theodoret of Cyr. Nevertheless Domnus was himself deposed and replaced by the monk Maximus, a former enemy of his uncle John. Domnus retired to the convent of St. Euthymius, near Jerusalem, where he had lived before his nomination to the See of Antioch.

Bibliography: Domnus (bishop). EUSEBIUS, *Historia ecclesiastica* 7.30; 32. R. AUBERT, *Dictionnaire d'histoire et de géographie ecclésiastiques*, ed. A. BAUDRILLART et al. (Paris 1912–) 14:644. G. BARDY, *Catholicisme. Hier, aujourd'hui et demain*, ed. G. JACQUEMET (Paris 1947–) 3:1014; *Paul de Samosate (Spicilegium sacrum Lovaniense* 4; 1923) 352–356. Domnus (patriarch). G. BARDY, *Catholicisme. Hier, aujourd'hui et demain* 3:1014–15; A. FLICHE and V. MARTIN, eds., *Histoire de l'église depuis les origines jusqu'à nos jours* (Paris 1935–) 4:208–236. C. J. VON HEFELE, *Histoire des conciles d'après les documents originaux*, tr. and continued by H. LECLERCQ (Paris 1907–38) 2.1:584–621.

[J. BEAUDRY]

DOMUS SANCTAE MARTHAE

The Domus Sanctae Marthae was built in 1996 to house the electors of the College of Cardinals gathered in conclave for a papal election. Pope John Paul II determined that the facilities in the Apostolic Palace, which had long been used to house the cardinals, were inadequate. Under the direction of the president of the Pontifical Commission for Vatican City, Cardinal Rosalio José Castillo Lara, the Domus Sanctae Marthae was built on the site of the old Santa Marta Hospice, which had been built by Pope Leo XIII and was a center of Allied diplomatic activity during World War II. It is situated in the Piazza Santa Marta opposite Saint Peter's Basilica, hard against the Vatican Wall, between the Paul VI Audience Hall and the Palazzo San Carlo. The cardinals will live, eat, and pray at the Domus Sanctae Marthae, but the voting sessions will be held twice each day in the Sistine Chapel. The new building of a basement and six floors comprises 130 apartments and a range of chapels, dining rooms, and meeting rooms. There are approximately 40 permanent residents, mainly priests working in the Secretariat of State, who would be housed elsewhere during a conclave. The Domus Sanctae Marthae also accommodates groups both large and small for meetings and for-

mal dinners on various occasions. The administration of the house is entrusted to the Daughters of Charity, whose presence in the Vatican City is of long standing.

[M. COLERIDGE]

DONATION OF CONSTANTINE

A spurious document, called also the *Constitutum Constantini,* composed most likely in the early 50s of the 8th century. It relies heavily on a genuine composition of the late 5th century, the so-called *Legenda s. Silvestri.* The Donation purports to be a constitutional grant of the Emperor CONSTANTINE I, by which he handed over to Pope SYLVSTER I imperial power, dignity and emblems, the LATERAN PALACE, and rulership over Rome and ''all provinces, localities and towns in Italy and the Western hemisphere.'' The grant was supposedly the Emperor's reward for the gift of Baptism and for his miraculous recovery from leprosy. Because the Emperor considered it inappropriate to reside in the same city with the successor of St. Peter, he removed his residence to CONSTANTINOPLE, which thereby became the *urbs regia* of the empire.

Composition and Application. The model upon which this forgery drew had already described the conversion of Constantine in vivid terms, and it enjoyed great popularity. What the forger in the 8th century did was to mold the contents of this novelistic product into something approaching a constitutional document. The oldest surviving ''copy'' of the forgery is preserved in Paris (Bib. Nat. Lat. 2777) and is indubitably of 8th-century origin. This spurious grant was very influential throughout the medieval period and served the papacy as a basis for a number of its claims. It was used first against the LOMBARDS by STEPHEN II in his negotiations with King PEPIN in 754. While the authenticity of this grant was only rarely impugned—as far as is known, only OTTO III called the document outright what it was—its validity was often questioned, especially by civil lawyers in the Italian universities. They maintained that Constantine had acted *ultra vires* by making such vast donations and grants. Indirectly the Donation stimulated the emergence of the thesis of inalienability, according to which no ruler was entitled to give away any of his essential governmental functions or any lands entrusted to him. This thesis gained great importance in the medieval kingdoms. The spurious nature of the grant was not exposed until the 15th century, when quite independently NICHOLAS OF CUSA and Lorenzo VALLA proved that it was a fabrication.

Place and Purpose. While with great likelihood the Donation can be assigned to the pontificate of Stephen II, the place of composition is not certain. But there are strong indications that it was fabricated in the papal chancery, the head of which was Christophorus. Many adverse judgments have been made on this document; but, like all medieval forgeries, it should be seen from the contemporary point of view and in its historic context. By the time of its composition the relations between the papacy and the BYZANTINE EMPIRE had reached the breaking point. The latter had not acknowledged the PRIMACY OF THE POPE, and in the immediately preceding decades imperial legislation favoring ICONOCLASM had gravely concerned the West, especially the papacy. Papal resistance to this legislation only brought forth further threatening measures on the part of Constantinople, which, in one way or another, went back to the Council of CHALCEDON (ch. 17, 28). According to ch. 17, the ecclesiastical status of a city is determined by its civil status. The application of this chapter entailed a diminution of the status of Rome and, therefore, of the pope, because the capital of the Empire, the *urbs regia*, was that city in which the emperor and his government resided. The author of the Donation wished to show *how*, in actual fact, Constantinople had become the *urbs regia*. In so doing the forger utilized the *Legenda s. Silvestri*, where this theme had already been touched upon. He presented the transfer of the government from Rome to Constantinople as a thing to which Sylvester had agreed.

Although—according to the Donation—Constantine had offered the imperial crown to Sylvester, the latter refused to wear it. It is clearly implied that if he had so wished, Sylvester could have worn it, and that therefore Constantinople had become the *urbs regia* through the volition and acquiescence of the Pope himself. Consequently, the Pope could withdraw this permission and retransfer the crown from Constantinople to Rome: for the seat of the imperial government was where the imperial crown was kept. There can be no doubt that this was the forger's principal aim. The forgery was directed exclusively against Byzantium, although by virtue of its comprehensiveness and vagueness it could be used in the West, as in fact it was. The forger dealt with no less a problem than that of legitimate rulership in the Roman-Christian world, i.e., of the ROMAN EMPIRE. The seat of the Empire was at Constantinople, whose orthodoxy, however, was in more than one way suspect. In "demonstrating" the historical changes ideologically, the author was compelled to constitute the pope a proper ruler in the West. And since no ruler could exist without governmental machinery, emblems, and territorial possessions, these too were granted, but were only a subsidiary feature of the document.

Clearly, for the exercise of governmental functions by the papacy, the constitutional and institutional enact-

ments were of great value, because they supplied the regal function of the pope and made him a true king and priest. The Donation was a construction whose obvious weakness was that it presented the regal function of the pope as derived from an imperial grant. When the full potentialities of the pope as the VICAR OF CHRIST were elaborated, the Donation could be dispensed with, as was done in fact by INNOCENT III.

Bibliography: Editions. C. B. COLEMAN, *Constantine the Great and Christianity* (New York 1914). C. MIRBT, *Quellen zur Geschichte des Papsttums* (4th ed. Tübingen 1924). Edition of the *Legenda s. Silvestri* in B. MOMBRIZIO, *Sanctuarium seu vitae sanctorum*, 2 v. (Paris 1910) 2:508–531. Literature. G. LÄHR, *Die konstantinische Schenkung in der abendländischen Literatur* (Berlin 1926). W. LEVISON, "Konstantinische Schenkung und Silvesterlegende," *Miscellanea Francesco Ehrle*, 5 v. (Rome 1924) 2:181–225. W. ULLMANN, *Growth of Papal Government in the Middle Ages* (2d ed. London 1962) 74–86. D. MAFFEI, "Cino da Pistoia e il Constitutum Constantini," *Annali d'Università di Macerata* 24 (1961) 95–115. H. M. KLINKENBERG, *Lexikon für Theologie und Kirche*, ed. J. HOFER and K. RAHNER, 10 v. (2d new ed. Freiburg1957-65) 6:483–484. S. WILLIAMS, "The Oldest Text of the *Constitutum Constantini*," *Traditio* 20 (1964) 448–461.

[W. ULLMANN]

DONATISM

A schismatic movement that affected the Church in North Africa during the 4th and 5th centuries. Donatism was primarily religious in origin and stemmed from an exaggerated insistence on the holiness of the minister in the confection of sacramental rites; it gradually became an ethnic and social problem that emphasized the enmity between the native Berber population and the Romans by origin or culture and the hatred of the laboring classes for the landowners.

History. It began with a dispute over the reconciliation of the *traditores*, or clerics and bishops who had handed over the sacred books to the imperial officials during the DIOCLETIAN PERSECUTION (303–305). When peace was restored to the Church, questions were raised regarding the validity of the ordinations conferred by bishops who had conformed with the imperial demands and later had been reconciled with the Church. In particular, the action of Bp. Mensurius of Carthage was challenged. He had satisfied the persecuting authorities by handing over heretical books. His action was considered immoral by the zealots who claimed that the tradition of the African Church demanded that true Christians should have offered themselves for martyrdom in the spirit of their predecessors during the Decian persecutions. These zealots received the support of DONATUS and of Bp. Secundus of Tigisi, the metropolitan of Numidia.

When Mensurius died in 311, the faithful and clergy of Carthage elected the archdeacon Caecilian, whose action in handing over the sacred books was also contested. Since one of his three consecrators was Bp. Felix of Aptonga, who likewise was accused as a *traditor,* 70 Numidian bishops under the influence of Donatus held a synod at Carthage and elected Majorinus in place of Caecilian.

Constantinian Intervention. Supported by the affluent widow Lucilla, who had been rebuked by Caecilian for her excessive zeal in the cult of the MARTYRS, the dissident faction addressed a letter to Emperor CONSTANTINE I demanding that judges be sent to settle the dispute between Caecilian and Majorinus for the See of Carthage. The emperor instructed Pope Miltiades to hold a synod in Rome (Oct. 2, 313), and the bishops of Gaul and Italy present at this assembly supported the claims of Caecilian. This judgment was rejected by the partisans of Majorinus in a second appeal to the emperor; and a new synod was convoked at Arles (Aug. 1, 314), which confirmed the Roman decision. To give the dissidents full satisfaction, Constantine allowed a third appeal, which was heard in a synod at Milan (Nov. 10, 316); but the results were the same. Caecilian's election and consecration were judged valid, and his possession of the See of Carthage was sustained.

Majorinus had died meanwhile, and Donatus had been elected in his place. He had energetically organized the Donatist church, spreading its teachings throughout North Africa and consecrating bishops for the sees. Appealing to the native Berber population, he stressed the need of sanctity in clerics and ministers of the Sacraments and employed the imperial repression of the Donatists to insist on their continuance of the North African tradition of martyrdom.

Circumcellions. In opposition to a Constantinian edict of 317 that had ordered the confiscation of Donatist churches and the exile of their leaders, a widespread revolt broke out; but in 321 the emperor granted the Donatists full liberty. The revolt, however, had produced a fanatical group of armed zealots called Circumcellions, who terrorized the countryside in favor of the Donatists in Carthage. Despite their stringent demands regarding the validity of baptism, an attempt at reconciliation was made by the Catholic bishop, Gratus of Carthage (*c.* 341), and in 347 the emperor Constantius II sent two legates, Macarius and Paul, to restore religious unity. They were accused of favoring the Catholic position, and their mission ended in repressive measures against the Donatists. Donatus died *c.* 355 and was replaced by Parmenian, an intelligent and active organizer. He was opposed by weak Catholic bishops, such as Restitutus of Carthage, who had signed the Arian formulary of Rimini, and Genethlius.

A new lease on life was given to Donatism under JULIAN THE APOSTATE (361–363), who recalled the Donat-

ist bishops from exile. In 371 the Donatists joined in the anti-Roman revolt of Firmus; in 388 a fanatical Donatist bishop, Optatus of Thamugadi, and bands of Circumcellions under Gildon staged a revolt that lasted until 398 and ended in the death of the two leaders. These revolts strengthened the ethnic and social motives of the Donatists and added to their list of martyrs. A serious split occurred in their ranks, however, when a relative of Donatus the Great, the deacon Maximianus, with 43 bishops objected to a policy of leniency toward dissidents; they were excommunicated by the Donatist primate. An attempt was made to heal the schism in 394 at the Council of Bagai, where the Donatists agreed to recognize the validity of Sacraments conferred by the Maximianists.

St. Augustine. Augustine began his campaign against the Donatists as a priest in Carthage by writing (393) an alphabetical psalm, *Psalmus contra partem Donati,* which gave a popular refutation of the Donatist doctrines. At the same time he wrote a controversial treatise, *Contra Epistulam Donati haeretici, liber unus,* which is now lost. Two letters of this period are extant: one to Maximinus, Donatist bishop of Sinitum, on the question of rebaptism (*Epist.* 23); another to Alipius of Tagaste (*Epist.* 29). In some of his sermons on the Psalms (*In psalm.* 25; 54) he deals with the violence of the Circumcellions.

Augustine's elevation to the episcopate made him a key figure in the anti-Donatist movement from 395 to 411. Under the Primate of Carthage, Aurelius, the third Council of Carthage met in 397 and considered the schismatic condition of the North African Church; in 398 Augustine produced his *Contra Epistolam Parmeniani* in three books, in which he defended the catholic, or universal, nature of the Church that contains both good and evil. Parmenian had attacked a Donatist writer, Tyconius, for bringing forward the same ideas. In approving the ideas of Tyconius, Augustine developed his teaching on the Church as the Body of Christ. He dealt with the rebaptism controversy and with the authority of CYPRIAN and the Council of Carthage of 256 in his *De Baptismo contra Donatistas* (*c.* 400). This was followed by *Contra Litteras Petiliani,* against the Donatist Petilian, bishop of Cirta. Augustine continued writing against the Donatists until 412, after which he turned to combat PELAGIANISM.

Conference at Carthage. In 411 a conference was convened at Carthage by imperial mandate to resolve the dispute. It was presided over by an imperial tribune, Marcellinus, and was attended by 286 Catholic bishops and 279 Donatist bishops. The Donatists used obstructionist tactics and wrangled over procedural problems before the true historical and theological problems could be discussed. In the debate Augustine made short work of his opponents, using arguments that he had been developing against them for more than a decade. The decision of the imperial commissioner favored the Catholic position. The Donatist churches were to be handed over to the Catholics unless they came over as whole communities. In this case, they would be welcomed as true Catholic Churches. Those who refused to obey were liable to the penalties of the civil law.

The Donatists pointed to the severe penalties of floggings, confiscations of property, and exile as evidence that they were the successors of the Church of the persecuted and that the Catholics were the successors of the tyrannical emperors. From the *Retractationes* it is clear that Augustine, despite the wavering support he gave to the policy of imperial coercion, felt doubts about submitting spiritual questions to secular adjudication and appealing to the civil law to support religious truth.

Decline of Donatism. In the 5th century Donatism declined as a result of internal schisms and of the Catholic pressure exerted by Augustine and the civil power. Radical elements under Optatus of Thamugadi opposed the moderate group led by such thinkers as Tyconius, Rogatus of Cartenna (Rogatists), and Claudius at Rome (Claudianists). A serious break came with the schism of the deacon Maximian against Primian, the Donatist bishop of Carthage, which resulted in warring synods: Cabarsussi in 393 for Maximian and the synod of Bagai for Primian. The events of 312 were repeated in the consecration of Maximian as a rival bishop, the holding of rival synods, and the issue of decrees of deposition. This provided Augustine with an unanswerable argument, since the Primianists had promised to recognize the Sacraments of the Maximianists if they returned to their sect. After 411 the Donatist cause declined gradually, but still had enough strength left to merit the attention of Pope GREGORY I (THE GREAT) (590–604). The Donatists finally disappeared in the Arab invasions.

Donatist Doctrine and Its Development. The errors of the Donatists were based on their teaching that heretics must be rebaptized. Using the teaching of Tertullian and Cyprian, they assumed that the part played by the minister in the administration of the Sacraments was substantial and not merely instrumental; therefore, they maintained that a minister without grace could not confer the Sacraments. Since they held that all outside the Donatist church lacked grace, they insisted on rebaptizing all who returned from heretical or schismatic sects. Holiness was required in the minister, and sanctity could only be obtained in the true Church.

Donatist teaching on the efficacy of the Sacraments led to a narrow idea of the Church. For them, the Church was an exclusive caste that should not be contaminated by contact with sinners, least of all with the infamous

traditores who had handed over the sacred books to the persecutors and had refused martyrdom, the desired goal of true believers. The reverence of the Donatists for the word of God in the Scriptures led them to maintain that to change one syllable or letter deserved the infliction of great punishment. Hence severe punishment awaited traitors who had surrendered these sacred books to be burned.

Anyone who communicated with the *traditores* was cut off from the Church and lost both his sacred character and the power to confer sanctity. The holy Church, in the Donatist view, contained no sinners; it was absolutely separated from the sinful world. For them, the sinful world was epitomized in the Roman Empire that Christian tradition represented as the city of evil. Even after Constantine, they still asserted that implacable hostility between the true Church and the Roman Empire. Since, as Donatists, they were the object of official persecution, they considered themselves to be the only true Church.

The Donatists following Cyprian made no distinction in the sequence of salvific action; they proclaimed one Church, one baptism, one salvation. As their idea of the Church was corporeal or spatial, they maintained that the validity or value of a Sacrament depended on the minister's actual public membership in the Church. Augustine distinguished between baptism received simply and baptism received usefully for salvation. His chief preoccupation was to ascertain the true subject of salvific acts. For the Donatists, the value of a Sacrament depended on the ecclesial position of the minister, as either inside or outside the local church. In actual fact the conferring of grace did not depend on his personal sanctity. The minister of the Sacrament could have personal sins; but as long as they were not public, he could not be expelled from the Church and the Sacraments he conferred were valid in its eyes.

Augustine distinguished two aspects of the Church that could be described as two concentric circles. The outer ring, or the *communio sacramentorum,* was the union in the Sacraments through the institution of the Church, into which all those who fulfilled the condition of baptism entered. This included even the Donatists. The inner ring was the *communio sanctorum,* or the communion of saints, whose members are united by the Holy Spirit in charity. A Sacrament, the institution of Christ administered by men, is not dependent on the quality of the man who administers it, for this would be to attribute the creation of a spiritual gift to a man. The Donatists had the sacramental act but not the grace that caused salvation. The *communio sacramentorum,* to which they belonged, was described by Augustine, under the influence of his Neoplatonist formation, as the plane of exterior, corporeal appearance where one could possess Christ bodily and yet be without the Spirit that brings charity.

For the Donatists, the Church is here and now without spot or blemish. They neglected to observe the tension that exists between the present state of the Church and its eschatological state. For Augustine, the Church is still the Church of sinners on Earth; it is composed of two parts, one of which has the Sacraments without grace, the other the Sacraments with grace. The advance in sacramental theology and ecclesiology made by Augustine in response to the Donatists was of great importance for the development of theology in the Middle Ages.

Bibliography: G. BAREILLE, *Dictionnaire de théologie catholique,* ed. A. VACANT et al., 15 v. (Paris 1903–50; Tables générales 1951–) 4.2:1701–28. J. RATZINGER and L. EUDING, *Lexikon für Theologie und Kirche,* ed. J. HOFER and K. RAHNER, 10 v. (2d, new ed. Freiburg 1957–65) 3:504–506. H. POPE, *St. Augustine of Hippo* (London 1937) 271–327. W. H. C. FREND, *The Donatist Church* (London 1952). J. P. BRISSON, *Autonomisme et christianisme dans l'Afrique romaine* (Paris 1958). J. KELLEHER, *St. Augustine's Notion of Schism in the Donatist Controversy* (Mundelin 1961). Y. M. J. CONGAR, Introd. to *Traités Anti-Donatistes,* v. 28 of *Oeuvres de S. Augustin* (Paris 1963). R. CRESPIN, *Ministère et sainteté* (Paris 1965). F. HOFMANN, *Der Kirchenbegriff des hl. Augustinus* (Munich 1933). J. RATZINGER, *Volk und Haus Gottes in Augustins Lehre von der Kirche* (Munich 1954). G. C. WILLIS, *Saint Augustine and the Donatist Controversy* (Society for Promoting Christian Knowledge; 1950). W. H. C. FREND, *Reallexikon für Antike und Christentum,* ed. T. KLAUSER (Stuttgart 1941 [1950]–) 4:128–147. S. L. GREENSLADE, *Schism in the Early Church* (New York 1953).

[D. FAUL]

DONATUS

4th-century North African schismatic bishop of Carthage (313–347). There is an unresolved problem regarding the true identity of Donatus, whose name is given to the schismatical movement that disturbed the Church in North Africa during the 4th and 5th centuries (*see* DONATISM). It is possible that he is identical with Donatus of Casae Nigrae, who apparently initiated the schism by supporting the usurping Bishop Majorinus against the legitimately elected Caecilian. This Donatus represented the schismatics at the Council of the Lateran in 313, called by Pope MILTIADES at the urging of Emperor CONSTANTINE I. Optatus of Milevis spoke of one Donatus as did Augustine until the conference of Carthage between the Catholics and Donatists in 411. There Augustine spoke of two Bishops Donatus; and after that Augustine carefully distinguished them in his *Retractationes* and in his book on heresies. Present-day scholars are inclined to identify the two figures.

Donatus the Great was a leader of intelligence and energy who directed the schismatic movement with great

shrewdness and with an eye to the social and ethnic factors that were important in spreading Donatism. When the imperial power interfered (347) to put down the outrages committed by Donatist terrorists (known as Circumcellions), Donatus was ousted from his see at Carthage by the imperial legates, Paul and Macarius. He was exiled to Gaul or Spain, where he died *c.* 350 or 355. He was succeeded by Bishop Parmenian.

Bibliography: W. H. C. FREND, *The Donatist Church* (New York 1952) 153–, 165–. AUGUSTINE, *Retract.* 1.21.3; *Haer.* 69.

[D. FAUL]

DONATUS OF BESANÇON, ST.

Bishop; d. *c.* 660. Donatus, descendant of a ducal family, was educated at LUXEUIL. As bishop of Besançon, he established the famous Saint Paul's Cloister (*Palatium*) and gave it a rule drawn from BENEDICT and COLUMBAN. Donatus's mother, Flavia, founded the monastery of Jussa-Moutiers or Saint-Marie, for which Donatus wrote a rule (*Regula ad virgines; Patrologia Latina* 87:273–98). Donatus assisted at the councils of Clichy (627) and Chalon-sur-Saône (*c.* 650). He is also mentioned in a charter of Clotaire III (658).

Feast: Aug. 7.

Bibliography: J. MABILLON, *Acta sanctorum ordinis S. Benedicti* (Venice 1733–1740), 2:320–322. *Acta Sanctorum* Aug. 2: 197–200. JONAS, *Vita s. Columbani, Patrologia Latina,* ed. J. P. MIGNE, 217 v. (Paris 1878–90) 87: 1024. J. L. BAUDOT and L. CHAUSSIN, *Vies des saints et des bienheureux selon l'ordre du calendrier avec l'historique des fêtes* (Paris 1935–1956), 8: 123–124. R. AIGRAIN, *Catholicisme* 3:1015–17. T. DE MOREMBERT, *Dictionnaire d'histoire et de géographie ecclésiastiques* (Paris 1912–), 14:648–649.

[B. F. SCHERER]

DONDERS, PETER, BL.

Redemptorist missionary priest; b. Oct. 27, 1809, Tilburg, the Netherlands; d. Jan. 14, 1887, Batavia, Suriname (formerly Dutch Guiana), South America; beatified May 23, 1982.

Born into a poor family, headed by Arnold Denis Donders and Petronella van den Brekel, he received little schooling and had to delay his vocation in order to help support the family by working in a factory. He was accepted as a domestic in the minor seminary of St. Michiels-Gestel, Holland, in the autumn of 1831 and the following year was admitted as a student. Having unsuccessfully sought entry into the Franciscans, Jesuits, and Redemptorists, he made his major seminary studies at

Oegstgeest, South Holland, and was ordained June 5, 1841. On Aug. 1, 1842, he departed for Suriname, arriving September 16. He labored there on the missions until his death. His first duties entailed preaching and ministering the sacraments to plantation slaves. In the course of eight years, he instructed and baptized 1,200.

The mission was ceded to the Dutch Redemptorists in 1865, and Donders entered that congregation on Nov. 1, 1866, making his profession to the first Redemptorist apostolic vicar (Johan Baptist Swinkels) on June 24, 1867 (age 57), at Paramaribo. He was dedicated particularly to the care of the 600 inmates of the leprosarium at Batavia, and he labored there for many years (1856–66, 1867–83, 1885–87) as priest and nurse. Endowed with a spirit of prayer and charity, he exhibited mercy to the most miserable and abandoned of all classes. In 1868 and 1869, he also learned the languages of and worked among the Arrowaks, Warros, Caribs and Maroons. In 1883, when his health began to fail, he was transferred to Paramaribo, then to Coronie, but he returned to Batavia in November 1885 to resume his previous work. He died in the leprosarium, was buried in Batavia, and later placed in a vault in the Cathedral in Paramaribo (1921).

Pope John Paul II praised Donders as ''an incentive for the renewal and flourishing of the missionary thrust which in the last century and in this one has made an exceptional contribution to the carrying out of the Church's missionary duty.''

Feast: Jan. 14 (Redemptorists).

Bibliography: *Acta Apostolicae Sedis* 74 (1982): 1205–7. *L'Osservatore Romano,* English edition, no. 24 (1982): 6–7. C. J. ANTONELLIS, *The Story of Peter Donders* (Boston 1982). J. CARR, *A Fisher of Men* (Dublin 1952). J. L. F. DANKELMAN, *Peerke Donders: schering en inslag van zijn leven* (Hilversum 1982). J. KRONENBURG, *An Apostle of the Lepers* (London 1930). B. L. J. RADEMAKER, *Petrus Donders* (Bussum, Netherlands 1956).

[A. SAMPERS]

DONG BODI, PATRICK, ST.

Franciscan seminarian, martyr; b. 1882, Guchengyin, Taiyüan Xian, Shanxi Province; d. July 9, 1900, Taiyüan, Shanxi Province, China. Patrick Dong Bodi (also written Tung or Tun) was the eldest of the four sons of the pious Christians Paul Dong Hongxi and Clare Wong. He began his studies for the priesthood at Dongergou in 1893, then continued at Taiyüan's major seminary (1895), where he was an acolyte known for his maturity and devotion to the Blessed Mother, and where he learned three European languages. He traveled throughout Europe with Bp. Francesco Fogolla (1897–99). Pat-

Peter Donders.

rick was preparing to enter the Franciscan novitiate at Tong-el-Kou when he was captured by the Boxers and beheaded. The rest of his family was martyred (Aug. 13, 1900), while praying in church. Patrick was beatified by Pope Pius XII (Nov. 24, 1946) and canonized (Oct. 1, 2000) by Pope John Paul II with Augustine Zhao Rong and companions.

Feast: July 4.

See Also: CHINA, MARTYRS OF, SS.

Bibliography: L. M. BALCONI, *Le Martiri di Taiyuen* (Milan 1945). *Acta Apostolicae Sedis* 47 (1955) 381–388. *Vita del b. A. Crescitelli* (Milan 1950). M. T. DE BLARER, *Les Bse Marie Hermine de Jésus et ses compagnes, franciscaines missionnaires de Marie, massacrées le 9 juillet 1900 à Tai-Yuan-Fou, Chine* (Paris 1947). *Les Vingt-neuf martyrs de Chine, massacrés en 1900, béatifiés par Sa Sainteté Pie XII, le 24 novembre, 1946* (Rome 1946). L. MINER, *China's Book of Martyrs: A Record of Heroic Martyrdoms and Marvelous Deliverances of Chinese Christians during the Summer of 1900* (Ann Arbor 1994). J. SIMON, *Sous le sabre des Boxers* (Lille 1955). C. TESTORE, *Sangue e palme sul fiume giallo. I beati martiri cinesi nella persecuzione della Boxe Celi Sud-Est, 1900* (Rome 1955). *L'Osservatore Romano,* Eng. ed. 40 (2000): 1–2, 10.

[K. I. RABENSTEIN]

Gaetano Donizetti.

DONIZETTI, GAETANO

Opera composer; b. Bergamo, Italy, Nov. 29, 1797; d. Bergamo, April 8, 1848. He studied music in Bergamo with Mayr and in Bologna with Pilotti and Mattei. While he was serving in the Austrian army, his first opera, *Enrico di Borgogna,* was performed in Venice (1818). He subsequently composed operas in rapid succession for various theaters throughout Europe, attaining international stature with *Anna Bolena* (Milan 1830). Though appointed in 1835 professor of counterpoint at the Royal College of Music in Naples, he settled in Paris in 1839. During a visit to Vienna in 1842, he wrote for the royal court two settings of the *Ave Maria,* a *Miserere,* two Masses, and a *Requiem* (for Bellini), in a "severe style," that was warmly received by German critics of the time. He composed also various cantatas; songs; and piano, orchestral, and chamber works. The most popular of his 64 operas are *Lucia di Lammermoor, La Favorita, La Fille du régiment* (an *opéra comique*), *L'Elisir d'amore,* and *Don Pasquale* (in *buffa* style). In spite of their dramatic and musical shortcomings, these works merit occasional revival because of their graceful melodies and the opportunity they offer for vocal virtuosity. The last few years of Donizetti's life were marred by mental and physical illness. He is buried in S. Maria Maggiore, Bergamo, where a monument by Vela was erected to his memory in 1855.

Bibliography: G. ZAVADINI, *Donizetti* (Bergamo 1948). G. BARBLAN, *Die Musik in Geschichte und Gegenwart,* ed. F. BLUME (Kassel-Basel 1949–) 3:678–684. H. S. EDWARDS et al., *Grove's Dictionary of Music and Musicians,* ed. E. BLOM, 9 v. (5th ed. London 1954) 2:733–736. D. J. GROUT, *A Short History of Opera,* 2 v. (2d, rev. and enl. ed. New York 1965). A. EINSTEIN, *Music in the Romantic Era* (New York 1947). J. S. ALLITT, *Donizetti in the Light of Romanticism and the Teaching of Johann Simon Mayr* (Shaftesbury 1991). W. ASHBROOK, "The Evolution of the Donizettian Tenor-Persona," *Opera Quarterly* 14/3 (1998) 25–32; "(Domenico) Gaetano (Maria) Donizetti," in *International Dictionary of Opera,* ed. C. S. LARUE, 2 v. (Detroit 1993) 354–359. H. BERLIOZ, "Berlioz on the Premiere of *La Favorite,*" introduced and tr. by E. T. GLASOW, *Opera Quarterly,* 14/3 (1998) 33–43. R. CELLETTI, "Il vocalismo Italiano da Rossini a Donizetti, Parte II: Bellini e Donizetti," *Analecta Musicologia* 7 (1969) 223–247. C. P. D. CRONIN, "Stefano Pavesi's *Ser Marcantonio* and Donizetti's *Don Pasquale,*" *Opera Quarterly* 11/2 (1995) 39–53. A. FISCHLER, "Gilbert and Donizetti," *Opera Quarterly* 11/1 (1995) 29–42. L. ZOPPELLI, "Narrative Elements in Donizetti's Operas," *Opera Quarterly* 10/1 (1993) 23–32.

[R. W. LOWE]

DONNE, JOHN

English poet and divine; b. London, 1572; d. there March 31, 1631. As Donne once said himself in *Biathanatos,* he had his "first breeding and conversation with men of a suppressed and afflicted Religion." On his mother's side, he was related to the More, Rastell, and HEYWOOD families, who had suffered severely for their adherence to the Old Faith (*see* MORE, THOMAS, ST.; MORE, SCHOOL OF). It is quite clear from his education that he was brought up as a Catholic, for he attended both Oxford and Cambridge, but went down without taking a degree, since he could not make the necessary religious commitments. He probably traveled on the Continent (1591?) and then went up to London to study at the Inns of Court, at Thavies Inn (1591) and Lincoln's Inn (1592–94), a course taken frequently by RECUSANTS at this time.

Religious Situation of the Period. There has been a good deal of speculation as to just how much his upbringing differed from that of the average Englishman of his means and connections at this period. To hazard even a guess about that, one has to remember the complexity of the Recusant situation at this time. In Donne's boyhood, in the seventh and eighth decades of the 16th century, some Catholics made token appearances at the Anglican parish churches, a course of action that brought upon them severe criticism from the leaders of the Recusant exiles on the Continent. Others did not pretend to conform, but nevertheless thought the English Mission of 1580 a mistake, because under the leadership of the Jesuits it boldly challenged the status quo, and thus militated against the hope that the Elizabethan government, reassured by the loyalty of the Catholics, might grant some amelioration of their hard circumstances. Not all the clergy in England by any means supported the English Mission. (*See* PERSONS, ROBERT; CAMPION, EDMUND, BL.; ELIZABETH I, QUEEN OF ENGLAND.)

Many, however, welcomed the mission and cooperated with it once they were satisfied that its purposes were strictly religious and not political. Donne's mother, a shadowy figure at best, would seem to have belonged to this group, for she held to the Old Faith even until her death in the deanery of St. Paul's, and so would Donne's younger brother Henry, for he lost his life from jail fever in Newgate as a result of having sheltered a priest. Moreover, Donne's uncle, Jasper Heywood, was a leader in the Jesuit effort, and it is reasonable to assume that the young Donne felt his influence. The fact that Donne seems to have had a special animus against the Jesuits, as expressed in *Ignatius His Conclave* (1611), would suggest that his uncle had put some pressure on his brilliant nephew to join him as a Jesuit.

Temperament and Character. A surviving picture of young Donne eloquently suggests a proud, ambitious, self-confident young man with a very hungry look about him, as he himself admitted, and a great thirst for learning and experience. It is quite clear that despite the handicap of his religion, he was ambitious for a career in public life. He had a number of most promising friends among the landed gentry and the wealthy professional classes, and his wit and brilliant address would enable him to make the most of any opportunities they opened to him. Although one must always be a little suspicious of the remembered sins of notable converts, there is no reason to doubt that Donne was a very gay young man about town. The character of his earliest verses would do nothing to diminish his reputation, and he seems to have done all the things fashionable young Elizabethans did, even to taking part in Essex's expeditions to Cadiz and the Azores in 1596 and 1597. Like other young men about town, too, Donne seems to have run through a substantial patrimony, and thus to have been left dependent on the favor of patrons, a situation by no means abnormal for young aspirants to a place at court.

Reversals and Brightening Career. During these years the brilliant young Donne was busily laying the foundations of a promising career. He may have been employed in the diplomatic service of Robert Cecil; he certainly became the secretary of Sir Thomas Egerton, the Lord Keeper, in 1597 and 1598. It is probable that at this time he conformed at least nominally to the Established Church. His prospects must certainly have seemed prom-

John Donne, engraving by W. Skelton Sculp. (CORBIS/Bettmann)

ising, for Sir Thomas was later to become the lord chancellor as Baron Ellesmere. At this juncture, however, one of the first of the dramatic ironies that punctuated the career of Donne interrupted his brilliant progress. For now the young poet who had cut such a dashing figure as a careless cynic in matters of love threw away his burgeoning career for love, when he not only won the niece of Lady Egerton, Ann More, but eloped with her in December 1601. Her father, in the heaviest tradition of the heavy father, not only had Donne imprisoned for a time, but also insisted that Egerton discharge his secretary; he himself did nothing to help the young couple. Years of privation and hardship followed for Donne and his growing family, in an exile from the great world enforced by poverty. Donne was quite literally in a desperate situation with all his consciousness of great powers doomed to rust unused. It says much for his charm that he found patrons and patronesses to help him in these dark days, and much, too, for the depth of his affection for his wife that it survived these frustrations. Some of his loveliest verses are usually thought to have been addressed to her.

Donne had been a great reader of theological literature even in his early man-about-town days. He seems never to have been in any way irreligious, but there is evidence that he was long uncertain as to the identity of the true church. Tradition has it that he found employment at some time between 1605 and 1607 aiding Bp. Thomas Morton in his controversies with Catholics; if so, Donne certainly must have swung clear out of his earlier religious orbit to undertake that role, and yet when in 1607 Morton offered him ecclesiastical preferment, he declined. At that point, religious allegiance could hardly have determined his action; that question must already have been settled, but apparently Donne still hoped for secular preferment at court. It may also have been true that, in view of his earlier career, he did not feel himself the right kind of person for holy orders. But his admirer King James made it clear that only in the Church would he offer preferment, and would do so gladly once Donne bowed to the inevitable. Donne yielded, was ordained in 1615, and preferment followed soon after. By that time he must have decided that he could with a clear conscience accept the Anglican position with regard to the national church and its spiritual headship. The death of his wife in 1617 seems to have wearied him with worldly ambition, and helped him to focus all his powers on the Anglican ministry. In 1621 King James nominated him dean of St. Paul's.

Donne's Religious Stance. If one takes his later verse, his devotional writings, and his sermons as a whole, it is clear that he accepted the position that the Church of England was the reasonable mean between the two extremes of Geneva and Rome, and that it was the duty of the Englishman to accept the religious settlement of his country. Such a decision would certainly solve the problem of divided religious and civic loyalties; indeed, if a man could accept it, he would find his religious and his civic loyalties knit up in a whole that would unify his world for him and give him a great sense of security and pride. There is no reason to doubt the sincerity of Donne's conviction, however slowly it was arrived at, and however convenient it proved to him in a worldly fashion.

And yet, though Donne accepted the THIRTY-NINE ARTICLES, he took a position much closer to Rome than to Geneva on the issue of predestination and good works. He moved back and forth from the Church Fathers to medieval doctors and authorities with more ease than did many of his colleagues, and he quoted medieval writers with a freedom that a man like John Foxe would hardly have tolerated. Some of his earlier devotional habits persisted, as may be seen (Helen Gardner has pointed this out) in the influence of ancient liturgical forms in poems like the *La Corona* series. In his devotional prose, too, the influence of earlier patterns of meditation has been detected. And in the "Holy Sonnets" and in the hymns, he approached the theme of death with rather more of Catholic uncertainty about the sureness of perseverance

unto the end than with Protestant confidence in his election. Clearly, that was an issue on which he had thought long, and on which he never lost a certain lack of confidence in himself, however encouraging he might be to his flock. But he certainly brought all his gifts of mind, imagination, intellectual passion, and eloquence to the service of the men and women who flocked to hear him preach in St. Paul's.

Reputation and Significance. After a century and a half of repudiation and then almost complete neglect, Donne's verse began to be appreciated at the end of the 19th century and won deeper regard with the advance of the 20th. Indeed, many things in Donne's verse especially commended themselves to the temper of the opening years of the 20th century. The highly dramatic, realistic, and brilliant expression of the reaction of a very complex self-awareness to the impact of various facets of Renaissance experience stirred the curiosity and the admiration of the post–World War I generation. The range of his conceits from near blasphemy almost to ecstasy, his candor about sex, his consciousness of a thoroughly upset intellectual world, his homeliness, his metaphysical sweep, his tough determination to bend all the resources of learning and language to the expression of a wide range of intellectual and passional purposes—all these appealed greatly to the generation of the 1920s. His analysis of almost every state of a wide-ranging and highly complex consciousness fascinated young people who had had their psychological awareness extended by Freud and Frazer. His rebellious daring, too, was highly attractive to a generation that was to prove less resolute in action than they had perhaps dreamed. His use of scientific data for imagery captured the attention of many who did not always realize that Donne's exploitation of science, like much of his use of scholastic philosophy, was only a means to an end. In the long run Donne cared much less about the external world than the internal, and God was always of much more concern to him than the world He had made.

But whatever the limitations of the understanding of Donne in the first two-fifths of the 20th century, there was no question of his prestige and his influence. Critics like T. S. Eliot joined scholars like the late Sir Herbert Grierson in making known to the general reading public the wonders of Donne, and poets like T. S. Eliot did not hesitate to claim the authority of Donne and his followers for their own innovations and experiments. Soon a host of lesser poets endeavored to imitate the techniques of Donne and his imitators, particularly the tension of wit in many of his apt but far-fetched comparisons, and the brilliant use of recondite learning intermixed with the commonplaces of human nature and the daily round on this quite mundane earth. The modern metaphysical movement is a striking example of how a scholarly revival can have a very stimulating effect not only on criticism but on creative work as well.

In spite of the great interest in religion of the present century, Donne's prose was much slower in making its way. Perhaps the sheer weight and volume of, say, the *LXXX Sermons* of 1640, dismayed all but the man interested in ideas, and, later on, in the development of prose style. Some of the finest work of recent years has centered on the study of Donne's prose. The application of the techniques of the new criticism has done a good deal to open up the majestic beauties of Donne's prose style, to say nothing of its liveliness and its pervasive wit. Donne in preaching to his congregation at St. Paul's preached himself, and one learns much more about the social and the personal factors in these great expressions of what was something like the central position of the Church of England in his time.

And yet in Donne the medieval background comes so often and so much alive in the Renaissance context that the Catholic reader may well find riches in his pages that most of the preacher's fellow Anglicans would miss. For to Donne the basic human issues were the issues that most mattered—how one could draw near to God in his own spirit, how he could forcibly concentrate his often distracted consciousness upon that high endeavor, how he could cooperate with the grace of God that God's purpose might be wholly fulfilled in him. Donne was far too persistently self-conscious ever to lose himself in the high contemplations of the mystics, but at his best he has caught a far-off gleam of their serene heights, and it is to their land that he would come, one feels, when all the preoccupations of this engaging world were washed away in death.

Bibliography: J. DONNE, *Poems*, ed. H. J. C. GRIERSON, 2 v. (Oxford 1912); 1 v. (1929); *Divine Poems*, ed. H. L. GARDNER (Oxford 1952); *Devotions upon Emergent Occasions*, ed. J. SPARROW (Cambridge, Eng. 1923); *ibid.*, ed. W. H. DRAPER (London 1926; pa. Ann Arbor 1959); *Sermons*, ed. G. R. POTTER and E. M. SIMPSON, 10 v. (Berkeley 1953–62); *LXXX Sermons . . . with Author's Life by Izaak Walton* (London 1640), enl. as I. WALTON, *Life of Dr. J. Donne* (London 1658); *The Lives of John Donne, Sir Henry Wotton, Richard Hooker, George Herbert and Robert Sanderson*, ed. S. B. CARTER (London 1951). E. W. GOSSE, *The Life and Letters of John Donne*, 2 v. (New York 1899; reprint Gloucester, Mass. 1959). T. S. ELIOT, *Selected Essays, 1917–1932* (new ed. New York 1950). *A Garland for John Donne, 1631–1931*, ed. T. SPENCER (Cambridge, Mass. 1931; reprinted Gloucester, Mass. 1958). J. B. LEISHMAN, *The Monarch of Wit: An Analytical and Comparative Study of the Poetry of John Donne* (5th ed. London 1962). A. STEIN, *John Donne's Lyrics: The Eloquence of Action* (Minneapolis 1962). J. WEBBER, *Contrary Music: The Prose Style of John Donne* (Madison 1963). E. S. LE COMTE, *Grace to a Witty Sinner: A Life of Donne* (New York 1965). J. CAREY, *John Donne: His Life, Mind, and Art* (New York 1981). P.R. SELLIN, *John Donne and* Calvinist *Views of Grace* (Amsterdam 1984).

[H. C. WHITE]

DONOSO, JUSTO

Chilean bishop, missionary, and scholar; b. Santiago, July 10, 1800; d. La Serena, 1868. He entered the Recoleta Dominicana in 1816 and was ordained in 1822. In October 1824, apostolic vicar MUZI granted him secularization. During 1828 to 1829 he visited the provinces of Aconcagua and Coquimbo where he did mission work and gave spiritual retreats. From 1829 to 1840, as pastor of Talca, he spent four months a year doing missionary work in the field. From 1840 to 1844 he was professor of theology at the seminary of Santiago, which he directed in 1843. In 1845 he took charge of the Diocese of Ancud and he was consecrated in 1849. He made his pastoral visitation, founded the seminary, and built the cathedral and several churches. In 1852 he went to the Diocese of La Serena where his work was similar to that in Ancud. In 1867 he was elected senator and minister of justice and education, a position he held for only a short time. In addition to being a man of action, he was a scholar and author of *Instituciones de derecho canónico americano, Diccionario teológico-canónico,* and *Manual del párroco americano.*

Bibliography: L. F. PRIETO DEL RÍO, *Diccionario biográfico del clero secular de Chile* (Santiago de Chile 1922) 189–191.

[A. M. ESCUDERO]

DONOSO CORTÉS, JUAN FRANCISCO MARÍA DE LA SALUD

Spanish statesman and writer on philosophy, politics, history, and theology; b. Valle de Serena (Extremadura), May 9, 1809; d. Paris, May 5, 1853. Donoso, son of a lawyer and landowner, studied civil law at the universities of Salamanca and Seville (1820–28). His student's zeal for the Enlightenment ended in skepticism tending to eclecticism. In 1832 he supported liberal constitutional monarchy under María Cristina against the Carlist absolutists. Having first taught literature at Cáceres (1829–30), he took up work in the Ministry of Justice in Madrid (1833). Between 1834 and 1838 he emerged as a leading political theorist of the moderate party. His writings and Atheneum lectures presented an influential synthesis of bourgeois LIBERALISM upholding the monarchy and the Church. He followed Cousin's eclecticism and Guizot's doctrinaire liberalism until about 1842, when he turned toward the quasi-theological TRADITIONALISM and conservatism of Joseph Marie de MAISTRE and Louis Gabriel Ambroise de BONALD, with whom he was later ranked. During Espartero's era (1840–43), he was an exile in France defending María Cristina's claims. As a deputy in the Cortes after 1843, he edited a conservative reform of the constitution, but in 1845 called for a liberal relationship of Church and State based on "mutual independence." In 1846 he became Marqués de Valdegamas, and in 1847 he entered the Spanish Academy with a beautiful address on the Bible.

Donoso experienced a "conversion" in 1847 because of his brother's death and his belief that a new era was beginning in which Europe would need a "dogmatic" philosophy and politics. He became fervently religious in thought and action, studied traditionalism and theology, and imitated the charity of St. VINCENT DE PAUL. He welcomed the liberal reforms of PIUS IX (1847) as a "dogmatic" example of "Catholic liberty" that presaged other papal teachings for modern society, but after the revolutions of 1848 he was persuaded that only conservative dictatorship and general religious revival—not liberal concessions—could save society from anarchy. His "Speech on Dictatorship" (1849) made him famous as Europe's theorist of reaction. Metternich, Frederick William IV, Pius IX, Guizot, Louis Napoleon, Ranke, Schelling, and Brownson all esteemed his ideas, and Veuillot and Montalembert became his friends.

Becoming an authoritarian democrat and rejecting middle-class liberalism, Donoso advocated a new order based on Catholic social teachings, which might be introduced through salutary reforms by vigilant governments but which would depend for success upon a moral and religious revival. This was a theme of his great parliamentary "Speech on Europe" (1850), in which he saw a rationalistic and materialistic Europe heading for revolutionary and socialistic "catastrophe"; in his view, only Catholicism could save civilization. As ambassador in Paris (1851–53) he hoped in vain that Louis Napoleon would sponsor a renewed "concert of Europe" and a pattern for conservative reform. After 1852 he expected the revolution eventually to spread around the world, to bring first demagogic anarchy, then a despotic and anti-Christian communist world-state, and finally socialistic anarchy and barbarism. If a religious renewal came in time, liberalism and socialism might turn Christian; otherwise, Christianity would rebuild world civilization on the ruins.

Donoso's *Ensayo sobre el catolicismo, el liberalismo, y el socialismo* (Barcelona 1851) was a prophetic criticism of rationalism, middle-class liberalism, and nascent socialism, but it also offered a theory of order based on theology. Conservative Catholics hailed it; liberal Catholics thought its "absolutes" and paradoxes misrepresented the Catholic position theologically, politically, and historically. His letter to Cardinal Fornari (1852) has been called his "syllabus of errors," anticipating the papal document. His letters to Montalembert (1849) pres-

ented St. Augustine's "two cities" as "Catholic civilization" vs. "philosophic civilization," and the *Ensayo* has been called his "City of God." His philosophy (or theology) of history drew also on Vico and the Apocalypse.

Bibliography: *Obras completas*, ed. J. JURETSCHKE, 2 v. (*Biblioteca de autores cristianos* 7; 1946). E. SCHRAMM, *Donoso Cortés: Leben und Werke eines spanischen Antiliberalen* (Hamburg 1935). P. D. WESTEMEYER, *Donoso Cortés: Staatsmann und Theologe* (Münster 1940). T. P. NEILL, *They Lived the Faith* (Milwaukee 1951) 242–266. P. R. VIERECK, *Conservatism* (New York 1956). J. CHAIX-RUY, *Donoso Cortés: Théologien de l'histoire et prophète* (Paris 1956). J. T. GRAHAM, *Donoso Cortés on Liberalism* (doctoral diss. microfilm; St. Louis U. 1957). B. MONSEGÚ, *Clave teológica de la historia según Donoso Cortés* (Badajoz 1958).

[J. T. GRAHAM]

DONUS, POPE

Pontificate: Nov. 2, 676 to Apr. 11, 678; b. Rome; d. Rome. In the controversy over MONOTHELITISM, Theodore, Patriarch of Constantinople, sent him a vague letter that urged unity but did not contain the expected profession of faith. But on Aug. 12, 678, Emperor CONSTANTINE IV POGONATUS sent a conciliatory letter asking Donus to dispatch representatives to a theological conference preparatory to a possible council. Donus was already dead but this council would mark the end of the schism between Constantinople and Rome. Archbishop Reparatus of Ravenna seems to have submitted to Donus, healing a schism created by his ambitious predecessor, Maurus. In Rome, Donus disbanded a monastery of Syrian Nestorians. He rebuilt and decorated several churches. A so-called Donus II (974) resulted from a chronicler's mistranslation of *Dominus papa* as *Donus papa*.

Bibliography: *Liber pontificalis*, ed. L. DUCHESNE (Paris 1886–1958) 1:348–349. P. JAFFÉ, *Regesta pontificum romanorum ab condita ecclesia ad annum post Christum natum 1198* (Graz 1956) 1:238. P. F. KEHR, *Regesta Pontificum Romanorum. Italia Pontificia* (Berlin 1906–35) 5:33. F. DÖLGER, *Corpus der griechischen Urkunden des Mittelalters und der neueren Zeit* (Munich 1924–32) 242. J. D. MANSI, *Sacrorum Conciliorum nova et amplissima collectio* (Graz 1960) 11:196–201. C. J. VON HEFELE, *Histoire des conciles d'après les documents originaux* (Paris 1907–38) 3.1:472. H. K. MANN, *The Lives of the Popes in the Early Middle Ages from 590 to 1304* (London 1902–32) 1.2. A. FLICHE and V. MARTIN, eds. *Histoire de l'église depuis les origines jusqu'à nos jours* (Paris 1935) 5. J. HALLER, *Das Papsttum* (Stuttgart 1950–53) 1. H. MAROT, *Dictionnaire d'histoire et de géographie ecclésiastiques*, ed. A. BAUDRILLART et al. (Paris 1912) 14:671–672. S. GASPARRI, *Dizionario biografico delgi italiani* 41 (Rome 1992). G. SCHWAIGER, *Lexikon für Theologie und Kirche*, 3d. ed. (1995). J. N. D. KELLY, *Oxford Dictionary of Popes* (New York 1986) 77.

[C. M. AHERNE]

Dr. Thomas A. Dooley. (©Bettmann/CORBIS)

DOOLEY, THOMAS ANTHONY

Doctor and humanitarian, who helped to organize the Medical International Corporation (MEDICO); b. St. Louis, Mo., Jan. 17, 1927; d. New York, N.Y., Jan. 18, 1961. As the son of a well-to-do St. Louis family, Dooley graduated from Notre Dame University, Ind., and the St. Louis University medical school. After two years' service as a U.S. Navy doctor in Indo-China, he resigned from the service and with three other former medical corpsmen offered to establish a privately financed medical mission in Laos. In 1958 the International Rescue Committee agreed to take Dr. Dooley's "Operation Laos" under its aegis, and MEDICO was organized to provide medical care in remote areas. Less than a year later, Dooley contracted melanoma, a rapidly diffusing form of cancer, which despite frequent hospitalization and an operation soon caused his death. Within five years, Dooley oversaw the establishment of seven hospitals in four Asian nations, and personally raised almost two million dollars for MEDICO. He made numerous speaking tours and published *Deliver Us From Evil* (1956), *The Edge of Tomorrow* (1958), *The Night They Burned the Mountain* (1960), and *Dr. Tom Dooley, My Story* (1960). On May 27, 1961, the U.S. Congress authorized the striking of the

Thomas A. Dooley medal in recognition of the Catholic missionary doctor's contributions to humanity.

Bibliography: A. W. DOOLEY, *Promises to Keep* (New York 1962).

[J. Q. FELLER]

DOORS, CHURCH

By virtue of their scale, location and materials church doors have provided opportunities for important and impressive artistic works throughout the Christian centuries, up to the Renaissance and beyond. Church doors received from pagan palaces and temples communicate the concept of monumentality, the architectural subdivision into rectangular panels framed with decorative designs, the familiar lions' masks supporting the knockers and the all-important method of casting the doors in bronze, which was favored over wood during the Middle Ages and the Italian Renaissance. From late Roman times came the special technique of bronze inlaid with silver.

Church doors have served simultaneously to glorify God and to instruct the illiterate; and, as the threshold to

Portal of the church of S. Marcello in Capua. The doorframe was probably carved in the 12th century. The painting is from a later date. (Alinari-Art Reference/Art Resource, NY)

Bronze doors, detail, engraved scenes of events or miracles wrought by the Archangel Michael, in the Sanctuary of S. Michele, Gargano, Monte S. Angelo, Italy, 1076. (Alinari-Art Reference/Art Resource, NY)

the sacred, they have prepared the faithful for their spiritual experience within. Accordingly, their themes have ranged from the fall of man and the lives of the Saints to the glory of Christ, and have reflected in their iconography and style changes in belief and artistic sensibility throughout the centuries.

Early Christian. The wooden doors of S. Sabina, Rome, the most celebrated and best preserved from this period (*c.* 432), consist of 28 panels in alternating larger and smaller pairs, of which 18 remain, and probably presented a *concordantia* of the two Testaments. The nonrealistic Crucifixion panel of these doors is one of the earliest examples of the subject in Christian art. Other panel themes of disputed identity are probably connected with imperial iconography. Iconographic and stylistic elements suggest an Oriental origin for the doors.

Byzantine. The most important of doors in bronze, a medium favored by Byzantium, is a series from the 11th century, all now in Italy. Executed mainly between 1062 and 1087 to the order of an Amalfian family, they are located at Amalfi, in the abbey church of Monte Cassino, St. Paul-Outside-the-Walls (badly preserved), S. Michele in Gargano on Monte S. Angelo, and Attrani and Salerno cathedrals. All are executed in the niello technique—the design is inlaid in the flat, bronze plaque in silver and gold. The Amalfi doors consist of 24 plaques attached to the wood and framed by metal bands. On 16 of these plaques, bronze crosses are nailed, and the four central panels represent Christ, the Virgin, St. Peter and St. Andrew in inlaid silver. Faces and extremities consist of silver in thin plates, on which details of the features have been delicately engraved.

The most beautiful of the doors in this category are those of the great church of S. Michele in Gargano, embodying a song of praise for the Archangel in 23 panels depicting his great deeds: he expels Adam from Eden,

Bronze doors by Edward Scharff for the church in Marienthal, Germany, 1950. The twenty vignettes are a pictorial rendering of the Creed.

rescues Isaac from sacrifice, struggles with Jacob, overcomes Lucifer, protects the three youths from the fire and appears to the bishop of Siponte. In the simple but expressive style, reflecting Byzantine manuscripts, the silver line flowing over the bronze adds sublimity to the remarkably moving figures. An inscription identifies the donor, Pantaleon of Amalfi, and states that the doors were cast in Constantinople in 1076. In 1087 Pantaleon's son presented to the church of Atrani a pair of bronze doors virtually identical to those of nearby Amalfi, the main difference being the substitution of St. Sebastian for St. Andrew. Also imitations of the Amalfi doors and likewise cast in Constantinople are the somewhat larger doors at Salerno.

These Byzantine doors inspired a further series made in Italy during the following century in which the niello technique is extensively replaced by relief in the bronze itself: Troia, Canosa, Trani, Pisa and Ravello. Among these doors the stylistic and iconographic debt to Byzan-

tine ivories is best exemplified in those of Trani, the work of Barisanus of Trani (1175).

Romanesque. Following the apocalyptic threat of the year 1000 the search for new artistic form in western Europe was reflected in a series of bronze doors found in Germany, Russia, Poland and Italy, which reveal the great initial indebtedness of Western medieval monumental sculpture to book illumination. Their new technique and concept of form are best exemplified in the doors cast for Archbishop Bernward of Hildesheim for the cathedral of St. Michael in 1015. They were the first sculptured bronze doors in the West to be cast in one piece since Roman times and probably were originally inspired by the doors of S. Sabina in Rome and S. Ambrosius in Milan. The two leaves of the door present Genesis scenes and episodes from Christ's life. They owe their style to Carolingian and Ottonian miniatures. The figures, widely spaced, seem lost in empty backgrounds, their three-dimensional heads recalling those in Limoges enamels. But the stories are effective in the narrative sense. The Fall is told with simplicity and charm; in the Expulsion, while Adam prepares to endure his fate Eve still glances backward as if hoping that God will recall His command.

Next to Hildesheim the other important center of bronze casting in Germany during the Ottonian period was Magdeburg, with which the doors of the cathedral of S. Sophia in Novgorod, originally intended for the Polish cathedral of Plock, are related. Latin and Cyrillic inscriptions, not all of the same date, clarify the representations, which constitute dramatic interpretations of religious beliefs. Old Testament scenes complement episodes from the life of Christ. Included are a number of allegorical figures whose significance is not clear. Choice of subject and iconography reveal the influence of French art, thus indicating artistic relations between regional divisions of medieval Europe.

Such relations are also exemplified among Italian doors, especially those of S. Zeno at Verona (end of 11th century and product of an Italian workshop), which are strongly influenced by Spanish miniatures.

Renaissance and Post-Renaissance. In the 13th century the architectural development of the portals of Gothic cathedrals caused a decline of sculptured doors, but the Italian Renaissance revived them. Most celebrated are the east bronze doors of the Baptistery of Florence, Ghiberti's masterpiece (1425–52), called by Michelangelo "Porta del Paradiso." Old Testament scenes are displayed in 16 large panels, with charming pictorial details, which complement the sculptor's earlier north doors (1403–24) devoted to the life of Christ. Their serene style reveals the master's excellence in combining the styles of goldsmith and sculptor.

Bibliography: H. LECLERCQ, *Dictionnaire d'archéologie chrétienne et de liturgie,* eds., F. CABROL, H. LECLERCQ and H. I. MARROU, 15 v. (Paris 1907–53) 14.1:1504–23. O. M. DALTON, *Byzantine Art and Archaeology* (Oxford 1911) 146–149, 616–620. J. BECKWITH, *The Art of Constantinople* (London 1961) 120. H. LEISINGER, *Romanesque Bronzes: Church Portals in Medieval Europe* (London 1956). A. CHASTEL, *Italian Art,* tr. P. and L. MURRAY (New York 1963) 121, 122, 162–163, 416, 491. J. WIEGAND, *Das altchristliche Hauptportal an der Kirche der hl. Sabina* (Trier 1900). E. H. KANTOROWICZ, "The King's Advent and the Enigmatic Panels in the Doors of Santa Sabina," *Art Bulletin,* 26 (1944) 207–231. A. GOLDSCHMIDT, *Die deutschen Bronzetüren des frühen Mittelalters* (Marburg 1926). A. BOECKLER, *Die Bronzetür von Verona* (Marburg 1932). E. N. ROGERS, *La Chapelle de Notre Dame du Haut à Ronchamp de Le Corbusier* (Milan 1956).

[G. GALAVARIS]

DÖPFNER, JULIUS

Cardinal; b. Hausen, Germany, Aug. 26, 1913; d. Munich, July 25, 1976. After courses in philosophy and theology in Rome, Döpfner was ordained to the priesthood there Oct. 29, 1939, for the Diocese of Würzburg. Two years later, he received a doctorate in theology at the Gregorian University, and was assigned to Schweinfurt, where he was chaplain to thousands of displaced person's from East Germany. During the postwar years, while on the staff of the diocesan seminary, he promoted cooperative housing for the numerous war refugees. Named bishop of Würzburg by PIUS XII, he was ordained in the local cathedral, Oct. 14, 1948. He was transferred to the Diocese of Berlin on Jan. 17, 1957, where he labored to achieve a sense of unity between the Catholics of West and East Berlin, and was renowned as a rebuilder of the churches destroyed during the war.

Created a cardinal by JOHN XXIII on Dec. 15, 1958, he was then named Archbishop of Munich and Freising. Here, as a leading figure of the German hierarchy, Döpfner had a significant role in the preparations for VATICAN COUNCIL II. In June of 1960, for example, he chaired the gathering of German bishops on preparations for the Council. Thereafter, he was named a member of the Central Preparatory Commission and, at the same time, to the Committee on Technical Arrangements. During the first session he became a member of the Secretariat for Extraordinary Matters and was also appointed to the Commission for Coordination. For the succeeding sessions, with cardinals AGAGIANIAN, Lercaro, and SUENENS, he was named by the Holy Father to the key post of Moderator of the Council.

Döpfner's is probably most important for his influence on the framing of *Lumen gentium,* especially because of his insistence on the need to go beyond a legalistic concept of the Church and to stress the Church *as mystery.* Sanctity, he pointed out, is bestowed on man through the mediation of Christ *and* of the Church, insofar as it is the primordial Sacrament of Christ. Later he was involved with a number of other cardinals in the delicate issues of religious freedom and the Church's relationship with Judaism.

Between the sessions of the Council, Döpfner organized and conducted numerous episcopal gatherings, notably the meeting of the European bishops at Fulda in August of 1963. When the Council ended, he continued to be associated with its programs. In 1963 he was named to the Commission for the Revision of the Code of Canon Law and became a familiar figure at the meetings of the Synod of Bishops.

Bibliography: H. FESQUET, *The Drama of Vatican II,* tr. B. MURCHLAND (New York 1967). *L'Osservatore Romano* English edition 31 (435) July 29, 1976, 8; 36 (436) Aug. 5, 1976, 2. H. VORGRIMLER et al., eds., *Commentary on the Documents of Vatican II* (New York 1967–69).

[P. F. MULHERN]

DORCHESTER, ABBEY OF

Former house of the CANONS REGULAR OF ST. AUGUSTINE, Oxfordshire, England, LINCOLN Diocese, present-day Oxford Diocese. Its patrons were SS. Peter, Paul, and Birinus. The abbey was founded *c.* 1140 by Bishop Alexander of Lincoln, who replaced the secular canons left from the bishopric before the time of the Conquest, with 13 Augustinian canons, probably of the Arrouasian congregation, to which the monastery remained affiliated. Canons from Dorchester colonized Lilleshall monastery (1143–48). Dorchester claimed the bones of the 7th-century St. BIRINUS. The large church was built mainly from the late 12th to the mid-14th century. Visitations after 1441 found an exceptionally disorderly community, numbering ten or 12. Its 1535 income was £190; the house was suppressed in 1536.

Bibliography: No known chartulary or chronicle. H. E. SALTER, ed., *Chapters of the Augustinian Canons* (Oxford 1922) 136, 277. A. H. THOMPSON, ed., *Visitations in the Diocese of Lincoln . . . 1420–1449,* 3 v. (Horncastle 1914–29); *Visitations in the Diocese of Lincoln* 1517–1531 3 v. (Hereford 1940–47). *The Victoria History of the County of Oxford,* ed. L. F. SALZMAN et al. (London 1907–) v. 2, 8. E. H. CORDEAUX and D. H. MERRY, *A Bibliography . . . Oxfordshire* (Oxford 1955).

[S. WOOD]

DORLAND, PETER (DORLANDUS)

Carthusian spiritual writer; b. 1454, Walcourt, Belgium; d. at the Zeelhem charterhouse near Diest (Brabant), Aug. 25, 1507. Nothing is known of his life except that he studied at Louvain University, entered the Carthusians at Zeelhem *c.* 1475, lived piously and humbly, and endured a long illness with great patience. Some 60 of his works in Latin are known, and of these seven have been published. The Carthusian Petreius edited (Cologne 1608) the first seven books of his *Chronicon Cartusiense,* which Dorland himself called *Corona Cartusiana;* it is a somewhat uncritical collection of pious stories. His hagiographical works are mostly sermons. His ascetical writings are partly monastic (on Carthusian observances), partly devotional (hymns, prayers, reflections on the rosary, the Passion, etc.), and partly on the spiritual life. His *Viola animae,* a dialogue between the Blessed Virgin and ''Dominicus'' (servant of the Lord), is notable for its literary excellence and, in spite of some dependence upon Ludolph of Saxony's *Vita Christi,* for its originality. In it Dorland made much of the idea, prominent in modern Mariology, that Mary at the foot of the Cross was the type and representative of the Church. Translations of the *Viola* have been published down to our own day. There is some evidence for crediting Dorland with the authorship of the famous allegorical play *Elckerlyc* (*Everyman* in English; *Jedermann* in German).

Bibliography: S. AUTORE, *Dictionnaire de théologie catholique,* ed. A. VACANT et al. (Paris 1903–50) 4.2:1782–85. L. MOEREELS, *Dictionnaire de spiritualité ascétique et mystique. Doctrine et histoire,* ed. M. VILLER et al. (Paris 1932–) 3:1646–51.

[B. DU MOUSTIER]

DORMITION OF THE VIRGIN

The phrase ''Dormition of the Virgin,'' which literally means the falling asleep of the Virgin, figuratively refers to MARY's death. From New Testament times Christians referred to death as sleep. St. Paul wrote of deceased Christians as ''those . . . who have fallen asleep through Jesus'' (1 Thes 4.14). The deep faith that Christians had in life after death and the resurrection when the body would be eternally reunited to the soul, led them to view death not as the end of everything but as a transition into another life in which the body fell asleep and rested until awakened into eternal glory. Thus they looked upon the death of the saints and martyrs with joy and commemorated the day of their ''falling asleep'' as their ''birthday'' into a new life.

Exactly when the Dormition of the Virgin first occupied the attention of the Christians is not known, but by the end of the 5th century the event was vigorously present in religious literature and the sacred liturgy.

The most vivid concern for Mary's dormition appeared in a body of apocryphal literature called by mod-

ern scholars the *Transitus Mariae*—the passing of Mary. These writings, some of which date back to at least the second half of the 5th century, were written to supply for the silence of Sacred Scriptures about Mary's death. They were highly imaginative and, by and large, fictitious. But they satisfied the yearning of Christians to know more about Mary's death. They describe in great detail Mary's last hours. Though they differ markedly from one another in length, language, and detail, they do manifest a similarity in narration that may be schematized thus: Mary's death is foretold by an angel or by Christ; some or all of the Apostles are miraculously gathered together to assist Mary and receive her blessing; Christ comes and takes Mary's soul into heaven; her body is carried by the Apostles to the valley of Josaphat for burial; the Jews plot to burn the body but are foiled by the Holy Spirit; the Apostles keep vigil at the grave; after a short or long period there is finally an assumption of Mary's body into paradise.

Such imaginative accounts of Mary's dormition, though not strictly historical, are not without value. Beneath their fiction they manifest the beliefs of the early Christians concerning the MOTHER OF GOD. In them especially is found early evidence of belief in the bodily ASSUMPTION OF MARY. This same belief is manifested in the liturgical feast of the Dormition of Mary.

As a liturgical feast the Dormition was celebrated at least as early as the end of the 6th century. At that time Emperor Maurice (582–602) decreed that the feast be celebrated on August 15 throughout the entire Byzantine Empire.

The Emperor's decree became a stabilizing factor in a development toward this feast that had begun early in the 5th century. At that time a feast in honor of the Blessed Mother of God was celebrated on August 15 at a Jerusalem church called Kathisma (meaning in Greek ''rest''). The feast did not commemorate any single prerogative of Mary, but all her perfections and privileges as the Mother of God. By the beginning of the 6th century one hears of a basilica in Gethsemane that claims to possess the cherished tomb of the Virgin Mary. It too celebrates Mary's feast of August 15, but, owing to the belief that Mary's tomb is there and to the widespread popularity of the apocryphal works on Mary's dormition, emphasis in the celebration is now put on Mary's death with its extraordinary circumstances.

With the Emperor's decree establishing the annual feast throughout the empire, preachers began to speak more often on Mary's dormition. From their discourses one gets a deeper insight to the meaning of the feast. Sermons by St. Modestus of Jerusalem (d. *c.* 634), St. Andrew of Crete (d. 740), and St. John Damascene (d. *c.*

750) show that the object of the feast was not only Mary's death but also the glorification of her soul and body.

The feast of the Dormition of Mary has continued to be celebrated in the Oriental liturgies to the present day, though it is now more commonly called the "Assumption" or the "Journey of the Blessed Mother of God into Heaven." The feast embodies belief in Mary's bodily Assumption.

The feast was adopted in Rome during the 7th century. Pope Sergius I (687–701) ordered a solemn procession to be celebrated on the feast. From its beginning in the West the feast centered on Mary's bodily glorification, and thus by the end of the 8th century the title had already been changed from the Dormition to the Feast of the Assumption.

For a discussion of theological opinion on the question of Mary's death, *see* ASSUMPTION OF MARY.

See Also: MARIAN FEASTS.

Bibliography: M. JUGIE, *La Mort et l'Assomption de la sainte Vierge: Étude historico-doctrinale* (*Studi e Testi* 114; Vatican City 1944). R. H. CHABOT, "Feasts in Honor of Our Lady," J. B. CAROL, ed., *Mariology,* 3 v. (Milwaukee 1954–61) 3:22–52. W. BURGHARDT, "The Testimony of the Patristic Age concerning Mary's Death," *Marian Studies* 8 (1957) 58–59. H. HOLSTEIN, "Le Développement du dogme marial," *Maria* 6 (1961) 241–293, bibliog. 291–293. M. R. JAMES, tr., *The Apocryphal New Testament: Being the Apocryphal Gospels, Acts, Epistles, and Apocalypses . . .* (Oxford 1924).

[D. F. HICKEY]

DOROTHEA VON MONTAU, ST.

Also called Dorothea of Prussia; first native saint of Prussia and Patroness of Prussia; b. village of Montau, 1347; d. 1394. Dorothea was the seventh child of a prosperous peasant household. When Dorothea was seven, she was scalded with hot water over most of her body, and while being nursed back to health, she experienced her first mystic vision of Christ, an experience that continued through her lifetime. Upon her recovery, Dorothea began a regimen of harsh mortifications of the flesh. She was compelled at age 17 to marry a weaponsmith from Gdansk, who was more than twice her age. Dorothea suffered physical, verbal, and emotional abuse at her husband's hands. She chafed at the need to comply with his wishes fearing that it would impede her relationship with God. She was said to have mourned the loss of her virginity and hated the birth of each of her children. Finally, after the birth of her ninth child, Dorothea was able to persuade her husband to agree to a life of marital chastity. Her husband died in 1390.

In 1391, Dorothea was accused of being a part of the Free Spirit movement. Her irregular behavior at Mass attracted attention because she was taken up in ecstasy in anticipation of receiving the Eucharist, and she often failed to stand during the elevation of the host. Although the charge of heresy was dropped, it became obvious that she needed a confessor to guide and counsel her. With the help of Johannes Marienwerder, she secured permission to build and dwell in an anchoress' cell.

After Dorothea's death in 1394, Johannes took it upon himself to spread her cult, and wrote an account of her life and visions. Numerous miracles were attributed to her, and her tomb became a local pilgrimage site. Dorothea was never officially canonized, but in 1976, Pope Paul VI confirmed her cult as saint based on long-standing veneration. In art, Dorothea is usually depicted holding a lantern and a rosary, and is often surrounded by arrows, meant to represent the many afflictions she suffered and overcame during her life.

Bibliography: J. VON MARIENWERDER, *The Life of Dorothea von Montau, A Fourteenth-Century Recluse,* Trans. by U. STARGARDT (Studies in Women and Religion 39; Lewiston, NY 1997). R. KIECKHEFER, *Unquiet Souls: Fourteenth-Century Saints and their Religious Milieu* (Chicago 1984). D. ELLIOTT, *Authorizing a Life: The Collaboration of Dorothea of Montau and John Marienwerder,* in *Gendered Voices: Medieval Saints and Their Interpreters,* ed. C. M. MOONEY (Philadelphia 1999).

[M. SAUER]

DOROTHEANS

(SSD, Official Catholic Directory #3790); formally known as the Institute of the Sisters of St. Dorothy, founded by (St.) Paola FRASSINETTI in 1834 at Quinto, Italy. This pontifical congregation, with its generalate in Rome, Italy, follows rules based on those of St. IGNATIUS OF LOYOLA. The first United States foundations were made in 1911 in New York and Providence, Rhode Island, at the invitation of Cardinal John Farley and Bishop Matthew Harkins, respectively. Its members work in schools, pastoral centers, and in outreach to homeless and immigrants. The U.S. provincialate is in Bristol, Rhode Island.

Bibliography: J. UMFREVILLE, *A Foundress in Nineteenth Century Italy* (New York 1939). M. DE PIRO, *Paula* (Fall River, Mass. 1958). M. DE PIRO et al., *A Golden Anniversary: North American Province* (Taunton, Mass. 1961).

[M. MORRIS/EDS.]

DOROTHEUS

The name of several ecclesiastics in the early and medieval church.

Dorotheus of Antioch, priest of the School of Antioch *c.* 300, was an authority on the Hebrew language and on Scripture, which he publicly explicated. He became an administrator in the imperial palace. He was admired by EUSEBIUS OF CAESAREA (*Histoire ecclesiastique* 7.32).

Dorotheus of Gaza, 6th-century monk of the convent of Seridon who founded a monastery near Gaza *c.* 535, gave extremely successful sermons to his monks on cenobitism and monastic virtues. His principal sources were BASIL of Caesarea and EVAGRIUS PONTICUS.

Dorotheus of Mytilene, 15th-century Byzantine bishop, d. before July 1444, worked tirelessly for union between the Greeks and Latins at the Council of Ferrara-FLORENCE and wrote a discourse on the siege of Constantinople in June 1422. Whether he wrote a session-by-session history of the Council of Florence is disputed.

Bibliography: J. QUASTEN et al., *Lexikon für Theologie und Kirche* (Freiburg 1957–65) 3:524–526. G. BARDY and V. LAURENT, *Catholicisme* 3:1039–40.

[P. ROCHE]

St. Dorothy, detail of a reliquary, Treasury, Cattedrale di Santa Eufemia, Grado, Italy, 14th century. (© Elio Ciol/Corbis-Bettmann)

DOROTHY, ST.

Died Caesarea, Cappadocia, *c.* 304. She is numbered among the martyrs of the DIOCLETIAN persecution. The *Passio* narrating her life is full of legendary material, stating that she was born in Caesarea, and that, after converting two women sent to make her apostatize, she was beheaded. She was greatly honored during the Middle Ages, became a favorite subject for German and Italian artists, and is represented holding a basket containing three roses and three apples and attended by an angel. Her feast was removed from the universal calendar in 1969.

Feast: Feb. 6.

Bibliography: *The Icelandic Legend of Saint Dorothy,* ed. K. WOLF (Toronto 1997). A. SCHRÖDER, *Dorothy,* tr. H. H. ROSENWALD (Recklinghausen, Germany 1967). R. VAN DOREN, *Dictionnaire d'histoire et de géographie ecclésiastiques* (Paris 1912–), 14:684. A. BUTLER, *The Lives of the Saints,* ed. H. THURSTON and D. ATTWATER (New York 1956) 1:261–262.

[E. G. RYAN]

DOSITHEUS OF SAMARIA

The name of one or more Samaritan heresiarchs placed variously between the third century B.C. and the first Christian century or even later, in Palestine. The sources—Jewish, Patristic, Samaritan, and Arabic—are confused as to the origins, beliefs, practices, and development of his sect (the Dositheans), and provide little information about their founder. It is possible that there were two sects (and even two heresiarchs) of the same name, an earlier one in the pre-Christian era that was characterized by a denial of resurrection of the dead and a later one in the Christian era that affirmed this doctrine. Perhaps, also, each was in consonance with the dominant Sadducean and Pharisaic convictions in this regard in the respective periods. In any case, the Dosithean heresy is the most prominent of the various Samaritan offshoots.

While it is difficult to determine the periods to which the various descriptions of the Dositheans apply, they are portrayed as strict observers of Levitical purity, possessors of a calendar of unvarying 30-day months, vegetarians, and ascetics. They are reported to have abolished the biblical fast days and to have substituted Elohim (God) for the Tetragrammaton (YHWH) in their Pentateuch in order to avoid the profanation of the Divine Name.

Bibliography: A. JÜLICHER, *Paulys Realenzyklopädie der klassischen Altertumswissenschaft,* ed. G. WISSOWA et al. (Stuttgart 1893–) 10:1608–09. J. MACDONALD, *Theology of the Samaritans* (London 1964) 34–36. S. KRAUS, ''Dosithée et les Dosithéens,'' *Revue des études latines* 42 (Paris 1901) 27–42. J. BOWMAN, ''The Importance of Samaritan Researches,'' *Annual of Leeds University, Oriental Society* 1 (1959) 43–45. M. GASTER, *The Samaritans: Their History, Doctrines and Literature* (London 1925) 66–67. J. A. MONTGOMERY, *The Samaritans* (Philadelphia 1907) 252–264. *The Jewish Encyclopedia,* ed. J. SINGER 13 v. (New York 1901–06) 4:643. *Encyclopaedia Judaica: Das Judentum in Geschichte und Gegenwart* 10 v. (Berlin 1928–34) 5:1202–05. K. SCHUBERT, *Lexikon für Theologie und Kirche,* ed. J. HOFER and K. RAHNER, 10 v. (2d, new ed. Freiburg 1957–65) 3:527–528.

[R. KRINSKY]

Fĕdor Mikhaĭlovich Dostoevskiĭ.

DOSTOEVSKIĬ, FĔDOR MIKHAĬLOVICH

Russian novelist; b. Moscow, Oct. 30, 1821; d. St. Petersburg, Jan. 28, 1881. His family, although impoverished, was of the nobility. His father Michael was physician to a Moscow orphanage; his gentle and pious mother died when he was 17 years old. Fĕdor received a deeply religious formation from her, and as a child he used to accompany her to churches and monasteries in Moscow, where the services impressed and attracted him. These early religious experiences were to become important factors in his life and writings.

In spite of his love for his mother, Fĕdor found the home atmosphere cold and depressing under his martinet father. In 1837, the boy was enrolled in the school of military engineering in St. Petersburg, but he disliked and even resented the studies and military regime. His main and growing interest was in literature and the humanities. He avidly read Russian, French, and English classics, especially Balzac and Dickens. A bitter quarrel with his father ended tragically when that harsh man was murdered by his own ill-treated serfs. Appalled and shocked, Fĕdor suffered the first of the epileptic seizures that were to become increasingly frequent. After graduation, he embarked on a writer's career, and his first short story,

"Bédnye lyúdi" (1846, Poor People), won immediate recognition.

Suffering and Self-Realization. Dostoevskiĭ's rising fame was soon eclipsed. In 1849, he was charged with having taken part in a socialist underground movement, although actually he had merely attended the group's meeting. Arrested, tried, and condemned to death, he was pardoned at the last instant in the very place of his impending execution. He was taken in chains to Siberia, where he endured four years of hard labor among common criminals. His health and nerves were wrecked, but his spirit remained unbroken. His only book, a New Testament given him by a charitable woman who visited prisoners, sustained him and led him to a deep penetration of Christian mysteries and of the meaning of suffering. After his release, he was still obliged to serve in a regiment on the Siberian border. There he married a young widow, Maria Isayeva. Soon estranged from her, Dostoevskiĭ began to gamble and went abroad with a young and beautiful girl, Polina Suslova. When she returned his passionate love with coldness and finally left him, he returned to Maria, who was dying of tuberculosis. Deep remorse assailed him after her death and his epilepsy grew worse.

It was, however, in this period of deep distress and self-examination that he began to write his major novels—the first, *Prestupleniye i Nakazaniye* (*Crime and Punishment*), was published in 1866. A year later he married his stenographer, Anna Snitkina, who brought her husband love, security, and understanding. In spite of his passion for gambling, and in spite of poverty and ill health, his newly found peace of mind enabled him to continue his writing; *Idiót* (1868, *The Idiot*), *Bésy* (1871–72, *The Possessed*), and *Brátya Karamázovy* (1879–80, *The Brothers Karamazov*) firmly established his fame.

The Quality of His Great Novels. Dostoevskiĭ's physical and mental afflictions deeply influenced his writings; his relationship with his father, for instance, was the seed of his frequent depiction in his novels of tensions and conflicts between father and son, murder, brutality, and guilt complex. But far more important are the deeply human quality of his novels and their constant spiritual theme: the struggle between good and evil, the problem of sin and salvation, the rebellion of the self-willed individualist who deems himself a superman (*Crime and Punishment*) pitted against God, whose justice he refuses to accept. These were the problems that haunted Dostoevskiĭ until he found the answer—in Christ, in His humility and love (*The Idiot*), in pity for fellow men through Christ as exemplified in the Russian monastic ideal (*The Brothers Karamazov*). If the law of love is rejected, man becomes not only bestial but monstrous (*The Possessed*). This monstrous image of man prophetically foreshadowed the excesses of the Russian Revolution.

Besides the major novels mentioned above, Dostoevskiĭ wrote a number of other works: *Igrók* (1866, *The Gambler*), *Zapíski iz podpolya* (1864, *Notes from Underground*), *Večnyj muž* (1870, *The Eternal Husband*), and others. He was not only a master of fiction but a precursor of modern depth psychology and an explorer of the sick and criminal mind. He betrayed in some of his writings a negative approach to Catholicism, not surprising, perhaps, in an author who was fervent, nationalistic, and militantly Russian Orthodox.

Bibliography: Latest editions of Dostoyevsky's works in Russian: *Vospominaniía* (Leningrad 1930) and *Sobranie sochinenti* (Moscow 1956–); *The Diary of a Writer,* tr. and ed. B. BRASOL, 2 v. (New York 1949); *Letters and Reminiscences,* tr. S. S. KOTELIANSKY and J. M. MURRY (New York 1923). Literature. A. G. DOSTOEVSKAYA, *Dostoevsky Portrayed by His Wife,* tr. and ed. S. S. KOTELIANSKY (New York 1926). J. S. COULSON, *Dostoevsky, a Self-Portrait* (New York 1962). L. DOSTOEVSKAIÂ, *Fyodor Dostoyevsky, a Study* (New Haven 1922). E. J. SIMMONS, *Dostoevsky: The Making of a Novelist* (London 1950). H. TROYAT, *Firebrand,* tr. N. GUTERMAN (New York 1946). M. SLONIM, *Three Loves of Dostoevsky* (London 1955). N. A. BERDIAEV, *Dostoievsky: An Interpretation,* tr. D. ATTWATER (New York 1934). V. I. IVANOV, *Freedom and the Tragic Life,* tr. N. CAMERON (New York 1952). V. SEDURO, *Dostoyevski in Russian Literary Criticism, 1846–1956* (New York 1957). R. GUARDINI, *L'Univers religieux de Dostoievski,* tr. H. ENGLEMAN and R. GIVORD (Paris 1947). H. DE LUBAC, *The Drama of Atheist Humanism,* tr. E. M. RILEY (London 1949).

[H. ISWOLSKY]

DOSWALD, HILARY JOSEPH

Prior general; b. Saulgau, Germany, Sept. 19, 1877; d. Rome, Italy, March 2, 1951. He was born of Swiss parents. After joining the Order of Calced CARMELITES at New Baltimore, Pa., in 1894, he was ordained Aug. 6, 1900, in Pittsburgh, Pa., by Bp. Richard Phelan. He helped found St. Cyril's College (now Mount Carmel High School) in Chicago, Ill., where he became principal, prior of the monastery, and pastor of St. Cyril's parish. In 1925 he was called to Rome as English-speaking assistant general of the Carmelite Fathers. In 1931 he became prior general of the order; he served in that capacity until his retirement to Whitefriars Hall, Washington, D.C., in 1947. He also acted as consultor of the Congregation of the Sacraments in Rome.

As prior general Doswald increased the order's membership by a third. The commissariate, or preprovince of Catalonia, Spain, was established (1932), the Carmelite mission in Indonesia became a vicariate apostolic (1935), and a mission was opened in Southern Rhodesia (1946). His circular letters to the order were contributions to Carmelite spiritual writing. Two spiritual works were issued trader his direction: *Life in Carmel* (1934), papers by the novice masters of the order, and *The Carmelite Directory of the Spiritual Life* (1951), a manual for novices. Doswald also republished the liturgical books of the order: a psalter adopting the new division of the Psalms (1933), a diurnal (1935), a Missal (1935), and a Breviary (1938).

[J. SMET]

DOUAI (DOUAY)

A city in the North of France memorable to English-speaking Catholics as a center of education and missionary activity during penal times. Following Queen Elizabeth I's accession in 1558 and her Protestant religious settlement, Catholic exiles took refuge there because of its newly founded university, its proximity to the English Channel, and its location in the safely Catholic part of the Spanish Netherlands. For these same reasons William ALLEN in 1568 chose Douai as the location of an English college for the education of priests. Though its later claim to be the first seminary founded after the Tridentine decrees on the formation of the clergy fails to take into account several earlier Italian seminaries, it was surely the first such institution in northern Europe.

From its small beginnings the English College grew rapidly and within ten years as many as 20 students were ordained annually. The first seminary priest to go to England was Louis Barlow (1574) and the first one to die for the faith was Bl. Cuthbert MAYNE (1577). The real beginning of the Catholic revival in England must be dated from those years. By the end of the century Douai had sent into England more than 400 priests of whom 103 merited the martyr's crown.

The very success of the seminary caused financial problems. In 1575 Pope Gregory XIII allotted a monthly pension and later Philip II of Spain promised an annual contribution, but the payment of this latter was erratic due to the religious wars in the Netherlands. These same wars forced the College in 1578 to move to Reims, a university town in that part of France under the protection of the dukes of Guise. It returned to Douai only in 1593.

One means of relieving the financial pressure was to found other such institutions. Douai rightly claims to be the mother of the English seminaries since the first students of the English colleges in Rome (1577) and Valladolid (1589) were old Douai men. In Douai itself there were Irish and Scotch seminaries before the end of the century. Soon after, the English Benedictines (1604) and Franciscans (1618) established houses of study there. The town was also the most important publishing center for those proscribed books that nourished the piety and sharpened the controversial skills of the English Catholics during these times. The most famous of these publications was the Douai Old Testament (2 v. 1609–10).

By this time the heroic period of the English College was over. Its founder and first president, William (later Cardinal) Allen, had been able to govern the seminary without rules, but his successors, Richard Barrett (1588–99) and Thomas WORTHINGTON (1599–1613), understandably lacked Allen's charismatic gifts. Both were plagued with debts and accused of being too favorable to the Jesuits, a charge that was repeated, with even less foundation, against almost every successive president. The English secular clergy were better satisfied with the administration of Matthew Kellison (1613–41), but he in turn was accused of favoring the dangerous teachings of Thomas White (alias Blacklo).

After 1622 Douai was under the supervision of the Congregation of Propaganda. The complaints about frequent visitations, the accusations of Jansenism, and the bickering for control among various factions of the English secular clergy that fills the correspondence of these years should not blind us to the solid if unspectacular results obtained throughout the 17th and 18th centuries. In an average year there were from 70 to 90 students, some of them laymen profiting from the humanities course in the minor seminary.

Douai was thus the alma mater not only of most of England's early bishops, but also of some of her outstanding Catholic laymen. The French Revolution in 1791 drove the seminary, along with most of the other British religious houses, back to England where the repeal of some of the harsher penal laws made it possible to continue the work of education at Crook Hall (later transferred to Ushaw) and St. Edmund's, Old Hall.

Bibliography: P. K. GUILDAY, *The English Catholic Refugees on the Continent, 1558–1795* (New York 1914). *The First and Second Diaries of the English College, Douay,* ed. FATHERS OF THE CONGREGATION OF THE LONDON ORATORY (London 1878). The remaining College Diaries are published in *Proceedings of the Catholic Record Society* 10–11 (1911); 28 (1928).

[T. H. CLANCY]

DOUBLE EFFECT, PRINCIPLE OF

The Principle of Double Effect is a rule of conduct frequently used in moral theology to determine when a person may lawfully perform an action from which two effects will follow, one bad and the other good.

Conditions. Theologians commonly teach that four conditions must be verified in order that a person may legitimately perform such an act. (1) The act itself must be morally good or at least indifferent. (2) The agent may not positively will the bad effect but may merely permit it. If he could attain the good effect without the bad effect, he should do so. The bad effect is sometimes said to be indirectly voluntary. (3) The good effect must flow from the action at least as immediately (in the order of causality, though not necessarily in the order of time) as the bad effect. In other words, the good effect must be produced directly by the action, not by the bad effect. Otherwise the agent would be using a bad means to a good end, which is never allowed. (4) The good effect must be sufficiently desirable to compensate for the allowing of the bad effect. In forming this decision many factors must be weighed and compared, with care and prudence proportionate to the importance of the case. Thus, an effect that benefits or harms society generally has more weight than one that affects only an individual; an effect sure to occur deserves greater consideration than one that is only probable; an effect of a moral nature has greater importance than one that deals only with material things.

Of these four conditions the first two are general rules of morality. A person is never allowed to perform a morally bad action. Nor may one ever positively will an evil effect of an action, even though the act would otherwise be lawful. Thus, a censor of books, who is allowed to read obscene literature, may not take deliberate pleasure in the evil thoughts arising in consequence, though he necessarily permits them to enter his mind. The third and fourth conditions enumerated above pertain specifically to the principle of the double effect.

Typical Situations. Situations calling for the application of this principle occur frequently in connection with pregnancy. Thus, a pregnant woman bearing a nonviable fetus is found to have a cancerous womb that will cause her death if it is not excised as soon as possible. The operation of hysterectomy is morally lawful, for this operation is permissible in itself as a normal means of saving the woman's life. She does not positively will the death of her child, but permits it as an unavoidable evil. Both the benefit to her health and the death of the child follow from the surgery with equal directness or immediacy in the order of CAUSALITY, though the death of the child is prior in the order of time. The woman's chance of restoration to health (the good effect) is sufficiently desirable to compensate for the death of the fetus (the bad effect), which would probably not survive even if the operation were not performed.

However, if the woman is suffering from kidney disease, heart trouble, or tuberculosis, which would be easier to care for if she were relieved of the pregnancy, it would be immoral to perform an abortion. In such a case the third condition for the proper use of the principle of the double effect would be lacking. The relief to the woman would come as an effect of the abortion, not directly as an effect of the surgery. Hence, a bad means would be employed to produce a good end.

Even if the woman's life would be gravely endangered unless an abortion were performed (a situation rarely verified in view of modern medical progress), it would be a grave violation of God's law to kill directly an innocent child to save her life.

The Old Testament (1 Mc 6) contains a striking example of a lawful application of the principle of the double effect. Eleazar, a Jew, was fighting in the army of the Maccabees against an enemy force. Seeing an elephant on which he believed the king of the opposing side was riding to battle, Eleazar ran under the beast and slew it, knowing that he himself would be crushed, but hoping that he would thus kill or disable the leader of the enemy. This narrative is told in the inspired book as something commendable.

Historical Development. The discussion of the principle in its technical details is comparatively recent in Catholic theology. St. THOMAS may have visualized it when he argued in the *Summa theologiae* (2a2ae, 64.7) that a person may kill an unjust aggressor when this is necessary to save his own life. One difficulty in the application of the principle to this case, however, is that it seems to lack the third condition, since the preservation of one's own life seems to follow from the killing of the aggressor. Hence, others would decide that in this case God gives permission to the victim to protect himself, if necessary, by a direct slaying of the unjust assailant.

The principle of the double effect was developed by the theologians of the 16th and 17th centuries, especially by the Salmanticenses. However, the greatest credit in modern times for the thorough exposition of this principle as a norm applicable to the whole field of moral theology is owed to the Jesuit theologian Jean Pierre GURY.

Applications. Actually, the principle of the double effect is often used in the ordinary affairs of human life by persons who are unaware of the speculative requirements of this principle but are acting on common sense. Thus, the aviator who tests planes in order to improve aeronautic equipment, the doctor who treats patients affected with contagious diseases, the policeman who attempts to capture an armed criminal—all these are lawfully using the principle of the double effect, the bad effect being the hazard they are incurring to their own life or health, the good effect being the benefit they are conferring on society.

Not only physical evils, such as danger to life and bodily welfare, but also spiritual evils, such as the occasions of SIN, can enter into the application of the principle of the double effect. Thus, a young couple soon to be married may be in the proximate occasion of SINS of impurity when they are together. Nevertheless, through a reasonable application of the principle of the double effect, such association may be permitted, the good effect, which consists in the normal benefits of lawful courtship with a view to marriage in the near future compensating for the spiritual danger. Of course, they must take suitable measures to avoid sin. However, company keeping involving the proximate danger of sin is wrong for a couple who have no intention of marrying, at least within a reasonable period, since there is no adequate reason to compensate for the moral danger.

Passive SCANDAL can also be justified at times by the use of the principle of the double effect. This means that for a sufficiently good reason one may perform a lawful action even though another person makes this action the occasion of sin. Thus, a priest is justified in visiting the sick in a hospital even though a man residing nearby, on seeing the priest, becomes enraged and blasphemes.

In modern warfare the principle of the double effect is frequently applicable. Thus, in waging a just war a nation may launch an air attack on an important military objective of the enemy even though a comparatively small number of noncombatants are killed. This evil effect can be compensated for by the great benefit gained through the destruction of the target. This would not be true if the number of noncombatants slain in the attack were out of proportion to the benefits gained, as is clear from the fourth condition explained above. Furthermore, if the direct purpose of the attack were to kill a large number of noncombatants so that the morale of the enemy would be broken and they would sue for peace, the attack would be sinful because the third condition for the lawful use of the principle would not be fulfilled. Instead it would be a case of the use of a bad means to obtain a good end.

Bibliography: THOMAS AQUINAS, *Summa theologiae*, 2a2ae, 64.7. Salamanca Collegium Fratrum Discalceatorum . . . , *Cursus theologicus*. . . , v. 7 (Paris 1877) 211–213. J. P. GURY, *Compendium theologiae moralis* (New York 1874), tract. 1, ch. 2, nn. 6–10. B. H. MERKELBACH, *Summa theologiae moralis*, 3 v. (Paris 1949) 1:173–177. O. LOTTIN, *Morale fondamentale* (Tournai 1954) 265–268. F. J. CONNELL, *Outlines of Moral Theology* (Milwaukee 1964) 22–24. J. MANGAN, ''An Historical Analysis of the Principle of the Double Effect,'' *Theological Studies* 10 (1949) 40–61.

[F. J. CONNELL]

DOUBLE TRUTH, THEORY OF

The theory of double truth proposes a proposition may be false according to reason (and philosophy) and at the same time be true according to faith (and theology), or vice versa. It implies that two propositions, one of which is contrary or contradictory to the other, can be true simultaneously. For example, the immortality of the human soul might be considered false in philosophy and true in theology; or, the mortality of the human soul and the immortality of the human soul might both be regarded as true, the first in philosophy, the second in theology.

Historically this theory derives from the teaching of 13th–century Latin Averroists as interpreted by some of their adversaries (*see* AVERROISM, LATIN). It can best be understood against the background of Aristotle's impact on Western Europe.

Heterodox Aristotelianism. During the 12th and 13th centuries, works of ARISTOTLE such as the *Metaphysics, Physics* and *De anima* were introduced into Europe in Latin translation, together with commentaries by Arabian thinkers. "The Philosopher," previously admired for his logical works, in time became identified with philosophy itself. As interpreted by Arabian thinkers, especially Averroës, Aristotle seemed to be saying that only one agent and possible intellect exists for all men (*see* INTELLECT, UNITY OF) and that the world is necessary and eternal. This implicit denial of personal immortality and creation contradicted the teachings of Christian faith. How, then, could a man be at once a philosopher and a Christian?

Ibn Rushd or AVERROËS (1126–98) had faced a similar problem in Muslim Spain. While he recognized the need of religion to maintain social order, Aristotle, to him, was the "exemplar that Nature found to show forth ultimate human perfection" (*In 3 de anima,* comm. 14). Could he say, then, that religion was true when its teachings differed from Aristotle's? In *The Accord between Religion and Philosophy* he answers that religion presents in an allegorical way, suitable to simple believers, the truth that philosophers grasp in purely intelligible fashion. For him there can be no double truth, for he says, "Truth could not be contrary to truth." There is only one truth, and the philosopher attains this, not in symbols, but as it is in itself.

That the absolute truth in its precise and perfect expression is identical with philosophical truth could not be professed by a Christian who accepted divine revelation. The Christian "Latin Averroist" or "heterodox Aristotelian," SIGER OF BRABANT (fl. 1277), was careful to identify truth with the Catholic faith. His own intention, as he repeatedly insists, is merely to report the philosophers' views, especially those of Aristotle, and not to assert them as true (*De aeternitate mundi,* 80b; *De anima intellectiva,* c. 7). Where the Philosopher's opinion is contrary to faith, Siger will give preference to faith. In any doubt,

FAITH must be adhered to since it exceeds all human reason (*De anima intellectiva,* cc. 3, 7). In his own work, however, Siger is concerned "not with miracles," but with what can be concluded through natural reason. He is only discussing "natural things in a natural way" (*ibid.,* c. 3).

Ecclesiastical Condemnation. Necessary conclusions of reason that contradict faith are not asserted as true by Siger or his fellow "Averroist," BOETHIUS OF SWEDEN (Dacia). But their position was interpreted as a doctrine of double truth by Bishop TEMPIER OF PARIS. In the prologue to the condemnation of March 7, 1277, he accused the Averroists of saying that what was true according to philosophy was not true according to the Catholic faith, "as if there were two contrary truths (*quasi sint due contrarie veritates*), and as if there were truth in the sayings of the accursed pagans contrary to the truth of sacred Scripture" (*Chartularium universitatis Parisiensis,* ed. H. Denifle and E. Chatelain, [Paris 1889–97] 1:543). Ever since this statement was written, the theory of double truth has been associated with the Averroists. Regardless of what the Averroists had actually said, it seemed to Bishop Tempier, as to THOMAS AQUINAS, that necessary conclusions of reason must be consonant with faith. An Averroist who said, "I necessarily conclude through reason that the intellect is one in number, but I firmly hold the opposite through faith," must, in Thomas's mind, be implying that faith is concerned with something false and impossible (*De unit. intell.* 5).

The irreverent implication that Thomas saw in the 13th–century Averroists was to become more explicit in JOHN OF JANDUN (d. 1328) and Pietro Pomponazzi (d. 1525). Both openly opposed philosophical conclusions to the truths of faith, but then added that the latter must be believed.

While the theory of double truth as stated in the 1277 condemnation does not seem to have been formally taught in the texts that are known to us, the Christian Averroists experienced a conflict they never resolved. Some 20th–century Christians have sensed a similar conflict: not between the teachings of faith and the conclusions of Averroës' Aristotle, but between teachings of faith and the conclusions of modern science. To Christians of any era whose faith seems menaced by the new learning of their time, St. Thomas would say: "Since faith rests upon infallible truth, and since the contrary of truth cannot be demonstrated, it is clear that proofs brought against faith are not demonstrations, but arguments capable of being answered" (*Summa theologiae* 1a, 1.8). He would add that "the truth of reason is not opposed to the truth of the Christian faith," for "every truth is from God" (*C. gent.* 1.7; *De ver.* 1.8).

See Also: FAITH AND REASON; SCHOLASTICISM; THOMISM; ARISTOTELIANISM; ARABIAN PHILOSOPHY.

Bibliography: É. GILSON, ''La Doctrine de la double vérité,'' *Études de philosophie médiévale* (Strasbourg 1921); *Reason and Revelation in the Middle Ages* (New York 1938); ''Boèce de Dacie et la double vérité,'' *Archives d'histoire doctrinale et littéraire du moyen-âge* 30 (1955) 81–99. P. F. MANDONNET, *Siger de Brabant et l'averroïsme latin au 13ᵐᵉ siècle* (2d ed. Louvain 1911). A. MAURER, ''Boetius of Dacia and the Double Truth,'' *Mediaeval Studies* 17 (1995) 233–39.

[B. H. ZEDLER]

DOUBT

Doubt is one of the states of mind that a knower can entertain toward some PROPOSITION. If the knower is unaware of the proposition altogether, he is in a state of IGNORANCE. If he either affirms or denies the proposition with no hesitancy, he possesses CERTITUDE. If he affirms or denies the proposition but with fear that he may be incorrect, he has an OPINION. If, on slight grounds, he is inclined either to affirm or deny, he has SUSPICION. Finally, he can decline either to affirm the proposition or deny it, in which case he is in a state of doubt (St. Thomas Aquinas, *Summa theologiae* 2a2ae, 2.1; *De ver.* 14.1). Thus doubt, in general, is a suspension of JUDGMENT concerning the TRUTH or FALSITY of a proposition.

Kinds of Doubt. When serious evidence is lacking both for and against the proposition, the doubt is called negative. When there is equally serious evidence for and against, the doubt is called positive.

Distinction is made also between speculative doubt and practical doubt. As the terms themselves suggest, the former pertains chiefly to abstract, objective truth or falsity, while the latter concerns a concrete act of conduct. The distinction is relevant principally in ETHICS and MORAL THEOLOGY. In these sciences speculative doubt bears on the objective morality of an action considered in itself. Practical doubt pertains to the lawfulness of someone's performing an action here and now. In some instances it is possible to solve a practical doubt without solving a speculative doubt on the same matter.

Also of moral relevance is the distinction between doubt of law and doubt of fact, which regard respectively the existence or meaning of a law and its applicability. The following discussion is concerned primarily with speculative doubt understood simply as the intellectual state of suspended judgment with no necessary association with moral science (*see* DOUBT, MORAL).

Role of Doubt. Most often doubt is taken unfavorably as signifying undesired and insoluble perplexity, or the deliberate despair of acquiring certitude, characteristic of skepticism. Yet doubt has also positive roles in preventing ERROR and in initiating philosophical inquiry. When cogent evidence or authority in support of a proposition is lacking, one *ought* to suspend judgment lest, under influences extrinsic to objective truth, the simple lack of truth (ignorance) become its positive corruption (error). Thus can doubt prevent error.

Similarly, doubt can promote the discovery of truth. In this role doubt is closely associated with WONDER in the genesis of KNOWLEDGE. Wonder is a kind of emotional shock, a species of fear that occurs when one confronts an effect, the cause of which he does not know (ST 1a2ae, 32.8; 41.4). Out of the initial state of wonder there arises a sort of doubt that is not a symptom of unbelief but a stimulus to investigation (ST 3a, 27.4 ad2; 30.4 ad 2). When this incipient doubt is elaborated into technically formulated difficulties against some position, the mind is in a state that Aristotle calls APORIA; metonymically, such difficulties are themselves called aporias (*dubitabilia* by THOMAS AQUINAS).

Both Aristotle and Aquinas make it incumbent on the philosopher to consider the aporias. If one has not looked carefully at a knot, they ask, how can he expect to untie it? Therefore, he who wishes to discover truth''ought to 'doubt well,' that is, to touch well on things that are dubitable,'' i.e., the aporias (*In 3 meta.* 1.339). Aporia, however, is not an end in itself but a means of defending and clarifying truth: ''the elimination of doubt is the goal of the truth seeker'' (*ibid.* 340). Moreover, aporia is sometimes hypothetical, a means of talking to one's adversaries, rather than a doubt (*ibid.* 342).

Methodical Doubt. The foregoing indicates that the older philosophers understood the methodical use of doubt. However, the term methodical doubt is usually associated with DESCARTES in his celebrated proposal to doubt all things as a prerequisite for establishing certitude (*Discourse on Method*, 4; *Meditations*, 1, 2). Scholastic philosophers maintain that Descartes's method logically leads to universal skepticism, even though Descartes himself was not a skeptic.

Among scholastics there is disagreement regarding the place doubt should have as a philosophical method, particularly in the critique of knowledge. Some exclude the possibility of doubting the first fact (one's own EXISTENCE), the first condition (the mind's ability to achieve truth), and the first principle (the principle of CONTRADICTION). Others maintain that such an attitude is open to the charge of excessive DOGMATISM and that it also arbitrarily singles out only three among many spontaneous and evidential certitudes. Hence, this group holds that all certitudes are subject to methodical doubt, but of a different kind than Descartes's.

To understand this view rightly, it is necessary to distinguish first between simple doubt and methodical doubt. Simple doubt is the mind's involuntary perplexity when confronted with a problem it is unable to solve. Methodical doubt, on the other hand, is an assumed attitude whereby one deliberately chooses to doubt as a means of promoting inquiry and establishing certitude. Such methodical doubt may be either real or fictitious. It is real when one actually suspends his judgment on a proposition. Apparently it was this sort of methodical doubt that Descartes attempted to use universally; yet to do so plunges one into a skepticism from which it is impossible to emerge. The doubt is fictitious when one attempts only to assume that the contradictory of a certitude is true and discovers that such an assumption is impossible to entertain. Only this latter sort of doubt can be applied to the first fact, condition, and principle, and to other immediately evident truths. Hence, universal real doubt is prohibited not because of any dogmatic presumptions, but because the very attempt to doubt some truths is absurd and self-defeating.

Doubt and Skepticism. SKEPTICISM differs from methodical doubt in accepting doubt as the final outcome of inquiry rather than as its beginning. Skepticism abandons the quest for truth, despairs of certitude, and adopts an attitude of permanent doubt. The skepticism that is of interest to philosophy is not the practical skepticism of indecisive persons, nor the shallow, affected skepticism of those who want only to avoid intellectual effort, but the speculative or doctrinal skepticism of some serious thinkers who say that definitive and certain answers cannot be given to the great problems of life and knowledge.

Speculative skepticism is absolute if it is an unqualified mistrust of human knowledge that questions not only certitude but even PROBABILITY. In an extreme form it professes to doubt everything—even the most immediate facts of existence and CONSCIOUSNESS. Skepticism is relative if it rejects the possibility of achieving reflex, scientific certitude, but recognizes probability and the necessity of accepting many things as certain in everyday life.

Skepticism may be universal or partial. Universal skepticism doubts all human knowledge, whatever its source. Partial skepticism doubts only some kinds of knowledge. Thus, PLATONISM is skeptical of sense knowledge; POSITIVISM is skeptical of supra-sensible truths; FIDEISM is skeptical of purely natural knowledge; RATIONALISM is skeptical of divinely revealed truth, and so forth.

See Also: DIALECTICS; KNOWLEDGE, THEORIES OF; EPISTEMOLOGY.

Bibliography: P. COFFEY, *Epistemology,* 2 v. (New York 1917; reprint 1958) 1:135–38. L. M. RÉGIS, *Epistemology,* tr. I. C. BYRNE (New York 1959). P. J. GLENN, *Criteriology* (St. Louis 1933). R. P. PHILLIPS, *Modern Thomistic Philosophy,* 2 v. (Westminster, Md. 1948) 2:8–38. J. MARITAIN, *Distinguish to Unite, or the Degrees of Knowledge,* tr. G. B. PHELAN from 4th French ed. (New York 1959).

[J. B. NUGENT]

DOUBT, MORAL

Uncertainty of mind concerning the morality of an action or the omission of an action. In other words, a person is not certain whether a particular course is sinful or lawful.

Kinds of Moral Doubt. Because many factors can enter into a moral problem, a person can frequently be doubtful as to whether a certain action, the performance of which he is considering, is lawful or unlawful; or he may be uncertain whether he is bound to perform a particular action or may lawfully omit it. The doubt is negative when the reasons for one side are very slight compared to those for the other side; it is positive when there are solid reasons for both law and liberty. When the reasons on both sides are about equal, there is said to be a strict doubt. Ordinarily, a negative doubt is to be disregarded.

A doubt of law (*dubium juris*) is concerned with the existence or scope of a certain law; for example, does the law of eucharistic fast forbid solid food for one complete hour before Holy Communion or will a period of 55 minutes suffice? A doubt of fact (*dubium facti*) is concerned with the performance or nonperformance of some particular act relating to the fulfillment or nonfulfillment of the law; for example, have I fasted the required period of time to receive Holy Communion lawfully?

A speculative doubt is concerned with the lawfulness or unlawfulness of an action in itself; for example, does double vasectomy prevent a man from marrying validly and lawfully? A practical doubt is concerned with the morality of an action if performed by oneself; for example, in view of the controversy, may I, a vasectomized person, be permitted to attempt marriage?

Course to be Followed by One in Doubt. When a person is in doubt about the morality of performing (or of omitting) an action, he must either follow the opinion for law or settle the doubt with practical certainty in favor of liberty before he performs (or omits) the action. In other words, when a person is uncertain whether or not it is sinful for him here and now to perform an action that may be forbidden (or to omit an action that may be commanded) and in that state of mind performs (or omits) the action in question, he thereby sins formally, for he shows that he does not care whether or not he offends God. This is true even though the course for liberty is not objectively forbidden. However, he may lawfully follow the course for liberty after he has come to sufficient practical certainty (even indirect certainty) that this course is permissible, even though objectively the opinion for liberty happens in fact to be erroneous. In this case, his conduct is only materially sinful.

Evidently, then, one who contemplates a particular course of conduct and doubts whether it is morally right or wrong is bound to seek further information—at least, if he wishes to follow the course for liberty. First, he should try to obtain direct certainty by investigating the problem himself or by seeking direction from some more learned person. However, if direct certainty is not available he may ordinarily apply reflex principles, such as "A doubtful law does not bind," or "In a doubt the possessor is to be favored." If, then, through a prudent use of such principles he obtains indirect certainty that he may lawfully act for liberty, he will not sin formally if he chooses this course. In such a case, the speculative doubt about the morality of the action in question remains, but the practical doubt has been solved in favor of liberty. Theologians differ as to the degree of probability required before one may follow the opinion for liberty, as can be seen by a study of the various moral systems.

See Also: DOUBT; REFLEX PRINCIPLES; MORALITY, SYSTEMS OF.

Bibliography: D. PRÜMMER, *Manuale theologiae moralis*, ed. E. M. MÜNCH (Barcelona 1945–56) 1:324–336. J. AERTNYS and C. A. DAMEN, *Theologia moralis* (Turin 1950) 1:79–89. N. ZALBA, *Theologiae moralis compendium* (Madrid 1958) 1:663–672.

[F. J. CONNELL]

DOUCELINE OF THE MIDI, ST.

Nun; b. Digne, France, *c.* 1214; d. Marseilles, France, Sept. 1, 1274. Known also as Donolina, Dulcelina, and Donzeline, she was the daughter of Berengier of Digne and Huguette of Barjols and came to live at Hyères after her mother's death (*c.* 1230). On the advice of her brother, HUGH OF DIGNE, a Franciscan, she founded near Hyères a house of BEGUINES, pious women, very often widows, who lived the ideal of St. FRANCIS but without constituting themselves as a religious order. They made a vow of perpetual chastity and vowed obedience for the period they would remain associated as Beguines, but they were not obliged to enclosure or to choir and they retained the disposition of their own possessions. About 1250, Douceline founded a second and larger house near Marseilles and then made a third foundation at Aix. She spent the last 20 years of her life in Mar-

seilles, and it is reported that during that time she was often favored by ECSTASIES while praying in the Franciscan church, and she is supposed to have died during one of them in 1274. She was immediately venerated as a saint, especially at the church of the Major in Marseilles, where her body rests beside that of her brother in a tomb given by William de la Font in 1278. The Beguines of Crotte-Vieille, dispersed after the Council of Vienne, regrouped near the site of the present-day Lenche, but the house was suppressed by the beginning of the 15th century for lack of vocations, and its possessions went to the Franciscans in 1419.

Feast: Sept. 1.

Bibliography: *La cronica de Salembene, Monumenta Germaniae Scriptores* (Berlin 1825), 32:554. *Chronica XXIV minorum generalium, Analecta Franciscana* 3 (1902) 405–406. J. H. ALBANÉS, *La Vie de sainte Douceline, fondatrixe des béguines de Marseille; composée au xiiie siècle en langue provençale* (Marseille 1879). A. CONSULTER, *Histoire Littéraire de la France* (Paris 1865) 29:526–546. H. MOUCHOT, "Une extatique du XIIIème s.: Douceline de Digne," *Revue Sextienne* 1 (1880) 45–65. A. MACDONNELL, *St. Douceline* (London 1905). G. MOUREY, *Sainte Douceline, béguine de Provence* (Paris 1922). A. SISTO, *Figure del primo francescanesimo in Provenza Ugo e Douceline di Digne* (Florence 1971). R. AIGRAIN, *Catholicisme* 3: 1049–1051. M. H. LAURENT, *Dictionnaire d'histoire et de géographie ecclésiastiques* (Paris 1912–), 14:740–741. B. DE GAIFFIER, *Dictionnaire de spiritualité ascétique et mystique,* ed. M. VILLERS (Paris 1932–), 3:1672–74.

[J. DAOUST]

DOUGHERTY, DENNIS

Cardinal, archbishop; b. Schuylkill County, Pa., Aug. 16, 1865; d. Philadelphia, Pa., May 31, 1951. He was the sixth of ten children of Patrick and Bridget (Henry) Dougherty, Irish immigrants who had settled in the coal mining area of Pennsylvania. He attended the public schools of Ashland and Girardville and at the age of 14 applied for admission to the diocesan seminary of Philadelphia. Although he passed the entrance examination, he was barred because of his youth. In September 1880 he entered Sainte-Marie College in Montreal, Canada. Two years later he transferred to St. Charles Borromeo Seminary, Overbrook, Pa., and in 1885 Abp. Patrick J. RYAN sent him to the North American College, Rome, to continue his studies.

On May 31, 1890, he was ordained by Cardinal Lucido Parocchi in the Basilica of St. John Lateran. When he returned to Philadelphia in September he was appointed professor at St. Charles Borromeo Seminary, where he taught in turn Latin, English, history, Greek, French, Hebrew, and dogmatic theology. He was also procurator of the seminary and one of the synodal examiners of the archdiocese. On April 7, 1903, Leo XIII appointed him bishop of NUEVA SEGOVIA in the Philippine Islands; Cardinal Francesco Satolli consecrated him in the Church of SS. John and Paul, Rome, on June 14, 1903.

Dougherty arrived in the Philippines in October 1903, with five Philadelphia priests: Edgar Cook, who died within a few years; James Carroll, who succeeded Dougherty in the Diocese of Nueva Segovia; John MacGinley, later bishop of Nueva Caceres and afterwards of Fresno, California; James McCloskey, later bishop of Zamboanga and Dougherty's successor to the See of Jaro; and Daniel Gercke, later bishop of Tucson, Arizona. It was the first great missionary effort of the diocesan priesthood of the U.S. beyond the boundaries of the country. The Nueva Segovia diocese had 997,629 Catholics, 110 parishes, and 171 parish priests, of whom 131 were native-born.

Dougherty rebuilt the façade of the cathedral, refurnished the diocesan seminary at Vigan, where American troops had been quartered, and dealt with the schism begun by Padre Gregorio Aglipay. This native priest had apostatized and started his own church in the diocese, with a following of native priests who protested that the Holy See had refused their petition for a native bishop. They had usurped ownership of church property, but the American civil authorities, fearful of disturbing the natives, had neglected to correct these abuses. However, they advised Dougherty that, as a test case, he should take legal action against Aglipay to prove the Church's claim to the properties in question. Dougherty refused; instead, he persuaded the American authorities that Aglipay had to substantiate his claims to the ecclesiastical property. The litigation dragged on for seven years, until the courts finally decided against Aglipay and returned all the properties to the Catholic Church. In 1907, Dougherty attended the provincial council of Manila. After one year he was transferred to the larger diocese of Jaro in the province of Iloilo, where he was installed on June 21, 1908.

In 1915 he was appointed bishop of BUFFALO. He returned to the U.S. to be installed on June 7, 1916, by Cardinal John Farley of New York. He soon liquidated the debt on the cathedral, established 15 new parishes, and revitalized the parochial school system. Two years later, Rome appointed him to the Archdiocese of PHILADELPHIA, where he was enthroned by Cardinal James Gibbons on July 10, 1918. During Dougherty's administration, 112 new parishes, 145 parochial schools, 53 Catholic high schools, four Catholic colleges, 12 hospitals, and 11 homes for the aged were established. He consecrated 15 bishops and ordained more than 2,000 priests. Benedict XV made him a cardinal priest on March 7, 1921, with the titular church of SS. Nereus and

Achilles. The French called him the "Cardinal of the Little Flower" because of his aid in her canonization. He died on the 61st anniversary of his ordination and was buried in the crypt of the archdiocesan Cathedral of SS. Peter and Paul.

Bibliography: H. J. NOLAN, "Cardinal Dougherty: an Appreciation," *Records of the American Catholic Historical Society of Philadelphia* 62 (1951) 135–141. *New York Times,* June 1, 1951, 23:1.

[J. F. CONNELLY]

DOUGLAS, GEORGE, BL.

Franciscan priest and martyr; b. Edinburgh, Scotland; d. hanged, drawn, and quartered at York, England, under Charles II, Sept. 9, 1587. Douglas was a schoolmaster at Rutland before his ordination at Paris, *c.* 1574. Ten years later he entered the English mission field and was arrested, but released. He was apprehended again at Ripton, Yorkshire, and condemned for "persuading to popery." Fr. Douglas was beatified by Pope John Paul II on Nov. 22, 1987 with George Haydock and Companions.

Feast of the English Martyrs: May 4 (England).

See Also: ENGLAND, SCOTLAND, AND WALES, MARTYRS OF.

Bibliography: R. CHALLONER, *Memoirs of Missionary Priests,* ed. J. H. POLLEN (rev. ed. London 1924). J. H. POLLEN, *Acts of English Martyrs* (London 1891). J. THADDEUS, *The Franciscans in England 1600–1859,*15 v. (London, 1898).

[K. I. RABENSTEIN]

DOUKHOBORS

Doubkhobors, or Spirit Wrestlers, originated in the 18th century in Kharkov and the villages of the Dnieper, Russia; in 1898 members of this mystical sect began migrating to Canada. When groups of Russian peasants rejected the authority of the Russian Orthodox Church, they appealed to the authority of the "inner light" in much the same way as do the Quakers (*see* FRIENDS, RELIGIOUS SOCIETY OF). They spurned priests, ritual, sacraments, oaths, icons, and military service. Refusal to bear arms brought them into conflict with the czar's government as well as with the established church. Despite their appeal to the individual conscience, the Doukhobors have allowed themselves to be ruled by a series of authoritarian and often dissolute spiritual leaders. They believe that the soul of Christ reappears in living beings or Messiahs. Saveli Kapustin became their first acknowledged leader in

1790. His son, Vasili Kalmikoff, and his grandson, Illarion Kalmikoff, inherited leadership of the sect, but both were alcoholics. The Doukhobors were finally banished to the Wet Mountains of the Caucasus.

Peter Vasilivich Verigin, a later Messiah, decided to lead his people out of Russia. Encouraged by Leo Tolstoy and aided by the English Quakers, he settled most of his followers in Saskatchewan, Canada, and later led them to British Columbia. He was assassinated in 1924. The Doukhobors split into several sects. The estimated 2,000 Sons of Freedom form the most radical branch; they engage in arson and nudism to protest the policies of the Canadian government. The Doukhobors reject the doctrine of the Trinity and baptism. They teach that Jesus was simply a wise man. They look to neither the Bible nor the church for religious authority. Doukhobors practice vegetarianism. Their altars hold only a pitcher of water, a dish of salt, and a loaf of bread. After a series of legal and economic setbacks from the 1930s–1960s, including the loss of land in Saskatchewan, arson, and forced assimilation, the Doukhobors regrouped and regained their vitality from the 1980s onward.

Bibliography: Doukhobor Research Committee, *The Doukhobors of British Columbia,* ed. H. B. HAWTHORN (Vancouver 1955). J. F. C. WRIGHT, *Slava Bohu: The Story of the Dukhobors* (New York 1940).

[W. J. WHALEN/EDS.]

DOWDALL, GEORGE

Archbishop of the primatial See of ARMAGH (schismatical 1543–52, and papal 1553–58); b. Drogheda, Ireland, 1487; d. London, Aug. 15, 1558. He was employed in archdiocesan court *c.* 1518 to 1520, and joined the CRUTCHED FRIARS in Ardee Priory *c.* 1522. He surrendered his priory to Henry VIII in 1539, became an official of Archbishop Cromer's court in the winter of 1539 to 1540, after the papal suspension of Cromer, and was consecrated archbishop of Armagh, on Henry's mandate, Nov. 28, 1543. He reported to Government on March 22, 1550, the "sedition" of his rival Robert Wauchop (papal archbishop March 23, 1545 to Nov. 10, 1550). He was removed from office by Government for rejecting Edwardian liturgy. After he had emigrated, he was appointed primate and archbishop by Julius III, March 1, 1553. Mary Tudor, still acting as "Head of the Church," recalled him to the see March 12, 1554, and appointed him to her commission of reform in April 1554. Her instructions to the Lord Deputy April 17, 1556, proclaiming papal supremacy, reconciled Dowdall's titles in papal and English law. But, protesting against the deputy's despoliation of Armagh in October 1557 during war with

the Irish, Dowdall was summoned Feb. 7, 1558, to appear before Mary in London. He died there six months later.

Bibliography: A. GWYNN, *The Medieval Province of Armagh, 1470–1545* (Dundalk, Ire. 1946).

[J. HURLEY]

DOWDALL, JAMES

Martyr; parentage and date of birth unknown; evidence of date of death conflicting. According to P. Bruodin he was executed on Sept. 20, 1600, but Challoner gives Aug. 13, 1599 as the date. Challoner's testimony is supported by Rev. Dr. G. Oliver's transcript from the Devon archives in the following entry for the 1599 Autumn assizes, "Jacobus Dowdall suspendatur etc., pro proditione." He was a merchant of Drogheda (Challoner says he was from Wexford) driven onto the Devonshire coast while returning from France to Ireland. In custody he rejected the Queen's spiritual supremacy while being questioned by William Bourchier, Earl of Bath. On receiving a report of the examination, Sir Robert Cecil had Dowdall committed to Exeter jail. On June 18, 1599, the Earl of Bath wrote to Cecil for instructions regarding him. By order of the Council he was tried and convicted of high treason after suffering the rack in an attempt to induce him to deny his faith.

Bibliography: D. MURPHY, *Our Martyrs* (Dublin 1896). R. CHALLONER, *Memoirs of Missionary Priests,* ed. J. H. POLLEN (rev. ed. London 1924).

[J. G. BARRY]

DOWLING, AUSTIN

Second archbishop of ST. PAUL, Minn.; b. New York City, April 6, 1868; d. St. Paul, Oct. 31, 1930. His parents, Daniel and Mary Teresa (Santry) Dowling, emigrants from Ireland, moved their family to Newport, R.I., where Austin attended the Academy of the Sisters of Charity. In 1887 he graduated with honors from Manhattan College, New York City; entered St. John's Seminary, Brighton, Mass.; and in 1890 was sent to The Catholic University of America, Washington, D.C., to complete his studies in theology. He was ordained for the Diocese of Providence, R.I., June 24, 1891, by Matthew Harkins, Bishop of Providence. A year later he received his licentiate in theology from The Catholic University, then served briefly as a curate in a Providence parish, after which he taught church history at St. John's Seminary in Brighton until 1896, when he became editor of the *Providence Visitor,* the diocesan newspaper. From 1898 to 1905 he did pastoral work in Providence and Warren, R.I., and on July 3, 1905, was named rector of the Cathedral of SS. Peter and Paul, Providence.

When DES MOINES, Iowa, was erected a diocese in 1911, Dowling was named first bishop and consecrated in Providence April 25, 1912. During his seven-year tenure in Des Moines, then a small rural diocese with but few priests to minister to large areas, Dowling worked constantly to build an extensive diocesan system of Catholic schools. Early in 1919 he was named to succeed John IRELAND as the second archbishop of St. Paul. After his installation in the Cathedral of St. Paul on March 25, he received the pallium in formal ceremonies on May 27 at the hands of his old friend, Abp. James J. KEANE of Dubuque, Iowa. In the same year Dowling helped to organize the NATIONAL CATHOLIC WELFARE CONFERENCE and was elected to its first administrative board, which he served as treasurer and as chairman of the department of education. He also organized and incorporated a bureau of Catholic charities in each of the Twin Cities during his first year in office. In September 1919 he announced a diocesan-wide drive for the Archbishop Ireland Educational Fund, with a goal of five million dollars. Although the goal was never fully realized, Dowling considered this drive one of his lasting achievements. Its revenue was used to construct Nazareth Hall, a new diocesan preparatory seminary built in 1922 to 1923, Cretin High School in St. Paul, and De La Salle High School in Minneapolis, and to open a diocesan teachers college for sisters and lay teachers in 1925 (discontinued in September 1950). On July 9, 1928, Dowling transferred the College of ST. THOMAS, founded in 1885 by Archbishop Ireland, from the control of diocesan priests to the Congregation of Holy Cross, an action which was revoked five years later by his successor, Abp. John Gregory MURRAY.

Throughout his life Dowling retained an interest in historical studies and often lectured on the history of the Reformation in England. His published sermons are polished and scholarly treatises. The last three years of his life were marked by recurrent circulatory and coronary attacks.

Bibliography: M. R. O'CONNELL, *The Dowling Decade in Saint Paul* (unpub. master's thesis; St. Paul Seminary 1955). J. M. REARDON, *The Catholic Church in the Diocese of Saint Paul* (St. Paul 1952) 436–505. A. DOWLING, *Occasional Sermons and Addresses,* ed. J. T. MCNICHOLAS (Paterson 1940). Archives, Archdiocese of St. Paul, "Dowling Papers, 1919–1930"; "Dowling Sermons, 1919–1930" (manuscripts and mimeographs). Archives, Catholic Historical Society of St. Paul, "Dowling Papers, 1919–1930."

[J. P. SHANNON]

DOWNSIDE ABBEY

Benedictine abbey 12 miles south of Bath, south England. The community originated in Douai (France) in 1607, moved to Downside in 1814, and became an abbey in 1900. Englishmen, unable to become monks in England, joined Benedictine houses in Spain and then moved to Douai in the Spanish Netherlands, seeking to found a monastery and work among English Catholics. Abbot Philip de Caverel of nearby SAINT-VAAST helped establish conventual life (1607), gave funds for building and endowment, and joined to the community (St. Gregory) a house of studies for his own monks who were members of the University of Douai. Augustine Bradshaw was the first prior. A school for boys (founded 1614–18) flourished until the French Revolution, averaging 50 students, all English until the last years. Six martyrs from the many monks who worked among Catholics in England were beatified in 1925: John ROBERTS, Ambrose BARLOW, George Gervase, Philip Powell, Maur Scott, and Thomas Pickering. By 1793, when the Revolutionary government closed it, St. Gregory was an accepted establishment of Douai, where its monks taught in the university. Half the monks and pupils escaped to England and in 1794 were joined by the rest, who had been imprisoned in Picardy for several months. They were at Acton Burnell in Shropshire on the estate of an alumnus, Sir Edward Smythe, until they purchased Mount Pleasant at Downside (1814), where they have since flourished.

The Divine Office is solemnly performed with a daily solemn Mass in the church. This edifice (330 feet long) possesses the relics of Bl. Oliver PLUNKET. The monastery was near completion in 1965. The monks engage in pastoral work, but their principal occupation is teaching in the abbey's school, one of England's leading public schools. The *Downside Review,* devoted to theological studies, is well known. Bernard ULLATHORNE, Bede POLDING, and Roger Bede VAUGHAN were Downside monks who helped establish the Church in Australia and ameliorate the lot of convicts there. EALING ABBEY (London) in 1955 and Worth Abbey (Sussex) in 1957 became independent houses with large schools. Outstanding monks of Downside include the historian Cardinal Aidan GASQUET, the scholar Cuthbert BUTLER, the liturgist Hugh Connolly, and John CHAPMAN.

Bibliography: B. HICKS, *H. E. Ford, First Abbot of Downside* (London 1947). B. SANKEY, *Dictionnaire d'histoire et de géographie ecclésiastiques,* ed. A. BAUDRILLART et al. (Paris 1912–) 14:767–768. L. H. COTTINEAU, *Répertoire topobibliographique des abbayes et prieurés,* 2 v. (Mâcon 1935–39) 1:998. O. L. KAPSNER, *A Benedictine Bibliography: An Author-Subject Union List,* 2 v. (2d ed. Collegeville, Minn. 1962) 2:203–204. m

[C. MCCANN]

DOWRY

"Dowry" was used in Church Law only in reference to institutes of women religious and never to marriage.

It consisted of a definite sum of money, or its equivalent, paid by a postulant to a religious community in which she wished to make religious profession.

The dowry had a threefold purpose. The principal purpose was to provide a means of support for the religious in the institute in which she was to become a member by religious profession. Secondly, the dowry served to provide a dependable financial income by which the religious community might enjoy a measure of permanent economic stability. The third aim was to provide an ''emergency fund'' if the religious should leave the convent; in this case the entire capital sum of the dowry had to be restored to the departing religious, thus providing a means for her temporary support during the period of transition to secular life. Although the 1983 Code of Canon Law does not mention ''dowry,'' it does state in ch. 702 §2, that the religious institute ''is to observe equity and the charity of the gospel toward a member who is separated from it.'' This applies to both men and women.

The necessity of a dowry depended partly upon the nature of the religious institute. The 1917 Code of Canon Law mandated that all postulants seeking admission to monasteries of nuns, i.e., those in which solemn vows were taken, were required to bring a dowry. It gave religious congregations, i.e., institutes with simple vows, more latitude in this respect, allowing them to determine in their constitutions whether a dowry is required. The members of these institutes were usually engaged in charitable or educational ministries from which they were able to derive an income that, in whole or in part, covered the cost of their material support.

The dowries were administered at the monastery or house of the habitual residence of the mother general or provincial. After the first profession of a religious, her dowry was to be invested in safe, lawful, and productive investments by the superioress with her council and with the consent of the local ordinary. If the house was subject to regulars, the consent of the regular was also required.

The principal of the dowry had to remain intact during the entire time of the religious profession of the nun or sister, and it could not be spent in any way before her death, not even for the building of a convent or the payment of debts. However, the interest or income from the invested dowries belonged to the institute and was intended to help pay for the support of the religious. Upon the death of a religious, her dowry was irrevocably acquired by the institute, even though she had taken only temporary vows. If for any reason a professed religious, either in solemn or simple vows, left the institute, her dowry had to be returned to her in its entirety, without the interest already earned.

Bibliography: T. M. KEALY, *Dowry of Women Religious* (*Catholic University of America Canon Law Studies* 134; Washington 1941) A. LARRAONA, ''De dote religiosarum in codice juris canonici,'' *Commentarium pre religiosis* 19 (1938) 19–30, 93–100.

[T. M. KEALY]

DOXOLOGY, BIBLICAL

Doxology, derived from the Greek δοξολογία (giving glory), is a prayer of praise and gratitude. The ordinary form most frequently appearing in the OT is that of an expression of blessing, introduced by the Hebrew word *bārûk* (blessed), for example, ''Blessed be Yahweh'' (2 Chr 9.8). The subject of the blessing may be expressed also by ''God'' or the ''Lord God'' [Ps 28(29).11; 40(41).14; 67(68).20, 36] or ''the Name of God'' [Gn 14.20; 24.27; Ps 17(18).47;71(72).19]. The introductory word of praise is often followed by reasons why God is blessed [1 Sm 25.39; 2 Sm 18.28; 1 Kgs 1.48; 8.56; 10.9; Ps 27(28).6; 123(124).6].

In the NT, the traditional OT form appears, but the subject is not only God as such, but God as Father and as Christ. However, no doxology to God as Holy Spirit appears. The traditional form is found in Lk 1.68; 2 Cor 1.3; Eph 1.3; 1 Pt 1.3, but the order is often changed (2 Cor 11.31; Rom 1.25; 9.5; 16.27), and the words ''forever,'' a common Hebraism (Tb 13.23), and AMEN are added (Gal 1.5; 1 Tm 1.17; Heb 13.21; 1 Pt 4.11). The OT form of doxology expressed as an invitation to ''give glory'' to God (Dt 32.43) occurs also in the NT (Lk 2.14; Phil 4.20; Jude 24–25; Rv 4.8, 11; 7.12).

Abbreviated hymns in the OT addressed in praise of God are usually referred in the NT to God the Father (Gal 1.3; Phil 4.20); but when the thought is fixed on Christ, the praise is directed to Him (Rom 9.5; 2 Pt 3.18; Rv 1.6; 5.9–13; 7.10). Again, in other passages it is Christ as Head of the Church and the mediator through whom honor, glory, and thanksgiving are given to the Father (Eph 3.21). St. Paul provides a norm for such hymns in the words: ''Whatsoever you do in word or in work, do all in the name of the Lord Jesus, giving thanks to God the Father through him'' (Col 3.17). In the original Greek of 1 Pt 4.11, the verb ''to be'' occurs in the indicative mood in the doxology, ''to him belong [ἐστίν] glory and dominion forever,'' a more fitting expression than the optative mood expressing a wish or desire.

The solemn command to praise God was probably addressed to the Israelites in their early history only in the flush of victory (Jgs 5.2, 9). With development of Temple liturgy, however, such hymns were sung when the ark of the covenant was carried in solemn procession while God's merciful acts of intervention in the history of the Israelites as the Chosen People of God were recounted

[Psalm 67(68)] and climaxed in recital by a glorious, ''Blessed be God'' [Ps 67(68).36]. In such liturgical celebrations, the Israelites were summoned by priests and Levites to bless the Lord [Ps 134(135).1–4, 19–20] with an exhortation to glorify God who is the almighty Lord of creation and defender of His People [Ps 135(136); 146(147B); etc.].

The great hymn of praise, the Hallel [Ps 112(113)–117(118)], that came to be embodied in the Jewish liturgy of the postexilic period, might also be considered an extended doxology. Especially significant are Ps 112(113).1–113(114).8, sung during the Paschal meal; Ps 113(114).9–117(118), sung after the meal; and Ps 117(118), the great processional hymn, chanted antiphonally by priests, people, and proselytes entering the Temple to thank God for victory and renewal of national life. Another of the magnificent extended doxologies is that of the canticle Benedicite Dominum (Dn 3.52–90). While not following the compressed form of doxology, these hymns of praise are redolent of the spirit of jubilant gratitude that marked the prayer life of the Israelites. Such songs came to be the common practice not only in their Temple worship, but also in their private lives [Ps 17(18).47; 33(34).2; 143(144).1–11; 145(146).2]. [See PRAYER (IN THE BIBLE)].

With such expressions of praise familiar to Jewish converts, fittingly similar ones were introduced into the primitive worship of the Christian community. In Eph 4.20–21, for instance, the doxology, after invoking the boundless generosity of God, praises the twofold instrument of God's glory, Christ and the Church. Hymns of praise to Christ stressed His divinity (Rom 9.5; 16.26; 1 Tm 3.16; 2 Tm 4.18; Eph 5.14). Perhaps the most elaborate is that of Rom 16.25–27, where the entire message of the epistle is gathered into one finale of jubilant praise of the power of God unto salvation, of the revelation of His plan of salvation in the Gospel, of salvation by faith in Jesus Christ, of the universality of salvation, of the Apostles' divine mission, and of the continuity with the OT—all reasons for glorifying God through Christ.

Bibliography: J. K. ELLIOT, ''The Language and Style of the Concluding Doxology to the Epistle to the Romans,'' in *Zeitschrift für die Neutestamentliche Wissenschaft und die Kunde der Älteren Kirche* 72 no. 1/2 (1981) 124–130. L.W. HURTADO, ''The Doxology at the End of Romans,'' in *New Testament Textual Criticism; its Significance for Exegesis* (Oxford 1981) 185–199. H. C. SCHMIDT-LAUBER, ''Die Verchristlichung der Psalmen durch das Gloria Patri,'' in *Zur Aktualität des Alten Testaments* (Frankfurt 1992) 317–329.

[M. R. E. MASTERMAN/EDS.]

DOXOLOGY, LITURGICAL

The Church has continued the biblical custom of concluding prayers with a short, hymnlike expression of praise to God.

Sometimes we find a simple laudatory acclamation to God without distinction of Persons. The Didache, for instance, concludes the Lord's Prayer with the doxology: ''For Thine is the power and the glory evermore'' (8.2) and it employs this formula as a refrain in liturgical prayers: ''To Thee be glory forever'' (9.2). Sometimes it is directed immediately to Jesus Christ: ''Hosanna deo David'' (Didache 10.6). Similar doxologies are found in the Martyrdom of Polycarp (20.2; 21), the Epistle of Barnabas (12.7), and the First Epistle of Clement (c.20).

The basic form of the ancient Christian doxology used by the Fathers and the liturgy depicted Christ as the source of the Father's glorification in the Spirit: ''Glory be to the Father through the Son in the Holy Spirit'' (Didache, 9.4; Clement of Alexandria, *Quis dives,* 42.2; Origen, *De oratione,* 33). Since supporters of ARIANISM used the phrase ''through the Son'' as a slogan of their SUBORDINATIONISM making the Son inferior to the Father, the leaders of the Catholic camp at Antioch (4th century) sponsored the use of the formula, ''Glory be to the Father and to the Son and to the Holy Spirit.'' This formula was derived from the baptismal formula (Mt 28.19), which expressed clearly the equality of the three Divine Persons (J. A. Jungmann, *The Mass of the Roman Rite,* 1:328). Thus this Little Doxology, as it is called, came to be used in the conclusion of psalms and elsewhere.

Every eucharistic prayer of the Mass concludes with a Trinitarian doxology that retains the emphasis on Christ's mediatorship: ''Through Him [Christ], and with Him, and in Him, all honor and glory is given to You, God the Father, in the unity of the Holy Spirit, forever and ever. Amen.'' This practice of summarizing the whole thematic upsweep of the Eucharistic Prayer—glorifying the Father through the Son's redemptive work in the Spirit—can be found as early as the 3rd century *Apostolic Tradition* of Hippolytus (6; B. Botte, ed. *La Tradition apostolique de saint Hippolyte: Essai de reconstitution* (*Liturgiegeschichtliche Quellen und Forschungen* 39; 1963, 18). But Hippolytus adds ''in Thy holy Church,'' thus indicating the earthly basis or vehicle of Christ's continued glorification of His Father.

The GLORIA in excelsis Deo is known as the Greater Doxology. Its author is unknown. It includes three parts: (1) the song of the angels at the Nativity (Lk 2.14), (2) praise of God the Father, and (3) an invocation of Christ with mention of the Holy Spirit. By the 6th century, the Gloria had been firmly established in the Roman Mass for some time [*Liber pontificalis,* ed. L. Duchesne, v. 1–2 (Paris 1886–92), v. 3 (Paris 1958) 1:56]. The *TE DEUM* is an extended doxology. It seems to be the work, not of St. Ambrose or St. Augustine, but of Niceta of Remesiana (d. 414), who apparently brought several different hymns together and fashioned them into one. The *Te decet laus* is a brief Trinitarian acclamation. It was prescribed by the Rule of St. Benedict (*Reg. Monast.* c.11), but it has disappeared from the Roman liturgy.

See Also: DOXOLOGY, BIBLICAL; TRISAGION.

Bibliography: J. A. JUNGMANN, *The Mass of the Roman Rite,* tr. F. A. BRUNNER, 2 v. (New York 1951–55) 1:328, 346–359. A. GERHARDS, ''La doxologie, un chapitre définitif de l'histoire du dogme,'' in *Trinité et Liturgie* (Rome 1984) 103–118. A. NOCENT, ''Les doxologies des prières eucharistiques,'' in *Gratias Agamus* (Freiburg 1992) 343–353. G. RAMSHAW-SCHMIDT, ''Our Final Praise: The Concluding Doxology,'' in *New Eucharistic Prayers,* ed. F. SENN (Mahwah, N.J. 1987) 210–213.

[E. J. GRATSCH/EDS.]

DOXOPATRES, NEILOS

Called Nilus the Archimandrite, Byzantine theologian of the first half of the 12th century. Neilos began his career as notary to the patriarch of Constantinople and subsequently became a high ecclesiastical official and head of the law school of the Eastern Roman Empire. In 1141 he was summoned by Roger II (1130–54) of Sicily to serve at his court. During his stay in Sicily (1142–43) he wrote at the request of Roger II a geographical-statistical survey of the succession of patriarchs of Constantinople, preceded by an epitome that constitutes a historical treatment of the origin and development of the five patriarchates, written entirely from the Eastern and anti-Roman point of view. He is believed to be identical with Joannes Doxopatres, author of a voluminous work on divine providence (*economia*), of which only two books have been preserved. The first deals with creation, anthropology, Paradise, and original sin; and the second with the Incarnation and Christology. He demonstrates a good knowledge of the early Greek Fathers and has left marginal glosses on the writings of St. Athanasius.

Bibliography: G. PARTHEY, ed., *Hieroclis synecdemus et notitiae graecae episcopatuum* (Berlin 1866) 266–308; H. G. BECK, *Kirche und theologische Literatur im byzantinischen Reich* (Munich 1959) 619–621. S. VAILHÉ, *Dictionnaire de théologie catholique,* ed. A. VACANT et al. (Paris 1903–50) 4.2:1820. A. MICHEL, *Lexikon für Theologie und Kirche,* ed. M. BUCHBERGER (Freiburg 1930–38) 3:433. G. MERCATI, *Per la storia dei manoscritti greci di Genova* (*Studi e Testi* 68; 1935) 75–79. V. LAURENT, *Échos d'Orient* 36 (1937) 5–30.

[G. LUZNYCKY]

DOYLE, JAMES WARREN

Irish bishop and patriot; b. near New Ross, County Wexford, Ireland, 1786; d. Carlow, Ireland, June 16, 1834. His parents were poor, but saw to his education through the college in New Ross run by the Augustinian Friars, an order which he then joined. He completed his studies at Coimbra, Portugal, where he had to endure severe temptations against faith while at the university. After his ordination (1809) he was assigned to teach logic at his old college in New Ross (1809–17), and was then appointed to the staff of Carlow College (1817–19). He became bishop of Kildare and Leighlin in 1819. As a bishop, Doyle actively identified himself with the cause of his oppressed coreligionists, and became a formidable antagonist of the Protestant archbishop of Dublin. He was a shrewd and powerful pamphleteer and opposed the Irish Establishment with vigor and persistence. On two occasions he was examined by Parliamentary committees on Irish affairs. He openly supported Daniel O'CONNELL, and joined the Catholic Association in Clare. In pastoral matters, the bishop was an ideal prelate and did much to elevate the tone of religion in his area by providing public sermons and retreats, and also by introducing religious confraternities and temperance societies. He built schools, opened libraries, and spared no effort to improve the education of the people.

Bibliography: D. O'CONNELL, *Correspondence of Daniel O'Connell,* ed. W. J. FITZPATRICK, 2 v. (London 1888). W. J. FITZPATRICK, *The Life, Times, and Correspondence of Dr. Doyle,* 2 v. (Dublin 1890). M. MACDONAGH, *Bishop Doyle, ''J. K. L.''* (London 1896).

[V. A. MCCLELLAND]

DRAKESTEIN, YVONNE BOSCH VAN

Noted Catholic lay leader; b. Holland, April 13, 1903; d. Combermere, Canada, Aug. 2, 1994. Daughter of Lucie Adele Cornelie Serraris and Jean Louis Paul Bosch van Drakestein van Hieuw-van-Amelsweerd, members of the Catholic aristocracy. Drakestein was baptized Yvonne Caroline. In 1927, after studying art history, she joined the Women of Nazareth, a group of committed lay women founded in Holland in 1921 by Jacques van Ginneken (*see* GRAIL). In 1929 she was sent to Java (now Indonesia) where she hoped to spend the rest of her life working with women.

Unexpectedly in 1932, Drakestein was sent to England to start the Grail, as the Women of Nazareth had become known. She did this with flair and flamboyance: colorful uniforms and banners, processions and marches, spectacular plays with 500 to 1200 participants in London's prestigious Royal Albert Hall, and a magazine called *Fire*. All witnessed that Christian ideals were alive and flourishing among Catholic youth.

A less glamorous period of consolidation came from 1939 to 1945 with the war. Grail members distributed leaflets and campaigns to sustain morale in bomb shelters; booklets bringing lay spirituality in attractive and readable form were published; papal encyclicals were simplified and distributed in millions; and the Grail became an inspiration to young women up and down the country through the national Girls Training Corps. Throughout this period, Caryll HOUSELANDER was a valued colleague of Drakestein: Houselander contributed regularly to the *Grail* magazine, and her *This War is the Passion* was published by the Grail.

Postwar Years. Another period of development took place after the war, beginning in 1949 when the English Grail became autonomous at the instigation of the hierarchy. After much heart-searching, Drakestein felt her responsibility was to remain in England and continue to develop what she had begun. Her Dutch colleagues returned to Holland. The rightness of her decision was born out by the development of the movement's work that was steady and manifold: the small remnant of a community was enlarged by a flow of English recruits. Grail training outlines were produced for parish groups of girls and women all over the country. Ahead of her time, Drakestein did for professional and middle-class women what her friend, Patrick Keegan of Young Christian Workers, was doing for the re-Christianization of the working class. Grail Family Circles developed for groups of married couples. Discussion material was backed up by weekend and longer courses at the new headquarters, Waxwell Farm House, Pinner, Middlesex. Drakestein emerged as a strong leader, with serendipity, farsightedness, and inspiration, although at times a little autocratic. Early on she recognized and encouraged individuals and movements preparing for the renewal of the Church through Vatican II. It was she who drew together a small group of translators who produced the Grail psalms, providing a ready translation with sanction from Rome for liturgical use for the English-speaking world in 1962.

During Vatican II she lived in Rome with the small Grail secretariat set up for the English and Welsh bishops. She made the most of this opportunity to meet key figures promoting *aggiornamento* in the Church. Back in England, she worked tirelessly to forward renewal: she advanced theologian and scripture scholar meetings; set up weekend and longer courses for clergy and lay people; encouraged Grail members to be active in the early catechetical movement; encouraged ecumenical relationships and liturgical reforms. The Grail expanded as the Grail Companions were admitted, single women with active commitment, some in secular occupation. This was followed by the formation of Grail Partners, married couples who made similar commitment. With Archbishop Derek John Worlock of Liverpool, Drakestein was in the vanguard when the vocation and status of secular institutes were developed in Rome; c. 710-711 of the *Codex Iuris Canonici* owe much to her vision and perseverance.

Drakestein stepped down as president in 1969, beginning what was probably the happiest period of her life. Her final 24 years she lived hidden and prayerful as a poustinik member of the Madonna House in Combermere, Ontario. She became a much loved confidante and wise woman to the many hurt and needy people seeking healing at Madonna House. Even during her last five years with Alzheimer's disease, she was an inspiration and support for her nurses and many visitors.

The English Grail to which Drakestein devoted much of her life continues to develop and flourish. The full-time community now shares responsibility for the Grail movement with the Companions and Partners on a more equal footing. New branches have been formed: Associates, a large number of people from all walks of life for whom the Grail is a spiritual lifeline; the Family Network, which organizes weeks and days for families; and the Grail Young Adults, which organizes meetings and activities for themselves and others. Together all these Grail people work for the refounding of the Church and renewal of society and the environment in a multitude of ways.

[C. WIDDICOMBE]

DRAMA, MEDIEVAL

The drama of the Middle Ages began as mimetic representations of religious history, in which clerics and subsequently laymen enacted the events of Holy Scripture, God's dealings with His people in the Old and New Testaments. Originally associated with the Church's annual festival of Easter Sunday, it was gradually expanded to include the events commemorated at other great feasts such as Christmas and the Epiphany, and even saints' days in some locales. From the 10th to the 13th centuries the plays were in Latin, the official language of the Roman liturgy, but in the 14th and 15th centuries a vernacular religious drama flourished in each of the western European countries, and in this stage of expansion was marked by the composition of cycles dramatizing the full range of scriptural events from Creation to the Last Judgment.

A second stage in the development of the medieval drama resulted in morality plays. These belong mainly to the 15th and 16th centuries and are distinguishable from the miracle plays by their extensive use of allegory and by the shift in subject matter, as the period advances, from religious truths to secular, and even political, indoctrination.

Finally, with the rise of the interludes as almost an inevitable corollary of the moralities, the medieval drama lost its original religious inspiration and concern. The allegorical element still continues in the interludes, but is progressively employed in the service of farce.

This survey traces the development of the early drama: the Latin liturgical drama, the vernacular mystery cycles, and dramatization of the saints' lives, or miracle plays (*see* MORALITY PLAYS).

The medieval religious drama was a creation of the Benedictine monks during the CAROLINGIAN RENAISSANCE (*see* BENEDICTINES). It was a phase of the literary and artistic work that accompanied the renovations of liturgical service books under CHARLEMAGNE's direction, and was preceded by many experiments of an essentially lyrical character that are known under the general name of tropes. Although many attempts have been made by historians to connect the liturgical drama with a secular theatrical tradition surviving from classical antiquity, there is little or no proof of such continuity. Evidence points to the collapse of the Roman theater even before the fall of the empire itself, and the seeds of its destruction were already present in its most flourishing days. The Roman citizen, even when he patronized the stage, looked with contempt upon the performers, most of whom were slaves and were barred from juridical and social privileges. The material of the performances was thoroughly obscene, evoking the disapproval even of a pagan emperor (MARCUS AURELIUS) and meriting the condemnation of many Christian leaders in the early days of the Church. During the barbarian invasions, when the Germanic peoples infiltrated or plundered the imperial territory, the newly arrived inhabitants ignored the decadent performances of the actors (*histriones* and *mimi*) as utterly alien to their own tribal customs of bardic recitations at military festivals. Though some type of informal entertainment by vagabond actors may have long survived the Roman theatrical institution, it is nevertheless probable that even the conception of public stage performance was lost in Italy and Western Europe from about A.D. 600.

Liturgical drama. Quasi-dramatic ceremonies within the Church, such as Holy Week observances at Jerusalem or the celebration of Mass itself, have often tempted historians to interpret it as drama, but the liturgical drama

Illumination from "Play of Daniel," medieval drama manuscript by Daniel Beauvais.

of the 10th century was a wholly new phenomenon. Dialogue and patterned movement do not constitute drama, without the presence of fictive impersonation, i.e., the assumption of roles by actors who pretend to be other than themselves. This was the fundamental thesis of Professor Karl Young (*The Drama of the Medieval Church, passim*) in his monumental study of the liturgical plays, and it remains valid as the essential criterion of drama.

Troping. The process of troping was at first a lyrical and musical embellishment of an established liturgical text, e.g., the INTROIT of the Mass. The trope was a commentary or explanation provided for the text and probably had greatest significance at the Introit, which strikes the theme for the Mass of a particular feast. Often an extract from the Old Testament Psalms, the Introit needed a New Testament counterpart to reveal its prefigurative or prophetic import. Even in the Gallican liturgy (*see* GALLICAN RITES), used in Frankish territory before Charlemagne's time, a prose preface recited by the priest had served this function. In the Carolingian period and thereafter, a choral prelude to the Introit psalm was substituted for the preface and chanted by the monastic choir. Thus the Introit for Easter Sunday, from the 138th Psalm, began with the 18th verse, "Resurrexi et adhuc tecum sum" and was "troped" by prefixing the angelic dialogue with the three Marys at the tomb beginning: "Quem queritis in sepulchro, Christicole?" The transition between trope and Introit proper was arranged in some such manner as that used at Limoges: "Alleluia, ad sepulcrum residens angelus nunciat resurrexisse Christum. En ecce completum est illud quod olim ipse per prophetam dixerat ad Patrem, taliter inquiens: Resurrexi," etc. (Young, 1:209).

For a century (c. 850–950) the tropes were merely chanted by the choir, which was divided into semichoruses to simulate dialogue. Only when individual clergymen took the roles of the angel and the Marys and acted out the little scene at the sepulcher was drama present. The earliest surviving copy of such a play is that in the *Regularis concordia,* a rule drawn up in England about 975 to create unity in monastic practices, but the custom was older than this date in French religious houses. As soon as genuine drama was present the scene was removed from the Mass and placed at the end of MATINS, the hour in the Divine Office that precedes the dawn. It was an appropriate time for the Easter play, which may have been attracted to this place in the recitation of the Office by the custom, already established in connection with Easter Matins, of raising up a cross that bad been "buried" on Good Friday after its veneration, the entombed cross sometimes being accompanied by a Sacred Host. This ceremony was known as the *Elevatio Crucis* and would he followed quite naturally by a dramatic representation of the Marys' visit to the sepulcher.

Easter Plays. The Easter drama in this simple form was known as the *Visitatio Sepulchri.* It was enlarged by two additional scenes, the approach of Peter and John to the tomb and the appearance of the risen Savior to Mary Magdalen. The first of these increments offered theatrical opportunities for dynamism as opposed to the nearly static effect of the original *Visitatio.* Peter and John raced to the sepulcher, John outrunning his companion, and, since no dialogue was provided by the scriptural accounts, the monastic chorus usually chanted a narrative commentary, the liturgical antiphon *Currebant duo simul,* and thus filled the silent interval with music. The angel was still present to point out the empty grave and to hold up the linen cloths that had bound the Sacred Body. In the Latin texts that survive from German monasteries, there is often a rubric directing the congregation to sing a vernacular Easter hymn at the close of this scene, its opening words being given as "Christ ist erstanden." The popular hymn might then be followed by the *Te Deum laudamus,*

if no other scene was enacted. The directions for the plays with Peter and John as characters include some indication of costume and a growing realism in the representation. The Apostles were to be clothed in red vestments (*dalmaticis rubeis*) and Peter was to limp visibly. The tomb might be a structure erected on the model of the sepulcher in the church of the Anastasis in Jerusalem, or the tomb of a wealthy donor who had provided in his will for the use of his monument within the church edifice for this theatrical purpose.

The last addition to the Easter play was the so-called *Hortulanus* scene, in which Christ appeared to Magdalen in the form of a gardener. It was probably not until the late 12th century that this climactic incident was introduced, and it seems to have been a French innovation. It provided for the first time a peripeteia within the acted play, a reversal of the emotional mood by a "recognition" or illumination, which is fundamental to dramatic structure conceived as a finished work of art. When the three scenes were integrated by this emotional reversal the lyric beauty of the three Marys' laments was balanced by the joy that followed the stunning revelation of Christ's identity. At times Mary Magdalen herself chanted the *Improperia* or reproaches from the Good Friday liturgy; or the well-known Easter sequence VICTIMAE PASCHALI LAUDES was divided between Mary and the Apostles, whose "Dic nobis, Maria, quid vidisti in via?" served as a fitting denouement to the now fully elaborated *Ludus paschalis.* The risen Lord's appearance was carefully provided for in the stage directions: at Saint-Benoît-sur-Loire the famous Fleury playbook contains the rubric that the actor impersonating Him should be clothed in a white garment tinged as with blood and that he was to carry the Cross through the monastery choir before appearing to Mary; that at his return he should be holding the Resurrection banner in his hand.

Further elaboration of the Easter dramatic observances can be considered incidental and occasional. In German liturgical manuscripts there was sometimes a scene prefixed to the *Visitatio Sepulchri,* in which the Marys stopped on the way to the tomb for purchase of ointments. A spice-merchant or *unguentarius* was featured in such an episode, but within the Latin drama he remained a dignified and quiet character. Only in the vernacular of a later time did he become a comic persona, caviling over the price of his wares and delaying the sale. In some churches a play called the *Peregrini* was performed at Vespers within Easter week, dramatizing the confrontation of Christ with the disciples on the road to Emmaus. This scene was likely to be performed in the nave of the church, a structure having been erected to serve as the inn where the breaking of the bread and the recognition of the Savior occurred.

Christmas Plays. The very widespread distribution and the frequency of liturgical drama at Easter are attested by the several hundred manuscripts of this play that still survive. In comparison with this quantity the number of extant Christmas plays is so small as to be negligible. That the Christmas texts are later than the Easter ones cannot be doubted, for it is not until the 11th century that Christmas tropes are found, and these are nondramatic choral elaborations of the Introit. Genuine drama, associated with Christmas Matins, very probably grew up some time during the same century. The simple nucleus of the text is a close imitation of the Easter *Visitatio Sepulchri.* For "Quem queritis in sepulchro?" now appears "Quem queritis in presepe [manger], pastores, dicite." The question is addressed to the shepherds who have come to Bethlehem, and the speakers are to be identified as the apocryphal midwives represented in legend and art as attending Mary. When the shepherds reply that they are seeking Christ the Savior, they are told that He is present—"Adest hic"—instead of receiving the negative answer given at the tomb, "Non est hic." The close verbal parallelism reveals the origin of the Christmas text in the much older Easter pattern, but the lyrical embellishment of the simple dialogue proceeded on its independent course as the Christmas plays became more elaborate. (Young, 2:4.)

When the dramatist saw fit to include the appearance of the angelic messenger to the shepherds in the field, he used St. Luke's account of the incident, ending with the choral *Gloria in excelsis Deo* chanted by the several clerics representing the heavenly host. The shepherds on their way to Bethlehem chanted an antiphon or hymn as processional, e.g., the *Pax in terris nunciatur* in the well-known play from Rouen. After the dialogue with the attendants at the crib, they might chant the beautiful hymn (originally a Mass sequence), *Salve, Virgo singularis,* paying honor to the Virgin Mother as they approached to adore the Child. The Holy Family was usually represented not by living actors but by statues placed about a crib or manger. Since the dramatic records of these plays are so few and meager, we cannot be sure whether there was any connection between these constructions used as stage props and the stable scenes erected, especially under Franciscan auspices, in public squares and churches at Christmas time. (*See* CRIB, CHRISTMAS.)

The number of Christmas plays built around the *Quem queritis in presepe?* is fewer than ten, as far as surviving manuscripts are witness. Undoubtedly there were some others of which we have no remains, for parish records in England contain references to liturgical plays at this season. There was also, however, a type of Christmas play connected with the office of Lauds, in which choirboys dressed as shepherds. Professor Young found only one instance of this practice, at Rouen, but Father Richard Donovan has discovered that the custom was widespread in France, and of special importance in Spain even into modern times. It may therefore more certainly be regarded as the typical Christmas play than the *Quem queritis* can be. Its kernel is the question and answer that make up one of the antiphons for Christmas Lauds (the second hour of the Divine Office). The following example is from Dax in France: "Pastores, dicite quidnam vidistis, et annunciate Christi nativitatem. . . . Infantem vidimus pannis involutum, et choros angelorum laudantes Salvatorem." (Donovan, 34). To this question chanted by the choir and answered by several boys dressed as shepherds there might be prefixed a journey to Bethlehem, so that the dialogue became a report upon this visit. The timing of the presentation seems to have varied in different localities, the most common practice being the chanting of Lauds (with the drama) immediately after the first Mass of Christmas.

Christmas-related Plays. Of much greater popularity than these Nativity plays were two other dramas closely related to the Christmas story, namely, the Procession of Prophets and the Offering of the Magi. The first of these has a curious development unique in the drama of the West, although there are historians who consider that the Byzantine liturgy (*see* BYZANTINE RITE) contained dramatic offices of this kind. Its origin is not a trope but a sermon, written in the 5th century, long associated erroneously with St. Augustine as author and incorporated into the office of Matins during the Christmas season as a homiletic reading. A leader summons various Prophets from the Old Testament to render their testimony to the Messiah, and each one is quoted in a few sentences, this Hebraic evidence being augmented by citation from a few Gentile figures like Vergil, Nabuchodonosor, and the Erythraean Sibyl. The basic speaker (Pseudo-Augustine) engages in a kind of imaginary dialogue with the Prophets and also with auditors who are indicated as the Jewish people refusing to accept Christ as Messiah. The dialogue and the monologues of each speaker form in their totality a recapitulation of Old Testament prevision of the Savior's coming and thus a summation of the Advent liturgy on the threshold of the great Christmas feast.

The obvious dramatic potentialities of this *lectio* were recognized and explored in a number of French monasteries from the 11th century, the oldest surviving text of a dramatized version coming to us from Saint-Martial at Limoges. Although originally no action occurred beyond the advance of each Prophet to the center of a platform or stage, the total effect of the solemn processional form and chanting appears to have been highly theatrical. The rubrics provide for costuming and makeup of considerable realism: Isaiah was to be bearded, Moses to wear a dalmatic and carry the Tables of the Law, Daniel to be dressed splendidly, Vergil to be crowned with ivy, and so on. Professor Martial Rose has recorded that modern performances of this play (in the vernacular versions) have an astonishing effect upon an audience, because the short homiletic pronouncements can become little fiery sermons of great eloquence and emotional power (Rose, 171). Some of the prophecies were delivered in the more elaborate Latin plays with accompanying action. Thus Nabuchodonosor consigned the three youths to a fiery "furnace" prepared in advance with cloth and oakum fiber ready to be ignited at the proper moment. Most popular of all such prophetic scenes was undoubtedly that of the Prophet Balaam, who rode in upon an ass, spurring it fiercely in the attempt to reach King Balak, but was prevented from completing his forbidden journey by an angel with drawn sword. This is the stuff of which theater is made, and a gradually perfected technique transformed the spectacles from homiletic to genuinely dramatic performance.

In addition to the Prophet play there was another drama associated with the Christmas season and destined to overshadow the popularity of the quiet Nativity scene. This was the *Officium stellae* celebrating the Epiphany to the Magi, which gave opportunity for splendid trappings in the royal garments, ceremonial, and gifts of the Oriental kings, and for the characterization of Herod as the ranting tyrant. Herod became the stellar role of liturgical drama, for his treachery and his rage transcended the conventional limits of stylized and hieratic speech and gesture. In one version he might express mere anxiety at the information that a Child had been born King of the Jews; in another he might threaten the Magi or cast them into prison; in several versions he would give vent to his fury and frustration by brandishing his sword on learning that the three Wise Men had eluded him after their visit to Bethlehem. All of this activity was a delight to the spectators even in the dignified performances within the church edifices, and it was to become a major comic attraction in the vernacular cycles when Herod could vent his spite and display his histrionic talents on a pageant wagon or in a public square.

From a literary point of view the Magi plays were among the most finished and artistic. The interview between Herod and the alien kings was sometimes cast into the form of Latin hexameters in the classical manner, closely imitating passages in Vergil's *Aeneid* in which the wandering Trojans are questioned concerning their home and their destination. The Magi offered their gifts to the Christ Child in solemn and decorous phrases, which in some texts have a patterned rhetoric that is genuinely lyrical. Herod himself was not confined to gesticulation and swordplay, but occasionally expressed his fear

in an eloquent stanza, or his anger in a threatening tag line that has been identified as a quotation from Sallust: "Incendium meum ruina extinguam."

International Scope. Within the limits of strictly liturgical drama, then, the countries of Western Europe show an almost identical series of expansions and elaborations. Since the medieval Latin language of the plays was an international idiom, there was free and extensive borrowing of texts without adaptation to the circumstances of national locales. So similar are the liturgical sources and the ecclesiastical customs upon which the dramas rest that we can infer the nature of any Latin play that happens not to survive in one or the other country. If a locale does not possess the remains of a *Hortulanus* scene, for example, one can reconstruct the missing material confidently by study of a French manuscript for the same chronological period. The case of England is peculiarly illustrative of this fact. Virtually no Latin texts survive from the British Isles for the liturgical plays because the 16th-century reformers were thoroughly hostile to this drama and destroyed the whole surviving corpus of monastic and cathedral manuscripts containing it. It is quite easy, however, to reconstruct the tradition for England by a study of local parish records of performances and of corresponding Continental texts for each phase of the development. French, German, and Spanish libraries withstood the antagonism of the Reformation forces and have yielded abundant treasures of this genre. Spain (and its New World colonies) preserved into the 20th century even the actual performances of the medieval plays in some locales. Puerto Rico, for example, abolished the remnants of its popular dramatic customs only in the 1950s, at the official restoration of the EASTER VIGIL observances and the revision of the Holy Week liturgy made by Rome at that time.

Mystery plays. The liturgical Latin drama must not be relegated to the centuries preceding the 13th, as though it were abandoned for a new interest in the vernacular and left to decay within monastic cloisters. The dramatized trope continued to be performed within the churches long after the great enterprise of mystery-play production had been undertaken by parish or civic guilds. The Latin plays had been the prerogative of monastic communities, on the one hand, and of the cathedral churches with their chapters of resident canons, on the other. In both cases the actors in the plays were clergymen who performed the dramatized liturgy in the very choirs of their churches as an extension of their regular duties in the choral chanting of the Divine Office. The vernacular mysteries were generically different in that they were the prerogative of laymen who supported, regulated, and acted them as parish activities. This guild enterprise should not be regarded as a competitive one, drawing the spectators out of the church and into the public squares, but rather as one supplementary to the church productions and associated with a different part of the liturgical year than either Christmas or Easter, namely with Corpus Christi.

The very term "secularization" of the drama, which occurs in so many histories of the 13th-century developments, is an unfortunate misnomer. It creates the impression of a growing irreverence and worldliness as the plays became more elaborate, as though they were no longer appropriate for association with church and clergy. On the contrary, the vernacular cycles were still the literary work of monks and cathedral canons, who were the only ones trained in the theological learning needed for these vast enterprises and usually the only ones who had the rhetorical and poetic skill for the actual composition. To the very end of the period in which the English, French, and German mystery cycles flourished they remained essentially a devotional exercise pervaded by the doctrines and the liturgical spirit of the Church, although increasing emphasis on spectacle, entertainment, and professional acting was the inevitable concomitant of experiment and experience. Comic incident and characterization, though often singled out for undue praise by modern critics, were the peripheral and accidental fringes of a cosmic narrative that related the history of God's people seriously and reverently.

Beginning of Mystery Cycles. Some of the liturgical plays at Christmas during the transition period (13th century) were already small cycles, including Prophets, Annunciation, Visitation, Nativity, Magi, and Herod elements. The Easter drama seems not to have reached a comparable degree of elaboration until the vernacular plays were written, and nothing but the most rudimentary beginnings of a Passion play belong to this Latin drama. France, which was the birthplace of so many experimental features of the drama from the 10th to the 12th centuries, provides virtually nothing in extant remains from the transition era. Germany possesses a manuscript that testifies to the existence of highly developed Christmas plays, the famous Benediktbeuern (*see* BEURON, ABBEY OF) text from Munich, embracing the whole narrative from the Prophets to the death of Herod. England's loss of all liturgical manuscripts, as mentioned above, presents a special problem in the assessment of its precyclic drama, but the state of its surviving vernacular cycles so clearly reveals the building of them in successive "layers" that one can infer the transitional Latin stage from the most primitive *stratum* of the English.

Corpus Christi Cycles. The attachment of plays to the post-Paschal season and especially to the feast of COR-PUS CHRISTI seems to have been a gradual achievement and not a uniform one. The earliest record of a complete cycle performed at this time of year is from Cividale in Italy, for Pentecost of the year 1298, and the record is duplicated there for the year 1303. The feast of Corpus Christi itself was extended to the universal Church early in the 14th century, and a procession seems to have been associated with it from the beginning as a solemn celebration. Most probably the plays were attracted to the grand festival because of the time of year, which was propitious for outdoor performances. They should not, however, be regarded as part of the procession, even though at times actors walked in it. The procession was a strictly religious observance, in which the Sacred Host was carried through the streets of a town accompanied by clergy and laity. The plays, which were much older, at least in their Latin form, than the Corpus Christi festival, became casually associated with this late spring holy day in northern England and in various places on the Continent. When this association occurred, the Latin plays of Christmas and Easter were translated into the vernacular and expanded by degrees into the entire story of salvation, from the scene in the Garden of Eden until the final Judgment.

The extant cycles of this kind in England are those of Chester, York, Wakefield, Coventry (a fragmentary text), and one conjecturally associated with the town of Lincoln. France has no really comparable texts but rather PASSION PLAYS, the earliest of which is the *Passion du Palatinus,* of the 14th century, lacking Old Testament and Nativity material altogether. In Germany both Corpus Christi plays and the distinct genre of Passion play flourished; the former, called *Frohnleichnamspiel,* is the pattern of the early 14th-century Vienna play as well as that of the Erlau Magdalen play, and the Eger and the Künzelzau cycles. The genuine Passion play, often containing only the Fall of Man, the Passion, and the Resurrection, can be found in such texts as the Donaueschingen, Redentin, Frankfurt, and Alsfeld plays. There is a Cornish cycle, probably based on Continental Breton models, which is of the Corpus Christi type, but strangely lacks a Nativity drama.

One of the greatest problems in the study of the cycles is the origin of the Old Testament plays. Since there are amazingly few Latin dramas on any Old Testament narratives, the composition of such texts is attributed to the period of vernacular expansion in the 14th century, and it is possible that they are as late as the 15th. All speculation on this problem must take account of the theory advanced by the French historian Marius Sepet, in a book entitled *Les Prophètes du Christ* (1878). Briefly, his idea was that the Old Testament plays in the vernacular cycles were incidents originally developed within the Latin Prophet plays (discussed above), subsequently detached to stand as small independent dramas and finally reunited into a much larger framework than that of the *Prophetae* procession. This hypothesis is closely related to the already rather advanced cyclic status of Latin Christmas plays in the transitional 13th century, and Sepet regarded the Old Testament material as controlled by the terminus in the Nativity of Christ. If the theory is correct, these narratives of the great Jewish leaders like Abraham and Moses must have been present in at least the earliest stage of vernacular cycle-building and perhaps already in the Latin era.

Sepet's book was hailed as a monumental contribution to medieval dramatic studies in his day and was accepted by almost all European scholars. The challenge to it has been largely an American phenomenon; even today, after practically a full century, Sepet's theory is referred to by European historians as the standard explanation of cyclic development. The point of attack from American critics has been Sepet's emphasis upon prophecy in the Old Testament material, whereas the vernacular plays are usually based upon the Patriarchs Adam, Noah, Abraham, and Moses. This is not the place for a full account of the controversy, but one may say that a flexible conception of prophecy, such as Sepet possessed, can embrace the figures of the Patriarchs, who were precursors and prefigurative types of Christ. The inclusion of them in a procession of witnesses to the Messiah is simply an extension of the "prophetic principle" (W. W. Greg's term) from the *Processus prophetarum* to the entire Old Testament span.

When the elaborate Christmas plays (perhaps already linked with Old Testament expansions) were united to the Easter plays and translated into English, French, or German for use at the Corpus Christi festival, a rather lengthy series of plays was available for production, even before the insertion of incidents from Christ's ministry, suffering, and Crucifixion. These inserted incidents were to form a second layer of composition added perhaps a generation later than the primitive stratum and detectable by the large amount of apocryphal legendary material, which stands out in relief against the liturgical character of the earlier work. The plays continued to be subjected to revision, polishing, and expansion, and thus a third layer of stratification is visible in a number of cycles, made significant by professional literary art, such as the use of the alliterative poetic line in the Towneley and York cycles. This visible stratification characterizes the English plays rather than the French and German, for those in France are so highly developed that the more primitive layers have been completely obscured and those in Germany seem to have progressed very slowly and retained the style of the first cyclic expansions without easily discernible revisions.

English and French Cycles. The city of Chester in northwestern England has long enjoyed the distinction of possessing the oldest extant English cycle, which was considered, according to some ancient records, to date from 1328. It has been the work of Professor F. M. Salter to challenge that priority by showing that the records containing the early dating are themselves 16th-century reconstructions of the historical case and quite in error. Salter has revised the estimate of the Chester cycle's age by dating it in the time of Sir Henry Francis, a monk of St. Werburgh's Abbey, about 1375. If this decision is correct, Chester's plays were first produced about the same time as those of York (1378), Beverley (1377), and Coventry (1392). It is probable that the second stratum in each cycle was the work of revisers about 1400, and that the literary embellishments of the final stage were completed by 1425 or 1430.

When a cycle spanned the entire biblical narrative, it might include 30 or 40 plays and thus require several days for its enactment. The magnitude of the enterprise can scarcely be grasped today, when revivals of the plays almost inevitably mean cutting of the text (e.g., of all the Old Testament scenes except that of the Fall) or selection of an individual play for a Christmas or Easter production. The problem of temporal disposition is only one of several gigantic technical difficulties in the representation, for the provision of actors, costumes, and stage props in such a performance must have taxed the ingenuity and the financial resources of a whole city. The disposition of space for the rapidly changing locales of a cycle was solved in various ways, the Continental solution differing markedly from the English method.

Manner of Staging. In France the outdoor stages were but the spatial extension of the interior scenes that had characterized the liturgical drama. The earliest extant French vernacular play is *Le Mystère d'Adam* (c. 1175), containing elaborate rubrics that indicate its method of staging. Since it was a miniature Old Testament cycle it needed a Garden of Eden, Heaven, Hell, and a place for the Prophets who rendered their testimonies to the Messiah. The top step or porch of a church (perhaps a side entrance) was used for the terrestrial Paradise, Heaven itself was within the church, while the ground level at the foot of the steps became the refuge for the rejected Adam and Eve and the Limbo to which they were finally led away. As the plays were expanded later, a series of *loca* or *sedes* was arranged in linear juxtaposition within view of a spectator-throng and capable even of attracting an audience to move in succession from one *sedes* to the next for the progressing action. The individual locality might be a raised scaffold provided with curtains and some furniture, a series of these structures lining a public square or even built into a large composite stage such as that of the well-known miniature in the Valenciennes *Passion* manuscript. France knew also the pageant wagon drawn through a town from one locale to another, at each of which an audience was gathered in expectation of a performance. Records from a few places like Béthune and Lille make it certain that such movable stages were known, but the stationary type was the norm for French theater.

In England the pageant wagon was known at York and Chester at least, and probably elsewhere. It has long been the accepted theory that such stages on wagons drawn from place to place were the regular English device. The theory has been challenged by Professor Martial Rose, who has suggested that some towns, notably Wakefield and Lincoln, probably used a single playing space, an outdoor theater in the round, with stationary scaffolds arranged on the circumference of a large circle. Pageant wagons were probably drawn up with stage and equipment used only in a single play, (e.g., Noah's prefabricated ark) and then removed after their moment had passed. The stationary scaffolds would have been designated for locales of recurring importance, e.g., Heaven, Jerusalem, and Nazareth. The validity of this hypothesis rests partly upon stage directions in the manuscripts that could not have been implemented without a large playing space and several *sedes;* it rests also upon statements in the parish or guild records that seem to support the notion of a single place rather than a series of designated stopping points. British historians of the drama have taken the lead in this effort to demonstrate that both mystery and morality plays were frequently performed in outdoor theaters in which rows of seats were constructed on a tiered hillside built artificially around an open grassy "place," this "place" serving as a flexible locality for scenes not assigned to one of the scaffolds or wagons.

The use of such a playing area and theater in the round would have enabled a small group of actors to perform an entire cycle with unity and continuity. On the other hand, the use of many pageant wagons drawn through a town in succession would have required a different actor for each role in every individual pageant. Professor Rose has argued that Wakefield had so small a population throughout the 15th century that it could not have supplied enough actors to duplicate the roles again and again in a series of pageant-wagon performances. It becomes highly probable that such a village as Wakefield would have entrusted its cycle to a single religious guild rather than to the civic trade guilds, at least until the 16th century. In York, on the other hand, a large and flourishing city, the craftsmen's groups were numerous and of great membership, thus making the theatrical venture of the pageant wagons a feasible and successful undertaking.

Acting and Care of Text. Civic and parish records make it clear that high standards of performance were established and maintained in the Corpus Christi plays. Although it would be erroneous to designate the mystery cycles as professional theater, since its actors were carpenters, bakers, merchants, and so forth, the civic pride of a town was nevertheless great enough to regulate efficiently and strictly the actors and the productions. The records of royal visits to a place like Coventry for the purpose of attending the Corpus Christi plays indicate the respect in which the enterprises were held. The season of Lent was often used as a time for tryouts and selection of actors. Undoubtedly there were individuals who, like Bottom the Weaver, wished to play all the parts, but regulations like those at York imposed heavy fines on those attempting more roles than were consonant with excellent performance. An actor who forgot his lines or read them indistinctly was subject to fine, and the guild responsible for a play was required under financial penalty to furnish its pageant wagon well and maintain it in good condition. Late arrival of a pageant at its playing locale was also penalized. Even the spectators were under surveillance to prevent carrying of weapons into the crowd or public demeanor capable of initiating riot or disorder.

In addition to the care bestowed upon the theatrical production itself there was also constant supervision of the text and frequent remodeling of its literary character. In some towns the manuscript of the cycle was copied and preserved by the local community of monks; in others it was the property of the civic officials, who deputed clerks to keep it in legible condition. In England during the 16th century, the disturbances of the Reformation focused attention upon the medieval dramatic manuscript wherever it had survived, and the struggle to control its possession and revision became a major issue, especially in the Archdiocese of York. During the 15th century, before such troubles developed, the revision of the plays was a matter of gradual literary embellishment. As mentioned previously, most of the cycles show a third layer of "stratification," that is, a rewriting or an addition of new scenes (*c.* 1420–30), distinguished by more mature characterization and greater prosodic sophistication than had marked either the primitive layer of vernacular translation from the Latin or the second level of apocryphal and legendary expansion.

Names of individual authors have not survived in English literary embellishment of this kind, but modern scholarship has found ways of designating the style of this or that reviser. "The Wakefield Master" is the best-known 15th-century author, distinguished for his late work in the Towneley plays, recognizable by the peculiarly complex stanza form he employed and by a vigorous comic spirit touched with sardonic wit. "The York

Realist'' is another such appellation, applied to the author of the York Passion plays and certain other dramas in the cycle, perhaps most notable for the richness and complexity of their diction. We are more fortunate in the search for authorial identity in Continental cycles. The great Passion plays of France have specific names attached to them: Eustache Mercadé, to whom the *Passion d'Arras* (*c.* 1440) is attributed; Arnoul Greban, choirmaster at Notre Dame Cathedral in Paris (*c.* 1450); and Jean Michel, who revised and expanded the work of his two predecessors (*c.* 1485).

Literary Quality and Popularity. Modern critics of the medieval plays have been slow to admit literary excellence in the vernacular compositions, even when they have accorded praise to the lyrical beauty and musical grandeur of the Latin liturgical drama. This area of study has been among the last to elicit the attention of stylistic analysts, who have retreated before the arduous tasks involved in the discrimination of dialect peculiarities, layers of incremental growth in the texts, and prosodic patterns of great freedom and complexity. Consistent and painstaking study is quite rewarding, however, and the extensive range of poetic expression in the monologues, dialogues, and choral chants reveals a variety of literary effects overlooked by social historians and students of merely ''theatrical'' possibilities in the plays.

As might well be expected, the lyrical cast of the Latin prototypes continues to mark the vernacular lines, so that many an Old Testament figure expresses his longing for the Messiah in melancholy, reflective laments reminiscent of the Advent liturgy. New Testament characters like the shepherds tending their flocks near Bethlehem transcend the limits of their peasant life and speech to pronounce ''Hail lyrics'' before the Holy Manger. Their lines are indebted to the sequences and hymns of the Mass and the Breviary, and complement the music of an angelic choir that has just rendered *Gloria in excelsis Deo.* Christ the Savior speaks from the Cross a reproach to His sinful and erring followers and one detects in His language and His cadences the poignant question of the Good Friday *Improperia*—''Popule meus, quid feci tibi?'' A full realization of the total artistry in these plays demands a synthesis of visual, musical, and verbal techniques comparable to those of modern spectacular performances designated by the term ''operatic,'' but shorn of the romantic extravagances of that form.

Suppression and Survival. The medieval cycles continued to draw the interest, attendance, and participation of European Catholics well into the Renaissance and Reformation periods. They survived into virtually modern times in many places on the Continent; even in England, where the hostility of reforming clergy and government

to the plays was especially strong, they were still important in the late 16th century. Several methods of eradicating them (see H. C. Gardiner, *Mysteries' End*) were undertaken wherever official anti-Catholic attitudes prevailed. One method was the recall of the playbook by an ecclesiastic, for instance, by Archbishop Grindal of York, for revision and ''correction.'' At times the manuscript was retained in custody and denied to the players, or offensive passages were canceled before return of the copy. A stronger method was the actual prohibition of the performances, and this method often provoked determined opposition to the Crown policies by the local mayor and town council. The city of Chester was involved in serious conflict of this type in 1575. Finally, a very successful way of supplanting the traditional festive enactments of the Corpus Christi plays was the composition of short biblical dramas, independent of the cycles, by writers of Protestant persuasion, often schoolmasters who substituted classroom milieu and Terentian style for the public square and the liturgical language.

This last-mentioned practice was of immense importance on the Continent, where a movement of Biblical drama flourished especially in German-speaking areas, led by playwrights such as Sixt Birck, George Macropedius, and Thomas Kirchmayer. England's John Bale, who had been a Carmelite friar before entering the Reformation controversy about 1535, wrote under the patronage of Thomas CROMWELL a series of religious plays imitative of medieval models but informed with a bitter anti-Catholic sentiment.

There was an authentic survival of the mystery plays in the Jesuit school drama of the 17th and 18th centuries. Our own times have seen sporadic revival of the religious medieval plays in many places. Gustave Cohen, the leading French historian of this dramatic form, has been responsible for performances by his students in Paris and its vicinity for many years. In England the interest generated by the York Festival in 1951, when a shortened version of the York cycle was produced, has supported further attempts of this kind, in revivals of the Towneley and Chester pageants. American academic groups made a few efforts in the 1950s, among them the production of the Beauvais Latin *Play of Daniel* in New York, which has been recorded by the Pro Musica singers. In Germany the best-known performance continues to be the world-famous Oberammergau Passion play, given every ten years.

Miracle plays. A distinct genre of medieval religious drama is the miracle play, which differs from the mysteries both in nature and in origin. It is a dramatization of a saint's life, with special emphasis upon the miraculous works performed by him and his sufferings leading to martyrdom. The materials of the life were drawn from the legendary accounts of popular saints, literature of a romantic and extravagant cast, with highly imaginative elements involved. Consequently, plays based upon these legends were markedly different in many ways from the strictly liturgical performances of narratives drawn from Holy Scripture. Indeed, plays dealing with the acts of New Testament saints, such as Paul or Mary Magdalen, should ordinarily be excluded from the category of ''miracle,'' because of the sobriety and restraint imposed upon them by their biblical source. The saint's legend in dramatic form, on the other hand, seems to have come into existence rather late in the history of Latin religious drama, probably not before the 12th century, when the Christmas and Easter plays were well established; the new genre flourished with a freedom produced by the semi-fictional nature of the material and by a more casual association with the liturgy than the earlier plays had possessed. France was its true home, and it prospered there.

Miracle Plays in Latin. The only Latin texts of such miracles now surviving are those of St. Nicholas. The cult of this saint flourished in central France in the late 11th and 12th centuries, resulting in dramatization of several different legends about his marvelous deeds in behalf of scholars, travelers, and the destitute. The best known of the legends to receive dramatic form is that of the three daughters whose poverty-stricken father cannot provide dowries for them. At a proposal of prostitution for the sake of the family's fortunes, made by the eldest daughter, a purse of gold is cast through the window by the saint, forestalling the threatened calamity. This play became known as the *Tres filiae,* of which one text survives from the German town of Hildesheim and one from the French Benedictine monastery of Fleury. The Latin verse of these plays is so highly lyrical as to suggest a basis in hymnody, perhaps from the Office of the saint's day. The *Te Deum* closing the Hildesheim play confirms the association with liturgical Matins, and the Fleury text ends with the antiphon *O Christi pietas,* which was ordinarily used in Lauds and Vespers of the feast. (*See* NICHOLAS OF MYRA, ST.)

Hildesheim and Fleury possessed also a play on the three students (*Tres clerici*) murdered by their landlord but restored to life by St. Nicholas. Still another legendary play of this type is the *Iconia Sancti Nicolai,* dramatized by the wandering scholar known to us under the name of Hilarius. (A similar text appears in the Fleury playbook.) In this legend a nonbeliever who has acquired an image of St. Nicholas commits his accumulated treasures to its protection, with a superstitious trust in what he regards as magic power. While he is away on a journey, thieves enter his house and steal the treasure. On his return he berates the saint and even scourges the image, but Nicholas himself forces the robbers to return the treasure. The chastened pagan hears him refer the miraculous achievement to God and, thus instructed, undergoes conversion to Christianity. Plays such as these had considerable potential for theatrical effect in costume, bizarre setting, and pantomime. The *Iconia* is of special importance because of the elaborate French play on the same story, written by Jean Bodel in the late 12th century, and distinguished as the earliest surviving miracle play in a vernacular language.

French Miracle Plays. The French dramatizations of the saintly narratives developed very naturally into more imaginative and highly exciting creations. Their connection with liturgical origins was even more tenuous than had been the association of Latin miracles, and the isolation of them from the great mystery cycles encouraged an exotic growth and exuberant spirit. Bodel's *Jeu de S. Nicolas,* mentioned above, contained a pagan king instead of the Latin *Barbarus,* a Crusade instead of a nondescript journey, and a series of tavern scenes for the drinking and gambling thieves, replacing the silent, furtive robbery of the legend. Indeed, the dimension of ''low life'' has much of the fabliau comic spirit and contends vigorously with the elevated religious scenes. Bodel's work is the product of a cultivated and flourishing artistic life in his native city of Arras, a milieu in which the long tradition of simple, liturgical drama could be joined with a vigorous school of sophisticated vernacular poetry.

Perhaps the most popular type of French miracle play was that which displayed the intercessory powers of the Blessed Virgin—*les miracles de Notre Dame.* About 40 of these are preserved in the Cangé manuscripts surviving from the early 15th century. Apparently written for performance by a guild (*puy*) dedicated to the Mother of God, these plays dealt with the lives of great sinners who obtained the grace of repentance and conversion through her intercession. The plots are often of sensational or erotic in character because of the sinful lives preceding the conversions, and must have exercised considerable fascination upon the spectators for this reason. Modern taste is sometimes shocked by the lurid contents of these narratives, or by the apparent ease with which the sinners secure forgiveness, but the plays are essentially religious and devout. The Anglo-Saxon reader needs, perhaps, to make allowance for a Gallic spirit that he often fails to understand.

The arts of poetry and of music figure prominently in these miracles. A regular feature of them is the singing of rondeaux in honor of the Blessed Virgin as she appears on the stage, the singing usually done by the Archangels Gabriel and Michael, who accompany her. The style and structure of these musical pieces are often quite elegant and vividly reminiscent of troubadour lyric verse and music. The manuscripts contain, in addition to these interpolated songs, a series of poems in honor of Mary, copied into the spaces between the plays. Known as *serventoys,* these pieces seem to have been produced in poetical contests sponsored by the *puy* and are usually the winning entries chosen for their excellence. The competitive nature of the phenomenon is indicated by the terms *couronnés* and *estrivés* appearing as designations for the ones copied into the little volumes. It is a curious fact that most of them have as subject the Annunciation rather than any other event of Mary's life, thus pointing to the one feast as the ordinary occasion for the miracle play and the literary contest.

Miracle Plays in England and Scotland. England is almost wholly destitute of saints' plays, with *miracles de Notre Dame* among its surviving medieval manuscripts, but records of performances clearly indicate that the genre was known and loved in that area. Moreover, saints' lives and Marian "miracles" are to be found extant in nondramatic form, e.g., in the work of John Lydgate and his early 15th-century contemporaries. The earliest record of a saint's play in England is that staged by the Anglo-Norman schoolmaster Geoffrey in honor of St. Katherine. The charming story of his ill-fated venture in borrowing vestments from St. Alban's Abbey for costumes and losing them in a fire is told by a contemporary historian, who notes that Geoffrey made restitution by becoming a monk of St. Alban's. The city of London, in which the vernacular mystery cycles seem not to have flourished, was known already in the 12th century for the production of miracle plays. Scattered records of performances from various other places tell us of dramas on St. Mary Magdalen in Norfolk, St. Thomas Becket at King's Lynn, St. Christiana in Kent, etc. Scotland, even more than England, was devoted to this genre, and its records are abundant—for St. Andrew, St. George, and, among others, St. Nicholas. The name of St. George must give us pause when it appears, for we cannot be certain whether dramatic records about his life refer to genuine miracle plays. Very probably many of them do, but account must be taken of St. George's appearance as a swashbuckling hero in the crude folk plays that are not Christian in origin, but are degenerate remains of pagan vegetation rituals. The mumming and sword plays are wholly independent of Christian drama, but it is likely that St. George was drawn into the folk dramas late in the Middle Ages by his association with a dragon-slaying and by his rescue of the Egyptian princess. He thus became one of a group including Captain Slasher, Giant Blunderbore, and the Turkish Champion, who figure prominently in these folk festival celebrations. Plays of this kind are an anomaly in a Christian society, and their crudity in language and technique indicates that they are distinct in origin and development from the "miracles," which had ecclesiastical and academic backgrounds.

See Also: AUTOS SACRAMENTALES.

Bibliography: General. E. K. CHAMBERS, *The Medieval Stage,* 2 v. (Oxford 1903; reprint 1948); *English Literature at the Close of the Middle Ages* (Oxford 1945). C. J. STRATMAN, *Bibliography of Medieval Drama* (Berkeley 1954). A. WILLIAMS, *The Drama of Medieval England* (East Lansing, Mich. 1961). K. YOUNG, *The Drama of the Medieval Church,* 2 v. (Oxford 1933). Special. H. CRAIG, *English Religious Drama of the Middle Ages* (Oxford 1955). R. B. DONOVAN, *The Liturgical Drama in Medieval Spain* (Toronto 1958). G. FRANK, *The Medieval French Drama* (Oxford 1954). H. C. GARDINER, *Mysteries' End* (Yale Studies in English 103; New Haven 1946). A. NICOLL, *Masks, Mimes and Miracles* (New York 1931). M. ROSE, ed., *The Wakefield Mystery Plays* (Garden City, N.Y. 1962). F. M. SALTER, *Medieval Drama in Chester* (Toronto 1955). R. SOUTHERN, *The Medieval Theatre in the Round* (New York 1958). G. COHEN, *Histoire de la mise en scène dans le théâtre religieux français du moyen âge* (new ed. rev. Paris 1951); *Le Théâtre en France au moyen âge* (rev. ed. Paris 1948). W. M. A. CREIZENACH, *Geschichte des neueren Dramas,* 5 v. (Halle 1893–1916) v. 1–2. E. PROSSER, *Drama and Religion in the English Mystery Plays: A Re-Evaluation* (Stanford Studies in Language and Literature 23; Stanford 1962). A. VALBUENA PRAT, *Historia de la literatura española,* 3 v. (4th ed. Barcelona 1953).

[E. C. DUNN]

DRAŠCOVIČ, GEORG DE TRAKOSĆAN

Theologian, cardinal, statesman; b. Biline, near Knin (southern Croatia), Feb. 5, 1525; d. Vienna, Jan. 31, 1587. His uncle, G. MARTINUZZI, sent him to pursue his education at Cracow, Vienna, Bologna, and Rome. He was bishop of Pécs from 1557 to 1563. He attended the Council of TRENT in 1561 as personal legate of Ferdinand I, and later represented the entire Hungarian Church. As leader of the liberal reform group at the Council, he fought for communion under both species and the abolition of clerical celibacy. Later, as bishop of Zagreb (1563–78), he founded the diocesan seminary and published the first polemical writing against CALVINISM. He defended the land against the Turks when he was viceroy of Croatia and Dalmatia (1567–78), and thus earned the title "father of his country and of the poor." He was also bishop of Kalocsa (1572–78) and Györ (1578–87), and royal governor and Hungarian imperial chancellor (1578–85). He was named a cardinal in 1585. In addition to his work against Calvinism, he translated the *Commonitorium* of Vincent of Lerins into Hungarian and edited some works of Lactantius.

Bibliography: K. ST. DRAGANOVIČ, *Lexikon für Theologie und Kirche,* ed. J. HOFER and K. RAHNER (2d, new ed. Freiburg

1957–65) 3:542–543. A. DUDITH, *Orationes quinque in concilio Tridentino habitae* (Halle 1743) appendix. D. FARLATI, *Illyricum sacrum* v.5–8, ed. G. COLETI (Venice 1751–1819) 5:539–545. J. KOLLER, *Historia episcopatus Quinqueecclesiarum* (Pozsony 1782–1806) 6:1–266.

[C. HENKEY]

DREAM

An illusory or hallucinatory psychic activity, particularly of a perceptual-visual nature, that occurs during sleep. It is essentially a psychological phenomenon with many philosophical, religious, and moral implications.

Meaning and Interpretation

People have always been fascinated by the mysterious phenomenon of dreams and, throughout history, have made innumerable attempts to penetrate behind the chaotic appearance of dreams and reach their hidden meaning. These attempts at interpretation were done on several levels, such as the religious, the philosophical, the psychological, and the clinical.

Early Civilizations. Almost all primitive and ancient peoples believed in the religious character of dreams. For them, dreams were vehicles of divine revelation. They imagined that, during sleep, the soul would leave the body, converse with other spirits and with gods, and receive their communications. In the Vedic religion there was the belief that the soul could get entangled in immoral actions. Therefore, after bad dreams, special rites of expiation were prescribed.

Divination through dreams (oneiromancy) was an important religious practice among the early peoples, particularly among the Assyro-Babylonians and Egyptians. Divination was carried out through incubation dreams in temples or through the private practice of magicians and dream interpreters. To facilitate the dream analysis, special handbooks were compiled containing oneirocritical rules and catalogues of dream symbols.

Greeks and Romans. In Greek literature there are many references to dreams. The practice of dream interpretation was a significant aspect of the Greek religious life. The Greek world knew several incubation temples, dedicated usually to Asclepius, god of medicine, in which the devotee spent the night and, through dreams, obtained pertinent information about his problems. The most famous of these incubation temples was that of Asclepius at Epidaurus. There were also professional dream interpreters (*oneirocritai*) for whom special manuals of interpretation were compiled from the fourth century B.C. The most famous of the preserved manuals is the *Oneirocritica* written by Artemidorus of Daldis in the second century A.D. Perhaps the oldest Greek treatise on dreams is a work contained in the Hippocratic corpus. Although the author of this work does not deny the religious meaning of dreams, he admits that some dreams may reflect the physiological conditions of the organism. Some Greek philosophers, such as the Pythagoreans, Socrates, the Platonists, and many Stoics, believed in oneiromancy; others, particularly Aristotle and the Epicureans, rejected it.

For PLATO, fantastic and lawless dreams can easily be aroused by the "wild beast in us." According to Plato, before going to bed, one should awaken his rational powers and collect himself in meditation in order to avoid the experience of bad dreams. Further, Plato thinks that prophetic inspirations are not granted by the divinity to sane people in a waking state, but to people whose intelligence is either demented or enthralled in sleep. However, only a sane man may interpret prophetic dreams.

ARISTOTLE discusses dreams in the three works of his *Parva naturalia: On Sleep and Wakefulness, On Dreams,* and *On Divination through Sleep.* Dreams are a natural phenomenon because they are experienced by everyone, even by animals. Aristotle teaches that not every psychic experience during sleep is a dream, but only those representations that are aroused during sleep by faint residuary movements left in the organism by actual sense perceptions. Dreams are illusions produced by the conceptual fantasy and easily affected by strong emotions and by bodily disturbances. According to Aristotle, prophetic dreams can be explained through coincidence or through natural causes: a plan of activity can be initiated in a dream and later carried out in the waking state; symptoms of an incipient disease can be perceived for the first time in a dream; other dreams may be explained through some natural telepathic ability.

Among the Romans, where divination through dreams was a standard practice, CICERO contested strongly the divine origin of dreams in his *De divinatione.* He claims that there is no connection between dreams and the natural course of events; a scientific method of foretelling the future through dreams is impossible; oneiromancy is a superstition, and dreams do not deserve the slightest degree of respect.

Christianity. The Christian attitude toward dreams was molded by the Bible and may be formulated in the following statements. (1) The dream may be a legitimate vehicle of divine revelation, in which case God Himself provides for proofs attesting the divine origin of dreams. He also takes care of dream interpretation. (2) The majority of dreams are natural phenomena lacking in any special religious meaning. (3) Superstitious divination through dreams is severely forbidden by God as an immoral practice.

The Fathers and Doctors of the Church do not add anything new to the Biblical teaching on dreams. Occasionally they attempt a philosophical or psychological explanation of dream phenomena that reflects the views of Greek philosophers, particularly of Aristotle. St. AUGUSTINE discusses the problem of dreams in one of his letters to Nebridius (*Patrologia Latina*, ed. J. P. Migne [Paris 1878–90] 33:71–73) and in *De Genesi ad litteram* (*Patrologia Latina* 34:470–479). He attempts to explain that superior powers produce dreams in man by energizing *latenter* (in a secret or unconscious way) those traces of activity imprinted by the mind in the organism during the waking state. The supernatural powers use such traces to bring about dreams reflecting their intentions. St. Augustine admits that some dreams may have a psychological significance insofar as they reflect physiological or mental conditions of the dreamer ("men . . . dream what they need"). St. THOMAS AQUINAS deals with dreams in connection with his discussion of superstition (*Summa theologiae* 2a2ae, 95.6). Dreams can be understood best by considering the four causes that produce them: first, the internal spiritual cause of dreams, namely, all the mental activities of the waking state that may recur in dreams; second, internal and corporal causes dependent on the physical disposition of the body; third, external corporal causes that include all environmental conditions, particularly those of the atmosphere; fourth, external spiritual causes—God, angels, and demons. The devil can also reveal future events in dreams to those who have entered into a special compact with him.

Jewish and Islamic Tradition. Dream interpretation through natural means and through divination played an important role in the early Talmudic and Islamic traditions. Many rabbis believed that nothing important happens to a man that is not communicated to him through dreams. They had a saying according to which "a dreamless life is a sinful life." Many of the revelations attributed to Muḥammad took place in dreams. Some medieval Islamic theologians enumerate interpretation of dreams among accepted theological methods.

Modern Psychology. From W. WUNDT on, psychologists have been interested in dreams, both in the psycho-physiological mechanisms that regulate the process of dreaming and in the value that dreams have for the understanding of human PERSONALITY. In the mid-20th century, few psychologists would deny any psychological meaning to dreams. Divergences begin when psychologists start to theorize about the meaning of dreams.

Freud's Theory. Sigmund FREUD bestowed scientific respectability upon dream analysis, particularly with his work on the *Interpretation of Dreams* (1900). An essential feature of psychoanalytical treatment is to bring to the surface the repressed unconscious experiences that are often the source of neurotic conflicts. The main method for uncovering the unconscious is free association. Dream analysis was conceived by Freud as a subsidiary technique to facilitate and expedite free association. Soon it became the royal road to the knowledge of the unconscious psychic life. According to Freud, every dream has a meaning insofar as it is an attempted wish-fulfillment involving repressed sexual infantile urges. Its biological function is to preserve sleep by channeling the unfulfilled infantile wishes, which would disturb the sleep, into disguised modes of wish-fulfillment. Freud called the mechanism that regulates the disguise the censor. It consists of all the inhibitory and repressive tendencies that try to prevent the unconscious from emerging into consciousness. It is because of the work of the censor that every dream presents a double aspect, namely, the manifest content or the external dress of imagery in which the dream is recalled, and the latent content or the hidden meaning fraught with repressed infantile wishes, mostly of a libidinal nature. According to Freud, the following important mechanisms take part in the elaboration of a dream. (1) Condensation occurs when several meanings of the latent content are compressed into a single image of the manifest content. (2) Displacement takes place when the emotional charge is detached from its natural object and directed to a secondary object. (3) Dramatization consists in expressing conceptual ideas with concrete and plastic images. (4) Symbolization involves a concrete representation through an image of another concrete but hidden image, as when, in Freud's mind, a pointed object seen in a dream represents the male sexual organ. Many dream symbols are, according to Freud, independent from any individual interpretation and possess a universal meaning. (5) Secondary elaboration is a dream mechanism that attempts to bring some order and logical understanding into a dream during the process of recalling it.

Jung's Theory. C. G. JUNG introduced new conceptual breadth into dream interpretation. He was the first to analyze the dreams of a person in a sequential series, treating them as a meaningful whole and interpreting them on the basis of an internal consistency. For Jung, dreams reveal not only repressed infantile libidinal wishes, but manifest the whole human personality with its positive and negative characteristics, its past experiences, present attitudes, and future strivings—including the personal and collective unconscious. They have a compensatory function in the sense that tendencies neglected during waking life come into action in dreams. The Jungian interpretation of dreams is flexible, varies with every personality type, and does not rely too strongly on free association and typical symbolism.

Adler's Theory. Alfred Adler views in dreams the manifestation of a person's specific style of life, his particular way of asserting himself within the frame of his community. In contrast to Freud and in accordance with Jung, Adler stresses the value of dreams in understanding not only past experiences, but also present problems and future plannings. Dreams are particularly useful in studying the lifestyle because they are more spontaneous and uninhibited and less under the control of the reality of everyday life. At times, they may exert a harmful influence on the personality; thus, when the lifestyle is inadequate and the personality weak, the work of imagination as it occurs in dreams may consolidate wrong personality attitudes. In the interpretation of dream images, Adler stresses both the typical and the individual.

Other Trends. Freudian views and techniques have come to be considered by many psychologists and psychiatrists as too one-sided and too narrow-minded to be of real value in understanding and in helping the human personality. There is thus a tendency to enlarge Freud's theories by enriching them with insights from Jung, Adler, W. Stekel, T. French, the existentialists (L. Binswanger), and the experimentalists (C. S. Hall). The holistic concept of human personality is being extended even to dream analysis. This can be seen in the increased use of the dream-series method and in the stress on the total human experience as projected in dreams—not only past events, but even present problems and attitudes and future strivings and goals. The language of dreams is said to express the unconscious and the conscious, the id and the ego forces, and the emotional, motivational, and cognitive layers of human personality. Hall finds the analysis of the manifest content of dreams much more rewarding than the delving into their latent content. M. Ullman considers the dream as one of the many roads leading toward the understanding of CONSCIOUSNESS. J. L. Moreno wishes to add to the manifest and latent content of dreams a new dimension that he calls the "actional" aspect of dream. Dream becomes one of the psychodramatic techniques used by Moreno: instead of telling his dreams, Moreno's patients are encouraged to act them out.

Moral Questions

None of the psychological techniques of dream analysis is by its nature immoral; a technique's goodness depends upon the total clinical context in which its methods are being applied. Moral evaluation of dreams is concerned with the problems of divination, of moral responsibility, and of use in the spiritual life.

Divination. Foretelling of the future by means of a dream is legitimate if one is sure that the dream comes from God. One's attitudes toward such dreams should be the same as in the case of private visions and revelations. When divine intervention in a dream is excluded, then divination is an act of superstition because it involves, either explicitly or implicitly, an attempt to predict the future by means of demonic powers. The gravity of sin depends upon the amount of awareness, the degree of certainly about the prediction, and the more or less explicit intention of regulating one's life according to dreams. Ignorance and an implicit belief in some infallible natural means of knowing secrets and predicting the future, such as telepathy and precognition, can easily excuse from sin.

Moral Responsibility. Neither merit nor demerit can be acquired through dream behavior. Man's critical and deliberative ability is so reduced during sleep that he is not morally responsible for whatever may happen, nor can he reasonably assume any antecedent responsibility (*in causa*) because there is no specific type of activity in human behavior that has a necessary connection with any of man's dreams.

Use in Spiritual Life. The old Platonic view that virtuous people have virtuous dreams found its echo in many ascetic authors and theologians, such as St. JOHN CLIMACUS, John CASSIAN, and Diego ALVAREZ DE PAZ. Even St. Thomas Aquinas states that "the virtuous come to have better visions in dreams than those who are not virtuous" (*Der ver.* 28.3 ad 7). Particularly in the area of chastity, some claim that absence of impure dreams is a sign of perfect and consummate virtue. P. Meseguer seems to favor this opinion, adducing as the psychological and theological explanation the so-called law of progressive impregnation; this measures the degree according to which the law of grace succeeds in permeating man's whole nature, even his unconscious tendencies. It is not quite certain whether or not this law can be applied to dreams. A person cannot talk about dreams in general, but only about dreams as he recalls them. It is known from research that the recall of dreams is regulated by selective factors rooted in the personality structure. Until more is known about the dynamics of dreams and about the relationship between conscious and unconscious life, great caution should regulate attempts to use dreams as a technique of spiritual guidance.

See Also: PSYCHOLOGY.

Bibliography: T. HOPFNER, *Paulya Realenzyklopädie der klassischen Altertumswissenschaft,* ed. G. WISSOWA et al. 6A.2 (1937) 2233–45. G. M. BOLLING, J. HASTINGS, ed. *Encyclopedia of Religion and Ethics* (Edinburgh 1908–27) 4:775–830; 5:28–40. S. FREUD, *The Interpretation of Dreams,* ed. and tr. J. STRACHEY and A. FREUD (London 1961; repr. of v.4–5 of standard ed. 1953). C. G. JUNG, *Psychology of the Unconscious,* tr. B. HINKLE (New York 1916; repr. 1963); *Symbols of Transformation: An Analysis of the Prelude to a Case of Schizophrenia,* tr. R. F. C. HULL (Bollingen Ser. 20; New York 1956) rev. ed. of *Psychology of the Unconscious.* A.

ADLER, *The Individual Psychology of Alfred Adler,* ed. H. L. and R. R. ANSBACHER (New York 1956). D. BROWER and L. E. ABT, eds., *Progress in Clinical Psychology* (New York 1952–) 4:239–257; 5:88–111. N. KLEITMAN, *Sleep and Wakefulness . . .* (Chicago 1939; rev. and enl. 1963). C. S. HALL, *The Meaning of Dreams* (New York 1953). R. LA ROCHE, *La Divination: Avec un supplément sur la superstition en Afrique Centrale* (Washington 1957). P. MESEGUER, *The Secret of Dreams,* tr. P. BURNS (Westminster, Md. 1960).

[A. M. CUK]

DREXEL, JEREMIAS

Jesuit educator, preacher, and spiritual writer; b. Augsburg, Aug. 15, 1581; d. Munich, April 19, 1638. A Lutheran by birth, he was converted in his youth, educated by the Jesuits, and in 1598 entered the Jesuit novitiate. He completed his philosophical and theological studies at Ingolstadt and became professor of humanities in Munich and Augsburg. He taught the Jesuit seminarians at Dillingen and then for 23 years was preacher at the court of the elector of Bavaria. During this period he accompanied Maximilian on his Bohemian campaign. From 1620 until his death he wrote some 20 works that were avidly read and zealously translated. His first work, *De aeternitate considerationes,* underwent four distinct English translations before 1710. Among the considerations, Drexel noted various representations of eternity—the natural, the Roman, and the Scriptural. Another of his works, *Heliotropium* (1627), translated into English in 1862, discussed man's recognition of the divine will and conformity to it.

Bibliography: P. BAILLY, *Dictionnaire de spiritualité ascétique et mystique. Doctrine et histoire,* ed. M. VILLER et al. (Paris 1932–) 3:1714–17. C. SOMMERVOGEL et al., *Bibliothèque de la Compagnie de Jésus,* 11 v. (Brussels-Paris 1890–1932) 3:181–205. B. DUHR, *Geschichte der Jesuiten in den Ländern deutscher Zunge,* 4 v. in 5 (St. Louis 1907–28) 2.2:444–449.

[D. M. BARRY]

DREXEL, KATHARINE MARIE, ST.

Foundress of the Blessed Sacrament for Indians and Colored People (later Sisters of the Blessed Sacrament); b. Nov. 26. 1858, Philadelphia, Pa.; d. March 3, 1955, Cornwell Heights, Pa.; beatified Nov. 20, 1988; canonized Oct. 1, 2000, the second U.S.-born saint, after Elizabeth Seton.

Granddaughter of Francis Martin Drexel, founder of a Philadelphia banking house, Katharine's Protestant mother, Hannah Jane (Langstreth) Drexel, died when Katharine was an infant; two years later her father Francis

Anthony Drexel married Emma M. Bouvier, who became a devoted mother to Katharine, her elder sister Elizabeth, and their stepsister Louise. Katharine was educated at home by private governesses, traveled in Europe and the U.S., was a Philadelphia debutante in 1879, and took part in many social activities.

The Church called upon the wealthy Drexel family to help implement the decrees of the Third Plenary Council of Baltimore (1884), which legislated for missionary activity among Native and African-Americans. Katharine had inherited a fortune at the death of her stepmother (1883) and father (1885). While recovering from an illness in a German spa in 1886, she recruited many priests and nuns for the Native American missions. During a visit to Rome she asked Leo XIII to recommend a religious order to which she could give her fortune on condition that it be used only for African- and Native Americans. When the pope challenged her to be their missionary herself, her vocation was decided. On Nov. 7, 1889 she began her novitiate with the Sisters of Mercy of Pittsburgh, Pa., and in 1891 she and a few companions founded the Sisters of the Blessed Sacrament for Indians and Colored People in a convent made over from the old Drexel summer home at Torresdale, Pa. Within a year there were 21 sisters.

Requests for help soon came from Southern centers for Blacks and from Native American missions in the Southwest. Mother Katharine built and maintained missions and staffed them with sisters. Later she opened schools and convents in Columbus, Oh.; Chicago, Ill.; Boston, Mass.; and Harlem, New York City. In 1915 she established Xavier University in New Orleans, La., which has been the only predominantly African-American Catholic institution of higher learning in the United States since its founding. By 1927 the university's growth led Mother Drexel to plan larger quarters. The new site and buildings, costing $600,000, were dedicated by Cardinal Dennis Dougherty in 1932. In 1935 Mother Drexel suffered a heart attack, but she continued her work, which included long day-coach trips to her 49 foundations in the Northeast, Midwest, and Deep South. At her golden jubilee in 1941, a letter from Pius XII described her work as "a glorious page in the annals of the Church." Although an invalid during her last years, she devoted herself to prayer until her death at 96. Her body is enshrined in the Philadelphia suburb of Bensalem, Pa.

At her death there were more than 500 sisters teaching in 63 schools throughout the country. She had spent more than $12 million of her inheritance on work for the disadvantaged minorities of the U.S. and the advancement of human rights. At the beginning of the 21st century, her work continued at 48 sites in 12 states and Haiti.

Katharine's cause, introduced in 1964 by John Cardinal Krol of Philadelphia, culminated Jan. 27, 2000, when the restoration of hearing to 17-month-old Robert Gutherman (May 1994) was declared a miracle wrought through her intercession.

Feast: March 3 (U.S.A.).

Bibliography: K. BURTON, *The Golden Door: The Life of Katharine Drexel* (New York 1957). C. M. DUFFY, *Katharine Drexel* (Philadelphia 1966). G. D. KITTLER, *Profiles in Faith* (New York 1962). P. LYNCH, *Sharing the Bread in Service: Sisters of the Blessed Sacrament* (Bensalem, Pa. 1998). E. TARRY, *Katharine Drexel, Friend of the Neglected.* (New York 1958).

[K. BURTON]

DREY, JOHANN SEBASTIAN VON

Systematic theologian and historian of dogma, Catholic Tübingen school; b. Killingen, near Ellwangen, Germany, Oct. 16, 1777; d. Tübingen, Feb. 19, 1853. Drey began theology studies in Augsburg (1797–99) and was ordained in 1801, having entered the seminary in Pfaffenhausen. In 1806 he began to teach philosophy of religion, mathematics, and physics at the Catholic secondary school in Rottweil; in 1812 he became professor of apologetics, dogma, and history of dogma in the newly founded university at Ellwangen. When it was closed in 1817, he transferred to the University of Tübingen, where he taught until 1846. With P. Gratz, J. G. Herbst, and J. HIRSCHER, he founded the *Tübinger theologische Quartalschrift* in 1819. Rome refused to approve the Württemberg government's designation of Drey as first bishop of Rottenburg in 1823.

As early as his first work, *Entwurf zu meinen Vorlesungen aus der Physik* (1806–13), Drey showed himself under the influence of the philosophy of F. SCHELLING. The development of his thought and scholarship is well mirrored in his *Mein Tagebuch über philosophische, theologische und historische Gegenstände* (1812–17), which reveals Drey as a representative of Romantic thought (e.g., his organic conception of history and tradition, his theory of thesis and antithesis), again heavily dependent on Schelling. In his *Revision des gegenwärtigen Zustandes der Theologie* (1812) he attacked both the scholasticism and Enlightenment of the 16th to the 18th centuries along the lines of the new Romantic view of the Middle Ages; at the same time he sought to reassess medieval scholasticism, to which he claimed theology must constantly return "if it would discover its beginnings as a science." In his *Geschichte des katholischen Dogmensystems* (1812–13) Drey appears as a classical example of the 19th-century theory of the development of DOGMA; from that time forward this idea of dogmatic evolution

St. Katharine Marie Drexel. (AP/Wide World Photos)

as the organic unfolding of the seed planted by Christ became a substantial component of his doctrinal system. Essentially this component is a combination of B. Gular's notion on the "revealedness" of the doctrines of revelation and Schelling's philosophy of history. In the two last-mentioned works, as also in his "Vom Geist und Wesen des Katholizismus" [*Theologische Quartalschrift* (Tübingen 1819)], Drey was concerned with the concept of tradition as the organic, living unfolding of historically given revelation; this notion is especially important for him as the explanation for the inner continuity of Christianity. He claimed that in modern Catholicism, the primitive Christian fact (which was given in Jesus) is still present. The basis of this interpretation of Drey's was the organic concept of history proper to Romanticism (i.e., the notion of the historical as the uninterrupted persistence and development of the primal). *See* HISTORY AND HISTORICITY; ROMANTICISM, PHILOSOPHICAL.

Drey's *Über den Satz der allein seligmachenden Kirche* (1822) restates his theory of thesis and antithesis and precludes both interdenominational indifferentism and pointless polemic, because various denominations, said Drey, are the necessary opposite poles to the Church and as such are built into the plan of history by God's predestination (*see* HISTORY, THEOLOGY OF). Drey's most important work was *Die Apologetik als wissenschaftliche*

Nachweisung der Göttlichkeit des Christentums (1838–47). Whereas Drey had initially joined SCHLEIER-MACHER in assigning to apologetics the task of crystallizing the generic essence of Christianity, in this work he came to the conviction that the true task of apologetics was to create—on the basis of the concrete model of revelation within the Catholic Church—the basis for all disciplines treating of revelation (*see* FUNDAMENTAL THEOLOGY). As for the foundations of religion, he opposed both the apriorism of the Enlightenment (i.e., his rejection of concrete historicity) and pure traditionalism (his rejection of an innate idea of God). Drey greatly influenced his pupils J. A. MÖHLER, J. KUHN, F. A. Staudenmaier, A. Berlage, and F. X. DIERINGER. His ideas are still influential in theological discussion on the Church, on Scripture and tradition, and on related topics.

See Also: HISTORIOGRAPHY, ECCLESIASTICAL

Bibliography: Works. *Dissertatio historico-theologica de origine et vicissitudine exomologeseos in ecclesia catholica* (Ellwangen 1815); *Kurze Einleitung in das Studium der Theologie* (Tübingen 1819); "Über den Satz der allein seligmachenden Kirche," *Der Apologet des Katholizismus,* ed. A. GRATZ, Heft 5 (Mainz 1822); *Neue Untersuchungen über die Constitutionen und Kanones der Apostel* (Tübingen 1832); *Die Apologetik als wissenschaftliche Nachweisung der Göttlichkeit des Christentums,* 3 v. (Mainz 1838–47; v.1–2, 2d ed. 1844–47). J. R. GEISELMANN, *Lexikon für Theologie und Kirche,* ed. J. HOFER and K. RAHNER (2d, new ed. Freiburg 1957–65) 3:573–574, for unedited MSS. Literature. S. LÖSCH, *Die Anfänge der Tübinger Theologischen Quartalschrift* (Rottenburg 1938). H. LOHMANN, *Die Philosophie der Offenbarung bei J. S. von Drey* (Diss. Freiburg 1953). W. RUF, *J. S. von Dreys System der Theologie als Begründung der Moraltheologie* (Diss. Freiburg 1958). F. LAUPHEIMER, *Die kultisch-liturgischen Anschauungen J. S. Dreys* (Diss. Tübingen 1959). H. J. BROSCH, *Das Übernatürliche in der katholischen Tübinger Schule* (Essen 1962), discussed by J. R. GEISELMANN, in *Theologische Quartalschrift* 143 (1963) 422–453. J. R. GEISELMANN, *Geist des Christentums und des Katholizismus* (Mainz 1940); *Lebendiger Glaube aus geheiligter Überlieferung* (Mainz 1942); *Die katholische Tübinger Schule* (Freiburg 1965); *Theologische Quartalschrift* 112 (1931) 88–89.

[M. CSÁKY]

DRISCOLL, JAMES F.

Educator, editor; b. Poultney, Vermont, Sept. 30, 1859; d. Yonkers, N.Y., July 5, 1922. Driscoll's early education was in the Vermont public schools. Later he studied at Montreal, Paris, and Rome, where his professors included the Semitic scholars Henri HYVERNAT and Ignazio Guidi. He joined the Society of St. Sulpice after being ordained at Rome in 1887. In 1889 he was appointed to the faculty of the Grand Seminaire, Montreal, Canada, and he taught dogmatic theology there until 1896, when he joined the faculty of the major seminary of the Archdiocese of New York at Dunwoodie, Yonkers, N.Y.

With the exception of the year spent as president of St. Austin's College, Washington, D.C., he remained at Dunwoodie until 1909, serving as professor of dogmatic theology (1896–98) and of Scripture and Semitic languages (1898–1901), and as rector (1902–09). In 1906, when the administration of the seminary passed from the Sulpicians to the New York archdiocesan clergy, Driscoll withdrew from the former and joined the latter.

During his rectorship, the *New York Review* began publication, with Driscoll as editor, and appeared every two months from June 1905 until publication ended in 1908. It drew its contributors from representatives of European as well as American scholarship, and compared favorably with the best European periodicals of the period. According to a notice that appeared in the last issue (May–June 1908), its early demise was caused by lack of Catholic interest and not by any "command of authority." In the same year Driscoll submitted his resignation as rector of the seminary; it was accepted at the end of the scholastic year (1908–09), and he was appointed pastor of St. Ambrose's Church in New York City. In 1910 he became pastor of St. Gabriel's Church, New Rochelle, N.Y., and he held that office until his death. Driscoll contributed many articles to the old *Catholic Encyclopedia,* and was one of the group of scholars responsible for the significant advance in U.S. Catholic theological thought made during the late 19th and early 20th centuries.

Bibliography: A. J. SCANLAN, *St. Joseph's Seminary, Dunwoodie, New York, 1896–1921* (New York 1922).

[M. M. BOURKE]

DROGO OF METZ

Leading churchman of the CAROLINGIAN REFORM; b. June 17, 801; d. Dec. 8, 855. In the aftermath of the revolt of Bernard of Italy, Emperor Louis the Pious forced Drogo, one of CHARLEMAGNE's illegitimate sons, to receive tonsure (818) and had him interned in a monastery. By 822 Louis changed his opinion about his half-brother and nominated him bishop of Metz with the approval of the clergy and laity of that city; Drogo was consecrated June 28, 823. Through all his political vicissitudes Louis found a loyal supporter in Drogo, whom he made his chief chaplain, a position that carried with it a great amount of supervision of ecclesiastical matters throughout the Frankish kingdom, and the title of archbishop. In 844, at the insistence of Emperor LOTHAIR I, Drogo, with a commission of 22 bishops, investigated the validity of the election of Pope SERGIUS II. The election was upheld, but the pope had to swear an oath of fidelity to Lothair and appoint Drogo the vicar of the apostolic see for all the Frankish kingdoms (*cunctis provinciis trans Alpes constitutis,* P. Jaffé, *Regesta pontificum romanorum ab condita ecclesia ad annum post Christum natum 1198,* P. Ewald, ed., 1:327–328). In October of the same year Drogo presided at a council held in Yütz, near THIONVILLE, but it is difficult to determine whether he acted as papal vicar. The effective exercise of this office was probably limited to the regions immediately subject to Lothair. The remaining years of the bishop's life were spent in the capable administration of his diocese and the abbeys entrusted to him. He met his death by drowning near the Abbey of Luxeuil.

Bibliography: *Drogo Sacramentary,* Paris, Bibliothèque nationale MS lat. 9428. H. LECLERCQ, *Dictionnaire d'archéologie chrétienne et de liturgie,* ed. F. CABROL, H. LECLERCQ, and H. I. MARROU (Paris 1907–53) 4.2:1540–49. L. ALPHEN, *Charlemagne et l'empire carolingien* (Paris 1947). P. VIARD, *Catholicisme. Hier, aujourd'hui et demain,* ed. G. JACQUEMET (Paris 1947–) 3:1090–91. T. SCHIEFFER, *Lexikon für Theologie und Kirche,* ed. J. HOFER and K. RAHNER (2d, new ed. Freiburg 1957–65) 3:575–576. A. DUMAS, *Dictionnaire d'histoire et de géographie ecclésiastiques,* ed. A. BAUDRILLART et al. (Paris 1912–) 14:799–802. J. B. PELT, ed., *Études sur la cathédrale de Metz* (Metz 1930) 1:51–112. K. GAMBER, *Codices liturgici latini antiquiores* (Spicilegium friburgense, subsidia 1; Fribourg 1963) 181.

[H. DRESSLER]

DROSTE ZU VISCHERING, CLEMENS AUGUST VON

Archbishop of Cologne; b. Münster (Westphalia), Germany, Jan. 21, 1773; d. Münster, Oct. 19, 1845. He came from a noble, conservative family, studied at the University of Münster, journeyed to Rome, and moved in the circle of Princess Amalia GALLITZIN previous to his ordination (1798) after insufficient theological training. He then assisted the vicar-general of Münster until 1807 and directed the administration of the diocese (1807–21). Because of differences with the Prussian government concerning the teachings of Georg HERMES, he resigned his post and led a retired life (1821–27), dedicated to asceticism, charity, and the direction of the Sisters of Charity of Münster (Clemens Sisters), founded by him (1808). After his brother Kaspar became bishop of Münster, he was consecrated his auxiliary (1827). On the recommendation of the Prussian crown prince he succeeded Ferdinand SPIEGEL as archbishop of COLOGNE (1836). Droste was zealous and deeply pious; but his autocratic, aloof, and inflexible character did not attract the Rhinelanders. His fideistic type of piety, severed from scientific theology, increased the harshness of his opposition to the followers of Hermes, whose rationalistic ideas had been condemned by Rome (1835). The COLOGNE MIXED MARRIAGE DISPUTE involved him in open conflict with PRUSSIA. When Droste renounced Spiegel's arrangements on

mixed marriages, he was imprisoned without trial (1837). Pope Gregory XVI solemnly protested this act of violence, Johann von GÖRRES was moved to compose his celebrated tract *Athanasius,* and German Catholics were roused to struggle for freedom against state overlordship in religious matters. King Friedrich Wilhelm IV (1840–61) restored peace with the Church. Droste received a personal apology, but had to surrender the administration of his see to Johannes von GEISSEL, his codajutor (1842). Thereafter Droste retired to Münster. The adherence of the "confessor bishop" to his convictions impressed contemporaries, but his bluntness intensified unnecessarily the Church-State conflict.

Bibliography: H. SCHRÖRS, *Die Kölner Wirren* (Berlin 1927). R. LILL, *Die Beilegung der Kölner Wirren 1840–1842* (Düsseldorf 1962). W. LIPGENS, *Neue deutsche Biographie* (Berlin 1953–) 4:133–135. W. MÜLLER, *Dictionnaire d'histoire et de géographie ecclésiastiques,* ed. A. BAUDRILLART et al. (Paris 1912–) 14:815–820.

[R. LILL]

DROUIN, HYACINTHE RENÉ (DROUVEN)

Dominican theologian; b. Toulon, *c.* 1680; d. Ivrée, Sept. 30, 1740. He entered the Dominican Order, Jan. 21, 1696, at Toulon, for the priory of Marseilles, and made his novitiate and was professed at Carpentras, Jan. 21, 1697. After completing his preparatory studies, he went to Paris for graduate work; there he taught at Saint-Jacques and was regent at Saint Honoré. In 1713 he received the Dominican degree of master of sacred theology. He entered into conflict with the Jesuits after the king named him professor of theology at the University of Caen in 1719. Later he taught for ten years at Chambéry; from 1730 he was in retirement at Ivrée. His chief work was *De re sacramentaria contra perduelles hereticos* (2 v. 1765).

Bibliography: R. COULON, *Dictionnaire de théologie catholique,* ed. A. VACANT et al. (Paris 1903–50) 4.2:1842–43. J. QUÉTIF and J. ÉCHARD, *Scriptores Ordinis Praedicatorum,* 5 v. (Paris 1719–23); repr. 2 v. in 4 (New York 1959) 3:696–699.

[T. MYERS]

DRUMGOOLE, JOHN CHRISTOPHER

Social worker, founder of the Mission of the Immaculate Virgin, Staten Island, N.Y.; b. Granard, County Longford, Ireland, Aug. 15, 1816; d. New York, N.Y., March 28, 1888. Coming to New York at the age of eight, he attended St. Patrick's Cathedral School, but was soon forced to leave to support his widowed mother. He worked as a shoemaker, a bookseller, and then as sexton at St. Mary's Church in New York City from 1844 until 1865. At the age of 49, Drumgoole entered Our Lady of Angels Seminary, Niagara, N.Y., and was ordained on May 22, 1869.

After parish work at St. Mary's, where he had been sexton, he became superintendent of St. Vincent's Home for Homeless Boys. By 1881 he had established the larger Mission of the Immaculate Virgin, first in Manhattan, and in the following year at Mt. Loretto, Staten Island, where he was able to care for 2,000 children. To finance his growing project, he founded St. Joseph's Union.

During the years of his activities, New York was filled with homeless children; as late as 1868 there were 40,000 uncared-for children in the city. Few laws existed to protect them and public money for their support was scarce. Many of them were Catholic children whose mothers had died in childbirth or as the result of epidemics. Many were sent by the authorities to homes where they were raised as Protestants. The homes and schools founded by Drumgoole to meet the situation were often imitated and brought him a world-wide reputation. He was influential also in the passage of a New York law that provided for homeless children to be placed in homes or in institutions of their own religion.

Bibliography: K. BURTON, *Children's Shepherd: The Story of John Christopher Drumgoole* (New York 1954).

[G. A. KELLY]

DRUNKENNESS

The condition of a person deprived of the use of reason or the control of his faculties by the consumption of alcohol or by means of some other intoxicating substance. In ordinary speech the term is usually applied to this condition when it has been induced by alcohol, but from a moral point of view it is irrelevant whether the intoxicant is alcohol, or whether it is taken by mouth in liquid or solid form, inhaled as a gas, or injected into the bloodstream. Until relatively modern times the only form of intoxicant in common use was alcoholic drink, and consequently older moralists considered drunkenness an offense against temperance consisting in the immoderate consumption of wine or other fermented drink. What was essential to the act and distinguished it from gluttony was the intoxicating effect of the substance ingested. But definitions of drunkenness applicable only to the excessive use of alcohol can no longer be regarded as satisfactory. The moral deformity of the act of getting drunk lies essentially in the unreasonable surrender of control over oneself and one's faculties. The chemical composition of the intoxicant, or its particular mode of affecting the nervous system, is of no moral significance so far as intoxication itself is concerned. What is said of the immoderate use of alcohol is equally true of the immoderate use of ether, narcotics, marijuana, barbiturates, sleeping pills, LSD (lysergic acid diethylamide), model-maker's glue, or other substances that produce an effect comparable to alcoholic intoxication.

Moral Classification. The extension of the concept of drunkenness to include intoxication brought on by other means than alcoholic drink raises a question regarding the propriety of considering it, as the classic moralists did, as an offense against temperance. It might seem more reasonable to classify it simply as a form of temporary mutilation, in which case its essential opposition would be to the virtue of charity or justice. Nevertheless, it is possible to defend and to retain the older classification, because, besides being a mutilation, drunkenness is also—and more formally—an unreasonable indulgence of the sense appetite. It is not necessarily a gratification of the sense of taste, for the pleasure involved in the actual drinking does not commonly account for the drinker's excess. He seeks other satisfactions—the feeling of relief from strain and tension, the feeling of ease in social situations, a sense of euphoria, or perhaps the alleviation of unpleasant feelings by forgetfulness or oblivion. The inordinateness of his act, from the point of view of temperance, consists in the fact that he is so attached to his sensory satisfactions that he is prepared to give up control of himself to achieve them.

Degrees of Drunkenness. Moralists commonly distinguish two degrees of drunkenness. A person is perfectly or absolutely drunk when he sinks into a stupor from which he cannot be aroused, or when he can no longer tell right from wrong, or when the inhibitions that usually hold his disorderly impulses in check are so weakened that he cannot control himself and is in proximate danger, if occasion offers, of doing something seriously wrong. In these cases an intoxicated person is said to be perfectly drunk, because he has lost the capacity to act as a responsible human being. On the other hand, if he has lost some measure of control over himself, yet has not reached absolute drunkenness as here defined, he is said to be imperfectly drunk.

Some authors would measure perfect drunkenness by a relative as well as an absolute standard. The amount of control over self that can be surrendered without losing one's capacity to act as a responsible moral agent depends to some extent upon circumstances. The temporary loss of the capacity to articulate distinctly or to walk steadily would be a relatively minor deprivation in some circumstances; in others, the condition could cause serious scandal. Similarly, a retardation in the speed of one's reflexes could matter little, but a person with retarded reflexes is a public menace when he is at the wheel of a car. In surrendering such capacities, which are not absolutely necessary in themselves but which are necessary for the responsible human behavior of an individual by reason of his circumstances, he becomes, in effect, perfectly drunk.

Moral Evaluation. It is generally admitted that drunkenness can be legitimately induced when it is necessary for purposes of health. It is then justified, as is any legitimate mutilation, by application of the principle of TOTALITY. The use of reason can be temporarily sacrificed in the interests of the whole man. The total anesthesia administered to a surgical patient would be an example in point. The use of sodium pentathol or some other similar drug in narcoanalysis would be another.

Imperfectly Voluntary Drunkenness. Drunkenness may be no sin at all, or less than a grave sin, when the conditions necessary for subjective responsibility are lacking. For example, if one becomes drunk by accident, or because he fails inculpably to advert to the excessive quantity of liquor he is consuming, there can be no grave sin. In the case of a habitual drunkard or an alcoholic, there may be reason to wonder whether the individual has the moral freedom necessary to resist the compulsion to drink (*see* RESPONSIBILITY).

Perfect Drunkenness. St. Paul in Gal 5.21 enumerates drunkenness among the works of the flesh and, here as in 1 Cor 6.10, declares that those guilty of it will be excluded from the kingdom of God. However, no absolutely compelling argument can be drawn from the Scriptures to show that isolated acts of drunkenness, uncomplicated by association with other kinds of wicked action, are mortally sinful. St. Thomas Aquinas as a younger man seems to have held that drunkenness was not per se a grave sin (see *In 2 sent.* 24.3.6.; *De malo* 7.4 ad 1; 2.8 ad 3). But if this indeed was his earlier opinion, he changed his mind on the subject and in the *Summa theologiae* declared unambiguously that drunkenness was mortally sinful. It may be that in his earlier statements he was misled, as were other scholastics, by an apocryphal text attributed to St. Augustine, according to which drunkenness was not a mortal sin except when indulged in frequently or for evil purpose. It was St. Thomas's later teaching that prevailed, however, and it represents the common doctrine of all Catholic moralists.

The reasons why perfect drunkenness is held to be mortally sinful are these: (1) It makes the exercise of reason temporarily impossible; and reason, besides being man's noblest faculty, is radically necessary to responsible moral action, to self-protection, to the performance of duty, and to the avoidance of evil. (2) It relaxes the inhibitions and so permits vicious inclinations to seek an outlet, thus exposing a man to the danger of sin. (3) The immoderate use of intoxicants exposes a man to the danger of addiction and to many other grave evil consequences of a personal and a social kind.

It is disputed among moralists whether perfect drunkenness may be venially sinful because of slightness (parvity) of matter, by which is meant the brevity of time during which an intoxicated person is without control of himself. Some authors (e.g., Lacroix and Noldin) held that a short loss of self-control (the limits of which are variously set at several minutes, half an hour, or even an hour) will excuse from mortal sin. Others have taken the position that the full malice of perfect drunkenness is realized even when one's self-possession is lost for a short time.

There is general agreement among moralists that a person is morally accountable for the sinful acts and the injustice that he foresees he is likely to commit when he allows himself to become intoxicated.

Imperfect Drunkenness. Imperfect drunkenness is per se no more than a venial sin. It could be a grave sin if indulged in for a gravely sinful purpose or if it caused serious scandal. On the other hand, it is no sin at all if there is sufficient reason for the indulgence, e.g., an acute attack of melancholy, a special occasion calling for something unusual in the way of festivity and joviality.

Remedy. For cases of recurrent excess in the use of intoxicants without the addiction or sickness factors that occur in the alcoholic, prayer and the frequent use of the Sacraments ought to be encouraged. An effort should be made to get at the root of the disorder, i.e., to discover why the individual is so strongly inclined to look to intoxicants for satisfaction, and to work out a more adequate solution to his problems. The total-abstinence pledge is sometimes helpful, but it should be recommended with some caution; if it does not appear likely that the person will be faithful to it, the pledge could do more harm than good. Some application of the program of ALCOHOLICS ANONYMOUS, particularly of the Twelve Steps, can be made to the cases of those who are not, strictly speaking, alcoholics. Membership in total abstinence societies has helped many.

See Also: SOBRIETY; TEMPERANCE (VIRTUE OF); TEMPERANCE MOVEMENTS.

Bibliography: THOMAS AQUINAS, *Summa Theologiae* 1a2ae, 88.5 ad 1; 2a2ae, 150. D. M. PRÜMMER, *Manuale theologiae moralis,* ed. E. M. MÜNCH (12th ed. Freiburg-Barcelona 1955) 2:668–673. T. ORTOLAN, *Dictionnaire de théologie catholique,* ed.

A. VACANT et al., (Paris 1903–50; Tables générales 1951–) 8.1: 246–248. J. C. FORD, *Man Takes a Drink* (New York 1955).

[P. K. MEAGHER]

DRURY, ROBERT, BL.

Priest and martyr; b. Buckinghamshire, England, 1567; d. hanged, drawn, and quartered at Tyburn (London) under James I, Feb. 26, 1607. Drury began his seminary studies at Rheims in 1588 and completed them at the English College at Valladolid, Spain, where he was ordained (1593). Upon his return to England, he worked chiefly in London.

His name is affixed to the appeal against archpriest Blackwell, which is dated Nov. 17, 1600, from Wisbeach Prison. On Nov. 5, 1602, the government invited these appellant priests to acknowledge their allegiance to the queen, which they did in the famous address of Jan. 21, 1603. The statement, drafted by Dr. William Bishop and signed by 13 leading priests, including Drury and Bl. Roger CADWALLADOR, acknowledged the queen as their lawful sovereign, repudiated the claim of the pope to release them from their duty of allegiance to her, and expressed their abhorrence of the forcible attempts already made to restore the Catholic religion and their determination to reveal any further conspiracies against the government that should come to their knowledge. In return they ingenuously stated that as they were ready to render to Caesar the things that were Caesar's, so they should be permitted to yield to the successor of Peter that obedience which Peter himself might have claimed under Christ's commission. Thus they hoped to distinguish between their several duties and obligations. Although the theological faculty of Louvain condemned their repudiation of papal power to depose the sovereign, the pope himself selected Dr. Bishop to revive episcopal authority in England in 1623.

Disappointingly, Elizabeth died within three months of the statement's signature, and James I was unsatisfied with purely civil allegiance. He thirsted for spiritual authority. With the assistance of an apostate Jesuit, a new oath of allegiance was crafted with a subtlety designed to trouble the conscience of Catholics and divide them on the lawfulness of taking it. It was imposed July 5, 1606, about the time of Drury's arrest.

Drury was condemned for his priesthood, but offered his life if he would take the new oath. A letter from Jesuit Fr. Persons was found on Drury condemning the oath (also condemned by Pope Paul V, Sept. 22, 1606). He died because his conscience would not permit him to take the oath.

A pious contemporary account of his martyrdom, entitled "A true Report of the Arraignment . . . of a Popish Priest named Robert Drewrie" (London, 1607; reprinted in the *Harleian Miscellany*) calls him a Benedictine and says he wore his monastic habit at the execution. He may have been a Benedictine oblate. Drury was beatified by Pope John Paul II on Nov. 22, 1987 with George Haydock and Companions.

Feast of the English Martyrs: May 4 (England).

See Also: ENGLAND, SCOTLAND, AND WALES, MARTYRS OF.

Bibliography: *A True Report of the Arraignment, Tryall, Conviction, and Condemnation, of a Popish Priest, Named Robert Drewrie . . .* (London 1607). R. CHALLONER, *Memoirs of Missionary Priests,* ed. J. H. POLLEN (rev. ed. London 1924). J. H. POLLEN, *Acts of English Martyrs* (London 1891).

[K. I. RABENSTEIN]

DRUTHMAR, ST.

Abbot; d. Feb. 15, 1046. A monk of LORSCH, he was made abbot of CORVEY, Westphalia, in 1014 by Emperor HENRY II, who had deposed the preceding abbot, Walo, as a result of complaints by Bishop Meinwerk of Paderborn. Druthmar gradually won over the lax monks by his learning and zeal, and the community became renowned for its strict observance of monastic discipline. His cult developed together with that of a preceding abbot, LUDOLF OF CORVEY (d. 983), when the two bodies were exhumed in 1100. A 17th-century statue in the choir of Corvey gives him the title of blessed.

Feast: Feb. 15, Aug. 13.

Bibliography: *Acta Sanctorum* June 1:526; Aug. 3:139–142. *Bibliotheca rerum Germanicarum,* ed. P. JAFFÉ, 6 v. (Berlin 1864–73) 1:37–39; 3:355. THIETMAR OF MERSEBURG, *Die Chronik,* ed. R. HOLTZMANN, *Monumenta Germaniae Scriptores rerum Germanicarum* (Berlin 1825–), 9:412–413. J. MABILLON, *Annales Ordinis S. Benedicti,* 6 v. (Lucca 1739–45) 4:224, 284, 346, 395, 439. R. AUBERT, *Dictionnaire d'histoire et de géographie ecclésiastiques* (Paris 1912–), 14:821–822.

[W. E. WILKIE]

DRUŻBICKI, GASPAR

Ascetical writer and preacher, who, with LANCICIUS, has been called the most notable of 17th-century Polish Jesuits; b. Sieradz, Jan 6, 1590; d. Posen, April 2, 1662. He entered the Society of Jesus in 1609. He taught for several years, part of the time instructing in logic at Lublin; he was then master of novices for seven years, and rector of the colleges at Kalisz, Ostrog, and Posen. In 1632 he wrote a brief defense of the society against a writer of the Cracow Academy. Twice he was provincial of the Polish province (1629–33, 1650–54), and participated in the seventh and tenth general congregations of the society.

Practically all of his voluminous ascetical writings in Latin and Polish, mostly treatises on the religious life and a series of meditations, were published after his death. A list of them occupies 12 columns in Sommervogel. An accurate chronology of their composition is impossible. Many of his works have been translated into German and English, and a Spanish translation of his treatise on religious vows has been found in the library at Guadalajara, Mexico.

Among his better known works are: *Exercitia tironum religiosorum in duodecim menses distributa; Vota religiosa seu tractatus de votis religiosis in communi et particulari; Lapis Lydius boni spiritus sive considerationes de soliditate verae virtutis;* and *Sublimitas perfectionis religiosae LXXIX discursibus explicata.* A collection of his *Opera Ascetica* was published at Kalisz and Posen *c.* 1686–91 and reedited with additions at Ingolstadt in 1732.

Bibliography: L. KOCH, ed., *Jesuiten-Lexikon* (Paderborn 1934) 458. C. SOMMERVOGEL et al., *Bibliothèque de la Compagnie de Jésus,* 11 v. (Brussels-Paris 1890–1932) 3:212–224. D. PAWLOWSKI, *Vita P. Gasparis Druzbicki, Poloni, Societatis Jesu* (1670).

[W. J. FULCO]

DRUZES

The Druzes are a schismatic Muslim sect, derived from ultra–Shī'ism (*see* SHĪ'ITES) and quartered largely in southern Lebanon and Hawrān (Hauran). The name (Ar., *Durūz,* sing. *Durzi*) stems from al-Darazī (from the Turkish word for tailor), a missionary (*dā'i*) of the Egyptian Fātimid caliph, al-Hākim (996–1021), who, while following the Isma'ili doctrine (*see* ISMAILIS) of the IMĀM as the supreme authority and guardian of ISLAM, proclaimed himself the incarnation of the Deity. Al-Darazi (d. 1019) introduced the Hākim cult into Wādi al-Taym, at the foot of Mt. Hermon; but it was another missionary, the Persian Hamzah al-Labbād (the Furrier), who gave Druzism its system of theology. This was an esoteric system (*Bātini*), giving the Sacred Writings an inner meaning, beyond the apparent, literal one. Hamzah died shortly after al-Hākim and was succeeded by al-Muqtana Bahā'-al-Dīn, whose letters to the Byzantine Emperor and the Christians suggest Syrian-Christian origin. Bahā'-al-Dīn introduced the doctrine that, during the "absence" (*ghaybah*) of al–Hākim, no part of the religion should be divulged or promulgated. Dictated by the urge for safety amid a hostile environment, the doctrine made of Druzism a closed corporate body. Only to the initiated few, *'uqqāl* (intelligent, sage), was given the knowledge and understanding of the Scriptures, kept hidden and in handwriting. The bulk of the community remained *juhhāl* (ignorant, uninitiated).

In accordance with the Shī'ite doctrine of dissimulation (*taqīyah*), Druzes profess Islam but do not observe prescribed Muslim prayers, fast during RAMADAN, undertake the holy pilgrimage to Mecca, or pray in a MOSQUE. Their religious meeting places are inconspicuous, secluded buildings (*khalwahs*) on hills outside their villages. Meetings are held Thursday evenings, for prayer, meditation, religious instruction, and discussion of current problems.

Bibliography: P. K. HITTI, *Lebanon in History* (2d ed. New York 1962); *The Origins of the Druze People and Religion* (New York 1928). N. BOURON, *Les Druzes: Histoire du Liban et de la montagne haouranaise* (Paris 1930). A. I. SILVESTRE DE SACY, *Exposé de la religion des Druzes,* 2 v. (Paris 1838).

[P. K. HITTI]

DRYBURGH, MONASTERY OF

Former Premonstratensian abbey on the Tweed River, about 50 miles south of Edinburgh in Berwickshire, Scotland; Diocese of Saint Andrew's. It was founded in 1150, probably by the Anglo-Norman Hugh de Moreville (d. 1162), constable of Scotland. The first PREMONSTRATENSIAN (or Norbertine) canons arrived in 1152 from Alnwick, an English daughterhouse of Newhouse, the first Premonstratensian foundation in England. Established on the site of an ancient Celtic monastery, Dryburgh joined the relatively new abbeys of MELROSE, JEDBURGH, and Kelso in Scotland's monastery-rich Border country. Adam Scotus (Adam of Dryburgh) was abbot, or at least coadjutor there (*c.* 1184–88), but his successors are little known. The poet Patrick Strode lived there, as did the poet and philosopher RALPH STRODE (*c.* 1354). The 14th-century Wars of Independence resulted in internal laxity of discipline at Dryburgh, and serious external destruction. In 1322 it was burned by King Edward II's retreating forces, and in 1385, when King Richard II raided Scotland, the abbey was again burned; this time it never fully revived. From 1509 on, the abbey was held in COMMENDATION, the Erskines soon becoming hereditary commendatory abbots. Dryburgh was attacked again in 1522, while in 1544 English raiders burned the entire monastery, except for the church, and the abbey was never rebuilt. Thereafter the number of canons in residence continually dwindled until only two remained in 1584. In 1604 King James VI (I) of Scotland and England erected Dryburgh and other temporalities into the Barony of Cardross. Since 1918 the ruins have been a national monument. Sir Walter Scott is buried there.

Bibliography: *Liber s. Marie de Dryburgh,* ed. J. SPOTTIS-WOODE (Bannatyne Club; Edinburgh 1847). D. G. MANUEL, *Dryburgh Abbey in the Light of Its Historical and Ecclesiastical Setting* (Edinburgh 1922). L. H. COTTINEAU, *Répertoire topobibliographique des abbayes et prieurés,* 2 v. (Mâcon 1935–39) 1:1003. *The Chronicle of Melrose,* ed. A. O. and M. O. ANDERSON (London 1936). N. BACKMUND, *Monasticon Praemonstratense,* 3 v. (Straubing 1949–56) 2:100–103. N. BACKMUND, "The Premonstratensian Order in Scotland," *Innes Review* 4 (1953) 24–41; *Dictionnaire d'histoire et de géographie ecclésiastiques,* ed. A. BAUDRILLART et al. (Paris 1912–) 14:823–824. *Dryburgh Abbey: Ministry of Works Official Guide-book,* ed. J. S. RICHARDSON and M. WOOD (2d ed. Edinburgh 1948).

[M. J. HAMILTON]

DUALISM

The name given to any theory, whether general or limited, that invokes two opposed and heterogeneous principles of explanation; as such, it differs from both MONISM and PLURALISM, at least when the latter involves more than two principles. The difficulties posed by the existence of EVIL, moral and physical, were the earliest source of dualistic theories. In modern times, dualism is espoused most frequently in dealing with the problem of KNOWLEDGE; here thought and being, mind and body, certitude and opinion seem to be dyads whose members are irreducible the one to the other. The problem of knowledge was the source of some early dualistic theories as well.

Early Theories. From earliest times it has seemed to many that there is no acceptable way in which GOOD and EVIL can be reduced to the same source. And, since both good and evil are found in the universe, the universe itself is not the product of one author. The evil in question can be physical, as, for example, defective structure of plant, animal, or human body, or it can be moral, the prevalence, temporary or permanent, of man's evil tendencies. Moral evil has, through the centuries, evoked the image of the human person as a battleground, a locus of conflicting tendencies, some good, others bad. A man can recognize and approve the right course and yet, as Ovid and St. Paul poignantly observe, pursue its opposite. Whence comes moral evil? What is the explanation of defective being? Whether one thinks of the moral question as a particularization of the physical or the physical as an extrapolation from the sense of moral evil, there is historically a link between the ethical and the ontological in du-

alism. The universe seems the result of a struggle between Good and Evil, Light and Darkness. Such dualism is to be found in Persia, in the teaching of ZOROASTER (ZARATHUSHTRA). In Christian times this same dualism is expressed in MANICHAEISM.

In its beginnings in Ionia, GREEK PHILOSOPHY sought a monistic explanation of the world. Thales, Anaximander, and Anaximenes may be seen as postulating a single underlying source of the multiple things of ordinary experience when they suggested, respectively, that water, the unlimited, or air is nature; yet, because they were physical philosophers and took change seriously, they held that there are many things. It is this assumption of natural philosophy that was challenged by PARMENIDES, the most uncompromising monist of antiquity. BEING is, NONBEING is not. This Parmenidean assertion entails the negation of change and multiplicity, for if being is said to come to be, it must come from either being or nonbeing. It cannot come from nonbeing; and, if from being, no change has occurred. Multiplicity is canceled out by the same logic. Given two things, they can differ in either being or nothing; but being is what they have in common, and if they differ in nothing, they are the same. This monism, then, is thorough: the one, being, is not the source of any later multiplicity (*see* UNITY). But if the doctrine of Parmenides must be called monistic, the seeds of dualism were present in the poem in which the great Eleatic set down his thought. The monistic doctrine just sketched is found in that part of the poem called the way of truth; a second part, the way of opinion, speaks of the world as it appears to man, and Parmenides there gives a cosmological doctrine not unlike those of his predecessors. This bifurcation between what really and truly is, on the one hand, and what appears, on the other, was to be developed by Plato; before turning to that, however, mention must be made of Pythagoreanism. PYTHAGORAS thought of physical things as numbers; the principles of number, the odd and even, were the principles of all things. This fundamental dualism led to a list of opposites, the so-called Pythagorean categories (see Aristotle, *Meta.* 985b 23–986b 1).

Platonic Dualism. Platonic dualism arose from Parmenides and Pythagoreanism; its motivations were at once ethical and epistemic. PLATO was struck by the non-empirical character of ethical ideals; for example, one need not encounter a perfect instance of justice in order to desire to be just; rather man judges some acts to be just because he recognizes in them an imitation of the IDEA of justice. So too, since man has never experienced perfect equality between physical things, his notion of equality cannot be derived from experience. Justice, equality, and gradually other natures come to be looked upon as ideals that phenomenal things strive to imitate. Add to this the recognition that true knowledge implies an unchanging object, an object unaffected by time, and one has two motives for Plato's assertion that above and beyond the material world where things imitate ideal natures and, being forever in flux, cannot be objects of true knowledge, there is another and better world, the world of Ideas. The Ideas are the subsistent ideals that phenomenal things imitate; they are the guarantee of true knowledge. Plato thus introduced a radical dualism. Only Ideas truly are, but the things of this world have an extenuated kind of being. Knowledge is of Ideas; phenomenal things can ground only opinion.

Aristotelian Dualism. Aristotle, Plato's pupil and colleague, thought that such arguments as Plato himself had formulated in the *Parmenides* were conclusive against the Ideas: the whole doctrine was a great mistake. Thus, in Aristotle's view, if there are things existing separately and apart from the material world, a better argument for their existence would have to be devised. In his famous analysis of moved movers, Aristotle proved that such movers demand a mover that is itself unmoved (*see* MOTION, FIRST CAUSE OF). This First Mover was then seen to have other attributes that reveal His being as personal; Christians have always and rightly observed that here Aristotle had in effect proved the existence of God.

The status of MATTER in Aristotle's philosophy raises the question whether his worldview is monistic or dualistic. That is, is everything in the cosmos reduced to the First Mover as to its cause, or is there something in the world that enjoys existence apart from the causality of the First Mover? Aristotle held that, so far as man can know, the world has always existed; thus motion has always existed and matter as well. The First Mover is PURE ACT; matter, what Aristotle called primary matter, is pure POTENCY. Does one have here two irreducibly different principles of the world man knows? It is important to see that this consequence does not follow because, in seeing so, one is better able to appreciate the difference between Aristotelian and Cartesian matter.

Aristotle's analysis of physical things, that is, of things that come to be as a term of a CHANGE, led him to maintain that physical things are composed of matter and form (*see* MATTER AND FORM). Roughly, matter is what survives a change and form is what the matter gains as the result of the change. These principles are not themselves things; that is, matter cannot exist except in material things, and form exists only in formed things. If matter exists only in material things, it is not an entity on the same level as the First Mover. A similar opposition in Aristotelian philosophy, it may be noted, is that between body and SOUL, particularly when one restricts the consideration to the soul whose operations are not bound up

with matter (*see* SOUL, HUMAN). Matter versus form, body versus human soul, material substance versus immaterial substance—these are the undeniable dualisms in Aristotle's doctrine.

Whether everything in the cosmos can be reduced to one principle is a question whose answer must be formulated carefully. Aristotle is quite clear as to the various meanings he ascribes to the term PRINCIPLE. It is commonly agreed among scholars that he taught that the First Mover is the ultimate final cause of everything in the cosmos, the good toward which all things tend. Some scholars have thought they could accept this conclusion and still doubt whether, for Aristotle, the First Mover is as well the efficient cause of everything. Against this doubt it can be argued that, unless there is an efficient causality comprehensive enough to fashion everything so that its *telos* is the First Mover, the order of the universe would be, on Aristotelian grounds, due to pure CHANCE. But this Aristotle explicitly denies. The sense of the Aristotelian view of the universe, then, would be that there is one principle on whom depend Earth and the heavens and everything therein. Therefore, all dualisms in Aristotle are, so to speak, regional and not universal.

Scholastic Dualism. In Christian times the most important new candidate for the title of dualism would be the contrast between nature and grace, between the natural and the supernatural. From a metaphysical point of view, however, the most important clarification of the difference between God and creature was had in the doctrine of essence and existence. The sources of this distinction can be found in the Greeks, but the document that forced subsequent discussion of it was the *De hebdomadibus* of BOETHIUS. Among the later scholastics who commented on this opusculum was St. THOMAS AQUINAS. *"Diversum est esse et id quod est,"* Boethius wrote, and St. Thomas, combining this with the Aristotelian doctrine of matter and form, understood its import as follows: "In substances composed of matter and form, there is a twofold composition of act and potency, the first of the substance itself that is composed of matter and form, the second of the already constituted substance and its existence (*esse*), which can also be said to be a composition resulting from what it is (*quod est*) and its existence (*esse*), or from 'that which is' (*quod est*) and 'that whereby it is' (*quo est*). Thus it is clear that the composition of act and potency is found in more things than the composition of form and matter. Form and matter divide natural substance but potency and act divide being in general" (*C. gent.* 2.54). Only in God is there no composition whatsoever. He is being essentially; everything else is being by PARTICIPATION. As *Ipsum Esse Subsistens,* God is the source of the essence and existence of all creatures. Thus, if all created being is divided by potency and act at least in the sense of essence and existence, the source of all created being is one, God, whose essence is His existence (*see* ESSENCE AND EXISTENCE; POTENCY AND ACT).

Cartesian Dualism. The division of reality into thought and extension is already implied in the methodical DOUBT that characterizes the philosophy of R. DESCARTES. In his effort to find an indubitable starting point, Descartes agreed to set aside anything about which doubt was at all possible. Sensible things, those of which man is aware by sensation, were first set aside, since it is in principle possible to think that one is deceived concerning shape, size, colors, etc. Man may even be deceived about his own body. But if any item of knowledge that might be substituted for *X* in "I think that *X*" can be thought of as possibly false, and therefore dubitable, man cannot doubt the existence of himself as a thinking something. Having reached an indubitable truth, the *cogito ergo sum*, Descartes moved rapidly to the assertion of the existence of God via a modified ONTOLOGICAL ARGUMENT. That done, God's veracity became the guarantee of the reality of the external world. Now, while everything may have seemed to be as it was before this step, the reasoning involved left Descartes with an unbridgeable gulf between the material world (*res extensa*) and mind (*res cogitans*). The difficulty became most acute, perhaps, when he attempted to establish the relation between soul and body, and this because of his general view of matter as a substance, a something in its own right, rather than as an element or component of substance. The unity of the human person posed the problem of making two substances, mind and body, into one substance—a problem that was destined never to be solved in Cartesian terms (*see* MIND-BODY PROBLEM).

The hope of Descartes was to fashion philosophy on the model of the most rigorous science, mathematics. For something to be certain, it must be clear and distinct. As the father of modern philosophy, Descartes bequeathed this ideal of rigor, the search for a method to achieve it, and an almost skeptical attitude toward sensation to a great line of followers. One of the most important thinkers in his wake was Immanuel Kant.

Kantian Dualism. Kant's critical philosophy introduced a dualism that is fundamentally epistemological. D. HUME had held that experience is insufficient ground for universal and necessary judgments such as those abounding in metaphysics. Kant agreed with this and asked whether there is a source of universality and necessity elsewhere than in experience. For him, some concepts are pure and a priori in the sense that, while formed in terms of what is experienced, they are not derived from what is experienced. Such concepts as cause, effect, and

substance are pure in this sense. Experience is possible because there are forms of sensuous intuition (space and time) and of understanding—subjective grooves, as it were, to which the matter of experience must conform in order to be known by man. Things as known, PHENOMENA, are an amalgam of subjective form and objective matter; NOUMENA are things in themselves, as such unknowable by man. This Kantian dualism has had a great impact on the philosophy of science; there Kant's theory of the forms of intuition and of understanding as what man imposes upon an amorphous and unknowable reality seems to many to explain the preponderance of theory and hypotheses in modern physical science.

Critique. Although it is possible to reduce the uses of the term "dualism" to a finite number of meanings, the term remains vague and of widely varying application. Abstractly speaking, there is little to be said for or against dualism. Whereas explanations of moral evil lead some to posit two equal principles, the one of good, the other of evil, the motive behind the reasoning is usually to deny that God is the cause of evil. The disadvantage is that God's causality seems thereby restricted and so too His preeminence. Physical dualisms, which often have epistemological sources, have the advantage of drawing a sharp distinction between the human and the nonhuman, between the spiritual and the corporeal. The disadvantage of so sharp a demarcation is that such a dualism is finally unable to account for the fact that man's vocabulary embraces the two spheres. In the final analysis, it seems that dualism is a second-order word; it is not so much a philosophical theory as a term to describe theories.

See Also: MONISM; PERSIAN RELIGION, ANCIENT; PLURALISM, PHILOSOPHICAL.

Bibliography: J. HASTINGS, ed., *Encyclopedia of Religion and Ethics*, 13 v. (Edinburgh 1908–27) 5:100–114. P. FOULQUIÉ and R. SAINT-JEAN, *Dictionnaire de la langue philosophique* (Paris 1962) 190–191. G. SEMPRINI, *Enciclopedia filosofica*, 4 v. (Venice-Rome 1957) 1:1741–44. J. HENNINGER et al., *Lexikon für Theologie und Kirche*, ed. J. HOFER and K. RAHNER, 10 v. (2d, new ed. Freiburg 1957–65) 3:582–589. G. MENSCHING and G. GLOEGE, *Die Religion in Geschichte und Gegenwart*, 7 v. (3d ed. Tübingen 1957–65) 2:272–276. R. EISLER, *Wörterbuch der philosophischen Begriffe*, 3 v. (4th ed. Berlin 1927–30) 1:294–296.

[R. M. MCINERNY]

DUBLIN REVIEW

A Catholic quarterly, founded by Nicholas WISEMAN, the future cardinal archbishop of Westminster, and Daniel O'Connell, the Irish politician, in May 1836 as a literary, historical, and religious journal. The name was misleading. Despite a green cover, its connection with Dublin itself was only nominal: it was always published in London. From 1837 to 1863 it was edited by a barrister, H. R. Bagshawe. Wiseman transferred ownership to Henry Edward MANNING, the future archbishop of Westminster, and Manning appointed William George WARD as editor, thus ensuring the continuity of the ultramontane tradition in which it had been founded. Ward retired in 1878, and the ownership passed to Herbert VAUGHAN, who appointed Cuthbert Hedley, O.S.B., as editor. He resigned on his appointment as bishop, and the editorship shortly afterwards passed to James Moyes, canon theologian of Westminster, who made it much more ecclesiastically oriented. Wilfrid WARD took over in 1906, and edited the *Dublin Review* until 1915. He gave it much greater scope, and through his wide range of contacts brought many distinguished authors to its pages. Not all of these authors were Roman Catholic, and some came from overseas, including the Italian priest-politician Luigi STURZO and Cardinal FAULHABER. Though from Vaughan's death in 1903 it belonged to the diocese of Westminster, the quarterly was published by the firm of Burns and Oates, for which Ward worked, and Burns and Oates from then on supplied the editor. These included several of the Catholic intellectuals of the day: the writer Sir Shane Leslie, the historian Denis Gwynn and the future editor of *The Tablet* Tom Burns. In the early years of the Second World War the review was edited by Christopher Dawson, supported by Barbara Ward, and used by them to promote the policies of the Sword of the Spirit, an organization they had helped to found to unite Christian opinion in Britain behind the government's war aims. In the years after the war, circulation of the *Dublin Review* was not high. In an attempt to renew interest, and to make it sound, perhaps, less ''foreign,'' the lawyer and journalist Norman St-John Stevas, later Baron St. John of Fawsley, changed the name to the *Wiseman Review* when he took over editorship in 1961. He changed it back again in 1964. Circulation, however, continued to decline and in 1969, at the request of the archbishop of Westminster, Cardinal Heenan, it was incorporated into the British Jesuit publication, *The MONTH*.

Bibliography: J. L. ALTHOLZ, *The Religious Press in Britain, 1760–1900* (Westport, Conn. 1989). J. J. DWYER, ''The Catholic Press, 1850–1950,'' in G. A. BECK, ed., *The English Catholics, 1850–1950* (London 1950) 475–514.

[M. J. WALSH]

DUBOIS, GUILLAUME

French cardinal, b. Brive-la-Gaillarde, Limousin, Sept. 6, 1656; d. Paris, Aug. 10, 1723. In 1672 he came to the college of St. Michel in Paris, received tonsure, and after his studies tutored in divers families. In 1683 he was assistant tutor and in 1687 tutor to the Duke of Chartres, son of the Duke of Orléans, brother of the king. He remained in the service of the duke afterward. In London in 1698, Dubois made valuable ties, and, when in 1715 his former student, now Duke of Orléans, became regent of LOUIS XV, Dubois was named to the Council of State. He secured, in 1716, an Anglo-French alliance against Spain, which Holland joined in 1717, and Austria, in 1718. In 1721 Spain, after military hostilities, signed an alliance with France. Dubois's policy also led to a peace with Sweden, Denmark, and Russia in 1721. Dubois had become foreign minister in September 1718. He was ordained March 3, 1720, and made archbishop of Cambrai June 9 of the same year. In December 1720 he secured the registry of the anti-Jansenist papal bull *UNIGENITUS*, and on July 16, 1721, was made cardinal, reluctantly on the part of Rome. He became prime minister in August 1722, and, when Louis XV was declared of age in 1723, Dubois continued to direct foreign policy. In December 1722 he was accepted into the Académie Française. Dubois was not known for either piety or morality. His revenue from ecclesiastical benefices was enormous. But venality was part of diplomacy, and he had no part in the corruption of his student, the Duke of Chartres. His enemies maligned him in pamphlets.

Bibliography: P. BLIARD, *Dubois, cardinal et premier ministre*, 2 v. (Paris 1901). P. MURET and P. SAGNAC, *La Prépondérance anglaise, 1715–1763* (Paris 1937), bibliography. J. L. AUJOL, *Le Cardinal Dubois: Ministre de la paix* (Paris 1948). R. CHALUMEAU, *Catholicisme. Hier, aujourd'hui et demain*, ed. G. JACQUEMET (Paris 1947–) 3:1134–36.

[W. E. LANGLEY]

DUBOIS, JOHN

Third bishop of New York; b. Paris, Aug. 24, 1764; d. New York City, Dec. 20, 1842. After graduating from the Collège Louis-le-Grand, Paris, where he had as fellow students Robespierre and Desmoulins, he entered the Seminary of St. Magloire in Paris and was ordained on Sept. 22, 1787. His work in Paris, as assistant to the curé of St. Sulpice and chaplain to a community of Sisters of Charity of St. Vincent de Paul, was cut short by the French Revolution, and in May 1791 he made his escape from France. Arriving in Norfolk, Va., in August 1791, with letters of introduction from Lafayette to prominent Virginians, he was for a time the house guest of James Monroe and received English lessons from Patrick Henry. While in Richmond, he celebrated Mass in the state house.

He soon became an American citizen and was assigned by Bp. John Carroll to missionary work at Norfolk

John Dubois.

and Richmond, Va. He built the first Catholic church in Frederick, Md., and used it as a base for missionary travels into Virginia and Pennsylvania. In 1807 he established a preparatory seminary at Emmitsburg, Md., and in the following year affiliated himself and his seminary with the Society of St. Sulpice. Before long the institution was expanded into Mt. St. Mary's College and Seminary for the education of theological students and laymen. Financial difficulties marked the early years of the college, during which he served simultaneously as president, treasurer, and professor. A disastrous fire in 1824 destroyed a new building on the point of completion. In addition, there were disagreements with his Sulpician superiors in Baltimore, who desired to reduce the institution to its original function as a minor seminary. Nevertheless, Mt. St. Mary's prospered, numbering among its alumni leading members of the American hierarchy, including Cardinal J. McCloskey and Archbishops J. Hughes and J. Purcell. It was also at Emmitsburg that Mother Elizabeth SETON, with the help of Dubois, founded her first convent of Sisters of Charity in May 1809.

In 1826, after severing his connection with the Sulpicians and beginning the reorganization of Mt. St. Mary's, he was appointed to the See of New York to succeed Bp. John Connolly. He was consecrated by Abp. Ambrose Maréchal in the Baltimore cathedral on Oct. 29, 1826.

Many difficulties awaited him in New York. His appointment was not viewed with favor by the predominantly Irish Catholic community there. Charges that he was a Frenchman, far from fluent in the English language, not a member of the New York clergy, and seemingly imposed on New York by Maréchal and the Sulpicians, caused friction for some years after he refuted them in a pastoral letter of July 1827. His vast diocese, which he toured on a 3,000-mile visitation in 1828, included the whole of New York State and half of New Jersey, about 150,000 Catholics, but only 18 priests and 12 churches. One of his most urgent needs was a seminary, and to obtain funds for one he went to Rome and Paris in 1829. Upon his return, with financial aid from the Congregation of Propaganda Fide and the Society for the Propagation of the Faith, he proceeded to erect a seminary at Nyack, N.Y. Two years later (1834), the building was destroyed by fire; it was uninsured and total loss resulted. His subsequent attempts to establish a seminary, in Brooklyn and in Lafargeville, N.Y., also ended in failure.

Another problem, common to American bishops of the day, was that of TRUSTEEISM, a system whereby laymen administered church finances. In 1834 the trustees of St. Patrick's Cathedral refused to receive a successor to their pastor, Thomas Levins, whom Dubois had suspended, and they threatened to withhold the bishop's salary. The situation lasted for three years. In the meantime, debilitated by the struggle and by attacks of crippling rheumatism, he asked for a coadjutor. In 1837 he received one with the right of succession in the person of John HUGHES, a former student of his at Mt. St. Mary's. Three strokes of paralysis early in 1838 so weakened his physical and mental vigor that when the cathedral trustees again defied him in 1839, it was Hughes upon whom he relied to quell the rebellion and to put an end to the abuses of trusteeism in the diocese. In the same year he reluctantly resigned the active government of his see to his coadjutor.

His administration was marked by a triple growth in the number of clergy and a quadrupling of churches. His seminary project, while not duplicating the success of Mt. St. Mary's, was soon to be realized under his successor, at Rose Hill, Fordham, N.Y.C., in 1840. Moreover, despite the initial resentment of his flock and his own imperious temper, Dubois had won the affection of his clergy and people. His body was interred at the entrance to old St. Patrick's Cathedral.

Bibliography: J. T. SMITH, *The Catholic Church in New York,* 2 v. (New York 1905) v. 1. C. G. HERBERMANN, "The Rt. Rev. John Dubois, D.D.," *Historical Records and Studies of the U.S. Catholic Historical Society of New York* 1 (1899) 278–355: *The Sulpicians in the United States* (New York 1916). M. M. MELINE and E. F. MC-SWEENEY, *The Story of the Mountain,* 2 v. (Emmitsburg, Md. 1911)

v. 1. J. W. RUANE, *The Beginnings of the Society of St. Sulpice in the United States, 1791–1829* (Catholic University of America, *Studies in American Church History* 22; Washington 1935). A. M. MELVILLE, *Elizabeth Bayley Seton 1774–1821* (New York 1951; reprint 1960). L. R. RYAN, *Old St. Peter's, the Mother Church of Catholic New York, 1785–1935* (U.S. Catholic Historical Society 15; New York 1935). M. P. CARTHY, *Old St. Patrick's New York's First Cathedral* (New York 1947).

[J. A. REYNOLDS]

DUBOIS, LOUIS ERNEST

Cardinal, archbishop of Paris; b. St-Calais (Sarthe), Sept. 1, 1856; d. Paris, Sept. 23, 1929. After studies at the seminary in Le Mans, he was ordained (1879), became curate in the Le Mans Diocese at Brûlon and then at Couture du Mans, editor of the diocesan bulletin *Semaine du fidèle* (1888), almoner of the Notre-Dame boarding school in Le Mans (1893), pastor in Le Mans (1895), and vicar-general (1898). As bishop of Verdun (1901–09), his adherence to the Holy See's directives in the crisis caused by the law separating Church and State (1905) merited his elevation to the archiepiscopal See of Bourges (1909). During World War I he dedicated his efforts especially to the *Union sacrée* and to patriotic works. In 1916 Benedict XV transferred him to the See of Rouen, and made him cardinal. The government sent Dubois to the Near East to strengthen French influence (1919–20). He succeeded Cardinal AMETTE in the See of Paris (1920). Further voyages in official capacities carried him to Poland (1924), the U.S. and Canada (1926), and Austria (1928). With his conciliatory spirit he established such diocesan cultural associations as the Gregorian Institute for plain chant, and Catholic committees for the theater, cinema, and radio; and inaugurated radio broadcasts of sermons. Christian syndicalism and the first specialized activities of CATHOLIC ACTION met his approval. He suffered bitter recrimination in his opposition to ACTION FRANÇAISE. He published several brochures on the religious history of the French region of Maine; *Vie de St Joseph* (1927); and *Paroles catholiques* (1928).

Bibliography: M. FLORISOONE, *Le Cardinal Dubois* (Paris 1929). H. L. ODELIN, *Le Cardinal Dubois: Souvenirs* (Paris 1931). J. RUPP, *Histoire de l'Église de Paris* (Paris 1948) 311–316. G. JACQUEMET, *Catholicisme. Hier, aujourd'hui et demain*, ed. G. JACQUEMET (Paris 1947–) 3:1136–38.

[R. LIMOUZIN-LAMOTHE]

DU BOS, CHARLES

French literary critic; b. Paris, Oct. 27, 1882; d. La Celle Saint-Cloud, Aug. 5, 1939. His mother was English, his grandmother American. He attended the Catholic Collège Gerson and the state *lycée,* Janson-de-Sailly. At Oxford University (1900–01) he lost his faith, influenced by the philosophy of Herbert SPENCER. At Florence and Berlin (1904–05) he studied philosophy and art criticism. Having met U.S. novelist Edith Wharton through their common friend Paul Bourget, Du Bos, together with André Gide, became active in her projects to aid war victims (1914–16), and after the war translated her *The House of Mirth* under the title *Chez les Heureux du Monde,* his first literary effort. He was Paris correspondent of the London *Athenaeum* (1919–21), supervisor of foreign writers at Plon's publishing firm (1922–27), literary advisor to the *Éditions Schiffrin* (1926–27), and secretary of the French Intellectual Union (1925–27). In 1927 he returned to the Catholic faith and attended Mass daily until his death.

While editing the Catholic quarterly, *Vigile,* Du Bos lectured at several universities in Germany, Italy, and Switzerland (1925–32). He taught at the University of Notre Dame and St. Mary's College, South Bend, Ind. (1937–39). Among his important works should be listed *Approximations* (7 ser., 1922–37), *Diary* (9 v., 1908–39), and *Journal Intime* (3 v., 1946–49). Depending on sympathy rather than on precise judgments, Du Bos's criticism aims at finding the creative source of a work. His *Diary,* revealing a remarkably wide range of close friendships with the artists of his time, manifests a striking and attractive personality and sensitively follows the course of his spiritual evolution.

Bibliography: A. P. BERTOCCI, *Charles Du Bos and English Literature* (New York 1949). M. A. GOUHIER, *Charles Du Bos* (Paris 1951). J. MOUTON, *Charles Du Bos: Sa relation avec la vie et avec la mort* (Paris 1954).

[M. LELEU]

DUBOURG, LOUIS WILLIAM VALENTINE

Bishop; b. Cap Français, Santo Domingo, Feb. 14, 1766; d. Besançon, France, Dec. 12, 1833. He was taken to France as an infant, made his classical studies at the Collège de Guyenne, and entered the Seminary of St. Sulpice in Paris in 1786. He was ordained probably in 1788, but records were destroyed in the French Revolution, which also forced his flight to Baltimore, Md., where he became a member of the Society of St. Sulpice in 1795. Bishop John CARROLL appointed him third president of Georgetown College (now University), Washington, D.C., in 1796, and he served until 1798, when he left to direct the Sulpician College in Cuba. Upon his return to Baltimore, he founded St. Mary's College (1803; University since 1805) and aided (Bl.) Elizabeth Bayley SETON's early endeavors in Maryland.

In 1812 Dubourg was appointed administrator of the Diocese of Louisiana, which had been without a bishop since 1801. The diocese was crippled by lack of staff and by the intrigues of Anthony de Sedella, a Capuchin angered by the Louisiana Purchase of 1803. Despite these troubles, Dubourg, with the aid of Ursuline nuns, assisted in the defense of New Orleans, La., against the British in 1815. On Sept. 24, 1815, Dubourg was consecrated bishop of Louisiana by Cardinal Joseph Doria-Pamfili in Rome. There he obtained recruits for his diocese, notably the Lazarist Fathers Felix de Andreis and Joseph Rosati. Sedella's machinations in New Orleans continued, however, and Dubourg settled in St. Louis, Mo., after his return to the U.S. on Jan. 5, 1818. During the next three years he undertook the construction of a cathedral in St. Louis and sought to promote education. A seminary was opened under Rosati, a girls' school was established at Florissant, Mo., under (Bl.) Philippine Duchesne, and St. Louis College (later University) was operated by the diocesan clergy. Once hostility waned in the South, however, Dubourg returned to New Orleans (1820), where even Sedella welcomed his arrival. There, in addition to founding new schools, he promoted northern Native American missions. During a visit to Washington, D.C., in 1822, he persuaded the U.S. War Department to support schools for the natives. At the same time he convinced the Maryland Jesuits, among whom was Rev. Pierre de Smet, to undertake mission work in Missouri, where they established the first school for Native American boys and later took over St. Louis College.

On March 25, 1824, Dubourg consecrated the Lazarist, Rosati, as coadjutor, but this followed a long period of dissension induced by Dubourg's recommendation of such alternate choices as Rev. Angelo Inglesi, a gifted adventurer who was but recently ordained. The rift caused by these events led to Dubourg's resignation, which was accepted in 1826. Leo XII then nominated Dubourg for the Diocese of Montauban, France. In France the bishop resumed writing, publishing his *Concordance for the Four Gospels* (1830). In 1833 he was promoted to the archbishopric of Besançon. Dubourg officiated but once in his new see; he died after a month in office.

Bibliography: Archives, Archdiocese of St. Louis. Archives, Congregation de Propaganda Fide.

[P. J. RAHILL]

DUBUQUE, ARCHDIOCESE OF

Metropolitan see embracing 30 counties in the northeast section of Iowa, an area of 17,403 square miles. Du-buque (Dubuquensis) was established as a diocese July 28, 1837, and created an archdiocese June 15, 1893. Since 1945 the metropolitan province has been coextensive with the state of Iowa and the suffragan sees have been those of DAVENPORT, SIOUX CITY, and DES MOINES. The city of Dubuque itself, named for its French Canadian founder, Julien Dubuque, has the smallest total population of any archdiocesan see city in the United States; the people in the city and county of Dubuque are preponderantly Catholic. Slightly more than 20 percent of the total population of the archdiocese is Catholic, largely of Irish, German, and Czech origin, but nationalism has virtually disappeared and technically no genuine national parishes exist.

Geographical Evolution. The Third Provincial Council of Baltimore, in petitioning (1837) for the creation of a diocese at Dubuque, was following a logical pattern in organizing the Church in the territory of the Louisiana purchase. The upper Mississippi region had previously been separated from the New Orleans, Louisiana, diocese, by the erection of the Diocese of St. Louis, Missouri (1826); in 1837 the still vast northern area was subdivided by organizing its northern part into the Diocese of Dubuque. The original diocesan boundaries included the area lying north of the state of Missouri and between the Mississippi and Missouri Rivers, that is, the area now comprised by the states of Iowa and Minnesota, and the eastern half of the states of North and South Dakota. Until the erection of the Dioceses of Chicago, Illinois, and Milwaukee, Wisconsin (1843), however, the eastern banks of the Mississippi both upstream and downstream from Dubuque were delegated to the care of the bishop of Dubuque by the far away bishops of St. Louis, Missouri, and Detroit, Michigan. In 1850, with the creation of the Diocese of St. Paul, Minnesota, the boundaries of the Diocese of Dubuque were reduced to coincide with those of the state of Iowa, which had been admitted to the Union in 1846. In 1881 the southern half of Iowa, embracing the four southern tiers of counties, became the Diocese of Davenport, the Diocese of Dubuque retaining the five northern tiers of counties. With the separation of its 24 western counties in 1902 to form the new Diocese of Sioux City, the area of the see of Dubuque had shrunk to about to about one-twelfth of its original size. The final reduction came in 1911 when the Diocese of Des Moines was created out of the western half of the Diocese of Davenport, and Clinton County was transferred to the Davenport diocese.

Early History. Before the area, at least in part, was formally opened for white settlement by land treaty with the Native Americans in 1833, Iowa and the territory to the north of it was almost devoid of white population, and even the Native Americans, mostly of the Dakota, Ho-

Chunk, Sauk, and Mesquakie tribes, numbered only a few thousand. The Reverend Jacques MARQUETTE and Louis Jolliet had passed by on the Mississippi River in 1673, and during the 1770s a French lead miner, Jean Marie Cardinal, came to the site of the present Dubuque; but the first permanent white settler in the area was Julien Dubuque. By the terms of his treaty with the Mesquakie people (1788) he undertook to work the lead mines, which became known as the ''Mines of Spain'' after the confirmation of his rights in 1796 by the Spanish governor of Louisiana; they were subsequently called ''the Dubuque Mines.'' Julien Dubuque was a Catholic French Canadian, and he was buried on a high bluff in a grave surmounted with a cross. The first records of a Catholic priest ministering in the area coincide with the real beginnings of white settlement during the 1830s. In 1832 a Flemish Jesuit, Charles Felix VAN QUICKENBORNE, visited the Half Breed Tract (Keokuk), and in 1833, Dubuque. While there, he met with the considerable number of Catholics in the Dubuque area, and a petition to Bishop Joseph Rosati, of St. Louis, was framed, requesting permission to build a church. A memorandum of the meeting, dated July 19, 1833, contains specific plans for a log church and a list of committee members. Although the Rev. Charles F. Fitzmaurice, who was living nearby at Galena, Illinois, had been given a considerable quantity of building materials and $1,100 in cash by the Dubuque Catholics, he died of cholera before the church could be built. Meanwhile, a log church was constructed under the leadership of the Methodists (1834), with the understanding that it was to be available on Sunday for use by other religious groups and during the week as a school.

The effective beginnings of organized Catholic parish life in the upper Mississippi region, however, were in large part the work of the Italian Dominican, Samuel MAZZUCHELLI, who appeared in Dubuque in 1835 and immediately began directing the building of a stone church, on a larger scale than that originally planned. He named it St. Raphael's; later he named two other parishes he did much to found, St. Michael's at Galena, and St. Gabriel's at Prairie du Chien. Mazzuchelli also formed St. Anthony's parish at Davenport and St. Paul's at Burlington. For several years after the establishment of the Diocese of Dubuque, Mazzuchelli was a vicar general and frequent companion of the first bishop, Jean Mathias LORAS, while continuing his missionary travels and the foundation of parishes. In 1838 the German Catholics at Ft. Madison and nearby Sugar Creek were visited from Quincy, Illinois, by a German priest, Augustus Brickweede. In the same year, two Jesuits, Pierre Jean DE SMET and Felix Verreydt, together with two lay brothers, came up the Missouri River from St. Louis to Council Bluffs, and for several years conducted a mission center among the Pottawatomi.

Bishop Loras. The first bishop of Dubuque was consecrated on Dec. 11, 1837 by Bishop Michael Portier in Mobile, Alabama. After appointing as vicar generals Rosati of St. Louis and, through him, Mazzuchelli, who was the only priest then living within his diocese, Loras sailed directly for Europe in search of priests and funds with which to build a diocese. Although disappointed in his effort to locate German and Irish volunteers, he found six Frenchmen, who sailed with him from France for New York in August 1838. Two were priests—Joseph CRETIN, his close friend and later named the first bishop of St. Paul, and J. A. M. Pelamourges, longtime pastor of Davenport, who later refused his appointment as episcopal successor to Cretin in St. Paul; the four others were subdeacons, Augustin Ravoux, Lucien Galtier, Regius Petiot, and James Causse. Loras made valuable contacts with the SOCIETY FOR THE PROPAGATION OF THE FAITH of his native Lyons, France, and with the LEOPOLDINEN STIFTUNG (LEOPOLDINE SOCIETY) of Vienna, Austria, from which he received large amounts of money in annual grants, as well as from the LUDWIG MISSIONSVEREIN (LUDWIG MISSION SOCIETY) of Munich.

On April 18, 1839, Loras, accompanied by Cretin and Mazzuchelli, formally entered Dubuque, and three days later the bishop enthroned himself in his still partially incomplete little cathedral. The same summer he traveled north to St. Anthony's Falls and Ft. Snelling, Minnesota, and, returning by canoe, visited Native American villages and white settlements along the way. In the autumn of 1839 he organized St. Raphael's College and Seminary, which occupied one floor of his residence. In 1843 the Sisters of Charity of the Blessed Virgin Mary and their chaplain, Terrence Donaghoe, transferred their community from Philadelphia, Pennsylvania, to Dubuque and opened a school for girls. In 1849 a group of Trappists from Mt. Melleray Abbey, County Waterford, Ireland, began New Melleray monastery near Dubuque on land given them by Loras. In 1850 the diocesan college and seminary were transferred to new buildings at Table Mound, just south of Dubuque, and renamed Mt. St. Bernard's. In 1851 the Brothers of the Sacred Heart arrived in Dubuque from Le Puy, France, and opened a school for boys.

Although Mazzuchelli, Petiot, Ravoux, Cretin, and others had considerable missionary success among the Native Americans, chiefly the Ho-Chunk at Festina near Ft. Atkinson, Iowa, and later in Minnesota, the French and native character of the population was soon limited to the outreaches of the diocese. Eastern Iowa was rapidly populated by native-born whites, for the most part Protestant, or Catholic immigrants from Ireland, Germany, and Luxembourg. Loras, who had learned considerable German as well as almost perfect English, having tried but failed to attract French settlers, heartily encouraged this Catholic immigration, and eastern Iowa, particularly the area around Dubuque, was soon dotted with new parishes. The first Irish parish there was founded by Mazzuchelli in 1840 at Makokiti (Garryowen) in Jackson County. The first German parish in the diocese was organized in western Dubuque County in 1846 by Loras, and the settlement was named New Vienna in gratitude to the Leopoldine Society of Vienna. In 1849 the Germans at Dubuque were allowed to build their own church, called at first Holy Trinity, and later named St. Mary's. Loras, using chiefly his own funds and at the insistence of the Irish, constructed St. Patrick's Church at Dubuque (1852–53) as an exclusively English-speaking mission of the cathedral. But the French were now only a small minority even in the cathedral parish, and the Irish at debt-free St. Patrick's were given a pastor and parish status only when, after severe reprimand in 1855, they assured the bishop of their support in the construction of a new and adequate cathedral.

After attending the Provincial Councils of Baltimore (1840, 1843, and 1849), Loras traveled again to Europe in search of priests and funds, and returned with five seminarians: three Frenchmen, Andrew Trevis, Philip Laurent, and Frederick Jean; a German, Mathias Michels; and an Irishman, Michael Lynch. In 1854 the bishop traveled by steamboat from St. Louis up the Missouri River to visit Council Bluffs on the western edge of his diocese, which since 1850 had been limited to the state of Iowa. In 1853, recognizing his own failing health and concerned to assure the future of a diocese difficult to govern, Loras had discussed with Cretin the possibility of asking Rome to name Clement Smyth (1810–57), prior of New Melleray monastery near Dubuque, as his coadjutor and successor. The appointment itself was made only in the spring of 1857, shortly after construction had begun on the long-anticipated new cathedral. Loras offered the first Mass in the unfinished structure on Christmas Day, 1857; he died on Feb. 19, 1858, a few days after its formal dedication.

Bishop Smyth. The second bishop's consecration, May 3, 1857, in St. Louis by Archbishop Peter R. Kenrick, inaugurated an Irish succession in Dubuque and was a frank recognition by Loras that the period of fruitful French predominance, born of necessity and a thin tradition, had passed. But the Civil War and the financial distress that preceded it clouded the whole episcopate of Smyth. Although he was successful in bringing many priests, mostly Irish, and chiefly from All Hallows College, Dublin, into his diocese, discontent among the French priests led many of them to leave the diocese; thus the number of clergy remained almost constant. The Catholic population showed slow but steady increase;

one of the few new parishes founded was St. Wenceslaus in the Czech settlement of Spillville. The Brothers of the Sacred Heart closed their school and left the city. Both the hospital and Mt. St. Bernard Seminary were allowed to lapse. During the Civil War, there was considerable pro-Southern sentiment at Dubuque, especially among the Catholic immigrants. Its most outspoken exponent was Dennis A. Mahoney, editor of the local Democratic newspaper and longtime friend and adviser of Loras, whose missionary years in Alabama and even as a slaveholder had made him something of a Southern sympathizer. Smyth, however, was an insistent supporter of the Union, and shortly after the assassination of Abraham Lincoln, he answered his critics in a stinging sermon. That same evening his coach house, carriage, and horses were destroyed by arson. While the bishop was absent on a Confirmation tour in Des Moines and other places in Iowa, a group of local citizens, both Protestant and Catholic, organized a manifestation of loyalty by having the coach house rebuilt and by purchasing a new carriage and pair of horses. The bishop died but a few months later and was buried beside his predecessor in the crypt of the cathedral, which he as coadjutor had seen to completion.

Bishop Hennessy. The third bishop and first archbishop, Irish-born John Hennessy (1825–1900), was consecrated Sept. 30, 1866, at Dubuque by Kenrick of St. Louis; he became an archbishop June 16, 1893. The long episcopate of this former pastor of St. Joseph, Missouri, corresponded with a period of prodigious growth after the Civil War. The networks of railroads, crossing Iowa for the first time, brought floods of new Catholic settlers, who came both from the East Coast and directly from Europe. Before and during the Civil War, widely separated areas had been visited by circuit-riding priests; but now, parishes with resident pastors began to appear in both rural and urban areas on land that the farsighted Loras had purchased. Even when southern Iowa was separated (1881) to form the new Diocese of Davenport, there were still 123 diocesan priests, 109 parishes, and 107 missions in what remained, or more than double the number in the whole state of Iowa at the close of the Civil War. Of the parishes still within the 30 counties of the archdiocese of Dubuque, 118 were founded during the time of Hennessy. The diocesan college, begun by Loras in 1839, was reorganized and reopened in 1873 as St. Joseph's College in the former marine hospital, built by Loras, and further additions were built in 1878 and 1884. Although in time almost all the priests of the diocese were American-born and alumni of this college, priests recruited from Ireland and Germany formed the great majority of the local clergy for many years. At a time when the bishops throughout the nation were deciding whether or not to form a system of parochial schools, Hennessy was an avid supporter of a Catholic school system. His motto was "A Parochial School for Every Parish," and his zeal in the pursuit of this goal would lay the foundation for an outstanding and extensive school system in which 60 percent of all parishes would eventually have their own parochial school. With this view in mind, he was very successful in influencing congregations of teaching sisters to settle within Iowa. Under his leadership and guidance, the Visitation Sisters, the Sisters of Mercy, the Presentation Sisters, the Franciscan Sisters of the Holy Family, the Sisters of the Holy Humility of Mary, and the Franciscan Sisters of the Immaculate Conception all established themselves in the diocese. During his almost 34 years in office, the archdiocese made the greatest advances in the number of Catholics, priests, and parishes.

Bishop John Joseph Keane. The appointment in 1900 of John Joseph Keane (1839–1918) as Dubuque's fourth bishop and second archbishop marked the first episcopacy of the Archdiocese of Dubuque in its present boundaries when Sioux City became a separate diocese in 1902. Under this former first rector of the Catholic University of America, St. Joseph's College was expanded, additional parishes were erected in the cities of Dubuque, Waterloo, and Mason City, and the Sisters of the Good Shepherd were encouraged to open a home for troubled girls. A system of deanery conferences and annual reports was begun. A number of priests of the archdiocese were formed into a mission band and assigned the work of conducting parish missions and retreats. Keane was a strenuous advocate of total abstinence and agitated vigorously for the enforcement of laws regulating the operation of taverns until the day of his death, June 27, 1918.

Bishop James John Keane. The fifth bishop and third archbishop, James John Keane (1857–1929), had been born at Joliet, Illinois; ordained Dec. 23, 1882 at St. Paul, Minnesota; and consecrated bishop of Cheyenne, Wyoming, Oct. 28, 1902; he was transferred to Dubuque Aug. 11, 1911. This first American-born ordinary of Dubuque was not related to his predecessor, John Joseph Keane, who conferred the pallium upon him in 1912. As a former president of St. Thomas College in St. Paul, the new archbishop took an effective interest in St. Joseph, the archdiocesan college, which was renamed first Dubuque College and later Columbia College. A systematic effort was made to educate a college faculty in the best universities of Europe and the United States. In 1917 a financial drive throughout the archdiocese provided the college with a much-enlarged endowment and a large grant was obtained from the Rockefeller Foundation. An archdiocesan newspaper, the *Witness,* was begun in 1921.

Bishop Beckman. Francis J. L. Beckman (1875–1948), sixth bishop and fourth archbishop, was born in Cincinnati, Ohio; ordained June 20, 1902; consecrated bishop of Lincoln, Nebraska, May 1, 1924; and served as apostolic administrator of Omaha from June 1926 to July 1928. He was named to Dubuque on Jan. 17, 1930, and administered until his resignation Nov. 11, 1946. When Beckman was transferred to Dubuque from Lincoln, which was then a suffragan see of Dubuque, the economic depression of the 1930s had already begun. Almost all his years as ordinary of Dubuque were passed under the shadow of economic crisis and war. Although St. Peter Claver mission for blacks was begun in Waterloo and the Society of the Divine Word bought property at Epworth for a college seminary, only a few quite exceptional pastors were able to undertake any new projects of construction. Beckman founded the Catholic Students' Mission Crusade and made every effort to encourage the growth of the laymen's retreat movement. He undertook to develop a museum of art and history at Columbia College. In 1937 the archdiocesan centennial was celebrated and two years later the centennial of the archdiocesan college; on that occasion the institution was renamed Loras College in honor of its founder. Beckman attracted national attention before the U.S. entry into World War II by his outspoken criticism of Communist Russia and U.S. policy toward Russia. In 1940 the *Witness* openly opposed the election of President Franklin D. Roosevelt to a third term, and Dubuque County, traditionally Catholic and Democratic, voted Republican. Although he publicly supported the noninterventionist movement called America First, once the United States declared war, Beckman showed himself fully loyal and sent 40 of his priests into the armed services as chaplains, by proportion a national record. In 1944 Bishop Henry P. Rohlman, of Davenport, a former priest of the Archdiocese of Dubuque, was named apostolic administrator and coadjutor archbishop with the right of succession. Two years later Beckman resigned and within another two years he died.

Bishop Rohlman. Henry P. Rohlman (1876–1957), seventh bishop and fifth archbishop, was born in Appelhülsen, Westphalia, Germany; ordained Dec. 21, 1901; consecrated bishop of Davenport, July 25, 1927; named apostolic administrator and coadjutor archbishop of Dubuque, June 15, 1944; and succeeded to the see Nov. 11, 1946. During the decade after the close of World War II, six mission parishes were given a resident pastor for the first time, and new parishes were erected in Waterloo, Ames, Evansdale, Dubuque, Cedar Rapids, and St. Ansgar. In 1954 priests of the archdiocese replaced the Franciscans at St. Mary's Church, Waterloo. The Loras College Chapel of Christ the King was built as a memorial to Aloysius H. Schmitt, the first chaplain killed in World War II, with funds collected through an archdiocesan drive. On Sept. 12, 1946, Edward A. Fitzgerald, former dean of studies at Loras College and pastor of St. Joseph Church, Elkader, was consecrated as auxiliary bishop of Dubuque. In October 1949 Bishop Leo Binz, coadjutor of Winona, Minnesota, was named coadjutor archbishop of Dubuque with the right of succession, and Fitzgerald was transferred to Winona; two years later Loras T. Lane was consecrated as auxiliary bishop of Dubuque. In the months before his resignation (Dec. 2, 1954), Rohlman headed a committee of the bishops of Iowa that conducted a statewide campaign among Iowa Catholics to build at Dubuque a theological seminary for the province of Dubuque. It was named Mt. St. Bernard Seminary and began operation in 1951. Theological courses were taught by Dominican fathers of the province of St. Albert the Great, whose *studiummgenerale* had been established nearby. In 1953 a seminary residence was built on the campus of Loras College and for the first time ecclesiastical and lay students of the college were housed in separate dormitories. During his three years of retirement before his death in 1957, Rohlman lived at the new Mt. St. Bernard Seminary.

Bishop Binz. The eighth bishop and sixth archbishop, Leo Binz (1900–79), was born at Stockton, Illinois; ordained March 15, 1924; consecrated coadjutor bishop and apostolic administrator of Winona, Dec. 21, 1942; named coadjutor archbishop of Dubuque, Oct. 15, 1949; and succeeded to the see Dec. 2, 1954. During the seven years before his transfer to St. Paul (Dec. 16, 1961), the system of Catholic parochial high schools was considerably reorganized, and interparochial high schools were formed at Cresco, Ossian, Gilbertville, Bellevue, Waukon, Waterloo, Cedar Rapids, Dubuque, Lansing, Mason City, and Cascade. At Loras College, the Wahlert Memorial Library (1959) and Beckman Residence Hall (1960) were constructed. The American Martyrs Retreat House was built at Cedar Falls. New parishes were erected at Cedar Rapids (two), Marshalltown, Reinbeck, Blairstown, and Springville, and St. Joseph's parish, Independence, was absorbed into St. John's parish. By arrangement with the state government of Iowa, chaplains were stationed at the public institutions at Anamosa, Independence, and Eldora. In October 1956 Lane was appointed bishop of Rockford, the first of the many bishops taken from among the clergy of Dubuque to be named to a diocese lying wholly east of the Mississippi River. In 1961 Binz himself was transferred to St. Paul, the see carved from the territory of Dubuque.

Bishop Byrne. James J. Byrne (1908–96), ninth bishop and seventh archbishop, was ordained June 3, 1933; consecrated auxiliary bishop of St. Paul, July 2, 1947; named bishop of Boise, Idaho, June 16, 1956; and became archbishop of Dubuque, March 19, 1962. The period of his administration, 1962–83, would witness great,

almost cataclysmic, changes in the Church, his archdiocese, and society in general. For the first time in the history of the archdiocese, the number of Catholics dramatically increased, but at the same time the numbers of clergy, Sisters and Brothers, greatly decreased. Known for his personal piety and special devotion to the Blessed Mother, Archbishop Byrne met these challenges with an equanimity derived from much private prayer. Although not prone to making changes, after attending all four sessions of Vatican II, he implemented all the liturgical and canonical directives out of loyalty to the pope and the magisterium of the Church. He was among the very first to establish a priest senate and to approve extraordinary Eucharistic ministers. Among other post-Vatican II innovations approved by Byrne were the establishment of a clergy personnel advisory board, an archdiocesan pastoral council, an office of pastoral planning, and the permanent diaconate. The greatest difficulties with which he had to deal were the resignation of his priests, the drastic drop in vocations both to the priesthood and the religious sisterhood, and the closing of Mt. St. Bernard Seminary in 1969. His retirement was accepted on Aug. 23, 1983, and death came Aug. 2, 1996.

Bishop Kucera. Daniel W. Kucera (1923–), tenth bishop and eighth archbishop, and first Benedictine elected to the see, was ordained May 26, 1949. As a member of the Benedictine Order at St. Procopius Abbey in Lisle, Illinois, he was chosen president of Illinois Benedictine College in 1959, elected abbot in 1964, and remained in that position until 1971 when he was again asked to serve as president of the college. On July 27, 1977, he was ordained auxiliary bishop of Joliet, then named bishop of Salina, Kansas, in 1980, and installed as archbishop of Dubuque on Feb. 23, 1984. During the years of his administration, Archbishop Kucera spent much of his time in weekend parish visitation to celebrate the Sunday liturgy, homilize, and meet the parishioners. He reorganized archdiocesan boards, among them a finance commission and worship commission. He established the Archbishop's Cabinet to better coordinate the work of the central offices of the archdiocese. The cabinet members represent all the functions and services of the archdiocese under four categories: the division of pastoral services, the division of administrative services, the division of finance and business services, and the division of education and formation. In 1984 he sold the stately archbishop's mansion and moved to a more humble residence, and, amid some controversy, approved a major renovation of the cathedral. During his administration, the archdiocese celebrated its 150th anniversary with the proclamation to "Remember, Rejoice, and Proclaim." Year-long celebrations culminated in a liturgy celebrated at the civic center in Dubuque by Archbishop Pio Laghi,

Vatican Pronuncio to the United States. A momentous change was made in 1987 when Kucera divided the archdiocese into three large areas—Dubuque, Cedar Rapids, and Waterloo—and appointed a vicar general to administer in each. Also, a woman religious was appointed chancellor and the directorships of two archdiocesan offices were given to lay persons. He retired to live in Colorado in 1995.

Bishop Hanus. Jerome George Hanus (1940–), the eleventh bishop and ninth archbishop, and second Benedictine, was born George A. Hanus, May 26, 1940, in Brainard, Nebraska. As a member of Conception Abbey in Missouri, he was ordained July 30, 1966. After several years as a professor at Conception, he was elected abbot in 1977. After ten years, he was appointed bishop of St. Cloud, Minnesota, then appointed coadjutor archbishop of Dubuque Aug. 23, 1994. Upon the retirement of Archbishop Kucera on Oct. 16, 1995, he succeeded to the see of Dubuque. Known as a "people person," he immediately implemented the Strategic Planning Process. Using modern technology, he spoke to all the members of the archdiocese by means of a video sent to every parish. Parishioners were given a chance to respond and express their views as regards the needs of the Church in the archdiocese. From these sources, he issued a vision statement in which he spelled out his plans and hopes for the future of the archdiocese. These plans include, among other things, an increased role of the laity in leadership positions in the parishes, schools, health care institutions, social agencies, and other parts of the Church in his diocese.

Bibliography: Archives, Archdiocese of Dubuque and Omaha. M. M. HOFFMANN, *Church Founders of the Northwest* (Milwaukee 1939); ed., *Centennial History of the Archdiocese of Dubuque* (Dubuque 1938).

[S. D. LUBY/L. C. OTTING]

DUCASSE, CURT JOHN

Early advocate of analytic method in American philosophy, adverbial realist, mind-body interactionist, and proponent of a non-Humean theory of causation; b. Angouleme, France, July 7, 1881; d. Providence, Rhode Island, Sept. 3, 1969.

After schooling in France and England, Ducasse completed his education at the University of Washington and Harvard (Ph.D. 1912). From 1912 to 1926 he taught at the University of Washington and from 1926 until his retirement at Brown University.

In *Causation and the Types of Necessity* (1924) Ducasse argued that causation is an irreducible and observable triadic relation, a non-Humean view that he

defended with ingenuity and precision throughout his career. In this first book he also defended analytic method in philosophy, saying that "[i]t is only with truths about such questions as the meaning of the term 'true' or 'real,' or 'good,' and the like . . . that philosophy is concerned." In 1929 he published *The Philosophy of Art,* a defense of the emotionalist theory of art and aesthetic appreciation. The realism and adverbial theory of perception so influential on his student Roderick M. Chisholm he first presented in articles in the early 1930s, elaborating it in an exchange with G. E. Moore in the 1940s. His Carus Lectures, *Nature, Mind and Death* (1951), constitute the most complete statement of his epistemology and metaphysics and include a classic defense of mind-body interactionism. His philosophy of religion, in the tradition of William James, was published as *A Philosophical Scrutiny of Religion* (1953). Ducasse defended the right to believe where there is a genuine option and no preponderance of evidence. He took seriously paranormal phenomena, especially in relation to survival of death; and *A Critical Examination of the Belief in a Life After Death* (1961) is a lucid and impartial philosophical discussion of the topic. Just before his death a number of Ducasse's articles published over 40 years were collected in *Truth, Knowledge and Causation* (1968). Ducasse's greatest contribution was his rigorous use of analytic method in the articulation of a systematic metaphysics and epistemology.

Bibliography: "A Symposium in Honor of C. J. Ducasse," *Philosophy and Phenomenological Research* 13.1 (1952). F. C. DOMMEYER, ed., *Current Philosophical Issues: Essays in Honor of Curt John Ducasse* (Springfield, Ill. 1966). "A Tribute to Curt John Ducasse, 1881–1969, from His Colleagues and Friends in Psychical Research," *Journal of the American Society for Psychical Research* 64.2 (1970).

[P. H. HARE]

DUCHEMIN, M. THERESA MAXIS, MOTHER

Co-Founder of Sisters, Servants of the Immaculate Heart of Mary; founding member of the Oblate Sisters of Providence; b. 1810, Baltimore, Md.; d. Westchester, Pa., Jan. 21, 1892. Theresa is the first U.S. born African American woman to become a religious. Her mother, Betsy, was a refugee from Haiti and was of mixed race; Betsy's grandfather was an African slave. During the Toussaint L'Overture Rebellion, which began in Haiti in 1791, all white persons and those of mixed race came under attack. Betsy was the only member of her family to escape from the island. She arrived in Baltimore in 1793 at the age of 10, and came under the protection of the Duchemin family. They provided a home for her, and procured for her training as a nurse.

Theresa was born of Betsy Duchemin and Arthur Howard, a British military officer who was visiting his U.S. relatives in an adjoining estate. Her parents were not married. Because of her illegitimacy, Theresa was raised in the African American, Catholic, and French-speaking community rather than in the white, Protestant, English-speaking community. Her participation in the community of Haitian refugees led Theresa to attend a school established for children of that community by Elizabeth Lange and Marie Magdalen Baras, also of Haitian origin.

In 1829, under the leadership of Rev. Jacques Joubert, these women, together with another Haitian immigrant, Rose Boegue, formed the Oblates Sisters of Providence, the first congregation of African American women in the U.S. Theresa, who was then a 19-year old student at the school, was admitted to the new congregation, thereby becoming the fourth founding member. At first the congregation flourished under the guidance of the Sulpician Fathers and with the support of the Archbishop of Baltimore, James Whitfield. The sisters' situation changed upon the death of Archbishop Whitfield and as the number of Haitian children dwindled. The poor African-American students could not afford to pay the tuition, and the sisters turned to manual labor activities to support their fledging community and ministry. The new Archbishop Samuel Eccleston, was not supportive of the congregation and ordered them to discontinue accepting new members.

During some of the congregation's most difficult times, Theresa served as General Superior. She explored a number of avenues for rescuing the congregation from its desperate situation. One approach was to change the congregation's name to the Sisters of St. Charles in the hope of gaining the sponsorship of the descendents of the colonial hero, Charles Carroll. Her efforts, however, were unsuccessful, and she came to believe that the congregation was fated to disband.

Shortly after completing her term as General Superior, Theresa came into contact with Rev. Louis Florent Gillet. A French-speaking Redemptorist from Belgium, Father Gillet followed the missionary inspiration of St. Alphonsus Liguori; he had arrived in the U.S. in 1843 and established a mission in the town of Monroe in the Detroit diocese. He had met Mother Theresa in Baltimore where he was happy to minister in French to the sisters at the Oblate convent. In 1845, realizing that he needed bilingual sisters to teach the French-Canadian children in Monroe, he asked Theresa to establish a congregation there. Theresa agreed, traveled to Monroe, and on Nov. 10, 1845 initiated community life with two other sisters, Charlotte Shaaff (also from the Oblates) and Theresa Renault. Louis and Theresa adapted the Redemptorist rule to the circumstances of the new congregation of sisters. It was the beginning of the Sisters, Servants of the Immaculate Heart of Mary (*see* IMMACULATE HEART OF MARY, SISTERS, SERVANTS OF THE).

Once she moved to Monroe, Theresa dropped the Duchemin name and did not refer to her African American background, separating herself from her earlier life in Baltimore. Only in the last years of her life did she share with the sisters the information about her African American roots. The bishops with whom she had contact, however, knew of her origins, and used that information to try to discredit her when they were dissatisfied with her activities.

After almost a decade of successful ministry and growth in Monroe, the congregation was caught into difficulties arising between the bishop, Peter Paul Lefevere and the Redemptorist Fathers. In 1854 the Redemptorist leadership decided that it was necessary to withdraw from the Detroit diocese. Bishop Lefevere fought irately against the decision, but the Redemptorists did indeed withdraw from Monroe. The bishop's reaction was to strive to eradicate all Alphonsian influences in the IHM congregation and to sever all Redemptorists' contacts with the IHM sisters. He appointed a diocesan priest, Rev. Edward Joos, to lead the congregation, supplanting the role of the superior as it was specified in the congregation's rule.

Pennsylvania Foundation. Theresa was eager to preserve the Alphonsian tradition to the congregation and to restore the place of the superior in the government of the congregation. She recognized this was not possible in Monroe. She therefore persuaded Bishop Lefevere to allow her to accept a mission in Pennsylvania, where the Redemptorist St. John Neumann was bishop. The ministry was to poor, Irish Catholic immigrant farmers, whose ethnicity and religion had doubly marginalized them in 19th century U.S. society. Theresa intended eventually to move the entire congregation to Pennsylvania, where they could develop their Alphonsian charism. In that effort she pressured to open another mission in Pennsylvania; Bishop Lefevere reacted to her persistence by sending Theresa away to Pennsylvania permanently. She encouraged some Redemptorist priests to write to sisters in Monroe, encouraging them to leave Michigan and come to Pennsylvania. These letters were intercepted and forwarded to Bishop Lefevere. His response was to dismiss those sisters he deemed to be disloyal and to declare the two convents separate congregations as of 1859. His correspondence with Bishop James Wood, Neumann's successor in Pennsylvania, condemning Theresa's assertiveness, indicates how much the racism of the times had influenced his appraisal.

Theresa struggled for years to reunite the members of the congregation. In an effort to remove herself as an obstacle to reunion, she left the Pennsylvania congregation and lived with the Grey Nuns of Ottawa. In 1868 she traveled from Ottawa, first to the Monroe congregation, and then to the Pennsylvania congregation, in the hope of readmission. Having been refused by the bishops of both dioceses, she was received back at Ottawa, where she remained as a guest of the Grey Nuns for 17 years. The bishops forbade the sisters in the IHM congregations to communicate with Theresa during most of these years, times of great isolation and loneliness for Theresa. In 1881 Sister Genevieve Morrisey from Scranton broke the silence and established a regular correspondence with Theresa. Theresa's letters are full of longing to return to her congregation and suggestions on how the return could be effected. In 1885, efforts by IHMs and Redemptorists succeeded in gaining permission for her return to the congregation at Westchester, PA, where she lived until her death on Jan. 21, 1892.

Bibliography: M. GANNON, ed. *Paths of Daring, Deeds of Hope: Letters by and about Mother Theresa Maxis Duchemin* (Scranton, PA, 1992). R. KELLY, *No Greater Service: The History of the Congregation of the Sisters, Servants of the Immaculate Heart of Mary* (Monroe, Mich. 1948). G. H. SHERWOOD, *The Oblates' One Hundred and One Years* (New York 1931). SISTERS, SERVANTS OF THE IMMACULATE HEART OF MARY, MONROE, MICHIGAN, *Building Sisterhood: A Feminist History of the Sisters, Servants of the Immaculate Heart of Mary* (Syracuse 1997).

[M. GANNON]

DUCHESNE, LOUIS

Historian of the early Church, hagiographer, archeologist, and prelate; b. Saint-Servan, France, Sept. 13, 1843; d. Rome, April 21, 1922. Duchesne made his theological studies in Rome, where he developed a keen interest in Christian archeology and the history of the early Church under the direction of G. B. de ROSSI. Ordained in 1867, he taught at the École S.-Charles de S.-Brieuc (1867–71) and then turned to higher studies at the École des Carmes and the École des Hautes Études in Paris (1871–73). Appointed a member of the École archéologique française de Rome, he was charged with scholarly missions and research in Epirus, Thessaly, Mt. ATHOS, and Asia Minor (1874–76), and accepted the chair of Church history at the Institut catholique of PARIS (1877–85). Criticism raised against his lectures on the development of pre-Nicene doctrine and the foundation of the ancient Church in France occasioned his resignation, and he was given a chair at the Ecole supérieur des lettres (1885–95). From 1895 to his death, he served as director of the École archéologique française de Rome. In 1900

Pope LEO XIII made Duchesne a prothonotary apostolic, and in 1910 he replaced Cardinal Mathieu as a member of the French Academy.

Duchesne's first publication was concerned with the 5th-century apologist MACARIUS MAGNES; then followed a study of the *LIBER PONTIFICALIS*. Possessed of a sharp critical sense, and capable of indefatigable research, combined with lucid and at times ironic exposition, Duchesne frequently provoked violent reaction by his intolerance of pious fraud in history, particularly in regard to claims of apostolic foundations of the Church in France. During the crisis over Modernism, his three-volume *Histoire ancienne de l'Église chrétienne* (Paris 1906–10) was put on the Index despite the fact that it had received an imprimatur before publication. It was translated into English as the *Early History of the Church* (3 v. London 1905–24), and has undergone six reprintings, serving as a standard introduction to the complex problems of the first five centuries of the Church's development. A fourth volume, *L'Église au VIième siècle*, though incomplete, was edited by II. Quentin (Paris 1925). Though many of Duchesne's opinions have to be modified in the light of new documents and research, his fundamental judgments, based on deep and solid investigation, have proved invaluable.

Duchesne edited the *Liber pontificalis* with a commentary (2 v. Paris 1886–92; 2d ed., C. Vogel, 1955–57); and with G. B. de Rossi he edited the MARTYROLOGY OF ST. JEROME (*Martyrologium Hieronymianum*) for the *Acta Sanctorum*, Nov. (1894) 2.1. He produced the *Les Fastes épiscopaux de l'ancienne Gaule* (3 v. Paris 1894–1915), the *"Liber Censuum" de l'Église romaine* (Paris 1905), *Les premiers temps de l'État pontifical 757–1073* (Paris 1898), the *Autonomies ecclésiastiques: Église séparées* (Paris 1905), and *Les origines du culte chrétien* (Paris 1889; Eng. ed., London 1903), all based on numerous studies of papal and early Church history and archeology that resulted from his discoveries of MSS and other unused sources. A conscientious historian and a sincere churchman, he suffered unflinchingly under the suspicions of the anti-Modernists, but continued his invaluable contributions to the study of the Church's origins and early development in all its phases.

Bibliography: J. COLIN, *Mgr. Duchesne* (Rome 1922). F. CABROL, "Mgr. L. D.: Son oeuvre historique," *Journal of Theological Studies* 24 (1922–23) 253–281, bibliog. E. DUPONT, *Mgr. Duchesne, chez lui, en Bretagne* (Rennes 1928). H. LECLERCQ, *Dictionnaire d'archéologie chrétienne et de liturgi*, ed. F. CABROL, H. LECLERCQ, and H. I. MARROU (Paris 1907–53) 6.2:2680–2735. G. BARDY, *Catholicisme. Hier, aujourd'hui et demain*, ed. G. JACQUEMET (Paris 1947–) 3:1144–46. C. VOGEL, *Lexikon für Theologie und Kirche*, ed. J. HOFER and K. RAHNER (2d, new ed. Freiburg 1957–65) 3:593. F. L. CROSS, *The Oxford Dictionary of the Christian Church* (London 1957) 425.

[F. X. MURPHY]

DUCHESNE, ROSE PHILIPPINE, ST.

Missionary, founder of the U.S. branch of the Society of the SACRED HEART; b. Grenoble, France, Aug. 29, 1769; d. St. Charles, Missouri, Nov. 18, 1852. Her father, Pierre François Duchesne, was active in the legal and political life of Grenoble, and in national life after 1797. Her mother, Rose (Perier) Duchesne, was from Dauphiné. In 1780 Philippine was sent to study at the Convent of the Visitation, Sainte-Marie-d'en-Haut, where she was attracted to religious life. Despite her father's opposition, she entered the Visitation Order on Sept. 10, 1788, but returned home in 1792 when, as a result of the French Revolution, religious were expelled from their convents. For ten years she devoted herself to charity, often sheltering priests persecuted by the revolutionary government, nursing the sick, and teaching the neglected children of Grenoble. When peace returned to France, she obtained possession of the convent of Sainte-Marie-d'en-Haut, which had been confiscated by the revolutionary government for a prison. In 1804, having failed in her efforts to bring the scattered Visitandine nuns back to their home, she and a few companions joined the Society of the Sacred Heart (founded in 1800 by St. Madeleine Sophie BARAT) and Sainte-Marie-d'en-Haut became the second convent of the new order.

In 1815 Mother Duchesne was transferred to Paris and founded the first convent of her order there. Three years later, she and four companions left France for the U.S., arriving at New Orleans, La., on May 29, 1818. Bp. William Du Bourg of Louisiana commissioned Mother Duchesne to open a school in St. Charles, Missouri, the first free school west of the Mississippi River for Catholic and non-Catholic children. In 1819 she built a convent at Florissant, Missouri, and operated a free parish school, a small orphanage, a short-lived school for native girls, and an academy for boarding pupils, along with a novitiate for U.S. members of the Sacred Heart Society. In 1827 Bishop Joseph Rosati welcomed her to St. Louis, Missouri, where John Mullanphy provided a house and 24 acres of land for an orphanage, academy, and parish school. At 72, she founded a mission school for Potawatomi native girls at Sugar Creek, Kansas. She did not teach the children, for she could not learn their language, but she nursed the sick among the Potawatomi, who called her Quah-kah-ka-num-ad, Woman-who-prays-always. In 1842, she was recalled to St. Charles, where she spent the remaining years of her life. She was beatified in 1940, and canonized by John Paul II on July 3, 1988.

Feast: Nov. 18.

Bibliography: L. CALLAN, *Philippine Duchesne* (Westminster, Md. 1957); *The Society of the Sacred Heart in North America* (New York 1937); *Philippine Duchesne, Frontier Missionary of the Sacred Heart* (Westminster, Md. 1965). C. COLLINS, M. A. GUSTE, and A. THOMPSONS, eds., *Rose Philippine Duchesne* (Washington, D.C. 1988). C. M. MOONEY, *Philippine Duchesne: A Woman with the Poor* (New York 1990).

[L. CALLAN]

DUELING

A duel is a prearranged contest between two persons with deadly weapons carried on according to certain conventions with the intent of settling a quarrel or vindicating a point of honor. It is not to be confused with an ordinary fight in self-defense or a sudden quarrel. Neither is it to be identified with a public duel in which, by agreement of authorities, two persons rather than two armies fight to settle a national dispute (as in the case of Hector and Achilles or of David and Goliath).

History. Dueling was unknown in the ancient world. Roman gladiatorial combats were not duels as such but rather forms of public entertainment. Dueling appears to have entered the European tradition by way of Germanic influence. Certain evidence from early Teutonic law indicates that private duels were occasioned by an affront to another's honor, but the real influence in the development of the practice of dueling was the tradition of judicial combat. On the assumption that God would not allow the guilty party to prevail over the innocent, the Teutonic peoples sanctioned a contest between two individuals involved in a dispute as a kind of judicial process. The practice passed into the customary law of the feudal period in many areas and lingered until more sophisticated forms of adjudication were evolved in the high Middle Ages.

However, the custom of privately settling a disagreement by personal combat lingered on, and feudal tournaments were not uncommonly used to satisfy revenge. By the 15th century the duel of honor, dueling in the modern sense, was well established in France and Spain. When dueling became common among the aristocratic classes in the 16th and 17th centuries, civil authorities began to legislate against the practice. In many countries the death sentence was extended to those participating in duels, and heavy penalties were imposed for those who assisted the contestants. In the 19th century, dueling persisted in many parts of Europe among politicians, journalists, and especially military officers. In the early 20th century the German military code still authorized resort to a duel in extreme cases.

Position of the Church. In the medieval period the Church opposed judicial combat and legislated against tournaments. Her teaching regarding private dueling was consistent and clear. As early as 855 the Council of Valence prohibited dueling, and the condemnation was repeated by many medieval popes. As the modern custom became more entrenched, Julius II, Leo X, Clement VII, and Pius IV condemned it, and the Council of TRENT imposed excommunication not only upon duelists and their seconds but also upon civil authorities who permitted dueling within their realms. Similar condemnations and prohibitions were repeated by Gregory XIII (1582), Clement VIII (1592), Alexander VII (1655), Benedict XIV (1752), Pius IX (1869), and Leo XIII (1891).

Under the 1917 *Code of Canon Law*, penalties attached to dueling included *ipso facto* excommunication simply reserved to the Holy See for duelists themselves, those who challenged or accepted a duel, those who offered help or encouraged them, those who were deliberately present, and those who did not, as far as they were able, prevent them (1917 *Codex iuris canonici* c.2351.1). Duelists and their seconds *ipso facto* contracted legal infamy (1917 *Codex iuris canonici* c.2351.2). Those who were killed in a duel were excluded from ecclesiastical burial and from solemn funeral rites unless some sign of repentance was given before death (1917 *Codex iuris canonici* cc.1240.1n4, 1241). A duel undertaken on the understanding that it would cease as soon as one party was wounded was also forbidden; and in 1925 the Congregation of the Council likewise condemned the kind of duels then prevalent among German students wherein the danger was assumed to be that of only a slight wound.

The reason for this legislation is obvious. Dueling is directly opposed to natural and divinely revealed law (Leo XIII, *Pastoralis officii*, Sept. 12, 1891). It deliberately involves the risk of death or serious wounds for oneself and an assault on the life of another without being an act of self-defense against an unjust aggressor. It therefore is an arbitrary attack on God's dominion over human life. Moreover, it is ineffective as a means of satisfying outraged honor. Killing a person who has offered insult prevents the retraction of the insult and one's restoration to proper respect. Allowing oneself to be killed after enduring insult accomplishes nothing.

Canons dealing with dueling were not included in the 1983 *Code of Canon Law*.

Bibliography: L. FALLETI, *Dictionnaire du droit canonique*, ed. R. NAZ, 7 v. (Paris 1935–65) 5:3–40. J. G. MILLINGEN, *History of Duelling* (London 1841). E. CAUCHEY, *Du duel*, 2 v. (Paris 1846). P. CHAIGNON, *Le Duel sous l'Ancien Regime* (Doctoral diss. unpub. U. of Rennes 1936). V. CATHREIN, *The Catholic Encyclopedia* (New York 1907–14) 5: 184–187. P. MIKAT, *Staatslexikon*, ed. Görres-Gesellschaft, 8 v. (6th new and enl. ed.. Freiburg 1957–63) 8:1008–09.

[J. C. WILLKE]

DUFAY, GUILLAUME

Dominant Renaissance composer of the Burgundian school; b. Hainault?, Flanders, *c.* 1400; d. Cambrai, Nov. 27, 1474. After serving first as a choirboy at Cambrai and later with the Malatesta family in Italy, Dufay held various posts, including that of singer in the papal choir (1428–33, 1435–37), before returning north to serve at the Burgundian court and as director of cathedral music in Cambrai. His reputation as the greatest composer of his day did much to make both places important music centers. Eight Masses definitely known to be his survive, as well as numerous Mass sections. Several Masses are of the *cantus firmus* type, based on either plainsong or secular melodies like his own chansons. His *Missa Caput*, based on a *cantus firmus* from the SARUM RITE, became the model for Masses on the same melody by Okeghem and Obrecht. At least 20 composers (including Busnois, Okeghem, Desprez, Morales, and Palestrina) wrote Masses on the material of his *Missa L'Homme Armé*. A lost *Requiem* was probably the earliest polyphonic REQUIEM MASS. Dufay's motets are of conspicuous merit, e.g., the complicated *Nuper rosarum flores*, written for the consecration of the *Duomo* in Florence; the impressive troped *Ave Regina Caelorum*, which he wished sung over his deathbed; and the lovely and tender *Alma Redemptoris Mater* (which paraphrases the plainsong with fine effect). His hymn settings, written *c.* 1430 for the papal choir but widespread in popularity, constitute a cycle for the entire Church year. There is also a large body of semi-sacred and secular music, including a slightly italianate *Vergine bella* that sets stanza one of Petrarch's celebrated poem; and a *Lamentatio sanctae matris Ecclesiae constantinopolitanae*, written *c.* 1454, on the fall of Constantinople.

Bibliography: *Opera omnia*, ed. G. DE VAN and H. BESSELER (*Corpus mensurabilis musicae*, ed. American Institute of Musicology 1–; 1947–). C. VAN DEN BORREN, *Guillaume Dufay: Centre de rayonnement de la polyphonie européenne* . . . (Brussels 1939); *Études sur le XVe siècle musical* (Antwerp 1941). H. BESSELER, *Die Musik in Geschichte und Gegenwart*, ed. F. BLUME (Kassel-Basel 1949–) 3:889–912. M. F. BUKOFZER, *Studies in Medieval and Renaissance Music* (New York 1950). R. BOCKHOLDT, *Die frühen Messenkompositionen von Guillaume Dufay*, 2 v. (Tutzing 1960). G. REESE, *Music in the Renaissance* (rev. ed. New York 1959). E. H. SPARKS, *Cantus Firmus in Mass and Motet* (Berkeley 1963). C. E. HAMM, *A Chronology of the Works of Guillaume Dufay*, (Princeton, N.J. 1964). C. BEATE, ''Metrum und Rhythmus in einigen Rondeaux von Guillaume Dufay: Anmerkungen zur Auffassung von Rhythmus und Metrum im 15. Jahrhundert,'' *Musiktheorie*, 12 (1997) 147–164. B. HAGGH, ''Guillaume Du Fay's Birthplace: Some Notes on a Hypothesis,'' *Revue Belge de Musicologie*, 51 (1997) 17–21. L. HOLFORD-STREVENS, ''Du Fay the Poet? Problems in the Texts of His Motets,'' in *Early Music History 16: Studies in Medieval and Early Modern Music*, ed. I. FENLON (Cambridge, Eng. 1997) 97–165. A.-M. MATHY, ''Guillaume Dufay et la culture Florentine au début du quattrocento,'' *Esercizi: Musica e Spetta-*

colo, 16–17 (1997–98) 5–31. A. E. PLANCHART, "Notes on Guillaume Du Fay's Last Works," *Journal of Musicology,* 13 (1995) 55–72. R. C. WEGMAN, "*Miserere supplicanti Dufay:* The Creation and Transmission of Guillaume Dufay's *Missa Ave regina celorum,*" *Journal of Musicology,* 13 (1995) 18–54. L. WELKER, "Dufay Songs in German Manuscripts," in *Music in the German Renaissance: Sources, Styles, and Contexts,* ed. J. KMETZ (Cambridge, Eng. 1994) 3–26.

[C. V. BROOKS]

DUFFY, FRANCIS PATRICK

Military chaplain; b. Cobourg, Ontario, Canada, May 2, 1871; d. New York City, June 26, 1932. He was the third of 11 children of Patrick and Mary (Ready) Duffy. He was educated at St. Michael's College, Toronto, Canada, and at St. Francis Xavier College, New York City. In 1894 he entered St. Joseph's Seminary, then at Troy, N.Y., and was ordained in Cobourg Sept. 6, 1896. After two years' study at The Catholic University of America, Washington, D.C., he was assigned as an instructor in philosophy at the new seminary at Dunwoodie, N.Y., where he remained until 1912. He was also an editor (1905–08) of the *New York Review,* which ceased publication during the Modernist crisis, and the author of articles in several major Catholic journals. In 1912 he founded Our Savior's parish, Bronx, N.Y. Two years later he became chaplain of the 69th Regiment of the New York National Guard. Following service on the Mexican border in 1916 to 1917, he accompanied the regiment to France, where he won the fame that made him the best-known American chaplain of World War I. After the war he served as president of the Catholic Summer School, Cliff Haven, N.Y., and as pastor (1920–32) of Holy Cross Church, Manhattan. In the presidential campaign of 1928 he helped prepare Gov. Alfred E. Smith's reply to Charles Marshall's aspersions on the loyalty of Catholics to the U.S. Duffy received many honors, including the Distinguished Service Cross, the Distinguished Service Medal, and the Legion of Honor. His memorial, placed in Times Square (1937), was the first statue of a priest ever erected on public property in the State of New York.

Bibliography: F. P. DUFFY, *Father Duffy's Story* (New York 1919). R. J. PURCELL, *Dictionary of American Biography,* ed. A. JOHNSON and D. MALONE (reissue New York 1957; suppl. 1958) 11.1:267–269.

[F. D. COHALAN]

DUFFY, MARY C.

Catholic laywoman, supreme regent of the Catholic Daughters of America; b. Ireland; d. Sept 24, 1962.

Brought to the United States as a child, Mary C. Duffy was a 1907 founding member of a New Jersey group of the Catholic Daughters of America (CDA). From her position as grand regent of Newark's Court Seton in 1911, Duffy rose quickly in the recently-formed national organization, soon becoming the New Jersey district deputy and then state regent for the CDA. Appointed as a national director, she became supreme vice regent from 1915–1923. She then led the CDA as supreme regent for 27 years between 1923–1950.

Duffy moved the CDA headquarters from Utica, N.Y. to New York City and guided the organization into a position of national prominence. During her first year as supreme regent, the CDA set aside a portion of membership dues, both to promote its national programs and to help needy projects and persons. Duffy traveled extensively to build up CDA membership, promoting the establishment of local groups or "courts," and encouraging them to form study clubs, forums, and legislative discussion groups. By 1926 she had established a junior branch of the CDA for young women.

Under her leadership, the CDA encouraged its members to learn about Catholic teachings and then apply them in a variety of relief programs for impoverished persons of the depression era. With Duffy's encouragement the CDA became actively involved in World War II relief projects at home and abroad. After the war it began a European family adoption program in cooperation with the War Relief Services of the National Catholic Welfare Council. Ill health forced her to retire in 1950 to South Orange, N.J.

Bibliography: *The American Catholic Who's Who 1962–1963,* 30th ed., vol. 15 (Grosse Point, Mich.): 123. Archives of the Catholic Daughters of the Americas, located at the Catholic University of America, Washington, D.C. Note *Share* magazine editions for the 50th, 60th, 70th, and 75th anniversaries of the CDA. G. J. HEBERT, *A History of the Catholic Daughters of the Americas: 1903–1986* (New York).

[C. D. CLEMENT]

DUGLIOLI, HELENA, BL.

Widow; b. Bologna, 1472; d. there, Sept. 23, 1520. After a pious and obedient childhood she married, in accordance with the wishes of her parents, when she was 17 years old. Benedetto dall' Oglio was 20 years her senior, but they lived in happy marriage and great piety for nearly 30 years. During her short widowhood, she devoted herself to a life of prayer and mortification. When she died at the age of 48, she was buried in the church of S. Giovanni di Monte. From the time of her death the people of Bologna venerated her for the holiness of her life. This spontaneous and continual veneration has been traced by Prosper Lambertini in the *Acta Sanctorum*. She was beatified by Pope LEO XII in 1828.

Feast: Sept. 23.

Bibliography: *Acta Sanctorum* Sept. 6:655–659. G. B. MELLONI, *Atti, o Memorie degli uomini illustri in Santità, nati o morti a Bologna* 5 v. (Bologna 1773–1818) 3:300–385, 436–445. J. BAUR, *Lexikon für Theologie und Kirche*² 3:596. A. BUTLER, *The Lives of the Saints* 3:627.

[G. M. GRAY]

DU HAMEL, JEAN BAPTISTE

Physicist, philosopher, and theologian; b. Vire, Normandy, June 11, 1624; d. Paris, Aug. 6, 1706. He studied at Caen and Paris, and in 1643 he entered the Congregation of the Oratory. After ordination he became professor of philosophy and moral theology at Saint-Magloire. In 1653 he left the Oratory and became pastor at Neuilly-sur-Marne. In 1663 he became chancellor of Bayeux. With the creation of the Academy of Sciences (1666), Du Hamel was made first secretary, a position he held for more than 30 years. Astronomer, mineralogist, chemist, physician, biologist, Du Hamel was well known to his contemporaries. He enjoyed the friendship and favor of Jean Baptiste COLBERT and other court personages. He notably contributed to the diffusion of Cartesian philosophy in France. Along with various scientific treatises, he wrote *De consensu veteris et novae philosophiae* (Paris 1663), a treatise on natural philosophy in which Greek and scholastic positions are compared with those of Descartes; *De mente humana* (Paris 1672); *Philosophia vetus et nova ad usum scholae accommodata* (Paris 1678), a widely used college textbook; *Theologia speculatrix et practica* (7 v. Paris 1690), abridged in five volumes for use as a seminary textbook; and an annotated edition of the Bible (Paris 1705).

Bibliography: A. VIALARD, *Le Premier secrétaire perpétuel de l'Académie des sciences: J. B. Duhamel* (Paris 1884). C. A. DUBRAY, *The Catholic Encyclopedia*, ed. C. G. HERBERMANN et al. (New York 1907–14) 5:187. A. GUNY, *Catholicisme. Hier, aujourd'hui et demain*, ed. G. JACQUEMET (Paris 1947–) 3:1157–58.

[F. C. LEHNER]

DU HOUX, JEANNE

Mystic and religious of the Visitation; b. Pinczon, Sept. 2. 1616; d. Colombier, Sept. 26, 1677. Jeanne was four when her mother died, and her stepmother treated her like a servant. From her earliest years she wanted to become a religious. In 1636, however, her father arranged her marriage to Hilarion de Forsans, Seigneur du Houx. Du Houx joined her in works of charity, but, says her biographer, she ''bore the married yoke with difficulty.'' After the early death of her husband, she entered the Visitation Convent at Colombier. Here for 30 years she divided her time between the cloister and the world, and only two days before her death was she fully professed in religion. During her married years her piety was of the active type, but during her years in the convent it became passive. Six years of despair at the Visitation ended in a vision of St. Jane Frances de Chantal on Dec. 12, 1646. The saint taught her abandonment. Bloody penances and fasts, devotion to the Holy Infancy after the pattern of Marguerite du Saint-Sacrement, and communications with the souls in purgatory characterized her spirituality. Because she alternated between reserve and enthusiasm regarding the controversial Jeanne des Anges at Loudon, her reputation suffers. While her emphasis on simplicity marks her as Salesian, the stress she places on ''putting on the spirit of Jesus Christ'' aligns her with the school of Bérulle.

Bibliography: E. CATTA, *Dictionnaire de spiritualité ascétique et mystique. Doctrine et histoire*, ed. M. VILLER et al. (Paris 1932–) 3:1769–73. M. SAINT-GAL DE PONS, ''Une mystique bretonne du 17ᵉ siècle,'' *La Vie spirituelle* 86 (1952) 167–178.

[J. VERBILLION]

DUKE, EDMUND, BL.

Priest and martyr; b. Kent, England; d. hanged, drawn, and quartered at Durham, May 27, 1590. Duke studied at Rheims and Rome, where he was ordained (1589). The following March 22, he was sent to the English Mission. He was arrested with BB. Richard HILL, John HOGG, and Richard HOLIDAY in the north of England soon after they landed at Tynemouth. They were caught during the hysteria following the defeat of the Spanish Armada. They were beatified by Pope John Paul II on Nov. 22, 1987 with George Haydock and Companions.

Feast of the English Martyrs: May 4 (England).

See Also: ENGLAND, SCOTLAND, AND WALES, MARTYRS OF.

Bibliography: R. CHALLONER, *Memoirs of Missionary Priests,* ed. J. H. POLLEN (rev. ed. London 1924). J. H. POLLEN, *Acts of English Martyrs* (London 1891).

[K. I. RABENSTEIN]

DULIA

From the Greek δουλεία (slavery, bondage) has been taken in a general sense in Christian theology to signify both the honor rendered to those whose excellence is deserving of respect and also the virtue disposing a person to render such honor (St. Thomas Aquinas, ST 2a2ae, 103.4). In a narrower sense, more in keeping with the etymology of the term, it is concerned with the reverence a slave owes to his master, and, by extension, with the reverence owed by a subject to a superior (*ibid.*). However, the offering of reverence of this kind is the function of the virtue St. Thomas called *observantia* [*see* REVERENCE (OBSERVANTIA)], and it is not commonly referred to as dulia. In the other and more general sense, dulia has different species according to the various kinds and degrees of excellence to which honor is due. Spiritual excellence is, absolutely speaking, greater than any other, and is therefore deserving of a special honor. Usage has come to restrict the term to the honor given to the saints, whose spiritual excellence is clearly established and not subject to loss, as distinguished from latria, or the honor given to God alone, and hyperdulia, or the honor given to the Blessed Virgin because of her unique excellence as the Mother of God.

See Also: SAINTS, DEVOTION TO THE.

[A. V. VESZELOVSZKY]

DUM ACERBISSIMAS

An apostolic letter of Pope Gregory XVI issued on Sept. 26, 1835, condemning the teaching of Georg HERMES that all theological investigations must be founded on positive doubt. In this brief His Holiness, recalling that he had already had to condemn errors of others, stated that he had ordered the books of Hermes to be investigated by skilled theologians. They found them to contain grave errors concerning the nature of faith, Sacred Scripture, tradition, revelation, the magisterium of the Church, the motives of credibility, and the arguments for the existence of God; about God's essence, holiness, justice and liberty, and the purpose of God's works; and concerning the necessity of grace, original sin, and the state of the first parents. For this reason the writings of Hermes were condemned and to be placed on the Index of prohibited books.

Bibliography: H. DENZINGER, *Enchiridion symbolorum*, ed. A. SCHÖNMETZER (Freiburg 1963) 2738–40.

[W. F. HOGAN]

DUMOULIN, JEAN (JOANNES MOLINAEUS)

Canonist and theologian; b. Ghent, 1525; d. Sept. 29, 1575. He studied and taught at Louvain where he was ap-

pointed to the chair of Canon Law by King Philip II on Aug. 9, 1557. A year later he became rector of that University of Louvain. He opposed the government's proposed subjection of certain abbeys to new bishoprics and went to Rome in 1573 to obtain the suppression of these new bishoprics. After returning unsuccessful, he was summoned before the council of bishops assembled in Mechelen to explain his actions. Because of this, and also for his writings, his orthodoxy was called into question. It is possible that these events caused him to lose his mind so that he was forced into seclusion where he let himself starve to death. Most noteworthy is his publication of the *Decretum* of IVO OF CHARTRES (Louvain 1562), which he considered to be a much better arrangement of the canons than that of Gratian.

Bibliography: G. PEPOINTE, *Dictionnaire de droit canonique*, ed. R. NAZ (Paris 1935–65) 5:67–70. H. HURTER, *Nomenclator literarius theologiae catholicae* (3d ed. Innsbruck 1903–13) 3:130–131.

[H. A. LARROQUE]

DUNDRENNAN, ABBEY OF

Former Cistercian abbey in Kirkcudbrightshire, Diocese of Galloway, Scotland, founded by DAVID I in 1142 and colonized from the English abbey of RIEVAULX. Being well endowed it quickly expanded, and two daughterhouses were founded from it, Glenluce in 1192 and Sweetheart (NEW ABBEY) in 1273. Its easy access to England across the Solway Firth made it particularly vulnerable to raids, and in 1299 the abbey sought £8,000 compensation for damages in recent English attacks. The distinguished theologian Thomas Livingstone was abbot of Dundrennan before becoming bishop of Dunkeld in 1440. It was from Dundrennan that Queen MARY STUART left Scotland in 1568, never to return. Erected into a temporal lordship in 1606, the abbey revenues were later annexed to the chapel royal at Stirling. It is now a ruin.

Bibliography: H. TALBOT, *The Cistercian Abbeys of Scotland* (London 1939). J. S. RICHARDSON, *The Abbey of Dundrennan, Berwickshire* (2d ed. Edinburgh 1948). D. E. EASSON, *Medieval Religious Houses: Scotland* (London 1957) 64.

[L. MACFARLANE]

DUNFERMLINE, ABBEY OF

Former Benedictine abbey in Fife, Scotland, in the old Diocese of Saint Andrews. Founded by Queen MARGARET *c.* 1074 and richly endowed by her and her two sons, Alexander I and DAVID I, it became the wealthiest and most renowned abbey in Scotland. It was colonized from Christ Church, Canterbury, before 1089, and again in 1128 when the prior of the English primatial church was appointed first abbot of Dunfermline. The abbey was dedicated to the Holy Trinity in 1150, although it was also known as Christ Church. The abbey contains the royal sepulchers of Margaret and her family and a number of later Scottish kings. It had three dependent priories—Coldingham, Urquhart, and PLUSCARDEN—in 1560 when it was desecrated by Reformers and its numerous properties were confiscated. The abbey church is still in use.

Bibliography: Edinburgh, Bannatyne Club, *Registrum de Dunfermelyn*, C. INNES, ed. (Edinburgh 1842). J. M. WEBSTER and A. A. M. DUNCAN, *Regality of D. Court Book, 1531–1538* (Dunfermline 1953). D. E. EASSON, *Medieval Religious Houses: Scotland* (London 1957) 51. G. W. S. BARROW, ''Scottish Rulers and the Religious Orders 1070–1153,'' *Transactions of the Royal Historical Society*, ser. 5, 3 (1953) 77–100; ''From Queen Margaret to David I: Benedictines and Tironians,'' *Innes Review*, 11 (1960) 22–38.

[L. MACFARLANE]

DUNGAL

A common Irish medieval name; L. Traube distinguishes four individuals of note called Dungal [*O Roma Nobilis* (Munich 1891) 332–337].

Dungal of Saint-Denis, d. after 827. A recluse at SAINT-DENIS, who arrived from Ireland *c.* 784, he wrote to CHARLEMAGNE *c.* 811 explaining a supposed double eclipse of the sun in a letter [*Monumenta Germaniae Historica: Epistolae* (Berlin 1826–) 4:570] showing an advanced knowledge of astronomy. In 827 he wrote against the ICONOCLASM put forth by CLAUDIUS OF TURIN (*Monumenta Germaniae Historica: Epistolae* Carol 2:583–585), quoting from GREGORY OF NYSSA, JOHN CHRYSOSTOM, AUGUSTINE, AMBROSE, and the poets Venantius FORTUNATUS, PAULINUS OF NOLA, and PRUDENTIUS. He is also supposed to have been the author of several Latin poems (*Monumenta Germaniae Historica: Poetae* lat aevi car 1:408–410), one of which is dedicated to HILDUIN, Abbot of Saint-Denis. His identification with Hibernicus Exul, author of a panegyric on Charlemagne's victory, is rejected by Esposito [*Journal of Theological Studies* 33 (London 1932) 119–131], who attributes five of the poems to Dicuil, an Irish monk and geographer of the period, rather than to Dungal.

Dungal of Pavia, who is known from a capitular of LOTHAIR I that in 823 ordered the youth of Milan and ten other towns to repair to a central school in Pavia and there receive instruction from Dungal, who was to be director of education in northern Italy.

Dungal (fl. 855), a companion of Sedulius Scotus. He was the author of a poem to a master Baldo, a scribe

of Salzburg (*Monumenta Germaniae Historica: Poetae* lat aevi car 1:412). His name appears also in a margin of the *Codex Bernensis* (Berne, Stadtbibliothek, MS 363, fol. 54a).

Dungal of Bobbio, 11th century. The oldest catalog of the library of the abbey at BOBBIO includes a list of 29 books donated by *Dungalus, praecipuus Scottorum* to COLUMBAN. Esposito [*Journal of Theological Studies* 32 (1931) 337–344], following Muratori, identifies Dungal of Pavia and Dungal of Bobbio, conjecturing that the head of the school at Pavia retired to Bobbio, bringing his library with him.

Bibliography: M. MANITIUS, *Geschichte der lateinischen Literatur des Mittelalters*, 3 v. (Munich 1911–31) 1:370–374, 392–393; 2:804; 3:106. J. F. KENNEY, *The Sources for the Early History of Ireland*, v. 1 *Ecclesiastical* (New York 1929), 1:516, 535, 538–542, 550, 559–560, 563, 796. L. BIELER, *Ireland, Harbinger of the Middle Ages* (New York 1963) 118; *Lexikon für Theologie und Kirche*, ed. J. HOFER and K. RAHNER, 10 v. (2d, new ed. Freiburg 1957–65) 3:600–601. C. MOONEY, *Dictionnaire d'histoire et de géographie ecclésiastiques*, ed. A. BAUDRILLART et al. (Paris 1912–) 14:1047–50.

[T. P. HALTON]

DUNIN, MARTIN VON

Archbishop of Gniezno and Poznań; b. Wal, near Rawa (Mazowiecka), Poland, Nov. 11, 1774; d. Poznań, Dec. 26, 1842. He came from an impoverished noble family and was ordained (1797) following studies at the German College in Rome. After serving at Gniezno as canon from 1808 and as chancellor from 1815, and at Poznań as canon and educational adviser to the Prussian government from 1824, he became in 1831 archbishop of the sees of Gniezno and Poznań (whose personal union ended after World War II).

Dunin did his utmost for peace and the easing of tensions between Prussia and its Polish subjects but came into open conflict over mixed marriages, then a crucial question for Prussian bishops. Even after Archbishop DROSTE ZU VISCHERING of Cologne was imprisoned, Dunin continued to oppose civil law by insisting that persons contracting mixed marriages promise to educate their children as Catholics. For this he was condemned to six months in prison, a sentence the king commuted to residence in Berlin (1839). When Dunin returned to his see without authorization, he was detained under house arrest at Colberg for ten months until King Friedrich Wilhelm IV (1840–61) came to the throne. The new ruler was sympathetic toward the Catholic Church and his Polish subjects. Dunin returned to his sees (August 1840), where he had been supported by clergy and faithful. During his remaining years Dunin maintained good relations with the royal house and left a reputation as a pious, benevolent, zealous pastor.

See Also: COLOGNE, MIXED MARRIAGE DISPUTE IN

Bibliography: F. POHL, *Martin von Dunin* (Marienburg 1843). H. BRÜCK, *Geschichte der katholischen Kirche in Deutschland im 19. Jahrhundert,* 4 v. (Mainz 1887–1908) 2:335–354. M. LAUBERT, *Die preussische Polenpolitik, 1772–1914* (3d ed. Cracow 1944). R. LILL, *Die Beilegung der Kölner Wirren, 1840–1842* (Düsseldorf 1962). B. STASIEWSKI, *Neue deutsche Biographie* (Berlin 1953–) 4:197–198. R. AUBERT, *Dictionnaire d'histoire et de géographie ecclésiastiques,* ed. A. BAUDRILLART et al. (Paris 1912–) 14:1050–52.

[R. LILL]

DUNNE, M. FREDERIC

First American CISTERCIAN (Trappist) abbot; b. Ironton, Ohio, April 25, 1874; d. Knoxville, Tenn., Aug. 4, 1948. When he applied at age 20 for admission to the Trappist Abbey of Gethsemani as a lay brother, Abbot Edward Chaix-Bourbon advised him to study for the priesthood. After overcoming language difficulties in a French-speaking community and a lack of previous formal education, he was ordained on March 1, 1901. Abbot Edmond Obrecht then gave him simultaneous appointments as vice president of Gethsemani College, guestmaster, postmaster, and prior of the monastery. Dunne held the last two offices for more than 30 years, and during Obrecht's long absences he was responsible for the entire abbey. On Feb. 6, 1935, he was elected as Obrecht's successor and fifth abbot of Gethsemani. At one point the community was reduced to 68 members by an influenza epidemic, but by 1948 Gethsemani held almost 200 monks, had made foundations in Georgia and Utah, had prepared for others in South Carolina and New York, and had modernized its monastery under the Trappist Rule.

Bibliography: M. RAYMOND, *The Less Traveled Road* (Milwaukee 1953). T. MERTON, *Waters of Siloe* (New York 1949). Archives, Gethsemani Abbey.

[M. R. FLANAGAN]

DUNNE, PETER MASTEN

Jesuit historian; b. San Jose, Calif., April 16, 1889; d. San Francisco, Calif., Jan. 15, 1957. He attended Santa Clara College, Santa Clara, Calif., and entered the Society of Jesus at Los Gatos, Calif., on July 20, 1906. After 15 years of study and teaching, he was ordained at Hastings, England, on Aug. 24, 1921. On his return to the U.S., he was assigned to the staff of the Jesuit magazine *America.* Teaching assignments then took him again to Santa Clara College and Los Gatos, where he published his first book, a biography of the San Francisco foundress of the Helpers of the Holy Souls, *Mother Mary of St. Bernard* (1929). After his transfer in 1930 to the University of San Francisco, Dunne completed his doctoral studies in 1934 under Herbert Eugene Bolton at the University of California, Berkeley. He subsequently wrote several works on Hispanic America and the Jesuit missions, including: *Pioneer Blackrobes on the East Coast* (1940), *Pioneer Jesuits in Northern Mexico* (1944), *A Padre Views Latin America* (1945), *Early Jesuit Missions in Tarahumara* (1948), *Andres Perez de Ribas: Pioneer Blackrobe of the West Coast* (1951), *Blackrobes in Lower California* (1952), and *Jacopo Sedlmayr: Missionary, Frontiersman, Historian* (1955). With John Francis Bannon, SJ, he wrote a textbook called *Latin America: An Historical Survey* (1947). His final work, *Juan Antonio Baltasar: Padre Visitador to the Sonora Frontier, 1744–1745* (1957), was published posthumously. He wrote also more than 50 articles and many book reviews. In 1955 Dunne was elected president of the Pacific Coast branch of the American Historical Association; and in 1956, on the occasion of his golden jubilee as a Jesuit, the University of San Francisco awarded him the honorary degree of doctor of laws.

[J. B. MCGLOIN]

DUNS SCOTUS, JOHN, BL.

Franciscan philosopher and theologian; b. Duns, Scotland, *c.* 1266; d. Cologne, Nov. 8, 1308. He is known by the scholastic titles of *Doctor subtilis, Doctor maximus,* and *Doctor Marianus.* This article describes his life and works and summarizes his principal doctrines.

LIFE AND WORKS

One of the most distinguished British thinkers of the late Middle Ages, John Duns Scotus was formed in the Augustinian-Franciscan tradition at Oxford and Paris. Although only 42 when he died, he created a new school of scholastic thought that had considerable influence on later thinkers even outside the Franciscan school (*see* SCOTISM).

Academic Career. As a boy Scotus was trained by his paternal uncle, Elias Duns, at the Franciscan friary in Dumfries, Scotland. At the age of 15 he entered the Franciscan Order and was sent to Oxford during the 1280s. Whether he went to Paris before or after his ordination on March 17, 1291 at Northampton is unknown, but it is likely that he went to Paris at some point in the late 1280s or early 1290s to participate in the lectorate program at the Parisian studium since doing so was a necessary condition for those seeking the mastership at Paris. At Paris during his lectorate, Scotus would have been acquainted with the various theologians then teaching either as bachelors or masters, including Gonsalvus Hispanus and Vital du Four. Thereafter, he returned to Oxford and lectured as a bachelor on the *Sentences* from 1297 to 1301, revising his work continuously. In 1302 he returned to Paris to complete the requirements for the degree, reading the *Sentences* for a second or possibly a third time, but in the following year he was forced to leave the university because he refused to subscribe to Philip the Fair's appeal to a General Council against Boniface VIII. After a brief exile, which may have been spent at Oxford, he returned to Paris armed with a letter of recommendation from the minister general of the order, his former master, Gonsalvo. He finally received the degree from the University of Paris in 1305 and lectured there as a regent master in the Franciscan chair until 1307. Toward the end of 1307 he was sent to Cologne, where he lectured until his death.

His body was originally buried in the Franciscan church in Cologne, near the altar of the Three Kings. Toward the end of the 16th century it was moved to the middle of the choir near the main altar. His remains were frequently authenticated in the 16th and 17th centuries, and most recently in 1954. Veneration of his remains has existed from "time immemorial" and canonical proceedings for his beatification were held in Cologne in 1706 and in Nola in 1710 and from 1905 to 1906. On Feb. 8, 1906, the bishop of Nola declared that the cult given to Bl. Duns Scotus was from time immemorial; although the Order of Friars Minor requested the Congregation of Rites to confirm this for the universal Church, nothing resulted. Finally, on March 20, 1993, Pope John Paul II confirmed the immemorial cult of John Duns Scotus, at the same time according the Subtle Doctor the title of blessed.

Authentic Writings. Not all the writings published by Luke Wadding in the *Opera omnia* can be considered authentic The definitive list of authentic works is possible only with the publication of the critical edition currently being produced by the Scotus Commission (*Opera omnia, studio et cura Commissionis scotisticae ad fidem codicum edita,* Vatican City 1950–) and the Scotus Project, located first at the Franciscan Institute and then at the Catholic University of America. By the year 2001, eleven volumes had appeared in the Vatican edition of Scotus's Oxford theological writings, while three volumes had appeared of his *Opera philosophica,* edited by the American team of scholars.

The most important of Scotus's writings are the commentaries on the *Sentences* of PETER LOMBARD, of which

John Duns Scotus. (The Library of Congress)

there are many versions (five of bk. 1, three of bk. 2, five of bk. 3, and two of bk. 4). The original lecture notes used at Oxford (*Lectura prima*) were definitively arranged by Scotus in an *Ordinatio* (commonly known as the *Opus Oxoniense*). Some of the same notes were used by Scotus in his Paris lectures (*Reportatio Parisiensis*), but entirely new questions and arguments were introduced with much greater attention being paid to more contemporary Parisian authors such as Godfrey of Fontaines. It is probable that Scotus also lectured on the *Sentences* at Cambridge before 1300 (*Reportatio Cantabrigiensis*). Among the philosophical writings printed by Wadding, the following are authentic: *Quaestiones super universalia* of Porphyry, *De praedicamentis, Super Perihermeneias, Super libros elenchorum, De anima,* and *Metaphysica* (lib.1–9). Other authentic writings include: the *Tractatus de primo principio, Theoremata,* certain *Quaestiones disputatae,* and the *Quodlibeta.*

It is certain that roughly half of the works ascribed to Scotus in the Wadding and Vivès editions are not authentic. At the time of Scotus's premature death, many of his writings were incomplete or imperfect. His disciples hastened to complete and arrange his works, thus creating some uncertainty about the authentic text. Scarcely 15 years after the death of Scotus, one of his disciples was already insisting on the need to compare the version then in circulation with Scotus's original. However, the authentic doctrine of Duns Scotus can be determined with reasonable accuracy from the numerous MSS.

PRINCIPAL DOCTRINES

Duns Scotus was a man of acute and subtle intelligence. Reared as he was after the condemnation of certain Averroist and Thomist doctrines (1277), he tried to construct a new synthesis of philosophical and theological thought drawn from the ancient tradition of AUGUSTINE, BONAVENTURE, AVICENNA, and the Oxford school of Franciscan thought. "Writing after the condemnation of 1277," writes É. Tilson. "which was for him an established fact, Duns Scotus finds himself in a different relationship to the philosophers than was Thomas Aquinas. In the advance of philosophical naturalism, the pressing matter seemed to him to be the defense of theological autonomy rather than the further assimilation of philosophy" (664). Describing the sources of Scotus's thought, Maurice O'FIHELY says that "he constantly relies on Avicenna among the philosophers, except where he is contrary to the faith, on Augustine among Catholic doctors, on Paul among the Apostles, and on John among the Evangelists" (*Annot. in Meta. Scoti* 4.1.16; ed. Wadding 4:579B). While O'Fihely's statement may be considered accurate enough for characterizing the more ancient and classical sources for Scotus's writings, the Subtle Doctor's texts show that his interpretation and appropriation of philosophical sources was governed to a large extent by the writings of Henry of Ghent, especially in reference to Avicenna.

An attentive study of Scotus's doctrine reveals the intimate unity of his philosophy and theology. Although his philosophical doctrines cannot be considered corollaries of Christian faith, it would be a mistake to think that his philosophy was developed independently of the faith. The primacy of being constitutes the basis of his epistemology and metaphysics; the primacy of will characterizes his ethics; and the notion of Infinite Being who is Love dominates his entire theology.

Philosophy. The main elements of Scotus's philosophy may be sketched under the headings of the univocity of being, matter and form, individuation, the formal distinction, God's existence, divine infinity, and morality and freedom.

Univocity of Being. The basic Scotistic thesis in the theory of knowledge is the univocity of being. For Scotus the primary object of the intellect is neither the divine essence, as many in the Augustinian tradition thought, nor the essence of material things, as most Aristotelians held, but pure being, *ens inquantum ens,* in the purest possible sense, perceived prior to every determination it might have in reality. This purity and universality of being can be predicated univocally of all things, and without it nothing can be understood. Although universal, this concept of being is not a genus differentiated into species, for there is nothing outside being to differentiate. Being as such is in every reality and in every aspect of reality. It is univocally predicated of Infinite Being and finite being, which are two intrinsic modes of the universality of being as such. Since Scotus's univocity of being is more epistemological than ontological, it would be erroneous to accuse him of PANTHEISM. He clearly taught the essential difference between finite and Infinite Being, and he rejected every theory of EMANATIONISM and pantheism.

Matter and Form. Having established the univocal character of being as the primary object of knowledge, the Subtle Doctor developed a metaphysics that contained many new elements, nuances, and clarifications of traditional Augustinianism. In his view, primary matter has also a different sense from that of Aristotelianism. While agreeing with his contemporaries that all material beings are composed of matter and form, he conceived both as positive and actual entities. Matter as distinct from nothing is a positive reality and therefore actually something. Hence, for Scotus primary matter is not a pure potentiality, as it is for the Aristotelians, but an actuality capable of receiving further perfection. The unity of the composite, although resulting from two entities, is not eliminated, since the two elements are essentially and not accidentally ordered to one another. The union is therefore substantial and not accidental. (*See* MATTER AND FORM.)

Individuation. Besides matter and form, Scotus held also that universality and particularity are metaphysical components of concrete reality. In every being there is to be found a common nature (*natura communis*) that is indifferent to universality and particularity. For a common nature to be rendered particular and individual, a distinct principle of individuality is required. Scotus called this principle, at various points in his writings, either positive entity, individual entity, individual difference or *haecceitas* ("thisness"). It is a distinct, positive modality of individuals by which the common nature is rendered individual.

For Scotus the individuating principle is conferred through the form, which actualizes matter more specifically (*see* INDIVIDUATION). The first form that matter receives in order to be a physical body is a corporeal form (*forma corporeitatis*). Without this, matter cannot be a "body," but with it matter is disposed to receive the higher form called "soul." Thus the form of corporeity is the ultimate actual, specific, individual determination prior to the entry of the soul into matter. It also remains for a time after the soul has left the body, thus preserving the substantial identity of the living and dead body.

Formal Distinction. While every being has a unity, not every being is simple, or devoid of multiplicity. For Scotus every concrete being has a multiplicity of metaphysical elements that are real, positive, and distinct. Some distinctions are real and independent of mental consideration; others depend exclusively on mental consideration. Between these two types of distinction Scotus recognized a third, the formal distinction (*distinctio formalis a parte rei*). This special kind of distinction arises from the concept of various elements that are objectively and formally different in themselves, although not really distinct. The foundation of this distinction lies in the different positive formalities (*formalitates*) that constitute the inner richness of a single being. For Scotus this kind of distinction is to be found between the soul and its powers and between the various powers (*see* FACULTIES OF THE SOUL). In his view, the intellect and will are not completely identified with the spiritual substance of the soul, as in the Augustinian tradition, nor are they really distinct as accidents from an underlying subject, as in the Thomistic tradition. Similar distinctions exist, according to Scotus, between the concepts of unity, truth, and goodness insofar as they are transcendental properties of being, and between the divine persons within the divine essence.

God's Existence. Scotus manifested even greater originality in his natural theology. He was not satisfied with Anselm's ONTOLOGICAL ARGUMENT. Yet in Anselm's attempt he saw valuable elements for a valid affirmation of an Infinite Being. Instead of beginning with the existence of things, as St. THOMAS AQUINAS had done, Scotus began with the essence and metaphysical properties of creatures. Seeing the intrinsic possibility of every created being, Scotus proved the possibility of a first efficient cause. Its actual existence is demonstrated by the principle of non-contradiction. Since created beings exist, it is absolutely certain that they can exist, even if they did not. The reason for this possibility cannot be found in nothing, for nothing cannot be a cause; to say that a thing has nothing for its cause is to say that it has no cause. Nor can creatures themselves be the cause of their own possibility, for they cannot cause anything before they exist. Therefore the cause of the intrinsic possibility of creatures must be found in a being distinct from all producible beings. This being either exists of itself or exists by reason of another. If its existence is of itself, it is possible of itself and the cause of all possibility. But if this being exists by reason of another, the series of prior causes cannot be infinite; otherwise the possibility of be-

ings would have no cause. Scotus therefore concluded that a necessary being exists, capable of producing all things that are possible. For Scotus the possibility of some being demonstrates the possibility of a necessary, uncaused being. But for him it is precisely the impossibility of being caused that justifies the assertion of its actual existence. For if this uncaused being did not exist in actuality, then (1) something can cause itself, or (2) there is no first cause but only mutual dependencies or (3) such a being is impossible. Scotus rejected the first hypothesis as absurd and the other two as previously excluded. Thus to admit the possibility of a first efficient cause is to admit the necessity of its actual existence.

Divine Infinity. For Scotus the essential characteristic of the first being is its infinity. It must be infinite because it is the first efficient cause of all finite beings. As the final cause of all, it must be infinite, for the natural love and desire rooted in each being are toward something infinite. As the most perfect being it cannot be other than infinite, for otherwise it would not be most perfect. Infinite being thus conceived must have intelligence and will in order to know and love before acting as efficient cause.

Morality and Freedom. The moral philosophy of Duns Scotus was strongly influenced by the condemnation of 1277 (*see* AVERROISM, LATIN). In opposition to Averroës, Scotus firmly asserted the absolute freedom of God's will and the preeminence of freedom in man. The objective norm of the moral law, for Scotus, is the divine essence, which always operates most reasonably and fittingly. Although he strongly asserted the absolute liberty of God, he did not imply that God could ever act capriciously or blindly. The norm of divine activity is the divine nature itself, which is essentially rational (*ens rationabilissime, ordinatissime volens*).

Applying this analysis to divine positive law governing mankind, Scotus maintained that God can command what was previously forbidden and forbid what had been commanded, thus altering the moral value of certain actions. At least he held that in the beginning God could have created a different rational relationship among values, provided they were consistent with the supreme goodness and lovableness of God. Consequently Scotus asserted that God can change or suspend the last seven commandments of the Decalogue, but not the first three, for this would be contrary to His supreme rationality. God cannot permit creatures to hate Him.

In man as in God, liberty is the supreme value. For Scotus, free will expresses the highest perfection of human nature—the primacy of this will is characteristic of his ethics. Since knowledge is prior to action, the intellect has a priority of origin. But since the will commands the intellect, and not vice versa, the will enjoys a superiority and primacy over the intellect. Although Scotus did not admit a real distinction between intellect and will, he saw human rationality as most perfectly expressed through love and voluntary activity.

Theology. The basic intuition of Scotus's theological speculation is the perception of God as the Infinite Being who is Love. Scotus made first a distinction between the knowledge God has of Himself (*theologia Dei*) and the knowledge man has of Him through revelation and theological speculation (*theologia nostra*). Consonant with the Franciscan tradition, Scotus emphasized the affective and practical role of theology rather than the abstract and speculative. For Scotus the purpose of theology is to love God above all things.

God's Infinite Love. The primary object of theology is God's own essence, which is love. The metaphysical concept of Infinite Being as "I am who am" (Ex 3.14) thus attains perfection in the biblical definition of God as love (1 Jn 4.8). Infinite Being, the proper modality of the very essence of God, is formally love, Infinite Love.

Between the essential and personal attributes of God and between the divine attributes themselves, Scotus introduced a formal distinction *a parte rei*. At the same time he insisted on the absolute simplicity of God. For him the notions (*rationes*) of Father, Son, and Holy Spirit are distinct from the notion of God. Similarly, the notions of divine wisdom and goodness are formally distinct in the divine essence itself.

Since God is love, everything has its origin in love. God created creatures not out of necessity but out of love, in order to communicate to others the fullness of His love. Although independent and full of love in Himself, He wished to manifest His goodness, happiness, and love to others in a most reasonable and orderly way. In this communication of God's love, Scotus distinguished a hierarchy of objects, even though God, being utterly simple, willed all creatures in a single act of His will. In this hierarchy, the highest manifestation of God's love and glory is the God-Man, Jesus Christ. From all eternity, God predestined Christ to be the sublime manifestation of the Trinity (*In 3 sent.* 7.3; *Report.* 3.7.4–6). All others predestined to glory are willed in relation to Christ, as "co-lovers" (*condiligentes*) of the Trinity. It is in view of this end that God wills the means, namely, grace. Nature, the lowest in the hierarchy, is directly ordained to the supernatural order of grace and glory.

Christology. The theology of Duns Scotus is essentially Christocentric in the sense that Christ, "God's greatest work," is the supreme glorifier of the Holy Trinity. Conscious of St. Paul's statement that "All things are from God, who has reconciled us to himself through Christ" (2 Cor. 5.18), Scotus developed a theological system of speculation consistent with the Christocentric spirituality of the Franciscan tradition. One can say that he supplied the theoretical and speculative structure for the spirituality lived by St. Francis and developed by St. Bonaventure.

For Scotus, the Incarnation in itself is a manifestation of God's infinite love and willed by God from all eternity independent of any foreknowledge of Adam's fall. However, Christ "would not have come as a mediator, as one who was to suffer, as one who was to redeem, unless someone had previously sinned" (*Report.* 3.7.5). In other words, the primary purpose of the Incarnation, for Duns Scotus, was the manifestation of God's love for man. The fact that Christ had to come as a Redeemer was secondary in the mind of God. Scotus could not admit that the greatest good, the Incarnation, was occasioned by an inferior good, the Redemption of mankind. God, however, having willed to create angels and men with freedom of choice, and having foreseen their fall, also willed to send Christ to redeem mankind by His suffering and death.

For Scotus, the Redemption is an expression of highest mercy, supreme justice, and infinite love. Mercy is manifest in the Persons of the Trinity, who sent the Word Incarnate, and in Christ, who offered Himself on the cross for man, alienated by sin. Justice is manifest both in repairing the damage caused by man and in the reconciliation of man with God. Above all, love radiates the entire drama of Redemption. When Scotus described the Passion of Christ and considered the blood that was shed, he strongly emphasized love as the formal element of Christ's merit. Scotus saw the Passion as the culmination of Christ's love for the Trinity and for mankind, the ultimate service predestined for him. By this service, Christ became the one and only mediator between God and man; He became man's unique means of salvation.

Scotus refused to explain the doctrine of the Redemption simply in terms of expiating man's sin and satisfying divine justice. For him, the Redemption could be understood only by the love that inflamed Christ's free will. This infinite love, freely given, calls forth a loving response from man. "I am of the opinion that he wished to redeem us in this fashion principally in order to draw us to his love" (*Oxon.* 3.20). The response of man's love, for Scotus, is thus included in the purpose of the Redemption, for through love man and Christ are "co-lovers" of the Holy Trinity.

Mariology. The title Marian Doctor indicates the special role of the Blessed Virgin in the theology of Duns Scotus. His Marian doctrine, still being developed by his disciples, brings together mother and son in all the mysteries of Christ. They were united in the Incarnation and Redemption by a single decree of divine predestination. As a result, mother and son were united, according to Scotus, in their life, mission, and privileges. One of Scotus's immediate disciples developed this to mean that Mary was predestined ''in the second degree after Christ'' for the Incarnation, Redemption, and Salvation. In this sublime view, the Incarnate Word is the firstborn, the greatest of beings, while Mary is the first of all women. Together with Christ, Mary is the efficient, final, and exemplary cause of all creation. In this doctrine, Christ is the glorifier of the Trinity, Mary the coglorifier; Christ is the Redeemer, Mary the co-redemptrix; Christ is the source of all grace, Mary the dispenser. While these conclusions are not explicitly stated in the writings of Scotus, they must be considered Scotistic.

Immaculate Conception. The name of Scotus is indissolubly associated with the doctrine of Mary's IMMACULATE CONCEPTION. One of his teachers at the University of Oxford, WILLIAM OF WARE, had earlier spoken in favor of this Marian privilege, but Scotus was perhaps the first to defend it in Paris (*Report.* 3.3.1). For the great doctors of the Middle Ages, the principal difficulty was that Mary—as all other descendants of Adam—had to be redeemed by Christ. Scotus admitted fully that ''Mary would greatly have needed Christ as a Redeemer, for she would have contracted original sin by reason of human propagation unless she had been preserved through the grace of the Mediator'' (*In 3 sent.* 18.13). Thus, for Scotus, Mary was preserved from all sin, actual and original, by reason of Christ's Redemption. This view was heatedly debated for five centuries before it was definitively declared a doctrine of Catholic faith.

Scotus considered Mary the trophy of the Redemption, the most perfect product of Christ's love of man. He established a principle in Mariological studies that contributed greatly to the scholastic development of Marian doctrine: ''We can with probability attribute to Mary all that has the greatest perfection, provided it is not opposed to the authority of the Church or the Scriptures'' (*In 3 sent.* 3.1).

Nature, Grace, and Glory. Since, for Scotus, the entire natural order is ordained to the supernatural, natural actions are rendered supernaturally meritorious by the modality of grace freely given by God. Nature finds its perfection and completion in grace, which God willed from all eternity to give man through Christ. For Scotus, the supernatural order does not transcend the natural order substantially and infinitely, as it does for St. Thomas, but only modally and determinately, because from eternity God intended the natural order to be perfected by grace.

Recognizing no real distinction between the soul and its powers, Scotus also recognized no real distinction between grace and charity. They are the same reality, a HABIT, whereby man's nature shares supernatural life and merits eternal salvation. However, Scotus recognized a formal distinction *a parte rei* between grace and charity, for grace signifies an ontological perfection, while charity signifies an operative modality. The object of grace is God, the lover and giver of gifts, while the object of charity is the lovableness of God in Himself. Thus, insofar as grace involves a certain imperfection, one does not say that God is grace but that He is charity, love.

For Scotus, the essence of eternal happiness consists in the beatific love of God. While remaining free, this love is inflexible and indefectible as a result of God's positive predetermined choice. The whole of Scotus's theology is dominated by the notion of love. The characteristic note of this love is its absolute freedom. As love becomes more perfect and intense, freedom becomes more noble and integral.

Evaluation. ''Perhaps there is no medieval doctor more misunderstood than this Scottish Franciscan,'' wrote A. GEMELLI. ''The very title of Subtle Doctor by which he is honored has an ironic ring. He was called an innovator, yet he followed the most ancient scholastic tradition, developing the intuitions of St. Augustine and incorporating compatible elements of Aristotelian doctrine. He was called a Franciscan who had lost the significance of love, yet his philosophy is founded on love. He was said to be a methodical saboteur, an insidious theologian, a precursor of voluntarism and immanentism, a 13th-century Kant, yet his realism is scholastic to an extreme, carefully avoiding any pretended autonomy of nature of the individual ego. His theories of the Blessed Virgin and the Incarnation received approval centuries later in the dogma of the Immaculate Conception and in devotion to the Kingship of Christ'' [*Il Francescanesimo,* 2d ed. (Milan 1933) 58–59].

This evaluation by a pioneer of neoscholasticism in Italy reveals the change brought about by research and historical criticism. In the first edition of *Histoire de la philosophie médiévale,* appearing in 1900, M. DE WULF described Scotus as a skeptic. In the 6th and last edition (Louvain 1936) Scotism was described as an original and forceful scholasticism, ''a homogeneous synthesis in which everything has been brought together in a wonderful unity'' (347–348). Similarly, M. GRABMANN considered Duns Scotus to be ''the last of the great personalities of scholasticism'' [*Die Geschichte der katholischen Theologie* (Freiburg im Breisgau 1933) 86–87].

The whole of scholasticism, and Scotus in particular, has profited greatly from the application of historical criticism to original sources. Historical criticism has made it possible to determine the genuine works of Scotus and to appreciate their original form. It has revealed the method by which he developed his system. It has shown that he was more in agreement than in disagreement with the great theologians of his time. Finally, it has corrected the misunderstanding concerning his relation to St. Thomas and concerning the Church's attitude toward these two thinkers.

Duns Scotus did not originate opposition to St. Thomas; it existed long before Scotus (*see* THOMISM). In any case, as De Wulf has pointed out, Duns Scotus did not criticize for the sake of criticism, but for the sake of constructing his own philosophical system, which was the culmination of an ancient Christian tradition.

See Also: SCHOLASTICISM.

Bibliography: Works. *Opera omnia:* ed. L. WADDING et al., 12 v. (Lyon 1639); 26 v. (Vivès; Paris 1891–95); critical ed. C. BALIĆ (Vatican City 1950–). *The De Primo Principio of John Duns Scotus,* ed. and tr. E. ROCHE (St. Bonaventure, N.Y. 1949). *Philosophical Writings,* ed. and tr. A. B. WOLTER (New York 1962). *Prologue de l'Ordinatio,* trans. G. SONDAG (Paris 1999). Literature. F. C. COPLESTON, *History of Philosophy,* v. 2. (Westminster, Md., 1946). A. B. EMDEN, *A Biographical Register of the University of Oxford to A.D. 1500* (Oxford 1957–59) 1:607–610; *A Biographical Register of the Scholars of the University of Cambridge before 1500* (Cambridge 1963) 198–201. E. BETTONI, *Enciclopedia Filosofica,* (Venice-Rome 1957) 4: 463–472. P. RAYMOND, *Dictionnaire de théologie catholique* (Paris 1950) 4.2:1865–1947. É. H. GILSON, *History of Christian Philosopphy in the Middle Ages* (New York 1955) 454–464, 763–768; *Jean Duns Scot: Introduction à ses positions fondamentales* (Paris 1952). O. SCHÄFER, *Bibliographia de vita, operibus et doctrina Iohannis Duns Scoti doctoris subtilis ac mariani, saec. XIX–XX* (Rome 1955); *Johannes Duns Scotus,* v. 22 (1953) of *Bibliographische Einführungen in das Studium der Philosophie,* ed. I. M. BOCHEŃSKI (Bern 1948–). B. DE SAINT-MAURICE, *John Duns Scot: A Teacher for Our Times,* tr. C. DUFFY (St. Bonaventure, N.Y. 1955). A. B. WOLTER, *The Transcendentals and Their Function in the Metaphysics of Duns Scotus* (Washington 1946). M. J. GRAJEWSKI, *The Formal Distinction of Duns Scotus* (Washington 1944). C. L. SHIRCEL, *The Univocity of the Concept of Being in the Philosophy of John Duns Scotus* (Washington 1942). J. K. RYAN and B. M. BONANSEA, eds., *John Duns Scotus 1265–1965* (Studies in Philosophy and the History of Philosophy, Washington 1965). S. D. DUMONT, ''Henry of Ghent and Duns Scotus,'' *Routledge History of Philosophy,* v. 3, *Medieval Philosophy* (London 1998). L. HONNEFELDER, *Ens inquantum ens: Der Begriff des Seienden als solchen als Gegenstand der Metaphysik nach der Lehre des Johannes Duns Scotus* (Münster 1989). W. A. FRANK and A. B. WOLTER, *Duns Scotus: Metaphysician* (West Lafayette, Ind. 1995). O. BOULNOIS, *Tre et représentation: une généalogie de la métaphysique moderne à l'époque de Duns Scot (XIIIe–XIVe siècle)* (Paris 1999). R. CROSS, *Duns Scotus,* v. 1 in the series *Great Medieval Thinkers,* ed. B. DAVIES, O.P. (Oxford 1999).

[C. BALÍC/T. B. NOONE]

DUNSTABLE, JOHN

Composer, singer, astronomer, and mathematician; b. Bedfordshire?, England, *c.* 1370; d. London, Dec. 24, 1453. His only recorded ecclesiastical appointment is a canonry at Hereford cathedral held (almost certainly *in absentia*) from 1419 to 1440. His treatise on astronomy is dated 1438, and another such treatise owned by him bears a notation that he was ''musician to the Duke of Bedford'' (John of Lancaster). As regent in France during the Hundred Years' War, the Duke spent considerable time in Paris, where Dunstable would have met both DUFAY and BINCHOIS, who are said by the poet Martin le Franc to have adopted Dunstable's *''contenance angloise.''* This refers to a peculiarly English style brought to a high degree of perfection by Dunstable, but noticeable also in the music of his greatest contemporaries. Basically, it is a texture from which all but unessential dissonances have been removed, and the resultant harmony sounds effortlessly radiant and crystal clear. Examples abound in his motets in honor of the Blessed Virgin Mary and in many of his settings of the Ordinary of the Mass. He was equally competent in the creation of complex isorhythmic structures, used in Mass sections and motets, though even here his fondness for consonance and freely flowing melody is never in doubt. He experimented boldly with the integration or pairing of Mass sections, and his cyclical Mass, *Rex saeculorum,* is one of the earliest of its kind. In all, some 60 of his works have survived and are available in a modern edition.

Bibliography: *Complete Works,* ed. M. F. BUKOFZER (Musica Britannica 8; New York 1953). M. F. BUKOFZER, ''English Church Music of the Fifteenth Century,'' *New Oxford History of Music,* ed. J. A. WESTRUP 11 v. (New York 1957–) 3:184–193. A. HUGHES, *Grove's Dictionary of Music and Musicians,* ed. E. BLOM, 9 v, (5th ed. London 1954) 2:808–810. *Baker's Biographical Dictionary of Musicians,* ed. N. SLONIMSKY (5th, rev. ed. New York 1958) 410. M. BENT, ''John Dunstable'' in *The New Grove Dictionary of Music and Musicians, vol. 5,* ed. S. SADIE (New York: Grove's Dictionaries of Music Inc., 1980) 720–725. J.-M. EVANS, ''A Unique Cantus Firmus Usage in a 15th-century English Mass Movement,'' *Early Music* 26 (1998), 469–476. D. FALLOWS, ''Dunstable, Bedyngham, and *O rosa bella,''* *The Journal of Musicology* 12 (1994), 287–305. D. M. RANDEL, ed. *The Harvard Biographical Dictionary of Music* (Cambridge, Massachusetts 1996) 230. B. SMITH, ''John Dunstable and Leonel Power: A Stylistic Comparison'' (Ph.D. diss. University of Sheffield, 1993).

[D. STEVENS]

DUNSTAN OF CANTERBURY, ST.

Benedictine, archbishop; b. Baltonsborough, Somerset, 909; d. May 19, 988. He came of a noble family living in the vicinity of Glastonbury, where he was educated by Irish clerics. Dunstan later joined the household of his uncle Athelm, Archbishop of Canterbury, and hence the court of King Athelstan. He made a private monastic profession to ALPHEGE (AELFHEAH), bishop of Winchester, was ordained by him, and went to live as a hermit at Glastonbury, practicing there the crafts of the scribe, embroiderer, and silversmith. In 940 King Edmund, after a narrow escape from death in a stag hunt, installed him as abbot of GLASTONBURY and gave financial help. Dunstan introduced the BENEDICTINE RULE, enlarged the church and monastic buildings, and added to the collection of books.

Under King Edwig, Dunstan was exiled for his reproof of Edwig's irresponsible conduct and went to Mont Blandin, Ghent, where he saw the reformed type of Continental monasticism. This, together with FLEURY, which was visited by St. ETHELWOLD's disciples, influenced the English monasteries in their way of life. The full flowering of this movement took place after Dunstan's recall by King EDGAR in 957. He became successively bishop of WORCESTER and London and archbishop of CANTERBURY (960). Thus began a fruitful collaboration between king and archbishop, which was regarded as a golden age by post-Conquest writers. Dunstan's influence can be seen in some of Edgar's laws: monks occupied several important sees and displaced secular canons in cathedrals, and the monasteries enjoyed royal protection. About 970 at WINCHESTER there was held a congress of secular and ecclesiastical magnates at which was promulgated the *Regularis concordia,* based on Continental customaries, which all agreed to observe. In recent years the importance of Saints Ethelwold and OSWALD OF YORK in the monastic revival in the south and midlands of England have been rightly stressed, but Dunstan himself seems to have reformed or refounded MALMESBURY, BATH, and Westminster, and, shortly before his death, to have perhaps introduced monks at Canterbury cathedral, at least as members of his household.

As archbishop he built many churches and corrected abuses, such as the neglect of celibacy by the clergy, and of fasting and justice by the laity. As an old man, he presided regularly in the courts and corrected manuscripts. His name appears on charters until the year of his death. But the reform of monasteries, which became centers of religion and vernacular culture and provided many bishops for England and missionaries for Scandinavia, is his principal title to fame. He was reputed to have cast bells and made organs, and was a patron saint of metalworkers. In art he is often portrayed holding the devil's nose in a pair of tongs.

Feast: May 19.

Bibliography: E. G. FLIGHT, *The True Legend of St. Dunstan and the Devil* (3d ed. London 1871). W. STUBBS, ed., *Memorials of Saint Dunstan (Rerum Brittanicarum medii aevi scriptores* 63; 1874). T. SYMONS, ed. and tr., *Regularis concordia* (New York 1953). E. S. DUCKETT, *Saint Dunstan of Canterbury* (New York 1955). D. KNOWLES, *The Monastic Order in England, 943–1216* (Cambridge 1940–). *English Historical Documents* v.1, ed. D. DOUGLAS (New York 1953–). E. JOHN, ''The Beginning of the Benedictine Reform in England,'' *Revue Benedictine* 73 (1963) 73–87. D. DALES, *Dunstan: Saint and Statesman* (Cambridge 1988). *St Dunstan: His Life, Times, and Cult,* ed. N. RAMSAY, M. SPARKS, and T. TATTON-BROWN (Woodbridge, Suffolk, UK 1992). D. T. RICE, *English Art, 871–1100* (Oxford 1952).

[H. FARMER]

DU PAC, GABRIEL DE BELLEGARDE

French Jansenist historian; b. Bellegarde (Aude), Oct. 17, 1717; d. Utrecht (Holland), Dec. 13, 1789. As a young lawyer he joined the Jansenist party and received appropriate ecclesiastical training from his teachers. He was soon named canon in Lyons, but lost his prebend because of his views. After going to Holland in 1751, he first lived at the seminary of Rijswijk, then at Utrecht. He was a zealous defender of the schismatic Church of Utrecht, but also undertook negotiations in Rome with a view to its reconciliation. As a professional historian, he carried on a wide correspondence in order to obtain documents. In this way he contributed considerably to the archives of the Ancienne Clérésie, which were to prove very precious, and are now preserved temporarily in the royal archives in Utrecht. He carefully published (with historical introductions, critical notes, and supplements) several works of others: Antoine Arnauld, B. Z. van Espen, A. Dorsanne, and the Acts of the Council of Pisa and of the Second Synod of Utrecht. His most important historical works are: *Mémoires historiques sur l'affaire de la bulle Unigenitus dans les Pays-Bas* (4 v., Brussels 1755), *Histoire abrégée de l'Église métropolitaine d'Utrecht* (Utrecht 1765; 3d ed., 1852), and the biographies of Van Espen and Arnauld. His *Mémoires historiques touchant l'Université de Louvain et les Églises des Pays-Bas, surtout depuis 1680–1713* is preserved in manuscript form in the archives of the Ancienne Clérésie.

Bibliography: J. DEDIEU, *Dictionnaire d'histoire et de géographie ecclésiastiques,* ed. A. BAUDRILLART et al. (Paris 1912) 7:848–850. F. C. DE VRIES, *Vredespogingen tusschen. . . Utrecht en Rome* (Assen 1930).

[L. CEYSSENS]

DUPANLOUP, FÉLIX ANTOINE PHILIBERT

Bishop of Orléans; b. Saint-Félix in Savoy, Jan. 3, 1802; d. Lacombe (Isère), France, Oct. 11, 1878. He was

Félix Antoine Philibert Dupanloup. (The Catholic University of America)

an illegitimate child whose mother, Anne Dechosal, was a poor young peasant and whose father was probably one of the higher French nobility. In Paris, where the boy lived with his mother from 1809, his intelligence impressed his teachers, who directed him toward the seminary. There he made valuable contacts in aristocratic and ecclesiastical circles and was ordained (Dec. 12, 1825). While he was a curate in the Parisian church of the Madeleine, his catechetical instructions were extremely successful. Obliged to abandon this work (1834), he thereupon became well known as a preacher. When named superior of the minor seminary of St. Nicholas (September 1837), he was able to utilize anew his pedagogical talents. His role some months later in the deathbed reconciliation of TALLEYRAND-PÉRIGORD made him famous. His polemical abilities were first revealed in 1844 when he came out in favor of freedom for Catholic secondary education. At first an opponent of LAMENNAIS and his followers, he slowly became attracted to MONTALEMBERT and his idea that defense of the Catholic Church in modern society is best conducted on the field of constitutional liberties. Thanks to his diplomatic skill, from 1848 he was the chief artisan of the Falloux Law (1850), but his energetic defense of this temporary solution of the school question brought about his rupture with Louis VEUILLOT, leader of the intransigent Catholics.

Dupanloup bowed to the entreaties of his friend Falloux after much hesitation and accepted the See of Orléans (April 1849). Endowed with a keen appreciation of the needs of souls and with the temperament of a leader, although at times too authoritarian, he excelled in his ability to arouse and direct the activity of subordinates. For two decades he dedicated himself to the betterment of his diocese, especially to the intellectual, spiritual, and pastoral improvement of his clergy. His proposed new solutions ranked him a pioneer in religious sociology and sacerdotal spirituality. A rigorous economy in the distribution of time permitted him to remain in close contact with the capital and to keep alert to the problems vexing France and the Church, while initiating numerous apostolic and charitable works in his diocese. All the quarrels that then beset the Church in France found him in the midst of the combat, particularly those concerning ULTRAMONTANISM and modern liberties. He sustained, often passionately, the Catholic liberals of the group connected with the *Correspondant* against the attacks of Veuillot. This made him a very controversial figure in that large segment of the clergy who looked upon Veuillot as an oracle, but it increased his prestige among the elite of French society, even the unbelievers, as was evident by his election to the French Academy (1854).

Dupanloup moved to the forefront of the European politico-religious scene from the time of the Italian war (1859) because of the role he assumed in defense of the papal temporal power by publishing numerous explosive brochures with the aid of friends. Persuaded thenceforth that he had a unique mission to fulfill, he threw himself with redoubled ardor into an unremitting struggle conducted simultaneously on two fronts: against the anticlericals in defense of the Church and religion, and against the extreme ultramontanes in defense of moderate ideas in the Church. His brochure *La convention du 15 septembre et l'encyclique du 8 décembre* (1865) appeased the tempest unleashed by the SYLLABUS OF ERRORS and met with favorable reaction throughout the world. His interventions in favor of Poland, Ireland, and the Eastern Churches popularized his name far beyond French borders. At the assemblies of bishops in Rome in 1862 and 1867, Dupanloup organized the resistance of the moderates and thereby avoided anti-liberal, ultramontane declarations at variance with public opinion. He also hoped to profit from his prestige and to enjoy an analogous role at VATICAN COUNCIL I; but he intervened maladroitly on the eve of the council's opening with his *Observations sur. . . l'infallibilité au futur concile* (Nov. 11, 1869), in which he amassed reasons against the opportuneness of a definition, although he admitted the doctrine. During the sessions he also alienated many otherwise sympathetic persons by the passionate manner in which he tried to alert his episcopal colleagues and, still more debatably, public opinion and the French government, against decisions that, in his mind, threatened a rupture between the Church and modern society. His feverish activity undoubtedly injured his cause more than it helped.

Elected to the French National Assembly (1871) and to the Senate (1875), Dupanloup devoted his closing years mainly to politics. For a while he advocated a restoration of the monarchy as the sole guarantee for the future of the Church; then he tried to orient the Third Republic in a direction as conservative and clerical as possible. This action obtained for the Church immediate advantages, notably the law extending freedom to higher education (1876), but it compromised the Church in the eyes of the radical left. Circumscribed in his contacts with the world, Dupanloup totally lacked appreciation of modern social problems.

His sermons, conferences, and parliamentary speeches were highly esteemed, although their eloquence was diffuse and replete with romantic rhetoric. Dupanloup's published writings, considerable in volume, enjoyed a wide international reading public, but they dealt mostly with matters of merely contemporary interest presented in the form of polemical brochures and pastoral works without great literary value. Most durable were his pedagogical writings, consisting of works on catechetical instruction, education for women (a field in which he was a pioneer), and especially his great six-volume tract, *De l'Education* (1850–66), which condensed the experience of one whom Ernest Renan called an "educator without equal."

Dupanloup was a man of action, impetuous, superficial in theology, too insistent on the sentimental aspects of religion, yet a great bishop passionately devoted to the Church and possessed with the idea of rebuilding a "Christianity," although his famed liberalism was in fact very moderate. Despite a degree of vanity and a taste for the game of politics, he was a true priest and a highly esteemed director of souls whose powers of inspiration were remarkable.

Bibliography: R. AUBERT, *Dictionnaire d'histoire et de géographie ecclésiastiques,* ed. A. BAUDRILLART et al. (Paris 1912–). 14:1070–1122, lists Dupanloup's writings, full bibliog.; "Mgr. Dupanloup et le Syllabus," *Revue d'histoire ecclésiastique* 51 (1956) 79–142, 471–512, 837–915; "Mgr. Dupanloup au début du concile du Vatican," *Miscellanea historiae ecclesiasticae* (Louvain 1961) 96–116. C. DE WARMONT, "F. A. Dupanloup," *The XIXth Century* 5 (1879) 219–246. F. LAGRANGE, *Life of Monseigneur Dupanloup* tr. LADY HERBERT, 2 v. (London 1885), detailed but too panegyrical. U. MAYNARD, *Mgr. Dupanloup et Mgr. Lagrange son historien* (Paris 1884) É. FAGUET, *Mgr. Dupanloup: Un grand évêque* (Paris 1914), useful for Dupanloup's personality. C. MARCILHACY, *Le, Diocèse d'Orléans sous l'épiscopat de Mgr. Dupanloup* (Paris 1962), excellent on diocesan activity. S. LÖSCH, *Döllinger und Frankreich* (Munich 1955) 230–347. F. BUISSON, ed., *Dictionnaire de pédagogie et d'instruction primaire,* 2 v. in 4 (Paris 1887–88) 1.1:742–747. M. PETERS, *Die Stellungnahme Felix Dupanloups zu den Fragen der Mädchenerziehung und Frauenbildung seiner Zeit* (Münster 1929).

[R. AUBERT]

DUPERRON, JACQUES DAVY

Cardinal, theologian, statesman; b. Berne, Switzerland (not St. Lô, Normandy), Nov. 25, 1556; d. Paris, 1618. His family was Norman. He was educated by his Calvinist father, went to Paris in 1573 after theological and humanist studies and gained fame as a learned man, being presented to Henry III in 1576. After reading the *Summa* of St. Thomas, he became a Catholic (1577–78) in a sincere conversion that nonetheless helped his career. Because of his talent as a speaker, he became reader for Henry III and, though not yet a priest, gave the funeral oration for Ronsard in 1586. He was ordained in 1591, had a part in the conversion of Henry IV in 1593, and with A. d' Ossat went to Rome in 1595 to obtain reconciliation and papal absolution for the king (*see* HENRY IV, KING OF FRANCE). Henry made him first chaplain and councilor of state, and in 1596 Duperron took possession of the See of Evreux, to which Henry had named him in 1591. He then devoted himself to combating CALVINISM, having studied the Fathers, scholastics, contemporary Catholic theologians, and Calvinist authors as well. After winning a public debate in Paris in 1597, he vanquished P. DUPLESSIS-MORNAY at Fontainebleau, June 4, 1600, before the king and a jury of Catholics and Calvinists. After he was made a cardinal in 1604, he represented France in Rome. In 1606 he became archbishop of Sens and grand chaplain of France, returning to France in 1607. In 1610 he became a member of the regency and in 1612 defended Robert BELLARMINE and papal authority against Parlement and E. RICHER. In 1615, for the French clergy, he delivered a harangue against an article of the Estates General of 1614. His harangue was attacked by James I of England, with whom, through I. Casaubon, Duperron had conducted an epistolary debate in 1611 and 1612 (ed. 1620), defending the legitimacy of the Church of Rome.

Duperron was ambitious and a subtle negotiator. He was essentially a polemicist and cannot be compared with the MAURISTS, for example, in his scholarship. Most of his writings, including a treatise on the Eucharist in 1622, were published posthumously.

Bibliography: C. CONSTANTIN, *Dictionnaire de théologie catholique,* ed. A. VACANT et al. (Paris 1903–50) 4.2:1953–60. J. CALVET, *Catholicisme. Hier, aujourd'hui et demain,* ed. G. JACQUE-

MET (Paris 1947–) 3:1183–84. K. HOFMANN, *Lexikon für Kirche*, ed. J. HOFER and K. RAHNER (2d, new ed. Freiburg 1957–65) 3:607. R. SNOEKS, *Dictionnaire d'histoire et de géographie ecclésiastiques*, ed. A. BAUDRILLART et al. (Paris 1912–) 14:1130–36.

[D. R. PENN]

DU PIN, LOUIS ELLIES

A prolific and influential Gallican theologian. b. Paris, June 17, 1657; d. Paris, June 6, 1719. Du Pin was doctor of theology of the Faculty of Paris, July 1, 1684 and Professor of Philosophy (1693) at the Collège Royal. The first volumes of his *Nouvelle Bibliothèque des Auteurs ecclésiastiques* (some 60 vols, 1686–1719) were considered too critical of the early Christian centuries and aroused opposition, notably from J. B. Bossuet and R. Simon. He was censured by the Archbishop of Paris (1693), but continued writing the *Bibliothèque*, which was put on the Index in 1757. Banished from Paris in 1704 for alleged Jansenism, he was removed from his Regius Professorship, but remained a respected and influential member of the Faculty of Theology. He was involved in the religious affairs of his age, especially in opposition to the Bull *Unigenitus*. Interested in Christian reunion, he took part in two projects involving other members of the Faculty of Theology: a proposal for union between the Russian and French Churches, in 1717, and a correspondence with the Archbishop of Canterbury, William Wake (1718–1719).

Besides his historical writings, his main works are theological and biblical: *De Antiqua Ecclesiæ Disciplina* (1686), *Traité de la doctrine chrétienne* (1703), put on the Index in 1688 et 1704, and *Prolégomènes sur la Bible* (1699). He also edited the works of St Optatus of Milevis (1700) and J. Gerson (1706).

Bibliography: P. PIERLING, *La Sorbonne et la Russie* (Paris 1882). N. SYKES, *William Wake* (Cambridge 1957). J. M. GRES-GAYER, ''Un théologien gallican, témoin de son temps: Louis Ellies Du Pin (1657–1719),'' *Revue d'Histoire de l'Église de France*, 72 (1986), 67–121; *Paris-Cantorbéry (1717–1720): Le Dossier d'un premier œcuménisme* (Paris 1989); ''Un théologien gallican et l'Écriture sainte: le 'Projet biblique' de L. Ellies Du Pin,'' in J. R. ARMOGATHE ed., *Le Grand Siècle et la Bible* (Paris 1989), 255–275; ''Le gallicanisme de L. Ellies Du Pin,'' *Lias* 18 (1991), 37–82; *Théologie et pouvoir en Sorbonne. La Faculté de Théologie de Paris et la bulle Unigenitus, 1714–1721* (Paris 1991). J. H. HAYES, ed., *Dictionary of Biblical Interpretation* (Nashville 1999).

[J. M. GRES-GAYER]

DUPLESSIS-MORNAY, PHILIPPE

Huguenot leader; b. Buhy, near Mantes-Gassicourt, Nov. 5, 1549; d. La-Forêt-sur-Sèvre, Poitou, Nov. 11, 1623. On the death of his Catholic father, he became a Protestant with his mother *c.* 1559. After brilliant studies in Paris, he traveled through much of Europe (1568–72), and returned to argue that France's policy should be anti-Spanish and anti-Hapsburg. He escaped the ST. BARTHOLOMEW'S DAY massacre, went to England, and returned to France in 1573. He became a councilor of Henry IV of Navarre, who sent him on an embassy to England and the Netherlands (1578–81). From 1588 he was the HUGUENOT leader, becoming in 1589 governor of Saumur, where he founded a Protestant academy in 1599 that Louis XIV suppressed in 1685. After Henry's conversion to Catholicism in 1593, Duplessis-Mornay's position declined, but he continued his keen anti-Catholic polemics, especially against the papacy and the Eucharist. In 1600 he lost a debate on the latter to J. DUPERRON and retired to Saumur. His appeal for tolerance, which would have improved the Huguenot position, was supported by an ecumenical spirit: his *Traité de la verité* (1581) attacked deists; as a moderate Huguenot, he could serve as a mediator with the king; he believed in an equality of all men for religious reasons; and he worked for a Protestant unity until the THIRTY YEARS' WAR. He has left many writings defending the religion of the Huguenots, and his *Memoires et correspondence,* 12 v. (Paris 1824–25).

Bibliography: R. PATRY, *Philippe du Plessis-Mornay* (Paris 1933). M. ANDRIEUX, *Henri IV* (Paris 1955). L. PFLEGER, *Lexikon für Theologie und Kirche*, ed. J. HOFER and K. RAHNER (2d, new ed. Freiburg (1957–65) 3:608. R. SNOEKS, *Dictionnaire d'histoire et de géographie ecclésiastiques*, ed. A. BAUDRILLART et al. (Paris 1912–) 14:1136–41. R. NÜRNBERGER, *Die Religion in Geschichte und Gegenwart* (3d ed. Tübingen 1957–65) 2:286–287.

[D. R. PENN]

DUPRAT, GUILLAUME

Bishop, Catholic reformer; b. Issoire, France, 1507; d. Beauregard, Oct. 22, 1560. His father, Antoine (1463–1535), was at first chancellor for the king of France, Francis I; ten years after his wife died, he became archbishop of Sens and abbot of St. Benoît-sur-Loire, and in 1527 cardinal. When his uncle, Thomas Duprat, Bishop of Clermont, died in 1528, Guillaume, at the age of 23, was elected his successor by the cathedral chapter. In 1545 he was sent by Francis I to the Council of Trent and there took part in the debates about Holy Scripture and tradition, and the nature and number of the Sacraments. He also fought strenuously against the plurality of benefices and for the duty of residence for bishops. Though he had heard of the Society of Jesus through the Minim S. Guiscard, his admiration of it grew when, at Trent, he met LE JAY, SALMERÓN and LAINEZ. In 1547, he founded the first Jesuit seminary in France by giving the Society his Hôtel de Clermont (later in Paris, the Collège Louis le Grand). Unfortunately, since the property did not belong to him personally but to the bishops of Clermont, this gift met with litigation for ten years, involving both Rome and the French parliament. In order to train preachers, he worked to reestablish the college of Billom and opened another at Mauriac.

Bibliography: P. BROUTIN, *Lexikon für Theologie und Kirche,* ed. J. HOFER and K. RAHNER (2d, new ed. Freiburg 1957–65) 3:609. P. TOURNIER, ''Monseigneur Guillaume du Prat au concile de Trente,'' *Études* 98 (1904) 289–307, 465–484, 622–644. H. JEDIN, *History of the Council of Trent,* tr. E. GRAF, v.1-2 (St. Louis 1957–60) 16, 65, 331, 341, 381, 387, 429, 464.

[P. BROUTIN]

DURA-EUROPOS

An ancient city on the right bank of the Middle Euphrates in modern Syria, the object of intensive archeological investigation from 1923 to 1934. From the 3d century B.C. to its destruction in the 3d century A.D. it was an important military and commercial center on the caravan route across the Syrian desert between the Mediterranean coast and Mesopotamia.

History. The older site of Dura was raised to importance by Nicanor, general of Alexander the Great, who established a military colony there in about 280 B.C. Its alternative name, Europos, has reference to the place of origin of Seleucus I or of members of the city's Macedonian garrison. Commercial development followed the military, and by 120 B.C. Dura-Europos was a flourishing caravan center. When the Romans under Trajan began their move through the Middle East in A.D. 116, the city fell into their hands and a triumphal arch was erected to commemorate the conquest. Although abandoned soon afterward, it was reestablished in 165 because of growing pressure from the Persians and was steadily strengthened until it became one of the most important Roman fortresses in the province of Syria. Following the Persian attack under Ardashir (224–241) the Romans stationed at Dura a *dux ripae,* i.e., a military commander for the whole Middle Euphrates area. Despite these increased defenses, however, the Persians besieged and captured Dura some time before A.D. 260, but after a brief period of occupancy abandoned the city. Julian the Apostate hunted lions in its ruins about A.D. 361.

In 1921 a Captain Murphy of the British Army, while digging trenches on the ancient site, uncovered some frescoes. Shortly thereafter, the American Egyptologist J. H. Breasted made surface explorations and took some photographs. In 1922 and 1923, F. V. Cumont, a Belgian historian, conducted the first archeological excavations.

In 1928, under the direction of M. I. Rostovtzeff, the French Academy of Inscriptions and Yale University began to collaborate on seasons of excavations in the ruins, but discontinued in 1934. About one-fourth of the city has been explored and enough found to reconstruct some of its history and to identify military installations; the palace of the *dux;* the acropolis; numerous temples to Persian, Greek, Babylonian, and Palmyrene gods; a Christian church; and a Jewish synagogue. The walls of most of these places of worship were profusely decorated with frescoes.

The Christian church. This was discovered near the city wall that faces the desert. In the final defense of the city, the Romans had strengthened the wall by building a ramp along it from the inside of the city. The tops of the houses protruding above the ramp were cut off, but since the parts buried under the earth-fill were preserved by the covering, the Christian church unearthed by Rostovtzeff in 1931 and 1932 was in fairly good condition. An inscription on the wall indicated that the building had been converted into a Christian meeting place in about A.D. 232. A vestibule that opened into a courtyard led to the interior, where to the left there was a large double room capable of holding about 100 people. A podium at one end of the room may have been used as a pulpit or as a predella for an altar. The room directly across from the entrance to the courtyard seems to have been simply a living room. To the right was the ''chapel,'' which abounded in wall frescoes. On the wall opposite the entrance were two bands of paintings, the lower one showing three women near a sarcophagus, the upper one depicting various miracles of Christ around the Lake of Galilee. Between the doors was a painting of David and Goliath, and to the right, one of the Samaritan woman at the well. A ''baptistery,'' i.e., a deep stone tub covered by a baldachin, occupied almost the entire end of the room. A representation of the Good Shepherd above one of Adam and Eve covered the backdrop of the ''baptistery.'' The style of these frescoes shows marked Greek influence, while their similarities to other early Christian art may indicate that the themes were imported from Antioch or Alexandria.

Synagogue. Found near the city wall, but north of the main gate, the SYNAGOGUE, which bore an inscription placing the final redecoration in A.D. 255, consisted of an open courtyard and a single room about 25 by 40 feet. The walls of the synagogue were covered with some 30 paintings arranged in three bands reaching from the ceiling to the wainscot above the stone seats. The topics, although taken from the OT, e.g., Abraham and Isaac, Moses, the Exodus, Ezechiel's Vision of the Dry Bones, Job, show a mixture of detail from rabbinic tradition. Various attempts have been made to suggest a common theme for all these paintings. The Dura synagogue obviously represents a sharp departure from the usual Jewish prohibition of pictorial art. The Talmud, however, contains a reference to a Rabbi Jochanan who allowed wall paintings, and floor mosaics are frequent in the ancient synagogues of Palestine.

Bibliography: M. I. ROSTOVTZEFF, *Dura-Europos and Its Art* (Oxford 1938). R. B. WISCHNITZER, *The Messianic Theme in the Paintings of the Dura Synagogue* (Chicago 1948). J. A. FISCHER, ''The Synagogue Paintings of Dura-Europos,'' *The Catholic Biblical Quarterly* 17 (1955) 189–195. YALE UNIVERSITY, *The Excavations at Dura-Europos: Final Reports, 4–5–6–8* (New Haven, Conn. 1943–59). A. L. PERKINS, *The Art of Dura-Europos* (Oxford 1973). C. HOPKINS and B. GOLDMAN, *The Discovery of Dura-Europos* (New Haven, Conn. 1979). A. R. BELLINGER, *The Excavations at Dura-Europos* (New York 1979). S. B. MATHESON, *Dura-Europos, the Ancient City and the Yale Collection* (New Haven, Conn. 1982). K. WEITZMANN and H. L. KESSLER, *The Frescoes of the Dura Synagogue and Christian Art* (Washington, D.C. 1990). J. GUTMANN, *The Dura-Europos Synagogue: A Re-evaluation (1932–1992)* (Atlanta, Ga. 1992).

[J. A. FISCHER/EDS.]

DURÁN, DIEGO

Dominican chronicler; b. Seville, Spain, 1537; d. Mexico, 1588. Little is known about Durán's life. He went to New Spain as a child and lived in Texcoco, where he learned Nahuatl. In May 1556 he entered the Order of Preachers in the monastery of St. Dominic, Mexico City. After serving some time in the Province of Oaxaca, he apparently returned to the Mexico City area. His chronicle was begun by 1574 and completed by 1581. Durán's title for the chronicle is not extant, but on the atlas is an inscription by a copyist: ''Historia de las Indias de N. i islas y tierra firme.'' Even that was corrupted in a 19th-century publication to *Historia de la Nueva España i Islas de Tierra Firme.*

The *Historia de las Indias* is divided into three treatises: on the Mexican calendar (finished in 1579); on Mexican religious ideas and practices; and on the history of Mexico from its origins through the conquest. Although it was not printed in the 16th century, the *Historia* was referred to by Juan de Tovar in a letter (*c.* 1586–88) to José de ACOSTA, and it was considered an excellent work by Agustín DÁVILA Y PADILLA. These fellow chroniclers were among the few who saw the MS before it was discovered in the National Library of Madrid in the 19th century. By 1880 most of the work had been published, but a complete critical edition still remains to be done. Durán based his history on pre-Hispanic pictographic MSS, particularly *Crónica X.* It bears great similarity to the works of Acosta and Tovar and is complementary to SAHAGÚN's *Historia general.* Durán had a more immediate knowledge of indigenous culture than most chroniclers, because of his childhood in Texcoco as well as his missionary work. He also had great sympathy for that culture and did not wish to destroy it. He did wish to Christianize it, and this, he said, was the reason for writing the history. He felt it imperative for the missionaries to understand the native religion if they were ever to be successful with evangelization.

Bibliography: D. DURÁN, *The Aztecs: The History of the Indies of New Spain,* tr. D. HEYDEN and F. HORCASITAS (New York 1964); *Historia de las Indias de Nueva-España y islas de tierra firme,* ed. J. FERNÁNDEZ RAMÍREZ, 2 v. and app. (Mexico City 1867–80).

[J. HERRICK]

DURAN, PROFIAT (EPHODI)

Jewish controversialist, exegete, and grammarian; b. *c.* 1350, in southern France or Spain; d. *c.* 1415, probably in the East. The Duran family, of which he was the most famous member, came, it seems, originally from Provence. His full Jewish name was Isaac ben Moses ha-Levi. The original spelling of the name Profiat was Profeit or Profet (i.e., prophet). As an anti-Christian writer he used the pseudonym Ephodi, from the initials of the Hebrew phrase, *'ănî prōpēt dûrān* (I am Profiat Duran).

Most of the first half of his life was spent in Catalonia, where he served for a while as tutor in the house of his friend, Hasdai CRESCAS. Here he witnessed the great Spanish persecution of the Jews in 1391, when many of them sought Baptism for the sake of remaining in Spain. But most of these Jews became Catholics merely in appearance, while they continued to practice their old religion in secret. Duran was one of these MARRANOS, as such Jews were called by the populace in contempt of their motive for professing Christianity. (The Spanish INQUISITION, begun in 1480, was aimed at these pseudoconverts from Judaism and Islam.)

Soon after his Baptism, however, Duran succeeded in leaving for Palestine, where he returned to the religion of his forefathers, and it is to this event that his most famous writing is related. In 1396 he wrote a letter known from its first words as *'al tehî ka'ăbôtèkā* (Be Not Like Thy Fathers). It was addressed to his friend, David Bonet Bongiorno, another new ''convert'' from Judaism who also had decided to flee to Palestine to escape persecution. The letter written after David, convinced by the eloquent Jewish convert, Paul of Burgos, that he should remain in the Catholic Church, informed Duran by letter of the reversal of his earlier decision. Duran's answer was a masterpiece of satire directed against the Jewish converts. So clever and biting was it that its true nature was at first not recognized by Christians, who published it, under the title *Alteca Boteca,* as a genuine defense of Christianity. The letter was first printed at Constantinople in 1554.

Of greater scientific value is Duran's *Maʿăśēh ʾēpōd* (*The Fashioning of the Ephod*), a Hebrew grammar, finished in 1403. This work, with its lexigraphical introduction, endeavored to base Hebrew grammar on philosophical linguistics, rather than on empirical examination of the language. Other writings of Duran include a minor astronomical work on the calendar, a commentary on the *Môrēh Nᵉbûkîm* (*Guide to the Perplexed*) of MAIMONIDES (Moses ben Maimon), and commentaries on several books of the Bible.

Bibliography: B. SULER, *Encyclopedia Judaica: Das Judentum in Geschichte und Gegenwart* (Berline 1928–34) 6:123–128. M. KAYSERLING, *The Jewish Encyclopedia,* ed. J. SINGER (New York 1901–06) 5:16. H. H. GRAETZ, *History of the Jews,* ed. B. LÖWY (Philadelphia 1891–98) 4:188–190. S. GRONEMANN, *De Profiatii Duranii (Efodaci)* (Breslau 1869). P. DURAN, *Maʾaseh Efod,* ed. J. FRIEDLÄNDER and J. KOHN (Vienna 1865), introduction 2–12.

[A. BRUNOT]

DURANDUS OF AURILLAC

French Dominican theologian; fl. 1330 to 1334. Born in the Diocese of Saint-Flour in the province of Auvergne, he joined the order at Clermont. The general chapter of the order held at Utrecht in 1330 assigned him on May 27 to lecture on the *Sentences* that very year at the University of Paris. He attended the meeting of masters in theology, held in the presence of Philip VI on Dec. 20, 1332, to discuss the heatedly debated question "whether the souls of the blessed possess the beatific vision before the day of the last judgment." This was occasioned by the personal opinion of JOHN XXII that they did not. Durandus signed a joint statement of the theologians opposing the pope's view on Jan. 2, 1333. He is credited with having written *Scripta in 4 libros sententiarum* and two *quodlibets,* but these have not yet been discovered. Therefore his significance as a theologian and Thomist cannot be determined. The dates commonly given for his death, 1380 and 1382, are not impossible but rather improbable. Quétif-Échard (1:587–588) and many others have identified this Durandus with a certain Durandellus, author of *Evidentiae contra Durandum,* a defense of Thomistic teaching against the views of DURANDUS OF SAINT-POURÇAIN. Since this work was composed *c.* 1330, Durandellus could conceivably be identified with the young Durandus of Aurillac. However, J. Koch has presented a strong case against this identification in favor of Nicholas of Saint-Victor, a disciple of JOHN OF NAPLES.

Bibliography: J. KOCH, "Durandus de S. Porciano, OP," *Beiträge zur Geschichte des Philosophie und Theologie des Mittelalters* 26 (1927) 240–369. A. BACCI, *Ex primordiis scholae thomisticae* (Rome 1928) 51–72. B. DECKER, *Lexikon für Theologie und Kirche,* ed. J. HOFER and K. RAHNER (2d, new ed. Freiburg 1957–65) 3:610. J. QUÉTIF and J. ÉCHARD, *Scriptores Ordinis Praedicatorum,* 5 v. (Paris 1719–23) 2:819–820. G. MOLLAT, *Dictionnaire d'histoire et de géographie ecclésiastiques,* ed. A. BAUDRILLART et al. (Paris 1912–) 14:1156. *Histoire littéraire de la France,* ed. Académie des Inscriptions et Belles-Lettres (1814–1941) 36 (1938) 515–517.

[J. J. PRZEZDZIECKI]

DURANDUS OF SAINT-POURÇAIN

Dominican bishop and scholastic theologian; b. Saint-Pourçain-sur-Sioule, Auvergne, France, *c.* 1275; d. Meaux, France, Sept. 10, 1334.

Life. At the age of 19 he entered the Dominican Order at Clermont for the province of France. By 1303 he was assigned to Saint-Jacques, Paris to study theology at the university. The first version of his commentary on the *Sentences* of PETER LOMBARD was written when he was a bachelor (1307–08), possibly under the influence of JAMES OF METZ. In these lectures he strongly opposed certain views of THOMAS AQUINAS, whom the Dominican Order had in 1286 commanded its members to study, promote, and defend. In 1309 the general chapter of the order insisted more strongly that all lectors, assistants, and students adhere faithfully to Thomistic teaching. At Paris the views of Durandus were immediately attacked by HARVEY NEDELLEC and PETER OF LA PALU. Consequently between 1310 and 1313 Durandus revised his commentary, mitigating many previous statements and omitting the most offensive passages; this was neither satisfactory to the order nor in accord with his own convictions. Nevertheless in 1312 he obtained permission to incept in theology as master, succeeding Yves of Caen (fl. 1303–14). Before completing his first year of teaching, 1312–13, he was called to Avignon by CLEMENT V to lecture in the papal Curia, succeeding WILLIAM OF PETER OF GODIN, who was created cardinal. Toward the end of 1313 the Dominican Master General, Berengar of Landorra (*c.* 1262–1330), appointed a theological commission headed by Harvey Nedellec to examine the writings of Durandus. Out of 93 questionable propositions extracted from the first and second redactions of Durandus's commentary on the *Sentences,* 91 were censured by the commission. Writing from Avignon in 1314, Durandus replied in his *Excusationes.* Between 1314 and 1317 he was continuously attacked in Paris by Harvey Nedellec. JOHN OF NAPLES, James of Lausanne (fl. 1303–22), Guy Terreni (*c.* 1260–1342), and Gerard of Bologna (d. 1317). Durandus replied to these attacks in three series of disputations *De quolibet [Quodlibet avenionensia tria* (ed. P. T. Stella,

Rome 1965)], held at Avignon, inveighing against "certain idiots" who charge him with Pelagianism (*See* PELAGIUS AND PELAGIANISM).

On Aug. 26, 1317, Durandus was appointed first bishop of Limoux, formerly a part of the Archdiocese of Narbonne; this diocese was suppressed on Feb. 13, 1318, when Durandus was named bishop of Le Puy en Velay, a diocese under the immediate jurisdiction of the pope. When Durandus attempted to enforce certain disciplinary decrees on the cathedral canons, whom he eventually excommunicated, he exceeded his jurisdiction. JOHN XXII then appointed him bishop of Meaux.

Although he was appointed to a commission of six theologians to examine 56 propositions taken from the commentary on the *Sentences* by WILLIAM OF OCKHAM, Durandus's name is absent from the final document censuring 51 of these propositions. Earlier historians saw in this absence proof of sympathy for Ockham and a refusal to participate in the condemnation. J. Koch, however, has given a simpler explanation: Durandus had left for Meaux before the process was completed.

Between 1317 and 1327 Durandus, free from jurisdiction of the Dominican Order, prepared a third and final version of his commentary of the *Sentences*. In the conclusion (Venice 1571, fol. 423r) he expressed regret that the first version had been circulated outside the order against his wishes, "before it had been sufficiently corrected" by him. He added that only this new version was to be recognized as edited and approved by him. Nevertheless, although he came closer in parts of this version to the "common teaching" of the schools, much was taken verbatim from the first draft and from the first Avignon *Quodlibet*. The final version, completed in 1327, abounded in compromises and contradictions.

In the jurisdictional dispute between John XXII and Philip VI of France, Durandus sided with the pope. For the parley at Vincennes between the two factions (1328) he composed a treatise of three questions, *De origine potestatum et jurisdictionum quibus populus regitur*. It was used extensively by the pope's spokesman for the occasion, Peter Bertrandi, Bishop of Autun, who published it with an additional question as his own composition after the death of Durandus.

Consulted by John XXII concerning the beatific vision for the just prior to the Last Judgment, Durandus composed his reply in 1333, *De visione Dei quam habent animae sanctorum ante judicium generale*. Displeased with the reply, John promptly submitted it to a theological commission, which found 11 objectionable statements (ChartUnParis 2:418). Although John retracted his private opinion on his deathbed and BENEDICT XII vindi-

cated Durandus in two treatises explicitly relating to him, Durandus did not live to see the vindication. He was buried in his cathedral church of St. Martin of Tours, his tomb being marked only with three bells on a Gothic shield.

Characteristic Teaching. In general Durandus was an orthodox theologian, although he was far from being a Thomist. In philosophical questions he manifested an independence of spirit more influenced by AUGUSTINE and BONAVENTURE than by ARISTOTLE and Aquinas. He has often been called a nominalist and precursor of Ockham, but the similarities are only incidental. At least there was no direct influence of one on the other.

Besides denying the real distinction between essence and existence in creatures, as did also Harvey Nedellec, Durandus rejected the reality of mental species and any real distinction between agent and possible intellect (*see* ESSENCE AND EXISTENCE; INTELLECT). For Durandus, the mind is essentially active and necessarily related to things as they physically exist without the mediation of impressed or expressed species (*see* SPECIES, INTENTIONAL). For him only individuals exist, receiving their individuality not from matter, but from the efficient cause exclusively (*see* INDIVIDUATION). Since the human intellect directly perceives individual realities, the apparent universality of ideas is a deceptive fabrication. Striving to avoid IDEALISM and exaggerated REALISM, he emphasized the direct perception of individual existents (*see* UNIVERSALS).

Durandus insisted, as did many of his contemporaries, that theology could not be a true science (*scientia*) in the strict sense of the term, for this would detract from the merit of FAITH, which adheres to revealed truths even though their contradictories cannot be proved false. In discussing the question of FREE WILL and GRACE, Durandus refused to acknowledge the universal causality of God's efficacious grace in human actions: God "is the cause of free actions only insofar as He creates and conserves free will" (*In two sent.* 37.1). The SACRAMENTS, according to Durandus, produce grace only as occasions and not as instrumental efficient causes; nor do they produce any real or permanent quality in the soul (*In four sent.* 4.5). He considered it probable that MATRIMONY is not a Sacrament in the true sense of the word, but only an institution of NATURAL LAW (*In four sent.* 26.3). Concerning the EUCHARIST he believed that by God's absolute power (*potentia absoluta*) Christ could be present in the Eucharist together with the substance of bread and wine (*In four sent.* 11.1; *see* TRANSUBSTANTIATION).

Influence. The prestige of Durandus was considerable in the later Middle Ages. In the 15th and 16th centuries theologians continued to read him and quote him, favorably and unfavorably. Many later Thomists, notably John CAPREOLUS, attacked the doctrines of Durandus vigorously. However, many editions of his commentary on the *Sentences* (3d version) were printed, beginning with the Paris edition of 1508. At some universities, Salamanca for example, "the chair of Durandus" rivaled that of St. Thomas and that of DUNS SCOTUS. His was the chair of NOMINALISM. At some late date an unknown quipster penned an epitaph for Durandus's tomb: "Here lies the hard Durandus beneath this hard slab. Should he be burned? I don't know nor do I care." Some historians believe that Durandus influenced Gabriel BIEL, Martin LUTHER, and later Reformers.

Bibliography: J. QUÉTIF and J. ÉCHARD, *Scriptores Ordinis Praedicatorum* (New York 1959) 1.2:586–587. J. KOCH, *Durandus de S. Porciano, O.P. (Beiträge zur Geschichte der Philosophie und Theologie des Mittelalters* 26.1; 1927); "Jakob von Metz, O.P., der Lehrer des Durandus de S. Porciano, O.P.,"*Archives d'histoire doctrinale et littéraire du moyen-âge* 4 (1929–30) 169–233. P. FOURNIER, "Durand de saint Pourçain," *Histoire littéraire de la France* 37 (1938) 1–38. P. GLORIEUX, *Répetoire des maîitres en théologie de Paris au XIIIᵉ siècle* (Paris 1933–34) 1:214–220; *La Litterature quodlibétique* (Paris 1935) 2:70–75. É. H. GILSON, *History of Christian Philosophy in the Middle Ages* Copleston 3. J. MÜLLER, "Quaestionen der ersten Redaktion von I und II Sent. des Durandus de S. Porciano in einer Hs. der Biblioteca Antoniana in Padua," *Divus Thomas* 19 (1941) 435–440. E. BETTONI, *Enciclopedia filosofica* 1:1767–68. B. DECKER, *Lexikon für Theologie und Kirche* (Freiburg 1957–65) 3:612. F. STEGMÜLLER, *Repertorium commentariorum in Sententias Petri Lombardi* (Würzburg 1947) 1:192–198. H. A. OBERMAN, *The Harvest of Medieval Theology: Gabriel Biel and Late Medieval Nominalism* (Cambridge, Mass. 1963).

[J. A. WEISHEIPL]

DURANDUS OF TROARN

Benedictine abbot; b. Neubourg, in Normandy, between 1005 and 1020; d. Troarn, near Caen, France, Feb. 11, 1088 or 1089. He was probably a monk at FONTENELLE (Saint-Wandrille) under his uncle, Abbot Gerard, and later studied at Sainte-Catherine-du-Mont at Rouen and at FÉCAMP. He is best remembered for his treatise *De corpore et sanguine Christi* (*Patrologia Latina*, ed. J. P. Migne, 149:1375–1424), written shortly before WILLIAM I (the Conqueror) made him abbot of the new foundation of Saint-Martin, TROARN, in 1059. This work, strongly influenced by PASCHASIUS RADBERTUS (d. 859) and primarily intended for the edification of souls, is one of the earliest replies to the Eucharistic teaching of BERENGARIUS, with whom the last of the nine sections is wholly concerned. Through the analysis of scriptural and patristic texts, many newly selected, Durandus propounded the Ambrosian doctrine of the conversion of the bread and wine into the identical Body and Blood of Christ and at-

tempted to explain away, with an argument already used by Guitmond, the Augustinian *praesentia spiritualis.* Only parts of his later Eucharistic poem of 800 verses survive.

Bibliography: J. MABILLON, *Annales ordinis S. Benedicti,* 6 v. (2d ed. Lucca 1739–45) 5:97. R. F. N. SAUVAGE, *L'Abbaye de Saint-Martin de Troarn au diocèse de Bayeux* (Caen 191). R. HEURTEVENT, *Durand de Troarn et les origines de l'hérésie bérengarienne* (Paris 1912). A. WILMART, "Distiques d'Hincmar sur l'eucharistie? Un Sermon oublié de S. Augustin sur le même sujet," *Revue Bénédictine* 40 (1928) 87–98. G. PORAS, *Dictionnaire d'histoire et de géographie ecclésiastiques,* ed. A. BAUDRILLART et al. (Paris 1912–) 14:1159–60.

[W. E. WILKIE]

DURANTI, WILLIAM THE ELDER

One of the most influential canonists of the Middle Ages, renowned liturgist, experienced judge and administrator, bishop of Mende; b. Puymisson, in Languedoc, between 1230 and 1237; d. Rome, Nov. 1, 1296. He obtained his doctorate in Bologna, taught briefly there and in Modena, and went to Rome soon after 1260. At first in the Service of Cardinal HOSTIENSIS, he was commissioned, probably under Pope Clement IV (1265–68) as one of the *auditores causarum sacri palatii,* the college of judges from which the tribunal of the Roman Rota later developed. In 1274 he helped in drafting the conciliar legislation of Pope Gregory X promulgated in the Second Council of Lyons. From 1278 on he held various high posts, including the governorship (1283), in the administration of Bologna and the Romagna, territories then newly acquired by the Papal States. Although elected bishop of Mende in 1285 and consecrated in 1286, he took possession of his see only in 1291. There he published instructions and constitutions for his clergy and revised the *Pontificale Romanum* (this revision became the model for the official Roman text of 1485). After declining the archbishopric of Ravenna offered to him by Boniface VIII in 1295, he served the Curia once more as provincial governor in the Papal States until his death.

To the lawyers of the later Middle Ages, Duranti was simply "the Speculator"—the author of the *Speculum iudiciale.* Into this comprehensive treatise on court procedure, first published between 1271 and 1276 (revised *c.* 1289), the author poured his encyclopedic learning on canon and civil law in general, and all the wealth of his judicial and administrative experience; each section is further illustrated with model forms. Enlarged in the 14th century by the *Additiones* of Joannes Andreae and Baldus, the book remained authoritative for centuries in the practice of ecclesiastical and civil courts; it was printed at least 50 times between 1473 and 1678. Duranti wrote also a *Speculum legatorum* (later incorporated in the revised version of his great work), a widely used *Repertorium sive Breviarium* of Canon Law and, after 1282, a very instructive commentary on the statutes of the Second Council of Lyons (ed. Simon Maioli, Fano 1569). His glosses on Gratian, on the decretals, and on a constitution of Pope Nicholas III seem to be lost. The *Rationale divinorum officiorum,* written between 1285 and 1291, was an original and lasting contribution to liturgy. It became a standard treatise on liturgical symbolism; it exists in 44 incunabula (first, 1459) and in many later editions.

Bibliography: W. DURANTI, *Le Pontifical de Guillaume Durand,* v.3 of *Le Pontifical romain au moyen-âge,* ed. M. ANDRIEU, 4 v. (*Studi et Testi* 86–88, 90; 1938–41); "Les Instructions et constitutions de Guillaume Durand . . . ," ed. J. BERTEHLÉ and M. VALMARY in *Mémoires de l'Academie des sciences et lettres de Montpellier,* 2d series, 3 (1900) 1–148, also pub. sep. Parts of the *Rationale* exist in tr., *The Symbolism of Churches and Church Ornaments,* ed. and tr. J. M. NEALE and B. WEBB (3d ed. London 1906); *Sacred Vestments,* ed. and tr. T. H. PASSMORE (London 1899). *Gesamtkatalog der Wiegendrucke* 7 (1938) 9101–62. J. F. VON SCHULTE, *Die Geschichte der Quellen und der Literatur des kanonischen Rechts* (Stuttgart 1875–80; repr. Graz 1956) 2:144–156. L. FALLETTI, *Dictionnaire de droit canonique,* ed. R. NAZ (Paris 1935–65) 5:1014–75.

[S. KUTTNER]

DURANTI, WILLIAM THE YOUNGER

Nephew of William Duranti, the Elder; b. Puymisson, France; d. Nicosia, Cyprus, July 1330. He was appointed bishop of Mende by BONIFACE VIII, Dec. 17, 1296. In 1305 CLEMENT V entrusted him, together with the abbot of Lombez, with the task of reporting on conditions in Italy. In 1307, at the pope's request, he likewise conducted an inquiry into the canonization cause of THOMAS OF CANTELUPE, Bishop of Hereford; in August 1308 he was a member of the commission investigating the TEMPLARS. The commission began operations Aug. 8, 1309, and completed its work June 5, 1311. At the Council of VIENNE, Duranti composed a lengthy memorandum criticizing abuses in the Church, especially the centralization of power in the papal court, to the detriment of the episcopate. According to the testimony of JOHN XXII, these criticisms were on the point of provoking a schism [A. Coulon, *Lettres secrètes et curiales de Jean XXII* (Paris 1900)]. The restriction placed on the right of episcopal election by cathedral chapter, promulgated by the constitution *Ex debito* (Sept. 15, 1316), brought a reaction from Duranti. His proposals at the Papal Curia occasioned the opening of an abortive investigation against him, but apparently his advisory position at the French court saved him. In March 1318, the pope granted benefices to Duranti's relatives, including his

brothers Bernard, William, and Pons [G. Mollat, *Lettres communes de Jean XXII* (Paris 1905) v.2, n. 6523–36, 6552, 6613, 6615]. In 1329 John XXII and Philip VI entrusted him and Peter of Palu, Patriarch of Jerusalem, with the delicate mission of organizing a crusade.

Bibliography: W. DURANTI, *Tractatus de modo concilii generalis celebrandi et corruptelis in Ecclesia reformandis* (Lyons 1531, 1534; Paris 1545, 1671), analyzed by P. VIOLLET, *Histoire littéraire de la France* (Paris), ed. Académie des Inscriptions et Belles-Lettres (1814–1941) 35:79–129; *Directorium chori,* in Bibl. de Mende, MS 2; Memoir on the Crusade (1330) in Paris, BN lat. 7470, fols. 117–123; *Acta Sanctorum* Oct. 1 (1765) 587–596; *Instructions et constitutions de Guillaume Durand, le Spéculateur,* ed. BERTHELÉ and VALMARY (Archives du département de l'Hérault. Documents et inventaire complémentaires 5.1; Montpellier 1900), additions to the work of his uncle, dating back to 1309; Report on the mission conducted in Italy in 1305–06, partially ed. R. DAVIDSOHN, *Forschungen zur älteren Geschichte von Florenz,* 4 v. (Berlin 1896–1908) 3:287–321. E. GÖLLER, "Zur Geschichte der italienischen Legation Durantis des Jüngeren von Mende," *Römische Quartalschrift für christliche Altertumskunde und für Kirchengeschichte* 19 (1905) 15–24. E. MÜLLER, *Das Konzil von Vienne* (Münster 1934), contains several errors.

[G. MOLLAT]

DURBIN, ELISHA JOHN

Missionary; b. near Boonesboro, Madison County, Ky., Feb. 1, 1800; d. Shelbyville, Ky., March 22, 1887. He was the son of John D. and Patience (Logsdon) Durbin. In 1816 he entered St. Thomas Seminary, Bardstown, Ky.; he was ordained Sept. 21, 1822, and then served at St. Joseph College and the cathedral parish, Bardstown. In 1824 he was given charge of the entire western and southwestern part of KENTUCKY, an area of more than 10,000 square miles, or about one-third of the state. From headquarters at Morganfield, Ky., he also served the Catholics on the Indiana and Illinois borders and after 1832 those of Nashville, Tenn. In 1873 he was finally relieved of the vast pastorate of Union County and placed at Princeton, Ky., to minister to the people living along the railroad. Later he moved to Bardstown and then was given the chaplaincy of the Franciscan sisters at Shelbyville, where he died. In 60 years of missionary life Durbin rode more than 500,000 miles on horseback and earned the titles "Patriarch-Priest of Kentucky" and "Apostle of Western Kentucky." He was buried in St. Louis cemetery, Louisville.

Bibliography: B. J. WEBB, *The Centenary of Catholicity in Kentucky* (Louisville 1884).

[J. H. SCHAUINGER]

DURHAM, ANCIENT SEE OF

The Ancient See of Durham was a northern English diocese (Lat. *Dunelmensis*) founded in 995 when Bishop Ealdhun, whose diocesan seat had been at Chester-le-Street, transferred the body of the venerated Northumbrian St. CUTHBERT from his cathedral there to nearby Durham city. The area had originally formed part of the See of Lindisfarne (established 635), but after the sack of the Abbey of LINDISFARNE (793) and further attacks by Danish invaders, the monks had removed the shrine of Cuthbert, and hence the diocesan seat, to Chester-le-Street (883). The newly founded See of Durham withstood Scottish attacks but yielded to the Normans under WILLIAM I (the Conqueror), whose appointment of Bishop Walcher (1071) initiated a series of important reforms, culminating in the replacement of the cathedral's chapter of secular canons by BENEDICTINES under his successor (1083). This made for a more stable diocesan organization and encouraged an enduring literary and artistic renaissance. The revival, however, carried for its bishops, who were made counts palatine, the added responsibility of the diocese's civil jurisdiction. Being in border territory, the bishops and the palatinate were often involved in conflict with either the Scottish or the English crown.

The present impressive cathedral at Durham was begun by Bishop William of St. Carilef in 1093 and was considerably enlarged by his successors, a number of whom, such as Hugh du Puiset (1153–95), Anthony BEK (1284–1311), RICHARD OF BURY (1333–45), and Thomas Hatfield (1345–81), were outstanding as administrators, statesmen, or men of letters. Though a stronghold of Benedictine monasticism, with its own liturgical rite, the diocese was also well supplied with houses of most of the other religious and mendicant orders, besides hospitals and collegiate churches. The see was reformed under Elizabeth in 1559, the first Anglican bishop being James Pilkington.

Bibliography: *Symeonis Monachi opera omnia,* ed. T. ARNOLD, 2 v. (*Rerum Britannicarum medii aevi scriptores,* 244 v. (London 1858–96; repr. New York 1964–), ordinarily called Rolls Series, 1882–85). T. D. HARDY, ed., *Registrum Palatinum Dunelmense,* 4 v. (ibid. 62; 1873–78). D. S. BOUTFLOWER, ed., *Fasti Dunelmenses* (Surtees Society 139; Durham 1926). R. SURTEES, *The History and Antiquities of the County Palatine of Durham,* 4 v. (London 1816–40). *The Victoria History of the County of Durham,* ed. W. PAGE (London 1905–) v. 2, 3. W. A. PANTIN, *Durham Cathedral* (London 1948) C. J. STRANKS, *This Sumptuous Church: The Story of Durham Cathedral* (London 1973). R. W. J. AUSTIN, *A Guide to the Pre-Reformation Cathedral Church & Abbey of Durham,* (Durham 1986). D. C. D. POCOCK and R. BILLINGHAM, *St. Cuthbert and Durham Cathedral: A Celebration,* 2nd rev. ed. (Durham 1995). S. PEDLEY, *The Cathedral Church of Christ and Blessed Mary the Virgin in Durham* (Norwich 1997).

[L. MACFARLANE/EDS.]

DURKHEIM, ÉMILE

Sociologist and moral philosopher; b. Épinal (Vosges), Lorraine, April 13, 1858; d. Fontainebleau, France, Nov. 15, 1917.

Life. Of Jewish origin, with rabbinical forebears, Durkheim early broke with the Judaic faith and, though deeply interested in religion as an institution, remained the rest of his life an agnostic. Following a brilliant career in the secondary school of his native province, he went to Paris in 1879 to enter the *École Normale Supérieure* in a class that included Pierre Janet and others destined to win equal note as scholars and scientists. Among Durkheim's teachers were the philosopher Émile BOUTROUX and the historian Fustel de Coulanges, from both of whom Durkheim acquired lasting interests and insights. Despite (or perhaps because of) a notable originality of mind and work, Durkheim finished nearer to the bottom than at the top of his class.

Undaunted, he began immediately a career of scholarship that eventually won him the chair of sociology at the Sorbonne and the honor of wide regard as one of the two seminal thinkers (the other being the German Max WEBER) on the theoretical nature of contemporary sociology. Durkheim's impact on cultural ANTHROPOLOGY, largely through such men as A. R. Radcliffe-Brown and Bronislaw Malinowski, was almost equally great. Also, through his inspiring lectures at the Sorbonne, beginning in 1902, he became a major influence on some of France's leading jurists, historians, and classicists. He was a distinguished teacher, nowhere more tellingly than through the pages of the illustrious journal *L'Année sociologique,* which he founded in 1896 primarily as a medium for the ideas of his students and in which appeared, during its all too brief life, works by such men as Marcel Mauss, Georges Davy, Paul Fauconnet, and Maurice Halbwachs.

Durkheim's mind was one of fascinating paradox. Politically liberal (he was an active Dreyfusard), he nevertheless constructed his sociology around the conservative values of solidarity and consensus; religiously agnostic, he became the author of the most convincing demonstration of the indispensability of religion to society ever written by a social scientist; utterly dedicated to science and to ethical neutrality in the study of human phenomena, he nevertheless made the moral element primary in all of his studies; a pluralist in his view of authority and a cosmopolitan in culture, he became known in World War I (in which he lost a son and many lifelong friends) as an ardent French nationalist.

Contributions. The most fundamental contribution of Durkheim to modern social thought was his insistence on the primacy of society to the individual. By this, he did not mean ethical primacy, for he had a persisting sense of the dignity and value of the individual. What he meant and tirelessly demonstrated through his research was that explanations of human behavior must be made in social terms, that is, in terms of man's relationship to cultural values, institutions, and social groups rather than in terms of individual instincts or climatic and geographical factors, all of which were widely employed in Durkheim's age as posited causes of social behavior. Durkheim sometimes went too far in his stress on society, as in his concepts of the *conscience collective* and *representations collective,* in which even with the most generous interpretation the identity of discrete human beings becomes blurred. But in his empirical studies—e.g., of suicide, industrial disorder, kinship, personality, and religion—society is seen not as a monolith but as a perspective of understanding. More than any other single figure in modern social science, Durkheim was responsible for the abandonment of explanations of society that were strictly psychobiological and physical.

In his first major work, *The Division of Labor in Society* (1893), he advanced his notable distinction between "mechanical solidarity" and "organic solidarity," the first representing the kind of moral order ingrained in tradition, kinship, and community, and the second representing the more impersonal type of order resulting from division of labor and mutual interdependence of specializations. His conclusion was that society, however developed in type it may be, cannot dispense with the "mechanical" ties of tradition; that even in such rationalistic and individualistic activities as legal contract, it is the "noncontractual foundations" of tradition and social authority that alone give contract its efficacy.

In his second work, *The Rules of Sociological Method* (1895), he dealt methodologically with the ways by which the elements of tradition and constraint in society become fixed in human personality and thought. It was in this work that Durkheim explicitly advanced the logical concepts deriving from the claimed priority of society, and it was this work above all others that drew the fire of his critics, most notably that of a French contemporary and critic, Gabriel Tarde.

Next came Durkheim's momentous study *Suicide* (1896), in which he brought to bear on a specific, empirical problem the method and perspective previously dealt with in largely theoretical or ethnological terms. The problem was how to account for the variable incidence of suicide in human society. Others had given explanations in terms of instinct, climate, terrain, race, nationality, etc. Durkheim, working from the premise of society's constraining effect on the individual, was able to show that suicide varies inversely with the degree of social and moral constraint in a population. He distinguished three main types of suicide: (1) egoistic, in which social cohesion is weak; (2) anomic, in which moral integration breaks down; and (3) altruistic (rare in modern society), in which group solidarity is so intense that an offending individual feels impelled to take his life as self-punishment. Although this theory of suicide has been modified by later studies, its basic orientation remains unchallenged, and Durkheim's study is regarded as a classic not only for its explanation of suicide but for the theory of personality and the social order in which it is set.

Durkheim's final major work was *The Elementary Forms of Religious Life* (1912), in many ways his most remarkable achievement. Still proceeding from the premise of society's anteriority to the individual and using the religion of the Australian aborigines as his material, he sought to show that the most fundamental conceptions of religion are subtilizations of social experience. He held the sovereign and universal characteristic of religion to be the distinction made by men between the sacred and the profane, a distinction that arises in, and is enjoined by, society. To Durkheim, it was from the felt power of the community that primitive man derived gradually his sense of a deity and of the binding power of the sacred. Agnostic though he was, Durkheim held religion to be man's most fundamental experience and religion and society to be but two sides of the same coin. In society, sanctified by religion, he saw the source of all man's major institutions and ideas. He was led even to advance a theory of the mind in these terms. Taking the problem of the origin of the categories of thought (time, mass, space, etc.) that David Hume and Immanuel Kant had posed, Durkheim proposed a solution in terms of the impact of society—its authority, its rituals, its totemic divisions, etc.—on primitive man.

No modern sociologist has exceeded, and only two or three have equaled, Durkheim's masterful combination of theory and empirical investigation. Uniting all of his investigations and theoretical insights is his notable concept of function. The central task of the sociologist, Durkheim declared, is to determine what function is performed by any element in the social system of which it is a part, what needs it fulfills, and what social ends it serves. Durkheim's emphasis on function had much to do with the subsequent demise in sociology and ethnology of pretentious schemes of evolutionism and diffusionism in which social and cultural traits were dealt with as isolated, abstracted elements without relation to contexts.

See Also: RELIGION (IN PRIMITIVE CULTURE); SOCIETY.

Bibliography: H. R. ALPERT, *Émile Durkheim and His Sociology* (New York 1939; reissue 1961). K. H. WOLFF, ed., *Émile

Durkheim, 1858–1917 (Columbus, OH 1960). R. A. NISBET, *Émile Durkheim* (Englewood Cliffs, NJ 1965).

[R. A. NISBET]

DUROCHER, MARIE ROSE, BL.

Foundress of the Congregation of the Sisters of the Holy Names of Jesus and Mary in Canada; b. St. Antoine, Quebec, Canada, Oct. 6, 1811; d. Longueuil, Quebec, Canada, Oct. 6, 1849.

The tenth of 11 children, Eulalie Mélanie Durocher was educated by the Sisters of the Congregation of Notre Dame at their convents in St. Denis and Montreal. From the age of 18, shortly after the death of her mother, she served as hostess, parish worker, nurse and homemaker in the Beloeil parish where her brother, Theophile, was pastor. For 13 years Durocher coordinated activities in the rectory, organized programs in religious education for children and young women of the parish, and cared for the poor and sick of the surrounding village. During the latter part of this period, with the assistance of the Oblates of Mary Immaculate who had recently arrived from France, Eulalie established the first Canadian parish Sodality.

In October 1843, at the request of Bishop Ignace Bourget, bishop of Montreal, Durocher, together with two companions, Mélodie Dufresne and Henriette Céré, founded the Congregation of the Sisters of the Holy Names of Jesus and Mary, at Longueuil. The purpose of the congregation, as stated in the 1850 *Chronicles*, was "to give religious education to the poorest and most abandoned children." The Oblates of Mary Immaculate helped the three women with the new foundation, offering spiritual guidance as well as financial and moral support. The new congregation adopted the habit and a modified form of the Constitutions of a Marseilles community of the same name, a group whom the Oblates had directed in France, and who were unable to send sisters to Canada to begin a new foundation. The Marseilles community later ceased to exist due to political upheaval in France. On Dec. 8, 1844, during the pontificate of GREGORY XVI, the Canadian congregation was canonically established, with Eulalie (Sister Marie Rose) as its first superior.

A woman of deep faith, practical wisdom and singleness of purpose, Sister Marie Rose overcame many obstacles to commit her congregation to its work with the poor and illiterate. Poor living conditions, misunderstanding from an Oblate pastor who had been a main source of support, and false reports about the congregation spread by a discontented priest of the diocese were the greatest challenges during these early years. Undaunted, Sister Marie Rose particularly addressed the needs of young women, whose religious education as well as overall education was sorely neglected in Quebec at this time. Using the congregation's limited resources to provide them with the best quality of education available, she even sent some sisters away for professional training to insure their thorough preparation for teaching. Through her numerous letters and frequent visits, Sister Marie Rose fostered a sense of unity among the sisters which enabled them to stay focused on their mission despite the hardships they endured.

When Sister Marie Rose died at 38 years of age, six years after its foundation, the community had 30 sisters teaching 384 students in four schools. In 1859 the first distant mission of the congregation was founded in Oregon. From 1931 on, the congregation spread beyond North America to Basutoland (Lesotho), Japan, Brazil, Peru, and Haiti. Sister Marie Rose was beatified by Pope John Paul II on May 23, 1982.

Feast: Oct. 6.

See Also: HOLY NAMES OF JESUS AND MARY, SISTERS OF THE.

Bibliography: "Sister Marie Rose Durocher," Archives, Sisters of the Holy Names of Jesus and Mary (Longueuil). F. ALLISON, *She Who Believed in Tomorrow* (Montreal 1981). J. BEAUDET. *Braise au coeur du pays* (Montreal 1982). C. MARIE, tr., *Beatificationis et Canonizationis Servae Dei Mariae Rosae Durocher*, 10 v., *Positio* (Vatican City 1975). P. DUCHAUSSOIS, *Rose of Canada* (Outremont 1934). G. DUVAL, *Par le chemin du roi: une femme est venue* (Montreal 1982). E. TERESA, *So Short a Day* (New York 1954). M. THERIAULT, "Foundress of the Sisters of the Holy Names of Jesus and Mary," *Vita Evangelica* (Ottawa 1975).

[P. A. PARACHINI]

DURROW, BOOK OF

In Trinity College, Dublin, a richly decorated vellum codex of the four Gospels, with Vulgate text and Old Latin Prefaces, written and decorated in the province of the Columban mission in Northumbria or Ireland, *c.* 675; 248 folios, 9½ by 6 inches in size. The Book of Durrow is the sole representative of a crucial phase in the development of Hiberno-Saxon art and the first manuscript to show the decorative structure characteristic of the later Insular Gospel books such as LINDISFARNE and KELLS. Pages devoted to symbols of the Evangelists and pages of pure ornament mark the opening of the codex and precede each Gospel. Beginnings of texts carry enlarged decorative initials or monograms. The ornamentation, expert and assured, is close to the Celtic and Saxon metalwork of the middle of the century. It includes interlace,

Celtic curvilinear designs, animal ornament, and rectilinear cellwork patterns; ornamental letters are outlined with red dots. The different groups of ornament are not yet intermixed as in the mature Hiberno-Saxon style and the script is not yet of the developed Insular ornamental majuscule form.

See Also: MANUSCRIPT ILLUMINATION.

Bibliography: *Codex Durmachensis,* ed. A. A. LUCE et al., 2 v. (New York 1960). S. F. H. ROBINSON, *Celtic Illuminative Art in the Gospel Books of Durrow, Lindisfarne and Kells* (Dublin 1908).

[R. L. S. BRUCE-MITFORD]

DUŠEK, JAN LADISLAV

Proto-Romanticist composer-virtuoso (also Dussek, Duschek, Dusík); b. Čáslav (Czaslau), Bohemia, Feb. 12, 1760; d. Saint-Germaine-en-Laye, France, March 20, 1812. As a child he studied piano and organ with his father, and later attended the Jesuit school in Jihlava (Iglau). After successful concert work in Amsterdam *c.* 1782, he appeared throughout Europe as piano and glass harmonica soloist and remained 11 years in London as virtuoso, teacher, composer, and publisher. From 1803 he was with Prince Ludwig Ferdinand of Prussia (himself a musician) until Ludwig's death in combat in 1806; from 1807 until his own death Dušek was in Talleyrand's service. He composed in the late classical vein for several instrumental combinations, but his piano works, which evolved side by side with the piano in its evolution from harpsichord and clavichord, are especially significant as anticipating severally the Romanticist styles of Schubert, Weber, Schumann, Liszt, Chopin, and Brahms. He was an "unacknowledged explorer" whose daring chromaticisms and modulations, long, singing phrases, and undulating accompaniments were absorbed into the characteristic expression of subsequent keyboard masters. Even his programmatic titles and descriptive directions (*con amore, sotto voce*) were prophetic.

Bibliography: Modern eds. of some of his works appear in *Musica antiqua Bohemica,* ed. J. RACEK, rev. A. NEMEC and J. PEKELSKY (Prague 1949–), v. 8, 22, 41, 46. H. TRUSCOTT, "D. and the Concerto," *Music Review* 16 (1955) 29–53. E. BLOM, "The Prophecies of D.," in *Classics: Major and Minor* (London 1958); *Grove's Dictionary of Music and Musicians,* ed. E. BLOM, 9 v. (5th ed. London 1954) 2:825–829. W. KAHL, *Die Musik in Geschichte und Gegenwart,* ed. F. BLUME (Kassel-Basel 1949–) 3:1007–10. H. A. CRAW, *A Biography and Thematic Catalog of the Works of J. L. Dussek (1760–1812)* (Ph.D. diss. University of Southern California 1964); "Dussek," in *The New Grove Dictionary of Music and Musicians,* ed. S. SADIE, v. 5 (New York 1980) 754–758. M. E. DOUTT, *The Concertos of Jan Ladislav Dussek (1760–1812)* (Ph.D. diss. University of Kentucky 1989). O. L. GROSSMAN, *The Solo Piano Sonatas of Jan Ladislav Dussek* (Ph.D. diss. Yale University 1975). D. M. RANDEL, ed., *The Harvard Biographical Dictionary of Music* (Cambridge, Mass. 1996) 233. N. SLONIMSKY, ed., *Baker's Biographical Dictionary of Musicians* (8th ed. New York 1992) 468.

[R. W. RICKS]

DUSMET, GIUSEPPE BENEDETTO, BL.

Cardinal, archbishop of Catania; b. Aug. 15, 1818, Palermo, Sicily, Italy; d. April 4, 1894, Catania, Sicily. Giuseppe, the son of the Marquis Luigi Dusmet and his noble wife Maria Dragonetti, was taught by the Benedictines of San Martino delle Scale at Badia from age five, then stayed to pronounce his vows (Aug. 10, 1840). He was ordained priest in 1842. After his election as prior in 1858, he reformed San Nicoló Abbey in Catania. He left the abbey in protest of government interference before it was closed like those of all religious orders. Although he was consecrated archbishop of Catania (March 10, 1861) and received the cardinal's red hat (1888), he remained a humble Benedictine monk at heart. Thereafter he was even more devoted to the poor, the suffering, and his order. During a cholera epidemic, he provided for those in need, and he ministered to victims of earthquake and epidemic in the streets. He played a large role in reforming the Roman Benedictine College of Sant'Anselmo and the Confederation of Benedictine Congregations. The cardinal's remains rest in Catania's cathedral. His cause was introduced by Archbishop Carmelo Patanè (Jan. 7, 1931), and he was declared venerable by Pope Paul VI (July 15, 1965) and beatified by John Paul II, Sept. 25, 1988. Dusmet is the patron of evangelical charity.

Bibliography: A Benedictine of Stanbrook Abbey, *A Sicilian Borromeo, the Servant of God, Joseph Benedict Dusmet, Archbishop of Catania and Cardinal of the Holy Roman Church* (London 1938). *Acta Apostolicae Sedis* (1988): 1092.

[K. I. RABENSTEIN]

DUTTON, JOSEPH BROTHER

Soldier, lay missionary; b. Stowe, Vt., April 27, 1843; d. Honolulu, Hawaii, March 26, 1931. He served as a lieutenant in the Union Army in the Civil War and worked for the War Department for some time afterward. His wife was faithless during their year of marriage and finally deserted him. For a time Dutton was inconsolable and sank into habitual dissipation. Subsequently he became a Catholic (1883) and, after spending two years as an oblate at the Trappist monastery of Our Lady of Gethsemani in Kentucky, he learned in 1886 of the work of Father Joseph DAMIEN in the leper settlement of Kalaupapa, Molokai Island, Hawaii. Deciding to do penance by helping with this work, he offered his services to the vicar apostolic of Hawaii and was accepted. From that time until his final illness in 1930, he never left the settlement. He worked closely with Damien up to Damien's death in 1888, and independently thereafter, nursing the lepers, improving their living conditions, and directing the Baldwin Home for leper boys. Dutton was honored by the U.S. Navy when the Atlantic Fleet in 1908 and the U.S. Battle Fleet in 1925 sailed in review before Kalawao in tribute to him. He bequeathed all his possessions to the Kalaupapa lepers.

Bibliography: C. J. DUTTON, *The Samaritans of Molokai* (New York 1932). J. FARROW, *Damien the Leper* (New York 1937).

[R. E. CARSON]

DUVERGIER DE HAURANNE, JEAN

Abbé de Saint-Cyran, whose writings, friendship with Cornelius O. JANSEN, and influence on Antoine Arnauld and PORT-ROYAL contributed to the rise of JANSENISM; b. Bayonne, France, 1581; d. Paris, Oct. 11, 1643. Duvergier (known more generally as Saint-Cyran) studied theology at the Jesuit College in Louvain under Leonard LESSIUS and Cornelius LAPIDE. With his fellow student Cornelius Jansen he retired to his family estate near Bayonne to make a methodical study of Scripture and the Fathers, especially St. Augustine (1611–16). He was ordained a priest (1618), and later created abbé de Saint-Cyran (1620), but lived in Paris. He became an intimate friend of BÉRULLE, whose book *Les Grandeurs de Jésus* he defended against the Jesuit François Garasse (1626). He was thus closely associated with the beginnings of the French Oratory.

When Richard Smith (1568–1655) was appointed vicar apostolic for England, Saint-Cyran gained European fame under the name of Petrus Aurelius by defending Smith against the Jesuits Edward Knott (1582–1656) and John Floyd (1572–1649), thereby giving wide publicity to Bérulle's ideas on the priesthood and the superiority of the secular over the regular clergy (1632). He made more enemies by defending Agnès Arnauld's *Chapelet du Saint Sacrement* (1627) and by his great success as a spiritual director. His open stand against the policies of Cardinal RICHELIEU and the extremism of his theology, which demanded perfect contrition for valid reception of the Sacrament of Reconciliation (Richelieu advocated the sufficiency of attrition), led to his imprisonment at Vincennes (May 14, 1638). Public opinion regarded him as a martyr. In prison Saint-Cyran continued his spiritual direction by letters and the visits of his penitents, among whom were magistrates, ladies of rank, priests and the su-

periors of monasteries, and his fellow prisoner, the German General Enkevort. He was freed on Feb. 6, 1643, shortly after Richelieu's death.

Saint-Cyran had close links with the VISITATION NUNS and had helped to found their house in Poitiers. Among his published letters is one addressed to Jane Francis de CHANTAL. Better known are his links with Port-Royal and the Abbesses Angélique and Agnès Arnauld. Their nephew Antoine Lemaître was the first solitary to retire near the monastery under Saint-Cyran's influence (1637). Most important for the subsequent history of Jansenism is his spiritual guidance of their youngest brother, Antoine Arnauld, who visited him at Vincennes (1638). Saint-Cyran's letters to Arnauld prove that he encouraged him to write *De la fréquente Communion*. He saw its success in 1643 and the first attacks on its doctrine. No evidence connects him with Jansen in the composition of *AUGUSTINUS* (1640).

Saint-Cyran's importance lies not in his dogmatic theology, but in his spiritual doctrine, which is to be found mainly in short treatises, such as *Théologie familière* (1639), *Le Coeur nouveau* (1642), *Vie d'Abraham, De la Pénitence* (1962), and in his letters of direction, some 150 of which were published after his death (1645 and 1647), and almost as many of which remained unpublished until 1962. Like Bérulle he insists on the dignity of the priest and is the first to have compared a priest to the Virgin Mary, saying that he is superior to the angels because he "produces and forms" the Body of Christ in the Eucharist, hence the necessity of vocation.

The Abbé de Saint-Cyran has much in common with Francis de Sales, whose person and teaching he venerated, when he views charity as the essence of piety; salvation to be worked out in the world by means of special graces for each state of life; obedience to grace; and the importance of a spiritual director. He recommends in particular what he calls the "beggar's prayer," showing God our defects without words. The influence of Jansenism, however, appears in his insistence on the small number of the elect, predestination without regard to merit, deferment of absolution (though here he claimed to follow Charles BORROMEO), and for some of his penitents, a spiritual renewal (*renouvellement*) that involved abstention from Communion for some weeks or even months. His *Lettres chrétiennes et spirituelles* (1645) influenced both PASCAL's theology and, through John WESLEY's translation (1760), Methodist piety.

The contradictions in his teaching often can be ascribed to his concern for the individual soul. His deep spirituality is reflected in his motto, *suivre Dieu*.

Bibliography: J. DUVERGIER DE HAURANNE, *Oeuvres chrétiennes et spirituelles*, 4 v. in 12 (Lyon 1679). J. ORCIBAL, *Saint-*

Antonín Dvořák.

Cyran et le Jansénisme (Paris 1961); *Les Origines du Jansénisme,* 5 v. (Louvain 1947–62); *Dictionnaire d'histoire et de géographie ecclésiastiques,* ed. A. BAUDRILLART, et al. (Paris 1912–) 14:1216–41. H. BRÉMOND, *Histoire littéraire du sentiment réligieux en France depuis la fin des guerres de religion jusqu'à nos jours* (Paris 1911–36) 4:36–175. L LAPORTE, *La Doctrine de Port-Royal,* 2 v. in 4 (Paris 1923–51) v. 1. L. COGNET, *Les Origines de la spiritualité française au XVIIᵉ siècle* (Paris 1949). C. CONSTANTIN, *Dictionnaire de théologie catholique,* ed. A. VACANT et al. (Paris 1903–50) 4.2:1967–75, bibliog.

[A. BARNES]

DVOŘÁK, ANTONÍN

Czech composer; b. Nelahozeves (Vltava), Sept. 8, 1841; d. Prague, May 1,1904. He studied the violin with his village schoolmaster, left home at 16 to enter the Prague organ school, supported himself as a violist and later organist at St. Adalbert's Church, and became professor of composition at Prague Conservatory. He frequently visited England to conduct his music, and from 1892 to 1895 he was artistic director of the National Conservatory in New York.

The popularity of his "American" works—the "New World" symphony, the "American" quartet, and the cello concerto—has overshadowed that of his other compositions. Since the 1950s increasing interest has been shown in his other symphonies, the piano quintet and string quartets, and his vocal music.

Dvořák's deep religious feeling is clearly shown in his sacred vocal works. His *Stabat Mater* (1876), the most popular of these, and his *Requiem* (1890), for soloists, chorus, and orchestra, are of oratorio dimensions; his *149th Psalm* and *Te Deum* are shorter. The oratorio *St. Ludmila* (1886) is uneven and often lapses into the "choir fodder" style of the Victorian oratorio. More noteworthy are his intimate Mass in D (1887) for soloists and chorus (originally with organ and low string accompaniment) and his *Biblical Songs* (1894) for voice and piano. The choral works contain most of the elements of Dvořák's style: folklike melodies, idiomatic vocal and instrumental writing, harmony that is rich without being cloying, and loose but coherent formal structure.

Bibliography: *Complete Works,* ed. O. ŠOUREK et al. (Prague 1955–); *Letters and Reminiscences,* ed. O. ŠOUREK, tr. R. F. SAMSOUR (Prague 1954). O. ŠOUREK, *Zivot a dílo Antonína Dvořáka,* 4 v. (1922–33); *Antonín Dvořák: His Life and Works* (New York 1954), abr. Eng. tr.; *Grove's Dictionary of Music and Musicians,* ed. E. BLOM, 9 v. (5th ed. London 1954) 2:831–845. A. ROBERTSON, *Dvořák* (London 1945). R. LONGYEAR, *The Larger Sacred Choral Works of Antonín Dvořák* (Master's diss. unpub. University of North Carolina 1954). G. CHASE, *America's Music* (New York 1955) 386–392. N. SLONIMSKY, ed., *Baker's Biographical Dictionary of Musicians* (5th ed. New York 1958) 415–416. M. BECKERMAN, ed. *Dvořák and His World* (Princeton, N.J. 1993). D. R. BEVERIDGE, "Dvořák's *Dumka* and the Concept of Nationalism in Music Historiography," *Journal of Musicological Research* 12 (1993) 303–325; ed. *Rethinking Dvořák: Views from Five Countries* (Oxford 1996). H. CROHN, "Antonín (Leopold) Dvořák," in *International Dictionary of Opera,* ed. C. S. LARUE, 2 v. (Detroit 1993) 370–373. M. IVANOV, *In Dvořák's Footsteps: Musical Journeys in the New World,* ed. L. KAREL, tr. S. SLAHOR (Kirksville, Mo. 1995). W. LANDOWSKA, "Thoughts on Modern Music: Tchaikovsky and Dvořák," in *Landowska on Music,* ed. and tr. D. RESTOUT, (New York 1964) 343–344. J. PARSONS, "*Rusalka,*" in *International Dictionary of Opera,* ed. C. S. LARUE, 2 v. (Detroit 1993) 1158–1160. J. C. TIBBETTS, *Dvořák in America* (Portland, Ore. 1993).

[R. M. LONGYEAR]

DWENGER, JOSESPH GERHARD

Second bishop of Fort Wayne, Ind.; b. Maria Stein, Ohio, Sept. 7, 1837; d. Fort Wayne, Jan. 22, 1893. His parents, Gerhard Henry and Maria Catherina (Wirdt) Dwenger, were immigrants from Ankum, Hanover, Prussia. Joseph lost his father at the age of three. His widowed mother moved to Cincinnati, Ohio, where Joseph attended Holy Trinity, the first German parochial school in the state. In 1849 his mother died of cholera, and young Joseph was cared for by the Society of the Precious Blood, which he entered five years later at Thompson, Ohio. He was sent to Mt. St. Mary's Seminary, Cincinnati, for the last two years of his preparation for the priesthood. By papal dispensation, he was ordained at 22 years of age on Sept. 4, 1859.

Dwenger's first assignment was the supervision of the society's seminary program, which had been under criticism by ecclesiastical authorities. He was instrumental in obtaining a site for St. Charles Seminary at Carthagena, Ohio, where he was rector until 1864. That year he was assigned the pastorates of Wapakoneta and St. Mary's, Ohio, with missions at Glynnwood and Celina. In 1866 he attended the Second Plenary Council of Baltimore as theologian to Abp. John B. Purcell and as representative of his society. He was occupied from 1868 to 1872 in giving missions in Ohio, Indiana, and Kentucky.

On April 14, 1872, Dwenger was consecrated by Purcell to succeed Bp. John H. Luers at Fort Wayne. He was not yet 35 years of age and was the youngest bishop in the U.S. For the next 20 years he labored to strengthen his young diocese. Having been orphaned himself, he took special interest in providing orphan asylums for boys in Lafayette, Ind., and for girls in Fort Wayne. He also developed a parochial school system, dividing the diocese into several school districts, and establishing a diocesan school board to conduct annual inspections in each parish. His system was adopted by the provincial synod of Cincinnati, and by the Third Plenary Council of Baltimore in 1884. This council selected him to present its decrees to the Holy Father for approval. He had previously gone to Rome and to Lourdes in 1874, as leader of the first national pilgrimage to these sites. During his last years, Dwenger's name was associated with the CAHENSLY controversy, and he was subjected to unfounded charges that were made against his patriotism.

Bibliography: H. J. ALERDING, *The Diocese of Fort Wayne, 1857-September 22, 1907* (Fort Wayne 1907). F. J. ZWIERLEIN, *Life and Letters of Bishop McQuaid* 3 v. (Rochester 1925–27) v. 2, 3.

[P. J. KNAPKE]

DWIGHT, TIMOTHY

Eminent Puritan divine and educator; b. Northampton, Mass., May 14, 1752; d. New Haven, Conn., Jan. 11, 1817. Jonathan EDWARDS was his maternal grandfather, to whom he owed much of his theology. He graduated from Yale at 17, and two years later was appointed tutor there. After excessive study almost ruined his eyesight and resulted in a serious illness, he resolved to enter the ministry (c. 1774). He served for about a year as chaplain in the Revolutionary Army (1777), but was forced to re-turn to Northampton to support his widowed mother and her ten children. In 1783 he accepted a call to become pastor of the Congregational Church at Greenfield Hill, Conn., where he soon became noted as an eloquent preacher, founder and head of a well-known academy, and knowledgeable gentleman farmer and poet. In 1795, when deism, skepticism, and even atheism had become widespread, Dwight was called to the presidency of Yale, where he preached a vigorous attack against "infidelity." The result was a revival of religion at Yale; in 1802 a third of the students professed conversion. By the time of his death, the Second GREAT AWAKENING was eloquent testimony to the success of his defense of evangelical Christianity. His works include the once-popular poems *The Conquest of Canaan* (1785), *The Triumph of Infidelity* (1788), and *Greenfield Hill* (1794); several hymns; and lectures published posthumously as *Theology, Explained and Defended,* (5 v. 1818–19). One of his sons, Sereno Edwards Dwight (1786–1850) edited the writings of Jonathan Edwards; a grandson, Timothy Dwight (1828–1916), was a Congregational clergyman and served as president of Yale (1886–98).

Bibliography: C. E. CUNNINGHAM, *Timothy Dwight 1752–1817* (New York 1942). H. E. STARR, *Dictionary of American Biography* 5:573–57.

[J. R. WILLIS]

DWIN

Dwin was an Armenian city south of modern Erivan and north of ancient Artaxata, of great importance from 428 to 894. Dwin, or Dvin, was built by King Chosroes II (331–339), who transferred his residence there from Artaxata for its purer air. In the 5th century the city was surrounded with a wall, and from 465 to 931 the Armenian patriarchs had a residence there. After the fall of the Arsacid dynasty, Dwin became the capital of Armenia, and both the Persian (marzban) and Arab (osdigan) governors resided there until the 10th century. Vardan Mamikonian (d. 451) built a church at Dwin in honor of Gregory the Illuminator with materials from the temple of Ormuzd; it was renovated in the 6th century. Catholicos Nerses III, called the Constructor, rebuilt the church of St. Sergius and erected a patriarchal residence that was eventually pillaged by the Arabs and destroyed in an earthquake. The 8th–century Arab ruler Abdul–Aziz, after sacking the city, enlarged its walls and rebuilt it. During the reign of the Bagratuni, Ani prospered and Dwin lost its political importance; it was destroyed by two earthquakes (862 and 894). What was left of the city was razed by the Tartars in the 10th century.

Dwin was the scene of several important synods. In 506 Catholicos Babgen I (502–510) condemned the teaching of Nestorius, and the heretics Acacius, Barsauma, and Babaï. In 554–555 Nerses II (548–557) officially repudiated the Council of CHALCEDON (451)], whose acts were interpreted in a Nestorian sense. In *c.* 592 Moses II (574–604) forbade his bishops to communicate with the Chalcedonians of the Byzantine Church; and in 607–608 the Armenian bishops met in synod at Dwin to select a successor to Moses II. While they anathematized the Council of Chalcedon, they hesitated to elect a new catholicos since a pro-Chalcedonian, Armenian catholicos was resident in the Byzantine province of Armenia. However, the Persian ruler forced the issue, and they selected Abraham I (607–615). In 648–649, Nerses III (641–661) called a synod to discuss reunion with the Byzantines as proposed by Emperor Constans II, but fear of Arab reprisal prevented the 17 bishops present from accepting the offer.

Bibliography: L. M. ALISHAN, *Ararat* (Venice 1890) 404–414, in Armenian. L. S. KOGYAN, *The Armenian Church* (Beirut 1961) 216–218, 249–251, in Armenian. V. HAROUTIUNIAN, *The Buildings at Dwin from the 5th to the 7th Centuries* (Erivan 1950), in Armenian. H. HÜBSCHMANN, *Die alt-armenischen Ortsnamen* (Strasbourg 1904); *Indogermanische Forschungen* 16 (1904) 197–490. A. GRILLMEIER and H. BACHT, *Das Konzil von Chalkedon: Geschichte und Gegenwart,* 3 v. (Würzburg 1951–54) 2:364–368. V. INGLISIAN, *Lexikon für Theologie und Kirche,* ed. J. HOFER and K. RAHNER, 10 v. (2d, new ed. Freiburg 1957–65) 3:531.

[N. M. SETIAN]

DYMPNA, ST.

In the 13th century the body of St. Dympna was discovered in the Flemish town of Gheel near Antwerp, and a number of epileptics and lunatics were allegedly restored to health. Thus, the saint became the patroness of the insane. At the close of the 13th century Gheel built an infirmary for the insane, and today the town is noted for its superior mental institution and the close personal care that the local population extends to its patients. All certain knowledge of the saint's life is lost, but popular legend depicts Dympna as an Irish, British, or Armorican princess. When her Christian mother died, says the legend, Dympna's pagan father attempted to seduce her. To escape his advances she went to Antwerp and settled as a solitary at Gheel. Her father followed her, and when she refused to return with him, he killed her.

Feast: May 15.

Bibliography: *Acta Sanctorum* May 3:475–495. A. BUTLER, *The Lives of the Saints,* ed. H. THURSTON and D. ATTWATER, (New York 1956) 2:320–321. H. DELEHAYE, *The Legends of the Saints,* tr. D. ATTWATER (New York 1962) 8, 77, 124.

[E. DAY]

DYNAMISM

Deriving from the Greek term δύναμις meaning power, dynamism is attributed to any philosophical system that explains the spatially extended appearances of things in terms of the activities of unextended forces. The system of G. W. LEIBNIZ represents a thorough dynamism of this type and contemporary physics gives support to a similar interpretation of the basic material of the universe. The term is used also to denote the active aspects of material being; in this meaning, some dynamism is involved in most philosophical explanations of CHANGE. Accordingly, a chronological survey of the dynamic aspects of matter in the major philosophies is here given, leading up to an exposition of the dynamism of Leibniz and that of modern thinkers.

Greek Origins. Pre-Socratics such as Thales and his Milesian followers posited one material from which all things come to be; they also invoked a dynamic process of transformation to explain the existence and interaction of the four basic elements (earth, air, fire and water). Of this group, Anaximenes posited rarefaction and condensation as the dynamic processes whereby air was alternately transformed into fire and condensed to water, or further condensed to stone. Other pre-Socratics affirmed the existence of different forces: EMPEDOCLES, for example, held that love and strife are the causes of the aggregation and segregation of basic elements, while DEMOCRITUS thought of atoms as being in motion in the void.

The Democritean form of atomism held that very small impenetrable substances alone exist and that these traverse empty space in rapid motion. This is classical MECHANISM, a philosophy describing matter as composed of inert particles completely dominated by motion from an extrinsic principle. Appearances are explained in terms of the various aggregations of particles and whatever appearances are not thus reducible to matter and motion are alleged to be subjective—contributions of an observer and not real aspects of matter. In such a mechanistic interpretation of the universe the dynamic principle assumes paramount importance, for it must account for most of the novelty in the universe.

Both Plato and Aristotle elaborated their explanations of dynamic processes in opposition to Democritean atomism. Plato posited two sources of action, one a soul that moves a living body as a whole (including a soul for each heavenly body and a soul of the whole universe), the other an ever-moving substance. The latter is the matter out of which bodies are ultimately constituted and in which qualitative forms (earthy, airy, fiery and watery) and quantitative forms (shapes) constantly come into being, combine with one another, dissociate and eventually pass away. Plato called this matter the receptacle to indicate its constant receptivity of sensible forms and space to indicate its function of locating material beings. In itself it is invisible and characterless, but it is filled with motions that account for the activity of the elements. Such activity is the basis for the constant flux or all-pervading change that is the mark of the Platonic sensible universe.

Aristotelian Dynamism. Aristotle admitted several sources of motion, including soul and active qualities (*see* QUALITY). His receiver of forms is called primary matter. Although invisible and characterless, like Plato's receptacle, unlike the latter it is not in motion, rather it is in combination with substantial form as part of a composite that has a NATURE (*see* MATTER AND FORM). Nature is defined as the principle or cause of motion and of rest and is conceived as a source of activity intrinsic to every kind of material agent from the smallest subsistent entity to man. Common language attests to this conception, for one speaks of the different natures of things as accounting for their various activities.

For Aristotle a related source of action in the universe is the natural tendency of bodies to move as a result of their heaviness or lightness. These tendencies account, for example, for the upward motion of fire and for the downward motion of earth and supply the Aristotelian answer to the problem of gravitation. Since such tendencies are characteristic of the four elementary bodies and produce motions that terminate in some natural PLACE, they would themselves result in rest did not something else also influence such natural processes. Thus the movement of the sun (and of other heavenly bodies) was used to explain the alternate warming and cooling of the sublunary region, composed of the four elements; the resulting qualitative changes were then invoked to explain the perpetual continuance of upward and downward motion. The movements of the heavenly bodies were themselves ascribed to a system of interconnected crystalline spheres, with the earth at the center of the system. An intelligent mover, somewhat like the Platonic souls, was assigned to each sphere; beyond this there was also an absolute Prime Mover, whose eternal existence is imitated by the perpetuity of change in the material universe. Thus the dynamic processes of things that act upon, and are transformed into, one another are actually in imitation of a divine dynamism, and this is ultimately the perduring thought of the Prime Mover about His own being.

Medieval Variations. Variations upon these types of Greek dynamism were many in medieval philosophy, with the greatest advance stemming from recognition of the Christian God as the Prime Mover from whom the universe originated by creation, and as the conserving

Michael Faraday engaged in a chemistry experiment.

force further directing events in accord with His will. The principle, "good is diffusive of itself," which Plato used in the *Timaeus* (in a different formulation) to explain why a universe exists at all, became the dominant explanation among the medievals for the coming-to-be of creatures. These cannot in any way be considered as necessary to God, for He is the summit of perfection and consequently in need of nothing. God is therefore the Supreme Good whose goodness overflows into the being of creatures. He gives them their being and their ability to act, and in so doing manifests His divine goodness in as many ways as possible. The dynamics of this overflow of goodness were worked out in a variety of ways, most of which attempted to avoid the PANTHEISM that could easily be implicit in this notion.

Atomistic Theories. In the 16th and 17th centuries thinkers such as G. GALILEI, R. DESCARTES and Sir Isaac Newton proposed explanations of the ultimate sources of action in the universe along atomistic lines. Thus Galileo held that qualities such as taste, odor, and color—since manifested through the action of the senses alone—are mere names. They have no objective existence, but are merely the resultant of the motions of small particles of matter impinging upon sense organs.

Descartes identified matter with extension and distinguished terrestrial matter from a subtle matter, or

ETHER, which is the dynamic principle imparting motion to terrestrial matter. Every body one perceives is composed, for Descartes, of other bodies so small as not to be perceptible, and its properties arise from the motions, sizes and shapes of such imperceptible bodies. Any apparent absence of terrestrial matter, in man-made vacuums for example, is accounted for by the ether, and this likewise explains the transmission of light and magnetism.

Newton also theorized that the extension, hardness, etc., of macroscopic bodies result from similar properties in the smallest particles of those bodies, and that heat, magnetism, color, and the like result from the motion of such particles. Newton's dynamism consisted of attractive and repulsive forces in matter, seemingly capable of ACTION at a distance. However, he admitted these into his system rather tentatively, conferring a mathematical rather than a physical status upon them, because of the philosophical difficulties involved in the concept of action at a distance.

Leibniz's Dynamism. Leibniz was aware of Newton's principle of gravitation and of his use, in the *Optics,* of attractive and repulsive forces within matter to account for the reflection and refraction of light corpuscles. In his own *Monadology,* Leibniz elaborated a different theory of reality according to which the elementary parts became formal atoms rather than material ones. He called these monads and held them to be immaterial. Leibniz argued that what others called matter is indefinitely divisible and consequently cannot account for the unity of the things one experiences. This unity can be accounted for, however, by monads, since these are simple, indivisible, unextended and inalterable by external agents (*see* MONAD).

Activities of Monads. Monads come into being by God's creation in an overflowing of His divinity and they act in accord with His regulative influence. Thus, although no one monad can act upon any other, God regulates them all so that whatever happens within one substance is coordinated with what happens in every other one. This conception is Leibniz's famous ''preestablished harmony.'' Moreover, several monads combine to form a composite; in this there is a chief monad and others, called body monads, that are subordinated to its activities. Apart from combining, the activities of monads include perceptions, which are living representations of the universe, and desires, which are tendencies to pass from one perception to another in order to secure ever more adequate perceptions of the universe. In composites the chief monad is aided by subordinate monads in achieving a maximum of clarity and distinctness in its perceptions.

Each monad is a center of action and each one differs from all others in its different capacity for perceptual operations. Since perception includes any structural correspondence of the monad to the universe, nonconscious monads can be said to have perceptions. A hierarchy consequently exists among monads, ascending from those capable of unconscious perceptions, to those having a memory that connects experience, to those having reflective knowledge. The last type is present in men, who are aware of their acts of perceiving and of the substantial self that perceives. The summit of this hierarchy of spiritual substances and spiritual activities is God, the Infinite Monad.

Epistemological Critique. In such a universe of spirit there can be no matter in the usual sense of the term. Nevertheless location, spatiality and temporality are undeniable facets of human experience. Leibniz held that ideas of size, figure and motion are imaginary and relative to human perceptions, although they are better founded than are qualities such as color, heat and the like. It is because of confused perceptions, both in the aggregated substances making up the composites of experience and also in the perceiving mind, that one imagines the world to be homogeneous and extended. In a similar manner space and time are based upon the coexistence and the successiveness of the multiplicity of monads; things are said to be near if one's perception of them is clear and far if it is not. Thus the mind's own act of perceiving gives rise to the notions of quantity, time and space.

Leibniz's dynamism is subject to the standard criticism of all reductionist philosophies. These cast aside sensory qualities and then pretend that such qualities do not exist, or are irrelevant, while maintaining that particles or fields (whose existence is inferred through qualities) are the only reality. If the means of detecting the substrata of appearances are illusory, what status can the substrata have? Furthermore, Leibniz's system eliminates EXTENSION and therefore LOCATION, both of which are indispensable to physical science.

Boscovich and Faraday. R. G. Boscovich was an avowed disciple of Leibniz. For him, indivisible, extensionless points were material and exerted forces of attraction and repulsion across the vacuums between them. These points never contact each other and the forces between them vary according to the distance.

Michael Faraday adduced experimental evidence to support the notion of centers of force underlying chemical reactions and electromagnetic and gravitational phenomena. He reasoned that chemical experiments show coexisting atoms to interact without touching each other; since they do affect one another, they can be thought of as surrounded by an atmosphere of force. Properties such as solidity, hardness, conduction, and the like must belong to the atmosphere of force. It follows that since the atmosphere of force is the matter of the elements, matter is wherever force is exerted; consequently it is wherever gravitational attraction exists. Later he modified his position by distinguishing actions at a distance that could be modified by changes in the intervening medium, and those (such as gravitation) that could not. On this basis electric and magnetic activities seem to involve some medium for their transmission.

Modern Theories. No medium has been discerned or invented to date that accounts for the radiation of light, electromagnetic phenomena in general, or the attractive force of gravitation. The conclusion of the dynamist type of analysis consists in the positing of fields of energy that spread out from centers of activity and exist, for example, between gravitationally related masses. Field and quantum theories in modern physics, however, present contrasting views: the first holds that energy is continuously present throughout the space where change occurs, whereas the second maintains that energy transformations take place discontinuously or by discrete jumps. Both theories are useful in interpreting different happenings on the microphysical level, but as yet there is no clear and consistent interpretation relevant to the macrophysical level. This fact is of great weight against those who would elaborate a philosophy holding that ENERGY is the only physical reality and that most of the appearances of things are purely subjective imaginings. The role of FORM in accounting for both appearances and continuous duration cannot be disregarded. Transfer of energy in fields and through quanta is part of present theoretical accounts of change; yet this need not be interpreted as a denial of substances, qualities and stable natures in the universe.

See Also: ATOMISM; PHILOSOPHY OF NATURE; HYLOMORPHISM; HYLOSYSTEMISM.

Bibliography: S. CARAMELLA, *Enciclopedia filosofica,* 4 v. (Venice-Rome 1957) 1:1583–93. D. NYS, *Cosmology,* tr., S. A. RAEMERS, 2 v. (Milwaukee 1942). J. D. COLLINS, *A History of Modern European Philosophy* (Milwaukee 1954). L. L. WHYTE, *Essay on Atomism* (New York 1960); ed., *Roger Joseph Boscovich . . .: Studies of His Life and Work . . .* (London 1962). H. V. GILL, *Roger Boscovich, S.J.* (Dublin 1941). *The Concept of Matter,* ed., E. MC-MULLIN, (Notre Dame 1963). G. W. LEIBNIZ, *The Monadology,* ed., H. W. CARR (Los Angeles 1930).

[F. J. COLLINGWOOD]

ISBN 0-7876-4008-5

90000